CurrentLaw

STATUTES

1995

VOLUME THREE

AUSTRALIA
The Law Book Company
Brisbane • Sydney • Melbourne • Perth

CANADA
Carswell
Ottawa • Toronto • Calgary • Montreal • Vancouver

Agents:
Steimatzky's Agency Ltd., Tel Aviv;
N. M. Tripathi (Private) Ltd., Bombay;
Eastern Law House (Private) Ltd., Calcutta;
M.P.P. House, Bangalore;
Universal Book Traders, Delhi;
Aditya Books, Delhi;
MacMillan Shuppan KK, Tokyo;
Pakistan Law House, Karachi

Current Law

STATUTES

1995

VOLUME THREE

SWEET & MAXWELL EDITORIAL TEAM
SARAH ANDREWS
MELANIE BHAGAT
ALA KUZMICKI
SOPHIE LOWE
CERI PICKERING

W. GREEN EDITORIAL TEAM
CHARLOTTE HALL
PETER NICHOLSON

LONDON

SWEET & MAXWELL

EDINBURGH

W. GREEN

1996

Published by
SWEET & MAXWELL LIMITED
of 100 Avenue Road, Swiss Cottage, London,
and W. GREEN LIMITED
of Alva Street, Edinburgh,
Typeset by MFK Information Services Limited, Hitchin, Herts.
and printed in Great Britain
by The Bath Press,
Somerset

ISBN This Volume only : 0 421 54780 4
As a set : 0 421 54800 2

CONTENTS

CHRONOLOGICAL TABLE

VOLUME THREE

Annotators' names are in italic

VOLUME THREE

INDEX OF SHORT TITLES

STATUTES 1995

(References are to chapter numbers of 1995)

GENEVA CONVENTIONS (AMENDMENTS) ACT 1995

(1995 c. 27)

ARRANGEMENT OF SECTIONS

An Act to make provision for the amendment of the Geneva Conventions Act 1957 to enable effect to be given to the Protocols additional to the Geneva Conventions of 1949 done at Geneva on 10 June 1977; and for connected purposes.   [19th July 1995]

PARLIAMENTARY DEBATES
Hansard, H.L. Vol. 564, cols. 1076, 1860, Vol. 565, col. 871.

INTRODUCTION
This Act alters the Geneva Conventions Act 1957 (c. 52) to give effect, *inter alia*, to the 1977 protocols to the Geneva Conventions of 1949 on the protection of victims of armed conflicts.

Amendment of section 1 of the 1957 Act

1.—(1) Section 1 (grave breaches of scheduled conventions) of the Geneva Conventions Act 1957 (in this Act referred to as "the 1957 Act") shall be amended as follows.

(2) In subsection (1) for the words from "any such" to "aforesaid" (in the second place it appears) there shall be substituted the words "a grave breach of any of the scheduled conventions or the first protocol shall be guilty of an offence and on conviction on indictment—

   (a) in the case of a grave breach involving the wilful killing of a person protected by the convention or protocol in question, shall be sentenced to imprisonment for life;

   (b) in the case of any other grave breach".

(3) After subsection (1) there shall be inserted the following subsection—

"(1A) For the purposes of subsection (1) of this section—

   (a) a grave breach of a scheduled convention is anything referred to as a grave breach of the convention in the relevant Article, that is to say—

      (i) in the case of the convention set out in the First Schedule to this Act, Article 50;

      (ii) in the case of the convention set out in the Second Schedule to this Act, Article 51;

      (iii) in the case of the convention set out in the Third Schedule to this Act, Article 130;

      (iv) in the case of the convention set out in the Fourth Schedule to this Act, Article 147; and

   (b) a grave breach of the first protocol is anything referred to as a grave breach of the protocol in paragraph 4 of Article 11, or paragraph 2, 3 or 4 of Article 85, of the protocol."

(4) In subsection (3)—

(a) for the words from the beginning to "jurisdiction" there shall be substituted the words "In Scotland, the sheriff shall have no jurisdiction"; and

(b) for the words "Attorney General" there shall be substituted the words "Director of Public Prosecutions".

(5) In subsection (4), for the words from the beginning to "applies)" there shall be substituted the words "If in proceedings for an offence under this section any question arises under Article 2 of any of the scheduled conventions or Article 1 or 3 of the first protocol (which relate to the circumstances in which the conventions and protocol apply)".

Amendment of section 6 of the 1957 Act

2.—(1) Section 6 of the 1957 Act shall be amended as follows.

(2) In subsection (1)—

(a) for the words "Army Council" there shall be substituted the words "Secretary of State"; and

(b) after paragraph (c) there shall be inserted the following paragraphs—

"(d) the sign of an equilateral blue triangle on, and completely surrounded by, an orange ground, being the international distinctive sign of civil defence;

(e) any of the distinctive signals specified in Chapter III of Annex I to the first protocol, being the signals of identification for medical units and transports."

(3) In subsection (2)—

(a) for the words "Board of Trade" there shall be substituted the words "Secretary of State"; and

(b) after paragraph (b) there shall be inserted the following paragraphs—

"(c) any design so nearly resembling the sign specified in subsection (1)(d) of this section as to be capable of being mistaken for that sign;

(d) any signal so nearly resembling any of the signals referred to in subsection (1)(e) of this section as to be capable of being mistaken for one of those signals."

(4) In subsection (3)—

(a) for the words "level 3" there shall be substituted the words "level 5";

(b) after the words "goods" there shall be inserted the words "or other article"; and

(c) after the word "designation," there shall be inserted the words "sign, signal,".

(5) After subsection (4) there shall be inserted the following subsection—

"(4A) Subsection (4) of this section shall apply in relation to a design reproducing or resembling the sign specified in paragraph (d) of subsection (1) of this section as it applies to designs reproducing or resembling an emblem specified in paragraph (b) or (c) of that subsection.

For the purposes of this subsection references in subsection (4) of this section to the passing of this Act shall be construed as references to the passing of the Geneva Conventions (Amendment) Act 1995."

(6) In subsection (6)—

(a) for the words "design or wording" there shall be substituted the words "design, wording, sign or signal"; and

(b) for the words from "any British" to the end there shall be substituted the words "—

(a) any British ship (within the meaning of the Merchant Shipping (Registration, etc.) Act 1993);

(b) any British-controlled aircraft or hovercraft (within the meaning of section 92 of the Civil Aviation Act 1982 or, as the case may be, that section as applied to hovercraft by virtue of provision made under the Hovercraft Act 1968).”

(7) In subsection (7)—

(a) after the word “proceedings” there shall be inserted the words “for an offence”; and

(b) for the words “Attorney General” there shall be substituted the words “Director of Public Prosecutions”.

Regulations

3. After section 6 of the 1957 Act there shall be inserted the following section—

“**Regulations**

6A.—(1) The Secretary of State may make regulations—

(a) granting the authority of the Secretary of State for the purposes of subsection (1) or (2) of section 6 of this Act to persons of any description prescribed in the regulations for the use of any emblem, designation, sign, signal, design or wording referred to in those subsections;

(b) making such provision as he may think appropriate for regulating the use for the purposes of any of the scheduled conventions, the first protocol or the second protocol of any emblem, designation, sign or signal;

and any authority granted by regulations under paragraph (a) of this subsection may be subject to such limitations and conditions as may be prescribed in the regulations.

(2) Paragraph (a) of the foregoing subsection is without prejudice to the Secretary of State’s power to give his authority under subsection (1) or (2) of section 6 of this Act otherwise than by regulations under this section.

(3) The power to make regulations under this section shall be exercisable by statutory instrument which shall be subject to annulment in pursuance of a resolution of either House of Parliament.”

Amendment of section 7 of the 1957 Act

4.—(1) Section 7 of the 1957 Act shall be amended as follows.

(2) In the definition of “protected internee”, after the word “Act” there shall be inserted the words “(including a person so protected by virtue of the first protocol)”.

(3) In the definition of “protected prisoner of war”, at the end, there shall be inserted the words “(including a person protected as a prisoner of war under the first protocol) or a person entitled under the first protocol to the same protection as a prisoner of war;”.

(4) After the definition of “protected prisoner of war” there shall be inserted the following definition—

“ ‘the first protocol’ means the Protocol, additional to the Geneva Conventions of 12 August 1949, relating to the Protection of Victims of International Armed Conflicts (Protocol I) done on 10 June 1977, the text of which is set out in the Fifth Schedule to this Act;”.

(5) In the definition of “the protecting power”, for the words from “or, as” to the end there shall be substituted the words “Schedule to this Act, the convention set out in the Fourth Schedule to this Act or the first protocol;”.

(6) After the definition of “the scheduled conventions” there shall be inserted the following definition—

“ ‘the second protocol’ means the Protocol, additional to the Geneva Conventions of 12 August 1949, relating to the Protection of Victims of Non-International Armed Conflicts (Protocol II) done on 10 June 1977, the text of which is set out in the Sixth Schedule to this Act.”

(7) After subsection (2) there shall be inserted the following subsections—

"(3) If the ratification by the United Kingdom of the first protocol or the second protocol is subject to any reservation or accompanied by a declaration—

(a) Her Majesty may by Order in Council certify that such a reservation or declaration has been made and the terms in which it was made; and

(b) the protocol shall for the purposes of this Act be construed subject to and in accordance with any reservation or declaration so certified.

(4) If such a reservation or declaration is withdrawn (in whole or part), an Order in Council under the foregoing subsection may certify that fact and revoke or amend any Order in Council containing the terms of that reservation or declaration.

(5) If the first protocol is further revised under Article 98 of the protocol, Her Majesty may by Order in Council amend the Fifth Schedule to this Act so as to ensure that the Schedule sets out the text of the protocol as in force in relation to the United Kingdom."

Repeals

5. The following provisions of the 1957 Act are hereby repealed, namely—

(a) in section 6—

(i) in subsection (1), the words "emblems or designations"; and

(ii) subsection (9) (which is spent); and

(b) in section 8(2), paragraphs (d) and (e) (which are obsolete).

Additional schedules to the 1957 Act

6. The provisions set out in the Schedule to this Act shall be inserted after the Fourth Schedule to the 1957 Act as the Fifth and Sixth Schedules to that Act.

Short title, commencement and extent

7.—(1) This Act may be cited as the Geneva Conventions (Amendment) Act 1995.

(2) This Act shall come into force on such day as Her Majesty may by Order in Council appoint.

(3) This Act extends to Northern Ireland.

(4) Section 8(2) of the 1957 Act (power to extend provisions to the Channel Islands, Isle of Man and colonies) shall apply in relation to the provisions of this Act as if they were contained in that Act.

SCHEDULE

Section 6   SCHEDULES TO BE INSERTED INTO THE 1957 ACT

"FIFTH SCHEDULE

PROTOCOL I

PROTOCOL ADDITIONAL TO THE GENEVA CONVENTIONS OF 12 AUGUST 1949, AND RELATING TO THE PROTECTION OF VICTIMS OF INTERNATIONAL ARMED CONFLICTS (PROTOCOL I)

PREAMBLE

The High Contracting Parties,

Proclaiming their earnest wish to see peace prevail among peoples,

Recalling that every State has the duty, in conformity with the Charter of the United Nations, to refrain in its international relations from the threat or use of force against the sovereignty, territorial integrity or political independence of any State, or in any other manner inconsistent with the purposes of the United Nations,

Believing it necessary nevertheless to reaffirm and develop the provisions protecting the victims of armed conflicts and to supplement measures intended to reinforce their application,

Expressing their conviction that nothing in this Protocol or in the Geneva Conventions of 12 August 1949 can be construed as legitimising or authorising any act of aggression or any other use of force inconsistent with the Charter of the United Nations,

Reaffirming further that the provisions of the Geneva Conventions of 12 August 1949 and of this Protocol must be fully applied in all circumstances to all persons who are protected by those instruments, without any adverse distinction based on the nature or origin of the armed conflict or on the causes espoused by or attributed to the Parties to the conflict,

Have agreed on the following:

PART I

GENERAL PROVISIONS

Article 1—General principles and scope of application

1. The High Contracting Parties undertake to respect and to ensure respect for this Protocol in all circumstances.

2. In cases not covered by this Protocol or by other international agreements, civilians and combatants remain under the protection and authority of the principles of international law derived from established custom, from the principles of humanity and from the dictates of public conscience.

3. This Protocol, which supplements the Geneva Conventions of 12 August 1949 for the protection of war victims, shall apply in the situations referred to in Article 2 common to those Conventions.

4. The situations referred to in the preceding paragraph include armed conflicts in which peoples are fighting against colonial domination and alien occupation and against racist régimes in the exercise of their right of self-determination, as enshrined in the Charter of the United Nations and the Declaration on Principles of International Law concerning Friendly Relations and Co-operation among States in accordance with the Charter of the United Nations.

Article 2—Definitions

For the purposes of this Protocol:
(a) "First Convention", "Second Convention", "Third Convention" and "Fourth Convention" mean, respectively, the Geneva Convention for the Amelioration of the Condition of the Wounded and Sick in Armed Forces in the Field of 12 August 1949; the Geneva Convention for the Amelioration of the Condition of Wounded, Sick and Shipwrecked Members of Armed Forces at Sea of 12 August 1949; the Geneva Convention relative to the Treatment of Prisoners of War of 12 August 1949; the Geneva Convention relative to the Protection of Civilian Persons in Time of War of 12 August 1949; "the Conventions" means the four Geneva Conventions of 12 August 1949 for the protection of war victims;
(b) "rules of international law applicable in armed conflict" means the rules applicable in armed conflict set forth in international agreements to which the Parties to the conflict are Parties and the generally recognised principles and rules of international law which are applicable to armed conflict;
(c) "Protecting Power" means a neutral or other State not a Party to the conflict which has been designated by a Party to the conflict and accepted by the adverse Party and has agreed to carry out the functions assigned to a Protecting Power under the Conventions and this Protocol;
(d) "substitute" means an organisation acting in place of a Protecting Power in accordance with Article 5.

Article 3—Beginning and end of application

Without prejudice to the provisions which are applicable at all times:
(a) the Conventions and this Protocol shall apply from the beginning of any situation referred to in Article 1 of this Protocol;

(b) the application of the Conventions and of this Protocol shall cease, in the territory of Parties to the conflict, on the general close of military operations and, in the case of occupied territories, on the termination of the occupation, except, in either circumstance, for those persons whose final release, repatriation or re-establishment takes place thereafter. These persons shall continue to benefit from the relevant provisions of the Conventions and of this Protocol until their final release, repatriation or re-establishment.

Article 4—Legal status of the Parties to the conflict

The application of the Conventions and of this Protocol, as well as the conclusion of the agreements provided for therein, shall not affect the legal status of the Parties to the conflict. Neither the occupation of a territory nor the application of the Conventions and this Protocol shall affect the legal status of the territory in question.

Article 5—Appointment of Protecting Powers and of their substitute

1. It is the duty of the Parties to a conflict from the beginning of that conflict to secure the supervision and implementation of the Conventions and of this Protocol by the application of the system of Protecting Powers, including, *inter alia*, the designation and acceptance of those Powers, in accordance with the following paragraphs. Protecting Powers shall have the duty of safeguarding the interests of the Parties to the conflict.

2. From the beginning of a situation referred to in Article 1, each Party to the conflict shall without delay designate a Protecting Power for the purpose of applying the Conventions and this Protocol and shall, likewise without delay and for the same purpose, permit the activities of a Protecting Power which has been accepted by it as such after designation by the adverse Party.

3. If a Protecting Power has not been designated or accepted from the beginning of a situation referred to in Article 1, the International Committee of the Red Cross, without prejudice to the right of any other impartial humanitarian organisation to do likewise, shall offer its good offices to the Parties to the conflict with a view to the designation without delay of a Protecting Power to which the Parties to the conflict consent. For that purpose it may, *inter alia*, ask each Party to provide it with a list of at least five States which that Party considers acceptable to act as Protecting Power on its behalf in relation to an adverse Party, and ask each adverse Party to provide a list of at least five States which it would accept as the Protecting Power of the first Party; these lists shall be communicated to the Committee within two weeks after the receipt of the request; it shall compare them and seek the agreement of any proposed State named on both lists.

4. If, despite the foregoing, there is no Protecting Power, the Parties to the conflict shall accept without delay an offer which may be made by the International Committee of the Red Cross or by any other organisation which offers all guarantees of impartiality and efficacy, after due consultations with the said Parties and taking into account the result of these consultations, to act as a substitute. The functioning of such a substitute is subject to the consent of the Parties to the conflict; every effort shall be made by the Parties to the conflict to facilitate the operations of the substitute in the performance of its tasks under the Conventions and this Protocol.

5. In accordance with Article 4, the designation and acceptance of Protecting Powers for the purpose of applying the Conventions and this Protocol shall not affect the legal status of the Parties to the conflict or of any territory, including occupied territory.

6. The maintenance of diplomatic relations between Parties to the conflict or the entrusting of the protection of a Party's interests and those of its nationals to a third State in accordance with the rules of international law relating to diplomatic relations is no obstacle to the designation of Protecting Powers for the purpose of applying the Conventions and this Protocol.

7. Any subsequent mention in this Protocol of a Protecting Power includes also a substitute.

Article 6—Qualified persons

1. The High Contracting Parties shall, also in peacetime, endeavour, with the assistance of the national Red Cross (Red Crescent, Red Lion and Sun) Societies, to train qualified personnel to facilitate the application of the Conventions and of this Protocol, and in particular the activities of the Protecting Powers.

2. The recruitment and training of such personnel are within domestic jurisdiction.

3. The International Committee of the Red Cross shall hold at the disposal of the High Contracting Parties the lists of persons so trained which the High Contracting Parties may have established and may have transmitted to it for that purpose.

4. The conditions governing the employment of such personnel outside the national territory shall, in each case, be the subject of special agreements between the Parties concerned.

Article 7—Meetings

The depositary of this Protocol shall convene a meeting of the High Contracting Parties, at the request of one or more of the said Parties and upon the approval of the majority of the said Parties, to consider general problems concerning the application of the Conventions and of the Protocol.

PART II

WOUNDED, SICK AND SHIPWRECKED

SECTION I—GENERAL PROTECTION

Article 8—Terminology

For the purposes of this Protocol:
(a) "wounded" and "sick" means persons, whether military or civilian, who, because of trauma, disease or other physical or mental disorder or disability, are in need of medical assistance or care and who refrain from any act of hostility. These terms also cover maternity cases, new-born babies and other persons who may be in need of immediate medical assistance or care, such as the infirm or expectant mothers, and who refrain from any act of hostility;
(b) "shipwrecked" means persons, whether military or civilian, who are in peril at sea or in other waters as a result of misfortune affecting them or the vessel or aircraft carrying them and who refrain from any act of hostility. These persons, provided that they continue to refrain from any act of hostility, shall continue to be considered shipwrecked during their rescue until they acquire another status under the Conventions or this Protocol;
(c) "medical personnel" means those persons assigned, by a Party to the conflict, exclusively to the medical purposes enumerated under sub-paragraph (e) or to the administration of medical units or to the operation or administration of medical transports. Such assignments may be either permanent or temporary. The term includes:
(i) medical personnel of a Party to the conflict, whether military or civilian, including those described in the First and Second Conventions, and those assigned to civil defence organisations;
(ii) medical personnel of national Red Cross (Red Crescent, Red Lion and Sun) Societies and other national voluntary aid societies duly recognised and authorised by a Party to the conflict;
(iii) medical personnel of medical units or medical transports described in Article 9, paragraph 2;
(d) "religious personnel" means military or civilian persons, such as chaplains, who are exclusively engaged in the work of their ministry and attached:
(i) to the armed forces of a Party to the conflict;
(ii) to medical units or medical transports of a Party to the conflict;
(iii) to medical units or medical transports described in Article 9, paragraph 2; or
(iv) to civil defence organisations of a Party to the conflict.
The attachment of religious personnel may be either permanent or temporary, and the relevant provisions mentioned under sub-paragraph (k) apply to them;
(e) "medical units" means establishments and other units, whether military or civilian, organised for medical purposes, namely the search for, collection, transportation, diagnosis or treatment—including first-aid treatment—of the wounded, sick and shipwrecked, or for

the prevention of disease. The term includes, for example, hospitals and other similar units, blood transfusion centres, preventive medicine centres and institutes, medical depots and the medical and pharmaceutical stores of such units. Medical units may be fixed or mobile, permanent or temporary;

(f) "medical transportation" means the conveyance by land, water or air of the wounded, sick, shipwrecked, medical personnel, religious personnel, medical equipment or medical supplies protected by the Conventions and by this Protocol;

(g) "medical transports" means any means of transportation, whether military or civilian, permanent or temporary, assigned exclusively to medical transportation and under the control of a competent authority of a Party to the conflict;

(h) "medical vehicles" means any medical transports by land;

(i) "medical ships and craft" means any medical transports by water;

(j) "medical aircraft" means any medical transports by air;

(k) "permanent medical personnel", "permanent medical units" and "permanent medical transports" mean those assigned exclusively to medical purposes for an indeterminate period. "Temporary medical personnel", "temporary medical units" and "temporary medical transports" mean those devoted exclusively to medical purposes for limited periods during the whole of such periods. Unless otherwise specified, the terms "medical personnel", "medical units" and "medical transports" cover both permanent and temporary categories;

(l) "distinctive emblem" means the distinctive emblem of the red cross, red crescent or red lion and sun on a white ground when used for the protection of medical units and transports, or medical and religious personnel, equipment or supplies;

(m) "distinctive signal" means any signal or message specified for the identification exclusively of medical units or transports in Chapter III of Annex I to this Protocol.

Article 9—Field of application

1. This Part, the provisions of which are intended to ameliorate the condition of the wounded, sick and shipwrecked, shall apply to all those affected by a situation referred to in Article 1, without any adverse distinction founded on race, colour, sex, language, religion or belief, political or other opinion, national or social origin, wealth, birth or other status, or on any other similar criteria.

2. The relevant provisions of Articles 27 and 32 of the First Convention shall apply to permanent medical units and transports (other than hospital ships, to which Article 25 of the Second Convention applies) and their personnel made available to a Party to the conflict for humanitarian purposes:

(a) by a neutral or other State which is not a Party to that conflict;

(b) by a recognised and authorised aid society of such a State;

(c) by an impartial international humanitarian organisation.

Article 10—Protection and care

1. All the wounded, sick and shipwrecked, to whichever Party they belong, shall be respected and protected.

2. In all circumstances they shall be treated humanely and shall receive, to the fullest extent practicable and with the least possible delay, the medical care and attention required by their condition. There shall be no distinction among them founded on any grounds other than medical ones.

Article 11—Protection of persons

1. The physical or mental health and integrity of persons who are in the power of the adverse Party or who are interned, detained or otherwise deprived of liberty as a result of a situation referred to in Article 1 shall not be endangered by any unjustified act or omission. Accordingly, it is prohibited to subject the persons described in this Article to any medical procedure which is not indicated by the state of health of the person concerned and which is not consistent with generally accepted medical standards which would be applied under similar medical circumstances to persons who are nationals of the Party conducting the procedure and who are in no way deprived of liberty.

2. It is, in particular, prohibited to carry out on such persons, even with their consent:

(a) physical mutilations;

(b) medical or scientific experiments;

(c) removal of tissue or organs for transplantation,

except where these acts are justified in conformity with the conditions provided for in paragraph 1.

3. Exceptions to the prohibition in paragraph 2(c) may be made only in the case of donations of blood for transfusion or of skin for grafting, provided that they are given voluntarily and without any coercion or inducement, and then only for therapeutic purposes, under conditions consistent with generally accepted medical standards and controls designed for the benefit of both the donor and the recipient.

4. Any wilful act or omission which seriously endangers the physical or mental health or integrity of any person who is in the power of a Party other than the one on which he depends and which either violates any of the prohibitions in paragraphs 1 and 2 or fails to comply with the requirements of paragraph 3 shall be a grave breach of this Protocol.

5. The persons described in paragraph 1 have the right to refuse any surgical operation. In case of refusal, medical personnel shall endeavour to obtain a written statement to that effect, signed or acknowledged by the patient.

6. Each Party to the conflict shall keep a medical record for every donation of blood for transfusion or skin for grafting by persons referred to in paragraph 1, if that donation is made under the responsibility of that Party. In addition, each Party to the conflict shall endeavour to keep a record of all medical procedures undertaken with respect to any person who is interned, detained or otherwise deprived of liberty as a result of a situation referred to in Article 1. These records shall be available at all times for inspection by the Protecting Power.

Article 12—Protection of medical units

1. Medical units shall be respected and protected at all times and shall not be the object of attack.

2. Paragraph 1 shall apply to civilian medical units, provided that they:
  (a) belong to one of the Parties to the conflict;
  (b) are recognised and authorised by the competent authority of one of the Parties to the conflict; or
  (c) are authorised in conformity with Article 9, paragraph 2, of this Protocol or Article 27 of the First Convention.

3. The Parties to the conflict are invited to notify each other of the location of their fixed medical units. The absence of such notification shall not exempt any of the Parties from the obligation to comply with the provisions of paragraph 1.

4. Under no circumstances shall medical units be used in an attempt to shield military objectives from attack. Whenever possible, the Parties to the conflict shall ensure that medical units are so sited that attacks against military objectives do not imperil their safety.

Article 13—Discontinuance of protection of civilian medical units

1. The protection to which civilian medical units are entitled shall not cease unless they are used to commit, outside their humanitarian function, acts harmful to the enemy. Protection may, however, cease only after a warning has been given setting, whenever appropriate, a reasonable time-limit, and after such warning has remained unheeded.

2. The following shall not be considered as acts harmful to the enemy:
  (a) that the personnel of the unit are equipped with light individual weapons for their own defence or for that of the wounded and sick in their charge;
  (b) that the unit is guarded by a picket or by sentries or by an escort;
  (c) that small-arms and ammunition taken from the wounded and sick, and not yet handed to the proper service, are found in the units;
  (d) that members of the armed forces or other combatants are in the unit for medical reasons.

Article 14—Limitations on requisition of civilian medical units

1. The Occupying Power has the duty to ensure that the medical needs of the civilian population in occupied territory continue to be satisfied.

2. The Occupying Power shall not, therefore, requisition civilian medical units, their equipment, their *matériel* or the services of their personnel, so long as these resources are necessary for the provision of adequate medical services for the civilian population and for the continuing medical care of any wounded and sick already under treatment.

3. Provided that the general rule in paragraph 2 continues to be observed, the Occupying Power may requisition the said resources, subject to the following particular conditions:
  (a) that the resources are necessary for the adequate and immediate medical treatment of the wounded and sick members of the armed forces of the Occupying Power or of prisoners of war;

(b) that the requisition continues only while such necessity exists; and
(c) that immediate arrangements are made to ensure that the medical needs of the civilian population, as well as those of any wounded and sick under treatment who are affected by the requisition, continue to be satisfied.

Article 15—Protection of civilian medical and religious personnel

1. Civilian medical personnel shall be respected and protected.
2. If needed, all available help shall be afforded to civilian medical personnel in an area where civilian medical services are disrupted by reason of combat activity.
3. The Occupying Power shall afford civilian medical personnel in occupied territories every assistance to enable them to perform, to the best of their ability, their humanitarian functions. The Occupying Power may not require that, in the performance of those functions, such personnel shall give priority to the treatment of any person except on medical grounds. They shall not be compelled to carry out tasks which are not compatible with their humanitarian mission.
4. Civilian medical personnel shall have access to any place where their services are essential, subject to such supervisory and safety measures as the relevant Party to the conflict may deem necessary.
5. Civilian religious personnel shall be respected and protected. The provisions of the Conventions and of this Protocol concerning the protection and identification of medical personnel shall apply equally to such persons.

Article 16—General protection of medical duties

1. Under no circumstances shall any person be punished for carrying out medical activities compatible with medical ethics, regardless of the person benefiting therefrom.
2. Persons engaged in medical activities shall not be compelled to perform acts or to carry out work contrary to the rules of medical ethics or to other medical rules designed for the benefit of the wounded and sick or to the provisions of the Conventions or of this Protocol, or to refrain from performing acts or from carrying out work required by those rules and provisions.
3. No person engaged in medical activities shall be compelled to give to anyone belonging either to an adverse Party, or to his own Party except as required by the law of the latter Party, any information concerning the wounded and sick who are, or who have been, under his care, if such information would, in his opinion, prove harmful to the patients concerned or to their families. Regulations for the compulsory notification of communicable diseases shall, however, be respected.

Article 17—Role of the civilian population and of aid societies

1. The civilian population shall respect the wounded, sick and shipwrecked even if they belong to the adverse Party, and shall commit no act of violence against them. The civilian population and aid societies, such as national Red Cross (Red Crescent, Red Lion and Sun) Societies, shall be permitted, even on their own initiative, to collect and care for the wounded, sick and shipwrecked, even in invaded or occupied areas. No one shall be harmed, prosecuted, convicted or punished for such humanitarian acts.
2. The Parties to the conflict may appeal to the civilian population and the aid societies referred to in paragraph 1 to collect and care for the wounded, sick and shipwrecked, and to search for the dead and report their location; they shall grant both protection and the necessary facilities to those who respond to this appeal. If the adverse Party gains or regains control of the area, that Party also shall afford the same protection and facilities for so long as they are needed.

Article 18—Identification

1. Each Party to the conflict shall endeavour to ensure that medical and religious personnel and medical units and transports are identifiable.
2. Each Party to the conflict shall also endeavour to adopt and to implement methods and procedures which will make it possible to recognise medical units and transports which use the distinctive emblem and distinctive signals.
3. In occupied territory and in areas where fighting is taking place or is likely to take place, civilian medical personnel and civilian religious personnel should be recognisable by the distinctive emblem and an identity card certifying their status.
4. With the consent of the competent authority, medical units and transports shall be marked by the distinctive emblem. The ships and craft referred to in Article 22 of this Protocol shall be marked in accordance with the provisions of the Second Convention.

5. In addition to the distinctive emblem, a Party to the conflict may, as provided in Chapter III of Annex I to this Protocol, authorise the use of distinctive signals to identify medical units and transports. Exceptionally, in the special cases covered in that Chapter, medical transports may use distinctive signals without displaying the distinctive emblem.

6. The application of the provisions of paragraphs 1 to 5 of this Article is governed by Chapters I to III of Annex I to this Protocol. Signals designated in Chapter III of the Annex for the exclusive use of medical units and transports shall not, except as provided therein, be used for any purpose other than to identify the medical units and transports specified in that Chapter.

7. This Article does not authorise any wider use of the distinctive emblem in peacetime than is prescribed in Article 44 of the First Convention.

8. The provisions of the Conventions and of this Protocol relating to supervision of the use of the distinctive emblem and to the prevention and repression of any misuse thereof shall be applicable to distinctive signals.

Article 19—Neutral and other States not Parties to the conflict

Neutral and other States not Parties to the conflict shall apply the relevant provisions of this Protocol to persons protected by this Part who may be received or interned within their territory, and to any dead of the Parties to that conflict whom they may find.

Article 20—Prohibition of reprisals

Reprisals against the persons and objects protected by this Part are prohibited.

SECTION II—MEDICAL TRANSPORTATION

Article 21—Medical vehicles

Medical vehicles shall be respected and protected in the same way as mobile medical units under the Conventions and this Protocol.

Article 22—Hospital ships and coastal rescue craft

1. The provisions of the Conventions relating to:
(a) vessels described in Articles 22, 24, 25 and 27 of the Second Convention,
(b) their lifeboats and small craft,
(c) their personnel and crews, and
(d) the wounded, sick and shipwrecked on board,
shall also apply where these vessels carry civilian wounded, sick and shipwrecked who do not belong to any of the categories mentioned in Article 13 of the Second Convention. Such civilians shall not, however, be subject to surrender to any Party which is not their own, or to capture at sea. If they find themselves in the power of a Party to the conflict other than their own they shall be covered by the Fourth Convention and by this Protocol.

2. The protection provided by the Conventions to vessels described in Article 25 of the Second Convention shall extend to hospital ships made available for humanitarian purposes to a Party to the conflict:
(a) by a neutral or other State which is not a Party to that conflict; or
(b) by an impartial international humanitarian organisation,
provided that, in either case, the requirements set out in that Article are complied with.

3. Small craft described in Article 27 of the Second Convention shall be protected even if the notification envisaged by that Article has not been made. The Parties to the conflict are, nevertheless, invited to inform each other of any details of such craft which will facilitate their identification and recognition.

Article 23—Other medical ships and craft

1. Medical ships and craft other than those referred to in Article 22 of this Protocol and Article 38 of the Second Convention shall, whether at sea or in other waters, be respected and protected in the same way as mobile medical units under the Conventions and this Protocol. Since this protection can only be effective if they can be identified and recognised as medical ships or craft, such vessels should be marked with the distinctive emblem and as far as possible comply with the second paragraph of Article 43 of the Second Convention.

2. The ships and craft referred to in paragraph 1 shall remain subject to the laws of war. Any warship on the surface able immediately to enforce its command may order them to stop, order

them off, or make them take a certain course, and they shall obey every such command. Such ships and craft may not in any other way be diverted from their medical mission so long as they are needed for the wounded, sick and shipwrecked on board.

3. The protection provided in paragraph 1 shall cease only under the conditions set out in Articles 34 and 35 of the Second Convention. A clear refusal to obey a command given in accordance with paragraph 2 shall be an act harmful to the enemy under Article 34 of the Second Convention.

4. A Party to the conflict may notify any adverse Party as far in advance of sailing as possible of the name, description, expected time of sailing, course and estimated speed of the medical ship or craft, particularly in the case of ships of over 2,000 gross tons, and may provide any other information which would facilitate identification and recognition. The adverse Party shall acknowledge receipt of such information.

5. The provisions of Article 37 of the Second Convention shall apply to medical and religious personnel in such ships and craft.

6. The provisions of the Second Convention shall apply to the wounded, sick and shipwrecked belonging to the categories referred to in Article 13 of the Second Convention and in Article 44 of this Protocol who may be on board such medical ships and craft. Wounded, sick and shipwrecked civilians who do not belong to any of the categories mentioned in Article 13 of the Second Convention shall not be subject, at sea, either to surrender to any Party which is not their own, or to removal from such ships or craft; if they find themselves in the power of a Party to the conflict other than their own, they shall be covered by the Fourth Convention and by this Protocol.

Article 24—Protection of medical aircraft

Medical aircraft shall be respected and protected, subject to the provisions of this Part.

Article 25—Medical aircraft in areas not controlled by an adverse Party

In and over land areas physically controlled by friendly forces, or in and over sea areas not physically controlled by an adverse Party, the respect and protection of medical aircraft of a Party to the conflict is not dependent on any agreement with an adverse Party. For greater safety, however, a Party to the conflict operating its medical aircraft in these areas may notify the adverse Party, as provided in Article 29, in particular when such aircraft are making flights bringing them within range of surface-to-air weapons systems of the adverse Party.

Article 26—Medical aircraft in contact or similar zones

1. In and over those parts of the contact zone which are physically controlled by friendly forces and in and over those areas the physical control of which is not clearly established, protection for medical aircraft can be fully effective only by prior agreement between the competent military authorities of the Parties to the conflict, as provided for in Article 29. Although, in the absence of such an agreement, medical aircraft operate at their own risk, they shall nevertheless be respected after they have been recognised as such.

2. "Contact zone" means any area on land where the forward elements of opposing forces are in contact with each other, especially where they are exposed to direct fire from the ground.

Article 27—Medical aircraft in areas controlled by an adverse Party

1. The medical aircraft of a Party to the conflict shall continue to be protected while flying over land or sea areas physically controlled by an adverse Party, provided that prior agreement to such flights has been obtained from the competent authority of that adverse Party.

2. A medical aircraft which flies over an area physically controlled by an adverse Party without, or in deviation from the terms of, an agreement provided for in paragraph 1, either through navigational error or because of an emergency affecting the safety of the flight, shall make every effort to identify itself and to inform the adverse Party of the circumstances. As soon as such medical aircraft has been recognised by the adverse Party, that Party shall make all reasonable efforts to give the order to land or to alight on water, referred to in Article 30, paragraph 1, or to take other measures to safeguard its own interests, and, in either case, to allow the aircraft time for compliance, before resorting to an attack against the aircraft.

Article 28—Restrictions on operations of medical aircraft

1. The Parties to the conflict are prohibited from using their medical aircraft to attempt to acquire any military advantage over an adverse Party. The presence of medical aircraft shall not be used in an attempt to render military objectives immune from attack.

2. Medical aircraft shall not be used to collect or transmit intelligence data and shall not carry any equipment intended for such purposes. They are prohibited from carrying any persons or cargo not included within the definition in Article 8, sub-paragraph (f). The carrying on board of the personal effects of the occupants or of equipment intended solely to facilitate navigation, communication or identification shall not be considered as prohibited.

3. Medical aircraft shall not carry any armament except small-arms and ammunition taken from the wounded, sick and shipwrecked on board and not yet handed to the proper service, and such light individual weapons as may be necessary to enable the medical personnel on board to defend themselves and the wounded, sick and shipwrecked in their charge.

4. While carrying out the flights referred to in Articles 26 and 27, medical aircraft shall not, except by prior agreement with the adverse Party, be used to search for the wounded, sick and shipwrecked.

Article 29—Notifications and agreements concerning medical aircraft

1. Notifications under Article 25, or requests for prior agreement under Articles 26, 27, 28 (paragraph 4), or 31 shall state the proposed number of medical aircraft, their flight plans and means of identification, and shall be understood to mean that every flight will be carried out in compliance with Article 28.

2. A Party which receives a notification given under Article 25 shall at once acknowledge receipt of such notification.

3. A Party which receives a request for prior agreement under Articles 26, 27, 28 (paragraph 4), or 31 shall, as rapidly as possible, notify the requesting Party:

(a) that the request is agreed to;

(b) that the request is denied; or

(c) of reasonable alternative proposals to the request. It may also propose a prohibition or restriction of other flights in the area during the time involved. If the Party which submitted the request accepts the alternative proposals, it shall notify the other Party of such acceptance.

4. The Parties shall take the necessary measures to ensure that notifications and agreements can be made rapidly.

5. The Parties shall also take the necessary measures to disseminate rapidly the substance of any such notifications and agreements to the military units concerned and shall instruct those units regarding the means of identification that will be used by the medical aircraft in question.

Article 30—Landing and inspection of medical aircraft

1. Medical aircraft flying over areas which are physically controlled by an adverse Party, or over areas the physical control of which is not clearly established, may be ordered to land or to alight on water, as appropriate, to permit inspection in accordance with the following paragraphs. Medical aircraft shall obey any such order.

2. If such an aircraft lands or alights on water, whether ordered to do so or for other reasons, it may be subjected to inspection solely to determine the matters referred to in paragraphs 3 and 4. Any such inspection shall be commenced without delay and shall be conducted expeditiously. The inspecting Party shall not require the wounded and sick to be removed from the aircraft unless their removal is essential for the inspection. That Party shall in any event ensure that the condition of the wounded and sick is not adversely affected by the inspection or by the removal.

3. If the inspection discloses that the aircraft:

(a) is a medical aircraft within the meaning of Article 8, sub-paragraph (j),

(b) is not in violation of the conditions prescribed in Article 28, and

(c) has not flown without or in breach of a prior agreement where such agreement is required, the aircraft and those of its occupants who belong to the adverse Party or to a neutral or other State not a Party to the conflict shall be authorised to continue the flight without delay.

4. If the inspection discloses that the aircraft:

(a) is not a medical aircraft within the meaning of Article 8, sub-paragraph (j),

(b) is in violation of the conditions prescribed in Article 28, or

(c) has flown without or in breach of a prior agreement where such agreement is required, the aircraft may be seized. Its occupants shall be treated in conformity with the relevant provisions of the Conventions and of this Protocol. Any aircraft seized which had been assigned as a permanent medical aircraft may be used thereafter only as a medical aircraft.

Article 31—Neutral or other States not Parties to the conflict

1. Except by prior agreement, medical aircraft shall not fly over or land in the territory of a neutral or other State not a Party to the conflict. However, with such an agreement, they shall be

respected throughout their flight and also for the duration of any calls in the territory. Nevertheless they shall obey any summons to land or to alight on water, as appropriate.

2. Should a medical aircraft, in the absence of an agreement or in deviation from the terms of an agreement, fly over the territory of a neutral or other State not a Party to the conflict, either through navigational error or because of an emergency affecting the safety of the flight, it shall make every effort to give notice of the flight and to identify itself. As soon as such medical aircraft is recognised, that State shall make all reasonable efforts to give the order to land or to alight on water referred to in Article 30, paragraph 1, or to take other measures to safeguard its own interests, and, in either case, to allow the aircraft time for compliance, before resorting to an attack against the aircraft.

3. If a medical aircraft, either by agreement or in the circumstances mentioned in paragraph 2, lands or alights on water in the territory of a neutral or other State not Party to the conflict, whether ordered to do so or for other reasons, the aircraft shall be subject to inspection for the purposes of determining whether it is in fact a medical aircraft. The inspection shall be commenced without delay and shall be conducted expeditiously. The inspecting Party shall not require the wounded and sick of the Party operating the aircraft to be removed from it unless their removal is essential for the inspection. The inspecting Party shall in any event ensure that the condition of the wounded and sick is not adversely affected by the inspection or the removal. If the inspection discloses that the aircraft is in fact a medical aircraft, the aircraft with its occupants, other than those who must be detained in accordance with the rules of international law applicable in armed conflict, shall be allowed to resume its flight, and reasonable facilities shall be given for the continuation of the flight. If the inspection discloses that the aircraft is not a medical aircraft, it shall be seized and the occupants treated in accordance with paragraph 4.

4. The wounded, sick and shipwrecked disembarked, otherwise than temporarily, from a medical aircraft with the consent of the local authorities in the territory of a neutral or other State not a Party to the conflict shall, unless agreed otherwise between that State and the Parties to the conflict, be detained by that State where so required by the rules of international law applicable in armed conflict, in such a manner that they cannot again take part in the hostilities. The cost of hospital treatment and internment shall be borne by the State to which those persons belong.

5. Neutral or other States not Parties to the conflict shall apply any conditions and restrictions on the passage of medical aircraft over, or on the landing of medical aircraft in, their territory equally to all Parties to the conflict.

SECTION III—MISSING AND DEAD PERSONS

Article 32—General principle

In the implementation of this Section, the activities of the High Contracting Parties, of the Parties to the conflict and of the international humanitarian organisations mentioned in the Conventions and in this Protocol shall be prompted mainly by the right of families to know the fate of their relatives.

Article 33—Missing persons

1. As soon as circumstances permit, and at the latest from the end of active hostilities, each Party to the conflict shall search for the persons who have been reported missing by an adverse Party. Such adverse Party shall transmit all relevant information concerning such persons in order to facilitate such searches.

2. In order to facilitate the gathering of information pursuant to the preceding paragraph, each Party to the conflict shall, with respect to persons who would not receive more favourable consideration under the Conventions and this Protocol:
  (a) record the information specified in Article 138 of the Fourth Convention in respect of such persons who have been detained, imprisoned or otherwise held in captivity for more than two weeks as a result of hostilities or occupation, or who have died during any period of detention;
  (b) to the fullest extent possible, facilitate and, if need be, carry out the search for and the recording of information concerning such persons if they have died in other circumstances as a result of hostilities or occupation.

3. Information concerning persons reported missing pursuant to paragraph 1 and requests for such information shall be transmitted either directly or through the Protecting Power or the Central Tracing Agency of the International Committee of the Red Cross or national Red Cross (Red Crescent, Red Lion and Sun) Societies. Where the information is not transmitted through the International Committee of the Red Cross and its Central Tracing Agency, each Party to the conflict shall ensure that such information is also supplied to the Central Tracing Agency.

4. The Parties to the conflict shall endeavour to agree on arrangements for teams to search for, identify and recover the dead from battlefield areas, including arrangements, if appropriate, for such teams to be accompanied by personnel of the adverse Party while carrying out these missions in areas controlled by the adverse Party. Personnel of such teams shall be respected and protected while exclusively carrying out these duties.

Article 34—Remains of deceased

1. The remains of persons who have died for reasons related to occupation or in detention resulting from occupation or hostilities and those of persons not nationals of the country in which they have died as a result of hostilities shall be respected, and the gravesites of all such persons shall be respected, maintained and marked as provided for in Article 130 of the Fourth Convention, where their remains or gravesites would not receive more favourable consideration under the Conventions and this Protocol.

2. As soon as circumstances and the relations between the adverse Parties permit, the High Contracting Parties in whose territories graves and, as the case may be, other locations of the remains of persons who have died as a result of hostilities or during occupation or in detention are situated, shall conclude agreements in order:

(a) to facilitate access to the gravesites by relatives of the deceased and by representatives of official graves registration services and to regulate the practical arrangements for such access;

(b) to protect and maintain such gravesites permanently;

(c) to facilitate the return of the remains of the deceased and of personal effects to the home country upon its request or, unless that country objects, upon the request of the next of kin.

3. In the absence of the agreements provided for in paragraph 2(b) or (c) and if the home country of such deceased is not willing to arrange at its expense for the maintenance of such gravesites, the High Contracting Party in whose territory the gravesites are situated may offer to facilitate the return of the remains of the deceased to the home country. Where such an offer has not been accepted the High Contracting Party may, after the expiry of five years from the date of the offer and upon due notice to the home country, adopt the arrangements laid down in its own laws relating to cemeteries and graves.

4. A High Contracting Party in whose territory the gravesites referred to in this Article are situated shall be permitted to exhume the remains only:

(a) in accordance with paragraphs 2(c) and 3, or

(b) where exhumation is a matter of overriding public necessity, including cases of medical and investigative necessity, in which case the High Contracting Party shall at all times respect the remains, and shall give notice to the home country of its intention to exhume the remains together with details of the intended place of reinterment.

PART III

METHODS AND MEANS OF WARFARE COMBATANT AND PRISONER-OF-WAR STATUS

SECTION I—METHODS AND MEANS OF WARFARE

Article 35—Basic rules

1. In any armed conflict, the right of the Parties to the conflict to choose methods or means of warfare is not unlimited.

2. It is prohibited to employ weapons, projectiles and material and methods of warfare of a nature to cause superfluous injury or unnecessary suffering.

3. It is prohibited to employ methods or means of warfare which are intended, or may be expected, to cause widespread, long-term and severe damage to the natural environment.

Article 36—New weapons

In the study, development, acquisition or adoption of a new weapon, means or method of warfare, a High Contracting Party is under an obligation to determine whether its employment would, in some or all circumstances, be prohibited by this Protocol or by any other rule of international law applicable to the High Contracting Party.

Article 37—Prohibition of perfidy

1. It is prohibited to kill, injure or capture an adversary by resort to perfidy. Acts inviting the confidence of an adversary to lead him to believe that he is entitled to, or is obliged to accord,

protection under the rules of international law applicable in armed conflict, with intent to betray that confidence, shall constitute perfidy. The following acts are examples of perfidy:

(a) the feigning of an intent to negotiate under a flag of truce or of a surrender;
(b) the feigning of an incapacitation by wounds or sickness;
(c) the feigning of civilian, non-combatant status; and
(d) the feigning of protected status by the use of signs, emblems or uniforms of the United Nations or of neutral or other States not Parties to the conflict.

2. Ruses of war are not prohibited. Such ruses are acts which are intended to mislead an adversary or to induce him to act recklessly but which infringe no rule of international law applicable in armed conflict and which are not perfidious because they do not invite the confidence of an adversary with respect to protection under that law. The following are examples of such ruses: the use of camouflage, decoys, mock operations and misinformation.

Article 38—Recognised emblems

1. It is prohibited to make improper use of the distinctive emblem of the red cross, red crescent or red lion and sun or of other emblems, signs or signals provided for by the Conventions or by this Protocol. It is also prohibited to misuse deliberately in an armed conflict other internationally recognised protective emblems, signs or signals, including the flag of truce, and the protective emblem of cultural property.

2. It is prohibited to make use of the distinctive emblem of the United Nations, except as authorised by that Organisation.

Article 39—Emblems of nationality

1. It is prohibited to make use in an armed conflict of the flags or military emblems, insignia or uniforms of neutral or other States not Parties to the conflict.

2. It is prohibited to make use of the flags or military emblems, insignia or uniforms of adverse Parties while engaging in attacks or in order to shield, favour, protect or impede military operations.

3. Nothing in this Article or in Article 37, paragraph 1(d), shall affect the existing generally recognised rules of international law applicable to espionage or to the use of flags in the conduct of armed conflict at sea.

Article 40—Quarter

It is prohibited to order that there shall be no survivors, to threaten an adversary therewith or to conduct hostilities on this basis.

Article 41—Safeguard of an enemy hors de combat

1. A person who is recognised or who, in the circumstances, should be recognised to be *hors de combat* shall not be made the object of attack.

2. A person is *hors de combat if:*
(a) he is in the power of an adverse Party;
(b) he clearly expresses an intention to surrender; or
(c) he has been rendered unconscious or is otherwise incapacitated by wounds or sickness, and therefore is incapable of defending himself;
provided that in any of these cases he abstains from any hostile act and does not attempt to escape.

3. When persons entitled to protection as prisoners of war have fallen into the power of an adverse Party under unusual conditions of combat which prevent their evacuation as provided for in Part III, Section 1, of the Third Convention, they shall be released and all feasible precautions shall be taken to ensure their safety.

Article 42—Occupants of aircraft

1. No person parachuting from an aircraft in distress shall be made the object of attack during his descent.

2. Upon reaching the ground in territory controlled by an adverse Party, a person who has parachuted from an aircraft in distress shall be given an opportunity to surrender before being made the object of attack, unless it is apparent that he is engaging in a hostile act.

3. Airborne troops are not protected by this Article.

SECTION II—COMBATANT AND PRISONER-OF-WAR STATUS

Article 43—Armed forces

1. The armed forces of a Party to a conflict consist of all organised armed forces, groups and units which are under a command responsible to that Party for the conduct of its subordinates, even if that Party is represented by a government or an authority not recognised by an adverse Party. Such armed forces shall be subject to an internal disciplinary system which, inter alia, shall enforce compliance with the rules of international law applicable in armed conflict.

2. Members of the armed forces of a Party to a conflict (other than medical personnel and chaplains covered by Article 33 of the Third Convention) are combatants, that is to say, they have the right to participate directly in hostilities.

3. Whenever a Party to a conflict incorporates a paramilitary or armed law enforcement agency into its armed forces it shall so notify the other Parties to the conflict.

Article 44—Combatants and prisoners of war

1. Any combatant, as defined in Article 43, who falls into the power of an adverse Party shall be a prisoner of war.

2. While all combatants are obliged to comply with the rules of international law applicable in armed conflict, violations of these rules shall not deprive a combatant of his right to be a combatant or, if he falls into the power of an adverse Party, of his right to be a prisoner of war, except as provided in paragraphs 3 and 4.

3. In order to promote the protection of the civilian population from the effects of hostilities, combatants are obliged to distinguish themselves from the civilian population while they are engaged in an attack or in a military operation preparatory to an attack. Recognising, however, that there are situations in armed conflicts where, owing to the nature of the hostilities an armed combatant cannot so distinguish himself, he shall retain his status as a combatant, provided that, in such situations, he carries his arms openly:

(a) during each military engagement, and

(b) during such time as he is visible to the adversary while he is engaged in a military deployment preceding the launching of an attack in which he is to participate.

Acts which comply with the requirements of this paragraph shall not be considered as perfidious within the meaning of Article 37, paragraph l(c).

4. A combatant who falls into the power of an adverse Party while failing to meet the requirements set forth in the second sentence of paragraph 3 shall forfeit his right to be a prisoner of war, but he shall, nevertheless, be given protections equivalent in all respects to those accorded to prisoners of war by the Third Convention and by this Protocol. This protection includes protections equivalent to those accorded to prisoners of war by the Third Convention in the case where such a person is tried and punished for any offences he has committed.

5. Any combatant who falls into the power of an adverse Party while not engaged in an attack or in a military operation preparatory to an attack shall not forfeit his rights to be a combatant and a prisoner of war by virtue of his prior activities.

6. This Article is without prejudice to the right of any person to be a prisoner of war pursuant to Article 4 of the Third Convention.

7. This Article is not intended to change the generally accepted practice of States with respect to the wearing of the uniform by combatants assigned to the regular, uniformed armed units of a Party to the conflict.

8. In addition to the categories of persons mentioned in Article 13 of the First and Second Conventions, all members of the armed forces of a Party to the conflict, as defined in Article 43 of this Protocol, shall be entitled to protection under those Conventions if they are wounded or sick or, in the case of the Second Convention, shipwrecked at sea or in other waters.

Article 45—Protection of persons who have taken part in hostilities

1. A person who takes part in hostilities and falls into the power of an adverse Party shall be presumed to be a prisoner of war, and therefore shall be protected by the Third Convention, if he claims the status of prisoner of war, or if he appears to be entitled to such status, or if the Party on which he depends claims such status on his behalf by notification to the detaining Power or to the

Protecting Power. Should any doubt arise as to whether any such person is entitled to the status of prisoner of war, he shall continue to have such status and, therefore, to be protected by the Third Convention and this Protocol until such time as his status has been determined by a competent tribunal.

2. If a person who has fallen into the power of an adverse Party is not held as a prisoner of war and is to be tried by that Party for an offence arising out of the hostilities, he shall have the right to assert his entitlement to prisoner-of-war status before a judicial tribunal and to have that question adjudicated. Whenever possible under the applicable procedure, this adjudication shall occur before the trial for the offence. The representatives of the Protecting Power shall be entitled to attend the proceedings in which that question is adjudicated, unless, exceptionally, the proceedings are held *in camera* in the interest of State security. In such a case the detaining Power shall advise the Protecting Power accordingly.

3. Any person who has taken part in hostilities, who is not entitled to prisoner-of-war status and who does not benefit from more favourable treatment in accordance with the Fourth Convention shall have the right at all times to the protection of Article 75 of this Protocol. In occupied territory, any such person, unless he is held as a spy, shall also be entitled, notwithstanding Article 5 of the Fourth Convention, to his rights of communication under that Convention.

Article 46—Spies

1. Notwithstanding any other provision of the Conventions or of this Protocol, any member of the armed forces of a Party to the conflict who falls into the power of an adverse Party while engaging in espionage shall not have the right to the status of prisoner of war and may be treated as a spy.

2. A member of the armed forces of a Party to the conflict who, on behalf of that Party and in territory controlled by an adverse Party, gathers or attempts to gather information shall not be considered as engaging in espionage if, while so acting, he is in the uniform of his armed forces.

3. A member of the armed forces of a Party to the conflict who is a resident of territory occupied by an adverse Party and who, on behalf of the Party on which he depends, gathers or attempts to gather information of military value within that territory shall not be considered as engaging in espionage unless he does so through an act of false pretences or deliberately in a clandestine manner. Moreover, such a resident shall not lose his right to the status of prisoner of war and may not be treated as a spy unless he is captured while engaging in espionage.

4. A member of the armed forces of a Party to the conflict who is not a resident of territory occupied by an adverse Party and who has engaged in espionage in that territory shall not lose his right to the status of prisoner of war and may not be treated as a spy unless he is captured before he has rejoined the armed forces to which he belongs.

Article 47—Mercenaries

1. A mercenary shall not have the right to be a combatant or a prisoner of war.
2. A mercenary is any person who:
(a) is specially recruited locally or abroad in order to fight in an armed conflict;
(b) does, in fact, take a direct part in the hostilities;
(c) is motivated to take part in the hostilities essentially by the desire for private gain and, in fact, is promised, by or on behalf of a Party to the conflict, material compensation substantially in excess of that promised or paid to combatants of similar ranks and functions in the armed forces of that Party;
(d) is neither a national of a Party to the conflict nor a resident of territory controlled by a Party to the conflict;
(e) is not a member of the armed forces of a Party to the conflict; and
(f) has not been sent by a State which is not a Party to the conflict on official duty as a member of its armed forces.

PART IV

CIVILIAN POPULATION

SECTION I—GENERAL PROTECTION AGAINST EFFECTS OF HOSTILITIES

Chapter I—basic rule and field of application

Article 48—Basic rule

In order to ensure respect for and protection of the civilian population and civilian objects, the Parties to the conflict shall at all times distinguish between the civilian population and combatants and between civilian objects and military objectives and accordingly shall direct their operations only against military objectives.

Article 49—Definition of attacks and scope of application

1. "Attacks" means acts of violence against the adversary, whether in offence or in defence.

2. The provisions of this Protocol with respect to attacks apply to all attacks in whatever territory conducted, including the national territory belonging to a Party to the conflict but under the control of an adverse Party.

3. The provisions of this Section apply to any land, air or sea warfare which may affect the civilian population, individual civilians or civilian objects on land. They further apply to all attacks from the sea or from the air against objectives on land but do not otherwise affect the rules of international law applicable in armed conflict at sea or in the air.

4. The provisions of this Section are additional to the rules concerning humanitarian protection contained in the Fourth Convention, particularly in Part II thereof, and in other international agreements binding upon the High Contracting Parties, as well as to other rules of international law relating to the protection of civilians and civilian objects on land, at sea or in the air against the effects of hostilities.

CHAPTER II—CIVILIANS AND CIVILIAN POPULATION

Article 50—Definition of civilians and civilian population

1. A civilian is any person who does not belong to one of the categories of persons referred to in Article 4A(1), (2), (3) and (6) of the Third Convention and in Article 43 of this Protocol. In case of doubt whether a person is a civilian, that person shall be considered to be a civilian.

2. The civilian population comprises all persons who are civilians.

3. The presence within the civilian population of individuals who do not come within the definition of civilians does not deprive the population of its civilian character.

Article 51—Protection of the civilian population

1. The civilian population and individual civilians shall enjoy general protection against dangers arising from military operations. To give effect to this protection, the following rules, which are additional to other applicable rules of international law, shall be observed in all circumstances.

2. The civilian population as such, as well as individual civilians, shall not be the object of attack. Acts or threats of violence the primary purpose of which is to spread terror among the civilian population are prohibited.

3. Civilians shall enjoy the protection afforded by this Section, unless and for such time as they take a direct part in hostilities.

4. Indiscriminate attacks are prohibited. Indiscriminate attacks are:

(a) those which are not directed at a specific military objective;

(b) those which employ a method or means of combat which cannot be directed at a specific military objective; or

(c) those which employ a method or means of combat the effects of which cannot be limited as required by this Protocol;

and consequently, in each such case, are of a nature to strike military objectives and civilians or civilian objects without distinction.

5. Among others, the following types of attacks are to be considered as indiscriminate:

(a) an attack by bombardment by any methods or means which treats as a single military objective a number of clearly separated and distinct military objectives located in a city, town, village or other area containing a similar concentration of civilians or civilian objects; and

(b) an attack which may be expected to cause incidental loss of civilian life, injury to civilians, damage to civilian objects, or a combination thereof, which would be excessive in relation to the concrete and direct military advantage anticipated.

6. Attacks against the civilian population or civilians by way of reprisals are prohibited.

7. The presence or movements of the civilian population or individual civilians shall not be used to render certain points or areas immune from military operations, in particular in attempts to shield military objectives from attacks or to shield, favour or impede military operations. The Parties to the conflict shall not direct the movement of the civilian population or individual civilians in order to attempt to shield military objectives from attacks or to shield military operations.

8. Any violation of these prohibitions shall not release the Parties to the conflict from their legal obligations with respect to the civilian population and civilians, including the obligation to take the precautionary measures provided for in Article 57.

CHAPTER III—CIVILIAN OBJECTS

Article 52—General protection of civilian objects

1. Civilian objects shall not be the object of attack or of reprisals. Civilian objects are all objects which are not military objectives as defined in paragraph 2.

2. Attacks shall be limited strictly to military objectives. In so far as objects are concerned, military objectives are limited to those objects which by their nature, location, purpose or use make an effective contribution to military action and whose total or partial destruction, capture or neutralisation, in the circumstances ruling at the time, offers a definite military advantage.

3. In case of doubt whether an object which is normally dedicated to civilian purposes, such as a place of worship, a house or other dwelling or a school, is being used to make an effective contribution to military action, it shall be presumed not to be so used.

Article 53—Protection of cultural objects and of places of worship

Without prejudice to the provisions of the Hague Convention for the Protection of Cultural Property in the Event of Armed Conflict of 14 May 1954, and of other relevant international instruments, it is prohibited:
  (a) to commit any acts of hostility directed against the historic monuments, works of art or places of worship which constitute the cultural or spiritual heritage of peoples;
  (b) to use such objects in support of the military effort;
  (c) to make such objects the object of reprisals.

Article 54—Protection of objects indispensable to the survival of the civilian population

1. Starvation of civilians as a method of warfare is prohibited.

2. It is prohibited to attack, destroy, remove or render useless objects indispensable to the survival of the civilian population, such as foodstuffs, agricultural areas for the production of foodstuffs, crops, livestock, drinking water installations and supplies and irrigation works, for the specific purpose of denying them for their sustenance value to the civilian population or to the adverse Party, whatever the motive, whether in order to starve out civilians, to cause them to move away, or for any other motive.

3. The prohibitions in paragraph 2 shall not apply to such of the objects covered by it as are used by an adverse Party:
  (a) as sustenance solely for the members of its armed forces; or
  (b) if not as sustenance, then in direct support of military action, provided, however, that in no event shall actions against these objects be taken which may be expected to leave the civilian population with such inadequate food or water as to cause its starvation or force its movement.

4. These objects shall not be made the object of reprisals.

5. In recognition of the vital requirements of any Party to the conflict in the defence of its national territory against invasion, derogation from the prohibitions contained in paragraph 2 may be made by a Party to the conflict within such territory under its own control where required by imperative military necessity.

Article 55—Protection of the natural environment

1. Care shall be taken in warfare to protect the natural environment against widespread, long-term and severe damage. This protection includes a prohibition of the use of methods or means of warfare which are intended or may be expected to cause such damage to the natural environment and thereby to prejudice the health or survival of the population.

2. Attacks against the natural environment by way of reprisals are prohibited.

Article 56—Protection of works and installations containing dangerous forces

1. Works or installations containing dangerous forces, namely dams, dykes and nuclear electrical generating stations, shall not be made the object of attack, even where these objects are military objectives, if such attack may cause the release of dangerous forces and consequent severe losses among the civilian population. Other military objectives located at or in the vicinity

of these works or installations shall not be made the object of attack if such attack may cause the release of dangerous forces from the works or installations and consequent severe losses among the civilian population.

2. The special protection against attack provided by paragraph 1 shall cease:

(a) for a dam or a dyke only if it is used for other than its normal function and in regular, significant and direct support of military operations and if such attack is the only feasible way to terminate such support;

(b) for a nuclear electrical generating station only if it provides electric power in regular, significant and direct support of military operations and if such attack is the only feasible way to terminate such support;

(c) for other military objectives located at or in the vicinity of these works or installations only if they are used in regular, significant and direct support of military operations and if such attack is the only feasible way to terminate such support.

3. In all cases, the civilian population and individual civilians shall remain entitled to all the protection accorded them by international law, including the protection of the precautionary measures provided for in Article 57. If the protection ceases and any of the works, installations or military objectives mentioned in paragraph 1 is attacked, all practical precautions shall be taken to avoid the release of the dangerous forces.

4. It is prohibited to make any of the works, installations or military objectives mentioned in paragraph 1 the object of reprisals.

5. The Parties to the conflict shall endeavour to avoid locating any military objectives in the vicinity of the works or installations mentioned in paragraph 1. Nevertheless, installations erected for the sole purpose of defending the protected works or installations from attack are permissible and shall not themselves be made the object of attack, provided that they are not used in hostilities except for defensive actions necessary to respond to attacks against the protected works or installations and that their armament is limited to weapons capable only of repelling hostile action against the protected works or installations.

6. The High Contracting Parties and the Parties to the conflict are urged to conclude further agreements among themselves to provide additional protection for objects containing dangerous forces.

7. In order to facilitate the identification of the objects protected by this Article, the Parties to the conflict may mark them with a special sign consisting of a group of three bright orange circles placed on the same axis, as specified in Article 16 of Annex I to this Protocol. The absence of such marking in no way relieves any Party to the conflict of its obligations under this Article.

Note: the reference in this paragraph to Article 16 of Annex I is to be read as a reference to Article 17 of that Annex, following the entry into force on 1 March 1994 of amendments to Annex I made under Article 98.

CHAPTER IV—PRECAUTIONARY MEASURES

Article 57—Precautions in attack

1. In the conduct of military operations, constant care shall be taken to spare the civilian population, civilians and civilian objects.

2. With respect to attacks, the following precautions shall be taken:

(a) those who plan or decide upon an attack shall:

(i) do everything feasible to verify that the objectives to be attacked are neither civilians nor civilian objects and are not subject to special protection but are military objectives within the meaning of paragraph 2 of Article 52 and that it is not prohibited by the provisions of this Protocol to attack them;

(ii) take all feasible precautions in the choice of means and methods of attack with a view to avoiding, and in any event to minimising, incidental loss of civilian life, injury to civilians and damage to civilian objects;

(iii) refrain from deciding to launch any attack which may be expected to cause incidental loss of civilian life, injury to civilians, damage to civilian objects, or a combination thereof, which would be excessive in relation to the concrete and direct military advantage anticipated;

(b) an attack shall be cancelled or suspended if it becomes apparent that the objective is not a military one or is subject to special protection or that the attack may be expected to cause incidental loss of civilian life, injury to civilians, damage to civilian objects, or a combination thereof, which would be excessive in relation to the concrete and direct military advantage anticipated;

(c) effective advance warning shall be given of attacks which may affect the civilian population, unless circumstances do not permit.

3. When a choice is possible between several military objectives for obtaining a similar military advantage, the objective to be selected shall be that the attack on which may be expected to cause the least danger to civilian lives and to civilian objects.

4. In the conduct of military operations at sea or in the air, each Party to the conflict shall, in conformity with its rights and duties under the rules of international law applicable in armed conflict, take all reasonable precautions to avoid losses of civilian lives and damage to civilian objects.

5. No provision of this Article may be construed as authorising any attacks against the civilian population, civilians or civilian objects.

Article 58—Precautions against the effects of attacks

The Parties to the conflict shall, to the maximum extent feasible:
(a) without prejudice to Article 49 of the Fourth Convention, endeavour to remove the civilian population, individual civilians and civilian objects under their control from the vicinity of military objectives;
(b) avoid locating military objectives within or near densely populated areas;
(c) take the other necessary precautions to protect the civilian population, individual civilians and civilian objects under their control against the dangers resulting from military operations.

CHAPTER V—LOCALITIES AND ZONES UNDER SPECIAL PROTECTION

Article 59—Non-defended localities

1. It is prohibited for the Parties to the conflict to attack, by any means whatsoever, non-defended localities.

2. The appropriate authorities of a Party to the conflict may declare as a non-defended locality any inhabited place near or in a zone where armed forces are in contact which is open for occupation by an adverse Party. Such a locality shall fulfil the following conditions:
(a) all combatants, as well as mobile weapons and mobile military equipment must have been evacuated;
(b) no hostile use shall be made of fixed military installations or establishments;
(c) no acts of hostility shall be committed by the authorities or by the population; and
(d) no activities in support of military operations shall be undertaken.

3. The presence, in this locality, of persons specially protected under the Conventions and this Protocol, and of police forces retained for the sole purpose of maintaining law and order, is not contrary to the conditions laid down in paragraph 2.

4. The declaration made under paragraph 2 shall be addressed to the adverse Party and shall define and describe, as precisely as possible, the limits of the non-defended locality. The Party to the conflict to which the declaration is addressed shall acknowledge its receipt and shall treat the locality as a non-defended locality unless the conditions laid down in paragraph 2 are not in fact fulfilled, in which event it shall immediately so inform the Party making the declaration. Even if the conditions laid down in paragraph 2 are not fulfilled, the locality shall continue to enjoy the protection provided by the other provisions of this Protocol and the other rules of international law applicable in armed conflict.

5. The Parties to the conflict may agree on the establishment of non-defended localities even if such localities do not fulfil the conditions laid down in paragraph 2. The agreement should define and describe, as precisely as possible, the limits of the non-defended locality; if necessary, it may lay down the methods of supervision.

6. The Party which is in control of a locality governed by such an agreement shall mark it, so far as possible, by such signs as may be agreed upon with the other Party, which shall be displayed where they are clearly visible, especially on its perimeter and limits and on highways.

7. A locality loses its status as a non-defended locality when it ceases to fulfil the conditions laid down in paragraph 2 or in the agreement referred to in paragraph 5. In such an eventuality, the locality shall continue to enjoy the protection provided by the other provisions of this Protocol and the other rules of international law applicable in armed conflict.

Article 60—Demilitarised zones

1. It is prohibited for the Parties to the conflict to extend their military operations to zones on which they have conferred by agreement the status of demilitarised zone, if such extension is contrary to the terms of this agreement.

2. The agreement shall be an express agreement, may be concluded verbally or in writing, either directly or through a Protecting Power or any impartial humanitarian organisation, and may consist of reciprocal and concordant declarations. The agreement may be concluded in peacetime, as well as after the outbreak of hostilities, and should define and describe, as precisely as possible, the limits of the demilitarised zone and, if necessary, lay down the methods of supervision.

3. The subject of such an agreement shall normally be any zone which fulfils the following conditions:
  (a) all combatants, as well as mobile weapons and mobile military equipment, must have been evacuated;
  (b) no hostile use shall be made of fixed military installations or establishments;
  (c) no acts of hostility shall be committed by the authorities or by the population; and
  (d) any activity linked to the military effort must have ceased.

The Parties to the conflict shall agree upon the interpretation to be given to the condition laid down in sub-paragraph (d) and upon persons to be admitted to the demilitarised zone other than those mentioned in paragraph 4.

4. The presence, in this zone, of persons specially protected under the Conventions and this Protocol, and of police forces retained for the sole purpose of maintaining law and order, is not contrary to the conditions laid down in paragraph 3.

5. The Party which is in control of such a zone shall mark it, so far as possible by such signs as may be agreed upon with the other Party, which shall be displayed where they are clearly visible, especially on its perimeter and limits and on highways.

6. If the fighting draws near to a demilitarised zone, and if the Parties to the conflict have so agreed, none of them may use the zone for purposes related to the conduct of military operations or unilaterally revoke its status.

7. If one of the Parties to the conflict commits a material breach of the provisions of paragraphs 3 or 6, the other Party shall be released from its obligations under the agreement conferring upon the zone the status of demilitarised zone. In such an eventuality, the zone loses its status but shall continue to enjoy the protection provided by the other provisions of this Protocol and the other rules of international law applicable in armed conflict.

CHAPTER VI—CIVIL DEFENCE

Article 61—Definitions and scope

For the purposes of this Protocol:
  (a) "civil defence" means the performance of some or all of the undermentioned humanitarian tasks intended to protect the civilian population against the dangers, and to help it to recover from the immediate effects, of hostilities or disasters and also to provide the conditions necessary for its survival. These tasks are:
    (i) warning;
    (ii) evacuation;
    (iii) management of shelters;
    (iv) management of blackout measures;
    (v) rescue;
    (vi) medical services, including first aid, and religious assistance;
    (vii) fire-fighting;
    (viii) detection and marking of danger areas;
    (ix) decontamination and similar protective measures;
    (x) provision of emergency accommodation and supplies;
    (xi) emergency assistance in the restoration and maintenance of order in distressed areas;
    (xii) emergency repair of indispensable public utilities;
    (xiii) emergency disposal of the dead;
    (xiv) assistance in the preservation of objects essential for survival;
    (xv) complementary activities necessary to carry out any of the tasks mentioned above, including, but not limited to, planning and organisation;
  (b) "civil defence organisations" means those establishments and other units which are organised or authorised by the competent authorities of a Party to the conflict to perform any of the tasks mentioned under sub-paragraph (a), and which are assigned and devoted exclusively to such tasks;

(c) "personnel" of civil defence organisations means those persons assigned by a Party to the conflict exclusively to the performance of the tasks mentioned under sub-paragraph (a), including personnel assigned by the competent authority of that Party exclusively to the administration of these organisations;

(d) "*matériel*" of civil defence organisations means equipment, supplies and transports used by these organisations for the performance of the tasks mentioned under sub-paragraph (a).

Article 62—General protection

1. Civilian civil defence organisations and their personnel shall be respected and protected, subject to the provisions of this Protocol, particularly the provisions of this Section. They shall be entitled to perform their civil defence tasks except in case of imperative military necessity.

2. The provisions of paragraph 1 shall also apply to civilians who, although not members of civilian civil defence organisations, respond to an appeal from the competent authorities and perform civil defence tasks under their control.

3. Buildings and *matériel* used for civil defence purposes and shelters provided for the civilian population are covered by Article 52. Objects used for civil defence purposes may not be destroyed or diverted from their proper use except by the Party to which they belong.

Article 63—Civil defence in occupied territories

1. In occupied territories, civilian civil defence organisations shall receive from the authorities the facilities necessary for the performance of their tasks. In no circumstances shall their personnel be compelled to perform activities which would interfere with the proper performance of these tasks. The Occupying Power shall not change the structure or personnel of such organisations in any way which might jeopardise the efficient performance of their mission. These organisations shall not be required to give priority to the nationals or interests of that Power.

2. The Occupying Power shall not compel, coerce or induce civilian civil defence organisations to perform their tasks in any manner prejudicial to the interests of the civilian population.

3. The Occupying Power may disarm civil defence personnel for reasons of security.

4. The Occupying Power shall neither divert from their proper use nor requisition buildings or *matériel* belonging to or used by civil defence organisations if such diversion or requisition would be harmful to the civilian population.

5. Provided that the general rule in paragraph 4 continues to be observed, the Occupying Power may requisition or divert these resources, subject to the following particular conditions:

(a) that the buildings or *matériel* are necessary for other needs of the civilian population; and

(b) that the requisition or diversion continues only while such necessity exists.

6. The Occupying Power shall neither divert nor requisition shelters provided for the use of the civilian population or needed by such population.

Article 64—Civilian civil defence organisations of neutral or other States not Parties to the conflict and international co-ordinating organisations

1. Articles 62, 63, 65 and 66 shall also apply to the personnel and *matériel* of civilian civil defence organisations of neutral or other States not Parties to the conflict which perform civil defence tasks mentioned in Article 61 in the territory of a Party to the conflict, with the consent and under the control of that Party. Notification of such assistance shall be given as soon as possible to any adverse Party concerned. In no circumstances shall this activity be deemed to be an interference in the conflict. This activity should, however, be performed with due regard to the security interests of the Parties to the conflict concerned.

2. The Parties to the conflict receiving the assistance referred to in paragraph 1 and the High Contracting Parties granting it should facilitate international co-ordination of such civil defence actions when appropriate. In such cases the relevant international organisations are covered by the provisions of this Chapter.

3. In occupied territories, the Occupying Power may only exclude or restrict the activities of civilian civil defence organisations of neutral or other States not Parties to the conflict and of international co-ordinating organisations if it can ensure the adequate performance of civil defence tasks from its own resources or those of the occupied territory.

Article 65—Cessation of protection

1. The protection to which civilian civil defence organisations, their personnel, buildings, shelters and *matériel* are entitled shall not cease unless they commit or are used to commit, outside

their proper tasks, acts harmful to the enemy. Protection may, however, cease only after a warning has been given setting, whenever appropriate, a reasonable time-limit, and after such warning has remained unheeded.

2. The following shall not be considered as acts harmful to the enemy:

  (a) that civil defence tasks are carried out under the direction or control of military authorities;

  (b) that civilian civil defence personnel co-operate with military personnel in the performance of civil defence tasks, or that some military personnel are attached to civilian civil defence organisations;

  (c) that the performance of civil defence tasks may incidentally benefit military victims, particularly those who are *hors de combat.*

3. It shall also not be considered as an act harmful to the enemy that civilian civil defence personnel bear light individual weapons for the purpose of maintaining order or for self-defence. However, in areas where land fighting is taking place or is likely to take place, the Parties to the conflict shall undertake the appropriate measures to limit these weapons to handguns, such as pistols or revolvers, in order to assist in distinguishing between civil defence personnel and combatants. Although civil defence personnel bear other light individual weapons in such areas, they shall nevertheless be respected and protected as soon as they have been recognised as such.

4. The formation of civilian civil defence organisations along military lines, and compulsory service in them, shall also not deprive them of the protection conferred by this Chapter.

Article 66—Identification

1. Each Party to the conflict shall endeavour to ensure that its civil defence organisations, their personnel, buildings and *matériel*, are identifiable while they are exclusively devoted to the performance of civil defence tasks. Shelters provided for the civilian population should be similarly identifiable.

2. Each Party to the conflict shall also endeavour to adopt and implement methods and procedures which will make it possible to recognise civilian shelters as well as civil defence personnel, buildings and *matériel* on which the international distinctive sign of civil defence is displayed.

3. In occupied territories and in areas where fighting is taking place or is likely to take place, civilian civil defence personnel should be recognisable by the international distinctive sign of civil defence and by an identity card certifying their status.

4. The international distinctive sign of civil defence is an equilateral blue triangle on an orange ground when used for the protection of civil defence organisations, their personnel, buildings and *matériel* and for civilian shelters.

5. In addition to the distinctive sign, Parties to the conflict may agree upon the use of distinctive signals for civil defence identification purposes.

6. The application of the provisions of paragraphs 1 to 4 is governed by Chapter V of Annex I to this Protocol.

7. In time of peace, the sign described in paragraph 4 may, with the consent of the competent national authorities, be used for civil defence identification purposes.

8. The High Contracting Parties and the Parties to the conflict shall take the measures necessary to supervise the display of the international distinctive sign of civil defence and to prevent and repress any misuse thereof.

9. The identification of civil defence medical and religious personnel, medical units and medical transports is also governed by Article 18.

Article 67—Members of the armed forces and military units assigned to civil defence organisations

1. Members of the armed forces and military units assigned to civil defence organisations shall be respected and protected, provided that:

  (a) such personnel and such units are permanently assigned and exclusively devoted to the performance of any of the tasks mentioned in Article 61;

  (b) if so assigned, such personnel do not perform any other military duties during the conflict;

  (c) such personnel are clearly distinguishable from the other members of the armed forces by prominently displaying the international distinctive sign of civil defence, which shall be as large as appropriate, and such personnel are provided with the identity card referred to in Chapter V of Annex I to this Protocol certifying their status;

  (d) such personnel and such units are equipped only with light individual weapons for the purpose of maintaining order or for self-defence. The provisions of Article 65, paragraph 3 shall also apply in this case;

(e)　such personnel do not participate directly in hostilities, and do not commit, or are not used to commit, outside their civil defence tasks, acts harmful to the adverse Party;

(f)　such personnel and such units perform their civil defence tasks only within the national territory of their Party.

The non-observance of the conditions stated in (e) above by any member of the armed forces who is bound by the conditions prescribed in (a) and (b) above is prohibited.

2. Military personnel serving within civil defence organisations shall, if they fall into the power of an adverse Party, be prisoners of war. In occupied territory they may, but only in the interest of the civilian population of that territory, be employed on civil defence tasks in so far as the need arises, provided however that, if such work is dangerous, they volunteer for such tasks.

3. The buildings and major items of equipment and transports of military units assigned to civil defence organisations shall be clearly marked with the international distinctive sign of civil defence. This distinctive sign shall be as large as appropriate.

4. The *matériel* and buildings of military units permanently assigned to civil defence organisations and exclusively devoted to the performance of civil defence tasks shall, if they fall into the hands of an adverse Party, remain subject to the laws of war. They may not be diverted from their civil defence purpose so long as they are required for the performance of civil defence tasks, except in case of imperative military necessity, unless previous arrangements have been made for adequate provision for the needs of the civilian population.

SECTION II—RELIEF IN FAVOUR OF THE CIVILIAN POPULATION

Article 68—Field of application

The provisions of this Section apply to the civilian population as defined in this Protocol and are supplementary to Articles 23, 55, 59, 60, 61 and 62 and other relevant provisions of the Fourth Convention.

Article 69—Basic needs in occupied territories

1. In addition to the duties specified in Article 55 of the Fourth Convention concerning food and medical supplies, the Occupying Power shall, to the fullest extent of the means available to it and without any adverse distinction, also ensure the provision of clothing, bedding, means of shelter, other supplies essential to the survival of the civilian population of the occupied territory and objects necessary for religious worship.

2. Relief actions for the benefit of the civilian population of occupied territories are governed by Articles 59, 60, 61, 62, 108, 109, 110 and 111 of the Fourth Convention, and by Article 71 of this Protocol, and shall be implemented without delay.

Article 70—Relief actions

1. If the civilian population of any territory under the control of a Party to the conflict, other than occupied territory, is not adequately provided with the supplies mentioned in Article 69, relief actions which are humanitarian and impartial in character and conducted without any adverse distinction shall be undertaken, subject to the agreement of the Parties concerned in such relief actions. Offers of such relief shall not be regarded as interference in the armed conflict or as unfriendly acts. In the distribution of relief consignments, priority shall be given to those persons, such as children, expectant mothers, maternity cases and nursing mothers, who, under the Fourth Convention or under this Protocol, are to be accorded privileged treatment or special protection.

2. The Parties to the conflict and each High Contracting Party shall allow and facilitate rapid and unimpeded passage of all relief consignments, equipment and personnel provided in accordance with this Section, even if such assistance is destined for the civilian population of the adverse Party.

3. The Parties to the conflict and each High Contracting Party which allow the passage of relief consignments, equipment and personnel in accordance with paragraph 2:

(a)　shall have the right to prescribe the technical arrangements, including search, under which such passage is permitted;

(b)　may make such permission conditional on the distribution of this assistance being made under the local supervision of a Protecting Power;

(c)　shall, in no way whatsoever, divert relief consignments from the purpose for which they are intended nor delay their forwarding, except in cases of urgent necessity in the interest of the civilian population concerned.

4. The Parties to the conflict shall protect relief consignments and facilitate their rapid distribution.

5. The Parties to the conflict and each High Contracting Party concerned shall encourage and facilitate effective international co-ordination of the relief actions referred to in paragraph 1.

Article 71—Personnel participating in relief actions

1. Where necessary, relief personnel may form part of the assistance provided in any relief action, in particular for the transportation and distribution of relief consignments; the participation of such personnel shall be subject to the approval of the Party in whose territory they will carry out their duties.

2. Such personnel shall be respected and protected.

3. Each Party in receipt of relief consignments shall, to the fullest extent practicable, assist the relief personnel referred to in paragraph 1 in carrying out their relief mission. Only in case of imperative military necessity may the activities of the relief personnel be limited or their movements temporarily restricted.

4. Under no circumstances may relief personnel exceed the terms of their mission under this Protocol. In particular they shall take account of the security requirements of the Party in whose territory they are carrying out their duties. The mission of any of the personnel who do not respect these conditions may be terminated.

SECTION III—TREATMENT OF PERSONS IN THE POWER OF A PARTY TO THE CONFLICT

CHAPTER I—FIELD OF APPLICATION AND PROTECTION OF PERSONS
AND OBJECTS

Article 72—Field of application

The provisions of this Section are additional to the rules concerning humanitarian protection of civilians and civilian objects in the power of a Party to the conflict contained in the Fourth Convention, particularly Parts I and III thereof, as well as to other applicable rules of international law relating to the protection of fundamental human rights during international armed conflict.

Article 73—Refugees and stateless persons

Persons who, before the beginning of hostilities, were considered as stateless persons or refugees under the relevant international instruments accepted by the Parties concerned or under the national legislation of the State of refuge or State of residence shall be protected persons within the meaning of Parts I and III of the Fourth Convention, in all circumstances and without any adverse distinction.

Article 74—Reunion of dispersed families

The High Contracting Parties and the Parties to the conflict shall facilitate in every possible way the reunion of families dispersed as a result of armed conflicts and shall encourage in particular the work of the humanitarian organisations engaged in this task in accordance with the provisions of the Conventions and of this Protocol and in conformity with their respective security regulations.

Article 75—Fundamental guarantees

1. In so far as they are affected by a situation referred to in Article I of this Protocol, persons who are in the power of a Party to the conflict and who do not benefit from more favourable treatment under the Conventions or under this Protocol shall be treated humanely in all circumstances and shall enjoy, as a minimum, the protection provided by this Article without any adverse distinction based upon race, colour, sex, language, religion or belief, political or other opinion, national or social origin, wealth, birth or other status, or on any other similar criteria. Each Party shall respect the person, honour, convictions and religious practices of all such persons.

2. The following acts are and shall remain prohibited at any time and in any place whatsoever, whether committed by civilian or by military agents:

    (a) violence to the life, health, or physical or mental well-being of persons, in particular:

        (i) murder;

        (ii) torture of all kinds, whether physical or mental;

        (iii) corporal punishment; and

        (iv) mutilation;

(b) outrages upon personal dignity, in particular humiliating and degrading treatment, enforced prostitution and any form of indecent assault;

(c) the taking of hostages;

(d) collective punishments; and

(e) threats to commit any of the foregoing acts.

3. Any person arrested, detained or interned for actions related to the armed conflict shall be informed promptly, in a language he understands, of the reasons why these measures have been taken. Except in cases of arrest or detention for penal offences, such persons shall be released with the minimum delay possible and in any event as soon as the circumstances justifying the arrest, detention or internment have ceased to exist.

4. No sentence may be passed and no penalty may be executed on a person found guilty of a penal offence related to the armed conflict except pursuant to a conviction pronounced by an impartial and regularly constituted court respecting the generally recognised principles of regular judicial procedure, which include the following:

(a) the procedure shall provide for an accused to be informed without delay of the particulars of the offence alleged against him and shall afford the accused before and during his trial all necessary rights and means of defence;

(b) no one shall be convicted of an offence except on the basis of individual penal responsibility;

(c) no one shall be accused or convicted of a criminal offence on account of any act or omission which did not constitute a criminal offence under the national or international law to which he was subject at the time when it was committed; nor shall a heavier penalty be imposed than that which was applicable at the time when the criminal offence was committed; if, after the commission of the offence, provision is made by law for the imposition of a lighter penalty, the offender shall benefit thereby;

(d) anyone charged with an offence is presumed innocent until proved guilty according to law;

(e) anyone charged with an offence shall have the right to be tried in his presence;

(f) no one shall be compelled to testify against himself or to confess guilt;

(g) anyone charged with an offence shall have the right to examine, or have examined, the witnesses against him and to obtain the attendance and examination of witnesses on his behalf under the same conditions as witnesses against him;

(h) no one shall be prosecuted or punished by the same Party for an offence in respect of which a final judgement acquitting or convicting that person has been previously pronounced under the same law and judicial procedure;

(i) anyone prosecuted for an offence shall have the right to have the judgement pronounced publicly; and

(j) a convicted person shall be advised on conviction of his judicial and other remedies and of the time-limits within which they may be exercised.

5. Women whose liberty has been restricted for reasons related to the armed conflict shall be held in quarters separated from men's quarters. They shall be under the immediate supervision of women. Nevertheless, in cases where families are detained or interned, they shall, whenever possible, be held in the same place and accommodated as family units.

6. Persons who are arrested, detained or interned for reasons related to the armed conflict shall enjoy the protection provided by this Article until their final release, repatriation or re-establishment, even after the end of the armed conflict.

7. In order to avoid any doubt concerning the prosecution and trial of persons accused of war crimes or crimes against humanity, the following principles shall apply:

(a) persons who are accused of such crimes should be submitted for the purpose of prosecution and trial in accordance with the applicable rules of international law; and

(b) any such persons who do not benefit from more favourable treatment under the Conventions or this Protocol shall be accorded the treatment provided by this Article, whether or not the crimes of which they are accused constitute grave breaches of the Conventions or of this Protocol.

8. No provision of this Article may be construed as limiting or infringing any other more favourable provision granting greater protection, under any applicable rules of international law, to persons covered by paragraph 1.

CHAPTER II—MEASURES IN FAVOUR OF WOMEN AND CHILDREN

Article 76—Protection of women

1. Women shall be the object of special respect and shall be protected in particular against rape, forced prostitution and any other form of indecent assault.

2. Pregnant women and mothers having dependant infants who are arrested, detained or interned for reasons related to the armed conflict, shall have their cases considered with the utmost priority.

3. To the maximum extent feasible, the Parties to the conflict shall endeavour to avoid the pronouncement of the death penalty on pregnant women or mothers having dependant infants, for an offence related to the armed conflict. The death penalty for such offences shall not be executed on such women.

Article 77—Protection of children

1. Children shall be the object of special respect and shall be protected against any form of indecent assault. The Parties to the conflict shall provide them with the care and aid they require, whether because of their age or for any other reason.

2. The Parties to the conflict shall take all feasible measures in order that children who have not attained the age of fifteen years do not take a direct part in hostilities and, in particular, they shall refrain from recruiting them into their armed forces. In recruiting among those persons who have attained the age of fifteen years but who have not attained the age of eighteen years, the Parties to the conflict shall endeavour to give priority to those who are oldest.

3. If, in exceptional cases, despite the provisions of paragraph 2, children who have not attained the age of fifteen years take a direct part in hostilities and fall into the power of an adverse Party, they shall continue to benefit from the special protection accorded by this Article, whether or not they are prisoners of war.

4. If arrested, detained or interned for reasons related to the armed conflict, children shall be held in quarters separate from the quarters of adults, except where families are accommodated as family units as provided in Article 75, paragraph 5.

5. The death penalty for an offence related to the armed conflict shall not be executed on persons who had not attained the age of eighteen years at the time the offence was committed.

Article 78—Evacuation of children

1. No Party to the conflict shall arrange for the evacuation of children, other than its own nationals, to a foreign country except for a temporary evacuation where compelling reasons of the health or medical treatment of the children or, except in occupied territory, their safety, so require. Where the parents or legal guardians can be found, their written consent to such evacuation is required. If these persons cannot be found, the written consent to such evacuation of the persons who by law or custom are primarily responsible for the care of the children is required. Any such evacuation shall be supervised by the Protecting Power in agreement with the Parties concerned, namely, the Party arranging for the evacuation, the Party receiving the children and any Parties whose nationals are being evacuated. In each case, all Parties to the conflict shall take all feasible precautions to avoid endangering the evacuation.

2. Whenever an evacuation occurs pursuant to paragraph 1, each child's education, including his religious and moral education as his parents desire, shall be provided while he is away with the greatest possible continuity.

3. With a view to facilitating the return to their families and country of children evacuated pursuant to this Article, the authorities of the Party arranging for the evacuation and, as appropriate, the authorities of the receiving country shall establish for each child a card with photographs, which they shall send to the Central Tracing Agency of the International Committee of the Red Cross. Each card shall bear, whenever possible, and whenever it involves no risk of harm to the child, the following information:

    (a) surname(s) of the child;

    (b) the child's first name(s);

    (c) the child's sex;

    (d) the place and date of birth (or, if that date is not known, the approximate age);

    (e) the father's full name;

    (f) the mother's full name and her maiden name;

    (g) the child's next-of-kin;

    (h) the child's nationality;

    (i) the child's native language, and any other languages he speaks;

(j) the address of the child's family;
(k) any identification number for the child:
(l) the child's state of health;
(m) the child's blood group;
(n) any distinguishing features;
(o) the date on which and the place where the child was found;
(p) the date on which and the place from which the child left the country;
(q) the child's religion, if any;
(r) the child's present address in the receiving country;
(s) should the child die before his return, the date, place and circumstances of death and place of interment.

CHAPTER III—JOURNALISTS

Article 79—Measures of protection for journalists

1. Journalists engaged in dangerous professional missions in areas of armed conflict shall be considered as civilians within the meaning of Article 50, paragraph 1.

2. They shall be protected as such under the Conventions and this Protocol, provided that they take no action adversely affecting their status as civilians, and without prejudice to the right of war correspondents accredited to the armed forces to the status provided for in Article 4A(4) of the Third Convention.

3. They may obtain an identity card similar to the model in Annex II of this Protocol. This card, which shall be issued by the government of the State of which the journalist is a national or in whose territory he resides or in which the news medium employing him is located, shall attest to his status as a journalist.

PART V

EXECUTION OF THE CONVENTIONS AND OF THIS PROTOCOL

SECTION I—GENERAL PROVISIONS

Article 80—Measures for execution

1. The High Contracting Parties and the Parties to the conflict shall without delay take all necessary measures for the execution of their obligations under the Conventions and this Protocol.

2. The High Contracting Parties and the Parties to the conflict shall give orders and instructions to ensure observance of the Conventions and this Protocol, and shall supervise their execution.

Article 81—Activities of the Red Cross and other humanitarian organisations

1. The Parties to the conflict shall grant to the International Committee of the Red Cross all facilities within their power so as to enable it to carry out the humanitarian functions assigned to it by the Conventions and this Protocol in order to ensure protection and assistance to the victims of conflicts; the International Committee of the Red Cross may also carry out any other humanitarian activities in favour of these victims, subject to the consent of the Parties to the conflict concerned.

2. The Parties to the conflict shall grant to their respective Red Cross (Red Crescent, Red Lion and Sun) organisations the facilities necessary for carrying out their humanitarian activities in favour of the victims of the conflict, in accordance with the provisions of the Conventions and this Protocol and the fundamental principles of the Red Cross as formulated by the International Conferences of the Red Cross.

3. The High Contracting Parties and the Parties to the conflict shall facilitate in every possible way the assistance which Red Cross (Red Crescent, Red Lion and Sun) organisations and the League of Red Cross Societies extend to the victims of conflicts in accordance with the provisions of the Conventions and this Protocol and with the fundamental principles of the Red Cross as formulated by the International Conferences of the Red Cross.

4. The High Contracting Parties and the Parties to the conflict shall, as far as possible, make facilities similar to those mentioned in paragraphs 2 and 3 available to the other humanitarian organisations referred to in the Conventions and this Protocol which are duly authorised by the respective Parties to the conflict and which perform their humanitarian activities in accordance with the provisions of the Conventions and this Protocol.

Article 82—Legal advisers in armed forces

The High Contracting Parties at all times, and the Parties to the conflict in time of armed conflict, shall ensure that legal advisers are available, when necessary, to advise military commanders at the appropriate level on the application of the Conventions and this Protocol and on the appropriate instruction to be given to the armed forces on this subject.

Article 83—Dissemination

1. The High Contracting Parties undertake, in time of peace as in time of armed conflict, to disseminate the Conventions and this Protocol as widely as possible in their respective countries and, in particular, to include the study thereof in their programmes of military instruction and to encourage the study thereof by the civilian population, so that those instruments may become known to the armed forces and to the civilian population.

2. Any military or civilian authorities who, in time of armed conflict, assume responsibilities in respect of the application of the Conventions and this Protocol shall be fully acquainted with the text thereof.

Article 84—Rules of application

The High Contracting Parties shall communicate to one another, as soon as possible, through the depositary and, as appropriate, through the Protecting Powers, their official translations of this Protocol, as well as the laws and regulations which they may adopt to ensure its application.

SECTION II—REPRESSION OF BREACHES OF THE CONVENTIONS AND OF THIS PROTOCOL

Article 85—Repression of breaches of this Protocol

1. The provisions of the Conventions relating to the repression of breaches and grave breaches, supplemented by this Section, shall apply to the repression of breaches and grave breaches of this Protocol.

2. Acts described as grave breaches in the Conventions are grave breaches of this Protocol if committed against persons in the power of an adverse Party protected by Articles 44, 45 and 73 of this Protocol, or against the wounded, sick and shipwrecked of the adverse Party who are protected by this Protocol, or against those medical or religious personnel, medical units or medical transports which are under the control of the adverse Party and are protected by this Protocol.

3. In addition to the grave breaches defined in Article 11, the following acts shall be regarded as grave breaches of this Protocol, when committed wilfully, in violation of the relevant provisions of this Protocol, and causing death or serious injury to body or health:
  (a) making the civilian population or individual civilians the object of attack;
  (b) launching an indiscriminate attack affecting the civilian population or civilian objects in the knowledge that such attack will cause excessive loss of life, injury to civilians or damage to civilian objects, as defined in Article 57, paragraph 2(a)(iii);
  (c) launching an attack against works or installations containing dangerous forces in the knowledge that such attack will cause excessive loss of life, injury to civilians or damage to civilian objects, as defined in Article 57, paragraph 2(a)(iii);
  (d) making non-defended localities and demilitarised zones the object of attack;
  (e) making a person the object of attack in the knowledge that he is *hors de combat*;
  (f) the perfidious use, in violation of Article 37, of the distinctive emblem of the red cross, red crescent or red lion and sun or of other protective signs recognised by the Conventions or this Protocol.

4. In addition to the grave breaches defined in the preceding paragraphs and in the Conventions, the following shall be regarded as grave breaches of this Protocol, when committed wilfully and in violation of the Conventions or the Protocol:
  (a) the transfer by the Occupying Power of parts of its own civilian population into the territory it occupies, or the deportation or transfer of all or parts of the population of the occupied territory within or outside this territory, in violation of Article 49 of the Fourth Convention;
  (b) unjustifiable delay in the repatriation of prisoners of war or civilians;
  (c) practices of *apartheid* and other inhuman and degrading practices involving outrages upon personal dignity, based on racial discrimination;
  (d) making the clearly recognised historic monuments, works of art or places of worship which constitute the cultural or spiritual heritage of peoples and to which special protec-

tion has been given by special arrangement, for example, within the framework of a competent international organisation, the object of attack, causing as a result extensive destruction thereof, where there is no evidence of the violation by the adverse Party of Article 53, sub-paragraph (b), and when such historic monuments, works of art and places of worship are not located in the immediate proximity of military objectives;

(e) depriving a person protected by the Conventions or referred to in paragraph 2 of this Article of the rights of fair and regular trial.

5. Without prejudice to the application of the Conventions and of this Protocol, grave breaches of these instruments shall be regarded as war crimes.

Article 86—Failure to act

1. The High Contracting Parties and the Parties to the conflict shall repress grave breaches, and take measures necessary to suppress all other breaches, of the Conventions or of this Protocol which result from a failure to act when under a duty to do so.

2. The fact that a breach of the Conventions or of this Protocol was committed by a subordinate does not absolve his superiors from penal or disciplinary responsibility, as the case may be, if they knew, or had information which should have enabled them to conclude in the circumstances at the time, that he was committing or was going to commit such a breach and if they did not take all feasible measures within their power to prevent or repress the breach.

Article 87—Duty of commanders

1. The High Contracting Parties and the Parties to the conflict shall require military commanders, with respect to members of the armed forces under their command and other persons under their control, to prevent and, where necessary, to suppress and to report to competent authorities breaches of the Conventions and of this Protocol.

2. In order to prevent and suppress breaches, High Contracting Parties and Parties to the conflict shall require that, commensurate with their level of responsibility, commanders ensure that members of the armed forces under their command are aware of their obligations under the Conventions and this Protocol.

3. The High Contracting Parties and Parties to the conflict shall require any commander who is aware that subordinates or other persons under his control are going to commit or have committed a breach of the Conventions or of this Protocol, to initiate such steps as are necessary to prevent such violations of the Conventions or this Protocol, and, where appropriate, to initiate disciplinary or penal action against violators thereof.

Article 88—Mutual assistance in criminal matters

1. The High Contracting Parties shall afford one another the greatest measure of assistance in connection with criminal proceedings brought in respect of grave breaches of the Conventions or of this Protocol.

2. Subject to the rights and obligations established in the Conventions and in Article 85, paragraph 1, of this Protocol, and when circumstances permit, the High Contracting Parties shall co-operate in the matter of extradition. They shall give due consideration to the request of the State in whose territory the alleged offence has occurred.

3. The law of the High Contracting Party requested shall apply in all cases. The provisions of the preceding paragraphs shall not, however, affect the obligations arising from the provisions of any other treaty of a bilateral or multilateral nature which governs or will govern the whole or part of the subject of mutual assistance in criminal matters.

Article 89—Co-operation

In situations of serious violations of the Conventions or of this Protocol, the High Contracting Parties undertake to act, jointly or individually, in co-operation with the United Nations and in conformity with the United Nations Charter.

Article 90—International Fact-Finding Commission

1. (a) An International Fact-Finding Commission (hereinafter referred to as "the Commission") consisting of fifteen members of high moral standing and acknowledged impartiality shall be established.

(b) When not less than twenty High Contracting Parties have agreed to accept the competence of the Commission pursuant to paragraph 2, the depositary shall then, and at intervals of five years thereafter, convene a meeting of representatives of those High Contracting Parties for the purpose of electing the members of the Commission. At the meeting, the representatives shall elect the members of the Commission by secret ballot from a list of persons to which each of those High Contracting Parties may nominate one person.

(c) The members of the Commission shall serve in their personal capacity and shall hold office until the election of new members at the ensuing meeting.

(d) At the election, the High Contracting Parties shall ensure that the persons to be elected to the Commission individually possess the qualifications required and that, in the Commission as a whole equitable geographical representation is assured.

(e) In the case of a casual vacancy, the Commission itself shall fill the vacancy, having due regard to the provisions of the preceding sub-paragraphs.

(f) The depositary shall make available to the Commission the necessary administrative facilities for the performance of its functions.

2. (a) The High Contracting Parties may at the time of signing, ratifying or acceding to the Protocol, or at any other subsequent time, declare that they recognise *ipso facto* and without special agreement, in relation to any other High Contracting Party accepting the same obligation, the competence of the Commission to enquire into allegations by such other Party, as authorised by this Article.

(b) The declarations referred to above shall be deposited with the depositary, which shall transmit copies thereof to the High Contracting Parties.

(c) The Commission shall be competent to:

(i) enquire into any facts alleged to be a grave breach as defined in the Conventions and this Protocol or other serious violation of the Conventions or of this Protocol;

(ii) facilitate, through its good offices, the restoration of an attitude of respect for the Conventions and this Protocol.

(d) In other situations, the Commission shall institute an enquiry at the request of a Party to the conflict only with the consent of the other Party or Parties concerned.

(e) Subject to the foregoing provisions of this paragraph, the provisions of Article 52 of the First Convention, Article 53 of the Second Convention, Article 132 of the Third Convention and Article 149 of the Fourth Convention shall continue to apply to any alleged violation of the Conventions and shall extend to any alleged violation of this Protocol.

3. (a) Unless otherwise agreed by the Parties concerned, all enquiries shall be undertaken by a Chamber consisting of seven members appointed as follows:

(i) five members of the Commission, not nationals of any Party to the conflict, appointed by the President of the Commission on the basis of equitable representation of the geographical areas, after consultation with the Parties to the conflict;

(ii) two *ad hoc* members, not nationals of any Party to the conflict, one to be appointed by each side.

(b) Upon receipt of the request for an enquiry, the President of the Commission shall specify an appropriate time-limit for setting up a Chamber. If any *ad hoc* member has not been appointed within the time-limit, the President shall immediately appoint such additional member or members of the Commission as may be necessary to complete the membership of the Chamber.

4. (a) The Chamber set up under paragraph 3 to undertake an enquiry shall invite the Parties to the conflict to assist it and to present evidence. The Chamber may also seek such other evidence as it deems appropriate and may carry out an investigation of the situation *in loco*.

(b) All evidence shall be fully disclosed to the Parties, which shall have the right to comment on it to the Commission.

(c) Each Party shall have the right to challenge such evidence.

5. (a) The Commission shall submit to the Parties a report on the findings of fact of the Chamber, with such recommendations as it may deem appropriate.

(b) If the Chamber is unable to secure sufficient evidence for factual and impartial findings, the Commission shall state the reasons for that inability.

(c) The Commission shall not report its findings publicly, unless all the Parties to the conflict have requested the Commission to do so.

6. The Commission shall establish its own rules, including rules for the presidency of the Commission and the presidency of the Chamber. Those rules shall ensure that the functions of the

President of the Commission are exercised at all times and that, in the case of an enquiry, they are exercised by a person who is not a national of a Party to the conflict.

7. The administrative expenses of the Commission shall be met by contributions from the High Contracting Parties which made declarations under paragraph 2, and by voluntary contributions. The Party or Parties to the conflict requesting an enquiry shall advance the necessary funds for expenses incurred by a Chamber and shall be reimbursed by the Party or Parties against which the allegations are made to the extent of fifty per cent of the costs of the Chamber. Where there are counter-allegations before the Chamber each side shall advance fifty per cent of the necessary funds.

Article 91—Responsibility

A Party to the conflict which violates the provisions of the Conventions or of this Protocol shall, if the case demands, be liable to pay compensation. It shall be responsible for all acts committed by persons forming part of its armed forces.

PART VI

FINAL PROVISIONS

Article 92—Signature

This Protocol shall be open for signature by the Parties to the Conventions six months after the signing of the Final Act and will remain open for a period of twelve months.

Article 93—Ratification

This Protocol shall be ratified as soon as possible. The instruments of ratification shall be deposited with the Swiss Federal Council, depositary of the Conventions.

Article 94—Accession

This Protocol shall be open for accession by any Party to the Conventions which has not signed it. The instruments of accession shall be deposited with the depositary.

Article 95—Entry into force

1. This Protocol shall enter into force six months after two instruments of ratification or accession have been deposited.

2. For each Party to the Conventions thereafter ratifying or acceding to this Protocol, it shall enter into force six months after the deposit by such Party of its instrument of ratification or accession.

Article 96—Treaty relations upon entry into force of this Protocol

1. When the Parties to the Conventions are also Parties to this Protocol, the Conventions shall apply as supplemented by this Protocol.

2. When one of the Parties to the conflict is not bound by this Protocol, the Parties to the Protocol shall remain bound by it in their mutual relations. They shall furthermore be bound by this Protocol in relation to each of the Parties which are not bound by it, if the latter accepts and applies the provisions thereof.

3. The authority representing a people engaged against a High Contracting Party in an armed conflict of the type referred to in Article 1, paragraph 4, may undertake to apply the Conventions and this Protocol in relation to that conflict by means of a unilateral declaration addressed to the depositary. Such declaration shall, upon its receipt by the depositary, have in relation to that conflict the following effects:

   (a) the Conventions and this Protocol are brought into force for the said authority as a Party to the conflict with immediate effect;

   (b) the said authority assumes the same rights and obligations as those which have been assumed by a High Contracting Party to the Conventions and this Protocol; and

   (c) the Conventions and this Protocol are equally binding upon all Parties to the conflict.

Article 97—Amendment

1. Any High Contracting Party may propose amendments to this Protocol. The text of any proposed amendment shall be communicated to the depositary, which shall decide, after consul-

tation with all the High Contracting Parties and the International Committee of the Red Cross, whether a conference should be convened to consider the proposed amendment.

2. The depositary shall invite to that conference all the High Contracting Parties as well as the Parties to the Conventions, whether or not they are signatories of this Protocol.

Article 98—Revision of Annex I

1. Not later than four years after the entry into force of this Protocol and thereafter at intervals of not less than four years, the International Committee of the Red Cross shall consult the High Contracting Parties concerning Annex I to this Protocol and, if it considers it necessary, may propose a meeting of technical experts to review Annex I and to propose such amendments to it as may appear to be desirable. Unless, within six months of the communication of a proposal for such a meeting to the High Contracting Parties, one third of them object, the International Committee of the Red Cross shall convene the meeting, inviting also observers of appropriate international organisations. Such a meeting shall also be convened by the International Committee of the Red Cross at any time at the request of one third of the High Contracting Parties.

2. The depositary shall convene a conference of the High Contracting Parties and the Parties to the Conventions to consider amendments proposed by the meeting of technical experts if, after that meeting, the International Committee of the Red Cross or one third of the High Contracting Parties so request.

3. Amendments to Annex I may be adopted at such a conference by a two-thirds majority of the High Contracting Parties present and voting.

4. The depositary shall communicate any amendment so adopted to the High Contracting Parties and to the Parties to the Conventions. The amendment shall be considered to have been accepted at the end of a period of one year after it has been so communicated, unless within that period a declaration of non-acceptance of the amendment has been communicated to the depositary by not less than one third of the High Contracting Parties.

5. An amendment considered to have been accepted in accordance with paragraph 4 shall enter into force three months after its acceptance for all High Contracting Parties other than those which have made a declaration of non-acceptance in accordance with that paragraph. Any Party making such a declaration may at any time withdraw it and the amendment shall then enter into force for that Party three months thereafter.

6. The depositary shall notify the High Contracting Parties and the Parties to the Conventions of the entry into force of any amendment, of the Parties bound thereby, of the date of its entry into force in relation to each Party, of declarations of non-acceptance made in accordance with paragraph 4, and of withdrawals of such declarations.

Article 99—Denunciation

1. In case a High Contracting Party should denounce this Protocol, the denunciation shall only take effect one year after receipt of the instrument of denunciation. If, however, on the expiry of that year the denouncing Party is engaged in one of the situations referred to in Article 1, the denunciation shall not take effect before the end of the armed conflict or occupation and not, in any case, before operations connected with the final release, repatriation or re-establishment of the persons protected by the Conventions or this Protocol have been terminated.

2. The denunciation shall be notified in writing to the depositary, which shall transmit it to all the High Contracting Parties.

3. The denunciation shall have effect only in respect of the denouncing Party.

4. Any denunciation under paragraph 1 shall not affect the obligations already incurred, by reason of the armed conflict, under this Protocol by such denouncing Party in respect of any act committed before this denunciation becomes effective.

Article 100—Notifications

The depositary shall inform the High Contracting Parties as well as the Parties to the Conventions, whether or not they are signatories of this Protocol, of:

(a) signatures affixed to this Protocol and the deposit of instruments of ratification and accession under Articles 93 and 94;

(b) the date of entry into force of this Protocol under Article 95;
(c) communications and declarations received under Articles 84, 90 and 97;
(d) declarations received under Article 96, paragraph 3, which shall be communicated by the quickest methods; and
(e) denunciations under Article 99.

Article 101—Registration

1. After its entry into force, this Protocol shall be transmitted by the depositary to the Secretariat of the United Nations for registration and publication, in accordance with Article 102 of the Charter of the United Nations.
2. The depositary shall also inform the Secretariat of the United Nations of all ratifications, accessions and denunciations received by it with respect to this Protocol.

Article 102—Authentic texts

The original of this Protocol, of which the Arabic, Chinese, English, French, Russian and Spanish texts are equally authentic, shall be deposited with the depositary, which shall transmit certified true copies thereof to all the Parties to the Conventions.

ANNEX I

[Note: the following text includes amendments to Annex I made under Article 98 of the Protocol which entered into force on 1st March 1994]

REGULATIONS CONCERNING IDENTIFICATION

Article 1—General provisions

1. The regulations concerning identification in this Annex implement the relevant provisions of the Geneva Conventions and the Protocol; they are intended to facilitate the identification of personnel, material, units, transports and installations protected under the Geneva Conventions and the Protocol.
2. These rules do not in and of themselves establish the right to protection. This right is governed by the relevant articles in the Conventions and the Protocol.
3. The competent authorities may, subject to the relevant provisions of the Geneva Conventions and the Protocol, at all times regulate the use, display, illumination and detectability of the distinctive emblems and signals.
4. The High Contracting Parties and in particular the Parties to the conflict are invited at all times to agree upon additional or other signals, means or systems which enhance the possibility of identification and take full advantage of technological developments in this field.

CHAPTER I—IDENTITY CARDS

Article 2—Identity card for permanent civilian medical and religious personnel

1. The identity card for permanent civilian medical and religious personnel referred to in Article 18, paragraph 3, of the Protocol should:
(a) bear the distinctive emblem and be of such size that it can be carried in the pocket;
(b) be as durable as practicable;
(c) be worded in the national or official language and, in addition and when appropriate, in the local language of the region concerned;
(d) mention the name, the date of birth (or, if that date is not available, the age at the time of issue) and the identity number, if any, of the holder;
(e) state in what capacity the holder is entitled to the protection of the Conventions and of the Protocol;
(f) bear the photograph of the holder as well as his signature or his thumbprint, or both;
(g) bear the stamp and signature of the competent authority;
(h) state the date of issue and date of expiry of the card;
(i) indicate, whenever possible, the holder's blood group, on the reverse side of the card.
2. The identity card shall be uniform throughout the territory of each High Contracting Party and, as far as possible, of the same type for all Parties to the conflict. The Parties to the conflict may be guided by the single-language model shown in Figure 1. At the outbreak of hostilities, they shall transmit to each other a specimen of the model they are using, if such model differs

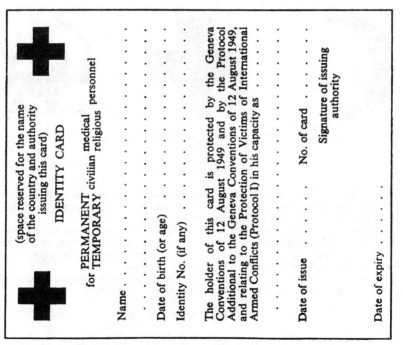

Fig. 1: Model of identity card (format: 74 mm × 105 mm)

from that shown in Figure 1. The identity card shall be made out, if possible, in duplicate, one copy being kept by the issuing authority, which should maintain control of the cards which it has issued.

3. In no circumstances may permanent civilian medical and religious personnel be deprived of their identity cards. In the event of the loss of a card, they shall be entitled to obtain a duplicate copy.

Article 3—Identity card for temporary civilian medical and religious personnel

1. The identity card for temporary civilian medical and religious personnel should, whenever possible, be similar to that provided for in Article 1 of these Regulations. The Parties to the conflict may be guided by the model shown in Figure 1.

2. When circumstances preclude the provision to temporary civilian medical and religious personnel of identity cards similar to those described in Article 2 of these Regulations, the said personnel may be provided with a certificate signed by the competent authority certifying that the person to whom it is issued is assigned to duty as temporary personnel and stating, if possible, the duration of such assignment and his right to wear the distinctive emblem. The certificate should mention the holder's name and date of birth (or if that is not available, his age at the time when the certificate was issued), his function and identity number, if any. It shall bear his signature or his thumbprint, or both.

CHAPTER II—THE DISTINCTIVE EMBLEM

Article 4—Shape

The distinctive emblem (red on a white ground) shall be as large as appropriate under the circumstances. For the shapes of the cross, the crescent or the lion and sun, the High Contracting Parties may be guided by the models shown in Figure 2.

Fig. 2: Distinctive emblems in red on a white ground

Article 5—Use

1. The distinctive emblem shall, whenever possible, be displayed on a flat surface, on flags or in any other way appropriate to the lay of the land, so that it is visible from as many directions and from as far away as possible, and in particular from the air.

2. At night or when visibility is reduced, the distinctive emblem may be lighted or illuminated.

3. The distinctive emblem may be made of materials which make it recognisable by technical means of detecting. The red parts should be painted on top of black primer paint in order to facilitate its identification, in particular by infrared instruments.

4. Medical and religious personnel carrying out their duties in the battle area shall, as far as possible, wear headgear and clothing bearing the distinctive emblem.

CHAPTER III—DISTINCTIVE SIGNALS

Article 6—Use

1. All distinctive signals specified in this Chapter may be used by medical units or transports.

2. These signals, at the exclusive disposal of medical units and transports, shall not be used for any other purpose, the use of the light signal being reserved (see paragraph 3 below).

3. In the absence of a special agreement between the Parties to the conflict reserving the use of flashing blue lights for the identification of medical vehicles, ships and craft, the use of such signals for other vehicles, ships and craft is not prohibited.

4. Temporary medical aircraft which cannot, either for lack of time or because of their characteristics, be marked with the distinctive emblem, may use the distinctive signals authorised in this Chapter.

Article 7—Light signal

1. The light signal, consisting of a flashing blue light as defined in the Airworthiness Technical Manual of the International Civil Aviation Organisation (ICAO) Doc. 9051, is established for the use of medical aircraft to signal their identity. No other aircraft shall use this signal. Medical aircraft using the flashing blue light should exhibit such lights as may be necessary to make the light signal visible from as many directions as possible.
2. In accordance with the provisions of Chapter XIV, para. 4 of the International Maritime Organisation (IMO) International Code of Signals, vessels protected by the Geneva Conventions of 1949 and the Protocol should exhibit one or more flashing blue lights visible from any direction.
3. Medical vehicles should exhibit one or more flashing blue lights visible from as far away as possible. The High Contracting Parties and, in particular, the Parties to the conflict which use lights of other colours should give notification of this.
4. The recommended blue colour is obtained when its chromaticity is within the boundaries of the International Commission on Illumination (ICI) chromaticity diagram defined bv the following equations:

green boundary $y = 0.065 + 0.805 \, x$;

white boundary $y = 0.400 - x$;

purple boundary $x = 0.133 + 0.600 \, y$.

The recommended flashing rate of the blue light is between sixty and one hundred flashes per minute.

Article 8—Radio signal

1. The radio signal shall consist of the urgency signal and the distinctive signal as described in the International Telecommunication Union (ITU) Radio Regulations (RR Articles 40 and N 40).
2. The radio message preceded by the urgency and distinctive signals mentioned in paragraph 1 shall be transmitted in English at appropriate intervals on a frequency or frequencies specified for this purpose in the Radio Regulations, and shall convey the following data relating to the medical transports concerned:
(a) call sign or other recognised means of identification;
(b) position;
(c) number and type of vehicles;
(d) intended route;
(e) estimated time *en route* and of departure and arrival, as appropriate;
(f) any other information, such as flight altitude, guarded radio frequencies, languages used and secondary surveillance radar modes and codes.
3. In order to facilitate the communications referred to in paragraphs 1 and 2, as well as the communications referred to in Articles 22, 23 and 25 to 31 of the Protocol, the High Contracting Parties, the Parties to a conflict, or one of the Parties to a conflict, acting in agreement or alone, may designate, in accordance with the Table of Frequency Allocations in the Radio Regulations annexed to the International Telecommunication Convention, and publish selected national frequencies to be used by them for such communications. The International Telecommunication Union shall be notified of these frequencies in accordance with procedures approved by a World Administrative Radio Conference.

Article 9—Electronic identification

1. The Secondary Surveillance Radar (SSR) system, as specified in Annex 10 to the Chicago Convention on International Civil Aviation of 7 December 1944, as amended from time to time, may be used to identify and to follow the course of medical aircraft. The SSR mode and code to be reserved for the exclusive use of medical aircraft shall be established by the High Contracting Parties, the Parties to a conflict, or one of the Parties to a conflict, acting in agreement or alone, in accordance with procedures to be recommended by the International Civil Aviation Organisation.
2. Protected medical transports may, for their identification and location, use standard aeronautical radar transponders and/or maritime search and rescue radar transponders.

It should be possible for protected medical transports to be identified by other vessels or aircraft equipped with secondary surveillance radar by means of a code transmitted by a radar transponder, e.g. in mode 3/A, fitted on the medical transports.

The code transmitted by the medical transport transponder should be assigned to that transport by the competent authorities and notified to all the Parties to the conflict.

3. It should be possible for medical transports to be identified by submarines by the appropriate underwater acoustic signals transmitted by the medical transports.

The underwater acoustic signal shall consist of the call sign (or any other recognised means of identification of medical transport) of the ship preceded by the single group YYY transmitted in morse on an appropriate acoustic frequency, e.g. 5kHz.

Parties to a conflict wishing to use the underwater acoustic identification signal described above shall inform the Parties concerned of the signal as soon as possible, and shall, when notifying the use of their hospital ships, confirm the frequency to be employed.

4. Parties to a conflict may, by special agreement between them, establish for their use a similar electronic system for the identification of medical vehicles, and medical ships and craft.

CHAPTER IV—COMMUNICATIONS

Article 10—Radiocommunications

1. The urgency signal and the distinctive signal provided for in Article 8 may precede appropriate radiocommunications by medical units and transports in the application of the procedures carried out under Articles 22, 23 and 25 to 31 of the Protocol.

2. The medical transports referred to in Articles 40 (Section II, No. 3209) and N 40 (Section III, No. 3214) of the ITU Radio Regulations may also transmit their communications by satellite systems, in accordance with the provisions of Articles 37, N 37 and 59 of the ITU Radio Regulations for the Mobile-Satellite Services.

Article 11—Use of international codes

Medical units and transports may also use the codes and signals laid down by the International Telecommunication Union, the International Civil Aviation Organisation and the International Maritime Organisation. These codes and signals shall be used in accordance with the standards, practices and procedures established by these Organisations.

Article 12—Other means of communication

When two-way radiocommunication is not possible, the signals provided for in the International Code of Signals adopted by the International Maritime Organisation or in the appropriate Annex to the Chicago Convention on International Civil Aviation of 7 December 1944, as amended from time to time, may be used.

Article 13—Flight plans

The agreements and notifications relating to flight plans provided for in Article 29 of the Protocol shall as far as possible be formulated in accordance with procedures laid down by the International Civil Aviation Organisation.

Article 14—Signals and procedures for the interception of medical aircraft

If an intercepting aircraft is used to verify the identity of a medical aircraft in flight or to require it to land in accordance with Articles 30 and 31 of the Protocol, the standard visual and radio interception procedures prescribed by Annex 2 to the Chicago Convention on International Civil Aviation of 7 December 1944, as amended from time to time, should be used by the intercepting and the medical aircraft.

CHAPTER V—CIVIL DEFENCE

Article 15—Identity card

1. The identity card of the civil defence personnel provided for in Article 66, paragraph 3, of the Protocol is governed by the relevant provisions of Article 2 of these Regulations.

2. The identity card for civil defence personnel may follow the model shown in Figure 3.

3. If civil defence personnel are permitted to carry light individual weapons, an entry to that effect should be made on the card mentioned.

REVERSE SIDE

Height	Eyes	Hair . . . . .

Other distinguishing marks or information:

. . . . . .
. . . . . .

Weapons . . . . . .

PHOTO OF HOLDER

Stamp	Signature of holder or thumbprint or both

FRONT

(space reserved for the name of the country and authority issuing this card)

IDENTITY CARD
for civil defence personnel

Name . . . .

Date of birth (or age) . . . . . .

Identity No. (if any) . . . . . .

The holder of this card is protected by the Geneva Conventions of 12 August 1949 and by the Protocol Additional to the Geneva Conventions of 12 August 1949, and relating to the Protection of Victims of International Armed Conflicts (Protocol I) in his capacity as . . . . . .

. . . . . .

Date of issue . . . . . .   No. of card . . . . . .

Signature of issuing authority . . . . . .

Date of expiry . . . . . .

Fig. 3: Model of identity card for civil defence personnel
(format: 74 mm × 105 mm)

Article 16—International distinctive sign

1. The international distinctive sign of civil defence provided for in Article 66, paragraph 4, of the Protocol is an equilateral blue triangle on an orange ground. A model is shown in Figure 4:

Fig. 4: Blue triangle on an orange ground

2. It is recommended that:
(a) if the blue triangle is on a flag or armlet or tabard, the ground to the triangle be the orange flag, armlet or tabard;
(b) one of the angles of the triangle be pointed vertically upwards;
(c) no angle of the triangle touch the edge of the orange ground.
3. The international distinctive sign shall be as large as appropriate under the circumstances. The distinctive sign shall, whenever possible, be displayed on flat surfaces or on flags visible from as many directions and from as far away as possible. Subject to the instructions of the competent authority, civil defence personnel shall, as far as possible, wear headgear and clothing bearing the international distinctive sign. At night or when visibility is reduced, the sign may be lighted or illuminated; it may also be made of materials rendering it recognisable by technical means of detection.

CHAPTER VI—WORKS AND INSTALLATIONS CONTAINING DANGEROUS FORCES

Article 17—International special sign

1. The international special sign for works and installations containing dangerous forces, as provided for in Article 56, paragraph 7, of the Protocol, shall be a group of three bright orange circles of equal size, placed on the same axis, the distance between each circle being one radius, in accordance with Figure 5 illustrated below.
2. The sign shall be as large as appropriate under the circumstances. When displayed over an extended surface it may be repeated as often as appropriate under the circumstances. It shall, whenever possible, be displayed on flat surfaces or on flags so as to be visible from as many directions and from as far away as possible.
3. On a flag, the distance between the outer limits of the sign and the adjacent sides of the flag shall be one radius of a circle. The flag shall be rectangular and shall have a white ground.
4. At night or when visibility is reduced, the sign may be lighted or illuminated. It may also be made of materials rendering it recognisable by technical means of detection.

Fig. 5: International special sign for works and installations containing dangerous forces

ANNEX II

IDENTITY CARD FOR JOURNALISTS ON DANGEROUS PROFESSIONAL MISSIONS

FRONT

(Name of country issuing this card)

(اسم القطر المصدر لهذه البطاقة)

(Nombre del país que expide esta tarjeta)

(Nom du pays qui a délivré cette carte)

(Название страны, выдавшей настоящее удостоверение)

IDENTITY CARD FOR JOURNALISTS
ON DANGEROUS PROFESSIONAL MISSIONS

بطاقة الهوية الخاصة بالصحفين
المكلفين بمهمات مهنة خطرة

TARJETA DE IDENTIDAD DE PERIODISTA
EN MISION PELIGROSA

CARTE D'IDENTITÉ DE JOURNALISTE
EN MISSION PÉRILLEUSE

УДОСТОВЕРЕНИЕ ЖУРНАЛИСТА,
НАХОДЯЩЕГОСЯ В ОПАСНОЙ
КОМАНДИРОВКЕ

NOTICE

This identity card is issued to journalists on dangerous professional missions in areas of armed conflicts. The holder is entitled to be treated as a civilian under the Geneva Conventions of 12 August 1949, and their Additional Protocol I. The card must be carried at all times by the bearer. If he is detained, he shall at once hand it to the Detaining Authorities, to assist in his identification.

ملاحظة

تعرّف هذه البطاقة للصحفين المكلفين بمهمة مهنة خطرة في مناطق النزاعات المسلحة. ويحق لحاملها أن يعامل معاملة المدنيين حسب اتفاقيات جنيف المؤرخة في ١٢ آب/أغسطس ١٩٤٩ وبروتوكولها الإضافي الأول. ويجب أن يحمل صاحب البطاقة بطاقته في كل وقت. فإذا اعتقل يجب أن يسلّم فوراً البطاقة للسلطة التي تحتجزه تسهيلاً لتحديد هويته.

NOTA

La presente tarjeta de identidad se expide a los periodistas en misión profesional peligrosa en zonas de conflictos armados. Su titular tiene derecho a ser tratado como persona civil conforme a los Convenios de Ginebra del 12 de agosto de 1949 y su Protocolo adicional I. El titular debe llevar la tarjeta consigo, en todo momento. En caso de ser detenido, la entregará inmediatamente a las autoridades que lo detengan a fin de facilitar su identificación.

AVIS

La présente carte d'identité est délivrée aux journalistes en mission professionnelle périlleuse dans des zones de conflit armé. Le porteur a le droit d'être traité comme une personne civile aux termes des Conventions de Genève du 12 août 1949 et de leur Protocole additionnel I. La carte doit être portée en tout temps par son titulaire. Si celui-ci est arrêté, il la remettra immédiatement aux autorités qui le détiennent afin qu'elles puissent l'identifier.

ПРИМЕЧАНИЕ

Настоящее удостоверение выдается журналистам, находящимся в опасных профессиональных командировках в районах вооруженного конфликта. Его обладатель имеет право на обращение с ним как с гражданским лицом в соответствии с Женевскими Конвенциями от 12 августа 1949 г. и Дополнительным Протоколом I к ним. Владелец настоящего удостоверения должен постоянно иметь его при себе. В случае задержания он немедленно вручает его задерживающим властям для содействия установлению его личности.

REVERSE SIDE

Issued by (competent authority)
(السلطة المختصة)
Expedido por (autoridad competente)
Délivrée par (autorité compétente)
Выдано (компетентным властям)

Photograph
of bearer
الصورة
Fotografía
del titular
Photographie
du porteur
Фотография
предъявителя

Place
المكان
Lugar
Lieu
Место

Date
التاريخ
Fecha
Date
Дата

(Official seal imprint)
(خاتم رسمي)
(Sello oficial)
(Timbre de l'autorité délivrant la carte)
(Официальная печать)

(Signature of bearer)
(توقيع حامل البطاقة)
(Firma del titular)
(Signature du porteur)
(Подпись владельца)

Name
الاسم
Apellidos
Nom
Фамилия

First names
الاسم
Nombre
Prénom
Имя, Отчество

Place & date of birth
مكان وتاريخ الميلاد
Lugar y fecha de nacimiento
Lieu & date de naissance
Дата и место рождения

Correspondent of
يعمل
Corresponsal de
Correspondant de
Корреспондент

Specific occupation
مهنة صاحب البطاقة
Categoría profesional
Catégorie professionnelle
Род занятий

Valid for
تصلح لـ
Válido para
Valable pour
Действительно

Height
الطول
Estatura
Taille
Рост

Eyes
العينان
Ojos
Yeux
Глаза

Weight
الوزن
Peso
Poids
Вес

Hair
الشعر
Cabello
Cheveux
Волосы

Blood type
فصيلة الدم
Grupo sanguíneo
Groupe sanguin
Группа крови

Rh factor
عامل ريزوس
Factor Rh
Facteur Rh
Rh-фактор

Religion (optional)
الديانة (اختياري)
Religión (optativo)
Religion (facultatif)
Религия (факультативно)

Fingerprints (optional)
(بصمات الأصابع (اختياري)
Huellas dactilares (optativo)
Empreintes digitales (facultatif)
Отпечатки пальцев (факультативно)

(Left forefinger)
(السبابة اليسرى)
(Dedo índice izquierdo)
(Index gauche)
(Левый указательный палец)

(Right forefinger)
(السبابة اليمنى)
(Dedo índice derecho)
(Index droit)
(Правый указательный палец)

Special marks of identification
علامات مميزة للتعرف
Señas particulares
Signes particuliers
Особые приметы

SIXTH SCHEDULE

PROTOCOL II

PROTOCOL ADDITIONAL TO THE GENEVA CONVENTIONS OF 12 AUGUST 1949, AND RELATING TO THE PROTECTION OF VICTIMS OF NON-INTERNATIONAL ARMED CONFLICTS (PROTOCOL II)

Preamble

The High Contracting Parties,

Recalling that the humanitarian principles enshrined in Article 3 common to the Geneva Conventions of 12 August 1949, constitute the foundation of respect for the human person in cases of armed conflict not of an international character,

Recalling furthermore that international instruments relating to human rights offer a basic protection to the human person,

Emphasising the need to ensure a better protection for the victims of those armed conflicts,

Recalling that, in cases not covered by the law in force, the human person remains under the protection of the principles of humanity and the dictates of the public conscience,

Have agreed on the following:

PART I

SCOPE OF THIS PROTOCOL

Article 1—Material field of application

1. This Protocol, which develops and supplements Article 3 common to the Geneva Conventions of 12 August 1949 without modifying its existing conditions of application, shall apply to all armed conflicts which are not covered by Article 1 of the Protocol Additional to the Geneva Conventions of 12 August 1949, and relating to the Protection of Victims of International Armed Conflicts (Protocol I) and which take place in the territory of a High Contracting Party between its armed forces and dissident armed forces or other organised armed groups which, under responsible command, exercise such control over a part of its territory as to enable them to carry out sustained and concerted military operations and to implement this Protocol.

2. This Protocol shall not apply to situations of internal disturbances and tensions, such as riots, isolated and sporadic acts of violence and other acts of a similar nature, as not being armed conflicts.

Article 2—Personal field of application

1. This Protocol shall be applied without any adverse distinction founded on race, colour, sex, language, religion or belief, political or other opinion, national or social origin, wealth, birth or other status, or on any other similar criteria (hereinafter referred to as "adverse distinction") to all persons affected by an armed conflict as defined in Article 1.

2. At the end of the armed conflict, all the persons who have been deprived of their liberty or whose liberty has been restricted for reasons related to such conflict, as well as those deprived of their liberty or whose liberty is restricted after the conflict for the same reasons, shall enjoy the protection of Articles 5 and 6 until the end of such deprivation or restriction of liberty.

Article 3—Non-intervention

1. Nothing in this Protocol shall be invoked for the purpose of affecting the sovereignty of a State or the responsibility of the government, by all legitimate means, to maintain or re-establish law and order in the State or to defend the national unity and territorial integrity of the State.

2. Nothing in this Protocol shall be invoked as a justification for intervening, directly or indirectly, for any reason whatever, in the armed conflict or in the internal or external affairs of the High Contracting Party in the territory of which that conflict occurs.

PART II

HUMANE TREATMENT

Article 4—Fundamental guarantees

1. All persons who do not take a direct part or who have ceased to take part in hostilities, whether or not their liberty has been restricted, are entitled to respect for their person, honour

27–45

and convictions and religious practices. They shall in all circumstances be treated humanely, without any adverse distinction. It is prohibited to order that there shall be no survivors.

2. Without prejudice to the generality of the foregoing, the following acts against the persons referred to in paragraph 1 are and shall remain prohibited at any time and in any place whatsoever:

(a) violence to the life, health and physical or mental well-being of persons, in particular murder as well as cruel treatment such as torture, mutilation or any form of corporal punishment;

(b) collective punishments;

(c) taking of hostages;

(d) acts of terrorism;

(e) outrages upon personal dignity, in particular humiliating and degrading treatment, rape, enforced prostitution and any form of indecent assault;

(f) slavery and the slave trade in all their forms;

(g) pillage;

(h) threats to commit any of the foregoing acts.

3. Children shall be provided with the care and aid they require, and in particular:

(a) they shall receive an education, including religious and moral education, in keeping with the wishes of their parents or, in the absence of parents, of those responsible for their care;

(b) all appropriate steps shall be taken to facilitate the reunion of families temporarily separated;

(c) children who have not attained the age of fifteen years shall neither be recruited in the armed forces or groups nor allowed to take part in hostilities;

(d) the special protection provided by this Article to children who have not attained the age of fifteen years shall remain applicable to them if they take a direct part in hostilities despite the provisions of sub-paragraph (c) and are captured;

(e) measures shall be taken, if necessary, and whenever possible with the consent of their parents or persons who by law or custom are primarily responsible for their care, to remove children temporarily from the area in which hostilities are taking place to a safer area within the country and ensure that they are accompanied by persons responsible for their safety and well-being.

Article 5—Persons whose liberty has been restricted

1. In addition to the provisions of Article 4, the following provisions shall be respected as a minimum with regard to persons deprived of their liberty for reasons related to the armed conflict, whether they are interned or detained:

(a) the wounded and the sick shall be treated in accordance with Article 7;

(b) the persons referred to in this paragraph shall, to the same extent as the local civilian population, be provided with food and drinking water and be afforded safeguards as regards health and hygiene and protection against the rigours of the climate and the dangers of the armed conflict;

(c) they shall be allowed to receive individual or collective relief;

(d) they shall be allowed to practise their religion and, if requested and appropriate, to receive spiritual assistance from persons, such as chaplains, performing religious functions;

(e) they shall, if made to work, have the benefit of working conditions and safeguards similar to those enjoyed by the local civilian population.

2. Those who are responsible for the internment or detention of the persons referred to in paragraph 1 shall also, within the limits of their capabilities, respect the following provisions relating to such persons:

(a) except when men and women of a family are accommodated together, women shall be held in quarters separated from those of men and shall be under the immediate supervision of women;

(b) they shall be allowed to send and receive letters and cards, the number of which may be limited by competent authority if it deems necessary;

(c) places of internment and detention shall not be located close to the combat zone. The persons referred to in paragraph 1 shall be evacuated when the places where they are interned or detained become particularly exposed to danger arising out of the armed conflict, if their evacuation can be carried out under adequate conditions of safety;

(d) they shall have the benefit of medical examinations;

(e) their physical or mental health and integrity shall not be endangered by any unjustified act or omission. Accordingly, it is prohibited to subject the persons described in this Article to any medical procedure which is not indicated by the state of health of the person concerned, and which is not consistent with the generally accepted medical standards applied to free persons under similar medical circumstances.

3. Persons who are not covered by paragraph 1 but whose liberty has been restricted in any way whatsoever for reasons related to the armed conflict shall be treated humanely in accordance with Article 4 and with paragraphs 1(a), (c) and (d), and 2(b) of this Article.

4. If it is decided to release persons deprived of their liberty, necessary measures to ensure their safety shall be taken by those so deciding.

Article 6—Penal prosecutions

1. This Article applies to the prosecution and punishment of criminal offences related to the armed conflict.

2. No sentence shall be passed and no penalty shall be executed on a person found guilty of an offence except pursuant to a conviction pronounced by a court offering the essential guarantees of independence and impartiality. In particular:

(a) the procedure shall provide for an accused to be informed without delay of the particulars of the offence alleged against him and shall afford the accused before and during his trial all necessary rights and means of defence;

(b) no one shall be convicted of an offence except on the basis of individual penal responsibility;

(c) no one shall be held guilty of any criminal offence on account of any act or omission which did not constitute a criminal offence, under the law, at the time when it was committed; nor shall a heavier penalty be imposed than that which was applicable at the time when the criminal offence was committed; if, after the commission of the offence, provision is made by law for the imposition of a lighter penalty, the offender shall benefit thereby;

(d) anyone charged with an offence is presumed innocent until proved guilty according to law;

(e) anyone charged with an offence shall have the right to be tried in his presence;

(f) no one shall be compelled to testify against himself or to confess guilt.

3. A convicted person shall be advised on conviction of his judicial and other remedies and of the time-limits within which they may be exercised.

4. The death penalty shall not be pronounced on persons who were under the age of eighteen years at the time of the offence and shall not be carried out on pregnant women or mothers of young children.

5. At the end of hostilities, the authorities in power shall endeavour to grant the broadest possible amnesty to persons who have participated in the armed conflict, or those deprived of their liberty for reasons related to the armed conflict, whether they are interned or detained.

PART III

WOUNDED, SICK AND SHIPWRECKED

Article 7—Protection and care

1. All the wounded, sick and shipwrecked, whether or not they have taken part in the armed conflict, shall be respected and protected.

2. In all circumstances they shall be treated humanely and shall receive, to the fullest extent practicable and with the least possible delay, the medical care and attention required by their condition. There shall be no distinction among them founded on any grounds other than medical ones.

Article 8—Search

Whenever circumstances permit, and particularly after an engagement, all possible measures shall be taken, without delay, to search for and collect the wounded, sick and shipwrecked, to protect them against pillage and ill-treatment, to ensure their adequate care, and to search for the dead, prevent their being despoiled, and decently dispose of them.

Article 9—Protection of medical and religious personnel

1. Medical and religious personnel shall be respected and protected and shall be granted all available help for the performance of their duties. They shall not be compelled to carry out tasks which are not compatible with their humanitarian mission.

2. In the performance of their duties medical personnel may not be required to give priority to any person except on medical grounds.

Article 10—General protection of medical duties

1. Under no circumstances shall any person be punished for having carried out medical activities compatible with medical ethics, regardless of the person benefiting therefrom.

2. Persons engaged in medical activities shall neither be compelled to perform acts or to carry out work contrary to, nor be compelled to refrain from acts required by, the rules of medical ethics or other rules designed for the benefit of the wounded and sick, or this Protocol.

3. The professional obligations of persons engaged in medical activities regarding information which they may acquire concerning the wounded and sick under their care shall, subject to national law, be respected.

4. Subject to national law, no person engaged in medical activities may be penalised in any way for refusing or failing to give information concerning the wounded and sick who are, or who have been, under his care.

Article 11—Protection of medical units and transports

1. Medical units and transports shall be respected and protected at all times and shall not be the object of attack.

2. The protection to which medical units and transports are entitled shall not cease unless they are used to commit hostile acts, outside their humanitarian function. Protection may, however, cease only after a warning has been given setting, whenever appropriate, a reasonable time-limit, and after such warning has remained unheeded.

Article 12—The distinctive emblem

Under the direction of the competent authority concerned, the distinctive emblem of the red cross, red crescent or red lion and sun on a white ground shall be displayed by medical and religious personnel and medical units, and on medical transports. It shall be respected in all circumstances. It shall not be used improperly.

PART IV

CIVILIAN POPULATION

Article 13—Protection of the civilian population

1. The civilian population and individual civilians shall enjoy general protection against the dangers arising from military operations. To give effect to this protection, the following rules shall be observed in all circumstances.

2. The civilian population as such, as well as individual civilians, shall not be the object of attack. Acts or threats of violence the primary purpose of which is to spread terror among the civilian population are prohibited.

3. Civilians shall enjoy the protection afforded by this Part, unless and for such time as they take a direct part in hostilities.

Article 14—Protection of objects indispensable to the survival of the civilian population

Starvation of civilians as a method of combat is prohibited. It is therefore prohibited to attack, destroy, remove or render useless, for that purpose, objects indispensable to the survival of the civilian population, such as foodstuffs, agricultural areas for the production of foodstuffs, crops, livestock, drinking water installations and supplies and irrigation works.

Article 15—Protection of works and installations containing dangerous forces

Works or installations containing dangerous forces, namely dams, dykes and nuclear electrical generating stations, shall not be made the object of attack, even where these objects are military objectives, if such attack may cause the release of dangerous forces and consequent severe losses among the civilian population.

Article 16—Protection of cultural objects and of places of worship

Without prejudice to the provisions of the Hague Convention for the Protection of Cultural Property in the Event of Armed Conflict of 14 May 1954, it is prohibited to commit any acts of hostility directed against historic monuments, works of art or places of worship which constitute the cultural or spiritual heritage of peoples, and to use them in support of the military effort.

Article 17—Prohibition of forced movement of civilians

1. The displacement of the civilian population shall not be ordered for reasons related to the conflict unless the security of the civilians involved or imperative military reasons so demand. Should such displacements have to be carried out, all possible measures shall be taken in order that the civilian population may be received under satisfactory conditions of shelter, hygiene, health, safety and nutrition.
2. Civilians shall not be compelled to leave their own territory for reasons connected with the conflict.

Article 18—Relief societies and relief actions

1. Relief societies located in the territory of the High Contracting Party, such as Red Cross (Red Crescent, Red Lion and Sun) organisations, may offer their services for the performance of their traditional functions in relation to the victims of the armed conflict. The civilian population may, even on its own initiative, offer to collect and care for the wounded, sick and shipwrecked.
2. If the civilian population is suffering undue hardship owing to a lack of the supplies essential for its survival, such as foodstuffs and medical supplies, relief actions for the civilian population which are of an exclusively humanitarian and impartial nature and which are conducted without any adverse distinction shall be undertaken subject to the consent of the High Contracting Party concerned.

Part V

Final Provisions

Article 19—Dissemination

This Protocol shall be disseminated as widely as possible.

Article 20—Signature

This Protocol shall be open for signature by the Parties to the Conventions six months after the signing of the Final Act and will remain open for a period of twelve months.

Article 21—Ratification

This Protocol shall be ratified as soon as possible. The instruments of ratification shall be deposited with the Swiss Federal Council, depositary of the Conventions.

Article 22—Accession

This Protocol shall be open for accession by any Party to the Conventions which has not signed it. The instruments of accession shall be deposited with the depositary.

Article 23—Entry into force

1. This Protocol shall enter into force six months after two instruments of ratification or accession have been deposited.
2. For each Party to the Conventions thereafter ratifying or acceding to this Protocol, it shall enter into force six months after the deposit by such Party of its instrument of ratification or accession.

Article 24—Amendment

1. Any High Contracting Party may propose amendments to this Protocol. The text of any proposed amendment shall be communicated to the depositary which shall decide, after consultation with all the High Contracting Parties and the International Committee of the Red Cross, whether a conference should be convened to consider the proposed amendment.
2. The depositary shall invite to that conference all the High Contracting Parties as well as the Parties to the Conventions, whether or not they are signatories of this Protocol.

Article 25—Denunciation

1. In case a High Contracting Party should denounce this Protocol, the denunciation shall only take effect six months after receipt of the instrument of denunciation. If, however, on the expiry of six months, the denouncing Party is engaged in the situation referred to in Article 1, the denunciation shall not take effect before the end of the armed conflict. Persons who have been deprived of liberty, or whose liberty has been restricted, for reasons related to the conflict shall nevertheless continue to benefit from the provisions of this Protocol until their final release.

2. The denunciation shall be notified in writing to the depositary, which shall transmit it to all the High Contracting Parties.

Article 26—Notifications

The depositary shall inform the High Contracting Parties as well as the Parties to the Conventions, whether or not they are signatories of this Protocol, of:
(a) signatures affixed to this Protocol and the deposit of instruments of ratification and accession under Articles 21 and 22;
(b) the date of entry into force of this Protocol under Article 23; and
(c) communications and declarations received under Article 24.

Article 27—Registration

1. After its entry into force, this Protocol shall be transmitted by the depositary to the Secretariat of the United Nations for registration and publication, in accordance with Article 102 of the Charter of the United Nations.

2. The depositary shall also inform the Secretariat of the United Nations of all ratifications and accessions received by it with respect to this Protocol.

Article 28—Authentic text

The original of this Protocol, of which the Arabic, Chinese, English, French, Russian and Spanish texts are equally authentic shall be deposited with the depositary which shall transmit certified true copies thereof to all the Parties to the Conventions."

INDEX

References in roman type are to sections of this Act: references in italics are to articles of the new Protocols of the Geneva Convention (*PI* and *PII*) set out in the Schedule

27–51

SALE OF GOODS (AMENDMENT) ACT 1995*

(1995 c. 28)

An Act to amend the law relating to the sale of unascertained goods forming part of an identified bulk and the sale of undivided shares in goods.

[19th July 1995]

PARLIAMENTARY DEBATES
Hansard, H.L. Vol. 563, col. 1453, Vol. 564, col. 1467, Vol. 565, col. 680, H.C. Vol. 263, col. 1283.

INTRODUCTION AND GENERAL NOTE
   This Act was introduced in the House of Lords sponsored by Lord Mustill. It implements the findings of the English and Scottish Law Commissions contained in their joint Report of July 1993 *Sale of Goods forming part of a bulk* (Law Com. No. 215; Scot. Law Com. No. 145) (H.C. 807) (the Report).
   The Report resulted from a request to the Law Commissions from a leading international commodity trade association to consider examining the law relating to the rights of purchasers of goods forming part of a larger bulk carried by the sea. The association's anxiety arose following a decision of the Commercial Court in Rotterdam in 1985 (*The Gosforth* S. en S. 1985 Nr. 91) during which the court referred in passing to the fact that under English law, which governed the contract, s.16 of the Sale of Goods Act 1979 (c. 54) (the 1979 Act) appeared to prevent property passing before the goods were ascertained.
   The Law Commissions carried out preliminary research to try to identify the extent of any problem in practice and received over 100 replies to its questionnaire, mainly from traders in goods such as grain, animal feedstuffs, vegetable oils and oilseeds or commodities—sugar, coffee, tea, cocoa, metals *etc.* Over 85 per cent said that they purchased goods while they were still part of a bulk, roughly divided equally between purchases on sea and on land. Some 10 per cent had had problems because the seller had gone into liquidation after being paid but before delivery.
   The consultation showed that there was support for reform of s.16 of the 1979 Act and of the Bills of Lading Act 1855 (c. 111). As the latter was regarded as the more pressing, the Law Commissions issued a report (*Rights of Suit in Respect of Carriage of Goods by Sea* (1991) Law Com. No. 196; Scot. Law Com. No. 130) which was implemented by the Carriage of Goods by Sea Act 1992 (c. 50). That Act made three changes:
   (a) it repealed the Bills of Lading Act 1855 thus removing the link between the acquisition of rights and the transfer of property;
   (b) sea waybills and ship's delivery orders were included among documents to which the Act applied;
   (c) it enabled regulations to be made to bring electronic data exchange within the scope of the Act.
   The Law Commissions also consulted on whether there should be a special rule for insolvency cases. Paragraphs 4.22 to 4.33 of the Report set out the arguments which were raised and the reasons why, in the event, the Law Commissions decided to take no action at present.
   During its second reading in the House of Lords (the Bill passed all stages in the Commons without debate) Lord Mustill explained that there were three situations where the property in goods may pass. The first is where the goods are identified conclusively at the time of the contract. They may be single items or several or in bulk. ("I will buy that bottle of wine"; or "I will buy all the grain in the holds of the ship Challenger"). The existing law, s.17(1) of the 1979 Act, prescribes that the property is transferred when the parties intend and s.18, Rule 1, says that, unless there is a different intention, property passes when the contract is made. This arrangement protects the buyer who has pre-paid against the seller's insolvency; even though the goods have not been delivered, they belong to him. It should be noted that if they are destroyed between contract and delivery through no fault of the seller or a carrier, the loss falls on the buyer because, by s.20 of the 1979 Act, risk passes with property unless otherwise agreed.
   The second situation where property in goods may pass is where goods are merely identified by a general description ("200 bottles of Beaujolais Villages 1992"). The seller may deliver any goods from any source. Here the law corresponds with common sense; s.16 of the 1979 Act says that until goods are identified they cannot be "appropriated" to the contract. The buyer cannot own the goods at the time of the contract because no one can be the owner of something when it

---

*Annotations by W.H. Thomas, Solicitor, Editor of The Encyclopedia of Consumer Law.

is impossible to know what he owns and there is no means of finding out. Until appropriation the pre-paying buyer has no protection against the seller's insolvency.

This Act deals with the third situation which Lord Mustill described as midway between the two extremes: the goods are identified at the time of the contract to the extent that they must come from a fixed and prescribed source – a group of items or a bulk of the same kind of goods – but no one specifies which items or which part of the bulk are involved ("I will buy 200 bottles of Beaujolais Villages 1992 now in your cellar"; or "I will buy 1,000 tonnes out of the cargo of grain in the holds of the ship Challenger"). The seller can only deliver goods from the prescribed source.

However, property cannot pass at the time of the contract. It is clear that the bottles of wine are there among the rest of the grain in the ship but until the bottles are physically separated, or the 1,000 tonnes of grain unloaded, there is no means of knowing whether a particular bottle or a given shovelful of grain has or has not been sold to the buyer.

The present Act attempts to remove a gap in the law by making a new rule on sales of goods out of bulk which would enable property in an undivided share in the bulk to pass before ascertainment of goods relating to specific sale contracts. This rule is contained by an amendment to s.18 of the 1979 Act. The amendment recognises, and puts into statutory form, the doctrine of "ascertainment by exhaustion" – which is a name for the situation where stock from which the goods are to be drawn is depleted successively by withdrawals until all that is left will satisfy the contract in question. Using the example of the Beaujolais quoted above, if bottles are removed from the cellar until there are only 200 left, at that moment it is possible to identify those 200 as the subject matter of the contract, and property passes to the buyer.

The Act also introduces a wholly new concept. Upon payment of all or part of the price, the buyer will become a co-owner with others having a claim on the entire bulk. Although there is no ownership of particular objects, the buyer will acquire an immediate undivided share. That interest as co-owner will prevail in an insolvency and protect commercial and private buyers alike. The previous law provided that the purchaser of a quantity of cargo shipped on board a particular ship did not obtain any rights of ownership when the goods were shipped, or when the bill of lading was delivered to him or when he paid for the goods. He had to wait until the ship docked, was unloaded and his share had been identified – either by physical delivery or by the process of exhaustion. The buyer was prejudiced in case of insolvency of the seller or damage to the goods.

These reforms are achieved by the insertion into the 1979 Act of two new sections. The newly inserted s.20A provides the basic rule on the passing of property in an undivided share in the bulk. The newly inserted s.20B modifies the legal consequences of owning goods in common so as to enable trading in the bulk goods to continue in the normal way. Amendments are also made to s.61 of the 1979 Act to include new definitions introduced by the Act.

The Act is essentially for the benefit of commercial traders although there are circumstances where individuals, dealing as consumers, may be assisted. Buying shares in horses or boats, for example, is not uncommon and the new rules would apply to such contracts.

COMMENCEMENT

The Act comes into force on September 19, 1995 and applies to England and Wales, Scotland and Northern Ireland.

ABBREVIATIONS

The 1979 Act: Sale of Goods Act 1979.

Unascertained goods forming part of an identified bulk

1.—(1) At the beginning of section 16 of the Sale of Goods Act 1979 ("the 1979 Act") there shall be added the words "Subject to section 20A below".

(2) In section 18 of the 1979 Act, at the end of rule 5 there shall be added the following—

"(3) Where there is a contract for the sale of a specified quantity of unascertained goods in a deliverable state forming part of a bulk which is identified either in the contract or by subsequent agreement between the parties and the bulk is reduced to (or to less than) that quantity, then, if the buyer under that contract is the only buyer to whom goods are then due out of the bulk—

    (a) the remaining goods are to be taken as appropriated to that contract at the time when the bulk is so reduced; and

    (b) the property in those goods then passes to that buyer.

(4) Paragraph (3) above applies also (with the necessary modifications) where a bulk is reduced to (or to less than) the aggregate of the quantities due to a single buyer under separate contracts relating to that bulk and he is the only buyer to whom goods are then due out of that bulk.".

(3) After section 20 of the 1979 Act there shall be inserted the following—

"Undivided shares in goods forming part of a bulk

20A.—(1) This section applies to a contract for the sale of a specified quantity of unascertained goods if the following conditions are met—

> (a) the goods or some of them form part of a bulk which is identified either in the contract or by subsequent agreement between the parties; and
>
> (b) the buyer has paid the price for some or all of the goods which are the subject of the contract and which form part of the bulk.

(2) Where this section applies, then (unless the parties agree otherwise), as soon as the conditions specified in paragraphs (a) and (b) of subsection (1) above are met or at such later time as the parties may agree—

> (a) property in an undivided share in the bulk is transferred to the buyer, and
>
> (b) the buyer becomes an owner in common of the bulk.

(3) Subject to subsection (4) below, for the purposes of this section, the undivided share of a buyer in a bulk at any time shall be such share as the quantity of goods paid for and due to the buyer out of the bulk bears to the quantity of goods in the bulk at that time.

(4) Where the aggregate of the undivided shares of buyers in a bulk determined under subsection (3) above would at any time exceed the whole of the bulk at that time, the undivided share in the bulk of each buyer shall be reduced proportionately so that the aggregate of the undivided shares is equal to the whole bulk.

(5) Where a buyer has paid the price for only some of the goods due to him out of a bulk, any delivery to the buyer out of the bulk shall, for the purposes of this section, be ascribed in the first place to the goods in respect of which payment has been made.

(6) For the purposes of this section payment of part of the price for any goods shall be treated as payment for a corresponding part of the goods.

Deemed consent by co-owner to dealings in bulk goods

20B.—(1) A person who has become an owner in common of a bulk by virtue of section 20A above shall be deemed to have consented to—

> (a) any delivery of goods out of the bulk to any other owner in common of the bulk, being goods which are due to him under his contract;
>
> (b) any dealing with or removal, delivery or disposal of goods in the bulk by any other person who is an owner in common of the bulk in so far as the goods fall within that co-owner's undivided share in the bulk at the time of the dealing, removal, delivery or disposal.

(2) No cause of action shall accrue to anyone against a person by reason of that person having acted in accordance with paragraph (a) or (b) of subsection (1) above in reliance on any consent deemed to have been given under that subsection.

(3) Nothing in this section or section 20A above shall—

> (a) impose an obligation on a buyer of goods out of a bulk to compensate any other buyer of goods out of that bulk for any shortfall in the goods received by that other buyer;

    (b) affect any contractual arrangement between buyers of goods out of a bulk for adjustments between themselves; or

    (c) affect the rights of any buyer under his contract.".

DEFINITIONS
    "action": 1979 Act, s.61(1).
    "appropriation": 1979 Act, s.18, r.5.
    "bulk": s.2(a).
    "buyer": 1979 Act, s.61(1).
    "contract": 1979 Act, ss.2(1), 61(1).
    "deliverable state": 1979 Act, s.61(5).
    "delivery": ss.2(b) and 1979 Act, 61(1).
    "goods": s.2(c) and 1979 Act, s.61(1).
    "price": 1979 Act, s.61(1).
    "property": 1979 Act, s.61(1).
    "specific goods": s.2(d) and 1979 Act, s.61(1).
    "unascertained goods": 1979 Act, s.18, r.5.

GENERAL NOTE
    Subsection (1) inserts words in s.16 of the 1979 Act paving the way for the insertion of the new s.20A. The Act only applies where there has been prepayment for goods.

Subs. (2)
    By adding to the existing r.5, this subsection gives statutory effect to the expression "ascertainment by exhaustion" which has been recognised by the courts in such cases as *Waite and James v. Midland Bank* (1926) 24 L1. L. Rep. 313, (1926) 31 Com. Cas. 172; *Karlshamns Olefabriker v. East Port Navigation Corp.; Elafi, The* [1981] 2 Lloyd's Rep. 629 at p. 683; [1982] 1 All E.R. 208, at p. 212.
    The new r.5(3) as added applies where there is one contract and one buyer. It means that a buyer's undivided share in the bulk at any time should be such a share as the quantity of goods paid for and due to the buyer out of the bulk at that time bears to the quantity of goods in the bulk at that time.
    The new r.5(4) as added extends its application to cases where there are two or more contracts in which the buyer is the same person and the bulk is reduced to or less than the total of goods covered by those contracts.
    The new rules are confined to goods in a deliverable state so as to avoid a clash with the existing rr.1 and 2 in s.18 of the 1979 Act. The existing opening words of s.18 also make it clear that the new rules will only apply where no different intention appears.

Subs. (3)
    This inserts the new ss.20A and 20B into the 1979 Act. Section 20A enables a buyer who has prepaid for a specified quantity of unascertained goods forming part of an identified bulk to acquire an undivided share in the bulk and become a common owner with other such buyers but before his goods have been ascertained. As the new section is concerned with the passing of property in an undivided share in a bulk, it is unnecessary and inappropriate to limit it to goods in a deliverable state.

Inserted s.20A(1) of the 1979Act
    This makes it clear that the new provision is concerned with quantity not shares expressed as fractions or percentages. The bulk must be identified and the buyer have paid some part of the price.

Inserted s.20A(2) of the 1979 Act
    This sets out the basic rule for the passing of property in an undivided share in the bulk. Assuming the bulk is identified, and the contract does not exclude the rule or provide for property to pass at a later date, property in an undivided share will pass as soon as the buyer has paid for all or some of the goods.

Inserted s.20A(3) and (4) of the 1979 Act
The buyer's undivided share at any time is, by subs.(3), such a share as the goods paid for and due to him bear to the quantity of goods in the bulk at that time. Subsection (4) makes it clear that the aggregate of the shares of two or more buyers can never exceed the whole of the bulk.

Inserted s.20A(5) of the 1979 Act
This provides that where a buyer has paid for only some of the goods, any deliveries to the buyer out of the bulk should be ascribed in the first place to the prepaid goods. The reference to "delivery" includes (because of an amendment to the definition of that word in s.6(1) of the 1979 Act by this Act) a reference to an appropriation of goods to the contract in such a way that property passes to the buyer.

Inserted s.20A(6) of the 1979 Act
In ss.20A(1)(b), 20A(3) and 20A(5) reference is made to the case where a buyer has paid for some only of the goods in the contract or due from the bulk. Because in practice part-payments would not normally be related to any proportion of the goods bought, this subsection provides that part-payments are to be treated as payments for part.
Subsection (3) also inserts a new s.20B which modifes the legal consequences of owning goods in common so as to enable trading in the bulk goods to continue in the normal way.

Inserted s.20B(1) of the 1979 Act
To give effect to this intention, each co-owner is deemed to have consented to deliveries to other co-owners of the quantities due to them; otherwise, the normal rules on co-ownership would severely restrict the division of bulk to meet the expectations of all parties. Subsection 20B(1)(b) makes it clear that each co-owner can deal with goods coming within his share without needing the consent of the others. The references to "delivery" include (because of an amendment to the definition of that word in s.61(1) of the 1979 Act by this Act) a reference to an appropriation of goods to the contract in such a way that property passes to the buyer.

Inserted s.20B(2) of the 1979 Act
This subsection protects liquidators or other insolvency office-holders who release goods to co-owning buyers in reliance on the deemed consent in s.20B(1) against any action by other co-owning buyers who may receive short delivery because there is insufficient bulk to meet all claims.

Inserted s.20B(3) of the 1979 Act
This has three effects. The new rules do not:
(a) impose any obligation on a buyer who takes delivery of goods out of bulk to compensate others who receive short delivery because of a shortage;
(b) affect any contractual arrangements between the buyers for adjustments between themselves;
(c) alter or diminish contractual rights of the buyer against the seller.

Additional provisions

2. In section 61(1) of the 1979 Act—
(a) after the definition of "action" there shall be inserted the following definition—
  " "bulk" means a mass or collection of goods of the same kind which—
   (a) is contained in a defined space or area; and
   (b) is such that any goods in the bulk are interchangeable with any other goods therein of the same number or quantity;";
(b) at the end of the definition of "delivery" there shall be added the words "except that in relation to sections 20A and 20B above it includes such appropriation of goods to the contract as results in property in the goods being transferred to the buyer;";

   (c) at the end of the definition of "goods" there shall be added the words "and includes an undivided share in goods;";

   (d) at the end of the definition of "specific goods" there shall be added the words "and includes an undivided share, specified as a fraction or percentage, of goods identified and agreed on as aforesaid".

GENERAL NOTE

This section inserts into s.61(1) of the 1979 Act a new definition of "bulk" and amends the existing definitions of "delivery", "goods" and "specific goods". The last two are included to make it clear that the sale of an undivided share in goods, or specific goods, is a sale of goods for the purposes of the 1979 Act.

Short title, commencement and extent

3.—(1) This Act may be cited as the Sale of Goods (Amendment) Act 1995.

(2) This Act shall come into force at the end of the period of two months beginning with the day on which it is passed; but nothing in this Act shall have effect in relation to any contract concluded before the coming into force of this Act.

(3) This Act extends to Northern Ireland.

GENERAL NOTE

The Act comes into force on 19 September, 1995 but has no retrospective effect on any contract concluded before that date.

INDEX

References are to sections

INSURANCE COMPANIES (RESERVES) ACT 1995

(1995 c. 29)

An Act to provide for the maintenance by insurance companies of reserves in respect of certain classes of business; and for connected purposes.

[19th July 1995]

PARLIAMENTARY DEBATES
Hansard, H.C. Vol. 255, col. 1373. H.L. Vol. 562, col. 1445, Vol. 564, cols. 146, 1442, 1895.

INTRODUCTION
This Act, *inter alia*, enables the Secretary of State to make regulations requiring insurance companies to maintain equalisation reserves in respect of specified types of business.

Equalisation reserve

1.—(1) After section 34 of the Insurance Companies Act 1982 there shall be inserted—

> **"General business: equalisation reserve**
> 34A.—(1) Every insurance company to which this section applies which carries on general business of a prescribed description shall maintain, in accordance with regulations made for the purposes of this section, a reserve (in this section referred to as an "equalisation reserve") in respect of its general business of that description.
>
> (2) Subject to subsection (3) below, this section applies to any insurance company to which this Part of this Act applies—
>> (a) whose head office is in the United Kingdom;
>> (b) whose business in the United Kingdom is restricted to reinsurance; or
>> (c) whose head office is not in a member State.
>
> (3) This section does not apply to an insurance company of a description prescribed for the purposes of this subsection.
>
> (4) Without prejudice to the generality of subsection (1) above, regulations made for the purposes of this section may make provision—
>> (a) as to the circumstances in which, and times at which, amounts are to be placed to, or taken from, an equalisation reserve;
>> (b) as to the determination of the amounts to be so placed or taken; and
>> (c) as to such other matters incidental to the maintenance of an equalisation reserve as the Secretary of State considers expedient."

(2) In section 32 of that Act (margin of solvency), after subsection (6) there shall be inserted—

> "(7) In applying subsection (5) above, the amount of the company's liabilities shall be taken to be increased by the amount of any reserve maintained under section 34A below."

Power to modify equalisation reserve requirements in relation to particular companies

2.—(1) Section 68 of the Insurance Companies Act 1982 (power to modify Part II in relation to particular companies) shall be amended as follows.

(2) In subsection (4), for "and 25 to 36" there shall be substituted "25 to 34 and 35 to 36".

(3) After that subsection there shall be inserted—

> "(4A) If regulations made for the purposes of this subsection so provide, the provisions to which this section applies shall also include

section 34A above and the provisions of regulations made for the purposes of that section."

Consequential amendments

3.—(1) Schedule 9A to the Companies Act 1985 and Schedule 9A to the Companies (Northern Ireland) Order 1986 (form and content of accounts of insurance companies and groups) shall be amended as follows.

(2) In Note (24) on the balance sheet format set out in Section B—

(a) after "Liabilities item C.5)" there shall be inserted—
   "This item shall comprise the amount of any reserve maintained by the company under section 34A of the Insurance Companies Act 1982."; and

(b) after "This item shall" there shall be inserted "also".

(3) For paragraph 50 there shall be substituted—

"Equalisation reserves

50. The amount of any reserve maintained—

(a) under section 34A of the Insurance Companies Act 1982 ("the 1982 Act"), or

(b) under regulation 76 of, and Schedule 14 to, the Insurance Companies Regulations 1994 ("the 1994 Regulations"),

shall be determined in accordance with regulations under section 34A of the 1982 Act or, as the case may be, in accordance with regulation 76 of, and Schedule 14 to, the 1994 Regulations.".

Short title, commencement and extent

4.—(1) This Act may be cited as the Insurance Companies (Reserves) Act 1995.

(2) Sections 1 and 3 of this Act shall come into force on such day as the Secretary of State may by order made by statutory instrument appoint.

(3) This Act extends to Northern Ireland.

INDEX

References are to sections

LANDLORD AND TENANT (COVENANTS) ACT 1995*

(1995 c. 30)

*Annotations by Suzanne Lloyd Holt and Sarah Thompson of Wragge & Co., Solicitors, Birmingham.

An Act to make provision for persons bound by covenants of a tenancy to be released from such covenants on the assignment of the tenancy, and to make other provision with respect to rights and liabilities arising under such covenants; to restrict in certain circumstances the operation of rights of re-entry, forfeiture and disclaimer; and for connected purposes.

[19th July 1995]

PARLIAMENTARY DEBATES
Hansard, H.C. Vol. 254, col. 799; Vol. 258, col. 485; Vol. 263, col. 1236. H.L. Vol. 564, col. 1087; Vol. 565, cols. 354, 1104, 1682.

INTRODUCTION AND GENERAL NOTE
This Act marks a very significant development in the area of landlord and tenant law by limiting the liability of both the original parties to the lease and of their assignees. Prior to the coming into force of the Act, the liability of parties to the lease was governed by two concepts: the doctrine of privity of contract and the doctrine of privity of estate. The distinction between the two was discussed and considered by the House of Lords in the case of *City of London Corp. v. Fell* [1994] 1 A.C. 458.

As a result of privity of contract, the original parties to the lease are liable to one another in respect of the covenants contained in the lease notwithstanding any transfer by them of their respective interests. As the covenants imposed on tenants are generally more onerous than those imposed on landlords, the potential liability as a result of the doctrine is greater for tenants. Depending on the actual wording of the lease document, this liability would extend to paying any increase in the rent on review and to yield up the premises in good repair on the expiration of the term.

It is a direct and primary liability; it is not in the nature of a guarantee (see *Baynton v. Morgan* (1888) 22 Q.B.D. 74 and *Allied London Investments v. Hambro Life Assurance* (1984) 269 E.G. 41). The liability is unaffected by any material change of the terms of the lease notwithstanding that the original party may not have consented or indeed known of the change or derived any benefit from it (see *Selous Street Properties v. Oronel Fabrics* (1984) 270 E.G. 643, *GUS Property Management v. Texas Homecare* (1993) 27 E.G. 130). The liability might extend beyond the end of the contractual lease term if the terms of the lease were sufficiently wide (see *London City Corp. v. Fell*; *Herbert Duncan v. Cluttons (A Firm)* (1993) 04 E.G. 115 where the liability was held to extend into the statutory continuation of the term pursuant to the provisions of Pt. II of the Landlord and Tenant Act 1954 (c. 56)). Further case law governed the enforcement of the covenants by assignees against the original parties (for example by an assignee of the original landlord against the original tenant).

The doctrine of privity of estate governed the position of assignees of both the landlord and the tenant to ensure that those assignees were bound by and could enforce the obligations contained in the lease, during the period that the assignee held the same interest of either the original landlord or the original tenant. The rules with regard to the running of covenants are contained partly in case law (*Spencer's case* (1583) 5 Co Rep 16) and partly in statute (ss.141 and 142 of the Law of Property Act 1925). For the assignee to be liable under a particular covenant, that covenant must touch and concern the land or have reference to the subject matter of the lease. Such covenants were contrasted with purely personal covenants. Whilst most significant covenants did generally touch and concern the land, it was a distinction which did prompt litigation (see, for example, *Hua Chiao Commercial Bank v. Chaiphua Industries* [1987] A.C. 99, *P. & A. Swift Investments v. Combined English Stores Group* [1988] 3 W.L.R. 313).

Another feature of the position was the chain of indemnity covenants between the original tenant and his successors in title (there was no such chain for the assignment of the reversion).

Each time the lease was assigned by the tenant, an indemnity would be implied by statute, as modified by any express agreement between the tenant and his assignee (s.77 of the Law of Property Act 1925 and s.24 of the Land Registration Act 1925). Under the terms of the indemnity, the assignee agreed with the tenant to pay all future rent and perform all the covenants in the lease for the residue of the term, irrespective of whether they touched and concerned the land. Thus the original tenant would have the benefit of an indemnity from his assignee, who in turn would have the benefit of an indemnity from his assignee. However, the chain could obviously break down in the event that one of the links in the chain was unable to meet its obligations and thus the original tenant was often only afforded minimal protection by such indemnities.

The position was made more complex by the fact that either on the grant of the lease or on an assignment, the landlord might obtain a guarantee to support the obligations of the original tenant/assignee. Further, on each assignment, the general practice was for the landlord of commercial premises to get a direct contractual covenant from the assignee that he would comply with the covenants in the lease.

As a result of the doctrines of privity of contract and estate and the general commercial practice, when the current landlord sought to recover any outstanding rent or damages for any other breach of covenant, he might well have a number of possible sources of recovery; the original tenant, intermediate assignees of the lease who had now parted with their interest in the premises (as a result of the direct covenant which had been given by the assignee at the time of the assignment of the premises to him), the current tenant and lastly any guarantors of any of these parties. Once a landlord had recovered the outstanding sums, questions would then arise as to the rights of indemnity which the paying party might have against all the other parties with a potential liability to the landlord. This would depend on the effectiveness of the chain of indemnity covenants and the quasi-contractual right to an indemnity in favour of the paying party (*Moule v. Garrett* (1872) LR 7 Ex 101).

Times of economic difficulty brought into sharp focus the position of the original tenant (and indeed of intermediate assignees who had extended their liability until the end of the term by contract and guarantors). Such tenants who thought that they had disposed of their interests in premises many years previously were being asked by landlords to comply with the covenants. Whilst they would have had some responsibility for the ability of their own assignee to perform the covenants, they would have had no influence over the choice of any subsequent assignees. The perceived injustice of this was exacerbated by the fact that landlords did not owe any "duty of care" to such tenants, in particular, the landlord was not under an obligation to notify the previous tenant when the current tenant began to default under the terms of the lease, was entitled to sue the original tenant before pursuing the current tenant and further the landlord was under no obligation to take steps to minimise the liability of any of the parties against whom he might recover (for example by investigating the financial status of the current tenant prior to the assignment); *Norwich Union Life Insurance Society v. Low Profile Fashions* (1992) 21 E.G. 104. Further, even if the original tenant was aware of this potential liability under the lease, it was a contingent liability which would be very difficult to quantify. This could make the planning and management of business and the winding up of estates problematic.

The concepts of privity of contract and estate were examined by the Law Commission and, in their Report published in 1988 (*Landlord and Tenant Law: Privity of Contract and Estate. Law Com. No. 174*), the Commission broadly recommended that privity of contract be abolished to achieve a "clean break" on the assignment of either the reversion or the lease and that such abolition should be retrospective. Further the Law Commission recommended that all the obligations in the lease should bind, and be enforceable by and against, the parties who were for the time being the landlord and tenant under the lease. There should be a single bargain for the letting of premises. The Commission advised that the distinction between covenants which touched and concerned the land and other covenants should be abolished, so that the parties would be bound by all covenants in the lease save to the extent that they were purely personal in nature.

This Act largely gives effect to the Law Commission recommendations although the abolition of the doctrine of privity of contract is not retrospective. The existing rules about privity will therefore be of relevance for many years to come. There were some very significant amendments to the Act as it was carried through Parliament, and therefore the Act itself bears little resemblance to the draft bill prepared by the Commission. Very broadly, the Act provides for the automatic release of tenants from their obligations under the lease on assignment and for the release of the landlord with the consent of either the tenant or the court. This release is available only to parties to leases granted after the commencement of the Act. In certain circumstances, a landlord may require a tenant to give a limited guarantee on assignment for the performance of his assignee. Certain protection is given to former tenants and guarantors, whose liability survives an assignment, in respect of leases granted both before and after the passing of the Act. In particular, the landlord must give tenants and guarantors notice that the current tenant has defaulted within six months of the relevant sum becoming due. If notice is not given, the landlord loses his right to recover against that party. If payment is made in full by a former tenant or guarantor, then they are entitled to call for an intermediate lease of the premises. In this way, they gain some control of the situation and of their potential liability. They then, in effect, become the landlord of the defaulting tenant and can take steps to enforce the covenants or ultimately forfeit the lease. Finally, the Act contains what is intended to be a complete statutory code for the transmission of the benefit and burden of covenants in relation to leases granted after the commencement of the Act.

COMMENCEMENT
    The Act will come into force on such day as the Lord Chancellor may appoint by order. As yet no statutory instrument with regard to the commencement of the Act has been made, but it is anticipated that the Act will come into force on January 1, 1996 (*Hansard*, H.C. Vol. 263, col. 1269).

Preliminary

Tenancies to which the Act applies

    1.—(1) Sections 3 to 16 and 21 apply only to new tenancies.
    (2) Sections 17 to 20 apply to both new and other tenancies.
    (3) For the purposes of this section a tenancy is a new tenancy if it is granted on or after the date on which this Act comes into force otherwise than in pursuance of—
    (a) an agreement entered into before that date, or
    (b) an order of a court made before that date.
    (4) Subsection (3) has effect subject to section 20(1) in the case of overriding leases granted under section 19.
    (5) Without prejudice to the generality of subsection (3), that subsection applies to the grant of a tenancy where by virtue of any variation of a tenancy there is a deemed surrender and regrant as it applies to any other grant of a tenancy.
    (6) Where a tenancy granted on or after the date on which this Act comes into force is so granted in pursuance of an option granted before that date, the tenancy shall be regarded for the purposes of subsection (3) as granted in pursuance of an agreement entered into before that date (and accordingly is not a new tenancy), whether or not the option was exercised before that date.
    (7) In subsection (6) "option" includes right of first refusal.

DEFINITIONS
    "commencement date": s.31.
    "new tenancy": s.1.
    "overriding leases": s.19.
    "tenancy": s.28.

GENERAL NOTE
    Throughout the Act (save in s.19), the draftsman has used the word "tenancy". This is synonymous with the word "lease" and this is confirmed in the definition section. A distinction is drawn between new and other tenancies. Section 1 provides that the principal provisions of the Act apply only to "new tenancies", with important exceptions relating to restrictions on the liability of former tenants and guarantors and the right to obtain an overriding lease (ss.17 to 20 of the Act).
    A new tenancy is one which is granted on or after the commencement date of the Act save those tenancies which are granted pursuant to an agreement or court order (an obvious example being an order under the provisions of Pt. II of the Landlord and Tenant Act 1954) made prior to the commencement date. Thus, as noted in the Introduction, the Act is *not* of retrospective effect. The subsequent provisions of s.1 deal with the determination of the date of grant of the tenancy.

Subs. (4)
    Subsection (4) deals with the date of grant of overriding leases pursuant to s.19 (intermediate leases which landlords are obliged to grant, if required to do so, by former tenants and guaran-

tors who have been called upon to pay and have paid rent and service charge due under the tenancy). The date of grant is determined by the provisions of s.20(1).

Subs. (5)

Certain variations of the terms of a tenancy (for example an extension of the term or where new premises are added to the demise) will operate as a surrender and regrant of a lease. This subsection provides that the date of the regrant will determine whether a tenancy falls within the definition of a new tenancy.

Subss. (6) and (7)

The position of tenancies granted pursuant to an option is dealt with in subs. (6). It is the date of the option, rather than the date of exercise of the option, which determines whether or not a tenancy is a new tenancy for the purposes of the Act. Subsection (7) provides that the term "option" covers a right of first refusal.

Covenants to which the Act applies

2.—(1) This Act applies to a landlord covenant or a tenant covenant of a tenancy—

    (a) whether or not the covenant has reference to the subject matter of tenancy, and

    (b) whether the covenant is express, implied or imposed by law,

but does not apply to a covenant falling within subsection (2).

    (2) Nothing in this Act affects any covenant imposed in pursuance of—

    (a) section 35 or 155 of the Housing Act 1985 (covenants for repayment of discount on early disposals);

    (b) paragraph 1 of Schedule 6A to that Act (covenants requiring redemption of landlord's share); or

    (c) paragraph 1 or 3 of Schedule 2 to the Housing Associations Act 1985 (covenants for repaying of discount on early disposals or for restricting disposals).

DEFINITIONS

    "landlord covenant": s.28.

    "tenant covenant": s.28.

GENERAL NOTE

The Act describes those covenants imposed on the landlord and tenant as "landlord" and "tenant" covenants respectively. Section 2 abolishes the distinction between covenants which "have reference to the subject matter" of the tenancy and those which do not for the purpose of the transmission of covenants under new tenancies. It applies to covenants which are express, implied or imposed by law. The term "covenant" is wide, as is clear from the definition section (s.28): it includes terms, conditions or obligations contained in the tenancy (which includes an agreement for a tenancy) or in a collateral agreement made either before or after the tenancy. However, the covenant must be one which "falls to be complied with by" the landlord/tenant of the premises demised by the tenancy. This is a central concept of the Act, which is discussed in the General Note to s.28.

There are three qualifications to this definition contained in subs. (2) which relates to covenants implied by the Housing Act 1985 (c. 68) and the Housing Associations Act 1985 (c. 69). These covenants will continue to bind the original tenants and their successors in title.

Transmission of covenants

Transmission of benefit and burden of covenants

3.—(1) The benefit and burden of all landlord and tenant covenants of a tenancy—

    (a) shall be annexed and incident to the whole, and to each and every part, of the premises demised by the tenancy and of the reversion in them, and

    (b) shall in accordance with this section pass on an assignment of the whole or any part of those premises or of the reversion in them.

(2) Where the assignment is by the tenant under the tenancy, then as from the assignment the assignee—

(a) becomes bound by the tenant covenants of the tenancy except to the extent that—

    (i) immediately before the assignment they did not bind the assignor, or

    (ii) they fall to be complied with in relation to any demised premises not comprised in the assignment; and

(b) becomes entitled to the benefit of the landlord covenants of the tenancy except to the extent that they fall to be complied with in relation to any such premises.

(3) Where the assignment is by the landlord under the tenancy, then as from the assignment the assignee—

(a) becomes bound by the landlord covenants of the tenancy except to the extent that—

    (i) immediately before the assignment they did not bind the assignor, or

    (ii) they fall to be complied with in relation to any demised premises not comprised in the assignment; and

(b) becomes entitled to the benefit of the tenant covenants of the tenancy except to the textent that they fall to be complied with in relation to any such premises.

(4) In determining for the purposes of subsection (2) or (3) whether any covenant bound the assignor immediately before the assignment, any waiver or release of the covenant (in whatever terms) is expressed to be personal to the assignor shall be disregarded.

(5) Any landlord or tenant covenant of a tenancy which is restrictive of the user of land shall, as well as being capable of enforcement against an assignee, be capable of being enforced against any other person who is the owner or occupier of any demised premises to which the covenant relates, even though there is no express provision in the tenancy to that effect.

(6) Nothing in this section shall operate—

(a) in the case of a covenant which (in whatever terms) is expressed to be personal to any person, to make the covenant enforceable by or (as the case may be) against any other person; or

(b) to make a covenant enforceable against any person if, apart from this section, it would not be enforceable against him by reason of its not having been registered under the Land Registration Act 1925 or the Land Charges Act 1972.

(7) To the extent that there remains in force any rule of law by virtue of which the burden of a covenant whose subject matter is not in existence at the time when it is made does not run with the land affected unless the covenantor covenants on behalf of himself and his assigns, that rule of law is hereby abolished in relation to tenancies.

DEFINITIONS
    "assignment": s.28.
    "covenant": s.28.
    "landlord": s.28.
    "landlord covenant": s.28.
    "reversion": s.28.
    "tenancy": s.28.
    "tenant": s.28.
    "tenant covenant": s.28.

GENERAL NOTE
    The aim of Parliament was that the Act should provide a complete and self-contained framework for new tenancies giving full effect to the Law Commission's recommendations with

regard to the transmission of covenants and rights of re-entry (*Hansard*, H.L. Vol. 565, col. 355). It will no longer be relevant to consider whether a covenant has "reference to the subject matter" of the tenancy (alternatively whether the covenant "touches and concerns" the land). The benefit and burden of all covenants will run on assignment subject to the provisions of s.3.

Subss. (1), (2) and (3)

Subsection (1) provides that the benefit and burden of both landlord and tenant covenants are annexed to the demised premises and to the reversion, and shall pass on an assignment in accordance with the provisions of the section. Subsections (2) and (3) deal with the position on assignments by the tenant and landlord respectively. The only covenants which do not pass at the date of the assignment are, first, those covenants which did not bind the assignor and, secondly, those covenants which do not "fall to be complied with" in relation to the premises. The concept of covenants which fall to be complied with in relation to a particular part of the demised premises is discussed in more detail in the General Note to the definition section (s.28). Pursuant to subss. (2)(b) and (3)(b), at the date of the assignment, the assignee becomes entitled to the benefit of the covenants contained in the tenancy.

Subs. (4)

Where there has been a personal release or waiver to the assignor of a landlord or tenant covenant, subs. (4) provides that this release or waiver is to be disregarded for the purposes of determining whether the covenant bound the assignor prior to the assignment, and therefore falls within the terms of subs. (2)(a)(i) or subs. (3)(a)(i).

The provisions with regard to the passing of the covenants should be read, in particular, with s.5 (the release of tenants on assignment), s.6 (the release of landlords on assignment), and s.9 (apportionment agreements), and the supplemental provisions of ss.23 and 24.

Subs. (5)

Subsection (5) is a surprising provision. It relates solely to user covenants and its effect appears to be that such covenants shall be enforceable not only against the landlord and tenant for the time being (and any former landlords and tenants who have not been released in accordance with the statutory provisions) but also against the owner or occupier of the premises. Whilst the tenant is likely to give a covenant restrictive of user in any tenancy, such covenants may also be given by landlords (for example in connection with other units in a shopping development). No definition is given of owner but this is presumably the owner of the interest from whom the landlord's own interest is derived – a head landlord or freeholder. The occupier would apparently include a subtenant or licensee of the tenant (whether lawful or unlawful). This subsection therefore contains an important extension of the enforceability of user covenants in a tenancy, which may be very significant for estate management by landlords.

Subs. (6)

Subsection (6) contains clarification and confirmation on two points. First, the section does not have the effect of making any covenant personal to one person enforceable against another. Secondly, the section does not make enforceable a covenant which would not be enforceable for want of registration under either the Land Registration Act 1925 or the Land Charges Act 1972.

Subs. (7)

Subsection (7) abolishes insofar as is necessary the rule contained in *Spencer's Case* (1583) 5 Co Rep 16a governing covenants made prior to January 1, 1926 to do some act relating to the land where the subject-matter is not in existence at the time the covenant was made (for example, to erect a new building). The position with regard to such covenants made after January 1, 1926 is governed by s.79(1) of the Law of Property Act 1925.

Transmission of rights of re-entry

4. The benefit of a landlord's right of re-entry under a tenancy—

(a) shall be annexed and incident to the whole, and to each and every part, of the reversion in the premises demised by the tenancy, and

(b) shall pass on an assignment of the whole or any part of the reversion in those premises.

DEFINITIONS
"assignment": s.28.
"landlord": s.28.
"reversion": s.28.
"tenancy": s.28.

GENERAL NOTE
A landlord's right to re-enter the premises is not a landlord covenant. Prior to the passing of the Act, the right passed with the reversion as a result of s.141 of the Law of Property Act 1925 but this provision does not apply to new tenancies (s.30(4)). In respect of new tenancies, s.4 provides that the right to re-enter is annexed to the whole and every part of the reversion and passes on an assignment of the whole or part of the reversion. The purpose of the section is therefore to treat each part as if it had been separately demised and the right to re-enter attached to each part.

Release of covenants on assignment

Tenant released from covenants on assignment of tenancy

5.—(1) This section applies where a tenant assigns premises demised to him under a tenancy.

(2) If the tenant assigns the whole of the premises demised to him, he—

(a) is released from the tenant covenants of the tenancy, and

(b) ceases to be entitled to the benefit of the landlord covenants of the tenancy,

as from the assignment.

(3) If the tenant assigns part only of the premises demised to him, then as from the assignment he—

(a) is released from the tenant covenants of the tenancy, and

(b) ceases to be entitled to the benefit of the landlord covenants of the tenancy,

only to the extent that those covenants fall to be complied with in relation to that part of the demised premises.

(4) This section applies as mentioned in subsection (1) whether or not the tenant is tenant of the whole of the premises comprised in the tenancy.

DEFINITIONS
"assignment": s.28.
"landlord": s.28.
"landlord covenant": s.28.
"tenancy": s.28.
"tenant": s.28.
"tenant covenant": s.28.

GENERAL NOTE
This section provides the release given to tenants under new tenancies who assign their interest in the demised premises. Subsection (1) provides that an assignment of the whole results in the automatic release of the tenant from the tenant covenants as from the date of the assignment. The section also deals with the corollary of this, namely, that the tenant is from the date of the assignment no longer entitled to the benefit of the landlord covenants. For the release to take effect, the assignment must not be an "excluded assignment", as defined by s.11.

As a result of the release, the only liability which the tenant may then have will be as a guarantor pursuant to an authorised guarantee agreement under s.16. The tenant will benefit from the restrictions on liability under such guarantees as set out in the general law (as applied by s.16(8)) and ss.17 and 18.

Subsection (3) covers the situation where the tenant assigns his interest in part only of the premises, and provides for a release only to the extent that those covenants fall to be complied with in relation to that part of the premises which has been assigned. Thus the assignor will still be liable for covenants either which do not relate to the part assigned, or which cannot be attributed to any specific part of the premises. To the extent that the assignor is not released from tenant covenants relating to the premises, he will be jointly and severally liable with his assignee in respect of the covenants pursuant to s.13(1) of the Act. In respect of "non-attributable" covenants, it is open to the tenant and his assignee to enter into an apportionment agreement binding on the landlord pursuant to the provisions of s.9.

Subsection (4) makes clear that the provisions of s.5 apply also where there has, prior to the relevant assignment, been an assignment/subletting of part.

Landlord may be released from covenants on assignment of reversion

6.—(1) This section applies where a landlord assigns the reversion in premises of which he is the landlord under a tenancy.

(2) If the landlord assigns the reversion in the whole of the premises of which he is the landlord—

(a) he may apply to be released from the landlord covenants of the tenancy in accordance with section 8; and

(b) if he is so released from all of those covenants, he ceases to be entitled to the benefit of the tenant covenants of the tenancy as from the assignment.

(3) If the landlord assigns the reversion in part only of the premises of which he is the landlord—

(a) he may apply to be so released from the landlord covenants of the tenancy to the extent that they fall to be complied with in relation to that part of those premises; and

(b) if he is, to that extent, so released from all of those covenants, then as from the assignment he ceases to be entitled to the benefit of the tenant covenants only to the extent that they fall to be complied with in relation to that part of those premises.

(4) This section applies as mentioned in subsection (1) whether or not the landlord is landlord of the whole of the premises comprised in the tenancy.

DEFINITIONS
"assignment": s.28.
"landlord": s.28.
"landlord covenants": s.28.
"reversion": s.28.
"tenancy": s.28.
"tenant": s.28.
"tenant covenants": s.28.

GENERAL NOTE
This section provides the release given to landlords from landlord covenants under new tenancies. In contrast to the position of tenants, there is no automatic release on an assignment of the reversion. The rationale for this is that tenants have no way of vetting the landlord's assignee and preventing assignment to a weak or nominee assignee (*Hansard*, H.C. Vol. 263, col. 1240). In order to obtain a release, the landlord must follow the procedure set out in s.8 of the Act. Section 6 sets out the consequences of any release which mirror those of a release of a tenant set out in s.5. Thus if he is released, the landlord ceases to be bound by the landlord covenants or entitled to the benefit of the tenant covenants as from the date of the assignment.

Subsection (2) deals with the position on an assignment of the reversion of the whole and subs. (3) with an assignment of part of the reversion. On an assignment of part, the release relates to the covenants only to the extent that they fall to be complied with in relation to that part of the demised premises. If he is released, the landlord will cease to have the benefit of the tenant covenants from the date of the assignment. Subsection (4) mirrors s.5(4). As with tenants, a landlord and his assignee will be jointly and severally liable under s.13 on any covenants in respect of which the landlord is not released, and can seek to apportion their liability under the procedure contained in s.9.

Former landlord may be released from covenants on assignment of reversion

7.—(1) This section applies where—

(a) a landlord assigns the reversion in premises of which he is the landlord under a tenancy, and

(b) immediately before the assignment a former landlord of the premises remains bound by a landlord covenant of the tenancy ("the relevant covenant").

(2) If immediately before the assignment the former landlord does not remain the landlord of any other premises demised by the tenancy, he may apply to be released from the relevant covenant in accordance with section 8.

(3) In any other case the former landlord may apply to be so released from the relevant covenant to the extent that it falls to be complied with in relation to any premises comprised in the assignment.

(4) If the former landlord is so released from every landlord covenant by which he remained bound immediately before the assignment, he ceases to be entitled to the benefit of the tenant covenants of the tenancy.

(5) If the former landlord is so released from every such landlord covenant to the extent that it falls to be complied with in relation to any premises comprised in the assignment, he ceases to be entitled to the benefit of the tenant covenants of the tenancy to the extent that they fall to be so complied with.

(6) This section applies as mentioned in subsection (1)—

(a) whether or not the landlord making the assignment is landlord of the whole of the premises comprised in the tenancy; and

(b) whether or not the former landlord has previously applied (whether under section 6 or this section) to be released from the relevant covenant.

DEFINITIONS
"assignment": s.28.
"landlord": s.28.
"landlord covenant": s.28.
"reversion: s.28.
"tenant": s.28.
"tenant covenant": s.28.

GENERAL NOTE
This section provides for the release of former landlords who are still bound by landlord covenants under a tenancy. The former landlord has the opportunity to apply for a release at the time of a subsequent assignment. This situation might arise in the following circumstances: where the former landlord did not apply for a release at the time of the assignment by him; the release was validly objected to by either the tenant or the court pursuant to the procedure laid down in s.8; the assignment by the former landlord was an excluded assignment as defined by s.11. Subsections (2) and (3) make it clear that the former landlord is entitled to apply for a complete release where he is no longer the landlord of any of the premises comprised in the tenancy, or a partial release in respect of those landlord covenants which fall to be complied with in relation to the premises to be assigned.

Subsections (4) and (5) confirm that, if the landlord does obtain a release, he will cease to be entitled to the benefit of the tenant covenants – subs. (4) dealing with a full release of all landlord covenants under the tenancy and subs. (5) with a partial release of the landlord. Subsection (6) states that the former landlord can seek a release under s.7 notwithstanding that the assignment which provides the opportunity for him to seek that release is not an assignment of the whole of the premises comprised in the tenancy, or that he has previously been unsuccessful in an application for a release.

Procedure for seeking release from a covenant under section 6 or 7

8.—(1) For the purposes of section 6 or 7 an application for the release of a covenant to any extent is made by serving on the tenant, either before or within the period of four weeks beginning with the date of the assignment in question, a notice informing him of—

(a) the proposed assignment or (as the case may be) the fact that the assignment has taken place, and

(b) the request for the covenant to be released to that extent.

(2) Where an application for the release of a covenant is made in accordance with subsection (1), the covenant is released to the extent mentioned in the notice if—

(a) the tenant does not, within the period of four weeks beginning with the day on which the notice is served, serve on the landlord or former landlord a notice in writing objecting to the release, or

(b) the tenant does so serve such a notice but the court, on the application of the landlord or former landlord, makes a declaration that it is reasonable for the covenant to be so released, or

(c) the tenant serves on the landlord or former landlord a notice in writing consenting to the release and, if he has previously served a notice objecting to it, stating that that notice is withdrawn.

(3) Any release from a covenant in accordance with this section shall be regarded as occurring at the time when the assignment in question takes place.

(4) In this section—

(a) "the tenant" means the tenant of the premises comprised in the assignment in question (or, if different parts of those premises are held under the tenancy by different tenants, each of those tenants);

(b) any reference to the landlord or the former landlord is a reference to the landlord referred to in section 6 or the former landlord referred to in section 7, as the case may be; and

(c) "the court" means a county court.

DEFINITIONS
"assignment": s.28.
"court": s.8(4).
"covenant": s.28.
"former landlord": ss.7, 8(4)(b).
"landlord": ss.6, 8(4)(b).
"tenant": ss.8(4)(a), 28.

GENERAL NOTE
This section sets out the procedure to be followed by a landlord or former landlord who wishes to be released from the landlord covenants. Until a release is given in accordance with the terms of the section, the landlord will continue to be liable under the landlord covenants and that liability could continue until the end of the term. The landlord and former landlord who has not obtained a release under this section will be jointly and severally liable in respect of the landlord covenants.

In order to achieve a release from the landlord covenants under either subs. (6) or (7), a landlord or former landlord must serve notice on the tenant either before or within four weeks of the date of the assignment, informing the tenant of the assignment and requesting the release from the covenants. The tenant has four weeks from the date of service of the notice to serve his notice objecting to the release. If he does not serve such a notice, then the landlord is released. If notice of objection is served, the landlord or former landlord must make an application to the county court for a declaration that it is reasonable for the covenants to be released. The landlord must give notice of the "assignment in question". The clear implication from this is that the identity of the assignee is known and disclosed to the tenant. The tenant will require this information so that he can take a view on whether to consent. If the assignment in question does not proceed, the landlord will have to serve a further notice in respect of any subsequent assignment.

The provisions of the section do not require the landlord to serve notice of the assignment on former landlords who have not been released, although they do have the right to seek a release on a subsequent assignment. The question therefore arises as to how the former landlord will know of his opportunity to apply for a release – a matter of some importance in view of the strict four-week time-limit. It seems that the only way that this can be dealt with is for the former landlord to obtain a contractual commitment from his assignees to inform him of subsequent assignments.

Subsection (2)(c) allows the tenant to give notice at any time consenting to the release or withdrawing any notice of objection. If consent to the release is not forthcoming from the tenant, then the onus moves to the landlord to make the necessary application to the court in order to secure the release. There is no guidance given as to the grounds on which the court might make or refuse to make such a declaration. Grounds on which a tenant might oppose the release are the financial strength of the assignee or, having regard to the extent and nature of the landlord covenants, where the ability (not just financial) of the assignee to comply with the landlord covenants is uncertain.

Section 18 provides for the form of the notice which will be prescribed by regulations to be made by the Lord Chancellor. See the General Note to s.18 regarding the form of notice. There is no provision in the Act allowing either the landlord any period longer than four weeks to serve notice of the assignment or similarly the tenant any longer period for serving notice of objection. The time-limits therefore seem to be strict, subject perhaps to any argument of waiver or estoppel. Provisions with regard to the service of any notice are set out in s.27 of the Act.

Subsection (3) provides that any release of the landlord or former landlord will take effect on the date of the assignment giving rise to the opportunity to seek the release.

Apportionment of liability between assignor and assignee

Apportionment of liability under covenants binding both assignor and assignee of tenancy or reversion

9.—(1) This section applies where—

(a) a tenant assigns part only of the premises demised to him by a tenancy;

(b) after the assignment both the tenant and his assignee are to be bound by a non-attributable tenant covenant of the tenancy; and

(c) the tenant and his assignee agree that as from the assignment liability under the covenant is to be apportioned between them in such manner as is specified in the agreement.

(2) This section also applies where—

(a) a landlord assigns the reversion in part only of the premises of which he is the landlord under a tenancy;

(b) after the assignment both the landlord and his assignee are to be bound by a non-attributable landlord covenant of the tenancy; and

(c) the landlord and his assignee agree that as from the assignment liability under the covenant is to be apportioned between them in such manner as is specified in the agreement.

(3) Any such agreement as is mentioned in subsection (1) or (2) may apportion liability in such a way that a party to the agreement is exonerated from all liability under a covenant.

(4) In any case falling within subsection (1) or (2) the parties to the agreement may apply for the apportionment to become binding on the appropriate person in accordance with section 10.

(5) In any such case the parties to the agreement may also apply for the apportionment to become binding on any person (other than the appropriate person) who is for the time being entitled to enforce the covenant in question; and section 10 shall apply in relation to such an application as it applies in relation to an application made with respect to the appropriate person.

(6) For the purposes of this section a covenant is, in relation to an assignment, a "non-attributable" covenant if it does not fall to be complied with in relation to any premises comprised in the assignment.

(7) In this section "the appropriate person" means either—

(a) the landlord of the entire premises referred to in subsection (1)(a) (or, if different parts of those premises are held under the tenancy by different landlords, each of those landlords), or

(b) the tenant of the entire premises referred to in subsection (2)(a) (or, if different parts of those premises are held under the tenancy by different tenants, each of those tenants),

depending on whether the agreement in question falls within subsection (1) or subsection (2).

DEFINITIONS

"appropriate person": s.9(7).

"assignment": s.28.

"covenant falling to be complied with": s.28(2).

"landlord": s.28.

"landlord covenant": s.28.

"non-attributable covenant": s.9(6).

"reversion": s.28.
"tenant": s.28.
"tenant covenant": s.28.

GENERAL NOTE

This section deals with the position where there is an assignment of part of either the tenancy or reversion, and how the liability under what is called a "non-attributable" covenant may be determined by the assignor and assignee. Subsection (1) states that the section applies to an assignment of part by the tenant; subs. (2) applies the section to the assignment of part by the landlord. The tenant/landlord and his assignee can agree that, as from the date of the assignment, liability under the non-attributable covenant is to be apportioned and, pursuant to subs. (3), this may extend to relieving one of the parties from all liability. This agreement would therefore govern the position between assignor and assignee. In the event that no apportionment agreement is reached, then the assignor and assignee will be jointly and severally liable under the covenant pursuant to the provisions of s.13.

A non-attributable covenant is one which does not fall to be complied with in relation to any premises comprised in the assignment. The test of whether a covenant does or does not fall to be complied with is contained in s.28(2) and (3); see further the General Note to that section. Examples of non-attributable covenants would be: a covenant by the tenant to repair the roof of a building where the tenant assigns part of the tenancy with regard to one floor within the building; a landlord's obligation to give the tenant access to facilities separate from the demised property (an example given by the Law Commission); subject to s.28(3), the covenant to pay rent, service charge, insurance premium or any other sums of money.

This section further provides that the assignor and assignee can ensure that such an apportionment agreement can become binding on third parties if the procedure set out in s.10 of the Act is followed. The third parties which can be bound are the "appropriate person" or any person who is for the time being entitled to enforce the covenant (for example, a mortgagee in possession pursuant to s.15). The appropriate person is defined in subs. (7). Where there is an agreement between the tenant and his assignee, the appropriate person will be the landlord or landlords of the demised premises. In the case of the landlord, the appropriate person will be the tenant or tenants.

Procedure for making apportionment bind other party to lease

10.—(1) For the purposes of section 9 the parties to an agreement falling within subsection (1) or (2) of that section apply for an apportionment to become binding on the appropriate person if, either before or within the period of four weeks beginning with the date of the assignment in question, they serve on that person a notice informing him of—

(a) the proposed assignment or (as the case may be) the fact that the assignment has taken place;

(b) the prescribed particulars of the agreement; and

(c) their request that the apportionment should become binding on him.

(2) Where an application for an apportionment to become binding has been made in accordance with subsection (1), the apportionment becomes binding on the appropriate person if—

(a) he does not, within the period of four weeks beginning with the day on which the notice is served under subsection (1), serve on the parties to the agreement a notice in writing objecting to the apportionment becoming binding on him, or

(b) he does so serve such a notice but the court, on the application of the parties to the agreement, makes a declaration that it is reasonable for the apportionment to become binding on him, or

(c) he serves on the parties to the agreement a notice in writing consenting to the apportionment becoming binding on him and, if he has previously served a notice objecting thereto, stating that the notice is withdrawn.

(3) Where any apportionment becomes binding in accordance with this section, this shall be regarded as occurring at the time when the assignment in question takes place.

(4) In this section—

"the appropriate persons" has the same meaning as in section 9;

"the court" means a county court;
"prescribed" means prescribed by virtue of section 27.

DEFINITIONS
"appropriate person": ss.9, 10(4).
"assignment": s.28.
"court, the": s.10(4).
"prescribed": s.27.

GENERAL NOTE
This section sets out the procedure for making an apportionment agreement under s.9 binding on certain third parties. The procedure is similar to that set out in s.8 with regard to the release of landlord covenants. Before or within four weeks of the assignment to which the apportionment agreement relates takes place, the parties to the agreement must serve on the appropriate person (or person entitled to enforce the covenant, see s.9(5)) a notice in the prescribed form. The notice will inform the appropriate person of the proposed assignment, the prescribed details of the apportionment agreement and their request that the apportionment should become binding on him.

As under s.8, the person receiving the notice has four weeks from the date of service to serve notice either objecting or consenting to the apportionment agreement. If an objection is made, then the parties to the agreement can apply to the county court for a declaration that it is reasonable for the agreement to become binding on the third party. No guidance is given as to the circumstances in which the court will make such a declaration but it is reasonable to anticipate that the nature of the non-attributable covenant and the likely prejudice to the respective parties will be taken into account.

Section 27 provides that the Lord Chancellor will make regulations with regard to the form of the notice to be served under s.10 and for the service of such notices. See further the General Note to s.27.

Where an apportionment agreement does become binding, either following consent from the third party or an application to the court, it takes effect from the date of the assignment.

Excluded assignments

Assignments in breach of covenant or by operation of law

11.—(1) This section provides for the operation of sections 5 to 10 in relation to assignments in breach of a covenant of a tenancy or assignments by operation of law ("excluded assignments").

(2) In the case of an excluded assignment subsection (2) or (3) of section 5—

(a) shall not have the effect mentioned in that subsection in relation to the tenant as from that assignment, but

(b) shall have that effect as from the next assignment (if any) of the premises assigned by him which is not an excluded assignment.

(3) In the case of an excluded assignment subsection (2) or (3) of section 6 or 7—

(a) shall not enable the landlord or former landlord to apply for such a release as is mentioned in that subsection as from that assignment, but

(b) shall apply on the next assignment (if any) of the reversion assigned by the landlord which is not an excluded assignment so as to enable the landlord or former landlord to apply for any such release as from that subsequent assignment.

(4) Where subsection (2) or (3) of section 6 or 7 does so apply—

(a) any reference in that section to the assignment (except where it relates to the time as from which the release takes effect) is a reference to the excluded assignment; but

(b) in that excepted case and in section 8 as it applies in relation to any application under that section made by virtue of subsection (3) above, any refe.. :ce to the assignment or proposed assignment is a reference to any sucn subsequent assignment as is mentioned in that subsection.

(5) In the case of an excluded assignment section 9—

(a) shall not enable the tenant or landlord and his assignee to apply for an agreed apportionment to become binding in accordance with section 10 as from that assignment, but

(b) shall apply on the next assignment (if any) of the premises or reversion assigned by the tenant or landlord which is not an excluded assignment so as to enable him and his assignee to apply for such an apportionment to become binding in accordance with section 10 as from that subsequent assignment.

(6) Where section 9 does so apply—

(a) any reference in that section to the assignment or the assignee under it is a reference to the excluded assignment and the assignee under that assignment; but

(b) in section 10 as it applies in relation to any application under section 9 made by virtue of subsection (5) above, any reference to the assignment or proposed assignment is a reference to any such subsequent assignment as is mentioned in that subsection.

(7) If any such subsequent assignment as is mentioned in subsection (2), (3) or (5) above comprises only part of the premises assigned by the tenant or (as the case may be) only part of the premises the reversion in which was assigned by the landlord on the excluded assignment—

(a) the relevant provision or provisions of section 5, 6, 7 or 9 shall only have the effect mentioned in that subsection to the extent that the covenants or covenant in question fall or falls to be complied with in relation to that part of those premises; and

(b) that subsection may accordingly apply on different occasions in relation to different parts of those premises.

DEFINITIONS
"assignment": s.28.
"excluded assignment": s.11(1).
"landlord": s.28.
"reversion": s.28.
"tenant": s.28.

GENERAL NOTE

This section modifies the provisions for the release of both landlords and tenants on "excluded assignments" for the purposes of ss.5 to 10. Excluded assignments are defined as assignments either in breach of covenant or by operation of law. An assignment in breach of covenant will be an assignment by the tenant in breach of the alienation provisions of the tenancy. Where the covenant is qualified, questions are therefore likely to arise as to whether the landlord has unreasonably withheld consent and, thus, whether the tenant has the benefit of the release notwithstanding that consent has not been given.

Examples of an assignment by operation of law are an assignment on the death of a joint tenant of the legal estate; on the bankruptcy of an individual tenant, the tenancy will vest in the trustee in bankruptcy; on the death of a tenant, the tenancy will vest in his executor at death or administrator from the date of grant of letters of administration.

Where there is an excluded assignment of either the tenancy or the reversion, the effect of s.11 is to defer the release (or in the case of the landlord the opportunity to request a release) to the next assignment which is not an excluded assignment.

Subsection (4) is not happily drafted but the effect seems to be that a subsequent release following an assignment which is not an excluded assignment, will not be retrospective. Thus, the date of the release and the date on which the application must be made under s.8 is determined by the date of the subsequent assignment.

Subsection (5) restricts the operation of an apportionment agreement entered into under s.9. The tenant/landlord and his assignee cannot apply for the apportionment agreement to become binding on a third party, until the next assignment which is not an excluded assignment. Pursuant to subs. (6)(b), the date of the application under s.10 and the date that the apportionment agreement becomes binding is determined by reference to the date of the subsequent assignment, not the excluded assignment. The position where the subsequent assignment relates only to part of the premises assigned under the excluded assignment is dealt with in subs. (7). Any release can relate only to those covenants which fall to be complied with in relation to the premises assigned under the subsequent assignment.

Third party covenants

Covenants with management companies etc.

12.—(1) This section applies where—

(a) a person other than the landlord or tenant ("the third party") is under a covenant of a tenancy liable (as principal) to discharge any function with respect to all or any of the demised premises ("the relevant function"); and

(b) that liability is not the liability of a guarantor or any other financial liability referable to the performance or otherwise of a covenant of the tenancy by another party to it.

(2) To the extent that any covenant of the tenancy confers any rights against the third party with respect to the relevant function, then for the purposes of the transmission of the benefit of the covenant in accordance with this Act it shall be treated as if it were—

(a) a tenant covenant of the tenancy to the extent that those rights are exercisable by the landlord; and

(b) a landlord covenant of the tenancy to the extent that those rights are exercisable by the tenant.

(3) To the extent that any covenant of the tenancy confers any rights exercisable by the third party with respect to the relevant functions, then for the purposes mentioned in subsection (4), it shall be treated as if it were—

(a) a tenant covenant of the tenancy to the extent that those rights are exercisable against the tenant; and

(b) a landlord covenant of the tenancy to the extent that those rights are exercisable against the landlord.

(4) The purposes mentioned in subsection (3) are—

(a) the transmission of the burden of the covenant in accordance with this Act; and

(b) any release from, or apportionment of liability in respect of, the covenant in accordance with this Act.

(5) In relation to the release of the landlord from any covenant which is to be treated as a landlord covenant by virtue of subsection (3), section 8 shall apply as if any reference to the tenant were a reference to the third party.

DEFINITIONS
"landlord covenant": s.28.
"relevant function": s.12(1)(a).
"tenant": s.28.
"tenant covenant": s.28.
"third party": s.12(1)(a).

GENERAL NOTE
Section 12 provides for the transmission and release of any covenant given by a party other than the landlord, tenant or guarantor, to discharge any function with respect to all or any of the demised premises. The side note refers to management companies but these are not mentioned elsewhere in the section. The present position with regard to such management companies is that, as they have no legal estate vested in them (either the reversion or the tenancy), their rights and obligations are determined entirely by the general law of contract. With regard to new tenancies, the position of such companies will be governed by the provisions of s.12. The broad effect of s.12 is to treat the rights and obligations of the management companies as landlord/tenant covenants (as appropriate) for the purpose of transmission of and any release from those covenants. For the purpose of the transmission of the benefit of a covenant, subs. (2) provides that, in respect of rights exercisable against the third party, the covenant shall be treated as a landlord or tenant covenant depending upon by whom the rights are exercisable. Presumably,

the third party will cease to have the benefits of those covenants on assignment in accordance with the provisions of ss.5 and 6 of the Act.

Subsection (3) deals with rights exercisable by the third party under any covenant for the purposes of transmission of the burden of the covenant, the release of the covenant and the apportionment of liability under the covenant (these purposes being set out in subs. (4)). If the rights are exercisable by the third party against the tenant, the relevant covenant is treated as a tenant covenant. Thus, on an assignment of the whole of the tenancy by the tenant, the tenant will obtain an automatic release from his obligations to his landlord and the third party.

Subsection (5) deals with the release of the landlord from any landlord covenant exercisable by the third party pursuant to subs. (3)(b). The provisions of s.8 apply, the third party being treated for these purposes as the tenant. Thus, if the landlord wishes to seek a release from this covenant on assignment, he must give the necessary notice to the third party.

Joint liability under covenants

Covenants binding two or more persons

13.—(1) Where in consequence of this Act two or more persons are bound by the same covenant, they are so bound both jointly and severally.

(2) Subject to section 24(2), where by virtue of this Act—

(a) two or more persons are bound jointly and severally by the same covenant, and

(b) any of the persons so bound is released from the covenant,

the release does not extend to any other of those persons.

(3) For the purpose of providing for contribution between persons who, by virtue of this Act, are bound jointly and severally by a covenant, the Civil Liability (Contribution) Act 1978 shall have effect as if—

(a) liability to a person under a covenant were liability in respect of damage suffered by that person;

(b) references to damage accordingly included a breach of a covenant of a tenancy; and

(c) section 7(2) of that Act were omitted.

DEFINITIONS
"covenant": s.28.

GENERAL NOTE
As a result of the provisions of the Act, the situation may arise where two or more people are bound by the same covenant. Examples of such cases are: where a tenant has been unable to obtain a release on an excluded assignment; where a landlord has failed to apply or applied unsuccessfully for a release on assignment; where there has been an assignment of part of the tenancy or reversion and no apportionment agreement in respect of the non-attributable covenants has become binding on the appropriate person. By virtue of subs. (1), where there are two or more persons bound, they are jointly and severally liable under the covenant.

Subs. (2)
Subsection (2) provides that the release of one of the persons jointly bound will not release any other person. This is subject to s.24(2) which does provide for the automatic release of a guarantor of the tenant when the tenant is himself released.

Subs. (3)
Subsection (3) provides that for the purposes of contribution between joint covenantors, the Civil Liability (Contribution) Act 1978 shall apply, the references to damage in the 1978 Act being construed as liability under a covenant. By subs. (3)(c), s.7(2) of the 1978 Act is treated as having been omitted for these purposes. However, as it is clear from s.1 that s.13 only applies to new tenancies (and indeed s.13 itself refers to parties jointly and severally bound "in consequence of this Act"), it is difficult to see the purpose of this section. All relevant obligations would have been assumed after January 1, 1979 in any event.

Abolition of indemnity covenants implied by statute

14. The following provisions (by virtue of which indemnity covenants are implied on the assignment of a tenancy) shall cease to have effect—

(a) subsections (1)(C) and (D) of section 77 of the Law of Property Act 1925; and

(b) subsections (1)(b) and (2) of section 24 of the Land Registration Act 1925.

DEFINITIONS
"tenancy": s.28.

GENERAL NOTE
This section abolishes the provisions of the Law of Property Act 1925 and the Land Registration Act 1925 which give rise to the chain of indemnity covenants on the assignment of the tenancy as briefly described in the Introduction, above. Very broadly, the purpose of the Act is to release tenants from the benefit and burden of covenants after they have assigned their interest, and an important aspect of that release is the abolition of the indemnity covenants. The provisions of the Law of Property Act 1925 deal with the indemnity given on an assignment of whole or part of a tenancy in unregistered land. The provisions of the Land Registration Act 1925 deal with the implied indemnity on the assignment of the whole or part of a tenancy with registered title. Whilst it is not stated expressly within s.14, the abolition clearly relates only to new tenancies pursuant to the provisions of ss.1 and 30(2).

Enforcement of covenants

Enforcement of covenants

15.—(1) Where any tenant covenant of a tenancy, or any right of re-entry contained in a tenancy, is enforceable by the reversioner in respect of any premises demised by the tenancy, it shall also be so enforceable by—

(a) any person (other that the reversioner) who, as the holder of the immediate reversion in those premises, is for the time being entitled to the rents and profits under the tenancy in respect of those premises, or

(b) any mortgagee in possession of the reversion in those premises who is so entitled.

(2) Where any landlord covenant of a tenancy is enforceable against the reversioner in respect of any premises demised by the tenancy, it shall also be enforceable against any person falling within subsection (1)(a) or (b).

(3) Where any landlord covenant of a tenancy is enforceable by the tenant in respect of any premises demised by the tenancy, it shall also be so enforceable by any mortgagee in possession of those premises under a mortgage granted by the tenant.

(4) Where any tenant covenant of a tenancy, or any right of re-entry contained in a tenancy, is enforceable against the tenant in respect of any premises demised by the tenancy, it shall also be so enforceable against any such mortgagee.

(5) Nothing in this section shall operate—

(a) in the case of a covenant which (in whatever terms) is expressed to be personal to any person to make the covenant enforceable by or (as the case may be) against any other person; or

(b) to make a covenant enforceable against any person if, apart from this section, it would not be enforceable against him by reason of its not having been registered under the Land Registration Act 1925 or the Land Charges Act 1972.

(6) In this section—

"mortgagee" and "mortgage" include "chargee" and "charge" respectively;

"the reversioner", in relation to a tenancy, means the holder for the time being of the interest of the landlord under the tenancy.

DEFINITIONS
"landlord": s.28.
"landlord covenant": s.28.
"mortgage": s.15(6).

"mortgagee": s.15(6).
"reversion": s.28.
"reversioner": s.15(6).
"tenancy": s.28.
"tenant covenant": s.28.

GENERAL NOTE

This section provides for the enforceability of covenants and the right of re-entry by and against parties other than the landlord and tenant under the tenancy. There are two categories of such persons referred to in the section. The first is the person who for the time being is entitled to the rents and profits under the tenancy. Normally that right would of course be vested in the landlord. However, where the landlord creates a further tenancy/lease of the premises after the grant of the relevant tenancy, that further tenancy gives to the second tenant the right to receive the rent of the premises until such time (if ever) that the second tenant is entitled to possession. This would be the position on the grant of an overriding lease under s.19.

The second category of person is the mortgagee in possession of either the tenancy or the reversion. A mortgagee will be considered to be in possession if he has actual possession of the mortgaged property or is in receipt of the rents from the property. Prior to the passing of the Act, a mortgagee in possession would have certain rights and liabilities with regard to the property and the mortgagor. The position with regard to the benefit and burden of covenants where the mortgaged property was leasehold was far from clear. Looking at the position of a mortgagee of the landlord's interest, a mortgagee in possession would be entitled to enforce covenants contained in a tenancy granted by his mortgagor pursuant to the statutory powers of leasing under s.99 of the Law of Property Act 1925 (see *The Municipal Permanent Investment Building Society v. Smith* (1888) 22 Q.B.D. 70). However, there were difficulties with regard to the enforcement of covenants against the mortgagee. The position is now clarified in respect of new tenancies. The covenants will now be enforceable by and against the mortgagee in possession. In practical terms, it is likely to mean that mortgagees will be even more reluctant to go into possession than they are at present.

Subsection (1) provides that the tenant covenants will be enforceable by the reversioner/mortgagee in possession against the tenant. Under subs. (2) these two categories of person also become liable to perform the landlord covenants contained in the lease.

Subsections (3) and (4) deal with the position of a mortgagee in possession of the tenant's interest and, in particular, state that such a mortgagee can enforce the landlord covenants in the tenancy and that any tenant covenant or right of re-entry shall be enforceable against a mortgagee in possession. Whilst the covenants under the tenancy become enforceable by and against the mortgagee in possession, it would appear that the mortgagee does not become bound by such covenants. As a result, it would appear that there would be no need for the mortgagee in possession of the landlord's interest to apply for a release under s.8.

Subsection (5) clarifies the extent of the section and provides that the section does not have the effect of making any covenant personal to one person more widely enforceable, and does not save any covenant which would have failed to be enforceable for want of registration.

Liability of former tenant etc. in respect of covenants

Tenant guaranteeing performance of covenant by assignee

16.—(1) Where on an assignment a tenant is to any extent released from a tenant covenant of a tenancy by virtue of this Act ("the relevant covenant"), nothing in this Act (and in particular section 25) shall preclude him from entering into an authorised guarantee agreement with respect to the performance of that covenant by the assignee.

(2) For the purposes of this section an agreement is an authorised guarantee agreement if—

(a) under it the tenant guarantees the performance of the relevant covenant to any extent by the assignee; and

(b) it is entered into in the circumstances set out in subsection (3); and

(c) its provisions conform with subsections (4) and (5).

(3) those circumstances are as follows—

(a) by virtue of a covenant against assignment (whether absolute or qualified) the assignment cannot be effected without the consent of the landlord under the tenancy or some other person;

(b) any such consent is given subject to a condition (lawfully imposed) that the tenant is to enter into an agreement guaranteeing the performance of the covenant by the assignee; and

(c) the agreement is entered into by the tenant in pursuance of that condition.

(4) An agreement is not an authorised guarantee agreement to the extent that it purports—

(a) to impose on the tenant any requirement to guarantee in any way the performance of the relevant covenant by any person other than the assignee; or

(b) to impose on the tenant any liability, restriction or other requirement (of whatever nature) in relation to any time after the assignee is released from that covenant by virtue of this Act.

(5) Subject to subsection (4), an authorised guarantee agreement may—

(a) impose on the tenant any liability as sole or principal debtor in respect of any obligation owed by the assignee under the relevant covenant;

(b) impose on the tenant liabilities as guarantor in respect of the assignee's performance of that covenant which are no more onerous than those to which he would be subject in the event of his being liable as sole or principal debtor in respect of any obligation owed by the assignee under that covenant;

(c) require the tenant, in the event of the tenancy assigned by him being disclaimed, to enter into a new tenancy of the premises comprised in the assignment—

(i) whose term expires not later than the term of the tenancy assigned by the tenant, and

(ii) whose tenant covenants are no more onerous than those of that tenancy;

(d) make provision incidental or supplementary to any provision made by virtue of any of paragraphs (a) to (c).

(6) Where a person ("the former tenant") is to any extent released from a covenant of a tenancy by virtue of section 11(2) as from an assignment and the assignor under the assignment enters into an authorised guarantee agreement with the landlord with respect to the performance of that covenant by the assignee under the assignment—

(a) the landlord may require the former tenant to enter into an agreement under which he guarantees, on terms corresponding to those of that authorised guarantee agreement, the performance of that covenant by the assignee under the assignment; and

(b) if its provisions conform with subsections (4) and (5), any such agreement shall be an authorised guarantee agreement for the purposes of this section; and

(c) in the application of this section in relation to any such agreement—

(i) subsections (2)(b) and (c) and (3) shall be omitted, and

(ii) any reference to the tenant or to the assignee shall be read as a reference to the former tenant or to the assignee under the assignment.

(7) For the purposes of subsection (1) it is immaterial that—

(a) the tenant has already made an authorised guarantee agreement in respect of a previous assignment by him of the tenancy referred to in that subsection, it having been subsequently revested in him following a disclaimer on behalf of the previous assignee, or

(b) the tenancy referred to in that subsection is a new tenancy entered into by the tenant in pursuance of an authorised guarantee agreement;

and in any such case subsections (2) to (5) shall apply accordingly.

(8) It is hereby declared that the rules of law relating to guarantees (and in particular those relating to the release of sureties) are, subject to its terms,

applicable in relation to any authorised guarantee agreement as in relation to any other guarantee agreement.

DEFINITIONS
"assignment": s.28.
"authorised guarantee agreement": s.16(2).
"disclaimer": s.178 and the Insolvency Act 1986, s.315.
"former tenant": s.16(6).
"tenancy": s.28.
"tenant": s.28.
"tenant covenant": s.28.

GENERAL NOTE
This section permits guarantees by the tenant of performance of the tenant covenants of the tenant's assignee, notwithstanding the anti-avoidance provisions contained in s.25. Such agreements, which can only be entered into in respect of new tenancies, are to be known as authorised guarantee agreements. However, not surprisingly, the circumstances in which such agreements can be entered into are heavily proscribed, the limitations being set out in subss. (3) and (4). Subsection (3) sets out three conditions. The first is that the assignment must require either the consent of the landlord or some other person (for example, the superior landlord) by virtue of the alienation covenant in the tenancy. The second condition is that the tenant enters an authorised guarantee agreement pursuant to a lawful condition for consent to the assignment. (The question whether it is lawful for the landlord to require a guarantee will be governed by the terms of the tenancy and the provisions of the Landlord and Tenant Act 1988. Section 22 of the Act allows the parties to new tenancies to enter an agreement setting out the conditions subject to which the landlord may grant consent. For a discussion of the implications of ss.16 and 22, see the General Note to s.22.) Thirdly, the tenant must enter into the agreement pursuant to that condition.

Subsection (4) places certain limitations on the scope of authorised guarantee agreements. Such a guarantee can only relate to the performance of the covenant by the tenant's assignee and cannot extend to any time after the release of that assignee pursuant to the Act. The permitted extent of such agreements is set out in subs. (5). First, it is clear from subs. (5)(a), that the tenant can enter such agreement as principal, not merely guarantor. If the tenant does enter into the agreement as principal, his liability is potentially greater because, for example, it will not be open to him to seek to limit his liability by reference to certain defences which might be available to the assignee. Subsection (5)(b) provides that the terms of the guarantee can be no more onerous than if the tenant had contracted as principal debtor in respect of any obligation owed by the assignee.

It has become common practice in the drafting of commercial leases to require guarantors (and others) to enter into a new tenancy of the premises on similar terms, in the event that the tenancy is disclaimed. A liquidator or trustee in bankruptcy has the power to disclaim a tenancy under ss.178 and 315 respectively of the Insolvency Act 1986 (c. 45). Subsection (5)(c) confirms this practice providing that the new tenancy cannot expire later than the term of the disclaimed tenancy, and the terms of the new tenancy cannot be any more onerous than those of the disclaimed tenancy. Further in subs. (7), it is made clear that an assignor can be required to enter into an authorised guarantee agreement, notwithstanding that he has been obliged to take the tenancy following the disclaimer of the previous tenancy. A tenant in these circumstances might only be able to rid himself of any continuing liability under the tenancy when he has assigned to a solvent tenant who then lawfully assigns.

The position of the former tenant is dealt with in subs. (6). Notwithstanding the automatic release of tenants generally under the Act, a former tenant may still have liability where the previous assignment was an excluded assignment under s.11. Such a tenant would be released on the next assignment (provided that the next assignment was not an excluded assignment). Subsection (6) provides that the landlord can require such a former tenant to enter into an authorised guarantee agreement where the tenant is entering such an agreement, and on the same terms as that agreement, and provided that the agreement meets the conditions set out in subss. (4) and (5). The provisions of subss. (5) and (6) should be read subject to the provisions of ss.17 and 18 which place certain further restrictions on the liability of guarantors under an authorised guarantee agreement.

Subsection (8) provides that the law of guarantees shall apply to agreements created by s.16. Particular reference is made to the release of guarantors/sureties. Subject to the terms of the guarantee, such a release will occur where there has been a substantial variation of the tenancy after the date of the guarantee. A recent application of this principle in the landlord and tenant context is the case of *Howard de Walden Estates v. Pasta Place* (1995) 22 E.G. 143.

Restriction on liability of former tenant or his guarantor for rent or service charge etc.

17.—(1) This section applies where a person ("the former tenant") is as a result of an assignment no longer a tenant under a tenancy but—

(a) (in the case of a tenancy which is a new tenancy) he has under an authorised guarantee agreement guaranteed the performance by his assignee of a tenant covenant of the tenancy under which any fixed charge is payable; or

(b) (in the case of any tenancy) he remains bound by such a covenant.

(2) The former tenant shall not be liable under that agreement or (as the case may be) the covenant to pay any amount in respect of any fixed charge payabie under the covenant unless, within the period of six months beginning with the date when the charge becomes due, the landlord serves on the former tenant a notice informing him—

(a) that the charge is now due; and

(b) that in respect of the charge the landlord intends to recover from the former tenant such amount as is specified in the notice and (where payable) interest calculated on such basis as is so specified.

(3) Where a person ("the guarantor") has agreed to guarantee the performance by the former tenant of such a covenant as is mentioned in subsection (1), the guarantor shall not be liable under the agreement to pay any amount in respect of any fixed charge payable under the covenant unless, within the period of six months beginning with the date when the charge becomes due, the landlord serves on the guarantor a notice informing him—

(a) that the charge is now due; and

(b) that in respect of the charge the landlord intends to recover from the guarantor such amount as is specified in the notice and (where payable) interest calculated on such basis as is so specified.

(4) Where the landlord has duly served a notice under subsection (2) or (3), the amount (exclusive of interest) which the former tenant or (as the case may be) the guarantor is liable to pay in respect of the fixed charge in question shall not exceed the amount specified in the notice unless—

(a) his liability in respect of the charge is subsequently determined to be for a greater amount,

(b) the notice informed him of the possibility that that liability would be so determined, and

(c) within the period of three months beginning with the date of the determination, the landlord serves on him a further notice informing him that the landlord intends to recover that greater amount from him (plus interest, where payable).

(5) For the purposes of subsection (2) or (3) any fixed charge which has become due before the date on which this Act comes into force shall be treated as becoming due on that date; but neither of those subsections applies to any such charge if before that date proceedings have been instituted by the landlord for the recovery from the former tenant of any amount in respect of it.

(6) In this section—

"fixed charge", in relation to a tenancy, means—

(a) rent,

(b) any service charge as defined by section 18 of the Landlord and Tenant Act 1985 (the words "of a dwelling" being disregarded for this purpose), and

(c) any amount payable under a tenant covenant of the tenancy providing for the payment of a liquidated sum in the event of a failure to comply with any such covenant;

"landlord", in relation to a fixed charge, includes any person who has a right to enforce payment of the charge.

DEFINITIONS

"assignment": s.28.
"authorised guarantee agreement": s.16.
"commencement date": s.31.
"fixed charge": s.17(4).
"former tenant": s.17(1).
"landlord": ss.17(4), 28.
"tenant": s.28.
"tenant covenant": s.28.

GENERAL NOTE

This section applies to former tenants and guarantors under both new and other tenancies as defined by s.1. It limits the liability of those parties in respect of any covenant under which any fixed charge is payable, this term being defined in subs. (4) as rent, service charge and liquidated damages for breach of covenant. The definition is discussed further below. In respect of new tenancies, the section specifically refers to former tenants as those who have entered into an authorised guarantee agreement. The second group of former tenants is those who are bound by a covenant to pay a fixed charge. This covers tenants under other tenancies (see s.1) who do not have the benefit of the automatic release and also tenants under new tenancies who have not been released because there has been an excluded assignment.

The protection granted to such former tenants is set out in subs. (2). The former tenant is not liable on the fixed charge covenant unless the landlord has served notice upon him within six months of the date that the fixed charge became due. The notice must state that the charge is due and that the landlord intends to recover that charge and (if appropriate) interest on that sum. Both the amount of the charge and the basis of interest claim must be specified. Subsection (3) grants exactly the same protection to any guarantor of the former tenant.

Subsection (4) sets out the procedure to be followed where the landlord seeks to recover a greater sum than that originally specified in the notice. (These provisions do not apply where the increase relates solely to interest.) This procedure will be particularly relevant in connection with service charge where at the end of the service charge year a balancing amount may be payable to the landlord. The subsection requires the landlord to serve a second notice claiming the greater amount, having given warning in the first notice that a larger sum might in fact be due. The landlord is required to serve the second notice within three months of the larger sum having been determined, giving details of the sum due and a calculation of any interest which the landlord seeks to recover.

In the event that the required notices are given, the landlord's right to recover the sums is protected. Whilst it is not expressly dealt with in the Act, it would appear that the landlord can then institute recovery proceedings at any time within the relevant limitation period. If the notices are not given, the right to recover for those sums against the former tenant or guarantor under a new or other tenancy is lost. A question may arise whether a guarantor having only secondary liability can be sued by the landlord if the landlord has failed to serve the proper notice on the tenant. In view of the wording used in the section ("shall not be liable"), it is thought that the landlord could not pursue the guarantor in these circumstances.

Subsection (5) has great practical importance in the immediate period after the Act comes into force. In respect of fixed charges which have become due before the Act comes into force, that commencement date is treated as the date on which the fixed charge becomes due. Therefore in respect of all outstanding rent and service charge as at that date, a landlord must serve a notice within six months on former tenants under former tenancies. This provision would not apply where the landlord has already commenced proceedings prior to the commencement date of the Act.

The protection granted by this section relates only to payment of fixed charges. This term is defined in subs. (6) as rent, service charge and any liquidated sum payable in the event of failure to comply with a tenant covenant. This last limb of the definition would seem to cover sums payable to the landlord in respect of repairs to the premises where the landlord has reserved the right to carry out the repairs himself and recover the cost as a debt or rent. (See, for example, *Hamilton v. Martell Securities* [1984] Ch. 266.) The section does not therefore cover sums due by way of unliquidated damages for breach of a tenant covenant such as breach of the user covenant.

Restriction of liability of former tenant or his guarantor where tenancy subsequently varied

18.—(1) This section applies where a person ("the former tenant") is as a result of an assignment no longer a tenant under a tenancy but—

   (a) (in the case of a new tenancy) he has under an authorised guarantee agreement guaranteed the performance by his assignee of any tenant covenant of the tenancy; or

   (b) (in the case of any tenancy) he remains bound by such a covenant.

   (2) The former tenant shall not be liable under the agreement or (as the case may be) the covenant to pay any amount in respect of the covenant to the extent that the amount is referable to any relevant variation of the tenant covenants of the tenancy effected after the assignment.

   (3) Where a person ("the guarantor") has agreed to guarantee the performance by the former tenant of a tenant covenant of the tenancy, the guarantor (where his liability to do so is not wholly discharged by any such variation of the tenant covenants of the tenancy) shall not be liable under the agreement to pay any amount in respect of the covenant to the extent that the amount is referable to any such variation.

   (4) For the purposes of this section a variation of the tenant covenants of a tenancy is a "relevant variation" if either—

   (a) the landlord has, at the time of the variation, an absolute right to refuse to allow it; or

   (b) the landlord would have had such a right if the variation had been sought by the former tenant immediately before the assignment by him but, between the time of that assignment and the time of the variation, the tenant covenants of the tenancy have been so varied as to deprive the landlord of such a right.

   (5) In determining whether the landlord has or would have had such a right at any particular time regard shall be had to all the circumstances (including the effect of any provision made by or under any enactment).

   (6) Nothing in this section applies to any variation of the tenant covenants of a tenancy effected before the date on which this Act comes into force.

   (7) In this section "variation" means a variation whether effected by deed or otherwise.

DEFINITIONS
   "assignment": s.28.
   "authorised guarantee agreement": s.16.
   "tenant covenant": s.28.
   "tenancy": s.28.
   "variation": s.18(7).

GENERAL NOTE
   The purpose of this section is to protect former tenants following an assignment or guarantors (whether under an authorised guarantee agreement or any other form of guarantee) from any increase in their liability as a result of a variation of the terms of the tenancy effected after the date the Act comes into force. As mentioned in the Introduction, the liability of an original tenant is a direct and primary liability. Thus, subject to the provisions of the Act, the original tenant will be liable for performance of covenants notwithstanding any variations which were made without his consent and from which he derived no benefit. The liability of intermediate tenants will generally be extended by contract to put them in the same position as the original tenant. With regard to the guarantees, the general principle is that a guarantor will be released from the guarantee on a variation, unless it is not substantial or cannot be prejudicial to the guarantor. However, the extent of the guarantee will depend on the wording of the document and, subject to the wording, may survive any variation. The basic protection is contained in subss. (2) and (3) which provide that the former tenant or guarantor will not be liable to pay any sum which is referable to a relevant variation of the tenant covenants, effected after the assignment by the former tenant.

   The term relevant variation is defined in subs. (4). The protection applies where the landlord had the absolute right to refuse the variation at the time the variation was made. For example, the landlord may agree to vary the alienation clause to allow the tenant greater freedom to sublet the premises, which may result in an increase in the rent payable either at the time of the variation or at review. Subject to any provision of the tenancy, the landlord would have an absolute right to refuse to allow that variation. The protection also applies where the landlord had the absolute right to refuse to allow the variation at the time of the assignment by the former tenant, but after that assignment had agreed to a variation of the tenancy which withdrew that right. In considering whether the provisions of the section apply, there will need to be an assessment of the effect on the rent or service charge of the variation which will no doubt involve expert valuation evidence.

Subsection (5) provides that in considering whether the landlord has or would have had a right to refuse to allow the variation, regard shall be had to all the circumstances including any statutory provisions. The effect of this is not entirely clear: a landlord's right to refuse any variation will depend on the contractual terms governing the relationship between the landlord and tenant, as set out in the tenancy and any collateral agreement. It is difficult to see what other circumstances might be relevant.

Overriding leases

Right of former tenant or his guarantor to overriding lease

19.—(1) Where in respect of any tenancy ("the relevant tenancy") any person ("the claimant") makes full payment of an amount which he has been duly required to pay in accordance with section 17, together with any interest payable, he shall be entitled (subject to and in accordance with this section) to have the landlord under that tenancy grant him an overriding lease of the premises demised by the tenancy.

(2) For the purposes of this section "overriding lease" means a tenancy of the reversion expectant on the relevant tenancy which—

(a) is granted for a term equal to the remainder of the term of the relevant tenancy plus three days or the longest period (less than three days) that will not wholly displace the landlord's reversionary interest expectant on the relevant tenancy, as the case may require; and

(b) (subject to subsections (3) and (4) and to any modifications agreed to by the claimant and the landlord) otherwise contains the same covenants as the relevant tenancy, as they have effect immediately before the grant of the lease.

(3) An overriding lease shall not be required to reproduce any covenant of the relevant tenancy to the extent that the covenant is (in whatever terms) expressed to be a personal covenant between the landlord and the tenant under that tenancy.

(4) If any right, liability or other matter arising under a covenant of the relevant tenancy falls to be determined or otherwise operates (whether expressly or otherwise) by reference to the commencement of that tenancy—

(a) the corresponding covenant of the overriding lease shall be so framed that that right, liability or matter falls to be determined or otherwise operates by reference to the commencement of that tenancy; but

(b) the overriding lease shall not be required to reproduce any covenant of that tenancy to the extent that it has become spent by the time that that lease is granted.

(5) A claim to exercise the right to an overriding lease under this section is made by the claimant making a request for such a lease to the landlord; and any such request—

(a) must be made to the landlord in writing and specify the payment by virtue of which the claimant claims to be entitled to the lease ("the qualifying payment"); and

(b) must be so made at the time of making the qualifying payment or within the period of 12 months beginning with the date of that payment.

(6) Where the claimant duly makes such a request—

(a) the landlord shall (subject to subsection (7)) grant and deliver to the claimant an overriding lease of the demised premises within a reasonable time of the request being received by the landlord; and

(b) the claimant—

(i) shall thereupon deliver to the landlord a counterpart of the lease duly executed by the claimant, and

(ii) shall be liable for the landlord's reasonable costs of and incidental to the grant of the lease.

(7) The landlord shall not be under any obligation to grant an overriding lease of the demised premises under this section at a time when the relevant tenancy has been determined; and a claimant shall not be entitled to the grant of such a lease if at the time when he makes his request—

(a) the landlord has already granted such a lease and that lease remains in force; or

(b) another person has already duly made a request for such a lease to the landlord and that request has been neither withdrawn nor abandoned by that person.

(8) Where two or more requests are duly made on the same day, then for the purposes of subsection (7)—

(a) a request made by a person who was liable for the qualifying payment as a former tenant shall be treated as made before a request made by a person who was so liable as a guarantor; and

(b) a request made by a person whose liability in respect of the covenant in question commenced earlier than any such liability of another person shall be treated as made before a request made by that other person.

(9) Where a claimant who has duly made a request for an overriding lease under this section subsequently withdraws or abandons the request before he is granted such a lease by the landlord, the claimant shall be liable for the landlord's reasonable costs incurred in pursuance of the request down to the time of its withdrawal or abandonment; and for the purposes of this section—

(a) a claimant's request is withdrawn by the claimant notifying the landlord in writing that he is withdrawing his request; and

(b) a claimant is to be regarded as having abandoned his request if—

(i) the landlord has requested the claimant in writing to take, within such reasonable period as is specified in the landlord's request, all or any of the remaining steps required to be taken by the claimant before the lease can be granted, and

(ii) the claimant fails to comply with the landlord's request,

and is accordingly to be regarded as having abandoned it at the time when that period expires.

(10) Any request or notification under this section may be sent by post.

(11) The preceding provisions of this section shall apply where the landlord is the tenant under an overriding lease granted under this section as they apply where no such lease has been granted; and accordingly there may be two or more such leases interposed between the first such lease and the relevant tenancy.

DEFINITIONS

"claimant": s.19(1).
"landlord": s.28.
"overriding lease": s.19(2).
"qualifying payment": s.19(5).
"relevant tenancy": s.19(1).

GENERAL NOTE

This section introduces novel protection for anyone who has made a payment pursuant to s.17 in respect of a liability under a new or other tenancy. If the payment has been made in full (including interest), the payor or "claimant" is entitled to call upon the landlord to grant to him an "overriding lease". This is in fact an intermediate lease (or tenancy) which is interposed between the interest of the landlord and the current tenant. The purpose of the overriding lease is to give to the claimant control over the defaulting tenant. The claimant becomes the immediate landlord of the tenant and, in the event that the current tenant defaults, can exercise the remedies available to the landlord, most importantly suing the tenant for outstanding rent and other sums or damages for breach of covenant, or (depending on the terms of the lease) forfeiture. However, as a corollary of the control which the overriding lease gives the claimant, he will also take on the burden of the covenants of the overriding lease and the claimant will need to consider whether he wishes to assume those obligations.

Subsection (1) sets out the circumstances in which the claimant can call upon the landlord to grant to him an overriding lease, namely following payment in full by the claimant to the landlord pursuant to the provisions of s.17.

Subsections (2) and (3) deal with the terms of the overriding lease and specifically the length of the term and the general principle that, subject to any agreement between the landlord and claimant, the terms of the overriding lease should mirror the existing lease. The overriding lease is to have a term of the remainder of the current lease plus three days. In the event that the landlord's reversionary interest is less than three days, then the section provides that the term of the overriding lease will be the longest term possible without displacing the landlord's own interest. The overriding lease will not contain any personal covenants between the landlord and tenant (subs. (3)). Subsection (4) covers the position where there is a specific obligation in the tenancy which is referable to the commencement date of the term of the tenancy. An example of this would be an obligation to carry out certain works of repair within six months of the commencement of the tenancy. The subsection provides that the timescale in the overriding lease will mirror that in the tenancy save to the extent that any covenant has become "spent".

The procedure for obtaining an overriding lease is set out in subs. (5). The claimant must make a request in writing to the landlord specifying what payment by the claimant gives rise to the right to an overriding lease. The request must be made within 12 months of the date of the payment and, as with other time-limits set out in the Act, there is no provision for extension of that time-limit. Once the request has been made, subs. (6) states that the landlord shall grant to the claimant an overriding lease within a "reasonable" time, the claimant providing the landlord with a duly executed counterpart and payment of the landlord's reasonable costs.

Subsection (7) deals with the exceptions to the principle that the landlord is to grant an overriding lease to a claimant. The first is where the lease has already been determined (perhaps as a result of the landlord exercising his right to forfeit the tenancy for breach of covenant). The second is where the landlord has already granted one overriding lease (although it is clear from subs. (11) that the landlord under an overriding lease may himself be obliged to grant one overriding lease). The third exception is where there is an extant request for an overriding lease by another claimant.

The question of priority between two requests for an overriding lease made on the same day is covered by subs. (8); former tenants take priority over guarantors and the party whose liability arose first in time takes priority over those whose liability arose later. Subsection (9) provides that a claimant must pay the reasonable costs of the landlord where a request for an overriding lease is withdrawn or cancelled. A request is withdrawn where the claimant gives the landlord notice in writing to that effect. A request is abandoned where the claimant fails to respond to the landlord's requirements for completion of the overriding lease within a reasonable period (as specified by the landlord).

Subsection (10) deals with the practical matter of service of documents under the section – they can be served by post. The service requirements are therefore different from those for service of notices under ss.8, 10 or 17 – see the General Note to s.27. Subsection (11) makes clear that a landlord who himself has been granted an overriding lease under the provisions of s.19 can be obliged to grant an overriding lease to any claimant following payment having been made to that landlord.

Overriding leases: supplementary provisions

20.—(1) For the purposes of section 1 an overriding lease shall be a new tenancy only if the relevant tenancy is a new tenancy.

(2) Every overriding lease shall state—

(a) that it is a lease granted under section 19, and

(b) whether it is or is not a new tenancy for the purposes of section 1;

and any such statement shall comply with such requirements as may be prescribed by rules made in pursuance of section 144 of the Land Registration Act 1925 (power to make general rules).

(3) A claim that the landlord has failed to comply with subsection (6)(a) of section 19 may be made the subject of civil proceedings in like manner as any other claim in tort for breach of statutory duty; and if the claimant under that section fails to comply with subsection (6)(b)(i) of that section he shall not be entitled to exercise any of the rights otherwise exercisable by him under the overriding lease.

(4) An overriding lease—

(a) shall be deemed to be authorised as against the persons interested in any mortgage of the landlord's interest (however created or arising); and

(b) shall be binding on any such persons;

and if any such person is by virtue of such a mortgage entitled to possession of the documents of title relating to the landlord's interest—

(i) the landlord shall within one month of the execution of the lease deliver to that person the counterpart executed in pursuance of section 19(6)(b)(i); and

(ii) if he fails to do so, the instrument creating or evidencing the mortgage shall apply as if the obligation to deliver a counterpart were included in the terms of the mortgage as set out in that instrument.

(5) It is hereby declared—

(a) that the fact that an overriding lease takes effect subject to the relevant tenancy shall not constitute a breach of any covenant of the lease against subletting or parting with possession of the premises demised by the lease or any part of them; and

(b) that each of sections 16, 17 and 18 applies where the tenancy referred to in subsection (1) of that section is an overriding lease as it applies in other cases falling within that subsection.

(6) No tenancy shall be registrable under the Land Charges Act 1972 or be taken to be an estate contract within the meaning of that Act by reason of any right or obligation that may arise under section 19, and any right arising from a request made under that section shall not be an overriding interest within the meaning of the Land Registration Act 1925; but any such request shall be registrable under the Land Charges Act 1972, or may be the subject of a notice or caution under the Land Registration Act 1925, as if it were an estate contract.

(7) In this section—

(a) "mortgage" includes "charge"; and

(b) any expression which is also used in section 19 has the same meaning as in that section.

DEFINITIONS

"estate contract": Land Charges Act 1972, s.2.
"mortgage": s.20(7).
"new tenancy": s.28.
"overriding interest": Land Registration Act 1925, s.3.
"overriding lease": s.19.
"relevant tenancy": s.19.

GENERAL NOTE

This section contains various supplemental provisions arising on the grant of overriding leases.

Subsection (1) provides that an overriding lease is a new tenancy for the purposes of the Act if the relevant tenancy was itself a new tenancy. Thus whilst an overriding lease can be granted out of both old and new tenancies, the provisions with regard to release of both landlords and tenants on assignment, only apply to overriding leases granted out of a new tenancy. It would seem therefore that these provisions will be of more assistance to a claimant in respect of a new tenancy to the extent that he will obtain the control without the burden of no release on assignment.

Subsection (2) requires that every overriding lease shall state in the document that it is an overriding lease and whether it is treated as an old or new tenancy, in accordance with any rules which may be made under the Land Registration Act 1925.

The sanctions against the landlord and claimant for failing to comply with the provisions of s.19(6) are contained in subs. (3). If a landlord fails to grant an overriding lease, he is open to a claim against him in tort for breach of statutory duty. A failure by the claimant to deliver the counterpart of the lease and pay the landlord's costs will prevent the claimant from exercising any of the rights granted to him under the overriding lease.

Subsection (4) provides that any mortgagee of a landlord's interest in the relevant tenancy is deemed, if necessary, to have given consent to the overriding lease and that the overriding lease is binding upon him. If the mortgagee is entitled to hold the title documents of the landlord's interest, then the landlord is obliged to pass to the mortgagee the counterpart of the overriding lease executed by the claimant within one month of execution. If the landlord fails to do this, the obligation to deliver up the counterpart is implied into the mortgage terms. If the landlord fails to comply with this implied term, there may be certain remedies available to the mortgagee, depending on the terms of the mortgage, including the right to make demand. It is notable that there is no similar provision to the effect that the overriding lease is binding on all superior landlords. Possibly this is because the draftsman thought that such a provision would be of limited practical effect. The superior lease clearly contemplated the grant of subtenancies/subleases as the relevant tenancy was created out of that interest. Further, it is difficult to see on what basis the superior landlord could successfully seek to forfeit the relevant tenancy on the basis of the alienation provisions contained in that tenancy. Whilst relief from forfeiture is always a matter within the discretion of the court, it would be virtually certain that the court would grant relief from forfeiture as the overriding lease had been entered into pursuant to a statutory obligation.

Subsection (5)(b) applies ss.16 (authorised guarantee agreements) and 17 and 18 (restrictions on the liability of former tenants and their guarantors) to overriding leases. On the assumption that the terms of the overriding lease entitle the claimant to assign the lease, subs. (5)(b) ensures that the claimant has the same protection/obligations available to others under the Act in his capacity as both tenant and landlord.

Subsection (6) deals with the question of the extent to which the right to an overriding lease under s.19 needs to be protected by registration against subsequent purchasers. The position needs to be considered in various stages. The right of the claimant to call for an overriding lease arises when he makes the relevant payment under s.17: this right is not registrable in respect of either registered or unregistered land. Once the request for an overriding lease has been made under s.19(5), the request – if the claimant wishes to protect his position against a purchaser of the landlord's interest – must be registered as an estate contract in unregistered land and, because it is not an overriding interest, must be protected by a notice or caution in registered land. Once the overriding lease has been granted, then the existing rules with regard to registration of leases will apply. The fact that a right to call for an overriding lease does not have to be registered will be of great practical importance on the sale of any reversion, particularly as the right to call for a lease is exercisable at any time in the 12 months after the qualifying payment. This is no doubt a matter which will be raised in preliminary enquiries.

Forfeiture and disclaimer

Forfeiture or disclaimer limited to part only of demised premises

21.—(1) Where—

(a) as a result of one or more assignments a person is the tenant of part only of the premises demised by a tenancy, and

(b) under a proviso or stipulation in the tenancy there is a right of re-entry or forfeiture for a breach of a tenant covenant of the tenancy, and

(c) the right is (apart from this subsection) exercisable in relation to that part and other land demised by the tenancy,

the right shall nevertheless, in connection with a breach of any such covenant by that person, be taken to be a right exercisable only in relation to that part.

(2) Where—

(a) a company which is being wound up, or a trustee in bankruptcy, is as a result of one or more assignments the tenant of part only of the premises demised by a tenancy, and

(b) the liquidator of the company exercises his power under section 178 of the Insolvency Act 1986, or the trustee in bankruptcy exercises his power under section 315 of that Act, to disclaim property demised by the tenancy,

the power is exercisable only in relation to the part of the premises referred to in paragraph (a).

DEFINITIONS

"assignment": s.28.
"disclaimer": s.178 and Insolvency Act 1986, s.315.
"tenancy": s.28.
"tenant": s.28.

GENERAL NOTE

Prior to the passing of the Act, it was not entirely clear whether a landlord was entitled to forfeit in part and thus a tenant could suffer forfeiture of his tenancy even though there had been no breach of covenant on his part (the issue arose in the case of *GMS Syndicate v. Gary Elliott (A Firm)* [1982] Ch. 1). It is now clear that the right to forfeit is limited to that part demised to the defaulting tenant.

Under subs. (2), the right to disclaim is similarly limited to that part of the premises of which the insolvent person is tenant.

Landlord's consent to assignments

Imposition of conditions regulating giving of landlord's consent to assignments

22. After subsection (1) of section 19 of the Landlord and Tenant Act 1927 (provisions as to covenants not to assign etc. without licence or consent) there shall be inserted—

"(1A) Where the landlord and the tenant under a qualifying lease have entered into an agreement specifying for the purposes of this subsection—

(a) any circumstances in which the landlord may withhold his licence or consent to an assignment of the demised premises of any part of them, or

(b) any conditions subject to which any such licence or consent may be granted,

then the landlord—

(i) shall not be regarded as unreasonably witholding his licence or consent to any such assignment if he withholds it on the ground (and it is the case) that any such circumstances exist, and

(ii) if he gives such licence or consent subject to any such conditions, shall not be regarded as giving it subject to unreasonable conditions;

and section 1 of the Landlord and Tenant Act 1988 (qualified duty to consent to assignment etc.) shall have effect subject to the provisions of this subsection.

(1B) Subsection (1A) of this section applies to such an agreement as is mentioned in that subsection—

(a) whether it is contained in the lease or not, and

(b) whether it is made at the time when the lease is granted or at any other time falling before the application for the landlord's licence or consent is made.

(1C) Subsection (1A) shall not, however, apply to any such agreement to the extent that any circumstances or conditions specified in it are framed by reference to any matter falling to be determined by the landlord or by any other person for the purposes of the agreement, unless under the terms of the agreement—

(a) that person's power to determine that matter is required to be exercised reasonably, or

(b) the tenant is given an unrestricted right to have any such determination reviewed by a person independent of both landlord and tenant whose identity is ascertainable by reference to the agreement,

and in the latter case the agreement provides for the determination made by any such independent person on the review to be conclusive as to the matter in question.

(1D) In its application to a qualifying lease, subsection (1)(b) of this section shall not have effect in relation to any assignment of the lease.

(1E) In subsections (1A) and (1D) of this section—

(a) "qualifying lease" means any lease which is a new tenancy for the purposes of section 1 of the Landlord and Tenant (Covenants) Act 1995 other than a residential lease, namely a lease by which a building or part of a building is let wholly or mainly as a single private residence; and

(b) references to assignment include parting with possession on assignment."

DEFINITIONS
"assignment": Landlord and Tenant Act 1927, s.19(1E).
"new tenancy": s.1.
"qualifying lease": Landlord and Tenant Act 1927, s.19(1E).

GENERAL NOTE
This section amends s.19 of the Landlord and Tenant Act 1927 which provides that where a lease contains a qualified covenant against alienation (that is, that such alienation requires the landlord's consent), such consent must not be unreasonably withheld. The amendment only applies to a "qualifying lease" namely a lease which is a new tenancy for the purposes of the Act (as defined in s.1) other than a residential lease. Pursuant to s.19(4) of the 1927 Act, the provisions will not apply to agricultural tenancies. The purpose of the amendment is to refine the statutory provisions restricting a landlord's right to refuse consent. The provisions allow the landlord a greater supervisory role in respect of assignment by allowing the landlord and tenant to agree the terms under which future assignments can be made. It does not affect the landlord's right to prohibit assignments absolutely.

Amendments to s.19 of the 1927 Act
Subsection (1A) of s.19 of the 1927 Act as now amended provides that a landlord may reasonably withhold consent where the circumstances in which he may do so have been set out in an agreement and he withholds consent on the ground that those circumstances exist (and they do). Similarly a landlord is entitled to impose conditions on the consent where they have been set out in the agreement and the landlord imposes the conditions in accordance with that agreement.

Subsection (1B) of the 1927 Act makes clear that the agreement need not be contained in the lease document itself or indeed entered into at the same time as the lease.

Subsection (1C) requires that where there is any discretion to be exercised by the landlord or some other third party with regard to the consent or conditions, the agreement must state that the discretion must be exercised reasonably. Alternatively, the tenant must have the right to have the decision reviewed by an independent third party whose determination is conclusive. If either of these conditions is not met, then the landlord is not entitled to rely upon the grounds or conditions set out in the agreement when considering an application from the tenant for licence to assign.

The effect of subs. (1D) is that s.19(1)(b) of the 1927 Act will not apply to long building leases which are qualifying leases. The interesting result seems to be that where there is a qualified covenant, consent will now be required throughout the term.

The provisions of s.22 are of great significance and will no doubt lead to changes in the drafting of alienation clauses in tenancies. Under s.22, the landlord can stipulate in advance the circumstances in which he will grant consent to assignment of the tenancy. It is likely to become common practice that a landlord will require that a tenant on assignment enter into an authorised guarantee agreement. The landlord will then be entitled to such an agreement irrespective of the financial status of the proposed assignee of the tenant. The landlord may also require that other criteria be met, for example that the profits/net assets of the proposed assignee are a specified multiple of the passing rent. If the proposed assignee does not meet these criteria, the landlord will be entitled to refuse consent whatever the circumstances of the particular application for licence to assign.

This can be contrasted with the position where there is no s.22 agreement and in particular with regard to the requirement by the landlord that the tenant enter into an authorised guarantee agreement. In the absence of a s.22 agreement, the application for the licence and the conditions which the landlord seeks to impose will have to be judged on its individual merits and by reference to the existing test of reasonableness. The landlord therefore has less control over the assignment and the benefits which might be secured on assignment. However, there may be a disincentive for the landlord to impose too stringent requirements on assignment: overly restrictive alienation provisions may adversely affect the level of rent on review.

Supplemental

Effects of becoming subject to liability under, or entitled to benefit of, covenant etc.

23.—(1) Where as a result of an assignment a person becomes by virtue of this Act, bound by or entitled to the benefit of a covenant, he shall not by virtue of this Act have any liability or rights under the covenant in relation to any time falling before the assignment.

(2) Subsection (1) does not preclude any such rights being expressly assigned to the person in question.

(3) Where as a result of an assignment a person becomes, by virtue of this Act, entitled to a right of re-entry contained in a tenancy, that right shall be exercisable in relation to any breach of a covenant of the tenancy occurring before the assignment as in relation to one occurring thereafter, unless by reason of any waiver or release it was not so exercisable immediately before the assignment.

DEFINITIONS
    "assignment": s.28.
    "covenant": s.28.

GENERAL NOTE
    This section deals with the effects of an assignee becoming bound by or entitled to the benefit of a covenant in a tenancy as a result of the Act. It therefore applies in respect of new tenancies and is part of the complete statutory code for such tenancies. The assignee will not have either the burden or benefit of the covenant in respect of any time prior to the assignment, save that the right to assign the benefits expressly is preserved by subs. (2). With regard to the right of re-entry, the assignee of the reversion may re-enter the premises on the basis of a breach of covenant occurring prior to the assignment (unless the right has been waived or released prior to the assignment).

Effects of release from liability under, or loss of benefit of, covenant

24.—(1) Any release of a person from a covenant by virtue of this Act does not affect any liability of his arising from a breach of the covenant occurring before the release.

(2) Where—

(a) by virtue of this Act a tenant is released from a tenant covenant of a tenancy, and

(b) immediately before the release another person is bound by a covenant of the tenancy imposing any liability or penalty in the event of a failure to comply with that tenant covenant,

then, as from the release of the tenant, that other person is released from the covenant mentioned in paragraph (b) to the same extent as the tenant is released from that tenant covenant.

(3) Where a person bound by a landlord or tenant covenant of a tenancy—

(a) assigns the whole or part of his interest in the premises demised by the tenancy, but

(b) is not released by virtue of this Act from the covenant (with the result that subsection (1) does not apply),

the assignment does not affect any liability of his arising from a breach of the covenant occurring before the assignment.

(4) Where by virtue of this Act a person ceases to be entitled to the benefit of a covenant, this does not affect any rights of his arising from a breach of the covenant occurring before he ceases to be so entitled.

DEFINITIONS
"assignment": s.28.
"covenant": s.28.
"landlord covenant": s.28.
"tenant": s.28.
"tenant covenant": s.28.

GENERAL NOTE
Section 24 of the Act deals with the effect of release from liability under the covenants contained in the lease. The release is not retrospective – there is a release from future liability only (subs. (1)). Subsection (2) deals with the position of guarantors. The release of the principal debtor, the tenant, also operates as a release of the guarantor and to the same extent.

Subsection (3) deals with the position where the landlord or tenant are not released on the assignment and therefore the provisions of subs. (1) do not apply. On an assignment of whole or part, the assignment does not affect any liability of the landlord or tenant which arose prior to that assignment. Such parties are not released from future liability at the date of the assignment and from that time will be jointly and severally liable with their assignee on the covenants pursuant to s.13.

Finally, subs. (4) deals with the benefit of any covenant on assignment. The assignor's right to sue for any breach of covenant prior to the assignment is not affected by the assignment. This seems to represent a change in the law. For example, prior to the Act, the current landlord alone was entitled to sue for breaches of the tenancy, even those which occurred before the assignment of the reversion to him (see s.141 of the Law of Property Act 1925 and *King, Re*; *Robinson v. Gray* [1963] Ch. 459).

Agreement void if it restricts operation of the Act

25.—(1) Any agreement relating to a tenancy is void to the extent that—
(a) it would apart from this section have effect to exclude, modify or otherwise frustrate the operation of any provision of this Act, or
(b) it provides for—
(i) the termination or surrender of the tenancy, or
(ii) the imposition on the tenant of any penalty, disability or liability,
in the event of the operation of any provision of this Act, or
(c) it provides for any of the matters referred to in paragraph (b)(i) or (ii) and does so (whether expressly or otherwise) in connection with, or in consequence of, the operation of any provision of this Act.

(2) To the extent that an agreement relating to a tenancy constitutes a covenant (whether absolute or qualified) against the assignment, or parting with the possession, of the premises demised by the tenancy or any part of them—
(a) the agreement is not void by virtue of subsection (1) by reason only of the fact that as such the covenant prohibits or restricts any such assignment or parting with possession; but
(b) paragraph (a) above does not otherwise affect the operation of that subsection in relation to the agreement (and in particular does not preclude its application to the agreement to the extent that it purports to regulate the giving of, or the making of any application for, consent to any such assignment or parting with possession).

(3) In accordance with section 16(1) nothing in this section applies to any agreement to the extent that it is an authorised guarantee agreement; but (without prejudice to the generality of subsection (1) above) an agreement is void to the extent that it is one falling within section 16(4)(a) or (b).

(4) This section applies to an agreement relating to a tenancy whether or not the agreement is—
(a) contained in the instrument creating the tenancy; or
(b) made before the creation of the tenancy.

DEFINITIONS
"assignment": s.28.
"authorised guarantee agreement": s.16.
"tenancy": s.28.

GENERAL NOTE
This section contains the anti-avoidance provisions. Any agreement which has the effect of
excluding, modifying or frustrating the operation of the Act is void. These words give the court
plenty of scope for ensuring that any schemes to circumvent the purpose of the Act are ineffec-
tive. The section extends to any agreements requiring the termination or surrender of the tenancy in question or imposing on the tenant some penalty or liability when the provisions of the Act
come into operation. This section will therefore prevent landlords from obtaining a direct
covenant on assignment from an assignee to perform the covenants for the residue of the term.
Subsection (2) confirms that the anti-avoidance provisions do not invalidate an agreement
which prohibits or restricts alienation, or agreements under s.22 of the Act.
Subsection (4) concerns authorised guarantee agreements and confirms that such agreements
are not void for imposing a liability on the former tenant at the time of the assignment. An
agreement is void to the extent that it seeks to require a guarantee for some person other than
the tenant's assignee. The anti-avoidance provisions apply to agreements relating to tenancies
whether or not they are contained in the same document as the tenancy or are made at the same
time as the tenancy.

Miscellaneous savings etc.

26.—(1) Nothing in this Act is to be read as preventing—
  (a) a party to a tenancy from releasing a person from a landlord covenant
      or a tenant covenant of the tenancy; or
  (b) the parties to a tenancy from agreeing to an apportionment of liability
      under such a covenant.
(2) Nothing in this Act affects the operation of section 3(3A) of the Landlord and Tenant Act 1985 (preservation of former landlord's liability until
tenant notified of new landlord).
(3) No apportionment which has become binding in accordance with section 10 shall be affected by any order or decision made under or by virtue of
any enactment not contained in this Act which relates to apportionment.

DEFINITIONS
"landlord covenant": s.28.
"tenancy": s.28.
"tenant covenant": s.28.

GENERAL NOTE
This provides confirmation that parties are not prevented by the terms of the Act from agreeing at any stage a release under any of the covenants contained in the tenancy, or from agreeing
inter se an apportionment of liability under the covenant. (The enforceability of such agreements in relation to non-attributable covenants is covered by s.9.)
Subsection (2) ensures that tenants do not lose the benefit of the protection granted to them
by the Landlord and Tenant Act 1985. Section 3(3A) of the 1985 Act provides that the landlord
of residential premises shall remain liable to the tenant for any breach of covenant until such
time as notice is given to the tenant of the assignment and of the new landlord's name and
address. Subsection (3) relates also to the question of apportionment and confirms that no
apportionment agreement as allowed by s.10 shall be affected by any decision under any other
statute. (Applications by tenants for apportionment of rents which become binding on the landlord can also be made under the Inclosure Act 1854 and the Landlord and Tenant Act 1927.)

Notices for the purposes of the Act

27.—(1) The form of any notice to be served for the purposes of section 8,
10, or 17 shall be prescribed by regulations made by the Lord Chancellor by
statutory instrument.
(2) The regulations shall require any notice served for the purposes of section 8(1) or 10(1) ("the initial notice") to include—
  (a) an explanation of the significance of the notice and the options avail-
      able to the person on whom it is served;

(b) a statement that any objections to the proposed release, or (as the case may be) to the proposed effect of the apportionment, must be made by notice in writing served on the person or persons by whom the initial notice is served within the period of four weeks beginning with the day on which the initial notice is served; and

(c) an address in England and Wales to which any such objections may be sent.

(3) The regulations shall require any notice served for the purposes of section 17 to include an explanation of the significance of the notice.

(4) If any notice purporting to be served for the purposes of section 8(1), 10(1) or 17 is not in the prescribed form, or in a form substantially to the same effect, the notice shall not be effective for the purposes of section 8, section 10 or section 17 (as the case may be).

(5) Section 23 of the Landlord and Tenant Act 1927 shall apply in relation to the service of notices for the purposes of section 8, 10 or 17.

(6) Any statutory instrument made under this section shall be subject to annulment in pursuance of a resolution of either House of Parliament.

General Note

This is an important section in the Act dealing with the form and content of the notices to be served under ss.8 (release of landlord on assignment), 10 (apportionment agreement) and 17 (restriction of liability of former tenants and guarantors). The notices will be prescribed by regulations to be made by the Lord Chancellor but the section sets out the essential elements of the notices.

Subsection (2) provides that for ss.8 and 10, the notice must explain the significance of the notice and the requirement that any objection to the release/apportionment agreement must be made within the statutory time-limits and state where such objections should be sent. With regard to a notice under s.17 the requirement is that the significance of the notice must be explained. The consequences of failing to follow the prescribed form or a form to substantially the same effect, are set out in subs. (4). The notice will not be effective for the purposes of the relevant sections of the Act.

Subsection (5) provides that s.23 of the Landlord and Tenant Act 1927 applies in relation to the service of notices under ss.8, 10 and 17. The terms of s.23 allow for personal service or service on the last known place of abode within the jurisdiction either by leaving the notice there or sending it by registered or recorded post.

Interpretation

28.—(1) In this Act (unless the context otherwise requires)—

"assignment" includes equitable assignment and in addition (subject to section 11) assignment in breach of a covenant of a tenancy or by operation of law;

"authorised guarantee agreement" means an agreement which is an authorised guarantee agreement for the purposes of section 16;

"collateral agreement", in relation to a tenancy, means any agreement collateral to the tenancy, whether made before or after its creation;

"consent" includes licence;

"covenant" includes term, condition and obligation, and references to a covenant (or any description of covenant) of a tenancy include a covenant (or a covenant of that description) contained in a collateral agreement;

"landlord" and "tenant", in relation to a tenancy, mean the person for the time being entitled to the reversion expectant on the term of the tenancy and the person so entitled to that term respectively;

"landlord covenant", in relation to a tenancy, means a covenant falling to be complied with the landlord of premises demised by the tenancy;

"new tenancy" means a tenancy which is a new tenancy for the purposes of section 1;

"reversion" means the interest expectant on the termination of a tenancy;

"tenancy" means any lease or other tenancy and includes—

    (a) a sub-tenancy, and

    (b) and agreement for a tenancy,

but does not include a mortgage term;

"tenant covenant", in relation to a tenancy, means a covenant falling to be complied with by the tenant of premises demised by the tenancy.

(2) For the purposes of any reference in this Act to a covenant falling to be complied with in relation to a particular part of the premises demised by a tenancy, a covenant falls to be so complied with if—

    (a) it in terms applies to that part of the premises, or

    (b) in its practical application it can be attributed to that part of the premises (whether or not it can also be so attributed to other individual parts of those premises).

(3) Subsection (2) does not apply in relation to covenants to pay money; and, for the purposes of any reference in this Act to a covenant falling to be complied with in relation to a particular part of the premises demised by a tenancy, a covenant of a tenancy which is a covenant to pay money falls to be so complied with if—

    (a) the covenant in terms applies to that part; or

    (b) the amount of the payment is determinable specifically by reference—

        (i) to that part, or

        (ii) to anything falling to be done by or for a person as tenant or occupier of that part (if it is a tenant covenant), or

        (iii) to anything falling to be done by or for a person as landlord of that part (if it is a landlord covenant).

(4) Where two or more persons jointly constitute either the landlord or the tenant in relation to a tenancy, any reference in this Act to the landlord or the tenant is a reference to both or all of the persons who jointly constitute the landlord or the tenant, as the case may be (and accordingly nothing in section 13 applies in relation to the rights and liabilities of such persons between themselves).

(5) References in this Act to the assignment by a landlord of the reversion in the whole or part of the premises demised by a tenancy are to the assignment by him of the whole of his interest (as owner of the reversion) in the whole or part of those premises.

(6) For the purposes of this Act—

    (a) any assignment (however effected) consisting in the transfer of the whole of the landlord's interest (as owner of the reversion) in any premises demised by a tenancy shall be treated as an assignment by the landlord of the reversion in those premises even if it is not effected by him; and

    (b) any assignment (however effected) consisting in the transfer of the whole of the tenant's interest in any premises demised by a tenancy shall be treated as an assignment by the tenant of those premises even if it is not effected by him.

GENERAL NOTE

This is the definition section within the Act. Subsection (1) contains the general definitions of terms used in the Act. The wide definitions of the terms "covenant" and "tenancy" should be noted.

Fundamental concepts in the Act are the tenant covenant and the landlord covenant. Such covenants are those which fall to be complied with by the tenant or landlord of the premises. The party which bears the burden of the covenant determines the type of covenant, *i.e.* where the burden falls on the tenant, it is described as a tenant covenant. Subsection (2) sets out the test to be applied to determine whether a covenant falls to be complied with in relation to a particular part of the premises. This is of importance in connection with any assignment of part of the tenancy or of the reversion and the conclusion of apportionment agreements under s.9. A covenant falls to be complied with in connection with a particular part of the premises if it expressly applies to that part of the premises, or as a matter of practicality it applies to that part of the premises. An example might be as follows: the demise comprises a two-storey office block and car park. Separate repairing covenants are given in respect of the block and car park and therefore these are covenants which expressly apply to each part. The tenant then assigns part of the tenancy, one floor in the office block. The lease contains a tenant covenant to clean the windows – that is a covenant which in its practical application can be attributed to each floor. However (repeating the example given in the General Note to s.9), an obligation to repair the roof would be a non-attributable covenant and would therefore need to be the subject of an apportionment agreement between the parties which they then might wish to make binding on the landlord.

Where the covenant concerned involves the payment of money, it can only fall to be complied with in relation to a particular part of the premises if it expressly applies to that part or the amount can be determined specifically in relation to that part.

Subsection (6) clarifies the definition of "assignment". An assignment does not need to be effected by the landlord/tenant; thus the term includes assignment by operation of law. It is not clear what this adds to the general definition contained in s.28(1).

Crown application

29. This Act binds the Crown.

Consequential amendments and repeals

30.—(1) The enactments specified in Schedule 1 are amended in accordance with that Schedule, the amendments being consequential on the provisions of this Act.

(2) The enactments specified in Schedule 2 are repealed to the extent specified.

(3) Subsections (1) and (2) do not affect the operation of—

(a) section 77 of, or Part IX or X of Schedule 2 to, the Law of Property Act 1925, or

(b) section 24(1)(b) or (2) of the Land Registration Act 1925,

in relation to tenancies which are not new tenancies.

(4) In consequence of this Act nothing in the following provisions, namely—

(a) sections 78 and 79 of the Law of Property Act 1925 (benefit and burden of covenants relating to land), and

(b) sections 141 and 142 of that Act (running of benefit and burden of covenants with reversion),

shall apply in relation to new tenancies.

(5) The Lord Chancellor may by order made by statutory instrument make, in the case of such enactments as may be specified in the order, such amendments or repeals in, or such modifications of, those enactments as appear to him to be necessary or expedient in consequence of any provision of this Act.

(6) Any statutory instrument made under subsection (5) shall be subject to annulment in pursuance of a resolution of either House of Parliament.

GENERAL NOTE

This section sets out the consequential amendments and repeals required as a result of the Act. The amendments and repeals are commented upon in the General Notes to Schedules 1 and 2.

Subsection (3) preserves the indemnities given by an assignee to the tenant on an assignment in both registered and unregistered land in respect of old tenancies. Subsection (4) provides that the statutory provisions with regard to the running of covenants contained in the Law of Property Act 1925 shall not apply to new tenancies. As noted in the General Note to s.3, the intention is that the Act should provide a complete statutory code for the transmission of the benefit and burden of the covenants for new tenancies. Subsection (5) grants power to the Lord Chancellor to make such further consequential amendments as he considers necessary by statutory instrument.

Commencement

31.—(1) The provisions of this Act come into force on such day as the Lord Chancellor may appoint by order made by statutory instrument.

(2) An order under this section may contain such transitional provisions and savings (whether or not involving the modification of any enactment) as appear to the Lord Chancellor necessary or expedient in connection with the provisions brought into force by the order.

GENERAL NOTE

No statutory instrument has yet been made under this provision but the Lord Chancellor's Department have indicated that commencement is very likely to be January 1, 1996.

Short title and extent

32.—(1) This Act may be cited as the Landlord and Tenant (Covenants) Act 1995.

(2) This Act extends to England and Wales only.

SCHEDULES

Section 30(1)   SCHEDULE 1

CONSEQUENTIAL AMENDMENTS

Trustee Act 1925 (c. 19)

1. In section 26 of the Trustee Act 1925 (protection against liability in respect of rents and covenants), after subsection (1) insert—

"(1A) Where a personal representative or trustee has as such entered into, or may as such be required to enter into, an authorised guarantee agreement with respect to any lease comprised in the estate of a deceased testator or intestate or a trust estate (and, in a case where he has entered into such an agreement, he has satisfied all liabilities under it which may have accrued and been claimed up to the date of distribution)—

(a) he may distribute the residuary real and personal estate of the deceased testator or intestate, or the trust estate, to or amongst the persons entitled thereto—

(i) without appropriating any part of the estate of the deceased, or the trust estate, to meet any future liability (or, as the case may be, any liability) under any such agreement, and

(ii) notwithstanding any potential liability of his to enter into any such agreement; and

(b) notwithstanding such distribution, he shall not be personally liable in respect of any subsequent claim (or, as the case may be, any claim) under any such agreement.

In this subsection "authorised guarantee agreement" has the same meaning as in the Landlord and Tenant (Covenants) Act 1995."

Law of Property Act 1925 (c. 20)

2. In section 77 of the Law of Property Act 1925 (implied covenants in conveyances subject to rents), for subsection (2) substitute—

"(2) Where in a conveyance for valuable consideration, other than a mortgage, part of land affected by a rentcharge is, without the consent of the owner of the rentcharge, expressed to be conveyed subject to or charged with the entire rent, paragraph (B)(i) of subsection (1) to this section shall apply as if, in paragraph (i) of Part VIII of the Second Schedule to this Act—

(a) any reference to the apportioned rent were to the entire rent; and

(b) the words "(other than the covenant to pay the entire rent)" were omitted.

(2A) Where in a conveyance for valuable consideration, other than a mortgage, part of land affected by a rentcharge is, without the consent of the owner of the rentcharge, expressed to be conveyed discharged or exonerated from the entire rent, paragraph (B)(ii) of subsection (1) of this section shall apply as if, in paragraph (ii) of Part VIII of the Second Schedule to this Act—

(a) any reference to the balance of the rent were to the entire rent; and

(b) the words ", other than the covenant to pay the entire rent," were omitted."

Landlord and Tenant Act 1954 (c. 56)

3. At the end of section 34 of the Landlord and Tenant Act 1954 (rent under new tenancy) insert—

"(4) It is hereby declared that the matters which are to be taken into account by the court in determining the rent include any effect on rent of the operation of the provisions of the Landlord and Tenant (Covenants) Act 1995."

4.—(1) The existing provisions of section 35 of that Act (other terms of new tenancy) shall constitute subsection (1) of that section.

(2) After those provisions insert—

"(2) In subsection (1) of this section the reference to all relevant circumstances includes (without prejudice to the generality of that reference) a reference to the operation of the provisions of the Landlord and Tenant (Covenants) Act 1995."

GENERAL NOTE

This Schedule contains the consequential amendments arising from the provisions of the Act. Paragraph 1 deals with the Trustee Act 1925 (c. 19). Section 26 of that Act is amended to add subs. (1A) which provides protection for personal representatives and trustees who have entered into an authorised guarantee agreement in accordance with s.16 of the Act. Such personal representatives and trustees are entitled to distribute the estate or trust estate to the beneficiaries without making a reserve, notwithstanding that there may be a contingent liability under the authorised guarantee agreement, and notwithstanding that a personal representative or trustee may subsequently be required to enter into an authorised guarantee agreement, provided that at the time of the distribution all sums due under the agreement have been paid. Further, the trustee or personal representative is released from personal liability in respect of any subsequent claim under such an agreement. Authorised guarantee agreements will only be entered into in connection with new tenancies; the position with regard to old tenancies will continue to be dealt with by s.26(1) of the Trustee Act 1925.

Paragraph 2 contains a consequential amendment with regard to the covenants to be implied in conveyances of land affected by rentcharges. The effect of the amendments is to remove the reference to leases in the implied covenants which deal with apportionment of the rents.

Paragraphs 3 and 4 provide for amendments to Pt. II of the Landlord and Tenant Act 1954. In determining the rent and terms of the tenancy on renewal under the 1954 Act, the court should take account of the effect of the operation of the Act. As a result, the court will consider any proposed amendments to the existing lease (and in particular the alienation provisions) not only by reference to the decision in *O'May v. City of London Real Property Co.* [1983] 2 A.C. 726 but also in the light of the changes introduced by the Act. It is therefore to be expected that the court will permit changes to the terms of the tenancy to reflect the automatic release of tenants from the tenant covenants and the provisions for authorised guarantee agreements. Similarly, the valuation consequences of the provisions of the Act and any amendments to the terms of the renewal lease as a result can be taken into account by the court when determining the rent.

Section 30(2)   SCHEDULE 2

REPEALS

Chapter	Short title	Extent of repeal
15 & 16 Geo. 5 c. 20.	Law of Property Act 1925.	In section 77, subsection (1)(C) and (D) and, in subsection (7), paragraph (c) and the "or" preceding it. In Schedule 2, Parts IX and X.
15 & 16 Geo. 5 c. 21.	Land Registration Act 1925.	Section 24(1)(b) and (2).

GENERAL NOTE

This Schedule deals with the consequential repeals as a result of the Act, namely the implied indemnity given by an assignee to the tenant on assignment with regard to the future performance of the covenants. The repealed statutory provisions deal with the position in both registered and unregistered land. As provided in s.30(2), the repeal operates only in respect of new tenancies.

INDEX

References are to sections and Schedules

NATIONAL HEALTH SERVICE (AMENDMENT) ACT 1995*

(1995 c. 31)

An Act to make provision in relation to persons disqualified, or subject to proceedings for disqualification, under section 46 of the National Health Service Act 1977; to make provision about the constitution of the tribunal under that section; to make corresponding provision for Scotland; and for connected purposes. [19th July 1995]

PARLIAMENTARY DEBATES
Hansard, H.C. Vol. 257, cols. 1025, 1360, Vol. 258, cols. 121, 479, Vol. 263, col. 1231. H.L. Vol. 563, col. 703, Vol. 564, cols. 892, 1442, Vol. 565, col. 15.

INTRODUCTION AND GENERAL NOTE

This Act amends the powers and constitution of the National Health Service Tribunal. The Tribunal, established under s.46 of and Sched. 9 to the National Health Service Act 1977 (c. 49), already had the power to disqualify general practitioners, dentists, pharmacists and ophthalmists from providing family health services. Although the Tribunal's powers are rarely invoked, and it considers only five or six cases a year, it nevertheless performs an important function. Family health services practitioners are independent contractors, whose terms of service do not allow for them to be removed from practice by the Family Health Service Authorities which hold their contracts. The relevant Authority, or any other person, may, however, make representations to the Tribunal that the continued inclusion of individual practitioners in its lists of those providing general medical, dental, ophthalmic and pharmaceutical services would be prejudicial to the efficiency of those services. The Tribunal could direct a practitioner's name be removed from the relevant list and also prevent its inclusion in similar lists held by other Authorities.

Until now, however, there was no procedure under which immediate action could be taken, even when the safety of patients was at risk. This Act fills an important gap in the Tribunal's powers by enabling it to suspend a practitioner immediately, pending the outcome of its inquiry, where this is necessary to protect patients. It also contains a new power for the Tribunal to prevent a disqualified or suspended practitioner being engaged in any capacity in the provision of the services he can no longer provide as a principal. The Act also removes the unrestricted

---

*Annotations by Gay Wilder, Beachcroft Stanleys.

right of appeal to the Secretary of State from a decision of the Tribunal, bringing it into line with other Tribunals, and increases its membership, to help expedite hearings.

ABBREVIATIONS
The 1977 Act : The National Health Service Act 1977.
The 1978 Act : The National Health Service (Scotland) Act 1978.

England and Wales

Disqualified practitioners: engagement in provision of services by others

1. In section 46(2) of the National Health Service Act 1977 (functions of Tribunal on finding that the inclusion of a person's name in a list under Part II of that Act would be prejudicial to the efficiency of the services to which the list relates) there shall be inserted at the end ", and
  (c) where they make a direction under paragraph (b) above, may also, if they think fit, declare that he is not fit to be engaged in any capacity in the provision of those services."

GENERAL NOTE
Section 46(2)(b) of the 1977 Act enables the National Health Service Tribunal, when directing a practitioner's name be removed from a list, also to direct his name be removed from or not included in any corresponding list kept by any other Health Authority. When doing so, s.1 provides the Tribunal with a new discretion to prevent that person practising as a locum, assistant or deputy for any other practitioner on those lists.

Interim suspension of practitioners

2.—(1) After section 49 of the National Health Service Act 1977 there shall be inserted the following sections—

"Applications for interim suspension
49A.—(1) A Health Authority who have made representations under section 46 above may, at any time before the case is disposed of by the Tribunal, apply to the Tribunal for a direction to be made under subsection (2) below in relation to the person to whom the case relates.
(2) If, on an application under this section, the Tribunal are satisfied that it is necessary to do so in order to protect patients, they shall direct that subsection (3) below shall apply to the person concerned as respects services of the kind to which the case in question relates.
(3) A person to whom this subsection applies shall—
  (a) be deemed to have been removed from any relevant list in which his name is included,
  (b) be disqualified for inclusion in any relevant list in which his name is not included, and
  (c) be deemed to be a person in relation to whom there is in force a declaration under section 46(2)(c) above concerning his fitness to be engaged in the provision of services of the relevant kind.
(4) A direction under subsection (2) above shall cease to have effect on the Tribunal's disposing of the case in connection with which it is made.
(5) In subsection (2) above, the reference to patients is to persons to whom services of the kind to which the case in question relates are, or may be, provided under this Part of this Act.

(6) In the application of subsection (3) above to any person—

(a) "relevant list" means a list prepared under this Part of this Act of persons undertaking to provide services of the kind to which the direction applying the subsection to him relates, and

(b) "services of the relevant kind" means services of the kind to which that direction relates.

Continuation of suspension pending appeal

49B.—(1) Where—

(a) on disposing of a case under section 46 above, the Tribunal make a direction under subsection (2)(b) of that section, and

(b) the person to whom the direction relates is a person to whom section 49A(3) above would, apart from this section, cease to apply on the disposal of the case,

the Tribunal may, if they consider it necessary to do so in order to protect patients, direct that that provision shall continue to apply to him as respects services of the kind to which the direction under section 46(2)(b) above relates.

(2) A direction under subsection (1) above shall cease to have effect—

(a) where no appeal against the direction under section 46(2)(b) above is brought, at the end of the period for bringing an appeal, and

(b) where an appeal against that direction is brought, when the appeal process has been exhausted.

(3) Where the power conferred by subsection (1) above is exercisable by virtue of a direction which is not coupled with a declaration under section 46(2)(c) above, section 49(A)(3) above shall have effect, in relation to the exercise of that power, with the omission of paragraph (c).

(4) In subsection (1) above, the reference to patients is to persons to whom services of the kind to which the direction under section 46(2)(b) above relates are, or may be, provided under this Part of this Act.

Sections 49A and 49B: procedure etc.

49C.—(1) Before making a direction under section 49A(2) or 49B(1) above in relation to any person, the Tribunal shall give him an opportunity—

(a) to appear before them, either in person or by counsel or solicitor or such other representative as may be prescribed, and

(b) to be heard and to call witnesses and produce other evidence.

(2) Regulations may—

(a) make provision for, or for the determination of, procedure in relation to determining applications under section 49A above or the exercise of the power conferred by section 49B(1) above, and

(b) provide for the functions of the Tribunal under section 49A or 49B above to be carried out, or to be carried out in prescribed circumstances, by the chairman or a deputy chairman of the Tribunal.

Suspension provisions in Scotland or Northern Ireland

49D.—(1) This section applies where, under any provisions in force in Scotland or Northern Ireland corresponding to section 49A or 49B above, a person ("the practitioner") is disqualified for inclusion in all lists prepared under the provisions in force there corresponding to the provisions of this Part of this Act of persons undertaking to provide services of one or more of the kinds specified in section 46(1) above, other than those in which his name is included.

(2) The practitioner shall, while he is so disqualified—

(a) be disqualified for inclusion in any list prepared under this Part of this Act of persons undertaking to provide services of the same kinds ("relevant list") in which his name is not included, and

(b) be deemed to have been removed from any relevant list in which his name is included.

Payments in consequence of suspension

49E.—(1) Regulations may provide for the making to persons to whom section 49A(3) or 49D(2) above applies of payments in consequence of the application of that provision.

(2) Regulations under subsection (1) above may provide for the determination by the Secretary of State in a prescribed manner of anything for which provision may be made by regulations under that subsection."

(2) In section 46(1) of that Act for "49" there shall be substituted "49C".

DEFINITIONS
"Health Authority": s.14(5).
"patients": ss.49A(5) and 49B(4) of the 1977 Act.
"relevant list": s.49A(6)(a) of the 1977 Act.
"services of the relevant kind": s.49A(6)(b) of the 1977 Act.

GENERAL NOTE

Subs. (1)

This subsection adds ss.49A–E to the 1977 Act to enable the interim suspension of practitioners, and contains the main provisions of this Act.

The new s.49A of the 1977 Act empowers the Tribunal, on the application of the Health Authority which has made representations to it, to suspend a practitioner pending the outcome of the substantive hearing. This is a discretionary power, to be exercised if the Tribunal is satisfied this is necessary to protect patients, but if a direction is made, the practitioner is then to be regarded as having been disqualified from any relevant list and unfit to provide services of the relevant kind in any capacity.

The new s.49B of the 1977 Act enables the Tribunal to prevent a practitioner from practising following its decision and pending any appeal. If a practitioner was suspended pending the Tribunal's decision and the Tribunal then disqualifies him from any relevant lists, it may also direct his suspension continue until the time for bringing an appeal expires or the appeal process is exhausted. If his suspension is continued, this will prevent him from working in any capacity if the Tribunal has also made a direction under s.46(2)(c) of the 1977 Act. Where such a direction has not been made, a suspension may be continued but will only prevent a person practising as a principal, not as a locum, assistant or deputy. An appeal must be brought within 28 days of the Tribunal decision. For appeals generally, see the General Note to s.3, below.

The new s.49C of the 1977 Act ensures that the practitioner has the right to be heard before a direction suspending him is made. The procedure for suspension applications may be provided for by Regulations. Specifically, Regulations may allow for these functions of the Tribunal to be carried out by the chairman or a deputy chairman so that the Tribunal can act quickly if patients are at risk.

The new s.49D of the 1977 Act provides that, while a practitioner is suspended under corresponding provisions in Scotland or Northern Ireland, he is also disqualified from any equivalent list in England and Wales. For the provisions in Scotland corresponding to ss.49A and 49B of the 1977 Act, see s.8 of this Act, below. See s.13 below for the position in Northern Ireland.

Suspension may remove a person's livelihood, before the full hearing and when nothing has been proved against him, and s.49E of the 1977 Act enables Regulations to provide for suspended practitioners to be paid.

Appeals against disqualification: removal of appeal to Secretary of State

3.—(1) In section 46 of the National Health Service Act 1977 (disqualification of persons providing services), subsection (3) (right of appeal to Secretary of State from direction of Tribunal) shall cease to have effect.

(2) In that section, for subsection (4) there shall be substituted—

"(4) Subject to subsection (5) below, where the Tribunal direct that the name of any person be removed from or not included in any list or lists, the Health Authority or Health Authorities concerned shall remove the name of the person concerned from the list or lists in question.

(5) Subsection (4) above shall not apply—

(a) where no appeal is brought against the decision to make the direction, until the end of the period for bringing an appeal, and

(b) where an appeal is brought against that decision, until the appeal process has been exhausted."

DEFINITIONS

"Health Authority or Health Authorities": s.14(5).

GENERAL NOTE

Subs. (1)

This brings an end to an anomaly by removing a practitioner's unrestricted right of appeal to the Secretary of State.

Subs. (2)

This provides that where the Tribunal directs that a practitioner be disqualified, the Health Authority or Health Authorities concerned shall remove his name from their lists when the time for bringing an appeal expires or, if an appeal is made, at the end of the appeal process.

A practitioner can appeal a Tribunal decision to the High Court on a point of law, and has 28 days to serve the notice of motion and enter the appeal. See s.11(1) and Sched. 1, para. 33(b) Tribunals and Inquiries Act 1992 (c. 53) and the Rules of the Supreme Court, Order 55.

Removal of disqualification

4.—(1) In section 47 of the National Health Service Act 1977 (power of the Tribunal or the Secretary of State to remove disqualification imposed by virtue of section 46 of that Act), in subsection (1), the words "or the Secretary of State" shall be omitted.

(2) In paragraph 8 of Schedule 14 to that Act (power of the Tribunal or the Secretary of State to remove disqualification imposed by virtue of section 42(8) of the National Health Service Act 1946), for "the Tribunal or the Secretary of State directs" there shall be substituted "the Tribunal direct".

GENERAL NOTE

Previously, either the Tribunal or the Secretary of State could remove a disqualification. This section removes the Secretary of State's power to reinstate and follows on from the removal of the right of appeal in s.3(1). The Tribunal alone shall consider applications for the reinstatement of disqualified practitioners, subject to the right of appeal on a point of law to the High Court—see the notes to s.3(2).

Procedure relating to disqualification

5.—(1) In section 49 of the National Health Service Act 1977 (regulations as to sections 46 to 48) the power conferred by paragraph (a) (under which regulations are to provide for prescribing the procedure for the holding of inquiries) shall include power to provide for the procedure to be determined under regulations.

(2) Accordingly, that provision shall be amended as follows—

(a) the words "prescribing the procedure for the holding of", "by the Tribunal" and "securing that" shall be omitted,

(b) after "48 above" there shall be inserted "to be held in accordance with such procedure as may be prescribed byor determined under the regulations", and
    (c) for "shall have" there shall be substituted "to have", for "that the hearing" there shall be substituted "for the hearing" and for "shall be" there shall be substituted "to be".

GENERAL NOTE
   This section amends s.49 of the 1977 Act which enables Regulations to be made to provide the procedure in accordance with which the Tribunal's inquiries are held. Section 49 of the 1977 Act is further repealed by s.14(2), below. The current Regulations are contained in the National Health Service (Service Committees and Tribunal) Regulations 1992 (S.I. No. 664 of 1992).

Constitution of the Tribunal

   6.—(1) Schedule 9 to the National Health Service Act 1977 (which makes provision about the tribunal under section 46 of that Act) shall be amended as follows.
   (2) For paragraphs 1 to 5 (constitution) there shall be substituted—
     "1. The Tribunal shall consist of—
        (a) a chairman appointed by the Lord Chancellor,
        (b) such number of deputy chairmen as the Lord Chancellor may appoint,
        (c) such number of persons as the Secretary of State may appoint for the purposes of this sub-paragraph,
        (d) such number of medical practitioners as the Secretary of State may appoint for the purposes of this sub-paragraph,
        (e) such number of medical practitioners having the qualifications prescribed under section 38 above as the Secretary of State may appoint for the purposes of this sub-paragraph,
        (f) such number of dental practitioners as the Secretary of State may appoint for the purposes of this sub-paragraph,
        (g) such number of ophthalmic opticians as the Secretary of State may appoint for the purposes of this sub-paragraph, and
        (h) such number of registered pharmacists as the Secretary of State may appoint for the purposes of this sub-paragraph.
     2. A person appointed as the chairman or a deputy chairman shall be a person who has a 10 year general qualification (within the meaning of section 71 of the Courts and Legal Services Act 1990).
     3. Any appointment for the purposes of paragraph 1(c) above shall be made after consultation with such associations of Health Authorities as the Secretary of State may recognise as representative of Health Authorities.
     4. Any appointment for the purposes of any sub-paragraphs (d) to (h) of paragraph 1 above shall be made after consultation with such organisations as the Secretary of State may recognise as representative of the profession or calling concerned."
   (3) After paragraph 5 there shall be inserted—

"Sittings of Tribunal
   5A.—(1) The functions of the Tribunal shall be exercised by three members consisting of—
        (a) the chairman or a deputy chairman,
        (b) a person appointed under paragraph 1(c) above, and
        (c) a person appointed under such one of sub-paragraphs (d) to (h) of paragraph 1 above as provides for the appointment of persons of the same profession or calling as that of the person concerned.
     (2) In sub-paragraph (1)(c) above, the reference to the person concerned is—

    (a) in the case of functions under section 46 above, to the person to whom the representations in question relate,

    (b) in the case of functions under section 47 above (or paragraph 8 of Schedule 14 to this Act), to the person whose disqualification is under consideration,

    (c) in the case of functions under section 49A above, to the person to whom the application in question relates, and

    (d) in the case of functions under section 49B above, to the person in relation to whom the application of section 49A(3) above may be continued.

    (3) In the case of functions under section 49A or 49B above, sub-paragraph (1) above is subject to section 49C(2)(b) above."

DEFINITIONS
"the person concerned": Sched. 9, para. 5A(2) of the 1977 Act.

GENERAL NOTE
    This section amends the constitution of the Tribunal by increasing its membership. It allows the appointment of permanent deputy chairmen and removes the restrictions on the number of lay and practitioner members who may be appointed. The Tribunal has occasionally been hampered by the unavailability of a chairman or members, a problem which these amendments seek to solve. The functions of the Tribunal shall be exercised by three members; the chairman or a deputy chairman, one lay member and a practitioner member of the same profession as the person concerned, subject to any Regulations made under s.49C(2)(b) of the 1977 Act.

Scotland

Disqualified practitioners: engagement in provision of services by others

    7. In section 29(3) of the National Health Service (Scotland) Act 1978 (functions of Tribunal on finding that the inclusion of a person's name in a list under Part II of that Act would be prejudicial to the efficiency of the services to which the list relates)—

    (a) the words "shall direct that his name be removed from that list" shall be paragraph (a);

    (b) the words "may also, if they think fit, direct that his name be removed from, or not be included in, any corresponding list kept by any other Health Board under this Part" shall be paragraph (b); and

    (c) there shall be added at the end—

        ", and

    (c) where they make a direction under paragraph (b) above, may also, if they think fit, declare that he is not fit to be engaged in any capacity in the provision of those services."

GENERAL NOTE
    Section 29(3) of the 1978 Act is the equivalent provision in Scotland to s.46(2) of the 1977 Act. This section amends s.29(3) of the 1978 Act to enable practitioners to be disqualified from practising in any capacity and corresponds to s.46(2)(c) of the 1977 Act. See the General Note to s.1, above.

Interim suspension of practitioners

    8. After section 32 of the National Health Service (Scotland) Act 1978 there shall be inserted the following sections—

"Applications for interim suspension

    32A.—(1) A Health Board who have made representations under section 29 may, at any time before the case is disposed of by the Tribunal, apply to the Tribunal for a direction to be made under subsection (2) below in relation to the person to whom the case relates.

    (2) If, on an application under this section, the Tribunal are satisfied that it is necessary to do so in order to protect patients, they shall direct

that subsection (3) below shall apply to the person concerned as respects services of the kind to which the case in question relates.

(3) A person to whom this subsection applies shall—

(a) be deemed to have been removed from any relevant list in which his name is included,

(b) be disqualified for inclusion in any relevant list in which his name is not included, and

(c) be deemed to be a person in relation to whom there is in force a declaration under section 29(3)(c) concerning his fitness to be engaged in the provision of services of the relevant kind.

(4) A direction under subsection (2) above shall cease to have effect on the Tribunal's disposing of the case in connection with which it is made.

(5) In subsection (2) above, the reference to patients is to persons to whom services of the kind to which the case in question relates are, or may be, provided under this Part of this Act.

(6) In the application of subsection (3) above to any person—

(a) "relevant list" means a list prepared under this Part of this Act of persons undertaking to provide services of the kind to which the direction applying the subsection to him relates, and

(b) "services of the relevant kind" means services of the kind to which that direction relates.

Continuation of suspension pending appeal

32B.—(1) Where—

(a) on disposing of a case under section 29, the Tribunal make a direction under subsection (3)(b) of that section, and

(b) the person to whom the direction relates is a person to whom section 32A(3) above would, apart from this section, cease to apply on the disposal of the case,

the Tribunal may, if they consider it necessary to do so in order to protect patients, direct that that provision shall continue to apply to him as respects services of the kind to which the direction under section 29(3)(b) relates.

(2) A direction under subsection (1) above shall cease to have effect—

(a) where no appeal against the direction under section 29(3)(b) is brought, at the end of the period for bringing an appeal, and

(b) where an appeal against that direction is brought, when the appeal process has been exhausted.

(3) Where the power conferred by subsection (1) above is exercisable by virtue of a direction which is not coupled with a declaration under section 29(3)(c), section 32(A)(3) shall have effect, in relation to the exercise of that power, with the omission of paragraph (c).

(4) In subsection (1) above, the reference to patients is to persons to whom services of the kind to which the direction under section 29(3)(b) relates are, or may be, provided under this Part of this Act.

Sections 32A and 32B: procedure etc.

32C.—(1) Before making a direction under section 32A(2) or 32B(1) in relation to any person, the Tribunal shall give him an opportunity—

(a) to appear before them, either—

(i) in person; or

(ii) by counsel or solicitor or such other representative as may be prescribed; and

(b) to be heard and to call witnesses and produce other evidence.

(2) Regulations may—

(a) make provision for, or for the determination of, procedure in relation to determining applications under section 32A or the exercise of the power conferred by section 32B(1), and

(b) provide for the functions of the Tribunal under section 32A or 32B to be carried out, or to be carried out in prescribed circumstances, by the chairman or a deputy chairman of the Tribunal.

Suspension provisions in England and Wales or in Northern Ireland

32D.—(1) This section applies where, under any provisions in force in England and Wales or in Northern Ireland corresponding to section 32A or 32B, a person ("the practitioner") is disqualified for inclusion in all lists prepared under the provisions in force there corresponding to the provisions of this Part of this Act of persons undertaking to provide services of oneor more of the kinds specified in section 29(1), other than those in which his name is included.

(2) The practitioner shall, while he is so disqualified—

(a) be disqualified for inclusion in any list prepared under this Part of this Act of persons undertaking to provide services of the same kinds ("relevant list") in which his name is not included, and

(b) be deemed to have been removed from any relevant list in which his name is included.

Payments in consequence of suspension

32E.—(1) Regulations may provide for the making to persons to whom section 32A(3) or 32D(2) applies of payments in consequence of the application of that provision.

(2) Regulations under subsection (1) above may provide for the determination by the Secretary of State in a prescribed manner of anything for which provision may be made by regulations under that subsection."

DEFINITIONS
"patients": ss.32A(5), 32B(4) of the 1978 Act.
"relevant list": s.32A(6)(a) of the 1978 Act.
"services of the relevant kind": s.32A(6)(b) of the 1978 Act.

GENERAL NOTE
Section 32 of the 1978 Act is the equivalent provision in Scotland to s.49 of the 1977 Act. This section adds ss.32A–E to the 1978 Act to enable the interim suspension of practitioners, which correspond to the provisions which were added to s.49 of the 1977 Act by s.2. See the General Note to s.2, above.

Appeals against disqualification: removal of appeal to Secretary of State

9.—(1) In section 29 of the National Health Service (Scotland) Act 1978 (disqualification of persons providing services), subsection (4) shall cease to have effect.

(2) In that section, for subsection (5) there shall be substituted—

"(5) Subject to subsection (5A) below, where the Tribunal direct that the name of any person be removed from or not included in any list or lists, the Health Board or Health Boards concerned shall remove the name of the person concerned from the list or lists in question.

(5A) Subsection (5) above shall not apply—

(a) where no appeal is brought against the decision to make the direction, until the end of the period for bringing an appeal, and

(b) where an appeal is brought against that decision, until the appeal process has been exhausted."

GENERAL NOTE
Section 29(4) of the 1978 Act was the equivalent provision in Scotland to s.46(3) of the 1977 Act. This section removes the right of appeal to the Secretary of State in Scotland as s.3 does in

England and Wales. See the General Note to s.3, above, and s.11(7)(b) and Sched. 1, para. 56(b) of the Tribunals and Inquiries Act 1992 for appeals on a point of law to the Court of Session.

Removal of disqualification

10.—(1) In section 30 of the National Health Service (Scotland) Act 1978 (power of the Tribunal or the Secretary of State to remove disqualification imposed by virtue of section 29 of that Act), in subsection (1), the words "or the Secretary of State" shall be omitted.

(2) In paragraph 6 of Schedule 15 to that Act (power of the Tribunal or the Secretary of State to remove disqualification imposed by virtue of section 43(8) of the National Health Service (Scotland) Act 1947), for the words "the Tribunal or the Secretary of State directs" there shall be substituted "the Tribunal direct".

GENERAL NOTE
Section 30 and Sched. 15, para. 6 of the 1978 Act are the equivalent provisions to s.47 and Sched. 14, para. 8 of the 1977 Act. This section removes the Secretary of State's power to reinstate, and makes similar amendments to the provisions in Scotland as are made to those in England and Wales by s.4. See the General Note to s.4, above.

Procedure relating to disqualification

11.—(1) In section 32 of the National Health Service (Scotland) Act 1978 (regulations as to sections 29 to 31) the power conferred by paragraph (a) (under which regulations are to provide for prescribing the procedure for the holding of inquiries) shall include power to provide for the procedure to be determined under regulations.

(2) Accordingly, that provision shall be amended as follows—
(a) for the words from the beginning to "by the Tribunal" there shall be substituted the words "for inquiries";
(b) after "31" there shall be inserted "to be held in accordance with such procedure as may be prescribed by or determined under the regulations";
(c) the words "securing that" shall be omitted;
(d) for "shall be", in both places where those words occur, there shall be substituted "to be";
(e) for "shall have" there shall be substituted "to have";
(f) for "that the hearing" there shall be substituted "for the hearing".

GENERAL NOTE
Section 32 of the 1978 Act is the Scottish equivalent to s.49 of the 1977 Act and enables Regulations to be made to provide the procedure in accordance with which the Tribunal's inquiries are held. This section makes amendments to the 1978 Act corresponding to those made to the 1977 Act by s.5. Section 32 of the 1978 Act is also further repealed by s.14(2). The current Regulations are contained in the National Health Service (Service Committees and Tribunal) (Scotland) Regulations 1992 (S.I. 1992 No. 434).

Constitution of the Tribunal

12.—(1) Schedule 8 to the National Health Service (Scotland) Act 1978 (which makes provision about the tribunal under section 29 of that Act) shall be amended as follows.

(2) For paragraphs 1 to 6 (constitution) there shall be substituted—
"1. The Tribunal shall consist of—
(a) a chairman appointed by the Lord President of the Court of Session,
(b) such number of deputy chairmen as may be so appointed,
(c) such number of persons as the Secretary of State may appoint for the purposes of this sub-paragraph,
(d) such number of medical practitioners as the Secretary of State may appoint for the purposes of this sub-paragraph,

(e) such number of medical practitioners having the qualifications prescribed under section 26 as the Secretary of State may appoint for the purposes of this sub-paragraph,

(f) such number of dental practitioners as the Secretary of State may appoint for the purposes of this sub-paragraph,

(g) such number of ophthalmic opticians as the Secretary of State may appoint for the purposes of this sub-paragraph, and

(h) such number of registered pharmacists as the Secretary of State may appoint for the purposes of this sub-paragraph.

2. A person appointed as the chairman or a deputy chairman shall be a practising—

(a) advocate; or

(b) solicitor,

of not less than ten years' standing.

3. Any appointment for the purposes of paragraph 1(c) above shall be made after consultation with such body as the Secretary of State may recognise as representative of Health Boards.

4. Any appointment for the purposes of any sub-paragraphs (d) to (h) of paragraph 1 above shall be made after consultation with such organisations as the Secretary of State may recognise as representative of the profession or calling concerned."

(3) After paragraph 7 there shall be added—

"8.—(1) The functions of the Tribunal shall be exercised by three members consisting of—

(a) the chairman or a deputy chairman,

(b) a person appointed under paragraph 1(c) above, and

(c) a person appointed under such one of sub-paragraphs (d) to (h) of paragraph 1 above as provides for the appointment of persons of the same profession or calling as that of the person concerned.

(2) In sub-paragraph (1)(c) above, the reference to the person concerned is—

(a) in the case of functions under section 29, to the person to whom the representations in question relate,

(b) in the case of functions under section 30 (or paragraph 6 of Schedule 15), to the person whose disqualification is under consideration,

(c) in the case of functions under section 32A, to the person to whom the application in question relates, and

(d) in the case of functions under section 32B, to the person in relation to whom the application of section 32A(3) may be continued.

(3) In the case of functions under section 32A or 32B, sub-paragraph (1) above is subject to section 32C(2)(b)."

DEFINITIONS

"the person concerned": Sched. 8, para. 8(2) of the 1978 Act.

GENERAL NOTE

Schedule 8 of the 1978 Act is the equivalent to Sched. 9 of the 1977 Act. This section makes similar amendments to the constitution of the Tribunal under the 1978 Act as are made to the 1977 Act by s.6. See the General Note to s.6, above.

Miscellaneous and supplementary

Orders in Council making corresponding provision for Northern Ireland

13. An Order in Council under paragraph 1(1)(b) of Schedule 1 to the Northern Ireland Act 1974 (legislation for Northern Ireland in the interim period) which states that it is made for purposes corresponding to those of sections 1, 2, 5 and 6 above—

    (a) shall not be subject to paragraph 1(4) and (5) of that Schedule (affirm-
ative resolution of both Houses of Parliament), but

    (b) shall be subject to annulment in pursuance of a resolution of either
House.

GENERAL NOTE

This is the only section of the Act which applies to Northern Ireland (s.14(6)). Corresponding
provisions to those contained in this Act may be made by Order in Council for Northern Ireland
and are subject to annulment rather than requiring positive approval from Parliament.

Short title, etc.

14.—(1) This Act may be cited as the National Health Service (Amendment) Act 1995.

(2) The enactments specified in the Schedule to this Act are hereby
repealed to the extent specified in the third column of that Schedule.

(3) Sections 1 to 12 above and subsection (2) above shall come into force
on such day as the Secretary of State may by order made by statutory instrument appoint; and different days may be so appointed for different purposes.

(4) An order under subsection (3) above may contain such transitional
provisions and savings as appear to the Secretary of State to be necessary or
expedient in connection with the coming into force of this Act.

(5) References in the amendments made by sections 2, 3 and 6 to a Health
Authority or to Health Authorities shall, until 1st April 1996, be construed as
references to a Family Health Services Authority or to Family Health Services Authorities.

(6) This Act, except section 13 above, subsection (1) above and this subsection, does not extend to Northern Ireland.

GENERAL NOTE

No Commencement Orders have been made to date but it is clear from the extended definition of Health Authority in subs. (5) that it is envisaged the Act will come into force before
April 1, 1996.

Section 14   SCHEDULE

REPEALS

Chapter	Short title	Extent of repeal
1977 c. 49.	The National Health Service Act 1977.	Section 46(3). In section 47, in subsection (1), the words "or the Secretary of State" and, in subsection (2), the words "or the Secretary of State, as the case may be,". In section 49, in paragraph (a), the words "prescribing the procedure for the holding of", "by the Tribunal or the Secretary of State", ", and for the making and determining of appeals to the Secretary of State under that procedure," "securing that", "and, in the case of an inquiry by, or appeal to, the Secretary of State before a person appointed by the Secretary of State", "or the person so appointed" and ", whether by the Tribunal or the person so appointed,"; in paragraph (b), the words "and on any person so appointed"; and, in paragraph (c), the words "and the Secretary of State".

Chapter	Short title	Extent of repeal
1978 c. 49.	The National Health Service (Scotland) Act 1978.	Section 29(4). In section 30, in subsection (1), the words "or the Secretary of State" and, in subsection (2), the words "or the Secretary of State, as the case may be,". In section 32, in paragraph (a), the words "or the Secretary of State", "and for the making and determining of appeals to the Secretary of State under that procedure,", "securing that", "and, in the case of an inquiry by, or appeal to, the Secretary of State, before a person appointed by the Secretary of State", "or the person so appointed" where those words first occur, and "whether by the Tribunal or the person so appointed,"; in paragraph (b), the words "and on any person so appointed"; and, in paragraph (c), the words "and the Secretary of State".
1995 c. 17.	The Health Authorities Act 1995.	In Schedule 1, paragraphs 34(c) and 63.

INDEX

OLYMPIC SYMBOL ETC. (PROTECTION) ACT 1995*

(1995 c. 32)

ARRANGEMENT OF SECTIONS

The Olympics association right

An Act to make provision about the use for commercial purposes of the Olympic symbol and certain words associated with the Olympic games; and for connected purposes. [19th July 1995]

PARLIAMENTARY DEBATES
Hansard, H.C. Vol. 253, col. 1357, Vol. 254, col. 636, Vol. 263, col. 1200. H.L. Vol. 561, col. 1638, Vol. 562, col. 1572, Vol. 563, cols. 706, 1207.

INTRODUCTION AND GENERAL NOTE
As the long title indicates, this Act, which received Royal Assent on July 19, 1995 and came into force on September 20, 1995, is intended to protect the Olympic symbol and various words associated with the Olympic Games from unauthorised commercial exploitation. The Act creates a quasi-property right, 'the Olympics Association right' which bears many similarities to a registered trade mark, although in some respects the protection is even more comprehensive (see General Note to s.1). The Act gives the person to be designated as proprietor of the right, the British Olympic Association, the exclusive right to use the controlled representation in the course of trade, thus giving statutory force to the common law rights of the Association. Prior to this Act, no 'property' rights existed in the Olympic symbol as such, or in its various associated

---

*Annotations by Alan Coulthard and Alison Firth.

words and motto. Apart from any underlying goodwill, there was no copyright or other tangible or intangible property rights in the symbols *per se*, although it was possible to have property rights in a copyright work, design or trade mark incorporating the symbols, providing, of course, that the statutory requirements for each of these rights were satisfied. Applications to register a design or trademark containing the symbols were accepted if they were part of a wider design and were not passed off as goods or services with an Olympic association.

Background

The debate concerning the protection of the Olympic symbols can be traced back to 1981 when the Nairobi Treaty, under the auspices of the World Intellectual Property Organisation, vested rights in the Olympic symbols in the International Olympic Committee. The Government was reluctant to sign this Treaty, as it was felt that it would be more suitable for the rights to be vested in a United Kingdom organisation. This was accepted by the International Olympic Committee, and, in addition to providing increased revenue opportunities, the Act also honours a commitment made by the Government in the course of the unsuccessful Manchester Olympic bid to regulate the use of the symbols in the UK. Not surprisingly, the Government decided to vest the rights in the British Olympic Association, which is a company limited by guarantee, established in accordance with the principles of the Olympic charter with a constitution which is approved by the International Olympic Committee. Its principal object is to promote the Olympic movement in the U.K. The British Olympic Association already owns and licenses trade marks that incorporate the Olympic rings together with a representation of the Union Jack. This enables the British Olympic Association to grant the right to use the trade marks to companies who sponsor the Olympic team, so as to enable them to use the trade mark for marketing purposes. None of these marks, however, has the same impact as the Olympic symbol and its associated words. The Act provides further marketing opportunities for the British Olympic Association which should generate significant extra funding. This is particularly important in view of the fact that the Association receives no Government funding, being entirely dependent on funds it receives from the private sector, whether through commerce or donations. The Act will allow further funds to be generated for the Association which will be utilised so as to develop further sporting achievement in Britain and to help ensure the continuing participation and success of British sportsmen and women in the Olympic games. (*Hansard*, H.C. Vol. 253, col. 1379.)

Structure of the Act

Section 1 creates the Olympic Association right, and grants the Secretary of State the power to decide upon the person responsible for exercising the right. Sections 2 and 3 determine, or make provision for determining, the subject-matter in which the right subsists, the powers of the person appointed proprietor of the right and the acts which constitute infringement of the right. Sections 4 and 5 provide for circumstances in which activities which would otherwise infringe the right, will not amount to infringement. Sections 6 and 7 are concerned with civil remedies for infringement of the Olympic Association right. Section 6 provides that the proprietor is entitled to recover the usual civil remedies available in respect of the infringement of a property right (*i.e.* damages, injunctions, accounts, etc.). Section 7 empowers the Secretary of State to make regulations introducing provisions equivalent to those in the Trade Marks Act 1994 (c.26), ss.15–20 (which provide for the remedies of delivery up of infringing goods, materials or articles, disposal of such matter, removal of offending signs, etc.). Section 7 also defines the terms infringing goods, infringing material and infringing articles for this purpose. Sections 8–10 provide for criminal offences and ss.11 and 12 deal with the remedy of forfeiture, pursuant to such offences. Section 13 amends the Registered Designs Act 1949 (c. 88), s.1 and the TMA, s.4 by providing that a design or trade mark consisting of, or containing a controlled representation will not be registrable unless the application is made by the proprietor or with his consent. Section 14 amends the Copyright, Designs and Patents Act 1988 (c. 48), s.213 by providing that design right does not subsist in a design which consists of or contains a controlled representation. Section 15 empowers the Secretary of State to make directions as to how the right should be exercised. Section 16 introduces a remedy for groundless threats of infringement proceedings similar to the provision contained in TMA, s.21, which was the first time this remedy was provided in a trade mark context. Section 17 deals with the burden of proof in civil proceedings, s.18 deals with interpretation and s.19 makes provision for the short title, commencement and extent of the Act.

COMMENCEMENT

This Act shall come into force on such day as the Secretary of State may appoint by order made by statutory instrument (s.19(2)). The relevant order was S.I. 1995 No. 2472, C. 48, and became effective on September 20, 1995.

ABBREVIATIONS

CDPA	:	Copyright, Designs and Patents Act 1988 (c. 48)
PA	:	Patents Act 1977 (c. 37)
RDA	:	Registered Designs Act 1949 (as amended) (c. 88). This appears as Sched. 4 to the CDPA
TMA	:	Trade Marks Act 1994 (c. 26)
1938 Act	:	Trade Marks Act 1938 (c. 22)

The Olympics association right

Creation

1.—(1) There shall be a right, to be known as the Olympics association right.

(2) The right shall carry with it the rights and remedies provided by this Act, which shall be exercisable by such person as the Secretary of State may by order made by statutory instrument appoint for the purposes of this subsection.

(3) An order under subsection (2) above which revokes a previous order under that subsection may contain such supplementary and transitional provision as the Secretary of State thinks fit.

(4) A statutory instrument containing an order under subsection (2) above shall be subject to annulment in pursuance of a resolution of either House of Parliament.

DEFINITIONS
"Olympics association right": s.2(1).

GENERAL NOTE
The right granted by subs. (1) is analogous to a registered trade mark, but in some respects the protection is even wider. In particular, there is no requirement for the 'mark' to be used by the proprietor in relation to goods or services, nor is there any danger of the mark being revoked for non-use as under s.46 TMA, or being declared invalid as under s.47 TMA. Furthermore, there is no limit on its duration nor is there any renewal requirement (compare ss.42, 43 of the TMA). In essence, the Act provides for an extremely wide-ranging right, with a number of rather esoteric defences to infringement in order to protect 'legitimate' uses of the various marks. Whether this is the most effective way of implementing this right remains to be seen.

Subs. (2)
Rights and remedies: For the 'rights' conferred see s.2, for infringements of these rights see s.3, for defences see s.4, for the power of the Secretary of State to provide for additional cases in which the rights are not infringed see s.5 and for the remedies available for infringement see ss.6 and 7.
By this Act: The right arises automatically as a result of the Act. There is no requirement of registration as for trade marks under the TMA.
Person: The 'person' in question is the British Olympic Association who thereby becomes the proprietor for the purposes of the Act (see s.2(2)(b)).
Secretary of State: The Secretary of State in question is the Secretary of State for National Heritage, who is also responsible for public lending rights. Other intellectual and industrial property matters come within the purview of the Department of Trade and Industry.

Rights conferred

2.—(1) The Olympics association right shall confer exclusive rights in relation to the use of the Olympic symbol, the Olympic motto and the protected words.

(2) Subject to sections 4 and 5 below, the rights conferred by subsection (1) above shall be infringed by any act done in the United Kingdom which—
  (a) constitutes infringement under section 3 below, and
  (b) is done without the consent of the person for the time being appointed under section 1(2) above (in this Act referred to as "the proprietor").

(3) The proprietor may exploit the rights conferred by subsection (1) above for gain, but may not make any disposition of, or of any interest in or over, them.

(4) This section shall not have effect to permit the doing of anything which would otherwise be liable to be prevented by virtue of a right—
  (a) subsisting immediately before the day on which this Act comes into force, or
  (b) created by—
      (i) the registration of a design under the Registered Designs Act 1949 on or after the day on which this Act comes into force, or
      (ii) the registration of a trade mark under the Trade Marks Act 1994 on or after that day.
(5) Consent given for the purposes of subsection (2)(b) above by a person appointed under section 1(2) above shall, subject to its terms, be binding on any person subsequently appointed under that provision; and references in this Act to doing anything with, or without, the consent of the proprietor shall be construed accordingly.

DEFINITIONS
  "infringed": s.3(1).
  "infringement": s.3(1).
  "Olympic motto": s.18(1).
  "Olympic symbol": s.18(1).
  "proprietor": subs. (2).
  "protected words": s.18(2), (3).

GENERAL NOTE
  This section deals with subsistence, territorial extent and ownership of the right. It provides that the Olympic association right subsists in the Olympic symbol, the Olympic motto "*Citius, altius, fortius*" and the protected words. These terms are all defined in the interpretation section (s.18). It also determines the nature of the rights which the proprietor has and the powers it has in respect of exploitation.

Subs. (1)
  Exclusive rights: The Olympics association right restricts to the proprietor (the British Olympic Association) the exclusive right to use the marks described in this subsection. As a result, the proprietor may, therefore, prevent others from using the marks in the ways described in s.3 (infringement) unless it gives consent (see also s.9 of the TMA). This consent will usually be given, if at all, in return for payment, thus deriving income for the proprietor. In this way, a proprietor can derive much more income than he would be able to do if he were confined to exploiting the intellectual property rights himself. Although it might be possible to mount a common law claim for passing off in the absence of a registered trade mark, such an action is inherently uncertain and, as a result, the unregistered mark is far less effective as a marketable asset (see S. Lane, *The Status of Licensing Common Law Marks* (1991)). In addition to the extra revenue the British Olympic Association might expect to gain, statutory protection also allows it to retain more control over the merchandise which it licenses, in order to prevent its reputation being tarnished by an association with shoddy goods or services.

Subs. (2)
  In the United Kingdom: The territorial scope of the Act is confined to the U.K., which includes Northern Ireland (s.19(3)). This provision confirms the usual intellectual property position, namely that the British Olympic Association can only sue in relation to infringements which take place in the U.K.
  And: Both paras. (a) and (b) must be satisfied for there to be an infringement.
  Consent: With the permission or licence of the proprietor. This expression is also used in s.9 TMA, s.60 PA (Patents) and s.180 CDPA (Rights in Performances). In other contexts, the word 'licence' is used: s.16 CDPA (Copyright), s.226 CDPA (Design Right) and s.7 RDA (Registered Designs), but it does not seem that there is any significant distinction between the two concepts.
  Person: See note to s.1(2) above.

Subs. (3)
  Although the word proprietor issued throughout this Act, a concept which suggests full ownership of the right conferred by subs. (1), it is clear from this subsection that the British Olympic Association has not been granted a full property right. The proprietor's status is, in effect, that of an exclusive licensee (see s.29(1) TMA).
  May exploit ... for gain: The proprietor is free to grant 'sub-licences' under this section but the question arises whether he is *only* entitled to grant licences for gain, *i.e.* can he grant 'free

licences'? This might be appropriate in some situations where the promotional value might enure to the benefit of the proprietor even if no financial rewards were forthcoming. A way round this would, of course, be to construe 'gain' so that it is not limited to financial reward, but this does leave open the dilemma as to whether the expression 'gain' is assessed objectively or subjectively. See also s.4(5)(b) below and s.92 TMA, for the use of 'gain' in a different context and the note to s.4(1) '*Honest practices*' for the objective/subjective debate. There is also no requirement that any licences should be in writing (*contra* s.28(2) TMA) nor is there any provision for licensees to bring infringement proceedings (*contra* ss.30, 31 TMA). As for the registration of a licence, this would seem to be precluded, since the Olympics Association right is not a trade mark within s.25 TMA, although a trade mark which consists of or contains a controlled representation, in so far the requirements of s.4(5) TMA (as inserted by s.13(2) below) are satisfied, could be registered by the licensee or British Olympic Association as proprietor. Thereupon, licensees of *that* mark could register their licences under s.25 at the Trade Marks Registry.

Disposition: Clearly the proprietor is unable to assign his rights, which suggests not only that the proprietor is merely an exclusive licensee rather than full owner but that the exclusive licence is personal to the proprietor alone. It is envisaged that a different person may subsequently be appointed as proprietor; see subs. (5).

Interest in or over: The final question left unresolved by this subsection is whether the British Olympic Association can grant an exclusive 'sublicence'. The point may be of little significance since there are no provisions corresponding to s.30 and s.31 TMA, but it has to be said that the position is by no means clear.

Subs. (4)

The effect of this section is to deny to the 'proprietor' or licensees a defence of statutory authority to infringement of a prior right or to infringement of a trade mark or design registered after commencement. See s.13 for the circumstances in which designs and trade marks containing the controlled representation can, in fact, be registered after the implementation date of this Act.

Subs. (5)

For equivalent provisions see also ss.28(3) and 29(2) TMA and s.92(2) CDPA.

Infringement

3.—(1) A person infringes the Olympics association right if in the course of trade he uses—

 (a) a representation of the Olympic symbol, the Olympic motto or a protected word, or

 (b) a representation of something so similar to the Olympic symbol or the Olympic motto as to be likely to create in the public mind an association with it,

(in this Act referred to as "a controlled representation").

(2) For the purposes of this section, a person uses a controlled representation if, in particular, he—

 (a) affixes it to goods or the packaging thereof,

 (b) incorporates it in a flag or banner,

 (c) offers or exposes for sale, puts on the market or stocks for those purposes goods which bear it or whose packaging bears it,

 (d) imports or exports goods which bear it or whose packaging bears it,

 (e) offers or supplies services under a sign which consists of or contains it, or

 (f) uses it on business papers or in advertising.

DEFINITIONS

"business": s.18(1).
"controlled representation": subs. (1).
"infringes": subs. (1).
"Olympics association right": ss.1(1), 2(1).
"Olympic motto": s.18(1).

"Olympic symbol": s.18(1).
"protected word": s.18(2).
"trade": s.18(1).
"uses": subs. (2).

GENERAL NOTE
    This provision corresponds with s.10 TMA, which is the section which has (not surprisingly) provoked the most litigation since the TMA came into force. See, in particular, *Wagamama v. City Centre Restaurants* [1995] F.S.R. 713, *Origins Natural Resources Inc. v. Origin Clothing* [1995] F.S.R. 280, *Mercury Communications v. Mercury Interactive* (U.K.) [1995] F.S.R. 850, *Bravado Merchandising Services v. Mainstream Publishing (Edinburgh), The Times*, November 20, 1995, *Barclays Bank v. R.B.S. Advanta, The Times*, February 8, 1996 and *British Sugar v. James Robertson, The Times*, February 17, 1996.

Subs. (1)
    In the course of trade: 'Trade' is defined in s.18(1) as including a business or profession, which is similar to the definition in s.103(1) TMA. This would include any kind of commercial activity such as buying, selling or leasing. In the infamously obscure s.4 of the Trade Marks Act 1938, the general first part of s.4(1) did not include any reference to 'in the course of trade' (see the Irish case of *Gallagher v. Health Education Bureau* [1982] F.S.R. 464, which held, on a similarly worded provision, that the use did not have to be 'in the course of trade'). However, it would not seem that the *Gallagher* principle could apply under this Act.
    Uses: Under the 1938 Act, there was only infringement if there was use as a *trade mark* (see s.9 TMA and for cases under the 1938 Act see *Mothercare U.K. v. Penguin Books* [1988] R.P.C. 113 and *Mars GB v. Cadbury* [1987] R.P.C. 387). Under the TMA this may not obtain. In *Bravado Merchandising* case (above) where Lord McCluskey held that use of the registered name of a pop group 'Wet Wet Wet', was a trade mark use within s.10 TMA (although he found for the defendant on other grounds). For an opinion on *Bravado Merchandising*, see Gredley's 'People you know, but can't quite name' [1996] ENT.LR (forthcoming). Conversely in *British Sugar v. James Robertson* (above), Jacob J. declined to limit the effects of s.10 TMA to 'trade mark'. The position is not clear under this Act. In view of wide purport it is by no means inevitable that it was intended to limit the protection of the symbols. Therefore it may well be that a description of a swimming pool as being 'Olympic-sized' by a sports centre, which is clearly not a trade mark use, could amount to infringement (subject to s.4 below). It is difficult to see how this position can be justified, and, indeed, led to some unnecessary amendments being tabled in relation to s.4.
    Representation: This would appear to suggest that a graphic representation of the Olympic symbols, etc. is required in order to infringe. It would not seem to be an infringement for a trader to use, for example, the protected words orally to advertise his goods. This was the case for trade marks under the 1938 Act. The requirement of visual use was omitted from the TMA.
    Subsection (1)(b): Whereas subs. (1)(a) corresponds with s.10(1) TMA, subs. (1)(b) corresponds with s.10(2) TMA (and s.5(2) in the context of relative grounds for refusal) apart, of course, from the fact that in both cases infringement does not depend on the representation being applied to identical or similar goods or services (since the Olympics association right does not depend on being applied to goods or services). It should, however, be noted that para. (b) does not apply to use of the protected words. In *Wagamama* (above) Laddie J. held that s.10(2) has not extended the concept of trade mark infringement to include association-based infringements where there is no confusion as to origin. In doing so, he rejected the Benelux interpretation of the Trade Mark Directive (1989/104/EEC) in spite of the fact that there was some evidence that the E.C. Commission had intended to incorporate the Benelux definition into the Directive (for further criticisms of his decision on this point see Kamperman Sanders, 'The Wagamama decision: back to the dark ages of trade mark law' [1996] 1 EIPR 3). Under this Act, however, there is no such ambiguity. The absence of any reference to confusion in this subsection would appear to have ensured that any use (even if not a trade mark use—see note under 'uses' above) of a representation similar to the Olympic symbols or motto will infringe if it evokes an association with it, irrespective as to whether there is any question as to confusion of origin. One wonders whether a record sleeve for a pop-song entitled 'Faster and Stronger' (note that translations are covered in s.18(3)) could potentially infringe under this section, so that its producer would have to establish a defence under s.4? Finally, the use of the expression '*in the public mind*' is not used in the TMA and is hardly likely to clarify matters, although it would seem to be an objective test.

Subs. (2)
    This provision is similar to s.10(4) of the TMA with the addition of para. (b). Reference should be made to the annotations to s.10(4) of the TMA in Current Law Statutes, 1994.

Limits on effect

4.—(1) The Olympics association right is not infringed by use of a controlled representation where—

(a) the use consists of use in a work of any of the descriptions mentioned in subsection (3) below, and

(b) the person using the representation does not intend the work to be used in relation to goods or services in circumstances which would involve an infringement of the Olympics association right,

provided the use is in accordance with honest practices in industrial or commercial matters.

(2) The Olympics association right is not infringed by use of a controlled representation where—

(a) the use consists of use of a work of any of the descriptions mentioned in subsection (3) below, and

(b) the use of the work is not in relation to goods or services,

provided the use of the representation is in accordance with honest practices in industrial or commercial matters.

(3) The descriptions of work referred to in subsections (1)(a) and (2)(a) above are a literary work, a dramatic work, a musical work, an artistic work, a sound recording, a film, a broadcast and a cable programme, in each case within the meaning of Part I of the Copyright, Designs and Patents Act 1988.

(4) For the purposes of subsection (2)(b) above, there shall be disregarded any use in relation to a work which—

(a) is of any of the descriptions mentioned in subsection (3) above, and

(b) is to any extent about the Olympic games or the Olympic movement.

(5) For the purposes of subsection (2)(b) above, use of a work in relation to goods shall be disregarded where—

(a) the work is to any extent about the Olympic games or the Olympic movement, and

(b) the person using the work does not do so with a view to gain for himself or another or with the intent to cause loss to another.

(6) In the case of a representation of a protected word, the Olympics association right is not infringed by use which is not such as ordinarily to create an association with—

(a) the Olympic games or the Olympic movement, or

(b) a quality ordinarily associated with the Olympic games or the Olympic movement.

(7) In the case of a representation of a protected word, the Olympics association right is not infringed by use which creates an association between the Olympic games or the Olympic movement and any person or thing where the association fairly represents a connection between the two, provided the use is in accordance with honest practices in industrial or commercial matters.

(8) The Olympics association right is not infringed by use of a controlled representation where—

(a) the use is in relation to goods which bear, or whose packaging bears, the representation,

(b) the goods are not infringing goods by virtue of paragraph (a) or (b) of section 7(2) below, and

(c) the use involves doing any of the things mentioned in section 3(2)(c) or (d) above.

(9) The Olympics association right is not infringed by use of a controlled representation where—

(a) the use is in relation to goods,

(b) the goods have been put on the market in the European Economic Area by the proprietor or with his consent, and

(c) the representation was used in relation to the goods when they were so put on the market.

(10) Subsection (9) above shall not apply where there exist legitimate reasons for the proprietor to oppose further dealings in the goods (in particular, where the condition of the goods has been changed or impaired after they have been put on the market).

(11) The Olympics association right is not infringed by use of a controlled representation where—

(a) the use is for the purposes of an undertaking, and

(b) the way in which the representation is used for the purposes of the undertaking is a way in which it has been continuously used for those purposes since a date prior to the commencement of this Act.

(12) In the case of a representation of a protected word, the Olympics association right is not infringed by use as part of—

(a) the name of a company, being a name which was the company's corporate name immediately before the day on which this Act comes into force, or

(b) the name under which a business is carried on, being a business which was carried on under that name immediately before the day on which this Act comes into force.

(13) The Olympics association right is not infringed by use of a controlled representation where the use—

(a) takes place under a right subsisting immediately before the day on which this Act comes into force, or

(b) is liable to be prevented by virtue of such a right.

(14) The Olympics association right is not infringed by use of a controlled representation where the use—

(a) takes place under a right created by—

(i) the registration of a design under the Registered Designs Act 1949 on or after the day on which this Act comes into force, or

(ii) the registration of a trade mark under the Trade Marks Act 1994 on or after that day, or

(b) is liable to be prevented by virtue of such a right.

(15) The Olympics association right is not infringed by use of a controlled representation for the purposes of—

(a) judicial or parliamentary proceedings, or

(b) a Royal Commission or statutory inquiry.

(16) In subsection (15) above—

"judicial proceedings" includes proceedings before any court, tribunal or person having authority to decide any matter affecting a person's legal rights or liabilities;

"parliamentary proceedings" includes proceedings of the Northern Ireland Assembly or of the European Parliament;

"Royal Commission" includes a Commission appointed for Northern Ireland by the Secretary of State in pursuance of the prerogative powers of Her Majesty delegated to him under section 7(2) of the Northern Ireland Constitution Act 1973; and

"statutory inquiry" means an inquiry held or investigation conducted in pursuance of a duty imposed or power conferred by or under an enactment.

(17) In this section, references to use of a work in relation to goods include use of a work on goods.

DEFINITIONS

"artistic work": subs. (3); CDPA, s.4.

"broadcast": subs. (3); CDPA, s.6.

"business": s.18(1).
"cable programme": subs. (3); CDPA, s.7.
"design": subs. (14); RDA, s.1.
"dramatic work": subs. (3); CDPA, s.3.
"film": subs. (3); CDPA, s.5.
"literary work": subs. (3); CDPA, s.3.
"musical work": subs. (3); CDPA, s.3.
"Olympics association right": s.2(1).
"protected word": s.18(2), (3).
"sound recording": subs. (3); CDPA, s.5.
"trade mark": subs. (14); TMA, s.1.
"use": s.3(2).
"work": subs. (3).

GENERAL NOTE
This section contains numerous defences to infringement. The intention is to allow existing, honest and legitimate uses which do not exploit an association with the Olympic movement to continue, whilst prohibiting dishonest traders who seek to exploit the association for their own gain. Some of the defences are virtually incomprehensible without reference to *Hansard*, and it is fair to say that the drafting and suitability of the defences was almost the entire subject matter of the debates in both the Commons and the Lords. For this reason, some references will be made to *Hansard* to explain what these provisions are intended to cover. See, in particular, *Hansard*, H.L. Vol. 562, cols. 1574 *et seq*, and H.C. Vol. 263, col. 1212. See also the notes to s.17(2) below on the burden of proof in relation to these defences.

Subs. (1)
This subsection is designed to allow the controlled representation to be used in a copyright work so long as it is not used for the purposes of thereby advertising a product or service. It was felt that it would be unacceptable censorship for the Act to prevent broadcasters, journalists, photographers and film makers from making reference to the Olympic games without the consent of the proprietor. However, it will not be possible for a trader to incorporate the controlled representation in a copyright work so as to avoid infringement when the use is to advertise or promote goods or services. Thus it is not intended that a person could use an artistic work incorporating a controlled representation on goods such as T-shirts, sports bags and equipment simply in order to sell that equipment. This would drive a coach and horses through the entire Act. Originally, subs. (1)(b) read: "the work is not one whose purpose is, or whose purposes include, the advertising or other promotion of goods or services", which was reasonably clear. However, it was amended in the Lords as a result of concerns that it might allow certain unfair practices to escape infringement. In particular, it was suggested that under the unamended provision, it might be possible for a T-shirt manufacturer to claim that his design incorporating the controlled representation was not included for the purposes of advertising or promoting the T-shirt, but simply to make it more commercially attractive. To avoid this loop-hole, the much wider version of subs. (1)(b) was adopted, which prevents the defence being raised in these circumstances.
Use in a work: See the notes under s.3(1) above on 'uses'. It does not seem that there needs to be use *as a trade mark* in a work for the subsection to operate.
In relation to: There is much law on the meaning of this provision in the context of the 1938 Act. See, for example, *Ind Coope & Co. v. Paine* [1983] R.P.C. 326 where the proprietor of 'John Bull' for beer was able to restrain the defendant (the proprietor of the mark for beer kits) from telling kit purchasers how to make 'John Bull' beer. In this context, the controlled representation only needs to be used in relation to goods or services in general, rather than in relation to specific goods or services for which a mark is registered. Furthermore, subs. (17), another consequential amendment, now makes it clear that the use of a work in relation to goods includes the use of a work on goods, thus covering the T-shirt example above.
Honest practices in industrial or commercial matters: This expression also appears in s.10(6) and s.11(2) TMA. The meaning of this phrase, in the context of s.10(6), was recently examined in *Barclays Bank v. R.B.S. Advanta* (above), where it was established that the test is objective and, it is suggested, the corresponding provision in s.11(2), use of one's own name, is likely to be treated as objective also, unlike the equivalent provision in s.8(a) of the 1938 Act which was treated subjectively in the *Mercury Communications* case (above).

Subs. (2)

This covers the situation where indirect infringement of the right is not present because the work incorporating the controlled representation is not itself used in relation to goods or services. See notes to subs. (1) above.

Subs. (3)

The sections of CDPA in which these categories of work are defined are listed above under the Definitions. See annotations to these definitions in Current Law Statutes, 1988.

Subs. (4)

This provision would allow, for example, trailers for television coverage of the Olympic games or merchandise promoting films about them.

Subs. (5)

This may be referred to as the 'Ken Livingstone provision', since it was introduced specifically to deal with a question raised by Mr Livingstone during one of the debates. In view of the expansion of subs. (1), it was thought that the use of a satirical cartoon featuring the Olympic games in a T-shirt design, as a campaign against the games would become an infringement, so this section was introduced specifically to allow this kind of use. Parody is not generally recognised as a defence to infringement of intellectual property rights in the U.K.: *Schweppes v. Wellington* [1984] F.S.R. 210; *Williamson Music v. Pearson Partnership* [1987] F.S.R. 97; *cf. Joy Music v. Sunday Pictorial Newspapers* [1960].

Gain: See also s.8 and s.92 TMA. The use of the word '*gain*' clearly refers to financial gain in this context, see the note to s.2(3) above.

Subs. (6)

During the debates, it was suggested that members of the Greek community who open small restaurants, or florists would have a defence under this subsection (which only applies to use of a protected word) on the basis that the use creates an association with their homeland rather than with the Olympic movement. As for the meaning of '*ordinarily*' one can only speculate! Simply limiting infringements to 'uses as a trade mark' would have obviated the need for this provision (see the notes on '*uses*' under s.3(1) above).

Subs. (7)

This would cover, for example, a hotelier who advertises accommodation as being within 5 minutes' walk of an Olympic Games venue. It would not cover a manufacturer who claimed that his products had been endorsed by the proprietor when they had not. Again this only applies to use of a protected word.

Honest practices in industrial or commercial matters: See s.10(6) TMA and the notes to subs. (1) above.

Subss. (9) and (10)

These two subsections correspond with s.12 of the TMA and ensure that the Olympics association right cannot act as an illegitimate fetter to free movement of goods within the EEA (contrary to Art. 30 of the E.C. Treaty, as extended). See the annotations relating to s.12 in Current Law Statutes, 1994.

Subs. (11)

This allows continuation of a pre-existing use, which is spared from infringement after commencement. For a similar provision, see TMA, Sched. 3, para. 4(2).

Subs. (12)

See s.11(2)(a) of the TMA and the *Mercury Communications* case (above). Note that there is no requirement of '*honesty*' here and that the use is confined to the use of a protected word.

Subs. (13)

This is the converse of s.2(4)(a). '*A right subsisting*' suggests an unregistered right such as copyright or a right which would be protected by the law of passing off, but presumably also refers to registered designs or trade marks or the right to use a varietal name for a plant.

Subs. (14)

This is the converse situation to that referred to in s.2(4)(b) above.

Subss. (15) and (16)
Since the Olympics association right, like a trademark but unlike copyright, is infringed only by activities carried out in the course of trade, this subsection may be otiose. For equivalent provisions, see ss.45, 46 of the CDPA.

Subs. (17)
See notes on '*In relation to*' under s.4(1) above.

Power to prescribe further limits on effect

5.—(1) The Secretary of State may by order made by statutory instrument specify additional cases in which the Olympics association right is not infringed.

(2) Without prejudice to the generality of subsection (1) above, the matters by reference to which a case may be specified under that subsection include—

(a) the description of controlled representation used, and
(b) the description of persons by whom a controlled representation is used.

(3) An order under this section may contain such supplementary and transitional provision and savings as the Secretary of State thinks fit.

DEFINITIONS
"controlled representation": s.3(1).
"Olympics association right": s.2(1).

GENERAL NOTE
This provision was one of the main amendments to the Bill as it passed through the House of Lords. It is designed to allow the Secretary of State, by order made by statutory instrument, to prescribe that certain categories of use of the controlled representation would not infringe the Olympics association right. Essentially, it provides a way of protecting uses of the representation, which are perceived as 'fair', yet which do not fall within the terms of any of the s.4 defences. See *Hansard*, H.L. Vol. 562, cols. 1572–1574. See also s.15 below.

Subs. (1)
Secretary of State: See notes to s.1(2) above.

Subs. (2)
Persons: In this section, the 'person' in question is not the same person as in the note to s.1(2) above. The person here refers to a user (or a group of users) of the controlled representation who would, were it not for this section, otherwise infringe the Olympics association right.

Remedies in relation to infringement

Action for infringement

6.—(1) An infringement of the Olympics association right shall be actionable by the proprietor.

(2) In an action for infringement, all such relief by way of damages, injunctions, accounts or otherwise shall be available to the proprietor as is available in respect of the infringement of a property right.

DEFINITIONS
"infringement": s.3(1).
"Olympics association right": ss.1(1) and 2(1).
"proprietor": s.2(2).

GENERAL NOTE
This provision is equivalent to s.14 of the TMA and s.96 of the CDPA, apart from the subtle change to 'of a property right' as opposed to 'any other property right'. The effect of this is to clarify that the Olympics association right is not, in fact, a property right, unlike a trade mark or a

copyright. This is also consistent with s.2(3) above which establishes that the right is not assignable. However, the proprietor is still entitled to all the remedies that are normally available in respect of the infringement of a property right, namely damages, injunctions and accounts. Although it is not explicit, it would also appear that infringements of the right are actionable *only* by the proprietor, so that licensees are unable to enforce the right. Compare TMA, ss.30, 31 and CDPA, s.101.

Orders in relation to infringing goods, material or articles

7.—(1) The Secretary of State may by regulations make, in relation to infringing goods, material and articles, provision corresponding to that made by the following provisions of the Trade Marks Act 1994 in relation to goods, material and articles which are infringing goods, material and articles for the purposes of that Act—

> section 15 (order for erasure etc. of offending sign),
> section 16 (order for delivery up of infringing goods, material or articles),
> section 18 (period after which remedy of delivery up not available),
> section 19 (order as to disposal of infringing goods, material or articles), and
> section 20 (jurisdiction in Scotland and Northern Ireland in relation to proceedings for an order under section 16 or 19).

(2) Goods are "infringing goods" for the purposes of this Act if they or their packaging bear a controlled representation and—

(a) the application of the representation to the goods or their packaging was an infringement of the Olympics association right,

(b) the goods are proposed to be imported into the United Kingdom and the application of the representation in the United Kingdom to them or their packaging would be an infringement of that right, or

(c) the representation has otherwise been used in relation to the goods in such a way as to infringe that right.

(3) Material is "infringing material" for the purposes of this Act if it bears a controlled representation and either—

(a) it is used for labelling or packaging goods, as a business paper, or for advertising goods or services, in such a way as to infringe the Olympics association right, or

(b) it is intended to be so used and such use would infringe that right.

(4) Articles are "infringing articles" for the purposes of this Act if they are articles—

(a) which are specifically designed or adapted for making copies of a controlled representation, and

(b) which a person has in his possession, custody or control, knowing or having reason to believe that they have been or are to be used to produce infringing goods or material.

(5) The power conferred by subsection (1) above shall be exercisable by statutory instrument which shall be subject to annulment in pursuance of a resolution of either House of Parliament.

(6) Nothing in subsection (2) above shall be construed as affecting the importation of goods which may lawfully be imported into the United Kingdom by virtue of an enforceable Community right.

DEFINITIONS
"controlled representation": s.3(1).
"infringe": s.3(1).
"infringing articles": subs. (4).
"infringing goods": subs. (2).
"infringing material": subs. (3).
"Olympics association right": s.2(1).

This section grants the Secretary of State the power to make regulations implementing certain provisions of the TMA (namely ss.15–16 and 18–20 inclusive) to provide further remedies for the proprietor. For detailed comments on the effects of these provisions if implemented, the reader should refer to the annotated version of the TMA (Current Law Statutes, 1994). The definitions of infringing goods, material and articles which are contained in s.17 of the TMA are inapplicable here, since these expressions have been defined in a slightly modified form in subss. (2)–(4), however, the effect is substantially the same.

Subs. (1)
Secretary of State: See notes to s.1(2) above.

Subs. (2)
United Kingdom: This includes Northern Ireland (s.19(3)).

Subs. (4)
Knowing or having reason to believe: In a copyright context, the phrase "having reason to believe" has been defined as "knowledge of facts from which a reasonable man would arrive at the relevant belief". See *LA Gear v. Hi-Tech Sports* [1992] F.S.R. 121 at 139. See also Laddie, Prescott and Vitoria, *The Modern Law of Copyright and Designs* (Butterworths 1995) at paras. 10.5–10.7.

Subs. (6)
See TMA, s.17(3) and CDPA, s.27(5).

Criminal sanctions

Offences in relation to goods

8.—(1) A person shall be guilty of an offence if with a view to gain for himself or another, or with intent to cause loss to another, and without the consent of the proprietor, he—
  (a) applies a controlled representation to goods or their packaging,
  (b) sells or lets for hire, offers or exposes for sale or hire or distributes goods which bear, or the packaging of which bears, such a representation, or
  (c) has in his possession, custody or control in the course of a business any such goods with a view to the doing of anything, by himself or another, which would be an offence under paragraph (b) above.
  (2) A person shall be guilty of an offence if with a view to gain for himself or another, or with intent to cause loss to another, and without the consent of the proprietor, he—
  (a) applies a controlled representation to material intended to be used—
      (i) for labelling or packaging goods,
      (ii) as a business paper in relation to goods, or
      (iii) for advertising goods,
  (b) uses in the course of a business material bearing such a representation for labelling or packaging goods, as a business paper in relation to goods, or for advertising goods, or
  (c) has in his possession, custody or control in the course of a business any such material with a view to the doing of anything, by himself or another, which would be an offence under paragraph (b) above.
  (3) A person shall be guilty of an offence if with a view to gain for himself or another, or with intent to cause loss to another, and without the consent of the proprietor, he—
  (a) makes an article specifically designed or adapted for making copies of a controlled representation, or
  (b) has such an article in his possession, custody or control in the course of a business,
knowing or having reason to believe that it has been, or is to be, used to produce goods, or material for labelling or packaging goods, as a business paper in relation to goods, or for advertising goods.

(4) It shall be a defence for a person charged with an offence under this section to show that he believed on reasonable grounds that the use of the representation in the manner in which it was used, or was to be used, was not an infringement of the Olympics association right.

(5) A person guilty of an offence under this section shall be liable—

(a) on summary conviction, to a fine not exceeding the statutory maximum, and

(b) on conviction on indictment, to a fine.

DEFINITIONS

"controlled representation": s.3(1).
"Olympics association right": s.2(1).
"proprietor": s.2(2).

GENERAL NOTE

This section creates a number of offences which are triable either way, although in both cases the sentence is limited to a fine. They mirror the offences contained in s.92 of the TMA. The annotations under that section of the TMA should be referred to for more detail of its provisions (Current Law Statutes, 1994).

Supplementary provisions as to summary proceedings in Scotland

9.—(1) Notwithstanding anything in section 331 of the Criminal Procedure (Scotland) Act 1975, summary proceedings in Scotland for an offence under this Act may be begun at any time within six months after the date on which evidence sufficient in the Lord Advocate's opinion to justify the proceedings came to his knowledge.

(2) For the purposes of subsection (1) above—

(a) a certificate of the Lord Advocate as to the date mentioned in that subsection shall be conclusive evidence, and

(b) proceedings in Scotland shall be deemed to be begun on the date on which a warrant to apprehend or to cite the accused is granted, if such warrant is executed without undue delay.

GENERAL NOTE

This section mirrors s.96 TMA and is self-explanatory. For a case on copyright which fell foul of the six months' time limit, see *Carmichael v. Sardar*, 1983 S.C.C.R. 423.

Partnerships and bodies corporate

10. Section 101 of the Trade Marks Act 1994 (offences committed by partnerships and bodies corporate) shall apply in relation to an offence under this Act as it applies in relation to an offence under that Act.

GENERAL NOTE

Section 101 fixes criminal liability upon partners (unless ignorant of, or attempting to prevent commission) and upon officers *de facto* of corporate bodies. See the annotation to s.101 TMA (Current Law Statutes, 1994).

Forfeiture of counterfeit goods, etc.

Forfeiture: England and Wales or Northern Ireland

11.—(1) Section 97 of the Trade Marks Act 1994 (which makes provision about the forfeiture of certain goods, material or articles which come into the possession of any person in connection with the investigation or prosecution of a relevant offence) shall also have effect with the following modifications.

(2) In subsection (1) (which describes the goods, material or articles concerned)—

(a) in paragraph (a), for "sign identical to or likely to be mistaken for a registered trade mark" there shall be substituted "representation within paragraph (a) or (b) of section 3(1) of the Olympic Symbol etc. (Protection) Act 1995", and

(b) in paragraphs (b) and (c), for "sign" there shall be substituted "representation".

(3) In subsection (7)(a) (power of court to direct release instead of destruction on condition that offending sign erased etc.) for "sign" there shall be substituted "representation".

(4) In subsection (8) (which defines "relevant offence") for "section 92 above (unauthorised use of trade mark etc. in relation to goods)" there shall be substituted "section 8 of the Olympic Symbol etc. (Protection) Act 1995".

GENERAL NOTE
The effect of s.97 is described in subs. (1) above. Equivalent provisions appear at s.35A RDA and ss.110 and 202 CDPA. See the annotation to s.97 TMA (Current Law Statutes, 1994).

Forfeiture: Scotland

12.—(1) Section 98 of the Trade Marks Act 1994 (which makes provision about the forfeiture of certain goods, material or articles on application by the procurator-fiscal or where a person is convicted of a relevant offence) shall also have effect with the following modifications.

(2) In subsection (1) (which describes the goods, material or articles concerned)—

    (a) in paragraph (a), for "sign identical to or likely to be mistaken for a registered trade mark" there shall be substituted "representation within paragraph (a) or (b) or section 3(1) of the Olympic Symbol etc. (Protection) Act 1995", and

    (b) in paragraphs (b) and (c), for "sign" there shall be substituted "representation".

(3) In subsection (13) (power of court to direct release instead of destruction on condition that offending sign erased etc.) for "sign" there shall be substituted "representation".

(4) In subsection (14), in the definition of "relevant offence", for "section 92 (unauthorised use of trade mark, &c. in relation to goods)" there shall be substituted "section 8 of the Olympic Symbol etc. (Protection) Act 1995".

GENERAL NOTE
Subsection (1) summarises the effect of s.98 TMA. For further detail, see the annotation to s.98 TMA (Current Law Statutes, 1994).

Restrictions on acquisition of competing rights

Registration of designs and trade marks

13.—(1) In section 1 of the Registered Designs Act 1949 (designs registrable under Act) there shall be inserted at the end—

    "(6) A design shall not be registered if it consists of or contains a controlled representation within the meaning of the Olympic Symbol etc. (Protection) Act 1995 unless it appears to the registrar—

    (a) that the application is made by the person for the time being appointed under section 1(2) of the Olympic Symbol etc. (Protection) Act 1995 (power of Secretary of State to appoint a person as the proprietor of the Olympics association right), or

    (b) that consent has been given by or on behalf of the person mentioned in paragraph (a) of this subsection."

(2) In section 4 of the Trade Marks Act 1994 (which specifies cases where a trade mark shall not be registered) there shall be inserted at the end—

    "(5) A trade mark which consists of or contains a controlled representation within the meaning of the Olympic Symbol etc. (Protection) Act 1995 shall not be registered unless it appears to the registrar—

    (a) that the application is made by the person for the time being appointed under section 1(2) of the Olympic Symbol etc. (Protection) Act 1995 (power of Secretary of State to appoint a person as the proprietor of the Olympics association right), or

    (b) that consent has been given by or on behalf of the person mentioned in paragraph (a) above."

(3) This section has effect in relation to applications for registration made on or after the day on which this Act comes into force.

DEFINITIONS
"controlled representation": s.3(1).
"design": subs. (1); RDA, s.1.
"Olympics association right": s.2(1).
"proprietor": s.2(2).
"trade mark": subs. (1); TMA, ss.1, 4.

GENERAL NOTE
This section amends s.1 of the RDA and s.4 of the TMA, by providing that a design consisting of or containing a controlled representation is not registrable under the RDA and a trade mark consisting of or containing a controlled representation is not registrable under the TMA. In both cases, there is an exception where the application for registration is made by the proprietor or is made with his consent. See also the note to s.2(4) above. The International Olympic Committee is not given any direct say in the matter, but is presumably protected via the constitution of the British Olympic Association (see Introduction and General Note).

Subs. (1)
   Person: See the note to s.1(2) above.
   Secretary of State: See the note to s.1(2) above.
   Consent: See the note to s.2(2) above.

Subs. (3)
   This provides that the exclusions in this section do not operate retrospectively.

Acquisition of design right

14.—(1) In section 213 of the Copyright, Designs and Patents Act 1988 (design right in original designs) after subsection (5) there shall be inserted—
   "(5A) Design right does not subsist in a design which consists of or contains a controlled representation within the meaning of the Olympic Symbol etc. (Protection) Act 1995."
   (2) Subsection (1) above has effect in relation to designs created on or after the day on which this Act comes into force.
   (3) For the purposes of subsection (2) above, a design is created on the first day on which—
   (a) it is recorded in a design document, or
   (b) an article is made to it.

DEFINITIONS
"controlled representation": s.3(1).
"design": subs. (1); CDPA, s.213(2).
"design document": subs. (3)(a); CDPA, s.263.
"design right": subs. (1), CDPA, s.213(1).
"original": subs. (1); CDPA, s.213(4).

GENERAL NOTE
Section 213 of the CDPA confers an unregistered, relatively short-term design right in the shape of articles or parts. The effect of this provision is to amend s.213 so as to deny design right protection to any design which consists of or contains a controlled representation. This amendment also precludes the British Olympic Association or its licensees from relying on any design right protection. It is not clear why the British Olympic Association or its licensees should be able to register designs pursuant to s.13 above but should be precluded from exercising any design right protection. There is no hint of the justification for this in any of the Parliamentary debates. In practice, the effect is likely to be limited, since design right does not extend to surface decoration.
   Or contains. Quaere whether this excludes design right for features of a design which are unconnected with the use of a controlled representation.

Subs. (2)
   This provides that the amendment does not operate retrospectively.

Miscellaneous

Power to give directions to proprietor

15.—(1) The proprietor shall comply with any directions given by the Secretary of State with respect to the exercise of the rights conferred by section 2(1) above.

(2) Directions under this section may be of a general or particular character and may be varied or revoked by subsequent directions.

(3) A transaction between any person and the proprietor in his capacity as such shall not be void by reason only that the transaction was carried out in contravention of a direction given under this section; and a person dealing with the proprietor shall not be concerned to see or enquire whether a direction under this section has been given or complied with.

GENERAL NOTE
    This section ensures that the Secretary of State retains some control over the activities of the proprietor by empowering him to make directions concerning the exercise of the Olympic association right. During the Parliamentary debates, it was suggested that this provision would allow traders who did not technically fall within one of the s.4 defences to complain to the Secretary of State, if they felt their activities did not take advantage of an Olympic connection. It was felt, however, that this placed an unduly onerous burden on the traders concerned, which was why the amendment which is now contained in s.5 appeared (see *Hansard*, H.L. Vol. 562, cols. 1572–1574). In the light of that amendment, it is difficult to imagine that much use will be made of this provision.

Subs. (1)
    Secretary of State: See the note to s.1(2) above.

Subs. (3)
    Person: See the note to s.5(2) above.
    Shall not be void: This rather odd provision has some hallmarks of the apparent authority of an agent. The effect of it would appear to be that a transaction entered into with the British Olympic Association will still be valid, notwithstanding that such a transaction is contrary to a direction given by the Secretary of State to the British Olympic Association.

Remedy for groundless threats of infringement proceedings

16.—(1) Where the proprietor threatens another with proceedings for infringement of the Olympics association right other than—
    (a) the application to goods or their packaging of a controlled representation,
    (b) the importance of goods to which, or to the packaging of which, such a representation has been applied, or
    (c) the supply of services under a sign which consists of or contains such a representation,
any person aggrieved may bring proceedings for relief under this section.

(2) The relief which may be applied for is any of the following—
    (a) a declaration that the threats are unjustifiable,
    (b) an injunction against the continuance of the threats, and
    (c) damages in respect of any loss he has sustained by the threats;

(3) A plaintiff under this section shall be entitled to the relief applied for unless the defendant shows that the acts in respect of which proceedings were threatened constitute (or if done would constitute) an infringement of the Olympics association right.

(4) The mere notification of the rights conferred by this Act shall not constitute a threat of proceedings for the purposes of this section.

DEFINITIONS
    "controlled representation": s.3(1).
    "infringement": s.3(1).
    "Olympics association right": s.2(1).
    "proprietor": s.2(2).

GENERAL NOTE
Section 16 is designed to protect traders from unjustified threats relating to 'secondary' infringements. It enables a 'person aggrieved' by threats to take the initiative by suing the proprietor, who then has the burden of justifying the threats: subs. (3). This provision corresponds with s.21 of the TMA which brought the remedy of a "threats action" into trade mark law for the first time. For comments on s.21 TMA, see Lim; 'The threats section in the U.K. Trade Marks Act 1994: can a person still wound without striking?' [1995] EIPR 138. See also s.70 PA, s.26 RDA and s.253 CDPA and the annotation to s.21 TMA (Current Law Statutes, 1994).

any person aggrieved includes the recipient of threats, suppliers whose goods the recipient fears to stock and so forth.

Burden of proof

17.—(1) Subject to subsection (2) below, if in any civil proceedings under this Act a question arises as to the use to which a controlled representation has been put, it shall be for the proprietor to show what use was made of it.

(2) If in any civil proceedings under this Act a question arises as to the application of any of subsections (1), (2) and (6) to (15) of section 4 above or any case specified under section 5 above, it shall be for the person who alleges that the subsection or case applies to show that it does.

DEFINITIONS
"controlled representation": s.3(1).
"proprietor": s.2(2).

GENERAL NOTE

Subs. (1)
This provision corresponds with s.100 TMA but, in this context, it is difficult to see why it is necessary. It was implemented in the TMA because of the problems a defendant faced under the 1938 Act in proving non-use, so as to effect a revocation of the mark. For the purposes of s.46 TMA, it is now made clear that the proprietor must establish that the mark is or was being used. The Olympic association right is exercisable irrespective of use by the proprietor and a revocation action is not possible against him. If it is self-evident that, in infringement proceedings, the proprietor must establish his case, then it is difficult to resist the impression that this provision is entirely otiose.

Subs. (2)
This establishes that the burden of proof in relation to any of the defences is on the defendant. There is no corresponding provision in relation to any of the defences in the TMA, which is probably because it was not necessary, suggesting that it was hardly necessary in relation to this statute either. It is also odd that nothing in this section apart from subs. (1) makes it clear that the burden of proof is on the plaintiff to prove elements of *infringement*, although it would seem very odd if this were not the case. On the whole, this section is not very well thought out.

General

Interpretation

18.—(1) In this Act—
"business" includes a trade or profession;
"controlled representation" has the meaning given by section 3(1) above;
"infringing articles" has the meaning given by section 7(4) above;
"infringing goods" has the meaning given by section 7(2) above;
"infringing material" has the meaning given by section 7(3) above;
"Olympic motto" means the motto of the International Olympic Committee, "Citius, altius, fortius";
"Olympic symbol" means the symbol of the International Olympic Committee, consisting of five interlocking rings;
"proprietor" has the meaning given by section 2(2) above; and
"trade" includes a business or profession.

(2) For the purposes of this Act each of the following is a protected word, namely, "Olympiad", "Olympiads", "Olympian", "Olympians", "Olympic" and "Olympics".

(3) In this Act, references to the Olympic motto or a protected word include the motto or word in translation into any language.

(4) In the application of this Act to Scotland—

"accounts" means count, reckoning and payment;

"declaration" means declarator;

"defendant" means defender;

"injunction" means interdict; and

"plaintiff" means pursuer.

GENERAL NOTE

Although only a definition section, this section contains several matters of interest in relation to infringement. Of particular interest is the provision in s.18(3) which provides that translations of the Olympic motto or a protected word are covered. This could cause particular problems in relation to the motto, since the words 'faster, higher and stronger' are very much in the public domain. Presumably, there will only be an infringement if the words are used in their entirety, particularly as there is no requirement that only a 'substantial part' of the phrase be taken. However, it could still be argued that using two of the three words might constitute a 'similar' representation for the purposes of s.3(1)(b). See also the example given in the note to s.3(1)(b) above. Translation into a language unfamiliar to the British public would also infringe.

Short title, commencement and extent

19.—(1) This Act may be cited as the Olympic Symbol etc. (Protection) Act 1995.

(2) This Act shall come into force on such day as the Secretary of State may by order made by statutory instrument appoint.

(3) This Act extends to Northern Ireland.

GENERAL NOTE

All the provisions of this Act were brought into force on September 20, 1995 pursuant to the Olympic Symbols etc. (Protection) Act 1995 (Commencement) Order 48 (S.I. 1995 No. 2472).

Subs. (2)

Secretary of State: See the note to s.1(2) above.

INDEX

References are to sections

LICENSING (SUNDAY HOURS) ACT 1995*

(1995 c. 33)

An Act to amend the provisions of the Licensing Act 1964 relating to permitted hours in licensed premises and clubs on Sundays and Good Friday; and for connected purposes.   [19th July 1995]

PARLIAMENTARY DEBATES
   Hansard, H.C. Vol. 254, col. 1013, Vol. 257, col. 1767, Vol. 263, col. 1340. H.L. Vol. 563, cols. 288, 1329, Vol. 564, cols. 670, 1718, Vol. 565, col. 530.
   The House of Commons Standing Committee discussed the Bill on March 14, 1995.

INTRODUCTION AND GENERAL NOTE
   This Act amends Pt. III of the Licensing Act 1964 (c. 26) to remove certain restrictions on the permitted hours during which intoxicating liquor may be sold, or supplied, on Sundays and Good Friday in licensed premises and registered clubs. The permitted hours on weekdays and Christmas Day will remain unchanged. The Act came into force on August 6, 1995.

ABBREVIATIONS
   The 1964 Act : Licensing Act 1964

Permitted hours in licensed premises

1.—(1) Section 60 of the Licensing Act 1964 (permitted hours in licensed premises) shall be amended as follows.

(2) For subsection (1)(b) (Sundays, Christmas Day and Good Friday) there shall be substituted—

   "(b) on Sundays, other than Christmas Day, and on Good Friday, the hours from twelve noon to half past ten in the evening; and

   (c) on Christmas Day, the hours from twelve noon to half past ten in the evening, with a break of four hours beginning at three in the afternoon.".

(3) In subsection (6) (off-licences), the words "or Good Friday" shall be omitted and at the end of that subsection there shall be added the words "and the permitted hours on Sundays, other than Christmas Day, shall begin at ten in the morning".

GENERAL NOTE
   The effect of these amendments to the 1964 Act is to permit the sale and supply of intoxicating liquor in licensed premises during the afternoon period on Sundays (except where Christmas Day falls on a Sunday) and Good Friday. The permitted hours in off-licensed premises are also amended with the effect that sales of intoxicating liquor from 10:00am until 10:30pm are permitted on Sundays (except where Christmas Day falls on a Sunday). On Good Friday in off-licensed premises sales of intoxicating liquor are permitted between 8:00am and 10:30pm.

Permitted hours in registered clubs

2.—(1) In section 62(1) of the Licensing Act 1964 (permitted hours in registered clubs)—

---

* Annotations by Matthew Pink, Solicitor, Clerk to the Justices North Gloucestershire Magistrates' Court.

(a) for paragraph (a) there shall be substituted—
"(a) on days other than Christmas Day, the general licensing hours;"; and
(b) in paragraph (b), for the words "Sundays, Christmas Day and Good Friday," there shall be substituted the words "Christmas Day,".

(2) In section 62(3) of that Act (notice of permitted hours) for the words "on Sundays, Christmas Day and Good Friday" there shall be substituted the words "on Christmas Day".

DEFINITIONS
"General Licensing Hours": Licensing Act 1964, s.60(5).

GENERAL NOTE
The effect of this amendment is that the permitted hours for the supply of intoxicating liquor in registered clubs on Sundays (except when Christmas Day falls on a Sunday), and Good Friday will be the same as the general licensing hours. The permitted hours for clubs on these days will therefore be from midday through to 10:30pm without a break.

Subsection (2) removes from s.62(3) of the 1964 Act the need for clubs to notify the Clerk to the Justices of the hours chosen by the club for supplying intoxicating liquor on Sundays and Good Friday. The need remains for the clubs to notify the Clerk of the hours chosen by the club to supply intoxicating liquor on Christmas Day.

Restriction orders

3. In section 67A(4) of the Licensing Act 1964 (restriction orders) for the words from "specify" to "and may" there shall be substituted the words—
"(a) specify any time between half past two and half past five in the afternoon on weekdays other than Good Friday, and between three and seven in the afternoon on Sundays and Good Friday, and
(b)".

GENERAL NOTE
The powers of the licensing justices and magistrates' courts to make restrictions orders are extended to include Sundays and Good Fridays between the hours from 3:00pm to 7:00pm so that alcohol may not be sold or supplied at those premises during the time specified in the order. There already exists powers given to the justices to make restriction orders for periods between 2:30pm and 5:30pm on other days of the week.

Consequential amendments and repeals

4.—(1) The amendments of the Licensing Act 1964 set out in Schedule 1 to this Act (which are consequential on sections 1 to 3) shall have effect.

(2) The enactments listed in Schedule 2 to this Act are hereby repealed to the extent specified in the third column of that Schedule.

Commencement

5. This Act shall come into force on such day as the Secretary of State may by order made by statutory instrument appoint.

GENERAL NOTE
An order, S.I. 1995 No. 1930 (C.37), was made on July 20, 1995 for the coming into force of this Act on August 6, 1995.

Short title and extent

6.—(1) This Act may be cited as the Licensing (Sunday Hours) Act 1995.
(2) This Act does not extend to Scotland or Northern Ireland.

SCHEDULES

SCHEDULE 1

CONSEQUENTIAL AMENDMENTS

1. The Licensing Act 1964 shall be amended as follows.

2. In section 51(2) (register of clubs), for the words "on Sundays, Christmas Day and Good Friday," there shall be substituted the words "on Christmas Day,".

3. In section 60(5) (permitted hours in licensed premises), for the words "(a) and (b)" there shall be substituted the words "(a) to (c)".

4. In section 68(1)(a) (extension of permitted hours in restaurants), for the words "Sundays, Christmas Day and Good Friday," there shall be substituted the words "Christmas Day,".

5. In section 87A (power to vary permit.ed hours in on-licensed vineyard premises)—
    (a) in subsection (4)—
        (i) for the words ", Christmas Day or" there shall be substituted the words ", other than Christmas Day, or on"; and
        (ii) in paragraph (b) for the word "five" there shall be substituted the word "nine"; and
    (b) after subsection (4) there shall be inserted—
      "(4A) In making an order under this section with respect to the permitted hours on Christmas Day, licensing justices may not so vary the hours as to make them—
      (a) begin before twelve noon; or
      (b) exceed in total more than five and a half hours.".

DEFINITIONS
"General Licensing Hours": Licensing Act 1964, s.60(5).

GENERAL NOTE

Para. 2
The Clerk to the Justices is required to keep a register of clubs holding registration certificates for premises in the area. This paragraph removes from s.51 of the 1964 Act the need for the register to show the hours on Sundays and Good Friday, if any, fixed as the permitted hours by or under the rules of the club as notified to the Clerk to the Justices. The register however must still show the hours for Christmas Day.

Para. 4
As a result of the changes made in this Act to the permitted hours there is no longer a need for a certificate under s.68 of the 1964 Act, which extends the permitted hours in the afternoon period, on Sundays (except where Christmas Day falls on a Sunday) and Good Friday. A certificate will be required for permission to sell liquor with meals on Christmas Day between the first and second parts of the general licensing hours. Licensees who currently hold a certificate for the afternoon period are advised to amend their notices which are displayed on the premises to reflect these changes. If a certificate has been granted for both the afternoon period and the evening period and the licensee no longer wishes to make use of the certificate insofar as the afternoon period is concerned, the licensee is advised to notify the police in accordance with s.69 of the Licensing Act 1964, and in order that the court's records can be amended notice should also be given to the Clerk to the Justices. It should be noted that the provisions relating to the extension of permitted hours for one hour in the evening following the general licensing hours remain unchanged, and therefore a s.68 certificate will still be required.

Para. 5
This paragraph extends from five-and-a-half to nine-and-a-half the total hours on Sundays and Good Friday for which an order may be granted in respect of a vineyard under s.87A of the 1964 Act.

SCHEDULE 2

REPEALS

Chapter	Short title	Extent of repeal
1964 c. 26.	The Licensing Act 1964	In section 60(6), the words "or Good Friday".
1988 c. 17.	The Licensing Act 1988	Section 1(2). In Schedule 1, paragraphs 1 and 4.

INDEX

References are to sections and Schedules

CHILD SUPPORT ACT 1995*

(1995 c. 34)

ARRANGEMENT OF SECTIONS

An Act to make provision with respect to child support maintenance and other maintenance; and to provide for a child maintenance bonus.

[19th July 1995]

PARLIAMENTARY DEBATES
Hansard, H.C. Vol. 257, col. 21; Vol. 260, col. 616; Vol. 263, col. 1342. H.L. Vol. 564, cols. 1185, 1356; Vol. 565, cols. 16, 31, 82, 154, 226, 870, 1246, 1318, 1841.

*Annotations by Professor N. J. Wikeley, Faculty of Law, University of Southampton; of Gray's Inn, Barrister

INTRODUCTION AND GENERAL NOTE

The Child Support Act 1991 came into force in April 1993. Lord Mackay of Ardbrecknish, the Minister of State for Social Security, in a masterly understatement, conceded when introducing the Child Support Bill 1995 that the Child Support Agency (CSA) "has had a less than comfortable time since its inception" (*Hansard*, H.L. Vol. 564, col. 1185). Others were less charitable. Lord Simon of Glaisdale, speaking from the cross-benches in the House of Lords, declared that the 1991 Act "has been an unprecedented legislative disaster. It has caused injustice; it has caused hardship; it has caused enormous public expense resulting in administrative chaos" (*ibid.*, col. 1190). For the Opposition, Baroness Hollis of Heigham argued that, "having ignored Parliamentary dissent, the Government found themselves overwhelmed by extra-parliamentary dissent and have created such a culture of resistance that the Act has become unenforceable" (*ibid.*, col. 1194).

There have been a number of developments in the child support system since April 1993, but none as far-reaching as the changes made by the 1995 Act. In December 1993 the House of Commons Social Security Committee issued a report on *The Operation of the Child Support Act* (see *First Report*, H.C. 69, Session 1993–94, and the Government's reply, Cm. 2469). This led to a number of modest changes in February 1994 (Child Support (Miscellaneous Amendments and Transitional Provisions) Regulations 1994 (S.I. 1994 No. 227)). These included a reduction in the carer component in the calculation of the maintenance requirement where older children were concerned, and adjustments to the protected income formula, as well as more flexible phasing-in provisions.

In October 1994 the Social Security Committee published a further report, *The Operation of the Child Support Act: Proposals for Change* (*Fifth Report*, H.C. 470, Session 1993–94). This was followed in January 1995 by a special report from the Parliamentary Commissioner for Administration (the Ombudsman), devoted to an investigation of complaints against the CSA (*Third Report*, H.C. 135, Session 1994–95). In the same month the Government published their reply to the Social Security Committee (Cm. 2743) and a White Paper, *Improving Child Support* (Cm. 2745), setting out more radical proposals for change. Some of the changes outlined in the White Paper were introduced by delegated legislation in April 1995. These included: an allowance in the formula for high travel-to-work costs; a broad brush allowance in the formula to take account of capital and property settlements; full allowance in exempt income for the housing costs of new partners and step-children; an upper limit for child support maintenance of 30 per cent of net income for current awards; and a reduction in the maximum level of maintenance payable under the formula (Child Support and Income Support (Amendment) Regulations 1995 (S.I. 1995 No. 1045)). These regulations also made various procedural changes, *e.g.* the suspension of fees and interest for two years from April 1995 and the introduction of two-yearly (as opposed to annual) periodic reviews.

The more significant proposals in the White Paper, some of which went beyond the recommendations of the Social Security Committee, required primary legislation, hence the need for the Child Support Act 1995. According to the Secretary of State for Social Security, "the main purpose of the Bill is to improve the system of child support so that it has greater acceptability and works better, to streamline the operations and to encourage greater compliance" (*per* Mr P. Lilley, *Hansard*, H.C. Vol. 257, col. 22). The most fundamental reform is the creation of a "departures system", allowing some flexibility in the application of the formula, albeit in narrowly defined situations (ss.1–9 and Scheds. 1 and 2). Other important measures include the introduction of a child maintenance bonus, payable when recipients of child support take up work of at least 16 hours a week (s.10), together with various changes to the system of reviews and appeals (ss.11–17). Private or non-benefit cases which fall outside the jurisdiction of the CSA, and which were supposed to be brought within its remit by 1996/97, are now excluded indefinitely from the operation of the 1991 Act (s.18).

The departures system

The central feature of the new Act is the departures system, which enables the Secretary of State to issue a direction modifying the application of the child support formula in prescribed cases. It would be a mistake to see this as a return to the type of discretion previously exercised by the courts. The White Paper made it clear that:

"The intention is that formula assessment should continue to be the norm; that the standard formula assessment should be the starting point even when a departure is allowed; and that departures should not be common ... Although the circumstances in which a departure can be allowed will be tightly specified, the process is *not* intended to be simply the application of a series of mechanical rules. The intention is that a departure will be allowed only when this seems fair, looking at a case in the round and taking account of all the circumstances including the financial position of both parents and the interests of the taxpayer" (para. 2.4).

Thus Mr Alistair Burt, the Under-Secretary of State for Social Security, was keen to stress that this latest measure was not meant to undermine the basic principles of the 1991 Act:

> "The Bill in no sense reflects any diminution of the Government's commitment to ensuring that parents support their children whenever they can afford to do so. However, we recognise that many of the problems with the operation of the child support scheme resulted from the universal application of a set formula for assessing maintenance. The Bill represents an opportunity to introduce a degree of flexibility so as to address certain special costs which it would be neither right nor realistic to include in the universal formula" (Standing Committee E, col. 3, March 28, 1995).

As one observer has commented, the departures system is in principle "the first major crack in the monolithic structure of child support, since it goes to the very heart of the philosophy of the legislation" (D.J. Roger Bird "Child Support: Reform or Tinkering?" [1995] Fam Law 112 at p.113). Schedule 2 lays down certain "gateways" to the departures system; in so far as they relate to travel-to-work costs and the effect of capital and property settlements, these build on the April 1995 adjustments to the formula. Some absent parents may qualify for no more than an allowance on the basis of the April 1995 changes; others may succeed in obtaining a more generous allowance under the departures system. Equally, some absent parents may receive an allowance under the April 1995 changes but then find this effectively withdrawn as a result of an application for a departure direction by the parent with care, arguing that the extra allowance is unduly generous in the circumstances. Schedule 2 also introduces new grounds for departures, relating to other types of "special expenses", which were not foreshadowed by the April 1995 amendments.

It is very difficult to predict how the departures system will actually operate in practice. What is clear is that, although its introduction represents a fundamental shift in Government policy towards child support, applications for departure directions under the new scheme will still be determined within the existing administrative and appellate structures, *i.e.* by an officer acting on behalf of the Secretary of State, with a right of appeal to a child support appeal tribunal (CSAT) and then to a Child Support Commissioner. Needless to say, legal aid will not be available.

The scheme of the Act

Sections 1–9 lay down the framework for the departures system by inserting ss.28A–28I into the 1991 Act. Section 1 inserts s.28A which makes provision for applications for departures directions, and also introduces Sched. 1; this inserts a new Sched. 4A into the 1991 Act, which makes supplementary and miscellaneous provisions in connection with such applications. This new Schedule includes one particularly important reform: it contains a regulation-making power which will enable certain categories of appeal to a CSAT to be heard by a chairman sitting alone (Sched. 4A, para. 9). Section 2 inserts s.28B, which enables the CSA to carry out a filtering process, known as a "preliminary consideration", of departure applications, in order to weed out hopeless cases. Section 3 inserts s.28C, which enables the Secretary of State to require an absent parent to meet a "regular payments condition" of child support maintenance while the application for a departure direction is being considered. Section 4 inserts s.28D, which provides for the Secretary of State to determine applications himself, or to refer them to a CSAT. Section 5, which inserts s.28E, lays down some very general principles which are to govern the exercise of the discretion in determining an application for a departure direction. Section 6, inserting s.28F, defines the circumstances in which a departure direction can be made. This section also introduces Sched. 2, which inserts Sched. 4B into the 1991 Act, which in turn provides for the cases in which a departure direction can be granted (Part I) and for controls on the provisions which may be included in departure directions (Part II). These cases include some of those in which the standard formula assessment has been unable to take into account certain special expenses, or the effect of capital or property transfers. Section 7 inserts s.28G and imposes a duty on a child support officer (CSO) to comply with a departure direction. Section 8 provides for a right of appeal to a CSAT against the Secretary of State's decision by adding s.28H to the 1991 Act. Section 9 inserts s.28I and makes various transitional provisions.

Section 10 provides for a child maintenance bonus to be paid in specified circumstances to people who have received child support while in receipt of income support or jobseeker's allowance.

Sections 11–15 deal with various aspects of reviews of maintenance assessments. Section 11 amends s.12 of the 1991 Act and enables an interim maintenance assessment to be made when a CSO conducts a review under the 1991 Act. Sections 12 and 13 amend ss.17 and 18 of the 1991 Act and enable a CSO carrying out a review to review maintenance assessments other than the assessment which was in force when the request for a review was made. Section 12 also confines the review process to changes which have been notified or which are otherwise known to have taken place. Section 14 amends s.18 and Sched. 1, para. 16 of the 1991 Act so as to allow a CSO to cancel maintenance assessments in certain circumstances. Section 15 substitutes a new s.19 for the original version in the 1991 Act in order to expand the powers of CSOs to conduct a review at their own instigation.

Sections 16 and 17 are both concerned specifically with appeals. Section 16 inserts a new s.20A into the 1991 Act providing for an appeal to lapse if, before the appeal is heard, a review decision is made which is the same as the decision which would have been reached on a successful appeal. Section 17 amends Sched. 4 to the 1991 Act to enable nominated officers to assist the Child Support Commissioners in their duties, by dealing with interlocutory matters.

Sections 18–24 make various miscellaneous changes. Section 18 concerns private cases which are outside the jurisdiction of the CSA. These are cases in which a written maintenance agreement made before April 5, 1993 or a maintenance order is in force and the parent with care is not in receipt of a relevant benefit. These cases were due to be taken on by the CSA in 1996/97. Their integration within the system is now deferred indefinitely. Section 19 amends s.11 of the 1991 Act so as to allow the Secretary of State not to proceed with an application for a maintenance assessment made on the basis of a benefit claim if he becomes aware that the benefit claim has been disallowed or withdrawn. Section 20 amends ss.27 and 28 of the 1991 Act to enable a declaration of parentage to be applied for after a maintenance assessment has been made. Section 21, inserting a new s.27A into the 1991 Act, permits the recovery of fees for DNA tests in certain cases. Section 22, which inserts a new s.41A into the 1991 Act, gives the Secretary of State the power to impose a financial penalty, as an alternative to interest, for the late payment of child support maintenance. Section 23, which inserts a new s.41B into the 1991 Act, allows the Secretary of State to reimburse overpayments of child support maintenance and to recover overpayments from those who have received them. Section 24 permits the Secretary of State to make compensation payments to recipients of family credit or disability working allowance whose child support maintenance is reduced because of changes to the child support legislation. Section 25 amends the Social Security Administration Act 1992 so as to clarify the Secretary of State's power to pay income support "gross", *i.e.* without regard to maintenance, and then to collect and retain any relevant maintenance.

Sections 26–30 concern supplementary matters. Section 26 specifies which regulations under the Act are subject to the affirmative resolution procedure (see also Sched. 3, para. 15, amending s.52(2) of the 1991 Act). Section 27 is the interpretation section (see below), while s.28 deals with financial provisions and s.29 makes provision for Northern Ireland. Section 30 details the short title, commencement (see below) and extent of the Act. It also introduces Sched. 3, which contains "minor and consequential amendments" (s.30(5)). Not all of these changes deserve to be consigned to such obscurity. Schedule 3, para. 5 amends s.20 of the 1991 Act so as to enable a CSAT to consider subsequent maintenance assessments or changes in circumstances when determining an appeal. Paragraph 9 amends s.30 of the 1991 Act so as to allow the CSA to charge a collection fee when offering collection services to non-CSA cases at some point in the future. Paragraph 10 amends s.33 of the 1991 Act and enables the Secretary of State to enter liability orders in the register of county court judgments. This is intended specifically as a compliance measure targeted at self-employed absent parents. Finally, para. 12 amends s.46 of the 1991 Act so as to allow the Secretary of State to exempt certain categories of parent with care from the operation of the reduced benefit penalty.

The use of powers to make delegated legislation

The Child Support Act 1995 contains more than 60 regulation-making powers. Over two-thirds of these relate to the departures system itself, the structure for which is laid down in ss.1 to 9 and Scheds. 1 and 2. The House of Lords Select Committee on the Scrutiny of Delegated Powers accepted that the Bill "does indeed lack flesh in important matters which will have a direct effect on those its provisions will touch" (*10th Report*, H.L. 71, Session 1994–1995). However, the Committee was persuaded by the Department of Social Security's arguments in favour of the extent of the delegated powers in the Bill. These referred primarily to the need for secondary legislation to provide sufficient flexibility and to ensure consistency of operation. In the light of these arguments, the Select Committee concluded that, unlike the recent Jobseekers Act 1995, there was no need to draw the House's attention to the Bill as a skeleton Bill on the ground that it inappropriately delegated powers.

The Appendix to the *10th Report* provides a full explanation of the reasons for the regulation-making powers in the Act, and reference is made to this source where appropriate in these annotations.

Administrative costs of the Act

According to the Explanatory and Financial Memorandum to the Bill, the administrative costs of the departures system are likely to be £3 million in 1995–1996, £22 million in 1996–1997,

£25 million in 1997–1998 and £15 million a year thereafter. It is also estimated that the departures system will require around 750 extra staff in the long term. The majority of these will be in the CSA, although some will be required in the Independent Tribunal Service, which is responsible for CSATs. The reforms to the reviews system are expected to save £5 million a year in 1996–1997, rising to £7 million in 1997–1998. Put another way, the saving will be "300 man-years". There will, however, be no savings in staff numbers, as CSA personnel will be redeployed to other work.

INTERPRETATION

General
Terms which appear in this Act which are also used in the 1991 Act are to be given the same meaning (s.27(2)). It follows that the relevant provisions of the 1991 Act, most notably s.54, must be consulted in order to ascertain the meaning of particular terminology. In addition, it should be noted that s.54 is amended by Sched. 3, para. 16 of this Act, which provides definitions for the following expressions: "application for a departure direction", "current assessment", "departure direction" and "parent with care".

Gender neutrality and "parent with care"
These annotations refer to the parent with care as "she" and the absent parent as "he", reflecting the most common arrangements in practice. The statutory provisions, of course, apply regardless of gender. In addition, these annotations use the expression "parent with care", rather than the statutory formulation "person with care". The latter is technically more accurate, as a person with care need not actually be that child's parent, but the former has become the more common usage. The specific statutory term "parent with care" is used in this Act only in ss.18 and 19.

COMMENCEMENT
Sections 29 (dealing with Northern Ireland) and 30 (short title, commencement, *etc.*, with the exception of subs. (5)) came into force on Royal Assent (July 19, 1995). The remaining provisions of the Act come into force as and when the Secretary of State so directs (s.30(4)): see also Child Support Act 1995 (Commencement No. 1) Order 1995 (S.I. 1995 No. 2302 (C.46)). The departures system will be piloted from April 1996, and may come into force properly in the autumn of 1996. The child maintenance bonus scheme will come into operation in April 1997; at the same time, it is expected that fees will be re-introduced and late payment penalties under s.22 will commence.

ABBREVIATIONS
10th Report	:	10th Report of the Select Committee on the Scrutiny of Delegated Powers (H.L. 71, Session 1994–95).
the 1991 Act	:	Child Support Act 1991.
CSA	:	Child Support Agency.
CSAT	:	child support appeal tribunal.
CSO	:	child support officer.
DWA	:	disability working allowance.
IMA	:	interim maintenance assessment.
MEF	:	maintenance enquiry form.
SSAA 1992	:	Social Security Administration Act 1992.
SSAT	:	social security appeal tribunal.
White Paper	:	*Improving Child Support* (Cm. 2745, 1995).

Application for a departure direction

Applications for departure directions

1.—(1) In the 1991 Act, insert after section 28—

"Departure from usual rules for determining maintenance assessments

Application for a departure direction
28A.—(1) Where a maintenance assessment ("the current assessment") is in force—
  (a) the person with care, or absent parent, with respect to whom it was made, or
  (b) where the application for the current assessment was made under section 7, either of those persons or the child concerned,

may apply to the Secretary of State for a direction under section 28F (a "departure direction").

(2) An application for a departure direction shall state in writing the grounds on which it is made and shall, in particular, state whether it is based on—

(a) the effect of the current assessment; or

(b) a material change in the circumstances of the case since the current assessment was made.

(3) In other respects, an application for a departure direction shall be made in such manner as may be prescribed.

(4) An application may be made under this section even though—

(a) an application for a review has been made under section 17 or 18 with respect to the current assessment; or

(b) a child support officer is conducting a review of the current assessment under section 16 or 19.

(5) If the Secretary of State considers it appropriate to do so, he may by regulations provide for the question whether a change of circumstances is material to be determined in accordance with the regulations.

(6) Schedule 4A has effect in relation to departure directions."

(2) Schedule 1 inserts in the 1991 Act a new Schedule 4A which makes supplemental provision with respect to procedural and other matters.

DEFINITIONS

"1991 Act, the": s.27(1).
"absent parent": ss.3(2) and 54 of the 1991 Act.
"current assessment": s.28A(1) of the 1991 Act.
"departure direction": s.28A(1) of the 1991 Act.
"maintenance assessment": s.54 of the 1991 Act.
"person with care": ss.3(3) and 54 of the 1991 Act.
"prescribed": s.54 of the 1991 Act.

GENERAL NOTE

This section, which inserts a new s.28A into the 1991 Act, introduces the system of departures from the formula provided for by the earlier Act. It also sets out who may apply for a departure direction and makes further procedural provision for such applications. Additional supplementary matters are dealt with in Sched. 4A to the 1991 Act, introduced by subs. (2) and Sched. 1 below. The actual grounds for departure directions are specified in Sched. 4B to the 1991 Act, introduced by s.6 and Sched. 2 below.

It will be noted that the new section does not specify any time-limit for making an application for a departure direction. As originally drafted, the Bill provided that an application made on the basis of the current assessment had to be made within 28 days, and would only be considered outside that time period if the applicant had good cause for the late application. Applications based on a change in circumstances were not to be subject to time-limits. This provision was deleted as a result of an Opposition amendment, agreed to by the Government, at the Report stage in the House of Lords (*Hansard*, H.L. Vol. 565, col. 1246). The result is that an application made later than 28 days from the issue of a maintenance assessment will be accepted even if there is no good cause for the delay. However, any departure direction which follows will not be backdated beyond the date of the application unless good cause can be shown. This will be achieved by bringing in regulations under s.28G(4) of the 1991 Act, inserted by s.7 (*per* Lord Mackay of Ardbrecknish, *ibid.*, col. 1248).

s.28A(1) of the 1991 Act

This allows for an application for a departure from the formula (a "departure direction") to be made by either the parent with care or the absent parent (or, in Scotland, a child aged over 12 years under s.7 of the 1991 Act) where there is a maintenance assessment in force. It is anticipated that the great majority of such applications will be made by absent parents.

s.28A(2) of the 1991 Act

This deals with the requirements for a valid application. First, it must be in writing. The CSA intends to provide a special form for such purposes, as may be prescribed under s.28A(3). Secondly, it must specify whether the application is in response to the existing assessment itself or is prompted by a material change in circumstances since that assessment was made. A "material change" has been described, rather predictably, as "a change that directly affects the position of the applicant in relation to special expenses in respect of which a departure either could be, or has been granted" (*per* Mr A. Burt, Standing Committee E, col. 19, March 28, 1995). The Secretary of State has a permissive power to specify what constitutes a "material change" in regulations made under s.28A(5), but there is no immediate intention to exercise this power.

s.28A(3) of the 1991 Act

Regulations will prescribe precisely how the written application under s.28A(2) must be made, *e.g.* that it should be signed by the applicant or representative.

s.28A(4) of the 1991 Act

This permits an application for a departure direction to be made even if an application for a review has been made or the child support officer is conducting a review. There is clearly some potential for confusion here when parallel applications for a review and a departure direction are under consideration, and so regulations may be made under Sched. 4A to the 1991 Act, paras. 2(c) and 6, inserted by Sched. 1, to deal with this eventuality. Provision for joint appeals may be made in regulations under Sched. 4A, para. 8.

s.28A(5) of the 1991 Act

The Government does not expect that it will be necessary to provide a definition of "material" for these purposes (*10th Report*, Appendix I, para. 7), so this is essentially a reserve power.

Preliminary consideration

2. In the 1991 Act, insert after section 28A—

"Preliminary consideration of applications

28B.—(1) Where an application for a departure direction has been duly made to the Secretary of State, he may give the application a preliminary consideration.

(2) Where the Secretary of State does so he may, on completing the preliminary consideration, reject the application if it appears to him—

   (a) that there are no grounds on which a departure direction could be given in response to the application; or

   (b) that the difference between the current amount and the revised amount is less than an amount to be calculated in accordance with regulations made by the Secretary of State for the purposes of this subsection and section 28F(4).

(3) In subsection (2)—

    "the current amount" means the amount of the child support maintenance fixed by the current assessment; and

    "the revised amount" means the amount of child support maintenance which, but for subsection (2)(b), would be fixed if a fresh maintenance assessment were to be made as a result of a departure direction allowing the departure applied for.

(4) Before completing any preliminary consideration, the Secretary of State may refer the current assessment to a child support officer for it to be reviewed as if an application for a review had been made under section 17 or 18.

(5) A review initiated by a reference under subsection (4) shall be conducted as if subsection (4) of section 17, or (as the case may be) subsection (8) of section 18, were omitted.

(6) Where, as a result of a review of the current assessment under section 16, 17, 18 or 19 (including a review initiated by a reference under subsection (4)), a fresh maintenance assessment is made, the Secretary of State—

(a) shall notify the applicant and such other persons as may be prescribed that the fresh maintenance assessment has been made; and

(b) may direct that the application is to lapse unless, before the end of such period as may be prescribed, the applicant notifies the Secretary of State that he wishes it to stand."

DEFINITIONS

"1991 Act, the": s.27(1).
"application for a departure direction": s.54 of the 1991 Act, as amended by Sched. 3, para. 16.
"child support maintenance": ss.3(6) and 54 of the 1991 Act.
"child support officer": ss.13 and 54 of the 1991 Act.
"current amount": s.28B(3) of the 1991 Act.
"current assessment": s.54 of the 1991 Act, as amended by Sched. 3, para. 16.
"departure direction": s.54 of the 1991 Act, as amended by Sched. 3, para. 16.
"maintenance assessment": s.54 of the 1991 Act.
"prescribed": s.54 of the 1991 Act.
"revised amount": s.28B(3) of the 1991 Act.

GENERAL NOTE

This section, which inserts a new s.28B into the 1991 Act, permits an application for a departure direction to be rejected without a full investigation. The purpose of this procedure "is to sift out those applications in which no qualifying ground is cited and to weed out those cases in which the departure application is flawed and will not go any further" (*per* Mr A. Burt, Standing Committee E, col. 44, March 30, 1995). Thus there are two bases on which an application may be rejected on such a preliminary consideration. The first is for want of grounds (s.28B(2)(a)), thereby avoiding the necessity of invoking the full procedure for determination, which would have involved seeking comments from the other parent. The second is where any consequential change in the maintenance assessment would be *de minimis* (s.28B(2)(b)). The latter possibility in effect mirrors the existing provision for limiting the impact of change of circumstances reviews (1991 Act, s.17(2) and (6)). However, while the effect of the drafting of the existing s.17 is in some respects obscure (see the annotations in Edwards and Jacobs, *Child Support: The Legislation* (1993)), the new provision makes it clear that an application can fall at the first hurdle without the other parent even being aware that it has been made. (Note that amendments to s.17 of the 1991 Act are made by s.12).

The Government's intention is that "this will be a quick, straightforward check of application forms, involving no discretionary judgments, and will be carried out by officers at a lower grade than those who will determine the applications and give departure directions on behalf of the Secretary of State" (*per* Lord Mackay of Ardbrecknish, *Hansard*, H.L. Vol. 565, col. 55, June 19, 1995).

s.28B(4) of the 1991 Act

Section 28B(4) enables a maintenance assessment, which is the subject of an application for a departure direction, to be referred to a child support officer for review under ss.17 or 18 of the 1991 Act, before the preliminary consideration under s.28B(1) has been completed. This allows errors in the original assessment to be identified so as not to confuse the operation of the departures system. On such a reference, the requirement to notify all other relevant persons is removed (s.28B(5)).

s.28B(6) of the 1991 Act

In the event that a fresh maintenance assessment is made following a review under ss.16 to 19 of the 1991 Act (including reviews initiated by a reference under s.28B(4)), the Secretary of State is obliged to notify the relevant parties (regulations under the power in s.28B(6)(a) will reflect the existing notification provisions in the Child Support (Maintenance Assessment Procedure) Regulations 1992 (S.I. 1992 No. 1813), regs. 11–16). The Secretary of State may also specify that the application is to lapse if the applicant does not notify him within a set period that he wishes it to stand. The prescribed period will be 14 days in the first instance (*10th Report*, Appendix I, para. 10).

Regulations may be made in order to provide for determining when the preliminary consideration of a departure application is to be taken to have been completed (Sched. 4A to the 1991 Act, para. 3, inserted by Sched. 1).

Imposition of a regular payments condition

3. In the 1991 Act, insert after section 28B—

"**Imposition of a regular payments condition**

28C.—(1) Where an application for a departure direction is made by an absent parent, the Secretary of State may impose on him one of the conditions mentioned in subsection (2) ("a regular payments condition").

(2) The conditions are that—

(a) the applicant must make the payments of child support maintenance fixed by the current assessment;

(b) the applicant must make such reduced payments of child support maintenance as may be determined in accordance with regulations made by the Secretary of State.

(3) Where the Secretary of State imposes a regular payments condition, he shall give written notice to the absent parent and person with care concerned of the imposition of the condition and of the effect of failure to comply with it.

(4) A regular payments condition shall cease to have effect on the failure or determination of the application.

(5) For the purposes of subsection (4), an application for a departure direction fails if—

(a) it lapses or is withdrawn; or

(b) the Secretary of State rejects it on completing a preliminary consideration under section 28B.

(6) Where an absent parent has failed to comply with a regular payments condition—

(a) the Secretary of State may refuse to consider the application; and

(b) in prescribed circumstances the application shall lapse.

(7) The question whether an absent parent has failed to comply with a regular payments condition shall be determined by the Secretary of State.

(8) Where the Secretary of State determines that an absent parent has failed to comply with a regular payments condition he shall give that parent, and the person with care concerned, written notice of his decision."

DEFINITIONS

"1991 Act, the": s.27(1).
"absent parent": ss.3(2) and 54 of the 1991 Act.
"application for a departure direction": s.54 of the 1991 Act, as amended by Sched. 3, para. 16.
"child support maintenance": ss.3(6) and 54 of the 1991 Act.
"current assessment": s.54 of the 1991 Act, as amended by Sched. 3, para. 16.
"departure direction": s.54 of the 1991 Act, as amended by Sched. 3, para. 16.
"person with care": ss.3(3) and 54 of the 1991 Act.
"a regular payments condition": s.28C(1) of the 1991 Act.

GENERAL NOTE

There is inevitably the risk that some absent parents may seek to use the departures system as a device for putting off compliance with their obligations under the 1991 Act. This section inserts s.28C into the earlier Act in an attempt to deter such behaviour. The new section provides that an application by an absent parent for a departure direction does not have to be considered unless he is making regular payments of maintenance. In effect, therefore, the new statutory procedure will only be open to those who demonstrate their good faith. The intention behind this provision is also that the parent with care should receive continuing maintenance while the absent parent and any new family do not suffer undue hardship.

The imposition of a regular payments condition while an application for a departure is considered does not affect the liability of the absent parent concerned for maintenance in accordance with the formula assessment in force. As the Under-Secretary of State for Social Security explained, "It simply allows him, temporarily, to pay at a lower amount until a decision is made on his application. If the application does not succeed, for whatever reason, he will be liable for the balance of the maintenance due for the period in which the regular payments condition applied. The balance will be calculated by deducting from the total of maintenance due for that period any payments actually made" (*per* Mr A. Burt, Standing Committee E, col. 62, March 30, 1995).

In addition, the regular payments condition is not designed to have any regard to arrears which may have built up: it relates solely to payments due after the date that the application was lodged (*10th Report*, Appendix I, para. 12).

s.28C(1) of the 1991 Act

This provides that, where an absent parent makes an application for a departure direction, the Secretary of State *may* impose a condition as to regular payments, which may either be at the rate of the existing assessment or at a reduced rate (s.28C(2)). Written notice of such a condition must be given in accordance with s.28C(3). The provision is deliberately drafted in terms of a discretionary power as some absent parents applying for a departure direction will in any event be making regular payments.

s.28C(2) of the 1991 Act

Regulations made under the power contained in s.28C(2)(b) will determine the "safe rate" or reduced rate of payments. "The intention is that, where a safe rate is appropriate (*e.g.*, if there is a special expense which reduces the income available to meet maintenance liability) it will reflect the likely assessment should a departure be allowed" (*10th Report*, Appendix I, para. 13). Such regulations are subject to the affirmative procedure (s.52(2) of the 1991 Act, as amended by Sched. 3, para. 15(a)).

s.28C(4) of the 1991 Act

A regular payments condition terminates once the application has been determined, or once it has failed, *i.e.* it lapses or is withdrawn, or the Secretary of State rejects it under a s.28B preliminary consideration (s.28C(5)).

s.28C(6) of the 1991 Act

This permits the Secretary of State to refuse to consider an application where the absent parent does not comply with the regular payments condition (determination of this question is also a matter for the Secretary of State to decide: s.28C(7)). In some circumstances, to be prescribed, the application itself may lapse. The intention, apparently, is to allow for a degree of flexibility so that, for example, an application will not lapse simply because the absent parent is late with one payment; however, regular default will lead to the application lapsing. In such a case, a further application—which itself would have to satisfy s.28A, introduced by s.1 above— would have to be made.

Determination of applications

4. In the 1991 Act, insert after section 28C—

"Determination of applications

28D.—(1) Where an application for a departure direction has not failed, the Secretary of State shall—
  (a) determine the application in accordance with the relevant provisions of, or made under, this Act; or
  (b) refer the application to a child support appeal tribunal for the tribunal to determine it in accordance with those provisions.

(2) For the purposes of subsection (1), an application for a departure direction has failed if—
  (a) it has lapsed or been withdrawn; or
  (b) the Secretary of State has rejected it on completing a preliminary consideration under section 28B.

(3) In dealing with an application for a departure direction which has been referred to it under subsection (1)(b), a child support appeal tribunal shall have the same powers, and be subject to the same duties, as would the Secretary of State if he were dealing with the application."

DEFINITIONS
"1991 Act, the": s.27(1).
"application for a departure direction": s.54 of the 1991 Act, as amended by Sched. 3, para. 16.

"child support appeal tribunal": ss.21 and 54 of the 1991 Act.
"departure direction": s.54 of the 1991 Act, as amended by Sched. 3, para. 16.

GENERAL NOTE

This section, inserting s.28D into the 1991 Act, provides that the Secretary of State can either determine the application himself or refer the matter to a CSAT for determination. The Secretary of State's power to determine applications for departure directions himself or to refer them to a CSAT arises only in respect of applications which have "not failed", *i.e.* ones which have not lapsed or been withdrawn, or been rejected on preliminary consideration under s.28B (s.28D(2)). The Government's intention is that a specialist group of staff within the CSA will act as departure officers and be responsible for considering such applications. "Staff employed on those duties will receive special training and the process of deciding applications for departures will be independent of the normal maintenance assessment process carried out by child support officers" (*per* Mr A. Burt, Standing Committee E, col. 55, March 30, 1995).

The alternative practice of referring matters to a tribunal without first instance adjudication has been borrowed from the social security jurisdiction (SSAA 1992, s.21(2)). In social security matters the power to make references is used rarely, and is confined principally to cases where there is a conflict of evidence which the adjudication officer feels unable to resolve on the papers (*e.g.* as to the reasons for a dismissal). It remains to be seen whether this power to refer is used more widely within the child support jurisdiction by staff acting on behalf of the Secretary of State. The Government anticipates that there may be a number of such cases in the early days of the departure scheme, but fewer when the system is well established. "Only where a case raises novel or particularly complex issues, and will clearly benefit from an oral hearing or the input of a legally qualified chairman, will it be referred to a tribunal for determination" (*per* Lord Mackay of Ardbrecknish, *Hansard*, H.L. Vol. 565, col. 60, June 19, 1995). Where an application is so referred, the CSAT is placed in the same position as the Secretary of State so far as their powers and duties are concerned (s.28D(3)).

Regulations may be made enabling the Secretary of State to determine a departure application where a person has failed to furnish information within a prescribed time limit (Sched. 4A, para. 4(2) to the 1991 Act, inserted by Sched. 1). Thus "a refusal to co-operate would be at that party's peril" (*per* Mr A. Burt, Standing Committee E, col. 71, March 30, 1995).

Matters to be taken into account

5. In the 1991 Act, insert after section 28D—

"Matters to be taken into account

28E.—(1) In determining any application for a departure direction, the Secretary of State shall have regard both to the general principles set out in subsection (2) and to such other considerations as may be prescribed.

(2) The general principles are that—

(a) parents should be responsible for maintaining their children whenever they can afford to do so;

(b) where a parent has more than one child, his obligation to maintain any one of them should be no less of an obligation than his obligation to maintain any other of them.

(3) In determining any application for a departure direction, the Secretary of State shall take into account any representations made to him—

(a) by the person with care or absent parent concerned; or

(b) where the application for the current assessment was made under section 7, by either of them or the child concerned.

(4) In determining any application for a departure direction, no account shall be taken of the fact that—

(a) any part of the income of the person with care concerned is, or would be if a departure direction were made, derived from any benefit; or

(b) some or all of any child support maintenance might be taken into account in any manner in relation to any entitlement to benefit.

(5) In this section "benefit" has such meaning as may be prescribed."

DEFINITIONS
"1991 Act, the": s.27(1).
"absent parent": ss.3(2) and 54 of the 1991 Act.
"application for a departure direction": s.54 of the 1991 Act, as amended by Sched. 3, para. 16.
"benefit": s.28E(5) of the 1991 Act.
"child": s.55 of the 1991 Act.
"child support maintenance": ss.3(6) and 54 of the 1991 Act.
"current assessment": s.54 of the 1991 Act, as amended by Sched. 3, para. 16.
"departure direction": s.54 of the 1991 Act, as amended by Sched. 3, para. 16.
"parent": s.54 of the 1991 Act.
"person with care": ss.3(3) and 54 of the 1991 Act.
"prescribed": s.54 of the 1991 Act.

GENERAL NOTE
This section, inserting s.28E into the 1991 Act, provides that decisions on applications for departure directions should take account of certain principles but must disregard certain other factors. Two general principles to be taken into account are specified in s.28E(2), although others may be prescribed under s.28E(1). The purpose of these general principles is said to be "to ensure that the system of departure directions does not undermine the basic intentions of the child support scheme" (*10th Report*, Appendix I, para. 14). As well as the general principles specified in s.28E(2) or in regulations under s.28E(1), the Secretary of State is required to take into account, when determining the application, any representations made by the parties (s.28E(3)). However, in making any such determination the Secretary of State must disregard the fact that any reduction or increase in the maintenance assessment would have implications for benefit entitlement (s.28E(4)).

s.28E(1) of the 1991 Act
This allows the Secretary of State to specify further general considerations in secondary legislation. The Government's intention is to use this power only if it is necessary to do so in order to ensure that discretion is used consistently in dealing with applications. One possibility is that regulations may provide that the Secretary of State, in considering a departure in a case where there was a court order before an assessment was made under the 1991 Act, should have regard to the level of the court order in deciding whether a departure direction was appropriate (*10th Report*, Appendix I, para. 16).

s.28E(2) of the 1991 Act
The first of these general principles, set out in s.28E(2)(a), reaffirms the principle of parental responsibility for the maintenance of children which is fundamental to the 1991 Act. This principle, if not all manifestations of its application under the child support scheme, presumably commands widespread support.

The second general principle is that where a parent has more than one child, his obligation to maintain each of them is equal (s.28E(2)(b)). In other words, his responsibility to his children with whom he lives cannot override his responsibility to his other children. Two observations may be made about this second principle.

First, the notion of equal treatment represents a subtle shift from the philosophy underlying the 1991 Act. The White Paper *Children Come First* (Cm. 1264–I, 1990) declared that where a parent had formed a second family, "he is liable to maintain all his own children. A fair and reasonable balance has to be struck between the interest of the children of a first family and the children of a second" (para. 2.1). Thus there was no explicit acceptance of the principle that a parent's obligation to maintain one child is no less than a duty to support any other(s). Indeed, some absent parents undoubtedly regard the operation of the child support scheme itself as inimical to this principle.

Secondly, this principle is still phrased in terms of parents' obligations as regards *their* children. A "parent" of a child means "any person who in law is the mother or father of the child" (1991 Act, s.54). That definition, which applies equally to this Act (s.27(2)), necessarily excludes from the concept of parenthood any step-parent, foster parent or other person who treats a child as their own. The Government's response to this omission is that, by definition, there is usually another father where step-children are concerned, and that a parent's primary responsibilities are to his natural children. Where special circumstances apply—*e.g.* the natural father of the step-children is dead—then it may be possible to obtain a departure direction (see Sched. 4B to the 1991 Act, para. 2(3)(f), inserted by Sched. 2). There remains, however, an uneasy fit between the principles embodied in the child support scheme and the social realities of repartnering and new families.

s.28E(4) of the 1991 Act
The purpose behind this provision is to protect the interests of the taxpayer by countering the risk that, if a parent with care is on benefit, any reduction in maintenance might be seen as justified, regardless of wider considerations, since benefit would necessarily increase to compensate in full or in part for the shortfall (*10th Report*, Appendix I, para. 15).

s.28E(5) of the 1991 Act
This allows the term "benefit", which appears in s.28E(4), to be defined in regulations. The intention is that it should reflect the benefits prescribed for the purposes of s.6 of the 1991 Act, *i.e.* income support, family credit, DWA and, from October 1996, income-based jobseeker's allowance.

Departure directions

6.—(1) In the 1991 Act, insert after section 28E—

"Departure directions
28F.—(1) The Secretary of State may give a departure direction if—
   (a) he is satisfied that the case is one which falls within one or more of the cases set out in Part I of Schedule 4B or in regulations made under that Part; and
   (b) it is his opinion that, in all the circumstances of the case, it would be just and equitable to give a departure direction.
(2) In considering whether it would be just and equitable in any case to give a departure direction, the Secretary of State shall have regard, in particular, to—
   (a) the financial circumstances of the absent parent concerned,
   (b) the financial circumstances of the person with care concerned, and
   (c) the welfare of any child likely to be affected by the direction.
(3) The Secretary of State may by regulations make provision—
   (a) for factors which are to be taken into account in determining whether it would be just and equitable to give a departure direction in any case;
   (b) for factors which are not to be taken into account in determining such a question.
(4) The Secretary of State shall not give a departure direction if he is satisfied that the difference between the current amount and the revised amount is less than an amount to be calculated in accordance with regulations made by the Secretary of State for the purposes of this subsection and section 28B(2).
(5) In subsection (4)—
   "the current amount" means the amount of the child support maintenance fixed by the current assessment, and
   "the revised amount" means the amount of child support maintenance which would be fixed if a fresh maintenance assessment were to be made as a result of the departure direction which the Secretary of State would give in response to the application but for subsection (4).
(6) A departure direction shall—
   (a) require a child support officer to make one or more fresh maintenance assessments; and

    (b) specify the basis on which the amount of child support mainten-
ance is to be fixed by any assessment made in consequence of the
direction.

    (7) In giving a departure direction, the Secretary of State shall comply
with the provisions of regulations made under Part II of Schedule 4B.

    (8) Before the end of such period as may be prescribed, the Secretary
of State shall notify the applicant for a departure direction, and such
other persons as may be prescribed—

    (a) of his decision in relation to the application, and

    (b) of the reasons for his decision."

(2) Schedule 2 inserts in the 1991 Act the new Schedule 4B which is
referred to in subsections (1)(a) and (7) of the new section 28F inserted by
this section.

GENERAL NOTE

This section, inserting s.28F and Sched. 4B into the 1991 Act, specifies the grounds on which a
departure direction may be given, enables regulations to be made concerning the contents of
such a direction, and requires a child support officer to reassess maintenance taking into account
the direction. The Government has made it clear that access to the departures system will not be
readily available:

    "We want to ensure that the departures system permits a reduction in maintenance for the
    small proportion of people who, because of their particular circumstances, feel that the
    formula bears especially hard on them and who have real difficulty in meeting their
    unavoidable costs at the same time as paying the assessed amount of maintenance.

    We do not want to return to the old levels of discretion which led to different people in
    virtually the same circumstances paying different amounts. If a large proportion of people
    qualify for departures, the widely-accepted principles behind the Child Support Act will be
    subverted and we risk creating a departures system that will collapse under its own weight.
    We shall tend towards tightness in the gateways wherever possible for that reason" (*per* Mr
    A. Burt, Standing Committee E, col. 4, March 28, 1995).

However, once access to the departures system has been secured, the Government has declared
that its intention is to allow the adjudicating authorities "freedom and flexibility to take all
relevant factors into account. If we draw regulations too tightly, there is a danger that we may
end up with the same difficulties of rigidity and inflexibility that the departure system is designed
to overcome" (*per* Mr A. Burt, Standing Committee E, col. 80, March 30, 1995). The tensions
between these two statements are explored further in the General Note to Sched. 2, inserting
Sched. 4B into the 1991 Act.

    In general terms, a departure direction can be given only if it would be "just and equitable" to
do so (s.28F(1)(b)). The DSS memorandum annexed to the *10th Report* notes (Appendix I, para.
18), perhaps with unintentional irony, that "although the use of the term 'just and equitable' in
this area is novel, it is a well recognised phrase in other legislation." This replaces (and provides a
better balance than) the notion of hardship to the absent parent, which the White Paper suggested would be a precondition for eligibility for a departure direction (para. 2.5). A direction
will not be given if its effect is to change the assessment by less than a minimum amount
(s.28F(4)). A direction requires a CSO to make a new maintenance assessment in accordance
with its provisions (s.28F(6)), and must be notified to all relevant persons (s.28F(8)).

s.28F(1) of the 1991 Act

    Two conditions have to be met before the Secretary of State is empowered to issue a depar-
ture direction. First, the case must fall within one of those situations specified in Pt. I of Sched.

4B to the 1991 Act (inserted by subs. (2) and Sched. 2 below), or in regulations under that Part. Secondly, the Secretary of State must be of the opinion that, in all the circumstances of the case, it would be "just and equitable" to make the proposed direction (see s.28F(2) and (3)). The latter criterion introduces an element of discretion notably absent from the 1991 Act as originally enacted. In addition, the general principles set out in s.28E of the 1991 Act, inserted by s.5, must be taken into account.

s.28F(2) of the 1991 Act

This contains further guidance as to what is meant by it being "just and equitable" to make a departure direction. The Secretary of State must have regard to the financial circumstances of both parties and to the welfare of *any* child likely to be affected by the direction (*i.e.* not just the child(ren) covered by the maintenance assessment in issue). The requirement to have regard to the welfare of the child is something of a belt and braces provision, as s.2 of the 1991 Act in any event requires the Secretary of State to have regard to this factor when considering any discretionary power conferred by the Act. Having said that, s.2 of the 1991 Act has no influence on the quantification of liability, and so the words of the heading to that section may "seem hollow indeed" (*per* Thorpe J., *R. v. Secretary of State for Social Security, ex p. Biggin* [1995] 1 F.L.R. 851 at 855). Further provision may be made by regulations under s.28F(3) as regards matters which are either relevant or to be disregarded in determining what is "just and equitable". Not surprisingly, however, the statute makes no attempt to structure the exercise of this discretion in terms of the weight to be accorded to particular factors. The breadth of this discretion can be highlighted by reference to other contexts in which the expression "just and equitable" appears in legislation. This phraseology was used in s.6 of the Law Reform (Married Women and Tortfeasors) Act 1935; according to Hilbery J., it meant that "exercising a judicial discretion in the matter I am intended to do that which I think is right between the parties" (*Daniel v. Rickett, Cockerell & Co. Ltd. and Raymond* [1938] 2 K.B. 322 at 326). Similarly, the Rent Act 1977 enables the courts to dispense with the requirement that a landlord serve a relevant notice before seeking possession on a mandatory ground, providing it is "just and equitable" to do so. This expression was considered by the Court of Appeal to be "of very wide import" (*Bradshaw v. Baldwin-Wiseman* (1985) 49 P. & C.R. 382). In this context this broad construction is fortified by the statutory directive in s.28F(1)(b) to consider "all the circumstances of the case". This will require the Secretary of State (and, on appeal, the CSAT: s.28H(4) of the 1991 Act, inserted by s.8) to undertake an extremely difficult and sensitive balancing exercise in some cases. For an attempt to resolve such issues in the context of applications under the Matrimonial Homes Act 1983, which enjoins the court to make "such order as it thinks just and reasonable having regard to [various factors] and to all the circumstances of the case", see *Kaur v. Gill* [1988] Fam. 110.

An indication of the Government's thinking behind the introduction of this provision was given by the Minister of State at the Committee stage in the House of Lords:

> "Let us suppose that an absent parent has requested a departure because he has a debt which costs him £25 a week to repay. It is clear that the debt is a reasonable one, that he has not been able to reschedule it and that he therefore has to meet the payments. On the face of it, he may qualify for a departure. However, perhaps we may suppose that he is a horse-racing enthusiast, a car enthusiast or something similar and has a part share in a racehorse which costs him £2,500 a year—not that I indulge in such activities, but I gather that it is pretty expensive. The parent may have other enthusiasms that cost him a great deal of money. The Secretary of State may consider that, in view of the circumstances of the case, it would not be just and equitable to allow a debt to reduce support for the absent parent's own child, when he is spending much more on an expensive hobby" (*per* Lord Mackay of Ardbrecknish, *Hansard*, H.L. Vol. 565, col. 83).

Put like this, few could disagree with the Minister. The practical difficulty will be the robustness (or otherwise) of the evidence which will be relied upon by staff in making such decisions.

s.28F(3) of the 1991 Act

This power enables the Secretary of State to specify which factors are to be either taken into account or disregarded when deciding whether it would be just and equitable to give a departure direction. "It is intended, for example, that the circumstances in which the parents stopped living together—and, in particular, any apportioning of blame for the break-up—should not be a factor in determining whether a departure was just and equitable" (*10th Report*, Appendix I, para. 19). One need not have access to a crystal ball to appreciate that many separated or divorced parents will perceive the departures system as inherently unjust and inequitable precisely because it does *not* consider such issues. As the regulations under this power will have a significant impact on access to the departures system, they will be subject to Parliamentary control by the affirmative procedure (s.52(2) of the 1991 Act, as amended by Sched. 3, para. 15(a)).

s.28F(4) of the 1991 Act
This requires the Secretary of State to reject applications where the maintenance assessment would only be changed by a *de minimis* amount. This reflects the provisions contained in ss.17(2) and (6) and 28B(2)(b) (introduced by s.2 above) of the 1991 Act.

s.28F(5) of the 1991 Act
These definitions mirror those in s.28B(3) of the 1991 Act, inserted by s.2 above, subject to certain drafting modifications in the case of the definition of "the revised amount".

s.28F(6) of the 1991 Act
A departure direction must require a child support officer to make the necessary fresh maintenance assessment(s) and must specify how that maintenance is now to be calculated. Where the departure relates to special expenses, they will be taken into account as part of the process for calculating assessable income. Maintenance will then be reassessed on the revised assessable income figure. Where the departure relates to a capital or property transfer, any allowance under the formula (*i.e.* following the April 1995 amendments) will be removed. An amount which represents the weekly value of the assets when the settlement was made will then be deducted from the maintenance otherwise payable (*White Paper*, paras. 2.12–2.13).

s.28F(7) of the 1991 Act
The scope of a departure direction may be limited in accordance with regulations made under Pt. II of Sched. 4B.

s.28F(8) of the 1991 Act
Before the end of such a period as may be prescribed. In view of the experience of the operation of the 1991 Act, the official explanation for this proviso needs no comment: "The Government is committed to prompt action on all departure applications and will seek to ensure that notifications of departure directions are issued quickly. However, it is sensible to allow some flexibility in setting out a time limit in this new and untested area" (*10th Report*, Appendix I, para. 19).

Effect and duration

7. In the 1991 Act, insert after section 28F—

"Effect and duration of departure directions

28G.—(1) Where a departure direction is given, it shall be the duty of the child support officer to whom the case is referred to comply with the direction as soon as is reasonably practicable.

(2) A departure direction may be given so as to have effect—
(a) for a specified period; or
(b) until the occurrence of a specified event.

(3) The Secretary of State may by regulations make provision for the cancellation of a departure direction in prescribed circumstances.

(4) The Secretary of State may by regulations make provision as to when a departure direction is to take effect.

(5) Regulations under subsection (4) may provide for a departure direction to have effect from a date earlier than that on which the direction is given."

DEFINITIONS
"1991 Act, the": s.27(1).
"child support officer": ss.13 and 54 of the 1991 Act.
"departure direction": s.54 of the 1991 Act, as amended by Sched. 3, para. 16.
"prescribed": s.54 of the 1991 Act.

GENERAL NOTE
This section, inserting s.28G into the 1991 Act, requires a CSO to comply with a departure direction "as soon as is reasonably practicable" (s.28G(1)). It also provides for a departure direction to be limited for a specified period or by reference to a specified event occurring (s.28G(2)). Regulations under s.28G(3) will be made enabling departure directions to be cancelled (*e.g.* because of a significant intervening change of circumstances which undermines the basis on which the original direction was made). Regulations will also allow the Secretary of State to

specify when a direction is to have effect, which may be backdated (s.28G(4) and (5)). The Government's intention is to provide that departure directions will normally be backdated to the date of the current assessment if the departure application immediately follows that assessment, or to the date of the application if it is based on a change in circumstances.

s.28G(1) of the 1991 Act

The duty on the CSO to comply with the departure direction "as soon as is reasonably practicable" clearly gives considerable scope for latitude: see by analogy *R. v. Secretary of State for Social Services, ex p. Child Poverty Action Group* [1990] 2 Q.B. 540, C.A., on the requirement to dispose of benefit claims, "so far as practicable", within 14 days (now SSAA 1992, s.21(1)).

s.28G(3) of the 1991 Act

A departure direction will apply indefinitely unless specifically limited in time or effect by the operation of the power in s.28G(2), which enables a direction to take account of foreseeable changes. The power to make regulations permitting cancellation of a direction is necessary in order to provide for unforeseen contingencies. For example, a direction based on travel to work costs would no longer be appropriate if the absent parent moved closer to his place of work (*10th Report*, Appendix I, para. 23).

s.28G(4) of the 1991 Act

A direction made in response to an application under s.28A(2)(a) (inserted by s.1 above) will normally take effect from the same date as the assessment, whereas a direction following a s.28A(2)(b) application will take effect from the date of the application or, in certain cases, from the date of the change in circumstances which forms the basis for the application (*10th Report*, Appendix I, para. 23). It should be noted that, where a maintenance assessment was made before the departures directions provisions came into force, any direction cannot be applied retrospectively before the date of the introduction of the departures system (s.28I(5) of the 1991 Act, inserted by s.9 below).

Appeals

8. In the 1991 Act, insert after section 28G—

"Appeals in relation to applications for departure directions

28H.—(1) Any qualifying person who is aggrieved by any decision of the Secretary of State on an application for a departure direction may appeal to a child support appeal tribunal against that decision.

(2) In subsection (1), "qualifying person" means—

   (a) the person with care, or absent parent, with respect to whom the current assessment was made, or

   (b) where the application for the current assessment was made under section 7, either of those persons or the child concerned.

(3) Except with leave of the chairman of a child support appeal tribunal, no appeal under this section shall be brought after the end of the period of 28 days beginning with the date on which notification was given of the decision in question.

(4) On an appeal under this section, the tribunal shall—

   (a) consider the matter—

      (i) as if it were exercising the powers of the Secretary of State in relation to the application in question; and

      (ii) as if it were subject to the duties imposed on him in relation to that application;

   (b) have regard to any representations made to it by the Secretary of State; and

   (c) confirm the decision or replace it with such decision as the tribunal considers appropriate."

DEFINITIONS

"1991 Act, the": s.27(1).

"absent parent": ss.3(2) and 54 of the 1991 Act.

"application for a departure direction": s.54 of the 1991 Act, as amended by Sched. 3, para. 16.

"child support appeal tribunal": ss.21 and 54 of the 1991 Act.

"current assessment": s.54 of the 1991 Act, as amended by Sched. 3, para. 16.
"departure direction": s.54 of the 1991 Act, as amended by Sched. 3, para. 16.
"person with care": ss.3(3) and 54 of the 1991 Act.
"qualifying person": s.28H(2) of the 1991 Act.

GENERAL NOTE

This section, inserting s.28H into the 1991 Act, provides for a right of appeal to a CSAT against any decision in relation to a departure direction. This is a somewhat unusual measure as there is virtually no precedent within the mainstream social security adjudication and appeals machinery for appeals against decisions of the Secretary of State to be heard by tribunals. (The sole exception relates to appeals to SSATs against certificates issued by the Secretary of State under the recoupment scheme: SSAA 1992, s.98). The right of appeal may be exercised by the absent parent, the parent with care or, in Scotland, a child who has made a s.7 application (s.28H(2)). The appeal must be brought within the standard child support scheme time-limit of 28 days (s.28H(3)), unless a CSAT chairman gives leave to appeal out of time. This contrasts with the standard three month time-limit for social security appeals. The CSAT will hear the application *de novo*, subject to the same powers and duties as those placed on the Secretary of State (s.28H(4)(a); see especially ss.28E and 28F of the 1991 Act, inserted by ss.5 and 6 above). The CSAT must consider any representations made by the Secretary of State (s.28H(4)(b)); these will presumably take the form of a written submission in the appeal papers, together with an oral contribution from the presenting officer at the hearing. The CSAT must either confirm the decision or replace it with the decision it thinks appropriate (s.28H(4)(c)). This may be contrasted with the rather limited powers available to a CSAT hearing an ordinary appeal in relation to a maintenance assessment. The general rule is that where an appeal is allowed, the CSAT "shall remit the case to the Secretary of State, who shall arrange for it to be dealt with by a child support officer" (1991 Act, s.20(3)). Clearly, however, implementation of the CSAT's revised decision will be a matter for the CSA. Appeals against departure directions may be heard concurrently with ordinary appeals against maintenance assessments (Sched. 4A to the 1991 Act, para. 8(2), inserted by Sched. 1 below).

The child support officer and any person aggrieved by a CSAT decision has a right of appeal on a point of law to a Child Support Commissioner (s.24(1) of the 1991 Act). This right is extended to the Secretary of State where decisions on departure directions are concerned: s.24(1A) of the 1991 Act, inserted by Sched. 3, para. 7 below. There is also the possibility, if a rather faint one given the existence of the statutory appeal mechanism, of an application for judicial review.

Transitional provisions

9. In the 1991 Act, insert after section 28H—

"Transitional provisions
28I.—(1) In the case of an application for a departure direction relating to a maintenance assessment which was made before the coming into force of section 28A, the period within which the application must be made shall be such period as may be prescribed.

(2) The Secretary of State may by regulations make provision for applications for departure directions to be dealt with according to an order determined in accordance with the regulations.

(3) The regulations may, for example, provide for—
(a) applications relating to prescribed descriptions of maintenance assessment, or
(b) prescribed descriptions of application,
to be dealt with before applications relating to other prescribed descriptions of assessment or (as the case may be) other prescribed descriptions of application.

(4) The Secretary of State may by regulations make provision—
(a) enabling applications for departure directions made before the coming into force of section 28A to be considered even though that section is not in force;
(b) for the determination of any such application as if section 28A and the other provisions of this Act relating to departure directions were in force; and

(c) as to the effect of any departure direction given before the coming into force of section 28A.

(5) Regulations under section 28G(4) may not provide for a departure direction to have effect from a date earlier than that on which that section came into force."

DEFINITIONS
"1991 Act, the": s.27(1).
"application for a departure direction": s.54 of the 1991 Act, as amended by Sched. 3, para. 16.
"departure direction": s.54 of the 1991 Act, as amended by Sched. 3, para. 16.
"maintenance assessment": s.54 of the 1991 Act.
"prescribed": s.54 of the 1991 Act.

GENERAL NOTE
This section, inserting s.28I into the 1991 Act, makes provision for transitional arrangements to cover cases where maintenance has been assessed before the introduction of the departure system. Given the difficulties which have faced the CSA since the 1991 Act came into force, it is obviously imperative that applications for departure directions with regard to existing cases are phased in on a realistic basis. Accordingly, s.28I(1) removes the 28-day time-limit for departure applications imposed by s.28A and enables other time-limits to be specified in regulations. Section 28I(2) allows regulations to make provision for phasing in such applications; these arrangements will presumably be more realistic than the targets which the CSA was originally set in 1993. Section 28I(3) makes it clear that phasing may be by type of maintenance assessment or by type of departure application. The system for handling departure applications will be piloted under regulations made by virtue of s.28I(4), although no change in the maintenance assessment itself will be possible until the full departure scheme comes into force (s.28I(5)).

s.28I(1) of the 1991 Act
This disapplies the normal 28-day time-limit for making departure directions during the transitional period. The Government's intention is to prescribe an alternative time-limit in regulations "that should be related in some way to the first date on which an application for a departure could be made by the applicant" (*per* Mr A. Burt, Standing Committee E, col. 145, April 4, 1995).

s.28I(2) and (3) of the 1991 Act
This permits a phased take-on of departure applications to avoid the problems that beset the CSA in 1993 when the child support scheme was established. Such phasing in will not affect the right to a departure from the outset of the new system (*i.e.* successful applications will be backdated to the first date from which a departure could have been authorised had the phasing in provisions not been operative). The criteria for phasing in have yet to be determined, but they are likely to include the oldest cases and those in which people are on protected incomes (*10th Report*, Appendix I, para. 26).

s.28I(4) of the 1991 Act
This permits the CSA to pilot the departures system before it comes fully into effect. The purpose is "to invite early applications which, although any resulting departure will not take effect until the system is introduced, will allow the staff to familiarise themselves with its operations and allow the early identification of difficulties in the regulations governing the scheme" (*per* Mr A. Burt, Standing Committee E, col. 145, April 4, 1995). It is intended that piloting will start as early as April 1996, but this may be an optimistic target given the problems the Government has encountered in introducing Jobseeker's Allowance on time.

s.28I(5) of the 1991 Act
Departure directions, unlike the 1991 Act itself, are not retrospective in their effect.

The child maintenance bonus

The child maintenance bonus

10.—(1) The Secretary of State may by regulations make provision for the payment, in prescribed circumstances, of sums to persons—
(a) who are or have been in receipt of child maintenance; and

(b) to or in respect of whom income support or a jobseeker's allowance is or has been paid.

(2) A sum payable under the regulations shall be known as "a child maintenance bonus".

(3) A child maintenance bonus shall be treated for all purposes as payable by way of income support or (as the case may be) a jobseeker's allowance.

(4) Subsection (3) is subject to section 617 of the Income and Corporation Taxes Act 1988 (which, as amended by paragraph 1 of Schedule 3, provides for a child maintenance bonus not to be taxable).

(5) The regulations may, in particular, provide for—

(a) a child maintenance bonus to be payable only on the occurrence of a prescribed event;

(b) a bonus not to be payable unless a claim is made before the end of the prescribed period;

(c) the amount of a bonus (subject to any maximum prescribed by virtue of paragraph (f)) to be determined in accordance with the regulations;

(d) enabling amounts to be calculated by reference to periods of entitlement to income support and periods of entitlement to a jobseeker's allowance;

(e) treating a bonus as payable wholly by way of a jobseeker's allowance or wholly by way of income support, in a case where amounts have been calculated in accordance with provision made by virtue of paragraph (d);

(f) the amount of a bonus not to exceed a prescribed maximum;

(g) a bonus not to be payable if the amount of the bonus which would otherwise be payable is less than the prescribed minimum;

(h) prescribed periods to be disregarded for prescribed purposes;

(i) a bonus which has been paid to a person to be treated, in prescribed circumstances and for prescribed purposes, as income or capital of hers or of any other member of her family;

(j) treating the whole or a prescribed part of an amount which has accrued towards a person's bonus—

(i) as not having accrued towards her bonus; but

(ii) as having accrued towards the bonus of another person.

(6) The Secretary of State may by regulations provide—

(a) for the whole or a prescribed part of a child maintenance bonus to be paid in such circumstances as may be prescribed to such person, other than the person who is or had been in receipt of child maintenance, as may be determined in accordance with the regulations;

(b) for any payments of a prescribed kind which have been collected by the Secretary of State, and retained by him, to be treated for the purposes of this section as having been received by the appropriate person as payments of child maintenance.

(7) In this section—

"appropriate person" has such meaning as may be prescribed;

"child" means a person under the age of 16;

"child maintenance" has such meaning as may be prescribed;

"family" means—

(a) a married or unmarried couple;

(b) a married or unmarried couple and a member of the same household for whom one of them is, or both are, responsible and who is a child or a person of a prescribed description;

(c) except in prescribed circumstances, a person who is not a member of a married or unmarried couple and a member of the same household for whom that person is responsible and who is a child or a person of a prescribed description;

"married couple" means a man and woman who are married to each other and are members of the same household; and "unmarried couple" means a man and woman who are not married to each other but are living together as husband and wife otherwise than in prescribed circumstances.

(8) For the purposes of this section, the Secretary of State may by regulations make provision as to the circumstances in which—

(a) persons are to be treated as being or not being members of the same household;

(b) one person is to be treated as responsible or not responsible for another.

DEFINITIONS

"appropriate person": subs. (7).
"child": subs. (7).
"child maintenance": subs. (7).
"child maintenance bonus": subs. (2).
"family": subs. (7).
"income support": s.54 of the 1991 Act.
"married couple": subs. (7).
"prescribed": s.54 of the 1991 Act.
"unmarried couple": subs. (7).

GENERAL NOTE

This provision is modelled on s.26 of the Jobseekers Act 1995, which introduced the "back to work bonus". This section introduces a child maintenance bonus for parents with care who receive child maintenance along with income support or income-based jobseeker's allowance (subss. (1) and (2)). The Government's intention is to use the regulation-making powers so that a flat-rate amount should accrue for each week in which maintenance is received and taken into account in the benefit assessment. This amount is likely to be £5 a week, or the actual amount of maintenance, if less. When the parent with care or her partner starts work, and benefit stops, the child maintenance bonus will be paid as a lump sum.

This bonus is to be treated as a payment of income support or jobseeker's allowance, thus bringing it within the scope of the common provisions and adjudication arrangements for those benefits (subs. (3)). The bonus is non-taxable (subs. (4)). The Government's intention is to prescribe a maximum lump sum of £1,000 (by regulations made under subs. (5)(f)).

The background to the child maintenance bonus lies in the longstanding controversy over the role of disregards in the child support scheme as well as in the social security system itself. The Government has consistently resisted attempts to permit parents with care on income support to retain a certain amount of maintenance before it is taken into account for the purposes of calculating entitlement to benefit. The Government's view is that such a disregard for income support claimants would act as a disincentive to work. The child maintenance bonus is, in effect, a form of postponed and aggregated disregard, although it remains to be seen how effective it is in terms of encouraging parents with care to come off benefit. According to one Opposition spokesperson, "the Government are merely offering a back to work bonus which will take at least four years to be arrived at, and gives the wrong money to the wrong mothers at the wrong time for the wrong reasons" (*per* Baroness Hollis of Heigham, *Hansard*, H.L. Vol. 564, col. 1195).

The scheme is largely to be defined by way of regulations, the first set of which are subject to the affirmative procedure (s.26(4)). As there is a strong social security element to the child maintenance bonus, this new scheme will come within the remit of the Social Security Advisory Committee (SSAA 1992, s.170(5)(ab), inserted by Sched. 3, para. 20 below). The child maintenance bonus will not commence until April 1997. According to the Explanatory and Financial Memorandum to the Bill, it is expected to increase benefit expenditure by £10 million in 1997–98 and by £20 million a year in the longer term.

Subs. (5)

These regulation-making powers replicate those relating to the back to work bonus, which are to be found in s.26(4) of the Jobseekers Act 1995 (see the annotations to that statute, 1995 ch. 18). The one exception is that the back to work bonus scheme has a regulation-making power enabling claimants to be kept informed of the amounts credited to them by way of a bonus. Such a power is absent from the child maintenance bonus scheme.

Subs. (6)(a)

Regulations made under this power will provide for special cases where payment of the bonus to a person other than the parent with care is appropriate, *e.g.* to the partner where the parent with care dies.

Subs. (6)(b)

This allows the child maintenance bonus to be paid where maintenance was not actually received by the parent with care. Typically this will cover cases where the parent with care receives benefit gross (*i.e.* inclusive of maintenance), and the Secretary of State is collecting and retaining such maintenance under s.25 of this Act, which inserts s.74A into the SSAA 1992.

Subs. (8)

This power is consequential upon the definitions in subs. (7). Similar provisions exist within the income support scheme (see Income Support (General) Regulations 1987 (S.I. 1987 No. 1971), regs. 15 and 16).

Reviews of maintenance assessments etc.

Reviews: interim maintenance assessments

11. In section 12 of the 1991 Act (interim maintenance assessments), for subsection (1) substitute—

"(1) This section applies where a child support officer—
(a) is required to make a maintenance assessment;
(b) is proposing to conduct a review under section 16, 17, 18 or 19; or
(c) is conducting such a review.

(1A) If it appears to the child support officer that he does not have sufficient information to enable him—
(a) in a case falling within subsection (1)(a), to make the assessment,
(b) in a case falling within subsection (1)(b), to conduct the proposed review, or
(c) in a case falling within subsection (1)(c), to complete the review,
he may make an interim maintenance assessment."

DEFINITIONS

"1991 Act, the": s.27(1).
"child support officer": ss.13 and 54 of the 1991 Act.
"interim maintenance assessment": ss.12 and 54 of the 1991 Act.
"maintenance assessment": s.54 of the 1991 Act.

GENERAL NOTE

This section amends s.12 of the 1991 Act, which governs the circumstances in which an interim maintenance assessment (IMA) may be made. A CSO may make an IMA if sufficient information is not available to make an ordinary maintenance assessment under the Act. An IMA will usually result in the setting of a higher figure for child support than under a standard assessment, and is therefore a form of sanction designed to encourage parties to comply with requests for information.

Under s.12(1) of the 1991 Act as originally enacted, a CSO could only make an IMA when "required to make a maintenance assessment". Problems were encountered where absent parents, who had been unemployed and in receipt of benefit, and so were only making a small contribution by way of child support, then stopped claiming benefit but declined to forward details of their new circumstances. This section substitutes a new s.12(1) and (1A), which enables an IMA to be imposed when a review is either being proposed or actually being conducted. The aim is clearly to use the threat or imposition of an IMA in such cases to ensure that the necessary information is forthcoming in order to make a correct assessment.

Reviews on change of circumstances

12.—(1) Section 17 of the 1991 Act (reviews on change of circumstances) is amended as follows.

(2) After subsection (2) insert—

"(2A) The Secretary of State shall refer to a child support officer any application under this section which is duly made."

(3) In subsection (3)—
(a) after "subsection (6)" insert ", or by virtue of subsection (7),"; and
(b) for "the review applied for" substitute "a review".

(4) After subsection (4) insert—

"(4A) Where a child support officer is conducting a review under this section, and the original assessment has ceased to have effect, he may continue the review as if the application for a review related to the original assessment and any subsequent assessment."

(5) For subsection (5) substitute—

"(5) In conducting a review under this section, the child support officer shall take into account a change of circumstance only if—

(a) he has been notified of it in such manner, and by such person, as may be prescribed; or

(b) it is one which he knows has taken place."

(6) In subsection (6)—

(a) for "any review" substitute "a review of the original assessment"; and

(b) after "maintenance assessment" insert "by reference to the circumstances of the case as at the date of the application under this section".

(7) After subsection (6) add—

"(7) On completing a review of any subsequent assessment under this section, the child support officer concerned shall make a fresh maintenance assessment except in such circumstances as may be prescribed.

(8) In this section "subsequent assessment" means a maintenance assessment made after the original assessment with respect to the same persons as the original assessment."

DEFINITIONS

"1991 Act, the": s.27(1).

"child support officer": ss.13 and 54 of the 1991 Act.

"maintenance assessment": s.54 of the 1991 Act.

"prescribed": s.54 of the 1991 Act.

"subsequent assessment": s.17(8) of the 1991 Act, inserted by subs. (7).

GENERAL NOTE

This section amends s.17 of the 1991 Act, which provides for reviews where there has been a change of circumstances since the maintenance assessment was made. The purposes of the amendments are two-fold. The first is to correct a technical defect in the original legislation, which meant that where a change of circumstances was not acted upon before other changes (*e.g.* in the legislation) were implemented, it became impossible to give effect to that change. The second is to allow reviews to be based only on reported changes, rather than requiring a complete investigation of the entire case on every review. Given the number of amendments made by this section, it might have been more helpful if an entirely new s.17 had been substituted by this section (see *e.g.* s.15 below, substituting a new s.19 in the 1991 Act).

During the Parliamentary debates, the Government also announced that, once these new review procedures are in place, the date for a periodical review will not be automatically reset. In future, therefore, reviews on changes of circumstances will not affect the normal periodical review cycle. This change, to be implemented through secondary legislation, will ensure that cases are subject to a full review at regular two-yearly intervals, regardless of intervening changes in circumstances (*per* Mr A. Burt, Standing Committee E, col. 164, April 25, 1995).

Subs. (2)

This makes explicit the fact that although an application for a s.17 review is made to the Secretary of State, it must then be referred to a CSO for consideration. This point was implicit in the original s.17.

Subs. (3)

This amends the existing s.17(3), which provides that a CSO shall not proceed with the review unless that it is likely that a fresh assessment would be required under s.17(6). That provision in turn allows for the effect of *de minimis* changes in the assessment amount below a prescribed figure to be disregarded. The amended wording effectively includes reviews of subsequent assessments. This allows the CSO not to proceed with the review unless, on the basis of the available information, it appears that a fresh assessment is needed.

Subs. (4)

The original s.17(1) applied only where there was a maintenance assessment in force. In some cases reviews are requested when the application was made sometime in the past and the assessment in force then is no longer the current assessment. This inserts s.17(4A), which seeks to deal with this jurisdictional problem. Where a number of assessments have been made in relation to the same people, s.17(4A) will enable a CSO to reconsider each assessment in turn on review.

Subs. (5)

The original s.17(5) required the CSO to carry out the review as if a fresh application had been made by the person in whose favour the original assessment was made. As amended, s.17(5) now requires the CSO merely to consider those changes of circumstances which have been notified by prescribed persons and in ways prescribed by regulations. CSOs must also take into account changes which they know to have taken place (*e.g.* age changes or changes in benefit rates, which affect the age allowances). The intention is that any party to an assessment can notify a change but that the notification will need to be in writing (*10th Report*, Appendix I, para. 30).

Subs. (6)

This amendment makes it clear that the *de minimis* check on the potential effect of any change in the assessment is made with reference to the assessment which was in force at the time the application for review was made.

Subs. (7)

This inserts s.17(7) and (8), which provide that, on completing a review of any later assessment, a CSO must make a fresh assessment, except in prescribed cases (*i.e.* those where the *de minimis* rule applies).

Continuation of reviews under section 18 of 1991 Act

13. In section 18 of the 1991 Act (reviews of decisions of child support officers), after subsection (6) insert—
"(6A) Where a child support officer is conducting a review under this section and the maintenance assessment in question ("the original assessment") is no longer in force, he may continue the review as if the application for a review related to the original assessment and any maintenance assessment made after the original assessment with respect to the same persons as the original assessment."

DEFINITIONS
"1991 Act, the": s.27(1).
"child support officer": ss.13 and 54 of the 1991 Act.
"maintenance assessment": s.54 of the 1991 Act.

GENERAL NOTE

Section 18 of the 1991 Act concerns requests for reviews from parties to a maintenance assessment based on grounds other than a change of circumstances. This amendment, inserting a new s.18(6A), has a parallel effect to the amendment made by s.12(4) above. The purpose, again, is to ensure that changes of circumstances can be given effect to even when the original assessment has been superseded. This amendment is needed to cover situations in which a review has not been carried out before another assessment is made. This could happen, for example, because of an exercise to implement policy changes or because of a backlog of work on the special CSA sections dealing with second-tier reviews. A further amendment to s.18 is made by s.14(1) below.

Cancellation of maintenance assessments on review

14.—(1) In section 18 of the 1991 Act (reviews of decisions of child support officers), after subsection (10) insert—
"(10A) If a child support officer conducting a review under this section is satisfied that the maintenance assessment in question was not

validly made he may cancel it with effect from the date on which it took effect."

(2) In paragraph 16 of Schedule 1 to the 1991 Act (termination of maintenance assessments), insert after sub-paragraph (4)—

"(4A) A maintenance assessment may be cancelled by a child support officer if he is conducting a review under section 16, 17, 18 or 19 and it appears to him—

(a) that the person with care with respect to whom the maintenance assessment in question was made has failed to provide him with sufficient information to enable him to complete the review; and

(b) where the maintenance assessment in question was made in response to an application under section 6, that the person with care with respect to whom the assessment was made has ceased to fall within subsection (1) of that section."

(3) In sub-paragraph (7) of paragraph 16 of Schedule 1 to the 1991 Act, after "sub-paragraph" insert "(4A),".

DEFINITIONS

"1991 Act, the": s.27(1).
"child support officer": ss.13 and 54 of the 1991 Act.
"maintenance assessment": s.54 of the 1991 Act.
"person with care": ss.3(3) and 54 of the 1991 Act.

GENERAL NOTE

These amendments give CSOs conducting reviews under the 1991 Act the power to cancel maintenance assessments in certain circumstances. This could be appropriate where the original assessment was made outwith the CSA's jurisdiction, or where a parent with care refuses to supply information in order for a review to be properly conducted. In the latter respect, these amendments mirror the broadened power given in s.11 to impose an interim maintenance assessment. The intention is that this step should only be taken "in exceptional cases where a parent with care is being deliberately obstructive" (*per* Mr J. Arbuthnot, Parliamentary Under-Secretary of State for Social Security, Standing Committee E, col. 166, April 25, 1995).

Subs. (1)

This inserts a new s.18(10A) into the 1991 Act, enabling a CSO to cancel an assessment from the date it was made where satisfied that it should not have been made.

Subs. (2)

This inserts a new para. 16(4A) into Schedule 1 to the 1991 Act. The amendment enables a CSO, who has asked the parent with care for information in order to carry out a review, to cancel the assessment where that information is not provided. This sanction only applies to 'private cases'; where the parent with care is a benefit claimant, the assessment cannot be cancelled on this basis (sub-para. (4A)(b)). In any event, a CSO carrying out a periodical review is not required to seek further information from a parent with care on income support (Child Support (Maintenance Assessment Procedure) Regulations 1992, S.I. 1992 No. 1813, reg. 17(6)), as her circumstances should already be known.

Reviews at instigation of child support officers

15. For section 19 of the 1991 Act substitute—

"Reviews at instigation of child support officers

19.—(1) Where a child support officer is not conducting a review under section 16, 17 or 18, he may nevertheless review—

(a) a refusal to make a maintenance assessment,
(b) a refusal to review a maintenance assessment under section 17,
(c) a maintenance assessment (whether or not in force),
(d) a cancellation of a maintenance assessment, or
(e) a refusal to cancel a maintenance assessment,

if he suspects that it may be defective for one or more of the reasons set out in subsection (2).

(2) The reasons are that the refusal, assessment or cancellation—

(a) was made in ignorance of a material fact;
(b) was based on a mistake as to a material fact; or
(c) was wrong in law.
(3) If, on completing such a review, the child support officer is satisfied that the refusal, assessment or cancellation is defective for one or more of those reasons, he may—
(a) take no further action;
(b) in the case of a maintenance assessment which has been cancelled, set aside the cancellation;
(c) make a maintenance assessment;
(d) make a fresh maintenance assessment;
(e) cancel the maintenance assessment in question.
(4) Where a child support officer sets a cancellation aside under subsection (3), the maintenance assessment in question shall have effect as if it had never been cancelled.
(5) Any cancellation of a maintenance assessment under this section shall have effect from such date as may be determined by the child support officer.
(6) Where a child support officer suspects that if an application for a review of a maintenance assessment were to be made under section 17 it would be appropriate to make one or more fresh maintenance assessments, he may review the maintenance assessment even though no application for its review has been made under that section.
(7) If, on completing a review by virtue of subsection (6), the child support officer is satisfied that it would be appropriate to make one or more fresh maintenance assessments, he may do so."

DEFINITIONS
"1991 Act, the": s.27(1).
"child support officer": ss.13 and 54 of the 1991 Act.
"maintenance assessment": s.54 of the 1991 Act.

GENERAL NOTE
Section 19 of the 1991 Act allows CSOs to review a maintenance assessment at their own instigation if they are satisfied that it was in some way defective, and to make a fresh assessment accordingly. This section substitutes an entirely new s.19, as it was found in practice that the original s.19, although a useful measure, was too narrowly drawn. In particular, the former s.19 made no allowance for reviewing CSO decisions which did not lead to assessments or for reviews of assessments which were no longer current.

s.19(1) of the 1991 Act
This widens the scope of the power of CSOs to initiate reviews under s.19. The original s.19 was confined to cases where there was a defective maintenance assessment actually in force.

s.19(2) of the 1991 Act
The grounds on which a s.19 review may now take place are the same as those under the original s.19.

s.19(3) of the 1991 Act
This lists the options open to the CSO when satisfied that a refusal, assessment or cancellation is defective; under the original version the only course of action available was to make a fresh assessment. If a cancellation is set aside under s.19(3)(b), the cancelled assessment is reinstated (s.19(4)). If a maintenance assessment is cancelled under s.19(3)(e), this is to take effect from such date as the CSO specifies (s.19(5)).

s.19(6) of the 1991 Act
This effectively permits CSOs to carry out a review under this section where they learn of a change of circumstances and suspect that, were a s.17 review requested, then one or more fresh assessments would follow. Any necessary re-assessments may be made by virtue of s.19(7).

Appeals

Lapse of appeals to child support appeal tribunals

16. In the 1991 Act, insert after section 20—

> **"Lapse of appeals**
>   20A.—(1) This section applies where—
>   (a) a person has brought an appeal under section 20; and
>   (b) before the appeal is heard, the decision appealed against is
>   reviewed under section 19.
>   (2) If the child support officer conducting the review considers that
> the decision which he has made on the review is the same as that which
> would have been made on the appeal had every ground of the appeal
> succeeded, the appeal shall lapse.
>   (3) In any other case, the review shall be of no effect and the appeal
> shall proceed accordingly."

DEFINITIONS
  "1991 Act, the": s.27(1).
  "child support officer": ss.13 and 54 of the 1991 Act.

GENERAL NOTE
  This is an important new provision relating to appeals. The section inserts a new s.20A into the
1991 Act which provides for an appeal to lapse if, before the appeal is heard, a review decision
under s.19 of the 1991 Act is made which is the same as the decision which would have been
reached on a successful appeal. This is designed to avoid unnecessary appeals, by enabling the
CSO to revise the earlier decision fully, so avoiding delay both for the party concerned and for
others awaiting the hearing of their appeals. This new power is modelled on s.29 of the SSAA
1992, which makes similar provision for appeals pending before SSATs. It should be noted,
however, that the power relates only to cases which have been the subject of a review under s.19
of the 1991 Act (note that a new s.19 has been substituted by s.15 above).

Determination of questions other than by Child Support Commissioners

17.—(1) In Schedule 4 to the 1991 Act (Child Support Commissioners),
insert after paragraph 4—

> *"Determination of questions by other officers*
>
>   4A.—(1) The Lord Chancellor may by regulations provide—
>   (a) for officers authorised—
>   (i) by the Lord Chancellor; or
>   (ii) in Scotland, by the Secretary of State,
>   to determine any question which is determinable by a Child Sup-
>   port Commissioner and which does not involve the determi-
>   nation of any appeal, application for leave to appeal or reference;
>   (b) for the procedure to be followed by any such officer in determin-
>   ing any such question;
>   (c) for the manner in which determinations of such questions by such
>   officers may be called in question.
>   (2) A determination which would have the effect of preventing an
> appeal, application for leave to appeal or reference being determined by
> a Child Support Commissioner is not a determination of the appeal,
> application or reference for the purposes of sub-paragraph (1)."

(2) In paragraph 7 of that Schedule (consultation with Lord Advocate), for "or 4(1) or (2)(b)" substitute "4(1) or (2)(b) or 4A(1)".

(3) In paragraph 8 of that Schedule (application of Schedule to Northern Ireland), in sub-paragraph (e), for "paragraphs 5" substitute "paragraphs 4A".

DEFINITION
"1991 Act, the": s.27(1).

GENERAL NOTE
　This amendment, as with that in s.16, follows a precedent set within the social security adjudication machinery. The section inserts a new para. 4A into Sched. 4 to the 1991 Act, providing for nominated officers to assist Child Support Commissioners in the exercise of their duties. This corrects an oversight in the 1991 Act. Nominated officers have operated for some years in the Office of the Social Security Commissioners, dealing with various interlocutory matters such as requests for extensions of time in which to make submissions (SSAA 1992, s.58(6)). Such a system clearly has beneficial effects in terms of both using judicial resources more efficiently and saving time for the parties.

Miscellaneous

Deferral of right to apply for maintenance assessment

18.—(1) In section 4 of the 1991 Act (right of person with care or absent parent to apply for maintenance assessment), insert at the end—
　　"(10) No application may be made at any time under this section with respect to a qualifying child or any qualifying children if—
　　　(a) there is in force a written maintenance agreement made before 5th April 1993, or a maintenance order, in respect of that child or those children and the person who is, at that time, the absent parent; or
　　　(b) benefit is being paid to, or in respect of, a parent with care of that child or those children.
　　(11) In subsection (10) "benefit" means any benefit which is mentioned in, or prescribed by regulations under, section 6(1)."
　(2) In section 7 of the 1991 Act (right of child in Scotland to apply for maintenance assessment), insert at the end—
　　"(10) No application may be made at any time under this section by a qualifying child if there is in force a written maintenance agreement made before 5th April 1993, or a maintenance order, in respect of that child and the person who is, at that time, the absent parent."
　(3) In section 8 of the 1991 Act (role of the courts with respect to maintenance for children), after subsection (3) insert—
　　"(3A) In any case in which section 4(10) or 7(10) prevents the making of an application for a maintenance assessment, and—
　　　(a) no application has been made for a maintenance assessment under section 6, or
　　　(b) such an application has been made but no maintenance assessment has been made in response to it,
　　subsection (3) shall have effect with the omission of the word "vary"."
　(4) In section 9 of the 1991 Act (maintenance agreements), at the beginning of subsection (3) insert "Subject to section 4(10)(a) and section 7(10)," and after subsection (5) insert—
　　"(6) In any case in which section 4(10) or 7(10) prevents the making of an application for a maintenance assessment, and—
　　　(a) no application has been made for a maintenance assessment under section 6, or
　　　(b) such an application has been made but no maintenance assessment has been made in response to it,
　　subsection (5) shall have effect with the omission of paragraph (b)."

(5) The Secretary of State may by order repeal any of the provisions of this section.

(6) Neither section 4(10) nor section 7(10) of the 1991 Act shall apply in relation to a maintenance order made in the circumstances mentioned in sub-section (7) or (8) of section 8 of the 1991 Act.

(7) The Secretary of State may by regulations make provision for section 4(10), or section 7(10), of the 1991 Act not to apply in relation to such other cases as may be prescribed.

(8) Part I of the Schedule to the Child Support Act 1991 (Commencement No. 3 and Transitional Provisions) Order 1992 (phased take-on of certain cases) is hereby revoked.

(9) At any time before 7th April 1997, neither section 8(3), nor section 9(5)(b), of the 1991 Act shall apply in relation to any case which fell within paragraph 5(2) of the Schedule to the 1992 order (pending cases during the transitional period set by that order).

DEFINITIONS
"1991 Act, the": s.27(1).
"absent parent": ss.3(2) and 54 of the 1991 Act.
"benefit": s.4(11) of the 1991 Act, inserted by subs. (1).
"child": s.55 of the 1991 Act.
"maintenance agreement": ss.9(1) and 54 of the 1991 Act.
"maintenance assessment": s.54 of the 1991 Act.
"maintenance order": ss.8(11) and 54 of the 1991 Act.
"parent": s.54 of the 1991 Act.
"parent with care": s.54 of the 1991 Act, as amended by Sched. 3, para. 16.
"person with care": ss.3(3) and 54 of the 1991 Act.
"prescribed": s.54 of the 1991 Act.
"qualifying child": ss.3(1) and 54 of the 1991 Act.

GENERAL NOTE
This section represents an admission of defeat by the Government. The original objective was to ensure that all cases of child maintenance came within the scope of the CSA by 1996/97. This section abandons that intention and so amends ss. 4, 7, 8 and 9 of the 1991 Act, and repeals Part I of the Schedule to the Child Support Act 1991 (Commencement No. 3 and Transitional Provisions) Order 1992 (S.I. 1992 No. 2644).

When the 1991 Act was brought into force, certain "non-benefit cases" were prevented from applying for a child support assessment until 1996/97 under the so-called phasing-in arrangements. This group comprised those cases where there was an existing court order or a written maintenance agreement made before April 5, 1993 and where the parent with care was not receiving income support, family credit or DWA. The effect of the amendments made by this section is that such cases will remain outside the CSA's jurisdiction, and so will continue to be able to use the court system. The Government has stated that the new CSA take-on date will be decided at some time in the future; it remains conceivable, of course, that these cases will *never* come within the ambit of the 1991 Act. The observations of the Under-Secretary of State for Social Security on the matter repay careful study:

"As currently envisaged we are deferring *sine die* the consideration of the cases. We will want the House to decide before such cases are brought back to the agency. It is not possible to say when that might be or when we believe that the House will be able to make that decision" (*per* Mr A. Burt, Standing Committee E, col. 180, April 25, 1995).

The reasoning behind this further deferral is a concern to ensure that the CSA can "concentrate on the effective introduction of the new departures system before a further tranche of work is taken on: it should be noted that this group of cases is likely to give rise to a substantial number of departure applications. It will remain open to parents to return to the Courts for a variation in an existing court order or to convert a written agreement to a court order and to vary it" (*10th Report*, Appendix I, para. 33). This option is perhaps more apparent than real given the legal fees which are likely to be involved and the restrictive nature of the legal aid eligibility test today.

Subs. (1)
This inserts new subss. (10) and (11) into s.4 of the 1991 Act. Section 4 provides the mechanism for parties to non-benefit cases to apply for a child support assessment. These amendments prohibit such an application in cases where there is in force a written maintenance agreement made before April 5, 1993, or a maintenance order (on which see s.8(11) of the 1991 Act), or

where a relevant benefit is paid to or for the parent with care. The benefits in question are those mentioned in (or in regulations under) s.6 of the 1991 Act, *i.e.* income support, family credit, DWA and, when it comes into force, income-based jobseeker's allowance. The new s.4(10) is disapplied (*i.e.* an application for child support assessment may be made) in cases where the courts have made maintenance orders which are solely for the costs of a child's education, or the extra costs of looking after a child with disabilities (subs. (6)). There is also a power to extend the exemption contained in s.4(10) of the 1991 Act to any other prescribed types of case (subs. (7)).

Subs. (2)
This makes parallel provision preventing applications by children in Scotland under s.7 of the 1991 Act in the same situations as those mentioned in s.4(10)(a) of the 1991 Act, inserted by subs. (1) above. There is also a power to extend the exemption contained in s.7(10) of the 1991 Act to any other prescribed types of case (subs. (7)).

Subs. (3)
This amendment to s.8 of the 1991 Act ensures that, where a case is outside the CSA's jurisdiction by virtue of ss.4(10) or 7(10) of the 1991 Act, inserted by subss. (1) and (2) above, the courts retain the power to vary the relevant maintenance order. The court's power is lost if there has been a successful application for an assessment under s.6 of the 1991 Act (*i.e.* as a "benefit case"). The effect of s.8(3) of the 1991 Act, as modified by this amendment, is that the court is still barred from making or reviving a maintenance order in such cases.

Subs. (4)
This amendment removes the restriction in s.9 of the 1991 Act which prevents a court from increasing the amount of maintenance payable when it makes a maintenance order varying a maintenance agreement. It does so in the same circumstances as those mentioned in subs. (3) above.

Subs. (5)
This provision is a Henry VIII clause, in that it allows the Secretary of State to repeal (but not to amend) any of the provisions of this section (*10th Report*, para. 9). The effect of any such repeal would be to bring the cases affected within the jurisdiction of the CSA. However, any Order effecting such an appeal is subject to the affirmative resolution procedure (see s.26(4) below), which the Delegated Powers Scrutiny Committee regarded as providing an adequate degree of Parliamentary control.

Subs. (7)
The government's intention is that this power to provide for exceptions to the deferral arrangements should apply to those parents whose court orders cannot be enforced or varied by the courts. It is not possible to define these cases in primary legislation since the inability of the courts to vary certain orders is, as yet, unclear (*10th Report*, Appendix I, para. 34).

Subs. (9)
This provision enables the courts to continue to make maintenance orders up until April 6, 1997 where an application was made to the court before April 5, 1993 and is still pending. This is in line with the existing transitional arrangements.

Non-referral of applications for maintenance assessments

19. In section 11 of the 1991 Act, after subsection (1) (referral of application for maintenance assessment to child support officer) insert—
  "(1A) Where—
    (a) an application for a maintenance assessment is made under section 6, but
    (b) the Secretary of State becomes aware, before referring the application to a child support officer, that the claim mentioned in subsection (1) of that section has been disallowed or withdrawn,
  he shall, subject to subsection (1B), treat the application as if it had not been made.
    (1B) If it appears to the Secretary of State that subsection (10) of section 4 would not have prevented the parent with care concerned from making an application for a maintenance assessment under that section he shall—

    (a) notify her of the effect of this subsection, and

    (b) if, before the end of the period of 28 days beginning with the day on which notice was sent to her, she asks him to do so, treat the application as having been made not under section 6 but under section 4.

(1C) Where the application is not preserved under subsection (1B) (and so is treated as not having been made) the Secretary of State shall notify—

    (a) the parent with care concerned; and

    (b) the absent parent (or alleged absent parent), where it appears to him that that person is aware of the application."

DEFINITIONS

"1991 Act, the": s.27(1).
"absent parent": ss.3(2) and 54 of the 1991 Act.
"child support officer": ss.13 and 54 of the 1991 Act.
"maintenance assessment": s.54 of the 1991 Act.
"parent": s.54 of the 1991 Act.
"parent with care": s.54 of the 1991 Act, as amended by Sched. 3, para. 16.

GENERAL NOTE

Section 11 of the 1991 Act provides for the Secretary of State to refer applications for maintenance assessments to CSOs for determination. Under the existing arrangements it is possible for women who are barred from applying to the CSA, because they have a pre-April 1993 maintenance agreement and are not in receipt of benefit, to obtain a maintenance application form by simply making a claim for benefit even though they do not have any entitlement to benefit. These amendments, inserting subss. (1A), (1B) and (1C) into s.11 of the 1991 Act, are a response to what the Government has described as this "problem of spurious claims for benefit, which involves unfair attempts to jump the queue and to usurp the system" (*per* Mr A. Burt, Standing Committee E, col. 182, April 25, 1995).

By virtue of these changes, the Secretary of State can disregard certain applications for maintenance assessments which are required to be made by benefit claimants under s.6 of the 1991 Act. The benefit claims in question currently concern those for income support, family credit and DWA. In October 1996 income-based jobseeker's allowance, introduced by the Jobseekers Act 1995, will be added to this list. A s.6 application is to be treated as not having been made where the Secretary of State becomes aware, before it is referred to a CSO, that the benefit claim has been disallowed or withdrawn (s.11(1A)). If this course is taken, the parent with care and, if aware of the application, the absent parent, must be duly notified (s.11(1C)).

Where a s.6 application for a maintenance assessment is disregarded on this basis, there is in principle nothing to prevent the parent with care from making a private application under s.4 of the 1991 Act, subject, of course, to the amendments made by s.18 above. Indeed, the Secretary of State is required to raise this possibility in appropriate cases (s.11(1B)). If a request is made in time under s.11(1B)(b), then the effective date of the assessment would be the date of the original application, so avoiding a potential loss of maintenance.

Disputed parentage

20.—(1) Section 27 of the 1991 Act (reference to court for declaration of parentage) is amended as set out in subsections (2) to (4).

(2) For subsection (1) substitute—

    "(1) Subsection (1A) applies in any case where—

    (a) an application for a maintenance assessment has been made, or a maintenance assessment is in force, with respect to a person ("the alleged parent") who denies that he is a parent of a child with respect to whom the application or assessment was made; and

    (b) a child support officer to whom the case is referred is not satisfied that the case falls within one of those set out in section 26(2).

(1A) In any case where this subsection applies, the Secretary of State or the person with care may apply to the court for a declaration as to whether or not the alleged parent is one of the child's parents."

(3) In subsection (2), for "(1)" substitute "(1A)".

(4) For subsection (3), substitute—

"(3) A declaration under this section shall have effect only for the purposes of—
(a) this Act; and
(b) proceedings in which a court is considering whether to make a maintenance order in the circumstances mentioned in subsection (6), (7) or (8) of section 8."

(5) Section 28 of the 1991 Act (power of Secretary of State to initiate or defend actions of declarator) is amended as set out in subsections (6) and (7).

(6) For subsection (1) substitute—

"(1) Subsection (1A) applies in any case where—
(a) an application for a maintenance assessment has been made, or a maintenance assessment is in force, with respect to a person ("the alleged parent") who denies that he is a parent of a child with respect to whom the application or assessment was made; and
(b) a child support officer to whom the case is referred is not satisfied that the case falls within one of those set out in section 26(2).

(1A) In any case where this subsection applies, the Secretary of State may bring an action for declarator of parentage under section 7 of the Law Reform (Parent and Child) (Scotland) Act 1986."

(7) In subsection (2), at the end insert "or in a maintenance assessment which is in force".

DEFINITIONS
"1991 Act, the": s.27(1).
"alleged parent": s.27(1)(a) of the 1991 Act, inserted by subs. (2), and s.28(1)(a) of the 1991 Act, inserted by subs. (6).
"child": s.55 of the 1991 Act.
"child support officer": ss.13 and 54 of the 1991 Act.
"maintenance assessment": s.54 of the 1991 Act.
"maintenance order": ss.8(11) and 54 of the 1991 Act.
"parent": s.54 of the 1991 Act.
"person with care": ss.3(3) and 54 of the 1991 Act.

GENERAL NOTE
Sections 27 and 28 of the 1991 Act allow the Secretary of State or parent with care to apply to court for a declaration of parentage (s.27, as regards England and Wales) and for the Secretary of State to initiate or defend an action of declarator (s.28, as regards Scotland). Those provisions therefore enable the court to make a declaration of parentage where the alleged parent denies that he is the parent. As originally drafted, ss.27 and 28 only allowed an application to the courts before a maintenance assessment had been made. If a paternity dispute arose after an assessment was in force, the only procedure was for the matter to go before a CSAT which would refer the question of paternity to the court for a declaration. There was anecdotal evidence that some absent parents were deliberately raising paternity as an issue after an assessment had been made in order to delay the proceedings. Whether or not this was the case, the existing procedure was unduly cumbersome. These amendments therefore streamline the procedure under ss.27 and 28 of the 1991 Act.

Subs. (2)
This amendment extends the existing conditions for England and Wales so that the Secretary of State or parent with care may apply to court for a declaration of parentage once an assessment is in force, as well as where a maintenance application has been made but not determined. This provision does not apply where the CSO is satisfied that the case falls within one of the straightforward categories of parentage specified in Cases A to F of s.26(2) of the 1991 Act.

Subs. (4)
Section 27(3) of the 1991 Act as originally enacted provided that a declaration under that section had effect only for the purposes of that Act. The new version of s.27(3) modifies this, so that a declaration of paternity is also effective where a court is considering any of the situations

specified in s.8(6)–(8) of the 1991 Act, *i.e.* ordering extra maintenance specifically for a disabled child, a child's educational expenses, or for maintenance above the formula limits.

Subss. (6) and (7)
These amendments apply to Scotland the principle underlying the change made by subs. (2) above, so that under s.28 of the 1991 Act the Secretary of State may bring or defend an action for declarator of parentage before or after a maintenance assessment has been made.

Fees for scientific tests

21. After section 27 of the 1991 Act insert—

> **"Recovery of fees for scientific tests**
> 27A.—(1) This section applies in any case where—
> (a) an application for a maintenance assessment has been made or a maintenance assessment is in force;
> (b) scientific tests have been carried out (otherwise than under a direction or in response to a request) in relation to bodily samples obtained from a person who is alleged to be a parent of a child with respect to whom the application or assessment is made;
> (c) the results of the tests do not exclude the alleged parent from being one of the child's parents; and
> (d) one of the conditions set out in subsection (2) is satisfied.
> (2) The conditions are that—
> (a) the alleged parent does not deny that he is one of the child's parents;
> (b) in proceedings under section 27, a court has made a declaration that the alleged parent is a parent of the child in question; or
> (c) in an action under section 7 of the Law Reform (Parent and Child) (Scotland) Act 1986, brought by the Secretary of State by virtue of section 28, a court has granted a decree of declarator of parentage to the effect that the alleged parent is a parent of the child in question.
> (3) In any case to which this section applies, any fee paid by the Secretary of State in connection with scientific tests may be recovered by him from the alleged parent as a debt due to the Crown.
> (4) In this section—
> "bodily sample" means a sample of bodily fluid or bodily tissue taken for the purpose of scientific tests;
> "direction" means a direction given by a court under section 20 of the Family Law Reform Act 1969 (tests to determine paternity);
> "request" means a request made by a court under section 70 of the Law Reform (Miscellaneous Provisions) (Scotland) Act 1990 (blood and other samples in civil proceedings); and
> "scientific tests" means scientific tests made with the object of ascertaining the inheritable characteristics of bodily fluids or bodily tissue.
> (5) Any sum recovered by the Secretary of State under this section shall be paid by him into the Consolidated Fund."

DEFINITIONS
"1991 Act, the": s.27(1).
"alleged parent": s.27(1)(a) of the 1991 Act, inserted by s.20(2) and s.28(1)(a) of the 1991 Act, inserted by s.20(6).
"bodily sample": s.27A(4) of the 1991 Act.
"child": s.55 of the 1991 Act.
"direction": s.27A(4) of the 1991 Act.
"maintenance assessment": s.54 of the 1991 Act.
"parent": s.54 of the 1991 Act.

"request": s.27A(4) of the 1991 Act.
"scientific tests": s.27A(4) of the 1991 Act.

GENERAL NOTE
This section inserts a new s.27A into the 1991 Act which enables fees for DNA testing to be recovered from an alleged parent who either does not deny parentage (s.27A(2)(a)) or is subsequently declared by a court to be the parent of the child in question (s.28A(2)(b) or (c)). This power applies to both "benefit cases", *i.e.* where an application has been made under s.6 of the 1991 Act, and to private applications under s.4 of the 1991 Act. Previously, if a court ordered DNA testing and required the CSA to pay the necessary fees, the Secretary of State would effectively be able to recoup this sum only if costs were awarded in the CSA's favour. This section provides for a more straightforward system of recovering DNA test fees (but see s.27A(1)(b) of the 1991 Act, discussed below).

s.27A(1)(b) of the 1991 Act
Otherwise than under a direction or in response to a request. The effect of this proviso is that where a court has ordered or requested that the test be carried out, the Secretary of State must apply to the court for fees to be included in the costs awarded, if paternity is established.

Arrears of child support maintenance: alternative to interest payments

22. In the 1991 Act, insert after section 41—

"Arrears: alternative to interest payments

41A.—(1) The Secretary of State may by regulations make provision for the payment by absent parents who are in arrears with payments of child support maintenance of sums determined in accordance with the regulations.

(2) A sum payable under any such regulations is referred to in this section as an "additional sum".

(3) Any liability of an absent parent to pay an additional sum shall not affect any liability of his to pay the arrears of child support maintenance concerned.

(4) The Secretary of State shall exercise his powers under this section and those under section 41(3) in such a way as to ensure that no absent parent is liable to pay both interest and an additional sum in respect of the same period (except by reference to different maintenance assessments).

(5) Regulations under subsection (1) may, in particular, make provision—

(a) as to the calculation of any additional sum;
(b) as to the time at which, and person to whom, any additional sum shall be payable;
(c) as to the circumstances in which, in a case where the Secretary of State has been acting under section 6, any additional sum may be retained by him;
(d) for the Secretary of State, in a case where he has been acting under section 6 and in such circumstances as may be prescribed, to waive any additional sum (or part of any additional sum).

(6) The provisions of this Act with respect to—

(a) the collection of child support maintenance;
(b) the enforcement of any obligation to pay child support maintenance,

shall apply equally to additional sums payable by virtue of regulations made under this section.

(7) Any sum retained by the Secretary of State by virtue of this section shall be paid by him into the Consolidated Fund."

DEFINITIONS
"1991 Act, the": s.27(1).
"absent parent": ss.3(2) and 54 of the 1991 Act.

"additional sum": s.41A(2) of the 1991 Act.
"child support maintenance": ss.3(6) and 54 of the 1991 Act.

GENERAL NOTE

Section 41(3) of the 1991 Act provides for interest to be charged on outstanding payments of child support maintenance. Detailed provisions are to be found in the Child Support (Arrears, Interest and Adjustment of Maintenance Assessments) Regulations 1992 (S.I. 1992 No. 1816). These highly complex rules have given rise to considerable operational difficulties. Hence this section inserts a new s.41A into the 1991 Act, enabling the Secretary of State to impose a financial penalty for late payment of child support maintenance as an alternative to interest on arrears. The option to charge interest under s.41 will thus be retained, although in practice the arrangements for charging interest were suspended for two years with effect from April 18, 1995: Child Support and Income Support (Amendment) Regulations 1995 (S.I. 1995 No. 1045), reg. 7.

The details of this penalty scheme will not be known until the relevant regulations are available. It seems likely that the penalty (known as an "additional sum") will be based on the size of the arrears and will be levied when the arrears total more than the liability for a specified period (*e.g.* three months) and when the arrears are above a specified minimum. It is clear, however, that an individual will not be required to pay both interest on arrears and an additional sum in respect of the same period (s.41A(4)). The regulation-making powers contained in s.41A(5) reflect those applying to interest payments, with the necessary adjustments. As is the case with interest payments, the general enforcement procedures apply equally to this additional sum (s.41A(6)).

Regulations made under this power are subject to the affirmative procedure (s.52(2) of the 1991 Act, as amended by Sched. 3, para. 15(b)).

These changes are in addition to two reforms made in April 1995 which relate to arrears. The first was that, where the absent parent returns the maintenance enquiry form (MEF) within four weeks of its issue, and provides sufficient basic information to enable the case to be dealt with by the CSA, the liability for maintenance starts eight weeks from the date of the issue of the MEF, rather than the date of issue itself (Child Support and Income Support (Amendment) Regulations 1995 (S.I. 1995 No. 1045), reg. 36). Secondly, where delay by the CSA has contributed to the arrears, only six months' arrears are now enforced if the absent parent pays his ongoing maintenance and maintains an agreement to repay the six months' arrears. This is an extra-statutory concession (*White Paper*, para. 6.4).

Repayment of overpaid child support maintenance

23. In the 1991 Act, insert after section 41A—

"Repayment of overpaid child support maintenance
41B.—(1) This section applies where it appears to the Secretary of State that an absent parent has made a payment by way of child support maintenance which amounts to an overpayment by him of that maintenance and that—
  (a) it would not be possible for the absent parent to recover the amount of the overpayment by way of an adjustment of the amount payable under a maintenance assessment; or
  (b) it would be inappropriate to rely on an adjustment of the amount payable under a maintenance assessment as the means of enabling the absent parent to recover the amount of the overpayment.

(2) The Secretary of State may make such payment to the absent parent by way of reimbursement, or partial reimbursement, of the overpayment as the Secretary of State considers appropriate.

(3) Where the Secretary of State has made a payment under this section he may, in such circumstances as may be prescribed, require the relevant person to pay to him the whole, or a specified proportion, of the amount of that payment.

(4) Any such requirement shall be imposed by giving the relevant person a written demand for the amount which the Secretary of State wishes to recover from him.

(5) Any sum which a person is required to pay to the Secretary of State under this section shall be recoverable from him by the Secretary of State as a debt due to the Crown.

(6) The Secretary of State may by regulations make provision in relation to any case in which—

(a) one or more overpayments of child support maintenance are being reimbursed to the Secretary of State by the relevant person; and

(b) child support maintenance has continued to be payable by the absent parent concerned to the person with care concerned, or again becomes so payable.

(7) For the purposes of this section any payments made by a person under a maintenance assessment which was not validly made shall be treated as overpayments of child support maintenance made by an absent parent.

(8) In this section "relevant person", in relation to an overpayment, means the person with care to whom the overpayment was made.

(9) Any sum recovered by the Secretary of State under this section shall be paid by him into the Consolidated Fund."

DEFINITIONS

"1991 Act, the": s.27(1).
"absent parent": ss.3(2) and 54 of the 1991 Act.
"child support maintenance": ss.3(6) and 54 of the 1991 Act.
"maintenance assessment": s.54 of the 1991 Act.
"prescribed": s.54 of the 1991 Act.
"relevant person": s.41B(8) of the 1991 Act.

GENERAL NOTE

This section, inserting a new s.41B into the 1991 Act, enables the Secretary of State to reimburse overpayments of child support maintenance and to recover overpayments from those who have received them. The section has been introduced because, under the existing legislation, absent parents who have overpaid maintenance may be repaid only by a reduction in their current maintenance assessment (Child Support (Arrears, Interest and Adjustment of Maintenance Assessments) Regulations 1992 (S.I. 1992 No. 1816), reg. 10). However, in some cases there may be no current assessment to reduce (*e.g.* because the relevant child has reached 16 years and is no longer at school). Equally it may take a very long time to effect full reimbursement by this method. The new power seeks to resolve this problem by giving the Secretary of State the power to make a full or partial reimbursement of overpaid maintenance in accordance with regulations. Any such reimbursement may be recovered from the parent with care (s.41B(3)). There are no plans to seek recovery from parents with care who are in receipt of income support or family credit (*per* Mr A. Burt, Standing Committee E, col. 192, April 25, 1995). According to the Explanatory and Financial Memorandum to the Bill, this provision is expected to increase benefit expenditure by £1 million a year.

s.41B(1) of the 1991 Act

This sets out the two situations in which direct repayment of overpaid child support maintenance is possible. The first—where it is simply not possible to effect recovery by adjustment to a maintenance assessment—is clear enough (s.41B(1)(a)). The second situation is much less straightforward; there is evidently considerable scope for discretion in determining whether the circumstances are such that it is "inappropriate" to rely on an adjustment to the maintenance assessment (s.41B(1)(b)).

s.41B(2) of the 1991 Act

Again, this provision vests the Secretary of State with a very broad discretion in that reimbursement may be in full or in part. According to the *Notes on Clauses*, partial reimbursement may be appropriate where some reduction in the current assessment can be made but it is not reasonable to repay the whole amount which has been overpaid in that manner.

s.41B(3) of the 1991 Act

Under the original scheme a parent with care was not asked to repay an overpayment of child support maintenance as repayment was effected by adjustment to the current assessment. This provision enables the Secretary of State to define the circumstances in which the "relevant person" (*i.e.* the person with care—s.41B(8)) who received the overpaid maintenance will be required to reimburse the CSA in full or in part. According to the *Notes on Clauses*, it is the Government's intention that recovery will only be considered appropriate in cases where the recipient secured additional income as a result of the overpayment. This will exclude cases where income support was being paid, as the overall level of income would have remained unchanged if the correct maintenance had been paid. It is also intended that the financial circumstances of the recipient will be considered. The Government has indicated that it is not the intention that recovery should be sought in all cases: "We propose to seek recovery only when the financial circumstances of the parent with care are such that it is reasonable to expect her to repay the overpaid maintenance—for example, if she has a reasonable income and low outgoings. If, however, her income is only marginally above benefit levels, recovery would probably not be considered appropriate" (*per* Mr A. Burt, Standing Committee E, cols. 192–193, April 25, 1995).

s.41B(6) of the 1991 Act
Regulations made under this power are subject to the affirmative procedure (s.52(2) of the 1991 Act, as amended by Sched. 3, para. 15(b)).

s.41B(7) of the 1991 Act
It is possible (but perhaps rare) that an overpayment may arise out of an invalid assessment. For example, it may subsequently transpire that the CSA had no jurisdiction to make the purported assessment (*e.g.* because the absent parent was not habitually resident in the United Kingdom, or there was already a written maintenance agreement made before April 5, 1993). This provision makes it clear that an absent parent who has overpaid maintenance because of an invalid assessment may still be entitled to recovery of such maintenance, subject at least to a favourable exercise of the Secretary of State's discretion.

Compensation payments

24.—(1) The Secretary of State may by regulations make provision for the payment by him, in prescribed circumstances and to or in respect of qualifying persons, of sums by way of compensation or partial compensation for any reduction which is attributable to one or more prescribed changes in child support legislation.

(2) For the purposes of this section—
"child support legislation" means—
(a) the provisions of the 1991 Act and this Act;
(b) any provision made under that Act or this Act; and
(c) such other provisions (if any) of primary or subordinate legislation with respect to child support maintenance as may be prescribed;
"compensation payment" means any sum payable under the regulations;
"qualifying person" means a person with care—
(a) with respect to whom a maintenance assessment ("the revised assessment" is in force or was made after the change or changes took effect;
(b) to or in respect of whom family credit or disability working allowance is or has been paid; and
(c) with respect to whom an earlier maintenance assessment was in force at the relevant time;
"reduction" means a reduction in the amount of child support maintenance payable under the revised assessment when compared with the amount payable under the earlier assessment; and
"relevant time" has such meaning as may be prescribed.

(3) The regulations may include provision—
(a) as to the calculation of the amount of any compensation payment;
(b) for any compensation payment to be made in instalments or as a lump sum;
(c) as to the manner in which any compensation payment is to be made;

(d) for a compensation payment which would otherwise be made under the regulations not to be made if the amount of the payment would be less than the prescribed minimum.

(4) The Secretary of State may by order provide that, for the purposes of specified provisions of the Social Security Administration Act 1992, a compensation payment is to be treated as if it were a payment of a benefit (as defined by section 191 of that Act) or of a benefit of a prescribed kind.

DEFINITIONS

"1991 Act, the": s.27(1).
"child support legislation": subs. (2).
"child support maintenance": ss.3(6) and 54 of the 1991 Act.
"compensation payment": subs. (2).
"family credit": s.54 of the 1991 Act.
"maintenance assessment": s.54 of the 1991 Act.
"person with care": ss.3(3) and 54 of the 1991 Act.
"prescribed": s.54 of the 1991 Act.
"qualifying person": subs. (2).
"reduction": subs. (2).
"relevant time": subs. (2).
"revised assessment": subs. (2).

GENERAL NOTE

This section enables the Secretary of State to make compensation payments to parents with care in receipt of family credit or DWA whose maintenance assessment is reduced as a result of changes in the child support legislation. Both family credit and DWA are paid for fixed periods of 26 weeks and are not subject to adjustment for changes in circumstances within the life of the award, except on very narrow grounds which do not apply here. Consequently this section empowers the Secretary of State to make regulations providing for sums to be paid by way of compensation in such cases. It is also for the Secretary of State to prescribe precisely which types of changes resulting in a reduction in maintenance will give rise to a right to compensation. In fact, compensation has already been paid on an extra-statutory basis to those parents with care whose maintenance assessments were reduced as a result of the changes in the regulations made in April 1995 (*Hansard*, H.L. Vol. 565, col. 246).

It does not necessarily follow that *full* compensation will be paid, as the section specifically provides for *partial* compensation as an alternative. It is the Government's intention that compensation will be calculated on the basis of *half* the reduction in the maintenance assessment for the period from the date of the reduction until the expiry of the award of family credit or DWA. This approach reflects the fact that the amount of maintenance being taken into account in a family credit assessment is always less than the maintenance assessment itself. There are two reasons for this: first, in many cases the amount of maintenance actually being paid at the time of the claim for family credit is less than the formal entitlement to maintenance. Secondly, the family credit assessment disregards the first £15 per week of any maintenance received. Thus the Government concluded that the fairest reflection of the real loss of maintenance would be at the rate of 50 per cent of the reduction in the assessment for the remainder of the family credit or DWA award (Standing Committee E, cols. 202–203, April 25, 1995).

This power is not needed in relation to income support, which is re-assessed immediately to take account of any change in the level of maintenance. Similarly, the necessary adjustments can be made swiftly to both housing benefit and council tax benefit (increasing them by 65 per cent and 20 per cent respectively of the amount of the reduction).

The first regulations made under this section will be subject to the affirmative procedure (s.26(4)(c) below). According to the Explanatory and Financial Memorandum to the Bill, this provision is expected to increase benefit expenditure by £1 million in 1995–1996.

Subs. (1)

The Secretary of State has the power to determine which changes to the child support legislation will actually trigger compensation payments. In particular, there is no commitment to compensate for all changes which could reduce maintenance payments.

Subs. (2)

Relevant time. The Government's intention is to prescribe this time as being the day before that on which the reduced maintenance assessment comes into force, rather than the date of the benefit claim (*10th Report*, Appendix I, para. 38).

Subs. (3)

As noted above, the Government's intention is to calculate compensation on the basis of half of the reduction in the maintenance assessment for the outstanding period of the benefit award. Payments will usually be by way of a lump sum, in the form of a Girocheque, and with a minimum payment of £5 (*10th Report*, Appendix I, para. 38).

Subs. (4)

This power allows the common administrative framework for social security payments (including the provisions as regards the recovery of overpayments) to be applied to compensation payments made under this section.

Payment of benefit where maintenance payments collected by Secretary of State

25. In the Social Security Administration Act 1992, insert after section 74—

"Payment of benefit where maintenance payments collected by Secretary of State

74A.—(1) This section applies where—

(a) a person ("the claimant") is entitled to a benefit to which this section applies;

(b) the Secretary of State is collecting periodical payments of child or spousal maintenance made in respect of the claimant or a member of the claimant's family; and

(c) the inclusion of any such periodical payment in the claimant's relevant income would, apart from this section, have the effect of reducing the amount of the benefit to which the claimant is entitled.

(2) The Secretary of State may, to such extent as he considers appropriate, treat any such periodical payment as not being relevant income for the purposes of calculating the amount of benefit to which the claimant is entitled.

(3) The Secretary of State may, to the extent that any periodical payment collected by him is treated as not being relevant income for those purposes, retain the whole or any part of that payment.

(4) Any sum retained by the Secretary of State under subsection (3) shall be paid by him into the Consolidated Fund.

(5) In this section—

"child" means a person under the age of 16;

"child maintenance", "spousal maintenance" and "relevant income" have such meaning as may be prescribed;

"family" means—

(a) a married or unmarried couple;

(b) a married or unmarried couple and a member of the same household for whom one of them is, or both are, responsible and who is a child or a person of a prescribed description;

(c) except in prescribed circumstances, a person who is not a member of a married or unmarried couple and a member of the same household for whom that person is responsible and who is a child or a person of a prescribed description;

"married couple" means a man and woman who are married to each other and are members of the same household; and

"unmarried couple" means a man and woman who are not married to each other but are living together as husband and wife otherwise than in prescribed circumstances.

(6) For the purposes of this section, the Secretary of State may by regulations make provision as to the circumstances in which—

   (a) persons are to be treated as being or not being members of the same household;

   (b) one person is to be treated as responsible or not responsible for another.

   (7) The benefits to which this section applies are income support, an income-based jobseeker's allowance and such other benefits (if any) as may be prescribed."

DEFINITIONS

   "child": s.74A(5) of the SSAA 1992.
   "child maintenance": s.74A(5) of the SSAA 1992.
   "claimant": s.74A(1)(a) of the SSAA 1992.
   "family": s.74A(5) of the SSAA 1992.
   "income-based jobseeker's allowance": s.191 of the SSAA 1992.
   "married couple": s.74A(5) of the SSAA 1992.
   "relevant income": s.74A(5) of the SSAA 1992.
   "spousal maintenance": s.74A(5) of the SSAA 1992.
   "unmarried couple": s.74A(5) of the SSAA 1992.

GENERAL NOTE

   A parent with care who is entitled to income support can ask for that benefit to be paid gross or net. If paid gross, she is paid the total amount of her maintenance and benefit entitlement in one payment. The maintenance is then collected by the Secretary of State and retained. If paid net, the onus is on the claimant to keep track of payments (not) made by the absent parent. The majority of claimants choose the former option, as it provides a regular and stable income and avoids the need to approach the Benefits Agency every time that maintenance is not paid on time.

   Section 74 of the SSAA 1992 is designed to ensure that an income support claimant does not receive a duplicate payment of benefit when other sources of income are not paid on time. This section, inserting a new s.74A into the SSAA 1992, has been drafted with a similar purpose in mind, but deals exclusively with maintenance cases. It provides that where the Secretary of State is collecting maintenance and income support or other relevant benefits are paid gross, the maintenance payments may then be retained by the Secretary of State (s.74A(1)–(3)). The provision applies to both child and spousal maintenance and to claimants who are receiving income support, income-based jobseeker's allowance or any other prescribed benefit (s.74A(7)). According to the *Notes on Clauses*, there is no current intention to prescribe any other benefits.

s.74A(5) of the SSAA 1992

   These definitions apply the same meanings as these terms carry in social security legislation (see the Social Security Contributions and Benefits Act 1992, s.137(1)).

Supplemental

Regulations and orders

   26.—(1) Any power under this Act to make regulations or orders shall be exercisable by statutory instrument.

   (2) Any such power may be exercised to make different provision for different cases, including different provision for different areas.

   (3) Any such power includes power—

   (a) to make such incidental, supplemental, consequential or transitional provision as appears to the Secretary of State to be expedient; and

   (b) to provide for a person to exercise a discretion in dealing with any matter.

   (4) Subsection (5) applies to—

   (a) the first regulations made under section 10;

(b) any order made under section 18(5);

(c) the first regulations made under section 24.

(5) No regulations or order to which this subsection applies shall be made unless a draft of the statutory instrument containing the regulations or order has been laid before Parliament and approved by a resolution of each House.

(6) Any other statutory instrument made under this Act, other than one made under section 30(4), shall be subject to annulment in pursuance of a resolution of either House of Parliament.

GENERAL NOTE

This is a standard provision as regards the use of statutory instruments under the Act. It applies only to regulation-making powers which are created by the Act otherwise than by amendments to the 1991 Act. Essentially the presumption is that statutory instruments are subject to the negative resolution procedure. The affirmative resolution procedure applies if the Secretary of State seeks to make an order repealing any part of s.18 of this Act (deferral of right to apply for maintenance assessment). This procedure also applies to regulations concerning the child maintenance bonus or compensation payments for loss of child support maintenance (subss. (4) and (5)). All other statutory instruments under the freestanding parts of this Act, with the exception of any commencement order under s.30(4), are subject to the negative resolution procedure (subs. (6)).

There are, however, a number of sections in this Act (notably ss.1 to 9 inclusive, inserting new ss.28A to 28I) which make wholesale changes to the text of the 1991 Act. Accordingly, these provisions are subject to different drafting arrangements as regards Parliamentary control of regulations. Within this latter group, regulations in respect of the following matters are made subject to the affirmative procedure (s.52(2) of the 1991 Act, amended by Sched. 3, para. 15): reduced payments under a regular payments condition (s.28C(2)(b) of the 1991 Act, inserted by s.3); factors relevant to whether it is "just and equitable" to make a departure direction (s.28F(3) of the 1991 Act, inserted by s.6(1)); collection fees for cases not within the CSA for assessment purposes (s.30(5A) of the 1991 Act, inserted by Sched. 3, para. 9); additional sums for arrears purposes (s.41A of the 1991 Act, inserted by s.22); repayment of overpaid child support maintenance (s.41B(6) of the 1991 Act, inserted by s.23) and the cases and controls for departure directions (Sched. 4B to the 1991 Act, inserted by s.6(2)).

Interpretation

27.—(1) In this Act "the 1991 Act" means the Child Support Act 1991.

(2) Expressions in this Act which are used in the 1991 Act have the same meaning in this Act as they have in that Act.

GENERAL NOTE

It follows from subs. (2) that reference should be made to ss.3, 54 and 55 of the 1991 Act for the definition of identical terms used in this Act.

Financial provisions

28. There shall be paid out of money provided by Parliament—

(a) any expenditure incurred by the Secretary of State under or by virtue of this Act;

(b) any increase attributable to this Act in the sums payable out of money so provided under or by virtue of any other enactment.

Provision for Northern Ireland

29.—(1) An Order in Council under paragraph 1(1)(b) of Schedule 1 to the Northern Ireland Act 1974 (legislation for Northern Ireland in the interim period) which states that it is made only for purposes corresponding to those of this Act—

(a) shall not be subject to paragraph 1(4) and (5) of that Schedule (affirmative resolution of both Houses of Parliament); but

(b) shall be subject to annulment in pursuance of a resolution of either House of Parliament.

(2) The Secretary of State may make arrangements with the Department of Health and Social Services for Northern Ireland with a view to securing, to the extent allowed for in the arrangements, that—

(a) the provision made by or under sections 10 and 24 ("the provision made for Great Britain"); and

(b) the provision made by or under any corresponding enactment having effect with respect to Northern Ireland ("the provision made for Northern Ireland"),

provide for a single system within the United Kingdom.

(3) The Secretary of State may make regulations for giving effect to any such arrangements.

(4) The regulations may, in particular—

(a) adapt legislation (including subordinate legislation) for the time being in force in Great Britain so as to secure its reciprocal operation with the provision made for Northern Ireland; and

(b) make provision to secure that acts, omissions and events which have any effect for the purposes of the provision made for Northern Ireland have a corresponding effect for the purposes of the provision made for Great Britain.

GENERAL NOTE

This section makes provision for Northern Ireland by reference to the powers contained in the Northern Ireland Act 1974 to make an Order in Council subject to negative resolution. It also enables a reciprocal agreement to be drawn up so that the provisions contained in ss.10 (child maintenance bonus) and 24 (compensatory payments to certain benefit claimants) can apply uniformly across the United Kingdom. In doing so the section follows the pattern of s.56 of the 1991 Act.

Short title, commencement, extent etc.

30.—(1) This Act may be cited as the Child Support Act 1995.

(2) This Act and the 1991 Act may be cited together as the Child Support Acts 1991 and 1995.

(3) Section 29 and this section (apart from subsection (5)) come into force on the passing of this Act.

(4) The other provisions of this Act come into force on such day as the Secretary of State may by order appoint and different days may be appointed for different purposes.

(5) Schedule 3 makes minor and consequential amendments.

(6) This Act, except for—

(a) sections 17, 27 and 29,

(b) this section, and

(c) paragraphs 1, 18, 19 and 20 of Schedule 3,

does not extend to Northern Ireland.

GENERAL NOTE

The commencement provisions are dealt with in the Introduction and General Note above. On the so-called "minor and consequential amendments", see further the General Note to Sched. 3, below.

SCHEDULES

      SCHEDULE 1

DEPARTURE DIRECTIONS

The following Schedule is inserted in the 1991 Act, after Schedule 4—

"SCHEDULE 4A

DEPARTURE DIRECTIONS

Interpretation

1. In this Schedule—
    "departure application" means an application for a departure direction;
    "regulations" means regulations made by the Secretary of State;
    "review" means a review under section 16, 17, 18 or 19.

Applications for departure directions

2. Regulations may make provision—
(a) as to the procedure to be followed in considering a departure application;
(b) as to the procedure to be followed when a departure application is referred to a child support appeal tribunal under section 28D(1)(b);
(c) for the giving of a direction by the Secretary of State as to the order in which, in a particular case, a departure application and a review are to be dealt with;
(d) for the reconsideration of a departure application in a case where further information becomes available to the Secretary of State after the application has been determined.

Completion of preliminary consideration

3. Regulations may provide for determining when the preliminary consideration of a departure application is to be taken to have been completed.

Information

4.—(1) Regulations may make provision for the use for any purpose of this Act of—
(a) information acquired by the Secretary of State in connection with an application for, or the making of, a departure direction;
(b) information acquired by a child support officer or the Secretary of State in connection with an application for, or the making of, a maintenance assessment.
(2) If any information which is required (by regulations under this Act) to be furnished to the Secretary of State in connection with a departure application has not been furnished within such period as may be prescribed, the Secretary of State may nevertheless proceed to determine the application.

Anticipation of change of circumstances

5.—(1) A departure direction may be given so as to provide that if the circumstances of the case change in such manner as may be specified in the direction a fresh maintenance assessment is to be made.
(2) Where any such provision is made, the departure direction may provide for the basis on which the amount of child support maintenance is to be fixed by the fresh maintenance assessment to differ from the basis on which the amount of child support maintenance was fixed by any earlier maintenance assessment made as a result of the direction.

Reviews and departure directions

6. Regulations may make provision—
(a) with respect to cases in which a child support officer is conducting a review of a maintenance assessment which was made as a result of a departure direction;
(b) with respect to cases in which a departure direction is made at a time when a child support officer is conducting a review.

Subsequent departure directions

7.—(1) Regulations may make provision with respect to any departure application made with respect to a maintenance assessment which was made as a result of a departure direction.

(2) The regulations may, in particular, provide for the application to be considered by reference to the maintenance assessment which would have been made had the departure direction not been given.

Joint consideration of departure applications and appeals

8.—(1) Regulations may provide for two or more departure applications with respect to the same current assessment to be considered together.
(2) A child support appeal tribunal considering—
(a) a departure application referred to it under section 28D(1)(b), or
(b) an appeal under section 28H,
may consider it at the same time as hearing an appeal under section 20 in respect of the current assessment, if it considers that to be appropriate.

Child support appeal tribunals

9.—(1) Regulations may provide that, in prescribed circumstances, where—
(a) a departure application is referred to a child support appeal tribunal under section 28D(1)(b), or
(b) an appeal is brought under section 28H,
the application or appeal may be dealt with by a tribunal constituted by the chairman sitting alone.
(2) Sub-paragraph (1) does not apply in relation to any appeal which is being heard together with an appeal under section 20.

Current assessments which are replaced by fresh assessments

10. Regulations may make provision as to the circumstances in which prescribed references in this Act to a current assessment are to have effect as if they were references to any later maintenance assessment made with respect to the same persons as the current assessment."

DEFINITIONS
"application for a departure direction": s.54 of the 1991 Act, as amended by Sched. 3, para. 16.
"child support maintenance": ss.3(6) and 54 of the 1991 Act.
"child support officer": ss.13 and 54 of the 1991 Act.
"current assessment": s.54 of the 1991 Act, as amended by Sched. 3, para. 16.
"departure application": Sched. 4A, para. 1 to the 1991 Act.
"maintenance assessment": s.54 of the 1991 Act.
"prescribed": s.54 of the 1991 Act.
"regulations": Sched. 4A, para. 1 to the 1991 Act.
"review": Sched. 4A, para. 1 to the 1991 Act.

GENERAL NOTE
This Schedule, introduced by s.1(2), makes supplemental provision with regard to procedural and other matters relating to departure directions by inserting Sched. 4A into the 1991 Act.

Sched. 4A to the 1991 Act

Para. 2
The regulation-making power in subpara. (a) will allow the CSA to operate the preliminary consideration procedure introduced by s.2 in the manner intended. Thus once a departure application is received, the other party will not be notified immediately. Notification will only take place if the application passes the sifting process and is regarded as meriting full consideration. At this juncture the other party will be able to make representations on the application. The other powers are concerned with CSAT procedures for determining applications (subpara. (b)), for deciding whether to deal with a review before or after a departure (subpara. (c)) and

for the reconsideration of a departure if further information becomes available (subpara. (d)). This may become necessary if an application has been determined under Sched. 4A, para. 4(2) of the 1991 Act, inserted by Sched. 1 to this Act, which enables the Secretary of State to proceed to determination in the absence of information being furnished within a prescribed period.

Para. 4
    This corresponds to the power contained in s.14 of the 1991 Act (see further the Child Support (Information, Evidence and Disclosure) Regulations 1992 (S.I. 1992 No. 1812)).

Para. 5
    This enables a departure direction to be made with prospective effect, anticipating a specific change of circumstances (*e.g.* an announced future increase in rail fares). This mirrors a similar provision with regard to anticipatory reviews under the social security legislation (SSAA 1992, s.25(1)(c)).

Para. 6
    Regulations made under this power will cover the various permutations which may arise where a case subject to a departure direction is subsequently reviewed by a CSO, and vice versa.

Para. 9
    Although hidden away towards the end of this Schedule, this provision is potentially of very great significance. It enables regulations to be made which may specify that appeals (or references) relating to departure directions must be heard by a CSAT chairman sitting alone (subpara. (1)). It is understood that such cases are likely as a matter of policy, initially at least, to be listed before a Full-Time Chairman. It is a requirement of appointment that a Full-Time Chairman must have a seven-year general qualification or, in Scotland, be an advocate or solicitor of seven years' standing (1991 Act, Sched. 3, para. 4(2)). Many Full-Time Chairmen have extensive experience of matrimonial work from their time in private practice. If the case is heard jointly with an appeal against a CSO's decision under s.20, a full CSAT consisting of a chairman and two other members must determine both matters (subpara. (2)).
    There is no precedent for this within the social security system, although of course both Full-Time and part-time SSAT chairmen, acting alone, do determine certain interlocutory matters outside of the hearing (*e.g.* requests for postponements and applications for leave to appeal). Precedents do, however, exist elsewhere in the tribunal system. For many years industrial tribunal chairmen have had jurisdiction to sit alone when dealing with certain non-contentious matters (*e.g.* making an order dismissing proceedings where the applicant has given written notice of abandonment of proceedings: Industrial Tribunals (Constitution and Rules of Procedure) Regulations 1993 (S.I. 1993 No. 2687), reg. 12(2)). More recently, and more controversially, amendments made by the Trade Union Reform and Employment Rights Act (TURERA) 1993 gave industrial tribunal chairmen the power to hear a wider range of cases sitting alone. Thus industrial tribunal chairmen may sit alone to determine claims under the Wages Act or for breach of contract: see the Employment Protection (Consolidation) Act 1978, s.128(2A)–(2F), inserted by TURERA 1993, s.36. This reform was prompted by the rise in the number of applications made to industrial tribunals. The Council on Tribunals expressed its reservations about this development in its Annual Report for 1992–1993 (H.C. 78, Session 1993–1994, paras. 2.25–2.27), although it was largely reassured by the fact that the matters to go before chairmen sitting alone were confined to legal issues.
    It seems clear that the prospect of a large number of appeals was also a factor in making the Government bring forward a similar proposal for CSATs in respect of departure directions. The Under-Secretary of State for Social Security stressed the need for the Independent Tribunal Service, the judicial body responsible for oversight of CSATs and related tribunals, to retain "some management flexibility. It will be easier to list applications for hearing by a chairman alone than to arrange a three-person tribunal" (*per* Mr A. Burt, Standing Committee E, col. 47, March 30, 1995). The precise range of appeals to go before chairmen sitting alone has yet to be finalised, but will almost certainly include appeals against a rejection of the application at the preliminary consideration stage under s.28B of the 1991 Act (inserted by s.2). It is to be hoped that the power introduced by para. 9(1) will not be widely used, not least because of the concern expressed by the Council on Tribunals in relation to industrial tribunals, namely that "some parties might think that they were not getting full measure from the tribunals if the hearing were to be conducted by a chairman sitting alone" (Annual Report for 1992–1993 (H.C. 78, Session 1993–1994, para. 2.26).

SCHEDULE 2

DEPARTURE DIRECTIONS: THE CASES AND CONTROLS

The following Schedule is inserted in the 1991 Act, after Schedule 4A—

"SCHEDULE 4B

DEPARTURE DIRECTIONS: THE CASES AND CONTROLS

PART I

THE CASES

General

1.—(1) The cases in which a departure direction may be given are those set out in this Part of this Schedule or in regulations made under this Part.

(2) In this Schedule "applicant" means the person whose application for a departure direction is being considered.

Special expenses

2.—(1) A departure direction may be given with respect to special expenses of the applicant which were not, and could not have been, taken into account in determining the current assessment in accordance with the provisions of, or made under, Part I of Schedule 1.

(2) In this paragraph "special expenses" means the whole, or any prescribed part, of expenses which fall within a prescribed description of expenses.

(3) In prescribing descriptions of expenses for the purposes of this paragraph, the Secretary of State may, in particular, make provision with respect to—

(a) costs incurred in travelling to work;

(b) costs incurred by an absent parent in maintaining contact with the child, or with any of the children, with respect to whom he is liable to pay child support maintenance under the current assessment;

(c) costs attributable to a long-term illness or disability of the applicant or of a dependant of the applicant;

(d) debts incurred, before the absent parent became an absent parent in relation to a child with respect to whom the current assessment was made—

(i) for the joint benefit of both parents;

(ii) for the benefit of any child with respect to whom the current assessment was made; or

(iii) for the benefit of any other child falling within a prescribed category;

(e) pre-1993 financial commitments from which it is impossible for the parent concerned to withdraw or from which it would be unreasonable to expect that parent to have to withdraw;

(f) costs incurred by a parent in supporting a child who is not his child but who is part of his family.

(4) For the purposes of sub-paragraph (3)(c)—

(a) the question whether one person is a dependant of another shall be determined in accordance with regulations made by the Secretary of State;

(b) "disability" and "illness" have such meaning as may be prescribed; and

(c) the question whether an illness or disability is long-term shall be determined in accordance with regulations made by the Secretary of State.

(5) For the purposes of sub-paragraph (3)(e), "pre-1993 financial commitments" means financial commitments of a prescribed kind entered into before 5th April 1993 in any case where—

(a) a court order of a prescribed kind was in force with respect to the absent parent and the person with care concerned at the time when they were entered into; or

(b) an agreement between them of a prescribed kind was in force at that time.

(6) For the purposes of sub-paragraph (3)(f), a child who is not the child of a particular person is a part of that person's family in such circumstances as may be prescribed.

Property or capital transfers

3.—(1) A departure direction may be given if—

(a) before 5th April 1993—

(i) a court order of a prescribed kind was in force with respect to the absent parent and either the person with care with respect to whom the current assessment was made or the child, or any of the children, with respect to whom that assessment was made, or

          (ii) an agreement of a prescribed kind between the absent parent and any of those persons was in force;

   (b) in consequence of one or more transfers of property of a prescribed kind—

          (i) the amount payable by the absent parent by way of maintenance was less than would have been the case had that transfer or those transfers not been made; or

          (ii) no amount was payable by the absent parent by way of maintenance; and

   (c) the effect of that transfer, or those transfers, is not properly reflected in the current assessment.

(2) For the purposes of sub-paragraph (1)(b), "maintenance" means periodical payments of maintenance made (otherwise than under this Act) with respect to the child, or any of the children, with respect to whom the current assessment was made.

(3) For the purposes of sub-paragraph (1)(c), the question whether the effect of one or more transfers of property is properly reflected in the current assessment shall be determined in accordance with regulations made by the Secretary of State.

4.—(1) A departure direction may be given if—

   (a) before 5th April 1993—

          (i) a court order of a prescribed kind was in force with respect to the absent parent and either the person with care with respect to whom the current assessment was made or the child, or any of the children, with respect to whom that assessment was made, or

          (ii) an agreement of a prescribed kind between the absent parent and any of those persons was in force;

   (b) in pursuance of the court order or agreement, the absent parent has made one or more transfers of property of a prescribed kind;

   (c) the amount payable by the absent parent by way of maintenance was not reduced as a result of that transfer or those transfers;

   (d) the amount payable by the absent parent by way of child support maintenance under the current assessment has been reduced as a result of that transfer or those transfers, in accordance with provisions of or made under this Act; and

   (e) it is nevertheless inappropriate, having regard to the purposes for which the transfer or transfers was or were made, for that reduction to have been made.

(2) For the purposes of sub-paragraph (1)(c), "maintenance" means periodical payments of maintenance made (otherwise than under this Act) with respect to the child, or any of the children, with respect to whom the current assessment was made.

Additional cases

5.—(1) The Secretary of State may by regulations prescribe other cases in which a departure direction may be given.

(2) Regulations under this paragraph may, for example, make provision with respect to cases where—

   (a) assets which do not produce income are capable of producing income;

   (b) a person's life-style is inconsistent with the level of his income;

   (c) housing costs are unreasonably high;

   (d) housing costs are in part attributable to housing persons whose circumstances are such as to justify disregarding a part of those costs;

   (e) travel costs are unreasonably high; or

   (f) travel costs should be disregarded.

Part II

Regulatory Controls

6.—(1) The Secretary of State may by regulations make provision with respect to the directions which may be given in a departure direction.

(2) No directions may be given other than those which are permitted by the regulations.

(3) Regulations under this paragraph may, in particular, make provision for a departure direction to require—

   (a) the substitution, for any formula set out in Part I of Schedule 1, of such other formula as may be prescribed;

   (b) any prescribed amount by reference to which any calculation is to be made in fixing the amount of child support maintenance to be increased or reduced in accordance with the regulations;

(c) the substitution, for any provision in accordance with which any such calculation is to be made, of such other provision as may be prescribed.

(4) Regulations may limit the extent to which the amount of the child support maintenance fixed by a maintenance assessment made as a result of a departure direction may differ from the amount of the child support maintenance which would be fixed by a maintenance assessment made otherwise than as a result of the direction.

(5) Regulations may provide for the amount of any special expenses to be taken into account in a case falling within paragraph 2, for the purposes of a departure direction, not to exceed such amount as may be prescribed or as may be determined in accordance with the regulations.

(6) No departure direction may be given so as to have the effect of denying to an absent parent the protection of paragraph 6 of Schedule 1.

(7) Sub-paragraph (6) does not prevent the modification of the provisions of, or made under, paragraph 6 of Schedule 1 to the extent permitted by regulations under this paragraph.

(8) Any regulations under this paragraph may make different provision with respect to different levels of income."

DEFINITIONS
"absent parent": ss.3(2) and 54 of the 1991 Act.
"applicant": Sched. 4B, para. 1(2) to the 1991 Act.
"application for a departure direction": s.54 of the 1991 Act, as amended by Sched. 3, para. 16.
"child": s.55 of the 1991 Act.
"child support maintenance": ss.3(6) and 54 of the 1991 Act.
"current assessment": s.54 of the 1991 Act, as amended by Sched. 3, para. 16.
"departure direction": s.54 of the 1991 Act, as amended by Sched. 3, para. 16.
"disability": Sched. 4B, para. 2(4)(b) to the 1991 Act.
"illness": Sched. 4B, para. 2(4)(b) to the 1991 Act.
"maintenance": Sched. 4B, paras. 3(2) and 4(2) to the 1991 Act.
"person with care": ss.3(3) and 54 of the 1991 Act.
"pre-1993 financial commitments": Sched. 4B, para. 2(5) to the 1991 Act.
"prescribed": s.54 of the 1991 Act.
"special expenses": Sched. 4B, para. 2(2) to the 1991 Act.

GENERAL NOTE
This Schedule, which inserts Sched. 4B into the 1991 Act, is the heart of the new Act. A parent with care or absent parent may apply for a departure direction under s.28A(1) of the 1991 Act (inserted by s.1). The Secretary of State may make a departure direction under s.28F(1) of the 1991 Act (inserted by s.6(1)) where two criteria are met. The first is that he is satisfied that the case falls within one or more of the cases set out in Part I of Sched. 4B below (or in regulations thereunder). The second is that it is "just and equitable" to make such a direction (see the General Note to s.6 above). In reaching a decision, the Secretary of State must also take into account the principles set out in s.28E of the 1991 Act, inserted by s.5.

Schedule 4B falls into two Parts. Part I provides for the cases in which a departure direction may be given. There are three broad categories: cases involving special expenses (para. 2), property or capital transfers (paras. 3 and 4) or additional cases (para. 5). In principle, all these grounds are available to both absent parents and parents with care. In practice, however, applications under the heads of special expenses or property or capital transfers will tend to be made by absent parents, while applications under the additional cases provisions are likely to be made by parents with care. It should be noted that these provisions give only the broadest outline; much of the detail is to appear in regulations.

Part II (*i.e.* para. 6) provides certain controls on the contents of such directions. This will enable limits to be set on the modifications to the provisions of the 1991 Act which may be effected by departure directions, and allow for these limits to vary according to the applicant's income.

Regulations made under this Schedule are subject to the affirmative procedure (s.52(2) of the 1991 Act, as amended by Sched. 3, para. 15(c)).

Para. 2
This paragraph allows a departure direction to be given where the applicant has special expenses which are not taken into account in the standard formula assessment. The requirement that it is "just and equitable" to make the direction also applies (s.28F(1)(b) of the 1991 Act, inserted by s.6(1)). If a departure direction is granted it is expected that the special expenses will

be added to the exempt and protected income, thus reducing assessable income. This treats the expenses in the same way as other expenses such as housing costs. The way the formula works means that the effect a departure has on an individual's actual liability will vary from case to case, depending on the assessment in force. Broadly, an absent parent with a lower disposable income will find greater relief than one with a higher income. Thus a parent on a protected income will find that 85 per cent of the amount added to exempt income will affect the maintenance assessment. A parent who is on an income above the protected income and who is paying the standard deduction rate will gain 50 per cent of the allowance (*10th Report*, Appendix I, Annex C, paras. 4 and 5).

In April 1995 the Government introduced some limited reforms allowing for regard to be had in specified circumstances to travel-to-work costs and the effects of property transfers (Child Support and Income Support (Amendment) Regulations 1995 (S.I. 1995 No. 1045), regs. 44, 45 and 57 and Scheds. 1 and 2). These two forms of special expenses reappear in these provisions (paras. 2(3)(a) and (e)), although the departures system will permit greater flexibility than the adjustments possible under the April 1995 changes.

The types of special expenses which may be considered under this paragraph are to be prescribed by the Secretary of State and may include (but not necessarily be confined to) those listed in subpara. (3). These are travel to work expenses (para. 2(3)(a)), contact costs (para. 2(3)(b)), costs relating to long-term illness or disability (para. 2(3)(c)), certain debts incurred before the relationship breakdown (para. 2(3)(d)), certain "pre-1993 financial commitments" (para. 2(3)(e)) and costs incurred in supporting certain other children (para. 2(3)(f)).

In principle, it will be open to both absent parents and parents with care to apply for a departure direction under these provisions. However, the special expenses have been selected because they reflect "where the greatest pressure points were to be found in the system" (*per* Mr A. Burt, *Hansard*, Vol. 260, col. 657), following a departmental review of representations made in connection with the Act. The categories chosen therefore reflect the principal grievances of absent parents. There is one glaring omission so far as parents with care are concerned: there is no mention of child care costs as being a potential special expense. It is true that the maintenance requirement makes some allowance for this in building into the formula calculation a carer element. However, parents with care who are single parents and reliant on commercially-provided child care will find this provides little tangible assistance.

Subpara. (3)(a). Travel to work costs are covered by the April 1995 amendments to the regulations, but only on the basis of the "straight-line distance". A person may apply for an allowance towards travel to work costs where the "straight-line distance" between home and work, multiplied by the number of journeys per week, is more than 150 miles. Under the formula an allowance is then made of 10p per mile for the distance above 150 miles. This concession is not available to those who receive assistance from their employer with travel costs or who are self-employed (Child Support and Income Support (Amendment) Regulations 1995 (S.I. 1995 No. 1045), reg. 57 and Sched. 2).

The category of special expenses under the departures system is not constrained by the "straight-line distance" rule. Hence a departure direction could take account of an applicant's actual travel to work costs, *e.g.* where a person lives and works on opposite sides of an estuary, or lives in a rural area where the road to work involves a significant detour around high ground. On the basis of 1991 Census data, the Government anticipate that less than 11.5 per cent of absent parents will qualify for a departure on this basis (*10th Report*, Appendix I, Annex B).

Subpara. (3)(b). A major grievance among some absent parents is that the costs of contact have not been recognised under the formula. This is primarily a problem for absent parents who find themselves living some distance from their ex-partner and their children. Again, the Government anticipate that only a minority of absent parents will benefit from this provision: information from the CSA computer indicates that 40 per cent of absent parents paying maintenance above the minimum amount live in the same postcode district as the parent with care, and a further 33 per cent live in the same area. Furthermore, not all absent parents maintain contact with their children. Overall, it is estimated that some 15 per cent of absent parents may live a relatively long distance from a child with whom they have contact (*10th Report*, Appendix I, Annex B).

Subpara. (3)(c). It is anticipated that only a very small minority of absent parents (perhaps 2–3 per cent) will qualify for a direction on this basis (*10th Report*, Appendix I, Annex B).

Subpara. (3)(d). The failure of the formula to allow for debts incurred during the former relationship has been a matter of controversy since the outset of the 1991 Act. This head of special expenses covers three different types of debt arising from the relationship which has broken down. Paragraph 2(3)(d)(i) covers debts incurred "for the joint benefit of both parents"; an example would be the cost of a loan for a kitchen re-fit (*10th Report*, Appendix I, Annex B, Example 7). Paragraph 2(3)(d)(ii) is self-explanatory; the DSS memorandum to the *10th Report* gives an example of £100 a month being paid after separation for the cost of a grand piano for a musically-gifted child (*ibid.*, Example 8). Paragraph 2(3)(d)(iii) could cover the situation where the debts were incurred for the benefit of a child who was a dependant at the time but is no longer dependent, and so is excluded from para. 2(3)(d)(ii). This provision might also be used to include step-children in certain circumstances.

Subpara. (3)(e). The particular kinds of commitment involved, whether under a court order or otherwise, are to be set out in regulations under para. 2(5). The intention is that this head should only apply "where a parent entered into a financial commitment before April 6, 1993 on the basis of a clear agreement about maintenance liability for the children. In the absence of such an agreement, there can be no argument that the financial commitment should be met to the detriment of support for the children. It is intended that provisions under this paragraph would exclude commitments such as business debts, debts which should have been repaid prior to liability under the Act commencing etc." (*10th Report*, Appendix I, para. 21).

Subpara. (3)(f). The scope of para. 2(3)(f) should be noted carefully. It provides that "special expenses" may include "costs incurred by a parent in supporting a child who is not his child but who is part of his family". Regulations will define the circumstances in which the latter condition is satisfied (para. 2(6)). The DSS *Notes for Guidance* indicate that the power may be used to cover grandchildren or the children of a widowed partner. To this extent it may include step-children. However, it seems that the Government will resist any attempt to broaden the scope of departures on this ground to all cases of step-children; rather, eligible cases will probably be confined to those exceptional cases where the natural parent is not available to pay maintenance, *e.g.* because he is in prison, is abroad and untraceable, or has died.

Subpara. (4)
  Dependants. Dependants for the purposes of para. 2(3)(c) will be limited to the immediate family of the applicant, *i.e.* partner, natural children and step-children living with him (*10th Report*, Appendix I, para. 21).
  Disability. This will have a "dictionary or common-sense definition" (*ibid.*); presumably this will be in identical or similar terms to the definition in s.8(9) of the 1991 Act, which defines a child as disabled "if he is blind, deaf or dumb or is substantially and permanently handicapped by illness, injury, mental disorder or congenital deformity or such other disability as may be prescribed". However, "it may be that experience will lead to a need for a more detailed definition of disability" (*10th Report*, Appendix I, para. 21). This might be by reference to receipt of a particular benefit, *e.g.* disability living allowance.
  Long-term. A long-term illness or disability will be one which is medically certified and expected to last at least 52 weeks (*ibid.*).

Subpara. (5). Regulations will prescribe the kinds of court order or agreement which an applicant must have had before a financial commitment can be considered for a departure direction under para. 2(3)(e).

Subpara. (6). The intention is to define "child" for the purposes of para. 2(3)(f) as step-children who are living in the applicant's household.

Para. 3
  A central criticism of the 1991 Act is that it fails to take any account of past financial settlements, especially the so-called "clean break". This point was made repeatedly during the debates on the 1991 Act, and especially in the House of Lords. Similarly, the House of Commons Social Security Committee had originally advocated some mechanism for taking into account capital settlements made in lieu of child maintenance (*Third Report*, H.C. 277–II, para. 72, Session 1990–1991). The Government's initial position was that it was both wrong in principle and impossible in practice to make any allowance under the formula for such settlements. This approach was later endorsed in a volte-face by the Social Security Committee (*First Report*, H.C. 69, Session 1993–1994, paras. 65–74). The Committee suggested that the only option for absent parents faced with an increased child maintenance bill, following an earlier property transfer, was to seek a variation of the existing order on the basis of changed circumstances. This possibility was firmly rebuffed by Booth J., sitting in the Family Division of the High Court, in *Crozier v. Crozier* [1994] Fam. 114 (but see also *Smith v. McInerney* [1994] 2 F.L.R. 1077, discussed by Miller (1995) 7 *Child and Family Law Quarterly* 152).

Absent parents and their lobbying groups continued to press the argument that the failure of the formula to take into account earlier property settlements amounted to injustice. In its further review, the Social Security Committee reverted to its original position and called upon the Secretary of State to take into account past property and capital settlements (*Fifth Report*, H.C. 470, Session 1993–1994). In its subsequent *White Paper*, the Government announced two reforms to deal with these sorts of cases. First, as from April 1995, the formula was amended to provide a broad-brush allowance in respect of property transfers. Thus an addition of £20, £40 or £60 is made to the weekly exempt income when the value of the settlement falls into one of three bands: between £5,000 and £9,999; between £10,000 and £24,999; and over £25,000: (Child Support and Income Support (Amendment) Regulations 1995 (S.I. 1995 No. 1045), reg. 44 and Sched. 1). The Government accepted that this might still not be entirely satisfactory: "It does not take account of such issues as the precise amount transferred, the way in which it was intended to divide the assets between the ex-partner and the child, or the exact age of the children at the time of the settlement" (*per* Mr A. Burt, Standing Committee E, col. 118, April 4, 1995).

The 1995 Act accordingly makes further allowance for such transfers. Either parent will be able to apply for a departure from the formula (as amended in April 1995) and have their case considered on a more discretionary basis. In practice, absent parents are likely to apply under para. 3 and parents with care under para. 4. It must, of course, still be "just and equitable" to make such a direction (s.28F(1)(b) of the 1991 Act, inserted by s.6(1)), and the principles laid down by s.28E of the 1991 Act (inserted by s.5) must be taken into account in reaching the decision.

The number of likely applications for departure directions on these grounds remains a matter of speculation. Official statistics suggest that approximately 12 per cent of absent parents were party to a property or capital transfer before 1993. Of these transfers, 75 per cent were for £5,000 or more and so would be eligible for consideration under the April 1995 broad-brush allowance in the formula (Standing Committee E, col. 132, April 4, 1995). An unknown number of these may seek further relief under the new provisions.

Subpara. (1). This sets out the three cumulative conditions which must be satisfied in order to depart from the formula. The first is that before April 5, 1993 a court order or relevant agreement applied to the parties involved (para. 3(1)(a)). Regulations will prescribe the precise forms of orders or agreements to be included for these purposes. Secondly, as a result of one or more transfers of property *either* the amount payable by way of maintenance was less than it would otherwise have been *or* no such maintenance was payable by the absent parent (para. 3(1)(b)). "Maintenance", in this context, means child maintenance (para. 3(2)). The third requirement is that the effect of the transfer(s) "is not properly reflected in the current assessment" (para. 3(1)(c)).

There are potential difficulties of interpretation with regard to each of these three conditions. First, as a matter of strict construction, there need be no connection between the pre-April 5, 1993 court order or agreement, under para. 3(1)(a), and the property transfer under para. 3(1)(b). This is because there is no direct linkage between these two provisions (contrast the wording in para. 4(1)(a) and 4(1)(b), which specifically states that "*in pursuance of* the court order or agreement" a transfer has been made (emphasis added)). In para. 3(1)(b) the "in consequence of" refers to the impact of the property transfer on the level of maintenance being paid (if any), not the effect of the court order in requiring such a transfer. There must at least be an argument that any attempt in regulations to make such a linkage would be *ultra vires*. There will, of course, in practice usually be a very direct link, but there might be some cases where transfers or settlements were made independently of, or in advance of, any court order or agreement. On the reading suggested here, such cases should still be eligible for consideration for a departure direction.

Secondly, under para. 3(1)(b)(ii), it will usually be fairly clear whether the absent parent is liable to pay any child maintenance as a consequence of the transfer. It is much less clear how it will be determined whether or not "the amount payable by the absent parent by way of maintenance was less than would have been the case had that transfer or those transfers not been made" (para. 3(1)(b)(i)). This issue may be straightforward where a genuinely nominal figure for maintenance is ordered following a clean break (*e.g.* 5p per year). But how is one to judge whether what may appear at first sight to be a more realistic amount (*e.g.* £20 per week) has nonetheless been depressed by the effect of a property transfer? Moreover, para. 3(1)(b) only applies where the effect of the property transfer is to reduce or to remove the liability to pay *child* maintenance (see para. 3(2)). Thus this dispensation will paradoxically not apply in the (admittedly rather unusual?) pre-1993 case where an absent parent agreed (i) to make a property transfer to his ex-wife; (ii) to pay *her* no or nominal maintenance; but (iii) agreed to pay child maintenance at a realistic rate. The precise way in which maintenance has been allocated in the past as between spousal and child maintenance may well depend on various extraneous considerations (*e.g.* whether the parent with care is working, tax advantages *etc.*), yet this distinction between the two forms of maintenance may now become crucial. However, a departure direction can be made under para. 4 (presumably on an application by the parent with care) in a pre-1993 case where (i) a property transfer was made under a court order or agreement; (ii) this had no effect on the absent parent's liability to pay child maintenance; (iii) the CSA maintenance assessment has been reduced to allow for that transfer (*i.e.* under the broad brush provisions in the regulations) and (iv) it is inappropriate for that reduction to take place, having regard to the purposes of the transfer.

Thirdly, a departure direction may be given where the effect of the transfer(s) "is not properly reflected in the current assessment" (para. 3(1)(c)), a matter which is to be determined in accordance with regulations made by the Secretary of State (see para. 3(3)). In many cases this may be the critical issue to determine. The Government's intention is that " 'properly reflected' means in accordance with normal best practice adopted by the Courts. This will probably be achieved by numerical tables of the kind best set out in secondary legislation. There may also be a need for a degree of flexibility to take account of variations in Court practice" (*10th Report*, Appendix I, para. 21). Those with experience of family law practice and litigation can only wait in wonder to see precisely what format these tables will take.

The requirement that it be "just and equitable" to make the direction applies throughout this paragraph (s.28F(1)(b) of the 1991 Act, inserted by s.6(1)), and regulations are promised which will provide further elucidation. According to the Minister of State, "We do not intend that those regulations should be comprehensive or overly restrictive: the decision-maker must be free to exercise his discretion as he sees fit. It may be that we will feel it necessary to include in the regulations some of the matters covered in Sections 25 and 25A of the Matrimonial Causes Act" (*per* Lord Mackay of Ardbrecknish, *Hansard*, H.L. Vol. 565, col. 114).

Para. 4

These provisions mirror those in para. 3, but relate to the case where an allowance has been made for a property or capital transfer in the formula (*i.e.* under the broad-brush provisions) but that transfer in fact contained no element for child maintenance, and so it was inappropriate for such an allowance to be made. Unlike para. 3, there is here a direct nexus between the court order and the transfer. Presumably applications under this paragraph will be made by parents with care.

Para. 5

This paragraph enables the Secretary of State to make provision for further cases of "special expenses" to be defined in regulations. These additional cases are not confined to the examples listed in para. 5(2). Given the nature of the heads listed, they are more likely to be invoked by the parent with care than the absent parent, although in principle either may apply.

Subpara. (2)(a) and (b). These are designed to cover the case in which an absent parent is contriving to adjust his income so as to minimise the amount that can be taken into account for child support purposes. The example was given of an absent parent who has "a large house in a stockbroker belt in the home counties with several luxury cars in the drive and the apparent trappings of wealth. The absent parent may be a director of his own company and may pay a low salary to himself and perhaps also a salary to a new partner" (per Mr A. Burt, Standing Committee E, col. 119, April 4, 1995).

Subpara. (2)(c) and (d). Until April 1995 housing costs for any new partner and step-children were disregarded, and the absent parent's housing costs had to be apportioned. Since the April 1995 amendments such reasonable housing costs have been allowed in full. Paragraph 5(2)(c) is essentially a counterbalance to that reform, in that it allows a departure direction to be made where the absent parent's housing costs are excessive, *e.g.* in terms of being over-accommodated or living in an unduly expensive area. There is a considerable body of case law on this concept in relation to restrictions on income support housing costs and housing benefit, but in both instances the definitions of excessive housing costs are much more fully defined (see *e.g.* Housing Benefit (General) Regulations 1987 (S.I. 1987 No. 1971), reg. 11). Paragraph 5(2)(d) is also a reaction to the April 1995 concessions to absent parents. It may be "just and equitable" to disregard part of the absent parent's housing costs if he moves in with a new partner who is an owner-occupier and has always paid her own mortgage (*per* Mr A. Burt, Standing Committee E, col. 119, April 4, 1995).

Subpara. (2)(e) and (f). Travel costs may give rise to a departure direction where, although allowed under the formula, they are unreasonably high or should otherwise be disregarded: "a parent with care might argue that the absent parent ... deliberately opted to move out of the city to benefit from the better quality of life offered by a rural location, in the knowledge that he could defray part of his travel costs through reduced maintenance payments" (*per* Mr A. Burt, Standing Committee E, col. 119, April 4, 1995).

Para. 6

This paragraph provides for regulations to be made defining the contents of departure directions. Thus only those directions permitted by the regulations may be included (para. 6(2)), and these may lay down how the formula is to be affected (para. 6(3)), limit the amount of the departure (para. 6(4)) and prescribe the maximum amount of "special expenses" to be taken into account (para. 6(5)). The purpose of the regulation-making power under para. 6(4) and (5) is to allow a degree of "dampening" on the effect of a departure direction, so that those on very high incomes, who retain a higher proportion of their income under the formal assessment and can thus afford to meet any special expenses, will not gain as much from departures as people on lower incomes (*10th Report*, Appendix I, para. 21 and Annex C). Regulations may also make different provision depending upon the level of income of the parent concerned (para. 6(8)). The paragraph also ensures that an absent parent is not to be deprived of the benefit of the protected income provisions in Sched. 1, para. 6 of the 1991 Act, as these can be modified to include special expenses within their definition (paras. 6(6) and (7)).

Section 30(5)   SCHEDULE 3

MINOR AND CONSEQUENTIAL AMENDMENTS

Income and Corporation Taxes Act 1988 (c. 1)

1. In section 617(2) of the Income and Corporation Taxes Act 1988 (social security and other benefits which are not treated as income for purposes of the Income Tax Acts), insert after paragraph (ac)—

"(ad) payments of a child maintenance bonus;

(ae) compensation payments made under regulations under section 24 of the Child Support Act 1995 or under any corresponding enactment having effect with respect to Northern Ireland;".

Child Support Act 1991 (c. 48)

2. The 1991 Act is amended as follows.

3.—(1) In section 14 (information required by Secretary of State), after subsection (1) insert—

"(1A) Regulations under subsection (1) may make provision for notifying any person who is required to furnish any information or evidence under the regulations of the possible consequences of failing to do so."

(2) In section 14, after subsection (2) insert—

"(2A) Where the Secretary of State has in his possession any information acquired by him in connection with his functions under this Act, he may—

(a) make use of that information for purposes of any of the benefit Acts or of the Jobseekers Act 1995; or

(b) disclose it to the Department of Health and Social Services for Northern Ireland for purposes of any enactment corresponding to any of those Acts and having effect with respect to Northern Ireland."

4. In section 18 (review of decisions by child support officers), after subsection (6)(b) insert "or".

5. In section 20 (appeals to child support appeal tribunals), after subsection (2) insert—

"(2A) A tribunal hearing an appeal under this section may, at the request of any party to the appeal, take into account—

(a) any later maintenance assessment made with respect to the same parties;

(b) any change in the circumstances of the case."

6. In section 21(1) (functions of child support appeal tribunals), add at the end "and have such other functions as are conferred by this Act".

7.—(1) Section 24 (appeal to Child Support Commissioner) is amended as follows.

(2) After subsection (1) insert—

"(1A) The Secretary of State may appeal to a Child Support Commissioner on a question of law in relation to any decision of a child support appeal tribunal made in connection with an application for a departure direction."

(3) In subsection (3), for paragraph (c) substitute—

"(c) on an appeal by the Secretary of State, refer the case to a child support appeal tribunal with directions for its determination; or

(d) on any other appeal, refer the case to a child support officer or, if he considers it appropriate, to a child support appeal tribunal with directions for its determination."

8.—(1) In section 25 (appeal from Child Support Commissioner on question of law), insert after subsection (3)—

"(3A) The Child Support Commissioner to whom an application for leave to appeal under this section is made shall specify as the appropriate court either the Court of Appeal or the Court of Session.

(3B) In determining the appropriate court, the Child Support Commissioner shall have regard to the circumstances of the case, and in particular the convenience of the persons who may be parties to the appeal."

(2) In the definition of "appropriate court" in subsection (4) of that section, for the words from "means" to "Session" substitute ", except in subsections (3A) and (3B), means the court specified in accordance with those subsections".

9. In section 30 (collection and enforcement of maintenance payments other than child support maintenance), at the end add—

"(5A) Regulations made under subsection (1) or (2) prescribing payments which may be collected by the Secretary of State may make provision for the payment to him by such person or persons as may be prescribed of such fees as may be prescribed."

10. In section 33 (liability orders), at the end add—

"(5) If the Secretary of State designates a liability order for the purposes of this subsection it shall be treated as a judgment entered in a county court for the purposes of section 73 of the County Courts Act 1984 (register of judgments and orders)."

11. In section 41 (retention by Secretary of State of arrears recovered by him in benefit cases) for subsection (2) substitute—

"(2) Where the Secretary of State recovers any such arrears he may, in such circumstances as may be prescribed and to such extent as may be prescribed, retain them if he is satisfied that the amount of any benefit paid to or in respect of the person with care of the child or children in question would have been less had the absent parent made the payment or payments of child support maintenance in question.

(2A) In determining for the purposes of subsection (2) whether the amount of any benefit paid would have been less at any time than the amount which was paid at that time, in a case where the maintenance assessment had effect from a date earlier than that on which it was made, the assessment shall be taken to have been in force at that time."

12. In section 46(5) (circumstances in which child support officer may give a reduced benefit direction), after "may" insert ", except in prescribed circumstances,".

13. In section 47 (fees), in subsections (1) and (2) in each case after "takes" insert ", or proposes to take,".

14. In section 48(1) (power of Secretary of State to confer right of audience), for "person authorised" substitute "officer of the Secretary of State who is authorised".

15. In section 52(2) (statutory instruments subject to affirmative resolution control)—

(a) after "12(2)," insert "28C(2)(b), 28F(3), 30(5A)";

(b) after "or (4)" insert "41A, 41B(6)"; and

(c) after "Schedule 1" insert "or under Schedule 4B".

16. In section 54 (interpretation), insert the following definitions in the appropriate places—

""application for a departure direction" means an application under section 28A;

"current assessment", in relation to an application for a departure direction, means (subject to any regulations made under paragraph 10 of Schedule 4A) the maintenance assessment with respect to which the application is made;

"departure direction" has the meaning given in section 28A; and

"parent with care" means a person who is, in relation to a child, both a parent and a person with care."

17. In paragraph 2 of Schedule 3 (constitution of child support appeal tribunals), add at the end—

"(4) This paragraph is subject to the provisions of any regulations made under paragraph 9 of Schedule 4A."

18.—(1) In Schedule 4 (Child Support Commissioners), after paragraph 2 insert—

"Expenses of other persons

2A.—(1) The Secretary of State may pay to any person required to attend at any proceedings before a Child Support Commissioner such travelling and other allowances as, with the consent of the Treasury, the Secretary of State may determine.

(2) In sub-paragraph (1), references to travelling and other allowances include references to compensation for loss of remunerative time.

(3) No compensation for loss of remunerative time shall be paid to any person under this paragraph in respect of any time during which he is in receipt of other remuneration so paid."

(2) In paragraph 8 of Schedule 4 (application of Schedule to Northern Ireland), after sub-paragraph (b) insert—

"(bb) paragraph 2A were omitted;".

19.—(1) In paragraph 3(2) of Schedule 5 (amendment of the House of Commons Disqualification Act 1975), after "Part I" insert "of Schedule 1".

(2) In paragraph 3(3) of Schedule 5, after "Part III" insert "of Schedule 1".

(3) In paragraph 4(1) of Schedule 5 (amendment of the Northern Ireland Assembly Disqualification Act 1975), after "Part I of" insert "Schedule 1 to".

Social Security Administration Act 1992 (c. 5)

20. In section 170(5) of the Social Security Administration Act 1992 (the Social Security Advisory Committee)—
  (a) in the definition of "the relevant enactments", after paragraph (aa) insert—
    "(ab) section 10 of the Child Support Act 1995;"; and
  (b) in the definition of "the relevant Northern Ireland enactments", after paragraph (aa) insert—
    "(ab) any enactment corresponding to section 10 of the Child Support Act 1995 having effect with respect to Northern Ireland; and".

GENERAL NOTE

This Schedule, introduced by s.30(5), makes various minor and consequential amendments.

Para. 5

This is an important amendment to s.20 of the 1991 Act which enables a CSAT to take account, if asked to do so during a hearing, of any further maintenance assessment made with respect to the same parties since that which is the subject of the appeal, and of any change in circumstances. From one perspective, given the delays that have dogged the processing of assessments, reviews and appeals, this is a welcome power. However, the new power may have significant resource implications in terms of the time which may have to be taken in determining appeals. Where the CSAT allows an appeal, the tribunal will still be required to remit the matter to a child support officer for implementation (s.20(3) of the 1991 Act). In such circumstances, the parties retain their right to seek a review of or appeal from those later assessments.

Para. 9

This amendment to s.30 of the 1991 Act is an enabling power which permits the CSA to charge a collection fee in specified circumstances. This is designed to deal with those private cases where a court order or maintenance agreement was made before April 1993, and where the parent with care does not receive income support, family credit or DWA. These cases will not now be taken on by the CSA in April 1996 for assessment purposes (see s.18). However, the CSA intends to offer a collection service in such cases, at a date yet to be decided, and this amendment allows the collection fee to be charged in such cases (*10th Report*, Appendix I, Annex D). Regulations made under this power are subject to the affirmative procedure (s.52(2) of the 1991 Act, as amended by Sched. 3, para. 15(a)).

Para. 10

This amendment gives the Secretary of State the power to apply for a liability order to be entered in the register of county court judgments. Even assuming a proper assessment has been made, the CSA has faced particular problems in securing effective enforcement action against self-employed absent parents, as deduction from earnings orders are impossible. It is thought that the threat of an entry in the register of county court judgments may act as an incentive for such absent parents to meet their liabilities, as an entry can result in difficulties in obtaining credit for both personal and business purposes. According to the Minister of State, "Liability orders will not be entered automatically in the register. When a liability order is granted, the absent parent will be warned that consideration will be given to making an application if the absent parent has not made arrangements to meet his liabilities within a reasonable period" (*Hansard*, H.L. Vol. 565, col. 260).

Para. 11

This amendment to s.41 of the 1991 Act relates to the provisions governing the circumstances in which the Secretary of State may retain arrears of maintenance where a higher amount of income support was paid than would have been had the maintenance been paid at the right time. It is intended to make it clear that the provisions apply to cases where it is either the parent with care or the absent partner who receives income support, and to arrears due for periods both before the date on which the assessment was made and later periods (*10th Report*, Appendix I, Annex D).

Para. 12

This apparently innocuous amendment represents a significant concession by the Government. Section 46 of the 1991 Act concerns the reduced benefit direction, or benefit penalty, which may be imposed where a parent with care fails to comply with the obligations under s.6 of that Act. Section 46(5) provides that if the CSO considers that there are no reasonable grounds for the failure to comply, "he may give a reduced benefit direction with respect to the parent". This, of course, imports a degree of discretion into the decision-making process, and requires consideration of the welfare of child under s.2 of the 1991 Act (see Ogus, Barendt and Wikeley, *The Law of Social Security* (4th ed., 1995), p.504).

The effect of this amendment is to preclude the CSO from making a reduced benefit direction "in prescribed circumstances". This amendment was brought forward by the Government in the House of Lords in response to an Opposition amendment (*Hansard*, H.L. Vol. 565, col. 1360). The Government's intention is to introduce regulations exempting parents with care who are disabled, or who have disabled children, from the operation of the benefit penalty. The reduced benefit direction will also be suspended in cases where the parent with care has deductions made from her income support *e.g.* to repay fuel debts (*per* Mr A. Mitchell, Parliamentary Under-Secretary of State for Social Security, *Hansard*, H.C. Vol. 263, col. 1350). It was also indicated that there is an official working party examining the requirement to co-operate and the process of implementing reduced benefit directions.

Para. 13

This amendment to s.47 of the 1991 Act allows fees to be charged in advance. As it is, fees have been suspended for two years from April 1995 (see the Child Support and Income Support (Amendment) Regulations 1995 (S.I. 1995 No. 1045), reg. 20).

Para. 14

This amendment to s.48 of the 1991 Act makes it clear that rights of audience, *e.g.* to conduct or defend proceedings in magistrates courts relating to child support matters, may only be conferred on departmental staff.

Para. 18

This amendment corrects an oversight in the 1991 Act. It makes provision for people attending hearings before a Child Support Commissioner to be paid travelling and other associated expenses (including loss of earnings: Sched. 4, para. 2A(2) of the 1991 Act). This brings the child support legislation in line with the mainstream social security provisions (SSAA 1992, Sched. 2, para. 7). However, the Social Security Commissioners have no power to make an award of costs, *e.g.* to cover legal expenses, in respect of hearings before them (*R(FC) 2/90*), and by analogy the same principle must apply to the Child Support Commissioners, who are the same individuals exercising a different jurisdiction.

INDEX

References are to sections and Schedules

CRIMINAL APPEAL ACT 1995*

(1995 c. 35)

---

*Annotations by Gary Scanlan, Senior Lecturer in Law, City University.

An Act to amend provisions relating to appeals and references to the Court of Appeal in criminal cases; to establish a Criminal Cases Review Commission and confer functions on, and make other provision in relation to, the Commission; to amend section 142 of the Magistrates' Courts Act 1980 and introduce in Northern Ireland provision similar to those of that section; to amend section 133 of the Criminal Justice Act 1988; and for connected purposes.

[19th July 1995]

PARLIAMENTARY DEBATES
Hansard, H.C. Vol. 256, col. 23, Vol. 258, col. 860, Vol. 263, col. 1352. H.L. Vol. 563, col. 1030, Vol. 564, cols. 298, 1470, 1519, 1591, Vol. 565, cols. 530, 942, Vol. 566, col. 186.

INTRODUCTION AND GENERAL NOTE
The Secretary of State for the Home Department (Mr Michael Howard), in introducing the Criminal Appeal Bill for its second reading on March 6, 1995, emphasised the importance of the Bill in the context of recent legislation relating to criminal justice. The Bill was intended, he said, to create "new and independent arrangements for identifying possible miscarriages of justice, and it will reinforce and extend the powers of the courts in criminal appeals. In so doing it implements some of the key recommendations made by the Royal Commission on Criminal Justice in July 1993".

The Bill is in four parts. Part I clarifies and strengthens the powers of the respective Courts of Appeal in England and Wales and in Northern Ireland. Part II establishes the new criminal cases review commission. Part III extends the powers of magistrates' courts to reopen cases and to rectify mistakes. Part IV is supplemental.

ABBREVIATIONS
    The 1968 Act : Criminal Appeal Act 1968.
    The 1980 Act : Criminal Appeal (Northern Ireland) Act 1980.
    The 1988 Act : Criminal Justice Act 1988.

PART I

THE COURT OF APPEAL

Leave to appeal etc.

1.—(1) In the Criminal Appeal Act 1968 ("the 1968 Act"), in section 1 (appeal against conviction), for subsection (2) (requirement of leave to appeal or certificate of trial judge unless appeal involves question of law only) substitute—
    "(2) An appeal under this section lies only—
      (a) with the leave of the Court of Appeal; or
      (b) if the judge of the court of trial grants a certificate that the case is fit for appeal."

(2) In the Criminal Appeal (Northern Ireland) Act 1980 ("the 1980 Act"), in section 1 (appeal against conviction subject to requirement of leave to appeal or certificate of trial judge unless appeal involves question of law only), for the words from "conviction" to the end substitute "conviction—
    (a) with the leave of Court; or
    (b) if the judge of the court of trial grants a certificate that the case is fit for appeal."

(3) In section 12 of the 1968 Act (appeal against verdict of not guilty by reason of insanity subject to requirement of leave to appeal or certificate of trial judge unless appeal involves question of law only), for the words from "against the verdict" to the end substitute "against the verdict—
    (a) with the leave of the Court of Appeal; or
    (b) if the judge of the court of trial grants a certificate that the case is fit for appeal."

(4) In section 12(1) of the 1980 Act (appeal against finding of not guilty on ground of insanity subject to requirement of leave to appeal or certificate of trial judge unless appeal involves question of law only), for the words from "against that finding" to the end substitute "to the Court of Appeal against the finding—
    (a) with the leave of the Court; or
    (b) if the judge of the court of trial grants a certificate that the case is fit for appeal."

(5) In section 15 of the 1968 Act (appeal against finding of disability), for subsection (2) (requirement of leave to appeal or certificate of trial judge unless appeal involves question of law only) substitute—
    "(2) An appeal under this section lies only—
    (a) with the leave of the Court of Appeal; or
    (b) if the judge of the court of trial grants a certificate that the case is fit for appeal."

(6) In section 13A of the 1980 Act (appeal against finding of unfitness to be tried), for subsection (2) (requirement of leave to appeal or certificate of trial judge unless appeal involves question of law only) substitute—
    "(2) An appeal under this section lies only—
    (a) with the leave of the Court; or
    (b) if the judge of the court of trial grants a certificate that the case is fit for appeal."

GENERAL NOTE

This section brings appeals against conviction based on questions of law alone into line with other appeals against conviction or sentence. The section now requires such appeals to be brought with leave, unless the trial judge has certified that the case is fit for appeal. Prior to the enactment of this section, appeals against conviction on questions of law alone could be made without leave. By way of contrast, an appeal which involved questions of fact or mixed fact and law always required leave. In essence the section will provide a filter mechanism for appeals on grounds of law alone which are wholly without merit. See the unreported case of *R. v. Tejendersingh* where the appellant sought to argue that an English court could not try him because, although the offence was committed in England, he was a foreigner. With the enactment of this section the Court of Appeal will not be required to consider such appeals without leave being granted.

Similar provision is made in respect of Northern Ireland and in respect of appeals with regard to the finding of insanity or disability.

Grounds for allowing and dismissing appeals

2.—(1) In section 2 of the 1968 Act (disposal of appeal against conviction), for subsection (1) (grounds on which Court of Appeal are to allow or dismiss appeal), including the proviso, substitute—
    "(1) Subject to the provisions of this Act, the Court of Appeal—
    (a) shall allow an appeal against conviction if they think that the conviction is unsafe; and
    (b) shall dismiss such an appeal in any other case."

(2) In section 2 of the 1980 Act (disposal of appeal against conviction), for subsection (1) (grounds on which Court of Appeal is to allow or dismiss appeal), including the proviso, substitute—
"(1) Subject to the provisions of this Act, the Court of Appeal—
(a) shall allow an appeal against conviction if it thinks that the conviction is unsafe; and
(b) shall dismiss such an appeal in any other case."

(3) In section 13 of the 1968 Act (disposal of appeal against verdict of not guilty by reason of insanity), for subsections (1) and (2) (grounds on which Court of Appeal are to allow or dismiss appeal) substitute—
"(1) Subject to the provisions of this section, the Court of Appeal—
(a) shall allow an appeal under section 12 of this Act if they think that the conviction is unsafe; and
(b) shall dismiss such an appeal in any other case."

(4) In section 12 of the 1980 Act (appeal against finding of not guilty on ground of insanity), for subsections (2) and (3) (grounds on which Court of Appeal is to allow or dismiss appeal) substitute—
"(2) Subject to subsection (4) below, the Court—
(a) shall allow an appeal under this section if it thinks that the finding is unsafe; and
(b) shall dismiss such an appeal in any other case."

(5) In section 16 of the 1968 Act (disposal of appeal against finding of disability), for subsection (1) (grounds on which Court of Appeal are to allow or dismiss appeal) substitute—
"(1) The Court of Appeal—
(a) shall allow an appeal under section 15 of this Act against a finding if they think that the finding is unsafe; and
(b) shall dismiss such an appeal in any other case."

(6) In section 13A of the 1980 Act (appeal against finding of unfitness to be tried), for subsection (3) and (4) (grounds on which Court of Appeal is to allow or dismiss appeal) substitute—
"(3) The Court—
(a) shall allow an appeal under this section if it thinks that the finding is unsafe; and
(b) shall dismiss such an appeal in any other case (except one to which subsection (5) below applies)."

GENERAL NOTE

This section requires the Court of Appeal to allow an appeal against conviction where the conviction is unsafe, and to dismiss an appeal in any other case. This new test for granting appeals applies also to appeals against verdicts and findings where the appellant is under a mental disability. This section endorses the proposals of the majority of The Runciman Committee (Chap. 10, paras. 27–34), that the previous multi-faceted grounds of appeal should be replaced by a single broad ground which would give an appellate court flexibility to consider all categories of appeal.

Accordingly, if the court is satisfied on whatever grounds, that the conviction is unsafe, it should allow the appeal outright.

Abolition of references by Secretary of State

3. Section 17 of the 1968 Act and section 14 of the 1980 Act (which provide for references by Secretary of State to Court of Appeal of cases tried on indictment) shall cease to have effect.

GENERAL NOTE

This section abolishes the powers of the Secretary of State to refer cases to the Court of Appeal.

Evidence

4.—(1) In section 23 of the 1968 Act (evidence)—
(a) in subsection (1) (power to receive evidence etc.), for paragraph (c) substitute—
"(c) receive any evidence which was not adduced in the proceedings from which the appeal lies.",
(b) for subsection (2) (duty to receive evidence in certain circumstances) substitute—
"(2) The Court of Appeal shall, in considering whether to receive any evidence, have regard in particular to—
(a) whether the evidence appears to the Court to be capable of belief;
(b) whether it appears to the Court that the evidence may afford any ground for allowing the appeal;
(c) whether the evidence would have been admissible in the proceedings from which the appeal lies on an issue which is the subject of the appeal; and
(d) whether there is a reasonable explanation for the failure to aduce the evidence in those proceedings.", and
(c) in subsection (3), after "any" insert "evidence of a".
(2) In section 25 of the 1980 Act (evidence)—
(a) in subsection (1) (power to receive evidence etc.), for paragraph (c) substitute—
"(c) receive any evidence which was not adduced at the trial.",
(b) for subsection (2) (duty to receive evidence in certain circumstances) substitute—
"(2) The Court of Appeal shall, in considering whether to receive any evidence, have regard in particular to—
(a) whether the evidence appears to the Court to be capable of belief;
(b) whether it appears to the Court that the evidence may afford any ground for allowing the appeal;
(c) whether the evidence would have been admissible at the trial on an issue which is the subject of the appeal; and
(d) whether there is a reasonable explanation for the failure to adduce the evidence at the trial.", and
(c) in subsection (3), after "any" insert "evidence of a".

GENERAL NOTE

This section implements a recommendation of the Royal Commission. Under s.23(2) of the Criminal Appeal Act 1968 (c. 11) (the 1968 Act), the Court of Appeal must under the conditions prescribed therein receive fresh evidence on hearing an appeal. One of the grounds under the above provision which permitted the appellate court to receive fresh evidence was if the court was satisfied that the evidence was likely to be credible. The Royal Commission was of the opinion that this ground was too high a threshold for the admission of fresh evidence. Accordingly the Commission recommended that the test be changed to require the Court of Appeal to hear evidence on appeal if it would be capable of belief. This formula gives the court greater scope for doing justice, providing a lower threshold for the admission of fresh evidence.

The section also deals with the general admissibility of fresh evidence. The Court of Appeal will receive fresh evidence, if, *inter alia*, there is a reasonable explanation for the failure to adduce it at the original trial, or it would have been admissible at the original trial.

Power to order investigations

5.—(1) After section 23 of the 1968 Act insert—

"Power to order investigations

23A.—(1) On an appeal against conviction the Court of Appeal may direct the Criminal Cases Review Commission to investigate and report to the Court on any matter if it appears to the Court that—

    (a) the matter is relevant to the determination of the case and ought, if possible, to be resolved before the case is determined;

    (b) an investigation of the matter by the Commission is likely to result in the Court being able to resolve it; and

    (c) the matter cannot be resolved by the Court without an investigation by the Commission.

(2) A direction by the Court of Appeal under subsection (1) above shall be given in writing and shall specify the matter to be investigated.

(3) Copies of such a direction shall be made available to the appellant and the respondent.

(4) Where the Commission have reported to the Court of Appeal on any matter which they have been directed under subsection (1) above to investigate, the Court—

    (a) shall notify the appellant and the respondent that the Commission have reported; and

    (b) may make available to the appellant and the respondent the report of the Commission and any statements, opinions and reports which accompanied it."

(2) After section 25 of the 1980 Act insert—

"Power to order investigations

25A.—(1) On an appeal against conviction the Court of Appeal may direct the Criminal Cases Review Commission to investigate and report to the Court on any matter if it appears to the court that—

    (a) the matter is relevant to the determination of the case and ought, if possible, to be resolved before the case is determined;

    (b) an investigation of the matter by the Commission is likely to result in the Court being able to resolve it; and

    (c) the matter cannot be resolved by the Court without an investigation by the Commission.

(2) A direction by the Court under subsection (1) above shall be given in writing and shall specify the matter to be investigated.

(3) Copies of such a direction shall be made available to the appellant and the respondent.

(4) Where the Commission have reported to the Court of Appeal on any matter which they have been directed under subsection (1) above to investigate, the Court—

    (a) shall notify the appellant and the respondent that the Commission have reported; and

    (b) may make available to the appellant and the respondent the report of the Commission and any statements, opinions and reports which accompanied it."

General Note

    By this section the Court of Appeal in England and Wales is enabled to commission investigations to be carried out by the Criminal Cases Review Commission (see General Note to s.8). On receiving a direction, the Commission must investigate and report its findings to the court.

    This power is exercisable by the Court of Appeal in England and Wales by virtue of a new s.23A of the Criminal Appeal Act 1968 and in respect of Northern Ireland by a new s.25A of the Criminal Appeal (Northern Ireland) Act 1980 (c. 47), both inserted by s.5 (see also s.15 below).

Powers exercisable by registrar

    6. After section 31 of the 1968 Act insert—

"Powers of Court under Part I which are exercisable by registrar

    31A.—(1) The powers of the Court of Appeal under this Part of this Act which are specified in subsection (2) below may be exercised by the registrar.

    (2) The powers mentioned in subsection (1) above are the following—

(a) to extend the time within which notice of appeal or of application for leave to appeal may be given;
(b) to order a witness to attend for examination; and
(c) to vary the conditions of bail granted to an appellant by the Court of Appeal or the Crown Court.

(3) No variation of the conditions of bail granted to an appellant may be made by the registrar unless he is satisfied that the respondent does not object to the variation; but, subject to that, the powers specified in that subsection are to be exercised by the registrar in the same manner as by the Court of Appeal and subject to the same provisions.

(4) If the registrar refuses an application on the part of an appellant to exercise in his favour any of the powers specified in subsection (2) above, the appellant shall be entitled to have the application determined by a single judge."

GENERAL NOTE

This section enables the Registrar of Criminal Appeals to exercise certain limited powers of the Court of Appeal in England and Wales. The powers exercisable by the Registrar are set out in subs.(2). The section is designed to reduce the burden on the judiciary without compromising the rights of appellants.

Appeals in cases of death

7.—(1) Immediately before section 45 of the 1968 Act insert—

"Appeals in cases of death

44A.—(1) Where a person has died—
(a) any relevant appeal which might have been begun by him had he remained alive may be begun by a person approved by the Court of Appeal; and
(b) where any relevant appeal was begun by him while he was alive or is begun in relation to his case by virtue of paragraph (a) above or by a reference by the Criminal Cases Review Commission, any further step which might have been taken by him in connection with the appeal if he were alive may be taken by a person so approved.

(2) In this section "relevant appeal" means—
(a) an appeal under section 1, 9, 12 or 15 of this Act; or
(b) an appeal under section 33 of this Act from any decision of the Court of Appeal on an appeal under any of those sections.

(3) Approval for the purposes of this section may only be given to—
(a) the widow or widower of the dead person;
(b) a person who is the personal representative (within the meaning of section 55(1)(xi) of the Administration of Estates Act 1925) of the dead person; or
(c) any other person appearing to the Court of Appeal to have, by reason of a family or similar relationship with the dead person, a substantial financial or other interest in the determination of a relevant appeal relating to him.

(4) Except in the case of an appeal begun by a reference by the Criminal Cases Review Commission, an application for such approval may not be made after the end of the period of one year beginning with the date of death.

(5) Where this section applies, any reference in this Act to the appellant shall, where appropriate, be construed as being or including a reference to the person approved under this section.

(6) The power of the Court of Appeal to approve a person under this section may be exercised by a single judge in the same manner as by the Court of appeal and subject to the same provisions; but if the single

judge refuses the application, the applicant shall be entitled to have the application determined by the Court of Appeal."
(2) After section 47 of the 1980 Act insert—

"Appeals in cases of death

47A.—(1) Where a person has died—
    (a) any relevant appeal which might have been begun by him had he remained alive may be begun by a person approved by the Court of Appeal; and
    (b) where any relevant appeal was begun by him while he was alive or is begun in relation to his case by virtue of paragraph (a) above or by a reference by the Criminal Cases Review Commission, any further step which might have been taken by him in connection with the appeal if he were alive may be taken by a person so approved.

(2) In this section "relevant appeal" means—
    (a) an appeal under section 1, 8, 9, 12 or 13A of this Act; or
    (b) an appeal under section 31 of this Act from any decision of the Court of Appeal on an appeal under any of those sections.

(3) Approval for the purposes of this section may only be given to—
    (a) the widow or widower of the dead person;
    (b) a person who is the personal representative (within the meaning of the Wills and Administration Proceedings (Northern Ireland) Order 1994) of the dead person; or
    (c) any other person appearing to the Court of Appeal to have, by reason of a family or similar relationship with the dead person, a substantial financial or other interest in the determination of a relevant appeal relating to him.

(4) Except in the case of an appeal begun by a reference by the Criminal Cases Review Commission, an application for such approval may not be made after the end of the period of one year beginning with the date of death.

(5) Where this section applies, any reference in this Act to the appellant shall, where appropriate, be construed as being or including a reference to the person approved under this section."

GENERAL NOTE
This section makes provision for appeals in the case of the death of a convicted person. It inserts a new s.44A into the 1968 Act and a new s.47A into the 1980 Act on behalf of convicted persons who have died. The section allows the Court of Appeal to approve an application to conduct an appeal on behalf of a dead person if the applicant meets the specified criteria. The time-limits for bringing an appeal under the section should be noted under ss.44A(4) and 47A(4) of the 1968 and 1980 Acts, respectively.
Under s.44A(3)(c) and s.47A(3)(c) of the 1968 and 1980 Acts respectively a party may apply for approval for the purposes of an appeal under either section by reason of a family or similar relationship with the deceased, or a substantial financial interest in the determination of the relevant appeal. This latter requirement or condition was explained by the Parliamentary Under Secretary of State for the Home Department, Mr Nicholas Baker, House of Commons Official Report, Standing Committee B, March 21, 1995, paras. 34–35 in the following vein:
"If a court imposes a financial penalty on a convicted person, and he dies before any appeal against that penalty is determined, the appeal is abated but the effect of the penalty continues to be felt by his widow or surviving family. That is why we are providing an avenue of appeal in such cases for a person such as the dead person's son or daughter, who may be suffering financial hardship and who will therefore have a financial interest in the determination of the appeal.
The inability to challenge a financial penalty in such circumstances was an issue in the case of *R. v. Kearley* (No. 2) [1994] 2 A.C. 414. The House of Lords held that a right of appeal under the Criminal Appeal Act 1968 was personal to the convicted person, and that if he died before the appeal was heard the right of appeal died with him. Kearley was convicted of drug trafficking offences, sentenced to custody and made subject to a confiscation order. He appealed against conviction and sentence. The Court of Appeal reduced the custodial sentence but

upheld the conviction and confiscation order. On further appeal, the House of Lords quashed some of the counts in the indictment and referred the case to the Court of Appeal to consider whether the confiscation order should be varied. Kearley was murdered before the case was relisted.

The House of Lords commented: "the rule that a convicted person's right of appeal abates with his death may lead to injustice if an individual's estate is obliged to suffer a wrongly imposed pecuniary penalty whether by way of a fine, confiscation order or an order for costs, since there exists no procedure for challenging the order and it must be for serious consideration by Parliament whether some machinery to alleviate such possible injustice should not be available".

Part II

The Criminal Cases Review Commission

The Commission

The Commission

8.—(1) There shall be a body corporate to be known as the Criminal Cases Review Commission.

(2) The Commission shall not be regarded as the servant or agent of the Crown or as enjoying any status, immunity or privilege of the Crown; and the Commission's property shall not be regarded as property of, or held on behalf of, the Crown.

(3) The Commission shall consist of not fewer than eleven members.

(4) The members of the Commission shall be appointed by Her Majesty on the recommendation of the Prime Minister.

(5) At least one third of the members of the Commission shall be persons who are legally qualified; and for this purpose a person is legally qualified if—

    (a) he has a ten year general qualification, within the meaning of section 71 of the Courts and Legal Services Act 1990, or

    (b) he is a member of the Bar of Northern Ireland, or solicitor of the Supreme Court of Northern Ireland, of at least ten years' standing.

(6) At least two thirds of the members of the Commission shall be persons who appear to the Prime Minister to have knowledge or experience of any aspect of the criminal justice system and of them at least one shall be a person who appears to him to have knowledge or experience of any aspect of the criminal justice system in Northern Ireland; and for the purposes of this subsection the criminal justice system includes, in particular, the investigation of offences and the treatment of offenders.

(7) Schedule 1 (further provisions with respect to the Commission) shall have effect.

General Note

One of the significant aspects of this Act is the creation of the Criminal Cases Review Commission, the purpose of which is to investigate, and, where appropriate to refer to the courts cases of possible wrongful conviction or sentence. Section 8 establishes this body as a body corporate, independent from the Crown. The section also provides for the appointment of the Commissioners who shall be at least 11 in number. The appointment of a commissioner is by Her Majesty on the recommendation of the Prime Minister. Subsections (5) and (6) determine the specified proportions of the members of the Commission who are to have particular experience or qualifications.

Schedule 1 to the Act makes further provision concerning the appointment and remuneration of members and employees of the Commission and about its decision-making powers. The Commission must submit both reports and accounts to the Secretary of State.

References to court

Cases dealt with on indictment in England and Wales

9.—(1) Where a person has been convicted of an offence on indictment in England and Wales, the Commission—

(a) may at any time refer the conviction to the Court of Appeal, and
(b) (whether or not they refer the conviction) may at any time refer to the Court of Appeal any sentence (not being a sentence fixed by law) imposed on, or in subsequent proceedings relating to, the conviction.

(2) A reference under subsection (1) of a person's conviction shall be treated for all purposes as an appeal by the person under section 1 of the 1968 Act against the conviction.

(3) A reference under subsection (1) of a sentence imposed on, or in subsequent proceedings relating to, a person's conviction on an indictment shall be treated for all purposes as an appeal by the person under section 9 of the 1968 Act against—
(a) the sentence, and
(b) any other sentence (not being a sentence fixed by law) imposed on, or in subseqent proceedings relating to, the conviction or any other conviction on the indictment.

(4) On a reference under subsection (1) of a person's conviction on an indictment the Commission may give notice to the Court of Appeal that any other conviction on the indictment which is specified in the notice is to be treated as referred to the Court of Appeal under subsection (1).

(5) Where a verdict of not guilty by reason of insanity has been returned in England and Wales in the case of a person, the Commission may at any time refer the verdict to the Court of Appeal; and a reference under this subsection shall be treated for all purposes as an appeal by the person under section 12 of the 1968 Act against the verdict.

(6) Where a jury in England and Wales has returned findings that a person is under a disability and that he did the act or made the omission charged against him, the Commission may at any time refer either or both of those findings to the Court of Appeal; and a reference under this subsection shall be treated for all purposes as an appeal by the person under section 15 of the 1968 Act against the finding or findings referred.

GENERAL NOTE
By this section the Criminal Cases Review Commission may refer to the Court of Appeal in England and Wales any conviction or sentence in any case which has been tried on indictment within England and Wales. The Commission may also refer to the Court of Appeal a verdict or finding arrived at any trial on indictment concerning a person suffering from a mental disability. The section further provides that any such reference as noted above must be treated for all purposes as an appeal by the person the subject of the conviction, sentence, verdict or finding.

Cases dealt with on indictment in Northern Ireland

10.—(1) Where a person has been convicted of an offence on indictment in Northern Ireland, the Commission—
(a) may at any time refer the conviction to the Court of Appeal, and
(b) (whether or not they refer the conviction) may at any time refer to the Court of Appeal any sentence (not being a sentence fixed by law) imposed on, or in subsequent proceedings relating to, the conviction.

(2) A reference under subsection (1) of a person's conviction shall be treated for all purposes as an appeal by the person under section 1 of the 1980 Act against the conviction.

(3) A reference under subsection (1) of a sentence imposed on, or in subsequent proceedings relating to, a person's conviction on an indictment shall be treated for all purposes as an appeal by the person under section 8 or 9 (as the case may be) of the 1980 Act against—
(a) the sentence, and
(b) any other sentence (not being a sentence fixed by law) imposed on, or in subsequent proceedings relating to, the conviction or any other conviction on the indictment.

(4) On a reference under subsection (1) of a person's conviction on an indictment the Commission may give notice to the Court of Appeal that any other conviction on the indictment which is specified in the notice is to be treated as referred to the Court of Appeal under subsection (1).

(5) On a reference under subsection (1) the Court of Appeal may not pass any sentence more severe than that passed by the Crown Court.

(6) Where a finding of not guilty on the ground of insanity has been recorded in Northern Ireland in the case of a person, the Commission may at any time refer the finding to the Court of Appeal; and a reference under this subsection shall be treated for all purposes as an appeal by the person under section 12 of the 1980 Act against the finding.

(7) Where a jury in Northern Ireland has returned a finding that a person is unfit to be tried, the Commission may at any time refer the finding to the Court of Appeal; and a reference under this subsection shall be treated for all purposes as an appeal by the person under section 13A of the 1980 Act against the finding.

GENERAL NOTE

By this section the Commission is given corresponding powers to those set out in s.9, noted above, concerning cases tried on indictment in Northern Ireland. The ambit of this section is the same as that of s.9 and will empower the Commission to refer verdicts or findings following trials on indictment relating to a person's mental disability. References in these cases will be made to the Court of Appeal in Northern Ireland.

Cases dealt with summarily in England and Wales

11.—(1) Where a person has been convicted of an offence by a magistrates' court in England and Wales, the Commission—

   (a) may at any time refer the conviction to the Crown Court, and

   (b) (whether or not they refer the conviction) may at any time refer to the Crown Court any sentence imposed on, or in subsequent proceedings relating to, the conviction.

(2) A reference under subsection (1) of a person's conviction shall be treated for all purposes as an appeal by the person under section 108(1) of the Magistrates' Courts Act 1980 against the conviction (whether or not he pleaded guilty).

(3) A reference under subsection (1) of a sentence imposed on, or in subsequent proceedings relating to, a person's conviction shall be treated for all purposes as an appeal by the person under section 108(1) of the Magistrates' Courts Act 1980 against—

   (a) the sentence, and

   (b) any other sentence imposed on, or in subsequent proceedings relating to, the conviction or any related conviction.

(4) On a reference under subsection (1) of a person's conviction the Commission may give notice to the Crown Court that any related conviction which is specified in the notice is to be treated as referred to the Crown Court under subsection (1).

(5) For the purposes of this section convictions are related if they are convictions of the same person by the same court on the same day.

(6) On a reference under this section the Crown Court may not award any punishment more severe than that awarded by the court whose decision is referred.

(7) The Crown Court may grant bail to a person whose conviction or sentence has been referred under this section; and any time during which he is released on bail shall not count as part of any term of imprisonment or detention under his sentence.

GENERAL NOTE
By this section the Commission may refer to the Crown Court any conviction or sentence in any case which has been tried summarily in England and Wales. The section provides for the Crown Court to grant bail, in appropriate cases, to a person who is the subject of a reference.

Cases dealt with summarily in Northern Ireland

12.—(1) Where a person has been convicted of an offence by a magistrates' court in Northern Ireland, the Commission—

(a) may at any time refer the conviction to a county court, and

(b) (whether or not they refer the conviction) may at any time refer to a county court any sentence imposed on, or in subsequent proceedings relating to, the conviction.

(2) A reference under subsection (1) of a person's conviction shall be treated for all purposes as an appeal by the person under Article 140(1) of the Magistrates' Courts (Northern Ireland) Order 1981 against the conviction (whether or not he pleaded guilty).

(3) A reference under subsection (1) of a sentence imposed on, or in subsequent proceedings relating to, a person's conviction shall be treated for all purposes as an appeal by the person under Article 140(1) of the Magistrates' Courts (Northern Ireland) Order 1981 against—

(a) the sentence, and

(b) any other sentence imposed on, or in subsequent proceedings relating to, the conviction or any related conviction.

(4) On a reference under subsection (1) of a person's conviction the Commission may give notice to the county court that any related conviction which is specified in the notice is to be treated as referred to the county court under subsection (1).

(5) For the purposes of this section convictions are related if they are convictions of the same person by the same court on the same day.

(6) On a reference under this section a county court may not award any punishment more severe than that awarded by the court whose decision is referred.

(7) The High Court may grant bail to a person whose conviction or sentence has been referred to a county court under this section; and any time during which he is released on bail shall not count as part of any term of imprisonment or detention under his sentence.

GENERAL NOTE
This section gives the Commission powers which correspond to those which are contained in s.11 (noted above), in respect of cases tried summarily in Northern Ireland. References under s.12 will be made to the county court. Any grant of bail to a person the subject of a reference will be made by the High Court.

Conditions for making of references

13.—(1) A reference of a conviction, verdict, finding or sentence shall not be made under any of sections 9 to 12 unless—

(a) the Commission consider that there is a real possibility that the conviction, verdict, finding or sentence would not be upheld were the reference to be made,

(b) the Commission so consider—

(i) in the case of a conviction, verdict or finding, because of an argument, or evidence, not raised in the proceedings which led to it or on any appeal or application for leave to appeal against it, or

(ii) in the case of a sentence, because of an argument on a point of law, or information, not so raised, and

(c) an appeal against the conviction, verdict, finding or sentence has been determined or leave to appeal against it has been refused.

(2) Nothing in subsection (1)(b)(i) or (c) shall prevent the making of a reference if it appears to the Commission that there are exceptional circumstances which justify making it.

GENERAL NOTE

This section sets out the criteria which must be satisfied before the Criminal Cases Review Commission may refer a conviction, verdict, finding or sentence, to the Court of Appeal in England and Wales. In referring a case the Commission must give reasons for the referral. Where it declines to refer a case, it must inform the applicant of its reasons for so doing (see s.14, below).

The criteria require the raising of new issues whether by way of argument or evidence if a conviction, verdict or finding is to be referred. These issues or matters must not have been raised at any relevant court proceedings. The criteria, however, are seemingly wide enough to permit a referral by the Commission based on new evidence or new argument which is based on matters or issues raised in the relevant court proceedings, but only if the new argument or evidence in the context of the whole case gives rise to a real possibility of the conviction, verdict, finding or sentence not being upheld on appeal. A case could therefore be referred if, *e.g.* incompetent advocacy prevented an important aspect of an applicant's case from being put to the jury at the first instance trial. It would appear that the criterion that there must be a "real possibility" that the conviction, verdict, finding or sentence will not be upheld means that that possibility must be a realistic one and not a mere possibility. This would appear to constitute a stringent criterion.

The Commission may not, unless there are exceptional circumstances, make a referral unless the convicted person has already appealed, or leave has been refused. Exceptional circumstances justifying a referral outside the facts of the above situations would be where evidence in another case or in respect of a co-defendant casts doubt upon the conviction of an individual, though the latter has not appealed against his conviction.

Further provisions about references

14.—(1) A reference of a conviction, verdict, finding or sentence may be made under any of sections 9 to 12 either after an application has been made by or on behalf of the person to whom it relates or without an application having been so made.

(2) In considering whether to make a reference of a conviction, verdict, finding or sentence under any of sections 9 to 12 the Commission shall have regard to—

(a) any application or representations made to the Commission by or on behalf of the person to whom it relates,

(b) any other representations made to the Commission in relation to it, and

(c) any other matters which appear to the Commission to be relevant.

(3) In considering whether to make a reference under section 9 or 10 the Commission may at any time refer any point on which they desire the assistance of the Court of Appeal to that Court for the Court's opinion on it; and on a reference under this subsection the Court of Appeal shall consider the point referred and furnish the Commission with the Court's opinion on the point.

(4) Where the Commission make a reference under any of sections 9 to 12 the Commission shall—

(a) give to the court to which the reference is made a statement of the Commission's reasons for making the reference, and

(b) send a copy of the statement to every person who appears to the Commission to be likely to be a party to any proceedings on the appeal arising from the reference.

(5) Where a reference under any of sections 9 to 12 is treated as an appeal against any conviction, verdict, finding or sentence, the appeal may be on any ground relating to the conviction, verdict, finding or sentence (whether or not the ground is related to any reason given by the Commission for making the reference).

(6) In every case in which—
(a) an application has been made to the Commission by or on behalf of any person for the reference under any of sections 9 to 12 of any conviction, verdict, finding or sentence, but
(b) the Commission decide not to make a reference of the conviction, verdict, finding or sentence,
the Commission shall give a statement of the reasons for the their decision to the person who made the application.

GENERAL NOTE
This section sets out the very wide powers of the Commission to refer a conviction, verdict, finding or sentence under Pt. II of the Act. It also prescribes the matters which the Commission should consider before making a referral. It is supplemental to s.13, above, and reference should be made to the General Note to that section.

Investigations and assistance

Investigations for Court of Appeal

15.—(1) Where a direction is given by the Court of Appeal under section 23A(1) of the 1968 Act or section 25A(1) of the 1980 Act the Commission shall investigate the matter specified in the direction in such manner as the Commission think fit.

(2) Where, in investigating a matter specified in such a direction, it appears to the Commission that—
(a) another matter (a "related matter") which is relevant to the determination of the case by the Court of Appeal ought, if possible, to be resolved before the case is determined by that Court, and
(b) an investigation of the related matter is likely to result in the Court's being able to resolve it,
the Commission may also investigate the related matter.

(3) The Commission shall—
(a) keep the Court of Appeal informed as to the progress of the investigation of any matter specified in a direction under section 23A(1) of the 1968 Act or section 25A(1) of the 1980 Act, and
(b) if they decide to investigate any related matter, notify the Court of Appeal of their decision and keep the Court informed as to the progress of the investigation.

(4) The Commission shall report to the Court of Appeal on the investigation of any matter specified in direction under section 23A(1) of the 1968 Act or section 25A(1) of the 1980 Act when—
(a) they complete the investigation of that matter and of any related matter investigated by them, or
(b) they are directed to do so by the Court of Appeal,
whichever happens first.

(5) A report under subsection (4) shall include details of any inquiries made by or for the Commission in the investigation of the matter specified in the direction or any related matter investigated by them.

(6) Such a report shall be accompanied—
(a) by any statements and opinions received by the Commission in the investigation of the matter specified in the direction or any related matter investigated by them, and
(b) subject to subsection (7), by any reports so received.

(7) Such a report need not be accompanied by any reports submitted to the Commission under section 20(6) by an investigating officer.

GENERAL NOTE
This section provides for the Criminal Cases Review Commission, following a direction by the Court of Appeal in either England and Wales or Northern Ireland, to conduct an investigation on behalf of the particular appellate court. The Commission has full discretion as to the manner in which such an investigation is to be carried out, and may investigate any other matters which it

considers will be likely to resolve the principal investigation. The section also prescribes the procedural matters that the Commission must follow during the investigation such as reporting the progress of any investigation to the relevant Court of Appeal.

Assistance in connection with prerogative of mercy

16.—(1) Where the Secretary of State refers to the Commission any matter which arises in the consideration of whether to recommend the exercise of Her Majesty's prerogative of mercy in relation to a conviction and on which he desires their assistance, the Commission shall—

(a) consider the matter referred, and

(b) give to the Secretary of State a statement of their conclusions on it; and the Secretary of State shall, in considering whether so to recommend, treat the Commission's statement as conclusive of the matter referred.

(2) Where in any case the Commission are of the opinion that the Secretary of State should consider whether to recommend the exercise of Her Majesty's prerogative of mercy in relation to the case they shall give him the reasons for their opinion.

GENERAL NOTE

This section makes provision for the Commission first to consider, and then to give to the Secretary of State, its conclusions on any matter referred to it by the Secretary of State arising out of any consideration of the exercise of the Royal Prerogative of mercy relating to a conviction.

Supplementary powers

Power to obtain documents etc.

17.—(1) This section applies where the Commission believe that a person serving in a public body has possession or control of a document or other material which may assist the Commission in the exercise of any of their functions.

(2) Where it is reasonable to do so, the Commission may require the person who is the appropriate person in relation to the public body—

(a) to produce the document or other material to the Commission or to give the Commission access to it, and

(b) to allow the Commission to take away the document or other material or to make and take away a copy of it in such form as they think appropriate,

and may direct that person that the document or other material must not be destroyed, damaged or altered before the direction is withdrawn by the Commission.

(3) The documents and other material covered by this section include, in particular, any document or other material obtained or created during any investigation or proceedings relating to—

(a) the case in relation to which the Commission's function is being or may be exercised, or

(b) any other case which may be in any way connected with that case (whether or not any function of the Commission could be exercised in relation to that other case).

(4) The duty to comply with a requirement under this section is not affected by any obligation of secrecy or other limitation on disclosure (including any such obligation or limitation imposed by or by virtue of an enactment) which would otherwise prevent the production of the document or other material to the Commission or the giving of access to it to the Commission.

DEFINITIONS

"appropriate person": s.22.

"Public Body": s.22.

GENERAL NOTE
The necessity to preserve evidence relevant to the Commission's investigations, or its considerations as to whether to make a referral, requires the Commission to have the ability to acquire evidence which is in the hands of third parties and which is documentary in form. Under s.17 the Commission is empowered to acquire access to documents or other material in the hands of a person serving in a public body, where such documents or materials may assist the Commission in carrying out its functions (note the documents and materials excluded from this section by s.18 noted below).

Government documents etc. relating to current or old cases

18.—(1) Section 17 does not apply to any document or other material in the possession or control of a person serving in a government department if the document or other material—

(a) is relevant to a case to which this subsection applies, and

(b) is in the possession or control of the person in consequence of the Secretary of State's consideration of the case.

(2) Subsection (1) applies to a case if the Secretary of State—

(a) is, immediately before the day on which the repeal by this Act of section 17 of the 1968 Act or of section 14 of the 1980 Act comes into force, considering the case with a view to deciding whether to make a reference under that section or whether to recommend the exercise of Her Majesty's prerogative of mercy in relation to a conviction by a magistrates' court, or

(b) has at any earlier time considered the case with a view to deciding whether to make such a reference or whether so to recommend.

(3) The Secretary of State shall give to the Commission any document or other material which—

(a) contains representations made to him in relation to any case to which this subsection applies, or

(b) was received by him in connection with any such case otherwise than from a person serving in a government department,

and may give to the Commission any document or other material which is relevant to any such case but does not fall within paragraph (a) or (b).

(4) Subsection (3) applies to a case if—

(a) the Secretary of State is, immediately before the day on which the repeal by this Act of section 17 of the 1968 Act or of section 14 of the 1980 Act comes into force, considering the case with a view to deciding whether to make a reference under that section or whether to recommend the exercise of Her Majesty's prerogative of mercy in relation to a conviction by a magistrates' court, or

(b) the Secretary of State has at any earlier time considered the case with a view to deciding whether to make such a reference, or whether so to recommend, and the Commission at any time notify him that they wish subsection (3) to apply to the case.

GENERAL NOTE
On the coming into force of the 1995 Act the Secretary of State will no longer be able to make a reference to the Courts of Appeal in either England and Wales or Northern Ireland. However, outstanding references will remain following the coming into force of the 1995 Act. In such cases s.18 provides that s.17 above relating to the power of the Commission to obtain documents and materials in carrying out of its functions, will not apply to documents and materials in the possession of the Secretary of State in connection with a reference by him to the Court of Appeal. However, documents or materials in possession of the Secretary of State which contain representations by him in relation to a case covered by s.18 or which was received by him otherwise than from a person serving in a government department must be surrendered to the Commission in the circumstances prescribed under s.18(4).

Power to require appointment of investigating officers

19.—(1) Where the Commission believe that inquiries should be made for assisting them in the exercise of any of their functions in relation to any case they may require the appointment of an investigating officer to carry out the inquiries.

(2) Where any offence to which the case relates was investigated by persons serving in public body, a requirement under this section may be imposed—

(a) on the person who is the appropriate person in relation to the public body, or

(b) where the public body has ceased to exist, on any chief officer of police or on the person who is the appropriate person in relation to any public body which appears to the Commission to have functions which consist of or include functions similar to any of those of the public body which has ceased to exist.

(3) Where no offence to which the case relates was investigated by persons serving in a public body, a requirement under this section may be imposed on any chief officer of police.

(4) A requirement under this section imposed on a chief officer of police may be—

(a) a requirement to appoint a person serving in the police force in relation to which he is the chief officer of police, or

(b) a requirement to appoint a person serving in another police force selected by the chief officer.

(5) A requirement under this section imposed on a person who is the appropriate person in relation to a public body other than a police force may be—

(a) a requirement to appoint a person serving in the public body, or

(b) a requirement to appoint a person serving in a police force, or in a public body (other than a police force) having functions which consist of or include the investigation of offences, selected by the appropriate person.

(6) The Commission may direct—

(a) that a person shall not be appointed, or

(b) that a police force or other public body shall not be selected,

under subsection (4) or (5) without the approval of the Commission.

(7) Where an appointment is made under this section by the person who is the appropriate person in relation to any public body, that person shall inform the Commission of the appointment; and if the Commission are not satisfied with the person appointed they may direct that—

(a) the person who is the appropriate person in relation to the public body shall, as soon as is reasonably practicable, select another person in his place and notify the Commission of the proposal to appoint the other person, and

(b) the other person shall not be appointed without the approval of the Commission.

DEFINITIONS

"appropriate person": s.22.
"police force": s.22.
"Public Body": s.22.

GENERAL NOTE

The Commission in carrying out its functions is empowered by this section to appoint investigating officers. These officers, usually senior police officers, are authorised to conduct inquiries with the object of assisting the Commission in carrying out its function in relation to any case. The Commission may stipulate that an investigating officer be someone from a public body, usually a police force, other than from the body which originally investigated the relevant offence, which resulted in the conviction, verdict, finding, or sentence and which is the subject matter of the Commission's consideration. Where no public body investigated the relevant offence the Commission may appoint a chief officer of police, who may himself appoint an investigating officer. The Commission or any commissioner investigating the possible miscarriage of justice retains full control over the investigations and the investigating officer. The Commission may direct what inquiries should be made and may if necessary supervise the investigation (see s.20 below). The Commission may order further inquiries to be made, the investigating officer must report back to the Commission or a commissioner regarding the result of his investigation.

Inquiries by investigating officers

20.—(1) A person appointed as the investigating officer in relation to a case shall undertake such inquiries as the Commission may from time to time reasonably direct him to undertake in relation to the case.

(2) A person appointed as an investigating officer shall be permitted to act as such by the person who is the appropriate person in relation to the public body in which he is serving.

(3) Where the chief officer of an England and Wales police force appoints a member of the Royal Ulster Constabulary as an investigating officer, the member appointed shall have in England and Wales the same powers and privileges as a member of the police force has there as a constable; and where the Chief Constable of the Royal Ulster Constabulary appoints a member of an England and Wales police force as an investigating officer, the member appointed shall have in Northern Ireland the same powers and privileges as a member of the Royal Ulster Constabulary has there as a constable.

(4) The Commission may take any steps which they consider appropriate for supervising the undertaking of inquiries by an investigating officer.

(5) The Commission may at any time direct that a person appointed as the investigating officer in relation to a case shall cease to act as such; but the making of such a direction shall not prevent the Commission from imposing a requirement under section 19 to appoint another investigating officer in relation to the case.

(6) When a person appointed as the investigating officer in relation to a case has completed the inquiries which he has been directed by the Commission to undertake in relation to the case, he shall—

(a) prepare a report of his findings,
(b) submit it to the Commission, and
(c) send a copy of it to the person by whom he was appointed.

(7) When a person appointed as the investigting officer in relation to a case submits to the Commission a report of his findings he shall also submit to them any statements, opinions and reports received by him in connection with the inquiries which he was directed to undertake in relation to the case.

DEFINITIONS
    "chief officer of police": s.22.
    "police force": s.22.

GENERAL NOTE
    This section is supplementary to s.19. It makes provision for the Commission to direct and supervise any investigation carried out by an investigating officer under s.19. The investigating officer is under an obligation to report his findings to the Commission and to any person appointing him (see also s.19(3) and (4) above).

Other powers

21.—(1) Sections 17 to 20 are without prejudice to the taking by the Commission of any steps which they consider appropriate for assisting them in the exercise of any of their functions including, in particular—

(a) undertaking, or arranging for others to undertake, inquiries, and
(b) obtaining, or arranging for others to obtain, statements, opinions and reports.

GENERAL NOTE

This section provides that notwithstanding the extensive powers given to the Commission to obtain evidence or conduct investigations in connection with the exercising of its functions under ss.17–20, these latter provisions do not preclude the Commission from a general power to obtain opinions, or to commission reports, or to take any other steps to assist itself in the exercise of its functions.

Meaning of "public body" etc

22.—(1) In sections 17, 19 and 20 and this section "public body" means—
(a) any police force,
(b) any government department, local authority or other body constituted for purposes of the public service, local government or the administration of justice, or
(c) any other body whose members are appointed by Her Majesty, any Minister or any government department or whose revenues consist wholly or mainly of money provided by Parliament or appropriated by Measure of the Northern Ireland Assembly.
(2) In sections 19 and 20 and this section—
(a) "police force" includes the Royal Ulster Constabulary and the Royal Ulster Constabulary Reserve and any body of constables maintained otherwise than by a police authority,
(b) references to the chief officer of police, in relation to the Royal Ulster Constabulary and the Royal Ulster Constabulary Reserve, are to the Chief Constable of the Constabulary and, in relation to a police force maintained otherwise than by a police authority, are to the chief constable, and
(c) references to an England and Wales police force are to a police force maintained under section 2 of the Police Act 1964, the metropolitan police force or the City of London police force.
(3) In section 18 and this section—
(a) references to a government department include a Northern Ireland department and the Office of the Director of Public Prosecutions for Northern Ireland, and
(b) "Minister" means a Minister of the Crown as defined by section 8 of the Ministers of the Crown Act 1975 but also includes the head of a Northern Ireland department.
(4) In sections 17, 19 and 20 "the appropriate person" means—
(a) in relation to a police force, the chief officer of police,
(b) in relation to the Crown Prosecution Service, the Director of Public Prosecutions,
(c) in relation to the Office of the Director of Public Prosecutions for Northern Ireland, that Director,
(d) in relation to the Serious Fraud Office, the Director of the Serious Fraud Office,
(e) in relation to the Inland Revenue, the Commisioners of Inland Revenue,
(f) in relation to the Customs and Excise, the Commissioners of Customs and Excise,
(g) in relation to any government department not within any of the preceding paragraphs, the Minister in charge of the department, and
(h) in relation to any public body not within any of the preceding paragraphs, the public body itself (if it is a body corporate) or the person in charge of the public body (if it is not).

(5) For the purposes of sections 17, 19 and 20—
(a) a justices' chief executive or justices' clerk appointed by, or a member of the staff of, a magistrates' courts committee shall be treated as serving in the committee, and
(b) a person authorised under section 57 of the Northern Ireland (Emergency Provisions) Act 1991 to exercise the powers conferred by Schedule 5 to that Act shall be treated as if he were serving in a public body and he were the appropriate person in relation to the body.

GENERAL NOTE
This section is a general definition section for ss.17–20 of the Act (see General Notes to the appropriate sections for commentary).

Disclosure of information

Offence of disclosure

23.—(1) A person who is or has been a member or employee of the Commission shall not disclose any information obtained by the Commission in the exercise of any of their functions unless the disclosure of the information is excepted from this section by section 24.
(2) A person who is or has been an investigating officer shall not disclose any information obtained by him in his inquiries unless the disclosure of the information is excepted from this section by section 24.
(3) A member of the Commission shall not authorise—
(a) the disclosure by an employee of the Commission of any information obtained by the Commission in the exercise of any of their functions, or
(b) the disclosure by an investigating office of any information obtained by him in his inquiries,
unless the authorisation of the disclosure of the information is excepted from this section by section 24.
(4) A person who contravenes this section is guilty of an offence and liable on summary conviction to a fine of an amount not exceeding level 5 on the standard scale.

GENERAL NOTE
Confidentiality in the carrying out of the Commission's functions will be necessary in many cases to protect both the applicant and third parties from publicity. Section 23 therefore provides that it is an offence for a member of the Commission, an employee of the Commission or a current or former investigating officer, to disclose any information obtained in connection with their involvement with the Commission. The section does, however, provide that it is lawful to disclose information so obtained in accordance with the terms of s.24 below. A Commissioner may not authorise an employee or investigating officer (presumably this term includes a former investigating officer) to disclose any information obtained as a result of involvement with the Commission's functions except in accordance with the terms of s.24.

Exceptions from obligations of non-disclosure

24.—(1) The disclosure of information, or the authorisation of the disclosure of information, is excepted from section 23 by this section if the information is disclosed, or is authorised to be disclosed—
(a) for the purposes of any criminal, disciplinary or civil proceedings,
(b) in order to assist in dealing with an application made to the Secretary of State for compensation for a miscarriage of justice,
(c) by a person who is a member or an employee of the Commission either to another person who is a member or an employee of the Commission or to an investigating officer,
(d) by an investigating officer to a member or an employee of the Commission,
(e) in any statement or report required by this Act,

(f) in or in connection with the exercise of any function under this Act, or

(g) in any circumstances in which the disclosure of information is permitted by an order made by the Secretary of State.

(2) The disclosure of information is also excepted from section 23 by this section if the information is disclosed by an employee of the Commission, or an investigating officer, who is authorised to disclose the information by a member of the Commission.

(3) The disclosure of information, or the authorisation of the disclosure of information, is also excepted from section 23 by this section if the information is disclosed, or is authorised to be disclosed, for the purposes of—

(a) the investigation of an offence, or

(b) deciding whether to prosecute a person for an offence,

unless the disclosure is or would be prevented by an obligation of secrecy or other limitation on disclosure (including any such obligation or limitation imposed by or by virtue of an enactment) arising otherwise than under that section.

(4) Where the disclosure of information is excepted from section 23 by subsection (1) or (2), the disclosure of the information is not prevented by any obligation of secrecy or other limitation on disclosure (including any such obligation or limitation imposed by or by virtue of an enactment) arising otherwise than under that section.

(5) The power to make an order under subsection (1)(g) is exercisable by statutory instrument which shall be subject to annulment in pursuance of a resolution of either House of Parliament.

GENERAL NOTE

This section enables the Commission, and any investigating officer to disclose, if the circumstances specified in the section are satisfied, information which would otherwise be subject to an obligation of secrecy. The disclosure or authorisation to disclose is also excepted from s.23 if the information is disclosed by an employee or investigating officer for the purposes of investigation of an offence, or in deciding whether to prosecute, unless the disclosure is prohibited by any provision in an enactment other than the 1995 Act.

Note that the Secretary of State is empowered by order to prescribe additional circumstances where disclosure of information may be permitted under s.24.

Consent to disclosure

25.—(1) Where a person on whom a requirement is imposed under section 17 notifies the Commission that any information contained in any document or other material to which the requirement relates is not to be disclosed by the Commission without his prior consent, the Commission shall not disclose the information without such consent.

(2) Such consent may not be withheld unless—

(a) (apart from section 17) the person would have been prevented by any obligation of secrecy or other limitation on disclosure from disclosure the information to the Commission, and

(b) it is reasonable for the person to withhold his consent to disclosure of the information by the Commission.

(3) An obligation of secrecy or other limitation on disclosure which applies to a person only where disclosure is not authorised by another person shall not be taken for the purposes of subsection (2)(a) to prevent the disclosure by the person of information to the Commission unless—

(a) reasonable steps have been taken to obtain the authorisation of the other person, or

(b) such authorisation could not reasonably be expected to be obtained.

GENERAL NOTE

This section provides that in the circumstances prescribed by the section a person who supplies information, documents or materials, to the Commission can require the Commission not to disclose any such matters unless they consent to such disclosure.

PART III

OTHER PROVISIONS

Powers of magistrates' courts to rectify mistakes

Extension of power of courts in England and Wales

26.—(1) Section 142 of the Magistrates' Courts Act 1980 (power of magistrates' courts to re-open cases to rectify mistakes etc.) shall be amended as follows.

(2) In subsection (1) (power, subject to subsection (4), to vary or rescind a sentence or other order), for the words from the beginning to "offender;" substitute "A magistrates' court may vary or rescind a sentence or other order imposed or made by it when dealing with an offender if it appears to the court to be in the interests of justice to do so;".

(3) After that subsection insert—

"(1A) The power conferred on a magistrates' court by subsection (1) above shall not be exercisable in relation to any sentence or order imposed or made by it when dealing with an offender if—
    (a) the Crown Court has determined an appeal against—
        (i) that sentence or order;
        (ii) the conviction in respect of which that sentence or order was imposed or made; or
        (iii) any other sentence or order imposed or made by the magistrates' court when dealing with the offender in respect of that conviction (including a sentence or order replaced by that sentence or order; or
    (b) the High Court has determined a case stated for the opinion of that court on any question arising in any proceeding leading to or resulting from the imposition or making of the sentence or order."

(4) In subsection (2) (power, subject to subsection (4), to direct that a person's case be re-heard by different justices where he pleaded not guilty or the court proceeded in his absence)—
    (a) for the words from "found guilty" to "section 11(1) above," substitute "convicted by a magistrates' court", and
    (b) omit ", subject to subsection (4) below,".

(5) After that subsection insert—

"(2A) The power conferred on a magistrates' court by subsection (2) above shall not be exercisable in relation to a conviction if—
    (a) the Crown Court has determined an appeal against—
        (i) the conviction; or
        (ii) any sentence or order imposed or made by the magistrates' court when dealing with the offender in respect of the conviction; or
    (b) the High Court has determined a case stated for the opinion of that court on any question arising in any proceeding leading to or resulting from the conviction."

(6) In subsection (3) (effect of directions under subsection (2)), for "finding of guilty" substitute "conviction".

(7) Omit subsection (4) (powers in subsection (1) and (2) to be exercisable only within 28 days of making of sentence or order or finding of guilty and only by similarly constituted court).

GENERAL NOTE

This section enables magistrates' courts, under s.142 of the Magistrates' Courts Act 1980 (c. 43), to reopen a case in order to rectify mistakes and to correct a miscarriage of justice. This power may be exercised by a magistrates' court irrespective of the plea made by the defendant at the relevant proceedings. The court may accordingly vary, rescind, or replace a sentence so imposed at those proceedings where it appears to be in the interests of justice.

Introduction of power in Northern Ireland

27.—(1) After Article 158 of the Magistrates' Courts (Northern Ireland) Order 1981 insert—

"Power to rectify mistakes etc.

Power of magistrates' court to re-open cases to rectify mistakes etc.

158A.—(1) A magistrates' court may vary or rescind a sentence or other order imposed or made by it when dealing with an offender if it appears to the court to be in the interests of justice to do so; and it is hereby declared that this power extends to replacing a sentence or order which for any reason appears to be invalid by another which the court has power to impose or make.

(2) The power conferred on a magistrates' court by paragraph (1) shall not be exercisable in relation to any sentence or order imposed or made by it when dealing with an offender if—

    (a) the county court has determined an appeal against—
        (i) that sentence or order;
        (ii) the conviction in respect of which that sentence or order was imposed or made; or
        (iii) any other sentence or order imposed or made by the magistrates' court when dealing with the offender in respect of that conviction (including a sentence or order replaced by that sentence or order); or
    (b) the Court of Appeal has determined a case stated for the opinion of that court on any question arising in any proceeding leading to or resulting from the imposition or making of the sentence or order.

(3) Where a person is convicted by magistrates' court and it subsequently appears to the court that it would be in the interests of justice that the case should be heard again by another resident magistrate or another justice of the peace (as the case may be), the court may so direct.

(4) The power conferred on a magistrates' court by paragraph (3) shall not be exercisable in relation to a conviction if—

    (a) the county court has determined an appeal against—
        (i) the conviction; or
        (ii) any sentence or order imposed or made by the magistrates' court when dealing with the offender in respect of the conviction; or
    (b) the Court of Appeal has determined a case stated for the opinion of that court on any question arising in any proceeding leading to or resulting from the conviction.

(5) Where a court gives a direction under paragraph (3)—

    (a) the conviction and any sentence or other order imposed or made in consequence of it shall be of no effect; and
    (b) Article 47 shall apply as if the trial of the person in question had been adjourned.

(6) Where a sentence or order is varied under paragraph (1), the sentence or other order, as so varied, shall take effect from the beginning of the day on which it was originally imposed or made, unless the court otherwise directs."

GENERAL NOTE

This section gives the magistrates' courts in Northern Ireland, the equivalent powers of magistrates' courts in England and Wales contained in s.142 of the Magistrates' Courts Act 1980, as amended by s.26 above.

Compensation for miscarriages of justice

Assessment of compensation

28. In section 133 of the Criminal Justice Act 1988 (compensation for miscarriages of justice), after subsection (4) insert—

"(4A) In assessing so much of any compensation payable under this section to or in respect of a person as is attributable to suffering, harm to reputation or similar damage, the assessor shall have regard in particular to—

(a) the seriousness of the offence of which the person was convicted and the severity of the punishment resulting from the conviction;

(b) the conduct of the investigation and prosecution of the offence; and

(c) any other convictions of the person and any punishment resulting from them."

GENERAL NOTE

Section 133 of the Criminal Justice Act 1988 provides for compensation to be paid to the victims of miscarriages of justice. By s.133(4) of the 1988 Act if the Secretary of State determines that there is a right to such compensation, the amount of that compensation shall be assessed by an assessor appointed by the Secretary of State. Section 28 of the 1995 Act inserts a new subs. (4A) into s.133 of the 1988 Act. It sets out the criteria to be adopted in the assessment of compensation for a miscarriage of justice in so far as the compensation payable under s.133 of 1988 Act relates to the suffering of harm to the reputation, or similar damage, of the person the victim of the miscarriage of justice. The criteria are not, however, exhaustive. The assessor is only required to have particular regard to the matters prescribed in subs. (4A) when making an assessment of compensation relating to damage to reputation or similar damage.

PART IV

SUPPLEMENTARY

Minor and consequential amendments and repeals

29.—(1) Schedule 2 (minor and consequential amendments) shall have effect.

(2) The enactments specified in Schedule 3 (which include spent provisions) are repealed to the extent specified in the third column of that Schedule.

Interpretation

30.—(1) In this Act—

"the 1968 Act" means the Criminal Appeal Act 1968,

"the 1980 Act" means the Criminal Appeal (Northern Ireland) Act 1980,

"the Commission" means the Criminal Cases Review Commission,

"enactment" includes an enactment comprised in Northern Ireland legislation, and

"investigating officer" means a person appointed under section 19 to carry out inquiries.

(2) In this Act "sentence"—

(a) in section 9 has the same meaning as in the 1968 Act,

(b) in section 10 has the same meaning as in Part I of the 1980 Act,

(c) in section 11 has the same meaning as in section 108 of the Magistrates' Courts Act 1980, and

(d) in section 12 has the same meaning as in Article 140(1) of the Magistrates' Courts (Northern Ireland) Order 1981.

Financial provision

31.—(1) There shall be paid out of money provided by Parliament—

(a) any expenditure of the Secretary of State incurred in connection with the Commission, and

(b) any increase attributable to this Act in the sums payable under any other Act out of money so provided.

(2) Any sums received by the Treasury under or by virtue of this Act (so far as not used as an appropriation in aid) shall be paid into the Consolidated Fund.

Commencement

32.—(1) This Act shall come into force on such day as the Secretary of State may by order made by statutory instrument appoint; and different days may be appointed for different provisions or for different purposes.

(2) An order under subsection (1) may include such transitional provisions and savings as appear to the Secretary of State to be necessary or desirable.

Extent

33.—(1) The provisions of Part I and III and of Schedules 2 and 3 have the same extent as the enactments which they amend or repeal.

(2) Section 8 and Schedule 1 and sections 13 to 25 extend only to England and Wales and Northern Ireland.

(3) Sections 9 and 11 extend only to England and Wales.

(4) Sections 10 and 12 extend only to Northern Ireland.

Short title

34. This Act may be cited as the Criminal Appeal Act 1995.

SCHEDULES

Section 8   SCHEDULE I

THE COMMISSION: FURTHER PROVISIONS

Membership

1. Her Majesty shall, on the recommendation of the Prime Minister, appoint one of the members of the Commission to be the chairman of the Commission.

2.—(1) Subject to the following provisions of this paragraph, a person shall hold and vacate office as a member of the Commission, or as chairman of the Commission, in accordance with the terms of his appointment.

(2) An appointment as a member of the Commission may be full-time or part-time.

(3) The appointment of a person as a member of the Commission, or as chairman of the Commission, shall be for a fixed period of not longer than five years.

(4) Subject to sub-paragraph (5), a person whose term of appointment as a member of the Commission, or as chairman of the Commission, expires shall be eligible for re-appointment.

(5) No person may hold office as a member of the Commission for a continuous period which is longer than ten years.

(6) A person may at any time resign his office as a member of the Commission, or as a chairman of the Commission, by notice in writing addressed to her Majesty.

(7) Her Majesty may at any time remove a person from office as a member of the Commission if satisfied—

(a) that he has without reasonable excuse failed to discharge his functions as a member for a continuous period of three months beginning not earlier than six months before that time,

(b) that he has been convicted of a criminal offence,

(c) that a bankruptcy order has been made against him, or his estate has been sequestrated or he has made a composition or arrangement with, or granted a trust deed for, his creditors, or

(d) that he is unable or unfit to discharge his functions as a member.

(8) If the chairman of the Commission ceases to be a member of the Commission he shall also cease to be chairman.

Members and employees

3.—(1) The Commission shall—

(a) pay to members of the Commission such remuneration,

(b) pay to or in respect of members of the Commission any such allowances, fees, expenses and gratuities, and

(c) pay towards the provision of pensions to or in respect of members of the Commission any such sums,

as the Commission are required to pay by or in accordance with directions given by the Secretary of State.

(2) Where a member of the Commission was, immediately before becoming a member, a participant in a scheme under section 1 of the Superannuation Act 1972, the Minister for the Civil Service may determine that his term of office as a member shall be treated for the purposes of the scheme as if it were service in the employment or office by reference to which he was a participant in the scheme; and his rights under the scheme shall not be affected by sub-paragraph (1)(c).

(3) Where—

(a) a person ceases to hold office as a member of the Commission otherwise than on the expiry of this term of appointment, and

(b) it appears to the Secretary of State that there are special circumstances which make it right for him to receive compensation,

the Secretary of State may direct the Commission to make to him a payment of such amount as the Secretary of State may determine.

4.—(1) The Commission may appoint a chief executive and such other employees as the Commission think fit, subject to the consent of the Secretary of State as to their number and terms and conditions of service.

(2) The Commission shall—

(a) pay to employees of the Commission such remuneration, and

(b) pay to or in respect of employees of the Commission any such allowances, fees, expenses and gratuities,

as the Commission may, with the consent of the Secretary of State, determine.

(3) Employment by the Commisssion shall be included among the kinds of employment to which a scheme under section 1 of the Superannuation Act 1972 may apply.

5. The Commission shall pay to the Minister for the Civil Service, at such times as he may direct, such sums as he may determine in respect of any increase attributable to paragraph 3(2) or 4(3) in the sums payable out of money provided by Parliament under the Superannuation Act 1972.

Procedure

6.—(1) The arrangement for the procedure of the Commission (including the quorum for meetings) shall be such as the Commission may determine.

(2) The arrangements may provide for the discharge, under the general direction of the Commission, of any function of the Commission—

(a) in the case of a function specified in sub-paragraph (3), by a committee consisting of not fewer than three members of the Commission, and

(b) in any other case, by any committee of, or by one or more of the members or employees of, the Commission.

(3) The functions referred to in sub-paragraph (2)(a) are—

(a) making a reference to a court under any of sections 9 to 12,

(b) reporting to the Court of Appeal under section 15(4),

(c) giving to the Secretary of State a statement under section 16(1)(b), and

(d) requiring the appointment of an investigating officer under section 19.

(4) The validity of any proceedings of the Commission (or of any committee of the Commission) shall not be affected by—

(a) any vacancy among the members of the Commission or in the office of chairman of the Commission, or

(b) any defect in the appointment of any person as a member of the Commission or as chairman of the Commission.

(5) Where—

(a) a document or other material has been produced to the Commission under section 17, or they have been given access to a document or other material under that section, and the Commission have taken away the document or other material (or a copy of it), and

(b) the person who produced the document or other material to the Commission, or gave them access to it, has notified the Commission that he considers that its disclosure to others may be contrary to the interests of national security,

the Commission shall, after consulting that person, deal with the document or material (or copy) in a manner appropriate for safeguarding the interests of national security.

Evidence

7. A document purporting to be—

(a) duly executed under the seal of the Commission, or

(b) signed on behalf of the Commission,

shall be received in evidence and, unless the contrary is proved, taken to be so executed or signed.

Annual reports and accounts

8.—(1) As soon as possible after the end of each financial year of the Commission, the Commission shall send to the Secretary of State a report on the discharge of their functions during that year.

(2) Such a report may include an account of the working of the provisions of sections 9 to 25 and recommendations relating to any of those provisions.

(3) The Secretary of State shall lay before each House of Parliament, and cause to be published, a copy of every report sent to him under sub-paragraph (1).

9.—(1) The Commission shall—

(a) keep proper accounts and proper records in relation to the accounts, and

(b) prepare a statement of accounts in respect of each financial year of the Commission.

(2) The statement of accounts shall contain such information and shall be in such form as the Secretary of State may, with the consent of the Treasury, direct.

(3) The Commission shall send a copy of the statement of accounts to the Secretary of State and to the Comptroller and Auditor General within such period after the end of the financial year to which the statement relates as the Secretary of State may direct.

(4) The Comptroller and Auditor General shall—

(a) examine, certify and report on the statement of accounts, and

(b) lay a copy of the statement of accounts and of his report before each House of Parliament.

10. For the purposes of this Schedule the Commission's financial year shall be the period of twelve months ending with 31st March; but the first financial year of the Commission shall be the period beginning with the date of establishment of the Commission and ending with the first 31st March which falls at least six months after that date.

Expenses

11. The Secretary of State shall defray the expenses of the Commission up to such amount as may be approved by him.

Section 29   SCHEDULE 2

<small>MINOR AND CONSEQUENTIAL AMENDMENTS</small>

The Army Act 1955 (c. 18)

1. In section 110 of the Army Act 1955 (powers of confirming officers), for the words from "is under" in subsection (1) to the end of the proviso to that subsection substitute "is unsafe, or by confirming the finding or sentence or referring the finding or sentence (or both) for confirmation to a higher confirming officer."

The Air Force Act 1955 (c. 19)

2. In section 110 of the Air Force Act 1955 (powers of confirming officers), for the words from "is under" in subsection (1) to the end of the proviso to that subsection substitute "is unsafe, or

by confirming the finding or sentence or referring the finding or sentence (or both) for confirmation to higher confirming officer."

The Public Records Act 1958 (c. 51)

3. In the First Schedule to the Public Records Act 1958 (definition of public records), in Part II of the Table at the end of paragraph 3, at the appropriate place insert—
"Criminal Cases Review Commission."

The Criminal Appeal Act 1968 (c. 19)

4.—(1) The Criminal Appeal Act 1968 shall be amended as follows.

(2) In section 5 (disposal of appeal against conviction on special verdict), in subsection (1), for "by a person in whose case" substitute "in a case where".

(3) In section 23 (evidence), in subsections (1) and (4), for the "purposes of" substitute "the purposes of an appeal under".

(4) Inspection 29 (effect of appeal on sentence), in subsection (2)(c), for "by the Secretary of State under section 17 of this Act" substitute "under section 9 of the Criminal Appeal Act 1995".

(5) In section 45 (construction of references to Court of Appeal and single judge)—
(a) in subsection (1) (references to Court of Appeal), after "II" insert "and section 44A", and
(b) in subsection (2) (references to single judge), for "and 44" substitute ", 31A, 44 and 44A".

The Courts-Martial (Appeals) Act 1968 (c. 20)

5.—(1) The Courts-Martial (Appeals) Act 1968 shall be amended as follows.

(2) In section 12 (disposal of appeal against conviction by court-martial), for subsection (1) (grounds on which Courts-Martial Appeal Court are to allow or dismiss appeal), including the proviso, substitute—
"(1) The Appeal Court—
(a) shall allow an appeal against conviction by court-martial if they think that the conviction is unsafe; and
(b) shall dismiss such an appeal in any other case.",
and, in the side-note, for "wrong in law, etc" substitute "unsafe".

(3) In section 28 (evidence)—
(a) in subsection (1) (power to receive evidence etc.), for paragraph (c) substitute—
"(c) receive any evidence which was not adduced at the trial.",
(b) for subsection (2) (duty to receive evidence in certain circumstances) substitute—
"(2) The Appeal Court shall, in considering whether to receive any evidence, have regard in particular to—
(a) whether the evidence appears to the Court to be capable of belief;
(b) whether it appears to the Court that the evidence may afford any ground for allowing the appeal;
(c) whether the evidence would have been admissible at the trial on an issue which is the subject of the appeal; and
(d) whether there is a reasonable explanation for the failure to adduce the evidence at the trial.", and
(c) in subsection (3), after "any" insert "evidence of a".

The Costs in Criminal Cases Act (Northern Ireland) 1968 (c. 10 (N.I.))

6. In section 4 of the Costs in Criminal cases Act (Northern Ireland) 1968 (costs awarded by Court of Appeal), at the end insert—
"(5) Where section 47A of the Criminal Appeal (Northern Ireland) Act 1980 (death of convicted person) applies, any reference in this section to the appellant includes the person approved under that section."

The Superannuation Act 1972 (c. 11)

7. In Schedule 1 to the Superannuation Act 1972 (kinds of employment to which a scheme under section 1 of that Act may apply) at the end of the list of "Royal Commissions and other Commissions" insert—
"Criminal Cases Review Commission."

The Juries Act 1974 (c. 23)

8. In Part I of Schedule 1 to the Juries Act 1974 (persons ineligible for jury service), in Group B, after the entry beginning "Members of the Parole Board" insert—

"Members and employees of the Criminal Cases Review Commission."

The Juries (Northern Ireland) Order 1974 (S.I. 1974/2143 (N.I. 6))

9. In Schedule 2 to the Juries (Northern Ireland) Order 1974 (exemptions from jury service), in the group headed "Persons concerned with administration of justice), at the end insert—
"Members and employees of the Criminal Cases Review Commission."

The House of Commons Disqualification Act 1975 (c. 24)

10. In the House of Commons Disqualification Act 1975, in Part II of Schedule 1 (bodies of which all members are disqualified), at the appropriate place insert—
"The Criminal Cases Review Commission".

The Northern Ireland Assembly Disqualification Act 1975 (c. 25)

11. In the Northern Ireland Assembly Disqualification Act 1975, in Part II of Schedule 1 (bodies of which all members are disqualified), at the appropriate place insert—
"The Criminal Cases Review Commission".

The Criminal Appeal (Northern Ireland) Act 1980 (c. 47)

12.—(1) The Criminal Appeal (Northern Ireland) Act 1980 shall be amended as follows.
(2) In section 16 (notice of appeal or application for leave), in subsection (1), omit "appeal or".
(3) In section 25 (evidence), in subsection (1), after "purposes of" insert "an appeal under".
(4) In section 26 (additional powers of Court), in subsection (1), after "purposes of" insert "an appeal under".
(5) In section 29 (computation of sentence), in subsection (3)(c), for "section 14 of this Act" substitute "section 10 of the Criminal Appeal Act 1995".
(6) In section 45 (powers of the Court of Appeal exercisable by single judge), after subsection (3A) insert—
"(3B) Subject to section 44(4) above, the power of the Court of Appeal to approve a person under section 47A of this Act may be exercised by a single judge of the Court."

The County Courts (Northern Ireland) Order 1980 (S.I. 1980/397 (N.I.3))

13. In Article 28(3) of the County Courts (Northern Ireland) Order 1980 (power of county court to increase punishment on appeal), after "1954" insert "but subject to section 12(6) of the Criminal Appeal Act 1995".

The Supreme Court Act 1981 (c. 54)

14. In section 48 of the Supreme Court Act 1981 (appeals to Crown Court), in subsection (4) (power to award more severe punishment), for "If" substitute "Subject to section 11(6) of the Criminal Appeal Act 1995, if".

The Prosecution of Offences Act 1985 (c. 23)

15. In section 21(1) of the Prosecution of Offences Act 1985 (interpretation of Part II), before the definition of "defendant's costs order" insert—
""accused" and "appellant", in a case where section 44A of the Criminal Appeal Act 1968 (death of convicted person) applies, include the person approved under that section;".

The Criminal Justice Act 1988 (c. 33)

16.—(1) The Criminal Justice Act 1988 shall be amended as follows.
(2) In section 32 (evidence through television links), in subsection (1A) (proceedings where section applies)—
(a) in paragraph (a), for "section 17 of the Criminal Appeal Act 1968" substitute "section 9 of the Criminal Appeal Act 1995", and
(b) in paragraph (b), for "and appeals to the Crown Court arising out of such proceedings" substitute ", appeals to the Crown Court arising out of such proceedings and hearings of references under section 11 of the Criminal Appeal Act 1995 so arising".
(3) In section 32A (video recordings of testimony from child witness), in subsection (1) (proceedings where section applies)—
(a) in paragraph (b), for "section 17 of the Criminal Appeal Act 1968" substitute "section 9 of the Criminal Appeal Act 1995", and
(b) in paragraph (c), for "and appeals to the Crown Court arising out of such proceedings" substitute ", appeals to the Crown Court arising out of such proceedings and hearings of references under section 11 of the criminal Appeal Act 1995 so arising".

(4) In section 133 (compensation for miscarriages of justice), in subsection (5) (meaning of "reversed" in relation to a conviction), in paragraph (b) (references), for sub-paragraph (i) substitute—
> "(i) under the Criminal Appeal Act 1995; or",

and omit sub-paragraph (iii).

The Legal Aid Act 1988 (c. 34)

17. In section 21 of the Legal Aid Act 1988 (availability of representation for the purposes of criminal proceedings), after subsection (10) insert—
> "(10A) Where section 44A of the Criminal Appeal Act 1968 (death of convicted person) applies, the reference in subsection (1) above to the convicted person shall be construed as a reference to the person approved under that section."

The Police and Criminal Evidence (Northern Ireland) Order 1989 (S.I. 1989/1341 (N.I. 12))

18.—(1) The Police and Criminal Evidence (Northern Ireland) Order 1989 shall be amended as follows.

(2) In Article 81 (evidence through television links), in paragraph (1A) (proceedings where Article applies)—
  (a) in sub-paragraph (a), for "section 14 of the Criminal Appeal (Northern Ireland) Act 1980" substitute "section 10 of the Criminal Appeal Act 1995", and
  (b) in sub-paragraph (b), for "and appeals to the county court rising out of such proceedings" substitute ", appeals to the county court arising out of such proceedings and hearings of references under section 12 of the Criminal Appeal Act 1995 so arising".

(3) In Article 81A (video recordings of testimony from child witnesses), in paragraph (1) (proceedings where Article applies)—
  (a) in sub-paragraph (b), for "section 14 of the Criminal Appeal (Northern Ireland) Act 1980" substitute "section 10 of the Criminal Appeal Act 1995", and
  (b) in sub-paragraph (c), for "and appeals to the county court arising out of such proceedings" substitute ", appeals to the county court arising out of such proceedings and hearings of references under section 12 of the Criminal Appeal Act 1995 so arising".

The Criminal Justice and Public Order Act 1994 (c. 33)

19. In section 51 of the Criminal Justice nad Public Order Act 1994 (intimidation etc. of witnesses, jurors and others), in subsection (9), in the definition of "the relevant period", for "reference under section 17 of the Criminal Appeal Act 1968" substitute "a reference under section 9 or 11 of the Criminal Appeal Act 1995".

Section 29   SCHEDULE 3

REPEALS

Chapter	Short title	Extent of repeal
1967 c. 13.	The Parliamentary Commissioner Act 1967.	In Schedule 3, in paragraph 7, the words "the Court of Appeal,".
1968 c. 19.	The Criminal Appeal Act 1968.	Section 17.
		In section 23(3), the words following "compellable".
1968 c. 20.	The Courts-Martial (Appeals) Act 1968.	In section 28(3), the words following "compellable".
1977 c. 45.	The Criminal Law Act 1977.	Section 44.
1980 c. 43.	The Magistrates' Courts Act 1980.	In section 142, in subsection (2), the words ", subject to subsection (4) below," and subsection (4).
1980 c. 47.	The Criminal Appeal (Northern Ireland) Act 1980.	Section 14.
		In section 16(1), the words "appeal or".
		In section 25(3), the words following "compellable".
		In section 44(4), the words "14 or".
1981 c. 54.	The Supreme Court Act 1981.	In Schedule 5, the entries relating to the Army Act 1955 and the Air Force Act 1955.

Chapter	Short title	Extent of repeal
S.I. 1986/595 (N.I. 4).	The Mental Health (Northern Ireland) Order 1986.	In Schedule 5, in Part I, the entry relating to section 14(1) of the Criminal Appeal (Northern Ireland) Act 1980.
1988 c. 33.	The Criminal Justice Act 1988.	In section 133(5)(b), sub-paragraph (iii) and the word "or" immediately preceding it.
1991 c. 25.	The Criminal Procedure (Insanity and Unfitness to Plead) Act 1991.	In Schedule 3, paragraphs 3(1) and 4.

INDEX

References are to sections and Schedules

CHILDREN (SCOTLAND) ACT 1995*

(1995 c. 36)

---

* Annotations by Kenneth McK. Norrie, LL.B., Ph.D., Professor of Law at the University of Strathclyde

CHAPTER 2

CHILDREN'S HEARINGS

Constitution of children's hearings

Qualifications, employment and duties of reporters

Safeguards for children

Conduct of proceedings at and in connection with children's hearing

Transfer etc. of cases

Appeals

CHAPTER 3

PROTECTION AND SUPERVISION OF CHILDREN

Children requiring compulsory measures of supervision

Preliminary and investigatory measures

Interpretation of Part II

93. Interpretation of Part II.

PART III

ADOPTION

94. Approval of adoption society for specific services.
95. Welfare of child paramount consideration.
96. Duty of adoption agency to consider alternatives to adoption.
97. Adoption by person married to natural parent.
98. Further amendments of the 1978 Act; and interpretation of Part III.

PART IV

GENERAL AND SUPPLEMENTAL

99. Registration of births by persons who are themselves children.
100. Inquiries into matters affecting children.
101. Panel for curators *ad litem*, reporting officers and safeguarders.
102. Removal of duty to report on operation of Children Act 1975.
103. Interpretation, rules, regulations and Parliamentary control.
104. Financial provision.
105. Extent, short title, minor and consequential amendments, repeals and commencement.

SCHEDULES:
    Schedule 1—Children's Panels.
    Schedule 2—Amendments of the Adoption (Scotland) Act 1978.
    Schedule 3—Transitional Provisions and Savings.
    Schedule 4—Minor and Consequential Amendments.
    Schedule 5—Repeals.

An Act to reform the law of Scotland relating to children, to the adoption of children and to young persons who as children have been looked after by a local authority; to make new provision as respects the relationship between parent and child and guardian and child in the law of Scotland; to make provision as respects residential establishments for children and certain other residential establishments; and for connected purposes.

[19th July 1995]

PARLIAMENTARY DEBATES
    Hansard, H.C. Vol. 252, col. 555, Vol. 259, col. 25, Vol. 263, col. 1739. H.L. Vol. 564, cols. 13, 37; Vol. 565, cols. 1109, 1200, 1792.
    The Bill was debated before the House of Commons Special Standing Committee C on January 25, February 6, 13, 21, 23 and 28, March 2, 7, 9 and 14, 1995. The Committee Stage in the House of Lords took place on June 6, 7 and 13, 1995.

INTRODUCTION AND GENERAL NOTE
    Scottish child law has been in a state of flux for some years now. Society has changed dramatically since the basic precepts of family law were laid down, and the position and status and role of children in our society is very different today from what it was earlier this century. Even less than 10 years ago, when the Law Reform (Parent and Child) (Scotland) Act 1986 (c. 9) was passed, it was considered appropriate to talk of the rights that parents had in and over their children. Now, society more and more sees children as individual persons in their own right and perceives the nature of the parent-child relationship as in essence one of responsibility rather than one of right. There has been a clear shift from parental rights to children's rights, a shift heralded in domestic law by the House of Lords decision in the case of *Gillick v. West Norfolk & Wisbech Area Health Authority* [1986] A.C. 112, and in international law, by the adoption on November 28, 1989 of the United Nations *Convention on the Rights of the Child* (28 International Legal Materials 1448). This Convention evidenced a growing awareness in the international community of the importance of children's rights, and its implementation by the British Government

(on December 16, 1991, a few months after the coming into force of the English Children Act 1989 (c. 41)) had the effect of rendering a number of provisions in the current Scots domestic law incompatible with the U.K.'s international obligations. Scots child law therefore required to move on, not only to take account of the change in the social perception of the status of children in Scotland, but also to allow Scots law to consist with the UN Convention. In 1992 the Scottish Law Commission produced their *Report on Family Law* (Scot. Law Com. No. 135, May 1992), in which many suggestions for major changes were made, and upon which Pt. I of the present Act is based.

In the field of child protection Scots law has had a bumpy few years of late. The children's hearing system, established by the Social Work (Scotland) Act 1968 (c. 49) and in operation since 1971, has been much admired on all sides and was free of significant criticism in its first 20 years. However, in the early 1990s there were a number of high-profile cases which highlighted some serious problems that did exist in the system. A number of inquiries were established to scrutinise various aspects of the system and to suggest possible improvements, and extremely useful reports followed. These included the Clyde Report (*Report of the Inquiry into the Removal of Children From Orkney in February 1991*: H.C. Papers 1992–1993, No. 195), the Kearney Report (*Report of the Inquiry into Child Care Policies in Fife*: H.C. Papers 1992–1993, No. 191), and the Finlayson Report (*Reporters to Children's Panels: Their Role, Function and Accountability*: Scottish Office, 1992). The Government reacted to these reports by producing the White Paper, *Scotland's Children: Proposals for Child Care Policy and Law* (1993, Cm. 2286). The bulk of Pt. II of this Act gives effect to the proposals contained therein. In addition, new rules are created in order to deal with the problems that led to the highly contentious litigation in the cases of *Sloan v. B* 1991 S.L.T. 530 (the Orkney case), *L., Petrs. (No. 1)* 1993 S.L.T. 1310 and *L., Petrs. (No. 2)* 1993 S.L.T. 1342 (the Ayrshire case), and *D v. Grampian Regional Council* 1995 S.L.T. 519.

Both in terms of drafting and substance, the Act that received Royal Assent on July 19, 1995 is infinitely better than the Bill presented to the House of Commons in November 1994. Many provisions of that Bill were hideously flawed, and it is a credit to the parliamentary process and the careful scrutiny given to the Bill by a number of MPs and peers that the vast majority of these flaws have been rectified. There were over 300 amendments made in the House of Lords alone. Flawed provisions do, however, remain, usually in those sections which were added at a very late stage when the opportunity for proper debate did not exist. Inevitably in an Act of this size and importance there will be certain provisions which do not meet the approval of all commentators. It seems to the present commentator, however, that there are at least two provisions, deliberately enacted and in the Bill from the very start, which undermine the whole philosophy upon which the Act purports to be based. First, the shift from parental rights to parental responsibilities cannot be taken seriously so long as a third of all fathers (namely the unmarried ones) are expressly absolved of their responsibilities. Secondly, the (correct) presumption that a children's hearing is a far more appropriate forum than a court to make long-term decisions in relation to children in need of supervision is undermined by the new power of the sheriff to substitute his own disposal for that of the children's hearing. In addition to these policy flaws there remain a number of drafting difficulties, which will be highlighted in the following annotations. Amongst the most noticeable of these is the fact that various provisions in Pt. II refer only to parental rights while other provisions refer only to parental responsibilities, as if the one were not inherently connected (as is made plain in Pt. I) to the other. There are wild fluctuations in how time is to be calculated, with different provisions requiring things to be done "within three days", or "not later than the third day after", or "up to 22 days" or "22 days after"; also, the phrase "relevant person", used throughout the Act, is given three quite separate definitions (ss.30(2), 86(4) and 93(2)). Both in determining time and in identifying the "relevant person", anyone dealing with particular provisions will have to take very great care that they do not use rules applicable to other provisions. The huge number of cross-references makes this a difficult Act to follow.

ARRANGEMENT OF THE ACT

Part I—Parents, Children and Guardians
Part I of the Act, dealing with private law matters, contains in many respects the most fundamental alterations to the law as it previously stood. Custody and access are replaced by "residence" and "contact", and a much more clearly defined list of orders available to a court in dealing with private law matters is set out. Replacing the appropriate provisions in the Law Reform (Parent and Child) (Scotland) Act 1986 (c. 9), this Part sets out the parental responsibilities and parental rights that mothers and some fathers will have in relation to their children, who is to

have these responsibilities and rights, and how they can be acquired. The important s.11 sets out the orders that a court can make in relation to parental responsibilities and parental rights, who can apply for them and on what terms such orders can be made. It is provided in s.11 that three "overarching principles" must inform the court's decision-making: that is to say (i) the welfare of the child is to be the court's paramount consideration, (ii) the child is to be given an opportunity to express views on the decisions the court has to make and the court will take appropriate account of these views, and (iii) the court will not make an order unless persuaded that to do so is better than making no order at all.

In addition, the law of guardianship in Scotland, which had sat uneasily with the indigenous offices of tutory and curatory and which had been left anchorless on the abolition of these offices, is at last clarified. It is made plain that a guardian is (in the absence of statutory provision defining it otherwise) a parent-substitute, with all the responsibilities and rights of a mother. Provisions in this Part set out the effect of guardianship and detail the rules for the appointment and termination of appointment of guardians. There is also a much needed modernisation of the rules on administration of children's property.

Part II—Promotion of Children's Welfare by Local Authorities and by Children's Hearings etc.

This is by far the largest Part of the Act, though the changes it introduces are, perhaps, less fundamental than those in Part I. Much of this Part is a re-enactment, and tidying, of the Social Work (Scotland) Act 1968 (c. 49), though a number of important amendments to the rules contained therein have been made. The duties that local authorities have towards children in their areas are specified and clarified; and in a significant change in terminology, designed to update the law and make it more accessible, the statute moves away from the notion of children "in care" to a notion of children being "looked after" or "accommodated" by local authorities. The aim here is to remove the stigma felt by many to attach to the notion of children "in care".

The children's hearing system survives much as it was before, though the legal provisions applicable to that system are significantly tidied and updated. A number of new powers are granted to children's hearings, though the philosophy behind the system remains, thankfully, intact. The most important changes in this Part are in the creation of a number of new orders that the court can make in relation to children who are in need of some form of supervision or protection. In particular the court is given power to make child assessment orders to assess the physical or emotional wellbeing of a child, child protection orders (which replace the old place of safety orders), and exclusion orders (excluding a named person from a child's home). Also, the court can make a parental responsibilities order, which replaces the local authorities' power to assume to themselves parental rights and powers.

As under Pt. I, there are three similar "overarching principles" which courts and children's hearings must apply whenever they are called upon under this Part to make decisions relating to children: (i) that the welfare of the child is the court's or children's hearing's paramount consideration, (ii) that the child is to be given an opportunity to express views on the decision the sheriff or children's hearing have to make and appropriate account will be taken of these views, and (iii) that the sheriff or children's hearing will not make an order unless persuaded that to do so is better for the child than making no order at all. The philosophy throughout the Act—and not only this Part—is that children are best looked after by their parents, that the state should interfere in the upbringing of children only when absolutely necessary for the protection of children's welfare, and that when such interference is necessary it should be to the minimum extent required to achieve its purpose.

Part III—Adoption

Part III of the Act and Sched. 2 amend the law of adoption as it is contained in the Adoption (Scotland) Act 1978 (c. 28) in a number of important respects. The most significant of these changes is the provision allowing a step-parent to adopt a child alone, without having to bring in her or his spouse (the natural parent) as a co-applicant. In addition, in order to bring Scots law into line with the UN Convention on the Rights of the Child, the child's welfare is made the paramount consideration in the whole adoption process.

Part IV—General and Supplemental

The normal general provisions are contained in this Part, though in addition there is an amendment to the Registration of Births, Deaths and Marriages (Scotland) Act 1965 (c. 49) to take account of the fact that some parents who will be obliged to register births are themselves children (i.e. persons under the age of 16 years). This undeniable fact, which has never been given express recognition in the law before, is reflected in various other provisions in Part I.

ABBREVIATIONS

The 1968 Act	: The Social Work (Scotland) Act 1968.
The 1986 Act	: The Law Reform (Parent and Child) (Scotland) Act 1986.

The 1971 Rules	: Reporter's Duties and Transmission of Information etc (Scotland) Rules (SI 1971, No. 525).
The 1986 Rules	: Children's Hearings (Scotland) Rules (SI 1986, No. 2291).
The UN Convention	: The United Nations *Convention on the Rights of the Child* (28 International Legal Materials 1448).
Scot. Law Com. No. 135	: Scottish Law Commission *Report on Family Law* (May 1992).

PART I

PARENTS, CHILDREN AND GUARDIANS

Parental responsibilities and parental rights

Parental responsibilities

1.—(1) Subject to section 3(1)(b) and (3) of this Act, a parent has in relation to his child the responsibility—

(a) to safeguard and promote the child's health, development and welfare;

(b) to provide, in a manner appropriate to the stage of development of the child—

(i) direction;

(ii) guidance,

to the child;

(c) if the child is not living with the parent, to maintain personal relations and direct contact with the child on a regular basis; and

(d) to act as the child's legal representative,

but only in so far as compliance with this section is practicable and in the interests of the child.

(2) "Child" means for the purposes of—

(a) paragraphs (a), (b)(i), (c) and (d) of subsection (1) above, a person under the age of sixteen years;

(b) paragraph (b)(ii) of that subsection, a person under the age of eighteen years.

(3) The responsibilities mentioned in paragraphs (a) to (d) of subsection (1) above are in this Act referred to as "parental responsibilities"; and the child, or any person acting on his behalf, shall have title to sue, or to defend, in any proceedings as respects those responsibilities.

(4) The parental responsibilities supersede any analogous duties imposed on a parent at common law; but this section is without prejudice to any other duty so imposed on him or to any duty imposed on him by, under or by virtue of any other provision of this Act or of any other enactment.

DEFINITIONS

"child": ss.1(2), 15(1).

"parent": s.15(1).

"parental responsibilities": s.1(3).

GENERAL NOTE

See Scot. Law Com. No. 135, paras. 2.1–2.13.

Though statute law before the passing of this Act was worded in terms of parental rights, it had long been understood that "parental rights exist for the benefit of the child and they are justified only in so far as they enable the parent to perform his duties towards the child" (per Lord Fraser of Tullybelton in *Gillick v. West Norfolk & Wisbech Area Health Authority* [1985] 3 WLR 830 at

841; see also Stair I, v, 1 and Erskine I, vi, 53). The aim of the current provision is to emphasise that a parent's primary relationship to her child is one of responsibility, and that this responsibility flows from being a parent. There are still parental rights recognised by the law and dealt with in s.2 below, but the change in terminology from rights alone to both responsibilities and rights is designed to remove the common misunderstanding, given credence by the terms of the 1986 Act, that parents have rights in, rather than duties and powers towards, their children.

Subs. (1)

This subsection tells us what mothers and some fathers are expected to do and how they are expected to act in relation to their children. Much of the language used in this subsection can be traced to the UN Convention on the Rights of the Child. That Convention is worded in terms of the child's rights while the present provision is worded in terms of the parents' responsibilities; the statute should, however, be interpreted in the light of the Convention since Parliament has clearly designed this Act to give effect to it.

There are four parental responsibilities which can shortly be referred to as the responsibilities: (1) to safeguard and promote the child's health, development and welfare, (2) to provide the child with direction and guidance, (3) to maintain personal relations and direct contact with the child, and (4) to act as the child's legal representative. It is provided that the parent must fulfil these responsibilities in so far as it is practicable for her to do so and in so far as it is in the interests of the child for her to do so. A parent need not act as the child's legal representative if it is not in the child's interests, say, to raise an action which has little chance of success. Nor need the parent do any more than is practicable in all the circumstances. So the responsibility, for example, to maintain direct contact with the child will be affected by where the child lives, how old she or he is, and whether the child her or himself wants to maintain contact. There will be no breach of this responsibility if the child lives in Australia and the parent living in Scotland can afford few long distance telephone calls.

Subject to s.3(1)(b). Section 3(1)(b) provides that a father who is not married to the child's mother will not have parental responsibilities or parental rights in relation to the child unless he obtains an order from the court granting them under s.11 below, or he enters into an agreement with the mother under s.4 below. If these requirements are not satisfied the father is absolved of his parental responsibilities. This position breaches the U.K.'s international obligations under the UN Convention, for reasons which are explored more fully in the General Note to s.3 below.

Direction and guidance. Art. 5 of the UN Convention requires that the parent or guardian of a child has a duty to provide appropriate direction and guidance to the child. Direction differs from guidance in that the former implies instruction while the latter implies advice. They are treated differently in the present statute with subs. (2) below providing that the parent is obliged to direct the child until the age of 16 and is obliged to guide the child until the age of 18.

Maintain personal relations and direct contact. This parental responsibility reflects the child's right, protected by Art. 9(3) of the UN Convention, to personal relations and direct contact with both parents on a regular basis. The exclusion of the unmarried father from this responsibility breaches the child's right under the Convention.

Legal representation. The responsibility of legal representation is the duty to act on behalf of the child in transactions having legal effect, such as entering into contracts, raising and defending actions, granting discharges etc.

Subs. (2)

Instead of specifying at what age the various parental responsibilities come to an end, the Act follows the rather clumsy approach previously adopted by the 1986 Act of defining a child differently depending upon which parental responsibility is at issue. All bar one of the parental responsibilities end when the child attains the age of 16 years. The exception is the responsibility to give guidance (i.e. advice), which lasts until the child is 18 years old. It is, however, difficult to see what content this responsibility has since the parental right to give guidance ends on the child's 16th birthday (see s.2(7) below).

Under the age of. A person attains a particular age at the beginning of the relevant anniversary of the date of her or his birth: Age of Legal Capacity (Scotland) Act 1991 (c. 50), s.6(1).

Subs. (3)

This subsection gives the child title to sue or defend in any proceeding relating to parental responsibilities. A child is given title to seek an order under s.11 below by subss. (3) and (5) of that section. This provision gives the child title to defend such an action, and title to sue or defend in any proceedings other than s.11 actions which will affect the exercise of parental responsibilities or which arise from such exercise, such as applications for parental responsibilities orders and child protection orders. It might also include actions by the child for breach of a parental responsibility. A breach of parental responsibilities has not yet been held to give rise to delictual liability in Scots law, though there is no reason in principle why it should not do so. There is nothing to stop a child suing a parent for damages in reparation, and if the child suffers a legally recognised loss through a failure by the parent in her duty to promote the child's welfare then liability might well be recognised. It would, however, be surprising if the Act intended to create a new form of liability but did so only here in relation to title to sue. The liability must be regarded as based on common law, and the effect of this provision is to put the child's title to sue in her or his own name beyond doubt.

Any person acting on his behalf. The child is not given any legal capacity by this Act that she or he does not otherwise have, and it follows that someone else will often have to act on behalf of the child in enforcing a parental responsibility. The legal representative of the child has title to sue under this provision but cannot be the only person included: if the action concerned liability arising out of legal representation, then that representative is hardly the appropriate person to join issue on behalf of the child. It is submitted that title to take a matter to court inheres in any person claiming to act on behalf of the child, even when they are not exercising any parental responsibility or parental right. The court will appoint a curator *ad litem* in such cases.

Subs. (4)
The common law is superseded by this Act in relation to parental responsibilities, and the duties that parents have towards their children are now to be found exclusively in this Act, or in other statutory provisions (such as the obligation of child support in the Child Support Act 1991 (c. 48), or the obligation to educate a child of school age in the Education (Scotland) Act 1980 (c. 44), s.30).

Parental rights

2.—(1) Subject to section 3(1)(b) and (3) of this Act, a parent, in order to enable him to fulfil his parental responsibilities in relation to his child, has the right—

(a) to have the child living with him or otherwise to regulate the child's residence;

(b) to control, direct or guide, in a manner appropriate to the stage of development of the child, the child's upbringing;

(c) if the child is not living with him, to maintain personal relations and direct contact with the child on a regular basis; and

(d) to act as the child's legal representative.

(2) Subject to subsection (3) below, where two or more persons have a parental right as respects a child, each of them may exercise that right without the consent of the other or, as the case may be, of any of the others, unless any decree or deed conferring the right, or regulating its exercise, otherwise provides.

(3) Without prejudice to any court order, no person shall be entitled to remove a child habitually resident in Scotland from, or to retain any such child outwith, the United Kingdom without the consent of a person described in subsection (6) below.

(4) The rights mentioned in paragraphs (a) to (d) of subsection (1) above are in this Act referred to as "parental rights"; and a parent, or any person acting on his behalf, shall have title to sue, or to defend, in any proceedings as respects those rights.

(5) The parental rights supersede any analogous rights enjoyed by a parent at common law; but this section is without prejudice to any other right so enjoyed by him or to any right enjoyed by him by, under or by virtue of any other provision of this Act or of any other enactment.

(6) The description of a person referred to in subsection (3) above is a person (whether or not a parent of the child) who for the time being has and is exercising in relation to him a right mentioned in paragraph (a) or (c) of subsection (1) above; except that, where both the child's parents are persons so described, the consent required for his removal or retention shall be that of them both.

(7) In this section, "child" means a person under the age of sixteen years.

DEFINITIONS
    "child": ss.2(7), 15(1).
    "parent": s.15(1).
    "parental responsibilities": s.1(3).
    "parental rights": s.2(4).

GENERAL NOTE
    See Scot. Law Com. No. 135, paras. 2.14–2.35.
    Under the 1986 Act the parental rights were "guardianship, custody or access", together with "any right or authority relating to the welfare or upbringing of a child conferred on a parent by any rule of law" (s.8). The aim of the present provision is to put all parental rights onto a statutory basis, to declare that they exist only for the purpose of enabling the parent to fulfil her parental responsibilities, and to set out as clearly as possible the content of each of these rights.

Subs. (1)
    The four parental rights are listed here, and there are no others: they may shortly be referred to as the rights (1) to regulate the child's residence, (2) to direct or guide her or his development and upbringing, (3) to maintain personal relations and contact with the child, and (4) to act as the child's legal representative. It will be noticed that all four reflect the parental responsibilities listed in s.1 above. So the right to have the child living with the parent exists in order that the parent has the practical power to safeguard and promote the child's health, development and welfare; the right to control the child's upbringing is granted in order to allow the parent to fulfil the obligation to provide direction and guidance; the right to maintain personal relations is granted to allow the parent to fulfil her obligation of maintaining personal relations; and the right to act as legal representative is granted to allow the fulfilling of the obligation to act as legal representative.
    In order to enable him to fulfil his parental responsibilities. The exercise of any particular parental right is valid only in so far as it is directed towards the fulfilling of one or more of the parental responsibilities.
    Has the right. As under the 1986 Act, the use of the word "right" in this context is inept since the interest recognised by this section is not a "right" in any normal sense of the word. An action to enforce the "right" will not be determined according to the strength of its validity but according to the welfare of the child; breach of the "right" will not give rise to an action for damages (*McKeen v. Chief Constable of Lothian and Borders Police* 1994 S.L.T. 93). Rather, the so-called parental rights are really more in the nature of powers or capabilities, that is to say the ability to act in ways that the law will recognise and give effect to. "Parental power" would have been a more apt phrase to use.
    Legal representative. A parent has the right to act as the child's legal representative, i.e. to enter into transactions having legal effect on behalf of the child. It sometimes happens, however, that the parent is herself a child (i.e. a person under the age of 16) and may well lack legal capacity to undertake legal transactions, whether on behalf of herself or of her child. (A father under the age of 16 would not have parental rights since he would not be married and the court is highly unlikely to grant such a father parental rights). Either this provision is inept in relation to the under-16-year-old mother, or it confers full legal capacity on such a person to act on behalf of her child. Neither of these interpretations is satisfactory. If the provision is inept, this runs the risk of a child of a mother under 16 having no legal representative until the court appoints one. And if a mother under the age of 16 has full capacity to enter into contracts on behalf of her child it would be a strange law which prohibited her from entering into contracts on her own behalf. The solution, though it is slightly clumsy, must be as follows. The process of acting as a legal representative is itself a transaction having legal effect; if a mother under 16 has no capacity to undertake a particular transaction it has to be undertaken by her own legal representative (i.e., normally, her own parent, or the baby's grandparent). The responsibility and the right to act as a child's legal representative passes through the young parent to the young parent's legal representatives, who therefore have the responsibility and the right to act on behalf not only of their own child but also of their filial grandchild. A mother under 16 can act on behalf of her child on terms which are not unreasonable and in circumstances in which it is common for persons of her age and circumstances to transact (Age of Legal Capacity (Scotland) Act 1991 (c. 50), s.2(1)).

Subs. (2)
    This replaces s.2(4) of the 1986 Act, and has the same effect. A person exercising one of the powers recognised by this section can do so on their own without consulting any other person with the same powers, and it follows that in cases of disagreement the advantage is given to the

person who takes the initiative. If, for example, married parents disagree as to the school the child is to attend, either can, against the wishes of the other, enrol the child into the school of their choice. However, s.6(1) below imposes an obligation on any person exercising a parental responsibility or parental right to have regard to the views of any other person with parental responsibilities and parental rights: see the General Note to that section. An alteration to the old s.2(4) is that this provision is made subject to the immediately following subsection.

Any decree or deed. The decree would be granted in terms of s.11; the deed would be one governed by the rules in s.7.

Subss. (3) and (6)

One of the most contentious areas of law in recent years has concerned international child abduction, and the problems of one parent removing the child from the jurisdiction before the court has resolved an issue of custody. Removal of a child from the jurisdiction in defiance of a court order, or without appropriate consent when there is a court order, is an offence (Child Abduction Act 1984 (c. 37), s.6). Removal or retention of a child away from her or his habitual residence is not permitted without the consent of a person with the parental right to have the child living with her or of a person with the parental right to maintain personal relations and contact with the child; and when both parents have either of these rights the consent of both is required for such removal or retention. This clarifies an issue which arose under the application of the Hague Convention on International Child Abduction (brought into our law by the Child Abduction and Custody Act 1985 (c. 60)), in which it was sometimes argued that a parent with parental rights who removed a child against the wishes of the other parent with parental rights was not acting wrongfully but was merely exercising her or his own rights (see *McKiver v. McKiver* 1995 S.L.T. 799). This argument will no longer be open since any person, including a parent with parental rights, must obtain the consent of both parents (if both have parental rights) before removing or retaining the child. A child wrongfully removed to a Hague Convention country will be returned to its habitual residence forthwith.

No person. This includes, but is not limited to, the person who has parental rights under this section.

Remove a child. In its terms this provision is wide enough to cover both a removal with an intention of permanency, and removal for a foreseeably short term, such as a holiday.

Habitually resident. See the General Note to s.14(1) below.

Retain any such child. The notion of retention has been dealt with in a number of cases raised under the Hague Convention on International Child Abduction and the present provision is likely to be interpreted consistently with that Convention, as enacted in the Child Abduction and Custody Act 1985 (c. 60). See for example *H. (Minors) (Abduction: Custody Rights), Re* [1991] 2 A.C. 476, *Findlay v. Findlay* 1994 S.L.T. 709.

Consent. It is not laid down how consent to the removal of the child is to be evidenced, and it can be assumed, therefore, that it is open to proof *prout de jure*. A number of cases have arisen under the Hague Convention, in which it is a defence to an application for the return of the child that the parent from whom she or he was removed consented to the removal. See for example *Zenel v. Haddow* 1993 S.L.T. 975. Acquiescence may infer consent.

Subs. (4)

Title to sue, or to defend, in any proceedings. Section 11(3) gives the parent title to seek an order under s.11, and this section gives the parent title to defend such an action, and title to sue or defend any other action which will affect the exercise of parental responsibilities or which arises from such exercise, such as, for example, a parental responsibilities order or a child protection order.

Parent. Though defined in s.15 as "genetic parent", it is clear that the context here requires the word to be limited to parent with parental responsibilities and parental rights (i.e. it initially excludes the father who is not married to the mother at the appropriate time).

Subs. (5)

Like s.1(4) in relation to parental responsibilities, s.2(5) ensures that parental rights come solely from the present Act or any other Act of Parliament and not from the common law, which is entirely superseded in so far as it existed before the coming into force of the present Act (thereby tidying up the confused position under s.8 of the 1986 Act).

Subs. (7)

All parental rights cease on the child's 16th birthday (including the right to give guidance, notwithstanding that the responsibility to give guidance lasts until the child's 18th birthday: see note to s.1(2) above).

Provisions relating both to parental responsibilities and to parental rights

3.—(1) Notwithstanding section 1(1) of the Law Reform (Parent and Child) (Scotland) Act 1986 (provision for disregarding whether a person's parents are not, or have not been, married to one another in establishing the legal relationship between him and any other person)—

    (a) a child's mother has parental responsibilities and parental rights in relation to him whether or not she is or has been married to his father; and

    (b) without prejudice to any arrangements which may be made under subsection (5) below and subject to any agreement which may be made under section 4 of this Act, his father has such responsibilities and rights in relation to him only if married to the mother at the time of the child's conception or subsequently.

(2) For the purposes of subsection (1)(b) above, the father shall be regarded as having been married to the mother at any time when he was a party to a purported marriage with her which was—

    (a) voidable; or

    (b) void but believed by them (whether by error of fact or of law) in good faith at that time to be valid.

(3) Subsection (1) above is without prejudice to any order made under section 11 of this Act or section 3(1) of the said Act of 1986 (provision analogous to the said section 11 but repealed by this Act) or to any other order, disposal or resolution affecting parental responsibilities or parental rights; and nothing in subsection (1) above or in this Part of this Act shall affect any other—

    (a) enactment (including any other provision of this Act or of that Act); or

    (b) rule of law,

by, under or by virtue of which a person may have imposed on him (or be relieved of) parental responsibilities or may be granted (or be deprived of) parental rights.

(4) The fact that a person has parental responsibilities or parental rights in relation to a child shall not entitle that person to act in any way which would be incompatible with any court order relating to the child or the child's property, or with any supervision requirement made under section 70 of this Act.

(5) Without prejudice to section 4(1) of this Act, a person who has parental responsibilities or parental rights in relation to a child shall not abdicate those responsibilities or rights to anyone else but may arrange for some or all of them to be fulfilled or exercised on his behalf; and without prejudice to that generality any such arrangement may be made with a person who already has parental responsibilities or parental rights in relation to the child concerned.

(6) The making of an arrangement under subsection (5) above shall not affect any liability arising from a failure to fulfil parental responsibilities; and where any arrangements so made are such that the child is a foster child for the purposes of the Foster Children (Scotland) Act 1984, those arrangements are subject to the provisions of that Act.

DEFINITIONS
    "parent": s.15(1).
    "parental responsibilities": s.1(3).
    "parental rights": s.2(4).
    "person": s.15(4).

GENERAL NOTE
    In *Marckx v. Belgium* [1980] 2 EHRR 330 the European Court of Human Rights held that Belgian legislation which drew a distinction between the "legitimate" and the "illegitimate" family constituted discrimination in violation of Art. 14 of the European Convention on Human Rights (ECHR), by virtue of the lack of any objective and reasonable justification for the difference in treatment accorded by Belgian law. In relation to Scots law the 1986 Act attempted to

remove all the civil disabilities attaching to the children of unmarried parents, and while it achieved that limited aim it did not, as is sometimes claimed, abolish the status of "illegitimacy". Apart from the various rules in relation to domicile and succession (see Wilkinson and Norrie *Parent and Child* (1993, W. Green) at pp. 5–10), the terminology is still used in, for example, the Adoption (Scotland) Act 1978 (c. 28) and can still be found in recent judicial dicta (see for example Lord Jauncey in *D v. Grampian Regional Council* 1995 S.L.T. 519 at p. 520). In addition and most importantly, under the 1986 Act the unmarried father was denied parental rights in relation to his child. The Scottish Law Commission (Scot. Law Com. No. 135 at paras 2.50 and 17.10) had recommended that the status of illegitimacy be abolished and with it the discrimination against unmarried fathers. The Government rejected that recommendation and the present provision re-enacts the 1986 Act, with minimal improvements (and indeed an added disadvantage) in the position of the unmarried father. In doing so, the U.K. remains in clear breach of its international obligations.

In *McMichael v. UK* February 24, 1995 (European Court of Human Rights) the applicant had argued that his exclusion from a children's hearing considering the case of his child, on the basis that he was not married to the mother, was discriminatory and therefore in violation of Art. 14 ECHR, but the Court unanimously held that the 1986 provisions were not discriminatory. The aim of the legislation was to identify meritorious fathers and the Court held that the conditions they had to satisfy before obtaining parental rights were proportionate to that legitimate aim. This decision may well be inconsistent with the Court's slightly earlier ruling in *Schmidt v. Germany* (1994) 18 EHRR 513 in which it was held that very weighty reasons would have to be established before the Court could accept that a difference of treatment based exclusively on the ground of sex was compatible with the ECHR. The *McMichael* case was not argued on that basis but on the basis of discrimination between unmarried and married men. The decision might well have been different had the questions asked in the case been these: why should men have to prove their parenting merit when women do not? And why is marriage in itself a determinant of paternal merit?

Even if it is conceded that married parents should be treated differently from unmarried parents, there is no justification in treating the children of unmarried parents differently from the children of married parents. Article 18 of the UN Convention on the Rights of the Child provides for the recognition of the principle that both parents have common responsibilities for the upbringing and development of the child. This is based on the proposition that all children have the right to look to at least two adults for protection and guidance (a proposition, incidentally, given explicit statutory recognition in the U.K. by s.13(5) of the Human Fertilisation and Embryology Act 1990 (c. 37)). The child of the unmarried father can look only to her or his mother. The present provision absolves the unmarried father from the responsibilities of safeguarding and promoting the child's health, development and welfare, of providing direction and guidance to the child, and of maintaining contact with the child. As such the present provision breaches Art. 18UN, frustrates the Scottish Law Commission's aim of abolishing the concept of illegitimacy, and (by absolving male parents of their responsibilities towards their children) undermines the whole philosophy of this Part of the Act that responsibilities rather than rights are the basic determinant of a parent's relationship with a child.

Subs. (1)

This subsection re-enacts, with insignificant changes in terminology, the provision previously contained in s.2 of the 1986 Act. All mothers will have full parental responsibilities and parental rights in relation to their children; fathers will have such responsibilities and rights only if married to the mother at the time of, or any time after, the child's conception. The truth is out, and this provision is expressly stated to be "notwithstanding s.1(1)" of the 1986 Act, i.e. even although that earlier provision says that children of unmarried parents are to be treated the same as children of married parents, the two classes of children are still to be treated differently, for the child of unmarried parents has a lesser legal relationship with her or his father than the child of married parents.

Time of the child's conception. It is always difficult to determine this accurately (for a discussion, see Wilkinson and Norrie *Parent and Child* (1993, W. Green) at pp. 129–131).

Subs. (2)

Again repeating the provision in s.2 of the 1986 Act, it is provided that the "marriage" which confers parental responsibilities and parental rights on fathers can be valid, voidable or void. It is not stated, but one can assume, that both regular and irregular marriages are covered (though there is always the difficulty in establishing when an irregular marriage occurred: see Clive *The Law of Husband and Wife in Scotland* (1992, W. Green) at pp. 57–64).

Believed by them . . . to be valid. In one respect the law is tightened up from the 1986 provisions and fewer fathers than previously will be able to rely on this provision to obtain parental responsibilities. A father will have automatic parental responsibilities and parental rights even when his "marriage" to the mother is void, so long as it was believed "by them", i.e. by both the father and the mother, to be valid. In other words, the husband in a void marriage will acquire parental responsibilities and parental rights only if both he and his wife are in good faith. Under s.2(2)(b) of the 1986 Act (and the common law before that: see Fraser *Parent and Child* (1906, W. Green) 3rd edn. at p. 27), the void marriage had to be believed to be valid "by him", that is by the father alone. The fact that the mother knew the marriage was void (say, because she knew she was already married) did not, under the 1986 Act, prevent the father obtaining parental rights; now, however, bad faith on the part of the mother alone will prevent the father from sharing parental responsibilities and parental rights with the mother. As in s.4(1) below, an unmarried father can be disadvantaged by the wrongdoing of the (equally married) mother.

Subs. (3)

It is enacted for the avoidance of doubt that notwithstanding the automatic conferral of parental responsibilities and parental rights under subs. (1) above, the court can make an order which confers such responsibilities and rights on another person, whether under this Act or another Act or any other rule of law. It may be noted here that when a court confers parental responsibilities and parental rights it is not conferring parenthood on the individual, but merely some of the consequences thereof.

Subs. (4)

This is a new provision, making plain what was implicit in the pre-1995 law, namely that the person with parental responsibilities or parental rights cannot exercise them in such a way as is inconsistent with either a court order or a supervision requirement imposed by a children's hearing. In respect of the children's hearing, this provision is important in emphasising that parental responsibilities and parental rights are effectively superseded in so far as the hearing decides by way of a supervision requirement. So, for example, when a hearing imposes a supervision requirement with a condition of residence, which it may do under s.70(3) below, this supersedes the parent's responsibility and right to determine the child's residence (but only for so long as the supervision requirement lasts).

Subs. (5)

The ultimate legal responsibility for exercising parental responsibilities and parental rights rests with the parent who has these responsibilities and rights, and that responsibility cannot be given up. Parents cannot (without judicial process) resign their parenthood. If the child is harmed as a result of the wrongful exercise of parental responsibilities and parental rights, it is the parent with these responsibilities and rights who must bear the blame. A parent may provide for the fulfilment of her responsibilities at a practical level by someone else, by a formal or an informal arrangement, but while the parent has parental responsibilities and parental rights that delegation does not amount to a delegation of liability.

Arrangement. An informal arrangement is envisaged here, and there is no provision, as there is in s.4 below, for the arrangement to be in any specified format or to be registered anywhere.

Subs. (6)

Following on from the previous subsection, this provides that liability for failure to fulfil parental responsibilities rests with the parent who has such responsibilities. So a parent who leaves the exercise of the responsibility and the right of, for example, legal representation to someone else cannot evade liability for any loss to the child's estate caused by the delegate. If the delegation amounts to the fostering of the child within the meaning of the Foster Children (Scotland) Act 1984 (c. 56) (i.e. private fostering rather than fostering as an aspect of local authority care) then that Act will govern the responsibilities of the foster carer (without, of course, prejudice to the liability of the parent under the current provision).

Acquisition of parental rights and responsibilities by natural father

4.—(1) Where a child's mother has not been deprived of some or all of the parental responsibilities and parental rights in relation to him and, by virtue of subsection (1)(b) of section 3 of this Act, his father has no parental responsibilities or parental rights in relation to him, the father and mother, whatever age they may be, may by agreement provide that, as from the appropriate date, the father shall have the parental responsibilities and parental rights which (in the absence of any order under section 11 of this Act affecting those responsibilities and rights) he would have if married to the mother.

(2) No agreement under subsection (1) above shall have effect unless—

(a) in a form prescribed by the Secretary of State; and

(b) registered in the Books of Council and Session while the mother still has the parental responsibilities and parental rights which she had when the agreement was made.

(3) The date on which such registration as is mentioned in subsection (2)(b) above takes place shall be the "appropriate date" for the purposes of subsection (1) above.

(4) An agreement which has effect by virtue of subsection (2) above shall, subject only to section 11(11) of this Act, be irrevocable.

DEFINITIONS
"child": s.15(1).
"parental responsibilities": s.1(3).
"parental rights": s.2(4).

GENERAL NOTE
Under the 1986 Act an unmarried father could obtain parental rights only by being appointed guardian by the testamentary deed of the mother in accordance with s.4 thereof or by being conferred parental rights by a court under s.3 thereof. In addition to these means (which are re-enacted in the present Act), this section provides another means by which a father, who is not married to the mother of the child or was not married to her at the time of the child's conception or subsequently, can acquire parental responsibilities and parental rights in relation to the child, and that is by entering into a registered agreement in prescribed form with the mother.

Subs. (1)
Where a child's mother has not been deprived. It is only mothers who still retain the full gamut of parental responsibilities and parental rights who have power to confer parental responsibilities and parental rights on unmarried fathers, and it follows that if those responsibilities and rights have been taken away from the mother, whether by private law means (an order under s.11 below) or by public law means (an order under s.86 below or under the Adoption (Scotland) Act 1978 (c. 28)) this section is inapplicable. On the other hand, a mother whose child is subject to a supervision requirement with a condition of residence has not "been deprived" of her parental responsibilities and parental rights; rather they have simply been suspended during the currency of the supervision requirement to the extent necessary to give effect to that requirement, and such a mother can enter into an agreement under this section with the father. While the thinking behind this rule is clear and understandable—a mother ought not to be able to confer upon the father that which she does not herself have—it does nevertheless limit the number of fathers who can acquire parental responsibilities and parental rights by this route, without any fault or influence on the part of the father. A mother, by her failure to fulfil her own parental responsibilities, can thereby create a situation in which the father cannot acquire those responsibilities without going to court.

Deprived of some or all. If the mother has been deprived even of only one of the parental responsibilities or parental rights (e.g. that of legal representation) the father loses the chance of acquiring any parental responsibilities and parental rights by an agreement under this section. This is because the agreement can confer only the full gamut, as opposed to a selection, of the parental responsibilities and parental rights and, again, the mother should not be able to give what she does not have.

His father. "Father" is not defined, though s.15(1) defines "parent" to mean "genetic father or mother". We may take "father" to mean "genetic father". It is generally only a child's genetic father who can acquire parental responsibilities and parental rights by registering an agreement under this section. It is not open, for example, to the husband or the cohabitant of the mother (or any other relative of the child) to acquire parental responsibilities and parental rights in this way, even when they have alimentary obligations towards the child. It follows that in order for the agreement to be effective, the father will have to establish that he is the legal father of the child concerning whom the agreement is made. This can be done either by relying on the presumption in s.5(1)(b) of the 1986 Act, the provision deeming paternity under s.28(3) of the Human Fertilisation and Embryology Act 1990 (c. 37) (even though this does not deem genetic paternity), or by proof in court in an action of declarator of paternity under s.7 of the 1986 Act. The registering of an agreement under this section may well operate to create a presumption of fact that the male party to the agreement is the father of the child.

Whatever age they may be. These words give legal capacity to any person old enough to be a parent to enter into such an agreement. It does not, however, confer upon an under-16-year-old parent any capacity to exercise parental responsibilities or parental rights which he does not otherwise have (see note to s.2(1) above for further comment on the child-parent). A child-parent who acquires parental responsibilities and parental rights by an agreement under this section will not be able to exercise any of them until such time as he has capacity to do so, and the effect of these words is limited to preserving the validity of an agreement entered into before either or both of the parties reaches the age of 16.

Agreement. The matter lies in the hands of the mother to allow the father to obtain responsibilities and rights; but she cannot force him to accept them. Nor can the father force the mother to allow him responsibilities and rights, and there is no provision for the dispensing with the mother's agreement (as in, for example, adoption).

As from the appropriate date. The agreement takes effect on the day the agreement is registered in terms of subs. (2) below (subs. (3)).

He would have if married to the mother. The agreement is non-negotiable in the sense that the mother cannot offer some parental responsibilities only or some parental rights only. Again it is to be emphasised that parental rights exist only in order to allow the fulfilment of parental responsibilities and this would be defeated if only rights or only responsibilities could be obtained by such an agreement. Nor is it open to the mother to confer one of the parental responsibilities with its reciprocal parental right. The agreement must confer on the father all the parental responsibilities listed in s.1(1) together with all the parental rights listed in s.2(1).

Subs. (2)
The agreement in terms of subs. (1) above must be in a form to be prescribed, and to be effective, the agreement has to be registered in the Books of Council and Session at a time when the mother retains her parental responsibilities and parental rights.

Subs. (4)
Once entered into, only the court can revoke the agreement and it can do so only when making an order under s.11(2)(a) or (b) (i.e. an order depriving a person of parental responsibilities or parental rights or an order conferring these responsibilities and rights on a person). As the revocation is done under the authority of s.11, the three overarching principles in s.11(7) must be taken into account by the court. The making of an order under s.11(2)(a) or (b) does not automatically revoke an agreement—rather the court must make an express decision to that effect, separate from its decision to make an order under either of these paragraphs.

Care or control of child by person without parental responsibilities or parental rights

5.—(1) Subject to subsection (2) below, it shall be the responsibility of a person who has attained the age of sixteen years and who has care or control of a child under that age, but in relation to him either has no parental responsibilities or parental rights or does not have the parental responsibility mentioned in section 1(1)(a) of this Act, to do what is reasonable in all the circumstances to safeguard the child's health, development and welfare; and in fulfilling his responsibility under this section the person may in particular, even though he does not have the parental right mentioned in section 2(1)(d) of this Act, give consent to any surgical, medical or dental treatment or procedure where—

(a) the child is not able to give such consent on his own behalf; and

(b) it is not within the knowledge of the person that a parent of the child would refuse to give the consent in question.

(2) Nothing in this section shall apply to a person in so far as he has care or control of a child in a school ("school" having the meaning given by section 135(1) of the Education (Scotland) Act 1980).

DEFINITIONS
"child": s.15(1).
"parental responsibilities": s.1(3).
"parental rights": s.2(4).
"person": s.15(4).
"school": Education (Scotland) Act 1980, s.135(1).

GENERAL NOTE
See Scot. Law Com. No. 135, para. 2.59.

The law as it stood before the making of this provision was very unclear as to the powers of persons who had the care and control of a child but no parental rights in relation to the child. The concept of a person acting *in loco parentis* was undeveloped in Scots law and is a description of fact rather than a distinct legal institution. Yet it frequently happens that a child falls into the care and control of such a person. For example, a neighbour may be looking after a child while a parent is in hospital, or a relative may be taking the child on holiday, or a baby sitter may be watching over the child for an evening, or a child-minder may be caring for the child during the day, or a foster carer may be caring for the child on an emergency and short-term basis; in addition, an unmarried father who lives in family with his child and the mother will often adopt a parenting role even when the law says he has no responsibility to do so. This provision imposes a measure of responsibility on any such person. It is implicit, though surprisingly not stated, that the power or right to act in such a way as is necessary to fulfil the responsibility is also conferred. It is expressly provided that a person with care or control of a child can consent to the child's medical treatment. What, in essence, is contemplated by this provision is a safeguarding power rather than an upbringing role.

Subs. (1)

A person who has care or control of a child under 16 has the responsibility to safeguard the child's health, development and welfare, even though she or he does not have that responsibility by way of parental responsibility or right. The responsibility expressly includes the power to consent to medical treatment when the child cannot give personal consent and when the person is unaware of any parental objection thereto.

Has attained the age of 16 years. This provision does not apply to persons under 16, such as, for example, a 15-year-old baby sitter (thus avoiding problems relating to the legal capacity of such a person). Notwithstanding a contrary assumption in the House of Lords debates on this clause (see *Hansard*, H.L., Vol.564, col.53) the provision does not require that all babysitters be over the age of 16 years, but merely provides a rule for those who are.

Care or control. Whether a child is in the care or control of another person is a question of fact, to be determined by all the circumstances, and these factual circumstances can change rapidly. Physical possession of and proximity to the child are clearly significant but not determining. It will cover informal temporary arrangements, such as weekends with grandparents or friends (but not, because of subs. (2) below, school trips), as well as longer term arrangements such as when an unmarried father cares for his child, or the child is being looked after by foster carers; and it is clearly wide enough also to cover the kidnapper.

Do what is reasonable. The responsibility to safeguard the child's health, development and welfare is not absolute and is merely one to use reasonable care. What is reasonable will depend on all the circumstances. A person with long-term care or control will have more extensive responsibilities towards the child's development than a person with care and control for a weekend.

Consent to any surgical, medical or dental treatment or procedure. This phrase reflects that used in s.2(4) of the Age of Legal Capacity (Scotland) Act 1991 (c. 50) and is to be given a wide interpretation. The power to give medical consent under this provision is, however, limited by its protective context. It will not include treatment designed for the benefit of others, such as circumcision or organ donation, nor elective treatment such as contraception or abortion (unless this can be shown to be necessary to safeguard the child's welfare). It may not cover cosmetic surgery (unless this is therapeutic). Experimental treatment for research cannot be consented to under this provision. Power to consent includes power to refuse, because "consent" is simply a shorthand way of expressing the power of medical decision-making (see notes to s.90 below). The reference to s.2(1)(d) (the right of legal representation) indicates that the exercise of the power of consent is an exercise of the right of legal representation rather than the responsibility to safeguard the child's health (this has importance for the purposes of how long the right to represent the child lasts: see the notes to s.15(5) below). If this is so (and it was assumed to be so in Scot. Law Com. No. 135 at para. 2.22) then the acquisition by the child of capacity to consent denies anyone else the right to consent on her or his behalf: this is made explicit by s.15(5) below.

The child is not able to give such consent. A child may not be able to give consent on her or his own behalf for practical reasons (e.g. unconsciousness after an accident) or legal reasons (i.e. incapacity). A child's capacity to consent to or to refuse medical treatment is governed by s.2(4) of the Age of Legal Capacity (Scotland) Act 1991 (c. 50) (see discussion in Wilkinson & Norrie *Parent and Child* (1993, W. Green) at pp. 182–187).

Not within the knowledge. The onus of proof lies on the person claiming that it is within the knowledge of the person with care or control of the child that the parent would refuse to give consent.

Would refuse. To deny the person with care or control the power to consent to medical treatment, it has to be shown that the parent would refuse consent, and not simply that the parent is likely to refuse consent. This is a high standard of proof and will only be satisfied in cases in which there is positive and unequivocal evidence, apparent before the need for consent arose, that the parent would not consent, for example if the parent, to the knowledge of the person with care or control of the child, had consistently refused to have the child innoculated.

Subs. (2)

The powers of teachers and school administrators are contained in the Education (Scotland) Act 1980 (c. 44), and are not enlarged by this section.

Views of children

6.—(1) A person shall, in reaching any major decision which involves—

(a) his fulfilling a parental responsibility or the responsibility mentioned in section 5(1) of this Act; or

(b) his exercising a parental right or giving consent by virtue of that section,

have regard so far as practicable to the views (if he wishes to express them) of the child concerned, taking account of the child's age and maturity, and to those of any other person who has parental responsibilities or parental rights in relation to the child (and wishes to express those views); and without prejudice to the generality of this subsection a child twelve years of age or more shall be presumed to be of sufficient age and maturity to form a view.

(2) A transaction entered into in good faith by a third party and a person acting as legal representative of a child shall not be challengeable on the ground only that the child, or a person with parental responsibilities or parental rights in relation to the child, was not consulted or that due regard was not given to his views before the transaction was entered into.

DEFINITIONS

"child": s.15(1).
"legal representative": s.15(5).
"parental responsibilities": s.1(3).
"parental rights": s.2(4).
"person": s.15(4).
"transaction": s.15(1); s.9 of the Age of Legal Capacity (Scotland) Act 1991.

GENERAL NOTE

Article 12 of the UN Convention on the Rights of the Child provides as follows:

"States parties shall assure to the child who is capable of forming his or her own views the right to express those views freely in all matters affecting the child, the views of the child being given due weight in accordance with the age and maturity of the child. For this purpose, the child shall in particular be provided the opportunity to be heard in any judicial and administrative proceedings affecting the child, either directly, or through a representative or an appropriate body, in a manner consistent with the procedural rules of national law".

The duty on courts and children's hearings making decisions in connection with children to take account of the views of children is dealt with in ss.11(7) and 16(2) respectively below. The present provision, following Scot. Law Com. No. 135 at paras. 2.60–2.66, attempts to give effect to art. 12 UN by directing that parents and others exercising parental responsibilities and parental rights are also to have regard to the views of the child and others with parental responsibilities and parental rights in making decisions which will affect the child. The difficulty lies in identifying how this provision can be enforced, or identifying what sanction could follow a failure to fulfil the obligation. In relation to decisions of the court or the children's hearing, the obligation to take account of the child's views can be enforced through the appeal mechanisms; but there is no judicial review of parental decisions and any decision made to the absence of consultation with the child or other person with parental responsibilities and parental rights will be given effect to. This is made explicit in relation to the entering into of transactions; other decisions too will remain effective. So, for example, a parental decision to send a 13-year-old child to one school rather than another will be an effective and valid exercise of a parental responsibility and parental right even although the child or other person has not been consulted.

Subs. (1)

A person fulfilling a parental responsibility or exercising a parental right or otherwise fulfilling a responsibility to safeguard the child's health, development and welfare will frequently have to make decisions which affect the child. In doing so the person is obliged by this provision to have regard to the child's views, taking account of her or his age and maturity. The child is not obliged to express views, but the wording suggests that the person making the decision is obliged to seek out, or at the very least to give the child the opportunity to express, her or his views. A child aged 12 or more is (rebuttably) presumed to be of sufficient age and maturity to form a view. In addition, the decision-maker must take account of the views of any other person with parental responsibilities and parental rights, though the fact that under s.2(2) above each person with parental rights can exercise these rights without the consent of the other renders the obligation of consultation one of symbolic and educative importance only.

Any major decision. Clearly not all decisions affecting a child will fall within this category. Decisions concerning what clothes the child is to wear, when she or he is to be home at night, or what she or he is to eat, are not major decisions. A decision by the parents to move house, which involves moving the child to another school is likely to be considered major, and sending the child to stay long term with a relative certainly is. To change the child's nationality is a major decision, as is a change in her or his domicile or habitual residence, for all these will affect the laws to which the child is subject. The appointment of a guardian is expressly made a major decision: s.7(6) below. Due to the unenforceability of s.6 as a whole, it is unlikely that there will be court proceedings on the question of what is or is not a major decision.

Have regard. The parent must have regard to the views of the child and other person with parental responsibilities and parental rights, but need not follow them. All the provision requires is that the parent seeks out and gives active consideration to any expressed views. These views are not determining, for other considerations, such as costs and practicality and the child's welfare may predominate. A child may desperately wish to attend a fee-paying school, but these wishes are meaningless if the parent cannot afford the fees.

So far as practicable. It may not be practicable to obtain the views of a child or other person on a particular matter and, if so, the obligation under this provision is not breached by a failure to do so. Indeed in circumstances in which it would not be practicable to give effect to any view expressed by the child, the obligation to have regard to such a view is so meaningless as to be non-existent.

If he wishes to express them. A child has no obligation to give views on matters relating to major decisions, and there will indeed be circumstances in which a child's welfare demands that she or he is not disturbed by being asked to make serious choices. It is cruel, for example, for separating parents to ask their young child to choose between them. Pressure should not be put on a child to express views which are difficult to form and awkward to express.

A child 12 years of age or more. Under the adoption legislation a child 12 years of age or over must consent to the adoption before an adoption order can be made (Adoption (Scotland) Act 1978 (c. 28), s.12(8)) and under the Age of Legal Capacity (Scotland) Act 1991 (c. 50), s.2(3), legal capacity to give or withhold that consent is granted at that age. This provision is similar, but not identical. There is a rebuttable presumption that the child of 12 or more is able to form (and express) a view on the matter at issue, but the provision does not give the child a veto, as is the case with adoption. The obligation is as effective for younger children who in fact can form and express a view; and if an older child cannot in fact form a view on the particular matter at issue then there is no obligation under this provision to seek out and have regard to her or his views.

Subs. (2)

This subsection protects the interests of third parties acting in good faith who transact with a person acting as a child's legal representative. If the legal representative has not consulted with, or had regard to the views of, the child or other person with parental responsibilities and parental rights in relation to the transaction, the transaction remains valid (unless it can be challenged on some other ground).

Child. A child for this purpose is a person under 16, otherwise she or he will not have a legal representative who is entitled to act because the child is incapable of so acting (see s.15(5) below).

Guardianship

Appointment of guardians

7.—(1) A child's parent may appoint a person to be guardian of the child in the event of the parent's death; but—

(a) such appointment shall be of no effect unless—

(i) in writing and signed by the parent; and

(ii) the parent, at the time of death, was entitled to act as legal representative of the child (or would have been so entitled if he had survived until after the birth of the child); and

(b) any parental responsibilities or parental rights (or the right to appoint a further guardian under this section) which a surviving parent has in relation to the child shall subsist with those which, by, under or by virtue of this Part of this Act, the appointee so has.

(2) A guardian of a child may appoint a person to take his place as guardian in the event of the guardian's death; but such appointment shall be of no effect unless in writing and signed by the person making it.

(3) An appointment as guardian shall not take effect until accepted, either expressly or impliedly by acts which are not consistent with any other intention.

(4) If two or more persons are appointed as guardians, any one or more of them shall, unless the appointment expressly provides otherwise, be entitled to accept office even if both or all of them do not accept office.

(5) Subject to any order under section 11 or 86 of this Act, a person appointed as a child's guardian under this section shall have, in respect of the child, the responsibilities imposed, and the rights conferred, on a parent by sections 1 and 2 of this Act respectively; and sections 1 and 2 of this Act shall apply in relation to a guardian as they apply in relation to a parent.

(6) Without prejudice to the generality of subsection (1) of section 6 of this Act, a decision as to the appointment of a guardian under subsection (1) or (2) above shall be regarded for the purposes of that section (or of that section as applied by subsection (5) above) as a major decision which involves exercising a parental right.

DEFINITIONS

"child": s.15(1).
"legal representative": s.15(5).
"parent": s.15(1).
"parental responsibilities": s.1(3).
"parental rights": s.2(4).
"person": s.15(4).

GENERAL NOTE

See Scot. Law Com. No. 135, paras. 3.1.–3.15.

Until the coming into force of the Age of Legal Capacity (Scotland) Act 1991 (c. 50), the word "guardian" was not a term of art with a uniform recognised meaning in Scots law, notwithstanding that it appeared in numerous statutes (each with its own, peculiar, definition). Since 1991 it has been clear that the primary (but not the only) meaning of the word "guardian" (as used, for example, in the 1986 Act) is "legal representative", in the way that tutor was prior to the Age of Legal Capacity (Scotland) Act 1991. However, ambiguity remained, and it was common to refer to parents as guardians when they were exercising the guardianship role, that is acting as the child's legal representative. Under s.4 of the 1986 Act, a parent could appoint a guardian to a child, but this was an appointment only of a legal representative and did not amount to the conferring of the right of, say, custody. Yet sometimes the word "guardian" was used to mean much more than legal representative, and in the common phrase "parent or guardian", the meaning is clearly understood to be parent on the one hand or parent-substitute with all the rights and duties of a parent on the other hand. The present Act, though nowhere defining "guardian", clarifies the position, and this section provides that "guardian", as appointed under the provisions of the Act, is a parent-substitute, with all the parental responsibilities and parental rights, and not only the responsibility and right of legal representation. The parent will never act as "guardian", but may act as "legal representative". It should be noted, however, that a guardian is a parent-substitute only for the purposes of parental responsibilities and parental rights as defined in ss.1 and 2 above, and not, for example, for the purposes of succession or the law of incest or the forbidden degrees of marriage. Guardians are no longer to be treated as trustees for the purposes of the Trusts Acts (Sched. 5 below), but any person acting as a child's legal representative will be subject to trust-like obligations.

This section deals with the powers of, and testamentary appointment of, guardians, while s.8 below deals with revocation and termination of guardianship, and s.11(2)(h) below deals with court appointment and removal of guardians.

Subs. (1)

This provision re-enacts, with some modification, the rules previously contained in s.4 of the 1986 Act, to the effect that a parent may appoint a person to act as guardian of the child by testamentary deed, and that the appointment does not affect the responsibilities and rights of the other parent.

A child's parent. Subs. (1) applies only to the genetic parent of the child who has the parental responsibility and the parental right of legal representation.

A person. Though the singular is used, normal principles of statutory interpretation (Interpretation Act 1978 (c. 30), s.6(c)) indicate that the singular can include the plural, and it follows that a parent can appoint more than one person to be the child's guardian. This is given further support by subs. (4) below, which would be meaningless if "a person" were interpreted as being restricted to the singular.

To be guardian. The equivalent provision under the 1986 Act (s.4) limited the appointee to the parental right of legal representation, but under the new provision the notion of "guardian" is significantly extended by subs. (5) below and the appointment of a person to be guardian has the effect of conferring all the parental responsibilities and parental rights on the appointee: the appointment of a person to be guardian is an appointment of a person to be parent-substitute of the child.

In the event of the parent's death. The appointment is testamentary in nature, in that it can only take effect as from the date of death of the parent. A parent cannot appoint a guardian to act during that parent's lifetime. The appointment can be made in a will or codicil thereto, or in a separate deed.

Entitled to act as legal representative. These words show a lingering confusion as to whether a guardian is a parent-substitute or a legal representative. Only a parent who has the responsibility and right of legal representation can appoint a guardian, but the appointment, according to subs. (5) below, will confer all the parental responsibilities and rights and not just that of legal representation. If a parent has only the responsibility and right of legal representation and has been denied the others then an appointment would seem to confer upon the appointee more power than the appointer her or himself has (*cf.* s.4(1) above, where a mother who has been denied any one of her parental responsibilities or parental rights is prohibited from agreeing to share parental responsibilities and parental rights with the father, because he would thereby acquire from her more than she had to give). However, the terms of subs. (5) below are clear and unambiguous, with the result that a parent who has the right of legal representation but not the right, say, to have the child living with him can appoint a guardian who will have both the right of legal representation and the right to determine the child's residence. This position is odd but, on the clear wording of the statute, unavoidable.

Survived until after the birth. A person may make such a testamentary appointment even though she or he dies before the birth of the child (following the old common law rule in relation to appointment of tutors: *Murray v. Merschall* (1555) Mor. 16226). However, it should be noted that the child must be conceived and in the womb before the death of the father making the appointment, otherwise the genetic father is not the father in legal terms: Human Fertilisation and Embryology Act 1990, s.28(6)(b).

A surviving parent. The surviving parent who has parental responsibilities and parental rights retains these responsibilities and rights notwithstanding the acquisition of responsibilities and rights by the appointee. There was no such provision in the 1986 Act, though it was certainly assumed to be the law. This provision is included, therefore, for the avoidance of doubt. Section 2(2) above is to be recalled, which allows any person with parental responsibilities or parental rights to exercise them without reference to any other person with the same responsibilities or rights.

Subs. (2)

This is a new provision. One of the flaws in the 1986 Act was that while it allowed parents to appoint guardians, it did not allow guardians to appoint guardians, and so if a child was unfortunate enough to lose a parent, who had appointed a guardian, and then to lose that guardian, the only way a further guardian could be appointed to such a child was by petition to the court. This flaw has now been remedied, in a way consistent with the whole format of this section, which is to give guardians all the parental responsibilities and parental rights of a parent. One of these rights is to appoint a guardian by testamentary deed, and a guardian, whether so appointed or appointed by the court, is now expressly given that right in this subsection.

A guardian. The office of guardianship must be subsisting in the guardian at the date of her or his death.

A person. As with subs. (1) above, the singular includes the plural.

Subs. (3)

Again, this is a new provision added for the avoidance of doubt. The office of guardian can be onerous and is not to be imposed on a person unwilling to accept the responsibilities of a parent-substitute. The appointment, therefore, only takes effect once it has been accepted by the nominee. (The rule may well be different with court appointments under s.11(2)(h), for there is no requirement under that section for the consent of any person before any parental responsibility or parental right be imposed upon them).

Accepted ... impliedly. Cases involving implied acceptance of the office of trusteeship may prove of use here: see Wilson and Duncan *Trusts, Trustees and Executors* (1975, W. Green) at pp. 244–246.

Subs. (4)

The appointment of more than one guardian is joint and several and any nominee can accept without affecting the nomination of the others. This provision reflects the law as it already stands (see Wilkinson and Norrie *Parent and Child* (1993, W. Green) at pp. 385–387), but puts it on a statutory basis and is for the avoidance of doubt, as recommended by the Scottish Law Commission (Scot. Law Com. No. 135, para. 3.9).

Subs. (5)

This important provision has the effect of showing that the "guardian" in today's law is a "parent-substitute". Once appointed, the guardian acquires all the parental responsibilities and parental rights that the parent is given under ss.1 and 2 of the present Act. The guardian is no longer simply the legal representative or, as she or he was known at common law, the tutor of the child, but has the full powers, duties, liabilities, responsibilities and rights of a parent. The guardian steps into the shoes of the parent (for the purposes of parental responsibilities and parental rights as defined in ss.1 and 2 above). The parent making the appointment cannot confer only some of the parental responsibilities or parental rights on the appointee.

Appointed under this section. These words suggest that the rule contained in this subsection applies only when the guardian is appointed by testamentary deed. But the same effect is achieved with court-appointed guardians (see the General Note to s.11(2)(h) below).

Subs. (6)

The effect of this provision is that the views of the child and any other person with parental responsibilities and parental rights must be sought and regard given to them according to the principles in s.6 above in relation to the appointment of a guardian. In other words, when a parent or guardian is drawing up a testamentary deed in which a guardian is to be appointed, she must have regard so far as practicable to the views (if she or he wishes to express them) of the other parent and of the child over whom a guardian is to be appointed, taking account of the child's age and maturity. As with the generality of s.6, this provision is more a pious hope than a legally enforceable obligation. If the child's or other parent's views are not sought, or ignored, then this will not be a ground for challenging the appointment. Section 6(2) saves the validity of "transactions" entered into by legal representatives, but that would not save the appointment of a guardian, which only with some difficulty could be described as an act of legal representation. The absence of a provision similar to that in s.6(2) might indicate that the appointment is not saved. However, it is likely that if Parliament intended that the child's or other parent's consent were a requirement for an appointment as guardian it would have made express provision for this, just as express provision is made for the child's consent to adoption (Adoption (Scotland) Act 1978, s.12(8)). Consent is not a condition precedent, and nor is consultation with the child. It is a hope and an expectation, but in legal terms nothing more. A child or parent who objects to the appointment will be able to apply to the court under s.11 below for the termination of the appointment or for the appointment of someone else. Such an application would only be successful, of course, if the court is persuaded that it is in the child's interests, but it will usually be against a child's interests (particularly when the child is older) to be given a guardian (that is a parent-substitute) to whom she or he objects.

Revocation and other termination of appointment

8.—(1) An appointment made under section 7(1) or (2) of this Act revokes an earlier such appointment (including one made in an unrevoked will or codicil) made by the same person in respect of the same child, unless it is clear (whether as a result of an express provision in the later appointment or by any necessary implication) that the purpose of the later appointment is to appoint an additional guardian.

(2) Subject to subsections (3) and (4) below, the revocation of an appointment made under section 7(1) or (2) of this Act (including one made in an unrevoked will or codicil) shall not take effect unless the revocation is in writing and is signed by the person making the revocation.

(3) An appointment under section 7(1) or (2) of this Act (other than one made in a will or codicil) is revoked if, with the intention of revoking the appointment, the person who made it—

(a) destroys the document by which it was made; or

(b) has some other person destroy that document in his presence.

(4) For the avoidance of doubt, an appointment made under section 7(1) or (2) of this Act in a will or codicil is revoked if the will or codicil is revoked.

(5) Once an appointment of a guardian has taken effect under section 7 of this Act, then, unless the terms of the appointment provide for earlier termination, it shall terminate only by virtue of—

(a) the child concerned attaining the age of eighteen years;

(b) the death of the child or the guardian; or

(c) the termination of the appointment by a court order under section 11 of this Act.

DEFINITIONS
"child": s.15(1).
"parent": s.15(1).

GENERAL NOTE
See Scot. Law Com. No. 135, para. 3.16.

The 1986 Act did not deal expressly with revocation and termination of guardianship, and the law on this point, rather untidily, was mostly to be found in the Trusts (Scotland) Act 1921 (c. 58), since guardians were trustees for the purposes of that Act, and the other Trusts Acts. Schedule 5 to the present Act removes guardianship from the Trusts Acts and this section aims to provide a complete code of when and how guardianship comes to an end (other than by court termination, which is dealt with under s.11(2)(h) below).

Subs. (1)
This introduces a presumption that a subsequent appointment will supersede a previously made appointment. The appointment, of course, does not take effect until the death of the appointer, and it would have been more apt to talk here of nomination rather than appointment. The nomination that takes effect is the latest in time and a new nomination has the effect of revoking an earlier nomination. It is, however, possible to appoint more than one person to be guardian, and this may be done in consecutive deeds. So it is provided that, so long as this is made clear, a subsequent deed can be interpreted as nominating an additional guardian rather than superseding the previous nomination.

Express provision... or by any necessary implication. If the intent is to nominate an additional guardian then it would be better if this were done expressly, but the provision allows such an intent to be indicated by necessary implication. The word "necessary" is likely to receive a strict interpretation. Interpretation of deeds is governed by the intent of the maker of the deed, and not by the welfare of the child (see for example *Spencer's Trs v. Ruggles* 1982 S.L.T. 165).

Subss. (2) and (3)
The nomination must be in writing and signed by the person making it (s.7(1)(a) and (2) above); likewise the revocation of the nomination must be in writing and signed by the person who made it. This is the only method by which a nomination contained in a will or codicil can be revoked. Alternatively, if the nomination does not appear in a will or codicil, it can be revoked by intentional destruction, either at the hands of the appointer or at the hands of someone else at the instigation of and in the presence of the appointer.

Subs. (4)
It is assumed that when a will which contains an appointment is revoked, the appointment too is revoked. If the appointer does not intend that result, she or he must make a new appointment

at the revocation of the will, or revoke the will in such a way that the appointment is preserved (e.g. by revoking the individual legacies in the will rather than the will itself).

Subs. (5)

An appointment, once it takes effect, is irrevocable: neither parents nor parent-substitutes can escape from their parental responsibilities and parental rights and the office of guardian (like the role of parent) is not one from which a person can resign. This clarifies the position from the old law, in which it was at least arguable that a guardian could resign by using the power of resignation contained in the Trusts (Scotland) Act 1921 (see Wilkinson and Norrie *Parent and Child* (1993 W. Green) at pp. 395–397).

Unless the terms of the appointment provide for earlier termination. These words suggest that, notwithstanding the fact that a testamentary appointment will confer upon the appointee all the responsibilities and rights of a parent (s.7(5) above), the appointment itself may allow the parent-substitute to escape from these responsibilities and rights earlier than a parent could, either by providing a power to resign or by specifying for how long the appointment is to last. Such a provision should, it is submitted, be interpreted very strictly since it will seldom be in the interests of the child to allow a person prematurely to escape her or his responsibilities towards the child. In the case of a court appointment it would only be in highly exceptional circumstances that the decree appointing a person as guardian would allow the person to relinquish the parental responsibilities and rights undertaken. In the absence of any such term, the appointment as guardian will terminate only when the child grows up, or when the child or guardian dies, or when the court orders termination under s.11 below.

Has taken effect. This will normally be on the moment of death, since the appointment is testamentary in nature. It might, however, be at some time after death if the acceptance of the office of guardian has not occurred before then (see s.7(3) above).

Eighteen years. This again shows that the appointment is as a parent-substitute and not simply as legal representative, because the parental responsibility and parental right of legal representation lasts only until the child is 16. Indeed, all that remains after the child's 16th birthday is the responsibility of providing guidance to the child and the guardian shall have no other legal responsibility.

Administration of child's property

Safeguarding of child's property

9.—(1) Subject to section 13 of this Act, this section applies where—

(a) property is owned by or due to a child;

(b) the property is held by a person other than a parent or guardian of the child; and

(c) but for this section, the property would be required to be transferred to a parent having parental responsibilities in relation to the child or to a guardian for administration by that parent or guardian on behalf of the child.

(2) Subject to subsection (4) below, where this section applies and the person holding the property is an executor or trustee, then—

(a) if the value of the property exceeds £20,000, he shall; or

(b) if that value is not less than £5,000 and does not exceed £20,000, he may, apply to the Accountant of Court for a direction as to the administration of the property.

(3) Subject to subsection (4) below, where this section applies and the person holding the property is a person other than an executor or trustee, then, if the value of the property is not less than £5,000, that person may apply to the Accountant of Court for a direction as to the administration of the property.

(4) Where the parent or guardian mentioned in subsection (1)(c) above has been appointed a trustee under a trust deed to administer the property concerned, subsections (2) and (3) above shall not apply, and the person holding the property shall transfer it to the parent or guardian.

(5) On receipt of an application under subsection (2) or (3) above, the Accountant of Court may do one, or (in so far as the context admits) more than one, of the following—

(a) apply to the court for the appointment of a judicial factor (whether or not the parent or guardian mentioned in subsection (1)(c) above) to administer all or part of the property concerned and in the event of the court making such an appointment shall direct that the property, or as the case may be part, concerned be transferred to the factor;

(b) direct that all or part of the property concerned be transferred to himself;

(c) direct that all or, in a case where the parent or guardian so mentioned has not been appointed by virtue of paragraph (a) above, part of the property concerned be transferred to the parent or guardian, to be administered on behalf of the child.

(6) A direction under subsection (5)(c) above may include such conditions as the Accountant of Court considers appropriate, including in particular a condition—

(a) that in relation to the property concerned no capital expenditure shall be incurred without his approval; or

(b) that there shall be exhibited annually to him the securities and bank books which represent the capital of the estate.

(7) A person who has applied under subsection (2) or (3) above for a direction shall not thereafter transfer the property concerned except in accordance with a direction under subsection (5) above.

(8) The Secretary of State may from time to time prescribe a variation in any sum referred to in subsections (2) and (3) above.

(9) In this section "child" means a person under the age of sixteen years who is habitually resident in Scotland.

DEFINITIONS
"child": s.9(9).
"parent": s.15(1).
"parental responsibilities": s.1(3).

GENERAL NOTE
It can sometimes happen that substantial amounts of property fall into the ownership or entitlement of a child, and before the enactment of this provision the child's parent, exercising the right of guardianship, or the child's guardian, had the right to administer that property on behalf of the child. That administration was, however, subject to the provisions of the Judicial Factors Act 1849 (c. 51), with the result that a parent or guardian who received property on behalf of the child was under the supervision of the Accountant of Court, and was obliged to lodge an inventory and to submit annual accounts (1849 Act, ss.3 and 4). Clearly this was frequently ignored, particularly when the sums involved were modest, and the Scottish Law Commission (Scot. Law Com. No. 135 at para. 4.17) suggested a scheme whereby the law impose the obligations of judicial factors on parents and guardians in only some appropriate cases. Their proposals are given effect to in this section. In summary, directions may (and sometimes must) be sought from the Accountant of Court as to the administration of the property that is due to be paid to the parent or guardian on behalf of the child. The Accountant of Court has various options and can make orders and attach conditions thereto, which must be followed by the person who sought the directions.

Subs. (1)
The section applies in any situation in which property which is owned by, or due to, a child is held by a person other than a parent or guardian and would be (but for this section) required to be transferred to a parent or guardian having the right to administer the property on the child's behalf. The most common situations in which this arises is with inheritance, awards of damages (dealt with in s.13 below) and awards under the Criminal Injuries Compensation Scheme, though the section is not limited to these situations.

A parent or guardian. The word "parent" in subs. (1)(b) refers to a parent with parental responsibilities and parental rights rather than to all genetic parents since the requirement is that the property be held by someone other than a person with parental responsibilities and parental rights.

Required to be transferred. The section applies only when the holder of property is required to pay it over to a parent with parental responsibilities or to a guardian. Not all property due to a child is required to be transferred to a parent or guardian for administration on behalf of the child. A child who earns money is normally entitled to have her or his earnings paid direct (though it would be unusual for the child to earn more than £5,000). Indeed a child who has legal capacity to grant a discharge to any person holding property on her or his behalf can be paid directly, and s.13 below, for example, is certainly based on the assumption that a discharge may sometimes be granted even before the age of 16.

Transferred to a parent ... or to a guardian. If the property is required to be transferred to someone other than a parent or guardian then this provision does not apply. In particular, the obligation may be to transfer the property to a trustee, for which, see subs. (4) below.

Subs. (2)

Under the previous law parents and guardians were treated as judicial factors no matter how modest the sums involved were, and the law was clearly frequently ignored with parents seldom submitting annual accounts. Indeed, when one considers the values of most children's property holding, the expense of fulfilling such an obligation was likely to be disproportionate and therefore against the child's economic welfare. The aim of s.9, therefore, is to ensure that the Accountant of Court becomes involved only when large amounts of money are involved. It is therefore provided that an executor or trustee holding property due to a child *must* apply to the Accountant of Court for directions when the amount exceeds £20,000 in value, and she or he *may* (but is not obliged to) apply for directions when the amount is less than £20,000 but exceeds £5,000. Though not stated, a necessary implication is that it would be incompetent to apply for directions when the sum involved is less than £5,000.

Subs. (3)

It is likely that most cases of a child becoming due amounts in excess of £5,000 will be as a result of inheritance, but there will sometimes be other situations, such as payments under the Criminal Injuries Compensation Scheme, or by gift. In any case other than that of an executor or trustee, if the amount due exceeds £5,000 the person holding the property has the discretion of applying to the Accountant of Court for directions. It is likely to be considered appropriate to seek directions if the sum involved is considerably in excess of £5,000, and while the person holding the property is not a legal representative and therefore not subject to the obligations contained in s.10 below, any person holding property on behalf of another is to some extent subject to the rules of trust law: it follows that the holder of the property is obliged to act as a reasonable and prudent trustee would act, and if loss is caused by a failure to seek directions the holder of the property may be liable to the child.

Subs. (4)

The obligation or discretion to make an application for directions to the Accountant of Court does not apply when the property holder is obliged to transfer the property to a parent or guardian who is a trustee under a trust deed to administer the property concerned. The property holder in that case must pay the property over directly to such a parent or guardian. This is because the child's interest in the property will be sufficiently protected by its being transferred into a trust and thereby subject to the rules of trust law.

Subs. (5)

If an application is made to the Accountant of Court he may either apply to the court for the appointment of a judicial factor, direct that the property be transferred to himself, or direct that the property be transferred to the parent or guardian; in each case so that it can be properly administered on behalf of the child.

May do one. The terms of the statute do not here admit of a discretion on the part of the Accountant of Court to do none of the listed acts. He may do one or he may do another or he may do more than one, but he must respond in one of the listed ways.

Apply to the court for the appointment of a judicial factor. If the Accountant of Court makes the application for such an appointment, the court is not obliged to grant it, nor to grant it in the terms in which the Accountant asks. If the court does make an appointment of a judicial factor then it must direct that the appropriate property be transferred to the factor. The factor will be subject, of course, to the rules in the Judicial Factors Act 1849.

The property concerned be transferred to himself. If the Accountant of Court directs that the property or part thereof be transferred to himself, then it shall be up to him to invest, administer or otherwise deal with the property on behalf of the child.

The property concerned be transferred to the parent or guardian. If the Accountant of Court directs that the property be transferred to the parent or guardian, then the parent or guardian must administer it on behalf of the child by exercising the responsibility and right of legal representation.

Subs. (6)

If the Accountant of Court has directed that all or part of the property concerned be transferred to the parent or guardian to be administered on behalf of the child, then he may include in that direction such conditions as he considers appropriate. The provision is wide in its terms, and paras. (a) and (b) give examples of the sorts of condition that might, in appropriate cases, be included.

Subs. (7)
If an application for directions has been made to the Accountant of Court, the person making the application must follow these directions in transferring the property. If he transfers the property otherwise than in accordance with the directions, say by paying direct to a parent or guardian instead of, as instructed, to the Accountant of Court, and loss is caused to the child thereby, that person may be called upon to pay again out of his own pocket the value of the property in accordance with the directions. This liability is not spelt out in the statute, but is analogous to the liability of a trustee who pays out to a wrong beneficiary to pay again to the correct beneficiary. See Wilson and Duncan *Trusts, Trustees and Executors* (1975, W. Green) at pp. 373–376.

Subs. (8)
The figures of £5,000 and £20,000 may be varied by the Secretary of State.

Subs. (9)
Child. The protections provided by this section are not required for persons who are able to administer their own property for themselves, and since the coming into effect of the Age of Legal Capacity (Scotland) Act 1991, this has been at age 16 at the latest and, sometimes, earlier. The responsibility and the right of legal representation lasts only until the child is 16 in any case (ss.1(2) and 2(7) above) or sometimes ends sooner (s.15(5) below).
Habitually resident. For the meaning of this phrase, see notes to s.14(1) below.

Obligations and rights of person administering child's property

10.—(1) A person acting as a child's legal representative in relation to the administration of the child's property—
   (a) shall be required to act as a reasonable and prudent person would act on his own behalf; and
   (b) subject to any order made under section 11 of this Act, shall be entitled to do anything which the child, if of full age and capacity, could do in relation to that property;
and subject to subsection (2) below, on ceasing to act as legal representative, shall be liable to account to the child for his intromissions with the child's property.
   (2) No liability shall be incurred by virtue of subsection (1) above in respect of funds which have been used in the proper discharge of the person's responsibility to safeguard and promote the child's health, development and welfare.

DEFINITIONS
"legal representative": s.15(5).

GENERAL NOTE
The previous law imposed a duty on all parents or guardians who administered the estate of a child to account to the child for their intromissions with the funds. The Scottish Law Commission felt that it was inappropriate to impose this duty on everyone, given that most parents and guardians will at some time have to manage very small sums on behalf of their children (see Scot. Law Com. No. 135 at para. 4.22). This present section attempts to balance the need to ensure that parents and guardians can be called to account in appropriate cases with the reality that most parents will control funds for the benefit of the child which are so small that the obligation to account is next to meaningless. It does so by imposing an obligation, similar to the obligation on trustees in managing trust funds for the benefit of beneficiaries, to act as a reasonable and prudent person would act on her or his own behalf, and to subject the parent or guardian to liability for failing so to act. In addition, it obliges the parent or guardian to account for intromissions, but exempts the parent or guardian from liability for using the child's fund for the promotion of the child's welfare.

Subs. (1)
The obligation imposed in para. (a) is to achieve the standard of the reasonable and prudent person acting as she or he would on her or his own behalf. This is an objective test, as it is in trust

law (see Norrie and Scobbie *Trusts* (1991, W. Green) at p. 141), and it is no defence for the legal representatives who have failed in this obligation to show that they acted as they would act on their own behalf: the question is not how they themselves would act in their own affairs, but how the reasonable and prudent person would act in her or his own affairs.

Paragraph (b) confers on the legal representative the right to do anything which the child would be able to do with her or his own property, had she or he been of full age and capacity. This has the effect of distancing the position of the legal representative both from the guardian of the previous law and from the trustee (Sched. 5 below removes the position of guardian from the operation of the Trusts Acts). Previously, a guardian had a primarily preservative function, particularly in relation to heritage, and this had the effect that property owned by the child could not be disposed of by the guardian, even when this was in the interests of the child. In trust law, trustees are subject to the same limitations, and they can be avoided only by going to the expense of petitioning the court. Now the rule for children is that their legal representatives can do all that the children could do if they were of full age and capacity.

Acting as a child's legal representative. This could be a parent with the parental responsibility and parental right of legal representation, or a guardian with such responsibility and right. Legal representation lasts, at most, until the child is 16 years old, for only before then is the child incapable of acting on her or his own behalf.

Subs. (2)

If the legal representative has used funds in the proper discharge of her or his responsibilities to safeguard and promote the child's health, development and welfare, that is the parental responsibility contained in s.1(1)(a), then the legal representative has no liability to account for such funds.

Proper discharge. The key word in this paragraph is "proper", and non-liability to account only arises if the parental responsibility has been discharged properly. If it has not then the legal representative will be under the obligation to account contained in subs. (1) above. So, for example, a parent who expends a child's money on private health care of that child will not be called to account if the expenditure is designed to safeguard and promote the child's health and welfare, but will be called to account if the expenditure is wasteful and harmful such as, for example, some forms of cosmetic surgery. Likewise a parent can expend the child's money on private schooling because this promotes the child's development, without being called to account (though if the expenditure is great, the reasonable and prudent person is likely to keep proper accounts). In practical terms the onus will be on the person alleging improper use of funds to show this.

Court Orders

Court orders relating to parental responsibilities etc.

11.—(1) In the relevant circumstances in proceedings in the Court of Session or sheriff court, whether those proceedings are or are not independent of any other action, an order may be made under this subsection in relation to—

    (a) parental responsibilities;
    (b) parental rights;
    (c) guardianship; or
    (d) subject to section 14(1) and (2) of this Act, the administration of a child's property.

(2) The court may make such order under subsection (1) above as it thinks fit; and without prejudice to the generality of that subsection may in particular so make any of the following orders—

    (a) an order depriving a person of some or all of his parental responsibilities or parental rights in relation to a child;
    (b) an order—
        (i) imposing upon a person (provided he is at least sixteen years of age or is a parent of the child) such responsibilities; and
        (ii) giving that person such rights;
    (c) an order regulating the arrangements as to—
        (i) with whom; or
        (ii) if with different persons alternately or periodically, with whom during what periods,

a child under the age of sixteen years is to live (any such order being known as a "residence order");

(d) an order regulating the arrangements for maintaining personal relations and direct contact between a child under that age and a person with whom the child is not, or will not be, living (any such order being known as a "contact order");

(e) an order regulating any specific question which has arisen, or may arise, in connection with any of the matters mentioned in paragraphs (a) to (d) of subsection (1) of this section (any such order being known as a "specific issue order");

(f) an interdict prohibiting the taking of any step of a kind specified in the interdict in the fulfilment of parental responsibilities or the exercise of parental rights relating to a child or in the administration of a child's property;

(g) an order appointing a judicial factor to manage a child's property or remitting the matter to the Accountant of Court to report on suitable arrangements for the future management of the property; or

(h) an order appointing or removing a person as guardian of the child.

(3) The relevant circumstances mentioned in subsection (1) above are—

(a) that application for an order under that subsection is made by a person who—

(i) not having, and never having had, parental responsibilities or parental rights in relation to the child, claims an interest;

(ii) has parental responsibilities or parental rights in relation to the child;

(iii) has had, but for a reason other than is mentioned in subsection (4) below no longer has, parental responsibilities or parental rights in relation to the child; or

(b) that although no such application has been made, the court (even if it declines to make any other order) considers it should make such an order.

(4) The reasons referred to in subsection (3)(a)(iii) above are that the parental responsibilities or parental rights have been–

(a) extinguished on the making of an adoption order;

(b) transferred to an adoption agency on the making of an order declaring the child free for adoption;

(c) extinguished by virtue of subsection (9) of section 30 of the Human Fertilisation and Embryology Act 1990 (provision for enactments about adoption to have effect with modifications) on the making of a parental order under subsection (1) of that section; or

(d) transferred to a local authority by a parental responsibilities order.

(5) In subsection (3)(a) above "person" includes (without prejudice to the generality of that subsection) the child concerned; but it does not include a local authority.

(6) In subsection (4) above—

"adoption agency" and "adoption order" have the same meanings as they are given, in section 18 of the Adoption (Scotland) Act 1978, by section 65(1) of that Act; and

"parental responsibilities order" has the meaning given by section 86(1) of this Act.

(7) Subject to subsection (8) below, in considering whether or not to make an order under subsection (1) above and what order to make, the court—

(a) shall regard the welfare of the child concerned as its paramount consideration and shall not make any such order unless it considers that it would be better for the child that the order be made than that none should be made at all; and

(b) taking account of the child's age and maturity, shall so far as practicable—

(i) give him an opportunity to indicate whether he wishes to express his views;

(ii) if he does so wish, give him an opportunity to express them; and

(iii) have regard to such views as he may express.

(8) The court shall, notwithstanding subsection (7) above, endeavour to ensure that any order which it makes, or any determination by it not to make an order, does not adversely affect the position of a person who has, in good faith and for value, acquired any property of the child concerned, or any right or interest in such property.

(9) Nothing in paragraph (b) of subsection (7) above requires a child to be legally represented, if he does not wish to be, in proceedings in the course of which the court implements that paragraph.

(10) Without prejudice to the generality of paragraph (b) of subsection (7) above, a child twelve years of age or more shall be presumed to be of sufficient age and maturity to form a view for the purposes both of that paragraph and of subsection (9) above.

(11) An order under subsection (1) above shall have the effect of depriving a person of a parental responsibility or parental right only in so far as the order expressly so provides and only to the extent necessary to give effect to the order; but in making any such order as is mentioned in paragraph (a) or (b) of subsection (2) above the court may revoke any agreement which, in relation to the child concerned, has effect by virtue of section 4(2) of this Act.

(12) Where the court makes a residence order which requires that a child live with a person who, immediately before the order is made does not have in relation to the child all the parental responsibilities mentioned in paragraphs (a), (b) and (d) of section 1(1), and the parental rights mentioned in paragraphs (b) and (d) of section 2(1), of this Act (those which he does not so have being in this subsection referred to as the "relevant responsibilities and rights") that person shall, subject to the provisions of the order or of any other order made under subsection (1) above, have the relevant responsibilities and rights while the residence order remains in force.

(13) Any reference in this section to an order includes a reference to an interim order or to an order varying or discharging an order.

DEFINITIONS

"adoption agency": Adoption (Scotland) Act 1978, s.65(1).
"adoption order": Adoption (Scotland) Act 1978, s.65(1).
"child": ss.2(7), 15(1).
"contact order": s.11(2)(d).
"parental responsibilities": s.1(3).
"parental responsibilities order": s.86(1).
"parental rights": s.2(4).
"person": ss.11(5), 15(4).
"residence order": s.11(2)(c).

GENERAL NOTE

See Scot. Law Com. No. 135, Part V.

In many respects this is the fundamental section of this Part, replacing the very much shorter s.3 of the 1986 Act (which similarly played a central role there). The old s.3 had much value, in its terseness and wideness, but its drawback was that it relied to a very great extent on the common law telling us what parental rights were, how they were to be exercised and how the court should resolve disputes. The present provision attempts to put all questions of parental responsibilities and parental rights on to a statutory basis. The court's powers to make orders are clearly spelt out, together with various supplementary rules relating to their effect. Issues of title, which had generated much case law under the 1986 Act, are dealt with similarly.

The major change effected by this section is the replacement of custody and access orders with the new concepts of residence and contact orders. This terminology follows that introduced in England by the Children Act 1989 (c. 41) and has important symbolic significance. The whole ethos of Part I is to move away from the common understanding that parents have a right to keep and to control their children and towards an understanding that mothers and some fathers have a responsibility to protect and guide their children and to maintain contact with them. Parental responsibilities and parental rights are governed by ss.1–6 above and this section allows the court to make orders regulating any issue in connection therewith, or in connection with guardianship (governed by ss.6–8 above), or the administration of children's property (ss.9–10 above).

Though the theoretical basis of the law has been changed, much of the old law will remain since the factors previously relevant to the determination of custody disputes will be those that are relevant to the determination of an application for a residence order, and the factors previously relevant to access will be those that are relevant to contact orders. The familiar welfare principle remains paramount, but further guidance is given to the court as to how it should come to its decisions.

Subs. (1)

In any proceedings in which the issue arises, the court can make an order relating to parental responsibilities or parental rights, guardianship, or administration of children's property. Any of the orders specified in subs. (2) below can be made whether the action is raised under this section or by any other means. So the court can make an order under this section when the issue before the court is primarily something other than whether an order relating to the child should be made. Typically this will be in a divorce action, but the terms of the section are wide and the court can make an order in any action, so long as the "relevant circumstances", set out in subs. (3) below, exist.

Subs. (2)

Under the old s.3(1) of the 1986 Act, the court was empowered to make any order relating to parental rights it thought fit; the present provision similarly empowers the court to make any order it thinks fit in relation to parental responsibilities and parental rights, guardianship, or administration of children's property and, without limiting that wide discretion, it lists a number of particular orders that can be made. Other orders, relating to these matters, which do not precisely fit into one or other of the stated orders, can be made. Any order can only be made in the "relevant circumstances" as defined in subs. (3) below and the court is obliged, in coming to its decision, to have regard to the three "overarching principles" listed in subs. (7) below.

Paragraph (a) allows the court to make an order depriving a person who has parental responsibilities or parental rights of some or all of these rights. The order will have to be explicit as to which responsibilities and rights are being removed, and this provision is to be read with subs. (11) below. That subsection creates an important change in the law. The old custody orders were assumed, unless joint custody was awarded (which was rare), to remove any rights of custody which existed in the person who was not awarded custody, even when this was not made plain in the court decree. Indeed, this was often their sole effect: when custody was awarded to one of the divorcing parents, it was giving that parent what she or he already had and taking away the right from the other parent. It is now required that for that result to follow the court must make a specific decision to that effect (taking account of the overarching principles in subs. (7) below) and the effect must be spelt out in the decree.

Paragraph (b), conversely, allows the court to impose parental responsibilities or confer parental rights on any person, and again the court must be explicit that this is what has been determined to be best for the child. It should be noted here that an order conferring parental responsibilities and parental rights does not confer the status of parenthood (for the purposes, for example, of succession or the obligations of aliment and child support) but merely imposes some of the consequences. The order can impose merely some of the parental responsibilities and rights on a person rather than them all: the generality of s.11(1) clearly allows for this and the competence of doing so is confirmed by s.103(1) below. If all the parental responsibilities and parental rights are to be conferred on a long-term basis, then the person is probably being appointed as a guardian, i.e. a parent-substitute, and as such the order is more properly one under para. (h) below than this one. This paragraph will be more appropriate when only a limited number of specific parental responsibilities or parental rights are being imposed or conferred.

The court can confer responsibilities and rights only on a person who is aged 16 years or more except in one situation; that is when the person under 16 is the child's parent (i.e. father, since mothers of whatever age have parental responsibilities and parental rights automatically under s.3(1)(a) above). The section is no authority, however, for giving an under-16-year-old parent legal capacity he does not otherwise have, and it will not be in the interests of any child to give the responsibility and right of legal representation in relation to a child to a boy-parent who lacks the capacity to act as such. Indeed, it is difficult to imagine a situation in which it would ever be in the child's interests to confer any parental responsibility or parental right on a father under the age of 16: though there is no age limit on a mother automatically acquiring those rights, that acquisition is an inevitable legal consequence to which the child's welfare is irrelevant.

Paragraph (c) allows the court to make what is termed a "residence order", which is an order regulating the arrangements as to with whom the child is to live. The terminology of the paragraph should be noted. Residence orders will not be made "in favour of" one parent or the other, for it is to be remembered that mothers and most fathers will already have the right (from s.2(1)(a) above) to have their children living with them in any case: the order will not be made simply to confer upon a parent that which she or he already has (for that would offend the "minimum interference principle" in subs. (7) below). Rather, the order will regulate, for the benefit of the child, the arrangements under which parents can exercise their rights. The paragraph is designed to give the court maximum flexibility in regulating these arrangements, and subparagraph (ii) permits residence orders to make arrangements whereby the child lives periodically with more than one person. The typical example will be divorcing parents with one of whom the child lives most of the time and with the other of whom the child lives (i.e. sleeps overnight) periodically. Unless parental responsibilities and parental rights have been removed from one parent, the effect of such an arrangement will be very different from an award of custody to one parent with residential access, say at weekends, being given to the other parent. Under that arrangement (common in the old law) the parent with custody had full rights in relation to the care and upbringing of the child, and the parent with access had minimal rights. Joint custody orders, though competent, were not favoured. This often left the parent with regular access in a very awkward position and the practice, for example, of many schools and medical practitioners was to refuse to divulge information about the child to the parent with access without the permission of the parent with custody. This inhibited the parent with access from playing a full role in the child's life. That role is now to be encouraged and the regulation of a child's residence will not in itself have the effect of minimising one parent's rights. If one parent wishes to be in sole control of the child's upbringing with sole decision-making powers, then she or he must apply for the removal of the other's parental responsibilities and parental rights under para. (a) above rather than through the arrangements regulating where the child is to live under this paragraph. The onus will be on the applicant, not to show why she or he should be in sole charge of the child's upbringing, but why the other should be denied responsibilities and rights (see also subs. (11) below).

A residence order can require the child to live with someone who does not have any parental responsibilities or parental rights, or has only the responsibility and right to maintain personal relations and direct contact with the child. If so, the order carries to that person all parental responsibilities and parental rights except those to maintain contact and to control residence (subs. (12) below). It would, however, normally be unwise to require the child to live with a person who does not have the right to determine the child's residence, and in most cases such a residence order ought not to be made unless combined with an order under para. (b) imposing parental responsibilities and parental rights on the person with whom the child is to live.

Paragraph (d) concerns what used to be called access and an order under this paragraph is to be termed a "contact order". The careful wording of this paragraph is designed to move away from the notion that parents have a right of access and to reiterate the idea that parents have a responsibility to maintain personal relations and direct contact with the child (s.1(1)(c) above). That responsibility is not removed by a residence order under para. (c) above and what this paragraph does is to allow the court to make an order regulating the fulfilment of that responsibility; in addition it can regulate the contact the child is to have with any other person who does not have the responsibility and right to maintain relations and contact with the child. Inevitably, previous decisions relating to access applications will remain of relevance in identifying the sorts of considerations the courts are likely to take into account in determining how best to regulate contact between the child and another person. As under the pre-1995 law (see *D. v. Strathclyde Regional Council* 1985 S.L.T. 114), a court order regulating contact will be inoperative during the subsistence of an inconsistent supervision requirement made under s.70 below. The discretion of a children's hearing to regulate contact (indeed their obligation to consider whether to do so under s.70(2) below) is not inhibited by a court order regulating contact, just as their power to impose a condition of residence is not inhibited by the granting by a court of a residence order.

Paragraph (e) allows the court to make an order regulating "any specific question" which has arisen in relation to parental responsibilities or rights, or guardianship, or the administration of a child's property. This is very wide and reflects the (implicit) position in the old s.3(1) of the 1986 Act. This provision could be used to allow the court to determine wherein the child's welfare lies in any situation in which there is dispute, for example in relation to medical treatment, schooling, religious upbringing, or any aspect of the child's lifestyle. Of course an order under this paragraph, as under all the others, is subject to the minimum intervention principle in subs. (7) below (one of the three "overarching principles"), and there are some situations in which this principle will be very useful. For example it will seldom be better for a child that a court regulates her or his religious upbringing than that the matter be left to be worked out between the child and the person with whom the child lives. On the other hand, there are some situations, such as consent to medical treatment, in which the court might have a very important role to play, and there have been many cases in England in which the courts were faced with difficult questions to resolve in that field: see for example, *B (A Minor) (Wardship: Sterilization), Re* [1988] A.C. 199 and *E (A Minor) (Medical Treatment), Re* [1991] 2 FLR 585 (sterilisation); *B (A Minor), Re* [1981] 1 W.L.R. 1421, *C (A Minor) (Wardship: Medical Treatment), Re* [1989] 2 All E.R. 782 and *J (A Minor) (Wardship, Medical Treatment), Re* [1990] 3 All E.R. 930 (life-saving or life-prolonging treatment); *R (A Minor) (Wardship: Medical Treatment), Re* [1991] 4 All E.R. 177 and *W (A Minor) (Medical Treatment: Court's Jurisdiction), Re* [1992] 4 All E.R. 627 (child refusing treatment).

Paragraph (f) allows the court to interdict the exercise of a parental responsibility or a parental right which it determines is against the welfare of the child. So, for example, the court could interdict a parent from consenting to, and doctors from performing, the sterilisation of a mildly mentally retarded child (see *D (A Minor) (Wardship: Sterilization), Re* [1976] 1 All E.R. 326). Or the court could interdict the legal representative from selling or dissipating a child's property, or putting it to improper purposes. It should be noted, however, that the court is exhorted to "endeavour to ensure that any order that it makes, or any determination by it not to make an order, does not adversely affect the position of a person who has, in good faith and for value, acquired any property of the child concerned, or any right or interest in such property" (subs. (8) below). So, for example, a parent who has improperly leased the child's property to a third party can be interdicted from doing so again or from continuing to do so, but the order must attempt to preserve the position of the bona fide third party (the lessee).

Paragraph (g) deals with a different situation from either s.9 above or s.13 below, though both provide the court with similar powers. Here the situation envisaged is that of a child who already owns and possesses property, and it is in the interests of the child that some appropriate person be appointed to manage that property on the child's behalf.

Paragraph (h) allows the court to appoint or remove a person as guardian of the child. Before the coming into force of this Act, s.5(2) of the Age of Legal Capacity (Scotland) Act 1991 (c. 50) provided that the only two ways in which a guardian could be appointed were by court order under s.3 of the 1986 Act or by testamentary deed under s.4 thereof. Schedule 4 to the present Act amends s.5(2) of the 1991 Act to read that the only way in which a guardian can be appointed is by testamentary deed under s.7 of the present Act. The omission of a reference to the present paragraph is surprising, but not fatal, and there is no doubt that court appointments are valid and the new wording of s.5(2) is inept. A person appointed guardian under this section will have all the parental responsibilities and parental rights conferred on a parent by ss.1 and 2 above, and will become, therefore, a parent-substitute. This is made plain in s.7(5) above in relation to appointment of guardians under that section, but is not stated in so many words here. However, there is nothing in the Act to indicate that the powers, duties, liabilities and role of guardian are different depending upon whether the person comes into that office by means of a court order under s.11 or by testamentary appointment under s.7, and had Parliament intended to change the law in that respect it would surely have done so expressly. The court can, of course, make the appointment of guardian subject to such conditions as it thinks fit.

Subs. (3)

Under the old law an order relating to parental rights could be sought by "any person claiming interest" (1986 Act, s.3(1)). This phrase gave rise to much dispute, both academic and judicial (see *A.B. v. M.* 1988 S.L.T. 652, *F v. F* 1991 S.L.T. 357, *D v. Grampian Regional Council* 1995 S.L.T. 519), and the case law was being developed even during the parliamentary passage of the Bill that became the present Act. The Bill was amended from a form very similar in effect to that in the 1986 Act to its present structure as a result of the House of Lords decision in *D v. Grampian Regional Council*, which was decided on March 9, 1995 while the Bill was being considered by the Special Standing Committee in the House of Commons. Subsections (3) and (4) are designed to give statutory effect to the decision in *D v. Grampian Regional Council* and to clarify other related issues that it raises.

An order under s.11 can be made by the court if an application for such an order has been made by a person falling within one of three separate classes, which will cover any person except those specified in subss. (4) and (5) below. (It should be noted that it makes no practical difference which class the applicant comes within, so long as she or he is not in one of the excluded classes in subss. (4) or (5) below). In addition, it is made clear that an order under s.11 can be made in any other action in which such an application has not been made but in which the court considers it appropriate (taking account of the overarching principles in subs. (7) below) to make the order.

A person. Excluded from the definition of "person" are local authorities (subs. (5) below), but nowhere are other non-natural persons excluded (*cf.* the terms of s.15(4) below under which only natural persons can have parental responsibilities and parental rights). While the typical applicant will be a natural person there is nothing to prevent an application by a corporate body which claims an interest. So, for example, an NHS Trust might seek a specific issues order to regulate the child's medical treatment over which some argument has arisen.

Who ... claims an interest. As in the pre-1995 law, title to seek an order is not subject to artificial limitations (see Wilkinson 1976 S.L.T. (News) 221 and 237) and technical issues of title tend to be subsumed into the substantive issue of the child's welfare (see Wilkinson and Norrie *Parent and Child* (1993, W. Green) at pp. 202–204). Title inheres under this subparagraph in unmarried fathers, grandparents, step-parents, siblings, other relatives and anyone else with a connection to or legitimate concern for the welfare of the child, such as foster carers (see *M v. Lothian Regional Council* 1990 S.L.T. 116 and *F v. F* 1991 S.L.T. 357). "A person who ... claims an interest" includes the child her or himself (subs. (5) below). Excluded from this paragraph are those who currently have parental responsibilities and parental rights, and those who used to, but no longer, have parental responsibilities and parental rights.

Has parental responsibilities or parental rights. This category includes any person who has such responsibilities and rights automatically, or has acquired them by any means whatsoever. (It does not include a local authority which has acquired parental responsibilities by means of a parental responsibilities order in its favour: subs. (5) below). The use of the word "or" suggests that this category includes a person who has one particular responsibility or right but not all of them, such as the responsibility or right to maintain contact with the child.

Has had, but ... no longer has. This category includes persons whose responsibilities and rights have been lost by private law means, such as a court order under the present section. So a person who is deprived of all parental responsibilities and parental rights under s.11(2)(a) above retains title to seek their restoration or to seek any other s.11 order. Excluded from this category are those who lose their parental responsibilities and parental rights by some public law process, specified in subs. (4) below.

Although no such application has been made. If the court is not dealing with an application under the present section but nevertheless considers that an order should be made it may make such an order. In certain actions, specified in s.12(1) below, the court is obliged to consider whether to make a s.11 order. In any other action the court may consider the question without any request to do so and may make any s.11 order that it considers should be made. This allows the court to act *ex proprio motu* or on the motion of any party in, for example, an action for divorce, judicial separation, declarator of marriage, nullity of marriage, parentage or non-parentage or any other action. This expands the jurisdiction of the Court of Session, which prior to the coming into force of this Act could deal with parental rights only in certain specified actions (Court of Session Act 1988 (c. 36), s.20, repealed in Sched. 5 below).

Subs. (4)

In *Beagley v. Beagley* 1984 S.C. (H.L.) 69 the House of Lords held that a person who had lost parental rights by means of a resolution under s.16 of the 1968 Act vesting parental rights and powers in a local authority had no title to seek their restoration by way of a custody application; and in *Borders Regional Council v. M* 1986 S.C. 63 the Inner House came to the same conclusion when parental rights were removed by an order freeing a child for adoption. These decisions pre-dated the 1986 Act, s.3(1) of which conferred title to seek an order relating to parental rights under that Act on "any person claiming interest". In *D v. Grampian Regional Council* 1994 S.L.T. 1038 the Inner House (by a majority) took the view that this overturned the earlier decisions and that "any person" meant precisely that and therefore included a mother whose parental rights had been removed by an order freeing the child for adoption. The House of Lords overruled this (1995 S.L.T. 519), holding that the phrase "any person" as it appeared in the 1986 Act could not be interpreted literally. They held that the removal of parental rights by an adoption order or by an order freeing a child for adoption under the Adoption (Scotland) Act 1978 removed title to seek an order relating to parental rights under the 1986 Act. There were, however, some difficulties with that decision, primarily that it was based very firmly on an analysis of the law of adoption, which rendered it unclear whether the same result would be reached in other situations in which parental rights had been removed by public law process (such as in particular by a parental rights resolution under s.16 of the Social Work (Scotland) Act 1968 (c. 49)). It is the purpose of this subsection (together with subs. (3) above) to give statutory effect to the House of Lords decision and to clarify the doubts that it raised.

The subsection sets out four categories of natural person who cannot seek a s.11 order. There are no others and the terms of subs. (3) above are wide enough to ensure that title inheres in any other person except either those mentioned here, or local authorities (subs. (5) below). The categories are persons whose parental responsibilities and parental rights have been removed by: (i) s.12(3) of the Adoption (Scotland) Act 1978 on the making of an adoption order; (ii) s.18(5) of the 1978 Act on the making of an order freeing a child for adoption; (iii) s.30(9) of the

Human Fertilisation and Embryology Act 1990 on the making of a parental order after a surrogacy arrangement; and (iv) s.86(1) below, on the making of a parental responsibilities order transferring those rights and responsibilities to a local authority (the equivalent of the old parental rights resolutions under s.16 of the 1968 Act). It may appear at first sight a little odd that a person whose parental responsibilities and parental rights are removed under s.11(2)(a) above can seek their restoration under s.11 while a person whose responsibilities and rights have been removed under s.86 below cannot, but there is a clear distinction to be drawn between the public law and the private law processes. It would lead to confusion and delay which would inevitably be detrimental to the child if both processes could be utilised, and the Act is sensible in separating them out so clearly.

There may be very exceptional circumstances in which this rule seems to work harshly. For example, an adopted child may in fact maintain a relationship of affection with her or his natural mother; if the adoptive parents die or otherwise become unable to look after the child the natural mother would be unable to seek a s.11 order. However, this harshness can be mitigated by other means. The natural mother is not prevented from adopting the child; the child her or himself can seek an order under s.11 conferring parental responsibilities and parental rights on the natural mother, as can any other person who claims an interest. For it is to be remembered that subss. (3) and (4) merely deny title, but they do not prevent the court from making any order at all in favour of any person whose title is denied.

Subs. (5)

The child concerned. The "person" who can raise an action under subs. (1) above is stated here to include the child concerning whom the application is made. The terms of the old s.3 of the 1986 Act were clearly wide enough to include the child, but the matter was occasionally doubted and this provision is enacted for the avoidance of that doubt. A child can seek an order, for example, removing the parental responsibilities and rights from her or his own parent or guardian, or an order regulating a specific question such as medical treatment. The provision does not, however, grant to a child any legal capacity to raise (or defend) an action that she or he would not otherwise have, and that capacity remains to be determined by the Age of Legal Capacity (Scotland) Act 1991. Section 2(1) of that Act gives to some children the capacity to raise or defend actions, for these acts are within the definition of "legal transaction" laid down by s.9 of that Act (and see also s.15(6) below).

A local authority. Excluded from the definition of "a person who . . . claims an interest" in subs. (3) above are local authorities. Part I of the present Act deals exclusively with private law matters, in respect of which local authorities have no standing. Local authorities' rights, duties, powers and interests are governed exclusively by Part II, which is the limit of their interest and role. It must follow from this, though it is not expressly stated, that the decision in *M v. Dumfries and Galloway Regional Authority* 1991 S.C.L.R. 481 (Sh. Ct.) is no longer good law (if it ever was). In that case a local authority was held to be entitled to rely upon s.3(2) of the 1986 Act to defend an action for delivery of a child whom they were keeping under no statutory authority. The local authority cannot raise an action under Part I and nor, it is submitted, can they rely on any rule or principle in Part I to achieve that which they cannot achieve by other means.

Subs. (7)

In making any decision about whether or not to make any order under this section, the court is obliged by this subsection to have regard to three quite distinct principles, which have been referred to above as the overarching principles.

Welfare of the child. The first overarching principle is that the welfare of the child concerned is to be the court's paramount consideration. (For the statute to require the court to regard welfare as "its paramount consideration" neatly sidesteps the rather sterile argument that arose in the negotiations before the adoption of the UN Convention on the Rights of the Child about whether welfare should be "a paramount consideration" or "the paramount consideration"). This welfare test is familiar and no different from that required under the old law contained in s.3(2) of the 1986 Act (on the application of the welfare test in custody disputes, see Wilkinson and Norrie *Parent and Child* (1993, W. Green) at pp. 206–225).

Shall not make any such order. The second overarching principle is that the court is prohibited from making any order unless it considers that making an order would be better for the child than making none (see Scot. Law Com. No. 135 at paras. 5.16–5.18). This is what might be called the "minimum intervention principle", under which it is assumed that matters are best left without court interference and that the onus is on the party seeking an order to persuade the court that it satisfies the welfare test. This was probably the position under the old law in any case (a good example is to be found in the judgment of Lord Gill in *Clayton v. Clayton* April 21, 1995, where he refused to make one of the orders sought in relation to the child's upbringing because he was not persuaded that the party who sought the order had proved it was "necessary"), but the current provision makes it absolutely plain. And it is a particularly important break on unnecessary orders, given the extension of the court's power to make orders even when not asked to do so (subs. (3)(b) above). The application of the principle is general. In relation to contact, for example, it will be presumed that the arrangements made by the parents themselves are better for the child than those the court could devise, though the presumption is always open to challenge. The principle will prevent a residence order being made in favour of a person who already has parental responsibilities and parental rights, such as a mother, because such an order will give her nothing she does not already have. If the aim of the application is to deny parental responsibilities and parental rights to the father then this must be done by means of an order under s.11(2)(a) rather than a residence order under s.11(2)(c) in favour of the mother (see subs. (11) below). This is an important practical difference from the old law when it was common to grant custody to a person who already had the legal right of custody as a means of denying custody to someone else.

One consequence of the minimum intervention principle which is not altogether satisfactory is that any particular decision may be made according to how the question comes before the court, rather than according to its merits in the abstract. For example, a person may seek an interdict against a child attending the services of some quasi-religious sect, and the court, adopting the principle of minimum intervention, may well refuse to grant the interdict (allowing the child to continue attending). If, on the other hand, the child raises the action seeking an interdict against the parents' attempts to prevent the attendance at the services of the sect the court may well again apply the principle of minimum intervention to refuse the interdict (effectively allowing the parents to continue to prevent the child attending). If the onus of satisfying the welfare test cannot be discharged then the unregulated position, whichever that is, will govern.

Shall... have regard... to the views... of the child. The third overarching principle is that the court should give the child the opportunity to express views on the matter the court is being asked to determine, and should have appropriate regard to any view expressed. This provision has been enacted in order to bring Scots law into line with Art. 12 of the UN Convention on the Rights of the Child (the terms of which are set out in the General Note to s.6 above), and is similar in its terms to s.6 of the Adoption (Scotland) Act 1978 (which is amended later in the current statute). The important change in the law here is that the child's views are to be taken into account in all actions before the court in which a s.11 order is being considered, with the result that for the first time in Scots law there is a requirement on the court to take account of the views of the child in determining whether to regulate residence and contact, and how to do so. There is no age limit, though it is provided by subs. (10) below that a child aged 12 or over is presumed capable of forming a view. This has the effect that the court should not take account of the views of a child over 12 only when persuaded (and the issue is a matter of fact) that the child is not of sufficient age and maturity to form a view. This certainly does not prevent the court taking account of the views of children under 12 and there have been cases in which the court has considered it proper to have regard to the expressed views of even very young children (see for example *Pow v. Pow* 1931 S.L.T. 485, which involved children of 10 and eight, and *Russell v. Russell* 1991 S.C.L.R. 429, which involved a five-year-old).

Similar, but not identical, provisions are to be found in s.6 above, which obliges a parent exercising a parental responsibility or parental right to have regard to the views of the child, and in s.95 below, which amends s.6 of the Adoption (Scotland) Act 1978, to oblige the court making an adoption order to have regard to the views of the child. The difference in s.6 above is that the parent must also have regard to the views of the other parent (which is not the case here) and the difference in s.95 is that there the court is obliged also to have regard to the child's racial origins and cultural and linguistic background (which is not the case here).

If he wishes to express them. There is no obligation on the child to express a view. The court should seek the child's opinion but must also be careful not to burden a child with undue pressure to make a decision and, in general, care ought also to be taken to ensure that the child understands that his or her views, if expressed, will help the judge decide but will not themselves decide the issue. No child should ever be made to feel, for example, that she or he has the burden of deciding which parent to live with. The child may speak directly to the judge (see subs. (9) below).

Subs. (8)
See the notes to subs. (2)(f) above.

Subs. (9)
In fulfilling his obligation to have regard to the views of the child concerned, the judge may speak directly to the child, who is not obliged (but is permitted) to speak through a legal representative with a right of audience to the court.

Subs. (10)
See the notes to subs. (7) above.

Subs. (11)
Parental responsibilities and parental rights continue in existence, once acquired, subject only to their express removal by the court acting under subs. (2)(a) or (h) above. Such removal is only to the extent specified by the court. So, for example, if a court denies a parent the right to regulate the child's residence (the right under s.(2)(1)(a) above) and nothing more, that parent remains subject to all the responsibilities listed in s.1 above and possessed of all the other rights listed in s.2 above. In addition, it is provided here that in making an order depriving a person of parental responsibilities or rights or imposing and conferring parental responsibilities and rights, the court can revoke an agreement under s.4 above giving an unmarried father parental responsibilities and rights.

Subs. (12)
See the notes to subs. (2)(c) above.

Subs. (13)
The court can make an interim order or can vary or discharge an order in the same circumstances as it can make a final order, and in particular the same overarching principles listed in subs. (7) above must be applied.

Restrictions on decrees for divorce, separation or annulment affecting children

12.—(1) In any action for divorce, judicial separation or declarator of nullity of marriage, the court shall, where this section applies, consider (in the light of such information as is before the court as to the arrangements which have been, or are proposed to be, made for the upbringing of each child by virtue of which it applies) whether to exercise with respect to him the powers conferred by section 11 or 54 of this Act.

(2) Where, in any case to which this section applies, the court is of the opinion that—

(a) the circumstances of the case require, or are likely to require, it to exercise any power under section 11 or 54 of this Act with respect to the child concerned;

(b) it is not in a position to exercise that power without giving further consideration to the case; and

(c) there are exceptional circumstances which make it desirable in the interests of that child that it should not grant decree in the action until it is in a position to exercise such a power,

it shall postpone its decision on the granting of decree in the action until it is in such a position.

(3) This section applies where a child of the family has not reached the age of sixteen years at the date when the question first arises as to whether the court should give such consideration as is mentioned in subsection (1) above.

(4) In this section "child of the family", in relation to the parties to a marriage, means—

(a) a child of both of them; or

(b) any other child, not being a child who is placed with them as foster parents by a local authority or voluntary organisation, who has been treated by both of them as a child of their family.

DEFINITIONS
"child": s.15(1).
"foster parent": Boarding Out and Fostering of Children Regulations 1985 (S.I. 1985 No. 1799).
"local authority": Local Government etc. (Scotland) Act 1994 (c. 39), s.2.

GENERAL NOTE

Under the Matrimonial Proceedings (Children) Act 1958 (c. 40) the court was obliged in actions for divorce, nullity of marriage or separation to consider the arrangements for the care and upbringing of the children involved (1958 Act, s.8), and it could commit the child to the care of an individual other than the parent or to the care of a local authority (1958 Act, s.10). These sections are now repealed (Sched. 5 below) and the current provision requires the court, in any matrimonial proceeding concerning a family in which there is a child, to consider whether to grant any of the s.11 orders and whether to refer the case of the child to the reporter under s.54.

Subs. (1)

In considering whether to make a s.11 order, account must be taken of the overarching principles in s.11(7) above; in addition, referring the child to the reporter is appropriate only when the court considers that one of the grounds of referral listed in s.52(2) below exists.

Subs. (2)

If the court believes that an order under s.11 or a reference under s.54 is required, or is likely to be required, but it is not in the position to make such an order without further consideration, and there are exceptional circumstances requiring the court to postpone granting decree for divorce, separation or nullity, then the court shall so postpone granting decree until it is able to decide whether and how to exercise a power under s.11 or s.54. This provision replaces s.8 of the Matrimonial Proceedings (Children) Act 1958, though the emphasis is significantly different. Under the 1958 Act the court was duty bound to refuse the matrimonial decree unless satisfied as to the arrangements for the care and upbringing of the child; under the present provision it may postpone its decision only in "exceptional circumstances".

Exceptional circumstances. These words suggest that the norm will be that the matrimonial decree will be granted even though the court is not in a position to exercise its powers in relation to the child. The circumstances must relate to the welfare of the child.

Subss. (3) and (4)

The court must consider whether to make a s.11 order or to make a referral to the reporter under s.54, or postpone deciding whether to grant a matrimonial decree only when a child, of the family concerning which the decree is being sought, has not reached the age of 16 at the date when the question first arises. "Child of the family" is defined to mean either a child of both parties to the marriage which is the subject of the action, or any other child who has been treated by both the parties as a child of their family.

A child of both of them. This includes the genetic child of both, the adopted child of both, the genetic child of one who is the adopted child of the other, and the child over whom both have a parental order under s.30 of the Human Fertilisation and Embryology Act 1990.

Any other child. There is no requirement (as there was, for example, in the unamended Family Law Act 1986: *Bradley v. Bradley* 1987 S.C.L.R. 62) that the child be related to one or other of the parties to the marriage. Children being boarded with the family under the Boarding Out and Fostering of Children Regulations 1985 (S.I. 1985 No. 1799) are excluded from these provisions.

Treated by both of them as a child of their family. The pre-1995 legislation talked of a child being "accepted" rather than "treated" as a child of the family, and that word gave rise to much judicial discussion in England (see Wilkinson and Norrie *Parent and Child* (1993, W. Green) at p. 240). All the legislation in which that phrase appeared is amended in Sched. 4 so that the word always used is now "treated". This requires, as acceptance did not, some positive act or course of conduct by the parties to the marriage, directed towards the child, indicating that she or he is regarded by the parties as a child of their family. The parties to the marriage must act in some way consistent with them having adopted a parenting role and accepting all the parental responsibilities and parental rights.

Awards of damages to children

13.—(1) Where in any court proceedings a sum of money becomes payable to, or for the benefit of, a child under the age of sixteen years, the court may make such order relating to the payment and management of the sum for the benefit of the child as it thinks fit.

(2) Without prejudice to the generality of subsection (1) above, the court may in an order under this section—

    (a) appoint a judicial factor to invest, apply or otherwise deal with the money for the benefit of the child concerned;

    (b) order the money to be paid—

        (i) to the sheriff clerk or the Accountant of Court; or

(ii) to a parent or guardian of that child,
to be invested, applied or otherwise dealt with, under directions of the court, for the benefit of that child; or
(c) order the money to be paid directly to that child.
(3) Where payment is made to a person in accordance with an order under this section, a receipt given by him shall be a sufficient discharge of the obligation to make the payment.

DEFINITIONS
  "child": s.15(1).
  "parent": s.15(1).

GENERAL NOTE
    An issue concerning a child may be before the court not only in matrimonial proceedings but also in proceedings in which a sum of money becomes payable to or for the benefit of the child, typically in an action for damages in which the child is the successful pursuer. Before the coming into force of this provision, there were rules allowing the Court of Session to appoint a judicial factor and allowing the sheriff court to direct payment of awards into court to be administered on behalf of the child. There was little reason for the procedures to be different depending upon which court was involved, and the Scottish Law Commission (Scot. Law Com. No. 135, para. 4.7) recommended that there should be common rules and that these rules should be contained in primary legislation. These recommendations are given effect to in this section, which confers wide discretionary powers on the Court of Session and the sheriff court, and makes provision for the granting of a discharge of the obligation to make payment. It is to be noted that the three overarching principles in s.11(7) do not apply here. While the minimum intervention principle is obviously inappropriate it is, perhaps, surprising that there is no requirement to have regard to the views of the child nor any reference to the interests of the child. Inevitably, however, the court in making decisions under this section that "it thinks fit" will regard the child's interests as, at the very least, always relevant.

Subs. (1)
    The provision is in the widest possible terms, covering any court proceedings in which, by any means, a sum of money becomes payable to or for the benefit of a person under the age of 16 years. The court is empowered to make any such order relating to the payment and management of the sum as it sees fit, so long as this is for the benefit of the person under 16.

Subs. (2)
    This provision lists the sorts of orders that the court can make, though the list is not exhaustive and the court can make any order under subs. (1) above that it considers will be for the benefit of the child. There are three basic sorts of order: (i) the appointment of a judicial factor, (ii) an order to pay the money to the sheriff clerk or the Accountant of Court or to a parent or guardian of the under-16-year old, or (iii) an order to pay the money direct to the person under the age of 16. The second form of order may contain directions by the court how to invest, apply or otherwise deal with the property, and the person who is paid the property must follow these directions.
    To be invested. Investments made in terms of this provision are not governed by the terms of the Trustee Investments Act 1961 (c. 62). The 1961 Act no longer defines "trustee" to include "guardian" (Sched. 5), and there is, quite deliberately (Scot. Law Com. No. 135, para. 4.8), no provision in the current statute subjecting the powers of investment in this section to the 1961 Act.
    Parent. Section 15(1) defines this word to mean "genetic father or mother", and it is nowhere limited for the purposes of the present section to parents with parental responsibilities or parental rights. The generality of s.13 requires that the court has the power to order payment to a parent, such as an unmarried father, who has no responsibility or right of legal representation, and any other interpretation of "parent" would render the definition in s.15 meaningless since this provision is the only one in Part I in a context other than parental responsibilities and parental rights (where the definition is inept since the genetic but unmarried father is excluded). However, it will seldom be in the interests of the child for this to be done unless such a parent were also given that responsibility and right, but extreme cases are not beyond the bounds of imagination and such an order would not be incompetent. In any case directions as to the investment or application of the money would be given, which the parent would have to follow, and the authority to do so would be the order under this section itself.
    Order the money to be paid directly to that person. The court can order that a sum of money falling due in the court proceedings to a person under the age of 16 can be paid directly to that

child. It is likely that the court would only consider this appropriate when the sum involved is relatively modest; and though there is no express limitation on the court's discretion, there is the practical limitation that a discharge of the obligation to make payment will have to be given (see subs. (3) below) and the person under 16 would need to have capacity to grant that discharge: it follows that a court ought not to order money to be paid direct to a person who has no legal capacity to grant a discharge for the payment.

Subs. (3)

Once payment has been made to a person (including the child) in terms of subs. (1) above, a receipt for that payment given by the person who receives it will be sufficient discharge. The only problematic case would be if the court ordered the money to be paid direct to the child, for this provision merely states the effect of the discharge and does not itself give capacity to grant a discharge. Section 2(1) of the Age of Legal Capacity (Scotland) Act 1991 grants capacity to a person under 16 to do that which is commonly done by persons of her or his age and circumstances and on terms which are not unreasonable. A discharge in the face of a court order for payment is unlikely to be considered unreasonable, and it might be an act commonly done by children who are the recipients of awards of damages. The terms of this subsection necessarily imply that a child under 16 could have capacity to grant the discharge, otherwise subs. (2)(c) above would be meaningless and could never be applied.

Jurisdiction and choice of law

Jurisdiction and choice of law in relation to certain matters

14.—(1) The Court of Session shall have jurisdiction to entertain an application for an order relating to the administration of a child's property if the child is habitually resident in, or the property is situated in, Scotland.

(2) A sheriff shall have jurisdiction to entertain such an application if the child is habitually resident in, or the property is situated in, the sheriffdom.

(3) Subject to subsection (4) below, any question arising under this Part of this Act—

(a) concerning—

(i) parental responsibilities or parental rights; or

(ii) the responsibilities or rights of a guardian,

in relation to a child shall, in so far as it is not also a question such as is mentioned in paragraph (b) below, be determined by the law of the place of the child's habitual residence at the time when the question arises;

(b) concerning the immediate protection of a child shall be determined by the law of the place where the child is when the question arises; and

(c) as to whether a person is validly appointed or constituted guardian of a child shall be determined by the law of the place of the child's habitual residence on the date when the appointment was made (the date of death of the testator being taken to be the date of appointment where an appointment was made by will), or the event constituting the guardianship occurred.

(4) Nothing in any provision of law in accordance with which, under subsection (3) above, a question which arises in relation to an application for, or the making of, an order under subsection (1) of section 11 of this Act falls to be determined, shall affect the application of subsection (7) of that section.

DEFINITIONS

"child": ss.9(9), 15(1).

"parental responsibilities": s.1(3).

"parental rights": s.2(4).

GENERAL NOTE

Jurisdiction in relation to many of the issues governed by Part I, in particular parental responsibilities and parental rights, remains governed by the Family Law Act 1986 (as amended to take account of the present statute). That Act does not, however, cover guardianship or the administration of children's property and this section provides the rules for these issues in relation to both jurisdiction and choice of law. In relation to both, the basic (though not the only) determinant is the child's habitual residence.

Subs. (1)

In questions concerning the administration of a child's property, the Court of Session will have jurisdiction either if the child is habitually resident in Scotland, or if the property concerned is situated in Scotland. The property can be either heritable or moveable property. As an issue of administration, "child" is limited to a person under the age of 16 years (s.9(9) above).

Habitual residence. For the meaning of this concept, see Anton and Beaumont, *Private International Law* (2nd ed. 1990, W. Green) at pp. 150–152. The concept has been discussed recently in a number of cases arising out of the Hague Convention on International Child Abduction: see *Dickson v. Dickson* 1990 S.C.L.R. 692, *J (A Minor) (Abduction), Re* [1990] 2 A.C. 562, *S (Minors), Re* [1994] 2 W.L.R. 228, *Findlay v. Findlay* [1994] S.L.T. 709. And see Crawford " 'Habitual Residence of the Child' as a Connecting Factor in Child Abduction Cases" 1992 J.R. 177.

Subs. (2)

In questions concerning the administration of a child's property, the sheriff will have jurisdiction either if the child is habitually resident in the sheriffdom, or if the property concerned is situated in the sheriffdom.

Subss. (3) and (4)

These subsections deal with choice of law, that is the question of which legal system is to apply to the determination of particular matters. The matters dealt with are the responsibilities and rights of parents and guardians, the immediate protection of the child, and the appointment of guardians.

In any question concerning the responsibilities and rights of parents or guardians, the court is obliged to apply the law of the child's habitual residence, which is determined at the time when the question arises. However, this rule must be read in the light of subs. (4) below which requires that the three overarching principles in s.11(7) above be given effect: the result is that no matter which law the Scottish court is applying, it must regard the child's welfare as its paramount consideration, must give the child the opportunity to express views on the matter at issue and take appropriate account of these views, and must not make any order unless it considers that making that order is better for the child than making none.

In any question concerning the immediate protection of the child, the law to be applied is the law of the place where the child actually is when the question arises. If a question of the child's immediate protection comes before the Scottish court then most likely the child will be in Scotland and Scots law will apply. It is however possible to envisage a situation in which a child is furth of Scotland and an issue concerning its immediate protection is brought before the Scottish court (though practically speaking the need for speedy enforcing of any protection will demand that the applicant take the case to the court of the place where the child actually is). "Child" here is defined in s.15(1) to mean a person under the age of 18 years.

In any question concerning the appointment or constitution of guardianship, the matter will be determined by the law of the child's habitual residence on the date when the appointment was made or event constituting the guardianship occurred. In Scots law a person can become guardian only by appointment, either by the parent or guardian (s.7 above) or by the court (s.11(2)(h) above) and in no other way (see the General Note to s.11(2)(h) above), but other systems may allow guardianship to be imposed upon an individual by facts and circumstances, rather as the law imposes a trust on constructive trustees. If an appointment as guardian is made by a parent or guardian in a will, the date of death shall be taken to be the date of appointment and the date, therefore, at which the child's habitual residence is determined for the purposes of choice of law.

Interpretation

Interpretation of Part I

15.—(1) In this Part of this Act—

"child" means, where the expression is not otherwise defined, a person under the age of eighteen years;

"contact order" has the meaning given by section 11(2)(d) of this Act;

"parent", in relation to any person, means, subject to Part IV of the Adoption (Scotland) Act 1978 and sections 27 to 30 of the Human

Fertilisation and Embryology Act 1990 and any regulations made under subsection (9) of the said section 30, someone, of whatever age, who is that person's genetic father or mother;

"parental responsibilities" has the meaning given by section 1(3) of this Act;

"parental rights" has the meaning given by section 2(4) of this Act;

"residence order" has the meaning given by section 11(2)(c) of this Act;

"specific issue order" has the meaning given by section 11(2)(e) of this Act; and

"transaction" has the meaning given by section 9 of the Age of Legal Capacity (Scotland) Act 1991 (except that, for the purposes of subsection (5)(b) below, paragraph (d) of the definition in question shall be disregarded).

(2) No provision in this Part of this Act shall affect any legal proceedings commenced, or any application made to a court, before that provision comes into effect; except that where, before section 11 of this Act comes into force, there has been final decree in a cause in which, as respects a child, an order for custody or access, or an order which is analogous to any such order as is mentioned in subsection (2) of that section, has been made, any application on or after the date on which the section does come into force for variation or recall of the order shall proceed as if the order had been made under that section.

(3) In subsection (2) above, the reference to final decree is to a decree or interlocutor which, taken by itself or along with previous interlocutors, disposes of the whole subject matter of the cause.

(4) Any reference in this Part of this Act to a person—

(a) having parental rights or responsibilities;

(b) acting as a legal representative; or

(c) being appointed a guardian,

is to a natural person only.

(5) Any reference in this Part of this Act to a person acting as the legal representative of a child is a reference to that person, in the interests of the child—

(a) administering any property belonging to the child; and

(b) acting in, or giving consent to, any transaction where the child is incapable of so acting or consenting on his own behalf.

(6) Where a child has legal capacity to sue, or to defend, in any civil proceedings, he may nevertheless consent to be represented in those proceedings by any person who, had the child lacked that capacity, would have had the responsibility to act as his legal representative.

GENERAL NOTE

This is the interpretation section, and is largely self-explanatory. To be noted, however, are the definitions of "child" and "parent".

Subs. (1)

Child. The definition of "child" is not helpful since each provision in Part I either defines the word itself or adopts by necessary implication a definition from another provision. So s.1 defines child as a person under the age of 16 years except in relation to the parental responsibility of providing guidance (when the age is 18); s.2 defines child as a person under the age of 16 years for all the parental rights; ss.3, 4, 6, 7 and 8 adopt by necessary implication these definitions; ss.5 and 9 expressly limit child to person under the age of 16; s.10, referring to the responsibility and right of legal representation, is implicitly limited to age 16; s.11 adopts by necessary implication the ages appropriate to the particular issue; ss.12 and 13 expressly limit child to persons under 16; and s.14 adopts by necessary implication the ages appropriate to the issue, with the sole exception of immediate protection under s.14(3)(b). That is the only provision with which the definition of "child" contained in s.15(1) is applicable.

Parent. This word is stated to mean, in cases other than those in which parenthood is determined by the Adoption (Scotland) Act 1978 or the Human Fertilisation and Embryology Act 1990, "genetic father or mother". This of course must be read subject to s.3(1)(b), which provides that the "father" (i.e. the genetic father) is not to have parental responsibilities and rights automatically. Whenever the word parent is used in circumstances other than in relation to parental responsibilities and parental rights the word refers to all mothers and fathers and not just those with these responsibilities and rights. The word is used in this way only in s.13(2). To be noted are the words "of whatever age", which provide recognition that a person under the age of 16 can be a parent. The position of such a child-parent, and her ability to exercise responsibilities and rights, is discussed in the notes to s.2(1), s.4(1) and s.11(2)(b) above.

Subss. (2) and (3)
    If proceedings are commenced before the coming into force of Part I they shall continue to be governed by the previous law. However, an application after the coming into force of Part I to vary or recall a custody or access order contained in a final decree granted before its coming into force will be governed by the new law. Final decrees are decrees disposing of all the issues.

Subs. (4)
    This provision emphasises the point discussed in the note to s.11(5) above, that is that Part I concerns private law and cannot be used in any way by local authorities. It is provided here that any reference in Part I of the Act to a person having parental responsibilities or parental rights or acting as legal representative or being appointed a guardian is to a natural person only. A local authority or corporate body cannot be appointed a child's guardian, and cannot be granted any parental responsibilities or rights. Though not expressed, it can be assumed that a local authority cannot be required (under Part I) to administer a child's property, for that is an act of legal representation.

Subs. (5)
    This is an important provision, clarifying a doubt created in 1991. Under the Age of Legal Capacity (Scotland) Act 1991 a child under the age of 16 is given legal capacity to enter into transactions of a kind that are not uncommon and on terms that are not unreasonable (1991 Act, s.2(1)). That Act did not affect the right of the parent to act as the child's legal representative, and the position seemed to be that a child could exercise a legal capacity (e.g. to purchase clothes with his or her own money) and the parent at the same time had the right to use the child's money to enter into transactions such as the purchase of clothes on the child's behalf. It is now made plain, however, that a person may act as a child's legal representative only when the child is incapable of acting on her or his own behalf. It follows that when a child acquires capacity under the 1991 Act before the age of 16, the parent or guardian who is the child's legal representative loses the right to act in relation to the particular transaction which the child has capacity to enter into her or himself. This applies not only to the entering into of contracts but also other legal transactions such as the giving or withholding of consent to medical treatment (assumed to be an issue of legal representation in s.5(1) above). A child under 16 can acquire capacity to consent in terms of s.2(4) of the 1991 Act and when she or he does so, the effect of this provision is to deny the parent or guardian any power or capacity to consent on the child's behalf. The exclusion in the definition of "transaction" (subs. (1) above) of the giving of consent having legal effect does not exclude medical consent from this provision: it merely prevents the tautology that would be inherent if it were included in para. (b) ("giving consent to [the giving by a person of any consent having legal effect]").

Subs. (6)
    A child's capacity to sue or defend in civil proceedings is governed by the 1991 Act and the effect of subs. (5) above is that the child's legal representative loses the right to sue or defend actions on behalf of the child when the child acquires capacity under that Act. This provision allows a child who has capacity to act for her or himself to consent to be represented in civil proceedings by a person who was her or his legal representative. This is limited to civil proceedings and cannot be relied upon by a child wishing someone to act on her or his behalf in some other transaction such as, for example, a contract (though the law of agency is available to a mature child). Nor can this provision be relied upon for the giving of consent to medical treatment, and that act must be performed by the child her or himself.

PART II

PROMOTION OF CHILDREN'S WELFARE BY LOCAL AUTHORITIES AND BY
CHILDREN'S HEARINGS ETC.

CHAPTER 1

SUPPORT FOR CHILDREN AND THEIR FAMILIES

Introductory

Welfare of child and consideration of his views

16.—(1) Where under or by virtue of this Part of this Act, a children's
hearing decide, or a court determines, any matter with respect to a child the
welfare of that child throughout his childhood shall be their or its paramount
consideration.

(2) In the circumstances mentioned in subsection (4) below, a children's
hearing or as the case may be the sheriff, taking account of the age and
maturity of the child concerned, shall so far as practicable—

(a) give him an opportunity to indicate whether he wishes to express his
views;

(b) if he does so wish, give him an opportunity to express them; and

(c) have regard to such views as he may express;

and without prejudice to the generality of this subsection a child twelve years
of age or more shall be presumed to be of sufficient age and maturity to form
a view.

(3) In the circumstances mentioned in subsection (4)(a)(i) or (ii) or (b) of
this section, no requirement or order so mentioned shall be made with
respect to the child concerned unless the children's hearing consider, or as
the case may be the sheriff considers, that it would be better for the child that
the requirement or order be made than that none should be made at all.

(4) The circumstances to which subsection (2) above refers are that—

(a) the children's hearing—

(i) are considering whether to make, or are reviewing, a supervision requirement;

(ii) are considering whether to grant a warrant under subsection
(1) of section 66, or subsection (4) or (7) of section 69, of this Act or
to provide under subsection (5) of the said section 66 for the continuation of a warrant;

(iii) are engaged in providing advice under section 60(10) of this
Act; or

(iv) are drawing up a report under section 73(13) of this Act;

(b) the sheriff is considering—

(i) whether to make, vary or discharge a parental responsibilities
order, a child assessment order or an exclusion order;

(ii) whether to vary or discharge a child protection order;

(iii) whether to grant a warrant under section 67 of this Act; or

(iv) on appeal, whether to make such substitution as is mentioned in section 51(5)(c)(iii) of this Act; or

(c) the sheriff is otherwise disposing of an appeal against a decision of a
children's hearing.

(5) If, for the purpose of protecting members of the public from serious
harm (whether or not physical harm)—

(a) a children's hearing consider it necessary to make a decision under or
by virtue of this Part of this Act which (but for this paragraph) would
not be consistent with their affording paramountcy to the consideration mentioned in subsection (1) above, they may make that decision;
or

(b) a court considers it necessary to make a determination under or by virtue of Chapters 1 to 3 of this Part of this Act which (but for this paragraph) would not be consistent with its affording such paramountcy, it may make that determination.

DEFINITIONS
"child": s.93(2)(a).
"child assessment order": ss.55(1), 93(1).
"child protection order": ss.57(1), 93(1).
"children's hearing": s.93(1).
"exclusion order": ss.76(12), 93(1).
"parental responsibilities order": ss.86(1), 93(1).
"supervision requirement": ss.70(1), 93(1).

GENERAL NOTE
The court, when deciding whether to make any Part I order under s.11 above, is obliged to have regard to the three overarching principles listed in s.11(7). The same three principles are applied by this section to the matters governed by Part II of the Act. An important difference, however, is that in Part II only the welfare principle applies to all matters, and the other two principles apply only in certain (differently) specified circumstances.

The overarching principles listed in this section apply in terms only to decisions and determinations of courts and children's hearings, notwithstanding that Part II allows other persons and bodies to make decisions that might significantly affect individual children. Local authorities are subject to similar principles under s.17 below; reporters on the other hand, who have various decision-making powers under Chapters 2 and 3 of Part II, are not governed by the overarching principles, though inevitably any decision they make will be strongly influenced by their views of the welfare of the child concerned.

Subs. (1)
The paramount consideration of a court or a children's hearing in determining or deciding any matter under Part II is the child's welfare. This does not mean to say that all other considerations are irrelevant, nor even that the decision must always be to favour the child's interests above those of all other persons. This is made plain in subs. (5) below. Rather, it simply means that the child's welfare is always the most important consideration and is likely, in most cases, to determine the issue to be resolved.

Any matter. These words are not to be read literally. The only matters that can be determined taking account of the child's welfare are the discretionary decisions that a court or a children's hearing may be called upon to make, such as whether to impose or to terminate a supervision requirement or whether to make or vary a parental responsibilities order or to grant a child protection order. Decisions of fact which a court has to make are not to be influenced by the child's welfare. So, for example, on an application before a sheriff under s.68 to determine whether or not a ground of referral has been established, the welfare of the child is irrelevant to that determination (though it is, of course, the paramount consideration in determining what steps a hearing should take in response to a finding that the grounds are established). A sheriff could not hold something in the order of the following: "the evidence is too finely balanced for me to determine whether or not the ground of referral has been made out, but the child's interests clearly demand that compulsory measures of supervision be imposed, and so I hold that this is enough to tip the balance towards a finding that the ground is established". Similarly, the welfare of the child will not determine whether the conditions for granting a child protection order, laid down in s.57 below, are satisfied, but will determine whether the order ought to be made or not.

Throughout his childhood. These words are to be compared with those in s.11(7) above in which the welfare test is made the paramount consideration in relation to parental responsibilities and parental rights but no limitation in terms of time is laid down, and with s.95 below, which amends s.6 of the Adoption (Scotland) Act 1978 to ensure that welfare, expressly "throughout the child's life", is the paramount consideration in the adoption process. For the purposes of the present section, childhood ends when the person reaches the age of 18 years (see the definition of "child" in s.93(2)(a) below) and the person's welfare until then must be taken into account. Even when the child reaches the age of 18, welfare is to be given broad scope and is not to be looked at as a short-term consideration. That of course is often little more than a pious hope. A children's hearing or a court can seldom predict how a child's life is going to develop beyond the immediate or, at best, medium term future, and they are not to be criticised if, in the long term and with hindsight, it is obvious that some other decision would have been preferable.

Subs. (2)

In some of their decisions or determinations, listed in subs. (4) below, the court or children's hearing must give the child the opportunity to express her or his views on the matter under consideration, and must take account of any views expressed in coming to these decisions or determinations. As with s.6 and s.11(7) above, this provision is designed to bring Scots law into line with art. 12 of the UN Convention on the Rights of the Child (quoted in the notes to s.6 above). There is little significant alteration to the law in relation to children's hearings, the whole point of which has always been to afford the child the opportunity to express views, and the important change lies in the application of this rule to the sheriff. As with s.11(7), there is no age limit, though it is similarly provided that a child aged 12 years or more is presumed capable of forming a view. This has the effect that the court or children's hearing need not take into account the views of a child over the age of 12 only when they are persuaded as a matter of fact that the child is not of sufficient maturity to form a view, and it certainly does not prevent the court or children's hearing taking account of the views of children under 12 when in fact the child under that age is capable of forming and expressing a view. The capacity of each child is to be judged individually.

Subs. (3)

This is the "minimum intervention principle", reflecting that contained in s.11(7)(a) above in relation to Part I. It applies to all those matters in which the child's views must be taken into account under subs. (2) above, except in relation to a children's hearing either providing advice to a sheriff as to whether a child protection order should be continued or drawing up a report in relation to certain orders that are proposed, and in relation to the disposal by the sheriff of most appeals from decisions of children's hearings. The only time this principle applies on appeal is when the sheriff is exercising his unfortunate power under s.51(5)(c)(iii) below to substitute his own disposal for that of the hearing: so both the children's hearing and the sheriff must apply this principle in deciding upon the appropriate disposal of a case. The minimum intervention principle amounts to a presumption that matters are best left as they are, and the practical effect of that is that the onus lies with the person seeking intervention by court order or decision of the children's hearing to justify why intervention is necessary: that justification will nearly always lie in the protection or enhancement of the child's welfare.

Subs. (5)

While the welfare of the child is the paramount consideration for both the children's hearing and the court, this must not be allowed to deny necessary protection to others, and this subsection permits the children's hearing or the court to make a decision or determination which will protect members of the public (implicitly, from the child concerned), even when the decision is not in the best interests of the child. It will, for example, seldom be in a child's best interests to be kept in secure accommodation, but a decision to this effect might be necessary in order to protect others. This provision is to be read with s.70(10) below, the notes to which reference should be made.

Serious harm (whether or not physical harm). The harm to which members of the public are to be protected from can be physical harm to person or to property, or emotional or psychological harm: in any case it must be serious harm. Serious harm is harm that is not trivial. The phrase ought to be interpreted strictly and this subsection should not be used lightly by either the children's hearing or the sheriff.

Duty of local authority to child looked after by them

17.—(1) Where a child is looked after by a local authority they shall, in such manner as the Secretary of State may prescribe—

   (a) safeguard and promote his welfare (which shall, in the exercise of their duty to him be their paramount concern);

   (b) make such use of services available for children cared for by their own parents as appear to the authority reasonable in his case; and

   (c) take such steps to promote, on a regular basis, personal relations and direct contact between the child and any person with parental responsibilities in relation to him as appear to them to be, having regard to their duty to him under paragraph (a) above, both practicable and appropriate.

(2) The duty under paragraph (a) of subsection (1) above includes, without prejudice to that paragraph's generality, the duty of providing advice and assistance with a view to preparing the child for when he is no longer looked after by a local authority.

(3) Before making any decision with respect to a child whom they are looking after, or proposing to look after, a local authority shall, so far as is reasonably practicable, ascertain the views of—

(a) the child;

(b) his parents;

(c) any person who is not a parent of his but who has parental rights in relation to him; and

(d) any other person whose views the authority consider to be relevant, regarding the matter to be decided.

(4) In making any such decision a local authority shall have regard so far as practicable—

(a) to the views (if he wishes to express them) of the child concerned, taking account of his age and maturity;

(b) to such views of any person mentioned in subsection (3)(b) to (d) above as they have been able to ascertain; and

(c) to the child's religious persuasion, racial origin and cultural and linguistic background.

(5) If, for the purpose of protecting members of the public from serious harm (whether or not physical harm) a local authority consider it necessary to exercise, in a manner which (but for this paragraph) would not be consistent with their duties under this section, their powers with respect to a child whom they are looking after, they may do so.

(6) Any reference in this Chapter of this Part to a child who is "looked after" by a local authority, is to a child—

(a) for whom they are providing accommodation under section 25 of this Act;

(b) who is subject to a supervision requirement and in respect of whom they are the relevant local authority;

(c) who is subject to an order made, or authorisation or warrant granted, by virtue of Chapter 2, 3 or 4 of this Part of this Act, being an order, authorisation or warrant in accordance with which they have responsibilities as respects the child; or

(d) who is subject to an order in accordance with which, by virtue of regulations made under section 33(1) of this Act, they have such responsibilities.

(7) Regulations made by the Secretary of State under subsection (1) above may, without prejudice to the generality of that subsection, include—

(a) provision as to the circumstances in which the child may be cared for by the child's own parents; and

(b) procedures which shall be followed in the event of the child's death.

DEFINITIONS

"accommodation": s.25(8).

"child": s.93(2)(a).

"local authority": Local Government etc. (Scotland) Act 1994, s.2.

"parental responsibilities": ss.1(3), 93(1).

"parental rights": ss.2(4), 93(1).

"relevant local authority": s.93(1).

"supervision requirement": ss.70(1), 93(1).

GENERAL NOTE

The notion of "children in care" under the 1968 Act has disappeared with the current legislation, and children are now to be "looked after" by local authorities rather than be in their "care". Replacing the much shorter s.20 of the 1968 Act, this section sets out, in general terms, the duties that local authorities have in relation to children who are being looked after by them, and how they are to go about fulfilling these duties. In addition, it defines the circumstances in which a child is being "looked after" for the purposes of the legislation. The drafting of the section is, in places, unhelpful, with terms remaining undefined (such as "parent"), with some provisions referring to persons with parental responsibilities while other provisions refer to persons with parental rights. Also unhelpful is the fact that there are shades of the three overarching principles listed in s.16 to guide local authorities, but they are not, for no apparent reason, identical in either wording or effect to those in s.16 which guide courts and children's hearings. The substance of a local authority's duties will be set out in regulations yet to be made.

Subss. (1) and (2)

The local authority is obliged to perform the listed duties in relation to children who are being looked after by them, in the manner prescribed in regulations. The basic duty is to safeguard and promote the child's welfare (*cf.* the parental responsibility in s.1(1) above to safeguard and promote the child's health, development and welfare), and that promotion includes, under subs. (2), the duty to advise and assist the child in preparing for the time when she or he is no longer being looked after by the local authority.

Looked after. A child is considered as being looked after by a local authority in the circumstances listed in subs. (6) below.

Direct contact between the child and any person with parental responsibilities. The duty here is to encourage the person with the parental responsibility under s.1(1)(c) to maintain personal relations and direct contact with the child to fulfil that responsibility. That person will have the right to do so under s.2(1)(c), with the result that the local authority is not permitted to inhibit the exercise of that right. "Promote" means encourage, but the duty to encourage contact is made subject to the paramount duty to safeguard and promote the child's welfare.

Subs. (3)

Local authorities will have to make a variety of different decisions in relation to children whom they look after, and before coming to their decision they must ascertain the views of the listed individuals on the matter being considered.

So far as reasonably practicable. A local authority must act reasonably in attempting to ascertain the views of the individual, but an inability to ascertain these views does not nullify the decision made. It would not be practicable to ascertain the views of a parent when that person was unknown, or when the individual's whereabouts were unknown, or when the individual was unable, for whatever reason, to express a view.

His parents. There is no definition in this Part of the Act of "parent", and there is no limitation to parents with parental responsibilities or parental rights. An unmarried father is often considered by the law to be a parent (for example, in relation to succession and aliment and child support): there is no reason to apply any other meaning to the word "parent" than the normal meaning of either mother or father irrespective of that person's marital status. "Parent" will, of course, include adoptive parent, person deemed parent by an order under ss.27, 28 or 30 of the Human Fertilisation and Embryology Act 1990, and parent presumed under s.5 or declared under s.7 of the 1986 Act.

Parental rights. It is surprising that the reference in para. (c) is not to parental responsibilities and parental rights, but the sloppy draftsmanship has no effect since a person who is not a parent cannot acquire parental rights in relation to a child unless she or he also acquires parental responsibilities.

Any other person. The local authority must act reasonably in determining whose views are relevant, and invariably any person who ordinarily has charge of or control over the child ought to be considered relevant. This would include any relative with whom the child is living, or any foster carer.

Subs. (4)

Having obtained the views they are obliged to obtain under subs. (3) above, the local authority must go on to make the decision concerning the child, and in doing so must have regard, so far as practicable, to the listed matters, including the views of the child.

Shall have regard. The obligation is to take account of the matters listed rather than necessarily to follow any views expressed. The decision must be made regarding the child's welfare as the authority's paramount concern (subs. (1) above).

The views … of the child concerned. This may be compared to s.16(2) above, under which sheriffs and children's hearings must have regard to the views of the child concerned. The terms of the provisions are not identical, however, in that there is no presumption here concerning the ability to express a view after the age of 12, as there is in s.16(2) (and, indeed, as there is in s.25(5) in relation to the local authority's powers to provide accommodation). This omission is unlikely to be a deliberate attempt to distinguish this situation from those others and it simply means that local authorities must exercise some care in determining whether any child is of sufficient age and maturity to express views.

The child's religious persuasion. It is the child's religious persuasion that is important here and not the persuasion of any parent or guardian of the child. The provision is inapplicable to children who are too young to be persuaded.

Racial origin and cultural and linguistic background. These matters are never determining of any decision that has to be made by a local authority looking after a child, but are always relevant.

Subs. (5)

This provision ensures that a local authority is not inhibited from taking necessary protective steps by any obligation contained in this section (such as the obligation to regard the child's welfare as paramount or the obligation to take account of the child's or other person's views). These obligations are qualified, but only to the extent necessary for protecting members of the public from "serious" harm. See the General Note to s.16(5) above.

Subs. (6)

This subsection defines the child who is being "looked after" by a local authority. It represents a substantial improvement from the 1968 Act, under which the child "in care" was defined as such by a number of different provisions. In all the circumstances described in each of the following paragraphs a child will be regarded as being "looked after" by a local authority, and the local authority will have all the duties and responsibilities in relation to the child listed in this Chapter of Part II.

Para. (a). A local authority may provide accommodation to a child under s.25 below when (i) no-one has parental responsibility for her or him; or (ii) when she or he is lost or abandoned; or (iii) when the person caring for the child is unable to provide suitable accommodation; or (iv) when the local authority consider that it would safeguard or promote the child's welfare for them to provide accommodation.

Para. (b). A child who is the subject of a supervision requirement, whether that requirement has a condition of residence with the local authority or not, is being "looked after" by the local authority.

Para. (c). A child who is the subject of a place of safety order, child protection order, parental responsibilities order, a warrant to apprehend or keep in a place of safety, under which the local authority have responsibilities in relation to the child, is being "looked after" by the local authority.

Para. (d). When a local authority has responsibilities over a child as a result of an order made by a court in another part of the U.K. and which has effect in Scotland as a result of regulations made under s.33, that child is being "looked after" by the local authority.

Subs. (7)

A child being looked after by a local authority may in fact remain in the care of her or his parents: regulations may provide for the circumstances in which this can occur. In addition, these regulations may prescribe the procedures to be followed in the event of the child's death: this was a matter previously governed by s.28 of the 1968 Act.

Duty of persons with parental responsibilities to notify change of address to local authority looking after child

18.—(1) Where a child is being looked after by a local authority, each natural person who has parental responsibilities in relation to the child shall, without unreasonable delay, inform that authority whenever the person changes his address.

(2) A person who knowingly fails to comply with the requirement imposed by subsection (1) above shall be liable on summary conviction to a fine of level 1 on the standard scale; but in any proceedings under this section it shall be a defence that—

(a) the change was to the same address as that to which another person who at that time had parental responsibilities in relation to the child was changing; and

(b) the accused had reasonable cause to believe that the other person had informed the authority of the change of address of them both.

DEFINITIONS
"child": s.93(2)(a).
"local authority": Local Government etc. (Scotland) Act 1994, s.2.
"parental responsibilities": ss.1(3), 93(1).

GENERAL NOTE
It is part of the local authority's duties, when they are looking after a child, to promote personal relations and direct contact between the child and anyone with parental responsibilities on a regular basis. They can do so effectively only when they know the address of the person with parental responsibilities. This section imposes upon a person with parental responsibilities the obligation to inform the local authority looking after the child of any change of address that she or he makes. Breach of that obligation is a criminal offence, but there is a defence if the accused was flitting with another person who also has parental responsibilities and the accused had reasonable cause to believe that the other person had informed the local authority of the change of address.

Looked after by a local authority. A child is "looked after" by a local authority in the circumstances described in s.17(6) above.

Provision of services

Local authority plans for services for children

19.—(1) Within such period after the coming into force of this section as the Secretary of State may direct, each local authority shall prepare and publish a plan for the provision of relevant services for or in respect of children in their area.

(2) References to "relevant services" in this section are to services provided by a local authority under or by virtue of—
(a) this Part of this Act; or
(b) any of the enactments mentioned in section 5(1B)(a) to (o) of the Social Work (Scotland) Act 1968 (enactments in respect of which Secretary of State may issue directions to local authorities as to the exercise of their functions).

(3) A local authority shall from time to time review the plan prepared by them under subsection (1) above (as modified, or last substituted, under this subsection) and may, having regard to that review, prepare and publish—
(a) modifications (or as the case may be further modifications) to the plan reviewed; or
(b) a plan in substitution for that plan.

(4) The Secretary of State may, subject to subsection (5) below, issue directions as to the carrying out by a local authority of their functions under subsection (3) above.

(5) In preparing any plan, or carrying out any review, under this section a local authority shall consult—
(a) every Health Board and National Health Service trust providing services under the National Health Service (Scotland) Act 1978 in the area of the authority;
(b) such voluntary organisations as appear to the authority—
    (i) to represent the interests of persons who use or are likely to use relevant services in that area; or
    (ii) to provide services in that area which, were they to be provided by the authority, might be categorised as relevant services;
(c) the Principal Reporter appointed under section 127 of the Local Government etc. (Scotland) Act 1994;
(d) the chairman of the children's panel for that area;
(e) such housing associations, voluntary housing agencies and other bodies as appear to the authority to provide housing in that area; and
(f) such other persons as the Secretary of State may direct.

DEFINITIONS
  "local authority": Local Government etc. (Scotland) Act 1994, s.2.
  "principal reporter": s.93(1).

GENERAL NOTE
  Local authorities have the obligation, introduced by this section, to prepare and publish and keep under review plans for their provision of services to children in their area.

Subs. (1)
  The obligation is absolute: each local authority must draw up, in consultation with the persons and bodies mentioned in subs. (5) below, plans setting out how they intend to provide those services towards children that they are legally obliged to provide. The plan concerns general policy rather than plans in relation to individual children.
  Relevant services. See subs. (2) below.
  Children in their area. This means children who are physically present in the local authority area. The domicile or habitual residence of the child is not relevant. "Children" means persons under the age of 18 years.

Subs. (2)
  This subsection indicates the services upon which plans must be prepared and published. These include services provided under this Part of this Act, such as services for disabled children provided under ss.23 and 24, the provision of accommodation to children under s.25, the provision of day care under s.27, and after care and training under ss.29 and 30.

Subs. (3)
  In addition to drawing up and publishing plans, local authorities are obliged to keep these plans under constant review and may make modifications to or substitutions for them. The Act does not require that reviews be at any stated period but merely that they be held "from time to time". Local authorities must act reasonably in interpreting that phrase. There is nothing to prevent local authorities reviewing some parts of their plans more frequently than other parts.

Subs. (4)
  The Secretary of State may direct how reviews are to be carried out, and when, but may not absolve the local authority from consulting those whom they are obliged to consult under subs. (5) below.

Subs. (5)
  This lists the bodies and persons whom the local authority are obliged to consult in drawing up their plans or in reviewing them. It is hoped that this duty of consultation will allow local authorities readily to identify gaps in their provision of services to children. There is no requirement that each body or person specified has to be consulted on every aspect of the plan. For example a National Health Service trust providing very limited services (say, dental services) need not be consulted in respect of that part of the plan relating to the provision of accommodation for children.

Publication of information about services for children

20.—(1) A local authority shall, within such period after the coming into force of this section as the Secretary of State may direct, and thereafter from time to time, prepare and publish information—
  (a) about relevant services which are provided by them for or in respect of children (including, without prejudice to that generality, services for or in respect of disabled children or children otherwise affected by disability) in their area or by any other local authority for those children; and

(b) where they consider it appropriate, about services which are provided by voluntary organisations and by other persons for those children, being services which the authority have power to provide and which, were they to do so, they would provide as relevant services.

(2) In subsection (1) above, "relevant services" has the same meaning as in section 19 of this Act.

DEFINITIONS
　"local authority": Local Government etc. (Scotland) Act 1994, s.2.
　"relevant services": s.19(2).

GENERAL NOTE
　In addition to the obligation to prepare and publish plans under s.19 above, local authorities are also obliged to prepare and publish information about services which they provide as "relevant services" (i.e. those described in s.19(2) above) for children in their area or which are provided for these children by other local authorities. Local authorities may also, where they consider it appropriate, publish information about services provided by voluntary organisations, such as Children First (the RSSPCC), Shelter (Scotland), adoption societies and churches when these services are such that, were the local authority to provide them, they would be "relevant services".
　Information. What must be provided are details about how the relevant services are provided and how access to these services can be obtained.

Co-operation between authorities

21.—(1) Where it appears to a local authority that an appropriate person could, by doing certain things, help in the exercise of any of their functions under this Part of this Act, they may, specifying what those things are, request the help of that person.

(2) For the purposes of subsection (1) above, persons who are appropriate are—
　(a) any other local authority;
　(b) a health board constituted under section 2 of the National Health Service (Scotland) Act 1978;
　(c) a national health service trust established under section 12A of that Act; and
　(d) any person authorised by the Secretary of State for the purposes of this section;
and an appropriate person receiving such a request shall comply with it provided that it is compatible with their own statutory or other duties and obligations and (in the case of a person not a natural person) does not unduly prejudice the discharge of any of their functions.

DEFINITIONS
　"local authorities": Local Government etc. (Scotland) Act 1994, s.2.

GENERAL NOTE
　This section permits the local authority to request help in the exercise of any function that they have under this Part of this Act from any of the persons specified in subs. (2). It also imposes an obligation on the person requested to provide help: that obligation is absolute unless the provision of the help is not compatible with the requested person's own statutory or other duties.

Promotion of welfare of children in need

22.—(1) A local authority shall—
　(a) safeguard and promote the welfare of children in their area who are in need; and

(b) so far as is consistent with that duty, promote the upbringing of such children by their families,

by providing a range and level of services appropriate to the children's needs.

(2) In providing services under subsection (1) above, a local authority shall have regard so far as practicable to each child's religious persuasion, racial origin and cultural and linguistic background.

(3) Without prejudice to the generality of subsection (1) above—

    (a) a service may be provided under that subsection—

        (i) for a particular child;

        (ii) if provided with a view to safeguarding or promoting his welfare, for his family; or

        (iii) if provided with such a view, for any other member of his family; and

    (b) the services mentioned in that subsection may include giving assistance in kind or, in exceptional circumstances, in cash.

(4) Assistance such as is mentioned in subsection (3)(b) above may be given unconditionally or subject to conditions as to the repayment, in whole or in part, of it or of its value; but before giving it, or imposing such conditions, the local authority shall have regard to the means of the child concerned and of his parents and no condition shall require repayment by a person at any time when in receipt of—

    (a) income support or family credit payable under the Social Security Contributions and Benefits Act 1992; or

    (b) an income-based jobseeker's allowance payable under the Jobseekers Act 1995.

DEFINITIONS
"child": s.93(2)(a).
"family": s.93(1).
"local authority": Local Government etc. (Scotland) Act 1994, s.2.

GENERAL NOTE
This section imposes upon local authorities an obligation to promote the welfare of children in need by providing a range and level of services appropriate to the children's needs. It is left to local authorities to determine how and to what extent these services are to be provided, but certain guidance is given here.

Subs. (1)
Section 1(1) above imposes upon mothers and some fathers the obligation to safeguard and promote the welfare of their children, and this provision imposes upon local authorities a similar obligation in relation to children in their area who are in need, to provide services appropriate to that need and to promote the upbringing of these children by their families.

Children ... who are in need. This phrase is defined in s.93(4)(a) below. "Need" refers to being in need of care and attention because the child is unlikely to achieve or maintain a reasonable standard of health or development without the provision of local authority services; or because her or his health or development is likely to be impaired without such services; or because she or he is disabled within the meaning of s.23(2) below; or because some other member of her or his family is disabled and that disability will adversely affect the child.

Promote the upbringing ... by their families. It is considered that a child's needs are best met by being brought up by her or his family (that is to say, by the person who has parental responsibility for the child and any other person with whom the child has been living: s.93(1) below) and local authorities must therefore provide such services as will promote, that is to say encourage and allow in practical terms, the child's family to bring up the child. The obligation to encourage is not an obligation to ensure, and the local authority may promote the upbringing of children by their families only in so far as this is consistent with their duty to safeguard and promote the welfare of children. This amounts to a presumption that in providing services for children these services are best directed towards the maintaining of the child at home, together with a recognition that sometimes a child's welfare can be safeguarded and promoted only by removing the child from her or his home in accordance with later provisions in this Act.

Subs. (2)
A local authority must be sensitive to the child's religious persuasion, racial origin and cultural and linguistic background and must take these matters into account in determining what services to provide in order to fulfil their obligations under subs. (1) above. The obligation, like that in s.17(4) above, is not absolute and a local authority need not, for example, provide social workers with the ability to speak all the languages native to all the children they provide services to. This subsection must not be used to provide either a greater or a lesser level of service for those of minority persuasions, origins or backgrounds than is provided to those of the majority in Scotland today.

Subs. (3)
The services that can be provided under subs. (1) above include services provided directly to children in need, or to the family as a whole of a child in need or to an individual member of the family of a child in need.
Assistance in kind. Goods may be provided, such as for example cooking equipment provided to the parent of a child in need.
In exceptional circumstances, in cash. There is no indication as to what circumstances would amount to exceptional but is likely to include circumstances in which the child's needs can be practically met in no other way.

Subs. (4)
This provision is designed to give the local authority maximum flexibility in the provision of assistance in kind or in cash, and it imposes upon the local authority the obligation to take account of the needs of the child and her or his parents in determining the conditions upon which assistance is given. The persons mentioned are not to be required to repay any assistance given, but there is no absolute obligation to give such assistance to such persons.
Parents. There is no limitation on this word to parents with parental responsibilities within the meaning of Part I of the Act. Both parents have legal obligations to maintain their child, and their means can be taken into account here whether or not they live with the child or have responsibilities towards the child under Part I.

Children affected by disability

23.—(1) Without prejudice to the generality of subsection (1) of section 22 of this Act, services provided by a local authority under that subsection shall be designed—
    (a) to minimise the effect on any—
        (i) disabled child who is within the authority's area, of his disability; and
        (ii) child who is within that area and is affected adversely by the disability of any other person in his family, of that other person's disability; and
    (b) to give those children the opportunity to lead lives which are as normal as possible.
(2) For the purposes of this Chapter of this Part a person is disabled if he is chronically sick or disabled or suffers from mental disorder (within the meaning of the Mental Health (Scotland) Act 1984).
(3) Where requested to do so by a child's parent or guardian a local authority shall, for the purpose of facilitating the discharge of such duties as the authority may have under section 22(1) of this Act (whether or not by virtue of subsection (1) above) as respects the child, carry out an assessment of the child, or of any other person in the child's family, to determine the needs of the child in so far as attributable to his disability or to that of the other person.

DEFINITIONS
"child": s.93(2)(a).
"family": s.93(1).
"local authority": Local Government etc. (Scotland) Act 1994, s.2.

GENERAL NOTE
See White Paper, *Scotland's Children: Proposals for Child Care Policy and Law* (Cm. 2286, August 1993), paras. 4.1–4.10.

The aim of this section is to ensure that, in carrying out their obligation to provide services to safeguard and promote the welfare of children in their area, local authorities take account of, and provide for the needs of, disabled children in their area. The nature of the service to be provided will, of course, depend upon the nature of the disability, but it must aim both to minimise the effect of the disability on the child, whether it is the child or a member of the child's family who has the disability, and to allow the child the opportunity to lead as normal a life as possible.

Subss. (1) and (2)
   Disabled child. A person is disabled if she or he is chronically sick or disabled or suffers from mental disorder within the meaning of the Mental Health (Scotland) Act 1984. "Chronic" means long term and continuously. "Sick or disabled" is to be given broad scope.

Subs. (3)
   An assessment of the child's needs created by the disability of the child or the member of her or his family must be carried out by the local authority, if requested to do so. The aim of this assessment will be for the local authority to identify the appropriate services that they have to provide to the child to fulfil their obligations under this Chapter in relation to the particular disabled child.
   Parent or guardian. Neither of these words is defined in this Part of the Act but they should be interpreted in the light of the reference to the child's family in subs. (1) above. "Parent" is not to be limited to parent with parental responsibilities or parental rights; "guardian" means a person appointed as parent-substitute to the child under s.7 or s.11 of the present Act.

Assessment of ability of carers to provide care for disabled children

24.—(1) Subject to subsection (2) below, in any case where—
   (a) a local authority carry out under section 23(3) of this Act an assessment to determine the needs of a disabled child, and
   (b) a person (in this section referred to as the "carer") provides or intends to provide a substantial amount of care on a regular basis for that child,
the carer may request the local authority, before they make a decision as to the discharge of any duty they may have under section 2(1) of the Chronically Sick and Disabled Persons Act 1970 or under section 22(1) of this Act as respects the child, to carry out an assessment of the carer's ability to continue to provide, or as the case may be to provide, care for that child; and if the carer makes such a request, the local authority shall carry out such an assessment and shall have regard to the results of it in making any such decision.

   (2) No request may be made under subsection (1) above by a person who provides or will provide the care in question—
   (a) under or by virtue of a contract of employment or other contract; or
   (b) as a volunteer for a voluntary organisation.

   (3) Where an assessment of a carer's ability to continue to provide, or as the case may be to provide, care for a child is carried out under subsection (1) above, there shall, as respects the child, be no requirement under section 8 of the Disabled Persons (Services, Consultation and Representation) Act 1986 (carer's ability to continue to provide care to be considered in any decision as respects provision of certain services for disabled persons) to have regard to that ability.

   (4) In this section "person" means a natural person.

DEFINITIONS
   "child": s.93(2)(a).
   "disabled child": s.23(2).
   "local authority": Local Government etc. (Scotland) Act 1994, s.2.

GENERAL NOTE
   Local authorities have obligations under s.22 above to provide services to children appropriate to their needs, and these needs will be affected both by the nature of any disabilities they suffer from and by the care that is provided to them by other persons. Provision was made under s.23(3) above for the assessment of the child's disability; this section provides for the assessment of the care that the child is receiving. It requires the local authority—if requested to do so—to make an assessment as to the ability to provide care for disabled children of those (natural)

persons who care for these children on a regular basis and requires the local authority to have regard to that assessment, once it has been carried out, in making their decisions as to how to fulfil their duties to provide services to disabled children in their area.

Subss. (1) and (2)

A person who provides a substantial amount of care on a regular basis to a disabled child, otherwise than by virtue of a contract or as a volunteer for a voluntary organisation, may request the local authority to assess her or his ability to provide that care. The local authority is then obliged to carry out that assessment and is further obliged to have regard to its results in determining how to provide services to the child under s.22 above.

Substantial amount of care on a regular basis. It is envisaged that the carer under this section is the main, or one of the main, carers of the child, without whose care the development or welfare of the child would be prejudiced.

Subs. (3)

Once they have carried out an assessment under subs. (1) above, the local authority is absolved from the obligation to take it into account in making decisions under the Disabled Persons (Services, Consultation and Representation) Act 1986 (c. 33) as to whether to provide any of its welfare services under that or any other enactment. Though not so obliged, it remains open to the local authority to take the assessment into account if they think fit.

Provision of accommodation for children, etc.

25.—(1) A local authority shall provide accommodation for any child who, residing or having been found within their area, appears to them to require such provision because—

(a) no-one has parental responsibility for him;

(b) he is lost or abandoned; or

(c) the person who has been caring for him is prevented, whether or not permanently and for whatever reason, from providing him with suitable accommodation or care.

(2) Without prejudice to subsection (1) above, a local authority may provide accommodation for any child within their area if they consider that to do so would safeguard or promote his welfare.

(3) A local authority may provide accommodation for any person within their area who is at least eighteen years of age but not yet twenty-one, if they consider that to do so would safeguard or promote his welfare.

(4) A local authority providing accommodation under subsection (1) above for a child who is ordinarily resident in the area of another local authority shall notify the other authority, in writing, that such provision is being made; and the other authority may at any time take over the provision of accommodation for the child.

(5) Before providing a child with accommodation under this section, a local authority shall have regard, so far as practicable, to his views (if he wishes to express them), taking account of his age and maturity; and without prejudice to the generality of this subsection a child twelve years of age or more shall be presumed to be of sufficient age and maturity to form a view.

(6) Subject to subsection (7) below—

(a) a local authority shall not provide accommodation under this section for a child if any person who—

(i) has parental responsibilities in relation to him and the parental rights mentioned in section 2(1)(a) and (b) of this Act; and

(ii) is willing and able either to provide, or to arrange to have provided, accommodation for him,

objects; and

(b) any such person may at any time remove the child from accommodation which has been provided by the local authority under this section.

(7) Paragraph (a) of subsection (6) above does not apply—

(a) as respects any child who, being at least sixteen years of age, agrees to be provided with accommodation under this section; or

(b) where a residence order has been made in favour of one or more persons and that person has, or as the case may be those persons have, agreed that the child should be looked after in accommodation provided by, or on behalf of, the local authority;

and paragraph (b) of that subsection does not apply where accommodation has been provided for a continuous period of at least six months (whether by a single local authority or, by virtue of subsection (4) above, by more than one local authority), unless the person removing the child has given the local authority for the time being making such provision at least fourteen days' notice in writing of his intention to remove the child.

(8) In this Part of this Act, accommodation means, except where the context otherwise requires, accommodation provided for a continuous period of more than twenty-four hours.

DEFINITIONS
  "child": s.93(2)(a).
  "local authority": Local Government etc. (Scotland) Act 1994, s.2.
  "parental responsibilities": ss.1(3), 93(1).
  "parental rights": ss.2(4), 93(1).
  "residence order": ss.11(2)(c), 93(1).

GENERAL NOTE
  This section replaces s.15 of the 1968 Act, and makes some substantial alterations to the law contained therein. In particular, the notion of a duty to "receive children into care" has been removed from the law, and replaced with the idea that local authorities must "look after" certain children and provide them with accommodation. The duties that local authorities have in looking after children are spelt out in s.17 above; one class of children to whom these duties are owed is that for whom the local authority provides accommodation for a continuous period of more than 24 hours. This section imposes upon local authorities a duty, and in some cases a power, to provide such accommodation for children in their area. The connection between the old s.15 and the old s.16 has been broken, with the result that parental responsibilities orders under s.86 below (replacing parental rights resolutions under the old s.16) are no longer dependent on the child being "in care" or "looked after" by the local authority: accommodation is provided to children who need accommodation, and parental responsibilities orders are granted in relation to children who need such orders.
  The old s.15 had always been awkwardly worded, and had become more so over the years as amendments and insertions were made and the present section simplifies the rules greatly.

Subs. (1)
  This subsection imposes upon local authorities the duty (and subs. (2) below in some cases confers upon them the power) to provide accommodation to children in their area. If accommodation is provided by a local authority, whether as a result of fulfilling their duty or exercising their power, then the local authority becomes subject to the obligations specified in s.17 above. Reflecting, without substantive change, s.15(1) of the 1968 Act (except for the change from "receiving into care" to "providing accommodation"), subs. (1) obliges the local authority to provide accommodation in the stated circumstances. The subsection is designed to deal with cases in which there is no-one able or willing to look after and provide appropriate care and accommodation for the child. It is in these circumstances that a duty, as opposed to the power in subs. (2) below, arises. If the duty is not fulfilled, a remedy is available in terms of a petition to the Court of Session under s.91 of the Court of Session Act 1868 to ordain the local authority to perform their statutory duty.
  Accommodation. This is defined in subs. (8) below to mean accommodation provided for a continuous period of more than 24 hours: in other words, it necessarily includes the provision of a place to sleep.
  Child. A child for these purposes is a person under the age of 18 years.
  Residing or having been found within their area. Mere physical presence of the child in the local authority area is sufficient to impose the duty or confer the power and the child's nationality, domicile or habitual residence is irrelevant, except that the provision of accommodation for a child ordinarily resident in the area of another local authority can be taken over by that other local authority under subs. (4) below.

Appears to them to require. The obligation to provide accommodation arises only when it appears to the local authority that one or more of the specified circumstances exists. It follows that a bona fide decision by the local authority as to whether these circumstances exist cannot be challenged except by way of judicial review.

Lost or abandoned. A child has been abandoned when she or he has been left to her or his fate. "Lost" means lost to the parent or guardian, who one can assume will be searching for the child, and does not mean lost in the sense that no-one can find the child.

Prevented ... for whatever reason. It is a matter of fact whether the person previously caring for the child is now prevented from providing suitable accommodation and the reason for that prevention is entirely irrelevant to the question of whether the fact exists. A parent may be imprisoned, or made homeless, or fall ill, or be no longer able to cope with the child: if she or he is "prevented", that is to say in fact cannot (in the view of the local authority), provide suitable accommodation or care, then the obligation under subs. (1) arises.

Subs. (2)

As well as the obligation to provide accommodation under subs. (1) the local authority has the power to provide accommodation under subs. (2) whenever they consider that to do so would safeguard or promote the welfare of the child. This will allow a local authority to provide, for example, respite care when a parent remains able to provide accommodation but it is in the interests of the child to spend some time away from home. The local authority may not exercise this power when the parent objects (subs. (6) below).

Subs. (3)

A local authority similarly have the power, but not the obligation, to provide accommodation to persons who are over the age of 18, but are not yet 21, when such provision would promote the young person's welfare. This allows local authorities to accommodate, for example, homeless young persons (though it does not oblige them to do so). Such a person is not a child, with the result that the local authority are not subject to the s.17 duties when they provide accommodation to such a person.

Subs. (4)

Reflecting and simplifying s.15(4) of the 1968 Act, this subsection allows the provision of accommodation for a child to be taken over by the local authority in whose area the child is ordinarily resident from the authority which have provided accommodation on the basis that the child was found within their area. Section 86 of the 1968 Act, which deals with disputes as to the child's residence for this purpose, remains in force.

Subs. (5)

This provision reflects that contained in s.6 above, in relation to parents fulfilling parental responsibilities or exercising parental rights, and reference to the notes to that section should again be made. This is an important addition to the law in this context, for under s.15 of the 1968 Act there was no such provision. It does not give the child a veto, but a voice which will be a heavy consideration in determining her or his welfare.

Subs. (6)

The provision of accommodation under this section is voluntary in the sense that the section does not permit such provision to be made against the wishes of a person with the responsibility and right to provide accommodation for the child. Consequently it is provided here, reflecting the rules contained in s.15(3) of the 1968 Act, that the local authority may not provide accommodation when a person who has parental responsibilities for the child is willing and able to take over the provision of that accommodation and objects to the local authority providing the accommodation. Such a person may (subject to the immediately following subsection) remove the child from accommodation at any time and the local authority cannot prevent that removal under this section.

Shall not provide. It would appear from these words that the local authority is prohibited from providing accommodation if the stated circumstances present themselves. That however is qualified by the words "under this section", and a local authority may provide accommodation under some other provision in the Act, even when a person with parental responsibilities towards the child objects (such as, for example, providing residential accommodation under a supervision requirement granted under s.70(3) below). If the local authority believes that the child's welfare would be threatened by being returned to a person with parental responsibilities, it will have to rely on the compulsory or emergency measures later in the Act to ensure the child's welfare.

Subs. (7)

The prohibition on providing accommodation to a child when the child's parent objects (para. (a) of subs. (6) above) does not apply when the child is at least 16 years old and she or he agrees to be provided with accommodation or when a person in whose favour a residence order has been made under s.11 above so agrees. It is, perhaps, unfortunate that the statute adopts an absolute age limit rather than some formula similar to that contained in the Age of Legal Capacity (Scotland) Act 1991, which recognises that some children below the age of 16 are mature enough to make their own decisions in many matters, but this approach does avoid disputes concerning whether the child is mature enough to make such a decision.

The power of a person with parental responsibilities, who is willing and able to provide accommodation, to remove the child from local authority accommodation (para. (b) of subs. (6) above) is qualified when the child has been provided with accommodation by one or more local authorities for a continuous period of six months: in that situation the person with parental responsibilities can remove the child only after having given the local authority at least 14 days written notice of their intention to remove the child. It is, at first sight, odd that para. (a) of subs. (6) above is not similarly qualified. That paragraph states that the local authority "shall not" provide accommodation when a person with parental responsibilities who is able and willing to provide accommodation objects, and since this is not qualified they seem to be prohibited from providing accommodation to the child during the 14 day period of notice. However, it is submitted that when a child has been in local authority accommodation for more than six months, the person with parental responsibilities is not "able" to provide accommodation during the 14 day period, with the result that all the conditions in para. (a) of subs. (6) are not satisfied, thus maintaining the local authority's obligation to provide accommodation. "Able" in that subsection means lack of legal constraint as well as practical ability.

Manner of provision of accommodation to child looked after by local authority

26.—(1) A local authority may provide accommodation for a child looked after by them by—

    (a) placing him with—

        (i) a family (other than such family as is mentioned in paragraph (a) or (b) of the definition of that expression in section 93(1) of this Act);

        (ii) a relative of his; or

        (iii) any other suitable person,

    on such terms as to payment, by the authority or otherwise, as the authority may determine;

    (b) maintaining him in a residential establishment; or

    (c) making such other arrangements as appear to them to be appropriate, including (without prejudice to the generality of this paragraph) making use of such services as are referred to in section 17(1)(b) of this Act.

(2) A local authority may arrange for a child whom they are looking after—

    (a) to be placed, under subsection (1)(a) above, with a person in England and Wales or in Northern Ireland; or

    (b) to be maintained in any accommodation in which—

        (i) a local authority in England and Wales could maintain him by virtue of section 23(2)(b) to (e) of the Children Act 1989; or

        (ii) an authority within the meaning of the Children (Northern Ireland) Order 1995 could maintain him by virtue of Article 27(2)(b) to (e) of that Order.

DEFINITIONS

    "accommodation": s.25(8).

    "child": s.93(2)(a).

"family": s.93(1).
"local authority": Local Government etc. (Scotland) Act 1994, s.2.
"residential establishment": s.93(1).

GENERAL NOTE
Under s.25 above local authorities have duties and sometimes powers to provide accommodation for children in need. This section sets out the different forms which that provision may take, and the aim of the section is to give as wide a range of options to the local authority as is possible.

Subs. (1)
The local authority may fulfil their obligation or exercise their right to provide accommodation by placing the child in a domestic familial situation (that is to say with foster carers), or with a relative of the child (that is to say someone with whom the child has a relationship of blood or affinity), or with any other suitable person (that is suitable to look after and provide accommodation for a child of the age and circumstances of the particular child). In addition the local authority may place the child in a residential establishment, or may make any other appropriate arrangements. These arrangements might well include allowing the parents of the child to provide accommodation for the child.

Subs. (2)
The person with whom the child is placed, or the accommodation provided, may be in England or Wales or in Northern Ireland.

Day care for pre-school and other children

27.—(1) Each local authority shall provide such day care for children in need within their area who—
(a) are aged five or under; and
(b) have not yet commenced attendance at a school,
as is appropriate; and they may provide such day care for children within their area who satisfy the conditions mentioned in paragraphs (a) and (b) but are not in need.
(2) A local authority may provide facilities (including training, advice, guidance and counselling) for those—
(a) caring for children in day care; or
(b) who at any time accompany such children while they are in day care.
(3) Each local authority shall provide for children in need within their area who are in attendance at a school such care—
(a) outside school hours; or
(b) during school holidays,
as is appropriate; and they may provide such care for children within their area who are in such attendance but are not in need.
(4) In this section—
"day care" means any form of care provided for children during the day, whether or not it is provided on a regular basis; and
"school" has the meaning given by section 135(1) of the Education (Scotland) Act 1980.

DEFINITIONS
"children": s.93(2)(a).
"local authority": Local Government etc. (Scotland) Act 1994, s.2.
"school": Education (Scotland) Act 1980, s.135(1).

GENERAL NOTE
This section governs the local authority's duty and power to provide day care for pre-school children.

Subs. (1)
Each local authority has a duty to provide day care for pre-school children in their area who are in need; in addition they have the power to provide day care for pre-school children who are not in need. "Need" is defined in s.93(4)(a) below; "day care" is defined in subs. (4) below. The

regulation of day care found in Part X of the Children Act 1989 does not apply to local authority provision of day care.

Subs. (2)

The local authorities are empowered to provide facilities for those adults who care for children on a day care basis or who accompany them at day care.

Subs. (3)

The local authorities are obliged to provide appropriate care outside school hours and during school holidays to school children in need ("need" again being defined in s.93(4)(a) below), and they are empowered to provide such care to school children who are not in need.

Removal of power to arrange for emigration of children

28. Section 23 of the Social Work (Scotland) Act 1968 (which provides a power for local authorities and voluntary associations, with the consent of the Secretary of State, to make arrangements for the emigration of children in their care) shall cease to have effect.

GENERAL NOTE

The power contained in s.23 of the 1968 Act to arrange for the emigration of a child in care had for many years been outdated and the exercise of the power was almost unknown. Local authorities can no longer deal with children in their care by removing them from the U.K., but must continue to look after them according to their duties under this Act. Schedule 5 below contains many other repeals from the 1968 Act and other Acts.

Advice and assistance for young persons formerly looked after by local authorities

After-care

29.—(1) A local authority shall, unless they are satisfied that his welfare does not require it, advise, guide and assist any person in their area over school age but not yet nineteen years of age who, at the time when he ceased to be of school age or at any subsequent time was, but who is no longer, looked after by a local authority.

(2) If a person within the area of a local authority is at least nineteen, but is less than twenty-one years of age and is otherwise a person such as is described in subsection (1) above, he may by application to the authority request that they provide him with advice, guidance and assistance; and they may, unless they are satisfied that his welfare does not require it, grant that application.

(3) Assistance given under subsection (1) or (2) above may include assistance in kind or in cash.

(4) Where a person—

(a) over school age ceases to be looked after by a local authority; or

(b) described in subsection (1) above is being provided with advice, guidance or assistance by a local authority,

they shall, if he proposes to reside in the area of another local authority, inform that other local authority accordingly provided that he consents to their doing so.

DEFINITIONS

"local authority": Local Government etc. (Scotland) Act 1994, s.2.

"school age": Education (Scotland) Act 1980, s.31.

GENERAL NOTE

See White Paper: *Scotland's Children: Proposals for Child Care Policy and Law* (Cm. 2286, August 1993) at paras. 3.36–3.40.

Children brought up by their parents can usually turn to them for advice, guidance and assistance, even after they reach full adulthood, but this is often not possible for persons who, while they were children, were looked after by local authorities. This section, in an important addition to the law, gives power to local authorities to continue to provide advice, guidance and assistance to young persons whom they looked after as children.

Subs. (1)

Local authorities are obliged to provide advice, guidance and assistance to any person under the age of 19 years but over school age who were, but are no longer, looked after by the local authority. This obligation is qualified in cases in which the person's welfare does not require such advice, guidance and assistance. It does not apply to children who were, but had ceased to be, looked after by a local authority before they ceased to be of school age, with the result that it might benefit a child about to cease to be of school age to continue to be looked after until that time: this might well be a relevant consideration for children's hearings deciding whether to terminate a supervision requirement under s.73(9) below.

Looked after. The definition of children who are or were "looked after" by a local authority is found in s.17(6) above.

Subs. (2)

In addition to the obligation under subs. (1) above, local authorities also have the power to provide advice, guidance and assistance to persons over the age of 19 years and under the age of 21 years who are no longer looked after by the local authority. That power can be exercised whenever application has been made to the local authority by the person seeking advice, guidance and assistance. The matter is entirely within the discretion of the local authority to grant or withhold what has been applied for, except that they have no power to provide it when satisfied that the person's welfare does not require it.

Subs. (3)

The assistance, whether given under the local authority's duty or power, may be goods or services or cash. Again, the matter is in the discretion of the local authority.

Subs. (4)

Where the local authority have a duty to provide advice, guidance and assistance under subs. (1) above, and the person to whom it is provided moves to another local authority area, the providing local authority must inform the new local authority, so long as the person consents to this being done.

Financial assistance towards expenses of education or training and removal of power to guarantee indentures etc.

30.—(1) Without prejudice to section 12 of the Social Work (Scotland) Act 1968 (general social welfare services of local authorities), a local authority may make—

(a) grants to any relevant person in their area to enable him to meet expenses connected with his receiving education or training; and

(b) contributions to the accommodation and maintenance of any such person in any place near where he may be—

(i) employed, or seeking employment; or

(ii) receiving education or training.

(2) Subject to subsection (3) below, a person is a relevant person for the purposes of subsection (1) above if—

(a) he is over school age but not yet twenty-one years of age; and

(b) at the time when he ceased to be of school age or at any subsequent time he was, but he is no longer, looked after by a local authority.

(3) A local authority making grants under paragraph (a), or contributions under paragraph (b)(ii), of subsection (1) above to a person may continue to make them, though he has in the meantime attained the age of twenty-one years, until he completes the course of education or training in question; but if, after he has attained that age, the course is interrupted by any circum-

stances they may only so continue if he resumes the course as soon as is practicable.

(4) Section 25 of the Social Work (Scotland) Act 1968 (which empowers a local authority to undertake obligations by way of guarantee under any indentures or other deed of apprenticeship or articles of clerkship entered into by a person in their care or under supplemental deeds or articles) shall cease to have effect.

DEFINITIONS
"local authority": Local Government etc. (Scotland) Act 1994, s.2.
"school age": Education (Scotland) Act 1980, s.31.

GENERAL NOTE
Local authorities have the power (to be exercised at their discretion) to make grants towards the expenses of education or training or to make contributions towards the accommodation and maintenance of "relevant persons" who are employed or seeking employment or are receiving education or training. "Relevant person" is defined in subs. (2) to be a person who is over school age but under the age of 21 years, and who was, but no longer is, being "looked after" by the local authority. Persons "looked after" by local authorities are defined in s.17(6) above. Grants and contributions can be continued after the person reaches 21 years until the relevant education or training is completed; but any interruption of that education or training after the person's 21st birthday will take away the local authority's power to make grants and contributions unless the course is recommenced as soon as practicable.

Local authorities will no longer have express power to guarantee indentures or apprenticeships or articles of clerkship in relation to young persons who are or were in their care. This repeals s.25 of the 1968 Act, though the power contained in that section is now subsumed into the more general power in this section.

Miscellaneous and General

Review of case of child looked after by local authority

31.—(1) Without prejudice to their duty under section 17(1)(a) of this Act, it shall be the duty of a local authority who are looking after a child to review his case at such intervals as may be prescribed by the Secretary of State.

(2) The Secretary of State may prescribe—

(a) different intervals in respect of the first such review and in respect of subsequent reviews;

(b) the manner in which cases are to be reviewed under this section;

(c) the considerations to which the local authority are to have regard in reviewing cases under this section.

DEFINITIONS
"child": s.93(2)(a).
"local authority": Local Government etc. (Scotland) Act 1994, s.2.

GENERAL NOTE
A local authority which is looking after a child must periodically review the child's case in order to determine whether the method adopted for the looking after of the child remains appropriate and whether any changes require to be made in the way the child is being looked after or the legislative provisions under which the child is being looked after. The intervals at which such reviews must be held will be specified by the Secretary of State, as well as the manner in which reviews are to be conducted and the considerations to be taken into account in these reviews.

Removal of child from residential establishment

32. A local authority, notwithstanding any agreement made in connection with the placing of a child in a residential establishment under this Chapter, or Chapter 4, of this Part of this Act by them—

(a) may, at any time; and

(b) shall, if requested to do so by the person responsible for the establishment,

remove a child so placed.

Definitions
"child": s.93(2)(a).
"local authority": Local Government etc. (Scotland) Act 1994, s.2.
"residential establishment": s.93(1).

General Note
The local authority which has provided accommodation for a child in a residential establishment must remove the child from the establishment if requested to do so by the manager of the establishment, and has the power to remove the child at any other time (if, presumably, they consider that to do so is in the child's best interests or in the interests of other persons in the establishment).

Effect of orders etc. made in different parts of the United Kingdom

33.—(1) The Secretary of State may make regulations providing for a prescribed order which is made by a court in England and Wales or in Northern Ireland, if that order appears to him to correspond generally to an order of a kind which may be made under this Part of this Act or to a supervision requirement, to have effect in prescribed circumstances and for prescribed purposes of the law of Scotland as if it were an order of that kind or, as the case may be, as if it were a supervision requirement.

(2) The Secretary of State may make regulations providing—

(a) for a prescribed order made under this Part of this Act by a court in Scotland; or

(b) for a supervision requirement,

if that order or requirement appears to him to correspond generally to an order of a kind which may be made under any provision of law in force in England and Wales or in Northern Ireland, to have effect in prescribed circumstances and for prescribed purposes of the law of England and Wales, or as the case may be of Northern Ireland, as if it were an order of that kind.

(3) Regulations under subsection (1) or (2)(a) above may provide for the order given effect for prescribed purposes to cease to have effect for those purposes, or for the purposes of the law of the place where the order was made, if prescribed conditions are satisfied.

(4) Where a child who is subject to a supervision requirement is lawfully taken to live in England and Wales or in Northern Ireland, the requirement shall cease to have effect if prescribed conditions are satisfied.

(5) Regulations under this section may modify any provision of—

(a) the Social Work (Scotland) Act 1968 or this Act in any application which the Acts may respectively have, by virtue of the regulations, in relation to an order made otherwise than in Scotland;

(b) the Children Act 1989 or the Children and Young Persons Act 1969 in any application which those Acts may respectively have, by virtue of the regulations, in relation to an order prescribed under subsection (2)(a) above or to a supervision requirement; or

(c) the Children (Northern Ireland) Order 1995 or the Children and Young Persons Act (Northern Ireland) 1968 in any application which they may respectively have, by virtue of the regulations, in relation to an order so prescribed or to a supervision requirement.

Definitions
"supervision requirement": ss.70(1), 93(1).

General Note
Regulations may provide that specified orders from courts in England and Wales or in Northern Ireland will have the effect of an order or supervision requirement made under Part II of the present Act, and that an order or supervision requirement made under Part II will have the effect of an order from a court in England and Wales or in Northern Ireland if the one appears to the Secretary of State to correspond to the other. Regulations may also provide for the termin-

ation of a supervision requirement if in prescribed circumstances the child who is subject to that requirement is taken to live in England and Wales or in Northern Ireland. Authority is given to make regulations to modify any of the statutory provisions listed in subs. (5).

Registration and inspection of certain residential grant-aided and independent schools etc.

34.—(1) Part IV of the Social Work (Scotland) Act 1968 (which makes provision as regards residential and other establishments) shall be amended in accordance with this section.

(2) In section 61 (restriction on carrying on of establishments)—

(a) for subsection (1) there shall be substituted—

"(1) In so far as the context admits, the following provisions of this Part of this Act apply—

(a) except in the case mentioned in paragraph (b) below, to any residential or other establishment the whole or a substantial part of whose functions is to provide persons with such personal care or support, whether or not combined with board and whether for reward or not, as may be required for the purposes of this Act or of the Children (Scotland) Act 1995;

(b) in the case of a residential establishment which is a grant-aided or independent school (as respectively defined in section 135 (1) of the Education (Scotland) Act 1980), to that establishment if any part of its functions are as described in paragraph (a) above.";

(b) in subsection (1A)—

(i) in paragraph (a) of the definition of "establishment", for the words "sections 61A and" there shall be substituted "section"; and

(ii) at the end of that definition there shall be added "but an establishment is not excluded for those purposes by paragraph (a) above by reason only of its being registrable by the Registrar of Independent Schools in Scotland;"; and

(c) in subsection (2), for the words "section 62(8) and (8A) below" there shall be substituted "sections 61A(1) and 62(8) and (8A) of this Act".

(3) For section 61A there shall be substituted—

"**Voluntary registration**

61A.—(1) A grant-aided or independent school, provided it is not a residential establishment the whole or a substantial part of whose functions is as described in subsection (1)(a) of section 61 of this Act, may be carried on by a person without his being registered in respect of it as mentioned in subsection (2) of that section; but he may if he wishes apply in accordance with section 62, or as the case may be 63, of this Act for such registration.

(2) Sections 62(8) and (8A) and 65 of this Act shall not apply in relation to establishments as respects which registration has been by virtue of subsection (1) above.".

(4) After section 62 there shall be inserted—

"**Certificate of registration as respects grant-aided or independent school**

62A. A certificate of registration granted under section 62 of this Act as respects an establishment which is a grant-aided, or independent, school shall relate to the whole of the establishment except so much as is used exclusively for educational purposes.".

(5) In section 65(1) (removal of persons from establishment), after the word "ought"—

(a) where it first occurs, there shall be inserted "(by virtue of subsections (2) and (3)) of section 61 of this Act)"; and

(b) where it occurs for the second time, there shall be inserted "(by virtue of the said subsections (2) and (3))".

(6) For section 67 there shall be substituted—

"Entry to examine state and management of establishments etc.
    67.—(1) A person duly authorised by a local authority may in the area of that authority, at all reasonable times, enter, for a relevant purpose—
    (a) any establishment as regards which a person is registered, or ought (by virtue of subsections (2) and (3) of section 61 of this Act) to be registered, under section 62 of this Act; or
    (b) any place which the person so authorised has reasonable cause to believe is being used as such an establishment,
and subsections (2A) to (2D), (4) and (5) of section 6 of this Act shall apply in respect of a person so authorised as they apply in respect of a person duly authorised under subsection (1) of that section.

    (2) "Relevant purpose" in subsection (1) above means—
    (a) the purpose of making such examinations into the state and management of the establishment or place, and the condition and treatment of the persons in it, as the person so authorised thinks necessary; or
    (b) the purpose of inspecting any records, or registers (in whatever form they are held) relating to the place, or to any person for whom, under or by virtue of this Act, section 7 (functions of local authorities) or 8 (provision of after-care services) of the Mental Health (Scotland) Act 1984, or Part II of the Children (Scotland) Act 1995, services are being or have been provided in the place.".

GENERAL NOTE
    Residential establishments carrying out functions under the present Act or the 1968 Act, grant-aided schools and independent schools are required to be registered with local authorities, and inspected regularly. The rules are contained in ss.61–68 of the 1968 Act and are described in detail in Wilkinson & Norrie *Parent and Child* (3rd ed., W. Green) at pp. 504–508. These rules are amended by the present section to take account of the provisions in this Act.

Welfare of children in accommodation provided for purposes of school attendance

    35. After section 125 of the Education (Scotland) Act 1980 there shall be inserted—

"Children and young persons in accommodation

Welfare of children and young persons in accommodation provided for purposes of school attendance
    125A. Where, for the purposes of his being in attendance at a school, a child or young person is provided with residential accommodation, in a place in or outwith that school, by—
    (a) an education authority, the board of management of a self-governing school or the managers of a grant-aided or independent school; or
    (b) by any other person in pursuance of arrangements made by any such authority, board of management or managers,
the authority, board of management or managers in question shall have the duty to safeguard and promote the welfare of the child or young person while he is so accommodated; and the powers of inspection exer-

cisable by virtue of section 66(1) of this Act shall include the power to inspect the place to determine whether his welfare is adequately safeguarded and promoted there.".

GENERAL NOTE
Adding a new s.125A to the Education (Scotland) Act 1980, this section ensures that those responsible for schools providing residential accommodation, whether within or outwith the school, have a duty to safeguard and promote the welfare of the child accommodated, and subjects them to the rules on inspection.

Welfare of certain children in hospitals and nursing homes etc.

36.—(1) Where a child is provided with residential accommodation by a person mentioned in subsection (3) below and it appears to the person that the child either—
  (a) has had no parental contact for a continuous period of three months or more; or
  (b) is likely to have no parental contact for a period which, taken with any immediately preceding period in which the child has had no such contact, will constitute a continuous period of three months or more,
the person shall (whether or not the child has been, or will be, so accommodated throughout the continuous period) so notify the local authority in whose area the accommodation is provided.

(2) A local authority receiving notification under subsection (1) above shall—
  (a) take such steps as are reasonably practicable to enable them to determine whether the child's welfare is adequately safeguarded and promoted while he is so accommodated; and
  (b) consider the extent to which (if at all) they should exercise any of their functions under this Act with respect to the child.

(3) The persons are—
  (a) any health board constituted under section 2 of the National Health Service (Scotland) Act 1978;
  (b) any national health service trust established under section 12A of that Act;
  (c) any person carrying on—
       (i) a private hospital registered under Part IV of the Mental Health (Scotland) Act 1984; or
       (ii) a nursing home in respect of which either he is registered under section 1(3) of the Nursing Homes Registration (Scotland) Act 1938 or exemption has been granted under section 6 or 7 of that Act.

(4) For the purposes of subsection (1) above, a child has parental contact only when in the presence of a person having parental responsibilities in relation to him.

(5) A person duly authorised by a local authority may in the area of that authority, at all reasonable times, enter for the purposes of subsection (2) above or of determining whether there has been compliance with subsection (1) above any such place as is mentioned in sub-paragraph (i) or (ii) of subsection (3)(c) above and may for those purposes inspect any records or registers relating to that place; and subsections (2A) to (2D) and (4) of section 6 of the Social Work (Scotland) Act 1968 (exercise of powers of entry and inspection) shall apply in respect of a person so authorised as they apply in respect of a person duly authorised under subsection (1) of that section.

DEFINITIONS
  "accommodation": s.25(8).
  "child": s.93(2)(a).
  "local authority": Local Government etc. (Scotland) Act 1994, s.2.
  "parental responsibilities": ss.1(3), 93(1).

GENERAL NOTE
Whenever a child is being accommodated, that is to say provided with accommodation for longer than 24 hours, by a health board, a national health service trust, a private hospital, or a nursing home, and the person providing that accommodation concludes that the child has not been visited personally by any person with parental responsibilities for the child for a period of more than three months, that person must inform the local authority of that fact. The local authority must then determine whether the child's welfare is adequately safeguarded and whether they ought to exercise any of their functions under the Act. This might include, for example, providing accommodation to the child under s.25 above, or giving information to the reporter under s.53 below. The local authority also has the power to enter certain premises to ensure that the obligation to inform them under this section is being properly carried out.

Modification of provisions of Children Act 1989 regarding disqualification from registration as child minder etc.

37. In paragraph 2 of Schedule 9 to the Children Act 1989 (which provides for regulations disqualifying certain persons from registration as a child minder or as a provider of day care for young children), at the end of sub-paragraph (1) there shall be added "unless he has—
(a) disclosed the fact to the appropriate local authority; and
(b) obtained their written consent.".

GENERAL NOTE
This addition to a part of the Children Act 1989 that applies to Scotland allows a person to be registered as a child minder when she or he would otherwise be disqualified, so long as both the stated conditions are satisfied.

Short-term refuges for children at risk of harm

38.—(1) Where a child appears—
(a) to a local authority to be at risk of harm, they may at the child's request—
    (i) provide him with refuge in a residential establishment both controlled or managed by them and designated by them for the purposes of this paragraph; or
    (ii) arrange for a person whose household is approved by virtue of section 5(3)(b) of the Social Work (Scotland) Act 1968 (provision for securing that persons are not placed in any household unless the household has prescribed approval) and is designated by them for the purposes of this paragraph to provide him with refuge in that household,
for a period which does not exceed the relevant period;
(b) to a person who carries on a residential establishment in respect of which the person is for the time being registered (as mentioned in section 61(2) of that Act), or to any person for the time being employed in the management of that establishment, to be at risk of harm, the person to whom the child so appears may at the child's request provide him with refuge, for a period which does not exceed the relevant period, in the establishment but shall do so only if and to the extent that the local authority within whose area the establishment is situated have given their approval to the use of the establishment (or a part of the establishment) for the purposes of this paragraph.
(2) The Secretary of State may by regulations make provision as to—
(a) designation, for the purposes of paragraph (a) of subsection (1) above, of establishments and households;
(b) application for, the giving of and the withdrawal of, approval under paragraph (b) of subsection (1) above;
(c) requirements (if any) which must be complied with while any such approval remains in force;
(d) the performance by a person mentioned in the said paragraph (b) of anything to be done by him under that paragraph;

(e) the performance by a local authority of their functions under this section; and

(f) the giving, to such persons or classes of person as may be specified in the regulations, of notice as to the whereabouts of a child provided with refuge under this section,

and regulations made under this subsection may include such incidental and supplementary provisions as he thinks fit.

(3) While a child is being provided with refuge under, and in accordance with regulations made under, this section, none of the enactments mentioned in subsection (4) below shall apply in relation to him unless the commencement of the period of refuge has followed within two days of the termination of a prior period of refuge so provided to him by any person.

(4) The enactments are—

(a) section 89 of this Act and, so far as it applies in relation to anything done in Scotland, section 83 of this Act; and

(b) section 32(3) of the Children and Young Persons Act 1969 (compelling, persuading, inciting or assisting any person to be absent from detention etc.), so far as it applies in relation to anything done in Scotland.

(5) References in this section to the relevant period shall be construed as references either to a period which does not exceed seven days or, in such exceptional circumstances as the Secretary of State may prescribe, to a period which does not exceed fourteen days.

(6) A child who is provided with refuge for a period by virtue of such arrangements as are mentioned in subsection (1)(a) above shall not be regarded as a foster child for the purposes of the Foster Children (Scotland) Act 1984 by reason only of such provision.

DEFINITIONS
"child": s.93(2)(a).
"local authority": Local Government etc. (Scotland) Act 1994, s.2.
"residential establishment": s.93(1).

GENERAL NOTE
See White Paper: *Scotland's Children: Proposals for Child Care Policy and Law* (Cm. 2286, August 1993) at paras. 5.21–5.22.

Local authorities and persons who run residential establishments may provide short-term refuge (i.e. for a period not exceeding seven, or exceptionally 14, days) to children who appear to be at risk of harm and who themselves request to be provided with such refuge. A child provided with such a refuge will not be regarded as a foster child for statutory purposes, and, in a significant alteration to the law, the person who provides such a refuge will not be subject to certain specified offences, including that under s.83 of the present Act (harbouring). The Secretary of State may make regulations providing for various matters in connection with such short-term refuges. There is no limitation on the source of the harm, nor its duration, nor its nature and it is likely, therefore, to be given wide scope. The only limitation is that the child her or himself requests refuge and this section does not, therefore, apply to children who are too young themselves to seek refuge, or who do not want to go to the relevant residential establishment.

A local authority which does provide such a refuge will frequently, if not invariably, be obliged to pass information concerning the child to the reporter in terms of s.53 below.

CHAPTER 2

CHILDREN'S HEARINGS

Constitution of children's hearings

Formation of children's panel and children's hearings

39.—(1) For every local government area there shall be a children's panel for the purposes of this Act, and any other enactment conferring powers on a children's hearing (or on such a panel).

(2) Schedule 1 to this Act shall have effect with respect to the recruitment, appointment, training and expenses of members of a children's panel and the establishment of Children's Panel Advisory Committees and joint advisory committees.

(3) Sittings of members of the children's panel (to be known as "children's hearings") shall be constituted from the panel in accordance with subsection (5) below.

(4) A children's hearing shall be constituted for the performance of the functions given to such a hearing by or by virtue of—

(a) this Act; or

(b) any other enactment conferring powers on a children's hearing.

(5) A children's hearing shall consist of three members, one of whom shall act as chairman; and shall not consist solely of male, or solely of female, members.

DEFINITIONS

"children's hearing": s.93(1).

"local government area": Local Government etc. (Scotland) Act 1994, s.2.

GENERAL NOTE

This section replaces much of ss.33 and 34 of the Social Work (Scotland) Act 1968 with little substantive alteration, except that the role of the local authority is minimised due to the system being administered on a national, rather than a regional, level. The section provides that in every local government area there shall be a children's panel, which is a panel of individuals recruited, appointed and trained in accordance with Sched. 1, and from whose numbers shall be constituted children's hearings to deal with the cases of individual children. These hearings consist of three panel members, at least one of whom must be a woman and at least one of whom must be a man.

Qualifications, employment and duties of reporters

Qualification and employment of reporters

40.—(1) The qualifications of a reporter shall be such as the Secretary of State may prescribe.

(2) A reporter shall not, without the consent of the Scottish Children's Reporter Administration, be employed by a local authority.

(3) The Secretary of State may make regulations in relation to the functions of any reporter under this Act and the Criminal Procedure (Scotland) Act 1975.

(4) The Secretary of State and the Lord Advocate may—

(a) by regulations empower a reporter, whether or not he is an advocate or solicitor, to conduct before a sheriff any proceedings which under this Chapter or Chapter 3 of this Part of this Act are heard by the sheriff;

(b) prescribe such requirements as they think fit as to qualifications, training or experience necessary for a reporter to be so empowered.

(5) In this section, "reporter" means—

(a) the Principal Reporter; or

(b) any officer of the Scottish Children's Reporter Administration to whom there is delegated, under section 131(1) of the Local Government etc. (Scotland) Act 1994, any of the functions which the Principal Reporter has under this or any other enactment.

GENERAL NOTE

This section replaces ss.36 and 36A of the 1968 Act. It deals with the qualifications and employment of children's reporters, taking account of the reorganisation of the reporters' service in the Local Government etc. (Scotland) Act 1994 (c. 39), but making little substantive change in the law. The service, to be known as the Scottish Children's Reporter Administration, is now run on a national basis, rather than being tied in to regional council areas, and the chief officer of the service is the Principal Reporter.

Subs. (1)

As under s.36(2) of the 1968 Act, the Secretary of State for Scotland is empowered to pre-scribe the qualifications of reporters.

Subs. (2)

This provision has its origins in s.36(5) of the 1968 Act, which prohibited reporters from being employed by local authorities in any capacity other than as reporter. Reporters are now employed by the Scottish Children's Reporter Administration and are prohibited from being employed in any capacity at all by local authorities. That prohibition could under the 1968 Act be removed in individual cases with the consent of the Secretary of State; under the present pro-vision the consent of the Scottish Children's Reporter Administration is required.

Subs. (3)

The functions of the reporter under the present Act (issues in relation to children's hearings) and under the Criminal Procedure (Scotland) Act 1975 (c. 21) (in relation to referrals and remits from the criminal courts to the children's hearing) will be governed by regulations to be made.

Subs. (4)

As under s.36A of the 1968 Act, the Secretary of State and the Lord Advocate may make regulations giving reporters a right of audience before the sheriff, and reporters will therefore be allowed to conduct cases whether or not they are legally qualified. Regulations may also provide for requirements for qualifications to be obtained before any individual reporter is given the right to conduct cases.

Subs. (5)

The term "reporter" means the Principal Reporter and any officer to whom he has delegated any of his functions under s.131(1) of the Local Government etc. (Scotland) Act 1994. Through-out the remainder of the Act the term "Principal Reporter" is used, but that is defined in s.93(1) in the same way as "reporter" is defined here. For the sake of simplicity, these annotations will refer only to "the reporter".

Safeguards for children

Safeguarding child's interests in proceedings

41.—(1) Subject to subsection (2) below, in any proceedings under this Chapter or Chapter 3 of this Part of this Act either at a children's hearing or before the sheriff, the hearing or, as the case may be, the sheriff—

(a) shall consider if it is necessary to appoint a person to safeguard the interests of the child in the proceedings; and

(b) if they, or he, so consider, shall make such an appointment, on such terms and conditions as appear appropriate.

(2) Subsection (1) above shall not apply in relation to proceedings under section 57 of this Act.

(3) Where a children's hearing make an appointment under subsection (1)(b) above, they shall state the reasons for their decision to make that appointment.

(4) The expenses of a person appointed under subsection (1) above shall—

(a) in so far as reasonably incurred by him in safeguarding the interests of the child in the proceedings, and

(b) except in so far as otherwise defrayed in terms of regulations made under section 101 of this Act,

be borne by the local authority—

(i) for whose area the children's panel from which the relevant children's hearing has been constituted is formed;

(ii) where there is no relevant children's hearing, within whose area the child resides.

(5) For the purposes of subsection (4) above, "relevant children's hearing" means, in the case of proceedings—

(a) at a children's hearing, that hearing;

(b) under section 68 of this Act, the children's hearing who have directed the application;

(c) on an appeal under section 51 of this Act, the children's hearing whose decision is being appealed against.

"child": s.93(2)(b).
"children's hearing": s.93(1).
"local authority": Local Government etc. (Scotland) Act 1994, s.2.

GENERAL NOTE
Safeguarders were introduced into the children's hearing system by s.66 of the Children Act 1975, coming into effect on June 30, 1985, with the insertion into the 1968 Act of a new s.34A. The present provision replaces the old s.34A, making some important alterations to the law, which are designed both to clarify and to strengthen the role of the safeguarder. The ground upon which a safeguarder can be appointed is substantially widened; power is given in s.42 below to make rules to deal with the functions of safeguarders.

Subs. (1)
In any proceedings conducted under either Chapter 2 or Chapter 3 of Part II of the Act, the sheriff or the children's hearing must consider whether the interests of the child make it necessary to appoint a safeguarder and, if it is considered necessary, must make such an appointment. Under s.34A(1)(c)(i) of the 1968 Act, appointment was permitted when there was, or might have been, a conflict of interest between the child and the parent. The present provision does not specify why the appointment of a safeguarder is necessary, except that it must be in the interests of the child, and the appointment can now be made whenever and for whatever reason the child's interests will be served by such an appointment. This might be because, for example, there is a conflict of interests between the parent and the child, or because there is a conflict of views between the family and the Social Work Department, or because this is the best way of giving the child a voice in the hearing.
Any proceedings. Except in relation to child protection orders (for which see subs. (2) below), the appointment of a safeguarder can be made in any proceedings before the sheriff or the children's hearing which are governed by Chapters 2 or 3. These words are, however, subject to the (unspoken) qualification that the outcome of the proceedings must not be a dispositive decision: it would, it is submitted, be incompetent to appoint a safeguarder in proceedings in which the sheriff or the children's hearing dispose of the case. For example, in proceedings before the sheriff under s.68 below to establish the grounds of referral a safeguarder could be appointed, but not if the sheriff discharges the referral under s.68(9); similarly if the hearing decide to discharge the referral under s.69(12) or to make a supervision requirement under s.70(1) or to terminate a supervision requirement under s.73(9), no safeguarder can be appointed. The typical proceedings before a sheriff in which a safeguarder is appointed are when grounds are found to be established, or when on appeal the sheriff remits the case back to a children's hearing for reconsideration, and, before a children's hearing, when the case is referred to the sheriff or when the hearing is continued for further investigation.
The hearing. Under the 1968 Act, the decision whether to appoint a safeguarder lay solely in the discretion of the chairman of the children's hearing (see the old s.34A(1)(c)). This was one of the very few decisions that was made by the chairman alone rather than by the hearing as a whole though there was no good reason why that should have been so, and (sensibly) this has now been changed so that under the present provision the matter is one for the hearing to decide. As always in relation to decisions of a children's hearing, a majority decision is sufficient. The decision is governed by the welfare principle in s.16(1) above, but not the other two overarching principles in s.16(2) or (3). Nevertheless in the context of a children's hearing, it will often be appropriate to discuss the possible appointment of a safeguarder with a child.

Subs. (2)
A safeguarder cannot be appointed in relation to proceedings for child protection orders. This reflects the fact that such proceedings are emergency proceedings which are required to be concluded as quickly as possible. A safeguarder can be appointed by a children's hearing arranged under s.65(2) when the child protection order comes to an end.

Subs. (3)
A children's hearing is required under the rules to state the reasons for any decision that they make. This subsection ensures that, in addition to stating why they have, for example, continued the hearing, they also state why they felt it necessary in the interests of the child to appoint a safeguarder. This was not necessary under the old law since there was only one reason why a safeguarder was appointed in any case, namely where there was a conflict of interest between

parent and child. Now there are many possible reasons (see notes to subs. (1) above), and a statement of the hearing's reason not only consists with their general duty to state reasons for their decisions but will in addition serve the useful purpose of indicating to the safeguarder the issues that she or he ought to address.

Subs. (4)

This replaces the old s.34A(3) under which expenses were paid by the local authority of the area from which the children's hearing was formed. This will generally continue to be the case, but there may now be no relevant children's hearing or at least not yet, before a safeguarder is appointed. One of the new powers granted to sheriffs by the present Act is to refer the case of a child to a children's hearing under s.54 below. At that point there will be no relevant children's hearing, and if the sheriff appoints a safeguarder in such proceedings it is the local authority within whose area the child lives which must bear the expenses of the safeguarder.

Subs. (5)

This replaces the old s.34A(4) and makes no substantive changes. It specifies the children's hearing which has appointed a safeguarder to any particular child in order to identify which local authority must bear the safeguarder's expenses.

Conduct of proceedings at and in connection with children's hearing

Power of Secretary of State to make rules governing procedure at children's hearing etc.

42.—(1) Subject to the following provisions of this Act, the Secretary of State may make rules for constituting and arranging children's hearings and other meetings of members of the children's panel and for regulating their procedure.

(2) Without prejudice to the generality of subsection (1) above, rules under that subsection may make provision with respect to—
  (a) the conduct of, and matters which shall or may be determined by, a business meeting arranged under section 64 of this Act;
  (b) notification of the time and place of a children's hearing to the child and any relevant person in relation to the child and to such other persons as may be prescribed;
  (c) how the grounds for referring the case to a children's hearing under section 65(1) of this Act are to be stated, and the right of the child and any such relevant person to dispute those grounds;
  (d) the making available by the Principal Reporter, subject to such conditions as may be specified in the rules, of reports or information received by him to—
      (i) members of the children's hearing;
      (ii) the child concerned;
      (iii) any relevant person; and
      (iv) any other person or class of persons so specified;
  (e) the procedure in relation to the disposal of matters arising under section 41(1) of this Act;
  (f) the functions of any person appointed by a children's hearing under section 41(1) of this Act and any right of that person to information relating to the proceedings in question;
  (g) the recording in writing of any statement given under section 41(3) of this Act;
  (h) the right to appeal to the sheriff under section 51(1)(a) of this Act against a decision of the children's hearing and notification to such persons as may be prescribed of the proceedings before him;
  (i) the right of the child and of any such relevant person to be represented at a children's hearing;
  (j) the entitlement of the child, of any such relevant person and of any person who acts as the representative of the child or of any such relevant person to the refund of such expenses, incurred by the child or as the case may be the person or representative, as may be prescribed in

connection with a children's hearing and with any proceedings arising from the hearing;
  (k) persons whose presence shall be permitted at a children's hearing.

This replaces and expands s.35(4) and (5) of the 1968 Act, empowering the Secretary of State to make rules for the constituting and arranging of children's hearings, for business meetings, for safeguarders and for regulating the procedure at children's hearings. The specified matters in subs. (2) are little different from those under the old law, except that under para. (a) it is provided that regulations will deal with the conduct of and matters to be determined by the new business meetings introduced by s.64.

Privacy of proceedings at and right to attend children's hearing

43.—(1) Subject to subsection (3) below, a children's hearing shall be conducted in private, and, subject to any rules made under section 42 of this Act, no person other than a person whose presence is necessary for the proper consideration of the case which is being heard, or whose presence is permitted by the chairman, shall be present.

(2) The chairman shall take all reasonable steps to ensure that the number of persons present at a children's hearing at any one time is kept to a minimum.

(3) The following persons have the right to attend a children's hearing—
  (a) a member of the Council on Tribunals, or of the Scottish Committee of that Council, in his capacity as such; and
  (b) subject to subsection (4) below, a bona fide representative of a newspaper or news agency.

(4) A children's hearing may exclude a person described in subsection (3) (b) above from any part or parts of the hearing where, and for so long as, they are satisfied that—
  (a) it is necessary to do so, in the interests of the child, in order to obtain the child's views in relation to the case before the hearing; or
  (b) the presence of that person is causing, or is likely to cause, significant distress to the child.

(5) Where a children's hearing have exercised the power conferred by subsection (4) above to exclude a person, the chairman may, after that exclusion has ended, explain to the person the substance of what has taken place in his absence.

DEFINITIONS
  "child": s.93(2)(b).
  "children's hearing": s.93(1).

GENERAL NOTE
Subsections (1)–(3) of this section replace without substantive alteration the first three subsections of s.35 of the 1968 Act, and aim to ensure that there are as few people as possible present at a children's hearing. The significant change in the law is contained in subss. (4) and (5), under which the children's hearing are given the power to exclude from the hearing journalists, who otherwise have an absolute right to attend.

Subs. (1)
A children's hearing is to be conducted in private, and members of the public are not permitted to attend. The only persons normally present will be those who are necessary for a proper consideration of the child's case, though exceptionally the chairman may permit the presence of other persons. The Secretary of State may make rules permitting other classes of person to attend.
  Necessary for the proper consideration of the case. The presence of those who have an obligation to attend is normally, but not always, necessary for the proper consideration of the case. In addition, social workers, safeguarders, interpreters if required, representatives, and anyone who can speak to reports on the child may well be considered necessary.
  Permitted by the chairman. The discretion to permit the presence of individuals who have no statutory right to attend a children's hearing rests solely with the chairman, who is guided in her

or his decision by subs. (2) below. Any decision made by the chairman cannot be challenged (see notes to s.51(1) below).

Subs. (2)

The chairman is obliged to keep the number of persons present at a children's hearing at any one time to a minimum. This does not entitle the chairman to exclude any person who has a right to attend, except for the reasons specified in any statutory provision which permits such exclusion (as in subs. (4) below or s.46 below); and this subsection does no more than exhort the chairman to minimise the number of those persons whose presence can be admitted under subs. (1) above on a discretionary basis. These will be, for the most part, observers rather than active participants, but individuals such as foster carers, unmarried fathers who are not "relevant persons", or other relatives may well have some role to play in helping the consideration of the case.

At any one time. The chairman can sanction an arrangement whereby parts only of the hearing take place in the presence of particular individuals.

Subs. (3)

This subsection lists the persons who have a right to attend a children's hearing and who cannot, therefore, be excluded. Paragraph (b) deals with journalists, but their right to attend is subject to subs. (4) below. Rules made under s.42(2)(k) above may give other individuals a right to attend. Under the 1986 Rules (S.I. 1986 No. 2291) safeguarders and representatives were given a right to attend by rr.12 and 14 respectively, and it is expected that the new rules will similarly so provide.

Subs. (4)

A journalist who would otherwise have the right to attend a hearing under subs. (3) above may be excluded from part or all of the hearing if the journalist's presence either (a) inhibits the child from expressing her or his views, or (b) is causing or is likely to cause significant distress to the child.

A children's hearing may. The decision to exclude a journalist lies with the whole hearing and not solely with the chairman. It is governed by the welfare principle in s.16(1) above.

It is necessary to do so. The exclusion under para. (a) is justified only when it is likely that the child will not express her or his views while the journalist is present. This may arise if the child is inhibited due to the large number of people present at the hearing, or if the child is afraid that the journalist will report her or his views, or if the matters being discussed are of a particularly personal nature.

Significant distress. A preference on the part of the child that the journalist be absent is not sufficient to justify exclusion under para. (b). The presence must cause or be likely to cause "significant" distress, though there is probably no requirement that that distress be of a long lasting nature, so long as it is severe at the moment.

Subs. (5)

If a journalist has been excluded from a hearing under the terms of subs. (4) above, the substance of what has taken place may be explained to the journalist by the chairman.

The chairman may. The right to explain rests with the chairman and there is no obligation on the chairman to do so. If, for example, the matters discussed were particularly personal the chairman may take the view that they should not be revealed to the journalist. If the journalist has been excluded because she or he has deliberately distressed the child, the chairman might properly take the view that the journalist has forfeited the right to an explanation. The decision whether to reveal to a journalist the substance of what occurred is to be determined by having regard only to the welfare of the child and should not be influenced by considerations of "freedom of the press" or "the public's right to know".

After that exclusion has ended. If the journalist has been excluded for the whole of the hearing, the explanation, if the chairman decides to give one, will be after the hearing's decision has been made and the rights of the family have been explained to them. Since the parent and child have a right to attend all parts of the hearing, the explanation to the excluded journalist should be made in their presence.

Prohibition of publication of proceedings at children's hearing

44.—(1) No person shall publish any matter in respect of proceedings at a children's hearing, or before a sheriff on an application under section 57, section 60(7), section 65(7) or (9), section 76(1) or section 85(1) of this Act, or on any appeal under this Part of this Act, which is intended to, or is likely to, identify—

(a) any child concerned in the proceedings or appeal; or

(b) an address or school as being that of any such child.

(2) Any person who contravenes subsection (1) above shall be guilty of an offence and shall be liable on summary conviction to a fine not exceeding level 4 on the standard scale in respect of each such contravention.

(3) It shall be a defence in proceedings for an offence under this section for the accused to prove that he did not know, and had no reason to suspect, that the published matter was intended, or was likely, to identify the child or, as the case may be, the address or school.

(4) In this section "to publish" includes, without prejudice to the generality of that expression,—

(a) to publish matter in a programme service, as defined by section 201 of the Broadcasting Act 1990 (definition of programme service); and

(b) to cause matter to be published.

(5) The requirements of subsection (1) above may, in the interests of justice, be dispensed with by—

(a) the sheriff in any proceedings before him;

(b) the Court of Session in any appeal under section 51(11) of this Act; or

(c) the Secretary of State in relation to any proceedings at a children's hearing,

to such extent as the sheriff, the Court or the Secretary of State as the case may be considers appropriate.

DEFINITIONS
"child": s.93(2)(b).
"children's hearing": s.93(1).

GENERAL NOTE
This section replaces, in rather stronger terms, s.58 of the 1968 Act, and it prohibits the publication of any matter either intended to or likely to identify any child, or her or his address or school, who is subject to proceedings at a children's hearing or before a sheriff in relation to child protection orders, exclusion orders, referrals from a children's hearing, rehearing of evidence, or an appeal. The omission of a reference to child assessment orders granted under s.55 is odd, and publication of the identity of the child in proceedings for such an order would appear not to be a criminal offence.

The prohibition is more extensive than that contained in the 1968 Act, and the section applies in England and Wales and in Northern Ireland (s.105(8) below).

Subs. (1)
Subject to subs. (3) below, the prohibition is absolute, and the offence created by this section is committed if the prohibited matter is intended to, or is likely to, identify the child, or her or his address or school. It may well follow from this that nothing at all can be published in relation to children from small country or island communities where there is only one school, while similar matters could be published in relation to children from urban communities.

No person. These words are to be given broad scope. The section is not limited to representatives of the media but includes individuals such as reporters, social workers, panel members, parents and relatives. Also covered will be publishers, broadcasters and distributors of material containing the information.

Publish. Subs. (4) below indicates some forms of publication covered by the prohibition, but the prohibition is wider. For one person to inform another person is not to "publish", which requires a more general communication, though it is not necessary that the communication be to a large number of individuals. The word ought to be interpreted in the light of its clear aim, which is to protect the privacy of children. This again is wider than the prohibition contained in the 1968 Act.

Any child concerned. This is not limited to the child referred to the children's hearing, but might include, for example, another child giving evidence or a child in the same household as the referred child and victim of a Sched. 1 offence: *McArdle v. Orr* [1993] S.L.T. 463.

Subs. (2)
Each such contravention. Every time prohibited material is published by an accused a new offence is committed which will attract the stated penalty. A single publication can constitute many offences if different people are involved in its production and distribution.

Subs. (3)

This defence did not exist in the 1968 Act, but it is necessary now since the prohibition has been extended to cover any person and can be used, for example, by a distributor of a newspaper which, unknown to him, carries the prohibited material. Those responsible for the contents of the material, such as newspaper editors, are unlikely to be able to rely on the defence in this subsection. The onus is on the accused to prove his own ignorance.

Subs. (5)

Under s.58(3) of the 1968 Act the Secretary of State could permit publication if it were in the interests of justice to do so. The present provision permits the sheriff to do so in relation to proceedings before him, the Court of Session to do so in relation to appeal proceedings before them, and the Secretary of State to do so in relation to proceedings at a children's hearing. The children's hearing themselves have no power to grant such a dispensation.

In the interests of justice. Dispensation can be given only in the interests of justice. In making their decision, however, sheriffs and the Court of Session must regard the child's welfare as their paramount consideration (s.16(1) above applies here as to any other decision affecting the child), and this has the result, it is submitted, that the publication ban can be lifted only when this is in the interests of justice *to the child*; circumstances in which this will be so are difficult to visualise but might, for example, cover the case of a child who wishes publicly to clear her or his name from an allegation made in a previous, unauthorised, publication. The Secretary of State is not governed by s.16, but the welfare of the child will in any case be a heavy consideration in his balancing of the interests of justice. If he does decide to lift the publication ban, this should be only in the most exceptional circumstances and only to the extent that is absolutely necessary to achieve the particular interests of justice that have been identified. The interests of persons other than the child may well be taken into account by the Secretary of State, but again it is difficult to visualise circumstances in which this would be appropriate. No dispensation was ever given by the Secretary of State under the equivalent provision in the 1968 Act (according to the Earl of Lindsay, speaking for the Government in the House of Lords Committee of the Whole House, June 7, 1995, col. 95).

Attendance of child and relevant person at children's hearing

45.—(1) Where a child has been notified in accordance with rules made under subsection (1) of section 42 of this Act by virtue of subsection (2)(b) of that section that his case has been referred to a children's hearing, he shall—

(a) have the right to attend at all stages of the hearing; and

(b) subject to subsection (2) below, be under an obligation to attend those stages in accordance with the notice.

(2) Without prejudice to subsection (1)(a) above and section 65(4) of this Act, where a children's hearing are satisfied—

(a) in a case concerned with an offence mentioned in Schedule 1 to the Criminal Procedure (Scotland) Act 1975, that the attendance of the child is not necessary for the just hearing of that case; or

(b) in any case, that it would be detrimental to the interests of the child for him to be present at the hearing of his case,

they may release the child from the obligation imposed by subsection (1)(b) above.

(3) Subject to subsection (2) above, the Principal Reporter shall be responsible for securing the attendance of the child at the hearing of his case by a children's hearing (and at any subsequent hearing to which the case is continued under section 69(1)(a) of this Act).

(4) On the application of the Principal Reporter, a children's hearing, if satisfied on cause shown that it is necessary for them to do so, may issue, for the purposes of subsection (3) above, a warrant under this subsection to find the child, to keep him in a place of safety and to bring him before a children's hearing.

(5) Where a child has failed to attend a children's hearing in accordance with such notice as is mentioned in subsection (1) above, they may, either on the application of the Principal Reporter or of their own motion, issue a war-

rant under this subsection, which shall have the same effect as a warrant under subsection (4) above.

(6) A child who has been taken to a place of safety under a warrant granted under this section shall not be kept there after whichever is the earlier of—

    (a) the expiry of seven days beginning on the day he was first so taken there; or

    (b) the day on which a children's hearing first sit to consider his case in accordance with subsection (7) below.

(7) Where a child has been found in pursuance of a warrant under this section and he cannot immediately be brought before a children's hearing, the Principal Reporter shall, wherever practicable, arrange a children's hearing to sit on the first working day after the child was so found.

(8) Subject to section 46 of this Act, a person who is a relevant person as respects a child shall, where a children's hearing are considering the case of the child—

    (a) have the right to attend at all stages of the hearing; and

    (b) be obliged to attend at all stages of the hearing unless the hearing are satisfied that it would be unreasonable to require his attendance or that his attendance is unnecessary for the proper consideration of the case.

(9) Any person who fails to attend a hearing which, under subsection (8)(b) above, he is obliged to attend shall be guilty of an offence and shall be liable on summary conviction to a fine not exceeding level 3 on the standard scale.

Definitions
    "child": s.93(2)(b).
    "children's hearing": s.93(1).
    "place of safety": s.93(1).
    "principal reporter": s.93(1).
    "relevant person": s.93(2)(b).
    "working day": s.93(1).

General Note
    This section replaces, with important alterations in substance, parts of s.40 and all of s.41 of the 1968 Act. It obliges the child and the parent to attend the children's hearing, makes it a criminal offence for the parent to fail to do so, and allows for the issuing of warrants to find, keep and bring the child before a children's hearing.

Subs. (1)
    The child who has been notified of the fact that a children's hearing has been arranged, whether to put grounds of referral to her or him, or to discuss established grounds or for a review of an existing supervision requirement, is granted the right and subjected to the obligation to attend all stages of the hearing, together with any continuations thereof. Granting the child the right to attend is an important improvement on the 1968 Act, which nowhere expressly granted to the child the right to attend her or his own hearing (though as Sheriff Kelbie pointed out in *Sloan v. B* 1991 S.L.T. 530 at p. 535A, the obligation to attend implicitly carried with it the right of the child to attend the hearing). Paragraph (a) of the present subsection puts the matter beyond any doubt, and additionally has the symbolic importance of emphasising that the hearing is the child's hearing.
    Notified. A child is notified when a notification in relevant form has been sent to her or his address. It is not notification to send it to any address at which the reporter is aware the child is not living (*Sloan v. B* 1991 S.L.T. 530, per Lord President Hope at p. 540I).
    The right to attend. If the child insists on attending, she or he cannot be excluded from any part of the hearing and that includes those parts from which she or he may not be obliged to attend in terms of subs. (2) below. The reporter must, therefore, always give the child the opportunity to attend, by inviting that attendance in the notice given.
    At all stages. This includes the stages at which the grounds are to be put, the case is considered, and the decision is made, together will all continuations and reviews. It does not, however, include business meetings arranged under s.64 below.

Under an obligation. If the child fails or is likely to fail to attend a hearing in circumstances in which she or he has not been relieved of that obligation under subs. (2) below, a warrant can be issued under the terms of subs. (4) or subs. (5) below.

Subs. (2)

Notwithstanding the child's obligation to attend all stages of the children's hearing consider-ing her or his case, the children's hearing may conduct all or any part of the proceedings in the absence of the child, if the child chooses not to exercise her or his right to attend and the hearing decide to release the child from the obligation to attend.

Without prejudice to subs. (1) above. The power to proceed in the absence of the child is expressly "without prejudice" to the child's right to attend, with the result that the children's hearing can do so only when the child has agreed not to be present (either expressly or impliedly): it is important to note that all this provision does is release the child from the obli-gation to attend and it does *not* deny the child the right to attend. The hearing cannot "exclude" the child in the way that they can "exclude" a journalist under s.43(4) above or a parent under s.46(1) below.

Without prejudice to ... s.65(4). The releasing of the child from the obligation to attend does not release the chairman from the obligation in s.65(4) below to explain the grounds to the child. It follows that it will seldom be appropriate to allow the child not to attend at that stage of the hearing at which grounds are to be put; and if this is done the hearing will be unable to proceed to a consideration of the case because there will have been no acceptance of the grounds on the part of the child. This resolves the difficulties created under the 1968 Act by the First Division's decision in *Sloan v. B* 1991 S.L.T. 530 (see Norrie, "Excluding Children from Children's Hear-ings" 1993 S.L.T. (News) 67; Wilkinson and Norrie *Parent and Child* (1993, W. Green) at pp. 464–467) which held that children could competently be excluded from that part of the hearing whenever a referral to the sheriff would be necessary in any case. The new wording allows the hearing to proceed in the absence of the child, but still requires an explanation of the grounds to be given to the child, with the result that the only time it would be appropriate to permit non-attendance from the part of the hearing at which grounds are to be put is when the child will be too young to understand and reference to the sheriff will be required in any case under s.65(9)(a) below.

Just hearing of that case. Under para. (a) the child can be permitted not to attend when her or his attendance is not necessary for a just consideration of the case. These words suggest that the major aim of this provision is to avoid the possibility of the child being inhibited or influenced in what she or he says by the presence of another person, though a secondary aim is probably the avoidance of distress to the child. It might also be used when the child is too young to make any meaningful contribution to the consideration of the case.

Detrimental to the interests of the child. Under para. (b) it would appear that the primary aim is to avoid distress to the child, but since it would clearly be detrimental to her or his interests to be influenced by the presence of another person that too must be an important factor.

May release the child. The decision to allow the child not to attend her or his hearing is gov-erned by s.16(1) and the paramount consideration of the children's hearing must therefore be the child's welfare. The decision cannot be appealed (see the General Note to s.51(1) below).

Subs. (3)

It is the reporter who is responsible for ensuring that the child is properly notified and attends the hearing, whether an initial hearing or a review hearing. To a large extent, however, the reporter is dependent upon the parent or social worker bringing the child to the hearing, and if there is reason to believe that this will not happen, for whatever reason, the reporter will be obliged to utilise the provisions of subs. (4) below.

Subs. (4)

This replaces s.40(4) of the 1968 Act and deals with the situation when the reporter believes that for some reason the child is unlikely to attend the hearing. In these circumstances, in order to allow her or him to fulfil the obligation under subs. (3) above, the reporter may apply to a children's hearing to issue a warrant to find the child, keep her or him in a place of safety, and bring her or him to a hearing. (Subs. (5) below deals with the situation in which the child has actually failed to attend the hearing).

A children's hearing. This will not be the children's hearing arranged to consider the child's case, otherwise subs. (5) below would be the appropriate authority under which the warrant is issued. A children's hearing arranged for some other purpose, or solely for this purpose, may issue the warrant under this subsection.

On cause shown. The reporter must have reason to believe that the child will not attend, or will be prevented from attending, the hearing without the utilisation of this provision, and must explain that reason to the children's hearing. The cause might be that the child has a history of non-attendance at hearings, or a belief that the child is at risk of being spirited away before the hearing.

It is necessary for them to do so. The reporter must persuade the children's hearing that it is necessary for a warrant to be issued, but necessity is to be interpreted in light of the purposes of the warrant, which is to allow the reporter to fulfil her or his obligation under subs. (3) above to ensure the child's attendance. A warrant under this section is not available to protect the child's interests or to ensure her or his safety in circumstances in which there is no suggestion of the child failing to attend.

Subs. (5)

If a hearing has been arranged but the child has failed to attend, then the children's hearing which had been arranged to consider the child's case are empowered to issue a warrant to find the child, keep her or him in a place of safety, and bring her or him to a hearing. Under the 1968 Act power to issue a warrant in these circumstances was contained in s.40(4), together with the power now governed by subs. (4) above. The present Act separates the two circumstances. Subsection (4) above applies when there is reason to believe that the child is unlikely to attend the hearing, while the present subsection applies when the child has in fact failed to attend the hearing. The practical difference is that the hearing under this subsection, but not under subs. (4) above, can issue the warrant on their own motion, as well as on the application of the reporter. The effect of the warrant, however, is the same under both subsections.

Subs. (6)

If a warrant has been issued by a children's hearing under either subs. (4) or subs. (5) above and the child has been taken to a place of safety, that warrant will last for only a limited period of time, and will terminate at the earlier of (a) the expiry of seven days from the day the child was first taken to the place of safety, or (b) the day on which a children's hearing first sit to consider the child's case.

The expiry of seven days. The seven days begin to run on the day the child is taken to a place of safety, and expire on midnight of the seventh day. So for example if a child is taken to a place of safety on a Monday, the period expires at midnight on the following Sunday.

Consider his case. In most cases in which a child has been taken to a place of safety under a warrant issued under this section, the cessation of the authority to detain will come about by the sitting of a children's hearing arranged in accordance with subs. (7) below, for seldom will seven days elapse before it is practicable to arrange a hearing.

Subs. (7)

It may be impossible to bring a child before a children's hearing immediately because of the lateness of the hour, because it is not a working day, or because there is no time to prepare any reports that will be necessary. Whatever the reason why the child is not brought to a hearing immediately after being found (notice, not taken to a place of safety, but found) a children's hearing must be arranged for the first working day thereafter. Due to the requirement in the Rules that the hearing members have three days notice of the hearing, in order to allow them time to give proper consideration to any reports submitted, a children's hearing arranged under this subsection will normally have to be continued under s.69(2) below. The hearing under this subsection brings any warrant issued under this section to an end (subs. (6) above), but that does not prevent the hearing deciding to grant a warrant under s.69(7) below.

Wherever practicable. A hearing is not incompetent just because it has been arranged more than one working day after the child was found, for it may not have been practicable to arrange a hearing. The reason may be, for example, because there is no reporter available to deal with the case or because parents or other relevant persons have to travel some distance.

First working day. "Working day" is defined in s.93(1) below. If the child is found on a Tuesday, she or he must, wherever practicable, be brought before a children's hearing on the following Wednesday; if found on a Friday she or he must, wherever practicable, be brought before a children's hearing on the following Monday.

Subss. (8) and (9)

These two subsections replace, with little substantive alteration, the provisions in s.41 of the 1968 Act. The "relevant person" has a right to attend the children's hearing and is indeed obliged so to attend. Failure to attend in breach of this obligation is a criminal offence for which the penalties are listed in subs. (9). The obligation does not, however, apply if the children's hearing are satisfied that it would be unreasonable to require the attendance of the relevant person or that such attendance is not necessary for the proper consideration of the case.

Relevant person. The definition of relevant person is found in s.93(2)(b) below, and it has a similar but not identical effect to the position under the 1968 Act. Under s.41 of that Act the parent of the child was obliged to attend the children's hearing, but "parent" was defined to include "guardian", which itself was defined to include any person who, *in the opinion of the court or children's hearing having cogniscance of the case*, had for the time being custody or charge of or control over the child. Section 93(2)(b) below, on the other hand, defines "relevant person" to mean any person with parental responsibilities or parental rights, however obtained, and any person who appears to have charge of or control over the child. The significant difference is that in the present Act it is not specified to whom it must appear that a person has charge of or control over the child, with the result that any person or body that deals with a "relevant person" must decide whether a particular individual comes within the definition. The practical effect of this is, it is submitted, that the reporter must notify any person who appears *to the reporter* to be a relevant person and is no longer entitled to wait for recognition by a children's hearing of a status that gives a right to attend. Any person who appears to a criminal court dealing with an offence under subs. (9) to have charge of or control over the child may be found guilty of non-attendance even when the children's hearing have not yet recognised the person as a relevant person.

At all stages. The right and obligation to attend the children's hearing extends to all stages of the hearing, that is to say the explanation of the grounds, the consideration of the case, and the making of the decision by the hearing, as well as any other part of the procedure, whether at an initial hearing or at a review hearing. There is, however, no right to attend a business meeting arranged under s.64 below.

Unless the hearing are satisfied. The hearing can determine that the attendance of the parent is unreasonable or unnecessary either when the parent does not show up or when the parent asks to be excused. Since failure to attend without this dispensation is a criminal offence (subs. (9)), the hearing ought to make a positive (and recorded) decision to this effect and ought not simply to proceed in the absence of the relevant person. A decision to proceed in the absence of the relevant person does no more than take away the legal obligation to attend: it does not take away the right to do so (unless a decision under s.46 below has been made) and a relevant person can still attend if she or he wishes even after the hearing have decided to proceed in her or his absence.

Power to exclude relevant person from children's hearing

46.—(1) Where a children's hearing are considering the case of a child in respect of whom a person is a relevant person, they may exclude that person, or that person and any representative of his, or any such representative, from any part or parts of the hearing for so long as is necessary in the interests of the child, where they are satisfied that—

(a) they must do so in order to obtain the views of the child in relation to the case before the hearing; or

(b) the presence of the person or persons in question is causing, or is likely to cause, significant distress to the child.

(2) Where a children's hearing exercise the power conferred by subsection (1) above, the chairman of the hearing shall, after that exclusion has ended, explain to any person who was so excluded the substance of what has taken place in his absence.

DEFINITIONS
"child": s.93(2)(b).
"children's hearing": s.93(1).

GENERAL NOTE
This provision grants a wholly new power to the children's hearing, with nothing analogous appearing in the 1968 Act. For some time it had been felt that the child's interests, and her or his right to speak freely, were not sufficiently protected. Sometimes a child and parent ought not to be in the same room, and sometimes the child's ability to voice opinions is inhibited by the parent's presence. Under the 1968 Act, while it was always open to the hearing to request a parent to withdraw from the hearing for a short period, such a request could not be enforced and these problems could be dealt with only by excluding the child from her or his own hearing. This

new provision entitles the hearing to exclude the parent or her or his representative for stated reasons.

Subs. (1)

Are considering. A children's hearing cannot proceed to a consideration of the child's case until the grounds of referral have been accepted or established (see wording of s.69(1) below) and it follows that the power to exclude a relevant person under this section is limited to that stage of the proceedings at which the case is being considered and *not* from the putting of the grounds. The need for a relevant person's acceptance of the grounds cannot, therefore, be avoided by excluding that person before the grounds are put.

They may exclude. The children's hearing are not obliged to exclude a person even when one of the grounds for exclusion exists. It is a matter in their discretion. The power to exclude rests with the hearing as a whole and not solely with the chairman. As usual decisions are made on a majority basis and the paramount consideration in making the decision is the welfare of the child (s.16(1) above).

In order to obtain the views of the child. It may frequently happen that a child is likely to speak more openly in the absence of a parent. This may be because there is a conflict of interest between the parent and the child, or because the child is embarrassed to talk about certain personal matters in front of a parent. This ground might also be used if the parent is disrupting the hearing or, due to the parent insisting on answering for the child, the child is being deprived of the chance to speak for her or himself.

Significant distress. The presence of both parent and child in the same room may sometimes cause the child significant distress. This will commonly be because the parent has abused the child and the child is afraid of the parent, but it might also be, for example, when the child is settled in an environment away from the parent and the security of that settlement would be disturbed by contact with the parent. Under the old law this could only be resolved by excluding the child; this section gives the children's hearing an option which will often be more appropriate.

Subs. (2)

This provision is to be compared with that in s.43(5), under which if a journalist has been excluded the chairman may explain to the journalist what took place in his absence. If, on the other hand, a parent or representative is excluded under subs. (1) above, the chairman has no option but to explain to such a person the substance of what took place in her or his absence. There will usually be little point in excluding a parent solely in order to allow a child to speak freely on matters she or he does not want her or his parents to know about and it should be made plain to both parent and child that the substance of what takes place must be revealed. It is not possible, therefore, to use the exclusion as a means of protecting the child's confidentiality against a parent.

Presumption and determination of age

47.—(1) Where a children's hearing has been arranged in respect of any person, the hearing—

(a) shall, at the commencement of the proceedings, make inquiry as to his age and shall proceed with the hearing only if he declares that he is a child or they so determine; and

(b) may, at any time before the conclusion of the proceedings, accept a declaration by the child, or make a fresh determination, as to his age.

(2) The age declared to, or determined by, a children's hearing to be the age of a person brought before them shall, for the purposes of this Part of this Act, be deemed to be the true age of that person.

(3) No decision reached, order continued, warrant granted or requirement imposed by a children's hearing shall be invalidated by any subsequent proof that the age of a person brought before them had not been correctly declared to the hearing or determined by them.

DEFINITIONS

"child": s.93(2)(b).

"children's hearing": s.93(1).

GENERAL NOTE

This provision replaces s.55 of the 1968 Act and makes no substantive alteration to the law contained therein.

Subs. (1)

The hearing (normally the chairman) opens the proceedings by asking the child or parent to state the child's age. The children's hearing have jurisdiction only over "children" and are permitted to proceed either to put grounds or to consider the case only when satisfied that the person is indeed a child. Their determination on this matter can change in the course of the hearing, though if it is subsequently determined that the person is not a child, this brings the proceedings to an automatic end.

That he is a child. A "child" for the purposes of chapters 2 and 3 of this Part of the Act is a person under the age of 16 years, or a person over that age but under the age of 18 years and currently subject to a supervision requirement.

Subs. (2)

If the hearing have determined that the child is a "child" within the terms of Part II then the age so determined shall be deemed to be the true age of the child until the hearing make a fresh determination of the child's age under subs. (1)(b) above.

Subs. (3)

Following on from subs. (2) above, under which a determination of age is treated as the child's true age whether it is or not, any decision, order, warrant or requirement made under Part II is not challengeable on the ground that the age determined by the hearing is not the child's true age.

Transfer etc. of cases

Transfer of case to another children's hearing

48.—(1) Where a children's hearing are satisfied, in relation to a case which they are hearing, that it could be better considered by a children's hearing constituted from a children's panel for a different local government area, they may at any time during the course of the hearing request the Principal Reporter to arrange for such other children's hearing to dispose of the case.

(2) Where a case has been transferred in pursuance of subsection (1) above, the grounds of referral accepted or established for the case shall not require to be further accepted or established for the purposes of the children's hearing to which the case has been transferred.

DEFINITIONS

"children's hearing": s.93(1).
"local government area": Local Government etc. (Scotland) Act 1994, s.2.
"principal reporter": s.93(1).

GENERAL NOTE

This provision replaces, with no substantive alteration, s.54 of the 1968 Act. It provides that when a children's hearing considers that the case would be better dealt with by a children's hearing in another local government area, they may request the reporter to arrange for the case to be transferred to that other area. Accepted or established grounds remain accepted or established before the new hearing.

Referral or remission to children's hearing where child guilty of an offence

49.—(1) In section 173 of the Criminal Procedure (Scotland) Act 1975 (reference or remission to children's hearing where child guilty of an offence: solemn proceedings), for subsections (1) to (3) there shall be substituted—

"(1) Where a person who is charged with an offence and pleads guilty to, or is found guilty of, that offence is a child who is not subject to a supervision requirement, the court on that plea or finding may—

(a) instead of making an order, remit the case to the Principal Reporter to arrange a children's hearing to dispose of the case; or

(b) request the Principal Reporter to arrange a children's hearing for the purpose of obtaining their advice as to the treatment of the child.

(2) Where a person, who is charged with an offence and pleads guilty to, or is found guilty of, that offence, is aged sixteen years or over and is subject to a supervision requirement, the court if it is—

    (a) the High Court, may; and

    (b) the sheriff court shall,

proceed in accordance with either paragraph (a) or (b) of subsection (1) above.

(3) Where a child who is charged with an offence and pleads guilty to, or is found guilty of, that offence—

    (a) is aged under sixteen years; and

    (b) is subject to a supervision requirement,

the court dealing with the case if it is—

      (i) the High Court, may; and

     (ii) the sheriff court, shall,

request the Principal Reporter to arrange a children's hearing for the purpose of obtaining their advice as to the treatment of the child.

(3A) Where a court has obtained the advice of a children's hearing in pursuance—

    (a) of paragraph (b) of subsection (1) above; or

    (b) of subsection (3) above,

the court, after consideration of the advice received from the children's hearing may, as it thinks proper, itself dispose of the case or remit the case as mentioned in paragraph (a) of the said subsection (1).".

(2) In section 372 of that Act (reference or remission to children's hearing where child guilty of an offence: summary proceedings), for subsections (1) to (3) there shall be substituted—

"(1) Where a person who is charged with an offence and pleads guilty to, or is found guilty of, that offence is a child who is not subject to a supervision requirement, the court on that plea or finding may—

    (a) instead of making an order, remit the case to the Principal Reporter to arrange a children's hearing to dispose of the case; or

    (b) request the Principal Reporter to arrange a children's hearing for the purpose of obtaining their advice as to the treatment of the child.

(2) Where a person, who is charged with an offence and pleads guilty to, or is found guilty of, that offence, is aged sixteen years or over and is subject to a supervision requirement, the court shall proceed in accordance with either paragraph (a) or (b) of subsection (1) above.

(3) Where a child who is charged with an offence and pleads guilty to, or is found guilty of, that offence—

    (a) is aged under sixteen years; and

    (b) is subject to a supervision requirement,

the court dealing with the case shall request the Principal Reporter to arrange a children's hearing for the purpose of obtaining their advice as to the treatment of the child.

(3A) Where a court has obtained the advice of a children's hearing in pursuance—

    (a) of paragraph (b) of subsection (1) above; or

    (b) of subsection (3) above,

the court, after consideration of the advice received from the children's hearing may, as it thinks proper, itself dispose of the case or remit the case as mentioned in paragraph (a) of the said subsection (1).".

DEFINITIONS

"child": s.93(2)(b).

"children's hearing": s.93(1).

"court": Criminal Procedure (Scotland) Act 1975, s.462(1).

"offence": Criminal Procedure (Scotland) Act 1975, s.462(1).

"principal reporter": s.93(1).
"supervision requirement": ss.70(1), 93(1).

GENERAL NOTE
Though in the majority of cases a child who commits an offence will be dealt with by having her or his case referred to a children's hearing instead of being prosecuted in a criminal court, there will be some situations in which the Crown or the procurator fiscal takes the decision that the appropriate course is to prosecute the child for the offence in the normal criminal courts. This might be, for example, because of the seriousness of the alleged offence, or because the child has committed a large number of offences, or because the children's hearing system has exhausted the good it can realistically do. If the child, on prosecution, pleads guilty or after trial is found guilty, the criminal court has the power and sometimes the duty, under the Criminal Procedure (Scotland) Act 1975, to seek advice from a children's hearing as to how it should dispose of the case (i.e. what sentence, if any, is appropriate), or to remit the case of the child to the children's hearing for disposal by them. Before the enactment of this provision, the rules governing remits for disposal and referrals for advice differed according to whether the child was being prosecuted under summary or under solemn procedure. The aim of the amendments in the present section is to harmonise the rules for both summary and solemn procedure and the new s.173 of the 1975 Act (substituted by subs. (1) here) is to all intents and purposes the same as the new s.372 thereof (substituted by subs. (2) here). The change to s.173 (solemn procedure) is not dramatic and is limited to an alteration of the position of young persons who are over the age of 16 and currently subject to a supervision requirement. The effect on s.372 (summary procedure) is far more substantive, in that the rules applicable are assimilated as far as possible to those applicable to solemn procedure.

Subs. (1)
This replaces the first three subsections of s.173 of the 1975 Act with four new subsections and deals with solemn procedure. The effect is that there are different rules governing remits and referrals from the court to the children's hearing depending upon which of four separate categories the child or young person falls into. The categories and their rules are as follows.
(A) Child under 16 not currently under supervision.
In this situation the court (that is to say the High Court or the sheriff court) has three choices: (i) it can dispose of the case itself; (ii) it can remit the case for disposal by a children's hearing; or (iii) it can refer the case to a children's hearing for advice as to how the court should dispose of the case. If the third option is chosen the advice the hearing give to the court is merely advice and does not oblige the court to follow it; and it can be of whatever nature the hearing consider appropriate. The hearing may advise the court to dispose of the case itself, suggesting which of the disposals that are open to the court is the most appropriate for the child, or it may advise the court to remit the case back to the hearing for disposal. The court must consider the advice obtained and having done so may either dispose of the case itself or remit it back to the hearing for their disposal, whether this consists with their advice or not.
(B) Child under 16 currently under supervision.
In this situation the High Court may either dispose of the case itself or, at its discretion, refer the case to a children's hearing for the purpose of obtaining advice as to how to dispose of the case (but may not, at this stage, remit the case for disposal by a children's hearing); the sheriff must refer the case to a children's hearing for such advice (and may, at this stage, neither dispose of the case himself nor remit the case to a children's hearing for disposal). On receiving advice the court (whether High Court or sheriff court) must consider the advice and may now either dispose of the case itself or remit it back to the hearing for their disposal.
(C) Child aged 16 or over currently under supervision.
In this situation the High Court can (i) dispose of the case itself; (ii) remit the case for disposal by a children's hearing; or (iii) refer the case to a children's hearing for advice as to how the court should dispose of the case. The sheriff court can (i) remit the case for disposal by a children's hearing or (ii) refer the case to a children's hearing for advice as to how the court should dispose of the case; the sheriff court cannot, at this stage, dispose of the case itself. On receiving advice the court (whether High Court or sheriff court) must consider the advice and may now either dispose of the case itself or remit it back to the hearing for their disposal.
(D) Child aged 16 or over not currently under supervision.
No referral or remit from a court of solemn jurisdiction to a children's hearing can be made in this situation and the court must itself dispose of the case without advice of the children's hearing.
It should be noted that none of the above rules applies when the sentence for the offence with which the child is charged is fixed by law: s.173(5) (unamended here).

Subs. (2)

This provision replaces the first three subsections of s.372 of the 1975 Act with four new subsections and deals with summary procedure (i.e. criminal proceedings conducted without a jury in the sheriff court or in the district court). The aim of this provision is to ensure that the rules governing remits and referrals from the court to the children's hearing are as similar as possible to the rules for solemn procedure, and the basic rules set out in subs. (1) above should be referred to. In categories (B) and (C) above, the applicable rule in summary proceedings is that governing the sheriff rather than the High Court. One difference does remain between summary and solemn procedure, for s.373 of the 1975 Act is neither amended nor repealed by the present provisions and applies only to summary proceedings. That section provides that, for a child in Category (D) above who is more than six months short of her or his 18th birthday, the court in summary proceedings may (but does not have to) request advice from the children's hearing and after considering that advice may itself either dispose of the case or (but only if this is what the hearing recommended in their advice) remit the case back to the hearing for them to dispose of it. This is the only circumstance in which a person who is not subject to a supervision requirement on her on his 16th birthday can be made subject to such a requirement thereafter. It is very rare indeed for a hearing to utilise this provision. If the person is less than six months short of her or his 18th birthday (or over that age), the court cannot remit for disposal or refer for advice and must therefore deal with the case itself.

Treatment of child's case on remission by court

50.—(1) Where a court has, under section 173, 372 or 373 of the Criminal Procedure (Scotland) Act 1975, remitted a case to a children's hearing for disposal, a certificate signed by the clerk of the court stating that the child or person concerned has pled guilty to, or has been found guilty of, the offence to which the remit relates shall be conclusive evidence for the purposes of the remit that the offence has been committed by the child or person.

(2) Where a court has under the said section 373 remitted a case to a children's hearing for disposal, the provisions of this Act shall apply to the person concerned as if he were a child.

DEFINITIONS

"child": s.93(2)(b) and Criminal Procedure (Scotland) Act 1975, s.462(1).
"children's hearing": s.93(1).
"court": Criminal Procedure (Scotland) Act 1975, s.462(1).
"offence": Criminal Procedure (Scotland) Act 1975, s.462(1).

GENERAL NOTE

Replacing, with no substantive alteration in the law, ss.56 and 57 of the 1968 Act, this section ensures that when a court remits a case to a children's hearing under the provisions in s.49 above, the ground of referral (being that the child has committed an offence: s.52(2)(i)) shall be treated as having been established. It follows that a children's hearing which is empowered by the remit to dispose of the case can move straight onto a consideration of the case and disposal thereof without having to put the ground to the child and parent for acceptance under s.65(3) below.

Subsection (2) is required since a person over 16 who is not currently under supervision (but who might be put under supervision by s.373 of the 1975 Act) is not a "child" for the purposes of the children's hearing provisions in the present Act. Such a person is to be treated as a child for these purposes if s.373 applies.

Appeals

Appeal against decision of children's hearing or sheriff

51.—(1) Subject to subsection (15) below, a child or a relevant person (or relevant persons) or both (or all)—

    (a) may, within a period of three weeks beginning with the date of any decision of a children's hearing, appeal to the sheriff against that decision; and

(b) where such an appeal is made, shall be heard by the sheriff.

(2) The Principal Reporter shall, in respect of any appeal under subsection (1) above, ensure that all reports and statements available to the hearing, along with the reports of their proceedings and the reasons for the decision, are lodged with the sheriff clerk.

(3) The sheriff may, on appeal under subsection (1) above, hear evidence from, or on behalf of, the parties in relation to the decision; and, without prejudice to that generality, the sheriff may—

    (a) examine the Principal Reporter;

    (b) examine the authors or compilers of any reports or statements; and

    (c) call for any further report which he considers may assist him in deciding the appeal.

(4) Where the sheriff decides that an appeal under this section has failed, he shall confirm the decision of the children's hearing.

(5) Where the sheriff is satisfied that the decision of the children's hearing is not justified in all the circumstances of the case he shall allow the appeal, and—

    (a) where the appeal is against a warrant to find and keep or, as the case may be, to keep a child in a place of safety, he shall recall the warrant;

    (b) where the child is subject to a supervision requirement containing a condition imposed under section 70(9) of this Act, he shall direct that the condition shall cease to have effect; and

    (c) in any case, he may, as he thinks fit—

        (i) remit the case with reasons for his decision to the children's hearing for reconsideration of their decision; or

        (ii) discharge the child from any further hearing or other proceedings in relation to the grounds for the referral of the case; or

        (iii) substitute for the disposal by the children's hearing any requirement which could be imposed by them under section 70 of this Act.

(6) Where a sheriff imposes a requirement under subsection (5)(c)(iii) above, that requirement shall for the purposes of this Act, except of this section, be treated as a disposal by the children's hearing.

(7) Where the sheriff is satisfied that an appeal under subsection (1) above against the decision of a children's hearing arranged under section 73(8) of this Act is frivolous, he may order that no subsequent appeal against a decision to continue (whether with or without any variation) the supervision requirement in question shall lie until the expiration of twelve months beginning with the date of the order.

(8) An appeal under subsection (1) above in respect of the issue of a warrant by a children's hearing shall be disposed of within three days of the lodging of the appeal; and failing such disposal the warrant shall cease to have effect at the end of that period.

(9) Where a child or a relevant person appeals under subsection (1) above against a decision of a children's hearing in relation to a supervision requirement, the child or the relevant person may make application to a children's hearing for the suspension of the requirement appealed against.

(10) It shall be the duty of the Principal Reporter forthwith to arrange a children's hearing to consider the application under subsection (9) above, and that hearing may grant or refuse the application.

(11) Subject to subsections (13) and (15) below, an appeal shall lie by way of stated case either on a point of law or in respect of any irregularity in the conduct of the case—

    (a) to the sheriff principal from any decision of the sheriff—

        (i) on an appeal under subsection (1) of this section;

        (ii) on an application made under section 65(7) or (9) of this Act;
    or

        (iii) on an application made under section 85(1) of this Act; and

(b) to the Court of Session from any decision of the sheriff such as is mentioned in sub-paragraphs (i) to (iii) of paragraph (a) above and, with leave of the sheriff principal, from any decision of the sheriff principal on an appeal under that paragraph; and the decision of the Court of Session in the matter shall be final.

(12) An appeal under subsection (11) above may be made at the instance of—

(a) the child or any relevant person, either alone or together; or

(b) the Principal Reporter on behalf of the children's hearing.

(13) An application to the sheriff, or as the case may be the sheriff principal, to state a case for the purposes of an appeal under subsection (11)(a) or (b) above shall be made within a period of twenty-eight days beginning with the date of the decision appealed against.

(14) On deciding an appeal under subsection (11) above the sheriff principal or as the case may be the Court of Session shall remit the case to the sheriff for disposal in accordance with such directions as the court may give.

(15) No appeal shall lie under this section in respect of—

(a) a decision of the sheriff on an application under section 57 of this Act; or

(b) a decision of a children's hearing continuing a child protection order under section 59(4) of this Act.

DEFINITIONS
"child": s.93(2)(b).
"children's hearing": s.93(1).
"principal reporter": s.93(1).
"relevant person": s.93(2)(b).
"supervision requirement": ss.70(1), 93(1).

GENERAL NOTE
Decisions of the children's hearing can be appealed against by the child or the parent, as can decisions of the sheriff. This section governs appeals and replaces, with some important alterations in the law, ss.49 and 50 of the 1968 Act. The basic principle remains that any decision of the children's hearing can be appealed to the sheriff, and any decision of the sheriff, whether on an application for finding established a ground of referral or in dealing with an appeal from the hearing's decision, can be appealed to the Court of Session on a point of law or in respect of procedural irregularity. The two major changes are: (i) the introduction of a new level of appeal to the sheriff principal, and (ii) the conferring upon the sheriff of a power, on appeal from a decision of the children's hearing, to substitute his own disposal for that of a hearing with whom he disagrees.

As under the old law, there is no appeal from the Court of Session to the House of Lords, and there are some decisions of the children's hearing which are not open to appeal at all. The power of the Secretary of State to terminate a supervision requirement, previously contained in s.52 of the 1968 Act, has not been re-enacted.

Subs. (1)
Within three weeks of a decision of the children's hearing, either the child or the relevant person, or both, can appeal against that decision to the sheriff, and the sheriff is obliged to hear the appellants. The reporter, of course, has no title or interest in appealing a decision of the hearing, but is the contradictor in any appeal made to the sheriff.

Relevant person. This is the person who has the right and obligation to attend the children's hearing and to dispute the grounds of referral. The right of appeal inheres in this person even when she or he did not attend the hearing.

Within a period of three weeks. The appeal must be made within 21 days of the date of the hearing's decision, the day of the decision being the first day (*S, Applicants* 1979 S.L.T. (Sh. Ct.) 37). So if a children's hearing make a decision on Wednesday, August 1, the appeal must be lodged on or before Tuesday, August 21.

Any decision. It is not, in fact, any decision that a hearing reach that can be appealed against. Under subs. (15) below no appeal can be had against a decision of the hearing to continue a child protection order under s.59(4) below. In addition to this, however, it had been established by the case law under the 1968 Act (in which the same words appeared) that appeals can be had only against dispositive decisions of the children's hearing or decisions on the granting or renewing of warrants. Decisions which are merely procedural steps in the process towards the making of a dispositive decision, such as decisions to direct the reporter to apply to the sheriff for a finding as to whether the grounds of referral are established, are not appealable (*H. v. McGregor* 1973 S.C. 95, *Sloan v. B* 1991 S.L.T. 530 at p. 545L), and confirmation that this remains the law can be found in subs. (5)(c)(iii) below which allows a sheriff to substitute his own disposal for that of the hearing—but that disposal must be one governed by s.70, which deals only with final dispositive decisions. Into the category of unappealable decisions will also fall decisions to exclude journalists or parents or representatives from part or all of the hearing, decisions to excuse the child from her or his obligation to attend, and decisions to continue the case to a subsequent hearing under s.69(1)(a) below. A decision to appoint a safeguarder under s.41 above is likely to be considered unappealable, as is a determination under s.70(7) that a supervision requirement be reviewed at some point during its currency, but the Act would have been better expressly to state this.

"Any decision" does include a dispositive decision of a children's hearing arranged to reconsider their decision after a sheriff has found that decision not justified, and the special rules for appeals in that case under s.51 of the 1968 Act have not been re-enacted.

Appeal to the sheriff. The old s.49 specified that the appeal would be to the sheriff in chambers, and this rule is now contained in s.93(5) below.

Subs. (2)

It is the responsibility of the reporter to ensure that there are lodged with the sheriff clerk all the appropriate documents relevant to the appeal, which includes all reports available to the hearing, reports of the proceedings at all the hearings, and the reasons for the decision which have been made or been caused to have been made by the chairman under r.9 of the 1986 Rules.

Subs. (3)

In hearing an appeal from a decision of the children's hearing the sheriff is permitted to hear evidence only from or on behalf of the parties to the appeal (that is the child and the relevant persons and the reporter) and in addition he may examine the reporter and the compilers of any reports he has received. This includes the chairman of the hearing who has drawn up the reasons for the decision. It is in the discretion of the sheriff whom he wants to examine and he may call for further reports, such as an updated social background report, educational report, medical report, or safeguarder's report.

Subs. (4)

If the appeal fails, the decision of the hearing is confirmed without variation. Any suspension of a supervision requirement granted under subs. (9) below will (though the Act does not tell us so) be lifted on the rejection of the appeal.

Subs. (5)

The grounds of appeal to the sheriff are not specified in the Act (as they were not in the 1968 Act) except for the rule in this subsection that the sheriff shall allow the appeal if the decision of the children's hearing is "not justified in all the circumstances of the case". These words (taken from s.49(5) of the 1968 Act) do not permit the sheriff to allow the appeal merely because he has a difference of opinion with the hearing as to the correct disposal of the case. It is perfectly conceivable that two different, even opposing, disposals are justifiable in the circumstances of a single case. Rather, the sheriff must be satisfied either that there was a procedural irregularity in the conduct of the case before the hearing, or that the hearing failed to give proper consideration to some factor in the case.

Once the sheriff has decided that the appeal is to be allowed, he must proceed according to one of the three options listed in para. (c). In addition, if the successful appeal is against a warrant to find or keep a child in a place of safety, the sheriff is obliged to recall the warrant. And if the supervision requirement contained an authorisation under s.70(9) to keep the child in secure accommodation, he is obliged to direct that that authorisation shall cease to have effect (though he will be entitled to grant such authorisation himself under para. (c)(iii), which allows him to do anything that the hearing can do under s.70). The three options open to the sheriff are:

(i) To remit the case back to the hearing for reconsideration. When the sheriff does this, he must give reasons for his decision, but he is not entitled to give any directions as to how the hearing should proceed with the case or dispose of it, for that would be to usurp the role of the children's hearing. His statement of reasons must be limited to a statement of why he has found the decision appealed against to be not justified in all the circumstances of the case.

(ii) To discharge the child from any further hearing or proceedings in respect of the grounds which led to the hearing whose decision is being appealed against. Any supervision requirement imposed in respect of these grounds will be terminated, together with any order attached thereto.

(iii) To make a supervision requirement in terms of s.70 below on whatever terms and conditions permitted by that section the sheriff considers appropriate. The overwhelming majority of appeals will concern cases in which a supervision requirement has been imposed or continued in any case, and the disposal of the sheriff under this subparagraph will therefore normally amount to a variation of its terms (for example removing a requirement that the child resides at a specified place, or varying a direction regulating contact between the child and another person). Appeals against discharge of a referral or termination of a supervision requirement are not incompetent, and on such appeals the sheriff can impose a supervision requirement on such terms and conditions as are available to the hearing under s.70. Though technically all the disposals open to the children's hearing are open to the sheriff, he will in practice be unable to adopt the very disposal previously adopted by the children's hearing themselves, for that would amount to an acceptance by the sheriff that that disposal was justifiable—in which case he must reject the appeal and allow the hearing's decision to stand.

The third option open to the sheriff did not (unlike the first and the second) exist in the 1968 Act, and its inclusion in the present Act was bitterly opposed by many. One cannot question the Government's good intention, which was to protect the hearing system from challenge on the basis that it is not judicial enough to satisfy the due process requirements in the European Convention on Human Rights, but nor can one doubt that the provision may in time destroy what Lord President Hope described in *Sloan v. B* 1991 S.L.T. 530 at p. 548E as the "genius" of the system under the 1968 Act, that is to say the complete separation of roles between the children's hearing and the court (though it must be admitted that Lord Hope himself supported the inclusion of this provision: see *Hansard* H.L. Vol. 565, col. 1150). Prior to the enactment of this provision the sheriff's role on allowing an appeal was limited to ordering the children's hearing to reconsider the case. It was for the hearing to reconsider the case and to determine the appropriate disposal in the light of the sheriff's findings, not the sheriff. The whole point of the system and its major justification is the recognition that the children's hearing is a far more appropriate forum than the court to discuss with a child and her or his family the problems and the options, and that ought to be sufficient answer to any challenge based on human rights law. There is no provision in the Act requiring the sheriff to conduct a sort of judicial children's hearing in order to identify the appropriate way forward for the child, and though he must apply the three overarching principles in s.16 (see s.16(4)(b)(iv) above) which, amongst other things, requires that the child be given an opportunity to express her or his views and have these views taken into account, the actual decision-making process is entirely judicial. If judicial decision-making is seriously considered to be more appropriate than letting a children's hearing make decisions then the whole children's hearing system ought to be abolished forthwith and all children in need of compulsory measures of supervision given the "benefit" of a judicial determination of their case: it is surely unfair to grant that "benefit" only to the small number of children whose cases happen to reach an appeal court. Of course in reality there is no benefit to a child whose future is to be determined by an inappropriate forum.

Not only is the provision bad in principle but it is likely to prove bad in practice. There is no doubt that practice will differ in different courts, some sheriffs being of the view that they are better qualified to make decisions than hearings, others being of the view that the hearing are in a better position to make appropriate decisions. Like a hearing, a sheriff will be obliged to state reasons for his decision (though the Act does not actually say this) and these reasons may in time work their way into the law reports. They will have no value as precedents, but their very existence will increase the formalisation of the whole children's hearing process, to the detriment of all the children who are involved in that process.

Subs. (6)

A supervision requirement substituted by the sheriff under subs. (5) above will be treated as a disposal of the children's hearing in relation to effect, duration, review and termination. Its date of making will be the date of the sheriff's decision.

Subs. (7)

Where a sheriff has rejected an appeal against a decision of the children's hearing at a review of a supervision requirement and he is satisfied that the appeal was "frivolous", he may prohibit for a period of 12 months any subsequent appeal against a subsequent decision to continue (with or without variation) the supervision requirement in respect of which the appeal was made. In other words, if the supervision requirement continued by a decision frivolously appealed against is reviewed at any time within 12 months of the sheriff's order, any decision at that review is not appealable until these 12 months have elapsed. An order under this subsection will prevent an appeal by anyone, even by those who did not join in the frivolous appeal.

An appeal... against a decision... under s.73(8). An order under this subsection can be made only in the context of an appeal from a decision of a hearing reviewing a supervision requirement and not from the decision which initially imposes it.

Frivolous. The Act does not define what a frivolous appeal is, but the aim of the provision is clear: it is to ensure that the courts are not cluttered by appeals which have no chance of success or which seek review when no change whatsoever has occurred in the child's circumstances since the last review and which are being brought by the child or parent simply in order to prolong the procedure.

Subs. (8)

If the appeal is against the hearing's issuing of a warrant, whether under s.45 above, s.66 below, or under any other provision in the Act permitting a children's hearing to grant a warrant, that appeal must be heard and disposed of within three days of its lodging and if it is not so disposed of the warrant shall cease to have effect.

At the end of that period. The first day is the day on which the appeal is lodged, and the end of the period of three days is the end of the third day. So if an appeal is lodged on a Monday it must be disposed of by the following Wednesday, otherwise the warrant shall cease to have effect at midnight on that day. Notice that the days here are not "working days", as is the case in, for example, s.45(7).

Subss. (9) and (10)

As under s.49(8) of the 1968 Act, the child or parent who appeals against a decision of the children's hearing imposing, continuing or varying a supervision requirement can apply to the hearing for the suspension of the requirement until the appeal has been heard. The application can be made immediately the appeal is lodged, but not before. It is the responsibility of the reporter to arrange a hearing to consider the application for suspension, and that hearing may grant or refuse the application. There is no indication as to what criteria the hearing should use to determine such an application, but the decision is clearly one governed by the welfare of the child as the paramount consideration (s.16(1) above). Though s.16(2) does not apply, good practice will be for the hearing to take account of any views expressed by the child in appropriate circumstances.

Forthwith. This means as soon as practically possible, rather than immediately (see *Viola v. Viola* 1988 S.L.T. 7 on the meaning of "forthwith" in the context of the Child Abduction and Custody Act 1985).

Subs. (11)

Replacing s.50 of the 1968 Act, this subsection allows for appeals from decisions of the sheriff, both in determining an appeal from a decision of the children's hearing and in determining whether grounds of referral have been established (whether on the initial application or at a review of the evidence). Title to appeal inheres in the child, all relevant persons, and the reporter. The reporter may appeal against a finding that the grounds of referral have not been established, but has no interest in appealing against a decision that the grounds are established; since she or he appeals "on behalf of the children's hearing" (subs. (12)(b) below), she or he can appeal against the sheriff's finding that the hearing's decision was not justified, but not against a confirmation of the hearing's decision.

In a significant change from the 1968 Act (not, incidentally, wholeheartedly supported by Lord Hope of Craighead in his maiden speech in the House of Lords: see *Hansard* H.L. Vol. 564, col. 41), a new level of appeal is added, from the sheriff to the sheriff principal. This is an additional rather than an alternative appeal, and appeal can be had from the sheriff's decision to the sheriff principal and then from the sheriff principal (with his consent) to the Court of Session, or direct from the sheriff to the Court of Session. It is to be expected that appeals direct to the Court of Session will occur when the point of law is particularly difficult or contentious, or raises an important matter of principle. Appeal, whether to the sheriff principal or to the Court of Session, is by way of stated case and is on a point of law or in respect of any irregularity in the conduct of the case. There is no appeal from the Court of Session to the House of Lords.

Subject to subsections (13) and (15). The right of appeal is lost if not exercised within 28 days (subs. (13) below); there are certain decisions which are unappealable (subs. (15) below).

Any irregularity in the conduct of the case. The irregularity refers to the conduct of the case before the sheriff or the sheriff principal since it is the sheriff's or sheriff principal's decision that is being appealed against. Irregularity in the conduct of the children's hearing is a ground of appeal to the sheriff but is not a ground of appeal from a decision of the sheriff. An irregularity may, for example, be when the sheriff refuses to hear one or other of the parties to the appeal, or has purported to make a disposal which is not open to him (such as affirming the hearing's decision and at the same time varying the supervision requirement).

To the sheriff principal. Appeal is to the sheriff principal of the sheriffdom in which the sheriff, from whose decision the appeal is being taken, sits.

Any decision. This is subject to subs. (15) which states that decisions of the sheriff granting child protection orders are not appealable.

To the Court of Session … with leave of the sheriff principal. Leave is not required to appeal from the sheriff to the sheriff principal nor direct from the sheriff to the Court of Session, but if an appeal has already been made from the sheriff to the sheriff principal, a further appeal to the Court of Session will require the leave of the sheriff principal. No guidance is given to the sheriff principal as to the circumstances in which it would be appropriate to grant or to withhold leave, but the aim of the provision (see *Hansard*, H.L. Vol. 565, col. 1152) is to ensure that the new appeal to the sheriff principal is not used simply as a delaying tactic. Leave ought to be refused, it is submitted, when an appeal to the sheriff principal has failed and it is his view that the ground of appeal put forward was not arguable. Leave ought to be granted if appeal to the Court of Session is necessary to resolve a difference which has arisen between sheriff principals.

Subs. (12)

The appeal against the sheriff's decision to either the sheriff principal or the Court of Session, and against the sheriff principal's decision to the Court of Session, can be made at the instance of the child or the relevant person, or by the reporter. The child or parent can appeal against a decision discharging the referral: although this would be unusual, it is competent, and might be appropriate, where the child is seeking the protection of a supervision requirement, or the parent is seeking to exercise parental control with the assistance of a supervision requirement. The reporter appeals on behalf of the children's hearing and so has interest to appeal only against a decision which alters or challenges the hearing's decision: she or he cannot appeal against the sheriff's confirmation of the decision under subs. (4) above.

Subs. (13)

An appeal from a decision of the sheriff or the sheriff principal is by way of stated case (subs. (11) above) and the application to state a case must be made within a period of 28 days from the date of the sheriff's or the sheriff principal's decision, otherwise the right of appeal is lost. The date of the decision is the first day, so if the decision is made on Wednesday, October 1, the application must be made on or before Tuesday, October 28.

Subs. (14)

Once the appeal has been decided the sheriff principal or the Court of Session must remit the case back to the sheriff for disposal.

In accordance with such directions as the court may give. The appeal court is only entitled to give procedural directions and cannot give any indication as to how the case should be finally disposed of. The sheriff may decide under subs. (5)(c)(iii) above to substitute for the hearing's disposal his own disposal, but the appeal court cannot give any directions that this should be done, nor which disposal would be appropriate. The wording of this subsection is the same as that in s.50(3) of the 1968 Act, and in the context of the earlier statute the Court of Session has held that no such directions can be given: *Kennedy v. A* 1986 S.L.T. 358. That case cannot be taken to have been overruled by the new, anomalous, power of the sheriff in subs. (5)(c)(iii).

Subs. (15)

This section specifies decisions which are not appealable: decisions of the sheriff to make a child protection order, and decisions of the children's hearing to continue a child protection order at an initial hearing arranged under s.59 below. It might be argued that by specifying these decisions the Act is indicating that all other decisions are appealable, including those characterised as unappealable in the notes to subs. (1) above. It is submitted, however, that this argument (*expressio unius est exclusio alterius*) is not good since the same wording is used in subs. (1) above as appeared in the 1968 Act and there is no indication other than the present subsection that the words are to be given a meaning different from that gleaned by the courts since 1968. This subsection lists, it is submitted, decisions which are unappealable in addition to those which have long been regarded as such, and was rendered necessary as a consequence of the creation of the new child protection orders with their own special appeal mechanisms.

CHAPTER 3

PROTECTION AND SUPERVISION OF CHILDREN

Children requiring compulsory measures of supervision

Children requiring compulsory measures of supervision

52.—(1) The question of whether compulsory measures of supervision are necessary in respect of a child arises if at least one of the conditions mentioned in subsection (2) below is satisfied with respect to him.

(2) The conditions referred to in subsection (1) above are that the child—

(a) is beyond the control of any relevant person;

(b) is falling into bad associations or is exposed to moral danger;

(c) is likely—

(i) to suffer unnecessarily; or

(ii) be impaired seriously in his health or development,

due to a lack of parental care;

(d) is a child in respect of whom any of the offences mentioned in Schedule 1 to the Criminal Procedure (Scotland) Act 1975 (offences against children to which special provisions apply) has been committed;

(e) is, or is likely to become, a member of the same household as a child in respect of whom any of the offences referred to in paragraph (d) above has been committed;

(f) is, or is likely to become, a member of the same household as a person who has committed any of the offences referred in paragraph (d) above;

(g) is, or is likely to become, a member of the same household as a person in respect of whom an offence under sections 2A to 2C of the Sexual Offences (Scotland) Act 1976 (incest and intercourse with a child by step-parent or person in position of trust) has been committed by a member of that household;

(h) has failed to attend school regularly without reasonable excuse;

(i) has committed an offence;

(j) has misused alcohol or any drug, whether or not a controlled drug within the meaning of the Misuse of Drugs Act 1971;

(k) has misused a volatile substance by deliberately inhaling its vapour, other than for medicinal purposes;

(l) is being provided with accommodation by a local authority under section 25, or is the subject of a parental responsibilities order obtained under section 86, of this Act and, in either case, his behaviour is such that special measures are necessary for his adequate supervision in his interest or the interest of others.

(3) In this Part of this Act, "supervision" in relation to compulsory measures of supervision may include measures taken for the protection, guidance, treatment or control of the child.

DEFINITIONS
　"child": s.93(2)(b).
　"children's hearing": s.93(1).
　"compulsory measures of supervision": s.93(1).

"local authority": Local Government etc. (Scotland) Act 1994, s.2.
"parental responsibilities": ss.1(3), 93(1).
"parental responsibilities order": ss.86(1), 93(1).
"relevant person": s.93(2)(b).

GENERAL NOTE

This important section sets out the grounds upon which a child can be referred to a children's hearing. It replaces s.32 of the 1968 Act, and while there has been some tidying of the wording there is little substantive alteration to the grounds themselves. It is a pity that the opportunity was not taken to simplify the wording to make the grounds more readily understandable to children and to lay people, especially since one of the most important duties of the chairman of the hearing is to explain the grounds to the family (s.63(3) below). The concept, for example, of "relevant person" is unlikely to prove readily understandable to many people unversed in the intricacies of the present Act. There is some confusion possible with this section adopting the terminology of "conditions" while other parts of the Act refer to "grounds" (see for example ss.65, 68 and 69). There is, however, no difference between conditions and grounds and what are commonly referred to as "the grounds of referral" (as in s.69(1 below) or, sometimes, the "grounds for referral" (as in s.68(8) below) are the conditions listed in subs. (2) of the present section and it is these conditions which must be explained by the chairman at the commencement of the proceedings in accordance with s.65(4) below. The existence of a ground of referral founds the jurisdiction of the children's hearing, which cannot consider the case of a child in order to determine whether compulsory measures of supervision are required unless one or more of them exists.

Subs. (1)

The satisfaction of one or more of the conditions in subs. (2) below or, to put it another way, the existence of one or more of the grounds of referral, will be established either by the child and the parent accepting that they exist (s.65(5) below) or by the sheriff finding that they exist on an application under either s.68 or s.85 below or by a court holding that they exist under s.54 below. The existence of one or more of the grounds of referral is not, however, in itself proof that compulsory measures of supervision are necessary; conversely, however, their absence is conclusive of a lack of any need for such measures. The existence of a ground of referral does no more than raise the question of whether or not compulsory measures of supervision are necessary, and that question can be answered either by the reporter deciding to take no further action (as she or he is permitted to do under s.56(4) below) or by a children's hearing arranged by the reporter under s.65(1) below. If no ground exists the question does not arise, the children's hearing have no jurisdiction, and no compulsory measures of supervision can be imposed; if a ground does exist then the hearing have jurisdiction to embark upon a consideration of the child's case in order to determine whether compulsory measures of supervision are required, and if so what form these measures should take.

Subs. (2)

This central provision lists the grounds of referral, and reflects to a very large degree the grounds that existed in s.32(2) of the 1968 Act. The only substantive alterations to the old law are to be found in para. (g) which extends the old incest ground to include male children and to include offences related to incest, and in para. (j) which introduces a wholly new ground of referral.

Para. (a). A "relevant person" is someone who has parental responsibilities or parental rights in relation to a child (however acquired), or who ordinarily has charge of, or control over, a child (s.93(2)(b) below). Such a person has the responsibility of providing control for the child, and if unable, for whatever reason, to exercise that control the child shall be considered to be beyond the control of such person. "Control" must, it is submitted, be interpreted in a manner appropriate to the particular child: the control required to be provided to a young child is very different from that to be provided to a teenager who is nearing 16.

Para. (b). This is identical to the old ground under s.32(2)(b) of the 1968 Act. Wilkinson and Norrie, *Parent and Child* (1993, W. Green) at p. 450 say of this ground: "Any association which may be harmful to the child's welfare in any, not only in its moral, aspect, may be regarded as bad. Moral danger is commonly equiperated with the risk of sexual corruption, but there is no warrant for restricting it to such cases. The mere commission of an offence does not, but the exposure to circumstances from which a habitual pattern of criminal conduct is likely to follow probably does, indicate moral danger. There are obvious hazards and difficulties in going beyond recognised categories such as sexual corruption and criminality, but a wide scope is clearly intended. Thus, exposure of a child to scenes of habitual drunkenness may involve moral danger or at least indicate that the child is falling into bad associations. Similarly, circumstances in which the child is likely to indulge in solvent abuse or to develop the habit of taking drugs or drinking to excess may be regarded as obnoxious to this condition".

Para. (c). This is worded differently from, but has the same effect as, s.32(2)(c) of the 1968 Act. "Parental care" is care provided by any person who has the parental responsibility of safeguarding and promoting the child's health, development and welfare. The reason for the lack of care is irrelevant, and the important point is the likelihood that such lack will cause the child to suffer unnecessarily (that is, avoidably) or seriously to impair her or his health or development. On "likelihood" in the context of the offence of wilful neglect of a child, see *H v. Lees, D v. Orr* 1994 S.L.T. 908; *McFadden v. Normand* 1995 Green's Fam. L. Bul. 15/7.

Para. (d). This replaces the first part of s.32(2)(d) of the 1968 Act and concerns children who have been victims of certain specified offences. In relation to the existence of this ground of referral, it is of no significance who perpetrated the offence, nor where the offence was perpetrated; these matters will, of course, be highly relevant to the final disposal of the child's case. Proof of this ground, though it is proof of a criminal offence, is on the civil standard, and this can be met even in the absence of a conviction: the issue at stake is the harm to the child rather than how it was perpetrated.

Para. (e). This replaces the second part of s.32(2)(d) of the 1968 Act, and provides a ground of referral in relation to a child who is, or is likely to become, a member of the same household as a child victim of the offences covered in para. (d) above. So if one child in a household is a victim of, say, physical abuse, all the children in that household can be referred to the children's hearing. This is based on the assumption, borne out by experience, that if one child in a household is threatened by a source of danger, that source is likely to have access to and constitute a threat to the other children in the household. Again it is to be emphasised that the existence of the ground of referral merely raises the question of whether compulsory measures of supervision are necessary and is not conclusive of that necessity. On the meaning of "household" in this context, and in the context of the following two paragraphs, see Norrie "The Meaning of 'Household' in Referrals to Children's Hearings" 1993 S.L.T. (News) 192.

Para. (f). This replaces the old s.32(2)(dd). A child who lives with a Sched. 1 offender may not be in need of compulsory measures of supervision, but the very existence of the offence raises the question. It will normally be essential to establish who the perpetrator is in order to establish that the child is a member of her or his household.

Para. (g). Under the old s.32(2)(e) female children who were members of the same household as female victims of the crime of incest could be referred to the children's hearing if both females were members of the same household as the perpetrator of that crime. This tortuous ground was not needed under the 1968 Act and while it has been slightly tidied up, it is not needed under the current legislation. The ground is expanded to allow it to bring boys as well as girls to a children's hearing, and it is further expanded to cover the offences related to incest which were created by the Incest and Related Offences (Scotland) Act 1968. However, all cases in which this ground would be applicable will be covered by para. (f) above since incest and the related offences are all now Sched. 1 offences and if the child is in the same household as the perpetrator, para. (f) is activated. It is obscure why incest and the related offences are given their own separate (and still opaque) paragraph, and chairmen will still suffer the difficulties of explaining this ludicrous and unnecessary ground to children. It was very seldom used under the 1968 Act (in 1993, out of a total of 13,395 referrals of girls, the ground was used in only 13 cases: *Statistical Bulletin*, Scottish Office, No. SWK (CH) 1994/18).

Para. (h). Before this ground can be made out, the child must, one assumes, be "of school age" (defined in s.93(1) below and s.31 of the Education (Scotland) Act 1980). "Reasonable excuse" is to be proved by the child or parent, and will usually mean a reason for which neither can be held responsible, such as illness. An exclusion order issued due to the child's disruptive behaviour does not constitute a reasonable excuse for not attending school. The fact that the child is being appropriately educated at home is, on the other hand, a reasonable excuse.

Para. (i) This is identical to the ground in s.32(2)(g) of the 1968 Act, and while the consideration and disposal of a case brought on this ground is no different from cases brought on any other ground, the establishment of this ground does raise some specialties. In particular, proof, if an application has been made to the sheriff to establish the ground, is on the criminal rather than the civil standard (see s.68(3)(b) below). The ground is applicable only to children who are above the age of criminal responsibility, which is eight years old (see *Merrin v. S* 1987 S.L.T. 193). And a child who has pleaded guilty to or been found guilty of an offence in a criminal court can have the case referred by the court to a children's hearing, in which case a certificate of the court will be considered conclusive proof for the purpose of establishing the ground of referral (s.50(1) above).

Para. (j). This is an entirely new ground of referral, and was designed to bring Scots law into line with art. 33 of the UN Convention on the Rights of the Child. That obliges States to take all appropriate measures to protect children from the illicit use of drugs. Usually under the old law children who misused drugs or alcohol could be referred under another ground in any case, such as being beyond parental control, or falling into bad associations, or lack of parental care. Drug and alcohol abuse is however a significant threat to the well-being of some children and the introduction of this ground serves to strengthen the concern rightly felt about the problem. Also, it may well be clearer as a ground in itself rather than evidence of another ground, and thus easier to establish.

Para. (k). This is the same as the old s.32(2)(gg).

Para. (l). This replaces the old s.32(2)(i) and takes account of the amendments in the law in other parts of the Act. The addition to the old law comes in the words "or the interest of others", but in practical terms this adds little since a child who harms the interests of others is inevitably harming her or his own interests as well.

Subs. (3)
This is, effectively, the same as subs. (3) in the old s.32. The words "may include" allow the children's hearing to dispose of a case by means of a form of supervision that provides only some of these elements.

Preliminary and investigatory measures

Provision of information to the Principal Reporter

53.—(1) Where information is received by a local authority which suggests that compulsory measures of supervision may be necessary in respect of a child, they shall—

(a) cause inquiries to be made into the case unless they are satisfied that such inquiries are unnecessary; and

(b) if it appears to them after such inquiries, or after being satisfied that such inquiries are unnecessary, that such measures may be required in respect of the child, give to the Principal Reporter such information about the child as they have been able to discover.

(2) A person, other than a local authority, who has reasonable cause to believe that compulsory measures of supervision may be necessary in respect of a child—

(a) shall, if he is a constable, give to the Principal Reporter such information about the child as he has been able to discover;

(b) in any other case, may give the Principal Reporter that information.

(3) A constable shall make any report required to be made under paragraph (b) of section 17(1) of the Police (Scotland) Act 1967 (duty to make reports in relation to commission of offences) in relation to a child to the Principal Reporter as well as to the appropriate prosecutor.

(4) Where an application has been made to the sheriff—

(a) by the Principal Reporter in accordance with a direction given by a children's hearing under section 65(7) or (9) of this Act; or

(b) by any person entitled to make an application under section 85 of this Act,

the Principal Reporter may request any prosecutor to supply him with any evidence lawfully obtained in the course of, and held by the prosecutor in connection with, the investigation of a crime or suspected crime, being evidence which may assist the sheriff in determining the application; and, subject to subsection (5) below, it shall be the duty of the prosecutor to comply with such a request.

(5) A prosecutor may refuse to comply with a request issued under subsection (4) above where he reasonably believes that it is necessary to retain the

evidence for the purposes of any proceedings in respect of a crime, whether the proceedings have been commenced or are to be commenced by him.

(6) The Lord Advocate may direct that in any specified case or class of cases any evidence lawfully obtained in the course of an investigation of a crime or suspected crime shall be supplied, without the need for a request under subsection (4) above, to the Principal Reporter.

(7) In subsections (3), (4) and (5) above "crime" and "prosecutor" have the same meanings respectively given by section 462 of the Criminal Procedure (Scotland) Act 1975.

DEFINITIONS
　"child": s.93(2)(b).
　"children's hearing": s.93(1).
　"compulsory measures of supervision": s.93(1).
　"constable": s.93(1) and Police (Scotland) Act 1967 (c.77).
　"crime": Criminal Procedure (Scotland) Act 1975, s.462.
　"local authority": Local Government etc. (Scotland) Act 1994, s.2.
　"principal reporter": s.93(1).
　"prosecutor": Criminal Procedure (Scotland) Act 1975, s.462.

GENERAL NOTE
　The reporter is dependent, for the proper carrying out of her or his functions under the Act, on receiving information concerning children from various sources, including local authorities, schools, welfare agencies and the police. The reporter's duty to respond to information obtained is governed by s.55 below; the present section deals with the rights and obligations of others to furnish the reporter with information which suggests that a child may be in need of compulsory measures of supervision. Subsections (1) and (2) replace, with no substantive alteration to the law, the provisions in s.37(1) and (1A) of the 1968 Act, subs. (3) replaces s.38(2), and the remaining subsections impose new obligations on the prosecuting authorities to pass on information and evidence to the reporter.

Subs. (1)
　An obligation is imposed here upon local authorities who receive information concerning children to investigate that information in order to determine whether it suggests that compulsory measures of supervision may be necessary, and to pass to the reporter that information and any other information that their investigations reveal. They may seek a child protection order under s.57(2) below if their investigations are being frustrated by the refusal of parents to allow them access to a child. The reporter will usually carry out an initial investigation too (s.56(1) below) and it is the reporter who decides whether it is necessary to arrange a children's hearing: it follows that the decision the local authority have to make under this provision is restricted to a determination of whether compulsory measures of supervision *may* be necessary, and they have neither power nor ability to determine that such measures are in fact necessary.

　Information ... which suggests. The obligations imposed on the local authority by this section only arise when the information they receive is of a nature which suggests that one or more of the grounds of referral under s.52(2) above exist, for otherwise the question of whether compulsory measures of supervision are necessary does not arise (s.52(1) above).

　Received by a local authority. Information is received by a local authority when any of their officers or agencies, or anyone acting on their behalf, come to hold information of the appropriate nature. This will include social work departments, education departments and local authority medical services, but it is not limited to these agencies and the phrase is to be given wide scope.

　Unless ... satisfied that such inquiries are unnecessary. Inquiries may be unnecessary because the question clearly arises as to whether compulsory measures of supervision are necessary (i.e. the information suggests that one or more of the grounds of referral exists) or because clearly no such question arises from the information (i.e. the information does not indicate that any of the grounds of referral exists).

Subs. (2)
　This permits any person other than a local authority to give to the reporter such information as she or he has which gives reasonable cause to believe that one or more of the grounds of referral exists in relation to a particular child. There is no limitation on who has the right to pass information to the reporter, and it may be a medical practitioner, law enforcement officer, school teacher, group leader, neighbour, relative, child protection agency or even the child her or him-

self. If the person with the information is a police officer, the right to give information to the reporter becomes a duty to give that information.

Reasonable cause to believe. The right or duty to give information exists only insofar as the person with the information has reasonable cause to believe that it indicates that one or more of the grounds of referral are made out. This suggests that there is no right to give information when there is no reasonable cause for that belief. It is clearly not the aim of the Act to discourage the passing of information concerning children to the reporter, even when investigations are likely to show that there is no cause for concern (see further *D v. NSPCC* [1977] 1 All E.R. 589), but these words ensure that a person acting maliciously in giving the reporter information is not completely immune to legal redress. In other words, the transmission of information to the reporter is an act which is protected by the defence of qualified privilege in the law defamation, and in order to establish liability the pursuer would have to show both malice on the part of the defender and want of probable cause (see Norrie, *Defamation and Related Actions in Scots Law* (1995) at pp.123–124).

Subs. (3)

When police officers are required to make reports to prosecutors in connection with the commission of offences, they are also required to make reports to the reporter if the report relates to a child. This replaces, without substantive alteration, s.38(2) of the 1968 Act.

In relation to a child. The child may be the perpetrator of the offence being reported, or the victim thereof.

Subs. (4)

This is a new and highly significant provision. Not only are the police obliged to pass information to the reporter to assist her or him in deciding whether it is necessary to arrange a children's hearing under s.65 below, but the prosecuting authorities are now also obliged to pass on to the reporter evidence they hold when the reporter is trying to establish a ground of referral before the sheriff (whether on an initial application to the sheriff or on a rehearing of the evidence). Previously the sharing of evidence with reporters was a matter of practice rather than statutory obligation on the prosecutor. The obligation of co-operation imposed by this subsection arises only when the evidence is such that it may assist the sheriff in determining whether the ground of referral is made out or not, and when the reporter has made a request to be supplied with such evidence.

Evidence. This might be information or property or evidence of any other nature.

Lawfully obtained. Evidence that has been obtained by the prosecutor unlawfully cannot be made available to the reporter.

A crime or suspected crime. There is no limitation on who the evidence relates to, so long as it is relevant to the existence of a ground of referral in relation to the child. So the evidence can refer to a crime or suspected crime of which the child is either the perpetrator or the victim, or of which the perpetrator or victim is a member of the same household as the child.

Subs. (5)

The obligation to supply the reporter with evidence in subs. (4) above suffers an exception when the prosecutor reasonably believes that he must retain the evidence for use in proceedings that he has commenced or is going to commence. The prosecutor has no obligation to retain the evidence and in many situations will be able to co-operate with the reporter. Refusal to comply with the reporter's request ought only to be made when it is essential in the interests of justice that the evidence be retained by the prosecutor.

Subs. (6)

The Lord Advocate is given the power to specify a case or type of case in which evidence obtained in the course of a criminal investigation will automatically be supplied to the reporter, even without a request. It is expected that evidence suggesting, for example, that a child has committed an offence will automatically be shared with the reporter.

Reference to the Principal Reporter by court

54.—(1) Where in any relevant proceedings it appears to the court that any of the conditions in section 52(2)(a) to (h), (j), (k) or (l) of this Act is satisfied with respect to a child, it may refer the matter to the Principal Reporter, specifying the condition.

(2) In this section "relevant proceedings" means—

(a) an action for divorce or judicial separation or for declarator of marriage, nullity of marriage, parentage or non-parentage;

(b) proceedings relating to parental responsibilities or parental rights within the meaning of Part I of this Act;

(c) proceedings for an adoption order under the Adoption (Scotland) Act 1978 or for an order under section 18 of that Act declaring a child free for adoption; and

(d) proceedings for an offence against section 35 (failure by parent to secure regular attendance by his child at a public school), 41 (failure to comply with attendance order) or 42(3) (failure to permit examination of child) of the Education (Scotland) Act 1980.

(3) Where the court has referred a matter to the Principal Reporter under subsection (1) above, he shall—

(a) make such investigation as he thinks appropriate; and

(b) if he considers that compulsory measures of supervision are necessary, arrange a children's hearing to consider the case of the child under section 69 of this Act; and subsection (1) of that section shall apply as if the condition specified by the court under subsection (1) above were a ground of referral established in accordance with section 68 of this Act.

DEFINITIONS

"adoption order": Adoption (Scotland) Act 1978, s.65(1).
"children's hearing": s.93(1).
"parental responsibilities": ss.1(3), 93(1).
"parental rights": ss.2(4), 93(1).
"principal reporter": s.93(1).

GENERAL NOTE

Though this section does have statutory antecedents, there was no provision analogous to the present section in the 1968 Act. Various statutes had permitted the court in specified circumstances to commit the child to the care of a local authority: see the Matrimonial Proceedings (Children) Act 1958 (c. 40), s.10 (actions of divorce or nullity of marriage or separation), the Guardianship Act 1973 (c. 29), s.11 (custody cases), and the Adoption (Scotland) Act 1978 (c. 28), s.26 (adoption applications). In each situation committal to care was on the basis that it was not appropriate for the child to remain in the care of either of her or his parents. All these provisions are repealed in Sched. 5 below, but a similar though more appropriate effect is achieved here. Instead of committing the child to the care of a local authority, the court is empowered to refer the case of a child to the reporter. The court may do so, not when it considers neither parent to be suitable to have the care of the child, but when during the course of any of the specified proceedings the court comes to be of the view that one of the grounds of referral exists in relation to that child. The committal to care provisions were not used very frequently and the replacement of the concept of care in Chapter 1 of this Part of the Act renders it more appropriate that the court directs its attention to the question of whether the child requires compulsory measures of supervision. The proceedings in which the court may exercise this power are, mostly, family proceedings and they do not include, for example, a criminal trial in which it becomes evident that a child has been the victim of a Sched. 1 offence.

Subs. (1)

It appears to the court. The court, which can be either the sheriff court or the Court of Session must make a positive determination that the ground of referral exists, and it will only be able to do so if there is sufficient evidence to suggest it. An unsubstantiated allegation by one party in the course of divorce proceedings would not, it is submitted, be sufficient. It is to be noted that subs. (3) below provides that if the court refers the matter to the reporter specifying the ground, the ground will be treated as having been established: this suggests that the ground must be established in the relevant proceedings with the sufficiency of evidence required for a sheriff to determine that a ground has been established on application of the reporter under s.68 below. This is, however, very different from the provision in s.50(1) above where a criminal court's certificate is conclusive of a child having committed an offence, since the whole purpose of these criminal proceedings would have been to establish the child's guilt. Courts will have to be very careful here to ensure that there is sufficient opportunity to challenge any evidence suggesting that the appropriate ground of referral exists, since the main purpose of the proceedings is not directed towards that finding.

Any of the conditions in s.52(2)(a) to (h), (j), (k) or (l). The only ground that the court cannot hold to be satisfied is subs. (2)(i), that is to say that the child has committed an offence.

With respect to a child. There is no limitation in relation to which child the court can make such a reference. The typical case will be in an action for divorce in which the parents are arguing about the child's residence and evidence is presented to the court which leads it to believe, for example, that there is a lack of parental care. Information may come to the attention of the court even when the child is not being argued over, such as in a divorce in which residence has already been agreed upon by the parties. It is possible for information to come to the attention of the court concerning a child with no connexion whatsoever with the parties, and the terms of the section are clearly wide enough to cover such a case. For example if during the course of an adoption application in relation to one child it is alleged that the natural parent who is withholding consent abused another child, that child could be referred to the reporter, so long as there is sufficient evidence to satisfy the court. The comment under "It appears to the court" should again be referred to.

May refer. The court has a discretion and is not obliged to refer the matter to the reporter, even when it appears that a ground of referral does exist. It may be appropriate not to refer the matter to the reporter when another option available to the court is likely to be better for the child, such as for example making a residence order under s.11 above in favour of someone other than the parties to the proceedings. The court's decision to refer the case to the reporter is one to which the welfare of the child is paramount under s.16(1), but it is not one to which the other two "overarching principles" in s.16(2) (regard to the child's views) and s.16(3) (the minimum intervention principle) apply: that does not, however, prohibit the court from applying these principles if to do so enhances the child's welfare.

Subs. (2)

The court cannot refer any matter to the reporter in proceedings other than those specified, though of course any person involved in other proceedings (including the judge) may provide the reporter with information under s.53(2) above. (If the reporter receives information under s.53 the immediately following subsection does not come into play).

Subs. (3)

If the court refers the case of a child to the reporter the reporter is obliged to make such investigations as she or he thinks appropriate and must arrange a children's hearing if she or he considers that compulsory measures of supervision are necessary. The ground specified by the court shall be regarded as being a ground established by the sheriff on an application by the reporter and the hearing will not, therefore, be obliged or entitled to put the ground of referral to the child or parent. The hearing will proceed immediately to a consideration of the child's case, and make a decision and disposal in accordance with ss.69 and 70 below. Note again the comment in subs. (1) above under "It appears to the court".

Child assessment orders

55.—(1) A sheriff may grant an order under this section for an assessment of the state of a child's health or development, or of the way in which he has been treated (to be known as a "child assessment order"), on the application of a local authority if he is satisfied that—

(a) the local authority have reasonable cause to suspect that the child in respect of whom the order is sought is being so treated (or neglected) that he is suffering, or is likely to suffer, significant harm;

(b) such assessment of the child is required in order to establish whether or not there is reasonable cause to believe that the child is so treated (or neglected); and

(c) such assessment is unlikely to be carried out, or be carried out satisfactorily, unless the order is granted.

(2) Where—

(a) an application has been made under subsection (1) above; and

(b) the sheriff considers that the conditions for making a child protection order under section 57 of this Act are satisfied,

he shall make such an order under that section as if the application had been duly made by the local authority under that section rather than this section.

(3) A child assessment order shall—

(a) specify the date on which the assessment is to begin;

(b) have effect for such period as is specified in the order, not exceeding seven days beginning with the date specified by virtue of paragraph (a) above;

(c) require any person in a position to produce the child to—

(i) produce him to any authorised person;

(ii) permit that person or any other authorised person to carry out an assessment in accordance with the order; and

(iii) comply with any other conditions of the order; and

(d) be carried out by an authorised person in accordance with the terms of the order.

(4) A child assessment order may—

(a) where necessary, permit the taking of the child concerned to any place for the purposes of the assessment; and

(b) authorise the child to be kept at that place, or any other place, for such period of time as may be specified in the order.

(5) Where a child assessment order makes provision under subsection (4) above, it shall contain such directions as the sheriff considers appropriate as to the contact which the child shall be allowed to have with any other person while the child is in any place to which he has been taken or in which he is being kept under a child assessment order.

(6) In this section "authorised person" means any officer of the local authority, and any person authorised by the local authority to perform the assessment, or perform any part of it.

DEFINITIONS

"child": s.93(2)(b).

"child protection order": ss.57(1), 93(1).

"local authority": Local Government etc. (Scotland) Act 1994, s.2.

GENERAL NOTE

One of the difficulties facing child care agencies responsible for ensuring the well-being of children is that they may well have suspicions of abuse or neglect but be unable to provide evidence, necessary for the application of many of the care mechanisms in the Act, without a medical examination or other assessment of the child. Medical examination or assessment can be carried out only with the consent of a person who has the right and capacity to provide that consent, though there has long been a suspicion that this requirement is often ignored in practice and children subjected to intimate examination without the appropriate consent being obtained. This section, following the model established by s.43 of the English Children Act 1989, introduces a wholly new form of order available to the court and is designed to allow an assessment to be made of a child's health or development or of the way in which she or he has been treated even in the absence of consent by the parent, and it authorises the removal of the child to the place where the assessment is to be carried out, and the keeping of the child there or elsewhere.

It is not made explicit in the Act what happens when the child her or himself is old enough to consent or refuse consent to medical examination (as it is, for example, when a supervision requirement contains a condition under s.70(5)(a) below that the child submit to medical treatment). Capacity to consent or refuse is governed by s.2(4) of the Age of Legal Capacity (Scotland) Act 1991, and the effect of that provision is expressly preserved by s.90 below. It follows (though it would have been better to express this) that an assessment cannot be carried out upon a child who refuses to submit to it, whenever the child is of sufficient mental maturity to understand the nature and consequences of the proposed procedure. A child assessment order under this section cannot authorise what would otherwise be an assault against the child, for otherwise s.2(4) of the 1991 Act would be compromised, contrary to the express terms of s.90 below. The order, therefore, permits an assessment to be carried out in the absence of parental consent but not in the absence of the capable child's own consent.

Child assessment orders have not proved popular in England, and local authorities there have been much more inclined to seek child protection orders. This may well eventuate in Scotland also. Sheriffs are obliged to make a child protection order when a child assessment order is sought but the conditions for the granting of a child protection order are established, and the difference between the conditions required for each will often be subtle. Under this section a child assessment order will be available when there is reasonable cause for suspecting that the child is at risk; under s.57(1) below a child protection order will be available when there are reasonable grounds for believing that the child is at risk. A local authority with reasonable cause for suspecting will usually have little difficulty in establishing reasonable grounds for believing. Whether the introduction of child assessment orders under this section adds significantly to the armoury of the law of child protection will depend upon how willing local authorities are to seek the less interventionist order: they may well feel that, for no other reason than their own protection, the more interventionist (but still temporary) order under s.57 ought to be sought. In which case the present section will have added little in practical terms.

Subs. (1)

A sheriff can grant a child assessment order if a local authority have applied for it and he is satisfied that the three specified conditions are made out. Paragraph (a) is satisfied when the local authority have reasonable cause to suspect that the child might be suffering harm; para. (b) is satisfied when an assessment is shown to be necessary to test that suspicion; and para. (c) requires that it be shown that the assessment would not be carried out properly without the order.

A sheriff may grant. Even though the sheriff is satisfied that the three conditions for the granting of the order exist, the matter is still within his discretion. His decision is governed by all three overarching principles in s.16, and so he must regard the welfare of the child as his paramount consideration, must give the child an opportunity to express views and take appropriate account of them, and must not make the order unless he considers that it would be better for the child that the order be made than that it not be made at all.

The state of a child's health or development. The child assessment order may be designed to assess the state of the child's current health or her or his development. Part of that assessment will inevitably include an assessment of what is necessary to ensure that the child attains the state of health or development that she or he should have.

Or of the way in which he has been treated. These words permit the assessment to be used to examine the child to see whether there is any evidence of past abuse or maltreatment, which would justify the utilisation of any of the protection procedures in the Act.

On the application of a local authority. Only local authorities have title to apply for child assessment orders.

Reasonable cause to suspect. Each case must be dealt with individually in determining whether the local authority's suspicions are founded on reasonable cause. Since the purpose of the order is to allow a testing of that suspicion, the level of suspicion is unlikely to be required to be high. An allegation of abuse, even when made anonymously, may well give reasonable cause for suspicion (unless clearly spurious) as might, for example, the failure of a very young child to thrive. It is likely that only in cases in which there is no cause whatsoever to suspect that the child is suffering will this condition not be satisfied.

Significant harm. Significant harm is harm that is serious and of a not minor or transient nature. It may be physical or emotional. *Cf.* s.57(1) below where the same phrase is used.

Subs. (2)

The conditions for the granting of a child protection order laid down in s.57 below are stricter than the conditions for the granting of a child assessment order in the sense that it must be shown in that section that there actually are reasonable grounds for believing the child is suffering significant harm, while the present provision requires that it be shown that there are grounds for suspicion and the assessment is necessary to test that suspicion. Nevertheless there may well be cases in which in establishing the grounds for the suspicion the local authority actually establish grounds for believing that the child is suffering significant harm. This subsection therefore provides that if the conditions for a child protection order are shown to be satisfied then an order under s.57 must be made rather than a child assessment order.

He shall make. These words suggest that the sheriff has no discretion but must make the child protection order if the conditions in s.57(1) below are found to be satisfied in an application under s.55(1). This, however, must be read in light of s.57(1) itself, which provides that the sheriff "may make" a child protection order. It is submitted that the words "he shall make" should be interpreted to mean that he must treat an application made under s.55 as if it were an application under s.57, so permitting the sheriff the discretion contained in the latter section. This, admittedly, involves some violence to the actual terms of the statute, but the alternative of giving the sheriff a discretion to make an order under s.57 when the application is made under s.57 but obliging him to make an order under s.57 when the application is made under s.55 is ludicrous, and an interpretation which avoids that result is to be preferred. A factor telling against this proposed interpretation, however, is the wording of s.76(8) below, which in relation to an application for an exclusion order provides a similar rule to that contained in this subsection, except that it is provided that the sheriff "may" rather than "shall" make an order under s.57. The principle behind the rule in both provisions is the same but the fact that different words are used might be taken to indicate a parliamentary intention that the provisions are to have a different effect; a more realistic explanation for the difference is, it is submitted, sloppy draftsmanship. "Shall", for the purposes of this subsection, means "may".

Subs. (3)

The child assessment order will last for a specified period of time, not exceeding seven days, and its effect will commence on a date that must be specified in the order. In addition, it will require any person who can produce the child to do so and to permit the assessment to be carried out as well as to comply with any conditions in the order. And the order will require an officer of the local authority who sought the order, or any person authorised by the local authority, to carry out the assessment in accordance with the terms of the order. That officer or person is referred to in this section as the "authorised person": subs. (6).

Require any person ... to ... comply with any other conditions. The order requires the local authority to carry out the assessment, and it may also require the person in a position to produce the child to do anything specified in the order in addition to producing the child. This might involve, for example, the giving of consent to a particular examination or treatment, though the order itself will normally be sufficient authority to carry out the examination or treatment.

Subss. (4) and (5)

In order to carry out the assessment the child may be taken to any place at which the assessment is to be carried out. The terms of subs. (4) suggest that if this is to happen authority to take the child there must be specified in the order. A child cannot be kept for longer than the order is specified to last (a maximum of seven days). If a child is taken to a place for the carrying out of an assessment the sheriff must consider whether to make directions as to the contact the child is to have with any other person while at the place of assessment. The provision is designed to ensure maximum flexibility: the sheriff may direct, for example, daily contact when the child is kept for a number of days, or he may direct that the child be accompanied at all times by a parent if, for example, the assessment is likely to last only a matter of hours. The three overarching principles in s.16 govern his decision on this as on other matters relating to child assessment orders.

Where necessary. The order can permit the taking of the child to a place only when the assessment cannot be carried out at the place where the child already is (that is to say, generally speaking, at home).

That place or any other place. The child can be kept in overnight accommodation for a number of days while the assessment itself takes place elsewhere, such as at a hospital.

Initial investigation by the Principal Reporter

56.—(1) Where the Principal Reporter receives information from any source about a case which may require a children's hearing to be arranged he shall, after making such initial investigation as he thinks necessary, proceed with the case in accordance with subsection (4) or (6) below.

(2) For the purposes of making any initial investigation under subsection (1) above, the Principal Reporter may request from the local authority a report on the child and on such circumstances concerning the child as appear to him to be relevant; and the local authority shall supply the report which may contain such information, from any person whomsoever, as the Principal Reporter thinks, or the local authority think, fit.

(3) A report requested under subsection (2) above may contain information additional to that given by the local authority under section 53 of this Act.

(4) The Principal Reporter may decide, after an initial investigation under subsection (1) above, that a children's hearing does not require to be arranged; and where he so decides—

    (a) he shall inform the child, any relevant person and the person who brought the case to his notice, or any of those persons, that he has so decided; and

(b) he may, if he considers it appropriate, refer the case to a local authority with a view to their making arrangements for the advice, guidance and assistance of the child and his family in accordance with Chapter 1 of this Part of this Act.

(5) Where the Principal Reporter has decided under subsection (4) above that a children's hearing does not require to be arranged, he shall not at any other time, on the basis solely of the information obtained during the initial investigation referred to in that subsection, arrange a children's hearing under subsection (6) below.

(6) Where it appears to the Principal Reporter that compulsory measures of supervision are necessary in respect of the child, he shall arrange a children's hearing to which he shall refer the case for consideration and determination.

(7) Where the Principal Reporter has arranged a children's hearing in accordance with subsection (6) above, he—

(a) shall, where he has not previously done so, request a report under subsection (2) above;

(b) may request from the local authority such information, supplementary or additional to a report requested under subsection (2) above, as he thinks fit;

and the local authority shall supply that report, or as the case may be information, and any other information which they consider to be relevant.

DEFINITIONS
"child": s.93(2)(b).
"children's hearing": s.93(1).
"family": s.93(1).
"local authority": Local Government etc. (Scotland) Act 1994, s.2.
"principal reporter": s.93(1).
"relevant person": s.93(2)(b).

GENERAL NOTE
This section replaces, with little alteration in content, the provisions previously contained in s.38(1) and s.39 of the 1968 Act. It specifies the actions the reporter must take on receiving information which has come to her or him under s.53 above or by any other means. The reporter must decide whether to make an initial investigation and must thereafter decide whether or not to arrange a children's hearing. These decisions are not governed by the overarching principles in s.16 above (which refers only to decisions made by a court or a children's hearing), but inevitably the reporter will be guided by her or his assessment of the child's welfare. The only change from the 1968 Act is contained in subss. (2) and (3) which permits the reporter to call for a report on the child's circumstances from the local authority in order to assist in the initial investigation the reporter is making before deciding whether to arrange a children's hearing. It had long been the practice of reporters to call for reports for that reason even before this Act, but the practice is put onto a statutory basis here, and the local authority are now obliged to conform to the reporter's request.

Subs. (1)
May require a children's hearing to be arranged. These words specify the type of information that will trigger the reporter's obligations under this section. A hearing is required to be arranged only if the investigation suggests that one or more of the grounds of referral in s.52 above exists. If the reporter receives information of any other nature her or his response is not governed by this section.

Such initial investigation as he thinks necessary. Having received information from whatever source, the first decision that the reporter must make is whether further investigation is needed. That investigation is to be directed to the question of whether or not a children's hearing requires to be arranged and no investigation is necessary when the reporter is of the view that she or he already has sufficient information to make that decision.

Subss. (2) and (3)
If the reporter decides that an initial investigation is required, then as part of that investigation she or he may request the local authority to draw up a social background report, detailing any

circumstances that she or he considers necessary, including information additional to that given by the local authority under the terms of s.53 above. The local authority are obliged to supply this report.

Subs. (4)

Having made such investigation as she or he thinks necessary, the reporter must then make a decision whether a children's hearing is required to be arranged. She or he is obliged by s.65(1) to arrange a hearing when satisfied that at least one of the grounds of referral exists *and* that compulsory measures of supervision are necessary, and she or he may decide that a children's hearing does not require to be arranged only when not satisfied of one or both of these elements. If not so satisfied the reporter's decision not to arrange a children's hearing must be intimated to someone. Just who must be informed, however, is unclear due to the opaque wording in para. (a). As originally drafted, the words "shall inform" appeared as "may inform", and this reflected the discretionary element in the words "or any of those persons". The latter words remain, suggesting a discretion while the amended words "shall inform" indicate an absolute obligation (s.39(1) of the 1968 Act, which this subsection replaces, qualified the obligation with the words "where he considers this to be the proper course"). The result seems to be an obligation to inform, but a discretion as to who is to be informed. The reporter must inform any one or more of the following persons of the decision that a children's hearing does not require to be arranged: (i) the child, (ii) any person with parental responsibilities or parental rights, or any person who ordinarily has charge of or control over the child, or (iii) the person who supplied the reporter with the information concerning the child in the first place. In addition, the reporter has the power, to be exercised when she or he considers it appropriate, to refer the case to a local authority for the purposes of the authority providing advice, guidance and assistance to the child and family under ss.16–38 above.

Subs. (5)

The effect of this provision is that the decision not to refer the child to a children's hearing cannot be retracted unless new circumstances, which are additional to those discovered in the course of the investigation to determine whether to arrange a hearing, come to the attention of the reporter. These new circumstances might indicate a quite different ground of referral, or they may concern the same—for example, when the decision not to arrange a children's hearing was made on the basis of a lack of evidence which has subsequently come to light. It is unclear when the decision is made and when, therefore, it becomes irrevocable. It is submitted that before the reporter's opinion can properly be characterised as a "decision", some step must be taken consequent upon it or pursuant to it. That step will normally be giving the intimation required under subs. (4) above: in other words the decision not to refer the child to a children's hearing is irrevocable only once the reporter has intimated that decision.

Subs. (6)

This provision is to be compared with, and is probably tautologous in light of, s.65(1) below. The later provision obliges the reporter to arrange a children's hearing when she or he is satisfied that compulsory measures of supervision are necessary *and* when at least one of the grounds of referral exists; the present provision obliges the reporter to arrange a children's hearing when it appears to her or him that compulsory measures of supervision are necessary. The reference to the grounds of referral in s.65(1) is otiose, since the question of whether compulsory measures of supervision are necessary arises only if at least one of these grounds exists (s.52(1) above), with the result that both that provision and this provision amount to exactly the same thing.

Subs. (7)

If a hearing is to be arranged by the reporter, she or he must request a report on the child from the local authority unless she or he has already done so as part of an initial investigation, and she or he may request any supplementary information. The local authority must provide such reports and information, and any other information concerning the child or her or his circumstances that they consider to be necessary. The reporter is not obliged to wait until the children's hearing is arranged before requesting such a report, and it will normally be sensible for her or him to make the request as soon as the decision to arrange a hearing has been made.

Measures for the emergency protection of children

Child protection orders

57.—(1) Where the sheriff, on an application by any person, is satisfied that—

(a) there are reasonable grounds to believe that a child—
> (i) is being so treated (or neglected) that he is suffering significant harm; or
> (ii) will suffer such harm if he is not removed to and kept in a place of safety, or if he does not remain in the place where he is then being accommodated (whether or not he is resident there); and

(b) an order under this section is necessary to protect that child from such harm (or such further harm),

he may make an order under this section (to be known as a "child protection order").

(2) Without prejudice to subsection (1) above, where the sheriff on an application by a local authority is satisfied—

(a) that they have reasonable grounds to suspect that a child is being or will be so treated (or neglected) that he is suffering or will suffer significant harm;

(b) that they are making or causing to be made enquiries to allow them to decide whether they should take any action to safeguard the welfare of the child; and

(c) that those enquiries are being frustrated by access to the child being unreasonably denied, the authority having reasonable cause to believe that such access is required as a matter of urgency,

he may make a child protection order.

(3) Without prejudice to any additional requirement imposed by rules made by virtue of section 91 of this Act, an application for a child protection order shall—

(a) identify—
> (i) the applicant; and
> (ii) in so far as practicable, the child in respect of whom the order is sought;

(b) state the grounds on which the application is made; and

(c) be accompanied by such supporting evidence, whether in documentary form or otherwise, as will enable the sheriff to determine the application.

(4) A child protection order may, subject to such terms and conditions as the sheriff considers appropriate, do any one or more of the following—

(a) require any person in a position to do so to produce the child to the applicant;

(b) authorise the removal of the child by the applicant to a place of safety, and the keeping of the child at that place;

(c) authorise the prevention of the removal of the child from any place where he is being accommodated;

(d) provide that the location of any place of safety in which the child is being kept should not be disclosed to any person or class of person specified in the order.

(5) Notice of the making of a child protection order shall be given forthwith by the applicant to the local authority in whose area the child resides (where that authority is not the applicant) and to the Principal Reporter.

(6) In taking any action required or permitted by a child protection order or by a direction under section 58 of this Act the applicant shall only act where he reasonably believes that to do so is necessary to safeguard or promote the welfare of the child.

(7) Where by virtue of a child protection order a child is removed to a place of safety provided by a local authority, they shall, subject to the terms and conditions of that order and of any direction given under section 58 of this Act, have the like duties in respect of the child as they have under section 17 of this Act in respect of a child looked after by them.

DEFINITIONS
"child": s.93(2)(b).
"local authority": Local Government etc. (Scotland) Act 1994, s.2.
"place of safety": s.93(1).
"principal reporter": s.93(1).
"relevant person": s.93(2)(b).

GENERAL NOTE
Under the 1968 Act a court or justice of the peace could, in the circumstances specified in s.37(2) thereof, authorise the removal of a child to a place of safety, and a constable could take a child to a place of safety even without such authorisation. A number of criticisms could be made of the law in that provision. For one thing, though the specified circumstances which justified a place of safety order were relatively clear, the Act gave no guidance to the court as to when in any particular case the making of an order was appropriate. It was not, for example, appropriate to remove a child from her or his parent every time the child was a victim of a Sched. 1 offence, though in every such case it would be competent to do so under s.37(2)(a). Another problem, which was illustrated by the Orkney case, was that the mechanisms for appealing against a place of safety order were inextricably linked to the hearing system itself, and the Act did not cater for families who were perfectly willing to attend a children's hearing but wished immediately to challenge the necessity for the removal of children from their homes. Again, the order available under the old s.37 was inflexible in that the only action it authorised was the taking of the child to a place of safety, and it did not authorise the taking of less drastic steps. If removal of the child were considered inappropriate no action could be taken to protect the child until the sitting of a children's hearing. As a result of these, and other, criticisms (see White Paper, *Scotland's Children: Proposals for Child Care Policy and Law* (Cm 2286, August 1993) at paras. 5.8–5.18), the whole procedure for the interim protection of the child has been radically remodelled, with the introduction of a new order, to be known as a child protection order, which is designed (i) to last for the shortest possible period of time, (ii) to include a speedy review mechanism, (iii) to be more flexible than the old place of safety order, and (iv) to have the conditions for its granting simplified and much more clearly directed towards the immediate need to protect the child from imminent harm. The main provisions are contained in ss.57–60, with supplementary provisions contained in ss.61 and 62.

Section 57 sets out the grounds upon which a child protection order can be granted, and specifies what actions it may authorise; s.58 deals with the directions that can be attached to a child protection order, and ss.59 and 60 deal with the various means by which the order can be reviewed and brought to an end. There are strict time-limits to be adhered to throughout. In summary, the procedure (assuming the child protection order authorises the removal of a child to a place of safety) is as follows:

STEP 1: A child protection order, once made, must be implemented within 24 hours, and if it is not, it shall *cease to have effect* (s.60(1) below).

STEP 2: Once implemented, the child protection order can be challenged by means of an application to the sheriff within two working days thereafter.

STEP 2A: If STEP 2 is not taken within two working days of the implementation of the child protection order, an initial children's hearing must be convened on the second working day in order to determine whether the child protection order should continue in effect: if no such initial hearing is held, or if the hearing does not continue the child protection order, it shall *cease to have effect* (s.60(6)(a) below).

STEP 2B: If the initial hearing continues the order it can be challenged by means of an application to the sheriff within two working days of the continuation and the same process as below will be followed from STEP 3 to STEP 5.

STEP 3: If the sheriff does not determine that application within three working days of it being made the child protection order shall *cease to have effect* (s.60(2) below).

STEP 4: If the sheriff determines that the conditions for the granting of the child protection order are not satisfied he shall *recall the order* (s.60(13) below); if he determines that the conditions are satisfied he will continue the child protection order until a children's hearing arranged under s.65(2) has commenced (s.60(12)(d) below).

STEP 5: On the commencement of a children's hearing arranged under s.65(2), which must be on the eighth working day after the implementation of the child protection order, the order shall *cease to have effect* (s.60(6)(e) below) and any further protection of the child that is necessary will be provided by the children's hearing system.

Whatever happens, a child protection order must come to an end at the latest on the eighth working day after its implementation. Before then the need for the child protection order will have been reviewed at least once (either by the sheriff or by an initial hearing) and often twice (by an initial hearing and then by the sheriff). Apart from these provisions for review, there is no appeal from the granting or refusal of a child protection order nor its continuation to the sheriff principal or the Court of Session (s.51(15) above); though not expressly excluded there is probably no appeal from the variation of a child protection order either, since the timescale will require the order coming to an end within a very few days of such variation. That consideration does not apply with a sheriff's decision to discharge a child protection order that has already been granted but the only interest in an appeal would lie in those seeking to protect the child and that protection is probably better provided by other means (such as arranging a children's hearing under s.65(1) below); nevertheless it is odd that the right of appeal against discharge of a child protection order is not either expressly excluded or provided for.

Subs. (1)

Any person may apply to the sheriff for him to make an order, to be known as a "child protection order". If the sheriff is satisfied both that one of the conditions in para. (a) is satisfied and that the making of the order is necessary to protect the child, he may grant such an order.

Any person. The applicant can be a local authority, a parent, a constable, or any other person, but will normally be the local authority.

There are reasonable grounds to believe. The sheriff must be satisfied that there is evidence to show that the child is being or will be harmed and that evidence must give reasonable ground for the belief. If there are grounds for suspicion but they do not reasonably give rise to the belief then the condition is not satisfied.

Suffering significant harm. The harm that the child must be suffering or threatened with is serious harm of a not minor, transient or superficial nature. It may be physical or emotional. The Act gives little guidance as to how serious this harm need be but it is submitted that, since the aim of the Act is to protect the child's welfare, harm will be significant only when it is clearly more serious than the potential trauma removal from home will almost inevitably cause a child.

Necessary to protect that child. Not only must the ground in para. (a) be satisfied but the sheriff must also be satisfied that the making of a child protection order is necessary to protect the child from the actual or threatened harm there mentioned. It is not assumed, as it was under the old law, that the making of the order is the only way to protect the child. There may be other, equally efficacious, means that are less traumatic for the child (such as the granting of an exclusion order under s.76 below), and the word "necessary" indicates to the court that a child protection order should not be granted unless this is the only, or is the most efficacious, or in the circumstances the most appropriate, means of protecting the child.

May make an order. Even if both paragraphs are satisfied, the sheriff retains a discretion, and he is guided in the exercise of that discretion by s.16(1), under which the welfare of the child must be his paramount consideration. It may well be the case that the making of an order does more harm (perhaps psychological) to the child than good. Welfare, as always, is to be given broad scope and is not limited to the immediate circumstances which would otherwise justify the granting of a child protection order. The other overarching principles in s.16 (*i.e.* having regard to the views of the child and the minimum intervention principle) do not apply to the making of a child protection order though curiously they do apply to the varying and discharging thereof (s.16(4)(b)(ii) above). There is, therefore, no presumption that a child protection order, when sought, ought not to be granted, but there is a presumption that, once granted, it ought not to be varied or discharged.

Subs. (2)

A child protection order can be made under subs. (1) above on the application of anyone so long as there are reasonable grounds to believe that the child is being or will be harmed. In addition, this subsection permits a local authority (but only a local authority) to apply for the granting of a child protection order (which, if granted, can be on the same terms and conditions as one granted under subs. (1) above) when they have reasonable grounds to suspect that the child is being or will be harmed, but the enquiries they are making are being frustrated by the denial to them of access to the child.

Frustrated by access to the child being unreasonably denied. The enquiries must be rendered wholly ineffectual in allowing the local authority to determine whether or not their suspicions are justified, due to the person with control over who has access to the child denying that access for no good cause. Merely hampering or making more difficult these enquiries will not be sufficient. Due to the local authority's various duties in relation to children it would appear that the onus of proving reasonable cause lies with those denying the local authority access (though the onus of proving reasonable grounds for suspicion will lie with the local authority).

Subs. (3)

Rules will specify the form of the application, but it must include information concerning the matters set out here.

Subs. (4)

A child protection order is much more flexible than the old place of safety order, since it can not only authorise the removal of the child to a place of safety but can also require, authorise or provide any of the other stated actions. This will in appropriate circumstances allow a child to be protected from a source of danger without necessarily removing her or him from her or his home.

Any one or more of the following. The child protection order can do only the things mentioned, and none other. The sheriff can make these subject to appropriate terms and conditions, but he cannot order anything not specified. For example the sheriff cannot, under this provision, exclude a person from the child's home.

Authorise the removal of the child ... [or] authorise the prevention of the removal of the child. It is to be noted that if the child protection order authorises the doing of any of the acts in paras. (b) or (c) then certain other provisions are activated which do not apply when the child protection order authorises only those acts in either para. (a) or para. (d). In particular an initial hearing under s.59 below will have to be held if an application to the sheriff to set aside or vary the order has not already been made, and the reporter has power to release the child from a place of safety under s.60(3) below.

Prevention of the removal of the child. This sort of order is not an order to detain the child against her or his will. The word "removal" suggests that the order prevents someone else from taking the child away, and does not authorise the prevention of the child leaving a place on her or his own instigation.

Subs. (5)

Once made, the applicant must inform the local authority and the reporter of the making of the child protection order. Though not expressed, it can be expected that any person obliged to do anything by the child protection order will also be informed of its making. "Forthwith" means as soon as practicable.

Subs. (6)

A child protection order must not be enforced automatically and unthinkingly, and the applicant is authorised or required to do certain acts only where he reasonably believes that the doing of them is necessary to safeguard or promote the welfare of the child. If the applicant acts without this belief then he is acting without statutory authority and can be subject to liability therefor. Though it is likely to be difficult to establish lack of reasonable belief after a child protection order has been granted, this is not impossible, if for example the original source of danger to the child has died or been imprisoned since the granting of the order.

Subs. (7)

A local authority who "looks after" a child is subject to various obligations under s.17 above. A child removed to a place of safety under subs. (4)(b) above is a child being "looked after" for these purposes (s.17(6)(c)).

Directions in relation to contact and exercise of parental responsibilities and parental rights

58.—(1) When the sheriff makes a child protection order, he shall at that time consider whether it is necessary to give a direction to the applicant for the order as to contact with the child for—

(a) any parent of the child;

(b) any person with parental responsibilities in relation to the child; and

(c) any other specified person or class of persons;

and if he determines that there is such a necessity he may give such a direction.

(2) Without prejudice to the generality of subsection (1) above, a direction under that subsection may—

(a) prohibit contact with the child for any person mentioned in paragraphs (a) to (c) of that subsection;

(b) make contact with the child for any person subject to such conditions as the sheriff considers appropriate to safeguard and promote the welfare of the child.

(3) A direction under subsection (1) above may make different provision in relation to different persons or classes of person.

(4) A person applying for a child protection order under section 57(1) or (2) of this Act may at the same time apply to the sheriff for a direction in relation to the exercise or fulfilment of any parental responsibilities or parental rights in respect of the child concerned, if the person considers such a direction necessary to safeguard or promote the welfare of the child.

(5) Without prejudice to the generality of subsection (4) above, a direction under that subsection may be sought in relation to—

(a) any examination as to the physical or mental state of the child;
(b) any other assessment or interview of the child; or
(c) any treatment of the child arising out of such an examination or assessment,

which is to be carried out by any person.

(6) The sheriff may give a direction sought under subsection (4) above where he considers there is a necessity such as is mentioned in that subsection; and such a direction may be granted subject to such conditions, if any, as the sheriff (having regard in particular to the duration of the child protection order to which it relates) considers appropriate.

(7) A direction under this section shall cease to have effect when—

(a) the sheriff, on an application under section 60(7) of this Act, directs that it is cancelled; or
(b) the child protection order to which it is related ceases to have effect.

DEFINITIONS
"child": s.93(2)(b).
"child protection order": ss.57(1), 93(1).
"parental responsibilities": ss.1(3), 93(1).
"parental rights": ss.2(4), 93(1).

GENERAL NOTE
The 1968 Act contained no provisions in relation to the access by a parent or guardian to a child removed to a place of safety and the matter remained in the hands of the local authority, until such time as a children's hearing was convened and made any provision therefor. This was regarded as one of the flaws in the system and this new section therefore imposes upon the sheriff an obligation to consider in all cases in which a child protection order is made the matter of contact between the parent or any other person and the child, and gives him the power to make a direction as to contact. In addition, the sheriff may also make a direction in relation to the exercise of parental responsibilities or parental rights, including directions as to medical examination and treatment of the child. There is no requirement for the sheriff to consider in every case whether this additional type of direction should be given, but the applicant is permitted to request the sheriff to give that matter consideration.

Subs. (1)
This provision imposes an obligation on a sheriff who makes a child protection order to give consideration to the question of whether he should give a direction as to contact, and grants him a discretion to give such an order if he believes that it is necessary. The direction is given to the applicant who, presumably, is then obliged to follow it. Such a direction is not the same as a contact order made under s.11 above and is more in the nature of a direction to one person to allow contact between the child and another person. A direction cannot be given here to a person who is not an applicant and if the applicant is not the person who will be looking after the child then a direction under this section will seldom be appropriate. The applicant will normally be the local authority and the direction under this subsection will be to the effect that, for example, a parent is to be allowed contact with a child who has been removed to a place of safety under s.57(4)(b) above.

Necessary to give a direction. The words "necessary" and "necessity" should be given a strict construction and the direction ought not to be given simply because the sheriff wants everything to remain within judicial control. The philosophy here, as in other parts of the Act, is that the court should get involved in directing children's lives only when not to do so would be against the child's interests. Necessity might arise, for example, when the applicant is minded to grant contact and the sheriff thinks that contact would not be in the child's best interests, or when the applicant cannot come to an agreement with a person who is seeking to have contact with the child.

Subs. (2)

The direction made by the sheriff may arrange contact, or may prohibit it or may subject it to such conditions as the sheriff considers appropriate. So the sheriff may direct that contact always be supervised, or he may direct where it is to take place or how often, or he may direct that any specified person or class of persons is not to have contact at all.

Subs. (3)

The aim of this provision is to ensure maximum flexibility in relation to contact for the benefit of the child. It may be appropriate to direct that contact, say, with a father be prohibited completely and that contact with a mother be supervised at all times.

Subs. (4)

It is important to note that a child protection order does not confer parental responsibilities and parental rights on the applicant and these remain with whomsoever had them before the making of the order. It follows that the direction applied for under this subsection as to the fulfilment of parental responsibilities or the exercise of parental rights will be a direction not to the applicant (unless the applicant otherwise has parental responsibilities or parental rights) as in subs. (1) above but to the person with the parental responsibilities or parental rights, and it will provide directions as to how these responsibilities and rights should be carried out. This subsection merely permits the applicant to request the sheriff to give such a direction, and the sheriff has no power to do so in the absence of such a request. The statute does not indicate the consequences of a failure to follow directions given under this subsection.

Subs. (5)

The applicant may request the sheriff to give any direction in relation to the fulfilment or exercise of parental responsibilities or parental rights and in particular in relation to medical examination and treatment. It is important to be aware of the precise effect of this. The sheriff *cannot* authorise examination or treatment under this provision, nor can he authorise the applicant to carry it out. Rather he can simply direct the parent or guardian to exercise her or his parental responsibilities and parental rights in a particular manner. This may include a direction that the parent, say, consents to medical treatment, but that would be competent only when the parent or guardian has the right to provide such consent. Section 90 below (to which reference should be made) preserves the child's capacity to consent or refuse consent under s.2(4) of the Age of Legal Capacity (Scotland) Act 1991 (c. 50), and s.15(5)(b) above ensures that a person with parental responsibilities and parental rights can consent only when the child cannot consent or refuse on her or his own behalf. It follows that a direction as to medical examination or treatment under the present section would be competent only when the child is too young to consent to that examination or treatment her or himself.

Subs. (6)

A direction to those with parental responsibilities and parental rights as to how they should exercise these responsibilities and rights is to be given only when necessary to safeguard or promote the welfare of the child. Such a direction might be necessary, for example, in order to ensure that a parent maintains beneficial contact with the child, or when a parent refuses to consent to an examination of the physical or mental state of the child and this is considered essential to allow for the proper identification of the child's needs. The sheriff must bear in mind in coming to his decision the duration of the order: a child protection order is designed to last only for the shortest possible period of time, and it follows that directions made in connection with it should not, except in cases of immediate necessity, deal irrevocably with matters of long-term significance. In all cases it will be for the applicant to show the existence of such a necessity.

Subs. (7)

The child protection order ... ceases to have effect. The direction cannot survive without the child protection order to which it is attached and it will cease to have effect whenever the child protection order ceases to have effect, for whatever reason. So any direction under this section, like the child protection order itself, can last for a maximum of eight working days (see the General Note to s.57 above).

Initial hearing of case of child subject to child protection order

59.—(1) This section applies where—
(a) a child in respect of whom a child protection order has been made—
    (i) has been taken to a place of safety by virtue of section 57(4)(b) of this Act; or
    (ii) is prevented from being removed from any place by virtue of section 57(4)(c) of this Act;
(b) the Principal Reporter has not exercised his powers under section 60(3) of this Act to discharge the child from the place of safety; and
(c) the Principal Reporter has not received notice, in accordance with section 60(9) of this Act, of an application under subsection (7) of that section.

(2) Where this section applies, the Principal Reporter shall arrange a children's hearing to conduct an initial hearing of the child's case in order to determine whether they should, in the interests of the child, continue the child protection order under subsection (4) below.

(3) A children's hearing arranged under subsection (2) above shall take place on the second working day after that order is implemented.

(4) Where a children's hearing arranged under subsection (2) above are satisfied that the conditions for the making of a child protection order under section 57 of this Act are established, they may continue the child protection order and any direction given under section 58 of this Act (whether with or without variation of the order or, as the case may be, the direction) until the commencement of a children's hearing in relation to the child arranged in accordance with section 65(2) of this Act.

(5) In subsection (3) above, section 60 and section 65(2) of this Act any reference, in relation to the calculation of any period, to the time at which a child protection order is implemented shall be construed as a reference—
(a) in relation to such an order made under paragraph (b) of subsection (4) of section 57 of this Act, to the day on which the child was removed to a place of safety in accordance with the order; and
(b) in relation to such an order made under paragraph (c) of that subsection, to the day on which the order was made,
and "implement" shall be construed accordingly.

DEFINITIONS
    "child": s.93(2)(b).
    "children's hearing": s.93(1).
    "child protection order": ss.57(1), 93(1).
    "place of safety": s.93(1).
    "principal reporter": s.93(1).
    "working day": s.93(1).

GENERAL NOTE
    A child protection order may, but will not necessarily, authorise the removal of the child from her or his home and the keeping of the child in a place of safety, or the prevention of the removal of the child from any specified place. Though the child protection order process has been designed to ensure that the order will last for only a short period of time (*i.e.* until the eighth working day after its implementation: s.60(6)(e) below) and that there is an opportunity to challenge the granting of the child protection order even before its termination, it was felt that in addition, if the child has been removed to a place of safety or is being prevented from being removed from a specified place, there should be an automatic review of the order at some time before the children's hearing arranged for the eighth working day. If there is an immediate application to the sheriff to set aside or vary the order then that process provides such a review; in the absence of such an application, this section provides that a review will be undertaken by a children's hearing. It should be noted that it is not the making of a child protection order itself

that activates this section, but the removal of a child to a place of safety or the prevention of the child from being removed from a specified place. If an application is made to the sheriff to have the order set aside or varied before this hearing commences, then the need for this initial hearing is obviated and it will not go ahead. The hearing must determine two questions: whether the conditions for the making of a child protection order are established, and, if so, whether the order should be continued in the interests of the child.

Subs. (1)

This sets out the circumstances in which an initial hearing must be arranged. These are that the child has been removed from her or his home and taken to a place of safety or is being prevented from being removed from any specified place where she or he is being accommodated, *and* that the child remains in the place of safety, *and* that no application to the sheriff to set aside or vary the child protection order has been notified to the reporter.

Subss. (2) and (3)

The obligations in these subsections are absolute. An initial hearing must be arranged and it must be held on the second working day after the implementation of the child protection order. It would be incompetent for the hearing to be held on the first working day, even if it were feasible to do so. If the hearing is not arranged or otherwise does not take place when this section applies, then the child protection order cannot be continued under subs. (4) below and it will, therefore, cease to have effect. (The Act does not actually say this, but it is an inevitable result of subs. (4) below permitting only a hearing arranged under subs. (2) to continue the child protection order. *Cf.* s.60(6)(a) in which it is provided that when the initial hearing that has been arranged does not continue the order it will cease to have effect, and s.60(2) which provides that if the sheriff does not determine an application to review the order within three working days it will cease to have effect).

A children's hearing. This will be a normal hearing to which all the rules relating to attendance and procedure apply. Its purpose, however, is limited to determining the two questions specified in the General Note above.

Second working day. The day of implementation is what can be called "day zero", the next day is the first working day after the implementation, and the day after that is the second working day. So, for example, if a child protection order is implemented on a Monday, the initial hearing must be convened on the immediately following Wednesday. If the child protection order is implemented on a Friday, the initial hearing must be convened on the immediately following Tuesday (Saturday and Sunday not being "working days": s.93(1) below). "Implementation" is defined in subs. (5) below.

Subs. (4)

The hearing must first decide whether they are satisfied that the conditions for the making of the child protection order, set out in s.57(1) above, exist or not. If they are so satisfied they must then go on to consider whether to continue the order and whether to vary it; if they are not so satisfied they have no authority to continue the order (which brings the order to an end: s.60(6)(a) below).

Conditions ... are established. It is not made clear whether the hearing has to determine that the conditions are established as at the time of the granting of the order, or as at the time they are looking at the matter, though the latter interpretation is probably to be preferred. Given the shortness of time between the making of the order and the initial hearing it is unlikely that there will be any significant change in circumstances, but extreme cases (such as death of the source of danger) are not beyond the realms of possibility.

May continue. Even when the hearing are satisfied that the conditions for the making of the child protection order are established, they need not continue it. They have a discretion, to be exercised by regarding the welfare of the child as paramount (s.16(1) above), in determining whether to continue the order or not. Generally speaking the order should be continued only when there remains a greater risk to the child in its termination than in its continuation. The fact that s.16(2) (requiring regard to be had to the views of the child) is not expressed to apply here does not mean that the hearing should not or cannot seek the child's views, for the very essence of the consideration of a child's case by a children's hearing, however the case comes to the hearing, is discussion with any child able and willing to discuss the matter. The continuation will be until either the sheriff recalls the child protection order under s.60(13) below or until a full hearing arranged under s.65(2) below has commenced.

Subs. (5)

The children's hearing under this section must meet on the second working day after the implementation of the child protection order which either authorises the removal of and keeping a child in a place of safety, or authorises the prevention of the removal of the child from a specified place. In relation to the former, "implementation" occurs on the day the child is removed, and in relation to the latter, "implementation" is deemed to occur on the day the order is made.

Duration, recall or variation of child protection order

60.—(1) Where, by the end of twenty-four hours of a child protection order being made (other than by virtue of section 57(4)(c) of this Act), the applicant has made no attempt to implement the order it shall cease to have effect.

(2) Where an application made under subsection (7) below has not been determined timeously in accordance with subsection (8) below, the order to which the application relates shall cease to have effect.

(3) A child shall not be—
(a) kept in a place of safety under a child protection order;
(b) prevented from being removed from any place by such an order; or
(c) subject to any term or condition contained in such an order or a direction given under section 58 of this Act,
where the Principal Reporter, having regard to the welfare of the child, considers that, whether as a result of a change in the circumstances of the case or of further information relating to the case having been received by the Principal Reporter, the conditions for the making of a child protection order in respect of the child are no longer satisfied or that the term, condition or direction is no longer appropriate and notifies the person who implemented the order that he so considers.

(4) The Principal Reporter shall not give notice under subsection (3) above where—
(a) proceedings before a children's hearing arranged under section 59(2) of this Act in relation to the child who is subject to the child protection order have commenced; or
(b) the hearing of an application made under subsection (7) of this section has begun.

(5) Where the Principal Reporter has given notice under subsection (3) above, he shall also, in such manner as may be prescribed, notify the sheriff who made the order.

(6) A child protection order shall cease to have effect—
(a) where an initial hearing arranged under section 59(2) of this Act does not continue the order under subsection (4) of that section;
(b) where an application is made to the sheriff under subsection (7) below, on the sheriff recalling such order under subsection (13) below;
(c) on the person who implemented the order receiving notice from the Principal Reporter that he has decided not to refer the case of a child who is subject to the order to a children's hearing arranged in accordance with section 65(2) of this Act;
(d) on the Principal Reporter giving notice in accordance with subsection (3) above in relation to the order that he considers that the conditions for the making of it are no longer satisfied; or
(e) where such order is continued under section 59(4) of this Act or subsection (12)(d) below, on the commencement of a children's hearing arranged under section 65(2) of this Act.

(7) An application to the sheriff to set aside or vary a child protection order made under section 57 of this Act or a direction given under section 58 of this Act or such an order or direction continued (whether with or without variation) under section 59(4) of this Act, may be made by or on behalf of—
(a) the child to whom the order or direction relates;
(b) a person having parental rights over the child;
(c) a relevant person;

(d) any person to whom notice of the application for the order was given by virtue of rules; or

(e) the applicant for the order made under section 57 of this Act.

(8) An application under subsection (7) above shall be made—

(a) in relation to a child protection order made under section 57, or a direction given under section 58, of this Act, before the commencement of a children's hearing arranged in accordance with section 59(2) of this Act; and

(b) in relation to such an order or direction continued (whether with or without variation) by virtue of subsection (4) of the said section 59, within two working days of such continuation,

and any such application shall be determined within three working days of being made.

(9) Where an application has been made under subsection (7) above, the applicant shall forthwith give notice, in a manner and form prescribed by rules, to the Principal Reporter.

(10) At any time which is—

(a) after the giving of the notice required by subsection (9) above; but

(b) before the sheriff has determined the application in accordance with subsection (11) below,

the Principal Reporter may arrange a children's hearing the purpose of which shall be to provide any advice they consider appropriate to assist the sheriff in his determination of the application.

(11) The sheriff shall, after hearing the parties to the application and, if he wishes to make representations, the Principal Reporter, determine whether—

(a) the conditions for the making of a child protection order under section 57 of this Act are satisfied; or

(b) where the application relates only to a direction under section 58 of this Act, the direction should be varied or cancelled.

(12) Where the sheriff determines that the conditions referred to in subsection (11)(a) above are satisfied, he may—

(a) confirm or vary the order, or any term or condition on which it was granted;

(b) confirm or vary any direction given, in relation to the order, under section 58 of this Act;

(c) give a new direction under that section; or

(d) continue in force the order and any such direction until the commencement of a children's hearing arranged in accordance with section 65(2) of this Act.

(13) Where the sheriff determines that the conditions referred to in subsection (11)(a) above are not satisfied he shall recall the order and cancel any direction given under section 58 of this Act.

DEFINITIONS

"child": s.93(2)(b).
"child protection order": ss.57(1), 93(1).
"children's hearing": s.93(1).
"parental rights": ss.2(4), 93(1).
"principal reporter": s.93(1).
"relevant person": s.93(2)(b).
"working day": s.93(1).

GENERAL NOTE

As explained more fully in the General Note to s.57, a child protection order is designed to last for as short a period of time as possible, and to give as much opportunity to challenge its implementation as is practicable. This important section sets out the circumstances in which the child protection order will cease to have effect, and prescribes the procedures to be followed in applications to set aside or vary the order. In addition, it permits the reporter to return the child home when her or his interests so require.

Subs. (1)

The child protection order is to be used as an emergency procedure designed to provide immediate protection to the child when this is necessary in her or his welfare. It follows that when the applicant delays in implementing the order, it can be assumed that the immediate necessity, previously argued for by the applicant, no longer exists, and it therefore ought to fall. The rule is therefore that the child protection order will cease to have effect unless an attempt to implement it is made within 24 hours of making the order.

Has made no attempt. The applicant can be said to make an attempt to implement the order when he takes necessary steps to that end. The nature of the attempt will of course vary with the nature of the order, and this provision specifically does not apply to an order preventing the removal of the child from a place where he is being accommodated. Implementation in that case is deemed to occur on the day the order is made (s.59(5)(b) above). It is difficult to see how the applicant can attempt to implement the keeping secret of the child's whereabouts if no-one attempts to find this out and it is submitted that here too implementation occurs on the obtaining of the order. The attempt might not be successful until after the 24 hours have passed, but that does not bring the order to an end so long as the attempt commences before then. So, for example, if a child protection order authorises the removal of a child to a place of safety the order ceases if the applicant does nothing for more than 24 hours, but it does not cease if the applicant attempts to obtain the child but the attempt is frustrated by the parents of the child spiriting her or him away or the child running away.

Time starts to run in relation to applications to the sheriff, and the arranging of the initial and the full hearings, from the successful implementation of the order.

Shall cease to have effect. If the order ceases to have effect the child is no longer subject to a child protection order with the result that there is no obligation on the reporter to arrange a children's hearing in terms of s.65(2) below. The reporter is still entitled, however, to arrange a hearing under s.65(1) below on the basis of the information obtained as a result of the child protection order. When the order ceases to have effect, any directions to the applicant made under s.58 above also cease to have effect.

Subs. (2)

In order to ensure the speedy resolution of applications to the sheriff to set aside or vary the child protection order, it is provided as an absolute rule that the order will cease to have effect if such an application has not been dealt with within three working days of its being made (subs. (8) below).

Subs. (3)

When a child is kept in a place of safety, or is prevented from being removed from a place, or is subjected to any term or condition, the reporter is obliged to keep a continual eye on the situation, and this subsection ensures that the child protection order will not justify that keeping or prevention or subjection when the reporter considers that the conditions for the granting of the child protection order or the giving of the directions are no longer satisfied. Where the reporter so considers, and notifies the person who implemented the order that she or he so considers, this provision takes away the authority to keep the child or prevent the child's removal and terminates the direction. It follows that the child must be returned home or freed, unless some other statutory authority to keep the child can be invoked. Subsection (6)(d) below provides that in the circumstances described the order shall cease to have effect. This means that there is no obligation on the reporter to arrange a children's hearing in terms of s.65(2) below, but she or he may still do so, in terms of s.65(1) below.

Conditions for the making. This refers to the conditions set out in s.57. The further evidence that comes to the attention of the reporter might suggest that the conditions are no longer satisfied or, implicitly, that they never were, in fact, satisfied. The reporter cannot come to that view unless there has been a change in circumstances or she or he has acquired further information (and she or he cannot, therefore, release a child simply because she or he disagrees with the sheriff who granted the order). Evidence that the child's welfare is suffering due to the implementation of the child protection order will be a persuasive (and usually sufficient) change in circumstances.

And notifies. The authority to keep the child or prevent her or him being removed comes to an end when the reporter's decision is notified to the person who implements the order, and not simply by the reporter making the decision.

Subs. (4)

The effect of this provision almost entirely detracts from the aim of subs. (3) above, which is to allow the reporter to react speedily to sudden changes in circumstances. It provides that the reporter cannot arrange for the return or release of the child after the commencement of any initial hearing that is held under s.59 above or the commencement of any application to the sheriff to set aside or vary the order. This means that the reporter's power to arrange for a release of the child lasts only until the second working day after the implementation of the child protection order and she or he cannot arrange for the child's release thereafter.

Subs. (5)

The sheriff who made the child protection order must be informed if the child is to be returned home or released by the reporter's decision under subs. (3) above.

Subs. (6)

The child protection order ceases to have effect (with the result that there is no authority to do any of the acts authorised under the order or an attached direction and the reporter is no longer obliged to arrange a children's hearing in terms of s.65(2) below) immediately on the happening of any of the listed events. Under para. (a) the child protection order ceases either when an initial hearing arranged under s.59 above does not continue the order or (though the statute does not say this) when an initial hearing which ought to have been arranged on the second working day after the implementation of the order did not in fact take place (see comments to s.59(2) above). Paragraph (b) provides that the effect of the sheriff recalling the order is that it shall cease to have effect. Paragraph (c) brings the child protection order to an end when the reporter notifies a decision not to refer the child's case to a children's hearing for consideration and disposal (*i.e.* when she or he has come to the view either that none of the grounds of referral exists or that, even if a ground does exist, compulsory measures of supervision are not necessary). Paragraph (d) brings the order to an end when the reporter notifies the person who implemented the order that the conditions for its making are no longer satisfied. Paragraph (e) ensures that the order ceases as soon as the full children's hearing commences: if the child's welfare requires that she or he be kept in a place of safety thereafter then the provisions in ss.66 and 67 below must be utilised: in other words the matter is in the hands of the children's hearing.

Subs. (7)

The application to the sheriff to set aside or vary a child protection order or an attached direction can be made within two working days of its implementation (*i.e.* before the holding of, and obviating the need for, an initial hearing) or within two working days of its continuation by an initial hearing. That application can be made by or on behalf of only the specified persons (and not, for example, a stranger to the child seeking to clear her or his name of an allegation of abuse against the child).

The child. The child will require the application to be made on her or his behalf when she or he has no capacity (determined by the Age of Legal Capacity (Scotland) Act 1991) to conduct civil proceedings, or when she or he does have that capacity but consents to be represented in proceedings by someone who used to be her or his legal representative (s.15(6) above).

A person having parental rights. It is surprising that the reference in para. (b) is not to a person with parental rights or parental responsibilities, for a person with parental responsibilities has as much interest in the child protection order as a person with parental rights. It may be noticed that s.58(1)(b) above (directions as to contact) refers only to a person with parental responsibilities. There is no practical result to this example of sloppy draftsmanship since all such persons come within the category described in the immediately following paragraph (rendering this paragraph entirely otiose).

A relevant person. This is defined to mean a person having parental responsibilities or parental rights or who ordinarily has charge of or control over the child (s.93(2)(b) below).

Subs. (8)

This sets out the strict time-limits within which an application to the sheriff to set aside or vary the child protection order must be made. If it is not made within these times then it is incompetent later to make it. The application must be made *either* before the commencement of an initial hearing (which is to be held on the second working day after implementation of the order in circumstances described in s.59(1) above) *or* if it was not made before then within two workings days of the continuation of the order by the initial hearing. In either situation, the sheriff must determine the application within three working days of its being made (so if the application is made, for example, on a Friday he must determine it on or before the following Wednesday). If he has not determined the application by then, the child protection order ceases to have effect (subs. (2) above).

Subs. (9)

Notice is necessary since if notice is not given to the reporter of an application to the sheriff to set aside or vary the child protection order within two working days of its implementation, and the order contains an authorisation to remove the child to a place of safety or to keep the child in a place, the reporter is obliged to arrange an initial hearing in terms of s.59 above.

Subs. (10)

This subsection introduces a wholly new type of advice hearing. The reporter is given the discretion to arrange a children's hearing (to which the normal rules of attendance and procedure apply) after an application has been made, but before the sheriff has determined the application, for variation or setting aside of a child protection order, in order that the hearing may provide the sheriff with advice to assist him in his decision. The effect of para. (a) is that this advice hearing may be held only when the application to the sheriff has been made before the commencement of an initial hearing under s.59 and an advice hearing would be incompetent when an application to the sheriff has been made after an initial hearing. This is sensible, since the initial hearing will have stated reasons for their decision and these reasons will be available to advise the sheriff if an application is made to him thereafter. The nature of the advice given is entirely for the children's hearing themselves to decide, but it should, of course, be directed towards the question of whether a child protection order remains in the child's best interests. Any advice the hearing gives must regard the welfare of the child as the paramount consideration (s.16(1) above) and must give the child an opportunity to express views and have regard so far as practicable to these views taking account of the child's age and maturity (s.16(2), as applied to this advice hearing by s.16(4)(a)(iii) above). The statute gives no guidance to the reporter as to how and when to exercise her or his discretion to arrange this advice hearing, and often the matter will be determined by the availability of time: this hearing does not interrupt the running of the three working days within which the sheriff must determine the application. It may well prove impractical in the generality of cases to arrange any advice hearing under this subsection.

Subs. (11)

The application may either request the sheriff to set aside the whole child protection order, which will terminate any directions as to contact or the exercise of parental responsibilities or parental rights given under s.58, or to vary the order, or to vary or cancel any such direction. The sheriff must hear the parties to the application and, if she or he wishes to make representations, the reporter.

The parties to the application. This refers to the parties to the application to set aside or vary the child protection order, which are the applicants themselves (being one of the persons specified in subs. (7) above), and the person who originally sought the child protection order together with any person who opposed its making.

The conditions for the making of a child protection order ... are satisfied. This means, it is submitted, currently satisfied as at the date the sheriff determines the issue rather than the date the child protection order was made. "The conditions" are all the conditions set out in s.57 and not simply the grounds upon which the order was granted set out in s.57(1), otherwise the statute would have limited it to that subsection. So for example the child protection order can be challenged here on the ground that the application was not made in the form specified in s.57(3): adopting the correct form is, it is submitted, one of the conditions for the making of a child protection order set out in s.57.

Subs. (12)

If the conditions for the making of a child protection order are held by the sheriff to be satisfied then he may do any of the acts listed. He is not entitled to do any other act, such as recalling the order. In deciding which option to adopt, the sheriff is governed by the three overarching principles in s.16, that is to say the paramountcy of the child's welfare, the requirement to have regard to the views of the child, and the minimum intervention principle. The last-mentioned amounts in this context to a presumption that the present order is to continue unvaried.

Subs. (13)

A finding that the conditions in s.57 have not been satisfied (*i.e.* all the conditions including but not limited to the grounds in s.57(1): see note to subs. (11) above) seems to oblige the sheriff to recall the order and cancel any directions attached to it. However, the words "shall recall the order" must be read in the light of s.16 above, which provides that the three overarching principles apply when "the sheriff is considering ... whether to ... discharge a child protection order" (s.16(4)(b)(ii)): these words have the effect, if they have any effect at all, of conferring a discretion on to the sheriff's decision. If the sheriff finds that the conditions in s.57 have not been satisfied it can be assumed that in the vast majority of cases it will be for the child's welfare to recall the order, but this would not be so if the condition not satisfied were a mere procedural condition (such as that in s.57(3)) and the ground upon which the order was made clearly still exists. In these circumstances the sheriff can, it is submitted, rely on s.16(1) to refuse to recall the order. The views of the child (s.16(2) above) should be taken into account but will never determine the issue and could not, it is submitted, subvert the apparent obligation to recall the order. The minimum intervention principle in s.16(3) amounts to a presumption that no recall will be pronounced unless the sheriff considers that it would be better for the child to pronounce recall than not to do so: this clearly confers a discretion on the sheriff, notwithstanding the words "shall recall the order" as they appear in the present subsection.

Emergency protection of children where child protection order not available

61.—(1) Where, on the application of any person, a justice of the peace is satisfied—

(a) both that the conditions laid down for the making of a child protection order in section 57(1) of this Act are satisfied and that it is probable that any such order, if made, would contain an authorisation in terms of paragraph (b) or (c) of subsection (4) of that section; but

(b) that it is not practicable in the circumstances for an application for such an order to be made to the sheriff or for the sheriff to consider such an application,

he may grant to the applicant an authorisation under this section.

(2) Where on the application of a local authority a justice of the peace is satisfied—

(a) both that the conditions laid down for the making of a child protection order in section 57(2) of this Act are satisfied and that it is probable that any such order, if made, would contain an authorisation in terms of paragraph (b) or (c) of subsection (4) of that section; but

(b) that it is not practicable in the circumstances for an application for such an order to be made to the sheriff or for the sheriff to consider such an application,

he may grant an authorisation under this section.

(3) An authorisation under this section may—

(a) require any person in a position to do so to produce the child to the applicant;

(b) prevent any person from removing a child from a place where he is then being accommodated;

(c) authorise the applicant to remove the child to a place of safety and to keep him there until the expiration of the authorisation.

(4) An authorisation under this section shall cease to have effect—

(a) twelve hours after being made, if within that time—

(i) arrangements have not been made to prevent the child's removal from any place specified in the authorisation; or

(ii) he has not been, or is not being, taken to a place of safety; or

(b) where such arrangements have been made or he has been so taken when—

(i) twenty-four hours have expired since it was so given; or

(ii) an application for a child protection order in respect of the child is disposed of,

whichever is the earlier.

(5) Where a constable has reasonable cause to believe that—

(a) the conditions for the making of a child protection order laid down in section 57(1) are satisfied;

(b) that it is not practicable in the circumstances for him to make an application for such an order to the sheriff or for the sheriff to consider such an application; and

(c) that, in order to protect the child from significant harm (or further such harm), it is necessary for him to remove the child to a place of safety,

he may remove the child to such a place and keep him there.

(6) The power conferred by subsection (5) above shall not authorise the keeping of a child in a place of safety for more than twenty-four hours from the time when the child is so removed.

(7) The authority to keep a child in a place of safety conferred by subsection (5) above shall cease on the disposal of an application in relation to the child for a child protection order.

(8) A child shall not be—

(a) kept in a place of safety; or

(b) prevented from being removed from any place,

under this section where the Principal Reporter considers that the conditions for the grant of an authorisation under subsection (1) or (2) above or the exercise of the power conferred by subsection (5) above are not satisfied, or that it is no longer in the best interests of the child that he should be so kept.

DEFINITIONS

"child": s.93(2)(b).

"child protection order": ss.57(1), 93(1).

"constable": s.93(1).

"local authority": Local Government etc. (Scotland) Act 1994, s.2.

"place of safety": s.93(1).

"principal reporter": s.93(1).

GENERAL NOTE

There may be situations in which either a sheriff is not available to grant a child protection order or it appears that a child's safety can be secured only by her or his immediate and summary removal from a source of danger. In these situations a child protection order, though designed to be granted quickly, might not be available quite quickly enough. This section therefore permits a justice of the peace to grant authorisations to do certain of the acts which could be authorised by a child protection order and permits police officers to remove a child from an immediate source of danger. To a large extent the section has been drafted to mirror the provisions in s.57 above, which sets out the conditions for the making of a child protection order, but this has led to certain anomalies in the present section since the emergency situation is not wholly analogous to the situation governed by s.57. Due to the very limited periods of time the authorisations under this provision can last, there are no provisions for review of or appeal from decisions.

Subs. (1)

When both conditions specified in s.57(1) above for the granting of a child protection order are satisfied, but it is not practicable to obtain such an order from a sheriff, then an authorisation may be granted by a justice of the peace to do any of the acts listed in subs. (3) below, so long as the justice of the peace is satisfied that had a child protection order been granted it is probable that it would have contained an authorisation under s.57(4)(b) (*i.e.* an authorisation to remove the child to a place of safety and to keep the child there) or an authorisation under s.57(4)(c) (*i.e.* an authorisation to prevent the removal of a child from any place where he is being accommodated).

Any person. There is no limitation on who may apply for an authorisation under this subsection, though normally it will be a local authority.

It is probable. This means more likely than not.

Not practicable. The only situation in which it would not be practicable to obtain a child protection order from a sheriff is when no sheriff is, for whatever reason, available in sufficient time to deal with whatever emergency has arisen. This eventuality is unlikely to occur in large urban areas such as Glasgow or Edinburgh in which there are many sheriffs, but it may occur more frequently in rural areas such as the Western or the Northern Isles.

May grant... an authorisation. In deciding whether to grant the authorisation the justice of the peace will be governed by the need to regard the welfare of the child as paramount (s.16(1) above) but, not being a sheriff, will not be governed by the requirement to have regard to the views of the child (s.16(2) above) or the minimum intervention principle (s.16(3) above). The grant is not of a child protection order, but merely of an authorisation to do certain acts. It follows that once the authorisation is made the procedures under ss.57–60 are not activated. It is, however, envisaged that a child protection order will be applied for as soon as possible after the granting of the authorisation under this section, and that authorisation comes to an end as soon as an application for a child protection order has been dealt with (subs. (4)(b)(ii) below).

Subs. (2)

This provision reflects that contained in s.57(2) above, whereby a child protection order can be granted if inquiries into the child's wellbeing are being frustrated by a failure to obtain access to the child. In these circumstances, and on the satisfaction of the same conditions as contained in subs. (1) above, a justice of the peace may grant an authorisation to do any of the acts listed in subs. (3) below. As in s.57(2), only a local authority can apply for an authorisation under this subsection. This provision is unlikely to be much used since investigations will seldom require to be carried out with the urgency that this section is designed to deal with.

Subs. (3)

The authorisation under this section may permit the carrying out of any of the listed acts. Paragraph (a) reflects para. (a) in s.57(4), para. (b) reflects para. (c) in s.57(4) and para. (c) reflects para. (b) in s.57(4). The only power in s.57(4) left out is the provision that the location of any place of safety in which the child is being kept should not be disclosed to any person. This power is not needed since the authorisation in this section is an emergency process and matters such as disclosure can be dealt with by the proper child protection order procedure which is likely to follow. It is not easy to understand why the justice of the peace is permitted under this subsection to authorise acts of the same nature as those listed in s.57(4)(a), (b) and (c) but according to subs. (1) above can do so only when he believes that a sheriff would authorise either of the acts in s.57(4)(b) or (c), but this untidiness is unlikely to have much practical effect.

Subs. (4)

This deals with the length of time for which the authorisation survives. Its effect is that the authorisation lasts for a maximum of 24 hours after its granting. If the act authorised is not carried out within 12 hours of being granted it cannot be carried out thereafter; if it is carried out within that time the authorisation for it lapses at the expiry of 24 hours, or on the disposal of an application for a child protection order (if earlier). There is no requirement to seek a child protection order after the obtaining of an authorisation under this section, but that will be the only way in which a child can be kept in a place of safety for longer than the periods provided here.

Subs. (5)

A child can be removed from, or kept away from, a source of immediate danger without any involvement of a sheriff or a justice of the peace by a police officer who has reasonable cause to believe that the conditions for the granting of a child protection order exist but it is not practicable in the circumstances for her or him to obtain a child protection order. However, she or he can only remove or keep a child if this is necessary to protect the child from significant harm. The necessity must be immediate, otherwise the provisions above concerning authorisations by a justice of the peace can be adopted. A police officer can, for example, step in and remove a child to a place of safety if she or he witnesses the child being beaten up by her or his parents, or a child is brought, say, to a female and child unit at a police station in a distressed state, or if the police officer comes across a child who has been expelled from the family home in conditions that create a risk of significant harm. On "significant harm" see the General Note to s.57(1) above.

Subs. (6)

If a child is taken to or kept in a place of safety by a police officer under the terms of subs. (5) above, she or he can be kept there only for a maximum period of 24 hours after first being removed from the source of danger. If the child is to be kept for any longer period than that, a child protection order under s.57 must be sought and obtained. This tightens up the old law under which the time-limits were not so strict (s.37(4) of the 1968 Act was expressed "where practicable").

Subs. (7)

If a child has been taken to or kept in a place of safety by a police officer under the terms of subs. (5) above, the authority to keep her or him there granted by that subsection lapses when a child protection order application has been determined. That determination supersedes subs. (6) above. If the application is successful, the authority to keep the child will be the child protection order; if the application is unsuccessful the child cannot be kept in the place of safety and must be released home forthwith.

Subs. (8)

As in s.60(3) above, the reporter has ultimate control over whether a child is kept in a place of safety, and the child cannot be kept in a place of safety or prevented from being removed from a place by any provision in this section if the reporter is of the view either (i) that it is no longer in the best interests of the child that she or he be kept there, or (ii) in cases of authorisation by a justice of the peace that the conditions for its granting are not satisfied, or (iii) in cases of emergency removal by a constable that the conditions specified in subs. (5) above for the exercise of that power of removal are not satisfied.

Regulations in respect of emergency child protection measures

62.—(1) The Secretary of State may make regulations concerning the duties in respect of a child of any person removing him to, and keeping him in, a place of safety under section 61 above.

(2) Regulations under this section may make provision requiring—

(a) notification of the removal of a child to be given to a person specified in the regulations;

(b) intimation to be given to any person of the place of safety at which a child is being kept;

(c) notification to be given to any person of the ceasing to have effect, under section 61(4)(a) of this Act, of an authorisation.

DEFINITIONS
"child": s.93(2)(b).
"place of safety": s.93(1).

GENERAL NOTE
In addition to the duties imposed by regulations made under this section, a local authority who provides accommodation for a child who is removed to and kept in a place of safety will also be subject to the duties in respect of that child set out in s.17 above: s.17(6)(c).

Children arrested by the police

Review of case of child arrested by police

63.—(1) Where the Principal Reporter has been informed by a constable, in accordance with section 296(3) of the Criminal Procedure (Scotland) Act 1975, that charges are not to be proceeded with against a child who has been detained in a place of safety in accordance with that section, the Principal Reporter shall, unless he considers that compulsory measures of supervision are not required in relation to the child, arrange a children's hearing to which he shall refer the case.

(2) A children's hearing arranged under subsection (1) above shall begin not later than the third day after the Principal Reporter received the information mentioned in that subsection.

(3) Where the Principal Reporter considers that a child of whose detention he has been informed does not require compulsory measures of supervision, he shall direct that the child shall no longer be kept in the place of safety.

(4) Subject to subsection (3) above, a child who has been detained in a place of safety may continue to be kept at that place until the commencement of a children's hearing arranged under subsection (1) above.

(5) Subject to subsection (6) below, a children's hearing arranged under subsection (1) above may—

(a) if they are satisfied that the conditions mentioned in subsection (2) of section 66 of this Act are satisfied, grant a warrant to keep the child in a place of safety; and

(b) direct the Principal Reporter to arrange a children's hearing for the purposes of section 65(1) of this Act,

and subsections (3) to (8) of the said section 66 shall apply to a warrant granted under this subsection as they apply to a warrant granted under subsection (1) of the said section 66.

(6) A child shall not be kept in a place of safety in accordance with a warrant granted under subsection (5) above where the Principal Reporter, having regard to the welfare of the child, considers that, whether as a result of a change in the circumstances of the case or of further information relating to the case having been received by the Principal Reporter—

(a) the conditions mentioned in section 66(2) of this Act are no longer satisfied in relation to the child; or

(b) the child is not in need of compulsory measures of supervision,

and where he does so consider he shall give notice to that effect to the person who is keeping the child in that place in accordance with the warrant.

DEFINITIONS

"child": s.93(2)(b).
"children's hearing": s.93(1).
"compulsory measures of supervision": s.93(1).
"constable": s.93(1).
"place of safety": s.93(1).
"principal reporter": s.93(1).

GENERAL NOTE

There was no provision analogous to this section in the 1968 Act, but it does replace those parts of s.296 of the Criminal Procedure (Scotland) Act 1975 (c. 21) that are repealed in Sched. 5 below. The aim is clearly to gather together as many as possible of the statutory provisions dealing with the reporter's duties to arrange children's hearings, but this provision significantly alters the rules previously contained in s.296 and produces in their place one of the most peculiar provisions in the present Act. The section was introduced into the Act at a late stage in the parliamentary process (the Report stage in the House of Lords, a fortnight before the Bill received the Royal Assent: see *Hansard*, H.L. Vol. 565, col. 1203) and, like other provisions in that category (see for example the disastrously drafted s.67 below), the lack of proper parliamentary scrutiny is quite apparent.

A child may come to the attention of the reporter as being potentially in need of compulsory measures of supervision not only by the provision of information under s.53 above, but also by being informed that the child is in a place of safety after having been apprehended by the police and detained in a place of safety in terms of s.296(2) of the Criminal Procedure (Scotland) Act 1975. The present section provides that in such circumstances a children's hearing must be arranged to determine whether the child is to continue to be kept in a place of safety and whether the child should be referred to a children's hearing. There are three significant changes to the law. First, the hearing must sit not later than the third day after the reporter receives the relevant information, rather than, as under s.37(4) of the 1968 Act, on the "first lawful day". Secondly, the provision in s.296(4)(c) permitting the child to be detained for up to seven days has not been re-enacted. And thirdly, the hearing which is held not later than the third day is to determine not only whether to grant a warrant to keep the child in a place of safety (as under the old s.37(4)) but also, bizarrely, whether a children's hearing should be arranged to put grounds of referral to the child and parent. In no other situation does the children's hearing have a role in deciding whether a child's case should be referred to a children's hearing, and that is a matter left entirely within the discretion of the reporter (even when the case is referred to her or him by a court under s.54 above). If this was seriously considered an appropriate role for the children's hearing to play, it is surprising that the role is granted only in the highly specialised circumstances governed by the present section.

Subs. (1)

The police are obliged by s.296(3) of the 1975 Act to inform the reporter whenever a child who has been arrested is detained in a place of safety. On being informed that the child is not to be charged with any offence, the reporter must consider whether, in her or his opinion, compulsory measures of supervision are required and must, subject to what is said below, arrange an initial children's hearing. That hearing's role is not to consider the child's case in terms of ss.65–70, but to decide whether a warrant needs to be granted and whether a full children's hearing requires to be arranged.

Unless he considers that compulsory measures of supervision are not required. The emphasis is quite deliberately to the effect that there is an obligation on the reporter to arrange an initial children's hearing, unless she or he is persuaded that compulsory measures are not required. In other words, the obligation exists whenever the reporter either believes that compulsory measures of supervision are required or is not convinced that they are not required.

Subs. (2)

The initial children's hearing arranged under this section must commence on or before the third day after the reporter becomes obliged under subs. (1) above to arrange the hearing. So if the reporter receives the appropriate information on a Monday, the first day after that is the Tuesday and the third day after is the Thursday: the hearing must commence on or before the Thursday. (*Cf.* many other provisions in the Act, *e.g.* s.51(8) and s.68(12), which talk of "within three days" and "the expiry of three days", which goes to the Wednesday rather than "the third day after" which goes to the Thursday).

Shall begin. The reference to a children's hearing "beginning" on a particular day is, in this context, inept. A children's hearing cannot be adjourned overnight (1986 Rules, r.9(2)); rather they can continue a case to another hearing. However, a continuation would not be appropriate in the context of the decisions that the limited hearing under this section must make and would indeed, it is submitted, be incompetent: the hearing that sits no later than the third day must make the two decisions for which the hearing has been arranged. This provision would have been more comprehensible, and more consistent with other provisions in the Act, had it said that the children's hearing will "take place" no later than the third day (*cf.*, for example, s.59(3) above: "A children's hearing ... shall take place on the second working day ...").

Subss. (3) and (4)

If the reporter is of the opinion that the child does not require compulsory measures of supervision, she or he is not obliged to arrange a children's hearing (subs. (1) above), but is obliged to direct that the child no longer be kept in the place of safety to which she or he was taken in pursuance of s.296 of the 1975 Act. If the reporter is of the opinion that the child does or may require compulsory measures of supervision, then the child may be kept in the place of safety until the children's hearing arranged under subs. (1) above commences, that is to say no longer than the third day after the reporter receives the relevant information (see subs. (2) above). If, in breach of the reporter's duty under subs. (1) above, no hearing has been timeously arranged, the child must be released on the third day.

Subs. (5)

This subsection lists the two decisions that the children's hearing arranged under this section must make: they may grant a warrant under para. (a) and they may give a direction under para. (b). Their decision is governed by the welfare principle set out in s.16(1) above. The children's hearing may decide to do neither, or to do both, or to give a direction under para. (b) but not grant a warrant under para. (a); but they cannot, it is submitted, grant a warrant under para. (a) without giving a direction under para. (b).

Grant a warrant. If the hearing are satisfied either (i) that there is reason to believe that the child will not attend any hearing of her or his case or will fail to comply with a requirement to undergo investigation, or (ii) that it is necessary to safeguard or promote her or his welfare that the child be kept in a place of safety, then the hearing may grant a warrant which will have the same effect as one granted under s.66(1) (*i.e.* one granted when the hearing arranged to consider the child's case have directed the reporter to make an application to the sheriff for proof of a ground of referral and the same conditions, in s.66(2), are satisfied).

Subsections (3) to (8) ... shall apply to a warrant granted under this subsection. It is to be noted that the effect of the warrant granted under this subsection is governed only by subss. (3) to (8) of s.66, and that its termination does not activate the sheriff's power to grant an additional warrant under s.67, as he may do at the termination of a warrant granted under s.66.

Direct the Principal Reporter. The second decision the children's hearing must make is whether or not to make a direction to the reporter to arrange a children's hearing under s.65(1) (*i.e.* to put grounds of referral to the child and parent). The hearing should so direct the reporter only when satisfied both that one or more of the grounds of referral in s.52 above has been established and that the child is in need of compulsory measures of supervision. The fact that the child has been arrested will indicate that the child may have committed an offence, and it would be appropriate for the hearing not to direct the reporter to arrange a children's hearing only when satisfied that, even if the ground is accepted or established, no compulsory measures of supervision will be required.

While it can be assumed that a reporter directed by a children's hearing to arrange a children's hearing must do so (though the Act does not actually say this), it is left entirely unclear from the terms of the statute whether the children's hearing are permitted expressly to direct the reporter *not* to arrange a children's hearing and whether the reporter can, in the absence of any direction to do so, nevertheless arrange a children's hearing. The discretion of the reporter has long been seen as an important element in the whole system and it is submitted that the terms of this section should be interpreted to limit that discretion only insofar as absolutely necessary to give effect to its wording. It follows (i) that the reporter retains a discretion to arrange a children's hearing even if the hearing arranged under this section do not direct him to do so, and (ii) that the hearing have no power expressly to direct the reporter not to arrange a children's hearing. The hearing's power under this paragraph is limited to directing the reporter to arrange a hearing or leaving the matter to the discretion of the reporter.

Subs. (6)

If, after having arranged an initial hearing in accordance with subs. (1) above, the reporter comes to the conclusion, due to a change in the child's circumstances or because of new information made available to her or him, that the grounds for granting a warrant to detain the child no longer exist *or* that the child is not in need of compulsory measures of care, the child cannot be kept in a place of safety and the reporter must give notice to that effect to the person keeping the child. It is a flaw in this provision that while the reporter must release the child from a place of safety when she or he comes to the view that compulsory measures of supervision are not necessary in the child's welfare, she or he remains obliged to arrange a children's hearing if the initial hearing, which did not have access to the new information, have so directed.

Business meeting preparatory to children's hearing

Business meeting preparatory to children's hearing

64.—(1) At any time prior to the commencement of proceedings at the children's hearing, the Principal Reporter may arrange a meeting with members of the children's panel from which the children's hearing is to be constituted under section 39(4) of this Act for those proceedings (any such meeting being, in this Part of this Act referred to as a "business meeting").

(2) Where a business meeting is arranged under subsection (1) above, the Principal Reporter shall give notice to the child in respect of whom the proceedings are to be commenced and any relevant person in relation to the child—

(a) of the arrangement of the meeting and of the matters which may be considered and determined by the meeting;

(b) of their right to make their views on those matters known to the Principal Reporter; and

(c) of the duty of the Principal Reporter to present those views to the meeting.

(3) A business meeting, subject to subsection (4) below—

(a) shall determine such procedural and other matters as may be prescribed by rules under subsection (1) of section 42 of this Act by virtue of subsection (2)(a) of that section; and

(b) may give such direction or guidance to the Principal Reporter in relation to the performance of his functions in relation to the proceedings as they think appropriate.

(4) Before a business meeting makes such a determination or gives such direction or guidance to the Principal Reporter, the Principal Reporter shall present, and they shall consider, any views expressed to him by virtue of subsection (2)(b) above.

(5) Subject to any rules made under section 42(1) of this Act by virtue of subsection (2)(a) of that section and with the exception of sections 44 and, as regards any determination made by the business meeting under subsection (3)(a) above, 51, the provisions of this Act which relate to a children's hearing shall not apply to a business meeting.

DEFINITIONS

"child": s.93(2)(b).
"children's hearing": s.93(1).
"principal reporter": s.93(1).
"relevant person": s.93(2)(b).

General Note

It had long been the practice in many panel areas for hearings to discuss, and make determinations on, procedural matters relating to a child's case before the meeting of the hearing was properly constituted with the child and family in attendance. Often such a meeting would make a determination that the child's presence at the proper hearing was unnecessary. Under the 1968 Act such meetings had no place in the statutory framework but, when the matter came to the attention of the court in *Sloan v. B* 1991 SLT 530, their validity received judicial sanction as involving no illegality or unfairness. That sanction was, however, expressly limited to those meetings doing no more than giving guidance to the reporter on such matters as who she or he should invite to the hearing, and the legally efficacious decision on attendance remained to be made and recorded by a properly constituted children's hearing (*per* Lord President Hope at p. 540). The present provision aims to put such meetings on a statutory basis, and to give the child and the parent a chance to express their views. It permits the reporter to arrange what is to be called a "business meeting" at which procedural and other matters can be discussed and determined before the start of the proper children's hearing and permits the child and the parent to make their views known on the matters to be discussed. Such meetings will be much more formal than the arrangements made in the past, where very often a decision would be made by a hearing concerning a case that was due to be considered the next day, and no notice of the fact that such a decision would be considered was given to anyone. It is likely that business meetings will not be arranged terribly frequently, though how useful they are will depend upon the matters they are permitted, by rules to be made, to discuss.

Subs. (1)

The reporter is given a discretion to arrange a business meeting of panel members in order for them to discuss and make decisions upon certain matters relating to the proper running of the full children's hearing when it is convened. The reporter is given no guidance as to when it would be appropriate to arrange such a meeting, and to a large extent this will depend upon the matters which the meeting is permitted to discuss (to be specified by rules made under s.42(1) above).

At any time prior to the commencement of the proceedings. The case of the child must have been referred to a children's hearing under s.65(1) or s.73(8) before a business meeting can be held and it would, it is submitted, be incompetent to hold such a meeting before the reporter has made such a referral.

A meeting with members of the children's panel. The meeting will be between panel members and the reporter. The child and her or his parent or representative will not be present. The panel members who conduct the business meeting need not be the same individuals as those who will constitute the children's hearing when it later meets, but they must be members of the same local authority area panel as that from which those individuals will be chosen. The reporter should always be present, for it is solely in order to guide and direct the reporter that the meeting is being held.

Subs. (2)

Unlike the informal meetings held before the commencement of this Act referred to in the General Note above, business meetings require to be intimated to those who have a right to attend the proper children's hearing. That notice must include intimation of the matters listed here. Rules made by the Secretary of State under s.42(1) above will determine how the views of the child and her or his parent are to be presented to the meeting and (probably) within what timescale the meetings are to be held. The implication is, though it is not stated, that failure to adhere to these requirements will invalidate the meeting (though that will have little practical effect since the proper children's hearing will then be able to make those decisions the meeting would otherwise have made).

Subs. (3)

The matters which are open to be discussed and determined by the business meeting will be specified in rules, but are likely to include decisions concerning the exclusion of any person from a children's hearing (where power to exclude exists), whether to proceed in the absence of any person who ought to but is likely to fail to attend, whether persons who have no absolute right to attend (such as unmarried fathers, grandparents, observers and the like) should be permitted to attend, and other matters relating to the conduct of the proper children's hearing. No dispositive decision will be possible at a business meeting and the purpose will be limited to giving the reporter direction or guidance as to how her or his functions are to be carried out. So, for example, if a business meeting decide to relieve the child of her or his obligation to attend at the proper children's hearing, they can direct the reporter not to arrange for the child to be brought to the hearing (so long as this is done in such a way as protects the child's right to attend if she or he so wishes).

Subs. (4)

If the child or parent has expressed views on the matters they have been informed will be discussed then the reporter must present these views to the meeting.

Subs. (5)

A business meeting is not a children's hearing. It follows that the rules relating to the constitution, conduct and procedure at children's hearings do not apply, subject to the stated exceptions. These are that s.44 above (prohibitions of publications of proceedings) and s.51 (appeals) apply. In relation to appeals it is difficult to see what decisions open to a business meeting could be subject to the appeal provisions in s.51 in any case. Under the 1968 Act there was no appeal from procedural decisions of the children's hearing (see the General Note to s.51(1) above) and the words "any determination made by a business meeting" cannot, it is submitted, grant a right of appeal under s.51 from decisions of such a meeting which, had they been taken by a proper children's hearing, would not be appealable.

The composition of a business meeting is not stated in the Act and the provisions relating to composition of children's hearings do not apply. There is no requirement that the meeting have at least one member of each sex, nor indeed that the meeting have three members: such matters are likely to be dealt with in the rules made by the Secretary of State under s.42(1) above.

Referral to, and disposal of case by, children's hearing

Referral to, and proceedings at, children's hearing

65.—(1) The Principal Reporter shall refer to the children's hearing, for consideration and determination on the merits, the case of any child in respect of whom he is satisfied that—

(a) compulsory measures of supervision are necessary, and

(b) at least one of the grounds specified in section 52(2) of this Act is established;

and he shall state such grounds in accordance with rules made under section 42(1) of this Act by virtue of subsection (2)(c) of that section.

(2) Where a referral is made in respect of a child who is subject to a child protection order made under section 57, and that order is continued under section 59(4) or 60(12)(d), of this Act, the Principal Reporter shall arrange for the children's hearing under subsection (1) above to take place on the eighth working day after the order was implemented.

(3) Where a referral is made in respect of a child who is subject to a supervision requirement, the children's hearing shall, before disposing of the referral in accordance with section 69(1)(b) or (c) of this Act, review that requirement in accordance with subsections (9) to (12) of section 73 of this Act.

(4) Subject to subsections (9) and (10) below, it shall be the duty of the chairman of the children's hearing to whom a child's case has been referred under subsection (1) above to explain to the child and the relevant person, at the opening of proceedings on the referral, the grounds stated by the Principal Reporter for the referral in order to ascertain whether these grounds are accepted in whole or in part by them.

(5) Where the chairman has given the explanation required by subsection (4) above and the child and the relevant person accept the grounds for the referral, the children's hearing shall proceed in accordance with section 69 of this Act.

(6) Where the chairman has given the explanation required by subsection (4) above and the child and the relevant person accept the grounds in part,

the children's hearing may, if they consider it appropriate to do so, proceed in accordance with section 69 of this Act with respect to those grounds which are accepted.

(7) Where the chairman has given the explanation required under subsection (4) above and either or both of the child and the relevant person—

(a) do not accept the grounds for the referral; or

(b) accept the grounds in part, but the children's hearing do not consider it appropriate to proceed with the case under subsection (6) above,

the hearing shall either direct the Principal Reporter to make an application to the sheriff for a finding as to whether such grounds for the referral as are not accepted by the child and the relevant person are established or shall discharge the referral.

(8) Subject to subsection (10) below, it shall be the duty of the chairman to explain to the child and to the relevant person the purpose for which the application to the sheriff is being made and to inform the child that he is under an obligation to attend the hearing before the sheriff.

(9) Where a children's hearing are satisfied that the child—

(a) for any reason will not be capable of understanding the explanation of the grounds for the referral required under subsection (4) above; or

(b) has not understood an explanation given under that subsection,

they shall either direct the Principal Reporter to make an application to the sheriff for a finding as to whether any of the grounds of the referral are established or discharge the referral.

(10) The acceptance by the relevant person of the grounds of the referral shall not be a requirement for a children's hearing proceeding under this section to consider a case where that person is not present.

DEFINITIONS
"child": s.93(2)(b).
"child protection order": ss.57(1), 93(1).
"compulsory measures of supervision": s.93(1).
"principal reporter": s.93(1).
"relevant person": s.93(2)(b).
"working day": s.93(1).

GENERAL NOTE
Sections 65 to 73 substantially tidy up the provisions they replace in the 1968 Act, though the changes in the law are neither numerous nor fundamental. The rules now contained in the present section were mostly to be found in the old s.42(1) (2) (3) (7) and (8), and the changes here are almost entirely terminological. The section deals with the referral by the reporter of the child's case to a children's hearing and the procedure for establishing whether or not the grounds of referral are accepted.

Subs. (1)
The reporter is obliged under s.56 above to determine, upon receipt of information concerning a child, whether a children's hearing requires to be arranged, and the present subsection obliges her or him to refer the case to a children's hearing when satisfied that compulsory measures of supervision are necessary and that at least one of the grounds of referral exists. The second limb of that test is redundant since the question of whether compulsory measures of supervision are necessary does not arise unless one or more of the grounds of referral exists (s.51(1) above). Nevertheless, the wording of this subsection serves to emphasise that the existence of the ground alone is not sufficient to create an obligation on the reporter to refer the case to a children's hearing. That obligation arises only when, in addition to the existence of the ground, the reporter is satisfied that compulsory measures of supervision are necessary in the interests of the child. The reporter may quite validly take the view that, while a ground exists (*e.g.* an isolated incident of shoplifting, or the kidnapping and abusing of a child of caring parents by a stranger) there is no necessity for the imposition of compulsory measures of supervision: in these circumstances, the reporter must proceed in accordance with s.56(4) and (5) above. If,

however, she or he is satisfied that compulsory measures of supervision are necessary, then the grounds must be stated in accordance with the rules, and the case referred to a children's hearing.

Subs. (2)

The reporter is also obliged to arrange a children's hearing whenever a child has been made subject to a child protection order under s.57 which is still effective on the eighth working day after its implementation. The nature of the obligation is to act as under subs. (1) above, that is to state grounds in accordance with the rules and to refer the case to a children's hearing. One major difference between this subsection and subs. (1) above is that here there is a strict time-table to be adhered to, and the children's hearing must take place on the eighth working day after the order was implemented.

The eighth working day. It would be incompetent for a children's hearing to take place before the eighth working day, even when this is practicable (though it would be so only when there is no application made to the sheriff to recall the child protection order under s.60(7) above) and any purported decision would be of no legal effect. "Working day" is defined in s.93(1) below to exclude Saturdays and Sundays, and December 25 and 26, and January 1 and 2. It follows that the children's hearing are obliged to sit on a day anything between 10 and 16 days after the implementation of the child protection order, depending upon (i) the day of the week it was implemented, and (ii) whether or not the specified holidays interrupt the running of the eight days.

Implemented. On implementation of a child protection order, see the notes to s.59(5) above.

Subs. (3)

It often happens that the reporter feels obliged to state grounds in respect of a child who is already subject to a supervision requirement, for example because new grounds evidence a deteriorating situation or indicate that the existing measures of supervision are not, or are no longer, appropriate. If that occurred under the 1968 Act then a child could find her or himself subject to two supervision requirements, for there was no provision requiring the original supervision requirement to be reviewed when new grounds were accepted or established and that would only be done if a review were due or had been called by a person able to call for it. This subsection is designed to avoid such untidiness by providing that whenever a children's hearing is arranged to put new grounds of referral to a child who is already subject to compulsory measures of supervision, the existing supervision requirement must be reviewed at the same time.

Before disposing of the referral. The "referral" means referral both in respect of a consideration of the new ground and a review of the current supervision requirement. The review of that requirement can take place at any time before the referral is finally disposed of, and there is no requirement that the review be conducted and determined separately from a consideration of the new grounds. It will normally be best for the children's hearing to look at the child's case as a whole, reviewing the existing supervision requirement as an integral part of their consideration of the new grounds and how to respond to them. The existence of the new grounds may itself justify the continuation or variation of an existing supervision requirement, and that outcome amounts to a disposal of the combined referral. It would be competent to deal with the review separately from a consideration of the new grounds, but this would be appropriate only when the grounds are to be sent to the sheriff for proof and the existing supervision requirement will lapse before the likely date of the hearing of the application before the sheriff. In that case, if the grounds are held established, the hearing arranged to consider and dispose of the case would appear to be obliged by this subsection to review again the current supervision requirement as part of their consideration of how to dispose of the present referral. Though this appears repetitive, it is perfectly appropriate that the final disposal takes account of the efficacy of the existing supervision requirement.

Subs. (4)

This provision replaces s.42(1) of the 1968 Act, and similarly provides that the chairman of the hearing has the duty of explaining to the child and her or his parent the grounds of referral, in order to ascertain whether these grounds are accepted or not. The wording is, however, a little different from the old s.42(1), presumably in an attempt to clarify some of the problematic issues that were identified by the case of *Sloan v. B* 1991 SLT 530.

Subject to subsections (9) and (10) below. The obligation to explain to the child does not apply where the children's hearing are satisfied that the child will not be capable of understanding the explanation (see subs. (9) below), and the obligation to explain to the parent will not apply where the parent has not attended the hearing, in breach of her or his obligation to do so under s.45(8) above (see subs. (10) below).

Explain. The duty of the chairman is not simply to read out the grounds as specified by the reporter, but to explain what these grounds mean. The implicit duty on the chairman is to check that the child and parent understand the nature of the grounds. Not only must the statement of facts be explained, but the statutory ground which the facts are alleged to amount to must be explained.

At the opening of the proceedings on the referral. The old s.42(1) obliged the chairman to explain the grounds "at the commencement of the children's hearing and before proceeding to the consideration of the case". The current wording probably creates the same obligation, but rather less clearly than before indicates that the whole proceedings are made up of various different parts: explanation of the grounds (required here), consideration of the case (required in s.69(1) below), and disposal of the referral (dealt with in s.69(2)–(13) and s.70 below). The proceedings still open with an explanation of the grounds and there can be no discussion of the grounds or any other consideration of the child's case until the grounds have been accepted under subs. (5) below or established under s.68(10) below.

In order to ascertain whether the grounds are accepted. The chairman must ask the child and parent to indicate whether they accept the grounds stated by the reporter as true or not.

Subs. (5)
The children's hearing can proceed to a consideration of the case under s.69(1) below only if the child and parent accept at least part of the stated grounds of referral. If the child does not understand the grounds, the hearing's options are listed in subs. (9) below; there is no provision dealing with the parents' lack of understanding but it seems clear that a parent who does not understand an explanation cannot give an acceptance of the ground.

The relevant person. Every relevant person who attends the hearing must be asked whether or not they accept the grounds of referral. The "relevant person" is defined in s.93(2)(b) to be any person who has parental responsibilities or parental rights, however acquired, and any person who ordinarily (other than by reason of employment) has charge of or control over the child. Under the 1968 Act a person who had custody or charge of or control over the child similarly had to accept the grounds of referral but, explicitly, had to be recognised by the children's hearing as having such charge or control. The present s.93(2)(b) requires that "it appears" that the person has charge of or control over the child, and in this context this must mean "it appears to the children's hearing". (In other contexts it must so appear to other persons: see notes to s.45(8) above.)

Subs. (6)
If the child and the parent accept the grounds in part but deny them in part, the children's hearing may proceed with the hearing in respect of the grounds that have been accepted. This might happen either when there are numerous grounds some of which are not accepted, or when the specified ground is accepted subject to alteration (*e.g.* accepting a theft but not of the amount specified, or accepting absence from school but not to the extent specified). So long as there is enough left in the accepted portion to amount to a ground of referral the hearing may proceed.

May proceed. The decision whether to proceed to a consideration of the accepted grounds under s.69, or alternatively to refer the grounds not accepted to the sheriff under subs. (7) below, is to be made by the hearing in the light of the welfare principle contained in s.16(1). It may, for example, be considered detrimental to the child to delay a consideration of her or his case; conversely there are situations in which it would be detrimental to the proper consideration of the child's case not to refer serious grounds to the sheriff.

With respect to those grounds which are accepted. If the children's hearing decide to proceed in respect of the grounds which are accepted, they cannot consider those grounds or portions thereof which have not been accepted in making their dispositive decision. Difficult questions of emphasis may arise if the hearing decide to proceed, for it is permitted to consider the whole of the child's "case", which might well include the fact that allegations have been made but are denied. The proper approach is to hold that any ground or part thereof which is denied and discharged is to be treated as not established fact. For example, a child may be referred to a hearing on the ground that he is beyond parental control and this may be accepted; in addition, there may be a number of offences specified as grounds which the child denies on the basis that while he was present he did not take part in the offences. If the hearing proceeds on the basis that the child is beyond parental control they cannot take into account the fact that offences have been committed, but they can, it is submitted, take into account the fact that the child is associating with persons who lead the child to the attention of the police.

Subs. (7)

This provision replaces the old s.42(2) of the 1968 Act. It provides that where either the child or the parent or both deny the grounds, or deny part thereof and the hearing consider that they cannot proceed on that basis, then the hearing have two options: they may either discharge the referral in whole, or they may direct the reporter to apply to the sheriff for a finding as to whether the grounds not accepted are made out. One of the difficulties facing children's hearings is that this decision has to be made only on the basis of the reports already presented to them. No discussion is permitted with the family in order to assist the hearing in determining which option is more appropriate, but the welfare principle in s.16(1), as always, governs the decision.

Either or both. Before the hearing can proceed in terms of s.69 the child and all the relevant persons must accept the grounds, and if any denies that they exist the hearing cannot proceed. On the "relevant person", see General Note to subs. (5) above.

Subs. (8)

This replaces part of the old s.42(3) of the 1968 Act, with no substantive change in the law. If the children's hearing decide to refer grounds to the sheriff for proof, either because they have been denied under subs. (7) above or because they are not understood by the child under subs. (9) below, the chairman of the hearing must explain to the child and the parent the purpose of the sheriff court hearing. It must also be explained to the child that she or he has an obligation (under s.68(4) below) to attend the hearing before the sheriff.

Subs. (9)

This replaces s.42(7) of the 1968 Act, with a change in wording, but little change in effect. Under the old law the wording suggested that the hearing had in every case to examine the child to determine her or his understanding (though this was not how the provision was normally applied in practice). The new provision reflects reality rather more. It is provided that where the children's hearing are satisfied that the child either will not be capable of understanding the explanation of the grounds or has not understood that explanation, they must either discharge the referral or direct the reporter to apply to the sheriff court for proof. That decision is, of course, governed by the welfare principle in s.16(1) above.

Children's hearing are satisfied. Though the obligation to explain the grounds of referral rests with the chairman of the children's hearing, the assessment that the child will not understand or has not understood the explanation is one to be made by the hearing as a whole, and in cases of disagreement amongst the hearing members a majority decision is sufficient. That decision is one of fact and not, therefore, one to which the welfare test in s.16(1) applies. Not being a dispositive decision, it is not appealable under s.51 above.

Will not be capable. In many cases the age of the child will make this quite obvious: a baby or toddler will clearly not understand any explanation. The wording suggests (as the 1968 Act did not) that the chairman is under no obligation to attempt an explanation in these circumstances, and this is confirmed by subs. (4) above (duty to explain) which is expressly made subject to the present subsection. It should be noted that it is not a ground in itself for relieving a child of the obligation to attend under s.45(2) above that the child will not understand the grounds of referral (though this, in addition to some other factor, may well indicate that it would be detrimental to the child's interests to attend): rather, the present provision simply means that the chairman is relieved of the obligation in subs. (4) above to attempt an explanation when the child obviously will not understand.

Has not understood. This provision can be relied upon only when an attempt has been made by the chairman to explain the grounds, but the hearing as a whole are satisfied that the attempt has failed. Whenever an application is made to the sheriff on the basis of this subsection it should be made plain which paragraph the children's hearing are relying upon to justify the application (*cf. Sloan v. B* 1991 SLT 530).

Subs. (10)

This replaces, with no substantive change, s.42(8) of the 1968 Act, though its wording is possibly not very apt. A children's hearing does not consider the case under this section, but under s.69. Nevertheless the purpose of the provision is clear. Parents have a duty to attend at all stages of a children's hearing and failure to do so can be a criminal offence (see s.45(8) and (9) above). It often happens however that parents do not attend and there is no power under the Act to bring them before a hearing. This subsection allows a hearing to go ahead even in the absence of parents who have breached their obligation to attend, by providing that if they do not attend their acceptance of the grounds of referral specified by the reporter is not required before the hearing can proceed to a consideration of the case. It is to be noted that this subsection is limited in its terms to "the relevant person", and the requirement of the child's acceptance of the grounds is not affected by the absence of the child. If the child is not present there can be no acceptance and the case must either be discharged or referred to the sheriff as under subs. (7) above, or rescheduled to allow for the child's attendance.

Warrant to keep child where children's hearing unable to dispose of case

66.—(1) Without prejudice to any other power enjoyed by them under this Part of this Act and subject to subsection (5) below, a children's hearing—

(a) arranged to consider a child's case under this Part of this Act; and

(b) unable to dispose of the case,

may, if they are satisfied that one of the conditions mentioned in subsection (2) below is met, grant a warrant under this subsection.

(2) The conditions referred to in subsection (1) above are–

(a) that there is reason to believe that the child may—

(i) not attend at any hearing of his case; or

(ii) fail to comply with a requirement under section 69(3) of this Act; or

(b) that it is necessary that the child should be kept in a place of safety in order to safeguard or promote his welfare.

(3) A warrant under subsection (1) above may require any person named in the warrant—

(a) to find and to keep or, as the case may be, to keep the child in a place of safety for a period not exceeding twenty-two days after the warrant is granted;

(b) to bring the child before a children's hearing at such times as may be specified in the warrant.

(4) A warrant under subsection (1) above may contain such conditions as appear to the children's hearing to be necessary or expedient, and without prejudice to that generality may—

(a) subject to section 90 of this Act, require the child to submit to any medical or other examination or treatment; and

(b) regulate the contact with the child of any specified person or class of persons.

(5) Subject to subsection (8) below, at any time prior to its expiry, a warrant granted under this section may, on an application to the children's hearing, on cause shown by the Principal Reporter, be continued in force, whether with or without variation of any condition imposed by virtue of subsection (4) above, by the children's hearing for such further period, not exceeding twenty-two days, as appears to them to be necessary.

(6) Where a children's hearing are satisfied that either of the criteria specified in section 70(10) of this Act are satisfied, they may order that, pending the disposal of his case, the child shall be liable to be placed and kept in secure accommodation within a residential establishment at such times as the person in charge of that establishment, with the agreement of the chief social work officer of the relevant local authority, considers necessary.

(7) Where a children's hearing grant a warrant under subsection (1) above or continue such a warrant under subsection (5) above, they may order that the place of safety at which the child is to be kept shall not be disclosed to any person or class of persons specified in the order.

(8) A child shall not be kept in a place of safety or secure accommodation by virtue of this section for a period exceeding sixty-six days from the day when he was first taken to a place of safety under a warrant granted under subsection (1) above.

DEFINITIONS
"chief social work officer": s.93(1).
"child": s.93(2)(b).
"children's hearing": s.93(1).
"place of safety": s.93(1).
"principal reporter": s.93(1).
"relevant local authority": s.93(1).
"residential establishment": s.93(1).
"secure accommodation": s.93(1).

GENERAL NOTE

A child whose case has been referred to a children's hearing has an obligation to attend that hearing (s.45(1) above), and if it appears that the child might not attend (or has failed to attend) a warrant can be issued under s.45(4) (or s.45(5)) to secure her or his attendance. This section allows a warrant to be granted when a children's hearing has been held with the child in attendance but for some other reason no disposal can be made. Such a warrant can be granted either to ensure the attendance of the child at a hearing or to ensure the child's attendance at some investigative clinic or hospital, or to ensure the child's safety in the meantime. The section replaces the provisions in s.40(7)–(8B) of the 1968 Act, and it contains some important tightening and tidying of the old rules. The makeup of this section is confusing and appears to overlap with certain other provisions, and for that reason must be read strictly and in the light of these other provisions. Subsection (1) sets out the circumstances in which the warrant may be granted, subs. (2) lays down the conditions for its granting, subs. (3) describes its effect, subs. (5) permits it to be continued, and subs. (8) limits the total length of time the child can be kept in a place of safety under a warrant granted under this section to 66 days.

Subs. (1)

Where a children's hearing has been arranged but that hearing are unable to dispose of the case, they may grant a warrant, if the conditions specified in subs. (2) below are met, and that warrant will be authority to keep the child in a place of safety and to bring the child to a children's hearing. The hearing may (one assumes – *cf.* s.45(5) where the point is made clear) grant such warrant either *ex proprio motu* or on the motion of the reporter.

Without prejudice to any other power. The existence of a power to grant a warrant under this section does not detract from any power to grant a warrant under any other section in Pt. II. Indeed, for reasons which will be explained in the next paragraph, wherever there seems to be a choice of which section to grant a warrant under, the power in this section must give way to the power in that other section.

Unable to dispose of the case. A case is disposed of when the children's hearing makes a dispositive decision, that is to say a decision to impose a supervision requirement or to discharge the referral or, on review, to continue or vary or terminate an existing supervision requirement. If they are unable to make such a decision then they are "unable to dispose of the case" and this section appears to be activated. This can occur when grounds of referral are denied and the hearing decide to direct the reporter to make an application to the sheriff (rather than to discharge the referral) or when the grounds are accepted or established or the case is being reviewed and after a consideration of the case the children's hearing feel that they do not have enough information to make an informed decision. Again, a children's hearing may consider themselves unable to dispose of a case because the child or parent breaches her or his obligation to attend and the hearing consider that attendance necessary for a proper consideration of the case. In all these circumstances, the hearing will be unable to dispose of the case and a warrant under this section might appear to be available. However, if the children's hearing are unable to dispose of the case because the child has failed to attend the hearing, a warrant, which can last a maximum of seven days, can be granted under s.45(5) above and it would, it is submitted, be incompetent to grant a warrant under the present provision (which could last initially for 22 days) due to the child's non-attendance. Also, if the children's hearing are unable to dispose of the case because they feel that they do not have enough information and they continue the case under s.69(2) below, a warrant, which can last for a maximum of 22 days, can be granted under s.69(7) below and it would similarly, it is submitted, be incompetent to grant a warrant under the present provision due to the hearing being continued for further investigation. It follows that a warrant under the present section is available not in all cases in which a children's hearing are unable to dispose of the case, but only when they are unable to do so because the grounds have been denied and they direct the reporter to make an application to the sheriff, or because the parent does not attend and the hearing consider that they cannot properly consider the case without the parent's attendance.

May . . . grant a warrant. The hearing is not obliged to grant a warrant under this section even when the conditions for its granting, set out in subs. (2) below, have been satisfied. The decision is one to which all three overarching principles in s.16 apply: the children's hearing must therefore regard the welfare of the child as their paramount consideration (s.16(1) above), they must take appropriate account of the child's views (s.16(2) and s.16(4)(a)(ii) above), and they must apply the minimum intervention principle (s.16(3) and s.16(4)(a)(ii) above). This last amounts to a presumption that no warrant should be granted, with the result that before granting it the hearing must be persuaded that the warrant is necessary to ensure the child's attendance at the hearing, or at the clinic, hospital or other establishment, or to ensure the child's safety in the meantime.

Subs. (2)

Replacing without substantive change s.40(7) of the 1968 Act, this subsection sets out the conditions, one or other of which must be satisfied before a warrant under subs. (1) above can be granted. These are (a) that the hearing are satisfied that there is reason to believe the child will not attend the next hearing or will fail to comply with a requirement that she or he attend a clinic, hospital, or other establishment for investigation under s.69(3) below, or (b) that it is necessary to safeguard and promote the child's welfare that she or he be kept in a place of safety. A history of non-attendance at children's hearings or at clinics *etc.* for investigation, or a threat by a parent to prevent the child attending at the hearing will usually be sufficient to satisfy (a); some other factor, such as the child's continued dangerous behaviour, or a continued threat to the child's wellbeing, will be necessary to satisfy (b).

Subs. (3)

The warrant granted under subs. (1) above may require a person to do one or other or both of the mentioned acts. The time specified in the warrant for the bringing of the child to a children's hearing may be after the 22 days in which she or he was kept in a place of safety, though in practical terms the hearing will usually be arranged during the child's residence in a place of safety.

Twenty-two days after the warrant is granted. If the warrant is granted on Wednesday June 1, the period will end at midnight on Wednesday June 22. It is to be noted that the 22 days commence when the warrant is granted and not when the child is found or first kept in a place of safety. So if a child is not found until the 21st day after the warrant is granted, she or he can be kept only for one further day (during which time, of course, the warrant may be continued under subs. (5) below).

Subs. (4)

The warrant can contain such conditions as the children's hearing think necessary or expedient. They may require the child to submit to any medical or other examination or treatment, though that examination or treatment cannot be carried out if a child who has capacity to do so under s.2(4) of the Age of Legal Capacity (Scotland) Act 1991 refuses to submit; and they may regulate the contact that the child is to have with any other person while the child is being kept in the place of safety.

Subs. (5)

A warrant granted by a children's hearing under subs. (1) above allows a child to be kept in a place of safety for a maximum period of 22 days. The present subsection allows that warrant to be continued by the children's hearing, with or without variation, for a further period of 22 days.

Subject to subsection (8) below. Subsection (8) provides that a child can be kept (under this section) for no longer than 66 days, with the result that the children's hearing can continue a warrant granted under this section only twice (or such number of times as does not exceed the limit).

At any time prior to its expiry. A warrant can be continued on any date before the expiry of the original 22 days, and the continuation will last for a maximum of 22 days from the date of continuation.

On cause shown. The reporter has the onus of showing why an application to continue the warrant should be granted by the hearing. This will be satisfied by showing that one of the conditions for its granting (in subs. (2) above) still exists and that it is in the interests of the child to remain in a place of safety; in addition an explanation as to why the case has not advanced ought to be given by the reporter. All three overarching principles in s.16 apply to decisions to continue warrants under this subsection.

Such further period … as appears to them to be necessary. While the warrant will normally permit the keeping of a child for up to 22 days, there is no reason why the hearing should not specify a shorter period, if this is appropriate in the child's interests.

Subs. (6)

In cases in which a children's hearing are satisfied that the conditions for authorising the child to be kept in secure accommodation (listed in s.70(10) below) are satisfied, the hearing may authorise the child to be kept there. As under s.70(9), the children's hearing do not order that the child be kept in secure accommodation, rather they merely authorise that this can be done if the chief social worker of the relevant local authority considers it necessary. The authorisation under this subsection cannot stand alone and it must be given in connection with a warrant under subs. (1) above: this is implicit from the wording of subs. (8) below which provides that a child may not be kept in a place of safety or in secure accommodation for more than 66 days after being taken to a place of safety under a warrant granted under subs. (1) above.

Subs. (7)

The children's hearing can order that the child's whereabouts not be disclosed to any named person or class of person. This is an important new power, which is also to be found in s.69(10), s.70(6) and s.73(11), and is designed as a protective measure. A children's hearing ought not to make an order under this subsection (or those other subsections) unless they are satisfied that there is a real need for it, that is to say that there is a realistic threat to the child's wellbeing from the named person or class of person.

Subs. (8)

This subsection does not do what it appears, at first sight, to do. It does not provide that a child must be released from a place of safety or secure accommodation having been kept there for a period of 66 days. Rather, all it does is to limit the power of the children's hearing to keep a child in a place of safety to 66 days. The child may be kept there for longer than 66 days if a sheriff at the end of the 66 days grants a warrant under s.67 below: and no limit is expressed on the number of times a warrant can be granted under that section.

Warrant for further detention of child

67.—(1) Where a child is being kept in a place of safety by virtue of a warrant granted under section 66 of this Act or under this subsection, the Principal Reporter at any time prior to the expiry of that warrant may apply to the sheriff for a warrant to keep the child in that place after the warrant granted under the said section 66 or, as the case may be, this subsection has expired.

(2) A warrant under subsection (1) above shall only be granted on cause shown and—

(a) shall specify the date on which it will expire; and

(b) may contain any such requirement or condition as may be contained in a warrant granted under the said section 66.

(3) Where the sheriff grants a warrant under subsection (1) above, he may also make an order under this subsection in such terms as are mentioned in subsection (6) or (7) of the said section 66; and any order under this subsection shall cease to have effect when the warrant expires.

(4) An application under subsection (1) above may be made at the same time as, or during the hearing of, an application which the Principal Reporter has been directed by a children's hearing to make under section 65(7) or (9) of this Act.

DEFINITIONS
    "child": s.93(2)(b).
    "children's hearing": s.93(1).
    "place of safety": s.93(1).
    "principal reporter": s.93(1).

GENERAL NOTE

This is another provision that was added into the Act at a very late stage (the Report stage in the House of Lords on July 5, 1995: see *Hansard*, H.L. Vol. 565, col. 1206), and like others in that category would have greatly benefited (as very many other provisions did) from further consideration before enactment.

Under the 1968 Act, warrants issued by a children's hearing under s.40(7) could last for 21 days and could be renewed under s.40(8) *once* by the children's hearing for a further 21 days, after which a sheriff could issue a warrant on similar terms under s.40(8A) for a further 21 days, after which the sheriff could renew his warrant *once* under s.40(8B) for a further 21 days: the result was that a child could never be kept in a place of safety under these various provisions for any longer than 84 days. These provisions have been somewhat modified by this and the immediately preceding section. Under s.66 above, a children's hearing can grant a warrant and continue it for such periods as do not exceed 66 days; under this section the sheriff can, on the expiry of the hearing's warrant, grant a warrant whose length we are not told and he can grant a further, unspecified, number of warrants thereafter.

Subs. (1)

If a child has been kept in a place of safety under a warrant granted under s.66 above (that is to say granted when the children's hearing have been unable to dispose of the case because they have directed the reporter to make an application for proof of a ground of referral to the sheriff) and that warrant is about to expire, the reporter can apply to the sheriff for a warrant under this section to keep the child where she or he is after the warrant granted by the children's hearing has expired.

At any time prior to the expiry of that warrant. An application to the sheriff under this section can be made at any time before the warrant granted by the children's hearing has expired, and this will include a time prior to any continuation of a warrant granted by the children's hearing. In other words, the reporter may, a few days after the initial granting of a warrant by a children's hearing under s.66(1) above, apply to the sheriff for a warrant, without again applying to the children's hearing for a continuation of their warrant under s.66(5) above. He must, however, show cause to the sheriff, and there will normally be good cause for bypassing the children's hearing in this manner only when subs. (4) below applies.

By virtue of a warrant granted ... under this subsection. A warrant granted under this subsection will expire when the sheriff says it will expire, and these words allow the reporter to apply to the sheriff for another warrant under this subsection whenever a previous warrant granted under this subsection is about to expire. There is a noticeable lack of any provision, such as was contained in s.40(8B) of the 1968 Act, that the sheriff can renew the warrant (or grant another warrant) "on one occasion only", and it would appear from that omission that the sheriff can grant as many warrants as he thinks fit. Reference should, however, be made to s.16(1) above, under which the child's welfare must be the sheriff's paramount consideration – it will seldom be in the child's interests to be kept in a place of safety, waiting to be brought to a children's hearing, for even as long as 66 days. In addition, the other two overarching principles in s.16 also apply to the sheriff's decision whether to grant a warrant under this subsection.

Subs. (2)

On cause shown. The reporter must show to the sheriff cause why a warrant ought to be granted by the sheriff under this section. Though it does not say so, it is submitted that an essential part of that cause must be the continued satisfaction of the conditions listed in s.66(2) for the granting of a warrant under s.66(1) above, for it is only after a warrant granted under that provision has ceased to have effect that this section comes into operation. Because the sheriff is obliged to regard the child's welfare as his paramount consideration (see General Note to subs. (1) above) it must be shown to his satisfaction that it is less detrimental to the child to be kept waiting for this length of time than to be released home. In addition, the reporter is probably also obliged to explain to the sheriff why the case has not advanced sufficiently after 66 days to allow the child to be brought before a children's hearing to consider her or his case.

Shall specify the date on which it will expire. These words appear to give the sheriff an unlimited discretion in specifying how long the warrant he grants under subs. (1) above will last, though because he must specify a date he cannot let it last indefinitely. There is no provision, as there is in s.66(3) above, that the warrant shall authorise the keeping of a child in a place of safety "for a period not exceeding 22 days after the warrant is granted" (and as there was in s.40(8A) of the 1968 Act). As such, this provision is unique in the Act, for every other provision in which either a children's hearing or a court can grant a warrant or make an order to detain a child is expressly made subject to strict and very clearly defined time-limits. This oversight would surely not have been made had this whole section been introduced into the Act at a much earlier stage, when its proper integration with s.66 above (upon which it is dependent) could have been assured.

May contain any such requirement or condition. Section 66(4) allows a warrant to contain such conditions as appear to be necessary or expedient, and in particular may require the child to submit to medical or other examination or treatment (see notes to s.66(4) above) and may regulate contact between the child and any other person. The sheriff must regard the child's welfare as his paramount consideration when deciding whether to make any such requirement or condition (s.16(1)), he must have regard to any views expressed by the child (s.16(2)), and he must not make any such requirement or condition unless persuaded that it is better for him to do so than not to do so (s.16(3)).

Subs. (3)

If a warrant is granted under this section the sheriff is able to order that the child be liable to be kept in secure accommodation, or that the address of the child be kept secret from any specified person or specified class of person (or, presumably, both). Such orders cease to have effect when the warrant the sheriff grants ceases to have effect.

Subs. (4)
   The usual case in which a warrant will be granted by a children's hearing under s.66 above is when they have directed the reporter to apply to the sheriff for proof of a ground of referral. Once that application has been heard by the sheriff the reporter will arrange a children's hearing to consider the child's case, but it might sometimes remain necessary to keep the child in a place of safety after the sheriff's decision until the hearing sits. If that is so, the reporter can apply to the sheriff for a warrant under this section in the same proceedings as those in which the ground of referral is sought to be proved. This is the situation (referred to in the General Note to subs. (1) above) in which it might be appropriate for the reporter to bypass the children's hearing and seek a warrant from a sheriff even before the power of the children's hearing under s.66 above to grant a warrant has been exhausted. A reporter can apply to the sheriff for a warrant under this provision only when the child is currently in a place of safety (for otherwise subs. (1) above does not apply), and it follows that a child who has been at home until the sheriff court hearing cannot be taken to a place of safety thereafter under this provision (the appropriate provision to deal with that situation is s.68(10)(b) below).

Application to sheriff to establish grounds of referral

   68.—(1) This section applies to applications under subsections (7) and (9) of section 65 of this Act and a reference in this section (except in subsection (8)) to "an application" is a reference to an application under either of those subsections.
   (2) An application shall be heard by the sheriff within twenty-eight days of its being lodged.
   (3) Where one of the grounds for the referral to which an application relates is the condition referred to in section 52(2)(i)—
   (a) the application shall be made to the sheriff who would have jurisdiction if the child were being prosecuted for that offence; and
   (b) in hearing the application in relation to that ground, the standard of proof required in criminal proceedings shall apply.
   (4) A child shall—
   (a) have the right to attend the hearing of an application; and
   (b) subject to subsection (5) below, be under an obligation to attend such hearing;
and without prejudice to the right of each of them to be legally represented, the child and the relevant person may be represented by a person other than a legally qualified person at any diet fixed by the sheriff for the hearing of the application.
   (5) Without prejudice to subsection (4)(a) above, the sheriff may dispense with the obligation imposed by subsection (4)(b) above where he is satisfied—
   (a) in an application in which the ground of referral to be established is a condition mentioned in section 52(2)(d), (e), (f) or (g) of this Act, that the obligation to attend of the child is not necessary for the just hearing of that application; and
   (b) in any application, that it would be detrimental to the interests of the child for him to be present at the hearing of the application.
   (6) Where the child fails to attend the hearing of an application at which his attendance has not been dispensed with under subsection (5) above, the sheriff may grant an order to find and keep the child; and any order under this subsection shall be authority for bringing the child before the sheriff and, subject to subsection (7) below, for keeping him in a place of safety until the sheriff can hear the application.
   (7) The child shall not be kept in a place of safety by virtue of subsection (6) above after whichever is the earlier of—
   (a) the expiry of fourteen days beginning with the day on which the child is found; or
   (b) the disposal of the application by the sheriff.
   (8) Where in the course of the hearing of an application—

(a) under section 65(7) of this Act, the child and the relevant person accept any of the grounds for referral to which the application relates, the sheriff shall; or

(b) under section 65(9) of this Act, the relevant person accepts any of the grounds for referral to which the application relates, the sheriff may, if it appears to him reasonable to do so,

dispense with the hearing of evidence relating to that ground and deem the ground to be established for the purposes of the application, unless he is satisfied that, in all the circumstances of the case, the evidence should be heard.

(9) Where a sheriff decides that none of the grounds for referral in respect of which an application has been made are established, he shall dismiss the application, discharge the referral to the children's hearing in respect of those grounds and recall, discharge or cancel any order, warrant, or direction under this Chapter of this Act which relates to the child in respect of those grounds.

(10) Where the sheriff, after the hearing of any evidence or on acceptance in accordance with subsection (8) above, finds that any of the grounds for the referral to which the application relates is, or should be deemed to be, established—

(a) he shall remit the case to the Principal Reporter to make arrangements for a children's hearing to consider and determine the case; and

(b) he may if he is satisfied that—

(i) keeping the child in a place of safety is necessary in the child's best interests; or

(ii) there is reason to believe that the child will run away before the children's hearing sit to consider the case,

issue an order requiring, subject to subsection (12) below, that the child be kept in a place of safety until the children's hearing so sit.

(11) An order issued under subsection (10) above may, if the sheriff is satisfied that either of the criteria mentioned in section 70(10) of this Act is fulfilled, provide that the child shall be liable to be placed and kept in secure accommodation within a residential establishment at such times as the person in charge of the establishment, with the agreement of the chief social work officer of the relevant local authority, considers necessary.

(12) A child shall not be kept in a place of safety by virtue of subsection (10)(b) above after whichever is the earlier of the following—

(a) the expiry of three days beginning with the day on which he is first so kept; or

(b) the consideration of his case by the children's hearing arranged under subsection (10)(a) above.

DEFINITIONS
"chief social work officer": s.93(1).
"child": s.93(2)(b).
"children's hearing": s.93(1).
"place of safety": s.93(1).
"principal reporter": s.93(1).
"relevant person": s.93(2)(b).

GENERAL NOTE
This section replaces s.42(3)–(6A) of the 1968 Act, with amendments in format but little substantive change. It deals with the procedure for applying to the sheriff for proof of grounds of referral, and with the sheriff's powers in dealing with such applications.

Subs. (1)
The section deals with applications made by the reporter at the direction of the children's hearing because the grounds of referral explained to the child and parent have not been accepted (s.65(7) above) by one or both, or will not be or have not been understood by the child (s.65(9) above) and the hearing have not considered it appropriate to discharge the referral.

Subs. (2)

The rules provide (r.4(1) of the 1971 Rules) that the reporter must lodge an application with the sheriff clerk within seven days of being directed to do so by the children's hearing, and, once lodged, this subsection lays down the time-limit for the hearing of the application by the sheriff. The Act does not specify what happens if the application is not heard within the 28 days, though it is understood that both the application and the referral to the children's hearing will fall in that eventuality.

Shall be heard. All that is required is that the hearing before the sheriff be commenced within 28 days rather than commenced and completed.

By the sheriff. The application will be heard by the sheriff in chambers: s.93(5) below.

Subs. (3)

Cases in which the ground of referral is that the child has committed a criminal offence are treated rather differently in a number of respects from all other cases (see General Note to s.52(2) above). This subsection provides a special jurisdictional rule for such cases, to the effect that the sheriff must hear the case who would have jurisdiction were the child being prosecuted for the offence. In addition, it is provided here that the standard of proof required is proof beyond reasonable doubt (rather than, as with all other grounds, the balance of probabilities). This is the only ground in which this standard applies, notwithstanding that other grounds may involve establishment of the commission of a criminal offence (*McGregor v. D* 1977 SLT 182; *Harris v. F* 1991 SLT 242). An application can be heard by the sheriff which covers a number of different grounds of referral at the same time, including that under s.52(2)(i) and other paragraphs of s.52(2).

Subs. (4)

A child has both the right and the obligation to attend the hearing before the sheriff, and if that obligation is breached an order may be granted under subs. (6) below for her or his finding and keeping in a place of safety. Both the child and the parent can be legally represented, and they may be represented by a person other than a legally qualified person: this gives them an equal right to the reporter, who may have a right of audience even when not legally qualified (see s.40(4) above). Since this section only applies to applications under s.65(7) or s.65(9) (see subs. (1) above) it follows that in applications to review the evidence under s.85 below, the child has neither right nor obligation to attend at the rehearing under that section.

Subs. (5)

Reflecting the power of the children's hearing to relieve the child of the obligation to attend the hearing under s.45(2) above, this subsection permits the sheriff to relieve the child of the obligation to attend the hearing of the application by the reporter to establish grounds of referral. The same considerations as apply to s.45(2) apply here, and the notes to that subsection should be referred to. The wording in para. (a) here is, rather untidily, different from the wording in para. (a) of s.45(2), in that there the reference is to a case involving a Sched. 1 offence while here the reference is to specific grounds (each of which involves a Sched. 1 offence). It is possible to interpret s.45(2)(a) to include a ground under s.52(2)(i), which is not mentioned here, where the child has committed a Sched. 1 offence, but apart from that the two provisions apply in the same circumstances and are to be interpreted in the same way. However, the purposes of the two processes (the court hearing evidence and the children's hearing considering the child's case) are different and it is clearly possible to envisage a case in which the child might properly be excused from the hearing of the evidence but not the consideration of her or his case (or vice versa).

Subss. (6) and (7)

If the child breaches her or his obligation to attend the sheriff court hearing, the sheriff may grant an order to find the child and keep her or him in a place of safety until the sheriff can hear the application. The decision to grant such an order is one to which the welfare principle in s.16(1) applies. A child kept in a place of safety under such an order must be released from that place on the earlier of either the expiry of 14 days after being taken there or the disposal of the application by the sheriff. There is no provision for the renewal of this order. This ensures that the hearing of the evidence takes place as soon after the child has been found as possible.

Expiry of 14 days beginning with the day on which the child is found. The day on which the child is found is the first day, and she or he must be released before the end of the 14th day.

Subs. (8)

This provision replaces s.42(6A) of the 1968 Act. It provides that the sheriff has the power to dispense with the hearing of evidence as to whether the ground is established and, instead of making a finding to that effect from the evidence, he is entitled to deem the ground to be established. Altering the previous law, the sheriff is *obliged* to dispense with hearing evidence where the child and the parent, who at the children's hearing denied the grounds of referral, now accept them; and, reflecting the previous law, the sheriff *may* dispense with hearing evidence if the child could not, or did not, understand the explanation of the grounds and the parent accepts the grounds. In either case he may hear evidence if in all the circumstances of the case he is satisfied that evidence should be heard.

In the course of the hearing. The sheriff can make his determination to dispense with evidence at any time, whether before any evidence is led or (in cases to which para. (b) applies) while evidence is being led. A parent who denied grounds before the hearing may, for example, accept the grounds when it is explained by the sheriff what it is that is being accepted or when she or he realises that the evidence is incontrovertible.

If it appears to him reasonable to do so. If the child could not, or did not, understand the grounds of referral it may be reasonable to dispense with evidence when all the parties who can accept are accepting and there is no-one denying or disputing the grounds. It might not be reasonable if for some reason it is not in the interests of the child that the evidence remains untested. The decision whether to dispense with evidence or to hear it is a decision governed by the welfare principle in s.16(1).

Subs. (9)

Replacing s.42(5) of the 1968 Act, this subsection provides that when the sheriff finds that none of the grounds is established he must discharge the referral and release the child from any order, warrant or direction she or he is subject to which relates to those grounds. The sheriff has no option in this case and cannot, for example, find that other grounds than those relating to the application have been established. If the evidence suggests the existence of other grounds the reporter may state these new grounds and arrange a children's hearing under s.65(1) above.

Subs. (10)

Where the sheriff has found the grounds, or any of them, established, or has deemed them to be established under the terms of subs. (8) above, he is obliged to remit the case back to the reporter for the arranging of a children's hearing to consider the child's case under s.66 below. In addition, if he is satisfied that the child's best interests require that she or he be kept in a place of safety or that there is reason to believe that the child will run away before the sitting of the children's hearing, the sheriff may issue an order requiring that the child be kept in a place of safety.

Subs. (11)

If the conditions for keeping the child in secure accommodation (listed in s.70(10) below) are satisfied, the sheriff can attach to an order granted under subs. (10) above an authorisation to keep the child in such accommodation. This does not require that the child be kept there, but authorises it if, in addition, the chief social work officer considers it necessary.

Subs. (12)

An order keeping the child in a place of safety issued by the sheriff, and any authorisation to keep the child in secure accommodation, loses effect at the earlier of (a) the expiry of three days or (b) the consideration of the child's case by the children's hearing.

The expiry of three days. It is to be noted that, in distinction from the provisions in the Act dealing with child protection orders, the time is expressed not in "working days" but simply in days. The first day is the day the child is first kept under the order granted in terms of subs. (10) (which will usually be the day that the order is made); the order ceases to have effect on the expiry of the third day. So for example when a child is first kept under this provision on a Monday the order ceases to have effect at the expiry of the immediately following Wednesday. If a child is first kept under this provision on a Friday the order ceases to have effect at the expiry of the immediately following Sunday.

The consideration of his case. The order expires when the children's hearing first consider the case under s.69 below, and not when the hearing disposes of the case. If the children's hearing decide to continue the hearing the order under this provision will have lapsed, and if the hearing decide that the child still requires to be kept in a place of safety they may grant a warrant to this effect under s.69(7) above.

Continuation or disposal of referral by children's hearing

69.—(1) Where the grounds of referral of the child's case stated by the Principal Reporter are accepted or are established in accordance with section 68 or section 85 of this Act, the children's hearing shall consider those grounds, any report obtained under section 56(7) of this Act and any other relevant information available to them and shall—

(a) continue the case to a subsequent hearing in accordance with subsection (2) below;

(b) discharge the referral of the case in accordance with subsection (12) below; or

(c) make a supervision requirement under section 70 of this Act.

(2) The children's hearing may continue the case to a subsequent hearing under this subsection where they are satisfied that, in order to complete their consideration of the case, it is necessary to have a further investigation of the case.

(3) Where a children's hearing continue the case under subsection (2) above, they may, for the purposes of the investigation mentioned by that subsection, require the child to attend, or reside at, any clinic, hospital or other establishment during a period not exceeding twenty-two days.

(4) Where a child fails to fulfil a requirement made under subsection (3) above, the children's hearing may, either on an application by the Principal Reporter or of their own motion, grant a warrant under this subsection.

(5) A warrant under subsection (4) above shall be authority—

(a) to find the child;

(b) to remove the child to a place of safety and keep him there; and

(c) where the place of safety is not the clinic, hospital or other establishment referred to in the requirement made under subsection (3) above, to take the child from the place of safety to such clinic, hospital or other establishment for the purposes of the investigation mentioned in subsection (2) above.

(6) A warrant under subsection (4) above shall be granted for such period as appears to the children's hearing to be appropriate, provided that no warrant shall permit the keeping of a child in a place of safety after whichever is the earlier of—

(a) the expiry of twenty-two days after the warrant is granted; or

(b) the day on which the subsequent hearing of the child's case by a children's hearing begins.

(7) Where a child's case has been continued under subsection (2) above and the children's hearing are satisfied that—

(a) keeping the child in a place of safety is necessary in the interests of safeguarding or promoting the welfare of the child; or

(b) there is reason to believe that the child may not attend the subsequent hearing of his case,

they may grant a warrant requiring that the child be taken to and kept in a place of safety.

(8) A warrant under subsection (7) above shall cease to have effect on whichever is the earlier of—

(a) the expiry of twenty-two days after the warrant is granted; or

(b) the day on which the subsequent hearing of the child's case by a children's hearing begins.

(9) A warrant under subsection (4) or (7) above may contain such conditions as appear to the children's hearing to be necessary or expedient, and without prejudice to that generality may—

(a) subject to section 90 of this Act, require the child to submit to any medical or other examination or treatment;

(b) regulate the contact with the child of any specified person or class of persons.

(10) Where a child is to be kept at a place of safety under a warrant granted under this section or is to attend, or reside at, any place in accordance with a requirement made under subsection (3) above, the children's hearing may order that such place shall not be disclosed to any person or class of persons specified in the order.

(11) Where a child is to reside in a residential establishment by virtue of a requirement made or warrant granted under this section, the children's hearing may, if satisfied that either of the criteria mentioned in section 70(10) of this Act is fulfilled, order that while the requirement or warrant remains in effect he shall be liable to be placed in secure accommodation within that establishment at such times as the person in charge of the establishment, with the agreement of the chief social work officer of the relevant local authority, considers necessary.

(12) Where a children's hearing decide not to make a supervision requirement under section 70 of this Act they shall discharge the referral.

(13) On the discharge of the referral of the child's case any order, direction, or warrant under Chapter 2, or this Chapter, of this Act in respect of the child's case shall cease to have effect.

DEFINITIONS
"chief social work officer": s.93(1).
"child": s.93(2)(b).
"children's hearing": s.93(1).
"place of safety": s.93(1).
"principal reporter": s.93(1).
"supervision requirement": s.93(1).

GENERAL NOTE
This section deals with matters previously dealt with in s.43 of the 1968 Act. It obliges the children's hearing to consider the case of the child once the grounds of referral have been accepted or established, sets out the options available to the hearing, and governs the procedures to be adopted when the option either of continuing the case or of discharging the referral is chosen.

Subs. (1)
This subsection replaces s.43(1) of the 1968 Act and obliges the children's hearing to consider the child's case once the grounds have been accepted under s.65(5) above, established under s.68(10) above, or established on a review of the evidence under s.85 below. The process of consideration must take into account the grounds of referral, any report and any other relevant information available to the hearing. The test of relevancy of the hearing's consideration is whether the matter is relevant to the question of what course should be taken in the child's best interests and the hearing are not limited to a narrow consideration of the grounds alone (*O. v. Rae* 1993 SLT 570, *per* Lord President Hope at p. 574). The grounds upon which the child has been referred to the hearing are central to the consideration of the case and are always relevant, but there may well be many other additional factors relevant to a determination of what, if any, measures of supervision are in the child's best interests. A child may competently be subject to compulsory measures of supervision which would not be justified simply because of the existence of a ground of referral when there are other significant concerns that do justify them. It is the strength of the system that the existence of a ground of referral merely raises the question of whether compulsory measures of supervision are necessary (s.52(1) above) but does not determine their nature; it is both questions which must be considered by the children's hearing.

Having given consideration to the circumstances of the child's case, the children's hearing must then decide which of the three listed options most appropriately meets the child's needs. These options are as follows. First, the hearing may decide under subs. (2) below to continue the case for further investigation on the basis that they do not have enough information to come to a proper decision. Having chosen this option the hearing can make a requirement under subs. (3) below and enforce it by means of a warrant granted under subs. (4) below; and they can also grant a warrant to ensure the child's safety until the next hearing under subs. (7) below. Secondly, the hearing may decide to discharge the referral under subs. (12) below, in which case any order, direction or warrant issued in respect of the child shall cease to have effect (subs. (13) below). Thirdly the hearing may impose a supervision requirement on the child, in accordance with s.70, considered in detail below.

The decision of which option to choose is one to which all three of the overarching principles in s.16 apply: the children's hearing must regard the child's welfare throughout her or his childhood as paramount, must have regard so far as practicable to the views (if she or he wishes to express them) of the child concerned, and must make no order imposing a supervision requirement or continuing the case or granting a warrant under this section unless they consider that it would be better for the child to do so than to make no order or requirement at all. Decisions are, as always, made on a majority basis, and no decision is made unless it attracts the support of at least two members of the hearing. It is possible that each member of the hearing will decide to do one of the three possibilities listed, in which case no decision has been made. Unless one of the hearing members then wishes to reconsider her or his decision (which is competent if the chairman so permits), the only option is to continue the hearing: there is no provision for the hearing failing to come to a decision and such failure due to disagreement amounts, it is submitted, to an agreement that the hearing must be continued.

Subs. (2)

This provision, repeated from s.43(3) of the 1968 Act, allows the hearing to continue the case to a subsequent hearing if further investigation is necessary. If, but only if, this option is chosen, subss. (3)–(11) below may come into play.

In order to complete their consideration of the case. The hearing's consideration of the case is completed only when they are in a position to make a decision as to what course of action is in the best interests of the child. It follows that a continuation is the proper course when the children's hearing are not in possession of sufficient information, and cannot obtain that information in the course of the current hearing, to make a dispositive decision.

Subs. (3)

Replacing s.43(4) of the 1968 Act, a children's hearing who continue a case under subs. (2) above may require the child to reside in or attend a clinic, hospital or other establishment during a period of not more than 22 days. As explained under subs. (2) above, continuation will be appropriate when further information is required and this subsection can be used only for the gathering of this information. A child may, for example, be required to reside in an assessment centre, or attend an educational psychologist, or even undergo medical examination during the period of continuation. If a requirement is made under this subsection, it may be enforced by means of a warrant granted under subs. (4) below.

During a period not exceeding 22 days. The 22 days start running on the day the investigation commences, which will usually be the day of the hearing which continues the case. If, however, a place at, say, an assessment centre is not available immediately, the 22 days will start running the day the child first attends or resides there.

Subs. (4)

Replacing s.43(5) of the 1968 Act, if a child does not attend or reside for investigation as required under subs. (3) above, a warrant may be granted. The decision is that of the children's hearing, which may make the decision to grant a warrant with or without an application to that effect by the reporter. The warrant under this subsection can, however, only be granted retrospectively, that is after the child has failed to fulfil the requirement, and no warrant can be granted on the basis that the child is likely to fail to fulfil the requirement.

Subs. (5)

This subsection indicates for what the warrant granted under subs. (4) above is authority.

Subs. (6)

There is no limit in time as to how long the warrant can be granted for, though it cannot authorise the keeping of a child in a place of safety for any more than 22 days after the granting of the warrant or after the beginning of the subsequent hearing, whichever is earlier. It is also to be remembered that the requirement to attend or reside at a clinic or hospital cannot exceed 22 days (subs. (3) above), so the warrant to enforce that requirement cannot last beyond the requirement itself.

Subs. (7)

This subsection overlaps the provisions contained in s.66(1) and (2) above, the General Notes to which reference should again be made. Though substantially similar, the main difference between s.66 and the present section is that here the warrant can last a maximum of 22 days and cannot be continued while under s.66 it can, with continuations, last a maximum of 66 days (or even longer if continued by a sheriff under s.67 above). It is therefore important to know under which provision the warrant is granted. As explained in the General Note to s. 66(1) above, that is not immediately clear. Under s.66 a warrant may be granted when the children's hearing are "unable to dispose of the case", while under the present subsection a warrant may be granted when the hearing continue the case under subs. (2) above. The difference lies in the fact that the present provision applies only after a children's hearing have considered the child's case under subs. (1) above and, after that consideration, have determined to continue the case for further investigation under subs. (2) above; s.66, on the other hand, applies when the children's hearing have not yet considered the case (because the grounds are denied or because the parent has not attended). That is not a case of continuation within the terms of subs. (2) above.

The grounds upon which the warrant under this subsection can be granted are specified in paras. (a) and (b): under para. (a) some factor indicating a threat to the child's welfare were she or he not to be kept in a place of safety ought to be shown, and under para. (b) a history of non-attendance will be sufficient as might, for example, a threat by a parent not to bring the child back to the continued hearing.

Subs. (8)

The warrant granted under subs. (7) above ceases to have effect either at the end of 22 days after it was granted or on the day a hearing convenes to consider the continued case. There is no provision for the renewal of a warrant granted under subs. (7) (*cf.* s.66(5) above), which is designed to ensure that a continued hearing takes place within a very short period of time. However, the continued hearing may decide again to continue the case on the ground that the investigations are not yet complete, and the granting of another warrant under subs. (7) above would appear to be competent. Indeed there is no limit to the number of times the hearing can continue the case, though clearly it is not in a child's interests to be kept indefinitely in a place of safety without a substantive decision as to her or his future. It is a flaw in the statute that there is no prohibition on multiple warrants being granted under this section beyond the 66-day period that limits warrants under s.66, though perhaps the real flaw lies in the confusing overlap in these provisions.

Subs. (9)

This is in the same terms as s.66(4) above, and reference should again be made to the notes to that subsection. The power applies whether the warrant is granted under subs. (4) above or subs. (7) above.

Subs. (10)

This provision gives the same power to the children's hearing granting a warrant under subs. (4) or subs. (7) as is contained in s.66(7) above, and reference should be made to the notes to that provision.

Subs. (11)

This is in similar terms to s.66(6) above, and the General Note to that section should again be referred to. It is to be remembered that this subsection is applicable only when the case has been continued, and the authorisation to keep the child in secure accommodation will not last beyond the commencement of the continued hearing or, if earlier, the cessation of the effect of a warrant or requirement under this section.

Subss. (12) and (13)

A children's hearing can make a supervision requirement under s.70 below only when they are satisfied that compulsory measures of supervision are necessary in the interests of the child. If, after a sufficient consideration of the child's case, taking account of the three overarching principles in s.16 above, they are not so satisfied their decision must be not to make a supervision requirement and they are obliged to discharge the referral. On that discharge all warrants to find and keep the child, orders as to assessments and investigations, directions as to contact, and any other order or requirement made under ss.39–85 in respect of the case based on the referral that is discharged, will cease to have effect.

Disposal of referral by children's hearing: supervision requirements, including residence in secure accommodation

70.—(1) Where the children's hearing to whom a child's case has been referred under section 65(1) of this Act are satisfied that compulsory measures of supervision are necessary in respect of the child they may make a requirement under this section (to be known as a "supervision requirement").

(2) A children's hearing, where they decide to make such a requirement, shall consider whether to impose any condition such as is described in subsection (5)(b) below.

(3) A supervision requirement may require the child—

(a) to reside at any place or places specified in the requirement; and

(b) to comply with any condition contained in the requirement.

(4) The place or, as the case may be, places specified in a requirement under subsection (3)(a) above may, without prejudice to the generality of that subsection, be a place or places in England or Wales; and a supervision requirement shall be authority for the person in charge of such a place to restrict the child's liberty to such extent as that person may consider appropriate, having regard to the terms of the requirement.

(5) A condition imposed under subsection (3)(b) above may, without prejudice to the generality of that subsection—

(a) subject to section 90 of this Act, require the child to submit to any medical or other examination or treatment;

(b) regulate the contact with the child of any specified person or class of persons.

(6) A children's hearing may require, when making a supervision requirement, that any place where the child is to reside in accordance with the supervision requirement shall not be disclosed to any person specified in the requirement under this subsection or class of persons so specified.

(7) A children's hearing who make a supervision requirement may determine that the requirement shall be reviewed at such time during the duration of the requirement as they determine.

(8) A supervision requirement shall be in such form as the Secretary of State may prescribe by rules.

(9) Where a children's hearing are satisfied—

(a) that it is necessary to make a supervision requirement which includes a requirement under subsection (3)(a) above that the child reside in a named residential establishment; and

(b) that any of the criteria specified in subsection (10) below are satisfied, they may specify in the requirement that the child shall be liable to be placed and kept in secure accommodation in that establishment during such period as the person in charge of that establishment, with the agreement of the chief social work officer of the relevant local authority, considers necessary.

(10) The criteria referred to in subsection (9) above are that the child—

(a) having previously absconded, is likely to abscond unless kept in secure accommodation, and, if he absconds, it is likely that his physical, mental or moral welfare will be at risk; or

(b) is likely to injure himself or some other person unless he is kept in such accommodation.

Definitions

"chief social word officer": s.93(1).
"child": s.93(2)(b).
"children's hearing": s.93(1).
"compulsory measures of supervision": s.93(1).
"relevant local authority": s.93(1).
"residential establishment": s.93(1).
"secure accommodation": s.93(1).
"supervision requirement": s.93(1).

General Note

Section 69 above deals with the situation where a children's hearing, after considering a child's case, either discharge the referral or continue the case for further investigation. The present section, replacing various parts of ss.44 and 58A of the 1968 Act, deals with the hearing's power, after having considering the child's case, to impose supervision requirements and grant secure accommodation authorisations. A number of important changes to the law have been made. Perhaps the most noticeable, but hardly the most significant in practical effect, is the scrapping of the distinction between supervision requirements imposed under the old s.44(1)(a) and those under the old s.44(1)(b), that is between supervision requirements requiring the child to submit to supervision and supervision requirements requiring the child to reside in a residential establishment. That distinction always was rather artificial, especially in the eyes of children required to live away from home but not in a residential establishment. The present section does not make the distinction, and the children's hearing may now impose a supervision requirement whenever they consider this necessary in the interests of the child, which requirement may or may not contain a condition that the child resides at a specified place, and which specified place may or may not be a residential establishment.

There are a number of other important changes in the law, including new provisions requiring the children's hearing to consider whether a condition in relation to contact should be imposed, allowing the hearing to impose a condition relating to medical examination or treatment, to require that the child's place of residence be kept confidential, and, importantly, to require that a review hearing be arranged within a specified time.

One provision which has not been re-enacted is the unhelpful obligation previously contained in s.44(2) of the 1968 Act, that in making a residential supervision requirement the children's hearing have regard to the religious persuasion of the child. If that matter is important to the child, then it will be a relevant consideration in determining which form of disposal best serves her or his welfare; if it is not important to the child, its importance to any other person is irrelevant.

Subs. (1)

A children's hearing to whom a child's case has been referred under s.65(1) above is obliged to consider that case in accordance with s.69(1) above and if, after that consideration, they come to the view that compulsory measures of supervision are required in respect of that child, they may make a supervision requirement. The wording of this provision is to be noted. If compulsory measures are deemed "necessary", the hearing "may" make a supervision requirement. There are no compulsory measures available to the children's hearing other than a supervision requirement, and the use of the permissive "may" might appear odd at first sight. However, this terminology allows the children's hearing to decide not to impose a supervision requirement in circumstances in which, though such a requirement is considered "necessary" it will not, in fact, succeed (for example in the case of a child nearing 16 who refuses to co-operate with any help offered). The decision whether to make a supervision requirement is one governed by all three overarching principles in s.16, and so while the child's welfare is the hearing's paramount consideration, they must also take into account the child's views, and must make no supervision requirement unless persuaded that it would be better to make the requirement than that none be made at all.

Subs. (2)

Subsection (3) below permits the children's hearing to impose conditions on to a supervision requirement, and this subsection requires the hearing to give consideration to the question of whether a condition relating to contact between the child and any other named person or class of persons should be made. The obligation is *not* to regulate contact in every case in which a supervision requirement is imposed, but simply to give consideration in every case as to whether a condition ought to be attached to the supervision requirement regulating contact.

In its terms the obligation to consider contact is limited to the initial making of a supervision requirement, and there is no such obligation when the children's hearing are considering whether to continue the supervision requirement at a review under s.73. However, if a condition relating to contact has been made, that condition will be reviewed when the supervision requirement is reviewed; in addition though there is no requirement to give the matter consideration at the review there is nothing to prevent the hearing from doing so.

Subs. (3)

Unlike s.44(1) of the 1968 Act there is now no technical difference in the current provisions between a non-residential supervision requirement and a residential supervision requirement. Instead, this subsection provides that a supervision requirement can require the child to reside at any place or places: this may be in a residential establishment, or with foster carers, or with relatives, or with one parent, or in any other place deemed to be in the best interests of the child. In addition the requirement can oblige the child to comply with any other specified condition. The decision whether to attach a condition to the supervision requirement is one to which all three overarching principles in s.16 apply, even though s. 16(4)(a)(i) refers only to the making or reviewing of supervision requirements, for the terms upon which the supervision requirement is made are, it is submitted, part of the consideration of whether to make it. There is no reason to deny an obligation to have regard to the child's views in relation to conditions when there is such an obligation in relation to the supervision requirement itself; and it is consistent with the principle of minimum intervention to allow the children's hearing to impose conditions only when they consider that that would be better than no conditions. At a review, any conditions are clearly open for consideration and all three of the s.16 principles are to be taken into account.

Specified in the requirement. If the hearing impose a supervision requirement with a requirement that the child reside somewhere, they must specify that place. The requirement cannot be to the effect that the child is to reside, say, "otherwise than with the parents", or "in an establishment chosen by the local authority", or "with foster carers selected by the local authority". The address of the child must be specified by the hearing, though it may be kept secret from any person under subs. (6) below. It is to be remembered that if a child is to be provided with accommodation by a local authority in a domestic familial context (*i.e.* with foster carers rather than in a residential establishment) the rules contained in the Boarding Out and Fostering of Children Regulations 1985 (S.I. 1985 No. 1799) must be adhered to.

Any condition. As under the old law the hearing can impose any condition they consider appropriate on the child, so long as, in their view, this is in the interests of the child. Such a condition may concern one of the matters mentioned in subs. (5) below, but it is not limited to these matters. The only limitation is that the condition must require something of the child. A children's hearing have no power to impose conditions on any other person, such as the parent or the local authority (though the placing of the child under supervision necessarily imposes the duty upon the local authority to "look after" the child in terms of s.17 above and to give effect to the supervision requirement under s.71 below). If the children's hearing decide to impose a condition they must do so expressly and it must be specified in the relevant form: a passage in the statement of reasons issued by the hearing is not a condition attached to the supervision requirement (see *Kennedy v. M* 1995 SLT 717).

Subs. (4)

This subsection replaces s.44(1A) of the 1968 Act. A supervision requirement which specifies the place of residence of the child may specify a place in England or Wales. If it does specify a place in England or Wales, it shall be authority for the person in charge of that place to restrict the child's liberty to such extent as is appropriate given the terms of the supervision requirement.

Subs. (5)

Under subs. (3) above a supervision requirement can impose any condition that the hearing consider appropriate. The two specified conditions here are, therefore, listed for the avoidance of doubt.

Require the child to submit to any medical or other examination or treatment. The aim of this provision is to ensure that there is legal authority to carry out medical examinations of children when this is necessary to determine what medical treatment she or he might need, and to ensure that such treatment as is necessary is given. This provision *does not* authorise medical examination for the purpose of gaining evidence in order to establish a ground of referral (for which, see s.55 above) nor for the purpose of completing an investigation into the child's needs when a case is continued under s.69(2) above (for which, see s.69(3) above): this requirement is attached to the disposal of the case and is imposed as one of the measures deemed necessary in the interests of the child. In determining whether to attach such a condition to a supervision requirement, the children's hearing must have regard to the three overarching principles in s.16 above; in addition, they should also be aware of s.90 below, to which this paragraph is made subject. Section 90 preserves the child's capacity to consent to or to refuse medical examination or treatment under s.2(4) of the Age of Legal Capacity (Scotland) Act 1991 and expressly provides that any examination or treatment the child is required to receive by a condition under this subsection can only be carried out if the child who has capacity to consent does consent. A children's hearing are not barred from imposing a condition of medical treatment on a refusing child, but such a condition will not provide legal authority for carrying it out. Rather, a child who refuses to submit in the face of such a condition will be treated as having breached that condition, and brought back to a children's hearing for a review under s.73(4)(b) below. A children's hearing ought to give especially careful consideration to the appropriateness of imposing such a requirement when they know that the child is refusing.

Regulate the contact with the child of any specified person. Whenever a supervision requirement is made, the children's hearing are obliged under subs. (2) above to give consideration to the question of whether they should make a condition regulating the contact that the child is to have with any specified person or class of person. If such a condition is to be made then it should be in clear and unambiguous terms. Such a condition will normally be appropriate when the child is required to live away from home and she or he wishes to maintain contact with her or his parents or guardians, but the condition may also be imposed when the child remains at home and the child's interests would be served by some other person, such as an absent unmarried father, or a previous foster carer to whom the child has become attached, having contact. This is, however, a slightly peculiar provision since the condition is in a supervision requirement over the child and it is only the child, in terms of subs. (3) above, who can be required to comply with the condition. The condition imposed by the children's hearing may purport to regulate contact between the child and another person, but steps can be taken to enforce that condition only when it is the child who breaches it. A parent's failure to maintain contact with the child when the children's hearing have considered it to be in the interests of the child will not automatically activate a review under s.73(4)(b) below, but it may well indicate to the local authority that a review should be requested in any case under s.73(4)(a).

Subs. (6)

This provision gives an important new power to the hearing. As part of a supervision requirement, the requirement that the child's residence not be disclosed will be potentially much longer lasting than the similar requirement under s.66(7) and s.69(10) above, though much the same considerations will come into play. A requirement under this subsection would be appropriate when contact between the child and the named person is considered to be harmful to the child, and it is also believed that there is a risk that the named person will attempt to make contact. The statute gives no indication as to when it would be appropriate for the children's hearing to exercise this power and there is nothing to prevent them from doing so for the benefit of someone other than the child, such as foster carers. If the person from whom details of the child's residence is to be kept is present at the hearing, care must be taken to ensure that the address is not mentioned and this might require that the person be excluded from part of the hearing (though such a reason for excluding a person does not fit into either of the grounds of exclusion under s.46(1) above). In addition, the person may be entitled to receive a statement of the decision and the grounds for the decision, and care should be taken to ensure that the address is not specified (though it must be specified on the actual supervision requirement).

Subs. (7)

This is another new provision and is a useful addition to the powers of the children's hearing. Under the old law the hearing themselves had no power to specify how long the supervision requirement was to last, and if the case indicated that supervision for a period of less than a year was appropriate, all the hearing could do was to express the hope to the Social Work Department that they would call for a review, or encourage the child and parent to call for a review at some time before the end of the year. Now the hearing may determine that a supervision requirement be reviewed at any time they determine during its currency.

Subss. (9) and (10)

These subsections replace s.58A of the 1968 Act with no substantive alteration, and they provide that the children's hearing can specify that the child be liable to be placed and kept in secure accommodation in a residential establishment during such periods as are considered necessary by the chief social work officer. The children's hearing have no power to require that the child be kept in secure accommodation; rather they simply authorise the placing of the child there. Before granting such an authorisation, the following conditions must be satisfied:

(1) the children's hearing must have made a supervision requirement with a requirement that the child resides in a named residential establishment, *and either*

(2) the child must have absconded from a residential establishment at least once before and is likely to do so again in circumstances in which her or his welfare will be put at risk, *or*

(3) the child is likely to injure either her or himself or some other person unless kept in secure accommodation.

The decision to make the child liable to be kept in secure accommodation is one to which the welfare principle in s.16(1) applies, though that is qualified to a certain extent by s.16(5) above (*cf.* s.1 of the English Children Act 1989 (c. 41), as interpreted by the Court of Appeal in *M. (A Minor) (Secure Accommodation), Re* [1995] 2 WLR 302), but not the other overarching principles in s.16(2) and (3). However, it might well be in the interests of the child her or himself to be kept in secure accommodation.

Injure himself or some other person. This refers to personal injuries, and not economic injuries such as damage to property. However, it can clearly be argued that a child who, for example, steals motor cars is likely to cause himself and others physical injury (since he will not have passed a driving test). A child who commits criminal offences that do not put either himself or other people at risk of physical injury probably does not come within this provision (unless it could be argued that the threat to moral welfare by persistent criminality amounts to an "injury": this is, it is submitted, too wide an interpretation of that word). This provision is to be read with s.16(5) above, which applies "whether or not" the harm threatened is physical.

Duties of local authority with respect to supervision requirements

71.—(1) The relevant local authority shall, as respects a child subject to a supervision requirement, give effect to the requirement.

(2) Where a supervision requirement provides that the child shall reside—

(a) in relevant accommodation; or

(b) in any other accommodation not provided by a local authority,

the relevant local authority shall from time to time investigate whether, while the child is so resident, any conditions imposed by the supervision requirement are being fulfilled; and may take such steps as they consider reasonable if they find that such conditions are not being fulfilled.

(3) In this section, "relevant accommodation" means accommodation provided by the parents or relatives of the child or by any person associated with them or with the child.

DEFINITIONS
"child": s.93(2)(b).
"children's hearing": s.93(1).
"relevant local authority": s.93(1).
"supervision requirement": s.93(1).

GENERAL NOTE
This section replaces s.44(5) of the 1968 Act and provides that a supervision requirement made by a children's hearing must be given effect to by the local authority for whose area the children's hearing sit. The nature of the obligations thereby imposed on the local authority will depend upon the terms of the supervision requirement and the conditions attached thereto. A requirement, for example, that the child reside in a specified residential establishment will oblige the local authority to provide a place in that residential establishment. If there is no requirement that the child resides in a particular place the duty of the local authority is to provide such supervision, guidance and support as the children's hearing have decided is necessary in the child's interests.

Subs. (1)
The obligation is absolute. If, for whatever reason, the supervision requirement or any of its conditions cannot be given effect to, the local authority must refer the case to the reporter under s.73(4) below for a review of the supervision requirement by the children's hearing under s.73(8) below.

Subs. (2)
This provision only applies when the supervision requirement requires the child under s.70(3)(a) above to reside in a specified place, but that place is not a residential establishment as defined in s.93(1). In such cases the local authority have an obligation to check that the conditions attached to the supervision requirement are being fulfilled.

Provides that the child shall reside. A supervision requirement that does not contain a requirement under s.70(3)(a) above is not one which provides that the child "shall reside" anywhere and this provision will not, therefore, apply.

Such steps as they consider reasonable. If, on investigation under this section, the local authority discover that any of the conditions attached to the supervision requirement are not being fulfilled, they must either provide such guidance and support as will allow for the fulfilment of the appropriate conditions, or call for a review under s.73(4) below.

Subs. (3)
Parents or relatives. Neither of these words is defined in the Act and both are to be given their natural meaning. "Parent" is not limited to "parent with parental responsibilities"; "relative" means any person with a relationship of blood or affinity with the child.

Any person associated with them or with the child. This phrase is probably to be given broad scope to mean any individual with a legitimate concern with the parents or with the child, such as friends or neighbours to whom the child has some emotional attachment.

Transfer of child subject to supervision requirement in case of necessity

72.—(1) In any case of urgent necessity, where it is in the interests of—

(a) a child who is required by a supervision requirement imposed under section 70(3)(a) of this Act to reside in a specific residential establishment or specific other accommodation; or

(b) other children in that establishment or accommodation,

the chief social work officer of the relevant local authority may direct that, notwithstanding that requirement, the child be transferred to another place.

(2) Any child transferred under subsection (1) above shall have his case reviewed, in accordance with section 73(8) of this Act, by a children's hearing within seven days of his transfer.

DEFINITIONS
"accommodation": s.25(8).
"chief social work officer": s.93(1).
"child": s.93(2)(b).
"children's hearing": s.93(1).
"relevant local authority": s.93(1).
"residential establishment": s.93(1).
"supervision requirement": s.93(1).

GENERAL NOTE
This section replaces s.44(6) and (7) of the 1968 Act, without making any substantive alteration in the law. It deals with the situation of a child who was obliged to reside in a specified place but in her or his interests has had to be transferred to another place immediately.

Subs. (1)
Urgent necessity. In other words, an immediate necessity which cannot wait until a children's hearing has been arranged under s.73(4) in order to decide whether the supervision requirement should be varied to allow the child to be moved to another place.

Residential establishment or specific other accommodation. This section applies to all children who are required under s.70(3)(a) to reside at a specified place as a term of their supervision requirement.

Of … other children. It may be in the interests of other children at the specified place that the child must be moved if, for example, the child poses a threat to other children residing at the specified place.

Subs. (2)
A review of the child's case, under s.73(8) below, by a children's hearing must be held within seven days of the child's transfer to another place. The purpose will be primarily to examine where the child is to reside in light of the breakdown of the placement previously determined by the children's hearing. It is, however, the whole supervision requirement, or to put it another way, the whole of the child's case, and not only the condition of residence that is to be reviewed.

His case reviewed. It is worthy of note that s.73(8) talks of the supervision requirement being reviewed, while this subsection talks of the child's case being reviewed. The two are, it is submitted, synonymous since the disposals available to the children's hearing conducting the review are identical however the review comes before them. The change in terminology signifies nothing more than sloppy draftsmanship (see further, General Note to s.73(9) below).

Within seven days of his transfer. The day the transfer takes place is the first day and the review hearing must take place on or before the seventh day.

Duration and review of supervision requirement

73.—(1) No child shall continue to be subject to a supervision requirement for any period longer than is necessary in the interests of promoting or safeguarding his welfare.

(2) Subject to any variation or continuation of a supervision requirement under subsection (9) below, no supervision requirement shall remain in force for a period longer than one year.

(3) A supervision requirement shall cease to have effect in respect of a child not later than on his attaining the age of eighteen years.

(4) A relevant local authority shall refer the case of a child who is subject to a supervision requirement to the Principal Reporter where they are satisfied that—

  (a) the requirement in respect of the child ought to cease to have effect or be varied;
  (b) a condition contained in the requirement is not being complied with; or
  (c) the best interests of the child would be served by their—
        (i) applying under section 86 of this Act for a parental responsibilities order;
        (ii) applying under section 18 of the Adoption (Scotland) Act 1978 for an order freeing the child for adoption; or
        (iii) placing the child for adoption,
  and they intend to apply for such an order or so place the child.

(5) Where the relevant local authority are aware that an application has been made and is pending, or is about to be made, under section 12 of the said Act of 1978 for an adoption order in respect of a child who is subject to a supervision requirement, they shall forthwith refer his case to the Principal Reporter.

(6) A child or any relevant person may require a review of a supervision requirement in respect of the child at any time at least three months after—

  (a) the date on which the requirement is made; or
  (b) the date of the most recent continuation, or variation, by virtue of this section of the requirement.

(7) Where a child is subject to a supervision requirement and, otherwise than in accordance with that requirement or with an order under section 11 of this Act, a relevant person proposes to take the child to live outwith Scotland, the person shall, not later than twenty-eight days before so taking the child, give notice of that proposal in writing to the Principal Reporter and to the relevant local authority.

(8) The Principal Reporter shall—

  (a) arrange for a children's hearing to review any supervision requirement in respect of a child where—
        (i) the case has been referred to him under subsection (4) or (5) above;
        (ii) the review has been required under subsection (6) above;
        (iii) the review is required by virtue of section 70(7) or section 72(2) of this Act;
        (iv) he has received in respect of the child such notice as is mentioned in subsection (7) above; or
        (v) in any other case, the supervision requirement will expire within three months; and
  (b) make any arrangements incidental to that review.

(9) Where a supervision requirement is reviewed by a children's hearing arranged under subsection (8) above, they may—

  (a) where they are satisfied that in order to complete the review of the supervision requirement it is necessary to have a further investigation of the child's case, continue the review to a subsequent hearing;
  (b) terminate the requirement;
  (c) vary the requirement;
  (d) insert in the requirement any requirement which could have been imposed by them under section 70(3) of this Act; or
  (e) continue the requirement, with or without such variation or insertion.

(10) Subsections (3) to (10) of section 69 of this Act shall apply to a continuation under paragraph (a) of subsection (9) above of a review of a supervision requirement as they apply to the continuation of a case under subsection (1)(a) of that section.

(11) Where a children's hearing vary or impose a requirement under subsection (9) above which requires the child to reside in any specified place or places, they may order that such place or places shall not be disclosed to any person or class of persons specified in the requirement.

(12) Where a children's hearing is arranged under subsection (8)(a)(v) above, they shall consider whether, if the supervision requirement is not continued, the child still requires supervision or guidance; and where a children's hearing consider such supervision or guidance is necessary, it shall be the duty of the local authority to provide such supervision or guidance as the child is willing to accept.

(13) Where a children's hearing is arranged by virtue of subsection (4)(c) or (5) above, then irrespective of what the hearing do under subsection (9) above they shall draw up a report which shall provide advice in respect of, as the case may be, the proposed application under section 86 of this Act or under section 18 of the said Act of 1978, or the proposed placing for adoption or the application, or prospective application, under section 12 of that Act, for any court which may subsequently require to come to a decision, in relation to the child concerned, such as is mentioned in subsection (14) below.

(14) A court which is considering whether, in relation to a child, to grant an application under section 86 of this Act or under section 18 or 12 of the said Act of 1978 and which, by virtue of subsection (13) above, receives a report as respects that child, shall consider the report before coming to a decision in the matter.

DEFINITIONS
    "child": s.93(2)(b).
    "children's hearing": s.93(1).
    "parental responsibilities order": ss.86(1), 93(1).
    "principal reporter": s.93(1).
    "relevant local authority": s.93(1).
    "relevant person": s.93(2)(b).
    "supervision requirement": s.93(1).

GENERAL NOTE
    A child is subject to compulsory measures of supervision for only a specified period of time which, unless the supervision requirement is renewed, cannot be for more than a year. This section replaces ss.47 and 48 of the 1968 Act and makes some fairly important amendments to the law, as well as tidying it up. It deals with the duration of supervision requirements, their review, and the powers of the children's hearing on review to terminate, vary or continue supervision requirements, and to draw up reports in certain circumstances.
    The substantive changes to the law are to be found in subs. (6), under which a review can be required by the child or parent at any time after three months from the making or last review of the requirement, subs. (7), which obliges notice to be given to the reporter if the child is being removed from Scotland, subs. (11), which permits the children's hearing to require that the child's address be kept secret, and subss. (13) and (14), which concern the reports that the hearing must draw up in certain circumstances. In addition to the rules relating to termination contained in this section, the court also now has the power under the Adoption (Scotland) Act 1978 (c. 28) to terminate supervision requirements on the making of adoption orders or orders freeing for adoption (see Sched. 2, paras. (7) and (11) below). However, the Secretary of State no longer has the power himself to terminate supervision requirements (s.51 of the 1968 Act is repealed in Sched. 5 and is not re-enacted).

Subs. (1)
    A child is to remain subject to a supervision requirement only for so long as her or his interests require that she or he be so subject and this subsection provides that she or he shall not continue to be subject to a supervision requirement when it is no longer necessary in her or his interests.

The effect of this provision is *not* to bring the supervision requirement automatically to an end when the child's interests are best served by the termination of the requirement, but rather to indicate to the local authority when they ought to require a review under subs. (4)(a) below, as well as to indicate to the children's hearing the paramount consideration to which they must direct their minds in determining whether or not a supervision requirement should be terminated under subs. (9)(b) below.

Subs. (2)
A supervision requirement, if it has not been reviewed within that time, will remain effective for one year. If no children's hearing has been arranged within that time (contrary to the reporter's obligation to do so under subs. (8)(a)(v) below) the supervision requirement automatically ceases to have effect on the anniversary of its being imposed, and to bring the child back into the system would then require new grounds of referral. If a children's hearing is arranged under any paragraph of subs. (8) below the requirement can be continued for another period of a year (or less if again reviewed before then).
A period longer than a year. A supervision requirement imposed, say, on June 3, will cease to have effect at midnight on June 2 of the following year.

Subs. (3)
A person cannot be subject to a supervision requirement after reaching the age of 18 years, and any subsisting requirement automatically ceases to have effect on the person's 18th birthday, even without the meeting of a hearing to terminate it. The reporter does, however, have an obligation to arrange a review within three months of the expiry of the supervision requirement (subs. (8)(a)(v) below): if this expiry would be effected by this subsection any continuation would last only until the child's 18th birthday. On the attaining of the age of 18 years, see the Age of Legal Capacity (Scotland) Act 1991 (c. 50), s.6.

Subs. (4)
The local authority which are responsible for giving effect to the supervision of the child may call for a review of the requirement by referring the case to the reporter. On such referral, the reporter then has an obligation under subs. (8) below to arrange a review hearing. This subsection replaces s.48(2) of the 1968 Act, but is more specific in that it sets out a number of circumstances in which the local authority are obliged to refer the case to the reporter to arrange a review. Paragraph (a) reflects the old s.47(1) and obliges a referral when the local authority are satisfied that the supervision requirement ought to be varied or terminated (due to some change in the child's circumstances since the supervision requirement was made or last reviewed). Paragraph (b), not expressed in the 1968 Act but reflecting practice, requires a referral when a condition in the supervision requirement is not being fulfilled. It does not matter why the condition is not being fulfilled, whether it is because of non-co-operation by the child, lack of resources of the local authority, or for any other reason. Paragraph (c) is a new provision, requiring a review whenever the local authority intends to do any of the listed acts. These acts are seen as acts which will significantly change the child's circumstances, so making it appropriate that a review of the child's case be held. A children's hearing arranged as a result of a referral under para. (c) must not only review the supervision requirement under subs. (9) below, but must also draw up a report under subs. (13) below.

Subs. (5)
In addition to their duty to refer the case to the reporter in the circumstances listed in subs. (4) above, a local authority also have the duty to refer the case to the reporter when they become aware that an adoption application has been or is about to be made in respect of the child, and the children's hearing will be obliged to draw up a report under subs. (13) below. It is to be remembered that the court that grants an adoption order now has the power to terminate a supervision requirement (see the Adoption (Scotland) Act 1978, s.12(9), as added by Sched. 2 of the present Act).
They shall forthwith. The word "forthwith" does not govern the obligation under subs. (4) above and it serves the function here of indicating that the case should be referred to the reporter as a matter of urgency. "Forthwith" means as soon as practicable.

Subs. (6)
Under the old s.48(4) the child or parent could require a review of the supervision requirement three months after the requirement was made or last varied or six months after it was continued at a review without variation. This new provision allows the child, or her or his parent, to call for a review at any time after three months from the imposition or last continuation of the supervision requirement, whether varied or not.

Relevant person. Defined in s.93(2)(b) below, this is the same person as is obliged under s.45(8) to attend the children's hearing considering the case of the child. If a child's circumstances have changed since the last review, it is possible that a different person comes within this category. The person who has, for the time being, charge of or control over the child is the person who can call for a review under this provision, whether or not that person was a "relevant person" at the time of the making of the supervision requirement or of its last review.

At least three months after. The months are calendar months and three months after the date on which the requirement was made, continued or varied is the day after the expiry of the three months. For example a supervision requirement made or continued on March 23, can be reviewed at the instance of the child or relevant person on or after June 24. The call for a review can be made at a time before the expiry of the three months, but the children's hearing cannot consider the case until after that expiry.

Subs. (7)

The jurisdiction of the children's hearing extends only to Scotland. This new provision obliges a relevant person who intends to remove a child subject to a supervision requirement from Scotland to notify the reporter at least 28 days before that removal. Notice is required only when the proposal is that the child be taken to live outwith Scotland and not merely for a holiday. Extended holidays may well cause problems here, and the test is probably one of whether the intention is to change the child's habitual residence. On receiving notice under this subsection, the reporter must then arrange a review of the supervision requirement under subs. (8)(iv) below and the children's hearing, by specifying a place of residence for the child within Scotland, may effectively prohibit the child's removal from the jurisdiction (if, as always, they consider that this is necessary in the interests of the child). Again, this provision is designed to ensure that a review takes place whenever there is, or is about to be, a significant change in the child's circumstances. It is, however, difficult to see how this provision can be enforced and a relevant person who removes the child without notice is subject to no penalty.

Subs. (8)

A review of a supervision requirement by the children's hearing must be arranged by the reporter whenever the child's case has been referred to her or him by the local authority under subss. (4) or (5) above, or a review has been requested by the child or parent under subs. (6) above, or the children's hearing have exercised their power under s.70(7) to specify a time at which the requirement must be reviewed, or the child has been moved from specified accommodation to other accommodation under s.72 above, or the reporter has received notice under subs. (7) above that a relevant person intends to remove the child outwith Scotland, or, if none of these circumstances apply, within three months of the expiry of the supervision requirement. In addition to these circumstances in which a children's hearing must be arranged by the reporter for a review, the supervision requirement over a child will also be reviewed whenever a children's hearing has been arranged in order to put new grounds of referral to the child and parent (s.65(3) above).

The Principal Reporter shall. The reporter is obliged to arrange a review and if the children's hearing is not arranged timeously the supervision requirement will lapse. The reporter, however, is not entitled to decide simply to let the supervision requirement lapse, for that would be usurping the role of the children's hearing as well as constituting a breach of statutory obligation. Once a child is under supervision the reporter has no power to decide that the child is no longer in need of compulsory measures of supervision.

Will expire within three months. A review hearing under para. (a)(v) must be arranged by the reporter not later than three months before the date on which the supervision requirement will cease to have effect, that is to say within three months of the child's 18th birthday or within three months of the anniversary of the imposition or last variation or continuation of the requirement or within three months of the date specified by the children's hearing under s.70(7) for a review.

Make any arrangements incidental to that review. In other words, the reporter must call for reports into the child's circumstances from the Social Work Department of the appropriate local authority, and any other reports in relation to the child that will be relevant to the children's hearing's consideration of the case.

Subs. (9)

Some provisions in the Act refer to the children's hearing considering the child's case (see *e.g.* s.69(2) above), some refer to the review of the child's case (see *e.g.* s.72(2) above), and this subsection requires a review of the supervision requirement. It would be appropriate to refer to a consideration of the child's case when there is no supervision requirement and to refer to a consideration of the supervision requirement when there is such a requirement, but the statute is not consistent in this. There is, however, no difference between a review of the child's case and a review of the supervision requirement, since the supervision requirement cannot properly be reviewed without a consideration of the whole of the child's case. The hearing must direct its mind to the question of whether the supervision requirement should be terminated, varied, or continued and they can do this only by considering the reports provided before the hearing, the discussion at the hearing, and all aspects of the case which indicate wherein the child's interests lie. Having considered the child's case, taking account of the effect the supervision requirement in its present form has had so far, and directing their minds to the question of whether it should be terminated, varied or continued without variation, the children's hearing may do one or other of the five options listed in this subsection.

The decision of which option to adopt at a review is one to which all three overarching principles in s.16 apply: the children's hearing must regard the welfare of the child as their paramount consideration, they must have regard so far as practicable to the views, if she or he wishes to express them, of the child concerned, and they may continue the supervision requirement only when they consider that to do so would be better than having no supervision requirement at all. In addition, the children's hearing at a review must pay regard to the rule in subs. (1) above that no child shall continue to be subject to a supervision requirement for any period longer than is necessary in the interests of promoting or safeguarding her or his welfare.

Subs. (10)

This subsection ensures that if, after having reviewed the child's case, the children's hearing feel that they need more information to make a proper decision and they continue the case to a subsequent hearing, the same powers to require the child to undergo investigative assessment and to be kept in a place of safety apply as when a hearing at which established grounds of referral are being considered is continued. The aim is to ensure that a hearing reviewing a supervision requirement have the same powers as the hearing which decided to impose a supervision requirement in the first place.

Subs. (11)

This reflects the power of the children's hearing under s.70(6) above, the General Note to which reference should be made.

Subs. (12)

If the review is arranged because the supervision requirement is about to expire (because it has lasted for a year or because the child is about to attain the age of 18) the children's hearing must consider whether voluntary supervision and guidance is still required for the child. If they do so determine, the local authority must offer such supervision and guidance to the child.

If the supervision requirement is not continued. If the review is other than because the child is about to attain the age of 18 and the children's hearing consider that the child still requires supervision and guidance, then a continuation of the supervision requirement will nearly always be the correct decision. If, however, the review is because the child is about to attain the age of 18, continuation will not really be an option and it is then that this provision will come into play.

Subs. (13)

This new provision follows on from the new requirement to arrange a children's hearing under subss. (4)(c) or (5) above, that is when the local authority intend to place the child for adoption or to apply for an order freeing the child for adoption or to apply for a parental responsibilities order, or they become aware that someone intends to apply to adopt the child. When a children's hearing is arranged for any of these reasons they are obliged to draw up a report to provide advice to the court in respect of that matter.

Irrespective of what the hearing do under subs. (9). A children's hearing arranged for this reason must review the supervision requirement in respect of the child (subs. (8) above provides that the reporter shall arrange a hearing to review any supervision requirement when a case has been referred to her or him under, *inter alia* subss. (4)(c) or (5) above) and it follows that the hearing must make a decision in respect of that requirement in the normal way.

Shall draw up a report. In addition to the decision that the children's hearing make in respect of the supervision requirement the hearing must also draw up a report. This report should be wider than the statement of reasons for the decision, which is limited to justifying the decision made in respect of the supervision requirement. Rather, the report should take the form of the hearing's opinion as to the appropriateness of the order that the court is being asked to make.

Or the proposed placing for adoption. It is not by means of a court order that a child is placed for adoption, and it is not, therefore, for the court that a report is drawn up in these circumstances. In this case there is no obligation under subs. (14) below on any court to consider the report, but it is implicit that the local authority take account of it in deciding whether to go ahead with the placement, otherwise there would be no point in the children's hearing drawing it up.

Subs. (14)

The court is obliged to consider the report drawn up by the children's hearing before making a decision as to whether to grant a parental responsibilities order under s.86 below or an order freeing the child for adoption under s.18 of the Adoption (Scotland) Act 1978 or an adoption order under s.12 thereof.

Further provision as respects children subject to supervision requirements

74. The Secretary of State may by regulations provide—
  (a) for the transmission of information regarding a child who is subject to a supervision requirement to any person who, by virtue of that requirement, has, or is to have, control over the child;
  (b) for the temporary accommodation, where necessary, of a child so subject; and
  (c) for the conveyance of a child so subject—
          (i) to any place in which, under the supervision requirement, he is to reside;
          (ii) to any place to which he falls to be taken under subsection (1) or (5) of section 82 of this Act; or
          (iii) to any person to whom he falls to be returned under subsection (3) of that section.

DEFINITIONS

"child": s.93(2)(b).
"supervision requirement": s.93(1).

GENERAL NOTE

This provision replaces s.45 of the 1968 Act. The Secretary of State is empowered to make regulations concerning the transmission of information regarding a child subject to a supervision requirement to any person who is to have control over the child, concerning the temporary accommodation of children subject to supervision requirements, and for the conveyance of children to places or persons.

Powers of Secretary of State with respect to secure accommodation

75.—(1) The Secretary of State may by regulations make provision with respect to the placing in secure accommodation of any child—
  (a) who is subject to a requirement imposed under section 70(3)(a) of this Act but not subject to a requirement under subsection (9) of that section; or
  (b) who is not subject to a supervision requirement but who is being looked after by a local authority in pursuance of such enactments as may be specified in the regulations.
  (2) Regulations under subsection (1) above may—
  (a) specify the circumstances in which a child may be so placed under the regulations;
  (b) make provision to enable a child who has been so placed or any relevant person to require that the child's case be brought before a children's hearing within a shorter period than would apply under regulations made under subsection (3) below; and
  (c) specify different circumstances for different cases or classes of case.
  (3) Subject to subsection (4) below and without prejudice to subsection (2)(b) above, the Secretary of State may prescribe—
  (a) the maximum period during which a child may be kept under this Act in secure accommodation without the authority of a children's hearing or of the sheriff;
  (b) the period within which a children's hearing shall be arranged to consider the case of a child placed in secure accommodation by virtue of

regulations made under this section (and different periods may be so prescribed in respect of different cases or classes of case).

(4) Subsection (8) of section 66 of this Act shall apply in respect of a child placed in secure accommodation under regulations made under this section as if such placing took place by virtue of that section.

(5) The Secretary of State may by regulations vary the period within which a review of a condition imposed under section 70(9) of this Act shall be reviewed under section 73 of this Act.

(6) The Secretary of State may by regulations make provision for the procedures to be applied in placing children in secure accommodation; and without prejudice to the generality of this subsection, such regulations may—

(a) specify the duties of the Principal Reporter in relation to the placing of children in secure accommodation;

(b) make provision for the referral of cases to a children's hearing for review; and

(c) make provision for any person with parental responsibilities in relation to the child to be informed of the placing of the child in secure accommodation.

DEFINITIONS
"child": s.93(2)(b).
"children's hearing": s.93(1).
"local authority": Local Government etc. (Scotland) Act 1994, s.2.
"parental responsibilities": ss.1(3), 93(1).
"principal reporter": s.93(1).
"secure accommodation": s.93(1).
"supervision requirement": s.93(1).

GENERAL NOTE
The Secretary of State is empowered to make regulations concerning the various matters listed in this section in respect of placing a child in secure accommodation who is subject to a supervision requirement with a condition of residence but for whom a children's hearing have not issued an authorisation for the placing in secure accommodation, or who is otherwise being looked after by the local authority under statutory authority. The 66-day limit for keeping a child in a place of safety (s.66(8) above) applies to children kept in secure accommodation under this provision.

Exclusion orders

Exclusion orders

76.—(1) Subject to subsections (3) to (9) below, where on the application of a local authority the sheriff is satisfied, in relation to a child, that the conditions mentioned in subsection (2) below are met, he may grant an order under this section (to be known as "an exclusion order") excluding from the child's family home any person named in the order (in this Part of this Act referred to as the "named person").

(2) The conditions are—

(a) that the child has suffered, is suffering, or is likely to suffer, significant harm as a result of any conduct, or any threatened or reasonably apprehended conduct, of the named person;

(b) that the making of an exclusion order against the named person—

(i) is necessary for the protection of the child, irrespective of whether the child is for the time being residing in the family home; and

(ii) would better safeguard the child's welfare than the removal of the child from the family home; and

(c) that, if an order is made, there will be a person specified in the application who is capable of taking responsibility for the provision of appropriate care for the child and any other member of the family who requires such care and who is, or will be, residing in the family home (in this section, sections 77 to 79 and section 91(3)(f) of this Act referred to as an "appropriate person").

(3) No application under subsection (1) above for an exclusion order shall be finally determined under this section unless—

(a) the named person has been afforded an opportunity of being heard by, or represented before, the sheriff; and

(b) the sheriff has considered any views expressed by any person on whom notice of the application has been served in accordance with rules making such provision as is mentioned in section 91(3)(d) of this Act.

(4) Where, on an application under subsection (1) above, the sheriff—

(a) is satisfied as mentioned in that subsection; but

(b) the conditions mentioned in paragraphs (a) and (b) of subsection (3) above for the final determination of the application are not fulfilled,

he may grant an interim order, which shall have effect as an exclusion order pending a hearing by the sheriff under subsection (5) below held within such period as may be specified in rules made by virtue of section 91(3)(e) of this Act.

(5) The sheriff shall conduct a hearing under this subsection within such period as may be specified in rules made by virtue of section 91(3)(e) of this Act, and, if satisfied at that hearing as mentioned in subsection (1) above, he may, before finally determining the application, confirm or vary the interim order, or any term or condition on which it was granted, or may recall such order.

(6) Where the conditions mentioned in paragraphs (a) and (b) of subsection (3) above have been fulfilled, the sheriff may, at any point prior to the final determination of the application, grant an interim order.

(7) An order under subsection (5) or (6) above shall have effect as an exclusion order pending the final determination of the application.

(8) Where—

(a) an application is made under subsection (1) above; and

(b) the sheriff considers that the conditions for making a child protection order under section 57 of this Act are satisfied,

he may make an order under that section as if the application had been duly made by the local authority under that rather than under this section.

(9) The sheriff shall not make an exclusion order if it appears to him that to do so would be unjustifiable or unreasonable, having regard to—

(a) all the circumstances of the case, including without prejudice to the generality of this subsection the matters specified in subsection (10) below; and

(b) any requirement such as is specified in subsection (11) below and the likely consequences in the light of that requirement of the exclusion of the named person from the family home.

(10) The matters referred to in subsection (9)(a) above are—

(a) the conduct of the members of the child's family (whether in relation to each other or otherwise);

(b) the respective needs and financial resources of the members of that family;

(c) the extent (if any) to which—

(i) the family home; and

(ii) any relevant item in that home,

is used in connection with a trade, business or profession by any member of the family.

(11) The requirement referred to in subsection (9)(b) above is a requirement that the named person (whether alone or with any other person) must reside in the family home, where that home—

(a) is or is part of an agricultural holding within the meaning of the Agricultural Holdings (Scotland) Act 1991; or

(b) is let, or is a home in respect of which possession is given, to the named person (whether alone or with any other person) by an employer as an incident of employment.

(12) In this Part of this Act—

"caravan" has the meaning given to it by section 29(1) of the Caravan Sites and Control of Development Act 1960;

"exclusion order", includes an interim order granted under subsection (4) above and such an order confirmed or varied under subsection (5) above and an interim order granted under subsection (6) above; except that in subsection (3) above and in section 79 of this Act, it does not include an interim order granted under subsection (4) above;

"family" has the meaning given in section 93(1) of this Act;

"family home" means any house, caravan, houseboat or other structure which is used as a family residence and in which the child ordinarily resides with any person described in subsection (13) below and the expression includes any garden or other ground or building attached to and usually occupied with, or otherwise required for the amenity or convenience of, the house, caravan, houseboat or other structure.

(13) The description of person referred to in the definition of "family home" in subsection (12) above, is a person who has parental responsibilities in relation to the child, or who ordinarily (and other than by reason only of his employment) has charge of, or control over him.

DEFINITIONS
"child": s.93(2)(b).
"family": s.93(1).
"local authority": Local Government etc. (Scotland) Act 1994, s.2.

GENERAL NOTE
It often happens that the protection of a child can only be achieved by separating that child from the adult who poses a threat to her or his wellbeing. Until the passing of the present Act, if the threatening adult lived in the same household as the child, that separation could only be achieved by removing the child from her or his home, either by means of the emergency provisions (place of safety orders) or by means of more long-term protective measures (supervision requirements with conditions of residence away from the source of danger). It had long been recognised that the removal of a child from her or his home environment would itself in most, if not all, cases, be a traumatic experience for the child and in some cases that trauma could counter or even outweigh any good the removal was designed to achieve. The highlighting of this fact by the Orkney case led it to be seen as a failing in the law that there was no procedure, similar to that contained in the Matrimonial Homes (Family Protection) (Scotland) Act 1981 (c. 59), for the exclusion of an abuser from the child's home (see White Paper *Scotland's Children: Proposals for Child Care Policy and Law* (Cm 2286, August 1993)). Sections 76 to 80 are designed to correct that perceived flaw, by giving sheriffs the right to grant exclusion orders excluding named individuals from the homes of particular children whenever this is necessary for the protection of individual children.

If a child needs protecting from a particular adult, there is in principle no difference between removing the child from the adult and removing the adult from the child; but in practice the two acts have hugely different consequences. For one thing the removal of the adult may well result in the denial of property rights, which is seldom a consideration with children. Also, removal of an adult may leave the child with no carer in the family home, which would require the child to be taken into care in any case. Again, removal of a child obliges the local authority to provide the child with accommodation whereas removal of an adult does not create any analogous obligation. For these, and other, reasons, the following sections were amongst the most keenly debated and controversial provisions in the whole of the Act. The aim of proponents of exclusion orders, to ensure that children are not disrupted in their lives unduly is, of course, worthy, but it is difficult to see what real benefit the present provisions will bring. There is little possibility of exclusion orders providing emergency protection for children on a short-term basis, for it is likely to be considered "unjustifiable or unreasonable" to exclude a person from her or his own home on the basis of unproven allegations alone, even when such allegations are sufficient to activate the other protection mechanisms in the Act. A child who needs long-term protection from a particular adult will not receive that protection by removing the adult for a period of no more than six months, which is the extent of the exclusion in the present provisions. On the other hand, the exclusion order might well prove of great use to protect a child from an adult who visits the family home regularly and who poses some risk to the child.

The draftsmen have modelled the provisions in ss.76–80 to a large extent on those in the Matrimonial Homes (Family Protection) (Scotland) Act 1981, to which very different considerations apply. As under that Act, interim orders may be made, and the sheriff is obliged to refuse to make an exclusion order in a number of stated circumstances. There is, however, rather more discretion given to sheriffs in the present provisions than in the 1981 Act, and it remains to be seen how willing sheriffs are to utilise their new powers.

Subs. (1)

A local authority can apply to the sheriff for the granting of an exclusion order, which will be granted if the conditions in subs. (2) below are satisfied, and which will have the effect, in terms of s.77(1) below, of excluding from the child's home any named person, preventing that person from entering the home, and suspending during its currency any rights of occupancy in the home that the named person has.

On the application of a local authority. It should be noted that some persons other than local authorities are entitled to seek an exclusion order under the terms of the Matrimonial Homes (Family Protection) (Scotland) Act 1981, which might be used as a means of protecting a child. The present provision, on the other hand, deals with the power of public authorities to protect children, and it is only a local authority which have title to seek an exclusion order under this Act. This is to be compared with s.57(1) above which entitles "any person" (including a local authority) to apply to the sheriff for a child protection order which will frequently have the effect of removing the child from her or his home. There is no indication given in the Act to local authorities as to when it would be appropriate for them to seek one order rather than the other, but there are at least two considerations which will encourage local authorities to seek a child protection order rather than an exclusion order. First, the burden of proof is rather less under s.57 than under the present section, in that the condition to be established in s.57 is "reasonable grounds for believing" that the child is suffering significant harm while in the present section the condition to be established is that the child is actually suffering significant harm as a matter of fact rather than as a matter of belief. Secondly, there are a number of defences to the granting of exclusion orders (see subss. (9)–(11) below) which do not apply to child protection orders, so that even when the conditions for both orders can be satisfied by the applicant local authority, the inclination is likely to be to seek the order which cannot be defended rather than the order which can be.

The sheriff. It is the sheriff within whose sheriffdom the family home is situated who has jurisdiction to make the exclusion order (s.80(2) below).

He may. Even if the local authority establishes the conditions to be satisfied under subs. (2) below (and the defences in subss. (9)–(11) below are not satisfied), the sheriff retains a discretion as to whether or not to grant the exclusion order. His decision is governed by all three of the overarching principles set out in s.16: the child's welfare must be his paramount consideration; he must give the child an opportunity to express views and take account of these views; and he must not make the exclusion order unless he considers that it would be better to make the order than that no order be made at all.

The child's family home. The order excludes the named person from the child's family home, that is to say from the place where the child normally lives with a person who has parental responsibilities in relation to the child.

Any person named in the order. The order can exclude any named person from the child's family home, and it is not limited to a relative of the child, nor to someone who is living in the home with the child. The exclusion order may well in practice prove most useful in protecting a child from a regular visitor to the family home, such as an ex-cohabitant of the mother, for it is likely to be easier to show that it is reasonable to exclude a visitor than to show that it is reasonable to exclude a person who lives in the home.

Subs. (2)

All three of the listed conditions must be satisfied, and the onus lies on the local authority to establish them.

Is necessary for the protection of the child. It must be shown by the applicant that the exclusion order is "necessary", but this word is not to be interpreted to mean that the exclusion order can be granted only when no other orders (such as a child protection order) are available to protect the child, for otherwise exclusion orders could never be granted. Rather it must be shown that without this order or any other order the child's welfare is at risk. It is submitted that an exclusion order is "necessary" when it is the most appropriate of the available means of protecting the child from significant harm.

Irrespective of whether the child is ... residing in the family home. An exclusion order may be necessary to allow a child to return home from a short-term refuge to which she or he has fled or been taken.

Would better safeguard the child's welfare. These words require that the sheriff undertakes a balancing of the respective merits and likely success of the different orders available to him (it being remembered that subs. (8) below permits him to make a child protection order even when asked for an exclusion order). An order excluding a regular visitor from the child's home will nearly always be better than removing the child from her or his home; the balance will be less obvious when the local authority's objective is to exclude a resident from the child's home.

There will be a person specified in the application who is capable of taking responsibility. The applicant local authority must name a person who is able to look after the child in the child's own home, and the sheriff must be satisfied that that person is both willing and able to provide that care at that place. An exclusion order will not, therefore, be appropriate in cases in which the threat to the child comes from her or his only carer, nor in cases in which both or all of the carers are alleged to be the source of danger to the child. Having been born out of the Orkney case, it is a nice irony that exclusion orders, had they been in existence then, could not have "protected" the Orkney children.

Subs. (3)

The final determination by the sheriff of the application for an exclusion order cannot be made until such time as the person to be excluded has been given an opportunity to be heard by the sheriff, either personally or through a representative, and the sheriff has given consideration to the views expressed by any person notified of the application under rules to be made. As a consequence, a final exclusion order (as opposed to an interim order made under subs. (4) below) is inappropriate as a means of providing emergency protection for the child. A final exclusion order will last for anything up to six months (see s.79(1) below) and it will, therefore, be appropriate only in those cases in which the child's interests are best served by excluding a person for that length of time. In addition, because exclusion orders are expressly mentioned in s.16(4)(b)(i), the sheriff must give the child an opportunity to express views and have appropriate regard to any views expressed.

Subss. (4), (5) and (6)

A final determination of the application can be made only when both (a) the conditions in subs. (2) above are satisfied and (b) the persons mentioned in subs. (3) above (and the child) have been given an opportunity to express views. This means that the final determination will invariably be too late to use an exclusion order as a means of emergency protection of the child. To deal with this point, the present subsections were introduced to allow immediate exclusion of someone suspected of abusing a child. They provide that where subs. (2) above is satisfied but subs. (3) above is not, an interim exclusion order can be made under subs. (4), and where subs. (3) is satisfied but subs. (2) is not (yet) satisfied an interim exclusion order can be made under subs. (6).

An interim exclusion order, once granted, has the same effect (described in s.77(1) below) as a final order, but its granting under subs. (4) (but not subs. (6)) will require the sheriff to hold a hearing under subs. (5) within a time specified in rules to be made. If such a hearing is not timeously held, the interim exclusion order will fall. At that hearing the sheriff must consider whether the conditions for the granting of an exclusion order in subs. (2) above remain satisfied, and if so he may confirm, vary or recall the order. It is not stated but the implication is clear that if not so satisfied he must recall the order. Presumably at this hearing the sheriff may also come to a final determination of the application, but if he does not do so the interim order will remain in effect on the terms laid down until the final determination. An interim order granted under subs. (6) can last up to six months (s.78 below).

Subs. (7)

Any interim order that the sheriff makes under subs. (6) above, or a continuation under subs. (5) above of an interim order made under subs. (4) above shall have the same effect (described in s.77(1) below) as a full exclusion order, and it shall last until the final determination of the application (or until six months after having been made if the application is not finally determined before then).

Subs. (8)

This subsection provides that if the conditions for the granting of a child protection order are established in an application for an exclusion order, the sheriff may treat the application as if it were an application for a child protection order. As pointed out in the notes to subs. (1) above, the conditions listed in subs. (2) above for the granting of an exclusion order are stricter than the conditions for the granting of a child protection order laid down in s.57 above. It follows that in every case in which the conditions in subs. (2) above have been satisfied, the conditions in s.57 will also have been satisfied (for proof that the child has been harmed will invariably include proof that there are reasonable grounds for believing that the child has been harmed) and the sheriff will be entitled to treat the application under this section as if it were an application under that section. In addition, the local authority may fail to satisfy the conditions in this section, but nevertheless succeed in satisfying the conditions in s.57: in that case too the sheriff may treat the application as if it had been made under s.57.

He may. The sheriff has a discretion and he is not obliged to treat the application as one for a child protection order even when the conditions for the granting of such an order have been made out (*cf.* General Note to s.55(2) above). If the conditions for both orders have been satisfied, the sheriff will decide according to which order is most likely to further the welfare of the child. If only the conditions for the granting of a child protection order have been satisfied then he will decide according to whether he considers that order rather than no order is more appropriate to the child's need for protection.

Subs. (9)

Following closely the terms in s.4(3) of the Matrimonial Homes (Family Protection) (Scotland) Act 1981, this and the immediately following two subsections prohibit the sheriff from making an exclusion order in circumstances in which it would be unjustifiable and unreasonable to do so, taking account of certain specified matters.

Unjustifiable or unreasonable. These are clearly the key words in this provision, as they are of the 1981 provision upon which this subsection is based. An exclusion order may well be "necessary" (as required in subs. (2)(b) above) but remain "unjustifiable or unreasonable", because while necessity is to be looked at from the point of view of the child, this provision requires the issue to be looked at from the point of view of the adult whom the local authority want excluded from the child's home. As explained in the General Note to subs. (2) above, an exclusion order may well be "necessary" even when other orders are available for the protection of the child, but the granting of an exclusion order might be considered unjustifiable or unreasonable when some other order is available. This cannot, however, be regarded as an automatic conclusion, otherwise there would always be a defence to an exclusion order under this provision. Rather, what is required from the sheriff is a weighing up of the respective interests of the child and the adult, and the respective effects that the different orders will have on both. If the detriment to the adult is disproportionate to the benefit to the child (bearing in mind, in making that assessment, that the child's welfare is paramount: s.16(1)) then an exclusion order under this section is likely to be considered unjustifiable or unreasonable.

Subs. (10)

The whole circumstances of the case are to be taken into account by the sheriff in determining whether it would be unjustifiable or unreasonable to make an exclusion order, and this subsection lists some of the circumstances which will always be relevant.

The conduct of the members of the child's family. The conduct is to be such as to suggest that an exclusion order should not be granted: it must, therefore, refer to conduct which suggests that members of the child's family are able to protect the child from the risk posed by the person the local authority are seeking to exclude.

Respective needs and financial resources. Every member of a child's family needs accommodation and it will seldom be justifiable or reasonable to exclude a person from her or his home when she or he has nowhere else to go. The reference to financial resources allows the sheriff to take account of the ability of the potentially excluded person to pay for alternative accommodation.

Subs. (11)

In deciding whether an exclusion order would be unjustifiable or unreasonable the sheriff must take account of any requirement (for the reasons listed in this subsection) that the potentially excluded person reside in the child's home and the likelihood of that person losing her or his entitlement to live there if the exclusion order is made.

Subs. (13)

The person with whom the child resides in the family home is defined here in the same way as "the relevant person" is defined throughout the rest of this Part of the Act (except for s.86), except that the reference is to a person with parental responsibilities rather than to a person with parental responsibilities or parental rights. This makes no difference since persons with parental responsibilities have such rights as are necessary to fulfil their responsibilities.

Effect of, and orders etc. ancillary to, exclusion order

77.—(1) An exclusion order shall, in respect of the home to which it relates, have the effect of suspending the named person's rights of occupancy (if any) and shall prevent him from entering the home, except with the express permission of the local authority which applied for the order.

(2) The sheriff, on the application of the local authority, may, if and in so far as he thinks fit, when making an exclusion order do any of the things mentioned in subsection (3) below.

(3) The things referred to in subsection (2) above are—

(a) grant a warrant for the summary ejection of the named person from the home;

(b) grant an interdict prohibiting the named person from entering the home without the express permission of the local authority;

(c) grant an interdict prohibiting the removal by the named person of any relevant item specified in the interdict from the home, except either—
　　(i) with the written consent of the local authority, or of an appropriate person; or
　　(ii) by virtue of a subsequent order of the sheriff;

(d) grant an interdict prohibiting the named person from entering or remaining in a specified area in the vicinity of the home;

(e) grant an interdict prohibiting the taking by the named person of any step of a kind specified in the interdict in relation to the child;

(f) make an order regulating the contact between the child and the named person,

and the sheriff may make any other order which he considers is necessary for the proper enforcement of a remedy granted by virtue of paragraph (a), (b) or (c) of this subsection.

(4) No warrant, interdict or order (except an interdict granted by virtue of paragraph (b) of subsection (3) above) shall be granted or made under subsection (2) above if the named person satisfies the sheriff that it is unnecessary to do so.

(5) Where the sheriff grants a warrant of summary ejection under subsection (2) above in the absence of the named person, he may give directions as to the preservation of any of that person's goods and effects which remain in the family home.

(6) The sheriff may make an order of the kind specified in subsection (3)(f) above irrespective of whether there has been an application for such an order.

(7) On the application of either the named person or the local authority, the sheriff may make the exclusion order, or any remedy granted under subsection (2) above, subject to such terms and conditions as he considers appropriate.

(8) In this Part of this Act references to a "relevant item" are references to any item within the home which both—

(a) is owned or hired by any member of the family concerned or an appropriate person or is being acquired by any such member or person under a hire purchase agreement or conditional sale agreement; and

(b) is reasonably necessary to enable the home to be used as a family residence,

but does not include any such vehicle, caravan or houseboat or such other structure so used as is mentioned in the definition of "family home" in section 76(12) of this Act.

DEFINITIONS
　"appropriate person": s.76(2)(c).
　"exclusion order": ss.76(12), 93(1).
　"family home": s.76(12).
　"local authority": Local Government etc. (Scotland) Act 1994, s.2.
　"named person": s.76(1).

GENERAL NOTE

Following on from the section above, this section sets out the effect of an exclusion order and lists various ancillary orders that the sheriff can make in connection with an exclusion order.

Subs. (1)

The effect of an exclusion order is to prevent the named person from entering the child's home over which the order has been made, and to suspend any right of occupancy that the named person has in that home. Entry into the home is permitted only with the express permission of the local authority.

Suspending the named person's rights of occupancy (if any). The order granted under s.76 can exclude any person from the child's home, whether or not that person has a right of occupancy. If the person does have a right of occupancy in that home, whether as owner, tenant or otherwise, then this is suspended for the currency of the exclusion order; if she or he has no such right then she or he can be prevented from entering into the home even with the permission of the occupier.

Exclusion order. This means an order granted under s.76(1) above, an interim order granted under s.76(4) above, the continuation granted under s.76(5) of such an interim order, and an interim order granted under s.76(6) above.

Subs. (2)

The sheriff may grant any of the warrants or interdicts or make any of the orders listed in subs. (3) below if he thinks fit. This differs somewhat from the provisions in the Matrimonial Homes (Family Protection) (Scotland) Act 1981, under which the sheriff is obliged to make some of these orders whenever he is requested to do so. Here, the matter lies entirely in the discretion of the sheriff, who must apply the three overarching principles in s.16 above in deciding whether to do any of these things. It is for the local authority which applies for the exclusion order to seek one of these ancillary orders, and to persuade the sheriff that the child's welfare would be advanced by the making of such an order.

Subs. (3)

Paragraphs (a) to (f) list the warrants, interdicts and orders that the sheriff can make ancillary to the making of an exclusion order. In addition, the sheriff can make any other order that is necessary for the proper enforcement of a warrant for summary ejection from the child's home, of an interdict prohibiting the named person entering the child's home, or of an interdict prohibiting the removal of items from the child's home. It is not clear why the statute does not permit orders necessary for the proper enforcement of the other interdicts in the subsection. Nor is it clear why para. (b) exists at all since the effect of the exclusion order is to prohibit in any case that which can be interdicted under that paragraph.

Relevant item. This is defined in subs. (8) below.

Vicinity of the home. The interdict can prohibit the named person only from a specified area in the vicinity of the child's home, and not elsewhere, such as, for example, in the vicinity of the child's school. This emphasises the essentially domestic nature of the protection afforded by an exclusion order.

Subs. (4)

The person excluded from the child's home is entitled to seek to persuade the sheriff not to make any of the ancillary orders in subs. (3) above (except one). The onus is on the person to satisfy the sheriff that such an order is unnecessary (unlike with the exclusion order itself, where the onus lies with the applicant to show that it is necessary). Only in relation to an order prohibiting the excluded person from entering the child's home without the local authority's permission is the excluded person not entitled to show that it is unnecessary. This is because such a prohibition is inherent in the exclusion order in any case, which will only have been made if the applicant local authority have established that it is necessary.

Unnecessary. This means unnecessary in light of the threat to the child. An order which is not needed to provide the child with protection is not necessary. So, for example, a warrant for the summary ejection of the excluded person from the child's home will be unnecessary if that person agrees to leave the home voluntarily, or is not in it. It will be unnecessary to grant any of the listed interdicts in situations in which there is no suggestion that the excluded person will perform any of the acts that can be interdicted.

Subs. (5)

Any of the ancillary orders can be made in relation to interim exclusion orders, made before the excluded person has been given the opportunity of being heard by the sheriff. If the ancillary order is one of summary ejection from the child's home, the sheriff may give directions of the nature specified. It is surprising in the light of the terms of subs. (6) below that no express power is given to the sheriff to give directions in the absence of any request to do so, but since the excluded person is *ex hypothesi* absent for the purposes of this subsection, it is unclear who else will make such a request and the implication must be that the sheriff can give directions *ex proprio motu.* There is no requirement that the directions under this subsection be sought by the local authority and any interested party to the exclusion order can, it is submitted, seek directions.

Subs. (6)
The sheriff can make an order regulating the contact between the child and the excluded person even when not requested to do so by the local authority. His determination to do so is governed by the three overarching principles in s.16 above.

Subs. (7)
Once the exclusion order (which includes interim orders and orders continuing interim orders) has been made, either the excluded person or the local authority can request the sheriff to subject that order to such terms and conditions as are appropriate. The sheriff's decision is governed by the three overarching principles in s.16: though s.16(4)(b)(i) refers in its terms only to the making of an exclusion order this includes, it is submitted, the conditions which are to be attached thereto.

Powers of arrest etc. in relation to exclusion order

78.—(1) The sheriff may, whether or not on an application such as is mentioned in subsection (2) below, attach a power of arrest to any interdict granted under section 77(2) of this Act by virtue of subsection (3) of that section.

(2) A local authority may at any time while an exclusion order has effect apply for such attachment of a power of arrest as is mentioned in subsection (1) above.

(3) A power of arrest attached to an interdict by virtue of subsection (1) above shall not have effect until such interdict, together with the attached power of arrest, is served on the named person.

(4) If, by virtue of subsection (1) above, a power of arrest is attached to an interdict, the local authority shall, as soon as possible after the interdict, together with the attached power of arrest, is served on the named person, ensure that there is delivered—
  (a) to the chief constable of the police area in which the family home is situated; and
  (b) where the interdict was granted by virtue of section 77(3)(e) of this Act, to the chief constable of the area in which the step or conduct which is prevented by the interdict may take place,
a copy of the application for the interdict and of the interlocutor granting the interdict together with a certificate of service of the interdict and, where the application to attach the power of arrest was made after the interdict was granted, a copy of that application and of the interlocutor above granting it and a certificate of service of the interdict together with the attached power of arrest.

(5) Where any interdict to which a power of arrest is attached by virtue of subsection (1) above is varied or recalled, the person who applied for the variation or recall shall ensure that there is delivered to each chief constable specified in subsection (4) above a copy of the application for such variation or recall and of the interlocutor granting the variation or recall.

(6) A constable may arrest without warrant the named person if he has reasonable cause for suspecting that person to be in breach of an interdict to which a power of arrest has been attached by virtue of subsection (1) above.

(7) Where a person has been arrested under subsection (6) above, the constable in charge of a police station may—
  (a) if satisfied there is no likelihood of that person further breaching the interdict to which the power of arrest was attached under subsection (1) above, liberate him unconditionally; or
  (b) refuse to liberate that person.
  (8) Such a refusal to liberate an arrested person as is mentioned in subsection (7)(b) above, and the detention of that person until his appearance in court by virtue of either subsection (11) below, or any provision of the Criminal Procedure (Scotland) Act 1975, shall not subject that constable to any claim whatsoever.
  (9) Where a person has been liberated under subsection (7)(a) above, the facts and circumstances which gave rise to the arrest shall be reported to the procurator fiscal forthwith.
  (10) Subsections (11) to (13) below apply only where—
  (a) the arrested person has not been released under subsection (7)(a) above; and
  (b) the procurator fiscal decides that no criminal proceedings are to be taken in respect of the facts and circumstances which gave rise to the arrest.
  (11) A person arrested under subsection (6) above shall, wherever practicable, be brought before the sheriff sitting as a court of summary criminal jurisdiction for the district in which he was arrested not later than in the course of the first day after the arrest, such day not being a Saturday, a Sunday or a court holiday prescribed for that court under section 10 of the Bail etc. (Scotland) Act 1980, on which the sheriff is not sitting for the disposal of criminal business.
  (12) Subsections (1) and (3) of section 3 of the Criminal Justice (Scotland) Act 1980 (intimation to a person named by the person arrested) shall apply to a person arrested under subsection (6) above as they apply to a person who has been arrested in respect of an offence.
  (13) Where a person is brought before the sheriff under subsection (11) above—
  (a) the procurator fiscal shall present to the court a petition containing—
      (i) a statement of the particulars of the person arrested under subsection (6) above;
      (ii) a statement of the facts and circumstances which gave rise to that arrest; and
      (iii) a request that the person be detained for a further period not exceeding two days;
  (b) the sheriff, if it appears to him that—
      (i) the statement referred to in paragraph (a)(ii) above discloses a *prima facie* breach of interdict by the arrested person;
      (ii) proceedings for breach of interdict will be taken; and
      (iii) there is a substantial risk of violence by the arrested person against any member of the family, or an appropriate person, resident in the family home,
    may order the arrested person to be detained for a period not exceeding two days; and
  (c) the sheriff shall, in any case in which paragraph (b) above does not apply, order the release of the arrested person from custody (unless that person is in custody in respect of some other matter);
and in computing the period of two days referred to in paragraphs (a) and (b) above, no account shall be taken of a Saturday, a Sunday or any holiday in the court in which proceedings for breach of interdict will require to be raised.
  (14) Where a person—
  (a) is liberated under subsection (7)(a) above; or

(b) is to be brought before the sheriff under subsection (11) above,
the procurator fiscal shall at the earliest opportunity, and, in the case of a
person to whom paragraph (b) above applies, before that person is brought
before the sheriff, take all reasonable steps to intimate to—
   (i) the local authority which made the application for the interdict;
   (ii) an appropriate person who will reside in, or who remains in residence
     in, the family home mentioned in the order; and
   (iii) any solicitor who acted for the appropriate person when the interdict
     was granted or to any other solicitor who the procurator fiscal has rea-
     son to believe acts for the time being for that person,
that he has decided that no criminal proceedings should be taken in respect
of the facts and circumstances which gave rise to the arrest of the named
person.

DEFINITIONS
   "appropriate person": s.76(2)(c).
   "constable": s.93(1).
   "family": s.93(1).
   "family home": s.76(12).
   "local authority": Local Government etc. (Scotland) Act 1994, s.2.
   "named person": s.76(1).

GENERAL NOTE
   The sheriff may, at his own hand or on application by the local authority either when the
exclusion order is applied for or at any time during its currency, attach a power of arrest to any
interdict which has been granted ancillary to the exclusion order itself. This section sets out the
applicable circumstances and the consequences of such a power of arrest.

Duration, variation and recall of exclusion order

   79.—(1) Subject to subsection (2) below, an exclusion order shall cease to
have effect on a date six months after being made.
   (2) An exclusion order shall cease to have effect on a date prior to the date
mentioned in subsection (1) above where—
   (a) the order contains a direction by the sheriff that it shall cease to have
     effect on that prior date;
   (b) the sheriff, on an application under subsection (3) below, recalls the
     order before the date so mentioned; or
   (c) any permission given by a third party to the spouse or partner of the
     named person, or to an appropriate person, to occupy the home to
     which the order relates is withdrawn.
   (3) The sheriff may, on the application of the local authority, the named
person, an appropriate person or the spouse or partner of the named person,
if that spouse or partner is not excluded from the family home and is not an
appropriate person, vary or recall an exclusion order and any warrant, interdict, order or direction granted or made under section 77 of this Act.
   (4) For the purposes of this section, partners are persons who live together
in a family home as if they were husband and wife.

DEFINITIONS
   "appropriate person": s.76(2)(c).
   "family home": s.76(12).
   "local authority": Local Government etc. (Scotland) Act 1994, s.2.
   "named person": s.76(1).

GENERAL NOTE
   This section deals with the duration, variation and recall of exclusion orders.

Subs. (1)
   Unless brought to an end earlier in terms of subs. (2) below, an exclusion order ceases to have
effect six months after it was made. There is nothing to prevent a local authority seeking a new

exclusion order immediately on the termination of the old (so long as the conditions in s.76(2) can again be satisfied).

Exclusion order. What is being referred to here is the final order made on an application under s.76(1) above, an interim order made under s.76(6) and a continuation granted under s.76(5) of an interim order made under s.76(4). The phrase does not include, for this purpose, an interim order made under s.76(4): see s.76(12) above.

A date six months after being made. It is six calendar months that are being referred to: an order made on February 6 comes to an end at midnight on the immediately following August 5; an order made on September 1 comes to an end at midnight on the immediately following February 28 or 29.

Subs. (2)

An exclusion order need not last six months if any of the three circumstances listed here applies, that is to say, if the sheriff directed on making the order that it should cease on some sooner date, or if the sheriff recalls the order on an application under subs. (3) below, or if the excluded person's spouse or heterosexual cohabitant (subs. (4)) or the person looking after the child becomes no longer entitled to occupy the child's home. This last might include, for example, the termination of a lease or the sale of the house during the currency of the exclusion order: it is appropriate to bring the order to an end in these circumstances since the child will no longer practically be able to live in the house the person is excluded from. It is unfortunate that the paragraph was not expressed more clearly in terms of the child's departure rather than the "appropriate person's" right.

Subs. (3)

There is no provision in the Act expressly granting a right of appeal to the sheriff principal or to the Court of Session from a decision of the sheriff to grant (or refuse) an exclusion order, though normal principles of appeal will apply (it is assumed in s.92 below in the legal aid provisions that there is an appeal from the sheriff in relation to exclusion orders). In addition, application can be made under this subsection to the sheriff for the variation or recall of an exclusion order and any order made ancillary to it. The Act gives no direction to the sheriff as to how to deal with such an application, except that the three overarching principles in s.16 above apply. It follows that a sheriff may competently recall an exclusion order if he considers that this is in the interests of the child, even when the conditions for its making remain satisfied. It is unclear why the subsection limits so carefully title to seek a variation or discharge in circumstances in which the child's welfare is paramount. It would have been more consistent with the advancement of the child's welfare to allow any person claiming an interest to make such an application (*cf.* s.11(3) above which entitles "any person who . . . claims an interest" to seek a private law order, s.86(5) below which entitles "any person claiming an interest" to seek a variation or discharge of a parental responsibilities order, and s.88(3) below which entitles "any person with an interest" to seek an order as to contact between a child subject to a parental responsibilities order and another person). There would seem to be nothing to prevent an unsuccessful applicant for recall making a fresh application immediately thereafter, and there is no provision, analogous to that contained in s.51(7) above in relation to appeals against decisions of children's hearings, to prevent frivolous applications.

The sheriff. It is the sheriff within whose sheriffdom the family home is situated who has jurisdiction to vary or recall the exclusion order: s.80(2) below.

Exclusion orders: supplementary provisions

80.—(1) The Secretary of State may make regulations with respect to the powers, duties and functions of local authorities in relation to exclusion orders.

(2) An application for an exclusion order, or under section 79(3) of this Act for the variation or recall of such an order or of any thing done under section 77(2) of this Act, shall be made to the sheriff for the sheriffdom within which the family home is situated.

DEFINITIONS
   "exclusion order": s.76(12).
   "family home": s.76(12).
   "local authority": Local Government etc. (Scotland) Act 1994, s.2.

GENERAL NOTE
Under subs. (1) the Secretary of State is given the power to make regulations concerning the powers, duties and functions of local authorities. Subsection (2) concerns jurisdiction.

Offences in connection with orders etc. for protection of children

Offences in connection with orders etc. for protection of children

81. A person who intentionally obstructs—
(a) any person acting under a child protection order;
(b) any person acting under an authorisation granted under section 61(1) or (2) of this Act; or
(c) a constable acting under section 61(5) of this Act,
shall, subject to section 38(3) and (4) of this Act, be guilty of an offence and shall be liable on summary conviction to a fine not exceeding level 3 on the standard scale.

DEFINITIONS
"child protection order": ss.57(1), 93(1).

GENERAL NOTE
It is an offence, which attracts the stated penalty, intentionally to obstruct any person acting under a child protection order made under s.57 above or under an authorisation granted by a justice of the peace when a sheriff is not available to make a child protection order, or to obstruct a constable removing a child to a place of safety and keeping her or him there.

Fugitive children and harbouring

Recovery of certain fugitive children

82.—(1) A child who absconds—
(a) from a place of safety in which he is being kept under or by virtue of this Part of this Act;
(b) from a place (in this section referred to as a "relevant place") which, though not a place of safety such as is mentioned in paragraph (a) above, is a residential establishment in which he is required to reside by virtue of section 70(3)(a) of this Act or a hospital or other institution in which he is temporarily residing while subject to such a requirement; or
(c) from a person who, by virtue of a supervision requirement or of section 74 of this Act, has control over him while he is being taken to, is awaiting being taken to, or (whether or not by reason of being on leave) is temporarily away from, such place of safety or relevant place,
may be arrested without warrant in any part of the United Kingdom and taken to the place of safety or as the case may be the relevant place; and a court which is satisfied that there are reasonable grounds for believing that the child is within any premises may, where there is such power of arrest, grant a warrant authorising a constable to enter those premises and search for the child using reasonable force if necessary.

(2) Without prejudice to the generality of subsection (1) above, a child who at the end of a period of leave from a place of safety or relevant place fails to return there shall, for the purposes of this section, be taken to have absconded.

(3) A child who absconds from a person who, not being a person mentioned in paragraph (c) of subsection (1) above, is a person who has control over him by virtue of a supervision requirement may, subject to the same provisions as those to which an arrest under that subsection is subject, be arrested as is mentioned in that subsection and returned to that person; and the provision in that subsection for a warrant to be granted shall apply as

respects such a child as it applies as respects a child mentioned in that subsection.

(4) If a child—

(a) is taken under subsection (1) above to a place of safety or relevant place; or

(b) is returned under subsection (3) above to a person,

but the occupier of that place of safety or of that relevant place, or as the case may be that person, is unwilling or unable to receive him, that circumstance shall be intimated forthwith to the Principal Reporter.

(5) Where intimation is required by subsection (4) above as respects a child, he shall be kept in a place of safety until—

(a) in a case where he is subject to a supervision requirement, he can be brought before a children's hearing for that requirement to be reviewed; or

(b) in any other case, the Principal Reporter has, in accordance with section 56(6) of this Act, considered whether compulsory measures of supervision are required in respect of him.

DEFINITIONS

"child": s.93(2)(b).
"children's hearing": s.93(1).
"constable": s.93(1).
"place of safety": s.93(1).
"principal reporter": s.93(1).
"residential establishment": s.93(1).
"supervision requirement": ss.70(1), 93(1).

GENERAL NOTE

This section replaces, with only minor amendments, ss.69 and 70 of the 1968 Act, and provides that a child who has absconded from a place of safety or residential establishment or from a person can be arrested without a warrant and returned to where she or he absconded from.

Subss. (1) and (2)

As well as permitting the child to be arrested without a warrant, subs. (1) also permits the court to grant a warrant authorising a police officer to enter premises and search for the child. There are two changes from the 1968 Act: the present provision permits the child's arrest anywhere in the U.K. rather than, as previously, in the U.K. or the Channel Islands (though the reference to the Channel Islands may be restored: see s.105(10) below); and the authorisation to enter premises expressly permits the police officer to use reasonable force.

A child who absconds. A child absconds when she or he removes her or himself from the relevant place. It expressly includes the child who fails to return to a place after a period of leave, and it is likely to include also the child who absents her or himself to prevent being taken in the first place to the relevant place.

Subs. (3)

The same provisions apply in relation to a child who absconds from the control of a person who has that control by virtue of a supervision requirement. This might be, for example, a foster carer or a relative. It would not apply to a child who is required to reside with a person who otherwise than under the supervision requirement has parental responsibilities or parental rights over her or him.

Subss. (4) and (5)

These provisions replace s.69(3) and (4) of the 1968 Act and have much the same effect. If the child cannot be returned to the place or person from whom she or he absconded due to unwillingness to receive the child back, the reporter must be informed and the child kept in a place of safety until a children's hearing has been arranged (if currently subject to a supervision requirement) or the reporter has considered whether compulsory measures of supervision are required (in any other case). One alteration from the 1968 provisions, the reason for which is not apparent, is the removal of the requirement to hold the children's hearing within seven days. The current wording suggests that a hearing should be arranged as soon as practicable, but it does not, unlike most other provisions of the Act, specify when that hearing should be arranged. The provision cannot be interpreted to permit a child to be kept in a place of safety indefinitely.

Harbouring

83. A person who—
(a) knowingly assists or induces a child to abscond in circumstances which render the child liable to arrest under subsection (1) or (3) of section 82 of this Act;
(b) knowingly and persistently attempts to induce a child so to abscond;
(c) knowingly harbours or conceals a child who has so absconded; or
(d) knowingly prevents a child from returning—
    (i) to a place mentioned in paragraph (a) or (b) of the said subsection (1);
    (ii) to a person mentioned in paragraph (c) of that subsection, or in the said subsection (3),
shall, subject to section 38(3) and (4) of this Act, to section 51(5) and (6) of the Children Act 1989 and to Article 70(5) and (6) of the Children (Northern Ireland) Order 1995 (analogous provision for England and Wales and for Northern Ireland), be guilty of an offence and liable on summary conviction to a fine not exceeding level 5 on the standard scale or to imprisonment for a term not exceeding six months or to both such fine and such imprisonment.

DEFINITIONS
"child": s.93(2)(b).

GENERAL NOTE
This section replaces s.71 of the 1968 Act, with no substantive change. It is a crime with the stated penalty to do any of the listed acts. This is qualified by s.38 above, under which local authorities can provide short-term refuges for children at risk of harm who seek such refuge.

Implementation of authorisations etc.

Implementation of authorisations etc.

84. Where an order, authorisation or warrant under this Chapter or Chapter 2 of this Part of this Act grants power to find a child and to keep him in a place of safety, such order, authorisation or warrant may be implemented as if it were a warrant for the apprehension of an accused person issued by a court of summary jurisdiction; and any enactment or rule of law applying to such a warrant shall, subject to the provisions of this Act, apply in like manner to the order, authorisation or warrant.

DEFINITIONS
"child": s.93(2)(b).
"place of safety": s.93(1).

GENERAL NOTE
This section specifies the effect of orders, authorisations and warrants granted under ss.39–85 of the present Act.

New evidence: review of establishment of grounds of referral

Application for review of establishment of grounds of referral

85.—(1) Subject to subsections (3) and (4) below, where subsection (2) below applies an application may be made to the sheriff for a review of a finding such as is mentioned in section 68(10) of this Act.
(2) This subsection applies where the sheriff, on an application made by virtue of subsection (7) or (9) of section 65 of this Act (in this section referred to as the "original application"), finds that any of the grounds of referral is established.
(3) An application under subsection (1) above may only be made where the applicant claims—

(a) to have evidence which was not considered by the sheriff on the original application, being evidence the existence or significance of which might materially have affected the determination of the original application;

(b) that such evidence—
   (i) is likely to be credible and reliable; and
   (ii) would have been admissible in relation to the ground of referral which was found to be established on the original application; and

(c) that there is a reasonable explanation for the failure to lead such evidence on the original application.

(4) An application under subsection (1) above may only be made by—

(a) the child in respect of whom the ground of referral was found to be established; or

(b) any person who is a relevant person in relation to that child.

(5) Where the sheriff on an application under subsection (1) above is not satisfied that any of the claims made in the application are established he shall dismiss the application.

(6) Where the sheriff is satisfied on an application under subsection (1) above that the claims made in the application are established, he shall consider the evidence and if, having considered it, he is satisfied that—

(a) none of the grounds of referral in the original application to which the application relates is established, he shall allow the application, discharge the referral to the children's hearing in respect of those grounds and proceed in accordance with subsection (7) below in relation to any supervision requirement made in respect of the child (whether or not varied under section 73 of this Act) in so far as it relates to any such ground; or

(b) any ground of referral in the original application to which the application relates is established, he may proceed in accordance with section 68(10) of this Act.

(7) Where the sheriff is satisfied as is mentioned in subsection (6)(a) above, he may—

(a) order that any supervision requirement so mentioned shall terminate—
   (i) immediately; or
   (ii) on such date as he may specify; or

(b) if he is satisfied that there is evidence sufficient to establish any ground of referral, being a ground which was not stated in the original application, find such ground established and proceed in accordance with section 68(10) of this Act in relation to that ground.

(8) Where the sheriff specifies a date for the termination of a supervision requirement in accordance with subsection (7)(a)(ii) above, he may, before such termination, order a variation of that requirement, of any requirement imposed under subsection (6) of section 70 of this Act, or of any determination made under subsection (7) of that section; and such variation may take effect—

(a) immediately; or

(b) on such date as he may specify.

(9) Where the sheriff orders the termination of a supervision requirement in accordance with subsection (7)(a) above, he shall consider whether, after such termination, the child concerned will still require supervision or guidance; and where he considers that such supervision or guidance will be necessary he shall direct a local authority to provide it in accordance with subsection (10) below.

(10) Where a sheriff has given a direction under subsection (9) above, it shall be the duty of the local authority to comply with that direction; but that duty shall be regarded as discharged where they offer such supervision or

guidance to the child and he, being a child of sufficient age and maturity to understand what is being offered, is unwilling to accept it.

DEFINITIONS
"child": s.93(2)(b).
"children's hearing": s.93(1).
"local authority": Local Government etc. (Scotland) Act 1994, s.2.
"relevant person": s.93(2)(b).
"supervision requirement": ss.70(1), 93(1).

GENERAL NOTE
Though the 1968 Act was designed to create a unified and comprehensive code for dealing with children who may be in need of compulsory measures of care, the very novelty of the system it set up meant that certain gaps and omissions were inevitable. Some of these gaps were filled by amending legislation (such as the provisions introduced by the Children Act 1975 (c. 72) relating to safeguarders); and some have been left to the imagination of the Court of Session. One such omission concerned what was to happen when new evidence came to light after the sheriff had found a ground of referral to exist, which cast doubt on that original finding. There was no provision in the 1968 Act permitting the reopening of the question of whether a ground of referral existed or not, and appeal from a sheriff's decision was available on a point of law only. In *R. v. Kennedy* 1993 S.L.T. 910 parents of a child subject to a supervision requirement, who had all along disputed the grounds of referral found established by the sheriff, petitioned the *nobile officium* for an order requiring the sheriff to consider anew whether or not the grounds of referral had been made out, in the light of new evidence (which took the form, in this case, of a retraction by the child of her original allegations against her father of sexual abuse). The Inner House held that such a petition was incompetent since to allow a rehearing would be a judicial supplement to the statutory procedure laid down in the 1968 Act. However, in *L, Petrs* (No. 1) 1993 S.L.T. 1310 and (No. 2) 1342 (the so-called "Ayrshire Child Abuse Case") a similar petition to the *nobile officium* was granted. The parents in that case had alleged that new expert evidence was available which cast considerable doubt on the original expert evidence upon which the sheriff had based his findings, and that there was currently a much greater awareness since the Clyde Report into the Orkney Case of the need to be especially careful in interviewing children alleged to be the victims of abuse, which awareness had not been shown in the present case. The Inner House accepted that this justified them ordering the sheriff to examine again the question of whether the ground of referral existed or not, but the procedure under which this rehearing took place and the effect it had on any extant supervision requirement had to be determined by the Court of Session without any statutory guidance.

The effect of these two cases (which are probably irreconcilable) was to leave the law in a state of considerable doubt. The level of evidence required to persuade the court to exercise the *nobile officium*, the effect on supervision requirements, the role of the Court of Session, the issue of title to sue, the availability of appeal, and many other matters remained to be determined. The present section is designed to put the process for re-examining the grounds of referral on to a statutory basis, to clarify the grounds upon which rehearings can take place, and to specify what is to happen to any supervision requirement that has been made on the basis of a ground of referral which is subsequently found not to have been made out. An appeal from any decision of the sheriff under this section can be made in terms of s.51(11) above to the sheriff principal or the Court of Session.

Subss. (1) and (2)
When a sheriff has found any ground of referral in relation to a child established, whether the application for proof had been made because the child or parent denies the ground or because the child has been found by the children's hearing to be too young to understand the ground, an application can be made to the sheriff by any of the persons specified in subs. (4) below to reconsider the establishment of that ground. Such an application can be made whenever the applicant makes the three claims listed in subs. (3) below. The section does not place any limitation on when this application can be made, except implicitly that it must be after such a finding has been made. However, it might be made either before a children's hearing have imposed a supervision requirement upon the child, or after (even, as in *L, Petrs*, some years after), or, indeed, after a children's hearing have decided that no supervision requirement is justified in the case. This last would be rare, but the section provides for a challenge to the sheriff's finding and not to the imposition of a supervision requirement, and it follows that the challenge is competent even when the children's hearing discharge the referral or terminate the supervision requirement. A challenge might be made in these circumstances as a means of clearing a person's name, unjustly impugned by the original sheriff's finding.

Finds that any of the grounds of referral is established. An application under this section cannot be made when there has been no finding by the sheriff, such as when the child and parent accept the ground but later wish to retract that acceptance. An application can be made when the sheriff has dispensed with hearing the evidence under s.68(8), for he still makes a finding in that situation.

Subs. (3)

The applicant under this section must claim and, if the application for a review of the establishment of the grounds is to be successful must establish, each of the three conditions listed in this subsection, that is to say that material evidence was not considered by the sheriff at the original proof hearing, that the evidence is likely to be credible and was admissible, and that there is a reasonable explanation for the failure to have led that evidence at the original hearing.

Evidence which was not considered. This might include evidence which the sheriff did not hear because he dispensed with hearing the evidence under s.68(8) above.

There is a reasonable explanation. This is a lesser test than the Court of Session required for an application under the *nobile officium*, for in *L, Petrs* it was held that evidence could be heard only if the circumstances which had arisen were "exceptional and unforeseen". A reasonable explanation might include the non-availability of the evidence, for whatever reason (so long as that reason is not directly attributable to the applicant), or because of new understandings which have developed since the original finding.

Subs. (4)

Title to seek a rehearing on the basis of new evidence inheres only in the child and in any relevant person (*i.e.* any person with parental responsibilities or parental rights, or any person who ordinarily has charge of or control over the child) and no other person can challenge a finding of the sheriff that a ground of referral in relation to the child exists.

Subs. (5)

The onus is on the applicant to establish, to the satisfaction of the sheriff, the validity of all three claims made under subs. (3) above, and that may be challenged by the reporter or any person who would have title to raise an action under this section. If any one or more of the claims is not established then the application must be dismissed. There is no provision for the hearing of evidence to establish these claims, and the sheriff must make his determination on the basis of argument put before him. This will be directed towards an examination of the nature of the evidence and how it has come to light, but the evidence itself will not be, at this stage, challengeable.

Subs. (6)

If the sheriff determines that all three of the claims made in subs. (3) above are established then the application for a review of the original finding will be granted, and the sheriff must then move on to consider the new evidence which the applicant claims to have. That consideration will take the same form as a consideration of evidence at an original hearing to establish grounds of referral under s.68 above. Having examined the evidence and heard such parties as are entitled to and wish to make representations to the sheriff, the sheriff must then decide whether the original ground, or any of the original grounds, of referral is, or are, established.

Paragraph (a). If the sheriff is satisfied that none of the original grounds of referral has been established he must discharge the referral. If the application has been made before any supervision requirement has been imposed by a children's hearing then none can be imposed thereafter in respect of these grounds, and if the child has already been made subject to a supervision requirement in respect of the grounds then on the discharge of the referral the sheriff must deal with that requirement in accordance with the rules in subs. (7) below.

Paragraph (b). If the sheriff is satisfied that any one or more of the original grounds of referral has been established he may remit the case to the reporter to arrange a children's hearing. The use of the permissive "may" here must be read in the light of s.68(10) above, under which the sheriff "shall" remit the case to the reporter on a finding that grounds of referral have been established. If the child is not currently under a supervision requirement in respect of the grounds found (again) to be established because a hearing has not yet been arranged then the sheriff has, it is submitted, a discretion only in the sense that he may decide not to remit the case to the reporter when the reporter is already in the process of arranging a children's hearing. If the child is not under a supervision requirement because the children's hearing discharged the referral in respect of the grounds now confirmed (but challenged, say, to clear someone's name) the sheriff may decide to remit the case back to the reporter if he thinks that the original decision of the children's hearing was not justified in all the circumstances of the case, or if the circumstances have changed sufficiently, or if new circumstances have come to light in the course of the rehearing, to justify the children's hearing looking at the matter afresh. Similarly, the sheriff will have a discretion when the child is currently subject to a supervision requirement in respect of the grounds confirmed to exist. A remit to the reporter in these circumstances will normally be redundant, but it might be appropriate when the child is already subject to a supervision requirement if the evidence presented to the sheriff satisfies him that the requirement ought to be reviewed.

Subs. (7)

When the original grounds of referral have been shown to be not made out, the sheriff must then go on to decide whether any other ground of referral is made out. If not, his choices are governed by para. (a) of this subsection, and if so, he must act in accordance with para. (b).

Under para. (a), if the child is currently subject to a supervision requirement, the sheriff may either terminate the supervision requirement immediately, or terminate it on a date he may specify. It is not within the discretion of the sheriff to do anything other than these two listed options, such as continuing the supervision requirement, for a child cannot be kept subject to a supervision requirement in the absence of an original ground of referral except where its termination is being postponed under this paragraph.

Under para. (b), if the sheriff determines that a ground of referral has been made out, though not the one originally established, then he may remit the case to the reporter to arrange a children's hearing for the consideration of the case based on that new established ground. As in subs. (6) above, the permissive "may" is to be read in light of the "shall" used in s.68(10) above. It is submitted that in all cases in which this paragraph applies the sheriff ought to remit the case to the reporter to arrange a children's hearing which in effect will be a review of the supervision requirement that the child is currently under (and which cannot be terminated under this paragraph: para. (a), which permits termination, is conjoined with this paragraph by "or"). If the sheriff has found a ground of referral to exist which is different from the original ground, then that amounts to a finding that the basis for the original supervision requirement was false and that requirement therefore stands in need of urgent review. If the child is, for whatever reason, not currently under a supervision requirement but a new ground is established then the question arises as to whether compulsory measures of supervision are required (see the terms of s.52(1) above). For the sheriff not to remit the case to the reporter for the arranging of a children's hearing would, in effect, be for the sheriff to answer that question and therefore to usurp the role of the children's hearing.

On such date as he may specify. The decision to postpone the termination of the supervision requirement must be made on the basis of the welfare of the child as expressed in s.16(1) above. It is to be noted that this was one of the effects of the Inner House's decision in *L, Petrs* (above), where it was considered to be against the children's interests to be returned home since they had been separated from their parents for a very long time and this is the sort of reason why a termination might appropriately be postponed. There is no limit specified for how long the sheriff can postpone the termination of the supervision requirement, but it is submitted that it would be inconsistent with the provisions determining the duration of supervision requirements contained in s.73 above to allow the sheriff to specify a date beyond the time at which a hearing must sit to review that requirement. Otherwise the sheriff would be prolonging an order, which was made upon the basis of false information, beyond its natural life. If the child's interests require further compulsory measures of supervision then new grounds can surely be formulated by the reporter.

Being a ground which was not stated in the original application. It is not necessary that the new ground which the sheriff finds established is one based on a different paragraph in s.52. Rather it must be based on different circumstances which amount to a ground of referral in accordance with any of these paragraphs. So the sheriff may find that the original ground (for example, the commission of the offence of assault) has not been made out but that a quite separate offence (say, that of theft) has been made out. Or the sheriff may find that the child has not been a victim of a Sched. 1 offence (a ground under s.52(2)(d) above) but lives in the same household as such a victim (a ground under s.52(2)(e) above).

There is nothing to prevent this finding being based on the same facts that founded the original finding: for example the sheriff may find that the facts do not justify a finding that the child has committed the offence of assault, but do justify a finding that the child has committed a breach of the peace.

Subs. (8)

If a sheriff is satisfied that none of the original grounds of referral are established but has decided, in the child's best interests, to postpone the termination of the supervision requirement, he may vary that requirement in any way he thinks fit (being guided again by the child's welfare), or vary any condition attached to it, or any requirement to keep the child's address secret, or any determination by the children's hearing concerning the length of time which the supervision requirement is to last. In other words, once the sheriff has determined that the supervision requirement is to be terminated, but that termination is to be postponed, every aspect of that requirement is under the control of, and open to variation by, the sheriff. There is no requirement that the sheriff takes account of the views of the child under s.16(2) above (nor, indeed, that the child attend at the rehearing), but good practice suggests that the sheriff should do so in appropriate circumstances.

Subs. (9)
   If a supervision requirement is to be terminated, the sheriff must go on to consider whether the child should be offered voluntary supervision and guidance. If he considers that such supervision and guidance is necessary for the child he must direct the local authority to provide it.
   A local authority. This provision is not limited to the local authority in whose area the child was first brought to a children's hearing but may be any local authority specified by the sheriff.

Subs. (10)
   The local authority directed under subs. (9) above to provide supervision and guidance must do so, but need not do so, when the child is unwilling to accept such supervision and guidance and the child is of sufficient age and maturity to understand what is being offered.

CHAPTER 4

PARENTAL RESPONSIBILITIES ORDERS, ETC.

Parental responsibilities orders

Parental responsibilities order: general

   86.—(1) On the application of a local authority the sheriff may make an order transferring (but only during such period as the order remains in force) the appropriate parental rights and responsibilities relating to a child to them; and any such order shall be known as a "parental responsibilities order".
   (2) A parental responsibilities order shall not be made unless the sheriff is satisfied that each relevant person either—
      (a) freely, and with full understanding of what is involved, agrees unconditionally that the order be made; or
      (b) is a person who—
            (i) is not known, cannot be found or is incapable of giving agreement;
            (ii) is withholding such agreement unreasonably;
            (iii) has persistently failed, without reasonable cause, to fulfil one or other of the following parental responsibilities in relation to the child, that is to say the responsibility to safeguard and promote the child's health, development and welfare or, if the child is not living with him, the responsibility to maintain personal relations and direct contact with the child on a regular basis; or
            (iv) has seriously ill-treated the child, whose reintegration into the same household as that person is, because of the serious ill-treatment or for other reasons, unlikely.
   (3) The reference in subsection (1) above to the appropriate parental rights and responsibilities relating to the child is to all parental rights and responsibilities except any right to agree, or decline to agree—
      (a) to the making of an application in relation to the child under section 18 (freeing for adoption) or 55 (adoption abroad) of the Adoption Act 1976, under section 18 or 49 of the Adoption (Scotland) Act 1978 or under Article 17, 18 or 57 of the Adoption (Northern Ireland) Order 1987 (corresponding provision for Scotland and Northern Ireland); or
      (b) to the making of an adoption order.

(4) A person is a relevant person for the purposes of this section if he is a parent of the child or a person who for the time being has parental rights in relation to the child.

(5) The sheriff may, in an order under this section, impose such conditions as he considers appropriate; and he may vary or discharge such an order on the application of the local authority, of the child, of any person who immediately before the making of the order is a relevant person or of any other person claiming an interest.

(6) An order under this section shall, if not first discharged by the sheriff, terminate on the occurrence of any of the following—

(a) the child attains the age of eighteen years;
(b) he becomes the subject—

　　(i) of an adoption order within the meaning of the Adoption (Scotland) Act 1978; or

　　(ii) of an order under section 18 (freeing for adoption) or 55 (adoption abroad) of the Adoption Act 1976, under section 18 or 49 of the said Act of 1978 or under Article 17, 18 or 57 of the Adoption (Northern Ireland) Order 1987 (corresponding provision for Scotland and Northern Ireland);

(c) an order is made for his return under Part I of the Child Abduction and Custody Act 1985; or
(d) a decision, other than a decision mentioned in section 25(2) of the said Act of 1985 (decisions relating to rights of access), is registered with respect to him under section 16 of that Act.

DEFINITIONS

"child": s.93(2)(a).
"local authority": Local Government etc. (Scotland) Act 1994, s.2.
"parental responsibilities": ss.1(3), 93(1).
"parental rights": ss.2(4), 93(1).

GENERAL NOTE

Under the provisions of ss.16–18A of the Social Work (Scotland) Act 1968 a local authority could in certain circumstances assume parental rights and powers over a child. This was achieved simply by the local authority passing a resolution, which had the effect of transferring the relevant rights and powers held by the parent in respect of whom the resolution was passed to the local authority themselves. The procedure was frequently, though not invariably, a prelude to adoption. There was no need for any court process before the resolution was made, though if the parent wished to challenge it this could be done by counter-notice which had the effect of putting the onus on the local authority to take the matter to the sheriff court for confirmation of the resolution. (See Wilkinson and Norrie *Parent and Child*, chap. 16 (1993, W. Green) for full details). These provisions, repealed in Sched. 5, are replaced with the present ss.86–89, which have followed the recommendations of the *Child Care Law Review* (Scottish Office, October 1990). The new rules represent a radical reshaping of the statutory procedure for local authority acquisition of parental responsibilities and parental rights. Among the most significant changes are the following: (1) power to make what is called a "parental responsibilities order" is vested solely in the sheriff and title to apply for such an order inheres solely in the local authority; (2) the grounds upon which such an order can be granted are very substantially simplified and clarified from the grounds upon which a local authority could assume parental rights and powers under the 1968 Act, though the effect of the order is to all intents and purposes the same as the effect of the old resolution; (3) the sheriff is given guidance as to how to come to his decision, for s.16 above provides that the sheriff must apply the three overarching principles listed there; (4) the limitation in the 1968 Act of the assumption provisions to those children statutorily "in care" is removed and the sheriff can make a parental responsibilities order over any child in his jurisdiction; (5) the order is made in relation to the child who needs to be looked after rather than in relation to a parent who has forfeited the right to bring up the child: this means that the order is available only when there is no suitable person available to look after the child (rather than, as before, when one of a number of persons had forfeited their right).

One noticeable feature of the current provisions is the extent to which things are left unsaid. For example, no section spells out the effect of the order on the parent's parental responsibilities and parental rights, and this is left to implication. Nor are the rights, powers, duties and responsibilities of the local authority in whose favour the order is made spelt out in Chap. 4 of this Part, and we must look both to other chapters in this Part and indeed to other Parts to delimit the extent of the local authority's role. Also, the definition of those parental rights which are transferred is, as we will see, unhelpful in the extreme. Again, contrasting sharply both with the equivalent English provisions (s.94 of the Children Act 1989) and with the provisions in the current statute in relation to children's hearings (s.51 above), there is no provision dealing with the right of appeal from the sheriff's decision. No right of appeal was laid down in the provisions under the 1968 Act dealing with the sheriff's confirmation of a local authority resolution but the competency of such appeals was never doubted (see Wilkinson and Norrie *Parent and Child* at pp. 440–441) and it can be assumed that the normal rules of appeals from decisions of the sheriff will apply to decisions under this Chapter also. (Though there is no express provision for legal aid for such appeals in s.92 below, that cannot be taken to suggest that no appeals are competent, for no legal aid is expressly provided in that section for the defending of an application under this section though there can be no doubt as to its availability).

Subs. (1)

A "parental responsibilities order" is an order which is made by a sheriff, on the application of a local authority, transferring the "appropriate parental rights and responsibilities" (defined in subs. (3) below) to the local authority. It is only a local authority who can apply for such an order, and not, for example the parent or the child. In addition, it is only to a local authority that the order can transfer parental rights and responsibilities. The statute does not expressly state from whom the rights and responsibilities are transferred, though implicitly it is each "relevant person" referred to in subs. (2) below and defined in subs. (4) below.

An order transferring. Bizarrely, there is no provision in the Act indicating the effect that a parental responsibilities order has on a relevant person's parental responsibilities and parental rights and we must assume an effect similar to that created by the old legislation. The word "transferring" indicates that the relevant person's parental responsibilities and parental rights are removed from that person and vested in the local authority. This was certainly the effect of a parental rights resolution under the 1968 Act and it would subvert the whole point of the order if the present provisions did not also have this effect. It is unfortunate that this important point has been left to implication, though it is submitted that the implication is inevitable. Confirmation that the order removes a person's parental responsibilities and parental rights can be found in s.11(4) above, which denies title to seek a s.11 order to a number of categories of individuals, including those whose responsibilities or rights have been "transferred" by this section: all are clearly meant to cover persons whose responsibilities and rights have been expressly removed. The use of the word "transferring" also suggests on first reading that the local authority obtains only those responsibilities and rights that the relevant person had immediately before the order was made, for there cannot be "transferred" from a person to a local authority that which the person does not have. (Under the 1968 legislation this was explicit in the terms of s.16(3) thereof). However, subs. (3) below provides that the local authority acquires under the order all parental rights and responsibilities except those listed, with the result that, in some cases, the word "transferring" is inapt. The effect of the order is to remove from each of the relevant persons such parental rights and parental responsibilities as they have and to confer on the local authority all the rights and responsibilities within the meaning of subs. (3) below.

The sheriff. The jurisdiction lies exclusively with the sheriff and the Court of Session cannot make a parental responsibilities order.

A child. Section 93(2)(a) defines child for this purpose as a person under the age of 18 and it follows that an order can be applied for under this section until the child reaches that age. See further, General Note to subs. (6) below.

Subs. (2)

Under the 1968 Act the conditions upon which the parental rights resolution could be passed were long and detailed, and there was some overlap both with the grounds for dispensing with parental agreement to adoption and with the grounds of referral to the children's hearing. The purpose of the new parental responsibilities order is often very different from the purpose of an adoption order (and the effect is radically different), but there are similarities and the order under this provision will very frequently be a step in the process to make long-term arrangements for the care and upbringing of the child. It was therefore considered appropriate to make the grounds upon which an order could be made similar to the rules in adoption. This subsection lists the conditions at least one of which have to be satisfied. They are, first, that every relevant person in relation to the child agrees to the making of the order unconditionally, freely and with full understanding of what is involved; or secondly that one of the stated circumstances in para. (b) exists. The circumstances in para. (b) are identical to the new grounds upon which consent to adoption can be dispensed with by the court, and reference should be made to the General Note to Sched. 2, para. 10 below. The nature of the two procedures is different, as are their aims, and the grounds must be interpreted and applied by the court in such a way as reflects this. It may well, for example, be unreasonable for a parent to withhold agreement to a parental responsibilities order but not be unreasonable for that parent to withhold consent to adoption (if, for example, the parental responsibilities order is designed to be temporary).

Shall not be made unless. The satisfaction of one or other of the stated conditions is mandatory before a parental responsibilities order can be made, but it does not follow that the making of the order is mandatory if one or both conditions is, in fact, satisfied. Rather, the sheriff must first determine as a matter of fact whether or not one of the conditions is satisfied. If it is not, he cannot make an order; if it is, he must then go on to determine, in the light of the three over-arching principles in s.16 above and, if the child is subject to a supervision requirement, the report from the children's hearing drawn up in terms of s.73(12) above, whether or not to make the order.

Each relevant person. The "relevant person" is defined in subs. (4) below. Under the 1968 Act the local authority resolution was passed in respect of a particular parent or guardian, and it did not affect the rights and duties of other parents and guardians. The current provisions, on the other hand, provide that the order is made in relation to the child and is available only when every parent and guardian of the child satisfies one or other of the conditions in this subsection. This emphasises that a parental responsibilities order should be sought only when there is no appropriate person who has the responsibility and right to look after the child. It follows that a parental responsibilities order cannot be made which removes one parent's rights and responsibilities but allows the other parent's rights and responsibilities to continue.

Agrees unconditionally that the order be made. Again to emphasise the closeness of this procedure to that of adoption, it is provided that the parental responsibilities order can be granted to the local authority if each one of the persons with rights in relation to the child agrees to its being terminated. There was no analogous provision in the 1968 Act, which was primarily concerned with forfeiture of parental rights rather than their voluntary surrender. If there is a relevant person who does not agree unconditionally to the making of the order, the order cannot be made, unless, in relation to that person, one of the four conditions in para. (b) exists.

Is not known, cannot be found, or is incapable of giving agreement. It will be in unusual circumstances only that a person with parental rights is not known: the usual case of the unknown parent is the unmarried father, but he does not have parental rights in any case. A person "cannot be found" when it is practically impossible to communicate with her or him. Incapacity can be either legal or factual, though in both cases it should be permanent, or at least long-term.

Is withholding such agreement unreasonably. There have been many cases in relation to the dispensation of parental agreement to adoption on the basis of identical wording in the Adoption (Scotland) Act 1978. Whether the ground exists is not to be determined by the welfare principle (*Central Regional Council v. M* 1991 SCLR 300), though that will of course govern the sheriff's decision whether, if this subparagraph is satisfied, the parental responsibilities order should be made. The test is an objective one of whether or not the reasonable parent would have withheld consent in the circumstances (*A & B, Petrs* 1971 SC(HL) 129).

"Two reasonable parents can perfectly reasonably come to opposite conclusions on the same set of facts without forfeiting their title to be regarded as reasonable. The question in any given case is whether a parental veto comes within the band of possible reasonable decisions and not whether it is right or mistaken. Not every reasonable exercise of judgment is right, and not every mistaken exercise of judgment is unreasonable. There is a band of decisions within which no court should seek to replace the individual's judgment with its own" (per Lord Hailsham in *W. (An Infant), Re* [1971] 2 All ER 49 at p. 56).

Has persistently failed, without reasonable excuse, to fulfil... parental responsibilities. On similar wording in s.16 of the 1968 Act, it has been held that "persistently" does not mean deliberately but repeatedly or continuously for some time (*Central Regional Council v. B* 1985 S.L.T. 413), but the words "without reasonable cause" suggest that some element must be present for which the person can be held responsible. A useful addition to the law is to specify which of the parental responsibilities must be neglected to satisfy this subparagraph.

Has seriously ill-treated the child. Ill-treatment is to be given wide scope, and covers abuse, neglect, and any treatment (or lack of it) which causes serious harm to the child. It might be constituted by either a single event or a course of conduct. Serious ill-treatment is the causing of "significant harm", as that phrase is used in s.57(2) above. In addition to serious ill-treatment it must be shown that there is little possibility that the child can be reintegrated back into the household of the person guilty of that ill-treatment. This subparagraph can apply even when the child has never been a member of the same household as the person who has seriously ill-treated her or him and "reintegration" should be interpreted to include "integration".

Subs. (3)

Subsection (1) above allows the sheriff to make an order transferring the "appropriate parental rights and responsibilities"; this section contains a singularly unhelpful definition of that phrase. To define the "appropriate parental rights and responsibilities" as "all parental rights and responsibilities" subject to stated exceptions tells us nothing more than which aspects of parental responsibility are not transferred to the local authority. The stated exceptions are not parental rights as defined by s.2(4) above which indicates that the phrase "all parental rights and responsibilities" is intended by this section to be wider than the parental responsibilities listed in s.1(1) and the parental rights listed in s.2(1) above. The phrase will certainly include these, but how much further it goes is not clear. "Parental rights and responsibilities" in this section may well include the duty of aliment (but not the duty of child support, since the terms of the Child Support Act 1991 would preclude local authorities being liable). It is surprising that there is no provision analogous to the now repealed s.17(6) of the 1968 Act to the effect that the person whose parental rights are removed is not thereby relieved of any liability to contribute to the maintenance of the child, and it would seem that such an obligation is within the meaning of the phrase "parental rights and responsibilities" and is now removed from the parent and imposed on the local authority. In addition to the responsibilities and rights defined in ss.1 and 2, the phrase "rights and responsibilities" will include the duties of local authorities spelt out in s.17 above. Also, the right and obligation of parents to attend a children's hearing considering the case of the child will be included in "parental rights and responsibilities" with the result that after the making of a parental responsibilities order, a representative of the local authority will be obliged to attend any children's hearing considering the case of the child who is the subject of the order, and the parents will have lost their right to attend.

Except... The local authority in whose favour a parental responsibilities order has been made does not obtain the right to agree to or to refuse to agree to the making of an adoption order, the making of an order freeing the child for adoption, or the making of an order vesting parental responsibilities and parental rights in a person who intends to adopt the child abroad. There is no substantive change in the law here from that contained in s.16(3) of the 1968 Act. These rights remain with the person to whom they attached before the making of the order.

Subs. (4)

The "relevant person" who must agree to the order under subs. (2)(a) above or fall within one of the circumstances in subs. (2)(b) above is defined in this subsection as belonging to one of two different classes.

(i) A parent. It is to be noted that "parent" is not defined for the purposes of Pt. II. The word probably means mother to the exclusion of father if the parents are not and never have been married, because an unmarried father will have no parental responsibilities and parental rights to be transferred (except the duty of aliment and child support). This would be consistent with the adoption legislation, with which the unmarried father has no right to agree or refuse to agree to the adoption of his child (*A. v. B.* 1955 SC 378, *A. & B. v. C.* 1987 SCLR 514: these cases are, however, inconsistent with the decision of the European Court of Human Rights in *Keegan v. Ireland* (1994) 18 EHRR 342 and are ripe for reconsideration).

(ii) A person who for the time being has parental rights. "Parental rights" are defined in s.93(1) to mean those rights listed in s.2(1) of the Act. It is surprising that the statute does not here refer to parental responsibilities and parental rights, as it does throughout Pt. I, given that s.2(1) explicitly states that parental rights exist only in order to enable the person to fulfil their parental responsibilities listed in s.1. The omission is likely to be the result of sloppy draftsmanship rather than any attempt to distinguish between a person with parental responsibilities and parental rights for the purposes of Pt. I and a person with parental rights for the purposes of Pt. II: it is to be noted that s.87(1) below talks of "the transferred responsibilities", which suggests that a person with parental rights is assumed to have responsibilities which can be transferred. It is submitted that any person who at the date of the court action has any (see s.103(1) below) or all of the parental rights or their concomitant responsibilities is a relevant person, who must agree to the order or fall within one of the specified circumstances, and whose rights can be transferred to the local authority under this order.

Subs. (5)

In making a parental responsibilities order the sheriff may impose such conditions as he considers appropriate. This might include, for example, conditions as to the child's residence or medical treatment or even the religious observances to which the child is to be subjected. A condition could determine the length of time the order is to last. The sheriff might also include conditions as to contact between the child and any other person: s.88 below, which deals with contact, applies both during the subsistence of a parental responsibilities order and when it is being made. The sheriff may also vary or discharge the order. His decision in relation to conditions, variation or discharge is to be made having regard to the three overarching principles in s.16, to which reference should be made.

On the application of the local authority. Under the old law the local authority could itself simply rescind the parental rights resolution that it had previously made. The philosophy of the current provision is that the order be kept within the hands of the court, and therefore not only is it only the sheriff who can make the order, but it is only the sheriff who can vary or discharge it. The local authority in whose favour the order has been made, but no other local authority, has title to apply for variation or discharge.

On the application ... of the child. The child too may apply for the variation or discharge of the order, and the wording suggests that the child can make such an application on her or his own behalf. Capacity to do so is, of course, determined by the Age of Legal Capacity (Scotland) Act 1991 and it is submitted that such an application by a child who is the subject of a parental responsibilities order can be regarded as a transaction that is commonly entered into by persons in their circumstances. Under the 1991 Act, "commonly" does not refer to numerical frequency (otherwise this new form of application could never be made a first time, however common it was for children to wish to make it): rather it means transactions that are not unusual or surprising in the circumstances (see Norrie, *The Age of Legal Capacity (Scotland) Act 1991* (1991) 36 JLSS 434). Children with capacity to raise or defend actions can authorise those who used to be their representatives to do so on their behalf: s.15(6) above.

Any person who immediately before ... is a relevant person. Though parental responsibilities and parental rights are removed from a person by the order, that person retains title to seek the variation or discharge of the order.

Any other person claiming an interest. This phrase is to be given wide scope. As in s.11(3) above title to seek the variation or discharge of a parental responsibilities order inheres in any person who has a legitimate concern in the wellbeing of, or established connection with, the child. Unlike s.11(3), there is no limitation excluding title from those whose parental responsibilities and parental rights have been removed by legal action. No such limitation is needed in this context since those who lose their responsibilities and rights by an order in this process have a legitimate claim to be able to use this process to challenge or alter that order.

Subs. (6)

The sheriff may discharge the order under subs. (5) above, but if this has not been done the order terminates on the occurrence of any of the listed events.

Child attains the age of eighteen years. "Child" is defined in s.93(2)(a) as a person under the age of 18 years and a parental responsibilities order remains in effect until the person reaches that age. It is, however, to be noted that on the child attaining the age of 16 years all the parental responsibilities except that to provide guidance come to an end (s.1(2) above), as do all the parental rights (s.2(7) above). The effect of a parental responsibilities order is not, it is submitted, to maintain on behalf of the local authority all these responsibilities and rights until the child is 18, otherwise the statute would have provided for them having more rights than parents. The order may last until the child is 18, but its effect can vary with time, just as the effect of the parent-child relationship varies with time. It follows that the local authority lose those responsibilities and rights in relation to a child that a parent would lose on the child's 16th birthday. However, the duties incumbent on a local authority contained in s.17 above remain until the child's 18th birthday and it can be assumed that the local authority also retain the rights necessary to fulfil their duties under that section.

He becomes the subject of an adoption order. The adoption supersedes and terminates the parental responsibilities order.

He becomes the subject ... of an order under s.18. An order freeing a child for adoption will vest the parental responsibilities and parental rights in the adoption agency (Adoption (Scotland) Act 1978, s.18(5), as amended by Sched. 2 below) and this supersedes and terminates the parental responsibilities order vesting those responsibilities and rights in the local authority (which may well be the adoption agency in any case).

He becomes the subject ... of an order ... under ... s.49. An order vesting parental responsibilities and parental rights in a person for the purpose of allowing that person to adopt the child abroad supersedes and terminates the parental responsibilities order.

An order is made for his return. An order by a Scottish or English court under the Hague Convention on the Civil Aspects of International Child Abduction will be to the effect that the child is returned to her or his habitual residence forthwith, and the parental responsibilities order cannot interfere with that process. The order for return therefore supersedes and terminates the parental responsibilities order.

A decision ... is registered. The registration in the Books of Council and Session of a custody (but not an access) decision, obtained from the appropriate authorities in any country which is a signatory to the European Convention on Recognition and Enforcement of Decisions Concerning Custody of Children, supersedes and terminates the parental responsibilities order. A custody decision for the purpose of that Convention is "a decision of an authority in so far as it relates to the care of the person of the child, including the right to decide on the place of his residence, or to the right of access to him" (Art. 1, para. 1 of the European Convention, enacted in the 1985 Act, Sched. 2).

Further provision as respects parental responsibilities orders

87.—(1) Subject to subsections (2) and (3) below, where a parental responsibilities order is made as respects a child it shall be the duty of the local authority which applied for it (in this section and in section 88 of this Act referred to as the "appropriate authority") to fulfil the transferred responsibilities while the order remains in force.

(2) Notwithstanding that a parental responsibilities order has been made as respects a child, the appropriate authority may allow, either for a fixed period or until the authority otherwise determine, the child to reside with a parent, guardian, relative or friend of his in any case where it appears to the authority that so to allow would be for the benefit of the child.

(3) Without prejudice to any other provision of this Part of this Act, where by virtue of subsection (2) above a child is residing with a person, the appropriate authority may by notice in writing to the person require him to return the child to them by a time specified in the notice; and service of such notice shall be effected either by the authority leaving it in the person's hands or by their sending it to him, at his and the child's most recent known address, by recorded delivery service.

(4) For the purposes of any application for a parental responsibilities order, rules shall provide for the appointment, in such cases as are prescribed by such rules—

(a) of a person to act as curator *ad litem* to the child in question at the hearing of the application, safeguarding the interests of the child in such manner as may be so prescribed; and

(b) of a person (to be known as a "reporting officer") to witness agreements to parental responsibilities orders and to perform such other duties as may be so prescribed,

but one person may, as respects the child, be appointed both under paragraph (a) and under paragraph (b) above; so however that, where the applicant is a local authority, no employee of theirs shall be appointed under either or both of those paragraphs.

(5) Rules may provide for a person to be appointed reporting officer before the application in question is made.

DEFINITIONS
"child": s.93(2)(a).
"local authority": Local Government etc. (Scotland) Act 1994, s.2.
"parental responsibilities order": ss.86(1), 93(1).

GENERAL NOTE
Under the 1968 Act it was only children who were "in care" who could be the subject of a resolution assuming parental rights, and that statute imposed various duties on local authorities in relation to children in their care (whether subject to such a resolution or not). The current provisions do not require that the child be "in care", and this section therefore indicates the duties that the local authority will be under in relation to the child in respect of whom a parental responsibilities order has been made at their instance. In addition, the section provides that in fulfilling their responsibilities towards the child, the local authority may permit the child to reside with certain individuals, though if they do so they can always require the return of the child from such an individual. Rules will provide for the appointment of a curator *ad litem* and a reporting officer.

Subs. (1)
Having obtained the order in their favour, the local authority are obliged to carry out their duties in relation to the child. The only duty specified here is the duty to "fulfil the transferred

responsibilities". It is surprising that the provision does not read "transferred responsibilities and rights" but it is submitted that a local authority are obliged to exercise the rights they obtain by means of a parental responsibilities order whenever this is necessary in the child's interests. In addition, the local authority will be subject to the duties in s.17 above, that is to say, the duty to safeguard and promote the child's welfare; the duty to make use of such services available to children cared for by their own parents as appears reasonable; and the duty to take practical and appropriate steps to promote personal relations and direct contact between the child and those with parental responsibilities. This last is inept in relation to children subject to a parental responsibilities order since the parent's responsibilities will have been removed and since contact is specifically dealt with in s.88 below.

Subs. (2)
This subsection replaces much of s.17 of the 1968 Act. In fulfilling their responsibilities towards the child the local authority are not obliged to accommodate the child in a residential establishment or with foster carers. Though this may well be the normal case after a parental responsibilities order has been made, it is open to the local authority to allow the child to reside with a parent, guardian, relative or friend of the child, so long as they consider that this would benefit the child.
Parent. There is no definition of this word in this Part of the Act, and though it may sometimes appropriately be defined to exclude the unmarried father (as for example in s.84(4) above), reading the word *ejusdem generis* with the immediately following words, there would be no reason so to restrict it in this context. Parent means parent, whether adoptive or genetic or presumed (under the 1986 Act) or deemed (under the Human Fertilisation and Embryology Act 1990 (c. 37)).
Guardian. This word is not defined, either here or elsewhere in the Act. It should be taken to mean, it is submitted, parent-substitute appointed as guardian under s.7 or s.11(2)(h) above.
Relative or friend. This means a person with some existing connection to the child, whether of blood or affinity in the former case or affection in the latter case.

Subs. (3)
The local authority in whose favour a parental responsibilities order has been made, and who have permitted the child to reside with a parent, guardian, relative or friend, may at any time call for the return to them of the child. They can do so only if the notice to that effect is in writing and specifies a time. No time-limit is laid down.

Subs. (4)
It is to be expected that in the course of the application for a parental responsibilities order a reporting officer, with similar functions to the reporting officer in an adoption petition, and a curator *ad litem* again with similar functions, may be appointed. Rules will govern the appointment and functions of these officers and the same person can be appointed to both offices.

Parental contact

88.—(1) This section applies where a parental responsibilities order is being made, or as the case may be is in force, as respects a child.
(2) The child shall, subject to subsection (3) below, be allowed reasonable contact by the appropriate authority with—
(a) each person who, immediately before the making of the parental responsibilities order, is a relevant person for the purposes of section 86 of this Act as respects the child; and
(b) where, immediately before that order was made—
(i) a residence order or contact order was in force with respect to the child, the person in whose favour the residence order or contact order was made;
(ii) a person was entitled to have the child residing with him under an order by a court of competent jurisdiction, that person.
(3) Without prejudice to subsection (4) below, on an application made to him by the child, by the appropriate authority or by any person with an inter-

est, the sheriff may make such order as he considers appropriate as to the contact, if any, which is to be allowed between the child and any person specified in the order (whether or not a person described in paragraphs (a) and (b) of subsection (2) above).

(4) A sheriff, on making a parental responsibilities order, or at any time while such an order remains in force as respects a child, may make an order under subsection (3) above as respects the child even where no application has been made to him in that regard.

(5) An order under this section may impose such conditions as the sheriff considers appropriate; and he may vary or discharge such an order on the application of the child, the appropriate authority or any person with an interest.

(6) An order under this section shall, if not first discharged by the sheriff, terminate when the parental responsibilities order to which it is referable does.

DEFINITIONS
"child": s.93(2)(a).
"contact order": ss.11(2)(d), 93(1).
"parental responsibilities order": ss.86(1), 93(1).
"relevant person": s.86(4).
"residence order": ss.11(2)(c), 93(1).

GENERAL NOTE
The 1968 Act was amended in 1983 to provide that a local authority which had assumed parental rights and powers could not terminate arrangements for access or refuse to make them without first giving the parent notice to that effect (1968 Act, s.17A), and on receipt of the notice the parent was entitled to apply to the sheriff for an access order (1968 Act, s.17B). The new procedure set out in this Chapter provides that the granting of a parental responsibilities order is in the hands of the sheriff in any case, and this section ensures that there is reasonable contact between the child and her or his parent, who, if dissatisfied with the arrangements made by the local authority, can apply to the sheriff for an order relating to contact.

Subs. (1)
Application can be made to the sheriff for an order relating to contact between the child and any named person at the time of the application for the making of a parental responsibilities order, or at any time while it is in force. This section governs such applications and imposes duties as to contact on the local authority.

Subs. (2)
The format of this subsection is interesting. Contact is not regarded here as a parental responsibility or parental right (though it is expressly stated to be such for the purposes of Pt. I of the Act); rather it is something which is to be "allowed" to the child. Decisions under this section should, therefore, be made looking at the situation through the eyes of the child rather than the parent. It is provided that the local authority are to allow the child reasonable contact (i) with any person who was a relevant person immediately before the making of the order, (ii) with any person in whose favour a residence order or a contact order was in force immediately before the making of the parental responsibilities order (though a residence order will make its holder a "relevant person" in any case), and (iii) with any person who was entitled to have the child residing with her or him under an order of a court of competent jurisdiction. Though the child must be allowed reasonable contact with the stated persons, there is nothing to prevent the local authority from allowing the child contact with other persons such as siblings, grandparents, foster carers and friends, so long as the authority are of the view that it is not against the child's interests to be allowed such contact.

Shall ... be allowed. The fact that the child is to be "allowed" contact suggests that the child will have some say in whether or not contact will take place. It is not a right of the relevant person, who cannot insist on contact under this section, even when an order under this section so provides. A child cannot be forced into contact with a person she or he wishes to have no contact with.

Reasonable contact. It is primarily for the local authority to determine what reasonable contact is. "Reasonable" is to be determined according to all relevant factors, including in particular the wishes of the child, the welfare of the child, the long-term plans for the child, and the nature of the relationship between the child and the appropriate person. If any person believes that reasonable contact is not being permitted, or that what the local authority claim is reasonable is not in fact so, then application to the sheriff can be made in terms of subs. (3) below.

Appropriate authority. Though this phrase is nowhere defined, it means the local authority to whom the appropriate parental rights and responsibilities have been transferred.

Relevant person. The two categories of person under s.86(4) who are included in this phrase are any person who is a parent and any person who has parental responsibilities or parental rights in relation to the child: the comments attached to both of these categories in the notes to s.86(4) above should be referred to. In addition, it is to be remembered that the child may, in the discretion of the local authority, be allowed contact with other people by the proper exercise of the local authority's parental responsibilities.

An order by a court of competent jurisdiction. A person entitled to have the child residing with her or him under a residence order granted by a Scottish court since the commencement of this Act will be covered by subpara. (i) and the present provision therefore will cover persons who have orders obtained under the pre-1995 legislation or orders of courts outwith Scotland.

Subs. (3)

If the child or appropriate person is not satisfied with the contact arrangements made by the local authority, or if the local authority feel that they cannot resolve a dispute, application can be made to the sheriff to make an order regulating contact with a child who is the subject of a parental responsibilities order. This subsection gives the sheriff a wide discretion to make any order that he considers appropriate as to contact, on an application by the child, the local authority, or any person having interest. In coming to his decision, the sheriff is obliged to have regard to all three of the overarching principles in s.16 above, notwithstanding that contact orders under s.88 are not mentioned by s.16, for an order relating to contact is either a part of the making of a parental responsibilities order or is the variation thereof, both of which processes are expressly covered by s.16.

Any person with an interest. This phrase is to be compared with "a person who ... claims an interest" as it appears in s.11(3) above and "any other person claiming an interest" as in s.86(5). It means a person with a legitimate concern for the welfare of, or established connection with, the child. Since the person whose parental responsibilities and parental rights have been removed will often be the person with whom contact would be most appropriate, there is no limitation, as there is in s.11(3), on who comes within this phrase. Persons whose responsibilities and rights are removed are excluded from using s.11 to obtain back some of these responsibilities and rights in order to prevent the present public law chapter being subverted by the use of private law remedies. That consideration does not apply in the interpretation of the phrase here and the fact that a person whose responsibilities and rights are removed by a parental responsibilities order is one of those with whom the child is to be allowed reasonable contact under subs. (2) above clearly gives that person interest to make an application under this subsection.

Whether or not a person described. The sheriff may make an order as to contact between the child and any named person, whether the applicant or otherwise. There is no limitation on who the sheriff may name.

Subs. (4)

A sheriff may make an order as to contact under subs. (3) above even when no application has been made to him to make such an order. This rule applies both when the sheriff is making the parental responsibilities order and at any time while such an order remains in force. However, he can make an order regulating contact under subs. (3) only when a matter relating to the parental responsibilities order is before him, such as when considering whether to make the order under s.86(1), or in reviewing the order under s.86(5). It is submitted that this is the extent of the sheriff's power under this provision to act *ex proprio motu* and that in particular he cannot make an order relating to contact under subs. (3) above if the need for such an order comes to his attention in some other process, such as, for example, a referral for proof from the children's hearing: to hold otherwise would be to confuse two quite separate procedures and indeed to usurp the role of the children's hearing.

Subs. (5)

Any order made as to contact may contain such conditions as the sheriff considers appropriate, he having come to his decision taking account of the three overarching principles in s.16 above (see subs. (3) above); and, on the same basis, he may vary or discharge the order on the application of any of the named parties.

Any person with an interest. As in subs. (3) above, this means any person with a legitimate concern for or established connection with the child – including the person whose parental responsibilities and parental rights were removed by the parental responsibilities order.

Subs. (6)

A contact order made under subs. (3) above is dependent for its existence on the parental responsibilities order to which it relates and it follows that when the latter ceases to have effect, so does the former. Any contact order made under s.11(2)(d) above, which will have been suspended during the currency of the parental responsibilities order, will be reactivated by the termination of the parental responsibilities order.

Offences in relation to parental responsibilities orders

89. Any person who, knowingly and without lawful authority or reasonable excuse—

(a) fails to comply with a notice under section 87(3) of this Act;

(b) harbours or conceals a child—

(i) as respects whom a parental responsibilities order has been made; and

(ii) who has run away, or been taken away or whose return is required by such a notice; or

(c) induces, assists or incites a child as respects whom any such order has been made to run away, or stay away, from a place where he is looked after or who takes away such a child from that place,

shall be guilty of an offence and liable, on summary conviction, to a fine not exceeding level 5 on the standard scale or to imprisonment for a term not exceeding six months or to both such fine and such imprisonment.

DEFINITIONS

"child": s.93(2)(a).

"parental responsibilities order": ss.86(1), 93(1).

GENERAL NOTE

Certain offences in relation to parental responsibilities orders are created by this section. Summary conviction carries the penalties listed. The offences are as follows: (i) failing to comply with a notice requiring the return of the child to the local authority which has allowed the child to reside with a parent, guardian, relative or friend; (ii) harbouring or concealing a child who is subject to a parental responsibilities order but who has run away or been taken away or whose return has been required by notice as in (i) above (subject to the defence in s.38 above of providing a short-term refuge for a child at risk of harm); and (iii) taking away or inducing, assisting or inciting a child who is subject to a parental responsibilities order to run away or stay away from the place where she or he is being looked after.

Miscellaneous

Consent of child to certain procedures

90. Nothing in this Part of this Act shall prejudice any capacity of a child enjoyed by virtue of section 2(4) of the Age of Legal Capacity (Scotland) Act 1991 (capacity of child with sufficient understanding to consent to surgical, medical or dental procedure or treatment); and without prejudice to that generality, where a condition contained, by virtue of—

(a) section 66(4)(a), section 67(2) or section 69(9)(a) of this Act, in a warrant; or

(b) section 70(5)(a) of this Act, in a supervision requirement,

requires a child to submit to any examination or treatment but the child has the capacity mentioned in the said section 2(4), the examination or treatment shall only be carried out if the child consents.

DEFINITIONS

"child": s.93(2)(a).

"supervision requirement": s.93(1).

GENERAL NOTE

Section 2(4) of the Age of Legal Capacity (Scotland) Act 1991 gives children under the age of 16 legal capacity to consent to any surgical, medical or dental treatment or procedure so long as that child is capable of understanding the nature and consequences of the proposed treatment or procedure. This section ensures that nothing in Pt. II of the present Act affects that capacity: so a child subject to a supervision requirement or an assessment order, or kept in a place of safety under a child protection order or a warrant, or subject to a parental responsibilities order, retains the capacity granted by the 1991 Act to the full extent there envisaged. Capacity to consent to medical treatment necessarily includes capacity to refuse consent, just as capacity to consent to adoption given by s.2(3) of the 1991 Act necessarily carries with it capacity to refuse. Lord James Douglas Hamilton accepted in the debate in the Special Standing Committee of the House of Commons that capacity to consent implied capacity to refuse (March 7, 1995, col. 532), as did Lord Fraser of Carmyllie in the Committee of the Whole House in the House of Lords (June 13, 1995, cols. 132–134).

In addition, this section protects the child's right to refuse examination or treatment (when she or he has capacity under the 1991 Act) even when a warrant granted under the specified sections contains a condition requiring such examination or treatment, or when a children's hearing make a supervision requirement with a condition attached that the child submits to such examination or treatment. Any force used against the child, even when such a condition has been made, would amount to assault. However, a children's hearing are not prohibited from imposing such a condition on a capable child: rather, any refusal on the part of the child to satisfy the condition would be a breach of a condition of the supervision requirement and treated in the way that any other breach would be. Such a condition attached to a warrant would be meaningless if the capable child refused the examination or treatment.

It is surprising that there is no express mention of the right of the capable child to refuse any examination or treatment required in terms of a child assessment order granted under s.55 above, but that omission cannot be taken to suggest that such an order be treated any differently from the warrants and requirements expressly mentioned here, for such an order clearly comes within the generality of the present section.

Procedural rules in relation to certain applications etc.

91.—(1) All proceedings to which this section applies are civil proceedings for the purposes of section 32 of the Sheriff Courts (Scotland) Act 1971 (power of Court of Session to regulate civil procedure in the sheriff court).

(2) Any reference in this Part of this Act to regulation or prescription by rules in relation to any proceedings to which this section applies shall be construed, unless the context otherwise requires, as a reference to regulation or prescription by rules made under the said section 32.

(3) Without prejudice to the generality of the said section 32, rules may make provision as to—

(a) the functions of a person appointed by the sheriff under section 41(1) of this Act and any right of that person to information relating to the proceedings;

(b) the circumstances in which any person who has been given notice in accordance with such rules of an application for a child assessment order, or any other person specified in the rules, may apply to the court to have that order varied or discharged;

(c) the persons to whom notice of the making of a child protection order shall be given by the applicant for that order, and without prejudice to that generality may in making such provision require such notice to be given to either or both of the child and any relevant person in relation to that child;

(d) the persons to whom notice of an application for an exclusion order or, under section 79(3) of this Act, for the recall or variation of such an order or of anything done under section 77(2) of this Act shall be given;

(e) the period within which a hearing shall be held under subsection (5) of section 76 of this Act after the granting of an order under subsection (4) of that section;

(f) the service of any exclusion order on the named person and the appropriate person within such period as may be specified in the rules.

(4) In relation to any proceedings to which this section applies, rules may permit a party to such proceedings, in such circumstances as may be specified

in the rules, to be represented by a person who is neither an advocate nor a solicitor.

(5) This section applies to any application made to the sheriff, and any other proceeding before the sheriff (whether on appeal or otherwise), under any provision of this Part of this Act.

DEFINITIONS
"child": s.93(2)(a).
"child assessment order": ss.55(1), 93(1).
"child protection order": ss.57(1), 93(1).
"exclusion order": ss.76(12), 93(1).

GENERAL NOTE
In the debate in the Committee of the Whole House in the House of Lords on June 13, 1995, Lord Fraser of Carmyllie said, at col. 135,
"Part II of the Bill contains a number of provisions for applications and appeals to be made to the sheriff. Some of these provisions contain rule-making powers while others do not. The purpose of this new clause is to ensure that adequate provision is made for all the sheriff court procedure rules necessary to ensure the effective implementation of the provisions of this legislation and, at the same time, to gather all of the provisions for the rules into one clause in the Bill to facilitate reference".

Legal aid in respect of certain proceedings

92. For section 29 of the Legal Aid (Scotland) Act 1986 substitute the following section—

> **"Legal aid in respect of certain proceedings relating to children**
> 29.—(1) This section applies to legal aid in connection with—
>   (a) proceedings before the sheriff (including, without prejudice to that generality, proceedings on an appeal to the sheriff principal from a decision of the sheriff) in respect of any matter arising under Chapter 2 or 3 of Part II of the Children (Scotland) Act 1995 (in this section referred to as "the 1995 Act"); or
>   (b) an appeal to the Court of Session in connection with such proceedings.
> (2) Subject to subsections (3) to (5) below, legal aid to which this section applies shall be available to a child and any relevant person in relation to him in connection with—
>   (a) proceedings before the sheriff on an application for a child protection order or child assessment order, or for the variation or recall of such an order;
>   (b) an appeal to the sheriff under section 51 of the 1995 Act against—
>   (i) a decision of a children's hearing to grant a warrant such as is mentioned in subsection (5)(a) of that subsection; or
>   (ii) any other decision of a children's hearing;
>   (c) an application—
>   (i) by virtue of section 65(7) or (9) of the 1995 Act for a finding as to whether the grounds for a referral are established; or
>   (ii) under section 85 of the 1995 Act for a review of such a finding;
>   (d) an appeal to the sheriff principal or to the Court of Session under section 51 of the 1995 Act.
> (3) Legal aid shall be available under subsection (2)(b)(i) above on an application made to the sheriff without inquiry into the resources of the child or the relevant person.
> (4) Legal aid shall be available under subsection (2)(a), (b)(ii) or (c) above on an application made to the sheriff if the sheriff is satisfied—
>   (a) that it is in the interests of the child that legal aid be made available; and

(b) after consideration of the financial circumstances of the child and any relevant person in relation to him that the expenses of the case cannot be met without undue hardship to the child or to any relevant person in relation to him or the dependants of any of them.

(5) Legal aid shall be available under subsection (2)(d) above on an application made to the Board if it is satisfied—

(a) after consideration of the financial circumstances of the child and any relevant person in relation to him that the expenses of the appeal cannot be met without undue hardship to the child or to any relevant person in relation to him or the dependants of any of them; and

(b) that the child, or as the case may be the relevant person, has substantial grounds for making or responding to the appeal and it is reasonable, in the particular circumstances of the case, that legal aid should be made available accordingly.

(6) The Board may require a person receiving legal aid under subsection (2)(d) above or subsection (9) below to comply with such conditions as it considers expedient to enable it to satisfy itself from time to time that it is reasonable for him to continue to receive such legal aid.

(7) Subject to subsection (8) below, legal aid to which this section applies shall be available in connection with proceedings before the sheriff on an application for an exclusion order (or for the variation or recall of such an order) to—

(a) a child;

(b) a relevant person in relation to a child;

(c) a person who is a named person, or will be such a person if the application is granted;

(d) a spouse or partner of a person mentioned in paragraph (c) above; and

(e) a person who is an appropriate person, or will be such a person if the application is granted.

(8) Legal aid shall be available under subsection (7) above on an application to the sheriff if the sheriff is satisfied after consideration of the financial circumstances of the applicant and, where the applicant is a child, of any relevant person or appropriate person in relation to him that the expenses of the case cannot be met without undue hardship to the applicant or any dependant of the applicant.

(9) Legal aid shall be available in connection with any appeal from a decision of the sheriff on an application for an exclusion order or for the variation or recall of such an order to any of the persons mentioned in paragraphs (a) to (e) of subsection (7) above on an application to the Board if it is satisfied—

(a) after consideration of the financial circumstances of the applicant and, where the applicant is a child, of any relevant person or appropriate person in relation to him, that the expenses of the appeal cannot be met without undue hardship to the applicant or any dependant of the applicant; and

(b) that the applicant has substantial grounds for making or responding to the appeal and that it is reasonable, in the particular circumstances of the case, that legal aid should be made available accordingly.

(10) Where in connection with any proceedings—

(a) the sheriff has been satisfied as is mentioned in subsection (4)(b) or subsection (8) above; or

(b) the Board has been satisfied as is mentioned in subsection (5)(a) or subsection (9)(a) above, and has made legal aid available to any person, it shall not be necessary for the sheriff or, as the case may be, the Board to be so satisfied in respect of an application for legal aid by such a person in connection with any subsequent proceedings arising from such proceedings.

(11) Legal aid to which this section applies shall consist of representation by a solicitor and, where appropriate, by counsel in any proceedings (including any appeal) mentioned in subsection (1) above and shall include all such assistance as is usually given by solicitor or counsel in the steps preliminary or incidental to such proceedings.

(12) In this section—

(a) "child" and "relevant person" have the meanings given by section 93(2)(b) of the 1995 Act;

(b) "child protection order", "child assessment order" and "exclusion order" have the meanings given by section 93(1) of that Act;

(c) "named person" and "appropriate person" have the meanings given by section 76 of that Act; and

(d) "partner" shall be construed in accordance with section 79(4) of that Act.".

DEFINITIONS
"child": s.93(2)(a).
"child assessment order": ss.55(1), 93(1).
"child protection order": ss.57(1), 93(1).
"exclusion order": ss.76(12), 93(1).
"relevant person": s.93(2)(b).

GENERAL NOTE
This is effectively a consolidating provision, replacing s.29 of the Legal Aid (Scotland) Act 1986 and taking account of the new rules in the present statute. It provides, very generally, that legal aid shall be made available to both the child and the "relevant person" (as defined in s.93(2)(b)) in all proceedings governed by Chaps. 2 and 3 of Pt. II of the present Act. In relation to proceedings before a sheriff on appeal against the granting by a children's hearing of a warrant to find and keep a child in a place of safety legal aid is available without inquiry into the resources of the child or the relevant person; in other proceedings their financial circumstances are to be taken into account. Legal aid is available for appeals from decisions of the sheriff only if there are "substantial grounds" (*i.e.* grounds which are not spurious) for making or responding to the appeal. In relation to exclusion orders legal aid is available not only to the child and the relevant person but also, if different, the "named person" (*i.e.* the person to be excluded), the spouse or heterosexual cohabitant of the named person, and the person who will look after the child in the family home during the exclusion; financial circumstances are again to be taken into account. Legal aid is available in proceedings on appeal but only if there are substantial grounds for making or responding to the appeal.

Interpretation of Part II

Interpretation of Part II

93.—(1) In this Part of this Act, unless the context otherwise requires,—
"accommodation" shall be construed in accordance with section 25(8) of this Act;
"chief social work officer" means an officer appointed under section 3 of the Social Work (Scotland) Act 1968;
"child assessment order" has the meaning given by section 55(1) of this Act;
"child protection order" has the meaning given by section 57(1) of this Act;
"children's hearing" shall be construed in accordance with section 39(3), but does not include a business meeting arranged under section 64, of this Act;

"compulsory measures of supervision" means, in respect of a child, such measures of supervision as may be imposed upon him by a children's hearing;

"constable" means a constable of a police force within the meaning of the Police (Scotland) Act 1967;

"contact order" has the meaning given by section 11(2)(d) of this Act;

"disabled" has the meaning given by section 23(2) of this Act;

"exclusion order" has the meaning given by section 76(12) of this Act;

"family", in relation to a child, includes—

(a) any person who has parental responsibility for the child; and

(b) any other person with whom the child has been living;

"local authority" means a council constituted under section 2 of the Local Government etc. (Scotland) Act 1994;

"local government area" shall be construed in accordance with section 1 of the said Act of 1994;

"parental responsibilities" has the meaning given by section 1(3) of this Act;

"parental responsibilities order" has the meaning given by section 86(1) of this Act;

"parental rights" has the meaning given by section 2(4) of this Act;

"place of safety", in relation to a child, means—

(a) a residential or other establishment provided by a local authority;

(b) a community home within the meaning of section 53 of the Children Act 1989;

(c) a police station; or

(d) a hospital, surgery or other suitable place, the occupier of which is willing temporarily to receive the child;

"the Principal Reporter" means the Principal Reporter appointed under section 127 of the said Act of 1994 or any officer of the Scottish Children's Reporter Administration to whom there is delegated, under section 131(1) of that Act, any function of the Principal Reporter under this Act;

"relevant local authority", in relation to a child who is subject to a warrant granted under this Part of this Act or to a supervision requirement, means the local authority for whose area the children's panel from which the children's hearing which granted the warrant or imposed the supervision requirement was formed;

"residence order" has the meaning given by section 11(2)(c) of this Act;

"residential establishment"—

(a) in relation to a place in Scotland, means an establishment (whether managed by a local authority, by a voluntary organisation or by any other person) which provides residential accommodation for children for the purposes of this Act or the Social Work (Scotland) Act 1968;

(b) in relation to a place in England and Wales, means a community home, voluntary home or registered children's home (within the meaning of the Children Act 1989); and

(c) in relation to a place in Northern Ireland, means a home provided under Part VIII of the Children (Northern Ireland) Order 1995, or a voluntary home, or a registered children's home (which have respectively the meanings given by that Order);

"school age" shall be construed in accordance with section 31 of the Education (Scotland) Act 1980;

"secure accommodation" means accommodation provided in a residential establishment, approved by the Secretary of State in accordance with regulations made under section 60(1)(bb) of the Social Work (Scotland) Act 1968 or under paragraph 4(2)(i) of Schedule 4

to the Children Act 1989, for the purpose of restricting the liberty of
children;

"supervision requirement" has the meaning given by section 70(1) of
this Act, and includes any condition contained in such a requirement or related to it;

"voluntary organisation" means a body (other than a public or local
authority) whose activities are not carried on for profit; and

"working day" means every day except—
      (a) Saturday and Sunday;
      (b) December 25th and 26th; and
      (c) January 1st and 2nd.

(2) For the purposes of—
(a) Chapter 1 and this Chapter (except this section) of this Part, "child"
means a person under the age of eighteen years; and
(b) Chapters 2 and 3 of this Part—
"child" means—
      (i) a child who has not attained the age of sixteen years;
      (ii) a child over the age of sixteen years who has not attained
the age of eighteen years and in respect of whom a supervision
requirement is in force; or
      (iii) a child whose case has been referred to a children's hear-
ing by virtue of section 33 of this Act;
and for the purposes of the application of those Chapters to a person
who has failed to attend school regularly without reasonable excuse
includes a person who is over sixteen years of age but is not over
school age; and
"relevant person" in relation to a child means—
      (a) any parent enjoying parental responsibilities or parental
rights under Part I of this Act;
      (b) any person in whom parental responsibilities or rights are
vested by, under or by virtue of this Act; and
      (c) any person who appears to be a person who ordinarily (and
other than by reason only of his employment) has charge of, or
control over, the child.

(3) Where, in the course of any proceedings under Chapter 2 or 3 of this
Part, a child ceases to be a child within the meaning of subsection (2) above,
the provisions of those Chapters of this Part and of any statutory instrument
made under those provisions shall continue to apply to him as if he had not so
ceased to be a child.

(4) Any reference in this Part of this Act to a child—
(a) being "in need", is to his being in need of care and attention because—
      (i) he is unlikely to achieve or maintain, or to have the opportuni-
ty of achieving or maintaining, a reasonable standard of health or
development unless there are provided for him, under or by virtue
of this Part, services by a local authority;
      (ii) his health or development is likely significantly to be
impaired, or further impaired, unless such services are so provided;
      (iii) he is disabled; or
      (iv) he is affected adversely by the disability of any other person
in his family;
(b) who is "looked after" by a local authority, shall be construed in
accordance with section 17(6) of this Act.

(5) Any reference to any proceedings under this Part of this Act, whether
on an application or on appeal, being heard by the sheriff, shall be construed
as a reference to such proceedings being heard by the sheriff in chambers.

Part III

Adoption

Approval of adoption society for specific services

94.—(1) In section 3 of the 1978 Act (approval of adoption societies)—
(a) for subsections (1) and (2) substitute—

"(1) Subject to any regulations made under section 9(1), a body which is a voluntary organisation may apply to the Secretary of State for his approval to its acting, or as the case may be continuing to act, as an adoption society, whether functioning generally or in relation to some service maintained, or to be maintained, as part of the Scottish Adoption Service and specified in the application (the service so specified being in this section and in section 4 referred to as the body's "specified service").

(1A) Application under subsection (1) shall be in such manner as may be specified in regulations made by the Secretary of State under this section.

(2) In considering an application under subsection (1), the Secretary of State shall take into account the matters relating to the applicant specified in subsections (3) to (5) and any other matters which appear to him to be relevant; and if, but only if, he is satisfied that, as the case may be, the applicant is likely to make, or is making, an effective contribution to the Scottish Adoption Service or to the applicant's specified service, he shall by notice to the applicant give the approval sought.

(2A) Approval under subsection (2) shall operate from such date as may be specified in the notice or, in the case of a renewal of approval, from the date of the notice.";
(b) in subsection (3)(a), the words ", including in particular its ability to make provision for children who are free for adoption" shall cease to have effect;
(c) in subsection (5), for the words "areas within which" substitute "geographical areas within which, the services as respects which";
(d) in subsection (6), after the word "Service" insert ", or as the case may be to the applicant's specified service"; and
(e) in subsection (7)—
　　(i) for the words "a period of" substitute "such period not exceeding"; and
　　(ii) after the word "operative" insert "as the Secretary of State may specify in the approval.".

(2) In section 4 of that Act (withdrawal of approval), after the word "Service" insert ", or as the case may be to the body's specified service,".

(3) In section 65(1) of that Act (interpretation), in the definition of "adoption society", after the word "for" insert ", or in connection with,".

Definitions
　"adoption society": Adoption (Scotland) Act 1978, s.65(1).

General Note
　Part III and Sched. 2 make various amendments to the law relating to adoption, as contained in the Adoption (Scotland) Act 1978. There seems no particular reason why some of these amendments are contained in Pt. III and some in Sched. 2, except that most (though not all) of the amendments in Pt. III are substantive while most (though not all) of the amendments in Sched. 2 are terminological. The most significant changes to the law of adoption are contained in s.95 below, which makes the welfare of the child the paramount consideration in all aspects of the adoption process, and s.97 which permits a step-parent to adopt a step-child without the spouse and natural parent joining in the application. In addition, in Sched. 2, para. 10, the grounds upon which parental agreement to adoption can be dispensed with are altered and para.

25 permits schemes to be prepared for the payment of allowances to persons who adopt a child. The present section concerns approval of specific adoption services.

Section 3 of the 1978 Act deals with the approval of adoption societies (*i.e.* adoption agencies other than local authorities) by the Secretary of State. Previously approval could be given only to bodies which provided the full range of adoption services covered by the 1978 Act. The effect of the amendments to s.3 contained in this section is to permit the approval of bodies (other than local authorities) which offer only specified services. This will allow separate bodies to be maintained as part of the Scottish Adoption Service which do not carry out all the functions necessary for that Service but which specialise in particular aspects thereof. The section also contains a number of consequential amendments. Reference should in addition be made to Sched. 2, para. 3, which inserts a new para. (aa) into s.3(3) of the 1978 Act. This provides that one of the factors to be taken into account by the Secretary of State in determining whether to grant approval is the body's procedures for dealing with complaints.

Welfare of child paramount consideration

95. For section 6 of the 1978 Act substitute—

"Duty to promote welfare of child
6.—(1) Without prejudice to sections 12(8) and 18(8), in reaching any decision relating to the adoption of a child, a court or adoption agency shall have regard to all the circumstances but—
 (a) shall regard the need to safeguard and promote the welfare of the child concerned throughout his life as the paramount consideration; and
 (b) shall have regard so far as practicable—
  (i) to his views (if he wishes to express them) taking account of his age and maturity; and
  (ii) to his religious persuasion, racial origin and cultural and linguistic background.
 (2) Without prejudice to the generality of paragraph (b) of subsection (1), a child twelve years of age or more shall be presumed to be of sufficient age and maturity to form a view for the purposes of that paragraph.".

DEFINITIONS
 "adoption agency": Adoption (Scotland) Act 1978, s.65(1).
 "child": Adoption (Scotland) Act 1978, s.65(1).
 "court": Adoption (Scotland) Act 1978, s.56.

GENERAL NOTE
 Section 6 of the 1978 Act previously provided that in reaching any decision relating to the adoption of the child both the court and the adoption agency had to give "first consideration" to the need to safeguard and promote the welfare of the child throughout his "childhood", giving "due consideration" to the wishes and feelings of the child having regard to his age and understanding and in so far as it was practicable to ascertain them. This section replaces these provisions with a new s.6, designed: (i) to harmonise the rules in relation to adoption decisions with those of other decisions relating to children, and (ii) to give effect to the provisions of the UN Convention on the Rights of the Child. Though dealing with the same matters as the old s.6 (*i.e.* the child's welfare and the child's wishes and feelings) the wording of the new s.6 is significantly different and more precise.
 Any decision. The obligations contained in the new s.6 apply to any decision that the court or adoption agency has to make in relation to the adoption process, and not merely in the granting of the adoption order itself. So it applies, for example, to the making of freeing orders by the court, placement decisions by the adoption agency, dispensing with parental agreement, authorising payments or rewards, and the termination of any supervision requirement the child is currently subject to. The obligation to treat the child's welfare as paramount is, however, limited to

the discretionary decisions the court has to make and not the procedural or technical decisions. So, for example, the child's welfare is paramount in deciding whether to make an adoption order, but is irrelevant to the question of whether the correct procedural requirements have been fulfilled; the child's welfare is paramount in deciding whether to dispense with parental agreement but is irrelevant to the question of whether a ground for dispensation exists.

Welfare ... as the paramount consideration. Under the old s.6 the welfare of the child was "the first consideration", and in *P. v. Lothian Regional Council* 1989 S.L.T. 739 the sheriff was criticised by the Inner House for interpreting this to mean "paramount". Other interests and circumstances were to be taken into account in adoption decisions, which required that the child's welfare, though always relevant and a matter of considerable importance, was not in every case determinative. This position, however, was not consistent with Art. 21 of the UN Convention on the Rights of the Child, which provides that "the best interests of the child shall be the paramount consideration" in adoption decisions, and the wording of the new s.6(1)(a) is designed to bring Scots law into line with the U.K.'s international obligations in this respect. In effect, welfare becomes a condition precedent to the granting of an adoption order and the court will be unable to make such an order unless satisfied that it is for the welfare of the child to do so. A positive finding by the court to this effect would seem to be necessary. Reference should also be made to Sched. 2, para. 16, which inserts a new s.24(3) into the 1978 Act, to the effect that no order can be made unless the court considers that it would be better for the child to make the order than not to make it (the principle of minimum intervention). This applies to decisions of the court, while s.6 applies to decisions of both the court and the adoption agency.

Throughout his life. The old s.6 obliged consideration to be given to the child's welfare throughout her or his childhood, which suggested that the court or adoption agency did not need to look beyond the child's 18th birthday in determining whether the adoption was in the child's best interests. The English court interpreted a similar English provision more broadly in *D. (A Minor) (Adoption Order: Validity), Re* [1991] 3 All ER 461 and made an adoption order a few days short of the child's 18th birthday when this was for the welfare of the child during his adult life, but that decision was predicated on the view that welfare during childhood was the first consideration and not a condition precedent to the granting of the order: other considerations, such as welfare after majority, could determine the issue. Welfare is now to be considered a condition precedent, but it is broadened to take account of the whole of the child's life. This is sensible. While the primary motivation of adoption is invariably to provide for the proper looking after and bringing up of a child, it does have life-long consequences (for example, in relation to succession, nationality and the forbidden degrees). It is therefore perfectly appropriate that the welfare of the child throughout her or his life should be considered. Welfare is to be regarded in the totality of the circumstances of the child's life and long-term benefits are not to be sacrificed in order to acquire short-term gains; but nor are short-term benefits to be dismissed as unimportant given that children's perception of timescale is very different from adults.

Shall have regard ... to the views ... of the child. The old s.6 obliged the court or adoption agency to "ascertain" the wishes and feeling of the child regarding any decision either had to make in relation to the proposed adoption of the child, and to give "due consideration" to them. The new s.6(1)(b) effects no substantive change, but the wording has been altered to consist with that used in ss.6 and 16(2) of the present Act which themselves are designed to ensure that Scots law consists in this regard with Art. 12 of the UN Convention on the Rights of the Child. As under the old law, there is a positive obligation on the part of the court or adoption agency to seek out these views. The obligation is to "have regard" to the views, and not necessarily to follow them. It is the child's welfare, rather than her or his wishes, that determines the matter – though clearly the older the child is the more her or his wishes will be indistinguishable from her or his welfare, and it is unlikely to be considered to be in the welfare of a child to make an adoption order in favour of applicants concerning whom the child expresses strong antipathy, or to place the child with such applicants. It should always be made clear to a child asked to express a view that any opinion given will not necessarily determine the issue but will merely assist the court or adoption agency in determining where the child's best interests lie.

So far as practicable. The child's views need to be sought only in so far as it is practicable to do so. *In C, Petrs* 1993 SCLR 14 the sheriff held that it was impracticable to ascertain the wishes and feelings of a six-year-old child when the prospective adopters refused to allow her to be interviewed, because they did not want her to know that she was adopted. This, however, is a highly unusual case and in general it is only with the very youngest of children, or with incapax children, that no effort need be made to seek the child's views. It should be borne in mind that it is possible to ascertain whether a child is happy and comfortable with prospective adopters even when the child is too young, or otherwise unable, to express a reasoned opinion.

If he wishes to express them. There is no obligation on the child to express a view if she or he would prefer not to do so. Immature children ought not to be made to feel burdened with heavy decisions.

Taking account of his age and maturity. There is no age limit attached to the obligation to have regard to the child's views, though clearly the regard that the court or adoption agency should pay to these views will lessen the younger the child is. It is presumed in a new subs. (2) to s.6 that once the child has reached the age of 12 years she or he will be sufficiently mature to form (and express) a view on the matter at hand. This is to be read with s.2(3) of the Age of Legal Capacity (Scotland) Act 1991, which confers capacity on a child aged 12 years or more to consent or withhold consent to the adoption order (which she or he may do under s.12(8) of the 1978 Act) or to an order freeing the child for adoption (s.18(8) of the 1978 Act); the present provision therefore applies to decisions in the adoption process other than these two. The new s.6(2) creates a presumption (which can be rebutted) of maturity in relation to children over 12 years of age; it does not create any presumption of lack of maturity in relation to children under 12, otherwise the whole point of s.6(1)(b)(i) would be negatived. There is no presumption one way or the other and each child must be assessed individually in order to determine what weight ought to be given to any views she or he has expressed.

Shall have regard ... to his ... racial origin and cultural and linguistic background. The obligation imposed here is *not* to match the child with adoptive parents of the same background as the child, but rather to be sensitive to any child's needs to be aware of her or his origins. It is difficult to see how this obligation can be enforced and there is no doubt that an adoption order, or other decision, made without regard to these matters is not challengeable on that ground alone (*cf. PH, Petrs*, March 10, 1995 in which a condition attached to the adoption order was to the effect that the children be brought up with an awareness of their cultural background – a breach of that condition is without legal consequence). Rather, this provision is to be read as setting out matters necessarily connected with the child's welfare and therefore always to be taken into account. It is better, for example, for an Asian child brought up by a European couple to be aware of Asian culture and history than to be brought up pretending that these things are irrelevant; it will seldom be in a child's best interests to be placed with prospective adopters who do not speak the language the child is most fluent in.

His religious persuasion. The obligation here is not to ensure that a child is placed with adopters of the same religious persuasion as the natural parent: the reference is to the child's religious persuasion. "Persuasion" requires an ability to be persuaded and this provision is applicable, therefore, only to children old enough to exercise judgment: there is no such thing as a Roman Catholic baby, or an Islamic baby. Unlike racial origin, religion is not passed on genetically but by those who bring up the child. Again the obligation is not enforceable as such but the child's religious beliefs are always relevant and must be taken into account in determining wherein her or his welfare lies. There is nothing here to prevent a child who adheres to one faith being placed with adopters who adhere to another or to none; but a factor telling against a placement would be the prospective adopters' unwillingness to permit a believing child to continue these religious observances to which she or he has become accustomed.

Duty of adoption agency to consider alternatives to adoption

96. After section 6 of the 1978 Act there shall be inserted—

"Duty to consider alternatives to adoption

6A. In complying with its duties under section 6 of this Act, an adoption agency shall, before making any arrangements for the adoption of a child, consider whether adoption is likely best to meet the needs of that child or whether for him there is some better, practicable, alternative; and if it concludes that there is such an alternative it shall not proceed to make those arrangements.".

DEFINITIONS
"adoption agency": Adoption (Scotland) Act 1978, s.65(1).
"child": Adoption (Scotland) Act 1978, s.65(1).

GENERAL NOTE
Section 53 of the Children Act 1975, as amended by Sched. 1 to the present Act, provides that when a court considers that a residence order would be more appropriate than an adoption order it shall direct that the adoption application be treated as an application for a residence order. The thinking behind that provision, which is directed to courts, is applied in the present provision, with a new s.6A inserted into the 1978 Act obliging adoption agencies making any arrangements in connection with the adoption of a child to give active consideration to alternatives to adoption to the meeting of the needs of the child. If these alternatives are both practicable and better than adoption then the agency is prohibited from making arrangements for the

adoption of the child. The implication is that the better alternatives ought then to be pursued. Adoption is the most radical order that a court can make in relation to a child, and in keeping with the philosophy in other parts of the present Act that the least intervention possible is the best intervention for the child, this provision aims, like that in s.53 of the Children Act 1975, to ensure that adoption is used only when that is the best means of enhancing the interests of the child. The security that adoption gives to a child will frequently be sufficient argument against the application of this section (and s.53 of the 1975 Act).

Arrangements. This will include placing the child with prospective adopters, seeking prospective adopters, and any other step in the adoption process carried out by the adoption agency.

Adoption by person married to natural parent

97.—(1) In section 12 of the 1978 Act (making of adoption orders)—

(a) in subsection (3), at the beginning, insert "Subject to subsection (3A)"; and

(b) after subsection (3) insert—

"(3A) Where the adoption order is made by virtue of section 15(1)(aa), its making shall not operate to extinguish the parental responsibilities and parental rights which immediately before the making of the order were vested in the natural parent to whom the adopter is married.".

(2) In section 15(1) of that Act (adoption by one person)—

(a) after paragraph (a) insert—

"(aa) not being a person who may make application by virtue of paragraph (b) below, is married to a person—

(i) who is the natural parent of the child concerned; and

(ii) in whom are vested parental responsibilities and parental rights in relation to the child,"; and

(b) in paragraph (b), at the beginning insert—

"not being a person who may make application by virtue of paragraph (aa) above,".

(3) In section 39 of that Act (status conferred by adoption), for subsection (1) substitute—

"(1) A child who is the subject of an adoption order shall be treated in law—

(a) where the adopters are a married couple, as if—

(i) he had been born as a legitimate child of the marriage (whether or not he was in fact born after the marriage was constituted); and

(ii) he were not the child of any person other than the adopters;

(b) where the adoption order is made by virtue of section 15(1)(aa) as if—

(i) he had been born as a legitimate child of the marriage between the adopter and the natural parent to whom the adopter is married (whether or not he was in fact born after the marriage was constituted); and

(ii) he were not the child of any person other than the adopter and that natural parent; and

(c) in any other case, as if—

(i) he had been born as a legitimate child of the adopter; and

(ii) he were not the child of any person other than the adopter.".

DEFINITIONS

"adoption order": Adoption (Scotland) Act 1978, s.65(1).

"child": Adoption (Scotland) Act 1978, s.65(1).

"parent": Adoption (Scotland) Act 1978, s.65(1).

"parental responsibilities": s.1(3) and the Adoption (Scotland) Act 1978, s.65(1).

"parental rights": s.2(4) and the Adoption (Scotland) Act 1978, s.65(1).

GENERAL NOTE

Under the previous law a married person could adopt a child only by means of a joint application with her or his spouse (subject to certain limited exceptions set out in s.15(1)(b) of the 1978 Act). It followed that for a child's step-parent to adopt the child the application had to be made by both the step-parent and the natural parent. Usually the natural parent had parental rights in any case but when the adoption order was made the natural parent lost all rights that flowed from parenthood and acquired rights under the adoption order. In other words, the natural parent had to adopt her or his own child and become thereby an adoptive parent. This clumsy and pointless arrangement was never satisfactory and rightly resented by many parents. The present section amends the appropriate provisions in the 1978 Act so that a child can now be adopted by means of a sole application by the person married to the natural parent. The natural parent no longer needs to join in the application and instead will retain the parental responsibilities and parental rights that she or he had before the adoption order is granted.

Subs. (1)

The unamended s.12 of the 1978 Act provided that the making of an adoption order operated to extinguish all parental rights and duties that vested in a parent or guardian of the child. This provision subjects that rule to the qualification that with step-parent adoptions, the parental responsibilities and parental rights which before the adoption vest in the natural parent who is the spouse of the adopter are left unaffected by the order. This means that the natural parent's relationship with the child continues to be governed by the general law of parent and child rather than by the law of adoption: she or he does not, in other words, become the child's adoptive parent.

Subs. (2)

Section 15 of the 1978 Act specifies the circumstances in which an adoption application can be made by one person rather than by a married couple. To those circumstances is added the situation of the applicant who is married to the natural parent of the child who has parental responsibilities and parental rights in relation to the child.

Natural parent. Though this term is not defined (and the word "natural" is removed from the rest of s.15 by Sched. 5 below) it means the genetic parent of the child (*cf.* the definition of "parent" for the purposes of Pt. I of the present Act as "genetic parent" given in s.15 above; "parent" is defined in the amended s.65(1) of the 1978 Act as a mother or father with parental responsibilities or parental rights). It follows that the adoptive parent of the child who marries again must join in any further adoption application made by the new spouse, as must a person who is parent by means of a parental order granted under s.30 of the Human Fertilisation and Embryology Act 1991. The position of a man deemed father under s.28 of the 1991 Act is slightly less obvious, for s.29 of that Act provides that a person deemed parent by s.27 or s.28 is parent for "all purposes". However, the current provisions must be taken to introduce an implicit exception to this, since a person deemed parent by s.28 of the 1991 Act is not deemed to be the genetic parent of the child and cannot, therefore, be described as the child's "natural" parent: the relationship, though recognised and valid for all purposes, is legal and artificial, and not natural.

In whom are vested ... A natural parent without parental responsibilities and parental rights cannot take advantage of this provision and must join in the application of her or his spouse to adopt her or his own child. The responsibilities and rights may vest automatically under s.3 above, or be conferred by the court under s.11 above; in either case it is only if the whole gamut of parental responsibilities and parental rights are vested that the parent comes within the terms of this provision. This provision is probably otiose since a person is not a "parent" for the purposes of the 1978 Act in any case unless she or he has parental responsibilities and parental rights (s.65(1), definition inserted by Sched. 2, para. 29 below).

Subs. (3)

Section 39 of the 1978 Act, which defines the status of the adopted child, is amended to reflect the above provisions. The substantive alteration is contained in the new s.39(1)(b), which provides that the child is to be treated as if born of the marriage between her or his natural parent with parental responsibilities and parental rights and the adopter, and of no other person. This is, of course, subject to the usual limitations to the adoption relationship, but they will apply only in relation to the adopter.

Further amendments of the 1978 Act; and interpretation of Part III

98.—(1) Schedule 2 to this Act, which contains further amendments of the 1978 Act, shall have effect.

(2) In this Part of this Act, "the 1978 Act" means the Adoption (Scotland) Act 1978.

PART IV

GENERAL AND SUPPLEMENTAL

Registration of births by persons who are themselves children

99.—(1) In paragraph (a) of section 14(1) of the Registration of Births, Deaths and Marriages (Scotland) Act 1965 (duty of father and mother to give information of particulars of birth), for the words "father or mother of the child" substitute "child's father or mother (whether or not they have attained the age of sixteen years)".

(2) Where, at any time after the coming into force of the Age of Legal Capacity (Scotland) Act 1991 but before the coming into force of subsection (1) above, a person mentioned in the said paragraph (a) who had not at that time attained the age of sixteen years purported to fulfil the duty mentioned in the said section 14(1), he shall be presumed to have had legal capacity to fulfil that duty.

(3) In section 18 of the said Act of 1965 (registration of birth of child born out of wedlock), after subsection (2) add—

"(3) A person under the age of sixteen years has legal capacity—

(a) to make a request, declaration or statutory declaration under subsection (1) or (2)(b) above if, in the opinion of the registrar; or

(b) to make an application under subsection (2)(c) above if, in the opinion of the sheriff,

that person understands the nature of the request or, as the case may be, of the declaration, statutory declaration or application; and without prejudice to the generality of this subsection a person twelve years of age or more shall be presumed to be of sufficient age and maturity to have such understanding.".

(4) Where, at any time after the coming into force of the Age of Legal Capacity (Scotland) Act 1991 but before the coming into force of subsection (3) above, a person who had not at that time attained the age of sixteen years made a request, declaration, statutory declaration or application mentioned in subsection (1) or (2) of the said section 18 in relation to a child in respect of whose birth an entry was consequently made under the said subsection (1) in a register of births, or as the case may be under the said subsection (2) in the Register of Corrections etc., the person shall be presumed to have had legal capacity to make the request, declaration, statutory declaration, or application in question.

GENERAL NOTE

It is a fact, which until the passing of this Act was given no formal legal recognition, that persons under the age of 16 years sometimes themselves become parents. Under the Age of Legal Capacity (Scotland) Act 1991 for most purposes a person has no legal capacity until reaching the age of 16; this, however, is subject to a number of stated exceptions. An exception not stated in that Act is capacity to register the birth of a child though, certainly with mothers, it was possible to argue that such registration was a transaction commonly undertaken by persons of the appropriate age and circumstances. Nevertheless an element of doubt existed and this section is designed to put beyond that doubt the legal capacity of a person, who becomes a parent before attaining the age of 16 years, to register the birth of her or his own child. It does so by amending the appropriate provision in the Registration of Births, Deaths and Marriages (Scotland) Act 1965 (c. 49) to make plain that the duty upon parents to give information concerning a birth applies whatever age the parent is. The new rule is given retrospective effect by subs. (2) according to which any person who purported to fulfil the duty in the 1965 Act before the coming into force of the present provision (but after the coming into force of the 1991 Act, which was on September 25, 1991) is presumed to have had that legal capacity which such a person would have now.

Subsection (3) amends s.18 of the 1965 Act. That section deals with the duty to register the birth of a child whose parents are not married (and will therefore deal with the vast majority of parents one or both of whom are under the age of 16). Such a person is given legal capacity to make the requests, declarations, or applications required by s.18 so long as she or he is of sufficient (mental) maturity to understand the nature of the request, declaration or application (in the opinion of the registrar or sheriff). It may be noted that there is no requirement of mental maturity to be fulfilled in order to acquire legal capacity to perform the duties in s.14 of the 1965 Act, capacity for which is given in subs. (1) hereof. A person aged 12 or more will be presumed to have sufficient understanding. That is a mere presumption: a person over 12 may be found to lack the appropriate understanding, and a person under 12 who is a parent may be found to have the appropriate understanding (though a parent under 12 years of age will be very rare indeed). The effect of subs. (4) is to give this rule retrospective effect as from September 25, 1991 (the date of the coming into force of the Age of Legal Capacity (Scotland) Act 1991).

Inquiries into matters affecting children

100. After section 6A of the Social Work (Scotland) Act 1968 there shall be inserted—

> **"Legal authority inquiries into matters affecting children**
>   6B.—(1) Without prejudice to section 6A(1) of this Act, a local authority may cause an inquiry to be held into their functions under this Act, or any of the enactments mentioned in section 5(1B) of this Act, in so far as those functions relate to children.
>   (2) The local authority may, before an inquiry under this section is commenced, direct that it be held in private; but where no such direction is given, the person holding the inquiry may if he thinks fit hold it, or any part of it, in private.
>   (3) Subsections (2) to (6) of section 210 of the Local Government (Scotland) Act 1973 (powers in relation to local inquiries) shall apply in relation to an inquiry under this section as they apply in relation to a local inquiry under that section, so however that, for the purposes of the application, any reference in those subsections to a Minister shall be construed as a reference to the local authority and any reference to an officer of his Department as a reference to an officer of that authority.
>   (4) The expenses incurred by a local authority in relation to an inquiry under this section (including such reasonable sum as the authority may determine for the services of any of their officers engaged in the inquiry) shall, unless the authority are of the opinion that those expenses should be defrayed in whole or in part by them, be paid by such party to the inquiry as they may direct; and the authority may certify the amount of the expenses so incurred;
>   (5) Any sum certified under subsection (4) above and to be defrayed in accordance with a direction under that subsection shall be a debt due by the party directed and shall be recoverable accordingly.
>   (6) The local authority may make an award as to the expenses of the parties at the inquiry and as to the parties by whom such expenses shall be paid.".

GENERAL NOTE
     This section introduces into the 1968 a new s.6B, giving local authorities the power to hold inquiries into any of their functions, as relates to children, under certain enactments (including Pt. II of the present Act (Sched. 5, para. 15(4)).

Panel for curators *ad litem*, reporting officers and safeguarders

101.—(1) The Secretary of State may by regulations make provision for the establishment of a panel of persons from whom—
     (a) curators *ad litem* may be appointed under section 58 of the Adoption (Scotland) Act 1978 or under section 87(4) of this Act;

(b) reporting officers may be appointed under those sections; and

(c) persons may be appointed under section 41(1) of this Act.

(2) Regulations under subsection (1) above may provide, without prejudice to the generality of that subsection—

(a) for the appointment, qualifications and training of persons who may be appointed to that panel; and

(b) for the management and organisation of persons available for appointment from that panel.

(3) Regulations under subsection (1) above may provide for the expenses incurred by persons appointed from the panel to be defrayed by a local authority.

GENERAL NOTE

The Secretary of State is given power to make regulations for the establishment of a panel of persons from whom curators *ad litem*, reporting officers, and safeguarders, who perform various functions under the Adoption (Scotland) Act 1978 and the present Act, may be appointed. There will be one panel of persons who are able to perform any of the stated roles, and sometimes a single person may be called upon to perform more than one of these roles. The regulations will also provide how persons are to be appointed to such a panel, and the qualifications and training necessary to perform the appropriate functions. It is expected that these regulations will be similar to but more extensive than the present regulations dealing with reporting officers in the adoption process (Act of Sederunt (Adoption of Children) 1984 (S.I. 1984 No. 1013)), and this will have the effect of enhancing quite significantly the position of the safeguarder in the children's hearing system.

Removal of duty to report on operation of Children Act 1975

102. Section 105 of the Children Act 1975 (which among other things provides that every five years there shall be laid before Parliament by the Secretary of State a report on the operation of such sections of that Act as are for the time being in force) shall cease to have effect.

GENERAL NOTE

The provisions of the Children Act 1975 which remain in effect are not important in comparison to the provisions of the present Act, but it was felt to be unduly onerous on local authorities to require them to draw up reports on the operation of the present Act. As a consequence the duty under s.105 of the 1975 Act has been repealed.

Interpretation, rules, regulations and Parliamentary control

103.—(1) Any reference in this Act, or in any enactment amended by this Act, to a person having, or to there being vested in him, parental responsibilities or parental rights shall, unless the context otherwise requires, be construed as a reference to his having, or to there being so vested, any of those rights or as the case may be responsibilities.

(2) Any reference in this Act to something being "prescribed" is, unless the context otherwise requires, a reference to its being prescribed by regulations; and any power conferred by this Act on the Secretary of State or the Lord Advocate to make rules or regulations shall be exercisable by statutory instrument which shall be subject to annulment in pursuance of a resolution of either House of Parliament.

(3) Rules or regulations made under this Act—

(a) may make different provision for different cases or classes of case; and

(b) may exclude certain cases or classes of case.

GENERAL NOTE

There are various references in the Act to persons having parental responsibilities, and various other references to persons having parental rights. Subsection (2) of this section provides that such references include persons who have one or more parental responsibility or parental right. Some provisions talk of persons having "parental responsibilities and parental rights" and that phrase suggests, it is submitted, a person with all these responsibilities and rights.

Financial provision

104. There shall be paid out of money provided by Parliament—
(a) any expenses of the Secretary of State incurred in consequence of the provisions of this Act; and
(b) any increase attributable to this Act in the sums payable out of money so provided under any other enactment.

Extent, short title, minor and consequential amendments, repeals and commencement

105.—(1) This Act, which subject to subsections (8) to (10) below extends to Scotland only—
(a) may be cited as the Children (Scotland) Act 1995; and
(b) except for subsections (1), (2) and (6) to (10) of this section, shall come into force on such day as the Secretary of State may by order made by statutory instrument appoint;
and different days may be appointed under paragraph (b) above for different purposes.

(2) An order under subsection (1)(b) above may contain such transitional and consequential provisions and savings as appear to the Secretary of State to be necessary or expedient in connection with the provisions brought into force.

(3) The transitional provisions and savings contained in Schedule 3 to this Act shall have effect but are without prejudice to sections 16 and 17 of the Interpretation Act 1978 (effect of repeals).

(4) Schedule 4 to this Act, which contains minor amendments and amendments consequential upon the provisions of this Act, shall have effect.

(5) The enactments mentioned in Schedule 5 to this Act (which include spent provisions) are hereby repealed to the extent specified in the third column of that Schedule.

(6) The Secretary of State may by order made by statutory instrument make such further amendments or repeals, in such enactments as may be specified in the order, as appear to him to be necessary or expedient in consequence of any provision of this Act.

(7) A statutory instrument containing an order under subsection (6) above shall be subject to annulment in pursuance of a resolution of either House of Parliament.

(8) Sections 18, 26(2), 33, 44, 70(4), 74, 82, 83, 93 and 104 of this Act and this section extend to England and Wales, and those sections and this section (except section 70(4)) also extend to Northern Ireland; but—
(a) subsection (4) of this section so extends—
(i) to England and Wales, only in so far as it relates to paragraphs 8, 10, 19, 31, 37, 41(1), (2) and (7) to (9), 48 to 52, 54 and 55 of Schedule 4; and
(ii) to Northern Ireland, only in so far as it relates to paragraphs 31, 37, 41(1), (2) and (7) to (9), 54, 55 and 58 of that Schedule; and
(b) subsection (5) of this section so extends—
(i) to England and Wales, only in so far as it relates to the entries in Schedule 5 in respect of Part V of the Social Work (Scotland) Act 1968, the Maintenance Orders (Reciprocal Enforcement) Act 1972, section 35(4)(c) of the Family Law Act 1986, the Children Act 1989, the Child Support Act 1991 and the Education Act 1993; and

(ii) to Northern Ireland, only in so far as it relates to the entries in that Schedule in respect of Part V of the Social Work (Scotland) Act 1968, the Maintenance Orders (Reciprocal Enforcement) Act 1972 and section 35(4)(c) of the Family Law Act 1986.

(9) This section, so far as it relates to the repeal of Part V of the Social Work (Scotland) Act 1968, also extends to the Channel Islands.

(10) Her Majesty may by Order in Council direct that any of the relevant provisions specified in the Order shall extend, with such exceptions, adaptations and modifications (if any) as may be specified in the Order, to any of the Channel Islands; and in this subsection "the relevant provisions" means sections 74, 82, 83 and 93 of this Act and any regulations made under section 74 of this Act.

SCHEDULES

Section 39(2)   SCHEDULE 1

CHILDREN'S PANELS

Appointment

1. The Secretary of State shall, for each local government area, appoint such number of members of children's panels as he considers appropriate and from among that number appoint a chairman and a deputy chairman.

2. A member of a children's panel shall hold office for such period as is specified by the Secretary of State, but may be removed from office by the Secretary of State at any time.

Children's Panel Advisory Committees

3. Subject to paragraph 8 below, each local authority shall form a body (to be known as a "Children's Panel Advisory Committee") consisting of two members nominated by the local authority and three members nominated by the Secretary of State.

4. The Secretary of State may at the request of the local authority provide for an increase in the membership of the Children's Panel Advisory Committee appointed under paragraph 3 above by such number, not exceeding five, of additional members as the authority specify in relation to their request, the additional members to be nominated as follows—

(a) the first, and any second or fourth additional member, by the Secretary of State;

(b) any third or fifth additional member, by the local authority.

5. The chairman of the Children's Panel Advisory Committee shall be appointed by the Secretary of State from among such of the members he has nominated as are resident in the local government area for which the panel is appointed.

6. It shall be the duty of the Children's Panel Advisory Committee—

(a) to submit names of possible panel members to the Secretary of State;

(b) to advise the Secretary of State, in so far as he requires advice, on the suitability of persons referred to him as potential panel members; and

(c) to advise the Secretary of State on such matters relating to the general administration of the panels as he may refer to them.

7. The Children's Panel Advisory Committee shall have power—

(a) to appoint sub-committees;

(b) to appoint to any such sub-committee a person who is not a member of the Children's Panel Advisory Committee; and

(c) to refer all or any of the duties set out in paragraph 6 above to any such sub-committee for their advice.

Joint Advisory Committees

8.—(1) Two or more local authorities may, instead of each acting under paragraph 3 above, make arrangements to form a Children's Panel Advisory Committee for their areas (a "joint advisory committee").

(2) A joint advisory committee shall not be formed in pursuance of arrangements made under sub-paragraph (1) above unless the authorities concerned have obtained the consent in writing of the Secretary of State.

(3) The Secretary of State may give a direction, in any case where a joint advisory committee has not been formed, to two or more local authorities requiring them to form a joint advisory committee; and they shall comply with any such direction.

(4) Paragraphs 3 to 7, 10(a) and 11(b) of this Schedule shall apply to a joint advisory committee as they apply in respect of a Children's Panel Advisory Committee and, for the purposes of those paragraphs the local authorities acting under sub-paragraph (1) above shall be regarded as a single local authority.

Recruitment and training of panel members

9. The Secretary of State may make such arrangements as he considers appropriate to recruit and train members, or possible members, of the children's panels.
    10. Each local authority shall make such arrangements as they consider appropriate—
    (a) to enable the Children's Panel Advisory Committee to obtain names for submission to the Secretary of State as potential panel members; and
    (b) to train panel members or potential panel members.

Expenses of panel members

11. A local authority may pay—
    (a) to a member or a potential member of a children's panel,
    (b) to a member of the Children's Panel Advisory Committee,
    (c) to any person appointed under paragraph 7 above,
such allowances as may be determined by the Secretary of State; and he may determine differently in relation to different cases or different classes of case.

Publication of list of members of children's panel

12. Each local authority shall publish a list of names and addresses of members of the children's panel for their area, and that list shall be open for public inspection at the principal offices of the local authority, and at any place where an electors list for the local government area is available for inspection.

Section 98(1)   SCHEDULE 2

GENERAL NOTE
    In addition to the amendments to the Adoption (Scotland) Act 1978 made in Pt. III above, this Schedule contains various other amendments to that Act. Most of the changes are terminological, to take account of the shift in Pt. I above from the notions of "custody" and "access" to "residence" and "contact", but in addition there are a number of important substantive changes, particularly in relation to the grounds for dispensing with parental agreement to adoption. The following notes refer only to the substantive changes in the law.

AMENDMENTS OF THE ADOPTION (SCOTLAND) ACT 1978

1. The Adoption (Scotland) Act 1978 shall be amended in accordance with this Schedule.
    2. In section 1(2) (facilities to be provided as part of adoption service)—
    (a) paragraph (a) shall cease to have effect; and
    (b) for paragraph (c) substitute—
        "(bb) counselling and assistance (but, without prejudice to sections 51 to 51B, not assistance in cash) to children who have been adopted and to persons who have adopted a child; and
        (c) counselling for other persons if they have problems relating to adoption.".
    3. In section 3(3) (factors to be considered by Secretary of State in considering application for approval of adoption society), after paragraph (a) insert—
        "(aa) the procedures in accordance with which the applicant deals with, or as the case may be proposes to deal with, complaints arising in relation to its exercise of its functions and, where the applicant is already an approved adoption society, the manner in which it deals with particular complaints,".
    4. Section 8 (direction where adoption society inactive or defunct) shall cease to have effect.
    5. In section 9 (regulations relating to an adoption agency's exercise of its functions)—
    (a) in subsection (2), at the end add—
        "including, without prejudice to the generality of this subsection, regulations as to procedures for dealing with complaints arising in relation to such exercise."; and
    (b) after subsection (3) insert—
        "(3A) Regulations under this section may make provision—
        (a) as to the determination by an adoption agency of whether, as regards a child for whose adoption it proposes to make arrangements, any such agreement as is mentioned in sections 16(1)(b)(i) and 18(1)(a) is likely to be forthcoming and as to a

period by the end of which, if they have determined that the agreement is unlikely to be forthcoming and if no application has been made for an adoption order in relation to the child, application for an order under section 18(1) shall require to be made in relation to him; and

(b) where the case of a child for whose adoption an adoption agency proposes to make arrangements is referred under section 73(4)(c)(ii) or (iii) of the Children (Scotland) Act 1995 to the Principal Reporter (within the meaning of Part II of that Act), as to circumstances in which and, on the occurrence of such circumstances, a period by the end of which, if no application has been made for an adoption order in relation to the child, application for an order under section 18(1) shall require to be made in relation to him.".

6. In section 11(3) (offence of receiving child illegally placed for adoption), for paragraph (c) substitute—

"(c) both receives a child placed with him in contravention of subsection (1) and knows that the placement is with a view to his adopting the child,".

7. In section 12 (adoption orders)—

(a) in subsection (1)—

(i) for the words "rights and duties relating" substitute "responsibilities and parental rights in relation"; and

(ii) at the end add—

"; except that an adoption order may be made in relation to a person who has attained the age of 18 years if the application for it was made before such attainment.";

(b) in subsection (2), for the words "rights and duties" substitute "responsibilities and parental rights";

(c) in subsection (3)—

(i) in paragraph (a), for the words "right or duty" substitute "responsibility or parental right"; and

(ii) in paragraph (b)(ii), for the words "rights and duties" substitute "responsibilities and parental rights"; and

(d) at the end add—

"(9) Where a court making an adoption order in relation to a child who is subject to a supervision requirement is satisfied that, in consequence of its doing so, compulsory measures of supervision in respect of the child are no longer necessary, it may determine that the child shall forthwith cease to be subject to that requirement.".

GENERAL NOTE

There are two important changes to the law here. First, para. 7(a)(ii) amends s.12 of the 1978 Act to permit the court to make an adoption order even after the adopted person's 18th birthday, so long as the application is made before that day. It sometimes happens that applications are made shortly before a child's 18th birthday and there was previously a temptation in these circumstances to rush things in order to meet the deadline that the birthday constituted. The present provision takes away the need for that rush. Secondly, para. 7(d) adds a new subs. (9) to s.12 and permits the court making an adoption order to terminate any supervision requirement the child may be under. Previously, a child subject to a supervision requirement who had been adopted had to have her or his case reviewed by a children's hearing, and while it was possible for the hearing to continue supervision even after the adoption order had been made this would occur in only highly exceptional circumstances. This provision allows the court making an adoption order to terminate the supervision requirement, so obviating the need for a merely technical review by the children's hearing. This provision is unusual in that it is the only situation in which a supervision requirement can be brought to an end by other than an appeal court or a children's hearing, and it is one of the examples of a slight shift of power from the hearing to the court that the Act creates. The court must make its decision on the basis of the welfare of the child as required by s.6 of the 1978 Act, since the decision under this new paragraph is, it is submitted, a "decision relating to the adoption of a child".

8. In section 14 (adoption by married couple)—

(a) in subsection (1), the words from "Subject" to "certain cases)" shall cease to have effect; and

(b) in subsection (2), after paragraph (b) add—

", or

(c) both of them were habitually resident in any of the places mentioned in paragraph (a) above throughout the period of one year which ends with the date of their application".

GENERAL NOTE
See General Note to para. 9, below.

9. In section 15 (adoption by one person)—
(a) in subsection (1), the words from "Subject" to "certain cases)" shall cease to have effect; and
(b) in subsection (2), after paragraph (b) add
", or
(c) he was habitually resident in any of the places mentioned in paragraph (a) above throughout the period of one year which ends with the date of his application".

GENERAL NOTE
Under the old law the court had jurisdiction to grant an adoption order in non-Convention cases only if the applicant or applicants were domiciled in the U.K., the Channel Islands or the Isle of Man (ss.14 and 15 of the 1978 Act). It is habitual residence rather than domicile that determines jurisdiction in most aspects of family law today, and the present paragraph amends these sections to reflect this, by providing that the court may make an adoption order if the applicants are either domiciled or habitually resident in the U.K., Channel Islands or Isle of Man for at least one year prior to the date of the application. For the meaning of "habitual residence", see General Note to s.14(2) above.

10. In section 16 (provision for parental agreement to adoption order)—
(a) for subsection (2) substitute—
"(2) The grounds mentioned in subsection (1)(b)(ii) are, that the parent or guardian—
(a) is not known, cannot be found or is incapable of giving agreement;
(b) is withholding agreement unreasonably;
(c) has persistently failed, without reasonable cause, to fulfil one or other of the following parental responsibilities in relation to the child—
(i) the responsibility to safeguard and promote the child's health, development and welfare; or
(ii) if the child is not living with him, the responsibility to maintain personal relations and direct contact with the child on a regular basis;
(d) has seriously ill-treated the child, whose reintegration into the same household as the parent or guardian is, because of the serious ill-treatment or for other reasons, unlikely."; and
(b) subsection (5) shall cease to have effect.

GENERAL NOTE
In many respects this paragraph contains the most significant of the changes in the law in this Schedule, though the effect is one of simplification and clarification rather than alteration. In a substituted s.16(2) of the 1978 Act are set out the grounds upon which agreement to the adoption order or freeing order by the parent or guardian can be dispensed with. Under the old s.16(2) there were six separate grounds, but these contained a certain overlap with each other and in some instances the same circumstances could amount to more than one of the grounds. The new s.16(2) sets out four quite distinct grounds, dealing with quite separate situations. The law is simplified by this change, but not tightened and there will be no situation in which agreement could have been dispensed with under the old law but cannot be dispensed with under the new.
In order to emphasise the closeness in aim between the adoption process and the procedure whereby parental responsibilities are transferred from the parent to the local authority, the grounds upon which agreement can be dispensed with are the same for both procedures (see General Note to s.86(2)(b) above).
Ground (a) is the same as the old ground contained in the original s.16(2)(a), except for the addition that the parent or guardian "is not known". Since unmarried fathers (the usual case of the unknown parent) have no right to consent in any case, and it is difficult to imagine a situation in which a child's guardian is unknown, it is likely that these words will be limited to foundlings. For the application of this ground in the old law, see Wilkinson and Norrie *Parent and Child* (1993, W. Green) at p. 536.
Ground (b) is the same as the old ground in the original s.16(2)(b). For the application of this ground under that law, see Wilkinson and Norrie at pp. 536–541.
Ground (c) replaces the ground in the old s.16(2)(c) but is more precise in that it defines which parental responsibilities have to be not fulfilled in order to justify dispensing with consent to adoption. This ground under the old law is discussed in Wilkinson and Norrie at pp. 541–543.
Ground (d) is an amalgamation of the old s.16(2)(f) and s.16(5), and does not substantively alter the law. The ground is discussed in Wilkinson and Norrie at p. 546.

The grounds specified under the old law that have not been expressly re-enacted are abandonment, neglect, and persistent ill-treatment. All of these can be brought within the ground contained in the new s.16(2)(c), that is failure to fulfil the appropriate parental responsibility.

11. In section 18 (making and effect of orders freeing for adoption)—
(a) in subsection (1), after the word "agency" insert "which is a local authority";
(b) for subsection (5) substitute—
"(5) On the making of an order under this section, the parental responsibilities and parental rights in relation to the child are transferred to the adoption agency.";
(c) for subsection (7) substitute—
"(7) Before making an order under this section in the case of a child whose father is not, and has not been, married to the mother and does not have any parental responsibilities or parental rights in relation to the child, the court shall satisfy itself in relation to any person claiming to be the father that—
(a) he has no intention of applying for, or, if he did so apply, it is likely that he would be refused, an order under section 11 of the Children (Scotland) Act 1995 (orders in relation to parental responsibilities and parental rights); and
(b) he has no intention of entering into an agreement with the mother under section 4(1) of that Act (acquisition by natural father by agreement of such responsibilities and rights), or, if he has such an intention, that no agreement under that subsection is likely to be made."; and
(d) at the end add—
"(9) Where a court making an order under this section in relation to a child who is subject to a supervision requirement is satisfied that, in consequence of its doing so, compulsory measures of supervision in respect of the child are no longer necessary, it may determine that the child shall forthwith cease to be subject to that requirement.".

GENERAL NOTE
Subparagraph (d) gives power to a court making an order freeing a child for adoption to terminate a supervision requirement that the child is currently under. See General Note to para. 7 above.

12. In section 19 (progress reports)—
(a) in subsection (1)—
(i) for the words "("the former parent")" substitute "(in this section and in section 20 referred to as the "relevant parent")"; and
(ii) for the words "did not do so" substitute—
"either—
(a) did not do so; or
(b) having done so, subsequently by written notice under this subsection to the adoption agency to which the parental responsibilities and parental rights have been transferred, has withdrawn such declaration.";
(b) in subsection (2)—
(i) for the words "in which the parental rights and duties were vested" substitute "to which the parental responsibilities and parental rights were transferred"; and
(ii) for the word "former", in both places where it occurs, substitute "relevant";
(c) in subsection (3)—
(i) for the word "former", wherever it occurs, substitute "relevant"; and
(ii) for the words "have his home with a person with whom he has been placed for adoption" substitute "be placed with a person with a view to his being adopted by that person"; and
(d) in subsection (4)—
(i) for the words "the former" substitute "the relevant";
(ii) after paragraph (b) add—
"but a declaration under this subsection may be withdrawn in the same way as may a declaration under subsection (6) of section 18, in which event the agency shall no longer be so released"; and
(iii) for the words "that former" substitute "that relevant".
13. In section 20 (revocation of order under section 18)—
(a) in subsection (1)—
(i) for the word "former" substitute "relevant"; and

(ii) for the words "rights and duties" substitute "responsibilities and parental rights";

(b) after subsection (1) insert—

"(1A) The adoption agency, at any time after the making of the order under section 18 when the conditions mentioned in paragraphs (a) and (b) of subsection (1) above are satisfied, may apply to the court which made the order for a further order revoking it.";

(c) in subsection (2)—

(i) for the words "the application" substitute "an application under subsection (1) or (1A)"; and

(ii) for the words "rights and duties" substitute "responsibilities and parental rights";

(d) for subsection (3) substitute—

"(3) Where an order freeing a child for adoption is revoked under this section, the court shall, by an order under section 11 of the Children (Scotland) Act 1995 determine on whom are to be imposed the parental responsibilities, and to whom are to be given the parental rights, in relation to the child.";

(e) in subsection (4)—

(i) for the words "if the application" substitute "if an application under subsection (1)"; and

(ii) in paragraph (a), for the word "former" substitute "relevant"; and

(f) in subsection (5), for the word "former" substitute "relevant".

General Note

Section 20(1) of the unamended 1978 Act permits the former parent of the child to apply to the court for the revocation of a freeing order made under s.18, so long as this is done within 12 months of the making of the order. Paragraph 13(b) adds a new subs. (1A) to s.20, giving the adoption agency a similar right to apply to the court for revocation, though there is no time-limit on the agency's right to do so. The conditions upon which the revocation can be made are the same as when the former parent makes the application (see s.20(1) of the 1978 Act).

The old s.20(3) provided that when a freeing order was revoked, the parental rights of the parents (which vested in the adoption agency on the making of the freeing order: s.18(5)) revived. This has been replaced by para. 13(d) with a new rule to the effect that on the revocation of the freeing order the court which revokes the order must then make an order under s.11 of the present Act determining who is to be given parental responsibilities and parental rights: such an order may, but will not necessarily, be made in favour of a person who had parental responsibilities and parental rights immediately before the making of the freeing order.

14. In section 21 (variation of order under section 18 so as to substitute one adoption agency for another)—

(a) in subsection (1)—

(i) for the words "rights and duties" substitute "responsibilities and parental rights"; and

(ii) for the words "in which they are vested under" substitute "to which they are transferred by virtue of"; and

(b) in subsection (3)—

(i) for the words "rights and duties" substitute "responsibilities and parental rights"; and

(ii) for the words "vested in" substitute "been transferred to".

15. After section 22 insert—

"Children subject to supervision requirements

22A.—(1) An approved adoption society shall refer the case of a child who is subject to a supervision requirement to the Principal Reporter where it is satisfied that the best interests of the child would be served by its placing the child for adoption and it intends so to place him.

(2) On a case being referred to him under subsection (1), the Principal Reporter shall arrange for a children's hearing to review the supervision requirement in question and shall make any arrangements incidental to that review.

(3) Subsections (9), (13) and (14) of section 73 of the Children (Scotland) Act 1995 (which provide, respectively, for acting on the review of a supervision requirement, a report by a children's hearing and consideration of that report) shall apply in relation to a children's hearing arranged under this section as those subsections apply in relation to one arranged by virtue of subsection (4)(c)(iii) of that section.

(4) In this section "Principal Reporter" has the same meaning as in Part II of the Children (Scotland) Act 1995.".

GENERAL NOTE

Section 73(4) of the present Act imposes upon local authorities, who are intending to apply for a freeing order or intending to place the child for adoption, an obligation, if the child is currently subject to a supervision requirement, to refer the case to the reporter; the reporter must then arrange a review hearing. The present provision inserts a new s.22A into the 1978 Act imposing an identical obligation on adoption societies (*i.e.* adoption agencies other than local authorities). The same obligations contained in s.73 above apply here; and the same potential problems exist. In particular, it is perfectly possible for the hearing to disagree with the plan drawn up by the adoption society (or local authority). The hearing, which has control over the child's place of residence, can prevent a child being placed, but it has no power to prevent the adoption society (or local authority) applying for a freeing order (though in its report to the court under s.73(13) the hearing has the chance to make its views known). Such disagreements can only be unsettling for the child, but her or his long-term interests must not be prejudiced by a rush to judgment. The hearing may in many situations disagree with other people's plans for the child and the adoption process is no different from, for example, a contact order made by a sheriff but the terms of which the hearing can depart from. Even in the adoption process the jurisdiction of the children's hearing over children who are subject to a supervision requirement is predominant.

16. In section 24 (restrictions on making adoption orders), for subsection (2) substitute—
   "(2) The court may make an adoption order in relation to a child even where it is found that the applicants have, as respects the child, contravened section 51.
   (3) In considering whether to make an adoption order or an order under section 18(1), the court shall regard the welfare of the child concerned as its paramount consideration and shall not make the order in question unless it considers that it would be better for the child that it should do so than that it should not.".

GENERAL NOTE

The old s.24(2) of the 1978 Act prohibited the court from making an adoption order if the applicant had breached the prohibitions against payments in relation to the adoption. The new s.24(2) introduced by this paragraph reverses this rule and the position now is that breach of the prohibitions against payments will be a criminal matter but that the adoption may still, in appropriate cases, go ahead. Since the welfare of the child is paramount there may well be situations in which a child's best interests are served by being adopted by applicants who have committed this criminal offence: were it otherwise, consideration of the offence rather than the child's interests would be paramount.

There is another important addition to the law in the form of a new s.24(3) to the 1978 Act. Reflecting the terminology in s.11(7) above, the court is bound by this new provision to regard the child's welfare as paramount, and to apply the minimum intervention principle in making either an adoption order or a freeing order. The reference to welfare is tautologous since it repeats (in different words but with no difference in substance) the principle in the amended s.6 of the 1978 Act (which applies more broadly than to the making of the adoption order or the freeing order). The minimum intervention principle is of little strength in adoption and cannot be used to justify keeping the child in a position of long-term fostering rather than being adopted, for the security given by the latter will always be a strong consideration and can easily outweigh the minimum intervention principle (see *C. (A Minor) (Adoption: Conditions), Re* [1988] 2 WLR 474, per Lord Ackner at p. 484).

17. In section 25(1) (making of interim order and preconditions for so doing)—
   (a) for the words "of sections 16(1) and 22(1) are complied with" substitute—
      "—
      (a) of section 16(1); and
      (b) in a case where the child was not placed with the applicant by an adoption agency, of section 22(1),
      are complied with"; and
   (b) for the words "vesting the custody of the child in" substitute "giving parental responsibilities and parental rights to".
18. After section 25 insert—

"Timetable for resolving question as to whether agreement to adoption order etc. should be dispensed with
   25A. In proceedings in which the question arises as to whether the court is satisfied as is mentioned in section 16(1)(b)(ii) or 18(1)(b), the court shall, with a view to determining the question without delay—
      (a) draw up a timetable specifying periods within which certain steps must be taken in relation to those proceedings; and

(b) give such directions as it considers appropriate for the purpose of ensuring, so far as is reasonably practicable, that the timetable is adhered to.".

GENERAL NOTE

A new s.25A of the 1978 Act provides that the court shall draw up a timetable for the taking of certain steps if parental agreement is to be dispensed with. This is to ensure speedy resolution of disputes, on the principle that it is in the interests of the child that matters not be delayed unduly. It will be for the court to determine the consequences of not adhering to the timetable.

19. In section 27 (restrictions on removal of a child by a parent or guardian who has agreed to an adoption order or to an order freeing the child for adoption)—

  (a) for subsections (1) and (2), substitute—

    "(1) Where—

      (a) an adoption agency has placed a child with a person with a view to his being adopted by the person; and

      (b) the consent of each parent or guardian of the child has been duly obtained to that placement (whether or not in knowledge of the identity of the person),

    any such parent or guardian shall not be entitled to remove the child from the care and possession of the person without the leave either of the adoption agency or of the court.

    (2) The reference in subsection (1) to consent having been duly obtained is to its having been obtained in accordance with such regulations as may be made by the Secretary of State for the purposes of this section."; and

  (b) in subsection (3), for the words "contravenes subsection (1) or (2)" substitute "removes a child in contravention of subsection (1)".

20. In section 28 (restriction on removal of child from care and possession of applicant for adoption order etc.)—

  (a) in subsection (4), for the words from ", in terms of" to the end substitute "under or by virtue of Chapter 2 or 3 of Part II of the Children (Scotland) Act 1995"; and

  (b) in subsection (5), the words "or of a voluntary organisation" and "or the organisation" shall cease to have effect.

21. Sections 32 to 37 (protected children) shall cease to have effect.

GENERAL NOTE

Under the old law the local authority had various duties in relation to children whom an applicant intended to adopt and who lived with the applicant. These children were known as protected children and the typical example was shown with step-parent adoptions. Step-parent adoptions are to be made easier (see s.97 above) and the notion of the "protected child" has little remaining use. Consequently the provisions concerning protected children are repealed. (See also Sched. 5 to the same effect).

22. In section 45(5) (restrictions as to persons to whom information contained in the Adopted Children Register or in certain other registers or books may be provided, including a restriction as to the minimum age which an adopted person must be for it to be provided to him), for the word "17" substitute "16".

GENERAL NOTE

This is a timely recognition that since the Age of Legal Capacity (Scotland) Act 1991 the age at which persons acquire capacity to control their own lives is 16.

23. In section 49(1) (adoption of children abroad), for the words "vesting in him the parental rights and duties relating" substitute "transferring to him the parental responsibilities and parental rights in relation".

24. In section 51 (prohibition on certain payments)—

  (a) in subsection (1), after the word "section" insert "and of section 51A(3)";

  (b) in subsection (2), for the words "the court may order any child in respect of whom the offence was committed" substitute "without prejudice to any power which the court has to make any other order in relation to the child as respects whom the offence was committed, it may order him";

  (c) in subsection (5)—

    (i) at the beginning insert "Subject to section 51B,"; and

    (ii) at the end add "(including any such payment made by virtue of section 51B)"; and

  (d) subsections (6)(a) and (7) to (11) shall cease to have effect.

25. After section 51 insert—

"Adoption allowances schemes

51A.—(1) Subject to subsection (2), an adoption agency which is—

(a) a local authority shall, within such period after the coming into force of this section as the Secretary of State may by order direct;

(b) an approved adoption society may,

prepare a scheme (in this section and in section 51B referred to as an "adoption allowances scheme") for the payment by the agency of allowances to any person who has adopted, or intends to adopt, a child in any case where arrangements for the adoption were made, or as the case may be are to be made, by the agency.

(2) The Secretary of State may make regulations as respects adoption allowances schemes; and without prejudice to the generality of this subsection such regulations may in particular make provision as to—

(a) the procedure to be followed by an agency in determining whether a person should be paid an allowance;

(b) the circumstances in which an allowance may be paid;

(c) the factors to be taken into account in determining the amount of an allowance;

(d) the procedure for review, variation and termination of allowances;

(e) the information about allowances which is to be supplied by an agency to a person who intends to adopt a child; and

(f) the procedure to be followed by an agency in drawing up, in making alterations to, or in revoking and replacing, an adoption allowances scheme.

(3) Section 51(1) shall not apply to any payment made in accordance with an adoption allowances scheme (including any such payment made by virtue of section 51B).

Transitional provisions as respects adoption allowances

51B. After the coming into force of section 51A—

(a) no scheme for the payment of allowances shall be submissible under subsection (5) of section 51; and

(b) a scheme which has been approved under that subsection of that section shall forthwith be revoked under subsection (6)(b) of that section, so however that where a person was before its revocation receiving payments made in accordance with that scheme he may continue to receive payments so made which, had there been no revocation, would have fallen to be made to him or he may agree to receive, instead of the continued payments, payments made in accordance with an adoption allowances scheme.".

GENERAL NOTE

This paragraph adds into the 1978 Act a new s.51A under which local authorities are obliged to, and adoption societies may, prepare schemes for the payment of allowances to adopters and persons intending to adopt. Regulations will govern the procedure for paying such allowances and for determining who should receive such allowances; and the payment of these allowances will not contravene the prohibition of payments in consideration of adoption contained in s.51. Such schemes are likely to be particularly useful to foster carers inhibited from adopting their charges because of the loss of foster allowances, and for the placement of children who for some reason, such as having special (and expensive) needs, are hard to place.

26. In section 58 (curators *ad litem* and reporting officers), in subsection (2)(c), for the words "rights and duties relating" substitute "responsibilities and parental rights in relation".

27. In section 59(4) (disapplication of provisions regarding rules), for the words ", 11 and 32 to 37" substitute "and 11".

28. In section 60(3) (affirmative procedure for certain orders), the words "or 51(9)" shall cease to have effect.

29. In section 65 (interpretation)—

(a) in subsection (1)—

(i) in the definition of "adoption order", in each of paragraphs (b) and (c), for the words "and 30 to 32" substitute "30 and 31";

(ii) after the definition of "child" insert—

"compulsory measures of supervision has the same meaning as in Part II of the Children (Scotland) Act 1995;";

(iii) in the definition of "guardian", paragraph (b) shall cease to have effect;

(iv) in the definition of "local authority", the words ", 35(1)" shall cease to have effect;

(v) after the definition of "overseas adoption" insert—

"parent means, irrespective of whether or not they are, or have been, married to each other—

(a) the mother of the child, where she has parental responsibilities or parental rights in relation to him;

(b) the father of the child where he has such responsibilities or rights; and

(c) both of his parents, where both have such responsibilities or rights;

"parental responsibilities" and "parental rights" have the meanings respectively given by sections 1(3) and 2(4) of the Children (Scotland) Act 1995 (analogous expressions being construed accordingly);";

(vi) in the definition of "relative" for the words from "and any person" to the end substitute "where he is not a parent within the meaning of this Act, and any person who would be a relative within the meaning of this definition if the father were such a parent;" and

(vii) after the definition of "specified order" insert—

"supervision requirement" has the same meaning as in Part II of the Children (Scotland) Act 1995;";

(b) in subsection (3), for the words "44 of the Social Work (Scotland) Act 1968" substitute "70 of the Children (Scotland) Act 1995"; and

(c) after subsection (5) add—

"(6) Any reference in this Act to a child being in, received into or kept in, care (whether or not such care is expressed as being the care of a local authority and except where the context otherwise requires) shall be taken to be a reference to his being looked after by a local authority and shall be construed in accordance with section 17(6) of the Children (Scotland) Act 1995; and any reference to the authority in whose care a child is, shall be construed accordingly.".

Section 105(3)　　　　　　　　　　　　SCHEDULE 3

TRANSITIONAL PROVISIONS AND SAVINGS

1. Where, immediately before the day appointed for the coming into force of section 25 of this Act, a child is by virtue of section 15 of the 1968 Act (duty of local authority to provide for orphans, deserted children etc.) in the care of a local authority, the child shall on and after that day be treated as if he had been provided with accommodation under (and within the meaning of) subsection (1) of the said section 25.

2. Sections 29 and 30 of this Act shall apply in respect of a person who, at the time when he ceased to be of school age (as defined in section 31 of the Education (Scotland) Act 1980) or at any subsequent time, was—

(a) in the care of a local authority by virtue of the said section 15 or of section 16 of the 1968 Act (assumption of parental rights and powers); or

(b) subject to a supervision requirement (within the meaning of section 44(1) of the 1968 Act),

as they apply in respect of a person who at such time was looked after (within the meaning of Part II of this Act) by a local authority.

3. Where the parental rights in respect of a child have, by a resolution under the said section 16 or under section 16A of the 1968 Act (duty of local authority in cases of necessity to assume parental rights and powers vested in a voluntary organisation), vested in a local authority and immediately before the day appointed for the coming into force of section 86 of this Act those rights remain so vested, the resolution shall on and after that day have effect as if it were a parental responsibilities order transferring the appropriate parental rights and responsibilities (as defined in subsection (3) of the said section 86) relating to the child to the authority; and any access order made under section 17B of the 1968 Act in relation to the child (with any order made under section 17C of that Act as respects the access order) being (in either case) an order which immediately before that day remains undischarged, shall on and after that day have effect as if it were an order made under section 88(3) of this Act as respects the child.

4. Where the parental rights in respect of a child have, by a resolution under the said section 16, vested in a voluntary organisation (as defined in section 93 of this Act) and immediately before the day mentioned in paragraph 3 above those rights remain so vested, the resolution shall, notwithstanding the repeal by this Act of the said section 16, continue to have effect until one of the following occurs

(a) the child attains the age of eighteen years;

(b) the resolution is rescinded by the local authority because it appears to them that their doing so would promote the child's welfare;

(c) the period of six months commencing with that day expires;

(d) an order is made by virtue of section 11(2)(b), or under section 86(1), of this Act in relation to the child;

(e) an order is made under section 12 (adoption order) or 18 (order freeing for adoption) of the Adoption (Scotland) Act 1978 in relation to the child.

5. Where the circumstance by virtue of which a resolution under the said section 16 ceases to have effect is that mentioned in sub-paragraph (c) of paragraph 4 above, the appropriate parental rights and responsibilities (defined as mentioned in paragraph 3 above) in relation to the child shall transfer forthwith to the local authority in whose area he resides; and for the purposes of sections 86(6) and 87 to 89 of this Act the transfer shall be deemed effected by a parental responsibilities order applied for by that authority.

6. While a resolution continues to have effect by virtue of paragraph 4 above, sections 17(3A) and (6) to (10), 17A, 17B, 17D, 17E and 20(3) of the 1968 Act (together with the code of practice last published under subsection (5) of the said section 17E) shall continue to have effect in relation to the child in question notwithstanding the repeal by this Act of those sections.

7. Where an order made under—

(a) section 10 (power of court in actions of divorce etc. to commit care of child to local authority) or 12 (power of court to provide for supervision of child) of the Matrimonial Proceedings (Children) Act 1958;

(b) section 11 of the Guardianship Act 1973 (orders relating to care and custody of children); or

(c) section 26 of the Adoption (Scotland) Act 1978 (provision for supervision or care where adoption order refused),

committed the care of the child to, or as the case may be placed the child under the supervision of, a local authority and immediately before the repeal by this Act of the section in question (the "relevant repeal") that order remained undischarged, the order shall continue to have effect notwithstanding the relevant repeal until one of the following occurs—

(i) the period of six months commencing with the date of the relevant repeal expires;

(ii) the Court of Session direct, or the sheriff directs, that the order be discharged; or

(iii) there is an event in consequence of which, but for the provisions (apart from this paragraph) of this Act, the order would have fallen to be discharged.

8.—(1) Where relevant proceedings in relation to a child have been commenced and on the relevant date have not been concluded, the provisions of Part III of the 1968 Act shall continue to apply to those proceedings until the proceedings are concluded, notwithstanding the repeal of any of those provisions by this Act.

(2) For the purposes of this paragraph, "relevant proceedings" means any proceedings at a children's hearing under Part III of the 1968 Act, any application to the sheriff under that Part for a warrant or under section 42(2)(c) of that Act to establish any ground of referral, and any appeal under section 49 or 50 of that Act; and a reference to the commencement, or to the conclusion, of such proceedings shall be construed in accordance with sub-paragraph (3) or, as the case may be, (4) below.

(3) Relevant proceedings are commenced when one of the following occurs—

(a) a children's hearing is arranged under section 37(4) or section 39(3) of the 1968 Act;

(b) an application under section 42(2)(c) of that Act is lodged;

(c) an appeal to the sheriff under section 49 of that Act is lodged;

(d) an application under section 50(2) of that Act is made.

(4) Relevant proceedings are concluded when one of the following occurs—

(a) the sheriff discharges the referral under section 42(5) of the 1968 Act;

(b) a children's hearing discharge the referral under section 43(2) of that Act;

(c) the period of three weeks after a children's hearing make a supervision requirement under section 44 of that Act or on remission to them under section 49(5) of that Act, expires provided that no appeal has been lodged within that period against that decision under section 49 of that Act;

(d) subject, as respects a decision under section 49(5)(b) of that Act, to head (c) above, the period of twenty eight days after the sheriff has disposed of an appeal under section 49(4), (5) or (6) of that Act expires provided that no application has been made within that period to him to state a case under section 50(2) of that Act;

(e) the period of twenty eight days after the sheriff has disposed of a case remitted to him under section 50(3) expires provided that no further application under the said section 50(2) has been made.

9. Where a child has been taken to a place of safety, or is being detained in such a place, in accordance with section 37(2) of the 1968 Act before the relevant date, and the first lawful day for the purposes of subsection (4) of that section is on or after that date, the child's case shall be proceeded with as if that day had been before the relevant date.

10.—(1) Where on the relevant date a child is subject to a supervision requirement imposed under section 44 of the 1968 Act, he shall be treated as if the requirement had been imposed under section 70 of this Act; and in calculating any period of time for the purposes of section 73 of this Act, that requirement shall be deemed to have been imposed on the day on which the requirement was imposed under the said section 44 or, as the case may be, was last reviewed or varied under the said Act of 1968.

(2) Where any relevant proceedings are concluded as mentioned in paragraph 8(4)(c) above, a supervision requirement imposed under section 44 of the 1968 Act shall have effect as if it were made under section 70 of this Act.

(3) Where before the relevant date, or in any relevant proceedings, the sheriff has in relation to a supervision requirement made an order under section 49(6) of the 1968 Act, that order shall have effect in relation to the supervision requirement deemed to have been made under section 70 of this Act as it would have had effect in relation to the supervision requirement made under section 44 of the 1968 Act.

11. In this Schedule—
"the 1968 Act" means the Social Work (Scotland) Act 1968;
"the relevant date" means the date on which the repeal of Part III of the 1968 Act by this Act takes effect; and
"relevant proceedings" shall be construed in accordance with paragraph 8(2) above.

<table>
<tr><td>**Section 105(4)**</td><td>SCHEDULE 4</td></tr>
</table>

Section 105(4)   SCHEDULE 4

MINOR AND CONSEQUENTIAL AMENDMENTS

Lands Clauses Consolidation (Scotland) Act 1845 (c. 19)

1.—(1) The Lands Clauses Consolidation (Scotland) Act 1845 shall be amended in accordance with this paragraph.

(2) In section 7 (which makes provision for certain persons to have full power to sell and convey land)—
(a) after the word "husbands," insert "persons who, within the meaning of Part I of the Children (Scotland) Act 1995, are entitled to act as the legal representatives of a child,";
(b) after the words "guardians for" the words "persons under a legal disability by reason of nonage" shall cease to have effect; and
(c) after the word "whether", the words "persons under legal disability by reason of nonage" shall cease to have effect;
(d) after the word "such" where it appears for the sixth time, insert "legal representatives,"; and
(e) after the word "such" where it appears for the seventh time, the words "persons under legal disability by reason of nonage" shall cease to have effect.

(3) In section 67 (certain payments to persons under a disability to be deposited with the Bank)—
(a) after the word "husband," insert "a person who, within the meaning of Part I of the Children (Scotland) Act 1995, is entitled to act as a legal representative of a child"; and
(b) the words "persons under legal disability by reason of nonage" shall cease to have effect.

(4) In section 69 (nomination of trustees to whom certain payments of under £200 may be paid)—
(a) the words "legal disability by reason of nonage" shall cease to have effect; and
(b) after the word "husbands," insert "legal representatives of a child (within the meaning of Part I of the Children (Scotland) Act 1995),".

(5) In section 70 (sums of under £20 to be paid to certain persons), after the word "husbands," insert "legal representatives of a child (within the meaning of Part I of the Children (Scotland) Act 1995),".

Judicial Factors (Scotland) Act 1849 (c. 51)

2.—(1) The Judicial Factors (Scotland) Act 1849 shall be amended in accordance with this paragraph.

(2) In section 1 (interpretation), the words from "the word "Guardian" to "years;" shall cease to have effect.

(3) In section 10 (duty of accountant to supervise judicial factors and others), for the words "guardians and tutors" substitute ", tutors".

(4) Section 25(2) (guardians to be subject to the provisions of the Act), shall cease to have effect.

(5) In section 27 (limitation by court of amount of caution), the words "guardians and" shall cease to have effect.

(6) In section 31 (power of court to remove tutors etc.), the word "guardian" shall cease to have effect.

(7) In section 32 (provisions of the Act not to alter existing powers, rights and duties of offices), the word "guardian," shall cease to have effect.

(8) In section 33 (power of accountant to obtain information from banks), the words "guardians or" shall cease to have effect.

(9) In section 34 (petitions for discharge of office), in both places where it occurs, the word "guardian," shall cease to have effect.

(10) In section 34A (act of sederunt to provide for other forms of discharge), for the words ", death or coming of age" substitute "or death".

(11) In section 36 (records held by accountant to be open to inspection), the word "guardianships," shall cease to have effect.

(14 In section 37 (accumulation of interest on accounts), the word "guardian," shall cease to have effect.

(13) In section 40 (act of sederunt to regulate *inter alia* application of the Act to offices other than judicial factors), in both places where it occurs, the word "guardians," shall cease to have effect.

Improvement of Land Act 1864 (c.114)

3. In section 24 of the Improvement of Land Act 1864 (representation of persons under disability in certain applications etc.), for the words from the beginning to "feoffee" where it last occurs substitute "Any person entitled to act as the legal representative of a person under legal disability by reason of non age or mental incapacity shall be entitled to act on behalf of that person for the purposes of this Act; and any trustee, judicial factor, executor or administrator shall, subject to any other enactment, have the same rights and powers for the purposes of this Act as if the property vested in or administered by him had been vested in him in his own right; but no such legal representative".

Judicial Factors (Scotland) Act 1880 (c. 4)

4. In section 3 of the Judicial Factors (Scotland) Act 1880 (interpretation), in the definition of "judicial factor"—
   (a) for the word "*absentis*," substitute "*absentis* and"; and
   (b) the words from "and" to "required," shall cease to have effect.

Heritable Securities (Scotland) Act 1894 (c. 44)

5. In section 13 of the Heritable Securities (Scotland) Act 1894 (persons to have powers conferred by Act where person subject to legal disability), for the words "and trustees" substitute "and—
   (a) any person entitled, within the meaning of Part I of the Children (Scotland) Act 1995, to act as the legal representative of a child; and
   (b) trustees".

Trusts (Scotland) Act 1921 (c. 58)

6. In section 2 of the Trusts (Scotland) Act 1921 (interpretation)—
   (a) in the definition of "trustee", the words "(including a father or mother acting as guardian of a child under the age of 16 years)" shall cease to have effect; and
   (b) after the definition of "trustee" insert—
      " "curator" and "tutor" shall have respectively the meanings assigned to these expressions by section 1 of the Judicial Factors Act 1849;
      "guardian" shall not include any person who, within the meaning of Part I of the Children (Scotland) Act 1995, is entitled to act as the legal representative of a child;".

Children and Young Persons (Scotland) Act 1937 (c. 37)

7.—(1) The Children and Young Persons (Scotland) Act 1937 shall be amended in accordance with this paragraph.
   (2) In section 12 (cruelty to persons under sixteen)—
   (a) in subsection (1), for the words from "has the custody" to "that age" substitute "who has parental responsibilities in relation to a child or to a young person under that age or has charge or care of a child or such a young person,";

(b) in subsection (2)(a), after the words "young person" insert "or the legal guardian of a child or young person"; and

(c) in subsection (4), for the words from "of whom" to "or care" substitute "and he had parental responsibilities in relation to, or charge or care of, that child or young person".

(3) In section 15 (causing or allowing persons under sixteen to be used for begging), in each of subsections (1) and (2), for the words "the custody" substitute "parental responsibilities in relation to, or having".

(4) In section 22 (exposing children under seven to risk of burning), for the words from "having the custody" to "seven years" substitute "and who has parental responsibilities in relation to a child under the age of seven years or charge or care of such a child".

(5) In section 27 (interpretation)—

(a) the first paragraph shall cease to have effect; and

(b) in the second paragraph, for the words "the custody of" substitute "parental responsibilities in relation to".

(6) In section 110(1) (interpretation)—

(a) after the definition of "local authority" insert—

" "parental responsibilities" has the same meaning as in section 1(3) of the Children (Scotland) Act 1995 and includes the responsibilities which a father would have as a parent but for the operation of section 3(1)(b) of that Act;";

(b) for the definition of "place of safety", substitute "'place of safety" has the meaning give by section 93(1) of the Children (Scotland) Act 1995;"; and

(c) for the definition of "residential establishment" substitute ""residential establishment" has the meaning given by the said section 93(1);".

Mines and Quarries Act 1954 (c. 70)

8. In section 182(1) of the Mines and Quarries Act 1954 (interpretation), in the definition of "parent", for the words from "means" to "and includes" substitute "means a parent of a young person or any person who is not a parent of his but who has parental responsibility for him (within the meaning of the Children Act 1989) or who has parental responsibilities in relation to him (within the meaning of section 1(3) of the Children (Scotland) Act 1995), and includes".

Matrimonial Proceedings (Children) Act 1958 (c. 40)

9. In section 11(1) of the Matrimonial Proceedings (Children) Act 1958 (reports as to arrangements for future care and upbringing of children), for the words from the beginning to "the court may" substitute "Where the court is considering any question relating to the care and upbringing of a child, it may".

Factories Act 1961 (c. 34)

10. In section 176(1) of the Factories Act 1961 (interpretation)—

(a) for the definition of "child" substitute—

" "child" means any person who is not over—

(a) compulsory school age (construed in accordance with section 277 of the Education Act 1993); or

(b) school age (construed in accordance with section 31 of the Education (Scotland) Act 1980);"

(b) in the definition of "parent", for the words from "means" to "and includes" substitute "means a parent of a child or young person or any person who is not a parent of his but who has parental responsibility for him (within the meaning of the Children Act 1989) or who has parental responsibilities in relation to him (within the meaning of section 1(3) of the Children (Scotland) Act 1995), and includes".

Education (Scotland) Act 1962 (c. 47)

11. In section 145(33) of the Education (Scotland) Act 1962 (interpretation), for the words "the actual custody of" substitute "parental responsibilities (within the meaning of section 1(3) of the Children (Scotland) Act 1995) in relation to, or has the care of,".

Registration of Births, Deaths and Marriages (Scotland) Act 1965 (c. 49)

12.—(1) The Registration of Births, Deaths and Marriages (Scotland) Act 1965 shall be amended in accordance with this paragraph.

(2) In section 20(3)(a) (re-registration of birth of person under sixteen), for sub-paragraphs (i) and (ii) substitute ", by any person (whether or not he has himself attained the age of sixteen years) having parental responsibilities in relation to that person;".

(3) In section 43 (recording of baptismal name or change of name or surname)—

(a) in subsection (3), the words from "In this" to the end shall cease to have effect;

(b) in subsections (6)(a) and (7), for the words "the parent or guardian" substitute "the qualified applicant";

(c) after subsection (9) insert—

"(9A) In this section "qualified applicant" means—

(a) where only one parent has parental responsibilities in relation to the child, that parent;

(b) where both parents have such responsibilities in relation to the child, both parents; and

(c) where neither parent has such responsibilities, any other person who has such responsibilities.

(9B) A person may be a qualified applicant for the purposes of this section whether or not he has attained the age of sixteen years"; and

(d) subsection (10) shall cease to have effect.

(4) In section 53(3)(c) (offence of failure by parent to give information concerning birth), after the word "fails" insert "without reasonable excuse".

(5) In section 56(1) (interpretation), after the definition of "parentage" insert—

" "parental responsibilities" has the meaning given in section 1(3) of the Children (Scotland) Act 1995;".

13. Where, at any time after the coming into force of the Age of Legal Capacity (Scotland) Act 1991 but before the coming into force of—

(a) sub-paragraph (2) of paragraph 12 of this Schedule, a person's mother or father, who had not at that time attained the age of sixteen years, purported to apply under section 20(3)(a) of that Act to re-register the person's birth, the mother, or as the case may be the father, shall be presumed to have had legal capacity to make the application; or

(b) sub-paragraph (3)(c) of that paragraph, a person who had not at that time attained the age of sixteen years purported to make an application under any provision of section 43 of that Act ("making an application" including for the purposes of this sub-paragraph, without prejudice to the generality of that expression, signing and delivering a certificate in accordance with subsection (3) of that section) the person shall be presumed to have had legal capacity to make the application.

Law Reform (Miscellaneous Provisions)(Scotland) Act 1966 (c. 19)

14. In section 8 of the Law Reform (Miscellaneous Provisions) (Scotland) Act 1966 (variation and recall of certain orders in respect of maintenance, custody etc.)—

(a) in subsection (1), after paragraph (c) insert—

"(cc) an order under section 11 of the Children (Scotland) Act 1995 (orders in respect of parental responsibilities etc.) or under any earlier enactment relating to the custody, care or supervision of a child, or access to a child;"; and

(b) in subsection (6), in the definition of "sheriff", in paragraph (a), for the words "or (c)" substitute ", (c) or (cc)".

Social Work (Scotland) Act 1968 (c. 49)

15.—(1) The Social Work (Scotland) Act 1968 shall be amended in accordance with this paragraph.

(2) In section 1(1) (duty of local authority to implement statutory duties not falling on other authorities), after the word "Act" insert "or Part II of the Children (Scotland) Act 1995".

(3) In section 4 (arrangements for provision of assistance to local authorities by other bodies), after "1984" insert "or Part II of the Children (Scotland) Act 1995".

(4) In section 5 (powers of the Secretary of State in relation to certain functions of local authorities)—

(a) in subsection (1) after the word "Act" insert "and Part II of the Children (Scotland) Act 1995";

(b) in subsection (1B)—

(i) before paragraph (o), the word "and" shall cease to have effect; and

(ii) at the end add "; and

(p) Part II of the Children (Scotland) Act 1995.";

(c) in subsection (2), in paragraph (c) for the words "and (o)" substitute ", (o) and (p)"; and

(d) for subsection (3) substitute—

"(3) Without prejudice to the generality of subsection (2) above, regulations under this section may make such provision as is mentioned in subsection (4) of this section as regards—

(a) the boarding out of persons other than children by local authorities and voluntary organisations, whether under any enactment or otherwise; and

(b) the placing of children under paragraph (a), or the making of arrangements in respect of children under paragraph (c), of section 26(1) of the Children (Scotland) Act 1995, by local authorities.

(4) The provision referred to in subsection (3) of this section is—

(a) for the recording—

(i) by local authorities and voluntary organisations, of information relating to those with whom persons are so boarded out, or who are willing to have persons so boarded out with them; and

(ii) by local authorities, of information relating to those with whom children are so placed or with whom such arrangements are made or who are willing to have children so placed with them or to enter into such arrangements;

(b) for securing that—

(i) persons are not so boarded out in any household unless it is for the time being approved by such local authority or voluntary organisation as may be prescribed by the regulations; and

(ii) children are not so placed or, in accordance with such arrangements, provided with accommodation, in any household unless it is for the time being approved by the local authority placing the child or as the case may be making the arrangements;

(c) for securing that, where possible, the person with whom a child is so placed or with whom such arrangements are made is either of the same religious persuasion as the child or gives an undertaking that the child shall be brought up in that persuasion;

(d) for securing—

(i) that a person who is, and the place in which he is, so boarded out by a local authority or voluntary organisation is supervised and inspected by that authority or organisation; and

(ii) that a child who is, and the place in which he is, so placed or, in accordance with such arrangements, provided with accommodation, by a local authority is supervised and inspected by that authority,

and that he shall be removed from the place in question if his welfare appears to require it.

(5) In subsections (3) and (4) of this section, "child" has the same meaning as in Chapters 2 and 3 of Part II of the Children (Scotland) Act 1995."

(5) In section 5B (requirement to establish complaints procedures)—

(a) in subsection (4), in paragraph (b), for the words "rights in respect of" substitute "responsibilities and parental rights (within the meaning of section 1(3) and section 2(4) respectively of the Children (Scotland) Act 1995) in relation to"; and

(b) in subsection (5), at the end of the definition of "child", the words from "and" to the end of the subsection shall cease to have effect.

(6) In section 6 (power to enter certain establishments to conduct examination)—

(a) in subsection (1)—

(i) in paragraph (a), after the word "1984" insert "or Part II of the Children (Scotland) Act 1995";

(ii) in paragraph (b), sub–paragraph (ii) shall cease to have effect;

(iii) in paragraph (c), after the word "person" insert ", other than a child,"; and

(iv) after paragraph (c) add—

"(cc) any place where a child is for the time being accommodated under paragraph (a) of, or by virtue of paragraph (c) of, section 26(1) of the Children (Scotland) Act 1995."; and

(b) in subsection (2), after the words "1984" insert "or Part II of the Children (Scotland) Act 1995".

(7) For subsection (1) of section 6A (power of the Secretary of State to hold inquiries), substitute—

"(1) Without prejudice to section 6B(1) of this Act, the Secretary of State may cause an inquiry to be held into—

(a) the functions of a local authority under this Act or any of the enactments mentioned in section 5(1B) of this Act;

(b) the functions of an adoption society, within the meaning of section 65 of the Adoption (Scotland) Act 1978;

(c) the functions of a voluntary organisation in so far as those functions relate to establishments to which sections 61 to 68 of this Act apply;

(d) the detention of a child under—
> (i) section 57 of the Children and Young Persons (Scotland) Act 1937; or
>
> (ii) section 206 or 413 of the Criminal Procedure (Scotland) Act 1975; or

(e) the functions of the Principal Reporter under Part III of the Local Government (Scotland) Act 1994, the Children (Scotland) Act 1995 or any other enactment."

(8) In section 9 (powers of the Secretary of State with regard to training etc.), in subsections (1) and (2), after the word "Act" insert "or Part II of the Children (Scotland) Act 1995".

(9) In section 10(1) (making of grants and loans for social work), for the words "and (l)" substitute ", (l) and (p)".

(10) In section 11(1) (local authority authorised by Secretary of State to purchase compulsorily land), in subsection (1), after the word "Act" insert "or Part II of the Children (Scotland) Act 1995".

(11) In section 12 (general social welfare services of local authorities), for the words from "be given" in subsection (1) to "a person" in subsection (2)(b) substitute—

", subject to subsections (3) to (5) of this section, be given in kind or in cash to, or in respect of, any relevant person.

(2) A person is a relevant person for the purposes of this section if, not being less than eighteen years of age, he is".

(12) in section 28 (burial or cremation)—

(a) in subsection (1), after the word "from," insert "or was a child being looked after by,"; and

(b) after subsection (2) add—

"(3) In subsection (1) of this section, the reference to a child being looked after by a local authority shall be construed in accordance with section 17(6) of the Children (Scotland) Act 1995.".

(13) In section 29 (power of local authority to defray expenses of parents etc. visiting persons accommodated by a local authority or attending certain funerals)—

(a) in subsection (1)—

> (i) for the words from "a person" to "respect" substitute—
> "—
>> (a) a person, other than a child, in the care of the authority or receiving assistance from the authority; or
>>
>> (b) a child who is being looked after by the authority,
>
> in respect";
>
> (ii) after the words "visiting the person" insert "or child"; and
>
> (iii) for the words "the person", where they occur for the second time, substitute "him";

(b) in subsection (2), for the words from "a person" to "for" substitute—
"—
>> (a) a person, other than a child, who had been in the care of the authority or receiving assistance from the authority; for
>>
>> (b) a child who had been looked after by the authority, for"; and

(c) after subsection (2), add—

"(3) In subsections (1) and (2) above, references to a child looked after by a local authority shall be construed as is mentioned in subsection (3) of section 28 of this Act.".

(14) Part III (children in need of compulsory measures of care) shall cease to have effect, with the exception of subsections (1) and (3) of section 31 and the amendments provided for by the said subsection (3) and contained in Schedule 2 to that Act.

(15) In section 59(1) (provision and maintenance of residential and other establishments) after the word "Act,", where it occurs for the second time insert "or under Part II of the Children (Scotland) Act 1995,".

(16) In section 68 (visiting of persons in establishments)—

(a) in subsection (2), for the words "in the care or under the supervision of the authority under Part II or Part III of this Act" substitute "being looked after by the authority"; and

(b) after subsection (3) add—

"(4) In subsection (2) of this section, the reference to children being looked after by a local authority shall be construed in accordance with section 17(6) of the Children (Scotland) Act 1995.".

(17) In section 78 (duty to make contributions in respect of children in care etc.)—

(a) in subsection (1)—

> (i) for the words "has been received into care under Part II of this Act" substitute "is being looked after by a local authority"; and
>
> (ii) in paragraph (a), for the words "his father and mother" substitute "any natural person who has parental responsibilities (within the meaning of section 1(3) of the Children (Scotland) Act 1995) in relation to him"; and

(b) for subsection (2) substitute—

"(2) This Part of this Act applies to any supervision requirement which, under paragraph (a) of section 70(3) of the Children (Scotland) Act 1995, requires the child concerned to reside in a place or places other than his own home.".

(18) In section 78A (recovery of contributions), in subsection (2)(a), for the words "in their care or under their supervision" substitute "looked after by them".

(19) In section 79 (recipients of contributions)—

(a) in subsection (1), for the words "in the care or under the supervision of" substitute "looked after by"; and

(b) in subsection (2), for the words "having the care or supervision of" substitute "looking after".

(20) In section 80 (enforcement of duty to make contributions)—

(a) in subsection (1), for the words from "received" to "requirement" substitute "looked after by a local authority";

(b) in subsection (4), for paragraphs (a) and (b) substitute "throughout the period during which he is looked after by a local authority";

(c) in subsection (5), for the words "is the maintainable child's father or mother" substitute ", being a natural person, has parental responsibilities (within the meaning of section 1(3) of the Children (Scotland) Act 1995) in relation to the maintainable child"; and

(d) in subsection (7), for the words "having the care or supervision of" substitute "looking after".

(21) In section 82(1) (recovery of arrears of contributions), for the words "having the care or supervision of" substitute "looking after".

(22) In section 83(2) (variation of trusts where person in whose care a child has been residing is for the time being residing in England, Wales or Northern Ireland), for the words "having the care or supervision of" substitute "looking after".

(23) After section 83 insert—

"References in this Part of this Act to child being looked after

83A. In this Part of this Act, references to a child being looked after by a local authority shall be construed in accordance with section 17(6) of the Children (Scotland) Act 1995".

(24) In section 86 (adjustments between local authorities as regards certain expenditure)—

(a) in subsection (1)—

(i) in paragraph (a), after the word "Act" insert ", or under section 25 of the Children (Scotland) Act 1995,"; and

(ii) in paragraph (b), for the words from "of services" to "Act" where it occurs for the second time, substitute ", or under or by virtue of Part II of the said Act of 1995, of services and facilities for a person ordinarily so resident (including, in the case of a child, any expenses incurred after he has ceased to be a child, and, in the event of another local authority taking over, under section 25(4) of that Act, the provision of accommodation for him,"; and

(b) in subsection (3), after the words "1989" insert "or provided with accommodation under paragraph (a) of, or by virtue of paragraph (c) of, section 26(1) of the Children (Scotland) Act 1995".

(25) In section 87 (charges which may be made for services and accommodation), in each of subsections (1) and (1A), after the words "1984" there shall be inserted "or under or by virtue of Part II of the Children (Scotland) Act 1995".

(26) Section 88 (duty of parents to notify change of address) shall cease to have effect.

(27) In section 90(1) (power to make regulations, orders or rules), the words "(other than orders under section 52 and 58 and Part V of this Act)" shall cease to have effect.

(28) In section 94(1) (interpretation)—

(a) the definition of "children's panel" and of "children's hearing" shall cease to have effect;

(b) the definition of "compulsory measures of care" shall cease to have effect;

(c) in the definition of "establishment", after the word "Act," insert "or of Part II of the Children (Scotland) Act 1995,";

(d) the definition of "guardian" shall cease to have effect;

(e) for the definition of "parent" substitute—

" "parent" means either parent or both parents, except that where the child was born out of wedlock and the parents have not subsequently married each other it means the natural mother but not the natural father;";

(f) the definition of "place of safety" shall cease to have effect;

(g) in the definition of "prescribed"—

(i) in paragraph (a), for the words "sections 3 and 36" substitute "section 3"; and

(ii) paragraph (b) shall cease to have effect;

(h) in the definition of "residential establishment", after the word "Act" insert "or of Part II of the Children (Scotland) Act 1995";

(i) the definition of "school age" shall cease to have effect;

(j) in the definition of "supervision requirement", for the words "section 44(1) of this Act" substitute "section 70(1) of the Children (Scotland) Act 1995"; and

(k) for the definition of "training school" substitute—

" "training school" has the meaning assigned to it by section 180(1) of the Children and Young Persons Act (Northern Ireland) 1968;".

(29) In section 97 (provisions of the Act which extend to England and Wales)—

(a) in subsection (1), the words "section 44(1) (except head (b)) and (1A)", "section 58" and "Part V" shall cease to have effect; and

(b) subsections (2) and (3) shall cease to have effect.

(30) In Schedule 2 (general adaptations of Part IV of Children and Young Persons (Scotland) Act 1937), for paragraph 1 substitute—

"1. Any reference to a child or to a young person shall be construed as a reference to a child as defined in section 93(2)(b) of the Children (Scotland) Act 1995.".

Children and Young Persons Act 1969 (c. 54)

16. In Schedule 5 to the Children and Young Persons Act 1969, paragraphs 57 and 65(1) (which relate to the provision of accommodation for children outside Scotland) shall cease to have effect.

Chronically Sick and Disabled Persons Act 1970 (c. 44)

17.—(1) The Chronically Sick and Disabled Persons Act 1970 shall be amended in accordance with this paragraph.

(2) In section 18(2) (information as to accommodation of younger with older persons), for the words "having functions under the Social Work (Scotland) Act 1968" substitute ", in respect of their functions both under the Social Work (Scotland) Act 1968 and under the Children (Scotland) Act 1995,".

(3) In section 29(2) (modifications of provisions of the Act in their application to Scotland)—

(a) in paragraph (a), at the end add "except that in the case of persons under eighteen years of age such references shall instead be construed as references to duties to disabled children (within the meaning of Chapter I of Part II of the Children (Scotland) Act 1995)"; and

(b) for paragraph (b) substitute—

"(b) any references to services provided under arrangements made by a local authority under the said section 29 shall be construed as references to services for—

(i) such chronically sick or disabled, or such mentally disordered, persons provided by virtue of the said section 12; or

(ii) such disabled children provided under section 23(1) of the said Act of 1995, by a local authority;".

Sheriff Courts (Scotland) Act 1971 (c. 58)

18.—(1) The Sheriff Courts (Scotland) Act 1971 shall be amended in accordance with this paragraph.

(2) In section 32(1) (power of Court of Session to regulate civil procedure in the sheriff court), after paragraph (i) insert—

"(j) permitting a person who is not an advocate or solicitor and is not represented by an advocate or solicitor to transmit, whether orally or in writing, the views of a child to the sheriff for the purposes of any enactment which makes provision (however expressed) for the sheriff to have regard to those views;".

(3) In section 37(2A) (remit to Court of Session), for the words "the custody" substitute "parental responsibilities or parental rights (within the meaning of sections 1(3) and 2(4) respectively of the Children (Scotland) Act 1995) in relation to a child or the".

Employment of Children Act 1973 (c. 24)

19. In section 2(2A) of the Employment of Children Act 1973 (supervision by education authorities), for paragraph (b) substitute—

"(b) in Scotland, if he has parental responsibilities (within the meaning of section 1(3) of the Children (Scotland) Act 1995) in relation to the child or care of him.".

Domicile and Matrimonial Proceedings Act 1973 (c. 45)

20.—(1) The Domicile and Matrimonial Proceedings Act 1973 shall be amended in accordance with this paragraph.

(2) In section 10 (ancillary and collateral orders)—

(a) in subsection (1)—

(i) for the words from the beginning to "in connection with" substitute "Where after the commencement of this Act an application is competently made to the Court of Session or to a sheriff court for the making, or the variation or recall, of an order which is ancillary or collateral to";

(ii) the words "as respects the person or property in question" shall cease to have effect; and

(b) after subsection (1) insert—

"(1A) For the purposes of subsection (1) above, references to an application for the making, or the variation or recall, of an order are references to the making, or the variation or recall, of an order relating to children, aliment, financial provision on divorce, judicial separation, nullity of marriage or expenses.".

(3) In paragraph 11 of Schedule 3 (sisting of consistorial action)—

(a) in sub-paragraph (1), in the definition of "the relevant order", for the words from "made" to the end substitute "relating to aliment or children"; and

(b) in sub-paragraph (3), for the words "custody of a child, and the education of a child" substitute "arrangements to be made as to with whom a child is to live, contact with a child, and any other matter relating to parental responsibilities within the meaning of section 1(3) of the Children (Scotland) Act 1995 or parental rights within the meaning of section 2(4) of that Act".

Land Compensation (Scotland) Act 1973 (c. 56)

21.—(1) The Land Compensation (Scotland) Act 1973 shall be amended in accordance with this paragraph.

(2) In section 35(3) (disturbance payments where modification of dwelling required for disabled person), in paragraph (a), after "1968" insert "or section 23 of the Children (Scotland) Act 1995".

(3) In section 80(1) (interpretation), in the definition of "disabled person"—

(a) after "means" insert "—

(a)"; and

(b) after "1972" insert "; and

(b) a child in need within the meaning of section 93(4)(a)(iii) of the Children (Scotland) Act 1995".

Local Government (Scotland) Act 1973 (c. 65)

22.—(1) The Local Government (Scotland) Act 1973 shall be amended in accordance with this paragraph.

(2) In section 56(9) (enactments exempted from repeal by virtue of that section), for paragraph (d) substitute—

"(d) paragraphs 3 and 8 of Schedule 1 to the Children (Scotland) Act 1995 (Children's Panel Advisory Committees and joint advisory committees);".

(3) In Schedule 25, paragraph 41 shall cease to have effect.

(4) In Schedule 27, paragraphs 185 and 187 shall cease to have effect.

Rehabilitation of Offenders Act 1974 (c. 53)

23.—(1) The Rehabilitation of Offenders Act 1974 shall be amended in accordance with this paragraph.

(2) In section 3 (special provision with respect to certain disposals by children's hearings)—

(a) for the words "Social Work (Scotland) Act 1968 is that mentioned in section 32(2)(g)" substitute "Children (Scotland) Act 1995 is that mentioned in section 52(2)(i)"; and

(b) for the words "to the satisfaction of the sheriff under section 42 of that Act, the acceptance or establishment" substitute "(or deemed established) to the satisfaction of the sheriff under section 68 or 85 of that Act, the acceptance, establishment (or deemed establishment)".

(3) In section 5 (rehabilitation periods for particular sentences)—

(a) in subsection (3)(b), for the words "43(2) of the Social Work (Scotland) Act 1968" substitute "69(1)(b) and (12) of the Children (Scotland) Act 1995";

(b) in subsection (5)(f), for the words "Social Work (Scotland) Act 1968" substitute "Children (Scotland) Act 1995";

(c) in subsection (10), for the words "Social Work (Scotland) Act 1968" substitute "Children (Scotland) Act 1995"; and

(d) subsection (10A) shall cease to have effect.

(4) In section 7(2) (limitations on rehabilitation)—
(a) for paragraph (c) substitute—
   "(c) in any proceedings relating to parental responsibilities or parental rights (within the meaning of section 1(3) and section 2(4) respectively of the Children (Scotland) Act 1995), guardianship, adoption or the provision by any person of accommodation, care or schooling for children under the age of 18 years;
   (cc) in any proceedings under Part II of the Children (Scotland) Act 1995;";
(b) paragraph (e) shall cease to have effect; and
(c) the words from "In the application" to the end shall cease to have effect.

Criminal Procedure (Scotland) Act 1975 (c. 21)

24.—(1) The Criminal Procedure (Scotland) Act 1975 shall be amended in accordance with this paragraph.
(2) Section 14 shall cease to have effect.
(3) In section 23 (which, as amended by the Criminal Justice (Scotland) Act 1995, provides for remand of persons under twenty-one in secure accommodation)—
(a) in sub-paragraph (i) of paragraph (a) of subsection (1), for the words "the Social Work (Scotland) Act 1968" substitute "Part II of the Children (Scotland) Act 1995"; and
(b) in paragraph (a) of subsection (4), for the words "the Social Work (Scotland) Act 1968" substitute "Part II of the Children (Scotland) Act 1995".
(4) In section 37 (power to order parent to give security for child's good behaviour) after subsection (3) add—
   "(4) In this section "parent" means either of the child's parents, if that parent has parental responsibilities or parental rights (within the meaning of sections 1(3) and 2(4) respectively of the Children (Scotland) Act 1995) in relation to him.".
(5) In section 39 (attendance at court of parent of child charged with an offence: solemn procedure)—
(a) for subsection (4) substitute—
   "(4) The parent or guardian whose attendance shall be required under this section shall be—
      (a) any parent who has parental responsibilities or parental rights (within the meaning of sections 1(3) and 2(4) respectively of the Children (Scotland) Act 1995) in relation to the child; or
      (b) the guardian having actual possession and control of him."; and
(b) in subsection (5), for the word "custody" substitute "care".
(6) In section 168 (power of court to refer child to reporter where accused convicted of certain offences: solemn proceedings)—
(a) in paragraph (c), the word "female" shall cease to have effect;
(b) in paragraph (ii), after the word "above" insert "or the person in respect of whom the offence so mentioned was committed"; and
(c) for the words "Part III of the Social Work (Scotland) Act 1968" substitute "Chapter 3 of Part II of the Children (Scotland) Act 1995".
(7) In section 171(2) (regard to be had to certain provisions in presumption of age of child: solemn proceedings)—
(a) for the words "application of the provisions of section 30(1) of the Social Work (Scotland) Act 1968" substitute "definition of a child for the purposes of Chapters 2 and 3 of Part II of the Children (Scotland) Act 1995"; and
(b) for the words "under Part V of that Act" substitute "by virtue of regulations made under that Act for the purpose of giving effect to orders made in different parts of the United Kingdom".
(8) In section 177 (directions by court in solemn proceedings as to conveyance of person to residential establishment), the words "provided by a local authority under Part IV of the Social Work (Scotland) Act 1968" shall cease to have effect.
(9) In section 296 (powers of police in relation to children apprehended)—
(a) in subsection (3), the words from "and the child" to the end shall cease to have effect; and
(b) subsection (4) shall cease to have effect.
(10) In section 304 (power to require parent to give security for child's good behaviour), after subsection (3) add—
   "(4) In this section "parent" means either of the child's parents, if that parent has parental responsibilities or parental rights (within the meaning of sections 1(3) and 2(4) respectively of the Children (Scotland) Act 1995) in relation to him.".
(11) In section 307 (attendance at court of parent of child charged with an offence: summary procedure)—
(a) for subsection (4) substitute—

"(4) The parent or guardian whose attendance shall be required under this section shall be—

    (a) any parent who has parental responsibilities or parental rights (within the meaning of sections 1(3) and 2(4) respectively of the Children (Scotland) Act 1995) in relation to the child; or

    (b) the guardian having actual possession and control of him."; and

(b) in subsection (5), for the word "custody" substitute "care".

(12) Section 323 shall cease to have effect.

(13) In section 329 (which, as amended by the Criminal Justice (Scotland) Act 1995, provides for remand of persons under twenty-one in secure accommodation)—

    (a) in sub-paragraph (i) of paragraph (a) of subsection (1), for the words "the Social Work (Scotland) Act 1968" substitute "Part II of the Children (Scotland) Act 1995"; and

    (b) in paragraph (a) of subsection (4), for the words "the Social Work (Scotland) Act 1968" substitute "Part II of the Children (Scotland) Act 1995".

(14) In section 364 (power of court to refer child to reporter where accused convicted of certain offences: summary proceedings)—

    (a) in paragraph (c), the word "female" shall cease to have effect;

    (b) in paragraph (ii), after the word "above" insert "or the person in respect of whom the offence so mentioned was committed"; and

    (c) for the words "Part III of the Social Work (Scotland) Act 1968" substitute "Chapter 3 of Part II of the Children (Scotland) Act 1995".

(15) In section 368(2) (regard to be had to certain provisions in presumption of age of child: summary proceedings)—

    (a) for the words "application of the provisions of section 30(1) of the Social Work (Scotland) Act 1968" substitute "definition of a child for the purposes of Chapters 2 and 3 of Part II of the Children (Scotland) Act 1995"; and

    (b) for the words "under Part V of that Act" substitute "by virtue of regulations made under that Act for the purpose of giving effect to orders made in different parts of the United Kingdom".

(16) In section 378 (directions by court in summary proceedings as to conveyance of person to residential establishment), the words "provided by a local authority under Part IV of the Social Work (Scotland) Act 1968" shall cease to have effect.

(17) In section 413 (detention of children found guilty in summary proceedings)—

    (a) in subsection (1), for the words "residential care" substitute "residential accommodation provided under Part II of the Children (Scotland) Act 1995";

    (b) in subsection (3)—

        (i) the definitions of "care" and of "the 1968 Act" shall cease to have effect; and

        (ii) after the definition of "the appropriate local authority" insert—

            "secure accommodation" has the meaning assigned to it in Part II of the Children (Scotland) Act 1995";

    (c) after subsection (3) insert the following subsection—

        "(3A) Where a child in respect of whom an order is made under this section is detained by the appropriate local authority, that authority shall have the same powers and duties in respect of the child as they would have if he were subject to a supervision requirement.";

    (d) in subsection (4), the words "within the meaning of the 1968 Act" shall cease to have effect;

    (e) in subsection (5), the words "(within the meaning of the 1968 Act)" shall cease to have effect;

    (f) in subsection (6), for the word "care" substitute "accommodation";

    (g) in subsection (6A), the words "within the meaning of the 1968 Act" shall cease to have effect;

    (h) in subsection (6B)—

        (i) for the words "care of" substitute "accommodation provided by"; and

        (ii) for the words "their care" substitute "that accommodation or any other such accommodation provided by that authority"; and

    (i) in subsection (6C)—

        (i) for the word "care", 'where it first occurs', substitute "accommodation provided by the appropriate local authority";

        (ii) in paragraph (a), for the word "care" substitute "accommodation"; and

        (iii) in paragraph (b), for the words "residential care" where they first occur substitute "detention in residential accommodation" and for those words where they secondly occur substitute "such detention".

(18) In section 462 (interpretation) in the definition of—

(a) "child", for the words "by section 30 of the Social Work (Scotland) Act 1968" substitute "for the purposes of Chapters 2 and 3 of Part II of the Children (Scotland) Act 1995";

(b) "children's hearing", for the words "by section 34(1) of the Social Work (Scotland) Act 1968" substitute "in Part II of the Children (Scotland) Act 1995";

(c) "place of safety", for the words "section 94(1) of the Social Work (Scotland) Act 1968" substitute "Part II of the Children (Scotland) Act 1995";

(d) "residential establishment", for the words from "has" to the end substitute "means an establishment within the meaning of that expression for the purposes of the Social Work (Scotland) Act 1968 or, as the case may be, of Part II of the Children (Scotland) Act 1995"; and

(e) "supervision requirement", for the words "by section 44(1) of the Social Work (Scotland) Act 1968" substitute "in Part II of the Children (Scotland) Act 1995".

Local Government (Scotland) Act 1975 (c. 30)

25. In section 23(2) of the Local Government (Scotland) Act 1975 (bodies subject to investigation by Commissioner for Local Administration in Scotland), for paragraph (d) substitute—

"(d) any Children's Panel Advisory Committee formed under paragraph 3, or joint advisory committee formed under paragraph 8, of Schedule 1 to the Children (Scotland) Act 1995;".

Children Act 1975 (c. 72)

26.—(1) The Children Act 1975 shall be amended in accordance with this paragraph.

(2) Sections 47 to 49 shall cease to have effect.

(3) In section 50 (payments towards maintenance for children), for the words from "custody" to "authority" substitute "a child under the age of sixteen is residing with and being cared for (other than as a foster child) by a person other than a parent of the child, a council constituted under section 2 of the Local Government (Scotland) Act 1994".

(4) In section 51 (restriction on removal of child where applicant has provided home for three years)—

(a) in subsection (1), for the words "custody of" substitute "a residence order in relation to";

(b) for subsection (2) substitute—

"(2) In any case where subsection (1) applies, and the child—

(a) was being looked after by a council constituted under section 2 of the Local Government etc. (Scotland) Act 1994 before he began to have his home with the applicant, and

(b) continues to be looked after by such a council,

the council by whom the child is being looked after shall not remove him from the applicant's care and possession except—

(i) with the applicant's consent;

(ii) with the leave of the court; or

(iii) in accordance with an order made, or authority or warrant granted, under Chapter 2 or 3 of Part II of the Children (Scotland) Act 1995."; and

(c) at the end add—

"(5) In this section "looked after" and "residence order" have the meanings given respectively by section 17(6) and section 11(2)(c) of the Children (Scotland) Act 1995; and "residence order" shall have the same meaning in sections 52 and 53 of this Act.".

(5) In section 52 (return of child taken away in breach of section 51), for the words "custody of" substitute "a residence order in relation to".

(6) Section 53 (custody order on application for adoption in Scotland) shall cease to have effect.

(7) In section 55 (interpretation and extent), for the words "sections 47 to 54", in both places where they occur, substitute "sections 50 to 53".

(8) Sections 73 to 84, 89, 99, 100, 102 and 103 shall cease to have effect.

(9) Section 107 (interpretation), except in so far as subsection (1) defines "adoption society", "child" and "voluntary organisation", shall cease to have effect.

(10) In Schedule 3 (minor and consequential amendments), paragraphs 52 to 57 shall cease to have effect.

Sexual Offences (Scotland) Act 1976 (c. 67)

27.—(1) The Sexual Offences (Scotland) Act 1976 shall be amended in accordance with this paragraph.

(2) In section 11(1) (causing or encouraging seduction, prostitution etc. of girls under sixteen), for the words "the custody" substitute "parental responsibilities (within the meaning of section 1(3) of the Children (Scotland) Act 1995), in relation to, or having".

(3) In section 14(1) (allowing child to be in brothel), for the words "the custody" substitute "parental responsibilities (within the meaning of section 1(3) of the Children (Scotland) Act 1995), in relation to, or having".

Education (Scotland) Act 1980 (c. 44)

28.—(1) The Education (Scotland) Act 1980 shall be amended in accordance with this paragraph.

(2) In section 36(3) (referral to reporter of case of irregular school attendance), for the words from "may" to the end substitute ", where no requirement arises under section 53(1) of the Children (Scotland) Act 1995 to give information about the child to the Principal Reporter, may under this subsection provide the Principal Reporter with such information.".

(3) In section 44—
(a) subsection (1) (referral by court to Principal Reporter of case involving offence against section 35) shall cease to have effect; and
(b) in subsection (2) (powers of court where no referral to Principal Reporter), for the words "subsection (1) above, make a direction" substitute "section 54(1) of the Children (Scotland) Act 1995, refer the matter to the Principal Reporter".

(4) In section 65B(6) (sending of report in relation to recorded child)—
(a) paragraph (a) shall cease to have effect; and
(b) at the end add—
"and the local authority as education authority shall also ensure that the local authority for the purposes of Part II of the Children (Scotland) Act 1995 receive such a copy.".

(5) In section 135(1) (interpretation)—
(a) in the definition of "parent", for the words "the actual custody of" substitute "parental responsibilities (within the meaning of section 1(3) of the Children (Scotland) Act 1995) in relation to, or has care of";
(b) the definition of "reporter of the appropriate local authority" shall cease to have effect;
(c) for the definition of "residential establishment" substitute—
" "residential establishment" has the meaning given by paragraph (a) of the definition of that expression in section 93(1) of the Children (Scotland) Act 1995;"; and
(d) for the definition of "supervision requirement" substitute—
" "supervision requirement" has the meaning given by section 70(1) of the said Act of 1995;".

Criminal Justice (Scotland) Act 1980 (c. 62)

29.—(1) The Criminal Justice (Scotland) Act 1980 shall be amended in accordance with this paragraph.

(2) In section 3 (right to have someone informed when arrested or detained), in subsection (5)(b), for the words "actual custody" substitute "care".

(3) In Schedule 7, paragraph 21 (which confers jurisdiction on a sheriff for the purposes of certain applications under section 42 of the Social Work (Scotland) Act 1968) shall cease to have effect.

Matrimonial Homes (Family Protection) (Scotland) Act 1981 (c. 59)

30. In section 22 of the Matrimonial Homes (Family Protection) (Scotland) Act 1981 (interpretation), in the definition of "child", for the word "accepted" substitute "treated".

Civil Jurisdiction and Judgments Act 1982 (c. 27)

31. In Schedule 9 to the Civil Jurisdiction and Judgments Act 1982 (excluded proceedings), after paragraph 2 insert—
"2A. Proceedings relating to parental responsibilities within the meaning of section 1(3) of the Children (Scotland) Act 1995 or parental rights within the meaning of section 2(4) of that Act.".

Health and Social Services and Social Security Adjudications Act 1983 (c. 41)

32. In Schedule 2 to the Health and Social Services and Social Security Adjudications Act 1983, paragraphs 4 to 6 and 8 (which amend provisions of the Social Work (Scotland) Act 1968 repealed by this Act) shall cease to have effect.

Mental Health (Scotland) Act 1984 (c. 36)

33.—(1) The Mental Health (Scotland) Act 1984 shall be amended in accordance with this paragraph.

(2) In section 10(1) (application of provisions relating to certain patients suffering from mental disorder)—

(a) in paragraph (a), sub-paragraph (i), and the word "or" immediately following that sub-paragraph, shall cease to have effect; and

(b) after paragraph (a) insert—

"(aa) a child or young person in relation to whom parental rights and responsibilities have been transferred to a local authority by virtue of section 86(1) of the Children (Scotland) Act 1995;".

(3) In section 54 (local authority to be deemed nearest relative of certain children and young persons), for paragraph (a) substitute—

"(a) the parental rights and responsibilities in relation to a patient who is a child or young person have been transferred to a local authority by virtue of section 86(1) of the Children (Scotland) Act 1995;".

(4) In section 55 (nearest relative of child under guardianship etc.)—

(a) for subsection (1) substitute—

"(1) Where—

(a) a guardian has been appointed for a child who has not attained the age of eighteen years; or

(b) there is in force a residence order, or a custody order, granted by a court in the United Kingdom, or an analogous order granted by a court outwith the United Kingdom (being an order which is entitled to recognition in Scotland), identifying a person as the person with whom a child under the age of sixteen years is to live,

that guardian or person shall, to the exclusion of any other person, be deemed to be the child's nearest relative.";

(b) for subsection (3) substitute—

"(3) In this section "guardian" does not include a guardian under this Part of this Act or, in relation to a child, a guardian whose appointment takes effect under section 7, or on an order under section 11(1), of the Children (Scotland) Act 1995 where there is a parent who has parental responsibilities and parental rights in relation to the child."; and

(c) subsection (4) shall cease to have effect.

Child Abduction Act 1984 (c. 37)

34. In section 6 of the Child Abduction Act 1984 (offence in Scotland of person connected with a child taking or sending that child out of United Kingdom)—

(a) in subsection (1)(a)(i), after the word "person" insert "or naming any person as the person with whom the child is to live";

(b) in subsection (2)(b), after the words "to him" insert "or naming him as the person with whom the child is to live"; and

(c) in subsection (3)(a)(i)(b), for the word "(whether" substitute "or who is named as the person with whom the child is to live (whether the award is made, or the person so named is named".

Foster Children (Scotland) Act 1984 (c. 56)

35.—(1) The Foster Children (Scotland) Act 1984 shall be amended in accordance with this paragraph.

(2) In section 2 (exceptions to definition of "foster child')—

(a) in subsection (1), for the words "in the care of a local authority or a voluntary organisation" substitute "being looked after by a local authority";

(b) in subsection (3), the words "within the meaning of the Social Work (Scotland) Act 1968" shall cease to have effect;

(c) in subsection (5), the words "; or (b) while he is a protected child within the meaning of section 32 of the said Act of 1978" shall cease to have effect; and

(d) after subsection (5) add—

"(6) The reference in subsection (1) above to a child being looked after by a local authority shall be construed as if it were a reference to which section 17(6) of the Children (Scotland) Act 1995 applies.".

(3) In section 3(4) (saving for Social Work (Scotland) Act 1968), for the words "the Social Work (Scotland) Act 1968" substitute "Part II of the Children (Scotland) Act 1995".

(4) In section 7(1) (persons disqualified from keeping foster children)—

(a) in paragraph (b), after the word "1968" insert "or under section 70 of the Children (Scotland) Act 1995"; and

(b) after paragraph (d) insert—

"(dd) his parental rights and parental responsibilities (within the meaning of the Children (Scotland) Act 1995) have been transferred, by an order under section 86(1) of that Act, to a local authority;".

(5) In section 12 (removal of foster children on complaint of local authority), for subsection (5) substitute—

"(5) For the purposes of section 25 of the Children (Scotland) Act 1995 (and for the reason mentioned in subsection (1)(c) of that section) a child removed under this section shall be regarded as requiring accommodation.".

(6) In section 13 (which makes provision as to the effect of a refusal to allow a visit to a foster child or to allow premises to be inspected), for the words from "sections" to the end substitute "section 55 of the Children (Scotland) Act 1995 (child assessment orders) as giving the local authority reasonable cause for the suspicion mentioned in subsection (1)(a) of that section).

(7) In section 21(1) (interpretation)—

(a) in the definition of "residential establishment', after the word "1968" insert "or of Part II of the Children (Scotland) Act 1995"; and

(b) for the definition of "supervision requirement', substitute—

" "supervision requirement" has the meaning given by section 70(1) of the Children (Scotland) Act 1995;".

Family Law (Scotland) Act 1985 (c. 37)

36. In section 2 of the Family Law (Scotland) Act 1985 (actions for aliment)—

(a) in subsection (2), for paragraph (c) substitute—

"(c) concerning parental responsibilities or parental rights (within the meaning of sections 1(3) and 2(4) respectively of the Children (Scotland) Act 1995) or guardianship in relation to children;"; and

(b) in subsection (4)(c), for sub–paragraph (iii) substitute—

"(iii) a person with whom the child lives or who is seeking a residence order (within the meaning of section 11(2)(c) of the Children (Scotland) Act 1995) in respect of the child.".

Child Abduction and Custody Act 1985 (c. 60)

37.—(1) The Child Abduction and Custody Act 1985 shall be amended in accordance with this paragraph.

(2) In section 9 (suspension of court's powers in cases of wrongful removal), for paragraph (d) substitute—

"(d) making, varying or discharging an order under section 86 of the Children (Scotland) Act 1995;".

(3) In section 20 (further provision as regards suspension of court's powers)—

(a) for paragraph (d) substitute—

"(d) in the case of proceedings for, or for the variation or discharge of, a parental responsibilities order under section 86 of the Children (Scotland) Act 1995, make, vary or discharge any such order;"; and

(b) in subsection (5), for the words "within the meaning of Part III of the Social Work (Scotland) Act 1968" substitute "(as defined in section 93(1) of the Children (Scotland) Act 1995)".

(4) In section 25 (termination of existing custody orders etc.), subsection (6) shall cease to have effect.

(5) In section 27(4) (interpretation), after the word "Wales" insert "or Scotland".

(6) In Schedule 3 (custody orders)—

(a) in paragraph 5—

(i) for the words "custody, care or control of a child or" substitute "residence, custody, care or control of a child or contact with, or";

(ii) in sub-paragraph (iii), for the words "tutory or curatory" substitute "guardianship";

(iii) in sub-paragraph (iv), for the words "16(8), 16A(3) or 18(3) of the Social Work (Scotland) Act 1968" substitute "86 of the Children (Scotland) Act 1995"; and

(iv) for sub-paragraph (v), substitute—

"(v) an order made, or warrant or authorisation granted, under or by virtue of Chapter 2 or 3 of Part II of the Children (Scotland) Act 1995 to remove the child to a place of safety or to secure accommodation, to keep him at such a place or in such accommodation, or to prevent his removal from a place where he is being accommodated (or an order varying or discharging any order, warrant or authorisation so made or granted);";

(b) for paragraph 6 substitute—

"6. A supervision requirement made by a children's hearing under section 70 of the Children (Scotland) Act 1995 (whether or not continued under section 73 of that Act) or made by the sheriff under section 51(5)(c)(iii) of that Act and any order made by a court in England and Wales or in Northern Ireland if it is an order which, by virtue of section 33(1) of that Act, has effect as if it were such a supervision requirement."; and

(c) paragraph 7 shall cease to have effect.

Law Reform (Parent and Child) (Scotland) Act 1986 (c. 9)

38.—(1) The Law Reform (Parent and Child) (Scotland) Act 1986 shall be amend in accordance with this paragraph.

(2) In section 1 (legal equality of children), for subsection (3) substitute—

"(3) Subsection (1) above is subject to subsection (4) below, to section 9(1) of this Act and to section 3(1)(b) of the Children (Scotland) Act 1995 (parental responsibilities and parental rights of natural father).".

(3) In section 6(2) (consent to taking of sample of blood), for the words from "guardian" to "custody or" substitute "any person having parental responsibilities (within the meaning of section 1(3) of the Children (Scotland) Act 1995) in relation to him or having".

Disabled Persons (Services, Consultation and Representation) Act 1986 (c. 33)

39.—(1) The Disabled Persons (Services, Consultation and Representation) Act 1986 shall be amended in accordance with this paragraph.

(2) In section 1(3) (regulations with respect to appointment of authorised representatives of disabled persons)—

(a) in paragraph (a), for the words from the beginning to "appoint" substitute—

"may provide for—

(i) any person who has parental responsibilities in relation to a disabled person under the age of sixteen ("parental responsibilities" having the meaning given by section 1(3) of the Children (Scotland) Act 1995); or

(ii) any other person who is entitled to act as the disabled person's legal representative (as defined in section 15(5) of the Children (Scotland) Act 1995), to appoint"; and

(b) in paragraph (b), for the words "in the care of" substitute "looked after by".

(3) In section 2 (rights of certain authorised representatives of disabled persons)—

(a) in subsection (3)(a), for the words "the words "the parent or guardian of" shall be inserted after the words "if so requested by";" substitute "for the words "by the disabled person" there shall be substituted the words "by any person appointed by virtue of regulations made under section 1(3)(a)(i) or (ii) of this Act";"; and

(b) in subsection (5), after paragraph (bb) insert—

"(bc) in Scotland, in accommodation provided by or on behalf of a local authority under Chapter 1 of Part II of the Children (Scotland) Act 1995, or".

(4) In section 13(8)(b) (limitation on requirement for assessment of needs)—

(a) for the words "his parent" substitute "any person having parental responsibilities in relation to him"; and

(b) after the word "request" insert "("parental responsibilities" having the meaning given in section 1(3) of the Children (Scotland) Act 1995)".

(5) In section 16 (interpretation)—
(a) in the definition of "disabled person", for paragraph (b) substitute—
  "(b) in relation to Scotland, means—
    (i) in the case of a person aged eighteen or over, one chronically sick or disabled or one suffering from mental disorder (being, in either case, a relevant person for the purposes of section 12 of the Social Work (Scotland) Act 1968); and
    (ii) in any other case, a disabled child ("disabled child" being construed in accordance with Chapter 1 of Part II of the Children (Scotland) Act 1995);";
(b) in the definition of "guardian", paragraph (b) shall cease to have effect;
(c) in the definition of "the welfare enactments", in paragraph (b), for the words "and sections 7 and 8 of the 1984 Act", substitute ", sections 7 and 8 of the 1984 Act and Chapter 1 of Part II of the Children (Scotland) Act 1995"; and
(d) the existing provisions as so amended shall be subsection (1) of the section and at the end of the section there shall be added—
  "(2A) In this Act as it applies in relation to Scotland, any reference to a child who is looked after by a local authority shall be construed in accordance with section 17(6) of the Children (Scotland) Act 1995.".

Legal Aid (Scotland) Act 1986 (c. 47)

40. In section 41 of the Legal Aid (Scotland) Act 1986 (interpretation)—
(a) in the definition of "legal aid", for the words "Part III of the Social Work (Scotland Act 1968" substitute "Chapter 2 or Chapter 3 of Part II of the Children (Scotland) Act 1995; and
(b) in the definition of "person", the existing words from "does" to the end shall be paragraph (a) and after that paragraph there shall be added—
  "; and
  (b) includes a person under the age of sixteen years.".

Family Law Act 1986 (c. 55)

41.—(1) The Family Law Act 1986 shall be amended in accordance with this paragraph.
(2) In section 1(1)(b) (meaning of "custody order")—
(a) for the words "custody, care or control of a child" substitute "residence, custody, care or control of a child, contact with or"; and
(b) in sub-paragraph (iv), for the words "for the custody of" substitute "giving parental responsibilities and parental rights in relation to".
(3) In section 13 (jurisdiction ancillary to matrimonial proceedings)—
(a) in subsection (2), for the words "under section 9(1) of the Matrimonial Proceedings (Children) Act 1958" substitute "in those proceedings"; and
(b) in subsection (4), for the words "under section 9(1) of the Matrimonial Proceedings (Children) Act 1958" substitute "in matrimonial proceedings where the court has refused to grant the principal remedy sought in the proceedings".
(4) In section 15 (duration, variation and recall of orders)—
(a) in subsection (1)(b), for the words "for the custody of" substitute "relating to the parental responsibilities or parental rights in relation to"; and
(b) in subsection (4), for the words from the beginning to "above" substitute "Where, by virtue of subsection (1) above, a child is to live with a different person".
(5) In section 17 (orders for delivery of child)—
(a) in subsection (3), for the words from "is the child" to "other party" substitute ", although not a child of both parties to the marriage, is a child of the family of those parties"; and
(b) at the end of the section add—
  "(4) In subsection (3) above, "child of the family" means any child who has been treated by both parties as a child of their family, except a child who has been placed with those parties as foster parents by a local authority or a voluntary organisation.".
(6) For section 26 (recognition: special Scottish rule), substitute—

"Recognition: special Scottish rule
  26. An order relating to parental responsibilities or parental rights in relation to a child which is made outside the United Kingdom shall be recognised in Scotland if the order was made in the country where the child was habitually resident.".
(7) In section 33(3) (power to order disclosure of child's whereabouts), for the words "for the custody of" substitute "relating to parental responsibilities or parental rights in relation to".
(8) In section 35(3) (power to restrict removal of child from jurisdiction), for the words "whose custody" substitute "whose care".

(9) In section 42 (interpretation)—

(a) in subsection (1), before the definition of "part of the United Kingdom" insert—

" "parental responsibilities" and "parental rights" have the meanings respectively given by sections 1(3) and 2(4) of the Children (Scotland) Act 1995;"; and

(b) in subsection (4)(b), for the words from "of one of the parties" to the end substitute "who has been treated by both parties as a child of their family, except a child who has been with those parties as foster parents by a local authority or a voluntary organisation;".

Housing (Scotland) Act 1987 (c. 26)

42. In section 61 of the Housing (Scotland) Act 1987 (exemption from secure tenant's right to purchase)—

(a) in subsection (4)(f)(iii) for the words "have left the care of" substitute "as children have been looked after by"; and

(b) after subsection (4) add—

"(4A) The reference in subsection (4)(f)(iii) above to children looked after by a local authority shall be construed in accordance with section 17(6) of the Children (Scotland) Act 1995.".

Criminal Justice (Scotland) Act 1987 (c. 41)

43. In section 49(4)(b) of the Criminal Justice (Scotland) Act 1987 (right to have someone informed when detained), for the words "actual custody" substitute "care".

Civil Evidence (Scotland) Act 1988 (c. 32)

44. In paragraph (a) of the definition of "civil proceedings" in section 9 of the Civil Evidence (Scotland) Act 1998 (interpretation)—

(a) the words "under section 42 of the Social Work (Scotland) Act 1968" shall cease to have effect;

(b) after the word "application" where it first occurs insert "under section 65(7) or (9) of the Children (Scotland) Act 1995";

(c) after the word "established," insert "or of an application for a review of such a finding under section 85 of that Act";

(d) after the word "application" where it occurs for the second time insert "or, as the case may be, the review"; and

(e) for the words "32(2)(g)" substitute "52(2)(i)".

Court of Session Act 1988 (c. 36)

45. In section 5 of the Court of Session Act 1988 (power to regulate procedure etc. by act of sederunt), after paragraph (e) insert—

"(ee) to permit a person who is not an advocate or solicitor and is not represented by an advocate or solicitor to transmit, whether orally or in writing, the views of a child to the Court for the purposes of any enactment which makes provision (however expressed) for the Court to have regard to those views;".

School Boards (Scotland) Act 1988 (c. 47)

46. In section 22(2) of the School Boards (Scotland) Act 1988 (interpretation), in the definition of "parent", for the word "custody" substitute "parental responsibilities (within the meaning of section 1(3) of the Children (Scotland) Act 1995) in relation to him or who has care".

Self-Governing Schools etc. (Scotland) Act 1989 (c. 39)

47. In section 80(1) of the Self-Governing Schools etc. (Scotland) Act 1989 (interpretation), in the definition of "parent", for the words "the actual custody" substitute "parental responsibilities (within the meaning of section 1(3) of the Children (Scotland) Act 1995) in relation to him or has care".

Children Act 1989 (c. 41)

48.—(1) The Children Act 1989 shall be amended in accordance with this paragraph.

(2) In section 31(7)(b)(iii) (restriction on applications for care and supervision orders), for the words "the Social Work (Scotland) Act 1968" substitute "Part II of the Children (Scotland) Act 1995".

(3) In section 51(7) (enactments which do not apply where a child is granted refuge), for paragraph (b) substitute—

"(b) sections 82 (recovery of certain fugitive children) and 83 (harbouring) of the Children (Scotland) Act 1995, so far as they apply in relation to anything done in England and Wales;".

(4) In section 79(e) (application of Part X to Scotland), for the words from "in whom" to "vested" substitute "having parental responsibilities (within the meaning of section 1(3) of the Children (Scotland) Act 1995) relating to the child".

(5) In Schedule 8 (privately fostered children), in paragraph 3(b), for the words "the Social Work (Scotland) Act 1968" substitute "Part II of the Children (Scotland) Act 1995".

Local Government and Housing Act 1989 (c. 42)

49.—(1) The Local Government and Housing Act 1989 shall be amended in accordance with this paragraph.

(2) In section 14(5) (restriction of effect of provisions of that section in relation to certain committees), for paragraph (d) substitute—

"(d) a Children's Panel Advisory Committee formed under paragraph 3, or a joint advisory committee formed under paragraph 8, of Schedule 1 to the Children (Scotland) Act 1995;".

Access to Health Records Act 1990 (c. 23)

50.—(1) The Access to Health Records Act 1990 shall be amended in accordance with this paragraph.

(2) In section 3(1) (right of access to health records), for paragraphs (c) and (d) substitute—

"(cc) where the patient is a child, a person having parental responsibility for him;".

(3) In section 4 (cases where right of access may be wholly excluded)—

(a) in subsection (1), for paragraphs (a) and (b) substitute "the patient is a child"; and

(b) in subsection (2), for the words "(1)(c) or (d)" substitute "(1)(cc)".

(4) In section 5(3) (access to records not to be given where record compiled on basis that access would not be available to particular applicant), for the words "(1)(c), (d), (e) or (f)" substitute "(1)(cc), (e) or (f)".

(5) In section 11 (interpretation), for the definition of "parental responsibility" substitute—

" "parental responsibility", in the application of this Act—

(a) to England and Wales, has the same meaning as in the Children Act 1989; and

(b) to Scotland, shall be construed as a reference to "parental responsibilities" within the meaning given by section 1(3) of the Children (Scotland) Act 1995.".

Horses (Protective Headgear for Young Riders) Act 1990 (c. 25)

51. In section 1(2)(a)(ii) (application), of the Horses (Protective Headgear for Young Riders) Act 1990, for the word "custody" substitute "parental responsibilities (within the meaning given by section 1(3) of the Children (Scotland) Act 1995) in relation to, or has".

Child Support Act 1991 (c. 48)

52.—(1) The Child Support Act 1991 shall be amended in accordance with this paragraph.

(2) In section 3(4)(d) (interpretation), for the words from "having" to the end substitute "with whom a child is to live by virtue of a residence order under section 11 of the Children (Scotland) Act 1995.".

(3) In section 5(1) (supplemental provisions as respects child support maintenance), the words "(or, in Scotland, parental rights over)", in both places where they occur, shall cease to have effect.

(4) In section 54 (interpretation)—

(a) for the definition of "parental responsibility" substitute—

" "parental responsibility", in the application of this Act—

(a) to England and Wales, has the same meaning as in the Children Act 1989; and

(b) to Scotland, shall be construed as a reference to "parental responsibilities" within the meaning given by section 1(3) of the Children (Scotland) Act 1995;"; and

(b) the definition of "parental rights" shall cease to have effect.

Age of Legal Capacity (Scotland) Act 1991 (c. 50)

53.—(1) The Age of Legal Capacity (Scotland) Act 1991 shall be amended in accordance with this paragraph.

(2) In section 1(3) (age of legal capacity)—

(a) in sub-paragraph (i) of paragraph (f), for the words "who has no guardian or whose guardian" substitute "in relation to whom there is no person entitled to act as his legal representative (within the meaning of Part I of the Children (Scotland) Act 1995), or where there is such a person"; and

(b) in paragraph (g), for sub-paragraphs (i) and (ii) substitute "exercising parental responsibilities and parental rights (within the meaning of sections 1(3) and 2(4) respectively of the Children (Scotland) Act 1995) in relation to any child of his.".

(3) In section 2 (exceptions to the general rule), after subsection (4) insert—

"(4A) A person under the age of sixteen years shall have legal capacity to instruct a solicitor, in connection with any civil matter, where that person has a general understanding of what it means to do so; and without prejudice to the generality of this subsection a person twelve years of age or more shall be presumed to be of sufficient age and maturity to have such understanding.

(4B) A person who by virtue of subsection (4A) above has legal capacity to instruct a solicitor shall also have legal capacity to sue, or to defend, in any civil proceedings.

(4C) Subsections (4A) and (4B) above are without prejudice to any question of legal capacity arising in connection with any criminal matter.".

(4) In section 5(1) (construction of references to "tutor")—

(a) the words "or tutory" shall cease to have effect; and

(b) for the words from "the guardian", where they first appear, to the end substitute "a person entitled to act as a child's legal representative (within the meaning of Part I of the Children (Scotland) Act 1995), and any reference to the tutory of such a child shall be construed as a reference to the entitlement to act as a child's legal representative enjoyed by a person by, under or by virtue of the said Part I.".

(5) In section 5(2) (restriction on appointment of guardian to person under sixteen), for the words from "section 3" to the end substitute "section 7 of the Children (Scotland) Act 1995.".

Armed Forces Act 1991 (c. 62)

54.—(1) The Armed Forces Act 1991 shall be amended in accordance with this paragraph.

(2) In paragraph (f) of section 17(4) (persons to whom notice of an application for an assessment order must be given)—

(a) after the word "order" insert "—
(i)"; and

(b) at the end insert "; or
(ii) under section 88 of the Children (Scotland) Act 1995".

(3) In paragraph (f) of section 18(7) (persons who may apply for variation etc. of assessment order)—

(a) after the word "order" insert "—
(i) "; and

(b) at the end insert "; or
(ii) under section 88 of the Children (Scotland) Act 1995".

(4) In section 21(4) (which makes provision in relation to a child returned to the United Kingdom under a protection order under that Act) for the words "Social Work (Scotland) Act 1968" substitute "Children (Scotland) Act 1995".

(5) In section 23(1) (interpretation)—

(a) in the definition of "contact order"—
(i) after the word "meaning" insert "—
(a) except in relation to an order made in Scotland,"; and
(ii) at the end, add "; and
(b) in relation to an order there made, given by section 11(2)(d) of the Children (Scotland) Act 1995."; and

(b) in the definition of "parental responsibility"—
(i) after the word "responsibility" " insert "—
(a) except in relation to Scotland,"; and
(ii) at the end add "; and
(b) in relation to Scotland, shall be construed as a reference to "parental responsibilities" within the meaning given by section 1(3) of the Children (Scotland) Act 1995;".

Tribunals and Inquiries Act 1992 (c. 53)

55. In paragraph 61 in column 2 of Schedule 1 to the Tribunals and Inquiries Act 1992 (which specifies certain tribunals in relation to social work in Scotland)—

(a) in sub-paragraph (a), for the words "Social Work (Scotland) Act 1968 (c. 49)" substitute "Children (Scotland) Act 1995 (c. 36)"; and

(b) in sub-paragraph (b), for the words "that Act" substitute "the Social Work (Scotland) Act 1968 (c. 49)".

Prisoners and Criminal Proceedings (Scotland) Act 1993 (c. 9)

56.—(1) The Prisoners and Criminal Proceedings (Scotland) Act 1993 shall be amended in accordance with this paragraph.

(2) In paragraph 8 of Schedule 3 (which provides for the definition of certain expressions in relation to the admission of documentary evidence in criminal proceedings), in the definition of "criminal proceedings"—

(a) the words "under section 42 of the Social Work (Scotland) Act 1968" shall cease to have effect;

(b) after the word "application" where it appears for the first time insert "under section 65(7) for (9) of the Children (Scotland) Act 1995";

(c) after the word "established" insert "or for a review of such a finding under section 85 of that Act"; and

(d) after the word "application", where it appears for the second time, insert "or, as the case may be, the review".

(3) In paragraph 1 of Schedule 6 (which provides for the definition of certain expressions in relation to transitional provisions), in the definition of "existing child detainee", for the words "section 30 of the Social Work (Scotland) Act 1968" substitute "section 93(2)(b) of the Children (Scotland) Act 1995".

Local Government etc. (Scotland) Act 1994 (c. 39)

57.—(1) The Local Government etc. (Scotland) Act 1994 shall be amended in accordance with this paragraph.

(2) In section 128 (establishment of Scottish Children's Reporter Administration)—

(a) in subsection (3), for the words from "the 1968 Act" to the end substitute "the Children (Scotland) Act 1995 and any other enactment conferring functions upon him"; and

(b) in subsection (8), for the words from "the 1968 Act" to the end substitute "the Children (Scotland) Act 1995 and any other enactment conferring functions upon him".

(3) In section 130 (annual reports by Principal Reporter) in sub-paragraph (i) of paragraph (a) of subsection (1), for the words "the 1968 Act and the Criminal Procedure (Scotland) Act 1975" substitute "the Children (Scotland) Act 1995 and any other enactment (except this Act) conferring functions upon him".

(4) In section 132 (duty of Administration to provide accommodation for children's hearings), for the words "section 34 of the 1968 Act" substitute "section 39 of the Children (Scotland) Act 1995".

Children (Northern Ireland) Order 1995 (SI 1995/755 (N.I.2))

58. In Article 70(7) of the Children (Northern Ireland) Order 1995 (enactments not to apply where child given refuge), in sub-paragraph (c), for the words "section 71 of the Social Work (Scotland) Act 1968" substitute "section 83 of the Children (Scotland) Act 1995".

Civil Evidence (Family Mediation) (Scotland) Act 1995 (c. 6)

59. In section 2 of the Civil Evidence (Family Mediation) (Scotland) Act 1995 (which provides for exceptions to the general inadmissibility of evidence concerning family mediation), in paragraph (d)(ii)—

(a) for the words "Part III of the Social Work (Scotland) Act 1968" substitute "Chapter 2 or 3 of Part II of the Children (Scotland) Act 1995"; and

(b) after the word "hearing" insert—

", before a sheriff or before a justice of the peace;

(iia) on any appeal arising from such proceedings as are mentioned in sub-paragraph (ii) above".

Criminal Justice (Scotland) Act 1995 (c. 20)

60. In section 20 of the Criminal Justice (Scotland) Act 1995 (construction of sections relating to the admissibility of certain evidence)—

(a) in subsection (3), in the definition of "criminal proceedings"—

(i) for the words from "under" to "application", where it appears for the first time, substitute "of an application made under Chapter 3 of Part II of the Children (Scotland) Act 1995"; and

(ii) after the word "child" insert "or for a review of such a finding"; and

(b) in subsection (5), after the words "1968" insert "or by virtue of Chapter 3 of Part II of the Children (Scotland) Act 1995".

Section 105(5)   SCHEDULE 5

REPEALS

Chapter	Short title	Extent of repeal
8 & 9 Vict. c. 19.	Lands Clauses Consolidation (Scotland) Act 1845.	In section 7, the words "persons under legal disability by reason of nonage" in each place where they occur. In section 67, the words "persons under legal disability by reason of nonage". In section 69, the words "persons under legal disability by reason of nonage".
12 & 13 Vict. c. 51.	Judicial Factors Act 1849.	In section 1, the words from "the word "Guardian" " to "years;". Section 25(2) In section 27, the words "guardians and". In section 31, the word "guardian,". In section 32, the word "guardian,". In section 33, the words "guardians or". In section 34, in both places where it occurs, the word "guardian,". In section 36, the word "guardianships,". In section 37, the word "guardian," In section 40, the word "guardians," in both places where it occurs.
27 & 28 Vict. c. 114.	Improvement of Land Act 1864.	In section 18, the words from "nor shall they" to the end. In section 21, the words from "or if the landowner" to "minors"; and the words "or circumstance" in both places where they occur.
43 & 44 Vict. c. 4.	Judicial Factors (Scotland) Act 1880.	In section 3, in the definition of "judicial factor", the words from "and" to "required".
7 Edw. 7 c. 51.	Sheriff Courts (Scotland) Act 1907.	Section 5(2C). Section 38C.
11 & 12 Geo. 5 c. 58.	Trusts (Scotland) Act 1921.	In section 2, in the definition of "trustee", the words from "guardian" to "years)".
1 Edw. 8 & 1 Geo 6 c. 37.	Children and Young Persons (Scotland) Act 1937.	In section 27, the first paragraph.
1 & 2 Geo. 6 c. 73.	Nursing Homes Registration (Scotland) Act 1938.	In section 4(1)(b)(iii), the words "custody or".
14 & 15 Geo. 6 c. 65.	Reserve and Auxiliary Forces (Protection of Civil Interests) Act 1951.	In section 8(1)(d), the words from "or any order" to the end.
6 & 7 Eliz. 2 c. 40.	Matrimonial Proceedings (Children) Act 1958.	Sections 8 to 10. Section 12.
1965 c. 49.	Registration of Births, Deaths and Marriages (Scotland) Act 1965.	In section 43, in subsection (3) the words from "In this" to the end; and subsection (10).
1968 c. 49.	Social Work (Scotland) Act 1968.	In section 5(1B), before paragraph (o), the word "and". In section 5B(5), the words from "and" at the end of the definition of child to the end of the subsection. Section 6(1)(b)(ii). Sections 15 to 26. Part III, except section 31(1) and (3). Part V. Section 88.

Chapter	Short title	Extent of repeal
		In section 90(1), the words "(other than orders under sections 52 and 58 and part V of this Act)".
		In section 94(1), the definition of "children's panel" and of "children's hearing"; the definitions of "compulsory measures of care", "guardian" and "place of safety"; in the definition of "prescribed", paragraph (b); and the definition of "school age".
		In section 97, in subsection (1), the words "section 44(1) (except head (b)) and (1A)", "section 58" and "Part V"; and subsections (2) and (3).
1969 c. 54.	Children and Young Persons Act 1969.	In Schedule 5, paragraphs 57 and 65(1).
1972 c. 18.	Maintenance Orders (Reciprocal Enforcement) Act 1972.	Section 4(3).
1972 c. 24.	Social Work (Scotland) Act 1972.	The whole Act.
1973 c. 29.	Guardianship Act 1973.	The whole Act.
1973 c. 65.	Local Government (Scotland) Act 1973.	In Schedule 25, paragraph 41. In Schedule 27, paragraphs 185 and 187.
1974 c. 53.	Rehabilitation of Offenders Act 1974.	Section 5(10A). In section 7(2), paragraph (e); and the words from "in the application" to the end.
1975 c. 21.	Criminal Procedure (Scotland) Act 1975.	Section 14. In section 168(c), the word "female". In section 177, the words "provided by a local authority under Part IV of the Social Work (Scotland) Act 1968". In section 296, in subsection (3), the words from "and the child" to the end; and subsection (4). Section 323. In section 364(c), the word "female". In section 378, the words "provided by a local authority under Part IV of the Social Work (Scotland) Act 1968". In section 413, in subsection (3), the definitions of "care" and of "the 1968 Act"; in subsection (4), the words "within the meaning of the 1968 Act"; in subsection (5), the words "(within the meaning of the 1968 Act)"; and in subsection (6A), the words "within the meaning of the 1968 Act". In Schedule 9, paragraphs 43 and 44.
1975 c. 72.	Children Act 1975.	Sections 47 to 49. Section 53. Sections 73 to 84. Sections 99 and 100. Section 102. Section 103. Section 105. Section 107, except the definitions, in subsection (1) of "adoption society", "child" and "voluntary organisation". In Schedule 3, paragraphs 52 to 57.

Chapter	Short title	Extent of repeal
1978 c. 28.	Adoption (Scotland) Act 1978.	In section 1(2), paragraph (a). In section 2, paragraph (d). In section 3(3)(a), the words "including in particular its ability to make provision for children who are free for adoption". Section 8. In section 12, in subsection (3)(b), the words "or by"; and in subsection (4) the word "—(a)" and paragraph (b). In section 14(1), the words from "Subject" to "certain cases)". In section 15, in subsection (1), the words from "Subject" to "certain cases)"; and in subsection (3), the word "natural" wherever it occurs. In section 16, subsection (5). Section 26. In section 28(5), the words "or of a voluntary organisation" and "or the organisation". Sections 32 to 37. In section 51, subsections 6(a) and (7) to (11). In section 60(3), the words "or 51(9)". In section 65(1), in the definition of "guardian", paragraph (b); and in the definition of "local authority", the words ", 35(1)". In Schedule 3, paragraphs 13, 14 and 15.
1980 c. 44.	Education (Scotland) Act 1980.	Section 44(1). In section 65B(6), paragraph (a). In section 135(1), the definition of "reporter of the appropriate local authority".
1980 c. 62.	Criminal Justice (Scotland) Act 1980.	In Schedule 7, paragraph 21.
1983 c. 33.	Solvent Abuse (Scotland) Act 1983.	The whole Act.
1983 c. 41.	Health and Social Services and Social Security Adjudications Act 1983.	Section 7. Section 8(1) and (4). In Schedule 2, paragraphs 4 to 6 and 8.
1984 c. 15.	Law Reform (Husband and Wife) (Scotland) Act 1984.	Section 3(2).
1984 c. 36.	Mental Health (Scotland) Act 1984.	In section 10(1)(a), sub-paragraph (i); and the word "or" immediately following that sub-paragraph. Section 55(4).
1984 c. 56.	Foster Children (Scotland) Act 1984.	In section 2, in subsection (3), the words "within the meaning of the Social Work (Scotland) Act 1968"; and in subsection (5), the words "; or (b) while he is a protected child within the meaning of section 32 of the said Act of 1978.".
1985 c. 37.	Family Law (Scotland) Act 1985.	In section 21, the words from "or an order" to "child".
1985 c. 60.	Child Abduction and Custody Act 1985.	In section 25, subsection (6). In Schedule 3, paragraph 7.
1986 c. 9.	Law Reform (Parent and Child) (Scotland) Act 1986.	Sections 2 to 4. In section 8, the definitions of "child" and "parental rights". In Schedule 1, paragraph 3.

Chapter	Short title	Extent of repeal
1986 c. 33.	Disabled Persons (Services, Consultation and Representation) Act 1986.	In section 16, in the definition of "guardian", paragraph (b).
1986 c. 55.	Family Law Act 1986.	In section 15(4), the words from "under section" to "1973".
		In section 17, in subsection (1), the words "Subject to subsection (2) below"; and subsection (2).
		In section 35(4)(c), the words "custody or".
1988 c. 32.	Civil Evidence (Scotland) Act 1988.	In section 9, in the definition of "civil proceedings", in paragraph (a), the words "under section 42 of the Social Work (Scotland) Act 1968".
1988 c. 36.	Court of Session Act 1988.	Section 20.
1989 c. 41.	Children Act 1989.	In Schedule 13, paragraph 13.
1989 c. 42.	Local Government and Housing Act 1989.	In Schedule 11, paragraph 15.
1991 c. 48.	Child Support Act 1991.	In section 5(1), the words "(or, in Scotland, parental rights over)" in both places where they occur.
		In section 54, the definition of "parental rights".
1991 c. 50.	Age of Legal Capacity (Scotland) Act 1991.	In section 5(1), the words "or tutory".
		In section 9, the definition of "parental rights".
		In Schedule 1, paragraphs 3 to 5 and 7 to 15.
1993 c. 9.	Prisoners and Criminal Proceedings (Scotland) Act 1993.	In paragraph 8 of Schedule 3, in the definition of "criminal proceedings", the words "under section 42 of the Social Work (Scotland) Act 1968".
1993 c. 35.	Education Act 1993.	In Schedule 19, paragraph 36.
1994 c. 39.	Local Government etc. (Scotland) Act 1994.	Section 139.
		In Schedule 13, paragraphs 76(6) and (10) to (25); 92(14)(b)(iii); 100(6)(b)(iv); 103; and 161(7)(c).

INDEX

ATOMIC ENERGY AUTHORITY ACT 1995*

(1995 c. 37)

Arrangement of Sections

An Act to make provision for the transfer of property, rights and liabilities of the United Kingdom Atomic Energy Authority to other persons; and for connected purposes. [8th November 1995]

Parliamentary Debates
Hansard, H.C. Vol. 256, col. 697; Vol. 257, col. 1128; Vol. 259, col. 175. H.L. Vol. 564, cols. 729, 1048; Vol. 566, cols. 14, 44, 82, 894, 1283.

Introduction and General Note
    This Act is intended to provide a framework for the privatisation of the activities of the Atomic Energy Authority's Commercial Division known as AEA Technology and for the sale of AEA Technology. The Act does not provide for privatisation of the Authority's other activities (see *Hansard*, H.C. Vol. 256, col. 697 and H.L. Vol. 564, col. 730).
    The Atomic Energy Authority was created by the Atomic Energy Authority Act 1954 (2 & 3 Eliz. 2, c.32) as a nuclear research and development organisation. In 1965 the Authority was authorised to carry out non-nuclear research and development, and from the outset non-nuclear work was done on a commercial basis. Under the Atomic Energy Authority Act 1971 (c.11), the Authority's isotopes production activities were transferred to Radiochemical Centre Limited which later became privatised as Amersham International plc. This Act also transferred the fuel

---

*Annotations by Gareth Jones, Solicitor, Nabarro Nathanson

processing activities to British Nuclear Fuels Limited. After the passing of the Atomic Energy Authority Act 1986 (c.3) the Authority's remaining funding support from the Consolidated Fund ceased. On April 1, 1994 the Authority was reorganised into three divisions: the Commercial Division (now known as AEA Technology), the Government Division—which manages the Authority's licensed nuclear activities, and the Services Division.

If privatised as a single entity AEA Technology would be one of the world's largest private sector engineering and science consultancies. In May 1992 the Monopolies & Mergers Commission reviewed the services provided by the Authority and concluded that the Authority's business activities should be transferred to the private sector. The Commission noted that there were a number of restrictions on the ability of AEA Technology to carry out its range of non-nuclear activities effectively.

This Act makes provision for the transfer of property, rights and liabilities of the Atomic Energy Authority. It provides for a scheme or schemes to facilitate the sale of AEA Technology by vesting all or parts of the Authority's Commercial Division in successor companies. The Act leaves open the method by which privatisation may take place. It provides for the business to be sold as a whole or in parts and provides for such sale or sales to be carried out by the Authority or by the Secretary of State. The Act specifically excludes both the transfer of any freehold land which is subject to a nuclear site licence and the transfer of any nuclear site licence.

The Act provides for the financial structure and control of the successor companies to AEA Technology after vesting and while they are publicly owned. The Act also makes provision for the tax consequences of transfers to successor companies and the tax effects of issuing securities and extinguishing liabilities. As regards pensions, there are powers to ensure that all employees transferred to a publicly owned successor company may remain in the Authority's scheme until privatisation and that new employees may join that scheme. On privatisation there will be a statutory duty on the seller to be satisfied that employees can join a pension scheme that is no less favourable than the Authority's scheme, although the mix of benefits is permitted to be different.

COMMENCEMENT
The Act came into effect immediately on receiving the Royal Assent on November 8, 1995.

ABBREVIATIONS
AEA: The Atomic Energy Authority of the United Kingdom.

Transfer of property, rights and liabilities of the Authority

Atomic Energy Authority to make schemes for transfer of property, rights and liabilities if so directed

1.—(1) If so directed by the Secretary of State under section 2(1) of this Act, the United Kingdom Atomic Energy Authority (in this Act referred to as "the Authority") shall make a scheme or schemes providing for the transfer to any person or persons of such property, rights and liabilities of the Authority as are specified in, or determined in accordance with, the scheme.

(2) In this Act a "transfer scheme" means a scheme made under subsection (1) above (including a scheme so made by virtue of section 2(3) of this Act).

(3) No transfer scheme may provide for the transfer of—

(a) a nuclear site licence (within the meaning of the Nuclear Installations Act 1965), or

(b) the fee simple estate in any land which, immediately before the day on which the scheme comes into force, consists of or is wholly or partly comprised in a site in respect of which such a licence held by the Authority is in force.

(4) The person or persons to whom anything is transferred by a transfer scheme may be or include one or more companies formed or acquired by the Authority or the Secretary of State for that purpose.

(5) Schedule 1 to this Act shall have effect with respect to transfer schemes.

(6) In the application of subsection (3)(b) above to Scotland, the reference to the fee simple estate shall be construed as a reference—

(a) in the case of feudal property, to the estate or interest of the proprietor of the *dominium utile*, or

(b) in the case of any property other than feudal property, to the estate or interest of the owner.

DEFINITIONS

"nuclear site licence": subs. (3) and the Nuclear Installations Act 1965, s.26(1).
"The Authority": s.13.
"transfer scheme": subs. (2) and s.13.

GENERAL NOTE

This section requires the Authority to make a transfer scheme or transfer schemes when so directed by the Secretary of State. The Secretary of State in practice is the Secretary of State for Trade and Industry and his power to direct is provided by section 2(1). In the House of Commons Committee there was considerable debate about the form privatisation should take, with the Opposition pressing for the Authority to be retained as a single entity. However, the Government made it clear that its intention was to preserve the possibility of multiple sales [Standing Committee D, March 23, 1995, col. 16].

Subs. (3)

A nuclear site licence or any land covered by such a licence is prevented from being included in a scheme.

Subs. (4)

This enables the Authority to form or acquire companies specifically for the purpose of privatisation.

Subs. (6)(a)

In Scottish law the full ownership (*dominium plenum*) of a piece of land may be sub-divided into superiority (*dominium directum* or direct ownership) and the feu (*dominium utile* or useful ownership). Sinclair, *Handbook of Conveyancing Practice in Scotland* (1986), Chap. 17.

Powers of Secretary of State

2.—(1) The Secretary of State may from time to time direct the Authority to make, before a date specified in the direction, a transfer scheme which relates to such property, rights and liabilities as are specified in, or determined in accordance with, the direction and contains such other provisions as may be so specified.

(2) A transfer scheme shall not take effect unless it is approved by the Secretary of State and by the Treasury; and the Secretary of State may modify such a scheme before approving it.

(3) If—

(a) the Secretary of State decides not to approve a scheme that has been submitted to him by the Authority (either with or without modifications), or

(b) the Secretary of State has given a direction under subsection (1) above and the Authority have failed, before the date specified in the direction, to submit the scheme for the approval of the Secretary of State,

the Secretary of State may himself make a transfer scheme with the consent of the Treasury.

(4) Subsections (1) to (3) above shall have effect subject to section 1(3) of this Act.

(5) Subject to subsection (6) below, the Secretary of State shall not approve or make a transfer scheme containing any provision in accordance with which any person other than—

(a) a company which is wholly owned by the Crown, or

(b) a wholly-owned subsidiary of the Authority,

becomes entitled or subject to any property, rights and liabilities unless it appears to the Secretary of State that the person has consented to the provisions of the scheme so far as they relate to him.

(6) Subsection (5) above shall not require the consent of any person to so much of a transfer scheme as—
(a) relates to property, rights or liabilities to which that person is already entitled or subject, and
(b) appears to the Secretary of State to be made for purposes that are no more than supplemental or incidental to the other provisions of the scheme.
(7) Before—
(a) declining to approve a transfer scheme, or
(b) modifying or making such a scheme,
the Secretary of State shall consult the Authority.
(8) The Secretary of State may—
(a) exercise his powers under this section,
(b) give any direction to the Authority under subsection (2) of section 3 of the Atomic Energy Authority Act 1954 (general power of Secretary of State to give directions to the Authority) which in his opinion is appropriate for the purpose of facilitating—
(i) any transfer effected or proposed to be effected under section 1 of this Act, or
(ii) the disposal of securities of a successor company, and
(c) do anything else which in his opinion is appropriate for that purpose,
whether or not the exercise of those powers, the giving of that direction or the doing of that thing is consistent with promoting or controlling the development of atomic energy.

DEFINITIONS
"the Authority": s.13.
"successor company": s.13.
"transfer scheme": s.12 and s.13.

GENERAL NOTE
This section prevents transfer schemes taking effect unless approved by the Secretary of State and the Treasury. It enables the Secretary of State to direct the Authority to prepare schemes, to modify them and to make a scheme himself in certain circumstances.

Subss. (5) and (6)
Require the Secretary of State to satisfy himself that schemes transfer property, or constitute rights or liabilities only with the consent of those affected.

Subs. (7)
Requires the Secretary of State to consult the Authority before modifying, rejecting or making a scheme.

Supplementary provisions as to the Authority's powers

3. Without prejudice to any powers of the Authority apart from this section, the Authority shall have power to do anything which in their opinion is appropriate for the purpose of facilitating—
(a) any transfer effected or proposed to be effected under section 1 of this Act, or
(b) the disposal of securities of a successor company.

DEFINITIONS
"the Authority": s.13.
"successor company": s.13.
"transfer scheme": s.1(2) and s.13.

GENERAL NOTE
This section gives the Authority discretion to do anything to facilitate a transfer under s.1 or the disposal of securities of a successor company. This discretion is not unlimited. S.2(2) makes transfer schemes subject to approval by the Secretary of State and the Treasury and s.7(2)

requires the Secretary of State and the Treasury to consent to any disposal by the Authority of the shares of a successor company.

Agreements with respect to transfer schemes

4.—(1) The Authority may enter into any such agreement as they think fit for the purpose of accepting or imposing contractual obligations with respect to, or to anything connected with, the manner in which their powers by virtue of section 1 of this Act are to be exercised.

(2) The Secretary of State may enter into such agreement as he thinks fit with respect to, or to anything connected with, the manner and circumstances in which his powers under or by virtue of section 2 of this Act are to be exercised.

(3) Any agreement under this section may, in particular, provide for the making of payments to the Authority or the Secretary of State (by way of consideration or otherwise) in respect of anything transferred or created in accordance with a transfer scheme.

(4) The consent of the Treasury shall be required for the making of an agreement under this section; and the consent of the Secretary of State shall also be required for the making by the Authority of an agreement under this section.

(5) Any sums received by the Secretary of State in pursuance of an agreement under this section shall be paid into the Consolidated Fund.

DEFINITION
    "transfer scheme": s.1(2) and s.13.

GENERAL NOTE
    This section provides for the Authority (subs. (1)) with the consent of the Secretary of State and the Treasury (subs. (4)) or the Secretary of State (subs. (2)), with the consent of the Treasury (subs. (4)) to enter into agreements in connection with transfer schemes.

Duty of Authority to assist Secretary of State in connection with transfer schemes

5.—(1) It shall be the duty of the Authority to furnish the Secretary of State with all such information and other assistance as he may require for the purposes of, or in connection with—
    (a) the exercise of any of his powers in relation to a transfer scheme or in relation to any agreement under section 4 of this Act, or
    (b) the making by him of a transfer scheme or of any such agreement.

(2) The obligation of the Authority under this section shall include a duty to secure, as far as practicable, that their subsidiaries furnish all such information and assistance as the Secretary of State may require for the purposes of, or in connection with, the exercise of any such power, or the making of any such scheme or agreement, as is mentioned in subsection (1) above.

(3) A duty under this section to furnish information or assistance, or to secure that it is furnished, shall be performed within such period after the requirement giving rise to the duty as the Secretary of State may allow.

DEFINITIONS
    "subsidiary": s.13 and Companies Act 1985, ss.736(1) and 736A.
    "transfer scheme": s.1(2) and s.13.

GENERAL NOTE
    This section places a duty on the Authority to provide any information required by the Secretary of State in connection with the exercise of his powers in relation to transfer schemes or agreements under s.4.

Successor companies

Successor companies

6. Schedule 2 to this Act (which relates to successor companies) shall have effect.

DEFINITION
"successor company": s.13.

Disposal by Authority or Secretary of State of shares in successor companies

7.—(1) In section 1 of the Atomic Energy (Miscellaneous Provisions) Act 1981 (extension of power of Authority and Secretary of State to dispose of shares), subsection (4) (which limits the power of the Authority to dispose of shares) and subsection (5) (which limits the power of the Secretary of State to dispose of shares) shall not apply in relation to shares in any successor company.

(2) The Authority shall not dispose of any securities of any successor company except with the consent of the Secretary of State and the Treasury.

DEFINITIONS
"shares": s.13.
"successor company": s.13.
"the Authority": s.13.

GENERAL NOTE
This section prevents the Authority from disposing of the shares of successor companies without the consent of the Treasury and the Secretary of State.

Financial arrangements relating to transfers

Taxation provisions

8. Schedule 3 to this Act (which relates to taxation) shall have effect.

Pensions

9. Schedule 4 to this Act (which relates to pensions) shall have effect.

Extinguishment of certain liabilities

Extinguishment of certain liabilities

10.—(1) Subject to subsection (2) below, the Secretary of State may, at any time after the coming into force of a transfer scheme, by order extinguish all or any of the liabilities of the Authority in respect of the principal of such relevant loans as may be specified in the order to such extent as may be so specified.

(2) The aggregate amount of the liabilities extinguished under subsection (1) above shall not exceed the aggregate of—
    (a) any sums received by the Secretary of State or the Authority in pursuance of agreements under section 4 of this Act, and

(b) any sums received by the Treasury, the Secretary of State or the Authority on the disposal of any securities of a successor company, or of rights to subscribe for such securities.

(3) The Secretary of State may by order extinguish all or any of the liabilities of a publicly owned successor company in respect of the principal of such relevant loans as may be specified in the order to such extent as may be so specified.

(4) Where any liabilities are extinguished under subsection (1) or (3) above, the assets of the National Loans Fund shall accordingly be reduced by amounts corresponding to the liabilities so extinguished.

(5) Where the Secretary of State has made an order under subsection (3) above and he considers it appropriate to do so, he may from time to time give a direction under this subsection to a successor company whose liabilities are extinguished by the order; and a company to which such a direction is given shall, as a consequence of the making of the order, issue such securities of the company as may be specified or described in the direction—
    (a) to the Treasury, the Secretary of State or the Authority, or
    (b) to any person entitled to require the issue of the securities following their initial allotment to the Treasury, the Secretary of State or the Authority.

(6) No direction may be given to a successor company under subsection (5) above at any time after that company has ceased to be publicly owned.

(7) Unless the Secretary of State otherwise determines in any particular case, where a company is directed to issue debentures in pursuance of this section—
    (a) the aggregate of the principal sums payable under the debentures to which the direction relates shall be equal to the aggregate of the sums the liability to repay which is extinguished by the order, and
    (b) the terms as to the payment of the principal sums payable on the debentures to which the direction relates, and as to the payment of interest on those principal sums, shall be the same as the corresponding terms of the loans specified in the order.

(8) For the purposes of subsection (7) above, any express or implied terms of a loan shall be disregarded in so far as they relate to the early discharge of liabilities to make repayments of principal and payments of interest.

(9) Paragraphs 1(4) and (5), 3 and 4 of Schedule 2 to this Act shall apply for the purposes of subsection (5) above as they apply for the purposes of paragraph 1 of that Schedule.

(10) The Secretary of State shall not exercise any power conferred on him by this section except with the consent of the Treasury.

(11) The power to make an order under this section shall be exercisable by statutory instrument subject to annulment in pursuance of a resolution of either House of Parliament.

(12) In this section "relevant loan"—
    (a) in relation to the Authority, means the Authority's commencing capital debt under section 1 of the Atomic Energy Authority Act 1986 and any loan made to the Authority under section 4 of that Act, and
    (b) in relation to a successor company, means—
        (i) any debt or loan mentioned in paragraph (a) above, if and to the extent that the liability to repay it is transferred to the company in accordance with a transfer scheme, and
        (ii) any loan made to that company by the Secretary of State under paragraph 11 of Schedule 2 to this Act.

DEFINITIONS
  "successor company": s.1(2) and s.13.
  "the Authority": s.13.
  "transfer scheme": s.1(2) and s.13.

"securities": s.13.
"relevant loan": subs. (12).
"company wholly owned by the Crown": s.13(2).
"publicly owned": s.13(3).

GENERAL NOTE
This section gives the Secretary of State the power (with the consent of the Treasury—subs. (10)) by order, to extinguish the National Loan Fund debt of the Authority, and such debts which have been transferred to a successor company by a scheme or which have been incurred by such a company while it is wholly owned by the Crown (see *Hansard*, H.L. Vol. 564, col. 732).

Membership of the Authority

Membership of the Authority

11.—(1) Section 1 of the Atomic Energy Authority Act 1954 shall be amended as follows.

(2) In subsection (2) (which provides that the Authority shall consist of a chairman and not less than seven nor more than fifteen other members) for "seven" there shall be substituted "four".

(3) In subsection (3) (which provides that all the members are to be appointed by the Secretary of State and that certain of them are to have certain experience) the words from "and of those members" to the end shall be omitted.

DEFINITION
"the Authority": s.13.

GENERAL NOTE
This section amends section 1 of the Atomic Energy Authority Act 1954 so as to reduce the minimum membership of the Authority to four and to dispense with the requirement for members to have specific experience. In response to Opposition queries, the Government explained in Committee [Standing Committee D, April 4, 1995, col. 136 and *Hansard*, H.L. Vol. 256, col. 756] that the intention was not to dispense with relevant experience, but to provide for more flexibility in the range of experience considered relevant.

Supplementary provisions

Expenses

12. There shall be paid out of money provided by Parliament any increase attributable to this Act in—

(a) the administrative expenses of the Secretary of State or the Treasury, or

(b) the sums which under any other Act are payable out of money so provided.

Interpretation

13.—(1) In this Act, unless the context otherwise requires—
"the Authority" means the United Kingdom Atomic Energy Authority;
"debentures" includes debenture stock;
"securities", in relation to a company, includes shares, debentures, bonds and other securities of the company, whether or not constituting a charge on the assets of the company;
"shares" includes stock;
"subsidiary" and "wholly-owned subsidiary" have the same meaning as in the Companies Act 1985;
"successor company" means any company which, at a time when it is wholly owned by the Crown or is a wholly-owned subsidiary of the Authority, becomes entitled or subject, in accordance with a transfer scheme, to any property, rights or liabilities;
"transfer scheme" has the meaning given by section 1 of this Act.

(2) A company shall be regarded for the purposes of this Act as wholly owned by the Crown at any time when none of the issued shares in the company is held otherwise than by, or by a nominee of, the Treasury or the Secretary of State.

(3) A successor company shall be regarded for the purposes of this Act as publicly owned at any time when it—

(a) is wholly owned by the Crown, or

(b) is a wholly-owned subsidiary of the Authority.

Short title and extent

14.—(1) This Act may be cited as the Atomic Energy Authority Act 1995.

(2) This Act extends to Northern Ireland.

SCHEDULES

Section 1(5)   SCHEDULE 1

TRANSFER SCHEMES: SUPPLEMENTARY PROVISIONS

Contents and effect of scheme

1.—(1) A transfer scheme may define the property, rights and liabilities to be transferred to a particular person—

(a) by specifying or describing the property, rights and liabilities in question,

(b) by referring to all (or all but so much as may be excepted) of the property, rights and liabilities comprised in a specified part of the Authority's undertaking, or

(c) partly in one way and partly in the other.

(2) A transfer scheme shall appoint the day on which it is to come into force.

(3) This Act shall have effect, in relation to any provision of a transfer scheme for the transfer of any property, rights or liabilities, so as to transfer the property, rights or liabilities, at the beginning of the day appointed for the coming into force of the scheme, and without further assurance, from the Authority to the person to whom they are allocated under the scheme and to vest them in that person; and the provisions of that scheme in relation to that transfer shall have effect from that time accordingly.

(4) This Act shall have effect, in relation to any provision of a transfer scheme for the creation, by virtue of paragraph 2 below, of any interest or right, so as to create the specified interests and rights, at the beginning of the day appointed for the coming into force of the scheme and without further assurance.

(5) The preceding provisions of this paragraph shall have effect subject to so much of a transfer scheme as provides for—

(a) the transfer of any of the property, rights or liabilities to be transferred in accordance with the scheme, or

(b) the creation of any of the rights or interests to be created in accordance with the scheme, to be effected by or under any agreement or instrument entered into or executed in pursuance of an obligation imposed by virtue of paragraph 2(1)(g) below.

(6) In their application to Scotland, sub-paragraphs (3) and (4) above shall have effect with the omission of the words "and without further assurance".

Division of Authority's undertaking by scheme

2.—(1) For the purposes of making any such division as the Authority consider appropriate of any of the property, rights and liabilities of the Authority between two or more persons (including any division between the Authority and any one or more other persons), a transfer scheme may contain provision—

(a) for the creation in favour of the Authority of an interest or right in or in relation to property transferred in accordance with that scheme to any person,

(b) for the creation, in favour of a person to whom any transfer is made, of an interest or right in or in relation to property so transferred to another,

(c) for giving effect to a transfer to any person by the creation, in favour of that person, of an interest or right in or in relation to property retained by the Authority,

(d) for rights and liabilities to be transferred so as to be enforceable by or against more than one transferee or by or against both one or more transferees and the Authority,

 (e) for rights and liabilities enforceable against more than one person in accordance with any provision falling within paragraph (d) above to be enforceable in different or modified respects by or against each or any of them,

 (f) for the creation of new rights and liabilities (including rights of indemnity and duties to indemnify) as between different transferees and as between any transferee and the Authority, and

 (g) without prejudice to paragraph (f) above, for imposing on any transferee or the Authority an obligation—

   (i) to enter into such written agreements with any other person on whom any corresponding obligation is, could be or has been imposed by virtue of this paragraph of this Schedule (whether in the same or a different scheme), or

   (ii) to execute such instruments in favour of any such person,

as may be specified or described in the scheme.

(2) A transfer scheme may contain such supplemental and incidental provision with respect to the interests, rights and liabilities of third parties in relation to anything to which the scheme relates as the Authority consider to be necessary or expedient for the purposes of any such division as is mentioned in sub-paragraph (1) above, or in connection with anything contained in the scheme by virtue of that sub-paragraph.

(3) The provision that may be contained in a transfer scheme by virtue of sub-paragraph (2) above shall include provision for interests, rights or liabilities to which any third party is entitled or subject in relation to anything to which the scheme relates to be modified in such respects or in such manner as may be specified or determined under the scheme.

(4) The provision that may be contained in a transfer scheme by virtue of sub-paragraph (1)(f) above shall include the creation of such rights and liabilities as the Authority think fit for the purpose of converting into a contract between the transferee under the scheme and the Authority any arrangements between different parts of the Authority's undertaking which exist immediately before the day on which the scheme comes into force.

(5) An obligation imposed on any person by virtue of sub-paragraph (1)(g) above shall be enforceable by the bringing, by any person with or in favour of whom the agreement or instrument is to be entered into or executed, of civil proceedings for an injunction or for interdict or for other appropriate relief.

(6) In relation to any transfer scheme made by the Secretary of State by virtue of section 2(3) of this Act, the first reference to the Authority in sub-paragraph (1) above, the reference to the Authority in sub-paragraph (2) above and the first such reference in sub-paragraph (4) above shall have effect as references to the Secretary of State.

Property to which a scheme may relate

3.—(1) The property, rights and liabilities that shall be capable of being transferred in accordance with a transfer scheme shall include—

 (a) property, rights and liabilities that would not otherwise be capable of being transferred or assigned by the Authority,

 (b) property acquired at a time after the making of the scheme and before it comes into force, and rights and liabilities which arise or may arise in respect of anything occurring after the making of the scheme,

 (c) property situated anywhere in the United Kingdom or elsewhere and rights and liabilities under the law of any part of the United Kingdom or of any country or territory outside the United Kingdom, and

 (d) rights and liabilities under enactments.

(2) The transfers authorised by sub-paragraph (1)(a) above, and the interests and rights that may be created in accordance with a transfer scheme, include transfers, interests and rights which are to take effect as if there were—

 (a) no such requirement to obtain any person's consent or concurrence,

 (b) no such liability in respect of a contravention of any other requirement, and

 (c) no such interference with any interest or right,

as there would be, in the case of any transaction apart from this Act, by reason of provisions having effect (whether under any enactment or agreement or otherwise) in relation to the terms on which the Authority are entitled or subject to any property, right or liability.

(3) Where apart from this sub-paragraph any person would have an entitlement, in consequence of anything done or likely to be done by or under this Act, to terminate, modify, acquire or claim an interest or right which is vested in the Authority at the passing of this Act or acquired by the Authority after that time, or to treat any such interest or right as modified or terminated, then—

(a) for the purposes of the transfer of the interest or right in accordance with a transfer scheme, that entitlement shall not be enforceable in relation to that interest or right until after its transfer in accordance with such a scheme, and

(b) without prejudice to the preceding provisions of this paragraph or to paragraph 5(2)(a) below, that entitlement shall be enforceable in relation to the interest or right after its transfer only in so far as the scheme contains provision for it to be transferred subject to the provisions conferring that entitlement.

(4) Subject to sub-paragraphs (5) and (6) below, nothing in sub-paragraph (1) or (2) above shall enable—

(a) any agreement or instrument entered into or executed in pursuance of an obligation imposed by virtue of paragraph 2(1)(g) above, or

(b) anything done under any such agreement,

to give effect to any transfer, or to create any interest or right, which could not apart from this paragraph have been made by or under that agreement or instrument.

(5) A transfer scheme may provide for—

(a) the transfers to which effect is to be given by or under any agreement or instrument entered into or executed in accordance with the scheme, or

(b) the interests or rights that are to be created by or under any such agreement or instrument, to include, to such extent as may be specified in the scheme, any such transfer, interest or right as is mentioned in sub-paragraph (2) above.

(6) A transfer scheme may provide that sub-paragraph (3) above shall apply in relation to the provisions of any agreement or instrument which is to be entered into or executed in accordance with the scheme, and in relation to any proposal for such an agreement or for the execution of such an instrument, as if the reference in sub-paragraph (3)(b) above to provision contained in the scheme included a reference to provision contained, in accordance with the scheme, in the agreement or instrument.

Certain debts owed to Secretary of State

4. No liability of the Authority in respect of the Authority's commencing capital debt under section 1 of the Atomic Energy Act 1986 or in respect of any loan made to them under section 4 of that Act shall be transferred by a transfer scheme except to a company which—

(a) is wholly owned by the Crown, or

(b) is a wholly-owned subsidiary of the Authority.

Supplementary provisions of schemes

5.—(1) A transfer scheme may contain supplemental, consequential and transitional provision for the purposes of, or in connection with, any transfer of property, rights or liabilities for which the scheme provides or in connection with any other provisions contained in the scheme; and any such provision may include different provision for different cases or different purposes.

(2) A transfer scheme may, in relation to transfers in accordance with the scheme, make provision, either generally or for such purposes as may be specified in the scheme—

(a) for the transferee to be treated as the same person in law as the Authority,

(b) for agreements made, transactions effected or other things done by or in relation to the Authority to be treated, so far as may be necessary for the purposes of or in connection with the transfers, as made, effected or done by or in relation to the transferee,

(c) for references in any agreement (whether or not in writing) or in any deed, bond, instrument or other document to, or to any member or officer of, the Authority to have effect, so far as may be necessary for the purposes of or in connection with any of the transfers, with such modifications as are specified in the scheme,

(d) for proceedings commenced by or against the Authority to be continued by or against the transferee, and

(e) for any such disputes as to the effect of the scheme as arise between different transferees, or between any transferee on the one hand and the Authority on the other, to be referred to such arbitration as may be specified in or determined under the scheme.

(3) Where any person is entitled, in consequence of any transfer made in accordance with a transfer scheme or in pursuance of any provision made under this paragraph, to possession of a document relating in part to the title to, or to the management of, any land or other property in England and Wales—

(a) the scheme may contain provision for treating that person as having given another person an acknowledgment in writing of the right of that other person to production of the document and to delivery of copies of the document, and

(b) section 64 of the Law of Property Act 1925 (production and safe custody of documents) shall have effect accordingly, and on the basis that the acknowledgment did not contain any such expression of contrary intention as is mentioned in that section.

(4) Where any person is entitled, in consequence of any transfer made in accordance with a transfer scheme or in pursuance of any provision made under this paragraph, to possession of a document relating in part to the title to, or to the management of, any land or other property in Scotland transferred in accordance with a transfer scheme, subsections (1) and (2) of section 16 of the Land Registration (Scotland) 1979 (omission of certain clauses in deeds) shall have effect in relation to the transfer as if the transfer had been effected by deed and as if from each of those subsections the words "unless specially qualified" were omitted.

(5) In this paragraph—
(a) references to a transfer include references to the creation in any person's favour of any interest or right, and references to a transferee shall be construed accordingly, and
(b) references to a person who is entitled, in consequence of any transfer, to possession of a document include references to the Authority in a case where the Authority are entitled to retain possession of any document following any transfer.

(6) Sub-paragraphs (2) to (4) above shall be without prejudice to the generality of sub-paragraph (1) above.

Proof of title by certificate

6.—(1) The Authority and any person to whom anything has been transferred in accordance with a transfer scheme may issue a joint certificate stating that—
(a) any property specified in the certificate, or
(b) any such interest in or right over any such property as may be so specified,
is property, or (as the case may be) an interest or right, which was intended to be and was vested by virtue of the scheme in such one of them as may be so specified; and any such certificate shall be conclusive evidence for all purposes of that fact.

(2) The Authority and any person to whom anything has been transferred in accordance with a transfer scheme may issue a joint certificate stating that any liability specified in the certificate is a liability which was intended to be, and was, vested by virtue of the scheme in such one of them as may be so specified.

(3) Any certificate under sub-paragraph (2) above—
(a) shall, if given with the concurrence of every person who is entitled to enforce the liability at the time of the giving of the certificate, be conclusive evidence for all purposes of the fact referred to in that sub-paragraph, and
(b) shall, in any other case, be conclusive evidence of that fact as between the persons giving or concurring in the giving of the certificate.

(4) If, after the end of the period of one month beginning with the date of a request from either the Authority or a transferee under a transfer scheme for the preparation of a joint certificate under sub-paragraph (1) or (2) above as respects any property, interest, right or liability, they have failed to agree on the terms of the certificate, they shall refer the matter to the Secretary of State and issue the certificate in such terms as he may direct.

(5) In this paragraph—
(a) references to a transfer include references to the creation in any person's favour of any interest or right, and references to a transferee shall be construed accordingly, and
(b) references to a transfer scheme include references to a modification agreement as defined in paragraph 8(7) below.

Duties in relation to foreign property etc.

7.—(1) It shall be the duty of the Authority and of any person to whom any foreign property, right or liability is transferred to take all such steps as may be requisite to secure that the vesting in the transferee, in accordance with the scheme, of the foreign property, right or liability is effective under the relevant foreign law.

(2) Until the vesting in the transferee in accordance with the scheme of any foreign property, right or liability is effective under the relevant foreign law, it shall be the duty of the Authority to hold that property or right for the benefit of, or to discharge that liability on behalf of, the transferee.

(3) Nothing in sub-paragraphs (1) and (2) above shall be taken as prejudicing the effect under the law of any part of the United Kingdom of the vesting in the transferee in accordance with the scheme of any foreign property, right or liability.

(4) The Authority shall have all such powers as may be requisite for the performance of their duties under this paragraph, but it shall be the duty of a person to whom a transfer is made in accordance with a transfer scheme to act on behalf of the Authority (so far as possible) in performing the duties imposed on them by this paragraph.

(5) Where—

(a) any foreign property, rights or liabilities are acquired or incurred by the Authority in respect of any other property, rights or liabilities, and

(b) by virtue of this paragraph the Authority holds the other property or rights for the benefit of another person or discharges the liability on behalf of another person,

the property, rights or liabilities acquired or incurred are immediately to become property, rights or liabilities of that other person; and the preceding provisions of this paragraph shall have effect accordingly in relation to the property, rights or liabilities acquired or incurred.

(6) References in this paragraph to any foreign property, right or liability are references to any property, right or liability as respects which any issue arising in any proceedings would have been determined (in accordance with the rules of private international law) by reference to the law of a country or territory outside the United Kingdom.

(7) Any expenses incurred by the Authority under this paragraph shall be met by the person to whom the transfer in question is made.

(8) Any obligation imposed under this paragraph shall be enforceable as if contained in a contract between the Authority and the person to whom the transfer in question is made.

Modification of scheme by agreement

8.—(1) This paragraph applies where any person to whom anything has been transferred in accordance with a transfer scheme agrees in writing with the Authority or another person to whom anything has been transferred in accordance with that or any other transfer scheme that, for the purpose of modifying the effect of the scheme or, as the case may be, of modifying the effect of either or both of the schemes—

(a) any of the property, rights or liabilities transferred in accordance with the scheme or either of them, and

(b) any or all of the property, rights or liabilities acquired or incurred since the transfer in respect of the transferred property, rights or liabilities,

should be transferred from one to the other as from a date appointed by the agreement.

(2) If—

(a) the agreement is entered into within the period of twelve months after the time when a transfer in accordance with a transfer scheme of property, rights or liabilities to any of its parties comes into force, and

(b) the Secretary of State, with the consent of the Treasury, has given his approval to the transfer for which the agreement provides and to its terms and conditions,

then the transfer for which the agreement provides shall take effect on the date appointed by the agreement in the like manner as a transfer for which provision is made by a transfer scheme.

(3) Subject to the approval of the Secretary of State and to sub-paragraph (4) below, the provisions that may be contained in a modification agreement shall include any such provision in relation to any transfer for which it provides as may be contained, in relation to any transfer for which a transfer scheme provides, in that scheme.

(4) Nothing in any modification agreement shall provide for any interests or rights to be created, as opposed to transferred, except as between persons who are parties to the agreement.

(5) Before—

(a) refusing his approval for the purposes of this paragraph, or

(b) giving his approval for those purposes in a case where the Authority are not a party to the proposed agreement,

the Secretary of State shall consult the Authority.

(6) In this paragraph references to a transfer in accordance with a transfer scheme include references to the creation of any interest, right or liability in accordance with such a scheme.

(7) In this paragraph and the following provisions of this Schedule "modification agreement" means any agreement providing for a transfer which is to take effect in accordance with sub-paragraph (2) above.

The Transfer of Undertakings (Protection of Employment) Regulations 1981

9.—(1) The 1981 regulations shall apply to any transfer of any undertaking or part of an undertaking in accordance with a transfer scheme or modification agreement as if (in so far as that would not otherwise be the case) the references in those regulations to the transferor were references to the person in whom that undertaking or part was vested immediately before the coming into force of the transfer.

(2) It shall be the duty of the Secretary of State, before—

(a) giving a direction under subsection (1) of section 2 of this Act,

(b) modifying a transfer scheme by virtue of subsection (2) of that section,

(c) making a transfer scheme by virtue of subsection (3) of that section, or

(d) approving a modification agreement,

to give such notice of his proposals to such persons as he considers appropriate for enabling any provisions of the 1981 regulations applicable to any transfer in accordance with the scheme or agreement to be complied with by the person who for the purposes of the regulations is the transferor in relation to that transfer.

(3) In this paragraph—

(a) "the 1981 regulations" means the Transfer of Undertakings (Protection of Employment) Regulations 1981, and

(b) "undertaking" has the same meaning as in the 1981 regulations.

Compensation

10.—(1) Where, in consequence of any provisions included in a transfer scheme for the purposes of any such division as is mentioned in paragraph 2(1) above, the interests, rights or liabilities of a third party are modified as mentioned in sub-paragraph (2) below, the third party shall be entitled to such compensation as may be just in respect of—

(a) any diminution attributable to that modification in the value of any of his interests or rights, or

(b) any increase attributable to that modification in the burden of his liabilities.

2. The modifications mentioned in sub-paragraph (1) above are modifications by virtue of which—

(a) an interest of the third party in any property is transformed into, or replaced by—

(i) an interest in only part of that property, or

(ii) separate interests in different parts of that property,

(b) a right of the third party against the Authority is transformed into, or replaced by, two or more rights which do not include a right which, on its own, is equivalent (disregarding the person against whom it is enforceable) to the right against the Authority, or

(c) a liability of the third party to the Authority is transformed into, or replaced by, two or more separate liabilities at least one of which is a liability enforceable by a person other than the Authority.

(3) Where—

(a) a third party would, apart from any provisions of a transfer scheme or paragraph 3(3) above, have become entitled to, or to exercise, any interest or right arising or exercisable in respect of the transfer or creation in accordance with such a scheme of any property, rights or liabilities, and

(b) the provisions of that scheme or of paragraph 3(3) above have the effect of preventing that person's entitlement to, or to exercise, that interest or right from arising on any occasion in respect of anything mentioned in paragraph (a) above, and

(c) provision is not made by a transfer scheme for securing that an entitlement to, or to exercise, that interest or right or an equivalent interest or right, is preserved or created so as to arise in respect of the first occasion when corresponding circumstances next occur after the coming into force of the transfers for which the scheme provides,

the third party shall be entitled to such compensation as may be just in respect of the extinguishment of the interest or right.

(4) A liability to pay compensation under this paragraph shall fall on the persons not being themselves third parties who, as the case may be—

(a) have interests in the whole or any part of the property affected by the modification in question,

(b) are subject to the rights of the person to be compensated which are affected by the modification in question,

(c) are entitled to enforce the liabilities of the person to be compensated which are affected by that modification, or

(d) benefit from the extinguishment of the entitlement mentioned in sub-paragraph (3) above,

and that liability shall be apportioned between those persons in such manner as may be appropriate having regard to the extent of their respective rights or liabilities or the extent of the benefit they respectively obtain from the extinguishment.

(5) Where any liability falls by virtue of sub-paragraph (4) above on the Authority, that sub-paragraph shall have effect subject to so much of any transfer scheme (including the one which gives rise to the liability) as makes provision for the transfer of that liability to any other person.

(6) Any dispute as to whether, or as to the person by whom, any compensation is to be paid under this paragraph, and any dispute as to the amount of any compensation to be paid by any person, shall be referred to and determined—

(a) where the claimant requires the matter to be determined in England and Wales or in Northern Ireland, by an arbitrator appointed by the Lord Chancellor, or

(b) where the claimant requires the matter to be determined in Scotland, by an arbiter appointed by the Lord President of the Court of Session.

(7) This paragraph shall have effect in relation to the provisions of any agreement or instrument entered into or executed in pursuance of an obligation imposed by virtue of paragraph 2(1)(g) above, and to any modification agreement, as it has effect in relation to the provisions of a transfer scheme.

(8) In this paragraph "third party", in relation to provisions capable of giving rise to compensation under this paragraph, means any person other than—

(a) the Authority or any of their wholly-owned subsidiaries,

(b) the Secretary of State,

(c) any successor company which is wholly owned by the Crown at the time in relation to which those provisions have effect, or

(d) any person whose consent to those provisions has been given for the purposes of section 2(5) of this Act or who has agreed to those provisions by virtue of being a party to a modification agreement.

DEFINITIONS

"the Authority": s.13.

"transfer scheme": s.1(2) and s.13.

"successor company": s.13.

"subsidiary" and "wholly-owned subsidiary": s.13 and Companies Act 1985 (c. 6), ss.736(1) and 736A.

"wholly-owned by the Crown": s.13.

"the 1981 regulations": para. 9(3)(a).

"undertaking": para. 9(3)(b) and the 1981 Regulations, Regulation 2(1).

"third party": para. 10(8).

"modification agreement": para. 8(7).

GENERAL NOTE

This Schedule contains detailed provisions on transfer schemes, including the payment of compensation to third parties whose interests or rights are extinguished or diminished in value on the transfer of assets or liabilities.

Section 6   SCHEDULE 2

SUCCESSOR COMPANIES

Initial Government holding in any successor company

1.—(1) As a consequence of the vesting in a successor company of property, rights and liabilities in accordance with a transfer scheme, that company shall issue such securities of the company as the Secretary of State may from time to time direct—

(a) to the Treasury or the Secretary of State, or

(b) to any person entitled to require the issue of the securities following their initial allotment, in accordance with directions of the Secretary of State, to the Treasury or the Secretary of State.

(2) As a consequence of the vesting referred to in sub-paragraph (1) above, any successor company which is a wholly-owned subsidiary of the Authority shall also issue such securities of the company as the Authority may with the consent of the Secretary of State from time to time direct—

(a) to the Authority, or

(b) to any person entitled to require the issue of the securities following their initial allotment to the Authority.

(3) No direction shall be given to a successor company under sub-paragraph (1) or (2) above at any time after that company has ceased to be publicly owned.

(4) Securities to be issued or allotted in pursuance of this paragraph shall be issued or allotted at such time or times, and (subject to sub-paragraph (5) below) on such terms, as may be specified in the direction.

(5) Any shares issued in pursuance of this paragraph—

(a) shall be of such nominal value as the Secretary of State may direct, and

(b) shall be issued as fully paid and treated for the purposes of the Companies Act 1985 as if they had been paid up by virtue of the payment to the company of their nominal value in cash.

(6) The Secretary of State may not exercise any power conferred on him by this paragraph, or dispose of any securities issued or of any rights to securities initially allotted to him in pursuance of this paragraph, without the consent of the Treasury.

Government investment in securities of successor company

2.—(1) The Treasury or, with the consent of the Treasury, the Secretary of State may at any time acquire—

(a) securities of a successor company, or

(b) rights to subscribe for any such securities.

(2) The Secretary of State may not dispose of any securities or rights acquired by virtue of this paragraph without the consent of the Treasury.

(3) Any expenses incurred by the Treasury or the Secretary of State in consequence of the provisions of this paragraph shall be paid out of money provided by Parliament.

Exercise of functions through nominees

3.—(1) The Treasury or, with the consent of the Treasury, the Secretary of State may, for the purposes of paragraph 1 or 2 above, appoint any person to act as the nominee, or one of the nominees, of the Treasury or the Secretary of State; and—

(a) securities of a company may be issued under paragraph 1 above to any nominee of the Treasury or of the Secretary of State appointed for the purposes of that paragraph or to any person entitled to require the issue of the securities following their initial allotment to any such nominee, and

(b) any such nominee appointed for the purposes of paragraph 2 above may acquire securities or rights under that paragraph,

in accordance with directions given from time to time by the Treasury or, with the consent of the Treasury, by the Secretary of State.

(2) Any person holding any securities or rights as a nominee of the Treasury or the Secretary of State by virtue of sub-paragraph (1) above shall hold and deal with them (or any of them) on such terms and in such manner as the Treasury or, with the consent of the Treasury, the Secretary of State may direct.

Payment of dividends etc. into Consolidated Fund

4. Any dividends or other sums received by the Treasury or the Secretary of State in right of, or on the disposal of, any securities or rights acquired by virtue of paragraph 1 or 2 above shall be paid into the Consolidated Fund.

Statutory accounts

5.—(1) The following provisions of this paragraph shall have effect for the purposes of any statutory accounts of a successor company.

(2) The vesting in the company effected by any transfer scheme shall be taken—

(a) to have been effected immediately after the end of the last financial year of the Authority to end before the coming into force of the scheme, and

(b) to have been a vesting of such property, rights and liabilities as are determined by or under the scheme.

(3) The value of any asset and the amount of any liability which is taken by virtue of sub-paragraph (2) above to have been vested in the company shall be taken to have been—

(a) in the case where the value or amount is determined by or under the transfer scheme, that value or amount, and

(b) in any other case, the value or amount assigned to the asset or liability for the purposes of the statements of account prepared by the Authority under section 4(3) of the Atomic Energy Authority Act 1954 in respect of their last financial year to end before the day on which the scheme comes into force.

(4) In this paragraph "statutory accounts", in relation to a company, means any accounts of that company prepared for the purposes of any provision of the Companies Act 1985 (including group accounts).

Distributable reserves of successor companies

6.—(1) Where statutory accounts of a successor company prepared as at any time would show the company as having net assets in excess of the aggregate of—

(a) its called-up share capital, and

(b) the amount, apart from any property, rights and liabilities to which the company has become entitled or subject in accordance with any transfer scheme, of its undistributable reserves,

then, for the purposes of section 263 of the Companies Act 1985 (profits available for distribution) and of the preparation as at that time of any statutory accounts of the company, that excess shall be treated, except so far as the Secretary of State may otherwise direct, as representing an excess of the company's accumulated realised profits over its accumulated realised losses.

(2) For the purposes of section 264 of the Companies Act 1985 (restriction on distribution of assets) so much of any excess of a company's net assets as falls, in accordance with a direction under this paragraph, to be treated otherwise than as representing an excess of the company's accumulated realised profits over its accumulated realised losses shall be treated (subject to any modification of that direction by a subsequent direction under this paragraph) as comprised in the company's undistributable reserves.

(3) A direction under this paragraph may provide, in relation to any amount to which it applies, that, on the realisation (whether before or after the company in question ceases to be publicly owned) of such profits and losses as may be specified or described in the direction, so much of that amount as may be determined in accordance with the direction is to cease to be treated as mentioned in sub-paragraph (2) above and is to fall to be treated as comprised in the company's accumulated realised profits.

(4) The Secretary of State shall not give a direction under this paragraph in relation to a successor company at any time after the company has ceased to be publicly owned.

(5) The consent of the Treasury shall be required for the giving of a direction under this paragraph.

(6) In this paragraph—

"called-up share capital" has the same meaning as in the Companies Act 1985;

"net assets" has the meaning given by subsection (2) of section 264 of that Act;

"undistributable reserves" has the meaning given by subsection (3) of that section;

and references in this paragraph, in relation to a company, to statutory accounts are references to accounts of that company prepared in respect of any period in accordance with the requirements of that Act, or with those requirements applied with such modifications as are necessary where that period is not an accounting reference period.

Dividends

7.—(1) Where a distribution is proposed to be declared during any accounting reference period of a successor company which includes a transfer date or before any accounts are laid or filed in respect of such a period, sections 270 to 276 of the Companies Act 1985 (accounts relevant for determining whether a distribution may be made by a company) shall have effect as if—

(a) references in section 270 to the company's accounts or to accounts relevant under that section, and

(b) references in section 273 to initial accounts,

included references to such accounts as, on the assumptions stated in sub-paragraph (2) below, would have been prepared under section 226 of that Act in respect of the relevant year (in this paragraph referred to as "the relevant accounts").

(2) Those assumptions are—

(a) that the relevant year had been a financial year of the successor company,

(b) that the vesting effected by this Act in accordance with the transfer scheme had been a vesting of all the property, rights and liabilities transferred to the company by that scheme and had been effected immediately after the beginning of that year,

(c) that the value of any asset and the amount of any liability of the Authority vested in the successor company by virtue of the transfer scheme had been the value or (as the case may be) amount determined by or under the transfer scheme or (if there is no such determination) the value or amount assigned to the asset or liability for the purposes of the statements of account prepared by the Authority under section 4(3) of the Atomic Energy Authority Act 1954 in respect of their financial year immediately preceding the relevant year,

(d) that any securities of the successor company issued or allotted before the declaration of the distribution had been issued or allotted before the end of the relevant year, and

(e) such other assumptions (if any) as may appear to the directors of the successor company to be necessary or expedient for the purposes of this paragraph.

(3) The relevant accounts shall not be regarded as statutory accounts for the purposes of paragraph 5 above.

(4) In this paragraph—
"accounting reference period" has the meaning given by section 224 of the Companies Act 1985;
"complete financial year" means a financial year ending with 31st March;
"the relevant year", in relation to any transfer date, means the last complete financial year ending before that date;
"a transfer date", in relation to a successor company, means the date of the coming into force of any transfer scheme in accordance with which any property, rights and liabilities are transferred to that company.

Application of Trustee Investments Act 1961

8.—(1) For the purpose of applying paragraph 3(b) of Part IV of Schedule 1 to the Trustee Investments Act 1961 (which provides that shares and debentures of a company shall not count as wider-range and narrower-range investments respectively within the meaning of that Act unless the company has paid dividends in each of the five years immediately preceding that in which the investment is made) in relation to investment in shares or debentures of a successor company during the calendar year in which the transfer date falls ("the first investment year") or during any year following that year, the successor company shall be deemed to have paid a dividend as there mentioned—
  (a) in every year preceding the first investment year which is included in the relevant five years, and
  (b) in the first investment year, if that year is included in the relevant five years and the successor company does not in fact pay such a dividend in that year.
(2) In sub-paragraph (1) above—
"the relevant five years" means the five years immediately preceding the year in which the investment in question is made or proposed to be made;
"the transfer date", in relation to a successor company, means the first date on which any transfer scheme in accordance with which any property, rights and liabilities are transferred to that company comes into force.

Accounts to be laid before Parliament

9. As soon as practicable after the holding of any general meeting of a successor company which is wholly owned by the Crown, the Secretary of State shall lay before each House of Parliament a copy of any accounts which, in accordance with any requirement of the Companies Act 1985, are laid before the company at that meeting, and of any documents which are annexed or attached to any such accounts.

Temporary restrictions on borrowing of companies

10.—(1) If the articles of association of a successor company confer on the Secretary of State powers exercisable with the consent of the Treasury for, or in connection with, restricting the sums of money which may be borrowed or raised during any period by the group to which that company belongs, those powers shall be exercisable in the national interest notwithstanding any rule of law and the provisions of any enactment.
(2) For the purposes of sub-paragraph (1) above an alteration of the articles of association of a successor company shall be disregarded if the alteration—
  (a) has the effect of conferring or extending any such power as is mentioned in that sub-paragraph, and
  (b) is made at a time when that company has ceased to be publicly owned.
(3) In this paragraph "group", in relation to a company, means that company and all of its subsidiaries taken together.

Government lending to the companies

11.—(1) Subject to paragraph 13 below, the Secretary of State may, with the approval of the Treasury, make loans of such amounts as he thinks fit to any successor company which is wholly owned by the Crown.
(2) Subject to section 10 of this Act, any loans which the Secretary of State makes under this paragraph shall be repaid to him at such times and by such methods, and interest thereon shall be paid to him at such rates and at such times, as he may, with the approval of the Treasury, from time to time direct.
(3) The Treasury may issue out of the National Loans Fund to the Secretary of State such sums as are required by him for making loans under this paragraph.
(4) Any sums received under sub-paragraph (2) above by the Secretary of State shall be paid into the National Loans Fund.

(5) It shall be the duty of the Secretary of State as respects each financial year—

(a) to prepare, in such form as the Treasury may direct, an account of sums issued to him in pursuance of sub-paragraph (3) above and of sums received by him under sub-paragraph (2) above and of the disposal by him of the sums so issued or received, and

(b) to send the account to the Comptroller and Auditor General not later than the end of the month of August in the following financial year;

and the Comptroller and Auditor General shall examine, certify and report on the account and shall lay copies of it and of his report before each House of Parliament.

Treasury guarantees for loans

12.—(1) Subject to paragraph 13 below, the Treasury may guarantee, in such manner and on such terms as they may think fit, the repayment of the principal of, the payment of interest on, and the discharge of any other financial obligation in connection with, any sums which are borrowed from a person other than the Secretary of State by any successor company which is wholly owned by the Crown.

(2) Immediately after a guarantee is given under this paragraph, the Treasury shall lay a statement of the guarantee before each House of Parliament; and immediately after any sum is issued for fulfilling a guarantee so given, the Treasury shall so lay a statement relating to that sum.

(3) Any sums required by the Treasury for fulfilling a guarantee under this paragraph shall be charged on and issued out of the Consolidated Fund.

(4) If any sums are issued in fulfilment of a guarantee given under this paragraph, the company whose obligations are so fulfilled shall make to the Treasury, at such times and in such manner as the Treasury may from time to time direct—

(a) payments of such amounts as the Treasury may so direct in or towards repayment of the sums so issued, and

(b) payments of interest on what is outstanding for the time being in respect of sums so issued at such rate as the Treasury may so direct.

(5) Any sums received under sub-paragraph (4) above by the Treasury shall be paid into the Consolidated Fund.

Limit on borrowing by certain successor companies

13.—(1) The aggregate amount outstanding by way of principal in respect of—

(a) money borrowed by the Authority the liability to repay which is transferred in accordance with a transfer scheme to any of the companies to which this sub-paragraph applies,

(b) money borrowed by any of those companies,

(c) money borrowed for the repayment of which any of those companies is a guarantor or surety, and

(d) sums issued by the Treasury in fulfilment of guarantees under paragraph 12 above,

shall not exceed 100 million.

(2) The companies to which sub-paragraph (1) above applies are successor companies which are wholly owned by the Crown and any such company's wholly-owned subsidiaries.

(3) In sub-paragraph (1)(a) above, the reference to money borrowed by the Authority includes a reference to the Authority's commencing capital debt under section 1 of the Atomic Energy Authority Act 1986.

(4) Borrowing between a successor company and any of its wholly-owned subsidiaries, or between two such subsidiaries, shall not be taken into account for the purposes of sub-paragraph (1) above.

Certain persons not to be treated as shadow directors

14. None of the following persons, that is to say—

(a) the Treasury,

(b) the Secretary of State, or

(c) the Authority,

shall be regarded for any purpose of the Companies Act 1985 as a shadow director, within the meaning of that Act, of any successor company which is publicly owned.

The House of Commons Disqualification Act 1975

15. In the House of Commons Disqualification Act 1975, in Part III of Schedule 1 (other disqualifying offices) there shall be inserted (at the appropriate place) the following entry—

"Director of a publicly owned successor company (within the meaning of the Atomic Energy Authority Act 1995)";

and the like insertion shall be made in Part III of Schedule 1 to the Northern Ireland Assembly Disqualification Act 1975.

DEFINITIONS
  "the Authority": s.13.
  "debentures": s.13.
  "securities": s.13.
  "shares": s.13.
  "successor company": s.13.
  "subsidiary": s.13 and Companies Act 1985, ss.736(1) and 736A.
  "transfer scheme": s.1(2) and s.13.
  "wholly-owned subsidiary": s.13 and Companies Act 1985, ss.736(1) and 736A.
  "publicly owned": s.13(3).
  "called-up share capital": para. 6(6).
  "net assets": para. 6(6).
  "undistributable reserves": para. 6(6).
  "accounting reference period": para. 7(4) and Companies Act 1985, s.224.
  "complete financial year": para. 7(4).
  "the relevant year": para. 7(4).
  "a transfer date": para. 7(4).
  "the relevant five years": para. 8(2).
  "the transfer date": para. 8(2).
  "group": para. 10(3).

GENERAL NOTE
This Schedule provides details of the financial arrangements for and controls on successor companies while they are publicly owned. Following the vesting in a successor company of properties, rights and liabilities, the Secretary of State may direct such a company to issue shares and other securities to him, the Treasury or the Authority. The Government will also be able to acquire, at any time, securities of a successor company. The Schedule also deals with statutory accounts, the definition of profits and the payment of dividends, and temporary restrictions on borrowing by the companies. Government loans to and Treasury guarantees for other loans obtained by successor companies wholly owned by the Crown will have an overall limit of £100 million.

Section 8   SCHEDULE 3

TAXATION PROVISIONS

PART I

CORPORATION TAX

Interpretation of Part I

1.—(1) In this Part of this Schedule—
  "the 1988 Act" means the Income and Corporation Taxes Act 1988;
  "the Corporation Tax Acts" has the meaning given by section 831(1)(a) of the 1988 Act;
  "the Gains Act" means the Taxation of Chargeable Gains Act 1992.
(2) This Part of this Schedule shall be construed as one with the Corporation Tax Acts.

General

2. If a transfer scheme transfers property, rights and liabilities to a successor company, then, subject to paragraph 3 and paragraphs 15 to 19 below, the following provisions shall apply for the purposes of the Corporation Tax Acts in their application in respect of any accounting period beginning on or after the date on which the transfer scheme comes into force, namely—
  (a) any trade or part of a trade carried on by the Authority which is transferred in accordance with the transfer scheme to the successor company shall be treated as having been, at the time of its commencement and at all times since that time, a separate trade carried on by that company,

(b) the trade or trades carried on by the successor company on and after the date on which the transfer scheme comes into force shall be treated as the same trade or trades as that which, by virtue of paragraph (a) above, is treated as carried on before that date,

(c) all property, rights and liabilities of the Authority which are transferred in accordance with the transfer scheme to the successor company shall be treated as having been, at the time when they became vested in the Authority and at all times since that time, property, rights and liabilities of that company, and

(d) anything done by the Authority in relation to property, rights and liabilities which are transferred in accordance with the transfer scheme to the successor company shall be treated as having been done by the company.

Chargeable gains: general

3. Paragraph 2 above shall not apply for the purposes of corporation tax on chargeable gains; and no provision included in a scheme by virtue of paragraph 5(2)(a) of Schedule 1 to this Act shall have effect for those purposes.

4.—(1) Section 171(1) of the Gains Act (which makes provision in relation to the disposal of assets from one member of a group of companies to another member of the group) shall not apply where the disposal in question is a disposal in accordance with a transfer scheme from the Authority to a wholly-owned subsidiary of the Authority.

(2) In sub-paragraph (1) above "disposal" shall be construed in accordance with section 21(2) of the Gains Act (which relates to part disposals).

Chargeable gains: group transactions

5.—(1) For the purposes of section 179 of the Gains Act (company ceasing to be a member of a group), where any subsidiary of the Authority ("the degrouped company") ceases, by virtue of a qualifying transaction, to be a member of a group of companies including the Authority, the degrouped company shall not, by virtue of that transaction, be treated under that section as having sold, and immediately reacquired, any asset acquired from a company which was at the time of acquisition a member of that group.

(2) Where, disregarding any preparatory transactions, a subsidiary of the Authority would be regarded for the purposes of section 179 of the Gains Act (and, accordingly, of this paragraph) as ceasing to be a member of a group of companies including the Authority by virtue of a qualifying transaction, it shall be regarded for those purposes as so doing by virtue of the qualifying transaction and not by virtue of any preparatory transactions.

(3) In this paragraph—

"preparatory transaction" means anything done under or by virtue of the Atomic Energy Authority Act 1954, the Atomic Energy (Miscellaneous Provisions) Act 1981 or this Act for the purposes of initiating, advancing or facilitating the qualifying transaction in question;

"qualifying transaction" means—

(a) the transfer of any property, rights or liabilities of the Authority in accordance with a transfer scheme, or

(b) the disposal by the Authority of any securities of a successor company.

(4) Expressions used in this paragraph and in section 179 of the Gains Act have the same meaning in this paragraph as they have in that section.

Chargeable gains: debts

6.—(1) Where—

(a) any debt owed to the Authority is transferred to a successor company in accordance with a transfer scheme, and

(b) the Authority would have been the original creditor in relation to that debt for the purposes of section 251 of the Gains Act (debts: general provisions),

the successor company shall be treated as the original creditor for those purposes.

(2) Where, in accordance with a transfer scheme, any obligations of the Authority under a guarantee of the repayment of a loan are transferred to a successor company, the successor company shall be treated for the purposes of section 253(4) of the Gains Act (relief for guarantors) as a person who gave the guarantee.

Securities issued in pursuance of Act

7.—(1) For the purposes of the Corporation Tax Acts, any securities of a company issued in pursuance of section 10 of, or paragraph 1 of Schedule 2 to, this Act shall be treated as having been issued for a new consideration equal—

(a) in the case of a share, to its nominal value, and

(b) in the case of a debenture, to the principal sum payable under the debenture.

(2) The liability of a successor company under any debentures issued as mentioned in sub-paragraph (1) above shall be treated for the purposes of the Corporation Tax Acts as having been incurred wholly and exclusively for the purposes of the trade carried on by the company.

Group relief

8.—(1) None of the following, namely—

(a) the existence of the powers of the Secretary of State or the Authority under the relevant provisions,

(b) any direction given by the Secretary of State under any of the relevant provisions or section 3 of the Atomic Energy Authority Act 1954 so far as that direction relates to a restructuring transfer, or

(c) any arrangements so far as relating to a restructuring transfer,

shall be regarded as constituting arrangements falling within subsection (1) or (2) of section 410 of the 1988 Act (arrangements for the transfer of a company to another group or consortium).

(2) Neither the existence of the powers of the Secretary of State or the Authority under the relevant provisions nor a direction given as mentioned in sub-paragraph (1)(b) above shall be regarded as constituting option arrangements for the purposes of paragraph 5B of Schedule 18 to the 1988 Act.

(3) In this paragraph—

"arrangements" has the meaning given by section 410(5) of the 1988 Act;

"the relevant provisions" means sections 1 to 6 and 10 of, and Schedules 1 and 2 to, this Act;

"a restructuring transfer" means—

(a) the transfer in accordance with a transfer scheme of property, rights and liabilities of the Authority to a company wholly owned by the Crown, or

(b) the transfer by the Authority to the Secretary of State or the Treasury or his or their nominee of shares of a successor company.

Leases

9.—(1) Section 35 of the 1988 Act (charge on lease granted at an undervalue) shall not apply in the case of any lease which, in accordance with a transfer scheme, is granted—

(a) to a successor company, or

(b) by a successor company to the Authority.

(2) Section 87 of the 1988 Act (taxable premiums) shall not apply where there is an amount which would have become chargeable in relation to any land but for sub-paragraph (1) above; and, accordingly, references to any such amount shall not be included in references in that section to the amount chargeable.

(3) In this paragraph "lease" has the same meaning as in Part II of the 1988 Act.

Sale and lease back

10. Subsections (1) and (2) of section 779 of the 1988 Act (sale and lease back) shall not apply where the liability of the transferor (within the meaning of that section) or of the person associated with that transferor is as a result of—

(a) the creation in favour of a successor company or the Authority in accordance with a transfer scheme of any interest or right,

(b) any other transaction for which a transfer scheme transferring property, rights and liabilities to a successor company provides, or

(c) the grant by a successor company ("the relevant company") to the Authority or to another successor company of any interest or right, at a time when the relevant company remains publicly owned, in a case where the ability of the relevant company to grant that interest or right derives from the vesting in the company in accordance with a transfer scheme of an estate or interest in land.

Leased assets

11.—(1) For the purposes of section 781 of the 1988 Act (assets leased to traders and others), where the interest of the lessor or the lessee under a lease, or any other interest in an asset, vests in a successor company or the Authority in accordance with a transfer scheme, the vesting shall be treated as being effected without any capital sum having been obtained in respect of that interest by the Authority or the successor company.

(2) Section 782 of the 1988 Act (deduction of payment under leases: special cases) shall not apply to any payments made by a successor company or the Authority—

(a) under any lease granted to a successor company or the Authority for the purposes of the creation in accordance with a transfer scheme of any leasehold interest, including, where effect has been given without the grant of a lease to the creation of a leasehold interest in accordance with such a scheme, any lease to which effect is so given, or

(b) under any lease—

    (i) which is granted to or by a successor company at a time when it remains publicly owned, and

    (ii) which is a lease of an asset which at any time before the creation of the lease was used by the Authority for the purposes of a trade carried on by the Authority and which was, when so used, owned by the Authority.

(3) In this paragraph "lease" and "asset" have the meanings given by section 785 of the 1988 Act and references to a leasehold interest are references to any such interest as may subsist under a lease.

Write-off of government investment

12.—(1) Subsection (1) of section 400 of the 1988 Act (write-off of government investment: restriction of tax losses) shall not have effect—

(a) in relation to any extinguishment by order under section 10 of this Act of—

    (i) any liabilities of the Authority, or

    (ii) any liabilities of a successor company which fall within section 10(12)(b)(i) of this Act, or

(b) in relation to any extinguishment by order under that section of any liabilities of a successor company which fall within section 10(12)(b)(ii) of this Act, if and to the extent that those liabilities are replaced by securities issued by the company in accordance with a direction under section 10(5) of this Act.

(2) Subsection (6) of section 400 of the 1988 Act shall apply in relation to any extinguishment of any liabilities of a successor company by an order under section 10 of this Act as if the reference to the body in question were a reference to the company whose liabilities are extinguished.

Modifications of transfer scheme

13. Where the effect of any transfer scheme is modified in pursuance of any agreement which takes effect under paragraph 8(2) of Schedule 1 to this Act, the Corporation Tax Acts and this Part of this Schedule shall have effect as if—

(a) the scheme originally made had been the scheme as modified, and

(b) anything done by or in relation to the person who without the modification became entitled or subject in accordance with the scheme to any property, rights or liabilities had, so far as relating to the property, rights or liabilities to which another person becomes entitled or subject in consequence of the modification, been done by or in relation to that other person.

PART II

CAPITAL ALLOWANCES

Interpretation of Part II

14.—(1) In this Part of this Schedule—

"the 1988 Act" means the Income and Corporation Taxes Act 1988;

"the Capital Allowances Acts" has the meaning given by section 832(1) of the 1988 Act.

(2) In any provision of this Part of this Schedule "the prescribed amount", in relation to any successor company, means such amount as may be specified by the Secretary of State by order for the purposes of that provision in its application to that company.

(3) This Part of this Schedule shall be construed as one with the Capital Allowances Acts.

Industrial buildings and structures

15. The Secretary of State may, for the purposes of section 3 of the Capital Allowances Act 1990 (writing-down allowances in respect of expenditure on industrial buildings and structures) by order make provision specifying—

(a) the amount to be taken for the purposes of subsection (3) of that section as the residue, on the date on which a transfer scheme comes into force, of any expenditure in relation to which any property vested in a successor company in accordance with that transfer scheme is a relevant interest for the purposes of that section, and

(b) the part of the period mentioned in subsection (3) of that section which is to be treated, in relation to any such property, as unexpired on that date.

Machinery and plant

16. For the purposes of Part II of the Capital Allowances Act 1990 (capital allowances in respect of machinery and plant) property which is vested in a successor company in accordance with a transfer scheme shall be treated as if—

    (a) it had been acquired by that company, for the purposes for which it is used by that company on and after the date on which the scheme comes into force, on that date, and

    (b) capital expenditure of the prescribed amount had been incurred on that date by that company on the acquisition of the property for the purposes mentioned in paragraph (a) above.

Scientific research

17.—(1) For the purposes of Part VII of the Capital Allowances Act 1990 (scientific research), a successor company in which an asset representing allowable scientific research expenditure is vested in accordance with a transfer scheme shall be treated as having incurred, on the date on which the transfer scheme comes into force, expenditure of a capital nature of the prescribed amount on the scientific research in question; and that research shall be taken to have been directly undertaken by the successor company or on its behalf.

(2) In sub-paragraph (1) above "allowable scientific research expenditure" means expenditure of a capital nature incurred by the Authority on scientific research directly undertaken by the Authority or on their behalf.

(3) In this paragraph "asset" and "scientific research" have the meaning given by subsection (1) of section 139 of the Capital Allowances Act 1990; and references to expenditure incurred on scientific research shall be construed in accordance with that subsection.

Patent rights

18.—(1) For the purposes of section 520 of the 1988 Act (allowances for expenditure on purchase of patent rights), a successor company in which any patent rights of the Authority are vested in accordance with a transfer scheme shall be treated as having incurred, on the date on which the transfer scheme comes into force, capital expenditure of the prescribed amount on the purchase of those patent rights for use in any trade in which they are, or are to be, used on or after that date.

(2) In this paragraph "patent rights" has the meaning given by section 533 of the 1988 Act.

Know-how

19.—(1) For the purposes of section 530 of the 1988 Act (disposal of know-how), a successor company in which any know-how of the Authority is vested in accordance with a transfer scheme shall be treated as having incurred, on the date on which the transfer scheme comes into force, capital expenditure of the prescribed amount on the acquisition of that know-how for use in any trade in which it is, or is to be, used on or after that date.

(2) Subsections (2) and (7) of section 531 of the 1988 Act (provisions supplementary to section 530) shall not apply in relation to any disposal from the Authority to a successor company in accordance with a transfer scheme.

(3) In this paragraph "know-how" has the meaning given by section 533(7) of the 1988 Act.

Connected persons

20. In Part II of the Capital Allowances Act 1990 (machinery and plant) and Chapter I of Part XIII of the 1988 Act (intellectual property) references to a transaction (however described) between connected persons within the meaning of section 839 of the 1988 Act shall not include references to—

    (a) a transfer to a successor company in accordance with a transfer scheme of any property, rights and liabilities, or

    (b) the creation in favour of a successor company or the Authority in accordance with a transfer scheme of any interest or right.

Orders under Part II

21.—(1) The Secretary of State shall not make an order under this Part of this Schedule in relation to any successor company except with the consent of the Treasury and at a time when the company is publicly owned.

(2) In exercising any power to make an order under this Part of this Schedule in relation to any asset vested in a successor company in accordance with a transfer scheme, the matters to which the Secretary of State shall have regard include such information as he considers appropriate as

to the price which the asset would fetch or have fetched if sold on the open market on the date on which the transfer scheme comes into force.

(3) Any power of the Secretary of State to make an order under this Part of this Schedule—

(a) shall be exercisable by statutory instrument, and

(b) shall include power to make different provision for different cases, including different provision in relation to different assets or descriptions of assets.

Modifications of transfer scheme

22. Where the effect of any transfer scheme is modified in pursuance of any agreement which takes effect under paragraph 8(2) of Schedule 1 to this Act, the Capital Allowances Acts and this Part of this Schedule shall have effect as if—

(a) the scheme originally made had been the scheme as modified, and

(b) anything done by or in relation to the person who without the modification became entitled or subject in accordance with the scheme to any property, rights or liabilities had, so far as relating to the property, rights or liabilities to which another person becomes entitled or subject in consequence of the modification, been done by or in relation to that other person.

PART III

STAMP DUTY AND STAMP DUTY RESERVE TAX

Transactions attracting exemptions

23. For the purposes of this Part of this Schedule a transaction is an exempt transaction if it is a transaction by virtue of which property, rights or liabilities are vested by or under this Act in any of the following persons, that is to say—

(a) the Authority,

(b) a company which is wholly owned by the Crown, and

(c) a wholly-owned subsidiary of the Authority.

Stamp duty

24.—(1) Subject to sub-paragraph (2) below, an exempt transaction shall not give rise to any charge to stamp duty except in so far as the charge to duty is on an instrument under this Act which is neither a transfer scheme nor an instrument that has been certified to the Commissioners of Inland Revenue by the Secretary of State to have been made—

(a) in pursuance of a transfer scheme, or

(b) by virtue of any provision of this Act, for the purpose of modifying the effect of such a scheme.

(2) No instrument which is certified as mentioned in sub-paragraph (1) above shall be taken to be duly stamped unless—

(a) it is stamped with the duty to which it would, but for that sub-paragraph, be liable, or

(b) it has, in accordance with section 12 of the Stamp Act 1891, been stamped with a particular stamp denoting that it is not chargeable with that duty or that it is duly stamped.

Stamp duty reserve tax

25. No agreement for the purposes of, or for purposes connected with giving effect to—

(a) so much of any transfer scheme as relates to an exempt transaction, or

(b) any exempt transaction to which effect is given by the modification of any transfer scheme,

shall give rise to a charge to stamp duty reserve tax.

DEFINITIONS

"the Authority": s.13.

"debentures": s.13.

"securities": s.13.

"shares": s.13.

"subsidiary": s.13 and Companies Act 1985 ss.736(1) and 736A.

"wholly-owned subsidiary": s.13.

"successor company": s.13.

"transfer scheme": s.13.

"publicly owned": s.13(3).

"a company wholly-owned by the Crown": s.13.

"the 1988 Act": para. 1. and para. 14(1).

"the Corporation Tax Acts": para. 1(1).
"the Gains Act": para. 1(1).
"disposal": para. 4(2).
"preparatory transaction": para. 5(3).
"qualifying transaction": para. 5(3).
"original creditor": para. 6(1).
"guarantor": para. 6(2).
"arrangements": para. 8(3).
"the relevant provisions": para. 8(3).
"a restructuring transfer": para. 8(3).
"lease": para. 9(3) and para. 11(3).
"asset": para. 11(3) and para. 17(3).
"leasehold interest": para. 11(3).
"the Capital Allowances Act": para. 14(1) and s.832(1) of the 1988 Act.
"the prescribed amount": para. 14(2).
"allowable scientific research expenditure": para. 17(2).
"scientific research": para. 17(3).
"patent rights": para. 18(2).
"know-how": para. 19(3).
"connected persons": para. 20.

GENERAL NOTE

This schedule makes provision for the tax consequences of a transfer of property, rights and liabilities to a successor company and the tax effects of issuing securities, and of extinguishing liabilities. It also provides a mechanism for determining future capital allowances in respect of any assets transferred to a successor company, and relieves the Authority and successor companies from the obligation to pay stamp duty or stamp duty reserve tax in respect of any transfer of property by or under a scheme. The provisions are intended to be tax neutral to a successor company [Standing Committee D, April 20, 1995 cols. 146 and 147. *Hansard*, H.L. Vol. 564, cols. 732 and 757].

Section 9   SCHEDULE 4

PENSIONS

Interpretation

1.—(1) In this Schedule—
"Authority pension scheme" means any pension scheme maintained by the Authority under paragraph 7(2)(b) of Schedule 1 to the Atomic Energy Authority Act 1954;
"participant", in relation to a pension scheme, means a person to whom pension rights are accruing under the scheme by virtue of his employment in a class or description of employment to which the scheme relates, and cognate expressions shall be construed accordingly.

(2) Any reference in this Schedule to a transfer scheme includes a reference to a modification agreement as defined in paragraph 8(7) of Schedule 1 to this Act.

Application of Authority pension schemes to employees of publicly owned successor companies

2.—(1) Subject to sub-paragraphs (2) and (4) below—
(a) no person who in consequence of a transfer scheme becomes an employee of a successor company (in this paragraph referred to as a "transferred employee") and who immediately before the coming into force of the transfer scheme is a participant in an Authority pension scheme, shall cease to be a participant in that scheme by reason only that he has ceased to be employed by the Authority, and
(b) no transferred employee who immediately before the coming into force of the transfer scheme is not a participant in such a pension scheme, but—
    (i) is eligible to become such a participant, or
    (ii) would have become eligible to become such a participant on attaining an age or fulfilling a condition specified in the scheme,
shall be precluded from being or, as the case requires, becoming eligible for participation in that scheme by reason only that he has ceased to be employed by the Authority.

(2) A transferred employee shall not by virtue of sub-paragraph (1) above be entitled to participate in an Authority pension scheme at any time after he has with his agreement become a participant—

(a) in a pension scheme maintained by the successor company of which he became an employee, or

(b) by virtue of his employment by that successor company, in a pension scheme maintained by any other person.

(3) An Authority pension scheme may apply to persons, other than transferred employees, who are employed by any publicly owned successor company, as well as to—

(a) transferred employees to whom the scheme is applicable by virtue of sub-paragraph (1) above, and

(b) persons to whom the scheme is applicable apart from the provisions of this Schedule.

(4) Where a successor company ceases to be publicly owned, no person employed by the company shall, from the time when it so ceases, be entitled to participate in any Authority pension scheme by virtue of his employment with the company.

Power of Secretary of State to require amendment of schemes

3.—(1) The Secretary of State may direct the Authority to make such amendments of any Authority pension scheme as may be specified in the direction for any of the following purposes—

(a) for providing that, in the case of any director or other officer of a publicly owned successor company who, immediately before he becomes such a director or other officer—

(i) is a participant in an Authority pension scheme, or

(ii) is not such a participant, but was or would have become eligible as mentioned in paragraph 2(1)(b)(i) or (ii) above,

the provisions of any Authority pension scheme having effect in relation to employees of the successor company shall have effect with such modifications as may be specified,

(b) for requiring or enabling funds to be transferred under an Authority scheme in cases where, by virtue of paragraph 2(4) above or on becoming in consequence of a transfer scheme employees of a person other than the Authority or a successor company, persons cease to be included in an Authority pension scheme and for prescribing the method of calculating the amounts to be transferred and the assumptions to be used in calculating those amounts, and

(c) for giving effect to paragraph 2 above.

(2) A direction under this paragraph may require the Authority to make such supplemental, consequential and transitional provision amending any Authority pension scheme as the Secretary of State considers appropriate.

(3) It shall be the duty of the Secretary of State, before giving a direction under this paragraph, to consult the Authority, the Treasury and persons appearing to him to represent the employees of the Authority likely to be affected by the direction.

(4) No direction under this paragraph affecting employees of a successor company may be given after that company has ceased to be publicly owned.

(5) Sub-paragraphs (1) to (4) above shall be without prejudice to the power of the Secretary of State to give directions under section 3 of the Atomic Energy Authority Act 1954.

Payments to Authority by successor companies

4. In respect of—

(a) any payments falling to be made by the Authority in consequence of the participation by virtue of paragraph 2 or 3 above in an Authority pension scheme of persons employed by any successor company or of directors or other officers of such a company, or

(b) the accruing liability of the Authority for any such payments,

the company shall pay to the Authority such sums as may be agreed between the company and the Authority or as, in default of such agreement, the Secretary of State may direct.

Establishment of pension scheme by successor company

5. Except with the consent of the Secretary of State, a publicly owned successor company shall not—

(a) establish or maintain any pension scheme, or

(b) enter into any arrangement under which employees of the company become eligible to participate, by reference to their employment with the company, in a pension scheme maintained by any other person.

Duties owed where employee transferred by scheme

6.—(1) Before the coming into force of any transfer scheme in consequence of which any employee of the Authority is to become the employee of a person ("the transferee") other than the Authority or a company which will, by virtue of that transfer scheme, be a successor company, the Authority shall, after such consultation as is required by sub-paragraph (5) below, satisfy themselves—

(a) that every person to whom the duty imposed by this sub-paragraph is owed will be afforded, and will be entitled to exercise (or, in a case falling within sub-paragraph (2)(b)(ii) below, entitled on attaining the age or fulfilling the condition to exercise), an option of becoming—

(i) a participant in a pension scheme maintained by the transferee, or

(ii) by virtue of his employment by the transferee, a participant in a pension scheme maintained by any other person, and

(b) that in his case the provisions of that scheme (taken as a whole) confer benefits which taking into account other benefits which he will obtain as a result of his employment by the transferee, are no less favourable than the benefits conferred by the provisions, as in force immediately before the coming into force of the transfer scheme, of the Authority pension scheme in which he is then or, as the case requires, would be entitled to become, a participant.

(2) The duty imposed by sub-paragraph (1) above shall be owed to every transferred employee who—

(a) is for the time being a participant in an Authority pension scheme, or

(b) is not for the time being such a participant but—

(i) is eligible to participate in an Authority pension scheme, or

(ii) would become eligible to participate in such a scheme on attaining an age or fulfilling a condition specified in the scheme.

(3) In sub-paragraph (2) above a "transferred employee", in relation to any transfer scheme, means any person who, in consequence of the scheme, becomes an employee of the transferee.

(4) In relation to any transfer scheme made by the Secretary of State by virtue of section 2(3) of this Act, the duty under sub-paragraph (1) above is owed by the Secretary of State instead of the Authority.

(5) The consultation required by this sub-paragraph is—

(a) in a case where the duty under sub-paragraph (1) above is owed by the Authority, consultation with the Secretary of State, the Treasury and persons appearing to the Authority to represent transferred employees, and

(b) in a case where that duty is owed by the Secretary of State, consultation with the Authority, the Treasury and persons appearing to the Secretary of State to represent transferred employees.

(6) Nothing in this paragraph shall be regarded as limiting the powers of the Authority or the Secretary of State in relation to the making of transfer schemes.

Duties owed where the successor company ceases to be publicly owned

7.—(1) Before a successor company ceases to be publicly owned, the relevant owner shall, after such consultation as is required by sub-paragraph (4) below, satisfy himself—

(a) that every person to whom the duty imposed by this sub-paragraph is owed will be afforded, and will be entitled to exercise (or, in a case falling within sub-paragraph (3)(b)(ii) below, entitled on attaining the age or fulfilling the condition to exercise), an option of becoming—

(i) a participant in a pension scheme maintained by the successor company, or

(ii) by virtue of his employment by that successor company, a participant in a pension scheme maintained by any other person, and

(b) that in his case the provisions of that scheme (taken as a whole) confer benefits which, taking into account other benefits which he will obtain as a result of his employment by the successor company, are no less favourable than the benefits conferred by the provisions, as in force immediately before the company ceases to be publicly owned, of the Authority pension scheme in which he is then or, as the case requires, would be entitled to become, a participant.

(2) In sub-paragraph (1) above, "the relevant owner" means—

(a) in relation to a company wholly owned by the Crown, the Secretary of State, and

(b) in relation to a wholly-owned subsidiary of the Authority, the Authority.

(3) The duty imposed by sub-paragraph (1) above shall be owed to every person employed by the successor company immediately before it ceases to be publicly owned who—

(a) is for the time being a participant in an Authority pension scheme, or

(b) is not for the time being such a participant but—

(i) is eligible to participate in an Authority pension scheme, or

(ii) would become eligible to participate in such a scheme on attaining an age or fulfilling a condition specified in the scheme.

(4) The consultation required by this sub-paragraph is—

(a) in a case where the company is wholly owned by the Crown, consultation with the Authority, the Treasury and persons appearing to the Secretary of State to represent employees of the company, and

(b) in a case where the company is a wholly-owned subsidiary of the Authority, consultation with the Secretary of State, the Treasury and persons appearing to the Authority to represent employees of the company.

(5) Nothing in this paragraph shall be regarded as limiting the powers of the Authority, the Treasury or the Secretary of State to dispose of any securities of a successor company.

DEFINITIONS

"the Authority": s.13.

"transfer scheme": s.13 and s.1(2).

"successor company": s.13.

"publicly owned": s.13(3).

"securities": s.13.

"Authority pension scheme": para. 1(1).

"participant": para. 1(1).

"transferred employee": para. 2(1).

"the relevant owner": para. 7(2).

"wholly owned by the Crown": s.13(2).

"subsidiary": s.13 and Companies Act 1985 ss.736(1) and 736A.

"wholly-owned subsidiary": s.13 and Companies Act 1985, ss.736(1) and 736A.

GENERAL NOTE

This Schedule enables Authority employees to remain in the Authority's pension schemes after transfer to a successor company and while those companies remain publicly owned. It provides the Secretary of State with powers to amend such pension schemes, to provide for such employees, and for contributions to be made to Authority schemes by successor companies. It also obliges the Secretary of State or the Authority (as the case may be) to be satisfied before sale, that the buyer will offer employees a pension scheme no less favourable than the Authority's pension scheme (*Hansard*, H.L. Vol. 564, col. 732).

INDEX

References are to sections and Schedules

CIVIL EVIDENCE ACT 1995*

(1995 c. 38)

An Act to provide for the admissibility of hearsay evidence, the proof of certain documentary evidence and the admissibility and proof of official actuarial tables in civil proceedings; and for connected purposes.

[8th November 1995]

PARLIAMENTARY DEBATES
Hansard, H.L. Vol. 564, col. 1048; Vol. 565, col. 217, 754, 1246. H.C. Vol. 263, col. 1566; Vol. 265, col. 201.

INTRODUCTION AND GENERAL NOTE

This Act enacts the Law Commission's proposals for the reform of the hearsay rule in civil proceedings, with minor amendments and one substantial addition. The Act has its genesis in the draft Bill appended to the Commission's Report (Law Com. No. 216), published in September 1993, to which general reference may be made. The main effect of the Act is to replace Part I of the Civil Evidence Act 1968 (c. 64) with new, simpler provisions.

In a system where the norm is for evidence to be given orally, on oath, in the presence of the court, a degree of suspicion naturally attaches to any attempt by a party to encourage the court to rely on statements made out of court, not on oath, not capable of being tested or evaluated by the process of cross-examination and observation to which other evidence is subject. This suspicion gave rise to the hearsay rule, which excludes such statements. It may be classically, or "narrowly" stated as follows: a statement, other than one made by a person while giving oral evidence in the proceedings, is inadmissible as evidence of the matter stated. Thus, an out-of-court statement may be admissible if the mere fact that it was made is of some relevance in the pro-

---

* Annotations by Mark Ockelton M.A., B.D., Barrister, Senior Lecturer in Law, The University of Leeds.

ceedings, but if the court is asked to rely on it, *i.e.* use it as evidence of the very matter stated, it is inadmissible as hearsay. Over the years a number of exceptions to the rule were developed or introduced by statute, allowing hearsay evidence in a variety of special cases where either there was no other evidence obtainable, or the out-of-court statement (or document) was likely to be especially reliable. In civil proceedings in particular, after the decline of civil jury trials, the hearsay rule was found to be unduly restrictive. Judges sitting in civil cases built up a body of expertise in the evaluation of evidence, and could be trusted to attribute appropriate weight to evidence that came to them indirectly. Following recommendations of the Law Reform Committee, Thirteenth Report, *Hearsay Evidence in Civil Proceedings*, Cmnd. 2964 (1966), Parliament enacted the Civil Evidence Act 1968 ("the 1968 Act"). Part I of that Act made all statements (whether hearsay or not) admissible, but restricted the mode of proof of multiple oral hearsay, with the result that statements made in documents, and first-hand oral hearsay ("A told me that X happened"), became admissible. Second-hand hearsay ("A told me that B told him that X happened") or multiple hearsay ("A told me that B told him that C told her . . .") might be admissible if it formed part of a business record. There were complex procedural rules; and there were provisions dealing with computerised records, which inevitably became quickly outdated. The 1968 Act was far from comprehensive in its abolition of the hearsay rule, and was never extended to magistrates' courts; new statutory exceptions to the hearsay rule continued to be created, for example in s.18 of the Solicitors Act 1974 (c. 47) and ss.7 and 96 of the Children Act 1989 (c. 41). In the criminal field too, substantial inroads have been made by statute into the hearsay rule, notably by the Criminal Evidence Act 1965 (c. 20), and ss.23–26 of the Criminal Justice Act 1988 (c. 33).

Judicial development of the hearsay rule has taken a contrary direction. In *Myers v. D.P.P.* [1965] A.C. 1001, the House of Lords held that the courts have no power to create new exceptions to the hearsay rule, and in *Bradford City Metropolitan Council v. K.* [1990] Fam. 140 the Court of Appeal insisted that the strict rules of evidence, including the hearsay rule, applied in civil proceedings not governed by the 1968 Act. Not only was the rule enforced, it was also enlarged. If the problem about hearsay evidence is seen as the merely formal one that the statements in question are not made on oath before the court, it is possible to confine the rule, as a matter of definition, to the formulation given in the previous paragraph. But if the problem is seen as the wider one of relying on the mind of a person not available for cross-examination, a wider definition may be inevitable, for there are many situations where the force of circumstantial evidence derives from the observation, by the witness, of the conduct of another person. The question appears to have been first raised by Parke B. in a famous passage in *Wright v. Doe d. Tatham* (1837) 7 Ad. & Ell. 313. The court was invited to admit letters, in normal terms, written to the testator by persons not available to be witnesses, as evidence that the testator was sane. The argument was that by acting in this way (writing to him in normal terms) the authors of the letters were demonstrating their contemporaneous belief that the testator was sane, and their act in writing was accordingly evidence on which the court should rely. Parke B. refused to admit the evidence for this purpose:

"[The testator's] election, in his absence, to some high and responsible office; the conduct of a physician who permitted a will to be executed by a sick testator; the conduct of a deceased sea captain on a question of seaworthiness, who, after examining every part of a vessel, embarked in it with his family; all these, when deliberately considered are . . . mere instances of hearsay evidence, mere statements, not on oath, but implied in or vouched by the actual conduct of persons . . .".

This view has now been endorsed by the House of Lords in *R. v. Kearley* [1992] 2 A.C. 228, holding that, although the relevance of such evidence must often be dubious, if it is relevant it is in principle inadmissible as hearsay. In *R. v. Kearley* itself K was charged with drug-dealing. While the police were in occupation of his flat there were several calls, by telephone and at the door, by persons asking for K and for drugs. A majority of the House held that police evidence of the calls was (even if relevant) inadmissible hearsay if tendered to prove that K was a supplier. A similar result, this time against the defendant, was reached in *R. v. Harry* (1988) 86 Cr.App.R. 105, C.A. There the accused, who was jointly charged, was not allowed to adduce evidence, similar to that in *R. v. Kearley*, to show that it was his co-defendant, not he, who was the supplier. Thus it is now clearly established that the hearsay rule is to be taken in this wider sense.

The Law Commission issued Consultation Paper No. 117, *The Hearsay Rule in Civil Proceedings* in 1991. The Report, Law Com. No. 216, reflects the views of the Commission after taking account of the views of respondents. The very question of the scope of the rule is treated somewhat casually in the report, with the unfortunate effect that the Bill enacted appears not to have carried out the Commission's aim of the abolition of the hearsay rule (Law Com. No. 216, para. 1.7). Undoubtedly, however, the present Act goes a long way towards that aim, and even further towards the general and laudable end that all relevant evidence should be admissible, so that the weight of the evidence as a whole can be properly assessed by the trier of fact.

Section 1 of the Act substantially abolishes the hearsay rule in civil proceedings. Sections 2–6 contain provisions for giving notice of intention to adduce hearsay evidence, and guidance on its evaluation. Section 7 preserves a few common-law exceptions to the hearsay rule. Sections 8 and 9 contain provisions as to the proof of documents. Section 10 makes the Ogden Tables admissible in certain proceedings. Sections 11–16 are supplementary. There is a Schedule of amendments and one of repeals.

Admissibility of hearsay evidence

Admissibility of hearsay evidence

1.—(1) In civil proceedings evidence shall not be excluded on the ground that it is hearsay.

(2) In this Act—

(a) "hearsay" means a statement made otherwise than by a person while giving oral evidence in the proceedings which is tendered as evidence of the matters stated; and

(b) references to hearsay include hearsay of whatever degree.

(3) Nothing in this Act affects the admissibility of evidence admissible apart from this section.

(4) The provisions of sections 2 to 6 (safeguards and supplementary provisions relating to hearsay evidence) do not apply in relation to hearsay evidence admissible apart from this section, notwithstanding that it may also be admissible by virtue of this section.

DEFINITIONS
"civil proceedings": s.11.
"oral evidence": s.13.
"hearsay": subs. (2).
"statement": s.13.

GENERAL NOTE

Subs. (1)
This is the principal reform introduced by the Act. Its purpose is to abolish the hearsay rule in civil proceedings. Its effect is, however, considerably reduced by the definition of "hearsay", for it is only the rule against hearsay *as defined* that is abolished.

Subs. (2)
This subsection contains, in para. (a), the definition of hearsay for the purposes of the Act, and, in para. (b), a provision indicating that in this Act, unlike the 1968 Act, admissibility does not depend on hearsay's being "first-hand". The definition adopted is the "narrow" one (see Introduction and General Note).

A statement is a way of using words; words can be used in other ways, for example greeting, promising, commanding. Gestures or acts can also be used to make a statement, for example by nodding or by using sign language; but the body can be used in many other ways, for example stepping onto a boat. A statement (or assertion) is a communication of some fact: a statement differs from other uses of language or acts in that it is capable of being true or false (rather than, at best, merely appropriate or inappropriate). The sea-captain envisaged by Parke B. in *Wright v. Doe d. Tatham* (above) would not be stating anything, expressly or impliedly, by stepping onto the vessel, nor were the callers in *R. v. Kearley* (above). Statements may be imputed to them for the purposes of the hearsay rule, but those imaginary communications of fact cannot be called "statements made", which is the phrase used in subs. (2)(a): the problem arises precisely because no statement was made. It follows that the hearsay rule in its "wide", or *Kearley* sense, excludes much evidence which does not consist of statements. Only such hearsay as does consist of statements is made admissible by this Act. Other ("wider") hearsay is still inadmissible at common law and, following *Bradford City Metropolitan Council v. K.* (above) cannot form the basis of any finding of fact. There is no discretion to admit it; nor, in proceedings to which the rules of evidence apply, may it be admitted by agreement. It is a pity that this subsection was enacted. Without it, "hearsay" could have been left to bear its meaning at common law, so that the abolition would be co-extensive with the rule itself.

Subss. (3) and (4)
Subsection (3) provides that the Act does not affect the admissibility of any evidence (whether hearsay or not) which would be admissible apart from s.1. Subsection (4) provides that ss.2–6,

the notice and guidance provisions, do not affect hearsay evidence admissible apart from this section, even if the evidence is also admissible under this section. The effect is that this Act leaves unchanged, existing statutory provisions making hearsay admissible (for example, the Bankers' Books Evidence Act 1879 (c. 11), or the Children Act 1989 (c. 41), ss.7 and 96). The régime prescribed by such Acts remains in force for the evidence in question. Further, the Ogden Tables, which are made admissible by s.10, are not subject to ss.2–6.

Safeguards in relation to hearsay evidence

Notice of proposal to adduce hearsay evidence

2.—(1) A party proposing to adduce hearsay evidence in civil proceedings shall, subject to the following provisions of this section, give to the other party or parties to the proceedings—

(a) such notice (if any) of that fact, and

(b) on request, such particulars of or relating to the evidence,

as is reasonable and practicable in the circumstances for the purpose of enabling him or them to deal with any matters arising from its being hearsay.

(2) Provision may be made by rules of court—

(a) specifying classes of proceedings or evidence in relation to which subsection (1) does not apply, and

(b) as to the manner in which (including the time within which) the duties imposed by that subsection are to be complied with in the cases where it does apply.

(3) Subsection (1) may also be excluded by agreement of the parties; and compliance with the duty to give notice may in any case be waived by the person to whom notice is required to be given.

(4) A failure to comply with subsection (1), or with rules under subsection (2)(b), does not affect the admissibility of the evidence but may be taken into account by the court—

(a) in considering the exercise of its powers with respect to the course of proceedings and costs, and

(b) as a matter adversely affecting the weight to be given to the evidence in accordance with section 4.

DEFINITIONS
"civil proceedings": s.11.
"court": s.11.
"hearsay": s.1(2).
"rules of court": s.11.

GENERAL NOTE
The admission of hearsay under the 1968 Act required, in theory, compliance with a procedure of detailed notice and counter-notice within prescribed time-limits. The complexity of this procedure (set out in R.S.C., Ord. 38, rr. 20–34) was probably one of the reasons why the Act could not be extended to magistrates' courts, although in practice the procedure was rarely followed exactly: much evidence was admitted after waiver of the notice requirements by the party entitled to benefit by them (see *Rover International v. Cannon Film Sales* [1987] 1 W.L.R. 1597). This Act substitutes a greatly simplified procedure. In particular the following features are to be noted. First, to avoid taking the other party by surprise, there is a general duty to give notice of the intention to rely on hearsay evidence: subs. (1). Secondly, the contents of the notice are not specified: if the party receiving the notice requires more details, he can ask for them (subs. (1)(b)). Thirdly, failure to comply with the notice requirements has no effect on admissibility, though there are other reasons why parties should follow the rules: subs. (4).

Subs. (1)
This subsection requires a party, who intends to introduce a hearsay statement under the Act, to give to the other parties "such notice as is reasonable and practicable in the circumstances", to enable those other parties to deal with any matters arising from the fact that the evidence will be hearsay. Paragraph (b) allows the recipient of a notice to require further particulars, still (because of the governing final phrases of the subsection) subject to reasonableness, practicality, and need. The terms of this provision are deliberately vague: it covers a great variety of proceed-

ings, both interlocutory and final, and can be adapted by the court to meet the needs of different situations. Sometimes the haste with which a hearing has to be arranged, or the risk of danger to a person who has provided information, may mean that it is either not practicable, or not reasonable, for any notice to be given: hence the words "(if any)" in para. (a). In the majority of cases, however, following the general practice of pre-trial disclosure in the High Court and the County Court, the duty to give notice under this subsection should impose no extra burden.

Subs. (2)

This subsection directs the general rule-making power of s.12 into two particular channels. First, some classes of proceedings, or of evidence, may be removed altogether from the ambit of the notice requirement. It is not at present clear how this power will be used; some classes of evidence are already exempt from the requirement because ss.2–6 do not apply to them: see s.1(3) and (4). It may well be appropriate to abandon any duty to give notice where proceedings are of such a nature that they may be nullified if the opposing party has advance notice of them. Secondly, rules may further define the requirements to give notice, including specifying time limits. It hardly needs to be said that the principle must be of minimum regulation: this power should not be used to create a régime with any of the complexities of that being replaced.

Subs. (3)

This subsection allows the notice requirements to be excluded by agreement of the parties or waived by the party to whom notice was to be given. If there are more than two parties to the action, the agreement will have to be by all, or the waiver by all those affected, before the party proposing to introduce the evidence is released from his duty to give notice. There appears to be no power under this subsection to dispense with or waive any requirements of the rules, if the basic requirement to give notice has not been excluded; but such a power may be in due course given by the rules themselves.

Subs. (4)

This subsection provides that failure to give notice, or to comply with rules as to notice, does not affect the admissibility of the evidence. The court may, however, take account of such failure in either or both of two possible ways. First, in directing the course of proceedings, for example the order in which evidence is to be heard, or by allowing an adjournment. In an extreme case it might be right to direct that the trial re-commence; and in any event the party at fault would no doubt be ordered to pay the costs so incurred. It is true that, in view of the likely long wait for a new hearing date, the party prejudiced may be unlikely to seek an adjournment or retrial; but the threat should be enough to ensure compliance with the rules in most cases. Secondly, the failure to give proper notice may be taken into account in assessing the weight to be given to the hearsay statement. If a party opponent is taken by surprise by the fact that the evidence is hearsay, so that he has little opportunity to investigate or test it, it may well be right, if it is on a contested matter, to attribute little weight to that evidence. The party adducing the evidence then has only himself to blame. In an extreme case the court might rule that the evidence be accorded no weight at all (see *T.S.B. Scotland v. James Mills (Montrose) Ltd. (in receivership)* 1992 S.L.T. 519). This would, however, be so close in effect to declaring the evidence inadmissible, that it would perhaps be regarded as against the spirit of this subsection.

Power to call witness for cross-examination on hearsay statement

3. Rules of court may provide that where a party to civil proceedings adduces hearsay evidence of a statement made by a person and does not call that person as a witness, any other party to the proceedings may, with the leave of the court, call that person as a witness and cross-examine him on the statement as if he had been called by the first-mentioned party and as if the hearsay statement were his evidence in chief.

DEFINITIONS
    "civil proceedings": s.11.
    "court": s.11.
    "oral evidence": s.13.

"hearsay": s.1(2).
"rules of court": s.11.
"statement": s.13.

GENERAL NOTE
This section enables rules of court to be made, under which, if the maker of a hearsay statement is not called as a witness by the party tendering the statement, any other party may call him as a witness and cross-examine him.

Even without this provision the court would have power, in the exercise of the general discretion to control proceedings, to allow a party to call a witness whose hearsay statement had been tendered by another party. That power would rarely satisfy the party against whom hearsay evidence had been adduced, however, because if the witness had given his evidence orally he could have been cross-examined on it, whereas the general rule is that a witness cannot be cross-examined by the party calling him. The abolition of the hearsay rule might therefore have been used unscrupulously to avoid the possibility of cross-examination. If a witness is available to give evidence but, despite a request by the party opponent, his evidence is tendered as hearsay, that would certainly be a factor to which the court would want to have regard in assessing the weight to be attached to his statement: s.4(2). Nevertheless it is proper that the party opponent should have the same opportunity of testing his accuracy and credibility as if he had made his statement from the witness-box. Hence the provisions of this section to make rules of court which, together with the provisions of ss.5 and 6, will have the effect of enabling a party, against whom hearsay evidence is tendered, to overcome the disadvantage that the statement is not made while giving oral evidence.

Considerations relevant to weighing of hearsay evidence

4.—(1) In estimating the weight (if any) to be given to hearsay evidence in civil proceedings the court shall have regard to any circumstances from which any inference can reasonably be drawn as to the reliability or otherwise of the evidence.

(2) Regard may be had, in particular, to the following—

(a) whether it would have been reasonable and practicable for the party by whom the evidence was adduced to have produced the maker of the original statement as a witness;

(b) whether the original statement was made contemporaneously with the occurrence or existence of the matters stated;

(c) whether the evidence involves multiple hearsay;

(d) whether any person involved had any motive to conceal or misrepresent matters;

(e) whether the original statement was an edited account, or was made in collaboration with another or for a particular purpose;

(f) whether the circumstances in which the evidence is adduced as hearsay are such as to suggest an attempt to prevent proper evaluation of its weight.

DEFINITIONS
"civil proceedings": s.11.
"court": s.11.
"hearsay": s.1(2).
"statement": s.13.
"the original statement": s.13.

GENERAL NOTE
This section makes provision for the performance of the court's task in assessing the weight, if any, to be given to hearsay evidence, in the process of fact-finding. As the Law Commission recognised, there are dangers in the production of a list of factors to be taken into account, such as that in subs. (2), particularly because the list may come to be seen as universally applicable, or complete. On the other hand, when this Act is brought into force it will apply in magistrates'

courts, where there is a high volume of work, a larger number of unrepresented parties and a majority of lay judiciary. The Law Commission therefore recommended the introduction of statutory guidelines as the lesser of two evils.

Subs. (1)

This subsection lays down the general injunction that the court shall have regard to *any* circumstances from which *any* inference can be drawn as to the reliability or otherwise of the evidence.

Subs. (2)

This subsection contains the list of factors to which, in particular, the court is to have regard. No indication is given as to whether the factors mentioned are suggestive of reliability or unreliability. The list seems to be of factors tending to make the evidence less weighty, except for some of those in para. (e): clearly the fact that the original statement was prepared for a particular purpose might diminish its usefulness for another purpose, but the fact that the statement was made in collaboration with another might well make it more reliable; and the fact that it was "an edited account" would appear for most purposes to be neutral. Paragraph (f) is of particular interest: it is provided by s.2(4)(b) that failure to give proper notice of intention to rely on hearsay evidence may be a factor which the court takes into account in assessing the evidence, presumably under this paragraph if the failure is thought to be deliberate, and under para. (a) if not.

The guidelines do not specifically allude to the accuracy or otherwise of copy of a document containing the hearsay statement, except incidentally in para. (c). This is in accord with the Act's approach to copy documents, tending to treat all copies, subject to their being "authenticated", as reliable (see s.8).

Supplementary provisions as to hearsay evidence

Competence and credibility

5.—(1) Hearsay evidence shall not be admitted in civil proceedings if or to the extent that it is shown to consist of, or to be proved by means of, a statement made by a person who at the time he made the statement was not competent as a witness.

For this purpose "not competent as a witness" means suffering from such mental or physical infirmity, or lack of understanding, as would render a person incompetent as a witness in civil proceedings; but a child shall be treated as competent as a witness if he satisfies the requirements of section 96(2)(a) and (b) of the Children Act 1989 (conditions for reception of unsworn evidence of child).

(2) Where in civil proceedings hearsay evidence is adduced and the maker of the original statement, or of any statement relied upon to prove another statement, is not called as a witness—

(a) evidence which if he had been so called would be admissible for the purpose of attacking or supporting his credibility as a witness is admissible for that purpose in the proceedings; and

(b) evidence tending to prove that, whether before or after he made the statement, he made any other statement inconsistent with it is admissible for the purpose of showing that he had contradicted himself.

Provided that evidence may not be given of any matter of which, if he had been called as a witness and had denied that matter in cross-examination, evidence could not have been adduced by the cross-examining party.

DEFINITIONS

"civil proceedings": s.11.
"hearsay": s.1(2).
"statement": s.13.
"the original statement": s.13.

GENERAL NOTE

This section makes provisions principally (see note to subs. (1)) relating to the competence and credibility of a person who is not called as a witness, but whose statement is admitted as hearsay evidence.

Subs. (1)

The Act is not intended to make admissible any statement which could not be received in evidence on the ground of the incompetence of the person making it. This section accordingly provides that a hearsay statement shall not be admissible if, at the time he made the statement, the person making it would not have been competent to be a witness (competence at the date of the proceedings is irrelevant). The requirements for a child to be competent are that "(a) he understands that it is his duty to speak the truth; and (b) he has sufficient understanding to justify his evidence being heard" (see Children Act 1989, s.96(2)). Note that, if the hearsay is multiple, each person involved must have been competent. So if W's evidence is of the form "A said that B said that X happened", then both A and B must have been competent at the time they made their respective statements.

The previous statement of a witness (see s.6) might fall foul of this provision, if he was too young, or mentally disordered, at the time he made the previous statement.

Subs. (2)

This subsection extends, to any person upon whose accuracy the court must depend if the hearsay statement is to be relied upon, the common-law rules by which credibility may be impeached or supported. Thus, again, if W's evidence is of the form "A said that B said that X happened", the credibility of A and of B may be supported or impeached by calling evidence, in exactly the same way, and subject to the same restriction on evidence relating to collateral issues, as if they had been called as witnesses. This subsection is to the same effect as s.7(1) of the 1968 Act, amended to reflect the simpler régime of this Act.

Previous statements of witnesses

6.—(1) Subject as follows, the provisions of this Act as to hearsay evidence in civil proceedings apply equally (but with any necessary modifications) in relation to a previous statement made by a person called as a witness in the proceedings.

(2) A party who has called or intends to call a person as a witness in civil proceedings may not in those proceedings adduce evidence of a previous statement made by that person, except—

(a) with the leave of the court, or

(b) for the purpose of rebutting a suggestion that his evidence has been fabricated.

This shall not be construed as preventing a witness statement (that is, a written statement of oral evidence which a party to the proceedings intends to lead) from being adopted by a witness in giving evidence or treated as his evidence.

(3) Where in the case of civil proceedings section 3, 4 or 5 of the Criminal Procedure Act 1865 applies, which make provision as to—

(a) how far a witness may be discredited by the party producing him,

(b) the proof of contradictory statements made by a witness, and

(c) cross-examination as to previous statements in writing,

this Act does not authorise the adducing of evidence of a previous inconsistent or contradictory statement otherwise than in accordance with those sections.

This is without prejudice to any provision made by rules of court under section 3 above (power to call witness for cross-examination on hearsay statement).

(4) Nothing in this Act affects any of the rules of law as to the circumstances in which, where a person called as a witness in civil proceedings is cross-examined on a document used by him to refresh his memory, that document may be made evidence in the proceedings.

(5) Nothing in this section shall be construed as preventing a statement of any description referred to above from being admissible by virtue of section 1 as evidence of the matters stated.

DEFINITIONS
  "civil proceedings": s.11.
  "court": s.11.

"document": s.13.
"oral evidence": s.13.
"hearsay": s.1(2).
"rules of court": s.11.
"statement": s.13.

GENERAL NOTE

This section governs the admissibility of the out-of-court (*i.e.* previous) statements of a person who *is* called as a witness.

Subs. (1)

This subsection allows any party to adduce, under s.1, evidence of previous statements of the witness, in order to prove the matter stated. Because this subsection is subject to the rest of the section, its effect is to give this right to any party other than the party calling the witness.

Subs. (2)

This subsection restricts the party calling a witness, from also adducing evidence of his previous statements, unless the purpose is to rebut a suggestion that his in-court evidence is a recent fabrication. For any other purpose he needs the leave of the court, as he would have done under the 1968 Act. This provision is intended "to prevent the pointless proliferation of previous consistent statements, which would needlessly prolong trials and increase costs" (Law Com. No. 216, para. 4.30). The closing words of the subsection make it clear that a witness statement, which under R.S.C. Ord. 38, r.2A may be adopted by a witness as his evidence-in-chief, does not count as a "previous statement" for these purposes.

Subs. (3)

This subsection preserves the rules in ss.3, 4 and 5 of the Criminal Procedure Act 1865 (c. 18), in so far as they apply to civil proceedings. Those sections contain rules about hostile witnesses (s.3), and procedural rules relating to the admissibility and proof of (s.4) a previous oral statement by a witness who does not admit he made it, and (s.5) a previous written statement before the maker of it can be contradicted by it.

Subs. (4)

The basic rule is that if the ambit of the cross-examination extends outside the part of the document used by the witness to refresh his memory, the party calling the witness can have the document made evidence (see *R. v. Britton* [1987] 1 W.L.R. 539, C.A. and *Senat v. Senat (K., H. and B. intervening)* [1965] P. 172).

Subs. (5)

This subsection specifically provides that where a previous statement becomes evidence under any of the rules made or retained by this section, it may be admitted, like any other out-of-court statement, as evidence of the matter stated (not merely as evidence that the statement was made). If, however, the statement is to be used as evidence of the matter stated, its admissibility will be governed by s.1, and it will accordingly be subject (where reasonable and practicable) to the notice provisions in s.2, as well as the guidance provisions in s.4 and potentially the competence rules of s.5.

Evidence formerly admissible at common law

7.—(1) The common law rule effectively preserved by section 9(1) and (2)(a) of the Civil Evidence Act 1968 (admissibility of admissions adverse to a party) is superseded by the provisions of this Act.

(2) The common law rules effectively preserved by section 9(1) and (2)(b) to (d) of the Civil Evidence Act 1968, that is, any rule of law whereby in civil proceedings—

(a) published works dealing with matters of a public nature (for example, histories, scientific works, dictionaries and maps) are admissible as evidence of facts of a public nature stated in them,

(b) public documents (for example, public registers, and returns made under public authority with respect to matters of public interest) are admissible as evidence of facts stated in them, or

(c) records (for example, the records of certain courts, treaties, Crown grants, pardons and commissions) are admissible as evidence of facts stated in them, shall continue to have effect.

(3) The common law rules effectively preserved by section 9(3) and (4) of the Civil Evidence Act 1968, that is, any rule of law whereby in civil proceedings—

    (a) evidence of a person's reputation is admissible for the purpose of proving his good or bad character, or

    (b) evidence of reputation or family tradition is admissible—

           (i) for the purpose of proving or disproving pedigree or the existence of a marriage, or

           (ii) for the purpose of proving or disproving the existence of any public or general right or of identifying any person or thing,

shall continue to have effect in so far as they authorise the court to treat such evidence as proving or disproving that matter.

Where any such rule applies, reputation or family tradition shall be treated for the purposes of this Act as a fact and not as a statement or multiplicity of statements about the matter in question.

(4) The words in which a rule of law mentioned in this section is described are intended only to identify the rule and shall not be construed as altering it in any way.

DEFINITIONS

    "civil proceedings": s.11.
    "court": s.11.
    "statement": s.13.

GENERAL NOTE

    This section provides for the supersession of some, and the preservation of other common-law exceptions to the hearsay rule. Where exceptions are preserved by this section the hearsay in question is admissible apart from s.1, so the notice and guidance provisions of ss.2–6 do not apply to it.

Subs. (1)

    This subsection abolishes the common law rule, under which a statement adverse to the interests of the person making it was admissible as an exception to the hearsay rule. Such statements are no longer to be given special treatment; they are admissible under s.1 and are subject to the notice and guidance provisions of ss.2–6.

Subs. (2)

    This subsection provides that three exceptions to the hearsay rule, expressly preserved by the 1968 Act, shall continue to have effect apart from s.1 of this Act. In the case of published works dealing with matters of a public nature (subs. (2)(a)), the notice provisions are not appropriate because the works are available to any party, and it is perhaps unlikely for there to be any real doubt about the evidential weight to be attached to the statements in such works. The need to preserve the common-law rules in subs. (2)(b) and (c) arises from the fact that the statutory exceptions preserved in s.14(3)(d) and (e) presuppose the existence of the common-law rules about public registers.

Subs. (3)

    This subsection continues the 1968 Act's clarification of the rules relating to reputation and family tradition. Reputation and tradition necessarily involve hearsay which is multiple or composite or both, and as a result it would be impossible to apply the notice and guidance provisions of ss.2–6 to each of the statements involved. This subsection accordingly provides that evidence of a person's reputation is admissible for the purpose of proving his good or bad character; that evidence of reputation or family tradition is admissible for the purposes mentioned in subs. (3)(b); and that, in either case, the reputation or tradition is to be treated for the purposes of the Act as a fact, not as a series of out-of-court statements each subject to ss.2–6.

Subs. (4)

    This subsection provides that the words in this section describing rules of law are not to be taken to alter those rules. It therefore follows that the Act's definition of "document" is not applicable in subs. (2)(b).

Other matters

Proof of statements contained in documents

8.—(1) Where a statement contained in a document is admissible as evidence in civil proceedings, it may be proved—
(a) by the production of that document, or
(b) whether or not that document is still in existence, by the production of a copy of that document or of the material part of it,
authenticated in such manner as the court may approve.

(2) It is immaterial for this purpose how many removes there are between a copy and the original.

DEFINITIONS
"civil proceedings": s.11.
"copy": s.13.
"court": s.11.
"document": s.13.
"statement": s.13.

GENERAL NOTE
The wording of this section follows that of s.27 of the Criminal Justice Act 1988 (c. 33). As with that section it does *not* have general application to the proof of documents, but only to the proof of statements contained in documents. Many documents are relevant in civil proceedings not for the statements they contain but because of the operative effect of the documents themselves, for example written contracts, licences, wills, bills of exchange, Land Registry certificates. Unless they fall within the provisions of s.9, the present Act has no effect on the general rules for the proof of such documents and their authentication. Even in the case of documents to which this section does apply, there is no provision here allowing oral evidence of the contents of a document.

The layout, if not the wording, of subs. (1) makes it clear that both original documents (subs. (1)(a)) and copies (subs. (1)(b)) are to be authenticated. No form of authentication is prescribed. It has been argued that a more precise provision along the lines of the equivalent Scottish legislation, would have been preferable, because otherwise there is the possibility of unfortunate variations between the practice of different courts and judges. This is doubtful for two reasons. First, no such difficulty has yet been observed in the operation of the 1988 Act. Secondly, the Scottish legislation in question, which provides merely that a copy, purporting to be authenticated by the person responsible for making it, shall be deemed to be a true copy and shall be treated as if it were the original, is in any event subject to the direction of the court to the contrary: Civil Evidence (Scotland) Act 1988 (c. 32), section 6(1).

Because of the broad definition of "copy" in s.13 and the provisions of subs. (2) (which reverses the common-law rule that a copy of a copy is not admissible in evidence), the copy before the court may be far removed from the original, perhaps as a manuscript transcript of a manuscript transcript. Nevertheless, if it is "authenticated", any potential defects go to its weight rather than its admissibility, following the general scheme of the Act.

Proof of records of business or public authority

9.—(1) A document which is shown to form part of the records of a business or public authority may be received in evidence in civil proceedings without further proof.

(2) A document shall be taken to form part of the records of a business or public authority if there is produced to the court a certificate to that effect signed by an officer of the business or authority to which the records belong.
For this purpose—
(a) a document purporting to be a certificate signed by an officer of a business or public authority shall be deemed to have been duly given by such an officer and signed by him; and
(b) a certificate shall be treated as signed by a person if it purports to bear a facsimile of his signature.

(3) The absence of an entry in the records of a business or public authority may be proved in civil proceedings by affidavit of an officer of the business or authority to which the records belong.

(4) In this section—
"records" means records in whatever form;
"business" includes any activity regularly carried on over a period of time, whether for profit or not, by any body (whether corporate or not) or by an individual;
"officer" includes any person occupying a responsible position in relation to the relevant activities of the business or public authority or in relation to its records; and
"public authority" includes any public or statutory undertaking, any government department and any person holding office under Her Majesty.
(5) The court may, having regard to the circumstances of the case, direct that all or any of the above provisions of this section do not apply in relation to a particular document or record, or description of documents or records.

DEFINITIONS
"business": subs. (4).
"civil proceedings": s.11.
"court": s.11.
"document": s.13.
"officer": subs. (4).
"public authority": subs. (4).
"records": subs. (4).

GENERAL NOTE
This section provides for "fast-track" proof of documents which are part of the records of a business or a public authority (as respectively defined). The cumbersome process of proof that had to be followed in respect of business records, and, in particular in the case of documents produced by computer, was seen as one of the least satisfactory features of the 1968 Act (the rules are in ss.4, 5 and 10 (the definition section) of that Act). The Law Commission recommended that there be no special rules for documents produced by computer (Law Com. No. 216, para. 4.43) and that the procedure for putting business records before the court should be greatly streamlined. It must be noted that this section, unlike ss.4 and 5 of the 1968 Act, and in contrast to s.8 of this Act, applies only to the proof of the documents themselves, and *not* to the proof of any facts stated in the documents (see the notes to s.8, and the final paragraph of this note).

Subs. (1)
This subsection provides that a document "shown to form part of" such records may be admitted in evidence without further proof. The phraseology makes it clear that, as would be expected, the burden of proof of admissibility under this section lies on the party adducing the document, but, because of subs. (2), that burden will in most cases be particularly easy to discharge.

Subs. (2)
This subsection deals with the method by which a document may be shown to fall within subs. (1), and so be eligible for fast-track proof. If a certificate is produced to the effect that the document in question is part of the records of a business or public authority, the document "shall be taken" to form part of such records, provided that the certificate purports (see para. (a)) to be a certificate signed (or—see para. (b)—signed in facsimile) by an officer of the business or authority to which the records belong. Thus, when such a certificate is produced, there is a conclusive presumption in favour of admissibility, unless the court decides that the relevant provisions shall not apply: see subs. (5). "Officer" is widely defined in subs. (4) to include not only a person holding a responsible position in relation to the concern as a whole, but also a person holding such a position in relation to its records.

Subs. (3)
This subsection provides that the absence of an entry in business or official records may be proved by an affidavit of an officer of the business or public authority to which the records

belong. The absence of an entry may be, in certain circumstances, as telling as the presence of an entry, but again it must be noted that *this* subsection makes no provision for the interpretation of such absence. This subsection is concerned only with the method by which the court comes to know that the entry does not occur in the record. Whether the reason for the absence is inefficiency of record-keeping or because nothing happened to cause an entry to be made, is a matter for the court to decide by weighing all the evidence, including the evidence appearing from the affidavit. If there is likely to be any dispute, the safer course will be to call the "officer" as a witness to give oral evidence of the accuracy of the system underlying the compilation of the records (*cf. R. v. Shone* (1982) 76 Cr.App.R. 72, C.A.; *R. v. Patel* [1981] 3 All E.R. 94, C.A.).

Subs. (4)

This subsection contains definitions for this section. "Records" is defined so as to include records in any form, but unfortunately, there is no further indication of what constitutes a record for the purposes of the section. The Law Commission's Report (Law Com. No. 216, para. 4.41) argues that the question "only goes to the *manner* of admission of the document", and that statements contained in documents that are not parts of "records" will be admissible under s.1. That is true; but it is not enough. Take the case of a cheque, which is a payable order and does not contain any statements: ss.1 and 8 therefore do not apply to it. Suppose further that it is drawn by a client of the bank, not in the course of any business activity of his, and is paid through the clearing system. If, after payment, it is produced from the custody of the bank, it will be a part of the bank's records, and this section may apply to it, but if it is produced from the custody of the customer this Act provides no assistance at all.

"Business" is defined so as to include any activity regularly carried out over a period of time by any body (corporate or otherwise) or an individual. Thus the activities of the honorary treasurer and secretary of a club will count as a "business" for these purposes, unless, of course, there has been a recent change of office-holder, in which case it may not be possible to show that the activity has been carried out for a period of time by *an* individual. For comment on the definition of "officer" see note to subs. (2).

Subs. (5)

This subsection allows the court to dispense with any of the provisions of this section. Such an exercise of discretion would be appropriate if, for example, other evidence before the court raised a real doubt as to the genuineness of the certificate produced under subs. (2).

The wording of the section should be observed with care. As indicated in the first paragraph of this note, s.9 is not concerned with any statements in the documents, but with the documents themselves. As the Law Commission point out (Law Com. No. 216, para. 4.42), "business and other records have long been treated as belonging to a class of evidence which can be regarded as likely to be reliable". Their reliability stems from a combination of various factors: pride in one's job or fear of losing it; regularity of practice leading to efficiency and accuracy; the possibility of cross-checks, balancing and audit, drawing attention to any inaccuracies. It is for this reason that statements in business documents were made admissible by s.4 of the 1968 Act even if the hearsay they contained was not "first-hand"; and, more recently, s.24 of the Criminal Justice Act 1988 renders a statement in a business document admissible even if the statement was not originally made in writing. Section 1 of the present Act removes the need for special treatment of statements in business documents, because all statements in documents are admissible in all proceedings to which the Act applies. As a result, this Act is able to go further than its predecessors, and recognise the special reliability of business documents by making them easy to prove, whether or not they contain statements. The result is as follows. If a business document is relied upon *other than* for any statement in it, it can be received in evidence under the provisions of this section. If, however, a party seeks to persuade the court to place reliance on statements in a business document, the provisions of this section would appear to replace (or fulfil) the authentication requirements of s.8, but the statements are still subject to the notice and guidance requirements of ss.2–6. This is almost what was intended by the Law Commission. In para. 4.38 of the Report (Law Com. No. 216) they write,

"Under our proposed Bill, business and other records will be admitted under clause [now section] 1. We intend that the court's approach to the reliability of the records should be governed by the same considerations as will apply to all other forms of hearsay evidence, namely the weighing provisions contained in clause [now section] 3."

The draft here enacted does not quite achieve that intention, because although it makes statements in business records subject to the same régime as all other statements, that régime only applies to statements, not to documentary evidence in general. The difficulty arises from the apparent assumption, in the extract quoted, that records are a "form of hearsay evidence".

"Hearsay" is confined by s.1(2) of this Act to statements: as explained in the note to s.8, and illustrated in the note to s.9(4), records may be (or include) statements, or they may not—in which case, ss.1–6 and 8 do not apply to them.

Admissibility and proof of Ogden Tables

10.—(1) The actuarial tables (together with explanatory notes) for use in personal injury and fatal accident cases issued from time to time by the Government Actuary's Department are admissible in evidence for the purpose of assessing, in an action for personal injury, the sum to be awarded as general damages for future pecuniary loss.

(2) They may be proved by the production of a copy published by Her Majesty's Stationery Office.

(3) For the purposes of this section—

(a) "personal injury" includes any disease and any impairment of a person's physical or mental condition; and

(b) "action for personal injury" includes an action brought by virtue of the Law Reform (Miscellaneous Provisions) Act 1934 or the Fatal Accidents Act 1976.

DEFINITIONS

"personal injury"; "action for personal injury": see subs. (3).

GENERAL NOTE

This section enacts clause 6(2) of the draft Bill attached to the Law Commission's Report on Structured Settlements and Interim and Provisional Damages (Law Com. No. 224 (1994)).

A court assessing lump sum damages for future pecuniary loss needs to look to the future and take into account various contingencies, including the probable length of the relevant life, in order to fix an appropriate sum. One method of calculation is the actuarial one, relying on the experience and skill of an actuary to calculate the effect of such matters as general life expectancy. The Government Actuary's Department produces and publishes tables, with explanatory notes, designed for this purpose, known as the "Ogden Tables". The tables themselves, however, are hearsay unless they are proved by an actuary giving evidence in court.

The Law Commission supports the actuarial method of calculation for lump sum damages, without intending that it should become compulsory or exclusive. This section therefore provides that an H.M.S.O. copy of the Ogden Tables is admissible in evidence. The court is then able to use the information contained in the tables to the extent it considers appropriate, supplementing that information with other factors pertaining to the particular case.

This section might well have been regarded as unnecessary, because s.1 makes the Tables admissible. It was felt, however, that the notice and guideline provisions of ss.2–6 of the Act are not appropriate to the Tables, which are readily available to all parties—though notice of intention to use them will probably have been given under Ord. 25, r.8(1)(b) or Ord. 18, r.12(1A) (see Law Com. No. 224, para. 2.13). This section therefore makes the Tables admissible without more ado, and when they are admissible under this section, ss.2–6 do not apply to them by virtue of s.1(4).

Unlike the other provisions of the Act, this section does not apply generally "in civil proceedings" but only admits the Tables "for the purpose of assessing, in an action for personal injury, the sum to be awarded as general damages for future pecuniary loss". "Personal injury" and "action for personal injury" have the extended meanings given by the definitions in subs. (3) but this section clearly does not cover the use of the Tables in for example, an action concerned with the correct calculation of an insurance premium. For those purposes, the Tables would have to be adduced under s.1, and would be subject to the notice and guideline provisions.

General

Meaning of "civil proceedings"

11. In this Act "civil proceedings" means civil proceedings, before any tribunal, in relation to which the strict rules of evidence apply, whether as a matter of law or by agreement of the parties.

References to "the court" and "rules of court" shall be construed accordingly.

GENERAL NOTE

This section defines "civil proceedings" for the purposes of the Act, and hence prescribes the ambit of all the substantive sections except s.10. Its effect is that ss.1–9 apply to all civil proceedings in courts whose procedure is governed by the strict rules of evidence, including civil proceedings in magistrates' courts, which are so governed: *Bradford City Metropolitan Council v. K.* [1990] Fam. 140. (The Civil Evidence Act 1968 was never extended to magistrates' courts, but the present Act is designed so that it can be: see notes to s.4). On the other hand, the Act does not apply to the proceedings of those statutory tribunals which as a matter of law are not bound by the strict rules of evidence, nor to other jurisdictions where hearsay has traditionally been received, for example coroners' courts and the Wardship Jurisdiction of the High Court (*Official Solicitor v. K.* [1965] A.C. 201). Where the admissibility of evidence is not a matter of law, it is open to the parties to agree that the strict rules of evidence shall apply; if (and only if) that has been done, ss.1–9 of this Act will apply to the proceedings.

Section 10 of this Act does *not* apply generally in "civil proceedings" (see notes to that section).

Provisions as to rules of court

12.—(1) Any power to make rules of court regulating the practice or procedure of the court in relation to civil proceedings includes power to make such provision as may be necessary or expedient for carrying into effect the provisions of this Act.

(2) Any rules of court made for the purposes of this Act as it applies in relation to proceedings in the High Court apply, except in so far as their operation is excluded by agreement, to arbitration proceedings to which this Act applies, subject to such modifications as may be appropriate.

Any question arising as to what modifications are appropriate shall be determined, in default of agreement, by the arbitrator or umpire, as the case may be.

DEFINITIONS

"civil proceedings": s.11.
"court": s.11.
"rules of court": s.11.

GENERAL NOTE

Subs. (1)

This subsection enlarges the powers to make Rules of Court (which, in accordance with the second sentence of s.11, include the rules of any proceedings to which ss.1–9 of the Act apply), so as to enable the making of any rules necessary or expedient to carry this Act into effect. Possible subjects for such rules are envisaged in ss.2(2) and 3.

Subs. (2)

This subsection provides that "arbitration proceedings to which this Act applies" are governed by the rules of the High Court made for the purposes of this Act. The "arbitration proceedings to which this Act applies" are those in which, by law or by agreement of the parties, the strict rules of evidence apply (see ss.11 and 10(3)(b) and notes). The effect of the rules of the High Court may in such proceedings be excluded by agreement of the parties, or modified either by agreement of the parties or (if the parties cannot agree) by the determination of the arbitrator or umpire that the modification is appropriate.

Interpretation

13. In this Act—
    "civil proceedings" has the meaning given by section 11 and "court" and
        "rules of court" shall be construed in accordance with that section;
    "document" means anything in which information of any description is
        recorded, and "copy", in relation to a document, means anything
        onto which information recorded in the document has been copied,
        by whatever means and whether directly or indirectly;

"hearsay" shall be construed in accordance with section 1(2);

"oral evidence" includes evidence which, by reason of a defect of speech or hearing, a person called as a witness gives in writing or by signs;

"the original statement", in relation to hearsay evidence, means the underlying statement (if any) by—

   (a) in the case of evidence of fact, a person having personal knowledge of that fact, or

   (b) in the case of evidence of opinion, the person whose opinion it is; and

"statement" means any representation of fact or opinion, however made.

GENERAL NOTE

This is the general definition section, and usefully includes references to other sections of the Act in which definitions occur. In using this section it must be noted that not all the words and phrases defined occur at the start of the defining paragraphs: "court", "rules of court" and "copy" are also defined here.

Savings

14.—(1) Nothing in this Act affects the exclusion of evidence on grounds other than that it is hearsay.

This applies whether the evidence falls to be excluded in pursuance of any enactment or rule of law, for failure to comply with rules of court or an order of the court, or otherwise.

(2) Nothing in this Act affects the proof of documents by means other than those specified in section 8 or 9.

(3) Nothing in this Act affects the operation of the following enactments—

   (a) section 2 of the Documentary Evidence Act 1868 (mode of proving certain official documents);

   (b) section 2 of the Documentary Evidence Act 1882 (documents printed under the superintendence of Stationery Office);

   (c) section 1 of the Evidence (Colonial Statutes) Act 1907 (proof of statutes of certain legislatures);

   (d) section 1 of the Evidence (Foreign, Dominion and Colonial Documents) Act 1933 (proof and effect of registers and official certificates of certain countries);

   (e) section 5 of the Oaths and Evidence (Overseas Authorities and Countries) Act 1963 (provision in respect of public registers of other countries).

DEFINITIONS

"court": s.11.
"document": s.13.
"hearsay": s.1(2).
"rules of court": s.11.

GENERAL NOTE

Subs. (1)

This subsection provides that nothing in the Act is to undermine the operation of rules excluding evidence on grounds other than that it is hearsay. There are various provisions in rules of court allowing the court to set limits or conditions on certain types of evidence, for example that adduced by expert witnesses. The present Act is not intended to allow such rules to be evaded by introducing the evidence as admissible hearsay.

Subs. (2)

This subsection specifically preserves the rules relating to the proof of documents (as distinct from the proof of statements in them) save where those rules are modified by the operation of ss.8 and 9 of this Act.

Subs. (3)

This subsection lists a number of statutory provisions, each of which provides a mode of proof of certain documentary sources and their contents. The subsection provides that "nothing in this Act" affects them; so the documents themselves are not subject to s.9 (proof of records of business or public authority), nor are statements in those documents admissible under s.1 or amenable to proof under s.8 of this Act.

Consequential amendments and repeals

15.—(1) The enactments specified in Schedule 1 are amended in accordance with that Schedule, the amendments being consequential on the provisions of this Act.

(2) The enactments specified in Schedule 2 are repealed to the extent specified.

GENERAL NOTE

This section introduces Schedules 1 and 2, which contain amendments and repeals. Not all the amendments in Sched. 1 are strictly "consequential": see General Note to that Schedule.

Short title, commencement and extent

16.—(1) This Act may be cited as the Civil Evidence Act 1995.

(2) The provisions of this Act come into force on such day as the Lord Chancellor may appoint by order made by statutory instrument, and different days may be appointed for different provisions and for different purposes.

(3) An order under subsection (2) may contain such transitional provisions as appear to the Lord Chancellor to be appropriate; and subject to any such provision, the provisions of this Act shall not apply in relation to proceedings begun before commencement.

(4) This Act extends to England and Wales.

(5) Section 10 (admissibility and proof of Ogden Tables) also extends to Northern Ireland.

As it extends to Northern Ireland, the following shall be substituted for subsection (3)(b)—

> "(b) "action for personal injury" includes an action brought by virtue of the Law Reform (Miscellaneous Provisions) (Northern Ireland) Act 1937 or the Fatal Accidents (Northern Ireland) Order 1977."

(6) The provisions of Schedules 1 and 2 (consequential amendments and repeals) have the same extent as the enactments respectively amended or repealed.

GENERAL NOTE

Subs. (1)

Despite its title, the ambit of the Act is restricted neither to civil process nor to matters of evidence alone. See General Note to Sched. 1.

Subss. (2) and (3)

As the Act is principally concerned with matters of procedure, it might be expected that its main provisions would come into force in such a way as to affect all proceedings after the commencement date, regardless of the date either of the events giving rise to the proceedings, or of the statements introduced under the Act. The Lord Chancellor has, however, made it clear (see *Hansard*, H.L. Vol. 564, col. 1058) that he is aware of the special need for sensitivity, in relation to cases that may have already been prepared on the basis of the rules of evidence as they were before the commencement of this Act. Hence the need for transitional provisions, as permitted by subs. (3). In any event it will be necessary to avoid retrospective effect on matters in Sched. 1 which relate to the definition of criminal offences.

Subs. (5)

The Act as a whole does not extend to Northern Ireland, because the hearsay rule is at present being considered by the Law Reform Advisory Committee for Northern Ireland. There is, however, no such hindrance to the extension of s.10 (suitably amended) to the province.

SCHEDULES

GENERAL NOTE

This Schedule makes amendments to a number of statutes. Few of the amendments are truly consequential. In the majority of cases the reason for amendment is that, in the statute as it stands, some word or words, such as "document" or "copy", is defined as having the same meaning as in the 1968 Act. As the relevant provisions of that Act are repealed by the present Act, amendment was certainly necessary; what was not necessary was the *changing* of the definition so as to be in line with the new Act, rather than *preserving* the definition by the insertion of words from the 1968 Act. The decision to make the change may well be the better option, but it is a deliberate decision, not one merely "consequential" on the provisions of this Act. It is to be noted that the definitions so altered are in a number of cases the definitions of elements of the criminal offence of failing to produce documents or the like: see paras. 4, 6, 8, 11, 13, 18, 19, 20. Further, despite the title of the Act, the amendments made by paras. 9, 12 and 15 relate to matters of criminal, not civil evidence.

Paragraphs 1–3 are of a different nature. The sections amended are those inserted in the Acts by s.3 of the Armed Forces Act 1986 (c. 21). There is no reference in them to any matters of civil evidence and it is difficult to see why it was thought appropriate to amend them by a Civil Evidence Act, or why the amendments are to be called "consequential". It must be admitted, however, that there is considerable convenience in having these offences defined in the much simpler terms of this Act. Lord Wilberforce raised the question (*Hansard*, H.L. Vol. 95, col. 1056) whether the new definitions unduly enlarged the scope of the offences. The position in fact seems to be the reverse. The previous definitions, though unwieldy, were extremely wide, and it is difficult to think of anything covered by the new phraseology that would not previously have founded a conviction. But the old definitions specifically included, in the definition of "record", "any program in a computer". A computer program, which consists of instructions, not information, does not fall within the amended definition of "document" (see subs. (3) of each of the substituted sections). Previously, then, a person to whom these Acts apply could have been guilty of an offence by tampering with a computer program; in future there can be no such offence until information is recorded.

CONSEQUENTIAL AMENDMENTS

Army Act 1955 (c. 18)

1. For section 62 of the Army Act 1955 (making of false documents) substitute—

"**Making of false documents**

62.—(1) A person subject to military law who—

(a) makes an official document which is to his knowledge false in a material particular, or

(b) makes in any official document an entry which is to his knowledge false in a material particular, or

(c) tampers with the whole or any part of an official document (whether by altering it, destroying it, suppressing it, removing it or otherwise), or

(d) with intent to deceive, fails to make an entry in an official document,

is liable on conviction by court-martial to imprisonment for a term not exceeding two years or any less punishment provided by this Act.

(2) For the purposes of this section—

(a) a document is official if it is or is likely to be made use of, in connection with the performance of his functions as such, by a person who holds office under, or is in the service of, the Crown; and

(b) a person who has signed or otherwise adopted as his own a document made by another shall be treated, as well as that other, as the maker of the document.

(3) In this section 'document' means anything in which information of any description is recorded.".

Air Force Act 1955 (c. 19)

2. For section 62 of the Air Force Act 1955 (making of false documents) substitute—

"**Making of false documents**

62.—(1) A person subject to air-force law who—

(a) makes an official document which is to his knowledge false in a material particular, or

(b) makes in any official document an entry which is to his knowledge false in a material particular, or

(c) tampers with the whole or any part of an official document (whether by altering it, destroying it, suppressing it, removing it or otherwise), or

(d) with intent to deceive, fails to make an entry in an official document,

is liable on conviction by court-martial to imprisonment for a term not exceeding two years or any less punishment provided by this Act.

(2) For the purposes of this section—

(a) a document is official if it is or is likely to be made use of, in connection with the performance of his functions as such, by a person who holds office under, or is in the service of, the Crown; and

(b) a person who has signed or otherwise adopted as his own a document made by another shall be treated, as well as that other, as the maker of the document.

(3) In this section 'document' means anything in which information of any description is recorded.".

Naval Discipline Act 1957 (c. 53)

3. For section 35 of the Naval Discipline Act 1957 (making of false documents) substitute—

"**Falsification of documents**

35.—(1) A person subject to this Act who—

(a) makes an official document which is to his knowledge false in a material particular, or

(b) makes in any official document an entry which is to his knowledge false in a material particular, or

(c) tampers with the whole or any part of an official document (whether by altering it, destroying it, suppressing it, removing it or otherwise), or

(d) with intent to deceive, fails to make an entry in an official document,

is liable to imprisonment for a term not exceeding two years or any less punishment authorised by this Act.

(2) For the purposes of this section—

(a) a document is official if it is or is likely to be made use of, in connection with the performance of his functions as such, by a person who holds office under, or is in the service of, the Crown; and

(b) a person who has signed or otherwise adopted as his own a document made by another shall be treated, as well as that other, as the maker of the document.

(3) In this section 'document' means anything in which information of any description is recorded.".

Gaming Act 1968 (c. 65)

4. In section 43 of the Gaming Act 1968 (powers of inspectors and related provisions), for subsection (11) substitute—

"(11) In this section—

'document' means anything in which information of any description is recorded, and

'copy', in relation to a document, means anything onto which information recorded in the document has been copied, by whatever means and whether directly or indirectly.".

Vehicle and Driving Licences Act 1969 (c. 27)

5.—(1) Section 27 of the Vehicle and Driving Licences Act 1969 (admissibility of records as evidence) is amended as follows.

(2) For subsection (2) substitute—

"(2) In subsection (1) of this section—

'document' means anything in which information of any description is recorded;

'copy', in relation to a document, means anything onto which information recorded in the document has been copied, by whatever means and whether directly or indirectly; and

'statement' means any representation of fact, however made.".

(3) In subsection (4)(b), for the words from "for the references" to the end substitute "for the definitions of 'document', 'copy' and 'statement' there were substituted '"document" and

"statement" have the same meanings as in section 17(3) of the Law Reform (Miscellaneous Provisions) (Scotland) Act 1968, and the reference to a copy of a document shall be construed in accordance with section 17(4) of that Act, but nothing in this paragraph shall be construed as limiting to civil proceedings the references to proceedings in subsection (1)'.".

Taxes Management Act 1970 (c. 9)

6. In section 20D of the Taxes Management Act 1970 (interpretation of ss.20 to 20CC), for subsection (3) substitute—
    "(3) Without prejudice to section 127 of the Finance Act 1988, in sections 20 to 20CC above 'document' means, subject to sections 20(8C) and 20A(1A), anything in which information of any description is recorded.".

Civil Evidence Act 1972 (c. 30)

7.—(1) Section 5 of the Civil Evidence Act 1972 (interpretation and application of Act) is amended as follows.
    (2) For subsection (1) (meaning of "civil proceedings" and "court") substitute—
    "(1) In this Act 'civil proceedings' means civil proceedings, before any tribunal, in relation to which the strict rules of evidence apply, whether as a matter of law or by agreement of the parties; and references to 'the court' shall be construed accordingly.".
    (3) For subsection (2) (application of High Court or county court rules to certain other civil proceedings) substitute—
    "(2) The rules of court made for the purposes of the application of sections 2 and 4 of this Act to proceedings in the High Court apply, except in so far as their application is excluded by agreement, to proceedings before tribunals other than the ordinary courts of law, subject to such modifications as may be appropriate.
    Any question arising as to what modifications are appropriate shall be determined, in default of agreement, by the tribunal.".

International Carriage of Perishable Foodstuffs Act 1976 (c. 58)

8. In section 15 of the International Carriage of Perishable Foodstuffs Act 1976 (admissibility of records as evidence), for subsection (2) substitute—
    "(2) In this section as it has effect in England and Wales—
    'document' means anything in which information of any description is recorded;
    'copy', in relation to a document, means anything onto which information recorded in the document has been copied, by whatever means and whether directly or indirectly; and
    'statement' means any representation of fact, however made.".
    (2A) In this section as it has effect in Scotland, "document" and "statement" have the same meanings as in section 17(3) of the Law Reform (Miscellaneous Provisions) (Scotland) Act 1968, and the reference to a copy of a document shall be construed in accordance with section 17(4) of that Act.
    (2B) In this section as it has effect in Northern Ireland, "document" and "statement" have the same meanings as in section 6(1) of the Civil Evidence Act (Northern Ireland) 1971, and the reference to a copy of a document shall be construed in accordance with section 6(2) of that Act.
    (2C) Nothing in subsection (2A) or (2B) above shall be construed as limiting to civil proceedings the references to proceedings in subsection (1) above.".

Police and Criminal Evidence Act 1984 (c. 60)

9.—(1) The Police and Criminal Evidence Act 1984 is amended as follows.
    (2) In section 72(1) (interpretation of provisions relating to documentary evidence), for the definition of "copy" and "statement" substitute—
    " 'copy', in relation to a document, means anything onto which information recorded in the document has been copied, by whatever means and whether directly or indirectly, and "statement' means any representation of fact, however made; and".

(3) In section 118(1) (general interpretation), in the definition of "document", for "has the same meaning as in Part I of the Civil Evidence Act 1968" substitute "means anything in which information of any description is recorded.".

Companies Act 1985 (c. 6)

10. In section 709 of the Companies Act 1985 (inspection, &c. of records kept by registrar), in subsection (3) (use in evidence of certified copy or extract), for the words from "In England and Wales" to the end substitute—

"In England and Wales this is subject, in the case of proceedings to which section 69 of the Police and Criminal Evidence Act 1984 applies, to compliance with any applicable rules of court under subsection (2) of that section (which relates to evidence from computer records).".

Finance Act 1985 (c. 54)

11.—(1) Section 10 of the Finance Act 1985 (production of computer records, &c.) is amended as follows.

(2) In subsection (1) (general scope of powers conferred in relation to assigned matters within meaning of Customs and Excise Management Act 1979), for the words from "were a reference" to the end substitute "were a reference to anything in which information of any description is recorded and any reference to a copy of a document were a reference to anything onto which information recorded in the document has been copied, by whatever means and whether directly or indirectly".

(3) In subsection (3) (documents within powers conferred by subsection (2)), for the words ", within the meaning of Part I of the Civil Evidence Act 1968," substitute ", within the meaning given by subsection (1) above,".

(4) In subsection (5) (scope of offences relating to false documents, &c.), for "the same meaning as in Part I of the Civil Evidence Act 1968" substitute "the meaning given by subsection (1) above".

(5) Omit subsection (7) (adaptation of references to Civil Evidence Act 1968).

Criminal Justice Act 1988 (c. 33)

12. In Schedule 2 to the Criminal Justice Act 1988 (supplementary provisions as to documentary evidence), for paragraph 5 (application of interpretation provisions) substitute—

"5.—(1) In Part II of this Act—

" 'document' means anything in which information of any description is recorded;

'copy', in relation to a document, means anything onto which information recorded in the document has been copied, by whatever means and whether directly or indirectly; and

'statement' means any representation of fact, however made.

(2) For the purposes of Part II of this Act evidence which, by reason of a defect of speech or hearing, a person called as a witness gives in writing or by signs shall be treated as given orally.".

Finance Act 1988 (c. 39)

13.—(1) Section 127 of the Finance Act 1988 (production of computer records, &c.) is amended as follows.

(2) In subsection (1) (general scope of powers conferred by or under Taxes Acts), for the words from "were a reference" to the end substitute "were a reference to anything in which information of any description is recorded and any reference to a copy of a document were a reference to anything onto which information recorded in the document has been copied, by whatever means and whether directly or indirectly".

(3) In subsection (3) (documents within powers conferred by subsection (2)), for the words ", within the meaning of Part I of the Civil Evidence Act 1968," substitute ", within the meaning given by subsection (1) above,".

(4) Omit subsection (5) (adaptation of references to Civil Evidence Act 1968).

Housing Act 1988 (c. 50)

14. In section 97 of the Housing Act 1988 (information, &c. for applicant), for subsection (4) substitute—

"(4) In this section 'document' means anything in which information of any description is recorded; and in relation to a document in which information is recorded otherwise than in legible form any reference to sight of the document is to sight of the information in legible form.".

Road Traffic Offenders Act 1988 (c. 53)

15. In section 13 of the Road Traffic Offenders Act 1988 (admissibility of records as evidence), for subsection (3) substitute—

"(3) In the preceding subsections, except in Scotland—
'copy', in relation to a document, means anything onto which information recorded in the document has been copied, by whatever means and whether directly or indirectly;
'document' means anything in which information of any description is recorded; and
'statement' means any representation of fact, however made.

(3A) In Scotland, in the preceding subsections "document" and "statement" have the same meanings as in section 17(3) of the Law Reform (Miscellaneous Provisions) (Scotland) Act 1968, and the reference to a copy of a document shall be construed in accordance with section 17(4) of that Act; but nothing in this subsection shall be construed as limiting to civil proceedings the references to proceedings in subsection (2) above.".

Children Act 1989 (c. 41)

16. In section 96(7) of the Children Act 1989 (evidence given by, or with respect to, children: interpretation), for the definition of "civil proceedings" and "court" substitute—
" 'civil proceedings' means civil proceedings, before any tribunal, in relation to which the strict rules of evidence apply, whether as a matter of law or by agreement of the parties, and references to 'the court' shall be construed accordingly;".

Leasehold Reform, Housing and Urban Development Act 1993 (c. 28)

17. In section 11(9) of the Leasehold Reform, Housing and Urban Development Act 1993 (right of qualifying tenant to certain information: interpretation), for the definition of "document" substitute—
" 'document' means anything in which information of any description is recorded, and in relation to a document in which information is recorded otherwise than in legible form any reference to sight of the document is to sight of the information in legible form;".

Finance Act 1993 (c. 34)

18. In Schedule 21 to the Finance Act 1993 (oil taxation: supplementary provisions as to information), in paragraph 14(1) (meaning of "document"), for the words from "has the same meaning" to the end substitute "means anything in which information of any description is recorded".

Vehicle Excise and Registration Act 1994 (c. 22)

19. In section 52 of the Vehicle Excise and Registration Act 1994 (admissibility of records as evidence), for subsections (3) to (5) substitute—

"(3) In this section as it has effect in England and Wales—
'document' means anything in which information of any description is recorded;
'copy', in relation to a document, means anything onto which information recorded in the document has been copied, by whatever means and whether directly or indirectly; and
'statement' means any representation of fact, however made.".

(4) In this section as it has effect in Scotland, "document" and "statement" have the same meanings as in section 17(3) of the Law Reform (Miscellaneous Provisions) (Scotland) Act 1968, and the reference to a copy of a document shall be construed in accordance with section 17(4) of that Act.

(5) In this section as it has effect in Northern Ireland, "document" and "statement" have the same meanings as in section 6(1) of the Civil Evidence Act (Northern Ireland) 1971, and the reference to a copy of a document shall be construed in accordance with section 6(2) of that Act.

(6) Nothing in subsection (4) or (5) limits to civil proceedings the references to proceedings in subsection (1).".

Value Added Tax Act 1994 (c. 23)

20. In section 96(1) of the Value Added Tax Act 1994 (general interpretative provisions), at the appropriate places insert—
"document" means anything in which information of any description is recorded; and
"copy", in relation to a document, means anything onto which information recorded in the document has been copied, by whatever means and whether directly or indirectly.

Section 15(2)   SCHEDULE 2

REPEALS

Chapter	Short title	Extent of repeal
1938 c. 28.	Evidence Act 1938.	Sections 1 and 2. Section 6(1) except the words from "Proceedings" to "references". Section 6(2)(b).
1968 c. 64.	Civil Evidence Act 1968.	Part I.
1971 c. 33.	Armed Forces Act 1971.	Section 26.
1972 c. 30.	Civil Evidence Act 1972.	Section 1. Section 2(1) and (2). In section 2(3)(b), the words from "by virtue of section 2" to "out-of-court statements". In section 3(1), the words "Part I of the Civil Evidence Act 1968 or". In section 6(3), the words "I and", in both places where they occur.
1975 c. 63.	Inheritance (Provision for Family and Dependants) Act 1975.	Section 21.
1979 c. 2.	Customs and Excise Management Act 1979.	Section 75A(6)(a). Section 118A(6)(a).
1980 c. 43.	Magistrates' Courts Act 1980.	In Schedule 7, paragraph 75.
1984 c. 28.	County Courts Act 1984.	In Schedule 2, paragraphs 33 and 34.
1985 c. 54.	Finance Act 1985.	Section 10(7)
1986 c. 21.	Armed Forces Act 1986.	Section 3.
1988 c. 39.	Finance Act 1988.	Section 127(5).
1990 c. 26.	Gaming (Amendment) Act 1990.	In the Schedule, paragraph 2(7).
1994 c. 9.	Finance Act 1994.	Section 22(2)(a). In Schedule 7, paragraph 1(6)(a).
1994 c. 23.	Value Added Tax Act 1994.	Section 96(6) and (7). In Schedule 11, paragraph 6(6)(a).
1995 c. 4.	Finance Act 1995.	In Schedule 4, paragraph 38.

INDEX

References are to sections and Schedules

CRIMINAL LAW (CONSOLIDATION) (SCOTLAND) ACT 1995*

(1995 c. 39)

ARRANGEMENT OF SECTIONS

PART I

SEXUAL OFFENCES

Incest and related offences

---

* Annotations by Christopher MacIntosh, LLB, LLM, Solicitor in Scotland, and of the Procurator Fiscal Service.

An Act to consolidate for Scotland certain enactments creating offences and relating to criminal law there. [8th November 1995]

PARLIAMENTARY DEBATES
Hansard, H.L. Vol. 565, col. 15; Vol. 566, cols. 384, 894; H.C. Vol. 265, col. 180.

INTRODUCTION AND GENERAL NOTE

This Act is a consolidation measure and makes no change to the existing law. This coverage is fairly wide and disparate covering sexual offences including homosexual offences, detention by customs officers, investigation of serious or complex fraud, drug trafficking and money laundering offences, false oaths, offensive weapons and vandalism. The opportunity has also been taken to relocate the provisions of the Criminal Procedure (Scotland) Act 1975 (c. 21), ss.59 and 312(L) which concern the ambit of the crime of reset, a matter of substantive law, into a statute dealing with matters of substantive law rather than procedure. The provisions appear here as s.51.

As the Act did not make any changes in the substantive law it did not receive the normal Parliamentary scrutiny appropriate to new legislation. Parliamentary references where given therefore relate to the passage of the superseded legislation.

PART I

SEXUAL OFFENCES

Incest and related offences

Incest

1.—(1) Any male person who has sexual intercourse with a person related to him in a degree specified in column 1 of the Table set out at the end of this subsection, or any female person who has sexual intercourse with a person related to her in a degree specified in column 2 of that Table, shall be guilty of incest, unless the accused proves that he or she—

(a) did not know and had no reason to suspect that the person with whom he or she had sexual intercourse was related in a degree so specified; or

(b) did not consent to have sexual intercourse, or to have sexual intercourse with that person; or

(c) was married to that person, at the time when the sexual intercourse took place, by a marriage entered into outside Scotland and recognised as valid by Scots law.

Table

Degrees of Relationship

Column 1	Column 2
1. *Relationships by consanguinity*	
Mother	Father
Daughter	Son
Grandmother	Grandfather
Grand-daughter	Grandson
Sister	Brother
Aunt	Uncle
Niece	Nephew
Great grandmother	Great grandfather
Great grand-daughter	Great grandson
2. *Relationships by adoption*	
Adoptive mother or former adoptive mother.	Adoptive father or former adoptive father.
Adopted daughter or former adopted daughter.	Adopted son or former adopted son.

(2) For the purpose of this section, a degree of relationship exists in the case of a degree specified in paragraph 1 of the Table—

(a) whether it is of the full blood or the half blood; and

(b) even where traced through or to any person whose parents are not or have not been married to one another.

(3) For the avoidance of doubt sexual intercourse between persons who are not related to each other in a degree referred to in subsection (1) above is not incest.

GENERAL NOTE

This section re-enacts s.2A of the Sexual Offences (Scotland) Act 1976 (c. 67), as inserted by the Incest and Related Offences (Scotland) Act 1986 (c. 36). Its effect is to confine the scope of the law of incest to the law governing the prohibited degrees of marriage with limited exceptions. Defences are provided that the accused did not know and had no reason to suspect that his partner was related to him in one of the prohibited degrees, or that he did not consent to intercourse or that the two were subject to a foreign marriage recognised as valid in Scotland. Blood relationships, whether full or half blood were covered to the same extent as the pre-existing law; relationships by adoption were brought into line with the law governing marriage; step relationships no longer fall within the law of incest, except as provided for in s.2.

Sexual intercourse

There is no definition in the Act, and the existing common law requires only penetration to any degree of the vagina by the penis; *Jas Simpson*, (1870) 1 COUP 437. It is restricted to heterosexual intercourse and other sexual acts involving penetration do not constitute incest. Conduct short of intercourse between persons within the prohibited degrees may amount to the crime of "shameless indecency": see *R. v. H.M. Advocate*, 1988 S.C.C.R. 254.

Male person and female person

With the development of medical knowledge the sex of a person is no longer a simple matter. What effect does a "sex change" have in law. The only Scottish case: *X, Petr.*, 1957 S.L.T. (Sh. Ct.) 61 is of little value as an authority but the indications are that the "biological test" rather than the wider "social" or "psychological" test would be preferred, *i.e.* gender is determined at birth. A similar approach is taken in English Law: *R. v. Tan* [1983] Q.B. 1953.

The European Court of Human Rights has grappled with the problem in *Rees v. U.K.* (No. 2/1985/88/135), *Cossey v. U.K.* (No. 16/1989/176/232) and *B. v. France* (No. 57/1990/248/319) the latest of which showed signs of acceptance that the attitude to and understanding of transsexuals and medical sex changes had altered, but there was no consensus between member states to overrule the two earlier cases which had accepted the biological test without critical comment. At present therefore "a man's a man for a' that".

Intercourse with step-child

2. Any step-parent or former step-parent who has sexual intercourse with his or her step-child or former step-child shall be guilty of an offence if that step-child is either under the age of 21 years or has at any time before attaining the age of 18 years lived in the same household and been treated as a child of his or her family, unless the accused proves that he or she—

(a) did not know and had no reason to suspect that the person with whom he or she had sexual intercourse was a step-child or former step-child; or

(b) believed on reasonable grounds that that person was of or over the age of 21 years; or

(c) did not consent to have sexual intercourse, or to have sexual intercourse with that person; or

(d) was married to that person, at the time when the sexual intercourse took place, by a marriage entered into outside Scotland and recognised as valid by Scots law.

GENERAL NOTE

Intercourse between step relations generally is not now covered by the law of incest. This section protects step children who are either under 21 or have lived "in family" with the person charged, before reaching the age of 18. Whether the child was treated as a member of the family or not appears to be an objective matter and is not necessarily determined by the actings of the accused or the child in that regard.

The same defences are provided as are provided for s.1. See also the cases of *R. v. H.M. Advocate*, 1988 S.C.C.R. 254 and *Advocate, H.M. v. R.K.*, 1994 S.C.C.R. 499 which indicate that where intercourse or acts falling short of intercourse occur between persons not caught by these provisions, or perhaps even where the accused manages to prove one of the statutory defences, particularly s.2(b), there may still be the crime of shameless indecency committed by either or both parties.

Intercourse of person in position of trust with child under 16

3.—(1) Any person of or over the age of 16 years who—

(a) has sexual intercourse with a child under the age of 16 years;

(b) is a member of the same household as that child; and

(c) is in a position of trust or authority in relation to that child,

shall be guilty of an offence, unless the accused proves that subsection (2) below applies in his or her case.

(2) This subsection applies where the accused—

(a) believed on reasonable grounds that the person with whom he or she had sexual intercourse was of or over the age of 16 years; or

(b) did not consent to have sexual intercourse, or to have sexual intercourse with that person; or

(c) was married to that person, at the time when the sexual intercourse took place, by a marriage entered into outside Scotland and recognised as valid by Scots law.

GENERAL NOTE

This section provides protection for children who do not come within the scope of ss.1 and 2, and who live in the same household as the accused. Foster children and those belonging to one party in an unmarried relationship would fall within this category.

There is no definition of what is meant by "a member of the same household". Some indication of the definition in regard to another statute is given in *McGregor v. Haswell*, 1983 S.L.T. 626, *re* the Social Work (Scotland) Act 1968, s.32: "a group of persons held together by a particular kind of tie who normally live together ... akin to a family unit".

A person may be a member of the household even though not physically present. This definition was approved by the Inner House in *A. v. Kennedy*, 1993 S.C.L.R. 107. It is a matter of fact and degree and a household may continue to constitute the same household even though some members leave and others join. Passage of time, the gender of members and their experiences do not necessarily change the identity of the household.

Position of trust or authority

This phrase is not defined but is obviously less restrictive than a person having custody over or control of the child. The fact that the person charged requires to be "a member of the same household" *and* in a position of trust or authority over the child narrows down the possibilities somewhat. See *Advocate, H.M. v. R.K.*, 1994 S.C.C.R. 499 which indicates that the crime of shameless indecency may be invoked to cover situations where intercourse occurs between persons whose family relationships are not caught by these provisions. In that case the intercourse occurred between a person and a girl who had been his foster daughter from the age of eight, the intercourse occurring after she had attained the age of 16. A plea to the relevancy of indictment was taken and repelled by the judge at first instance. The matter was not appealed and the decision remains that of a single judge of the High Court.

Proceedings and penalties for offences under sections 1 to 3

4.—(1) Proceedings in respect of an offence under section 1, 2 or 3 of this Act may be brought on indictment or, if the Lord Advocate so directs, on a summary complaint before the sheriff.

(2) Summary proceedings in pursuance of this section may be commenced at any time within the period of 6 months from the date on which evidence sufficient in the opinion of the Lord Advocate to justify the proceedings comes to his knowledge.

(3) Subsection (3) of section 136 of the Criminal Procedure (Scotland) Act 1995 (date of commencement of summary proceedings) shall have effect for

the purposes of subsection (2) above as it has effect for the purposes of that section.

(4) For the purposes of subsection (2) above, a certificate of the Lord Advocate as to the date on which the evidence in question came to his knowledge is conclusive evidence of the date on which it did so.

(5) Subject to subsection (6) below, a person guilty of an offence under section 1, 2 or 3 of this Act shall be liable—

(a) on conviction on indictment, to imprisonment for any term of imprisonment up to and including life imprisonment; and

(b) on summary conviction, to imprisonment for a term not exceeding '3' months.

(6) Before passing sentence on a person convicted of any such offence, the court shall—

(a) obtain information about that person's circumstances from an officer of a local authority or otherwise and consider that information; and

(b) take into account any information before it which is relevant to his character and to his physical and mental condition.

(7) In subsection (6) above, "local authority" has the meaning assigned to it by section 1(2) of the Social Work (Scotland) Act 1968.

General Note

Subss. (2), (3) and (4)

The time bar for summary proceedings is set out in subs. (2) which provides for a period of six months from when sufficient evidence in the opinion of the Lord Advocate becomes available. A certificate by him of that date is conclusive. Section 136(3) of the Criminal Procedure (Scotland) Act 1995 provides that proceedings are deemed to be commenced on the date on which a warrant to apprehend or to cite is granted where the warrant is executed without undue delay.

Subs. (6)

The obligation upon the sentencing court to obtain a background report applies in respect of all persons, not only those under 21 or those who have not previously served a term of imprisonment.

Offences against children

Intercourse with girl under 16

5.—(1) Any person who has unlawful sexual intercourse with any girl under the age of 13 years shall be liable on conviction on indictment to imprisonment for life.

(2) Any person who attempts to have unlawful sexual intercourse with any girl under the age of 13 years shall be liable on conviction on indictment to imprisonment for a term not exceeding two years or on summary conviction to imprisonment for a term not exceeding three months.

(3) Without prejudice to sections 1 to 4 of this Act, any person who has, or attempts to have, unlawful sexual intercourse with any girl of or over the age of 13 years and under the age of 16 years shall be liable on conviction on indictment to imprisonment for a term not exceeding two years or on summary conviction to imprisonment for a term not exceeding three months.

(4) No prosecution shall be commenced for an offence under subsection (3) above more than one year after the commission of the offence.

(5) It shall be a defence to a charge under subsection (3) above that the person so charged—

(a) had reasonable cause to believe that the girl was his wife; or

(b) being a man under the age of 24 years who had not previously been charged with a like offence, had reasonable cause to believe that the girl was of or over the age of 16 years.

(6) In subsection (5) above, "a like offence" means an offence under—

(a) subsection (3) above; or

(b) section 4(1) or 10(1) of the Sexual Offences (Scotland) Act 1976 or section 5 or 6 of the Criminal Law Amendment Act 1885 (the enactments formerly creating the offences mentioned in subsection (3) above and section 10(1) of this Act); or

(c) section 6 of the Sexual Offences Act 1956 (the provision for England and Wales corresponding to subsection (3) above), or with an attempt to commit such an offence; or

(d) section 9(1) of this Act.

(7) For the purposes of subsection (4) above, a prosecution shall be deemed to commence on the date on which a warrant to apprehend or to cite the accused is granted, if such warrant is executed without undue delay.

GENERAL NOTE

This section replaces ss.3 and 4 of the Sexual Offences (Scotland) Act 1976 (c. 67).

Subs. (1)

It is the practice to charge the common law crime of rape where the girl is under the age of 12, consent being irrelevant: see *Jas Burtnay* (1822) Alison I, 214; *C. v. H.M. Advocate*, 1987 S.C.C.R. 104. The statutory offence is used where the girl is between the ages of 12 and 13.

Subs. (4)

This subsection imposes a time bar on indictment. The former provision could be read so as to suggest that an indictment had to be served prior to the expiry of 12 months from the date of the offence. It is now made clear that appearance on Petition will prevent the time period running.

The Criminal Procedure (Scotland) Act 1995, s.136, will apply the six months time bar to offences triable *only* summarily.

Subs. (5)

This subsection provides a number of defences the proof whereof lies on the person charged. The defences relate only to subs. (3), a girl between the ages of 13 and 16, they do not apply in the case of subs. (1).

Reasonable cause

The accused should be able to point to some information which it was reasonable for him to accept and not merely rely on the appearance of the girl: *Advocate, H.M. v. Hoggan* 1893 1 Adam 1.

Previously charged

These words have not been judicially defined and could apply to a charge by the police or on Petition or complaint. While none of these involve adjudication by the court they can at least be said to put someone "on notice" and as the defence may be said to be based to some extent on naivete and good faith it may be held that even a charge of any of the types enumerated without a trial or adjudication will be sufficient to disable the accused from using this defence.

Subs. (6)

This subsection defines what is a "like" offence for the purposes of subs. (5).

Indecent behaviour towards girl between 12 and 16

6. Any person who uses towards a girl of or over the age of 12 years and under the age of 16 years any lewd, indecent or libidinous practice or behaviour which, if used towards a girl under the age of 12 years, would have constituted an offence at common law shall, whether the girl consented to such practice or behaviour or not, be liable on conviction on indictment to imprisonment for a term not exceeding two years or on summary conviction to imprisonment for a term not exceeding three months.

GENERAL NOTE

This section re-enacts the Sexual Offences (Scotland) Act 1976, s.5. There is no provision for defences akin to those available under s.5(5) of this Act with the strange result that a person charged with committing sexual acts short of intercourse with a girl aged 15 may find himself in a worse position than if he had intercourse with the girl and would have available to him the defences under s.5(5). See s.15 which provides a defence in the case of a person charged with indecent assault against a girl under 16. The type of behaviour envisaged by this section constitutes a common law crime if committed in respect of children below the age of puberty. See, however, *Batty v. H.M. Advocate*, 1995 S.C.C.R. 525 in which it is observed that such behaviour may constitute a common law crime even after the child attains the age of puberty if the relationship between the person charged and the child is such that the additional element of shamelessness is present. The significance of this lies in the penalties which can be imposed. The offence under this section carries a maximum sentence of two years' imprisonment. Batty received five years' imprisonment.

Procuring, prostitution etc.

Procuring

7.—(1) Any person who procures or attempts to procure—

(a) any woman under 21 years of age or girl to have unlawful sexual intercourse with any other person or persons in any part of the world; or

(b) any woman or girl to become a common prostitute in any part of the world; or

(c) any woman or girl to leave the United Kingdom, with intent that she may become an inmate of or frequent a brothel elsewhere; or

(d) any woman or girl to leave her usual place of abode in the United Kingdom, with intent that she may, for the purposes of prostitution, become an inmate of or frequent a brothel in any part of the world,

shall be liable on conviction on indictment to imprisonment for a term not exceeding two years or on summary conviction to imprisonment for a term not exceeding three months.

(2) Any person who—

(a) by threats or intimidation procures or attempts to procure any woman or girl to have any unlawful sexual intercourse in any part of the world; or

(b) by false pretences or false representations procures any woman or girl to have any unlawful sexual intercourse in any part of the world; or

(c) applies or administers to, or causes to be taken by, any woman or girl any drug, matter or thing, with intent to stupefy or overpower so as thereby to enable any person to have unlawful sexual intercourse with such woman or girl,

shall be liable on conviction on indictment to imprisonment for a term not exceeding two years or on summary conviction to imprisonment for a term not exceeding three months.

(3) A man who induces a married woman to permit him to have sexual intercourse with by impersonating her husband shall be deemed to be guilty of rape.

(4) A constable may arrest without a warrant any person whom he has good cause to suspect of having committed, or of attempting to commit, any offence under subsection (1) above.

GENERAL NOTE
This section re-enacts ss.1, 2 and 17 of the Sexual Offences (Scotland) Act 1976.

Subs. (1)

Procuring
The English case of *R. v. Christian* (1913) 23 COX c.c 541 states that some active step was required. The subsection does not appear to be aimed at brothel-keepers who simply allow women to enter the brothel to ply their trade, but rather persons who by persuasion or trickery or some other action impose their will on the women.

Attempt to procure
Where procuring has taken place with the intent that sexual intercourse take place but none has taken place there may be a conviction, in English law, for "attempted procuring": *R. v. Johnston* [1964] 2 Q.B. 404.

To procure a woman for a single act of lewdness with oneself is not to procure her to become a common prostitute: see *R. v. Morris-Lowe* [1985] 1 W.L.R. 29. One cannot attempt to "procure" for prostitution, a person whom one reasonably believes to be a prostitute already: *R. v. Brown (R.A.)* [1984] 1 W.L.R. 1211.

Common prostitute

This includes a woman who offers her body commonly for acts of lewdness short of actual intercourse for payment: see *R. v. De Munck* [1918] 1 K.B. 635; *R. v. Webb* [1964] 1 Q.B. 357; *Smith v. Sellers* 1978 JC 79. It is not necessary that sexual services offered are actually provided: see *R. v. McFarlane* [1994] 2 W.L.R. 494.

Subs. (2)

Where a woman who had been tricked by a man into going through a bigamous marriage with him and had sexual intercourse with him claimed criminal injuries compensations on the basis that a contravention of the forerunner of s.7(2)(b) had occurred, it was held that even assuming that this section applied it was not a crime of violence and thus did not qualify under CICB rules for compensation: *Gray v. Criminal Injuries Compensation Board*, 1993 S.L.T. 28.

Abduction and unlawful detention

8.—(1) Any person who, with intent that any unmarried girl under the age of 18 years should have unlawful sexual intercourse with men or with a particular man, takes or causes to be taken such girl out of the possession and against the will of her father or mother, or any other person having the lawful care or charge of her, shall be liable on conviction on indictment to imprisonment for a term not exceeding two years or on summary conviction to imprisonment for a term not exceeding three months.

(2) It shall be a defence to any charge under subsection (1) above that the person so charged had reasonable cause to believe that the girl was of or over the age of 18 years.

(3) Any person who detains any woman or girl against her will—

(a) in or upon any premises with intent that she may have unlawful sexual intercourse with men or with a particular man; or

(b) in any brothel,

shall be liable on conviction on indictment to imprisonment for a term not exceeding two years or on summary conviction to imprisonment for a term not exceeding three months.

(4) Where a woman or girl is in or upon any premises for the purpose of having unlawful sexual intercourse, or is in a brothel, a person shall be deemed to detain such woman or girl in or upon such premises or brothel if, with intent to compel or induce her to remain in or upon the premises or brothel, he withholds from her any wearing apparel or other property belonging to her or, where wearing apparel has been lent or otherwise supplied to the woman or girl by or by the direction of such person, he threatens the woman or girl with legal proceedings if she takes away with her the wearing apparel so lent or supplied.

(5) No legal proceedings, whether civil or criminal, shall be taken against a woman or girl mentioned in subsection (4) above for taking away or being found in possession of any such wearing apparel as was necessary to enable her to leave such premises or brothel mentioned in that subsection.

GENERAL NOTE

This section re-enacts ss.8 and 9 of the Sexual Offences (Scotland) Act 1976. There are no reported Scottish cases on the sections or indeed on their forerunners, ss.7 and 8 of the Criminal Law Amendment Act 1885 (c. 69), with the exception of one civil matter *Abinet v. Fleck* (1894) 2 S.L.T. 30 which adds nothing to the jurisprudence.

Permitting girl to use premises for intercourse

9.—(1) Any person who, being the owner or occupier of any premises, or having, or acting or assisting in, the management or control of any premises, induces or knowingly suffers any girl of such age as is mentioned in this subsection to resort to or be in or upon such premises for the purpose of having unlawful sexual intercourse with men or with a particular man—

(a) if such girl is under the age of 13 years, shall be liable on conviction on indictment to imprisonment for life; and

(b) if such girl is of or over the age of 13 years and under the age of 16 years, shall be liable on conviction on indictment to imprisonment for a term not exceeding two years or on summary conviction to imprisonment for a term not exceeding three months.

(2) It shall be a defence to a charge under this section that the person so charged, being a man under the age 24 years who had not previously been charged with a like offence, had reasonable cause to believe that the girl was of or over the age of 16 years.

(3) In subsection (2) above, "a like offence" means an offence under—

(a) subsection (1) above; or

(b) section 5(3) of this Act; or

(c) section 4(1) or 10(1) of the Sexual Offences (Scotland) Act 1976 or section 5 or 6 of the Criminal Law Amendment Act 1885 (the enactments formerly creating the offences mentioned in paragraphs (a) and (b) above).

GENERAL NOTE

This is a re-enactment of the Sexual Offences (Scotland) Act 1976, s.10. The offence may be committed even if the premises are the girl's home. In *R. v. Webster* (1885) 16 Q.B. 134 the mother of the girl knew that she had come home with a man and had intercourse with him in the house, and was convicted of an offence under this section of "knowingly suffering". Unlawful intercourse means intercourse outwith marriage: *R. v. Chapman* [1959] 1 Q.B. 100. Similar provision is made by the Mental Health (Scotland) Act 1984, s.106(1)(b), for women who are mental defectives.

Seduction, prostitution, etc., of girl under 16

10.—(1) If any person having parental responsibilities (within the meaning of section 1(3) of the Children (Scotland) Act 1995), in relation to, or having charge or care of a girl under the age of 16 years causes or encourages—

(a) the seduction or prostitution of;

(b) unlawful sexual intercourse with; or

(c) the commission of an indecent assault upon,

her he shall be liable on conviction on indictment to imprisonment for a term not exceeding two years or on summary conviction to imprisonment for a term not exceeding three months.

(2) For the purposes of this section, a person shall be deemed to have caused or encouraged the matters mentioned in paragraphs (a) to (c) of subsection (1) above upon a girl who has been seduced or indecently assaulted, or who has had unlawful sexual intercourse or who has become a prostitute, if he has knowingly allowed her to consort with, or to enter or continue in the employment of, any prostitute or person of known immoral character.

(3) Subsections (1) and (2) above shall apply to a contravention of section 6 of this Act in like manner as they apply to an indecent assault, and any reference to the commission of such an assault or to being indecently assaulted shall be construed accordingly.

(4) Where on the trial of any offence under this Part of this Act it is proved to the satisfaction of the court that the seduction or prostitution of a girl under the age of 16 years has been caused, encouraged or favoured by her father, mother or guardian it shall be in the power of the court to divest such person of all authority over her, and to appoint any person or persons willing to take charge of such girl to be her guardian until she has attained the age of 21 years, or such lower age as the court may direct.

(5) The High Court of Justiciary shall have the power from time to time to rescind or vary an order under subsection (4) above by the appointment of any other person or persons as such guardian, or in any other respect.

General Note
This section re-enacts the Sexual Offences (Scotland) Act 1976, s.11.

Parental responsibilities
These responsibilities are laid out in the Children (Scotland) Act 1995, s.1(3), and cover promotion of the child's health development and welfare and provision of guidance and direction. Any person having these responsibilities in relation to the child is covered by this provision—not simply a parent.

Encourages
See *R. v. Drury (Alfred)* (1974) 60 Cr.App.R. 195.

Trading in prostitution and brothel-keeping

11.—(1) Every male person who—
(a) knowingly lives wholly or in part on the earnings of prostitution; or
(b) in any public place persistently solicits or importunes for immoral purposes,
shall be liable on conviction on indictment to imprisonment for a term not exceeding two years or on summary conviction to imprisonment for a term not exceeding six months.

(2) If it is made to appear to a court of summary jurisdiction by information on oath that there is reason to suspect that any house or any part of a house is used by a female for purposes of prostitution, and that any male person residing in or frequenting the house is living wholly or in part on the earnings of the prostitute, the court may issue a warrant authorising a constable to enter and search the house and to arrest that male person.

(3) Where a male person is proved to live with or to be habitually in the company of a prostitute, or is proved to have exercised control, direction or influence over the movements of a prostitute in such a manner as to show that he is aiding, abetting or compelling her prostitution with any other person, or generally, he shall, unless he can satisfy the court to the contrary, be deemed to be knowingly living on the earnings of prostitution.

(4) Every female who is proved to have, for the purposes of gain, exercised control, direction or influence over the movements of a prostitute in such a manner as to show that she is aiding, abetting or compelling her prostitution with any other person, or generally, shall be liable to the penalties set out in subsection (1) above.

(5) Any person who—
(a) keeps or manages or acts or assists in the management of a brothel; or
(b) being the tenant, lessee, occupier or person in charge of any premises, knowingly permits such premises or any part thereof to be used as a brothel or for the purposes of habitual prostitution; or
(c) being the lessor or landlord of any premises, or the agent of such lessor or landlord, lets the same or any part thereof with the knowledge that such premises or some part thereof are or is to be used as a brothel, or is wilfully a party to the continued use of such premises or any part thereof as a brothel,
shall be guilty of an offence.

(6) A person convicted of an offence under subsection (5) above shall be liable—
(a) in the sheriff court to a fine not exceeding level 4 on the standard scale or to imprisonment for a term not exceeding six months; and
(b) in the district court to a fine not exceeding level 3 on the standard scale or to imprisonment for a term not exceeding three months,
or, in either case, to both such fine and imprisonment.

GENERAL NOTE
This section is derived from ss.12 and 13 of the Sexual Offences (Scotland) Act 1976.

Subs. (1)
See *Soni v. H.M. Advocate*, 1970 S.L.T. 275 and cases referred to therein.
Persistent. This requires two separate acts: see *Dale v. Smith* [1967] 1 W.L.R. 700.
Immoral purposes. This refers to sexual conduct and may not apply to a man who importunes a woman for the purpose of intercourse with himself: *Crook v. Edmondson* [1966] 2 Q.B. 81.

Subs. (3)
See *Soni v. H.M Advocate*, above. See generally the Civic Government (Scotland) Act 1982 (c. 45), s.46 and *White v. Allan*, 1985 S.L.T. 396.

Subs. (5)
Manages or assists in the management. See *Vaughan v. Smith*, 1919 J.C. 9.
Brothel. See *Singleton v. Ellison* [1895] 1 Q.B. 607, *Milne v. McNicol*, (unrep.), High Court of Justiciary, February 1965 (referred to in *Gordon's Criminal Law*, 2nd Ed, at para. 36.26). See also s.13(10) of this Act. See generally Gordon.

Allowing child to be in brothel

12.—(1) If any person having parental responsibilities (within the meaning of section 1(3) of the Children (Scotland) Act 1995), in relation to, or having charge or care of a child who has attained the age of four years and is under the age of 16 years, allows that child to reside in or to frequent a brothel, he shall be liable on conviction on indictment, or on summary conviction, to a fine not exceeding level 2 on the standard scale or alternatively, or in default of payment of such a fine, or in addition thereto, to imprisonment for a term not exceeding six months.

(2) Nothing in this section shall affect the liability of a person to be indicted under section 9 of this Act, but upon the trial of a person under that section it shall be lawful for the jury, if they are satisfied that he is guilty of an offence under this section, to find him guilty of that offence.

Homosexual offences

Homosexual offences

13.—(1) Subject to the provisions of this section, a homosexual act in private shall not be an offence provided that the parties consent thereto and have attained the age of eighteen years.

(2) An act which would otherwise be treated for the purpose of this Act as being done in private shall not be so treated if done—
  (a) when more than two persons take part or are present; or
  (b) in a lavatory to which the public have, or are permitted to have, access whether on payment or otherwise.

(3) A male person who is suffering from mental deficiency which is of such a nature or degree that he is incapable of living an independent life or of guarding himself against serious exploitation cannot in law give any consent which, by virtue of subsection (1) above, would prevent a homosexual act from being an offence; but a person shall not be convicted on account of the incapacity of such a male person to consent, of an offence consisting of such an act if he proves that he did not know and had no reason to suspect that male person to be suffering from such mental deficiency.

(4) In this section, a "homosexual act" means sodomy or an act of gross indecency or shameless indecency by one male person with another male person.

(5) Subject to subsection (3) above, it shall be an offence to commit or to be party to the commission of, or to procure or attempt to procure the commission of a homosexual act—
  (a) otherwise than in private;

(b) without the consent of both parties to the act; or

(c) with a person under the age of eighteen years.

(6) It shall be an offence to procure or attempt to procure the commission of a homosexual act between two other male persons.

(7) A person who commits or is party to the commission of an offence under subsection (5) or subsection (6) above shall be liable on conviction on indictment to imprisonment for a term not exceeding two years or to a fine or to both and on summary conviction to imprisonment for a term not exceeding 3 months, or to a fine not exceeding the prescribed sum (within the meaning of section 225(8) of the Criminal Procedure (Scotland) Act 1995).

(8) It shall be a defence to a charge of committing a homosexual act under subsection (5)(c) above that the person so charged being under the age of 24 years who had not previously been charged with a like offence, had reasonable cause to believe that the other person was of or over the age of 18 years.

(9) A person who knowingly lives wholly or in part on the earnings of another from male prostitution or who solicits or importunes any male person for the purpose of procuring the commission of a homosexual act within the meaning of subsection (4) above shall be liable—

(a) on summary conviction to imprisonment for a term not exceeding six months; or

(b) on conviction on indictment to imprisonment for a term not exceeding two years.

(10) Premises shall be treated for the purposes of sections 11(1) and 12 of this Act as a brothel if people resort to it for the purposes of homosexual acts within the meaning of subsection (4) above in circumstances in which resort thereto for heterosexual practices would have led to its being treated as a brothel for the purposes of those sections.

(11) No proceedings for—

(a) the offences mentioned in subsections (5) and (6) above; and

(b) any offence under subsection (9) above which consists of soliciting or importuning any male person for the purpose of procuring the commission of a homosexual act,

shall be commenced after the expiration of twelve months from the date on which that offence was committed.

DEFINITIONS

"Homosexual act": subs. (4).

"in private": subs. (2).

GENERAL NOTE

This section re-enacts s.80 of the Criminal Justice (Scotland) Act 1980, as amended. The original provision decriminalised certain acts when certain conditions were fulfilled. Acts which did not fall within the protection of the section could be prosecuted at common law using the crimes of sodomy, shameless indecency or lewd practices. See generally *Gordon's Criminal Law op. cit.* s.11 and 2nd Supplement.

Miscellaneous

Power, on indictment for rape, etc., to convict of other offences

14. If, in the trial of an indictment for rape or an offence under section 5(1) of this Act, the jury—

(a) are not satisfied that the accused is guilty of the charge or of an attempt to commit the charge; but

(b) are satisfied that the accused is guilty of an offence under section 5(2) or (3) or 7(2) or (3) of this Act, or of an indecent assault, the jury may acquit the accused of the charge mentioned in paragraph (a) above, and find him guilty of such offence as is mentioned in paragraph (b) or of an indecent assault, and the accused shall be liable to be punished in the same manner as if he had been convicted upon an indictment for such offence or for indecent assault.

GENERAL NOTE

This section replaces s.15 of the Sexual Offences (Scotland) Act 1976. A conviction on the alternative charges is competent even where the indictment does not set forth the statute; see *Advocate, H.M. v. McLaren*, (1897) 2 Adam 395, *Advocate, H.M. v. Barbour* (1887) 1 White 466, *cf.* L.J.C. McDonald in *Advocate, H.M. v. Henderson* (1888) 2 White 157.

Where however the indictment contains only a charge of attempted rape the section does not apply: see *Townsend v. H.M. Advocate*, (1914) 7 Adam 378.

Defence to charge or indecent assault

15. It shall be a defence to a charge of indecent assault committed against a girl under the age of 16 years that the person so charged has reasonable cause to believe that the girl was his wife.

GENERAL NOTE

The corresponding English legislation to the forerunner of this section (s.6 of the Sexual Offences (Scotland) Act 1976) makes the need for "actual belief" explicit. See *R. v. Banks* [1916] 2 K.B. 621 and *R. v. Harrison* (1938) 26 Cr.App.R. 166.

Power of search

16.—(1) If it appears to a justice on information on oath by any parent, relative or guardian of any woman or girl, or any other person who, in the opinion of the justice, is *bona fide* acting in the interest of any woman or girl, that there is reasonable cause to suspect that such woman or girl is unlawfully detained for immoral purposes by any person in any place within the jurisdiction of the justice, he may issue a warrant authorising any person named therein to search for, and, when found, to take to and detain in a place of safety, such woman or girl until she can be brought before a justice, and the justice before whom such woman or girl is brought may cause her to be delivered up to her parents or guardians, or otherwise dealt with as circumstances may permit and require.

(2) The justice issuing such warrant may, by the same or any other warrant, cause any person accused of so unlawfully detaining such woman or girl to be apprehended and brought before a justice, and proceedings to be taken for punishing such person according to law.

(3) A woman or girl shall be deemed to be unlawfully detained for immoral purposes is she is so detained for the purpose of having unlawful sexual intercourse with men or with a particular man, and she—

(a) is under the age of 16 years; or
(b) if of or over the age of 16 years and under the age of 18 years, is so detained against her will, or against the will of her father or mother or of any other person having the lawful care or charge of her; or
(c) if of or over the age of 18 years, is so detained against her will.

(4) Any person authorised by warrant under this section to search for any woman or girl so detained as aforesaid may enter (if need be by force) any house, building, or other place specified in the warrant, and may remove the woman or girl therefrom.

(5) Every warrant issued under this section shall be addressed to and executed by a constable, who shall be accompanied by the parent, relative, or

guardian or other person giving the information, if that person so desires, unless the justice directs otherwise.

(6) In this section, "justice" has the same meaning as in section 307 of the Criminal Procedure (Scotland) Act 1995.

Liability to other criminal proceedings

17. This Part of this Act shall not exempt any person from any proceedings for an offence which is punishable at common law, or under any enactment other than this Part, but nothing in this Part of this Act shall enable a person to be punished twice for the same offence.

PART II

SPORTING EVENTS: CONTROL OF ALCOHOL ETC. ETC.

GENERAL NOTE

This Part of the Act is derived from Pt. V of the Criminal Justice (Scotland) Act 1980 (which was enacted as a result of the Report of the McElhone Working Group on Football Crowd Behaviour), and the Sporting Events (Control of Alcohol etc.) Act 1985, both as amended and provides mechanisms for the control of alcohol at sporting events when the event or ground is designated by the Secretary of State.

PARLIAMENTARY DEBATES FOR THE SPORTING EVENTS (CONTROL OF ALCOHOL ETC.) ACT 1985 (c. 57)
    Hansard, H.C. Vol. 81, col. 919; Vol. 82, col. 333; Vol. 83, col. 758; H.L. Vol. 465, col. 1313; Vol. 466, cols. 322 and 751.

Designation of sports grounds and sporting events

18.—(1) Subject to subsection (2) below, the Secretary of State may for the purposes of this Part of this Act by order designate—

(a) a sports ground or a class of sports ground;

(b) a sporting event, or a class of sporting event, at that ground or at any of that class of ground;

(c) a sporting event, or a class of sporting event, taking place outside Great Britain.

(2) An order under this section shall not apply to a sporting event at which all the participants take part without financial or material reward and to which all spectators are admitted free of charge; but this subsection is without prejudice to the order's validity as respects any other sporting event.

(3) The power to make an order under subsection (1) above shall be exercisable by statutory instrument which shall be subject to annulment in pursuance of a resolution of either House of Parliament.

DEFINITIONS
    "sports ground": s.23.
    "sporting event": s.23.

GENERAL NOTE
    The power to designate applies to all sporting events except amateur events to which admission is free, including events outwith Great Britain.

Alcohol on vehicles

19.—(1) Where a public service vehicle or railway passenger vehicle is being operated for the principal purpose of conveying passengers for the whole or part of a journey to or from a designated sporting event, then—

(a) any person in possession of alcohol on the vehicle shall be guilty of an offence and liable on summary conviction to imprisonment for a period not exceeding 60 days or a fine not exceeding level 3 on the standard scale or both;

(b) if alcohol is being carried on the vehicle and the vehicle is on hire to a person, he shall, subject to subsection (7) below, be guilty of an offence and liable on summary conviction to a fine not exceeding level 3 on the standard scale; and

(c) any person who is drunk on the vehicle shall be guilty of an offence and liable on summary conviction to a fine not exceeding level 2 on the standard scale.

(2) Notwithstanding section 92 of the Licensing (Scotland) Act 1976 (restriction on carriage of alcoholic liquor in crates on contract carriages), but subject to subsection (7) below, if the operator of a public service vehicle which is being operated as mentioned in subsection (1) above, either by himself or by his employee or agent permits alcohol to be carried on the vehicle, the operator and, as the case may be, the employee or agent shall be guilty of an offence and liable on summary conviction to a fine not exceeding level 3 on the standard scale.

(3) This subsection applies to a motor vehicle which is not a public service vehicle but which is adapted to carry more than 8 passengers and is being operated for the principle purpose of conveying two or more passengers for the whole or part of a journey to or from a designated sporting event.

(4) Any person in possession of alcohol on a vehicle to which subsection (3) above applies shall be guilty of an offence and liable on summary conviction to imprisonment for a period not exceeding 60 days or a fine not exceeding level 3 on the standard scale or both.

(5) Any person who is drunk on a vehicle to which subsection (3) above applies shall be guilty of an offence and liable on summary conviction to a fine not exceeding level 2 on the standard scale.

(6) Any person who permits alcohol to be carried on a vehicle to which subsection (3) above applies and—

(a) is the driver of the vehicle; or

(b) where he is not its driver, is the keeper of the vehicle, the employee or agent of the keeper, a person to whom it is made available (by hire, loan or otherwise) by the keeper or the keeper's employee or agent, or

the employee or agent of a person to whom it is so made available,

shall, subject to subsection (7) below, be guilty of an offence and liable on summary conviction to a fine not exceeding level 3 on the standard scale.

(7) Where a person is charged with an offence under subsection (1)(b), (2) or (6) above, it shall be a defence for him to prove that the alcohol was carried on the vehicle without his consent or connivance and that he did all he reasonably could to prevent such carriage.

DEFINITIONS

"alcohol": s.23; Licensing (Scotland) Act 1976 (c. 66), s.139.
"operation": s.23.
"public service vehicle": s.23.
"railway passenger vehicle": s.23.
"standard scale": Criminal Procedure (Scotland) Act 1995 (c. 46), s.225.
"the 1980 Act": Criminal Justice (Scotland) Act 1980 (c. 62).

GENERAL NOTE

Subs. (2)

This section makes the operator vicariously liable for the actings of his employee or agent. There is a defence of "due diligence" contained in subs. (7).

Subss. (3), (4), (5) and (6)

These subsections create similar provisions to subss. (1) and (2), applicable to vehicles falling outwith the definition of "public service vehicle" or "railway passenger vehicle" but adapted to carry more than eight passengers and being operated for the purpose of taking two or more people to a designated event. These provisions were added to the 1980 Act by the Public Order Act 1986.

Sporting events: controls

20.—(1) Any person who—
(a) is in possession of a controlled container in; or
(b) while in possession of a controlled container, attempts to enter,
the relevant area of a designated sports ground at any time during the period of a designated sporting event shall be guilty of an offence and liable on summary conviction to imprisonment for a period not exceeding 60 days or to a fine not exceeding level 3 on the standard scale or both.

(2) Any person who—
(a) is in possession of alcohol in; or
(b) while in possession of alcohol, attempts to enter,
the relevant area of a designated sports ground at any time during the period of a designated sporting event, shall be guilty of an offence and liable on summary conviction to imprisonment for a period not exceeding 60 days or to a fine not exceeding level 3 on the standard scale or both.

(3) Any person who has entered the relevant area of a designated sports ground and is in possession of a controlled article or substance at any time during the period of a designated sporting event shall be guilty of an offence.

(4) Any person who, while in possession of a controlled article or substance, attempts to enter the relevant area of a designated sports ground at any time during the period of a designated sporting event at the ground shall be guilty of an offence.

(5) A person guilty of an offence under subsection (3) or (4) above shall be liable on summary conviction to imprisonment for a period not exceeding 60 days or to a fine not exceeding level 3 on the standard scale or both.

(6) It shall be a defence for a person charged with an offence under subsection (3) or (4) above to show that he had been lawful authority to be in possession of the controlled article or substance.

(7) Any person who—
(a) is drunk in; or
(b) while drunk, attempts to enter,
the relevant area of a designated sports ground at any time during the period of a designated sporting event shall be guilty of an offence and liable on summary conviction to a fine not exceeding level 2 on the standard scale.

(8) In this section—
"controlled article or substance" means—
(a) any article or substance whose main purpose is the emission of a flare for purposes of illuminating or signalling (as opposed to igniting or heating) or the emission of smoke or a visible gas; and in particular it includes distress flares, fog signals, and pellets and capsules intended to be used as fumigators or for testing pipes, but not matches, cigarette lighters or heaters; and
(b) any article which is a firework.
"controlled container" means any bottle, can or other portable container, whether open or sealed, which is, or was, in its original manufactured state, capable of containing liquid and is made from such material or is of such construction, or is so adapted, that if it were thrown at or propelled against a person it would be capable of causing some injury to that person; but the term does not include a container holding a medicinal product for a medicinal purpose.
"medicinal product" and "medicinal purpose" have the meanings assigned to those terms by section 130 of the Medicines Act 1968.

Definitions
"controlled article or substance": subs. (8).
"controlled container": subs. (8).
"relevant area": s.23.

This section provides for offences of being in possession of a controlled container, alcohol, controlled article or substance or being drunk, while in or attempting to enter, the relevant area of a designated sports ground. The definition of controlled articles, substances and containers covers items which would be likely to cause injury to a person. There is a defence of "lawful authority" in subs. (7).

Police powers of enforcement

21. For the purpose of enforcing the provisions of this Part of this Act, a constable shall have the power without warrant—

(a) to enter a designated sports ground at any time during the period of a designated sporting event;

(b) to search a person who he has reasonable grounds to suspect is committing or has committed an offence under this Part of this Act;

(c) to stop and search a vehicle where he has reasonable grounds to suspect that an offence under section 19 of this Act is being or has been committed;

(d) to arrest a person who he has reasonable grounds to suspect is committing or has committed an offence under this Part of this Act;

(e) to seize and detain—

    (i) with its contents (if any), a controlled container as defined in section 20(8) of this Act, or

    (ii) with its contents, any other container if he has reasonable grounds to suspect that those contents are or include alcohol.

GENERAL NOTE

This section contains the powers of the police to employ the provisions of this Part of the Act. Apart from the power to enter a designated sports ground the use of the powers require the constable to have "reasonable grounds to suspect"—an objective test which if not met will render the use of the powers unlawful and any evidence recovered as a result thereof inadmissible.

Presumption as to contents of container

22. Section 127 of the Licensing (Scotland) Act 1976 (presumption as to contents of container) shall apply for the purposes of any trial in connection with an alleged contravention of any provision of this Part of this Act as it applies for the purposes of any trial in connection with an alleged contravention of any provision of that Act.

GENERAL NOTE

The most important provisions in s.127 of the Licensing (Scotland) Act 1976 for the purposes of this section are that any liquid found in a container which is sealed or open, shall be presumed to conform to the description of the liquid on the container. No notice is required of the prosecutor's intention to rely on the presumption since the Law Reform (Miscellaneous Provisions) (Scotland) Act 1990, but the defence may lead evidence to rebut the presumption if they give seven days' notice of their intention to do so to the prosecutor.

The definition of "alcohol" in s.139(1) of the Licensing (Scotland) Act 1976, at that time did not include "any liquor which ... is found to be of an original gravity not exceeding 1016 degrees and to be of a strength not exceeding 2 degrees of proof ...". Where therefore the Crown sought to rely on the presumption where the objects in question were bottles of cider which were labelled as "strong cider fermented to full strength" but gave no indication of gravity or strength of the liquid, there was insufficient evidence that what was in the bottles was "alcohol": *Tudhope v. McDonald*, 1986 S.C.C.R. 32; see also *Grieve v. Hamilton*, 1987 S.C.C.R. 317. The present definition provides for exclusion by reference to strength—not exceeding 0.5% of ethyl alcohol by volume (at a temperature of 20 degrees celsius): see *Davenport v. Wilson*, High Court of Justiciary, November 1, 1994, Crown Office Circular A5/95, where the label in question read

"Grant's Vodka 35cl 37.5% vol". The court held that the label indicated that the bottle contained 37.5% of something by volume and the description of the contents as vodka led to the obvious conclusion that the words related to the alcoholic content of the liquor inside the bottle.

Interpretation of Part II

23. In this Part of this Act, unless the context otherwise requires—
   "advertised" means announced in any written or printed document or in any broadcast announcement;
   "alcohol" means alcoholic liquor as defined in section 139 of the Licensing (Scotland) Act 1976;
   "designated" means designated by the Secretary of State by order under section 18 of this Act, and "designated sporting event" includes a sporting event designated under section 9(3)(a) of the Sporting Events (Control of Alcohol) Etc. Act 1985;
   "keeper", in relation to a vehicle, means the person having the duty to take out a licence for it under section 1(1) of the Vehicles Excise and Registration Act 1994;
   "period of a designated sporting event" means the period commencing two hours before the start and ending one hour after the end of a designated sporting event, except that where the event is advertised as to start at a particular time but is delayed or postponed in includes, and where for any reason an event does not take place it means, the period commencing two hours before and ending one hour after, that particular time;
   "public service vehicle" has the same meaning as in the Public Passenger Vehicles Act 1981 and "operator" in relation to such a vehicle means—
        (a) the driver if he owns the vehicle; and
        (b) in any case the person for whom the driver works (whether under a contract of employment or any other description of contract personally to do work);
   "railway passenger vehicle" has the same meaning as in the Licensing (Scotland) Act 1976;
   "relevant area" means any part of a sports ground—
        (a) to which spectators attending a designated sporting event are granted access on payment; or
        (b) from which a designated sporting event may be viewed directly;
   "sporting event" means any physical competitive activity at a sports ground, and includes any such activity which has been advertised as to, but does not, take place; and
   "sports ground" means any place whatsoever which is designed, or is capable of being adapted, for the holding of sporting events in respect of which spectators are accommodated.

PART III

DETENTION BY CUSTOMS OFFICERS

GENERAL NOTE
   Sections 24 and 25 re-enact the provisions of ss.48 and 49 of the Criminal Justice (Scotland) Act 1989 which introduced with appropriate modifications the same powers granted to police officers by ss.2 and 3 of the Criminal Justice (Scotland) Act 1980, for customs officers. Section 26 re-enacts a new power introduced in s.50 of the 1987 Act.

Detention and questioning by customs officers

24.—(1) Where an officer has reasonable grounds for suspecting that a person has committed or is committing an offence punishable by imprisonment relating to an assigned matter, the officer may, for the purpose of facilitating the carrying out of investigations—

(a) into the offence; and

(b) as to whether criminal proceedings should be instigated against the person,

detain that person and take him as quickly as is reasonably practicable to a customs office or other premises and may thereafter for that purpose take him to any other place and, subject to the following provisions of this section, the detention may continue at the customs office or, as the case may be, the other premises or place.

(2) Detention under subsection (1) above shall be terminated not more than six hours after it beings or (if earlier)—

(a) when the person is arrested;

(b) when he is detained in pursuance of any other enactment or subordinate instrument; or

(c) where there are no longer such grounds as are mentioned in the said subsection (1),

and when a person has been detained under subsection (1) above, he shall be informed immediately upon the termination of his detention in accordance with this subsection that his detention has been terminated.

(3) Where a person has been detained under subsection (1) above, he shall not thereafter be detained under that subsection on the same grounds or on any grounds arising out of the same circumstances.

(4) Where a person has previously been detained in pursuance of any other enactment or subordinate instrument, he may not be detained under subsection (1) above on the same grounds or on grounds arising from the same circumstances as those which led to his earlier detention.

(5) At the time when an officer detains a person under subsection (1) above, he shall inform the person of his suspicion, of the general nature of the offence which he suspects has been or is being committed and of the reason for the detention; and there shall be recorded—

(a) the place where detention begins and the customs office or other premises to which the person is taken;

(b) any other place to which the person is, during the detention, thereafter taken;

(c) the general nature of the suspected offence;

(d) the time when detention under subsection (1) above begins and the time of the person's arrival at the customs office or other premises;

(e) the time when the person is informed of his rights in terms of subsection (8) below and of section 25(1) of this Act and the identity of the officer so informing him;

(f) where the person requests such intimation to be sent as is specified in the said section 25(1), the time when such request is—

(i) made;

(ii) complied with; and

(g) the time of the person's release from detention or, where instead of being released he is—

(i) further detained under section 26 of this Act, the time of commencement of the further detention; or

(ii) arrested in respect of the alleged offence, the time of such arrest.

(6) Where a person is detained under subsection (1) above, an officer may—

(a) without prejudice to any existing rule of law as regards the admissibility in evidence of an answer given, put questions to him in relation to the suspected offence;

(b) exercise the same powers of search as are available following an arrest.

(7) An officer may use reasonable force in exercising any power conferred by subsection (1) or (6)(b) above.

(8) A person detained under subsection (1) above shall be under no obligation to answer any question other than to give his name and address, and an officer shall so inform him both on so detaining him and on arrival at the customs office or other premises.

(9) In this section and in sections 25 and 26 of this Act "assigned matter" and "officer" have the meanings given to them by section 1 of the Customs and Excise Management Act 1979, and "customs office" means a place for the time being occupied by Her Majesty's Customs and Excise.

DEFINITIONS
"assigned matter": subs. (9); Customs and Excise Management Act 1979, s.1.
"Customs office": subs. (9).
"officers": subs. (9); Customs and Excise Management Act 1979, s.1.

GENERAL NOTE
See generally for the case law under the 1980 Act, s.2, Renton Brown's *Criminal Procedure* (5th Ed), paras. 5–13 et seq.

The powers under the section can be exercised by a police officer or any other person who is authorised by a customs officer under powers of delegation provided in the Customs and Excise Management Act 1979. So, where a suspect was detained by a police officer on the instructions of a customs officer, there was no breach of the section, and although the 1979 Act, s.8(1)(b), provided that a certificate by a Commissioner, to show that a person was acting under their authority, was sufficient evidence of the fact, the appropriate evidence could also be provided parole: *Montes v. H.M. Advocate*, 1990 S.C.C.R. 645.

Right to have someone informed when detained

25.—(1) Without prejudice to section 17 the Criminal Procedure (Scotland) Act 1995 (intimation to solicitor following arrest), a person who, not being a person in respect of whose detention subsection (2) below applies, is being detained under section 24 of this Act and has been taken to a customs office or other premises or place shall be entitled to have intimation of his detention and of the customs office or other premises or place sent to a solicitor and to one other person reasonably named by him without delay or, where some delay is necessary in the interest of the investigation or the prevention of crime or the apprehension of offenders, with no more delay than is so necessary; and the person shall be informed of such entitlement—

(a) on arrival at the customs office or other premises; or

(b) where he is not detained until after such arrival, on such detention.

(2) Without prejudice to the said section 17, an officer shall, where a person who is being detained as is mentioned in subsection (1) above appears to him to be a child, send without delay such information as is mentioned in that subsection to that person's parent if known; and the parent—

(a) in a case where there is reasonable cause to suspect that he has been involved in the alleged offence in respect of which the person has been detained, may; and

(b) in any other case shall,

be permitted access to the person.

(3) The nature and extent of any access permitted under subsection (2), above shall be subject to any restriction essential for the furtherance of the investigation or the well-being of the person.

(4) In subsection (2) above—

(a) "child" means a person under 16 years of age; and
(b) "parent" includes a guardian and any person who has the care of a child.

DEFINITIONS
"child": subs. (4)(a).
"customs office": s.24(9).
"officer": s.24(9).
"parent": subs. (4)(b).

Detention in connection with certain drug smuggling offences

26.—(1) Where an officer has reasonable grounds for suspecting—
(a) that a person has committed or is committing a relevant offence; and
(b) that, in connection with the commission of such an offence, a controlled drug is secreted in the person's body,
a superior officer may, notwithstanding that the person has been or is being detained in pursuance of any other enactment or subordinate instrument, authorise the detention of the person at a customs office or other premises in accordance with this section.

(2) Subject to subsection (7) below, where a person is detained under subsection (1) above or is further detained in pursuance of a warrant under subsection (4) below he shall—
(a) provide such specimens of blood or urine for analysis;
(b) submit to such intimate searches, to be carried out by a registered medical practitioner;
(c) submit to such other test or examinations prescribed by the Secretary of State by regulations made under this paragraph to be carried out by, or under the supervision of, a registered medical practitioner,
as the officer may reasonably require; and regulations under paragraph (c) above shall be made by statutory instrument subject to annulment in pursuance of a resolution of either House of Parliament.

(3) Subject to subsection (4) below, detention under subsection (1) above shall be terminated not more than 24 hours after it begins, or (if earlier)—
(a) when the person is arrested;
(b) when he is detained in pursuance of any other enactment or subordinate instrument; or
(c) where there are no longer such grounds as are mentioned in subsection (1),
and, when a person has been detained under subsection (1), he shall, unless further detained in pursuance of a warrant under subsection (4) below, be informed immediately upon the termination of his detention in accordance with this subsection that his detention has been terminated.

(4) Where a person is detained under subsection (1) above and either—
(a) he has failed or refused—
(i) to provide a specimen in pursuance of paragraph (a) of subsection (2) above; or
(ii) to submit to any search, test or examination referred to in paragraph (b) or (c) of that subsection; or
(b) as a result of anything done in pursuance of the said subsection (2) the officer continues to have reasonable grounds for suspecting—
(i) that the person has committed or is committing a relevant offence; and
(ii) that a controlled drug is secreted in the person's body,
the procurator fiscal may, at the request of a superior officer, apply to the sheriff for a warrant for the further detention of the person at a customs office or other premises for an additional period of not more than 7 days; and if the sheriff is satisfied that there has been such failure or refusal as is mentioned in paragraph (a) above or, as the case may be, that there are reasonable grounds

as mentioned in paragraph (b) above he may grant a warrant for such further detention.

(5) Detention in pursuance of a warrant under subsection (4) above shall be terminated at the end of the period of 7 days mentioned in that subsection or (if earlier)—

(a) when the person is arrested;

(b) when he is detained in pursuance of any other enactment or subordinate instrument; or

(c) where there are no longer such grounds as are mentioned in paragraph (b) of that subsection,

and when a person has been detained in pursuance of a warrant under subsection (4), he shall be informed immediately on the termination of his detention in accordance with this subsection that his detention has been terminated.

(6) Subject to subsection (7) below, the question whether it is to be a specimen of blood or a specimen of urine which is to be provided in pursuance of subsection (2) above shall be decided by the officer making the requirement.

(7) A person may be required, in pursuance of subsection (2) above—

(a) to provide a specimen of blood; or

(b) to submit to any search, test or examination,

only if a registered medical practitioner is of the opinion that there are no medical reasons for not making such a requirement; and, if a requirement to provide a specimen of blood is made, the specimen may be taken only by a registered medical practitioner.

(8) Subsections (3), (5), (6) and (8) of section 24 of this Act shall apply in respect of a person detained under this section as they apply in respect of a person detained under the said section 24; and, except as regards a requirement under subsection (2) above, an officer may use reasonable force in exercising any power conferred by this section.

(9) Section 25 of this Act shall, subject to the following modifications, apply in respect of a person detained under this section as it applies to a person detained under section 24 of this Act—

(a) any delay in informing a solicitor and one other person of such detention as is mentioned in subsection (1) of the said section 25 shall not extend longer than the period of 24 hours from the start of the detention, and shall only be permitted on the authorisation of a superior officer;

(b) the person detained shall be entitled to consult a solicitor at any time without delay, and he shall be informed of such entitlement at the commencement of the detention, but, if a superior officer considers it necessary in the interest of the investigation or the prevention of crime or the apprehension of offenders, he may authorise a delay not extending longer than the period of 24 hours from the start of the detention; and

(c) paragraph (a) of subsection (2) of the said section 25 shall cease to apply at the end of the period of 24 hours from the start of the detention,

but any delay authorised by virtue of this subsection shall be for no longer than is necessary in the interest of the investigation or the prevention of crime or the apprehension of offenders.

(10) Without prejudice to section 20(2) of the Interpretation Act 1978, the references in section 24(5) of this Act to section 25(1) of this Act shall be construed as including references to subsection (9) above; and the requirement to record certain matters under the said section 24(5) shall include a requirement to record the time when a person detained makes a request to consult a solicitor and the time when the solicitor is contacted for the purpose of arranging a consultation.

(11) In this section—

"controlled drug" has the meaning assigned by section 2 of the Misuse of Drugs Act 1971;

"intimate search" means a search which consists of the physical examination of a person's body orifices;

"relevant offence" means an offence involving a controlled drug under any of the following provisions of the Customs and Excise Management Act 1979—

(a) section 50(2) or (3) (importation etc. of prohibited goods);
(b) section 68(2) (exportation etc. of prohibited goods);
(c) section 170(1) (possession or dealing with prohibited goods);
(d) section 170(2) (being concerned in evasion or attempt at evasion of a prohibition);

"superior officer" means an officer of the grade of senior executive officer or above.

DEFINITIONS
"controlled drug": subs. (11).
"intimate search": subs. (11).
"officer": s.24.
"relevant offence": subs. (11).
"superior officer": subs. (11).

GENERAL NOTE
These powers are intended to deal with situations where persons are suspected of smuggling controlled drugs by having them secreted in their bodies.

Subs. (1)
The powers can only be exercised by a person who has been commissioned by the Commissioners of Customs and Excise. A police officer may not exercise these powers (unless so commissioned): see *Montes v. H.M. Advocate*, above.

Subs. (2)
An "intimate search" must be carried out by a medical practitioner. The safeguards provided for such searches under the Police and Criminal Evidence Act 1984, s.55, are absent from this section. Although the subsection requires a detainee to submit to examination and search and provide specimens, it is not specifically made an offence for him to fail or refuse to do so. Failure or refusal, however, may lead to the original 24-hour detention being extended by the Sheriff by up to seven days under subs. (4).

PART IV

INVESTIGATION OF SERIOUS OR COMPLEX FRAUD

GENERAL NOTE
Sections 27 to 30 re-enact ss.51 to 54 of the Criminal Justice (Scotland) Act 1987 as amended by the Criminal Justice and Public Order Act 1994. They provide for investigative powers to be exercised by a nominee of the Lord Advocate in the event of a direction being given by him when a suspected offence may involve serious or complex fraud.

Lord Advocate's direction

27.—(1) Where it appears to the Lord Advocate—
(a) that a suspected offence may involve serious or complex fraud; and
(b) that, for the purpose of investigating the affairs or any aspect of the affairs of any person, there is good reason to do so,
he may give a direction under this section.

(2) The Lord Advocate may also give a direction under this section by virtue of section 4(2B) of the Criminal Justice (International Co-operation) Act 1990 or on a request being made to him by the Attorney-General of the Isle of Man, Jersey or Guernsey acting under legislation corresponding to this Part of this Act.

(3) Where a direction is given under this section, this Part of this Act shall apply as regards the investigation of the offence; and any person (other than a constable) nominated by the Lord Advocate either generally or in respect of a particular case (in this Part of this Act referred to as "a nominated officer") shall be entitled to exercise the powers and functions conferred by this Part of this Act.

(4) A direction under this section shall be signed by the Lord Advocate.

GENERAL NOTE

"*Serious or complex fraud*". These concepts are not defined in any way.

"*nominated officer*". It was anticipated that this would be a member of the Procurator Fiscal Service or a person with specialised knowledge such as an accountant. He would be acting on behalf of the Lord Advocate who would be answerable for his acts and omissions.

Subs. (3)

This subsection was added to the 1987 Act by the Criminal Justice and Public Order Act 1994, s.164(3). The same conditions require to be met before the Lord Advocate issues a direction by virtue of the Criminal Justice (International Cooperation) Act 1990 (c. 5) in relation to an offence or suspected offence in a foreign country.

Powers of investigation

28.—(1) A nominated officer may by notice in writing require the person whose affairs are to be investigated ("the person under investigation") or any other person who he has reason to believe has relevant information to answer questions or otherwise furnish information with respect to any matter relevant to the investigation at a specified place and either at a specified time or forthwith.

(2) A nominated officer may by notice in writing require the person under investigation or any other person to produce at such place as may be specified in the notice and either forthwith or at such time as may be so specified any specified documents which appear to a nominated officer to relate to any matter relevant to the investigation or any documents of a specified description which appear to him so to relate; and—

(a) if any such documents are produced, a nominated officer may—
    (i) take copies or extracts from them;
    (ii) require the person producing them to provide an explanation of any of them;

(b) if any such documents are not produced, a nominated officer may require the person who was required to produce them to state, to the best of his knowledge and belief, where they are.

(3) Where, on a petition presented by the procurator fiscal, the sheriff is satisfied, in relation to any documents, that there are reasonable grounds for believing—

(a) that—
    (i) a person has failed to comply with an obligation under this section to produce them;
    (ii) it is not practicable to serve a notice under subsection (2) above in relation to them; or
    (iii) the service of such a notice in relation to them might seriously prejudice the investigation; and

(b) that they are on premises specified in the petition,

he may issue such a warrant as is mentioned in subsection (4) below.

(4) The warrant referred to in subsection (3) above is a warrant authorising a constable together with any other persons named in the warrant—

(a) to enter (using such force as is reasonably necessary for the purpose) and search the premises; and

(b) to take possession of any documents appearing to be documents of the description specified in the petition or to take in relation to any documents so appearing any other steps which may appear to be necessary for preserving them and preventing interference with them.

(5) A statement by a person in response to a requirement imposed by virtue of this section may only be used in evidence against him—

(a) in a prosecution for an offence under section 44(2) of this Act; or

(b) in a prosecution for some other offence where in giving evidence he makes a statement inconsistent with it.

(6) A person shall not under this section be required to disclose any information or produce any document which is an item subject to legal privilege within the meaning of section 33 of this Act; except that a lawyer may be required to furnish the name and address of his client.

(7) No person shall be bound to comply with any requirement imposed by a person exercising power by virtue of a nomination under section 27(3) of this Act unless he has, if required to do so, produced evidence of his authority.

(8) Any evidence obtained by the Lord Advocate by virtue of section 4(2B) of the Criminal Justice (International Co-operation) Act 1990 shall be furnished by him to the Secretary of State for transmission to the overseas authority in compliance with whose request (in the following subsections referred to as the "relevant request") it was so obtained.

(9) If, in order to comply with the relevant request, it is necessary for that evidence to be accompanied by any certificate, affidavit or other verifying document, the Lord Advocate shall also furnish for transmission such document of that nature as appears to him to be appropriate.

(10) Where any evidence obtained by virtue of section 4(2B) of the said Act of 1990 consists of a document, the original or a copy shall be transmitted and where it consists of any other article, the article itself or a description, photograph or other representation of it shall be transmitted, as may be necessary in order to comply with the relevant request.

(11) In this section—

"documents" includes information recorded in any form and, in relation to information recorded otherwise than in legible form, references to its production include references to producing a copy of the information in legible form;

"evidence", in relation to a relevant request, includes documents and other articles; and

"premises" has the same meaning as in section 33 of this Act.

(2) This section and sections 27 and 29 of this Act shall apply to England and Wales and Northern Ireland; and for the purposes of such application any reference—

(a) to the sheriff shall be construed as a reference to a justice of the peace; and

(b) to a petition presented by the procurator fiscal shall be construed—

(i) in England and Wales as a reference to an information laid by a nominated officer;

(ii) in Northern Ireland as a reference to a complaint laid by a nominated officer.

DEFINITIONS
"documents": subs. (11).
"evidence": subs. (11).
"premises": subs. (11); s.33.

GENERAL NOTE
This section contains the investigative powers of the nominated officer which extend to interrogating and obtaining documents from the "suspect" or any other person believed to have relevant information, under pain of punishment for non-compliance. It also provides "back up"

powers to obtain warrants via the Procurator Fiscal when the investigation would otherwise be impeded. The application for a warrant need not be intimated to the suspect or haver: *Harris, Petr.*, 1993 S.C.C.R. 881.

Subs. (6)
    See *R. v. Central Criminal Court, ex p. Francis and Francis* [1989] A.C. 346, a case on the English provisions corresponding with s.33 of this Act where it was held that items otherwise within legal privilege lost that status where their possession was intended to further a criminal purpose. Where a judge granted warrants in terms wider than apparently justified by the investigation and failed to consider legal privilege and its effect on certain material and without giving reasons for granting such intrusive powers, the warrants were quashed: *R. v. Southampton Crown Court, ex p. J. and P.* [1993] Crim.L.R. 962.

Offences in relation to investigations under section 28

29.—(1) Where any person—
  (a) knows or suspects that an investigation under section 28 of this Act is being carried out or is likely to be carried out; and
  (b) falsifies, conceals, destroys or otherwise disposes of, or causes or permits the falsification, concealment, destruction or disposal of documents which he knows or suspects or has reasonable grounds to suspect are or would be relevant to such an investigation,
he shall be guilty of an offence.
    (2) In proceedings against a person for an offence under subsection (1) above, it shall be a defence to prove—
  (a) that he did not know or suspect that by acting as he did he was likely to prejudice the investigation; or
  (b) that he had lawful authority or reasonable excuse for acting as he did.
    (3) A person guilty of an offence under subsection (1) above shall be liable—
  (a) on conviction on indictment, to imprisonment for a term not exceeding seven years or to a fine or to both; and
  (b) on summary conviction, to imprisonment for a term not exceeding six months or to a fine not exceeding the statutory maximum or to both.
    (4) Any person who fails to comply with a requirement imposed on him under the said section 28 shall be guilty of an offence and liable on summary conviction to imprisonment for a term not exceeding six months or to a fine not exceeding level 5 on the standard scale or to both.
    (5) In proceedings against a person for an offence under subsection (4) above, it shall be a defence to prove that he had a reasonable excuse for acting as he did.

GENERAL NOTE
    Failure to comply with a requirement to provide information makes one liable to summary conviction only. The more serious offences of concealing, etc., documents or causing and permitting same are punishable on indictment. Statutory defences are provided for an accused on whom lies the burden of proving them.

Subs. (4)
    It is not a reasonable excuse for a person served with a notice under s.28 and refusing to answer questions or furnish information, that she is married to the person under investigation although the Act makes no change to the law on admissibility of evidence: see *R. v. Director of the Serious Fraud Office, ex p. Johnson (Malcolm Keith)* [1993] C.O.D. 58.

Disclosure of information

30.—(1) Where any information subject to an obligation of secrecy under the Taxes Management Act 1970 has been disclosed by the Commissioners of Inland Revenue or an officer of those Commissioners for the purposes of any prosecution of an offence relating to inland revenue, that information may be disclosed by the Lord Advocate for the purposes of any prosecution of an offence—

(a) in respect of which a direction has been given under section 27(1)(a) of this Act; or

(b) relating to inland revenue,

but not otherwise.

(2) Where any information is subject to an obligation of secrecy imposed by or under any enactment other than an enactment contained in the Taxes Management Act 1970, the obligation shall not have effect to prohibit the disclosure of that information to a nominated officer but any information disclosed by virtue of this subsection may only be disclosed by the Lord Advocate for the purpose of a prosecution in Scotland or elsewhere.

(3) Without prejudice to his power to enter into an agreement apart from this subsection, the Lord Advocate may enter into an agreement for the supply of information to or by him subject, in either case, to an obligation not to disclose the information concerned otherwise than for a specified purpose.

(4) Subject to subsections (1) and (2) above and to any provision of an agreement for the supply of information which restricts the disclosure of the information supplied, information obtained by a nominated officer may be disclosed—

(a) to any government department, or any Northern Ireland Department, or other authority or body discharging its functions on behalf of the Crown (including the Crown in right of Her Majesty's Government in Northern Ireland);

(b) to any competent authority;

(c) for the purposes of any prosecution in Scotland or elsewhere; and

(d) for the purposes of assisting any public or other authority for the time being designated for the purpose of this paragraph by an order made by the Secretary of State to discharge any functions which are specified in the order.

(5) The following are competent authorities for the purposes of subsection (4) above—

(a) an inspector appointed under Part XIV of the Companies Act 1985 or Part XV of the Companies (Northern Ireland) Order 1986;

(b) the Accountant in Bankruptcy;

(c) an Official Receiver;

(d) the Official Receiver for Northern Ireland;

(e) a person appointed to carry out an investigation under section 55 of the Building Societies Act 1986;

(f) a body administering a compensation scheme under section 54 of the Financial Services Act 1986;

(g) an inspector appointed under section 94 of that Act;

(h) a person exercising powers by virtue of section 106 of that Act;

(j) an inspector appointed under section 177 of that Act or any corresponding enactment having effect in Northern Ireland;

(k) a person appointed by the Bank of England under section 41 of the Banking Act 1987 to carry out an investigation and make a report;

(l) a person exercising powers by virtue of section 44(2) of the Insurance Companies Act 1982;

(m) any body having supervisory, regulatory or disciplinary functions in relation to any profession or any area of commercial activity; and

(n) any person or body having, under the law of any country or territory outside the United Kingdom, functions corresponding to any of the functions of any person or body mentioned in any of the foregoing paragraphs.

(6) An order under subsection (4)(d) above may impose conditions subject to which, and otherwise restrict the circumstances in which, information may be disclosed under that paragraph.

PART V

DRUG TRAFFICKING

Investigations and disclosure of information

GENERAL NOTE
These provisions were introduced by the Criminal Justice (Scotland) Act 1987 and contain powers of investigation and search and offences of prejudicing investigations, acquisition or use (assisting others to acquire or use) of proceeds of drugs trafficking, failure to disclose suspicion or knowledge of money laundering and "tipping off". The powers are draconian and far reaching in their effects.

Order to make material available

31.—(1) The procurator fiscal may, for the purpose of an investigation into drug trafficking, apply to the sheriff for an order under subsection (2) below in relation to particular material or material of a particular description.

(2) If on such an application the sheriff is satisfied that the conditions in subsection (4) below are fulfilled, he may, subject to section 35(11) of this Act, make an order that the person who appears to him to be in possession of the material to which the application relates shall—
  (a) produce it to a constable or person commissioned by the Commissioners of Customs and Excise for him to take away; or
  (b) give a constable or person so commissioned access to it,
within such period as the order may specify.

(3) The period to be specified in an order under subsection (2) above shall be seven days unless it appears to the sheriff that a longer or shorter period would be appropriate in the particular circumstances of the application.

(4) The conditions referred to in subsection (2) above are—
  (a) that there are reasonable grounds for suspecting that a specified person has carried on, or has derived financial or other rewards from, drug trafficking;
  (b) that there are reasonable grounds for suspecting that the material to which the application relates—
    (i) is likely to be of substantial value (whether by itself or together with other material) to the investigation for the purpose of which the application is made; and
    (ii) does not consist of or include items subject to legal privilege; and
  (c) that there are reasonable grounds for believing that it is in the public interest, having regard—
    (i) to the benefit likely to accrue to the investigation if the material is obtained; and
    (ii) to the circumstances under which the person in possession of the material holds it,
  that the material should be produced or that access to it should be given.

(5) Where the sheriff makes an order under subsection (2)(b) above in relation to material on any premises he may, on the application of the procurator fiscal, order any person who appears to him to be entitled to grant entry to the premises to allow a constable or person commissioned as aforesaid to enter the premises to obtain access to the material.

(6) Provision may be made by rules of court as to—
  (a) the discharge and variation of orders under this section, and

(b) proceedings relating to such orders.

(7) Where the material to which an application under this section relates consists of information contained in a computer—

(a) an order under subsection (2)(a) above shall have effect as an order to produce the material in a form in which it can be taken away and in which it is visible and legible; and

(b) an order under subsection (2)(b) above shall have effect as an order to give access to the material in a form in which it is visible and legible.

(8) An order under subsection (2) above—

(a) shall not confer any right to production of, or access to, items subject to legal privilege;

(b) shall have effect notwithstanding any obligation as to secrecy or other restriction upon the disclosure of information imposed by statute or otherwise; and

(c) may be made in relation to material in the possession of an authorised government department.

DEFINITIONS
"drug trafficking": s.43(1); Proceeds of Crime (Scotland) Act 1995, s.49(2).
"items subject to legal privilege": s.33.
"premises": s.33.

GENERAL NOTE
This section entitles the court to make a "production order" on the application of the Procurator Fiscal if the conditions under subs. (4) are fulfilled.

Subs. (1)
There is no requirement that any person has been charged or placed on petition and the provisions would apply equally before and after conviction.

Subs. (2)
See *Harris, Petr.*, 1993 S.C.C.R. 881 for a case under similar provisions in relation to the investigation into serious or complex fraud, equivalent to ss.28–30 of this Act. There, the High Court of Justiciary held that intimation of application for a warrant to obtain material held by a third party in relation to a person under investigation, need not be intimated to the "suspect".

Subs. (4)
All the conditions require to be met.

Subs. (8)
The only items which are excluded from the scope of the section are those covered by legal privilege. No other "obligation" of confidentiality or secrecy will prevent an order being made. It may therefore apply to public bodies such as legal authorities, and government departments such as the Department of Social Security and the Inland Revenue.

Authority for search

32.—(1) The procurator fiscal may, for the purpose of an investigation into drug trafficking, apply to the sheriff for a warrant under this section in relation to specified premises.

(2) On such application the sheriff may issue a warrant authorising a constable, or person commissioned by the Commissioners of Customs and Excise, to enter and search the premises if the sheriff is satisfied—

(a) that an order made under section 31 of this Act in relation to material on the premises has not been complied with; or

(b) that the conditions in subsection (3) below are fulfilled; or

(c) that the conditions in subsection (4) below are fulfilled.

(3) The conditions referred to in subsection (2)(b) above are—

(a) that there are reasonable grounds for suspecting that a specified person has carried on, or has derived financial or other rewards from, drug trafficking; and

   (b) that the conditions in subsection (4)(b) and (c) of section 31 of this Act are fulfilled in relation to any material on the premises; and

   (c) that it would not be appropriate to make an order under that section in relation to the material because—

> (i) it is not practicable to communicate with any person entitled to produce the material; or
>
> (ii) it is not practicable to communicate with any person entitled to grant access to the material or entitled to grant entry to the premises on which the material is situated; or
>
> (iii) the investigation for the purposes of which the application is made might be seriously prejudiced unless a constable or person commissioned as aforesaid could secure immediate access to the material.

(4) The conditions referred to in subsection (2)(c) above are—

   (a) that there are reasonable grounds for suspecting that a specified person has carried on, or has derived financial or other rewards from, drug trafficking; and

   (b) that there are reasonable grounds for suspecting that there is on the premises material relating to the specified person or to drug trafficking which is likely to be of substantial value (whether by itself or together with other material) to the investigation for the purpose of which the application is made, but that the material cannot at the time of the application be particularised; and

   (c) that—

> (i) it is not practicable to communicate with any person entitled to grant entry to the premises; or
>
> (ii) entry to the premises will not be granted unless a warrant is produced; or
>
> (iii) the investigation for the purpose of which the application is made might be seriously prejudiced unless a constable or person commissioned as aforesaid arriving at the premises could secure immediate entry to them.

(5) Where a constable or person commissioned as aforesaid has entered premises in the execution of a warrant issued under this section, he may seize and retain any material, other than items subject to legal privilege, which is likely to be of substantial value (whether by itself or together with other material) to the investigation for the purpose of which the warrant was issued.

DEFINITIONS
   "drug trafficking": s.43(1); Proceeds of Crime (Scotland) Act 1995, s.49(2).
   "items subject to legal privilege": s.33.
   "premises": s.33.

GENERAL NOTE
   This section allows the Sheriff on the application of the Procurator Fiscal to grant a warrant to enter and search premises for material to which s.31 relates but when an order under s.31 has not been complied with or it would not be appropriate to make such an order for the reasons set out in subs. (3)(c) or (4)(c).

Interpretation of sections 31 and 32

33. In sections 31 and 32 of this Act—
   "items subject to legal privilege" means—

> (a) communications between a professional legal adviser and his client; or

(b) communications made in connection with or in contemplation of legal proceedings and for the purposes of these proceedings,
being communications which would in legal proceedings be protected from disclosure by virtue of any rule of law relating to the confidentiality of communications; and
"premises" includes any place and, in particular, includes—
(a) any vehicle, vessel, aircraft or hovercraft;
(b) any offshore installation within the meaning of section 1 of the Mineral Workings (Offshore Installations) Act 1971; and
(c) any tent or movable structure.

GENERAL NOTE
   The definition of "items subject to legal privilege" rests on the existing law on privileged communications which does not cover communications intended for the purpose of furthering a criminal act or to obtain advice thereon: see *McCowan v. Wright* (1852) 15 D. 229; *R. v. Central Criminal Court, ex p. Francis and Francis* [1989] A.C. 346. Communications with any person, not only legal advisers, may be covered by part (b) of the definition so long as these are communications for the purposes or in contemplation of legal proceedings.

Prosecution by order of the Commissioners of Customs and Excise

   34.—(1) Summary proceedings for a specified offence may be instituted by order of the Commissioners and shall, if so instituted, be commenced in the name of an officer.
   (2) In the case of the death, removal, discharge or absence of the officer in whose name any proceedings for a specified offence were commenced, those proceedings may be continued by another officer.
   (3) Where the Commissioners investigate, or propose to investigate, any matter with a view to determining—
   (a) whether there are grounds for believing that a specified offence has been committed; or
   (b) whether a person should be prosecuted for a specified offence,
that matter shall be treated as an assigned matter within the meaning of the Customs and Excise Management Act 1979.
   (4) Nothing in this section shall be taken—
   (a) to prevent any person (including any officer) who has power to arrest, detain or prosecute any person for a specified offence from doing so; or
   (b) to prevent a court from proceeding to deal with a person brought before it following his arrest by an officer for a specified offence, even though the proceedings have not been instituted by an order made under subsection (1) above.
   (5) In this section—
"the Commissioners" means the Commissioners of Customs and Excise;
"officer" means a person commissioned by the Commissioners; and
"specified offence" means—
   (a) an offence under section 36, 37, 38, 39 or 40 of this Act or section 14 of the Criminal Justice (International Co-operation) Act 1990 (concealing or transferring proceeds of drug trafficking);
   (b) attempting to commit, conspiracy to commit or incitement to commit, any such offence; or
   (c) any other offence of a kind prescribed in regulations made by the Secretary of State for the purposes of this section.
   (6) Regulations under subsection (5) above shall be made by statutory instrument subject to annulment in pursuance of a resolution of either House of Parliament.

  "commissioners": subs. (5).
  "officer": subs. (5).
  "specified offence": subs. (5).

General Note
  This section allows summary proceedings for "specified offences" to be commenced by a person commissioned by the Commissioners of Customs and Excise but it remains competent for proceedings to be brought by the Procurator Fiscal.

Disclosure of information held by government departments

35.—(1) Subject to subsection (4) below, the Court of Session may on an application by the Lord Advocate order any material mentioned in subsection (3) below which is in the possession of an authorised government department to be produced to the Court within such period as the Court may specify.

(2) The power to make an order under subsection (1) above is exercisable if—

  (a) the powers conferred on the Court by subsection (1) of section 28 of the Proceeds of Crime (Scotland) Act 1995 are exercisable by virtue of subsection (2) of section 29 of that Act; or

  (b) those powers are exercisable by virtue of subsection (3) of the said section 29 and the Court has made a restraint order (within the meaning of section 28 of that Act) which has not been recalled.

(3) The material referred to in subsection (1) above is any material which—

  (a) has been submitted to an officer of an authorised government department by a person who holds, or has at any time held, realisable property (within the meaning of section 4 of the said Act of 1995);

  (b) has been made by an officer of an authorised government department in relation to such a person; or

  (c) is correspondence which passed between an officer of an authorised government department and such a person,

and an order under that subsection may require the production of all such material or of a particular description of such material, being material in the possession of the department concerned.

(4) An order under subsection (1) above shall not require the production of any material unless it appears to the Court of Session that the material is likely to contain information that would facilitate the exercise of the powers conferred on the Court by section 28 of the said Act of 1995 or paragraph 1 or 12 of Schedule 1 to that Act or on an administrator appointed under subparagraph (1) of the said paragraph 1.

(5) The Court may by order authorise the disclosure to such an administrator of any material produced under subsection (1) above or any part of such material; but the Court shall not make an order under this subsection unless a reasonable opportunity has been given for an officer of the department to make representations to the Court.

(6) Material disclosed in pursuance of an order under subsection (5) above may, subject to any conditions contained in the order, be further disclosed for the purposes of the functions under the said Act of 1995 of the administrator or the High Court.

(7) The Court of Session may by order authorise the disclosure to a person mentioned in subsection (8) below of any material produced under subsection (1) above or any part of such material; but the Court shall not make an order under this subsection unless—

  (a) a reasonable opportunity has been given for an officer of the department to make representations to the Court; and

(b) it appears to the Court that the material is likely to be of substantial value in exercising functions relating to drug trafficking.

(8) The persons referred to in subsection (7) above are—

(a) a constable;

(b) the Lord Advocate or any procurator fiscal; and

(c) a person commissioned by the Commissioners of Customs and Excise.

(9) Material disclosed in pursuance of an order under subsection (7) above may, subject to any conditions contained in the order, be further disclosed for the purposes of functions relating to drug trafficking.

(10) Material may be produced or disclosed in pursuance of this section notwithstanding any obligation as to secrecy or other restriction upon the disclosure of information imposed by statute or otherwise.

(11) An order under subsection (1) above and, in the case of material in the possession of an authorised government department, an order under section 31(2) of this Act may require any officer of the department (whether named in the order or not) who may for the time being be in possession of the material concerned to comply with such order; and any such order shall be served as if the proceedings were civil proceedings against the department.

(12) The person on whom an order under subsection (1) above is served—

(a) shall take all reasonable steps to bring it to the attention of the officer concerned; and

(b) if the order is not brought to that officer's attention within the period referred to in subsection (1) above, shall report the reasons for the failure to the Court of Session,

and it shall also be the duty of any other officer of the department in receipt of the order to take such steps as are mentioned in paragraph (a) above.

DEFINITIONS
"Authorised Government Department": s.43(1).
"drug trafficking": s.43(1).

GENERAL NOTE
This section provides procedures by which the Court of Session may on the application of the Lord Advocate require a government department to produce material in the department's possession to the court, if that material is material to which the Proceeds of Crime (Scotland) Act 1995 applies, relating to appointment of an administrator, making restraint orders, etc. The material may be disclosed to an administrator on the order of the court.

Offences

Offence of prejudicing investigation

36.—(1) A person who, knowing or suspecting that an investigation into drug trafficking is taking place, does anything which is likely to prejudice the investigation is guilty of an offence.

(2) In proceedings against a person for an offence under subsection (1) above, it is a defence to prove—

(a) that he did not know or suspect, or have reasonable grounds to suspect, that by acting as he did he was likely to prejudice the investigation; or

(b) that he had lawful authority or reasonable excuse for acting as he did.

(3) Nothing in subsection (1) above makes it an offence for a professional legal adviser to disclose any information or other matter—

(a) to, or to a representative of, a client of his in connection with the giving by the adviser of legal advice to the client; or

(b) to any person—

(i) in contemplation of, or in connection with, legal proceedings; and

(ii) for the purpose of those proceedings.

(4) Subsection (3) above does not apply in relation to any information or other matter which is disclosed with a view to furthering any criminal purpose.

(5) A person guilty of an offence under subsection (1) above shall be liable—

(a) on conviction on indictment, to imprisonment for a term not exceeding five years or to a fine or to both; and

(b) on summary conviction, to imprisonment for a term not exceeding six months or to a fine not exceeding the statutory maximum or to both.

GENERAL NOTE

This section provides for the somewhat widely drawn offence of "doing anything" likely to prejudice an investigation. Knowledge or suspicion that an investigation is taking place is a pre-requisite to conviction but the person charged need not have intended to prejudice the investigation, the test being purely objective—was the act likely to do so? There are no bounds on the type of conduct which could fall within the definition save that it would appear that only an act of commission rather than omission would be struck at by the section. There is a proviso for a professional legal advisor disclosing information to his client or to others, which information would be subject to legal privilege in terms of s.33. Statutory defences are provided in subs. (2), para. (b) of which is fairly familiar. Paragraph (a) however, seems a little confusing. It appears that an accused may escape conviction only if he did not *know* that his conduct was likely to prejudice the investigation *and* that he had no such suspicion *and* that there were no reasonable grounds for suspicion.

Acquisition, possession or use of proceeds of drug trafficking

37.—(1) A person is guilty of an offence if, knowing that any property is, or in whole or in part directly or indirectly represents, another person's proceeds of drug trafficking, he acquires or uses that property or has possession of it.

(2) It is a defence to a charge of committing an offence under this section that the person charged acquired or used the property or had possession of it for adequate consideration.

(3) For the purposes of subsection (2) above—

(a) a person acquires property for inadequate consideration if the value of the consideration is significantly less than the value of the property; and

(b) a person uses or has possession of property for inadequate consideration if the value of the consideration is significantly less than the value of his use or possession of the property.

(4) The provision for any person of services or goods which are of assistance to him in drug trafficking shall not be treated as consideration for the purposes of subsection (2) above.

(5) Where a person discloses to a constable or to a person commissioned by the Commissioners of Customs and Excise a suspicion or belief that any property is, or in whole or in part directly or indirectly represents, another person's proceeds of drug trafficking, or discloses to a constable or a person so commissioned any matter on which such a suspicion or belief is based—

(a) the disclosure shall not be treated as a breach of any restriction upon the disclosure of information imposed by statute or otherwise; and

(b) if he does any act in relation to the property in contravention of subsection (1) above, he does not commit an offence under this section if—

(i) the disclosure is made before he does the act concerned and the act is done with the consent of the constable or person so commissioned, or

(ii) the disclosure is made after he does the act, but on his initiative and as soon as it is reasonable for him to make it.

(6) For the purposes of this section having possession of any property shall be taken to be doing an act in relation to it.

(7) In proceedings against a person for an offence under this section, it is a defence to prove that—

(a) he intended to disclose to a constable or a person so commissioned such a suspicion, belief or matter as is mentioned in subsection (5) above; but

(b) there is reasonable excuse for his failure to make the disclosure in accordance with paragraph (b) of that subsection.

(8) In the case of a person who was in employment at the relevant time, subsections (5) and (7) above shall have effect in relation to disclosures, and intended disclosures, to the appropriate person in accordance with the procedure established by his employer for the making of such disclosures as they have effect in relation to disclosures, and intended disclosures, to a constable or a person so commissioned.

(9) A person guilty of an offence under this section is liable—

(a) on summary conviction, to imprisonment for a term not exceeding six months or to a fine not exceeding the statutory maximum or to both; or

(b) on conviction on indictment, to imprisonment for a term not exceeding fourteen years or to a fine or to both.

(10) No constable, person so commissioned or other person shall be guilty of an offence under this section in respect of anything done by him in the course of acting in connection with the enforcement, or intended enforcement, of any provision of this Act or of any other enactment relating to drug trafficking or the proceeds of such trafficking.

DEFINITIONS

"drug trafficking": s.43(1).
"inadequate consideration": subs. (3).
"possession": subs. (6).
"proceeds of drug trafficking": s.38(2).

GENERAL NOTE

This section provides for the offence of knowingly acquiring, using or possessing property which represents another person's proceeds of drug trafficking. There is a defence provided that the property was acquired, etc., for adequate consideration: see generally, 1994 J.L.S. 132, *Money Laundering and Scottish Solicitors*, A.N. Brown.

Subss. (2)–(4)

The statutory defence is contained in these subsections. Note that inadequate consideration is defined in terms of being "significantly" less than the value of the property. No further guidance is given. Consideration which is given for assistance in drug trafficking is excluded from the calculation.

Subs. (5)

This subsection provides for the protection of those passing on suspicions to the enforcement agencies, in that such disclosures are "ring fenced" as regards alleged breaches of obligations imposed, by public or private law. Protection is also provided for a person who makes a disclosure and then continues with a transaction with the consent of the enforcement agencies. This subsection will provide some relief for professional advisers such as accountants, bankers, solicitors and the like.

Subs. (6)

Although somewhat inelegantly expressed this appears to be a declaration that "doing an act in relation to property" includes possession of the property rather than a definition of possession for the purposes of the section. This interpretation is given added weight by the terms of subs. (5).

Subs. (8)

This subsection provides protection for an employee who makes a disclosure to the "appropriate person" under internal reporting procedures which are required to be put in place in terms of the Money Laundering Regulations 1993 (S.I. 1993 No. 1933).

Offence of assisting another to retain the proceeds of drug trafficking

38.—(1) Subject to subsection (3)(b) below, a person shall be guilty of an offence if, knowing or suspecting that another person (in this section referred to as "A") is a person who carries on, or has carried on, or has derived financial or other rewards from, drug trafficking, he enters into, or is otherwise concerned in, an arrangement whereby—

(a) the retention or control, by or on behalf of A, of A's proceeds of drug trafficking is facilitated (whether by concealment, removal from the jurisdiction, transfer to nominees or otherwise); or

(b) A's proceeds of drug trafficking—

(i) are used to secure that funds are placed at A's disposal; or

(ii) are used for A's benefit to acquire property by way of investment.

(2) In this section, references to proceeds of drug trafficking shall be construed as including any property which, whether in whole or in part, directly or indirectly constitutes such proceeds.

(3) Where a person discloses to a constable or to a person commissioned by the Commissioners of Customs and Excise a suspicion or belief that any funds or investments are derived from or used in connection with drug trafficking or discloses to a constable or a person so commissioned any matter on which such a suspicion or belief is based—

(a) the disclosure shall not be treated as a breach of any restriction imposed by statute or otherwise on the disclosure of information; and

(b) if the disclosure relates to an arrangement entry into which, or concern in which, by the person would (but for this paragraph) contravene subsection (1) above, he does not commit an offence under that subsection if—

(i) the disclosure is made before, with the consent of the constable or as the case may be of the person so commissioned, he enters into, or becomes concerned in, that arrangement; or

(ii) though made after he enters into, or becomes concerned in, that arrangement, it is made on his own initiative and as soon as it is reasonable for him to do so.

(4) In proceedings against a person for an offence under subsection (1) above, it shall be a defence to prove—

(a) that he did not know or suspect that the arrangement related to any person's proceeds of drug trafficking; or

(b) that he did not know or suspect that by the arrangement the retention or control by or on behalf of A of any property was facilitated or, as the case may be, that by the arrangement any property was used as mentioned in subsection (1) above; or

(c) that—

(i) he intended to disclose to a constable or to a person commissioned as aforesaid such a suspicion, belief or matter as is mentioned in subsection (3) above in relation to the arrangement; but

(ii) there is reasonable excuse for his failure to make disclosure in accordance with paragraph (b) of that subsection.

(5) In the case of a person who was in employment at the relevant time, subsections (3) and (4) above shall have effect in relation to disclosures, and intended disclosures, to the appropriate person in accordance with the procedure established by his employer for the making of such disclosures as they

have effect in relation to disclosures, and intended disclosures, to a constable or a person commissioned as aforesaid.

(6) A person guilty of an offence under subsection (1) above shall be liable—

(a) on conviction on indictment, to imprisonment for a term not exceeding fourteen years or to a fine or to both; and

(b) on summary conviction, to imprisonment for a term not exceeding six months or to a fine not exceeding the statutory maximum or to both.

GENERAL NOTE

This section provides for the offence of knowingly or suspectingly assisting a person to launder or secure his drug trafficking proceeds. It is of particular relevance to financial institutions and other professional advisors whose remit covers finance and investment.

Subs. (1)

The amount of knowledge which triggers an offence under the section may be little more than a fleeting doubt about the probity of a transaction. There is no need for the suspicion to be reasonable. The terms "concerned" and "arrangement" are fairly imprecise with the obvious intention that the net of the offence is cast very widely indeed.

Subs. (3)

The effect of this subsection is identical to s.37(3). The Criminal Justice (Scotland) Act 1987, s.43 (the forerunner of this section), as originally enacted, provided only protection from breach of contractual obligation, but an amendment by the Criminal Justice Act 1993, s.19(2) and (3) extended the protection to obligations imposed by statute or otherwise.

Subs. (4)

The subsection provides for defences, the burden of proof of which lies on the accused on a balance of probabilities.

Subs. (5)

See the General Note to s.37(8).

Failure to disclose knowledge or suspicion of money laundering

39.—(1) A person is guilty of an offence if—

(a) he knows, or suspects, that another person is engaged in drug money laundering;

(b) the information, or other matter, on which that knowledge or suspicion is based came to his attention in the course of his trade, profession, business or employment; and

(c) he does not disclose the information or other matter to a constable or to a person commissioned by the Commissioners of Customs and Excise as soon as is reasonably practicable after it comes to his attention.

(2) Subsection (1) above does not make it an offence for a professional legal adviser to fail to disclose any information or other matter which has come to him in privileged circumstances.

(3) It is a defence to a charge of committing an offence under this section that the person charged had a reasonable excuse for not disclosing the information or other matter in question.

(4) Where a person discloses to a constable or a person so commissioned—

(a) his suspicion or belief that another person is engaged in drug money laundering; or

(b) any information or other matter on which that suspicion or belief is based,

the disclosure shall not be treated as a breach of any restriction imposed by statute or otherwise.

(5) Without prejudice to subsection (3) or (4) above, in the case of a person who was in employment at the relevant time, it is a defence to a charge of committing an offence under this section that he disclosed the information or

other matter in question to the appropriate person in accordance with the procedure established by his employer for the making of such disclosures.

(6) A disclosure to which subsection (5) above applies shall not be treated as a breach of any restriction imposed by statute or otherwise.

(7) In this section "drug money laundering" means doing any act which constitutes an offence under—

(a) section 37 or 38 of this Act; or

(b) section 14 of the Criminal Justice (International Co-operation) Act 1990 (concealing or transferring proceeds of drug trafficking),

or, in the case of an act done otherwise than in Scotland, would constitute such an offence if done in Scotland.

(8) For the purposes of subsection (7) above, having possession of any property shall be taken to be doing an act in relation to it.

(9) For the purposes of this section, any information or other matter comes to a professional legal adviser in privileged circumstances if it is communicated, or given, to him—

(a) by, or by a representative of, a client of his in connection with the giving by the adviser of legal advice to the client;

(b) by, or by a representative of, a person seeking legal advice from the adviser; or

(c) by any person—

(i) in contemplation of, or in connection with, legal proceedings; and

(ii) for the purpose of those proceedings.

(10) No information or other matter shall be treated as coming to a professional legal adviser in privileged circumstances if it is communicated or given with a view to furthering any criminal purpose.

(11) A person guilty of an offence under this section shall be liable—

(a) on summary conviction, to imprisonment for a term not exceeding six months or a fine not exceeding the statutory maximum or to both, or

(b) on conviction on indictment, to imprisonment for a term not exceeding five years or a fine, or to both.

GENERAL NOTE

The section, a re-enactment of s.43A of the Criminal Justice (Scotland) Act 1987 as inserted by the Criminal Justice Act 1993, s.19(1), provides for the offence of failing to disclose knowledge or suspicion of money laundering which has come to a person in the course of a trade, business, profession or employment. There are exceptions for legal advisers where the information given to them is privileged, and also a defence of reasonable excuse. The other provisions of the section mirror provisions in the foregoing sections of the Act.

Tipping-off

40.—(1) A person is guilty of an offence if—

(a) he knows or suspects that a constable or a person commissioned by the Commissioners of Customs and Excise is acting, or is proposing to act, in connection with an investigation which is being, or is about to be, conducted into drug money laundering within the meaning of subsections (7) and (8) of section 39 of this Act; and

(b) he discloses to any other person information or any other matter which is likely to prejudice that investigation, or proposed investigation.

(2) A person is guilty of an offence if—

(a) he knows or suspects that a disclosure has been made to a constable, or a person so commissioned, under section 37, 38 or 39 of this Act; and

(b) he discloses to any other person information or any other matter which is likely to prejudice any investigation which might be conducted following the disclosure.

(3) A person is guilty of an offence if—

(a) he knows or suspects that a disclosure of a kind mentioned in section 37(8), 38(5) or 39(5) of this Act has been made; and

(b) he discloses to any person information or any other matter which is likely to prejudice any investigation which might be conducted following the disclosure.

(4) Nothing in subsections (1) to (3) above makes it an offence for a professional legal adviser to disclose any information or other matter—

(a) to, or to a representative of, a client of his in connection with the giving by the adviser of legal advice to the client; or

(b) to any person—

(i) in contemplation of, or in connection with, legal proceedings; and

(ii) for the purpose of those proceedings.

(5) Subsection (4) above does not apply in relation to any information or other matter which is disclosed with a view to furthering any criminal purpose.

(6) In proceedings against a person for an offence under subsection (1), (2) or (3) above, it is a defence to prove that he did not know or suspect that the disclosure was likely to be prejudicial in the way mentioned in that subsection.

(7) A person guilty of an offence under this section shall be liable—

(a) on summary conviction, to imprisonment for a term not exceeding six months or a fine not exceeding the statutory maximum or to both, or

(b) on conviction on indictment, to imprisonment for a term not exceeding five years or a fine, or to both.

(8) No constable, person so commissioned or other person shall be guilty of an offence under this section in respect of anything done by him in the course of acting in connection with the enforcement, or intended enforcement, of any provision of this Act or of any other enactment relating to drug trafficking or the proceeds of such trafficking.

GENERAL NOTE

This section provides for the offences of "tipping off" in three situations. Where the person charged knows or suspects that (a) an investigation is being conducted into drug money laundering and action is proposed or taken by the enforcement agencies, *or* (b) a disclosure has been made to a constable or other person under ss.37–39 of the Act *or* (c) a disclosure is made to the appropriate person by a person in employment in terms of the said sections *and* he discloses information or other matter which is likely to prejudice the (or any) investigation. There is an exception provided for a legal adviser in terms of privileged communications and a defence of having no knowledge or suspicion that the disclosure was likely to be prejudicial. The burden of proof lies on the person charged.

Offences relating to controlled drugs: fines

41.—(1) Without prejudice to section 211(7) of the Criminal Procedure (Scotland) Act 1995 (fines) but subject to section 10(3)(a) of the Proceeds of Crime (Scotland) Act 1995, where a person is convicted on indictment of an offence to which this section relates and sentenced in respect of that offence to a period of imprisonment or detention, the Court where—

(a) paragraph (b) below does not apply shall, unless it is satisfied that for any reason it would be inappropriate to do so, also impose a fine;

(b) it makes a confiscation order under section 1(1) of the Proceeds of Crime (Scotland) Act 1995 as regards the person, may also impose a fine.

(2) In determining the amount of a fine imposed under paragraph (a) of subsection (1) above, the Court shall have regard to any profits likely to have

been made by the person from the crime in respect of which he has been convicted.

(3) This section relates to an offence which is a drug trafficking offence within the meaning of the said last mentioned Act of 1995.

(4) Where in any proceedings a fine has been imposed by virtue of subsection (1) above as regards a person and a period of imprisonment or detention is imposed on him in default of payment of its amount (or as the case may be of an instalment thereof), that period shall run from the expiry of any other period of imprisonment or detention (not being one of life imprisonment or detention for life) imposed on him in the proceedings.

(5) The reference in subsection (4) above to "any other period of imprisonment or detention imposed" includes (without prejudice to the generality of the expression) a reference to such a period imposed on default of payment of a fine (or instalment thereof) or of a confiscation order (or instalment thereof); but only where that default has occurred before the warrant for imprisonment is issued for the default in relation to the fine imposed by virtue of subsection (1) of this section.

GENERAL NOTE

This section relates to a person who is convicted on indictment in either the Sheriff Court or High Court of a drug trafficking offence and is sentenced to imprisonment or detention. The court must impose a fine unless it would be inappropriate to do so or unless it imposes a confiscation order. If it does impose a confiscation order it may also impose a fine. The court in imposing the fine should have regard to the profits *likely* to have been made by the person from the crime of which he has been convicted. Imprisonment or detention in default of payment of such a fine is served consecutively to the sentence or sentences imposed in the proceedings, including any sentence imposed for default on a fine or confiscation order where the default occurs before the warrant for imprisonment is issued in relation to the fine referred to in subs. (1).

Extension of certain offences to Crown servants and exemptions for regulators etc.

42.—(1) The Secretary of State may by regulations provide that, in such circumstances as may be prescribed, sections 36 to 40 of this Act shall apply to such persons in the public service of the Crown, or such categories of person in that service, as may be prescribed.

(2) Section 39 of this Act shall not apply to—

(a) any person designated by regulations made by the Secretary of State for the purpose of this paragraph; or

(b) in such circumstances as may be prescribed, any person who falls within such category of person as may be prescribed for the purpose of this paragraph.

(3) The Secretary of State may designate, for the purpose of paragraph (a) of subsection (2) above, any person appearing to him to be performing regulatory, supervisory, investigative or registration functions.

(4) The categories of person prescribed by the Secretary of State, for the purpose of paragraph (b) of subsection (2) above, shall be such categories of person connected with the performance by any designated person of regulatory, supervisory, investigative or registration functions as he considers it appropriate to prescribe.

(5) In this section—

"the Crown" includes the Crown in right of Her Majesty's Government in Northern Ireland; and

"prescribed" means prescribed by regulations made by the Secretary of State.

(6) The power to make regulations under this section shall be exercisable by statutory instrument.

(7) Any such instrument shall be subject to annulment in pursuance of a resolution of either House of Parliament.

GENERAL NOTE

This section provides power to the Secretary of State by statutory instrument to bring servants of the Crown within the terms of ss.36–40 and to exclude others from the provisions of s.39 either wholly or in particular circumstances. See S.I. 1994 No. 1808 made under the Criminal Justice (Scotland) Act 1987.

Interpretation of Part V

43.—(1) In this Part of this Act (except where the context otherwise requires)—

"authorised government department" means a government department which is an authorised department for the purposes of the Crown Proceedings Act 1947;

"confiscation order" means an order under section 1(1), 11(4), 12(3) or 13 of the Proceeds of Crime (Scotland) Act 1995; and

"drug trafficking" has the same meaning as in the said Act of 1995.

(2) This Part of this Act shall (except where the context otherwise requires) be construed as one with the Criminal Procedure (Scotland) Act 1995.

(3) This Part of this Act applies to property whether it is situated in Scotland or elsewhere.

(4) References in this Part of this Act—

(a) to offences include a reference to offences committed before the commencement of section 1 of the Criminal Justice (Scotland) Act 1987; but nothing in this Act imposes any duty or confers any power on any court in or in connection with proceedings against a person for an offence to which that section relates instituted before the commencement of that section;

(b) to anything received in connection with drug trafficking include a reference to anything received both in that connection and in some other connection; and

(c) to property held by a person include a reference to property vested in the interim or permanent trustee in his sequestration or in his trustee in bankruptcy or liquidator.

GENERAL NOTE

Practitioners should note the extended definitions of "offences" to include, (a) those committed before the 1987 Act came into force but not those in respect of which proceedings have commenced prior to that date, (b) anything received in connection with drug trafficking to cover something with a "dual connection" and (c) property, including that vested in a trustee in bankruptcy or sequestration or liquidator.

PART VI

MISCELLANEOUS AND GENERAL

False oaths etc.

False statements and declarations

44.—(1) Any person who—

(a) is required or authorised by law to make a statement on oath for any purpose; and

(b) being lawfully sworn, wilfully makes a statement which is material for that purpose and which he knows to be false or does not believe to be true,

shall be guilty of an offence and liable on conviction to imprisonment for a term not exceeding five years or to a fine or to both such fine and imprisonment.

(2) Any person who knowingly and wilfully makes, otherwise than on oath, a statement false in a material particular, and the statement is made—

(a) in a statutory declaration; or

(b) in an abstract, account, balance sheet, book, certificate, declaration, entry, estimate, inventory, notice, report, return or other document which he is authorised or required to make, attest or verify by, under or in pursuance of any public general Act of Parliament for the time being in force; or

(c) in any oral declaration or oral answer which he is authorised or required to make by, under or in pursuance of any public general Act of Parliament for the time being in force; or

(d) in any declaration not falling within paragraph (a), (b) or (c) above which he is required to make by an order under section 2 of the Evidence (Proceedings in Other Jurisdictions) Act 1975,

shall be guilty of an offence and liable on conviction to imprisonment for a term not exceeding two years or to a fine or to both such fine and imprisonment.

(3) Any person who—

(a) procures or attempts to procure himself to be registered on any register or roll kept under or in pursuance of any Act of Parliament for the time being in force of persons qualified by law to practise any vocation or calling; or

(b) procures or attempts to procure a certificate of the registration of any person on any such register or roll,

by wilfully making or producing or causing to be made or produced either verbally or in writing, any declaration, certificate or representation which he knows to be false or fraudulent, shall be guilty of an offence and be liable on conviction to imprisonment for a term not exceeding 12 months or to a fine or to both such fine and imprisonment.

(4) Subsection (2) above applies to any oral statement made for the purpose of any entry in a register kept in pursuance of any Act of Parliament as it applies to the statements mentioned in that subsection.

DEFINITIONS

"statutory declaration": s.46(4).

GENERAL NOTE

This section, together with ss.45 and 46, re-enacts most of the False Oaths (Scotland) Act 1933 (c. 20) along with s.42 of the Criminal Justice (Scotland) Act 1949.

Subs. (1)

The provisions here overlap substantially with the common law crime of perjury. Where there is a choice between the common law charge and the statutory charge it is the invariable practice to charge the common law crime.

Material for that purpose. In relation to the crime of perjury it has been held that if a statement is relevant and competent evidence then it is "material", no matter how trivial or insignificant: see Lord Advocate's Reference (No. 1 of 1985) 1987 S.L.T. 187.

Does not believe to be true. It has been held that where a witness makes a statement or when he does not know whether or not it is true, that amounts to the crime of perjury: see *Simpson v. Tudhope*, 1988 S.L.T. 297. An affirmation or declaration made in lieu of an oath is treated likewise: see s.46(1)(b).

Subs. (2)

Knowingly and wilfully. This is to be contrasted with "wilfully" as used in subs. (1): see *Waugh v. Mentiplay*, 1938 J.C. 117. The statement made in *Simpson v. Tudhope* would not be in breach of this subsection as it was not made in the knowledge of its falsity.

Provisions supplementary to section 44

45.—(1) Any person who aids, abets, counsels, procures or suborns another person to commit an offence against section 44 of this Act shall be liable to be proceeded against, indicted, tried and punished as if he were a principle offender.

(2) Any person who incites or attempts to procure or suborn another person to commit an offence against that section shall be guilty of an offence and be liable on conviction to imprisonment or to a fine or to both such fine and imprisonment.

(3) Nothing in section 44 and 46(1) of this Act and subsections (1) and (2) above shall affect the common law relating to the crime of perjury or to any crime or offence involving falsehood, fraud or wilful imposition, or the liability of any person to be prosecuted for any such crime or offence, provided that no person shall be liable in respect of the same matter to be punished both at common law and under these sections.

(4) Where the making of a false statement is not only an offence under the said sections 44 or 46(1) or under subsection (1) or (2) above, but also by virtue of some other Act is a corrupt practice or subjects the offender to any forfeiture or disqualification or to any penalty other than imprisonment or a fine, the liability of the offender under these sections shall be in addition to and not in substitution for his liability under such other Act.

(5) Where the making of a false statement is by any other Act whether passed before or after the commencement of this Act, made punishable on summary conviction, proceedings may be taken either under such other Act or under this Act.

GENERAL NOTE

Subs. (3)
Proceedings for actions which amount to a crime at common law and to an offence under the Act, may be taken either at common law or under the Act, but not both.

Subs. (4)
The accused may suffer an additional penalty of forfeiture on disqualification or the like where the "false statement" makes him liable to such under other legislation.

Proceedings

46.—(1) For the purposes of any proceedings at common law for perjury or of any proceedings for a contravention of section 44(1) of this Act—
  (a) the forms and ceremonies used in administering an oath shall be immaterial if the court or person before whom the oath is taken has power to administer an oath for the purpose of verifying the statement in question, and if the oath has been administered in a form and with ceremonies which the person taking the oath has accepted without objection or has declared to be binding on him;
  (b) an affirmation or declaration made in lieu of an oath shall be of the like effect in all respects as if it had been made on oath.

(2) Where an offence against section 44 of this Act is committed in any place outside the United Kingdom, the offender may be proceeded against, tried and punished in any place in Scotland where he was apprehended or is in custody as if the offence had been committed in that place; and for all purposes incidental to or consequential on the trial or punishment of the offence, it shall be deemed to have been committed in that place.

(3) Any summary criminal proceedings for an offence against section 44 of this Act may, notwithstanding anything in the Criminal Procedure (Scotland) Act 1995, be commenced at any time within one year from the date of the commission of the offence, or within three months from the date when evidence sufficient in the opinion of the Lord Advocate to justify the proceedings comes to his knowledge whichever period last expires; and for the purposes of this section a certificate purporting to be signed by or on behalf of the Lord Advocate as to the date on which such evidence as aforesaid came to his knowledge shall be conclusive evidence thereof.

(4) In sections 44 and 45 of this Act and in this section, the expression "statutory declaration" means a declaration made by virtue of the Statutory

Declarations Act 1835 or of any enactment (including subordinate legislation) applying or extending the provisions of that Act.

GENERAL NOTE
Whichever period last expires. There does not appear to be a definite "prescriptive period" for
summary proceedings under s.44, until sufficient evidence in the opinion of the Lord Advocate
comes to his notice.

Offensive weapons

Prohibition of the carrying of offensive weapons

47.—(1) Any person who without lawful authority or reasonable excuse,
the proof whereof shall lie on him, has with him in any public place any
offensive weapon shall be guilty of an offence, and shall be liable—
  (a) on summary conviction, to imprisonment for a term not exceeding six
      months or a fine not exceeding the statutory maximum, or both;
  (b) on conviction on indictment, to imprisonment for a term not exceed-
      ing two years or a fine, or both.
  (2) Where any person is convicted of an offence under subsection (1)
above the court may make an order for the forfeiture or disposal of any
weapon in respect of which the offence was committed.
  (3) A constable may arrest without warrant any person whom he has
reasonable cause to believe to be committing an offence under subsection (1)
above, if the constable is not satisfied as to that person's identity or place of
residence, or has reasonable cause to believe that it is necessary to arrest him
in order to prevent the commission by him of any other offence in the course
of committing which an offensive weapon might be used.
  (4) In this section "public place" includes any road within the meaning of
the Roads (Scotland) Act 1984 and any other premises or place to which at
the material time the public have or are permitted to have access, whether on
payment or otherwise; and "offensive weapon" means any article made or
adapted for use for causing injury to the person, or intended by the person
having it with him for such use by him.

DEFINITIONS
  "public place": subs. (4).
  "offensive weapon": subs. (4).
  "statutory maximum": Criminal Procedure (Scotland) Act 1995, s.225.

GENERAL NOTE
  This section is a re-enactment of s.1 of the Prevention of Crime Act 1953 as amended by the
Criminal Justice Act 1988 and the Roads (Scotland) Act 1984. The amendment made by the
Public Order Act 1986 has not been re-enacted: see the General Note to subs. (4).

Subs. (1)
  Lawful authority. This phrase would cover, for example, a police officer carrying a truncheon
or a soldier carrying a gun or bayonet. There appears little scope for growth in the case law here
having regard to the definition of "offensive weapon". Tools required by tradesmen, etc., should
not come within the definition.
  Reasonable excuse. It is not a reasonable excuse that the person who has the offensive weapon
with him fears attack by others and carries the weapon for self protection. *Grieve v. MacLeod*,
1967 S.L.T. 70 concerned a taxi driver who carried with him in his cab a piece of rubber hose with
a metal attachment at one end as a means of self defence against violent attacks by passengers.
The High Court held that one of the purposes of the 1953 Act was to ensure that ordinary citizens
do not, unless in exceptional circumstances, take the law into their own hands, and there was no
reasonable excuse in this particular case. This case however concerned an unspecific fear of
possible attack at some point in the future. A fear of imminent attack such as would justify
someone acting in self defence would however be considered differently. For example, a person
being chased by another who is wielding a weapon, may be justified in picking up an article to
defend himself. Indications of this approach appear in *McGovern v. Allan* (High Court of Justiciary, October 22, 1987, unrep., referred to in Sheils, *Offensive Weapons* (Edinburgh 1992))

and *Miller v. Douglas*, 1988 S.C.C.R. 565, in both of which the accused had been under attack and had armed himself with a weapon. The attack had, however, in both cases passed and the accused continued to carry the weapon. Reasonable excuse was therefore not made out by the accused in either case. See also *Kincaid v. Tudhope*, 1983 S.C.C.R. 389. A person who deliberately puts himself into the position of having to defend himself, say by seeking out a person or persons of violent disposition, may not benefit from this defence: see *Malnik v. D.P.P.* [1989] Crim.L.R. 451.

The reasonable excuse is referrable not simply to carrying a weapon but to carrying it in a public place. Where a person carried a broken bottle in a public place with the intent to commit suicide it was held that he did not have a reasonable excuse. It therefore is not sufficient for the person charged to prove simply that the reason for carrying the weapon is not in itself unlawful: see *Bryan v. Mott* (1975) 62 Cr.App.R. 71.

Conversely, where a person was carrying a flail in a public place on his way to a martial arts class, the fact that he waved the flail about in the public place did not take him out of the category of a person having a reasonable excuse: see *Glendinning v. Guild*, 1987 S.C.C.R. 304.

Where someone forgets that they have with them an article to which the section applies that may amount to a reasonable excuse, according to *R. v. McCalla* (1988) 152 J.P. 481, but *cf.* observations by the court in *McKee v. MacDonald*, 1995 S.C.C.R. 513. It does *not* amount to a "good reason" under s.49: *Lister v. Lees*, 1994 S.C.C.R. 548.

Carrying an offensive weapon as part of a fancy dress costume may amount to a reasonable excuse: *Houghton v. Chief Constable of Greater Manchester* (1987) 84 Cr.App.R. 319.

See *Lister v. Lees*, 1994 S.C.C.R. 549 (referred to in the General Note to s.49), where the approach taken by the court was to have regard to the general purpose of the legislation and, where the legislation contains a general prohibition, to determine whether the reason advanced by the person charged appears to constitute a justifiable exception to the general prohibition. *Has with him.* See *R. v. Cugullere* [1961] 1 W.L.R. 858 in which it was held that this expression means "knowingly had with him". This approach is consistent with principle in Scots Law. Any alternative interpretation would mean that the offence could be committed without *mens rea*. However, *quaere*: the situation where a person charged knowingly carries something to which the section applies but subsequently "forgets" that they have the article with them. In *R. v. McCalla* (1988) 152 J.P. 481, it was held that while this situation may amount to a reasonable excuse it does not allow the person charged to say that he did not "knowingly" have the article with him: see also *Lister v. Lees, McKee v. MacDonald* above; *Gill v. Lockhart*, 1987 S.C.C.R. 599. See *Smith v. H.M. Advocate*, High Court of Justiciary, October 26, 1995, Crown Office Circular A19/95, where the knowledge required for possession of a firearm was held to extend only to knowledge that an *object* was possessed and not that the object was a firearm.

Subs. (4)

Public place. A discotheque (*Owens v. Crowe*, 1994 S.C.C.R. 310) and the common stairs and landings of blocks of flats, where there were no barriers to entry (*Knox v. Anderton* (1983) 76 Cr.App.R. 156) have been held to be public places. A treatment cubicle in a hospital is not a public place: see *Normand v. Donnelly*, 1993 S.C.C.R. 639.

Where the person charged has the offensive weapon in a car in a public place then the weapon is in a public place: see *Murdoch v. Carmichael*, 1993 S.C.C.R. 444; *Grieve v. MacLeod* above. In both cases the point seems to have been assumed and was not argued: see *Bates v. D.P.P.* (1993) 157 J.P. 1004.

Where a person is found with an offensive weapon in a private place and there is evidence from which the inference can be drawn that he must have passed through a public place with the weapon the accused may be convicted: see *Normand v. Donnelly* above.

Offensive weapon

These are divided into three categories, as follows.

Made…for causing injury. This would include, *inter alia*, daggers, flick knives, nunchaca sticks (*Houston v. Snape*, 1993 S.C.C.R. 995, *Tudhope v. O'Neil*, 1982 S.C.C.R. 45, *Hemming v. Annan*, 1982 S.C.C.R. 432), commonly referred to as class one or category one offensive weapons.

The fact that a dagger is contained in a sheath does not take away from its essential classification: *Houston v. Snape*, above. Where the manufacture of an article is prohibited as it is a dangerous weapon it is *per se* an offensive weapon: *Tudhope v. O'Neil, Houston v. Snape* above. Where an article has two purposes, one for causing personal injury and the other an innocent purpose, then it cannot fall into this category: *Woods v. Heywood*, 1988 S.C.C.R. 434 (where the article was a machete). In *McKee v. MacDonald* above, an imitation police truncheon made as a souvenir and not possessing the offensive qualities of "the real thing" was held not to fall into this category.

Adapted for use .... This could cover any number of ordinary household objects which have been altered or adapted in some way. The adaption must have been made, although not necessarily by the person charged, with the intention of making the article more suitable for use. In *McLaughlin v. Tudhope*, 1987 S.C.C.R. 456 a kitchen implement with a potato peeler at one end and a knife at the other was carried by the accused. The potato peeling blade was missing as was the cover for the knife. The Appeal Court held that, there being no evidence as to who had removed the parts of the implement or that they had been removed in the course of adapting the knife for causing injury, the implement did not fall to be classified as an offensive weapon.

Intended ... for such use. In many cases the intention will require to be inferred from evidence of proved actings of the accused, the type of weapon, the type of place in which the accused has the weapon, the time of day or night, whether the blade is exposed, etc.: see generally *Lopez v. McNab*, 1978 J.C. 41, *Owens v. Crowe* above, *Kane v. H.M. Advocate*, 1988 S.C.C.R. 585, *Murdoch v. Carmichael* (above); *Ralston v. Lockhart*, 1986 S.C.C.R. 400.

The definition of offensive weapon contained in the 1953 Act was amended by the Public Order Act 1986, s.42(2) and s.2, by the addition after the words "or intended by the person having it with him for such use by him" of the words "or by some other persons". These additional words were not re-enacted in this Act. The gap caused by the omission of the words is partially filled by the concept of art and part guilt but it is possible to conceive of situations where a person has a weapon for use by another person and the evidence does not show concert between the "haver" and the person for whose use the weapon was intended.

Where the evidence of intention comes from the mouth of the person charged and the making of the statement by him is corroborated, that is the clearest evidence of intention and needs no further corroboration, despite the fact that it comes from only a single source, *i.e.* the person charged: *Normand v. Matthews*, 1993 S.C.C.R. 856.

Search for offensive weapons

48.—(1) Where a constable has reasonable grounds for suspecting that any person is carrying an offensive weapon and has committed or is committing an offence under section 47 of this Act, the constable may search that person without warrant, and detain him for such time as is reasonably required to permit the search to be carried out; and he shall inform the person of the reason for such detention.

(2) Any person who—

(a) intentionally obstructs a constable in the exercise of the constable's powers under subsection (1) above; or

(b) conceals from a constable acting in the exercise of those powers an offensive weapon,

shall be guilty of an offence and liable on summary conviction to a fine not exceeding level 4 on the standard scale.

(3) A constable may arrest without warrant any person who he has reason to believe has committed an offence under subsection (2) above.

(4) In this section, "offensive weapon" has the same meaning as in the said section 47.

DEFINITIONS

"Level 4 on the standard scale": Criminal Procedure (Scotland) Act 1995, s.225.
"offensive weapon": subs. (4), s.47(4).

GENERAL NOTE

Subs. (2)

Where police officers mistakenly told a suspect that she was being arrested, rather than being detained for search under s.23 of the Misuse of Drugs Act 1971, a search which followed thereon was found to be illegal: *Wither v. Reid*, 1980 J.C. 7.

Subs. (4)

For conviction under this part of the section there must be an active step of concealment to prevent discovery of the offensive weapon by the searching officer. So where the accused at a football match had been passed a razor by another and put it into his pocket, prior to being spoken to by the police there was no breach of the section: *Burke v. MacKinnon*, 1983 S.C.C.R. 23. Where, however, an accused person is aware that police officers are going to search him and takes active steps either to obstruct the police officers or conceal an article to which the section applies, he may be guilty of an offence under the section: see *Normand v. McCutcheon*, 1993 S.C.C.R. 709 (a case decided under the Misuse of Drugs Act 1971, s.23, which is in similar terms). The case of *Dunne v. Normand* unrep., referred to in *Normand v. McCutcheon* confirmed that one could be in breach of s.23 in respect of actings carried out *before* being spoken to by the police. There the appellant had torn up a reefer cigarette and thrown it to the ground when he saw the police approach him. It was apparent from the Sheriff's Note, although not made the subject of a finding in fact, that the appellant knew that the police were going to use their powers under the section. See also *Annan v. McIntosh*, 1993 S.C.C.R. 938 (another case decided under s.23 of the Misuse of Drugs Act 1971) in which it was held that it was not necessary to libel that an article which the accused put into his mouth was or was suspected to be a controlled drug.

Offence of having in public place article with blade or point

PARLIAMENTARY DEBATES FOR THE CARRYING OF KNIVES ETC. (SCOTLAND) ACT 1993 (C. 13)
   Hansard, H.C. Vol. 220, col. 1283; Vol. 221, col. 1378; H.L. Vol. 544, col. 1213; Vol. 545, cols. 443, 701, 866.

GENERAL NOTE
   These sections are a re-enactment of the substantive provisions of the Carrying of Knives etc. (Scotland) Act 1993 (c. 13) which was introduced and enacted in response to public fears regarding the prevalence of knives being carried in public and the perceived inadequacies of the existing law (principally the Prevention of Crime Act 1953) to deal with the problem. The Criminal Justice Act 1988 (c. 33) had introduced almost identical provisions for England and Wales and Northern Ireland but did not extend these provisions to Scotland.

   49.—(1) Subject to subsections (4) and (5) below, any person who has an article to which this section applies with him in a public place shall be guilty of an offence and liable—
   (a) on summary conviction, to imprisonment for a term not exceeding six months or a fine not exceeding the statutory maximum or both; and
   (b) on conviction on indictment, to imprisonment for a term not exceeding two years or a fine or both.
   (2) Subject to subsection (3) below, this section applies to any article which has a blade or is sharply pointed.
   (3) This section does not apply to a folding pocketknife if the cutting edge of its blade does not exceed three inches (7.62 centimetres).
   (4) It shall be a defence for a person charged with an offence under subsection (1) above to prove that he had good reason or lawful authority for having the article with him in the public place.
   (5) Without prejudice to the generality of subsection (4) above, it shall be a defence for a person charged with an offence under subsection (1) above to prove that he had the article with him—
   (a) for use at work;
   (b) for religious reasons; or
   (c) as part of any national costume.
   (6) Where a person is convicted of an offence under subsection (1) above the court may make an order for the forfeiture of any article to which the offence relates, and any article forfeited under this subsection shall (subject to section 193 of the Criminal Procedure (Scotland) Act 1995 (suspension of forfeiture etc., pending appeal)) be disposed of as the court may direct.
   (7) In this section "public place" includes any place to which at the material time the public have or are permitted access, whether on payment or otherwise.

DEFINITIONS
   "public place": subs. (7).
   "statutory maximum": Criminal Procedure (Scotland) Act 1995, s.225(8).

GENERAL NOTE
This section creates a general prohibition qualified by a proviso and allows an accused person certain defences, the burden of the proof of which lies on him.

Subs. (1)
See the commentary and case law referred to in the General Note to s.47(1).

Subs. (2)
This subsection defines the general prohibition and is very wide in its terms, extending to any article which has a blade *or* is sharply pointed. There is no requirement for the article to have been made, adapted or intended to be used, to cause personal injury, as is required under s.47. In *Lister v. Lees*, 1994 S.C.C.R. 548 the accused had with him in a railway station a nine-inch long metal spike, which appeared to have at one time formed part of an ornamental railing, and he was convicted of a contravention of the forerunner to this section. It would not be difficult to list a myriad of ordinary household or garden articles which comply with the definition.

Subs. (3)
This subsection creates a proviso to the general prohibition. In *Normand v. Walker*, 1994 S.C.C.R. 875 the Crown sought to argue before the Appeal Court that this was a proviso to which s.312(v) of the Criminal Procedure (Scotland) Act 1975 (now s.138(4) of and Sched. 3, para. 16 to the Criminal Procedure (Scotland) Act 1995 for summary proceedings; s.64(6) for solemn proceedings) applied and that therefore the non-application of the proviso need not be the subject of proof by the prosecution and the burden of proof lay on the accused to show that the proviso applied. However, as the Crown had not given proper notice of their intention to rely on this argument when applying for a stated case, the court refused to entertain the ground of appeal based thereon. The court gave a broad hint that due to the difficulty in reconciling the case law on s.312(v) it may be necessary for a full bench to consider the point, were the court required to do so.

The subsection takes account of Council Directive 80/181 (Approximation of Laws Relating to Units of Measurement) and alters the imperial measurement of three inches contained in the 1993 Act to 6.72 centimetres.

The proviso does not extend to *all* articles where the cutting edge of the blade does not exceed 6.72 centimetres (three inches) but *only* to folding pocket knives of this description. In *Stewart v. Friel*, 1995 S.C.C.R. 492 the knife in question had a blade the cutting edge of which did not exceed three inches, which was capable of being folded into the handle. The knife however was fitted with a device which was designed, until it had been overcome, to prevent the blade from being folded. That, it was held, took the knife out of the category of folding pocket knife as it had a feature additional to those mentioned in the subsection. It was more properly called a lock knife or locking knife.

Where two police officers gave evidence that the cutting edge of the blade of a folding pocket knife did exceed three inches, using, in court, an ordinary ruler (borrowed from the Sheriff Clerk!) that was sufficient evidence without any further evidence about certification of the ruler as being accurate: *Normand v. Walker* above.

Subs. (4)
The subsection creates a defence of "good reason" or lawful authority. The burden of proof is on the accused.

"Good reason" may be compared and contrasted with the expression contained in s.47, "reasonable excuse". In *Lister v. Lees* above, the Appeal Court agreed with judgment of the English Court of Criminal Appeal in *D.P.P. v. Gregson* (1993) 96 Cr.App.R. 240 to the effect that "good reason" was quite different from "reasonable excuse". Unfortunately, neither court gave an indication of how the interpretation of the expressions differed and in *Lister* the court stated that the same approach falls to be adopted in considering whether a reason falls within the ambit of either expression. That is, whether the reason advanced appears to constitute a justifiable exception to the general prohibition contained in the legislation. In taking this approach the court should avoid making any moral judgment (the accused in *Lister* had a spike with him for the purpose of opening tins of glue the vapours of which he wished to inhale).

See the General Note to s.47(1) for cases on "reasonable excuse" and "lawful authority". The time at which the accused must prove that he had "good reason" is when he is proved to have the article with him. In *Lister* the accused had used the spike and had no further reason for having it with him. He claimed that he had forgotten to throw it away. The court held that, while it was an explanation, it did not constitute a "good reason" for the accused having the spike with him at the material time. See also *Gill v. Lockhart*, 1987 S.C.C.R. 599 and *McKee v. MacDonald*, 1995 S.C.C.R. 513.

Subs. (5)

This subsection gives particular examples of reasons for having an article, to which the section applies, in a public place which will amount to a defence if proved by the accused. It is expressly provided that this is without prejudice to the generality of subs. (4). It is enough for the person charged to satisfy the court that any of the reasons in subs. (5) apply without going through the further hoop of subs. (4) and proving "good reason" or "lawful authority" as well.

Subs. (7)

See General Note to s.47(4).

Extension of constable's power to stop, search and arrest without warrant

50.—(1) Where a constable has reasonable grounds for suspecting that a person has with him an article to which section 49 of this Act applies and has committed or is committing an offence under subsection (1) of that section, the constable may search that person without warrant and detain him for such time as is reasonably required to permit the search to be carried out.

(2) A constable who detains a person under subsection (1) above shall inform him of the reason for his detention.

(3) Where a constable has reasonable cause to believe that a person has committed or is committing an offence under section 49(1) of this Act and the constable—

(a) having requested that person to give his name or address or both—
  (i) is not given the information requested; or
  (ii) is not satisfied that such information as is given is correct; or

(b) has reasonable cause to believe that it is necessary to arrest him in order to prevent the commission by him of any other offence in the course of committing which an article to which that section applies might be used,

he may arrest that person without warrant.

(4) Any person who—

(a) intentionally obstructs a constable in the exercise of the constable's powers under subsection (1) above; or

(b) conceals from a constable acting in the exercise of those powers an article to which section 49 of this Act applies,

shall be guilty of an offence and liable on summary conviction to a fine not exceeding level 3 on the standard scale.

(5) Where a constable has reasonable cause to believe that a person has committed or is committing an offence under subsection (4) above he may arrest that person without warrant.

DEFINITIONS

"Level 3 on the standard scale": Criminal Procedure (Scotland) Act 1995, s.225.

GENERAL NOTE

This section is in almost identical terms to s.48 (which applies to offensive weapons). Despite the slight differences in structure there is no difference in meaning between both sections. The penalty for contravention of s.50 is a fine not exceeding Level 3 on the standard scale whereas s.48 carries a Level 4 penalty. The comments at s.48 apply equally to this section.

Reset

Reset

51. Criminal resetting of property shall not be limited to the receiving of property taken by theft or robbery, but shall extend to the receiving of property appropriated by breach of trust and embezzlement and by falsehood, fraud and wilful imposition.

GENERAL NOTE
This section appears oddly out of place here, being derived directly from s.312(1) of the Criminal Procedure (Scotland) Act 1975, although strictly speaking it deals with matters of substantive law rather than procedure.

"*Receiving*". On whether one can be guilty of reset without actually being in possession of the goods, being "privy to the retention", see *Advocate, H.M. v. Browne* (1903) 6F.(J)24; *Clark v. H.M. Advocate*, 1965 S.L.T. 250; *McNeil v. H.M. Advocate*, 1968 J.C. 29.

Vandalism

Vandalism

52.—(1) Subject to subsection (2) below, any person who, without reasonable excuse, wilfully or recklessly destroys or damages any property belonging to another shall be guilty of the offence of vandalism.

(2) It shall not be competent to charge acts which constitute the offence of wilful fire-raising as vandalism under this section.

(3) Any person convicted of the offence of vandalism shall be liable on summary conviction—

    (a) in the district court, to imprisonment for a term not exceeding 60 days, or to a fine not exceeding level 3 on the standard scale, or to both;

    (b) in the sheriff court—

        (i) for a first such offence, to imprisonment for a term not exceeding 3 months, or to a fine not exceeding the prescribed sum (within the meaning of section 225(8) of the Criminal Procedure (Scotland) Act 1995), or to both; and

        (ii) for any subsequent such offence, to imprisonment for a term not exceeding 6 months, or to the fine mentioned in sub-paragraph (i) above, or to both.

DEFINITIONS
"Level 3 on the standard scale": Criminal Procedure (Scotland) Act 1995, s.225(2).

GENERAL NOTE
This section repeats the wording of the Criminal Justice (Scotland) Act 1980, s.78, which introduced a statutory offence covering part of the area dealt with by the common law crime of malicious mischief. The maximum penalty for the offence differs according to whether proceedings are taken in the District or the Sheriff Court and, if in the latter court, whether it is a first or subsequent *such* offence.

Subs. (1)
Without reasonable excuse. See *McDougall v. Ho*, 1985 S.C.C.R. 199 where the accused was charged with a contravention of s.78 of the 1980 Act in that he had damaged the windscreen of a car. His defence was that he thought the people in the car were responsible for damage to his shop which had occurred a very short time beforehand. His actions were said by him to have been carried out in an attempt to stop the car from leaving the scene. He was acquitted at trial and the Crown appeal was refused, the court being at pains to point out that it was a narrow case turning on its own facts and that the decision was not considered to afford any guidance on principle. It was, however, held that the trial court had been entitled to conclude that the Crown had not demonstrated that the excuse was not a reasonable one. For a case in which the facts appear fairly similar but the accused was convicted see *Murray v. O'Brien*, 1994 S.L.T. 105 where the Appeal Court held that the Justice was entitled to conclude that no reasonable excuse had been established.

Wilfully or recklessly. The *mens rea* for the common law crime of malicious mischief apart from intention, requires that the accused should have known that he was likely to cause damage or that he showed a deliberate disregard of, or even indifference to, the property: see *Ward v. Robertson*, 1938 J.C. 32; 1938 S.L.T. 165.

In *Black v. Allan*, 1985 S.C.C.R. 11 three men were charged with a contravention of s.78 of the 1980 Act. They had engaged in horseplay resulting in one of them jumping on to the back of another, being pushed off and falling against and smashing a plate glass window. The third man was not involved in the breaking of the window although he had been engaged in the previous horseplay. All three were convicted and in quashing the convictions the Appeal Court referred with approval to the definition of reckless in *Allan v. Patterson*, 1980 J.C. 57 and declared that the section was *not* simply a restatement of the common law crime of malicious mischief. While that may well be the case in terms of the other defining words of the offence it is difficult to see what the difference is between the *mens rea* defined in *Ward v. Robertson* and that in *Allan v. Patterson*.

Destroys or damages. The offence of vandalism requires that property is destroyed or damaged. This is not the case with malicious mischief which can be committed where there is no damage to property but only economic loss: see *Advocate, H.M. v. Wilson*, 1984 S.L.T. 1178 (switching off machinery at a power station leading to financial loss due to non-production of electricity) and *Peter Penman*, High Court, March 1984 unrep. (deflating a vehicle tyre).

Subs. (2)

It would appear to be competent to change acts which constitute the "offence" of culpable and reckless fireraising under the section. A complaint raised in breach of the subsection should be dismissed as incompetent and it will not be possible to obtain a conviction for the common law crime of wilful fireraising under the provisions of the Criminal Procedure (Scotland) Act 1995, Sched. 3, para. 14 as applied by s.64(6) for solemn proceedings and s.138(4) for summary proceedings.

General

Short title, commencement and extent

53.—(1) This Act may be cited as the Criminal Law (Consolidation) (Scotland) Act 1995.

(2) This Act shall come into force on 1 April 1996.

(3) Subject to subsection (4) below, this Act extends only to Scotland.

(4) Section 35(10) to (12) of this Act extends also to England and Wales and sections 27 to 29 of this Act and this section extend also to England and Wales and Northern Ireland.

TABLE OF DERIVATIONS

Notes:

1. This Table shows the derivation of the provisions of the Bill.

2. The following abbreviations are used in the Table:—

Acts of Parliament

1933	=	False Oaths (Scotland) Act 1933 (c. 20)
1976	=	Sexual Offences (Scotland) Act 1976 (c. 67)
1980	=	Criminal Justice (Scotland) Act 1980 (c. 62)
1987	=	Criminal Justice (Scotland) Act 1987 (c. 41)
1988	=	Criminal Justice Act 1988 (c. 33)
1993	=	Criminal Justice Act 1993 (c. 36)
1994	=	Drug Trafficking Act 1994 (c. 37)
1995	=	Criminal Justice (Scotland) Act 1995 (1995 c. 20)
1995CP	=	Criminal Justice (Consequential Provisions) (Scotland) Act (1995 c. 40)
1995CLC	=	Criminal Law (Consolidation) (Scotland) Act 1995 (1995 c. 39)

Provision	Derivation
1	1976 s.2A; Incest and Related Offences (Scotland) Act 1986 (c. 36) s.1
2	1976 s.2B; Incest and Related Offences (Scotland) Act 1986 (c. 36) s.1
3	1976 s.2C; Incest and Related Offences (Scotland) Act 1986 (c. 36) s.1
4	1976 s.2D; Incest and Related Offences (Scotland) Act 1986 (c. 36) s.1; 1987 Sch. 2
5(1), (2)	1976 s.3
(3)–(7)	1976 s.4; Incest and Related Offences (Scotland) Act 1986 (c. 36) Sch. 1 §.4; Criminal Justice (Scotland) Act 1995 (c. 20) Sch. 6 §
6	1976 s.5
7(1)	1976 s.1
(2), (3)	1976 s.2
(4)	1976 s.17
8(1), (2)	1976 s.8
(3)–(5)	1976 s.9
9	1976 s.10
10	1976 s.11
11(1)–(4)	1976 s.12
(5), (6)	1976 s.13(1)
12	1976 s.14; Criminal Procedure (Scotland) Act 1975 (c. 21) Sch. 7A; Criminal Law Act 1977 (c. 45) Sch. 11
13	1980 s.80; Mental Health (Scotland) Act 1984 (c. 36) Sch. 5; Criminal Justice and Public Order Act 1994 (c. 33) ss.145(2), 146(2)
14	1976 s.15
15	1976 s.6
16	1976 s.18
17	1976 s.19
18	1980 s.68; Sporting Events (Control of Alcohol etc.) Act 1985 (c. 57) s.10
19(1)	1980 s.69
(2)	1980 s.70
(3)–(6)	1980 s.70A; Public Order Act 1986 (c. 64) Sch. 1 §.10
(7)	1980 s.71; Public Order Act 1986 (c. 64) Sch. 1 §.11
20(1)	1980 s.72(1)
(2)	1980 s.73
(3)–(6)	1980 s.72A(1)–(4); Public Order Act 1986 (c. 64) Sch. 1 §.14
(7)	1980 s.74
(8)	1980 ss.72(2), (3), 72A(5); Public Order Act 1986 (c. 64) Sch. 1 §.14
21	1980 s.75; Public Order Act 1986 (c. 64) Sch. 1 §.12
22	1980 s.76; Law Reform (Miscellaneous Provisions) (Scotland) Act 1990 (c. 40) Sch. 8 §.30
23	1980 s.77; Sporting Events (Control of Alcohol etc.) Act 1985 (c. 57) s.10; Public Order Act 1986 (c. 64) Sch. 1 §.13
24	1987 s.48; Criminal Justice and Public Order Act 1994 (c. 33) s.129(4), (5)
25	1987 s.49; Criminal Justice and Public Order Act 1994 (c. 33) s.129(6); Children (Scotland) Act 1995 (c. 36) Sch. 3 §.[39]
26	1987 s.50
27	1987 s.51; Criminal Justice and Public Order Act 1994 (c. 33) s.164(3)
28	1987 s.52; 1988 Sch. 15 §.117; Criminal Justice and Public Order Act 1994 (c. 33) s.164(4)

Provision	Derivation
29	1987 s.53
30	1987 s.54; 1988 Sch. 15 §.111; S.I. 1989/2405 Sch. 9 Pt. II §.58
31	1987 s.38; 1988 Sch. 5 §.23
32	1987 s.39
33	1987 s.40
34	1987 s.40A; 1993 s.20(2)
35	1987 s.41
36	1987 s.42; 1993 s.26(2)
37	1987 s.42A; 1993 s.17(1)
38	1987 s.43; 1993 s.19(2), (3)
39	1987 s.43A; 1993 s.19(1)
40	1987 s.43B; 1993 s.19(1)
41	1987 s.44
42	1987 s.46A; 1993 Sch. 4 §.2
43	1987 s.47(1)(part)–(4)
44(1) (2) (3) (4)	1933 s.1; Criminal procedure (Scotland) Act 1975 s.221(1) 1933 s.2; Evidence (Proceedings in Other Jurisdictions) Act 1975 (c. 35) Sch.1 1933 s.3 Criminal Justice (Scotland) Act 1949 (c. 94) s.42(1)
45(1), (2) (3)–(5)	1933 s.4 1933 s.6
46(1) (2) (3) (4)	1933 s.7(1) 1933 s.5 Criminal Justice (Scotland) Act 1949 (c. 94) s.42(2) 1933 s.7(2)
47	Prevention of Crime Act 1953 (c. 14) s.1; Criminal Procedure (Scotland) Act 1975 (c. 21) ss.193A, 298B; Roads (Scotland) Act 1984 (c. 54) Sch. 9 §.42; Criminal Justice Act 1988 (c. 33) Sch. 8 §.16
48	1980 s.4
49	Carrying of Knives (Scotland) Act 1993 (c. 13) s.1; Council Directive 80/181 (Approximation of Laws Relating to Units of Measurement)
50	Carrying of Knives (Scotland) Act 1993 (c. 13) s.2
51	Criminal Procedure (Scotland) Act 1975 (c. 21) s.59
52	1980 s.78
53(1), (2) (3), (4)	Drafting 1987 s.72(1), (4)

TABLE OF DESTINATIONS

FALSE OATHS (SCOTLAND) ACT 1933
(C.20)

1933	1995
s.1	s.44(1)
2	44(2)
3	44(3)
4	45(1), (2)
5	46(2)
6	45(3)–(5)
7(1)	46(1)
(2)	46(2)

CRIMINAL JUSTICE (SCOTLAND) ACT 1949
C.94

1949	1995
s.42(1)	s.44(4)
(2)	46(2)

PREVENTION OF CRIME ACT 1953
(C.14)

1953	1995
s.1	s.47

CRIMINAL PROCEDURE (SCOTLAND) ACT 1975
(C.21)

1975	1995
s.59	s.51
193A	47
221(1)	44(1)
298B	47
Sched.7A	12

EVIDENCE (PROCEEDINGS IN OTHER JURISDICTIONS) ACT 1975
(C.35)

1975	1995
Sched. 1	s.44(2)

SEXUAL OFFENCES (SCOTLAND) ACT 1976
(C.67)

1976	1995	1976	1995	1976	1995
s.1	s.7(1)	s.4	s.5(3)–(7)	s.12	s.11(1)–(4)
2	7(2),(3)	5	6	13(1)	11(5), (6)
2A	1	6	15	14	12
2B	2	8	8(1), (2)	15	14
2C	3	9	8(3)–(5)	17	7(4)
2D	4	10	9	18	16
3	5(1), (2)	11	10	19	17

CRIMINAL LAW ACT 1977
(C.45)

1977	1995
Sched. 11	s.12

TABLE OF DESTINATIONS

CRIMINAL JUSTICE (SCOTLAND) ACT 1980
(c.62)

1980	1995	1980	1995	1980	1995
s.4	s.48	s.72(1)	s.20(1)	s.74	s.20(7)
68	18	(2)	20(8)	75	21
69	19(1)	(3)	20(8)	76	22
70	19(2)	72A(1)–(4)	20(3)–(6)	77	23
70A	19(3)–(6)	(5)	20(8)	78	52
71	19(7)	73	20(2)	80	13

MENTAL HEALTH (SCOTLAND) ACT 1984
(c.36)

1984	1995
Sched. 5	s.13

ROADS (SCOTLAND) ACT 1984
(c.54)

1984	1995
Sched. 9, para. 42	s.47

SPORTING EVENTS (CONTROL OF ALCOHOL ETC.) ACT 1985
(c.57)

1985	1995
s.10	ss.18, 23

INCEST AND RELATED OFFENCES (SCOTLAND) ACT 1986
(c.36)

1986	1995
s.1	ss.1, 2, 3, 4
Sched. 1, para. 4	s.5(3)–(7)

PUBLIC ORDER ACT 1986
(c.64)

1986	1995
Sched. 1,	
para. 10	s.19(3)–(6)
para. 11	19(7)
para. 12	21
para. 13	23
para. 14	ss.20(3)–(6), 20(8)

TABLE OF DESTINATIONS

CRIMINAL JUSTICE (SCOTLAND) ACT 1987
(c.41)

1987	1995	1987	1995	1987	1995
s.38	s.31	s.43	s.38	s.49	s.25
39	32	43A	39	50	26
40	33	43B	40	51	27
40A	34	44	41	52	28
41	35	46A	42	53	29
42	36	47(1)part–(4)	43	54	30
42A	37	48	24	72(1)	53(3)

CRIMINAL JUSTICE ACT 1988
(c.33)

1988	1995
Sched. 5,	
para. 23	s.31
Sched. 8,	
para. 16	47
Sched. 15,	
para. 111	30
para. 117	28

LAW REFORM (MISCELLANEOUS PROVISIONS) (SCOTLAND) ACT 1990
(c.40)

1990	1995
Sched. 8,	
para. 30	s.22

CARRYING OF KNIVES (SCOTLAND) ACT 1993
(c.13)

1993	1995
s.1	s.49
2	50

CRIMINAL JUSTICE ACT 1993
(c.36)

1993	1995
s.17(1)	s.37
19(1)	ss.39, 40
19(2), (3)	s.38
20(2)	34
26(2)	36
Sched. 4,	
para. 2	42

CRIMINAL JUSTICE AND PUBLIC ORDER ACT 1994
(c.33)

1994	1995
s.129(4), (5)	s.24
129(6)	25
145(2)	13
146(2)	13
164(3)	27
164(4)	28

TABLE OF DESTINATIONS

INDEX

References are to sections

ADOPTION,
  relationship by: incest, 1(1)

CHILDREN, OFFENCES AGAINST,
  allowing child to be in brothel, 12
  girls under 18: procurement, 8
  indecent behaviour towards girl between 12
    and 16, 6
  intercourse with girl over 13 and under 16,
    5(3)
    commencement of prosecutions, 5(4),
      5(7)
    defences, 5(5)–(6)
  intercourse with girl under 13, 5(1)–(2)
  permitting girl to use premises for inter-
    course, 9
  prostitution of girl under 16
  seduction of girl under 16, 10
COMMENCEMENT, 53(2)
CUSTOMS AND EXCISE,
  detention and questioning by customs
    officers,
    drug smuggling offences, 26
    power of, 24
    right to inform solicitor and one other
      person, 25
  drug trafficking,
    detention and questioning, 26
    summary proceedings, 34
  see also DRUG TRAFFICKING,

DRUG TRAFFICKING,
  authority for search, 32
  detention and questioning by customs offi-
    cers, 26
  disclosure of information held by govern-
    ment departments, 35
  interpretation, 33, 43
  investigation: order to make material avail-
    able, 31
  offences,
    Crown servants, 42
    fines following conviction, 41
    money laundering, failure to disclose
      knowledge or suspicion, 39
    prejudicing investigation, 36
    proceeds of,
      acquisition, possession or use of, 37
      assisting another to retain, 38
    regulators, 42
    tipping-off, 40
  summary proceedings by Commissioners of
    Customs and Excise, 34
DRUNKENNESS,
  controlled containers, 20

DRUNKENNESS—*cont.*
  designated sporting events,
    in or attempting to enter, 20(7)
    on vehicle going to or from, 19

EXTENT, 53(3)–(4)

FALSE STATEMENTS AND DECLARATIONS,
  offence, 44
    aiding and abetting, 45
    proceedings, 46
FIREWORKS, 20(3), 20(8)
FRAUD,
  investigation of serious or complex disclos-
    ure of information, 30
  Lord Advocate's direction, 27
  nominated officer's powers, 28
  offences in relation to, 29

HOMOSEXUAL OFFENCES,
  consent of mentally deficient person, 13(3)
  consenting parties over 18 in private, 13(1)
  defence, 13(8)
  homosexual act, meaning of, 13(4)
  living on earning of male prostitute, 13(9)
  offences, 13(5)
  private acts, 13(2)
  proceedings, time limit, 13(11)

INCEST,
  defences, 1(1)(a)–(c)
  degree of relationship, 1(2)
  offence, 1(1)
  penalties, 4(1)(5)–(7)
  person in position of trust, 3
  proceedings, 4(1)–(4)
  with step-child, 2
  Table of Relationship, 1(1)
INDECENT ASSAULT,
  defence to charge, 15

LICENSING,
  designated sporting events,
    control of alcohol, 20
    journeys to and from, 19

MARRIAGE,
  foreign: incestuous relations within,
    1(1)(c), 2(d)
  impersonating husband, 7(3)

39–59

CRIMINAL PROCEDURE
(CONSEQUENTIAL PROVISIONS)
(SCOTLAND) ACT 1995*

(1995 c. 40)

An Act to make provision for repeals, consequential amendments, transitional and transitory matters and savings in connection with the consolidation of enactments in the Criminal Procedure (Scotland) Act 1995, the Proceeds of Crime (Scotland) Act 1995 and the Criminal Law (Consolidation) (Scotland) Act 1995.   [8th November 1995]

PARLIAMENTARY DEBATES
Hansard, H.L. Vol. 565, col. 15; Vol. 566, cols. 385, 582, 894. H.C. Vol. 265, col. 183.

INTRODUCTION AND GENERAL NOTE
 The Scots criminal practitioner has had much to think about following recent legislation: the Criminal Justice (Scotland) Act 1995 (c.20) made substantial amendments to the criminal justice system as respects criminal proceedings. Thereafter followed the Criminal Law (Consolidation) (Scotland) 1995 (c.39), the Criminal Procedure (Consequential Provisions) (Scotland) Act 1995 (c.40), the Proceeds of Crime (Scotland) Act 1995 (c.43) and the Criminal Procedure (Scotland) Act 1995 (c.46).
 It would be very tempting to ignore the Consequential Provisions Act as being merely "technical law" in that it makes provision for repeals, consequential amendments, transitional and transitory matters and savings in connection with the consolidation of various enactments. However, the Consequential Provisions Act does form part of the series of new Acts, and the greater view can only be obtained by understanding the constituent parts of the change now being brought about.

---

*Annotations by Robert S. Shiels, Solicitor in the Supreme Courts of Scotland.

The Consequential Provisions Act contains seven sections and six Schedules and it is proposed now to outline briefly the nature and effect of each.

Section 1: Interpretation
It is unusual to have the interpretation section at the commencement of an Act. The section provides that the Criminal Procedure (Scotland) Act 1995 is the Principal Act and it, taken with the other new Acts, constitutes the consolidating Acts.

Section 2: Continuity of the law
The consolidating Acts when taken together do not produce a revolution or a fundamental attack on the criminal justice system of Scotland. An enormous number of individual aspects are, however, changed, sometimes for the effect of the change but often in name to improve the working of the law. Section 2 is statutory confirmation that the change is not intended to affect the continuity of the law. The principle is asserted in subs. (1) and thereafter subss. (2), (3) and (4) underpin the idea that there is or ought to be a smooth progress to the new legislation.

Section 3: Rationalisation of penalties
Criminal offences in statutes are often a reaction to perceived *lacunae* in the options available to prosecutors. The policy decisions prior to such legislation are thus directed at a specific problem. The result is that the statutory criminal law has developed on an *ad hoc* basis with no consistent approach to penalties. The development of sentencing as a coherent and rational subject in itself has required a rationalisation of penalties, hence this section.
Subsection (1) provides that Sched. 1 to the Act shall have effect for the purpose of setting or altering or enabling the Secretary of State to set or alter the various aspects of penalties in statutes.
The *minutiae* of the changes provided for in Sched. 1 reflect the wide variety of statutory provisions to which the rationalising scheme is applied, *e.g.* para. 1 of Sched. 1 deals with amendments relating to penalties and mode of trial for offences made triable only summarily. These offences are made triable only by reason of s.292 of the Principal Act and are specified in Pt. 1 to Sched. 1.
Subsection (2) provides that Sched. 2 to the Act shall have effect for the purpose of amending the enactments specified there.
Schedule 2 is divided into three parts, all of which increase certain penalties. Part 1 concerns offences made triable only summarily. Part II deals with named summary offences and Pt. 3 concerns some summary offences not dealt with in Sched. 1.

Section 4: Transitional, transitory and savings
Section 4 provides that Sched. 3 shall have effect. That Schedule in essence ensures the continuity of the law either by general rules of universal application or specific rules flowing from sections of given Acts.
Practitioners will require to be aware of the possibilities inherent in the changes, *e.g.* para. 2 of Sched. 3 provides that:
"any document made served or issued after this Act comes into force which contains a reference to any of the repealed enactments shall be construed, except so far as the contrary intention appears, as referring to, as the context may require, including a reference to the corresponding provision of the consolidating Act".
Accordingly, there may be on at least one occasion after April 1, 1996 the service of a certificate of routine evidence in terms of s.26 of and Sched. 1 to the Criminal Justice (Scotland) Act 1980 (c.62) notwithstanding the repeal of that Act of 1980. Paragraph 2 of Sched. 3 operates to provide for an implied reference to s.280 of and Sched. 9 to the Principal Act.

Section 5: Minor and consequential amendments
Section 5 provides that Sched. 4 shall have effect and while many amendments are certainly necessary as a consequence of the repeal of *e.g.* the Criminal Procedure (Scotland) Act 1975 (c.21), not all of the changes are minor. Paragraph 3 so alters the existing law of children to require a register of children found guilty of offences to be kept for every summary court. Again, para. 63 amends the law of legal aid to add to the category of cases with circumstances in which criminal legal aid is available automatically.

Section 6: Repeals
Subsection (1) provides that Sched. 5 shall have effect for the repeals specified in it and it is this authority that ends the life of some old friends, *e.g.* the Summary Jurisdiction (Scotland) Act 1954 (c.48), and a few new ones, *e.g.* the Carrying of Knives etc. (Scotland) Act 1993 (c.13).
Subsection (2) provides that Sched. 6 shall have effect in connection with some sections of the Criminal Procedure (Scotland) Act 1975 specified there. The section provides that the repeal of

the specified sections shall not revive any rule of law or practice having effect before the coming into force of the Criminal Procedure (Scotland) Act 1887 (c.35).

Section 7: Commencement
Subsection (2) provides that this Act shall come into force on April 1, 1996.

ABBREVIATIONS
The Principal Act: Criminal Procedure (Scotland) Act 1985 (c.46).

Interpretation

1. In this Act—
"the consolidating Acts" means the Principal Act, the Proceeds of Crime (Scotland) Act 1995, the Criminal Law (Consolidation) (Scotland) Act 1995 and, so far as it reproduces the effect of the repealed enactments, this Act;
"the Principal Act" means the Criminal Procedure (Scotland) Act 1995"; and
"the repealed enactments" means the enactments repealed by this Act.

Continuity of the law

2.—(1) The substitution of the consolidating Acts for the repealed enactments does not affect the continuity of the law.

(2) Anything done or having effect as if done under or for the purposes of a provision of the repealed enactments has effect, if it could have been done under or for the purposes of the corresponding provision of the consolidating Acts, as if done under or for the purposes of that provision.

(3) Any reference, whether express or implied, in any enactment, instrument or document to a provision of the consolidating Acts shall, so far as the context permits, be construed as including, in relation to the times, circumstances and purposes in relation to which the corresponding provision of the repealed enactments has effect, a reference to that corresponding provision.

(4) Any reference, whether express or implied, in any enactment, instrument or document to a provision of the repealed enactments shall be construed, so far as is required for continuing its effect, as including a reference to the corresponding provision of the consolidating Acts.

Rationalisation of penalties

3.—(1) Schedule 1 to this Act shall have effect for the purpose of setting or altering or enabling the Secretary of State to set or alter the penalties or maximum penalties in respect of certain offences or classes or descriptions of offences.

(2) Schedule 2 to this Act shall have effect for the purpose of amending the enactments there specified for the purposes of and in accordance with the provisions of the said Schedule 1.

Transitional, transitory and savings

4. The transitional provisions, transitory modifications and savings contained in Schedule 3 to this Act shall have effect.

Minor and consequential amendments

5. The enactments mentioned in Schedule 4 to this Act shall have effect subject to the amendments there specified being amendments consequential on this Act.

Repeals

6.—(1) The enactments mentioned in Schedule 5 to this Act are hereby repealed to the extent specified in the third column of that Schedule.

(2) Without prejudice to section 16(1)(a) of the Interpretation Act 1978, the repeal by this Act of the provisions of the Criminal Procedure (Scotland) Act 1975 specified in Schedule 6 to this Act shall not revive any rule of law or practice having effect before the coming into force of the Criminal Procedure (Scotland) Act 1887.

Short title, interpretation, commencement and extent

7.—(1) This Act may be cited as the Criminal Procedure (Consequential Provisions) (Scotland) Act 1995.

(2) This Act shall come into force on 1 April 1996.

(3) Subject to subsections (4) and (5) below, this Act extends to Scotland only.

(4) Paragraph 5 of Schedule 3 to this Act and this section also extend to England and Wales and Northern Ireland.

(5) Any amendment contained in Schedule 4 to this Act of any enactment which extends to England and Wales or Northern Ireland shall also so extend.

SCHEDULES

Section 3(1)   SCHEDULE 1

SETTING AND ALTERATION OF CERTAIN PENALTIES

Amendments relating to penalties and mode of trial for offences made triable only summarily

1.—(1) The enactments specified in column 2 of Part I of Schedule 2 to this Act (which relate to the modes of trial of, and the maximum penalties for, the offences which are by section 292 of the Principal Act made triable only summarily) shall continue to have effect subject to the amendments specified in column 3 of that Part.

(2) The said amendments have the effect of altering the maximum penalties available on summary conviction of those offences as well as making alterations consequential on their becoming triable only summarily; and in that Part, column 4 shows the maximum penalties resulting from the amendments.

Penalties on summary conviction for offences triable either summarily or on indictment

2.—(1) Where an offence created by a relevant enactment may be tried either on indictment or summarily, the penalty or maximum penalty on summary conviction shall, to the extent that it included, immediately before the commencement of section 55 of the Criminal Justice Act 1982, a penalty or maximum penalty mentioned in column 1 of the Table below, be amended so as to substitute as a maximum penalty the corresponding penalty set forth in column 2 thereof (unless provision is expressly made by any enactment for a larger penalty or maximum penalty on summary conviction)—

Column 1	Column 2
Penalty or maximum penalty at commencement of section 55 of Criminal Justice Act 1982	New maximum penalty
1. Fine (other than a fine specified in paragraph 3 below, or a fine in respect of each period of a specified length during which a continuing offence is committed).	1. Fine not exceeding the prescribed sum.
2. Imprisonment for a period exceeding 3 months.	2. Imprisonment for a period not exceeding 3 months.
3. Fine in respect of a specified quantity or number of things.	3. Fine not exceeding the prescribed sum in respect of each such quantity or number.
4. Fine exceeding £100 in respect of each period of a specified length during which a continuing offence is committed.	4. Fine not exceeding £100 in respect of each such period.

(2) Where by virtue of a relevant enactment, a person summarily convicted of any offence to which sub-paragraph (1) above relates would, apart from this paragraph, be liable to a fine or a

maximum fine of one amount in the case of a first conviction and of a different amount in the case of a second or subsequent conviction, sub-paragraph (1) above shall apply irrespective of whether the conviction is a first, second or subsequent one.

(3) Sub-paragraph (1) above is without prejudice to section 5 of the Principal Act (6 months' imprisonment competent for certain offences).

(4) In this paragraph "relevant enactment" means an enactment contained in the Criminal Law Act 1977 or in any other Act (including this Act).

(5) Sub-paragraph (1) of paragraph 7 below shall not affect so much of any enactment as (in whatever words) provides for a person to be made liable, on summary conviction, to a fine or a maximum fine for each period of a specified length during which a continuing offence is committed.

(6) Where an enactment to which sub-paragraph (1) of the said paragraph 7 below applies provides for a person to be made liable to a penalty or a maximum penalty on summary conviction of an offence triable either on indictment or summarily which includes a fine or a maximum fine in respect of a specified quantity or a specified number of things, that sub-paragraph shall apply to that fine or maximum fine.

(7) Sub-paragraph (1) above shall not apply on summary conviction of any of the offences mentioned in sub-paragraph (2) of paragraph 11 below.

Increase of fines for certain summary offences

3.—(1) The enactments specified in column 2 of Part II of Schedule 2 to this Act, which relate to the maximum fines for the offences mentioned (and broadly described) in column I of that Schedule, shall have effect as if the maximum fine that may be imposed on summary conviction of any offence so mentioned were a fine not exceeding the amount specified in column 4 of that Schedule instead of a fine not exceeding the amount specified in column 3 of that Schedule (being the amount of the maximum fine in respect of the offence immediately before the passing of the Criminal Law Act 1977), but this sub-paragraph shall not alter the maximum daily fine, if any, provided for by any of those enactments.

(2) In section 203 of the Local Government (Scotland) Act 1973 (offences against byelaws), except as applied to byelaws made under any provision contained in a local or private Act other than by a local authority, for any reference to £20 there shall be substituted a reference to £50.

(3) Subject to sub-paragraph (4) below, this sub-paragraph applies to any pre-1949 enactment however framed or worded which—

(a) as regards any summary offence makes a person liable on conviction thereof to a fine of, or not exceeding, a specified amount less than £50 which has not been altered since the end of 1948 (and is not altered by this Act); or

(b) confers power by subordinate instrument to make a person, as regards any summary offence (whether or not created by the instrument), liable on conviction thereof to a fine of, or a maximum fine of, less than £50 which has not been altered since the end of 1948 (and is not altered by this Act).

(4) Sub-paragraph (3) above does not apply to any offence to which section 292(2)(b) of the Principal Act applies (offences triable only summarily other than by virtue of express provision).

(5) Every enactment to which sub-paragraph (3) above applies shall have effect as if for the specified amount less than £50 there mentioned there were substituted—

(a) £25 if the specified amount is less than £20; or

(b) £50 if the specified amount is not less than £20.

(6) Where, by virtue of any enactment to which sub-paragraph (3) above applies by virtue of sub-sub-paragraph (a) of that sub-paragraph, a person convicted, of a summary offence would, apart from this paragraph, be liable to a fine, or maximum fine, of one amount in the case of a first conviction and of a different amount in the case of a second or subsequent conviction, sub-paragraph (5) above shall apply separately in relation to each specified amount less than £50, even if this produces the same instead of different amounts for different convictions.

(7) Sub-paragraph (3) above does not apply to so much of any enactment as in whatever words, makes a person liable or provides for a person to be made liable, on summary conviction, to a fine or a maximum fine for each period of a specified length during which a continuing offence is committed.

(8) Where an enactment to which sub-paragraph (3) above applies provides or confers a power to provide for, on conviction of an offence triable only summarily, a fine or a maximum fine in respect of a specified quantity or a specified number of things, "the specified amount" for the purposes of subsection (5) above is the fine or maximum fine so provided or for which provision may be made.

(9) In sub-paragraph (3) above "pre-1949 enactment" means an enactment passed before 1st January 1949 or an enactment passed on or after that date which whether directly or, through

successive re-enactments, indirectly re-enacts with or without modification an enactment passed before that date.

(10) In this paragraph, "enactment" does not include an enactment contained in an order, regulation or other instrument made under an Act.

Penalties for first and subsequent convictions of summary offences to be the same

4.—(1) Subject to sub-paragraphs (2) to (4) and (6) below, this paragraph applies where any enactment—

(a) makes a person liable on conviction of an offence triable only summarily to a penalty or a maximum penalty; or

(b) confers a power by subordinate instrument to make a person liable on conviction of an offence triable only summarily (whether or not created by the instrument) to a penalty or a maximum penalty,

which is different in the case of a second or subsequent conviction from the penalty or maximum penalty provided or for which provision may be made in the case of a first conviction.

(2) Where the penalty or maximum penalty for an offence to which section 292(2)(b) of the Principal Act applies has not been altered by any enactment passed or made after 29th July 1977 (the date of the passing of the Criminal Law Act 1977), this paragraph applies as if the amount referred to in sub-paragraph (5)(a) below were the greatest amount to which a person would have been liable on any conviction immediately before that date.

(3) Where any enactment—

(a) provides or confers a power to provide for a penalty or a maximum penalty which would, but for the operation of paragraph 3(5) above, be different in the case of a second or subsequent conviction from the penalty or maximum penalty provided for or for which provision may be made in the case of a first conviction; and

(b) otherwise fulfils the conditions of sub-paragraph (1) above;

this paragraph applies to that penalty or maximum penalty as if the amount referred to in sub-paragraph (5)(a) below were the greatest amount to which a person would have been liable or could have been made liable on any conviction immediately before 17th July 1978 (the date of coming into force of section 289C of the Criminal Procedure (Scotland) Act 1975).

(4) This paragraph does not apply to—

(a) section 5(3) of the Principal Act (imprisonment for certain offences);

(b) section 78 of the Criminal Justice (Scotland) Act 1980 (vandalism); or

(c) an enactment mentioned in Part III of Schedule 2 to this Act.

(5) Where this paragraph applies the maximum penalty to which a person is or may be made liable by or under the enactment in the case of any conviction shall be either or both of—

(a) a fine not exceeding the greatest amount;

(b) imprisonment for a term not exceeding the longest term (if any),

to which an offender would have been liable or could have been made liable on any conviction (whether the first or a second or subsequent conviction) by or under the enactment immediately before the relevant date.

(6) This paragraph does not affect the penalty which may be imposed in respect of an offence committed before the relevant date.

(7) In sub-paragraphs (5) and (6) above "the relevant date" means—

(a) in relation to an offence created by or under an Act or, as the case may be, to conviction of such an offence, 11th April 1983; and

(b) in relation to an offence created under a subordinate instrument or, as the case may be, to conviction of such an offence, 12th October 1988.

Increases of fines for certain summary offences

5.—(1) Subject to sub-paragraphs (3) to (8) and (10) below, this paragraph applies where any Act passed on or before 29th July 1977 (the date of the passing of the Criminal Law Act 1977)—

(a) makes a person liable on conviction of an offence triable only summarily to a fine or a maximum fine which is less than £1,000; or

(b) confers a power by subordinate instrument to make a person liable on conviction of an offence triable only summarily (whether or not created by the instrument) to a fine or a maximum fine which is less than £1,000, or a fine or a maximum fine which shall not exceed an amount of less than £1,000,

and the fine or maximum fine which may be imposed or, as the case may be, for which the subordinate instrument may provide has not been altered by any provision mentioned in sub-paragraph (2) below.

(2) The provisions referred to in sub-paragraph (1) above are—

(a) paragraph 1 above;

(b) paragraph 3 above (except where paragraph 4(3) above applies);

(c) section 30(3) of the Criminal Law Act 1977;

(d) an enactment passed or made after 29th July 1977 and before 11th April 1983.

(3) In the case of an offence to which section 292(2)(b) of the Principal Act applies, sub-paragraphs (2)(a) to (c) above do not apply and the fine or the maximum fine referred to in sub-paragraph (9) below is the fine or the maximum fine for the offence immediately before 29th July 1977 as amended, where applicable, by paragraph 4 above.

(4) This paragraph also applies where any enactment—

(a) is contained in a consolidation Act passed after 29th July 1977 and before 11th April 1983; and

(b) otherwise fulfils the conditions of sub-paragraph (1) above as amended by sub-paragraph (3) above where it applies; and

(c) is a re-enactment (with or without modification) of an enactment passed on or before 29th July 1977.

(5) Subject to sub-paragraph (10) below, where an Act provides or confers a power to provide for, on conviction of an offence triable only summarily, a fine or a maximum fine in respect of a specified quantity or a specified number of things, that fine or maximum fine is the fine or, as the case may be, the maximum fine for the purposes of this paragraph.

(6) Where an Act to which this paragraph applies provides or confers a power to provide different fines or maximum fines in relation to different circumstances or persons of different descriptions, such fines or maximum fines are to be treated separately for the purposes of this paragraph.

(7) This paragraph also applies where the penalties or maximum penalties provided or for which provision may be made by or under an Act on first and on second or subsequent conviction of an offence have been made the same by operation of paragraph 4 above; and in that case the fine or the maximum fine referred to in sub-paragraph (9) below is the maximum fine to which a person is or may be made liable by virtue of that paragraph.

(8) This paragraph does not apply in the case of—

(a) so much of any Act as (in whatever words) makes a person liable or provides for a person to be made liable to a fine or a maximum fine for each period of a specified length during which a continuing offence is committed;

(b) section 67(3) of the Transport Act 1962;

(c) sections 42(1) and 47(1) of the Road Traffic Act 1988;

(d) an enactment mentioned in Schedule 1 to the British Railways Act 1977 to the extent that the enactment was amended by section 13(1) of that Act;

(e) an enactment mentioned in Part III of Schedule 2 to this Act or in Schedule 2 to the Criminal Justice Act 1982.

(9) Where this paragraph applies, the fine or, as the case may be, the maximum fine to which a person is or may be made liable by or under the Act shall be increased to the amount shown in column 2 of the Table below opposite the band in column 1 within which the fine or the maximum fine referred to in sub-paragraph (1) above falls.

Column 1	Column 2
Fine or maximum fine	Increased amount
Under £25	£25
Under £50 but not less than £25	£50
Under £200 but not less than £50	£200
Under £400 but not less than £200	£500
Under £1,000 but not less than £400	£1,000

(10) Where an Act to which this paragraph applies provides or confers a power to provide for, on conviction of an offence triable only summarily, a fine or a maximum fine in respect of a specified quantity or a specified number of things but also provides or confers a power to provide for an alternative fine or maximum fine as regards the offence, sub-paragraph (9) above shall have effect to increase—

(a) the alternative fine; and

(b) any amount that the Act provides or confers a power to provide for as the maximum which a fine as regards the offence may not exceed,

as well as the fine or maximum fine which it has effect to increase by virtue of sub-paragraph (5) above.

Standard scale: amendment of enactments

6.—(1) Subject to sub-paragraph (5) below, where—

(a) an enactment to which sub-paragraph (2) below applies either—

(i) makes a person liable on conviction of an offence triable only summarily (whether created by that enactment or otherwise) to a fine or a maximum fine; or

(ii) confers a power by subordinate instrument to make a person liable on conviction of an offence triable only summarily (whether or not created by the instrument) to a fine or a maximum fine; and

(b) the amount of the fine or the maximum fine is, whether by virtue of that enactment or otherwise, an amount shown in the second column of the standard scale,

for the reference in the enactment to the amount of the fine or maximum fine there shall be substituted a reference to the level on the standard scale shown in the first column thereof as corresponding to the amount in the second column thereof referred to in sub-sub-paragraph (b) above.

(2) This sub-paragraph applies to an enactment in any Act passed before 11th April 1983.

(3) Subject to sub-paragraph (4) below, where an Act provides or confers a power to provide for, on conviction of an offence triable only summarily, a fine or a maximum fine in respect of a specified quantity or a specified number of things, that fine or maximum fine is the fine or, as the case may be, the maximum fine for the purposes of this paragraph.

(4) Where an Act provides or confers a power to provide for, on conviction of an offence triable only summarily, a fine or a maximum fine in respect of a specified quantity or a specified number of things but also provides or confers a power to provide for an alternative fine or maximum fine as regards the offence the fine or the maximum fine for the purposes of this paragraph is—

(a) the alternative fine; and

(b) any amount that the Act provides or confers a power to provide for as the maximum which a fine as regards the offence may not exceed,

as well as the fine or maximum fine referred to in sub-paragraph (3) above.

(5) Sub-paragraph (1) above does not apply to so much of any Act as (in whatever words) makes a person liable or provides for a person to be made liable to a fine or a maximum fine for each period of a specified length during which a continuing offence is committed.

(6) Where an enactment to which sub-paragraph (2) above applies confers a power such as is mentioned in sub-paragraph (1)(a)(ii) above, the power shall be construed as a power to make a person liable to a fine or, as the case may be, a maximum fine of the amount corresponding to the level on the standard scale to which the enactment refers by virtue of sub-paragraph (1) above or of a lesser amount.

(7) Subject to sub-paragraph (9) below, where under a relevant subordinate instrument the fine or maximum fine on conviction of a summary offence specified in the instrument is an amount shown in the second column of the standard scale, the reference in the instrument to the amount of the fine or maximum fine shall be construed as a reference to the level in the first column of the standard scale corresponding to that amount.

(8) In sub-paragraph (7) above, "relevant subordinate instrument" means any instrument made by virtue of an enactment after 30th April 1984 and before 12th October 1988 (the date of commencement of section 66 of the Criminal Justice (Scotland) Act 1987).

(9) Sub-paragraph (7) above shall not affect so much of any instrument as (in whatever words) makes a person liable on summary conviction to a fine not exceeding a specified amount for each period of a specified length during which a continuing offence is continued after conviction or the occurrence of any other specified event.

(10) Where there is—

(a) under any enactment (however framed or worded) contained in an Act passed before 12th October 1988,

(b) under any instrument (however framed or worded) made by virtue of such an enactment,

a power to provide by subordinate instrument that a person, as regards any summary offence (whether or not created by the instrument) shall be liable on conviction to a fine, a person may be so made liable to a fine not exceeding a specified level on the standard scale.

(11) Sub-paragraph (10) above has effect in relation to exercises of powers before as well as after 12th October 1988.

Statutory maximum as penalty in respect of summary conviction for offences in subordinate instruments

7.—(1) Where there is, under any enactment (however framed or worded) contained in an Act passed before the relevant date, a power by subordinate instrument to create a criminal offence triable either on indictment or summarily the maximum fine which may, in the exercise of the power, be authorised on summary conviction shall, by virtue of this paragraph, be the statutory maximum (unless some larger maximum fine can be authorised on summary conviction of such an offence by virtue of an enactment other than this sub-paragraph).

(2) Where there is, under any enactment (however framed or worded) contained in an Act passed before the relevant date, a power to create offences triable either on indictment or summarily by subordinate instrument, the maximum fine on summary conviction for such an offence may be expressed as a fine not exceeding the statutory maximum.

(3) Sub-paragraphs (1) and (2) above shall have effect in relation to any exercise of such power before as well as after the relevant date.

(4) Where an offence created by a subordinate instrument made before the relevant date may be tried either on indictment or summarily, the maximum fine which may be imposed on summary conviction shall by virtue of this sub-paragraph be the statutory maximum (unless the offence is one for which by virtue of the instrument a larger maximum fine may be imposed on summary conviction).

(5) Where a person summarily convicted of any offence to which sub-paragraph (4) above relates would, apart from this paragraph, be liable to a fine or to a maximum fine of an amount in the case of a first conviction and of a different amount in the case of a second or subsequent conviction, sub-paragraph (4) above shall apply irrespective of whether the conviction is a first, second or subsequent one.

(6) Sub-paragraph (4) above shall not affect so much of any instrument as (in whatever words) makes a person liable on summary conviction to a fine not exceeding a specified amount for each period of a specified length during which a continuing offence is continued after conviction or the occurrence of any other specified event.

(7) Nothing in this paragraph shall affect the punishment for an offence committed before the relevant date.

(8) In this paragraph "the relevant date" means 12th October 1988 (the date of commencement of section 66 of the Criminal Justice (Scotland) Act 1987).

Fines under secondary subordinate instruments

8.—(1) This paragraph applies to any instrument (however framed or worded) which—

(a) was made before 11th April 1983 (the date of commencement of Part IV of the Criminal Justice Act 1982); and

(b) confers on any authority other than a harbour authority a power by subordinate instrument to make a person, as regards any summary offence (whether or not created by the latter instrument), liable on conviction to a maximum fine of a specified amount not exceeding £1,000,

but does not affect so much of any such instrument as (in whatever words) confers a power by subordinate instrument to make a person liable on conviction to a fine for each period of a specified length during which a continuing offence is continued.

(2) The maximum fine to which a subordinate instrument made by virtue of an instrument to which this paragraph applies may provide that a person shall be liable on conviction of a summary offence is—

(a) if the specified amount is less than £25, level 1 on the standard scale;

(b) if it is £25 or more but less than £50, level 2;

(c) if it is £50 or more but less than £200, level 3;

(d) if it is £200 or more but less than £400, level 4; and

(e) if it is £400 or more, level 5.

(3) Subject to sub-paragraph (5) below, where an instrument to which this paragraph applies confers a power by subordinate instrument to make a person, as regards a summary offence, liable on conviction to a fine in respect of a specified quantity or a specified number of things, that shall be treated for the purposes of this paragraph as being the maximum fine to which a person may be made liable by virtue of the instrument.

(4) Where an instrument to which this paragraph applies confers a power to provide for different maximum fines in relation to different circumstances or persons of different descriptions, the amount specified as those maximum fines are to be treated separately for the purposes of this paragraph.

(5) Where an instrument to which this paragraph applies confers a power by subordinate instrument to make a person, as regards a summary offence, liable on conviction to a fine in respect of a specified quantity or a specified number of things but also confers a power by subordinate instrument to make a person, as regards such an offence, liable on conviction to an alternative fine, this paragraph shall have effect in relation—

(a) to the alternative fine; and

(b) to any amount that the instrument specifies as the maximum fine for which a subordinate instrument made in the exercise of the power conferred by it may provide,

as well as in relation to the fine mentioned in sub-paragraph (3) above.

*Fines on summary conviction for offences under subordinate instruments: conversion to
references to levels on scale*

9.—(1) Where an instrument which was made under an enactment on or after 11th April 1983
but before 12th October 1988 (the date of commencement of section 54 of the Criminal Justice
Act 1988) confers on any authority other than a harbour authority a power by subordinate
instrument to make a person liable on summary conviction to a fine of an amount shown in the
second column of the standard scale, as that scale had effect when the instrument was made, a
reference to the level in the first column of the standard scale which then corresponded to that
amount shall be substituted for the reference in the instrument conferring the power to the
amount of the fine.

(2) This paragraph shall not affect so much of any instrument as (in whatever words) makes a
person liable on summary conviction to a maximum fine not exceeding a specified amount for
each period of a specified length during which a continuing offence is continued.

Part III of Schedule 2

10.—(1) The enactments specified in column 1 of Part III of Schedule 2 to this Act, which
relate to the penalties or the maximum penalties for the offences mentioned in those enactments, shall be amended in accordance with the amendments specified in column 2 of that Part,
which have the effect of altering the penalties on summary conviction of the said offences and
placing the fines on a level on the standard scale; and in that Part column 3 shows the penalties or,
as the case may be, maximum penalties resulting from the amendments.

(2) Sub-paragraph (1) above does not affect the penalty which may be imposed in respect of
an offence committed before 11th April 1983.

*Alteration of penalties on summary conviction of certain offences under the Misuse of Drugs
Act 1971*

11.—(1) The Misuse of Drugs Act 1971 shall be amended as follows—
(a) in the entries in Schedule 4 showing the punishment that may be imposed on persons
summarily convicted of offences mentioned in sub-paragraph (2)(b) below, for "6
months" there shall be substituted "3 months"; and
(b) in the entry in Schedule 4 relating to section 5(2)—
(i) for "6 months" (being the maximum punishment on summary conviction of an
offence under that section where a Class B drug was involved) there shall be substituted "3 months", and
(ii) for "6 months" being the maximum punishment on summary conviction of such
an offence where a Class C drug was involved there shall be substituted "3 months".
(2) The offences to which (as provided in paragraph 2(7) above) paragraph 2(1) above does
not apply are—
(a) offences under section 5(2) of the Misuse of Drugs Act 1971 (having possession of a controlled drug) where the controlled drug in relation to which the offence was committed
was a Class B or Class C drug;
(b) offences under the following provisions of that Act, where the controlled drug in relation
to which the offence was committed was a Class C drug, namely—
(i) section 4(2) (production, or being concerned in the production, of a controlled
drug);
(ii) section 4(3) (supplying or offering a controlled drug or being concerned in the
doing of either activity by another);
(iii) section 5(3) (having possession of a controlled drug with intent to supply it to
another);
(iv) section 8 (being the occupier, or concerned in the management, of premises and
permitting or suffering certain activities to take place there);
(v) section 12(6) (contravention of direction prohibiting practitioner etc. from possessing, supplying etc. controlled drugs); or
(vi) section 13(3) (contravention of direction prohibiting practitioner etc. from prescribing, supplying etc. controlled drugs).
(3) In this paragraph "controlled drug", "Class B drug" and "Class C drug" have the same
meaning as in the Misuse of Drugs Act 1971.

Transitional provisions and savings

12.—(1) The following transitional provisions and savings relating to the provisions contained
in this Schedule shall have effect.

(2) For the purposes of paragraph 3(2) above, any provision in force at 17th July 1978 (the date of coming into force of subsection (3) of section 289C of the Criminal Procedure (Scotland) Act 1975) which—

   (a) is contained in any byelaw made by virtue of section 203 of the Local Government (Scotland) Act 1973 but not that section as applied to byelaws made under any provision contained in a local or private Act other than by a local authority; and

   (b) specified £20 as the maximum fine which may be imposed on summary conviction in respect of a contravention of, or offence under, any byelaw mentioned in that provision,

shall have effect as if it specified £50 instead, but with no change by virtue of this sub-paragraph in the maximum daily fine, if any, for which it provides.

(3) Paragraph 5 above does not affect the penalty which may be imposed in respect of an offence committed before 11th April 1983.

SCHEDULE 2

INCREASE IN CERTAIN PENALTIES

PART I

OFFENCES MADE TRIABLE ONLY SUMMARILY, AND RELATED AMENDMENTS

(1) Offence	(2) Enactment	(3) Amendment	(4) Penalties
NIGHT POACHING ACT 1828 (C. 69) Offences under section 1 (taking or destroying game or rabbits by night or entering land for that purpose).	Section 1.	For the words from "such offender" onwards substitute "he shall be liable on summary conviction to a fine not exceeding level 3 on the standard scale".	Level 3 on the standard scale.
PUBLIC MEETING ACT 1908 (C. 66) Offences under section 1(1) (endeavour to break up a public meeting).	Section 1(1).	After "offence" add "shall on summary conviction be liable to imprisonment for a term not exceeding 6 months or to a fine not exceeding level 5 on the standard scale or to both".	6 months or level 5 on the standard scale or both.
POST OFFICE ACT 1953 (C. 36) Offences under section 56 (criminal diversions of letters from addressee).	Section 56(1).	For the words "guilty" onwards substitute "liable on summary conviction to a fine not exceeding level 4 on the standard scale or to imprisonment for a term not exceeding six months or to both".	Level 4 on the standard scale or 6 months or both.

(1) Offence	(2) Enactment	(3) Amendment	(4) Penalties
BETTING, GAMING AND LOTTERIES ACT 1963 (C. 2) Offences under the following provisions – section 7 (restriction of betting on dog racecourses); section 10(5) (advertising licensed betting offices); section 11(6) (person holding bookmaker's or betting agency permit employing a person disqualified from holding such a permit); section 18(2) (making unauthorised charges to bookmakers on licensed track); section 19 (occupiers of licensed tracks not to have any interest in bookmaker thereon); section 21 (betting with young persons); section 22 (betting circulars not to be sent to young persons).	Section 52.	For paragraphs (a) and (b) of subsection (2) (penalties for certain offences) substitute "on summary conviction to a fine not exceeding level 5 on the standard scale or to imprisonment for a term not exceeding six months or to both".	Level 5 on the standard scale or 6 months or both.
THEATRES ACT 1968 (C. 54) Offences under section 6 (provocation of breach of the peace by means of public performance of play).	Section 6(2).	For paragraphs (a) and (b) substitute "on summary conviction to a fine not exceeding level 5 on the standard scale or to imprisonment for a term not exceeding six months or to both".	6 months or level 5 on the standard scale or both.

Part II

Increase of fines for certain summary offences

(1) Enactment creating offence	(2) Penalty enactment	(3) Old maximum fine	(4) New maximum fine
PROTECTION OF ANIMALS (SCOTLAND) ACT 1912 (C. 14) Offences under section 1(1) (inflicting or unnecessary suffering on, and cruelty to, animals).	Section 1(1) (as amended by section 3 of the Protection of Animals (Amendment) Act 1954).	£50	Level 4 on the standard scale.
PROTECTION OF ANIMALS ACT 1934 (C. 21) Offences under section 1(1) (prohibition of certain public contests, performances and exhibitions with horses or bulls).	Section 2.	£100	Level 4 on the standard scale.
PUBLIC ORDER ACT 1936 (1 Edw. 8 & 1 Geo. 6) (C. 6) Offences under section 1(1) (wearing uniform signifying association with political organisation).	Section 7(2).	£50	Level 4 on the standard scale.
CHILDREN AND YOUNG PERSONS (SCOTLAND) ACT 1937 (C. 37) Offences under section 46(2) (publication of matters identifying juveniles in court proceedings).	Section 46(2).	£50	Level 4 on the standard scale.
CINEMATOGRAPH FILMS (ANIMALS) ACT 1937 (C. 59) Offences under section 1(1) (prohibition of films in production of which suffering has been caused to animals).	Section 1(3).	£100	Level 4 on the standard scale.
ARCHITECTS REGISTRATION ACT 1938 (C. 54) Offences under section 1 (unregistered persons using title of architect).	Section 3.	£50	Level 4 on the standard scale.
NURSING HOMES REGISTRATION (SCOTLAND) ACT 1938 (C. 73) Any offence under the Act for which no express penalty is provided, except an offence under section 1(4).	Section 8 (as amended by Schedule 3 to the Criminal Justice Act 1967).	£20	Level 4 on the standard scale.

(1) Enactment creating offence	(2) Penalty enactment	(3) Old maximum fine	(4) New maximum fine
FIRE SERVICES ACT 1947 (C. 41) Offences under section 31(1) (giving false fire alarm).	Section 31(1) (as amended by Schedule 3 to the Criminal Justice Act 1967).	£50	Level 4 on the standard scale.
NATIONAL ASSISTANCE ACT 1948 (C. 29) Offences under section 55(2) (obstruction).	Section 55(2) (as amended by Schedule 3 to the Criminal Justice Act 1967).	£10 for a first offence and £20 for a second or subsequent offence.	Level 4 on the standard scale.
AGRICULTURE (SCOTLAND) ACT 1948 (C. 45) Offences under section 50(1) (prohibition of night shooting and use of spring traps).	Section 50(2).	£20 for a first offence and £50 for a second or subsequent offence.	Level 3 on the standard scale.
Offences under section 50A(1) (open trapping of hares and rabbits).	Section 50A(2).	£20 for a first offence and £50 for a second or subsequent offence.	Level 3 on the standard scale.
DOCKING AND NICKING OF HORSES ACT 1949 (C. 70) Offences under section 1(1) (prohibition of docking or nicking horses).	Section 1(3).	£25	Level 3 on the standard scale.
Offences under section 2(3) (offences in connection with importation of docked horses).	Section 2(3).	£25	Level 3 on the standard scale.
Offences under section 2(4) (making of false statement).	Section 2(4).	£25	Level 3 on the standard scale.
COCKFIGHTING ACT 1952 (C. 59) Offences under section 1(1) (possession of appliances for use in fighting of domestic fowl).	Section 1(1).	£25	Level 3 on the standard scale.

(1) Enactment creating offence	(2) Penalty enactment	(3) Old maximum fine	(4) New maximum fine
DOGS (PROTECTION OF LIVESTOCK) ACT 1953 (C. 28) Offences under section 1(1) (owning or keeping a dog which worries livestock).	Section 1(6) (as amended by Schedule 3 to the Criminal Justice Act 1967).	£20 for a first offence and £50 for a second or subsequent offence in respect of the same dog.	Level 3 on the standard scale.
PESTS ACT 1954 (C. 68) Offences under section 12 (spreading of myxomatosis).	Section 12.	£20 for a first offence and £50 for a second or subsequent offence in respect of the same dog.	Level 3 on the standard scale.
ANIMAL (CRUEL POISONS) ACT 1962 (C. 26) Offences under section 1 (offences in connection with use of prohibited poison for destroying animals).	Section 1.	£50	Level 3 on the standard scale.
POLICE (SCOTLAND) ACT 1967 (C. 77) Offences under section 41(1) (assaults on constable etc.), where the offender has not, within the period of two years immediately preceding the offence been convicted of an offence against the section.	Section 41(1).	£50	Level 4 on the standard scale.
SEA FISHERIES (SHELLFISH) ACT 1967 (C. 83) Offences under section 7(4) (using prohibited fishing implements etc. in an area of fishery or oyster bed to which section applies).	Section 7(4).	£2 for a first offence, £5 for a second offence and £10 for a third or subsequent offence.	Level 3 on the standard scale.
ABORTION ACT 1967 (C. 87) Offences under section 2(3) (contravening or failing to comply with regulations as to notification).	Section 2(3).	£100	Level 5 on the standard scale.
AGRICULTURE (MISCELLANEOUS PROVISIONS) ACT 1968 (C. 34) Offences under the following provisions— section 1(1) (prevention of unnecessary pain and distress to livestock); section 2(2) (breach of regulations with respect to welfare of livestock).	Section 7(1).	£100 for a first offence and £200 for a second or subsequent offence.	Level 4 on the standard scale.

(1) Enactment creating offence	(2) Penalty enactment	(3) Old maximum fine	(4) New maximum fine
SOCIAL WORK (SCOTLAND) ACT 1968 (C. 49) Offences under section 6(5) (obstructing officer in exercise of power under section 6).	Section 6(5).	£10 for a first offence and £50 for a second or subsequent offence.	Level 4 on the standard scale.
Offences under section 60(3) (failure to comply with regulations etc. in respect of the control of residential and other establishments).	Section 60(3).	£50 for a first offence and £100 for a second or subsequent offence.	Level 4 on the standard scale.
Offences under section 61(3) (carrying on establishment without registration).			
Offences under section 62(6) (failure to comply with a condition of the registration of an establishment).	Section 62(6).	£50 for a first offence and £100 for a second or subsequent offence.	Level 4 on the standard scale.
Offences under section 65(4) (obstructing officer in exercise of power under section 65).	Section 65(4).	£10 for a first offence and £50 for a second or subsequent offence.	Level 4 on the standard scale.
GAMING ACT 1968 (C. 65) Offences under section 8(5) (gaming in a street or public place).	Section 8(5).	£50.	Level 4 on the standard scale.
EMPLOYERS' LIABILITY (COMPULSORY INSURANCE ACT 1969 (C. 57) Offences under section 4(3) (offences in relation to certificates of insurance).	Section 4(3).	£50.	Level 3 on the standard scale.
Offences under section 5 (employer failing to insure employee).	Section 5.	£200.	Level 4 on the standard scale.
CONSERVATION OF SEALS ACT 1970 (C. 30) Any offence under the Act, except an offence under section 11(7).	Section 5(2).	£50 for a first offence and £100 for a second or subsequent offence.	Level 4 on the standard scale.
MISUSE OF DRUGS ACT 1971 (C. 38) Offences under section 17(3) (failure to comply with notice requiring information relating to prescribing supply etc. of drugs).	Schedule 4.	£100.	Level 3 on the standard scale.

(1) Enactment creating offence	(2) Penalty enactment	(3) Old maximum fine	(4) New maximum fine
POISONS ACT 1972 (C. 66) Any offence under section 8(1) (contravention of provisions of sections 1 to 7, other than section 6(4), or of the Poisons rules).	Section 8(1).	£50.	Level 4 on the standard scale.
Offences under section 6(4) (using title etc. falsely to suggest entitlement to sell poison).	Section 6(4).	£20.	Level 2 on the standard scale.
Offences under section 9(8) (obstructing an inspector etc.).	Section 9(8).	£5.	Level 2 on the standard scale.
HEALTH AND SAFETY AT WORK ETC. ACT 1974 (C. 37) Offences under the following provisions— section 33(1)(d) (contravening requirement imposed by or under section 14 or obstructing any person in exercise of his powers under section 14); section 33(1)(e) (contravening requirement imposed by inspector) where the requirement contravened was imposed under section 20; section 33(1)(f) (prevening etc, any other person from appearing before inspector); section 33(1)(h) (intentionally obstructing an inspector); section 33(1)(n) (falsely pretending to be an inspector).	Section 33(2).	£400.	Level 5 on the standard scale.
SALMON AND FRESHWATER FISHERIES ACT 1975 (C. 51) Offences against any provision of the Act not specified in the table in Part I of Schedule 4.	Paragraph 1(2) of Schedule 4.	£50 for a first offence and £100 for a second or subsequent offence.	Level 4 on the standard scale.
Offences under section 1 (fishing with certain instruments for salmon, trout or freshwater fish and possessing certain instruments for fishing for such fish) if not acting with another.	The Table in Part I of Schedule 4.	£50 for a first offence and £100 for a second or subsequent offence.	Level 4 on the standard scale.
Offences under section 19(2) (fishing for salmon during the annual close season or weekly close time).	The said Table.	£100 for a first offence and £200 for a second or subsequent offence.	Level 4 on the standard scale.

(1) Enactment creating offence	(2) Penalty enactment	(3) Old maximum fine	(4) New maximum fine
Offences under section 19(4) (fishing for trout during the annual close season or weekly close time).	The said Table.	£100 for a first offence and £200 for a second or subsequent offence.	Level 4 on the standard scale.
Offences under section 19(6) (fishing for freshwater fish during the annual close season for freshwater fish and fishing for eels by means of a rod and line during that season).	The said Table.	£100 for a first offence and £200 for a second or subsequent offence.	Level 4 on the standard scale.
Offences under section 19(7) (fishing for rainbow trout during the annual close season for rainbow trout and fishing for eels by means of a rod and line during that season).	The said Table.	£100 for a first offence and £200 for a second or subsequent offence.	Level 4 on the standard scale.
Offences under section 21 (prohibition on use of certain devices at certain times).	The said Table.	£100 for a first offence and £200 for a second or subsequent offence.	Level 4 on the standard scale.
Offences under section 27 (fishing for fish otherwise than under the authority of a licence and possessing an unlicensed instrument with intent to use it for fishing) if not acting with another.	The said Table.	£50 for a first offence and £100 for a second or subsequent offence.	Level 4 on the standard scale.

PART III

FINES TO BE ALTERED OTHER THAN IN ACCORDANCE WITH PARAGRAPHS 4 AND 5 OF SCHEDULE 1

(1) Enactment	(2) Amendment	(3) New penalty
MILITARY LANDS ACT 1892 (C. 43) Section 17(2) (offences against byelaws).	For "five pounds" substitute "level 2 on the standard scale".	Level 2 on the standard scale.
PROTECTION OF ANIMALS (SCOTLAND) ACT 1912 (C. 14) Section 7 (selling poisoned grain or placing on any land matter rendered poisonous).	For "ten pounds" substitute "level 4 on the standard scale".	Level 4 on the standard scale.
LAND DRAINAGE (SCOTLAND) ACT 1930 (C. 20) Section 4 (obstruction of person exercising power of entry).	For "twenty pounds" substitute "level 3 on the standard scale".	Level 3 on the standard scale.
LAND DRAINAGE (SCOTLAND) ACT 1941 (C. 13) Section 2(2) (obstruction of person exercising power of entry).	For "twenty pounds" substitute "level 3 on the standard scale".	Level 3 on the standard scale.
PUBLIC HEALTH (SCOTLAND) ACT 1945 (C. 15) Section 1(5) (contravention of regulations as to treatment and spread of certain deseases).	For "one hundred pounds" substitute "level 5 on the standard scale".	Level 5 on the standard scale and £50 per day during which the offence continues.
FIRE SERVICES ACT 1947 (C. 41) Section 14(5) (improper use of fire hydrant).	For "ten pounds" substitute "level 2 on the standard scale".	Level 2 on the standard scale.
Section 30(2) (obstructing a member of a fire brigade).	For "twenty-five pounds" substitute "level 3 on the standard scale".	Level 3 on the standard scale.
RADIOACTIVE SUBSTANCES ACT 1948 (C. 37) Section 8(1) (obstruction of person exercising power of entry).	For the words from "twenty pounds" to the end substitute "level 4 on the standard scale".	Level 4 on the standard scale.
Section 8(3) (other summary offences under Act).	For the words from "one hundred pounds" where first occurring to "one hundred pounds" where secondly occurring substitute "level 4 on the standard scale".	Level 4 on the standard scale or 3 months or both.

(1) Enactment	(2) Amendment	(3) New penalty
RIVERS (PREVENTION OF POLLUTION) (SCOTLAND) ACT 1951 (C. 66)		
Section 21 (obstruction of person exercising power of entry).	For the words from "five pounds" to the end substitute "level 3 on the standard scale".	Level 3 on the standard scale.
LAND DRAINAGE (SCOTLAND) ACT 1958 (C. 24)		
Section 11(4) (obstruction of person exercising power of entry)	For the words from "five pounds" to the end substitute "level 3 on the standard scale".	Level 3 on the standard scale.
BETTING, GAMING AND LOTTERIES ACT 1963 (C. 2)		
Section 28(10) (disclosing information about bookmaker's business).	For "one hundred pounds" substitute "level 4 on the standard scale".	Level 4 on the standard scale.
PLANT VARIETIES AND SEEDS ACT 1964 (C. 14)		
Section 25(9) (obstructing an authorised person)	For "twenty pounds" substitute "level 3 on the standard scale".	Level 3 on the standard scale.
Section 27(1) (tampering with samples).	For "one hundred pounds" substitute "level 5 on the standard scale".	Level 5 on the standard scale or 3 months or both.
AGRICULTURE AND HORTICULTURE ACT 1964 (C. 28)		
Section 20(1) (obstruction, etc. of authorised officer).	For "twenty pounds" substitute "level 3 on the standard scale".	Level 3 on the standard scale.
Section 20(2) (offences under Part III).	For the words from "one hundred pounds" to "two hundred and fifty pounds" substitute "level 5 on the standard scale".	Level 5 on the standard scale or 3 months or both.
INDUSTRIAL AND PROVIDENT SOCIETIES ACT 1965 (C. 12)		
Section 61 (general offences).	For "five pounds" substitute "level 3 on the standard scale".	Level 3 on the standard scale.
RIVERS (PREVENTION OF POLLUTION) (SCOTLAND) ACT 1965 (C. 13)		
Section 11(2) (unauthorised disclosure of information).	For the words from "one hundred pounds" to the end substitute "level 5 on the standard scale".	Level 5 on the standard scale.
FORESTRY ACT 1967 (C. 10)		
Section 24(4) (failure to comply with felling licence).	For "£50" substitute "level 5 on the standard scale".	Level 5 on the standard scale.

(1) Enactment	(2) Amendment	(3) New penalty
Section 46(5) (offences against byelaws).	In paragraph (a) for "£10" substitute "level 2 on the standard scale", and in paragraph (b) for "£5" substitute "level 2 on the standard scale".	Level 2 on the standard scale and 50 pence per day during which the offence continues.
Section 48(3) (obstruction of Forestry Commission officers).	For "£5" substitute "level 3 on the standard scale".	Level 3 on the standard scale.
POLICE (SCOTLAND) ACT 1967 (C. 77)		
Section 43(1) (impersonating a police officer).	For "fifty pounds" substitute "level 4 on the standard scale".	Level 4 on the standard scale or 3 months.
Section 44(5) (offences by constables).	For "ten pounds" substitute "level 3 on the standard scale".	Level 3 on the standard scale or 60 days.
AGRICULTURE (MISCELLANEOUS PROVISIONS) ACT 1968 (C. 34)		
Section 7(2) (obstructing officer authorised to carry out welfare inspections).	For "twenty pounds" substitute "level 3 on the standard scale".	Level 3 on the standard scale.
SALE OF VENISON (SCOTLAND) ACT 1968 (C. 38)		
Section 1(4) (contravention of provisions regarding registration of venison dealers).	For "£20" substitute "level 3 on the standard scale".	Level 3 on the standard scale.
Section 2(4) (failure to keep records, etc.).	For "£20" substitute "level 2 on the standard scale".	Level 2 on the standard scale.
SEWERAGE (SCOTLAND) ACT 1968 (C. 47)		
Section 44 (failure to provide information, etc.).	For "£20" substitute "level 3 on the standard scale".	Level 3 on the standard scale.
Section 48(9) (obstruction of person having right of entry).	For "£20" substitute "level 3 on the standard scale".	Level 3 on the standard scale and £5 per day which the offence continues.
Section 50(3) (unauthorised disclosure of information).	For the words from "£100" to the end substitute "level 5 on the standard scale".	Level 5 on the standard scale.
TRANSPORT ACT 1968 (C. 73)		
Section 97A(1) (tachograph offences).	For "£200" substitute "level 4 on the standard scale".	Level 4 on the standard scale.
Section 97A(2) (failure by employer to secure compliance with section 97A(1)(a)).	For "£200" substitute "level 4 on the standard scale".	Level 4 on the standard scale.

(1) Enactment	(2) Amendment	(3) New penalty
ROAD TRAFFIC (FOREIGN VEHICLES) ACT 1972 (C. 27)		
Section 3(1) (disobeying prohibition on a goods vehicle).	For "£200" substitute "level 5 on the standard scale".	Level 5 on the standard scale.
EDUCATION (SCOTLAND) ACT 1980 (C. 44)		
Section 43(1) (contravention of section 35, 41 or 42).	For the words from "in the case" where first occurring to "£50" where thirdly occurring substitute "to a fine not exceeding level 3 on the standard scale".	Level 3 on the standard scale or 1 month or both.
Section 66(3) (obstruction of inspectors).	For the words from "£20" to "£50" substitute "level 4 on the standard scale".	Level 4 on the standard scale or 3 months or both.
Section 98(2) (failure to register independent school, etc.).	For the words "£20" to "£50" substitute "level 4 on the standard scale".	Level 4 on the standard scale or 3 months or both.
Section 101(2) (using disqualified premises).	For the words from "£20" to "£50" substitute level 4 on the standard scale.	Level 4 on the standard scale or 3 months or both.
Section 101(3) (disqualified person acting as proprietor of independent school, etc.).	For the words from "£20" to "£50" substitute "level 4 on the standard scale".	Level 4 on the standard scale or 3 months or both.
WATER (SCOTLAND) ACT 1980 (C. 45)		
Section 38(7) (obstruction of person exercising power of entry).	For "£25" substitute "level 3 on the standard scale".	Level 3 on the standard scale.
Section 64(2) (failure to provide information, etc.).	For "£25" substitute "level 3 on the standard scale".	Level 3 on the standard scale.
Section 72(3) (penalty which may be provided for contravention of byelaws).	For "the sum of £400" substitute "level 4 on the standard scale".	Level 4 on the standard scale and £50 per day during which the offence continues.
Section 93(7) (failure to provide information, etc.).	For "£200" substitute "level 4 on the standard scale".	Level 4 on the standard scale and £20 per day during which the offence continues.

(1) Enactment	(2) Amendment	(3) New penalty
Paragraph 10(3) of Schedule 4 (offences relating to construction of reservoirs).	For the words from "£50" where first occurring to "continued" substitute "level 3 on the standard scale".	Level 3 on the standard scale.
Paragraph 28 of Schedule 4 (obstruction of person exercising power of entry).	For the words "£25" substitute "level 3 on the standard scale".	Level 3 on the standard scale.

SCHEDULE 3

Transitional Provisions, Transitory Modifications and Savings

Part I

General and Miscellaneous

General saving for old savings

1. The repeal by this Act of an enactment previously repealed subject to savings (whether or not in the repealing enactment) does not affect the continued operation of those savings.

Documents referring to repealed enactments

2. Any document made served or issued after this Act comes into force which contains a reference to any of the repealed enactments shall be construed, except so far as the contrary intention appears, as referring or, as the context may require, including a reference to the corresponding provision of the consolidating Acts.

Provisions relating to the coming into force of other provisions

3.—(1) The repeal by this Act of a provision providing for or relating to the coming into force of a provision reproduced in the consolidating Acts does not affect the operation of the first provision, in so far as it remains capable of having effect, in relation to the enactment reproducing the second provision.

(2) The repeal by this Act of a power to make provision or savings in preparation for or in connection with the coming into force of a provision reproduced in the consolidating Acts does not affect the power, in so far as it remains capable of having effect, in relation to the enactment reproducing the second provision.

Part II

Specific Provisions

Local government reform

4.—(1) At any time before 1 April 1996 or the coming into force of section 1 of the Local Government etc. (Scotland) Act 1994, whichever is the later, in section 206 of the Principal Act, for subsection (6) there shall be substituted the following subsection—

"(6) In this section the expression "police authority" means a regional or islands council, except that where there is an amalgamation scheme under the Police (Scotland) Act 1967 in force it means a joint police committee."

(2) Until the date on which paragraph 71 of Schedule 13 to the said Act of 1994 comes into force, the reference in section 17(5)(a) of the Proceeds of Crime (Scotland) Act 1995 to a joint police board shall be construed as a reference to a joint police committee.

The Principal Reporter

5. Until the coming into force of section 127 of the Local Government etc. (Scotland) Act 1994, for any reference in any provision of the Principal Act to the Principal Reporter there shall be substituted a reference to the reporter of the local authority in whose area any child referred to in that provision resides.

Penalties

6.—(1) The repeal by this Act of any enactment—
(a) by virtue of which the penalty which may be imposed in respect of any offence is altered; but
(b) which provides that the penalty in respect of such an offence committed before a particular date shall not be so altered,
shall not affect the penalty which may be imposed in respect of an offence mentioned in paragraph (b) above.

(2) The periods of imprisonment set forth in subsection (2) of section 219 of the Principal Act shall apply to the non-payment of any sum imposed under that section by a court under a statute or order passed or made before 1 June 1909, notwithstanding that that statute or order fixes any other period of imprisonment.

District court procedure

7. The repeal by this Act of section 4 of the District Courts (Scotland) Act 1975 shall not affect the rules of procedure and practice in the district court.

Detention of children in summary proceedings

8. Notwithstanding the repeal by Schedule 2 of the Criminal Justice (Scotland) Act 1987 of section 58A of the Children and Young Persons (Scotland) Act 1937, any child who, before 1 April 1988 (the date of commencement of section 59 of the said Act of 1987), had been ordered to be detained pursuant to the directions of the Secretary of State under section 413 of the Criminal Procedure (Scotland) Act 1975—
(a) shall, while so detained after such date, continue to be deemed to be in legal custody; and
(b) may at any time be released conditionally or unconditionally by the Secretary of State, and any such child conditionally released shall be liable to recall on the directions of the Secretary of State and if he fails to comply with any condition of his release he may be apprehended without warrant and taken to the place from which he was released.

Effect of probation and absolute discharge

9. Subsections (1) and (2) of section 246 of the Principal Act shall not affect the operation, in relation to an offender as mentioned in those subsections, of any enactment which was in force as at the commencement of section 9(3)(b) of the Criminal Justice (Scotland) Act 1949 and is expressed to extend to persons dealt with under section 1(1) of the Probation of Offenders Act 1907 as well as to convicted persons.

Restriction on discharge of hospital order

10. Until the coming into force of section 54 of the Criminal Justice (Scotland) Act 1995, in section 59 of the Principal Act for the words "without limit of time" there shall be substituted the words "either without limit of time or during such period as may be specified in the order".

Aiding and abetting

11. Subsection (2) of section 293 of the Principal Act shall not apply in respect of any offence committed before 1 October 1987 (the date of commencement of section 64 of the Criminal Justice (Scotland) Act 1987).

Penal servitude and hard labour

12.—(1) Any enactment which confers power on a court to pass a sentence of penal servitude in any case shall be construed, subject to sub-paragraph (3) below, as conferring power to pass a sentence of imprisonment for a term not exceeding the maximum term of penal servitude for which a sentence could have been passed in that case immediately before 12 June 1950.
(2) Any enactment which confers power on a court to pass a sentence of imprisonment with hard labour in any case shall be construed as conferring power to pass a sentence of imprisonment for a term not exceeding the term for which a sentence of imprisonment with hard labour could have been passed in that case immediately before 12 June 1950.
(3) Nothing in sub-paragraph (1) above shall be construed as empowering a court, other than the High Court, to pass a sentence of imprisonment for a term exceeding two years.

Supervised attendance orders

13.—(1) In section 235 of the Principal Act, paragraph (b) of subsection (3) shall also apply to an offender where, having been convicted of an offence, he has had imposed on him a fine which (or any part or instalment of which) he has failed to pay and the court, prior to 1 April 1991 (the date of commencement of section 62 of the Law Reform (Miscellaneous Provisions) (Scotland) Act 1990), has imposed on him a period of imprisonment under paragraph (a) of subsection (1) of section 219 of the Principal Act but he has not served any of that period of imprisonment.
(2) Where, in respect of an offender, a court makes a supervised attendance order in circumstances where paragraph (b) of the said subsection (3) applies as mentioned in sub-paragraph (1) above, the making of that order shall have the effect of discharging the sentence of imprisonment imposed on the offender.

Hearsay evidence

14. Nothing in the sections 259 to 261 of the Principal Act shall apply to—
(a) proceedings commenced; or

(b) where the proceedings consist of an application to the sheriff by virtue of section 42(2)(c) of the Social Work (Scotland) Act 1968 or by virtue of Chapter 3 of Part II of the Children (Scotland) Act 1995, an application made,

before sections 17 to 20 of the Criminal Justice (Scotland) Act 1995 came into force; and, for the purposes of paragraph (a) above, solemn proceedings are commenced when the indictment is served.

Confiscation of proceeds of crime, etc.

15.—(1) Where a person is charged with an offence in relation to which provision is made by Part I of the Proceeds of Crime (Scotland) Act 1995, being an offence committed before the coming into force of Chapter I of Part II of the Criminal Justice (Scotland) Act 1995, Part I of the said Proceeds of Crime (Scotland) Act shall not affect the powers of the court in the event of his being convicted of the offence.

(2) Where a person is charged with an offence committed before the coming into force of Part II of the Proceeds of Crime (Scotland) Act 1995, in the event of his being convicted of the offence, the court shall be entitled to exercise the powers conferred by section 223 or section 436 of the Criminal Procedure (Scotland) Act 1975, but not the powers conferred by that Part.

(3) Paragraph (b) of section 2(4) of the Proceeds of Crime (Scotland) Act 1995 shall not apply in the case of an offence committed before the coming into force of Chapter I of Part II of the Criminal Justice (Scotland) Act 1995.

(4) In any case in which, notwithstanding the coming into force of the Bankruptcy (Scotland) Act 1985, the Bankruptcy (Scotland) Act 1913 applies to a sequestration, paragraph 1(2) of Schedule 2 to the Proceeds of Crime (Scotland) Act 1995 shall have effect as if for sub-sub-paragraphs (a) and (b) thereof there were substituted the following paragraphs—

"(a) property comprised in the whole property of the debtor which vests in the trustee under section 97 of the Bankruptcy (Scotland) Act 1913,

(b) any income of the bankrupt which has been ordered, under subsection (2) of section 98 of that Act, to be paid to the trustee or any estate which, under subsection (1) of that section, vests in the trustee,",

and paragraph 1(3) of that Schedule shall have effect as if, for the reference in it to the said Act of 1985, there were substituted a reference to the said Act of 1913.

(5) In any case in which a petition in bankruptcy was presented, or a receiving order or adjudication in bankruptcy was made, before 29 December 1986 (the date on which the Insolvency Act 1986 came into force), paragraph 2(2) to (5) of Schedule 2 to the Proceeds of Crime (Scotland) Act 1995 shall have effect with the following modifications—

(a) for references to the bankrupt's estate for the purposes of Part IX of the said Act of 1986 there are substituted references to the property of the bankrupt for the purposes of the Bankruptcy Act 1914;

(b) for references to the said Act of 1986 and to sections 280(2)(c), 286, 339, and 423 of that Act there are respectively substituted references to the said Act of 1914 and to sections 26(2), 8, 27 and 42 of that Act;

(c) the references in subsection (4) to an interim receiver appointed as there mentioned include, where a receiving order has been made, a reference to the receiver constituted by virtue of section 7 of the said Act of 1914, and

(d) subsection (2)(b) is omitted.

(6) In any case in which a winding up of a company commenced, or is treated as having commenced, before 29 December 1986, paragraph 3(2) to (6) of the said Schedule 2 shall have effect with the substitution for references to the said Act of 1986 of references to the Companies Act 1985.

(7) In any case in which a receiver was appointed as is mentioned in sub-paragraph (1) of paragraph 4 of the said Schedule 2 before 29 December 1986, sub-paragraphs (2) to (4) of that paragraph have effect with the substitution for references to the said Act of 1986 of references to the Companies Act 1985.

Criminal Justice (Scotland) Act 1995 (c. 20)

16.—(1) Any enactment repealed by this Act which has been amended by any provision of the Criminal Justice (Scotland) Act 1995 which has not been brought into force at the commencement of this Act shall, notwithstanding such repeal, continue to have effect until such provision is brought into force as if it had not been so repealed or amended.

(2) Any provision of the consolidating Acts which re-enacts any enactment contained in the said Criminal Justice (Scotland) Act which has not been brought into force at the commencement of this Act shall be of no effect until such enactment is brought into force.

(3) The repeal by this Act of any enactment contained in the Criminal Justice (Scotland) Act 1995 which has not been brought into force shall not have effect until such enactment is brought into force.

Children (Scotland) Act 1995 (c. 36)

17. Any enactment repealed by this Act which has been amended by any provision of the Children (Scotland) Act 1995 which has not been brought into force at the commencement of this Act shall, notwithstanding such repeal, continue to have effect until such provision is brought into force as if it had not been so repealed or amended.

False oaths

18. Where an offence mentioned in section 45(5) of the Criminal Law (Consolidation) (Scotland) Act 1995 is, by any Act passed before 28 June 1933, as originally enacted, made punishable only on summary conviction, it shall remain only so punishable.

SCHEDULE 4

MINOR AND CONSEQUENTIAL AMENDMENTS

Jurors (Scotland) Act 1825 (c. 22)

1. In section 3 of the Jurors (Scotland) Act 1825 (sheriff principal to maintain lists of potential jurors)
   (a) the existing provision shall become subsection (1);
   (b) in that subsection, for the word "designations" there shall be substituted "addresses"; and
   (c) after that subsection there shall be inserted the following subsections—

   "(2) For the purpose of maintaining lists of potential jurors under subsection (1) above, a sheriff principal may require any person in the sheriff court district in question who appears to him to be qualified and liable to serve as a juror to provide such information, and in such form, as the Secretary of State may by order prescribe.

   (3) A statutory instrument containing an order prescribed by virtue of subsection (2) above shall be subject to annulment pursuant to a resolution of either House of Parliament.

   (4) Any person who fails to comply with a requirement under subsection (2) above shall be guilty of an offence and liable on summary conviction to a fine not exceeding level 1 on the standard scale.

   (5) In proceedings against a person for an offence under subsection (4) above it is a defence to prove that he had reasonable excuse for the failure."

Bankers' Books Evidence Act 1879 (c. 11)

2. In section 6 of the Bankers' Books Evidence Act 1879 (case in which banker not compellable to produce book), after the word "1988" there shall be inserted the words "or Schedule 8 to the Criminal Procedure (Scotland) Act 1995".

The Children and Young Persons (Scotland) Act 1937 (c. 37)

3.—(1) The Children and Young Persons (Scotland) Act 1937, shall be amended as follows.
(2) After 62 there shall be inserted the following section—

"Register of children found guilty of offences
    63. In addition to any other register required by law, a separate register of children found guilty of offences and of children discharged on bond or put on probation shall be kept for every summary court by the chief constable or other person charged with the duty of keeping registers of convictions. The register shall apply to children of such age, and shall include such particulars, as may be directed by the Secretary of State, and it shall be the duty of the keeper of the register, within seven days after any such child has been dealt with by the court, to transmit a copy of the entry relating to the child to the education authority for the area in which the child resides."
(3) Before section 104 there shall be added the following section—

"Proof of age a defence
    103. Where a person is charged with an offence under this Act in respect of a person apparently under a specified age, it shall be a defence to prove that the person was actually of or over that age."

The Trade Marks Act 1938 (c. 22)

4. In section 58B of the Trade Marks Act 1938 (delivery up of offending goods and material), in subsection (6) for the words "Chapter II of Part II of the Criminal Justice (Scotland) Act 1995" there shall be substituted the words "Part II of the Proceeds of Crime (Scotland) Act 1995."

The Backing of Warrants (Republic of Ireland) Act 1965 (c. 45)

5. In section 8(1)(b) of the Backing of Warrants (Republic of Ireland) Act 1965 (rules of court), for the words "section 457ZA of the Criminal Procedure (Scotland) Act 1975" there shall be substituted the words "section 306 of the Criminal Procedure (Scotland) Act 1995".

Social Work (Scotland) Act 1968 (c. 49)

6.—(1) The Social Work (Scotland) Act 1968 shall be amended as follows.

(2) In subsection (1B) of section 5 (powers of Secretary of State), for paragraph (f) there shall be substituted the following paragraph—

"(f) section 51 of the Criminal Procedure (Scotland) Act 1995;".

(3) In subsection (1) of section 6A (power to hold inquiries) for sub-paragraph (ii) of paragraph (d) there shall be substituted—

"(ii) section 44 or 208 of the Criminal Procedure (Scotland) Act 1995;".

(4) In subsection (1) of section 27 (supervision and care of certain persons)—

(a) after paragraph (a) there shall be inserted the following paragraphs—

"(aa) making available to any children's hearing such reports relating to persons aged 16 and 17 years in relation to the commission of an offence, as the hearing may require for the disposal of a case;

(ab) making available to any procurator fiscal or the Lord Advocate such reports as the procurator fiscal or the Lord Advocate may request in relation to persons who are charged with an offence;";

(b) in paragraph (b)(iii) for the words "the Community Service by Offenders (Scotland) Act 1978" there shall be substituted the words "section 238 of the Criminal Procedure (Scotland) Act 1995";

(c) in paragraph (b)(iv) for the words "section 62 of the Law Reform (Miscellaneous Provisions) (Scotland) Act 1990" there shall be substituted the words "section 235 of the said Act of 1995"; and

(d) after sub-paragraph (iv) of paragraph (b) there shall be inserted the following sub-paragraphs—

"(v) without prejudice to sub-paragraphs (i) to (iv) above, persons in their area who are subject to a supervision and treatment order made under section 57(2)(d) of the Criminal Procedure (Scotland) Act 1995; and

(vi) persons in their area aged 16 and 17 years who are subject to a supervision requirement imposed in relation to the commission of any offence by that person; and

(vii) persons in their area who are charged with, but not prosecuted for, any offence and are referred to the local authority by the procurator fiscal or the Lord Advocate; and".

Sea Fisheries Act 1968 (c. 77)

7. In section 13(2) of the Sea Fisheries Act 1968 (power to award compensation), for "£400" there shall be substituted the words "level 5 on the standard scale".

European Communities Act 1972 (c. 68)

8. In subsection (1) of section 11 of the European Communities Act 1972 (making a false statement before the European Court) for the words "section 1 of the False Oaths (Scotland) Act 1933" there shall be substituted the words "section 44(1) of the Criminal Law (Consolidation) (Scotland) Act 1995".

Fair Trading Act 1973 (c. 41)

9. In subsection (3) of section 129 of the Fair Trading Act 1973 (time-limit for prosecutions)—

(a) for the words "section 331 of the Criminal Procedure (Scotland) Act 1975" there shall be substituted the words "section 136 of the Criminal Procedure (Scotland) Act 1995" and

(b) for the words "subsection (3) of the said section 331" there shall be substituted the words "subsection (3) of the said section 136".

Fatal Accidents and Sudden Deaths Inquiry (Scotland) Act 1976 (c. 14)

10. In section 2(3) of the Fatal Accidents and Sudden Deaths Inquiry (Scotland) Act 1976 for "£25" there shall be substituted the words "level 3 on the standard scale".

Freshwater and Salmon Fisheries (Scotland) Act 1976 (c. 22)

11. In subsection (9) of section 1 of the Freshwater and Salmon Fisheries (Scotland) Act 1976 for the words "the operation of section 312(o) of the Criminal Procedure (Scotland) Act 1975" there shall be substituted the words "paragraph 10 of Schedule 3 to the Criminal Procedure (Scotland) Act 1995".

Restrictive Trade Practices Act 1976 (c. 34)

12.—(1) The Restrictive Trade Practices Act 1976 shall be amended as follows.
(2) In subsection (3) of section 39 (time limit for prosecution) the words "section 331 of the Criminal Procedure (Scotland) Act 1975" there shall be substituted the words "section 136 of the Criminal Procedure (Scotland) Act 1995".
(3) In subsection (6) of section 41 (time limit for prosecution of offences relating to disclosure of documents)—
(a) for the words "section 331 of the Criminal Procedure (Scotland) Act 1975" there shall be substituted the words "section 136 of the Criminal Procedure (Scotland) Act 1995"; and
(b) for the words "subsection (3) of the said section 331" there shall be substituted the words "subsection (3) of the said section 136".

International Carriage of Perishable Foodstuffs Act 1976 (c. 58)

13. In subsection (2) of section 12 of the International Carriage of Perishable Foodstuffs Act 1976 for the words "section 331 of the Criminal Procedure (Scotland) Act 1975" there shall be substituted the words "section 136 of the Criminal Procedure (Scotland) Act 1995".

Marriage (Scotland) Act 1977 (c. 15)

14. In subsection (3) of section 24 of the Marriage (Scotland) Act 1977 for the words "section 331 of the Criminal Procedure (Scotland) Act 1975 (date of commencement of summary proceedings)" there shall be substituted the words "section 136 of the Criminal Procedure (Scotland) Act 1995 (time limit for certain offences)".

Refuse Disposal (Amenity) Act 1978 (c. 3)

15. In subsection (3) of section 2 of the Refuse Disposal (Amenity) Act 1978 for the words "section 462(1) of the Criminal Procedure (Scotland) Act 1975" there shall be substituted the words "section 307(1) of the Criminal Procedure (Scotland) Act 1995".

Adoption (Scotland) Act 1978 (c. 28)

16. In subsection (1) of section 37 of the Adoption (Scotland) Act 1978, for the words "sections 14 and 323 of the Criminal Procedure (Scotland) Act 1975" there shall be substituted the words "section 47 of the Children and Young Persons (Scotland) Act 1975".

Interpretation Act 1978 (c. 30)

17. In Schedule 1 to the Interpretation Act 1978—
(a) in paragraph (b) of the definition of "the standard scale" for the words "section 289G of the Criminal Procedure (Scotland) Act 1975" there shall be substituted the words "section 225(1) of the Criminal Procedure (Scotland) Act 1995"; and
(b) in paragraph (b) of the definition of "statutory maximum" for the words "section 289B(6) of the Criminal Procedure (Scotland) Act 1975" there shall be substituted the words "section 225(8) of the Criminal Procedure (Scotland) Act 1995".

Customs and Excise Management Act 1979 (c. 2)

18.—(1) The Customs and Excise Management Act 1979 shall be amended as follows.
(2) In subsection (6) of section 118A (duty of revenue traders to keep records), in paragraph (d) for the words "Schedule 3 to the Prisoners and Criminal Evidence (Scotland) Act 1993"

there shall be substituted the words "Schedule 8 to the Criminal Procedure (Scotland) Act 1995".

(3) In subsection (3) of section 118C (search warrant) for the words "section 462 of the Criminal Procedure (Scotland) Act 1975" there shall be substituted the words "section 307 of the Criminal Procedure (Scotland) Act 1995".

(4) In subsection (1) of section 118D (order for access to certain information) for the words "section 462 of the Criminal Procedure (Scotland) Act 1975" there shall be substituted the words "section 307 of the Criminal Procedure (Scotland) Act 1995".

(5) In subsection (2) of section 171, in paragraph (b) for the words from "section 289B" to the end of the paragraph there shall be substituted the words "subsection (8) of section 225 of the Criminal Procedure (Scotland) Act 1995 (£5,000 or other sum substituted by order under subsection (4) of that section)".

Customs and Excise Duties (General Reliefs) Act 1979 (c. 3)

19. In subsection (3) of section 15 of the Customs and Excise Duties (General Reliefs) Act 1979, in paragraph (b) for the words from "section 289B" to the end of the paragraph there shall be substituted the words "subsection (8) of section 225 of the Criminal Procedure (Scotland) Act 1995 (£5,000 or other sum substituted by order under subsection (4) of that section)".

Alcoholic Liquor Duties Act 1979 (c. 4)

20. In subsection (1) of section 4 of the Alcoholic Liquor Duties Act 1979, in the definition of "the prescribed sum", in paragraph (b) for the words from "section 289B" to the end of the paragraph there shall be substituted the words "subsection (8) of section 225 of the Criminal Procedure (Scotland) Act 1995 (£5,000 or other sum substituted by order under subsection (4) of that section)".

Hydrocarbon Oil Duties Act 1979 (c. 5)

21. In subsection (1) of section 27 of the Hydrocarbon Oil Duties Act 1979, in the definition of "the prescribed sum", in paragraph (b) for the words from "section 289B" to the end of the paragraph there shall be substituted the words "subsection (8) of section 225 of the Criminal Procedure (Scotland) Act 1995 (£5,000 or other sum substituted by order under subsection (4) of that section)".

Credit Unions Act 1979 (c. 34)

22. In subsection (1) of section 31 of the Credit Unions Act 1979, in the definition of "statutory maximum", in paragraph (b) for the words from "section 289B" to the end of the paragraph there shall be substituted the words "subsection (8) of section 225 of the Criminal Procedure (Scotland) Act 1995".

Estate Agents Act 1979 (c. 38)

23. In subsection (1) of section 33 of the Estate Agents Act 1979, in the definition of "the statutory maximum", in paragraph (b) for the words "section 289B of the Criminal Procedure (Scotland) Act 1975" there shall be substituted the words "subsection (8) of section 225 of the Criminal Procedure (Scotland) Act 1995".

Ancient Monuments and Archaeological Areas Act 1979 (c. 46)

24.—(1) The Ancient Monuments and Archaeological Areas Act 1979 shall be amended as follows.

(2) In section 59, for the words "section 331 of the Criminal Procedure (Scotland) Act 1975" there shall be substituted the words "section 136 of the Criminal Procedure (Scotland) Act 1995".

(3) In subsection (1) of section 61, in the definition of "the statutory maximum" in sub-paragraph (i) of paragraph (b) for the words from "section 289B" to the end of the sub-paragraph there shall be substituted the words "subsection (8) of section 225 of the Criminal Procedure (Scotland) Act 1995 (that is to say £5,000 or another sum fixed by order under subsection (4) of that section for that purpose)".

Isle of Man Act 1979 (c. 58)

25. In subsection (4) of section 5 of the Isle of Man Act 1979, for the words "section 462(1) of the Criminal Procedure (Scotland) Act 1975" there shall be substituted the words "section 307(1) of the Criminal Procedure (Scotland) Act 1995".

Reserve Forces Act 1980 (c. 9)

26. In subsection (2) of section 144 of the Reserve Forces Act 1980, in paragraph (b) for the words "section 289B of the Criminal Procedure (Scotland) Act 1975" there shall be substituted the words "section 225(8) of the Criminal Procedure (Scotland) Act 1995".

Protection of Trading Interests Act 1980 (c. 11)

27. In subsection (5) of section 3 of the Protection of Trading Interests Act 1980, in paragraph (b) for the words "section 289B of the Criminal Procedure (Scotland) Act 1975" there shall be substituted the words "section 225(8) of the Criminal Procedure (Scotland) Act 1995".

Competition Act 1980 (c. 21)

28. In subsection (7) of section 19 of the Competition Act 1980, in paragraph (b) for the words "section 289B of the Criminal Procedure (Scotland) Act 1975" there shall be substituted the words "section 225(8) of the Criminal Procedure (Scotland) Act 1995".

Licensed Premises (Exclusion of Certain Persons) Act 1980 (c. 32)

29. In subsection (2) of section 1 of the Licensed Premises (Exclusion of Certain Persons) Act 1980, in paragraph (c) for the words from "sections" to "1975" there shall be substituted the words "sections 228, 246(2) and (3) and 247 of the Criminal Procedure (Scotland) Act 1995".

Water (Scotland) Act 1980 (c. 45)

30. In subsection (4) of section 75 of the Water (Scotland) Act 1980, for the words "section 289B(6) of the Criminal Procedure (Scotland) Act 1975" there shall be substituted the words "section 225(8) of the Criminal Procedure (Scotland) Act 1995".

Solicitors (Scotland) Act 1980 (c. 46)

31. In subsection (1) of section 25A of the Solicitors (Scotland) Act 1980 (rights of audience) for the words from "section 250" to "1975" there shall be substituted the words "section 103(8) of the Criminal Procedure (Scotland) Act 1995 (right of solicitor to appear before single judge)".

Law Reform (Miscellaneous Provisions) (Scotland) Act 1980 (c. 55)

32.—(1) The Law Reform (Miscellaneous Provisions) (Scotland) Act 1980 shall be amended as follows.

(2) After subsection (5) of section 1 (persons excused from jury service for good reason) there shall be inserted the following subsection—

"(5A) Where the clerk of court has, under subsection (5) above, excused a person from jury service in any criminal proceedings he shall, unless he considers there to be exceptional circumstances which make it inappropriate to do so, within one year of the date of that excusal cite that person to attend for jury service in criminal proceedings."

(3) In subsection (6) of that section, for paragraph (c) there shall be substituted the following—

"(c) section 85(8) or 88(7) of the Criminal Procedure (Scotland) Act 1995,".

(4) In Schedule 1 (ineligibility for and disqualification and excusal from jury service)—

(a) in Part I (persons ineligible), in paragraph (p) of Group B for the words "section 462(1) of the Criminal Procedure (Scotland) Act 1975" there shall be substituted the words "section 307(1) of the Criminal Procedure (Scotland) Act 1995";

(b) in Part II (persons disqualified from jury service), at the end of paragraph (b) there shall be inserted—

"(c) in respect of jury service in any criminal proceedings, persons who are on bail in or in connection with criminal proceedings in any part of the United Kingdom."; and

(c) in Part III (persons excusable as of right), at the end of Group D there shall be inserted—

."GROUP DD

Members of certain religious bodies

In respect of jury service in any criminal proceedings, practising members of religious societies or orders the tenets or beliefs of which are incompatible with jury service."

Criminal Justice (Scotland) Act 1980 (c. 62)

33. In subsection (10) of section 80 of the Criminal Justice (Scotland) Act 1980, for the words "section 289B of the 1975 Act" there shall be substituted the words "section 225(8) of the Criminal Procedure (Scotland) Act 1995".

Local Government, Planning and Land Act 1980 (c. 65)

34. In subsection (14) of section 167 of the Local Government, Planning and Land Act 1980, in paragraph (b) of the definition of "the statutory maximum" for the words "section 289B of the Criminal Procedure (Scotland) Act 1975" there shall be substituted the words "section 225(8) of the Criminal Procedure (Scotland) Act 1995".

Animal Health Act 1981 (c. 22)

35. In subsection (2) of section 92 of the Animal Health Act 1981, for the words "section 284 of the Criminal Procedure (Scotland) Act 1975" there shall be substituted the words "section 7(6) of the Criminal Procedure (Scotland) Act 1995".

Contempt of Court Act 1981 (c. 49)

36.—(1) Section 15 of the Contempt of Court Act 1981 (penalties for contempt in Scottish proceedings) shall be amended as follows.

(2) In subsection (2)—

(a) in paragraph (a) for "£500" there shall be substituted the words "level 4 on the standard scale"; and

(b) in paragraph (b) for "£200" there shall be substituted the words "level 4 on the standard scale".

(3) For subsections (3) and (4) there shall be substituted the following—

   "(3) The following provisions of the Criminal Procedure (Scotland) Act 1995 shall apply in relation to persons found guilty of contempt of court in Scottish proceedings as they apply in relation to persons convicted of offences—

      (a) in every case, section 207 (restrictions on detention of young offenders);

      (b) in any case to which paragraph (b) of subsection (2) above does not apply, sections 58, 59 and 61 (persons suffering from mental disorder);

   and in any case to which the said paragraph (b) does apply, subsection (5) below shall have effect."

(4) In subsection (5)—

(a) for the words "section 286 of the Criminal Procedure (Scotland) Act 1975" there shall be substituted the words "section 7(9) and (10) of the Criminal Procedure (Scotland) Act 1995"; and

(b) for the words "section 376(1)" there shall be substituted the words "section 58(1)".

The Matrimonial Homes (Family Protection) (Scotland) Act 1981 (c. 59)

37. In section 17 of the Matrimonial Homes (Family Protection) (Scotland) Act 1981 (procedure after arrest)—

(a) in subsection (2) for the words "section 10 of the Bail (Scotland) Act 1980" there shall be substituted the words "section 8 of the Criminal Procedure (Scotland) Act 1995"; and

(b) in subsection (3) for the words from the beginning to "1980" there shall be substituted the words "Subsections (1) to (3) of section 15 of the said Act of 1995".

Betting and Gaming Duties Act 1981 (c. 63)

38. In subsection (1) of section 33 of the Betting and Gaming Duties Act 1981 in the definition of "the prescribed sum", in paragraph (b) for the words from "section 289B" to the end of the paragraph there shall be substituted the words "subsection (8) of section 225 of the Criminal Procedure (Scotland) Act 1995 (£5,000 or other sum substituted by order under subsection (4) of that section)".

Civil Aviation Act 1982 (c. 16)

39. In subsection (1) of section 105 of the Civil Aviation Act 1982, in the definition of "the statutory maximum" for paragraph (b) there shall be substituted the following—

   "(b) in Scotland, the prescribed sum within the meaning of subsection (8) of section 225 of the Criminal Procedure (Scotland) Act 1995 (that is to say £5,000 or another sum fixed by order under subsection (4) of that section);".

Oil and Gas Enterprise Act 1982 (c. 23)

40. In subsection (1) of section 28 of the Oil and Gas Enterprise Act 1982, in the definition of "the statutory maximum" for paragraph (b) there shall be substituted the following—

   "(b) in Scotland, the prescribed sum within the meaning of subsection (8) of section 225 of the Criminal Procedure (Scotland) Act 1995 (that is to say £5,000 or another sum fixed by order under subsection (4) of that section);".

Iron and Steel Act 1982 (c. 25)

41. In subsection (1) of section 37 of the Iron and Steel Act 1982, in the definition of "the statutory maximum" for paragraph (b) there shall be substituted the following—

"(b) in Scotland, the prescribed sum within the meaning of subsection (8) of section 225 of the Criminal Procedure (Scotland) Act 1995 (that is to say £5,000 or another sum fixed by order under subsection (4) of that section);".

Civil Jurisdiction and Judgments Act 1982 (c. 27)

42. In subsection (4A) of section 18 of the Civil Jurisdiction and Judgments Act 1982 (enforcement of U.K. judgments in other parts of U.K.) for the words from "Part I of the Criminal Justice (Scotland) Act 1987" to the end there shall be substituted the words "the Proceeds of Crime (Scotland) Act 1995".

Aviation Security Act 1982 (c. 36)

43. In subsection (1) of section 38 of the Aviation Security Act 1982, in the definition of "the statutory maximum" for paragraph (b) there shall be substituted the following—

"(b) in Scotland, the prescribed sum within the meaning of subsection (8) of section 225 of the Criminal Procedure (Scotland) Act 1995 (that is to say £5,000 or another sum fixed by order under subsection (4) of that section);".

Civic Government (Scotland) Act 1982 (c. 45)

44.—(1) The Civic Government (Scotland) Act 1982 shall be amended as follows.

(2) In subsection (8) of section 51, in the definition of "prescribed sum" for the words "section 289B of the Criminal Procedure (Scotland) Act 1975" there shall be substituted the words "section 225(8) of the Criminal Procedure (Scotland) Act 1995".

(3) In subsection (3) of section 52, for the words "section 289B of the Criminal Procedure (Scotland) Act 1975" there shall be substituted the words "section 225(8) of the Criminal Procedure (Scotland) Act 1995".

Insurance Companies Act 1982 (c. 50)

45.—(1) The Insurance Companies Act 1982 shall be amended as follows.

(2) In subsection (3) of section 14, in paragraph (b)(ii) for the words "section 289B of the Criminal Procedure (Scotland) Act 1975" there shall be substituted the words "section 225(8) of the Criminal Procedure (Scotland) Act 1995".

(3) In subsection (2) of section 71, in paragraph (b)(ii) for the words "section 289B of the Criminal Procedure (Scotland) Act 1975" there shall be substituted the words "section 225(8) of the Criminal Procedure (Scotland) Act 1995".

(4) In subsection (1) of section 81, in paragraph (b)(ii) for the words "section 289B of the Criminal Procedure (Scotland) Act 1975" there shall be substituted the words "section 225(8) of the Criminal Procedure (Scotland) Act 1995".

(5) In subsection (4) of section 92, for the words "section 74 of the Criminal Procedure (Scotland) Act 1975" there shall be substituted the words "section 70 of the Criminal Procedure (Scotland) Act 1995".

(6) In subsection (4) of section 94 for the words "section 331 of the Criminal Procedure (Scotland) Act 1975" there shall be substituted the words "section 136 of the Criminal Procedure (Scotland) Act 1995".

(7) In subsection (5) of that section for the words "section 331 of the said Act of 1975" there shall be substituted the words "section 136 of the said Act of 1995".

Industrial Development Act 1982 (c. 52)

46. In Schedule 1 to the Industrial Development Act 1982, in paragraph 4(2) for the words "section 331 of the Criminal Procedure (Scotland) Act 1975" there shall be substituted the words "section 136 of the Criminal Procedure (Scotland) Act 1995".

Car Tax Act 1983 (c. 53)

47. In Schedule 1 to the Car Tax Act 1983, in paragraph 7(3) for the words "section 462 of the Criminal Procedure (Scotland) Act 1975" there shall be substituted the words "section 307 of the Criminal Procedure (Scotland) Act 1995".

Telecommunications Act 1984 (c. 12)

48.—(1) The Telecommunications Act 1984 shall be amended as follows.

(2) In subsection (2) of section 81, for the words from "section 310" to "1975 Act" there shall

be substituted the words "section 134 of the Criminal Procedure (Scotland) Act 1995 (in this section referred to as "the 1995 Act")".

(3) In subsection (8) of that section, for the words from "and section 452(4)(a)" to the end there shall be substituted the words "and section 182(5)(a) to (e) of the 1995 Act shall apply to appeals under this section as it applies to appeals such as are mentioned in section 176(1) of that Act".

(4) In Schedule 3 (penalties and mode of trial under the Wireless Telegraphy Act 1949), in paragraph 3(b) for the words "Chapter II of Part II of the Criminal Justice (Scotland) Act 1995" there shall be substituted the words "Part II of the Proceeds of Crime (Scotland) Act 1995".

Road Traffic Regulation Act 1984 (c. 27)

49. In subsection (2) of section 110 of the Road Traffic Regulation Act 1984—
(a) for the words "section 331 of the Criminal Procedure (Scotland) Act 1975" there shall be substituted the words "section 136 of the Criminal Procedure (Scotland) Act 1995"; and
(b) for the words "section 331" where they second occur there shall be substituted the words "section 136".

Mental Health (Scotland) Act 1984 (c. 36)

50.—(1) The Mental Health (Scotland) Act 1984 shall be amended as follows.
(2) In section 60 (effect of hospital orders)—
(a) in subsection (1) for the words "section 175 or 376 of the Criminal Procedure (Scotland) Act 1975" there shall be substituted the words "section 58 of the Criminal Procedure (Scotland) Act 1995"; and
(b) in subsection (3) for the words "section 178(3) or 379(3) of the said Act of 1975" there shall be substituted the words "section 59(3) of the said Act of 1995".

(3) In subsection (1) of section 61 (effect of guardianship orders) for the words "section 175 or 376 of the Criminal Procedure (Scotland) Act 1975" there shall be substituted the words "section 58 of the Criminal Procedure (Scotland) Act 1995".

(4) In subsection (1) of section 62 (effect of restriction orders), for the words "section 178 or 397 of the Criminal Procedure (Scotland) Act 1975" there shall be substituted the words "section 59 of the Criminal Procedure (Scotland) Act 1995".

(5) In subsection (3) of section 69 (persons ordered to be kept in custody during Her Majesty's pleasure), for the words from "an order" to the end there shall be substituted "a hospital order together with a restriction order".

(6) In subsection (7) of section 71 (removal to hospital of persons serving sentences of imprisonment etc.), in paragraph (a) for the words from "section 174" to "1975" there shall be substituted the words "section 54, 57, 118 or 190 of the Criminal Procedure (Scotland) Act 1995".

(7) In section 73 (provision as to persons removed to hospital while awaiting trial etc.)—
(a) in subsection (1), for the words from "section 174ZC" to "1975" there shall be substituted the words "section 53, 57, 58 or 59 of the Criminal Procedure (Scotland) Act 1995"; and
(b) in subsection (3)—
(i) in paragraph (a), for the words "section 175(7) or 376(10) of the said Act of 1975" there shall be substituted the words "section 58(8) of the said Act of 1995"; and
(ii) in paragraph (b) for the words "section 183, 184, 384 or 385 of the said Act of 1975" there shall be substituted the words "section 228 or 230 of the said Act of 1995".

(8) In section 76 (interpretation of Part VI) for the words "section 178(3) or 379(3) of the Criminal Procedure (Scotland) Act 1975" there shall be substituted the words "section 59(3) of the Criminal Procedure (Scotland) Act 1995".

(9) After section 121 there shall be inserted the following section—

"Warrants for arrest of escaped mental patients.
121A.—(1) On an application being made to a justice alleging that any person is a convicted mental patient liable to be retaken under section 18, 38(7) or 138 of the Mental Health Act 1983, section 28, 44 or 121 of the this Act or section 30 or 108 of the Mental Health Act (Northern Ireland) 1961 (retaking of mental patients who are absent without leave or have escaped from custody), the justice may issue a warrant to arrest him and bring him before any sheriff.

(2) Where a person is brought before a sheriff in pursuance of a warrant for his arrest under this section, the sheriff shall, if satisfied that he is the person named in the warrant and if satisfied that he is a convicted mental patient as mentioned in subsection (1) above, order him to be kept in custody or detained in a place of safety pending his admission to hospital.

(3) Section 137 of the Mental Health Act 1983 and section 107 of the Mental Health Act (Northern Ireland) 1961 (custody, conveyance and detention of certain mental patients)

shall apply to a convicted mental patient required by this section to be conveyed to any place or to be kept in custody or detained in a place of safety as they apply to a person required by or by virtue of the said Act of 1983 or 1961, as the case may be, to be so conveyed, kept or detained.

(4) In this section—

"convicted mental patient" means a person liable after being convicted of an offence to be detained under Part III of the Mental Health Act 1983, Part VI of this Act, Part III of the Mental Health Act (Northern Ireland) 1961 or section 52, 59(1) to (10) or 60 of the Criminal Procedure (Scotland) Act 1995 in pursuance of a hospital order or transfer direction together with an order or direction restricting his discharge or a person liable to be detained under section 38 of the said Act of 1983;

"place of safety" has the same meaning as in Part III of the said Act of 1983 or Part III of the said Act of 1961 or section 297 of the said Act of 1995, as the case may be."

(10) In section 125—

(a) in the definition of "hospital order" and "guardianship order" for the words "section 175 or 376 of the Criminal Procedure (Scotland) Act 1975" there shall be substituted the words "section 58 of the Criminal Procedure (Scotland) Act 1995";

(b) in the definition of "restriction order" for the words "section 178 or 379 of the Criminal Procedure (Scotland) Act 1975" there shall be substituted the words "section 59 of the Criminal Procedure (Scotland) Act 1995"; and

(c) in subsection (4) for the words from "section 174" to "1975" there shall be substituted the words "section 54, 57, 58 or 59 of the Criminal Procedure (Scotland) Act 1995".

Video Recordings Act 1984 (c. 39)

51. In subsection (1) of section 16C of the Video Recordings Act 1984 (sheriff's jurisdiction), for the words "section 287 of the Criminal Procedure (Scotland) Act 1975" there shall be substituted the words "section 9 of the Criminal Procedure (Scotland) Act 1995".

Repatriation of Prisoners Act 1984 (c. 47)

52. The Schedule to the Repatriation of Prisoners Act 1984 shall be amended as follows—

(a) in paragraph 4(2) for the words "section 207 or 415 of the Criminal Procedure (Scotland) Act 1975" there shall be substituted the words "section 207 of the Criminal Procedure (Scotland) Act 1995";

(b) in paragraph 5(3) for "1975" there shall be substituted "1995".

Foster Children (Scotland) Act 1984 (c. 56)

53.—(1) The Foster Children (Scotland) Act 1984 shall be amended as follows.

(2) In section 7, in paragraph (c) of subsection (1) for the words "Criminal Procedure (Scotland) Act 1975" there shall be substituted the words "Criminal Procedure (Scotland) Act 1995".

(3) In section 13 for the words "sections 14 and 323 of the Criminal Procedure (Scotland) Act 1975" there shall be substituted the words "section 47 of the Children and Young Persons (Scotland) Act 1937".

Rent (Scotland) Act 1984 (c. 58)

54. In subsection (1) of section 115 of the Rent (Scotland) Act 1984, in the definition of—

(a) "the standard scale" for the words "section 289G of the Criminal Procedure (Scotland) Act 1975" there shall be substituted the words "section 225(1) of the Criminal Procedure (Scotland) Act 1995"; and

(b) "the statutory maximum" for the words "section 289B(6) of the Criminal Procedure (Scotland) Act 1975" there shall be substituted the words "section 225(8) of the Criminal Procedure (Scotland) Act 1995".

Police and Criminal Evidence Act 1984 (c. 60)

55. In subsection (3) of section 75 of the Police and Criminal Evidence Act 1984—

(a) for the words "section 392 of the Criminal Procedure (Scotland) Act 1975" there shall be substituted the words "section 247 of the Criminal Procedure (Scotland) Act 1995"; and

(b) for the words "section 182 or section 183 of the said Act of 1975" there shall be substituted the words "section 228 or section 246(3) of the said Act of 1995".

Companies Act 1985 (c. 6)

56.—(1) The Companies Act 1985 shall be amended as follows.

(2) In section 440, for the words "section 52 of the Criminal Justice (Scotland) Act 1987" there

shall be substituted the words "section 28 of the Criminal Law (Consolidation) (Scotland) Act 1995".

(3) In subsection (3) of section 731, for the words "section 331 of the Criminal Procedure (Scotland) Act 1975" there shall be substituted the words "section 136 of the Criminal Procedure (Scotland) Act 1995".

(4) In subsection (4) of section 734, for the words "section 74 of the Criminal Procedure (Scotland) Act 1975" there shall be substituted the words "section 70 of the Criminal Procedure (Scotland) Act 1995".

Surrogacy Arrangements Act 1985 (c. 49)

57. In subsection (6) of section 4 of the Surrogacy Arrangements Act 1985, for the words "section 331(1) of the Criminal Procedure (Scotland) Act 1975" there shall be substituted the words "section 136(1) of the Criminal Procedure (Scotland) Act 1995".

The Bankruptcy (Scotland) Act 1985 (c. 66)

58.—(1) The Bankruptcy (Scotland) Act 1985 shall be amended as follows.

(2) In section 5(4) (meaning of qualified creditor), for the words "or by section 114(1) of the Criminal Justice (Scotland) Act 1995" there shall be substituted the words "or by section 49(1) of the Proceeds of Crime (Scotland) Act 1995".

(3) In section 7(1) (meaning of apparent insolvency), in the definition of "confiscation order", for the words "or by section 114(1) of the Criminal Justice (Scotland) Act 1995" there shall be substituted the words "or by section 49(1) of the Proceeds of Crime (Scotland) Act 1995".

(4) In subsection (2) of section 55 (effect of discharge of bankrupt on certain liabilities), after paragraph (a) there shall be inserted the following paragraphs—

"(aa) any liability to pay a fine imposed in a district court;

(ab) any liability under a compensation order within the meaning of section 249 of the Criminal Procedure (Scotland) Act 1995;".

(5) In subsection (2) of section 68, for the words "section 331 of the Criminal Procedure (Scotland) Act 1975" there shall be substituted the words "section 136 of the Criminal Procedure (Scotland) Act 1995".

Animals (Scientific Procedures) Act 1986 (c. 14)

59. In subsection (4) of section 26 of the Animals (Scientific Procedures) Act 1986, for the words "section 331 of the Criminal Procedure (Scotland) Act 1975" there shall be substituted the words "section 136 of the Criminal Procedure (Scotland) Act 1995".

Consumer Safety (Amendment) Act 1986 (c. 29)

60.—(1) The Consumer Safety (Amendment) Act 1986 shall be amended as follows.

(2) In subsection (3) of section 7, for "1975" there shall be substituted "1995".

(3) In section 10 for the words "section 452(4)(a) to (e) of the Criminal Procedure (Scotland) Act 1975" there shall be substituted the words "section 182(5)(a) to (e) of the Criminal Procedure (Scotland) Act 1995".

Insolvency Act 1986 (c. 45)

61. In subsection (3) of section 431 of the Insolvency Act 1986, for the words "section 331 of the Criminal Procedure (Scotland) Act 1975" there shall be substituted the words "section 136 of the Criminal Procedure (Scotland) Act 1995".

Company Directors Disqualification Act 1986 (c. 46)

62. In subsection (1) of section 8 of the Company Directors Disqualification Act 1986, for the words "section 52 of the Criminal Justice (Scotland) Act 1987" there shall be substituted the words "section 28 of the Criminal Law (Consolidation) (Scotland) Act 1995".

Legal Aid (Scotland) Act 1986 (c. 47)

63.—(1) The Legal Aid (Scotland) Act 1986 shall be amended as follows.

(2) In subsection (4) of section 21, for the words "section 462 of the Criminal Procedure (Scotland) Act 1975" there shall be substituted the words "section 307 of the Criminal Procedure (Scotland) Act 1995".

(3) In subsection (1) of section 22 (circumstances in which criminal legal aid automatically available), after paragraph (d) there shall be inserted the following paragraphs—

"(da) in relation to any proceedings under solemn or summary procedure whereby the court determines (whether or not on a plea by the accused person) whether he is insane so that his trial cannot proceed or continue;

(db) in relation to an examination of facts held under section 55 of the Criminal Procedure (Scotland) Act 1995 and the disposal of the case following such examination of facts;

(dc) in relation to any appeal under section 62 or 63 (appeal by, respectively, accused or prosecutor in case involving insanity) of that Act of 1995;"

(4) In subsection (2) of section 23, for the words from "section 41(2)(b)" to the end there shall be substituted the words "section 204(4)(b) of the Criminal Procedure (Scotland) Act 1995".

(5) In subsection (1) of section 25 (legal aid in criminal appeals)—

(a) after the word "sentence" there shall be inserted the words ", other disposal"; and

(b) at the end there shall be inserted the words "other than an appeal in relation to which section 22(1)(dc) of this Act applies".

(6) In subsection (2) of that section—

(a) in paragraph (a) after the word "below," there shall be inserted the words "the Board is satisfied"; and

(b) for paragraph (b) and the preceding "and" there shall be substituted the following paragraphs—

"(b) in the case of an appeal under section 106(1) or 175(2) of the Criminal Procedure (Scotland) Act 1995, leave to appeal is granted; and

(c) in the case of an appeal under any other provision of that Act, where the applicant is the appellant, the Board is satisfied that in all the circumstances of the case it is in the interests of justice that the applicant should receive criminal legal aid."

(7) After the said subsection (2) there shall be inserted the following subsection—

"(2A) Where the Board has refused an application for criminal legal aid on the ground that it is not satisfied as mentioned in subsection (2)(c) above the High Court may, at any time prior to the disposal of an appeal, whether or not on application made to it, notwithstanding such refusal determine that it is in the interests of justice that the applicant should receive criminal legal aid in connection with the appeal, and the Board shall forthwith make such legal aid available to him."

(8) For subsection (5) there shall be substituted the following subsections—

"(5) Subsections (2)(a), (3) and (4) above shall apply to an application for criminal legal aid in connection with consideration under section 107, 180 or 187 of the Criminal Procedure (Scotland) Act 1995 whether to grant leave to appeal as if—

(a) in subsection (2)(a), for the words "of the appeal" there were substituted the words "in connection with consideration whether to grant leave to appeal"; and

(b) in subsection (4), after the word "is" there were inserted the words "subject to leave being granted,".

(6) Subsections (2)(a) and (c) and (2A) to (4) above shall apply to an application for criminal legal aid in connection with a petition to the *nobile officium* of the High Court of Justiciary (whether arising in the course of any proceedings or otherwise) as they apply for the purposes of subsection (1) above.

(7) Subsections (2)(a), (3) and (4) above shall apply to an application for criminal legal aid in connection with a reference by the Secretary of State under section 124 of the Criminal Procedure (Scotland) Act 1995 as they apply for the purposes of subsection (1) above."

(9) In subsection (3) of section 30 (application of section 25 to legal aid in contempt proceedings),—

(a) before the words "Section 25" there shall be inserted the words "Subsections (2)(a) and (c), (2A) to (4) and (6) of";

(b) for the words "it applies" there shall be substituted the words "they apply";

(c) after the word "sentence" there shall be substituted the words ", other disposal";

(d) after the word "application" there shall be inserted the following paragraph—

"(za) in subsection (2a) of that section, the reference to the High Court shall include a reference to the Court of Session;"; and

(e) in paragraph (b) for the word "(5)" there shall be substituted the word "(6)".

(10) In subsection (2) of section 35, for the words "section 331 of the Criminal Procedure (Scotland) Act 1975" there shall be substituted the words "section 136 of the Criminal Procedure (Scotland) Act 1995".

Social Security Act 1986 (c. 50)

64. In subsection (5) of section 56 of the Social Security Act 1986—

(a) for the words "section 331 of the Criminal Procedure (Scotland) Act 1975" there shall be substituted the words "section 136 of the Criminal Procedure (Scotland) Act 1995"; and

(b) for the words "section 331 of the said Act of 1975" there shall be substituted the words "section 136 of the said Act of 1995".

Building Societies Act 1986 (c. 53)

65. In subsection (5) of section 111 of the Building Societies Act 1986, for the words "section 331(3) of the Criminal Procedure (Scotland) Act 1975" there shall be substituted the words "section 136(3) of the Criminal Procedure (Scotland) Act 1995".

Financial Services Act 1986 (c. 60)

66. In subsection (4) of section 203 of the Financial Services Act 1986, for the words "section 74 of the Criminal Procedure (Scotland) Act 1975" there shall be substituted the words "section 70 of the Criminal Procedure (Scotland) Act 1995".

Banking Act 1987 (c. 22)

67.—(1) The Banking Act 1987 shall be amended as follows.

(2) In subsection (3) of section 97, for the words "section 331 of the Criminal Procedure (Scotland) Act 1975" there shall be substituted the words "section 136 of the Criminal Procedure (Scotland) Act 1995"

(3) In subsection (4) of section 98, for the words "section 74 of the Criminal Procedure (Scotland) Act 1975" there shall be substituted the words "section 70 of the Criminal Procedure (Scotland) Act 1995".

Consumer Protection Act 1987 (c. 43)

68. In subsection (8) of section 17 of the Consumer Protection Act 1987, for the words from "and section 452(4)(a) to (e)" to the end there shall be substituted the words "and section 182(5)(a) to (e) of the Criminal Procedure (Scotland) Act 1995 shall apply to an appeal under this subsection as it applies to a stated case under Part X of that Act".

The Criminal Justice Act 1988 (c. 33)

69.—(1) The Criminal Justice Act 1988 shall be amended as follows.

(2) In section 74(2)(c) (meaning of realisable property) for the words "Chapter II of Part II of the Criminal Justice (Scotland) Act 1995" there shall be substituted the words "Part II of the Proceeds of Crime (Scotland) Act 1995".

(3) In subsection (10) of section 77 (restraint orders) for the words "Part II of the Criminal Justice (Scotland) Act 1995" there shall be substituted the words "the Proceeds of Crime (Scotland) Act 1995".

(4) In section 89(2)(b) (compensation), for sub-paragraph (ii) there shall be substituted the following sub-paragraph—

"(ii) an order of the Court of Session under section 32, 33, 34 or 35 of the Proceeds of Crime (Scotland) Act 1995."

The Copyright, Designs and Patents Act 1988 (c. 48)

70.—(1) The Copyright, Designs and Patents Act 1988 shall be amended as follows.

(2) In section 108(6) (order for delivery up in criminal proceedings) for the words "Chapter II of Part II of the Criminal Justice (Scotland) Act 1995" there shall be substituted the words "Part II of the Proceeds of Crime (Scotland) Act 1995".

(3) In section 199(6) (order for delivery up in criminal proceedings) for the words "Chapter II of Part II of the Criminal Justice (Scotland) Act 1995" there shall be substituted the words "Part II of the Proceeds of Crime (Scotland) Act 1995".

Road Traffic Offenders Act 1988 (c. 53)

71.—(1) The Road Traffic Offenders Act 1988 shall be amended as follows.

(2) In subsection (5) of section 6 (time limit for commencement of summary proceedings), for the words "section 331 of the Criminal Procedure (Scotland) Act 1975" there shall be substituted the words "section 136 of the Criminal Procedure (Scotland) Act 1995".

(3) In subsection (6) of section 24 (alternative verdicts) for the words "sections 61, 63, 64, 312 and 457A of the Criminal Procedure (Scotland) Act 1975" there shall be substituted the words "sections 295, 138(4), 256 and 293 of and Schedule 3 to the Criminal Procedure (Scotland) Act 1995".

(4) In subsection (2) of section 31 (taking account of endorsation) for the words "section 357(1) of the Criminal Procedure (Scotland) Act 1975" there shall be substituted the words "section 166(1) to (6) of the Criminal Procedure (Scotland) Act 1995".

(5) In subsection (6) of section 32 (extracts of licensing records) for the words "section 357(1) of the Criminal Procedure (Scotland) Act 1975" there shall be substituted the words "section 166(1) to (6) of the Criminal Procedure (Scotland) Act 1995".

(6) After section 33 of the Road Traffic Offenders Act 1988 (fine and imprisonment), there shall be inserted the following section—

"Forfeiture of vehicles: Scotland.

33A.—(1) Where a person commits an offence to which this subsection applies by—

(a) driving, attempting to drive, or being in charge of a vehicle; or

(b) failing to comply with a requirement made under section 7 of the Road Traffic Act 1988 (failure to provide specimen for analysis or laboratory test) in the course of an investigation into whether the offender had committed an offence while driving, attempting to drive or being in charge of a vehicle, or

(c) failing, as the driver of a vehicle, to comply with subsections (2) and (3) of section 170 of the Road Traffic Act 1988 (duty to stop and give information or report accident),

the court may, on an application under this subsection, make an order forfeiting the vehicle concerned, and any vehicle forfeited under this subsection shall be disposed of as the court may direct.

(2) Subsection (1) above applies—

(a) to an offence under the Road Traffic Act 1988 which is punishable with imprisonment; and

(b) to an offence of culpable homicide.

(3) An application under subsection (1) above shall be at the instance of the prosecutor made when he moves for sentence (or, if the person has been remitted for sentence under section 195 of the Criminal Procedure (Scotland) Act 1995) made before sentence is pronounced.

(4) Where—

(a) the court is satisfied, on an application under this subsection by the prosecutor—

　　(i) that proceedings have been, or are likely to be, instituted against a person in Scotland for an offence to which subsection (1) above applies allegedly committed in the manner specified in paragraph (a), (b) or (c) of that subsection; and

　　(ii) that there is reasonable cause to believe that a vehicle specified in the application is to be found in a place or in premises so specified; and

(b) it appears to the court that there are reasonable grounds for thinking that in the event of the person being convicted of the offence an order under subsection (1) above might be made in relation to the vehicle,

the court may grant a warrant authorising a person named therein to enter and search the place or premises and seize the vehicle.

(5) Where the court has made an order under subsection (1) above for the forfeiture of a vehicle, the court or any justice may, if satisfied on evidence on oath—

(a) that there is reasonable cause to believe that the vehicle is to be found in any place or premises; and

(b) that admission to the place or premises has been refused or that a refusal of such admission is apprehended,

issue a warrant of search which may be executed according to law.

(6) In relation to summary proceedings, the reference in subsection (5) above to a justice includes a reference to the sheriff and to a magistrate.

(7) Part II of the Proceeds of Crime (Scotland) Act 1995 shall not apply in respect of a vehicle in relation to which this section applies.

(8) This section extends to Scotland only."

(7) In subsection (3) of section 46 (combination of disqualification and endorsement with probation etc)—

(a) in paragraph (b) for the words from "section 182" to the end there shall be substituted the words "section 228 (probation) or 246(2) or (3) (absolute discharge) of the Criminal Procedure (Scotland) Act 1995"; and

(b) for the words from "section 191" to the end of the subsection there shall be substituted the words "section 247 of that Act shall not apply".

(8) In section 60—

(a) in subsection (4) for the words "section 315 of the Criminal Procedure (Scotland) Act 1975" there shall be substituted the words "section 140 of the Criminal Procedure (Scotland) Act 1995";

(b) in subsection (5) for the words "Part II" there shall be substituted the words "Part IX"; and

(c) in subsection (6)—

(i) in paragraph (b) for the words "section 312" where they first occur there shall be substituted the words "section 140(4)";

(ii) in that paragraph for the words "paragraphs (a) to (z) of section 312 of" there shall be substituted the words "section 255 of and Schedule 3 to"; and

(iii) paragraph (c) shall cease to have effect.

(9) In subsection (7) of section 64 (commencement of proceedings against owner of vehicle) for the words "section 331(1) of the Criminal Procedure (Scotland) Act 1975" there shall be substituted the words "section 136(1) of the Criminal Procedure (Scotland) Act 1995".

(10) In subsection (1) of section 89 (interpretation), in the definition of "court of summary jurisdiction" for the words "section 462(1) of the Criminal Procedure (Scotland) Act 1975" there shall be substituted the words "section 307(1) of the Criminal Procedure (Scotland) Act 1995".

Prevention of Terrorism (Temporary Provisions) Act 1989 (c. 4)

72.—(1) The Prevention of Terrorism (Temporary Provisions) Act 1989 shall be amended as follows.

(2) In section 15 (supplementary provisions relating to arrest and detention)—

(a) in subsection (7) for paragraph (a) there shall be substituted the following paragraph—

"(a) section 135(3) of the Criminal Procedure (Scotland) Act 1995;"; and

(b) in subsection (8) for the words "Section 295(1) of the Criminal Procedure (Scotland) Act 1975" there shall be substituted the words "Section 22(1) and (3) of the Criminal Procedure (Scotland) Act 1995".

(3) In Schedule 4—

(a) in paragraph 16—

(i) in sub-paragraph (1), paragraph (b) shall cease to have effect;

(ii) in sub-paragraph (2)(b) the words "where granted under sub-paragraph (1)(a) above," shall cease to have effect; and

(iii) in sub-paragraphs (5) and (6), the words "or arrestment", in each place where they occur, shall cease to have effect; and

(b) after paragraph 16 there shall be inserted the following paragraph—

"16A.—(1) On the application of the prosecutor, the court may, in respect of moveable property affected by a restraint order (whether such property generally or particular such property), grant warrant for arrestment if the property would be arrestable if the person entitled to it were a debtor.

(2) A warrant under sub-paragraph (1) above shall have effect as if granted on the dependence of an action for debt at the instance of the prosecutor against the person and may be executed, recalled, loosed or restricted accordingly.

(3) The fact that an arrestment has been executed under sub-paragraph (2) above in respect of property shall not prejudice the exercise of an administrator's powers under or for the purposes of this Part of this Schedule in respect of that property.

(4) No arrestment executed under sub-paragraph (2) above shall have effect once, or in so far as, the restraint order affecting the property in respect of which the warrant for such arrestment has been granted has ceased to have effect in respect of that property; and the prosecutor shall apply to the court for an order recalling, or as the case may be, restricting the arrestment accordingly."

(c) in paragraph 19 (enforcement in Scotland of orders made elsewhere in the British Isles)—

(i) in sub-paragraph (5), for the words "and 16" there shall be substituted ", 16 and (subject to sub-paragraph (5A) below) 16A"; and

(ii) after sub-paragraph (5) there shall be inserted the following sub-paragraph—

"(5A) In its application by virtue of sub-paragraph (5) above paragraph 16A above shall have effect with the following modifications—

(a) for the references to the prosecutor there shall be substituted references to the Lord Advocate; and

(b) for the references to the court there shall be substituted references to the Court of Session."

Extradition Act 1989 (c. 33)

73. In subsection (13) of section 10 of the Extradition Act 1989 (bail in connection with appeal)—

(a) for the words "section 446(2) of the Criminal Procedure (Scotland) Act 1975" there shall be substituted the words "section 177(2) and (3) of the Criminal Procedure (Scotland) Act 1995"; and

(b) for the words "section 444" there shall be substituted the words "section 176".

Companies Act 1989 (c. 40)

74.—(1) The Companies Act 1989 shall be amended as follows.

(2) In subsection (4) of section 44 (jurisdiction and procedure for offences) for the words "section 74 of the Criminal Procedure (Scotland) Act 1975" there shall be substituted the words "section 70 of the Criminal Procedure (Scotland) Act 1995".

(3) In subsection (4) of section 91 (jurisdiction and procedure for offences) for the words "section 74 of the Criminal Procedure (Scotland) Act 1975" there shall be substituted the words "section 70 of the Criminal Procedure (Scotland) Act 1995".

Prisons (Scotland) Act 1989 (c. 45)

75.—(1) The Prisons (Scotland) Act 1989 shall be amended as follows.

(2) In subsection (1) of section 11 (removal of prisoners for judicial and other purposes), for the words "section 279 of the 1975 Act" there shall be substituted the words "section 132 of the 1995 Act".

(3) In subsection (3) of section 21 (transfer to prison of young offenders) for the words "the 1975 Act" where they first occur there shall be substituted the words "the 1995 Act".

(4) In section 39 (prison rules)—

(a) in subsection (5), for the words "section 279 of the 1975 Act" there shall be substituted the words "section 132 of the 1995 Act"; and

(b) in subsection (7), for the words "section 206 of the 1975 Act" there shall be substituted the words "section 208 of the 1995 Act".

(5) For subsection (3) of section 40 (persons unlawfully at large) there shall be substituted the following subsection—

"(3) In this section—

(a) any reference to a person sentenced to imprisonment shall be construed as including a reference to any person sentenced or ordered to be detained under section 44, 205 or 208 of the 1995 Act;

(b) any reference to a prison shall be construed as including a reference to a place where the person is liable to be detained under the sentence or order; and

(c) any reference to a sentence shall be construed as including a reference to an order under the said section 44."

(6) After section 40 there shall be added the following section—

"Warrants for arrest of escaped prisoners

40A.—(1) On an application being made to a justice alleging that any person is an offender unlawfully at large from a prison or other institution to which this Act or, as the case may be the Prison Act 1952 or the Prison Act (Northern Ireland) 1953 applies in which he is required to be detained after being convicted of an offence, the justice may issue a warrant to arrest him and bring him before any sheriff.

(2) Where a person is brought before a sheriff in pursuance of a warrant for his arrest under this section, the sheriff shall, if satisfied that he is the person named in the warrant and if satisfied that he is an offender unlawfully at large as mentioned in subsection (1) above, order him to be returned to the prison or other institution where he is required or liable to be detained."

(7) In subsection (1) of section 43 (interpretation) for the definition of "the 1975 Act" there shall be substituted the following—

" "the 1995 Act" means the Criminal Procedure (Scotland) Act 1995;".

The Criminal Justice (International Co-operation) Act 1990 (c. 5)

76.—(1) The Criminal Justice (International Co-operation) Act 1990 shall be amended as follows.

(2) In subsection (6) of section 9 (enforcement of overseas forfeiture orders) for the words from "an offence", in the second place where they occur, to the end there shall be substituted the words "an offence to which Part VI of the Criminal Justice Act 1988 applies or an offence to which Part I of the Proceeds of Crime (Scotland) Act 1995 applies or an offence in respect of which a suspended forfeiture order may be made under section 18 of the said Act of 1995".

(3) In paragraph 2 of Schedule 1, for the words "section 320 of the Criminal Procedure (Scotland) Act 1975" there shall be substituted the words "section 156 of the Criminal Procedure (Scotland) Act 1995".

Computer Misuse Act 1990 (c. 18)

77. In subsection (7) of section 13 of the Computer Misuse Act 1990, for the words "section 331 of the Criminal Procedure (Scotland) Act 1975" there shall be substituted the words "section 136 of the Criminal Procedure (Scotland) Act 1995".

Law Reform (Miscellaneous Provisions) (Scotland) Act 1990 (c. 40)

78. In subsection (4) of section 20 of the Law Reform (Miscellaneous Provisions) (Scotland) Act 1990 (destination of fine imposed for professional misconduct) for the words "section 203 of the Criminal Procedure (Scotland) Act 1975" there shall be substituted the words "section 211(5) of the Criminal Procedure (Scotland) Act 1995".

The Northern Ireland (Emergency Provisions) Act 1991 (c. 24)

79. In section 50(2) of the Northern Ireland (Emergency Provisions) Act 1991 (realisable property, value and gifts), for paragraph (e) there shall be substituted the following paragraph—
"(e) Part II of the Proceeds of Crime (Scotland) Act 1995".

Criminal Justice Act 1991 (c. 53)

80.—(1) The Criminal Justice Act 1991 shall be amended as follows.
(2) In subsection (3) of section 24 (deduction of fines from income support)—
(a) in paragraph (a) for the words "section 196(2) of the Criminal Procedure (Scotland) Act 1975" there shall be substituted the words "section 211(4) of the Criminal Procedure (Scotland) Act 1995";
(b) in paragraph (b) for the words "section 66 of the Criminal Justice (Scotland) Act 1980" there shall be substituted the words "section 252 of the Criminal Procedure (Scotland) Act 1995"; and
(c) in paragraph (c) for the words "section 403(1)(a) or (b) of the Criminal Procedure (Scotland) Act 1975" there shall be substituted the words "section 222(1)(a) or (b) of the Criminal Procedure (Scotland) Act 1995".
(3) In paragraph 6(5)(a)(i) of Schedule 3 (reciprocal enforcement of community service orders) for the words "evidence on oath" there shall be substituted the word "information".

Dangerous Dogs Act 1991 (c. 65)

81. In subsection (9) of section 4 of the Dangerous Dogs Act 1991 (destruction and disqualification orders)—
(a) for the words "section 411 of the Criminal Procedure (Scotland) Act 1975" there shall be substituted the words "section 221 of the Criminal Procedure (Scotland) Act 1995"; and
(b) for the words "Part II" there shall be substituted the words "Part XI".

Social Security Administration Act 1992 (c. 5)

82. In subsection (7) of section 116 of the Social Security Administration Act 1992—
(a) for the words "section 331 of the Criminal Procedure (Scotland) Act 1975" there shall be substituted the words "section 136 of the Criminal Procedure (Scotland) Act 1995"; and
(b) for the words "section 331 of the said Act of 1975" there shall be substituted the words "section 136 of the said Act of 1995".

Timeshare Act 1992 (c. 35)

83. In subsection (3) of section 11 of the Timeshare Act 1992 (prosecution time limit), for the words "section 331 of the Criminal Procedure (Scotland) Act 1975" there shall be substituted the words "section 136 of the Criminal Procedure (Scotland) Act 1995".

Friendly Societies Act 1992 (c. 40)

84. In subsection (5) of section 107 of the Friendly Societies Act 1992 (prosecution time limit), for the words "section 331(1) of the Criminal Procedure (Scotland) Act 1975" there shall be substituted the words "section 136(1) of the Criminal Procedure (Scotland) Act 1995".

Trade Union and Labour Relations (Consolidation) Act 1992 (c. 52)

85. In subsection (6) of section 45A of the Trade Union and Labour Relations (Consolidation) Act 1992 (prosecution time limit), for the words "section 331 of the Criminal Procedure (Scot-

land) Act 1975" there shall be substituted the words "section 136 of the Criminal Procedure (Scotland) Act 1995".

Prisoners and Criminal Proceedings (Scotland) Act 1993 (c. 9)

86.—(1) The Prisoners and Criminal Proceedings (Scotland) Act 1993 shall be amended as follows.

(2) Subject to any specific amendment under this paragraph, for the words "1975 Act" where they occur there shall be substituted the words "1995 Act".

(3) In subsection (1) of section 5 (fine defaulters) for paragraph (a) there shall be substituted the following paragraph—

"(a) under section 219 of the 1995 Act (imprisonment for non-payment of fine) or, by virtue of that section, under section 207 of that Act (detention of young offenders);".

(4) Section 6 (application of Part to young offenders etc) shall be amended as follows—

(a) in paragraph (a) for the words "section 207(2) or 415(2)" there shall be substituted the words "section 207(2)";

(b) for the words "section 205" there shall be substituted the words "section 205(1) to (3)";

(c) for the words "section 206" where they occur there shall be substituted the words "section 208"; and

(d) for the words "section 207(2)" there shall be substituted the words "section 207(2)".

(5) In section 7 (children detained in solemn proceedings) for the words "section 206" where they occur there shall be substituted the words "section 208".

(6) In section 11 (duration of licence)—

(a) in subsection (3), for the words "section 212A" there shall be substituted the words "section 209"; and

(b) in paragraph (b) of that subsection, for the words from "the" in the second place where it occurs to the end there shall be substituted—

"there has elapsed—

(i) a period (reckoned from the date on which he was ordered to be returned to prison under or by virtue of subsection (2)(a) of that section) equal in length to the period between the date on which the new offence was committed and the date on which he would (but for his release) have served the original sentence in full; or

(ii) subject to subsection (4) below, a total period equal in length to the period for which he was so ordered to be returned to prison together with, so far as not concurrent with that period, any term of imprisonment to which he was sentenced in respect of the new offence,

whichever results in the later date.

(4) In subsection (3)(b) above, "the original sentence" and "the new offence" have the same meanings as in section 16 of this Act."

(7) Section 14 (supervised release of short term prisoners) shall be amended as follows—

(a) in subsection (2)—

(i) for the words "section 212A(1)" there shall be substituted the words "section 209(1)"; and

(ii) for the words "section 212A(2) to (6)" there shall be substituted the words "section 209(3) to (7)";

(b) in subsection (3) for the words "section 212A(2)" there shall be substituted the words "section 209(3)"; and

(c) in subsection (5) for the words "section 212A(5)(b)" there shall be substituted the words "section 209(6)(b)".

(8) In subsection (4) of section 15 (variation of supervised release order) for the words "section 212A(2)(b)" there shall be substituted the words "section 209(3)(b)"

(9) In section 16 (commission of offence by released prisoner)—

(a) in subsection (6), for the words "section 254(3) or 453C(1)" there shall be substituted the words "section 118(4) or 189(1) and (2)"; and

(b) for subsection (7) there shall be substituted the following subsection—

"(7) Where an order under subsection (2) or (4) above is made in respect of a person released on licence—

(a) the making of the order shall have the effect of revoking the licence; and

(b) if the sentence comprising—

(i) the period for which the person is ordered to be returned to prison; and

(ii) so far as not concurrent with that period, any term of imprisonment to which he is sentenced in respect of the new offence, is six months or more but less than four years, section 1(1) of this Act shall apply in respect of that sentence as if for the word "unconditionally" there were substituted the words "on licence"."

(10) In subsection (1) of section 27 (interpretation of Part I), for the words "section 212A" where they occur there shall be substituted the words "section 209".

(11) In section 46 (interpretation) the definition of "the 1975 Act" shall cease to have effect and at the end there shall be inserted the following definition—

" "the 1995 Act" means the Criminal Procedure (Scotland) Act 1995".

Agriculture Act 1993 (c. 37)

87. In subsection (5) of section 52 of the Agriculture Act 1993 (prosecution time limit) for the words "section 331 of the Criminal Procedure (Scotland) Act 1975" there shall be substituted the words "section 136 of the Criminal Procedure (Scotland) Act 1995".

Railways Act 1993 (c. 43)

88. In subsection (5) of section 148 of the Railways Act 1993 (prosecution time limit) for the words "section 331 of the Criminal Procedure (Scotland) Act 1975" there shall be substituted the words "section 136 of the Criminal Procedure (Scotland) Act 1995".

Finance Act 1994 (c. 9)

89.—(1) The Finance Act 1994 shall be amended as follows.

(2) In subsection (2) of section 22 (records and rules of evidence), in paragraph (d) for the words "Schedule 3 to the Prisoners and Criminal Proceedings (Scotland) Act 1993" there shall be substituted the words "Schedule 8 to the Criminal Procedure (Scotland) Act 1995".

(3) In subsection (3) of section 25 (order for production of documents), for the words "section 462 of the Criminal Procedure (Scotland) Act 1975" there shall be substituted the words "section 308 of the Criminal Procedure (Scotland) Act 1995".

(4) In Schedule 7 (insurance premium tax)—

(a) in paragraph 1(6)(d), for the words "Schedule 3 to the Prisoners and Criminal Proceedings (Scotland) Act 1993" there shall be substituted the words "Schedule 8 to the Criminal Procedure (Scotland) Act 1995"; and

(b) in paragraph 4(2), for the words "section 462 of the Criminal Procedure (Scotland) Act 1975" there shall be substituted the words "section 308 of the Criminal Procedure (Scotland) Act 1995".

Vehicle Excise and Registration Act 1994 (c. 22)

90.—(1) The Vehicle Excise and Registration Act 1994 shall be amended as follows.

(2) In subsection (1) of section 32 (effect of certain orders) for paragraph (b) there shall be substituted the following paragraph—

"(b) or an order under section 228 of the Criminal Procedure (Scotland) Act 1995 placing him on probation or under 246(3) of that Act discharging him absolutely, or".

(3) In subsection (1) of section 41 (effect of certain orders) for paragraph (b) there shall be substituted the following paragraph—

"(b) or an order under section 228 of the Criminal Procedure (Scotland) Act 1995 placing him on probation or under 246(2) or (3) of that Act discharging him absolutely, or".

(4) In subsection (4) of section 48 (time limit for proceedings) for the words "section 331 of the Criminal Procedure (Scotland) Act 1975" there shall be substituted the words "section 136 of the Criminal Procedure (Scotland) Act 1995".

Value Added Tax Act 1994 (c. 23)

91. In Schedule 11 of the Value Added Tax Act 1994—

(a) in paragraph 10(3) (power of entry and search) for the words "section 462 of the Criminal Procedure (Scotland) Act 1975" there shall be substituted the words "section 308 of the Criminal Procedure (Scotland) Act 1995"; and

(b) in paragraph 11(1) (access to certain information) for the words "section 462 of the Criminal Procedure (Scotland) Act 1975" there shall be substituted the words "section 308 of the Criminal Procedure (Scotland) Act 1995".

Trade Marks Act 1994 (c. 26)

92.—(1) The Trade Marks Act 1994 shall be amended as follows.

(2) In subsection (1) of section 96 (prosecution time limit) for the words "section 331 of the

Criminal Procedure (Scotland) Act 1975" there shall be substituted the words "section 136 of the Criminal Procedure (Scotland) Act 1995".

(3) In section 98 (forfeiture)—

(a) in subsection (2) for the words "section 310 of the Criminal Procedure (Scotland) Act 1975" there shall be substituted the words "section 134 of the Criminal Procedure (Scotland) Act 1995";

(b) in subsection (6) for the words "Criminal Procedure (Scotland) Act 1975" there shall be substituted the words "Criminal Procedure (Scotland) Act 1995";

(c) in subsection (9) for the words "section 452(4)(a) to (e) of the Criminal Procedure (Scotland) Act 1975" there shall be substituted the words "section 182(5)(a) to (e) of the Criminal Procedure (Scotland) Act 1995"; and

(d) in subsection (11) for the words "Criminal Procedure (Scotland) Act 1975" there shall be substituted the words "Criminal Procedure (Scotland) Act 1995".

Criminal Justice and Public Order Act 1994 (c. 33)

93.—(1) The Criminal Justice and Public Order Act 1994 shall be amended as follows.

(2) In subsection (5) of section 25 (restriction on bail) in the definition of "the relevant enactments", for paragraph (b) there shall be substituted the following paragraph—

"(b) as respects Scotland, sections 205(1) to (3) and 208 of the Criminal Procedure (Scotland) Act 1995;".

(3) In section 102 (provision of prisoner escorts)—

(a) in paragraph (b) of subsection (3), for the words "Criminal Procedure (Scotland) Act 1975" there shall be substituted the words "Criminal Procedure (Scotland) Act 1995"; and

(b) in subsection (6)—

(i) in the definition of "hospital order", for the words "section 174, 174A, 175, 375A or 376 of the Act of 1975" there shall be substituted the words "section 53, 54 or 58 of the Act of 1995"; and

(ii) in the definition of "warrant", for the words "Act of 1975" there shall be substituted the words "Act of 1995".

(4) In subsection (4) of section 104 (powers and duties of prison custody officers), for the words "section 395(2) of the Criminal Procedure (Scotland) Act 1975" there shall be substituted the words "section 212 of the Criminal Procedure (Scotland) Act 1995".

(5) In subsection (1) of section 117 (interpretation of Chapter), in the definition of "prisoner" for the words "section 215 or 426 of the Criminal Procedure (Scotland) Act 1975" there shall be substituted the words "section 295 of the Criminal Procedure (Scotland) Act 1995".

(6) In section 138 (which supplements section 137 relating to cross-border powers of arrest)—

(a) in subsection (2), for the words from "subsections (2) to (7)" to "1993" there shall be substituted the words "subsections (2) to (8) of section 14 (detention and questioning at police station), subsections (1), (2) and (4) to (6) of section 15 (rights of person arrested or detained) and section 18 (prints, samples etc. in criminal investigations) of the Criminal Procedure (Scotland) Act 1995";

(b) in subsection (6)—

(i) for the words "sections 2 and 3 of the Criminal Justice (Scotland) Act 1980" there shall be substituted the words "sections 14 and 15 of the said Act of 1995";

(ii) in paragraph (a), for the words "in section 2" there shall be substituted the words "in section 14" and for the words "in subsections (4) and (7)" there shall be substituted the words "in subsections (6) and (9)"; and

(iii) in paragraph (b), for the words "in section 3(1)" there shall be substituted the words "in subsections (1) and (2) of section 15".

The Drug Trafficking Act 1994 (c. 37)

94.—(1) The Drug Trafficking Act 1994 shall be amended as follows.

(2) In subsection (7) of section 4 (assessing the proceeds of drug trafficking), for paragraphs (b) and (c) there shall be substituted the following—

"(b) the Proceeds of Crime (Scotland) Act 1995;".

(3) In subsection (3) of section 6 (meaning of realisable property) for paragraph (e) there shall be substituted the following—

"(e) Part II of the Proceeds of Crime (Scotland) Act 1995 (forfeiture of property used in crime);"

(4) In subsection (2) of section 18 (compensation) for sub-paragraph (ii) of paragraph (b) there shall be substituted the following—

"(ii) an order of the Court of Session under section 32, 33, 34 or 35 of the Proceeds of Crime (Scotland) Act 1995 (recognition and enforcement of orders under this Act and inhibition and arrestment of property affected by restraint orders);".

(5) In subsection (10) of section 26 (restraint orders) for the words from "Part I" to the end of the subsection there shall be substituted the words "the Proceeds of Crime (Scotland) Act 1995, and in relation to such an order "realisable property" has the same meaning as in that Act".

(6) In section 37 (recognition and enforcement of certain Scottish orders and functions)—
 (a) in subsection (1)—
  (i) after the words "expedient for the purpose" there shall be inserted the words "in connection with a drug trafficking offence within the meaning of the Proceeds of Crime (Scotland) Act 1995";
  (ii) in paragraph (a) for the words "Part I of the Criminal Justice (Scotland) Act 1987" there shall be substituted the words "that Act";
  (iii) in each of paragraphs (a) and (b) where they occur, the words "that Part of" shall cease to have effect;
 (b) in subsection (2)—
  (i) in paragraph (a), in sub-paragraph (i) for the words "section 13 of the Criminal Justice (Scotland) Act 1987" there shall be substituted the words "Schedule 1 to the Proceeds of Crime (Scotland) Act 1995" and in sub-paragraph (ii) the words "Part I of" shall cease to have effect;
  (ii) in each of paragraphs (b) and (c) where they occur, the words "that Part of" shall cease to have effect.

(7) In subsection (2) of section 48 (interpretation of Part II), in paragraph (a) for the words "Part I of the Criminal Justice (Scotland) Act 1987" there shall be substituted the words "the Proceeds of Crime (Scotland) Act 1995".

Local Government etc. (Scotland) Act 1994 (c. 39)

95.—(1) The Local Government etc. (Scotland) Act 1994 shall be amended as follows.

(2) In subsection (1) of section 127 (the Principal Reporter), for the words "Criminal Procedure (Scotland) Act 1975" there shall be substituted the words "Criminal Procedure (Scotland) Act 1995".

(3) In each of subsections (3) and (8) of section 128 (Scottish Children's Reporter Administration), for the words "Criminal Procedure (Scotland) Act 1975" there shall be substituted the words "Criminal Procedure (Scotland) Act 1995".

(4) In subsection (1) of section 130 (annual report of Principal Reporter), for the words "Criminal Procedure (Scotland) Act 1975" there shall be substituted the words "Criminal Procedure (Scotland) Act 1995".

Deregulation and Contracting Out Act 1994 (c. 40)

96. In subsection (2) of section 2 of the Deregulation and Contracting Out Act 1994, for paragraph (b) there shall be substituted the following paragraph—
 "(b) section 292(6) and (7) of the Criminal Procedure (Scotland) Act 1995,".

Children (Scotland) Act 1995 (c. 36)

97.—(1) The Children (Scotland) Act 1995 shall be amended as follows.

(2) In subsection (2) of section 45 (attendance of child etc. at hearing), in paragraph (a) for the words "Schedule 1 of the Criminal Procedure (Scotland) Act 1975" there shall be substituted the words "Schedule I of the Criminal Procedure (Scotland) Act 1995".

(3) In section 50 (treatment of child's case on remission by court)—
 (a) in subsection (1), for the words "section 173, 372 or 373 of the Criminal Procedure (Scotland) Act 1975" there shall be substituted "section 49 of the Criminal Procedure (Scotland) Act 1995"; and
 (b) in subsection (2), for the words "the said section 373" there shall be substituted "subsection (7) of the said section 49".

(4) In subsection (2) of section 52 (children requiring compulsory supervision)—
 (a) in paragraph (d) for the words "Schedule 1 of the Criminal Procedure (Scotland) Act 1975" there shall be substituted the words "Schedule 1 of the Criminal Procedure (Scotland) Act 1995"; and
 (b) in paragraph (g), for the words "sections 2A to 2C of the Sexual Offences (Scotland) Act 1976" there shall be substituted "sections 1 to 3 of the Criminal Law (Consolidation) (Scotland) Act 1995".

(5) In subsection (7) of section 53 (information for Principal Reporter) for the words "section 462 of the Criminal Procedure (Scotland) Act 1975" there shall be substituted the words "section 307 of the Criminal Procedure (Scotland) Act 1995".

(6) In section 63(1) (duty of Principal Reporter where informed by constable of detention of a child) for the words "section 296(3) of the Criminal Procedure (Scotland) Act 1975" there shall be substituted "section 43(5) of the Criminal Procedure (Scotland) Act 1995".

(7) In section 78 (powers of arrest)—

(a) in subsection (8), for the words "Criminal Procedure (Scotland) Act 1975" there shall be substituted the words "Criminal Procedure (Scotland) Act 1995";

(b) in subsection (11), for the words "section 10 of the Bail etc, (Scotland) Act 1980" there shall be substituted the words "section 8 of the said Act of 1995"; and

(c) in subsection (12), for the words "Subsections (1) and (3) of section 3 of the Criminal Justice (Scotland) Act 1980" there shall be substituted the words "Subsections (1), (2) and (4) of section 15 of the said Act of 1995".

Pensions Act 1995 (c. 26)

98. In subsection (5) of section 100 of the Pensions Act 1995 (warrants) for the words "Criminal Procedure (Scotland) Act 1975" there shall be substituted the words "Criminal Procedure (Scotland) Act 1995".

Note

99. The amendments made by this Schedule to—

(a) the Sea Fisheries Act 1968;

(b) the Fatal Accidents and Sudden Deaths Inquiry (Scotland) Act 1976; and

(c) section 15(2) of the Contempt of Court Act 1981,

are in substitution for amendments made to those enactments by section 56 of and Schedule 7 to the Criminal Justice Act 1988 which are repealed by this Act.

Section 6   SCHEDULE 5

REPEALS

Chapter	Short title	Extent of repeal
11 Geo. 4 & 1 Wm. 4 c. 69	The Court of Session Act 1830	Section 18
50 & 51 Vict. c. 35	The Criminal Procedure (Scotland) Act 1887	The whole Act
4 & 5 Geo. 5 c. 58	The Criminal Justice Administration Act 1914	Section 28(3)
12, 13 & 14 Geo. 6, c. 94	The Criminal Justice (Scotland) Act 1949	The whole Act
1 & 2 Eliz. 2, c. 14	The Prevention of Crime Act 1953	Section 1
2 & 3 Eliz. 2, c. 48	The Summary Jurisdiction (Scotland) Act 1954	The whole Act
1968 c. 49	The Social Work (Scotland) Act 1968	Section 31(1)
1975 c. 20	The District Courts (Scotland) Act 1975	Sections 2 to 4 Section 6 In Schedule 1, paragraph 27
1975 c. 21	The Criminal Procedure (Scotland) Act 1975	The whole Act
1977 c. 45	The Criminal Law Act 1977	In Schedule 6, the entries relating to the Criminal Procedure (Scotland) Act 1975 In Schedule 7, paragraph 2 Schedule 11
1978 c. 29	The National Health Service (Scotland) Act 1978	In Schedule 16, paragraph 41

Chapter	Short title	Extent of repeal
1978 c. 49	The Community Service by Offenders (Scotland) Act 1978	Sections 1 to 8 Sections 10 to 13 Section 15 In Schedule 2, paragraphs 2 and 3
1979 c. 16	The Criminal Evidence Act 1979	In section 1(1) the words "sections 141 and 346 of the Criminal Procedure (Scotland) Act 1975"
1980 c. 4	The Bail (Scotland) Act 1980	The whole Act
1980 c. 62	The Criminal Justice (Scotland) Act 1980	Sections 1 to 3 Sections 4 to 7 Sections 9 to 43 Section 45(1) Sections 46 to 50 Sections 52 to 54 Sections 58 to 67 Part V Sections 78 and 80 Schedules 1 to 4 In Schedule 7, paragraphs 25 to 78
1981 c. 45	The Forgery and Counterfeiting Act 1981	Section 26
1982 c. 48	The Criminal Justice Act 1982	Part IV Schedules 6 and 7
1982 c. 49	The Transport Act 1982	In section 40, paragraph (c) of subsection (5)
1984 c. 39	The Video Recordings Act 1984	Section 20
1985 c. 66	The Bankruptcy (Scotland) Act 1985	In section 5(4) the words "by section 1(1) of the Criminal Justice (Scotland) Act 1987" In section 7(1) the words "by section 1(1) of the Criminal Justice (Scotland) Act 1987"
1985 c. 73	The Law Reform (Miscellaneous Provisions) (Scotland) Act 1985	Section 21 Sections 36 and 37 Section 40 Section 43 Section 45 In Schedule 2, paragraphs 16 to 20 and paragraph 23 In Schedule 3, paragraphs 1, 3 and 4
1987 c. 41	The Criminal Justice (Scotland) Act 1987	Part I Sections 56 to 68 In Schedule 1, paragraphs 4 to 18
1988 c. 53	The Road Traffic Offenders Act 1988	In section 60, paragraph (c) of subsection (6)
1988 c. 54	The Road Traffic (Consequential Provisions) Act 1988	In Schedule 3, paragraph 34
1990 c. 5	The Criminal Justice (International Co-operation) Act 1990	Section 15 In Schedule 4, paragraph 5
1990 c. 40	The Law Reform (Miscellaneous Provisions) (Scotland) Act 1990	Sections 56 and 57 Section 62 Schedule 6
1991 c. 53	The Criminal Justice Act 1991	In Schedule 3, paragraph 8
1991 c. 62	The Armed Forces Act 1991	In Schedule 2, paragraph 9(2)
1993 c. 9	The Prisoners and Criminal Proceedings (Scotland) Act 1993	Section 8 Section 14(1) Sections 28 to 35 Sections 37 to 43 In section 46, the definition of "the 1975 Act"

Chapter	Short title	Extent of repeal
		Schedules 3 and 4
		In Schedule 5, paragraph 1
1993 c. 13	The Carrying of Knives etc. (Scotland) Act 1993	The whole Act
1993 c. 36	The Criminal Justice Act 1993	Sections 68 and 69
		In Schedule 5, paragraph 2
1994 c. 33	The Criminal Justice and Public Order Act 1994	Section 47(4)
		In section 129, subsections (1) to (3)
		Section 132
		In section 157, subsection (7)
1994 c. 37	The Drug Trafficking Act 1994	In section 37, the words "that Part of" where they occur and in paragraph (a)(ii) of subsection (2) the words "Part I of".
1995 c. 20	The Criminal Justice (Scotland) Act 1995	The whole Act
1995 c. 36	The Children (Scotland) Act 1995.	Section 49
		In Schedule 4, paragraphs 24, 27 and 29.

Section 6(2)

SCHEDULE 6

PROVISIONS REPEALED WITH SAVINGS

In section 43, the words from "and it shall not be necessary" to the end.
Section 45.
Section 46.
Section 47.
Section 52.
Section 53.
In section 54 the words from "and it shall not be necessary to specify" to the end.
In section 55, the words "it shall not be necessary to set forth the document or any part of it in such indictment".
Section 56.
Section 57.
In section 109, the words from the beginning to "except that".
In section 111, the words "it shall not be necessary that a new warrant should be granted for the incarceration of the accused, but".
Section 124 (except the proviso).
Section 222.

INDEX

References are to sections and Schedules

LAW REFORM (SUCCESSION) ACT 1995*

(1995 c. 41)

An Act to amend the law relating to the distribution of the estates of deceased persons and to make provision about the effect of the dissolution or annulment of marriages on wills and appointments of guardians.

[8th November 1995]

PARLIAMENTARY DEBATES
Hansard, H.L. Vol. 561, cols. 502, 1309; Vol. 562, col. 1409; Vol 563, col. 1366. H.C. Vol. 261, col. 811; Vol. 265, col. 199.

INTRODUCTION AND GENERAL NOTE

This Act originates from two Law Commission reports, *Family Law: Distribution on Intestacy* (Law Com. No. 187) and *Family Law: The Effect of Divorce on Wills* (Law Com. No. 217). Sections 1 and 2 of the Act give effect to recommendations from the earlier report, relating to the distribution of estates on intestacy and partial intestacy. The Commission was concerned that its recommendations should reflect changes in the nature and ownership of property and in the demography of the population that had occurred since the law of distribution on intestacy had last been reviewed by the Morton Committee in 1951. The Commission's main recommendation was that where a spouse survived the intestate, the surviving spouse should receive the entire estate regardless of its size or whether there were surviving issue or not. Although the Commission acknowledged that such a reform would be contentious, it considered that there were considerable advantages to be gained by simplifying and reducing the expense of administering the estates of intestates, and ensuring that surviving spouses were adequately provided for. The Commission considered that the interests of surviving issue would be adequately protected by the Inheritance (Provision for Family and Dependants) Act 1975 (c. 63). However, the proposed reform was rejected on the basis that it would not be appropriate to exclude other members of the family in all cases, and especially where the deceased left surviving issue by an earlier marriage (see *Hansard*, H.L. Vol. 561, col. 503).

The first two sections of this Act do, however, give effect to the Commission's other recommendations. Under s.1 the "hotchpot" rule in relation to intestacy and partial intestacy is repealed, and a "survivorship" clause is inserted so that a surviving spouse who does not live for more than 28 days from the date of the deceased's death is treated as not having survived the deceased. Section 2 amends s.1 of the Inheritance (Provision for Family and Dependants) Act 1975, enabling cohabitants of the deceased in certain circumstances to make a claim for reasonable financial provision under that Act.

Sections 3 and 4 of this Act give effect to the recommendations of the later Law Commission Report on the effect of the dissolution or annulment of a marriage on a will and on a testamentary appointment of a guardian respectively.

Sections 5 and 6 of this Act cover repeals, the title of the Act and its extent.

---

* Annotations by Jake Gavin, of Inner Temple, Barrister.

ABBREVIATIONS
1975 Act: Inheritance (Provision for Family and Dependants) Act 1975 (c. 63).
1837 Act: Wills Act 1837 (c. 26).

Distribution of estates

Intestacy and partial intestacy

1.—(1) In the Administration of Estates Act 1925 ("the 1925 Act"), in section 46 (succession on intestacy) the following subsection shall be inserted after subsection (2)—

"(2A) Where the intestate's husband or wife survived the intestate but died before the end of the period of 28 days beginning with the day on which the intestate died, this section shall have effect as respects the intestate as if the husband or wife had not survived the intestate."

(2) The following provisions of the 1925 Act (which require certain payments made by an intestate, and certain interests acquired under a will of an intestate, to be brought into account) shall cease to have effect—

(a) in section 47 (statutory trusts in favour of issue and other relatives of intestate), subsection (1)(iii);

(b) in section 49 (partial intestacy), in subsection (1) paragraphs (aa) and (a), and subsections (2) and (3).

(3) Subsections (1) and (2) above have effect as respects an intestate dying on or after 1st January 1996.

(4) In section 50 of the 1925 Act (construction of documents), the references in subsection (1) to Part IV of that Act and to the foregoing provisions of that Part shall, in relation to an instrument inter vivos made or a will or codicil coming into operation on or after 1st January 1996 (but not in relation to instruments inter vivos made or wills or codicils coming into operation earlier), be construed as including references to this section.

(5) In this section "intestate" shall be construed in accordance with section 55(1)(vi) of the 1925 Act.

GENERAL NOTE

Subs. (1)
The effect of this subsection is to insert a survivorship clause to the rules on intestacy so that the surviving spouse should only inherit on intestacy if he or she survives the deceased by 28 days. This reflects the common practice of inserting such a clause into a will, thereby ensuring that the family of one spouse does not arbitrarily inherit the bulk of the property of the other spouse where both die simultaneously or within a short time of each other, as for example in a road accident.

Subs. (2)
Under this subsection the "hotchpot" rules on total and partial intestacy under ss.47 and 49 of the Administration of Estates Act 1925 (c. 23) respectively are repealed. The intention behind this section was to reduce the difficulties faced by lay personal representatives and to avoid consequences which probably would not have been in accordance with the deceased's intentions (*Hansard*, H.L. Vol. 561, col. 503).

Para. (a)
Section 47 of the Administration of Estates Act 1925 sets out the trusts on which the residuary estate is to be held where Pt. IV of that Act directs that it is to be held on the statutory trusts for the issue of the intestate. Under s.47(1)(iii), where the property held on the statutory trusts for issue was divisible into shares (*i.e.* there were more than one issue entitled), any money or property which had been paid to such a child by the intestate by way of advancement or on the

marriage of that child, or settled by the intestate for the benefit of the child, was taken, subject to any contrary intention expressed or appearing from the circumstances of the case, to have been so paid or settled towards the satisfaction of the share of the residuary estate held on statutory trusts to which the child would have been entitled. Such advancements or settlements can now, for the purposes of intestacy, be ignored.

Para. (b)

Where a person dies leaving a will which only effectively disposes of part of his property under s.49 of the Administration of Estates Act 1925 (as amended by the Intestates' Estates Act 1952 (c. 64), s.3), Pt. IV of the Act has effect in respect of the undisposed property. Accordingly, that part of the deceased's property is administered as if the deceased had died intestate. Under s.49(1)(aa) of the 1925 Act, where the deceased was survived by a spouse, the fixed net sum payable to the surviving spouse under the intestacy provisions of Pt. IV of the 1925 Act was reduced by the value of any beneficial interests to which the surviving spouse became entitled from the part of the deceased's estate that was effectively disposed of by the will. Section 49(1) (a) extended the hotchpot provisions of s.47 (now repealed by s.1(2)(a) of this Act) to beneficial interests acquired by issue of the deceased under the will of the deceased, but did not affect the beneficial interests acquired by any other person. These two paragraphs are now repealed.

Section 49(2) defined beneficial interests under a will to include a beneficial interest acquired by virtue of the exercise by the will of a *general* power of appointment, but not a *special* power of appointment. Section 49(3) empowered a personal representative to employ a duly qualified valuer for the purposes of s.49(1)(aa) where necessary.

Subs. (4)

Under s.50 of the Administration of Estates Act 1925, references to Statutes of Distribution made in an instrument *inter vivos*, or a will coming into operation, were to be construed after the commencement of that Act as references to Pt. IV of that Act. Accordingly, in respect of an instrument *inter vivos* or a will or codicil coming into operation on or after January 1, 1996, references in s.50(1) of the 1925 Act to Pt. IV of that Act are now to be construed as including s.1 of this Act.

Subs. (5)

Section 55(1)(vi) of the 1925 Act defined an intestate as including "a person who leaves a will but dies intestate as to some beneficial interest in his real or personal estate".

Application for financial provision by person who lived with deceased as husband or wife

2.—(1) The Inheritance (Provision for Family and Dependants) Act 1975 shall be amended as follows.

(2) In section 1 (application for financial provision from deceased's estate), in subsection (1) (persons who may apply) the following paragraph shall be inserted after paragraph (b)—

"(ba) any person (not being a person included in paragraph (a) or (b) above) to whom subsection (1A) below applies;".

(3) In that section, the following subsection shall be inserted after subsection (1)—

"(1A) This subsection applies to a person if the deceased died on or after 1st January 1996 and, during the whole of the period of two years ending immediately before the date when the deceased died, the person was living—

(a) in the same household as the deceased, and

(b) as the husband or wife of the deceased."

(4) In section 3 (matters to which court is to have regard in exercising its powers to make orders), the following subsection shall be inserted after subsection (2)—

"(2A) Without prejudice to the generality of paragraph (g) of subsection (1) above, where an application for an order under section 2 of this Act is made by virtue of section 1(1)(ba) of this Act, the court shall, in addition to the matters specifically mentioned in paragraphs (a) to (f) of that subsection, have regard to—

(a) the age of the applicant and the length of the period during which the applicant lived as the husband or wife of the deceased and in the same household as the deceased;

(b) the contribution made by the applicant to the welfare of the family of the deceased, including any contribution made by looking after the home or caring for the family."

GENERAL NOTE

Subss. (1), (2) and (3)

The effect of s.1(1), (2) and (3) of this Act is to enable surviving cohabitants to make a claim for financial provision under s.1 of the Inheritance (Provision for Family and Dependants) Act 1975 (the 1975 Act), regardless of whether the deceased died intestate or not. Although formerly a cohabitant of the deceased could make a claim, such a claim had to be made under s.1(1)(e) of the 1975 Act. The cohabitant of the deceased had therefore to satisfy the court that immediately before the death of the deceased he or she had been wholly or partly maintained by the deceased. Under this amendment, there is no need to prove any such dependency: the claiming cohabitant has to show that during the whole period of two years prior to the death of the deceased he or she was living in the same household as the deceased as the husband or wife of the deceased, this is the same basis on which cohabitants may make claims under the Fatal Accidents Act 1976 (c. 30). It is intended that this amendment shall take effect only in respect of cohabitants living "as husband and wife" and not for cohabitants of the same sex (*Hansard*, H.L. Vol. 561, col. 511).

The definition of "reasonable financial provision" given in s.1(2) of the 1975 Act remains the same for cohabitants as for other applicants, apart from spouses. Therefore the distinction between claims made by claimants married to (but not judicially separated from) the deceased at the time of his or her death and claims by claimants not married to, or judicially separated from, the deceased remains.

Subs. (4)

The amendments to the 1975 Act under this section retain the distinction between a claimant married to the deceased at the time of his death and a claimant not married to the deceased at the time of his death in the definition of "reasonable financial provision" under s.1(2) of the 1975 Act (see note to s.2 above). In contrast, the effect of subs. (4) is to equate the position of a cohabitant with that of a spouse or former spouse when specifying the matters to which the court is to have regard in exercising its powers under s.2 of the 1975 Act. Under subs. (4) of this Act, where an application is made by a cohabitant pursuant to subs. (3) above, the court should have regard to the same matters that it would when considering a claim by a spouse or former spouse of the deceased (substituting the length of cohabitation for the duration of the marriage).

Effect of dissolution or annulment of marriage

Effect of dissolution or annulment of marriage on will

3.—(1) In section 18A of the Wills Act 1837 (effect of dissolution or annulment of marriage on will), in subsection (1) for paragraphs (a) and (b) (abrogation of appointment of spouse as executor and lapse of devise or bequest to spouse) there shall be substituted—

"(a) provisions of the will appointing executors or trustees or conferring a power of appointment, if they appoint or confer the power on the former spouse, shall take effect as if the former spouse had died on the date on which the marriage is dissolved or annulled, and

(b) any property which, or an interest in which, is devised or bequeathed to the former spouse shall pass as if the former spouse had died on that date,".

(2) Subsection (1) above has effect as respects a will made by a person dying on or after 1st January 1996 (regardless of the date of the will and the date of the dissolution or annulment).

GENERAL NOTE

This section amends the "lapse" rule of s.18A of the Wills Act 1837 (c. 26) (as inserted by the Administration of Justice Act 1982 (c. 53) and substituted by the Family Law Act 1986 (c. 55)). Under that section, where a decree of a court annuls or dissolves a testator's marriage (or his marriage is dissolved or annulled and the divorce or annulment is entitled to recognition in England and Wales by virtue of Pt. II of the Family Law Act 1986), the testator's will took effect as if any appointment of the former spouse as executor and or trustee of the will were omitted, and a devise or bequest to the former spouse lapsed.

The Commission considered that there was a defect in the lapse provision in that in certain circumstances it could defeat the testator's presumed intentions. It would, for example, defeat a gift to a spouse with a gift over to a third party in the event of the spouse pre-deceasing the testator, as illustrated by the case of *Sinclair, decd., Re* [1985] Ch. 446 C.A. If the testator divorced his or her spouse, under the provisions of s.18A of the 1837 Act both the gift to the spouse and the gift over to the third party would lapse. Likewise, where a testator bequeaths property to a spouse "jointly" with other beneficiaries the whole gift would fail due to the testator's divorce.

Subs. (1)
Para. (a)
In order to achieve consistency, a testamentary provision conferring a power of appointment (either general or special) on a spouse, is now revoked on the dissolution or annulment of the testator's marriage, as well as those provisions appointing a spouse as executor or trustee. Since the former spouse is treated as if he or she had died on the date of the dissolution or annulment of the marriage, if the will contains provision for a substitute appointee or conferee in the event that the spouse pre-deceases the testator, such provision will now take effect on the dissolution or annulment of the marriage rather than lapsing.

Para. (b)
By treating the former spouse as having died on the date of the dissolution or annulment of the marriage, the potential problems highlighted in *Re Sinclair* above are now avoided. Under s.18A of the 1837 Act it was expressly provided that the lapse provision for appointments and bequests was subject to a contrary intention appearing in the will. The Law Commission recommended that such provision should remain in any reform. The Commission's draft Bill, on which this Act is based does not in fact contain such express provision. However, from the Lord Chancellor's summary of the Bill at its second reading (*Hansard*, Vol. 561, col. 504), the intention appeared to be for the proposed reforms to take effect subject to any contrary intention appearing in the will.

Effect of dissolution or annulment of marriage on appointment of guardian

4.—(1) In section 6 of the Children Act 1989 (revocation of appointment of guardian) the following subsection shall be inserted after subsection (3)—

"(3A) An appointment under section 5(3) or (4) (including one made in an unrevoked will or codicil) is revoked if the person appointed is the spouse of the person who made the appointment and either—

(a) a decree of a court of civil jurisdiction in England and Wales dissolves or annuls the marriage, or

(b) the marriage is dissolved or annulled and the divorce or annulment is entitled to recognition in England and Wales by virtue of Part II of the Family Law Act 1986,

unless a contrary intention appears by the appointment."

(2) Subsection (1) above has effect as respects an appointment made by a person dying on or after 1st January 1996 (regardless of the date of the appointment and the date of the dissolution or annulment).

GENERAL NOTE
Under this section an appointment of a spouse as a testamentary guardian of a child is, subject to any expressed contrary intention, automatically revoked on the dissolution or annulment of the marriage. Where the child concerned is a child of the testator *and* of the former spouse, the former spouse will already have parental responsibility of the child and this is not affected by the dissolution or annulment. This section will therefore have no effect on the former spouse's parental responsibility. If the child is not a child of the former spouse (*i.e.* a step-child), the Law Commission considered that if the step-parent did not already have parental responsibility by the date of the dissolution or annulment of the marriage, then it was unlikely that a testator

would wish the former spouse to be so appointed on his or her death after that date. This amendment is made to the Children Act 1989 (c. 41) rather than to the Wills Act 1837, since an appointment of a guardian in the event of death need not be made by will, but may be by any written instrument signed and dated by the appointor (Children Act 1989, s.5(5)).

Supplemental

Repeals

5. The enactments mentioned in the Schedule to this Act are repealed in accordance with that Schedule.

Citation and extent

6.—(1) This Act may be cited as the Law Reform (Succession) Act 1995.
(2) This Act extends to England and Wales only.

Section 5   SCHEDULE

REPEALS

Chapter	Short title	Extent of repeal
7 Will. 4 & 1 Vict. c. 26.	The Wills Act 1837.	Section 18A(3).
15 & 16 Geo. 5 c. 23.	The Administration of Estates Act 1925.	Section 47(1)(iii). In section 49, in subsection (1) paragraphs (aa) and (a), and subsections (2) and (3).
15 & 16 Geo. 6 & 1 Eliz. 2 c. 64.	The Intestates' Estates Act 1952.	Section 3(2).

The repeal in the Wills Act 1837 has effect as respects a will made by a person dying on or after 1st January 1996 and the other repeals have effect as respects an intestate (within the meaning of section 1) dying on or after that date.

INDEX

References are to sections and Schedules

PRIVATE INTERNATIONAL LAW
(MISCELLANEOUS PROVISIONS) ACT 1995*

(1995 c. 42)

ARRANGEMENT OF SECTIONS

PART I

INTEREST ON JUDGMENT DEBTS AND ARBITRAL AWARDS

PART II

VALIDITY OF MARRIAGES UNDER A LAW WHICH PERMITS POLYGAMY

PART III

CHOICE OF LAW IN TORT AND DELICT

PART IV

SUPPLEMENTAL

An Act to make provision about interest on judgment debts and arbitral awards expressed in a currency other than sterling; to make further provision as to marriages entered into by unmarried persons under a law which permits polygamy; to make provision for choice of law rules in tort and delict; and for connected purposes.   [8th November 1995]

PARLIAMENTARY DEBATES
   Hansard, H.L. Vol. 559, cols. 830, 1205; Vol. 562, col. 1409; Vol. 563, col. 1359. H.C. Vol. 261, col. 558; Vol. 265, col. 200.

INTRODUCTION AND GENERAL NOTE
   This Act introduces reforms aimed at modifying and clarifying private international law (conflict of law) rules in three areas:

---

*Annotations by Barry Rodger, lecturer in law, University of Strathclyde.

(a) the payment in England and Wales of interest on judgment debts and arbitral awards expressed in foreign currency (Pt. I);

(b) the validity under the law of England and Wales and the law of Scotland of marriages which are actually monogamous but which were entered into under a law which permits polygamy (Pt. II); and

(c) the choice of law to be applied where an action is brought in a part of the U.K. in respect of a tort or delict committed abroad or in another part of the U.K. (Pt. III).

The reforms have stemmed from the English and Scottish Law Commissions' four programmes for review of aspects of private international law including the law of domicile, for which no provision is made here. The provisions in the Act have resulted from (a) consultation on the Law Commissions' original provisional proposals in the three areas and (b) consultation on the Law Commissions' draft legislation. The Act was a House of Lords Bill passed under the Jellicoe procedure and involved a Special Public Bill Committee stage.

However, there are misgivings as to the simultaneous reform in Pts. II and III of English and Scots common law rules, particularly as inadequate consideration is given to the distinctive legal traditions in the separate jurisdictions for private international law.

COMMENCEMENT
See s.16 for the commencement dates for the three parts.

ABBREVIATIONS
Dicey and Morris: Dicey and Morris, The Conflict of Laws (12th edn.), Sweet & Maxwell.
Cheshire and North: Cheshire and North, Private International Law (12th edn.), Butterworth.
The Report: The Law Commission Report relating to the Part in which the reference is made (see the Introductory General Note for each part).
Working Paper/Consultative Document: The Law Commission Working Paper/Consultative Document relating to the Part in which the reference is made (see the Introductory General Note for each Part).
Morris: Morris, The Conflict of Laws (4th edn.), Sweet & Maxwell.
Special Public Bill Committee: see s.5(1).
Anton and Beaumont: Anton and Beaumont, Private International Law (2nd edn.), W. Green & Son.

PART I

INTEREST ON JUDGMENT DEBTS AND ARBITRAL AWARDS

GENERAL NOTE
The need for these reforms was identified by the Law Commission in its report on *Private International Law; Foreign Money Liabilities* (Law Com. No. 124; Cmnd. 9064). Part IV of the report recommended procedural changes in the method of awarding interest on foreign-currency judgment debts and arbitral awards in England and Wales in the light of developments in the rules allowing judgments in foreign currency.

The Law Commission was first requested to consider the general issue of foreign money liabilities in 1972. A Working Party was established and produced Working Paper No. 80 in 1981. However, in the interim there had been considerable judicial development of the law in the area. In 1972, the accepted rule was that an English court could only give judgment in English currency (see *United Railways of Havana and Regla Warehouses, Re* [1961] A.C. 1007). The amount due to the plaintiff had to be converted from foreign currency into sterling and the exchange rate was calculated as at the date the cause of action arose. However, judicial development allowed for arbitral awards to be made in foreign currency (*Jugoslovenska Oceanska Plovidba v. Castle Investment Co. Inc.* [1974] Q.B. 292), and most importantly the House of Lords held, in 1975 in *Miliangos v. Frank (George) (Textiles)* [1976] A.C. 443, that it was competent for English courts to give judgment for a sum of money in a foreign currency. In addition, conversion into sterling, for means of enforcement, could be authorised as at the date of judgment as opposed to the earlier breach-date rule. This decision related specifically to claims for money due under contracts governed by a foreign law, but the principles have since been applied to a wide range of issues (see Law Com. No. 124, Pts. II and III; *Dicey and Morris*, pp. 1583–1590; *Cheshire and North*, pp. 97–105. For the updated Scottish position, see Maher, *Foreign Currency Judgments: The Scottish Experience* [1995] I.C.L.Q. 72).

The Law Commission Working Paper No. 80 comprised a survey and reappraisal of both the law and the procedure across the field of foreign money liabilities and formed the provisional view that no specific legislation should be proposed. The question of interest on foreign currency judgments had not been canvassed in the Working Paper. However, after consultation it appeared that, as a result of *Miliangos*, the automatic application of the normal rules on interest gave rise to an anomaly that the Law Commission considered ought to be remedied. Interest may be awarded in an action for payment in a foreign currency at a rate which may be different from the English rate for sterling. However, interest on a judgment in foreign currency had to be paid at the appropriate English statutory rate for judgment debts (Practice Direction [1976] 1 All E.R. 669 as amended by Practice Direction [1977] 1 All E.R. 544). As the Report stated, "the judicial development of the rules concerning interest on foreign currency claims to the date of judgment has not been matched by legislative change relating to the rate of interest that automatically runs on foreign-currency judgment debts" (para. 4.8). The Law Commission recognised that this could cause injustice, as the English statutory rate is fixed in relation to the strength of sterling which may be at variance with the strength of the relevant foreign currency. Accordingly, legislation was proposed (para. 4.9; see Appendix A) to enable the High Court and county courts, in the case of a foreign-currency judgment, to order at their discretion that a specified rate of interest, other than the one prescribed under the Judgments Act 1838 (c. 110), should apply to the judgment. This proposal was extended to include arbitral awards (para. 4.7). Further, "in order to assimilate the rules governing the award of interest on foreign-currency claims to the date of the judgment to those applicable to interest on judgment debts in foreign currency" (para. 4.12) the rate of interest to be awarded could be variable. The problem with this latter proposal is the further anomaly that this could create as between foreign-currency judgment debts and sterling judgment debts upon which the courts have no power to award variable rates of interest. However, the law on interest on sterling judgment debts was considered outwith the remit of the Law Commission and the proposal for variable rates of interest has not been implemented in Pt. I of the Act.

The reform in Pt. I applies only to England and Wales. The provisions have been considered widely as technical but fairly uncontroversial. They implement substantially the Law Commission's recommendations for procedural reform relating to interest on judgment debts and arbitral awards. The provisions allow, in the case of judgments in a foreign currency, for the rate of interest payable on the judgment to be in the discretion of the court or arbitrator. Accordingly, for foreign-currency judgments, interest no longer requires to be awarded at the fixed statutory rate for judgments in sterling. The policy of this Part departs from the Law Commission proposals in one major respect. The Act does not provide for payment of interest on a variable basis. The main purpose of the reforms in Pt. I is to treat sterling and foreign-currency judgments on an equal basis. By s.35A(6) of the Supreme Court Act 1981 (c. 54) and s.69(1) of the County Courts Act 1984 (c. 28), the High Court and the county courts respectively have power to order that interest up to the date of judgment should be calculated at a variable rate, and it is relatively straightforward for a judge in these circumstances to assess the total interest payable up to judgment. This contrasts with the situation where the statutory rate of interest on judgments payable in sterling is fixed at the date of judgment, by reference to the Statutory Order then in force, and is not varied thereafter. The present difference in the rules on variable rates of interest before and after judgment in respect of sterling debts is to be retained and applied to foreign currency debts for the practical reasons of convenience of calculation and ease of execution, and to ensure equal treatment with sterling judgments. This latter aspect is outwith the scope of the present Act, although reform has been suggested to allow for variable rates of interest for sterling judgments.

Interest on judgment debts generally

1.—(1) In the Administration of Justice Act 1970, after section 44 (interest on judgment debts) there shall be inserted the following section—

"Interest on judgment debts expressed in currencies other than sterling
44A.—(1) Where a judgment is given for a sum expressed in a currency other than sterling and the judgment debt is one to which section 17 of the Judgments Act 1838 applies, the court may order that the interest rate applicable to the debt shall be such rate as the court thinks fit.

(2) Where the court makes such an order, section 17 of the Judgments Act 1838 shall have effect in relation to the judgment debt as if the rate specified in the order were substituted for the rate specified in that section."

(2) Subsection (1) above does not apply in relation to a judgment given before the commencement of this section.

GENERAL NOTE

This section empowers the High Court to order that a sum awarded by a judgment given by that court which is expressed in foreign currency should carry interest at such rate, determined as the court thinks fit, as is specified in the order. The court has discretion to set a certain fixed rate of interest to apply to the judgment debt. The rate specified in the order has effect instead of the statutory rate which would otherwise apply.

A weakness in s.1, and ss.2 and 3, is that they do not indicate the basis for the court to determine the applicable interest rate and this may affect practitioners in determining the size of any payments into court. However, the *prima facie* rule clearly applied in the exercise of that discretion is that interest should be awarded at the rate applicable to that currency (see *Shell Tankers (U.K.) v. Astro Comino Armadora S.A.*; *Pacific Colocotronis, The* [1981] 2 Lloyd's Rep. 40; cf. *Helmsing Schiffahrts GmbH v. Malta Drydocks Corp.* [1977] 2 Lloyd's Rep. 444. See also Law Com. No. 124, Pts. II and III, particularly at para. 2.33; *Dicey and Morris*, pp. 1583–1590; *Cheshire and North*, pp. 97–105, *Judgments in Foreign Currencies: Extension of the Miliangos Rule* [1979] M.L.R. 452, at pp. 456–457).

Subs. (1)

Section 17 of the Judgments Act 1838, as originally enacted, provided that: "... every judgment debt shall carry interest at the rate of four pounds per centum per annum from the time of entering up the judgment ... until the same be satisfied, and such interest may be levied under a writ of execution on such judgment". Under s.44 of the Administration of Justice Act 1970 (c. 31) the rate may, by order, be replaced by the rate specified in the order.

Subsection (1) inserts a new s.44A to make provision for interest on foreign-currency judgment debts. The policy of Pt. I is to allow for a fixed rate of interest to be awarded. However, subs. (1) makes no explicit reference to "such fixed rate of interest" and may appear ambiguous. It becomes clearer on analysis of s.17 of the Judgments Act 1838. Subsection (2) of the new s.44A of the Supreme Court Act 1981 provides that s.17 of the Judgments Act 1838 shall apply to the foreign-currency judgment as if the rate of interest ordered by the court were substituted for the rate specified in that section. The new s.44A substitutes for the rate fixed by order "such rate as the court decides" and, taken in the context of its substitution for a fixed rate, this rate is also to be considered as fixed. It would have been simpler for a precise provision to be inserted although there were concerns that this would cast doubt on earlier statutory provisions, none of which refer to a fixed rate of interest.

Subs. (2)

This is self-explanatory; s.1 applies only to foreign-currency judgments after commencement of this section.

Interest on county court judgment debts

2. In section 74 of the County Courts Act 1984 (interest on judgment debts etc.), after subsection (5) there shall be inserted the following subsection—

"(5A) The power conferred by subsection (1) includes power to make provision enabling a county court to order that the rate of interest applicable to a sum expressed in a currency other than sterling shall be such rate as the court thinks fit (instead of the rate otherwise applicable)."

GENERAL NOTE

This section amends s.74 of the County Courts Act 1984 so that provision can be made by order conferring a similar power on county courts to that in s.1. The same considerations, as under s.1, apply to the issues of a fixed rate of interest and the determination of the level of interest.

Interest on arbitral awards

3.—(1) In the Arbitration Act 1950, for section 20 (interest on awards) there shall be substituted the following section—

"Interest on awards

20.—(1) A sum directed to be paid by an award shall, unless the award otherwise directs, carry interest as from the date of the award.

(2) The rate of interest shall be—
  (a) the rate for judgment debts specified in section 17 of the Judgments Act 1838 at the date of the award; or
  (b) if the power under subsection (3) below is exercised, the rate specified in the award.

(3) Where the sum is expressed in a currency other than sterling, the award may specify such rate as the arbitrator or umpire thinks fit instead of the rate mentioned in subsection (2)(a) above."

(2) Subsection (1) above does not apply in relation to an award made before the commencement of this section.

General Note
This section amends the Arbitration Act 1950 (c. 27) in order to give a similar power to arbitrators as given to the High Court under s.1 and the same considerations apply.

Part I: consequential amendments

4.—(1) In section 24(1) of the Crown Proceedings Act 1947 (interest on debts etc.), after the word "interest)" there shall be inserted the words "and section 44A of the Administration of Justice Act 1970 (which enables the court to order an appropriate rate for a judgment debt expressed in a currency other than sterling)".

(2) In Schedule 11 to the Agricultural Holdings Act 1986, in paragraph 22 (interest on awards), for the words "same rate as a judgment debt" there shall be substituted the words "same rate as that specified in section 17 of the Judgments Act 1838 at the date of the award".

A corresponding amendment shall be deemed to have been made in paragraph 20B of Schedule 6 to the Agricultural Holdings Act 1948 in relation to any case to which it continues to apply.

(3) In section 10(3) of the Drug Trafficking Act 1994 (interest on sums unpaid under confiscation orders), for the words from "that" to the end there shall be substituted the words "the same rate as that specified in section 17 of the Judgments Act 1838 (interest on civil judgment debts)".

General Note
This section introduces consequential amendments required by Pt. I and it would have been simpler for these to have been placed in a separate schedule.

Subs. (1)
This provision ensures that s.1 applies to judgment debts in a foreign-currency due to or from the Crown. Schedule 2, para. 21 of the County Courts Act 1984 extended the provisions on interest on debts and damages under s.69 of that Act to judgments given in proceedings by or against the Crown in the county courts.

Subs. (2)
These amendments relate to arbitrations under each statute.

Subs. (3)
This is a curious provision in a statute amending private international law. The rationale for Pt. I lies in normal private international law actions in which judgment is given in foreign currency and where it is more appropriate, on grounds of justice to the plaintiff, to grant interest at the foreign rate. No similar justifications arise here and, in any event, neither s.4 of the Drug Trafficking Act 1994 which provides the criteria for assessment of the proceeds of drug trafficking or s.5 on the amount to be recovered under the confiscation order provide for orders in foreign currency, although, arguably, s.39 on external confiscation orders may be relevant.

PART II

VALIDITY OF MARRIAGES UNDER A LAW WHICH PERMITS POLYGAMY

General Note
The need for these reforms was identified by the Law Commission and the Scottish Law Commission in their joint report on *Private International Law: Polygamous Marriages—Capacity to*

Contract a Polygamous Marriage and Related Issues (Law Com. No. 146; Scot. Law Com. No. 96: Cmnd. 9595). The Report considered a number of issues pertinent to polygamous marriages and, in particular, the law relating to capacity to enter such marriages. A joint consultative document had previously been published on September 13, 1982 (Law Commission Working Paper No. 83; Scottish Law Commission Consultative Memorandum No. 56). This consultative document had considered four main issues:
  (a) the rules governing capacity to contract a polygamous marriage;
  (b) the continued existence in the law, generally, of the concept of the potentially polygamous marriage;
  (c) the choice of law rules relating in general to capacity to marry and in particular to enter into a polygamous marriage; and
  (d) the reform of the law of domicile.
The Report deals only with the first two issues. It was considered more appropriate to deal with the third issue as part of the choice of law rules on marriage generally (see Choice of Law Rules in Marriage, Working Paper No. 89; Consultative Memorandum No. 64 (1985); Fentiman (1986) 6 O.J.L.S. 353; see also the Convention on Celebration and Recognition of the Validity of Marriages (1978), Hague Conference of Private International Law). Reform of the law of domicile was also tackled separately, being reviewed by the Joint Report: *Private International Law: The Law of Domicile* (1987) (Law Com. No. 168 and Scot. Law Com. No. 107 (Cm. 200)). The treatment of these topics by the Law Commissions is indicative of the piecemeal reform of the rules in private international law for marriage (see for instance, the Matrimonial Proceedings (Polygamous Marriages) Act 1972 (c. 38) based on the report on Polygamous Marriages (1971), Law Com. No. 42). As Anton and Beaumont point out, "Legislators and judges in the United Kingdom have not found it easy to devise satisfactory solutions to private international law questions presented by polygamous or potentially polygamous marriages" (pp. 444–445). The reform produced in this Part is mainly limited to the first issue considered in the consultative document, that is to say the capacity of a person domiciled in England and Wales, and Scotland respectively, to enter a potentially polygamous marriage. Outwith the scope of the provisions in Pt. II are the issue of the effect of a second valid polygamous marriage (see below) and proposals to recognise the validity of Muslim marriages solemnised in a U.K. mosque without the need to attend a registry office.

It should be noted at this stage that the Report uses the expression "polygamous marriage" to signify not only an actually polygamous marriage (where either party has more than one spouse) but also a marriage which is potentially polygamous, in that although monogamous, it is celebrated in a form which permits either party to take an additional spouse. In most cases it will be the man who will have capacity to take another spouse and the principal reason is that Islamic law is polygynous, not polyandrous.

In effect, for England and Wales, Pt. II abolishes the distinctive treatment of a potentially polygamous marriage in the context of an English or Welsh domiciliary, in which case the marriage is either *de facto* monogamous or actually polygamous. Indeed, the Report, considering the concept of potentially polygamous marriages in England and Wales, observed that matrimonial relief (para. 3.3) is available, under s.47 of the Matrimonial Causes Act 1973 (c. 18) which abrogated the rule in *Hyde v. Hyde* (1866) L.R. 1 R&D. The Report (para. 3.5) considered whether there were circumstances in which the law distinguishes between monogamous marriages and potentially polygamous marriages. The only possibility was in the field of succession, but *Chaudhry v. Chaudhry* [1976] Fam. 148, suggested that there would in fact be equal treatment. The only difference lies in the possibility that the marriage will become polygamous. The problem then becomes twofold: (a) What is the validity of the second or subsequent marriage and (b) what remedy is open to the first wife (see General Note to s.5(1) below). The Report concluded on this point (para. 3.6) that English law appears to draw no distinction now between monogamous and potentially polygamous marriages as part of the movement in favour of recognising polygamous marriages in a pluralist society, and, accordingly, no legislative reform measures were required. The position in Scotland was noted to be less clear-cut and this shall be considered in fuller detail under the present law of Scotland below.

The Present Law

England and Wales
  The choice of law rules governing capacity to contract a polygamous marriage abroad fall within the choice of law rules relating to marriage generally. However, this does not apply should one of the parties be domiciled in England and Wales.
  In the case of a party domiciled in England or Wales there are internal rules on capacity to contract a polygamous marriage.

(a) For marriages celebrated on or before July 31, 1971, it is assumed that the common law provides that a person domiciled in England and Wales cannot validly contract a marriage abroad under a law which permits polygamy (the "lex loci celebrationis") (see Law Com. No. 42, para. 18 and *Hansard*, H.L., Vol. 331, cols. 1192–1193. See also Stone, *Capacity for Polygamy— Judicial Rectification of Legislative Error* [1983] Fam. Law 76, at p. 77).

(b) Marriages celebrated after July 31, 1971 are affected by the enactment of s.4 of the Matrimonial Proceedings (Polygamous Marriages) Act 1972 (c. 38), now embodied in s.11 of the Matrimonial Causes Act 1973, the relevant parts of which are as follows:
"A marriage celebrated after 31st July 1971 shall be void on the following grounds, that is to say ...
(b) that at the time of the marriage either party was already lawfully married; ...
(d) in the case of a polygamous marriage entered into outside England and Wales, that either party was at the time of the marriage domiciled in England and Wales. For the purposes of paragraph (d) of this subsection a marriage may be polygamous although at its inception neither party has any spouse additional to the other".

This section was considered in *Hussain v. Hussain* [1983] Fam. 26, which involved a marriage in Pakistan, the law of which permitted polygamy. At the time of the marriage, the husband was domiciled in England and the wife was domiciled in Pakistan. The wife subsequently petitioned for a decree of judicial separation and it was argued for the husband that this must be a potentially polygamous marriage, and accordingly void under s.11(d) of the 1973 Act. However, it was held that the husband did not lack capacity by reason of s.11(d) and the marriage was valid. Because a man domiciled in England lacks capacity to take more than one wife (by virtue of s.11(b) of the 1973 Act) and a wife is not allowed by Muslim law to have more than one husband, the marriage was not potentially polygamous such as to fall within s.11(d). The reasoning in this decision has been criticised (see Carter, *Classification of a Marriage as monogamous or polygamous: a point of statutory interpretation* 1982 BYBIL at p. 298), although the decision on policy grounds was welcomed as the consequences of an opposing decision would be serious.
"It would mean that all marriages contracted abroad by people domiciled in the country, in accordance with the local law would be void, if that law permitted polygamy in any form. The repercussions on the Muslim community alone in this country would be widespread and profound" (per the Court of Appeal in *Hussain v. Hussain* at pp. 32–33).

However, there are limitations on the scope of the decision in *Hussain v. Hussain* which can produce anomalous results with a knock-on effect on a range of practical consequences which flow from the validity of a marriage: succession, taxation, social security benefits, matrimonial relief, legitimacy, citizenship and immigration (see Pts. IV and VI of the Consultative Document). The decision is restricted to marriages entered into after July 31, 1971 by men domiciled in England and Wales. Most importantly, the distinction in treatment of women under the decision is clearly discriminatory. On the approach advocated in *Hussain*, s.11(d) would render void a marriage between a woman domiciled in England and Wales and a foreign domiciled man whose personal law allows him to have more than one wife (*cf. Radwan v. Radwan* (No. 2) [1973] Fam. 35). Accordingly, the principal recommendation made by the Report was for legislation to place beyond doubt the rules governing capacity to enter all polygamous marriages.

Scotland
It is unclear under Scots law what law governs the capacity of a person to enter into either a polygamous or potentially polygamous marriage abroad (see *Anton and Beaumont* pp. 448–449; Report at paras. 2.11–2.12). The Report stated that parties must be free by both their domicile and the *lex loci celebrationis* (para. 4.9). The law is undeveloped and although there exists dicta to the effect that a person domiciled in Scotland does not have capacity to enter into a potentially polygamous marriage abroad (per Lord Mackay, *obiter dictum* in *Lendrum v. Chakravarti* [1929] S.L.T. 96 at p. 99), in view of the Court of Appeal's decision in *Hussain*, and the potential injustice that could be caused, it is uncertain that a Scottish court would hold such a rule to be part of Scots law. The principal recommendation of the Report was that a Scots domiciliary should have capacity to marry under a law which permits polygamy. The Report considered that a married domiciled Scot cannot enter a second marriage and that it is likely to be the case that an unmarried domiciled Scot cannot enter a valid polygamous marriage abroad with a person who already has a spouse. The Report also confirmed that Scottish consultation was opposed to granting capacity to Scottish domiciliaries to enter actually polygamous marriages (at para. 4.9).

In Pt. III of the Report, the Law Commissions considered the concept of the potentially polygamous marriage in Scotland. Earlier dicta suggest a polygamous marriage (potential or actual) would not be recognised under Scots law (per Lord Brougham in *Warrender v. Warrender* (1835) 2 Sh. & MacL. 154, 201, but see *Polygamy—A New Approach* 1970 Jur. Rev. 135 and see also *Prawdziclazarska v. Prawdziclazarska* 1954 S.C. 98). There is no more recent authority in Scots law although influence may be derived from both the Matrimonial Proceedings

(Polygamous Marriages) Act 1972 (which provides that the Scottish courts are no longer precluded from granting matrimonial relief in relation to a marriage entered into under a law which permits polygamy, whether the marriage is potentially or actually polygamous, see s.2(3)) and the acceptance in English law that a change in domicile can, effectively, turn a potentially polygamous marriage into a monogamous marriage (*Ali v. Ali* [1968] P. 564). The Report considered it necessary to make provision that a marriage which is valid by the law of Scotland and which is only potentially polygamous (in the sense that, although entered into under a law permitting polygamy, neither spouse has in fact married someone else—a *de facto* monogamous marriage) has, so long as it remains monogamous, the same legal effects for all purposes of the law of Scotland as a marriage entered into under a law which does not permit polygamy.

The Report recommended that such a reform should have retrospective effect but should not attempt to regulate past effects. The rule would have no application if the husband took a second wife and this would be regulated by the existing law on the recognition of actually polygamous marriages. However, importantly, there is no Scottish authority on the effect of a second marriage, by the husband, on the first wife. This recommendation has been implemented substantially, along with the earlier proposal, in s.7 in Pt. II and the implications will be considered in the commentary to that section.

Reforms Introduced by Pt. II
Part II of the Act is relatively uncontroversial and recognised as sensible and overdue although the inelegant drafting may produce further anomalous results.

England and Wales
As stated above, Pt. II only introduces reform to one area of the treatment of polygamous marriages, namely the validity of a marriage entered into under a law which permits polygamy where either party is domiciled in England and Wales, and is based principally upon the Law Commissions' recommendations and draft clauses. Sections 5 and 6 must be read together as s.6 provides the rule in s.5 with retrospective effect and consequently requires to make further provision for the effect of subsequent marriages and also the effect on other ancillary issues prior to the commencement of this Part.

Scotland
The reform in s.7 makes similar provision under Scots law for potentially polygamous marriages, but extends this to confirm that potentially polygamous marriages will have all the consequences of marriage under Scots law. Given the concern of the Law Commissions (para. 2.15) that uncertainty in rules of law, particularly relative to status, is undesirable, it is surprising that s.7 has implemented the recommendation of the Commissions for the reform in respect of Scottish domiciliaries not to be declared to be retrospective. Further, there appears to be insufficient provision for subsequent marriage by a party to the potentially polygamous first marriage.

Validity in English law of potentially polygamous marriages

5.—(1) A marriage entered into outside England and Wales between parties neither of whom is already married is not void under the law of England and Wales on the ground that it is entered into under a law which permits polygamy and that either party is domiciled in England and Wales.

(2) This section does not affect the determination of the validity of a marriage by reference to the law of another country to the extent that it falls to be so determined in accordance with the rules of private international law.

GENERAL NOTE
This section applies only to England and Wales. This corrects the anomaly of the discriminatory treatment afforded to women domiciled in England and Wales as a result of *Hussain v. Hussain* [1983] Fam. 26. There was, however, no change proposed on the internal rule which does not allow an English or Welsh domiciliary to contract an actually polygamous marriage (at para. 4.7; Consultative Document at paras. 5.4–5.7).

Subs. (1)
This gives effect to the principal recommendation in the Report that a marriage entered into by a man or woman domiciled in England and Wales which is not actually polygamous should not be void by reason only of the fact that it is celebrated in polygamous form.

The reform introduced by this subsection is merely a partial change and in the case of an unmarried man and woman marrying abroad in a polygamous form, subs. 5(1) or subs. 5(1) in combination with the existing law ensures the marriage is now valid and will be treated, even though potentially polygamous, as a valid monogamous marriage. In effect, this eradicates the concept of potentially polygamous marriages in English law but does not purport to affect a second, valid polygamous marriage (see s.6 below).

This subsection has no application to marriages celebrated in England and Wales, as such marriages are not entered into under a law which permits polygamy.

An important omission from this provision is the consideration of the effect of an actually polygamous marriage on a prior marriage which has been validated under this provision (see also s.6(2) below). This problem arises from the interaction of the choice of law rule governing capacity generally and the internal rule for capacity of English and Welsh domiciliaries. The difficulty was already apparent as a result of *Hussain v. Hussain* (above). The problematic situation would arise if the husband, originally of English domicile, and having married in a country which permits polygamy, later acquires a domicile in a country which permits polygamy and remarries there. This has been further extended by this provision to the situation where the wife has English or Welsh domicile and the husband returns to the country of his domicile and remarries. This subsection makes no provision in respect of the second marriage but two important issues may arise: (a) the validity of the second or subsequent marriage, and (b) the availability of remedies to the first wife.

The Report found little authority as to the purported validity of the second marriage (para. 4.14, see *Nabi v. Heaton* [1981] 1 W.L.R. 1052 and *Att.-Gen. (Ceylon) v. Reid* [1965] A.C. 720), although it would appear that, given the modern attitude to polygamous marriages, such a marriage may be recognised under the normal rules of recognition of polygamous marriages (see *Cheshire and North*, pp. 621–626; Morris, pp. 174–179; *Sehda, Re* [1978] 3 All E.R. 385; *Shahnaz v. Rizwan* [1964] 2 All E.R. 993).

Regarding matrimonial relief for the first wife if the husband subsequently married again in polygamous form, the Law Commissions believed (para. 4.17, following *Quoraishi v. Quoraishi* [1985] F.L.R. 780) that the wife could obtain a divorce on the basis of the Matrimonial Causes Act 1973, s.47 (para. 2.7).

This would not necessarily apply if the wife is domiciled in England or Wales and the husband is domiciled in a country which permits polygamy. The wording here is that "either party is domiciled in England ..." and the clause applies equally if only the wife is domiciled in England (*cf. Quoraishi v. Quoraishi* above).

The issue of matrimonial relief is obviously linked to the issue of the validity of the subsequent marriage and although the general policy is to avoid limping marriages, neither did the Report recommend nor has this section inserted a provision to make such a marriage void, in light of wider policy on polygamous marriages. However, as Lord Coleraine suggested, "It seems entirely anomalous that a monogamous marriage could exist unchanged when there is a valid polygamous marriage to which one of the parties to the monogamous marriage is also a party" (p. 32 of Minutes of Evidence taken before the Special Public Bill Committee, HL, January 18, 1995, HMSO HL Paper 36).

The first wife may have grounds for seeking a divorce under the Matrimonial Causes Act 1973. It would appear to be difficult for the first wife to petition for divorce on the grounds of adultery (para. 4.16) since intercourse has not taken place between parties who are not married (see *Onobrauche v. Onobrauche* (1978) 122 SJ 210 and also because of the husband's foreign domicile, *Att.-Gen. (Ceylon) v. Reid* [1965] A.C. 720). It is also uncertain that the taking of a second wife by the husband would necessarily constitute unreasonable behaviour on his part under s.1(2)(b) or (c) of the 1973 Act (see the Report, para. 4.17 and *Quoraishi v. Quoraishi*; Lipstein, 1983 Journal de droit international *Clunet* 807, 809).

This subsection could have been improved by stating that it is without prejudice to the rights of either party under the 1973 Act, but, surprisingly, the Report concluded that there were no difficulties in practice, and, accordingly subs. 5(1) does not deal with the second marriage at all.

Subs. (2)

This provides that subs. (1) relates to the internal law of England and Wales. Accordingly, subs. (1) does not apply where, under the relevant choice of law rule, the law of another country is applied for the purpose of determining the validity of a marriage (see paras. 1.5 and 2.1–2.3 of the Report). This corresponds to s.14(1) of the Matrimonial Causes Act 1973.

Application of section 5 to prior marriages

6.—(1) Section 5 above shall be deemed to apply, and always to have applied, to any marriage entered into before commencement which is not excluded by subsection (2) or (3) below.

(2) That section does not apply to a marriage a party to which has (before commencement) entered into a later marriage which either—

(a) is valid apart from this section but would be void if section 5 above applied to the earlier marriage; or

(b) is valid by virtue of this section.

(3) That section does not apply to a marriage which has been annulled before commencement, whether by a decree granted in England and Wales or by an annulment obtained elsewhere and recognised in England and Wales at commencement.

(4) An annulment of a marriage resulting from legal proceedings begun before commencement shall be treated for the purposes of subsection (3) above as having taken effect before that time.

(5) For the purposes of subsections (3) and (4) above a marriage which has been declared to be invalid by a court of competent jurisdiction in any proceedings concerning either the validity of the marriage or any right dependent on its validity shall be treated as having been annulled.

(6) Nothing in section 5 above, in its application to marriages entered into before commencement—

(a) gives or affects any entitlement to an interest—

(i) under the will or codicil of, or on the intestacy of, a person who died before commencement; or

(ii) under a settlement or other disposition of property made before that time (otherwise than by will or codicil);

(b) gives or affects any entitlement to a benefit, allowance, pension or other payment—

(i) payable before, or in respect of a period before, commencement; or

(ii) payable in respect of the death of a person before that time;

(c) affects tax in respect of a period or event before commencement; or

(d) affects the succession to any dignity or title of honour.

(7) In this section "commencement" means the commencement of this Part.

GENERAL NOTE

This section deals with the retrospective effect of the rule in s.5 together with the consideration of the effect of the application of s.5 to prior marriages and ancillary issues. A further issue which has not been addressed by this provision is the validity of the first marriage in the interim period prior to one of the parties entering a subsequent marriage. This may have important implications, particularly for legitimacy of children and succession rights but no such protections were considered by the Report or implemented in this subsection.

Subs. (1)

This implements the recommendation in para. 2.33(b) of the Report and extends the rule laid down by s.5(1) to marriages celebrated before the date on which this Part comes into force and deems it always to have applied to such marriages. This does not affect marriages that are valid apart from the Act. This provision may not be beneficial to parties who had taken legal advice that their marriage was invalid, but it was considered that this class of people was not significant in number. In any event, there are saving provisions for such parties if they remarried under subs. (2), and also possibly under the Matrimonial Causes Act 1973 (see s.5(1) above).

Subs. (2)

This essentially implements, in modified form, the recommendation in para. 2.33(d) of the Report and attempts to make provision for subsequent marriages prior to commencement (*cf.* s.5(1)). It governs the case in which a party has entered, in a polygamous form of ceremony, into a marriage which was then in fact monogamous but which is void under the present law, and has subsequently entered into a marriage with some other person, both marriages having been celebrated before the commencement of the Act. A marriage which falls outside the scope of *Hussain v. Hussain* (above) (one entered into on or before July 31, 1971 by a man or woman domiciled in England or Wales or at any time before the commencement date by a woman so domiciled in the case of a marriage to a man the law of whose domicile permits him to have more than one wife) should not be validated if either party to the marriage has subsequently entered into another marriage with a different partner which would be rendered invalid by the retrospective validation of the first marriage.

Paragraph (a) applies where the later marriage is valid under the present law and, in that case, in general, the earlier marriage is not to be validated by s.5(1). Exceptionally, the earlier marriage may be validated if the later marriage was to be recognised as valid irrespective of the earlier marriage. This could create uncertainty, as it is unclear in any event which marriages would be void as a result of the application of s.5 and creates the same status problem for first wives in pre-commencement potentially polygamous marriages.

Paragraph (b) makes provision for the situation in which, prior to commencement, a party has entered into two marriages, both in polygamous form and both void under the present law on that ground only. The effect of this subsection and subs. 6(1) is to validate only the later marriage.

Subs. (3)
This gives effect to the recommendation in para. 2.33(c) of the Report that the changes implemented in s.5(1) should not validate marriages which have been annulled before commencement.

Subs. (6)
This provides for the preservation of existing rights in respect of property and certain other matters arising in the context of marriages which were celebrated before commencement and gives effect to the recommendation in para. 2.33(e) of the Report. This subsection has no effect in relation to a marriage whose validity is not dependent upon s.5(1).

Validity and effect in Scots law of potentially polygamous marriages

7.—(1) A person domiciled in Scotland does not lack capacity to enter into a marriage by reason only that the marriage is entered into under a law which permits polygamy.

(2) For the avoidance of doubt, a marriage valid by the law of Scotland and entered into—

(a) under a law which permits polygamy; and

(b) at a time when neither party to the marriage is already married,

has, so long as neither party marries a second spouse during the subsistence of the marriage, the same effects for all purposes of the law of Scotland as a marriage entered into under a law which does not permit polygamy.

GENERAL NOTE
This section applies only to Scotland.

Subs. (1)
This subsection makes provision corresponding to s.5 in relation to the law of Scotland and provides that a person domiciled in Scotland is not to be held to lack capacity to enter into marriage by reason only that the marriage is entered into under a law which permits polygamy. This implements the recommendations in para. 2.34 of the Report. It will apply only to unmarried persons, as a married person domiciled in Scotland would not have capacity to marry and it will only apply to marriages outside the U.K.

The major difference between this provision and the English equivalent under ss.5 and 6 is that the Scottish provision is not expressly retrospective. The provision is not intended to be retrospective as it was considered by the Report that there was no need, as Scots law was undeveloped in this regard. On the other hand it was considered "most unlikely that the courts now in Scotland would suddenly create an incapacity for potential polygamy in the light of *Hussain* and the developments in England". Strangely this provision was considered sufficient to clarify the law although it was accepted that the intention was not to prejudice the validity of existing marriages (*per* Dr Eric Clive, Scottish Law Commission, January 19, 1995, Special Public Bill Committee, p. 45; see Report at para. 2.16). The drafting here is ambiguous (although the term adopted "does" has greater declaratory effect than the term "shall" as used in the Report draft bill) and creates uncertainty as to their status for parties who entered potentially polygamous marriages prior to commencement. In addition to the concerns about the effect of subsequent marriages both after and prior to commencement, this provision lacks the benefits of the retrospective effect of the equivalent provisions for England and Wales.

Subs. (2)
This provision extends the scope of subs. (1) and provides for the effects of a potentially polygamous marriage under Scots law, the present law being unclear and unsatisfactory in this

regard. It implements para. 3.7 of the Report and effectively states that potentially polygamous marriages which are *de facto* monogamous shall be regarded as effective marriages for all purposes including divorce, aliment, succession and social security. Typical of the partial approach to polygamous marriage reform, the subsection leaves many questions unanswered. The subsection does not prevent a second, actually polygamous, marriage but neither indicates whether, for instance, it would be adultery for a man validly married in polygamous form to have intercourse with a second wife to whom he was also validly married. (Social security benefits are treated differently for actually polygamous marriages: see the Social Security Act 1975, s.162(b) and S.I. 1975 No. 561.)

The insertion of the term "valid by the law of Scotland" is curious and appears to add nothing to the substantive provision. Similar comments as those in subs. (1) apply to the failure to make this provision retrospective in terms of the effect this may have on status, although, similar to s.6(6), this is appropriate for other purposes.

Part II: supplemental

8.—(1) Nothing in this Part affects any law or custom relating to the marriage of members of the Royal Family.

(2) The enactments specified in the Schedule to this Act (which contains consequential amendments and amendments removing unnecessary references to potentially polygamous marriages) are amended in accordance with that Schedule.

(3) Nothing in that Schedule affects either the generality of any enactment empowering the making of subordinate legislation or any such legislation made before the commencement of this Part.

GENERAL NOTE

This ensures that the reforms in Pt. II are not to affect any rule or custom in relation to the marriage of members of the Royal Family, and introduces the minor and consequential amendments to other legislation made by the Schedule to the Act. Those amendments have the same extent as the enactments being amended.

PART III

CHOICE OF LAW IN TORT AND DELICT

GENERAL NOTE

The reforms in Pt. III originate from the joint Report of the Law Commission and the Scottish Law Commission, *Private International Law: Choice of Law in Tort and Delict* (Law Com. No. 193: Scot. Law Com. No. 129). The provisions in Pt. III although based principally on the Report's recommendations and draft Bill, contain important modifications in the legislative scheme for choice of law rules in tort and delict and the differences shall be outlined where appropriate. This is important given Lord Wilberforce's view that "it is difficult to separate principle from detail" in this subject. Lord Wilberforce was a particularly vehement opponent of statutory reform of these choice of law rules, considering that this subject was better left to the flexibility of the common law. Indeed, Pt. III has been recognised as the most controversial aspect of the Act and this is confirmed in the varying evidence given to the Special Public Bill Committee.

Present Law

(See *Morris*, pp. 280–296; *Cheshire and North*, pp. 533–549; *Dicey and Morris*, pp. 1480–1544; *Anton and Beaumont*, pp. 396–414.)

In an action for a tort or delict committed abroad, the approach adopted by both the Scottish and the English courts (and the courts of Northern Ireland) has placed significant emphasis upon the application of the *lex fori* (law of the forum) in order to determine the rights and liabilities of the parties. However, the existing differences in approach merit separate examination.

England and Wales and Northern Ireland

The applicable choice of law rule is based on a passage from the judgment of Willes J. in *Phillips v. Eyre* (1870) L.R. 6 Q.B. 1 at pp. 28–29:

> "As a general rule, in order to found a suit in England for a wrong alleged to have been committed abroad, two conditions must be fulfilled. First, the wrong must be of such a character that it would have been actionable if committed in England ... Secondly, the act must not have been justifiable by the place where it was done."

It appears that the rights and liabilities of the parties in an action in England and Wales, or in Northern Ireland, on a foreign tort are determined by the internal law of the *lex fori*. (This is the first branch of the rule and is derived from *The Halley* (1868) L.R. 2 P.C. 193, as approved by the House of Lords in *Boys v. Chaplin* [1971] A.C. 356.) The application of the *lex fori* is subject to the qualification that the action will succeed only to the extent that civil liability also exists, as between the same parties, under the *lex loci delicti* (see Working Paper No. 97, 1984, pp. 20–26. The earlier case of *Machado v. Fontes* [1897] 2 Q.B. 231, held that criminal liability under the *lex loci delicti* was sufficient, but this was overruled by a majority in *Boys v. Chaplin*; *per* Lord Hodson at p. 377, Lord Guest at p. 381 and Lord Wilberforce at pp. 388–389).

It is generally accepted that the rule in *Phillips v. Eyre* has been modified by the House of Lords in *Boys v. Chaplin* (see, for example, *McGregor* (1970) 33 M.L.R. 1, *Karsten* [1951] A.C. 356). The crucial issue in that case concerned whether damages should be assessed according to English or Maltese law. It is difficult to extract any *ratio* from the case, although it is assumed that the double actionability rule is to be applied with flexibility, and that the rule may be departed from under special circumstances. Rule 203(2) of Dicey and Morris is based on the judgments of Lords Hodson and Wilberforce and modelled on the American Restatement 2nd, s.145. It provides: But a particular issue between the parties may be governed by the law of the country which, with respect to that issue, has the most significant relationship with the occurrence and the parties.

Lords Guest and Donavon in *Boys v. Chaplin* applied English law by classifying the issue as procedural, and Lord Pearson applied English law as the substantive law on the basis that the forum plays the substantive role. Lord Hodson applied English law on the basis of a proper law-type exception to the general rule of Willes J. and Lord Wilberforce accepted the normal rule but applied English law due to the desirability of making the rule flexible enough to "take account of the varying interests and considerations of policy which may arise when one or more foreign elements are present" (p. 910. Both the latter approaches have elements of proper law thinking and are influenced by the American Restatement 2nd).

Despite the uncertainty as to the nature and extent of the exception provided for by *Boys v. Chaplin*, Lord Wilberforce's judgment has been regarded as authoritative and has been followed in subsequent cases (see *Church of Scientology of California v. Commissioner of Metropolitan Police* (1976) 120 S.J. 690, *Coupland v. Arabian Gulf Oil Co.* [1983] 1 W.L.R. 1136, *Armagas v. Mundogas S.A.* [1986] A.C. 717, *Johnson v. Coventry Churchill International* [1992] 3 All E.R. 14), allowing for a limited proper law flexible exception to the general rule (to apply the law of the country with which the occurrence and the parties had the most significant relationship). This is not necessarily an accurate reflection of the position adopted by Lord Wilberforce and many questions remain unanswered as to the scope of this exceptional departure from the general rule.

On the basis that the rule in *Phillips v. Eyre* is accepted as the choice of law rule, a key issue involves the effect of the requirement of double actionability on the determination of which substantive law is to apply. Under English private international law, the double actionability rule appeared in all cases (even with the use of the flexible exception) to be predicated on the application of the *lex fori*, as accepted by the findings of the Working Party and Dicey and Morris. The *lex loci delicti* apparently played the more subsidiary role, in that it acquired actionability by the *lex loci delicti* only and thereafter the issue was determined by the *lex fori* (*cf.* the opinions in *Boys v. Chaplin* of Lords Pearson and Wilberforce with Lords Guest and Hodge. Indeed on the basis that the *lex fori* is the substantive law under the double actionability rule, the debate in *Boys v. Chaplin* seems unnecessary).

However, the scope of the exception to the general rule was reconsidered by the Privy Council decision in *Red Sea Insurance Co. v. Bouygues SA* [1994] 3 All E.R. 749 ("*Red Sea*"). This both confirmed and extended the approach developed by Lord Wilberforce in *Boys v. Chaplin* and has arguably made significant changes to the structure of the law. It raised directly the question whether a claimant might succeed on a claim founded on a foreign tort in circumstances in which the wrong is actionable by the *lex loci* but not under the *lex fori*. The significance of the *Red Sea* decision is that it decided that the flexible exception apparently grafted on to the double actionability test by *Boys v. Chaplin* operates as an exception to both limbs of that test (see Rodger, *Bouygues and Scottish Choice of Law Rules in Delict, Reconsidering McElroy v. McAllister* 1995 SLPQ 58; Blaikie, *Foreign Torts and Choice of Law Flexibility* 1995 S.L.T. 23 and Briggs, *The Halley: Holed but still afloat* [1995] L.Q.R. 18). Prior to *Red Sea*, there was authority only in favour of its operation as an exception to the second limb: *Johnson v. Coventry Churchill International*, "[T]o limit the rule so as to enable an English court to apply English law would be in conflict with the degree of flexibility envisaged by Lord Wilberforce" (*per* Lord Slynn at p. 762). The Privy Council provided that the departure from the general rule would be warranted to avoid injustice (a) with regard to a particular issue, (b) which should be governed by the law of the country which, with respect to that issue, had the most significant relationship with the occurrence and the issue. Further extending *Boys v. Chaplin*, the Privy Council held that the exception may in rare cases apply to the whole case and not merely a particular issue. In *Red Sea*, the Privy Council applied the *lex loci delicti* as the substantive applicable law.

Further issues require to be outlined at this stage. First, when a tort is committed in England, Wales or Northern Ireland, the courts will apply the law of the forum to any claim arising (see *Szalatnay-Stacho v. Fink* [1947] K.B. 1). It is uncertain whether the flexibility introduced by *Boys v. Chaplin*, even as extended by *Red Sea*, would allow the displacement of the *lex fori* in these circumstances. (Part III does not make separate provision for U.K. torts/delicts; see particularly s.9.) Related is the determination of the place of a tort, in order to identify the law of the place of a tort. In the case where different elements or facts of the tort occur in two or more countries, the question is more difficult than should they occur in one country. The problem has been considered in cases involving application for leave to serve the writ out of the jurisdiction, and although of doubtful authority on choice of law rules, the solution has been to apply the fictional test of ascertaining where in substance the cause of action arose (see *Metall und Rohstoff AG v. Donaldson Lufkin and Jenrette Inc.* [1990] 1 Q.B. 391). Although Pt. III concerns the choice of law rules, rules on jurisdiction influence the cases which are brought before the courts. For torts committed abroad, the *lex loci* is likely to be the *forum conveniens* (*Cordoba Shipping Co. v. National State Bank, Elizabeth, New Jersey; Albaforth, The* [1984] 2 Lloyd's Rep. 91) and the discretionary doctrine of *forum non conveniens* may be applied (see Lord Goff in *Spiliada Maritime Corp. v. Cansulex; Spiliada, The* [1987] A.C. 460, at pp. 474–484). However, this may not be exercised in cases, for example, under the Brussels Convention on Jurisdiction and Enforcement of Judgments 1968 (see *Harrod's (Buenos Aires), Re* [1991] 4 All E.R. 334 (C.A.) and also Fentiman, *Jurisdiction, Discretion and the Brussels Convention* 26 Cornell Intl. LJ 59, at pp. 69–72 (1993)).

Scotland

The same general rule as to double actionability prevails in Scotland although it appears even more rigid in its application, see *McElroy v. McAllister* (1949 S.C. 110) and also *Goodman v. L. & N.W. Railway Co.* (1877) 14 S.L.R. 449. Lord Thomson stated in *McElroy v. McAllister* that "actionability under the *lex loci delicti* seems to me, in principle, a *sine qua non*" (p. 118). The cases of *Naftalin v. LMS Railway* 1933 S.C. 259 and the subsequent seven judge decision in *McElroy v. McAllister*, have firmly established the rule in Scotland as not only requiring actionability in the abstract but that the specific *jus actionis* must be available both under Scots law (*lex fori*) and the *lex loci delicti* (see *James Burrough Distillers v. Speymalt Whisky Distributors* 1989 S.L.T. 561). The action will only succeed to the extent that the specific heads of damage sought are recoverable under both systems of law. Accordingly, less emphasis is given to the *lex fori* as the applicable substantive law and the predominant role will be given to the *lex loci delicti* in determining the rights of the parties, subject to the availability of the same type of claim under the *lex fori* (see Working Paper No. 84, 1984, at p. 33).

Further, the decisions in *Boys v. Chaplin* and *Red Sea* and the exceptions to the general rule embodied therein have uncertain status in Scots law. Until the strict double actionability rule in *McElroy v. McAllister* is overturned by more than seven judges in the Court of Session or the House of Lords in a Scottish appeal, it remains good law.

The comments raised above regarding delicts/torts committed within the forum and the place of the delict/tort have equal validity.

Defects in the present law and the need for reform

There are three principal defects identified in the present law although this is a particularly controversial issue (see Pt. III of the Consultation Paper, paras. 2.6–2.11 of the Report and Lord Mackay of Clashfern at pp. 4–5, Special Public Bill Committee, January 16, 1995; see also Thomson, *Delictual Liability in Scottish Private International Law* (1976) 25 ICLQ 873; Carter, *Torts in English Private International Law* (1981) 52 BYBIL 9). Generally, however, particularly in the field of torts/delicts which nowadays occur with greater frequency across national frontiers, the private international law of tort/delict "can no longer rest content with solutions designed for nineteenth-century conditions" (*Morris* p. 277).

(1) The law is anomalous and parochial and it is out of step with almost every other area of private international law which allow for the exclusive application of an appropriate foreign law rather than concurrent application with the *lex fori*.

"A general rule such as the rule of 'double actionability', which imposes the use of the law of the forum as an additional limitation to an action is parochial in appearance in that it presupposes that it is inherently just for the rules of the English or Scottish domestic law of tort or delict to be indiscriminately applied regardless of the foreign elements of the relevant facts" (*per* Lord Mackay at p. 4 of the Special Public Bill Committee).

The argument is that the use of the *lex fori* is unprincipled and contrary to the ethos of private international law (excepting matters of procedure and subject to overriding public policy considerations).

Those in favour of retaining the common law rules and a role for the *lex fori* would argue that this is required to prevent courts from applying foreign laws which have radically different purposes from that of the forum (see for instance Lord Lester of Herne Hill, memorandum, pp. 39–40, Special Public Bill Committee, above). A related argument is that the bounds of involuntary obligations under tort/delict have a public interest element and that, accordingly, it is not inappropriate for the *lex fori* to be incorporated as part of the choice of law rule. The crux of the opposition to legislative reform is the concern that U.K. courts should not provide remedies for foreign torts/delicts unknown to the law of the forum. In any event, the rules on jurisdiction, particularly the doctrine of *forum non conveniens*, may eliminate cases where application of the *lex fori* is inappropriate at the jurisdiction stage.

However, a related argument in favour of statutory reform is that judgments of foreign courts applying a foreign law of tort/delict may in any case be applied indirectly under various enforcement schemes (for example, the Brussels and Lugano Conventions, the Administration of Justice Act 1920 (c. 81), the Foreign Judgments (Reciprocal Enforcement) Act 1933 (c. 13)).

(2) The second defect in the present rule on double actionability is that it can, at least in theory, lead to injustice. It is unfair to plaintiffs/pursuers as defendants/defenders may take advantage of any defence available under either law. This is exemplified by *McAllister v. McElroy* and although there is little reported injustice, this may be the result of cases settling on the basis of the present law. It is arguable that this possibility of injustice is remote under English rules which provide for flexible exceptions to the general rule, but there is certainly no doubt in Scotland as to the need for reform of the double actionability rule.

(3) The present law is uncertain. The *Red Sea* decision extended the exception to the rule on double actionability derived from *Boys v. Chaplin* in two significant ways, namely to be applicable to the first limb of the rule in *Phillips v. Eyre* and also to be applicable to the whole case. However, Lord Slynn accepted in *Red Sea* that many questions needed to be resolved as to the ambit of the exception and that the decision in *Red Sea* only answered two of these. Accordingly, the uncertainty for litigants is unsatisfactory, particularly as to whether the exception can be used to apply a third law other than the *lex fori* or *lex loci*. There is also doubt as to the authority in *Boys v. Chaplin* for the decision in *Red Sea*. Further, the status of the exceptions is uncertain in Scotland and would require litigation in the House of Lords.

The present law is not easily accessible for the fictional lawyer in Wigan and Inverness (see Mr Justice Brooke, Evidence to the Special Public Bill Committee, pp. 9–17). The need for certainty is important both before an event happens, particularly for insurance purposes, and after the event in order to avoid the expense and delay of litigation. The exceptions provided are preferable to a strict double actionability rule but there are suggestions of rule-selection and it is more appropriate to adopt traditional jurisdiction-selecting rules. It is also argued that *Red Sea* ensures the necessary flexibility in the law and that statutory reform is not required, although little guidance is given as to the exercise of the discretion. The desired balance between certainty and flexibility is a recurrent theme in the provisions of Pt. III.

The reformed choice of law rule

Part III enacts a choice of law regime similar to that approved by the Law Commissions' Report, although there are major modifications which will be highlighted. In 1984, the Commissions published a Consultation Paper on *Private International Law; Choice of Law in Tort and Delict* (Working Paper No. 87, Consultative Memorandum No. 62). Part IV of the Paper canvassed four basic options for reform of the choice of law rules in tort and delict: to apply (1) the law of the forum; (2) various kinds of rule-selection approach, selecting the applicable law on the basis of the particular issue in question in the light of the interests of the various countries whose laws fell to be considered; (3) the law of the place of the wrong, the *lex loci delicti*, with a proper law (*i.e.* the law of the place with the closest and most real connection) exception: Model 1; (4) the proper law with presumptions in certain types of case: Model 2. Options (1) and (2) were rejected by the Consultation Paper.

The two models produced were differing attempts to strike the balance between certainty and predictability with the need for flexibility to allow justice to be done in the individual case. The Law Commissions recommended the adoption of Model 1, with minor modifications, to combine the certainty of a general rule, that the *lex loci delicti* should apply, with the flexibility of a proper law exception, and this has been substantially adopted in the provisions of Pt. III (see Carter *Choice of Law in Tort and Delict* 1991 (107) L.Q.R. 405; North, *Choice of Law Revised* 1991 42 NILQ 183; Sood, *Torts Abroad: Double Actionability Rule* 1992 89 WJLS 23). The principal aims of the reforms introduced are to achieve flexibility without undue uncertainty and to end the automatic application of the *lex fori* and the double actionability rule. In the drafting of the provisions we can see the difficulties inherent in adopting a rule and exception approach, particularly the problems of definition and specificity when trying to balance two conflicting aims in statutory reform.

Part III is innovative in providing for one applicable law to be used for determining issues relating to tort or delict (however, see s.12(1) below which allows for segregation of issues) in place of the existing common law rule of double actionability. The general rule is that the applicable law is that of the country where the events constituting the delict occurred—the *lex loci delicti*. This should promote uniformity and discourage forum-shopping and is likely to accord with any expectations the parties may have. Guidelines are provided in s.11 for determining the *lex loci delicti* and this is generally the place where the plaintiff/pursuer was injured. This may reduce the problems involved in the difficult concept of "the place of the tort/delict".

The Law Commissions acknowledged that in certain cases the application of this law would be inappropriate (para. 3.3) and s.12 of Pt. III provides for an exceptional rule of displacement of the *prima facie* applicable law in the interests of flexibility and justice. The difference between this rule and exception reform and Model 2, the proper law approach, will be dependent upon the interpretation placed upon the threshold criteria in s.12, and the use of the term "substantial" in s.12 should strike the balance in favour of certainty and application of the *lex loci delicti* in most cases.

By a combination of ss.9 and 11, the courts of the U.K. may be required to give remedies on the basis of a foreign law which may be an unknown form of tort/delict under the law of the forum (this is partly dependent upon the forum's characterisation of issues as tortious/delictual under s.9. Under the Brussels Convention, cf. *Kalfelis v. Bankhaus Schröder, Münchmeyer, Hengst & Co.* [1988] E.C.R. 5565 and *Kleinwort Benson v. City of Glasgow District Council* [1994] 4 All E.R. 865). This is the most controversial aspect of the reforms introduced, and Lord Wilberforce in particular, was opposed to English courts adjudicating upon matters which were not wrongs according to the law of England (particularly foreign laws of privacy. See Proceedings of the Special Public Bill Committee, p. 8, January 16, 1995). In any event, as foreign judgments may be enforced, subject to public policy, this reform may be viewed as encouraging litigation directly in the U.K. fora. Further, the applicable law will generally be that law where the effects are produced, even for those who carry out activities in the U.K. and in compliance with the relevant domestic laws. This has been criticised although it is not inappropriate to have recourse to the law of the country where the effects are produced, as a case involving foreign elements provides the rationale for invoking the rules on private international law, again subject to public policy in s.14. (This is relevant in examples of foreign investors' claims against a U.K. auditor (although s.11(2)(c) may be applicable), international product liability, unfair competition and "nuisance" or environmental damages claims.) Potential liability under foreign law should accordingly be considered, particularly as the Act makes no distinction between wholly foreign torts/delicts, and torts/delicts with some elements in the U.K.

A final point is that, although the Act attempts to reduce the uncertainties in the application of the flexible exception at common law, the wording of ss.11 and 12 contains both inconsistencies and various terms which are open to judicial interpretation. An important procedural point is that Pt. III does not enact an obligatory choice of law scheme. It remains open to the parties to agree to apply the law of the forum.

Particular torts, delicts and issues

There is no special provision for U.K. torts for which the general rules apply equally (s.9(6)). The application of the new rules to defamation claims was considered particularly controversial and these have been excluded from the ambit of Pt. III (s.13). The operation of the doctrine of *renvoi* has been excluded but provision is made for the segregation of issues under the rule of displacement of the general rule (s.9(5)). However, Pt. III makes no specific provision for particular issues referred to in the Report (paras. 3.34–3.54; see s.12(1) below). Neither the Report nor Pt. III makes provision for restitutionary/unjustified enrichment claims and this may prove problematic, particularly under s.9(2) below.

Purpose of Part III

9.—(1) The rules in this Part apply for choosing the law (in this Part referred to as "the applicable law") to be used for determining issues relating to tort or (for the purposes of the law of Scotland) delict.

(2) The characterisation for the purposes of private international law of issues arising in a claim as issues relating to tort or delict is a matter for the courts of the forum.

(3) The rules in this Part do not apply in relation to issues arising in any claim excluded from the operation of this Part by section 13 below.

(4) The applicable law shall be used for determining the issues arising in a claim, including in particular the question whether an actionable tort or delict has occurred.

(5) The applicable law to be used for determining the issues arising in a claim shall exclude any choice of law rules forming part of the law of the country or countries concerned.

(6) For the avoidance of doubt (and without prejudice to the operation of section 14 below) this Part applies in relation to events occurring in the forum as it applies in relation to events occurring in any other country.

(7) In this Part as it extends to any country within the United Kingdom, "the forum" means England and Wales, Scotland or Northern Ireland, as the case may be.

(8) In this Part "delict" includes quasi-delict.

GENERAL NOTE

This introduces the concept of "the applicable law" which is to govern the determination of issues characterised as relating to tort (in England and Wales and Northern Ireland) or delict (in Scotland). The choice of law rules in Pt. III are to be applied in determining what is the applicable law.

Subs. (2)

This provides that characterisation (or classification) of an issue as tortious or delictual is a matter for the forum, and the method of dealing with this will be of central importance to the reforms introduced in this Part. The Commissions' draft Bill annexed to the Report was clearer and provided that the principles of classification were to be applied, notwithstanding that the matter is not actionable as a tort/delict under the law which would have been applied by the forum, apart from the provisions of the Bill and any rules of private international law. This was drafted to prevent the first branch of *Phillips v. Eyre* resurfacing as a rule of characterisation. The question remains whether this subsection has continued the partial application of the old rule by adapting the choice of law rule to become a rule of characterisation. It is possible that the courts will adopt a "half-way house" approach by characterising as issues relating to tort or delict for private international law purposes if there are sufficient similarities with claims available under the *lex fori* (see *Bonacina, Re* [1912] 2 Ch. 394). This is both a difficult task and contrary to the intention behind the reforms and it is hoped that the difficult process of characterisation will be carried out without reference to the *lex fori* by reference to the term "for the purposes of private international law". Although this would allow claims for unknown torts/delicts such as unfair competition and privacy, and this is a wide change of policy, it is an inevitable consequence of abolishing the rule in the Halley. However, public policy under s.14(3)(a)(i) may still have an important residual role in this regard.

It is unclear how enrichment claims will fall to be dealt with by the courts. The developing and under-developed area of the law of unjustified enrichment to use the normal European (and increasingly now Scots) term, or restitution, as it is more commonly called in England, is now seen as a separate area of the law of obligations, distinct from both contract and delict (see for instance, Birks, *Introduction to the Law of Restitution*, Oxford, 1985; Burrows, *The Law of Restitution*, Butterworth; Stewart, *The Law of Restitution in Scotland*, W. Green/Sweet and Maxwell, 1992, Supplement 1995). Although the law of unjustified enrichment or restitution was at one time seen as being based on a theory of implied contract ("quasi-contract") it seems clear that certainly today it cannot be covered by a scheme of choice of law rules designed for either contract or delict. Accordingly, neither the choice of law rules in the Contracts (Applicable Law) Act 1990 nor the rules in this Part of the Act apply. The choice of law rules applicable to enrichment claims are therefore common law rules. It is, as yet, a matter of considerable debate what they are and should be. It has been suggested on the one hand (Blaikie, *Unjust Enrichment and the Conflict of Laws* 1984 JR 112 at p. 125) that the appropriate rule is the proper law of the obligation to transfer the enrichment. (The issue concerning, for example, a question of contribution between two wrongdoers is particularly relevant under s.12 which allows for depecage.) On the other hand it has been suggested (Stewart, *The Law of Restitution in Scotland* at p. 211) that the appropriate rule is the *lex loci condictionis* (see also Dicey and Morris, rule 170(2) and generally, Bird, *Choice of Law* in Rose Ed., *Characterisation and the Conflict of Laws*, Mansfield Press, 1995). Two specialised aspects of the law of unjustified enrichment raise especially difficult problems. Where a legal system holds that there are situations where an enrichment should be transferred to someone even though that enrichment was not at the expense (or fully at the expense) of that person, there is a particularly difficult problem of classification. English law recognises this as a category of enrichment for wrongs. However, "wrong" in this context does not necessarily imply tortious conduct. The position in Scots law is yet to be worked out. Some examples have been classified under recompense, which is definitely part of the law of unjustified enrichment, these are namely where a defender has used property of the pursuer even though the pursuer has lost nothing thereby, for example a moveable where the pursuer neither intended to hire it out or to use it at that time (see Gloag and Henderson, *The Law of Scotland* (10th edn. (1995) ed. Wilson and Forte at p. 484). On the other hand a number of cases dealing with infringement of intellectual property rights have typically been treated by the Scots courts as delictual actions, disregarding the fact that they may also be enrichment actions (*e.g. James Burroughs Distillers v. Speymalt Whisky Distributors* 1989 SLT 561; see also s.11(1) below). It is difficult fully to bring the Scots law for other examples into the category used in England, enrichment for "wrongs" (*c.f.* Blackie, *Enrichment and Wrongs in Scots Law* (1992) Acta Juridica 23–47; Stewart, Supplement at 3.8), and it may be that the Scots law could be developed with a category similar to that in German law, which looks not at the quality of the conduct but at the interests involved. It is in any event the case that an enrichment claim is analytically distinct from a delictual claim. Sometimes it is stated that the distinction is because an enrichment claim is "result-oriented" whereas delict is "act-oriented" (Stewart (above) at 207). However, as far as private international law is concerned, such a distinction is no longer a relevant one, given the rules under Pt. III for determination of the applicable law. Interesting guidance may be found for this matter in cases involving jurisdiction under the Civil Jurisdiction and Judgments Act 1982 in forthcoming judgments in *Barclays Bank v. Glasgow District Council* [1994] 4 All ER C.A. and *Kleinwort Benson v. Glasgow District Council, The Times,* April 17, 1995 (see also *Strathaird Farms v. GA Chattaway & Co* 1993 SLT (Sh Ct) 36). A second area of difficulty is cases of breach of contract where the pursuer makes a gain through breaking the contract. Such claims are recognised in a number of legal systems, although, as yet, not in either Scots or English law (*Teacher v. Calder* (1899) 1 F (HL) 39). Such claims are properly enrichment claims, but might be characterised as contract claims as arising from breach of contract.

Subs. (3)
   The operation of the rules for choice of law in tort and delict introduced in this Part do not extend to the determination of issues arising in a "defamation claim" as defined in s.13(2).

Subs. (4)
   This expands upon the provision in subs. (2) above. Once the court of the forum has characterised the issue as relating to tort or delict, the applicable law alone will determine whether an actionable tort or delict has occurred together with any other substantive issues. The *lex fori* no longer plays a residual role (s.10). Accordingly, in a claim arising from a foreign tort/delict which is not recognised or is unknown under the *lex fori*, or is of a different character to a tort/delict under the *lex fori*, but which is characterised as relating to tort or delict under subs. (2), the foreign applicable law alone will determine any issues arising (subject to s.12(2)).

Subs. (5)
   This implements the recommendations of the Report at para. 3.56, that *renvoi* should be excluded. A reference to the applicable law is a reference to the internal law of that country and not to its rules of private international law. The application of *renvoi*, in whatever form, would have created uncertainty and would not accord with the reasonable expectations of parties. However, as the Act, as amended from the Law Commissions' recommendations, now allows for the segregation of issues, difficult situations may arise. For instance, if the issue of inter-spousal immunities were to be segregated and referred to a substantially more appropriate law, for instance, the law of the domicile of the parties according to the law of the forum, that law would determine the issue, even if the purported applicable law would refer the question to another personal law.

Subs. (6)
   The new rules for determining the applicable law apply equally to torts/delicts which are committed within the U.K. Accordingly, the courts of the forum can apply another U.K. law or a foreign law as "the applicable law" in such a situation. The Law Commissions recommended that there should be a proviso for torts and delicts occurring within the U.K. (paras. 3.14–3.19). However, this provision is logical and fits in with the overall statutory scheme. Section 11 provides the rules for determining generally where a tort or delict occurred and it would be strange to predetermine this issue for presumed U.K. torts/delicts, or to retain a common law rule of the place of the tort/delict. Such a provision in any case would be discriminatory and contrary to the spirit of the reforms which seeks to locate the most appropriate law to apply. This provision combined with subs. (2) and s.11 seeks to ensure that actions may be brought in respect of

foreign torts/delicts where the injury is suffered outwith the U.K. as a result of acts or omissions within the U.K. (subject to public policy).

Subs. (7)
This clarifies the references to the "forum" due to the alternative fora available. However subs. (5) and s.11(1) require more precise definition of the phrase "the law of the country" for a unitary state like the U.K., where the law of the country can mean the law of England and Wales or Northern Ireland or Scotland; although see s.11(1).

Subs. (8)
This subsection is intended to define the ambit of "delict" in Scots law for these purposes. This form of wording has been used elsewhere (The Brussels Convention Art. 5(3), as implemented by the Civil Jurisdiction and Judgments Act 1982). It is doubtful, however, if it adds anything to the word "delict" on its own. In modern Scots law, whatever may have earlier been the position (which is debatable), the term delict is now a generic term, comprehending liability for intentional conduct, liability for negligent conduct and all forms of strict or stricter liability. In some systems, notably the French, following a classification developed by writers on the *ius commune* in the seventeenth and eighteenth centuries, the term delict is confined to intentional conduct, and quasi-delict is used for negligent conduct (and by extension for delicts of strict or stricter liability). This distinction is supported in some academic Scots writing. Other academic Scots writing propounds a different, indeed, diametrically opposite distinction, confining "quasi-delict" to the two examples of strict liability received into Scots common law from Roman Law, the *actio de effusis vel dejectis*, and the praetorian edict *nautae caupones stabularii* (insofar as not modified by the Hotel Proprietors Act 1956), and leaving as delict all the rest (see on this academic debate: Bell's *Principles of the Law of Scotland* at p. 533; Stein, *The actio de Effusis Vel dejectis and the Concept of Quasi-Delict in Scots Law* 1955 ICLQ 356; Stewart, *Smith's Question Mark, Walker's Exhortation and Quasi-Delict* 1990 JR 71; Lord Fraser in *Junior Books v. Veitchi Co.* 1982 SLT 492 at p. 494). Since, however, it is clear that in modern Scots law, delict is a generic term, this debate is not of significance in the present context. Moreover, it is doubtful if there is any situation in this general field arising in another legal system where that system would characterise the area of law as within "delict" or within "quasi-delict" when Scots law would not characterise it as coming within its modern generic classification, delict, and, in any event a Scottish court in characterising an issue as delictual for the purposes of private international law is not restricted to exactly analogous delictual claims.

Abolition of certain common law rules

10. The rules of the common law, in so far as they—
(a) require actionability under both the law of the forum and the law of another country for the purpose of determining whether a tort or delict is actionable; or
(b) allow (as an exception from the rules falling within paragraph (a) above) for the law of a single country to be applied for the purpose of determining the issues, or any of the issues, arising in the case in question,
are hereby abolished so far as they apply to any claim in tort or delict which is not excluded from the operation of this Part by section 13 below.

GENERAL NOTE
This abolishes certain common law rules applicable in relation to claims other than defamation claims.
Paragraph (a) abolishes the rule, commonly known in England and Wales as the rule in *Phillips v. Eyre* (1870) LR 6 Q.B. 1 and in Scotland as the rule in *McElroy v. McAllister* (1949) S.C. 110.
Paragraph (b) abolishes the rules in *Boys v. Chaplin* [1971] A.C. 356 and *Red Sea (Red Sea Insurance Co. v. Bouygues SA)* [1994] 3 All E.R. 749.
The intention of this provision was that other rules of private international law applying in particular classes of case (such as torts/delicts committed on the high seas) would not be affected by the Act, but this could have been specified and made clearer.

Choice of applicable law: the general rule

11.—(1) The general rule is that the applicable law is the law of the country in which the events constituting the tort or delict in question occur.

(2) Where elements of those events occur in different countries, the applicable law under the general rule is to be taken as being—

- (a) for a cause of action in respect of personal injury caused to an individual or death resulting from personal injury, the law of the country where the individual was when he sustained the injury;
- (b) for a cause of action in respect of damage to property, the law of the country where the property was when it was damaged; and
- (c) in any other case, the law of the country in which the most significant element or elements of those events occurred.

(3) In this section "personal injury" includes disease or any impairment of physical or mental condition.

GENERAL NOTE

A new general rule is laid down, that the applicable law for determining the issues arising in a claim should *prima facie* be that of the place where the tort or delict that is the subject of the claim occurred—the *lex loci delicti*. Where the relevant events occurred in two or more countries, the tort or delict is taken to have occurred in the country where the plaintiff/pursuer was injured (if the claim is for a cause of action for personal injury), where property was damaged (if the claim is for a cause of action for damage to property) or, in other cases, where the most significant elements in the sequence of events constituting the tort or delict in question occurred. This should generally reduce the difficulties under the common law for localising the place of the tort/delict. The new choice of law scheme does not apply to torts/delicts on the high seas for which English/Scottish maritime law respectively applies (see Report at para. 3.27; *Dicey and Morris*, pp. 1535–1539; *Anton and Beaumont*, pp. 410–411). The provisions do cover torts/delicts on or over territorial waters (see Report at para. 3.26; *Dicey and Morris*, pp. 1539–1542).

This section, together with s.12 strives to achieve the balance between certainty and flexibility in the new choice of law rule. However, the meaning to be ascribed to certain phrases in s.11 remains unclear.

Subs. (1)

The general rule provided here is subject to s.12, under which the general rule may be displaced. The applicable law is that of the country where the "events" occur but this need not be all the events constituting the tort/delict as long as "elements" of those events do not occur in other countries. This provision is aimed essentially at torts/delicts where the damage occurred, and the place of the event giving rise to it occur, wholly or mainly in one country. The meaning and relationship of the term "events" here and "elements of those events" in subs. (2) is unclear. The reference to "country" makes no specific provision for unitary states such as the U.K., although it is generally accepted as meaning the territory of a particular jurisdiction even where such a jurisdiction constitutes part only of a unitary state, and also may prove problematic in relation to offshore installations (see the Oil and Gas (Enterprise) Act 1982 (c. 23) and the Continental Shelf Territorial Sea Civil Jurisdiction (Offshore Activities) Order 1987 (S.I. 1987 No. 2197)).

This section makes it possible for the courts of the forum to adjudicate on alleged infringements of intellectual property rights (IPRs) conferred by foreign laws according to the law of the place where the alleged infringement occurred. (This is subject to the rules on jurisdiction, see *Shevill v. Presse Alliance SA* [1995] All E.R. (EC) 289 and the territorial limitations on the granting of interlocutory remedies.) U.K. legislation will continue to apply to alleged infringements of U.K. IPRs by virtue of s.13(4) but will continue to have no application to alleged infringements outside the U.K. because of its territorial limitations.

Subs. (2)

This provision is aimed at cross-border torts/delicts and seeks to provide guidelines to identify the applicable law. The threshold of significance of the elements in another country required in order to remove the case from the basic rule in subs. (1) is unclear, although it suggests (see below) that the courts will require to look to the law of the place where the harm was suffered, even if all other events constituting the tort/delict occur in one country (including the forum. See para. (c) and the possibility of displacement under s.12). The certainty of the provisions in paras. (a) and (b) for personal injury and damage to property respectively is an improvement although the general and more vague wording for other cases under para. (c) detracts from the value of this provision.

Paragraphs (a) and (b) provide that the applicable law is the law of the country of the place of damage (*cf.* the alternative rules of jurisdiction under the Brussels and Lugano Conventions which provide for jurisdiction in the place of acting or the place of damage; *Bier BV v. Mines de*

Potasse D'Alsace SA [1976] E.C.R. 1735). Paragraph (b) will be particularly relevant in cases of cross-border nuisance or environmental damage.

Paragraph (c) is a catch-all provision for cases not involving personal injury or damage to property and is a rather uncertain *locus delicti* rule. The Working Paper produced detailed rules for each possible tort/delict but the Report was opposed to producing codified rules and the Act does not provide for such rules. The "most significant elements" rule does not specify whether emphasis is to be placed on the place of acting or where the harm occurred. Difficult questions are likely to arise under this provision, together with s.12, as to auditors' liability to foreign investors.

Subs. (3)
This is not an exhaustive definition, but the general rule as detailed under subs. (2)(a) for personal injury cases extends particularly to "nervous shock" cases, and this would seem to include third party nervous shock. This may have interesting results in cases which involve third party nervous shock cases such as *Alcock v. Chief Constable of South Yorkshire Police* [1992] 1 A.C. 310, as it may lead to the application of a different law from that applicable in the case of the primary victim which would be the law of the place where the physical injury was suffered and which engendered the shock.

Choice of applicable law: displacement of general rule

12.—(1) If it appears, in all the circumstances, from a comparison of—
  (a) the significance of the factors which connect a tort or delict with the country whose law would be the applicable law under the general rule; and
  (b) the significance of any factors connecting the tort or delict with another country,
that it is substantially more appropriate for the applicable law for determining the issues arising in the case, or any of those issues, to be the law of the other country, the general rule is displaced and the applicable law for determining those issues or that issue (as the case may be) is the law of that other country.

The factors that may be taken into account as connecting a tort or delict with a country for the purposes of this section include, in particular, factors relating to the parties, to any of the events which constitute the tort or delict in question or to any of the circumstances or consequences of those events.

GENERAL NOTE
The general rule may be displaced under this provision in any case in which it seems to be substantially more appropriate, having regard to the respective connecting factors, for the applicable law governing a claim, or particular issues arising in a claim, to be the law of another country. This section creates a second new choice of law rule which enables better justice to be done in cases where the general rule is thought to give a less appropriate answer. This provision is the key to the balance being struck between certainty and flexibility under the statutory scheme. The section contains a threshold for application of the "proper law" exception to the general rule and the level of the threshold dictates the balance of the new rules towards a degree of certainty under s.11 or flexibility. If the threshold is not interpreted as being difficult to overcome, then the "proper law" exception under s.12 will become the norm and the *lex loci delicti* rules under s.11 will become a rule of last resort if it is impossible to determine the most appropriate law. It is submitted that, notwithstanding the lack of clarity in the terminology under s.12, or s.11, the threshold is at a satisfactory high level to provide advisers with some certainty and that the rule of displacement under s.12 should be exceptional. This would also accord with the direction of the new rules, particularly when the suggested alternative applicable law is the *lex fori*. Where there are multiple parties to an action, the application of this section could lead to different applicable laws for each case (see the Report para. 3.54).

Subs. (1)

Threshold
The courts are hereby enabled to carry out a comparative exercise in order to determine whether the general rule should be displaced. However, comparisons with the "common law exception" are unlikely to be of much use as that relates to the "double actionability rule" and not a *prima facie* choice of law rule as here.

The court is to undertake a comparison of the "significance of the factors" which connect the tort/delict with the relevant countries. A non-exhaustive definition of factors is given in subs. (2). This subsection adds to the confusion for practitioners required to give advice as to the distinction between "events" under s.11 which is likely to encompass physical occurrences and outcomes as opposed to the broader term of "factors" in this subsection. The Working Paper suggested that the exception should apply only when there was an insignificant connection with the applicable law under the general rule. This subsection can be seen as a compromise between the aims of certainty and flexibility. However, the words which embody the threshold for application of the law of another country, "substantially more appropriate", suggest that the threshold will be difficult to overcome, particularly to prevent resort to the *lex fori* for separated issues which would to some extent damage the general policy of Pt. III. The term "appropriate" is derived from the *forum non conveniens* rule under jurisdiction where it concerns litigational convenience but should not allow arguments here as to ease of proving foreign law or arguments as to the better law to apply for the availability of compensation. It is uncertain whether the courts should apply this rule of displacement in a difficult case such as *Boys v. Chaplin* [1971] A.C. 356, and to this extent the statutory scheme is no more certain than the common law (see subs. (2) below).

Separation of issues—depecage
This does not affect issues of procedure (see s.14(3)(b)) which are separately dealt with by the *lex fori*. This provision, allowing for issues to be separated in a similar form to that advocated by Lords Hodson and Wilberforce in *Boys v. Chaplin*, reduces the certainty of the provisions in this part and makes it more complex for advisers. There is no general separation of issues but only where there is a more appropriate law to determine an issue using the threshold. The Working Paper and Report were opposed to the separation of issues fearing this may upset the balance of substantive rules in one system and allow for the use of a mixture of rules favourable to the case from more than one legal system. This provision should not lead to rule-selection by the courts looking at the purpose or policy of the relevant rules (subs. (2) below). The most likely situation where this may be invoked involves the separation of interspousal immunity from liability, although it may equally apply to issues such as vicarious liability, defences and immunities including contributory negligence, contractual defences to claims in tort/delict, prescription and limitation of actions, contribution and indemnity and subrogation (see Report, Pt. III, paras. 3.34–3.54. See also, for instance, Scot. Law Com. No. 115, *Report on Civil Liability— Contribution* at paras. 3.100–3.103).

Subs. (2)
This outlines the factors that may be taken into account in assessing whether it is substantially more appropriate for the general rule to be displaced. However, it is not an exhaustive list and may add to the uncertainty under subs. (1). The factors likely to be taken into account are the factual connections referred to together with residual factors such as the interests of justice, the expectation of the parties and the interests of legal certainty (*cf.* Art. 4 of the 1980 Rome Convention). In particular, it is unclear whether the common law approach for identifying the best connected law under the exception to *Phillips v. Eyre* 1870 L.R. 6 Q.B. 1 will be followed. This would include reference to the policy and purpose of the relevant competing rules of law (see *Johnson v. Coventry Churchill International* [1992] 3 All E.R. 14, relying upon the approaches of Lords Hodson and Wilberforce in *Boys v. Chaplin*) leading to complexity, unpredictability and a pro-forum bias. In addition this may lead to divergent approaches in the different jurisdictions due to the differing common law rules. The provision lacks guidance as to the exercise of the discretion, and in particular, there are no criteria as to the significance of the various factors although prioritising factors in the abstract may have proved an impossible exercise (*cf.* Working Paper, paras. 4.134–4.135).

Exclusion of defamation claims from Part III

13.—(1) Nothing in this Part applies to affect the determination of issues arising in any defamation claim.
  (2) For the purposes of this section "defamation claim" means—
  (a) any claim under the law of any part of the United Kingdom for libel or slander or for slander of title, slander of goods or other malicious falsehood and any claim under the law of Scotland for verbal injury; and

(b) any claim under the law of any other country corresponding to or otherwise in the nature of a claim mentioned in paragraph (a) above.

GENERAL NOTE
This was the most contentious issue during the passage of the Bill in Parliament. Defamation actions are now excluded from the operation of the Act and the common law rules of private international law will continue to apply to the issues arising in such claims (see *Cheshire and North*, pp. 555–556; *Norrie*, Chap. 13 of Defamation and Related Issues in Scots Law).

The Report had recommended a proviso to the application of the new choice of law rules for defamation cases in order to provide that where the statement was originally published in the U.K., the relevant law of the U.K. would apply regardless of where the statement was subsequently published and the alleged harm suffered (para. 3.33). Earlier versions of the Bill rejected this solution, similar to that for torts/delicts committed in the U.K., in favour of an internationalist approach under which the new rules on choice of law would apply. Defamation issues are particularly likely to cross national boundaries and partly due to U.K. media interests, concerns over the availability of suitable defences under foreign laws, and the combination of the application of foreign law with generous forum quantification, defamation claims were considered suitable to be treated as a special case, to be excluded from the new rules. Emphasis was placed on the freedom of expression in the U.K. although the possibility of enforcement of a foreign judgment in a defamation case remains (subject to public policy) together with the public policy provision under s.14(3)(a)(i).

Subs. (2)
Paragraph (a) defines the term "defamation claim" and ensures that the common law rules continue to apply as between the laws of the different jurisdictions in the U.K.

Paragraph (b) provides that similar claims under foreign laws are similarly excluded. This may involve difficult problems of characterisation in tandem with the provisions of s.9(2), particularly in relation to foreign privacy or confidentiality laws. The principle of Pt. III should not be restricted too far, and although possibly unrecognised by common law or statute in this country, such foreign laws should generally be applicable in appropriate cases under the rules provided in Pt. III.

Transitional provision and savings

14.—(1) Nothing in this Part applies to acts or omissions giving rise to a claim which occur before the commencement of this Part.

(2) Nothing in this Part affects any rules of law (including rules of private international law) except those abolished by section 10 above.

(3) Without prejudice to the generality of subsection (2) above, nothing in this Part—
  (a) authorises the application of the law of a country outside the forum as the applicable law for determining issues arising in any claim in so far as to do so—
      (i) would conflict with principles of public policy; or
      (ii) would give effect to such a penal, revenue or other public law as would not otherwise be enforceable under the law of the forum; or
  (b) affects any rules of evidence, pleading or practice or authorises questions of procedure in any proceedings to be determined otherwise than in accordance with the law of the forum.

(4) This Part has effect without prejudice to the operation of any rule of law which either has effect notwithstanding the rules of private international law applicable in the particular circumstances or modifies the rules of private international law that would otherwise be so applicable.

GENERAL NOTE
This ensures that the reform does not have retrospective effect and saves the effect of various procedural and other rules, the application of principles of public policy and certain mandatory domestic rules.

Subs. (1)

The reference is to "acts or omissions" rather than to the harm suffered to allow behaviour to be modified prospectively to take account of the legislation, otherwise past acts or omissions may have been actionable if the harm was suffered after commencement.

Subs. (2)

Section 10 does not abolish existing common law rules, for instance, for torts/delicts committed on the high seas.

Subs. (3)

Paragraph (a). (i) Public policy. Public policy has not been defined in this provision. Reference can be made to the body of common law rules in private international law for a variety of purposes such as enforcement of judgments. The Act does not codify these rules and different considerations may apply. There was concern that the application of public policy may be too narrow, based on the established rules, and in the Scottish context, Lord Cooper in *McElroy v. McAllister* (1949) S.C. 110 stated that "a liability recognised in the place of wrong should be enforced unless to do so would be utterly repugnant to the distinctive policy of the forum". This provision should not become an "unruly horse" allowing a modified form of the rule in *The Halley* (1868) L.R. 2 P.C. 193 to resurface and filter the application of foreign laws. This exception does not require the foreign law to be acceptable to the law of the forum. Characterisation of foreign rules is to be undertaken under s.9(2) and recourse to this escape route from the application of the *lex fori* will remain exceptional within the scheme of Pt. III. This is another provision under which there may be divergent approaches in the different jurisdictions.

(ii) Public laws. The law relating to enforcement of foreign penal or revenue law is fairly well-established. In England there is division of opinion as to whether the courts will refuse to enforce all public laws (*per* Lord Denning in *Att.-Gen. of New Zealand v. Ortiz* [1984] AC 1) or whether the court will only refuse if enforcement is contrary to actual policy in the case. The amended provision simply ensures that to the extent that there is such an exception, it is not affected by the Act, revising an earlier rule that no such public law should be applied. There is no authority in Scotland on this matter and it is unclear how to apply the distinction between public and private law (see *Anton and Beaumont*, pp. 105–106). No definition is provided for a concept derived from continental legal thinking.

Paragraph (b) ensures that the rules of the forum continue to apply to procedural issues.

Subs. (4)

This ensures the continued application of mandatory rules of law, *i.e.* the operation of common law or statutory rules forming part of the law of the forum that apply to exclude or modify the effects of the choice of law rules contained in Pt. III (for instance, U.K. legislation will continue to apply to alleged infringements of U.K. IPRs; see Fawcett, *Evasion of Law and Mandatory Rules in Private International Law* (1990) 49 CLJ 44). The Working Paper described such domestic rules as

> "so important that as a matter of construction or policy they must apply in any action before a court of the forum, even where the issues are in principle governed by a law selected by a choice of law rule" (para. 4.5).

The mandatory rules of other countries will continue to be enforced as part of the applicable law to govern the issue or issues under ss.11 or 12. However, as this provision makes no reference to the mandatory rules as being of the forum, the possibility remains for the application of mandatory rules of a third country, for instance the law of the place of acting (*cf.* Art. 7(1) of the Rome Convention and s.2(2) of the Contracts (Applicable Law) Act 1990).

Crown application

15.—(1) This Part applies in relation to claims by or against the Crown as it applies in relation to claims to which the Crown is not a party.   .

(2) In subsection (1) above a reference to the Crown does not include a reference to Her Majesty in Her private capacity or to Her Majesty in right of Her Duchy of Lancaster or to the Duke of Cornwall.

(3) Without prejudice to the generality of section 14(2) above, nothing in this section affects any rule of law as to whether proceedings of any description may be brought against the Crown.

GENERAL NOTE
This deals with the application of the provisions of Pt. III to the Crown.

PART IV

SUPPLEMENTAL

Commencement

16.—(1) Part I shall come into force on such day as the Lord Chancellor may by order made by statutory instrument appoint; and different days may be appointed for different provisions.
(2) Part II shall come into force at the end of the period of two months beginning with the day on which this Act is passed.
(3) Part III shall come into force on such day as the Lord Chancellor and the Lord Advocate may by order made by statutory instrument appoint; and different days may be appointed for the commencement of Part III as it extends to England and Wales, Scotland or Northern Ireland.

GENERAL NOTE
This enables Pts. I and III to be brought into force by order. Part II comes into force two months after Royal Assent.

Modification of Northern Ireland Act 1974

17. An Order in Council under paragraph 1(1)(b) of Schedule 1 to the Northern Ireland Act 1974 (legislation for Northern Ireland in the interim period) which contains a statement that it is only made for purposes corresponding to the purposes of any provision of Part II shall not be subject to paragraph 1(4) and (5) of that Schedule (requirement for affirmative resolution procedure) but shall be subject to annulment in pursuance of a resolution of either House of Parliament.

GENERAL NOTE
Northern Ireland legislation made for purposes corresponding to anything in Pt. II is to be subject to the negative resolution procedure rather than the affirmative resolution procedure.

Extent

18.—(1) Any amendment made by this Act has the same extent as the enactment being amended.
(2) In Part II, sections 5 and 6 extend to England and Wales only, section 7 extends to Scotland only and section 8 extends to England and Wales and Scotland.
(3) Part III extends to England and Wales, Scotland and Northern Ireland.

Short title

19. This Act may be cited as the Private International Law (Miscellaneous Provisions) Act 1995.

Section 8(2) SCHEDULE

CONSEQUENTIAL AND MINOR AMENDMENTS RELATING TO PART II

Matrimonial Proceedings (Polygamous Marriages) Act 1972 (c. 38)

1.—(1) Section 2 of the Matrimonial Proceedings (Polygamous Marriages) Act 1972 (matrimonial relief etc. in relation to polygamous marriages: Scotland) shall be amended as follows.

(2) In subsection (1), for the words "the marriage" onwards there shall be substituted the words "either party to the marriage is, or has during the subsistence of the marriage been, married to more than one person".

(3) For subsection (3) there shall be substituted—

"(3) Provision may be made by rules of court—

(a) for requiring notice of proceedings brought by virtue of this section to be served on any additional spouse of a party to the marriage in question; and

(b) for conferring on any such additional spouse the right to be heard in the proceedings,

in such cases as may be specified in the rules."

Matrimonial Causes Act 1973 (c. 18)

2.—(1) The Matrimonial Causes Act 1973 shall be amended as follows.

(2) In section 11 (grounds on which a marriage is void), for the words "may be polygamous although" there shall be substituted the words "is not polygamous if".

(3) In section 47 (matrimonial relief and declarations in respect of polygamous marriage)—

(a) in subsection (1), for the words "the marriage" onwards there shall be substituted the words "either party to the marriage is, or has during the subsistence of the marriage been, married to more than one person"; and

(b) for subsection (4) there shall be substituted—

"(4) Provision may be made by rules of court—

(a) for requiring notice of proceedings brought by virtue of this section to be served on any additional spouse of a party to the marriage in question; and

(b) for conferring on any such additional spouse the right to be heard in the proceedings,

in such cases as may be specified in the rules."

Matrimonial Homes Act 1983 (c. 19)

3. In section 10 of the Matrimonial Homes Act 1983 (interpretation), for subsection (2) there shall be substituted—

"(2) It is hereby declared that this Act applies as between the parties to a marriage notwithstanding that either of them is, or has at any time during the marriage's subsistence been, married to more than one person."

Social Security Contributions and Benefits Act 1992 (c. 4)

4.—(1) The Social Security Contributions and Benefits Act 1992 shall be amended as follows.

(2) In section 121(1)(b) (regulations as to application of provisions of Parts I to VI to polygamous marriages), for the words following "section" there shall be substituted the words "applies, a marriage during the subsistence of which a party to it is at any time married to more than one person is to be treated as having, or as not having, the same consequences as any other marriage."

(3) In section 147(5) (regulations as to application of provisions of Part IX to polygamous marriages), for the words following "in which" there shall be substituted the words "a marriage during the subsistence of which a party to it is at any time married to more than one person is to be treated for the purposes of this Part of this Act as having, or not having the same consequences as any other marriage."

GENERAL NOTE

Paragraph 1

Section 2 of the 1972 Act applies only to Scotland. This amendment is necessary under s.7(2) of Pt. II.

Subpara. (1). This amendment makes provision in order that the courts in Scotland should not be precluded from entertaining proceedings and granting such decrees as are mentioned in subs. (2) by reason only that either party to the marriage has, during the marriage, been married to another person.

Subpara. (3). This amendment allows for procedural rights to any additional spouse during proceedings under s.2 of the 1972 Act.

Paragraph 2

Section 47 of the 1973 Act applies only to England and Wales and these are identical amendments to those provided for Scotland under para. 1.

Paragraph 3

This amendment deletes the reference to a potentially polygamous marriage as being unnecessary as a result of s.5 of Pt. II. This Act extends only to England and Wales. There is no similar interpretation provision in the Scottish legislation: the Matrimonial Homes (Scotland) Act 1981 as amended by the Law Reform (Miscellaneous Provisions) (Scotland) Act 1990.

Paragraph 4

These amendments also delete the references to "a marriage celebrated under a law which permits polygamy" as being unnecessary.

INDEX

References are to sections and Schedule

PROCEEDS OF CRIME (SCOTLAND) ACT 1995*

(1995 c. 43)

ARRANGEMENT OF SECTIONS

PART I

CONFISCATION OF THE PROCEEDS OF CRIME

Confiscation orders

Exercise of powers

Compensation

Investigation and disclosure of information

PART II

FORFEITURE OF PROPERTY USED IN CRIME

*Annotations by Alastair N. Brown LL.B, Solicitor and Senior Procurator Fiscal Depute, Edinburgh

PART III

RESTRAINT ORDERS

PART IV

RECIPROCAL ARRANGEMENTS FOR ENFORCEMENT OF ORDERS

PART V

MISCELLANEOUS AND GENERAL

An Act to consolidate as regards Scotland certain enactments relating to the confiscation of the proceeds of, and forfeiture of property used in, crime.

[8th November 1995]

PARLIAMENTARY DEBATES
Hansard, H.L. Vol. 564, col. 1466; Vol. 565, col. 15; Vol. 566, cols. 383, 894. H.C. Vol. 265, col. 179.
Joint Committee on Consolidation Bills, Session 1994–1995, 5th Report, H.L. 74–I, II, H.C. 552–I, II, June 21, 1995.

INTRODUCTION AND GENERAL NOTE
This Act is the culmination of several years of work carried out by the Scottish Law Commission ("the SLC") on the subjects of the confiscation of the proceeds of crime and the forfeiture of its instrumentalities. The Criminal Justice (Scotland) Act 1995 (c. 20) gave statutory form to the recommendations made by the SLC in their *Report on Confiscation and Forfeiture* (SLC Report No. 147), together with certain additions. So far as the present Act is concerned, as the draftsman explained to the Joint Committee on Consolidation Bills, it
    "...draws together Part I of the 1987 Act which provides for the confiscation of the proceeds of drug trafficking and Part II of the 1995 Act which makes provision for the confiscation or forfeiture of all other crimes. These are specialised provisions which are unlikely

to be used in the majority of prosecutions and it seems appropriate to preset them as a discrete code" (Joint Committee on Consolidation Bills, Session 1994–95, 5th Report, H.L. Paper 74–II, H.C. 552–II, p. 7).

Part I deals with confiscation in relation to the proceeds of drug trafficking and the benefit obtained from other crimes (there are some important differences in the law between these two), Pt. II with forfeiture and Pt. III with restraint orders. Part IV deals with international enforcement and Pt. V with miscellaneous matters.

PART I

As the House of Commons Home Affairs Committee noted, "the most readily obvious internationally organised criminal activity is drug production and drug trafficking. The size of the drug economy is enormous" (House of Commons Home Affairs Committee, Third Report, *Organised Crime* (July 1995) H.C. 18–I, para. 19). That fact has, over the last decade or so, led governments throughout the world to enact legislation and enter into treaties designed to attack the financial motivation for drug trafficking. The most notable of these is the 1988 UN Convention Against Illicit Traffic in Narcotic Drugs and Psychotropic Substances ("the 1988 UN Drugs Convention"). The most complete and up-to-date account of the international instruments is to be found in Dr W. Gilmore's *Dirty Money* (Council of Europe Press, 1995).

There are two major justifications for this strategy. First, it is regarded as unacceptable that criminals should benefit from their crimes. And, secondly, the received wisdom is that one of the most effective ways of stopping the flow of illegal drugs is to intercept the profits generated by drugs.

The strategy has two parts. First, substantial efforts are directed to identifying the proceeds of crime as they enter the financial system and making that system an unfriendly environment for the criminal. This is the money laundering legislation and that part of the strategy is of little significance in the present Act. Secondly, however, since it would be unrealistic to think that it would be possible to stop all proceeds from getting into the system, it is necessary to overcome commercial or legal confidentiality in order to trace the funds, to provide a restraint mechanism under which the property of the suspect can be frozen; and to provide a mechanism for confiscating the proceeds of a suspect who has been convicted of a profit generating crime. This aspect, known commonly but inaccurately as "drug profit confiscation" was the subject of Pt. I of the Criminal Justice (Scotland) Act 1987 (c. 41).

It is increasingly clear that profit motivated criminals do not confine their activities to drug trafficking. Internationally, that fact informed the approach taken in the Council of Europe Convention on Laundering, Search, Seizure and Confiscation of the Proceeds from Crime ("the Laundering Convention"), which was opened for signature on November 8, 1990 and to which the U.K. is a party. Under that Convention, the "predicate offences" (that is, offences which have produced the benefit which is to be attacked) upon which the operation of the Laundering Convention is based, should include drug trafficking, terrorist offences, organised crime, violent crimes, offences involving the sexual exploitation of children and young persons, extortion, kidnapping, environmental offences, economic fraud, insider trading and other serious offences. Parliament provided English law with a confiscation mechanism in respect of non-drug-related crimes in Pt. VI of the Criminal Justice Act 1988 (c. 33). With this Act, a Scottish equivalent is brought into operation.

The 1987 Act was based very closely on the Drug Trafficking Offences Act 1986 (c. 32) (DTOA), but there were certain important differences and the divergence between Scots and English law has increased with innovations made in the Scottish approach by the present Act and by amendments made to English law which have not been followed by Scots law (and which, accordingly, are not considered in any detail here). The differences between the two bodies of legislation mean that English case law, whilst it is in some respects helpful, has the potential to be seriously misleading and therefore requires to be handled with considerable care. English cases are cited in these annotations but the rider "if the Scottish courts follow English authority" is implied in every case.

It is important to understand the nature of the confiscation order. There are two approaches which are commonly used in legal systems for the confiscation of the proceeds of crime. The first of these is "property confiscation" under which ownership rights in specific property which is derived directly or indirectly from offences are transferred to the state. Under the second, which is "value confiscation", there is a requirement to pay a sum of money based on an assessment of the value of property derived directly or indirectly from crime. Scots law, like English law and the laws of many other member states of the Council of Europe, operates value confiscation.

The first requirement which the law enforcement authorities have, is for a means of investigating the financial aspects of crime. Such a means of investigation is provided for by ss.18 and 19 of the present Act. Under s.18 the Crown can obtain an order requiring the production of material and, under s.19, a search warrant. Equivalent provision is made for drug trafficking cases by ss.31 and 32 of the Criminal Law (Consolidation) (Scotland) Act 1995 (c. 39).

Once assets have been identified by investigation, the authorities will wish to prevent them from being put out of the reach of the court. Pt. III of the Act (see below) therefore provides for restraint orders.

If an accused person is convicted it is open to the prosecutor to seek a confiscation order. Following the model of the 1987 Act, it is only the prosecutor's motion that can trigger the making of such an order.

Again following the 1987 Act, the court has a discretion whether or not to make a confiscation order. This is to be contrasted with s.2 of the Drug Trafficking Act 1994 (c. 37) under which an English court has no discretion, but is obliged to make an order where prosecutor requests one (provided the other criteria are met). The Scottish Law Commission consulted on the options and report (SLC Report, para. 6.4), that consultees were unanimous in thinking that the discretion should be retained. Moreover, the court has a discretion about the amount of any confiscation order. The mechanism provided by the Act for calculation sets *maxima* but it is for the court to decide what figure within these *maxima* is appropriate. Some guidance as to the approach likely to be taken by the court is to be found in *H.M. Advocate v. McLean*, 1993 S.C.C.R. 917 where Lord Sutherland took into account the facts that the accused was dealing with substantial sums of cash in circumstances which were not satisfactorily explained, that the deemed proceeds of drug trafficking were substantially in excess of the realisable property and that if the Crown had not sought a confiscation order he would have been obliged in terms of section 44 of the Criminal Justice (Scotland) Act 1987 to impose a fine which would have been "very substantial" having regard to the value of the cannabis in relation to the offence of which the accused had been convicted.

DTOA and the 1987 Act did not prescribe any particular standard of proof in relation to confiscation. Accordingly, it became necessary in *R. v. Dickens* [1990] 2 W.L.R. 1384 for the Court of Appeal to determine what the standard was. The Court reasoned that the context of DTOA and the nature of the penalties which were likely to be imposed made it clear that the standard of proof required is the criminal standard, namely proof beyond reasonable doubt. This decision was to provoke a considerable debate and in due course the Criminal Justice Act 1993 (c. 36) ss.7 and 27 were to reverse *Dickens* and apply the civil standard of proof in English cases. The reasoning was essentially that confiscation is reparative rather than penal, but this was found unconvincing by the SLC in relation to Scottish confiscation orders (SLC Report, para. 2.16). The Commission noted (SLC Report, para. 2.17) that to deprive a person of property, the use of which he has been enjoying, albeit wrongly, as his own is to punish him. They also noted the observation of Sir Thomas Bingham, M.R. in *Barretto, Re* [1994] 2 W.L.R. 149 at 155 that the confiscation provisions of DTOA are "in a broad sense penal, inflicting the vengeance of society on those who have transgressed in this field". They concluded that confiscation cannot satisfactorily be characterised as either exclusively reparative or exclusively penal (SLC Report, para. 2.17) and, because they were not prepared to share the view that confiscation is merely reparative, they recommended that the standard of proof which should apply in Scotland is the criminal standard (SLC Report, para. 6.5).

Almost by definition, the taking of benefit from crime is a covert activity. It is rare (though not entirely unknown) for the police to be fortunate enough to recover full accounts from a drug trafficker and in many cases more or less sophisticated steps will have been taken to launder the benefit in a way which conceals its provenance. Proof of benefit from crime is, therefore, often likely to be difficult and Parliament has provided the Crown with two ways to make it easier. These are, first, the Prosecutor's Statement and, second, certain assumptions.

The Prosecutor's Statement is dealt with in s.9 which applies in both drug trafficking and non-drug cases. Where the prosecutor applies for the making of a confiscation order he may lodge with the clerk of court, a statement as to matters relevant to the assessment of the value of the accused's proceeds of drug trafficking (s.9(1)(a)) or to determining whether and by how much the accused has benefited from the commission of some other offence (s.9(1)(b)) as the case may be. Although no statutory form is prescribed for such statements, they have in the past been reminiscent of the pursuer's pleadings in a civil action. Some idea of the detail into which the Crown has gone may be gained from the judgment in *McLean*. Whether this rigorous approach will be maintained in future where confiscation is being sought not only in High Court drug trafficking cases, but also in summary cases in the sheriff courts is a matter for conjecture. It may be that in non-drug cases, where confiscation is in most cases limited to the benefit from the crime or crimes charged, a less rigorous accounting exercise will be required than in relation to drug trafficking where the proceeds which are relevant always include everything the accused has received in the past six years. Certainly there is English authority which would allow the courts to adopt a less conservative approach than has been the habit in Scotland hitherto. In *R. v. Small* (1989) 88 Cr.App.R. 184 C.A. the accused had never filled in a tax return, had no records, would give no proper details of his financial position and had recently spent large amounts of money. The judge made a confiscation order for £10,000 and said that he could only guess at the figure, an approach which was upheld on appeal. Again, in *R. v. Comiskey* (1991) 93 Cr.App.R. 227 C.A. the prosecution calculated the proceeds of drug trafficking by multiplying the street value of the drugs with which the defendant was caught, by the number of importations they had established that he had made. The sentencing judge took the view that the amounts suggested by the Crown were "probably reasonable" and made an order on that basis, which was upheld on appeal. Moreover, it is worth bearing in mind the case of *R. v. Atkinson (Michael Frederick)* [1992] Crim.L.R. 749 in which the judge was satisfied that the value of the proceeds was greater than the amount shown in the prosecutor's statement, and it was held that he was entitled to make an order in the higher sum.

Where a prosecutor's statement is lodged, and served on the accused, the court may require the accused to "indicate, within such period as the court may specify, to what extent he accepts each allegation in the statement, and, in so far as he does not accept any such allegation to indicate the basis of such non-acceptance" (s.9(3)). The prosecutor's statement and the answers produced by the defence serve to focus the dispute for a hearing.

The second assistance to the Crown comes in the form of assumptions as to the provenance of assets provided for by ss.2 and 3 of the present Act. These assumptions apply in all drug trafficking cases and in some non-drug cases.

The approach taken by the Crown to the calculation of drug trafficking proceeds is described in Lord Sutherland's judgment in *McLean* at page 921 B–C:

"The general approach taken by the Crown is set out in Schedule 1. The first section calculates the increase in net assets for each year. The second section calculates total withdrawals from building society and bank accounts with an adjustment for payments which have already been taken into account by reason of increasing assets or reducing liabilities. The sum of net increase in assets and withdrawals constitutes known expenditure. From this is deducted for each year the total known income. The balance constitutes expenditure which cannot be explained by known legitimate transactions and, *using the assumption contained in section 3(2), is deemed to be the proceeds of drug trafficking*" (Emphasis added).

It is evident that the Crown has focused substantially upon expenditure, upon the basis that expenditure must be funded from somewhere. Allowance is made for the funding of expenditure out of capital and out of legitimate income. It is then left to the accused to demonstrate, if he can, that the assumption that the expenditure was funded out of drug trafficking proceeds is incorrect. On this approach, the importance of the assumptions is to make the link between unexplained income and crime. On this critical matter, the legislation shifts the burden of proof to the defence.

Clearly the procedure for the making of a confiscation order could take some time and might, as in *McLean*, involve a hearing. To allow for that, s.10 permits the postponement of the making of a confiscation order for up to six months from the date of conviction.

Section 11 deals with the situation in which it turns out at some later date that the proceeds or benefit from the offence or the value of the realisable property is greater than was thought at the time the confiscation order was made and permits an application for a new confiscation order within six years of the making of the original order. Section 12 permits an application for a reduction in a confiscation order where it appears that the value of the realisable property is less than was thought. Section 13 permits an application for the making of a confiscation order in a case where although no order was made, it can be shown that the offender has benefited or derived proceeds from crime and the information necessary to make a confiscation order was not available at the time of the imposition of the original sentence. Section 14 applies the provisions relating to fines to the collection of confiscation orders.

PART II

As well as considering confiscation of the proceeds of crime, the Scottish Law Commission also considered, and made recommendations about, the forfeiture of what the Council of Europe Explanatory Report on the Laundering Convention refers to as the "instrumentalities" of crime, by which is meant items of property used in the commission of crime or intended to be so used. Part II completely recasts the law on this subject and introduces a new order, known as a "suspended forfeiture order", which is at the heart of the new legislative scheme.

By s.21, a suspended forfeiture order will be available where, in respect of any offence, the accused is convicted (whether in solemn or summary proceedings) or where in summary proceedings he is discharged absolutely. The prosecutor will be able to ask for an order under solemn procedure upon moving for sentence and under summary procedure upon the conviction of the accused. At that time he will have to tell the court of the identity of any person whom he knows or reasonably suspects to have an interest in the property. Before making the order the court will have to be "satisfied" (the Act does not say to what standard) that:

"property which was at the time of the offence or of the accused's apprehension in his ownership or possession or under his control—

(a) has been used for the purpose of committing, or facilitating the commission of, any offence; or

(b) was intended to be used for that purpose".

The first effect of the making of a suspended forfeiture order will be that the property is taken into the possession of or placed under the control of the clerk of court until either the order is recalled, or the property is forfeited and disposed of. The prosecutor will have to intimate the making of the order immediately in writing to any person named in the order as someone thought to have an interest in the property and will have to notify that person that he may be entitled to apply for the order to be recalled or for a direction that he is entitled to compensation under s.26. If the property includes heritage the prosecutor will have to cause a certified copy of the order to be recorded in the General Register of Sasines or Land Register of Scotland. In addition, if the court directs, the prosecutor will have to insert notice of the order in the Edinburgh Gazette or other publication.

In many cases the property will be perishable, dangerous, worthless or intrinsically pernicious (in the sense that its mere possession is unlawful). Where the prosecutor certifies that such is the case, it will, by s.24, be forfeited immediately after the making of the suspended forfeiture order. In other cases, forfeiture will take effect only after the passage of a period of time. Forfeiture will take effect in the case of heritable property, six months after the copy of the suspended forfeiture order is registered and in the case of moveable property 60 days after the making of the suspended forfeiture order. This delay will allow an opportunity for a third party having an interest in the property to vindicate that interest and secure the recall of the order, as provided for by s.25. If recall does not take place, the clerk of court will be able to grant a certificate as to forfeiture and that certificate will be conclusive evidence of the vesting of the property in the Crown and the necessary link in title in the case of heritage.

A further innovation is the application of the restraint order mechanism to property liable to forfeiture, by s.30, though, of course, in the case of forfeitable property, the restraint order will be more limited than in relation to a case concerning the confiscation of benefit from crime.

PART III

Part III of the Act adopts and adapts the "restraint order" mechanism created by the 1987 Act and applies it to both confiscation and forfeiture cases. A restraint order interdicts those affected by it from dealing with their property and allows the Crown to use inhibition and arrestment to "freeze" property more effectively. The intended effect was described by Otton J. in *Re M* [1992] 1 All E.R. 537 thus:

"The property to which the Restraint Order applies is no longer to be considered a part of the defendant's estate. He holds only notional title to such properties. All dealings with such property are to be held in abeyance until such time as the defendant is acquitted or a Confiscation Order is made and satisfied".

There are two obvious problems associated with restraint orders. The first is that some estates will include assets which require active management if they are to retain their value, and to provide for this s.34 and Sched. 1 provide for the appointment of administrators. The nearest analogous office is that of receiver. The more pressing problem, especially from the perspective of the third party affected in some way by a restraint order, is the serious hardship which will sometimes be caused by the absolute nature of the order. To meet this, the Act provides in s.31 for the variation and recall of restraint orders but, as will be seen from that section, the conditions for such action are stringent.

PART IV

Part IV of the Act deals with reciprocal arrangements for the enforcement of orders made by courts outwith Scotland. The importance of this has to do with the way in which criminals of any sophistication deal with the proceeds of their crimes.

The successful criminal faces a dilemma. He has what might be a very large amount of money but cannot explain how he came by it. If, as is entirely possible, he is suspected of particular crimes for other reasons, or known to the police in general, the possession of that money will certainly increase police interest in him and might be a significant factor in linking him with the offences which he has committed. He therefore wishes to deal with his proceeds in such a way as to retain their control and use but also to give them an appearance of legitimacy. In short, he wishes to launder his proceeds, and that process will often involve cross-border transactions. In the fullest study so far carried out, Beare and Schneider identified an international dimension in 80 per cent of all laundering schemes (M.E. Beare and S. Schneider, *Tracing of Illicit Funds:*

Money Laundering in Canada, Ministry of the Solicitor General of Canada, 1990, p. xxiii). This is reflected in the fact that a significant proportion of requests for investigative assistance by foreign authorities in Scotland relates to establishing audit trails in respect of "dirty" money.

The problem which this cross border dimension creates (and which the launderer intends it to create) for the law enforcement authorities is that the mechanisms for cross-border co-operation in law enforcement are a great deal slower and more cumbersome than those for transferring funds electronically across the world. Tracing the source of funds held by a criminal, or finding them in a financial secrecy jurisdiction in which he has hidden them, can present major difficulties. It is therefore essential for a legal system to take steps to enable foreign restraint and confiscation orders to be enforced domestically. Pt. IV provides the means whereby Scots law responds to that need and complements a series of bilateral mutual legal assistance treaties (most of which relate only to drugs cases) negotiated by the U.K. as well as the Laundering Convention and the 1988 UN Drugs Convention.

PART V
Part V deals with the usual miscellaneous matters at the end of an Act, but also makes provision for the interaction of this legislation with insolvency law and for confiscation where the offender dies before sentence.

COMMENCEMENT
This Act comes into force on April 1, 1996.

ABBREVIATIONS
DTOA   : Drug Trafficking Offences Act 1986.
SLC Report   : Scottish Law Commission "Report on Confiscation and Forfeiture" (SLC No. 147).
The 1987 Act : Criminal Justice (Scotland) Act 1987.
The 1975 Act : Criminal Procedure (Scotland) Act 1975.

PART I

CONFISCATION OF THE PROCEEDS OF CRIME

Confiscation orders

General provision

1.—(1) Subject to the provisions of this Part, where in respect of any offence to which this Part applies—
  (a) the accused is convicted, whether in solemn or summary proceedings; or
  (b) in the case of summary proceedings (without proceeding to conviction) an order is made discharging him absolutely,
the court, on the application of the prosecutor, may make an order (a "confiscation order") requiring the accused to pay such sum as the court thinks fit.
  (2) This Part applies to any offence which has been prosecuted—
  (a) on indictment; or
  (b) on summary complaint if the offence is punishable by a fine of an amount greater than the amount corresponding to level 5 on the standard scale or by imprisonment for a period longer than 3 months or by both such fine and imprisonment,
but it does not apply to an offence under Part III of the 1989 Act (financial assistance for terrorism).
  (3) A confiscation order shall not be made unless the court orders some other disposal (including an absolute discharge) in respect of the accused.
  (4) Except where the offence is a drug trafficking offence, the court may make a confiscation order against an accused only if it is satisfied that he has benefited from the commission of the offence concerned.
  (5) The sum which a confiscation order requires an accused to pay in the case of a drug trafficking offence shall be an amount not exceeding—
  (a) subject to paragraph (b) below, what the court assesses to be the value of the proceeds of the person's drug trafficking; or

(b) if the court is satisfied that the amount that might be realised in terms of this Act at the time the confiscation order is made has a value less than that of the proceeds of the person's drug trafficking, what it assesses to be that amount.

(6) The sum which a confiscation order requires an accused to pay in the case of an offence not mentioned in subsection (5) above, must not exceed the lesser of—

(a) the amount of the benefit—
       (i) from the commission of the offence; or
       (ii) where section 2(4) of this Act applies, from the commission of the offence and any other offence, not being a drug trafficking offence, to which this Part of this Act applies; and

(b) the amount that might be realised at the time the order is made.

(7) Any application under this section shall be made—

(a) in proceedings on indictment, when the prosecutor moves for sentence or, if the accused is remitted for sentence under section 195 of the 1995 Act, before sentence is pronounced; and

(b) in summary proceedings, following the conviction of the accused.

(8) For the purposes of any appeal or review, a confiscation order is a sentence.

GENERAL NOTE

This section empowers the court, on the application of the prosecutor, to impose upon a person convicted of one of a specified range of offences an order known as a "confiscation order", which requires the accused to pay such sum as the court thinks fit. The offences in respect of which the order can be made are, with the exception of terrorist offences, all offences prosecuted on indictment and those offences prosecuted on summary complaint, in respect of which the available penalty exceeds the normal summary *maxima*. The upper limit of a confiscation order is (a) the value of the proceeds of drug trafficking or benefit from other crime, or (b) the amount which might be realised, whichever is less.

Subs. (1)

Any offence to which this Part applies. It is not open to the Court to make a confiscation order in relation to every offence of which a person might be convicted, nor even in relation to every offence which might generate proceeds. Subsection (2) sets out the offences to which the power applies.

The court... may. The Act follows the 1987 Act, and diverges from its English equivalents, in giving the court a discretion.

On the application of the prosecutor. The Scottish Law Commission took the view (SLC Report, para. 6.3) that the prosecutor's involvement would in practice be essential because only he would have the information necessary for an inquiry into the financial profile of the offender and that to oblige the court to make an enquiry where the prosecutor did not seek one would be to oblige it to waste its time. The commentator on *R. v. Bragason* [1988] Crim.L.R. 778 called attention to "...the absurdity of making the Act mandatory in every case where the offender is convicted of a drug trafficking offence, even where it is obvious from the start that the offender has no realisable assets". The Scottish Law Commission also took the view that even to give the court a discretion to consider confiscation *ex proprio motu* (as the English courts have under s.2(1)(b) of the Drug Trafficking Act 1994) would be to oblige the court to consider the matter pointlessly. They went on to say:

"[i]t is to be expected that a Scottish public prosecutor, who is required to act in the public interest and subject to the supervision of the Lord Advocate, would exercise his discretion only after careful consideration of all the relevant circumstances" (SLC Report, para. 6.3).

Requiring the accused to pay such sum as the court thinks fit. (i) *R. v. Porter* [1990] 1 W.L.R. 1260 makes it clear that joint and several confiscation orders are not appropriate. (ii) A confiscation order is an order requiring the accused to pay money and does not directly confiscate anything. It is at the enforcement stage that the property of the accused may be directly attacked (as to which, see s.14). (iii) The court has a discretion as to the amount of the order, within the *maxima* provided for in subs. (5). There is no lower limit. This is in line with the policy which was applied in the 1987 Act and contrasts with the 1988 Act which, in relation to non-drug-related crime in England and Wales, required that a threshold of £10,000 be reached before confiscation could be ordered. The Scottish Law Commission reviewed this (SLC Report, paras. 3.7 and 3.8) and concluded that the principle that the offender should not be allowed to retain any benefit from his crime must apply whatever the amount of the benefit. They considered that any prescribed amount would be "arbitrary and artificial". The Commission also expressed confidence that the Crown would seek confiscation only after careful consideration of all the circumstances, including the amount of the proceeds which might be confiscated. The Crown Office gave an indication of its approach to this matter to the Scottish Affairs Committee when it pointed out that pursuing small confiscation orders can cause a strain on the resources of the law enforcement authorities (Scottish Affairs Committee, *Drug Abuse in Scotland*, H.C. 62–III, para. 975, evidence of Mr N. McFadyen) and explained that it has been the practice of the Crown Office to concentrate its own time and resources, and those of the police, on seeking confiscation where realisable assets have been identified which can go to satisfying a confiscation order (Scottish Affairs Committee, *Drug Abuse in Scotland*, H.C. 62–II, Memorandum submitted by the Crown Office, p. 32).

Subs. (2)

This Part applies to any offence which has been prosecuted . . . (b) on summary complaint if the offence is punishable by a fine of an amount greater than the amount corresponding to level 5 on the standard scale or by imprisonment for a period longer than three months. Level 5 on the standard scale is at present £5,000 (Criminal Procedure (Scotland) Act 1995, s.225(1)).

The Scottish Law Commission noted (SLC Report, para. 3.2) Gilmore's observation that the Laundering Convention "contains an implicit invitation for [confiscation] legislation to be as broad in scope as possible" (W.C. Gilmore, *International Efforts to Combat Money Laundering*, Cambridge International Documents Series, 1992, Vol. 4, p. xv). They noted that offences from which substantial benefits are likely to be derived are usually prosecuted on indictment but are sometimes prosecuted on summary complaint in the sheriff court. English law has identified the offences in respect of which magistrates' courts can make confiscation orders by enacting a list in Pt. I of Sched. 4 to the Criminal Justice Act 1988. The Scottish Law Commission considered, however, that a better approach would be to make confiscation available in all those cases for which Parliament has provided an enhanced summary penalty. They considered it reasonable to assume that Parliament provides such penalties because it considers the particular offences to be especially lucrative or particularly serious. The effect of the legislation will be that, without further legislation, any offence for which Parliament provides such a penalty will be within the ambit of the confiscation mechanism.

Among the offences thus included will be all of those listed in Pt. I of Sched. 4 to the Criminal Justice Act 1988 but also many environmental offences, which carry a maximum penalty of £20,000 (see A.N. Brown, *Confiscation: A New Way to Make the Polluter Pay* (1995) 8 Green's Environmental Law Bulletin 2), trading standards offences, health and safety at work offences and most of the offences under the Misuse of Drugs Act 1971.

But it does not apply to an offence under Part III of the 1989 Act. The 1989 Act is the Prevention of Terrorism (Temporary Provisions) Act 1989 (c. 4) which contains its own confiscation provisions.

Subs. (3)

The Scottish Law Commission commented (SLC Report, para. 5.2):

"Although we consider a confiscation order to be in some degree penal in character we do not think it would be appropriate for an order to be the only sentence or other means of dealing with the offender to be ordered by the court. For the court only to make a confiscation order would be to indicate to the public that an offence of the kind concerned would be tolerated if the offender could be parted from his proceeds."

Gane has made a similar point, noting that it would be "invidious if those with substantial assets which could be confiscated could thereby hope to avoid other penalties such as imprisonment" (Criminal Justice (Scotland) Act 1987, Current Law Statutes Annotated 1987 Vol. 2, 41–9).

Subs. (4)

The proposition that a confiscation order can only be made where the offender has benefited from the crime arises inevitably from the fact that the purpose of such an order is to deprive the offender of that benefit. The exception for drug trafficking cases arises because there are assumptions under s.3 which operate to deprive the offender not only of the benefit from the particular crime of which he has been convicted but also of other drug crime over the preceding six years, even if he has not been convicted of that crime. It might easily be that he had no benefit from the particular offence (for example, if he has been convicted of possession with intent to supply) but substantial benefit from earlier offences.

Drug trafficking offence. By s.46(5) this expression is defined so as to include a wide range of drug-related offences.

Subs. (5)

The value of the proceeds of the person's drug trafficking. If the English authorities are to be followed, "proceeds" will be regarded as synonymous with gross proceeds, and no deduction will be made for running costs (*R. v. Smith* [1989] 1 W.L.R. 765). The terms of s.3(1) are consistent with this approach.

The amount that might be realised in terms of this Act. This expression is almost synonymous with "realisable property", as to which see s.4. However, "the amount that might be realised" applies only to the accused and to the calculation of a confiscation order, whereas "realisable property" applies also to the property of those who have received certain types of gift, as to which see s.6.

The amount of the benefit in respect of which it is made. The measure for non-drug-related crime is subtly different from that which applies in drugs cases. In drugs cases, the focus is on "proceeds", a word which implies positive income. In a drug trafficking case, or any other case involving the sale of a commodity or service (for example, pornography or prostitution) such positive income will be likely to exist. "Benefit", however, is a wider concept, developed by the Scottish Law Commission under reference to the requirement in the Laundering Convention that measures be adopted to permit the confiscation of proceeds, defined as "any economic advantage from criminal offences".

The Commission, of course, were considering only non-drug-related crime. As noted above, the requirement of the Laundering Convention as regards confiscation of proceeds goes further than positive income and defines "proceeds" in terms which the Commission have rendered by "benefit". In an appropriate case the way might have been open for the Scottish courts to interpret "proceeds" widely in the drug trafficking context, so as to include, for example, the provision of services or facilities to one who has assisted in trafficking, but the use of the words "proceeds" and "benefit" in apparent distinction within subs. (5) might make such an interpretation more difficult.

Subs. (6)

The provision that an application in solemn procedure is to be made when the prosecutor moves for sentence or, on a remit to the High Court, before sentence is pronounced, is derived from s.1(1) of the 1987 Act (SLC Report, para. 6.4). That section, however, applied in a situation in which *only* the High Court could make a confiscation order. Now that the sheriff court may also make confiscation orders, the provision in relation to remits seems unnecessary unless Crown Counsel are to have the opportunity to seek confiscation in cases where the procurator fiscal has refrained from doing so.

The reference to the conviction of the accused in summary proceedings is necessitated by the implicit, rather than explicit, nature of the motion for sentence in summary procedure (SLC Report, para. 6.4).

Subs. (7)

Subsection (7) avoids the contentious issue of whether confiscation is a penalty by equiparating confiscation with a sentence for the purposes of appeal, and hence making the usual avenues of appeal against sentence available, but offering no general principle.

Benefit from commission of offence

2.—(1) For the purposes of this Part of this Act, an accused shall be held to have benefited from the commission of an offence if in connection with its commission he has obtained, directly or indirectly, any property or other economic advantage.

(2) Subject to subsection (4) below, in determining whether an accused has benefited from the commission of an offence and, if he has, the amount referred to in section 1(6)(a)(i) of this Act, the court may make the following assumptions, except in so far as he proves either of them, on the balance of probabilities, to be incorrect—

　　(a) that any property or other economic advantage which has been obtained by him since the relevant date has been obtained in connection with the commission of the offence; and

(b) that any expenditure by him since the relevant date was met out of property or other economic advantage obtained in connection with the commission of the offence.

(3) In subsection (2) above "the relevant date" means—

(a) the date of the offence; or

(b) if the offence is found to have been committed over a period of time, the date occurring at the beginning of that period.

(4) Where—

(a) the application for the confiscation order has been made in respect of two or more offences; or

(b) during the relevant period the accused has been convicted of at least one other offence to which this Part of this Act applies,

the court may, in determining the amount referred to in section 1(6)(a)(ii) of this Act, make the assumptions set out in subsection (5) below, except in so far as the accused proves either of those assumptions, on the balance of probabilities, to be incorrect.

(5) Those assumptions are—

(a) that any property or economic advantage which has been obtained by the accused during the relevant period has been obtained in connection with the commission of an offence to which this Part of this Act applies; and

(b) that any expenditure by him during the relevant period was met out of property or other economic advantage obtained in connection with the commission of such an offence.

(6) In subsections (4) and (5) above, "the relevant period" means the period of six years ending with the date on which proceedings were instituted against the accused for the offence in respect of which the application for the confiscation order has been made.

(7) In this Act, "property" means any property wherever situated, whether heritable or moveable or whether corporeal or incorporeal.

GENERAL NOTE

Section 2 applies only in non-drug-related cases. It defines the concept of "benefit" and provides for the making of certain assumptions in relation to the proof of the amount of benefit.

Subs. (1)

Directly or indirectly. The scope of the definition of benefit is deliberately wide.

Property. Property is defined by subs. (4) so as to include property wherever situated, whether heritable or moveable or whether corporeal or incorporeal. It is, therefore, not necessary that the property should be in Scotland and there exists a substantial and expanding network of bilateral mutual legal assistance treaties with other countries designed, *inter alia*, to help identify and recover such property held overseas.

Other economic advantage. This will enable the courts to strike at the benefit derived from offences such as those concerned with the environment or health and safety at work where the gain is to be measured in terms of compliance costs not incurred rather than payment received. The Scottish Law Commission included among their examples the obtaining of services by fraud, the evasion of an obligation to make a payment and the obtaining of a reward in the form of a free holiday (SLC Report, para. 4.3).

Subs. (2)

The court may make. Whereas the movement in English law has been to oblige the court to make the assumptions, the Scottish court retains its discretion.

The following assumptions. The assumptions provided for by subs. (2) are variations on two of the assumptions which are made in drug trafficking cases as a result of s.3 and which are considered in greater detail there. The Scottish Law Commission reviewed experience with the use of assumptions in drugs cases and concluded that these two assumptions could properly be applied to non-drug-related cases (SLC Report, paras. 6.7–6.9). As the Commission pointed out, the source of any property or economic advantage should be within the knowledge of the accused (SLC Report, para. 6.9). We might indeed go further and suggest that it is likely to be peculiarly within his knowledge. The transfer of the tactical burden at least to the accused in such circumstances is consistent with such cases as *Milne v. Whaley*, 1975 S.L.T. (Notes) 75.

Subs. (4)

Subsection (4) permits the court to make the assumptions set out in subs. (5) (which are modified versions of those set out in subs. (2)) in relation to the six years immediately preceding the institution of proceedings, provided that the application for a confiscation order is made in respect of at least two offences or that the accused has during that six years been convicted of an offence to which Pt. I applies and except insofar as the accused proves them to be incorrect.

In so providing, the Act goes beyond the Scottish Law Commission's scheme and follows the approach taken by the Proceeds of Crime Act 1995 for England and Wales. On the face of it, it applies a modified version of the rules applying to drug trafficking with the additional protection for the accused that it only comes into play if he is convicted of at least two offences. There are, however, grounds for uneasiness about the principle of this, especially in relation to the requirement that the accused should have been convicted during the six years. As a protection, this is of very limited value in view of the wide scope of the application of the Act in terms of s.1(2). However, since the accused will already have been sentenced in respect of that offence (perhaps even by a financial penalty and almost always with that possibility), it is arguable that to make assumptions about its proceeds (which in effect is part of what is provided for) and to take them into account in assessing a confiscation order is to penalise the accused for a second time in respect of that offence.

The six-year period derives ultimately from the limitation period in English law (see Earl Ferrers, *Hansard*, H.L. Vol. 540, col. 748 and SLC Report, para. 7.8).

Assessing the proceeds of drug trafficking

3.—(1) For the purposes of this Act—
- (a) any payments or other rewards received by a person at any time (whether before or after the commencement of this Act) in connection with drug trafficking carried on by him or another are his proceeds of drug trafficking, and
- (b) the value of his proceeds of drug trafficking is the aggregate of the values of the payments or other rewards.

(2) Without prejudice to section 9 of this Act the court may, in making an assessment as regards a person under section 1(5) of this Act, make the following assumptions, except in so far as any of them may be shown to be incorrect in that person's case—
- (a) that any property appearing to the court—
  - (i) to have been held by him at any time since his conviction; or, as the case may be,
  - (ii) to have been transferred to him at any time since a date six years before his being indicted, or being served with the complaint, was received by him, at the earliest time at which he appears to the court to have held it, as a payment or reward in connection with drug trafficking carried on by him;
- (b) that any expenditure of his since the date mentioned in paragraph (a)(ii) above was met out of payments received by him in connection with drug trafficking carried on by him, and
- (c) that, for the purpose of valuing any property received or assumed to have been received by him at any time as such a reward, he received the property free of any other interests in it.

(3) Subsection (2) above does not apply if the only offence by virtue of which the assessment is being made is an offence under section 14 of the Criminal Justice (International Co-operation) Act 1990 or section 37 or 38 of the Criminal Law (Consolidation) (Scotland) Act 1995.

(4) The court shall, in making an assessment as regards a person under section 1(5) of this Act, leave out of account any of his proceeds of drug trafficking that are shown to the court to have been taken into account in a case where a confiscation order (whether under this Act or under and within the meaning of—
- (a) section 2 of the 1994 Act; or
- (b) any corresponding provision in Northern Ireland),
has previously been made against him.

GENERAL NOTE

This section is concerned with the assessment of the proceeds of drug trafficking. It provides that the value of the proceeds of drug trafficking is the aggregate of the value of the payments or other rewards received by the relevant person at any time in connection with drug trafficking carried on by him or another. The section does not limit itself to drug trafficking carried on within Scotland or even the U.K. and applies to payments or rewards received both before and after the commencement of the Act. This retrospective effect was, in its DTOA manifestation, at issue before the European Court of Human Rights in *Welch v. U.K.* [1995] E.H.R.R. 247 and the Court held that it constituted a breach of the Convention to the extent that it applied to payments received before the DTOA came into force. The essential difference, however, is that there was no such provision before the DTOA. So far as the present Act is concerned, the 1987 Act, which has been in force since 1988, contained a provision to the same effect in s.3(1) and it follows that the present legislation is to be distinguished from the *Welch* case. The only residual significance that case has in terms of its particular circumstances would be in a case in which the Crown sought to prove the receipt of payments, etc. in respect of drug trafficking before the commencement of the 1987 Act, which is unlikely.

By subs. (4) proceeds which are already the subject of a confiscation order anywhere in the U.K. are to be left out of account.

Subs. (1)

Any payments or rewards received... at any time. In *R. v. Taylor (Ronald), The Times,* December 7, 1995, the defendant had been convicted in 1986 of conspiracy to import cannabis during the period from 1970 to 1979. That conviction preceded the DTOA and accordingly, although he was fined £234,000, there could be no confiscation order. In 1994 he was again convicted, this time in relation to the importation of cannabis on several occasions between 1990 and 1993. A confiscation order was made in a total sum of £15,311,729 which took account not only of the proceeds of the drug trafficking between 1990 and 1993 (£3,740,086) but also of the proceeds of the trafficking during the 1970s (£11,571,643). It was argued on his behalf in the Court of Appeal that the trial judge was purporting to exercise a power in connection with proceedings against the appellant for a drug trafficking offence instituted before the commencement of the DTOA. The court, however, founding on s.2(5) of the DTOA (which was in equivalent, but not identical, terms to subs. (4) of the present Act) upheld both elements of the confiscation order.

Drug trafficking. Drug Trafficking is defined by s.49(2) and (3) in terms of the contravention of specified statutory provisions or the corresponding laws of another country.

Subs. (2)

Without prejudice to section 9 of this Act. Section 9 deals with the prosecutor's statement and provides that in certain circumstances the accused is to be treated as accepting the prosecutor's averments. That mechanism and the assumptions provided for by s.3 are intended to work together, not as alternatives.

The court... may make the following assumptions. As in relation to non-drug-related crime, the court has the discretion whether or not to make the assumptions. In *R. v. Redbourne* [1992] 1 W.L.R. 1182 the Court of Appeal said that the judge must have some reason to suspect that the defendant has benefited from drug trafficking before making the assumptions and that it is neither necessary nor sensible to apply any standard of proof to the question whether such reason to suspect exists. Presumably there will in most cases be material in the evidence upon which the accused has been convicted to give such reason for suspicion and there plainly was in *Redbourne.*

It may be noted that s.6 of the Drug Trafficking Act 1994 has removed the discretion of English judges as to the making of the assumptions.

Except in so far as any of them may be shown to be incorrect. In non-drug-related cases s.2 permits the assumptions to be made unless the accused proves them, on the balance of probabilities, to be incorrect. In drug trafficking cases the accused must "show" them to be incorrect, which was the wording used in s.3(2) of the 1987 Act. In *McClean* Lord Sutherland proceeded on the basis that the wording in the 1987 Act required the accused to prove the incorrectness of the assumptions on a balance of probabilities (see p. 921B) and that was also the approach taken by the trial judge in *Redbourne* and approved by the Court of Appeal in *R. v. Dickens* [1990] 2 W.L.R. 1384 at p. 1389. It may be that there is scope for the argument that some other standard applies in view of the difference between ss.2 and 3 but in light of this case law it is unlikely that such an argument would succeed.

Subs. (3)

Section 14 of the Criminal Justice (International Co-operation) Act 1990. Section 14 of the Criminal Justice (International Co-operation) Act 1990 creates two money laundering offences.

Section 14(1) makes it an offence for a person to conceal or disguise any property which is, or in whole or in part represents, his proceeds of drug trafficking for the purpose of avoiding prosecution for a drug trafficking offence or the making or enforcement in his case of a confiscation order; or to convert or transfer that property or remove it from the jurisdiction with such a purpose. Section 14(2) makes it an offence for a person who knows or has reasonable grounds to suspect that any property is, or in whole or in part directly or indirectly represents, another person's proceeds of drug trafficking, to conceal or disguise that property or convert or transfer that property or remove it from the jurisdiction for the purpose of assisting any person to avoid a prosecution for a drug trafficking offence or the making or enforcement of a confiscation order.

Realisable property

4.—(1) In this Act "realisable property" means, subject to subsection (2) below—
  (a) the whole estate wherever situated of a person—
      (i) against whom proceedings have been instituted for an offence to which this Part of this Act applies; or
      (ii) in respect of whom a restraint order has been made by virtue of section 29(3) of this Act;
  (b) the whole estate wherever situated of a person to whom any person whose whole estate is realisable by virtue of paragraph (a) above has (directly or indirectly and whether in one transaction or in a series of transactions) made a gift caught by this Part of this Act or, as the case may be, an implicative gift;
  (c) any other property in the possession or under the control of a person mentioned in paragraph (a) or (b) above; and
  (d) any income or estate vesting in a person mentioned in paragraph (a) or (b) above.
(2) Property is not realisable if—
  (a) held on trust by a person mentioned in subsection (1)(a) or (b) above for a person not so mentioned;
  (b) a suspended forfeiture order is in force in respect of the property; or
  (c) it is, for the time being, subject to a restraint order made in respect of other proceedings.
(3) For the purposes of this Part of this Act, the amount that might be realised at the time a confiscation order is made in respect of a person is—
  (a) in relation to an offence which is not a drug trafficking offence, subject to section 7(5) of this Act, the total value at that time of all his realisable property, and of all gifts caught by this Part which have been made by him, less any amount due by him at that time in respect of any compensation order under section 249 of the 1995 Act made before the confiscation order; and
  (b) in relation to a drug trafficking offence, the total value at that time of all his realisable property and all implicative gifts which have been made by him.
(4) In assessing the value of realisable property (other than money) of a person in respect of whom it proposes to make a confiscation order, the court shall have regard to the likely market value of the property at the date on which the order would be made; but it may also have regard to any security or real burden which would require to be discharged in realising the property or to any other factors which might reduce the amount recoverable by such realisation.
(5) In assessing the value of realisable property of a person whose estate has been sequestrated, or who has been adjudged bankrupt in England and Wales or Northern Ireland, the court shall take into account the extent to which the property is subject to, as the case may be, sequestration or bankruptcy procedure by virtue of paragraph 1 or 2 of Schedule 2 to this Act.
(6) Without prejudice to section 2(7) of this Act, the court may, for the purposes of section 1(5)(b) of this Act, disregard the amount (or part of the

amount) of an implicative gift if it considers it improbable that such amount (or part) could be realised.

GENERAL NOTE

This section defines "realisable property" and provides rules for its valuation. The concept of "realisable property" is of significance both to the assessment of the level of confiscation orders and to the effect of restraint orders.

Subs. (1)

The Scottish Law Commission considered that the correct approach to the specification of the property which might be realised for the purpose of satisfying a confiscation order would be to adopt "a broad definition with the fewest possible exceptions" (SLC Report, para. 4.9). This was to ensure that restraint orders are effective, bearing in mind that they are likely to be obtained before it is possible to make a careful appreciation of the extent of the benefit or proceeds of the crime, that the maximum property is available to satisfy a confiscation order and to prevent the use of third parties to circumvent restraint orders. To that end, the subsection includes in the definition of "realisable property": (a) the whole estate of a person against whom proceedings have been instituted or against whom proceedings are to be instituted within 28 days (under reference to s.29(3)); (b) the whole estate wherever situated of a person to whom such a person has made a gift which is "caught" by Pt. I of the Act or is an implicative gift; (c) any property in the possession of or under the control of a person mentioned in (a) or (b); and (d) any income or estate vesting in such a person.

The Commission did not think it likely that the property of innocent third parties would in practice be used to satisfy confiscation orders, partly because the Act provides a means in s.31 for such persons to obtain the variation and recall of restraint orders.

By subss. (4) and (5) the court may take into account the value of any security over property and must take into account the extent to which the property is subject to sequestration or bankruptcy.

The whole estate. The Act departs from that part of the 1987 Act definition which related to the capacity to exercise certain powers over property, for the reasons set out by the Scottish Law Commission in para. 4.12 of their Report. The expression is not now defined and presumably bears its ordinary, well understood but unextended meaning.

Wherever situated. The property need not be in Scotland or even in the U.K. Serious profit-motivated criminals are very likely to launder their proceeds overseas and indeed 80 per cent of all laundering schemes in a Canadian study had an international dimension (M.E. Beare and S. Schneider, *Tracing of Illicit Funds: Money Laundering in Canada*, Ministry of the Solicitor General of Canada, 1990, p. xxiii). Moreover the Financial Action Task Force, established by the G7 countries to assess the results of co-operation undertaken to prevent the utilisation of the banking system and financial institutions for money laundering, and to consider additional preventive efforts, has said that "the stage of drugs cash movements between countries is crucial in the detection of money laundering" (FATF Recommendations, reproduced in MacQueen, *Money Laundering*, Hume Papers on Public Policy, Vol. 1, No. 2, Edinburgh University Press, 1993, p. 28).

Against whom proceedings have been instituted. The institution of proceedings is defined by s.49(6) as the earliest occurring of arrest, charge, grant of a warrant to arrest, grant of a warrant to cite, first calling of the case in summary proceedings, intimation of a petition or service of an indictment or complaint.

An offence to which this Part of this Act applies. The offences to which Pt. I applies are set out in s.1(2).

A restraint order … made by virtue of section 29(3). Section 29(3) deals with restraint orders made before proceedings are commenced.

A gift caught by this Part of this Act. This expression refers to non-drug-related cases and is defined in s.5.

Implicative gift. This expression is the counterpart for drugs cases of gifts caught by Pt. I. It is defined in s.6.

Subs. (2)

Subsection (2) deals with three necessary exceptions to the inclusion of property within the category of realisable property.

Suspended forfeiture order. Suspended forfeiture orders are introduced by ss.21, 24 and 25 and are orders which take effect to forfeit the instrumentalities of crime if within specified times they are not recalled.

Subs. (3)

The two parts of subs. (3) mirror each other and provide in effect that the amount which might be realised is the aggregate of the accused's own realisable property and gifts, either caught by Pt. I of the Act or implicative, as the case may be. In the case of non-drug-related crime, the amount of any compensation order falls to be deducted but such orders are, for obvious reasons, unlikely to be made in drug trafficking cases.

Gifts caught by Part I

5.—(1) A gift is caught by this Part of this Act if—
(a) it was made by the accused—
    (i) in contemplation of, or after, the commission of the offence; or, if more than one,
    (ii) in contemplation of any of the offences or after the commission of the earlier or the earliest of the offences,
to which the proceedings mentioned in section 4(1)(a)(i) of this Act for the time being relate, not being drug trafficking offences; or
(b) where subsection (4) of section 2 of this Act applies, it was made by the accused within the relevant period within the meaning of subsection (6) of that section.
(2) The value of a gift caught by this Part of this Act shall be assessed in accordance with section 7 of this Act.
(3) At any time before the realisation of property which is or represents a gift caught by this Part of this Act, the recipient of the gift may apply to the court for an order under this subsection, and, if the court is satisfied, on the balance of probabilities—
(a) that the person received the gift not knowing, not suspecting and not having reasonable grounds to suspect that the gift was made in contemplation of, or after, the commission of the offence or, if more than one, in contemplation of any of the offences or after the commission of the earlier or the earliest of the offences to which the proceedings for the time being relate; and
(b) that he was not associated with the giver in the commission of the offence; and
(c) that he would suffer hardship if the application were not granted,
it may make an order declaring that the gift or a part of the gift shall not be caught by this Part of this Act and that the property or part of the property of the recipient of the gift shall not be, or shall cease to be, realisable for the purposes of this Part of this Act and, if a confiscation order has already been made, varying that order accordingly, where necessary.
(4) An appeal shall lie to the High Court at the instance of—
(a) the applicant against the refusal;
(b) the prosecutor against the granting,
of an application under subsection (3) above, and the High Court in determining such an appeal may make such order as could have been made by the court on an application under that subsection.
(5) The procedure in an appeal under this section shall be the same as the procedure in an appeal against sentence.

General Note

It is necessary to strike at gifts made by the accused in order to defeat the fairly obvious expedient of the criminal putting his proceeds or benefit from crime into the hands of a third party so as to avoid restraint or confiscation. However, as soon as property in the hands of a third party, unconvicted and unprosecuted, is affected by the Act, significant questions arise and it is necessary to attempt to strike a fair balance between the needs of the criminal justice system in relation to property which has at some point been in the possession of the offender and which might well represent benefit from crime and the needs of innocent third parties. Third parties who are not innocent are, of course, not intended to be protected and indeed they might well be guilty of money laundering offences.

Section 5 deals with gifts in non-drug-related cases.

Subs. (1)

Subsection (1) defines the gifts caught by the Act. They are those made by the accused in contemplation of, or after the commission of, the offence.

The proceedings mentioned in section 4(1)(a)(i). This refers to the prosecution in respect of the predicate (non-drug trafficking) offence.

Where subsection (4) of section 2 ... applies. Section 2(4) deals with the situation in which the application for a confiscation order relates to two or more offences and the accused has been convicted within the previous six years of at least one other offence to which Pt. I applies.

The relevant period. As provided by section 2(6), the relevant period is the six years before the commencement of proceedings.

Subs. (3)

Subsection (3) provides a means for the recipient of the gift to obtain an order which would take the gift out of the category of gifts caught by the Act, but in order to do so he must prove, on a balance of probabilities, that he received it without knowing, suspecting or having reasonable grounds to suspect that it was made in contemplation or after the commission of the offence(s), that he was not associated with the giver in the commission of the offence and that he would suffer hardship if the application were not granted. By subs. (4) an appeal lies to the High Court, the procedure being (in terms of subs. (5)) that applicable to an appeal against sentence.

Implicative gifts

6.—(1) In this Act references to an "implicative gift" are references to a gift (whether made before or after the commencement of this Act)—

(a) made not more than six years before the date on which, in respect of a person suspected of, or charged with, a drug trafficking offence, the proceedings were commenced or a restraint order was made (whichever first occurs); or

(b) made at any time if the gift was of property—

(i) received by the giver in connection with drug trafficking carried on by him or another, or

(ii) which, in whole or in part, directly or indirectly represented in the giver's hands property received by him in that connection.

(2) The value of an implicative gift shall be assessed in accordance with section 7 of this Act.

(3) Where the court is satisfied, on the application of a person in receipt of an implicative gift made before or after a confiscation order has been made—

(a) that the person received the gift not knowing, not suspecting and not having reasonable grounds to suspect that the giver was in any way concerned in drug trafficking; and

(b) that he is not, and has never been, associated with the giver in drug trafficking; and

(c) that he would suffer hardship if the application were not granted,

it may make an order declaring that the gift or a part of the gift shall not be an implicative gift and that the property or part of the property of the recipient of the gift shall not be, or shall cease to be, realisable for the purposes of this Part of this Act and, if a confiscation order has already been made, varying that order accordingly, where necessary.

(4) An appeal shall lie to the High Court at the instance of—

(a) the applicant against the refusal;

(b) the prosecutor against the granting,

of an application under subsection (3) above on the ground that there has been a miscarriage of justice.

(5) The procedure in an appeal under this section shall be the same as the procedure in an appeal against sentence.

GENERAL NOTE

Section 6 applies the scheme contained in s.5 to drug trafficking cases, using the term "implicative gift", derived from the 1987 Act.

Subs. (1)

"Implicative gift" is defined as a gift made not more than six years before the commencement of proceedings or the making of a restraint order, or made at any time if it is of property received by the giver in connection with drug trafficking or which represents such property.

Gifts: valuation

7.—(1) In assessing the value of—

(a) a gift caught by this Part of this Act; or

(b) an implicative gift,

the court shall, subject to subsections (4) to (6) below, take it to be the greater of the values specified in subsections (2) and (3) below.

(2) The value specified in this subsection is the value of the gift when received adjusted to take account of subsequent changes in the value of money.

(3) The value specified in this subsection is both of the following—

(a) the likely market value, on the date on which the confiscation order is to be made, of—

(i) the gift, if retained; or

(ii) where the recipient of the gift retains only part of it, the retained part, and any property or part of any property which, directly or indirectly, represents the gift; or

(iii) where the recipient of the gift retains no part of it, any property or part of any property which, directly or indirectly, represents the gift; and

(b) the value of any other property and any other economic advantage which by reason of the making of the gift the recipient of the gift has obtained, directly or indirectly, prior to the date on which the confiscation order is to be made, adjusted to take account of subsequent changes in the value of money.

(4) The circumstances in which the accused is to be treated as making a gift include those where he transfers an interest in property to another person directly or indirectly for a consideration the value of which is significantly less than the value of that interest at the time of transfer; and in those circumstances the value of the gift shall be the difference between the value of that consideration and the value of that interest at the time of transfer, adjusted to take account of subsequent changes in the value of money.

(5) Where a gift was in the form of money and the recipient of the gift shows that, on the balance of probabilities, the money or any of it has not been used to purchase goods or services or to earn interest or any other return, the value of the gift or such part of it as has not been so used shall be taken to be the face value of the money or, as the case may be, unused amount of the money.

(6) The court may, notwithstanding the foregoing provisions of this section, disregard the amount (or part of the amount) of a gift caught by this Part of this Act if it considers it improbable that such amount (or part) could be realised.

General Note

Section 7 provides the rules for the assessment of the value of a gift caught by Pt. I or of an implicative gift. By subs. (1) that value is to be the greater of the values specified in subss. (2) and (3).

Subs. (2)

No guidance is given in the Act as to how changes in the value of money are to be calculated but the Scottish Law Commission pointed out that inflation tables, as printed in textbooks on damages, are often used in civil cases (SLC Report, para. 4.22).

Making of confiscation orders

8.—(1) If the court decides to make a confiscation order, it shall determine the amount to be payable thereunder before making any decision as to—
    (a) imposing a fine on the accused;
    (b) making any order involving any payment by him.
(2) Where a court makes a confiscation order against an accused in any proceedings, it shall, in respect of any offence of which he is convicted in those proceedings, take account of the order before—
    (a) imposing any fine on him;
    (b) making any order involving any other payment by him,
but subject to that, the court shall leave the order out of account in determining the appropriate sentence or other manner of dealing with the accused.
(3) No enactment restricting the power of a court which deals with an accused in a particular way from dealing with him also in any other way shall, by reason only of the making of a confiscation order (or the postponement of a decision as regards making such an order), have the effect of restricting the court in dealing with the accused in any way it considers appropriate in respect of an offence.
(4) Where a court makes both a confiscation order and a compensation order under section 249 of the 1995 Act against the same person in the same proceedings in relation to the same offence and the offence involves the misappropriation of property, it shall direct that the compensation shall be paid first out of any sums applied towards the satisfaction of the confiscation order.

GENERAL NOTE
    Section 8 establishes the relationship between confiscation orders and other penalties. In particular, subs. (4) gives effect to paras. 5.17 to 5.24 of the Scottish Law Commission Report, by requiring that, where a compensation order is also made, and that compensation order relates to the misappropriation of property, the compensation is to be paid first out of any sums applied towards the satisfaction of the confiscation order. As the Scottish Law Commission pointed out, "in such a case the benefit obtained from the offence by the offender will consist of or include assets lost by the victim". It would be entirely unjust to the victim if the effect of a confiscation order was to make a compensation order unenforceable, perhaps because it exhausted the whole property of the offender. The effect would be to benefit the Treasury to the disadvantage of the victim of the crime. Otherwise, confiscation takes precedence over any other financial penalty.

Statements relevant to making confiscation orders

9.—(1) Where the prosecutor applies for the making of a confiscation order, the prosecutor may lodge with the clerk of court a statement as to any matters relevant—
    (a) in connection with a drug trafficking offence, to the assessment of the
        value of the accused's proceeds of drug trafficking; and
    (b) in connection with any other offence—
            (i) to determining whether the accused has benefited for the pur-
        poses of section 1(6)(a) of this Act; or
            (ii) to an assessment of the value of the accused's benefit from the
        commission of the offence.
(2) Without prejudice to section 256 of the 1995 Act, if the accused accepts to any extent any allegation in the statement lodged under subsection (1) above, the court may, for the purpose of such determination or assessment as is mentioned in paragraph (a) or (b) of that subsection, treat his acceptance as conclusive of the matters to which it relates.
(3) Where—
    (a) a statement is lodged under subsection (1) above; and

(b) the court is satisfied that a copy of that statement has been served on the accused,

the court may require the accused to indicate, within such period as the court may specify, to what extent he accepts each allegation in the statement and, in so far as he does not accept any such allegation, to indicate the basis of such non-acceptance.

(4) If the accused fails in any respect to comply with a requirement under subsection (3) above, he may be treated for the purposes of this section as accepting every allegation in the statement apart from any allegation in respect of which he has complied with the requirement.

(5) Without prejudice to section 256 of the 1995 Act, where—

(a) there is lodged with the clerk of court by the accused a statement as to any matters relevant to determining the amount that might be realised at the time the confiscation order is made; and

(b) the prosecutor accepts to any extent any allegation in the statement, the court may, for the purposes of that determination, treat that acceptance as conclusive of the matters to which it relates.

(6) Without prejudice to section 10(1) of this Act, where—

(a) any allegation in the statement lodged under subsection (1) above is challenged by the accused, or

(b) the basis of the non-acceptance by the accused of any such allegation is challenged by the prosecutor,

the court shall consider the matters being challenged at a hearing.

(7) Where the judge presiding at a hearing held under subsection (6) above is not the trial judge he may, on the application of either party, if he considers that it would be in the interests of justice to do so, adjourn the hearing to a date when the trial judge is available.

(8) No acceptance by a person under this section that any payment or other reward was received by him in connection with drug trafficking carried on by him or another shall be admissible in evidence in any proceedings, whether in Scotland or elsewhere, in respect of an offence.

GENERAL NOTE

Section 9, which applies in both drug trafficking and non-drug-related cases, allows the prosecutor to lodge a statement with the court in connection with the assessment of the value of the proceeds of drug trafficking or of the benefit from other crime. The procedure contemplated is as follows: (a) the prosecutor applies for the making of a confiscation order and lodges his statement (subs. (1)); (b) the court specifies a period within which the defence answer the prosecutor's statement (subs. (3)); (c) within that period the defence lodge answers (subss. (3) and (4)); (d) the prosecutor, if he chooses, accepts some or all of the allegations in the defence's answers (subs. (5)); and (e) a hearing takes place (subs. (6)).

No statutory form is prescribed for prosecutors' statements but they have in the past been reminiscent of the pursuer's pleadings in a civil action, and the answers lodged by the defence have followed that example and recalled the form of the defender's answers in such a case. However, beyond the prosecutor's option of accepting some or all of the defence allegations, there is no provision for adjustment of either the statement or answers in relation to confiscation and the civil analogy should not, therefore, be pressed too far.

Some idea of the detail into which the Crown has gone may be gained from the judgment in *McLean* 1993 S.C.C.R. 917. Whether this rigorous approach will be maintained in future where confiscation is being sought not only in High Court drug trafficking cases but also in summary cases in the sheriff courts is a matter for conjecture. It may be that in non-drug-related cases, where confiscation is limited to the benefit from the crime or crimes charged, a less rigorous accounting exercise will be required than in relation to drug trafficking or repeated offending of some other sort, in both of which cases the proceeds which are relevant include everything the accused has received in the past six years.

Subs. (1)

The lodging of a statement is a matter for the prosecutor's discretion. In the more simple cases there will be sufficient material in the evidence which has been led in proof of the substantive offence to enable the court to assess the appropriate level for a confiscation order.

Subs. (3)

Where a statement is lodged and served on the accused the court may require the accused to indicate to what extent he accepts the allegations in the prosecutor's statement and, insofar as he does not accept any particular allegation, to indicate the basis of such non-acceptance.

Within such period as the court may specify. There is no provision for extension of the period allowed to the defence to answer the prosecutor's statement and it is therefore arguable that any such extension would be incompetent.

Indicate. This word appeared in the 1987 Act. Its precise meaning is unclear. However, it seems to be somewhat less demanding than the word "specify" would have been and, when used in combination with the words "the basis of such non-acceptance", it perhaps eases the burden on the defence in relation to the detail required of them in answering the prosecutor's statement.

The basis of such non-acceptance. This seems to rule out both bare denials and the use of the formula "not known and not admitted". It is arguable that on any point where the defence answers did not go beyond one of these responses they would be irrelevant.

Subs. (4)

The effect of failing adequately to indicate the basis of non-acceptance of particular Crown allegations or of failing to lodge answers within the period allowed, will be that the accused may be treated as accepting those allegations in the former case and all of the Crown's allegations in the latter. By s.9(2), acceptance of the Crown's allegations is conclusive.

Subs. (6)

There was no provision made in the 1987 Act for a hearing but it is hard to see how else the court could make the various assessments required of it and so the practice grew up. The Act does not offer a procedure for such hearings and it remains to be seen whether such provision will be made by Act of Adjournal.

Nor does the Act say anything about onus at such hearings. It seems clear enough that it will be for the Crown to prove that the offender had proceeds or benefit from crime but matters are more complicated when the court comes to consider whether it is the value of proceeds or benefit which is the appropriate measure or whether the realisable property is less and therefore takes precedence. The English courts have held in *R. v. Ilsemann* (1990) 12 Cr.App.R.(S.) 398 that once the prosecution has proved the benefit it is up to the accused to prove that his realisable property is less.

Subs. (7)

Adjournment, of a trial at least, is a matter for the discretion of the presiding judge. Presumably that discretion remains even though it has been thought necessary to give that judge a specific power to adjourn so that the confiscation hearing can proceed before the trial judge.

Postponed confiscation orders

10.—(1) If the court considers—

(a) that it has some, but not sufficient, relevant information for the purpose of enabling it to come to a decision as to whether to make a confiscation order; or

(b) that it does not have sufficient relevant information to enable it to come to a decision as to the amount to be payable under the confiscation order,

it may, subject as the case may be to subsection (6) or (10) below, postpone that decision for a period not exceeding 6 months after the date of conviction for the purpose of enabling further information to be obtained.

(2) Without prejudice to sections 201 and 202 of the 1995 Act, the court may notwithstanding postponement under subsection (1) above and subject to subsection (3) below, proceed, on the prosecutor's motion therefor, to sentence or to otherwise deal with the accused in respect of the conviction.

(3) Where the court proceeds as mentioned in subsection (2) above—

(a) no fine shall be imposed on the accused; and

(b) no order shall be made involving any other payment by him,

in relation to the conviction before the decision whether to make a confiscation order is taken.

(4) Where in the case of conviction on indictment a decision has been postponed under subsection (1) above for a period, any intention to appeal under

section 106 of the 1995 Act against conviction or against both conviction and any sentence passed during that period in respect of the conviction, shall be intimated under section 109(1) of the 1995 Act not within 2 weeks of the final determination of the proceedings but within 2 weeks of—

(a) in the case of an appeal against conviction where there has been no such sentence, the day on which the period of postponement commences;

(b) in any other case, the day on which such sentence is passed in open court.

(5) Notwithstanding any appeal of which intimation has been given by virtue of subsection (4) above, a person may appeal under section 106 of the 1995 Act against the confiscation order (if the decision is to make one) or against any other sentence passed, after the period of postponement, in respect of the conviction.

(6) If during the period of postponement intimation is given by virtue of subsection (4) above by the person, the High Court may, on the application of the prosecutor, extend that period to a date up to 3 months after the date of disposal of the appeal.

(7) This subsection applies where in the case of summary conviction a decision has been postponed under subsection (1) above for a period.

(8) Where subsection (7) above applies and the offender appeals under section 175 of the 1995 Act against conviction or against both conviction and any sentence passed during the period of postponement—

(a) his application for a stated case shall be made not within one week of the final determination of the proceedings but within one week of the day mentioned in paragraph (a) or (b) of subsection (4) above;

(b) his draft stated case shall be prepared and issued not within 3 weeks of the final determination of the proceedings but within 3 weeks of the said day.

(9) Where subsection (7) above applies, then, notwithstanding any appeal against conviction or sentence or both, the offender may appeal under section 175(2)(b), and the prosecutor may appeal under section 175(3)(b), of the 1995 Act against any confiscation order or against any other sentence passed, after the period of postponement, in respect of the conviction.

(10) Where subsection (7) above applies, then, if during the period of postponement the offender applies for a stated case or lodges a note of appeal, the High Court may, on the application of the prosecutor, extend the period of postponement to a date up to 3 months after the date of disposal of the appeal.

GENERAL NOTE

Section 10 follows the scheme of the 1987 Act in allowing the court to postpone its decision in relation to a confiscation order for a period of up to six months so as to allow more complete information to be obtained. 110 days, for example, is a very short period within which to try to produce a reliable financial profile of an offender, especially where he has taken steps to launder his proceeds of crime and even more so where he has done so in another jurisdiction. This is not to say that the power to postpone is confined to custody cases.

Where a postponement does occur, it can have consequences for appeals and the section makes provision in that regard also.

Subs. (1)

Subsection (1) contains the power to postpone. It arises in two situations. The first is that in which the court has insufficient information to decide whether to make a confiscation order at all and the second is that in which the court has insufficient information to come to a decision as to the amount to be payable.

Some, but not sufficient, relevant information. It is not open to the Crown to seek a postponement so that it can investigate whether or not to seek a confiscation order. In terms of s.1(7) the prosecutor must ask for such an order at the time of moving for sentence. The Act is silent on how much information is required to constitute "some, but not sufficient". No doubt the *de minimis* rule would apply.

Subs. (2)

The court may notwithstanding postponement ... proceed ... to sentence. The Scottish Law Commission and their consultees thought that a confiscation order should not operate to reduce any sentence of imprisonment imposed in respect of the same offence and also that it would be unfair to keep the accused in ignorance of the length of such a sentence until after a postponed confiscation hearing (SLC Report, para. 6.25–6.26).

Subs. (3)

In view of the fact that the accused's financial position will be fundamentally altered by a confiscation order it would not make sense to impose any other financial penalty before determining the amount to be paid under a confiscation order.

Subs. (4)

The postponement of a confiscation order would delay the final determination of proceedings. In order not to delay appeals against conviction, having regard, for example, to the needs of trial judges in relation to their Reports for the High Court. In *Smith v. H.M. Advocate*, 1983 S.C.C.R. 30 the Lord Justice-General (Emslie) called attention (in the context of an inadequately stated ground of appeal) to the Crown's need for an opportunity to consider its position and to the trial judge's need in his report to explain and deal with the alleged misdirection. Both of these considerations argue with equal force for ensuring that the taking of such an appeal is brought to the attention of the Crown and the trial judge as soon as possible after the events which are to be aired before the High Court.

Subs. (5)

Since subs. (4) has to apply to appeals against both conviction and sentence, this saving provision is required to preserve the position where an accused appeals against conviction but has no basis to complain about sentence until a confiscation order is made which he wishes to have reviewed either alone or in combination with the rest of his sentence.

Subs. (6)

Where during a postponement there is a supervening appeal against conviction the High Court may extend the postponement until three months after the disposal of the appeal. One obvious benefit will be to avoid the need for a confiscation hearing where the conviction for the predicate offence is in doubt. There is no point in holding a five-day inquiry into the complicated financial affairs of a convicted accused if there is any real chance that the High Court will overturn the conviction and render the whole exercise nugatory. The provisions of s.230A(1) of the 1975 Act by which a judge of the High Court is to consider whether there exist arguable grounds of appeal and otherwise to refuse leave to appeal will presumably mean that the possibility of the overturning of the conviction in an appeal which survives that sift must be very real.

Subss. (7), (8), (9) and (10)

These subsections make equivalent provision in relation to summary appeals.

Increase in benefit or realisable property

11.—(1) This section applies where the court which made a confiscation order is satisfied, on an application made by the prosecutor, that at the time the application is made—

    (a) in the case of a drug trafficking offence, the value of the proceeds of the person's drug trafficking, or the amount that might be realised, is greater than—

        (i) the value of the proceeds of his drug trafficking; or, as the case may be,

        (ii) the amount that might be realised; or

    (b) in any other case, the benefit for the purposes of section 1(6)(a) of this Act, or the amount that might be realised, is greater than—

        (i) the benefit; or, as the case may be,

        (ii) the amount that might be realised,

which was taken into account when the order was made.

(2) The considerations by reference to which the court may be satisfied as mentioned in subsection (1) above shall include—

    (a) the value of the proceeds of the person's drug trafficking or, as the case may be, the benefit was greater than was taken into account when the confiscation order was made or has increased in value since the confiscation order was made; or

(b) further proceeds of drug trafficking have or benefit has been obtained since the confiscation order was made; or

(c) the value of realisable property was greater than was taken into account when the confiscation order was made; or

(d) any realisable property taken into account at the time when the confiscation order was made has subsequently increased in value; or

(e) that the amount, or part of the amount, of a gift which was disregarded under section 7(6) of this Act could now be realised.

(3) An application under subsection (1) above shall be made as soon as is reasonably practicable after the relevant information becomes available to the prosecutor but in any event within 6 years commencing with the date when the person was convicted of the offence.

(4) Where this section applies—

(a) the court may make a new confiscation order for the payment of such sum as appears to the court to be appropriate having regard to what is now shown to be the benefit or the amount that might be realised; and

(b) if the earlier confiscation order has not been satisfied then the court, in making the new confiscation order, shall recall the earlier order and may take into account the amount unpaid (including any interest payable by virtue of section 15(1) of this Act) under the earlier order.

(5) Subsection (4) above applies to an offence which is not a drug trafficking offence notwithstanding that any matters in relation to the making of the confiscation order are, by virtue of section 9(2) or (5) of this Act, to be treated as conclusive.

(6) Section 9 of this Act shall, subject to any necessary modifications, apply in relation to the making of a new confiscation order in pursuance of this section as it applies where the prosecutor has applied for the making of a confiscation order under section 1 of this Act.

(7) The assumptions mentioned in, as the case may be, section 3(2) or 2(2) and (5) of this Act shall not apply for the purposes of this section.

GENERAL NOTE

The Scottish Law Commission pointed out that, in view of the difficulties which face prosecutors in ascertaining the value of the benefit from crime and the value of the accused's realisable property, it is necessary to make provision for three situations which can arise. The first is that in which a confiscation order has been made but it then appears that one or other of the relevant amounts is greater than was taken into account when the order was made (SLC Report, para. 7.1). It is this situation which is addressed by s.11.

The first attempt to deal with this was by s.17 of the Criminal Justice (International Co-operation) Act 1990. That provision applied only to drugs-related cases and was to be described by the Scottish Law Commission as "a somewhat cumbersome procedure". It represented the translation into Scots law of a procedure developed under reference to English law and contained in s.16 of the 1990 Act. The Commission examined that procedure and recommended its replacement.

Section 11 allows the court, on the application of the prosecutor (subs. (1)), to make a new confiscation order. The section makes use of concepts such as the value of the proceeds of a person's drug trafficking and realisable property which have been considered where they first appear in the Act and which, for that reason, are not elaborated here.

The application of the assumptions which may be made in the original assessment is excluded by subs. (7). This is likely to limit the practical application of s.11 to a very considerable extent. It was done because of a fear that to allow the application of the assumptions up to six years after the making of the confiscation order (and hence up to 12 years after the earliest events about which they might be made) would be oppressive (SLC Report, para. 7.11).

Subs. (1)

The court which made a confiscation order. The application requires to be made to the original sentencing court and not to any other. In the case of the sheriff court, the normal rule is that an offence may be tried within the sheriffdom in which it is committed and not merely within the sheriff court district (Criminal Procedure (Scotland) Act 1995, s.4(2)). It is thought that the concept of the unity of the sheriffdom would probably allow a sheriff sitting in Edinburgh, for example, to consider an application made in relation to an order made in Linlithgow and there would be an obvious utility in that if that sheriff had himself made the order in the first place. However, the point does not seem to have been considered and would presumably arise only rarely.

Is satisfied. The standard of proof is not specified. It is thought that the analogy with the making of the original confiscation order is so close as to demand the criminal standard and this was certainly the intention of the Scottish Law Commission. Subsection (2) sets out the considerations by reference to which the court may be satisfied.

On an application by the prosecutor. Under the 1990 Act an administrator could apply but the Scottish Law Commission thought that unnecessary (SLC Report, para. 7.4).

Subs. (2)
The considerations ... shall include. The list in subs. (2) is not exhaustive.

Subs. (3)
An application ... shall be made as soon as reasonably practicable. The Scottish Law Commission thought that the prosecutor should apply as soon as reasonably practicable after he obtains the information which prompts the application in order to prevent undue delay in the making of an application (SLC Report, para. 7.8). The Act does not provide a means of checking whether this standard is met nor a sanction for failure. No doubt the Crown will act in a manner which it believes to be proper but the jurisprudence on undue delay in other contexts makes it clear that there is always likely to be room for conflicting views on the matter.

But in any event within six years. The six-year period was selected for no better reason than the undesirability of having different periods for Scotland and England. The Scottish Law Commission were decidedly lukewarm about the reasoning which led to the selection of the six-year period in the first place (SLC Report, para. 7.8).

Subs. (4)
In the event of the prosecutor satisfying the court as to the matters in subs. (1), this subsection allows the court to make a new confiscation order and, in the event of the original order being outstanding, to recall that order but take account of any payments made under it.

Realisable property inadequate to meet payments under confiscation order

12.—(1) This section applies where the court which made a confiscation order is satisfied on the balance of probabilities, on an application made to it by the accused or the prosecutor, that the value of the realisable property is inadequate to meet any amount unpaid (including any interest payable by virtue of section 15(1) of this Act) under the confiscation order.

(2) When considering whether the value of the realisable property is inadequate the court—

(a) shall, unless already taken into account under section 4(5) of this Act, take into account the extent to which property of a person whose estate has been sequestrated or who has been adjudged bankrupt is or has been included in the bankrupt's estate for the purposes of the Bankruptcy (Scotland) Act 1985 or Part IX of the Insolvency Act 1986; and

(b) may disregard any inadequacy which appears to it to be attributable, wholly or partly, to anything done by the accused for the purpose of protecting the realisable property from realisation.

(3) Where this section applies, the court shall recall the confiscation order and make a new confiscation order for the payment of such sum of a lesser amount than that for which the original order was made which appears to the court to be appropriate having regard to—

(a) the value of the realisable property as determined under subsection (1) above; and

(b) any amount paid in pursuance of the original order.

(4) Section 9 of this Act shall, subject to any necessary modifications, apply in relation to an application under this section as it applies where the prosecutor has applied for the making of a confiscation order under section 1 of this Act.

GENERAL NOTE

The second situation identified by the Scottish Law Commission as requiring provision is that in which the value of the realisable property is inadequate to meet an outstanding balance on the confiscation order. Such a situation might arise if, for example, an asset was accidentally destroyed or damaged. In the case of an investment, an adverse market movement could have a similar effect. Provision was made for such a situation in s.25 of the 1987 Act but the Scottish Law Commission considered the scheme of that section to be unnecessarily complex (SLC Report, para. 7.12). Section 12 allows the court to recall the confiscation order and substitute an order for a lesser amount.

Subs. (1)

The court which made a confiscation order. It is thought that this phrase has the same meaning as in s.11(1).

Is satisfied on the balance of probabilities. This was the standard which would have applied had there ever been an application to the Court of Session under s.25 of the 1987 Act. It may be justified on the basis that the effect of the section is to mitigate a penalty, not to impose or increase one.

On an application made ... by the accused or the prosecutor. Since s.14 applies to the enforcement of confiscation orders the provisions which apply to fines; failure to meet a confiscation order can result in the imposition of the alternative sentence of imprisonment. If the accused's realisable property is truly reduced below the level required to pay the confiscation order he has a very real incentive to apply for a reduction.

Confiscation orders where proceeds of crime discovered at later date

13.—(1) This section applies where no confiscation order has been made in relation to an offence under section 1 or 10 of this Act.

(2) Where the court, on an application made to it by the prosecutor under this section, is satisfied—

    (a) that a person convicted of—

          (i) an offence other than a drug trafficking offence has benefited in connection with the commission of the offence concerned; or

          (ii) a drug trafficking offence was in receipt of the proceeds of drug trafficking in respect of that offence;

    (b) that the information necessary to enable a confiscation order to be made on the date on which an application under section 1 of this Act was or could have been made was not available to the prosecutor,

it may make a confiscation order in relation to that person.

(3) An application under this section shall be made as soon as is reasonably practicable after the relevant information becomes available to the prosecutor but in any event not later than 6 years after the date when the person was convicted of the offence.

(4) In determining the sum to be payable under a confiscation order made in pursuance of this section, the court shall take into account—

    (a) any order involving any payment by the offender;

    (b) any suspended forfeiture order or an order for forfeiture under any other enactment made in respect of the offender,

which forms part of the sentence already imposed for the offence concerned.

(5) Sections 1(3) and 8(1), (2) and (4) of this Act shall not apply in relation to a confiscation order made in pursuance of this section.

(6) Section 9 of this Act shall, subject to any necessary modifications, apply in relation to the making of a confiscation order in pursuance of this section as it applies where the prosecutor has applied for the making of a confiscation order under section 1 of this Act.

(7) Where the court makes a confiscation order in pursuance of this section and a compensation order has been made under section 249 of the 1995 Act in respect of misappropriation of property by the offender, the court shall direct that compensation shall first be paid out of any sums applied towards

the satisfaction of the confiscation order to the extent of any sums outstanding in respect of the compensation order.

(8) The assumptions mentioned in, as the case may be, section 2(2) and (5) or 3(2) of this Act shall not apply for the purposes of this section.

(9) In determining the sum to be payable as mentioned in subsection (4) above in connection with a drug trafficking offence, the court may take into account any payment or other reward received by the offender on or after the date of conviction, but only if the prosecutor satisfies the court that it was received by the offender in connection with drug trafficking carried on by the offender or another on or before that date.

(10) In this section "the court" means the court which had jurisdiction in respect of the offence concerned to make a confiscation order under section 1 of this Act.

GENERAL NOTE

Section 13 deals with the third, and perhaps the most controversial, of the Scottish Law Commission's situations in which variation is appropriate—that in which no confiscation order is made on conviction but benefit is discovered later. One possibility, contemplated by subs. (9), is that rewards for drug trafficking carried out before conviction are received after conviction.

As in s.11, the application of the assumptions is excluded.

Subs. (2)
    The court. By subs. (10) jurisdiction is given to "the court which had jurisdiction in respect of the offence concerned to make a confiscation order".
    The information necessary to enable a confiscation order to be made ... was not available to the prosecutor. Section 13 does not come into operation merely because the prosecutor has had second thoughts or has realised that he forgot to ask for a confiscation order. He has to satisfy the court that the information was not available to him. In some cases this may be because the accused concealed his benefit effectively. In others, it may be because a reporting agency had the information but did not pass it on to the procurator fiscal.

Subs. (3)
    This subsection is identical to s.11(3) and is in the Act for the same reasons.

Subs. (4)
    Since the accused will have been sentenced on the basis that there was not to be a confiscation order, the court must take into account any financial penalty which was imposed and any order for forfeiture, both of which affect his realisable property and which may have in fact affected his benefit from the offence. The obligation is to "take into account", not necessarily to deduct. How such a financial penalty will affect a confiscation order under s.13 will depend on the particular circumstances of the case.

Application of provisions relating to fines to enforcement of confiscation orders

14.—(1) Section 211(3) to (6) of the 1995 Act and the other provisions of that Act specified in subsection (2) below shall, subject to the qualifications mentioned in that subsection, apply in relation to confiscation orders as they apply in relation to fines; and section 91 of the Magistrates' Courts Act 1980 and Article 96 of the Magistrates' Courts (Northern Ireland) Order 1981 (provisions relating to transfer of fines from Scotland etc.) shall be construed accordingly.

(2) The provisions of the 1995 Act mentioned in subsection (1) above are—
    (a) section 214, provided that—
        (i) any allowance under that section of time (or further time) for payment; or
        (ii) any order of payment by instalments,
    shall be without prejudice to the exercise by any administrator appointed in relation to the confiscation order of his powers and duties under this Act; and the court may, pending such exercise, postpone

any decision as to refusing or allowing time (or further time) for payment or, as the case may be, making an order of payment by instalments;
(b) section 215, subject to the like proviso as in paragraph (a) above;
(c) section 216, but as if subsection (1)—
(i) gave the prosecutor an opportunity to be heard at any enquiry thereunder; and
(ii) applied whether the offender was in prison or not;
(d) section 217;
(e) section 218(2) and (3);
(f) section 219, provided that—
(i) where a court imposes a period of imprisonment both in respect of a fine and of a confiscation order the amounts in respect of which the period is imposed shall, for the purposes of subsection (2) of that section, be aggregated; and
(ii) before imposing a period of imprisonment to which there is a liability by virtue of that section the court shall, if an administrator has been appointed in relation to the confiscation order, require a report from him as to whether and in what way he is likely to exercise his powers and duties under this Act and shall take that report into account; and the court may, pending such exercise, postpone any decision as to such imposition;
(g) section 220, except that the reference in subsection (1) of that section to the person paying a sum to the governor of the prison under conditions prescribed by rules made under the Prisons (Scotland) Act 1989 shall be construed as including a reference to an administrator appointed in relation to the confiscation order making such payment under this Act in respect of the person;
(h) section 221, provided that an order of recovery by civil diligence shall not be made under the section where an administrator is appointed in relation to the confiscation order;
(i) section 222; except that for the purposes of that section "confiscation order" in subsection (1) above shall be construed as including such an order within the meaning of the 1994 Act or of any corresponding provision in Northern Ireland;
(j) section 223;
(k) section 224.

(3) Where a court, by virtue of subsection (1) above, orders the sum due under a confiscation order to be recovered by civil diligence under section 221 of the 1995 Act, any arrestment executed by a prosecutor under subsection (2) of section 33 of this Act shall be deemed to have been executed by the court as if that subsection authorised such execution.

(4) Where in any proceedings a confiscation order has been made as regards a person and a period of imprisonment or detention is imposed on him in default of payment of its amount (or as the case may be of an instalment thereof), that period shall run from the expiry of any other period of imprisonment or detention (not being one of life imprisonment or detention for life) imposed on him in the proceedings.

(5) The reference in subsection (4) above to "any other period of imprisonment or detention imposed" includes (without prejudice to the generality of the expression) a reference to such a period on default of payment of a fine (or instalment thereof); but only where that default had occurred before the warrant for imprisonment is issued for the default in relation to the order.

GENERAL NOTE
By s.14, confiscation orders are enforced as if they were fines, except that it is possible for administrators to be appointed who will realise assets. By subs. (4) any period of imprisonment imposed in default of payment is to run consecutively to the sentence imposed in respect of the

offence of which the accused was convicted. To seek no time to pay and the imposition of the alternative is, therefore, not likely to be regarded as an attractive option.

The Scottish Law Commission noted that English law has been amended so that service of a term of imprisonment in default of payment does not expunge the liability to pay the confiscation order. However, they were not persuaded by the reasoning which led to that change and, on the basis that "if confiscation is regarded as a criminal financial penalty, there is no other case in which imprisonment in default of payment of such a penalty does not extinguish the obligation to pay", they recommended against going down that road (SLC Report, para. 8.5). Section 14 follows that recommendation.

Interest on sums unpaid under confiscation orders

15.—(1) If any sum required to be paid by a person under a confiscation order is not paid when it is required to be paid (whether forthwith on the making of the order or at a time specified under section 214(1) of the 1995 Act) that person shall be liable to pay interest on that sum for the period for which it remains unpaid and the amount of the interest shall for the purposes of enforcement be treated as part of the amount to be recovered from him under the confiscation order.

(2) The sheriff may, on the application of the prosecutor, increase the term of imprisonment or detention fixed in respect of the confiscation order under section 214(2) of the 1995 Act if the effect of subsection (1) above is to increase the maximum period applicable in relation to the order under section 219(2) of the 1995 Act.

(3) The rate of interest under subsection (1) above shall be the rate payable under a decree of the Court of Session.

GENERAL NOTE

Section 15 provides for interest on outstanding sums under confiscation orders, at the rate applicable to a civil decree in the Court of Session, and for an increase in the period of imprisonment in default of payment where the addition of the interest takes the amount into the next band for calculation of such periods.

Exercise of powers

Exercise of powers by court or administrator

16.—(1) This section applies to the powers as regards realisable property conferred on the court by sections 28, 29, 31, 32 and 33 of and paragraphs 1, 4, and 12 of Schedule 1 to this Act in relation to confiscation orders and on an administrator by that Schedule.

(2) Subject to the following provisions of this section, the powers shall be exercised with a view to making available for satisfying the confiscation order or, as the case may be, any confiscation order that may be made in the case of a person mentioned in section 4(1)(a) of this Act the value for the time being of realisable property held by any person by the realisation of such property.

(3) In the case of realisable property held by a person by virtue only of having received a gift made directly or indirectly by the accused which is caught by this Part of this Act, the powers shall be exercised with a view to realising no more than the value of the gift as assessed under section 7 of this Act.

(4) The powers shall be exercised with a view to allowing any person other than a person mentioned in paragraph (a) and, in relation to a drug trafficking offence, paragraph (b) of section 4(1) of this Act or the recipient of any such gift to retain or recover the value of any property held by him.

(5) An order may be made or other action taken in respect of a debt owed by the Crown.

(6) In exercising those powers, no account shall be taken of any obligations of such a person or of the recipient of any such gift which conflict with the obligation to satisfy the confiscation order.

(7) Subsections (2) to (6) of section 31 of the 1994 Act (exercise of powers by High Court etc.) shall apply as regards the powers conferred on the court by sections 35, 36, 37 and 38 of this Act as those subsections apply as regards the powers conferred on the High Court (within the meaning that expression has in relation to England and Wales) by the sections mentioned in subsection (1) of the said section 31.

GENERAL NOTE
Section 16 requires to be read with Sched. 1 and deals with administrators. The provisions relating to administrators do not depart from the arrangements set out in the 1987 Act.

Subs. (1)
Subsection (1) gives effect to Sched. 1.

Subs. (2)
Subsection (2) states the objective of the appointment of an administrator, which is to make available for satisfying a confiscation order the realisable property held by any person by the realisation of that property.

Subss. (3) and (4)
Where a person has received a gift caught by the Act or an implicative gift the administrator's powers are to be exercised with a view to realising no more than the value of the gift.

Subs. (6)
The obligation to satisfy a confiscation order takes precedence over other obligations and accordingly the administrator is to give priority to a confiscation order over other debts. This is hard on the ordinary creditors of the accused. It must be recalled, however, that any payment which such creditors might receive would be made out of the proceeds of crime and also that one who extends credit to anyone always does so at his own risk. These considerations perhaps go some way towards mitigating the harshness of the provision. It should also be recalled that ss.44 and 45 introduce special rules in the case of sequestration and in relation to the accused's family home.

Subs. (7)
Sections 35 to 38 of this Act deal with reciprocal arrangements for the enforcement of orders made in England and Wales. Section 31 of the 1994 Act deals with the exercise by the (English) High Court (which is a civil court), county court or receiver of the powers available under English law for the realisation of property. Subsections (2) to (6) of s.31 of the 1994 Act are in almost the same terms as subss. (2) to (6) of s.16 of this Act. The effect of subs. (7) seems, therefore, to be to apply the same principles to the enforcement of English orders in Scotland as apply to the enforcement of English orders in England and to Scottish orders in Scotland.

Compensation

Compensation

17.—(1) Subject to subsection (3) below, if proceedings are instituted against a person for an offence to which this Part of this Act applies, and either—

(a) the proceedings do not result in his conviction for any such offence, or
(b) where he is convicted of one or more such offences—

(i) the conviction or convictions concerned are quashed (and no conviction for any such offence is substituted); or
(ii) he is pardoned by Her Majesty in respect of the conviction or convictions concerned,

the court may, on an application by a person who held property which was realisable property, order compensation to be paid to the applicant if, having regard to all the circumstances, it considers it appropriate to do so.

(2) Subsection (1) above is without prejudice to any right which may otherwise exist to institute proceedings in respect of delictual liability disclosed by

such circumstances as are mentioned in paragraphs (a) and (b) of subsection (3) below.

(3) The court shall not order compensation to be paid under subsection (1) above in any case unless satisfied—

    (a) that there has been some serious default on the part of a person concerned in the investigation of the offence or offences concerned, being a person mentioned in subsection (5) below, and that, but for that default, the proceedings would not have been instituted or continued; and

    (b) that the applicant has suffered loss or damage in consequence of anything done in relation to the property under section 28, 29, 31, 32, 33 or 42 of or Schedule 1 to this Act or by virtue of section 37 of the 1994 Act (recognition and enforcement in England and Wales of orders and functions under this Act).

(4) The amount of compensation to be paid under this section shall be such as the court thinks just in all the circumstances of the case.

(5) Compensation payable under this section shall be paid, where the person in default was—

    (a) a constable of a police force within the meaning of the Police (Scotland) Act 1967, by the police authority or joint police board for the police area for which that force is maintained;

    (b) a constable other than is mentioned in paragraph (a) above, but with the powers of such a constable, by the body under whose authority he acts;

    (c) a procurator fiscal or was acting on behalf of the Lord Advocate, by the Lord Advocate;

    (d) a person commissioned by the Commissioners of Customs and Excise, by those Commissioners; and

    (e) an officer of the Commissioners of Inland Revenue, by those Commissioners.

(6) An application for compensation under this section shall be made not later than three years after the conclusion of the proceedings in respect of which the confiscation order was made; and subsection (6) of section 29 of this Act shall apply for the purpose of determining when proceedings are concluded for the purposes of this subsection as it applies for the purposes of that section.

(7) In this section, "the court" means the Court of Session or the sheriff exercising his civil jurisdiction.

GENERAL NOTE

The power to freeze the whole estate of the accused and of an alleged recipient of an implicative gift carries with it the potential to do enormous damage to those estates and to the estates of others which might be affected by some mischance. Accordingly Parliament has provided a means by which the civil court may be asked to order compensation. The ability of the civil court to do so is, however, very limited.

By subs. (1), the payment of compensation, even to a third party, depends on the acquittal of the accused, the quashing of his conviction or the grant of a pardon. There is no comfort under the Act for one who has lost where the accused is convicted, though subs. (2) preserves the ordinary law of delict and a remedy might exist there. Also by subs. (1), compensation may only be ordered "if, having regard to all the circumstances, [the court] considers it appropriate to do so". These words perhaps state the obvious, but subs. (3) requires the applicant to satisfy what may prove to be a most difficult set of criteria. First, the applicant has to satisfy the court that there has been "serious default" on the part of a person involved in the investigation of the offences. It is not clear what the effect of the word "serious" will be but it might well require more than mere negligence. The adjective is applied to the default and not to the loss. It might mean that recklessness must be proved or perhaps even malice.

The class of persons involved in the investigation whose default can give rise to compensation is limited to those mentioned in subs. (5) and these are essentially police officers, procurators fiscal and customs officers.

It must further be proved that, but for the default, the proceedings would not have been instituted or continued. This makes it clear that the default must have been in relation to something quite fundamental to the prosecution and it also raises interesting questions of proof, having regard to the reluctance the courts have traditionally shown to ordering the discovery of prosecution papers (see for example, *Friel Petr.*, 1981 S.L.T. 113). Presumably that reluctance will be reduced where such discovery is required in order to adjudicate on a claim that there has been default such as to bring the section into play.

Investigation and disclosure of information

Order to make material available

18.—(1) The procurator fiscal may, for the purpose of an investigation into whether a person has benefited from the commission of an offence to which this Part of this Act applies and as to the amount of that benefit, apply to the sheriff for an order under subsection (2) below in relation to particular material or material of a particular description.

(2) If on such an application the sheriff is satisfied that the conditions in subsection (4) below are fulfilled, he may, subject to section 20(11) of this Act, make an order that the person who appears to him to be in possession of the material to which the application relates shall—

(a) produce it to a constable for him to take away; or

(b) give a constable access to it,

within such period as the order may specify.

(3) The period to be specified in an order under subsection (2) above shall be seven days unless it appears to the sheriff that a longer or shorter period would be appropriate in the particular circumstances of the application.

(4) The conditions referred to in subsection (2) above are—

(a) that there are reasonable grounds for suspecting that a specified person has benefited from the commission of an offence to which this Part of this Act applies;

(b) that there are reasonable grounds for suspecting that the material to which the application relates—

(i) is likely to be of substantial value (whether by itself or together with other material) to the investigation for the purpose of which the application is made; and

(ii) does not consist of or include items subject to legal privilege; and

(c) that there are reasonable grounds for believing that it is in the public interest, having regard—

(i) to the benefit likely to accrue to the investigation if the material is obtained; and

(ii) to the circumstances under which the person in possession of the material holds it,

that the material should be produced or that access to it should be given.

(5) Where the sheriff makes an order under subsection (2)(b) above in relation to material on any premises he may, on the application of the procurator fiscal, order any person who appears to him to be entitled to grant entry to the premises to allow a constable to enter the premises to obtain access to the material.

(6) An application under subsection (1) or (5) above may be made *ex parte* in chambers.

(7) Provision may be made by rules of court as to—

(a) the discharge add variation of orders under this section, and

(b) proceedings relating to such orders.

(8) Where the material to which an application under this section relates consists of information contained in a computer—

(a) an order under subsection (2)(a) above shall have effect as an order to produce the material in a form in which it can be taken away and in which it is visible and legible; and

(b) an order under subsection (2)(b) above shall have effect as an order to give access to the material in a form in which it is visible and legible.

(9) An order under subsection (2) above—

(a) shall not confer any right to production of, or access to, items subject to legal privilege;

(b) shall have effect notwithstanding any obligation as to secrecy or other restriction upon the disclosure of information imposed by statute or otherwise; and

(c) may be made in relation to material in the possession of an authorised government department;

and in this subsection "authorised government department" means a government department which is an authorised department for the purposes of the Crown Proceedings Act 1947.

(10) In this section—

(a) "items subject to legal privilege" and "premises" have the same meanings as in section 33 of the Criminal Law (Consolidation) (Scotland) Act 1995; and

(b) references to a person benefiting from the commission of an offence to which this Part of this Act applies, in relation to conduct which is not such an offence but which would have been if it had occurred in Scotland, shall be construed in accordance with section 2 of this Act as if that conduct had so occurred.

(11) This section and sections 19 and 20 of this Act do not apply to investigations into drug trafficking.

GENERAL NOTE

Section 18 provides for what have become known as "inspection orders" in relation to non-drug-related cases. Such orders are made by the sheriff on the application of the procurator fiscal and their effect is that a person in possession of certain material must produce it to a constable for him to take away or give him access to it. The provisions owe much to ss.8 to 10 of the Police and Criminal Evidence Act 1984 ("PACE") and reached the present Act through the DTOA and the 1987 Act. The 1987 Act provisions were considered by E.C. Brown in *Tracing Drug Money* 1990, S.L.T. (News) 157. Equivalent provision is made for drug trafficking cases by s.31 of the Criminal Law (Consolidation) (Scotland) Act 1995.

Subs. (1)

The procurator fiscal may … apply to the sheriff. The procedure may be made *ex parte* in chambers (subs. (6)) and no opportunity is afforded to the suspect or the holder of material to oppose the application.

For the purpose of an investigation into whether a person has benefited from the commission of an offence. Mitchell, Hinton and Taylor have suggested that orders in drug trafficking cases are available, under the English legislation, not only for financial investigation into benefit derived but also as an intelligence gathering tool, to identify evidence for a prosecution and to gather evidence for contempt proceedings in relation to breach of restraint orders (A.R. Mitchell, M.G. Hinton and S.M.E. Taylor, *Confiscation*, Sweet & Maxwell, 1992, p. 11). The present provision is very much more limited in its scope.

An offence to which this part of this Act applies. The basic definition is contained in s.1(2). This must, however, be read subject to two qualifications. The first is that subs. (10)(b) extends the inspection order mechanism to offences committed other than in Scotland which would have been offences to which Pt. I applies had they been committed in Scotland. The second is that subs. (11) disapplies s.18 to investigations into drug trafficking.

Particular material or material of a particular description. The amount of specification required of a procurator fiscal as to the material sought is not clear. The use of the word "particular" suggests that some specification is needed. However, presumably holders of material will prefer to be subject to a s.18 order to the alternative, which is to be subject to full search warrant under s.19(2) where the material cannot at the time of the application be particularised.

Subs. (2)
The effect of the order is that, within seven days or such other period as the court fixes (subs. (3)), the holder of material must either give it to a constable for him to take away (in a visible and legible form if it is held on computer (subs. (8)) or give a constable access to it (again in a visible and legible form). Mitchell *et al.* have suggested that "Usually the application will be to take the material away to be examined later by the constable with, if necessary, the assistance of accountants" (*op. cit.*, p. 14). Certainly, if there is any expectation that the material will be used as evidence, it will have to be taken possession of.
Such orders are not the same as search warrants. They are better characterised as orders of court addressed to particular persons to do specific things. It is suggested, therefore, that the jurisprudence on search warrants is of limited value in understanding these provisions and also that mechanisms such as warrants of concurrence, which accompany search warrants, are at best of doubtful competence.

Subs. (4)
Before making an order, the sheriff must be satisfied that all of the conditions are satisfied. The conditions themselves are derived directly from s.8 of PACE.
The material ... is likely to be of substantial value ... to the investigation. This expression was originally introduced into PACE in order to prevent "fishing expeditions" (M.D.A. Freeman, *Police and Criminal Evidence Act 1984*, Scottish Current Law Statutes Annotated (1984), p. 60–34).
Does not consist of or include items subject to legal privilege. See subs. (10)(a) and s.33 of the Criminal Law (Consolidation) (Scotland) Act 1995. In *R. v. Central Criminal Court, ex p. Francis and Francis* [1989] A.C. 346 the House of Lords held, in relation to such orders under the DTOA, that items otherwise subject to privilege are not so subject if held with the intention (not necessarily on the part of the holder) of furthering a criminal purpose. Money laundering would be an obvious example of such a purpose.

Authority for search

19.—(1) The procurator fiscal may, for the purpose of an investigation into whether a person has benefited from the commission of an offence to which this Part of this Act applies and as to the amount of that benefit, apply to the sheriff for a warrant under this section in relation to specified premises.

(2) On such application the sheriff may issue a warrant authorising a constable to enter and search the premises if the sheriff is satisfied—
   (a) that an order made under section 18 of this Act in relation to material on the premises has not been complied with; or
   (b) that the conditions in subsection (3) below are fulfilled; or
   (c) that the conditions in subsection (4) below are fulfilled.

(3) The conditions referred to in subsection (2)(b) above are—
   (a) that there are reasonable grounds for suspecting that a specified person has benefited from the commission of an offence to which this Part of this Act applies; and
   (b) that the conditions in section 18(4)(b) and (c) of this Act are fulfilled in relation to any material on the premises; and
   (c) that it would not be appropriate to make an order under that section in relation to the material because—
      (i) it is not practicable to communicate with any person entitled to produce the material; or
      (ii) it is not practicable to communicate with any person entitled to grant access to the material or entitled to grant entry to the premises on which the material is situated; or
      (iii) the investigation for the purposes of which the application is made might be seriously prejudiced unless a constable could secure immediate access to the material.

(4) The conditions referred to in subsection (2)(c) above are—
   (a) that there are reasonable grounds for suspecting that a specified person has benefited from the commission of an offence to which this Part of this Act applies; and

(b) that there are reasonable grounds for suspecting that there is on the premises material relating to the specified person, or to the question whether that person has so benefited or the amount of that benefit, which is likely to be of substantial value (whether by itself or together with other material) to the investigation for the purpose of which the application is made, but that the material cannot at the time of the application be particularised; and

(c) that—

    (i) it is not practicable to communicate with any person entitled to grant entry to the premises; or

    (ii) entry to the premises will not be granted unless a warrant is produced; or

    (iii) the investigation for the purpose of which the application is made might be seriously prejudiced unless a constable arriving at the premises could secure immediate entry to them.

(5) Where a constable has entered premises in the execution of a warrant issued under this section, he may seize and retain any material, other than items subject to legal privilege, which is likely to be of substantial value (whether by itself or together with other material) to the investigation for the purpose of which the warrant was issued.

(6) Subsection (10) of section 18 of this Act shall apply for the purposes of this section as it applies for the purposes of that section.

GENERAL NOTE

Section 19 provides for a search warrant in relation to non-drug cases. The wording of the section is derived from s.39 of the 1987 Act and, ultimately, from PACE. It therefore represents an application in Scots law of rules which were developed originally for an English law context and which are unfamiliar to Scottish practitioners. Equivalent provision is made for drug trafficking cases by s.32 of the Criminal Law (Consolidation) (Scotland) Act 1995.

Subs. (1)

The purpose for which a search warrant may be granted under this section is limited in the same way as the purpose for which a s.18 order may be made.

Subs. (2)

As Stoddart has pointed out in relation to warrants under s.39 of the 1987 Act, the circumstances in which an order may be granted are alternatives (C.N. Stoddart, *Criminal Warrants*, Butterworths, 1991, p. 71). No further conditions are imposed on the granting of a warrant where a s.18 order has not been complied with.

Subs. (3)

Subsection (3) sets out the second set of circumstances in which a s.19 warrant can be granted. Essentially, they arise where a s.18 order could be obtained (subs. (3)(b)) but would be inappropriate for the reasons set out in subs. (3)(c).

Subs. (4)

The final set of circumstances in which a warrant can be granted arise where the material sought cannot be particularised.

Disclosure of information held by government departments

20.—(1) Subject to subsection (4) below, the Court of Session may on an application by the Lord Advocate order any material mentioned in subsection (3) below which is in the possession of an authorised government department to be produced to the Court within such period as the Court may specify.

(2) The power to make an order under subsection (1) above is exercisable if—

(a) the powers conferred on the Court by section 28(1)(a) of this Act are exercisable by virtue of section 29(2) of this Act; or

(b) those powers are exercisable by virtue of section 29(3) of this Act and the Court has made a restraint order which has not been recalled.

(3) The material referred to in subsection (1) above is any material which—
(a) has been submitted to an officer of an authorised government department by a person who holds, or has at any time held, realisable property;
(b) has been made by an officer of an authorised government department in relation to such a person; or
(c) is correspondence which passed between an officer of an authorised government department and such a person;
and an order under that subsection may require the production of all such material or of a particular description of such material, being material in the possession of the department concerned.

(4) An order under subsection (1) above shall not require the production of any material unless it appears to the Court of Session that the material is likely to contain information that would facilitate the exercise of the powers conferred on the Court by section 28(1)(a) of or paragraph 1 or 12 of Schedule 1 to this Act or on an administrator appointed under paragraph 1(1) of that Schedule.

(5) The Court may by order authorise the disclosure to such an administrator of any material produced under subsection (1) above or any part of such material; but the Court shall not make an order under this subsection unless a reasonable opportunity has been given for an officer of the department to make representations to the Court.

(6) Material disclosed in pursuance of an order under subsection (5) above may, subject to any conditions contained in the order, be further disclosed for the purposes of the functions under this Act of the administrator or the High Court.

(7) The Court of Session may by order authorise the disclosure to a person mentioned in subsection (8) below of any material produced under subsection (1) above or any part of such material; but the Court shall not make an order under this subsection unless—
(a) a reasonable opportunity has been given for an officer of the department to make representations to the Court; and
(b) it appears to the Court that the material is likely to be of substantial value in exercising functions relating to the investigation of crime.

(8) The persons referred to in subsection (7) above are—
(a) a constable;
(b) the Lord Advocate or any procurator fiscal; and
(c) an officer within the meaning of the Customs and Excise Management Act 1979.

(9) Material disclosed in pursuance of an order under subsection (7) above may, subject to any conditions contained in the order, be further disclosed for the purposes of functions relating to the investigation of crime or whether any person has benefited from the commission of an offence to which this Part of this Act applies or the amount of that benefit.

(10) Material may be produced or disclosed in pursuance of this section notwithstanding any obligation as to secrecy or other restriction upon the disclosure of information imposed by statute or otherwise.

(11) An order under subsection (1) above and, in the case of material in the possession of an authorised government department, an order under section 18(2) of this Act may require any officer of the department (whether named in the order or not) who may for the time being be in possession of the material concerned to comply with such order; and any such order shall be served as if the proceedings were civil proceedings against the department.

(12) Where any requirement is included in any order by virtue of subsection (11) above, the person on whom the order is served—
(a) shall take all reasonable steps to bring it to the attention of the officer concerned; and

(b) if the order is not brought to that officer's attention within the period referred to in subsection (1) above, shall report the reasons for the failure to the Court of Session,

and it shall also be the duty of any other officer of the department in receipt of the order to take such steps as are mentioned in paragraph (a) above.

(13) In this section "authorised government department" means a government department which is an authorised department for the purposes of the Crown Proceedings Act 1947; and subsection (10) of section 18 of this Act shall apply for the purposes of this section as it applies for the purposes of that section.

GENERAL NOTE

This section provides a means by which material in the hands of government departments can be obtained. It follows exactly the scheme of s.41 of the 1987 Act.

PART II

FORFEITURE OF PROPERTY USED IN CRIME

Suspended forfeiture order

21.—(1) This section applies where in respect of any offence—
   (a) the accused is convicted, whether in solemn or summary proceedings; or
   (b) in the case of summary proceedings, (without proceeding to conviction) an order is made discharging him absolutely.

(2) Where this section applies, the court may, if it is satisfied on the application of the prosecutor that any property which was at the time of the offence or of the accused's apprehension in his ownership or possession or under his control—
   (a) has been used for the purpose of committing, or facilitating the commission of, any offence; or
   (b) was intended to be used for that purpose,
make an order (a "suspended forfeiture order") in respect of that property.

(3) Any application under this section shall be made—
   (a) in proceedings on indictment, when the prosecutor moves for sentence or if the accused is remitted for sentence under section 195 of the 1995 Act, before sentence is pronounced; and
   (b) in summary proceedings, following upon the conviction of the accused or, as the case may be, the finding that he committed the offence with which he was charged.

(4) If the prosecutor knows or reasonably suspects the identity of a person (other than the accused) as being the owner of, or otherwise having an interest in, the property to which the suspended forfeiture order relates, he shall intimate that fact to the court on making the application and the order shall name that person as a person having an interest or suspected of having an interest in the property.

(5) Any reference in this Part of this Act to facilitating the commission of an offence shall include a reference to the taking of any steps after it has been committed for the purpose of disposing of any property to which it relates or of avoiding apprehension or detection.

(6) Where, by itself, the use of property constitutes an offence in whole or in part, that property shall be regarded for the purpose of subsection (2)(a) above as used for the purpose of committing the offence, unless the enactment which created the offence expressly excludes the application of this section.

(7) Subject to subsection (8) below, where the accused is convicted of an offence under any enactment, the court shall not be precluded from making a

suspended forfeiture order in respect of any property by reason only that the property would not be liable to forfeiture under that enactment.

(8) Subsection (7) above shall not apply—

(a) if the enactment concerned expressly excludes the application of this section; or

(b) to any property which has been used or has been intended to be used as mentioned in subsection (2)(a) or (b) above in relation to the offence of which the accused has been convicted, if the enactment concerned specifies the category of property which is to be liable to forfeiture thereunder, and the category so specified does not include the category of property which has been used or has been intended to be used as aforesaid.

(9) Where the court makes both a suspended forfeiture order and a compensation order under section 249 of the 1995 Act against the same accused in the same proceedings, it may order that, in the event of the property subject to the suspended forfeiture order being forfeited under section 24 of this Act, the proceeds of sale of that property shall be first directed towards satisfaction of the compensation order.

(10) As soon as may be after a suspended forfeiture order has been made, the prosecutor—

(a) shall notify in writing any person named in the order in pursuance of subsection (4) above that the order has been made, and that the person so notified may be entitled to apply to the court for—

(i) the order to be recalled under section 25 of this Act; or

(ii) a direction under section 26 of this Act; and

(b) if the property in respect of which the order has been made includes heritable property in Scotland, shall cause a certified copy of the order to be recorded in the General Register of Sasines or as the case may be registered in the Land Register of Scotland; and

(c) if the court directs him to do so, shall insert a notice in the Edinburgh Gazette or in such other newspaper or journal as appears to the court to be appropriate specifying the terms of the suspended forfeiture order.

(11) Any property in respect of which a suspended forfeiture order is made shall be taken into the possession of or placed under the control of the clerk of court until—

(a) the order is recalled; or

(b) the property is forfeited to the Crown and disposed of under section 24 of this Act or forfeited to another person under that section.

(12) For the purposes of any appeal or review a suspended forfeiture order is a sentence.

(13) In this section "the court" does not include a district court, whether or not constituted by a stipendiary magistrate.

GENERAL NOTE

Section 21 provides for the "suspended forfeiture order" and sets out the conditions which must be satisfied before it can be made.

Subs. (2)

Where this section applies. See subs. (1).

The court may. As a result of subs. (13) "the court" does not include the district court. The Scottish Law Commission's reasoning for this recommendation was that:

"... while our proposed scheme is not unduly complex, it is of such a character that it would not be reasonable to impose it on the district court. It involves not only the making of suspended forfeiture orders in relation to any kind of property, but also the adjudication of third parties' claims, the recall of suspended forfeiture orders and, where the property of third parties has been disposed of, the awarding of compensation" (SLC Report, para. 12.2).

It will be recalled that Judges of the High Court of Justiciary and sheriffs exercise a civil jurisdiction as well as a criminal one, albeit under different procedure from that in which they will make suspended forfeiture orders. They are, therefore, familiar with the law relating to property of all kinds and have experience in dealing with litigation about competing claims to property. The district court does not have these advantages. Since the power to make suspended forfeiture orders is discretionary, it is important that it is exercised only by those properly equipped to do so.

If it is satisfied. The Act is silent as to standard of proof, despite the Scottish Law Commission's expressed view that "it is important to make clear provision as to the standard of proof which the prosecutor must attain before the court may be satisfied that the conditions have been met" (SLC Report, para. 13.5). The Commission thought that the criminal standard should apply, and since forfeiture is plainly a penalty it seems likely that the courts will apply that standard in fact.

The same requirement, that the court be "satisfied", appeared in ss.223 and 436 of the 1975 Act and does not seem to have caused significant problems. In *Donnelly v. H.M. Advocate*, 1984 S.C.C.R. 93, £1,047 found hidden with drug paraphernalia in the house of a drug trafficker was ordered to be forfeited under s.223 on the basis that:

"... the judge was entitled to be satisfied that the money found concealed in the flat in association with the paraphernalia of drug trafficking and, indeed, the cannabis resin, was intended to be used by the appellant for the purpose of committing an offence ... The intention was there to be seen and it arises as a reasonable inference from the material which was before the trial judge" (*per* Lord Justice-General (Emslie) at p. 95).

On the application of the prosecutor. The Scottish Law Commission recommended that the making of a suspended forfeiture order should only be competent on the application of the prosecutor upon the basis that the prosecutor "will be the best judge of whether a suspended forfeiture order will create undesirable difficulties" (SLC Report, para. 13.2).

Any property. The Scottish Law Commission considered that there is no reason in principle why heritable and incorporeal property should not be liable to forfeiture as well as corporeal moveable property (SLC Report, para. 12.4), noting that heritage and incorporeal moveables can be forfeited under ss.13 and 20 of the Prevention of Terrorism (Temporary Provisions) Act 1989. The effect of the present Act is to remove the practical difficulties which stood in the way of forfeiture of such property under the general powers.

Which was at the time of the offence or of the accused's apprehension in his ownership, possession or under his control. The effect of these words is to widen the circumstances under which forfeiture can take place. Under the 1975 Act the property had to be possessed or controlled by the accused at the time of his apprehension, so that if he was not arrested at all (as might happen in relation to an otherwise respectable newsagent selling obscene material) property could not be forfeited. Similarly, if arrest was delayed and the property was disposed of in the meantime, forfeiture was not competent. Again, property which the accused owned but neither possessed nor controlled could not be forfeited. These loopholes are now closed and the difficulties which arose in *Reid v. Houston*, 1992 S.C.C.R. 442 (in which forfeiture of the accused's cohabitee's car was upheld on the basis that it was certainly freely available to the accused and under his control at the time of the offence and that there was nothing to show that the relationship had changed by his arrest a month later) should not recur.

Has been used for the purpose of committing, or facilitating the commission of, any offence. This expression occurred in the 1975 Act and the courts have taken it literally. Something which is used to make a crime easier to commit, and especially something without which it would not have been possible to commit the crime, is liable to forfeiture. So in *McQueeney v. Carmichael*, 1991 S.C.C.R. 221 a van in which the accused was loading with stolen property was forfeited and Lord Allanbridge said (at p. 222):

"... we are of the view that if criminals use cars or vehicles or vans for the purpose of committing or facilitating the commission of an offence then they are liable to have that vehicle forfeited ... [The appellant] would not have been able to carry out this offence without the use of his van and if he is prepared to use what he calls a valuable van then he does so at his own risk."

Lord Allanbridge was to use very similar language in *Wallace v. MacDougall*, 1991 S.C.C.R. 962. The Lord Justice-General (Emslie) had perhaps set the tone in *Carruthers v. MacKinnon*, 1986 S.C.C.R. 643. In that case the appellant could not have committed the offence of theft without a vehicle. He was on income support and so the Sheriff admonished him but ordered forfeiture of the vehicle, which was said to be worth £1,000. The Lord Justice-General described the appellant as "extremely lucky to be dealt with in that way". The basis of the appeal was that the forfeiture of an asset worth £1,000 was out of proportion to the crime, especially as the property stolen had been recovered. It seems that the Lord Justice-General doubted the truth of the claim that the car was worth £1,000 but he dismissed the appeal "resoundingly" with the observation that:

> "... any fine which would have met the circumstances of the case would have required the disposal of the motor car anyway in order to pay the fine. So in the end the sheriff has saved the appellant the trouble of attempting to find a market for the vehicle ...".

By subs. (5), facilitating the commission of an offence includes disposal of property after an offence and also the taking of steps to avoid apprehension or detection.

Subs. (6)

The example which the Scottish Law Commission had in mind was that of disqualified driving, where the driving of the car by the accused, he being disqualified, is enough to constitute the offence. This subsection therefore applies *Woods Petr.*, 1994 S.L.T. 197 (and *R. v. Highbury Corner Magistrates' Court, ex p. Di Matteo* [1991] 1 W.L.R. 1374), rather than *Findlay v. McNaughtan*, 1991 S.C.C.R. 321. However the Criminal Procedure (Consequential Provisions) (Scotland) Act 1995, Sched. 4, para. 71(6) now provides that forfeiture under the present Act does not apply to certain road traffic cases. Instead, it inserts a new section 33A in the Road Traffic Offenders Act 1988.

Subs. (7)

By this subsection the fact that there is a power of forfeiture attached to a statute under which the accused is convicted and that the specific power would not apply to the particular property is not a bar to forfeiture under the general power under the present Act. This must, however, be read subject to subs. (8).

Subs. (9)

There is an obvious injustice in a victim not receiving compensation whilst the Treasury gets the benefit of the sale of a forfeited asset belonging to the accused. The need to ensure that the entitlement of victims to be compensated is not defeated by the Treasury's entitlement to the proceeds of forfeited articles is dealt with by providing that a court which both awards compensation and orders forfeiture of an article will be able to order that the proceeds of sale should first be directed to satisfaction of the compensation order. The court retains a discretion in this because in most cases it will be appropriate that the offender should both lose the asset and pay compensation. It would be unacceptable if offenders could have their liability mitigated by having the compensation order "set off" against forfeiture in any way and the intention seems to be that such orders should only be made where the victim is otherwise unlikely to receive compensation.

Forfeiture: district court

22.—(1) Where, in respect of any offence tried in the district court, the accused is convicted or (without proceeding to conviction) an order is made discharging him absolutely the court may, if it is satisfied on the application of the prosecutor that any moveable property which was at the time of the offence or of the accused's apprehension in his ownership or possession or under his control—

    (a) has been used for the purpose of committing, or facilitating the commission of, any offence; or

    (b) was intended to be used for that purpose,

order that the property shall be forfeited to and vest in the Crown or such other person as the court may direct.

(2) Any application under subsection (1) above shall be made following upon the conviction of the accused or, as the case may be, the finding that he committed the offence with which he was charged.

(3) Where, by itself, the use of property constitutes an offence in whole or in part, that property shall be regarded for the purpose of subsection (1)(a) above as used for the purpose of committing the offence, unless the enactment which created the offence expressly excludes the application of this section.

(4) Subject to subsection (5) below, where the accused is convicted of an offence under any enactment, the court shall not be precluded from making

an order under subsection (1) above in respect of any property by reason only that the property would not be liable to forfeiture under that enactment.

(5) Subsection (4) above shall not apply—

(a) if the enactment concerned expressly excludes the application of this section; or

(b) to any property which has been used or has been intended to be used as mentioned in subsection (1)(a) or (b) above in relation to the offence of which the accused has been convicted, if the enactment concerned specifies the category of property which is to be liable to forfeiture thereunder, and the category so specified does not include the category of property which has been used or has been intended to be used as aforesaid.

(6) Where the court makes—

(a) an order under subsection (1) above that property shall be forfeited to the Crown; and

(b) a compensation order under section 249 of the 1995 Act,

against the same accused in the same proceedings, it may order that the proceeds of sale of the property forfeited by virtue of subsection (1) above shall be first directed towards satisfaction of the compensation order.

(7) For the purposes of any appeal or review an order under subsection (1) above is a sentence.

(8) In this section "the court" means the district court.

GENERAL NOTE

Section 22 applies to the district court the same scheme as s.21 applies to other courts, except that the element of suspension of the forfeiture order is omitted for the reasons discussed above (see s.21(2)).

Warrant to search for and seize property

23.—(1) Where—

(a) the sheriff is satisfied, on an application being made to him by the prosecutor—

(i) that proceedings have been, or are likely to be, instituted against a person in Scotland for an offence; and

(ii) that there is reasonable cause to believe that property specified in the application is to be found in a place or in premises specified in the application; and

(b) it appears to him that there are reasonable grounds for thinking that in the event of the person being convicted of the offence a suspended forfeiture order might be made in relation to the property,

he may grant a warrant authorising a person named therein to enter and search the place or premises and seize the property.

(2) Where a court has made a suspended forfeiture order in respect of any property, if it is satisfied on the application of the prosecutor—

(a) that there is reasonable cause to believe that the property is to be found in any place or premises; and

(b) that admission to the place or premises has been refused or that it is reasonably believed that such admission will be refused,

it may grant a warrant authorising a person named therein to enter and search the place or premises and seize the property.

(3) An application for a warrant under subsection (2) above may be made at the same time as an application for a suspended forfeiture order.

GENERAL NOTE

It has always been the case that courts could grant a warrant to search for property which they have ordered to be forfeited (1975 Act, ss.224 and 437). Subsection (2) makes such provision for the case in which a suspended forfeiture order has been made. However, subs. (1) introduces a power for a sheriff to grant a warrant for search and seizure where proceedings are at least likely to be commenced and there are reasonable grounds for thinking that, in the event of conviction, a suspended forfeiture order might be made. This, of course, will only be practicable in most cases in relation to corporeal moveables and such property will often be seized as productions in any event, presumably on the basis of *Mauchline v. Stevenson* (1878) 4 Couper 20, in which Lord Young commented (at p. 27) that "the statutory forfeiture of prohibited articles implies in the officer a power of seizure when he finds the offence being committed". However, the Scottish Law Commission took note of the fact that some items of property such as motor vehicles, ships and aircraft can be removed from the jurisdiction with relative ease and recommended that a power to grant such a warrant should be introduced (SLC Report, para. 16.6–16.8).

Forfeiture of property subject to suspended forfeiture order

24.—(1) Subject to the following provisions of this section, property in respect of which a suspended forfeiture order has been made shall be forfeited to and vest in the Crown, or such other person as the court may direct, as follows—

(a) heritable property situated in Scotland shall be forfeited at the end of the period of 6 months commencing with the date on which a certified copy of the suspended forfeiture order is recorded in the General Register of Sasines or, as the case may be, registered in the Land Register of Scotland;

(b) heritable property situated outside Scotland shall be forfeited at the end of the period of six months commencing with the date of the making of the suspended forfeiture order;

(c) moveable property shall be forfeited at the end of the period of 60 days commencing with the date of the making of the suspended forfeiture order.

(2) Notwithstanding subsection (1)(c) above, moveable property which is certified by the prosecutor as being—

(a) of a perishable or dangerous nature;

(b) of no commercial value; or

(c) property which cannot lawfully be sold, supplied or possessed,

shall be forfeited immediately after the making of the suspended forfeiture order.

(3) If an application for recall or variation of the suspended forfeiture order concerned has been made under section 25 of this Act, there shall be no forfeiture of property mentioned in paragraph (a), (b) or (c) of subsection (1) above unless and until whichever is the later of the following occurs—

(a) the application is finally disposed of in favour of the prosecutor; or

(b) the period mentioned in that paragraph has expired.

(4) Without prejudice to subsection (2) above, in the event of an appeal against conviction or sentence, there shall be no forfeiture of property until whichever is the later of the following occurs—

(a) the appeal, if it is proceeded with, is determined in favour of the prosecutor; or

(b) the period mentioned in paragraph (a) or, as the case may be, (b) or (c) of subsection (1) above has expired.

(5) Property which has been forfeited to the Crown under this section shall be dealt with by the Crown in such manner as seems to it to be appropriate.

(6) A certificate by the clerk of court that property was forfeited to and vested in the Crown, or another person, under this section on the date specified in the certificate shall be conclusive evidence of that fact; and, in the case of a certificate in respect of heritable property situated in Scotland, the prosecutor shall, forthwith, cause a certified copy of the certificate to be recorded in the General Register of Sasines or, as the case may be, registered in the Land Register of Scotland.

GENERAL NOTE

The essence of the suspended forfeiture order is that it does not take effect until a given period of time has elapsed, so as to afford those claiming an interest in property an opportunity to seek the recall of the order. Section 24 governs the relevant periods of time. In respect of heritable property situated in Scotland the period is six months from the recording of the certified copy of the suspended forfeiture order, whilst in relation to heritable property situated outside Scotland the period is to be six months from the making of the order. For moveable property the period is to be 60 days. The period of six months reflects the period which an innocent owner of property has in England to seek the return of property subject to a deprivation order under s.43(4) of the Powers of Criminal Courts Act 1973, and also the desire of the Scottish Law Commission to be cautious in relation to heritage, whilst the shorter period in relation to moveable property is to avoid unnecessary storage charges (SLC Report, para. 14.3).

One problem which is raised by this section relates to property outwith Scotland. There is no doubt that the Scottish courts have power under Pt. II of the present Act to order the forfeiture of property which is situated outwith Scotland and subs. (1)(b) makes provision for the taking of effect of an order in relation to what is referred to as "heritable property situated outside Scotland". It is not clear, however, how this is supposed to work.

In the first place, none of Pt. II applies outside Scotland. Accordingly, notwithstanding subs. (1)(b) and (c), an order by a Scottish court in relation to either heritable or moveable property situated and remaining outside Scotland cannot be effective. Some mechanism would need to be created in the law of the country in which the property is situated to give effect to the Scottish order. Section 42 provides for the making of provision, by Order in Council, for the enforcement of suspended forfeiture orders in England and Wales but that might prove difficult to carry out and is, in any event, restricted to that jurisdiction.

For one thing, the expression "heritable property situated outside Scotland" is probably a contradiction in terms. "Heritable property" is a term of art in Scots law and does not exist as a concept elsewhere. Moreover, the concept of *dominium* which underlies the Scots lawyer's understanding of landownership is entirely alien to English law and those systems derived from it. As Mackenzie and Phillips have put it, in English law "no subject can own land ... but he is allowed the use of the land by the Crown. What the subject owns is a series of rights and duties in relation to that piece of land" (J. MacKenzie and M. Phillips, *A Practical Approach to Land Law*, Blackstone Press Ltd, 1982, p. 2). It is no accident that s.43 of the Powers of Criminal Courts Act 1973, which deals with forfeiture of instrumentalities in English law, speaks only of depriving the offender of his rights in the property concerned. Accordingly, not only does heritable property not exist as a concept south of the border, or anywhere else in the common law world, but there is not even any very workable equivalent. The drafting of an Order in Council might, therefore, prove difficult. This annotator is not qualified to comment on the position in other legal traditions but it would be surprising if other systems of land law were not equally incompatible with the order contemplated.

Moreover, it is a standard condition in the U.K.'s mutual legal assistance treaties with other states that assistance may be refused if the state whose assistance is requested considers that the request, if granted, would seriously impair its sovereignty. One might imagine that such a question would be likely to arise in relation to the vesting of some of that foreign state's territory in the British Crown by order of a Scottish criminal court and that the displeasure with which the making of such an order would be regarded would be at least equal to that which has met some of the more outrageous claims to extraterritorial criminal jurisdiction which have from time to time been made by U.S. law.

Subs. (1)
Such other person as the court may direct. The Scottish Law Commission only contemplated that property would vest in the Crown. The purpose of these words is to retain what the Lord Advocate (speaking in the context of the Criminal Justice (Scotland) Bill 1995) called "the existing flexibility to allow the court to direct that property may be vested in another person ... for example ... the police authorities as a reward for what they had done in a particular case" (Lord Rodger of Earlsferry, *Hansard*, H.L. Vol. 560, col. 513). The flexibility spoken of is the provision under ss.223(1) and 436(1) of the 1975 Act that property forfeited is to be disposed of as the court directs. It is relatively common for English courts to order that property be handed over to police forces in the way contemplated by the Lord Advocate but rare in the extreme for Scottish courts to give explicit directions about the disposal of property. It remains to be seen whether Scottish prosecutors will begin to invite courts to make such directions.

Recall or variation of suspended forfeiture order

25.—(1) The court shall, on an application being made to it under this section by a person other than the accused, recall a suspended forfeiture order in relation to any property or an interest in property if—

(a) it is satisfied by the applicant on the balance of probabilities that he is the owner of the property or otherwise has an interest in it; and

(b) subsection (2) or subsection (3) below is applicable.

(2) This subsection applies if the court is not satisfied by the prosecutor that—

(a) where the applicant was the owner of or otherwise had an interest in the property before the commission of the offence in connection with which the suspended forfeiture order was made, he—

    (i) knew or ought to have known that the property was intended to be used for the purpose of committing, or facilitating the commission of, the offence, and

    (ii) did not take all the steps which were reasonable for him to take to prevent such intended use; or

(b) where he has become the owner of, or has otherwise acquired an interest in, the property after the commission of the offence, the applicant knew or ought to have known that the property had been intended to be, or had been, so used.

(3) This subsection applies if the court is satisfied as mentioned in subsection (2) above, but it appears to the court that, in all the circumstances of the case, forfeiture of the property would be excessive or inappropriate.

(4) Where an order ("a recalling order") recalling a suspended forfeiture order relates to heritable property situated in Scotland, the prosecutor shall, as soon as may be after the recalling order has been made, cause a certified copy of the recalling order to be recorded in the General Register of Sasines or, as the case may be, registered in the Land Register of Scotland.

(5) Where the prosecutor believes that the person named in the suspended forfeiture order in pursuance of section 21(4) of this Act is not the owner of, or does not otherwise have an interest in, the property concerned then—

(a) if he does not know who the true owner is, or who otherwise truly has the interest, he may apply to the court under this section for an order varying the suspended forfeiture order by deleting that name from it;

(b) if he does know or reasonably suspects the identity of the true owner or the person who otherwise truly has the interest ("the correct person"), he may apply to the court under this section for an order varying the suspended forfeiture order by substituting the name of the correct person for that of the person so named.

(6) Where no person is named in the suspended forfeiture order in pursuance of section 21(4) of this Act but the prosecutor later comes to believe that a person is, or may be, the owner of, or otherwise has or may have an interest in, the property concerned, he may apply to the court for an order varying the suspended forfeiture order by naming that person as a person having or being suspected of having such an interest.

(7) The court shall grant any application made in pursuance of subsection (5) or (6) above; and sections 21(10) and 24 of this Act shall apply in relation to an order varying a suspended forfeiture order in accordance with an application under subsection (5) or (6) above as they apply in relation to a suspended forfeiture order.

(8) An application under this section may be made at any time before the property concerned is forfeited to the Crown or another person under section 24 of this Act.

(9) The court shall not be entitled in considering any application under this section to review the sentence passed, or any probation order or order of discharge made, in respect of the offence concerned otherwise than as provided by this section.

(10) In this section "the court" means the court which made the suspended forfeiture order.

GENERAL NOTE

This section deals with the recall of a suspended forfeiture order at the instance of a person other than the accused where that person is the owner of the property or has some other interest in it. It also deals with variation of an order at the instance of the prosecutor where his information as to ownership changes.

Subs. (1)

The court. By subs. (10), application is to be made to the court which made the suspended forfeiture order.

Shall ... recall a suspended forfeiture order. If the criteria are satisfied the court has no discretion. Where a recalling order is made, subs. (9) prevents the court from altering the remainder of the original sentence.

On an application being made. By subs. (8), an application can be made at any time before forfeiture takes effect in terms of s.24.

If it is satisfied by the applicant on the balance of probabilities. It is for the applicant to prove, to the civil standard, that he has an interest in the property, not for the Crown to prove that he does not. Thereafter, the onus passes to the Crown. The applicant will presumably have to do better than the accused in *Carruthers v. MacKinnon*, 1986 S.C.C.R. 643. In attempting to persuade the court that the value of his forfeited car made the sentence excessive, he produced a receipt which was incomplete and which referred to a car with a different registration mark. The High Court considered that this document was not worth the paper it was written on.

Subs. (2)

If the applicant satisfies the court that he is the owner of the property or otherwise has an interest in it, the court must consider whether either subs. (2) or subs. (3) is satisfied. Subsection (2) allows the prosecutor to resist recall by proving that the applicant was blameworthy in the matter in respect that he knew or should have known that the offender intended to use the property for crime and did not take reasonable steps to prevent that use. An example of the kind of situation in which a prosecutor is likely to be successful is to be found in *Reid v. Houston*, 1992 S.C.C.R. 442, where a car which was, in name at least, the property of the accused's cohabitee was freely available to him for theftuous expeditions.

If the court is not satisfied by the prosecutor. The Scottish Law Commission contemplated that the prosecutor would be required to prove the matters set out in the subsection to the criminal standard, since they involve attributing "blameworthiness ... tainted with criminality" (SLC Report, para. 15.5) but the Act is silent on this matter.

Did not take all the steps which were reasonable for him to take. What will amount to "all the steps which were reasonable for him to take" will be a question of fact in each case but the formula is very close to part of the defence provision in s.24(1)(b) of the Trade Descriptions Act 1968, ("took all reasonable precautions and exercised all due diligence") and the case law on that section may be a fair starting point for interpretation. It must be remembered, however, that the onus is on the defence in relation to the 1968 Act provision and that the other matters which are to be proved differ.

The case law includes the following. *Kinchin v. Haines* [1979] Crim.L.R. 329 concerned a coal merchant who knew that the coal in his sacks was not the correct weight and did nothing to correct the position. He was convicted and his conviction upheld. *Sheratt v. Geralds the American Jewellers* (1970) 114 S.J. 147, D.C. and *Sutton London Borough Council v. Perry Sanger & Co.* (1971) 135 J.P.N. 239 both concerned traders who relied, without checking, on information from those who supplied goods to them. Both were convicted and their convictions upheld. In *Aitchison v. Reith and Anderson (Dingwall and Tain)* 1974 J.C. 12 the managing director of the accused company of auctioneers, recognising that a technical description of a car was something his company was not qualified to assess, instructed that it be checked. His subordinate relied upon the outward appearance of the vehicle. It was held that the defence had not been made out. By analogy with these cases it may be argued that a person who knows or ought to know that the accused intends to use the property for crime will not be able to get an order recalled if he simply relied on the accused's undertaking not to do so. He will have to take positive steps to prevent that use.

Where he has become the owner of ... the property after ... the offence the applicant knew ... that the property had been so used. For an example, see *Woods Petr.*, 1994 S.L.T. 197 in which, one week after his offence, the accused sold the car which he had used to commit it to his brother, who knew that the offence had been committed. The High Court considered that the critical question was whether the brother had purchased the car in good faith and for value and took the view that his knowledge of the offence meant that he was put on his enquiry as to the consequences were he to purchase the car in light of what had occurred. In *Woods* the court declined to disturb the order for forfeiture.

Subs. (3)

Even if the Crown proves the matters specified in subs. (2), the effect of subs. (3) is to leave it open to the court to make a recalling order if it considers that "in all the circumstances" forfeiture would be excessive or inappropriate. It is possible for a situation to arise in which the owner of a valuable piece of property had a fair idea what the accused was going to do with it and took some, but insufficient, steps to prevent him. Whilst the Crown could prove the matters necessary to prevent the making of a recalling order the court might take the view that the loss to the owner was out of all proportion to his culpability. As the Scottish Law Commission put it "the forfeiture of the property would be penal rather than preventative and would be an excessive or inappropriate penalty for the applicant to pay" (SLC Report, para. 15.9). This subsection allows the court to reflect that by making a recalling order anyway.

Property wrongly forfeited: return or compensation

26.—(1) Where the court, on an application being made to it by a person other than the accused—

(a) is satisfied by the applicant on the balance of probabilities that in relation to any property forfeited to the Crown or another person under section 24 of this Act or by virtue of an order for forfeiture made under any other enactment he was the owner of, or a person otherwise having an interest in, the property immediately before such forfeiture; and

(b) subsection (3) or (4) below is applicable,

it shall make an order under subsection (2) below.

(2) An order under this subsection shall direct the Crown or, as the case may be, the other person, if the applicant—

(a) was the owner of the property, to return it to him if reasonably practicable to do so or, if not, to pay compensation to him of an amount determined under subsection (5) below; or

(b) otherwise had an interest in the property, to pay compensation to him of an amount corresponding to the value of such interest.

(3) This subsection applies if the court is not satisfied that—

(a) where the applicant was the owner of or otherwise had an interest in the property before the commission of the offence in connection with which the suspended forfeiture order or order for forfeiture was made, he knew or ought to have known that the property was intended to be used for the purpose of committing, or facilitating the commission of, the offence, and did not take all the steps which were reasonable for him to take to prevent such intended use; or

(b) where the applicant has become the owner of, or has otherwise acquired an interest in, the property after the commission of the offence, he knew or ought to have known that the property had been intended to be, or had been, so used.

(4) This subsection applies if the court is satisfied as mentioned in subsection (3) above, but it appears to the court that, in all the circumstances of the case, forfeiture of the property would be excessive or inappropriate.

(5) For the purposes of subsection (2) above, the amount determined under this subsection shall be an amount equal to the amount of any consideration received for the property or the value of any such consideration at the time of the disposal, or, if no consideration was received, an amount equal to the value of the property at the time of the disposal.

(6) An application under subsection (1) shall be made not later than three years after the date on which the property was forfeited as mentioned in subsection (1)(a) above.

(7) Where, after property has been forfeited by virtue of section 24 of this Act, the prosecutor comes to believe that the person named in the suspended

forfeiture order in pursuance of section 21(4) of this Act is not the owner of, or a person otherwise having an interest in, the property concerned, then—

    (a) whether he knows who the true owner was, or who the person truly with the interest was, or not, he shall forthwith notify the court in writing of that belief; and

    (b) if he does know or reasonably suspects the identity of the person who was the true owner or who truly had the interest, he shall forthwith notify that person in writing that he may be entitled to apply to the court for a direction under this section.

(8) Where no person has been named in the suspended forfeiture order in pursuance of section 21(4) of this Act or in a variation order under section 25(5) of this Act but, after the property concerned has been forfeited under section 24 of this Act, the prosecutor comes to believe that a person was or might have been the owner of, or otherwise had or might have had an interest in, the property concerned, he shall forthwith notify—

    (a) the court of his belief; and

    (b) that person in writing that he may be entitled to apply to the court for a direction under this section.

(9) The court shall not be entitled in considering any application under this section to review the sentence passed, or any probation order or order of discharge made, in respect of the offence concerned otherwise than as provided by this section.

(10) In this section "the court" means the court which made the suspended forfeiture order or order for forfeiture.

This section addresses the situation in which a third party claims an interest in property which has already been forfeited. The criteria which are to be satisfied mirror those provided for by s.25 in relation to recalling orders. The action to be taken in the event of the satisfaction of those criteria is the return of the property or the payment of compensation.

Appeal against court decision under section 25(1) or 26(1)

27.—(1) An appeal shall lie to the High Court of Justiciary at the instance of—

    (a) the applicant against the refusal;

    (b) the prosecutor against the granting,

of an application under section 25(1) or 26(1) of this Act, and the High Court in determining such an appeal may make such order as could have been made by the court on an application under that section.

(2) The procedure in an appeal under this section shall be the same as the procedure in an appeal against sentence.

(3) Where a suspended forfeiture order relating to heritable property situated in Scotland is recalled on appeal to the High Court of Justiciary, the prosecutor shall, as soon as may be after the appeal has been disposed of, cause a certified copy of the interlocutor of the Court to be recorded in the General Register of Sasines or, as the case may be, registered in the Land Register of Scotland.

GENERAL NOTE
This section gives both the third party who applies for a recalling order or compensation and the prosecutor a right of appeal to the High Court.

Subs. (2)
This subsection applies the procedure relevant to an appeal against sentence. This will cause no real difficulty in an appeal by an applicant. It is, however, not clear whether the procedure

applicable to a prosecutor's appeal will be that which applies to a defence appeal against sentence or that which applies to the Lord Advocate's appeal against sentence.

PART III

RESTRAINT ORDERS

Restraint orders

28.—(1) The court may, on the application of the prosecutor, make an order (in this Part of this Act referred to as a "restraint order") in the circumstances mentioned in—

(a) section 29(2) or (3) of this Act interdicting—
>   (i) any person named in the order from dealing with his realisable property; or
>   (ii) that person and any person named in the order as appearing to the court to have received from him a gift caught by Part I of this Act or, as the case may be, an implicative gift from dealing with their own, or the other's, realisable property,
>   (whenever that property was acquired and whether it is described in the order or not); and

(b) section 30(1) of this Act interdicting any person named in the order from dealing with any property which is, or is liable to be, the subject of a suspended forfeiture order.

(2) A restraint order made under subsection (1)(a) above may contain conditions and exceptions to which the interdict shall be subject and in particular—

(a) may provide for the release to the person named in the order of such reasonable living expenses as the court thinks fit; and

(b) shall provide for the release of property in so far as it is required to meet reasonable legal expenses payable or likely to be payable in relation to proceedings—
>   (i) as regards the offence by virtue of which the restraint order has been made; or
>   (ii) as regards a confiscation order made on conviction of the offence.

(3) A restraint order shall—

(a) be made on an *ex parte* application which shall be heard in chambers; and

(b) without prejudice to the time when it becomes effective, be intimated to each person affected by it.

(4) For the purposes of this Part of this Act, dealing with property includes (without prejudice to the generality of the expression)—

(a) making a payment to any person in reduction of the amount of a debt;

(b) removing the property from the jurisdiction of the court; and

(c) transferring or disposing of the property.

(5) Where the court has made a restraint order (including a restraint order made under and within the meaning of the 1994 Act), a constable or a person commissioned by the Commissioners of Customs and Excise may, for the purpose of preventing any property subject to the order being removed—

(a) in the case of a restraint order made in connection with a drug trafficking offence (including a drug trafficking offence within the meaning of the 1994 Act) from Great Britain;

(b) in any other case, the jurisdiction of the court,
seize that property.

(6) Property seized under subsection (5) above shall be dealt with in accordance with the directions of the court which made the order.

(7) In this Part of this Act, "the court" means where, as regards the criminal proceedings in question, a trial diet or a diet fixed for the purposes of section 76 of the 1995 Act is intended to be held, is being or has been held—
    (a) in the High Court of Justiciary, the Court of Session;
    (b) in the sheriff court, a sheriff of that court exercising his civil jurisdiction.

(8) The court may, where it has granted a restraint order, interdict a person not subject to that order from dealing with property affected by it while it is in force.

(9) Subsections (2)(a) and (3)(a) above shall apply in relation to an interdict under subsection (8) above as they apply in relation to subsection (1) above; and subsections (1), (2), (4) and (5) of section 31 of this Act shall apply in relation to an interdict under subsection (8) above as they apply in relation to a restraint order.

(10) Without prejudice to the time when it becomes effective, an interdict under subsection (8) above shall be intimated to each person affected by it.

GENERAL NOTE

Restraint orders were first introduced by the DTOA and were based on English Mareva injunctions. The English case law on restraint orders assumes the developed jurisprudence which surrounds such injunctions in English law but much of that jurisprudence has no application in Scotland. In particular, it is doubtful whether the Scottish courts have the power at common law to make an order for disclosure of the nature and location of assets such as is frequently associated with Mareva injunctions (see *T, Re* [1992] 1 W.L.R. 949) and the legislation does not provide them with the statutory power to do so. It was held in *O, Re* [1991] 2 W.L.R. 475 that the power to make an order for disclosure was inherent in the English legislation but that depended on the specific terms of s.37 of the Supreme Court Act 1981.

Subs. (1)

The court. Restraint orders are matters for the civil courts, since they affect property rights. By subs. (7) the Court of Session has jurisdiction where the High Court is the trial court and the sheriff has jurisdiction where the sheriff court is the trial court.

On the application of the prosecutor. The application is, by subs. (3), to be made *ex parte* and in chambers.

Realisable property. See s.4.

A gift caught by Part I of this Act or ... an implicative gift. See ss.5 and 6 respectively.

A suspended forfeiture order. See s.21.

Subs. (2)

Reasonable living expenses. English restraint orders typically make provision for an exception for the reasonable living expenses of defendants, in terms of the Rules of the Supreme Court, Ord. 115, r. 4(1). Scottish restraint orders have not, in the past, usually made such exception, not least because the accused has usually been a remand prisoner with his living expenses being met by the Scottish Prison Service. However, the extension of the ambit of confiscation orders means that restraint orders are likely to be used more widely than in relation to drug traffickers alone and it may be that there will be some cases in which accused persons are at liberty and wish to make such applications. It must be kept clearly in view that English cases on living expenses are decided against a background of the Rules of Court and the jurisprudence on Mareva injunctions and will not necessarily be directly applicable as statements of principle which ought to apply in Scotland. Mitchell, Hinton and Taylor have said (*op. cit.* p. 38) that the English practice is to allow living expenses at a standard rate or as calculated from what is known about the defendant's (actual) living expenses. The latter basis for calculation might, however, present the accused with a dilemma. The higher he claims his usual living expenses have been, the greater the revenue expenditure the Crown can legitimately attribute to him when calculating his benefit from crime and the greater that benefit will be assessed to be (see Introductory Note above). It is also worth noting that Mann L.J. pointed out in *Peters, Re* [1988] 3 All E.R. 46 that exceptions for living expenses must always be subject to the need to leave sufficient property to satisfy any eventual confiscation order. Since in the past Scottish confiscation orders have tended to exhaust the accused's realisable property, as happened in *McLean*, the scope for such exceptions may be limited.

Reasonable legal expenses. It was held in *P., Re, W. Re* [1990] T.L.R. 299 that where a restraint order is subject to the legal expenses exception it is proper for the order to direct taxation of his legal costs after verdict.

Subs. (4)

Dealing with property. The definition of "dealing with property" represents an extension of the wording in the 1987 Act to meet the requirements of the Laundering Convention (SLC Report, para. 9.10). Since it is expressed to be without prejudice to the generality of the expression it is probable that burdening the property with any security would also be prohibited.

Restraint orders in relation to realisable property

29.—(1) A restraint order under section 28(1)(a) of this Act may be made in the circumstances mentioned in either subsection (2) or (3) below.

(2) For the purposes of this subsection, the circumstances are—

(a) proceedings have been instituted against an accused in Scotland for an offence to which Part I of this Act applies;

(b) the proceedings have not been concluded; and

(c) either a confiscation order has been made or it appears to the court that, in the event of his conviction of the offence, there are reasonable grounds for thinking that a confiscation order may be made in those proceedings.

(3) For the purposes of this subsection, the circumstances are that the court is satisfied that—

(a) it is proposed to institute proceedings within 28 days against a person suspected of such an offence and it appears to the court that, in the event of his conviction of the offence, there are reasonable grounds for thinking that a confiscation order may be made in those proceedings; or

(b) the prosecutor has made, or proposes within 28 days to make, an application under section 11 or, as the case may be, section 13 of this Act in relation to that person in respect of the offence, and it appears to the court that there are reasonable grounds for thinking that the application may be granted.

(4) Where the court has made a restraint order in the circumstances mentioned in subsection (3)(a) or (b) above and no proceedings have been instituted or application made within 28 days as mentioned in that subsection, the prosecutor shall forthwith apply to the court for the recall of the order and the court shall grant the application.

(5) When proceedings for the offence or, as the case may be, proceedings on an application under section 11 or 13 of this Act are concluded, the prosecutor shall forthwith apply to the court for recall of the order and the court shall grant the application.

(6) For the purposes of this section, proceedings are concluded as regards an offence where—

(a) the trial diet is deserted *simpliciter*;

(b) the accused is acquitted or, under section 65 or 147 of the 1995 Act, discharged or liberated;

(c) the High Court of Justiciary or, as the case may be, the sheriff sentences or otherwise deals with him without making a confiscation order and without postponing a decision as regards making such an order;

(d) after such postponement as is mentioned in paragraph (c) above, the High Court of Justiciary or, as the case may be, the sheriff decides not to make a confiscation order;

(e) his conviction is quashed; or

(f) a confiscation order made in the proceedings is satisfied (whether by payment of the amount due under the order or by the accused serving imprisonment in default).

(7) For the purposes of this section, proceedings on an application under section 11 or 13 of this Act are concluded—

(a) when the application is refused; or

(b) where the application is granted, when a confiscation order made in the proceedings is satisfied (whether by payment of the amount due under the order or by the accused serving imprisonment in default).

GENERAL NOTE

Section 29 makes provision for the circumstances in which a restraint order may be made in relation to realisable property. By subs. (2) an order may be made whilst proceedings are current and by subs. (3) an order may be made whilst proceedings are contemplated. By subs. (5) the order is to be recalled when the proceedings are concluded.

Subs. (2)

Three criteria must all be met before a restraint order can be made under subs. (2). Proceedings must have been instituted, they must not have been concluded and either a confiscation order must have been made or there must be reasonable grounds for thinking that one may be made.

Proceedings have been instituted. Section 49(6) defines the institution of proceedings for the purposes of the present Act.

Proceedings have not been concluded. See subs. (6).

Subs. (3)

The criteria for a restraint order under subs. (3) are alternatives, though in each case the court must be satisfied that there are reasonable grounds for thinking that a confiscation order may be made. Either it must be proposed to institute proceedings within 28 days or alternatively there must have been an application for an increase in a confiscation order or for the making of an order where one was not originally made or it must be proposed to make such an application within 28 days.

Subs. (5)

The prosecutor has an obligation to seek the recall of the restraint order when the proceedings which have been the basis of its making are concluded and the court must grant the application. It should be noted that, as a result of subs. (6)(f) the proceedings will not be concluded where a confiscation order is made until that order is satisfied.

Restraint orders in relation to forfeitable property

30.—(1) A restraint order may be made in respect of a person under section 28(1)(b) where—

(a) proceedings have been instituted against him in Scotland for an offence;

(b) the proceedings have not been concluded; and

(c) a suspended forfeiture order has been made in respect of the property concerned or it appears to the court that, in the event of his conviction of the offence, there are reasonable grounds for thinking that a suspended forfeiture order may be made in those proceedings.

(2) A restraint order may also be made where the court is satisfied that it is proposed to institute proceedings in respect of an offence within 28 days and it appears to the court that, in the event of his conviction of the offence, there are reasonable grounds for thinking that a suspended forfeiture order may be made in those proceedings.

(3) Where the court has made a restraint order by virtue of subsection (2) above, and no proceedings have been instituted within 28 days as mentioned in that subsection, the prosecutor shall forthwith apply to the court for the recall of the order and the court shall grant the application.

(4) When proceedings for the offence are concluded, the prosecutor shall forthwith apply to the court for recall of the order and the court shall grant the application.

(5) For the purposes of this section, proceedings are concluded as regards an offence where—

(a) the trial is deserted *simpliciter*;

(b) the accused is acquitted or, under section 65 or 147 of the 1995 Act, discharged or liberated;

   (c) the High Court of Justiciary or, as the case may be, the sheriff sentences or otherwise deals with him without making a suspended forfeiture order;

   (d) his conviction is quashed;

   (e) a suspended forfeiture order made in the proceedings is recalled or varied so as to exclude from forfeiture any property to which the restraint order relates; or

   (f) the property, or part of the property, to which the restraint order relates is forfeited.

GENERAL NOTE

Section 30 applies the same scheme for forfeitable property that s.29 applies for realisable property. The only significant difference is that, for obvious reasons, there is no equivalent to applications to increase confiscation orders or impose them where they were not originally imposed.

Variation and recall of restraint orders

31.—(1) Subject to subsections (2) and (3) below, the court may, at the instance of—

   (a) the prosecutor, at any time vary or recall a restraint order in relation to any person or to any property;

   (b) any person having an interest, at any time vary or recall a restraint order in relation to the person or to any property.

(2) On an application made under subsection (1)(b) above by a person named in a restraint order as having received a gift caught by Part I of this Act or, as the case may be, an implicative gift, the court may recall the order in relation to that person if it is satisfied on the balance of probabilities—

   (a) that he received the gift not knowing, not suspecting and not having reasonable grounds to suspect that the gift was made in contemplation of, or after, the commission of the offence or if more than one, in contemplation of any of the offences or after the commission of the earlier or the earliest of the offences to which the proceedings for the time being relate; and

   (b) that he was not associated with the giver in the commission of the offence; and

   (c) that he would suffer hardship if the order were not recalled.

(3) Where an application has been made under subsection (1) above for the variation or recall of a restraint order, any property in relation to which the restraint order was made shall not be realised during the period beginning with the making of the application and ending with the determination of the application by the court.

(4) The court may, where it has recalled a restraint order as mentioned in subsection (1)(b) or (2) above, order that property of the person at whose instance it was recalled shall cease to be realisable or, as the case may be, liable to forfeiture.

(5) The prosecutor or any person having an interest may reclaim or appeal to the Court of Session against an interlocutor refusing, varying or recalling or refusing to vary or recall a restraint order, within such period as may be prescribed by Act of Sederunt.

(6) Where, in relation to a restraint order which is recalled, interdict has been granted under section 28(8) of this Act, the clerk of court shall, on the restraint order being recalled, forthwith so inform each person so interdicted.

GENERAL NOTE

A restraint order is intended to be a temporary measure, designed to maintain the status quo until the court is in a position to make an order in relation to confiscation or forfeiture. Some mechanism is needed for the recall of such an order once its purpose has been served. Moreover, since a restraint order can affect the property rights of third parties it is necessary to provide some means of adjusting the order so as to minimise hardship to the blameless whilst maintaining the effectiveness of the order in general. This section therefore makes provision for variation and recall.

Subs. (1)

The court may. Variation or recall is discretionary except where proceedings are concluded (as to which see s.29(5)). The kind of judgment which the court will have to exercise appears from *Peters, Re* [1989] C.O.D. 180 C.A. in which a restraint order was varied to allow specific payments in relation to the defendant's son's education. In matrimonial proceedings he was ordered to pay his wife a lump sum of £25,000. The order was varied to enable that payment to be made. The prosecutor appealed and it was held that it was permissible to vary the order so as not to disrupt the son's education but that the anticipatory discharge of liabilities which would arise only after the outcome of the trial was known was contrary to the terms and underlying purpose of the legislation.

At the instance of ... any person having an interest. The accused will always have an interest though applications for variation by the accused are not likely to be very sympathetically received for obvious reasons. Other persons will have to demonstrate their interest before they can apply for variation or recall.

Subs. (2)

A gift caught by Part I. See s.5.

An implicative gift. See s.6.

The court may recall the order in relation to that person. Where the order is recalled in relation to a person, subs. (4) requires that such a person's property should cease to be realisable.

If it is satisfied on the balance of probabilities. The subsection places the onus on the applicant to satisfy the court, to the civil standard, that the criteria for recall are met and this will often be difficult to do. Subsection (2)(a) requires the applicant to demonstrate not only that he did not know or suspect the link between the gift and crime but also that, objectively, he had no reasonable grounds to suspect that link. The gift of a valuable asset or its transfer at obvious undervalue will often in itself constitute such grounds, by analogy with the law of reset. It will be recalled that Alison says (i, p.330):

"Certainly it is not requisite that the prisoner should have been informed by direct evidence that the goods were stolen: it is sufficient if they were received under circumstances which could have left no doubt in any reasonable mind, that they had been thus acquired ... it is sufficient if circumstances are proved which to persons of an ordinary understanding, and situated as the panel was, must have led to the conclusion that they were theftuously acquired".

He cites purchase at a discount as an example of a criminative circumstance.

Subsection (2)(b) requires the applicant to demonstrate his own innocence of involvement in the offence. Furthermore, subs. (2)(c), which may well be the hardest to meet in practice, requires him to demonstrate that he would suffer hardship if the order were not recalled in relation to him. The difficulty which this presents is that temporary inability to use what was received gratuitously, or at undervalue, is difficult to characterise as hardship.

Inhibition of property affected by restraint order or by interdict

32.—(1) On the application of the Lord Advocate, the Court of Session may in respect of heritable realisable property in Scotland affected by a restraint order (whether such property generally or particular such property) grant warrant for inhibition against any person interdicted by the order or, in relation to that property, under section 28(8) of this Act; and subject to the provisions of this Part of this Act, the warrant—

(a) shall have effect as if granted on the dependence of an action for debt at the instance of the Lord Advocate against the person and may be executed, recalled, loosed or restricted accordingly; and

(b) shall have the effect of letters of inhibition and shall forthwith be registered by the Lord Advocate in the Register of Inhibitions and Adjudications.

(2) Section 155 of the Titles to Land Consolidation (Scotland) Act 1868 (effective date of inhibition) shall apply in relation to an inhibition for which warrant has been granted under subsection (1) above as that section applies to an inhibition by separate letters or contained in a summons.

(3) In the application of section 158 of that Act of 1868 (recall of inhibition) to such an inhibition as is mentioned in subsection (2) above, references in

that section to a particular Lord Ordinary shall be construed as references to any Lord Ordinary.

(4) The fact that an inhibition has been executed under subsection (1) above in respect of property shall not prejudice the exercise of an administrator's powers under or for the purposes of this Part of this Act in respect of that property.

(5) No inhibition executed under subsection (1) above shall have effect once, or in so far as, the restraint order affecting the property in respect of which the warrant for the inhibition has been granted has ceased to have effect in respect of that property; and the Lord Advocate shall—

(a) apply for the recall, or as the case may be restriction, of the inhibition; and

(b) ensure that the recall, or restriction, of an inhibition on such application is reflected in the Register of Inhibitions and Adjudications.

GENERAL NOTE

This section makes inhibition available as an ancillary to a restraint order but only upon application to the Court of Session. There seems to be no reason why such application should not be made even where the restraint order itself is appropriately obtained in the sheriff court.

Arrestment of property affected by restraint order

33.—(1) On the application of the prosecutor, the court may, in respect of moveable property affected by a restraint order (whether such property generally or particular such property), grant warrant for arrestment if the property would be arrestable if the person entitled to it were a debtor.

(2) A warrant under subsection (1) above shall have effect as if granted on the dependence of an action for debt at the instance of the prosecutor against the person and may be executed, recalled, loosed or restricted accordingly.

(3) The fact that an arrestment has been executed under subsection (2) above in respect of property shall not prejudice the exercise of an administrator's powers under or for the purposes of this Act in respect of that property.

(4) No arrestment executed under subsection (2) above shall have effect once, or in so far as, the restraint order affecting the property in respect of which the warrant for such arrestment has been granted has ceased to have effect in respect of that property; and the prosecutor shall apply to the court for an order recalling, or as the case may be, restricting the arrestment accordingly.

GENERAL NOTE

This section makes arrestment available, as if on the dependence.

Administrators

34. Schedule 1 to this Act shall have effect as regards the appointment of administrators under this Act.

GENERAL NOTE

This section gives effect to Sched. 1 which contains detailed provision as to administrators.

PART IV

RECIPROCAL ARRANGEMENTS FOR ENFORCEMENT OF ORDERS

Recognition and enforcement of orders made in England and Wales

35.—(1) An order to which this section applies shall, subject to this section and section 36 of this Act, have effect in the law of Scotland but shall be enforced in Scotland only in accordance with this section and that section.

(2) A receiver's functions under or for the purposes of section 77, 80 or 81 of the 1988 Act or section 26, 29 or 30 of the 1994 Act shall, subject to this section and section 36 of this Act, have effect in the law of Scotland.

(3) If an order to which this section applies is registered under this section—

(a) the Court of Session shall have, in relation to its enforcement, the same power;

(b) proceedings for or with respect to its enforcement may be taken, and

(c) proceedings for or with respect to any contravention of such an order (whether before or after such registration) may be taken,

as if the order had originally been made in that Court.

(4) Nothing in this section enables any provision of an order which empowers a receiver to do anything in Scotland under section 80(3)(a) of the 1988 Act or section 29(3)(a) of the 1994 Act to have effect in the law of Scotland.

(5) The orders to which this section applies are orders of the High Court—

(a) made under section 77, 78 or 81 of the 1988 Act or section 26, 29, 30 or 59 of the 1994 Act;

(b) relating to the exercise by that Court of its powers under those sections; or

(c) relating to receivers in the performance of their functions under the said section 77, 78 or 81 of the 1988 Act or the said section 26, 29 or 30 of the 1994 Act,

but not including an order in proceedings for enforcement of any such order.

(6) References in this section to an order under—

(a) section 77 of the 1988 Act include references to a discharge under section 76(4) of that Act; or

(b) section 26 of the 1994 Act include references to a discharge under section 25(5) of that Act,

of such an order.

(7) In this section and in section 36 of this Act, "order" means any order, direction or judgment (by whatever name called).

(8) Nothing in any order of the High Court under section 80(6) of the 1988 Act or section 29(6) of the 1994 Act prejudices any enactment or rule of law in respect of the recording of deeds relating to heritable property in Scotland or the registration of interests in such property.

(9) In this Part, "High Court" means the High Court of England and Wales.

GENERAL NOTE

This section provides for the reciprocal enforcement of orders made in England and Wales under the Criminal Justice Act 1988 and the Drug Trafficking Act 1994.

Subs. (1)

An order to which this section applies. By subs. (7), "order" means any order, direction or judgment, by whatever name it is called. The orders referred to are, by subs. (5), the following orders of the English High Court.

(a)

Act	Section	Nature of Order
Criminal Justice Act 1988	77	Restraint Order
Criminal Justice Act 1988	78	Charging Order
Criminal Justice Act 1988	81	Directions as to application of proceeds of realisation of estate
Drug Trafficking Act 1994	26	Restraint Order
Drug Trafficking Act 1994	29	Appointment of a receiver and associated orders

Act	Section	Nature of Order
Drug Trafficking Act 1994	30	Directions as to application of proceeds of realisation of estate
Drug Trafficking Act 1994	59	Order that government departments should disclose information

   (b) Orders relating to the exercise by that court of its powers under the sections specified in (a).
   (c) Orders relating to receivers in the performance of their functions under those sections.

Subs. (3)
   Subsection (3) places an order to which the section applies and which is registered in the Court of Session on the same footing as if it had been made by the Court of Session in the first place.

Provisions supplementary to section 35

   36.—(1) The Court of Session shall, on application made to it in accordance with rules of court for registration of an order to which section 35 of this Act applies, direct that the order shall, in accordance with such rules, be registered in that Court.
   (2) Subsections (1) and (3) of section 35 of this Act and subsection (1) above are subject to any provision made by rules of court—
     (a) as to the manner in which and conditions subject to which that section applies are to be enforced in Scotland;
     (b) for the sisting of proceedings for enforcement of such an order;
     (c) for the modification or cancellation of the registration of such an order if the order is modified or revoked or ceases to have effect.
   (3) This section and section 35 of this Act are without prejudice to any enactment or rule of law as to the effect of notice or the want of it in relation to orders of the High Court.
   (4) The Court of Session shall have the like power to make an order under section 1 of the Administration of Justice (Scotland) Act 1972 (extended power to order inspection of documents etc.) in relation to proceedings brought or likely to be brought under—
     (a) Part VI of the 1988 Act; or
     (b) the 1994 Act,
in the High Court as if those proceedings were brought or were likely to be brought in the Court of Session.
   (5) The Court of Session may, additionally, for the purpose of—
     (a) assisting the achievement in Scotland of the purposes of orders to which section 35 of this Act applies;
     (b) assisting receivers performing functions thereunder or for the purposes of section 77, 80 or 81 of the 1988 Act or section 26, 29 or 30 of the 1994 Act,
make such orders and do otherwise as seems to it appropriate.
   (6) A document purporting to be a copy of an order under or for the purposes of—
     (a) Part VI of the 1988 Act; or
     (b) the 1994 Act,
by the High Court and to be certified as such by a proper officer of that Court shall, in Scotland, be sufficient evidence of the order.

GENERAL NOTE
   This section empowers the Court of Session to direct that the English orders referred to in s.35 be registered and to make such other orders as seem to the court to be appropriate to assist the enforcement of those English orders.

Inhibition of Scottish property affected by order registered under section 35

37.—(1) On the application of the Lord Advocate, the Court of Session may in respect of heritable realisable property in Scotland affected by a restraint order registered under section 35 of this Act (whether such property generally or particular such property) grant warrant for inhibition against any person with an interest in that property; and the warrant—

(a) shall have effect as if granted on the dependence of an action for debt at the instance of the Lord Advocate against the person and may be executed, recalled, loosed or restricted accordingly;

(b) shall have the effect of letters of inhibition and shall forthwith be registered by the Lord Advocate in the Register of Inhibitions and Adjudications.

(2) Section 155 of the Titles to Land Consolidation (Scotland) Act 1868 (effective date of inhibition) shall apply in relation to an inhibition for which warrant has been granted under subsection (1) above as that section applies to an inhibition by separate letters or contained in a summons.

(3) In the application of section 158 of that Act of 1868 (recall of inhibition) to such an inhibition as is mentioned in subsection (2) above, references in that section to a particular Lord Ordinary shall be construed as references to any Lord Ordinary.

(4) The fact that an inhibition has been executed under subsection (1) above, in respect of property shall not prejudice the exercise of a receiver's powers under or for the purposes of—

(a) section 77, 80 or 81 of the 1988 Act; or

(b) section 26, 29 or 30 of the 1994 Act,

in respect of that property.

(5) No inhibition executed under subsection (1) above shall have effect once, or in so far as, the restraint order affecting the property in respect of which the warrant for the inhibition has been granted has ceased to have effect in respect of that property; and the Lord Advocate shall—

(a) apply for the recall, or as the case may be restriction, of the inhibition; and

(b) ensure that the recall, or restriction, of an inhibition on such application is reflected in the Register of Inhibitions and Adjudications.

(6) Any power of the Court of Session to recall, loose or restrict inhibitions shall, in relation to an order containing an inhibition under subsection (1) above and without prejudice to any other consideration lawfully applying to the exercise of the power, be exercised with a view to achieving the purposes specified in section 80 of the 1988 Act or, as the case may be, section 31 of the 1994 Act.

GENERAL NOTE
This section provides for the use of inhibition in relation to English orders registered in the Court of Session.

Arrestment of Scottish property affected by order registered under section 35

38.—(1) On the application of the Lord Advocate, the Court of Session may, in respect of moveable property affected by a restraint order registered under section 35 of this Act (whether such property generally or particular such property), grant warrant for arrestment if the property would be arrestable if the person entitled to it were a debtor.

(2) A warrant under subsection (1) above shall have effect as if granted on the dependence of an action for debt at the instance of the Lord Advocate against the person and may be executed, recalled, loosed or restricted accordingly.

(3) The fact that an arrestment has been executed under subsection (2) above in respect of property shall not prejudice the exercise of a receiver's powers under or for the purposes of—
- (a) section 77, 80 or 81 of the 1988 Act; or
- (b) section 26, 29 or 30 of the 1994 Act,

in respect of that property.

(4) No arrestment executed under subsection (2) above shall have effect once, or in so far as, the restraint order affecting the property in respect of which the warrant for such arrestment has been granted has ceased to have effect in respect of that property; and the Lord Advocate shall apply to the Court of Session for an order recalling, or as the case may be, restricting the arrestment accordingly.

(5) Any power of the Court of Session to recall, loose or restrict arrestments shall, in relation to an arrestment proceeding upon a warrant under subsection (1) above and without prejudice to any other consideration lawfully applying to the exercise of the power, be exercised with a view to achieving the purposes specified in section 80 of the 1988 Act or, as the case may be, section 31 of the 1994 Act.

GENERAL NOTE
This section provides for the use of arrestments in relation to English orders registered in the Court of Session.

Enforcement of Northern Ireland orders

39.—(1) Her Majesty may by Order in Council provide that, for the purposes of Part III of and Schedules 1 and 2 to this Act, this Act shall have effect as if—
- (a) references to confiscation orders included a reference to orders made by courts in Northern Ireland which appear to Her Majesty to correspond to confiscation orders;
- (b) references to—
  - (i) offences to which Part I of this Act applies; or
  - (ii) drug trafficking offences,

  included a reference to any offence under the law of Northern Ireland (not being an offence to which that Part applies) which appears to Her Majesty to correspond to such an offence; and
- (c) such other modifications were made as may be specified in the Order in Council, being modifications which appear to Her Majesty to be requisite or desirable having regard to procedural differences which may for the time being exist between Scotland and Northern Ireland; and without prejudice to the generality of this paragraph modifications may include provision as to the circumstances in which proceedings in Northern Ireland are to be treated for the purposes of those sections as instituted or as concluded.

(2) An Order in Council under this section may provide for the provisions mentioned in subsection (1) above to have effect in relation to anything done or to be done in Northern Ireland subject to such further modifications as may be specified in the Order.

(3) An Order in Council under this section may contain such incidental, consequential and transitional provisions as Her Majesty considers expedient.

(4) An Order in Council under this section may, in particular, provide for section 18 of the Civil Jurisdiction and Judgements Act 1982 (enforcement of United Kingdom judgments in other parts of the United Kingdom) not to apply in relation to such orders made in connection with drug trafficking offences as may be prescribed by the Order.

(5) An Order in Council under this section shall be subject to annulment in pursuance of a resolution of either House of Parliament.

GENERAL NOTE
This section provides for the making of Orders in Council to give effect in Scotland to orders made in Northern Ireland.

Enforcement of orders made outside United Kingdom

40.—(1) Her Majesty may by Order in Council—

(a) direct in relation to a country or territory outside the United Kingdom designated by the Order that, subject to such modifications as may be specified, Part I of this Act and Part III of this Act so far as it relates to realisable property shall apply in relation to external confiscation orders and to proceedings which have been or are to be instituted in the designated country and may result in an external confiscation order being made there;

(b) make—

(i) such provision as to evidence or proof of any matter for the purposes of this section and section 41 of this Act; and

(ii) such incidental, consequential and transitional provision,

as appears to Her Majesty to be expedient.

(2) In this Part of this Act—

"designated country" means a country or territory designated by an Order in Council made under this section; and

"external confiscation order" means an order made by a court in a designated country for the purpose of recovering payments or other rewards or property or other economic advantage received in connection with—

(a) an offence corresponding with or similar to an offence to which Part I of this Act applies; or

(b) drug trafficking,

or the value of such payments, property, reward or economic advantage.

(3) An Order in Council under this section may make different provision for different cases or classes of case.

(4) The power to make an Order in Council under this section includes power to modify Part I of this Act or Part III of this Act so far as it relates to realisable property in such a way as to confer power on a person to exercise a discretion.

(5) An Order in Council under this section shall be subject to annulment in pursuance of a resolution of either House of Parliament.

GENERAL NOTE
This section provides for the making of Orders in Council to give effect in Scotland to orders made in countries with which the U.K. has arrangements as described in the Introductory Note. The approach under the 1987 Act has been to apply the relevant parts of the 1987 Act subject to such modifications as are necessary given the international context. The countries to which the arrangements apply have been designated in the Confiscation of the Proceeds of Drug Trafficking (Designated Countries and Territories) (Scotland) Order 1991 and the modifications to it (S.I. 1991 No. 1467 as amended by S.I. 1992 No. 1733, 1993 No. 1806 and 1993 No. 3156). The necessary modifications have been made by Sched. 2 to that Order. It is understood that a new Order in Council will be made to reflect the position under the present Act and to consolidate the list of countries which are designated. In *J.L., Re* (*The Times*, May 4, 1994) Judge J. held that the equivalent English Order was operative notwithstanding the fact that the proceedings in the foreign country were civil proceedings *in rem* (which is the approach to confiscation used in the USA).

As at August 1, 1994, the U.K. had bilateral confiscation arrangements in force in relation to drug trafficking, or in relation to all crimes including drug trafficking, with the USA, Switzerland, Canada, Australia, Gibraltar, Mexico, the Bahamas, Spain, Hong Kong, the Cayman Islands, Saudi Arabia, Bahrain, Sweden, Anguilla, Ecuador, Barbados, Nigeria, Colombia, Uruguay, Argentina and the Netherlands. Such arrangements existed but had still to be brought into force with Bermuda, Malaysia, Italy, Montserrat, Guyana, Panama, South Africa, India, Panama, the British Virgin Islands and Paraguay.

Countries which had ratified the Laundering Convention and with which the U.K. had multilateral arrangements under that were Bulgaria, Finland, the Netherlands, Italy and Switzerland. Countries which had ratified the 1988 UN Drugs Convention and with which the U.K. therefore had multilateral arrangements in relation to drug trafficking were as follows: Afghanistan, Antigua and Barbuda, Argentina, Armenia, Australia, Azerbaijan, Bahamas, Bahrain, Bangladesh, Barbados, Belarus, Bhutan, Bolivia, Bosnia and Herzegovina, Brazil, Brunei, Bulgaria, Burkina Faso, Burma, Burundi, Cameroon, Canada, Chile, China, Colombia, Costa Rica, Croatia, Cyprus, Czech Republic, Denmark, Dominica, Dominican Republic, El Salvador, Equador, Egypt, Fiji, Finland, France, Germany, Ghana, Greece, Grenada, Guatemala, Guinea, Guyana, Honduras, India, Iran, Italy, Ivory Coast, Japan, Jordan, Kenya, Latvia, Luxembourg, Macedonia, Madagascar, Malaysia, Mauritania, Mexico, Monaco, Morocco, Nepal, Netherlands, Nicaragua, Niger, Nigeria, Oman, Pakistan, Panama, Paraguay, Peru, Poland, Portugal, Qatar, Romania, Russian Federation, Saint Vincent, Saudi Arabia, Senegal, Seychelles, Sierra Leone, Slovakia, Slovenia, Spain, Sri Lanka, Sudan, Suriname, Sweden, Syria, Togo, Tunisia, Uganda, Ukraine, United Arab Emirates, USA, Venezuela, Yugoslavia and Zambia. Arrangements also existed with Guernsey, Jersey and the Isle of Man.

Registration of external confiscation orders

41.—(1) On an application made by or on behalf of the Government of a designated country, the Court of Session may register an external confiscation order made there if—
  (a) it is satisfied that at the time of registration the order is in force and not subject to appeal;
  (b) it is satisfied, where the person against whom the order is made did not appear in the proceedings, that he received notice of the proceedings in sufficient time to enable him to defend them; and
  (c) it is of the opinion that enforcing the order in Scotland would not be contrary to the interests of justice.
(2) In subsection (1) above "appeal" includes—
  (a) any proceedings by way of discharging or setting aside a judgment; and
  (b) an application for a new trial or a stay of execution.
(3) The Court of Session shall cancel the registration of an external confiscation order if it appears to the court that the order has been satisfied by payment of the amount due under it or by the person against whom it was made serving imprisonment in default of payment or by any other means.

GENERAL NOTE
  This section makes provision in relation to foreign confiscation orders equivalent to that for English orders made by s.36.

Enforcement of Scottish orders in England and Wales

42.—(1) Her Majesty may by Order in Council make such provision as Her Majesty considers expedient for the purpose—
  (a) of enabling property in England and Wales which is realisable property to be used or realised for the payment of any amount payable under a confiscation order made in connection with an offence to which Part I of this Act applies;
  (b) of securing that, where no such confiscation order has been made, property in England and Wales which is realisable property is available, in the event that such an order is so made, to be used or realised for the payment of any amount payable under it; and
  (c) of enabling the enforcement in England and Wales of restraint orders, suspended forfeiture orders and forfeiture orders under any enactment other than the 1989 Act.
· (2) Without prejudice to the generality of the power conferred by subsection (1) above, an Order in Council under this section may—

(a) provide that, subject to any specific conditions, such description of orders made under or for the purposes of Part I, II or III of this Act so far as it relates to realisable property shall have effect in the law of England and Wales;

(b) provide that, subject to any specified conditions, the functions of a person appointed under Schedule 1 to this Act shall have effect in the law of England and Wales;

(c) make provision—

(i) for the registration in the High Court of such descriptions of orders made under or for the purposes of Part I, II or III of this Act so far as it relates to realisable property as may be specified; and

(ii) for the High Court to have, in relation to the enforcement of orders made under or for the purposes of Part I, II or III of this Act so far as it so relates which are so registered, such powers as may be specified; and

(d) make provision as to the proof in England and Wales of orders made under or for the purposes of Part I, II or III of this Act so far as it so relates.

(3) In subsection (2) above "specified" means specified in an Order in Council under this section.

(4) An Order in Council under this section may amend or apply, with or without modifications, any enactment.

(5) An Order in Council under this section may contain such incidental, consequential and transitional provisions as Her Majesty considers expedient.

(6) An Order in Council under this section shall be subject to annulment in pursuance of a resolution of either House of Parliament.

GENERAL NOTE

This section provides for the making of Orders in Council in relation to the enforcement of Scottish orders in England and Wales. Under the 1987 Act, the relevant Order was the Drug Trafficking Offences (Enforcement in England and Wales) Order 1988 (S.I. 1988 No. 593) but it is to be expected that a new Order will now be required.

Order in Council as regards taking of action in designated country

43.—(1) Her Majesty may by Order in Council make such provision in connection with the taking of action in a designated country in consequence of the making of a restraint order, confiscation order or suspended forfeiture order under this Act or a forfeiture order under any other enactment as appears to Her Majesty to be expedient.

(2) Without prejudice to the generality of subsection (1) above, the provision contained in an Order in Council made under this section may include a direction that in such circumstances as may be specified proceeds arising out of action taken in a designated country with a view to satisfying a confiscation order which are retained there shall nevertheless be treated as reducing the amount payable under the confiscation order to such extent as may be specified.

(3) An Order in Council under this section may amend or apply, with or without modifications, any enactment.

(4) Subsections (1)(b), (3) and (5) of section 40 of this Act shall apply in respect of Orders in Council under this section as they apply in respect of Orders in Council under that section.

GENERAL NOTE

This section is a general Order-making power in relation to the taking of action in a foreign jurisdiction.

PART V

MISCELLANEOUS AND GENERAL

Sequestration etc. of person holding realisable or forfeitable property

44.—(1) Schedule 2 to this Act shall have effect in relation to the sequestration, bankruptcy, winding up or receivership of persons or, as the case may be, companies holding realisable or forfeitable property.

(2) In this section and in that Schedule "forfeitable property" means property which is or is liable to be the subject of a suspended forfeiture order.

GENERAL NOTE
This section gives effect to Sched. 2, which makes provisions necessary for the interaction of confiscation and forfeiture with insolvency law.

Disposal of family home under Part I or II

45.—(1) This section applies where—
(a) a confiscation order has been made in relation to any person and the prosecutor has not satisfied the court that—
(i) in the case of an order made in connection with a drug trafficking offence, the person's interest in his family home has been acquired by means of the proceeds of drug trafficking; or
(ii) in any other case, the person's interest in his family home has been acquired by means of the benefit derived from the commission of the offence concerned; or
(b) a person's family home has been forfeited to the Crown under section 24 of this Act.

(2) Where this section applies, then, before the Crown disposes of any right or interest in the person's family home it shall—
(a) obtain the relevant consent; or
(b) where it is unable to do so, apply to the court for authority to carry out the disposal.

(3) On an application being made to it under subsection (2)(b) above, the court, after having regard to all the circumstances of the case including—
(a) the needs and financial resources of the spouse or former spouse of the person concerned;
(b) the needs and financial resources of any child of the family;
(c) the length of the period during which the family home has been used as a residence by any of the persons referred to in paragraph (a) or (b) above,
may refuse to grant the application or may postpone the granting of the application for such period (not exceeding 12 months) as it may consider reasonable in the circumstances or may grant the application subject to such conditions as it may prescribe.

(4) Subsection (3) above shall apply—
(a) to an action for division and sale of the family home of the person concerned; or
(b) to an action for the purpose of obtaining vacant possession of that home,
brought by the Crown as it applies to an application under subsection (2)(b) above and, for the purposes of this subsection, any reference in the said subsection (3) to the granting of the application shall be construed as a reference to the granting of decree in the action.

(5) In this section—
"family home", in relation to any person (in this subsection referred to as "the relevant person") means any property in which the relevant person has or had (whether alone or in common with any other person) a right or interest, being property which is occupied as a

residence by the relevant person and his or her spouse or by the relevant person's spouse or former spouse (in any case with or without a child of the family) or by the relevant person with a child of the family;

"child of the family" includes any child or grandchild of either the relevant person or his or her spouse or former spouse, and any person who has been treated by either the relevant person or his or her spouse or former spouse as if he or she were a child of the relevant person, spouse or former spouse, whatever the age of such a child, grandchild or person may be; and

"relevant consent" means in relation to the disposal of any right or interest in a family home—

(a) in a case where the family home is occupied by the spouse or former spouse of the relevant person, the consent of the spouse or, as the case may be, of the former spouse, whether or not the family home is also occupied by the relevant person;

(b) where paragraph (a) above does not apply, in a case where the family home is occupied by the relevant person with a child of the family, the consent of the relevant person.

GENERAL NOTE

The Scottish Law Commission noted that, although the nature of property would as a general rule be irrelevant to questions in relation to a confiscation order, concerns could arise in the situation in which an offender's family is living in a family home which had in fact been acquired lawfully. They noted that insolvency legislation imposes restrictions on the sale of a bankrupt's family home and noted English case law to the effect that compensation orders should not be made where their effect would be to require the sale of the family home. They considered that protections for the family home equivalent to those in the Bankruptcy (Scotland) Act 1985 would be appropriate (SLC Report, paras. 4.15–4.18). This section enacts such protections. Their essence is that where a confiscation order has been made or a person's family home forfeited, the Crown is not entitled to dispose of any right or interest in the family home without either the consent of the family members involved or the consent of the court.

Subs. (1)

Subsection (1) defines the circumstances in which the section applies. In the case of a confiscation order the section applies unless the prosecutor satisfies the court that the accused's interest in his family home was acquired with the fruits of his crime. The section applies in all forfeiture cases involving the family home.

The prosecutor has not satisfied the court. The Act is silent as to the standard of proof. The Scottish Law Commission draft Bill (clause 36, SLC Report, p. 240) explicitly required proof beyond reasonable doubt.

Family home. This is defined in subs. (5). It is primarily any property in which the person to whom a confiscation order relates ("the relevant person") resides with his spouse or a child of the family (which expression is defined widely by subs. (5)). Property occupied by a former spouse is also covered. Mere cohabitees are not protected.

Subs. (2)

Where the section applies the Crown must first seek consent. If it cannot get consent it must apply to the court.

The relevant consent. This is defined by subs. (5). Where a relevant person's spouse occupies the property it is that spouse's consent which must be sought. Where the relevant person occupies the property with his child, it is the relevant person's consent which must be sought.

Subs. (3)

This subsection defines the court's powers on an application for its authority to carry out the disposal of a family home and also (by subs. (4)) where the Crown brings an action for division and sale in respect of such a home or to obtain vacant possession. The subsection also sets out the criteria which the court must apply.

Forfeiture of property where accused has died

46.—(1) This section applies where at any time after criminal proceedings have been instituted against an accused for an offence to which Part I of this

Act applies and before the accused has been sentenced or otherwise dealt with in the proceedings he dies.

(2) The Court of Session, if it is satisfied beyond reasonable doubt on an application being made to it by the Lord Advocate—

(a) that the accused committed the offence; and

(b) that there is property—

(i) which the accused had obtained, directly or indirectly, in connection with the commission of the offence or, as the case may be, in connection with drug trafficking; or

(ii) which is a gift caught by Part I of this Act or, as the case may be, an implicative gift,

may, subject to subsection (5) below, make an order which shall have the effect of forfeiting that property.

(3) The Court of Session may, without prejudice to any other power available to it, at any time before the determination of the case, allow an amendment of the application under subsection (2) above if the amendment is of a type which could competently have been made in an indictment or complaint under section 96 or 159 of the 1995 Act in the criminal proceedings.

(4) An application under subsection (2) above shall be made as soon as is reasonably practicable after the relevant information becomes available to the Lord Advocate, but, in any event, within 6 years commencing with the date of death of the accused.

(5) An application under subsection (2) above in relation to property such as is mentioned in paragraph (b)(ii) of that subsection shall be served on the recipient of the gift and, if he satisfies the Court on the balance of probabilities—

(a) that he received the gift not knowing, not suspecting and not having reasonable grounds to suspect that the gift was made in contemplation of, or after, the commission of the offence or, if more than one, in contemplation of any of the offences or after the commission of the earlier or the earliest of the offences to which the proceedings for the time being relate; and

(b) that he was not associated with the giver in the commission of the offence; and

(c) that he would suffer hardship if the application were granted,

the Court may refuse to make an order as mentioned in that subsection; and in the application of this subsection to an implicative gift, any reference to the commission of the offence shall be construed as a reference to the drug trafficking and the reference in paragraph (b) above to the earlier or earliest of more than one offence shall be construed as a reference to the beginning of the drug trafficking.

(6) Where property has been forfeited under this section, then, if the Court of Session, on an application being made to it is satisfied by the applicant on the balance of probabilities that he was the owner of, or otherwise had an interest in, the property immediately before such forfeiture, it shall make an order under subsection (7) below.

(7) An order under this subsection shall direct the Crown, if the applicant—

(a) was the owner of the property, to return it to him if it is reasonably practicable to do so or, if not, to pay compensation to him of an amount determined under subsection (8) below; or

(b) otherwise had an interest in the property, to pay compensation to him of an amount corresponding to the value of such interest.

(8) For the purposes of subsection (7) above, the amount determined under this subsection shall be an amount equal to the amount of any consideration received for the property or the value of any such consideration at the time of the disposal, or, if no consideration was received, an amount equal to the value of the property at the time of the disposal.

(9) Property which has been forfeited under this section shall be dealt with by the Crown in such manner as seems to it to be appropriate.

(10) Where a restraint order is not in force in respect of a person when he dies in the circumstances mentioned in subsection (1) above, the Court of Session may, on the application of the Lord Advocate, in so far as the property concerned is—

(a) heritable property in Scotland, make an order inhibiting any person; and

(b) moveable property, grant warrant for arrestment if the property would be arrestable if the person entitled to it were a debtor.

(11) Paragraphs (a) and (b) of subsection (1) and subsections (2) to (5) of section 32 of this Act shall, subject to any necessary modifications, apply for the purposes of subsection (10)(a) above as they apply for the purposes of that section.

(12) Subsections (2) to (4) of section 33 of this Act shall, subject to any necessary modifications, apply for the purposes of subsection (10)(b) above as they apply for the purposes of that section.

(13) Proceedings under this section are civil proceedings for the purposes of section 10 of the Law Reform (Miscellaneous Provisions) (Scotland) Act 1968.

GENERAL NOTE

A number of countries have addressed the issue of the accused who dies before a confiscation order can be made. In such a case, if confiscation cannot be achieved (as it could not under the 1987 Act) the accused's heirs could live on the proceeds of his crimes and might do so in some luxury. It seemed to the Scottish Law Commission that this was unacceptable (SLC Report, para. 19.2). This section makes provision enabling the Lord Advocate to obtain a restraint order and the forfeiture of the property.

Subs. (1)

This subsection defines the ambit of the provisions. They apply where criminal proceedings have been instituted but where the accused dies before he can be sentenced.

Subs. (2)

The Court of Session. The question with the heirs of a deceased accused resolves itself into one of entitlement to property. That is an essentially civil question, and one which is potentially complex. The Court of Session is therefore selected as the appropriate forum (SLC Report, para. 19.9).

If it is satisfied beyond reasonable doubt. The criminal standard is not the obvious one for application in the Court of Session but since what the Lord Advocate has to prove is that the deceased committed the offence and that there is property which he obtained as a result of the offence, and since these matters would have had to be proved to the criminal standard against the accused, it is appropriate that that standard should also apply against the heirs. The alternative would be to make it easier for the Crown to obtain the property of a dead criminal than of a living one (SLC Report, paras. 19.11–19.15). However, since the proceedings are civil, the more relaxed civil rules of evidence will apply.

That the accused committed the offence. This must be proved from scratch. An extract conviction, where the accused dies after conviction but before sentence, is not given any status as evidence.

That there is property . . . which the accused had obtained . . . in connection with the commission of the offence . . . or which is a gift. The property affected is that which would have been in issue under Pt. I of the Act had the accused lived. However, the prosecutor's statement mechanism and the various assumptions which would have been available against the accused himself have no place in an application under this section.

An order which shall have the effect of forfeiting the property. The order forfeits the property at once. It is not a suspended forfeiture order.

Subs. (4)

Applications time bar six years after the death of the accused.

Subs. (5)
Where the application relates to what is proved beyond doubt to be a gift in terms of s.5 or s.6, the onus is transferred to the recipient to prove on a balance of probabilities the matters which he would have to prove if seeking the recall of a restraint order.

Construction of certain enactments

47.—(1) Section 28 of the Bankruptcy Act 1914 (effect of order of discharge) shall have effect as if amounts payable under confiscation orders were debts excepted under subsection (1)(a) of that section.

(2) In section 1(2)(a) of the Rehabilitation of Offenders Act 1974 (failure to pay fines etc. not to prevent person becoming rehabilitated) the reference to a fine or other sum adjudged to be paid by or on a conviction does not include a reference to an amount payable under a confiscation order.

(3) Section 55(2) of the Bankruptcy (Scotland) Act 1985 (discharge of debtor not to release him from liabilities in respect of fines, etc.) shall have effect as if the reference to a fine included a reference to a confiscation order.

(4) Section 281(4) of the Insolvency Act 1986 (discharge of bankrupt not to release him from liabilities in respect of fines, etc.) shall have effect as if the reference to a fine included a reference to a confiscation order.

Service and notice

48. Subject to the provisions of this Act, provision may be made by rules of court as to the giving of notice required for the purposes of this Act in so far as it is connected with drug trafficking or the effecting of service so required; and different provision may be so made for different cases or classes of case and for different circumstances or classes of circumstance.

Interpretation

49.—(1) In this Act, unless the context otherwise requires—
"the 1988 Act" means the Criminal Justice Act 1988;
"the 1989 Act" means the Prevention of Terrorism (Temporary Provisions) Act 1989;
"the 1994 Act" means the Drug Trafficking Act 1994;
"the 1995 Act" means the Criminal Procedure (Scotland) Act 1995;
"accused" includes a person against whom criminal proceedings have been instituted in relation to the commission of an offence and a person convicted of an offence;
"clerk of court" includes the sheriff clerk;
"confiscation order" means an order made under section 1(1), 11(4), 12(3) or 13 of this Act;
"interest", in relation to property, includes right;
"property" has the meaning assigned by section 2 of this Act;
"realisable property" has the meaning assigned by section 4 of this Act;
"restraint order" means an order made under section 28 of this Act;
"suspended forfeiture order" means an order made under section 21(2) of this Act.

(2) In this Act, "drug trafficking" means, subject to subsections (3) and (4) below, doing or being concerned in any of the following, whether in Scotland or elsewhere—

(a) producing or supplying a controlled drug where the production or supply contravenes section 4(1) of the Misuse of Drugs Act 1971;

(b) transporting or storing such a drug where possession of it contravenes section 5(1) of that Act;

(c) importing or exporting such a drug where the importation or exportation is prohibited by section 3(1) of that Act;

(d) producing, supplying, transporting, storing, importing or exporting such a drug in contravention of a corresponding law ("corresponding law" having the meaning assigned by section 36(1) of that Act);

(e) manufacturing or supplying a scheduled substance within the meaning of section 12 of the Criminal Justice (International Co-operation) Act 1990 where the manufacture or supply is an offence under that section;

(f) acquiring, having possession of or using property in contravention of section 37 of the Criminal Law (Consolidation) (Scotland) Act 1995;

(g) concealing or transferring the proceeds of drug trafficking in contravention of section 14 of the said Act of 1990;

(h) using any ship for illicit traffic in controlled drugs in contravention of section 19 of the said Act of 1990.

(3) Drug trafficking also includes, whether in Scotland or elsewhere, entering into or being otherwise concerned in any arrangement whereby—

(a) the retention or control by or on behalf of another person of the other person's proceeds of drug trafficking is facilitated, or

(b) the proceeds of drug trafficking by another person are used to secure that funds are placed at the other person's disposal or are used for the other person's benefit to acquire property by way of investment.

(4) In paragraphs (e) to (g) of subsection (2) above, references to conduct in contravention of the enactments mentioned in those paragraphs include conduct which would contravene the enactments if it took place in Scotland.

(5) In this Act a "drug trafficking offence" means any of the following—

(a) an offence under—

　　(i) section 4(2) (production, or being concerned in production, of controlled drug);

　　(ii) section 4(3) (supply of, or offer to supply, or being concerned in supply of, controlled drug);

　　(iii) section 5(3) (possession of controlled drug with intent to supply); or

　　(iv) section 20 (assisting in, or inducing commission of, certain drug related offences punishable under foreign law),

of the Misuse of Drugs Act 1971;

(b) in connection with a prohibition or restriction on importation and exportation having effect by virtue of section 3 of the said Act of 1971, an offence under section 50(2) or (3) (improper importation), 68(2) (improper exportation) or 170 (fraudulent evasion of duty etc.) of the Customs and Excise Management Act 1979;

(c) an offence under section 37 of the Criminal Law (Consolidation) (Scotland) Act 1995;

(d) an offence under section 38 of the said Act of 1995;

(e) an offence under section 12, 14 or 19 of the Criminal Justice (International Co-operation) Act 1990;

(f) an offence of conspiring, inciting or attempting to commit an offence mentioned in paragraph (a), (b), (c) or (e) above.

(6) For the purposes of this Act proceedings for an offence are instituted against a person—

(a) on his arrest without warrant;

(b) when he is charged with the offence without being arrested;

(c) when a warrant to arrest him is granted;

(d) when a warrant to cite him is granted;

(e) in summary proceedings, on the first calling of the case; or

(f) when a petition is intimated to him or an indictment or a complaint is served on him,

and, where the application of this subsection would result in there being more than one time for the institution of proceedings, they shall be taken to be instituted at the earliest of those times.

(7) Any reference in this Act to a conviction of an offence includes a reference to a finding that the offence has been committed.

Short title, commencement and extent

50.—(1) This Act may be cited as the Proceeds of Crime (Scotland) Act 1995.

(2) This Act shall come into force on 1 April 1996.

(3) Subject to subsections (4) and (5) below, this Act extends only to Scotland.

(4) Section 44 of and Schedule 2 to this Act and this section extend to England and Wales as well as to Scotland.

(5) Section 42 of this Act extends only to England and Wales.

SCHEDULES

Section 34　　　　　　　　　　　SCHEDULE 1

ADMINISTRATORS

Appointment of administrators

1.—(1) On the application of the prosecutor the court may as regards property—

(a) affected by a restraint order or a suspended forfeiture order, appoint a person to manage, or otherwise deal with, the property; or

(b) where a suspended forfeiture order or a confiscation order has been made, appoint a person (or empower an appointee under paragraph (a) above) to realise the property,

in accordance with the court's directions and may (whether on making the appointment or from time to time) require any person having possession of the property to give possession of it to the appointee (any such appointee being in this Act referred to as an "administrator").

(2) A requirement under sub-paragraph (1) above—

(a) subject to paragraph (b) below, may relate to the property generally or to particular such property and may be subject to such exceptions and conditions as may be specified by the court;

(b) shall relate to property mentioned in paragraph (b) of section 4(1) of this Act only if expressly stated so to do and then only in so far as the person in whom such property is vested is named in the requirement as being subject to it.

(3) On a requirement being imposed under sub-paragraph (1) above—

(a) the clerk of court shall forthwith notify—

(i) the person in respect of whom the restraint order, or as the case may be the suspended forfeiture order or confiscation order, has been made; and

(ii) any other person named in the requirement as being subject to it; and

(b) any dealing of or with such person in relation to the property shall be of no effect in a question with the administrator unless whoever dealt with the person had, at the time when the dealing occurred, no knowledge of the appointment.

(4) The court, at the instance of any person having an interest, may at any time—

(a) vary or withdraw a requirement imposed under sub-paragraph (1) above; or

(b) without prejudice to paragraph 4 below or to the powers and duties of an administrator pending a decision under this sub-sub-paragraph, on cause shown, remove the administrator from office.

(5) On the death or resignation of the administrator, or on his removal from office under sub-paragraph (4)(b) above or paragraph 5 below, the court shall appoint a new administrator.

(6) Such of the property (if any) as was, by virtue of paragraph 2(3) below, vested in the administrator who has died, resigned or been removed shall forthwith vest in the new administrator; and any requirement imposed under sub-paragraph (1) above shall, on the person subject to the requirement being notified in writing of the appointment by the appointee, apply in relation to the appointee instead of in relation to his predecessor.

(7) The administration of property by an administrator shall be deemed continuous notwithstanding any temporary vacancy in that office.

(8) Any appointment under this paragraph shall be on such conditions as to caution as the accountant of court may think fit to impose; but the premium of any bond of caution or other security thereby required of the administrator shall be treated as part of his outlays in his actings as such.

(9) Without prejudice to paragraph 5 below, section 6 of the Judicial Factors (Scotland) Act 1889 (supervision of judicial factors) shall not apply in relation to an appointment under this section.

Functions of administrators

2.—(1) Subject to paragraph 5 below, an administrator—

(a) shall be entitled to take possession of, and if appointed (or empowered) under paragraph 1(1)(b) above where a confiscation order has been made shall as soon as practicable take possession of, the property as regards which he has been appointed and of any document which both—

(i) is in the possession or control of the person (in this paragraph referred to as "A") in whom the property is vested (or would be vested but for an order made under sub-paragraph (3) below); and

(ii) relates to the property or to A's assets, business or financial affairs;

(b) shall be entitled to have access to, and to copy, any document relating to the property or to A's assets, business or financial affairs and not in such possession or control as is mentioned in sub-sub-paragraph (a) above;

(c) may bring, defend or continue any legal proceedings relating to the property;

(d) may borrow money in so far as it is necessary to do so to safeguard the property and may for the purposes of such borrowing create a security over any part of the property;

(e) may, if the administrator considers that to do so would be beneficial for the management or realisation of the property—

(i) carry on any business of A;

(ii) exercise any right of A as holder of securities in a company;

(iii) grant a lease of the property or take on lease any other property; or

(iv) enter into any contract, or execute any deed, as regards the property or as regards A's business;

(f) may, where any right, option or other power forms part of A's estate, make payments or incur liabilities with a view to—

(i) obtaining property which is the subject of; or

(ii) maintaining,

the right, option or power;

(g) may effect or maintain insurance policies as regards the property on A's business;

(h) where he has been appointed under paragraph 1(1)(b) above may, where A has an uncompleted title to any heritable estate, complete title thereto;

Provided that completion of title in A's name shall not validate by accretion any unperfected right in favour of any person other than the administrator;

(j) may sell, purchase or exchange property or discharge any security for an obligation due to A:

Provided that it shall be incompetent for the administrator or an associate of his (within the meaning of section 74 of the Bankruptcy (Scotland) Act 1985) to purchase any of A's property in pursuance of this paragraph;

(k) may claim, vote and draw dividends in the sequestration of the estate (or bankruptcy or liquidation) of a debtor of A and may accede to a voluntary trust deed for creditors of such a debtor;

(l) may discharge any of his functions through agents or employees;

Provided that the administrator shall be personally liable to meet the fees and expenses of any such agent or employee out of such remuneration as is payable to the administrator by virtue of paragraph 6(1) and (3) below;

(m) may take such professional advice as he may consider requisite for the proper discharge of his functions;

(n) may at any time apply to the court for directions as regards the discharge of his functions;

(o) may exercise any power specifically conferred on him by the court, whether such conferral was at the time of his appointment or on his subsequent application to the court in that regard; and

(p) may do anything incidental to the above powers and duties.

(2) Subject to the proviso to sub-paragraph (1)(j) above—

(a) a person dealing with an administrator in good faith and for value shall not require to determine whether the administrator is acting within the powers mentioned in that subsection; and

(b) the validity of any title shall not be challengeable by reason only of the administrator having acted outwith those powers.

(3) The exercise of a power mentioned in any of sub-paragraphs (1)(c) to (k) above shall be in A's name except where and in so far as an order made by the court under this sub-paragraph (either on its own motion or on the application of the administrator) has vested the property in the administrator (or in his predecessor in that office).

Money received by administrator

3.—(1) Subject to sub-paragraph (2) below, all money received by an administrator in the exercise of his functions shall be deposited by him, in the name (unless vested in the administrator by virtue of paragraph 2(3) above) of the holder of the property realised, in an appropriate bank or institution.

(2) The administrator may at any time retain in his hands a sum not exceeding £200 or such other sum as may be prescribed by the Secretary of State by regulations made by statutory instrument.

(3) In sub-paragraph (1) above, "appropriate bank or institution" means a bank or institution mentioned in section 2(1) of the Banking Act 1979 or for the time being specified in Schedule 1 to that Act.

Application of proceeds of realisation and other sums

4.—(1) This paragraph applies only to an administrator appointed to realise property where a confiscation order has been made.

(2) Subject to sub-paragraph (3) below, sums in the hands of an administrator which are—

(a) proceeds of a realisation of property under paragraph 1 above, and

(b) other property held by the person in respect of whom the confiscation order was made,

shall first be applied in payment of any expenses to the payment of which a person is entitled under paragraph 5(2) of Schedule 2 to this Act and then shall, after such payments (if any) as the court may direct have been made out of those proceeds and sums, be applied on the person's behalf towards the satisfaction of the confiscation order.

(3) If, after the amount payable under the confiscation order has been fully paid, any such proceeds and sums remain in the hands of the administrator, he shall distribute them—

(a) among such of those who held property which has been realised under this Act, and

(b) in such proportions,

as the court may, after giving such persons an opportunity to be heard as regards the matter, direct.

(4) The receipt of any sum by a sheriff clerk on account of an amount payable under a confiscation order shall reduce the amount so payable, but the sheriff clerk shall apply the money—

(a) first, in payment of any expenses to the payment of which a person is entitled under paragraph 5(2) of Schedule 2 to this Act but which were not paid to him under sub-paragraph (2) above;

(b) next, in payment of the administrator's remuneration and expenses;

(c) next, in reimbursement of any sums paid by the Lord Advocate under paragraph 8(2) below;

(d) next, in accordance with any direction given by the court under section 8(4) or 13(7) of this Act,

and the balance shall be payable and recoverable (or as the case may be disposed of) under section 211(5) or (6) of the 1995 Act (destination of fines) as applied by section 14 of this Act.

Supervision of administrators

5.—(1) The accountant of court shall supervise the performance by administrators of the functions conferred on them by Part I of this Act; and in particular an administrator proposing to exercise functions conferred by any of paragraphs 2(1)(c) to (p) above shall first obtain the consent of the accountant of court to such exercise.

(2) If it appears to the accountant of court that an administrator has, without reasonable cause, failed to perform a duty imposed on him by any provision of section 16 of this Act or of this Schedule, he shall report the matter to the court which, after giving the administrator an opportunity to be heard as regards the matter, may remove the administrator from office, censure him or make such other order as the circumstances of the case may appear to the court to require.

Accounts and remuneration of administrator

6.—(1) The administrator shall keep such accounts in relation to his intromissions with the property as regards which he is appointed as the court may require and shall lodge these accounts with the accountant of court at such times as may be fixed by the court in that regard; and the accountant of court shall audit the accounts and issue a determination as to the amount of outlays and, on the basis mentioned in sub-paragraph (3) below, remuneration payable to the administrator in respect of those intromissions.

(2) Not later than two weeks after the issuing of a determination under sub-paragraph (1) above, the administrator or the Lord Advocate may appeal against it to the court.

(3) The basis for determining the amount of remuneration payable to the administrator shall be the value of the work reasonably undertaken by him, regard being had to the extent of the responsibilities involved.

(4) The accountant of court may authorise the administrator to pay without taxation an account in respect of legal services incurred by the administrator.

Effect of appointment of administrator on diligence

7. Without prejudice to sections 32 and 33 of this Act—

(a) no arrestment or poinding of property executed on or after an appointment as regards the property under paragraph 1 above shall be effectual to create a preference for the arrester or poinder and any such property so arrested or poinded, or the proceeds of sale thereof, shall be handed over to the administrator;

(b) no poinding of the ground in respect of property on or after such appointment shall be effectual in a question with the administrator except for the interest on the debt of a secured creditor, being interest for the current half-yearly term and arrears of interest for one year immediately before the commencement of that term;

(c) it shall be incompetent on or after such appointment for any other person to raise or insist in an adjudication against the property or to be confirmed as executor-creditor on that property; and

(d) no inhibition on property which takes effect on or after such appointment shall be effectual to create a preference for the inhibitor in a question with the administrator.

Further provision as to administrators

8.—(1) Where an administrator takes any action—

(a) in relation to property as regards which he has not been appointed, being action which he would be entitled to take if he had been so appointed,

(b) believing, and having reasonable grounds for believing, that he is entitled to take that action in relation to that property,

he shall not be liable to any person in respect of any loss or damage resulting from his action except in so far as the loss or damage is caused by his negligence.

(2) Any amount due in respect of the remuneration and expenses of an administrator appointed under this Schedule shall, unless in a case where a confiscation order has been made there are sums available to be applied in payment of it under paragraph 4(4)(b) above, be paid by the Lord Advocate.

(3) Any disposal of property under paragraph 1 above to a person taking in good faith shall vest the ownership of the property in that person.

Discharge of administrator

9. After an administrator has lodged his final accounts under paragraph 6(1) above, he may apply to the accountant of court to be discharged from office; and such discharge, if granted, shall have the effect of freeing him from all liability (other than liability arising from fraud) in respect of any act or omission of his in exercising the functions conferred on him by this Act.

Compensation

10.—(1) Where the court, on an application made to it by a person other than the accused or the recipient of a gift caught by Part I of this Act or an implicative gift, is satisfied on the balance of probabilities that in relation to any property realised under paragraph 1 above he was the owner of, or a person otherwise having an interest in, the property immediately before such realisation, it shall make an order directing the Crown to pay to that person compensation of an amount equal to the consideration received for the property or, as the case may be, interest or the value of any such consideration at the time of such realisation, or, if no consideration was received, an amount equal to the value of the property or interest at the time of the realisation.

(2) An application under this paragraph shall be made not later than three years after the conclusion of the proceedings in respect of which the confiscation order was made.

(3) Subsection (6) of section 29 of this Act shall apply for the purpose of determining for the purposes of this paragraph whether proceedings are concluded as it applies for the purposes of that section.

Rules of court as regards accountant of court's supervision etc of administrators

11. Without prejudice to section 5 of the Court of Session Act 1988 (power to regulate procedure etc. by Act of Sederunt), provision may be made by rules of court as regards (or as regards any matter incidental to) the accountant of court's powers and duties under this Act in relation to the functions of administrators.

Power to facilitate realisation

12.—(1) Without prejudice to any enactment or rule of law in respect of the recording of deeds relating to heritable property or the registration of interests therein, the court, to facilitate realisation under paragraph 1 above, may—
  (a) order any person (in this paragraph referred to as "A") holding an interest in property, not being such person (in this paragraph referred to as "B") as is mentioned in paragraph (a) or (b) of section 4(1) or section 21 of this Act, to make such payment to an administrator appointed to realise estate comprising an interest of B in that property as the court may direct and may, subject to such payment being made—
      (i) authorise the administrator to transfer B's interest to A or to discharge it in favour of A; or
      (ii) itself by order transfer or discharge B's interest; or
  (b) by order—
      (i) transfer A's interest to B; or
      (ii) discharge it in favour of B,
on the administrator making such payment to A out of that estate in respect of A's interest as the court may direct.
  (2) The court may make such incidental provision in relation to any exercise of powers conferred on it by sub-paragraph (1) above as it considers appropriate; but it shall not exercise those powers without giving such persons as hold an interest in the property reasonable opportunity to make representations to it in that regard.

Section 44   SCHEDULE 2

SEQUESTRATION ETC. OF PERSONS HOLDING REALISABLE OR FORFEITABLE PROPERTY

Sequestration of person holding realisable or forfeitable property

1.—(1) Where the estate of a person who holds realisable or forfeitable property is sequestrated—
  (a) property, other than heritable property situated in Scotland, for the time being subject to a restraint order made before the date of sequestration (within the meaning of section 12(4) of the 1985 Act) and heritable property situated in Scotland for the time being subject to a restraint order recorded in the General Register of Sasines or, as the case may be, registered in the Land Register of Scotland before such date of sequestration; and
  (b) any proceeds of property realised by virtue of paragraph 1 of Schedule 1 to this Act for the time being in the hands of an administrator appointed under that paragraph,
is excluded from the debtor's estate for the purposes of that Act.
  (2) Where an award of sequestration has been made, the powers conferred on the court by sections 28 to 33 and 35 to 38 of and the said Schedule 1 to this Act or on an administrator appointed under paragraph 1 of that Schedule shall not be exercised in relation to—
  (a) property comprised in the whole estate of the debtor (within the meaning of section 31(8) of the 1985 Act); or
  (b) any income of the debtor which has been ordered, under subsection (2) of section 32 of that Act, to be paid to the permanent trustee or any estate which, under subsection (10) of section 31 of that Act or subsection (6) of the said section 32 of that Act, vests in the permanent trustee,
and it shall not be competent to submit a claim in relation to the confiscation order to the permanent trustee in accordance with section 48 of that Act.
  (3) Nothing in the 1985 Act shall be taken as restricting, or enabling the restriction of, the exercise of the powers so conferred.
  (4) Where, during the period before sequestration is awarded, an interim trustee stands appointed under section 2(5) of the 1985 Act and any property in the debtor's estate is subject to

a restraint order, the powers conferred on the interim trustee by virtue of that Act do not apply to property for the time being subject to the restraint order.

(5) Where the estate of a person is sequestrated and he has directly or indirectly made a gift caught by Part I of this Act or an implicative gift—

(a) no decree shall, at any time when proceedings as regards an offence to which Part I of this Act applies or, as the case may be, a drug trafficking offence have been instituted against him and have not been concluded or when property of the person to whom the gift was made is subject to a restraint order, be granted under section 34 or 36 of the 1985 Act (gratuitous alienations and unfair preferences) in respect of the making of the gift; and

(b) any decree granted under either of the said sections 34 and 36 after the conclusion of the proceedings shall take into account any realisation under this Act of property held by the person to whom the gift was made.

Bankruptcy in England and Wales of person holding realisable or forfeitable property

2.—(1) Where a person who holds realisable or forfeitable property is adjudged bankrupt—

(a) property, other than heritable property situated in Scotland, for the time being subject to a restraint order made before the order adjudging him bankrupt and heritable property situated in Scotland for the time being subject to a restraint order recorded in the General Register of Sasines or, as the case may be, registered in the Land Register of Scotland before the order adjudging him bankrupt was made; and

(b) any proceeds of property realised by virtue of paragraph 1 of Schedule 1 to this Act for the time being in the hands of an administrator appointed under that paragraph,

is excluded from the bankrupt's estate for the purposes of Part IX of the Insolvency Act 1986.

(2) Where a person has been adjudged bankrupt, the powers conferred on the court by sections 28 to 33 and 35 to 38 of and the said Schedule 1 to this Act or on an administrator appointed under paragraph 1 of that Schedule shall not be exercised in relation to—

(a) property for the time being comprised in the bankrupt's estate for the purposes of the said Part IX;

(b) property in respect of which his trustee in bankruptcy may (without leave of the court) serve a notice under section 307, 308 or 308A of the Insolvency Act 1986 (after-acquired property and tools, clothes, etc. exceeding value of reasonable replacement and certain tenancies); and

(c) property which is to be applied for the benefit of creditors of the bankrupt by virtue of a condition imposed under section 280(2)(c) of the Insolvency Act 1986.

(3) Nothing in the Insolvency Act 1986 shall be taken as restricting, or enabling the restriction of, the exercise of the powers so conferred.

(4) Where, in the case of a debtor, an interim receiver stands appointed under section 286 of the Insolvency Act 1986 and any property of the debtor is subject to a restraint order the powers conferred on the receiver by virtue of that Act do not apply to property for the time being subject to the restraint order.

(5) Where a person is adjudged bankrupt and has directly or indirectly made a gift caught by Part I of this Act or an implicative gift—

(a) no order shall, at any time when proceedings for an offence to which Part VI of the Criminal Justice Act 1988 applies or, as the case may be a drug trafficking offence have been instituted against him and have not been concluded or when property of the person to whom the gift was made is subject to a restraint order, be made under section 339 or 423 of the Insolvency Act 1986 (avoidance of certain transactions) in respect of the making of the gift, and

(b) any order made under either of those sections after the conclusion of the proceedings shall take into account any realisation under this Act of property held by the person to whom the gift was made.

Winding up of company holding realisable or forfeitable property

3.—(1) Where realisable or forfeitable property is held by a company and an order for the winding up of the company has been made or a resolution has been passed by the company for the voluntary winding up, the functions of the liquidator (or any provisional liquidator) shall not be exercisable in relation to—

(a) property, other than heritable property situated in Scotland, for the time being subject to a restraint order made before the relevant time and heritable property situated in Scotland for the time being subject to a restraint order recorded in the General Register of

Sasines or, as the case may be, registered in the Land Register of Scotland before the relevant time; and
(b) any proceeds of property realised by virtue of paragraph 1 of Schedule 1 to this Act for the time being in the hands of an administrator appointed under that paragraph.

(2) Where, in the case of a company, such an order has been made or such a resolution has been passed, the powers conferred on the court by sections 28 to 33 and 35 to 38 of and the said Schedule 1 to this Act or on an administrator appointed under paragraph 1 of that Schedule shall not be exercised in relation to any realisable or forfeitable property held by the company in relation to which the functions of the liquidator are exercisable—
(a) so as to inhibit the liquidator from exercising those functions for the purpose of distributing any property held by the company to the company's creditors; or
(b) so as to prevent the payment out of any property of expenses (including the remuneration of the liquidator or any provisional liquidator) properly incurred in the winding up in respect of the property.

(3) Nothing in the Insolvency Act 1986 shall be taken as restricting, or enabling the restriction of, the exercise of the powers so conferred.

(4) For the purposes of the application of Parts IV and V of the Insolvency Act 1986 (winding up of registered companies and winding up of unregistered companies) to a company which the court has jurisdiction to wind up, a person is not a creditor in so far as any sum due to him by the company is due in respect of a confiscation order (whether under this Act or under and within the meaning of section 2 of the Drug Trafficking Act 1994 or any corresponding provision in Northern Ireland).

(5) Where an order for the winding up of a company has been made or a resolution has been passed by a company for its voluntary winding up and before the relevant time the company has directly or indirectly made a gift caught by Part I of this Act or an implicative gift—
(a) no order or, as the case may be, decree shall, at any time when proceedings as regards an offence to which that Part applies or, as the case may be a drug trafficking offence have been instituted against the company and have not been concluded or when property of the person to whom the gift was made is subject to a restraint order, be made under section 238 or 239 of the Insolvency Act 1986 (transactions at an undervalue and preferences) or granted under section 242 or 243 of that Act (gratuitous alienations and unfair preferences) in respect of the making of the gift; and
(b) any order made under either of the said sections 242 and 243 or decree granted under either of the said sections 242 or 243 after the conclusion of the proceedings shall take into account any realisation under Part I of this Act of property held by the person to whom the gift was made.

(6) In this paragraph—
"company" means any company which may be wound up under the Insolvency Act 1986; and
"the relevant time" means—
(a) where no order for the winding up of the company has been made, the time of the passing of the resolution for voluntary winding up;
(b) where such an order has been made and, before the presentation of the petition for the winding up of the company by the court, such a resolution had been passed by the company, the time of the passing of the resolution; and
(c) in any other case where such an order has been made, the time of the making of the order.

Property subject to floating charge

4.—(1) Where any property held subject to a floating charge by a company is realisable or forfeitable property and a receiver has been appointed by, or on the application of, the holder of the charge, the powers of the receiver in relation to the property so held shall not be exercisable in relation to—
(a) so much of it, not being heritable property situated in Scotland, as is for the time being subject to a restraint order made before the appointment of the receiver and so much of it, being heritable property situated in Scotland, as is for the time being subject to a restraint order recorded in the General Register of Sasines or, as the case may be, registered in the Land Register of Scotland before such appointment; and
(b) any proceeds of property realised by virtue of paragraph 1 of Schedule 1 to this Act for the time being in the hands of an administrator appointed under that paragraph.

(2) Where, in the case of a company, such an appointment has been made, the powers conferred on the court by sections 28 to 33 and 35 to 38 of and the said Schedule 1 to this Act or on an administrator appointed under paragraph 1 of that Schedule shall not be exercised in relation to

any realisable property held by the company in relation to which the powers of the receiver are exercisable—
  (a) so as to inhibit the receiver from exercising his powers for the purpose of distributing any property held by the company to the company's creditors; or
  (b) so as to prevent the payment out of any property of expenses (including the remuneration of the receiver) properly incurred in the exercise of the receiver's powers in respect of the property.
  (3) Nothing in the Insolvency Act 1986, shall be taken as restricting, or enabling the restriction of, the exercise of the powers so conferred.
  (4) In this paragraph—
    "company" has the same meaning as in paragraph 3 above; and
    "floating charge" includes a floating charge within the meaning given by section 462 of the Companies Act 1985 (power of incorporated company to create floating charge).

Insolvency practitioners dealing with property subject to restraint order

  5.—(1) Without prejudice to the generality of any enactment contained in the Insolvency Act 1986 or in the 1985 Act, where
  (a) any person acting as an insolvency practitioner seizes or disposes of any property in relation to which his functions are, because that property is for the time being subject to a restraint order, not exercisable; and
  (b) at the time of the seizure or disposal he believes, and has reasonable grounds for believing, that he is entitled (whether in pursuance of a court order or otherwise) to seize or dispose of that property,
he shall not be liable to any person in respect of any loss or damage resulting from the seizure or disposal except in so far as the loss or damage is caused by the insolvency practitioner's negligence; and the insolvency practitioner shall have a lien on the property, or the proceeds of its sale, for such of his expenses as were incurred in connection with the liquidation, sequestration or other proceedings in relation to which the seizure or disposal purported to take place and for so much of his remuneration as may reasonably be assigned for his actings in connection with those proceedings.
  (2) Any person who, acting as an insolvency practitioner, incurs expenses—
  (a) in respect of such realisable property as is mentioned in sub-paragraph (1)(a) above and in so doing does not know and has no reasonable grounds to believe that the property is for the time being subject to a restraint order; or
  (b) other than in respect of such realisable property as is so mentioned, being expenses which, but for the effect of a restraint order, might have been met by taking possession of and realising the property,
shall be entitled (whether or not he has seized or disposed of that property so as to have a lien under sub-paragraph (1) above) to payment of those expenses under paragraph 4(2) or (4)(a) of Schedule 1 to this Act.
  (3) In the foregoing provisions of this paragraph, the expression "acting as an insolvency practitioner" shall be construed in accordance with section 388 (interpretation) of the said Act of 1986 except that for the purposes of such construction the reference in subsection (2)(a) of that section to a permanent or interim trustee in a sequestration shall be taken to include a reference to a trustee in a sequestration and subsection (5) of that section shall be disregarded; and the expression shall also comprehend the official receiver acting as receiver or manager of the property.

Interpretation

  6.—(1) In this Schedule "the 1985 Act" means the Bankruptcy (Scotland) Act 1985.
  (2) References in this Schedule to the conclusion of proceedings, except for the purposes of paragraph 2(5) above, shall be construed—
  (a) as regards property subject to a restraint order under section 28(1)(a) of this Act, in accordance with section 29(6) of this Act; and
  (b) as regards property subject to a restraint order under section 28(1)(b) of this Act, in accordance with section 30(5) of this Act.
  (3) References in this Schedule to property held by a person include a reference to property vested in the interim or permanent trustee in his sequestration or in his trustee in bankruptcy or liquidation.

GENERAL NOTE
  The draftsman explained part of this Schedule to the Joint Committee on Consolidation Bills as follows:
  "... where a person is in insolvency, of any description, the powers of an administrator appointed under the Act will not be exercisable ... it has always been the intention that the two regimes, in relation to drug trafficking and other offences, should operate in the same way. There would be no point in the court having power to appoint an administrator in those circumstances since the administrator could not do anything ...".

TABLE OF DERIVATIONS

Notes:

1. This Table shows the derivation of the provisions of the Bill.
2. The following abbreviations are used in the Table:—

Acts of Parliament

1987	=	*Criminal Justice (Scotland) Act 1987 (c. 41)*
1988	=	*Criminal Justice Act 1988 (c. 33)*
1993	=	*Criminal Justice Act 1993 (c. 36)*
1994	=	*Drug Trafficking Act 1994 (c. 37)*
1995	=	*Criminal Justice (Scotland) Act 1995 (1995 c. 20)*
1995 CP	=	*Criminal Procedure (Consequential Provisions) (Scotland) Act (1995 c. 40)*
1995 CLC	=	*Criminal Law (Consolidation) (Scotland) Act 1995 (1995 c. 39)*

Provision	Derivation
1(1)	1987 s.1(1); 1995 s.70(1), Sch. 5 §.2
(2)	1987 s.1(2); 1995 s.70(2), Sch. 5 §.2
(3)	1987 s.1(2B); 1995 s.70(3), Sch. 5 §.2
(4)	1995 s.70(4)
(5)	1987 s.1(1); 1995 s.70(5), Sch. 5 §.2
(6)	1987 s.1(2A); 1995 s.70(6), Sch. 5 §.2
(7)	1987 s.1(4); 1995 s.70(7)
2	1995 s.71
3	1987 s.3; 1994 Sch. 1 §.12; 1995 Sch. 5 §.4
4(1)	1987 s.5(1); 1995 s.72(1), Sch. 5 §.6
(2)	1987 s.5(2); 1995 s.72(2), Sch. 5 §.6
(3)	1987 s.5(4); 1995 s.72(3), Sch. 5 §.6
(4)	1987 s.5(5); 1995 s.72(4), Sch. 5 §.6
(5)	1987 s.5(5); 1995 s.72(5), Sch. 5 §.6
(6)	1987 s.5(7); 1995 Sch. 5 §.6
5(1)	1995 s.73(1)
(2)	1995 s.73(2)(part)
(3)	1995 s.73(6)
(4)	1995 s.73(7)
(5)	1995 s.73(8)
6(1)	1987 s.6(1); Law Reform (Miscellaneous Provisions) (Scotland) Act 1990 (c. 40) Sch. 8 §.37; 1995 Sch. 5 §.7
(2)	1987 s.6(2)(part); 1995 Sch. 5 §.7
(3)	1987 s.5(7A); 1995 Sch. 5 §.6
(4)	1987 s.5(7B); 1995 Sch. 5 §.6
(5)	1987 s.5(7C); 1995 Sch. 5 §.6
7(1)	1987 s.6(2)(part); 1995 s.73(2)(part), Sch. 5 §.7
(2)	1987 s.6(2)(part); 1995 s.73(2)(part), Sch. 5 §.7
(3)	1987 s.6(2)(part); 1995 s.73(2)(part), Sch. 5 §.7
(4)	1987 s.6(3); 1995 s.73(3), Sch. 5 §.7
(5)	1987 s.6(3A); 1995 s.73(4), Sch. 5 §.7
(6)	1995 s.73(5)
8(1)	1987 s.1(2C); 1995 s.74(1), Sch. 5 §.2
(2)	1987 s.1(2D); 1995 s.74(2), Sch. 5 §.2
(3)	1987 s.1(5); 1995 s.74(3), Sch. 5 §.2
(4)	1987 s.1(2E); 1995 s.74(4), Sch. 5 §.2
9(1)	1987 s.4(1)(part); 1995 s.75(1), Sch. 5 §.5
(2)	1987 s.4(1)(part); 1995 s.75(2), Sch. 5 §.5
(3)	1987 s.4(2); 1995 s.75(3), Sch. 5 §.5

Provision	Derivation
9(4)	1987 s.4(3); 1995 s.75(4)
(5)	1987 s.4(4); 1995 s.75(5), Sch. 5 §.5
(6)	1987 s.4(6); 1995 s.75(6), Sch. 5 §.5
(7)	1995 s.75(7)
(8)	1987 s.4(5)
10	1987 s.2; 1995 s.76, Sch. 5 §.3
11	1987 s.6A; 1995 s.77, Sch. 5 §.8
12	1987 s.25; 1995 s.78, Sch. 23
13(1)	1987 s.6B(1); 1995 s.79(1), Sch. 5 §.8
(2)	1987 s.6B(2); 1995 s.79(2), Sch. 5 §.8
(3)	1987 s.6B(3); 1995 s.79(3), Sch. 5 §.8
(4)	1987 s.6B(4); 1995 s.79(4), Sch. 5 §.8
(5)	1987 s.6B(7); 1995 s.79(5), Sch. 5 §.8
(6)	1987 s.6B(6); 1995 s.79(6), Sch. 5 §.8
(7)	1987 s.6B(9); 1995 s.79(7), Sch. 5 §.8
(8)	1987 s.6B(8); 1995 s.79(8), Sch. 5 §.8
(9)	1987 s.6B(5); 1995 Sch. 5 §.8
(10)	1987 s.6B(10); 1995 s.79(9), Sch. 5 §.8
14	1987 s.7; 1994 Sch. 1 §.13; 1995 s.80, Sch. 5 §.9
15	Criminal Justice (International Co-operation) Act 1990 (c. 5) s.15; 1995 s.81
16	1987 s.23; 1995 s.82, Sch. 5 §.21
17(1)	1987 s.26(1); 1995 s.83(1), Sch. 5 §.24
(2)	1987 s.26(1A); 1995 s.83(2), Sch. 5 §.24
(3)	1987 s.26(2); 1995 s.83(3), Sch. 5 §.24
(4)	1987 s.26(3); 1995 s.83(4), Sch. 5 §.24
(5)	1987 s.26(4); 1995 s.83(5), Sch. 5 §.24
(6)	1987 s.26(6), 47(5); 1995 s.83(6), Sch. 5 §.24
(7)	1987 s.47(1); 1995 s.83(7), Sch. 5 §.33
18	1995 s.18
19	1995 s.19
20	1995 s.20
21	1995 s.84
22	1995 s.85
23	1995 s.86
24	1995 s.87
25	1995 s.88
26	1995 s.89
27	1995 s.90
28(1)	1987 s.8(1); 1995 s.91(1), Sch. 5 §.11
(2)	1987 s.8(2); 1995 s.91(2), Sch. 5 §.11
(3)	1987 s.8(7); 1995 s.91(3), Sch. 5 §.11
(4)	1987 s.8(8); 1995 s.91(4), Sch. 5 §.11
(5)	1987 s.10(1); 1994 Sch. 1 §.14; 1995 s.91(5)
(6)	1987 s.10(2); 1995 s.91(6)
(7)	1987 s.8(9); 1995 s.91(7), Sch. 5 §.11
(8)	1987 s.12(1); 1995 s.91(8), Sch. 5 §.14
(9)	1987 s.12(2); 1995 s.91(9)
(10)	1987 s.12(3); 1995 s.91(10), Sch. 5 §.14
29(1)	1995 s.92(1); Drafting
(2)	1987 s.8(3); 1995 s.92(2), Sch. 5 §.11
(3)	1987 s.8(4); 1995 s.92(3), Sch. 5 §.11
(4)	1987 s.8(5); 1995 s.92(4), Sch. 5 §.11
(5)	1987 s.8(6); 1995 s.92(5), Sch. 5 §.11
(6)	1987 s.47(5); 1995 s.92(6), Sch. 5 §.33
(7)	1987 s.8(10); 1995 s.92(7), Sch. 5 §.11
30	1995 s.93
31	1987 s.9; 1995 s.94, Sch. 5 §.11
32	1987 s.11; 1995 s.95, Sch. 5 §.12

Provision	Derivation
33	1987 s.11A; 1995 s.96, Sch. 5 §.13
34	1995 s.97; Drafting
35	1987 s.27; 1994 Sch. 1 §.18; 1995 s.98
36	1987 s.28; 1994 Sch. 1 §.19; 1995 s.99
37	1987 s.28A; 1995 s.100, Sch. 5 §.25
38	1987 s.28B; 1995 s.101, Sch. 5 §.25
39(1)	1987 s.29(1); 1995 s.102(1)
(2)	1987 s.29(2); 1995 s.102(2)
(3)	1987 s.29(3); 1995 s.102(3)
(4)	1987 s.29(3A); 1993 s.22(2)
(5)	1987 s.29(4); 1993 s.21(3); 1995 s.102(4)
40	1987 s.30; Law Reform Miscellaneous Provisions (Scotland) Act 1990 (c. 40) s.63; 1993 s.21(3); 1995 s.103
41	1987 s.30A; Law Reform Miscellaneous Provisions (Scotland) Act 1990 (c. 40) s.63; 1995 s.104
42	1995 s.105
43	1987 s.32; 1995 s.106, Sch. 5 §.27
44	1995 s.107; Drafting
45	1987 s.7A; 1995 s.108, Sch. 5 §.10
46	1987 s.37A; 1995 s.109, Sch. 5 §.32
47(1)	1987 s.45(1); 1995 s.110(4)
(2)	1987 s.45(2); 1995 s.110(5)
(3)	1987 s.45(5); 1995 s.110(7)
(4)	1987 s.45(4); 1995 s.110(6)
48	1987 s.46
49(1)	1995 s.111(1)
(2)	1987 s.1(6); 1988 Sch. 5 §.19; 1990 Sch. 4 §.5; 1993 s.24(13)
(3)	1987 s.1(6)
(4)	1987 s.1(7); 1993 s.24(15)
(5)	1987 s.1(6); 1990 Sch. 4 §.5; 1993 s.24(14)
(6)	1987 ss.5(3), 8(12); 1995 s.111(3), Sch. 5 §s.6, 11
(7)	1987 s.47(6); 1995 s.111(4), Sch. 5 §.33
50(1), (2)	Drafting
(3)–(5)	1995 s.115(4)–(6)
Sch. 1	
§.1	1987 s.13; 1995 Sch. 3 §.1, Sch. 5 §.15
§.2	1987 s.14; 1995 Sch. 3 §.2, Sch. 5 §.16
§.3	1987 s.15; 1995 Sch. 3 §.3
§.4	1987 s.16; 1988 Sch. 5 §.21; 1995 Sch. 3 §.4, Sch. 5 §.17
§.5	1987 s.17; 1995 Sch. 3 §.5, Sch. 5 §.18
§.6	1987 s.18; 1995 Sch. 3 §.6, Sch. 5 §.19
§.7	1987 s.19; 1995 Sch. 3 §.7
§.8	1987 s.20; 1995 Sch. 3 §.8, Sch. 5 §.20
§.9	1987 s.21; 1995 Sch. 3 §.9
§.10	1987 s.26(5), (6), 47(5); 1995 Sch. 3 §.10
§.11	1987 s.22; 1995 Sch. 5 §.11
§.12	1987 s.24; 1995 Sch. 5 §.12
Sch. 2	1
§.1	1987 s.33; Housing Act 1988 (c. 50) Sch. 17 §.81; 1995 Sch. 4 §.1, Sch. 5 §.28
§.2	1987 s.34; 1988 Sch. 5 §.22; Housing Act 1988 (c. 50) Sch. 17 §.81; 1995 Sch. 4 §.2, Sch. 5 §.29
§.3	1987 s.35; 1995 Sch. 4 §.3, Sch. 5 §.30
§.4	1987 s.36; 1995 Sch. 4 §.4, Sch. 5 §.31
§.5	1987 s.37; 1995 Sch. 4 §.5, Sch. 5 §.32
§.6	1987 s.47(1), (4); 1995 Sch. 4 §.6

TABLE OF DESTINATIONS

CRIMINAL JUSTICE (SCOTLAND) ACT 1987
(c.41)

TABLE OF DESTINATIONS

HOUSING ACT 1988
(c.50)

1988	1995
Sched. 17,	Sched. 2,
para. 81	para. 1
	para. 2

CRIMINAL JUSTICE (INTERNATIONAL CO-OPERATION) ACT 1990
(c.5)

1990	1995
s.15	s.15
Sched. 4,	
para. 5	49(2)–(5)

LAW REFORM (MISCELLANEOUS PROVISIONS) (SCOTLAND) ACT 1990
(c.40)

1990	1995
s.63	ss.40, 41
Sched. 8,	
para. 37	s.6(1)

CRIMINAL JUSTICE ACT 1993
(c.36)

1993	1995
s.21(3)........	ss.39(5), 40
22(2)........	s.39(4)
24(13)	49(2)
(14)	49(5)
(15)	49(4)

DRUG TRAFFICKING ACT 1994
(c.37)

1994	1995
Sched. 1,	
para. 12	s.3
para. 13	14
para. 14	28(5)
para. 18	35
para. 19	36

CRIMINAL JUSTICE (SCOTLAND) ACT 1995
(C.20)

INDEX

References are to sections and Schedules

STATUTE LAW (REPEALS) ACT 1995

(1995 c. 44)

An Act to promote the reform of the statute law by the repeal, in accordance
with recommendations of the Law Commission and the Scottish Law
Commission, of certain enactments which (except in so far as their effect is
preserved) are no longer of practical utility, and to make other provision in
connection with the repeal of those enactments.   [8th November 1995]

PARLIAMENTARY DEBATES
   Hansard, H.L. Vol. 563, col. 581; Vol. 564, col. 1542; Vol. 565, col. 410. H.C. Vol. 265, col. 185.

INTRODUCTION
   This Act follows the recommendations of the two Law Commissions in seeking to reform
statutory law. Certain enactments considered unnecessary, are now repealed, except where
their effect is preserved.

Repeals and associated provisions

1.—(1) The enactments mentioned in Schedule 1 to this Act are hereby
repealed to the extent specified in the third column of that Schedule.
   (2) Schedule 2 to this Act shall have effect.

Extent

2.—(1) This Act extends to England and Wales, Scotland and Northern
Ireland.
   (2) Any repeal by this Act of an enactment which extends to the Isle of
Man shall also extend there.
   (3) Subject to subsection (2) above, this Act does not repeal any enactment
so far as the enactment forms part of the law of a country outside the United
Kingdom; but Her Majesty may by Order in Council provide that the repeal

by this Act of any enactment specified in the Order shall on a date so specified extend to any of the Channel Islands or any colony.

Short title

3. This Act may be cited as the Statute Law (Repeals) Act 1995.

SCHEDULES

Section 1

SCHEDULE 1

REPEALS

PART I

BEDFORDSHIRE, NOTTINGHAM, NOTTINGHAMSHIRE, WARWICKSHIRE AND DERWENT VALLEY WATER BOARD

Chapter or Number	Short title	Extent of repeal
	Group 1 – Bedfordshire	
35 Geo. 3. c. 87 (1795).	An Act for dividing, allotting, and inclosing the open and common fields, meadows, closes, commonable lands, pastures, commons, and waste grounds, within the several parishes of Saint Paul, Saint Peter, and Saint Cuthbert, in the town of Bedford, in the county of Bedford.	The whole Act.
37 Geo. 3. c. 53 (1797).	An Act for dividing, allotting, and inclosing, the open and common fields, pastures, commons, and waste grounds, within the parish of Saint Mary, in the town of Bedford, in the county of Bedford.	The whole Act.
43 Geo. 3. c. cxxviii (1803).	An Act for the improvement of the town of Bedford in the county of Bedford, and for rebuilding the bridge over the river Ouse in the said town.	The whole Act.
50 Geo. 3. c. lxxxii (1810).	An Act for amending and enlarging the powers of [the Act 43 Geo. 3. c. cxxviii].	The whole Act.
55 Geo. 3. c. xxx (1815).	An Act for rebuilding Tempsford Bridge in the county of Bedford.	The whole Act.
16 & 17 Vict. c. cviii.	Midland Railway (Leicester and Hitchin) Act 1853.	Section 47.
26 & 27 Vict. c. 32.	Local Government Supplemental Act 1863.	In the Schedule, the order relating to Bedford.

Chapter or Number	Short title	Extent of repeal
29 & 30 Vict. c. 107.	Local Government Supplemental Act 1866 (No. 4).	In the Schedule, the order relating to Bedford.
40 & 41 Vict. c. xxii.	Local Government Board's Provisional Orders Confirmation (Horbury &c.) Act 1877.	Sections 2 to 4. In the Schedule, the order relating to Luton.
53 & 54 Vict. c. clxxxviii.	Electric Lighting Orders Confirmation (No. 3) Act 1890.	In the Schedule, the Bedford Electric Lighting Order 1890.
56 & 57 Vict. c. viii.	Tramways Orders (1892) Confirmation Act 1893.	In the Schedule, the Bedford and Kempston Tramways Order 1892.
58 & 59 Vict. c. lxvii.	Electric Lighting Orders Confirmation (No. 2) Act 1895.	In the Schedule, the Luton Corporation Electric Lighting Order 1895 except Articles 1, 2 and 5 and Schedule 1.
59 & 60 Vict. c. ccxxxvi.	Local Government Board's Provisional Orders Confirmation (No. 13) Act 1896.	In the Schedule, the Counties of Bedford and Huntingdon (Swineshead and Tilbrook) Order 1896.
60 & 61 Vict. c. lxxi.	Local Government Board's Provisional Orders Confirmation (No. 6) Act 1897.	In the Schedule, the Biggleswade Rural Order 1897.
60 & 61 Vict. c. lxxv.	Local Government Board's Provisional Orders Confirmation (No. 10) Act 1897.	In the Schedule, the Counties of Bedford and Hertford (Caddington &c.) Order 1897 and the County of Hertford (Holwell &c.) Order 1897.
63 & 64 Vict. c. cxcix.	Tramways Orders Confirmation (No. 2) Act 1900.	In the Schedule, the Bedford Corporation Tramways Order 1900.
1 Edw. 7. c. ccxxxiii.	Biggleswade Water Act 1901.	Sections 23, 25, 30 and 38. Section 40(1) to (3). Section 40(4) from "All works" to "Provided always that". Section 40(6), (8) and (9). Section 41(2), (3), (6) and (7). Section 84.
2 Edw. 7. c. lxxxii.	Local Government Board's Provisional Orders Confirmation (No. 8) Act 1902.	In the Schedule, the Biggleswade Joint Hospital Order 1902.
2 Edw. 7. c. lxxxiii.	Local Government Board's Provisional Orders Confirmation (No. 9) Act 1902.	In the Schedule, the Linslade Order 1902.
2 Edw. 7. c. cvii.	Bedford Corporation Water Act 1902.	The whole Act.
1903 Cd. 1574.	Leighton Buzzard and Hitchin Light Railway Order 1903.	The whole Order.
5 Edw. 7. c. cxciv.	Tramways Orders Confirmation (No. 2) Act 1905.	In the Schedule, the Luton Corporation Tramways Order 1905 except Articles 1, 3, 4, 8(1) and 9(1) to (4) and (8).
6 Edw. 7. c. cxx.	Local Government Board's Provisional Orders Confirmation (No. 8) Act 1906.	In the Schedule, the Counties of Bedford and Hertford (Alteration of County Boundaries) Order 1906.
7 Edw. 7. c. clvi.	Local Government Board's Provisional Orders Confirmation (No. 6) Act 1907.	In the Schedule, the Dunstable (Extension) Order 1907.

Chapter or Number	Short title	Extent of repeal
S.R. & O. 1910 No. 837.	Borough of Bedford Wards Order 1910.	The whole Order.
1 & 2 Geo. 5. c. lxxxvii.	Luton Corporation Act 1911.	Section 72.
—	Bedford (Alteration of Electoral Divisions) Order 1921.	The whole Order.
S.R. & O. 1926 No. 172.	Bedford (Alteration of Electoral Divisions) Order 1926.	The whole Order.
17 & 18 Geo. 5. c. lxxxix.	Bedford Corporation Act 1927.	Sections 9, 23, 27, 28, 36 to 62 and 64 to 77. The Schedule.
S.R. & O. 1927 No. 1267.	Biggleswade Joint Hospital Order 1927.	The whole Order.
S.R. & O. 1928 No. 729.	Luton Tramways Extension of Time Order 1928.	The whole Order.
S.R. & O. 1930 No. 596.	Luton Tramways Extension of Time Order 1930.	The whole Order.
S.R. & O. 1931 No. 660.	Luton Tramways Extension of Time Order 1931.	The whole Order.
S.R. & O. 1933 No. 1231.	South Bedfordshire Order 1933.	The whole Order.
S.R. & O. 1934 No. 89.	County of Bedford (Electoral Divisions) Order 1934.	The whole Order.
S.R. & O. 1934 No. 101.	North Bedfordshire Review Order 1934.	The whole Order.
—	Order in Council dated 15 July 1935 for confirming a scheme altering wards etc. in Bedford.	The whole Order.
26 Geo. 5 & 1 Edw. 8. c. viii.	Ministry of Health Provisional Order Confirmation (Bedford Joint Hospital District) Act 1936.	The whole Act.
S.R. & O. 1936 No. 281.	Biggleswade Joint Hospital Amendment Order 1936.	The whole Order.
S.R. & O. 1936 No. 424.	County of Bedford (Electoral Divisions) Order 1936.	The whole Order.
1 Edw. 8 & 1 Geo. 6. c. vii.	Ministry of Health Provisional Order Confirmation (Bedford) Act 1937.	The whole Act.
S.R. & O. 1938 No. 987.	Bedford Joint Hospital Amendment Order 1938.	The whole Order.
S.R. & O. 1938 No. 1266.	Biggleswade Joint Hospital Amendment Order 1938.	The whole Order.
S.I. 1951 No. 1071.	Bedford Water Order 1951.	The whole Order except Articles 1, 3, 4, 6 and 7.
S.I. 1951 No. 2149.	Bedford (Amendment of Local Enactments) Order 1951.	The whole Order.
4 & 5 Eliz. 2. c. lxiv.	Bedford Corporation Act 1956.	The whole Act.

Chapter or Number	Short title	Extent of repeal
S.I. 1956 No. 855.	Bedford Water Order 1956.	The whole Order.
1961 c. xlii.	Great Ouse Water Act 1961.	Sections 3, 5 to 7, 9 to 34 and 40. Section 41(1) and (2). Section 42(1) to (3). Sections 43, 50, 53, 55, 56, 70, 73(3), 79 to 96, 114 to 130 and 132. Section 133(1) and (4) to (6). Section 134(2) to (9), (10)(b) and (12). Sections 135, 136, 138 to 142, 145 and 147. Schedules 1 to 4.
S.I. 1961 No. 866.	Bedford (Amalgamation of Funds) Order 1961.	The whole Order.
1964 c. xxxiii.	Bedford Corporation Act 1964.	The whole Act.
S.I. 1964 No. 169.	Luton Order 1963.	The whole Order except Articles 1, 3, 4, 5, 51 and 57 and Schedule 5.
S.I. 1965 No. 23.	Counties of Bedford and Buckingham (Leighton-Linslade) Order 1965.	The whole Order.
S.I. 1965 No. 138.	County Borough of Luton (Wards) Order 1965.	The whole Order.
S.I. 1965 No. 568.	Great Ouse Water Order 1965.	The whole Order.
S.I. 1966 No. 69.	Bedfordshire Water Board Order 1966.	Articles 3 to 13, 15 to 18, 20(2) to (6) and 21 to 44. Part II of Schedule 1. Schedules 2, 3, 5 and 6.
S.I. 1967 No. 1786.	Bedford (Borough of Bedford) Order 1967.	The whole Order.
1969 c. xlvi.	Bedford Corporation Act 1969.	The whole Act.
S.I. 1970 No. 81.	County of Bedford (Electoral Divisions) Order 1970.	The whole Order.
S.I. 1971 No. 2169.	Great Ouse Water Order 1971.	Articles 8 to 13, 17, 18, 20 to 29, and 34 to 36. The Schedule.
S.I. 1972 No. 1924.	Lee Valley Water Order 1972.	Articles 15(b) and 16. In Part I of Schedule 3, the references to sections 6, 7, 14, 20 and 82 of the Great Ouse Water Act 1961. Part II of Schedule 3.

Chapter or Number	Short title	Extent of repeal
	Group 2 – Nottingham	
7 Geo. 3. c. *36* (1767).	An Act for dividing and inclosing the open fields, meadows, common pastures and commonable lands lying south of the turnpike road leading from Nottingham to Alfreton within the liberties and townships of Lenton and Radford in the county of Nottingham.	The whole Act.
36 Geo. 3. c. 152 (1796).	An Act for raising, maintaining, and keeping in repair the road from the north end of the bridge, commonly called the Old Trent Bridge, to the west end of Saint Mary's churchyard by way of Hollow Stone, in the parish of Saint Mary, in the town of Nottingham, and for erecting and maintaining such and so many flood bridges upon the said road as may be necessary to carry off the flood water, and for widening and improving the entrance into the town of Nottingham by way of Hollow Stone.	The whole Act except section 52.
36 Geo. 3. c. *114* (1796).	An Act for dividing and inclosing the forest, commons and waste lands within the liberties and townships of Lenton and Radford in the county of Nottingham.	The whole Act.
6 Will. 4. c. xlv (1836).	An Act for establishing a general cemetery in the town and county of the town of Nottingham.	The whole Act.
2 & 3 Vict. c. *28* (1839).	An Act for inclosing certain lands called the West Croft and Burton Leys, in the parish of Saint Mary in the town and county of the town of Nottingham.	The whole Act.
2 & 3 Vict. c. lxvi (1839).	An Act for forming a canal and other works within and near certain lands called the West Croft, in the parish of Saint Mary in the town and county of the town of Nottingham.	The whole Act except sections 6 to 9 and 11 to 15.

Chapter or Number	Short title	Extent of repeal
2 & 3 Vict. c. *32* (1839).	An Act for inclosing, allotting, and improving certain open fields in the parish of Saint Mary in the town and county of the town of Nottingham.	The whole Act except sections 28, 32, 53 and 55 to 58.
7 & 8 Vict. c. 7 (1844).	An Act for altering and amending [the Act 2 & 3 Vict. c. *28*].	The whole Act.
7 & 8 Vict. c. lvii (1844).	An Act for amending the provisions of [the Act 2 & 3 Vict. c. lxvi]; and for making certain improvements within the said town [of Nottingham].	The whole Act.
8 & 9 Vict. c. xix.	Nottingham Waterworks Act 1845.	The whole Act except sections 7, 40, 43, 45 and 46.
8 & 9 Vict. c. 7 (1845).	An Act for inclosing lands in the parish of Saint Mary in the town and county of the town of Nottingham.	The whole Act except sections 53, 54, 59, 70, 97 to 99 and 173 to 175.
16 & 17 Vict. c. xi.	Nottingham Gas Act 1853.	The whole Act.
17 & 18 Vict. c. x.	Nottingham Waterworks Amendment Act 1854.	The whole Act.
21 & 22 Vict. c. ix.	Nottingham Gas Amendment Act 1858.	The whole Act.
23 & 24 Vict. c. 118.	Local Government Supplemental Act 1860 (No. 2).	In the Schedule, the order relating to Nottingham.
26 & 27 Vict. c. 32.	Local Government Supplemental Act 1863.	In the Schedule, the order relating to Nottingham.
26 & 27 Vict. c. xli.	Nottingham Gas Amendment Act 1863.	The whole Act.
27 & 28 Vict. c. cix.	Nottingham Gas Act 1864.	The whole Act.
28 & 29 Vict. c. 108.	Local Government Supplemental Act 1865 (No. 5).	In the Schedule, the order relating to Nottingham.
30 & 31 Vict. c. x.	Nottingham Improvement Act 1867.	The whole Act.
30 & 31 Vict. c. lxxv.	Wilford Bridge Act 1867.	The whole Act.
33 & 34 Vict. c. cxiv.	Local Government Supplemental Act 1870.	In the Schedule, the order relating to Nottingham.
35 & 36 Vict. c. xcii.	Local Government Board's Provisional Orders Confirmation Act 1872.	In the Schedule, the order relating to Nottingham.
35 & 36 Vict. c. cv.	Nottingham and Leen District Sewerage Act 1872.	The whole Act.
36 & 37 Vict. c. lxxxii.	Local Government Board's Provisional Orders Confirmation Act 1873 (No. 2).	In the Schedule, the two orders relating to Nottingham.

Chapter or Number	Short title	Extent of repeal
36 & 37 Vict. c. ccv.	Nottingham Gas Act 1873.	The whole Act.
37 & 38 Vict. c. i.	Local Government Board's Provisional Orders Confirmation Act 1874.	In the Schedule, the order relating to Nottingham.
37 & 38 Vict. c. cxxxvi.	Nottingham Corporation (Gas) Act 1874.	The whole Act.
37 & 38 Vict. c. cxxxvii.	Nottingham Waterworks Act 1874.	The whole Act.
37 & 38 Vict. c. cxciv.	Nottingham Improvement Act 1874.	The whole Act except— (a) section 1; (b) section 88 from "The Markets and Fairs Clauses Act" to "limits of the borough"; (c) sections 89 to 93 and 110.
38 & 39 Vict. c. ccxi.	Local Government Board's Provisional Orders Confirmation (Abingdon, Barnsley &c.) Act 1875.	In the Schedule, the order relating to Nottingham.
39 & 40 Vict. c. xvi.	Local Government Board's Provisional Orders Confirmation (Briton Ferry, &c.) Act 1876.	In the Schedule, the two orders relating to Nottingham.
39 & 40 Vict. c. cxcviii.	Local Government Board's Provisional Orders Confirmation (Bingley, &c.) Act 1876.	In the Schedule, the order relating to Nottingham and the Nottingham and Leen District Sewerage Board.
39 & 40 Vict. c. ccxxxv.	Local Government Board's Provisional Orders Confirmation (Artisans and Labourers Dwellings) Act 1876.	In the Schedule, the order relating to Nottingham.
40 & 41 Vict. c. xxxi.	Nottingham Borough Extension Act 1877.	The whole Act except sections 1, 3, 55, 56(2)(D) and 59.
40 & 41 Vict. c. 10.	Chesterfield Estate (Nottingham Sewage) Act 1877.	The whole Act.
40 & 41 Vict. c. lxxvii.	Local Government Board's Provisional Orders Confirmation (Altrincham, &c.) Act 1877.	In the Schedule, the order relating to Nottingham.
40 & 41 Vict. c. cxxiv.	Tramways Orders Confirmation Act 1877.	In the Schedule, the Nottingham and District Tramways Order 1877 except Articles 1, 3, 4 and 30.
41 & 42 Vict. c. xlv.	Nottingham Waterworks Act 1878.	The whole Act.
41 & 42 Vict. c. xci.	Nottingham Improvement Act 1878.	The whole Act except sections 1 and 6 and Schedule 1.
42 & 43 Vict. c. xi.	Nottingham Waterworks Act 1879.	The whole Act except sections 1, 2 and 4 so far as unrepealed.
42 & 43 Vict. c. cciv.	Nottingham Improvement Act 1879.	The whole Act except sections 1, 3, 26, 29, 30, 37, 39 and 47 to 52 and Schedules 2 and 3.
43 and 44 Vict. c. ccviii.	Nottingham Corporation Loans Act 1880.	The whole Act.
44 & 45 Vict. c. cii.	Local Government Board's Provisional Orders Confirmation (Birmingham, Tame, and Rea, &c.) Act 1881.	In the Schedule, the order relating to Nottingham.

Chapter or Number	Short title	Extent of repeal
45 & 46 Vict. c. lix.	Local Government Board's Provisional Orders Confirmation (Artisans and Labourers Dwellings) Act 1882.	The whole Act.
45 & 46 Vict. c. lxii.	Local Government Board's Provisional Orders Confirmation (No. 4) Act 1882.	In the Schedule, the order relating to Nottingham.
45 & 46 Vict. c. ccxvii.	Nottingham Corporation Act 1882.	The whole Act except sections 1, 2 and 78.
46 & 47 Vict. c. lxxviii.	Nottingham Corporation Act 1883.	The whole Act except sections 1, 3, 13, 14, 19, 26 so far as unrepealed and 30.
47 & 48 Vict. c. cxii.	Tramways Orders Confirmation (No. 1) Act 1884.	In the Schedule, the Nottingham Tramways Order 1884.
47 & 48 Vict. c. ccxiv.	Local Government Board's Provisional Orders Confirmation (No. 7) Act 1884.	In the Schedule, Articles 2 and 3 of the order relating to Nottingham.
50 & 51 Vict. c. xcix.	Local Government Board's Provisional Orders Confirmation (No. 3) Act 1887.	In the Schedule, the order relating to Nottingham.
52 & 53 Vict. c. cxiii.	Local Government Board's Provisional Orders Confirmation (No. 11) Act 1889.	In the Schedule, the order relating to Nottingham.
53 & 54 Vict. c. cxci.	Electric Lighting Orders Confirmation (No. 6) Act 1890.	In the Schedule, the Nottingham Electric Lighting Order 1890.
55 & 56 Vict. c. lxviii.	Local Government Board's Provisional Orders Confirmation Act 1892.	In the Schedule, the order relating to Nottingham.
55 & 56 Vict. c. ccxxiii.	Local Government Board's Provisional Orders Confirmation (No. 12) Act 1892.	In the Schedule, the Nottingham Order 1892.
57 & 58 Vict. c. xxi.	Local Government Board's Provisional Orders Confirmation (No. 3) Act 1894.	In the Schedule, the Nottingham Order 1894.
57 & 58 Vict. c. clxxviii.	Nottingham Corporation Act 1894.	The whole Act.
59 & 60 Vict. c. ci.	Local Government Board's Provisional Orders Confirmation (No. 6) Act 1896.	Section 2. In the Schedule, the Basford (Selston) Order 1896.
59 & 60 Vict. c. clxxi.	Local Government Board's Provisional Orders Confirmation (No. 22) Act 1896.	In the Schedule, the Nottingham Order 1896.
60 & 61 Vict. c. cc.	Nottingham Corporation Water Act 1897.	The whole Act except sections 1, 2, 4, 6, 9, 11 to 14 and 25 to 27 and the Schedule.
60 & 61 Vict. c. ccxxxviii.	Nottingham Improvement Act 1897.	The whole Act except sections 1 and 17.
61 & 62 Vict. c. lxxi.	Nottingham Corporation Act 1898.	The whole Act.

Chapter or Number	Short title	Extent of repeal
61 & 62 Vict. c. lxxxi.	Local Government Board's Provisional Orders Confirmation (No. 8) Act 1898.	The whole Act.
62 & 63 Vict. c. ci.	Nottingham Corporation Act 1899.	The whole Act except sections 1, 3, 28, 29 and 32 and Schedule 1.
62 & 63 Vict. c. cclxxiii.	Tramways Orders Confirmation (No. 2) Act 1899.	In the Schedule, the Ilkeston Corporation Tramways Order 1899.
63 & 64 Vict. c. cxxxii.	Nottingham Corporation Act 1900.	The whole Act.
2 Edw. 7. c. ccxxxiii.	Nottingham Corporation Act 1902.	The whole Act except sections 1, 3, 5(3) and (7), 6(4) and (5), 18, 21 and 23.
3 Edw. 7. c. ccii.	Nottinghamshire and Derbyshire Tramways Act 1903.	The whole Act except— (a) sections 1 and 3; (b) section 101(1) to (7), (10) and (15); (c) section 102(1), (2), (4), (5), (10) and (13); (d) section 104(1), (3), (13), (15), (17) and (18).
5 Edw. 7. c. clxxv.	Nottingham Corporation Act 1905.	The whole Act except sections 1, 3, 23(2) and (5), 28, 29, 33 and the Schedule.
6 Edw. 7. c. lx.	Nottinghamshire and Derbyshire Tramways Act 1906.	The whole Act except sections 1 and 8.
8 Edw. 7. c. ci.	Nottinghamshire and Derbyshire Tramways Act 1908.	The whole Act except— (a) sections 1, 2 and 46; (b) section 52(1), (3), (5), (6), (9), (10) and (13) to (16).
10 Edw. 7 & 1 Geo. 5. c. xliv.	Nottingham Corporation Act 1910.	The whole Act.
1 & 2 Geo. 5. c. lxxxviii.	Nottinghamshire and Derbyshire Tramways Act 1911.	The whole Act.
3 & 4 Geo. 5. c. cxiii.	Nottingham Corporation Act 1913.	The whole Act except— (a) sections 1 and 4; (b) section 22(2) and (3); (c) section 23(1) to (5) and (9); (d) section 26(1), (2), (4), (5) and (7).
5 & 6 Geo. 5. c. lxvi.	Nottingham Corporation (Trent Navigation Transfer) Act 1915.	Sections 4, 6, 7, 11, 18 to 21, 23, 25 to 27, 29 to 31 and 34. Section 28 except as it applies to the Trent Navigation Act 1906.
7 & 8 Geo. 5. c. xi.	Nottinghamshire and Derbyshire Tramways Act 1917.	The whole Act.
10 & 11 Geo. 5. c. lxvi.	Nottingham Corporation Act 1920.	The whole Act except— (a) sections 1 and 4; (b) section 16(1), (2), (4), (5), (8) and (10).
12 & 13 Geo. 5. c. xv.	Nottingham Corporation (Trent Navigation) Act 1922.	The whole Act except sections 1, 3 and 8.

Chapter or Number	Short title	Extent of repeal
12 & 13 Geo. 5. c. xxviii.	Nottinghamshire and Derbyshire Tramways Act 1922.	The whole Act.
13 & 14 Geo. 5. c. iv.	Ministry of Health Provisional Orders Confirmation (No. 1) Act 1923.	In the Schedule, the Nottingham Order 1923.
13 & 14 Geo. 5. c. c.	Nottingham Corporation Act 1923.	The whole Act except sections 1, 4, 16, 25, 26, 28(2), 29 and 138.
15 & 16 Geo. 5. c. cix.	Nottingham Corporation Act 1925.	The whole Act except— (a) sections 1, 3 and 4; (b) section 15(2), (3), (5), (7) and (8); (c) section 16; (d) section 26(1) to (7) and (11); (e) section 28(1) to (7) and (11).
18 & 19 Geo. 5. c. xciii.	Nottinghamshire and Derbyshire Traction Act 1928.	The whole Act.
19 & 20 Geo. 5. c. lxi.	Nottingham Corporation Act 1929.	The whole Act except sections 1, 3 to 9, 13, 14(2), 32(2), 38 and 69.
20 & 21 Geo. 5. c. cxiv.	Nottingham Corporation Act 1930.	The whole Act.
21 & 22 Geo. 5. c. lxvii.	Public Works Facilities Scheme (Nottingham Corporation) Confirmation Act 1931.	In the Schedule, the Nottingham Corporation (Waterworks) Scheme 1931 except— (a) Articles 1, 3 and 4; (b) Article 8 from "Provided that" to "may require."; (c) Articles 9, 10, 16 and 17(5) and (6).
22 & 23 Geo. 5. c. lxxx.	Nottingham Corporation Act 1932.	The whole Act.
23 & 24 Geo. 5. c. xxxi.	Nottinghamshire and Derbyshire Traction Company (Trolley Vehicles) Order Confirmation Act 1933.	The whole Act.
24 & 25 Geo. 5. c. li.	Nottingham Corporation (Trolley Vehicles) Order Confirmation Act 1934.	The whole Act.
25 & 26 Geo. 5. c. cxix.	Nottingham Corporation Act 1935.	The whole Act.
26 Geo. 5 & 1 Edw. 8. c. xxviii.	Nottinghamshire and Derbyshire Traction Act 1936.	The whole Act.
1 & 2 Geo. 6. c. xcv.	Nottingham Corporation Act 1938.	Sections 2, 5 to 16, 18, 20 to 22, 23(1), 25, 26, 31, 34, 36, 37, 39, 40, 43, 45 to 59, 61 to 69, 71 to 78, 80, 82, 83, 86, 88. The Schedule.
10 & 11 Geo. 6. c. xi.	Nottinghamshire and Derbyshire Traction Act 1947.	The whole Act.
10 & 11 Geo. 6. c. xxxvi.	Nottingham Corporation Act 1947.	The whole Act except— (a) sections 1, 3, 4, 13, 15(2), 16, 17, 24 and 25; (b) section 47 as it extends, applies and amends section 32(2) of the Nottingham Corporation Act 1929 and sections 29, 44 and 81 of the Nottingham Corporation Act 1938; (c) sections 48, 51 and 53.

Chapter or Number	Short title	Extent of repeal
15 & 16 Geo. 6 & 1 Eliz. 2. c. xxxiii.	Nottingham Corporation Act 1952.	The whole Act except sections 1, 3, 5, 6, 15(3), 21, 25, 27(2), 28, 30, 32 and 37 to 59.
15 & 16 Geo. 6 & 1 Eliz. 2. c. xlv.	Nottinghamshire and Derbyshire Traction Act 1952.	The whole Act.
S.I. 1953 No. 1152.	Nottingham Water Order 1953.	Articles 3, 4 and 5. The Schedule.
S.I. 1957 No. 1638.	Nottingham Water Order 1957.	The whole Order except Articles 1, 2 and 8.
S.I. 1957 No. 2003.	Nottingham Water (No. 2) Order 1957.	The whole Order.
S.I. 1958 No. 1593.	Nottingham Water Order 1958.	Articles 3, 4 and 7. The Schedule.
S.I. 1959 No. 583.	Leicester and Nottingham Water Order 1959.	The whole Order.
S.I. 1960 No. 418.	Nottingham Water Order 1960.	The whole Order.
S.I. 1966 No. 63.	Nottingham Water Order 1966.	The whole Order.
S.I. 1966 No. 1389.	Nottingham (River Derwent) Water Order 1966.	Articles 4, 5, 7 and 11. Schedule 1 except so far as it refers to paragraph 10 of Schedule 3 to the Water Act 1945. Schedule 2.
1971 c. vii.	Nottingham Corporation Act 1971.	The whole Act.

Group 3 – Nottinghamshire

Chapter or Number	Short title	Extent of repeal
9 Geo. 3. c. 62 (1769).	An Act to rebuild the shire hall of the county of Nottingham; and for using the guildhall of the town and county of Nottingham for the purposes of a shire hall in the meantime.	The whole Act.
13 Geo. 3. c. 96 (1773).	An Act for the sale of certain charity estates therein mentioned, and to apply the money to arise therefrom in the building of a town hall and shambles in the town of Newark-upon-Trent; and in the purchasing of lands and hereditaments for enlarging the churchyard of the said town, and for opening the avenues thereto; and for laying out the residue of the money in purchasing other lands, to be settled to the charitable uses therein mentioned.	The whole Act.

Chapter or Number	Short title	Extent of repeal
3 & 4 Will. 4. c. i (1832).	An Act for raising money to pay compensation for damages committed within the Hundred of Broxtowe in the county of Nottingham during the late riots and tumults therein.	The whole Act.
15 & 16 Vict. c. i.	Mansfield Gas Act 1852.	The whole Act except sections 4 and 32.
29 & 30 Vict. c. xxxi.	Newark Gas Act 1866.	Section 38.
33 & 34 Vict. c. ii.	Mansfield Water Act 1870.	Sections 8, 20, 21, 27, 41 and 42.
37 & 38 Vict. c. lxxxvii.	Gas and Water Orders Confirmation Act 1874.	In the Schedule, the Retford Gas Order 1874 except Articles 1, 7 and 15 and the Schedule.
38 & 39 Vict. c. lxiii.	Worksop Waterworks Act 1875.	Section 56.
38 & 39 Vict. c. clxxv.	Local Government Board's Provisional Orders Confirmation (Aberdare, &c.) Act 1875.	In the Schedule, the order relating to Hucknall Torkard.
40 & 41 Vict. c. cxxxi.	Gas and Water Orders Confirmation (Abingdon, &c.) Act 1877.	In the Schedule, the Mansfield Gas Order 1877.
41 & 42 Vict. c. clxxii.	Sutton-in-Ashfield Local Board Gas Act 1878.	The whole Act.
41 & 42 Vict. c. cxcvii.	Mansfield Commissioners Gas Act 1878.	The whole Act.
46 & 47 Vict. c. cxxxvi.	Local Government Board's Provisional Orders Confirmation (No. 5) Act 1883.	In the Schedule, the order relating to Hucknall-under-Huthwaite.
47 & 48 Vict. c. lxxv.	Local Government Board's Provisional Orders Confirmation (Poor Law) (No. 10) Act 1884.	In the Schedule, the order relating to Marnham and South Clifton.
48 & 49 Vict. c. i.	Local Government Board's Provisional Orders Confirmation Act 1885.	In the Schedule, the order relating to Mansfield.
51 & 52 Vict. c. cviii.	Water Orders Confirmation (No. 2) Act 1888.	In the Schedule, the Mansfield Water Order 1888.
54 & 55 Vict. c. cxxii.	Newark Corporation Act 1891.	Section 78(1) to (3), (5) and (6).
58 & 59 Vict. c. xci.	Local Government Board's Provisional Orders Confirmation (No. 12) Act 1895.	In the Schedule, the Counties of Derby and Nottingham (Kirkby-in-Ashfield and Pinxton) Order 1895 and the County of Nottingham (Bole and West Burton) Order 1895.
59 Vict. (Sess. 2). c. ii.	Gas and Water Orders Confirmation Act 1895 Session 2.	In the Schedule, Articles 30 and 41 of the Newark Gas Order 1895.
61 & 62 Vict. c. xxxi.	Local Government Board's Provisional Orders Confirmation (No. 1) Act 1898.	In the Schedule, the Hucknall Torkard Order 1898.

Chapter or Number	Short title	Extent of repeal
62 & 63 Vict. c. xxxiv.	Electric Lighting Orders Confirmation (No. 1) Act 1899.	In the Schedule, the Worksop Electric Lighting Order 1899.
62 & 63 Vict. c. xxxv.	Electric Lighting Orders Confirmation (No. 2) Act 1899.	In the Schedule, the Mansfield Corporation Electric Lighting Order 1899.
62 & 63 Vict. c. cxxxvi.	Electric Lighting Orders Confirmation (No. 11) Act 1899.	In the Schedule, the East Retford Electricity Supply Order 1899.
63 & 64 Vict. c. xxii.	Electric Lighting Orders Confirmation (No. 2) Act 1900.	In the Schedule, the Newark Electric Lighting Order 1900.
1901 Cd. 651.	Mansfield and District Light Railways Order 1901.	The whole Order.
2 Edw. 7. c. lxviii.	Electric Lighting Orders Confirmation (No. 3) Act 1902.	In the Schedule, the Hucknall Torkard Electric Lighting Order 1902.
4 Edw. 7. c. xlix.	Kirkby-in-Ashfield Urban District Council (Gas) Act 1904.	The whole Act except sections 1 and 10 and the Schedule.
4 Edw. 7. c. clxxix.	Electric Lighting Orders Confirmation (No. 8) Act 1904.	In the Schedule, the Sutton-in-Ashfield Urban District Electric Lighting Order 1904.
5 Edw. 7. c. ci.	Mansfield Corporation Act 1905.	Section 64.
6 Edw. 7. c. ci.	Local Government Board's Provisional Orders Confirmation (No. 2) Act 1906.	In the Schedule, the Sutton-in-Ashfield Order 1906.
7 Edw. 7. c. liv.	Electric Lighting Orders Confirmation (No. 1) Act 1907.	In the Schedule, the Newark Electric Lighting (Amendment) Order 1907.
7 Edw. 7. c. cxiv.	Electric Lighting Orders Confirmation (No. 3) Act 1907.	Section 6. Section 8 so far as it repeals the Mansfield Woodhouse Electric Lighting Order 1904. In the Schedule, the Mansfield (Extension to Mansfield Woodhouse) Electric Lighting Order 1907.
1907 Cd. 3487.	Mansfield and District Light Railways (Extensions) Order 1907.	The whole Order.
8 Edw. 7. c. cxlix.	Local Government Board's Provisional Orders Confirmation (No. 9) Act 1908.	In the Schedule, Articles 1(1), (3) and (4) and 3 to 12 of the Sutton-in-Ashfield Order 1908.
9 Edw. 7. c. xxvi.	Worksop Waterworks Act 1909.	Section 14. The Schedule.
10 Edw. 7 & 1 Geo 5. c. xl.	Worksop Urban District Council Act 1910.	The whole Act.
9 & 10 Geo. 5. c. xxxix.	Newark Gas Act 1919.	Sections 53, 54, 58, 63 and 65.
1920 Cmd. 355.	Mansfield and District Light Railways (Extensions) Order 1920.	The whole Order.
S.R. & O. 1921 No. 567.	Newark Gas (Charges) Order 1921.	The whole Order.

Chapter or Number	Short title	Extent of repeal
S.R. & O. 1924 No. 609.	Mansfield Corporation Gas Order 1924.	The whole Order except— (a) Articles 1, 3, 8(1), 30(1), (4) and (5) and 31(1), (5) and (6); (b) Schedule 1.
15 & 16 Geo. 5. c. xcviii.	Mansfield Corporation Act 1925.	Section 24.
S.R. & O. 1926 No. 243.	Newark Gas Order 1926.	The whole Order except Articles 1 and 10 and Schedule 2. Schedule 2 so far as it saves— (a) section 38 of the Newark Gas Act 1866; (b) Articles 30 and 41 of the Newark Gas Order 1895; (c) sections 53, 54, 58, 63 and 65 of the Newark Gas Act 1919; (d) the Newark Gas (Charges) Order 1921.
S.R. & O. 1926 No. 1665.	Mansfield and District Light Railways (Extensions &c.) Order 1926.	The whole Order.
19 & 20 Geo. 5. c. lxxvi.	Mansfield District Traction Act 1929.	The whole Act.
S.R. & O. 1934 No. 1418.	Mansfield Gas Order 1934.	The whole Order.
1 Edw. 8 & 1 Geo. 6. c. xxxvi.	Mansfield District Traction Act 1937.	The whole Act.
S.R. & O. 1939 No. 723.	Sutton-in-Ashfield Gas Order 1939.	The whole Order.
S.R. & O. 1939 No. 749.	Mansfield Gas Order 1939.	The whole Order.
S.I. 1958 No. 2280.	Newark Corporation Water Order 1958.	Articles 3 to 5. Article 7. The Schedule.
S.I. 1961 No. 2143.	Worksop Water Order 1961.	Articles 6 and 7. The Schedule.
S.I. 1962 No. 1281.	Mansfield Water Order 1962.	Articles 3, 4 and 7. The Schedule.
S.I. 1963 No. 1332.	Central Nottinghamshire Water Board Order 1963.	Articles 3 and 25.

Group 4 – Warwickshire

6 & 7 Will. & Mar. c. *1* (1694).	An Act for rebuilding the town of Warwick and for determining differences touching houses burnt or demolished by reason of the late dreadful fire there.	The whole Act.
54 Geo. 3. c. xlv (1814).	An Act for providing a convenient house, with suitable accommodations, for His Majesty's judges at the assizes for the county of Warwick.	The whole Act.

Chapter or Number	Short title	Extent of repeal
7 Geo. 4. c. iv (1826).	An Act for maintaining and repairing the bridge over the river Avon, at or near Stratford-upon-Avon, in the county of Warwick, and for widening and improving the approaches thereto.	The whole Act.
15 & 16 Vict. c. 69.	Public Health Supplemental Act 1852 (No. 2).	Section 5.
20 & 21 Vict. c. lxvii.	Stratford-upon-Avon Gas Act 1857.	The whole Act.
26 & 27 Vict. c. xxxiii.	Rugby Waterworks Act 1863.	Sections 24 and 39.
30 & 31 Vict. c. xvii.	Stratford-upon-Avon Gas Act 1867.	The whole Act.
34 & 35 Vict. c. clxxxviii.	Sewage Utilisation Supplemental Act 1871.	Section 2. In the Schedule, the order relating to Hillmorton.
35 & 36 Vict. c. clviii.	Tramways Orders Confirmation Act 1872 (No. 4).	In the Schedule, the Leamington and Warwick Tramways Order 1872.
39 & 40 Vict. c. cci.	Local Government Board's Provisional Orders Confirmation (Bath &c.) Act 1876.	In the Schedule, the order relating to Warwick.
41 & 42 Vict. c. cix.	Local Government Board's Provisional Orders Confirmation (Belper Union &c.) Act 1878.	In the Schedule, the order relating to the Rugby Rural Sanitary Authority.
42 & 43 Vict. c. xliii.	Local Government Board's Provisional Orders Confirmation (Ashton-under-Lyne &c.) Act 1879.	In the Schedule, the orders relating to the Rugby and Southam Rural Sanitary Authorities.
42 & 43 Vict. c. cxix.	Stratford-upon-Avon Borough Act 1879.	Sections 2 to 29, 31, 32, 34 to 53, 55 to 77, 80, 81, 87 to 90, 93 to 95, 97 and 98. Schedules 2 and 3.
42 & 43 Vict. c. cxciii.	Tramways Orders Confirmation Act 1879.	In the Schedule, the Leamington and Warwick Tramways Order 1879.
44 & 45 Vict. c. i.	Local Government Board's Provisional Orders Confirmation (Godalming &c.) Act 1881.	In the Schedule, the Stratford-upon-Avon Order 1881.
45 & 46 Vict. c. c.	Water Orders Confirmation Act 1882.	In the Schedule, Articles 13 and 14 of the Kenilworth Water Order 1882.
45 & 46 Vict. c. cxxxviii.	Tramways Orders Confirmation (No. 1) Act 1882.	In the Schedule, the Leamington and Warwick Tramways (Amendment) Order 1882.
45 & 46 Vict. c. ccxxx.	East Warwickshire Waterworks Act 1882.	Sections 2, 4, 5, 7 to 24, 38, 55 and 73.
46 & 47 Vict. c. xc.	Local Government Board's Provisional Orders Confirmation (No. 6) Act 1883.	In the Schedule, the order relating to Stratford-upon-Avon.
47 & 48 Vict. c. ccx.	Local Government Board's Provisional Orders Confirmation (No. 4) Act 1884.	In the Schedule, the Warwick Joint Hospital District Order 1884.
48 & 49 Vict. c. ci.	Local Government Board's Provisional Orders Confirmation (No. 4) Act 1885.	In the Schedule, the order relating to Atherstone Rural Sanitary Authority.

Chapter or Number	Short title	Extent of repeal
51 & 52 Vict. c. lxi.	Local Government Board's Provisional Orders Confirmation (No. 3) Act 1888.	In the Schedule, the Stratford-upon-Avon Order 1888.
53 & 54 Vict. c. ccxxxvii.	Local Government Board's Provisional Orders Confirmation (No. 11) Act 1890.	The whole Act.
55 & 56 Vict. c. cxcviii.	Local Government Board's Provisional Orders Confirmation (No. 7) Act 1892.	In the Schedule, the Warwick Joint Hospital District Order 1892.
58 & 59 Vict. c. lxxxvi.	Local Government Board's Provisional Orders Confirmation (No. 5) Act 1895.	In the Schedule, the County of Warwick (Stoneton) Order 1895.
59 & 60 Vict. c. xxix.	Local Government Board's Provisional Orders Confirmation (No. 4) Act 1896.	In the Schedule, the Stratford-upon-Avon Order 1896.
59 & 60 Vict. c. lxxv.	Local Government Board's Provisional Orders Confirmation (No. 3) Act 1896.	In the Schedule, the County of Gloucester (Batsford) Order 1896 and the County of Warwick (Oldberrow) Order 1896.
59 & 60 Vict. c. civ.	Local Government Board's Provisional Orders Confirmation (No. 9) Act 1896.	In the Schedule, the Warwick Joint Hospital District Order 1896.
60 & 61 Vict. c. ccxiv.	East Warwickshire Waterworks Act 1897.	The whole Act.
62 & 63 Vict. c. xxi.	Nuneaton and Chilvers Coton Urban District Council Waterworks Act 1899.	Sections 2 to 4 and 17.
62 & 63 Vict. c. xxxvi.	Electric Lighting Orders Confirmation (No. 4) Act 1899.	In the Schedule, the Rugby Electric Lighting Order 1899.
62 & 63 Vict. c. cxxv.	Electric Lighting Order Confirmation (No. 18) Act 1899.	The whole Act.
62 & 63 Vict. c. ccxxvi.	Worcestershire County Council (Transfer of the Parish of Yardley) Act 1899.	The whole Act.
63 & 64 Vict. c. xlix.	Electric Lighting Orders Confirmation (No. 5) Act 1900.	In the Schedule, the Nuneaton and Chilvers Coton Electric Lighting Order 1900.
63 & 64 Vict. c. cxcix.	Tramways Orders Confirmation (No. 2) Act 1900.	In the Schedule, the Warwick Tramways Order 1900.
1 Edw. 7. c. xxxix.	Electric Lighting Orders Confirmation (No. 4) Act 1901.	In the Schedule, the Stratford-upon-Avon Electric Lighting Order 1901.

Chapter or Number	Short title	Extent of repeal
1 Edw. 7. c. clxxxi.	Tramways Orders Confirmation (No. 2) Act 1901.	In the Schedule, the Leamington Tramways Order 1901.
1 Edw. 7. c. cclxix.	Rugby Water and Improvement Act 1901.	Sections 3, 5 to 7, 9, 10, 43 to 61, 65, 68, 69, 71, 72, 75 to 78, 80, 81, 83 to 85, 87, 88, 90 to 112, 115 to 128, 134 to 144, 147 to 150, 155 to 168 and 170 to 179. Schedules 1 and 2.
2 Edw. 7. c. lxxxi.	Local Government Board's Provisional Orders Confirmation (No. 5) Act 1902.	In the Schedule, the Stratford-upon-Avon Order 1902.
3 Edw. 7. c. lxi.	Local Government Board's Provisional Orders Confirmation (No. 4) Act 1903.	Section 2 as it applies to Stratford-upon-Avon. In the Schedule, the Stratford-upon-Avon Order 1903.
4 Edw. 7. c. xxvii.	Nuneaton and Chilvers Coton Urban District Council (Prevention of Floods) Act 1904.	The whole Act except sections 1 and 13 to 15.
5 Edw. 7. c. lxxv.	Local Government Board's Provisional Orders Confirmation (No. 9) Act 1905.	In the Schedule, the Rugby Joint Hospital Order 1905.
5 Edw. 7. c. cxiii.	Electric Lighting Orders Confirmation (No. 5) Act 1905.	Section 6. In the Schedule, the Stratford-upon-Avon Electric Lighting Order 1901 (Amendment) Order 1905.
6 Edw. 7. c. cxvii.	Education Board Provisional Orders Confirmation (Kesteven &c.) Act 1906.	In the Schedule, the order relating to Warwickshire.
7 Edw. 7. c. cliii.	Local Government Board's Provisional Orders Confirmation (No. 3) Act 1907.	In the Schedule, the Rugby Joint Hospital Order 1907.
2 & 3 Geo. 5. c. cxxxv.	Local Government Board's Provisional Orders Confirmation (No. 9) Act 1912.	In the Schedule, the Stratford-upon-Avon Order 1912.
9 & 10 Geo. 5. c. xliii.	Nuneaton Corporation Act 1919.	The whole Act.
11 & 12 Geo. 5. c. xci.	Nuneaton Corporation Act 1921.	Sections 2 to 7, 9, 11, 15, 22, 28 to 30, 32 and 34 to 52. The Schedule.
13 & 14 Geo. 5. c. lxxv.	Rugby Urban District Council Act 1923.	The whole Act except sections 1, 4, 5, 8, 9, 30, 35 to 38, 40 and 168 and Schedule 1.
14 & 15 Geo. 5. c. xx.	Ministry of Health Provisional Order Confirmation (Stratford-upon-Avon Extension) Act 1924.	The whole Act.
19 & 20 Geo. 5. c. xliv.	Leamington and Warwick Traction Act 1929.	The whole Act.
S.R. & O. 1929 No. 336.	Rugby Urban (Public Health) Order 1929.	The whole Order.
S.R. & O. 1929 No. 438.	Rugby Rural (Urban Powers) Order 1929.	The whole Order.

Chapter or Number	Short title	Extent of repeal
21 & 22 Geo. 5. c. ix.	Ministry of Health Provisional Order Confirmation (Gloucestershire, Warwickshire and Worcestershire) Act 1931.	The whole Act.
S.R. & O. 1931 No. 261.	Borough of Nuneaton (Extension) Order 1931.	The whole Order.
S.R. & O. 1931 No. 270.	Borough of Warwick Order 1931.	The whole Order.
—	Rugby Urban District (Extension) Order 1931.	The whole Order.
S.R. & O. 1932 No. 104.	County of Warwick (Electoral Divisions) Order 1932.	The whole Order.
S.R. & O. 1932 No. 185.	Warwickshire Review Order 1932.	The whole Order.
S.R. & O. 1932 No. 667.	Order in Council consequential upon the grant of a charter of incorporation to Rugby	The whole Order.
23 & 24 Geo. 5. c. v.	Ministry of Health Provisional Order Confirmation (Rugby Joint Hospital District) Act 1933.	The whole Act.
23 & 24 Geo. 5. c. xli.	Rugby Corporation Act 1933.	The whole Act.
23 & 24 Geo. 5. c. xci.	Ministry of Health Provisional Order Confirmation (Warwick) Act 1933.	The whole Act.
S.R. & O. 1933 No. 339.	Borough of Rugby (Public Health &c.) Order 1933.	The whole Order.
25 & 26 Geo. 5. c. iv.	Ministry of Health Provisional Order Confirmation (Leicester and Warwick) Act 1935.	The whole Act.
25 & 26 Geo. 5. c. vi.	Ministry of Health Provisional Order Confirmation (Gloucester and Warwick) Act 1935.	The whole Act.
S.R. & O. 1935 No. 1099.	Warwick Joint Hospital Amendment Order 1935.	The whole Act.
1 & 2 Geo. 6. c. ix.	Ministry of Health Provisional Order Confirmation (Nuneaton Extension) Act 1938.	The whole Act.
S.R. & O. 1938 No. 387.	Warwick Joint Hospital Amendment Order 1938.	The whole Order.
S.I. 1954 No. 1653.	Borough of Nuneaton (Food) Order 1954.	The whole Order.
4 Eliz. 2. c. xii.	Nuneaton Corporation Act 1955.	The whole Act.
4 & 5 Eliz. 2. c. lxxviii.	Rugby Corporation Act 1956.	The whole Act.
S.I. 1956 No. 446.	Warwickshire and Coventry (Boundaries) Order 1956.	The whole Order.

Chapter or Number	Short title	Extent of repeal
S.I. 1956 No. 1229.	Leamington Water Order 1956.	The whole Order except Articles 1 to 3.
S.I. 1960 No. 154.	North East Warwickshire Water Board Order 1960.	The whole Order except Articles 1, 3, 14(2), 39(1) and 40 and Schedules 5 and 7.
S.I. 1961 No. 2193.	Rugby Joint Water Board Order 1961.	The whole Order except Articles 1, 2, 14(2) and 21(1) and Schedule 4.
S.I. 1962 No. 348.	North East Warwickshire Water Board Order 1962.	The whole Order.
S.I. 1962 No. 637.	Borough of Rugby (Wards) Order 1962.	The whole Order.
S.I. 1962 No. 1282.	Rugby (Amendment of Local Enactment) Order 1962.	The whole Order.
S.I. 1963 No. 38.	South Warwickshire Water Board Order 1963.	The whole Order except Articles 1, 2, 22 and 23(1) and Schedule 4.
S.I. 1964 No. 680.	North East Warwickshire Water Board Order 1964.	Article 3 and the Schedule.
S.I. 1966 No. 472.	South Warwickshire Water Board (Clifford Chambers) Water Order 1966.	The Schedule except so far as it refers to paragraph 10 of Schedule 3 to the Water Act 1945.
S.I. 1966 No. 799.	South Warwickshire Water Board (Wellesbourne Mountford Airfield) Water Order 1966.	Articles 3(2) and 4 and the Schedule.
S.I. 1967 No. 375.	Rugby and South Warwickshire Water Order 1966.	The whole Order except Articles 1 to 3, 4(1), 6, 8 to 12, 13(1) to (5) and 26 to 28.
S.I. 1968 No. 166.	Rugby Joint Water Board (Charges) Order 1968.	The whole Order.
S.I. 1969 No. 166.	South Warwickshire Water Board (Charges) Order 1969.	The whole Order.
S.I. 1969 No. 919.	South Warwickshire Water Board Order 1969.	The whole Order.
S.I. 1969 No. 1227.	Rugby Joint Water Board Order 1969.	The whole Order.
S.I. 1969 No. 1483.	South Warwickshire Water Board (Offchurch) Water Order 1969.	The whole Order except Articles 1, 2 and 7 and the Schedule.
S.I. 1969 No. 1672.	South Warwickshire Water Board and Coventry (Variation of Limits) Order 1969.	The whole Order.
1970 c. vi.	Warwickshire County Council Act 1970.	The whole Act.
S.I. 1970 No. 995.	North East Warwickshire Water Board Order 1970.	The whole Order.
S.I. 1971 No. 430.	North East Warwickshire Water Board (Charges) Order 1971.	The whole Order.
S.I. 1971 No. 1509.	Coventry, Birmingham and Rugby Water Order 1971.	The whole Order except Articles 1, 2 and 4 and Schedule 2.

Chapter or Number	Short title	Extent of repeal
S.I. 1972 No. 1270.	Rugby Joint Water Board Order 1972.	The whole Order.
S.I. 1973 No. 587.	North East Warwickshire Water Board (Charges) Order 1973.	The whole Order.
S.I. 1973 No. 2127.	Rugby Joint Water Board (Extension of Operation of Byelaws) Order 1973.	The whole Order.

Group 5 – Derwent Valley Water Board

Chapter or Number	Short title	Extent of repeal
62 & 63 Vict. c. cclxix.	Derwent Valley Water Act 1899.	Sections 2, 3, 5 to 23, 28, 32 to 36, 38 to 44, 48, 49, 51, 56, 57, 61, 63, 77 to 80, 83, 89, 94, 96, 97, 101, 107, 111 to 114, 116, 117 and 119. Section 121 from "Incorporation of Acts;" to "county council;". Section 129. Schedules 1 and 2.
1 Edw. 7. c. lxxx.	Derwent Valley Water Act 1901.	Sections 2, 3, 5 to 8, 12 to 14, 16 to 18, 21, 26 to 29, 31 to 33 and 35.
4 Edw. 7. c. cxcvi.	Derwent Valley Water Act 1904.	Sections 2, 3, 5, 7, 8, 14, 15, 17, 19, 20, 31, 33 to 35, 37 to 40, 43, 44, 46, 47 and 49. The Schedule.
9 Edw. 7. c. lxiii.	Derwent Valley Water Act 1909.	The whole Act except sections 1 and 3 to 6.
2 & 3 Geo. 5. c. xxxviii.	Derwent Valley Water Act 1912.	The whole Act except sections 1, 2 and 3.
10 & 11 Geo. 5. c. clxv.	Derwent Valley Water Act 1920.	Sections 2, 3, 5 to 10, 12 to 17, 19, 22 to 24, 31, 32(12), 38 to 45, 49 and 53.
14 & 15 Geo. 5. c. lxxiii.	Ministry of Health Provisional Orders Confirmation (No. 7) Act 1924.	In the Schedule, the Derwent Valley Water Order 1924.
17 & 18 Geo. 5. c. lxx.	Derwent Valley Water Act 1927.	Sections 2, 3, 5 to 7, 9 to 12, 14, 17 to 19, 22 and 24.
25 & 26 Geo. 5. c. cv.	Derwent Valley Water Act 1935.	Sections 2, 3, 8, 9, 14, 16 to 20 and 22.
1 & 2 Geo. 6. c. lxii.	Derwent Valley Water Act 1938.	Sections 2, 4, 5, 7 to 9, 11, 13, 15, 16, 17(1), 19 to 23, 26 and 27.
7 & 8 Geo. 5. c. xviii.	Derwent Valley Water Act 1944.	Sections 2, 3, 7, 8, 10, 11(1), 12, 14 to 16, 25(1), 39, 40, 53, 55 to 60, 63 and 64.
S.I. 1949 No. 324.	Derwent Valley Water Order 1949.	The whole Order.
S.I. 1955 No. 1174.	Derwent Valley Water Order 1955.	Articles 3, 4, 5(2) and 6 to 9. The Schedule.
S.I. 1957 No. 330.	Derwent Valley Water Order 1956.	Articles 3, 7 to 9, 11 and 12(2). The Schedule except so far as it refers to paragraph 10 of Schedule 3 to the Water Act 1945.
S.I. 1959 No. 1794.	Derwent Valley Water Board (Drought) Order 1959.	The whole Order.
S.I. 1965 No. 1174.	Derwent Valley Water Order 1965.	The whole Order.

Chapter or Number	Short title	Extent of repeal
S.I. 1969 No. 1526.	Derwent Valley Water Order 1969.	The whole Order.

PART II

OVERSEAS JURISDICTION

Chapter	Short title	Extent of repeal

Group 1 – Associated States

Chapter	Short title	Extent of repeal
1969 c. 29.	Tanzania Act 1969.	Section 6(3)(a) and (4).
1971 c. 77.	Immigration Act 1971.	In section 8(4)(b), the words "associated state,".
1973 c. 27.	Bahamas Independence Act 1973.	In section 3(1)(a), the words "or an associated state". Section 7(3).
1978 c. 15.	Solomon Islands Act 1978.	Section 6(4).
1979 c. 43.	Crown Agents Act 1979.	In section 7, the words "or associated state". In Schedule 3, in Part I, paragraph 1, the words "or associated state".
1979 c. 60.	Zimbabwe Act 1979.	In section 4(5), the words "of any associated state or".
1980 c. 2.	Papua New Guinea, Western Samoa and Nauru (Miscellaneous Provisions) Act 1980.	Section 1(3).
1980 c. 67.	Anguilla Act 1980.	Section 1(1). Section 2(2).
1981 c. 52.	Belize Act 1981.	Section 4(5). In section 5(2), the words "or an associated state".
1981 c. 53.	Deep Sea Mining (Temporary Provisions) Act 1981.	In section 1(5)(b), the words "or an associated state".
1981 c. 61.	British Nationality Act 1981.	Section 53(6). In section 53(7), the words "and (6)".
1982 c. 16.	Civil Aviation Act 1982.	In section 64(2) and (6)(b), the words "or an associated state". In section 65(3)(b), the words "or an associated state". In section 69A(7)(c), the words "or of an associated state". In section 70, the words "or (b) between the United Kingdom and any associated state," and "or state". In section 84(2)(a) and (4), the words "or an associated state".
1983 c. 6.	British Nationality (Falkland Islands) Act 1983.	Section 5(5) from "and it is hereby declared" onwards.

Chapter	Short title	Extent of repeal

Group 2 – Other Repeals

Chapter	Short title	Extent of repeal
11 Will. 3. c. 12.	An Act to Punish Governors of Plantations in this Kingdom for Crimes by them committed in the Plantations.	The whole Act.
42 Geo. 3. c. 85.	Criminal Jurisdiction Act 1802.	In section 1, the words "the said recited Act passed in the reign of King William aforesaid, or" and ", or either of them,".
33 & 34 Vict. c. 90.	Foreign Enlistment Act 1870.	Section 33.
48 & 49 Vict. c. 49.	Submarine Telegraph Act 1885.	In section 6(5), the words "or in a supreme court in India".
1 Edw. 8 & 1 Geo. 6. c. 16.	Regency Act 1937.	In section 2(2), the words "and to the Government of India".
2 & 3 Geo. 6. c. 65.	Prize Act 1939.	Section 4(1)(c).
5 & 6 Geo. 6. c. 17.	Anglo-Venezuelan Treaty (Island of Patos) Act 1942.	The whole Act.
7 & 8 Geo. 6. c. 7.	Prize Salvage Act 1944.	Section 2(1)(b).
9 & 10 Geo. 6. c. 45.	United Nations Act 1946.	In section 1(2), the words "British India" and "and territories in India."
1967 c. 58.	Criminal Law Act 1967.	In Schedule 2, paragraph 15(1) from the beginning to "and".
1967 c. 71.	Aden, Perim and Kuria Muria Islands Act 1967.	The whole Act.

PART III

SCOTTISH LOCAL ACTS

Chapter or Number	Short title	Extent of repeal

Group 1 – Glasgow Police Acts

Chapter or Number	Short title	Extent of repeal
29 & 30 Vict. c. cclxxiii.	Glasgow Police Act 1866.	The whole Act.
36 & 37 Vict. c. xxxviii.	Glasgow Police Act 1873.	The whole Act.
38 & 39 Vict. c. liii.	Glasgow Police Act 1875.	The whole Act.
40 & 41 Vict. c. cxxviii.	General Police and Improvement (Scotland) Act 1862 Order Confirmation (Glasgow) Act 1877.	The whole Act.
40 & 41 Vict. c. clxvii.	Glasgow Police Act 1877.	The whole Act.
42 & 43 Vict. c. cxxiii.	Glasgow Municipal Act 1879.	The whole Act.
45 & 46 Vict. c. xix.	Glasgow Corporation and Police Act 1882.	The whole Act.
48 & 49 Vict. c. xv.	Glasgow Police Act 1885.	The whole Act.

Chapter or Number	Short title	Extent of repeal
53 & 54 Vict. c. ccxxi.	Glasgow Police (Amendment) Act 1890.	The whole Act.
54 & 55 Vict. c. xxxvii.	Glasgow Police (Sewage &c.) Act 1891.	The whole Act.
55 & 56 Vict. c. clxv.	Glasgow Police (Further Powers) Act 1892.	The whole Act.
58 & 59 Vict. c. cxliii.	Glasgow Corporation and Police Act 1895.	The whole Act.
1 Edw. 7. c. clxiii.	Glasgow Corporation (Police) Order Confirmation Act 1901.	The whole Act.
3 Edw. 7. c. clii.	Glasgow Corporation (Police) Order Confirmation Act 1903.	The whole Act.
4 Edw. 7. c. clxxi.	Glasgow Corporation (Police) Order Confirmation Act 1904.	The whole Act.
5 Edw. 7. c. cxxvii.	Glasgow Corporation Order Confirmation Act 1905.	In the Schedule— (a) Article 73 of the Order; (b) Article 74 of the Order; (c) Article 79 of the Order, so far as relating to (i) the Glasgow Police Act 1866, (ii) the Glasgow Corporation and Police Act 1882, (iii) the Glasgow Police Act 1885, (iv) the Glasgow Police (Amendment) Act 1890 and (v) the Glasgow Police (Sewage &c.) Act 1891.
7 Edw. 7. c. cxlvi.	Glasgow Corporation Act 1907.	Sections 43 and 70(3).
2 & 3 Geo. 5. c. cxlix.	Glasgow Corporation Order Confirmation Act 1912.	In the Schedule, Article 22 of the Order.
4 & 5 Geo. 5. c. clxxviii.	Glasgow Corporation Order Confirmation Act 1914.	In the Schedule, Articles 4(1) and (2), 11 and 17 of the Order.
9 & 10 Geo. 5. c. xcvi.	Glasgow Corporation Order Confirmation Act 1919.	In the Schedule, Articles 10, 12 and, so far as relating to Article 28 of the Glasgow Corporation and Police Act 1895, Article 35 of the Order.
11 & 12 Geo. 5. c. xv.	Glasgow Corporation Order Confirmation Act 1921.	In the Schedule, Articles 10(3) and 23 of the Order.
15 & 16 Geo. 5. c. cxxxi.	Glasgow Boundaries Act 1925.	In section 31, from the beginning to the words "Act of 1866 and", the word "respectively" and the words "said section 43 and the".
17 & 18 Geo. 5. c. lix.	Glasgow Corporation Order Confirmation Act 1927.	In the Schedule, Articles 76 and 77 of the Order.
20 & 21 Geo. 5. c. xxxvii.	Glasgow Corporation Act 1929.	Sections 20, 22(2) and (4), 30 and 31.
20 & 21 Geo. 5. c. clxxvii.	Glasgow Corporation Act 1930.	Section 39.
24 & 25 Geo. 5. c. lxix.	Glasgow Corporation Order Confirmation Act 1934.	In the Schedule, Article 47 of the Order.
12 & 13 Geo. 6. c. xix.	Glasgow Corporation Order Confirmation Act 1949.	In the Schedule, Article 6 of the Order.

Chapter or Number	Short title	Extent of repeal
2 Eliz. 2. c. i.	Glasgow Corporation (Water &c.) Order Confirmation Act 1953.	In the Schedule, Article 12 of the Order.
S.I. 1956 No. 1996.	Police (Local Enactments) (Scotland) Order 1956.	In the Schedule, all entries in cols. 1, 2 and 3 relating to the Glasgow Police Act 1866.
5 & 6 Eliz. 2. c. xiv.	Glasgow Corporation Order Confirmation Act 1957.	In the Schedule, Article 9 of the Order.
9 & 10 Eliz. 2. c. xxxix.	Glasgow Corporation Order Confirmation Act 1961.	In the Schedule, Article 9 of the Order.
1964 c. xliii.	Glasgow Corporation Consolidation (Water, Transport and Markets) Order Confirmation Act 1964.	In the Schedule, Article 73 of the Order.
1965 c. ii.	Glasgow Corporation Order Confirmation Act 1965.	In the Schedule, Article 8 of the Order.
1970 c. i.	Glasgow Corporation Order Confirmation Act 1970.	In the Schedule, Article 16 of the Order.

Group 2 – Dog Warden Acts

Chapter or Number	Short title	Extent of repeal
1976 c. xxxii.	East Kilbride District Council Order Confirmation Act 1976.	The whole Act.
1977 c. xxii.	City of Glasgow District Council Order Confirmation Act 1977.	The whole Act.
1978 c. xix.	Monklands District Council Order Confirmation Act 1978.	The whole Act.
1979 c. xvii.	Stirling District Council Order Confirmation Act 1979.	The whole Act.
1979 c. xx.	Kilmarnock and Loudoun District Council Order Confirmation Act 1979.	The whole Act.
1980 c. iv.	Inverness District Council Order Confirmation Act 1980.	The whole Act.
1980 c. v.	Kirkcaldy District Council Order Confirmation Act 1980.	The whole Act.
1980 c. vi.	Lochaber District Council Order Confirmation Act 1980.	The whole Act.
1980 c. vii.	Strathkelvin District Council Order Confirmation Act 1980.	The whole Act.
1980 c. viii.	West Lothian District Council Order Confirmation Act 1980.	The whole Act.
1981 c. iii.	Cumnock and Doon Valley District Council Order Confirmation Act 1981.	The whole Act.
1981 c. iv.	Dunfermline District Council Order Confirmation Act 1981.	The whole Act.

Chapter or Number	Short title	Extent of repeal
1981 c. xxxiii.	Midlothian District Council Order Confirmation Act 1981.	The whole Act.

Group 3 – Other Repeals

Chapter or Number	Short title	Extent of repeal
20 & 21 Geo. 5. c. xix.	Lanarkshire, Renfrewshire and Dunbartonshire Education Authorities Order Confirmation Act 1929.	The whole Act.
15 & 16 Geo. 6 & 1 Eliz. 2. c. xvii.	Kilmarnock Corporation Order Confirmation Act 1952.	The whole Act.
15 & 16 Geo. 6 & 1 Eliz. 2. c. lii.	Hamilton Burgh Order Confirmation Act 1952.	The whole Act.
1970 c. xxxv.	Fife County Council Order Confirmation Act 1970.	The whole Act.
1970 c. lviii.	Stirling County Council Order Confirmation Act 1970.	The whole Act.
1971 c. xxvii.	Dunbarton County Council Order Confirmation Act 1971.	The whole Act.
1974 c. ii.	Ayr County Council Order Confirmation Act 1974.	The whole Act.
1974 c. xv.	Fife County Council Order Confirmation Act 1974.	The whole Act.
S.I. 1978 No. 584.	Fife County Council Order Confirmation Act 1974 (Application of Provisions) (No. 1) Order 1978.	The whole Order.
S.I. 1978 No. 585.	Fife County Council Order Confirmation Act 1974 (Application of Provisions) (No. 2) Order 1978.	The whole Order.

PART IV

STATUTORY CITATION

Chapter	Short title	Extent of repeal
59 & 60 Vict. c. 14.	Short Titles Act 1896.	Section 1. Schedule 1. In Schedule 2, the entries relating to the following groups of Acts:— Bank Notes Acts 1826 to 1852. Bankruptcy Acts 1883 to 1890. Bankruptcy (Scotland) Acts 1856 to 1881. Baths and Washhouses Acts 1846 to 1882. Births, Deaths, and Marriages (Scotland) Acts 1854 to 1860.

Chapter	Short title	Extent of repeal
		Births and Deaths Registration (Ireland) Acts 1863 to 1880.
		Bridges Acts 1740 to 1815.
		Bridges (Ireland) Acts 1813 to 1875.
		British Subjects Acts 1708 to 1772.
		Building Societies Acts 1874 to 1894.
		Burial Grounds (Scotland) Acts 1855 to 1886.
		Charitable Trusts Acts 1853 to 1894.
		Companies Acts 1862 to 1893.
		Congested Districts Board (Ireland) Acts.
		Copyright Acts 1734 to 1888.
		Coroners (Ireland) Acts 1829 to 1881.
		County Courts (Ireland) Acts 1851 to 1889.
		County Infirmaries (Ireland) Acts 1805 to 1833.
		Drainage and Improvement of Lands (Ireland) Acts 1863 to 1892.
		Drainage and Navigation (Ireland) Acts 1842 to 1857.
		Durham County Palatine Acts 1836 to 1889.
		East India Company (Money) Acts 1786 to 1858.
		East India Loans Acts 1859 to 1893.
		Education (Scotland) Acts 1872 to 1893.
		Elementary Education Acts 1870 to 1893.
		Endowed Schools Acts 1869 to 1889.
		Fisheries (Ireland) Acts 1842 to 1895.
		Government Annuities Acts 1829 to 1888.
		Herring Fisheries (Scotland) Acts 1821 to 1890.
		Highway Acts 1835 to 1885.
		International Copyright Acts.
		Judicature (Ireland) Acts 1877 to 1888.
		Juries Acts 1825 to 1870.
		Justiciary Court (Scotland) Acts 1783 to 1892.
		Labourers (Ireland) Acts 1883 to 1892.
		Lancaster County Palatine Acts 1794 to 1871.
		Licensing (Ireland) Acts 1833 to 1886.
		Life Assurance Companies Acts 1870 to 1872.
		Lunacy (Scotland) Acts 1857 to 1887.
		Lunacy (Ireland) Acts 1821 to 1890.
		Matrimonial Causes Acts 1857 to 1878.
		Medical Acts.
		Merchandise Marks Acts 1887 to 1894.
		Metropolis Management Acts 1855 to 1893.
		Municipal Corporations (Ireland) Acts 1840 to 1888.
		Naval Enlistment Acts 1835 to 1884.
		Patents, Designs, and Trade Marks Acts 1883 to 1888.
		Petroleum Acts 1871 to 1881.
		Police Acts 1839 to 1893.
		Police (Scotland) Acts 1857 to 1890.
		Post Office Acts 1837 to 1895.
		Post Office (Duties) Acts 1840 to 1891.
		Post Office (Management) Acts 1837 to 1884.

Chapter	Short title	Extent of repeal
		Post Office (Money Orders) Acts 1848 to 1883.
		Post Office (Offences) Acts 1837 and 1884.
		Post Office Savings Bank Acts 1861 to 1893.
		Prison Acts 1865 to 1893.
		Prisons (Scotland) Acts 1860 to 1887.
		Prisons (Ireland) Acts 1826 to 1884.
		Public Libraries Acts 1892 and 1893.
		Public Libraries (Ireland) Acts 1855 to 1894.
		Public Libraries (Scotland) Acts 1887 and 1894.
		Public Money Drainage Acts 1846 to 1856.
		Salmon Fisheries (Scotland) Acts 1828 to 1868.
		Salmon and Freshwater Fisheries Acts 1861 to 1892.
		Small Debt (Scotland) Acts 1837 to 1889.
		Solicitors Acts 1839 to 1894.
		Solicitors (Ireland) Acts 1849 to 1881.
		Superannuation Acts 1834 to 1892.
		Trustee Savings Banks Acts 1863 to 1893.
		Trusts (Scotland) Acts 1861 to 1891.
		Universities and College Estates Acts 1858 to 1880.
		Weights and Measures Acts 1878 to 1893.
		Yeomanry Acts 1802 to 1826.
11 & 12 Geo. 6. c. 62.	Statute Law Revision Act 1948.	Section 5. Schedule 2.
1951 c. 1 (N.I.)	Short Titles Act (Northern Ireland) 1951.	Section 1. The Schedule.
1964 c. 80.	Statute Law Revision (Scotland) Act 1964.	The whole Act.
1977 c. 18.	Statute Law (Repeals) Act 1977.	Section 3. Schedule 3.
1978 c. 45.	Statute Law (Repeals) Act 1978.	Section 2. Schedule 3.

PART V

TRANSPORT

Chapter	Short title	Extent of repeal

Group 1 – Pilotage Orders Confirmation Acts

Chapter	Short title	Extent of repeal
54 & 55 Vict. c. xlvii.	Pilotage Orders Confirmation (No. 2) Act 1891.	The whole Act.
56 & 57 Vict. c. xxxvi.	Pilotage Orders Confirmation Act 1893.	The whole Act.
60 & 61 Vict. c. clvii.	Pilotage Order Confirmation Act 1897.	The whole Act.
2 Edw. 7. c. lxxvi.	Pilotage Order Confirmation Act 1902.	The whole Act.
3 & 4 Geo. 5. c. clxv.	Pilotage Order (London) Confirmation Act 1913.	The whole Act.
10 & 11 Geo. 5. c. ciii.	Pilotage Orders Confirmation (No. 1) Act 1920.	The whole Act.

Chapter	Short title	Extent of repeal
10 & 11 Geo. 5 c. civ.	Pilotage Orders Confirmation (No. 2) Act 1920.	The whole Act.
10 & 11 Geo. 5. c. cxxiv.	Pilotage Orders Confirmation (No. 3) Act 1920.	The whole Act.
11 & 12 Geo. 5. c. vi.	Pilotage Orders Confirmation (No. 1) Act 1921.	The whole Act.
11 & 12 Geo. 5. c. xvi.	Pilotage Orders Confirmation (No. 2) Act 1921.	The whole Act.
11 & 12 Geo. 5. c. lv.	Pilotage Orders Confirmation (No. 3) Act 1921.	The whole Act.
11 & 12 Geo. 5. c. lvi.	Pilotage Orders Confirmation (No. 4) Act 1921.	The whole Act.
11 & 12 Geo. 5. c. lxxi.	Pilotage Orders Confirmation (No. 6) Act 1921.	The whole Act.
11 & 12 Geo. 5. c. lxxii.	Pilotage Orders Confirmation (No. 7) Act 1921.	The whole Act.
11 & 12 Geo. 5. c. cxii.	Pilotage Orders Confirmation (No. 5) Act 1921.	The whole Act.
12 & 13 Geo. 5. c. xiii.	Pilotage Orders Confirmation (No. 2) Act 1922.	The whole Act.
12 & 13 Geo. 5. c. xxxvii.	Pilotage Orders Confirmation (No. 1) Act 1922.	The whole Act.
12 & 13 Geo. 5. c. xxxviii.	Pilotage Orders Confirmation (No. 3) Act 1922.	The whole Act.
1976 c. xxi.	Stornoway Harbour Order Confirmation Act 1976.	In the Schedule, Part VII of the Order.

Group 2 – Other Repeals

Chapter	Short title	Extent of repeal
1975 c. 36.	Air Travel Reserve Fund Act 1975.	The whole Act.
1978 c. 8.	Civil Aviation Act 1978.	The whole Act.
1980 c. 66.	Highways Act 1980.	In section 18(8), the word "rural".
1982 c. 16.	Civil Aviation Act 1982.	In section 48(7)(a), the words from "and" to "a council". Section 60(3)(k). In Schedule 14, paragraph 11. In Schedule 15, paragraph 20.
1985 c. 67.	Transport Act 1985.	In section 35(4)(a), the words from ", not being a licence" to "suspension". Section 39(4) from "(not being" onwards. Section 89(6)(a)(i).

PART VI

MISCELLANEOUS

Chapter or Number	Short title	Extent of repeal

Group 1 – General Repeals

Chapter or Number	Short title	Extent of repeal
48 Geo. 3. c. 128.	Regimental Accounts Act 1808.	The whole Act.
57 Geo. 3. c. 93.	Distress (Costs) Act 1817.	The whole Act.
60 Geo. 3 & 1 Geo. 4. c. 1.	Unlawful Drilling Act 1819.	In section 1, the words from "or to be punished" to "shall be had" where they first appear.
7 & 8 Geo. 4. c. 17.	Distress (Costs) Act 1827.	The whole Act.

Chapter or Number	Short title	Extent of repeal
2 & 3 Vict. c. 47.	Metropolitan Police Act 1839.	Sections 35 to 37.
8 & 9 Vict. c. 113.	Evidence Act 1845.	Section 4.
37 & 38 Vict. c. 81.	Great Seal (Offices) Act 1874.	Section 4 from "There shall be paid" to the end. Section 7. In section 9, the proviso.
38 & 39 Vict. c. 16.	Regimental Exchange Act 1875.	The whole Act.
48 & 49 Vict. c. 72.	Housing of the Working Classes Act 1885.	The whole Act as it applies in England and Wales.
54 & 55 Vict. c. 40.	Brine Pumping (Compensation for Subsidence) Act 1891.	The whole Act.
10 & 11 Geo. 5. c. 43.	Firearms Act 1920.	The whole Act.
11 & 12 Geo. 5. c. 7.	Tribunals of Inquiry (Evidence) Act 1921.	In section 1(1), the words "(whether before or after the commencement of this Act)".
15 & 16 Geo. 5. c. 58.	Greenwich Hospital (Disused Burial Ground) Act 1925.	The whole Act.
26 Geo. 5 & 1 Edw. 8. c. 49.	Public Health Act 1936.	Section 309(4). Section 315. In section 326(6), the words "isolation hospital committee".
2 & 3 Geo. 6. c. 72.	Landlord and Tenant (War Damage) Act 1939.	In section 6(1), the words "or a notice of retention". In section 6(4), the words "in respect of a notice of disclaimer or a notice to elect". In section 6(5), the words "a notice of retention". In section 15, the words ", a notice of retention", "or retention", and ", notice of retention", wherever occurring.
2 & 3 Geo. 6. c. 89.	Trading with the Enemy Act 1939.	Section 17(2) and (3).
2 & 3 Geo. 6. c. 107.	Patents, Designs, Copyright and Trade Marks (Emergency) Act 1939.	In section 1(2), the words from "or has at any time" to "been,". In section 2(1)(a), the words from "or has at any time" to "been,".
4 & 5 Geo. 6. c. 41.	Landlord and Tenant (War Damage) (Amendment) Act 1941.	Section 1(9). Section 2(1) to (4). In section 2(5), from the beginning to "Act, and" and the word "said". Section 2(6) to (8). Sections 3 to 9. In section 10(1), from ", and" to the end. Section 10(2) and (3). In section 11, from ", and any proceedings" to the end. Section 16. Section 17(5). The Schedule, so far as it relates to modifications of section 6 of the Landlord and Tenant (War Damage) Act 1939.

Chapter or Number	Short title	Extent of repeal
5 & 6 Geo. 6. c. 9 (N.I.).	Landlord and Tenant (War Damage) Act (Northern Ireland) 1941.	In section 6(1), the words "or a notice of retention". In section 6(4), the words "in respect of a notice of disclaimer or a notice to elect". In section 6(5), the words "a notice of retention or". In section 14, the words ", a notice of retention", "or retention" and ", notice of retention", wherever occurring. Part III. Section 36. Section 38(3).
1965 c. 18.	War Damage Act 1965.	Section 1(2).
1966 c. 39.	Land Registration Act 1966.	The whole Act.
1968 c. 28 (N.I.).	Criminal Justice (Miscellaneous Provisions) Act (Northern Ireland) 1968.	In Schedule 2, the entry relating to the Evidence Act 1845.
1969 c. 48.	Post Office Act 1969.	In Schedule 9, paragraph 17(2)(a) and (5)(c).
1971 c. 54.	Land Registration and Land Charges Act 1971.	Section 2(6).
1972 c. 70.	Local Government Act 1972.	In section 243(4), the words "of election or".
1980 c. 25.	Insurance Companies Act 1980.	In Schedule 3, paragraphs 16 and 19.
1982 c. 50.	Insurance Companies Act 1982.	In Schedule 5, paragraph 22(b) and (e).
1989 c. 24.	Social Security Act 1989.	In Schedule 7, paragraph 27. In Schedule 8, paragraph 12(3) and (4).
S.I. 1989 No. 438.	Community Charges (Administration and Enforcement) Regulations 1989.	Regulation 39(9).
S.I. 1989 No. 1058.	Non-Domestic Rating (Collection and Enforcement) (Local Lists) Regulations 1989.	Regulation 14(9).
1990 c. 8.	Town and Country Planning Act 1990.	In section 252(12), the word "rural". In Schedule 14, in paragraph 1(2)(b)(ii), the word "rural" wherever it appears.
S.I. 1992 No. 613.	Council Tax (Administration and Enforcement) Regulations 1992.	Regulation 45(9).

Group 2 – Bank of England

Chapter or Number	Short title	Extent of repeal
3 Geo. 1. c. 8.	Bank of England Act 1716.	The whole Act.
4 Geo. 3. c. 49. (1764)	An Act to enable the Governor and Company of the Bank of England to purchase Houses and Ground for opening a Passage for Carriages, from Cornhill to the Bank, and making more commodious several other Passages leading thereto; and for enlarging the Buildings of the said Bank, and making the same more commodious.	The whole Act.

Chapter or Number	Short title	Extent of repeal
5 Geo. 3 c. 91. (1765)	An Act for vesting certain Glebe Lands belong to the Rectory of the Parish Church of Saint Christopher, in the City of London, in the Governor and Company of the Bank of England; and for making a Recompence to the Rector of the said Parish, and his Successors, in lieu thereof; and for obviating certain Doubts in an Act passed in the Thirty third Year of the Reign of His late Majesty, for widening certain Streets, Lanes, and Passages, within the City of London.	The whole Act except so far as it purports to obviate certain doubts in the Act of 33 Geo. 2. c. 30 (1759) for widening certain streets, lanes and passages within the City of London.
6 Geo. 3. c. 76. (1766)	An Act to enable the Governor and Company of the Bank of England to purchase certain Houses and Ground contiguous and near to the Bank; and for making certain Avenues leading thereto more commodious.	The whole Act.
21 Geo. 3. c. 71. (1781)	An Act for vesting the Parish Church of Saint Christopher le Stocks, in the City of London, and the Materials and Site thereof and the Churchyard thereto adjoining, in the Governor and Company of the Bank of England, and their Successors for ever; and for uniting the said Parish to the Parish of Saint Margaret Lothbury, in the said City.	The whole Act.
33 Geo. 3. c. 15. (1793)	An Act to enable the Governor and Company of the Bank of England to purchase certain Houses and Ground contiguous to the Bank of England.	The whole Act.
39 & 40 Geo. 3. c. lxxxix. (1800)	An Act to empower the Governor and Company of the Bank of England to purchase certain Houses and Ground contiguous to the Bank of England and to enable them to improve certain Avenues adjacent thereto.	The whole Act.

SCHEDULE 2

CONSEQUENTIAL AND CONNECTED PROVISIONS

Unlawful Drilling Act 1819 (c. 1)

1. In section 1 of the Unlawful Drilling Act 1819 (prohibition on unauthorised meetings of persons for the purpose of being trained, or of practising military exercise—
    (a) (in its application to Great Britain) for the words "the lieutenant, or two justices of the peace for any county or riding" substitute "a Secretary of State, or any officer deputed by him for the purpose";
    (b) (in its application to Northern Ireland) for the words "the lieutenant, or two justices of the peace for any county or riding" substitute "a Secretary of State";
    (c) (in its application to Great Britain and Northern Ireland) for the words "be transported" substitute "imprisonment".

Conveyancing (Scotland) Act 1874 (c. 94)

2. In section 51 of the Conveyancing (Scotland) Act 1874, after "1948" there shall be inserted "or
    (c) the Supreme Court of Aden before 30th November 1967,".

Aden, Perim and Kuria Muria Islands Act 1967 (c. 71)

3. The repeal by this Act of the Aden, Perim and Kuria Muria Islands Act 1967 shall not affect the continued operation of—
    (a) section 4 of that Act (Aden Widows' and Orphans' Pension Fund), and
    (b) any regulations under that section,
in accordance with section 2(3) of the Overseas Pensions Act 1973 (certain repealed provisions to have effect as schemes under section 2 of that Act).

INDEX

References are to sections and Schedules

GAS ACT 1995*

(1995 c. 45)

An Act to amend Parts I and III of the Gas Act 1986; to make provision for requiring the owners of certain gas processing facilities to make them available to other persons; and for connected purposes.

[8th November 1995]

PARLIAMENTARY DEBATES
Hansard, H.C. Vol. 260, col. 180; Vol. 256, col. 574; H.L. Vol. 564, cols. 595, 1266; Vol. 565, cols. 410, 491, 755, 781, 824; Vol. 566, col. 748.
The Bill was considered in Standing Committee A from 21st March to 27th April 1995.

INTRODUCTION AND GENERAL NOTE
This Act is a major reform of legislation relating to the gas supply industry in the United Kingdom. The Act provides a number of amendments to the regime created on privatisation of the industry by the Gas Act 1986 (c. 44) ("the 1986 Act"). Amendments are made to Pt. I of the 1986 Act, to create a new licensing framework for the gas industry. The "public gas supplier" formerly licensed under s.7, and the authorised suppliers formerly licensed under s.8 are replaced as the competitive market develops.

---

*Annotations by Stephen R. Dow and Professor Thomas Wälde, University of Dundee.

A relatively short Act (containing 18 sections and 6 Schedules), it will nonetheless have a major effect on the structure of the industry as it moves towards full competition. The Act provides for the separate licensing of "gas suppliers", who will sell gas to consumers; "public gas transporters", who will operate the pipeline network; and "gas shippers", who will arrange with public gas transporters for appropriate amounts of gas to be moved through the network.

The functions of the Director General of Gas Supply ("the Director") are amended to take account of the new licensing framework. The Director will be responsible for the issue of licences, and provision is made for standard conditions except where circumstances otherwise dictate, in which case the standard conditions may be modified.

The Act also takes a further step in liberalising the gas supply industry, by creating rights of third party access to gas processing facilities.

The Act is a reaction to the changing nature of the gas industry since privatisation. The underlying theme is the creation of competition—the Act restructures the industry with the aim of building on the level of competition created by the 1986 Act.

ABBREVIATIONS
Gas Act 1986: the 1986 Act.

Introductory

General duties under 1986 Act

1. For section 4 of the Gas Act 1986 ("the 1986 Act") there shall be substituted the following section—

"General duties of Secretary of State and Director

4.—(1) The Secretary of State and the Director shall each have a duty to exercise the functions assigned to him by or under this Part in the manner which he considers is best calculated—

    (a) to secure that, so far as it is economical to meet them, all reasonable demands in Great Britain for gas conveyed through pipes are met;

    (b) to secure that licence holders are able to finance the carrying on of the activities which they are authorised or required by their licences to carry on; and

    (c) to secure effective competition in the carrying on of activities the carrying on of which is required to be licensed under section 7A below.

(2) Subject to subsection (1) above, the Secretary of State and the Director shall each have a duty to exercise the functions assigned to him by or under this Part in the manner which he considers is best calculated—

    (a) to protect the interests of consumers of gas conveyed through pipes in respect of the prices charged and the other terms of supply, the continuity of supply, the quality of the gas supply services provided and the exercise of rights under this Part to enter their premises;

    (b) to promote efficiency and economy on the part of persons authorised by or under this Part to carry on any activities, and the efficient use of gas conveyed through pipes; and

    (c) to secure effective competition—

        (i) in the conveyance of gas through pipes to pipe-line systems and to areas to which it has not previously been so conveyed;

        (ii) in the supplying and laying of service pipes; and

        (iii) in the carrying on of activities ancillary to those mentioned in subsection (1)(c) above;

and a duty to take into account, in exercising those functions, the effect on the environment (whether by way of pollution or otherwise) of activities connected with the conveyance of gas through pipes.

(3) In performing his duty under subsection (2) above to exercise functions assigned to him in the manner which he considers is best calculated to protect the interests of consumers of gas conveyed through

pipes in respect of the quality of the gas supply services provided, the Secretary of State or, as the case may be, the Director shall take into account, in particular, the interests of those who are chronically sick, disabled or of pensionable age.

(4) In this section 'environment' and 'pollution', in relation to the environment, shall be construed in accordance with section 1 of the Environmental Protection Act 1990.

(5) In this Part, unless the context otherwise requires, 'licence' means a licence under section 7 or 7A below and 'licence holder' shall be construed accordingly."

DEFINITIONS
"Director": Gas Act 1986, s.1(1).

GENERAL NOTE
This section amends the general duties of the Secretary of State and the Director, creating broadly similar duties. Perhaps the most significant change is the insertion of s.4(1)(c), the duty to secure effective competition, mirroring similar provisions in the Electricity Act 1989 (c. 29), creating the Director General of Electricity Supply. The insertion of s.4(4) is also significant, clearly demonstrating how the link to environmental protection legislation is found.

Duties under 1986 Act with respect to safety

2. After section 4 of the 1986 Act there shall be inserted the following section—

"Duties of Secretary of State and Director with respect to safety

4A.—(1) Subject to section 4(1) above, the Secretary of State and the Director shall each have a duty to exercise the functions assigned to him by or under this Part in the manner which he considers is best calculated to protect the public from dangers arising from the conveyance of gas through pipes or from the use of gas conveyed through pipes.

(2) In performing his duty under subsection (1) above, the Secretary of State or, as the case may be, the Director shall consult with and take into account any advice offered by the Health and Safety Executive.

(3) It shall also be the duty of the Director—

(a) in conjunction with the Health and Safety Executive, to prepare and from time to time revise a document setting out such means as may, with the approval of the Health and Safety Commission, be agreed between the Director and that Executive for securing co-operation and the exchange of information between them; and

(b) without prejudice to the effect or operation of any relevant statutory provisions (within the meaning of Part I of the Health and Safety at Work etc. Act 1974), to exercise the functions assigned to him by or under this Part in accordance with any agreement contained in that document.

(4) As soon as practicable after agreement is reached for the purposes of—

(a) the preparation of a document in accordance with subsection (3) above, or

(b) any revision of a document prepared in accordance with that subsection,

the Director shall send a copy of the document or, as the case may be, of the revised version of it to the Secretary of State, and the Secretary of State shall lay the copy before each House of Parliament."

GENERAL NOTE
This section adds a new dimension to duties of the Secretary of State and the Director, creating a duty to exercise functions in a manner best calculated to protect the public from dangers

arising from conveyance of gas through pipes, or the use of gas so conveyed. In addition he must consult with and take into account advice offered by the Health and Safety Executive. This section develops from s.4(2)(c) of the 1986 Act, clarifying the duty and aiming to strengthen the protection of the public.

Licensing of activities relating to gas

Prohibition on unlicensed activities

3.—(1) For section 5 of the 1986 Act there shall be substituted the following section—

"Licensing of activities relating to gas

Prohibition on unlicensed activities

5.—(1) Subject to section 6A below and Schedule 2A to this Act, a person who—
  (a) conveys gas through pipes to any premises, or to a pipe-line system operated by a public gas transporter;
  (b) supplies to any premises gas which has been conveyed to those premises through pipes; or
  (c) arranges with a public gas transporter for gas to be introduced into, conveyed by means of or taken out of a pipe-line system operated by that transporter,
shall be guilty of an offence unless he is authorised to do so by a licence.
  (2) The exceptions to subsection (1) above which are contained in Schedule 2A to this Act shall have effect.
  (3) A person guilty of an offence under this section shall be liable—
  (a) on summary conviction to a fine not exceeding the statutory maximum;
  (b) on conviction on indictment, to a fine.
  (4) No proceedings shall be instituted in England and Wales in respect of an offence under this section except by or on behalf of the Secretary of State or the Director.
  (5) Any reference in this Part to the conveyance by any person of gas through pipes to any premises is a reference to the conveyance by him of gas through pipes to those premises with a view to the gas being supplied to those premises by any person, or being used in those premises by the holder of a licence under section 7A(2) below."

(2) After Schedule 2 to that Act there shall be inserted, as Schedule 2A, the provisions of Schedule 1 to this Act (exceptions to prohibition on unlicensed activities).

(3) Section 6 of that Act (which is superseded by this section) shall cease to have effect.

GENERAL NOTE
  This section is the basis of regulation of the gas industry, restricting licensed activities to those persons authorised by licence. Formerly the restriction was on gas supplied to premises (1986 Act, s.5), however with the alterations to the licensing regime, it is also necessary to include conveyance to the network operated by the public gas transporter (s.5(1)(a)). Section 5(1)(c) completes the picture, preventing any person acting as a gas shipper unless authorised under the Act. The new Sched. 2A contains exceptions to the prohibition on unlicensed activities. Note that supply to premises with annual demand in excess of two million therms will not require a licence, but rather notification to the Secretary of State.

Exemptions from prohibition

4. For section 6A of the 1986 Act there shall be substituted the following section—

"Exemptions from prohibition

6A.—(1) The Secretary of State may, after consultation with the Director, by order grant exemption from paragraph (a), (b) or (c) of section 5(1) above—

(a) either to a person or to persons of a class;

(b) either generally or to such extent as may be specified in the order; and

(c) either unconditionally or subject to such conditions as may be so specified.

(2) An exemption granted to persons of a class, and the revocation of such an exemption, shall be published in such manner as the Secretary of State considers appropriate for bringing it to the attention of persons of that class.

(3) An exemption, unless previously revoked in accordance with any term contained in the exemption, shall continue in force for such period as may be specified in or determined by or under the exemption.

(4) Without prejudice to the generality of paragraph (c) of subsection (1) above, conditions included by virtue of that paragraph in an exemption may require any person carrying on any activity in pursuance of the exemption—

(a) to comply with any direction given by the Secretary of State or the Director as to such matters as are specified in the exemption or are of a description so specified;

(b) except in so far as the Secretary of State or the Director consents to his doing or not doing them, not to do or to do such things as are specified in the exemption or are of a description so specified; and

(c) to refer for determination by the Secretary of State or the Director such questions arising under the exemption as are specified in the exemption or are of a description so specified.

(5) If any condition of an exemption granted to persons of a class is not complied with by any person of that class, the Secretary of State may give to that person a direction declaring that the exemption is revoked, so far as relating to that person, to such extent and as from such date as may be specified in the direction."

GENERAL NOTE

This section permits the Secretary of State, after consultation with the Director, to grant exemptions from the prohibition on unlicensed activities. The section allows considerable discretion, ranging from control of the person(s) who may benefit, to the insertion of conditions into the exemption, to the removal of exemption from any person or member of a class of exempted persons. It is likely that the section will also restrict recourse to judicial review (s.6A(4)(c)).

Licensing of public gas transporters

5. For section 7 of the 1986 Act there shall be substituted the following section—

"Licensing of public gas transporters

7.—(1) In this Part 'public gas transporter' means the holder of a licence under this section except where the holder is acting otherwise than for purposes connected with—

(a) the carrying on of activities authorised by the licence;

(b) the conveyance of gas through pipes which—

(i) are situated in an authorised area of his; or

(ii) are situated in an area which was an authorised area of his, or an authorised area of a previous holder of the licence, and were so situated at a time when it was such an area; or

    (c) the conveyance through pipes of gas which is in the course of being conveyed to or from a country or territory outside Great Britain.

(2) Subject to subsection (3) below, the Director may grant a licence authorising any person to do either or both of the following, namely—

    (a) to convey gas through pipes to any premises in an authorised area of his, that is to say, so much of any area specified in the licence or an extension of the licence as is not specified in a subsequent licence or extension granted under this section to another person; and

    (b) to convey gas through pipes either to any pipe-line system operated by another public gas transporter, or to any pipe-line system so operated which is specified in the licence or an extension of the licence.

(3) A licence shall not be granted under this section to a person who is the holder of a licence under section 7A below.

(4) The Director may, with the consent of the licence holder, direct that any licence under this section shall have effect—

    (a) as if any area or pipe-line system specified in the direction were specified in the licence;

    (b) in the case of a licence under subsection (2)(a) above, as if it were also a licence under subsection (2)(b) above and any pipe-line system specified in the direction were specified in the licence; or

    (c) in the case of a licence under subsection (2)(b) above, as if it were also a licence under subsection (2)(a) above and any area specified in the direction were specified in the licence;

and references in this Part to, or to the grant of, an extension under this section, or an extension of such a licence, shall be construed as references to, or to the giving of, such a direction.

(5) Before granting a licence or extension under this section, the Director shall give notice—

    (a) stating that he proposes to grant the licence or extension;

    (b) stating the reasons why he proposes to grant the licence or extension; and

    (c) specifying the time from the date of publication of the notice (not being less than two months or, in the case of an extension, such shorter time as may be prescribed) within which representations or objections with respect to the proposed licence or extension may be made,

and shall consider any representations or objections which are duly made and not withdrawn.

(6) A notice under subsection (5) above shall be given—

    (a) by publishing the notice in such manner as the Director considers appropriate for bringing it to the attention of persons likely to be affected by the grant of the licence or extension; and

    (b) by sending a copy of the notice to the Secretary of State, to the Health and Safety Executive and to any public gas transporter whose area includes the whole or any part of the area proposed to be specified in the licence or extension.

(7) A licence or extension under this section shall not specify any area which is specified in an earlier licence or extension granted under this section to another public gas transporter unless the Director considers that the applicant intends to carry on the activities authorised by the licence in a substantial part of that area.

(8) A licence or extension under this section shall not specify any area which is situated within 23 metres from a main of another public gas transporter unless—

(a) the other public gas transporter has consented in writing to the area being so specified; or

(b) no premises connected to the main are situated in the area and the Director considers—

(i) that the main is not, and is not intended to be, a relevant main;

(ii) that the other public gas transporter is not performing his duty under section 9(1) or 10(2) or (3) below in relation to any premises situated in the area; or

(iii) that the configuration of the main and of the surrounding area is such that it would be appropriate to specify the area in the licence or extension.

(9) As soon as practicable after the granting of a licence under this section, the public gas transporter shall publish, in such manner as the Director considers appropriate for bringing it to the attention of persons who are likely to do business with the transporter, a notice—

(a) stating that the licence has been granted; and

(b) explaining that, as a result, it might be necessary for those persons to be licensed under section 7A below.

(10) In this section—

(a) 'relevant main' has the same meaning as in section 10 below;

(b) references to an area specified in a licence or direction include references to an area included in an area so specified; and

(c) references to a pipe-line system specified in a licence or direction include references to a pipe-line system of a description, or situated in an area, so specified.

(11) Any reference in this Part (however expressed) to activities authorised by a licence under this section shall be construed without regard to any exception contained in Schedule 2A to this Act."

GENERAL NOTE

This section creates the position of public gas transporter, replacing the former s.7. The pipe-line network is a natural monopoly and this section seeks to allow the Director a degree of control over the activities of pipeline operators. In an echo of the recommendations of the Monopolies and Mergers Commission investigations into the gas supply industry (MMC, London HMSO 1993), the holder of a public gas transportation licence may not also be the holder of a gas supply licence or a gas shipping licence (s.7(3)). The section seeks to overcome the potential imbalance created by the former regime under which the public gas supplier (a position now abolished) could operate as transport network operator and also as a supplier to consumers. The MMC recommended divestment of the two businesses, which recommendation was not implemented. This section creates a licensing system which separates the two activities.

Licensing of gas suppliers and gas shippers

6.—(1) After section 7 of the 1986 Act there shall be inserted the following section—

"Licensing of gas suppliers and gas shippers

7A.—(1) Subject to subsection (3) below, the Director may grant a licence authorising any person to do either or both of the following, namely—

(a) to supply, to any premises specified in the licence, gas which has been conveyed through pipes to those premises; and

(b) to supply, to any premises at a rate which, at the time when he undertakes to give the supply, he reasonably expects to exceed 2,500 therms a year, gas which has been conveyed through pipes to those premises.

(2) Subject to subsection (3) below, the Director may grant a licence authorising any person to arrange with any public gas transporter for gas to be introduced into, conveyed by means of or taken out of a pipe-line

system operated by that transporter, either generally or for purposes connected with the supply of gas to any premises specified in the licence.

(3) A licence shall not be granted under this section to a person who is the holder of a licence under section 7 above.

(4) The Director may, with the consent of the licence holder, direct that any licence under this section shall have effect—

(a) as if any premises specified in the direction were specified in the licence; or

(b) in the case of a licence under subsection (1)(b) above, as if it were also a licence under subsection (1)(a) above and any premises specified in the direction were specified in the licence,

and references in this Part to, or to the grant of, an extension under this section, or an extension of such a licence, shall be construed as references to, or to the giving of, such a direction.

(5) Subsection (4) above shall not apply in relation to a licence under subsection (1) above which authorises only the supply to premises of gas which has been conveyed to the premises otherwise than by a public gas transporter.

(6) The Director may, with the consent of the licence holder, direct that any licence under this section shall have effect as if any premises specified in the direction were not specified in the licence; and references in this Part to, or to the grant of, a restriction under this section, or a restriction of such a licence, shall be construed as references to, or to the giving of, such a direction.

(7) In this section references to premises specified in a licence or direction include references to premises of a description, or situated in an area, so specified.

(8) The Director shall not, in any licence under subsection (1) above, or in any extension or restriction of such a licence, specify any premises by description or area if he is of the opinion that the description or area has been so framed as—

(a) in the case of a licence or extension, artificially to exclude from the licence or extension; or

(b) in the case of a restriction, artificially to include in the restriction,

premises likely to be owned or occupied by persons who are chronically sick, disabled or of pensionable age, or who are likely to default in the payment of charges.

(9) If the holder of a licence under subsection (1) above applies to the Director for a restriction of the licence, or for the revocation of the licence in accordance with any term contained in it, the Director shall, subject to subsection (8) above, accede to the application if he is satisfied that such arrangements have been made as—

(a) will secure continuity of supply for all relevant consumers; and

(b) in the case of each such consumer who is supplied with gas in pursuance of a contract, will secure such continuity on the same terms as nearly as may be as the terms of the contract.

(10) A person is a relevant consumer for the purposes of subsection (9) above if—

(a) immediately before the restriction or revocation takes effect, he is being supplied with gas by the holder of the licence; and

(b) in the case of a restriction, his premises are excluded from the licence by the restriction;

and in that subsection 'contract' does not include any contract which, by virtue of paragraph 8 of Schedule 2B to this Act, is deemed to have been made.

(11) In this Part 'gas supplier' and 'gas shipper' mean respectively the holder of a licence under subsection (1) above, and the holder of a licence under subsection (2) above, except (in either case) where the

holder is acting otherwise than for purposes connected with the carrying on of activities authorised by the licence.

(12) Any reference in this Part (however expressed) to activities authorised by a licence under subsection (1) above shall be construed without regard to any exception contained in Schedule 2A to this Act."

(2) Subject to subsections (3) to (6) below, no domestic supply licence shall authorise the supply of gas to any premises before the relevant date, that is to say, 1st January 1999 or, if the Secretary of State by order so provides, such earlier date (not earlier than 1st January 1998) as may be determined by or under the order.

(3) Subsection (2) above shall not apply in relation to a domestic supply licence in so far as it relates to—

(a) any premises to which subsection (4) below applies; or

(b) any premises to which that subsection has ceased to apply at any time and which are situated in an area which has not, at that or any later time, ceased to be an authorised area of a particular public gas transporter.

(4) This subsection applies to any premises at any time if, at that time, the public gas transporter in whose authorised area the premises are situated is an associate of the holder of the domestic supply licence in question.

(5) Subsection (2) above shall not apply in relation to a domestic supply licence in so far as it relates to any premises to which gas is conveyed otherwise than by a public gas transporter.

(6) In so far as a domestic supply licence relates to premises which are situated in any area specified in an order made by the Secretary of State, subsection (2) above shall apply in relation to the licence as if for the relevant date there were substituted such earlier date as may be determined, in relation to that area, by or under the order.

(7) Any reference in this section to a domestic supply licence includes a reference to an extension of such a licence (within the meaning of Part I of the 1986 Act).

(8) In this section—

"domestic supply licence" means a licence granted under subsection (1) (a) of section 7A of the 1986 Act, a licence having effect as such a licence by virtue of a direction given under subsection (4)(b) of that section, or a licence treated as so granted by virtue of a scheme made under paragraph 4 or 16 of Schedule 5 to this Act;

"public gas transporter", and "authorised area" in relation to such a transporter, have the same meanings as in Part I of that Act.

(9) For the purposes of this section a public gas transporter is an associate of the holder of a domestic supply licence if—

(a) both of them are companies registered under the Companies Act 1985 and are limited by shares; and

(b) either one company is wholly owned by the other or both companies are wholly owned by the same person.

(10) An order under this section may—

(a) provide for anything falling to be determined under the order to be determined by the Director; and

(b) make such supplementary or incidental provision as the Secretary of State considers necessary or expedient.

(11) An order under this section shall be made by statutory instrument which shall be subject to annulment in pursuance of a resolution of either House of Parliament.

GENERAL NOTE

This section completes the restructuring of licensed activities, providing for licences for gas suppliers (persons selling piped gas to consumers) and gas shippers (persons arranging with a public gas transporter for gas to be moved through the pipelines). A person may hold either or both types of licence. These licences replace the former category of authorised suppliers (any authorised person other than the public gas supplier). The alterations to the regulatory regime are made in view of the introduction of full competition in the gas supply market from April 1, 1998. Given the Director's duty to secure that licence, holders are able to finance their activities (s.4(1)(b)), it remains to be seen whether applicants with no previous experience of the industry or access to supplies will be granted licences.

The Director has so far not restricted the issue of supply licences.

Licences: general

7. After section 7A of the 1986 Act there shall be inserted the following section—

"Licences: general

7B.—(1) An application for a licence or an extension or restriction of a licence shall be made in such form and manner, and shall contain, or be accompanied by, such information and documents and such fee (if any), as may be prescribed.

(2) Within the prescribed period after the making of an application for a licence or an extension or restriction of a licence, the applicant shall—

(a) publish a notice of the application in the prescribed manner; and

(b) in the case of an application for a licence or extension under section 7 above, give notice of the application to any public gas transporter whose authorised area includes the whole or any part of the area to which the application relates.

(3) A licence or an extension or restriction of a licence shall be in writing and, unless revoked or suspended in accordance with any term contained in it, a licence shall continue in force for such period as may be specified in or determined by or under the licence.

(4) A licence may include—

(a) such conditions (whether or not relating to the activities authorised by the licence) as appear to the Director to be requisite or expedient having regard to the duties imposed by section 4 or 4A above;

(b) such conditions requiring arrangements to be made with respect to the provision of special services for meeting the needs of consumers of gas conveyed through pipes who are chronically sick, disabled or of pensionable age as appear to the Director to be requisite or expedient having regard to those duties;

(c) conditions requiring the rendering to the Director of a payment on the grant of the licence or payments during the currency of the licence or both of such amount or amounts as may be determined by or under the licence; and

(d) conditions requiring the holder to furnish the Council in such manner and at such times with such information—

(i) as appears to the Director to be requisite or expedient for the purpose of facilitating the exercise by the Council of the functions assigned to it by this Part; or

(ii) as may be reasonably required by the Council for that purpose.

(5) Without prejudice to the generality of paragraph (a) of subsection (4) above—

(a) conditions included by virtue of that paragraph in a licence may—

(i) require the holder to comply with any direction given by the Director or the Secretary of State as to such matters as are specified in the licence or are of a description so specified;

(ii) require the holder, except in so far as the Director or the Secretary of State consents to his doing or not doing them, not to do or to do such things as are specified in the licence or are of a description so specified; and

(iii) provide for the determination by the Director, the Secretary of State or the Health and Safety Executive of such questions arising under the licence, or under any document specified or described in the licence, as are specified in the licence or are of a description so specified; and

(b) conditions included by virtue of that paragraph in a licence under section 7 above may require the holder, in such circumstances as are specified in the licence—

(i) so to increase his charges for the conveyance of gas as to raise such amounts as may be determined by or under the conditions; and

(ii) to pay the amounts so raised to such holders of licences under section 7A above as may be so determined.

(6) Conditions included in a licence may—

(a) impose requirements by reference to designation, acceptance or approval by the Director, the Secretary of State or the Health and Safety Executive; and

(b) provide for references in the conditions to any document specified or described in the licence to operate as references to that document as revised or re-issued from time to time.

(7) Conditions included in a licence may contain provision for the conditions to—

(a) have effect or cease to have effect at such times and in such circumstances as may be determined by or under the conditions; or

(b) be modified in such manner as may be specified in the conditions at such times and in such circumstances as may be so determined.

(8) Any provision included in a licence by virtue of subsection (7) above shall have effect in addition to the provision made by this Part with respect to the modification of the conditions of a licence.

(9) As soon as practicable after granting a licence or an extension or restriction of a licence, the Director shall send a copy of the licence or extension or restriction—

(a) to the Health and Safety Executive; and

(b) in the case of a licence or extension under section 7 above, to any public gas transporter whose authorised area previously included the whole or any part of the area specified in the licence or extension.

(10) Any sums received by the Director under or by virtue of this section shall be paid into the Consolidated Fund."

GENERAL NOTE

This section clarifies the Director's powers in respect of licensing. For example, licences may be issued subject to conditions (s.7B(4)); and conditions may oblige the holder to comply with directions given by the Director or the Secretary of State (s.7B(5)). Considerable discretion is given to the Director under the framework outlined in the Act—precise and detailed regulation will be dealt with on a day-to-day basis outwith the Act.

The licence, as a contract between the authorised person and the Director, may only be varied by mutual agreement—or after the intervention of the Monopolies and Mergers Commission.

Standard conditions of licences

8.—(1) For section 8 of the 1986 Act there shall be substituted the following section—

"Standard conditions of licences

8.—(1) Subject to subsections (2) and (3) and sections 23(2), 26(1A) and 27(2) below, each condition which by virtue of section 8(2) of the Gas Act 1995 is a standard condition for the purposes of—

    (a) licences under section 7 above;
    (b) licences under subsection (1) of section 7A above; or
    (c) licences under subsection (2) of that section,
shall be incorporated (that is to say, incorporated by reference) in each licence under that section or, as the case may be, that subsection.

    (2) Subsection (1) above shall not apply in relation to a licence under section 7A(1) above which authorises only the supply to premises of gas which has been conveyed to the premises otherwise than by a public gas transporter.

    (3) Subject to the following provisions of this section, the Director may, in granting a licence, modify any of the standard conditions to such extent as he considers requisite to meet the circumstances of the particular case.

    (4) Before making any modifications under subsection (3) above, the Director shall give notice—
    (a) stating that he proposes to make the modifications and setting out their effect;
    (b) stating the reasons why he proposes to make the modifications; and
    (c) specifying the time (not being less than 28 days from the date of publication of the notice) within which representations or objections with respect to the proposed modifications may be made,
and shall consider any representations or objections which are duly made and not withdrawn.

    (5) A notice under subsection (4) above shall be given—
    (a) by publishing the notice in such manner as the Director considers appropriate for the purpose of bringing the notice to the attention of persons likely to be affected by the making of the modifications; and
    (b) by sending a copy of the notice to the Secretary of State, to the Health and Safety Executive and to the Council.

    (6) If, within the time specified in the notice under subsection (4) above, the Secretary of State directs the Director not to make any modification, the Director shall comply with the direction.

    (7) The Director shall not make any modifications under subsection (3) above of a condition of a licence under subsection (1) or (2) of section 7A above unless he is of the opinion that the modifications are such that no other holder of such a licence would be unduly disadvantaged in competing with other holders of such licences (including the holder of the licence).

    (8) The modification under subsection (3) above of a condition of a licence shall not prevent so much of the condition as is not so modified being regarded as a standard condition for the purposes of this Part.

    (9) In this section 'modify' includes fail to incorporate and 'modification' shall be construed accordingly."

    (2) Such conditions as may be determined by the Secretary of State before the appointed day, and published by him in such manner as he considers appropriate, in relation to—
    (a) licences under section 7 of the 1986 Act (licensing of public gas transporters);
    (b) licences under subsection (1) of section 7A of that Act (licensing of gas suppliers and gas shippers); or
    (c) licences under subsection (2) of that section;
shall be standard conditions for the purposes of licences under that section or, as the case may be, that subsection.

GENERAL NOTE

    This section deals with standard conditions for licences. It is envisaged that each of the three types of licence will be issued subject to the standard conditions, which will be determined by the

Secretary of State (s.8(2)). The Director is, however, empowered (s.8(1)(4)) to make modifications to the standard conditions as he considers requisite to meet the circumstances of the particular case. Modifications would require that no other holder of that licence type suffers a competitive disadvantage, although there is no requirement that the Director give reasons for granting a modification to the terms. The section accordingly gives considerable discretionary power to the Director.

Miscellaneous

The gas code

9.—(1) After section 8A of the 1986 Act there shall be inserted the following section—

"*The gas code*

The gas code
8B. The provisions of Schedule 2B to this Act (which relate to rights and obligations of licence holders and consumers and related matters) shall have effect."
(2) After Schedule 2A to that Act there shall be inserted, as Schedule 2B, the provisions of Schedule 2 to this Act (the gas code).
(3) Section 15 of and Schedule 5 to that Act (which are superseded by this section) shall cease to have effect.
(4) If the Secretary of State is satisfied that any of the provisions of paragraphs 22 and 27(3) of Schedule 2B to the 1986 Act have been or will be superseded by regulations under section 18 or 18A of that Act, he may by order made by statutory instrument provide that those provisions shall cease to have effect as from such date after the coming into force of the regulations as may be specified in the order.

GENERAL NOTE
This section deals with the Gas Code. It should not be confused with the Network Code to be produced by a public gas transporter. The Gas Code (formerly the "public gas supply code") is updated in line with the licensing arrangements.

Other amendments of Part I of 1986 Act

10.—(1) Schedule 3 to this Act (which contains other amendments of Part I of the 1986 Act) shall have effect.
(2) Subject to subsection (3) below, the provisions of sections 33A to 33E of the 1986 Act (standards of performance) shall cease to have effect at the end of the period of four years beginning with the appointed day.
(3) The Secretary of State may by order provide that subsection (2) above shall have effect as if the period there mentioned ended on such day, not earlier than that on which it would otherwise end and not later than two years after the making of the order, as may be specified in the order.
(4) An order under subsection (3) above may be made so as to apply—
(a) either in relation to all of the provisions mentioned in subsection (2) above or in relation to such of those provisions as may be specified in the order; and
(b) either generally or in relation to gas supply services provided in such areas as may be so specified.

(5) An order under subsection (3) above shall be made by statutory instrument which shall be subject to annulment in pursuance of a resolution of either House of Parliament.

Amendments of Part III of 1986 Act

11.—(1) In subsection (2) of section 62 of the 1986 Act (exclusion of certain agreements from Restrictive Trade Practices Act 1976), for paragraph (b) there shall be substituted the following paragraph—

> "(b) is or was an agreement containing provisions relating to, or to activities connected with, the supply otherwise than under a licence granted under section 7A(1) above of gas won under the authority of a petroleum production licence;".

(2) After subsection (2) of that section there shall be inserted the following subsections—

> "(2A) The said Act of 1976 shall not apply, and shall be deemed never to have applied, to any agreement which—
>> (a) is or was made on or after 2nd March 1995;
>> (b) is or was an agreement containing provisions relating to, or to activities connected with—
>>> (i) the introduction of gas into;
>>> (ii) the taking out of gas from; or
>>> (iii) the use by gas shippers of,
>> a pipe-line system or storage facility operated by a public gas transporter; and
>> (c) is specified, or is of a description specified, in an order made by the Secretary of State and satisfies such conditions as may be so specified.
>
> (2B) Before making an order under subsection (2) or (2A) above, the Secretary of State shall consult the Director and the Director General of Fair Trading."

(3) In subsection (3) of that section—
(a) after the words "subsection (2)" there shall be inserted the words "or (2A)"; and
(b) after the words "the Secretary of State" there shall be inserted the words ", the Director or the Director General of Fair Trading".

(4) In subsection (6) of that section, after the definition of "gas" there shall be inserted the following definitions—

> " 'gas shipper' and 'public gas transporter' have the same meanings as in Part I of this Act;".

(5) Subsection (7) of that section shall cease to have effect.

(6) Section 63 of the 1986 Act (restrictions on use of certain information) shall cease to have effect.

(7) In section 64 of that Act (provisions as to orders), in subsection (2), the words "20(9)" shall cease to have effect.

GENERAL NOTE

This section amends Pt. III of the 1986 Act, excluding certain agreements from the Restrictive Trade Practices Act 1976 (c. 34). The agreements affected relate to the gas supply industry—it is clear that activities under the authority of a petroleum production licence are not covered by this section. In effect, the section removes application of the 1976 Act from the vast majority of gas supply activities.

Acquisition of rights to use gas processing facilities

12.—(1) In the case of any gas processing facility operated otherwise than by a public gas transporter, any person may, after giving the owner of the facility not less than 28 days' notice, apply to the Secretary of State for directions under this section which would secure to the applicant a right to have processed by the facility, during a period specified in the application, quantities so specified of gas which—

(a) is of a kind so specified; and

(b) is of, or of a kind similar to, the kind which the facility is designed to process.

(2) Where an application is made under subsection (1) above, it shall be the duty of the Secretary of State—

(a) to decide whether the application is to be adjourned (so as to enable negotiations or further negotiations to take place), considered further or rejected;

(b) to give notice of his decision to the applicant; and

(c) in the case of a decision that the application is to be considered further, to give to the owner of the facility, to any person who has a right to have gas processed by the facility, and to the Health and Safety Executive, notice that the application is to be so considered and an opportunity of being heard about the matter.

(3) Where, after further considering an application under subsection (1) above, the Secretary of State is satisfied that the giving of directions under this section would not prejudice the efficient operation of the facility, or the processing by the facility of—

(a) the quantities of gas which the owner of the facility or any associate of the owner requires or may reasonably be expected to require to be processed by the facility for the purposes of any business carried on by him; and

(b) the quantities of gas which any person who is not such an associate and has a right to have gas processed by the facility is entitled to require to be so processed in the exercise of that right,

the Secretary of State may give such directions to the owner of the facility.

(4) Directions under this section may—

(a) specify the terms on which the Secretary of State considers the owner of the facility should enter into an agreement with the applicant for all or any of the following purposes—

(i) for securing to the applicant the right to have processed by the facility, during the period specified in the directions and in the quantities so specified, gas which is of a kind so specified;

(ii) for securing that the exercise of that right is not prevented or impeded;

(iii) for regulating the charges which may be made for the processing of gas by virtue of that right;

(iv) for securing to the applicant such ancillary or incidental rights as the Secretary of State considers necessary or expedient, which may include the right to have a pipe-line of his connected to the facility by the owner;

(b) specify the sums or the method of determining the sums which the Secretary of State considers should be paid by way of consideration for any such right; and

(c) require the owner, if the applicant pays or agrees to pay those sums within a period specified in that behalf in the directions, to enter into an agreement with him on the terms so specified.

(5) Section 22 of the 1986 Act (effect of directions) shall apply in relation to any directions under this section as it applies in relation to any directions under section 19 or 21(1) of that Act; and in subsection (4) of that section as applied by this subsection, the reference to the Director shall be construed as a reference to the Secretary of State.

(6) In this section—

"gas" means any substance which is or (if it were in a gaseous state) would be gas within the meaning of Part I of the 1986 Act;

"gas processing facility" means any facility which carries out gas processing operations;

"gas processing operation" means any of the following operations, namely—

    (a) purifying, blending, odorising or compressing gas for the purpose of enabling it to be introduced into a pipe-line system operated by a public gas transporter or to be conveyed to an electricity generating station, a gas storage facility or any place outside Great Britain;

    (b) removing from gas for that purpose any of its constituent gases, or separating from gas for that purpose any oil or water, and

    (c) determining the quantity or quality of gas which is or is to be so introduced, or so conveyed, whether generally or by or on behalf of a particular person,

and "process", in relation to gas, shall be construed accordingly;

"owner", in relation to a gas processing facility, includes a lessee and any person occupying or having control of the facility;

"pipe-line" has the same meaning as in the Pipe-lines Act 1962;

"public gas transporter" has the same meaning as in Part I of the 1986 Act.

(7) For the purposes of this section a person is an associate of the owner of a gas processing facility if—

  (a) both of them are companies; and

  (b) one of the companies has control of the other, or both are under the control of the same person or persons;

and subsections (2) to (5) of section 416 of the Income and Corporation Taxes Act 1988 shall apply for the purposes of paragraph (b) above as they apply for the purposes of Part XI of that Act.

(8) In relation to any time before the appointed day, this section shall have effect as if for the words "public gas transporter", in each place where they occur, there were substituted the words "public gas supplier".

GENERAL NOTE

This section introduces an entirely new concept, that of third party access to gas processing facilities. A shipper or supplier can apply for access to offshore pipelines under the Petroleum and Submarine Pipelines Act 1975 (c. 74), s.23; and to onshore pipelines by virtue of the now amended s.19 of the Gas Act 1986 (or s.10 of the Pipelines Act 1962 (c. 58), depending on owner of the pipeline). Prior to this section, there was no right to seek access to processing facilities. In line with experience of other third party access rights, it is likely that the greatest influence of this section will be to promote agreement—it is only after the failure of negotiations that the section will come into play. The final step in the gas supply process, namely access to gas storage facilities, cannot be obtained under this section but may be sought under the network code agreement with a public gas transporter.

Supplemental

Duty of Director to advise etc.

13. It shall be the duty of the Director General of Gas Supply, where either he considers it expedient or he is requested by the Secretary of State to do so, to give information, advice and assistance to the Secretary of State with respect to any matter in respect of which any function of the Secretary of State under this Act is exercisable.

GENERAL NOTE

This section simply reinforces the independence of the Director, giving him the right to give unsolicited advice or information to the Secretary of State.

Financial provisions

14. There shall be paid out of money provided by Parliament any increase attributable to this Act in the sums payable out of money so provided under any other Act.

Interpretation

15. In this Act—
"the 1986 Act" means the Gas Act 1986;
"the appointed day" means the day appointed under section 18(2) below.

Minor and consequential amendments

16.—(1) The enactments and instrument specified in Schedule 4 to this Act shall have effect subject to the amendments there specified (being minor amendments or amendments consequential on the preceding provisions of this Act).

(2) The Secretary of State may by order make such consequential modifications of any provision contained in any public general Act passed before the appointed day as appear to him necessary or expedient in respect of—
(a) any reference in that provision to a public gas supplier;
(b) any reference in that provision (in whatever terms) to a person authorised to supply gas through pipes by virtue of section 7 or 8 of the 1986 Act; or
(c) any reference in that provision (in whatever terms) to a person carrying on a gas undertaking or to such an undertaking.

(3) The Secretary of State may by order make such consequential modifications of any provision contained in—
(a) any Act passed before the appointed day which is not a public general Act; or
(b) any subordinate legislation (within the meaning of the Interpretation Act 1978) made before that day,
as appear to him necessary or expedient.

(4) An order under subsection (2) or (3) above shall be made by statutory instrument which shall be subject to annulment in pursuance of a resolution of either House of Parliament.

Transitional provisions, savings and repeals

17.—(1) The transitional provisions and savings contained in Schedule 5 to this Act shall have effect; but those provisions and savings are without prejudice to sections 16 and 17 of the Interpretation Act 1978 (effect of repeals).

(2) In that Schedule, unless the context otherwise requires, expressions which are also used in the 1986 Act have the same meanings as in that Act.

(3) The Secretary of State may by order make such other transitional provisions and savings as appear to him necessary or expedient.

(4) An order under subsection (3) above shall be made by statutory instrument which shall be subject to annulment in pursuance of a resolution of either House of Parliament.

(5) The enactments specified in Schedule 6 to this Act are hereby repealed to the extent specified in the third column of that Schedule.

Short title, commencement and extent

18.—(1) This Act may be cited as the Gas Act 1995.
(2) This Act, except—
(a) this section;
(b) sections 8(2), 11(1) to (5), 12 and 13;
(c) section 17(1) and (2) and Schedule 5; and

(d) so far as relating to the repeal of section 62(7) of the 1986 Act, section 17(5) and Schedule 6,

shall come into force on the appointed day, that is to say, such day as the Secretary of State may by order made by statutory instrument under this subsection appoint.

(3) Without prejudice to section 13 of the Interpretation Act 1978 (anticipatory exercise of powers), any power conferred on the Secretary of State or the Director by a provision of this Act which comes into force by virtue of subsection (2) above may be exercised before the appointed day provided that nothing done in the exercise of that power has effect before that day.

(4) Section 12 above shall come into force on such day as the Secretary of State may by order made by statutory instrument under this subsection appoint.

(5) This Act, except—

(a) this section;

(b) subsections (1) to (6) of section 11;

(c) paragraphs 1 to 3, 6, 7, 23 and 30 of Schedule 5 and section 17(1) and (2) so far as relating to those paragraphs; and

(d) Schedule 6 and section 17(5) so far as relating to the repeals of paragraph 1 of Schedule 5 to the Fair Trading Act 1973 and sections 62(7) and 63 of and paragraph 15(4) of Schedule 7 to the 1986 Act,

does not extend to Northern Ireland.

SCHEDULES

Section 3(2)   SCHEDULE 1

[SCHEDULE 2A TO 1986 ACT]

EXCEPTIONS TO PROHIBITION ON UNLICENSED ACTIVITIES

Conveyance or supply by landlords etc.

1. Section 5(1) of this Act is not contravened by a person—

(a) conveying within a building or part of a building in which he has an interest; or

(b) supplying for use in such a building or part of a building,

gas supplied to the building by a person authorised to supply it by or under section 6A or 7A of this Act or this Schedule.

Conveyance or supply to associated companies

2. Section 5(1) of this Act is not contravened by a company conveying or supplying gas to any premises occupied by a subsidiary or holding company of the company, or by a subsidiary of a holding company of the company.

Conveyance or supply of propane or butane

3.—(1) Section 5(1) of this Act is not contravened by a person conveying or supplying to any premises gas which consists wholly or mainly of propane or butane.

(2) In the case of a supply, this paragraph does not apply unless—

(a) the contract for the supply contains provisions empowering a person authorised by the supplier to enter the premises where in his opinion it is necessary to do so for the purpose of averting danger to life or property;

(b) those provisions are in terms approved for the purposes of this paragraph by the Secretary of State; and

(c) the gas is conveyed to the premises otherwise than by a public gas transporter.

Conveyance for supply to large consumers

4. Section 5(1) of this Act is not contravened by a person conveying gas to any premises at any time if they are supplied with gas at a rate which, at any time within the period of 12 months immediately preceding that time, he reasonably expected to exceed 75,000 therms a year.

Supply to very large consumers

5.—(1) Sub-paragraph (2) below applies where a person (in this paragraph referred to as a "supplier") notifies the Director—

(a) that he proposes to undertake a supply of gas to any premises at a rate in excess of 2,000,000 therms a year (in this paragraph referred to as "the required rate"); or

(b) that, in such circumstances as may be described in the notification, he would undertake a supply of gas to any premises, at a rate in excess of the required rate, for such period as may be so described.

(2) Section 5(1) of this Act is not contravened by a supply of gas to the premises (or, as the case may require, a supply of gas to the premises in the circumstances and for the period described in the notification) unless, within six weeks of receiving the notification, the Director notifies the supplier either—

(a) that he is of the opinion that the rate of supply to those premises would be unlikely to exceed the required rate; or

(b) that he is unable to form an opinion as to whether the rate of supply to those premises would or would not be likely to exceed the required rate.

(3) Where a supplier has given the Director a notification under sub-paragraph (1)(a) above and—

(a) the rate of supply to the premises to which the notification relates fails to exceed the required rate for three successive periods of twelve months;

(b) the supplier fails to furnish the Director with such information as he may require for the purpose of determining whether the condition in paragraph (a) above is fulfilled; or

(c) the supplier fails to afford to the Director such facilities as he may require for the purpose of verifying any information furnished in pursuance of such a requirement as is mentioned in paragraph (b) above,

the Director may direct that the supplier's notification shall be treated as invalid for the purposes of that sub-paragraph except as regards gas previously supplied.

(4) As soon as practicable after receiving a notification under sub-paragraph (1) above, giving a notification under sub-paragraph (2) above or giving a direction under sub-paragraph (3) above, the Director shall send a copy of the notification or direction to the Health and Safety Executive.

GENERAL NOTE

The exception to prohibition on unlicensed activities is relevant to s.3 above. This Schedule exempts suppliers within the same building; or to subsidiaries; or to the (specialised) propane or butane markets. It recognises commercial reality. Further, there is an exemption for suppliers to large and very large consumers, where notice must first be given to the Director.

Section 9(2)   SCHEDULE 2

[SCHEDULE 2B TO 1986 ACT]

THE GAS CODE

Preliminary

1.—(1) In this Schedule, unless the context otherwise requires—

"the appointed day" means the day appointed under section 18(2) of the Gas Act 1995;

"connect", in relation to any premises, means connect to a main of a public gas transporter, whether directly or by means of a service pipe, and "disconnect" and "re-connect" have corresponding meanings except that they also include discontinuing or, as the case may be, resuming the conveyance of gas to the premises;

"consumer" means a person who is supplied with gas conveyed to particular premises (in this Schedule referred to as his premises) by a public gas transporter;

"relevant gas supplier" and "relevant gas shipper", in relation to a consumer, mean respectively any gas supplier who is supplying him with gas conveyed to his premises and any gas shipper who has made arrangements in pursuance of which gas is conveyed to those premises.

(2) In so far as the provisions of this Schedule, other than paragraphs 20 to 22 below, apply in relation to a public gas transporter, gas supplier or gas shipper, they shall have effect subject to any conditions of his licence.

Consumption of gas to be ascertained by meter

2.—(1) Every consumer shall take his supply through a meter—
(a) the use of which does not contravene section 17 of this Act; and
(b) which is of a type appropriate for registering the quantity of gas supplied.
(2) In default of the consumer's doing so or agreeing to do so—
(a) the public gas transporter may disconnect or, as the case may be, refuse to connect his premises; and
(b) any relevant gas supplier may cut off the supply of gas to his premises.

Meters to be kept in proper order

3.—(1) Every consumer shall at all times, at his own expense, keep all meters—
(a) which belong to him, or which are lent or hired to him and are owned otherwise than by the public gas transporter or a relevant gas supplier; and
(b) by which the quantity of gas supplied is registered,
in proper order for correctly registering the quantity of gas.
(2) In default of the consumer's doing so—
(a) the public gas transporter may disconnect his premises; and
(b) any relevant gas supplier may cut off the supply of gas to his premises.
(3) In the case of any consumer, the public gas transporter or any relevant gas supplier shall at all times, without charge to the consumer, keep any meter which is owned by him and is lent or hired to the consumer in proper order for correctly registering the quantity of gas supplied.
(4) Sub-paragraph (3) above is without prejudice to any remedy the transporter or supplier may have against the consumer for failure to take proper care of the meter.
(5) In the case of any consumer, the public gas transporter, any relevant gas supplier and any relevant gas shipper—
(a) shall have power to remove, inspect and re-install any meter by which the quantity of gas supplied is registered; and
(b) shall, while any such meter is removed, fix a substitute meter on the premises;
and, subject to sub-paragraph (6) below, the cost of removing, inspecting and reinstalling a meter and of fixing a substitute meter shall be defrayed by the transporter, supplier or shipper.
(6) Where such a meter is removed for the purpose of being examined by a meter examiner in accordance with section 17 of this Act, the expenses incurred in removing, examining and re-installing the meter and fixing a substitute meter shall be defrayed as follows—
(a) if the examination is carried out at the request of any person and the meter is found in proper order, by that person;
(b) if the meter is not so found, by the person required by sub-paragraph (1) or (3) above to keep the meter in proper order.
(7) A meter is found in proper order for the purposes of sub-paragraph (6) above if it is found to register correctly or to register erroneously to a degree not exceeding the degree permitted by regulations under section 17 of this Act.
(8) Nothing in this paragraph shall apply in relation to any meter which, in pursuance of an agreement falling within section 17(14) of this Act, is used for ascertaining the quantity of gas supplied to a consumer if either—
(a) the agreement was entered into before the appointed day; or
(b) the public gas transporter and each relevant gas shipper have agreed that the meter should be kept in proper order by a person other than the consumer.

Meter as evidence of quantity of gas supplied

4.—(1) This paragraph applies where a consumer is supplied with gas through a meter at a rate not exceeding 75,000 therms a year.
(2) Subject to sub-paragraph (3) below, the register of the meter shall be prima facie evidence of the quantity of gas supplied.
(3) Where the meter is found, when examined by a meter examiner appointed under section 17 of this Act, to register erroneously to a degree exceeding the degree permitted by regulations under that section, the meter shall be deemed to have registered erroneously to the degree so

found since the relevant date, except in a case where it is proved to have begun to do so on some later date.

(4) In sub-paragraph (3) above "the relevant date" means—

  (a) the penultimate date on which, otherwise than in connection with the examination, the register of the meter was ascertained; or

  (b) if regulations so provide, such other date as may be determined by or under the regulations.

Installation of meters in new premises etc.

5.—(1) This paragraph applies where a meter is to be used to register the quantity of gas supplied to a consumer and—

  (a) gas has not previously been conveyed by the public gas transporter to the consumer's premises;

  (b) a new or substituted pipe is to be laid between the transporter's main and the meter; or

  (c) the meter is to be installed in a different position.

(2) Subject to sub-paragraph (3) below, the meter shall be installed as near as practicable to the public gas transporter's main, but within a building comprised in the premises.

(3) The meter may be installed otherwise than within a building comprised in the premises if it is installed either—

  (a) in accommodation of a type and construction approved by the public gas transporter by an approval given in relation to premises generally, or to any class or description of premises; or

  (b) in a separate meter house or other accommodation outside a building comprised in the premises which is approved by the transporter in the case of those particular premises.

(4) If the requirements of this paragraph are not complied with, the public gas transporter may refuse to connect or, as the case may be, disconnect the consumer's premises.

Meters for disabled persons

6. Where, in the case of any consumer, the public gas transporter or a relevant gas supplier, for the purpose of meeting the needs of a disabled person—

  (a) alters the position of any gas meter which is owned by the transporter supplier and is lent or hired to the consumer; or

  (b) replaces such a meter with one which has been specially adapted,

the transporter or supplier shall not charge the consumer for the alteration or replacement.

Recovery of gas charges etc.

7.—(1) Sub-paragraphs (3) and (4) below apply where—

  (a) a demand in writing is made by a gas supplier for the payment of any of the charges due to him from a consumer in respect of the supply of gas to the consumer's premises, or to any premises previously owned or occupied by him; and

  (b) the consumer does not pay those charges within 28 days after the making of the demand.

(2) Sub-paragraph (3) below also applies where—

  (a) a request in writing is made by a gas supplier for the provision of a deposit by way of reasonable security for the payment of the charges due to him from a consumer in respect of the supply of gas to the consumer's premises; and

  (b) the consumer does not provide such a deposit, or agree to take his supply through a pre-payment meter, within 7 days after the making of the request.

(3) If the supplier is a relevant supplier, he may, after giving not less than 7 days' notice of his intention—

  (a) cut off the supply to the consumer's premises by disconnecting the service pipe at the meter or by such other means as he thinks fit; and

  (b) recover any expenses incurred in so doing from the consumer.

(4) If—

  (a) the supplier is not a relevant supplier but another supplier ("the new supplier") is such a supplier; and

  (b) the supplier has assigned to the new supplier his right to recover any of the charges due to him from the consumer,

sub-paragraph (3) above shall apply as if any reference to the supplier were a reference to the new supplier.

(5) The powers conferred by sub-paragraphs (3) and (4) above shall not be exercisable as respects any charges or deposit the amount of which is genuinely in dispute.

Deemed contracts in certain cases

8.—(1) Where a gas supplier supplies gas to a consumer otherwise than in pursuance of a contract, the supplier shall be deemed to have contracted with the consumer for the supply of gas as from the time ("the relevant time") when he began so to supply gas to the consumer.

(2) Where—

(a) the owner or occupier of any premises takes a supply of gas which has been conveyed to those premises by a public gas transporter in pursuance of arrangements made with the transporter by a gas shipper, or by a person authorised to make the arrangements by an exemption granted under section 6A of this Act;

(b) that supply is not made by a gas supplier, or by a person authorised to make it by an exemption granted under section 6A of this Act or an exception contained in Schedule 2A to this Act; and

(c) a supply of gas so conveyed has been previously made by a gas supplier,

the owner or occupier shall be deemed to have contracted with the appropriate supplier for the supply of gas as from the time ("the relevant time") when he began to take such a supply; but nothing in this sub-paragraph shall be taken to afford a defence in any criminal proceedings.

(3) In sub-paragraph (2) above "the appropriate supplier" means—

(a) the gas supplier who previously supplied gas to the premises or, if more than one, the gas supplier who last supplied gas to the premises; or

(b) where that supplier's licence has been assigned generally, or has been assigned so far as relating to the premises, the person to whom the licence was so assigned; or

(c) where that supplier's licence has been revoked on his application, or has been so restricted on his application as to exclude the premises, the gas supplier with whom that supplier made arrangements for securing continuity of supply to the premises.

(4) Sub-paragraphs (1) and (2) above shall not apply in any case where gas is supplied or, as the case may be, a supply of gas is taken at a rate which is reasonably expected to exceed 2,500 therms a year.

(5) If a gas supplier at any time so elects, sub-paragraph (4) above shall have effect, so far as relating to him and to supplies begun to be made or taken after that time, as if the reference to 2,500 therms were a reference to 75,000 therms.

(6) If a gas supplier at any time withdraws an election under sub-paragraph (5) above, sub-paragraph (4) above shall have effect, so far as relating to him and to supplies begun to be made or taken after that time, without the modification made by sub-paragraph (5) above.

(7) The express terms and conditions of a contract which, by virtue of sub-paragraph (1) or (2) above, is deemed to have been made shall be provided for by a scheme made under this paragraph.

(8) Each gas supplier shall make, and from time to time revise, a scheme for determining the terms and conditions which are to be incorporated in the contracts which, by virtue of sub-paragraph (1) or (2) above, are to be deemed to have been made; but this sub-paragraph shall not apply in any case where it is reasonably expected that neither of those sub-paragraphs will apply.

(9) The terms and conditions so determined may include terms and conditions for enabling the gas supplier to determine, in any case where the meter is not read immediately before the relevant time, the number of therms or kilowatt hours which are to be treated as supplied to the consumer, or taken by the owner or occupier of the premises, during the period beginning with the relevant time and ending with—

(a) the time when the meter is first read after the relevant time; or

(b) the time when the supplier ceases to supply gas to the consumer, or the owner or occupier ceases to take a supply of gas,

whichever is the earlier.

(10) A scheme under this paragraph may make different provisions for different cases or classes of cases, or for different areas, determined by, or in accordance with, the provisions of the scheme.

(11) As soon as practicable after a gas supplier makes a scheme under this paragraph, a revision of such a scheme, an election under sub-paragraph (5) above or a withdrawal under sub-paragraph (6) above of such an election, he shall—

(a) publish, in such manner as he considers appropriate for bringing it to the attention of persons likely to be affected by it, a notice stating the effect of the scheme, revision, election or withdrawal;

(b) send a copy of the scheme, revision, election or withdrawal to the Director and to the Council; and

(c) if so requested by any other person, send such a copy to that person without charge to him.

Supplies of gas illegally taken

9.—(1) Where any person takes a supply of gas which is in the course of being conveyed by a public gas transporter, the transporter shall be entitled to recover from that person the value of the gas so taken.

(2) Where—

(a) any person at premises which have been reconnected in contravention of paragraph 11(1) below takes a supply of gas which has been conveyed to those premises by the public gas transporter; and

(b) the supply is taken otherwise than in pursuance of a contract made with a gas supplier, or deemed to have been made with such a supplier by virtue of paragraph 8 above or paragraph 19 of Schedule 5 to the Gas Act 1995,

the transporter shall be entitled to recover from that person the value of the gas so taken.

(3) Each public gas transporter shall make, and from time to time revise, a scheme providing for the manner in which, and the persons by whom, the number of therms or kilowatt hours represented by a supply of gas taken in such circumstances as are mentioned in sub-paragraph (1) or (2) above is to be determined for the purposes of that sub-paragraph.

(4) Sub-paragraphs (10) and (11) of paragraph 8 above shall apply in relation to a scheme under this paragraph as they apply in relation to a scheme under that paragraph.

(5) In this paragraph—

"gas supplier" includes a person authorised to supply gas by an exemption granted under section 6A of this Act or an exception contained in Schedule 2A to this Act;

"value", in relation to any gas taken in such circumstances as are mentioned in sub-paragraph (1) or (2) above, means the amount which, if the gas had been taken in such circumstances as are mentioned in sub-paragraph (2) of paragraph 8 above, could reasonably be expected to have been payable in respect of the gas under a contract deemed to have been made by virtue of that sub-paragraph.

Injury to gas fittings and interference with meters

10.—(1) If any person intentionally or by culpable negligence—

(a) injures or allows to be injured any gas fitting provided by a public gas transporter or gas supplier, or any service pipe by which any premises are connected to such a transporter's main;

(b) alters the index to any meter used for measuring the quantity of gas conveyed or supplied by such a transporter or supplier; or

(c) prevents any such meter from duly registering the quantity of gas conveyed or supplied,

he shall be guilty of an offence and liable on summary conviction to a fine not exceeding level 3 on the standard scale.

(2) In the case of any offence under sub-paragraph (1) above, the transporter or supplier may disconnect the premises of, or cut off the supply of gas to, the person so offending.

(3) Where any person is prosecuted for an offence under sub-paragraph (1)(b) or (c) above, the possession by him of artificial means for causing an alteration of the index of the meter or, as the case may be, for preventing the meter from duly registering shall, if the meter was in his custody or under his control, be prima facie evidence that the alteration or prevention was intentionally caused by him.

Restoration of supply without consent

11.—(1) Where a consumer's premises have been disconnected by a public gas transporter, or a supply of gas to a consumer's premises has been cut off by a gas supplier, otherwise than in the exercise of a power conferred by—

(a) paragraph 20, 21 or 22 below;

(b) regulations under section 18(2) or 18A(1) of this Act; or

(c) regulations under section 15 of the Health and Safety at Work etc. Act 1974 (health and safety regulations),

no person shall, without the relevant consent, reconnect the premises or restore the supply.

(2) If any person acts in contravention of sub-paragraph (1) above—

(a) he shall be guilty of an offence and liable on summary conviction to a fine not exceeding level 3 on the standard scale; and

(b) the transporter or supplier may again disconnect the premises or, as the case may be, cut off the supply.

(3) In this paragraph "the relevant consent" means—

(a) where the premises are reconnected, the consent of the public gas transporter to whose main the reconnection is made;

(b) where the supply is restored, the consent of the supplier who cut of the supply, or the consent of a person who is or is about to become a relevant gas supplier.

Failure to notify connection or disconnection of service pipe

12.—(1) No person shall connect any meter with a service pipe through which gas is conveyed to any premises by a public gas transporter, or disconnect any meter from any such pipe, unless he has given—

(a) in a case where gas is supplied to the premises by a relevant gas supplier whose name and address are known to him, to the supplier; and

(b) in any other case, to the transporter,

so that it is received by the supplier or transporter at least 48 hours before he does so, notice in the prescribed form of his intention to do so.

(2) Subject to sub-paragraph (3) below, a notice under sub-paragraph (1) above shall contain—

(a) details of the time and place of the proposed connection or disconnection; and

(b) such other information as may be prescribed.

(3) In so far as it is not reasonably practicable for a notice under sub-paragraph (1) above to contain any information required by sub-paragraph (2)(b) above, it shall be a sufficient compliance with that requirement if the information is given to the relevant gas supplier or, as the case may be, the public gas transporter within 48 hours after the connection or disconnection is effected.

(4) If any person acts in contravention of this paragraph, he shall be guilty of an offence and liable on summary conviction to a fine not exceeding level 3 on the standard scale.

Failure to notify disconnection of meter

13.—(1) Subject to sub-paragraph (2) below, this paragraph applies where any meter through which gas has been supplied to any premises is completely disconnected, that is to say, is disconnected both from the service pipe and from all other pipes within the premises.

(2) This paragraph does not apply where the meter—

(a) is disconnected for the purposes of an examination under section 17 of this Act or an inspection under paragraph 3(5) above; or

(b) is disconnected for a particular purpose (whether repair or repositioning of the meter, detection of a gas leak or otherwise) and is intended to be reconnected.

(3) Except in so far as it is not reasonably practicable for him to do so, the person making the disconnection shall—

(a) ascertain the name and address of the owner of the meter; and

(b) inform that owner of the disconnection and of the address at which the meter will be available for collection.

(4) If any person fails to comply with sub-paragraph (3) above, he shall be guilty of an offence and liable on summary conviction to a fine not exceeding level 2 on the standard scale.

Failure to maintain shipping arrangements

14.—(1) Where—

(a) any arrangements for the conveyance of gas by a public gas transporter to a consumer's premises at a rate reasonably expected to exceed 2,500 therms a year have been made by a gas shipper, or by a person authorised to make the arrangements by an exemption granted under section 6A of this Act; and

(b) those arrangements have ceased to operate and have not been replaced by arrangements made for the like purpose,

the transporter may, after giving 21 days' notice to the relevant persons, disconnect the premises.

(2) The relevant persons for the purposes of sub-paragraph (1) above are—

(a) the occupier, or the owner of the premises if they are unoccupied; and

(b) any gas supplier who, to the knowledge of the transporter, has contracted to supply gas to the premises.

(3) The notice required to be given by sub-paragraphs (1) and (2)(a) above may, in the case of unoccupied premises the owner of which is unknown to the public gas transporter and cannot be ascertained after diligent inquiry, be given by affixing it upon a conspicuous part of the premises.

Maintenance etc. of service pipes

15.—(1) A public gas transporter shall carry out any necessary work of maintenance, repair or renewal of any service pipe by which gas is conveyed by him to a consumer's premises, whether or not the service pipe was supplied and laid at the transporter's expense.

(2) The cost of any work carried out in accordance with sub-paragraph (1) above shall be defrayed as follows—
- (a) if the work was made necessary by any intentional act or culpable negligence of the consumer and the transporter so requires, by the consumer;
- (b) in any other case, by the transporter.

Alterations etc. of burners on change of calorific value

16.—(1) This paragraph applies where there is a change in the properties of any gas which is conveyed by a public gas transporter to a consumer's premises at a rate not exceeding 75,000 therms a year.

(2) It shall be the duty of the public gas transporter to take without charge to the consumer such steps as may be necessary to alter, adjust or replace the burners in appliances at the premises which burn that gas in such manner as to secure that the gas can be burned with safety and efficiency.

Use of antifluctuators and valves

17.—(1) Where a consumer uses gas for working or supplying a compressor, that is to say—
- (a) an engine, gas compressor or other similar apparatus; or
- (b) any apparatus liable to produce in any main of the public gas transporter a pressure less than atmospheric pressure,

he shall, if so required by the transporter by notice, fix in a suitable position and keep in use an appliance provided by him which will effectually prevent pressure fluctuation in the transporter's pipe-line system and any other inconvenience or danger being caused to persons by reason that he and they are supplied with gas conveyed through the same system.

(2) Where a consumer uses for or in connection with the consumption of gas—
- (a) any air at high pressure ("compressed air"); or
- (b) any gaseous substance not conveyed by the public gas transporter ("extraneous gas"),

he shall, if so required by the transporter by notice, fix in a suitable position and keep in use an appliance provided by him which will effectually prevent the admission of the compressed air or extraneous gas into the service pipe or into any main through which gas is conveyed by the transporter.

(3) Where a person is required by this paragraph to keep in use any appliance, he shall at his own expense keep it in proper order and repair, and repair, renew or replace it if it is not in proper order or repair.

(4) A consumer shall not be entitled to use a compressor, or any apparatus for using compressed air or extraneous gas, unless he has given to the public gas transporter not less than 14 days' notice of his intention to do so; but this sub-paragraph shall not apply to the use of any compressor or apparatus which was lawfully in use immediately before the appointed day.

(5) If a consumer makes default in complying with any provision of this paragraph, the public gas transporter may disconnect the consumer's premises.

(6) The public gas transporter shall have power to disconnect, remove, test and replace any appliance which a consumer is required by this paragraph to keep in use, and any expenses incurred by the transporter under this sub-paragraph shall, if the appliance is found in proper order and repair, be paid by the transporter, but otherwise shall be paid by the consumer.

Improper use of gas

18. If a consumer improperly uses or deals with gas so as to interfere with the efficient conveyance of gas by the public gas transporter (whether to the consumer or to any other person), the transporter may, if he thinks fit, disconnect the consumer's premises.

No obligation to restore supply where consumer in default

19.—(1) This paragraph applies where—
- (a) a consumer's premises have been disconnected by a public gas transporter in pursuance of paragraph 2(2)(a), 3(2)(a), 5(4), 10(2) or 11(2)(b), 14(1), 17(5) or 18 above; or

(b) a supply of gas to a consumer's premises has been cut off by a gas supplier in pursuance of paragraph 2(2)(b), 3(2)(b), 7(3) or (4), 10(2) or 11(2)(b) above.

(2) The transporter or supplier shall not be under any obligation to reconnect the consumer's premises or, as the case may be, resume the supply of gas to the consumer's premises until the consumer either is no longer an owner or occupier of the premises or—

(a) has made good the default, or remedied the matter, in consequence of which the premises were disconnected or the supply was cut off; and

(b) has paid the reasonable expenses of disconnecting and reconnecting the premises or, as the case may be, of cutting off the supply and restoring the supply.

(3) In this paragraph "consumer", in relation to a disconnection or cutting off under paragraph 11(2)(b) above, means—

(a) the owner of the premises at the time when the reconnection was made, or the supply was restored, without the relevant consent—

(i) if the premises were unoccupied at that time, or

(ii) if that reconnection or restoration of supply was made by him or on his behalf; and

(b) the occupier of the premises at that time in any other case;

and in this sub-paragraph "relevant consent" has the same meaning as in paragraph 11 above.

Notified escapes of gas

20.—(1) Where any gas escapes from any pipe of a public gas transporter, or from any pipe or other gas fitting used by a consumer to whose premises gas is conveyed by such a transporter, the transporter—

(a) shall, immediately after being informed of the escape, prevent the gas from escaping (whether by disconnecting any premises or otherwise); and

(b) shall take any other steps necessary to avert danger to life or property.

(2) If a public gas transporter—

(a) fails, within 12 hours after being so informed, effectually to prevent the gas from escaping; or

(b) fails to comply with sub-paragraph (1)(b) above,

he shall be guilty of an offence and liable on summary conviction to a fine not exceeding level 3 on the standard scale.

(3) In any proceedings for an offence under sub-paragraph (2)(a) above it shall be a defence for the public gas transporter to prove—

(a) that it was not reasonably practicable for him effectually to prevent the gas from escaping within the said period of 12 hours; and

(b) that he did effectually prevent the escape as soon as it was reasonably practicable for him to do so.

(4) In any proceedings for an offence under sub-paragraph (2)(b) above it shall be a defence for the public gas transporter to prove that he took all such steps to avert danger to life or property as were reasonably practicable.

(5) It shall be the duty of any public gas transporter, gas supplier or gas shipper to take any steps necessary to ensure that, if he is informed by any person ("the informant") of an escape of gas (other than one, in the case of a transporter, that he is required by sub-paragraph (1) above to prevent), he passes the information on, without avoidable delay, either—

(a) to a responsible person, that is to say, a person appearing to him—

(i) to be responsible (whether under that sub-paragraph or otherwise) for preventing the escape; or

(ii) to be a public gas transporter within whose authorised area the gas is escaping; or

(b) to a nominated person, that is to say, a person nominated by a responsible person to receive information about escapes of gas on his behalf.

(6) There shall be a sufficient compliance with sub-paragraph (5) above if the transporter, supplier or shipper is satisfied that the informant—

(a) intends to pass the information on, without avoidable delay, to a nominated person; and

(b) is in a position to do so.

(7) References in sub-paragraphs (5) and (6) above to the passing on of information to a nominated person are references to the passing on of information to that person in such manner (if any) as may be specified by the responsible person by whom that person was nominated.

Suspected escapes of gas

21.—(1) Where a public gas transporter has reasonable cause to suspect that gas conveyed by him which has escaped has entered, or may enter any premises, the transporter shall take any steps necessary to avert danger to life or property.

(2) If a public gas transporter fails to comply with sub-paragraph (1) above, he shall be guilty of an offence and liable on summary conviction to a fine not exceeding level 3 on the standard scale.

(3) In any proceedings for an offence under sub-paragraph (2) above it shall be a defence for the public gas transporter to prove that he took all such steps to avert danger to life or property as were reasonably practicable.

Entry for preventing escapes of gas etc.

22.—(1) Where a public gas transporter has reasonable cause to suspect—
(a) that gas conveyed by him is escaping, or may escape, in any premises; or
(b) that gas so conveyed which has escaped has entered, or may enter, any premises,
any officer authorised by the transporter may, on production of some duly authenticated document showing his authority, enter the premises, inspect the gas fittings, carry out any work necessary to prevent the escape and take any other steps necessary to avert danger to life or property.

(2) Where a public gas transporter has reasonable cause to suspect—
(a) that gas conveyed through pipes by some other person is escaping, or may escape, in any premises in an authorised area of his; or
(b) that gas so conveyed which has escaped has entered, or may enter, any premises in such an area,
any officer authorised by the transporter may, on production of some duly authenticated document showing his authority, enter the premises and take any steps necessary to avert danger to life or property.

(3) In this paragraph any reference to any officer authorised by a public gas transporter includes a reference to any officer authorised by another such transporter with whom the transporter has made arrangements for officers authorised by the other transporter to discharge any functions of the transporter under paragraphs 20 and 21 above.

Entry during continuance of supply

23.—(1) Any officer authorised by a public gas transporter may at all reasonable times, on the production of some duly authenticated document showing his authority, enter a consumer's premises for the purpose of—
(a) inspecting gas fittings;
(b) ascertaining the quantity of gas conveyed to the premises;
(c) exercising the power conferred on the transporter by paragraph 3(5) above;
(d) performing the duty imposed on the transporter by paragraph 15 or 16 above;
(e) exercising the power conferred on the transporter by paragraph 17(6) above; or
(f) in the case of premises where the transporter has reason to believe that a compressor or compressed air or extraneous gas is being used, inspecting the premises and ascertaining whether the provisions of paragraph 17 above are being complied with.

(2) Any officer authorised by a relevant gas supplier or relevant gas shipper may at all reasonable times, on the production of some duly authenticated document showing his authority, enter a consumer's premises for the purpose of—
(a) inspecting gas fittings;
(b) ascertaining the quantity of gas supplied or conveyed to the premises; or
(c) exercising the power conferred on the supplier or shipper by paragraph 3(5) above.

(3) In this paragraph "compressor", "compressed air" and "extraneous gas" have the same meanings as in paragraph 17 above, and any reference to a relevant gas supplier or relevant gas shipper includes a reference to a person who has been or is about to become such a supplier or shipper.

Entry on discontinuance of supply

24.—(1) This paragraph applies where—
(a) a public gas transporter or gas supplier is authorised by any provision of this Act to disconnect any premises, or, as the case may be, to cut off or discontinue the supply of gas to any premises;
(b) a person occupying premises supplied with gas by a gas supplier ceases to require a supply of gas; or

(c) a person entering into occupation of any premises previously supplied with gas by a gas supplier does not take a supply of gas.

(2) Any officer authorised by the public gas transporter or gas supplier, after 24 hours' notice to the occupier, or to the owner of the premises if they are unoccupied, may at all reasonable times, on production of some duly authenticated document showing his authority, enter the premises for the purpose of—

(a) disconnecting the premises, or cutting off or discontinuing the supply of gas to the premises; or

(b) removing any meter or other gas fitting owned by the transporter or supplier.

(3) The notice required to be given by sub-paragraph (2) above may, in the case of unoccupied premises the owner of which is unknown to the public gas transporter or gas supplier and cannot be ascertained after diligent inquiry, be given by affixing it upon a conspicuous part of the premises not less than 48 hours before the premises are entered.

Entry following discontinuance of supply

25.—(1) This paragraph applies where a consumer's premises have been disconnected by a public gas transporter, or a supply of gas to a consumer's premises has been cut off by a gas supplier, otherwise than in the exercise of a power conferred by—

(a) paragraph 20, 21 or 22 above;

(b) regulations under section 18(2) or 18A(1) of this Act; or

(c) regulations under section 15 of the Health and Safety at Work etc. Act 1974 (health and safety regulations).

(2) Any officer authorised by the public gas transporter or gas supplier may at all reasonable times, on production of some duly authenticated document showing his authority, enter the premises for the purpose of ascertaining whether the premises have been reconnected, or the supply has been restored, without the relevant consent.

(3) In this paragraph "the relevant consent" has the same meaning as in paragraph 11 above.

Entry for removing fittings and meters

26.—(1) This paragraph applies where—

(a) a person occupying premises supplied with gas through a meter or other gas fitting owned by a public gas transporter or gas supplier ceases to take a supply through that meter or fitting; or

(b) a person entering into occupation of any premises previously supplied with gas through a meter or other gas fitting so owned does not take a supply of gas through that meter or fitting.

(2) Any officer authorised by the public gas transporter or gas supplier, after 24 hours' notice to the occupier, or to the owner of the premises if they are unoccupied, may at all reasonable times, on production of some duly authenticated document showing his authority, enter the premises for the purpose of removing the meter or other gas fitting.

(3) Sub-paragraph (3) of paragraph 24 above applies for the purposes of this paragraph as it applies for the purposes of that paragraph.

Entry for replacing, repairing or altering pipes

27.—(1) Any officer authorised by a public gas transporter, after 7 clear days' notice to the occupier of any premises, or to the owner of any premises which are unoccupied, may at all reasonable times, on production of some duly authenticated document showing his authority, enter the premises for the purpose of—

(a) placing a new pipe in the place of any existing pipe which has already been lawfully placed; or

(b) repairing or altering any such existing pipe.

(2) The notice required to be given by sub-paragraph (1) above may, in the case of unoccupied premises the owner of which is unknown to the public gas transporter and cannot be ascertained after diligent inquiry, be given by affixing it upon a conspicuous part of the premises.

(3) In cases of emergency arising from defects in any pipes entry may be made under sub-paragraph (1) above without the notice required to be given by that sub-paragraph, but notice of the entry and the justification for it shall then be given as soon as possible after the occurrence of the emergency.

Provisions as to powers of entry

28.—(1) No officer shall be authorised by a public gas transporter, gas supplier or gas shipper to exercise any powers of entry conferred by this Schedule unless—

(a) the transporter, supplier or shipper has taken all reasonable steps to ensure that he is a fit and proper person to exercise those powers; or

(b) in cases of emergency, those powers are powers conferred by paragraph 22 above.

(2) Where in pursuance of any powers of entry conferred by this Schedule, entry is made on any premises by an officer authorised by a public gas transporter, gas supplier or gas shipper—

(a) the officer shall ensure that the premises are left no less secure by reason of the entry; and

(b) the transporter, supplier or shipper shall make good, or pay compensation for, any damage caused by the officer, or by any person accompanying him in entering the premises, in taking any action therein authorised by this Schedule, or in making the premises secure.

(3) Any officer exercising powers of entry conferred by this Schedule may be accompanied by such persons as may be necessary or expedient for the purpose for which the entry is made, or for the purposes of sub-paragraph (2) above.

(4) If any person intentionally obstructs any officer exercising powers of entry conferred by this Schedule, he shall be guilty of an offence and liable on summary conviction to a fine not exceeding level 3 on the standard scale.

(5) The Rights of Entry (Gas and Electricity Boards) Act 1954 (entry under a justice's warrant) shall apply in relation to any powers of entry conferred by this Schedule.

Gas meters and fittings not to be subject to distress

29.—(1) Any gas meter which is connected to a service pipe, and any gas fitting in a consumer's premises which is owned by a public gas transporter or gas supplier and is marked or impressed with a sufficient mark or brand indicating its owner—

(a) shall not be subject to distress or be liable to be taken in execution under process of any court or any proceedings in bankruptcy against the person in whose possession it may be; and

(b) shall be deemed not to be a landlord's fixture, notwithstanding that it may be fixed or fastened to any part of the premises in which it may be situated.

(2) In the application of sub-paragraph (1)(a) above to Scotland, for the word "distress" and the words "in bankruptcy against" there shall be substituted respectively the word "poinding" and the words "for the sequestration of the estate of".

GENERAL NOTE

This Schedule contains details of the Gas Code, referred to in s.9 above. The code mainly deals with technical matters, including metering; disconnection and reconnection; maintenance of service pipes; escapes of gas; entry to premises served by gas supply *etc*. The code is simply updated in line with the revised licensing system.

Section 10(1)   SCHEDULE 3

OTHER AMENDMENTS OF PART I OF 1986 ACT

Assignment of licences

1. After section 8 of the 1986 Act there shall be inserted the following section—

"Assignment of licences

8AA.—(1) A licence shall be capable of being assigned either generally or—

(a) in the case of a licence under section 7 above, so far as relating to the whole or any part of an authorised area or any specified pipe-line system;

(b) in the case of a licence under section 7A above, so far as relating to any specified premises,

but only if it includes a condition authorising such assignment.

In this subsection 'specified' means specified in the licence, or of a description, or situated in an area, so specified.

(2) A licence shall not be capable of being assigned except with the consent of the Director.

(3) In deciding whether to give his consent under subsection (2) above, the Director shall apply the same criteria as he would apply if—

(a) in the case of a general assignment, he were deciding whether to grant a corresponding licence to the assignee;

(b) in the case of any other assignment, he were deciding whether—

(i) to grant to the assignee a licence corresponding to so much of the licence as is proposed to be assigned; and

(ii) to grant to the assignor a licence corresponding to so much of the licence as is proposed to be retained.

(4) Subject to subsection (5) below, a consent under subsection (2) above may be given subject to compliance with—

    (a) such modification or other conditions as the Director considers necessary or expedient for the purpose of protecting the interests of consumers; and

    (b) such incidental or consequential modification conditions as he considers necessary or expedient,

and in the case of an assignment other than a general assignment, modification conditions may make as respects so much of the licence as is proposed to be retained by the assignor provision different from that made as respects so much of the licence as is proposed to be assigned.

(5) The Director shall—

    (a) give the Health and Safety Executive not less than 28 days' notice of any proposal of his to give a consent under subsection (2) above; and

    (b) give that Executive and the Secretary of State not less than 28 days' notice of any proposal of his to impose a modification condition;

and if, before the expiry of the time specified in a notice given to the Secretary of State under paragraph (b) above, the Secretary of State directs the Director not to impose the condition, the Director shall comply with the direction.

(6) A licence may include conditions which must be complied with before the licence can be assigned.

(7) An assignment, or purported assignment, of a licence shall be void—

    (a) if the licence is not capable of assignment;

    (b) if the assignment, or purported assignment, is in breach of a condition of the licence; or

    (c) if there has, before the assignment or purported assignment, been a contravention of a condition subject to compliance with which the consent required by subsection (2) above is given.

(8) A licence shall not be capable of being assigned under or by virtue of any other provision of this Act.

(9) In this section—

    'assignment' includes any form of transfer and cognate expressions shall be construed accordingly;

    'modification condition' means a condition requiring or otherwise providing for the making of modifications to the conditions of a licence.

(10) Any reference in this section to 'assignment' shall be construed in Scotland as a reference to assignation."

Modification or removal of certain limits

2.—(1) In subsection (1) of section 8A of the 1986 Act (modification or removal of the 25,000 therm limits), for the words "section 4(2)(d) or 8(5)(b) above or section 10(5) or 14(3) or (4)(b) below" there shall be substituted the words "section 10(8) or (12) below, paragraph 4 of Schedule 2A to this Act or paragraph 4, 8 or 16 of Schedule 2B to this Act".

(2) Subsections (3) and (4) of that section shall cease to have effect.

Powers and duties of public gas transporters

3. For section 9 of the 1986 Act there shall be substituted the following section—

"Powers and duties of public gas transporters

General powers and duties

9.—(1) It shall be the duty of a public gas transporter as respects each authorised area of his—

    (a) to develop and maintain an efficient and economical pipe-line system for the conveyance of gas; and

    (b) subject to paragraph (a) above, to comply, so far as it is economical to do so, with any reasonable request for him to connect to that system, and convey gas by means of that system to, any premises.

(2) It shall also be the duty of a public gas transporter to avoid any undue preference or undue discrimination—

    (a) in the connection of premises to any pipe-line system operated by him; or

    (b) in the terms on which he undertakes the conveyance of gas by means of such a system.

(3) The following provisions shall have effect, namely—

    (a) Schedule 3 to this Act (which provides for the acquisition of land by public gas transporters); and

(b) Schedule 4 to this Act (which relates to the breaking up of streets and bridges by such transporters)."

Duty to connect certain premises

4. For section 10 of the 1986 Act there shall be substituted the following section—

"Duty to connect certain premises

10.—(1) Subsection (2) below applies to any premises in an authorised area of a public gas transporter which—

(a) are situated within 23 metres from a relevant main of the transporter; or

(b) could be connected to any such main by a pipe supplied and laid, or proposed to be supplied and laid, by the owner or occupier of the premises.

(2) Subject to the provisions of this Part and any regulations made under those provisions, a public gas transporter shall, on being required to do so by the owner or occupier of any premises to which this subsection applies—

(a) in the case of premises falling within paragraph (a) of subsection (1) above, connect the premises to the relevant main, and supply and lay any pipe that may be necessary for that purpose; and

(b) in the case of premises falling within paragraph (b) of that subsection, connect the premises to the relevant main by the pipe there mentioned;

and in the following provisions of this section 'connect', in relation to any premises, means connect to a relevant main of a public gas transporter and 'connection' shall be construed accordingly.

(3) Subject to the provisions of this Part and any regulations made under those provisions, where any premises are connected (whether by virtue of subsection (2) above or otherwise), the public gas transporter shall maintain the connection until such time as it is no longer required by the owner or occupier of the premises.

(4) Where any person requires a connection in pursuance of subsection (2) above, he shall serve on the public gas transporter a notice specifying—

(a) the premises in respect of which the connection is required; and

(b) the day (not being earlier than a reasonable time after the service of the notice) upon which the connection is required to be made.

(5) Where any pipe is supplied and laid by a public gas transporter in pursuance of subsection (2)(a) above, the cost of supplying and laying the pipe shall, if and to the extent that the transporter so requires and the conditions of his licence so allow, be defrayed by the person requiring the connection.

(6) Where at any time a public gas transporter connects any premises under subsection (2)(b) above—

(a) the pipe supplied and laid by the owner or occupier of the premises; and

(b) any rights of the owner or occupier which relate to the laying, maintenance, repair, alteration or removal of the pipe,

shall at that time vest in and become property or rights of the transporter.

(7) The Director may, with the consent of the Secretary of State, make provision by regulations for entitling a public gas transporter to require a person requiring a connection in pursuance of subsection (2) above to pay to the transporter an amount in respect of the expenses of the laying of the main used for the purpose of making that connection if—

(a) the connection is required within the prescribed period after the laying of the main;

(b) a person for the purpose of connecting whose premises the main was laid has made a payment to the transporter in respect of those expenses;

(c) the amount required does not exceed any amount paid in respect of those expenses by such a person or by any person previously required to make a payment under the regulations; and

(d) the transporter has not recovered those expenses in full.

(8) Nothing in subsection (2) or (3) above shall be taken as requiring a public gas transporter to connect, or maintain the connection of, any premises if the supply of gas to those premises is likely to exceed 75,000 therms in any period of twelve months.

(9) Nothing in subsection (2) or (3) above shall be taken as requiring a public gas transporter to connect, or to maintain the connection of, any premises if—

(a) he is prevented from doing so by circumstances not within his control;

(b) circumstances exist by reason of which his doing so would or might involve danger to the public, and he has taken all such steps as it was reasonable to take both to prevent the circumstances from occurring and to prevent them from having that effect; or

(c) in the case of premises falling within paragraph (b) of subsection (1) above, the pipe supplied and laid by the owner or occupier of the premises is not fit for the purpose.

(10) Where—

(a) any person requires a connection to be made or maintained in pursuance of subsection (2) or (3) above;

(b) the making or maintenance of the connection would involve a new or increased supply of gas to the premises in question;

(c) the public gas transporter reasonably expects that, if the connection were made or maintained, gas would be supplied to the premises in question at a rate exceeding 2,500 therms a year; and

(d) the new or increased supply is such that the connection cannot be made or maintained without the laying of a new main, or the enlarging of an existing main, or the construction or enlarging of any other works required for the conveyance of gas,

the transporter may, if he thinks fit, refuse to make or maintain the connection unless that person enters into a written contract with the transporter to make such payments to him as he may reasonably require having regard to the expense to be incurred in laying or enlarging the main or constructing or enlarging the other works and the extent to which it is reasonable to expect that the transporter will recover that expense from elsewhere.

(11) If and to the extent that regulations made by the Director with the consent of the Secretary of State so provide, subsection (10) above shall have effect as if—

(a) the reference in paragraph (d) to the laying of a new main, the enlarging of an existing main or the construction or enlarging of any other works required for the conveyance of gas included a reference to a new main which had previously been laid, an existing main which had previously been enlarged or any other works required for the conveyance of gas which had previously been constructed or enlarged;

(b) the reference to the expense to be incurred in laying or enlarging the main or constructing or enlarging the other works included a reference to the expense which had been so incurred; and

(c) the reference to the extent to which it is reasonable to expect that the transporter will recover that expense from elsewhere included a reference to the extent to which the transporter had been able so to recover that expense.

(12) Subject to subsection (13) below, in this section 'relevant main', in relation to a public gas transporter, means any distribution main in his authorised area which is being used for the purpose of giving a supply of gas to any premises in that area at a rate not exceeding 75,000 therms a year.

(13) Any pipe which—

(a) vests in and becomes the property of a public gas transporter by virtue of subsection (6) above; and

(b) apart from this subsection, would be a relevant main for the purposes of this section,

shall be such a main if, and only if, it has been declared to be such a main by the transporter.

(14) A public gas transporter shall make a declaration under subsection (13) above in respect of each pipe falling within that subsection which is fit for the purpose of being a relevant main; and a declaration under that subsection shall not be capable of being revoked."

Power to require security

5. For section 11 of the 1986 Act there shall be substituted the following section—

"Power to require security

11.—(1) Where any person requires a connection in pursuance of paragraph (a) of section 10(2) above and a pipe falls to be supplied and laid by the public gas transporter in pursuance of that paragraph—

(a) the transporter may require that person to give him reasonable security for the payment to him of all money which may become due to him in respect of the supply and laying of the pipe; and

(b) if that person fails to give such security or, where any security given by him has become invalid or insufficient, fails to provide alternative or additional security, the transporter may if he thinks fit refuse to supply and lay the pipe for so long as the failure continues.

(2) Where any amount is deposited with a public gas transporter by way of security in pursuance of this section, the transporter shall pay interest on that amount, at such rate as may from time to time be fixed by the transporter with the approval of the Director, in respect of the period during which it remains in the hands of the transporter.

(3) In this section 'connection' shall be construed in accordance with section 10(2) above."

Methods of calculating therms

6. For section 12 of the 1986 Act there shall be substituted the following section—

"*Gas conveyed by public gas transporters*

Methods of calculating therms

12.—(1) Except in prescribed cases, the number of therms or kilowatt hours conveyed by a public gas transporter to premises, or to pipe-line systems operated by other public gas transporters, shall be calculated in the prescribed manner—

    (a) on the basis of calorific values of the gas determined by the transporter in accordance with regulations under this section, or so determined by another public gas transporter and adopted by the transporter in accordance with such regulations; or

    (b) if and to the extent that regulations under this section so provide and the transporter thinks fit, on the basis of declared calorific values of the gas;

and regulations under this section shall be made by the Director with the consent of the Secretary of State.

(2) In this Part—

    'calorific value', in relation to any gas, means the number of megajoules (gross) which would be produced by—

        (a) the combustion of one cubic metre of the gas measured at a temperature of 15°C and a pressure of 1013.25 millibars; or

        (b) if regulations under this section so provide, the combustion of one kilogram of the gas,

    containing in either case, if the Director so determines, such an amount of water vapour as is specified in the determination;

    'declared calorific value', in relation to any gas conveyed by a public gas transporter, means a calorific value declared by the transporter in accordance with regulations under this section, or so declared by another public gas transporter and adopted by the transporter in accordance with such regulations.

(3) Regulations under this section may make provision as to the manner in which prescribed information with respect to the making of calculations in accordance with the regulations is to be made available to other licence holders and to the public.

(4) Regulations under this section made for the purposes of subsection (1)(a) above may make provision—

    (a) for requiring determinations of calorific values of gas conveyed by public gas transporters to be made on the basis of samples of gas taken at such places or premises, at such times and in such manner as the Director may direct;

    (b) for requiring such determinations to be made at such places or premises, at such times and in such manner as the Director may direct;

    (c) as to the manner in which the results of such determinations are to be made available to other licence holders and to the public;

    (d) for requiring such premises, apparatus and equipment as the Director may direct to be provided and maintained by public gas transporters for the purpose of making such determinations;

    (e) for requiring public gas transporters to carry out tests of apparatus and equipment so provided and maintained by them; and

    (f) for requiring the results of such tests to be notified to the Director or to any person appointed under section 13(1) below, and to be made available to other licence holders and to the public.

(5) Regulations under this section made for the purposes of subsection (1)(b) above may make provision—

    (a) for requiring declarations of calorific values of gas conveyed by public gas transporters to be made at such times and in such manner as the Director may direct;

    (b) as to the times when such declarations are to take effect, and as to the manner in which the calorific values declared are to be made available to other licence holders and to the public;

    (c) for imposing requirements on public gas transporters as to the correlation between—

        (i) the calorific values of the gas conveyed by them for any period; and

        (ii) the calorific values declared by them for that period;
- (d) for requiring public gas transporters to carry out tests of gas for the purpose of ascertaining whether they are complying with the requirements of regulations made by virtue of paragraph (c) above;
- (e) for requiring such tests to be carried out at such places or premises, at such times and in such manner as the Director may direct; and
- (f) for requiring the results of such tests to be notified to the Director or to any person appointed under section 13(1) below, and to be made available to other licence holders and to the public.

(6) Subject to subsection (7) below, the Director may by notice in writing require a public gas transporter to give to the Director, or to any person appointed by him for the purpose, within such time and at such place as may be specified in the notice, such information as the Director may reasonably require for the purpose of making regulations under this section or section 13 below or of giving directions under such regulations.

(7) A public gas transporter shall not be required under subsection (6) above to give any information which he could not be compelled to give in evidence in civil proceedings before the court; and in this subsection 'the court' means—
- (a) in relation to England and Wales, the High Court;
- (b) in relation to Scotland, the Court of Session."

Calorific values: tests of apparatus etc.

7. For section 13 of the 1986 Act there shall be substituted the following section—

"Calorific values: tests of apparatus etc.

13.—(1) The Director shall appoint competent and impartial persons—
- (a) to carry out tests of apparatus and equipment provided and maintained by public gas transporters in pursuance of regulations made by virtue of subsection (4)(d) of section 12 above for the purpose of ascertaining whether they comply with the regulations;
- (b) to carry out tests of gas conveyed by public gas transporters where the number of therms or kilowatt hours falls to be calculated in accordance with subsection (1)(b) of that section for the purpose of ascertaining whether the transporters are complying with the requirements of regulations made by virtue of subsection (5)(c) of that section; and
- (c) generally to assist the Director in exercising his functions under, or under regulations made under, this section or that section.

(2) Regulations under this section, which shall be made by the Director with the consent of the Secretary of State, may make provision—
- (a) for requiring such tests as are mentioned in subsection (1)(b) above to be carried out at such places or premises as the Director may direct;
- (b) for requiring such premises, apparatus and equipment as the Director may direct to be provided and maintained by public gas transporters for the purpose of carrying out such tests;
- (c) for requiring samples of gas to be taken by public gas transporters at such places or premises, at such times and in such manner as the Director may direct; and
- (d) for requiring samples of gas so taken to be provided by public gas transporters, for the purpose of carrying out such tests, at such places or premises, at such times and in such manner as the Director may direct.

(3) Regulations under this section may make provision—
- (a) for persons representing the public gas transporter concerned to be present during the carrying out of such tests as are mentioned in subsection (1) above;
- (b) as to the manner in which the results of such tests are to be made available to other licence holders and to the public; and
- (c) for conferring powers of entry on property owned or occupied by public gas transporters for the purpose of carrying out such tests and otherwise for the purposes of this section or section 12 above.

(4) There shall be paid out of money provided by Parliament to persons appointed under subsection (1) above who are members of the Director's staff such remuneration and such allowances as may be determined by the Director with the approval of the Treasury, and such pensions as may be so determined may be paid out of money provided by Parliament to or in respect of such persons.

(5) Every person who is a public gas transporter during any period shall pay to the Director such proportion (if any) as the Director may determine of—
- (a) any sums paid by him under subsection (4) above in respect of that period; and

(b) such part of his other expenses for that period as he may with the consent of the Treasury determine to be attributable to his functions under section 12 above or this section;

and any liability under this subsection to pay to the Director sums on account of pensions (whether paid by him under subsection (4) above or otherwise) shall, if the Director so determines, be satisfied by way of contributions calculated, at such rate as may be determined by the Treasury, by reference to remuneration.

(6) Any sums received by the Director under this section shall be paid into the Consolidated Fund."

Fixing of tariffs

8. Section 14 of the 1986 Act (fixing of tariffs) shall cease to have effect.

Determination of disputes

9. Section 14A of the 1986 Act (which is superseded by paragraph 26 below) shall cease to have effect.

Billing disputes

10.—(1) In subsection (2) of section 15A of the 1986 Act (billing disputes), for the words "public gas supplier and a tariff customer" there shall be substituted the words "gas supplier and a domestic customer".

(2) In subsection (8) of that section—
(a) for the words "public gas supplier" there shall be substituted the words "gas supplier"; and
(b) for the words "tariff customer" there shall be substituted the words "domestic customer".

(3) After subsection (9) of that section there shall be inserted the following subsection—

"(10) In this Part 'domestic customer' means a person who is supplied by a gas supplier with gas conveyed to particular premises at a rate which is reasonably expected not to exceed 2,500 therms a year."

Promotion of efficient use of gas

11. Section 15B of the 1986 Act (which is superseded by paragraph 36 below) shall cease to have effect.

Standards of quality

12. For section 16 of the 1986 Act there shall be substituted the following section—

"Gas conveyed by public gas transporters and others

Standards of quality

16.—(1) The Director—
(a) shall, after consultation with public gas transporters and with the consent of the Secretary of State, by regulations prescribe standards of pressure and purity to be complied with by public gas transporters in conveying gas to premises; and
(b) may, after such consultation and with such consent, so prescribe other standards with respect to the properties, condition and composition of gas so conveyed.

(2) The Director—
(a) shall, after consultation with such persons and organisations as he considers appropriate and with the consent of the Secretary of State, by regulations prescribe standards of pressure and purity to be complied with by persons in supplying to premises gas which is conveyed through pipes to the premises otherwise than by a public gas transporter or in accordance with paragraph 1 of Schedule 2A to this Act; and
(b) may, after such consultation and with such consent, so prescribe other standards with respect to the properties, condition and composition of such gas so supplied.

(3) The Director shall appoint competent and impartial persons to carry out tests of—
(a) gas which is conveyed by a public gas transporter; and
(b) gas which is supplied by any person (a 'relevant supplier') to premises and is conveyed through pipes to the premises otherwise than by such a transporter or in accordance with paragraph 1 of Schedule 2A to this Act,

for the purpose of ascertaining whether it conforms with the standards prescribed under this section.

(4) Regulations under this section may make provision—

(a) for requiring such tests to be carried out at such places as the Director may direct;

(b) for requiring such premises, apparatus and equipment as the Director may direct to be provided and maintained by public gas transporters and relevant suppliers for the purpose of carrying out such tests;

(c) for persons representing the public gas transporter or relevant supplier concerned to be present during the carrying out of such tests;

(d) for the manner in which the results of such tests are to be made available to the public; and

(e) for conferring powers of entry on property of public gas transporters and relevant suppliers for the purpose of deciding where tests are to be carried out and otherwise for the purposes of this section.

(5) There shall be paid out of money provided by Parliament to persons appointed under subsection (3) above who are members of the Director's staff such remuneration and such allowances as may be determined by the Director with the approval of the Treasury, and such pensions as may be so determined may be paid out of money provided by Parliament to or in respect of those persons.

(6) Every person who is a public gas transporter or relevant supplier during any period shall pay to the Director such proportion (if any) as the Director may determine of—

(a) any sums paid by him under subsection (5) above in respect of that period; and

(b) such part of his other expenses for that period as he may with the consent of the Treasury determine to be attributable to his functions in connection with the testing of gas for the purposes of this section;

and any liability under this subsection to pay to the Director sums on account of pensions (whether paid by him under subsection (5) above or otherwise) shall, if the Director so determines, be satisfied by way of contributions calculated, at such rate as may be determined by the Treasury, by reference to remuneration.

(7) Any sums received by the Director under this section shall be paid into the Consolidated Fund."

Meter testing and stamping

13. For section 17 of the 1986 Act there shall be substituted the following section—

"Meter testing and stamping

17.—(1) No meter shall be used for the purpose of ascertaining the quantity of gas supplied through pipes to any person unless it is stamped either by, or on the authority of, a meter examiner appointed under this section or in such other manner as may be authorised by regulations under this section.

(2) Subject to subsections (3) to (5) below, it shall be the duty of a meter examiner who is a member of the Director's staff, on being required to do so by any person and on payment of the requisite fee—

(a) to examine any meter used or intended to be used for ascertaining the quantity of gas supplied to any person; and

(b) to stamp, or authorise the stamping of, that meter.

(3) A meter examiner shall not stamp, or authorise the stamping of, any meter unless he is satisfied that it is of such pattern and construction and is marked in such manner as is approved by the Director and that the meter conforms with such standards as may be prescribed for the purposes of this subsection.

(4) A meter examiner may stamp or authorise another person to stamp a meter, notwithstanding that he has not himself examined it, if—

(a) the meter was manufactured or repaired by the person submitting it to the examiner;

(b) that person has obtained the consent of the Director to his submission; and

(c) any conditions subject to which the consent was given have been satisfied.

(5) A meter examiner may authorise another person to stamp a meter, notwithstanding that he has not himself examined it, if—

(a) the meter was manufactured or repaired by that person;

(b) that person has obtained the consent of the Director to his stamping of the meter; and

(c) any conditions subject to which the consent was given have been satisfied.

(6) The Director shall appoint competent and impartial persons as meter examiners for the purposes of this section.

(7) There shall be paid out of money provided by Parliament to meter examiners who are members of the Director's staff such remuneration and such allowances as may be deter-

mined by the Director with the approval of the Treasury, and such pensions as may be so determined may be paid out of money provided by Parliament to or in respect of such examiners.

(8) All fees payable to meter examiners who are members of the Director's staff for the performance of functions conferred by or under this section shall be paid to the Director; and any sums received by him under this subsection shall be paid into the Consolidated Fund.

(9) Regulations under this section, which shall be made by the Director with the consent of the Secretary of State, may make provision—

(a) for re-examining meters already stamped, and for the cancellation of stamps in the case of meters which no longer conform with the prescribed standards and in such other circumstances as may be prescribed;

(b) for requiring meters to be periodically overhauled; and

(c) for the revocation of any approval given by the Director to any particular pattern or construction of meter, and for requiring existing meters of that pattern or construction to be replaced within such period as may be prescribed for the purposes of this subsection.

(10) The fees to be paid to meter examiners who are members of the Director's staff for the performance of functions conferred by or under this section, and the persons by whom they are to be paid, shall be such as the Director may with the approval of the Treasury, from time to time determine, and a determination under this subsection may—

(a) make different provision for different areas or in relation to different cases or different circumstances; and

(b) make such supplementary, incidental or transitional provision as the Director considers necessary or expedient.

(11) If any person supplies gas through a meter which has not been stamped under this section, he shall be guilty of an offence and liable on summary conviction to a fine not exceeding level 3 on the standard scale.

(12) Where the commission by any person of an offence under subsection (11) above is due to the act or default of some other person, that other person shall be guilty of the offence; and a person may be charged with and convicted of the offence by virtue of this subsection whether or not proceedings are taken against the first-mentioned person.

(13) In any proceedings for an offence under subsection (11) above it shall be a defence for the person charged to prove that he took all reasonable steps and exercised all due diligence to avoid committing the offence.

(14) The preceding provisions of this section shall not have effect in relation to the supply of gas to a person under any agreement providing for the quantity of gas supplied to him to be ascertained by a meter designed for rates of flow which, if measured at a temperature of 15°C and a pressure of 1013.25 millibars, would exceed 1600 cubic metres an hour.

(15) Regulations under this section may provide that subsection (14) above shall have effect as if for the number of cubic metres an hour which is for the time being applicable for the purposes of that subsection there were substituted such lower number of cubic metres an hour as the Director considers appropriate."

Safety regulations

14.—(1) In subsection (2) of section 18 of the 1986 Act (safety regulations)—

(a) in paragraph (a), after the words "gas fitting, or" there shall be inserted the words "any part of the gas system on the premises, that is to say," and after the words "used for the" there shall be inserted the words "conveyance or"; and

(b) in paragraph (c), for the words from "gas supply system" to the end there shall be substituted the words "gas system on the premises, or disconnect the premises or, if the premises are not connected, to signify the refusal of the relevant authority to convey gas or, as the case may be, allow gas to be conveyed to the premises".

(2) In subsection (4) of that section—

(a) in paragraph (a), for the words "part of any gas supply system" there shall be substituted the words "any part of any gas system";

(b) in paragraph (b), for the words "restoring the supply of gas to any premises where it has been cut off there shall be substituted the words "reconnecting any premises which have been disconnected"; and

(c) in paragraph (c), for the word "supplied" there shall be substituted the word "conveyed" and for the words "give or, as the case may be, allow a supply" there shall be substituted the words "convey gas or, as the case may be, allow gas to be conveyed".

(3) In subsection (8) of that section, for paragraphs (a) and (b) there shall be substituted the words "any reference to a gas operator were a reference to the relevant authority".

(4) For subsection (9) of that section there shall be substituted the following subsections—

"(9) In this section 'the relevant authority'—

(a) in relation to dangers arising from the conveyance of gas by a public gas transporter, or from the use of gas conveyed by such a transporter, means that transporter; and

(b) in relation to dangers arising from the conveyance of gas by a person other than a public gas transporter, or from the use of gas conveyed by such a person, means the Secretary of State.

(10) Where the relevant authority is a public gas transporter, any reference in this section to any officer authorised by the authority includes a reference to any officer authorised by another such transporter with whom the authority has made arrangements for officers authorised by the other transporter to discharge any functions of the authority under this section.

(11) Except in cases of emergency, no officer shall be authorised by a public gas transporter to exercise any powers of entry conferred by regulations under this section unless the transporter has taken all reasonable steps to ensure that he is a fit and proper person to exercise those powers."

Gas escape regulations

15. After section 18 of the 1986 Act there shall be inserted the following section—

"Gas escape regulations

18A.—(1) The Secretary of State may by regulations make provision—

(a) for empowering any officer authorised by a public gas transporter, if the transporter has reasonable cause to suspect—

(i) that gas conveyed by the transporter is escaping, or may escape, in any premises; or

(ii) that gas so conveyed which has escaped has entered, or may enter, any premises,

to enter the premises, to carry out any work necessary to prevent the escape of gas and to take any other steps necessary to avert danger to life or property; and

(b) for empowering any officer so authorised, if the transporter has reasonable cause to suspect—

(i) that gas conveyed through pipes by some other person is escaping, or may escape, in any premises; or

(ii) that gas so conveyed which has escaped has entered, or may enter, any premises,

to enter the premises and take any steps necessary to avert danger to life or property.

(2) Subsections (5) to (7) and (11) of section 18 above shall apply for the purposes of this section as if—

(a) any reference to subsection (2) of that section were a reference to subsection (1) above;

(b) any reference to the relevant authority were a reference to a public gas transporter;

(c) any reference to subsection (5) of that section were a reference to that subsection as applied by this subsection; and

(d) the reference in subsection (11) of that section to regulations under that section were a reference to regulations under this section.

(3) The Rights of Entry (Gas and Electricity Boards) Act 1954 (entry under a justice's warrant) shall apply in relation to any powers of entry conferred by regulations made under subsection (1) above.

(4) Any reference in this section to any officer authorised by a public gas transporter includes a reference to any officer authorised by another such transporter with whom the transporter has made arrangements for officers authorised by the other transporter to discharge any functions under this section of officers authorised by the transporter."

Acquisition of rights to use pipe-line systems

16. For section 19 of the 1986 Act there shall be substituted the following section—

"Use by other persons of public gas transporter's pipe-line systems"

Acquisition of rights to use pipe-line systems

19.—(1) In the case of a pipe-line system operated by a public gas transporter, any person may, after giving the transporter not less than 28 days' notice, apply to the Director for directions under this section which would secure to the applicant a right of a description specified in the application to have conveyed by the system gas which—

(a) is of a kind so specified; and

(b) is of, or of a kind similar to, the kind which the system is designed to convey.

(2) Where an application is made under subsection (1) above, it shall be the duty of the Director—

(a) to decide whether the application is to be adjourned (so as to enable negotiations or further negotiations to take place), considered further or rejected;

(b) to give notice of his decision to the applicant;

(c) in the case of a decision that the application is to be considered further, to give to the transporter, to the Health and Safety Executive and to any person who has a right to have gas conveyed by the pipe-line system, notice that the application is to be so considered and an opportunity of being heard about the matter.

(3) Where, after further considering an application under subsection (1) above, the Director is satisfied that the giving of directions under this section would not prejudice the efficient operation of the pipe-line system, or the conveyance by the system of—

(a) the quantities of gas which the public gas transporter requires or may reasonably be expected to require to be conveyed by the system to enable the transporter to comply with the conditions of his licence and to perform his contractual obligations;

(b) the quantities of gas which any person who has a right to have gas conveyed by the system is entitled to require to be so conveyed in the exercise of that right,

the Director may give such directions to the transporter.

(4) Directions under this section may—

(a) specify the terms on which the Director considers the public gas transporter should enter into an agreement with the applicant for all or any of the following purposes—

(i) for securing to the applicant the right to have conveyed by the pipe-line system, for the period specified in the directions and in the quantities so specified or determined by or under the directions, gas which is of a kind so specified;

(ii) for securing that the exercise of that right is not prevented or impeded;

(iii) for regulating the charges which may be made for the conveyance of gas by virtue of that right;

(iv) for securing to the applicant such ancillary or incidental rights as the Director considers necessary or expedient, which may include the right to have a pipe-line of his connected to the pipe-line system by the transporter;

(b) specify the sums or the method of determining the sums which the Director considers should be paid by way of consideration for any such right; and

(c) require the transporter, if the applicant pays or agrees to pay those sums within a period specified in that behalf in the directions, to enter into an agreement with him on the terms so specified.

(5) In giving any directions under this section, the Director shall apply the principle that the public gas transporter should be entitled to receive by way of charges for the conveyance of gas by virtue of the right—

(a) the appropriate proportion of the costs incurred by the transporter in administering, maintaining and operating his pipe-line system; and

(b) a return equal to the appropriate proportion of the return received by the transporter (otherwise than by virtue of the right) on the capital value of the system (including so much of that return as is set aside to meet the need from time to time to renew the system).

(6) In subsection (5) above 'the appropriate proportion' means such proportion as properly—

(a) reflects the use made of the public gas transporter's pipe-line system by virtue of the right as compared with the use made of that system for other purposes; and

(b) takes into account the sums paid by way of consideration for the right and any sums paid in respect of the pipe-line system (whether by the applicant or by any other person) in pursuance of directions under section 21(1) below.

(7) Any reference in this section to a right to have gas of any kind conveyed by a pipe-line system includes a reference to a right to introduce into, or take out of, such a system gas of that kind."

Construction of pipe-lines

17. Section 20 of the 1986 Act (construction of pipe-lines) shall cease to have effect.

Increase of capacity etc. of pipe-lines

18.—(1) For subsection (1) of section 21 of the 1986 Act (increase of capacity etc. of pipe-lines) there shall be substituted the following subsection—

"(1) If in the case of a pipe-line system operated by a public gas transporter it appears to the Director, on the application of a person other than the transporter, that the system can and should be modified—

    (a) by installing in it a junction through which another pipe-line may be connected to the system; or

    (b) by modifying apparatus and works associated with a high pressure pipe-line so as to increase the capacity of the pipe-line,

then, subject to subsection (3) below, the Director may, after giving to the transporter an opportunity of being heard about the matter and giving to the Health and Safety Executive notice of his proposed directions, give directions to the transporter in accordance with subsection (2) below in consequence of the application."

(2) In subsection (2) of that section—

    (a) for the words "public gas supplier" there shall be substituted the words "public gas transporter";

    (b) for the words "for the purpose of defraying the cost of" there shall be substituted the words "by way of consideration for"; and

    (c) for the words "the supplier", in both places where they occur, there shall be substituted the words "the transporter".

(3) In subsection (3) of that section, for the word "pipe-line", in each place where it occurs, there shall be substituted the words "pipe-line system".

(4) After subsection (3) of that section there shall be inserted the following subsection—

    "(3A) In giving any directions under this section, the Director shall apply the principle that, in so far as the following, namely—

        (a) the cost of carrying out the modifications; and

        (b) a reasonable element of profit,

will not be recoverable by the public gas transporter from elsewhere, the transporter should be entitled to receive them by way of consideration for carrying out the modifications."

(5) After subsection (4) of that section there shall be inserted the following subsection—

    "(5) In this section—

        'high pressure pipe-line' means any pipe-line which has a design operating pressure exceeding 7 bar gauge;

        'pipe-line' has the same meaning as in the Pipe-lines Act 1962."

Effect of directions as respects pipe-lines

19. In subsection (1) of section 22 of the 1986 Act (effect of directions), for the words "19, 20(4) or 21(1)" there shall be substituted the words "19 or 21(1)".

Construction of pipe-lines by public gas transporters

20. After section 22 of the 1986 Act there shall be inserted the following section—

"Construction of pipe-lines

22A.—(1) A public gas transporter shall not at any time execute in an authorised area of another public gas transporter any works for the construction of a pipe-line unless—

    (a) he has given the other transporter a notice stating that he intends to construct the pipe-line;

    (b) he has consulted with that transporter as to exactly where in that area the proposed pipe-line is to be located, having regard to the location of other pipe-lines in that area; and

    (c) he has consulted with that transporter as to the manner in which—

        (i) the safety of the pipe-line is to be secured; and

        (ii) any escapes of gas (actual or suspected) from the pipe-line are to be dealt with.

(2) A notice under subsection (1)(a) above shall—

    (a) specify the points between which the proposed pipe-line is to run and be accompanied by a map (drawn to an appropriate scale) on which is delineated the route which it is proposed to take;

    (b) specify the length, diameter and operating pressure of the proposed pipe-line and the kind of gas which it is designed to convey; and

    (c) contain such other particulars (if any) as may be prescribed.

(3) In this section—

    'construction', in relation to a pipe-line, includes placing;

    'pipe-line' has the same meaning as in the Pipe-lines Act 1962.

(4) For the purposes of this section the execution of works in land for the purpose of determining whether or not it is suitable for the placing in it of a pipe-line and the carrying

out of surveying operations for the purpose of settling the route of a proposed pipe-line shall be deemed not to constitute the execution of works for the construction of a pipe-line."

Modification of licences by agreement

21. For section 23 of the 1986 Act there shall be substituted the following section—

"Modification of licences

Modification by agreement

23.—(1) Subject to the following provisions of this section, the Director may—

(a) modify the conditions of a particular licence; or

(b) modify the standard conditions of licences under section 7 above, licences under subsection (1) of section 7A above or licences under subsection (2) of that section.

(2) Where at any time the Director modifies under subsection (1)(b) above the standard conditions of licences under section 7 above, licences under subsection (1) of section 7A above or licences under subsection (2) of that section, he—

(a) shall also make (as nearly as may be) the same modifications of those conditions for the purposes of their incorporation in licences under that section or, as the case may be, that subsection granted after that time; and

(b) may make such incidental or consequential modifications as he considers necessary or expedient of any conditions of licences under that provision granted before that time.

(3) Before making modifications under this section, the Director shall give notice—

(a) stating that he proposes to make the modifications and setting out their effect;

(b) stating the reasons why he proposes to make the modifications; and

(c) specifying the time (not being less than 28 days from the date of publication of the notice) within which representations or objections with respect to the proposed modifications may be made,

and shall consider any representations or objections which are duly made and not withdrawn.

(4) A notice under subsection (3) above shall be given—

(a) by publishing the notice in such manner as the Director considers appropriate for the purpose of bringing the notice to the attention of persons likely to be affected by the making of the modifications; and

(b) by sending a copy of the notice to the holder of the licence or, as the case may be, the relevant licence holders, to the Secretary of State, to the Health and Safety Executive and to the Council.

(5) If, within the time specified in the notice under subsection (3) above, the Secretary of State directs the Director not to make any modification, the Director shall comply with the direction.

(6) The Director shall not make any modifications under subsection (1)(a) above unless—

(a) the holder of the licence has consented to the modifications; and

(b) in the case of standard conditions of a licence under subsection (1) or (2) of section 7A above, the Director is of the opinion that the modifications—

(i) are requisite to meet the circumstances of the particular case; and

(ii) are such that no other holder of such a licence would be unduly disadvantaged in competing with other holders of such licences (including the holder of the licence).

(7) The Director shall not make any modifications under subsection (1)(b) above unless—

(a) the percentage given by each of subsections (8) and (9) below is not less than 90 per cent;

(b) the percentage given by subsection (8) below is not less than 90 per cent and no relevant activities have been carried on by relevant licence holders; or

(c) subsection (10) below applies.

(8) The percentage given by this subsection is the fraction given by the following formula expressed as a percentage, namely—

$$\frac{C}{C+N}$$

where—

C = the number of consenting holders;

N = the number of non-consenting holders.

(9) The percentage given by this subsection is the fraction given by the following formula expressed as a percentage, namely—

$$\frac{C}{C + N}$$

where—

C = the volume of gas to which relevant activities carried on by consenting holders relate;

N = the volume of gas to which relevant activities carried on by non-consenting holders relate,

as estimated (in each case) by the Director on the basis of the information available to him.

(10) This subsection applies where the Director is of the opinion—

(a) that the effect of the standard conditions is such as to impose a burden affecting relevant licence holders in the carrying on of activities to which the modifications relate;

(b) that the modifications would remove or reduce the burden without removing any necessary protection; and

(c) in the case of a licence under subsection (1) or (2) of section 7A above, that the modifications are such that no holder of such a licence would be unduly disadvantaged in competing with other holders of such licences.

(11) Where at any time the Director modifies standard conditions under subsection (2)(a) above for the purposes of their incorporation in licences under section 7 or 7A(1) or (2) above granted after that time, he shall publish the modifications in such manner as he considers appropriate.

(12) In this section, in relation to modifications of standard conditions under subsection (1)(b) above—

'consenting holder' means a relevant licence holder who has consented to the modifications;

'non-consenting holder' means a relevant licence holder who has not so consented;

'relevant activity' means an activity to which the modifications relate and which is carried on in the period of twelve months immediately preceding the making of the modifications;

'relevant licence holder' means a licence holder whose licence incorporates the standard conditions."

Modification references to Monopolies Commission

22.—(1) For subsection (1) of section 24 of the 1986 Act (modification references to Monopolies Commission) there shall be substituted the following subsections—

"(1) The Director may make to the Monopolies and Mergers Commission (in this Part referred to as "the Monopolies Commission") a reference which is so framed as to require the Commission to investigate and report on the questions—

(a) whether any matters which relate to—

(i) the carrying on of activities authorised or required by a particular licence, or

(ii) the storage of gas on terms which have been determined by the holder of a particular licence under section 7 above, or could have been determined by the holder if he had thought fit or had been required to determine them by or under a condition of the licence,

and which are specified in the reference operate, or may be expected to operate, against the public interest; and

(b) if so, whether the effects adverse to the public interest which those matters have or may be expected to have could be remedied or prevented by modifications of the relevant conditions, that is to say, the conditions of the licence.

(1A) The Director may make to the Monopolies Commission a reference which is so framed as to require the Commission to investigate and report on the questions—

(a) whether any matters which relate to the carrying on of activities authorised or required by—

(i) licences under section 7 above,

(ii) licences under subsection (1) of section 7A above which incorporate the standard conditions, or

(iii) licences under subsection (2) of that section,

and which are specified in the reference operate, or may be expected to operate, against the public interest; and

(b) if so, whether the effects adverse to the public interest which those matters have or may be expected to have could be remedied or prevented by modifications of the relevant conditions, that is to say, the standard conditions of licences under that section or, as the case may be, that subsection."

(2) In subsection (3) of that section, for the words "conditions of the authorisation" there shall be substituted the words "relevant conditions".

(3) In subsection (4) of that section, for the words "the public gas supplier" there shall be substituted the words "the holder of the licence or, as the case may be, the relevant licence holders".

(4) After subsection (4) of that section there shall be inserted the following subsection—

"(4A) The Director shall also send a copy of a reference under subsection (1A) above, or a variation of such a reference, to the Secretary of State; and if, before the end of the period of 28 days beginning with the day on which he receives the copy of the reference or variation, the Secretary of State directs the Monopolies Commission not to proceed with the reference or, as the case may require, not to give effect to the variation, the Commission shall comply with the direction."

(5) In subsection (6) of that section, for the words "section 4" there shall be substituted the words "sections 4 and 4A(1) and (2)".

(6) After subsection (7) of that section there shall be inserted the following subsection—

"(8) In this section and sections 25 and 26 below—

'relevant conditions' has the meaning given by subsection (1) or (1A) above;

'relevant licence holder'—

(a) in relation to a reference under subsection (1A) above, means the holder of a licence to which the reference relates;

(b) in relation to modifications of relevant conditions within the meaning given by that subsection, means the holder of a licence which incorporates the conditions."

Reports on modification references

23.—(1) In subsection (1)(c) of section 25 of the 1986 Act (reports on modification references), for the words "the conditions of the authorisation" there shall be substituted the words "the relevant conditions".

(2) In subsection (2) of that section, for the words "public gas supplier" there shall be substituted the words "holder of the licence or, as the case may be, any of the relevant licence holders".

(3) In paragraph (a) of subsection (5) of that section, for the words "such a report, send a copy of it to the public gas supplier" there shall be substituted the words "a report on a reference under section 24(1) above, send a copy of it to the licence holder".

(4) After that subsection there shall be inserted the following subsection—

"(5A) Subject to subsection (6) below, the Director shall—

(a) on receiving a report on a reference under section 24(1A) above, send a copy of it to the Secretary of State; and

(b) not less than 14 days after that copy is received by the Secretary of State—

(i) send another copy to the Council and to each relevant licence holder; and

(ii) not less than 24 hours after complying with sub-paragraph (i) above, publish the copy sent to the Council in such manner as he considers appropriate for bringing the report to the attention of persons likely to be affected by it."

(5) In subsection (6) of that section—

(a) after the words "subsection (5)" there shall be inserted the words "or (5A)"; and

(b) for the words from "the copy of the report" to the end there shall be substituted the words "the copy of the report, or (as the case may be) each copy of the report, to be sent and published as mentioned in paragraph (b) of that subsection".

Modification following report

24.—(1) In subsection (1) of section 26 of the 1986 Act (modification following report), for the words "the conditions of the authorisation", in both places where they occur, there shall be substituted the words "the relevant conditions".

(2) After that subsection there shall be inserted the following subsection—

"(1A) Where at any time the Director modifies under subsection (1) above the standard conditions of licences under section 7 above, licences under subsection (1) of section 7A above or licences under subsection (2) of that section, he—

(a) shall also make (as nearly as may be) the same modifications of those conditions for the purposes of their incorporation in licences under that section or, as the case may be, that subsection granted after that time; and

(b) may make such incidental or consequential modifications as he considers necessary or expedient of any conditions of licences under that provision granted before that time;

and the above reference to subsection (1) above is a reference to that subsection as it applies in relation to a report on a reference under section 24(1A) above."

(3) In subsection (4) of that section, for the words "public gas supplier" there shall be substituted the words "holder of the licence or, as the case may be, the relevant licence holders, to the Health and Safety Executive".

(4) After that subsection there shall be inserted the following subsection—

"(5) Where at any time the Director modifies standard conditions under subsection (1A)(a) above for the purposes of their incorporation in licences under section 7 or 7A(1) or (2) above granted after that time, he shall publish the modifications in such manner as he considers appropriate."

Modification by order under other enactments

25. For section 27 of the 1986 Act there shall be substituted the following section—

"Modification by order under other enactments

27.—(1) Where in the circumstances mentioned in subsection (3) or (4) below the Secretary of State by order exercises any of the powers specified in Parts I and II of Schedule 8 to the Fair Trading Act 1973 or section 10(2)(a) of the Competition Act 1980, the order may also provide for the modification of—

(a) the conditions of a particular licence; or

(b) the standard conditions of licences under section 7 above, licences under subsection (1) of section 7A above or licences under subsection (2) of that section,

to such extent as may appear to him to be requisite or expedient for the purpose of giving effect to or of taking account of any provision made by the order.

(2) Where at any time the Secretary of State modifies under subsection (1)(b) above the standard conditions of licences under section 7 above, licences under subsection (1) of section 7A above or licences under subsection (2) of that section, he—

(a) shall also make (as nearly as may be) the same modifications of those conditions for the purposes of their incorporation in licences under that section or, as the case may be, that subsection granted after that time; and

(b) may, after consultation with the Director, make such incidental or consequential modifications as he considers necessary or expedient of any conditions of licences under that provision granted before that time.

(3) Subsection (1) above shall have effect where—

(a) the circumstances are as mentioned in section 56(1) of the said Act of 1973 (order on report on monopoly reference), or in section 10(1) of the said Act of 1980 (order on report on competition reference); and

(b) the monopoly situation exists in relation to, or (as the case may be) the anti-competitive practice relates to—

(i) the carrying on of activities authorised or required by a licence; or

(ii) the storage of gas on terms which have been determined by the holder of a licence under section 7 above, or could have been determined by the holder if he had thought fit or had been required to determine them by or under a condition of the licence.

(4) Subsection (1) above shall also have effect where—

(a) the circumstances are as mentioned in section 73(1) of the said Act of 1973 (order on report on merger reference); and

(b) at least one of the two or more enterprises—

(i) which ceased to be distinct enterprises; or

(ii) in the application of that provision as it has effect by virtue of section 75(4)(e) of that Act, which would cease to be distinct enterprises,

was or, as the case may be, is engaged in the carrying on of activities authorised or required by a licence.

(5) Where at any time the Secretary of State modifies standard conditions under subsection (2)(a) above for the purposes of their incorporation in licences granted after that time, he shall publish those modifications in such manner as he considers appropriate.

(6) In this section expressions which are also used in the said Act of 1973 or the said Act of 1980 have the same meanings as in that Act."

Determination of certain disputes

26. After section 27 of the 1986 Act there shall be inserted the following section—

"Determination of disputes

Determination of certain disputes

27A.—(1) Subject to subsection (2) below, any dispute arising under section 9(1)(b) or (2), 10 or 11 above, regulations under section 10 above, or any provision of paragraphs 2, 3, 15 or 16 of Schedule 2B to this Act, between a public gas transporter or gas supplier and a person who is, or wishes to become, a domestic customer—

    (a) may be referred to the Director by either party, or with the agreement of either party, by the Council; and

    (b) on such a reference, shall be determined by order made either by the Director, or if he thinks fit by an arbitrator (or in Scotland arbiter) appointed by him.

(2) No dispute which—

    (a) arises under section 9(1)(b) above and relates to the connection of any premises to a pipe-line system operated by a public gas transporter; or

    (b) arises under section 10 above, or regulations under that section, and relates to the connection of any premises to a main of such a transporter,

may be referred to the Director after the end of the period of 12 months beginning with the time when the connection is made.

(3) Any person making an order under subsection (1) above shall include in the order his reasons for reaching his decision with respect to the dispute.

(4) The practice and procedure to be followed in connection with any such determination shall be such as the Director may consider appropriate.

(5) Where any dispute between a public gas transporter and a person requiring a connection to a main of the transporter falls to be determined under this section, the Director may give directions as to the circumstances in which, and the terms on which, the transporter is to connect or (as the case may be) to maintain the connection pending the determination of the dispute.

(6) Where any dispute between a gas supplier and a person requiring a supply of gas falls to be determined under this section, the Director may give directions as to the circumstances in which, and the terms on which, the supplier is to give or (as the case may be) to continue to give the supply pending the determination of the dispute.

(7) Where any dispute arising under section 11(1) above falls to be determined under this section, the Director may give directions as to the security (if any) to be given pending the determination of the dispute.

(8) Any direction under subsection (5), (6) or (7) above may be expressed to apply either in relation to a particular case or in relation to a class of case.

(9) An order under this section—

    (a) may include such incidental, supplemental and consequential provision (including provision requiring either party to pay a sum in respect of the costs or expenses incurred by the person making the order) as that person considers appropriate; and

    (b) shall be final and—

        (i) in England and Wales, enforceable, in so far as it includes such provision as to costs or expenses, as if it were a judgment of a county court; and

        (ii) in Scotland, enforceable as if it were an extract registered decree arbitral bearing a warrant for execution issued by the sheriff.

(10) In including in an order under this section any such provision as to costs or expenses, the person making the order shall have regard to the conduct and means of the parties and any other relevant circumstances."

Orders for securing compliance with certain provisions

27.—(1) In subsections (1), (2) and (4) of section 28 of the 1986 Act (orders for securing compliance with certain provisions), for the words "public gas supplier" there shall be substituted the words "licence holder".

(2) In subsection (5) of that section—

(a) for the words "section 4" there shall be substituted the words "section 4 or 4A";

(b) for the words "public gas supplier" there shall be substituted the words "licence holder"; and

(c) for the word "supplier", in the second place where it occurs, there shall be substituted the words "licence holder".

(3) In subsections (6) and (7) of that section, for the words "public gas supplier" there shall be substituted the words "licence holder".

(4) After subsection (7) of that section there shall be inserted the following subsection—

"(7A) Without prejudice to the generality of the power conferred by subsection (1) above, the provision that may be made in a final order includes, in particular, the imposition by the Director on the licence holder to whom the order relates of a requirement to pay to the Director a monetary penalty of such amount as may be appropriate, in all the circumstances of the case, in respect of the contravention in question."

(5) In subsection (8) of that section—

(a) in the definition of "relevant condition", for the words "public gas supplier" there shall be substituted the words "licence holder" and for the word "authorisation" there shall be substituted the word "licence"; and

(b) for the definition of "relevant requirement" there shall be substituted the following definition—

" 'relevant requirement', in relation to a licence holder, means any requirement imposed on him by or under section 9(1) or (2), 10(2), (3) or (14), 11(2), 12(1) or (6), 18(11), 22A(1) or 27A(5) or (6) above or section 33B, 33BB, 33D or 33E below or any provision of paragraphs 3, 6, 15, 16, 20(5) and 28(2) of Schedule 2B to this Act."

(6) After that subsection there shall be inserted the following subsection—

"(9) Any sums received by the Director by way of monetary penalty under this section shall be paid into the Consolidated Fund."

Procedural requirements

28. In subsections (2) to (4), (6) and (7) of section 29 of the 1986 Act (procedural requirements), for the words "public gas supplier", in each place where they occur, there shall be substituted the words "licence holder".

Validity and effect of orders

29.—(1) In subsection (1) of section 30 of the 1986 Act (validity and effect of orders), for the words "public gas supplier" there shall be substituted the words "licence holder".

(2) For subsection (2) of that section there shall be substituted the following subsection—

"(2) On any such application the court, if satisfied that the making or confirmation of the order was not within those powers or that the interests of the licence holder have been substantially prejudiced by a failure to comply with those requirements—

(a) may quash the order or any provision of the order; or

(b) if and to the extent that the application related to so much of an order as imposes a monetary penalty, may substitute a monetary penalty of such lesser amount as the court considers appropriate in all the circumstances of the case."

Duty of Director to investigate certain matters

30.—(1) In subsections (1) and (2) of section 31 of the 1986 Act (duty of Director to investigate certain matters), for the words "an enforcement matter" there shall be substituted the words "a reserved matter".

(2) For subsection (3) of that section there shall be substituted the following subsections—

"(3) In this section and section 32 below "reserved matter" means any matter—

(a) in respect of which any functions of the Director under section 28 above are or may be exercisable; and

(b) which has not been designated by the Director as a matter which is to be investigated by the Council.

(4) A designation under subsection (3) above may be made—

(a) either generally or in relation to matters of a particular class or a particular matter; and

(b) either unconditionally or subject to such conditions as may be specified in the designation.

(5) Conditions specified in a designation under subsection (3) above may contain provision for the designation to cease to have effect, either generally or in relation to matters of a particular class or a particular matter, in such circumstances as may be determined by or under the conditions."

Duty of Council to investigate certain matters

31.—(1) For subsection (2) of section 32 of the 1986 Act (duty of Council to investigate certain matters) there shall be substituted the following subsection—

"(2) This subsection applies to any matter (not being a reserved matter) in respect of which any functions of the Director under this Part are or may be exercisable."

(2) In subsections (3) and (5) of that section, the words "paragraph (a) of" shall cease to have effect.

(3) In subsection (4) of that section, the word "already" shall cease to have effect.

(4) Subsections (6) and (7) of that section shall cease to have effect.

Preliminary investigation by Council of certain disputes

32. In subsection (1) of section 32A of the 1986 Act (preliminary investigation by Council of certain disputes), for the words "section 14A" there shall be substituted the words "section 27A".

Power of Council to investigate other matters

33.—(1) In subsection (2) of section 33 of the 1986 Act (power of Council to investigate other matters), for the words "public gas suppliers" there shall be substituted the words "gas suppliers".

(2) In subsection (3) of that section, the words "but nothing in this subsection shall require the Council to send any such copy to the Director" shall cease to have effect.

(3) After that subsection there shall be inserted the following subsection—

"(4) References in this section to gas suppliers include references to persons supplying gas which they are authorised to supply by paragraph 1 of Schedule 2A to this Act."

Standards of performance in individual cases

34.—(1) In subsection (1) of section 33A of the 1986 Act (standards of performance in individual cases), for the words "public gas suppliers to tariff customers" there shall be substituted the words "gas suppliers to domestic customers".

(2) In subsection (2) of that section, for the words "the public gas suppliers" there shall be substituted the words "gas suppliers".

(3) In subsection (3) of that section—

(a) for the words "public gas suppliers", in each place where they occur, there shall be substituted the words "gas suppliers";

(b) for the words "tariff customers" there shall be substituted the words "domestic customers"; and

(c) at the beginning of paragraph (d) there shall be inserted the words "if the Director is of the opinion that the differences are such that no gas supplier would be unduly disadvantaged in competing with other gas suppliers,".

(4) In subsection (4) of that section—

(a) for the words "public gas supplier" there shall be substituted the words "gas supplier"; and

(b) for the words "tariff customer" there shall be substituted the words "domestic customer".

(5) Subsections (10) and (11) of that section shall cease to have effect.

Overall standards of performance

35.—(1) In subsection (1) of section 33B of the 1986 Act (overall standards of performance), for the words "public gas suppliers" there shall be substituted the words "gas suppliers".

(2) In subsection (2) of that section, for the words "the public gas suppliers" there shall be substituted the words "gas suppliers".

(3) For subsection (3) of that section there shall be substituted the following subsections—

"(3) Different standards may be determined for different gas suppliers if the Director is of the opinion that the differences are such that no gas supplier would be unduly disadvantaged in competing with other gas suppliers.

(3A) Standards may be determined either as respects the provision of gas supply services generally or as respects the provision of such services to customers of a particular class or description."

(4) In subsection (4) of that section, for the words "public gas supplier" there shall be substituted the words "gas supplier".

Standards for promoting efficient use of gas

36. After section 33B of the 1986 Act there shall be inserted the following section—

"Standards for promoting efficient use of gas

33BB.—(1) The Director may, after consulting gas suppliers and persons or bodies appearing to him to be representative of persons likely to be affected, from time to time—

(a) determine such standards of performance in connection with the promotion of the efficient use of gas by consumers as, in his opinion, ought to be achieved by gas suppliers; and

(b) arrange for the publication, in such form and in such manner as he considers appropriate, of the standards so determined.

(2) Different standards may be determined for different gas suppliers if the Director is of the opinion that the differences are such that no gas supplier would be unduly disadvantaged in competing with other gas suppliers.

(3) Each gas supplier shall, in such form and manner and with such frequency as the Director may direct, take steps to inform his customers of—

(a) the standards determined under this section which are applicable to that supplier; and

(b) that supplier's level of performance as respects those standards."

Information with respect to levels of performance

37.—(1) In subsection (1) of section 33C of the 1986 Act (information with respect to levels of performance), for the words "public gas suppliers", in each place where they occur, there shall be substituted the words "gas suppliers".

(2) In subsection (2) of that section—

(a) for the words "public gas supplier" there shall be substituted the words "gas supplier"; and

(b) for the words "section 15B or 33B" there shall be substituted the words "section 33B or 33BB".

(3) In subsection (3) of that section, for the words "public gas supplier" there shall be substituted the words "gas supplier".

(4) In subsection (4) of that section, for the words "public gas suppliers" there shall be substituted the words "gas suppliers".

Information to be given to customers about overall performance

38.—(1) In subsection (1) of section 33D of the 1986 Act (information to be given to customers about overall performance), for the words "public gas supplier" there shall be substituted the words "gas supplier".

(2) After subsection (2) of that section there shall be inserted the following subsection—

"(3) Where the standards of performance mentioned in subsection (1) above relate to the provision of gas supply services to customers of a particular class or description, the reference in that subsection to the supplier's customers shall be construed as a reference to such of his customers as are of that class or description."

Procedures for dealing with complaints

39.—(1) In subsection (1) of section 33E of the 1986 Act (procedures for dealing with complaints)—

(a) for the words "public gas supplier" there shall be substituted the words "gas supplier who is authorised to supply gas to domestic customers and whose licence incorporates the standard conditions"; and

(b) for the words "tariff customers or potential tariff customers" there shall be substituted the words "domestic customers or potential domestic customers".

(2) In subsections (2), (3), (4) and (6) of that section, for the words "public gas supplier", in each place where they occur, there shall be substituted the words "gas supplier".

General functions of Director

40.—(1) In subsection (1) of section 34 of the 1986 Act (general functions of Director), for the words "activities connected with the supply of gas through pipes" there shall be substituted the following paragraphs—

"(a) such activities as are mentioned in section 5(1) above; and

(b) activities ancillary to such activities (including in particular the storage of gas, the provision and reading of meters and the provision of pre-payment facilities)."

(2) In subsection (2) of that section, for the words "the supply of gas through pipes, and the persons providing such supplies" there shall be substituted the following paragraphs—

"(a) the carrying on of such activities as are mentioned in subsection (1) above; and

(b) the persons by whom such activities are carried on,".

(3) In subsection (4) of that section, after the words "function of the Director" there shall be inserted the words "or the Secretary of State."

(4) After that subsection there shall be inserted the following subsection—

"(5) The Director shall have power to make agreements with the Health and Safety Commission for the Director to perform on behalf of that Commission or the Health and Safety Executive (with or without payment) any of the functions of that Commission or, as the case may be, that Executive."

Publication of information and advice

41. In subsection (1) of section 35 of the 1986 Act (publication of information and advice), for the words "tariff customers and potential tariff customers of public gas suppliers" there shall be substituted the words "customers and potential customers of gas suppliers".

Keeping of register

42.—(1) In subsection (1) of section 36 of the 1986 Act (keeping of register)—
(a) for the words "section 6 above" there shall be substituted the words "paragraph 5 of Schedule 2A to this Act"; and
(b) for the words "authorisations under section 7 or 8" there shall be substituted the words "licences under section 7 or 7A".
(2) In subsection (2) of that section—
(a) for the words "section 6 above" there shall be substituted the words "paragraph 5 of Schedule 2A to this Act";
(b) after the words "particular class" there shall be inserted the words "and every direction under subsection (5) of that section";
(c) for the words "authorisation under section 7 or 8" there shall be substituted the words "licence under section 7 or 7A"; and
(d) for the words "such an authorisation" there shall be substituted the words "such a licence".

Functions with respect to competition

43. After section 36 of the 1986 Act there shall be inserted the following section—

"Functions with respect to competition

36A.—(1) If and to the extent that he is requested by the Director General of Fair Trading to do so, it shall be the duty of the Director to exercise the functions of that Director under Part III of the Fair Trading Act 1973 ('the 1973 Act') so far as relating to courses of conduct which are or may be detrimental to the interests of consumers of gas conveyed through pipes, whether those interests are economic or interests in respect of health, safety or other matters; and references in that Part to that Director shall be construed accordingly.

(2) There are hereby transferred to the Director (so as to be exercisable concurrently with the Director General of Fair Trading)—
(a) the functions of that Director under sections 44 and 45 of the 1973 Act;
(b) the functions of that Director under sections 50, 52, 53, 86 and 88 of that Act; and
(c) the functions of that Director under sections 56A to 56G of that Act,
so far as relating to monopoly situations which exist or may exist in relation to commercial activities connected with the carrying on of activities to which this subsection applies; and references in Part IV and sections 86, 88 and 133 of that Act to that Director shall be construed accordingly.

(3) There are hereby transferred to the Director (so as to be exercisable concurrently with the Director General of Fair Trading) the functions of that Director under sections 2 to 10 and 16 of the Competition Act 1980 ('the 1980 Act') so far as relating to courses of conduct which have or are intended to have or are likely to have the effect of restricting, distorting, or preventing competition in connection with the carrying on of activities to which this subsection applies; and references in those sections and in section 19 of that Act to that Director shall be construed accordingly.

(4) Subsections (2) and (3) above apply to—
(a) such activities as are mentioned in section 5(1) above; and
(b) activities ancillary to such activities as are so mentioned (including in particular the storage of gas, the provision and reading of meters and the provision of pre-payment facilities).

(5) Before either Director first exercises in relation to any matter functions transferred by any of the following provisions, namely—
(a) paragraph (a) of subsection (2) above;
(b) paragraph (b) of that subsection;
(c) paragraph (c) of that subsection; and

(d) subsection (3) above,

he shall consult the other Director; and neither Director shall exercise in relation to any matter functions transferred by any of those provisions if functions transferred by that provision have been exercised in relation to that matter by the other Director.

(6) It shall be the duty of the Director, for the purpose of assisting the Monopolies Commission in carrying out an investigation on a reference made to them by the Director by virtue of subsection (2) or (3) above, to give to the Commission—

(a) any information which is in his possession and which relates to matters falling within the scope of the investigation and—

(i) is requested by the Commission for that purpose; or

(ii) is information which in his opinion it would be appropriate for that purpose to give to the Commission without any such request; and

(b) any other assistance which the Commission may require and which it is within his power to give, in relation to any such matters,

and the Commission shall, for the purposes of carrying out any such investigation, take into account any information given to them for that purpose under this subsection.

(7) If any question arises as to whether subsection (2) or (3) above applies to any particular case, that question shall be referred to and determined by the Secretary of State; and no objection shall be taken to anything done under—

(a) Part IV or section 86 or 88 of the 1973 Act; or

(b) sections 2 to 10 of the 1980 Act,

by or in relation to the Director on the ground that it should have been done by or in relation to the Director General of Fair Trading.

(8) Section 93B of the 1973 Act (offences of supplying false or misleading information to the Secretary of State, the Director General of Fair Trading or the Monopolies Commission in connection with their functions under Parts IV, V, VI or VIII of the 1973 Act or under the 1980 Act) shall have effect, so far as relating to functions exercisable by the Director by virtue of subsection (2) or (3) above, as if the reference in subsection (1)(a) of that section to the Director of Fair Trading included a reference to the Director.

(9) Expressions used in this section which are also used in the 1973 Act or the 1980 Act have the same meanings as in that Act.

(10) Any reference in this Part to functions of the Director under this Part, or to functions assigned to him by or under this Part, includes a reference to functions transferred to the Director by subsection (2) or (3) above."

Functions with respect to gas measuring equipment etc.

44. After section 36A of the 1986 Act there shall be inserted the following section—

"Functions with respect to gas measuring equipment etc.

36B.—(1) If and to the extent that the Secretary of State so directs, the functions of the Secretary of State under section 6 of the Weights and Measures Act 1985 (testing of standards and equipment) so far as relating to—

(a) any article used or proposed to be used as a standard of a unit of measurement in relation to gas;

(b) any measuring equipment, or other metrological equipment, for use in relation to gas; or

(c) any article for use in connection with any such equipment,

shall be exercisable by the Director concurrently with the Secretary of State; and references in that section to the Secretary of State shall be construed accordingly.

(2) Any sums received by the Director by virtue of this section shall be paid into the Consolidated Fund."

Maximum prices for reselling gas

45. For section 37 of the 1986 Act there shall be substituted the following section—

"Maximum prices for reselling gas

37:—(1) The Director shall from time to time direct that the maximum prices at which gas supplied by gas suppliers may be resold—

(a) shall be such as may be specified in the direction; or

(b) shall be calculated by such method and by reference to such matters as may be so specified,

and shall publish directions under this section in such manner as in his opinion will secure adequate publicity for them.

(2) A direction under this section may—

(a) require any person who resells gas supplied by a gas supplier to furnish the purchaser with such information as may be specified or described in the direction; and

(b) provide that, in the event of his failing to do so, the maximum price applicable to the resale shall be such as may be specified in the direction, or shall be reduced by such amount or such percentage as may be so specified.

(3) Different directions may be given under this section as respects different classes of cases, which may be defined by reference to areas or any other relevant circumstances.

(4) If any person resells any gas supplied by a gas supplier at a price exceeding the maximum price determined by or under a direction under this section and applicable to the resale—

(a) the amount of the excess; and

(b) if the direction so provides, interest on that amount at a rate specified or described in the direction,

shall be recoverable by the purchaser.

(5) Nothing in this section shall apply in relation to the resale of gas for use in a motor vehicle which is constructed or adapted to use gas as fuel for its propulsion."

Power to require information etc.

46.—(1) In subsection (1) of section 38 of the 1986 Act (power to require information etc.)—

(a) for the words "public gas supplier" there shall be substituted the words "licence holder"; and

(b) the words from "but no person" to the end shall cease to have effect.

(2) After that subsection there shall be inserted the following subsections—

"(1A) Where a licence has been or is to be revoked or suspended, or has expired or is about to expire by effluxion of time, and it appears to the Director, having regard to the duties imposed by section 4 or 4A above, to be requisite or expedient to do so for any purpose connected with the revocation, suspension or expiry, the Director may, with the consent of the Secretary of State, by notice signed by him—

(a) require the licence holder to produce, at a time and place specified in the notice, to the Director, or to any person so specified, any records which are specified or described in the notice and are in the licence holder's custody or under his control; or

(b) require the licence holder to furnish to the Director, or to any person specified in the notice, such information as may be specified or described in the notice, and specify the time, the manner and the form in which any such information is to be furnished.

(1B) No person shall be compelled for any such purpose as is mentioned in subsection (1) or (1A) above to produce any documents or records which he could not be compelled to produce in civil proceedings before the court or, in complying with any requirement for the furnishing of information, to give any information which he could not be compelled to give in evidence in such proceedings."

(3) In subsections (2) and (4) of that section, after the words "subsection (1)" there shall be inserted the words "or (1A)".

Duty to consider representations and give reasons

47. After section 38 of the 1986 Act there shall be inserted the following section—

"Duty to consider representations and give reasons

38A.—(1) The Secretary of State may by order exercise any one or more of the powers conferred by subsections (2) to (4) below.

(2) This subsection confers power to provide that, before the Director makes a specified decision in relation to a licence holder, the Director—

(a) shall give to the licence holder a written notice stating—

(i) that he is considering making the decision and the reasons why he is considering doing so; and

(ii) that the licence holder may, within a period specified in the notice, make written representations to him or, if the licence holder so requests, make oral representations to a person appointed by him for the purpose; and

(b) shall consider any representations which are duly made and not withdrawn.

(3) This subsection confers power to provide that, where the Director makes a specified decision in relation to a licence holder, the Director shall as soon as practicable give to the licence holder a written notice explaining why it appeared to him to be appropriate to make the decision.

(4) This subsection confers power to provide that, where a specified decision made or proposed to be made in relation to a licence holder will or may materially affect any speci-

fied person, any provision made by virtue of subsection (2) or (3) above shall, with any specified modifications, apply in relation to that person.

(5) Nothing in any order made under this section shall require the Director to disclose any information the disclosure of which he considers would or might seriously and prejudicially affect the interests of a particular individual or body of persons, whether corporate or unincorporate.

(6) An order under this section—

(a) may make different provision in relation to different cases or different circumstances; and

(b) shall be made by statutory instrument which shall be subject to annulment in pursuance of a resolution of either House of Parliament.

(7) In this section—

'decision' means any decision under this Part, or under a condition of a licence, other than a decision to make a provisional order under section 28 above;

'specified', in relation to an order under this section, means specified in the order or of a description so specified;

and references to a licence holder include references to an applicant for a licence."

Annual and other reports

48. After subsection (2) of section 39 of the 1986 Act (annual and other reports) there shall be inserted the following subsection—

"(2A) Every such report shall also include—

(a) a general statement as to the extent to which, during the year to which it relates, there has been effective competition in the carrying on of activities the carrying on of which is required to be licensed under section 7A above; and

(b) a general survey of developments during that year in respect of such competition."

General duty of Council to advise Director

49. In section 40 of the 1986 Act (general duty of Council to advise Director), the words "which relates to tariff customers and" shall cease to have effect.

General restrictions on disclosure of information

50.—(1) After subsection (1) of section 42 of the 1986 Act (general restrictions on disclosure of information) there shall be inserted the following subsections—

"(1A) Subsection (1) above does not apply to any disclosure of information if—

(a) the disclosure is required by a notice under subsection (1) or (1A) of section 38 above;

(b) the information has been obtained in pursuance of a notice under subsection (1A) of that section; or

(c) the disclosure is made by one licence holder to another and is required either by a condition of the disclosing licence holder's licence, or by the other licence holder for purposes connected with the carrying on of relevant activities.

(1B) In subsection (1A) above 'relevant activities', in relation to a licence holder, means—

(a) activities which he is authorised by his licence to carry on; and

(b) in the case of a public gas transporter, such activities as are mentioned in section 7(1)(b) and (c) above."

(2) After subsection (3) of that section there shall be inserted the following subsection—

"(3A) The Secretary of State may by order provide that any of subsections (1A) to (3) above shall have effect subject to such modifications as are specified in the order."

Making of false statements etc.

51. After subsection (1) of section 43 of the 1986 Act (making of false statements etc.) there shall be inserted the following subsection—

"(1A) Any person who with intent to deceive—

(a) impersonates an officer of a public gas transporter, gas supplier or gas shipper for the purpose of obtaining entry to any premises; or

(b) for that purpose makes any statement or does any act calculated falsely to suggest that he is an officer, or an authorised officer, of such a transporter, supplier or shipper,

shall be guilty of an offence and liable on summary conviction to a fine not exceeding level 4 on the standard scale."

Service of notices etc.

52.—(1) In subsection (1) of section 46 of the 1986 Act (service of notices etc.), the words "Subject to subsection (2) below" shall cease to have effect.

(2) For subsections (2) and (3) of that section there shall be substituted the following subsections—

"(2) Without prejudice to subsection (1) above, where this subsection applies in relation to a public gas transporter or gas supplier, any notice to be given to or served on the transporter or supplier under—

(a) any condition of his licence;

(b) any provision of Schedule 2B to this Act; or

(c) in the case of a transporter, section 10 above,

may be given or served by delivering it at, or sending it in a prepaid letter to, an appropriate office of the transporter or supplier.

(3) Subsection (2) above applies in relation to a public gas transporter if he divides his authorised area into such areas as he thinks fit and—

(a) in the case of each area, fixes offices of his which are to be appropriate offices in relation to notices relating to matters arising in that area; and

(b) publishes in each area, in such manner as he considers adequate, the addresses of the offices fixed by him for that area.

(4) Subsection (2) above applies in relation to a gas supplier if he divides the premises specified in his licence into such areas as he thinks fit and—

(a) in the case of each area, fixes offices of his which are to be appropriate offices in relation to notices relating to matters arising in that area;

(b) publishes in each area, in such manner as he considers adequate, the addresses of the offices fixed by him for that area; and

(c) endorses on every demand note for gas charges payable to him the addresses of the offices fixed for the area in question.

(5) In this section references to premises specified in a licence include references to premises of a description, or situated in an area, so specified."

Provisions as to regulations

53.—(1) In subsection (3) of section 47 of the 1986 Act (provisions as to regulations)—

(a) for paragraph (aa) there shall be substituted the following paragraph—

"(aa) provide for anything falling to be determined under the regulations to be determined—

(i) by the Director or by such other person as may be prescribed by the regulations; and

(ii) in accordance with such procedure and by reference to such matters and to the opinion of such persons as may be so prescribed;" and

(b) in paragraph (b), after the words "the Secretary of State" there shall be inserted the words "or, as the case may be, the Director".

(2) In subsection (5) of that section, after the words "the Secretary of State" there shall be inserted the words ", the Director".

(3) For subsection (7) of that section there shall be substituted the following subsection—

"(7) Any power to make regulations conferred by this Part on the Secretary of State or the Director shall be exercisable by statutory instrument which shall be subject to annulment in pursuance of a resolution of either House of Parliament; and the Statutory Instruments Act 1946 shall apply to any such power so conferred on the Director as if he were a Minister of the Crown."

Interpretation of Part I and savings

54.—(1) In subsection (1) of section 48 of the 1986 Act (interpretation of Part I and savings)—

(a) in the definition of "authorised area", for the word "supplier" there shall be substituted the word "transporter";

(b) in the definition of "distribution main", for the word "supplier", in each place where it occurs, there shall be substituted the word "transporter";

(c) after that definition there shall be inserted the following definition—

" 'domestic customer' has the meaning given by section 15A(10) above;";

(d) after the definition of "gas fittings" there shall be inserted the following definition—

" 'gas supplier' and 'gas shipper' have the meanings given by section 7A(11) above;";

(e) after the definition of "kilowatt hour" there shall be inserted the following definitions—

" 'licence' and 'licence holder' have the meanings given by section 4(5) above;";

(f) after the definition of "notice" there shall be inserted the following definitions—

" 'officer', in relation to any person, includes any servant or agent of that person, and any officer or servant of such an agent;

'owner', in relation to any premises or other property, includes a lessee, and cognate expressions shall be construed accordingly;"

(g) in the definition of "prescribed", for the words "(except in section 33A above)" there shall be substituted the words "made, unless the context otherwise requires, by the Secretary of State";

(h) for the definition of "public gas supplier" there shall be substituted the following definition—

" 'public gas transporter' has the meaning given by section 7(1) above;";

(i) the definition of "regulations" shall cease to have effect;

(j) immediately before the definition of "subsidiary" there shall be inserted the following definitions—

" 'service pipe' means a pipe, other than a distribution main of a public gas transporter, which is used for the purpose of conveying gas from such a main to any premises, and includes part of any such pipe;

'storage', in relation to gas, means storage in, or in a facility which is connected (directly or indirectly) to, a pipe-line system operated by a public gas transporter;" and

(k) the definition of "tariff customer" shall cease to have effect.

(2) After subsection (1) of that section there shall be inserted the following subsection—

"(1A) In this Part any reference to an officer authorised by any person includes, in relation to an officer who is an officer or servant of an agent of that person, an officer who, in accordance with the terms of any written authority given by that person to the agent, is authorised by the agent on behalf of that person."

(3) In subsection (2) of that section, for paragraphs (a) and (b) there shall be substituted the words "to the supply of gas (directly or indirectly) to a public gas transporter, gas supplier or gas shipper".

(4) For subsection (3) of that section there shall be substituted the following subsections—

"(2A) In relation to any time after 31st December 1999—

(a) references in this Part to 2,500, 75,000 and 2 million therms shall be construed as references to 73,200, 2,196,000 and 58 million kilowatt hours respectively; and

(b) other references in this Part to therms, and references in this Part to therms or kilowatt hours, shall be construed as references to kilowatt hours.

(2B) A person is of pensionable age for the purposes of this Part if—

(a) he has attained pensionable age (within the meaning given by the rules in paragraph 1 of Schedule 4 to the Pensions Act 1995); or

(b) in the case of a man born before 6th April 1955, he is the same age as a woman who has attained pensionable age (within the meaning so given).

(3) Nothing in this Part relating to the modification of a licence shall authorise the inclusion in a licence of any condition other than one such as is mentioned in section 7B above or, in the case of a modification under section 27 above, as would be so mentioned if the references to the Director in subsection (4)(a), (b) and (d) of section 7B were references to the Secretary of State."

The Director General of Gas Supply

55. In paragraph 10 of Schedule 1 to the 1986 Act (the Director General of Gas Supply), after the words "the Director", in the first place where they occur, there shall be inserted the words "(other than the making of a statutory instrument)".

Acquisition of land by public gas transporters

56. In Schedule 3 to the 1986 Act (acquisition of land by public gas suppliers)—

(a) for the words "public gas supplier", in each place where they occur, there shall be substituted the words "public gas transporter";

(b) for the words "public gas supplier's", in each place where they occur, there shall be substituted the words "public gas transporter's"; and

(c) for the words "the supplier", in each place where they occur, there shall be substituted the words "the transporter".

Power of public gas transporters to break up streets, bridges etc.

57.—(1) In Schedule 4 to the 1986 Act (power of public gas suppliers to break up streets, bridges etc.)—

(a) for the words "public gas supplier", in each place where they occur, there shall be substituted the words "public gas transporter"; and

(b) for the words "the supplier", in each place where they occur, there shall be substituted the words "the transporter".

(2) In sub-paragraph (1) of paragraph 1 of that Schedule, for the words from "placing in" to the end there shall be substituted the following paragraphs—

"(a) placing pipes, conduits, service pipes, cables, sewers and other works, and pressure governors, ventilators and other apparatus, in or under any street; and

(b) from time to time repairing, altering or removing any such works or apparatus placed in or under any street (whether by him or by any other person)."

(3) After sub-paragraph (3) of that paragraph there shall be inserted the following sub-paragraphs—

"(4) The Secretary of State shall by regulations provide that, in such cases and to such extent as may be provided by the regulations, a public gas transporter shall pay, by way of compensation for any loss sustained by any person in consequence of the exercise of those powers, such sum as may be determined in accordance with the regulations.

(5) No regulations may be made under sub-paragraph (4) above which amend, or re-enact with modifications, regulations previously made under that sub-paragraph."

(4) In paragraph 3(2) of that Schedule, for the words "giving a supply of" there shall be substituted the word "conveying".

GENERAL NOTE

Dealing mainly with amendments to Part I of the 1986 Act, this Schedule covers assignment of licences; duties of a public gas transporter; conveyance; testing and metering of equipment *etc.* These are mainly technical amendments—given that the pipeline network is a natural monopoly, it is appropriate that there be regulation in the public interest. This Schedule also modifies the third party access rights granted under s.19 of the 1986 Act, adding details to the tariff calculations, as well as modifying the manner in which references are made to the MMC under s.24, in line with the new licensing arrangements.

Section 16(1).   SCHEDULE 4

MINOR AND CONSEQUENTIAL AMENDMENTS

Interpretation

1. In this Schedule "public gas transporter" has the same meaning as in Part I of the 1986 Act.

Enactments relating to statutory undertakers etc.

2.—(1) A public gas transporter shall be deemed to be a statutory undertaker and his undertaking a statutory undertaking for the purposes of the following enactments, namely—

  (i) the Public Health Act 1925;

  (ii) the Public Health Act 1936;

  (iii) the Acquisition of Land (Authorisation Procedure) (Scotland) Act 1947;

  (iv) section 4 of the Requisitioned Land and War Works Act 1948;

  (v) the National Parks and Access to the Countryside Act 1949;

  (vi) the Reserve and Auxiliary Forces (Protection of Civil Interests) Act 1951;

  (vii) the Landlord and Tenant Act 1954;

  (viii) the Opencast Coal Act 1958;

  (ix) the Flood Prevention (Scotland) Act 1961;

  (x) section 17(10) of the Public Health Act 1961;

  (xi) the Pipe-lines Act 1962;

  (xii) Schedule 3 to the Harbours Act 1964;

  (xiii) section 40 of the Forestry Act 1967;

  (xiv) section 50 of the Agriculture Act 1967;

  (xv) sections 38 and 66 of the Countryside (Scotland) Act 1967;

  (xvi) the New Towns (Scotland) Act 1968;

  (xvii) section 11 of and paragraph 6 of Schedule 2 to the Countryside Act 1968;

  (xviii) section 22 of the Sewerage (Scotland) Act 1968;

  (xix) sections 19, 37, 45, 46, 108(2), 117 to 119, 121, 154(3), 170 to 172, 175, 181, 195(6), 198(3), 199(2), 202(3), 205, 211, 212, 214, 216 to 230, 233(7), 242, 266(6)(b) and 275(2) of, and Schedule 8, paragraphs 1 to 3 of Schedule 17 and Schedule 18 to, the Town and Country Planning (Scotland) Act 1972;

  (xx) section 51 of the Land Compensation Act 1973;

  (xxi) sections 47 and 67 of the Land Compensation (Scotland) Act 1973;

  (xxii) section 73 of the Control of Pollution Act 1974;

(xxiii) the Welsh Development Agency Act 1975;
(xxiv) sections 15(3) and 26 of the Local Government (Miscellaneous Provisions) Act 1976;
(xxv) the Development of Rural Wales Act 1976;
(xxvi) section 9(3) of the Inner Urban Areas Act 1978;
(xxvii) the Ancient Monuments and Archaeological Areas Act 1979;
(xxviii) Parts XII and XVI and section 120 of the Local Government, Planning and Land Act 1980;
(xxix) the Highways Act 1980;
(xxx) the New Towns Act 1981;
(xxxi) the Acquisition of Land Act 1981;
(xxxii) the Civil Aviation Act 1982;
(xxxiii) section 30 of the Local Government (Miscellaneous Provisions) Act 1982;
(xxxiv) the Roads (Scotland) Act 1984;
(xxxv) the Building Act 1984;
(xxxvi) sections 283(2) and 296 of the Housing Act 1985;
(xxxvii) section 21 of the Road Traffic Act 1988.
(xxxviii) section 9 of the Enterprise and New Towns (Scotland) Act 1990;
(xxxix) section 7(5) of the Natural Heritage (Scotland) Act 1991.

(2) References to public gas suppliers in the following enactments shall have effect as references to a public gas transporter, namely—
(a) section 17(1)(b) of the Requisitioned Land and War Works Act 1945;
(b) the Local Government (Omnibus Shelters and Queue Barriers) (Scotland) Act 1958;
(c) section 7A(4)(b)(ii) of the Mines (Working Facilities and Support) Act 1966;
(d) section 109(2)(d) of the Transport Act 1968;
(e) section 204(2)(a) of the Town and Country Planning (Scotland) Act 1972;
(f) sections 73(11)(c) and 74(11)(b) of the Highways Act 1980;
(g) section 48(6)(c) of the Civil Aviation Act 1982;
(h) paragraph 3 of Schedule 5 to the Road Traffic Regulation Act 1984;
(i) section 80(3)(b) of the Building Act 1984;
(j) section 91 of the Planning (Listed Buildings and Conservation Areas) Act 1990;
(k) section 39 of the Planning (Hazardous Substances) Act 1990;
(l) section 52(1) of the Coal Mining Subsidence Act 1991;
(m) section 209(3)(b) of and paragraph 1(5)(e) of Schedule 13 to the Water Industry Act 1991;
(n) section 208(3)(b) of and paragraph 1(4)(e) of Schedule 22 to the Water Resources Act 1991;
(o) paragraph 1(1)(e) of Schedule 6 to the Land Drainage Act 1991.

(3) The reference in Schedule 4 to the Public Health Act 1961 to gas undertakers shall have effect as a reference to a public gas transporter.

(4) References in the Landlord and Tenant Act 1927 to a statutory company shall be deemed to include references to a public gas transporter.

(5) References to public utility undertakers in the Civil Defence Act 1939 shall be deemed to include references to a public gas transporter.

(6) References to public utility undertakers in the Highways Act 1980 shall be deemed to include references to a public gas transporter.

(7) Paragraph 23 of Schedule 2 to the Telecommunications Act 1984 (undertakers' works) shall apply to a public gas transporter for the purposes of any works carried out by him.

(8) The reference in section 82(4) of the Building Act 1984 (provisions with respect to demolition orders) to a person authorised by an enactment to carry on an undertaking for the supply of gas shall be construed as a reference to a public gas transporter.

(9) References to public undertakers in section 125(7) of, and paragraphs 9 and 10 of Schedule 8 to, the Housing (Scotland) Act 1987 shall be deemed to include references to a public gas transporter.

(10) In the following enactments, namely—
(a) section 39 of the Opencast Coal Act 1958;
(b) paragraph 2 of Schedule 6 to the Gas Act 1965;
(c) the New Towns (Scotland) Act 1968;
(d) sections 195(6), 214 to 227, 266(6)(b) and 275(2) of, and Schedule 8 to, the Town and Country Planning (Scotland) Act 1972;
(e) the Welsh Development Agency Act 1975;
(f) the Development of Rural Wales Act 1976;
(g) the New Towns Act 1981;
(h) section 9 of the Enterprise and New Towns (Scotland) Act 1990;

(i) section 7(5) of the Natural Heritage (Scotland) Act 1991,

"the appropriate Minister", in relation to a public gas transporter, shall mean the Secretary of State for Trade and Industry.

(11) In the following enactments, namely—

(a) the Pipe-lines Act 1962;

(b) Schedule 3 to the Harbours Act 1964;

(c) section 121 of the Highways Act 1980; and

(d) the Acquisition of Land Act 1981,

"the appropriate Minister", in relation to a public gas transporter, shall mean the Secretary of State.

Public Health Act 1936 (c.49)

3. In section 229 of the Public Health Act 1936 (power of statutory undertakers to supply water, gas or electricity to baths etc. on favourable terms), the word "gas", in both places where it occurs, shall cease to have effect.

Statistics of Trade Act 1947 (c.39)

4.—(1) In relation to gas, subsection (5)(b) of section 9 of the Statistics of Trade Act 1947 (restriction on disclosure of information obtained under that Act) shall have effect as if the references to the total quantity or value of any articles produced, sold or delivered included a reference to each of the following, that is to say—

(a) the total quantity or value of gas which is supplied in Great Britain;

(b) the total quantity or value of gas which in Great Britain is supplied—

(i) for the same purposes, or for different purposes but in similar quantities;

(ii) to premises appearing to the Secretary of State to be of the same description; or

(iii) on terms appearing to the Secretary of State to be similar as respects continuity of supply;

(c) the total quantity of gas which in Great Britain is conveyed or shipped to premises for supply purposes, or is stored; and

(d) the total quantity of gas which in Great Britain is conveyed or shipped to or from, or is stored in, facilities or pipe-line systems appearing to the Secretary of State to be of the same description.

(2) If different areas of Great Britain are specified for any purposes of this paragraph by order made by the Secretary of State, this paragraph shall have effect for those purposes as if any reference to Great Britain included a reference to each of those areas.

(3) An order under this paragraph shall be made by statutory instrument which shall be subject to annulment in pursuance of a resolution of either House of Parliament.

(4) In this paragraph—

"convey" means convey through pipes;

"for supply purposes", in relation to any conveyance or shipment of gas to any premises, means with a view to the gas being supplied to the premises, or being used in the premises by the holder of a licence under section 7A(2) of the 1986 Act;

"gas" and "public gas transporter" have the same meanings as in Part I of the 1986 Act;

"store" means store in, or in a facility which is connected (directly or indirectly) to, a pipe-line system operated by a public gas transporter;

"supply", in relation to gas, means supply to premises to which the gas has been conveyed, other than supply (directly or indirectly) to a public gas transporter, gas supplier or gas shipper.

(5) For the purposes of this paragraph—

(a) gas is shipped if, in pursuance of arrangements made with a public gas transporter, it is introduced into, conveyed by means of or taken out of a pipe-line system operated by that transporter; and

(b) any reference to the shipment of gas to any premises, or to or from any facilities or pipe-line systems, shall be construed accordingly.

Rights of Entry (Gas and Electricity Boards) Act 1954 (c.21)

5.—(1) In subsection (2) of section 1 of the Rights of Entry (Gas and Electricity Boards) Act 1954 (restriction on exercise of rights of entry), for the words "public gas supplier" there shall be substituted the words "gas operator".

(2) In subsection (1) of section 2 of that Act—

(a) in paragraph (a), for the words "public gas supplier" there shall be substituted the words "gas operator";

(b) in that paragraph, after the words "a supplier" there shall be inserted the words "or operator"; and

(c) for the words "the supplier or his employee", in both places where they occur, there shall be substituted the words "the operator or supplier or any employee of the operator or supplier".

(3) In paragraph (a) of subsection (3) of that section, for the words "public gas supplier" there shall be substituted the words "gas operator".

(4) In section 3 of that Act—

(a) for the definition of 'employee' there shall be substituted the following definition—
  " 'employee' means—
     (a) in relation to a gas operator, an officer, servant or agent of the operator and any servant or officer of such an agent; and
     (b) in relation to an electricity supplier, an officer, servant or agent of the supplier;" and

(b) for the definition of 'public gas supplier' there shall be substituted the following definition—
  " 'gas operator' means a public gas transporter, gas supplier or gas shipper within the meaning of Part I of the Gas Act 1986;".

Pipe-lines Act 1962 (c.58)

6.—(1) In section 58(1) of the Pipe-lines Act 1962 (exclusion of application of Act to pipe-lines of certain statutory bodies), for paragraph (a) there shall be substituted the following paragraph—

"(a) a public gas transporter within the meaning of Part I of the Gas Act 1986;"

(2) After that section there shall be inserted the following sections—

"**Avoidance of damage by buildings etc to pipe-lines of a public gas transporter**

58A.—(1) Notwithstanding subsection (4) of section 58 of this Act, but subject to subsection (2) of this section, the references to a pipe-line in sections 27(1) and 31(1) of this Act (protection of pipe-lines imperilled by buildings, structures or deposits) shall include references to any pipe-line operated by a public gas transporter other than one laid in a street or a service pipe.

(2) The application by virtue of subsection (1) of this section of sections 27(1) and 31(1) of this Act to a particular part of any pipe-line shall be dependent upon there having been previously deposited with every local authority in whose area the part lies by the public gas transporter a map (drawn to an appropriate scale) showing the route taken by the part.

(3) A local authority holding a map relating to a pipe-line operated by a public gas transporter shall keep the map at their offices, and shall secure that it is open to inspection by any person at all reasonable times free of charge.

(4) In this section—
  'local authority' means—
     (a) in England, the council of a county, district or London borough, and the Common Council of the City of London;
     (b) in Wales, the council of a county or county borough; and
     (c) in Scotland, a council constituted under section 2 of the Local Government etc. (Scotland) Act 1994;
  'public gas transporter' and 'service pipe' have the same meanings as in Part I of the Gas Act 1986;
  'street' has the same meaning as in Part III of the New Roads and Street Works Act 1991.

(5) In relation to any time before 1st April 1996, the definition of 'local authority' in subsection (4) of this section shall have effect as if—

(a) in paragraph (b), for the words 'county borough' there were substituted the word 'district'; and

(b) in paragraph (c), for the words 'a council constituted under section 2 of the Local Government etc. (Scotland) Act 1994' there were substituted the words 'an islands or district council'.

(6) In its application to Scotland this paragraph shall have effect with the substitution for any reference to a street of a reference to a road within the meaning of Part IV of the New Roads and Street Works Act 1991.

Exclusion of application of Act to construction of small pipes

58B.—(1) In relation to the construction, by any person other than a public gas transporter, of a pipe to which this section applies—

(a) references in sections 1 to 14 of this Act to a pipe-line shall be construed as not including references to such a pipe; and

(b) references in those sections to pipe-line works shall be construed as not including references to works executed in connection with the construction of such a pipe.

(2) This section applies to any pipe—

(a) by which any premises are proposed to be connected to a distribution main of a public gas transporter; and

(b) by which gas is proposed to be conveyed to premises at a rate which is not expected to exceed 75,000 therms in any period of twelve months.

(3) The Secretary of State may, after consulting the Director General of Gas Supply, by order amend subsection (2) above by substituting—

(a) where the limit is for the time being expressed by reference to a number of therms—

(i) such lower number of therms as he considers appropriate; or

(ii) such lower limit, expressed by reference to a number of kilowatt hours, as he considers appropriate; or

(b) where the limit is for the time being expressed by reference to a number of kilowatt hours, such lower number of kilowatt hours as he considers appropriate.

(4) An order under subsection (3) above shall be made by statutory instrument which shall be subject to annulment in pursuance of a resolution of either House of Parliament.

(5) In this section 'distribution main' and 'public gas transporter' have the same meanings as in Part I of the Gas Act 1986.

(6) In relation to any time after 31st December 1999, the reference in subsection (2) above to 75,000 therms shall be construed as a reference to 2,196,000 kilowatt hours.

(7) This section is without prejudice to anything in section 58 of this Act."

Gas Act 1965 (c.36)

7.—(1) In Part II of the Gas Act 1965 for the words "public gas supplier", in each place where they occur, there shall be substituted the words "public gas transporter".

(2) In subsection (2) of section 32 of that Act, for the words "public gas supplier" there shall be substituted the words " 'public gas transporter' ".

(3) In paragraph 14(1) of Schedule 2 to that Act, for the words "public gas suppliers" there shall be substituted the words "public gas transporters".

Local Government (Scotland) Act 1966 (c.51)

8. In paragraph (b) of subsection (4) of section 18 of the Local Government (Scotland) Act 1966 (rating of certain office premises), for the word "supplier" there shall be substituted the word "transporter".

Post Office Act 1969 (c.48)

9. In paragraph (ca) of subsection (1A) of section 7 of the Post Office Act 1969 (powers of Post Office), for the words "public gas supplier" there shall be substituted the words "gas supplier".

Health and Safety at Work etc. Act 1974 (c.37)

10.—(1) Part I of the Health and Safety at Work etc. Act 1974 ("the 1974 Act") shall have effect as if section 58A of the Pipe-lines Act 1962 and section 22A(1)(c) of and paragraphs 17, 20 and 21 of Schedule 2B to the 1986 Act—

(a) were existing statutory provisions within the meaning of Part I of the 1974 Act; and

(b) were specified in the third column of Schedule 1 to that Act.

(2) Without prejudice to the generality of subsection (1) of section 15 of the 1974 Act (health and safety regulations), regulations under that section may repeal or modify any of the provisions mentioned in sub-paragraph (1) above.

(3) Nothing in sub-paragraph (1) above shall affect the operation of section 18 of the 1974 Act (enforcement of relevant statutory provisions) in relation to any time before such day as the Secretary of State may by order made by statutory instrument appoint, and different days may be appointed for different purposes.

Energy Act 1976 (c.76)

11.—(1) In subsection (1) of section 9 of the Energy Act 1976 (liquefaction of offshore natural gas), for the words from "except" to the end there shall be substituted the words "except where—

(a) methane or ethane is liquefied for the purpose of enabling it to be stored;

(b) the process of liquefaction is carried out by a public gas transporter within the meaning of Part I of the Gas Act 1986; or

(c) small quantities of liquid methane or ethane are produced in the course of a gas processing operation within the meaning of section 12 of the Gas Act 1995."

(2) In subsection (2) of section 12 of that Act (disposal of gas by flaring, etc), for the words "except gas supplied by a public gas supplier" there shall be substituted the words "except gas conveyed through pipes to premises by a public gas transporter".

Water (Scotland) Act 1980 (c.45)

12. In paragraph (c) of the proviso to section 36 of Schedule 4 to the Water (Scotland) Act 1980 (provisions to be incorporated in orders relating to water undertakings), for the words—

(a) "gas undertakers" there shall be substituted the words "public gas transporter (within the meaning of Part I of the Gas Act 1986)"; and

(b) "those undertakers" there shall be substituted the words "such public gas transporter".

Bankruptcy (Scotland) Act 1985 (c.66)

13. In paragraph (a) of subsection (4) of section 70 of the Bankruptcy (Scotland) Act 1985 (supplies by utilities), for the words "public gas supplier" there shall be substituted the words "gas supplier".

Insolvency Act 1986 (c.45)

14.—(1) For paragraph (a) of subsection (3) of section 233 of the Insolvency Act 1986 (supplies of gas, water, electricity etc.) there shall be substituted the following paragraph—

"(a) a supply of gas by a gas supplier within the meaning of Part I of the Gas Act 1986;".

(2) Paragraph (a) of subsection (5) of that section shall cease to have effect.

(3) For paragraph (a) of subsection (4) of section 372 of that Act (supplies of gas, water, electricity etc.) there shall be substituted the following paragraph—

"(a) a supply of gas by a gas supplier within the meaning of Part I of the Gas Act 1986;".

(4) Paragraph (a) of subsection (5) of that section shall cease to have effect.

Consumer Protection Act 1987 (c.43)

15.—(1) In paragraph (c) of subsection (7) of section 10 of the Consumer Protection Act 1987 (the general safety requirement), for the words "section 6, 7 or 8" to the end there shall be substituted the following words "section 7A of the Gas Act 1986 (licensing of gas suppliers and gas shippers) or paragraph 5 of Schedule 2A to that Act (supply to very large customers an exception to prohibition on unlicensed activities)."

(2) In paragraph (c) of subsection (7) of section 11 of that Act (safety regulations), for the words "section 6, 7 or 8" to the end there shall be substituted the following words "section 7A of the Gas Act 1986 (licensing of gas suppliers and gas shippers) or paragraph 5 of Schedule 2A to that Act (supply to very large customers an exception to prohibition on unlicensed activities)."

Road Traffic (Driver Licensing and Information Systems) Act 1989 (c.22)

16. In paragraph 8 of Schedule 5 to the Road Traffic (Driver Licensing and Information Systems) Act 1989 (driver information systems: undertakers' works)—

(a) in the definition of "relevant undertaker", for the words "public gas supplier" there shall be substituted the words "public gas transporter"; and

(b) in the definition of "undertaker's works", for the words "supplying gas as a public gas supplier" there shall be substituted the words "conveying gas as a public gas transporter".

Electricity Act 1989 (c.29)

17.—(1) In paragraph 3 of Schedule 4 to the Electricity Act 1989 (other powers etc. of licence holders)—

(a) in sub-paragraph (1)(b), for the words "under the control of a public gas supplier" there shall be substituted the words "operated by a public gas transporter";

(b) in sub-paragraph (2), for the words "public gas supplier" there shall be substituted the words "public gas transporter".

(2) In sub-paragraph (1)(a) of paragraph 4 of that Schedule, for the words "public gas supplier" there shall be substituted the words "public gas transporter".

(3) In paragraph 12 of that Schedule, for the words "public gas supplier" there shall be substituted the words "public gas transporter".

Town and Country Planning Act 1990 (c.8)

18.—(1) In section 252 of the Town and Country Planning Act 1990 (procedure for making orders)—

(a) in paragraph (b) of subsection (2), for the words "public gas supplier" there shall be substituted the words "public gas transporter";

(b) in subsection (4), for the words "public gas supplier" there shall be substituted the words "public gas transporter"; and

(c) in subsection (5), for the word "supplier" there shall be substituted the word "transporter".

(2) In subsection (3) of section 262 of that Act (meaning of 'statutory undertakers'), for the words "public gas supplier" there shall be substituted the words "public gas transporter".

(3) In subsection (2) of section 265 of that Act (meaning of 'the appropriate Minister'), for the words "public gas supplier" there shall be substituted the words "public gas transporter".

(4) In subsection (1) of section 336 of that Act (interpretation), for the words "public gas supplier" there shall be substituted the words "public gas transporter".

Enterprise and New Towns (Scotland) Act 1990 (c.35)

19. In section 9(5) of the Enterprise and New Towns (Scotland) Act 1990 (powers of entry: meanings of certain expressions), for the words "Schedule 7 to the Gas Act 1986" there shall be substituted the words "Schedule 4 to the Gas Act 1995".

Natural Heritage (Scotland) Act 1991 (c.28)

20. In section 7 of the Natural Heritage (Scotland) Act 1991 (powers of entry)—

(a) in subsection (5), the words from "(within" to the end shall cease to have effect; and

(b) after subsection (5) there shall be inserted—

"(5A) In subsection (5) above, "appropriate Minister" has the same meaning as in section 213(1) of the Town and Country Planning (Scotland) Act 1972; but this subsection is subject to paragraph 2(10) of Schedule 4 to the Gas Act 1995.".

Central Rating Lists Regulations 1994 (S.I. 1994/3121)

21. In Part 3 of the Schedule to the Central Rating Lists Regulations 1994, for the words "public gas supplier", in both places where they occur, there shall be substituted the words "public gas transporter".

GENERAL NOTE

Minor and consequential amendments are made; perhaps the most important are in relation to the Pipelines Act 1962, s.58, relating to avoidance of damage by buildings to pipelines of a public gas transporter.

Section 17(1)   SCHEDULE 5

TRANSITIONAL PROVISIONS AND SAVINGS

PART I

PUBLIC GAS SUPPLIERS' AUTHORISATIONS

Preliminary

1.—(1) The provisions of this Part of this Schedule have effect as respects each person who is a public gas supplier immediately before the appointed day (in this Part of this Schedule referred to as "the public gas supplier") for the purpose of securing that his authorisation under section 7 of the 1986 Act has effect on and after that day as if it were—

(a) a licence under that section (licensing of public gas transporters) granted to one of the persons mentioned in sub-paragraph (2) below;

(b) a licence under subsection (1) of section 7A of that Act (licensing of gas suppliers) granted to the other of those persons; and

(c) a licence under subsection (2) of that section (licensing of gas shippers) granted to the person mentioned in paragraph (b) above.

(2) The persons referred to in sub-paragraph (1) above are—

(a) the public gas supplier; and

(b) such one of his associates as may be nominated by him for the purposes of this sub-paragraph (in this Part of this Schedule referred to as the nominated associate).

(3) For the purposes of this paragraph a company is an associate of the public gas supplier if—

(a) the company is registered under the Companies Act 1985 and is limited by shares; and

(b) either the company is wholly owned by the supplier or the supplier is wholly owned by the company.

Duty of public gas supplier to nominate associates and make transfer scheme

2.—(1) Before such date as the Secretary of State may direct, the public gas supplier shall—

(a) make such nomination as he thinks fit for the purposes of sub-paragraph (2) of paragraph 1 above; and

(b) make a scheme for the division of all his property, rights and liabilities between the persons mentioned in that sub-paragraph.

(2) Such a scheme may—

(a) define the property, rights and liabilities to be allocated to the nominated associate—

    (i) by specifying or describing the property, rights and liabilities in question;

    (ii) by referring to all (or all but as much as may be excepted) of the property, rights and liabilities comprised in a specified part of the public gas supplier's undertaking; or

    (iii) partly in the one way and partly in the other;

(b) provide that any rights or liabilities specified or described in the scheme shall be enforceable either by or against either, or by or against both, of the persons mentioned in paragraph 1(2) above;

(c) impose on either of those persons an obligation to enter into such written agreements with, or execute such other instruments in favour of, the other of those persons as may be specified in the scheme; and

(d) make such supplemental, incidental and consequential provision as the supplier considers appropriate.

(3) Without prejudice to the generality of sub-paragraph (2)(d) above, such a scheme may, in relation to transfers or transactions effected in pursuance of the scheme, make provision, either generally or for specified purposes—

(a) for the transfers or transactions to be regarded as taking place in a specified order; and

(b) for the nominated associate to be treated as the same person in law as the public gas supplier.

(4) An obligation imposed by a provision included in such a scheme by virtue of sub-paragraph (2)(c) above shall be enforceable by civil proceedings by the other person for an injunction or for interdict or for any other appropriate relief or remedy.

(5) A transaction of any description which is effected in pursuance of such a provision as is mentioned in sub-paragraph (4) above—

(a) shall have effect subject to the provisions of any enactment which provides for transactions of that description to be registered in any statutory register; but

(b) subject to that, shall be binding on all other persons, notwithstanding that it would, apart from this sub-paragraph, have required the consent or concurrence of any other person.

(6) Where a lease of any land is granted in pursuance of such a provision as is mentioned in sub-paragraph (4) above, any right of pre-emption or other like right affecting that land—

(a) shall not become exercisable by reason of the grant of the lease; but

(b) shall have effect as if the lessee were the same person in law as the lessor.

Functions of Secretary of State in relation to nominations and transfer scheme

3.—(1) If the public gas supplier fails, before the date specified in the Secretary of State's direction under paragraph 2 above, to make a nomination for the purposes of sub-paragraph (2) of paragraph 1 above, the Secretary of State may himself make a nomination for the purposes of that sub-paragraph.

(2) A scheme under paragraph 2 above shall not take effect unless it is approved by the Secretary of State; and the Secretary of State may if he thinks fit, before approving such a scheme, make such modifications of the scheme as he considers appropriate for the purpose of securing that the scheme makes such provision, and only such provision, as he considers requisite or expedient for the purposes of this Part of this Schedule.

(3) If, in relation to such a scheme—

(a) the public gas supplier fails, before the date specified in the Secretary of State's direction under paragraph 2 above, to submit the scheme for the approval of the Secretary of State; or

(b) the Secretary of State decides not to approve the scheme that has been submitted to him by the supplier because (even with modifications) it would not make such provision, and only such provision, as he considers requisite or expedient for the purposes of this Part of this Schedule,

the Secretary of State may himself make the scheme.

Duty of Secretary of State to make licensing scheme

4.—(1) As soon as practicable after the date specified in the Secretary of State's direction under paragraph 2 above and in any event before the appointed day, the Secretary of State shall make a scheme providing for the public gas supplier's authorisation under section 7 of the 1986 Act to have effect as mentioned in paragraph 1(1) above.

(2) In making a scheme under this paragraph, the Secretary of State shall have regard to the provisions of the scheme made under paragraph 2 above.

(3) Subject to sub-paragraph (4) below, a scheme under this paragraph shall provide that each condition which by virtue of section 8(2) of this Act is a standard condition for the purposes of—

(a) licences under section 7 of the 1986 Act;

(b) licences under subsection (1) of section 7A of that Act; or

(c) licences under subsection (2) of that section,

shall be incorporated in the licence treated as granted under that section or, as the case may be, the licence treated as granted under that subsection.

(4) Such a scheme may provide that each licence which is treated as so granted (including the terms and conditions which are derived from the authorisation and the standard conditions which are incorporated by virtue of sub-paragraph (3) above) shall have effect with—

(a) such incidental, consequential and supplementary amendments as appear to the Secretary of State to be necessary or expedient;

(b) such amendments as the Secretary of State thinks fit for varying the period of notice required for the revocation of the licence in accordance with any term contained in it; and

(c) such other amendments (if any) as may be agreed between the Secretary of State and the public gas supplier;

and such a scheme may also make such transitional provision as appears to the Secretary of State to be necessary or expedient.

(5) As soon as practicable after making a scheme under this paragraph, the Secretary of State shall publish the text of each licence which by virtue of the scheme is treated as granted under section 7 or 7A(1) or (2) of the 1986 Act; and any text so published shall be treated as authoritative unless the contrary is shown.

Information etc. for purposes of Secretary of State's functions

5.—(1) It shall be the duty of the public gas supplier to provide the Secretary of State with all such information and other assistance as he may require for the purposes of or in connection with the exercise of any function conferred on him by paragraph 3 or paragraph 4(1) to (4) above.

(2) The Secretary of State shall not exercise any function conferred on him by paragraph 3 or paragraph 4(1) to (4) above except after consultation with the public gas supplier.

Effect of schemes

6.—(1) Subject to the provisions of paragraph 7 below, on the appointed day all property, rights and liabilities—

(a) to which immediately before that day the public gas supplier was entitled or subject; and

(b) which are allocated to the nominated associate by the scheme under paragraph 2 above,

shall become by virtue of this paragraph property, rights and liabilities of that associate.

(2) On the appointed day the public gas supplier's authorisation under section 7 of the 1986 Act shall have effect as provided for by the scheme under paragraph 4 above.

Supplementary provisions as to transfers

7.—(1) The provisions of Schedule 10 to the Electricity Act 1989 (supplementary provisions as to transfers under sections 66 and 67 of that Act) shall apply—

(a) with the modifications made by sub-paragraph (2) below; and

(b) to the extent mentioned in those provisions as modified by that sub-paragraph, to any transfer which is effected by paragraph 6 above; and that paragraph shall have effect subject to those provisions as so modified.

(2) The provisions of that Schedule shall apply as if—

(a) paragraphs 2(4) and (5), 3 and 6(2), and in paragraphs 4(4)(b) and 8(1) and (2) the words "or of a direction under paragraph 2(4) above", were omitted;

(b) any reference to transfers effected in pursuance of a transfer scheme were references to transfers effected by paragraph 6 above in pursuance of the scheme under paragraph 2 above;

(c) any reference to the transferor were a reference to the public gas supplier;

(d) any reference to a transfer of all property, rights and liabilities comprised in a specified part of the transferor's undertaking were a reference to a transfer of all (or all but as much as may be excepted) of the property, rights and liabilities comprised in a specified part of the supplier's undertaking;

(e) any reference to the transferee of a specified part or any other part of the transferor's undertaking were a reference to a transferee of a specified part or any other part of the supplier's undertaking; and

(f) any reference to the transfer date were a reference to the appointed day.

(3) For the purposes of sub-paragraphs (1) and (2)(b), (d) and (e) above, any property, rights or liabilities retained by the public gas supplier in pursuance of the scheme under paragraph 2 above shall be deemed to be transferred to the supplier by paragraph 6 above in pursuance of the scheme.

Shares issued to public gas supplier by transferee

8. Any shares issued to the public gas supplier by the transferee in pursuance of the scheme under paragraph 2 above—

(a) shall be of such nominal value as may be specified in or determined under the scheme;

(b) shall be issued or allotted on such terms as may be so specified or determined; and

(c) shall be issued as fully paid and treated for the purposes of the Companies Act 1985 as if they had been paid up by virtue of the payment to the transferee in cash of their nominal value and, if the scheme so provides, such premium as may be so specified or determined.

Statutory accounts

9.—(1) This paragraph has effect for the purposes of any statutory accounts of the transferee, that is to say, any accounts prepared by the transferee for the purpose of any provision of the Companies Act 1985 (including group accounts).

(2) Subject to sub-paragraph (3) below, the value or amount to be assigned to any asset or liability which is vested in the transferee by virtue of paragraph 6 above shall be—

(a) the value or amount (if any) assigned to the asset or liability for the purposes of the corresponding statement of accounts prepared by the public gas supplier in respect of the last complete accounting year of the supplier to end before the appointed day; or

(b) if the asset or liability is part only of an asset or liability to which a value or amount is so assigned, so much of that value or amount as may be determined by or under the scheme under paragraph 2 above; or

(c) if no value or amount is given by paragraph (a) or (b) above or the value or amount so given is inappropriate in all the circumstances of the case, such value or amount as may be determined, on the basis of the supplier's accounting records, by or under that scheme.

(3) The amount to be included in respect of any item shall be determined as if so much of anything done by the public gas supplier (whether by way of acquiring, revaluing or disposing of any asset or incurring, revaluing or discharging any liability, or by carrying any amount to any provision or reserve, or otherwise) as may be determined by or under the scheme under paragraph 2 above had been done by the transferee.

(4) Without prejudice to the generality of the preceding provisions of this paragraph, the amount to be included from time to time in any reserves of the transferee as representing the transferee's accumulated realised profits shall be determined as if such proportion of any profits realised and retained by the public gas supplier as is determined by or under the scheme under paragraph 2 above had been realised and retained by the transferee.

(5) In this paragraph, in relation to the public gas supplier—

"accounting records" means accounting records kept by the supplier in pursuance of section 221 of the Companies Act 1985;

"complete accounting year" means a financial year of the supplier determined in accordance with section 223 of that Act.

Corporation tax

10.—(1) Any shares issued to the public gas supplier by the transferee in pursuance of the scheme under paragraph 2 above shall be treated for the purposes of the Corporation Tax Acts as if they had been issued wholly in consideration of a subscription paid to the transferee (and attributable equally between those shares) of an amount equal to the difference between—

(a) the value, on the appointed day, of the property, rights and liabilities vested in the transferee by paragraph 6 above; and

(b) the principal sum payable under any debentures issued to the supplier by the transferee in pursuance of the scheme.

(2) The value required to be determined for the purposes of sub-paragraph (1)(a) above is market value, as defined in section 272 of the Taxation of Chargeable Gains Act 1992.

(3) Any debenture issued to the public gas supplier by the transferee in pursuance of the scheme under paragraph 2 above shall be treated for the purposes of the Corporation Tax Acts as if it had been issued—

(a) wholly in consideration of a loan made to the transferee of an amount equal to the principal sum payable under the debenture; and

(b) wholly and exclusively for the purposes of the trade or business carried on by the transferee.

(4) For the purposes of Chapter II of Part VI of the Income and Corporation Taxes Act 1988 (definition of distributions), where in the case of any transfer under paragraph 6 above any consideration given or treated as given in respect of a security relating to—

(a) any liability; or

(b) the use of the principal to which any liability, being a liability to interest or an equivalent liability, relates,

would fall (apart from this sub-paragraph) to be regarded for those purposes as new consideration received by the public gas supplier, that consideration shall be treated instead, to the extent that it relates to so much of the liability as falls in consequence of the transfer to be discharged by the transferee, as if it were new consideration received by the transferee.

Petroleum revenue tax and gas levy

11. Where any transfer is effected by paragraph 6 above, the transferee shall be treated—

(a) for the purposes of section 10(1)(a) of the Oil Taxation Act 1975; and

(b) for the purposes of the Gas Levy Act 1981,

as if it were the same person in law as the public gas supplier.

Consequential modifications of rating provisions

12.—(1) This paragraph applies where any transfer effected by paragraph 6 above is a transfer of a hereditament which, immediately before the appointed day, falls within the description set out in Part 3 of the Schedule to the Central Rating Lists Regulations 1994.

(2) The Secretary of State may by order make such modifications of that Part of that Schedule, and of the British Gas plc (Rateable Values) Order 1994, as may appear to him necessary or expedient as a consequence of the transfer.

(3) An order under this paragraph which is made after the appointed day may have effect as from that day or any later day.

(4) Where, by virtue of sub-paragraph (3) above, an order under this paragraph has effect from a day earlier than that on which it is made, any necessary alteration shall be made with effect from that earlier day to any central rating list in which the hereditament is shown.

(5) An order under this paragraph shall be made by statutory instrument which shall be subject to annulment in pursuance of a resolution of either House of Parliament.

PART II

OTHER TRANSITIONAL PROVISIONS AND SAVINGS

Approvals under section 5(3)

13. Any approval—

(a) which has been given by the Secretary of State for the purposes of section 5(3) of the 1986 Act (approval of contract for supply of propane or butane); and

(b) which is in force immediately before the appointed day,
shall have effect on and after that day as if it had been given for the purposes of paragraph 3 of Schedule 2A to that Act.

Notifications under section 6

14.—(1) This paragraph applies where any notification given, or having effect as if given, to the Secretary of State under section 6(1) of the 1986 Act (exceptions to section 5) by any person ("the gas supplier") is in force immediately before the appointed day.

(2) The notification shall have effect on and after the appointed day as if it had been given to the Director under paragraph 5(1) of Schedule 2A to the 1986 Act (exceptions to prohibition on unlicensed activities).

(3) Before the appointed day, such one or more of the following as may be requisite to meet the particular circumstances of the case, namely—

(a) an exemption under section 6A of the 1986 Act (exemptions from prohibition) which is an exemption from section 5(1)(a) of that Act; and

(b) a licence under section 7A(2) of that Act (licensing of gas shippers),

shall be granted to the gas supplier, to come into force on that day, by the Secretary of State or, as the case may be, by the Director.

Applications for authorisation under section 7

15.—(1) This paragraph applies where—

(a) an application has been made to the Secretary of State under section 7 of the 1986 Act (authorisation of public gas suppliers) by any person ("the applicant"); and

(b) the application is not determined before the appointed day.

(2) Subject to the following provisions of this paragraph, the application shall have effect on and after the appointed day as if it were an application to the Director (in such terms as may be specified by the applicant for the purposes of this sub-paragraph) for—

(a) a licence under section 7 of the 1986 Act (licensing of public gas transporters) to be granted to one of the persons mentioned in sub-paragraph (3) below;

(b) a licence under subsection (1) of section 7A of that Act (licensing of gas suppliers) to be granted to the other of those persons; and

(c) a licence under subsection (2) of that section (licensing of gas shippers) to be granted to the person mentioned in paragraph (b) above.

(3) The persons referred to in sub-paragraph (2) above are—

(a) the applicant; and

(b) such one of his associates as may be nominated by him for the purposes of this sub-paragraph.

(4) Sections 7, 7A and 7B of the 1986 Act shall apply in relation to the application, and any licence granted or proposed to be granted on the application, as if subsections (5) and (6) of section 7, and subsections (1) and (2) of section 7B, were omitted.

(5) No licence shall be granted on the application except with the consent of the Secretary of State; and before giving his consent the Secretary of State shall consult—

(a) the Health and Safety Executive; and

(b) any public gas transporter whose authorised area includes the whole or any part of the area to which the application relates.

(6) For the purposes of this paragraph a company is an associate of the applicant if—

(a) the company is registered under the Companies Act 1985 and is limited by shares; and

(b) either the company is wholly owned by the applicant or the applicant is wholly owned by the company.

(7) Any reference in this paragraph to a licence of any description includes a reference to an extension of such a licence.

Individual authorisations under section 8

16.—(1) The provisions of this paragraph have effect as respects each person who holds, or is treated as holding, an authorisation under section 8 of the 1986 Act (authorisation of persons other than public gas suppliers) which is in force immediately before the appointed day (a "gas supplier") for the purpose of securing that the authorisation has effect on and after that day as if it were such one or more of the following as may be requisite to meet the particular circumstances of the case, namely—

(a) an exemption from section 5(1)(a) of that Act granted under section 6A of that Act (exemptions from prohibition);

(b) a licence granted under section 7A(1) of that Act (licensing of gas suppliers), or an exemption from section 5(1)(b) of that Act granted under section 6A of that Act; and

(c) a licence granted under section 7A(2) of that Act (licensing of gas shippers).

(2) As soon as practicable after the passing of this Act, and in any event before the appointed day, the Secretary of State shall make a scheme providing for each gas supplier's authorisation under section 8 of the 1986 Act to have effect as mentioned in sub-paragraph (1) above.

(3) Subject to sub-paragraphs (4) and (5) below, a scheme under this paragraph shall provide that each condition which by virtue of section 8(2) of this Act is a standard condition for the purposes of—

(a) licences under subsection (1) of section 7A of the 1986 Act; or

(b) licences under subsection (2) of that section,

shall be incorporated in any licence treated as granted under that subsection.

(4) Sub-paragraph (3) above shall not apply in relation to a licence treated as granted under section 7A(1) of the 1986 Act which authorises only the supply to premises of gas which has been conveyed to the premises otherwise than by a public gas transporter.

(5) A scheme under this paragraph may provide that any licence which is treated as granted under section 7A(1) or (2) of the 1986 Act and any exemption which is treated as granted under section 6A of that Act (including the terms and conditions which are derived from the authorisation and, in the case of a licence, the standard conditions which are incorporated by virtue of sub-paragraph (3) above) shall have effect with—

(a) such incidental, consequential and supplementary amendments as appear to the Secretary of State to be necessary or expedient;

(b) such amendments relating to the revocation or suspension of the licence or exemption as the Secretary of State thinks fit; and

(c) such other amendments (if any) as may be agreed between the Secretary of State and the gas supplier concerned;

and such a scheme may also make such transitional provision as appears to the Secretary of State to be necessary or expedient.

(6) A scheme under this paragraph may make different provisions for different cases or classes of cases determined by, or in accordance with, the provisions of the scheme.

(7) As soon as practicable after making a scheme under this paragraph, the Secretary of State shall publish, as respects each different case or class of case—

(a) the text of any exemption which by virtue of the scheme is treated as granted under section 6A of the 1986 Act; and

(b) the text of any licence which by virtue of the scheme is treated as granted under section 7A(1) or (2) of that Act;

and any text so published shall be treated as authoritative unless the contrary is shown.

(8) It shall be the duty of each gas supplier to provide the Secretary of State with all such information and other assistance as he may require for the purposes of or in connection with the exercise of any function conferred on him by sub-paragraphs (1) to (6) above.

(9) The Secretary of State shall not exercise any function conferred on him by sub-paragraphs (1) to (6) above except after consultation with such gas suppliers as he considers appropriate.

(10) On the appointed day each gas supplier's authorisation under section 8 of the 1986 Act shall have effect as provided for by the scheme under this paragraph.

Class authorisations under section 8

17.—(1) Subject to sub-paragraph (2) below, any authorisation granted under section 8 of the 1986 Act to persons of a class which is in force immediately before the appointed day shall have effect on and after that day as if it—

(a) were an exemption from such one or more of paragraphs (a), (b) and (c) of section 5(1) of that Act as may be requisite to meet the particular circumstances of the case; and

(b) had been granted under section 6A of that Act on the same terms and subject to the same conditions as those on or subject to which it had been granted as an authorisation under the said section 8.

(2) If, in the case of any such authorisation as is mentioned in sub-paragraph (1) above, the Secretary of State is satisfied that exemption from such one or more of paragraphs (a), (b) and (c) of section 5(1) of the 1986 Act as may be requisite to meet the particular circumstances of the case will be granted under section 6A of that Act as from the appointed day, he may by order direct that that sub-paragraph shall not apply in relation to the authorisation.

(3) An order under this paragraph shall be made by statutory instrument which shall be subject to annulment in pursuance of a resolution of either House of Parliament.

Gas shipping arrangements already made

18.—(1) Any arrangement—

(a) which any person has made with a public gas supplier for gas to be introduced into, conveyed by means of or taken out of a pipe-line system operated by that supplier; and

(b) which is in force immediately before the appointed day,

shall be treated for the purposes of section 5(1)(c) of the 1986 Act as if it had been made on that day with the supplier's transport successor.

(2) In this Part of this Schedule "transport successor", in relation to a public gas supplier, means the person who becomes a public gas transporter by virtue of the scheme made by or in relation to that supplier under Part I of this Schedule.

Former tariff customers

19.—(1) This paragraph applies where immediately before the appointed day a public gas supplier ("the public gas supplier") is supplying tariff customers with gas.

(2) The supplier's supply successor shall be deemed to have contracted with those customers for the supply of gas as from that day.

(3) The express terms and conditions of a contract which, by virtue of sub-paragraph (2) above, is deemed to have been made shall be provided for by the scheme made under this paragraph.

(4) Before such date as the Secretary of State may direct, the public gas supplier shall make a scheme for determining the terms and conditions which are to be incorporated in the contracts which, by virtue of sub-paragraph (2) above, are to be deemed to have been made.

(5) A scheme under this paragraph may—

(a) make different provisions for different cases or classes of cases, or for different areas, determined by, or in accordance with, the provisions of the scheme; and

(b) make such supplemental, incidental, consequential and transitional provisions as the public gas supplier considers appropriate.

(6) A scheme under this paragraph shall not take effect unless it is approved by the Secretary of State; and the Secretary of State may modify such a scheme before approving it.

(7) If, in relation to such a scheme—

(a) the public gas supplier fails, before the date specified in the Secretary of State's direction under sub-paragraph (4) above, to submit the scheme for the approval of the Secretary of State; or

(b) the Secretary of State decides not to approve the scheme that has been submitted to him by the supplier (either with or without modifications),

the Secretary of State may himself make the scheme.

(8) It shall be the duty of the public gas supplier to provide the Secretary of State with all such information and other assistance as he may require for the purposes of or in connection with the exercise of any function conferred on him by sub-paragraph (6) or (7) above.

(9) The Secretary of State shall not exercise any function conferred on him by sub-paragraph (6) or (7) above except after consultation with the public gas supplier.

(10) A scheme made under this paragraph shall be published in the London and Edinburgh Gazettes before the appointed day and shall come into operation on that day; and conclusive evidence of a scheme so made may be given in all courts of justice and in all legal proceedings whatever by the production of a copy of either of those Gazettes purporting to contain it.

(11) In this Part of this Schedule "supply successor", in relation to a public gas supplier, means the person who becomes a gas supplier by virtue of a scheme made by or in relation to that public gas supplier under Part I of this Schedule.

Connection charges

20.—(1) Sub-paragraph (2) below applies where—

(a) a public gas supplier has been required under subsection (1) (duty to supply certain premises) of section 10 of the 1986 Act to give a supply of gas to any premises; and

(b) the required supply is not given before the appointed day.

(2) The requirement shall have effect on and after the appointed day as if it were—

(a) a request made to the supplier's supply successor for a supply of gas; and

(b) if the premises are not connected to a relevant main, a requirement made of the supplier's transport successor under subsection (2)(a) of section 10 requiring him to connect the premises to such a main and supply and lay any pipe that may be necessary for that purpose.

(3) Sub-paragraph (4) below applies to any regulations—

(a) which have been made, or have effect as if made, by the Secretary of State under subsection (4) (connection charges) of section 10; and

(b) which are in force immediately before the appointed day.

(4) Regulations to which this sub-paragraph applies shall have effect on and after the appointed day as if—

(a) they had been made by the Director;

(b) any reference to a public gas supplier were a reference to a public gas transporter;

(c) any reference to a supply of gas were a reference to a connection to a relevant main;

(d) the reference to subsection (1) of section 10 were a reference to subsection (2) of that section; and

(e) anything done before the appointed day by or in relation to a public gas supplier had been done on that day by or in relation to the supplier's transport successor.

(5) Expressions used in this paragraph have the same meanings as in section 10.

Promotion of efficient use of gas

21. Any determination or direction—

(a) which has been made as respects a public gas supplier, or given to such a supplier, under section 15B of the 1986 Act (promotion of the efficient use of gas); and

(b) which is in force immediately before the appointed day,

shall have effect on and after that day as if it had been made as respects, or given to, the supply successor of that supplier under section 33BB of that Act.

Meter testing and stamping

22.—(1) Any regulations—

(a) which have been made, or have effect as if made, by the Secretary of State under section 17 of the 1986 Act (meter testing and stamping); and

(b) which are in force immediately before the appointed day,

shall have effect on and after that day as if they had been made by the Director and as if any reference in them to the Secretary of State were a reference to the Director.

(2) Any approval, consent or authorisation—

(a) which has been given by the Secretary of State under section 17 of the 1986 Act, or under regulations made, or having effect as if made, under that section; and

(b) which is in force immediately before the appointed day,

shall have effect on and after that day as if it had been given by the Director.

Restrictions on use of certain information

23. Notwithstanding the repeal by this Act of section 63 of the 1986 Act (restrictions on use of certain information), any direction given by the Secretary of State to the holder of an authorisation under section 7 of that Act shall continue to have effect so far as it relates to any relevant negotiations (within the meaning of the said section 63) which took place before the appointed day.

Recovery of gas charges etc.

24.—(1) Where—

(a) such a demand as is mentioned in paragraph 7(5) of Schedule 5 to the 1986 Act (recovery of gas charges etc.) has been made by a public gas supplier; and

(b) the payment demanded is not made before the appointed day,

paragraph 7(1) of Schedule 2B to the 1986 Act shall have effect as if the demand had been made by the supplier's supply successor on the day on which it was made by the supplier.

(2) Where—

(a) such a notice of intention as is mentioned in paragraph 7(5) of Schedule 5 to the 1986 Act has been given by a public gas supplier; and

(b) the supply of gas is not cut off before the appointed day,

paragraph 7(3) of Schedule 2B to the 1986 Act shall have effect as if the notice had been given by the supplier's supply successor on the day on which it was given by the supplier.

Use of antifluctuators and valves

25. Any notice—

(a) which has been given by a public gas supplier under sub-paragraph (1) or (2) of paragraph 8 (use of antifluctuators and valves) of Schedule 5 to the 1986 Act; and

(b) which is in force immediately before the appointed day,

shall have effect on and after that day as if it had been given on that day under sub-paragraph (1) or, as the case may be, sub-paragraph (2) of paragraph 17 of Schedule 2B to that Act by the supplier's transport successor.

Restoration of supply without consent

26.—(1) Where—

(a) a supply of gas to any premises has been cut off by a public gas supplier under paragraph 8 (use of antifluctuators and valves) or paragraph 9 (improper use of gas) of Schedule 5 to the 1986 Act; and

(b) the supply is not restored before the appointed day,

each of paragraphs 11 and 25 of Schedule 2B to that Act shall have effect as if those premises had been disconnected on that day by the supplier's transport successor otherwise than in the exercise of such a power as is mentioned in sub-paragraph (1) of that paragraph.

(2) Where—

(a) a supply of gas to any premises has been cut off by a public gas supplier otherwise than under paragraph 8 or 9 of Schedule 5 to the 1986 Act and otherwise than in the exercise of a power conferred by regulations under section 18(2) of that Act; and

(b) the supply is not restored before the appointed day,

each of paragraphs 11 and 25 of Schedule 2B to that Act shall have effect as if a supply of gas to those premises had been cut off on that day by the supplier's supply successor otherwise than in the exercise of such a power as is mentioned in sub-paragraph (1) of that paragraph.

Failure to notify connection or disconnection of service pipe

27. Any notice—

(a) which has been given to a public gas supplier under sub-paragraph (1) of paragraph 12 (failure to notify connection or disconnection of service pipe) of Schedule 5 to the 1986 Act; and

(b) which is in force immediately before the appointed day,

shall have effect on and after that day as if it had been given on that day under sub-paragraph (1) of paragraph 12 of Schedule 2B to that Act to the supplier's transport successor.

Entry warrants

28.—(1) Any warrant—

(a) which has been granted under section 2(1) of the Rights of Entry (Gas and Electricity Boards) Act 1954 (warrant to authorise entry) for the purpose of enabling an employee of a public gas supplier to enter any premises, in accordance with paragraph 15(1)(b) of Schedule 5 to the 1986 Act, in order to ascertain the quantity of gas supplied to those premises; and

(b) which is in force immediately before the appointed day,

shall have effect on and after that day as if it had been granted for the purpose of enabling an employee of the supplier's supply successor who is authorised by him for the purpose to enter those premises, in accordance with paragraph 23(1)(b) of Schedule 2B to the 1986 Act, in order to ascertain the quantity of gas supplied to the premises.

(2) Sub-paragraph (3) below applies to any warrant—

(a) which has been granted under section 2(1) of the Rights of Entry (Gas and Electricity Boards) Act 1954 for the purpose of enabling an employee of a public gas supplier to enter any premises in order to cut off or discontinue the supply of gas to those premises in accordance with paragraph 16(1) of Schedule 5 to the 1986 Act; and

(b) which is in force immediately before the appointed day.

(3) Any warrant to which this sub-paragraph applies shall have effect on and after the appointed day as if it had been granted as two separate warrants—

(a) one for the purpose of enabling an employee of the supplier's transport successor who is authorised by him for the purpose to enter the premises, in accordance with sub-paragraph (2) of paragraph 24 of Schedule 2B to the 1986 Act, in order to disconnect the premises; and

(b) the other for the purpose of enabling an employee of the supplier's supply successor who is authorised by him for the purpose to enter the premises, in accordance with that sub-paragraph, in order to cut off or discontinue the supply to the premises.

(4) In this paragraph "employee" has the same meaning as in the Rights of Entry (Gas and Electricity Boards) Act 1954.

Street works notices

29. Any notice—

(a) which has been given by a public gas supplier in England and Wales under section 54, 55 or 57 of the New Roads and Street Works Act 1991, or in Scotland under section 113, 114 or 116 of that Act; and

(b) which is in force immediately before the appointed day,

shall have effect on and after that day as if it had been given by the public gas supplier's transport successor.

Restrictive trade practices

30.—(1) In relation to any supply of gas before the appointed day, the reference in subsection (2) of section 62 of the 1986 Act (exclusion of agreements from Restrictive Trade Practices Act 1976) to a supply of gas otherwise than under a licence granted under section 7A(1) of the 1986 Act shall have effect—

(a) in the case of a supply before 23rd August 1986, as a reference to a supply of gas otherwise than in performance of any duty imposed by the Gas Act 1972; and

(b) in the case of a supply on or after that date, as a reference to a supply of gas otherwise than under an authorisation granted under section 7 of the 1986 Act.

(2) In relation to any introduction or taking out of gas, or any use of a system or facility, before the appointed day, subsection (2A) of section 62 of the 1986 Act shall have effect as if—

(a) the reference to a public gas transporter were a reference to a public gas supplier; and

(b) the reference to gas shippers were a reference to any persons.

Rating provisions

31. Nothing in this Act shall affect the operation of the following, namely—

(a) sections 19 and 33 of and Schedules 3 and 6 to the General Rate Act 1967 and Schedule 3 to the Local Government Act 1974, so far as those provisions of those Acts continue to have effect in relation to periods ending before 1st April 1990;

(b) the Valuation for Rating (Plant and Machinery) Regulations 1989, so far as those Regulations continue to have effect for the purpose of determining the rateable values of hereditaments for days falling before 1st April 1995;

(c) the Central Rating Lists Regulations 1989, so far as those Regulations continue to have effect in relation to periods ending before 1st April 1995; and

(d) the Central Rating Lists Regulations 1994, so far as those Regulations have effect in relation to periods ending before the appointed day.

GENERAL NOTE

Transitional provisions are dealt with, of which the most important refer to the continuation of business of the former public gas supplier. The critical issue becomes the separation of the transportation function from the supply function—divestment may be to an associate company. It is understood that the Department of Trade and Industry expect that divestment will be to a single company, as to allow otherwise may prejudice existing and continuing contractual relationships in the industry. In addition, transitional provisions are made in respect of other authorisations under the 1986 Act.

Section 17(5)   SCHEDULE 6

REPEALS

Chapter	Short title	Extent of repeal
26 Geo. 5 & 1 Edw. 8 c. 49.	Public Health Act 1936.	In section 229, the word "gas", in both places where it occurs.
1973 c. 41.	Fair Trading Act 1973.	In Schedule 5, paragraph 1.
1986 c. 44.	Gas Act 1986.	Section 6. In section 8A, subsections (3) and (4). Sections 14, 14A and 15. Section 15B. Section 20. In section 32, in subsections (3) and (5), the words "paragraph (a) of", in subsection (4), the word "already", and subsections (6) and (7). In section 33(3), the words "but nothing in this subsection shall require the Council to send any such copy to the Director". In section 33A, subsections (10) and (11).

Chapter	Short title	Extent of repeal
		In section 38(1), the words from "but no person" to the end.
		In section 40, the words "which relates to tariff customers and".
		In section 46(1), the words "Subject to subsection (2) below".
		In section 48(1), the definitions of "regulations" and "tariff customer".
		Section 62(7).
		Section 63.
		In section 64(2), the words "20(9)".
		Schedule 5.
		In Schedule 7, paragraphs 2, 4, 5, 6(2) and (26)(h), 15(4), 17, 20, 26(1) and 31.
1986 c. 45.	Insolvency Act 1986.	Section 233(5)(a).
		Section 372(5)(a).
1991 c. 22.	New Roads and Street Works Act 1991.	In Schedule 8, paragraph 120.
1991 c. 28.	Natural Heritage (Scotland) Act 1991.	In section 7(5), the words from "(within" to the end.
1992 c. 15.	Offshore Safety Act 1992.	In section 2(3)(b), the words "so far as relating to standards affecting safety" and the words "so far as so relating".
1992 c. 43.	Competition and Service (Utilities) Act 1992.	Sections 15 and 16.
		Section 19.
		Section 38.
		Section 53(1).
		In Schedule 1, paragraphs 5, 6 and 9(3).
1993 c. 1.	Gas (Exempt Supplies) Act 1993.	Sections 1 and 2.
1994 c. 19.	Local Government (Wales) Act 1994.	In Schedule 16, paragraph 78.
1994 c. 39.	Local Government etc. (Scotland) Act 1994.	In Schedule 13, paragraph 149.
1994 c. 40.	Deregulation and Contracting Out Act 1994.	In Schedule 16, paragraphs 11 to 13.

INDEX

References are to sections and Schedules

CRIMINAL PROCEDURE (SCOTLAND) ACT 1995*

(1995 c. 46)

ARRANGEMENT OF SECTIONS

PART I

CRIMINAL COURTS

JURISDICTION AND POWERS

The High Court

Solemn courts: general

The sheriff

District courts

Sittings of sheriff and district courts

Territorial jurisdiction: general

PART II

POLICE FUNCTIONS

Lord Advocate's instructions

Detention and questioning

---

* Annotations by Iain Bradley, Solicitor in Scotland and Robert S. Shiels, Solicitor in Scotland.

An Act to consolidate certain enactments relating to criminal procedure in Scotland. **[8th November 1995]**

PARLIAMENTARY DEBATES
    Hansard, H.L. Vol. 565, col. 14; Vol. 566, cols. 384, 581, 894. H.C. Vol. 265, col. 181.

INTRODUCTION AND GENERAL NOTE
    It has been said that it takes lawyers five years to change a habit: if that is correct then the memory of the Criminal Procedure (Scotland) Act 1975 will linger on for some time, most probably in the reference to the very familiar sections. The Criminal Procedure (Scotland) Act 1995 is a consolidating provision so that much of the legal landscape remains the same even though the reference to individual parts has changed.
    The Criminal Procedure (Scotland) Act 1995 has to be seen as part of a substantial Government policy to consolidate Scots criminal law, evidence and procedure. The Criminal Justice (Scotland) Act 1995 amended some aspects of the law of evidence and procedure and made new provisions in relation to attacking the proceeds of crime.
    Once the Criminal Procedure (Scotland) Act 1975 (c.21) had been amended the law was consolidated in the Criminal Procedure (Scotland) Act 1995. The complete package of contemporary legislation must be seen to include also the Criminal Law (Consolidation) (Scotland) Act

1995 (c.39), the Criminal Law (Consequential Provisions) (Scotland) Act 1995 (c.40) and the Proceeds of Crime (Scotland) Act 1995 (c.43). The mechanics of the application of much of the law is to be found in the Act of Adjournal (Criminal Procedure Rules) 1996.

Consideration of the new law is restricted in this note to the Criminal Procedure (Scotland) Act 1995. Comprehensive annotations follow and those should help practitioners round the details of Act but there is benefit in knowing the structure of the Act itself: the parts are set out with general reference to some of the interesting sections.

Part I
Sections 1 to 11 make various provisions in regard to the jurisdiction and powers of the criminal courts of Scotland. There is virtually nothing new in this Part, merely a re-ordering of existing powers.

Part II
Sections 12 to 22 make provision for police functions. The power of the Lord Advocate to issue instructions to a chief constable in regard to the reporting of matters continues to provide an important constitutional safeguard, especially when seen in the context of the proviso to s.17(3) of the Police (Scotland) Act 1967 (c.77). The additional provisions reflect the original provision in law resulting from the Criminal Justice (Scotland) Act 1980 (c.62) as interpreted in subsequent case law.

Part III
Sections 23 to 33 consolidate the law of bail: it is the result of this consolidation that several Acts are no longer required, including the Bail etc. (Scotland) Act 1980 (c.4).

Part IV
Sections 34 to 40 deal with the peculiarly Scottish procedure of judicial examination. Sheriff Gerald Gordon referred to the pre-1980 judicial examination as an "empty ritual": see *The Criminal Justice (Scotland) Act 1980* (1981) (W. Green, Edinburgh) p. xviii. Whether very much more is now achieved is debatable but it is nevertheless the start of criminal proceedings leading for many to trial in a criminal court.

Part V
Sections 41 to 51 are provisions dealing with children and young persons in the capacity of offenders. Reference might also be made to the Children (Scotland) Act 1995 (c.36) which forms an important additional part of current legislation.

Part VI
Sections 52 to 63 make provision for various aspects of mental disorder. Perhaps the most substantial change in the whole of this Act is the introduction in s.55 of examination of facts. This permits evidence to be led (by either party) in order that the court can determine whether it is satisfied beyond reasonable doubt that the accused did the act or made the omission constituting the offence, and if it is satisfied on the balance of probabilities that there are no grounds for acquitting him. This procedure can only follow where an accused is found to be insane: s.54(1). However, it now allows for an examination of circumstances where hitherto no trial would have taken place.

Part VII
Sections 64 to 102 set out the procedural stages and requirement for trial by jury. By s.12 of and Sched. 4 to the Criminal Justice (Scotland) Act 1980 there was abolished the mandatory diet in solemn proceedings and in its place there was established as required the preliminary diet. The new provision includes a first diet for solemn procedure in the sheriff court and a preliminary diet as required for solemn procedure in the High Court of Justiciary. Another change in nomenclature is the demise of the "section 102 letter"; the procedure where the accused desires to plead guilty is now found in s.76.

Part VIII
Sections 103 to 132 deal with appeals from solemn proceedings. Undoubtedly the major reform in this regard is the need to receive the grant of leave to appeal from a single judge in chambers: see s.105. The pressure that this rule puts on getting the ground of appeal stated

correctly at the outset cannot be over-emphasised. Carefully thought-out appeals against conviction are unlikely to be weeded out early on, but speculative appeals against summary sentences may be much reduced.

Part IX

Sections 133 to 172 replicate generally the rules for summary prosecutions that apply for solemn prosecutions. In the Criminal Procedure (Scotland) Act 1975 the division between solemn and summary procedure was more marked than under this Act, *e.g.* the various latitudes and implied terms are now contained in Sched. 3 and apply equally to indictments and complaints by ss.64(6) and 138(4) respectively.

Part X

Sections 173 to 194 replicate generally the rules for summary appeals that apply for solemn appeals. Those familiar with the work of appellate judges will know that numerically the heaviest burden is, or was until the passing of this Act, the appeals against summary sentences. The single judge shift will undoubtedly affect the volume but the concession that two judges may deal with this class of case will be welcomed: s.173(2).

Part XI

Sections 195 to 254 deal with a wide range of post-conviction issues. On occasions the detail of the sections overwhelms the inherent excitement. However, practitioners may look forward to the implementation of s.197 which requires courts at first instance to have regard to sentencing opinions pronounced on statutory authority. It would be crass merely to offer a percentage discount on sentence for a guilty plea but explicit recognition for an acceptance of responsibilities may have a marked effect on summary business.

Part XII

Sections 255 to 286 make provision for evidential matters. There is no attack on the general requirement for a sufficiency of evidence but it is clear from the wide range of provisions that those advising accused persons will require at the earliest opportunity after receiving instructions to narrow the issues and agree evidence accordingly. That is especially the case for routine evidence of the type covered by certificates in terms of s.281 of and Sched. 9 to this Act.

Part XIII

Sections 287 to 303 cover a wide variety of matters. The fixed penalty system, under ss.303 and 304, will probably and properly keep out of court a wide variety of minor infringements at the least serious end of criminal behaviour.

Part XIV

Sections 304 to 310 deal with general points but mention must be made of the establishment of the Criminal Courts Rules Council. It is true that many other bodies take an interest in criminal law but this body has the function of keeping under general review the procedures and practices of the courts exercising criminal jurisdiction in Scotland and that in itself is progress: see s.304(9).

Sched. 1

Section 21 and Sched. 1 give constables powers to take offenders into custody in relation to the offences against children under the age of 17 years.

Sched. 2

Petitions and indictments may be in a form set out in Sched. 2: see ss.34(1)(a) and 64(2)(a) respectively. The Schedule sets out examples of indictments. Given that the changes are discretionary in regard to the contents of the Schedule, the real question with a variance from an example is whether a change is relevant, not whether it coincides with such an example. Reference may also be made to Sched. 5.

Sched. 3

The structure of the 1975 Act was such that identical provisions were made for solemn proceedings and summary proceedings respectively. This duplication was felt to be unnecessary and by ss.64(6) and 138(4) the contents of Sched. 3 have effect as regards indictments and complaints. This Schedule will repay careful reading regularly by court practitioners because of the complexity of the provisions that frequently render pleas to the relevancy, for example, unnecessary and assist with more efficient pleading.

Sched. 4

The regime of supervision and treatment orders was introduced by s.50 of and Sched. 2 to the Criminal Justice (Scotland) Act 1995. The development is simply repeated in this Act.

Sched. 5

This Schedule provides forms of change in addition to those in Sched. 2. Questions may be raised as to why the Schedules are separate or what benefit is conferred by them in any event. Further, several of the forms are clearly anachronistic, for example by reference to assault "to the great effusion of blood".

Sched. 6

By s.231(1), this Schedule has effect in relation to the discharge and amendment of probation orders.

Sched. 7

Supervised attendance orders have been developed as an alternative to imprisonment and such orders have been extended by s.235 and Sched. 7.

Sched. 8

This Schedule makes provision regarding the admissibility in criminal proceedings of copy documents and of evidence contained in business documents. It should be noted that the Schedule has, by para. 8, definitions of terms that are not contained in the main interpretation section.

Sched. 9

Proof of routine or incontrovertible evidence is tedious and expensive and this Schedule provides for the increased use of certificates as to these matters. The consolidating nature of this legislation is such that this Schedule has a far wider range of subject-matters that may be covered by certificates.

Sched. 10

This Schedule must be read in the context of s.292 and the effect is to establish a narrow range of offences triable only summarily.

ABBREVIATIONS

The 1975 Act : Criminal Procedure (Scotland) Act 1975 (c.21).
The 1980 Act : Bail (Scotland) Act 1980 (c.4).
The 1984 Act : Mental Health (Scotland) Act 1984 (c.36).
The 1993 Act : Prisoners and Criminal Proceedings (Scotland) Act 1993 (c.9).

PART I

CRIMINAL COURTS

JURISDICTION AND POWERS

The High Court

Judges in the High Court

1.—(1) The Lord President of the Court of Session shall be the Lord Justice General and shall perform his duties as the presiding judge of the High Court.

(2) Every person who is appointed to the office of one of the Senators of the College of Justice in Scotland shall, by virtue of such appointment, be a Lord Commissioner of Justiciary in Scotland.

(3) If any difference arises as to the rotation of judges in the High Court, it shall be determined by the Lord Justice General, whom failing by the Lord Justice Clerk.

(4) Any Lord Commissioner of Justiciary may preside alone at the trial of an accused before the High Court.

(5) Without prejudice to subsection (4) above, in any trial of difficulty or importance it shall be competent for two or more judges in the High Court to preside for the whole or any part of the trial.

DEFINITIONS
"High Court": s.307(1).
"Lord Commissioner of Justiciary": s.307(1).

GENERAL NOTE
With one exception, the origins of this section are probably more a matter of legal history than a concern for practitioners. Section 1(5), reflecting the collegiate nature of Scottish judges, permits in any trial of difficulty or importance that it shall be competent for two or more judges in the High Court of Justiciary to provide for the whole or any part of the trial. Such problems tend to arise at short notice and while judges are on circuit but there are still a number of instances of this happening: see *Advocate, H.M. v. Cairns*, 1967 J.C. 37; *Advocate, H.M. v. MacKenzie*, 1970 S.L.T. 81; *MacNeil v. H.M. Advocate*, 1986 S.C.C.R. 288 and *Copeland v. H.M. Advocate*, 1987 S.C.C.R. 232.

Fixing of High Court sittings

2.—(1) The High Court shall sit at such times and places as the Lord Justice General, whom failing the Lord Justice Clerk, may, after consultation with the Lord Advocate, determine.

(2) Without prejudice to subsection (1) above, the High Court shall hold such additional sittings as the Lord Advocate may require.

(3) Where an accused has been cited to attend a sitting of the High Court, the prosecutor may, at any time before the commencement of his trial, apply to the Court to transfer the case to another sitting of the High Court; and a single judge of the High Court may—
(a) after giving the accused or his counsel an opportunity to be heard; or
(b) on the joint application of all parties,
make an order for the transfer of the case.

(4) Where no cases have been indicted for a sitting of the High Court or if it is no longer expedient that a sitting should take place, it shall not be necessary for the sitting to take place.

(5) If any case remains indicted for a sitting which does not take place in pursuance of subsection (4) above, subsection (3) above shall apply in relation to the transfer of any other such case to another sitting.

DEFINITIONS
"High Court": s.307(1).
"order": s.307(1).
"prosecutor": s.307(1).

Solemn courts: general

Jurisdiction and powers of solemn courts

3.—(1) The jurisdiction and powers of all courts of solemn jurisdiction, except so far as altered or modified by any enactment passed after the commencement of this Act, shall remain as at the commencement of this Act.

(2) Any crime or offence which is triable on indictment may be tried by the High Court sitting at any place in Scotland.

(3) The sheriff shall, without prejudice to any other or wider power conferred by statute, not be entitled, on the conviction on indictment of an accused, to pass a sentence of imprisonment for a term exceeding three years.

(4) Subject to subsection (5) below, where under any enactment passed or made before 1st January 1988 (the date of commencement of section 58 of the Criminal Justice (Scotland) Act 1987) an offence is punishable on convic-

tion on indictment by imprisonment for a term exceeding two years but the enactment either expressly or impliedly restricts the power of the sheriff to impose a sentence of imprisonment for a term exceeding two years, it shall be competent for the sheriff to impose a sentence of imprisonment for a term exceeding two but not exceeding three years.

(5) Nothing in subsection (4) above shall authorise the imposition by the sheriff of a sentence in excess of the sentence specified by the enactment as the maximum sentence which may be imposed on conviction of the offence.

(6) Subject to any express exclusion contained in any enactment, it shall be lawful to indict in the sheriff court all crimes except murder, treason, rape and breach of duty by magistrates.

DEFINITIONS
"crime": s.307(1).
"offence": s.307(1).
"sentence": s.307(1).

GENERAL NOTE
The maximum sentence of imprisonment that a sheriff may impose after conviction on indictment is, for most practical purposes, three years: s.3(3). However, that power must be read with the terms of s.219(8) in mind for that requires a sheriff to remit a case to the High Court of Justiciary for sentence where a period of imprisonment in default of payment is in contemplation and that period exceeds three years.

The sheriff

Territorial jurisdiction of sheriff

4.—(1) Subject to the provisions of this section, the jurisdiction of the sheriffs, within their respective sheriffdoms shall extend to and include all navigable rivers, ports, harbours, creeks, shores and anchoring grounds in or adjoining such sheriffdoms and includes all criminal maritime causes and proceedings (including those applying to persons furth of Scotland) provided that the accused is, by virtue of any enactment or rule of law, subject to the jurisdiction of the sheriff before whom the case or proceeding is raised.

(2) Where an offence is alleged to have been committed in one district in a sheriffdom, it shall be competent to try that offence in a sheriff court in any other district in that sheriffdom.

(3) It shall not be competent for the sheriff to try any crime committed on the seas which it would not be competent for him to try if the crime had been committed on land.

(4) The sheriff shall have a concurrent jurisdiction with every other court of summary jurisdiction in relation to all offences competent for trial in such courts.

DEFINITIONS
"court of summary jurisdiction": s.307(1).
"crime": s.307(1).
"offence": s.307(1).

GENERAL NOTE
The ancient lineage of this provision has not been tested much in court: however, in *Lewis v. Blair*, (1858) 3 Irv. 16 the sheriff had jurisdiction to try a foreign sailor for an offence committed by him aboard a foreign vessel lying within the sheriff's territory, upon a seaman engaged on that vessel.

The sheriff: summary jurisdiction and powers

5.—(1) The sheriff, sitting as a court of summary jurisdiction, shall continue to have all the jurisdiction and powers exercisable by him at the commencement of this Act.

(2) The sheriff shall, without prejudice to any other or wider powers conferred by statute, have power on convicting any person of a common law offence—

  (a) to impose a fine not exceeding the prescribed sum;

  (b) to ordain the accused to find caution for good behaviour for any period not exceeding 12 months to an amount not exceeding the prescribed sum either in lieu of or in addition to a fine or in addition to imprisonment;

  (c) failing payment of such fine, or on failure to find such caution, to award imprisonment in accordance with section 219 of this Act;

  (d) to impose imprisonment, for any period not exceeding three months.

(3) Where a person is convicted by the sheriff of—

  (a) a second or subsequent offence inferring dishonest appropriation of property, or attempt thereat; or

  (b) a second or subsequent offence inferring personal violence,

he may, without prejudice to any wider powers conferred by statute, be sentenced to imprisonment for any period not exceeding six months.

(4) It shall be competent to prosecute summarily in the sheriff court the following offences—

  (a) uttering a forged document;

  (b) wilful fire-raising;

  (c) robbery; and

  (d) assault with intent to rob.

DEFINITIONS

"caution": s.307(1).
"court of summary jurisdiction": s.307(1).
"fine": s.307(1).
"offence": s.307(1).
"prescribed sum, the": s.225(8) [*i.e.* £5,000].

GENERAL NOTE

The enhanced penalty competent on conviction by a sheriff of a second or subsequent offence inferring personal violence has led to challenges as to what is meant by "inferring personal violence". Section 5(3) repeats the terms of s.290 of the 1975 Act against which several appeals were taken.

The appellate judges have construed the term strictly and in favour of appellants so that threats or hints of violence are insufficient: see *Adair v. Morton*, 1972 S.L.T. (Notes) 70; *Sharp v. Tudhope*, 1986 S.C.C.R. 64; *Hemphill v. Donnelly*, 1992 S.C.C.R. 770; and *McMahon v. Lees*, 1993 S.L.T. 593.

The previous convictions which in effect authorise the enhanced penalty must be libelled by the Crown in the Notice of Previous Convictions and laid before the court: *Sim v. Lockhart*, 1994 S.L.T. 1063.

District courts

District courts: area, constitution and prosecutor

6.—(1) Each commission area shall be the district of a district court, and the places at which a district court sits and, subject to section 8 of this Act, the days and times when it sits at any given place, shall be determined by the local authority; and in determining where and when a district court should sit, the local authority shall have regard to the desirability of minimising the expense and inconvenience occasioned to those directly involved, whether as parties or witnesses, in the proceedings before the court.

(2) The jurisdiction and powers of the district court shall be exercisable by a stipendiary magistrate or by one or more justices, and no decision of the court shall be questioned on the ground that it was not constituted as required by this subsection unless objection was taken on that ground by or

on behalf of a party to the proceedings not later than the time when the proceedings or the alleged irregularity began.

(3) All prosecutions in a commission area shall proceed at the instance of the procurator fiscal.

(4) The procurator fiscal for an area which includes a commission area shall have all the powers and privileges conferred on a district prosecutor by section 6 of the District Courts (Scotland) Act 1975.

(5) The prosecutions authorised by the said Act of 1975 under complaint by the procurator fiscal shall be without prejudice to complaints at the instance of any other person entitled to make the same.

(6) In this section—

"commission area" means the area of a local authority;

"justice" means a justice of the peace appointed or deemed to have been appointed under section 9 of the said Act of 1975; and

"local authority" means a council constituted under section 2 of the Local Government (Scotland) Act 1994.

DEFINITIONS
"commission area": s.6(6).
"complaint": s.307(1).
"district prosecutor": s.26(1) of the District Courts (Scotland) Act 1975.
"justice": s.6(6).
"local authority": s.6(6).
"procurator fiscal": s.307(1).

GENERAL NOTE
This section is derived from several parts of the District Courts (Scotland) Act 1975 which brought about very substantial change to the existing system of lay courts of summary criminal jurisdiction. The extensive commentary on the District Courts (Scotland) Act 1975 by Dr. Enid A. Marshall in Current Law Statutes Annotated, encapsulated the details of the then old system which was to replace it. This section consolidates these matters.

District court: jurisdiction and powers

7.—(1) A district court shall continue to have all the jurisdiction and powers exercisable by it at the commencement of this Act.

(2) Where several offences, which if committed in one commission area could be tried under one complaint, are alleged to have been committed in different commission areas, proceedings may be taken for all or any of those offences under one complaint before the district court of any one of such commission areas, and any such offence may be dealt with, heard, tried, determined, adjudged and punished as if the offence had been wholly committed within the jurisdiction of that court.

(3) Except in so far as any enactment (including this Act or an enactment passed after this Act) otherwise provides, it shall be competent for a district court to try any statutory offence which is triable summarily.

(4) It shall be competent, whether or not the accused has been previously convicted of an offence inferring dishonest appropriation of property, for any of the following offences to be tried in the district court—

(a) theft or reset of theft;

(b) falsehood, fraud or wilful imposition;

(c) breach of trust or embezzlement,

where (in any such case) the amount concerned does not exceed level 4 on the standard scale.

(5) A district court when constituted by a stipendiary magistrate shall, in addition to the jurisdiction and powers mentioned in subsection (1) above, have the summary criminal jurisdiction and powers of a sheriff.

(6) The district court shall, without prejudice to any other or wider powers conferred by statute, be entitled on convicting of a common law offence—

(a) to impose imprisonment for any period not exceeding 60 days;

    (b) to impose a fine not exceeding level 4 on the standard scale;

    (c) to ordain the accused (in lieu of or in addition to such imprisonment or fine) to find caution for good behaviour for any period not exceeding six months and to an amount not exceeding level 4 on the standard scale;

    (d) failing payment of such fine or on failure to find such caution, to award imprisonment in accordance with section 219 of this Act,

but in no case shall the total period of imprisonment imposed in pursuance of this subsection exceed 60 days.

    (7) Without prejudice to any other or wider power conferred by any enactment, it shall not be competent for a district court, as respects any statutory offence—

    (a) to impose a sentence of imprisonment for a period exceeding 60 days;

    (b) to impose a fine of an amount exceeding level 4 on the standard scale; or

    (c) to ordain an accused person to find caution for any period exceeding six months or to an amount exceeding level 4 on the standard scale.

    (8) The district court shall not have jurisdiction to try or to pronounce sentence in the case of any person—

    (a) found within its jurisdiction, and brought before it accused or suspected of having committed any offence at any place beyond its jurisdiction; or

    (b) brought before it accused or suspected of having committed within its jurisdiction any of the following offences—

        (i) murder, culpable homicide, robbery, rape, wilful fire-raising, or attempted wilful fire-raising;

        (ii) theft by housebreaking, or housebreaking with intent to steal;

        (iii) theft or reset, falsehood fraud or wilful imposition, breach of trust or embezzlement, where the value of the property is an amount exceeding level 4 on the standard scale;

        (iv) assault causing the fracture of a limb, assault with intent to ravish, assault to the danger of life, or assault by stabbing;

        (v) uttering forged documents or uttering forged bank or banker's notes, or offences under the Acts relating to coinage.

    (9) Without prejudice to subsection (8) above, where either in the preliminary investigation or in the course of the trial of any offence it appears that the offence is one which—

    (a) cannot competently be tried in the court before which an accused is brought; or

    (b) in the opinion of the court in view of the circumstances of the case, should be dealt with by a higher court,

the court may take cognizance of the offence and commit the accused to prison for examination for any period not exceeding four days.

    (10) Where an accused is committed as mentioned in subsection (9) above, the prosecutor in the court which commits the accused shall forthwith give notice of the committal to the procurator fiscal of the district within which the offence was committed or to such other official as is entitled to take cognizance of the offence in order that the accused may be dealt with according to law.

DEFINITIONS
    "fine": s.307(1).
    "level 4": s.225(2) [*i.e.* £2,500].
    "offence": s.307(1).
    "procurator fiscal": s.307(1).
    "prosecutor": s.307(1).
    "sentence": s.307(1).
    "standard scale": s.225(1).
    "stipendiary magistrate": s.5 of the District Courts (Scotland) Act 1975.

GENERAL NOTE
This section provides for the jurisdictions and powers of the District Court. It is worth assert-ing that the additional jurisdiction conferred on a stipendiary magistrate by s.7(5) allows for the prosecution of more serious matters in the District Court.

Sittings of sheriff and district courts

Sittings of sheriff and district courts

8.—(1) Notwithstanding any enactment or rule of law, a sheriff court or a district court—
  (a) shall not be required to sit on any Saturday or Sunday or on a day which by virtue of subsection (2) or (3) below is a court holiday; but
  (b) may sit on any day for the disposal of criminal business.
  (2) A sheriff principal may in an order made under section 17(1)(b) of the Sheriff Courts (Scotland) Act 1971 prescribe in respect of criminal business not more than 10 days, other than Saturdays and Sundays, in a calendar year as court holidays in the sheriff courts within his jurisdiction; and may in the like manner prescribe as an additional court holiday any day which has been proclaimed, under section 1(3) of the Banking and Financial Dealings Act 1971, to be a bank holiday either throughout the United Kingdom or in a place or locality in the United Kingdom within his jurisdiction.
  (3) Notwithstanding section 6(1) of this Act, a sheriff principal may, after consultation with the appropriate local authority, prescribe not more than 10 days, other than Saturdays and Sundays, in a calendar year as court holidays in the district courts within his jurisdiction; and he may, after such consul-tation, prescribe as an additional holiday any day which has been proclaimed, under section 1(3) of the said Banking and Financial Dealings Act 1971, to be a bank holiday either throughout the United Kingdom or in a place or locality in the United Kingdom within his jurisdiction.
  (4) A sheriff principal may in pursuance of subsection (2) or (3) above prescribe different days as court holidays in relation to different sheriff or district courts.

Territorial jurisdiction: general

Boundaries of jurisdiction

9.—(1) Where an offence is committed in any harbour, river, arm of the sea or other water (tidal or otherwise) which runs between or forms the bound-ary of the jurisdiction of two or more courts, the offence may be tried by any one of such courts.
  (2) Where an offence is committed on the boundary of the jurisdiction of two or more courts, or within the distance of 500 metres of any such bound-ary, or partly within the jurisdiction of one court and partly within the juris-diction of another court or courts, the offence may be tried by any one of such courts.
  (3) Where an offence is committed against any person or in respect of any property in or on any carriage, cart or vehicle employed in a journey by road or railway, or on board any vessel employed in a river, loch, canal or inland navigation, the offence may be tried by any court through whose jurisdiction the carriage, cart, vehicle or vessel passed in the course of the journey or voyage during which the offence was committed.
  (4) Where several offences, which if committed in one sheriff court district could be tried under one indictment or complaint, are alleged to have been committed by any person in different sheriff court districts, the accused may be tried for all or any of those offences under one indictment or complaint before the sheriff of any one of such sheriff court districts.

(5) Where an offence is authorised by this section to be tried by any court, it may be dealt with, heard, tried, determined, adjudged and punished as if the offence had been committed wholly within the jurisdiction of such court.

DEFINITIONS
"complaints": s.307(1).
"indictment": s.307(1).
"offence": s.307(1).
"sheriff court districts": s.307(1).

GENERAL NOTE
There seem to have been few modern authorities on the issue of jurisdiction, although the older cases may still provide assistance should doubts arise: see *Lewis v. Blair*, (1858) 3 Irv. 16; *Witherington*, (1881) 4 Couper 475; *Mortensen v. Peters*, (1906) 5 Adam 121 and *Lipsey v. Mackintosh*, (1913) 7 Adam 182.

Crimes committed in different districts

10.—(1) Where a person is alleged to have committed in more than one sheriff court district a crime or crimes to which subsection (2) below applies, he may be indicted to the sheriff court of such one of those districts as the Lord Advocate determines.

(2) This subsection applies to—

(a) a crime committed partly in one sheriff court district and partly in another;

(b) crimes connected with each other but committed in different sheriff court districts;

(c) crimes committed in different sheriff court districts in succession which, if they had been committed in one such district, could have been tried under one indictment.

(3) Where, in pursuance of subsection (1) above, a case is tried in the sheriff court of any sheriff court district, the procurator fiscal of that district shall have power to prosecute in that case even if the crime was in whole or in part committed in a different district, and the procurator fiscal shall have the like powers in relation to such case, whether before, during or after the trial, as he has in relation to a case arising out of a crime or crimes committed wholly within his own district.

DEFINITIONS
"crime": s.307(1).
"procurator fiscal": s.307(1).
"sheriff court district": s.307(1).

Certain offences committed outside Scotland

11.—(1) Any British citizen or British subject who in a country outside the United Kingdom does any act or makes any omission which if done or made in Scotland would constitute the crime of murder or of culpable homicide shall be guilty of the same crime and subject to the same punishment as if the act or omission had been done or made in Scotland.

(2) Any British citizen or British subject employed in the service of the Crown who, in a foreign country, when acting or purporting to act in the course of his employment, does any act or makes any omission which if done or made in Scotland would constitute an offence punishable on indictment shall be guilty of the same offence and subject to the same punishment, as if the act or omission had been done or made in Scotland.

(3) A person may be proceeded against, indicted, tried and punished for an offence to which this section applies—

(a) in any sheriff court district in Scotland in which he is apprehended or is in custody; or

(b) in such sheriff court district as the Lord Advocate may determine, as if the offence had been committed in that district, and the offence shall, for all purposes incidental to or consequential on the trial or punishment thereof, be deemed to have been committed in that district.

(4) Any person who—

(a) has in his possession in Scotland property which he has stolen in any other part of the United Kingdom; or

(b) in Scotland receives property stolen in any other part of the United Kingdom,

may be dealt with, indicted, tried and punished in Scotland in like manner as if he had stolen it in Scotland.

DEFINITIONS
  "crime": s.307(1).
  "offence": s.307(1).
  "sheriff court district": s.307(1).

PART II

POLICE FUNCTIONS

Lord Advocate's instructions

Instructions by Lord Advocate as to reporting of offences

12. The Lord Advocate may, from time to time, issue instructions to a chief constable with regard to the reporting, for consideration of the question of prosecution, of offences alleged to have been committed within the area of such chief constable, and it shall be the duty of a chief constable to whom any such instruction is issued to secure compliance therewith.

DEFINITIONS
  "offence": s.307(1).

GENERAL NOTE
  This section repeats the terms of s.9 of the 1975 Act which, in turn, derived from the Criminal Justice (Scotland) Act 1949 (c.94), s.33. The Lord Advocate's authority to appoint or remove procurators fiscal and delineate their territorial jurisdictions, is found in the Sheriff Courts and Legal Officers (Scotland) Act 1927 (c.35), s.1(2). By s.12 of that Act the Lord Advocate may also after consultation with the Treasury, by Order direct, notwithstanding the terms of any Act of Parliament, that any sheriff court proceedings for contraventions thereof shall proceed at the instance of the procurator fiscal. The Sheriff Courts (Prosecutions for Poaching) Order 1938 is the only instance in which this power has been exercised.

Detention and questioning

Powers relating to suspects and potential witnesses

13.—(1) Where a constable has reasonable grounds for suspecting that a person has committed or is committing an offence at any place, he may require—

(a) that person, if the constable finds him at that place or at any place where the constable is entitled to be, to give his name and address and may ask him for an explanation of the circumstances which have given rise to the constable's suspicion;

(b) any other person whom the constable finds at that place or at any place where the constable is entitled to be and who the constable believes has information relating to the offence, to give his name and address.

(2) The constable may require the person mentioned in paragraph (a) of subsection (1) above to remain with him while he (either or both)—

(a) subject to subsection (3) below, verifies any name and address given by the person;

(b) notes any explanation proffered by the person.

(3) The constable shall exercise his power under paragraph (a) of subsection (2) above only where it appears to him that such verification can be obtained quickly.

(4) A constable may use reasonable force to ensure that the person mentioned in paragraph (a) of subsection (1) above remains with him.

(5) A constable shall inform a person, when making a requirement of that person under—

(a) paragraph (a) of subsection (1) above, of his suspicion and of the general nature of the offence which he suspects that the person has committed or is committing;

(b) paragraph (b) of subsection (1) above, of his suspicion, of the general nature of the offence which he suspects has been or is being committed and that the reason for the requirement is that he believes the person has information relating to the offence;

(c) subsection (2) above, why the person is being required to remain with him;

(d) either of the said subsections, that failure to comply with the requirement may constitute an offence.

(6) A person mentioned in—

(a) paragraph (a) of subsection (1) above who having been required—

    (i) under that subsection to give his name and address; or

    (ii) under subsection (2) above to remain with a constable,

fails, without reasonable excuse, to do so, shall be guilty of an offence and liable on summary conviction to a fine not exceeding level 3 on the standard scale;

(b) paragraph (b) of the said subsection (1) who having been required under that subsection to give his name and address fails, without reasonable excuse, to do so shall be guilty of an offence and liable on summary conviction to a fine not exceeding level 2 on the standard scale.

(7) A constable may arrest without warrant any person who he has reasonable grounds for suspecting has committed an offence under subsection (6) above.

DEFINITIONS

"constable": s.307(1) and s.51(1) of the Police (Scotland) Act 1967 (c.77).
"offence": s.307(1).

GENERAL NOTE

The provisions of s.1 of the 1980 Act, after minor re-numbering of subsections, are re-enacted to form s.13. This section deals with the preliminary stages of police enquiries many of which will never develop into criminal proceedings. It gives a general power to police officers, when they have reasonable cause to suspect that an offence either has occurred or is in the course of commission, to demand information from certain members of the public. Two distinct categories of person are affected by these provisions, those who may have committed an offence, and those who are potential witnesses to an offence.

Powers In Relation To Suspects

Subsection (1)(a) relates to any person whom the officer suspects is guilty of such an offence (whether it is an arrestable offence or not), and empowers the constable to demand that person's particulars and an explanation for the conduct which has given rise to suspicion. Note that at this early stage no caution of any sort need be administered and it seems likely that any reply would be admissible subject to the ordinary rules of evidence.

If however, suspicions were sufficiently tangible for the constable to feel a caution to be appropriate, then the s.13 procedure would not be appropriate; the proper approach would be to caution with a view to charging (in the case of non-arrestable offences) or, where the offence could attract a sentence of imprisonment, to consider whether the circumstances would justify the use of the power of detention now specified in s.14 of the Act (the statutory successor to s.2 of the 1980 Act), or arrest.

In the exercise of his power under subs. (1)(a) an officer must first explain the nature of his suspicion and may then require the potential suspect to remain while the veracity of his particulars is established (provided this can be done quickly) and any explanation given may be noted. It will be observed that in terms of subs. (6) failure to provide particulars or to remain while the explanation given is noted by the officer constitutes an offence which attracts arrest without warrant; nonetheless a suspect is under no more of an obligation to give an explanation than an officer is to note it.

Doubtless a suspect's failure to offer an account may well serve to heighten the constable's existing suspicions. On an equally pragmatic level an officer's failure to note an explanation given in response to a s.13 requirement would no doubt attract adverse comment in any subsequent proceedings.

Unlike s.14 below (which has re-enacted the provisions of s.2 of the 1980 Act), where strict adherence to the six hour detention period is demanded, no time limit is stipulated in s.13 for the completion of these initial enquiries, except that the procedure for verifying personal particulars must be capable of being completed quickly (see subs. (3)). While a suspect can be caused to remain for that verification to be made rapidly, it must be emphasised that he cannot be restrained under s.13 while his explanation is examined—that is the role of statutory detention.

What then is the status of the suspect who is required to remain in terms of s.13(2) or, worse, restrained at the scene by a constable using his powers under s.13(4)? It might reasonably be felt, not least by the hapless suspect, that he is not at liberty to go and is in the officer's custody. However, reference to s.295 of the Act suggests that legal custody or detention only occurs when a person is required to be taken, or is held for the purpose of being taken, to a place for the purposes of the Act. It is notable that s.13(2) studiously avoids use of the word "detain" and the meaning of being required "to remain" for the limited purposes of the section must surely be something more dilute than detention. It is submitted that the precise status of the suspect is by no means clearly established.

Powers In Relation To Potential Witnesses

Subsection (1)(b) applies to persons whom the officer has reason to believe may, wittingly or unwittingly, have information to offer about the offence. It seems that this could extend to the circumstances in which the officer exercised his powers in relation to the suspect under subs. (1)(a): for example, the witness could be a bystander at the time when the suspect gave an explanation to the constable, given if he had not witnessed the offence giving rise to the enquiry.

First however, a general explanation of the nature of the alleged offence being investigated must be given by the officer to the potential witness. The officer is also obliged to inform the other party of the belief that he or she possesses information relevant to that investigation and that failure to provide personal particulars in those circumstances is an offence.

Police powers in pursuit of requirements under subs. (1)(b) are more limited than those applicable to suspects, for subs. (4) allows the use of reasonable force to ensure that a suspect remains until the enquiries specified in subs. (2) are quickly completed or noted as the case may be. No force may be employed to cause a witness to remain at the scene. All that can lawfully be demanded of a witness is that he provides his name and address, albeit failure to give these particulars will render him liable to immediate arrest (subs. (7)).

Restrictions On Use Of Section 13 Powers

Most obviously an officer can only resort to using his powers under s.13 when he has reasonable cause to suspect that an offence has been committed or is ongoing.

The Act does not attempt to define what would constitute "reasonable cause" and nor need it do so. The phrase has been minutely examined by the courts, albeit usually in the context of the Road Traffic Acts. Suffice to say that the suspicions formed by the officer need not rest upon personal ocular observation; they can stem from the observations of other persons, from "information received" or from prior knowledge of the suspect's habits and background, as well as general knowledge of the area being policed.

It will be appreciated that some of the factors giving rise to cause to suspect, may well be inadmissible as evidence, but that would not disentitle the officer from forming his suspicion. The general considerations are discussed in *McNicol v. Peters*, 1969 S.L.T. (J.) 261, notably in Lord Wheatley's judgment at pp.265 and 266, from which it can also be seen that even an ill-founded suspicion can still constitute reasonable cause to suspect. Lord Wheatley returned to this topic in *Dryburgh v. Galt*, 1981 S.C.C.R. 27 at p.29 noting:

" ... the fact that the information on which the police officer formed his suspicion turns out to be ill-founded does not in itself necessarily establish that the police officer's suspicion was unfounded. The circumstances known to the police officer at the time he formed his suspicion constitute the criterion, not the facts as subsequently ascertained."

Nonetheless the Crown will have to establish objectively that the factors which exercised the constable's suspicions would reasonably create a cause to suspect an offence without, at that stage, amounting to sufficient grounds for detention or arrest or charge.

The section is equally silent on the question of defining "any place" or "a place where the constable is entitled to be". The phrases serve to differentiate between the locus of the offence (where the officer can proceed on his enquiries armed with his suspicions) at the time of the offence or later, and elsewhere, in which latter case a right to information may depend upon the legitimacy of the officer's presence there. For example, the constable may be in a public place, or in a private place where access has been gained by warrant, by invitation or for an unrelated legitimate purpose: each of these different situations may subtly impinge upon the ability of the constable to exercise his powers under s.13. It will also be borne in mind that the degree of restraint used to ensure that the suspect remains, must be reasonable.

If it is established that the force employed was unreasonable, *i.e.* excessive or inappropriate, or both, then that might well nullify any subsequent evidence and constitute a criminal assault upon the suspect.

There is a dearth of case authorities dealing with this section, a fact which serves to underline its preliminary nature in the scale of proceedings.

Detention and questioning at police station

14.—(1) Where a constable has reasonable grounds for suspecting that a person has committed or is committing an offence punishable by imprisonment, the constable may, for the purpose of facilitating the carrying out of investigations—

(a) into the offence; and

(b) as to whether criminal proceedings should be instigated against the person,

detain that person and take him as quickly as is reasonably practicable to a police station or other premises and may thereafter for that purpose take him to any other place and, subject to the following provisions of this section, the detention may continue at the police station or, as the case may be, the other premises or place.

(2) Detention under subsection (1) above shall be terminated not more than six hours after it begins or (if earlier)—

(a) when the person is arrested;

(b) when he is detained in pursuance of any other enactment; or

(c) where there are no longer such grounds as are mentioned in the said subsection (1),

and when a person has been detained under subsection (1) above, he shall be informed immediately upon the termination of his detention in accordance with this subsection that his detention has been terminated.

(3) Where a person has been released at the termination of a period of detention under subsection (1) above he shall not thereafter be detained, under that subsection, on the same grounds or on any grounds arising out of the same circumstances.

(4) Subject to subsection (5) below, where a person has previously been detained in pursuance of any other enactment, and is detained under subsection (1) above on the same grounds or on grounds arising from the same circumstances as those which led to his earlier detention, the period of six hours mentioned in subsection (2) above shall be reduced by the length of that earlier detention.

(5) Subsection (4) above shall not apply in relation to detention under section 41(3) of the Prisons (Scotland) Act 1989 (detention in relation to introduction etc. into prison of prohibited article), but where a person was detained under section 41(3) immediately prior to his detention under subsection (1) above the period of six hours mentioned in subsection (2) above shall be reduced by the length of that earlier detention.

(6) At the time when a constable detains a person under subsection (1) above, he shall inform the person of his suspicion, of the general nature of the offence which he suspects has been or is being committed and of the reason for the detention; and there shall be recorded—
(a) the place where detention begins and the police station or other premises to which the person is taken;
(b) any other place to which the person is, during the detention, thereafter taken;
(c) the general nature of the suspected offence;
(d) the time when detention under subsection (1) above begins and the time of the person's arrival at the police station or other premises;
(e) the time when the person is informed of his rights in terms of subsection (9) below and of subsection (1)(b) of section 15 of this Act and the identity of the constable so informing him;
(f) where the person requests such intimation to be sent as is specified in section 15(1)(b) of this Act, the time when such request is—
(i) made;
(ii) complied with; and
(g) the time of the person's release from detention or, where instead of being released he is arrested in respect of the alleged offence, the time of such arrest.
(7) Where a person is detained under subsection (1) above, a constable may—
(a) without prejudice to any relevant rule of law as regards the admissibility in evidence of any answer given, put questions to him in relation to the suspected offence;
(b) exercise the same powers of search as are available following an arrest.
(8) A constable may use reasonable force in exercising any power conferred by subsection (1), or by paragraph (b) of subsection (7), above.
(9) A person detained under subsection (1) above shall be under no obligation to answer any question other than to give his name and address, and a constable shall so inform him both on so detaining him and on arrival at the police station or other premises.

DEFINITIONS
"constable": s.307 and s.51(1) of the Police (Scotland) Act 1967.
"offence": s.307(1).
"offence punishable by imprisonment": s.307(6).
"prison": s.307(1).

GENERAL NOTE
This section regulates the practice of removing persons to, and detaining persons at police stations, for the purposes of questioning in relation to specified allegations of criminal conduct prior to charge.
The provisions were originally contained in s.2 of the Criminal Justice (Scotland) Act 1980 (c.62) and followed upon the recommendations of the Thomson Committee (II Chap. 3, recs. 3 to 13). A fixed six hour period of detention was then introduced along with a statutory form of caution distinct from the familiar common law caution. The intention was to allow time for further enquiry by the police where there was reasonable cause to suspect the commission of a crime but insufficient evidence immediately available to press charges. Detention was not, and should not be, regarded as a means of delaying arrest and charge; as soon as it is clear that sufficient evidence exists to arrest a suspect, detention has to be terminated. Note that while detention must be terminated at the point when a sufficiency of evidence is obtained, or within six hours (whichever is earlier), neither the 1980 Act nor this Act require that arrest must follow. However as a safeguard against oppressive use of detention powers it remains the case that only one period of detention will be permitted on the same or related grounds (see subs. (3)).
One of the benefits of s.2 detention was that it introduced both clarity and flexibility to the previously grey area between voluntary attendance, when (in theory at least) a person being

interviewed was free to leave the police station at any time, and arrest. Deprivation of liberty is unlikely to be an individual's preferred option; nonetheless it should be appreciated that statutory detention in the form provided by s.14 has the merit of establishing a suspect's legal status beyond doubt both in his mind and in the minds of those responsible for his detention.

Lawful Detention
The elements needed to constitute a lawful detention are not presented chronologically in s.14 but for convenience this course has been followed in the discussion below.

Grounds for Detention
Subs. (1) requires that the constable detaining a suspect must have reasonable grounds for suspecting that he has committed, or is in the course of committing, an imprisonable offence (for discussion of the factors underpinning "reasonable cause to suspect" see note to s.13 above), see *Wilson and Nolan v. Robertson*, 1986 S.C.C.R. 700. In contrast to s.13 powers (the right to require personal particulars from suspects and potential witnesses, and an explanation of circumstances from suspects) which can be exercised in relation to any offence, s.14 detention is only permissible when the offence under investigation can attract a term of imprisonment on conviction.

It will be seen that the section is not a preventative one, *i.e.* detention cannot be used to inquire into an offence which has yet to occur. In reality this distinction may be more apparent than real; often matters may have advanced sufficiently to consider that contemplation has blossomed into preparation and, accordingly, an attempt at the suspected offence can be established.

Secondly, the only valid purpose of the detention is to assist in the investigation of the matter at hand. If those inquiries can be shown objectively to have been capable of completion without the necessity of detaining the suspect, then logically, procedures should be regarded as vitiated—that is a determination which commonsense suggests it would be difficult for a court to reach.

Information To Be Given To A Detainee
Subsection (6) requires the constable to outline to the suspect the grounds for detention, namely the nature of his suspicions and general details of the offence suspected. It is certain that these steps must be taken at the time when the suspect is detained though, in practice, the grounds will undoubtedly be repeated when the place of detention is reached.

Subsection (9) obliges the officer, before undertaking any questioning of the detainee, to administer the statutory form of caution both when initially detaining the suspect and when presenting him at the place of detention. The statutory caution requires a detainee to furnish his name and address; otherwise he is under no obligation to answer any further questions. Note that in *Tonge v. H.M. Advocate*, 1982 S.C.C.R. 313 the Appeal Court stressed the desirability of administering a common law caution prior to interviews conducted during the six hour detention period.

Best practice also dictates that the statutory caution described above should be administered at the earliest opportunity although failure to do so will not inevitably damage a Crown case fatally. In *Scott v. Howie*, 1993 S.C.C.R. 81 the appellant was detained under s.2 of the 1980 Act on suspicion of housebreaking and conveyed to a police office. No statutory caution in terms of s.2(7) (the statutory precursor of s.14(9)), was administered but such a caution was given at the office, as was a common law caution, following which the appellant made a statement whose contents the Crown founded upon. The admitted absence of a statutory caution at the time of detention in the street was not fatal in this instance. However, there can be no doubt that any effort to lead evidence of statements made by the detainee between being stopped by the officers and his arrival at the police office would have foundered on the grounds of inadmissibility.

Reasonable force may be used to effect detention and at that time, or later, to search the suspect's person (see subss. (1), (7) and (8)).

From the moment of detention a suspect is to be regarded as being in legal custody (see s.295 below).

Removal To A Police Office Or Other Premises
Once detained, the objective has to be to ensure the swift removal of the suspect to a police station or other premises (usually detention will be continued at a police station but that is not demanded by s.14(1)). One of the operational limitations of s.2 of the 1980 Act was that the detainee could only be taken to either a police station or other premises and, once there, could not be removed elsewhere. This could create practical difficulties, for example, in organising a swift identification parade or in detaining individuals for an offence which had been investigated by another officer or had occurred in another police division or area.

It will be remembered also that these powers of detention can only be exercised by "a constable", and are not available to other law enforcement agencies whose powers, if any, are derived on the basis of individual statutory provisions.

Section 14(1) incorporates amendments which were made to s.2 of the 1980 Act by the Criminal Justice and Public Order Act 1994 (c.33), s.129(1). These go some way to answering the logistical difficulties mentioned above. It is now permissible to remove a suspect from the establishment where he has originally been detained to another police office, or other place, for the purpose of facilitating the investigation. So a suspect could be moved between police offices or, say, from a local trading standards office once detained, to a police office for photographing and fingerprinting. A valuable degree of flexibility has been created, but it will be borne in mind that a record of the detention procedures and times, sufficient to comply with the provisions of s.15 has to be maintained (see the notes to s.15 below) and all such inquiries are subject to the six hour time limit stipulated in s.14(2).

Different considerations apply to removal of detainees between jurisdictions in Great Britain and these are examined below.

The requirement to take the accused "as quickly as is reasonably practicable" does not mean that an accused must be conveyed to the closest police station. Operational factors may make detention at a more distant station appropriate. See *Menzies v. H.M. Advocate*, 1995 S.C.C.R. 550 (suspect detained near Airdrie conveyed to Dunfermline).

The Time Factors

Subsection (2) provides that the period of detention shall not exceed six hours. The 1980 Act contained provisions identical to those now found in subss. (a) and (c) but subs. (b), which re-enacts provisions contained in s.129 of the Criminal Justice and Public Order Act 1994, represents a significant alteration to the old six hour rule.

Generally the period of detention (six hours or less) will end with the suspect being arrested and charged or, alternatively, released without charge at that time if the grounds of suspicion have not been made out in that time. In the latter case the police or the Crown would not be barred subsequently from preferring charges arising from the grounds of detention: they would in terms of s.14(3) be unable to detain again using the statutory detention to be found in s.14. In theory, at the conclusion of the six hour detention period a suspect could remain voluntarily at the police office (or other premises used) when not then arrested and charged—it may fairly be assumed that this is, at best, an improbable scenario.

The end of the six hour detention clearly represents a procedural watershed, for at that point (subject to subs. (b) discussed later) the suspect's status must change to that of a prisoner or a citizen free to return to his own affairs. If procedures laid out in s.14 are complied with, then it would seem that evidence collected during that time will be admissible, despite any subsequent want of procedure; see *Grant v. H.M. Advocate*, 1990 S.C.C.R. 618 where arrest did not occur till some twenty minutes after the end of detention and replies made within the six hours were objected to. The Appeal Court held that subsequent laxity in compliance with formal requirements would not in themselves vitiate what had gone before.

It should not be forgotten that the cross-border enforcement provisions contained in Pt. X of the Criminal Justice and Public Order Act 1994 introduce in s.138(6)(a) an allowable period of four hours detention calculated from the time of arrival at a police station outside Scotland, in circumstances described in s.137 of that Act, *i.e.* where a person is detained in England or Wales for an offence previously committed (or attempted) in Scotland.

So far as Northern Ireland is concerned, quite different provisions, found in s.137(7)(d) apply. A suspect found there and detained in connection with an offence in Scotland can either be taken to the nearest convenient police station in Scotland, or to the nearest designated police station in Northern Ireland, as soon as reasonably practicable (on arrest elsewhere in Great Britain in relation to a Scottish crime, the arresting officer's duty is to take the arrested person either to the nearest convenient police station in Scotland or to a police station within the sheriffdom where the offence is being investigated).

When recourse is had to these cross-border provisions, it should be stressed that it is only competent to convey the detainee to a police office, or to police offices; the references in s.14 of the 1995 Act to "other premises" must then be disregarded.

Lastly, it is worthy of note that the powers of cross-border enforcement bear a surprising, and doubtless unintended, resemblance to the doctrine of hot pursuit which operated in the Scottish and English Borders during the times of the reivers.

Section 14 Detention And Other Statutory Powers

As has been mentioned, the inclusion of subs. (b) has substantially affected the previously clear cut operation of s.14. Now detention under the Act may be only a prelude to further statutory periods of detention. The provisions of the Prevention of Terrorism (Temporary Provisions) Act 1989 (c.4) and the Customs and Excise Management Act 1979 (c.2) as augmented by the Criminal Justice (Scotland) Act 1987 (c.41), ss. 48 to 50, spring to mind. Indeed it will be noted that the Customs legislation cited is a refinement of the 1980 Act's detention provisions and is generally directed against drug smuggling offences.

Subsection (4) requires that a period of detention under any other enactment upon the same grounds, shall be deducted from the six hour period ordinarily available under s.14. A like provision is made specifically in regard to the Prisons (Scotland) Act 1989 (c.45). Section 41(3) of that Act permits temporary detention within a prison for the purpose of investigating the introduction (*i.e.* smuggling) of forbidden materials by persons into prisons.

Details To Be Recorded

In addition to the obligation upon the detaining officer to disclose the nature of his suspicions and the reason for detention, subs. (6) stipulates other requirements which must be complied with by the officer and other police officers who become involved in the detention process later. It is an absolute requirement that (i) the time and place at which detention began, (ii) the general nature of the suspected offence, (iii) the time of arrival at the police office or other premises used for detention, (iv) the time, or times, at which the detainee was informed of his right to refuse to answer questions except those requiring his personal particulars (pursuant to subs. (9)) and his right to request that his solicitor and another person be advised of the fact of his detention as provided by s.15 of the Act, and the particulars of the officer who intimates this information, (v) the times when the above requests were made by the detainee and fulfilled by the police, and (vi) the time when detention terminated and/or the time of arrest should be recorded. All of these requirements simply echo the provisions contained in s.2(4) of the 1980 Act; it should be noted however that the corollary of the new power in subs. (1) of this Act to remove the detainee from the police office to "any other place", is that subs. (6)(b) demands that the "other place" should be specified in the record if such a power is exercised (although not statutorily required, it would be prudent to record fully the times of removal to that "other place" and return to the police office).

The practice adopted by Scottish police forces is for the detention forms which constitute the record of detention (stipulated now in subs. (6)), to be raised and maintained at police offices from the moment a detainee arrives there. It follows of course that initially the forms raised will necessarily have a retrospective effect since the detention process will have been initiated elsewhere: consequently it is sound practice for the detaining officer to note the time of initiating detention in his notebook.

In *Cummings v. H.M. Advocate*, 1982 S.C.C.R. 108 the only record produced to show that a statutory caution had been administered was contained in the officer's notebook. This was held to constitute a record sufficient for the purposes of s.2(4) of the 1980 Act. Nevertheless it is sound practice to ensure that the terms of the statutory caution in subs. (9) are repeated at the police office when documentation is raised.

Purpose Of Detention

While s.2(5) of the 1980 Act did broadly specify the avenues of inquiry which could be followed during detention, reference now has to be made to ss.18 and 19 of the 1995 Act to appreciate the wide-ranging powers which can be exercised (see notes to ss.18 and 19 below). Subsection (7) preserves the right to question and search the detainee.

Rights of person arrested or detained

15.—(1) Without prejudice to section 17 of this Act, a person who, not being a person in respect of whose custody or detention subsection (4) below applies—

(a) has been arrested and is in custody in a police station or other premises, shall be entitled to have intimation of his custody and of the place where he is being held sent to a person reasonably named by him;

(b) is being detained under section 14 of this Act and has been taken to a police station or other premises or place, shall be entitled to have intimation of his detention and of the police station or other premises or place sent to a solicitor and to one other person reasonably named by him,

without delay or, where some delay is necessary in the interest of the investigation or the prevention of crime or the apprehension of offenders, with no more delay than is so necessary.

(2) A person shall be informed of his entitlement under subsection (1) above—

(a) on arrival at the police station or other premises; or

(b) where he is not arrested, or as the case may be detained, until after such arrival, on such arrest or detention.

(3) Where the person mentioned in paragraph (a) of subsection (1) above requests such intimation to be sent as is specified in that paragraph there shall be recorded the time when such request is—

(a) made;

(b) complied with.

(4) Without prejudice to the said section 17, a constable shall, where a person who has been arrested and is in such custody as is mentioned in paragraph (a) of subsection (1) above or who is being detained as is mentioned in paragraph (b) of that subsection appears to him to be a child, send without delay such intimation as is mentioned in the said paragraph (a), or as the case may be paragraph (b), to that person's parent if known; and the parent—

(a) in a case where there is reasonable cause to suspect that he has been involved in the alleged offence in respect of which the person has been arrested or detained, may; and

(b) in any other case shall,

be permitted access to the person.

(5) The nature and extent of any access permitted under subsection (4) above shall be subject to any restriction essential for the furtherance of the investigation or the well-being of the person.

(6) In subsection (4) above—

(a) "child" means a person under 16 years of age; and

(b) "parent" includes guardian and any person who has the actual custody of a child.

DEFINITIONS

"child": s.307(1) as restricted by subs. (6) below.

"constable": s.307(1) and Police (Scotland) Act 1967 (c.77), s.51(1).

"parent": subs. (6) below.

GENERAL NOTE

This section specifies the extent to which arrested or detained persons are entitled to have other persons informed of their circumstances and whereabouts. This must be intimated to the subject as soon as he is presented at the station charge bar or at whatever other place he is being lawfully held in custody. Note that the entitlement does not extend to those attending voluntarily. Section 14(6) requires that the procedure be properly documented at the time of arrival at the police station or "other place", not before.

There are some important differences in the obligations the police are placed under by this section when dealing with arrested, as distinct from detained, persons.

Arrested Persons

In the case of arrested persons, subs. (1)(a) only deals with the right to have friends or relatives told this information and, while the arrested person has to be advised of his right to have a named person told of his circumstances, the police can, when there are legitimate grounds for doing so, delay such a notification. Section 17 makes it mandatory for the arrested person to be advised immediately of his right to have a legal representative (whether personally nominated by the person or acting as the duty solicitor under the Legal Aid Scheme) informed of his status and whereabouts. While that section stipulates that the arrested person must be informed of this right immediately on arrest, it does not demand immediate intimation to the solicitor who is named. Nevertheless an unexplained delay in notification would risk an unfavourable interpretation in subsequent proceedings. There is no obligation upon the solicitor to attend the police station (or other named premises) when notification is received from the police.

It should be noted that separate, more extensive, provisions are made in regard to children, and these are discussed below.

Detained Persons

Subsection (1)(b) relates to suspects detained in terms of s.14. Their rights to intimation differ from those applicable to arrested persons. At the time of detention at a police office or other place, the detainee must be informed of his entitlement to have his circumstances made known to a reasonably named person and to a solicitor. This right applies equally to situations where the subject is held at a police office or elsewhere but greater latitude is permitted in delaying the implementation of the detainee's demands. Informing either the detainee's reasonably named person or his solicitor, or both, can be delayed. Normally notifications requested by the suspect must be acted upon swiftly, in order to comply with the spirit of the Act unless, as subs. (1) stipulates, there are plausible grounds relative to the matter under investigation or affecting the prospects of apprehending others or relating to the prevention of crime (this last being an undefined catch-all) which justify a temporary withholding of notification.

Section 15 As Applied To Children

These provisions apply to children aged between eight and 16 years since s.41 statutorily repeats the common law concept of nonage; see also *Merrin v. S*, 1987 S.L.T. 193 and the general discussion there of the absence of dole in children under eight years.

In the context of s.15 it will be observed that the definition of "child" found in subs. (6) is narrower than that contained in the Interpretation section (s.308), which in turn refers back to the provisions of the Children (Scotland) Act 1995 (c.36). The narrower definition in subs. (6) has the effect of ensuring that identical provisions apply to all those aged 16 years or more. That section apart, the 1995 Act and Pt. II of the Children (Scotland) Act 1995, s.93(2)(b) adhere to the definition of a "child" as either a person less than 16 years old, or a person over the age of 16 years and less than 18 years old who is subject to a supervision requirement.

Subsection (4) places a positive onus upon the police when they think that the person in custody is a child, to take active steps to contact the child's parent or guardian and allow access to the child. This is the case even when it is suspected that the parent or guardian was involved in the offence which gave rise to the child's detention in the first place: subs. (5) allows access to the child to be limited (and, arguably, even refused) where this is essential to the further investigation of the offence under scrutiny or for the safety of the parent or guardian, or both. It is submitted that the grounds for any restriction upon, or refusal of, access in these circumstances should be fully noted by the officers involved. Failure to adhere to these requirements arose in the case of *Advocate, H.M. v. G.B. and D.J.M.*, 1991 S.C.C.R. 533 and a confession obtained by the police was withheld from the jury.

Generally the Act proceeds on the basis that children arrested for offences shall be liberated to appear at court rather than being detained in custody. See s.43 below which sets out the procedures following the arrest of a child.

Observations

Curiously while s.15 demands that the suspect be informed of these rights and (together with s.14(6)(e) and (f)) that a record of the person and solicitor named be kept along with the times of notification, it is not necessary to record when notification is wilfully delayed or the reasons for so doing. It is submitted that where a departure from the usual practice of notification occurs, this should only be done when the following factors are *all* present; (a) the suspect has been informed of his rights of intimation, and (b) has elected names which are deemed unreasonable or as inexpedient (broadly not in the interests of justice for the reasons expressed in subs. (1)) at that time, and (c) has been informed that such intimation will not be made and advised of the grounds for that decision. The suspect cannot simply be left in the dark if the spirit of s.15 is to have any meaning. As was remarked earlier, it would be expedient, with an eye to later proceedings, that the grounds for delaying notification to the suspect's solicitor or friend be recorded along with the other details stipulated in s.14(6) and subs. (3). Failure to comply with the terms of this section would taint any admissions, prints or samples subsequently obtained from the accused. Adapting the *ratio* in *Grant v. H.M. Advocate*, 1989 S.C.C.R. 618 (see notes to s.14 above) suggests that evidence obtained from the accused beforehand would still be admissible.

Drunken persons: power to take to designated place

16.—(1) Where a constable has power to arrest a person without a warrant for any offence and the constable has reasonable grounds for suspecting that that person is drunk, the constable may, if he thinks fit, take him to any place designated by the Secretary of State for the purposes of this section as a place suitable for the care of drunken persons.

(2) A person shall not by virtue of this section be liable to be detained in any such place as is mentioned in subsection (1) above, but the exercise in his case of the power conferred by this section shall not preclude his being charged with any offence.

DEFINITIONS
"constable": s.307(1) and s.51(1) of the Police (Scotland) Act 1967.
"offence": s.307(1).

GENERAL NOTE
More in hope than expectation this section repeats the provisions, word for word, of s.5 of the 1980 Act. The original intention of the section was to enable drunken persons to be dealt with other than by criminal prosecution and it gave the police the option of conveying the offender to a designated place for detoxification. The section can only be applied where such designated places exist and to date only pilot schemes have operated.

While a constable may choose to exercise his powers to deliver a drunkard to a designated place, neither he nor the staff there have any power to compel the subject to remain there. It will also be noted that conveyance to a place is entirely without prejudice to any further proceedings arising from the arrest. It is of interest that this section does not require the offence giving rise to arrest to be one specifically of drunkenness, or to have been committed in a public place, only that the offender offended while apparently drunk. That said, the scope of the powers of arrest for common law offences committed by a drunken offender remains hazy: plainly a common law offence witnessed by a constable would qualify, but what is the position when the suspicion of an offence stems from *ex parte* statements?

Certain statutory powers of arrest of drunken persons do exist. For example, the Civic Government (Scotland) Act 1982 (c.45), s.50(1) created an offence of being drunk and incapable, suggesting a more advanced state of intoxication and incapacity than mere drunkenness, while s.50(5) relates to possession of a firearm or crossbow in a public place while drunk.

The Criminal Justice (Scotland) Act 1980 confined itself to dealing with drunkenness: s.69(c) related to drunken persons on public passenger vehicles en route to designated sporting events; s.74 to drunkenness at a designated sports ground during the currency of a designated sporting event. These provisions are now to be found in Pt. 2 of the Criminal Law (Consolidation) (Scotland) Act 1995 (c.39). In the absence of local or centrally funded provision of designated places s.16 is destined to be moribund.

Arrest: access to solicitor

Right of accused to have access to solicitor

17.—(1) Where an accused has been arrested on any criminal charge, he shall be entitled immediately upon such arrest—
  (a) to have intimation sent to a solicitor that his professional assistance is required by the accused, and informing the solicitor—
      (i) of the place where the person is being detained;
      (ii) whether the person is to be liberated; and
      (iii) if the person is not to be liberated, the court to which he is to be taken and the date when he is to be so taken; and
  (b) to be told what rights there are under—
      (i) paragraph (a) above;
      (ii) subsection (2) below; and
      (iii) section 35(1) and (2) of this Act.
(2) The accused and the solicitor shall be entitled to have a private interview before the examination or, as the case may be, first appearance.

GENERAL NOTE
It is mandatory that an accused person, following arrest, must be informed (i) of his right to have a solicitor informed of this development and that the solicitor's services are required (ii) of his right to a private interview with his solicitor which is to be accorded to him prior to the first court appearance on the charges and (iii) where applicable, of his right to have a solicitor of his choosing present at judicial examination and, if need be, for that examination to be delayed up to 48 hours to permit the attendance of that solicitor.

There is no obligation upon the solicitor to attend immediately or, indeed, at all but legal advice must be available before the accused's court appearance.

It will be noted that while a request by the accused to have a solicitor informed of his arrest must be acted upon by the police, there is no similar entitlement to have friends or relatives told of his circumstances though this should ordinarily be permitted; see the discussion in Notes to s.15 above regarding "Arrested Persons".

Prints and samples

Prints, samples etc. in criminal investigations

18.—(1) This section applies where a person has been arrested and is in custody or is detained under section 14(1) of this Act.

(2) A constable may take from the person fingerprints, palm prints and such other prints and impressions of an external part of the body as the constable may, having regard to the circumstances of the suspected offence in respect of which the person has been arrested or detained, reasonably consider it appropriate to take.

(3) Subject to subsection (4) below, all record of any prints or impressions taken under subsection (2) above, all samples taken under subsection (6) below and all information derived from such samples shall be destroyed as soon as possible following a decision not to institute criminal proceedings against the person or on the conclusion of such proceedings otherwise than with a conviction or an order under section 246(3) of this Act.

(4) The duty under subsection (3) above to destroy samples taken under subsection (6) below and information derived from such samples shall not apply—

(a) where the destruction of the sample or the information could have the effect of destroying any sample, or any information derived therefrom, lawfully held in relation to a person other than the person from whom the sample was taken; or

(b) where the record, sample or information in question is of the same kind as a record, a sample or, as the case may be, information lawfully held by or on behalf of any police force in relation to the person.

(5) No sample, or information derived from a sample, retained by virtue of subsection (4) above shall be used—

(a) in evidence against the person from whom the sample was taken; or

(b) for the purposes of the investigation of any offence.

(6) A constable may, with the authority of an officer of a rank no lower than inspector, take from the person—

(a) from the hair of an external part of the body other than pubic hair, by means of cutting, combing or plucking, a sample of hair or other material;

(b) from a fingernail or toenail or from under any such nail, a sample of nail or other material;

(c) from an external part of the body, by means of swabbing or rubbing, a sample of blood or other body fluid, of body tissue or of other material;

(d) from the inside of the mouth, by means of swabbing, a sample of saliva or other material.

(7) A constable may use reasonable force in exercising any power conferred by subsection (2) or (6) above.

(8) Nothing in this section shall prejudice—

(a) any power of search;

(b) any power to take possession of evidence where there is imminent danger of its being lost or destroyed; or

(c) any power to take prints, impressions or samples under the authority of a warrant.

DEFINITIONS

"constable": s.307(1) and Police (Scotland) Act 1967 (c.77), s.51(1).
"in custody": s.295.

GENERAL NOTE

This section is derived from the Prisoners and Criminal Proceedings (Scotland) Act 1993 (c.9), s.28, which gave effect to the recommendations of the Scottish Law Commission's *Report on Evidence: Blood Group Tests, DNA Tests and Related Matters*, Paper No. 120, 1989. The current provisions were intended to give clearer expression to the extent of police powers (those contained in s.2(5)(c) of the 1980 Act being somewhat indeterminate) and to apply equally to arrested suspects and to those detained under s.14 of the 1995 Act. Section 18 does give more extensive sampling powers to the police in subs. (6) than were previously available under the 1980 Act, but note that these can only be exercised after authorisation by a senior police officer, *i.e.* an officer of inspector rank or higher. The tenor of the Act might suggest that the authorising officer should not be involved in the investigation but this is not expressly stated.

The section stops short of permitting the procuring of evidence by methods which case law has defined as invasive, for example, internal physical examinations, endoscopic or colonoscopic examinations. It remains the case that such extreme invasions of bodily privacy, which involve entering the suspect's body, still require the authority of a sheriff's warrant which has to be obtained by the procurator fiscal. An application for a warrant of this kind can be made at any time, but the court will take account of the nature of the examination or sampling proposed, the degree of physical invasion involved (when set against the public interest in the detection of crime), the stage which proceedings have reached and whether, at that time, there is a *prima facie* justification for the application. (See *Hay v. H.M. Advocate*, 1968 S.L.T. 334; *Advocate, H.M. v. Milford*, 1973 S.L.T. 12; *McGlennan v. Kelly*, 1989 S.L.T. 832; *Smith v. Cardle*, 1993 S.C.C.R. 609; *Hughes v. Normand*, 1993 S.L.T. 113).

Subs. (1)

This stipulates that the section applies to all persons arrested or detained by the police.

Subs. (2)

The reference to an "external part of the body" suggests that physical measurement of a suspect (as in *Smith v. Cardle*), would be permissible using s.18 powers but the obtaining of dental impressions (as in *Hay v. H.M. Advocate*) would not and would normally demand a sheriff's warrant. However subs. (8)(b) by implication permits urgent steps to be taken in situations where delay would create a real risk of evidence being irretrievably lost; the legitimacy, or otherwise, of such steps would fall to be considered in any subsequent proceedings.

Subss. (3) and (4)

Superficially, subs. (3) re-enacts the terms of s.2(1)(c) of the 1980 Act which provided for the destruction of fingerprint forms in the event either of their being no proceedings against the accused, or his acquittal following such proceedings. It will be noted that a decision not to proceed against an accused person will not always be because there is an insufficiency of evidence: the Crown may in broad terms decide that prosecution would not be in the public interest for a variety of reasons, or might opt to deal with the matter by way of a warning. It is in these situations, especially where proceedings are maintained against other accused, that intractable problems arise now because of the interaction of subss. (3) and (4).

Subsection (3) refers to "all information derived from such samples" and would seem to be more rigorous than the earlier provisions of s.2(1)(c) of the 1980 Act. The later provision suggests that data obtained as a result of such samples, which could arguably have been retained even after the destruction of the sample material under the 1980 Act, must also be destroyed. Yet while subs. (3) might momentarily be viewed as clarifying the law in this grey area, the terms of subs. (4) serve to qualify and obscure the position.

Subsection (4)(a) permits the retention of the samples, or the information derived from them, where to destroy such would itself "destroy" similar information obtained in relation to a person still accused. Presumably then, sample evidence gathered at an early stage in proceedings from suspect A against whom charges are later dropped, could still be preserved for use as evidence against suspect B now to be prosecuted. In such a situation there would be no obligation upon the police to destroy A's samples at all: they would only be precluded from using them as evidence in any other proceedings against A (see subs. (5) below).

Subsection (4)(b) also militates against the general requirement to destroy samples when no proceedings are to follow. In this case both samples and the data derived from them could be preserved to update existing data held by the police about the person concerned, albeit these could not be deployed *directly* in evidence or in the investigation of crime. Since the technology now exists to extract DNA from body samples of the sort specified in subs. (6), this is an issue of no small importance.

There has of course been no judicial interpretation as yet of these subsections.

Subs. (5)

The implications of this provision are discussed above in the Notes to subss. (3) and (4). This appears to open the way to the preservation of databanks derived from samples of previously convicted persons.

Subs. (6)

The samples which can be taken by a police officer, are those deemed to be of a non-invasive nature. In practice these are generally obtained by police casualty surgeons and while subs. (7) permits the use of reasonable physical force to recover the necessary samples, it is likely that doctors would assist in the procedures in the absence of the suspect's consent, only when a sheriff's warrant had been obtained by the procurator fiscal.

Prints, samples etc. in criminal investigations: supplementary provisions

19.—(1) This section applies where a person convicted of an offence—
(a) has not, since the conviction, had a sample, print or impression taken from him; or
(b) has (whether before or after the conviction) had a sample, print or impression taken from him but it was not suitable for the means of analysis for which it was taken or, though suitable, was insufficient (either in quantity or in quality) to enable information to be obtained by that means of analysis.

(2) Where this section applies, a constable may, within the permitted period—
(a) take from the convicted person fingerprints, palmprints and such other prints and impressions of an external part of the body as the constable reasonably considers it appropriate to take; and
(b) with the authority of an officer of a rank no lower than inspector, take from the person any sample mentioned in any of paragraphs (a) to (d) of subsection (6) of section 18 of this Act by the means specified in that paragraph in relation to that sample.

(3) A constable—
(a) may require the convicted person to attend a police station for the purposes of subsection (2) above;
(b) may, where the convicted person is in legal custody by virtue of section 295 of this Act, exercise the powers conferred by subsection (2) above in relation to the person in the place where he is for the time being.

(4) In subsection (2) above, "the permitted period" means—
(a) in a case to which paragraph (a) of subsection (1) above applies, the period of one month beginning with the date of the conviction;
(b) in a case to which paragraph (b) of that subsection applies, the period of one month beginning with the date on which a constable of the police force which instructed the analysis receives written intimation that the sample, print or impression was unsuitable or, as the case may be, insufficient as mentioned in that paragraph.

(5) A requirement under subsection (3)(a) above—
(a) shall give the person at least seven days' notice of the date on which he is required to attend;
(b) may direct him to attend at a specified time of day or between specified times of day.

(6) Any constable may arrest without warrant a person who fails to comply with a requirement under subsection (3)(a) above.

DEFINITIONS
"constable": s.307(1) and s.51(1) of the Police (Scotland) Act 1967.

GENERAL NOTE

This section gives the police a general power in the course of investigations or after the conviction of an accused, within the permitted period of one month specified in subs. (4), to obtain fingerprints or samples of the sort specified in s.18. The power can be utilised within that time in two distinct situations; (i) when no such samples have been taken since conviction (subs. (1)(a)) and (ii) when the materials obtained in the course of detention or arrest of the person have been either insufficient or deficient for the purposes of analysis (subs. (1)(b)).

As with s.18 a proposal to seek samples of head hair, mouth swabs, nail clippings or scrapings can only proceed after clearance from a senior police officer.

The Permitted Period (subs. (4))

The timescale in the event of conviction is unambiguous—one month from the date of that conviction. This would apply equally in the cases of the imposition of a money fine or caution, probation as defined in s.228 below or a deferment of sentence. Subsection (4)(a) provides for an opportunity to correct acts of omission.

Subsection (4)(b), which applies to suspects under investigation and to those convicted of offences, is by its nature much less precise; the one month timescale is effective from the date upon which the police force instructing a forensic or fingerprint examination of samples previously obtained from the suspect, receives written intimation of their unsuitability. Note that a verbal report to the same effect would not start the clock ticking. It should also be appreciated that subs. (4)(b) does not provide a remedy for situations where no samples had been taken from the suspect; the subsection only operates when samples taken are later found to be defective.

Police Powers Under S.19

The police are entitled, within the permitted period, to require that the accused makes himself available for sampling purposes if he is at liberty or to have access to him for those purposes if he is in custody. No notice need be given to a remand or serving prisoner of the police intention to exercise such powers, but subs. (3)(b) curiously makes it clear that the sampling procedures must be executed, "in the place where he is for the time being": this suggests that the sampling must be carried out in the penal establishment in which the accused is serving his sentence.

A person at large is entitled to no less than seven days notice of the requirement that he attend at a specified place and may also be directed to attend on a particular day and time (or days and times).

Failure to attend the nominated police station as demanded under s.19(3) renders the subject liable to arrest without warrant, but the Act does not treat such a failure as an offence. A further issue which is unresolved in the Act is the position when a suspect does attend as required, but samples are not sufficient for analysis or indeed no samples are taken at all. It is submitted that in the former case the whole procedure in subs. (4)(b) could be invoked anew, but in the latter, the suspect would have fulfilled his obligation and could not be subjected to the procedure again. Note also that subs. (5) is peremptory and is not qualified by any reasonableness test.

It will be necessary if the power of arrest in subs. (6) is to be invoked, that the police can demonstrate that notice of the requirement has been lawfully served upon the subject.

Use of prints, samples etc.

20. Without prejudice to any power to do so apart from this section, prints, impressions and samples lawfully held by or on behalf of any police force or in connection with or as a result of an investigation of an offence and information derived therefrom may be checked against other such prints, impressions, samples and information.

GENERAL NOTE

This section preserves the existing rights of the police to collate and compare fingerprint impressions of accused persons and authorises such operations in relation to other samples lawfully obtained by the police (see the notes to s.18(3) and (4) above).

Schedule 1 offences

Schedule 1 offences: power of constable to take offender into custody

21.—(1) Without prejudice to any other powers of arrest, a constable may take into custody without warrant—
   (a) any person who within his view commits any of the offences mentioned in Schedule 1 to this Act, if the constable does not know and cannot ascertain his name and address;
   (b) any person who has committed, or whom he had reason to believe to have committed, any of the offences mentioned in that Schedule, if the constable does not know and cannot ascertain his name and address or has reasonable ground for believing that he will abscond.
(2) Where a person has been arrested under this section, the officer in charge of a police station may—
   (a) liberate him upon a written undertaking, signed by him and certified by the said officer, in terms of which that person undertakes to appear at a specified court at a specified time; or
   (b) liberate him without any such undertaking; or
   (c) refuse to liberate him, and such refusal and the detention of that person until his case is tried in the usual form shall not subject the officer to any claim whatsoever.
(3) A person in breach of an undertaking given by him under subsection (2)(a) above without reasonable excuse shall be guilty of an offence and liable to the following penalties—
   (a) a fine not exceeding level 3 on the standard scale; and
   (b) imprisonment for a period—
         (i) where conviction is in the district court, not exceeding 60 days; or
         (ii) in any other case, not exceeding 3 months.
(4) The penalties provided for in subsection (3) above may be imposed in addition to any other penalty which it is competent for the court to impose, notwithstanding that the total of penalties imposed may exceed the maximum penalty which it is competent to impose in respect of the original offence.
(5) In any proceedings relating to an offence under this section, a writing, purporting to be such an undertaking as is mentioned in subsection (2)(a) above and bearing to be signed and certified, shall be sufficient evidence of the terms of the undertaking given by the arrested person.

DEFINITIONS
"constable": s.307(1) and s.51(1) of the Police (Scotland) Act 1967.

GENERAL NOTE
   This section repeats the provisions contained in ss.18(1) and 294(1) of the 1975 Act relating to offences against children under the age of 17 years. The relevant offences are found in Sched. 1 to the 1995 Act which now reflects the consolidating amendments contained in the Criminal Law (Consolidation) (Scotland) Act 1995 (c.39).
   Section 136(2) preserves the six month timebar provision in relation to statutory proceedings which are prosecuted summarily. It is often forgotten that common law offences involving bodily injury to a child, or lewd, indecent or libidinous practices towards a child (specified in paras. 2 and 3 of Sched. 1) must also be commenced within six months of the contravention. Powers to liberate persons charged with a Sched. I offence are vested in the officer in charge of the police station to which the accused has been brought. The powers, and penalties for failure to comply with the terms of any undertaking imposed, are identical to those contained in s.22 below, but note that liberation can be utilised for potentially more serious charges under s.21: liberation under s.22 is only competent if the charges preferred could be tried summarily.

Evidential Provisions

In proceedings for breach of the terms of a written undertaking made under s.21(2)(a) or the more commonplace provision under s.22(1)(a) below, the Act provides that a copy thereof certified and signed by the liberating officer, shall suffice as proof of the facts contained in it. In entering into such an undertaking an accused person is, in effect, placing himself in a special capacity. Once the court is satisfied as to the terms of the undertaking and that the accused failed to obtemper them, the onus of proof then falls upon an accused to make out reasonable grounds on the balance of probabilities for his failure to attend.

Penalties

Ordinarily the statutory maximum penalties of imprisonment or fine are laid down in s.3 (Sheriff Solemn), s.5(2) (Sheriff summary) and s.7(7) (District Courts) and cannot be exceeded *in cumulo*. Exceptions to this generality are provided in ss.21(4) and 22(4) in relation to breach of written undertakings and s.27(5) in regard to breach of bail conditions. In either case the sentence imposed can be added to that imposed for the substantive matter, even if this results in a cumulative sentence or fine higher than that which the Court could normally impose. See *Kelso v. Crowe*, 1992 S.C.C.R. 415—sentencing principles where contravention of bail conditions occur.

Police liberation

Liberation by police

22.—(1) Where a person has been arrested and charged with an offence which may be tried summarily, the officer in charge of a police station may—

(a) liberate him upon a written undertaking, signed by him and certified by the officer, in terms of which the person undertakes to appear at a specified court at a specified time; or

(b) liberate him without any such undertaking; or

(c) refuse to liberate him.

(2) A person in breach of an undertaking given by him under subsection (1) above without reasonable excuse shall be guilty of an offence and liable on summary conviction to the following penalties—

(a) a fine not exceeding level 3 on the standard scale; and

(b) imprisonment for a period—

(i) where conviction is in the district court, not exceeding 60 days; or

(ii) where conviction is in the sheriff court, not exceeding 3 months.

(3) The refusal of the officer in charge to liberate a person under subsection (1)(c) above and the detention of that person until his case is tried in the usual form shall not subject the officer to any claim whatsoever.

(4) The penalties provided for in subsection (2) above may be imposed in addition to any other penalty which it is competent for the court to impose, notwithstanding that the total of penalties imposed may exceed the maximum penalty which it is competent to impose in respect of the original offence.

(5) In any proceedings relating to an offence under this section, a writing, purporting to be such an undertaking as is mentioned in subsection (1)(a) above and bearing to be signed and certified, shall be sufficient evidence of the terms of the undertaking given by the arrested person.

GENERAL NOTE

This section permits the officer in charge of a police station, at his discretion, to liberate an accused person pending the submission of a report to the procurator fiscal, or to liberate him to appear at a named court on a specified future occasion, or to hold the person in custody for appearance at court on the next lawful day. These powers only apply when the charges preferred are capable of being prosecuted summarily, but the fact that a written undertaking has been entered into in no way commits the Crown to proceed summarily. Since a suspect has to consent to abide by the specified terms of an undertaking, it is equally open to him to refuse them and in that event it would be incompetent to proceed in terms of subs. (1)(a). The accused would either have to be detained in custody or be liberated for report.

Evidential Provisions
These are identical to those contained in s.21. See the notes on "Evidential Provisions" in that section.

Penalties (subs. (4))
The implications of this provision mirror those in s.21. Refer to the notes on "Penalties" in that section.

PART III

BAIL

Bail applications

23.—(1) Any person accused on petition of a crime which is by law bailable shall be entitled immediately, on any occasion on which he is brought before the sheriff prior to his committal until liberated in due course of law, to apply to the sheriff for bail, and the prosecutor shall be entitled to be heard against any such application.

(2) The sheriff shall be entitled in his discretion to refuse such application before the person accused is committed until liberated in due course of law.

(3) Where an accused is admitted to bail without being committed until liberated in due course of law, it shall not be necessary so to commit him, and it shall be lawful to serve him with an indictment or complaint without his having been previously so committed.

(4) Where bail is refused before committal until liberation in due course of law on an application under subsection (1) above, the application for bail may be renewed after such committal.

(5) Any sheriff having jurisdiction to try the offence or to commit the accused until liberated in due course of law may, at his discretion, on the application of any person who has been committed until liberation in due course of law for any crime or offence, except murder or treason, and having given the prosecutor an opportunity to be heard, admit or refuse to admit the person to bail.

(6) Where a person is charged on complaint with an offence, any judge having jurisdiction to try the offence may, at his discretion, on the application of the accused and after giving the prosecutor an opportunity to be heard, admit or refuse to admit the accused to bail.

(7) An application under subsection (5) or (6) above shall be disposed of within 24 hours after its presentation to the judge, failing which the accused shall be forthwith liberated.

(8) This section applies whether or not the accused is in custody at the time he appears for disposal of his application.

DEFINITIONS
　"bail": s.307(1).
　"complaint": s.307(1).
　"judge": s.307(1).
　"offence": s.307(1).
　"prosecutor": s.307(1).

GENERAL NOTE

Subs. (1)
　"*On petition*": This makes it clear that s.23(1) to (5) applies only to those accused at the outset of solemn procedure.

"*A crime which is by law bailable*": By s.24(1) all crimes are bailable except murder, treason and any others for which the Lord Advocate or the High Court admit the accused to bail. In *Boyle, Petr.*, 1993 S.C.C.R. 251 an accused on a murder charge was admitted to bail.

"*On any occasion on which he is brought before the sheriff*": This makes it certain that the accused must be present at the time of the application to the sheriff.

"*Prior to his committal until liberated in due course of law*": An application for bail cannot be after such committal on this wording.

"*The prosecutor shall be entitled to be heard*": The Crown attitude is crucial but not conclusive, having regard to s.23(2). For examples, see *Advocate, H.M. v. Saunders*, (1913) 7 Adam 76 and *Mackintosh v. McGlinchey*, 1921 J.C. 75.

Subs. (2)

"*His discretion*": The decision is one for the sheriff although the Crown attitude is crucial. There is no presumption in favour of the Crown on this question. The decision is based on attitude and is not amenable to proof.

There are important aspects to which, broadly, the court will have regard when exercising this discretion: (1) the more serious the crime the less willing the court is to allow bail, unless the Crown offers no objection: *Rennie v. Dickson*, (1907) 5 Adam 372; (2) the previous record of the accused is an important factor: *MacLeod v. Wright*, 1969 J.C. 12; (3) the attitude of the Crown; (4) no fixed abode weighs heavily but is not in itself sufficient to determine the question: *Advocate, H.M. v. Docherty*, 1958 S.L.T. (Notes) 50; (5) breach of earlier bail, which tends to suggest a contempt for earlier judicial fairness; (6) evidence that the accused will intimidate or threaten witnesses if released.

Subs. (3)

Ordinarily, committal for further examination is followed thereafter by committal until liberated in due course of law. This provision makes it clear that the latter need not necessarily follow the former.

Subs. (4)

A single application for bail is not provided for by this section: an application may be made at the stage of committal for further examination and may be renewed later when the accused next appears. Such an appearance may be for committal until liberated in due course of law or it may be for the purpose of such an application by arrangement.

Subs. (5)

"*Jurisdiction*": This may be territorial or in terms of statutory powers: see ss.4 and 5.

Subs. (6)

"*On complaint*": This extends shrieval discretion referred to in earlier subsections to "any judge having jurisdiction for the offence". For a definition of "judge", see s.308(1).

Subs. (8)

This subsection rehearses the provision in s.28(3) of the 1975 Act.

Bail and bail conditions

24.—(1) All crimes and offences except, subject to subsection (2) below, murder and treason are bailable.

(2) Nothing in this Act shall affect the right of the Lord Advocate or the High Court to admit to bail any person charged with any crime or offence.

(3) It shall not be lawful to grant bail or release for a pledge or deposit of money, and—

    (a) release on bail may be granted only on conditions which subject to subsection (6) below, shall not include a pledge or deposit of money;

    (b) liberation may be granted by the police under section 21, 22 or 43 of this Act.

(4) In granting bail the court or, as the case may be, the Lord Advocate shall impose on the accused—

    (a) the standard conditions; and

    (b) such further conditions as the court or, as the case may be, the Lord Advocate considers necessary to secure—

        (i) that the standard conditions are observed; and

(ii) that the accused makes himself available for the purpose of participating in an identification parade or of enabling any print, impression or sample to be taken from him.

(5) The standard conditions referred to in subsection (4) above are conditions that the accused—

(a) appears at the appointed time at every diet relating to the offence with which he is charged of which he is given due notice;

(b) does not commit an offence while on bail;

(c) does not interfere with witnesses or otherwise obstruct the course of justice whether in relation to himself or any other person; and

(d) makes himself available for the purpose of enabling enquiries or a report to be made to assist the court in dealing with him for the offence with which he is charged.

(6) The court or, as the case may be, the Lord Advocate may impose as one of the conditions of release on bail a requirement that the accused or a cautioner on his behalf deposits a sum of money in court, but only where the court or, as the case may be, the Lord Advocate is satisfied that the imposition of such condition is appropriate to the special circumstances of the case.

(7) In any enactment, including this Act and any enactment passed after this Act—

(a) any reference to bail shall be construed as a reference to release on conditions in accordance with this Act or to conditions imposed on bail, as the context requires;

(b) any reference to an amount of bail fixed shall be construed as a reference to conditions, including a sum required to be deposited under subsection (6) above;

(c) any reference to finding bail or finding sufficient bail shall be construed as a reference to acceptance of conditions imposed or the finding of a sum required to be deposited under subsection (6) above.

(8) In this section and sections 25 and 27 to 29 of this Act, references to an accused and to appearance at a diet shall include references respectively to an appellant and to appearance at the court on the day fixed for the hearing of an appeal.

DEFINITIONS
    "bail": s.307(1).
    "crime": s.307(1).
    "diet": s.307(1).
    "High Court": s.307(1).
    "offences": s.307(1).
    "standard conditions, the": s.24(5).

GENERAL NOTE
    The standard conditions referred to in s.24(5) are undoubtedly the commonest conditions of bail. However, the deposit of a sum of money in court, while unusual, is not unknown: see *Adam v. Kirichenko*, 1995 G.W.D. 26–1373 for a recent example.
    Two points of practice may be worth mentioning. First, the evidence of matters in s.28(3) to (8) is routine evidence under s.280(1) of and Sched. 9 to this Act and may thus be embodied in a certificate for service on the accused. Secondly, the grant of bail under this section must be read in conjunction with the provisions for bail under s.112 of this Act in relation to appeals.

Bail conditions: supplementary

25.—(1) The court shall specify in the order granting bail, a copy of which shall be given to the accused—

(a) the conditions imposed; and

(b) an address, within the United Kingdom (being the accused's normal place of residence or such other place as the court may, on cause shown, direct) which, subject to subsection (2) below, shall be his proper domicile of citation.

(2) The court may on application in writing by the accused while he is on bail alter the address specified in the order granting bail, and this new address shall, as from such date as the court may direct, become his proper domicile of citation; and the court shall notify the accused of its decision on any application under this subsection.

(3) In this section "proper domicile of citation" means the address at which the accused may be cited to appear at any diet relating to the offence with which he is charged or an offence charged in the same proceedings as that offence or to which any other intimation or document may be sent; and any citation at or the sending of an intimation or document to the proper domicile of citation shall be presumed to have been duly carried out.

DEFINITIONS
"bail": s.307(1).
"order": s.307(1).
"proper domicile of citation": s.25(3).

GENERAL NOTE
The importance for the Crown of this provision lies in the terms of s.25(2) which allows service of the citation to appear at any diet on the accused at the "proper domicile of citation". The importance for the accused lies in his release but there is a balancing factor of providing such a domicile of citation: change is possible on application but failure to observe the requirements has serious consequences, or may have: *McMahon v. MacPhail*, 1991 S.C.C.R. 470. Further, the evidence of the points in this section is routine evidence under s.280(1) of and Sched. 9 to this Act and may thus be embodied in a certificate for service on the accused.

Bail: circumstances where not available

26.—(1) Notwithstanding sections 23, 24 (except subsection (2)), 30, 32, 33 and 112 of this Act, a person who in any proceedings has been charged with or convicted of—
(a) attempted murder;
(b) culpable homicide;
(c) rape; or
(d) attempted rape,
in circumstances where this section applies shall not be granted bail in those proceedings.

(2) This section applies where—
(a) the person has previously been convicted by or before a court in any part of the United Kingdom of any offence specified in subsection (1) above or of murder or manslaughter; and
(b) in the case of a previous conviction of culpable homicide or of manslaughter—
(i) he was sentenced to imprisonment or, if he was then a child or young person, to detention under any of the relevant enactments;
(ii) a hospital order was imposed in respect of him;
(iii) an order having the same effect as a hospital order was made in respect of him under section 57(2)(a) of this Act; or
(iv) an order having equivalent effect to an order referred to in sub-paragraph (ii) or (iii) above has been made in respect of him by a court in England and Wales.

(3) This section applies whether or not an appeal is pending against conviction or sentence or both.

(4) In this section—
"conviction" includes—
(a) a finding that a person is not guilty by reason of insanity;

(b) a finding under section 55(2) of this Act;

(c) a finding under section 4A(3) of the Criminal Procedure (Insanity) Act 1964 (cases of unfitness to plead) that a person did the act or made the omission charged against him; and

(d) a conviction of an offence for which an order is made placing the offender on probation or discharging him absolutely or conditionally;

and "convicted" shall be construed accordingly; and

"the relevant enactments" means—

(a) as respects Scotland, sections 205(1) to (3) and 208 of this Act;

(b) as respects England and Wales, section 53(2) of the Children and Young Persons Act 1933; and

(c) as respects Northern Ireland, section 73(2) of the Children and Young Persons Act (Northern Ireland) 1968.

DEFINITIONS

"bail": s.307(1).

"conviction": s.26(4).

"hospital order": s.58(4).

"relevant enactments, the": s.26(4).

GENERAL NOTE

Section 26(1) of the 1975 Act provided that all crimes except murder and treason are bailable. Where an accused is brought before a sheriff or justice of the peace on any charge other than murder or treason, the sheriff or justice of the peace may release the accused on bail.

This section, which is derived from s.3 of the Criminal Justice (Scotland) Act 1995, extends the list of circumstances which are not bailable.

This section applies to bail applications in proceedings where an accused is charged with, or convicted of, one of four crimes, namely attempted murder, culpable homicide, rape or attempted rape. Bail must be refused in these proceedings if the accused already has a conviction for murder, manslaughter or one of the four above-mentioned crimes.

Breach of bail conditions: offences

27.—(1) Subject to subsection (7) below, an accused who having been granted bail fails without reasonable excuse—

(a) to appear at the time and place appointed for any diet of which he has been given due notice; or

(b) to comply with any other condition imposed on bail,

shall, subject to subsection (3) below, be guilty of an offence and liable on conviction to the penalties specified in subsection (2) below.

(2) The penalties mentioned in subsection (1) above are—

(a) a fine not exceeding level 3 on the standard scale; and

(b) imprisonment for a period—

(i) where conviction is in the district court, not exceeding 60 days; or

(ii) in any other case, not exceeding 3 months.

(3) Where, and to the extent that, the failure referred to in subsection (1) (b) above consists in the accused having committed an offence while on bail (in this section referred to as "the subsequent offence"), he shall not be guilty of an offence under that subsection but, subject to subsection (4) below, the court which sentences him for the subsequent offence shall, in determining the appropriate sentence or disposal for that offence, have regard to—

(a) the fact that the offence was committed by him while on bail and the number of bail orders to which he was subject when the offence was committed;

(b) any previous conviction of the accused of an offence under subsection (1)(b) above; and

(c) the extent to which the sentence or disposal in respect of any previous conviction of the accused differed, by virtue of this subsection, from that which the court would have imposed but for this subsection.

(4) The court shall not, under subsection (3) above, have regard to the fact that the subsequent offence was committed while the accused was on bail unless that fact is libelled in the indictment or, as the case may be, specified in the complaint.

(5) Where the maximum penalty in respect of the subsequent offence is specified by or by virtue of any enactment, that maximum penalty shall, for the purposes of the court's determination, by virtue of subsection (3) above, of the appropriate sentence or disposal in respect of that offence, be increased—

(a) where it is a fine, by the amount for the time being equivalent to level 3 on the standard scale; and

(b) where it is a period of imprisonment—
    (i) as respects a conviction in the High Court or the sheriff court, by 6 months; and
    (ii) as respects a conviction in the district court, by 60 days,
notwithstanding that the maximum penalty as so increased exceeds the penalty which it would otherwise be competent for the court to impose.

(6) Where the sentence or disposal in respect of the subsequent offence is, by virtue of subsection (3) above, different from that which the court would have imposed but for that subsection, the court shall state the extent of and the reasons for that difference.

(7) An accused who having been granted bail in relation to solemn proceedings fails without reasonable excuse to appear at the time and place appointed for any diet of which he has been given due notice (where such diet is in respect of solemn proceedings) shall be guilty of an offence and liable on conviction on indictment to the following penalties—

(a) a fine; and

(b) imprisonment for a period not exceeding 2 years.

(8) At any time before the trial of an accused under solemn procedure for the original offence, it shall be competent—

(a) to amend the indictment to include an additional charge of an offence under this section;

(b) to include in the list of witnesses or productions relating to the original offence, witnesses or productions relating to the offence under this section.

(9) The penalties provided for in subsection (2) above may be imposed in addition to any other penalty which it is competent for the court to impose, notwithstanding that the total of penalties imposed may exceed the maximum penalty which it is competent to impose in respect of the original offence.

(10) A court which finds an accused guilty of an offence under this section may remit the accused for sentence in respect of that offence to any court which is considering the original offence.

(11) In this section "the original offence" means the offence with which the accused was charged when he was granted bail or an offence charged in the same proceedings as that offence.

DEFINITIONS
"bail": s.307(1).
"level 3": s.225(2) [*i.e.* £1,000].
"offence": s.307(1).
"original offence, the": s.27(11).
"sentence": s.307(1).
"standard scale": s.225(1).
"subsequent offence, the": s.27(3).

GENERAL NOTE
Subss. (1) and (2)

These subsections create the main offences of breaching bail conditions and to the extent that they replicate s.3(1) and (2) of the Bail, etc. (Scotland) Act 1980 they are not new. What is new is the increase in the maximum fine to level three on the standard scale; *i.e.* from £200 to £1,000.

There has been an extensive number of decisions in regard to bail. Some of these are of a general nature. In *Aitchison v. Tudhope*, 1981 S.C.C.R. 1 it was held that in the absence of challenge to the special capacity the Crown does not require to prove that the bail order was still in force. In *Rowley v. H.M. Advocate*, 1983 S.C.C.R. 413 it was held that the fact that the accused had been acquitted of the charges in respect of which he had been placed on bail was irrelevant. In *MacNeill v. Smith*, 1984 S.L.T. (Sh.Ct.) 63 it was held that the court minutes must refer to grants of bail. In *Advocate, H.M. v. Crawford*, 1985 S.L.T. 242 it was held that special conditions must be referred to explicitly on the face of the copy of the bail order served on the accused. In *McGinn v. H.M. Advocate*, 1991 S.L.T. 266 it was held that the provisions related to breaches of bail conditions regardless of whether the subsequent proceedings were solemn or summary.

Some of the decisions are more particular to the terms of the legislation: for example, it is an offence to fail without reasonable excuse to comply with any condition (other than attending timeously) imposed on bail: see s.3(1)(b) of the 1980 Act. In *Mayo v. Neizer*, 1994 S.L.T. 931 it was held that bail orders continue in force for so long as the accused is at liberty even if as an appellant he abandons an appeal against sentence and awaits arrest on a consequent warrant. In *Fitzpatrick v. Normand*, 1994 S.L.T. 1263 it was held that recall or modification of a bail order must be the subject of an express decision of the court.

Breach of bail conditions: arrest of offender, etc.

28.—(1) A constable may arrest without warrant an accused who has been released on bail where the constable has reasonable grounds for suspecting that the accused has broken, is breaking, or is likely to break any condition imposed on his bail.

(2) An accused who is arrested under this section shall wherever practicable be brought before the court to which his application for bail was first made not later than in the course of the first day after his arrest, such day not being, subject to subsection (3) below, a Saturday, a Sunday or a court holiday prescribed for that court under section 8 of this Act.

(3) Nothing in subsection (2) above shall prevent an accused being brought before a court on a Saturday, a Sunday or such a court holiday where the court is, in pursuance of the said section 8, sitting on such day for the disposal of criminal business.

(4) Where an accused is brought before a court under subsection (2) or (3) above, the court, after hearing the parties, may—

   (a) recall the order granting bail;

   (b) release the accused under the original order granting bail; or

   (c) vary the order granting bail so as to contain such conditions as the court thinks it necessary to impose to secure that the accused complies with the requirements of paragraphs (a) to (d) of section 24(5) of this Act.

(5) The same rights of appeal shall be available against any decision of the court under subsection (4) above as were available against the original order of the court relating to bail.

(6) For the purposes of this section and section 27 of this Act, an extract from the minute of proceedings, containing the order granting bail and bearing to be signed by the clerk of court, shall be sufficient evidence of the making of that order and of its terms and of the acceptance by the accused of the conditions imposed under section 24 of this Act.

Bail: monetary conditions

29.—(1) Without prejudice to section 27 of this Act, where the accused or a cautioner on his behalf has deposited a sum of money in court under section 24(6) of this Act, then—

    (a) if the accused fails to appear at the time and place appointed for any diet of which he has been given due notice, the court may, on the motion of the prosecutor, immediately order forfeiture of the sum deposited;

    (b) if the accused fails to comply with any other condition imposed on bail, the court may, on conviction of an offence under section 27(1)(b) of this Act and on the motion of the prosecutor, order forfeiture of the sum deposited.

(2) If the court is satisfied that it is reasonable in all the circumstances to do so, it may recall an order made under subsection (1)(a) above and direct that the money forfeited shall be refunded, and any decision of the court under this subsection shall be final and not subject to review.

(3) A cautioner, who has deposited a sum of money in court under section 24(6) of this Act, shall be entitled, subject to subsection (4) below, to recover the sum deposited at any diet of the court at which the accused appears personally.

(4) Where the accused has been charged with an offence under section 27(1)(b) of this Act, nothing in subsection (3) above shall entitle a cautioner to recover the sum deposited unless and until—

    (a) the charge is not proceeded with; or

    (b) the accused is acquitted of the charge; or

    (c) on the accused's conviction of the offence, the court has determined not to order forfeiture of the sum deposited.

(5) The references in subsections (1)(b) and (4)(c) above to conviction of an offence shall include references to the making of an order in respect of the offence under section 246(3) of this Act.

Bail review

30.—(1) This section applies where a court has refused to admit a person to bail or, where a court has so admitted a person, the person has failed to accept the conditions imposed or that a sum required to be deposited under section 24(6) of this Act has not been so deposited.

(2) A court shall, on the application of any person mentioned in subsection (1) above, have power to review its decision to admit to bail or its decision as to the conditions imposed and may, on cause shown, admit the person to bail or, as the case may be, fix bail on different conditions.

(3) An application under this section, where it relates to the original decision of the court, shall not be made before the fifth day after that decision and, where it relates to a subsequent decision, before the fifteenth day thereafter.

(4) Nothing in this section shall affect any right of a person to appeal against the decision of a court in relation to admitting to bail or to the conditions imposed.

DEFINITIONS
    "bail": s.307(1).

GENERAL NOTE
    This section applies in a number of separate circumstances: *e.g.* the court may have refused to admit a person to bail. For the general guidelines as to the allowance or refusal of bail, see *Smith v. M.*, 1982 S.L.T. 421. Alternatively, a court may have so admitted a person but the person has failed to accept the conditions imposed: for a special condition that was challenged see *Brawls v. Walkingshaw*, 1994 S.C.C.R. 7. Also, a court may have required the deposit of a sum of money but that has not been done. In any or all of these circumstances, a person may seek to have the

original decision reviewed within modest statutory time-limits and yet otherwise appeal the original decision.

Bail review on prosecutor's application

31.—(1) On an application by the prosecutor at any time after a court has granted bail to a person the court may, where the prosecutor puts before the court material information which was not available to it when it granted bail to that person, review its decision.

(2) On receipt of an application under subsection (1) above the court shall—

(a) intimate the application to the person granted bail;

(b) fix a diet for hearing the application and cite that person to attend the diet; and

(c) where it considers that the interests of justice so require, grant warrant to arrest that person.

(3) On hearing an application under subsection (1) above the court may—

(a) withdraw the grant of bail and remand the person in question in custody; or

(b) grant bail, or continue the grant of bail, either on the same or on different conditions.

(4) Nothing in the foregoing provisions of this section shall affect any right of appeal against the decision of a court in relation to bail.

DEFINITIONS
"bail": s.307(1).
"diet": s.307(1).
"prosecutor": s.307(1).

GENERAL NOTE
This section enables the prosecutor to apply to the court to reconsider a decision to grant bail. Application must be made on the basis of information relevant to the decision to grant bail which was not available to the court when the decision was taken. Subsection (2) describes the procedure to be followed on receipt of an application by a prosecutor. Subsection (3) specifies the options available to the court on hearing the prosecutor's application.

Bail appeal

32.—(1) Where an application for bail—

(a) after committal until liberation in due course of law; or

(b) by a person charged on complaint with an offence,

is refused or where the applicant is dissatisfied with the amount of bail fixed, he may appeal to the High Court which may, in its discretion order intimation to the Lord Advocate or, as the case may be, the prosecutor.

(2) Where, in any case, an application for bail is granted, or, in summary proceedings an accused is ordained to appear, the public prosecutor, if dissatisfied—

(a) with the decision allowing bail;

(b) with the amount of bail fixed; or

(c) in summary proceedings, that the accused has been ordained to appear,

may appeal to the High Court, and the applicant shall not be liberated, subject to subsection (7) below, until the appeal by the prosecutor is disposed of.

(3) Written notice of appeal shall be immediately given to the opposite party by a party appealing under this section.

(4) An appeal under this section shall be disposed of by the High Court or any Lord Commissioner of Justiciary in court or in chambers after such inquiry and hearing of parties as shall seem just.

(5) Where an applicant in an appeal under this section is under 21 years of age, section 51 of this Act shall apply to the High Court or, as the case may be,

the Lord Commissioner of Justiciary when disposing of the appeal as it applies to a court when remanding or committing a person of the applicant's age for trial or sentence.

(6) In the event of the appeal of the public prosecutor under this section being refused, the court may award expenses against him.

(7) When an appeal is taken by the public prosecutor either against the grant of bail or against the amount fixed, the applicant to whom bail has been granted shall, if the bail fixed has been found by him, be liberated after 72 hours from the granting of the application, whether the appeal has been disposed of or not, unless the High Court grants an order for his further detention in custody.

(8) In computing the period mentioned in subsection (7) above, Sundays and public holidays, whether general or court holidays, shall be excluded.

(9) When an appeal is taken under this section by the prosecutor in summary proceedings against the fact that the accused has been ordained to appear, subsections (7) and (8) above shall apply as they apply in the case of an appeal against the granting of bail or the amount fixed.

(10) Notice to the governor of the prison of the issue of an order such as is mentioned in subsection (7) above within the time mentioned in that subsection bearing to be sent by the Clerk of Justiciary or the Crown Agent shall be sufficient warrant for the detention of the applicant pending arrival of the order in due course of post.

DEFINITIONS
   "bail": s.307(1).
   "Clerk of Justiciary": s.307(1).
   "complaint": s.307(1).
   "governor": s.307(1).
   "High Court": s.307(1).
   "Lords Commissioner of Justiciary": s.307(1).
   "order": s.307(1).
   "prison": s.307(1).
   "prosecutor": s.307(1).

GENERAL NOTE
   The essence of this section in the most general of terms is that, by subs. (1), the accused may appeal a refusal of bail and by subs. (2) the Crown may appeal the grant of bail. Each party appealing must give written notice to the other side, by subs. (3). Disposal of the appeal may be by the High Court or a single judge in court or in chambers: subs. (4).

Bail: no fees exigible

33. No clerks fees, court fees or other fees or expenses shall be exigible from or awarded against an accused in respect of his application for bail or of the appeal of such application to the High Court.

DEFINITIONS
   "bail": s.307(1).
   "High Court": s.307(1).

PART IV

PETITION PROCEDURE

Warrants

Petition for warrant

34.—(1) A petition for warrant to arrest and commit a person suspected of or charged with crime may be in the forms—
   (a) set out in Schedule 2 to this Act; or
   (b) prescribed by Act of Adjournal,

or as nearly as may be in such form; and Schedule 3 to this Act shall apply to any such petition as it applies to the indictment.

(2) If on the application of the procurator fiscal, a sheriff is satisfied that there is reasonable ground for suspecting that an offence has been or is being committed by a body corporate, the sheriff shall have the like power to grant warrant for the citation of witnesses and the production of documents and articles as he would have if a petition charging an individual with the commission of the offence were presented to him.

GENERAL NOTE

Solemn proceedings are generally initiated by the presentation of a petition to a sheriff in chambers. The petition may be put before the court along with the person accused of the crime, or the Crown may petition for a warrant to arrest the accused: on occasion where several accused are involved the petition may take both forms. Offences committed by corporate bodies can in terms of subs. (2) also be initiated by way of the same petition procedure and, when granted by the court, give the same powers to the Crown as would a petition against an individual accused. Prior to the enactment of s.74(7) of the 1975 Act the form of petition used for offences committed by such bodies was derived from the Criminal Justice (Scotland) Act 1949, s.40(7); indeed until the Second World War solemn proceedings against companies or other corporate bodies were unknown.

The crimes charged are narrated in the third person and s.40 of the 1995 Act requires that the principal petition must be signed by the prosecutor (normally a fiscal or a fiscal depute) and by a sheriff, both of whom must have a jurisdiction derived from one or more of the charges libelled. Subsection (1) refers to the forms of indictments set out in Sched. 2 to the Act. It will be noted that these charges originated in the Criminal Procedure (Scotland) Act 1887 (c.35) and many are arcane, obsolescent or obsolete (it has to be doubted that the Crown would ever libel a crime euphemistically as an "attempt to ravish" or "ravish" now—the charge would be one of attempted rape or rape).

As a matter of course the warrant granted by the court will authorise (i) the arrest of the accused and require that he be brought before the court for examination, (ii) the search of his abode or other premises for the purpose of such arrest and to gather evidence, (iii) the citation of witnesses and the production to the Crown of documentary and label productions, and (iv) after examination, his committal for further examination or until liberated in due course of law (technically the first-mentioned step is unnecessary in situations where the petition is of even date with the first appearance of the accused or where the accused is a body corporate).

Judicial examination

Judicial examination

35.—(1) The accused's solicitor shall be entitled to be present at the examination.

(2) The sheriff may delay the examination for a period not exceeding 48 hours from and after the time of the accused's arrest, in order to allow time for the attendance of the solicitor.

(3) Where the accused is brought before the sheriff for examination on any charge and he or his solicitor intimates that he does not desire to emit a declaration in regard to such a charge, it shall be unnecessary to take a declaration, and, subject to section 36 of this Act, the accused may be committed for further examination or until liberated in due course of law without a declaration being taken.

(4) Nothing in subsection (3) above shall prejudice the right of the accused subsequently to emit a declaration on intimating to the prosecutor his desire to do so; and that declaration shall be taken in further examination.

(5) Where, subsequent to examination or further examination on any charge, the prosecutor desires to question the accused as regards an extrajudicial confession, whether or not a full admission, allegedly made by him to or in the hearing of a constable, which is relevant to the charge and as regards which he has not previously been examined, the accused may be brought before the sheriff for further examination.

(6) Where the accused is brought before the sheriff for further examination the sheriff may delay that examination for a period not exceeding 24 hours in order to allow time for the attendance of the accused's' solicitor.

(7) Any proceedings before the sheriff in examination or further examination shall be conducted in chambers and outwith the presence of any co-accused.

(8) This section applies to procedure on petition, without prejudice to the accused being tried summarily by the sheriff for any offence in respect of which he has been committed until liberated in due course of law.

DEFINITIONS
"constable": s.307(1) and s.51(1) of the Police (Scotland) Act 1967.
"procurator": s.307(1).
"sheriff": s.4(1) and (4).

GENERAL NOTE
The process of judicial examination is often a part of petition procedure and its origins can be found in the Criminal Procedure (Scotland) Act 1887. After the passing of the Criminal Evidence Act 1898 (c.36) the practice of making "no plea; no declaration" became almost universal and while it remains competent for an accused to make a judicial declaration, it is now a rare event.

As with all petition procedure, judicial examination is held in private, outwith the presence of any co-accused or their agents.

The right of an accused person to emit a judicial declaration is preserved by s.35(4) of the 1995 Act and this can be made at any time before service of the indictment. The terms of a previously prepared statement can be declared by an accused provided that the words used are truly his own; it is not permissible for another person, even his solicitor, to edit or style the declaration since this may alter its sense or character (see *Carmichael v. Armitage*, 1982 S.C.C.R. 475).

A rare modern example of a declaration being made and not properly recorded either to meet the statutory requirements of s.20B of the 1975 Act or even the common law standards which prevailed prior to the 1980 Act is found in *Robertson v. H.M. Advocate*, 1995 S.C.C.R. 153, discussed in the notes to s.37 below.

Subsection (5) affords the prosecutor an opportunity then, or at a later time, to question the accused either about the contents of such a declaration or about any new admission made to, or heard by, a police officer which is deemed relevant to the charge libelled on the petition.

The prosecutor's right to examine upon any new material certainly can be exercised at any time before service of the indictment and arguably, by inference from *Frame v. Houston*, 1995 S.C.C.R. 436, up until the trial commences.

Section 17(2) of the 1995 Act stipulates that the accused shall be entitled to a private interview with his solicitor prior to judicial examination or court appearance and s.35(2), in effect, places the court under an obligation to ensure that access to legal advice has been offered. There is no requirement that an accused person must have had such a private interview or be legally represented at his judicial examination, but the court has to draw the accused's attention to his right to such services. Failure to do so may vitiate any admissions made in the course of the declaration by an accused without benefit of legal representation: see *Advocate, H.M. v. Goodall*, (1888) 2 White 1.

Subsection (6) gives the sheriff a discretion to delay the first examination for a further 24 hours to allow for the attendance of the agent nominated by the accused. Until the first examination has been concluded it is not competent for the accused to apply for bail.

There is no obligation upon the Crown to seek to judicially examine an accused in any petition case; the procedure for conduct of judicial examinations is laid out in s.36 of the Act and ss.37 and 38 specify the form of the record of proceedings. Additional provisions are found in the Act of Adjournal (Criminal Procedure Rules).

Judicial examination: questioning by prosecutor

36.—(1) Subject to the following provisions of this section, an accused on being brought before the sheriff for examination on any charge (whether the first or a further examination) may be questioned by the prosecutor in so far as such questioning is directed towards eliciting any admission, denial, explanation, justification or comment which the accused may have as regards anything to which subsections (2) to (4) below apply.

(2) This subsection applies to matters averred in the charge, and the particular aims of a line of questions under this subsection shall be to determine—

(a) whether any account which the accused can give ostensibly discloses a defence; and

(b) the nature and particulars of that defence.

(3) This subsection applies to the alleged making by the accused, to or in the hearing of a constable, of an extrajudicial confession (whether or not a full admission) relevant to the charge, and questions under this subsection may only be put if the accused has, before the examination, received from the prosecutor or from a constable a written record of the confession allegedly made.

(4) This subsection applies to what is said in any declaration emitted in regard to the charge by the accused at examination.

(5) The prosecutor shall, in framing questions in exercise of his power under subsection (1) above, have regard to the following principles—

(a) the question should not be designed to challenge the truth of anything said by the accused;

(b) there should be no reiteration of a question which the accused has refused to answer at the examination; and

(c) there should be no leading questions,

and the sheriff shall ensure that all questions are fairly put to, and understood by, the accused.

(6) The accused shall be told by the sheriff—

(a) where he is represented by a solicitor at the judicial examination, that he may consult that solicitor before answering any question; and

(b) that if he answers any question put to him at the examination under this section in such a way as to disclose an ostensible defence, the prosecutor shall be under the duty imposed by subsection (10) below.

(7) With the permission of the sheriff, the solicitor for the accused may ask the accused any question the purpose of which is to clarify any ambiguity in an answer given by the accused to the prosecutor at the examination or to give the accused an opportunity to answer any question which he has previously refused to answer.

(8) An accused may decline to answer a question under subsection (1) above; and, where he is subsequently tried on the charge mentioned in that subsection or on any other charge arising out of the circumstances which gave rise to the charge so mentioned, his having so declined may be commented upon by the prosecutor, the judge presiding at the trial, or any co-accused, only where and in so far as the accused (or any witness called on his behalf) in evidence avers something which could have been stated appropriately in answer to that question.

(9) The procedure in relation to examination under this section shall be prescribed by Act of Adjournal.

(10) Without prejudice to any rule of law, on the conclusion of an examination under this section the prosecutor shall secure the investigation, to such extent as is reasonably practicable, of any ostensible defence disclosed in the course of the examination.

(11) The duty imposed by subsection (10) above shall not apply as respects any ostensible defence which is not reasonably capable of being investigated.

DEFINITIONS

   "constable": s.307(1) and s.51(1) of the Police (Scotland) Act 1967.

   "prosecutor": s.307(1).

GENERAL NOTE

Section 35(7) provides that judicial examination is to be conducted in chambers outwith the presence of any other accused. It is not mandatory that the accused be legally represented at his judicial examination but it is the norm.

In terms of s.39, charges arising from other sheriff court jurisdictions can competently be included in the petition before the sheriff and the accused can be examined upon all charges.

The procedures specified in s.36 are recognisably derived from s.20A of the 1975 Act but the 1995 Act incorporates the amendments introduced by s.10(1) of the Criminal Justice (Scotland) Act 1995 (c.20): in summary these allow more direct questioning of the accused, require the Crown to make reasonable enquiry into any defence tendered by an accused in the course of his examination and, accordingly, oblige the presiding sheriff to impart additional information to the accused in the course of the judicial admonition which must precede any examination.

The prosecutor is not obliged to conduct a judicial examination at either the first or the further examination stage, but if he elects to do so he must adhere to the provisions laid down in s.36.

The role of the defence solicitor is still a reactive one; he may only consult with his client when the accused requests advice or intervene through the sheriff, as provided by subs. (7), to clarify ambiguities or to solicit answers to questions previously unanswered by the accused. Regulation of the proceedings remains the responsibility of the presiding sheriff.

At no time is an oath administered to the accused and nor can he be cross-examined, facts which following *Morrison v. H.M. Advocate*, 1990 S.C.C.R. 235 at 248E, the trial judge should make known to the jury at trial.

Subs. (1)

The revised terms of subs. (1) now make reference to the prosecutor's function to be able to question the accused about the charge with a view to securing any "admission" as well as any "denial, explanation, justification or comment" the accused may offer. On a strict interpretation of the 1980 Act's provisions the Crown could not directly ask an accused whether he admitted the charge in whole or part, only whether he denied the allegations entirely or not. Such a literal reading hardly lent clarity to the proceedings; indeed one means of complying with such a rigourous interpretation was to question the accused using a double negative ("Is there any part of the charge you do not deny?") then relieve the confusion with the obvious question ("Do you admit the charge or any part of it?"). Such circumlocutions should now be unnecessary but the radical nature of this apparently small amendment should not be under-estimated: an accused may now be asked questions which are directly aimed to achieve his self-incrimination, and his failure to answer (as subs. (8) provides) can be commented upon if he leads evidence at trial. Moreover his position can be still worse if he simply declines to answer any question put at judicial examination and fails to lead evidence at his trial, since s.32 of the Criminal Justice (Scotland) Act 1995, which repealed s.141(1)(b) of the 1975 Act and now effectively entitles the prosecutor to comment upon such a failure.

Subs. (2)

The scope of the prosecutor's questions in relation to the charge itself are restricted to eliciting whether the accused will advance any sort of defence at the examination. A greater (but still limited) latitude is available to the procurator fiscal when the accused is alleged to have uttered an extrajudicial admission: see the discussion relative to subs. (3) below.

It is of note that subs. (2) is explicitly drafted more broadly than was s.20A(1)(a) of the 1975 Act. As well as the generally understood defences of self-defence, alibi, incrimination and consent it could be argued that temporary insanity, certain forms of automatism, lawful authority or coercion could each equally constitute a defence.

Once a possible defence is stated at judicial examination subs. (10) below places a limited obligation upon the Crown to investigate its substance. Note however that there is no *compulsitor* upon the Crown, and no timescale specified for the conduct of these enquiries or even a duty to report findings to the court. Nonetheless it would be imprudent to ignore this provision if only because it would then be open to the accused at his trial to found upon any lack of diligence in investigating the defence tendered. It is submitted that in terms of subs. (2)(b) the fiscal can justifiably question the accused to obtain sufficient information to allow the Crown to fulfil the statutory duty imposed by subs. (10), namely, investigation of the defence revealed by the examination. During the Committee stage of the Bill the Lord Advocate reiterated that if the procurator fiscal discovered evidence at this stage of proceedings which might assist the accused, then it would be the Crown's duty to make the fact known to the defence (*Hansard*, January 12, 1995, Vol. 560, col. 369).

Subs. (3)

In addition to questions about the charge itself and any defence which the accused may then wish to tender as provided by subs. (1) and (2), the fiscal may also examine the accused upon any extrajudicial utterance made by him to, or within earshot of, a police officer. Note that the Crown may choose whether or not to put these alleged words to the accused and may elect not to do so, particularly when the reply is either mixed, self-serving or discloses previous convictions or references to matters not libelled. See *Advocate, H.M. v. Cafferty*, 1984 S.C.C.R. 444.

The 1996 Act of Adjournal stipulates that examination about such extrajudicial admissions can only occur if the presiding sheriff has first received a copy of the text of admissions already served on the accused; this does no more than codify the existing practice.

Although the usual procedure is for the procurator fiscal to examine initially upon the charges on the petition and any appropriate defences before questioning about any alleged replies, there is no statutory necessity to follow this chronology; the only requirements are that the "confession", partial or full, must be served upon the accused in written form prior to the examination for questioning to be permitted and the rules of the 1996 Act of Adjournal are obeyed.

Normally the statement of extrajudicial confessions is annexed to the copy petition served on the accused, though this is not a mandatory requirement. It will have to (i) specify the wording averred to have been used by the accused; (ii) identify the police officer in whose hearing the words were uttered and, by inference, the time and place of the event in order to qualify as legitimate material for the purposes of subs. (3). Where the accused has been interviewed on tape by the police this is usually indicated on the statement of extrajudicial admissions. When the accused has made a voluntary statement which is incriminating, it is the practice to annex a copy of it to the petition and question him about its contents and the circumstances in which it was made.

All of this raises the intractable issue of what does, or does not, constitute an extrajudicial confession: this is particularly problematical when the statement made is in part self-serving or is a veiled attack on the complainer's character (see *Morrison v. H.M. Advocate*, 1990 S.C.C.R. 235 discussed in the notes to subs. (8) below).

In *McKenzie v. H.M. Advocate*, 1982 S.C.C.R. 544 objection was taken by the agent at the examination, to a reply attributed to the accused on the grounds that it was not a confession. The sheriff allowed questioning by the fiscal and permitted the agent to clarify at the conclusion of the questioning. It is submitted that there is no *locus* for such an objection by the agent at this stage in proceedings; it is then solely a matter for judicial discretion. The appropriate time for objection is if, or when, either party (or a co-accused) seeks to found upon the transcript of judicial examination at the trial. The fairness and admissibility of the transcript can be properly weighed then and, in any event, such an approach excludes the possibility of the trial judge being called upon to review the earlier decision of the sheriff who presided at the examination. See also *Moran v. H.M. Advocate*, 1990 S.C.C.R. 40; 1990 S.L.T. 756.

Subss. (5), (6) and (7)

Judicial examination is not an opportunity for the Crown to cross-examine the accused. Subsection (5) underlines the role of the sheriff to ensure the fair conduct of proceedings. The accused must be informed by the sheriff (i) of the right to consult the solicitor appearing with him prior to answering questions and (ii) that the Crown will be under an obligation to investigate, so far as practicable, any defence disclosed during the examination. It is submitted that a judicial failure to admonish the accused with due regard to subss. (6), (8) and (10) would render the resultant transcript of proceedings inadmissible.

Note however that the solicitor's role in the examination is reactive; he may not initiate a consultation with his client during questioning by the fiscal and may only ask questions of his client as permitted by subs. (7). While that subsection does not expressly stipulate it, the practice has developed of giving leave to the defence solicitor to question at the conclusion of the fiscal's examination.

Subs. (8)

The object of judicial examination is to cause the accused at the earliest stage in proceedings to state his defence both as a means of focusing the issues and as a deterrent to the introduction of spurious lines of defence at the trial. While the accused is entitled to keep his own counsel at the examination, this may work to his disadvantage at his trial when other parties can utilise the provisions of subs. (8) to undermine his defence case. However the 1996 Act of Adjournal rule 5.5(4) imposes possible limits upon the freedom of others to comment upon contrasts in the accused's position at judicial examination and in his evidence at trial. It is now a matter for the trial judge to consider whether such comments can be made to the jury by other parties, or the judge himself, having regard to the terms of the original petition charges and the libel now before the court. To assist in the judge's deliberations, the prosecutor must be able to provide the original petition or a certified copy.

A number of issues flow from this reform; first, it would seem to be good practice for the Crown as a matter of course to include a certified copy of the petition and, by implication, a certified copy of the written record of any extrajudicial admissions referred to during the examination. Secondly, the provision suggests that before either the prosecutor or other accused invoke the right to comment under s.36(8), they should seek the authority of the presiding judge to do so. Thirdly, if the judge resolves to comment it would seem sensible, to say the least, to refer to the original petition and canvass the views of the parties, including the co-accused, before hand and outwith the presence of the jury.

Support for this reading can be found in Chap. 25 of the 1996 Rules, for rule 25.1(3) permits the trial judge to release copies to the jury of any written record of confession (appropriately edited) referred to during judicial examination.

It must be stressed that subs. (8) only comes into play when the accused leads evidence, from himself or other witnesses, at his trial. An accused who has declined to comment at examination and has not led evidence at trial is outwith the subsection's scope. See *Walker v. H.M. Advocate*, 1985 S.C.C.R. 150 and *Dempsey v. H.M. Advocate*, 1995 S.C.C.R. 431.

In *Walker* it was held on appeal that the statutory provisions of the 1975 Act, s.20A(5) were wrongly applied, the accused having maintained silence throughout and left the Crown to prove its case. Even then note, that while it was conceded that the trial judge had misdirected the jury, this did not in the circumstances, constitute a miscarriage of justice. Nonetheless where the judge does direct the attention of the jury to the operation of subs. (8) this must be done with restraint and without undue emphasis; see *McEwan v. H.M. Advocate*, 1990 S.C.C.R. 401.

It is common for an accused during examination to decline to answer questions and to state that this has been done on the advice of his solicitor. This stock reply does not protect an accused from unfavourable comment should he choose to lead evidence at his trial. Thus the judge's direction in *Gilmour v. H.M. Advocate*, 1982 S.C.C.R. 590 at 604, that such conduct at judicial examination could not be considered as relevant evidence is much too favourable to the accused. See *Alexander v. H.M. Advocate*, 1988 S.C.C.R. 542.

Subsection (8) does not deal with the potentially intractable situation where an accused, at judicial examination, responds to questioning by providing a self-serving account and founds upon it at trial without leading further evidence. Just such a situation arose in *Morrison*, above, a seven judge decision, which deals (it is hoped) definitively with the approach to mixed statements, or qualified admissions, including extrajudicial confessions. The law is stated at 247F to 248E and is discussed fully by Dr D.B. Griffiths, in *Confessions* (Edinburgh 1994) at pp.90 to 97: Dr Griffiths' comment that *Morrison* "is a difficult case and is always going to remain so", defies contradiction.

Prudence dictates that at trial the presiding judge would do well simply to echo and endorse the "Morrison formula" cited above. See *Smith v. H.M. Advocate*, 1994 S.C.C.R. 72 (conviction quashed), *MacLeod v. H.M. Advocate*, 1995 S.L.T. 145 and *Harley v. H.M. Advocate*, 1995 S.C.C.R. 595 (convictions upheld despite failure to follow *Morrison* explicitly). Opinion has been reserved however as to whether founding upon exculpatory answers given in the course of a judicial examination would be sufficient to meet the burden of proof resting upon an accused in charges under the Prevention of Corruption Act 1906 (c.34) (*Ridler v. H.M. Advocate*, 1995 S.C.C.R. 655).

Section 32 of the Criminal Justice (Scotland) Act 1995 which repealed s.141(1)(b) of the 1975 Act now entitles the prosecutor, but not co-accused, to comment upon the accused's failure to lead evidence. The removal of this long-standing prohibition introduces a much more telling weapon into the prosecutor's armoury than s.36(8) of the 1995 Act allows. Will the defence opt for even the emptiest transcript of judicial examination to be read, and, arguably, lead defence "evidence" as a means of precluding weighty adverse comment by the Crown: will the Crown adopt the same course or even refrain from judicial examination altogether to counter such a tactic?

Subss. (10) and (11)
See the discussion in the notes to subs. (2) above.

Judicial examination: record of proceedings

37.—(1) The prosecutor shall provide for a verbatim record to be made by means of shorthand notes or by mechanical means of all questions to and answers and declarations by the accused in examination, or further examination, under sections 35 and 36 of this Act.

(2) A shorthand writer shall—

(a) sign the shorthand notes taken by him of the questions, answers and declarations mentioned in subsection (1) above and certify the notes as being complete and correct; and

(b) retain the notes.

(3) A person recording the questions, answers and declarations mentioned in subsection (1) above by mechanical means shall—

(a) certify that the record is true and complete;

(b) specify in the certificate the proceedings to which the record relates; and

(c) retain the record.

(4) The prosecutor shall require the person who made the record mentioned in subsection (1) above, or such other competent person as he may specify, to make a transcript of the record in legible form; and that person shall—

(a) comply with the requirement;

(b) certify the transcript as being a complete and correct transcript of the record purporting to have been made and certified, and in the case of shorthand notes signed, by the person who made the record; and

(c) send the transcript to the prosecutor.

(5) A transcript certified under subsection (4)(b) above shall, subject to section 38(1) of this Act, be deemed for all purposes to be a complete and correct record of the questions, answers and declarations mentioned in subsection (1) above.

(6) Subject to subsections (7) to (9) below, within 14 days of the date of examination or further examination, the prosecutor shall—

(a) serve a copy of the transcript on the accused examined; and

(b) serve a further such copy on the solicitor (if any) for that accused.

(7) Where at the time of further examination a trial diet is already fixed and the interval between the further examination and that diet is not sufficient to allow of the time limits specified in subsection (6) above and subsection (1) of section 38 of this Act, the sheriff shall (either or both)—

(a) direct that those subsections shall apply in the case with such modifications as to time limits as he shall specify;

(b) subject to subsection (8) below, postpone the trial diet.

(8) Postponement under paragraph (b) of subsection (7) above alone shall only be competent where the sheriff considers that to proceed under paragraph (a) of that subsection alone, or paragraphs (a) and (b) together, would not be practicable.

(9) Any time limit mentioned in subsection (6) above and subsection (1) of section 38 of this Act (including any such time limit as modified by a direction under subsection (7) above) may be extended, in respect of the case, by the High Court.

(10) A copy of—

(a) a transcript required by paragraph (a) of subsection (6) above to be served on an accused or by paragraph (b) of that subsection to be served on his solicitor; or

(b) a notice required by paragraph (a) of section 38(1) of this Act to be served on an accused or on the prosecutor,

shall be served in such manner as may be prescribed by Act of Adjournal; and a written execution purporting to be signed by the person who served such transcript or notice, together with, where appropriate, the relevant post office receipt shall be sufficient evidence of service of such a copy.

GENERAL NOTE

This section provides that the record of proceedings at any judicial declaration or judicial examination is to be noted in shorthand or mechanically recorded. In either case it then becomes the responsibility of the prosecutor to effect service upon the accused and his agent of a transcript of the proceedings duly certified as complete and accurate by the person appointed to transcribe the record by the prosecutor. Service must be effected within 14 days of the hearing unless as subs. (7) allows, a trial diet occurs within that time or either the prosecutor or the accused have in terms of s.38 sought rectification of the transcript: in either of these events the sheriff has power to modify the timescale laid out in subs. (6) or, alternatively, postpone the trial diet. The High Court can review the sheriff's decision.

The Act of Adjournal (Criminal Procedure Rules) Chap. 5 regulates the use of both shorthand and tape transcription; applications for rectification of transcripts are to be in the form specified in these Rules.

In *Robertson v. H.M. Advocate*, 1994 S.C.C.R. 152 the previous provisions under s.20B of the 1975 Act were considered. The appellant by Minute of Notice took objection to the competency of proceedings following failure by the Crown either to record his declaration or to serve it upon him prior to the trial diet: he alleged that this could prejudice his case and nullified any proceedings.

While it is of note that the charge which had formed the subject matter of the petition had not been libelled in the subsequent indictment, and the likelihood of prejudice would be slim, the Appeal Court considered the much more fundamental issue of whether or not the provisions of the section were obligatory (in which event the Crown's non-compliance must result in a nullity) or directory in character.

The court in a majority decision took the latter view but it has to be said that even then that conclusion was reached with little common agreement on either the approach or terminology to be adopted. The best that can be said is that while some statutory provisions are so fundamental that failure to comply creates a nullity, s.20B (or its statutory successor) s.37 of the 1995 Act are not such provisions.

Judicial examination: rectification of record of proceedings

38.—(1) Subject to subsections (7) to (9) of section 37 of this Act, where notwithstanding the certification mentioned in subsection (5) of that section the accused or the prosecutor is of the opinion that a transcript served under paragraph (a) of subsection (6) of that section contains an error or is incomplete he may—

  (a) within 10 days of service under the said paragraph (a), serve notice of such opinion on the prosecutor or as the case may be the accused; and

  (b) within 14 days of service under paragraph (a) of this subsection, apply to the sheriff for the error or incompleteness to be rectified,

and the sheriff shall within 7 days of the application hear the prosecutor and the accused in chambers and may authorise rectification.

  (2) Where—

  (a) the person on whom notice is served under paragraph (a) of subsection (1) above agrees with the opinion to which that notice relates the sheriff may dispense with such hearing;

  (b) the accused neither attends, nor secures that he is represented at, such hearing it shall, subject to paragraph (a) above, nevertheless proceed.

  (3) In so far as it is reasonably practicable so to arrange, the sheriff who deals with any application made under subsection (1) above shall be the sheriff before whom the examination or further examination to which the application relates was conducted.

  (4) Any decision of the sheriff, as regards rectification under subsection (1) above, shall be final.

GENERAL NOTE
    The procedure for the rectification of errors in, or addition of materials omitted from, the transcript of judicial examination or any declaration are found in this section. If the parties concur that such rectification or amendment is required, then no hearing is necessary; otherwise the prosecutor is obliged to be represented at any hearing though an accused or his agent need not attend. Reference should be made to the 1996 Act of Adjournal for styles of forms and notices.

Judicial examination: charges arising in different districts

    39.—(1) An accused against whom there are charges in more than one sheriff court district may be brought before the sheriff of any one such district at the instance of the procurator fiscal of such district for examination on all or any of the charges.
    (2) Where an accused is brought for examination as mentioned in subsection (1) above, he may be dealt with in every respect as if all of the charges had arisen in the district where he is examined.
    (3) This section is without prejudice to the power of the Lord Advocate under section 10 of this Act to determine the court before which the accused shall be tried on such charges.

DEFINITIONS
    "procurator fiscal": s.307(1).
    "sheriff court district": s.307(1).

GENERAL NOTE
    The Lord Advocate's discretion to select which sheriff court shall exercise jurisdiction over offences arising from more than one jurisdiction is preserved by this section.

Committal

Committal until liberated in due course of law

    40.—(1) Every petition shall be signed and no accused shall be committed until liberated in due course of law for any crime or offence without a warrant in writing expressing the particular charge in respect of which he is committed.
    (2) Any such warrant for imprisonment which either proceeds on an unsigned petition or does not express the particular charge shall be null and void.
    (3) The accused shall immediately be given a true copy of the warrant for imprisonment signed by the constable or person executing the warrant before imprisonment or by the prison officer receiving the warrant.

GENERAL NOTE
    The petition should correspond with the forms prescribed in Scheds. 2 and 3 of the Act or as near as may be; see s.34 above and the general note thereto.

PART V

CHILDREN AND YOUNG PERSONS

Age of criminal responsibility

    41. It shall be conclusively presumed that no child under the age of eight years can be guilty of any offence.

DEFINITIONS
    "child": s.307(1) and s.93(2)(b) of the Children (Scotland) Act 1995.

GENERAL NOTE
    This provision repeats the presumption of nonage found in the Children and Young Persons (Scotland) Act 1937 (c.37), s.55. See also Macdonald (5th ed., Edinburgh 1948), p. 271.
    Consequently proceedings against a child aged less than eight years are incompetent and should be disposed of by means of a plea in bar of trial at a first diet in sheriff and jury proceedings or a preliminary diet in the High Court (refer to ss.71 to 73 below).

Prosecution of children

42.—(1) No child under the age of 16 years shall be prosecuted for any offence except on the instructions of the Lord Advocate, or at his instance; and no court other than the High Court and the sheriff court shall have jurisdiction over a child under the age of 16 years for an offence.
    (2) Where a child is charged with any offence, his parent or guardian may in any case, and shall, if he can be found and resides within a reasonable distance, be required to attend at the court before which the case is heard or determined during all the stages of the proceedings, unless the court is satisfied that it would be unreasonable to require his attendance.
    (3) Where the child is arrested, the constable by whom he is arrested or the police officer in charge of the police station to which he is brought shall cause the parent or guardian of the child, if he can be found, to be warned to attend at the court before which the child will appear.
    (4) For the purpose of enforcing the attendance of a parent or guardian and enabling him to take part in the proceedings and enabling orders to be made against him, rules may be made under section 305 of this Act, for applying, with the necessary adaptations and modifications, such of the provisions of this Act relating to summary proceedings as appear appropriate for the purpose.
    (5) The parent or guardian whose attendance is required under this section is—
    (a) the parent who has parental responsibilities or parental rights (within the meaning of sections 1(3) and 2(4) respectively of the Children (Scotland) Act 1995) in relation to the child; or
    (b) the guardian having actual possession and control of him.
    (6) The attendance of the parent of a child shall not be required under this section in any case where the child was before the institution of the proceedings removed from the care or charge of his parent by an order of a court.
    (7) Where a child is to be brought before a court, notification of the day and time when, and the nature of the charge on which, the child is to be so brought shall be sent by the chief constable of the area in which the offence is alleged to have been committed to the local authority for the area in which the court will sit.
    (8) Where a local authority receive notification under subsection (7) above they shall make such investigations and submit to the court a report which shall contain such information as to the home surroundings of the child as appear to them will assist the court in the disposal of his case, and the report shall contain information, which the appropriate education authority shall have a duty to supply, as to the school record, health and character of the child.
    (9) Any child detained in a police station, or being conveyed to or from any criminal court, or waiting before or after attendance in such court, shall be prevented from associating with an adult (not being a relative) who is

charged with any offence other than an offence with which the child is jointly charged.

(10) Any female child shall, while detained, being conveyed or waiting as mentioned in subsection (9) above, be kept under the care of a woman.

DEFINITIONS

"child": s.307(1) and s.93(2)(b) of the Children (Scotland) Act 1995.
"constable": s.307(1) and s.51(1) of the Police (Scotland) Act 1967.
"High Court": s.307(1).
"local authority": s.307(1).
"parent or guardian": s.42(5) below and in relation to "guardian" only, note also s.307(1).

GENERAL NOTE

While it is theoretically the case that reports of criminal offences committed by children will be submitted to the procurator fiscal in the first instance, administrative directions from the Lord Advocate instruct that such reports involving child offenders aged under 16 years will, ordinarily, be referred to the principal reporter for his consideration. Even where there are factors which merit the submission of a report to the procurator fiscal, the police are still required in terms of s.38(2) of the Social Work (Scotland) Act 1968 (c.49) to furnish a copy of the report to the appropriate reporter. Thereafter it is a matter for discussion between the procurator fiscal and the reporter whether the case should be retained for criminal prosecution or dealt with under the previously-mentioned Act.

When the case is retained by the procurator fiscal to initiate a prosecution, it is mandatory in terms of subs. (1) that any proceedings must occur in the sheriff court or a higher court. Rule 6.3 of the 1996 Act of Adjournal enacts that criminal proceedings can only be raised by the procurator fiscal who is, of course, required to comply with the Lord Advocate's directions. The spirit of s.15 of the 1995 Act (which enacts special provisions in regard to the detention of a child, and parental access to a child held in custody) is echoed in s.54: subss. (9) and (10) contain provisions to segregate children from adult offenders while remanded in custody or awaiting trial at court. Oddly, it is not deemed necessary to separate the child entirely from adult accused. Subsection (9) stops short of this and permits detention in custody, or in the court precincts, and transportation to or from court appearances, in the company of adult co-accused or relatives (whether the relatives are, or are not, accused persons).

In a similar spirit, s.142 of the Act stipulates that summary proceedings against a child must be held in private and in different rooms, or on different days, from the criminal courts in which adults appear. The sole exception to this rule is when the child appears on the same complaint or petition as an adult accused; in that event the case has to proceed in the usual "adult" court. The corollary of these provisions so far as an adult co-accused is concerned, is that when charged along with a child on a summary complaint he will necessarily appear in the sheriff, not the district, court.

The scope of s.142 (which replaces s.366(1) of the 1975 Act) extends to appearances from custody, cited diets and trials but it has been held to be directory rather than mandatory in character: failure by the court to obtemper its provisions would not nullify any subsequent conviction; see *Heywood v. B.*, 1993 S.C.C.R. 554. It is likely that the provisions of s.42 would equally be construed as being directory in nature. Similarly the 1996 Act of Adjournal, Rule 6.8 indicates that steps should be taken by the court to avoid children attending hearings from mixing with each other by appropriate scheduling of cases and providing suitable supervision of waiting facilities.

Subss. (3), (7) and (8)

Subsection (3) instructs the police to notify the parent or guardian of the child of the impending court appearance and, wherever practicable, to require parental attendance at the court on the appropriate date. Unreasonable failure to attend the court by a parent or guardian after receipt of such notice can attract criminal penalties and, accordingly, the police should warn of this fact when giving notice of the court date.

Where the child is already in the care of the local authority or has a guardian as a result of a court order, the police are under no duty to advise the parent (defined in subs. (5)(a)) of the proceedings. The date and time of the child's court appearance, and the nature of charges must also be communicated by the police to the local authority within whose boundaries the court is situated. In the event of a finding of guilt, that authority will be responsible for preparing background reports about the child's circumstances for the court.

The 1996 Act of Adjournal, Rule 6.5 contains extensive rules governing the procedures to be followed during a child's appearance before the court in relation to summary matters.

Arrangements where children arrested

43.—(1) Where a person who is apparently a child is apprehended, with or without warrant, and cannot be brought forthwith before a sheriff, a police officer of the rank of inspector or above or the officer in charge of the police station to which he is brought, shall inquire into the case, and, subject to subsection (3) below, shall liberate him on a written undertaking being entered into by him or his parent or guardian that he will attend at the hearing of the charge.

(2) An undertaking mentioned in subsection (1) above shall be signed by the child or, as the case may be, the parent or guardian and shall be certified by the officer mentioned in that subsection.

(3) A person shall not be liberated under subsection (1) where—

(a) the charge is one of homicide or other grave crime;

(b) it is necessary in his interest to remove him from association with any reputed criminal or prostitute; or

(c) the officer has reason to believe that his liberation would defeat the ends of justice.

(4) Where a person who is apparently a child having been apprehended is not liberated as mentioned in subsection (1) above, the police officer referred to in that subsection shall cause him to be kept in a place of safety other than a police station until he can be brought before a sheriff unless the officer certifies—

(a) that it is impracticable to do so;

(b) that he is of so unruly a character that he cannot safely be so detained; or

(c) that by reason of his state of health or of his mental or bodily condition it is inadvisable so to detain him,

and the certificate shall be produced to the court before which he is brought.

(5) Where a person who is apparently a child has not been liberated as mentioned in subsection (1) above but has been kept under subsection (4) above, and it is decided not to proceed with the charge against him, a constable shall so inform the Principal Reporter.

(6) Any person, who without reasonable excuse is in breach of an undertaking entered into by him under subsection (1) above after having been given due notice of the time and place of the diet, shall be guilty of an offence, and liable on summary conviction in addition to any other penalty which it is competent for the court to impose on him, to a fine not exceeding level 3 on the standard scale.

(7) In any proceedings relating to an offence under this section, a writing, purporting to be such an undertaking as is mentioned in subsection (1) above and bearing to be signed and certified, shall be sufficient evidence of the undertaking given by the accused.

DEFINITIONS

"child": s.307(1) and s.93(2)(b) of the Children (Scotland) Act 1995.

"parent or guardian": s.42(5) and in relation to "guardian" only also refer to s.307(1).

"place of safety": s.307(1) and s.93(1) of the Children (Scotland) Act 1995.

"Principal Reporter": s.93(1) of the Children (Scotland) Act 1995.

GENERAL NOTE

This section repeats the provisions previously contained in ss.295 and 296 of the 1975 Act but account has been taken of the introduction of the Children (Scotland) Act 1995. It is still to be generally assumed that a child who is arrested for a criminal offence will be brought before a court without delay, or be liberated on his undertaking, or that of his parent or guardian, to appear at court on a specified date. Subsection (2) stipulates that the undertaking must be given in writing, be signed by the child or his parent or guardian and be countersigned by a senior police officer. In the absence of a reasonable excuse, breach of that undertaking renders the signatory liable to prosecution in terms of subs. (7). The terms of the undertaking can be proved by production of a certified copy of the order at trial and it is submitted that the signatory is in a position of special capacity. The Act does not specify the form the undertaking should take, though subs. (8) clearly envisages that it will be a written undertaking.

In more serious cases as defined in subs. (3), the first effort should be to bring the child before a sheriff forthwith. If that is not practicable, then the senior police officer involved must first endeavour to obtain accommodation for the child in a place of safety, namely a local authority residential establishment, a community home, a hospital, surgery or "other suitable place" whose occupier is willing to take in the child.

Note that while the statutory definition of "a place of safety" in the Children (Scotland) Act, s.93(1) includes a police station, this does not hold good for the purposes of s.43(4) of the 1995 Act—police stations are expressly excluded as acceptable accommodation for this purpose. The reason for this apparent anomaly is found later in subs. (4) which stipulates the conditions which must prevail before a child can be held in police custody pending his appearance before the court: broadly, if it is not practical to convey the child to a suitable place of safety or such a place is not available, or the child's character is unruly and militates against his safe detention in an available place of safety, or there are medical grounds which raise concern for his well-being, then continued detention in a police station will be justified. The senior police officer must then certify the reasons for resorting to detention of the child in police custody rather than the preferred option of a place of safety and that certificate must be produced to the court when the child first appears. It will be noted that during such a period of detention, the police are still obliged to keep the child segregated from adult prisoners (see the notes to s.42(9) above).

If the procurator fiscal decides not to proceed with charges against the child, subss. (6) and (7) contain saving provisions to enable the child to be detained pending initial investigation by the principal reporter (see s.56(1) and (6) of the Children (Scotland) Act 1995) and consideration if necessary by a children's hearing within seven days.

Detention of children

44.—(1) Where a child appears before the sheriff in summary proceedings and pleads guilty to, or is found guilty of, an offence to which this section applies, the sheriff may order that he be detained in residential accommodation provided under Part II of the Children (Scotland) Act 1995 by the appropriate local authority for such period not exceeding one year as may be specified in the order in such place (in any part of the United Kingdom) as the local authority may, from time to time, consider appropriate.

(2) This section applies to any offence in respect of which it is competent to impose imprisonment on a person of the age of 21 years or more.

(3) Where a child in respect of whom an order is made under this section is detained by the appropriate local authority, that authority shall have the same powers and duties in respect of the child as they would have if he were subject to a supervision requirement.

(4) Where a child in respect of whom an order is made under this section is also subject to a supervision requirement, subject to subsection (6) below, the supervision requirement shall be of no effect during any period for which he is required to be detained under the order.

(5) The Secretary of State may, by regulations made by statutory instrument subject to annulment in pursuance of a resolution of either House of Parliament, make such provision as he considers necessary as regards the detention in secure accommodation of children in respect of whom orders have been made under this section.

(6) Where a child is detained in residential accommodation in pursuance of an order under—

(a) subsection (1) above, he shall be released from such detention not later than the date by which half the period specified in the order has (following commencement of the detention) elapsed but, without prejudice to subsection (7) below, until the entire such period has so elapsed may be required by the local authority to submit to supervision in accordance with such conditions as they consider appropriate;

(b) subsection (1) above or (8) below, the local authority may at any time review his case and may, in consequence of such review and after having regard to the best interests of the child and the need to protect members of the public, release the child—

(i) for such period and on such conditions as the local authority consider appropriate; or

(ii) unconditionally.

(7) Where a child released under paragraph (a) or (b)(ii) of subsection (6) above is subject to a supervision requirement, the effect of that requirement shall commence or, as the case may be, resume upon such release.

(8) If, while released under paragraph (a) or (b) of subsection (6) above (and before the date on which the entire period mentioned in the said paragraph (a) has, following the commencement of the detention, elapsed), a child commits an offence to which this section applies and (whether before or after that date) pleads guilty to or is found guilty of it a court may, instead of or in addition to making any other order in respect of that plea or finding, order that he be returned to the residential accommodation provided by the authority which released him and that his detention in that accommodation or any other such accommodation provided by that authority shall continue for the whole or any part of the period which—

(a) begins with the date of the order for his return; and

(b) is equal in length to the period between the date on which the new offence was committed and the date on which that entire period elapses.

(9) An order under subsection (8) above for return to residential accommodation provided by the appropriate local authority—

(a) shall be taken to be an order for detention in residential accommodation for the purpose of this Act and any appeal; and

(b) shall, as the court making that order may direct, either be for a period of detention in residential accommodation before and to be followed by, or to be concurrent with, any period of such detention to be imposed in respect of the new offence (being in either case disregarded in determining the appropriate length of the period so imposed).

(10) Where a local authority consider it appropriate that a child in respect of whom an order has been made under subsection (1) or (8) above should be detained in a place in any part of the United Kingdom outside Scotland, the order shall be a like authority as in Scotland to the person in charge of the place to restrict the child's liberty to such an extent as that person may consider appropriate having regard to the terms of the order.

(11) In this section—

"the appropriate local authority" means—

(a) where the child usually resides in Scotland, the local authority for the area in which he usually resides;

(b) in any other case, the local authority for the area in which the offence was committed; and

"secure accommodation" has the meaning assigned to it in Part II of the Children (Scotland) Act 1995.

DEFINITIONS
"appropriate local authority": s.44(11).
"child": s.307(1) and s.93(2)(b) of the Children (Scotland) Act 1995.
"offence": s.307(1).
"residential accommodation": s.307(1).
"secure accommodation": s.44(11) and s.93(1) of the Children (Scotland) Act 1995.
"supervision requirement": s.307(1) and s.70(1) of the Children (Scotland) Act 1995.

GENERAL NOTE
This section enables a sheriff sitting summarily to impose a term of detention in residential accommodation of up to one year when an offence, for which imprisonment could competently be imposed upon an adult, is held or admitted to have been committed by a child. The sheriff may then consider immediate use of his powers under s.44 or, in the first instance (and more usually), refer the case under s.49 of the Act to the Principal Reporter for the advice of a children's hearing: when the child is already under a supervision requirement, s.49(3)(b) stipulates that the advice of a children's hearing must be obtained.

Only a minority of cases will be likely to merit a disposal in terms of s.44 without first obtaining the advice of a children's hearing. The use of s.44 powers is perhaps an indication that the paramount consideration in sentencing has been public safety and the preservation of good order rather than the well-being of the child. Most cases involving juveniles found guilty of offences will continue to require the advice of a children's hearing.

Statutory duties of local authority
When the sheriff either with, or less usually without, advice of a children's hearing imposes detention under s.44, it is then the duty of the Scottish local authority within whose area the child lives, to provide such accommodation at a place within the United Kingdom selected by the authority. However if the child is not ordinarily resident in Scotland then this responsibility falls upon the local authority within whose area the offence was committed. It is not explicitly stated in the Act, but it seems reasonable to assume that, in the event of offences being committed in a number of jurisdictions, responsibility for providing suitable accommodation would rest with the local authority within whose area the sheriff court making the order was situated.

Subsection (3) provides that the powers and responsibilities of a local authority given charge of such a child will be the same as those regulating supervision requirements and reference to s.70(4) of the Children (Scotland) Act shows that this includes such restrictions on the child's liberty as are deemed appropriate.

Where supervision requirements are imposed by a children's hearing, the hearing can direct that the child resides in residential accommodation or (in more extreme cases) in such accommodation but under secure conditions (see s.70(3) and (8) of the Children (Scotland) Act 1995). Subsection (1) of the 1995 Act states that the court can order that the child "be detained" in residential accommodation, while subs. (5) deals with the regulation of secure accommodation. It is unfortunate that the same phraseology has not been employed consistently in both pieces of legislation, but the provisions of subs. (6) suggest that what is envisaged is placement of the child in secure accommodation and not simply local authority residential care. A measure of support for this reading can be found in subs. (8), albeit that the subsection is concerned with the treatment of those who re-offend.

Subsection (10) permits the Scottish local authority exercising jurisdiction to remit the child into the custody of persons elsewhere in the United Kingdom when this is felt appropriate. The persons then assuming responsibility for the charge of the child have the same duties and powers as would be vested in an individual under s.44 in Scotland.

Early release provisions and effect of further offences
In a manner similar to s.16 of the Prisoners and Criminal Proceedings (Scotland) Act 1993 (c.9) (which deals with the commission of offences by released prisoners during remission), subs. (6) affords a child an opportunity of remission of at least half of the period of detention. This concession can be rescinded if it is established that a further offence has been committed during the remission period and the timescale of the original detention order has not expired (in practice it may be difficult to re-apply the unexpired portion of the detention period since the sentence imposed under s.44 by the sheriff may have been relatively short).

In the event of re-offending being established the court can apply a full range of disposals but subs. (8) makes it competent to return the child to the residential accommodation from which he was earlier released there to serve the unexpired portion of that earlier detention, calculated according to subs. (8). This re-imposition of the order can be instead of, or in addition to, any disposal resulting from the later offence which had been committed during the early release period. Subsection (9) adds that the remaining portion of the original detention order may be served prior to, or concurrent with, the period of detention imposed for the later offence.

Section 44 and existing supervision requirements
    Where the child appearing before the court is already the subject of a supervision requirement made by a children's hearing, subs. (4) provides for the suspension of that requirement until the appropriate period of detention has been served by the child.
    On release from detention (either at the expiry of the full term of detention imposed by the court, or earlier in accordance with subs. (6)(a)), the pre-existing supervision requirement can be resumed. However, even when detention has been imposed by the court, the local authority still has a statutory duty to review the case of any child subject to a supervision requirement (see s.72(6) of the Children (Scotland) Act 1995) and has a discretionary power under the 1995 Act to conduct such a review for children detained by way of a s.44 order—see subs. (6)(b). Indeed, theoretically, such a s.44 review could constitute the first contact between the hearing and the child offender since, as was noted earlier, the statutory obligation upon the sentencing sheriff to seek the advice of a children's hearing before imposing a period of detention upon the child only applies to children who were already subject to a current supervision requirement.
    When reviewing the case of a child detained under a s.44 order, the hearing may, following subs. (6) discharge it altogether or vary its terms once due regard has been paid to both the interests of the child and the protection of the public.

Security for child's good behaviour

45.—(1) Where a child has been charged with an offence the court may order his parent or guardian to give security for his co-operation in securing the child's good behaviour.   ·
    (2) Subject to subsection (3) below, an order under this section shall not be made unless the parent or guardian has been given the opportunity of being heard.
    (3) Where a parent or guardian has been required to attend and fails to do so, the court may make an order under this section.
    (4) Any sum ordered to be paid by a parent or guardian on the forfeiture of any security given under this section may be recovered from him by civil diligence or imprisonment in like manner as if the order had been made on the conviction of the parent or guardian of the offence with which the child was charged.
    (5) In this section "parent" means either of the child's parents, if that parent has parental responsibilities or parental rights (within the meaning of sections 1(3) and 2(4) respectively of the Children (Scotland) Act 1995) in relation to him.

DEFINITIONS
    "child": s.307(1) and s.93(2)(b) of the Children (Scotland) Act 1995.
    "offence": s.307(1).
    "parent": s.45(5) and ss.1(3), 2(4) and 3(5) of the Children (Scotland) Act 1995.
    "guardian": s.307(1).

GENERAL NOTE
    This section permits the court to require caution to be found by the parent or *de facto* guardian of the child as a surety for parental co-operation in assuring the future good conduct of the child. Such a condition can only be imposed after the parent or guardian has been given an opportunity to be heard by the court, but it has been ruled unnecessary for a formal citation to attend there to have been served upon him; notification made by a police officer would probably suffice. See *White v. Jeans* (1911) 6 Adam 489 and *Montgomery v. Grey* (1915) 7 Adam 681. Note that subs. (2) does not stipulate that the parent must have been heard, only that the opportunity to be heard has been given. The court under subs. (3) can order attendance by the parent or guardian and require a finding of security, even in the absence of the person concerned. Failure by the parent or guardian to ensure the orderly conduct of the child can result in forfeiture of the amount of security. This can be recovered by civil diligence or by the imprisonment of the guarantor.

Presumption and determination of age of child

46.—(1) Where a person charged with an offence is brought before a court other than for the purpose of giving evidence, and it appears to the court that he is a child, the court shall make due enquiry as to the age of that person, and for that purpose shall take such evidence as may be forthcoming at the hearing of the case, and the age presumed or declared by the court to be the age of that person shall, for the purposes of this Act or the Children and Young Persons (Scotland) Act 1937, be deemed to be the true age of that person.

(2) The court in making any inquiry in pursuance of subsection (1) above shall have regard to the definition of child for the purposes of this Act.

(3) Where in an indictment or complaint for—

(a) an offence under the Children and Young Persons (Scotland) Act 1937;

(b) any of the offences mentioned in paragraphs 3 and 4 of Schedule 1 to this Act; or

(c) an offence under section 1, 10(1) to (3) or 12 of the Criminal Law (Consolidation) (Scotland) Act 1995,

it is alleged that the person by or in respect of whom the offence was committed was a child or was under or had attained any specified age, and he appears to the court to have been at the date of the commission of the alleged offence a child, or to have been under or to have attained the specified age, as the case may be, he shall for the purposes of this Act or the Children and Young Persons (Scotland) Act 1937 or Part I of the Criminal Law (Consolidation) (Scotland) Act 1995 be presumed at that date to have been a child or to have been under or to have attained that age, as the case may be, unless the contrary is proved.

(4) Where, in an indictment or complaint for an offence under the Children and Young Persons (Scotland) Act 1937 or any of the offences mentioned in Schedule 1 to this Act, it is alleged that the person in respect of whom the offence was committed was a child or was a young person, it shall not be a defence to prove that the person alleged to have been a child was a young person or the person alleged to have been a young person was a child in any case where the acts constituting the alleged offence would equally have been an offence if committed in respect of a young person or child respectively.

(5) An order or judgement of the court shall not be invalidated by any subsequent proof that—

(a) the age of a person mentioned in subsection (1) above has not been correctly stated to the court; or

(b) the court was not informed that at the material time the person was subject to a supervision requirement or that his case had been referred to a children's hearing by virtue of regulations made under the Children (Scotland) Act 1995 for the purpose of giving effect to orders made in different parts of the United Kingdom.

(6) Where it appears to the court that a person mentioned in subsection (1) above has attained the age of 17 years, he shall for the purposes of this Act or the Children and Young Persons (Scotland) Act 1937 be deemed not to be a child.

(7) In subsection (3) above, references to a child (other than a child charged with an offence) shall be construed as references to a child under the age of 17 years; but except as aforesaid references in this section to a child shall be construed as references to a child within the meaning of section 307 of this Act.

<small>DEFINITIONS
"child": s.307(1) and s.93(2)(b) of the Children (Scotland) Act 1995. Note that a more restricted definition is employed in relation to subs. (3) only by virtue of subs. (7).
"offence": s.307(1).</small>

GENERAL NOTE

This section repeats the provisions found in the 1975 Act as amended and, in effect, contains saving provisions to prevent proceedings in which children are involved either as witnesses or as accused, being invalidated on account of error as to a child's age. The savings only operate to cure a want of procedure and cannot cure a nullity (note that in addition to the provisions of s.46 which relate specifically to children, the 1995 Act, s.307(7) contains a general saving presumption covering adult persons whose age becomes a material factor during criminal proceedings).

Subss. (1), (5) and (6)

The subsections relate to the age of child offenders appearing before the court and extend to children aged under 16 years, and to any youth up to 18 years of age who at the time of appearing before the court was already the subject of a supervision requirement.

The court should if possible question the child as a means of establishing his age and assess the age by reference to his appearance. Additionally if evidence is led, that too can be scrutinised for indications of the offender's age. The court can then legitimately hold the offender's age to be established and consider the options for disposal of the case if the offence is admitted or proved. Note that if it is concluded on the basis of all the available material that the offender is 17 years old and it is not disclosed that he is subject to local authority supervision, the court can lawfully treat him as a young offender. Subsection (5) enacts that findings or orders pronounced by the court in circumstances where the court has had to deduce the child's age will not be voided if it is subsequently discovered that the court was misled.

Subss. (3) and (7)

These subsections apply when a child is either accused of an offence or is the victim of an offence. The effect of subs. (7) is to distinguish between those who meet the statutory definition of a "child" as promulgated by the 1995 Act and those who fulfil the narrower statutory definition of a "child" found in the Children and Young Persons (Scotland) Act 1937. In relation to the offences specified in Sched. 1 to the 1995 Act: in the first case an offender can be aged 17 years or more and continue to be treated as a "child" within the meaning of the 1995 Act provided he is still the subject of a supervision order. However, as a victim the complainer is to be regarded as a child only until his seventeenth birthday is attained. A rebuttable presumption exists that the complainer in the statutory offences specified in subs. (3) was a child at the time of the incident libelled. Similarly where it is averred in a libel that the accused was a "child" in terms of the 1995 Act's statutory definition at the time of committing an offence, and this allegation appears to be confirmed by his bearing and physical appearance, it will be presumed that the offender's age has been established.

Subs. (4)

This subsection prevents the introduction of purely technical defences in cases involving victims who are either children or young persons.

When charged with contravening either of the statutory provisions specified in relation to a child or a young person, an accused cannot base a defence upon a discrepancy between the age of the victim, as stated in the libel, and the actuality when, in either case, an offence would have been committed.

Restriction on report of proceedings involving children

47.—(1) Subject to subsection (3) below, no newspaper report of any proceedings in a court shall reveal the name, address or school, or include any particulars calculated to lead to the identification, of any person under the age of 16 years concerned in the proceedings, either—

(a) as being a person against or in respect of whom the proceedings are taken; or

(b) as being a witness in the proceedings.

(2) Subject to subsection (3) below, no picture which is, or includes, a picture of a person under the age of 16 years concerned in proceedings as mentioned in subsection (1) above shall be published in any newspaper in a context relevant to the proceedings.

(3) The requirements of subsections (1) and (2) above shall be applied in any case mentioned in any of the following paragraphs to the extent specified in that paragraph—

(a) where a person under the age of 16 years is concerned in the proceedings as a witness only and no one against whom the proceedings are taken is under the age of 16 years, the requirements shall not apply unless the court so directs;

(b) where, at any stage of the proceedings, the court, if it is satisfied that it is in the public interest so to do, directs that the requirements (including the requirements as applied by a direction under paragraph (a) above) shall be dispensed with to such extent as the court may specify; and

(c) where the Secretary of State, after completion of the proceedings, if satisfied as mentioned in paragraph (b) above, by order dispenses with the requirements to such extent as may be specified in the order.

(4) This section shall, with the necessary modifications, apply in relation to sound and television programmes included in a programme service (within the meaning of the Broadcasting Act 1990) as it applies in relation to newspapers.

(5) A person who publishes matter in contravention of this section shall be guilty of an offence and liable on summary conviction to a fine not exceeding level 4 of the standard scale.

(6) In this section, references to a court shall not include a court in England, Wales or Northern Ireland.

DEFINITIONS
"witness": s.307(1).

GENERAL NOTE
There is a general prohibition upon identifying anyone involved in criminal proceedings as a victim, a witness or an accused when that person is aged less than 16 years of age. The prohibition is intended to prevent the publication or broadcasting of the person's particulars, home address or educational background as well as any details of the circumstances of the case which would be sufficient to establish this information. It extends to photographs of the child, but not of other persons however closely related to the child. Such prohibitions remain in force until the child reaches 16 years of age. See *Caledonian Newspapers, Petrs.*, 1995 S.C.C.R. 576 and the general discussion there of the scope of s.169 of the 1975 Act, whose terms are echoed by s.47 of the 1995 Act.

Subsection (3) permits a relaxation of this prohibition where; (i) the accused is older than 16 years and the child appears as a witness only, not as a victim, though even here it must be noted that the court can direct that the provisions of subs. (1) are to apply; (ii) the court decides during the proceedings that it is in the public interest to identify the person concerned and stipulates the extent of material which may be published or broadcast; (iii) the Secretary of State decides after proceedings are concluded that it is in the public interest for such information, as specified, to be disseminated.

Note that the Act of Adjournal (Criminal Procedure Rules) Rule 6.9 requires the court to specify the persons whose identities are to be protected or, alternatively may be revealed, along with suitable directions in that regard.

Extent
These provisions do not extend to reports of proceedings arising outwith Scotland. The section does apply to any report of such Scottish proceedings published or broadcast in Scotland or elsewhere in Great Britain. The penalties for contravening s.47 are found in subs. (5).

Power to refer certain children to reporter

48.—(1) A court by or before which a person is convicted of having committed an offence to which this section applies may refer—

(a) a child in respect of whom an offence mentioned in paragraph (a) or (b) of subsection (2) below has been committed; or

(b) any child who is, or who is likely to become, a member of the same household as the person who has committed an offence mentioned in

paragraph (b) or (c) of that subsection or the person in respect of whom the offence so mentioned was committed,
to the Principal Reporter, and certify that the offence shall be a ground established for the purposes of Chapter 3 of Part II of the Children (Scotland) Act 1995.

(2) This section applies to an offence—

(a) under section 21 of the Children and Young Persons (Scotland) Act 1937;

(b) mentioned in Schedule 1 to this Act; or

(c) in respect of a person aged 17 years or over which constitutes the crime of incest.

DEFINITIONS
"offence": s.307(1).
"Principal Reporter": s.93(1) of the Children (Scotland) Act 1995.

GENERAL NOTE
Section 48 entitles the court before which a person is convicted of an offence specified in subs. (2) to take immediate account of the harm done to the child victim, or the risk, or potential risk, of harm to any child who stays or may stay in the same household as the offender. This power also extends to the households of persons convicted of incest.

With a view to preserving the moral and physical well-being of such children, the court is empowered to certify the grounds for a supervision order to be established, without there being any need for a children's hearing to be constituted to consider the matter. The task of the hearing is confined to consideration in terms of ss.69 and 70 of the Children (Scotland) Act 1995, of the measures necessary to safeguard the welfare of the child or children.

Reference or remit to children's hearing

49.—(1) Where a child who is not subject to a supervision requirement pleads guilty to, or is found guilty of, an offence the court—

(a) instead of making an order on that plea or finding, may remit the case to the Principal Reporter to arrange for the disposal of the case by a children's hearing; or

(b) on that plea or finding may request the Principal Reporter to arrange a children's hearing for the purposes of obtaining their advice as to the treatment of the child.

(2) Where a court has acted in pursuance of paragraph (b) of subsection (1) above, the court, after consideration of the advice received from the children's hearing may, as it thinks proper, itself dispose of the case or remit the case as mentioned in paragraph (a) of that subsection.

(3) Where a child who is subject to a supervision requirement pleads guilty to, or is found guilty of, an offence the court dealing with the case if it is—

(a) the High Court, may; and

(b) the sheriff court, shall,

request the Principal Reporter to arrange a children's hearing for the purpose of obtaining their advice as to the treatment of the child, and on consideration of that advice may, as it thinks proper, itself dispose of the case or remit the case as mentioned in subsection (1)(a) above.

(4) Where a court has remitted a case to the Principal Reporter under this section, the jurisdiction of the court in respect of the child shall cease, and his case shall stand referred to a children's hearing.

(5) Nothing in this section shall apply to a case in respect of an offence the sentence for which is fixed by law.

(6) Where a person who is—

(a) not subject to a supervision requirement;

(b) over the age of 16; and

(c) not within six months of attaining the age of 18,

is charged summarily with an offence and pleads guilty to, or has been found guilty of, the offence the court may request the Principal Reporter to arrange a children's hearing for the purpose of obtaining their advice as to the treatment of the person.

(7) On consideration of any advice obtained under subsection (6) above, the court may, as it thinks proper—

(a) itself dispose of the case; or
(b) where the hearing have so advised, remit the case to the Principal Reporter for the disposal of the case by a children's hearing.

<small>DEFINITIONS</small>
"child": s.307(1) and s.93(2)(b) of the Children (Scotland) Act 1995.
"children's hearing": s.93(1) of the Children (Scotland) Act 1995.
"High Court": s.307(1).
"offence": s.307(1).
"Principal Reporter": s.93(1) of the Children (Scotland) Act 1995.
"supervision requirement": s.307(1) and ss.70(1) and 93(1) of the Children (Scotland) Act 1995.

<small>GENERAL NOTE</small>
When a child not currently the subject of a supervision requirement admits, or is held to have committed an offence, the court effectively has three options; proceeding to an immediate disposal of the case, or remitting the case to a children's hearing either for their advice or for their consideration and disposal. Subsections (6) and (7) extend these provisions to youths aged up to 17½ years who are convicted on summary complaint. Once the case is remitted to a hearing for disposal, the court's involvement ceases.

In cases where the child is the subject of a supervision requirement, and thus can be aged up to 17½ years old, admits or is found guilty of an offence in the sheriff court, the court must obtain the advice of a children's hearing. On receipt of the hearing's advice the court can dispose of the case or remit the child to the hearing for their decision and disposal. Note that as subs. (3)(b) reads, this procedure would apply equally to summary or solemn cases but that the provisions of s.44 of the Act (which empower a sheriff sitting summarily to order detention of up to one year's duration in residential accommodation) derogate from this general requirement.

Section 208 of the Act empowers solemn courts to impose periods of detention following conviction on indictment.

When the child is convicted before the High Court it is in the discretion of the court to obtain the advice of a children's hearing except where the conviction is for murder since, in that event, the sentence provided by s.205 is a mandatory one of life imprisonment.

Children and certain proceedings

50.—(1) No child under 14 years of age (other than an infant in arms) shall be permitted to be present in court during any proceedings against any other person charged with an offence unless his presence is required as a witness or otherwise for the purposes of justice.

(2) Any child present in court when, under subsection (1) above, he is not to be permitted to be so shall be ordered to be removed.

(3) Where, in any proceedings in relation to an offence against, or any conduct contrary to, decency or morality, a person who, in the opinion of the court, is a child is called as a witness, the court may direct that all or any persons, not being—

(a) members or officers of the court;
(b) parties to the case before the court, their counsel or solicitors or persons otherwise directly concerned in the case;
(c) *bona fide* representatives of news gathering or reporting organisations present for the purpose of the preparation of contemporaneous reports of the proceedings; or
(d) such other persons as the court may specially authorise to be present,

shall be excluded from the court during the taking of the evidence of that witness.

(4) The powers conferred on a court by subsection (3) above shall be in addition and without prejudice to any other powers of the court to hear proceedings *in camera*.

(5) Where in any proceedings relating to any of the offences mentioned in Schedule 1 to this Act, the court is satisfied that the attendance before the court of any person under the age of 17 years in respect of whom the offence is alleged to have been committed is not essential to the just hearing of the case, the case may be proceeded with and determined in the absence of that person.

(6) Every court in dealing with a child who is brought before it as an offender shall have regard to the welfare of the child and shall in a proper case take steps for removing him from undesirable surroundings.

DEFINITIONS
"child": as defined in subs. (1).
"witness": s.307(1).

GENERAL NOTE
The provisions of this section are of a directory character and non-compliance would not render the proceedings null.

It will be noted that ss.271 and 272 of the 1995 Act allow for applications to be made for a child's evidence to be taken by a commissioner, relayed to the court by means of a remote closed-circuit television link, or to be taken in court while the child is screened from sight of the accused.

Remand and committal of children and young persons

51.—(1) Where a court remands or commits for trial or for sentence a person under 21 years of age who is charged with or convicted of an offence and is not released on bail or ordained to appear, then, except as otherwise expressly provided by this section, the following provisions shall have effect—
(a) subject to paragraph (b) below, if he is under 16 years of age the court shall, instead of committing him to prison, commit him to the local authority in whose area the court is situated to be detained—
(i) where the court so requires, in secure accommodation within the meaning of Part II of the Children (Scotland) Act 1995; and
(ii) in any other case, in a suitable place of safety chosen by the authority;
(b) if he is a person of over 16 years of age, or a child under 16 years of age but over 14 years of age who is certified by the court to be unruly or depraved, and the court has been notified by the Secretary of State that a remand centre is available for the reception from that court of persons of his class or description, he shall be committed to a remand centre instead of being committed to prison.
(2) Where any person is committed to a local authority or to a remand centre under any provision of this Act, that authority or centre shall be specified in the warrant, and he shall be detained by the authority or in the centre for the period for which he is committed or until he is liberated in due course of law.
(3) Where any person has been committed to a local authority under any provision of this Act, the court by which he was committed, if the person so committed is not less than 14 years of age and it appears to the court that he is unruly or depraved, may revoke the committal and commit the said person—
(a) if the court has been notified that a remand centre is available for the reception from that court of persons of his class or description, to a remand centre; and
(b) if the court has not been so notified, to a prison.
(4) Where in the case of a person under 16 years of age who has been committed to prison or to a remand centre under this section, the sheriff is satisfied that his detention in prison or a remand centre is no longer necess-

ary, he may revoke the committal and commit the person to the local authority in whose area the court is situated to be detained—
   (a) where the court so requires, in secure accommodation within the meaning of Part II of the Children (Scotland) Act 1995; and
   (b) in any other case, in a suitable place of safety chosen by the authority.

DEFINITIONS
   "commits for trial": s.307(1).
   "local authority": s.307(1).
   "place of safety": s.307(1) of the 1995 Act and, in relation to children see s.93(1) of the Children (Scotland) Act 1995.
   "prison": s.307(1).
   "remand": s.307(1).
   "remand centre": s.307(1).
   "secure accommodation": s.93(1) of the Children (Scotland) Act 1995.

GENERAL NOTE
   Section 51 applies equally to summary or solemn proceedings and specifies the forms of remand facilities which are to be utilised when persons under 21 years of age are held in custody awaiting trial or remanded for sentence by the court. The aim, so far as practicable, is not to resort to use of remand facilities either before or after any trial unless the circumstances of the case, or the offender, make this unavoidable.
   In discussing s.43 of the Act it was noted that when it was felt that ordaining or liberating a child to appear at the first diet of the case was considered inappropriate, the options available to the police thereafter would be to remand a child to a place of safety, unless his conduct or circumstances militated against that form of detention. The more stringent restrictions upon the child's liberty, produced by detaining him in police cells pending his appearance before the court from custody could only be justified by the production to the court, on first appearance, of an unruly certificate. A similar philosophy is applied by the courts when it is felt that a child or young person must be remanded in custody for trial or sentence; the broad objective is then to remand the offender to an establishment most suited to the offender's circumstances and so far as possible, to minimise the rigour of the remand regime.

Children Under 16 Years
   Prior to the child's appearance from custody before the sheriff, the procurator fiscal and the principal reporter (or their deputes) should already have considered whether such an appearance is necessary or whether the child can instead be referred to the reporter in custody or liberated for the reporter to arrange a later children's hearing. Such a consultation process also applies when the offender is aged between 16 and 17 years and six months old and is the subject of a supervision requirement, but failure on the part of the procurator fiscal to consult with the reporter in these circumstances would not vitiate proceedings: see s.46(5) above.
   Section 51 only takes effect when the procurator fiscal, having weighed the interests of the child and the broad public interest, elects to retain the case. If the child has been detained in police cells, the procurator fiscal will receive the unruly certificate from the police and has to produce it to the sheriff when the child appears from custody (following s.142 of the 1995 Act it will be observed that in summary proceedings such an appearance should not occur in an adult court (unless there is an adult co-accused) and must be held in private).
   Should the procurator fiscal decide that bail will be opposed because of the nature of the offence or the unruliness of the child, he should have established with the local authority before the case is called, whether suitable remand facilities are available. This information should be put before the court in conjunction with a motion to remand the child in custody. In the absence of suitable accommodation, the court, if it refuses bail, will have no option but to consider whether the child is unruly, and if so, certify the child unruly and remand him to a remand institution or an adult prison albeit subs. (4) does permit later variation of the order. It is submitted that while the nature of the offence may well point to the child being unruly or depraved that is not the test; it is the nature of the child himself which should be assessed by the court.
   It ought to be clearly established whether the child is or is not in custody pending trial, since the warrant issued by the court will specify either the centre to which the child is remanded or identify the local authority into whose charge he is placed and (following subs. (1)(a)) the nature of the accommodation to be provided—a place of safety, residential or secure accommodation. The important factor is whether the child is granted bail, and is at liberty, or remanded in custody, since this has an obvious bearing upon the timescale and competency of later proceedings;

see ss.65 and 147 of the 1995 Act which re-enact the familiar provisions of ss.101 and 331A of the 1975 Act regarding prevention of delay in proceedings, *i.e* the 110 day and 40 day rules respectively. The warrant issued by the court will not conclusively determine whether a child is in custody or not, that is ultimately an issue of fact in each case, but the warrant will assuredly be a highly persuasive determining factor.

These comments apply with even greater force when the child appearing before the court is already the subject of a residential supervision order: it is then vital that it is determined whether the child is bailed, and returns to the care of the local authority to continue the current supervision order, or is remanded to secure accommodation provided by the local authority as a preferred alternative to a remand or prison place. It is also essential that the local authority seek a review of the case in terms of subs. (4), should the circumstances of the offender change.

The complications which can arise are amply illustrated in *K. v. H.M. Advocate*, 1991 S.C.C.R. 343, where the child was "bailed" to reside at a List D school which in fact contained both secure and residential accommodation. K was bailed to reside in the school's secure unit, instead of being either remanded into the care of the local authority or certified unruly and remanded. The court's well-meant intention was to substitute an earlier warrant which had remanded K to an adult prison with a more suitable regime but, on any view, K was not at liberty and the provisions (then) of s.110 applied, since the bail order had had no practical effect (the solution would have been for the local authority, if it was in agreement, to seek review of the warrant as subs. (4) provides in the 1995 Act).

See also *W.C. v. H.M. Advocate* (High Court of Justiciary, March 2, 1995, unreported); following a petition appearance upon a rape charge and refusal of bail, C was held in custody in a remand institution. A review hearing later allowed bail subject to residence in a List D school; although the bail order did not stipulate it, C was kept in secure accommodation by staff solely in execution of the order, and only the issue of instructions by the procurator fiscal for the child's liberation (which were acted upon on the 109th day) stopped the 110 days running. A petition to the *nobile officium* was refused since *de facto* liberty had been obtained before the expiry of the 110 days.

Note that once a child has been certified unruly by the sheriff it is doubtful whether it can be revoked by anyone, even the certifying sheriff, or formally appealed. In *W.C. v. H.M. Advocate* (High Court of Justiciary, March 3, 1995, unreported), the child was certified unruly and remanded in a remand institution after absconding from the local authority home to which he had earlier been bailed. A petition to the *nobile officium* for revocation of the certification was lodged, but the High Court doubted that such an order would be competent; in the absence of Crown opposition the court used its inherent equitable powers to grant a bail order specifying residence in a secure unit. The principles which prompted this decision appear in conflict with the *ratio* in *K. v. H.M. Advocate* above.

A similar situation arose in *Y., Petr.*, 1995 S.C.C.R. 457, with the court ruling that a petition to the *nobile officium* was not a competent means for review of an unruly certificate.

Nevertheless the court substituted a bail order requiring Y to reside in the secure unit of a List D school.

PART VI

MENTAL DISORDER

Committal of mentally disordered persons

Power of court to commit to hospital an accused suffering from mental disorder

52.—(1) Where it appears to the prosecutor in any court before which a person is charged with an offence that the person may be suffering from mental disorder, it shall be the duty of the prosecutor to bring before the court such evidence as may be available of the mental condition of that person.

(2) Where a court remands or commits for trial a person charged with any offence who appears to the court to be suffering from mental disorder, and the court is satisfied that a hospital is available for his admission and suitable for his detention, the court may, instead of remanding him in custody, commit him to that hospital.

(3) Where an accused is committed to a hospital as mentioned in subsection (2) above, the hospital shall be specified in the warrant, and if the responsible medical officer is satisfied that he is suffering from mental disorder of a nature or degree which warrants his admission to a hospital under Part V of the Mental Health (Scotland) Act 1984, he shall be detained in the hospital specified in the warrant for the period for which he is remanded or the period of committal, unless before the expiration of that period he is liberated in due course of law.

(4) When the responsible medical officer has examined the person so detained he shall report the result of that examination to the court and, where the report is to the effect that the person is not suffering from mental disorder of such a nature or degree as aforesaid, the court may commit him to any prison or other institution to which he might have been committed had he not been committed to hospital or may otherwise deal with him according to law.

(5) No person shall be committed to a hospital under this section except on the written or oral evidence of a registered medical practitioner.

(6) Without prejudice to subsection (4) above, the court may review an order under subsection (2) above on the ground that there has been a change of circumstances since the order was made and, on such review—

(a) where the court considers that such an order is no longer required in relation to a person, it shall revoke the order and may deal with him in such way mentioned in subsection (4) above as the court thinks appropriate;

(b) in any other case, the court may—
    (i) confirm or vary the order; or
    (ii) revoke the order and deal with him in such way mentioned in subsection (4) above as the court considers appropriate.

(7) Subsections (2) to (5) above shall apply to the review of an order under subsection (6) above as they apply to the making of an order under subsection (2) above.

DEFINITIONS
"commits for trial": s.307(1).
"hospital": s.307(1).
"offence": s.307(1).
"order": s.307(1).
"prison": s.307(1).
"prosecutor": s.307(1).
"registered medical practitioner": s.2 of the Medicine Act 1968.
"responsible medical officer": s.307(1).

GENERAL NOTE
This section amends and consolidates the existing provisions of the court to commit to a specified hospital at the pre-trial stage an accused who appears to be suffering from a mental disorder. The section makes express provision for review of that committal.

Subs. (1)
The breadth of the definition of the word "prosecutor" should be noted for in solemn proceedings it includes Crown counsel. The flexibility implied by this is such that relevant evidence may be brought at what would otherwise be the trial diet in the High Court of Justiciary. The procedure is not contingent on a conviction because of the phrase "is charged with": see *Herron v. McCrimmon*, 1969 S.L.T.(Sh.Ct.) 37 for circumstances in which a summary complaint was deserted *pro loco et tempore* to place the accused on petition and yet the phrase was still satisfied.

Whether a person may be suffering from "mental disorder" is a medical question for those qualified to answer the question but that is frequently the most difficult point: in *Allan v. H.M. Advocate*, 1983 S.C.C.R. 183 four psychiatrists divided on precisely that aspect and, if the accused was so suffering, what the best method of disposal would be.

A similar division is apparent in *Jessop v. Robertson*, 1989 S.C.C.R. 600 (Sh.Ct.) where it was held by a sheriff that: (1) a written report that had been produced by the prosecutor but was not spoken to by a witness at the proof was not admissible; (2) there was an onus on any person alleging unfitness by reason of insanity to satisfy the court of that allegation by corroborated evidence on a balance of probabilities; and (3) in the circumstances of medical division the unfitness had not been proved; and the accused was called upon to plead.

Subs. (5)

The evidence required for committal should be the "written or oral" evidence of a registered medical practitioner. Given that a proof is held then on *Jessop v. Robertson*, above, the meaning of that phrase would seem to be "oral evidence supplemented, if necessary, by written evidence".

Subs. (6)

Subsection (2) permits the receiving hospital to have the accused examined and if the responsible medical officer is satisfied that the accused is suffering from a disorder of the requisite degree then the accused is detained. If the responsible medical officer is not so satisfied then under subs. (3) the accused can be committed by the court to any prison or other institution.

Subsection (6) introduces a degree of flexibility into the system. Under the previous law there was no express provision to permit any variation of the committal to hospital or for its revocation except in the circumstances identified in subs. (3), that is, immediately following initial examination. The new flexibility provides for fluctuating degrees of mental disorder and for a change of hospital to meet the requirements of the accused. Review, variation and revocation may be by the court at any time.

Interim hospital orders

Interim hospital orders

53.—(1) Where, in the case of a person to whom this section applies the court is satisfied on the written or oral evidence of two medical practitioners (complying with subsection (2) below and section 61 of this Act)—
  (a) that the offender is suffering from mental disorder within the meaning of section 1(2) of the Mental Health (Scotland) Act 1984; and
  (b) that there is reason to suppose—
        (i) that the mental disorder from which the offender is suffering is such that it may be appropriate for a hospital order to be made in his case; and
        (ii) that, having regard to section 58(5) of this Act, the hospital to be specified in any such hospital order may be a State hospital,
the court may, before making a hospital order or dealing with the offender in some other way, make an order (to be known as "an interim hospital order") authorising his admission to and detention in a state hospital or such other hospital as for special reasons the court may specify in the order.

(2) Of the medical practitioners whose evidence is taken into account under subsection (1) above at least one shall be employed at the hospital which is to be specified in the order.

(3) An interim hospital order shall not be made in respect of an offender unless the court is satisfied that the hospital which is to be specified in the order, in the event of such an order being made by the court, is available for his admission thereto within 28 days of the making of such an order.

(4) Where a court makes an interim hospital order it shall not make any other order for detention or impose a fine or pass sentence of imprisonment or make a probation order or a community service order in respect of the offence, but may make any other order which it has power to make apart from this section.

(5) The court by which an interim hospital order is made may include in the order such direction as it thinks fit for the conveyance of the offender to a place of safety and his detention therein pending his admission to the hospital within the period of 28 days referred to in subsection (3) above.

(6) An interim hospital order—
  (a) shall be in force for such period, not exceeding 12 weeks, as the court may specify when making the order; but

(b) may be renewed for further periods of not more than 28 days at a time if it appears to the court on the written or oral evidence of the responsible medical officer that the continuation of the order is warranted,

but no such order shall continue in force for more than six months in all and the court shall terminate the order if it makes a hospital order in respect of the offender or decides, after considering the written or oral evidence of the responsible medical officer, to deal with the offender in some other way.

(7) An interim hospital order may be renewed under subsection (6) above without the offender being brought before the court if he is represented by counsel or a solicitor and his counsel or solicitor is given an opportunity of being heard.

(8) If an offender absconds from a hospital in which he is detained in pursuance of an interim hospital order, or while being conveyed to or from such a hospital, he may be arrested without warrant by a constable and shall, after being arrested, be brought as soon as practicable before the court which made the order; and the court may thereupon terminate the order and deal with him in any way in which it could have dealt with him if no such order had been made.

(9) When an interim hospital order ceases to have effect in relation to an offender the court may deal with him in any way (other than by making a new interim hospital order) in which it could have dealt with him if no such order had been made.

(10) The power conferred on the court by this section is without prejudice to the power of the court under section 200(1) of this Act to remand a person in order that an inquiry may be made into his physical or mental condition.

(11) This section applies to any person—

(a) convicted in the High Court or the sheriff court of an offence punishable with imprisonment (other than an offence the sentence for which is fixed by law);

(b) charged on complaint in the sheriff court if the sheriff is satisfied that he did the act or made the omission charged but does not convict him; or

(c) remitted to the sheriff court from the district court under section 58(10) of this Act if the sheriff is satisfied as mentioned in paragraph (b) above.

(12) In this section "the court" means—

(a) the High Court, as regards a person—
(i) convicted on indictment in that court; or
(ii) convicted on indictment in the sheriff court and remitted for sentence to the High Court; and

(b) the sheriff court, as regards a person—
(i) convicted in the sheriff court and not remitted as mentioned in paragraph (a)(ii) above; or
(ii) referred to in paragraph (b) or (c) of subsection (11) above.

DEFINITIONS
"constable": s.307(1).
"court": s.53(12).
"fine": s.307(1).
"interim hospital order": s.53(1).
"medical practitioner": s.61(1).
"mental disorder": s.1(2) of the Mental Health (Scotland) Act 1984.
"probation order": s.307(1).
"responsible medical officer": s.307(1).
"sentence": s.307(1).
"State hospital": s.307(1).

GENERAL NOTE
The interim nature of the hospital orders made under this section is emphasised by the time-limits specified in s.53(6).

Insanity in bar of trial

Insanity in bar of trial

54.—(1) Where the court is satisfied, on the written or oral evidence of two medical practitioners, that a person charged with the commission of an offence is insane so that his trial cannot proceed or, if it has commenced, cannot continue, the court shall, subject to subsection (2) below—
  (a) make a finding to that effect and state the reasons for that finding;
  (b) discharge the trial diet and order that a diet (in this Act referred to as an "an examination of facts") be held under section 55 of this Act; and
  (c) remand the person in custody or on bail or, where the court is satisfied—
    (i) on the written or oral evidence of two medical practitioners, that he is suffering from mental disorder of a nature or degree which warrants his admission to hospital under Part V of the Mental Health (Scotland) Act 1984; and
    (ii) that a hospital is available for his admission and suitable for his detention,
make an order (in this section referred to as a "temporary hospital order") committing him to that hospital until the conclusion of the examination of facts.
(2) Subsection (1) above is without prejudice to the power of the court, on an application by the prosecutor, to desert the diet *pro loco et tempore.*
(3) The court may, before making a finding under subsection (1) above as to the insanity of a person, adjourn the case in order that investigation of his mental condition may be carried out.
(4) The court which made a temporary hospital order may, at any time while the order is in force, review the order on the ground that there has been a change of circumstances since the order was made and, on such review—
  (a) where the court considers that such an order is no longer required in relation to a person, it shall revoke the order and may remand him in custody or on bail;
  (b) in any other case, the court may—
    (i) confirm or vary the order; or
    (ii) revoke the order and make such other order, under subsection (1)(c) above or any other provision of this Act, as the court considers appropriate.
(5) Where it appears to a court that it is not practicable or appropriate for the accused to be brought before it for the purpose of determining whether he is insane so that his trial cannot proceed, then, if no objection to such a course is taken by or on behalf of the accused, the court may order that the case be proceeded with in his absence.
(6) Where evidence is brought before the court that the accused was insane at the time of doing the act or making the omission constituting the offence with which he is charged and he is acquitted, the court shall—
  (a) in proceedings on indictment, direct the jury to find; or
  (b) in summary proceedings, state,
whether the accused was insane at such time as aforesaid, and, if so, to declare whether he was acquitted on account of his insanity at that time.
(7) It shall not be competent for a person charged summarily in the sheriff court to found on a plea of insanity standing in bar of trial unless, before the first witness for the prosecution is sworn, he gives notice to the prosecutor of the plea and of the witnesses by whom he proposes to maintain it; and where

such notice is given, the court shall, if the prosecutor so moves, adjourn the case.

   (8) In this section, "the court" means—

   (a) as regards a person charged on indictment, the High Court or the sheriff court;

   (b) as regards a person charged summarily, the sheriff court.

DEFINITIONS
   "bail": s.307(1).
   "court": s.54(8).
   "examination of the facts": s.307(1).
   "medical practitioner": s.61(1).
   "temporary hospital order": s.54(1)(c).

GENERAL NOTE
   It is interesting to note, by way of a preliminary, that s.52 is concerned with "mental disorder", s.53 is concerned with "mental disorder within the meaning of s.1(2) of the Mental Health (Scotland) Act 1984" and s.54 is concerned with "insanity".
   However, s.54 requires a court in both solemn and summary proceedings, following a finding that a person is insane so that a trial cannot proceed or continue, to hold an examination of the facts ("EOF") relating to the charges. The section further provides for the court to remand in custody or on bail, or to commit such a person to hospital under a temporary hospital order, until the conclusion of the EOF.
   The new procedure very much contrasts with the previous law under which, when a person was found insane in bar of trial, no attempt was made by the court to examine the evidence as to whether the accused did the act with which he is charged. The new procedure requires that there be an examination of the relevant facts. It gives effect to certain recommendations contained in the Second Thomson Report on Criminal Procedure (Cmnd. 6218 (1975)). The only circumstances in which an EOF cannot be held are when the Crown applies for and the court agrees to the diet being deserted *pro loco et tempore*.
   The novelty of these proceedings is accentuated by the possibility that the hearing to determine insanity may in some circumstances proceed in the absence of the accused: see s.54(5).
   In relation to solemn proceedings, s.54 should be read together with s.67. The latter section sets out the statutory requirements on the Crown for the witnesses and for intimation in writing of the details of the witnesses and where they can be contacted for the purposes of precognition. For that reason the accused or those advising him should have clear intimation of the availability of the two medical practitioners who may give evidence for the Crown of insanity. If the illness has developed immediately prior to the trial then such medical practitioners may be called with leave of the court: see s.67(5). If the defence seek to raise the issue then they must intimate the details of the two medical practitioners: see s.78(4).
   In relation to summary proceedings, the approach to the issue is necessarily different. There appears to be no duty on the Crown to intimate the issue in advance of the trial although one would hope that such an important matter would be intimated in the interests of justice. In any event, an adjournment for inquiry at the first calling in terms of s.145(1) would undoubtedly follow where there had been no intimation. The accused or those advising him are under a clear duty to give notice: see s.54(7).
   Finally, it should be noted that for the purposes of s.54(1) a report in writing purporting to be signed by a medical practitioner may, subject to the provisions of s.61, be received in evidence without proof of the signature or qualifications of the practitioner: but the court may, in any case, require the practitioner by whom such a report was signed be called to give oral evidence; s.61(3).

Examination of facts

Examination of facts

   55.—(1) At an examination of facts ordered under section 54(1)(b) of this Act the court shall, on the basis of the evidence (if any) already given in the trial and such evidence, or further evidence, as may be led by either party, determine whether it is satisfied—

(a) beyond reasonable doubt, as respects any charge on the indictment or, as the case may be, the complaint in respect of which the accused was being or was to be tried, that he did the act or made the omission constituting the offence; and

(b) on the balance of probabilities, that there are no grounds for acquitting him.

(2) Where the court is satisfied as mentioned in subsection (1) above, it shall make a finding to that effect.

(3) Where the court is not so satisfied it shall, subject to subsection (4) below, acquit the person of the charge.

(4) Where, as respects a person acquitted under subsection (3) above, the court is satisfied as to the matter mentioned in subsection (1)(a) above but it appears to the court that the person was insane at the time of doing the act or making the omission constituting the offence, the court shall state whether the acquittal is on the ground of such insanity.

(5) Where it appears to the court that it is not practical or appropriate for the accused to attend an examination of facts the court may, if no objection is taken by or on behalf of the accused, order that the examination of facts shall proceed in his absence.

(6) Subject to the provisions of this section, section 56 of this Act and any Act of Adjournal the rules of evidence and procedure and the powers of the court shall, in respect of an examination of facts, be as nearly as possible those applicable in respect of a trial.

(7) For the purposes of the application to an examination of facts of the rules and powers mentioned in subsection (6) above, an examination of facts—

(a) commences when the indictment or, as the case may be, complaint is called; and

(b) concludes when the court—

(i) acquits the person under subsection (3) above;

(ii) makes an order under subsection (2) of section 57 of this Act; or

(iii) decides, under paragraph (e) of that subsection, not to make an order.

DEFINITIONS
"examination of facts": s.54(1)(b).
"offence": s.307(1).

GENERAL NOTE

Section 54 establishes the competency of an examination of facts ("EOF") and s.55 specifies the procedure and powers of the court, its findings, and a number of detailed ancillary matters. An EOF is to be held along the lines of a trial as far as possible and, again emphasising the novelty, it may proceed in certain circumstances in the absence of the accused.

It seems important to stress that an EOF need not necessarily be a matter wholly separate from a trial in the conventional sense. Section 54(1) refers to "a person charged with the commission of an offence" being insane "so that his trial cannot proceed or, if it has commenced, cannot continue". On that approach it is easy to imagine under solemn procedure a trial commencing in the ordinary way and after the jury has heard some evidence the defence lawyers (or others) intimating that there is concern about the accused's health. Thereafter, a medical examination might produce the necessary evidence leading the court to make the essential finding (s.54(1)(a)) and the trial diet being discharged and an EOF then being held (s.54(1)(b)). It follows from the discharge of the trial diet and the terms of s.55 that the jury is released.

Thereafter, at the EOF the court must consider both any evidence already given in the trial and the evidence led at the EOF itself, by either party. The court must then determine whether it is satisfied that the accused did the act or made the omission constituting the offence and that there are no grounds for his acquittal. The standard for the first determination is beyond reasonable doubt and for the second it is on a balance of probabilities (s.54(1)(a) and (b)).

If the court is not satisfied that these standards have been made out the accused is acquitted (s.54(3)) but acquittal on the grounds of insanity is competent and if so determined should be stated (s.54(4)).

Examination of facts: supplementary provisions

56.—(1) An examination of facts ordered under section 54(1)(b) of this Act may, where the order is made at the trial diet, be held immediately following the making of the order and, where it is so held, the citation of the accused and any witness to the trial diet shall be a valid citation to the examination of facts.

(2) Where an examination of facts is ordered in connection with proceedings on indictment, a warrant for citation of an accused and witnesses under section 66(1) of this Act shall be sufficient warrant for citation to an examination of facts.

(3) Where an accused person is not legally represented at an examination of facts the court shall appoint counsel or a solicitor to represent his interests.

(4) The court may, on the motion of the prosecutor and after hearing the accused, order that the examination of facts shall proceed in relation to a particular charge, or particular charges, in the indictment or, as the case may be, complaint in priority to other such charges.

(5) The court may, on the motion of the prosecutor and after hearing the accused, at any time desert the examination of facts *pro loco et tempore* as respects either the whole indictment or, as the case may be, complaint or any charge therein.

(6) Where, and to the extent that, an examination of facts has, under subsection (5) above, been deserted *pro loco et tempore*—

    (a) in the case of proceedings on indictment, the Lord Advocate may, at any time, raise and insist in a new indictment; or

    (b) in the case of summary proceedings, the prosecutor may at any time raise a fresh libel,

notwithstanding any time limit which would otherwise apply in respect of prosecution of the alleged offence.

(7) If, in a case where a court has made a finding under subsection (2) of section 55 of this Act, a person is subsequently charged, whether on indictment or on a complaint, with an offence arising out of the same act or omission as is referred to in subsection (1) of that section, any order made, under section 57(2) of this Act shall, with effect from the commencement of the later proceedings, cease to have effect.

(8) For the purposes of subsection (7) above, the later proceedings are commenced when the indictment or, as the case may be, the complaint is served.

DEFINITIONS
    "complaint": s.307(1).
    "diet": s.307(1).
    "examination of facts": s.54(1)(b).
    "indictment": s.307(1).
    "order": s.307(1).
    "prosecutor": s.307(1).

GENERAL NOTE
    This section makes supplementary provisions for examinations of facts ("EOF"): the most important aspects that arise are probably that existing powers of citation for the trial diet are valid for citation for the EOF (s.56(1) and (2)) and that any time-limits that might constrain the Crown following an EOF being deserted *pro loco et tempore* are disapplied (s.56(6)).

Disposal in case of insanity

Disposal of case where accused found to be insane

57.—(1) This section applies where—
(a) a person is, by virtue of section 54(6) or 55(3) of this Act, acquitted on the ground of his insanity at the time of the act or omission; or
(b) following an examination of facts under section 55, a court makes a finding under subsection (2) of that section.

(2) Subject to subsection (3) below, where this section applies the court may, as it thinks fit—
(a) make an order (which shall have the same effect as a hospital order) that the person be detained in such hospital as the court may specify;
(b) in addition to making an order under paragraph (a) above, make an order (which shall have the same effect as a restriction order) that the person shall, without limit of time, be subject to the special restrictions set out in section 62(1) of the Mental Health (Scotland) Act 1984;
(c) make an order (which shall have the same effect as a guardianship order) placing the person under the guardianship of a local authority or of a person approved by a local authority;
(d) make a supervision and treatment order (within the meaning of paragraph 1(1) of Schedule 4 to this Act); or
(e) make no order.

(3) Where the offence with which the person was charged is murder, the court shall make orders under both paragraphs (a) and (b) of subsection (2) above in respect of that person.

(4) Sections 58(1), (2) and (4) to (7) and 59 and 61 of this Act shall have effect in relation to the making, terms and effect of an order under paragraph (a), (b) or (c) of subsection (2) above as those provisions have effect in relation to the making, terms and effect of, respectively, a hospital order, a restriction order and a guardianship order as respects a person convicted of an offence, other than an offence the sentence for which is fixed by law, punishable by imprisonment.

(5) Schedule 4 to this Act shall have effect as regards supervision and treatment orders.

DEFINITIONS
"examination of facts": s.54(1)(b).
"medical practitioner": s.61(1).
"new supervising officer": Sched. 4, para. 7(1)(b).
"order": s.307(1).
"relevant sheriff court": Sched. 4, para. 3(2)(b).
"supervised person": Sched. 4, para. 1(1).
"supervising officer": Sched. 4, para. 1(1).
"supervision and treatment order": Sched. 4, para. 1(1).

GENERAL NOTE
This section specifies the disposals available to a court at an examination of facts ("EOF") in both solemn and summary proceedings, and to a court acquitting a person on the grounds of insanity at the time of the commission of the offence charged. It provides for the making of a hospital order, with or without a restriction order, a guardianship order, a new disposal (the Supervision and Treatment Order) in which the recipient resides in the community under the supervision of a social worker and for the purposes of treatment under a medical practitioner, and, finally, the making of no order at all.

Section 57 thus provides a court with a wider range of disposals than was available under the previous law when dealing with an accused who is unfit to plead. Only two observations need to be made in regard to these disposals. First, the new disposal of a Supervision and Treatment Order is only new to Scotland as it has been provided for in the Criminal Procedure (Insanity and Unfitness to Plead) Act 1991 (c.25) for England and Wales. The extensive arrangements for the new disposal are set out in Sched. 4 to this Act. Secondly, in only one disposal is the discretion of the court restricted. When the charge is one of murder the court must impose a hospital order and a restriction order without limit of time (s.57(3)).

Hospital orders and guardianship

Order for hospital admission or guardianship

58.—(1) Where a person is convicted in the High Court or the sheriff court of an offence, other than an offence the sentence for which is fixed by law, punishable by that court with imprisonment, and the following conditions are satisfied, that is to say—

(a) the court is satisfied, on the written or oral evidence of two medical practitioners (complying with section 61 of this Act) that the grounds set out in—
   (i) section 17(1); or, as the case may be
   (ii) section 36(a),
of the Mental Health (Scotland) Act 1984 apply in relation to the offender;

(b) the court is of the opinion, having regard to all the circumstances including the nature of the offence and the character and antecedents of the offender and to the other available methods of dealing with him, that the most suitable method of disposing of the case is by means of an order under this section,

subject to subsection (2) below, the court may by order authorise his admission to and detention in such hospital as may be specified in the order or, as the case may be, place him under the guardianship of such local authority or of such other person approved by a local authority as may be so specified.

(2) Where the case is remitted by the sheriff to the High Court for sentence under any enactment, the power to make an order under subsection (1) above shall be exercisable by that court.

(3) Where in the case of a person charged summarily in the sheriff court with an act or omission constituting an offence the court would have power, on convicting him, to make an order under subsection (1) above, then, if it is satisfied that the person did the act or made the omission charged, the court may, if it thinks fit, make such an order without convicting him.

(4) An order for the admission of a person to a hospital (in this Act, referred to as "a hospital order") shall not be made under this section in respect of an offender or of a person to whom subsection (3) above applies unless the court is satisfied that that hospital, in the event of such an order being made by the court, is available for his admission thereto within 28 days of the making of such an order.

(5) A State hospital shall not be specified in a hospital order in respect of the detention of a person unless the court is satisfied, on the evidence of the medical practitioners which is taken into account under paragraph (a) of subsection (1) above, that the offender, on account of his dangerous, violent or criminal propensities, requires treatment under conditions of special security, and cannot suitably be cared for in a hospital other than a State hospital.

(6) An order placing a person under the guardianship of a local authority or of any other person (in this Act referred to as "a guardianship order") shall not be made under this section unless the court is satisfied—

(a) after taking into consideration the evidence of a mental health officer, that it is necessary in the interests of the welfare of the person that he should be placed under guardianship; and

(b) that that authority or person is willing to receive that person into guardianship.

(7) A hospital order or guardianship order shall specify the form of mental disorder, being mental illness or mental handicap or both, from which, upon the evidence taken into account under paragraph (a) of subsection (1) above, the offender is found by the court to be suffering; and no such order shall be made unless the offender is described by each of the practitioners, whose evidence is taken into account as aforesaid, as suffering from the same form of mental disorder, whether or not he is also described by either of them as suffering from the other form.

(8) Where an order is made under this section, the court shall not pass sentence of imprisonment or impose a fine or make a probation order or a community service order in respect of the offence, but may make any other order which the court has power to make apart from this section; and for the purposes of this subsection "sentence of imprisonment" includes any sentence or order for detention.

(9) The court by which a hospital order is made may give such directions as it thinks fit for the conveyance of the patient to a place of safety and his detention therein pending his admission to the hospital within the period of 28 days referred to in subsection (4) above; but a direction for the conveyance of a patient to a residential establishment shall not be given unless the court is satisfied that the authority is willing to receive the patient therein.

(10) Where a person is charged before the district court with an act or omission constituting an offence punishable with imprisonment, the district court, if it appears to it that that person may be suffering from mental disorder, shall remit him to the sheriff court in the manner provided by section 7(9) and (10) of this Act, and the sheriff court shall, on any such remit being made, have the like power to make an order under subsection (1) above in respect of him as if he had been charged before that court with the said act or omission as an offence, or in dealing with him may exercise the like powers as the district court.

DEFINITIONS
  "guardianship order": s.58(6).
  "High Court": s.307(1).
  "hospital order": s.58(4).
  "local authority": s.307(1).
  "medical practitioner": s.61(1).
  "offence": s.307(1).
  "sentence": s.307(1).
  "sentence of imprisonment": s.58(8).
  "State hospital": s.307(1).

GENERAL NOTE
  This section provides for the making of orders for hospital admission or guardianship and to the extent that it re-enacts s.175 of the 1975 Act nothing new is set out here: some parts of this section have been taken from other parts of the 1975 Act.
  The section is in the generality for the admission of a person to a hospital but there is a requirement (s.58(7)) that an order made under the section specifies the form of mental disorder "being mental illness or mental handicap or both", from which the person is suffering and each medical practitioner must give evidence that the person is "suffering from the same form of mental disorder, whether or not he is also described by either of them as suffering from the other form".
  The section is specific in regard to a State hospital not being named in a hospital order unless the court is satisfied on medical evidence that the accused "on account of his dangerous, violent or criminal propensities, requires treatment under conditions of special security, and cannot suitably be cared for in a hospital other than a State hospital".
  Finally, it should be noted that for the purposes of s.58(1)(a) a report in writing purporting to be signed by a medical practitioner may, subject to the provisions of s.61, be received in evidence without proof of the signature or qualifications of the practitioner; but the court may, in any case, require the practitioner by whom such a report was signed be called to give oral evidence: s.61(3).

Hospital orders: restrictions on discharge

59.—(1) Where a hospital order is made in respect of a person, and it appears to the court—

(a) having regard to the nature of the offence with which he is charged;

(b) the antecedents of the person; and

(c) the risk that as a result of his mental disorder he would commit offences if set at large,

that it is necessary for the protection of the public from serious harm so to do, the court may, subject to the provisions of this section, further order that the person shall be subject to the special restrictions set out in section 62(1) of the Mental Health (Scotland) Act 1984, without limit of time.

(2) An order under this section (in this Act referred to as "a restriction order") shall not be made in the case of any person unless the medical practitioner approved by the Health Board for the purposes of section 20 or section 39 of the Mental Health (Scotland) Act 1984, whose evidence is taken into account by the court under section 58(1)(a) of this Act, has given evidence orally before the court.

(3) Where a restriction order is in force in respect of a patient, a guardianship order shall not be made in respect of him; and where the hospital order relating to him ceases to have effect by virtue of section 60(3) of the Mental Health (Scotland) Act 1984 on the making of another hospital order, that order shall have the same effect in relation to the restriction order as the previous hospital order, but without prejudice to the power of the court making that other hospital order to make another restriction order to have effect on the expiration of the previous such order.

DEFINITIONS

"hospital order": s.58(4).

"mental disorder": s.1(2) of the Mental Health (Scotland) Act 1984.

"offence": s.307(1).

"restriction order": s.59(2).

GENERAL NOTE

Section 59 makes provision to restrict the discharge of hospital orders made under s.58. As a court may make a further hospital order that amounts to a person being subject to statutory special restrictions without limit of time, the tests to be met are suitably high. Indeed, the aspects of risk and protection in s.59(1) are redolent of the concerns latent in the terms of s.58(5).

Appeals against hospital orders

60. Where a hospital order, interim hospital order (but not a renewal thereof), guardianship order or a restriction order has been made by a court in respect of a person charged or brought before it, he may without prejudice to any other form of appeal under any rule of law (or, where an interim hospital order has been made, to any right of appeal against any other order or sentence which may be imposed), appeal against that order in the same manner as against sentence.

DEFINITIONS

"guardianship order": s.58(6).

"hospital order": s.58(4).

"interim hospital order": s.53(1).

"restriction order": s.59(2).

"sentence": s.307(1).

GENERAL NOTE

This section conjoins the right of appeal formerly to be found in ss.280 and 443 of the 1975 Act. The right of appeal against these orders is treated as an appeal against sentence so that, for example, an appeal against a finding on fact under s.55(2) by the court cannot be appealed under s.60. Appeals against findings and orders are dealt with by ss.62 and 63.

Medical evidence

Requirements as to medical evidence

61.—(1) Of the medical practitioners whose evidence is taken into account under sections 53(1), 54(1) and 58(1)(a) of this Act, at least one shall be a practitioner approved for the purposes of section 20 or section 39 of the Mental Health (Scotland) Act 1984 by a Health Board as having special experience in the diagnosis or treatment of mental disorder.

(2) Written or oral evidence given for the purposes of the said section 58(1)(a) shall include a statement as to whether the person giving the evidence is related to the accused and of any pecuniary interest which that person may have in the admission of the accused to hospital or his reception into guardianship.

(3) For the purposes of the said sections 54(1) and 58(1)(a) a report in writing purporting to be signed by a medical practitioner may, subject to the provisions of this section, be received in evidence without proof of the signature or qualifications of the practitioner; but the court may, in any case, require that the practitioner by whom such a report was signed be called to give oral evidence.

(4) Where any such report as aforesaid is tendered in evidence, otherwise than by or on behalf of the accused, then—

(a) if the accused is represented by counsel or solicitor, a copy of the report shall be given to his counsel or solicitor;

(b) if the accused is not so represented, the substance of the report shall be disclosed to the accused or, where he is a child under 16 years of age, to his parent or guardian if present in court;

(c) in any case, the accused may require that the practitioner by whom the report was signed be called to give oral evidence, and evidence to rebut the evidence contained in the report may be called by or on behalf of the accused,

and where the court is of the opinion that further time is necessary in the interests of the accused for consideration of that report, or the substance of any such report, it shall adjourn the case.

(5) For the purpose of calling evidence to rebut the evidence contained in any such report as aforesaid, arrangements may be made by or on behalf of an accused person detained in a hospital or, as respects a report for the purposes of the said section 54(1), remanded in custody for his examination by any medical practitioner, and any such examination may he made in private.

DEFINITIONS
"hospital": s.307(1).
"medical practitioner": s.61(1).
"mental disorder": s.58(7).

GENERAL NOTE
The purpose of this section must be to ensure that medical practitioners who give evidence on the mental health of the accused do so in the capacity of skilled witnesses, or at least one of them must to meet the terms of s.61(1). It may be that in practice two general practitioners of medicine might be able properly to recognise mental disorder, for the purposes of this section one of the medical practitioners must have the statutory qualification in regard to diagnosis or treatment.

Appeals under Part VI

Appeal by accused in case involving insanity

62.—(1) A person may appeal to the High Court against—

(a) a finding made under section 54(1) of this Act that he is insane so that his trial cannot proceed or continue, or the refusal of the court to make such a finding;

(b) a finding under section 55(2) of this Act; or

(c) an order made under section 57(2) of this Act.

(2) An appeal under subsection (1) above shall be—

(a) in writing; and

(b) lodged——

    (i) in the case of an appeal under paragraph (a) of that subsection, not later than seven days after the date of the finding or refusal which is the subject of the appeal;

    (ii) in the case of an appeal under paragraph (b), or both paragraphs (b) and (c) of that subsection, not later than 28 days after the conclusion of the examination of facts;

    (iii) in the case of an appeal under paragraph (c) of that subsection against an order made on an acquittal, by virtue of section 54(6) or 55(3) of this Act, on the ground of insanity at the time of the act or omission, not later than 14 days after the date of the acquittal;

    (iv) in the case of an appeal under that paragraph against an order made on a finding under section 55(2), not later than 14 days after the conclusion of the examination of facts,

or within such longer period as the High Court may, on cause shown, allow.

(3) Where the examination of facts was held in connection with proceedings on indictment, subsections (1)(a) and (2)(b)(i) above are without prejudice to section 74(1) of this Act.

(4) Where an appeal is taken under subsection (1) above, the period from the date on which the appeal was lodged until it is withdrawn or disposed of shall not count towards any time limit applying in respect of the case.

(5) An appellant in an appeal under this section shall be entitled to be present at the hearing of the appeal unless the High Court determines that his presence is not practicable or appropriate.

(6) In disposing of an appeal under subsection (1) above the High Court may——

(a) affirm the decision of the court of first instance;

(b) make any other finding or order which that court could have made at the time when it made the finding or order which is the subject of the appeal; or

(c) remit the case to that court with such directions in the matter as the High Court thinks fit.

(7) Section 60 of this Act shall not apply in relation to any order as respects which a person has a right of appeal under subsection (1)(c) above.

DEFINITIONS
"examination of facts": s.54(1)(b).
"High Court": s.307(1).
"order": s.307(1).

GENERAL NOTE
Under the previous law, ss.174(1) and 375(2) of the 1975 Act enabled a court to find a person insane in bar of trial. An accused person had no right of appeal either against such a finding or against the refusal of any plea or motion that such a finding should be made. The only exception was where the finding was made at a preliminary diet in solemn proceedings in which event the accused had a right of appeal by s.76A(1) of the 1975 Act.

The new section provides the accused under solemn or summary procedure with rights of appeal in relation to any findings, or the refusal to make a finding, that the accused is insane in bar of trial and against findings made by, and orders made at, examinations of fact. Although such appeals must be made in comparatively short periods of time, longer periods may be allowed by the High Court of Justiciary on cause shown. The appellate judges have a broad range of powers to affirm or vary decisions and orders appealed against and to remit cases with directions.

Appeal by prosecutor in case involving insanity

63.—(1) The prosecutor may appeal to the High Court on a point of law
against—
  (a) a finding under subsection (1) of section 54 of this Act that an accused
      is insane so that his trial cannot proceed or continue;
  (b) an acquittal on the ground of insanity at the time of the act or omission
      by virtue of subsection (6) of that section;
  (c) an acquittal under section 55(3) of this Act (whether or not on the
      ground of insanity at the time of the act or omission); or
  (d) any order made under section 57(2) of this Act.
  (2) An appeal under subsection (1) above shall be—
  (a) in writing; and
  (b) lodged—
          (i) in the case of an appeal under paragraph (a) or (b) of that
      subsection, not later than seven days after the finding or, as the case
      may be, the acquittal which is the subject of the appeal;
          (ii) in the case of an appeal under paragraph (c) or (d) of that
      subsection, not later than seven days after the conclusion of the
      examination of facts,
      or within such longer period as the High Court may, on cause shown,
      allow.
  (3) Where the examination of facts was held in connection with proceedings on indictment, subsections (1)(a) and (2)(b)(i) above are without prejudice to section 74(1) of this Act.
  (4) A respondent in an appeal under this subsection shall be entitled to be
present at the hearing of the appeal unless the High Court determines that his
presence is not practicable or appropriate.
  (5) In disposing of an appeal under subsection (1) above the High Court
may—
  (a) affirm the decision of the court of first instance;
  (b) make any other finding or order which that court could have made at
      the time when it made the finding or order which is the subject of the
      appeal; or
  (c) remit the case to that court with such directions in the matter as the
      High Court thinks fit.
  (6) In this section, "the prosecutor" means, in relation to proceedings on
indictment, the Lord Advocate.

Definitions
  "examination of facts": s.54(1)(b).
  "High Court": s.307(1).
  "order": s.307(1).
  "prosecutor": s.63(6).

General Note
  Under the previous law, ss.174(1) and 375(2) of the 1975 Act enabled a court to find a person
insane in bar of trial. The Crown had no right of appeal against such a finding unless it had been
made at a preliminary diet in solemn proceedings, in which event the Crown had a right of appeal
by s.76A(1) of the 1975 Act.
  This section now provides the Crown with a right of appeal similar to those given to the
accused under s.62. The Crown may appeal against a finding of insanity in bar of trial, against a
trial verdict of acquittal on the ground of insanity, against any acquittal at an examination of
facts and against an order made at an examination of facts. In each of these the appeal may be
only on a point of law.

PART VII

SOLEMN PROCEEDINGS

The indictment

Prosecution on indictment

64.—(1) All prosecutions for the public interest before the High Court or before the sheriff sitting with a jury shall proceed on indictment in name of Her Majesty's Advocate.

(2) The indictment may be in the forms—
(a) set out in Schedule 2 to this Act; or
(b) prescribed by Act of Adjournal,
or as nearly as may be in such form.

(3) Indictments in proceedings before the High Court shall be signed by the Lord Advocate or one of his deputes.

(4) Indictments in proceedings before the sheriff sitting with a jury shall be signed by the procurator fiscal, and the words "By Authority of Her Majesty's Advocate" shall be prefixed to the signature of the procurator fiscal.

(5) The principal record and service copies of indictments and all notices of citation, lists of witnesses, productions and jurors, and all other official documents required in a prosecution on indictment may be either written or printed or partly written and partly printed.

(6) Schedule 3 to this Act shall have effect as regards indictments under this Act.

DEFINITIONS
"High Court": s.307(1).
"indictment": s.307(1).
"procurator fiscal": s.307(1).

GENERAL NOTE
The provisions dealing with the latitudes as to time, place, capacity and implied terms previously contained in ss.43 to 67 of the 1975 Act, in relation to solemn proceedings, and s.311 relative to summary proceedings, are now incorporated in Sched. 3 to the 1995 Act. It remains a moot point what practical benefit is derived from preserving the indictment styles of the 1887 Act as Sched. 2 does.

Section 287 of the 1995 Act makes provision for the maintenance of indictment proceedings in the event of the death of, or demission of office by, the Lord Advocate. Section 288 below entitles the Lord Advocate to be advised of, and be heard in relation to any proposed private prosecution: see *X. v. Sweeney*, 1982 S.C.C.R. 161 which proceeded by Bill of Criminal Letters, the Lord Advocate not objecting, following formal intimation by the Crown to the accused of no further proceedings.

Prevention of delay in trials

65.—(1) Subject to subsections (2) and (3) below, an accused shall not be tried on indictment for any offence unless the trial is commenced within a period of 12 months of the first appearance of the accused on petition in respect of the offence; and, failing such commencement within that period, the accused shall be discharged forthwith and thereafter he shall be for ever free from all question or process for that offence.

(2) Nothing in subsection (1) above shall bar the trial of an accused for whose arrest a warrant has been granted for failure to appear at a diet in the case.

(3) On an application made for the purpose, the sheriff or, where an indictment has been served on the accused in respect of the High Court, a single judge of that court, may on cause shown extend the said period of 12 months.

(4) Subject to subsections (5) to (9) below, an accused who is committed for any offence until liberated in due course of law shall not be detained by virtue of that committal for a total period of more than—
  (a) 80 days, unless within that period the indictment is served on him, which failing he shall be liberated forthwith; or
  (b) 110 days, unless the trial of the case is commenced within that period, which failing he shall be liberated forthwith and thereafter he shall be for ever free from all question or process for that offence.

(5) Subject to subsection (6) below, a single judge of the High Court, may, on an application made to him for the purpose, for any sufficient cause extend the period mentioned in subsection (4)(a) above.

(6) An application under subsection (5) above shall not be granted if the judge is satisfied that, but for some fault on the part of the prosecution, the indictment could have been served within the period of 80 days.

(7) A single judge of the High Court may, on an application made to him for the purpose, extend the period mentioned in subsection (4)(b) above where he is satisfied that delay in the commencement of the trial is due to—
  (a) the illness of the accused or of a judge;
  (b) the absence or illness of any necessary witness;
  (c) any other sufficient cause which is not attributable to any fault on the part of the prosecutor.

(8) The grant or refusal of any application to extend the periods mentioned in this section may be appealed against by note of appeal presented to the High Court; and that Court may affirm, reverse or amend the determination made on such application.

(9) For the purposes of this section, a trial shall be taken to commence when the oath is administered to the jury.

(10) In calculating the period of 12 months specified in subsections (1) and (3) above there shall be left out of account any period during which the accused is detained, other than while serving a sentence of imprisonment or detention, in any other part of the United Kingdom or in any of the Channel Islands or the Isle of Man in any prison or other institution or place mentioned in subsection (1) or (1A) of section 29 of the Criminal Justice Act 1961 (transfer of prisoners for certain judicial purposes).

DEFINITIONS
  "High Court": s.307(1).
  "indictment": s.307(1).
  "offence": s.307(1).
  "prison": s.307(1).

GENERAL NOTE
  The provisions of this section restate the terms of s.101 of the 1975 Act and impose time-limits upon the commencement of solemn proceedings. Failure on the part of the Crown to take proper account of these mandatory provisions can, on rare occasions, be cured retrospectively, but generally the section's terms are strictly construed. Existing case law, of which there is, unsurprisingly, a substantial volume given the mandatory finality of s.101 of the 1975 Act, will still be authoritative.
  Two distinct time scales are specified by s.65: the rules applicable to custody proceedings on indictment which demand service of any indictment within 80 days of full committal and the commencement of those proceedings within 110 days (subs. (4)); and the prescriptive one year period within which those persons liberated on petition bail must be brought to trial (subs. (1)). If the relevant time-limits are not met by the Crown, proceedings will ordinarily fall.

Subss. (1), (2) and (3)
  It is hard to believe that this provision against delay in solemn cases where the accused has been admitted to bail was introduced as recently as 1980 by s.6 of the Criminal Justice (Scotland) Act of that year.
  Service of any indictment should be effected not less than 29 days before the assigned diet of trial (see s.66(6) below) unless the accused has opted to plead guilty by way of an accelerated

plea under s.76 of the 1995 Act. Such accelerated proceedings apart, for practical purposes sheriff and jury proceedings are now activated by the calling of the indictment at the first diet, a mechanism introduced by ss.66 and 71 of the 1995 Act. Until this formal step has been taken the Crown has not begun to comply with the terms of s.65(1) in those proceedings.

Note that the one year period commences from the date of the accused's first appearance on the relative petition, whether he is committed for further examination, as is usual, or fully committed and halts, in terms of subs. (9), when the jury is put on oath at the trial diet (by contrast, calculation of the 80 and 110 day periods in solemn custody cases only runs from the date of full committal). It will be seen that s.66 does not make mandatory provision of first diets in proceedings before the High Court, but that a preliminary diet can be fixed by way of the procedures laid out in s.72.

Application for an extension of the one year period can be made by either the prosecutor or the defence and is considered by the judge of first instance (a sheriff or in High Court cases a High Court judge sitting alone), whose decision can be appealed to the High Court by way of note of appeal. Many of the issues referred to in the case law are likely to be aired at first or preliminary diets rather than at the trial diet itself in future.

Extension of the one year time bar (subs. (3))

Any such motion will be considered by a single judge and can be granted on cause shown, a less strict test than is applied to motions to extend the 110 day period in custody; see subss. (6) and (7) which in custody cases requires that any delay shall not be the fault of the prosecutor.

The judge does not have an absolute discretion when considering a motion to extend the 12 month period; in *Advocate, H.M. v. Brown*, 1984 S.C.C.R. 347 it was held that the sheriff acted unreasonably in granting a defence motion to adjourn the trial, but refusing an unopposed Crown motion for an extension.

A degree of fault on the part of the Crown would not be fatal to an application for extension of the year period (*Mallison v. H.M. Advocate*, 1987 S.C.C.R. 320), but certainly failure to serve an indictment at a domicile of citation would attract particularly rigorous scrutiny (*Advocate, H.M. v. Swift*, 1984 S.C.C.R. 216; 1985 S.L.T. 26). However, failure on the part of the police to execute service of an indictment timeously or to comply with express instructions are not faults of the prosecutor; see *Welsh v. H.M. Advocate*, 1985 S.C.C.R. 404; *Advocate, H.M. v. Davies*, 1993 S.C.C.R. 645; *Coutts v. H.M. Advocate*, 1992 S.C.C.R. 87. Equally, failure to intimate a change of domicile of citation which resulted in service being unsuccessful at the accused's former address could not count against the Crown (*Black v. H.M. Advocate*, 1990 S.C.C.R. 609).

Pressure of business alone will not justify an extension and even when administrative difficulties are founded upon, the court is under an obligation to make enquiry into their nature (see *Dobbie v. H.M. Advocate*, 1986 S.L.T. 648; *Fleming v. H.M. Advocate*, 1992 S.C.C.R. 575). Note that in *Rudge v. H.M. Advocate*, 1989 S.C.C.R. 105 a Crown motion in such circumstances was granted and one persuasive factor was the lack of real prejudice being demonstrated. In *Beattie v. H.M. Advocate*, 1995 S.C.C.R. 606 where a Crown motion to extend the 110 day period was granted, the Court of Appeal disfavoured the view that the non-availability of the trial judge was itself sufficient cause for extending the statutory time-limits. The court was critical of the lack of enquiry made by the trial judge as to possible alternatives and emphasised that the tests involved in extending the 110 day period are more exacting than those applicable to extending the one year period.

Miscalculation of the time bar period on the Crown's part was rejected by the Appeal Court as a valid ground for extension in *Lyle v. H.M. Advocate*, 1992 S.L.T. 467, as has a realisation too late that essential corroborative evidence had not been secured; see *Stewart v. H.M. Advocate*, 1994 S.L.T. 518 where a successful Crown application for extension was overturned on appeal when it was conceded that such additional evidence could have been obtained within the statutory year. Detention in England and consequent absence which necessitated an extension was, on the facts, regarded as attributable to the accused, not the Crown (*Duffy v. H.M. Advocate*, 1991 S.C.C.R. 685). Subsection (10) provides some statutory clarification in this area, by enacting that periods of remand served elsewhere in the United Kingdom shall interrupt the advance of the year time bar, an issue which had surfaced (and caused judicial calls for just such a reform) in *Advocate, H.M. v. Rowan*, 1994 S.C.C.R. 801. In *Rowan* the Court of Appeal considered a Crown appeal against a refusal of extension of the year period where R was in custody in England on other matters, and the English authorities lacked any powers to transfer him to Scotland; the appeal was allowed and this anomalous situation resulted in the amendment of the Criminal Justice (Scotland) Act 1995, s.15 at the Report Stage (*Hansard*, H.L. Vol. 561, col. 39).

While an application for extension may be presented orally to the court, the defence are entitled to be heard (*Sandford v. H.M. Advocate*, 1986 S.C.C.R. 573) and to have warning of the motion to be made, albeit no formal notice is necessary (*Ferguson v. H.M. Advocate*, 1992 S.C.C.R. 480; *Cation v. H.M. Advocate*, 1992 S.C.C.R. 480). These last two cases also serve as warnings to the Crown of the risks associated with excusing witnesses without first securing the agreement of the defence: in both cases appeals against extensions of the year period were successful. By contrast see *Berry v. H.M. Advocate*, 1989 S.L.T. 71 where delays in notifying the Crown that a witness on the indictment could not be excused, or his evidence be agreed, resulted in an extension of time which was upheld on appeal.

Persistent illness or absence of co-accused may not justify extensions if the Crown have not considered proceeding against the accused who is present on his own (*Mejka v. H.M. Advocate*, 1993 S.L.T. 1321; 1993 S.C.C.R. 978).

Where an accused has appeared on successive petitions, the court has to look to each petition individually in order to determine the effective date of the year time bar (*Ross v. H.M. Advocate*, 1990 S.C.C.R. 182).

It is possible for the time bar to be extended retrospectively (*Advocate, H.M. v. M.*, 1986 S.C.C.R. 624) and as subs. (2) provides the accused's failure to appear at a first or preliminary diet, or a trial diet, immediately stops the operation of the time bar.

While the provisions of s.65 do not apply directly to private prosecutions by way of a Bill of Criminal Letters, in *G.M.C. v. Forsyth*, 1995 S.C.C.R. 553, the court had regard to the spirit of the statutory provisions in refusing a Bill presented 14 months after proceedings were deserted by the Crown.

The Note of Appeal in relation to an application for extension of the 12 month period should be on Form 8.1–A of the Act of Adjournal (Criminal Procedure Rules).

Subss. (4) to (7)

Unlike the 12 month time bar in solemn bail cases which runs from the date of the first appearance on the petition, calculation of the 80 and 110 day time limits begins from the date of full committal. The 80 and 110 day rules are vigorously enforced by the courts and applications for extension of either period will not succeed if failure to serve the indictment, or delay in starting the trial, was occasioned by a fault of the Crown. Failure to serve the indictment timeously in custody cases will not itself bar proceedings; the Crown can either apply to the court for an extension of the 80 day period or elect to liberate the accused as soon as possible thereafter and certainly before the 110th day. It is difficult to envisage circumstances which would merit extension of the 80 days to allow service of an indictment except perhaps illness of the accused, but see *Farrell v. H.M. Advocate*, 1985 S.L.T. 58.

It is well-decided that a period of remand beyond 80 days without an indictment being served will not *per se* preclude proceedings until the provisions of subs. (4)(b) become operative (see *Advocate, H.M. v. McCann* 1977 S.L.T. (Notes) 19, and *W.C. v. H.M. Advocate*, High Court of Justiciary, March 2, 1995, unreported, which is discussed in notes to s.51 above).

The 80 day limit is peremptory and while it may exceptionally be extended, it cannot be interrupted. By contrast, it is essential to grasp that the 110 day period can be interrupted either by a liberation of the accused as noted above, or by the imposition of a sentence of imprisonment: to count towards calculation of the 110 days, the period spent in custody has to be referable solely to the committal order giving rise to the indictment charges (*Advocate, H.M. v. Boyle*, 1972 S.L.T. (Notes) 16; *Harley v. H.M. Advocate*, 1970 S.L.T. (Notes) 6); and where two or more petitions are conjoined on an indictment, the dates of each committal have to be weighed separately in any calculation (*Ross v. H.M. Advocate*, 1990 S.C.C.R. 182). Similarly where the 110 days are interrupted by a term of imprisonment, they recommence at the prisoner's earliest release date and not by reference to the working practices of the prison authorities which, in the past, released prisoners whose liberation date fell during a weekend, on the Friday before (*Brown v. H.M. Advocate*, 1988 S.C.C.R. 577).

The fact that an indictment has been served after the lapse of 80 days does not vitiate the proceedings or undermine the validity of any indictment served after that time, though the period of detention in excess of the statutory 80 days may give rise to a civil claim against the Crown (see *McCluskey v. H.M. Advocate*, 1993 S.L.T. 897).

Extension of the 110 day period (subs. (7))

Applications for such extensions can only be considered by a High Court judge and, as subs. (7) indicates, can only be granted where no fault for the delay attaches to the Crown. See *Beattie v. H.M. Advocate*, 1995 S.C.C.R. 606 discussed above.

So in *Advocate, H.M. v. McTavish*, 1974 S.L.T. 246 a Crown motion for extension, to enable the completion of further forensic tests and to allow further treatment of the accused's mental illness, in circumstances where the Crown was admittedly able to proceed to trial upon the matters libelled in the petition was rejected. In *Advocate, H.M. v. Bickerstaff*, 1926 J.C. 65 where trial had been unable to proceed due to the accused's supervening insanity, a Full Bench held the delay as being attributable to the accused, not the Crown. Illness of the judge and of co-accused permitted three extensions (upheld on appeal) in *Young v. H.M. Advocate*, 1990 S.C.C.R. 315, the High Court itself admitting the accused to bail on a murder charge. Two extensions of time, once on the motion of a co-accused and once on Crown motion because of illness of a witness, were allowed in *Johnston (R.) v. H.M. Advocate*, 1993 S.C.C.R. 295. Perhaps the most contentious use of these provisions in which no fault was felt to lie with the Crown is found in *Gildea v. H.M. Advocate*, 1983 S.C.C.R. 144 where an extension was granted on account of a case scheduled earlier in the assize having taken longer than could reasonably be foreseen.

Appeals from decisions under subs. (5) or (6) proceed in terms of subs. (8) of the 1995 Act and Rule 8(1)–(3) in the 1996 Act of Adjournal. Form 8.1–B is used.

Service and lodging of indictment, etc.

66.—(1) When a sitting of the sheriff court or of the High Court has been appointed to be held for the trial of persons accused on indictment—

(a) where the trial diet is to be held in the sheriff court, the sheriff clerk; and

(b) where the trial diet is to be held in the High Court, the Clerk of Justiciary,

shall issue a warrant to officers of law to cite the accused, witnesses and jurors, in such form as may be prescribed by Act of Adjournal, or as nearly as may be in such form, and such warrant authenticated by the signature of such clerk, or a duly certified copy thereof, shall be a sufficient warrant for such citation.

(2) The execution of the citation against an accused, witness or juror shall be in such form as may be prescribed by Act of Adjournal, or as nearly as may be in such form.

(3) A witness may be cited by sending the citation to the witness by ordinary or registered post or by the recorded delivery service and a written execution in the form prescribed by Act of Adjournal or as nearly as may be in such form, purporting to be signed by the person who served such citation together with, where appropriate, the relevant post office receipt shall be sufficient evidence of such citation.

(4) The accused shall be served with a copy of the indictment and of the list of the names and addresses of the witnesses to be adduced by the prosecution.

(5) Except in a case to which section 76 of this Act applies, the prosecutor shall on or before the date of service of the indictment lodge the record copy of the indictment with the clerk of court before which the trial is to take place, together with a copy of the list of witnesses and a copy of the list of productions.

(6) Except where the indictment is served under section 76(1) of this Act, a notice shall be served on the accused with the indictment calling upon him to appear and answer to the indictment—

(a) where the case is to be tried in the sheriff court, at a first diet not less than 15 clear days after the service of the indictment and not less than 10 clear days before the trial diet; and

(b) at a trial diet (either in the High Court or in the sheriff court) not less than 29 clear days after the service of the indictment and notice.

(7) Service of the indictment, lists of witnesses and productions, and any notice or intimation to the accused, and the citation of witnesses, whether for precognition or trial, may be effected by any officer of law.

(8) No objection to the service of an indictment or to the citation of a witness shall be upheld on the ground that the officer who effected service or executed the citation was not at the time in possession of the warrant of citation, and it shall not be necessary to produce the execution of citation of an indictment.

(9) The citation of witnesses may be effected by any officer of law duly authorised; and in any proceedings, the evidence on oath of the officer shall, subject to subsection (10) below, be sufficient evidence of the execution of the citation.

(10) A court shall not issue a warrant to apprehend a witness who fails to appear at a diet to which he has been duly cited unless the court is satisfied that the witness received the citation or that its contents came to his knowledge.

(11) No objection to the competency of the officer who served the indictment to give evidence in respect of such service shall be upheld on the ground that his name is not included in the list of witnesses served on the accused.

(12) Any deletion or correction made before service on the record or service copy of an indictment shall be sufficiently authenticated by the initials of the person who has signed, or could by law have signed, the indictment.

(13) Any deletion or correction made on a service copy of an indictment, or on any notice of citation, postponement, adjournment or other notice required to be served on an accused shall be sufficiently authenticated by the initials of any procurator fiscal or of the person serving the same.

(14) Any deletion or correction made on any execution of citation or notice of other document requiring to be served shall be sufficiently authenticated by the initials of the person serving the same.

DEFINITIONS
"Clerk of Justiciary": s.307(1).
"diet": s.307(1).
"High Court": s.307(1).
"indictment": s.307(1).
"officer of law": s.307(1).
"prosecutor": s.307(1).
"sheriff clerk": s.307(1).
"witness": s.307(1).

GENERAL NOTE
The provisions relating to service of indictments, citations and proof of service were spread over ss.58, 69 to 73, 75 and 78 in the 1975 Act but are now brought together in s.66 of the 1995 Act.

Service of the indictment upon the accused is the event which dictates the timetable for the proceedings and, as subs. (6) indicates, must be effected not less than 29 clear days before the assigned trial diet in High Court cases, and not less than 15 days before the now mandatory first diet in sheriff and jury cases. It is difficult to see what practical purpose is achieved by the lodging of the record copy of the indictment with the clerk of court, as subs. (5) requires other than confirming the expectation of a forthcoming first diet or trial; this is still contingent upon lawful and timeous service of the indictment upon the accused. In dealing with the statutory predecessor of subs. (5), s.78(1) of the 1975 Act (which stipulated lodging of the record copy of the indictment not less than 10 clear days before trial), in *Advocate, H.M. v. Graham*, 1985 S.L.T. 498, the High Court in an appeal from a preliminary diet held that the provision was directory, not mandatory, in nature and that a failure by the Crown to comply with the section's provisions did not nullify the proceedings.

Provisions relating to service of indictments
Rule 2.2.–(2) of the 1996 Act of Adjournal specifies a number of acceptable methods of service of indictments including in subpara. (2)(d) a means of service for accused who have no proper domicile of citation, a useful provision to deal with the circumstances described in the notes to s.65(4) to (7) above or where an accused has never appeared on petition at all.

Subsection (8) enacts that it is unnecessary for the officer serving the indictment to have seen the warrant to cite mentioned in subs. (1). However, failure to serve an indictment is undoubtedly fatal to any proceedings on that indictment (*McAllister v. H.M. Advocate*, 1985 S.C.C.R. 36; 1985 S.L.T. 399) and cannot be cured by the accused's appearance (*Hester v. MacDonald*, 1961 S.C. 370). In such circumstances the warrant for committal of an accused would not fall and nor would any bail order granted earlier to the accused albeit, in custody cases, the provisions of s.65(4) against delay in proceedings would still have to be obtempered by the Crown (see *Jamieson v. H.M. Advocate*, 1990 S.C.C.R. 137; 1990 S.L.T. 845).

In *Bryson v. H.M. Advocate*, 1961 S.L.T. 289, an accused bailed to a domicile was subsequently remanded in custody for further charges, but the indictment was served at his original domicile not at the prison, a procedure which was upheld. Service of an indictment without giving the requisite 29 clear days notice stipulated in subs. (6) would not create a nullity and in the absence of an objection to service, which should be taken at a preliminary diet (or at the first diet in Sheriff and jury cases), trial could proceed: furthermore the *induciae* can be waived and it can be argued that this has occurred in the absence of a preliminary challenge (see *Advocate, H.M. v. McDonald*, 1984 S.L.T. 426).

Proof of service
An indictment must be served by an officer of law in the presence of a witness in one of the manners specified in Rule 2.2 of the 1996 Act of Adjournal, namely; (i) by personal service; (ii) by leaving it in the hands of a member of the accused's family, an inmate or employee at the domicile of citation; or (iii) by delivery through, or affixing to the door of the domicile. Similar provisions apply in situations where the accused has no domicile of citation in which event service can be effected at the address which the officer has reasonable cause to believe is occupied by the accused or by personal service.

The execution of service completed by the officer should comply with Form 2.6–A shown in the Appendix to the 1996 Act of Adjournal and be returned to the prosecutor: the execution will in all likelihood require to be produced to the court if the accused fails to appear at any diet before an arrest warrant will be granted. In *Welsh v. H.M. Advocate*, 1986 S.L.T. 664 a dispute arose as to whether the police could have served the indictment as claimed, since (it was alleged) the building had been demolished. The claim was refuted by the officers but the court noted that even if the accused's assertion had been correct, there would have been a failure to inform the court of a change of domicile.

It is competent in terms of subs. (8) and (11) for the officers effecting service of the indictment to be heard in evidence without their particulars being added to the indictment, a useful provision in the event of later additional charges for failure to appear at a lawful diet.

Witnesses for precognition or trial can be cited in conformity with subs. (3) but in the event of a failure to appear at trial, it may be difficult to persuade the court to grant an arrest warrant, as subs. (10) allows, unless an execution of personal service conforming to Form 2.6–E of the 1996 Act of Adjournal can be exhibited. However the same Act of Adjournal has introduced a new Form 8.2–D, a reply form to be returned by witnesses cited in indictment cases acknowledging citation and this should be taken into account in the event of non-appearance and, incidentally, may alert the Crown at an early stage to any potential shortcomings in citation (it must be doubted that precognition mentioned in subs. (7) can be regarded as "a diet" for the purposes of subs. (10); it is submitted that a warrant for arrest could not properly be sought following failure to appear for precognition, except precognition on oath. The relevant forms of petition for authority to precognosce on oath, are Forms 29.1–A and 29.1–B in the above Act of Adjournal).

For purposes of computation of time, note that in the case of the time limits specified in subs. (6), s.75 enacts that where the final day falls on a *dies non*, the effective date for calculation is the next working day.

Witnesses

67.—(1) The list of witnesses shall consist of the names of the witnesses together with an address at which they can be contacted for the purposes of precognition.

(2) It shall not be necessary to include in the list of witnesses the names of any witnesses to the declaration of the accused or the names of any witnesses to prove that an extract conviction applies to the accused, but witnesses may be examined in regard to these matters without previous notice.

(3) Any objection in respect of misnomer or misdescription of—
   (a) any person named in the indictment; or
   (b) any witness in the list of witnesses,
shall be intimated in writing to the court before which the trial is to take place, to the prosecutor and to any other accused, where the case is to be tried in the sheriff court, at or before the first diet and, where the case is to be tried in the High Court, not less than ten clear days before the trial diet; and, except on cause shown, no such objection shall be admitted at the trial diet unless so intimated.

(4) Where such intimation has been given or cause is shown and the court is satisfied that the accused making the objection has not been supplied with sufficient information to enable him to identify the person named in the indictment or to find such witness in sufficient time to precognosce him

before the trial, the court may grant such remedy by postponement, adjournment or otherwise as appears to it to be appropriate.

(5) Without prejudice to—

(a) any enactment or rule of law permitting the prosecutor to examine any witness not included in the list of witnesses; or

(b) subsection (6) below,

in any trial it shall be competent with the leave of the court for the prosecutor to examine any witness or to put in evidence any production not included in the lists lodged by him, provided that written notice, containing in the case of a witness his name and address as mentioned in subsection (1) above, has been given to the accused not less than two clear days before the day on which the jury is sworn to try the case.

(6) It shall be competent for the prosecutor to examine any witness or put in evidence any production included in any list or notice lodged by the accused, and it shall be competent for an accused to examine any witness or put in evidence any production included in any list or notice lodged by the prosecutor or by a co-accused.

DEFINITIONS

"diet": s.307(1).
"High Court": s.307(1).
"indictment": s.307(1).
"prosecutor": s.307(1).
"witness": s.307(1).

GENERAL NOTE

Section 67 anticipates that the identity and particulars of most witnesses will be known to the Crown sufficiently early for inclusion in the indictment served upon the accused. Experience suggests otherwise; in custody cases particularly, increasing reliance has been placed upon the use of the provisions of s.81 of the 1975 Act both for adding witnesses and productions to the indictment. Those provisions are now re-enacted as s.67(5) of the 1995 Act.

The introduction of first diets in sheriff and jury cases and optional preliminary diets in High Court cases now means that any objection to inadequate identification, or misdescription of witnesses must be notified in writing to the prosecutor and co-accused, (a) at or prior to the first diet, or (b) 10 days before the High Court trial diet. Section 75 provides that where the last day of the period falls on a *dies non*, the effective date for calculation purposes will be the next working day (this provision is quite separate from the matters which can be raised by way of provisional diet in the High Court in terms of s.72(1) and (6)). Failure to give such notice timeously will have to be justified to the court at the trial diet but it has to be said that it would be difficult for a court to refuse an objection under subs. (4), even at that late stage, in view of the potential for prejudice to an accused. The remedy is adjournment of the trial or postponement if necessary in the interests of justice (*Vetters v. H.M. Advocate*, 1944 J.C. 138), but the court might well have to consider extending the time-limits upon proceedings dictated by s.65 and, *in extremis*, consider whether the Crown should be held at fault (see s.65(3) and (7) above).

Subs. (5)

As was noted above, the provisions of s.81 in regard to late intimation of witnesses and productions have been preserved in s.67(5) of the 1995 Act: provided due notice has been given to the accused, such evidence can be added to the indictment with leave of the court. However while an error in describing a witness in a s.67 notice is probably capable of being remedied by amendment in the course of proceedings, given the grounds of amendment in s.96 of the Act, a misdescription of a production either in the list of productions or, later, in a s.67 notice, cannot be so remedied. In *Advocate, H.M. v. Swift*, 1983 S.C.C.R. 204 an error in the original list of productions was corrected in a s.81 notice which itself misdescribed the production. The sheriff held the terms of s.81 to be peremptory and held evidence arising from the production, a tape, to be inadmissible. It is observed that it would still be open to parties to have such evidence admitted by way of a Minute of Agreement in the course of the trial if they were so minded.

Subsection (5)(a) entitles the prosecutor to examine certain witnesses without having given intimation to the accused. The most obvious categories of witnesses covered by this concession are co-accused whose pleas have been accepted prior to, or during trial, or even by way of an accelerated plea following service of a common indictment (see *Monaghan v. H.M. Advocate*,

1984 S.L.T. 262), witnesses cited by any of the accused, witnesses led in replication in accordance with s.269 of the 1995 Act, police officers proving service of an indictment (s.66(11)), and the officials specified in subs. (2) above.

Productions

68.—(1) The list of productions shall include the record, made under section 37 of this Act (incorporating any rectification authorised under section 38(1) of this Act), of proceedings at the examination of the accused.

(2) The accused shall be entitled to see the productions according to the existing law and practice in the office of the sheriff clerk of the district in which the court of the trial diet is situated or, where the trial diet is to be in the High Court in Edinburgh, in the Justiciary Office.

(3) Where a person who has examined a production is adduced to give evidence with regard to it and the production has been lodged at least eight days before the trial diet, it shall not be necessary to prove—

(a) that the production was received by him in the condition in which it was taken possession of by the procurator fiscal or the police and returned by him after his examination of it to the procurator fiscal or the police; or

(b) that the production examined by him is that taken possession of by the procurator fiscal or the police,

unless the accused, at least four days before the trial diet, gives in accordance with subsection (4) below written notice that he does not admit that the production was received or returned as aforesaid or, as the case may be, that it is that taken possession of as aforesaid.

(4) The notice mentioned in subsection (3) above shall be given—

(a) where the accused is cited to the High Court for the trial diet, to the Crown Agent; and

(b) where he is cited to the sheriff court for the trial diet, to the procurator fiscal.

DEFINITIONS
"diet": s.307(1).
"High Court": s.307(1).
"procurator fiscal": s.307(1).
"sheriff clerk": s.307(1).

GENERAL NOTE
The list of productions must include the judicial examination (if any) and by implication the executions of service, to show compliance by the Crown with the terms of s.37(6) and (10). In *Advocate, H.M. v. Cafferty*, 1984 S.C.C.R. 444, the terms of s.78(2), the identical provision in the 1975 Act were held to be mandatory and when objection was taken to the competency of the proceedings during the trial, the sheriff deserted the diet *pro loco et tempore*, reserving the right of the Crown to re-raise proceedings. Failure by the Crown to lodge the transcript of judicial examination is a matter which should be raised timeously at the first diet in sheriff and jury cases or by way of a preliminary diet in cases indicted before the High Court (the problems associated with the late lodging or misdescription of productions are discussed in the notes to s.67 above).

Subsection (3) contains presumptions that, (i) productions examined after their recovery by the police or lodging with the procurator fiscal were produced to the witness in the same condition as when recovered or lodged and (ii) that the articles produced to the witness were those seized by the police or the procurator fiscal. The presumption only applies to productions lodged not less than eight days prior to trial. Notice of a challenge to the presumption must be served in accordance with subs. (4) not less than four days before the trial.

Note that in *Livingston v. H.M. Advocate*, 1991 S.C.C.R. 350 examination of productions and their comparison against the accused's fingerprint forms, which necessitated a motion for the removal of articles from the court during the course of a trial for that purpose, was upheld on appeal. This was viewed as a matter within the discretion of the trial judge, albeit an exceptional procedure. In that case the Lord Justice General (at 356C) echoed the view expressed in *William Turner Davies, Petr.*, 1973 S.L.T. (Notes) 36 by the Lord Justice Clerk at p.37, that after service of an indictment;

"the productions... are lodged with the sheriff clerk who has a duty to retain them in his custody and make them available at the trial. At that stage, the only body with the authority to allow the productions to be inspected and examined is the court, and the proper procedure is to make application to the court thereanent. It is then for the court to decide whether the application should be granted or refused."

Davies had petitioned the *nobile officium* for authority for a defence expert to examine gloves lodged by the Crown as productions before the trial began, but the same principles apply both prior to, and during, trial. The court has to weigh the potential prejudice to the accused in the preparation and presentation of his case against the public interest in the effective prosecution of crime. See also *MacNeil v. H.M. Advocate*, 1986 S.C.C.R. 288, where productions listed in the indictment had not been lodged it was held that objection should have been taken before the jury was sworn and the appropriate remedy in the event of prejudice was an adjournment.

The procedures regulating the access of jurors to productions are discussed in the notes to s.99 below.

Notice of previous convictions

69.—(1) No mention shall be made in the indictment of previous convictions, nor shall extracts of previous convictions be included in the list of productions annexed to the indictment.

(2) If the prosecutor intends to place before the court any previous conviction, he shall cause to be served on the accused along with the indictment a notice in the form set out in an Act of Adjournal or as nearly as may be in such form, and any conviction specified in the notice shall be held to apply to the accused unless he gives, in accordance with subsection (3) below, written intimation objecting to such conviction on the ground that it does not apply to him or is otherwise inadmissible.

(3) Intimation objecting to a conviction under subsection (2) above shall be given—

(a) where the accused is cited to the High Court for the trial diet, to the Crown Agent; or

(b) where the accused is cited to the sheriff court for the trial diet, to the procurator fiscal,

at least five clear days before the first day of the sitting in which the trial diet is to be held.

(4) Where notice is given by the accused under section 76 of this Act of his intention to plead guilty and the prosecutor intends to place before the court any previous conviction, he shall cause to be served on the accused along with the indictment a notice in the form set out in an Act of Adjournal or as nearly as may be in such form.

(5) Where the accused pleads guilty at any diet, no objection to any conviction of which notice has been served on him under this section shall be entertained unless he has, at least two clear days before the diet, given intimation to the procurator fiscal of the district to the court of which the accused is cited for the diet.

DEFINITIONS
"extract of previous conviction": s.307(1).
"indictment": s.307(1).
"prosecutor": s.307(1).

GENERAL NOTE
The Notice of Previous Convictions which the Crown may place before the court in the event of conviction of the accused should conform to Form 8.3 in the 1996 Act of Adjournal.

Broadly these provisions repeat those found in s.68 of the 1975 Act, but subs. (5) now appears as a distinct (and clearer) requirement than heretofore. At any diet at which the accused pleads guilty, apart from the trial diet itself where subs. (3) demands five clear days' notice of any disputed conviction, the accused must give not less than two clear days' notice of any conviction libelled which he disputes: accordingly subs. (5) is relevant to the circumstances of accelerated pleas tendered under s.76 (the successor to s.102 of the 1975 Act), and to pleas tendered at any first diet or preliminary diet (see ss.71 and 72 of the 1995 Act).

Previous convictions which are under appeal should not be libelled (*McCall v. Mitchell* (1911) 6 Adam 303) and no previous conviction omitted from the Notice should be taken into account by the court considering sentence, unless it is disclosed in a social enquiry or other report before the court (*Sharp v. Stevenson* 1948 S.L.T. (Notes) 79).

Although the provisions of subs. (1) appear to be absolute, they must be read in conjunction with s.101(2) of the 1995 Act which permits the leading of evidence of an accused's previous convictions where it is a necessary element of proof of the substantive charge.

The anomalous position of previous convictions libelled against bodies corporate and any named officer in the indictment against that body is discussed in the notes to s.70 below.

Proceedings against bodies corporate

70.—(1) This section applies to proceedings on indictment against a body corporate.

(2) The indictment may be served by delivery of a copy of the indictment together with notice to appear at the registered office or, if there is no registered office or the registered office is not in the United Kingdom, at the principal place of business in the United Kingdom of the body corporate.

(3) Where a letter containing a copy of the indictment has been sent by registered post or by the recorded delivery service to the registered office or principal place of business of the body corporate, an acknowledgement or certificate of the delivery of the letter issued by the Post Office shall be sufficient evidence of the delivery of the letter at the registered office or place of business on the day specified in such acknowledgement or certificate.

(4) A body corporate may, for the purpose of—

(a) stating objections to the competency or relevancy of the indictment or proceedings; or

(b) tendering a plea of guilty or not guilty; or

(c) making a statement in mitigation of sentence,

appear by a representative of the body corporate.

(5) Where at the trial diet the body corporate does not appear as mentioned in subsection (4) above, or by counsel or a solicitor, the court shall, on the motion of the prosecutor, if it is satisfied that subsection (2) above has been complied with, proceed to hear and dispose of the case in the absence of the body corporate.

(6) Where a body corporate is sentenced to a fine, the fine may be recovered in like manner in all respects as if a copy of the sentence certified by the clerk of the court were an extract decree of the Court of Session for the payment of the amount of the fine by the body corporate to the Queen's and Lord Treasurer's Remembrancer.

(7) Nothing in section 77 of this Act shall require a plea tendered by or on behalf of a body corporate to be signed.

(8) In this section, "representative", in relation to a body corporate, means an officer or employee of the body corporate duly appointed by it for the purpose of the proceedings; and a statement in writing purporting to be signed by the managing director of, or by any person having or being one of the persons having the management of the affairs of the body corporate, to the effect that the person named in the statement has been appointed the representative of the body corporate for the purpose of any proceedings to which this section applies shall be sufficient evidence of such appointment.

DEFINITIONS
"diet": s.307(1).
"fine": s.307(1).
"indictment": s.307(1).
"prosecutor": s.307(1).
"representative": s.70(8).

GENERAL NOTE
Provisions in s.70 refer to prosecution on indictment. Section 143 of the Act deals with summary prosecutions of partnerships, trustees in their corporate capacity and companies. A number of statutory provisions, namely the Insurance Companies Act 1982 (c.50), s.92(4), the Companies Act, 1985 (c.6), s.734(4), the Financial Services Act 1986 (c.60), s.203(4), the Banking Act 1987 (c.22), s.98(4) and the Companies Act 1989 (c.40), ss.44(4) and 91(4) extended the terms of s.74 of the 1975 Act to unincorporated bodies. In the absence of contrary provisions, s.70 of the 1995 Act is similarly extended.

Once the court is satisfied that an indictment has been lawfully served upon a limited company or incorporation, it is entitled, on the motion of the prosecutor, to proceed to consider the evidence at a trial diet and dispose of the case at that time even if the body is unrepresented (it seems implicit from the reference to "the trial diet" in subs. (5) that a failure to appear at any earlier diet has to be treated as a plea of not guilty). If the body prosecuted does elect to make an appearance at any diet, this can be made on its behalf by an authorised representative and need not be by a solicitor or counsel.

The prosecutor may opt to prosecute the corporate body alone, proceed against a responsible officer of the company, or both. In the absence of specific statutory provision in regard to the previous convictions of bodies corporate, the general rules expressed in ss.69 and 101(7) would appear to apply. However if proceedings are taken solely against an officer of the company as its responsible representative, it would surely be inequitable to libel against him previous convictions incurred by the company.

Subsection (6) enacts that fines imposed upon bodies corporate are recoverable by civil diligence.

Pre-trial proceedings

First diet

71.—(1) At a first diet the court shall, so far as is reasonably practicable, ascertain whether the case is likely to proceed to trial on the date assigned as the trial diet and, in particular—

(a) the state of preparation of the prosecutor and of the accused with respect to their cases; and

(b) the extent to which the prosecutor and the accused have complied with the duty under section 257(1) of this Act.

(2) In addition to the matters mentioned in subsection (1) above the court shall, at a first diet, consider any matter mentioned in any of paragraphs (a) to (d) of section 72(1) of this Act of which a party has, not less than two clear days before the first diet, given notice to the court and to the other parties.

(3) At a first diet the court may ask the prosecutor and the accused any question in connection with any matter which it is required to ascertain or consider under subsection (1) or (2) above.

(4) The accused shall attend a first diet of which he has been given notice and the court may, if he fails to do so, grant a warrant to apprehend him.

(5) A first diet may proceed notwithstanding the absence of the accused.

(6) The accused shall, at the first diet, be required to state how he pleads to the indictment, and section 77 of this Act shall apply where he tenders a plea of guilty.

(7) Where at a first diet the court concludes that the case is unlikely to proceed to trial on the date assigned for the trial diet, the court—

(a) shall, unless having regard to previous proceedings in the case it considers it inappropriate to do so, postpone the trial diet; and

(b) may fix a further first diet.

(8) Subject to subsection (7) above, the court may, if it considers it appropriate to do so, adjourn a first diet.

(9) In this section "the court" means the sheriff court.

DEFINITIONS
"court": subs. (9).
"prosecutor": s.307(1).

GENERAL NOTE

Mandatory first diets for sheriff and jury cases were introduced by s.13 of the Criminal Justice (Scotland) Act 1995 (c.20). Separate provision is made for preliminary diets as an optional procedure in High Court cases.

Mandatory first diets require to be held not less than 15 clear days after service of the indictment upon the accused, and not less than 10 clear days before trial (s.66(6)(a)) at which time the court is obliged to ascertain the state of readiness of all parties for the pending trial and the extent of evidence capable of being agreed by them. Section 71 has a dual purpose; first to reduce the incidence of unforeseen adjournments or cancellations of trial (a reform aided by the right of the Crown to seek a warrant under subs. (4) if the accused is absent without authority); secondly, to restrict the length and expense of trials, and inconvenience to witnesses, by focusing the parties' attention at an early stage upon the duty to seek agreement of uncontentious evidence. Note that s.78(3)(b) anticipates that notices of incrimination and special defences will be lodged at or prior to the first diet.

The powers and duties of the sheriff in conducting a first diet are identical to those given to the High Court for the optional preliminary diets introduced in s.72 of the Act.

It will be noted that the court has a discretion to grant a warrant for the accused's arrest should he fail to appear, but subs. (5) also permits the diet to proceed in his absence. Obviously a first diet can continue against an accused notwithstanding the absence of co-accused, but matters become more problematical when the provisions of subs. (6) are considered. Is it intended that all accused are to tender pleas at the conclusion of the hearing or that pleas only be recorded from the accused who are present in court? The only clue may be offered by the references in subs. (6) to s.77 which enacts that an accused, other than a body corporate, shall tender a guilty plea by subscribing its terms in the record, and the use of the word "states" in the subsection both which tend to suggest that in the absence of an accused the court has two options; either to issue a warrant or continue the case in terms of subs. (7) to a further first diet against the absent accused or all accused.

In this context it is perhaps curious that the provisions against delay found in s.65 restate the familiar requirement that the calculation of the statutory time-bars is solely by reference to the commencement of the trial (s.65(9)), and pays no heed to the timing of a first, or a preliminary, diet. No doubt delay occasioned by the need to hold further first diets could be a factor the courts might address when it is necessary to consider extension of statutory time-bars: nonetheless great care will have to be taken to ensure that any postponements under subs. (7), or further first diets (which must still occur at least 10 clear days before trial), do not prejudice compliance with the time constraints imposed in s.65. By contrast, s.72(4), in allowing postponement of trial diets after a preliminary diet in High Court cases, enacts that any delay produced shall not count towards "any time-limit".

Mandatory first diets (then called pleading diets) were abolished by s.12 of the Criminal Justice (Scotland) Act 1980 (c.62) when it was perceived that they had been reduced to mere formal appearances. The new first diets are essential elements in retaining public confidence in the courts and it is to be hoped that the Bench exercises its powers in subs. (1) to (3) vigorously. Note however that the court can apply no *compulsitor* upon parties who do not enter into the spirit of s.258(1) and that that provision does not apply to accused who are unrepresented. It is debatable how far the court can venture in its enquiries under s.71 or s.72 where an accused is not legally represented.

Appeal procedures

Appeals arising from decisions of the court at first diets or preliminary diets are considered by the High Court under s.74 of the Act: in the event of an appeal, part, or all of the postponement period can be discounted by the High Court from any time bar calculation and, by implication, this can be done with retrospective effect. Appeals must be raised within two days upon Form 9.12 given in the Act of Adjournal and, if need be, abandoned by Form 9.17. Note that decisions to adjourn the first, or preliminary, diet or to postpone the trial diet cannot be appealed under s.74 (see subs. (2)(a)) but that such decisions can be challenged by an accused in an appeal against conviction or sentence (s.106) and by the Lord Advocate in an appeal against an unduly lenient sentence (s.108).

Preliminary diet: notice

72.—(1) Subject to subsections (4) and (5) below, where a party to a case which is to be tried in the High Court within the appropriate period gives written notice to the court and to the other parties—

    (a) that he intends to raise—

(i) a matter relating to the competency or relevancy of the indictment; or

(ii) an objection to the validity of the citation against him, on the ground of any discrepancy between the record copy of the indictment and the copy served on him, or on account of any error or deficiency in such service copy or in the notice of citation;

(b) that he intends—

(i) to submit a plea in bar of trial;

(ii) to apply for separation or conjunction of charges or trials;

(iii) to raise a preliminary objection under section 255 of this Act; or

(iv) to make an application under section 278(2) of this Act;

(c) that there are documents the truth of the contents of which ought to be admitted, or that there is any other matter which in his view ought to be agreed;

(d) that there is some point, as regards any matter not mentioned in paragraph (a) to (c) above, which could in his opinion be resolved with advantage before the trial and that he therefore applies for a diet to be held before the trial diet,

the court shall in a case to which paragraph (a) above applies, and in any other case may, order that there be a diet before the trial diet, and a diet ordered under this subsection is in this Act referred to as a "preliminary diet".

(2) A party giving notice under subsection (1) above shall specify in the notice the matter or, as the case may be, the grounds of submission or the point to which the notice relates.

(3) The fact that a preliminary diet has been ordered on a particular notice under subsection (1) above shall not preclude the court's consideration at that diet of any other such notice as is mentioned in that subsection, which has been intimated to the court and to the other parties at least 24 hours before that diet.

(4) Subject to subsection (5) below, the court may on ordering a preliminary diet postpone the trial diet for a period not exceeding 21 days; and any such postponement (including postponement for a period which by virtue of the said subsection (5) exceeds 21 days) shall not count towards any time limit applying in respect of the case.

(5) Any period mentioned in subsection (4) above may be extended by the High Court in respect of the case.

(6) In subsection (1) above, "appropriate period" means as regards notice—

(a) under paragraph (a) of that subsection, the period of 15 clear days after service of the indictment;

(b) under paragraph (b) of that subsection, the period from service of the indictment to 10 clear days before the trial diet; and

(c) under paragraph (c) or (d) of that subsection, the period from service of the indictment to the trial diet.

<small>DEFINITIONS</small>
"High Court": s.307(1).
"indictment": s.307(1).

<small>GENERAL NOTE</small>
Unlike first diets in sheriff and jury cases, preliminary diets which now apply only to High Court cases are not compulsory in any case; preliminary diets are initiated by service of a notice in the manner specified in Chap. 9 of the 1996 Act of Adjournal on Form 9.1. Subsection (6) provides several different timescales to be met, under reference to the interval from service of the indictment to the days leading to the trial. Yet the reasons for these differing time-limits are unclear particularly when it is seen that subs. (3) allows any other form of notice to be considered also on 24 hours' notice to other parties.

Note that unlike the Sheriff court procedure, where a preliminary diet is fixed the court can, at that diet, both order postponement of the trial diet up to 21 days (beyond the date when the indictment should otherwise call), and deduct that period from computation of any statutory time-limit. Subsection (5) suggests that the same court as distinct from the Court of Appeal can further extend the period of postponement as necessary.

Subsection (1)(a) stipulates that a preliminary diet must be held to consider any issue of competency or relevancy or want of proper citation, but that any other written motion for such a diet to consider matters arising from subs. (1)(b), (c) or (d) is at the discretion of the court. Section 74 of the Act regulates appeal procedures both from first diets in the sheriff court and preliminary diets in the High Court. It is not clear however whether a decision by a High Court judge *not* to order a preliminary diet can be appealed by this route. Section 74(1) refers to appeal against "a decision at a first diet or a preliminary diet", but if there has been a decision by the court not to hold a preliminary diet then it would seem that appeal would be to the *nobile officium* (refer also to the notes "Appeal Procedures" in s.71 above).

Subsection (1)(b)(iv) refers to the striking out of parts of a judicial transcript. Plainly there will be matters under this head which are only capable of a decision on fairness and admissibility when set in the context of evidence at a trial in which situation s.278 of the Act applies (see too the discussion in notes to s.36 above): however it would be open to the court conducting a preliminary diet to consider what relationship or similarity there was between the charges libelled in the petition and the indictment charges and, accordingly the propriety of excluding all, or part of the judicial examination transcript from the indictment.

Potentially the right of parties to identify to the court under subs. (1)(c) documents which it is felt should be agreed, or evidence of formal facts which are not in dispute, could help diminish the length of trials and, perhaps, focus the issues before the court more effectively. Of course the court is not obliged to fix a diet in these circumstances and there is no duty upon other parties to agree such evidence at all. Preliminary diets were not made mandatory in the High Court largely because of the logistical problems involved in processing and administering them in the limited time before trial.

Section 73 below enacts that at the conclusion of a preliminary diet an accused is called upon to plead; this assumes that objections to competency or relevancy have been repelled.

In the event of postponement, s.82 provides that the original warrant of committal shall remain in force.

Preliminary diet: procedure

73.—(1) Where a preliminary diet is ordered, subject to subsection (2) below, the accused shall attend it, and he shall be required at the conclusion of the diet to state how he pleads to the indictment.

(2) The court may permit the diet to proceed notwithstanding the absence of an accused.

(3) At a preliminary diet the court shall, in addition to disposing of any matter specified in a notice given under subsection (1) of section 72 of this Act or referred to in subsection (3) of that section, ascertain, so far as is reasonably practicable, whether the case is likely to proceed to trial on the date assigned as the trial diet and, in particular—

    (a) the state of preparation of the prosecutor and of the accused with respect to their cases; and

    (b) the extent to which the prosecutor and the accused have complied with the duty under section 257(1) of this Act.

(4) At a preliminary diet the court may ask the prosecutor and the accused any question in connection with any matter specified in a notice under subsection (1) of the said section 72 or referred to in subsection (3) of that section or which it is required to ascertain under subsection (3) above.

(5) Where at a preliminary diet the court concludes that the case is unlikely to proceed to trial on the date assigned for the trial diet, the court—

    (a) shall, unless having regard to previous proceedings in the case it considers it inappropriate to do so, postpone the trial diet; and

    (b) may fix a further preliminary diet.

(6) Subject to subsection (5) above, the court may, if it considers it appropriate to do so, adjourn a preliminary diet.

(7) Where an objection is taken to the relevancy of the indictment under subsection (1)(a)(i) of the said section 72, the clerk of court shall minute whether the objection is sustained or repelled and sign the minute.

(8) In subsection (1) above, the reference to the accused shall, without prejudice to section 6(c) of the Interpretation Act 1978, in any case where there is more than one accused include a reference to all of them.

<small>DEFINITIONS</small>
  "indictment": s.307(1).
  "prosecutor": s.307(1).

<small>GENERAL NOTE</small>
  This section sets out the options available to the court in dealing with preliminary diets. As has been noted, subs. (1) proceeds on the basis that pleas to competency or relevancy have been repelled and that the diet has not simply been adjourned. In dealing with a matter raised as a preliminary diet the court then has the same powers as a sheriff exercises under s.71; the court has then to ascertain the readiness of the parties and the extent of evidence which the parties feel to be capable of agreement.
  Subsection (2) permits preliminary diets to proceed in the absence of an accused, but as was noted in the discussion of s.71 it is not clear whether this provision is to enable a diet to proceed to its trial diet despite the absence of one, or all, accused (in which case pleas in accordance with subs. (1) would have to be tendered in absence) or simply to enable a diet to proceed in respect of those accused present at the time. It seems to be that in the case of High Court proceedings the first interpretation is to be preferred; the diets are not compulsory (unlike sheriff solemn first diets), they can be called on relatively short notice making intimation on an accused personally a problem, and may have to be heard in the High Court in Edinburgh rather than within the sheriffdom where the assize is due to convene for the trial diet. Certainly it was recognised that scheduling preliminary diets in all High Court cases would pose logistical difficulties of a much greater sort than arise in sheriff solemn cases. In any event if the court deemed it necessary that all accused should be present at the preliminary diet, subs. (b) would allow the fixing of a further diet for that purpose, or simply an adjournment, procedures which cannot be appealed under s.74(2).
  It is important to note that in contrast to the similar sheriff court procedures, s.72(4) entitles the High Court to postpone a trial diet when ordering that a preliminary diet be fixed and discount all, or part, of the time thereafter from time-bar calculations.
  The reference in subs. (3) to fulfilling the demands of s.258(1) of the Act (duty to seek agreement of evidence) does not apply to accused who are unrepresented (see s.258(2)).
  Incidental procedural matters are regulated by Rule 9.10 in the 1996 Act of Adjournal and the whole proceedings must be recorded or noted in shorthand in accordance with s.93 of the Act.

Appeals in connection with preliminary diets

74.—(1) Without prejudice to—
  (a) any right of appeal under section 106 or 108 of this Act; and
  (b) section 131 of this Act,
and subject to subsection (2) below, a party may with the leave of the court of first instance (granted either on the motion of the party or *ex proprio motu*) in accordance with such procedure as may be prescribed by Act of Adjournal, appeal to the High Court against a decision at a first diet or a preliminary diet.
  (2) An appeal under subsection (1) above—
  (a) may not be taken against a decision to adjourn the first or, as the case may be, preliminary diet or to postpone the trial diet;
  (b) must be taken not later than 2 days after the decision.
  (3) Where an appeal is taken under subsection (1) above, the High Court may postpone the trial diet for such period as appears to it to be appropriate and may, if it thinks fit, direct that such period (or some part of it) shall not count towards any time limit applying in respect of the case.
  (4) In disposing of an appeal under subsection (1) above the High Court—
  (a) may affirm the decision of the court of first instance or may remit the case to it with such directions in the matter as it thinks fit; and

(b) where the court of first instance has dismissed the indictment or any part of it, may reverse that decision and direct that the court of first instance fix a trial diet, if it has not already fixed one as regards so much of the indictment as it has not dismissed.

DEFINITIONS
"first diet": s.71(1).
"High Court": s.307(1).
"preliminary diet": s.72(1).

GENERAL NOTE
Refer to the discussion "*Appeal procedures*" in the notes to s.71 above. Parties can competently appeal decisions at a first diet or preliminary diet *ex proprio motu*, or with leave of the court. Subsection (4)(b) refers to the appellate court's power to fix a trial diet if this has not been done; this provision would appear to deal with situations where an indictment has been dismissed on grounds of competency or relevancy and, accordingly, no trial diet fixed.

Computation of certain periods

75. Where the last day of any period mentioned in section 66(6), 67(3), 72 or 74 of this Act falls on a Saturday, Sunday or court holiday, such period shall extend to and include the next day which is not a Saturday, Sunday or court holiday.

GENERAL NOTE
The timescales specified in s.66(6) refer both to the dates within which a first diet must occur in the Sheriff court and the time lapse from service of an indictment until trial; in either event the due date is extended to the next working day. A similar provision covers the time-limit for service of a notice objecting to the description of witnesses in that indictment. The section's reference to s.72 is understandable in that subs. (6) defines "the appropriate period" for notice of the matters to be raised at a preliminary diet. It will be appreciated that s.75's terms do not interfere in any way with the provisions in s.65 against delay.

Plea of guilty

Procedure where accused desires to plead guilty

76.—(1) Where an accused intimates in writing to the Crown Agent that he intends to plead guilty and desires to have his case disposed of at once, the accused may be served with an indictment (unless one has already been served) and a notice to appear at a diet of the appropriate court not less than four clear days after the date of the notice; and it shall not be necessary to lodge or give notice of any list of witnesses or productions.

(2) In subsection (1) above, "appropriate court" means—

(a) in a case where at the time of the intimation mentioned in that subsection an indictment had not been served, either the High Court or the sheriff court; and

(b) in any other case, the court specified in the notice served under section 66(6) of this Act on the accused.

(3) If at any such diet the accused pleads not guilty to the charge or pleads guilty only to a part of the charge, and the prosecutor declines to accept such restricted plea, the diet shall be deserted *pro loco et tempore* and thereafter the cause may proceed in accordance with the other provisions of this Part of this Act; except that in a case mentioned in paragraph (b) of subsection (2) above the court may postpone the trial diet and the period of such postponement shall not count towards any time limit applying in respect of the case.

DEFINITIONS
"High Court": s.307(1).
"indictment": s.307(1).
"witnesses": s.307(1).

GENERAL NOTE

Section 76 re-enacts the familiar accelerated plea provisions of s.102 of the 1975 Act. Although the statute requires written intimation of a proposed plea by the accused to the Crown agent, it is customary for the letter intimating the terms of the plea to be sent to the procurator fiscal at whose instance the petition charges were raised. It is of course competent to serve an indictment without any prior petition but in that event it will be difficult to negotiate a satisfactory plea practically.

On receipt of a letter, the procurator fiscal is under a duty to comply with the Procurator Fiscal Service's Book of Regulations and deliver the letter along with a report outlining his views on its merits, or otherwise, to the Crown agent. While the section stipulates that the letter be sent to the Crown agent, the Crown as a matter of course indicate the date of its receipt by the procurator fiscal to the court when the plea of guilt is recorded, since this may have a bearing upon any sentence; this is particularly pertinent now given the terms of s.196 of the Act which allows courts a discretion to consider as a sentencing parameter, the point in proceedings at which a plea was tendered.

It will be observed that a plea tendered prior to service of any indictment leaves the issue open as to whether the plea should be heard before a sheriff or in the High Court (subs. (2)(a)) and the choice of forum may be a material factor in the plea tendered; by contrast, once an indictment has been served, subs. (2)(b) enacts that a s.76 letter will only have the effect of accelerating the hearing before that court. Rule 10.1–(2) of the 1996 Act of Adjournal provides that cases set down for trial in the High Court, and by necessary inference, charges in which the High Court has exclusive jurisdiction—treason, murder and rape, can be called for disposal in the High Court sitting in Edinburgh instead of at the sitting originally scheduled elsewhere in Scotland.

If the plea offered by the accused is acceptable to the Crown, a notice conforming to the style of Form 10.1–A where no indictment has yet been served, or Form 10.1–B, when an indictment has still to be served, will accompany the indictment now served upon the accused. Cases in which a s.76 plea is offered prior to service of an indictment (see subs. (2)(a)) will ordinarily proceed upon an edited indictment which does not include lists of productions and witnesses; this is not an absolute requirement, but obviously economises on Crown resources. Cases which have simply been brought forward after service of the indictment competently proceed on the full indictment previously served on the accused.

Subsection (3) works to the benefit of the Crown; if, at the accelerated diet the accused reneges on his plea, the court can postpone the trial diet and discount the period of the postponement in any calculation of statutory time-bars. This concession only applies to cases proceeding under subs. (2)(b), *i.e.* where an accelerated plea has been offered after service of the indictment. Note however that Rule 10.1–(3) of the 1996 Act of Adjournal only permits such a postponement when all of the accused have tendered s.76 notices and all are present at the accelerated diet and the court grants the postponement in response to a motion made at that time. It is difficult to envisage practical instances in which these circumstances would apply: it may arise where one (or more) accused recants on a "package" deal involving a number of the accused, thus rendering the totality unacceptable to the Crown. Ordinarily the Crown would probably accept pleas from other accused and elect to proceed to trial later against the recalcitrant accused and a subs. (3) motion for postponement could then be made quite properly.

The Induciae

This section proceeds upon an *induciae* between service of the edited form of indictment, and its calling, of four clear days. The *induciae* can be waived by the accused but in *McKnight v. H.M. Advocate*, 1991 S.C.C.R. 751 where the accused pleaded to an indictment served upon him 10 minutes beforehand, the Court of Appeal doubted the wisdom of proceeding in such a summary fashion and indicated that the Crown should be hesitant to accept pleas tendered in such circumstances. It may be said too that with the current re-evaluation by the Appeal Court of the relationship between criminal practitioners and clients (see, for example, *Anderson v. H.M. Advocate*, 1996 S.L.T. 155), it could be regarded as imprudent to advise clients to waive the four day *induciae*.

Withdrawal of the Plea

A plea tendered at the accelerated diet can be withdrawn competently at a later diet, but the court would have to be satisfied that the accused had substantially misunderstood his position and had been prejudiced by that misunderstanding. See *Healy v. H.M. Advocate*, 1990 S.C.C.R. 110, where the indictment had been read over to the accused by the sheriff at the first diet and accepted by the accused who sought to withdraw her plea before a different sheriff at the diet of deferred sentence; and *Paul v. H.M. Advocate*, (1914) 7 Adam 343 where the accused sought to change his plea following upon a remit to the High Court for sentence.

Plea of guilty

77.—(1) Where at any diet the accused tenders a plea of guilty to the indictment or any part thereof he shall do so in open court and, subject to section 70(7) of this Act, shall, if he is able to do so, sign a written copy of the plea; and the judge shall countersign such copy.

(2) Where the plea is to part only of the charge and the prosecutor does not accept the plea, such non-acceptance shall be recorded.

(3) Where an accused charged on indictment with any offence tenders a plea of guilty to any other offence of which he could competently be found guilty on the trial of the indictment, and that plea is accepted by the prosecutor, it shall be competent to convict the accused of the offence to which he has so pled guilty and to sentence him accordingly.

DEFINITIONS
"diet": s.307(1).
"indictment": s.307(1).
"prosecutor": s.307(1).

GENERAL NOTE
This section substantially re-enacts the provisions of s.103 of the 1975 Act. Obviously if for some reason the accused is unable to subscribe his plea, the court is under an additional responsibility to ensure that the plea as recorded reflects his intention. Thereafter the judge is required to countersign the plea on the same papers; failure to do so constitutes a nullity (see *Advocate, H.M. v. MacDonald* (1896) 3 S.L.T. 317).

Prosecutor's refusal of pleas
There is no obligation upon the prosecutor to accept a plea of guilt to the libel (indeed, historically, in capital crimes the Crown always elected to prove its case when a guilty plea was offered).

The rules for such eventualities were stated in *Strathern v. Sloan*, 1937 J.C. 76 at 80 but had little practical impact once the 1980 Act abolished mandatory pleading diets. The re-introduction of mandatory first diets, and preliminary diets, in ss.71 and 72 of the 1995 Act may render that judgment more topical. If a guilty plea is tendered at the earlier diet but refused by the Crown, the minute should record that the plea was tendered and rejected; it should not record the plea as one of not guilty. At the trial diet the accused should not be called upon to plead *de novo*, in the interim, unless the prosecutor has decided to accept the plea previously tendered (it will be appreciated that the terms of s.196, which have already been discussed in the notes to s.76 above, may well make it advantageous to tender partial pleas at a first diet even if, at that juncture, they are not acceptable to the Crown). If the trial proceeds, and the plea previously tendered becomes acceptable to the Crown, the accused should then be called upon to state his plea publicly. No reference in the course of a trial should be made by the Crown to the fact that such a plea has been preferred.

Notice by accused

Special defences, incrimination and notice of witnesses, etc.

78.—(1) It shall not be competent for an accused to state a special defence or to lead evidence calculated to exculpate the accused by incriminating a co-accused unless—
  (a) a plea of special defence or, as the case may be, notice of intention to lead such evidence has been lodged and intimated in writing in accordance with subsection (3) below—
      (i) where the accused is cited to the High Court for the trial diet, to the Crown Agent; and
      (ii) where he is cited to the sheriff court for the trial diet, to the procurator fiscal,
    and to any co-accused not less than 10 clear days before the trial diet; or

(b) the court, on cause shown, otherwise directs.

(2) Subsection (1) above shall apply to a defence of automatism or coercion as if it were a special defence.

(3) A plea or notice is lodged and intimated in accordance with this subsection—

(a) where the accused is cited to the High Court for the trial diet, by lodging the plea or notice with the Clerk of Justiciary and by intimating the plea or notice to the Crown Agent and to any co-accused not less than 10 clear days before the trial diet;

(b) where the accused is cited to the sheriff court for the trial diet, by lodging the plea or notice with the sheriff clerk and by intimating it to the procurator fiscal and to any co-accused at or before the first diet.

(4) It shall not be competent for the accused to examine any witnesses or to put in evidence any productions not included in the lists lodged by the prosecutor unless—

(a) written notice of the names and addresses of such witnesses and of such productions has been given—

(i) where the case is to be tried in the sheriff court, to the procurator fiscal of the district of the trial diet at or before the first diet; and

(ii) where the case is to be tried in the High Court, to the Crown Agent at least ten clear days before the day on which the jury is sworn; or

(b) the court, on cause shown, otherwise directs.

(5) A copy of every written notice required by subsection (4) above shall be lodged by the accused with the sheriff clerk of the district in which the trial diet is to be held, or in any case the trial diet of which is to be held in the High Court in Edinburgh with the Clerk of Justiciary, at or before the trial diet, for the use of the court.

DEFINITIONS
"Clerk of Justiciary": s.307(1).
"High Court": s.307(1).
"procurator fiscal": s.307(1).

GENERAL NOTE
Section 78 stipulates the periods of notice to be given by the accused to the prosecutor, and any co-accused of any defence, special defence, list of witnesses or productions. Note that different periods of notice apply in sheriff and jury and High Court cases and that these procedures have to be seen in the context of the preliminary diets and first diets introduced by ss.71 and 72 of the 1995 Act.

Service of Lists and Notices in Sheriff Solemn cases
Section 71 now stipulates that a first diet has to occur not less than 15 clear days after service of an indictment and not more than 10 days before the trial diet. Section 78(4) enacts that any lists of witnesses or productions (other than those included in the indictment by the prosecutor) must be served upon the Crown, and a copy lodged with the court, no later than at the first diet. Note that there is no obligation to serve these lists upon any co-accused. Failure to lodge the lists timeously renders the examination of either productions or witnesses incompetent unless, in terms of subs. (4)(b), the accused can show cause for this failure. This timescale demands earlier action on the part of the accused than heretofore; s.82(2) of the 1975 Act only stipulated three clear days' notice of witnesses and productions to the prosecutor in any solemn case, calculated by reference to the date on which the jury was sworn.

It will be recalled that at the first diet the sheriff is obliged to enquire as to the state of preparation of the parties for trial (s.71(1)(a)). Accordingly it may be expected that later lodging of lists will entail a considerable burden in persuading the court that these should still be received. The same can be said for notices of special defences (extended to include defences of coercion and automatism): these have to be served upon the prosecutor and any co-accused at or before the first diet though, again, a discretion is open to the court to permit late lodging on cause shown.

A special defence is a fact which if established must necessarily lead to the acquittal of the accused upon the libel (*Adam v. McNeill*, 1971 S.L.T. (Notes) 80); thus pleas of diminished responsibility or provocation, which may rest heavily upon technical or medical evidence, and which it might reasonably be supposed would initiate further investigation by the Crown, need not be intimated prior to trial. Equally it is not necessary to serve notice incriminating a co-accused (*McShane v. H.M. Advocate*, 1989 S.C.C.R. 687; *Collins v. H.M. Advocate*, 1991 S.C.C.R. 898), or to lodge an alibi when it is to be asserted that the accused was at the *locus* for an innocent purpose (*Balsillie v. H.M. Advocate*, 1993 S.C.C.R. 760).

It remains open to the prosecutor to waive timeous notice, and to the court to consider the broad interests of justice when assessing whether due cause has been shown for notices to be received late, but such an assessment must surely now take account of any potential prejudice to co-accused since they too are entitled to timeous notification. In *Lowson v. H.M. Advocate*, 1943 J.C. 141, where a list of defence witnesses had not been lodged due to a change of trial venue, the trial judge disallowed the evidence on the view (shared by the procurator fiscal who had objected), that there was no discretion to permit examination of unintimated witnesses; the Lord Justice-General (at 145) while noting that the provisions existed to prevent the introduction of evidence which the prosecutor has no means of meeting, stated:

> "But I am clear that rules, being conceived in the interests of the prosecution, may competently, and should, be waived where the interests of justice are better served by waiving them than by insisting on them."

Despite the apparent mandatory nature of many of the 1995 Act's provisions this broad principle should still hold good.

Service of Lists and Notices in the High Court
The absence of mandatory first diets in the High Court has meant that a simple time-limit is imposed in these cases; any list of witnesses or productions and any notice must be served not less than 10 clear days before the trial diet. As with sheriff solemn cases, the accused is obliged to serve notices upon any co-accused, but need not intimate lists of witnesses or productions to them (see Chap. 11 of the 1996 Act of Adjournal). Section 72(6) specifies the "appropriate period" applicable to the variety of circumstances which can give rise to a preliminary diet but it has to be borne in mind that the need to lodge lists or notices proceeds entirely without reference to the timetable of any preliminary diet.

Preliminary pleas

79.—(1) Except by leave of the court on cause shown, no application, matter or point mentioned in subsection (1) of section 72 of this Act or that subsection as applied by section 71 of this Act shall be made, raised or submitted by an accused unless his intention to do so has been stated in a notice under the said subsection (1) or, as the case may be, under subsection (2) of the said section 71.

(2) No discrepancy, error or deficiency such as is mentioned in paragraph (a)(ii) of subsection (1) of the said section 72 or that subsection as applied by the said section 71 shall entitle the accused to object to plead to the indictment unless the court is satisfied that the discrepancy, error or deficiency tended substantially to mislead and prejudice the accused.

DEFINITIONS
"indictment": s.307(1).

GENERAL NOTE
No objection to competency or relevancy of an indictment, claim of want of lawful citation, application for separation of charges or trials, or objection to a special capacity libelled shall be entertained once the first diet has passed in sheriff solemn cases, or after lapse of the "appropriate period" specified in s.72(6). The intention of the section is to ensure that all preliminary matters are resolved before any case calls for trial; see generally ss.71(2) and 72(1) which apply the provisions of the latter section to sheriff and jury proceedings.

After the time for preliminary pleas to be stated has passed, the court will only exceptionally permit such pleas to be stated later if it is clear that the accused was not afforded an earlier opportunity (see *McAllister v. H.M. Advocate*, 1985 S.C.C.R. 36 where there had been a total failure to serve the indictment on the accused and hence no notice of preliminary plea could be stated) or substantial prejudice would otherwise result; for example, a tholed assize or other fundamental nullity, or failure by the Crown to lodge the judicial examination as a production (refer to *Advocate, H.M. v. Cafferty*, 1984 S.C.C.R. 347 discussed in the notes to s.68).

Alteration, etc, of diet

Alteration and postponement of trial diet

80.—(1) Where an indictment is not brought to trial at the trial diet and a warrant for a subsequent sitting of the court on a day within two months after the date of the trial diet has been issued under section 66(1) of this Act by the clerk of court, the court may adjourn the trial diet to the subsequent sitting, and the warrant shall have effect as if the trial diet had originally been fixed for the date of the subsequent sitting.

(2) At any time before the trial diet, a party may apply to the court before which the trial is to take place for postponement of the trial diet.

(3) Subject to subsection (4) below, after hearing all the parties the court may discharge the trial diet and either fix a new trial diet or give leave to the prosecutor to serve a notice fixing a new trial diet.

(4) Where all the parties join in an application to postpone the trial diet, the court may proceed under subsection (3) above without hearing the parties.

(5) Where there is a hearing under this section the accused shall attend it, unless the court permits the hearing to proceed notwithstanding the absence of the accused.

(6) In subsection (5) above, the reference to the accused shall, without prejudice to section 6(c) of the Interpretation Act 1978, in any case where there is more than one accused include a reference to all of them.

DEFINITIONS
    "indictment": s.307(1).
    "prosecutor": s.307(1).

GENERAL NOTE
    This section now consolidates the amendment made to the 1975 Act by the Criminal Justice (Scotland) Act 1995, Sched. 6, para. 24, the primary effect of which is to permit an adjournment of up to two months in any solemn case (previously s.77 of the 1975 Act granted such a length of adjournment only in High Court cases; sheriff solemn cases could be adjourned only for one month).
    The purpose of s.80 is to postpone the trial of a case while keeping the existing indictment alive. This avoids the expense of preparing and serving a fresh indictment and, with the arrival of first and preliminary diets introduced by ss.71(1) and 72(1) of the 1995 Act, will obviate the need for repetition of those diets. Although adjournments have customarily been obtained in the past by calling the indictment during the sitting (rather than by way of a preliminary diet), it has to be said that the provisions of s.80(1) are a second-best expedient to deal with the sorts of unforeseen events the occurrence of which seems to be one of the few certainties in any solemn sitting. If it can be anticipated that a trial cannot proceed, and the Crown wish to preserve the indictment, it is probably better to have the case postponed by way of s.71(7) in the sheriff court, or s.72(4) in the High Court. It is statutorily provided by s.72(4) that the period of postponement, in the High Court only, may be discounted from any time-bar calculation (see notes to s.65 above) but it could well be that when either a postponement or adjournment of trial is sought, the parties may seek an extension of the relevant time-bar provision; indeed, agreement to an adjournment might well depend upon an assent to an extension of the time-bar.
    An element of duplication occurs when the terms of ss.71 and 72 are compared against subs. (2) since all refer to postponement of the trial but the grounds for postponement under the former sections are identified by the court as a result of enquiry at the preliminary diet, whereas in a s.80, any of the parties can initiate an application for such postponement. From a technical stance, a s.80 adjournment could only be granted when a later sitting had already been warranted in accordance with the terms of s.66(1) of the Act and in the absence of such a sitting would simply not be competent; ss.71 and 72 proceed without reference to future sittings of the court though no doubt in practice the dates of future sittings would be taken into account.

Chapter 12 of the 1996 Act of Adjournal specifies the procedures to be followed. Where an application for postponement is to be moved it should be in the style of Form 12.2.–A; joint applications proceed on Form 12.2.–B. It is possible for hearings under s.80 to proceed without the presence of the accused being required but, in that event, it falls to the prosecutor to intimate the new diet to the accused (Rule 12.1.–(4)): see *Advocate, H.M. v. Carruthers*, 1994 S.L.T. 900, a case where the Crown failed to intimate properly but, notwithstanding, all accused duly appeared for trial and took objection to further procedure.

The tenor of the section can also be seen in Rule 12.5.–(1) which enables the court, on being satisfied that there were no other cases in the sitting in which the case had been postponed, to carry over the citation of jurors to the new trial diet.

It is not merely semantic to stress that s.80 provides for adjournment to a *sitting* within the coming two-month period. The adjournment can only be granted under s.80 when a warrant has already been granted for a subsequent sitting. While it is equally competent to adjourn to a specific date within a sitting, this commits the Crown to calling the indictment on that date come what may, failing which the instance will fall. The prudent course is to adjourn to the relevant sitting which commences on a given date. In *Advocate, H.M. v. Smith*, 1993 S.C.C.R. 987 a diet was adjourned in error to a *dies non*, the sitting commencing the day after. The Crown sought a Bill of Advocation to alter the date but also prepared and served a fresh, identical, indictment. The Appeal Court held that the instance fell once the adjournment was allowed, but upheld the Crown's decision to re-indict, noting the absence of any prejudice to the accused's case (see also *Advocate, H.M. v. Dow*, 1992 S.L.T. 577, a further example of the use of "dual indictments").

Any warrant for committal will remain in force when a diet is postponed under subs. 80(1): see s.82 below and Rule 12.1.–(6).

Procedure where trial does not take place

81.—(1) Where at the trial diet—
(a) the diet has been deserted *pro loco et tempore* for any cause; or
(b) an indictment is for any cause not brought to trial and no order has been given by the court postponing such trial or appointing it to be held at a subsequent date at some other sitting of the court,
it shall be lawful at any time within nine clear days after the last day of the sitting in which the trial diet was to be held to give notice to the accused on another copy of the indictment to appear to answer the indictment at a further diet either in the High Court or in the sheriff court when the charge is one that can be lawfully tried in that court, notwithstanding that the original citation to a trial diet was to a different court.

(2) Without prejudice to subsection (1) above, where a trial diet has been deserted *pro loco et tempore* and the court has appointed a further trial diet to be held on a subsequent date at the same sitting the accused shall require to appear and answer the indictment at that further diet.

(3) The prosecutor shall not raise a fresh libel in a case where the court has deserted the trial *simpliciter* and its decision in that regard has not been reversed on appeal.

(4) The notice referred to in subsection (1) above shall be in the form prescribed by Act of Adjournal or as nearly as may be in such form.

(5) The further diet specified in the notice referred to in subsection (1) above shall be not earlier than nine clear days from the giving of the notice.

(6) On or before the day on which notice referred to in subsection (1) above is given, a list of jurors shall be prepared, signed and kept by the sheriff clerk of the district to which the notice applies in the manner provided in section 85(1) and (2) of this Act.

(7) The warrant issued under section 66(1) of this Act shall be sufficient warrant for the citation of accused and witnesses to the further diet.

DEFINITIONS
  "High Court": s.307(1).
  "indictment": s.307(1).
  "prosecutor": s.307(1).
  "witness": s.307(1).

GENERAL NOTE
The terms of s.127 of the 1975 Act have been extended in this section of the 1995 Act. Where an indictment has been deserted *pro loco et tempore* or has not called for trial, it is open to the Crown to preserve the terms of the indictment already served upon the accused and serve a notice along with a copy of the indictment fixing a new trial diet on a shortened *induciae*. Like the provisions for adjournment of trial contained in s.80 above, this procedure has the advantage of avoiding preparation of a new indictment.

Section 127 of the 1975 Act demanded that service of a notice under the section had to be effected within nine clear days after the abortive trial diet; the equivalent provision in the 1995 Act stipulates that such notice should be served within nine clear days after the final day of the sitting in which the case had been due to proceed. Thereafter an *induciae*, of a further nine clear days is necessary before the case can proceed to trial. While the terms of the original indictment remain extant, this has to be confirmed to the accused by serving a copy of it on him along with the notice intimating the new diet. It is essential that any s.67(5) notices, which add witnesses or productions to the original indictment, are served anew; obviously this can be done most economically by effecting service along with the notice and copy indictment.

The form of the original indictment will remain unaltered (except insofar as added to by s.67 notices) but note that s.81(1) permits the calling of the indictment in a different forum; so irrespective of where the indictment was to be called originally, the accused can be called to trial in either a sheriff and jury court or in the High Court, the only limitation being that the charges must be ones which can be competently heard before that court. It is a necessary condition of proceedings under s.81 that the sheriff clerk, in compliance with subs. (6), has prepared and makes available a list of jurors by the time the s.81 notice is served on the accused.

Desertion or postponement where accused in custody

82. Where—
(a) a diet is deserted *pro loco et tempore*;
(b) a diet is postponed or adjourned; or
(c) an order is issued for the trial to take place at a different place from that first given notice of,
the warrant of committal on which the accused is at the time in custody till liberated in due course of law shall continue in force.

GENERAL NOTE
This section keeps the original committal warrant extant in circumstances where the indictment served has not proceeded to trial or a plea.

Circumstances giving rise to the need to keep the original warrant alive occur in cases of postponement under ss.71(7) and 72(4), s.74(3), adjournment of a trial diet by s.80(1) and desertion *pro loco et tempore* in terms of s.81(1)(a); s.82(c) relates both to situations in which the prosecutor alters the forum of trial (s.81(1)), or the court, before trial, in accordance with s.83 below, grants the prosecutor's motion to transfer the trial to another sheriff court in the sheriffdom.

Transfer of sheriff court solemn proceedings

83.—(1) Where an accused person has been cited to attend a sitting of the sheriff court the prosecutor may, at any time before the commencement of his trial, apply to the sheriff to transfer the case to a sheriff court in any other district in that sheriffdom.

(2) On an application under subsection (1) above the sheriff may—
(a) after giving the accused or his counsel or solicitor an opportunity to be heard; or
(b) on the joint application of the parties,
make an order for the transfer of the case.

DEFINITIONS
"prosecutor": s.307(1).

GENERAL NOTE
This provision was introduced into the 1975 Act by Sched. 6, para. 41 of the Criminal Justice (Scotland) Act 1995 and is untested. The most obvious use of this section is to permit the transfer of a case to a court equipped to take the evidence of a child via a live television link (see s.271(9)

and (10) below), but the section is widely drafted and could, for example, be used to enable the transfer of a sitting to another sheriff court in the sheriffdom if a previous sitting had badly overrun.

Jurors for sittings

Juries: returns of jurors and preparation of lists

84.—(1) For the purposes of a trial, the sheriff principal shall return such number of jurors as he thinks fit or, in relation to a trial in the High Court, such other number as the Lord Justice Clerk or any Lord Commissioner of Justiciary may direct.

(2) The Lord Justice General, whom failing the Lord Justice Clerk, may give directions as to the areas from which and the proportions in which jurors are to be summoned for trials to be held in the High Court, and for any such trial the sheriff principal of the sheriffdom in which the trial is to take place shall requisition the required number of jurors from the areas and in the proportions so specified.

(3) Where a sitting of the High Court is to be held at a town in which the High Court does not usually sit, the jury summoned to try any case in such a sitting shall be summoned from the list of potential jurors of the sheriff court district in which the town is situated.

(4) For the purpose of a trial in the sheriff court, the clerk of court shall be furnished with a list of names from lists of potential jurors of the sheriff court district in which the court is held containing the number of persons required.

(5) The sheriff principal, in any return of jurors made by him to a court, shall take the names in regular order, beginning at the top of the list of potential jurors in each of the sheriff court districts, as required; and as often as a juror is returned to him, he shall mark or cause to be marked, in the list of potential jurors of the respective sheriff court districts the date when any such juror was returned to serve; and in any such return he shall commence with the name immediately after the last in the preceding return, without regard to the court to which the return was last made, and taking the subsequent names in the order in which they are entered, as directed by this subsection, and so to the end of the lists respectively.

(6) Where a person whose name has been entered in the lists of potential jurors dies, or ceases to be qualified to serve as a juror, the sheriff principal, in making returns of jurors in accordance with the Jurors (Scotland) Act 1825, shall pass over the name of that person, but the date at which his name has been so passed over, and the reason therefor, shall be entered at the time in the lists of potential jurors.

(7) Only the lists returned in accordance with this section by the sheriffs principal to the clerks of court shall be used for the trials for which they were required.

(8) The persons to serve as jurors at sittings of the High Court shall be listed and their names and addresses shall be inserted in one roll to be signed by the judge, and the list made up under this section shall be known as the "list of assize".

(9) When more than one case is set down for trial at a sitting of the High Court, it shall not be necessary to prepare more than one list of assize, and such list shall be authenticated by the signature of a judge of the Court, and shall be the list of assize for the trial of all parties cited to that particular sitting; and the persons included in such list shall be summoned to serve generally for the trials of all the accused cited to the sitting, and only one general execution of citation shall be returned against them; and a copy of the list of assize, certified by one of the clerks of court, shall have the like effect, for all purposes for which the list may be required, as the principal list of assize authenticated as aforesaid.

(10) No irregularity in—

(a) making up the lists in accordance with the provisions of this Act;
(b) transmitting the lists;
(c) the warrant of citation;
(d) summoning jurors; or
(e) in returning any execution of citation,

shall constitute an objection to jurors whose names are included in the jury list, subject to the ruling of the court in relation to the effect of an objection as to any criminal act by which jurors may be returned to serve in any case contrary to this Act or the Jurors (Scotland) Act 1825.

DEFINITIONS
"High Court": s.307(1).
"Lord Commissioner of Justiciary": s.307(1).
"Lord Justice Clerk": s.307(1).
"Lord Justice General": s.1(1).

GENERAL NOTE
This section lays out the administrative procedures to be followed in drawing up and maintaining a list of assize. Particularly note that subs. (9) makes it competent for those who have served on a jury during the sitting to be balloted for later trials in the sitting.
Rule 13.1 of the 1996 Act of Adjournal requires the clerk of court to pay heed to the postponement or adjournment of trials under s.74(5), the postponement of trial following upon the withdrawal of an accelerated plea of guilty (s.76(3)) and the alteration and postponement of a trial during a sitting, when drawing up lists of jurors.

Juries: citation and attendance of jurors

85.—(1) It shall not be necessary to serve any list of jurors upon the accused, but on and after the date of the service of an indictment, a list of jurors prepared under the directions of the clerk of the court before which the trial is to take place shall be kept in the office of the sheriff clerk of the district in which the court of the trial diet is situated, and the accused shall be entitled to have a copy supplied to him on application free of charge.

(2) Such list shall contain not less than 30 names, and shall be headed "List of Assize for the Sitting of the High Court of Justiciary (or, the Sheriff Court of........at.........) on the........... of........... ."

(3) It shall not be necessary to summon all the jurors contained in any list of jurors under this Act, but it shall be competent to summon such jurors only, commencing from the top of the list, as may be necessary to ensure a sufficient number for the trial of the cases which remain for trial at the date of the citation of the jurors, and such number shall be fixed by the clerk of the court in which the trial diet is to be called, or in any case in the High Court by the Clerk of Justiciary, and the jurors who are not so summoned shall be placed upon the next list issued, until they have attended to serve.

(4) The sheriff clerk of the sheriffdom in which a sitting of the High Court is to be held or the sheriff clerk of the sheriff court district in which any juror is to be cited where the citation is for a trial before a sheriff, shall fill up and sign a proper citation addressed to each such juror, and shall cause the same to be transmitted to him by letter, sent to him at his place of residence as stated in the lists of potential jurors by registered post or recorded delivery or to be served on him by an officer of law; and a certificate under the hand of such sheriff clerk of the citation of any jurors or juror in the manner provided in this subsection shall be a legal citation.

(5) The sheriff clerk of the sheriffdom in which a sitting of the High Court is to be held shall issue citations to the whole jurors required for the sitting, whether the jurors reside in that or in any other sheriffdom.

(6) Persons cited to attend as jurors may, unless they have been excused in respect thereof under section 1 of the Law Reform (Miscellaneous Provisions) (Scotland) Act 1980, be fined up to level 3 on the standard scale if they fail to attend in compliance with the citation.

(7) A fine imposed under subsection (6) above may, on application, be remitted—
 (a) by a Lord Commissioner of Justiciary where imposed in the High Court;
 (b) by the sheriff court where imposed in the sheriff court,
and no court fees or expenses shall be exigible in respect of any such application.
 (8) A person shall not be exempted by sex or marriage from the liability to serve as a juror.

DEFINITIONS
 "Clerk of Justiciary": s.307(1).
 "High Court": s.307(1).
 "indictment": s.307(1).
 "Lord Commissioner of Justiciary": s.307(1).
 "sheriff clerk": s.307(1).

GENERAL NOTE
 The accused is entitled to apply for, and receive from the sheriff clerk, a copy of the list of assize relative to the sitting to which he has been indicted (subs. (1)).
 The form of citation of jurors is Form 13.2.–A in the 1996 Act of Adjournal; the execution of service of citation is Form 13.2.–B.
 Subsection (5) is authority for jurors at any sitting of the High Court to be drawn from any sheriffdom. Failure to appear for jury service on lawful citation is an offence attracting a fine of level three on the standard scale.

Jurors: excusal and objections

 86.—(1) Where, before a juror is sworn to serve, the parties jointly apply for him to be excused the court shall, notwithstanding that no reason is given in the application, excuse that juror from service.
 (2) Nothing in subsection (1) above shall affect the right of the accused or the prosecutor to object to any juror on cause shown.
 (3) If any objection is taken to a juror on cause shown and such objection is founded on the want of sufficient qualification as provided by section 1(1) of the Law Reform (Miscellaneous Provisions) (Scotland) Act 1980, such objection shall be proved only by the oath of the juror objected to.
 (4) No objection to a juror shall be competent after he has been sworn to serve.

DEFINITIONS
 "prosecutor": s.307(1).

GENERAL NOTE
 The right of peremptory challenge to a number of jurors without showing cause was abolished by s.8 of the Criminal Justice (Scotland) Act 1995 and subs. (1) was substituted; where parties concur, jurors can still be excused without cause being shown, a measure largely intended to enable patently unsuitable or unfit jurors to be relieved of possible selection without open challenge. Although the obvious time for such an agreement to be reached is when the assize presents itself for ballot, the section does not rule out an earlier agreement between parties after the list of assize has been inspected. The court has no power to intervene in the matter.
 Subsection (2) preserves the traditional right of challenge on cause shown to a juror selected in the ballot. "Cause shown" has to relate to the juror personally and to his inability to try the case impartially or without importing personal knowledge of the circumstances of the alleged offence or of the parties listed in the indictment. So in *Advocate, H.M. v. Devine* (1962) 78 S.C. Rep. 173, objection on the basis that a juror had already served on a jury in the same assize dealing with a similar incident to that now libelled at the same *locus*, and might thus be against the accused, was repelled.
 In *McCadden v. H.M. Advocate*, 1985 S.C.C.R. 282 the court disfavoured any suggestion that vetting of a jury was permissible. Objections to jurors must be stated as subs. (4) provides, before the jury is sworn; thereafter they cannot be entertained (also see *McArthur v. H.M. Advocate*, 1902 S.L.T. 310).

The Law Reform (Miscellaneous Provisions) (Scotland) Act 1980 (c.55), s.1(1) broadly enacts that persons aged between 18 and 65 years, ordinarily resident in the United Kingdom and registered as an elector are qualified for jury service; those persons exempted, barred or disqualified from jury service are detailed in Sched. I to that Act.

Non-availability of judge

Non-availability of judge

87.—(1) Where the court is unable to proceed owing to the death, illness or absence of the presiding judge, the clerk of court may convene the court (if necessary) and—

(a) in a case where no evidence has been led, adjourn the diet and any other diet appointed for that sitting to—

(i) a time later the same day, or a date not more than seven days later, when he believes a judge will be available; or

(ii) a later sitting not more than two months after the date of the adjournment; or

(b) in a case where evidence has been led—

(i) adjourn the diet and any other diet appointed for that sitting to a time later the same day, or a date not more than seven days later, when he believes a judge will be available; or

(ii) with the consent of the parties, desert the diet *pro loco et tempore.*

(2) Where a diet has been adjourned under sub-paragraph (i) of either paragraph (a) or paragraph (b) of subsection (1) above the clerk of court may, where the conditions of that subsection continue to be satisfied, further adjourn the diet under that sub-paragraph; but the total period of such adjournments shall not exceed seven days.

(3) Where a diet has been adjourned under subsection (1)(b)(i) above the court may, at the adjourned diet—

(a) further adjourn the diet; or

(b) desert the diet *pro loco et tempore.*

(4) Where a diet is deserted in pursuance of subsection (1)(b)(ii) or (3)(b) above, the Lord Advocate may raise and insist in a new indictment, and—

(a) where the accused is in custody it shall not be necessary to grant a new warrant for his incarceration, and the warrant or commitment on which he is at the time in custody till liberation in due course of law shall continue in force; and

(b) where the accused is at liberty on bail, his bail shall continue in force.

DEFINITIONS

"bail": s.307(1).

"indictment ": s.307(1).

GENERAL NOTE

This section provides powers to the clerk of court, in the event of illness or death of the presiding judge, to convene the court and defer the business of the sitting to a later date or dates.

Two different situations are envisaged: first where no evidence has been led (subs. (1)(a)), the clerk may in the absence of an available judge adjourn any such case for a maximum of seven days on the assumption that the presiding judge can within that time return to business, or alternatively, *ex proprio motu* adjourn the sitting for up to two months. Subsection (2) discussed below, limits the scale of these adjournments to a total of seven days.

On the other hand, where evidence has already been led (subs. (1)(b)) the options are to adjourn cases in the sitting up to seven days, or with consent of the parties, desert the diet *pro loco et tempore.* If any of the parties will not agree to desertion, then resort has to be had to an adjournment up to seven days of the trial; in terms of subs. (3) it only becomes competent (in the absence of the parties' concurrence) for the clerk to desert the diet after the first adjournment under subs. (1)(b)(i) has elapsed. To complicate matters further, subs. (2) limits the use of an administrative adjournment by the clerk to a total period of seven days.

Once a diet has been adjourned in these circumstances, or indeed, another judge has deserted the case due to the continued unavailability of the trial judge, subs. (4) entitles the Lord Advocate to re-raise the proceedings. Any bail order or warrant of committal remains in force.

Circumstances of the sort described in s.67 would surely entitle the Crown to seek an extension of the time-limits prescribed by s.65 above, since no fault for the delay could be ascribed to the Crown.

Jury for trial

Plea of not guilty, balloting and swearing of jury, etc.

88.—(1) Where the accused pleads not guilty, the clerk of court shall record that fact and proceed to ballot the jury.

(2) The jurors for the trial shall be chosen in open court by ballot from the list of persons summoned in such manner as shall be prescribed by Act of Adjournal, and the persons so chosen shall be the jury to try the accused, and their names shall be recorded in the minutes of the proceedings.

(3) It shall not be competent for the accused or the prosecutor to object to a juror on the ground that the juror has not been duly cited to attend.

(4) Notwithstanding subsection (1) above, the jurors chosen for any particular trial may, when that trial is disposed of, without a new ballot serve on the trials of other accused, provided that—

   (a) the accused and the prosecutor consent;

   (b) the names of the jurors are contained in the list of jurors; and

   (c) the jurors are duly sworn to serve on each successive trial.

(5) When the jury has been balloted, the clerk of court shall inform the jury of the charge against the accused—

   (a) by reading the words of the indictment (with the substitution of the third person for the second); or

   (b) if the presiding judge, because of the length or complexity of the indictment, so directs, by reading to the jury a summary of the charge approved by the judge,

and copies of the indictment shall be provided for each member of the jury without lists of witnesses or productions.

(6) After reading the charge as mentioned in subsection (5) above and any special defence as mentioned in section 89(1) of this Act, the clerk of court shall administer the oath in common form.

(7) The court may excuse a juror from serving on a trial where the juror has stated the ground for being excused in open court.

(8) Where a trial which is proceeding is adjourned from one day to another, the jury shall not be secluded during the adjournment, unless, on the motion of the prosecutor or the accused or *ex proprio motu* the court sees fit to order that the jury be kept secluded.

DEFINITIONS
   "prosecutor": s.307(1).

GENERAL NOTE
   This section deals with the selection of a trial jury from the list of assize prepared beforehand. Chapter 14 of the Act of Adjournal 1996 regulates the mechanics of the ballot and Forms 14.3.–A and 14.3.–B respectively stipulate the oath or affirmation to be administered to all jurors. While parties can concur to excuse jurors without showing cause (see the notes to s.86 above), in any other case objection to a juror serving on the jury must be on cause shown: the right to peremptory challenge of jurors has been abolished. It remains the case that a juror who is not exempted or disqualified from service by the provisions of the Law Reform (Miscellaneous Provisions) (Scotland) Act 1980, s.1 must serve on the jury unless he can give reason in terms of subs. (7) why he should be excused. Ordinarily personal knowledge of the circumstances of the case, or of the accused or witnesses would be telling factors but ultimately the determining factor has to be whether the court can be assured that the juror can try the accused according to the evidence, without importing outside knowledge or prejudice; if there is any doubt, fairness dictates that the juror should not be called upon to serve. In *Hay v. H.M. Advocate*, 1995 S.C.C.R.

639 an appeal was taken founding on the fact that two of the jurors had knowledge of the accused (a fact made known to the clerk and the sheriff by five of the assize) while a third juror had had dealings with an associate of the accused; no challenge had been given to the selection of the jury. The Appeal Court noted that the sheriff followed the guidance given in *Pullar v. H.M. Advocate,* 1993 S.C.C.R. 514 and emphasised (at 643C) that the issues raised in the appeal should properly have been aired prior to the trial; the appeal against conviction was dismissed.

Before the jury is empanelled, the clerk of court is required to have made the assembled assize aware of the particulars of the accused and of any witness named in the charges on the indictment and to have advised them to inform him of any prior knowledge of these parties which they have (*Pullar v. H.M. Advocate*).

The presiding judge should also make enquiry of the jurors once the indictment has been read to them and before evidence is led, if they know of any reason why they should not serve (*Spink v. H.M. Advocate,* 1989 S.C.C.R. 413 and also *Russell v. H.M. Advocate,* 1992 S.L.T. 25).

Subsection (4) re-enacts the rarely-used provision of s.132 of the 1975 Act: a jury which has just concluded a trial can be selected to sit in the following case in the sitting without the necessity of a ballot. However, this abbreviated procedure can only be used where; (i) the accused and the Crown consent and thus have no challenge on cause shown and; (ii) the jurors themselves pronounce no personal knowledge of the case, the accused or witnesses. Furthermore it is implicit that the whole of that prior jury must serve in the new case and subs. (4)(c) stipulates that the jury must be put on oath anew. A consent to the use of this shortened procedure can be withdrawn by an objection from the accused which is stated before the jury has been sworn (*Daniel or Donald Stuart, Re* (1829) Bell's Notes 237). Chapter 14 of the Act of Adjournal provides a short form of minute, recording the particulars of the jury by reference to the record of proceedings of the previous trial.

While subs. (5)(b) allows for a summary form of the indictment charges approved by the judge to be read to the jury, it is interesting to note that this is not a matter which has to be addressed expressly at either a first, or preliminary diet (the same observation could equally be made in relation to the provision in s.89(2) which allows for a condensed version of any special defence to be read to the jury instead of the notice intimated to the court).

Unempanelled jurors are not released until evidence is begun and the trial is lawfully under way.

Subsection (8) is broadly drafted. The statutory authority for the overnight accommodation of jurors who are deliberating upon their verdict is contained in s.99(4) below. Hence subs. (8) would appear to be intended for use at earlier points in the trial, while evidence is still being led.

Jury to be informed of special defence

89.—(1) Subject to subsection (2) below, where the accused has lodged a plea of special defence, the clerk of court shall, after informing the jury, in accordance with section 88(5) of this Act, of the charge against the accused, and before administering the oath, read to the jury the plea of special defence.

(2) Where the presiding judge on cause shown so directs, the plea of special defence shall not be read over to the jury in accordance with subsection (1) above; and in any such case the judge shall inform the jury of the lodging of the plea and of the general nature of the special defence.

(3) Copies of a plea of special defence shall be provided for each member of the jury.

DEFINITIONS
"judge": s.307(1).

GENERAL NOTE
Special defences require to be notified to the court and other parties in accordance with s.78 of the Act; in sheriff solemn cases, intimation has to be given at or before the first diet (s.78(3)(b)) while in High Court cases, where preliminary diets are not mandatory, such intimation has to be made not less than 10 clear days before trial. The 1995 Act in s.78(2) adds defences of coercion and automatism to the existing categories of special defence which require advance notice (examples of defences of automatism are found in *Sorley v. H.M. Advocate,* 1992 S.L.T. 867 and *Ross v. H.M. Advocate,* 1991 S.L.T. 564).

Once the indictment is read to the jury by the clerk of court, the next procedure is to read the terms of any special defence over to the jury. Failure to read over the special defence will not necessarily amount to a miscarriage of justice; see *Moar v. H.M. Advocate*, 1949 J.C. 31. Indeed it is often asserted that the only purpose of a notice of special defence is to give notice to the Crown of a possible line of defence evidence and, accordingly, the reading over of the terms of a notice which may not ultimately form a part of the defence case is both unnecessary and likely to confuse. Refer to *Mullen v. H.M. Advocate*, 1978 S.L.T. (Notes) 33. Nonetheless the provisions of s.89 are unequivocal: the terms of the notice must be made known to the jury before the trial begins. Subsection (2) allows the judge following a motion by one or other of the parties to withhold the full terms of the notice from the jury and to substitute a condensed account of the notice's meaning. In this context it has to be assumed that the terms of subs. (3), which instructs the distribution of copies of the notice of special defence, would not be adhered to, since that would appear to defeat the purpose of editing the original notice as lodged.

A plea of insanity must always be made known to the jury since the accused's state of mind at the time of the commission of the crime is a fundamental issue. It is not proper to read over a notice of incrimination of a co-accused; see *Collins v. H.M. Advocate*, 1991 S.C.C.R. 898.

Death or illness of jurors

90.—(1) Where in the course of a trial—

(a) a juror dies; or

(b) the court is satisfied that it is for any reason inappropriate for any juror to continue to serve as a juror,

the court may in its discretion, on an application made by the prosecutor or an accused, direct that the trial shall proceed before the remaining jurors (if they are not less than twelve in number), and where such direction is given the remaining jurors shall be deemed in all respects to be a properly constituted jury for the purpose of the trial and shall have power to return a verdict accordingly whether unanimous or, subject to subsection (2) below, by majority.

(2) The remaining jurors shall not be entitled to return a verdict of guilty by majority unless at least eight of their number are in favour of such verdict and if, in any such case, the remaining jurors inform the court that—

(a) fewer than eight of their number are in favour of a verdict of guilty; and

(b) there is not a majority in favour of any other verdict,

they shall be deemed to have returned a verdict of not guilty.

GENERAL NOTE

This section regulates the composition of the jury which, of course, must comprise of 15 people at the outset of the trial, and stipulates that a majority verdict in any case requires eight of the jury at least to favour a guilty verdict. Once the trial has begun, the size of the jury can be reduced by reason of death, illness or other suitable cause (including misconduct by a juror himself) but in no case can the trial proceed with a jury numbering less than 12 persons. Recent experience in long-running trials might have suggested that the preservation of jurors' numbers is no small feat; see for example the sheriff's note in *MacDonald v. H.M. Advocate*, 1995 S.C.C.R. 663 which lends an insight into the major logistical problems experienced in lengthy trials.

The subsection does not of course require that the trial must proceed with a reduced number of jurors though that is the normal procedure; it would be open to the court to consider motions to desert the trial diet and to exercise such powers as were competent to the court under s.65 of the Act to extend statutory time-bars.

The procedure to be followed when the jury seeks guidance on the calculation of their verdict is described in *Kerr v. H.M. Advocate*, 1992 S.C.C.R. 281; 1992 S.L.T. 1031, where the trial judge was handed a slip of paper from the jury showing a split verdict, eight for acquittal, seven (the arithmetical majority) for guilt and after further direction a conviction resulted; quashed on appeal.

Trial

Trial to be continuous

91. Every trial shall proceed from day to day until it is concluded unless the court sees cause to adjourn over a day or days.

GENERAL NOTE
Although it is generally the case that trials will continue from day to day until concluded, this section affords the presiding judge an element of discretion in allowing for variations from that norm when appropriate. See *MacDonald v. H.M. Advocate*, 1995 S.C.C.R. 663 for an insight into the conduct of longer trials.

Section 102 below permits the interruption of proceedings to receive the verdict in another case.

Trial in presence of accused

92.—(1) Without prejudice to section 54 of this Act, and subject to subsection (2) below, no part of a trial shall take place outwith the presence of the accused.

(2) If during the course of his trial an accused so misconducts himself that in the view of the court a proper trial cannot take place unless he is removed, the court may order—

    (a) that he is removed from the court for so long as his conduct makes it necessary; and

    (b) that the trial proceeds in his absence,

but if he is not legally represented the court shall appoint counsel or a solicitor to represent his interests during such absence.

(3) From the commencement of the leading of evidence in a trial for rape or the like the judge may, if he thinks fit, cause all persons other than the accused and counsel and solicitors to be removed from the court-room.

DEFINITIONS
"judge": s.307(1).

GENERAL NOTE
The hearing of evidence in all cases should occur in the presence of the accused unless he so misconducts himself as to necessitate his removal from the court. In *Aitken v. Wood*, 1921 J.C. 84 magistrates examined alleged injuries on the complainer's arm in private. The conviction was quashed. See also *Livingston v. H.M. Advocate*, 1991 S.C.C.R. 350; 1992 S.L.T. 481, where the removal of productions from the court for expert examination during the trial was held not to breach the general prohibition then contained in s.145 of the 1975 Act. In *McColl v. H.M. Advocate*, 1989 S.C.C.R. 229; 1989 S.L.T. 691 the clerk of court was called to the jury room and was asked for guidance upon the judge's directions which he gave; the conviction was quashed. See also *Kerr v. H.M. Advocate*, 1992 S.C.C.R. 281; 1992 S.L.T. 1031 discussed in the notes to s.90 above.

While the courts are generally public courts, subs. (3) permits the presiding judge in cases involving a charge of rape or other charges of a sexual nature, to close the court to the public from the outset of proceedings. Further provisions in regard to the line of questioning permissible in sexual offences are to be found at s.274 below. Specifically in relation to the evidence of children it will also be recalled that s.50(3) enables the court to be cleared of all but the immediately interested parties during the hearing of that evidence.

Record of trial

93.—(1) The proceedings at the trial of any person who, if convicted, is entitled to appeal under Part VIII of this Act, shall be recorded by means of shorthand notes or by mechanical means.

(2) A shorthand writer shall—

    (a) sign the shorthand notes taken by him of such proceedings and certify them as being complete and correct; and

    (b) retain the notes.

(3) A person recording such proceedings by mechanical means shall—

    (a) certify that the record is true and complete;

    (b) specify in the certificate the proceedings or, as the case may be, the part of the proceedings to which the record relates; and

(c) retain the record.

(4) The cost of making a record under subsection (1) above shall be defrayed, in accordance with scales of payment fixed for the time being by Treasury, out of money provided by Parliament.

(5) In subsection (1) above "proceedings at the trial" means the whole proceedings including, without prejudice to that generality—
   (a) discussions—
      (i) on any objection to the relevancy of the indictment;
      (ii) with respect to any challenge of jurors; and
      (iii) on all questions arising in the course of the trial;
   (b) the decision of the court on any matter referred to in paragraph (a) above;
   (c) the evidence led at the trial;
   (d) any statement made by or on behalf of the accused whether before or after the verdict;
   (e) the judge's charge to the jury;
   (f) the speeches of counsel or agent;
   (g) the verdict of the jury;
   (h) the sentence by the judge.

DEFINITIONS
"judge": s.307(1).

GENERAL NOTE
A shorthand or recorded record of the entire proceedings in all solemn cases must be maintained and preserved lest a call is made (in terms of s.94) for them to be produced. Additionally Chap. 14 of the Act of Adjournal 1996 enacts that the trial judge is obliged to preserve and authenticate his own notes of evidence and produce them (or a certified copy) to the High Court when requested. The same rules stipulate that where reliance is placed on a recording of the proceedings instead of shorthand notes, the clerk of court must record the fact in his minutes of proceedings.

On appeal in *Kyle v. H.M. Advocate*, 1987 S.C.C.R. 116, weight was placed by the appellant upon the apparent inconsistency of a part of the judge's charge, the shorthand notes having been certified as accurate. In fact the terms of the notes suggested that the shorthand writer had some doubts about the accuracy of that section of the transcription; the High Court held that while the notes had to be so certified, the court was not bound to accept them as such and that, in any event, no miscarriage of justice had occurred.

However the absence of a shorthand record altogether has been held to have left the Appeal Court in doubt as to additional directions given to the jury, the sheriff having re-convened the court in the absence of the shorthand writer in breach of the provisions of s.274(1) of the 1975 Act. The aggravated element of the conviction which had been the reason for further directions was quashed and a lesser conviction substituted (see *McLaughlan v. H.M. Advocate*, 1995 G.W.D. 38–1935).

Transcripts of record and documentary productions

94.—(1) The Clerk of Justiciary may direct that a transcript of a record made under section 93(1) of this Act, or any part thereof, be made and delivered to him for the use of any judge.

(2) Subject to subsection (3) below, the Clerk of Justiciary shall, if requested to do so by—
   (a) the Secretary of State; or
   (b) any other person on payment of such charges as may be fixed for the time being by Treasury,
direct that such a transcript be made and sent to the person who requested it.

(3) The Secretary of State may, after consultation with the Lord Justice General, by order made by statutory instrument provide that in any class of proceedings specified in the order the Clerk of Justiciary shall only make a direction under subsection (2)(b) above if satisfied that the person requesting the transcript is of a class of person so specified and, if purposes for which the transcript may be used are so specified, intends to use it only for such a

purpose; and different purposes may be so specified for different classes of proceedings or classes of person.

(4) Where subsection (3) above applies as respects a direction, the person to whom the transcript is sent shall, if purposes for which that transcript may be used are specified by virtue of that subsection, use it only for such a purpose.

(5) A statutory instrument containing an order under subsection (3) above shall be subject to annulment in pursuance of a resolution of either House of Parliament.

(6) A direction under subsection (1) or (2) above may require that the transcript be made by the person who made the record or by such competent person as may be specified in the direction; and that person shall comply with the direction.

(7) A transcript made in compliance with a direction under subsection (1) or (2) above—

(a) shall be in legible form; and

(b) shall be certified by the person making it as being a correct and complete transcript of the whole or, as the case may be, the part of the record purporting to have been made and certified, and in the case of shorthand notes signed, by the person who made the record.

(8) The cost of making a transcript in compliance with a direction under subsection (1) or (2)(a) above shall be defrayed, in accordance with scales of payment fixed for the time being by the Treasury, out of money provided by Parliament.

(9) The Clerk of Justiciary shall, on payment of such charges as may be fixed for the time being by the Treasury, provide a copy of any documentary production lodged in connection with an appeal under this Part of this Act to such of the following persons as may request it—

(a) the prosecutor;

(b) any person convicted in the proceedings;

(c) any other person named in, or immediately affected by, any order made in the proceedings; and

(d) any person authorised to act on behalf of any of the persons mentioned in paragraphs (a) to (c) above.

DEFINITIONS
"Clerk of Justiciary": s.307(1).
"judge": s.307(1).
"Lord Justice General": s.307(1).

GENERAL NOTE
The effect of certification of a transcript of evidence as correct was raised in *Kyle v. H.M. Advocate*, 1987 S.C.C.R. 116. See the discussion in the notes to s.93 above.

Verdict by judge alone

95.—(1) Where, at any time after the jury has been sworn to serve in a trial, the prosecutor intimates to the court that he does not intend to proceed in respect of an offence charged in the indictment, the judge shall acquit the accused of that offence and the trial shall proceed only in respect of any other offence charged in the indictment.

(2) Where, at any time after the jury has been sworn to serve in a trial, the accused intimates to the court that he is prepared to tender a plea of guilty as libelled, or such other plea as the Crown is prepared to accept, in respect of any offence charged in the indictment, the judge shall accept the plea tendered and shall convict the accused accordingly.

(3) Where an accused is convicted under subsection (2) above of an offence—

(a) the trial shall proceed only in respect of any other offence charged in the indictment; and

(b) without prejudice to any other power of the court to adjourn the case or to defer sentence, the judge shall not sentence him or make any other order competent following conviction until a verdict has been returned in respect of every other offence mentioned in paragraph (a) above.

DEFINITIONS
"indictment": s.307(1).
"judge": s.307(1).
"offence": s.307(1).
"prosecutor": s.307(1).

GENERAL NOTE
Section 95 deals with situations in the course of a trial in which the jury is not called upon to reach a verdict upon the evidence, either because the Crown has withdrawn a charge (subs. (1)) or acceptable pleas have been tendered (subs. (2)). In the latter case, it is implicit that acceptance of pleas tendered is signified by the prosecutor subscribing his minute of acceptance following the signatures of the accused and the presiding judge. Subsection (2) also deals with the tendering of a partial plea in circumstances where other charges remain outstanding against the accused. In that situation, where the prosecutor is maintaining the other charges on the libel, care must be taken to ensure that the prosecutor's endorsement is restricted solely to the charges in relation to which the plea was tendered.

It will be noted that the onus of assenting to the pleas tendered strictly lies with the trial judge, not with the jury. No sentence can competently be pronounced until a verdict is reached on all the charges on the indictment.

In determining sentence, the court may take account of the point in the proceedings at which a plea or pleas were tendered (see s.196 below).

Amendment of indictment

96.—(1) No trial shall fail or the ends of justice be allowed to be defeated by reason of any discrepancy or variance between the indictment and the evidence.

(2) It shall be competent at any time prior to the determination of the case, unless the court see just cause to the contrary, to amend the indictment by deletion, alteration or addition, so as to—

(a) cure any error or defect in it;

(b) meet any objection to it; or

(c) cure any discrepancy or variance between the indictment and the evidence.

(3) Nothing in this section shall authorise an amendment which changes the character of the offence charged, and, if it appears to the court that the accused may in any way be prejudiced in his defence on the merits of the case by any amendment made under this section, the court shall grant such remedy to the accused by adjournment or otherwise as appears to the court to be just.

(4) An amendment made under this section shall be sufficiently authenticated by the initials of the clerk of the court.

DEFINITIONS
"indictment": s.307(1).

GENERAL NOTE
Schedule 3 of the Act states the general rules concerning latitudes in time and place, implied terms and implied alternatives. Section 96 re-enacts the provisions contained in s.123 of the 1975 Act relating to the power of amendment of an indictment in the course of a trial. The Crown may seek leave to amend the terms of the libel at a first, or preliminary, diet to meet any preliminary objection, but s.96 deals with such motions in the course of trial. While wide powers of amendment are available to the Crown this is qualified by the provisos that; (i) they cannot be used to introduce an essential requisite into a criminal charge—a fundamentally defective libel cannot

be cured (*Stevenson v. McLevy*, (1879) 4 Couper 196 where the libel lacked a *locus delicti*) and (ii) they must not change the character of the charge to such a degree as to prejudice the accused's defence on the merits (see subs. (3)). Any amendment has to be justified to the court, and while amendment of either the libel or the description of a witness can be craved, amendment of the description of a production in the indictment is not competent (see *Advocate, H.M. v. Swift*, 1983 S.C.C.R. 204 discussed in the notes to s.67(5)).

Amendment of an indictment which omitted the accused's name in one of the three charges (the murder charge), when he had been correctly described in the instance, has been allowed (*Keane v. H.M. Advocate*, 1986 S.C.C.R. 491); the decision might have been quite different if there had been other accused on the indictment.

In the event that amendment is allowed by the court, the remedy for the accused is ordinarily adjournment. The presiding judge's decision on the issue will only be overturned on appeal if the Appeal Court is satisfied that the public interest or the interest of the accused has been adversely affected (see *Cumming v. Frame*, (1909) 6 Adam 57).

No case to answer

97.—(1) Immediately after the close of the evidence for the prosecution, the accused may intimate to the court his desire to make a submission that he has no case to answer both—

(a) on an offence charged in the indictment; and

(b) on any other offence of which he could be convicted under the indictment.

(2) If, after hearing both parties, the judge is satisfied that the evidence led by the prosecution is insufficient in law to justify the accused being convicted of the offence charged in respect of which the submission has been made or of such other offence as is mentioned, in relation to that offence, in paragraph (b) of subsection (1) above, he shall acquit him of the offence charged in respect of which the submission has been made and the trial shall proceed only in respect of any other offence charged in the indictment.

(3) If, after hearing both parties, the judge is not satisfied as is mentioned in subsection (2) above, he shall reject the submission and the trial shall proceed, with the accused entitled to give evidence and call witnesses, as if such submission had not been made.

(4) A submission under subsection (1) above shall be heard by the judge in the absence of the jury.

DEFINITIONS
  "indictment": s.307(1).
  "judge": s.307(1).
  "offence": s.307(1).

GENERAL NOTE
  The no case to answer submission was introduced into Scots criminal law by the Criminal Justice (Scotland) Act 1980, s.19 and the terms of that section are repeated in s.97 above. A common law submission could always be made at the conclusion of evidence, before the judge's charge but a s.97 submission, unlike the common law type, is concerned only with the sufficiency of evidence, not its quality. The submission is made outwith the presence of the jury and can relate to any, or all, of the charges on the indictment. Note that s.97 refers to "an offence" not "a charge" on the indictment; so where a number of offences are libelled as part of one charge a submission can competently be made upon each offence: the Crown cannot, by creative draftsmanship, withhold the right of an accused to make a s.97 motion (see *Cordiner v. H.M. Advocate*, 1991 S.C.C.R. 652).

  It will be observed that a submission can be made in regard to the charge libelled or any other offence which is implied by the libel but, in practical terms, the starting point will be the sufficiency, or otherwise, of the charge libelled before proceeding to a consideration of any alternative charge.

  If in terms of subs. (3) the accused's submissions are rejected, he has to decide whether or not to lead evidence, a dilemma heightened by the introduction of the prosecutor's right to comment upon the failure of the accused to lead evidence (see s.32 of the Criminal Justice (Scotland) Act 1995). It remains to be seen what use will be made of this provision and to what effect. What is the position if the judge incorrectly rejects a submission of no case to answer and the accused then leads evidence which confirms the Crown case? The problem was recognised but not addressed in *Little v. H.M. Advocate*, 1983 S.C.C.R. 56. The same problems occurred in *Mackie v. H.M. Advocate*, 1994 S.C.C.R. 277 and there the judge read the elements of the charge as a unity in what was, by any standard, a complex libel.

It is permissible for the Crown to submit to the jury at the conclusion of evidence that the withdrawal of charges at the submission stage does not necessarily reflect adversely upon prosecution witnesses; it is however one step too far to suggest that the accused might still have committed the offences of which he had been acquitted earlier (see *Dudgeon v. H.M. Advocate*, 1988 S.C.C.R. 147). In that case the improper remarks of the prosecutor were held to have been cured by the directions of the trial judge and no miscarriage to have resulted.

Defence to speak last

98. In any trial the accused or, where he is legally represented, his counsel or solicitor shall have the right to speak last.

Seclusion of jury to consider verdict

99.—(1) When the jury retire to consider their verdict, the clerk of court shall enclose the jury in a room by themselves and, except in so far as provided for, or is made necessary, by an instruction under subsection (4) below, neither he nor any other person shall be present with the jury after they are enclosed.

(2) Except in so far as is provided for, or is made necessary, by an instruction under subsection (4) below, until the jury intimate that they are ready to return their verdict—

(a) subject to subsection (3) below, no person shall visit the jury or communicate with them; and

(b) no juror shall come out of the jury room other than to receive or seek a direction from the judge or to make a request—
　　(i) for an instruction under subsection (4)(a), (c) or (d) below; or
　　(ii) regarding any matter in the cause.

(3) Nothing in paragraph (a) of subsection (2) above shall prohibit the judge, or any person authorised by him for the purpose, communicating with the jury for the purposes—

(a) of giving a direction, whether or not sought under paragraph (b) of that subsection; or

(b) responding to a request made under that paragraph.

(4) The judge may give such instructions as he considers appropriate as regards—

(a) the provision of meals and refreshments for the jury;

(b) the making of arrangements for overnight accommodation for the jury and for their continued seclusion if such accommodation is provided;

(c) the communication of a personal or business message, unconnected with any matter in the cause, from a juror to another person (or vice versa); or

(d) the provision of medical treatment, or other assistance, immediately required by a juror.

(5) If the prosecutor or any other person contravenes the provisions of this section, the accused shall be acquitted of the crime with which he is charged.

(6) During the period in which the jury are retired to consider their verdict, the judge may sit in any other proceedings; and the trial shall not fail by reason only of his so doing.

DEFINITIONS
　"judge": s.307(1).
　"prosecutor": s.307(1).

GENERAL NOTE

Until the point at which the jury is directed to retire to consider its verdict, all proceedings in a trial must take place in the presence of the accused (see s.92). Once the jury withdraws to the jury room, s.99 stipulates that no contact should be made with its members unless the jury requests directions or has need to seek assistance from the court. The provisions of s.99 are mandatory and conduct constituting a breach (subs. (5)) is fatal to any conviction.

Subss. (2) and (3)

Unfortunately the cases arising from s.153 (the statutory predecessor to s.99) tend to suggest that in their zeal to provide for the seclusion of the jury, officers of the court have on occasion overlooked the obligations (now) created by s.92 and trespassed into matters which should have been dealt with in open court.

It is the jury's right to examine productions referred to in the evidence but subject to any directions given by the court. The procedure to be followed is laid out in *Hamilton v. H.M. Advocate*, 1980 J.C. 66; the Lord Justice Clerk (at 69) stated:

"If the jury make a request to see a production, this request should be communicated to the clerk of court who should inform counsel on both sides and then refer the matter to the trial judge for his decision."

A practice has developed, in part to delay the jury's deliberations as little as possible and to avoid the need to reconvene the court repeatedly, of trial judges clarifying with the parties which productions can, and which cannot, be given to the jury on request. This is done in open court immediately after the jury retires and has the merit of focusing this issue even before the need arises and commits parties' views to the shorthand notes. There is no statutory authority for this procedure but, it is submitted, it complies with the directions in *Hamilton*. Support for this reading can be found in *Bertram v. H.M. Advocate*, 1990 S.C.C.R. 394, where the judge in his charge permitted access to all productions admitted in evidence during the trial. See also *Martin v. H.M. Advocate*, 1989 S.C.C.R. 546 where the sheriff gave directions which were inspecific and were acted upon by the clerk of court without reference to the parties and *Boyle v. H.M. Advocate*, 1990 S.C.C.R. 480 where productions not spoken of in evidence were given to the jurors in error. Once the error was appreciated, the sheriff gave further directions to the jury to ignore the content of these productions; the conviction was upheld in the circumstances.

It is clear that the question of access to productions is one upon which parties should be heard; it is not an administrative matter to be resolved between the clerk of court and the presiding judge. The complex issues which can surface are amply illustrated by *Collins v. H.M. Advocate*, 1991 S.C.C.R. 898 where the trial judge withheld statements by various of the accused on the grounds that they could be misapplied and wrongly used as evidence against other accused.

In the past, difficulty has also been caused by the interpretation of the provisions against contact being made with the jury room (subs. (2)). In *Brownlie v. H.M. Advocate* (1966) S.C.C.R. Supp. 14, the clerk of court on the judge's instructions went to the jury room door and asked if the jury had understood the judge's direction. This had followed earlier difficulty and further directions. The appeal, which had founded upon both the recall of the jury for further directions and the judge's actions in causing the clerk to communicate with the jury was refused. The right of the judge to recall the jury for further directions was upheld in *McBeth v. H.M. Advocate* (1976) S.C.C.R. Supp. 123.

In *Cunningham v. H.M. Advocate*, 1984 S.C.C.R. 40 written requests for directions were delivered to the judge in chambers in the presence of both counsel and dealt with by further written directions; these events occurred outwith the presence of the accused and were not recorded in the shorthand notes. While the conviction was quashed, the court held that the Crown was not at fault and gave authority for fresh proceedings, surely the only just solution in the circumstances. *McColl v. H.M. Advocate*, 1989 S.C.C.R. 229 is a rare example of communication of an order so extreme as to constitute a miscarriage, a decision the Court of Appeal reached after granting authority to parties to precognosce the clerk of court. The clerk had given formal directions to the jurors on the instructions of the presiding judge and the court did not reconvene; no record existed of the communings between the clerk and the jurors, all of which had occurred outwith the presence of the accused. It was by no means clear whether the circumstances had been brought to the attention of both counsel but the lack of a record of proceedings was critical and the verdict was overturned.

A novel problem (but one likely to concern courts in the future) arose in *Matthewson v. H.M. Advocate*, 1989 S.C.C.R. 101 when the jury asked to be shown parts of a video tape produced in evidence. The only operator available was the procurator fiscal depute who, in the presence of counsel for one of the accused and the clerk, showed a juror how to operate the video recorder, the jury having had to return to the court in order to view the tape. The jury also sought assistance from the court in *Moir v. H.M. Advocate*, 1993 S.C.C.R. 1191 to "hear if possible ... all or part of the evidence given by [J]." Plainly at that stage in proceedings the witness could not be recalled and, in the absence of a transcript, the judge had declined to read over his own notes of evidence lest this influence the jury's own recall. The Appeal Court (at 1197) followed *Hamilton v. H.M. Advocate*, 1938 S.L.T. 333 at 337 and held that the notes could have been read if the judge so chose, but that the issue was one which fell to the judge's discretion in determining the best way to conduct the case and not subject to review by the Appeal Court.

Subs. (4)

At earlier stages in the proceedings, arrangements for accommodating jurors overnight during adjournments of trial can be made (s.88(8)) and it is presumed that the requirements of subs. (4) would then be applied to those situations. Once the jury has been charged there is no doubt that its deliberations should be interrupted only for the purposes of subs. (4). It is implicit that the jury should be unhindered in its deliberations and should in no way be pressured directly or indirectly to hasten to a verdict. See *McKenzie v. H.M. Advocate*, 1986 S.C.C.R. 94 and *Love v. H.M. Advocate*, 1995 S.C.C.R. 501.

Subs. (6)

This provision was introduced by the Prisoners and Criminal Proceedings (Scotland) Act 1993 (c. 9), s.40(1) into the 1975 Act as s.155A. Section 91 enacts that trials shall proceed from day to day until concluded, while the marginal note stipulates "Trial to be continuous". Technical objections as to want of procedure of the sort raised in *Boyle v. H.M. Advocate* above should not occur. The logical corollary of subs. (6) is s.102 below which permits other proceedings to be interrupted for the taking of a verdict, deal with the requests of, or issue further directions to, the jury in a prior trial. Section 158 of the Act allows summary proceedings to be interrupted for the same purposes.

Verdict and conviction

Verdict of jury

100.—(1) The verdict of the jury, whether the jury are unanimous or not, shall be returned orally by the foreman of the jury unless the court directs a written verdict to be returned.

(2) Where the jury are not unanimous in their verdict, the foreman shall announce that fact so that the relative entry may be made in the record.

(3) The verdict of the jury may be given orally through the foreman of the jury after consultation in the jury box without the necessity for the jury to retire.

GENERAL NOTE

The jury's verdict can be returned competently in court immediately on conclusion of the judge's charge; it is not essential that they retire to the jury room (subs. (3)) or deliberate for any length of time (*Crowe v. H.M. Advocate*, 1989 S.C.C.R. 681).

The verdict should be delivered orally to the court, a written verdict being competent only when the court has previously directed that the verdict be given to the court in that form. In part this ensures that all proceedings occur within the view and hearing of the accused; see *Kerr v. H.M. Advocate*, 1992 S.C.C.R. 281; S.L.T. 1031 discussed in the notes to s.90. It has been held in *Neil v. H.M. Advocate*, 1948 J.C. 12 that the judge is not obliged to explain the meaning of the not proven verdict on the grounds that it is well understood in Scotland, but this is surely debatable.

On rare occasions the nature of evidence can be such as to require the withdrawal of the not proven verdict from the jury; see *Reid v. H.M. Advocate*, 1947 S.L.T. 156. The presiding judge is obliged to explain the meaning of a majority verdict to the jury and it must be made clear that at least eight of the jury are minded to convict: the jury will only be asked whether the verdict is unanimous or by a majority and no further enquiry should be made into the arithmetic involved (*Pullar v. H.M. Advocate*, 1993 S.C.C.R. 514). The manner of calculating a majority has to be well understood by jurors particularly because of the availability (usually) of three verdicts and because the size of the jury can be reduced in certain circumstances to consist of as few as 12 jurors (s.90(1)). Refer to *Affleck v. H.M. Advocate*, 1987 S.C.C.R. 150.

Once the verdict has been recorded by the clerk of court, read back to them and assented as correct, it cannot be subject to further consideration by the trial court, the verdict being finally pronounced (see *McGarry v. H.M. Advocate*, 1959 J.C. 30). It has been held however that failure to read back a verdict to the jury is not itself fatal to the conviction (*Torri v. H.M. Advocate*, 1923 J.C. 52).

Previous convictions: solemn proceedings

101.—(1) Previous convictions against the accused shall not be laid before the jury, nor shall reference be made to them in presence of the jury before the verdict is returned.

(2) Nothing in subsection (1) above shall prevent the prosecutor—

(a) asking the accused questions tending to show that he has been convicted of an offence other than that with which he is charged, where he is entitled to do so under section 266 of this Act; or

(b) leading evidence of previous convictions where it is competent to do so under section 270 of this Act, and nothing in this section or in section 69 of this Act shall prevent evidence of previous convictions being led in any case where such evidence is competent in support of a substantive charge.

(3) Previous convictions shall not be laid before the presiding judge until the prosecutor moves for sentence, and in that event the prosecutor shall lay before the judge a copy of the notice referred to in subsection (2) or (4) of section 69 of this Act.

(4) On the conviction of the accused it shall be competent for the court, subject to subsection (5) below, to amend a notice of previous convictions so laid by deletion or alteration for the purpose of curing any error or defect.

(5) An amendment made to the notice of previous convictions shall not be to the prejudice of the accused.

(6) Any conviction which is admitted in evidence by the court shall be entered in the record of the trial.

(7) Where a person is convicted of an offence, the court may have regard to any previous conviction in respect of that person in deciding on the disposal of the case.

(8) Where any such intimation as is mentioned in section 69 of this Act is given by the accused, it shall be competent to prove any previous conviction included in a notice under that section in the manner specified in section 285 of this Act, and the provisions of the said section shall apply accordingly.

DEFINITIONS
"judge": s.307(1).
"previous conviction": s.307(5).
"prosecutor": s.307(1).

GENERAL NOTE

The previous convictions of the accused should not normally be made known to the court until a conviction is recorded and the prosecutor moves for sentence. There are two accepted exceptions to this general rule: first where proof of the conviction is an essential to proof of the substantive charge (for example, driving while disqualified, or contravening the provisions of the Firearms Act 1968 (c. 27), s.21, or prison-breaking—see *Russell v. H.M. Advocate*, 1991 S.C.C.R. 785 and *Varey v. H.M. Advocate*, 1986 S.L.T. 321); secondly when the accused has represented himself to be of good character or impugned the character of prosecution witnesses, the complainer or the prosecutor (see ss.266(4) and 270(1)). The prosecutor is also under a duty not to question the accused in a fashion calculated to show that he has been involved in other criminal charges which are not before the court.

The consequences of revealing previous convictions, even when this is done by the prosecutor, are not necessarily fatal; much depends on the circumstances in which the section's provisions were breached, whether the information was wilfully elicited or was imparted unexpectedly, what objection, if any, was offered to the evidence and who sought the evidence in the first place. The approach adopted by the Court of Appeal is to consider whether a miscarriage of justice has occurred (having regard, *inter alia*, to any steps taken by the trial judge to address the issue, or consciously avoid it, in his charge) and then to consider whether the breach constituted a sufficiently substantial miscarriage to merit the quashing of the conviction or amendment of the verdict. So in *McCuaig v. H.M. Advocate*, 1982 S.C.C.R. 125 where a police officer in response to a question from the trial judge read over the full terms of a charge preferred to him, making reference to the accused's previous convictions, it was held that no substantial miscarriage had occurred. Similarly in *Binks v. H.M. Advocate*, 1984 S.C.C.R. 335; 1985 S.L.T. 59 where in reading a statement given by the accused, a Customs officer during his examination-in-chief read the phrase "I don't want to go back to jail again", the court took the view that the mere disclosure of a previous conviction might be of little or no significance in the circumstances of the case. See generally *Kepple v. H.M. Advocate*, 1936 J.C. 76 and *Advocate, H.M. v. McIlwain* 1965 S.L.T. 311.

By contrast a very similar reply to caution and charge elicited by the prosecutor in *Graham v. H.M. Advocate*, 1984 S.L.T. 67 was held to be deliberate and fatal to conviction. Compare *McAvoy v. H.M. Advocate*, 1991 S.C.C.R. 123 in which the prosecutor asked a police officer about "known associates" of the accused a question, which though criticised by the Appeal Court, was held not to have breached the provisions. The central issue in studying the conduct of the prosecutor is whether the disclosure came about as a result of calculation or unacceptable want of care on his part, or whether it occurred unexpectedly or as part of a wilful ploy by a witness or co-accused. See *Deeney v. H.M. Advocate*, 1986 S.C.C.R. 393 where a witness mentioned that the accused was on licence at the time of offences, an answer not anticipated from the Crown's question and which was held not to have breached the section's provisions. More recently in *Robertson v. H.M. Advocate*, 1995 S.C.C.R. 497 where a Crown witness repeatedly referred to the accused being provided accommodation by SACRO (Scottish Association for Care and Resettlement of Offenders), using only the acronym and without divulging the objects of the organisation, the disclosure was held to be accidental and to have been dealt with sensitively in the judge's charge to the jury.

It will be noted that the section bars any reference to an accused's previous convictions (unless the provisions of subs. (2) apply) but this cannot guard against wilful conduct on the part of co-accused or defence witnesses; in such circumstances this is almost certain to be prejudicial but the court will not rush to hold that a miscarriage has occurred. See *Slane v. H.M. Advocate*, 1984 S.L.T. 293. In the first instance the judge presiding at the trial has to decide whether to mention such inadmissible evidence in order to direct that it be disregarded or whether, in the whole circumstances, it is more discreet, and effective, to say nothing at all and in so doing avoid resurrecting the objectionable evidence (see *Fyfe v. H.M. Advocate*, 1989 S.C.C.R. 429; 1990 S.L.T. 50 and *Gallagher v. H.M. Advocate*, 1992 G.W.D. 6–355).

Interruption of trial for other proceedings

102.—(1) When the jury have retired to consider their verdict, and the diet in another criminal cause has been called, then, subject to subsection (3) below, if it appears to the judge presiding at the trial to be appropriate, he may interrupt the proceedings in such other cause—

(a) in order to receive the verdict of the jury in the preceding trial, and thereafter to dispose of the case;

(b) to give a direction to the jury in the preceding trial upon any matter upon which the jury may wish a direction from the judge or to hear any request from the jury regarding any matter in the cause.

(2) Where in any case the diet of which has not been called, the accused intimates to the clerk of court that he is prepared to tender a plea of guilty as libelled or such qualified plea as the Crown is prepared to accept, or where a case is remitted to the High Court for sentence, then, subject to subsection (3) below, any trial then proceeding may be interrupted for the purpose of receiving such plea or dealing with the remitted case and pronouncing sentence or otherwise disposing of any such case.

(3) In no case shall any proceedings in the preceding trial take place in the presence of the jury in the interrupted trial, but in every case that jury shall be directed to retire by the presiding judge.

(4) On the interrupted trial being resumed the diet shall be called *de novo*.

(5) In any case an interruption under this section shall not be deemed an irregularity, nor entitle the accused to take any objection to the proceedings.

DEFINITIONS
"High Court": s.307(1).
"judge": s.307(1).

This section and, in some circumstances, s.99(6) fall to be read in conjunction. While s.91 of the Act requires that the trial shall proceed from day to day, procedural difficulties can develop when it is necessary to interpose other solemn business. See for example *Boyle v. H.M. Advocate*, 1990 S.C.C.R. 480. These problems became yet more acute when a jury trial had spilled over from a previous sitting; then the disposal of business called to the later (delayed) sitting often demanded dexterity of a high order. Section 102 admits a degree of flexibility into the administration of court business but it will be noted that when a jury trial is interrupted to deal with other business before the court, that jury is to be excluded until the fresh business is concluded.

The section also enables a jury in a later trial to be empanelled while an earlier jury deliberates, a provision which may assist on occasion to utilise court time more effectively.

Rule 14.8. of the 1996 Act of Adjournal enacts that a minute of continuation shall be entered in the minutes of the interrupted trial; Rule 14.9.–(1) permits other matters, which have been deferred for sentence to await the outcome of the jury trial, to be called once a verdict has been reached in that trial without the need to adjourn.

It will be observed that it is still necessary to call the diet anew after any such interruption (subs. (4)).

PART VIII

APPEALS FROM SOLEMN PROCEEDINGS

Appeal sittings

103.—(1) The High Court shall hold both during session and during vacation such sittings as are necessary for the disposal of appeals and other proceedings under this Part of this Act.

(2) Subject to subsection (3) below, for the purpose of hearing and determining any appeal or other proceeding under this Part of this Act three of the Lords Commissioners of Justiciary shall be a quorum of the High Court, and the determination of any question under this Part of this Act by the court shall be according to the votes of the majority of the members of the court sitting, including the presiding judge, and each judge so sitting shall be entitled to pronounce a separate opinion.

(3) For the purpose of hearing and determining any appeal under section 106(1)(b) to (e) of this Act, or any proceeding connected therewith, two of the Lords Commissioners of Justiciary shall be a quorum of the High Court, and each judge shall be entitled to pronounce a separate opinion; but where the two Lords Commissioners of Justiciary are unable to reach agreement on the disposal of the appeal, or where they consider it appropriate, the appeal shall be heard and determined in accordance with subsection (1) above.

(4) Subsections (1) and (2) above shall apply to cases certified to the High Court by a single judge of the said court and to appeals by way of advocation in like manner as they apply to appeals under this Part of this Act.

(5) The powers of the High Court under this Part of this Act—
  (a) to extend the time within which intimation of intention to appeal and note of appeal may be given;
  (b) to allow the appellant to be present at any proceedings in cases where he is not entitled to be present without leave; and
  (c) to admit an appellant to bail,
may be exercised by any judge of the High Court, sitting and acting wherever convenient, in the same manner as they may be exercised by the High Court, and subject to the same provisions.

(6) Where a judge acting under subsection (5) above refuses an application by an appellant to exercise under that subsection any power in his favour, the appellant shall be entitled to have the application determined by the High Court.

(7) Subject to subsection (5) above and without prejudice to it, preliminary and interlocutory proceedings incidental to any appeal or application may be disposed of by a single judge.

(8) In all proceedings before a judge under section (5) above, and in all preliminary and interlocutory proceedings and applications except such as are heard before the full court, the parties may be represented and appear by a solicitor alone.

DEFINITIONS
"appellant": s.132.
"bail": s.307(1).
"High Court" s.307(1).
"judge": s.307(1).
"Lords Commissioners of Justiciary": s.307(1).
"sentence": s.132.

GENERAL NOTE
The structure of the 1975 Act in regard to solemn appeals was to deal with the right of appeal (ss.228 *et seq.*) and then to consider procedure at the hearing (ss.245 *et seq.*). The 1995 Act considers the sitting of the High Court of Justiciary to deal with appeals and then the law of appeals in general.

One of the most potent changes for practitioners in the appeal court is the quorum of the High Court of Justiciary. By s.245 of the 1975 Act the quorum for "any appeal" was three and the simple logic was that in the event of division there would be a majority. Commendable as this approach is, there was for nearly all appeals no possibility of division because of judicial uniformity in approach, especially to sentencing.

The fundamental split between appeals against conviction and appeals against sentence is now reflected in the necessary quorum. For any appeal under Pt. VIII of the 1995 Act the quorum is three judges except that for appeals against sentence alone the quorum is two judges.

The effect of this change, especially when taken with the requirement to obtain leave to appeal, is likely to reduce dramatically the extent of appellate business in the High Court of Justiciary and to reduce the time waiting for appeals to appear on the roll.

The quorum is one judge in relation to the matters of extending the time within which intimation of intention to appeal and note of appeal may be given, of allowing the appellant to be present at any proceedings in cases where leave is necessary and to admit the appellant to bail.

Power of High Court in appeals

104.—(1) Without prejudice to any existing power of the High Court, it may for the purposes of an appeal under section 106(1) or 108 of this Act—
   (a) order the production of any document or other thing connected with the proceedings;
   (b) hear any additional evidence relevant to any alleged miscarriage of justice or order such evidence to be heard by a judge of the High Court or by such other person as it may appoint for that purpose;
   (c) take account of any circumstances relevant to the case which were not before the trial judge;
   (d) remit to any fit person to enquire and report in regard to any matter or circumstance affecting the appeal;
   (e) appoint a person with expert knowledge to act as assessor to the High Court in any case where it appears to the court that such expert knowledge is required for the proper determination of the case.

(2) The evidence of any witnesses ordered to be examined before the High Court or before any judge of the High Court or other person appointed by the High Court shall be taken in accordance with the existing law and practice as to the taking of evidence in criminal trials in Scotland.

(3) The appellant or applicant and the respondent or counsel on their behalf shall be entitled to be present at and take part in any examination of any witness to which this section relates.

"appellant": s.132.
"High Court": s.307(1).
"judge": s.307(1).

GENERAL NOTE

The central question in appeals against conviction is whether there has been a miscarriage of justice: s.106(3). The essence of s.104 is to allow the High Court of Justiciary, in addition to any existing powers, statutory powers relating to the investigation of an allegation of a miscarriage of justice. The substance of s.104(1) is essentially that of s.252 of the 1975 Act although it is an indication of how allegations have developed that s.104(2) and (3) clarifies doubts, if there were any, about the manner of taking additional evidence in the presence of the appellant and his lawyer.

Appeal against refusal of application

105.—(1) When an application or applications have been dealt with by a judge of the High Court, under section 103(5) of this Act, the Clerk of Justiciary shall—

  (a) notify to the applicant the decision in the form prescribed by Act of Adjournal or as nearly as may be in such form; and

  (b) where all or any of such applications have been refused, forward to the applicant the prescribed form for completion and return forthwith if he desires to have the application or applications determined by the High Court as fully constituted for the hearing of appeals under this Part of this Act.

(2) Where the applicant does not desire a determination as mentioned in subsection (1)(b) above, or does not return within five days to the Clerk the form duly completed by him, the refusal of his application or applications by the judge shall be final.

(3) Where an applicant who desires a determination by the High Court as mentioned in subsection (1)(b) above—

  (a) is not legally represented, he may be present at the hearing and determination by the High Court of the application;

  (b) is legally represented, he shall not be entitled to be present without leave of the court.

(4) When an applicant duly completes and returns to the Clerk of Justiciary within the prescribed time the form expressing a desire to be present at the hearing and determination by the court of the applications mentioned in this section, the form shall be deemed to be an application by the applicant for leave to be so present, and the Clerk of Justiciary, on receiving the form, shall take the necessary steps for placing the application before the court.

(5) If the application to be present is refused by the court, the Clerk of Justiciary shall notify the applicant; and if the application is granted, he shall notify the applicant and the Governor of the prison where the applicant is in custody and the Secretary of State.

(6) For the purpose of constituting a Court of Appeal, the judge who has refused any application may sit as a member of the court, and take part in determining the application.

DEFINITIONS

"clerk of justiciary": s.307(1).
"High Court": s.307(1).
"judge": s.307(1).

GENERAL NOTE

Under s.103(5) the quorum is one judge in relation to the matters of extending the time within which intimation of intention to appeal and note of appeal may be given, of allowing the appellant to be present at any proceedings in cases where leave is necessary and to admit the appellant to bail.

Section 105 prescribes the procedure to appeal against a refusal of an application under s.103(5). Such an appeal (not being an appeal against sentence) requires to be heard by three judges. It is strange to see that for the purposes of constituting a Court of Appeal, the judge who has refused any application may sit as a member of the court, and take part in determining the application: s.105(6).

Right of appeal

106.—(1) Any person convicted on indictment may, with leave granted in accordance with section 107 of this Act, appeal in accordance with this Part of this Act, to the High Court—

(a) against such conviction;
(b) subject to subsection (2) below, against the sentence passed on such conviction;
(c) against his absolute discharge or admonition;
(d) against any probation order or any community service order;
(e) against any order deferring sentence; or
(f) against both such conviction and, subject to subsection (2) below, such sentence or disposal or order.

(2) There shall be no appeal against any sentence fixed by law.

(3) By an appeal under subsection (1) above a person may bring under review of the High Court any alleged miscarriage of justice in the proceedings in which he was convicted, including any alleged miscarriage of justice on the basis of the existence and significance of additional evidence which was not heard at the trial and which was not available and could not reasonably have been made available at the trial.

(4) Any document, production or other thing lodged in connection with the proceedings on the trial of any person who, if convicted, is entitled or may be authorised to appeal under this Part of this Act, shall, in accordance with subsections (5) to (9) below, be kept in the custody of the court in which the conviction took place.

(5) All documents and other productions produced at the trial of a convicted person shall be kept in the custody of the court of trial in such manner as it may direct until any period allowed under or by virtue of this Part of this Act for lodging intimation of intention to appeal has elapsed.

(6) Where no direction is given as mentioned in subsection (5) above, such custody shall be in the hands of the sheriff clerk of the district of the court of the second diet to whom the clerk of court shall hand them over at the close of the trial, unless otherwise ordered by the High Court on an intimation of intention to appeal being lodged, and if within such period there has been such lodgement under this Part of this Act, they shall be so kept until the appeal, if it is proceeded with, is determined.

(7) Notwithstanding subsections (5) and (6) above, the judge of the court in which the conviction took place may, on cause shown, grant an order authorising any of such documents or productions to be released on such conditions as to custody and return as he may deem it proper to prescribe.

(8) All such documents or other productions so retained in custody or released and returned shall, under supervision of the custodian thereof, be made available for inspection and for the purpose of making copies of documents or productions to a person who has lodged an intimation of intention to appeal or as the case may be, to the convicted person's counsel or agent, and to the Crown Agent and the procurator fiscal or his deputes.

(9) Where no intimation of intention to appeal is lodged within the period mentioned in subsection (6) above, all such documents and productions shall be dealt with as they are dealt with according to the existing law and practice at the conclusion of a trial; and they shall be so dealt with if, there having been such intimation, the appeal is not proceeded with.

DEFINITIONS
"community service order": s.238.
"High Court": s.307(1).
"indictment": s.307(1).
"judge": s.307(1).
"probation order": s.228.
"procurator fiscal": s.307(1).
"sentence": s.307(1).
"sheriff court": s.307(1).

GENERAL NOTE
Subs. (1)
　Section 106 relies heavily on the terms of s.228 of the 1975 Act but with several crucial differences. The most important in law and in practice is undoubtedly the qualification that an appeal under s.106 must be "with leave granted in accordance with s.107 of this Act". Reference may be made to that section and the General Note to it for a full understanding of this new hurdle to be cleared.
　Assuming that leave has been granted, an appeal against conviction alone is possible under s.106(1)(a) and against conviction and sentence under s.106(1)(f).The hearing of these appeals will be by three judges: s.103(2). Further assuming that leave has been granted, an appeal against sentence and other similar disposals is possible under s.106(1)(b) to (e) inclusive. The hearing of these appeals will be by two judges: s.103(2).

Subs. (2)
　There is no appeal against any sentence fixed by law. The clearest example of this is the sentence of imprisonment for life for murder: s.205(1).

Subs. (3)
　The terms of this subsection are identical to those of s.228(2) of the 1975 Act and they identify the test for appeals *viz.* "the alleged miscarriage of justice in the proceedings". The essential question for appeals is this: has there been a miscarriage of justice? Other tests in other jurisdictions may be directed to whether a conviction is unsafe and unsatisfactory but the terms of the statute dictate the correct approach. However, the statute does not and has never provided a definition of what a miscarriage of justice is in law. At best it is said to include "any alleged miscarriage of justice on the basis of the existence and significance of additional evidence which was not heard at the trial and which was not available and could not reasonably have been made available at the trial". The case law, discussion and writing on this vexed topic is enormous even in a small jurisdiction such as Scotland. Moreover, the continuity of the present test through several changes in the statute means legal events since the passing of the Criminal Appeal (Scotland) Act 1926 (c.15) are relevant: to quote *Renton and Brown* (5th ed.) at para. 11–33 on p. 196,
　　"it seems, however, that matters which constituted grounds of appeal under the old law will continue to do so, and in particular that circumstances which formerly were classified as miscarriages of justice will continue to be so classified, although they may not necessarily lead to a successful appeal."
　Discussion in relation to the predecessors of s.106(3) is frequently linked to the predecessors of s.118 which provided for what the High Court of Justiciary "may" do by way of disposing of the appeal against conviction. The word in parenthesis is still to be regarded as crucial because in *McCraig v. H.M. Advocate*, 1982 S.C.C.R. 125 the statute was interpreted as allowing the court a general discretion to refuse an appeal where there has been a miscarriage of justice, but it is not regarded by the court as sufficient to warrant quashing the conviction. The circumstances in which the court will exercise its discretion to refuse or allow an appeal were set out in *McAvoy v. H.M. Advocate*, 1983 S.L.T. 16, especially *per* Lord Dunpark at pp. 21–22. Further regard to Renton and Brown (5th ed.) from para. 11–33 at p. 196, to para. 11–45a at p. 207 gives an indication of the substantial body of case law, all of which is likely to remain relevant under the 1975 Act.
　Returning to the partial definition of miscarriage of justice in s.106(3), there can be said to be three separate heads for further thought. First, the alleged miscarriage of justice may be based on "the existence and significance of additional evidence". The meaning of "additional" in solemn proceedings is the evidence which was not laid before the judge: see Lord McCluskey *Criminal Appeals* (1992) at p. 161, where it is also pointed out that the further qualification of the evidence being that which was "not heard at the trial" means that evidence might be adduced in a so-called "trial within a trial" and not adduced before a jury.
　Secondly, that additional evidence must have been unavailable. It is not simply a matter of fact because in trials with several accused no one accused can be compelled to give evidence. The

evidence of one accused is not available to a co-accused. Lord McCluskey concludes, *ibid.*, at p. 163 that the test of "availability" must be considered from the standpoint of the appellant, taking full account of what was practicable to him at the trial.

Thirdly, the partial definition raises the aspect of reasonable availability. The simple view here is that if an accused person elects, as he is entitled to do, not to give evidence at his own trial he will not be able to persuade the High Court of Justiciary that evidence which he could have given was not reasonably available at the trial: *McDonald v. H.M. Advocate*, 1987 S.C.C.R. 153. However, the problem of what in context is reasonable raises many issues, partially of definition and partially, it has to be said, of professional assessment: at what point does a solicitor cease preparation for a solemn case? *McCarroll v. H.M. Advocate*, 1949 J.C. 10 prohibits criticism of one's lawyer as a ground for alleging a miscarriage of justice, but contemporary doubts about the correctness of the rigidity of that approach suggest a sea change in this regard.

Subss. (4) to (9)

The remaining subsections of s.106 are concerned with the custody of trial documents, productions and related matters. The emphasis in Scotland on real evidence means that there are or can be a substantial quantity of material to be kept safe for the possible consideration of the appellate judges or until such time as it seems reasonable to consider that there is not to be an appeal.

Sentence

The foregoing note is directed principally to any alleged miscarriage of justice in relation to conviction but it is competent to bring under review of the High Court of Justiciary any alleged miscarriage of justice, including one which arises in relation to sentence on the basis of additional evidence not reasonably available at the trial: see *Renton and Brown* (5th ed.) para. 11–47, at p. 208. At any rate in appeals against sentence the test is no longer (as before 1980) whether the sentence was harsh and oppressive but whether it was excessive: *Addison v. Mackinnon*, 1983 S.C.C.R. 52; *Donaldson v. H.M. Advocate*, 1983 S.C.C.R. 216. A bald statement that a sentence is excessive might reasonably be said to be lacking in specification. There must be an indication of the circumstances to be relied on. One important reason for that is to allow the trial judge or the sheriff to report fully upon them for the appellate judges.

Leave to appeal

107.—(1) The decision whether to grant leave to appeal for the purposes of section 106(1) of this Act shall be made by a judge of the High Court who shall—

    (a) if he considers that the documents mentioned in subsection (2) below disclose arguable grounds of appeal, grant leave to appeal and make such comments in writing as he considers appropriate; and

    (b) in any other case—

        (i) refuse leave to appeal and give reasons in writing for the refusal; and

        (ii) where the appellant is on bail and the sentence imposed on his conviction is one of imprisonment, grant a warrant to apprehend and imprison him.

(2) The documents referred to in subsection (1) above are—

    (a) the note of appeal lodged under section 110(1)(a) of this Act;

    (b) in the case of an appeal against conviction or sentence in a sheriff court, the certified copy or, as the case may be, the record of the proceedings at the trial;

    (c) where the judge who presided at the trial furnishes a report under section 113 of this Act, that report; and

    (d) where, by virtue of section 94(1) of this Act, a transcript of the charge to the jury of the judge who presided at the trial is delivered to the Clerk of Justiciary, that transcript.

(3) A warrant granted under subsection (1)(b)(ii) above shall not take effect until the expiry of the period of 14 days mentioned in subsection (4) below without an application to the High Court for leave to appeal having been lodged by the appellant under that subsection.

(4) Where leave to appeal is refused under subsection (1) above the appellant may, within 14 days of intimation under subsection (7) below, apply to the High Court for leave to appeal.

(5) In deciding an application under subsection (4) above the High Court shall—

(a) if, after considering the documents mentioned in subsection (2) above and the reasons for the refusal, the court is of the opinion that there are arguable grounds of appeal, grant leave to appeal and make such comments in writing as the court considers appropriate; and

(b) in any other case—

(i) refuse leave to appeal and give reasons in writing for the refusal; and

(ii) where the appellant is on bail and the sentence imposed on his conviction is one of imprisonment, grant a warrant to apprehend and imprison him.

(6) Consideration whether to grant leave to appeal under subsection (1) or (5) above shall take place in chambers without the parties being present.

(7) Comments in writing made under subsection (1)(a) or (5)(a) above may, without prejudice to the generality of that provision, specify the arguable grounds of appeal (whether or not they are contained in the note of appeal) on the basis of which leave to appeal is granted.

(8) Where the arguable grounds of appeal are specified by virtue of subsection (7) above it shall not, except by leave of the High Court on cause shown, be competent for the appellant to found any aspect of his appeal on any ground of appeal contained in the note of appeal but not so specified.

(9) Any application by the appellant for the leave of the High Court under subsection (8) above—

(a) shall be made not less than seven days before the date fixed for the hearing of the appeal; and

(b) shall, not less that seven days before that date, be intimated by the appellant to the Crown Agent.

(10) The Clerk of Justiciary shall forthwith intimate—

(a) a decision under subsection (1) or (5) above; and

(b) in the case of a refusal of leave to appeal, the reasons for the decision, to the appellant or his solicitor and to the Crown Agent.

DEFINITIONS
"bail": s.307(1).
"High Court": s.307(1).
"judge": s.307(1).

GENERAL NOTE
It is probably more convenient in seeking to understand the full import of this section to consider the law under the headings of, on the one hand, leave to appeal and, on the other, application for leave to appeal. Separate consideration of the hearing must be made.

Leave to appeal
The procedure of seeking leave to appeal existed prior to this change of the law to the extent that leave to appeal was required for an appeal arising out of a preliminary diet: s.76A(1) of the 1975 Act. However, under the previous law leave to appeal was not required for any appeal after conviction and now that such leave is required there can be said to have been a major change in the law.

Section 106 allows a right of appeal to any person convicted on indictment and such appeal may be against conviction or sentence or both. The right of appeal is conditional on a ground of leave to appeal by a judge of the High Court of Justiciary in terms of s.107. Before the judge can decide the grant he must have documents before him and these are specified as the note of appeal, the certified copy or actual record of proceedings for a sheriff court trial, a judge's report and a transcript of the charge to the jury by the judge, as necessary: subs. (2). Having considered these documents the judge must decide whether they disclose arguable grounds of appeal:

subs. (1)(a). The action that follows such a decision depends on which way the decision goes. Before considering the alternatives the turning point requires analysis: what are "arguable grounds of appeal"?

To answer that question one might start with "High Court of Justiciary Practice Note" dated March 29, 1985 (*Renton and Brown* (5th ed.) Appendix G. at p. 905). There, judicial criticism is directed predominantly at grounds of appeal which are found in notes of appeal to be "wholly unspecific". The examples given in the Note are, first, an allegation of "misdirection" without any specification whatever. Secondly, "insufficient evidence" without any specification of the particular point, if any, which is to be taken. Examples are also given in relation to appeals against sentence where the ground of appeal is "more often than not equally uninformative" with a bare allegation of a sentence being excessive or severe.

The Practice Note indicated in terms that it was intended to remind practitioners that grounds of appeal must be stated with sufficient specification to identify the particular criticism of the conviction or sentence which the appellant hopes to present at the hearing.

It can readily be seen that appellate judges require detail in the grounds of appeal such as allows some insight as to the appellant's complaint. Detail alone may not take matters far: although the allegation of a miscarriage of justice is the only ground of appeal, there are various particular grounds of appeal, which are commonly advanced as a basis for the conclusion that there has been a miscarriage of justice.

Lord McCluskey in *Criminal Appeals* (1992) at pp. 177–189 discusses some of the possible types or categories of appeal: it may be that there is alleged to have been a misdirection by the presiding judge (by omission, with an error of law, or regarding corroboration), that the conduct of the trial judge, the prosecutor or the defence advocate was improper, that the proceedings were incompetent or that there were some other irregularities. There are ample precedents for all these allegations. In short, "arguable grounds of appeal" are such to indicate, in Lord McCluskey's words, *ibid.* at p. 177, "clarity, accuracy, brevity and comprehensiveness" and which invite a conclusion that there has been in law a miscarriage of justice.

The judge of the High Court of Justiciary who will consider the documents to decide whether they disclose arguable grounds of appeal does so in chambers without the parties being present: subs.107(6). If the judge considers that the documents do disclose arguable grounds of appeal he then grants leave to appeal and he makes such comments in writing as he considers appropriate: subs.107(1)(a). If the judge considers that the documents do not disclose arguable grounds of appeal he then refuses leave to appeal and he gives reasons in writing for the refusal: subs. (1)(b)(i).

The appellant, who is at this stage on bail and who had a sentence of imprisonment imposed on conviction, will then be the subject of a warrant to apprehend granted by the judge and on implementation the appellant will be imprisoned: subs. (1)(b)(ii).

The warrant to apprehend and imprison under subs. (1)(b)(ii) shall not take effect until the expiry of the period of 14 days during which period the appellant may, in effect, appeal by making an application to the High Court of Justiciary: subs. (4). If no such application is to be made then the appellant's solicitor has the time available to arrange for the client to surrender to the warrant.

Application for leave to appeal

There can be no doubt that this change in law will end any practice, if there is one, of lodging broad and vague grounds of appeal against conviction or sentence to be supplemented with speculative advocacy before the appellate judges. A clear ground will require to be formulated at a far earlier point in the procedure.

There are no statutory grounds for the reason for, in effect, appealing the decision of the single judge in chambers. The provision merely states that if leave to appeal is refused under subs. (1) then the appellant may within 14 days of intimation apply to the High Court of Justiciary for leave to appeal against the original conviction or sentence or both: subs. (4).

Who decides the application in terms of subs. (4) depends on what is at issue, namely, on appeal against conviction, sentence or conviction and sentence. By s.103(2) "for the purpose of hearing and determining any appeal or other proceeding under this Part of this Act" the quorum is three judges, except that by s.103(3) for appeals against sentence alone the quorum is two judges.

The various judges of the High Court of Justiciary who must consider the documents to decide whether they disclose arguable grounds of appeal do so in chambers without the parties being present: subs. (6).

In deciding the application the judges must consider the documents that had been before the single judge in chambers and also consider the reasons for the earlier refusal but thereafter, if the court is of the opinion that there are arguable grounds of appeal, then the court should grant leave to appeal and make such comments in writing as the court considers appropriate:

subs. (5)(a). In any other case, leave to appeal will be refused with reasons in writing and a warrant to apprehend and imprison is to be granted if appropriate: subs. (5)(b).

Hearing of appeal

Regard must be paid to the comments in writing made either by the single judge in chambers by subs. (1)(a) or by a greater number of judges in chambers by subs. (5)(a). The importance of the comments in writing lies in the possibility that they "may specify the arguable grounds of appeal (whether or not they are contained in the note of appeal) on the basis of which leave to appeal is granted": subs. (7).

It is very easy to imagine on the wording of subs. (1)(a) a single judge in chambers granting leave to appeal, not on the original grounds in the note of appeal, but on the basis of comments in writing which amend, alter or distil the original grounds in the note of appeal. The new grounds of appeal, having been specified, in effect dictate the ground of appeal to be argued at the hearing: subs. (8).

The appellant who wishes to found any aspect of his appeal on any ground of appeal contained in the note of appeal but not so specified in the comments in writing provided under subs. (1)(a) or subs. (5)(a) may seek leave of the High Court of Justiciary to do so: subs. (8). Application for such leave under subs. (8) must be made not less than seven days before the date fixed for the hearing of the appeal: subs. (9). It is not immediately clear from a reading of the statute as to whom an application under subs. (8) will be directed. As it is not so much an appeal as a request to broaden an approach to an appeal it may simply be returned to those who made the comments in writing under subss. (1)(a) or (5)(a).

Lord Advocate's appeal against sentence

108. Where a person has been convicted on indictment, the Lord Advocate may appeal against the sentence passed on conviction or against any probation order or any community service order or against the person's absolute discharge or admonition or against any order deferring sentence—

(a) if it appears to the Lord Advocate that, as the case may be—

(i) the sentence is unduly lenient;

(ii) the making of the probation order or community service order is unduly lenient or its terms are unduly lenient;

(iii) to dismiss with an admonition or to discharge absolutely is unduly lenient; or

(iv) the deferment of sentence is inappropriate or on unduly lenient conditions; or

(b) on a point of law.

DEFINITIONS
    "community service order": s.238.
    "indictment": s.307(1).
    "probation order": s.228.

GENERAL NOTE

As there was no tariff for sentences in the criminal courts of Scotland the selection of the appropriate sentence was clearly a matter for the individual discretion of the sentencer: *Strawhorn v. Mcleod*, 1987 S.C.C.R. 413. The present Act invites the High Court of Justiciary, in appropriate circumstances, to pronounce an opinion on the sentence or other disposal or order which is appropriate in any similar case: ss.118(7) and 189(7).

In this developing line, the Crown right of appeal against an unduly lenient sentence can only proceed in circumstances where "it appears" that a sentence is unduly lenient: s.228A of the 1975 Act as amended, and now s.108 of the present Act.

Accordingly, having regard to judicial dicta on earlier occasions, it appeared to the Lord Advocate that the supply of class A controlled drugs to young teenagers was a crime that merited a sentence that was not a community service order, and the High Court of Justiciary agreed. The original sentence was quashed and in its place a period of three years detention in a young offender institution was imposed: *Advocate, H.M. v. McPhee*, 1994 S.L.T. 1292.

Intimation of intention to appeal

109.—(1) Subject to section 111(2) of this Act and to section 10 of the Proceeds of Crime (Scotland) Act 1995 (postponed confiscation orders), where a person desires to appeal under section 106(1)(a) or (f) of this Act, he shall within two weeks of the final determination of the proceedings, lodge with the Clerk of Justiciary written intimation of intention to appeal which shall identify the proceedings and be in as nearly as may be the form prescribed by Act of Adjournal.

(2) A copy of intimation given under subsection (1) above shall be sent to the Crown Agent.

(3) On intimation under subsection (1) above being lodged by a person in custody, the Clerk of Justiciary shall give notice of the intimation to the Secretary of State.

(4) Subject to subsection (5) below, for the purposes of subsection (1) above and section 106(5) to (7) of this Act, proceedings shall be deemed finally determined on the day on which sentence is passed in open court.

(5) Where in relation to an appeal under section 106(1)(a) of this Act sentence is deferred under section 202 of this Act, the proceedings shall be deemed finally determined on the day on which sentence is first so deferred in open court.

(6) Without prejudice to section 10 of the said Act of 1995, the reference in subsection (4) above to "the day on which sentence is passed in open court" shall, in relation to any case in which, under subsection (1) of that section, a decision has been postponed for a period, be construed as a reference to the day on which that decision is made, whether or not a confiscation order is then made or any other sentence is then passed.

DEFINITIONS
    "Clerk of Justiciary": s.307(1).
    "sentence": s.307(1).

GENERAL NOTE
    It is crucial to recall that the right of appeal under s.106(1) relates to all convictions on indictment. It is as important to know that all appeals following conviction on indictment are initiated in the justiciary office and not in the sheriff court. The intimation of an intention to appeal required under this section is important for it gives an office in Edinburgh notice of an appeal from a trial that may have occurred in any one of the sheriff courts of Scotland or one of the towns where the High Court has been on circuit. Those who may be required to produce notes or reports can thus be put on notice.

Note of appeal

110.—(1) Subject to section 111(2) of this Act—
  (a) within six weeks of lodging intimation of intention to appeal or, in the case of an appeal under section 106(1)(b) to (e) of this Act, within two weeks of the passing of the sentence (or, as the case may be, of the making of the order disposing of the case or deferring sentence) in open court, the convicted person may lodge a written note of appeal with the Clerk of Justiciary who shall send a copy to the judge who presided at the trial and to the Crown Agent; or, as the case may be,
  (b) within four weeks of the passing of the sentence in open court, the Lord Advocate may lodge such a note with the Clerk of Justiciary, who shall send a copy to the said judge and to the convicted person or that person's solicitor.

(2) The period of six weeks mentioned in paragraph (a) of subsection (1) above may be extended, before it expires, by the Clerk of Justiciary.

(3) A note of appeal shall—
  (a) identify the proceedings;
  (b) contain a full statement of all the grounds of appeal; and
  (c) be in as nearly as may be the form prescribed by Act of Adjournal.

(4) Except by leave of the High Court on cause shown, it shall not be competent for an appellant to found any aspect of his appeal on a ground not contained in the note of appeal.

(5) Subsection (4) above shall not apply as respects any ground of appeal specified as an arguable ground of appeal by virtue of subsection (7) of section 107 of this Act.

(6) On a note of appeal under section 106(1)(b) to (e) of this Act being lodged by an appellant in custody the Clerk of Justiciary shall give notice of that fact to the Secretary of State.

DEFINITIONS
    "Clerk of Justiciary": s.307(1).
    "judge": s.307(1).

GENERAL NOTE
    Three periods of time are envisaged by this section. First, for all solemn appeals written intimation of intention to appeal should be lodged within two weeks of the final determination with the Clerk of Justiciary by s.109(1). Alternatively, and secondly, if the appeal is only against sentence then the period is two weeks: subs. (1)(a). It is clear that if conviction is accepted fewer papers are required and less preparatory work is necessary. Thirdly, if the Crown wishes to appeal (against, for example, what appears to be an unduly lenient sentence) a note of appeal must be lodged within four weeks: subs. (1)(b).
    Those lodging notes of appeal must have regard to two important points. The note of appeal must contain a full statement of all the grounds of appeal: subs. (3)(b). There are a number of reported cases that emphasise the importance of specification; see, for example, *Mitchell v. H.M. Advocate*, 1991 S.C.C.R. 216. The previous importance is accentuated by the new requirement to disclose arguable grounds of appeal in the note of appeal for the consideration of a single judge in chambers to obtain leave to appeal: s.107(1)(a) and (2)(a).
    Further, it is not competent, except by leave of the High Court of Justiciary on cause shown, for an appellant to found any aspect of his appeal on a ground not contained in the note of appeal: subs. (4). The narrow approach is also emphasised earlier in the Act: s.107(8).

Provisions supplementary to sections 109 and 110

111.—(1) Where the last day of any period mentioned in sections 109(1) and 110(1) of this Act falls on a day on which the office of the Clerk of Justiciary is closed, such period shall extend to and include the next day on which such office is open.

(2) Any period mentioned in section 109(1) or 110(1)(a) of this Act may be extended at any time by the High Court in respect of any convicted person; and an application for such extension may be made under this subsection and shall be in as nearly as may be the form prescribed by Act of Adjournal.

DEFINITIONS
    "Clerk of Justiciary": s.307(1).
    "High Court": s.307(1).

Admission of appellant to bail

112.—(1) Subject to subsection (2) below, the High Court may, if it thinks fit, on the application of a convicted person, admit him to bail pending the determination of—
    (a) his appeal; or
    (b) any relevant appeal by the Lord Advocate under section 108 of this Act.

(2) The High Court shall not admit a convicted person to bail under subsection (1) above unless—
    (a) where he is the appellant and has not lodged a note of appeal in accordance with section 110(1)(a) of this Act, the application for bail

states reasons why it should be granted and sets out the proposed grounds of appeal; or
(b) where the Lord Advocate is the appellant, the application for bail states reasons why it should be granted,
and, in either case, the High Court considers there to be exceptional circumstances justifying admitting the convicted person to bail.

(3) A person who is admitted to bail under subsection (1) above shall, unless the High Court otherwise directs, appear personally in court on the day or days fixed for the hearing of the appeal.

(4) Where an appellant fails to appear personally in court as mentioned in subsection (3) above, the court may—
  (a) if he is the appellant—
    (i) decline to consider the appeal; and
    (ii) dismiss it summarily; or
  (b) whether or not he is the appellant—
    (i) consider and determine the appeal; or
    (ii) without prejudice to section 27 of this Act, make such other order as the court thinks fit.

(5) For the purposes of subsections (1), (3) and (4) above, "appellant" includes not only a person who has lodged a note of appeal but also one who has lodged an intimation of intention to appeal.

DEFINITIONS
"appellant": s.112(5).
"bail": s.307(1).
"High Court": s.307(1).

GENERAL NOTE
This section follows earlier authorities that allowed the High Court of Justiciary, if it thought fit, to admit an appellant to bail pending determination of the appeal. It is, however, for the appellant to show cause why he should be admitted to bail: *Young v. H.M. Advocate*, 1946 J.C. 5. The provision, however, should be read in the context of s.26 of this Act for if the appellant has previously been convicted of murder, culpable homicide or rape or attempted murder or attempted rape then bail shall not be granted if that person has been charged with or convicted of attempted murder, culpable homicide, rape or attempted rape.

Judge's report

113.—(1) As soon as is reasonably practicable after receiving the copy note of appeal sent to him under section 110(1) of this Act, the judge who presided at the trial shall furnish the Clerk of Justiciary with a written report giving the judge's opinion on the case generally and on the grounds contained in the note of appeal.

(2) The Clerk of Justiciary shall send a copy of the judge's report—
  (a) to the convicted person or his solicitor;
  (b) to the Crown Agent; and
  (c) in a case referred under section 124(3) of this Act, to the Secretary of State.

(3) Where the judge's report is not furnished as mentioned in subsection (1) above, the High Court may call for the report to be furnished within such period as it may specify or, if it thinks fit, hear and determine the appeal without the report.

(4) Subject to subsection (2) above, the report of the judge shall be available only to the High Court, the parties and, on such conditions as may be prescribed by Act of Adjournal, such other persons or classes of persons as may be so prescribed.

DEFINITIONS
"Clerk of Justiciary": s.307(1).
"High Court": s.307(1).
"judge": s.307(1).

Applications made orally or in writing

114. Subject to any provision of this Part of this Act to the contrary, any application to the High Court may be made by the appellant or respondent as the case may be or by counsel on his behalf, orally or in writing.

DEFINITIONS
  "appellant": s.132.
  "High Court": s.307(1).

Presentation of appeal in writing

115.—(1) If an appellant, other than the Lord Advocate, desires to present his case and his argument in writing instead of orally he shall, at least four days before the diet fixed for the hearing of the appeal—

(a) intimate this desire to the Clerk of Justiciary;

(b) lodge with the Clerk of Justiciary three copies of his case and argument; and

(c) send a copy of the intimation, case and argument to the Crown Agent.

(2) Any case or argument presented as mentioned in subsection (1) above shall be considered by the High Court.

(3) Unless the High Court otherwise directs, the respondent shall not make a written reply to a case and argument presented as mentioned in subsection (1) above, but shall reply orally at the diet fixed for the hearing of the appeal.

(4) Unless the High Court otherwise allows, an appellant who has presented his case and argument in writing shall not be entitled to submit in addition an oral argument to the court in support of the appeal.

DEFINITIONS
  "appellant": s.132.
  "Clerk of Justiciary": s.307(1).
  "High Court": s.307(1).

Abandonment of appeal

116.—(1) An appellant may abandon his appeal by lodging with the Clerk of Justiciary a notice of abandonment in as nearly as may be the form prescribed by Act of Adjournal; and on such notice being lodged the appeal shall be deemed to have been dismissed by the court.

(2) A person who has appealed against both conviction and sentence (or, as the case may be, against both conviction and disposal or order) may abandon the appeal in so far as it is against conviction and may proceed with it against sentence (or disposal or order) alone.

DEFINITIONS
  "appellant": s.132.
  "Clerk of Justiciary": s.307(1).
  "sentence": s.132.

Presence of appellant or applicant at hearing

117.—(1) Where an appellant or applicant is in custody the Clerk of Justiciary shall notify—

(a) the appellant or applicant;

(b) the Governor of the prison in which the appellant or applicant then is; and

(c) the Secretary of State,

of the probable day on which the appeal or application will be heard.

(2) The Secretary of State shall take steps to transfer the appellant or applicant to a prison convenient for his appearance before the High Court at such reasonable time before the hearing as shall enable him to consult his legal adviser, if any.

(3) A convicted appellant, notwithstanding that he is in custody, shall be entitled to be present if he desires it, at the hearing of his appeal.

(4) When an appellant or applicant is to be present at any diet—

(a) before the High Court or any judge of that court; or

(b) for the taking of additional evidence before a person appointed for that purpose under section 104(1)(b) of this Act, or

(c) for an examination or investigation by a special commissioner in terms of section 104(1)(d) of this Act,

the Clerk of Justiciary shall give timeous notice to the Secretary of State, in the form prescribed by Act of Adjournal or as nearly as may be in such form.

(5) A notice under subsection (4) above shall be sufficient warrant to the Secretary of State for transmitting the appellant or applicant in custody from prison to the place where the diet mentioned in that subsection or any subsequent diet is to be held and for reconveying him to prison at the conclusion of such diet.

(6) The appellant or applicant shall appear at any diet mentioned in subsection (4) above in ordinary civilian clothes.

(7) Where the Lord Advocate is the appellant, subsections (1) to (6) above shall apply in respect of the convicted person, if in custody, as they apply to an appellant or applicant in custody.

(8) The Secretary of State shall, on notice under subsection (4) above from the Clerk of Justiciary, ensure that sufficient male and female prison officers attend each sitting of the court, having regard to the list of appeals for the sitting.

(9) When the High Court fixes the date for the hearing of an appeal or of an application under section 111(2) of this Act, the Clerk of Justiciary shall give notice to the Crown Agent and to the solicitor of the convicted person, or to the convicted person himself if he has no known solicitor.

DEFINITIONS
"appellant": s.132.
"Clerk of Justiciary": s.307(1).
"diet": s.307(1).
"governor": s.307(1).
"High Court": s.307(1).
"judge": s.307(1).

Disposal of appeals

118.—(1) The High Court may, subject to subsection (4) below, dispose of an appeal against conviction by—

(a) affirming the verdict of the trial court;

(b) setting aside the verdict of the trial court and either quashing the conviction or, subject to subsection (2) below, substituting therefor an amended verdict of guilty; or

(c) setting aside the verdict of the trial court and quashing the conviction and granting authority to bring a new prosecution in accordance with section 119 of this Act.

(2) An amended verdict of guilty substituted under subsection (1) above must be one which could have been returned on the indictment before the trial court.

(3) In setting aside, under subsection (1) above, a verdict the High Court may quash any sentence imposed on the appellant (or, as the case may be, any disposal or order made) as respects the indictment, and—

(a) in a case where it substitutes an amended verdict of guilty, whether or not the sentence (or disposal or order) related to the verdict set aside; or

(b) in any other case, where the sentence (or disposal or order) did not so relate,

may pass another (but not more severe) sentence or make another (but not more severe) disposal or order in substitution for the sentence, disposal or order so quashed.

(4) The High Court may, subject to subsection (5) below, dispose of an appeal against sentence by—

(a) affirming such sentence; or

(b) if the Court thinks that, having regard to all the circumstances, including any additional evidence such as is mentioned in section 106(3) of this Act, a different sentence should have been passed, quashing the sentence and passing another sentence whether more or less severe in substitution therefor,

and, in this subsection, "appeal against sentence" shall, without prejudice to the generality of the expression, be construed as including an appeal under section 106(1)(c) to (e), and any appeal under section 108, of this Act; and other references to sentence shall be construed accordingly.

(5) In relation to any appeal under section 106(1) of this Act, the High Court shall, where it appears to it that the appellant committed the act charged against him but that he was insane when he did so, dispose of the appeal by—

(a) setting aside the verdict of the trial court and substituting therefor a verdict of acquittal on the ground of insanity; and

(b) quashing any sentence imposed on the appellant (or disposal or order made) as respects the indictment and—

(i) making, in respect of the appellant, any order mentioned in section 57(2)(a) to (d) of this Act; or

(ii) making no order.

(6) Subsections (3) and (4) of section 57 of this Act shall apply to an order made under subsection (5)(b)(i) above as they apply to an order made under subsection (2) of that section.

(7) In disposing of an appeal under section 106(1)(b) to (f) or 108 of this Act the High Court may, without prejudice to any other power in that regard, pronounce an opinion on the sentence or other disposal or order which is appropriate in any similar case.

(8) No conviction, sentence, judgment, order of court or other proceeding whatsoever in or for the purposes of solemn proceedings under this Act—

(a) shall be quashed for want of form; or

(b) where the accused had legal assistance in his defence, shall be suspended or set aside in respect of any objections to—

(i) the relevancy of the indictment, or the want of specification therein; or

(ii) the competency or admission or rejection of evidence at the trial in the inferior court,

unless such objections were timeously stated.

DEFINITIONS
"appeal against sentence": s.118(4).
"High Court": s.307(1).
"sentence": s.307(1).

GENERAL NOTE
Appeal against conviction
Subsection (1) is concerned with appeals against conviction following solemn proceedings. The High Court of Justiciary may dispose of an appeal by affirming the verdict of the trial court: subs. (1)(a). Alternatively, the High Court of Justiciary may dispose of an appeal by setting aside the verdict of the trial court: subs. (1)(b) and (c). What follows after setting aside the verdict depends on what has gone wrong and how that is to be corrected.

The High Court of Justiciary may set aside the verdict and quash the conviction and that may be done where the irregularity was substantial: *e.g. Gardiner v. H.M. Advocate*, 1978 S.L.T. 118. Alternatively, the High Court of Justiciary may set aside the verdict and substitute therefor an amended verdict of guilty: *e.g. Salmond v. H.M. Advocate*, 1991 S.C.C.R. 43 in which it was clear that the jury held some criminal behaviour proved but returned an incorrect verdict owing to a misunderstanding of the law.

The High Court of Justiciary may set aside the verdict of the trial court and quash the conviction and grant, on statutory grounds, authority to bring a new prosecution: *e.g. Mackenzie v. H.M. Advocate*, 1982 S.C.C.R. 499 through many cases to *McDade v. H.M. Advocate*, 1994 S.C.C.R. 627.

The setting aside of the verdict of the trial court and the quashing of the conviction in the context of a misdirection to the jury does not necessarily lead to the grant of authority to bring a new prosecution. In *Farooq v. H.M. Advocate*, 1993 S.L.T. 1271 the ages of child witnesses and the generally unsatisfactory nature of the evidence resulted in such authority being refused. The power in subs. (1) to set aside the verdict of the court necessarily requires a comparable power to deal with the question of sentence. Subsection (3) allows variation of sentence but whenever a sentence is varied a substituted sentence may only be the same or less than the original sentence. An appeal against conviction alone does not allow a variation of sentence for the imposition of a more severe sentence: *cf.* the earlier position, *e.g.* in *O'Neil v. H.M. Advocate*, 1976 S.L.T. (Notes) 7.

Appeals against sentence
Subsection (4) is concerned with appeals against sentence following solemn proceedings. The High Court of Justiciary may dispose of an appeal by affirming the sentence complained of: subs. (4)(a). Alternatively, the High Court of Justiciary may dispose of an appeal by quashing the sentence complained of and passing another sentence "whether more or less severe" in substitution. In doing the latter, the High Court of Justiciary may have regard to additional evidence such as that mentioned in s.106(3) of this Act.

An example of a more severe sentence being substituted is to be found in *Donnelly v. H.M. Advocate*, 1988 S.C.C.R. 386 where 18 months' detention was quashed and two years' detention substituted for a youth who had a CS gas canister at a football match. In contrast, a less serious sentence was substituted in *McIntyre v. H.M. Advocate*, 1994 G.W.D. 28–1687 where 20 years' imprisonment was quashed and was substituted with 14 years' imprisonment for culpable homicide for throwing or pouring acid on another.

Supplementary provisions
In relation to any appeal under s.160(1) of this Act, the High Court of Justiciary is required to set aside the verdict of the trial court and quash the sentence and make an order where it appears that the appellant committed the act charged against him but that he was insane when he did so: subss. (5) and (6). When disposing of appeals against sentence generally, the High Court of Justiciary may pronounce an opinion on the sentence or other disposal or order which is appropriate in any similar case: subs. (7).

Two other matters may have important consequences for appeals. First, no conviction, sentence, judgment, order of court or other proceedings whatsoever in or for the purposes of solemn proceedings shall be quashed for want of form: subs. (8)(A).

Secondly, and similarly, no conviction, sentence, judgment, order of court or other proceeding whatsoever in or for the purposes of solemn proceedings, where the accused had legal assistance in his defence, shall be suspended or set aside in respect of any objection to, either, the relevancy of the indictment, or the want of specification, or, the competency or admission or rejection of evidence at trial in the lower court, unless such objections were timeously stated: subs. (8)(b)(i) and (ii).

The concept of timeous objection was to be found in s.454 of the 1975 Act in relation to summary trials and it was said to be "special to summary trials": Renton and Brown (5th ed.) para. 14–61 at p. 300. For a recent case of how the section worked, see *McPherson v. McNaughton*, 1992 S.L.T. 600.

Provision where High Court authorises new prosecution

119.—(1) Subject to subsection (2) below, where authority is granted under section 118(1)(c) of this Act, a new prosecution may be brought charging the accused with the same or any similar offence arising out of the same facts; and the proceedings out of which the appeal arose shall not be a bar to such new prosecution.

(2) In a new prosecution under this section the accused shall not be charged with an offence more serious than that of which he was convicted in the earlier proceedings.

(3) No sentence may be passed on conviction under the new prosecution which could not have been passed on conviction under the earlier proceedings.

(4) A new prosecution may be brought under this section, notwithstanding that any time limit, other than the time limit mentioned in subsection (5) below, for the commencement of such proceedings has elapsed.

(5) Proceedings in a prosecution under this section shall be commenced within two months of the date on which authority to bring the prosecution was granted.

(6) In proceedings in a new prosecution under this section it shall, subject to subsection (7) below, be competent for either party to lead any evidence which it was competent for him to lead in the earlier proceedings.

(7) The indictment in a new prosecution under this section shall identify any matters as respects which the prosecutor intends to lead evidence by virtue of subsection (6) above which would not have been competent but for that subsection.

(8) For the purposes of subsection (5) above, proceedings shall be deemed to be commenced—

(a) in a case where a warrant to apprehend or to cite the accused is executed without unreasonable delay, on the date on which the warrant is granted; and

(b) in any other case, on the date on which the warrant is executed.

(9) Where the two months mentioned in subsection (5) above elapse and no new prosecution has been brought under this section, the order under section 118(1)(c) of this Act setting aside the verdict shall have the effect, for all purposes, of an acquittal.

(10) On granting authority under section 118(1)(c) of this Act to bring a new prosecution, the High Court shall, after giving the parties an opportunity of being heard, order the detention of the accused person in custody or admit him to bail.

(11) Subsections (4)(b) and (7) to (9) of section 65 of this Act (prevention of delay in trials) shall apply to an accused person who is detained under subsection (10) above as they apply to an accused person detained by virtue of being committed until liberated in due course of law.

DEFINITIONS
"High Court": s.307(1).
"offence": s.307(1).
"prosecutor": s.307(1).
"sentence": s.307(1).

GENERAL NOTE
Subs. (1)
There have been a considerable number of new prosecutions on statutory authority in its earlier form: see, *e.g. Mackenzie v. H.M. Advocate*, 1982 S.C.C.R. 499, *King v. H.M. Advocate*, 1985 S.C.C.R. 322, *McGhee v. H.M. Advocate*, 1991 S.C.C.R. 510, and *Allison v. H.M. Advocate*, 1994 S.C.C.R. 464. The grant of such authority does not mean that the Crown is bound to initiate new proceedings: see *e.g. Sinclair v. H.M. Advocate*, 1990 S.C.C.R. 412.

Subs. (2)

In a new prosecution under s.119 the accused is not to be *charged* with an offence more serious than that of which he was convicted in the earlier proceedings. The clearest example of this restriction is the case of Daniel Boyle. He had been charged with murder and after trial in the High Court of Justiciary at Glasgow he was convicted of culpable homicide in November 1991. He was sentenced to 10 years' detention. He appealed against conviction and that verdict was set aside in July 1992: *Boyle v. H.M. Advocate*, 1993 S.L.T. 577. The High Court of Justiciary, in setting aside that verdict, granted authority to the Crown to bring a new prosecution in accordance with s.254(1)(c) of the 1975 Act.

A new indictment with a charge of murder was served on Boyle on July 30, 1992 for trial on August 31, 1992 but the trial diet was overtaken by an appeal by the Crown against a decision at a preliminary diet: see s.76A of the 1975 Act. The Crown appeal arose in this way: at the preliminary diet the accused argued that the jury, having returned a verdict of culpable homicide, had barred the Crown from indicting Boyle for the more serious crime of murder. The Crown argued otherwise.

At the preliminary diet the judge held that the action of the Crown was competent in law but unfair in the circumstances and dismissed the indictment. The Crown appeal from the preliminary diet was allowed, it being for the Crown not the court to decide any charges brought, and the indictment for murder was remitted to the trial court to proceed: *Advocate, H.M. v. Boyle*, 1992 S.C.C.R. 939.

Thereafter, Boyle petitioned the *nobile officium* of the High Court of Justiciary to complain that that court had exceeded its own authority in the original appeal in setting aside certain charges on the indictment which Boyle had been convicted of but had not appealed. The petition was refused: *Boyle, Petr.*, 1992 S.L.T. 1085.

For the sake of completeness it should be added that at the adjourned trial diet in November 1992 the trial was again adjourned to January 1993 because of difficulties that the Crown had with citing witnesses. Boyle had been in custody since August 1991 and he again petitioned the *nobile officium* of the High Court of Justiciary, this time for bail. That was granted (unusually for those on a murder charge) in terms of s.35 of the 1975 Act: *Boyle, Petr.*, 1993 S.C.C.R. 251. Daniel Boyle was acquitted at his second murder trial.

Subs. (3)

This provision ensures that at a second trial in the event of conviction a sentence cannot competently be passed if it could not have been passed on conviction under the earlier proceedings.

Subs. (4)

This provision permits a new prosecution notwithstanding any existing time-limits except for that in subs. (5).

Subs. (5)

Proceedings in a prosecution under s.119 must be commenced within two months of the date on which authority to bring the prosecution was granted. Authority for a new prosecution was granted in *Maillie v. H.M. Advocate*, 1993 S.C.C.R. 535. Delay in implementing a subsequent petition warrant results in that petition being dismissed: *Friel v. Mailley*, 1993 S.C.C.R. 928.

Subss. (6) to (11)

The remaining subsections make sundry provisions in relation to the grant of authority for a new prosecution. The competency by subs. (10) of bail for the accused reflects the position that Boyle found himself in and that resulted in his petition to the *nobile officium*: see *Boyle, Petr.*, 1993, above.

Appeals: supplementary provisions

120.—(1) Where—
    (a) intimation of the diet appointed for the hearing of the appeal has been made to the appellant;
    (b) no appearance is made by or on behalf of an appellant at the diet; and
    (c) no case or argument in writing has been timeously lodged,
the High Court shall dispose of the appeal as if it had been abandoned.

    (2) The power of the High Court to pass any sentence under this Part of this Act may be exercised notwithstanding that the appellant (or, where the

Lord Advocate is the appellant, the convicted person) is for any reason not present.

(3) When the High Court has heard and dealt with any application under this Part of this Act, the Clerk of Justiciary shall (unless it appears to him unnecessary so to do) give to the applicant if he is in custody and has not been present at the hearing of such application notice of the decision of the court in relation to the said application.

(4) On the final determination of any appeal under this Part of this Act or of any matter under section 103(5) of this Act, the Clerk of Justiciary shall give notice of such determination—

(a) to the appellant or applicant if he is in custody and has not been present at such final determination;

(b) to the clerk of the court in which the conviction took place; and

(c) to the Secretary of State.

DEFINITIONS
"appellant": s.132.
"diet": s.307(1).
"High Court": s.307(1).

GENERAL NOTE
These supplementary provisions in practice are important because a not inconsiderable number of appeals are refused for want of insistence. The appellant cannot, however, fail to meet any obligation placed on him and expect to have the court overlook it. In *Manson, Petr.*, 1991 S.L.T. 96 the petitioner sought to have heard an appeal against sentence which had been dismissed for want of insistence. Manson claimed not to have been notified of the date of appeal but he had failed to notify the court of a change of address as required by s.2(2) of the 1980 Act and the petition was refused.

Suspension of disqualification, forfeiture, etc.

121.—(1) Any disqualification, forfeiture or disability which attaches to a person by reason of a conviction shall not attach—

(a) for the period of four weeks from the date of the verdict against him; or

(b) where an intimation of intention to appeal or, in the case of an appeal under section 106(1)(b) to (e) or 108 of this Act, a note of appeal is lodged, until the appeal, if it is proceeded with, is determined.

(2) The destruction or forfeiture or any order for the destruction or forfeiture of any property, matter or thing which is the subject of or connected with any prosecution following upon a conviction shall be suspended—

(a) for the period of four weeks after the date of the verdict in the trial; or

(b) where an intimation of intention to appeal or, in the case of an appeal under section 106(1)(b) to (e) or 108 of this Act, a note of appeal is lodged, until the appeal, if it is proceeded with, is determined.

(3) This section does not apply in the case of any disqualification, destruction or forfeiture or order for destruction or forfeiture under or by virtue of any enactment which makes express provision for the suspension of the disqualification, destruction or forfeiture or order for destruction or forfeiture pending the determination of an appeal against conviction or sentence.

(4) Where, upon conviction, a fine has been imposed on a person or a compensation order has been made against him under section 249 of this Act, then, for a period of four weeks from the date of the verdict against such person or, in the event of an intimation of intention to appeal (or in the case of an appeal under section 106(1)(b) to (e) or 108 of this Act a note of appeal) being lodged under this Part of this Act, until such appeal, if it is proceeded with, is determined—

(a) the fine or compensation order shall not be enforced against that person and he shall not be liable to make any payment in respect of the fine or compensation order; and

(b) any money paid by that person under the compensation order shall not be paid by the clerk of court to the person entitled to it under subsection (9) of the said section 249.

DEFINITIONS
"fine": s.307(1).

Fines and caution

122.—(1) Where a person has on conviction been sentenced to payment of a fine and in default of payment to imprisonment, the person lawfully authorised to receive the fine shall, on receiving it, retain it until the determination of any appeal in relation to the conviction or sentence.

(2) If a person sentenced to payment of a fine remains in custody in default of payment of the fine he shall be deemed, for the purposes of this Part of this Act, to be a person sentenced to imprisonment.

(3) An appellant who has been sentenced to the payment of a fine, and has paid it in accordance with the sentence, shall, in the event of his appeal being successful, be entitled, subject to any order of the High Court, to the return of the sum paid or any part of it.

(4) A convicted person who has been sentenced to the payment of a fine and has duly paid it shall, if an appeal against sentence by the Lord Advocate results in the sentence being quashed and no fine, or a lesser fine than that paid, being imposed, be entitled, subject to any order of the High Court, to the return of the sum paid or as the case may be to the return of the amount by which that sum exceeds the amount of the lesser fine.

DEFINITIONS
"appellant": s.132.
"fine": s.307(1).
"High Court": s.307(1).

Lord Advocate's reference

123.—(1) Where a person tried on indictment is acquitted or convicted of a charge, the Lord Advocate may refer a point of law which has arisen in relation to that charge to the High Court for their opinion; and the Clerk of Justiciary shall send to the person and to any solicitor who acted for the person at the trial, a copy of the reference and intimation of the date fixed by the Court for a hearing.

(2) The person may, not later than seven days before the date so fixed, intimate in writing to the Clerk of Justiciary and to the Lord Advocate either—

(a) that he elects to appear personally at the hearing; or
(b) that he elects to be represented thereat by counsel,

but, except by leave of the Court on cause shown, and without prejudice to his right to attend, he shall not appear or be represented at the hearing other than by and in conformity with an election under this subsection.

(3) Where there is no intimation under subsection (2)(b) above, the High Court shall appoint counsel to act at the hearing as *amicus curiae*.

(4) The costs of representation elected under subsection (2)(b) above or of an appointment under subsection (3) above shall, after being taxed by the Auditor of the Court of Session, be paid by the Lord Advocate.

(5) The opinion on the point referred under subsection (1) above shall not affect the acquittal or, as the case may be, conviction in the trial.

DEFINITIONS
"Clerk of Justiciary": s.307(1).
"High Court": s.307(1).
"indictment": s.307(1).

GENERAL NOTE
There is no appeal against acquittal in solemn proceedings: see the terms of s.106(1) of this Act. It is incompetent in such proceedings to advocate either a verdict of acquittal by a jury, or an acquittal by a judge on a submission of no case to answer. However, should there then be a doubt about the law to be applied then the Lord Advocate may invoke the reference procedure provided by s.123.

A few such references have been taken on a diverse range of points of law: see *Advocate's (Lord) Reference No. 1 of 1983*, 1984 S.C.C.R. 62 (taped interviews), *Advocate's (Lord) Reference No. 1 of 1985*, 1987 S.L.T. 187 (perjury), *Advocate's (Lord) Reference No. 1 of 1992*, 1992 S.L.T. 1010 (building societies), *Advocate's (Lord) Reference No. 2 of 1992*, 1992 S.C.C.R. 960 (joke as motive) and *Advocate's (Lord) Reference No. 1 of 1994*, 1995 S.L.T. 248 (supply of a controlled drug).

The costs of representation elected under s.123(2)(b) are, after being taxed by the Auditor of the Court of Session, paid by the Lord Advocate: s.123(4).

Finality of proceedings and Secretary of State's reference

124.—(1) Nothing in this Part of this Act shall affect the prerogative of mercy.

(2) Subject to subsection (3) below, every interlocutor and sentence pronounced by the High Court under this Part of this Act shall be final and conclusive and not subject to review by any court whatsoever and it shall be incompetent to stay or suspend any execution or diligence issuing from the High Court under this Part of this Act.

(3) The Secretary of State on the consideration of any conviction of a person or the sentence (other than sentence of death) passed on a person who has been convicted, may, if he thinks fit, at any time, and whether or not an appeal against such conviction or sentence has previously been heard and determined by the High Court, refer the whole case to the High Court and the case shall be heard and determined, subject to any directions the High Court may make, as if it were an appeal under this Part of this Act.

(4) The power of the Secretary of State under this section to refer to the High Court the case of a person convicted shall be exercisable whether or not that person has petitioned for the exercise of Her Majesty's mercy.

(5) This section shall apply in relation to a finding under section 55(2) and an order under section 57(2) of this Act as it applies, respectively, in relation to a conviction and a sentence.

DEFINITIONS
"High Court": s.307(1).
"sentence": s.132.

GENERAL NOTE
Subs. (1)
The prerogative of mercy remains unaffected by the provisions in Pt. VIII of the 1995 Act. Precisely what this subsection means, in the context of subs. (3), is a matter of some interest. Some assistance may be found in *Advocate, H.M. v. Waddell*, 1976 S.L.T. (Notes) 61 and C. Gane *The Effect of a Pardon in Scots Law* 1980 J.R. 18.

Subs. (2)
In its essentials, this provides for a discretionary reference of a conviction or the sentence to the High Court of Justiciary. Thereafter the case should be heard as if it was an appeal under this Part of this Act. The Secretary of State may refer the whole case to the court: *Slater v. H.M. Advocate*, 1928 J.C. 94; and *Higgins v. H.M. Advocate*, 1956 J.C. 69. A particular point may be referred to the court for its opinion on that point: *Gallacher v. H.M. Advocate*, 1951 J.C. 38. The reference may be "at any time" and in *Preece v. H.M. Advocate* [1981] Crim.L.R. 783 the reference was seven years after conviction. The provision confers absolute discretion on the Secretary of State: *Leitch v. Secretary of State for Scotland*, 1983 S.L.T. 394. A petition to the *nobile officium* cannot supersede the purpose of this provision: *Windsor, Petr.*, 1994 S.L.T. 604.

Subs. (4)

This indicates that the power of the Secretary of State to refer a case is independent of any Royal prerogative of mercy which the Crown itself may exercise.

Subs. (5)

The reference applies equally to orders that may be made at or following examinations of facts.

Reckoning of time spent pending appeal

125.—(1) Subject to subsection (2) below, where a convicted person is admitted to bail under section 112 of this Act, the period beginning with the date of his admission to bail and ending on the date of his readmission to prison in consequence of the determination or abandonment of—

(a) his appeal; or, as the case may be,

(b) any relevant appeal by the Lord Advocate under section 108 of this Act,

shall not be reckoned as part of any term of imprisonment under his sentence.

(2) The time, including any period consequent on the recall of bail during which an appellant is in custody pending the determination of his appeal or, as the case may be, of any relevant appeal by the Lord Advocate under section 108 of this Act shall, subject to any direction which the High Court may give to the contrary, be reckoned as part of any term of imprisonment under his sentence.

(3) Subject to any direction which the High Court may give to the contrary, imprisonment of an appellant or, where the appellant is the Lord Advocate, of a convicted person—

(a) who is in custody in consequence of the conviction or sentence appealed against, shall be deemed to run as from the date on which the sentence was passed;

(b) who is in custody other than in consequence of such conviction or sentence, shall be deemed to run or to be resumed as from the date on which his appeal was determined or abandoned;

(c) who is not in custody, shall be deemed to run or to be resumed as from the date on which he is received into prison under the sentence.

(4) In this section references to a prison and imprisonment shall include respectively references to a young offenders institution or place of safety or, as respects a child sentenced to be detained under section 208 of this Act, the place directed by the Secretary of State and to detention in such institution, centre or place of safety, or, as respects such a child, place directed by the Secretary of State and any reference to a sentence shall be construed as a reference to a sentence passed by the court imposing sentence or by the High Court on appeal as the case may require.

DEFINITIONS

"bail": s.307(1).

"prison": s.307(1).

"sentence": s.132.

"young offender's institution": s.307(1).

Extract convictions

126. No extract conviction shall be issued—

(a) during the period of four weeks after the day on which the conviction took place, except in so far as it is required as a warrant for the detention of the person convicted under any sentence which has been pronounced against him; nor

(b) where an intimation of intention to appeal or, in the case of an appeal under section 106(1)(b) to (e) or 108 of this Act, a note of appeal is lodged, until the appeal, if it is proceeded with, is determined.

DEFINITIONS
"extract conviction": s.307(1).
"sentence": s.132.

Forms in relation to appeals

127.—(1) The Clerk of Justiciary shall furnish the necessary forms and, instructions in relation to intimations of intention to appeal, notes of appeal or notices of application under this Part of this Act to—
(a) any person who demands them; and
(b) to officers of courts, governors of prisons, and such other officers or persons as he thinks fit.
(2) The governor of a prison shall cause the forms and instructions mentioned in subsection (1) above to be placed at the disposal of prisoners desiring to appeal or to make any application under this Part of this Act.
(3) The governor of a prison shall, if requested to do so by a prisoner, forwarded on the prisoner's behalf to the Clerk of Justiciary any intimation, note or notice mentioned in subsection (1) above given by the prisoner.

DEFINITIONS
"Clerk of Justiciary": s.307(1).
"governor": s.307(1).
"prison": s.307(1).

Fees and expenses

128. Except as otherwise provided in this Part of this Act, no court fees, or other fees or expenses shall be exigible from or awarded against an appellant or applicant in respect of an appeal or application under this Part of this Act.

Non-compliance with certain provisions may be waived

129.—(1) Non-compliance with—
(a) the provisions of this Act set out in subsection (3) below; or
(b) any rule of practice for the time being in force under this Part of this Act relating to appeals,
shall not prevent the further prosecution of an appeal if the High Court or a judge thereof considers it just and proper that the non-compliance is waived or, in the manner directed by the High Court or judge, remedied by amendment or otherwise.
(2) Where the High Court or a judge thereof directs that the non-compliance is to be remedied, and the remedy is carried out, the appeal shall proceed.
(3) The provisions of this Act referred to in subsection (1) above are:—
section 94
section 103(1), (4), (6) and (7)
section 104(2) and (3)
section 105
section 106(4)
section 111
section 114
section 115
section 116

section 117
section 120(1), (3) and (4)
section 121
section 122
section 126
section 128.

(4) This section does not apply to any rule of practice relating to appeals under section 60 of this Act.

DEFINITIONS
    "High Court": s.307(1).
    "judge": s.307(1).

GENERAL NOTE
    This general saving power permits an appeal against conviction or sentence to proceed notwithstanding non-compliance with the rules specified in s.129(3) if it appears just and proper to proceed or if a consequential problem can be remedied.

Bill of suspension not competent

130. It shall not be competent to appeal to the High Court by bill of suspension against any conviction, sentence, judgement or order pronounced in any proceedings on indictment in the sheriff court.

DEFINITIONS
    "indictment": s.307(1).
    "sentence": s.132.

GENERAL NOTE
    The origins of this section lie in the Criminal Appeal (Scotland) Act 1926 which, by s.13, abolished appeal by suspension, but appeal by advocation from the sheriff in solemn procedure remained competent. A bill of suspension for an appeal by a witness found in contempt in the course of solemn proceedings in the sheriff court was held competent in *Butterworth v. Herron*, 1975 S.L.T. (Notes) 56. This was later over-ruled when five judges held in *George Outram & Co. v. Lees*, 1992 S.L.T. 32 that the correct mode of appeal was a petition to the *nobile officium*.

Prosecution appeal by bill of advocation

131.—(1) Without prejudice to section 74 of this Act, the prosecutor's right to bring a decision under review of the High Court by way of bill of advocation in accordance with existing law and practice shall extend to the review of a decision of any court of solemn jurisdiction.

(2) Where a decision to which a bill of advocation relates is reversed on the review of the decision the prosecutor may, whether or not there has already been a trial diet at which evidence has been led, proceed against the accused by serving him with an indictment containing, subject to subsection (3) below, the charge or charges which were affected by the decision.

(3) The wording of the charge or charges referred to in subsection (2) above shall be as it was immediately before the decision appealed against.

DEFINITIONS
    "High Court": s.307(1).
    "prosecutor": s.307(1).

GENERAL NOTE
    An example of the use of this power is found in *Advocate, H.M. v. Sinclair*, 1987 S.L.T. 161 where a shrieval decision to desert an indictment *pro loco et tempore* was successfully challenged by the Crown.

Interpretation of Part VIII

132. In this Part of this Act, unless the context otherwise requires—
"appellant" includes a person who has been convicted and desires to
appeal under this Part of the Act;
"sentence" includes any order of the High Court made on conviction
with reference to the person convicted or his wife or children, and
any recommendation of the High Court as to the making of a
deportation order in the case of a person convicted and the power
of the High Court to pass a sentence includes a power to make any
such order of the court or recommendation, and a recommendation
so made by the High Court shall have the same effect for the purposes of Articles 20 and 21 of the Aliens Order 1953 as the certificate and recommendation of the convicting court.

PART IX

SUMMARY PROCEEDINGS

General

Application of Part IX of Act

133.—(1) This Part of this Act applies to summary proceedings in respect
of any offence which might prior to the passing of this Act, or which may
under the provisions of this or any Act, whether passed before or after the
passing of this Act, be tried summarily.

(2) Without prejudice to subsection (1) above, this Part of this Act also
applies to procedure in all courts of summary jurisdiction in so far as they
have jurisdiction in respect of—

(a) any offence or the recovery of a penalty under any enactment or rule
of law which does not exclude summary procedure as well as, in
accordance with section 211(3) and (4) of this Act, to the enforcement
of a fine imposed in solemn proceedings; and

(b) any order *ad factum praestandum*, or other order of court or warrant
competent to a court of summary jurisdiction.

(3) Where any statute provides for summary proceedings to be taken
under any public general or local enactment, such proceedings shall be taken
under this Part of this Act.

(4) Nothing in this Part of this Act shall—

(a) extend to any complaint or other proceeding under or by virtue of any
statutory provision for the recovery of any rate, tax, or impost whatsoever; or

(b) affect any right to raise any civil proceedings.

(5) Except where any enactment otherwise expressly provides, all prosecutions under this Part of this Act shall be brought at the instance of the
procurator fiscal.

DEFINITIONS
    "court of summary jurisdiction": s.5(1) and (2) and s.307(1).
    "offence": s.307(1).
    "statute": s.307(1).
    "summarily": s.5(1) and (2) and s.7(5) and (6).

GENERAL NOTE
    Part IX of the Act regulates the procedure in all summary cases including proceedings raised
under local enactments as well as statutory provisions which apply generally. Revenue offences

involving the Inland Revenue and H.M. Customs and Excise only adopt the procedures in Pt. IX of the Act insofar as expressly stipulated within their relevant statutes.

It will be seen that subs. (2)(a) provides that summary provisions also apply to the enforcement of monetary fines imposed following solemn convictions and to the enforcement of fines imposed by other courts in Scotland, England and Wales unless such a jurisdiction is specifically excluded.

Incidental applications

134.—(1) This section applies to any application to a court for any warrant or order of court—
  (a) as incidental to proceedings by complaint; or
  (b) where a court has power to grant any warrant or order of court, although no subsequent proceedings by complaint may follow thereon.

(2) An application to which this section applies may be made by petition at the instance of the prosecutor in the form prescribed by Act of Adjournal.

(3) Where it is necessary for the execution of a warrant or order granted under this section, warrant to break open shut and lockfast places shall be implied.

DEFINITIONS
  "complaint": s.307(1).

GENERAL NOTE
  This section determines that the form specified in the 1996 Act of Adjournal (Form 16.4.–A) shall be used for applications to the court by the prosecutor or the accused when summary proceedings have begun (subs. (1)(a)) or when the prosecutor, in carrying out his investigative role, seeks a search warrant, or other warrant, from a sheriff or magistrate even before any person has been charged with an offence (subs. (1)(b)); this latter provision will doubtless remain the most common use of this section. Examples of the range of warrants sought, can be found in *Carmichael, Complainer*, 1993 S.L.T. 305 (to precognosce a complainer on oath); *Frame v. Houston*, 1992 S.L.T. 205 (warrant for hair samples of accused sought after indictment served); *Normand, Complainer*, 1992 S.L.T. 478 (warrant at common law to inspect bankers' books before proceedings have begun).
  Summary warrants to apprehend which are used to commence proceedings and empower the arrest of a known accused are granted under s.139(1)(c) below.
  In addition to the statutory power of apprehension and search enacted in s.135 below, a multiplicity of statutes contain their own express powers of search, detention and arrest, notably the Misuse of Drugs Act 1971, the Road Traffic Act 1988 and the Firearms Act 1968: these express provisions override the general powers contained in s.134.
  In *Douglas v. Procurator Fiscal, Kirkcaldy* (High Court, November 1991) the procurator fiscal resorted to incidental application procedure to have citations as defence witnesses for himself and the Law Officers rescinded on the grounds that they had no evidence to offer pertinent to the case; the accused, on appeal, stated that citations had been served because he had a separate grievance against the procurator fiscal. His appeal by advocation was refused.
  Note that where one of the parties has declined to make a joint application to the court to alter a diet as enabled by s.137 below, s.137(4) permits the use of an incidental application to put the matter before the court for consideration.

Warrants of apprehension and search

135.—(1) A warrant of apprehension or search may be in the form prescribed by Act of Adjournal or as nearly as may be in such form, and any warrant of apprehension or search shall, where it is necessary for its execution, imply warrant to officers of law to break open shut and lockfast places.

(2) A warrant of apprehension of an accused in the form mentioned in subsection (1) above shall imply warrant to officers of law to search for and to apprehend the accused, and to bring him before the court issuing the

warrant, or before any other court competent to deal with the case, to answer to the charge on which such warrant is granted, and, in the meantime, until he can be so brought, to detain him in a police station, police cell, or other convenient place.

(3) A person apprehended under a warrant or by virtue of power under any enactment or rule of law shall wherever practicable be brought before a court competent to deal with the case not later than in the course of the first day after he is taken into custody.

(4) The reference in subsection (3) above to the first day after he is taken into custody shall not include a Saturday, a Sunday or a court holiday prescribed for that court under section 8 of this Act; but nothing in this subsection shall prevent a person being brought before the court on a Saturday, a Sunday or such a court holiday where the court is, in pursuance of the said section 8, sitting on such day for the disposal of criminal business.

(5) A warrant of apprehension or other warrant shall not be required for the purpose of bringing before the court an accused who has been apprehended without a written warrant or who attends without apprehension in answer to any charge made against him.

DEFINITIONS
"officers of law": s.307(1).

GENERAL NOTE
As subs. (5) makes clear, the provisions of this section are intended to initiate proceedings against an accused whose identity is known to the prosecutor but who, for one reason or another, has not been apprehended and brought before the court to answer the charge against him. Rule 16.5.–(1) of the 1996 Act of Adjournal stipulates that such warrants are to follow the styles shown as Forms 16.5–A and B (Warrants to apprehend following a failure to appear at a diet are granted under s.150 of the Act).

While the power granted by warrant under subs. (2) is to arrest the accused, it is competent for the prosecutor instead to exercise a discretion to invite the accused to appear at a specified court or police station on a given date and thus avoid the pains of arrest; see *Spowart v. Burr* (1895) 1 Adam 539. It was held in *Young v. Smith*, 1981 S.L.T.(Notes) 101; 1981 S.C.C.R. 85 that where an accused attended voluntarily in response to such an invitation the warrant had not been executed. Similarly failure to respond to such an invitation with the result that a warrant is executed, cannot work to the benefit of the accused (*Young v. McLeod*, 1993 S.C.C.R. 479 where pleas of undue delay were repelled).

The wording of subss. (3) and (4) paraphrases the terms of s.321(3) of the 1975 Act and, following *Robertson v. MacDonald*, 1992 S.C.C.R. 916; 1993 S.L.T. 1337, would appear to be directory rather than mandatory in its effect. In *Robertson*, the accused had been arrested upon a petition warrant, granted at Wick Sheriff Court, in Glasgow. He was conveyed to Wick and made his appearance on summary complaint four days later when he took objection to the competency of proceedings. Albeit a breach of the subsection had occurred, the court upheld Crown submissions that itself did not vitiate proceedings.

Time limit for certain offences

136.—(1) Proceedings under this Part of this Act in respect of any offence to which this section applies shall be commenced—
   (a) within six months after the contravention occurred;
   (b) in the case of a continuous contravention, within six months after the last date of such contravention,
and it shall be competent in a prosecution of a contravention mentioned in paragraph (b) above to include the entire period during which the contravention occurred.

(2) This section applies to any offence triable only summarily and consisting of the contravention of any enactment, unless the enactment fixes a different time limit.

(3) For the purposes of this section proceedings shall be deemed to be commenced on the date on which a warrant to apprehend or to cite the accused is granted, if the warrant is executed without undue delay.

DEFINITIONS
"offence": s.307(1).

GENERAL NOTE

The peremptory nature of these provisions in the 1975 Act inevitably produced a substantial volume of case law. Section 136 appears to re-enact the terms of s.331 of the 1975 Act which applied a six-month time bar to the raising of summary prosecutions of statutory offences; however subs. (2) now restricts the operation of the provisions to cases which are triable summarily only, and to statutory enactments which contain their own express time bar provisions.

Note that this time-bar provision, which now applies to a more limited number of statutory offences than were affected by s.331 of the 1975 Act, does not apply to the libelling of common law charges except assaults on children. While pleas to the competency of summary proceedings on the grounds of time bar should now be less commonplace, it may be noted that a delay on the part of the Crown in initiating proceedings could well justify a plea of *mora*. (For *mora* see generally *Tudhope v. McCarthy*, 1985 J.C. 48; 1985 S.L.T. 395; *McFarlane v. Jessop*, 1988 S.L.T. 596; 1988 S.C.C.R. 186; *Connachan v. Douglas*, 1990 S.L.T. 563; 1990 S.C.C.R. 101).

Proceedings will normally be commenced by the postal service of a citation and service copy complaint upon the accused, but can also be started by an initiating warrant or by obtaining an assigned diet within the six-month period for a diet outwith that period; the question of whether the prosecutor has complied with the statutory timebar provisions has to be approached differently in each of these situations. Service by post of a complaint timeously to call at a diet within the six-month date offers no difficulty; the proceedings commence on the date of posting of the complaint. The same rule applies to the service of a complaint to call at a diet after the expiry of six-months; in that event the proceedings are still competent, provided that the complaint is sent and received within the six-month date and calls at the cited diet (see *Keily v. Tudhope*, 1986 S.C.C.R. 351; 1987 S.L.T. 99; *Orr v. Lowdon*, 1987 S.C.C.R. 515): it is desirable that the prosecutor is able to produce an execution of service of the complaint in that latter situation.

Different considerations apply when the prosecutor elects to proceed instead by way of either an initiating warrant or by a warrant to cite the accused to an assigned diet. The grant of either form of warrant signals the commencement of the proceedings and to preserve those proceedings the warrant must in either case be executed without undue delay. It must be emphasised however that while an initiating warrant may well be a valid basis for proceedings months later (if the prosecutor can show that there was no undue delay on his part, a matter discussed later), in the case of a warrant to cite the complaint will either stand or fall on the date of the assigned diet (*Tudhope v. Buckner*, 1985 S.C.C.R. 352).

If service has not been effected upon the accused prior to the diet then the complaint necessarily falls. The only option available to the prosecutor should he learn of difficulty in effecting service of a warrant to cite, is to withdraw the warrant and reraise by means of an initiating warrant if this can be done before the expiry of the timebar.

Once an initiating warrant or a warrant to cite has been obtained, any undue delay in its execution must not be attributable to the actions (or inactions) of the prosecutor. Generally, reported cases have focused upon what constitutes "undue delay" and it has to be stressed that even where a warrant to cite an accused to a diet outwith the six-month period is granted timeously, the prosecutor must still effect service of the complaint swiftly. The onus of proof of "no undue delay" rests with the Crown and if facts are in dispute, the court should hear evidence of the steps taken to execute the warrant (*McCartney v. Tudhope*, 1985 S.C.C.R. 373; 1986 S.L.T. 159). An incorrect address in the instance of the complaint and frustrated efforts to serve at the correct address by post and personally were held not to constitute "undue delay"; see *McKay v. Normand*, 1995 G.W.D. 39–1995.

Computation of Time

The six-month period is calculated *de die in diem* and not *de momento in momentum* (see *Tudhope v. Lawson*, 1983 S.C.C.R. 435; *Lees v. Lovell*, 1992 S.L.T. 967; 1992 S.C.C.R. 557 following *Keenan v. Carmichael*, 1991 S.C.C.R. 680), *i.e.* excluding the date of offence.

In the exceptional circumstances produced by the death, illness or absence of the judge, which has interrupted a part-heard trial, s.151(2) permits a new prosecution of a statutory complaint raised within two months of its desertion, notwithstanding the usual timebar on statutory proceedings.

Undue Delay

Warrants are sought for arrest or for the assignment of a diet for a date usually outwith the normal prescriptive period. Undue delay where established is fatal to proceedings on that complaint and the result of such a finding is to preclude any further proceedings on a statutory (but not a common law) charge. The delay has to be attributable to the prosecutor alone and will be assessed according to the facts of each case. The presiding judge has a broad discretion in deciding the issue. Execution of the warrant extends to any action taken by the prosecutor to effect citation whether by post or other means (*Lockhart v. Bradley*, 1977 S.L.T. 5); "undue delay" was defined in *Smith v. Peter Walker and Son (Edinburgh)*, 1978 J.C. 44.

Examples of undue delay are found in *Carmichael v. Sardar and Sons*, 1983 S.C.C.R. 433 (unexplained period of six days), *Harvey v. Lockhart*, 1991 S.C.C.R. 83; 1992 S.L.T. 68 (14 days but the sheriff had erred in reaching a decision without hearing explanations for the delay), *Robertson v. Carmichael*, 1993 S.C.C.R. 841 (four days unexplained and not investigated).

Undue delay was not established in *Stagecoach v. MacPhail*, 1986 S.C.C.R. 184 (seven days between warrant to cite and service), *Anderson v. Lowe*, 1991 S.C.C.R. 712 (warrant mislaid in Sheriff Clerk's office for three days), *Buchan v. McNaughtan*, 1990 S.C.C.R. 688; 1991 S.L.T. 410 (delay attributed to conduct of accused), *Young v. MacPhail*, 1991 S.C.C.R. 630; 1992 S.L.T. 98 (a warrant granted for accused then serving a prison sentence in England not being executed until his date of release), *McGlennan v. Singh*, 1993 S.C.C.R. 341 (16 days lapsed from grant of warrant till its execution, but the sheriff had moved too summarily in finding against the Crown).

The period to be taken into account in assessing delay is from the date of granting of the warrant until its execution, not the time from the expiry of the prescriptive period until the execution of the warrant (see *MacNeill v. Cowie*, 1984 S.C.C.R. 449; *McNellie v. Walkingshaw*, 1990 S.C.C.R. 428; 1991 S.L.T. 892) but it must be emphasised that the issue of delay will only arise where service is effected outwith the six-month time-bar period.

Reduction of Proceedings to Summary Complaint

The recent judgment in *Gardner v. Lees*, 1996 G.W.D. 5–253 which concerned a reduction to summary proceedings more than a year after the original appearance on petition is one of some moment. The Appeal Court founding upon the provisions against delay in solemn proceedings in the 1975 Act (s.101(1)) which are repeated as s.65(1) of the 1995 Act held that these applied to all proceedings initiated by a petition: in effect a further timebar provision applicable to a limited category of summary complaints appears to have developed. Contrary to the tenor of the rest of Pt. IX of the Act where emphasis is placed upon the commencement of proceedings on the complaint, *Gardner v. Lees* requires calculation of this time-bar by reference to both the date of the first petition appearance and the date of conclusion (not commencement) of the trial. This judgment overturned *MacDougall v. Russell*, 1985 S.C.C.R. 441 and *Whitelaw v. Dickinson*, 1993 S.C.C.R. 164 and is likely to give rise to a substantial volume of case law. See *Normand v. Walker*, Crown Office Circular A2/96, where, on appeal under s.101(5) of the 1975 Act, it was held competent to extend the year time-bar applicable to such a summary complaint.

Alteration of diets

137.—(1) Where a diet has been fixed in a summary prosecution, it shall be competent for the court, on a joint application in writing by the parties or their solicitors, to discharge the diet and fix an earlier diet in lieu.

(2) Where the prosecutor and the accused make joint application to the court (orally or in writing) for postponement of a diet which has been fixed, the court shall discharge the diet and fix a later diet in lieu unless the court considers that it should not do so because there has been unnecessary delay on the part of one of more of the parties.

(3) Where all the parties join in an application under subsection (2) above, the court may proceed under that subsection without hearing the parties.

(4) Where the prosecutor has intimated to the accused that he desires to postpone or accelerate a diet which has been fixed, and the accused refuses, or any of the accused refuse, to make a joint application to the court for that purpose, the prosecutor may make an incidental application for that purpose under section 134 of this Act; and after giving the parties an opportunity to be heard, the court may discharge the diet and fix a later diet or, as the case may be, an earlier diet in lieu.

(5) Where an accused had intimated to the prosecutor and to all the other accused that he desires such postponement or acceleration and the prosecutor refuses, or any of the other accused refuse, to make a joint application to the court for that purpose, the accused who has so intimated may apply to the court for that purpose; and, after giving the parties an opportunity to be heard, the court may discharge the diet and fix a later diet or, as the case may be, an earlier diet in lieu.

DEFINITIONS
"diet": s.307(1).
"prosecutor": s.307(1).

GENERAL NOTE
This section provides procedures for applications to the court for alteration of summary diets on joint motion, and for such applications to be made by a party in the absence of agreement of all parties. Subsection (1) permits acceleration of a diet by means of a joint written application; subs. (2) relates to joint applications to postpone a summary diet and gives expression to the right of the court to refuse such an application which, unlike a motion for acceleration, can be made either orally or in writing. Where all parties concur in making a written application timeously, the court can dispose of it administratively. Note however that the court's power to refuse an application for postponement on grounds of unnecessary delay by one of the parties suggests that a hearing would be required before the motion could be decided by the court.

Subsections (4) and (5) respectively provide for the prosecutor and the accused to make application individually to the court for variation of the diet in situations where other parties will not concur. The prosecutor should make application by way of an incidental application (see s.134 above) while the accused, although it is not stipulated in subs. (5), can petition using Form 16.7 provided in the 1996 Act of Adjournal.

Complaints

Complaints

138.—(1) All proceedings under this Part of this Act for the trial of offences or recovery of penalties shall be instituted by complaint signed by the prosecutor or by a solicitor on behalf of a prosecutor other than the procurator fiscal.

(2) The complaint shall be in the form—

(a) set out in Schedule 5 to this Act; or

(b) prescribed by Act of Adjournal,

or as nearly as may be in such form.

(3) A solicitor may appear for and conduct any prosecution on behalf of a prosecutor other than the procurator fiscal.

(4) Schedule 3 to this Act shall have effect as regards complaints under this Act.

DEFINITIONS
"complaint": s.307(1).
"judge": s.307(1).
"procurator fiscal": s.307(1).
"prosecutor": s.307(1).

GENERAL NOTE
The complaint will ordinarily proceed at the instance of the procurator fiscal having jurisdiction over a locus where it is alleged an offence was committed. Section 138 also permits other authorised prosecutors (for example the local education authority) to initiate proceedings by a complaint and to prosecute such cases.

The form of complaint should correspond to Form 16.1.–A in the 1996 Act of Adjournal, a style identical to the format used under the 1975 Act. The citation form now shown in Form 16.1.–B is similarly familiar. Examples of statutory charges are given in Sched. 5 to the Act which in turn adopts the somewhat esoteric charges listed as indictment styles in Sched. 2; Sched. 5 may lack some of the colour of the earlier schedule but at least has the merit of being of some practical (if limited) use. More importantly, the provisions of Sched. 3 in relation to implied terms and alternative verdicts, which were previously contained in s.312 of the 1975 Act are applied to all summary complaints.

Essential Elements of a Complaint
The principal complaint has to be signed by the prosecutor but only the citation form to the accused need be signed (1996 Act of Adjournal Rule 16.2.–(1)). Rule 16.2.–(2) suggests that signature of any part of the papers sent to an accused as a service copy complaint would be sufficient to render proceedings competent. Failure by the prosecutor to sign the principal complaint creates a nullity (*Lowe v. Bee*, 1989 S.C.C.R. 476): loss of the principal complaint has till

now been held to be fatal to proceedings and could not be remedied by seeking to substitute a certified copy (*McSeveney v. Annan*, 1990 S.C.C.R. 573; *Wilson v. Carmichael*, 1991 S.C.C.R. 587; 1992 S.L.T. 54; *Scott v. MacKay*, 1983 S.C.C.R. 210). However, s.157 of the Act now permits the substitution of a certified copy of the complaint in the event of such loss.

A discrepancy between the libel in the principal complaint and the service copy is no more than a technical defect unless it can be shown that the variation has caused substantial prejudice (*Fletcher v. Webster*, 1991 S.L.T. 256; 1991 S.C.C.R. 379 following *Dunsmore v. Threshie* (1896) 2 Adam 202).

Rule 16.1. above directs that the copy complaint should include a reply form and a means form, which again are familiar in appearance; failure to include these two forms will not vitiate proceedings on that complaint (Rule 16.3.).

It will be noted that this section does not require a complaint to include notices of penalty; such notices were previously essential to any sentence upon conviction of a statutory offence on summary complaint. The complaint should include any previous convictions to be founded upon by the prosecutor in the event of a conviction of the accused; previous convictions are discussed in notes to s.166 below.

Although it is statutorily enacted that any proceedings must be initiated by the procurator fiscal or an authorised prosecutor, the cases of *Thomson v. Scott*; *Walker v. Emslie* (1899) 3 Adam 102 and *Hill v. Finlayson* (1883) 5 Couper 284 support the view that the court itself has an inherent power to appoint a prosecutor *pro hac vice* to conduct those proceedings in the event of the death, illness or unavoidable absence of the prosecutor.

Complaints: orders and warrants

139.—(1) On any complaint under this Part of this Act being laid before a judge of the court in which the complaint is brought, he shall have power on the motion of the prosecutor—

(a) to pronounce an order assigning a diet for the disposal of the case to which the accused may be cited as mentioned in section 141 of this Act;

(b) to grant warrant to apprehend the accused where this appears to the judge expedient;

(c) to grant warrant to search the person, dwelling-house and repositories of the accused and any place where he may be found for any documents, articles, or property likely to afford evidence of his guilt of, or guilty participation in, any offence charged in the complaint, and to take possession of such documents, articles or property;

(d) to grant any other order or warrant of court or warrant which may be competent in the circumstances.

(2) The power of a judge under subsection (1) above—

(a) to pronounce an order assigning a diet for the disposal of the case may be exercised on his behalf by the clerk of court;

(b) to grant a warrant to apprehend the accused shall be exercisable notwithstanding that there is power whether at common law or under any Act to apprehend him without a warrant.

DEFINITIONS
    "complaint": s.307(1).
    "judge": s.307(1).
    "prosecutor": s.307(1).

GENERAL NOTE
    As subs. (2)(a) provides, cited diets are normally assigned administratively by the clerk of court, the judge initially needing only to be involved in considering the grant of an expediency warrant (subs. (1)(b)) or an initiating warrant (subs. (1)(c)). It is the responsibility of the prosecutor to indicate to the clerk whether a specific date for the complaint to be called is needed; the complaint itself will show whether an assigned diet is craved and it then falls to the prosecutor to ensure that service is effected timeously (see notes to s.136 above).

When the prosecutor decides to begin proceedings by means of an initiating warrant the practice is for the complaint to be considered by the judge in chambers without hearing the prosecutor; it is unusual, but perfectly competent for the judge to require the prosecutor to specify the grounds which lie behind the application for a warrant. Commonly an initiating warrant will be necessary in order to obtain the accused's fingerprints or other samples in an admissible fashion or to place him before an identification parade.

As its name suggests, an expediency warrant is granted at the discretion of the court where a complaint is already current before the court and serves to keep the proceedings on it alive, provided that there are then reasonable grounds for believing that the complaint has been validly served: such a warrant cannot be used to validate a defect in the service of a complaint or as a means of overcoming a statutory timebar which would otherwise nullify the proceedings. In *Heywood v. McLennan*, 1994 S.C.C.R. 1 where a complaint had been continued without plea, and later was established not to have been served, the depute moved to desert the case *pro loco et tempore* and sought an initiating warrant on that complaint. In such circumstances the proper course should have been to raise a fresh complaint craving an initiating warrant, the first complaint having fallen. See also *Lees v. Malcolm*, 1992 S.C.C.R. 589.

The extent of the procurator fiscal's common law power to apply for a search warrant as part of his investigative role, before proceedings are initiated, was discussed in *MacNeill, Complainer,* 1983 S.C.C.R. 450.

Citation

Citation

140.—(1) This Act shall be a sufficient warrant for the citation of the accused and witnesses in a summary prosecution to any ordinary sitting of the court or to any special diet fixed by the court or any adjournment thereof.

(2) Such citation shall be in the form prescribed by Act of Adjournal or as nearly as may be in such form and shall, in the case of the accused, proceed on an induciae of at least 48 hours unless in the special circumstances of the case the court fixes a shorter induciae.

(3) This section shall apply to the citation of witnesses for precognition by the prosecutor where a judge on the application of the prosecutor deems it expedient to grant warrant to cite witnesses for precognition in regard to any offence which may be competently tried in the court of that judge, and whether or not any person has at the time of such application been charged with such offence.

DEFINITIONS
"diet": s.307(1).
"judge": s.307(1).
"prosecutor": s.307(1).

GENERAL NOTE
Chapter 16 of the 1996 Act of Adjournal provides that the citation of an accused shall be by Form 16.1–B while witnesses should be cited by post using Form 16.6–A and, personally, by Form 16.6–C. Omission of the date of the diet from the accused's citation creates a nullity (*Beattie v. MacKinnon*, 1977 J.C. 64).

As with solemn witness citations, the Act of Adjournal envisages that any witness cited post-ally to attend, will acknowledge receipt of the citation by returning a pre-paid envelope with a further form (Form 16.6–B) within 14 days of citation. The objective of this reform, particularly now that intermediate diets are to be mandatory in summary cases (see s.148 below), is to enable parties to be in a position to advise the court confidently about their readiness for trial; however well-intended this provision may be, serious doubts must remain as to its practical worth. No citation of a witness or an accused is valid until the principal complaint has been signed (*Stewart v. Lang* (1894) 1 Adam 493).

Subsection (2) prescribes an *induciae* in the case of service of a citation upon an accused of at least 48 hours. This period, in the case of postal citation, is reckoned from 24 hours after the time of posting (see s.141(6) below). The *induciae* can of course be waived by the accused or, exceptionally, be reduced by the court itself on cause shown, but must not be so shortened as to prejudice the accused in the conduct of his defence. No such time scale is applied to the citation of witnesses but Rule 16.6 in the Act of Adjournal plainly envisages a greater period of notice being given to witnesses.

Subsection (3) provides a mechanism for the prosecutor to obtain a warrant to cite witnesses for precognition even before any proceedings are active before the court. Both petition and summary warrants as a matter of course give power to the prosecutor to cite for precognition but subs. (3) enables the Crown to make preliminary investigations even before proceedings are initiated; it is usual to petition the court by way of an incidental application in circumstances where it is believed that witnesses will not attend for precognition voluntarily. This procedure is rarely used.

Manner of citation

141.—(1) The citation of the accused and witnesses in a summary prosecution to any ordinary sitting of the court or to any special diet fixed by the court or to any adjourned sitting or diet shall be effected by delivering the citation to him personally or leaving it for him at his dwelling-house or place of business with a resident or, as the case may be, employee at that place or, where he has no known dwelling-house or place of business, at any other place in which he may be resident at the time.

(2) Notwithstanding subsection (1) above, citation may also be effected—

(a) where the accused or witness is the master of, or a seaman or person employed in a vessel, if the citation is left with a person on board the vessel and connected with it;

(b) where the accused is a partnership, association or body corporate—

(i) if the citation is left at its ordinary place of business with a partner, director, secretary or other official; or

(ii) if it is cited in the same manner as if the proceedings were in a civil court; or

(c) where the accused is a body of trustees, if the citation is left with any one of them who is resident in Scotland or with their known solicitor in Scotland.

(3) Subject to subsection (4) below, the citation of the accused or a witness to a sitting or diet or adjourned sitting or diet as mentioned in subsection (1) above shall be effective if it is signed by the prosecutor and—

(a) in the case of the accused, sent by post in a registered envelope or through the recorded delivery service; and

(b) in the case of a witness, sent by ordinary post,

to the dwelling-house or place of business of the accused or witness or, if he has no known dwelling-house or place of business, to any other place in which he may be resident at the time.

(4) Where the accused fails to appear at a diet or sitting or adjourned diet or sitting to which he has been cited in the manner provided by this section, subsections (3) and (5) to (7) of section 150 of this Act shall not apply unless it is proved to the court that he received the citation or that its contents came to his knowledge.

(5) The production in court of any letter or other communication purporting to be written by or on behalf of an accused who has been cited as mentioned in subsection (3) above in such terms as to infer that the contents of such citation came to his knowledge, shall be admissible as evidence of that fact for the purposes of subsection (4) above.

(6) When the citation of any person is effected by post in terms of this section or any other provision of this Act to which this section is applied, the induciae shall be reckoned from 24 hours after the time of posting.

(7) It shall be sufficient evidence that a citation has been sent by post in terms of this section or any other provision of this Act mentioned in subsection (6) above, if there is produced in court a written execution, signed by the person who signed the citation in the form prescribed by Act of Adjournal, or as nearly as may be in such form, together with the post office receipt for the relative registered or recorded delivery letter.

DEFINITIONS
  "diet": s.307(1).
  "prosecutor": s.307(1).

Subsections (3) and (7) continue the existing practices governing postal service of summary complaints. The date of postal citation is the date of posting, not receipt of the citation (*Lockhart v. Bradley*, 1977 S.L.T. 5). No warrant for citation exists until the principal complaint is signed and the citation with the complaint has also been signed (see the discussion "Essential Elements of a Complaint" in notes to s.138 above and *Stewart v. Lang* (1894) 1 Adam 493).

Section 150 entitles the court to grant a warrant to arrest an accused following failure to appear at a diet to which he has been cited or notified to appear. The prosecutor must satisfy the court that service has been validly effected in accordance with this section and may found upon the recorded delivery execution of service of the complaint or any letter sent by, or on behalf of the accused which indicates the accused's awareness of the diet (see *Aitchison v. Wringe*, 1985 S.L.T. 449; 1985 S.C.C.R. 134; *Orr v. Lowdon*, 1987 S.C.C.R. 515). In certain statutory enactments it may be competent to proceed to trial in the absence of the accused (s.150(5)) but again this is contingent upon the court being satisfied that the accused knew of the diet.

In the case of limited companies, partnerships or other bodies, citation can be effected at the home of a responsible officer of that entity at his home address as well as at the place of business (*Kirkcudbright Scallop Gear Ltd. v. Walkingshaw*, 1994 S.C.C.R. 372).

Kelly v. Rae, 1917 J.C. 12 is still authority for the view that neither the accused apprehended *in flagrante delicto*, or his agent, need receive a copy complaint at least when the accused has been brought before the first available custody court; the case is mentioned tentatively since no previous convictions could be put before the court, and, it has to be said, that any conviction would be liable to be quashed if it was shown that the defence had suffered substantial prejudice as a result of this omission.

Children

Summary proceedings against children

142.—(1) Where summary proceedings are brought in respect of an offence alleged to have been committed by a child, the sheriff shall sit either in a different building or room from that in which he usually sits or on different days from those on which other courts in the building are engaged in criminal proceedings: and no person shall be present at any sitting for the purposes of such proceedings except—

   (a) members and officers of the court;

   (b) parties to the case before the court, their solicitors and counsel, and witnesses and other persons directly concerned in that case;

   (c) *bona fide* representatives of news gathering or reporting organisations present for the purpose of the preparation of contemporaneous reports of the proceedings;

   (d) such other persons as the court may specially authorise to be present.

(2) A sheriff sitting summarily for the purpose of hearing a charge against, or an application relating to, a person who is believed to be a child may, if he thinks fit to do so, proceed with the hearing and determination of the charge or application, notwithstanding that it is discovered that the person in question is not a child.

(3) When a sheriff sitting summarily has remanded a child for information to be obtained with respect to him, any sheriff sitting summarily in the same place—

   (a) may in his absence extend the period for which he is remanded provided that he appears before a sheriff or a justice at least once every 21 days;

   (b) when the required information has been obtained, may deal with him finally,

and where the sheriff by whom he was originally remanded has recorded a finding that he is guilty of an offence charged against him it shall not be necessary for any court which subsequently deals with him under this subsection to hear evidence as to the commission of that offence, except in so far as it may consider that such evidence will assist the court in determining the manner in which he should be dealt with.

(4) Any direction in any enactment that a charge shall be brought before a juvenile court shall be construed as a direction that he shall be brought before the sheriff sitting as a court of summary jurisdiction, and no such direction shall be construed as restricting the powers of any justice or justices to entertain an application for bail or for a remand, and to hear such evidence as may be necessary for that purpose.

(5) This section does not apply to summary proceedings before the sheriff in respect of an offence where a child has been charged jointly with a person who is not a child.

DEFINITIONS
"justice": s.307(1).
"offence": s.307(1).
"sheriff": s.5(1).

GENERAL NOTE
Section 42 stipulates that where criminal offences alleged to have been committed by children are prosecuted by the criminal courts, rather than being referred to the Principal Reporter, such offences must be prosecuted in the sheriff court or a higher court (see generally the discussion in the notes to s.42 above). This stipulation does not extend to cases in which a co-accused is over 16 years old; in that event the proceedings can be taken in any court if it is felt that referring the child to the Children's Panel is inappropriate and proceedings must be taken against both parties.

The District Court will not have jurisdiction over complaints against juvenile offenders but subs. (4) provides that this is without prejudice to any right of a justice (as defined in s.307(1) this includes sheriffs, stipendiary magistrates and justices of the peace) to determine applications for bail or remand.

The object of subs. (1) is to ensure that the juvenile criminal proceedings brought against children are conducted in court facilities distinct from those used in the course of summary proceedings against young persons and adults. This is intended to prevent the child coming into contact with older offenders and means that a separate juvenile court should convene to hear any custody, diet or trial business whose accused are solely children. The provision is directory in character and non-observance of it is not fatal to a finding of guilt (*Heywood v. B.*, 1994 S.C.C.R. 554).

Chapter 6 of the 1996 Act of Adjournal also provides that efforts be made to prevent the mixing of children attending any juvenile court hearing.

In addition to requiring separate courts for juvenile hearings, s.142 enacts that those proceedings will not be held in open court; access is restricted to the parties specified by subs. (1)(a) to (c) and is otherwise at the discretion of the court.

Subsection (2) preserves the validity of any finding made by a court which has proceeded on the mistaken belief that the accused, or one of the accused, is a child.

Subsection (3) provides for an administrative continuation of a juvenile's case by another sheriff in the absence of the sheriff who made the original remand for information and, in situations where the latter sheriff is unavailable at the time of receipt of that information, his colleague may dispose of the case. A period of remand of a juvenile can exceed 21 days provided that the child is brought before a justice at least once every 21 days.

Companies

Prosecution of companies, etc.

143.—(1) Without prejudice to any other or wider powers conferred by statute, this section shall apply in relation to the prosecution by summary procedure of a partnership, association, body corporate or body of trustees.

(2) Proceedings may be taken against the partnership, association body corporate or body of trustees in their corporate capacity, and in that event any penalty imposed shall be recovered by civil diligence in accordance with section 221 of this Act.

(3) Proceedings may be taken against an individual representative of a partnership, association or body corporate as follows:—

(a) in the case of a partnership or firm, any one of the partners, or the manager or the person in charge or locally in charge of its affairs;

(b) in the case of an association or body corporate, the managing director or the secretary or other person in charge, or locally in charge, of its affairs,

may be dealt with as if he was the person offending, and the offence shall be deemed to be the offence of the partnership, association or body corporate.

DEFINITIONS
"offence": s.307(1).

GENERAL NOTE
See generally the notes to s.70 above.

An unincorporated company may be charged in the name of the company or the partners' names or both (*City and Suburban Dairies v. Mackenna*, 1918 J.C. 105). The same approach can be followed against partnerships.

Proceedings against a registered club can be taken against its office bearers (*Burnette v. Mackenna*, 1917 J.C. 20).

It is competent to proceed against directors of a limited company or against a manager or employee locally responsible for its affairs (*Bean v. Sinclair*, 1930 J.C. 31) but previous convictions libelled against the company cannot be used against that individual (*Campbell v. Mac-Pherson* (1910) 6 Adam 394). A manager can competently represent the company at any diet (*McAlpine v. Ronaldson* (1901) 3 Adam 405).

Amendment of the complaint where the company is incorrectly named is problematical; see *Hoyers (U.K.) v. Houston*, 1991 S.L.T. 934; 1991 S.C.C.R. 919 where the description of the accused was amended at the trial diet, by which time a new complaint would have been time-barred. In *Ralston v. Carmichael*, 1995 G.W.D. 38–1933 a complaint against "Henry Ralston Ltd" was amended to "Henry Ralston" when it was discovered that the limited company did not exist; an appearance and correspondence had already passed before the amendment was sought and it could not be contended that prejudice was caused by the amendment. The issues are whether the error in the name or designation is trivial and if an appearance is made in answer to the complaint (*Poli v. Thomson* (1910) 5 Adam 261); in that event amendment is competent.

For service of citations against bodies corporate, see s.141 above.

First diet

Procedure at first diet

144.—(1) Where the accused is present at the first calling of the case in a summary prosecution and—
(a) the complaint has been served on him, or
(b) the complaint or the substance thereof has been read to him, or
(c) he has legal assistance in his defence,
he shall, unless the court adjourns the case under the section 145 of this Act and subject to subsection (4) below, be asked to plead to the charge.

(2) Where the accused is not present at a calling of the case in a summary prosecution and either—
(a) the prosecutor produces to the court written intimation that the accused pleads not guilty or pleads guilty and the court is satisfied that the intimation has been made or authorised by the accused; or
(b) counsel or a solicitor, or a person not being counsel or a solicitor who satisfies the court that he is authorised by the accused, appears on behalf of the accused and tenders a plea of not guilty or a plea of guilty,
subsection (3) below shall apply.

(3) Where this subsection applies—
(a) in the case of a plea of not guilty, this Part of this Act except section 146(2) shall apply in like manner as if the accused had appeared and tendered the plea; and
(b) in the case of a plea of guilty, the court may, if the prosecutor accepts the plea, proceed to hear and dispose of the case in the absence of the accused in like manner as if he had appeared and pled guilty, or may, if

it thinks fit, continue the case to another diet and require the attendance of the accused with a view to pronouncing sentence in his presence.

(4) Any objection to the competency or relevancy of a summary complaint or the proceedings thereon, or any denial that the accused is the person charged by the police with the offence shall be stated before the accused pleads to the charge or any plea is tendered on his behalf.

(5) No objection or denial such as is mentioned in subsection (4) above shall be allowed to be stated or issued at any future diet in the case except with the leave of the court, which may be granted only on cause shown.

(6) Where in pursuance of subsection (3)(b) above the court proceeds to hear and dispose of a case in the absence of the accused, it shall not pronounce a sentence of imprisonment or of detention in a young offenders institution, remand centre or other establishment.

(7) In this section a reference to a plea of guilty shall include a reference to a plea of guilty to only part of the charge, but where a plea of guilty to only part of a charge is not accepted by the prosecutor it shall be deemed to be a plea of not guilty.

(8) It shall not be competent for any person appearing to answer a complaint, or for counsel or a solicitor appearing for the accused in his absence, to plead want of due citation or informality therein or in the execution thereof.

(9) In this section, a reference to the first calling of a case includes a reference to any adjourned diet fixed by virtue of section 145 of this Act.

Definitions
    "complaint": s.307(1).
    "diet": s.307(1).
    "imprisonment": s.308.
    "prosecutor": s.307(1).
    "sentence": s.307(1).
    "young offenders institution": s.307(1).

General Note
    Appearance at a first diet cures any deficiency in citation (subs. (8)); the accused can make an appearance in person, by way of attendance at court by a solicitor or other authorised representative or by letter. Want of form, which is curable by appearance, should not be confused with a nullity; an unsigned complaint (*Lowe v. Bee*, 1989 S.C.C.R. 476), a complaint which failed to specify a date or locus or in which the court had no jurisdiction (*McMillan v. Grant*, 1924 J.C. 13; *Duffy v. Ingram*, 1987 S.C.C.R. 286) or a missing principal complaint (*McSeveney v. Annan*, 1990 S.C.C.R. 573) are all fundamental procedural defects which cannot be remedied. Note in the last instance, the terms of s.157 which appear to permit the use of a certified copy complaint to preserve proceedings.
    Before any plea is tendered any plea in bar, plea to the competency or relevancy (including any allegation of undue delay in executing any warrant to apprehend or cite), notice that the accused disputes having been cautioned and charged with the offences libelled should be stated (subs. (4)), as should any objection to the libelling of a special capacity (s.255).

Mental Disorder
    Section 52 expressly, and s.145 impliedly, require both the prosecutor and the court to ensure that the accused is not suffering any mental disorder and the diet should be adjourned without plea for the purpose of investigation (in the former section the prosecutor should place medical evidence before the court; in the latter the court itself may adjourn without plea, to enable the prosecutor to obtain a medical report). Until the issue is resolved, any continuation is to be treated as a first diet (subs. (9)).

Pleas to Competency and Relevancy and Special Capacity
    Subsection (5) stipulates that any such pleas must normally be stated at the first diet, though subs. (9) has the effect of permitting a continuation without plea under s.145, to permit proper formulation of any such objections. After the first diet, any objection can only be heard on cause shown; in *Advocate, H.M. v. Bell* (1892) 3 White 313, the court at a second diet was held to be

entitled to consider such objections not previously stated where otherwise a gross injustice would result. See also *McLeay v. Hingston*, 1994 S.L.T. 720; 1994 S.C.C.R. 116 where objection to a complaint devoid of a locus was stated only part way through a trial, the Appeal Court noting that the case could have been adjourned pending resolution of an appeal, the sheriff having repelled objections and granted leave to appeal. The introduction of mandatory intermediate diets in all summary cases (see s.148 below) may serve to limit the late introduction of any such motion.

The Appeal Court has indicated that it is primarily a matter for the discretion of the trial judge whether or not to entertain late pleas to competency, relevancy or capacity (which of course necessarily involve the withdrawal of any pleas previously tendered in regard to the charges) and that that discretion will only be reviewed in light of fundamental objections (*Henderson v. Ingram*, 1982 S.C.C.R. 135). See also *Scott v. Annan*, 1981 S.C.C.R. 172; 1982 S.L.T. 90; *Wimpey Homes Holdings v. Lees*, 1993 S.L.T. 564.

The principal ground for consideration of a plea to relevancy of a complaint is whether the libel is sufficiently specific to give the defence fair notice of the offences (*Clydesdale Group v. Normand*, 1994 S.L.T. 1302).

If a preliminary plea is wholly sustained, then the complaint falls. In the event that the complaint is upheld in whole or part, ordinarily the accused should then be called upon to plead to the charges (a continuation without plea, for example to obtain further instructions, would be competent in terms of s.145). It is important to note that even if the defence move for, or are granted, leave to appeal against the decision relating to the preliminary plea (by way of s.174 below), a plea of guilty or not guilty should be tendered and recorded and a trial diet assigned as necessary (see *Lafferty v. Jessop*, 1989 S.L.T. 846; 1989 S.C.C.R. 451 and *Jessop v. First National Securities*, 1988 S.C.C.R. 1). Note that in the latter case having decided the issue of relevancy, the sheriff, no doubt conscious that his decision was likely to be appealed, canvassed the views of parties and decided to issue a written note of his judgment. Procedurally the proper course would have been to give no decision and continue the case to a later diet for the judgment or, alternatively, give his decision and defer any written comment for his Report, should an appeal be taken against the judgment and the call upon the accused to plead.

Although the court may continue a case for the personal appearance of the accused for sentence (subs. (3)(b)), it does not follow that sentence is contingent upon such an appearance (see *Taylor v. Lees*, 1993 S.C.C.R. 947). The only stricture upon sentence in absence is stated in subs. (6); a sentence of imprisonment or detention can only be imposed when an accused is personally present.

The prosecutor is never obliged to accept a plea of guilty either to the whole or part of a complaint: (*Kirkwood v. Coalburn District Cooperative Society*, 1930 J.C. 38). However where a plea of guilt is tendered, it has been held that appeal by way of bill of suspension will rarely be appropriate; see *Aitken v. Reith*, 1996 G.W.D. 2–79 where following a letter plea of guilty and a personal appearance for sentence, the accused subsequently claimed to have been unaware that he had been charged with dangerous, rather than careless, driving and had been too timid to withdraw his plea at the deferred diet.

Adjournment for inquiry at first calling

145.—(1) Without prejudice to section 150(1) to (7) of this Act, at the first calling of a case in a summary prosecution the court may, in order to allow time for inquiry into the case or for any other cause which it considers reasonable, adjourn the case under this section, for such period as it considers appropriate, without calling on the accused to plead to any charge against him but remanding him in custody or on bail or ordaining him to appear at the diet thus fixed; and, subject to subsections (2) and (3) below, the court may from time to time so adjourn the case.

(2) Where the accused is remanded in custody, the total period for which he is so remanded under this section shall not exceed 21 days and no one period of adjournment shall, except on special cause shown, exceed 7 days.

(3) Where the accused is remanded on bail or ordained to appear, no one period of adjournment shall exceed 28 days.

DEFINITIONS
"bail": s.307(1).
"diet": s.307(1).
"remand": s.307(1).

General Note
The court's power to continue a case without plea on the motion of a party or *ex proprio motu* is preserved. However where an accused is remanded in custody in relation to the complaint before the court, no continuation should exceed seven days save on cause shown, and the total period of continuations cannot exceed 21 days (subs. (2)). It will be remembered that the period involved in any such continuation has to be included in the calculation of time spent in custody awaiting summary trial since the bringing of the complaint (see s.147 below).

The maximum period of adjournment allowed at any one time in cases where the accused is bailed or ordained to appear is 28 days (subs. (3)). A continuation without plea for debate would appear not to be subject to the time limit imposed by subs. (3) following the *ratio* in *Pearson v. Crowe*, 1994 S.L.T. 378, but is obviously affected by the strictures imposed in custody cases by subs. (2).

Plea of not guilty

146.—(1) This section applies where the accused in a summary prosecution—
(a) pleads not guilty to the charge; or
(b) pleads guilty to only part of the charge and the prosecutor does not accept the partial plea.

(2) The court may proceed to trial at once unless either party moves for an adjournment and the court considers it expedient to grant it.

(3) The court may adjourn the case for trial to as early a diet as is consistent with the just interest of both parties, and the prosecutor shall, if requested by the accused, furnish him with a copy of the complaint if he does not already have one.

(4) Where the accused is brought before the court from custody the court shall inform the accused of his right to an adjournment of the case for not less than 48 hours and if he requests such adjournment before the prosecutor has commenced his proof, subject to subsection (5) below, the adjournment shall be granted.

(5) Where the court considers that it is necessary to secure the examination of witnesses who otherwise would not be available, the case may proceed to trial at once or on a shorter adjournment than 48 hours.

(6) Where the accused is in custody, he may be committed to prison or to legalised police cells or to any other place to which he may lawfully be committed pending trial—
(a) if he is neither granted bail nor ordained to appear; or
(b) if he is granted bail on a condition imposed under section 24(6) of this Act that a sum of money is deposited in court, until the accused or a cautioner on his behalf has so deposited that sum.

(7) The court may from time to time at any stage of the case on the motion of either party or *ex proprio motu* grant such adjournment as may be necessary for the proper conduct of the case, and where from any cause a diet has to be continued from day to day it shall not be necessary to intimate the continuation to the accused.

(8) It shall not be necessary for the prosecutor to establish a charge or part of a charge to which the accused pleads guilty.

(9) The court may, in any case where it considers it expedient, permit any witness for the defence to be examined prior to evidence for the prosecution having been led or concluded, but in any such case the accused shall be entitled to lead additional evidence after the case for the prosecution is closed.

Definitions
"bail": s.307(1).
"diet": s.307(1).
"legalised police cells": s.307(1).
"prison": s.307(1).
"prosecutor": s.307(1).

GENERAL NOTE

Provided that any preliminary pleas have been repelled, the accused should then be called upon to plead to the charges still current on the complaint. The prosecutor may, but is not obliged to, accept any partial pleas tendered. Subject to the exceptional provisions of subs. (5), in custody cases the accused is entitled to an *induciae* of 48 hours before his trial occurs, an *induciae* which he may waive, but his right to which the court must make known to him; failure to do so will almost certainly vitiate any conviction (see *Ferguson v. Brown*, 1942 J.C. 113). The refusal of an adjournment which is needed, in order to enable the accused to lead evidence in support of his alibi defence once trial has begun, may constitute oppression; *McKellar v. Dickson* (1898) 2 Adam 504.

In accordance with subs. (2), the court can proceed to trial immediately unless any of the parties moves for an adjournment. In practice, such a peremptory diet of trial is rare though subs. (5) allows for such a trial then or within 48 hours, where this is essential to secure witnesses' evidence even in custody cases. It is perfectly competent to adjourn the trial once such evidence has been heard or at any point in any summary trial (subs. (7)).

Subsection (6) permits a remand in custody in cases where bail is either not granted or not sought, or more unusually, where a sum of money bail is required to be deposited with the court as an additional bail condition in terms of s.24(6).

Subsection (9) echoes the little-used terms of s.337(h) of the 1975 Act and permits the calling of defence evidence prior to, or during, Crown evidence. It is suggested that this provision envisages the leading of defence evidence, a preferable alternative to the Crown, as an expedient means of assisting the defence, calling defence witnesses during the Crown case formally, then leaving the defence to lead the witness' evidence in cross-examination.

Pre-trial procedure

Prevention of delay in trials

147.—(1) Subject to subsections (2) and (3) below, a person charged with an offence in summary proceedings shall not be detained in that respect for a total of more than 40 days after the bringing of the complaint in court unless his trial is commenced within that period, failing which he shall be liberated forthwith and thereafter he shall be for ever free from all question or process for that offence.

(2) The sheriff may, on application made to him for the purpose, extend the period mentioned in subsection (1) above and order the accused to be detained awaiting trial for such period as he thinks fit where he is satisfied that delay in the commencement of the trial is due to—

(a) the illness of the accused or of a judge;

(b) the absence or illness of any necessary witness; or

(c) any other sufficient cause which is not attributable to any fault on the part of the prosecutor.

(3) The grant or refusal of any application to extend the period mentioned in subsection (1) above may be appealed against by note of appeal presented to the High Court; and that Court may affirm, reverse or amend the determination made on such application.

(4) For the purposes of this section, a trial shall be taken to commence when the first witness is sworn.

DEFINITIONS

"complaint": s.307(1).
"High Court": s.307(1).
"judge": s.307(1).
"offence": s.307(1).
"prosecutor": s.307(1).
"sheriff": s.5(1).
"witness": s.307(1).

GENERAL NOTE
This section preserves the provisions introduced into the 1975 Act by s.14(2) of the Criminal Justice (Scotland) Act 1980 to limit the period of remand affecting persons awaiting summary trial. A person remanded in custody in terms of s.146(6) may only be held in custody pending trial for 40 days in relation to that complaint.

Note that the period only begins from "the bringing of the complaint" so a period on remand following an appearance on petition would not, it is submitted, be included in calculation of the 40 days, notwithstanding the recent decision in *Gardner v. Lees*, 1996 G.W.D. 5–253 which dealt with a non-custodial reduction of petition proceedings to summary proceedings.

Similarly, the period spent in custody must be attributable wholly to matters awaiting trial; a person serving a sentence, or a person remanded for trial but who then becomes a serving prisoner thus effectively interrupting the remand period, cannot benefit from the protection of the provisions against delay in trial. However in *Lockhart v. Robb*, 1988 S.C.C.R. 381 it was held by the sheriff that a remand for pre-sentencing reports on another complaint did not interrupt the running of 40 days in a custody complaint.

In calculating the 40 day period, the whole of the day on which the remand order is made is discounted, while the whole of the final day is included: see *Hazlett v. McGlennan*, 1992 S.C.C.R. 799; 1993 S.L.T. 74 and the discussion "Computation of Time" in notes to s.136 above. As subs. (4) enacts, the period expires when the trial begins. In *Grugen v. Jessop*, 1988 S.C.C.R. 182 the accused took a Bill of Advocation founding upon the actions of the prosecutor who commenced his trial on the fortieth day, in the knowledge that the trial would have to be adjourned only part-heard due to the known unavailability of Crown witnesses. The Appeal Court refused the Bill and declined to hold these procedures to be an abuse of process.

The court on application can extend the 40 day period on the grounds specified in subs. (2); considerations similar to those applying to s.65(4) in solemn procedure are relevant. Appeal to the High Court against such extension proceeds on Form 17.1 while Rule 17.1.–(2) of the 1996 Act of Adjournal stipulates service of copies of the Form upon the prosecutor and the clerk of court.

Intermediate diet

148.—(1) The court may at any time, as respects a case which is, adjourned for trial, fix a diet (to be known as an intermediate diet) for the purpose of ascertaining, so far as is reasonably practicable, whether the case is likely to proceed to trial on the date assigned as the trial diet and, in particular—

   (a) the state of preparation of the prosecutor and of the accused with respect to their cases;

   (b) whether the accused intends to adhere to the plea of not guilty; and

   (c) the extent to which the prosecutor and the accused have complied with the duty under section 257(1) of this Act.

(2) Where at an intermediate diet the court concludes that the case is unlikely to proceed to trial on the date assigned for the trial diet, the court—

   (a) shall, unless having regard to previous proceedings in the case it considers it inappropriate to do so, postpone the trial diet; and

   (b) may fix a further intermediate diet.

(3) Subject to subsection (2) above, the court may, if it considers it appropriate to do so, adjourn an intermediate diet.

(4) At an intermediate diet, the court may ask the prosecutor and the accused any question for the purposes mentioned in subsection (1) above.

(5) The accused shall attend an intermediate diet of which he has received intimation or to which he has been cited unless—

   (a) he is legally represented; and

   (b) the court considers that there are exceptional circumstances justifying him not attending.

(6) A plea of guilty may be tendered at the intermediate diet.

(7) The foregoing provisions of this section shall have effect as respects any court prescribed by the Secretary of State by order, in relation to proceedings commenced after such date as may be so prescribed, with the following modifications—

   (a) in subsection (1), for the word "may" there shall be substituted "shall, subject to subsection (1A) below,"; and

(b) after subsection (1) there shall be inserted the following subsections—
"(1A) If, on a joint application by the prosecutor and the accused made at any time before the commencement of the intermediate diet, the court considers it inappropriate to have such a diet, the duty under subsection (1) above shall not apply and the court shall discharge any such diet already fixed.

(1B) The court may consider an application under subsection (1A) above without hearing the parties.".

(8) An order under subsection (7) above shall be made by statutory instrument, which shall be subject to annulment in pursuance of a resolution of either House of Parliament.

DEFINITIONS
"diet": s.307(1).
"prosecutor": s.307(1).

GENERAL NOTE
Intermediate diets were introduced in 1980 in an attempt to avoid the waste of scarce court resources, and needless inconvenience to the public, caused by the large proportion of trials which did not proceed at trial diets.

Mandatory, as distinct from optional, intermediate diets in summary procedure were introduced by s.14 of the Criminal Justice (Scotland) Act 1995. The purposes of these diets are now extended as are the duties of the courts in disposing of them: the diet is to ascertain the state of preparation of the prosecutor and the accused, and whether the matter is indeed to proceed to trial (it will be observed that s.196 of the Act permits the court, when determining sentence, to take account of the stage in proceedings at which a guilty plea was tendered and s.257 obliges parties to seek to identify evidence which is felt to be capable of agreement).

When it is evident at the intermediate diet that the trial is unlikely to proceed, the court may then (if it is felt that the case should continue) postpone the trial to a new diet and, if appropriate, fix a further intermediate diet (subs. (2)). As an alternative at the intermediate diet the court may adjourn the diet for further preparation (subs. (3)), a procedure which allows the trial diet to be retained. It is open to parties by a prior joint application to discharge the intermediate diet fixed, but care has to be exercised to ensure that the trial diet itself is preserved.

Given the mandatory nature of intermediate diets it is clear that failure to call the complaint at that diet will cause the instance to fall. See *McDonald v. Knight*, 1990 S.C.C.R. 641, which related to the near-equivalent procedures in the 1975 Act.

Alibi

149. It shall not be competent for the accused in a summary prosecution to found on a plea of alibi unless he gives, at any time before the first witness is sworn, notice to the prosecutor of the plea with particulars as to time and place and of the witnesses by whom it is proposed to prove it; and, on such notice being given, the prosecutor shall be entitled, if he so desires, to an adjournment of the case.

DEFINITIONS
"prosecutor": s.307(1).
"witness": s.307(1).

GENERAL NOTE
Schedule 6, para. 121 of the Criminal Justice (Scotland) Act 1995 introduced only one small clarifying amendment to s.339 of the 1975 Act, which carried over into s.149 of the current Act. An alibi has now to be intimated before the first witness is sworn, whereas in the 1975 Act intimation had to be made "prior to the examination of the first witness".

Failure of accused to appear

Failure of accused to appear

150.—(1) This section applies where the accused in a summary prosecution fails to appear at any diet of which he has received intimation, or to which he has been cited other than a diet which, by virtue of section 148(5) of this Act, he is not required to attend.

(2) The court may adjourn the proceedings to another diet, and order the accused to attend at such diet, and appoint intimation of the diet to be made to him.

(3) The court may grant warrant to apprehend the accused.

(4) Intimation under subsection (2) above shall be sufficiently given by an officer of law, or by letter signed by the clerk of court or prosecutor and sent to the accused at his last known address by registered post or by the recorded delivery service, and the production in court of the written execution of such officer or of an acknowledgement or certificate of the delivery of the letter issued by the Post Office shall be sufficient evidence of such intimation having been duly given.

(5) Where the accused is charged with a statutory offence for which a sentence of imprisonment cannot be imposed in the first instance, or where the statute founded on or conferring jurisdiction authorises procedure in the absence of the accused, the court, on the motion of the prosecutor and upon being satisfied that the accused has been duly cited, or has received due intimation of the diet where such intimation has been ordered, may subject to subsections (6) and (7) below, proceed to hear and dispose of the case in the absence of the accused.

(6) Unless the statute founded on authorises conviction in default of appearance, proof of the complaint must be led to the satisfaction of the court.

(7) In a case to which subsection (5) above applies, the court may, if it considers it expedient, allow counsel or a solicitor who satisfies the court that he has authority from the accused so to do, to appear and plead for and defend him.

(8) An accused who without reasonable excuse fails to attend any diet of which he has been given due notice, shall be guilty of an offence and liable on summary conviction—

(a) to a fine not exceeding level 3 on the standard scale; and

(b) to a period of imprisonment not exceeding—
    (i) in the district court, 60 days; or
    (ii) in the sheriff court, 3 months.

(9) The penalties provided for in subsection (8) above may be imposed in addition to any other penalty which it is competent for the court to impose, notwithstanding that the total of penalties imposed may exceed the maximum penalty which it is competent to impose in respect of the original offence.

(10) An accused may be dealt with for an offence under subsection (8) above either at his diet of trial for the original offence or at a separate trial.

DEFINITIONS
    "complaint": s.307(1).
    "diet": s.307(1).
    "imprisonment": s.307(6).
    "offence": s.307(1).
    "officer of law": s.307(1).
    "prosecutor": s.307(1).

GENERAL NOTE
    Section 141, which specifies the methods of citation of accused, and this section which deals with the consequences of a failure by an accused to appear at a summary diet need to be considered together. Intimation of any diet can be made by notice sent by registered or recorded post, by personal service of such a notice by an officer of law, or by the fixing of the diet in the accused's presence. While s.141 relates to the way in which proceedings are launched, s.150 has general application once a complaint has been placed before the court until the proceedings are concluded.

The failure by an accused to attend a diet of which he has been given notice lawfully, entitles the prosecutor to seek an apprehension warrant in terms of s.150 and to libel a further complaint founding upon failure to appear. The penalties disclosed in subs. (8) are in addition to any penalty the court may impose on the original complaint and, cumulatively, the penalties exacted on the original and second complaint can competently exceed the statutory ceilings fixed in summary proceedings; these are defined in s.5(2) and (3) for the sheriff court, and in s.7(6) and (7) in relation to the district court.

On proof of citation or notice of a diet being produced to the court, the prosecutor may seek a warrant to apprehend the accused. The court may grant a warrant or continue the diet to a later diet and order intimation of the diet on the accused as provided by subs. (2). This underlines the importance of the Crown being able to exhibit evidence of service of the complaint or of intimation of the diet when required by the court. See *Beattie v. Mackinnon*, 1977 J.C. 64 where no date of citation had been placed on the accused's citation and service copy complaint, a fact unknown to the court when a warrant to apprehend was granted following an apparent failure to appear.

The court is not obliged to issue a warrant following failure to appear by the accused (subs. (2) permits adjournment of proceedings) but must pronounce some order and cannot simply refrain from action; see *Skeen v. Sullivan*, 1980 S.L.T. (Notes) 11. Equally the prosecutor can only proceed under this section to take a warrant, when he is satisfied that service of the complaint has been effected and, hence, that it is validly before the court for further procedure; see *Lees v. Malcolm*, 1992 S.L.T. 1137; 1992 S.C.C.R. 589 where a fresh complaint was raised to maintain proceedings, and *Heywood v. McLennan*, 1994 S.C.C.R. 1 where efforts were made to "convert" an unserved complaint into an initiating warrant, despite the complaint having fallen.

Subsections (5), (6) and (7) provide for trial proceedings in the absence of the accused only once the court is satisfied that the accused has either been cited or received an intimation of the diet deemed necessary by the court.

Non-availability of judge

Death, illness or absence of judge

151.—(1) Where the court is unable to proceed owing to the death, illness or absence of the presiding judge, it shall be lawful for the clerk of court—
  (a) where the diet has not been called, to convene the court and adjourn the diet;
  (b) where the diet has been called but no evidence has been led, to adjourn the diet; and
  (c) where the diet has been called and evidence has been led—
      (i) with the agreement of the parties, to desert the diet *pro loco et tempore*; or
      (ii) to adjourn the diet.

(2) Where, under subsection (1)(c)(i) above, a diet has been deserted *pro loco et tempore*, any new prosecution charging the accused with the same or any similar offence arising out of the same facts shall be brought within two months of the date on which the diet was deserted notwithstanding that any other time limit for the commencement of such prosecution has elapsed.

(3) For the purposes of subsection (2) above, a new prosecution shall be deemed to commence on the date on which a warrant to apprehend or to cite the accused is granted, if such warrant is executed without undue delay.

DEFINITIONS
  "judge": s.307(1).
  "offence": s.307(1).

GENERAL NOTE
  The purpose of this section is to provide for the adjournment, or desertion *pro loco et tempore*, of summary proceedings where the court cannot proceed due to the death, illness or absence of the "presiding judge", a phrase equally applicable to sheriff or district court proceedings. Similar provisions, taking due account of differences in procedure, apply to solemn proceedings by s.87 above.

In summary proceedings the court has a common law authority to fix a new diet when a judge is taken ill during a trial and therefore the possibility of postponement of a trial, for that same reason, was acknowledged in s.331A(2)(a) of the 1975 Act. However until the passage of s.30 of the Criminal Justice (Scotland) Act 1995, no statutory provision existed in summary cases to regulate proceedings in the event of the death of a judge.

Desertion of the diet necessarily means that the instance in the complaint falls. To preserve the public interest, particularly in cases which would otherwise be time-barred in accordance with s.136 above, subs. (2) permits the re-raising of any proceedings deserted in terms of s.151. In that event proceedings can be initiated anew, but must be effected upon the accused without undue delay (for "undue delay" see generally the notes to s.136 above).

A separate provision dealing with the illness or death of a judge in the course of preparation of an appeal by stated case is found at s.176(4).

Trial diet

Desertion of diet

152.—(1) It shall be competent at the diet of trial, at any time before the first witness is sworn, for the court, on the application of the prosecutor, to desert the diet *pro loco et tempore*.

(2) If, at a diet of trial, the court refuses an application by the prosecutor to adjourn the trial or to desert the diet *pro loco et tempore*, and the prosecutor is unable or unwilling to proceed with the trial, the court shall desert the diet *simpliciter*.

(3) Where the court has deserted a diet *simpliciter* under subsection (2) above (and the court's decision in that regard has not been reversed on appeal), it shall not be competent for the prosecutor to raise a fresh libel.

DEFINITIONS
  "diet": s.307(1).
  "prosecutor": s.307(1).
  "trial": s.307(1).
  "witness": s.307(1).

GENERAL NOTE
  The terms of s.338A of the 1975 Act are preserved. Section 147(4) of this Act enacts that a trial begins when the first witness is sworn; until that time it is open to the prosecutor to move the court to desert the diet *pro loco et tempore*, or to move to adjourn the trial. Once either of these motions has been made however, the court can refuse the motion and, instead, desert the trial *simpliciter*, a step which brings proceedings to an end. In some instances the Crown might better achieve its purpose simply by not calling the case for trial at all, since, although the instance in the current complaint would fall, the right to proceed might still be retained. It remains the case, as subs. (3) states, that the unreasonable refusal by the judge of a Crown motion to adjourn or desert *pro loco et tempore* can still be appealed.

  In *Tudhope v. Gough*, 1982 S.C.C.R. 157 it was held competent for the Crown to move to desert *pro loco* even after the refusal of a motion to adjourn. A more novel, but inappropriate, use of desertion *simpliciter* is found in *MacLeod v. Williamson*, 1993 S.L.T. 144 where the sheriff did so *ex proprio motu* having overheard witnesses during an adjournment and having drawn the nature of the eavesdropping to the attention of the prosecutor.

  The Appeal Court indicated that if the sheriff had come to the view that he could no longer preside over the trial, he should have discharged the trial diet and fixed a new diet to go before another sheriff; desertion *simpliciter* was invalid. In a similar vein, see *Carmichael v. Monaghan*, 1986 S.C.C.R. 598.

  In *McMahon v. Hamilton*, 1992 S.C.C.R. 351, the prosecutor deserted one of two charges on a complaint *simpliciter*, a plea of not guilty being recorded for the second charge. Issue was thereafter taken with the competency of proceeding on the latter charge. The plea to competency was repelled but the Appeal Court, rather than express any view on the competency of deserting a charge (as distinct from a complaint) *simpliciter* elected to treat both charges as live and to treat the minuting of the pleas as *pro non scripto*: it remains unresolved whether such a motion is competent or not, though the simplest solution is surely to accept a plea of not guilty to the charge in normal circumstances.

See *Normand v. West*, 1992 S.C.C.R. 76 as an example of an unreasonable refusal by the court to permit an adjournment in the absence of essential witnesses.

Trial in presence of accused

153.—(1) Without prejudice to section 150 of this Act, and subject to subsection (2) below, no part of a trial shall take place outwith the presence of the accused.

(2) If during the course of his trial an accused so misconducts himself that in the view of the court a proper trial cannot take place unless he is removed, the court may order—

(a) that he is removed from the court for so long as his conduct makes it necessary; and

(b) that the trial proceeds in his absence,

but if he is not legally represented the court shall appoint counsel or a solicitor to represent his interests during such absence.

DEFINITIONS
   "trial": s.307(1).

GENERAL NOTE
   Subject to the statutory enactments which permit trial in the absence of the accused (see s.150(5)), it is generally the case that any trial can only competently proceed in the accused's presence (see *Aitken v. Wood*, 1921 J.C. 84) for justice to be seen to be done. Section 153 introduces a further exception to the generality in circumstances where the accused so misconducts himself as to preclude proper conduct of the case. In that event the accused can be removed from the court and trial continue with the accused represented by his solicitor or counsel, or if he has not been legally represented, by an agent appointed by the court to act on his behalf, during the period of absence. This provision does not, of course, resolve what action the court may take at the conclusion of the trial to deal with any contempt.

   The equivalent provision in solemn proceedings is found at s.92(2) above.

Proof of official documents

154.—(1) Any letter, minute or other official document issuing from the office or in the custody of any of the departments of state or government in the United Kingdom the production of which in evidence is required in any summary prosecution, and which according to the rules and regulations applicable to such departments may be competently produced, shall when produced be received as *prima facie* evidence of the matter contained in it without being produced or sworn to by any witness, and a copy thereof bearing to be certified by any person having authority to certify it shall be treated as equivalent to the original, and no proof of the signature of the person certifying such copy, or of his authority to certify it shall he necessary.

(2) Any order by any of the departments of state or government or any local authority or public body made under powers conferred by any statute, or a print or copy of such order, shall when produced in a summary prosecution be received in evidence of the due making, confirmation, and existence of the order without being sworn to by any witness and without any further or other proof.

(3) Subsection (2) above is without prejudice to any right competent to the accused to challenge any order such as is mentioned in that subsection as being *ultra vires* of the authority making it or on any other competent ground.

(4) Where an order such as is mentioned in subsection (2) above is referred to in the complaint it shall not be necessary to enter it in the record of the proceedings as a documentary production.

(5) The provisions of this section are in addition to, and not in derogation of, any powers of proving documents conferred by statute, or existing at common law.

DEFINITIONS
    "complaint": s.307(1).
    "existing": s.307(1).
    "witness": s.307(1).

GENERAL NOTE
    Subsection (1) provides for the admissibility as evidence, without the need for supporting parole evidence, of official documents in the course of summary proceedings. It will be noted that either the document or a copy can be used provided it is certified appropriately. These provisions are without prejudice to any express statutory provisions.
    Bye-laws lack the probative status of Acts of Parliament and require to be tabled as part of the prosecution case (*Herkes v. Dickie*, 1958 J.C. 51). In *Johnston v. MacGillivray*, 1993 S.L.T. 120, a challenge to the validity of the statutory instrument under which the accused was charged was intimated at a preliminary diet. The sheriff ordered evidence from the accused to substantiate the plea. Although the Appeal Court did not rule on the procedure, it was recommended that the Crown should first be called upon to lead its evidence. The case was returned to the sheriff with a direction to call upon the accused to plead and fix a trial if necessary. See also *Neizer v. Johnston*, 1993 S.C.C.R. 772 and the statutory presumption in Sched. 3, para. 12 to the Act: accordingly if issue is taken with the statute or order under which a charge is libelled, this must be stated prior to trial.

Punishment of witness for contempt

155.—(1) If a witness in a summary prosecution—
(a) wilfully fails to attend after being duly cited; or
(b) unlawfully refuses to be sworn; or
(c) after the oath has been administered to him refuses to answer any question which the court may allow; or
(d) prevaricates in his evidence,
he shall be deemed guilty of contempt of court and be liable to be summarily punished forthwith for such contempt by a fine not exceeding level 3 on the standard scale or by imprisonment for any period not exceeding 21 days.

(2) Where punishment is summarily imposed as mentioned in subsection (1) above, the clerk of court shall enter in the record of the proceedings the acts constituting the contempt or the statements forming the prevarication.

(3) Subsections (1) and (2) above are without prejudice to the right of the prosecutor to proceed by way of formal complaint for any such contempt where a summary punishment, as mentioned in the said subsection (1), is not imposed.

(4) Any witness who, having been duly cited in accordance with section 140 of this Act—
(a) fails without reasonable excuse, after receiving at least 48 hours' notice, to attend for precognition by a prosecutor at the time and place mentioned in the citation served on him; or
(b) refuses when so cited to give information within his knowledge regarding any matter relative to the commission of the offence in relation to which such precognition is taken,
shall be liable to the like punishment as is provided in subsection (1) above.

DEFINITIONS
    "prosecutor": s.307(1).
    "witness": s.307(1).

GENERAL NOTE
    In minuting the act which constituted the contempt, care must be taken to specify in detail the nature of the misconduct; see *Strang v. Annan*, 1991 S.L.T. 676; *Sze v. Wilson*, 1992 S.L.T. 569; 1992 S.C.C.R. 54. Since s.155(1) refers to punishment "forthwith", there is no necessity to obtain social enquiry reports and the punishment imposed is not a "sentence" (see *Forrest v. Wilson*, 1993 S.C.C.R. 631; 1994 S.L.T. 490 and the statutory definition of "sentence" at s.307(1)).

Although subs. (4) refers back to the provisions of subs. (1), it would appear that the same comments would apply.

The factors justifying precognition on oath are set out in *Carmichael, Complainer*, 1992 S.C.C.R. 553, where a Bill of Advocation followed refusal of an application to precognosce on oath. Precognition on oath applications by the defence proceed by way of s.291 below.

Apprehension of witness

156.—(1) Where a witness, having been duly cited, fails to appear at the diet fixed for his attendance and no just excuse is offered by him or on his behalf, the court may, if it is satisfied that he received the citation or that its contents came to his knowledge, issue a warrant for his apprehension.

(2) Where the court is satisfied by evidence on oath that a witness is not likely to attend to give evidence without being compelled so to do, it may issue a warrant for his apprehension.

(3) A warrant of apprehension of a witness in the form mentioned in section 135(1) of this Act shall imply warrant to officers of law to search for and apprehend the witness, and to detain him in a police station, police cell, or other convenient place, until—

(a) the date fixed for the hearing of the case; or
(b) the date when security to the amount fixed under subsection (4) below is found,

whichever is the earlier.

(4) A witness apprehended under a warrant under subsection (1) or (2) above shall, wherever practicable, be brought immediately by the officer of law who executed that warrant before a justice, who shall fix such sum as he considers appropriate as security for the appearance of the witness at all diets.

DEFINITIONS
"diet": s.307(1).
"justice": s.307(1).
"officers of law": s.307(1).
"witness": s.307(1).

GENERAL NOTE
Rule 18.3 and Form 18.3 in the 1996 Act of Adjournal provide the form of warrant for the apprehension of a witness.

Record of proceedings

157.—(1) Proceedings in a summary prosecution shall be conducted summarily *viva voce* and, except where otherwise provided and subject to subsection (2) below, no record need be kept of the proceedings other than the complaint, or a copy of the complaint certified as a true copy by the procurator fiscal, the plea, a note of any documentary evidence produced, and the conviction and sentence or other finding of the court.

(2) Any objection taken to the competency or relevancy of the complaint or proceedings, or to the competency or admissibility of evidence, shall, if either party desires it, be entered in the record of the proceedings.

DEFINITIONS
"complaint": s.307(1).
"procurator fiscal": s.307(1).

GENERAL NOTE
The Criminal Justice (Scotland) 1995, Sched. 6, para. 128 added the words "or a copy of the complaint certified as true by a procurator fiscal" to s.359 of the 1975 Act. Presumably it is

intended that the loss of a complaint which had vitiated proceedings previously, can now be cured.

Interruption of summary proceedings for verdict in earlier trial

158. Where the sheriff is sitting in summary proceedings during the period in which the jury in a criminal trial in which he has presided are retired to consider their verdict, it shall be lawful, if he considers it appropriate to do so, to interrupt those proceedings—

(a) in order to receive the verdict of the jury and dispose of the cause to which it relates;

(b) to give a direction to the jury on any matter on which they may wish one from him, or to hear a request from them regarding any matter,

and the interruption shall not affect the validity of the proceedings nor cause the instance to fall in respect of any person accused in the proceedings.

DEFINITIONS
"sheriff": s.307(1).

GENERAL NOTE
This section was introduced by the Prisoners and Criminal Proceedings (Scotland) Act 1993 (c. 9) s.40. It provides for more efficient use of court time by enabling the sheriff to deal with summary business while a jury charged by him earlier is considering its verdict. Chapter 18 of the 1996 Act of Adjournal makes provision for the interruption of summary proceedings on conviction of the accused, to enable the court to consider conviction or sentence in other cases proceeding before the court.

Section 102 of this Act enacts equivalent provisions relative to the interruption of sheriff and jury trials.

Amendment of complaint

159.—(1) It shall be competent at any time prior to the determination of the case, unless the court see just cause to the contrary, to amend the complaint or any notice of previous conviction relative thereto by deletion, alteration or addition, so as to—

(a) cure any error or defect in it;

(b) meet any objection to it; or

(c) cure any discrepancy or variance between the complaint or notice and the evidence.

(2) Nothing in this section shall authorise an amendment which changes the character of the offence charged, and, if it appears to the court that the accused may in any way be prejudiced in his defence on the merits of the case by any amendment made under this section, the court shall grant such remedy to the accused by adjournment or otherwise as appears to the court to be just.

(3) An amendment made under this section shall be sufficiently authenticated by the initials of the clerk of the court.

DEFINITIONS
"complaint": s.138 and Sched. 5.
"offence": s.307(1).
"previous conviction": s.307(5).

GENERAL NOTE
The Act permits wide powers of amendment to a summary complaint but subject to the proviso that the amendment proposed must not alter the character of the offence charged, and cannot be used to validate a complaint which is radically defective in its essentials (*Stevenson v. McLevey* (1879) 4 Couper 196; *Lowe v. Bee*, 1989 S.C.C.R. 476).

The court cannot amend the complaint *ex proprio motu* in the absence of such a motion from the prosecutor (*Grant v. Lockhart*, Crown Office Circular A3/91). The refusal or grant of a proposed amendment rests in the discretion of the trial judge and will not readily be interfered with by the Appeal Court (*Cumming v. Frame* (1909) 6 Adam 57). Such a motion can be made at any point in the case prior to the determination of proceedings (see *Cochrane v. The West Calder Cooperative Society*, 1978 S.L.T. (Notes) 22 and *Matheson v. Ross* (1885) 5 Couper 582, where the date libelled was found to be incorrect after the close of the Crown case, the accused not being prejudiced and declining an adjournment). The point in the proceedings at which amendment is moved can itself be significant; in *MacArthur v. MacNeill*, 1986 S.C.C.R. 552; 1987 S.L.T. 299 the Crown sought to amend a road traffic complaint, substituting failure to supply a blood specimen in a libel which originally averred failure to provide breath specimens at the close of evidence, a manoeuvre which the Appeal Court held to have changed the character of the offence (compare with *Fenwick v. Valentine*, 1993 S.C.C.R. 892; 1994 S.L.T. 485).

Amendment of the Preamble and Instance

Adding a heading to the complaint to read "Under the Summary Jurisdiction (Scotland) Acts 1864 and 1881, and the Criminal Procedure (Scotland) Act 1887 "by amendment, was allowed in *Finlayson v. Bunbury* (1898) 2 Adam 478; correction of the heading on a complaint which referred to a District Court jurisdiction when the accused had been cited to, and the case called in, the relevant sheriff court was upheld on appeal (*Doonin Plant v. Lees*, 1993 S.C.C.R. 511; 1994 S.L.T. 313).

Altering the name of the accused even after the statutory time bar has expired was allowed in *Hoyers (U.K.) v. Houston*, 1991 S.L.T. 934; 1991 S.C.C.R. 919 and see also *Ralston v. Carmichael*, 1995 G.W.D. 38–1933 discussed in Notes to s.143 above. More curiously in *Montgomery Transport v. Walkingshaw*, 1992 S.C.C.R. 17 the complainers brought a Bill of Suspension following a guilty plea to a complaint which, it was later discovered, had libelled the wrong section of the statute albeit the narrative accurately set out the offence: they argued the complaint to be a nullity, but the High Court treated it as merely irrelevant and capable of amendment noting that the complainers had not taken objection before the sheriff.

However in *Lockhart v. British School of Motoring*, 1982 S.C.C.R. 118, amendment to the libel was refused on the grounds that, if allowed, it would deprive co-accused of a statutory defence. Amendment to change the identity of the accused was refused in *Valentine v. Thistle Leisure*, 1983 S.C.C.R. 515; by contrast, amendment of a nature which altered the capacity of the accused was allowed on appeal in *Tudhope v. Chung*, 1985 S.C.C.R. 139.

Amendment of Offence Dates

See *Matheson v. Ross* cited above. In *Duffy v. Ingram* (also cited above), where the offence date was omitted in the first charge and adopted in the second charge and detailed as "said 30 November 1985" in the last charge on the complaint, an objection to relevancy was repelled by the sheriff who allowed amendments to cure the defects in the libel.

Amendment of Locus

It is generally competent to amend the locus stated in a summary charge so as to bring the libel into accord with the evidence, and amendment should be permitted unless it alters the nature of the charge. Amendment is permissible even if it involves including a locus outwith the court's jurisdiction (see *Craig v. Keane*, 1981 S.C.C.R. 166; 1982 S.L.T. 198 and, more generally, *Belcher v. MacKinnon*, 1987 S.L.T. 298).

In *Herron v. Gemmell*, 1975 S.L.T. (Notes) 93 the sheriff refused an amendment to add "Glasgow" to the specification "on the road on the Glasgow Inner Ring Road, at a part thereof near Charing Cross underpass" a decision which was overturned on appeal.

A more radical amendment in *Brown v. McLeod*, 1986 S.C.C.R. 615 had the effect of extending the locus to include driving between two towns. In response, the sheriff offered the defence the opportunity of an adjournment to lead additional evidence in light of the amendment but this was declined. His decision was upheld on appeal. Similarly in *Tudhope v. Fulton*, 1986 S.C.C.R. 567 amendment of the *locus delicti*, where the offence was failure to provide breath specimens at an incorrectly specified police office, was allowed on appeal; this follows reasoning similar to that employed in *Belcher v. MacKinnon* cited above.

Amendment and Statutory Offences

Amendment may be used to alter an incorrectly specified contravention of statute or regulations, but must not change the nature of the offence libelled. In *MacKenzie v. Brougham*, 1984 S.C.C.R. 434; 1985 S.L.T. 276, the charge narrated the statute and regulations contravened but omitted reference to the precise regulation which created a criminal offence and was poorly specified; it was held that the complaint was not a nullity and could be cured by amendment. The broad test to be applied is whether the charge as specified affords the defence fair notice of what the Crown was seeking to prove; see *Blair v. Keane*, 1981 S.L.T. (Notes) 4; *Clydesdale Group v. Normand*, 1993 S.C.C.R. 958; 1994 S.L.T. 1302.

In *Sterling-Winthrop Group v. Allan*, 1987 S.C.C.R. 25, a prosecution under the Health and Safety at Work etc. Act 1974 (c. 37), objections to the relevancy of charges were repelled by the sheriff. Before the Appeal Court the Crown sought, and were permitted, to amend the charges to meet the objections previously stated. Even where a repealed statute has been libelled, amendment of the charge to make reference to the correct statutory provision is permissible, despite the greater penalties which can be imposed. See *Cook v. Jessop*, 1990 S.C.C.R. 211, where a charge of harbouring an escaper from an approved school was made, contrary to the Children and Young Persons (Scotland) Act 1937, a statute which had been repealed and replaced by the Social Work (Scotland) Act 1968: it will be noted however that the libel gave clear warning of the character of the offence and there could be little cause to argue prejudice or lack of specification of the *species facti* (see also *High-Clad Roofing v. Carmichael*, "The Scotsman" Law Reports February 24, 1989, where the wrong regulation under the Factories Act 1961 (c. 34) had been libelled).

Schedule 3 of the Act contains the provisions relating to latitudes in time and place and alternative verdicts which previously appeared in s.312 of the 1975 Act. Particularly, the terms of paras. 11 to 14 are of significance in relation to the libelling of statutory offences.

The Nomen Juris

It is well accepted that the charge in an indictment need not specify the *nomen juris* of the alleged crime, it being sufficient that the facts described in the libel are relevant and set forth a crime known to the law of Scotland (*Cameron v. H.M. Advocate*, 1971 S.L.T. 333 (piracy)). By the same token, since it is the *species facti* which indicate the nature of the crime complained of, and not the *nomen juris* attached, it follows that amendment of the *nomen juris* is competent (see *Dyce v. Aitchison*, 1985 S.C.C.R. 184 (contempt of court libelled)).

No case to answer

160.—(1) Immediately after the close of the evidence for the prosecution, the accused may intimate to the court his desire to make a submission that he has no case to answer both—

(a) on an offence charged in the complaint; and

(b) on any other offence of which he could be convicted under the complaint were the offence charged the only offence so charged.

(2) If, after hearing both parties, the judge is satisfied that the evidence led by the prosecution is insufficient in law to justify the accused being convicted of the offence charged in respect of which the submission has been made or of such other offence as is mentioned, in relation to that offence, in paragraph (b) of subsection (1) above, he shall acquit him of the offence charged in respect of which the submission has been made and the trial shall proceed only in respect of any other offence charged in the complaint.

(3) If, after hearing both parties, the judge is not satisfied as is mentioned in subsection (2) above, he shall reject the submission and the trial shall proceed, with the accused entitled to give evidence and call witnesses, as if such submission had not been made.

DEFINITIONS
"complaint": s.307(1).
"judge": s.307(1).
"offence": s.307(1).

GENERAL NOTE
The sufficiency in law of evidence presented by the prosecution falls to be considered at the close of the Crown case. The criteria for acceptance or rejection of a no case to answer submission were set out in *Williamson v. Wither*, 1981 S.C.C.R. 214, but the court must also assess the admissibility at that stage of evidence led in support of the prosecution case (see *Jessop v. Kerr*, 1989 S.C.C.R. 417) and make known the result of this assessment.

The court must give both parties the opportunity to make submissions before reaching a decision on sufficiency, and cannot consider the issue in the absence of a motion from the accused (*Stewart v. Lowe*, 1991 S.C.C.R. 317—a case in which the sheriff had rejected a submission without having heard from the prosecutor, and convicted the accused without first hearing from the defence agent; see also *Taylor v. Douglas*, 1984 S.L.T. 69). Where a number of submissions are advanced, the court is obliged to determine upon them all, rather than dismissing the case upon a consideration of only one. Consideration of all submissions avoids needless duplication of appeal procedures in the event of the Crown successfully appealing the court's original decision on sufficiency (*Lockhart v. Milne*, 1992 S.C.C.R. 864). In *Duffin v. Normand*, 1993 S.C.C.R. 864, the court having rejected a submission under the section, and there being no defence evidence, proceeded to convict without hearing further from the parties: the court is obliged to hear submissions at the close of evidence upon the quality of evidence, an issue which cannot be considered at the time of a s.160 submission. The conviction was quashed.

The form of questions to be posed in stated cases challenging decisions on submissions of no case to answer are discussed in the commentary to *Cassidy v. Normand*, 1994 S.C.C.R. 325, while guidance on the form of the stated case itself is given in *Keane v. Bathgate*, 1983 S.L.T. 651, since at that stage in the case the court cannot state findings-in-fact.

It will be noted that in *Tudhope v. Stewart*, 1986 S.L.T. 659; 1986 S.C.C.R. 384 it was held that use of a no case to answer submission, founding upon the inadmissibility of evidence which had earlier been led without objection, was inappropriate (see also *Skeen v. Murphy*, 1978 S.L.T. (Notes) 2 which states that, as a general rule, objections to the admissibility of evidence should be taken at the time when that evidence is tendered).

Defence to speak last

161. In any trial the accused or, where he is legally represented, his counsel or solicitor shall have the right to speak last.

GENERAL NOTE
"... There is no doubt that the panel is entitled to the last word in criminal trials ..." *Watson v. Stuart* (1878) 4 Couper 67. See also *Duffin v. Normand* discussed in the notes to s.160 above.

Verdict and conviction

Judges equally divided

162. In a summary prosecution in a court consisting of more than one judge, if the judges are equally divided in opinion as to the guilt of the accused, the accused shall be found not guilty of the charge or part thereof on which such division of opinion exists.

DEFINITIONS
"judge": s.307(1).

GENERAL NOTE
Where two judges sit and reach different verdicts, no conviction can follow (*Dorward v. Mackay* (1870) 1 Couper 392).

Conviction: miscellaneous provisions

163.—(1) Where imprisonment is authorised by the sentence of a court of summary jurisdiction, an extract of the finding and sentence in the form prescribed by Act of Adjournal shall be a sufficient warrant for the apprehension and commitment of the accused, and no such extract shall be void or liable to be set aside on account of any error or defect in point of form.

(2) In any proceedings in a court of summary jurisdiction consisting of more than one judge, the signature of one judge shall be sufficient in all warrants or other proceedings prior or subsequent to conviction, and it shall not be necessary that the judge so signing shall be one of the judges trying or dealing with the case otherwise.

DEFINITIONS
"court of summary jurisdiction": s.307(1).
"imprisonment": s.307(1).
"judge": s.307(1).

Conviction of part of charge

164. A conviction of a part or parts only of the charge or charges libelled in a complaint shall imply dismissal of the rest of the complaint.

DEFINITIONS
   "complaint": s.307(1).

"Conviction" and "sentence" not to be used for children

165. The words "conviction" and "sentence" shall not be used in relation to children dealt with summarily and any reference in any enactment, whether passed before or after the commencement of this Act, to a person convicted, a conviction or a sentence shall in the case of a child be construed as including a reference to a person found guilty of an offence, a finding of guilt or an order made upon such a finding as the case may be.

DEFINITIONS
   "child": s.307(1) and the Children (Scotland) Act 1995 s.93(2)(b).
   "enactment": s.307(1).
   "finding of guilt": s.307(8).
   "sentence": s.307(1).

Previous convictions: summary proceedings

166.—(1) This section shall apply where the accused in a summary prosecution has been previously convicted of any offence and the prosecutor has decided to lay a previous conviction before the court.

(2) A notice in the form prescribed by Act of Adjournal or as nearly as may be in such form specifying the previous conviction shall be served on the accused with the complaint where he is cited to a diet, and where he is in custody the complaint and such a notice shall be served on him before he is asked to plead.

(3) The previous conviction shall not be laid before the judge until he is satisfied that the charge is proved.

(4) If a plea of guilty is tendered or if, after a plea of not guilty, the accused is convicted the prosecutor shall lay the notice referred to in subsection (2) above before the judge, and—

   (a) in a case where the plea of guilty is tendered in writing the accused shall be deemed to admit any previous conviction set forth in the notice, unless he expressly denies it in the writing by which the plea is tendered;

   (b) in any other case the judge or the clerk of court shall ask the accused whether he admits the previous conviction,
and if such admission is made or deemed to be made it shall be entered in the record of the proceedings; and it shall not be necessary for the prosecutor to produce extracts of any previous convictions so admitted.

(5) Where the accused does not admit any previous conviction, the prosecutor unless he withdraws the conviction shall adduce evidence in proof thereof either then or at any other diet.

(6) A copy of any notice served on the accused under this section shall be entered in the record of the proceedings.

(7) Where a person is convicted of an offence, the court may have regard to any previous conviction in respect of that person in deciding on the disposal of the case.

(8) Nothing in this section shall prevent the prosecutor—

  (a) asking the accused questions tending to show that the accused has been convicted of an offence other than that with which he is charged, where he is entitled to do so under section 266 of this Act; or

  (b) leading evidence of previous convictions where it is competent to do so—

        (i) as evidence in support of a substantive charge; or

        (ii) under section 270 of this Act.

DEFINITIONS

"complaint": s.307(1).
"diet": s.307(1).
"judge": s.307(1).
"offence": s.307(1).
"previous conviction": s.307(1).
"prosecutor": s.307(1).

GENERAL NOTE

The general principles of placing previous convictions before the court are discussed in the notes to s.101 above. Unless adducing a previous conviction is necessary to prove the substantive charge, or the accused has either attacked the character of Crown witnesses or misrepresented his own character, no reference can be made to the accused's criminal record until he has been convicted.

Any previous convictions to be founded upon by the Crown for the purposes of sentence must accompany the citation and service copy complaint (see Rule 16.1.–(4) and Form 16.1–E in the 1996 Act of Adjournal) and have to be laid before the court by the prosecutor; see *Clark v. Connell*, 1952 J.C. 119; 1952 S.L.T. 421; convictions which have not been libelled cannot be considered by the court (*Adair v. Hill*, 1943 J.C. 9) except where they are referred to in a social enquiry report prepared for the purpose of sentence (*Sharp v. Stevenson*, 1948 S.L.T. (Notes) 79; *Sillars v. Copeland*, 1966 C.L.R. 686); in such circumstances the accused should be afforded the opportunity of admitting or denying such additional convictions.

It will be noted that subs. (4)(a) continues the presumption that any convictions not expressly disputed by the accused when tendering a letter plea are held to be admitted. Difficulty can arise where the plea contained in a letter is rejected by the prosecutor; care then has to be taken to ensure that any schedule of convictions is not retained with the complaint at any subsequent diet, though this has been held not to amount to laying of convictions before the court by the prosecutor (see *O'Neill v. Tudhope*, 1984 S.L.T. 424; 1984 S.C.C.R. 276).

The use of extract convictions as evidence in support of a substantive charge, for example the Road Traffic Act 1988 (c. 52) s.103 (driving while disqualified) has generated a considerable volume of case law. The cardinal rule is that so far as practicable, the extract used must disclose only the minimum necessary to prove the currency of a disqualification and nothing more (see *Mitchell v. Dean*, 1979 S.L.T. (Notes) 12; *Boustead v. McLeod*, 1979 S.L.T. (Notes) 48) but note also *Moffat v. Robertson*, 1983 S.C.C.R. 392 in which a defence appeal against conviction, founding upon the use of an extract conviction which libelled both driving without a licence and without insurance, was held *not* to be prejudicial.

The general principles applicable to the disclosure either wilfully or inadvertently by the prosecutor are discussed in the notes to s.101; see also *Kerr v. Jessop*, 1991 S.C.C.R. 27, an instance of questioning too far and thus breaching the provision and *Carmichael v. Monaghan*, 1986 S.C.C.R. 598; 1987 S.L.T. 338, where the sheriff's decision that there had been a breach by the unanticipated revelation that the accused had been apprehended in relation to a means warrant, was overruled.

Refer to s.285 in relation to proof of previous convictions by means of a certificate completed on behalf of the Chief Constable and s.286, which provides means by which the service of extract convictions upon the accused can be treated as sufficient evidence.

Forms of finding and sentence

  167.—(1) Every sentence imposed by a court of summary jurisdiction shall unless otherwise provided be pronounced in open court in the presence of the accused, but need not be written out or signed in his presence.

  (2) The finding and sentence and any order of a court of summary jurisdiction, as regards both offences at common law and offences under any enactment, shall be entered in the record of the proceedings in the form, as nearly as may be, prescribed by Act of Adjournal.

(3) The record of the proceedings shall be sufficient warrant for all execution on a finding, sentence or order and for the clerk of court to issue extracts containing such executive clauses as may be necessary for implement thereof.

(4) When imprisonment forms part of any sentence or other judgement, warrant for the apprehension and interim detention of the accused pending his being committed to prison shall, where necessary, be implied.

(5) Where a fine imposed by a court of summary jurisdiction is paid at the bar it shall not be necessary for the court to refer to the period of imprisonment applicable to the non-payment thereof.

(6) Where several charges at common law or under any enactment are embraced in one complaint, a cumulo penalty may be imposed in respect of all or any of such charges of which the accused is convicted.

(7) A court of summary jurisdiction may frame—

(a) a sentence following on conviction; or

(b) an order for committal in default of payment of any sum of money or for contempt of court,

so as to take effect on the expiry of any previous sentence or order which, at the date of the later conviction or order, the accused is undergoing.

(8) It shall be competent at any time before imprisonment has followed on a sentence for the court to alter or modify it; but no higher sentence than that originally pronounced shall be competent, and—

(a) the signature of the judge or clerk of court to any sentence shall be sufficient also to authenticate the findings on which such sentence proceeds; and

(b) the power conferred by this subsection to alter or modify a sentence may be exercised without requiring the attendance of the accused.

DEFINITIONS

"complaint": s.307(1).
"court of summary jurisdiction": s.307(1).
"enactment": s.307(1).
"fine": s.307(1).
"imprisonment": s.307(6).
"judge": s.307(1).
"offences": s.307(1).
"prison": s.307(1).
"sentence": s.307(1).

GENERAL NOTE

While sentence is normally pronounced in the accused's presence this does not apply to the circumstances covered by s.150(5) or, arguably, where the accused misconducts himself in the course of his trial (s.153(2)) provided he is legally represented. Section 144(6) of the Act provides that sentences of imprisonment or detention cannot be imposed in the absence of the accused.

Subsection (6) enacts that *cumulo* sentences can be imposed in relation to all the charges libelled on a complaint; conversely if the Crown elects to place on separate complaints, matters which could properly have been incorporated in one complaint, then consecutive sentences should not be imposed; *Kesson v. Heatly*, 1964 J.C. 40. See also *Noble v. Guild*, 1987 S.C.C.R. where a delay in imposing a sentence of imprisonment rendered it incompetent to apply imprisonment consecutive to a term which by then was already being served. However, where an accused was sentenced on indictment to 18-months' detention and had outstanding fines, the Appeal Court upheld the imposition of the alternative periods of detention in lieu of the fines, these being effective consecutive to each other, and to the 18-months' sentence (*Cartledge v. McLeod*, 1988 S.L.T. 389; 1988 S.C.C.R. 129).

The appropriateness and effect upon eligibility for licence of consecutive terms of detention were discussed in *Clayton, Petr.*, 1992 S.L.T. 404.

Section 218(2) sets out the table of fines and alternative periods of imprisonment applicable to proceedings under the Act. The minimum period of imprisonment which can be imposed summarily is five days (see s.205).

Caution

168.—(1) This section applies with regard to the finding, forfeiture, and recovery of caution in any proceedings under this Part of this Act.

(2) Caution may be found by consignation of the amount with the clerk of court, or by bond of caution signed by the cautioner.

(3) Where caution becomes liable to forfeiture, forfeiture may be granted by the court on the motion of the prosecutor, and, where necessary, warrant granted for the recovery of the caution.

(4) Where a cautioner fails to pay the amount due under his bond within six days after he has received a charge to that effect, the court may—

(a) order him to be imprisoned for the maximum period applicable in pursuance of section 219 of this Act to that amount or until payment is made; or

(b) if it considers it expedient, on the application of the cautioner grant time for payment; or

(c) instead of ordering imprisonment, order recovery by civil diligence in accordance with section 221 of this Act.

DEFINITIONS
"imprisonment": s.306(7).
"prosecutor": s.307(1).

Detention in precincts of court

169.—(1) Where a court of summary jurisdiction has power to impose imprisonment or detention on an offender it may, in lieu of so doing and subject to subsection (2) below, order that the offender be detained within the precincts of the court or at any police station, till such hour, not later than eight in the evening on the day on which he is convicted, as the court may direct.

(2) Before making an order under this section a court shall take into consideration the distance between the proposed place of detention and the offender's residence (if known to, or ascertainable by, the court), and shall not make any such order under this section as would deprive the offender of a reasonable opportunity of returning to his residence on the day on which the order is made.

DEFINITIONS
"court of summary jurisdiction": s.307(1).
"impose imprisonment or detention": s.307(1).
"imprisonment": s.307(6).

GENERAL NOTE
This is a rarely-used sentencing provision and would appear to escape the restrictions placed upon the imposition of sentences of imprisonment or detention contained in s.203(1) and (2) below. The 1996 Act of Adjournal stipulates that the order of detention under this section shall correspond to Form 18.6.

Miscellaneous

Damages in respect of summary proceedings

170.—(1) No judge, clerk of court or prosecutor in the public interest shall be found liable by any court in damages for or in respect of any proceedings taken, act done, or judgment, decree or sentence pronounced in any summary proceedings under this Act, unless—

(a) the person suing has suffered imprisonment in consequence thereof; and

(b) such proceedings, act, judgment, decree or sentence has been quashed; and

(c) the person suing specifically avers and proves that such proceeding, act, judgment, decree or sentence was taken, done or pronounced maliciously and without probable cause.

(2) No such liability as aforesaid shall be incurred or found where such judge, clerk of court or prosecutor establishes that the person suing was guilty of the offence in respect whereof he had been convicted, or on account of which he had been apprehended or had otherwise suffered, and that he had undergone no greater punishment than was assigned by law to such offence.

(3) No action to enforce such liability as aforesaid shall lie unless it is commenced within two months after the proceeding, act, judgment decree or sentence founded on, or in the case where the Act under which the action is brought fixes a shorter period, within that shorter period.

(4) In this section "judge" shall not include "sheriff", and the provisions of this section shall be without prejudice to the privileges and immunities possessed by sheriffs.

DEFINITIONS
"imprisonment": s.307(6).
"judge": ss.170(6) and 307(1).
"prosecutor": s.307(1).
"sentence": s.307(1).

GENERAL NOTE
In the conduct of proceedings on indictment the Lord Advocate, and subordinates appointed by him to prepare and conduct such proceedings, enjoy absolute privilege and thus immunity from actions for damages (see *Hester v. MacDonald*, 1961 J.C. 370; 1961 S.L.T. 414). This immunity extends to procurators fiscal in solemn proceedings but is restricted in summary proceedings by the operation of s.170: the right to seek damages from the criminal authorities in relation to any summary proceedings is available to an accused person who can satisfy all the requirements of subs. (1); see *Graham v. Strathern*, 1924 S.C. 699. Any proceedings must be commenced within two months of the conduct complained of or any shorter period specifically stated. Subsection (2) provides immunity from civil liability for court officials only while they are proceeding under the Act (*Graham v. Strathern* at 724; *Ferguson v. MacDonald* (1885) 12 Rettie 1083).

See *Bell v. McGlennan*, 1992 S.L.T. 237, where proceedings were held to have been competently raised against the prosecutor as vicariously liable over the retention of property as evidence in a case which did not proceed, due to the intervention of the statutory time bar.

Recovery of penalties

171.—(1) All penalties, for the recovery of which no special provision has been made by any enactment may be recovered by the public prosecutor in any court having jurisdiction.

(2) Where a court has power to take cognisance of an offence the penalty attached to which is not defined, the punishment therefore shall be regulated by that applicable to common law offences in that court.

DEFINITIONS
"offence": s.307(1).
"prosecutor": s.307(1).

GENERAL NOTE
Unless it is expressly stipulated to the contrary by statute, the public prosecutor holds a general title to prosecute for the recovery of penalties (subs. (1)). In the absence of any express provision, the competent punishment in summary proceedings shall be dictated by reference to the penalties applicable to common law offences (see s.219(2)).

Forms of procedure

172.—(1) The forms of procedure for the purposes of summary proceedings under this Act and appeals therefrom shall be in such forms as are prescribed by Act of Adjournal or as nearly as may be in such forms.

(2) All warrants (other than warrants of apprehension or search), orders of court, and sentences may be signed either by the judge or by the clerk of court, and execution upon any warrant, order of court, or sentence may proceed either upon such warrant, order of court, or sentence itself or upon an extract thereof issued and signed by the clerk of court.

(3) Where, preliminary to any procedure, a statement on oath is required, the statement may be given before any judge, whether the subsequent procedure is in his court or another court.

DEFINITIONS
  "judge": s.307(1).
  "sentence": s.307(1).

GENERAL NOTE
  The 1996 Act of Adjournal substantially revises the format of many forms to be utilised in criminal proceedings.
  Although subs. (2) provides that all warrants (except those for apprehension or search) may be subscribed by the judge or the clerk of court, and that extracts thereof shall be equally valid, this presupposes that the order or warrant must first have been granted by a judge (see *Skeen v. Ives Cladding*, 1976 S.L.T. (Notes) 31). Failure to complete proper minutes of proceedings and thus maintain a proper record of the proceedings is a fundamental defect (*Heywood v. Stewart* C.O. Circ. A54/91).

PART X

APPEALS FROM SUMMARY PROCEEDINGS

General

Quorum of High Court in relation to appeals

173.—(1) For the purpose of hearing and determining any appeal under this Part of this Act, or any proceeding connected therewith, three of the Lords Commissioners of Justiciary shall be a quorum of the High Court, and the determination of any question under this Part of this Act by the court shall be according to the votes of the majority of the members of the court sitting, including the presiding judge, and each judge so sitting shall be entitled to pronounce a separate opinion.

(2) For the purpose of hearing and determining appeals under section 175(2)(b) or (c) of this Act, or any proceeding connected therewith, two of the Lords Commissioners of Justiciary shall be a quorum of the High Court, and each judge shall be entitled to pronounce a separate opinion; but where the two Lords Commissioners of Justiciary are unable to reach agreement on the disposal of the appeal, or where they consider it appropriate, the appeal shall be heard and determined in accordance with subsection (1) above.

DEFINITIONS
  "High Court": s.307(1).
  "judge": s.307(1).
  "Lords Commissioners of Justiciary": s.307(1).

GENERAL NOTE
  Part X of this Act is concerned with appeals from summary proceedings. For the purpose of hearing and determining any appeal under this Part of this Act the quorum of judges is three: s.173(1). However, for the purpose of hearing and determining appeals against sentence or against absolute discharge or admonition or any probation order or any community service

order or any order deferring sentence the quorum of judges is two: s.173(2). This provision, particularly the latter, is likely to reduce the considerable burden that has been placed on appellate judges because of the enormous increase in appeals, and especially appeals against summary sentences.

Appeals relating to preliminary pleas

174.—(1) Without prejudice to any right of appeal under section 175(1) to (6) or 191 of this Act, a party may, with the leave of the court (granted either on the motion of the party or *ex proprio motu*) and in accordance with such procedure as may be prescribed by Act of Adjournal, appeal to the High Court against a decision of the court of first instance (other than a decision not to grant leave under this subsection) which relates to such objection or denial as is mentioned in section 144(4) of this Act; but such appeal must be taken not later than two days after such decision.

(2) Where an appeal is taken under subsection (1) above, the High Court may postpone the trial diet (if one has been fixed) for such period as appears to it to be appropriate and may, if it thinks fit, direct that such period (or some part of it) shall not count towards any time limit applying in respect of the case.

(3) If leave to appeal under subsection (1) above is granted by the court it shall not proceed to trial at once under subsection (2) of section 146 of this Act; and subsection (3) of that section shall be construed as requiring sufficient time to be allowed for the appeal to be taken.

(4) In disposing of an appeal under subsection (1) above the High Court may affirm the decision of the court of first instance or may remit the case to it with such directions in the matter as it thinks fit; and where the court of first instance had dismissed the complaint, or any part of it, may reverse that decision and direct that the court of first instance fix a trial diet (if it has not already fixed one as regards so much of the complaint as it has not dismissed.)

DEFINITIONS
   "diet": s.307(1).
   "High Court": s.307(1).

GENERAL NOTE
   Section 184(4) of this Act follows on the provision in s.334(2A) of the 1975 Act. These subsections require any objection to the competency, relevancy of a summary complaint or the proceedings thereon, or any denial that the accused is the person charged by the police with the offence shall be stated before the accused pleads to the charge or any plea is tendered on his behalf.
   Section 174(1) allows "a party" with leave of the court to appeal to the High Court of Justiciary against a decision of the court of first instance which relates to such objection or denial as is mentioned in s.144(4). This appeal must be taken within two days after that decision.
   Practitioners should remember that there are two hurdles in relation to appeals relating to preliminary pleas. First, appeal must be made with the leave of the court although such leave may be either on the motion of the party or *ex proprio motu*. Secondly, a note of appeal is required to be lodged with the sheriff clerk. For the procedure under the 1975 Act, see Act of Adjournal (Consolidation) 1988 rr. 34 and 35. Form 17 of Sched. 1 sets out the angle for the note of appeal.
   For examples of the substantive and procedural complexities that can arise in this regard see *Johnston v. MacGillivray*, 1993 S.L.T. 120 and *McLeay v. Hingston*, 1994 S.L.T. 720.
   Subsections (2), (3) and (4) make consequential provision for postponing the trial diet, allowing time for the appeal and setting out the powers of the High Court of Justiciary in relation to affirming the decision at first instance or remitting the case with directions.

Right of appeal

175.—(1) This section is without prejudice to any right of appeal under section 191 of this Act.

(2) Any person convicted, or found to have committed an offence, in summary proceedings may, with leave granted in accordance with section 180 or,

as the case may be, 187 of this Act, appeal under this section to the High Court—

(a) against such conviction, or finding;

(b) against the sentence passed on such conviction;

(c) against his absolute discharge or admonition or any probation order or any community service order or any order deferring sentence; or

(d) against both such conviction and such sentence or disposal or order.

(3) The prosecutor in summary proceedings may appeal under this section to the High Court on a point of law—

(a) against an acquittal in such proceedings; or

(b) against a sentence passed on conviction in such proceedings.

(4) The prosecutor in such proceedings, in any class of case specified by order made by the Secretary of State under this subsection, may appeal to the High Court against the sentence passed on such conviction or, whether the person has been convicted or not, against any probation order or any community service order or against the person's absolute discharge or admonition or against any order deferring sentence if it appears to the prosecutor that, as the case may be—

(a) the sentence is unduly lenient;

(b) the making of the probation order or community service order is unduly lenient or its terms are unduly lenient;

(c) to dismiss with an admonition or to discharge absolutely is unduly lenient; or

(d) the deferment of sentence is inappropriate or on unduly lenient conditions.

(5) By an appeal under subsection (2) above or, as the case may be, against acquittal under subsection (3) above, an appellant may bring under review of the High Court any alleged miscarriage of justice in the proceedings including, in the case of an appeal under the said subsection (2), any alleged miscarriage of justice on the basis of the existence and significance of additional evidence which was not heard at the trial and which was not available and could not reasonably have been made available at the trial.

(6) The power of the Secretary of State to make an order under subsection (4) above shall be exercisable by statutory instrument; and any order so made shall be subject to annulment in pursuance of a resolution of either House of Parliament.

(7) Where a person desires to appeal under subsection (2)(a) or (d) or (3) above, he shall pursue such appeal in accordance with sections 176 to 179, 181 to 185, 188, 190 and 192(1) and (2) of this Act.

(8) A person who has appealed against both conviction and sentence, may abandon the appeal in so far as it is against conviction and may proceed with it against sentence alone, subject to such procedure as may be prescribed by Act of Adjournal.

(9) Where a convicted person or as the case may be a person found to have committed an offence desires to appeal under subsection (2)(b) or (c) above, or the prosecutor desires so to appeal by virtue of subsection (4) above, he shall pursue such appeal in accordance with sections 186, 189(1) to (6), 190 and 192(1) and (2) of this Act; but nothing in this section shall prejudice any right to proceed by bill of suspension, or as the case may be advocation, against an alleged fundamental irregularity relating to the imposition of sentence.

(10) Where any statute provides for an appeal from summary proceedings to be taken under any public general or local enactment, such appeal shall be taken under this Part of this Act.

DEFINITIONS

    "community service order": s.238.

    "offence": s.307(1).

"probation order": s.228.
"prosecutor": s.307(1).
"sentence": s.307(1).

GENERAL NOTE
Subs. (1)
The right of appeal from summary proceedings to the High Court of Justiciary may be exercised without prejudice to an appeal by suspension or advocation on the ground of miscarriage of justice: see s.191.

Subs. (2)
Section 175 relies heavily on the terms of s.442 of the 1975 Act but with several crucial differences. The most important in law and in practice is undoubtedly the qualification that an appeal under s.175 must be "with leave granted in accordance with s.180 or, as the case may be, s.187 of this Act". Reference should be made to these two sections and the General Notes to them.
Assuming that leave has been granted, an appeal against conviction alone is possible under s.175(1)(a) and against sentence under s.175(1)(b) and against orders by way of sentence under s.175(1)(c) or against both conviction and sentence or orders under s.175(1)(d).
Appeals in terms of s.175(1)(a) and s.175(1)(d) will be heard by three judges: s.173(1). Appeals in terms of s.175(1)(b) and s.175(1)(c) will be heard by two judges: s.173(2).

Subs. (3)
This provision allows for a Crown appeal against acquittal on a point of law or against a sentence passed on conviction, again on a point of law. The second head appears to be designed to catch incompetent sentences.

Subs. (4)
This subsection equates with the Lord Advocate's appeal against sentence under s.108 of this Act, but there is a crucial distinction. A sentence passed after conviction on indictment must appear to the Lord Advocate to be unduly lenient. A sentence passed after conviction on summary complaint must appear to the prosecutor to be unduly lenient and it must be "in any class of case specified by order made by the Secretary of State". This last restriction is likely to curb the enthusiasm of prosecutors by being limited to a very narrow range of classes, if any.

Subs. (5)
The terms of this subsection are identical to those of s.442(2) of the 1975 Act and they identify the test for appeals, *viz.* "the alleged miscarriage of justice in the proceedings". This is the test for appeals under solemn procedure: see s.106(3) of this Act. Thus for all criminal appeals the essential question is this: has there been a miscarriage of justice?
As with solemn procedure, there is no definition in s.175 of what a miscarriage of justice is in law. Having regard to subs. (5) it can be said to include "any alleged miscarriage of justice on the basis of the existence and significance of additional evidence which was not heard at the trial and which was not available and could not reasonably have been made available at the trial".
Many of the considerations arising out of this section have direct parallels in the solemn procedure. There are separate authorities dealing with alleged miscarriage of justice and the partial definition: see, *e.g. Craven v. MacPhail*, 1990 S.C.C.R. 558 and *Carr v. Lees*, 1993 S.C.C.R. 316. These cases, however, frequently illustrate the section rather than elucidate it.

Stated case

Stated case: manner and time of appeal

176.—(1) An appeal under section 175(2)(a) or (d) or (3) of this Act all be by application for a stated case, which application shall—
  (a) be made within one week of the final determination of the proceedings;
  (b) contain a full statement of all the matters which the appellant desires to bring under review and, where the appeal is also against sentence or disposal or order, the ground of appeal against that sentence or disposal or order; and

(c) be signed by the appellant or his solicitor and lodged with the clerk of court,

and a copy of the application shall, within the period mentioned in paragraph (a) above, be sent by the appellant to the respondent or the respondent's solicitor.

(2) The clerk of court shall enter in the record of the proceedings the date when an application under subsection (1) above was lodged.

(3) The appellant may, at any time within the period of three weeks mentioned in subsection (1) of section 179 of this Act, or within any further period afforded him by virtue of section 181 (1) of this Act, amend any matter stated in his application or add a new matter; and he shall intimate any such amendment, or addition, to the respondent or the respondent's solicitor.

(4) Where such an application has been made by the person convicted, and the judge by whom he was convicted dies before signing the case or is precluded by illness or other cause from doing so, it shall be competent for the convicted person to present a bill of suspension to the High Court and to bring under the review of that court any matter which might have been brought under review by stated case.

(5) The record of the procedure in the inferior court in an appeal mentioned in subsection (1) above shall be as nearly as may be in the form prescribed by Act of Adjournal.

GENERAL NOTE

Subs. (1)

An application for a stated case is an application for a document that sets forth "the particulars of any matters competent for review which the appellant desires to bring under the review of the High Court, and of the facts, if any, proved in the case, and any point of law decided, and the grounds of the decision": subs. (2).

The nature and content of a stated case is emphasised because of the requirement in subs. (1)(b) that the application for a stated case contain "a full statement of all the matters which the appellant desires to bring under review". If the application does not have a comprehensive and accurate description of the point at issue the stated case will in the fullness of time reflect that.

Superficial applications can be held not to have met the requirements of the section: hence "insufficient evidence for conviction" did not lead to a stated case being issued: *Galloway v. Hillary*, 1983 S.C.C.R. 119. An allegation of insufficient evidence must proceed to highlight the part of the evidence said to be insufficient: *Durant v. Lockhart*, 1986 S.L.T. 312 and *Anderson v. McClory*, 1991 S.C.C.R. 571.

It may be that notwithstanding the brevity of an application a sheriff can state a case although not obliged to do so. The High Court of Justiciary would then proceed to hear an appeal: *Dickson v. Valentine*, 1988 S.C.C.R. 325.

A further concern arising from applications for stated cases that do not contain full statements relates to the hearing of the appeal. An application for a stated case, and in turn the stated case itself, that does not properly focus the real issue can unduly hamper those presenting the appeal. In *Walton v. Crowe*, 1993 S.C.C.R. 885 an attempt by the appellant to raise an issue which had not been mentioned in the application was refused. That restriction can also apply to the Crown: *Normand v. Walker*, 1994 S.C.C.R. 875.

The main practical problem is the failure to meet the requirements of subs. (1)(b) about a full statement. Making an application within one week of the final determination is less of a general problem: see subs. (1)(a) which must be read with s.194(3) for the meaning of "final determination".

Subs. (3)

The draft stated case that follows from a proper application may on authority be amended or added to and if that is done there must be intimation to the other side.

Subs. (4)

This authority makes it clear that an appeal cannot proceed on the basis of a draft stated case. Either there is a signed stated case to found the appeal or there is not. If there is no stated case in the terms set out in this subsection then the correct mode is a bill of suspension.

Procedure where appellant in custody

177.—(1) If an appellant making an application under section 176 of this Act is in custody, the court of first instance may—

(a) grant bail;

(b) grant a sist of execution;

(c) make any other interim order.

(2) An application for bail shall be disposed of by the court within 24 hours after such application has been made.

(3) If bail is refused or the appellant is dissatisfied with the conditions imposed, he may, within 24 hours after the judgment of the court, appeal against it by a note of appeal written on the complaint and signed by himself or his solicitor, and the complaint and proceedings shall thereupon be transmitted to the Clerk of Justiciary, and the High Court or any judge thereof, either in court or in chambers, shall, after hearing parties, have power to review the decision of the inferior court and to grant bail on such conditions as the Court or judge may think fit, or to refuse bail.

(4) No clerks' fees, court fees or other fees or expenses shall be exigible from or awarded against an appellant in custody in respect of an appeal to the High Court against the conditions imposed or on account of refusal of bail by a court of summary jurisdiction.

(5) If an appellant who has been granted bail does not thereafter proceed with his appeal, the inferior court shall have power to grant warrant to apprehend and imprison him for such period of his sentence as at the date of his bail remained unexpired and, subject to subsection (6) below, such period shall run from the date of his imprisonment under the warrant or, on the application of the appellant, such earlier date as the court thinks fit, not being a date later than the date of expiry of any term or terms of imprisonment imposed subsequently to the conviction appealed against.

(6) Where an appellant who has been granted bail does not thereafter proceed with his appeal, the court from which the appeal was taken shall have power, where at the time of the abandonment of the appeal the person is in custody or serving a term or terms of imprisonment imposed subsequently to the conviction appealed against, to order that the sentence or, as the case may be, the unexpired portion of that sentence relating to that conviction should run from such date as the court may think fit, not being a date later than the date on which any term or terms of imprisonment subsequently imposed expired.

(7) The court shall not make an order under subsection (6) above to the effect that the sentence or, as the case may be, unexpired portion of the sentence shall run other than concurrently with the subsequently imposed term of imprisonment without first notifying the appellant of its intention to do so and considering any representations made by him or on his behalf.

Definitions

"bail": s.307(1).

"Clerk of Justiciary": s.307(1).

"High Court": s.307(1).

"order": s.307(1).

General Note

This section sets out the immediate procedure if the appellant makes an application for a stated case and is in custody. If bail is sought an application would be disposed of within 24 hours of such an application or, if refused, a note of appeal may be lodged to review the decision to refuse: subss. (2) and (3).

Appeals are frequently not pursued despite the initial enthusiasm. Where the appellant is at liberty when he abandons his appeal the warrant to imprison him in accordance with his sentence shall run from the date of his imprisonment under the warrant or, on application, such earlier date as the court thinks fit, not being a date later than the date of expiry of any term of imprisonment imposed subsequently to the conviction appealed against: subs. (5).

This may be contrasted with the circumstances where the appellant is in custody when he abandons his appeal, then the unexpired portion of that sentence should run from such date as the court thinks fit, not being a date later than the date on which any term of imprisonment subsequently imposed expired: subs. (6).

Subsection (7) gives statutory effect to *Proudfoot v. Wither*, 1990 S.L.T. 742 and requires sentences under subs. (6) to be served concurrently but if the court is minded to do otherwise then the appellant must be notified and the court must consider any representations he wishes to make.

Stated case: preparation of draft

178.—(1) Within three weeks of the final determination of proceedings in respect of which an application for a stated case is made under section 176 of this Act—
   (a) where the appeal is taken from the district court and the trial was presided over by a justice of the peace or justices of the peace, the Clerk of Court; or
   (b) in any other case the judge who presided at the trial,
shall prepare a draft stated case, and the clerk of the court concerned shall forthwith issue the draft to the appellant or his solicitor and a duplicate thereof to the respondent or his solicitor.

(2) A stated case shall be, as nearly as may be, in the form prescribed by Act of Adjournal, and shall set forth the particulars of any matters competent for review which the appellant desires to bring under the review of the High Court, and of the facts, if any, proved in the case, and any point of law decided, and the grounds of the decision.

DEFINITIONS
   "judge": s.307(1).

Stated case: adjustment and signature

179.—(1) Subject to section 181(1) of this Act, within three weeks of the issue of the draft stated case under section 178 of this Act, each party shall cause to be transmitted to the court and to the other parties or their solicitors a note of any adjustments he proposes be made to the draft case or shall intimate that he has no such proposal.

(2) The adjustments mentioned in subsection (1) above shall relate to evidence heard or purported to have been heard at the trial and not to such additional evidence as is mentioned in section 175(5) of this Act.

(3) Subject to section 181(1) of this Act, if the period mentioned in subsection (1) above has expired and the appellant has not lodged adjustments and has failed to intimate that he has no adjustments to propose, he shall be deemed to have abandoned his appeal; and subsection (5) of section 177 of this Act shall apply accordingly.

(4) If adjustments are proposed under subsection (1) above or if the judge desires to make any alterations to the draft case there shall, within one week of the expiry of the period mentioned in that subsection or as the case may be of any further period afforded under section 181(1) of this Act, be a hearing (unless the appellant has, or has been deemed to have, abandoned his appeal) for the purpose of considering such adjustments or alterations.

(5) Where a party neither attends nor secures that he is represented at a hearing under subsection (4) above, the hearing shall nevertheless proceed.

(6) Where at a hearing under subsection (4) above—
   (a) any adjustment proposed under subsection (1) above by a party (and not withdrawn) is rejected by the judge; or
   (b) any alteration proposed by the judge is not accepted by all the parties,
that fact shall be recorded in the minute of the proceedings of the hearing.

(7) Within two weeks of the date of the hearing under subsection (4) above or, where there is no hearing, within two weeks of the expiry of the period

mentioned in subsection (1) above, the judge shall (unless the appellant has been deemed to have abandoned the appeal) state and sign the case and shall append to the case—

(a) any adjustment, proposed under subsection (1) above, which is rejected by him, a note of any evidence rejected by him which is alleged to support that adjustment and the reasons for his rejection of that adjustment and evidence; and

(b) a note of the evidence upon which he bases any finding of fact challenged, on the basis that it is unsupported by the evidence, by a party at the hearing under subsection (4) above.

(8) As soon as the case is signed under subsection (7) above the clerk of court—

(a) shall send the case to the appellant or his solicitor and a duplicate thereof to the respondent or his solicitor; and

(b) shall transmit the complaint, productions and any other proceedings in the cause to the Clerk of Justiciary.

(9) Subject to section 181(1) of this Act, within one week of receiving the case the appellant or his solicitor, as the case may be, shall cause it to be lodged with the Clerk of Justiciary.

(10) Subject to section 181(1) of this Act, if the appellant or his solicitor fails to comply with subsection (9) above the appellant shall be deemed to have abandoned the appeal; and subsection (5) of section 177 of this Act shall apply accordingly.

DEFINITIONS
  "Clerk of Justiciary": s.307(1).
  "judge": s.307(1).

GENERAL NOTE
  Section 179 consolidates s.448 of the 1975 Act which had been much amended. There are only two practical points which need to be emphasised. First, many appeals are deemed to be abandoned because adjustments are not lodged or because the appellant does not intimate that he has no adjournment to propose. This requirement still exists in subs. (3). Similarly, within one week of receiving the stated case itself it should be lodged with the Clerk of Justiciary: subs. (9). Failure to comply with that requirement also results in an appeal being deemed to be abandoned: subs. (10).
  Secondly, adjustments must relate to the evidence heard or purported to have been heard at trial: subs. (2). However, if any adjustments are rejected by the judge then reasons for that rejection must be given: subs. (7)(a).
  Where reasons are not given the case may be remitted for the purpose of having reasons given. That was done in *Owens v. Crowe*, 1994 S.C.C.R. 310 and on reporting the sheriff gave sound reasons.

Leave to appeal against conviction etc.

180.—(1) The decision whether to grant leave to appeal for the purposes of section 175(2)(a) or (d) of this Act shall be made by a judge of the High Court who shall—

(a) if he considers that the documents mentioned in subsection (2) below disclose arguable grounds of appeal, grant leave to appeal and make such comments in writing as he considers appropriate; and

(b) in any other case—

(i) refuse leave to appeal and give reasons in writing for the refusal; and

(ii) where the appellant is on bail and the sentence imposed on his conviction is one of imprisonment, grant a warrant to apprehend and imprison him.

(2) The documents referred to in subsection (1) above are—

(a) the stated case lodged under subsection (9) of section 179 of this Act; and

(b) the documents transmitted to the Clerk of Justiciary under subsection (8)(b) of that section.

(3) A warrant granted under subsection (1)(b)(ii) above shall not take effect until the expiry of the period of 14 days mentioned in subsection (4) below without an application to the High Court for leave to appeal having been lodged by the appellant under that subsection.

(4) Where leave to appeal is refused under subsection (1) above the appellant may, within 14 days of intimation under subsection (10) below, apply to the High Court for leave to appeal.

(5) In deciding an application under subsection (4) above the High Court shall—

(a) if, after considering the documents mentioned in subsection (2) above and the reasons for the refusal, the court is of the opinion that there are arguable grounds of appeal, grant leave to appeal and make such comments in writing as the court considers appropriate; and

(b) in any other case—

(i) refuse leave to appeal and give reasons in writing for the refusal; and

(ii) where the appellant is on bail and the sentence imposed on his conviction is one of imprisonment, grant a warrant to apprehend and imprison him.

(6) The question whether to grant leave to appeal under subsection (1) or (5) above shall be considered and determined in chambers without the parties being present.

(7) Comments in writing made under subsection (1)(a) or (5)(a) above may, without prejudice to the generality of that provision, specify the arguable grounds of appeal (whether or not they are contained in the stated case) on the basis of which leave to appeal is granted.

(8) Where the arguable grounds of appeal are specified by virtue of subsection (7) above it shall not, except by leave of the High Court on cause shown, be competent for the appellant to found any aspect of his appeal on any ground of appeal contained in the stated case but not so specified.

(9) Any application by the appellant for the leave of the High Court under subsection (8) above—

(a) shall be made not less than seven days before the date fixed for the hearing of the appeal; and

(b) shall, not less that seven days before that date, be intimated by the appellant to the Crown Agent.

(10) The Clerk of Justiciary shall forthwith intimate—

(a) a decision under subsection (1) or (5) above; and

(b) in the case of a refusal of leave to appeal, the reasons for the decision,

to the appellant or his solicitor and to the Crown Agent.

DEFINITIONS
"bail": s.307(1).
"High Court": s.307(1).
"judge": s.307(1).

GENERAL NOTE

This section mirrors so far as possible the provisions for solemn appeals which are to be found in s.107. Reference therefore might conveniently be made to the general note to that section.

Leave to appeal

The requirement to obtain a grant of appeal is likely to reduce substantially the number of summary appeals against conviction and, separately, appeals against conviction and sentence actually heard in court. For many years a considerable volume of these sorts of cases have got to a hearing more in hope than expectation of a setting aside of the conviction.

Section 175(2)(a) and (d) has provided for a right of appeal against conviction and, separately, appeal against conviction and sentence. The right of appeal is conditional on a grant of leave to appeal by a judge of the High Court of Justiciary in terms of s.180. Before the judge can decide the grant he must have documents before him and these are specified as the stated case, the complaint, the productions and any other proceedings: subs. (2). Having considered these documents the judge must decide whether they disclose arguable grounds of appeal: subs. (1)(a). The action that follows such a decision depends on which way the decision goes.

In the General Note to s.107 some thought was given to what is meant by "arguable grounds of appeal". On the principle that the greater (solemn procedure) includes the lesser (summary procedure) the considerations in relation to s.107 also apply to s.180. There are two procedural differences that may affect the meaning of "arguable grounds of appeal". First, in solemn procedure the presence of a jury means that there are aspects, *e.g.* the judge's charge to the jury, that do not apply to summary appeals: Renton and Brown (5th ed.) para. 11–38 at p. 199–200 sets out the law on the point.

Secondly, the pivotal role of the stated case in summary appeals is emphasised repeatedly in the case law, and the scrutiny applied to its terms gives rise to different issues: *e.g.* the nature of irregularity will be different: Renton and Brown (5th ed.) para. 16–28 at p. 337.

To return to the appeal, the judge of the High Court of Justiciary who must consider the documents to decide whether they disclose arguable grounds of appeal does so in chambers without the parties being present: subs. (6). If the judge considers that the documents do disclose arguable grounds of appeal he then grants leave to appeal and he makes such comments in writing as he considers appropriate: subs. (1)(a). If the judge considers that the documents do not disclose arguable grounds of appeal he then refuses leave to appeal and he gives reasons in writing for the refusal: subs. (1)(b)(i). The appellant, who is at this stage on bail and the sentence imposed on his conviction was one of imprisonment, will then be the subject of a warrant to apprehend granted by the judge and on implementation the appellant will be imprisoned: subs. (1)(b)(ii).

The warrant to apprehend and imprison under subs. (1)(b)(ii) shall not take effect until the expiry of the period of 14 days during which period the appellant may, in effect, appeal by making an application to the High Court of Justiciary: subs. (4). If no such application is to be made then the appellant's solicitor has the time available to arrange for the client to surrender to the warrant.

Application for leave to appeal

The refusal of leave to appeal by a single judge in chambers may therefore be followed by an application to the High Court of Justiciary for leave to appeal: subs. (4). This is in effect an appeal in itself. Who decides the application depends on what is at issue, namely an appeal against conviction, sentence or both.

By s.173(1) "for the purpose of hearing and determining any appeal under this Part of this Act or any proceeding connected therewith" the quorum is three judges, except that by s.173(2) for appeals against sentence alone the quorum is two judges. Accordingly, an application in terms of subs. (4) will generally be decided by three judges unless the appeal concerns sentence alone, in which event the quorum is two.

The various judges of the High Court of Justiciary who must consider the documents to decide whether they disclose arguable grounds of appeal do so in chambers without the parties being present: subs. (6). In deciding the application the judges must consider the documents that had been before the single judge in chambers and also consider the reasons for the earlier refusal but, thereafter, if the court is of the opinion that there are arguable grounds of appeal then the court should grant leave to appeal and make such comments in writing as the court considers appropriate: subs. (5)(a).

In any other case, leave to appeal will be refused with reasons in writing, and a warrant to apprehend and imprison is to be granted if appropriate: subs. (5)(b).

Hearing of appeal

Regard must be paid to the comments in writing made either by the single judge in chambers by subs. (1)(a) or by a greater number of judges in chambers by subs. (5)(a). The importance of the comments in writing lies in the possibility that they "may specify the arguable grounds of appeal (whether or not they are contained in the note of appeal) on the basis of which leave to appeal is granted": subs. (7).

It is very easy to imagine on the wording of subs. (1)(a) a single judge in chambers granting leave to appeal, not on the original ground in the note of appeal, but on the basis of comments in writing which amend, alter or distil the original grounds in the note of appeal. The new grounds of appeal, having been specified, in effect dictate the ground of appeal to be argued at the hearing: subs. (8).

The appellant who wishes to found any aspect of his appeal on any ground of appeal contained in the stated case but not so specified in the comments in writing provided under subs. (1)(a) or subs. (5)(a) may seek leave to do so: subs. (8). Application for such leave under subs. (8) must be made not less than seven days before the date fixed for the hearing of the appeal: subs. (9). It is not immediately clear from a reading of the statute as to whom an application under subs. (8) will be directed. As it is not so much an appeal as a request to broaden an approach to an appeal, it may simply be returned to those who made the comments in writing under subs. (1)(a) or subs. (5)(a).

Stated case: directions by High Court

181.—(1) Without prejudice to any other power of relief which the High Court may have, where it appears to that court on application made in accordance with subsection (2) below, that the applicant has failed to comply with any of the requirements of—
   (a) subsection (1) of section 176 of this Act; or
   (b) subsection (1) or (9) of section 179 of this Act,
the High Court may direct that such further period of time as it may think proper be afforded to the applicant to comply with any requirement of the aforesaid provisions.

(2) Any application for a direction under subsection (1) above shall be made in writing to the Clerk of Justiciary and shall state the ground for the application, and, in the case of an application for the purposes of paragraph (a) of subsection (1) above, notification of the application shall be made by the appellant or his solicitor to the clerk of the court from which the appeal is to be taken, and the clerk shall thereupon transmit the complaint, documentary productions and any other proceedings in the cause to the Clerk of Justiciary.

(3) The High Court shall dispose of any application under subsection (1) above in like manner as an application to review the decision of an inferior court on a grant of bail, but shall have power—
   (a) to dispense with a hearing; and
   (b) to make such enquiry in relation to the application as the court may think fit,
and when the High Court has disposed of the application the Clerk of Justiciary shall inform the clerk of the inferior court of the result.

DEFINITIONS
   "Clerk of Justiciary": s.307(1).
   "High Court": s.307(1).

GENERAL NOTE
   The complex arrangements for applying for a stated case and thereafter attending to adjustments and hearings will all be done within a short time frame: see s.176(1) and s.179(1) to (9). A pragmatic power is granted to the High Court of Justiciary to afford an appropriate further time to comply with these arrangements: s.181(1). An application for a grant is made in writing: subs. 181(2). A hearing is not necessary and the High Court may make enquiry: subs. (5).

Stated case: hearing of appeal

182.—(1) A stated case under this Part of this Act shall be heard by the High Court on such date as it may fix.

(2) For the avoidance of doubt, where an appellant, in his application under section 176(1) of this Act (or in a duly made amendment or addition to that application), refers to an alleged miscarriage of justice, but in stating a case under section 179(7) of this Act the inferior court is unable to take the allegation into account, the High Court may nevertheless have regard to the allegation at a hearing under subsection (1) above.

(3) Except by leave of the High Court on cause shown, it shall not be competent for an appellant to found any aspect of his appeal on a matter not

contained in his application under section 176(1) of this Act (or in a duly made amendment or addition to that application).

(4) Subsection (3) above shall not apply as respects any ground of appeal specified as an arguable ground of appeal by virtue of subsection (7) of section 180 of this Act.

(5) Without prejudice to any existing power of the High Court, that court may in hearing a stated case—

 (a) order the production of any document or other thing connected with the proceedings;

 (b) hear any additional evidence relevant to any alleged miscarriage of justice or order such evidence to be heard by a judge at the High Court or by such other person as it may appoint for that purpose;

 (c) take account of any circumstances relevant to the case which were not before the trial judge;

 (d) remit to any fit person to enquire and report in regard to any matter or circumstance affecting the appeal;

 (e) appoint a person with expert knowledge to act as assessor to the High Court in any case where it appears to the court that such expert knowledge is required for the proper determination of the case;

 (f) take account of any matter proposed in any adjustment rejected by the trial judge and of the reasons for such rejection;

 (g) take account of any evidence contained in a note of evidence such as is mentioned in section 179(7) of this Act.

(6) The High Court may at the hearing remit the stated case back to the inferior court to be amended and returned.

DEFINITIONS
 "judge": s.307(1).
 "single court": s.307(1).

GENERAL NOTE
    It remains the position (notwithstanding earlier strictures) that if in an application for a stated case a miscarriage of justice is alleged but for some reason has not been dealt with in the stated case itself, the High Court of Justiciary at a hearing of the appeal may still have regard to the earlier allegation: subs. (2). An appellant cannot himself found on a matter not contained in the application for a stated case without the leave of the court: subs. (3). However, if the appellant wishes to extend his position beyond any ground of appeal specified as an arguable ground of appeal then he may not do so: subs. (4).
    Prior to disposing of the appeal the High Court of Justiciary has a wide range of powers to assist in attaining justice: subs. (5).

Stated case: disposal of appeal

183.—(1) The High Court may, subject to subsection (3) below and to section 190(1) of this Act, dispose of a stated case by—

 (a) remitting the cause to the inferior court with its opinion and any direction thereon;

 (b) affirming the verdict of the inferior court;

 (c) setting aside the verdict of the inferior court and either quashing the conviction or, subject to subsection (2) below, substituting therefor an amended verdict of guilty; or

 (d) setting aside the verdict of the inferior court and granting authority to bring a new prosecution in accordance with section 185 of this Act.

(2) An amended verdict of guilty substituted under subsection (1)(c) above must be one which could have been returned on the complaint before the inferior court.

(3) The High Court shall, in an appeal—

(a) against both conviction and sentence, subject to section 190(1) of this Act, dispose of the appeal against sentence; or

(b) by the prosecutor, against sentence, dispose of the appeal,

by exercise of the power mentioned in section 189(1) of this Act.

(4) In setting aside, under subsection (1) above, a verdict the High Court may quash any sentence imposed on the appellant as respects the complaint, and—

(a) in a case where it substitutes an amended verdict of guilty, whether or not the sentence related to the verdict set aside; or

(b) in any other case, where the sentence did not so relate,

may pass another (but not more severe) sentence in substitution for the sentence so quashed.

(5) For the purposes of subsections (3) and (4) above, "sentence" shall be construed as including disposal or order.

(6) Where an appeal against acquittal is sustained, the High Court may—

(a) convict and, subject to subsection (7) below, sentence the respondent;

(b) remit the case to the inferior court with instructions to convict and sentence the respondent, who shall be bound to attend any diet fixed by the court for such purpose; or

(c) remit the case to the inferior court with their opinion thereon.

(7) Where the High Court sentences the respondent under subsection (6)(a) above it shall not in any case impose a sentence beyond the maximum sentence which could have been passed by the inferior court.

(8) Any reference in subsection (6) above to convicting and sentencing shall be construed as including a reference to—

(a) convicting and making some other disposal; or

(b) convicting and deferring sentence.

(9) The High Court shall have power in an appeal under this Part of this Act to award such expenses both in the High Court and in the inferior court as it may think fit.

(10) Where, following an appeal, other than an appeal under section 175(2)(b) or (3) of this Act, the appellant remains liable to imprisonment or detention under the sentence of the inferior court, or is so liable under a sentence passed in the appeal proceedings the High Court shall have the power where at the time of disposal of the appeal the appellant—

(a) was at liberty on bail, to grant warrant to apprehend and imprison or detain the appellant for a term, to run from the date of such apprehension, not longer than that part of the term or terms of imprisonment or detention specified in the sentence brought under review which remained unexpired at the date of liberation;

(b) is serving a term or terms of imprisonment or detention imposed in relation to a conviction subsequent to the conviction appealed against, to exercise the like powers in regard to him as may be exercised, in relation to an appeal which has been abandoned, by a court of summary jurisdiction in pursuance of section 177(6) of this Act.

DEFINITIONS

"High Court": s.307(1).

"sentence": s.183(5).

GENERAL NOTE

The general approach to disposing of appeals by way of stated case in s.183 is very similar to the general approach to disposing of solemn appeals in s.118. Reference may be made to the General Note to that section.

It should be emphasised that the different nature of the procedure means that the cause under this section may be remitted to the lower court with any necessary direction: subs. (1)(a). This includes an instruction to convict where an appeal against acquittal has been successful: subs. (6)(b).

Abandonment of appeal

184.—(1) An appellant in an appeal such as is mentioned in section 176(1) of this Act may at any time prior to lodging the case with the Clerk of Justiciary abandon his appeal by minute signed by himself or his solicitor, written on the complaint or lodged with the clerk of the inferior court, and intimated to the respondent or the respondent's solicitor, but such abandonment shall be without prejudice to any other competent mode of appeal, review, advocation or suspension.

(2) Subject to section 191 of this Act, on the case being lodged with the Clerk of Justiciary, the appellant shall be held to have abandoned any other mode of appeal which might otherwise have been open to him.

DEFINITIONS
"Clerk of Justiciary": s.307(1).

New prosecution

Authorisation of new prosecution

185.—(1) Subject to subsection (2) below, where authority is granted under section 183(1)(d) of this Act, a new prosecution may be brought charging the accused with the same or any similar offence arising out of the same facts; and the proceedings out of which the stated case arose shall not be a bar to such prosecution.

(2) In a new prosecution under this section the accused shall not be charged with an offence more serious than that of which he was convicted in the earlier proceedings.

(3) No sentence may be passed on conviction under the new prosecution which could not have been passed on conviction under the earlier proceedings.

(4) A new prosecution may be brought under this section, notwithstanding that any time limit (other than the time limit mentioned in subsection (5) below) for the commencement of such proceedings has elapsed.

(5) Proceedings in a prosecution under this section shall be commenced within two months of the date on which authority to bring the prosecution was granted.

(6) In proceedings in a new prosecution under this section it shall, subject to subsection (7) below, be competent for either party to lead any evidence which it was competent for him to lead in the earlier proceedings.

(7) The complaint in a new prosecution under this section shall identify any matters as respects which the prosecutor intends to lead evidence by virtue of subsection (6) above which would not have been competent but for that subsection.

(8) For the purposes of subsection (5) above, proceedings shall be deemed to be commenced—

(a) in a case where such warrant is executed without unreasonable delay, on the date on which a warrant to apprehend or to cite the accused is granted; and

(b) in any other case, on the date on which the warrant is executed.

(9) Where the two months mentioned in subsection (5) above elapse and no new prosecution has been brought under this section, the order under section 183(1)(d) of this Act setting aside the verdict shall have the effect, for all purposes, of an acquittal.

(10) On granting authority under section 183(1)(d) of this Act to bring a new prosecution, the High Court may, after giving the parties an opportunity of being heard, order the detention of the accused person in custody; but an accused person may not be detained by virtue of this subsection for a period of more than 40 days.

Appeals against sentence

Appeals against sentence only

186.—(1) An appeal under section 175(2)(b) or (c), or by virtue of section 175(4), of this Act shall be by note of appeal, which shall state the ground of appeal.

(2) The note of appeal shall, where the appeal is—

(a) under section 175(2)(b) or (c) be lodged, within one week of—

    (i) the passing of the sentence; or

    (ii) the making of the order disposing of the case or deferring sentence,

with the clerk of the court from which the appeal is to be taken; or

(b) by virtue of section 175(4) be so lodged within four weeks of such passing or making.

(3) The clerk of court on receipt of the note of appeal shall—

(a) send a copy of the note to the respondent or his solicitor; and

(b) obtain a report from the judge who sentenced the convicted person or, as the case may be, who disposed of the case or deferred sentence.

(4) Subject to subsection (5) below, the clerk of court shall within two weeks of the passing of the sentence or within two weeks of the disposal or order against which the appeal is taken—

(a) send to the Clerk of Justiciary the note of appeal, together with the report mentioned in subsection (3)(b) above, a certified copy of the complaint, the minute of proceedings and any other relevant documents; and

(b) send copies of that report to the appellant and respondent or their solicitors.

(5) Where a judge—

(a) is temporarily absent from duty for any cause;

(b) is a temporary sheriff; or

(c) is a justice of the peace,

the sheriff principal of the sheriffdom in which the judgment was pronounced may extend the period of two weeks specified in subsection (4) above for such period as he considers reasonable.

(6) Subject to subsection (4) above, the report mentioned in subsection (3)(b) above shall be available only to the High Court, the parties and, on such conditions as may be prescribed by Act of Adjournal, such other persons or classes of persons as may be so prescribed.

(7) Where the judge's report is not furnished within the period mentioned in subsection (4) above or such period as extended under subsection (5) above, the High Court may extend such period, or, if it thinks fit, hear and determine the appeal without the report.

(8) Section 181 of this Act shall apply where an appellant fails to comply with the requirement of subsection (2)(a) above as they apply where an applicant fails to comply with any of the requirements of section 176(1) of this Act.

(9) An appellant under section 175(2)(b) or (c), or by virtue of section 175(4), of this Act may at any time prior to the hearing of the appeal abandon his appeal by minute, signed by himself or his solicitor, lodged—

(a) in a case where the note of appeal has not yet been sent under subsection (4)(a) above to the Clerk of Justiciary, with the clerk of court;

(b) in any other case, with the Clerk of Justiciary,

and intimated to the respondent.

(10) Sections 176(5), 177 and 182(5)(a) to (e) of this Act shall apply to appeals under section 175(2)(b) or (c), or by virtue of section 175(4), of this Act as they apply to appeals under section 175(2)(a) or (d) of this Act, except

that, for the purposes of such application to any appeal by virtue of section 175(4), references in subsections (1) to (4) of section 177 to the appellant shall be construed as references to the convicted person and subsections (6) and (7) of that section shall be disregarded.

DEFINITIONS
"High Court": s.307(1).
"judge": s.307(1).
"sentence": s.307(1).

GENERAL NOTE
A brief glance at the vast number of criminal cases reported in Green's Weekly Digest will reveal that in all probability the single biggest category of cases is appeals against summary sentences. Whether this remains the position is open to doubt with the new procedure.

A note of appeal stating the ground of appeal commences the action: subs. (1). Merely to complain of an excessive sentence will not suffice and the High Court of Justiciary is very likely to support sheriffs who complain of minimal specification: *Campbell v. MacDougall*, 1991 S.C.C.R. 218.

Leave to appeal against sentence

187.—(1) The decision whether to grant leave to appeal for the purposes of section 175(2)(b) or (c) of this Act shall be made by a judge of the High Court who shall—

(a) if he considers that the note of appeal and other documents sent to the Clerk of Justiciary under section 186(4)(a) of this Act disclose arguable grounds of appeal, grant leave to appeal and make such comments in writing as he considers appropriate; and

(b) in any other case—
   (i) refuse leave to appeal and give reasons in writing for the refusal; and
   (ii) where the appellant is on bail and the sentence imposed on his conviction is one of imprisonment, grant a warrant to apprehend and imprison him.

(2) A warrant granted under subsection (1)(b)(ii) above shall not take effect until the expiry of the period of 14 days mentioned in subsection (3) below without an application to the High Court for leave to appeal having been lodged by the appellant under that subsection.

(3) Where leave to appeal is refused under subsection (1) above the appellant may, within 14 days of intimation under subsection (9) below, apply to the High Court for leave to appeal.

(4) In deciding an application under subsection (3) above the High Court shall—

(a) if, after considering the note of appeal and other documents mentioned in subsection (1) above and the reasons for the refusal, it is of the opinion that there are arguable grounds of appeal, grant leave to appeal and make such comments in writing as he considers appropriate; and

(b) in any other case—
   (i) refuse leave to appeal and give reasons in writing for the refusal; and
   (ii) where the appellant is on bail and the sentence imposed on his conviction is one of imprisonment, grant a warrant to apprehend and imprison him.

(5) The question whether to grant leave to appeal under subsection (1) or (4) above shall be considered and determined in chambers without the parties being present.

(6) Comments in writing made under subsection (1)(a) or (4)(a) above may, without prejudice to the generality of that provision, specify the argu-

able grounds of appeal (whether or not they are contained in the note of appeal) on the basis of which leave to appeal is granted.

(7) Where the arguable grounds of appeal are specified by virtue of subsection (6) above it shall not, except by leave of the High Court on cause shown, be competent for the appellant to found any aspect of his appeal on any ground of appeal contained in the note of appeal but not so specified.

(8) Any application by the appellant for the leave of the High Court under subsection (7) above—

(a) shall be made not less than seven days before the date fixed for the hearing of the appeal; and

(b) shall, not less that seven days before that date, be intimated by the appellant to the Crown Agent.

(9) The Clerk of Justiciary shall forthwith intimate—

(a) a decision under subsection (1) or (4) above; and

(b) in the case of a refusal of leave to appeal, the reasons for the decision, to the appellant or his solicitor and to the Crown Agent.

DEFINITIONS
"bail": s.307(1).
"High Court": s.307(1).
"judge": s.307(1).
"sentence": s.307(1).

GENERAL NOTE
The procedure to be followed in regard to appeals against summary sentences necessarily requires leave to appeal. The note of appeal containing the ground of appeal is placed before a single judge in chambers along with, principally, the trial judge's report: subs. (1)(a). There is consideration and determination without the parties being present: subs. (5). As there is no longer the opportunity to explain or expand upon the grounds of appeal by advocacy the written note of appeal assumes far greater significance: such a note no longer merely initiates an appeal, it is now the substance of the leave to appeal. When leave to appeal is refused further application can be made: subs. (3) which follows identical procedure under, *e.g.* s.180(3).

Disposal of appeals

Setting aside conviction or sentence: prosecutor's consent or application

188.—(1) Without prejudice to section 175(3) or (4) of this Act, where—

(a) an appeal has been taken under section 175(2) of this Act or by suspension or otherwise and the prosecutor is not prepared to maintain the judgment appealed against he may, by a relevant minute, consent to the conviction or sentence or, as the case may be, conviction and sentence ("sentence" being construed in this section as including disposal or order) being set aside either in whole or in part; or

(b) no such appeal has been taken but the prosecutor is, at any time, not prepared to maintain the judgment on which a conviction is founded or the sentence imposed following such conviction he may, by a relevant minute, apply for the conviction or sentence or, as the case may be, conviction and sentence to be set aside.

(2) For the purposes of subsection (1) above, a "relevant minute" is a minute, signed by the prosecutor—

(a) setting forth the grounds on which he is of the opinion that the judgment cannot be maintained; and

(b) written on the complaint or lodged with the clerk of court.

(3) A copy of any minute under subsection (1) above shall be sent by the prosecutor to the convicted person or his solicitor and the clerk of court shall—

(a) thereupon ascertain and note on the record, whether that person or solicitor desires to be heard by the High Court before the appeal, or as the case may be application, is disposed of; and

(b) thereafter transmit the complaint and relative proceedings to the Clerk of Justiciary.

(4) The Clerk of Justiciary, on receipt of a complaint and relative proceedings transmitted under subsection (3) above, shall lay them before any judge of the High Court either in court or in chambers who, after hearing parties if they desire to be heard, may—

(a) set aside the conviction or the sentence, or both, either in whole or in part and—

(i) award such expenses to the convicted person, both in the High Court and in the inferior court, as the judge may think fit;

(ii) where the conviction is set aside in part, pass another (but not more severe) sentence in substitution for the sentence imposed in respect of that conviction; and

(iii) where the sentence is set aside, pass another (but not more severe) sentence; or

(b) refuse to set aside the conviction or sentence or, as the case may be, conviction and sentence, in which case the complaint and proceedings shall be returned to the clerk of the inferior court.

(5) Where an appeal has been taken and the complaint and proceedings in respect of that appeal returned under subsection (4)(b) above, the appellant shall be entitled to proceed with the appeal as if it had been marked on the date of their being received by the clerk of the inferior court on such return.

(6) Where an appeal has been taken and a copy minute in respect of that appeal sent under subsection (3) above, the preparation of the draft stated case shall be delayed pending the decision of the High Court.

(7) The period from an application being made under subsection (1)(b) above until its disposal under subsection (4) above (including the day of application and the day of disposal) shall, in relation to the conviction to which the application relates, be disregarded in any computation of time specified in any provision of this Part of this Act.

DEFINITIONS
"complaint": s.307(1).
"High Court": s.307(1).
"prosecutor": s.307(1).
"relevant minute": s.188(2).
"sentence": s.188(1)(a).

GENERAL NOTE
A set of procedural or other circumstances may have arisen resulting in a clear and unequivocal miscarriage of justice having occurred so that the Crown would not wish to maintain a judgment. This section provides for a conviction being set aside with the prosecutor's consent or on the prosecutor's application depending on the circumstances.

Disposal of appeal against sentence

189.—(1) An appeal against sentence by note of appeal shall be heard by the High Court on such date as it may fix, and the High Court may, subject to section 190(1) of this Act, dispose of such appeal by—

(a) affirming the sentence; or

(b) if the Court thinks that, having regard to all the circumstances, including any additional evidence such as is mentioned in section 175(5) of this Act, a different sentence should have been passed, quashing the sentence and, subject to subsection (2) below, passing another sentence, whether more or less severe, in substitution therefor.

(2) In passing another sentence under subsection (1)(b) above, the Court shall not in any case increase the sentence beyond the maximum sentence which could have been passed by the inferior court.

(3) The High Court shall have power in an appeal by note of appeal to award such expenses both in the High Court and in the inferior court as it may think fit.

(4) Where, following an appeal under section 175(2)(b) or (c), or by virtue of section 175(4), of this Act, the convicted person remains liable to imprisonment or detention under the sentence of the inferior court or is so liable under a sentence passed in the appeal proceedings, the High Court shall have power where at the time of disposal of the appeal the convicted person—

(a) was at liberty on bail, to grant warrant to apprehend and imprison or detain the appellant for a term, to run from the date of such apprehension, not longer than that part of the term or terms of imprisonment or detention specified in the sentence brought under review which remained unexpired at the date of liberation; or

(b) is serving a term or terms of imprisonment or detention imposed in relation to a conviction subsequent to the conviction in respect of which the sentence appealed against was imposed, to exercise the like powers in regard to him as may be exercised, in relation to an appeal which has been abandoned, by a court of summary jurisdiction in pursuance of section 177(6) of this Act.

(5) In subsection (1) above, "appeal against sentence" shall, without prejudice to the generality of the expression, be construed as including an appeal under section 175(2)(c), and any appeal by virtue of section 175(4), of this Act; and without prejudice to subsection (6) below, other references to sentence in that subsection and in subsection (4) above shall be construed accordingly.

(6) In disposing of any appeal in a case where the accused has not been convicted, the High Court may proceed to convict him; and where it does, the reference in subsection (4) above to the conviction in respect of which the sentence appealed against was imposed shall be construed as a reference to the disposal or order appealed against.

(7) In disposing of an appeal under section 175(2)(b) to (d), (3)(b) or (4) of this Act the High Court may, without prejudice to any other power in that regard, pronounce an opinion on the sentence or other disposal or order which is appropriate in any similar case.

DEFINITIONS
"appeal against sentence": s.189(5).
"High Court": s.307(1).
"sentence": s.307(1).

GENERAL NOTE
Subs. (1)
The sole test for appeals is whether there has been a miscarriage of justice and the question in relation to sentence is whether the sentence complained of is excessive: *Addison v. Mackinnon,* 1983 S.C.C.R. 52; *Donaldson v. H.M. Advocate,* 1983 S.C.C.R. 216. The High Court of Justiciary may affirm the sentence or quash it and impose another of greater or lesser severity. The latter option is not often used to increase a summary sentence although it has been done: *Briggs v. Guild,* 1987 S.C.C.R. 141.

Disposal of appeal where appellant insane

190.—(1) In relation to any appeal under section 175(2) of this Act, the High Court shall, where it appears to it that the appellant committed the act charged against him but that he was insane when he did so, dispose of the appeal by—

(a) setting aside the verdict of the inferior court and substituting therefor a verdict of acquittal on the ground of insanity; and

(b) quashing any sentence imposed on the appellant as respects the complaint and—
  (i) making, in respect of the appellant, any order mentioned in section 57(2)(a) to (d) of this Act; or
  (ii) making no order.

(2) Subsection (4) of section 57 of this Act shall apply to an order made under subsection (1)(b)(i) above as it applies to an order made under subsection (2) of that section.

Miscellaneous

Appeal by suspension or advocation on ground of miscarriage of justice

191.—(1) Notwithstanding section 184(2) of this Act, a party to a summary prosecution may, where an appeal under section 175 of this Act would be incompetent or would in the circumstances be inappropriate, appeal to the High Court, by bill of suspension against a conviction or, as the case may be, by advocation against an acquittal on the ground of an alleged miscarriage of justice in the proceedings.

(2) Where the alleged miscarriage of justice is referred to in an application under section 176(1) of this Act, for a stated case as regards the proceedings (or in a duly made amendment or addition to that application), an appeal under subsection (1) above shall not proceed without the leave of the High Court until the appeal to which the application relates has been finally disposed of or abandoned.

(3) Sections 182(5)(a) to (e), 183(1)(d) and (4) and 185 of this Act shall apply to appeals under this section as they apply to appeals such as are mentioned in section 176(1) of this Act.

(4) This section is without prejudice to any rule of law relating to bills of suspension or advocation in so far as such rule of law is not inconsistent with this section.

Appeals: miscellaneous provisions

192.—(1) Where an appellant has been granted bail, whether his appeal is under this Part of this Act or otherwise, he shall appear personally in court at the diet appointed for the hearing of the appeal.

(2) Where an appellant who has been granted bail does not appear at such a diet, the High Court shall either—
  (a) dispose of the appeal as if it had been abandoned (in which case subsection (5) of section 177 of this Act shall apply accordingly); or
  (b) on cause shown permit the appeal to be heard in his absence.

(3) No conviction, sentence, judgement, order of court or other proceeding whatsoever in or for the purposes of summary proceedings under this Act—
  (a) shall be quashed for want of form; or
  (b) where the accused had legal assistance in his defence, shall be suspended or set aside in respect of any objections to—
    (i) the relevancy of the complaint, or to the want of specification therein; or
    (ii) the competency or admission or rejection of evidence at the trial in the inferior court,
  unless such objections were timeously stated.

(4) The provisions regulating appeals shall, subject to the provisions of this Part of this Act, be without prejudice to any other mode of appeal competent.

(5) Any officer of law may serve any bill of suspension or other writ relating to an appeal.

GENERAL NOTE
    First, highly pedantic points cannot be taken on procedural or other matters as no conviction, sentence, judgment, order of court or other proceedings in or for the purposes of summary proceedings can be quashed for want of form: subs. (3)(a).
    Secondly, the failure to object timeously to the relevancy of the complaint or to the want of specification or to the competency or admission or rejection of evidence prevents later suspension of a conviction or sentence if the accused had legal assistance: subs. (3)(b).
    These two matters (now applicable to solemn and also summary procedure) serve to emphasise the need to conduct a trial thoroughly at first instance.

Suspension of disqualification, forfeiture etc.

193.—(1) Where upon conviction of any person—
  (a) any disqualification, forfeiture or disability attaches to him by reason of such conviction; or
  (b) any property, matters or things which are the subject of the prosecution or connected therewith are to be or may be ordered to be destroyed or forfeited,
if the court before which he was convicted thinks fit, the disqualification, forfeiture or disability or, as the case may be, destruction or forfeiture or order for destruction or forfeiture shall be suspended pending the determination of any appeal against conviction or sentence (or disposal or order).
    (2) Subsection (1) above does not apply in respect of any disqualification, forfeiture or, as the case may be, destruction or forfeiture or order for destruction or forfeiture under or by virtue of any enactment which contains express provision for the suspension of such disqualification, forfeiture or, as the case may be, destruction or forfeiture or order for destruction or forfeiture pending the determination of any appeal against conviction or sentence (or disposal or order).
    (3) Where, upon conviction, a fine has been imposed upon a person or a compensation order has been made against him under section 249 of this Act—
  (a) the fine or compensation order shall not be enforced against him and he shall not be liable to make any payment in respect of the fine or compensation order; and
  (b) any money paid under the compensation order shall not be paid by the clerk of court to the entitled person under subsection (9) of that section,
pending the determination of any appeal against conviction or sentence (or disposal or order).

Computation of time

194.—(1) If any period of time specified in any provision of this Part of this Act relating to appeals expires on a Saturday, Sunday or court holiday prescribed for the relevant court, the period shall be extended to expire on the next day which is not a Saturday, Sunday or such court holiday.
    (2) Where a judge against whose judgment an appeal is taken—
  (a) is temporarily absent from duty for any cause;
  (b) is a temporary sheriff; or
  (c) is a justice of the peace,

the sheriff principal of the sheriffdom in which the court at which the judgment was pronounced is situated may extend any period specified in sections 178(1) and 179(4) and (7) of this Act for such period as he considers reasonable.

(3) For the purposes of sections 176(1)(a) and 178(1) of this Act, summary proceedings shall be deemed to be finally determined on the day on which sentence is passed in open court; except that, where in relation to an appeal—

(a) under section 175(2)(a) or (3)(a); or

(b) in so far as it is against conviction, under section 175(2)(d),

of this Act sentence is deferred under section 202 of this Act, they shall be deemed finally determined on the day on which sentence is first so deferred in open court.

PART XI

SENTENCING

General

Remit to High Court for sentence

195.—(1) Where at any diet in proceedings on indictment in the sheriff court, sentence falls to be imposed but the sheriff holds that any competent sentence which he can impose is inadequate so that the question of sentence is appropriate for the High Court, he shall—

(a) endorse upon the record copy of the indictment a certificate of the plea or the verdict, as the case may be;

(b) by interlocutor written on the record copy remit the convicted person to the High Court for sentence; and

(c) append to the interlocutor a note of his reasons for the remit,

and a remit under this section shall be sufficient warrant to bring the accused before the High Court for sentence and shall remain in force until the person is sentenced.

(2) Where under any enactment an offence is punishable on conviction on indictment by imprisonment for a term exceeding three years but the enactment either expressly or impliedly restricts the power of the sheriff to impose a sentence of imprisonment for a term exceeding three years, it shall be competent for the sheriff to remit the accused to the High Court for sentence under subsection (1) above; and it shall be competent for the High Court to pass any sentence which it could have passed if the person had been convicted before it.

(3) When the Clerk of Justiciary receives the record copy of the indictment he shall send a copy of the note of reasons to the convicted person or his solicitor and to the Crown Agent.

(4) Subject to subsection (3) above, the note of reasons shall be available only to the High Court and the parties.

DEFINITIONS
"Clerk of Justiciary": s.307(1).
"diet": s.307(1).
"enactment": s.307(1).
"High Court": s.307(1).
"indictment": s.307(1).
"sentence": s.307(1).

GENERAL NOTE
Subs. (1)
This subsection reproduces the terms of s.104(1) of the 1975 Act in requiring a remit where "the sheriff holds that any competent sentence which he can impose is inadequate so that the

question of sentence is appropriate for the High Court". This contrasts with the original position in s.31 of the Criminal Procedure (Scotland) Act 1887 (c.35) which required a remit if the sheriff held that if the case was "of so grave a nature" that the question of punishment should be disposed of by the High Court of Justiciary. Care must be taken that the plea and remit are properly authenticated: *Advocate, H.M. v. Galloway*, (1894) 1 Adam 375 and *Advocate, H.M. v. McDonald*, (1896) 3 S.L.T. 317. The sheriff who remits the accused merely means the sheriff who has the duty to sentence: *Borland v. H.M. Advocate*, 1976 S.L.T. (Notes) 12.

Subs. (2)

This subsection reproduces the terms of s.104(1A) of the 1975 Act as amended. The maximum competent sentence must be considered by the sheriff before remit, and where there are two or more indictments, each indictment must be considered separately. Where the maximum sentence which could be imposed on an indictment was within the competence of the sheriff then he must deal with that indictment: *Advocate, H.M. v. Anderson*, 1946 J.C. 81. Each of several indictments must be considered separately: *Advocate, H.M. v. Stern*, 1974 S.L.T. 2.

Sentence following guilty plea

196. In determining what sentence to pass on, or what other disposal or order to make in relation to, an offender who has pled guilty to an offence, a court may take into account—

(a) the stage in the proceedings for the offence at which the offender indicated his intention to plead guilty, and

(b) the circumstances in which that indication was given.

DEFINITIONS

"sentence": s.307(1).

GENERAL NOTE

This section emphasises the need for subtlety at the sentencing stage of criminal procedure. It is certain that, notwithstanding a long criminal record, any accused is entitled to go to trial and that is not to be held against the accused at the sentencing stage: *Young v. H.M. Advocate*, 1995 S.C.C.R. 418.

However, it has been said that it is generally irrelevant for sentencing purposes whether an accused pleads guilty or not guilty: D. Kelly *Criminal Sentences* (1993) at p.6. In particular, it has been held that to operate a policy of discounting on sentences for guilty pleas would fetter judicial discretion to consider each case on its own merits: *Strawhorn v. Mcleod*, 1987 S.C.C.R. 413. That view can be contrasted directly with the English practice of giving a percentage reduction: *R. v. Williams* [1983] Crim.L.R. 693.

The reality of court business is that a guilty plea does amount to a saving of court and judicial time and may well result in a substantial saving of public funds. It is doubtful whether one can infer full remorse merely from a guilty plea but the results of such a plea very properly can be acknowledged and this section permits a court to take such a plea into account in determining a sentence. The court may do so in either or both of two sets of circumstances.

Subs. (a)

The court may take into account the stage in the proceedings for the offence at which the offender indicated his intention to plead guilty. There are various stages from arrest to a letter of intention to plead guilty to an instruction to a solicitor at which the intention may be stated: see *Backdating Sentences and Imprisonment* (1995) 40 J.L.S. 383 and especially at p. 384 for a discussion of these stages and various authorities.

Subs. (b)

The court may take into account the circumstances in which the indication was given. Context is important because a guilty plea may save children from giving evidence: *Khaliq v. H.M. Advocate*, 1984 S.C.C.R. 483. Similar considerations must apply to other vulnerable witnesses but there can be little thought for an accused who puts such witnesses to the test and then pleads guilty at the end of the Crown case without having diminished the Crown case in any way.

Sentencing guidelines

197. Without prejudice to any rule of law, a court in passing sentence shall have regard to any relevant opinion pronounced under section 118(7) or section 189(7) of this Act.

Sections 254 and 455 of the 1975 Act (and now ss.118 and 189 of this Act) provided powers for the disposal of appeals by the High Court of Justiciary. These powers were concerned only with the individual appeal then before the court. On one view, for the court to give an exposition of sentencing policy in generality for similar cases would be *ultra vires*. However, by ss.118(7) and 189(7) of this Act the High Court of Justiciary may pronounce an opinion in relation to similar cases. By s.197, in sentencing a court must have regard to any such opinion.

Form of sentence

198.—(1) In any case the sentence to be pronounced shall be announced by the judge in open court and shall be entered in the record in the form prescribed by Act of Adjournal.

(2) In recording a sentence of imprisonment, it shall be sufficient to minute the term of imprisonment to which the court sentenced the accused, without specifying the prison in which the sentence is to be carried out; and an entry of sentence, signed by the clerk of court, shall be full warrant and authority for any subsequent execution of the sentence and for the clerk to issue extracts for the purposes of execution or otherwise.

(3) In extracting a sentence of imprisonment, the extract may be in the form set out in an Act of Adjournal or as nearly as may be in such form.

DEFINITIONS
"sentence": s.307(1).

Power to mitigate penalties

199.—(1) Subject to subsection (3) below, where a person is convicted of the contravention of an enactment and the penalty which may be imposed involves—

(a) imprisonment;

(b) the imposition of a fine;

(c) the finding of caution for good behaviour or otherwise whether or not imposed in addition to imprisonment or a fine,

subsection (2) below shall apply.

(2) Where this subsection applies, the court, in addition to any other power conferred by statute, shall have power—

(a) to reduce the period of imprisonment;

(b) to substitute for imprisonment a fine (either with or without the finding of caution for good behaviour);

(c) to substitute for imprisonment or a fine the finding of caution;

(d) to reduce the amount of the fine;

(e) to dispense with the finding of caution.

(3) Subsection (2) above shall not apply—

(a) in relation to an enactment which carries into effect a treaty, convention, or agreement with a foreign state which stipulates for a fine of a minimum amount; or

(b) to proceedings taken under any Act relating to any of Her Majesty's regular or auxiliary forces.

(4) Where, in summary proceedings, a fine is imposed in substitution for imprisonment, the fine—

(a) in the case of an offence which is triable either summarily or on indictment, shall not exceed the prescribed sum; and

(b) in the case of an offence triable only summarily, shall not exceed level 4 on the standard scale.

(5) Where the finding of caution is imposed under this section—

(a) in respect of an offence which is triable only summarily, the amount shall not exceed level 4 on the standard scale and the period shall not exceed that which the court may impose under this Act; and

(b) in any other case, the amount shall not exceed the prescribed sum and the period shall not exceed 12 months.

DEFINITIONS
"fine": s.307(1).
"indictment": s.307(1).
"level 4": s.225(2). [*i.e.* £2,500].
"prescribed sum": s.225(8).
"standard scale": s.225(1).

Pre-sentencing procedure

Remand for inquiry into physical or mental condition

200.—(1) Without prejudice to any powers exercisable by a court under section 201 of this Act, where—
(a) the court finds that an accused has committed an offence punishable with imprisonment; and
(b) it appears to the court that before the method of dealing with him is determined an inquiry ought to be made into his physical or mental condition,
subsection (2) below shall apply.
(2) Where this subsection applies the court shall—
(a) for the purpose of inquiry solely into his physical condition, remand him in custody or on bail;
(b) for the purpose of inquiry into his mental condition (whether or not in addition to his physical condition), remand him in custody or on bail or, where the court is satisfied—
(i) on the written or oral evidence of a medical practitioner, that the person appears to be suffering from a mental disorder; and
(ii) that a hospital is available for his admission and suitable for his detention,
make an order committing him to that hospital,
for such period or periods, no single period exceeding three weeks, as the court thinks necessary to enable a medical examination and report to be made.
(3) where the court is of the opinion that a person ought to continue to be committed to hospital for the purpose of inquiry into his mental condition following the expiry of the period specified in an order for committal to hospital under paragraph (b) of subsection (2) above, the court may—
(a) if the condition in sub-paragraph (i) of that paragraph continues to be satisfied and a suitable hospital is available for his continued detention, renew the order for such further period not exceeding three weeks as the court thinks necessary to enable a medical examination and report to be made; and
(b) in any other case, remand the person in custody or on bail in accordance with subsection (2) above.
(4) An order under subsection (3)(a) above may, unless objection is made by or on behalf of the person to whom it relates, be made in his absence.
(5) Where, before the expiry of the period specified in an order for committal to hospital under subsection (2)(b) above, the court considers, on an application made to it, that committal to hospital is no longer required in relation to the person, the court shall revoke the order and may make such other order, under subsection (2)(a) above or any other provision of this Part of this Act, as the court considers appropriate.
(6) Where an accused is remanded on bail under this section, it shall be a condition of the order granting bail that he shall—

(a) undergo a medical examination by a duly qualified registered medical practitioner or, where the inquiry is into his mental condition, and the order granting bail so specifies, two such practitioners; and

(b) for the purpose of such examination, attend at an institution or place, or on any such practitioner specified in the order granting bail and, where the inquiry is into his mental condition, comply with any directions which may be given to him for the said purpose by any person so specified or by a person of any class so specified,

and, if arrangements have been made for his reception, it may be a condition of the order granting bail that the person shall, for the purpose of the examination, reside in an institution or place specified as aforesaid, not being an institution or place to which he could have been remanded in custody, until the expiry of such period as may be so specified or until he is discharged therefrom, whichever first occurs.

(7) On exercising the powers conferred by this section to remand in custody or on bail the court shall—

(a) where the person is remanded in custody, send to the institution or place in which he is detained; and

(b) where the person is released on bail, send to the institution or place at which or the person by whom he is to be examined,

a statement of the reasons for which it appears to the court that an inquiry ought to be made into his physical or mental condition, and of any information before the court about his physical or mental condition.

(8) On making an order of committal to hospital under subsection (2)(b) above the court shall send to the hospital specified in the order a statement of the reasons for which the court is of the opinion that an inquiry ought to be made into the mental condition of the person to whom it relates, and of any information before the court about his mental condition.

(9) A person remanded under this section may appeal against the refusal of bail or against the conditions imposed and a person committed to hospital under this section may appeal against the order of committal within 24 hours of his remand or, as the case may be, committal, by note of appeal presented to the High Court, and the High Court, either in court or in chambers, may after hearing parties—

(a) review the order and grant bail on such conditions as it thinks fit; or

(b) confirm the order; or

(c) in the case of an appeal against an order of committal to hospital, revoke the order and remand the person in custody.

(10) The court may, on cause shown, vary an order for committal to hospital under subsection (2)(b) above by substituting another hospital for the hospital specified in the order.

(11) Subsection (2)(b) above shall apply to the variation of an order under subsection (10) above as it applies to the making of an order for committal to hospital.

DEFINITIONS
  "bail": s.307(1).
  "hospital": s.307(1).
  "registered medical practitioner": s.2 of the Medical Act 1983 (c.54).

Power of court to adjourn case before sentence

201.—Where an accused has been convicted or the court has found that he committed the offence and before he has been sentenced or otherwise dealt with, subject to subsection (3) below, the court may adjourn the case for the purpose of enabling inquiries to be made or of determining the most suitable method of dealing with his case.

(2) Where the court adjourns a case solely for the purpose mentioned in subsection (1) above, it shall remand the accused in custody or on bail or ordain him to appear at the adjourned diet.

(3) A court shall not adjourn the hearing of a case as mentioned in subsection (1) above for any single period exceeding—
(a) where the accused is remanded in custody, three weeks; and
(b) where he is remanded on bail or ordained to appear, four weeks or, on cause shown, eight weeks.

(4) An accused who is remanded under this section may appeal against the refusal of bail or against the conditions imposed within 24 hours of his remand, by note of appeal presented to the High Court, and the High Court, either in court or in chambers, may, after hearing parties—
(a) review the order appealed against and either grant bail on such conditions as it thinks fit or ordain the accused to appear at the adjourned diet; or
(b) confirm the order.

DEFINITIONS
"bail": s.307(1).
"diet": s.307(1).
"remand": s.307(1).

GENERAL NOTE
The antecedent provisions conjoined for this section have produced a considerable number of authorities, those provisions being ss.179 and 380 of the 1975 Act as amended. The principal point to note is that it is of paramount importance for courts at first instance to have in mind the clear statutory distinction between adjourning a case before sentence and deferring sentence. In *Advocate, H.M. v. Clegg,* 1991 S.L.T. 192 it was held that to obtain various reports for sentencing the correct approach is to adjourn the case and not to defer sentence, a distinction that was emphasised in *McRobbie v. H.M. Advocate,* 1990 S.C.C.R 767.

The necessity of abiding by the statutory time-limits was shown in *Wilson v. Donald,* 1993 S.L.T. 31 because, while the continuation was recorded as a deferred sentence, the obtaining of a DVLA printout during a period greater than three weeks was an adjournment to which the time-limits applied. This point was applied in *Holburn v Lees,* 1993 S.C.C.R. 426 and *Burns v. Wilson,* 1993 S.C.C.R. 418 although it was held that convictions were unaffected by these appeals on procedural points although the sentences were suspended: see also *McCulloch v. Scott,* 1993 S.L.T. 901.

A further distinction became apparent in *Douglas v. Jamieson,* 1993 S.L.T. 816 and *Douglas v. Peddie,* 1993 S.C.C.R. 717 where it was held that with a combination of guilty and not guilty pleas leading to an adjourned trial diet the court was exercising its power at common law to adjourn at any stage when it seemed appropriate to do so. See also *Mcleod v. Hutton* (Sh.Ct.), 1993 S.C.C.R. 747.

The statutory distinction was also held not to apply in *Johnstone v. Lees,* 1994 S.L.T. 551 where an adjournment of eight weeks to await the outcome of other cases was deemed competent at common law. A continuation for a proof of a previous conviction is a matter at common law: *Burns v. Lees,* 1994 S.C.C.R. 780.

In the authorities cited, objection to the competency of the various proceedings was taken timeously and to delay without explanation a complaint about competency may amount to acquiescence especially with a long passage of time and a payment of fines as ordered: *Storie v. Friel,* 1993 S.C.C.R. 955.

Finally, in *Long v. H.M. Advocate,* 1984 S.C.C.R. 161 it was held that review of the court's decision on bail (s.30 of the 1975 Act and this Act) had no application to bail in relation to the power of the court to adjourn a case before sentence.

Deferred sentence

202.—(1) It shall be competent for a court to defer sentence after conviction for a period and on such conditions as the court may determine.

(2) If it appears to the court which deferred sentence on an accused under subsection (1) above that he has been convicted during the period of deferment, by a court in any part of Great Britain of an offence committed during

that period and has been dealt with for that offence, the court which deferred sentence may—

(a) issue a warrant for the arrest of the accused; or

(b) instead of issuing such a warrant in the first instance, issue a citation requiring him to appear before it at such time as may be specified in the citation,

and on his appearance or on his being brought before the court it may deal with him in any manner in which it would be competent for it to deal with him on the expiry of the period of deferment.

(3) Where a court which has deferred sentence on an accused under subsection (1) above convicts him of another offence during the period of deferment, it may deal with him for the original offence in any manner in which it would be competent for it to deal with him on the expiry of the period of deferment, as well as for the offence committed during the said period.

DEFINITIONS
"sentence": s.307(1).

GENERAL NOTE
It is of paramount importance for courts at first instance to have in mind the clear statutory distinction between adjourning a case before sentence and deferring sentence. Regard might be had to the cases in the General Note to s.201 of this Act for the authorities arising from this distinction. The note by A.D. Smith on *Deferred Sentences in Scotland* 1968 S.L.T.(Notes) 153 is still of interest.

In *Valentine v. Parker*, 1992 S.C.C.R. 695 an appeal was taken during a deferred sentence but in the absence of the court papers the sheriff held the calling of the case on the appropriate date for consideration was incompetent. A Crown Bill of Advocation was passed and it was held by the High Court of Justiciary that the deferred sentence had been superceded by the appeal proceedings and the case was remitted to the sheriff for sentence.

Reports

203.—(1) Where a person specified in section 27(1)(b)(i) to (vi) of the Social Work (Scotland) Act 1968 commits an offence, the court shall not dispose of the case without obtaining from the local authority in whose area the person resides a report as to—

(a) the circumstances of the offence; and

(b) the character of the offender, including his behaviour while under the supervision, or as the case may be subject to the order, so specified in relation to him.

(2) In subsection (1) above, "the court" does not include a district court.

(3) Where, in any case, a report by an officer of a local authority is made to the court with a view to assisting the court in determining the most suitable method of dealing with any person in respect of an offence, a copy of the report shall be given by the clerk of the court to the offender or his solicitor.

DEFINITIONS
"local authority": s.307(1).
"offence": s.307(1).

GENERAL NOTE
This section requires the court to obtain a report targeted on new offences by an offender who is subject to statutory supervision. The circumstances of the new offences are an aspect distinct from the offender's behaviour on supervision.

Imprisonment, etc.

Restrictions on passing sentence of imprisonment or detention

204.—(1) A court shall not pass a sentence of imprisonment or of detention in respect of any offence, nor impose imprisonment, or detention, under section 214(2) of this Act in respect of failure to pay a fine, on an accused who is not legally represented in that court and has not been previously sentenced to imprisonment or detention by a court in any part of the United Kingdom, unless the accused either—

(a) applied for legal aid and the application was refused on the ground that he was not financially eligible; or

(b) having been informed of his right to apply for legal aid, and having had the opportunity, failed to do so.

(2) A court shall not pass a sentence of imprisonment on a person of or over twenty-one years of age who has not been previously sentenced to imprisonment or detention by a court in any part of the United Kingdom unless the court considers that no other method of dealing with him is appropriate; and for the purpose of determining whether any other method of dealing with such a person is appropriate the court shall obtain (from an officer of a local authority or otherwise) such information as it can about the offender's circumstances; and it shall also take into account any information before it concerning the offender's character and physical and mental condition.

(3) Where a court of summary jurisdiction passes a sentence of imprisonment on any such person as is mentioned in subsection (2) above, the court shall state the reason for its opinion that no other method of dealing with him is appropriate, and shall have that reason entered in the record of the proceedings.

(4) The court shall, for the purpose of determining whether a person has been previously sentenced to imprisonment or detention by a court in any part of the United Kingdom—

(a) disregard a previous sentence of imprisonment which, having been suspended, has not taken effect under section 23 of the Powers of Criminal Courts Act 1973 or under section 19 of the Treatment of Offenders Act (Northern Ireland) 1968;

(b) construe detention as meaning—

(i) in relation to Scotland, detention in a young offenders institution or detention centre;

(ii) in relation to England and Wales a sentence of youth custody, borstal training or detention in a young offender institution or detention centre; and

(iii) in relation to Northern Ireland, detention in a young offenders centre.

(5) This section does not affect the power of a court to pass sentence on any person for an offence the sentence for which is fixed by law.

(6) In this section—

"legal aid" means legal aid for the purposes of any part of the proceedings before the court;

"legally represented" means represented by counsel or a solicitor at some stage after the accused is found guilty and before he is dealt with as referred to in subsection (1) above.

DEFINITIONS

"court of summary jurisdiction": s.307(1).
"fine": s.307(1).
"impose imprisonment": s.307(1).
"legal aid": s.204(6).
"legally represented": s.204(6).
"offence": s.307(1).
"sentence": s.307(1).

GENERAL NOTE

This section conjoins the provisions in ss.41 and 42 of the 1980 Act. The intention remains to ensure so far as possible that no one is given a custodial sentence for the first time without having professional assistance at the time the sentence is imposed, or at least at one of the court appearances at which sentence is being considered. The existing restrictions are on a summary court's power to impose imprisonment or detention on all offenders who have not previously received sentences of imprisonment or detention on a previous occasion.

Two authorities are worth considering here. First, the duty (in subs. (2)) to obtain information from a local authority "or otherwise" is not fulfilled by obtaining information from the prosecution or the defence: *Auld v. Herron*, 1969 J.C. 4. It should be noted that the duty is qualified by the phrase "such information as it can" although that is not defined. Secondly, the imprisonment or detention relates only to the U.K. and that necessarily excludes the Republic of Ireland: *Mawhinney v. H.M. Advocate*, 1950 S.L.T. 135. It is difficult to see why imprisonment or detention elsewhere is excluded in this way but it may be information bearing on the accused's character.

Punishment for murder

205.—(1) Subject to subsections (2) and (3) below, a person convicted of murder shall be sentenced to imprisonment for life.

(2) Where a person convicted of murder is under the age of 18 years he shall not be sentenced to imprisonment for life but to be detained without limit of time and shall be liable to be detained in such place, and under such conditions, as the Secretary of State may direct.

(3) Where a person convicted of murder has attained the age of 18 years but is under the age of 21 years he shall not be sentenced to imprisonment for life but to be detained in a young offenders institution and shall be liable to be detained for life.

(4) On sentencing any person convicted of murder a judge may make a recommendation as to the minimum period which should elapse before, under section 1(4) of the Prisoners and Criminal Proceedings (Scotland) Act 1993, the Secretary of State releases that person on licence.

(5) When making a recommendation under subsection (4) above, the judge shall state his reasons for so recommending.

(6) Notwithstanding subsection (2) of section 106 of this Act it shall be competent to appeal under paragraph (b) or (f) of subsection (1) of that section against a recommendation made under subsection (4) above; and for the purposes of such appeal (including the High Court's power of disposal under section 118(4)(b) of this Act) the recommendation shall be deemed part of the sentence passed on conviction.

DEFINITIONS
"judge": s.307(1).
"sentence": s.307(1).

GENERAL NOTE
The recommendation permitted by subs. (4) appears to be fairly common now. A good example is *Birrell v. H.M. Advocate*, 1993 S.C.C.R. 812 where previous convictions were held not to be a factor of significance in this case. The important factors had been the method used to commit the crime, the degree of planning and premeditation and the ruthlessness exhibited in the acts which had been perpetrated. A recommendation of a minimum of 15 years was held to be correctly decided. A similar period was imposed on appeal in *Casey v. H.M. Advocate*, 1994 S.L.T. 54 where it was observed by the Appeal Court that it would not expect a recommendation to be made for a period of less than 12 years.

Minimum periods of imprisonment

206.—(1) No person shall be sentenced to imprisonment by a court of summary jurisdiction for a period of less than five days.

(2) Where a court of summary jurisdiction has power to impose imprisonment on an offender, it may, if any suitable place provided and certified as mentioned in subsection (4) below is available for the purpose, sentence the offender to be detained therein, for such period not exceeding four days as

the court thinks fit, and an extract of the finding and sentence shall be delivered with the offender to the person in charge of the place where the offender is to be detained and shall be a sufficient authority for his detention in that place in accordance with the sentence.

(3) The expenses of the maintenance of offenders detained under this section shall be defrayed in like manner as the expenses of the maintenance of prisoners under the Prisons (Scotland) Act 1989.

(4) The Secretary of State may, on the application of any police authority, certify any police cells or other similar places provided by the authority to be suitable places for the detention of persons sentenced to detention under this section, and may by statutory instrument make regulations for the inspection of places so provided, the treatment of persons detained therein and generally for carrying this section into effect.

(5) No place certified under this section shall be used for the detention of females unless provision is made for their supervision by female officers.

(6) In this section the expression "police authority" has the same meaning as in the Police (Scotland) Act 1967.

DEFINITIONS
  "court of summary jurisdiction": s.307(1).
  "imprisonment": s.307(1).
  "police authority": s.206(6).

Detention of young offenders

207.—(1) It shall not be competent to impose imprisonment on a person under 21 years of age.

(2) Subject to section 205(2) and (3) of this Act and to subsections (3) and (4) below, a court may impose detention (whether by way of sentence or otherwise) on a person, who is not less than 16 but under 21 years of age, where but for subsection (1) above the court would have power to impose a period of imprisonment; and a period of detention imposed under this section on any person shall not exceed the maximum period of imprisonment which might otherwise have been imposed.

(3) The court shall not under subsection (2) above impose detention on an offender unless it is of the opinion that no other method of dealing with him is appropriate; and the court shall state its reasons for that opinion, and, except in the case of the High Court, those reasons shall be entered in the record of proceedings.

(4) To enable the court to form an opinion under subsection (3) above, it shall obtain from an officer of a local authority or otherwise such information as it can about the offender's circumstances; and it shall also take into account any information before it concerning the offender's character and physical and mental condition.

(5) A sentence of detention imposed under this section shall be a sentence of detention in a young offenders institution.

DEFINITIONS
  "imprisonment": s.307(1).
  "local authority": s.307(1).
  "young offender's institution": s.307(1).

GENERAL NOTE
  The correct approach for the court in deciding the issue of detention for a young offender is to ask, in terms of subs. (3), what methods of dealing with the accused are appropriate. If the court is of the opinion that no method other than detention is appropriate then detention should be imposed: see *Milligan v. Jessop*, 1988 S.C.C.R. 137; *Dunsmore v. Allan*, 1991 S.C.C.R. 946 and *Divers v. Friel*, 1994 S.L.T. 247 in which the approaches were flawed. Having formed the opinion

that no other method of dealing with the accused is appropriate, the court is required to state its reasons for that opinion and those reasons shall be entered in the record of proceedings. For the effect of failure to obtemper an earlier version of this subsection, see *Binnie v. Farrell*, 1972 S.L.T. 212. The common reasons so stated are "character, gravity or nature of the offence" and "previous record of the accused", variations of which were used in *Dunsmore v. Allan*, above. Some support for these are to be found in s.214(4) of this Act.

Detention of children convicted on indictment

208. Subject to section 205 of this Act, where a child is convicted on indictment and the court is of the opinion that no other method of dealing with him is appropriate, it may sentence him to be detained for a period which it shall specify in the sentence; and the child shall during that period be liable to be detained in such place and on such conditions as the Secretary of State may direct.

DEFINITIONS
  "child": s.307(1).
  "indictment": s.307(1).
  "sentence": s.307(1).

GENERAL NOTE
  The correct approach for the court in deciding the issue of detention for a child convicted on indictment is the same as that for young offenders, namely to ask what methods of dealing with the child are appropriate. If the court is of the opinion that no method other than detention is appropriate then the child shall be detained for a specified period.
  In *R.J.K. v. H.M. Advocate*, 1993 S.L.T. 237 it was held that (in relation to s.206 of the 1975 Act from which this section is derived) the sentence of detention "without limit of time" is a specified sentence and the absence of those words from the section did not impose any restriction on a court to pass such a sentence. Such a sentence, however, is in effect a life sentence: *R.F. v. H.M. Advocate*, 1994 S.C.C.R. 71.

Supervised release orders

209.—(1) Where a person is convicted of an offence and is sentenced to imprisonment for a term of not less than twelve months but less than four years, the court on passing sentence may, if it considers that it is necessary to do so to protect the public from serious harm from the offender on his release, make such order as is mentioned in subsection (3) below.

(2) A court shall, before making an order under subsection (1) above, consider a report by a relevant officer of a local authority about the offender and his circumstances and, if the court thinks it necessary, hear that officer.

(3) The order referred to in subsection (1) above (to be known as a "supervised release order") is that the person, during a relevant period—

(a) be under the supervision either of a relevant officer of a local authority or of a probation officer appointed for or assigned to a petty sessions area (such local authority or the justices for such area to be designated under section 14(4) or 15(1) of the Prisoners and Criminal Proceedings (Scotland) Act 1993);

(b) comply with;
        (i) such requirements as may be imposed by the court in the order; and
        (ii) such requirements as that officer may reasonably specify,
    for the purpose of securing the good conduct of the person or preventing, or lessening the possibility of, his committing a further offence (whether or not an offence of the kind for which he was sentenced); and

(c) comply with the standard requirements imposed by virtue of subsection (4)(a)(i) below.

(4) A supervised release order—
(a) shall—

(i) without prejudice to subsection (3)(b) above, contain such requirements (in this section referred to as the "standard requirements"); and

(ii) be as nearly as possible in such form,

as may be prescribed by Act of Adjournal;

(b) for the purposes of any appeal or review constitutes part of the sentence of the person in respect of whom the order is made; and

(c) shall have no effect during any period in which the person is subject to a licence under Part I of the said Act of 1993.

(5) Before making a supervised release order as respects a person the court shall explain to him, in as straightforward a way as is practicable, the effect of the order and the possible consequences for him of any breach of it.

(6) The clerk of the court by which a supervised release order is made in respect of a person shall—

(a) forthwith send a copy of the order to the person and to the Secretary of State; and

(b) within seven days after the date on which the order is made, send to the Secretary of State such documents and information relating to the case and to the person as are likely to be of assistance to a supervising officer.

(7) In this section—

"relevant officer" has the same meaning as in Part I of the Prisoners and Criminal Proceedings (Scotland) Act 1993;

"relevant period" means such period as may be specified in the supervised release order, being a period—

(a) not exceeding twelve months after the date of the person's release; and

(b) no part of which is later than the date by which the entire term of imprisonment specified in his sentence has elapsed; and

"supervising officer" means, where an authority has or justices have been designated as is mentioned in subsection (3)(a) above for the purposes of the order, any relevant officer or, as the case may be, probation officer who is for the time being supervising for those purposes the person released.

(8) This section applies to a person sentenced under section 207 of this Act as it applies to a person sentenced to a period of imprisonment.

DEFINITIONS
"local authority": s.307(1).
"relevant officer": s.209(7).
"relevant period": s.209(7).
"supervised release order": s.209(3).
"supervising officer": s.209(7).

Consideration of time spent in custody

210.—(1) A court, in passing a sentence of imprisonment or detention on a person for an offence, shall—

(a) in determining the period of imprisonment or detention, have regard to any period of time spent in custody by the person on remand awaiting trial or sentence, or spent in custody awaiting extradition to the United Kingdom;

(b) specify the date of commencement of the sentence; and

(c) if the person—

(i) has spent a period of time in custody on remand awaiting trial or sentence; or

(ii) is an extradited prisoner for the purposes of this section, and the date specified under paragraph (b) above is not earlier than the date on which sentence was passed, state its reasons for not specifying an earlier date.

(2) A prisoner is an extradited prisoner for the purposes of this section if—

(a) he was tried for the offence in respect of which his sentence of imprisonment was imposed—

      (i) after having been extradited to the United Kingdom; and

      (ii) without having first been restored to the state from which he was extradited or having had an opportunity of leaving the United Kingdom; and

(b) he was for any period in custody while awaiting such extradition.

(3) In this section "extradited to the United Kingdom" means returned to the United Kingdom—

(a) in pursuance of extradition arrangements (as defined in section 3 of the Extradition Act 1989);

(b) under any law which corresponds to that Act and is a law of a designated Commonwealth country (as defined in section 5(1) of that Act);

(c) under that Act as extended to a colony or under any corresponding law of a colony;

(d) in pursuance of arrangements with a foreign state in respect of which an Order in Council under section 2 of the Extradition Act 1870 is in force; or

(e) in pursuance of a warrant of arrest endorsed in the Republic of Ireland under the law of that country corresponding to the Backing of Warrants (Republic of Ireland) Act 1965.

DEFINITIONS

"sentence": s.307(1).

GENERAL NOTE

The obligation placed on a court by this section is to "have regard to any period of time spent in custody by the person awaiting trial or sentence, or spent in custody awaiting extradition to the United Kingdom".

In effect, it is submitted, the court should have such a period in mind when selecting a sentence: it does not follow that such a period should be deducted automatically or that the sentence passed should be backdated to a commencement date that in effect deducts the period in mind. In practice, however, many sentences are backdated to a suitable commencement date: for a survey of the very considerable number of authorities on this point see *Backdating Sentences of Imprisonment* (1995) 40 J.L.S. 383.

Fines

Fines

211.—(1) Where an accused who is convicted on indictment of any offence (whether triable only on indictment or triable either on indictment or summarily other than by virtue of section 292(6) of this Act) would apart from this subsection be liable to a fine of or not exceeding a specified amount, he shall by virtue of this subsection be liable to a fine of any amount.

(2) Where any Act confers a power by subordinate instrument to make a person liable on conviction on indictment of any offence mentioned in subsection (1) above to a fine or a maximum fine of a specified amount, or which shall not exceed a specified amount, the fine which may be imposed in the exercise of that power shall by virtue of this subsection be a fine of an unlimited amount.

(3) Any sentence or decree for any fine or expenses pronounced by a sheriff court or district court may be enforced against the person or effects of any party against whom the sentence or decree was awarded—

(a) in the district where the sentence or decree was pronounced; or

(b) in any other such district.

(4) A fine imposed by the High Court shall be remitted for enforcement to, and shall be enforceable as if it had been imposed by—
- (a) where the person upon whom the fine was imposed resides in Scotland, the sheriff for the district where that person resides; and
- (b) where that person resides outwith Scotland, the sheriff before whom he was brought for examination in relation to the offence for which the fine was imposed.

(5) Any fine imposed in the High Court on the accused, and on a juror for non-attendance, and any forfeiture for non-appearance of a party, witness or juror in the High Court shall be payable to and recoverable by the Treasury, except where the High Court orders that the whole or any part of the fine shall be otherwise disposed of.

(6) All fines and expenses imposed in summary proceedings under this Act shall be paid to the clerk of court to be accounted for by him to the person entitled to such fines and expenses, and it shall not be necessary to specify in any sentence the person entitled to payment of such fines or expenses unless it is necessary to provide for the division of the penalty.

(7) A court in determining the amount of any fine to be imposed on an offender shall take into consideration, amongst other things, the means of the offender so far as known to the court.

DEFINITIONS
"fine": s.307(1).
"High Court": s.307(1).
"indictment": s.307(1).
"sentence": s.307(1).
"witness": s.307(1).

GENERAL NOTE
This section presumes as a generality the proposition that fines following conviction on indictment are unlimited subject to statutory maxima for certain offences. It is of some interest that the only item which is specified as being required to be taken into consideration in imposing a fine is "the means of the offender so far as known to the court": subs. (7).

Fines in summary proceedings

212.—(1) Where a court of summary jurisdiction imposes a fine on an offender, the court may order him to be searched, and any money found on him on apprehension or when so searched or when taken to prison or to a young offenders institution in default of payment of the fine, may, unless the court otherwise directs and subject to subsection (2) below, be applied towards payment of the fine, and the surplus if any shall be returned to him.

(2) Money shall not be applied as mentioned in subsection (1) above if the court is satisfied that it does not belong to the person on whom it was found or that the loss of the money will be more injurious to his family than his imprisonment or detention.

(3) When a court of summary jurisdiction, which has adjudged that a sum of money shall be paid by an offender, considers that any money found on the offender on apprehension, or after he has been searched by order of the court, should not be applied towards payment of such sum, the court, shall make a direction in writing to that effect which shall be written on the extract of the sentence which imposes the fine before it is issued by the clerk of the court.

(4) An accused may make an application to such a court either orally or in writing, through the governor of the prison in whose custody he may be at that time, that any sum of money which has been found on his person should not be applied in payment of the fine adjudged to be paid by him.

(5) A person who alleges that any money found on the person of an offender is not the property of the offender, but belongs to that person, may

apply to such court either orally or in writing for a direction that the money should not be applied in payment of the fine adjudged to be paid, and the court after enquiry may so direct.

(6) A court of summary jurisdiction, which has adjudged that a sum of money shall be paid by an offender, may order the attendance in court of the offender, if he is in prison, for the purpose of ascertaining the ownership of money which has been found on his person.

(7) A notice in the form prescribed by Act of Adjournal, or as nearly as may be in such form, addressed to the governor of the prison in whose custody an offender may be at the time, signed by the judge of a court of summary jurisdiction shall be a sufficient warrant to the governor of such prison for conveying the offender to the court.

DEFINITIONS
"court of summary jurisdiction": s.307(1).
"fine": s.307(1).

Remission of fines

213.—(1) A fine may at any time be remitted in whole or in part by—
(a) in a case where a transfer of fine order under section 222 of this Act is effective and the court by which payment is enforceable is, in terms of the order, a court of summary jurisdiction in Scotland, that court; or
(b) in any other case, the court which imposed the fine or, where that court was the High Court, by which payment was first enforceable.

(2) Where the court remits the whole or part of a fine after imprisonment has been imposed under section 214(2) or (4) of this Act, it shall also remit the whole period of imprisonment or, as the case may be, reduce the period by an amount which bears the same proportion to the whole period as the amount remitted bears to the whole fine.

(3) The power conferred by subsection (1) above shall be exercisable without requiring the attendance of the accused.

DEFINITIONS
"court of summary jurisdiction": s.307(1).
"fine": s.307(1).
"High Court": s.307(1).

GENERAL NOTE
In *Tudhope v. Furphy*, 1982 S.C.C.R. 575 a sheriff held *inter alia* that he has power to reduce or extinguish a compensation order in circumstances where it had subsequently been discovered that the payee had died before the order was made.

Fines: time for payment and payment by instalments

214.—(1) Where a court has imposed a fine on an offender or ordered him to find caution the court shall, subject to subsection (2) below, allow him at least seven days to pay the fine or the first instalment thereof or, as the case may be, to find caution; and any reference in this section and section 216 of this Act to a failure to pay a fine or other like expression shall include a reference to a failure to find caution.

(2) If on the occasion of the imposition of a fine—
(a) the offender appears to the court to possess sufficient means to enable him to pay the fine forthwith; or
(b) on being asked by the court whether he wishes to have time for payment, he does not ask for time; or
(c) he fails to satisfy the court that he has a fixed abode; or
(d) the court is satisfied for any other special reason that no time should be allowed for payment,

the court may refuse him time to pay the fine and, if the offender fails to pay, may exercise its power to impose imprisonment and, if it does so, shall state the special reason for its decision.

(3) In all cases where time is not allowed by a court for payment of a fine, the reasons of the court for not so allowing time shall be stated in the extract of the finding and sentence as well as in the finding and sentence itself.

(4) Where time is allowed for payment of a fine or payment by instalments is ordered, the court shall not, on the occasion of the imposition of a fine, impose imprisonment in the event of a future default in paying the fine or an instalment thereof unless the offender is before it and the court determines that, having regard to the gravity of the offence or to the character of the offender, or to other special reason, it is expedient that he should be imprisoned without further inquiry in default of payment; and where a court so determines, it shall state the special reason for its decision.

(5) Where a court has imposed imprisonment in accordance with subsection (4) above, then, if at any time the offender asks the court to commit him to prison, the court may do so notwithstanding subsection (1) of this section.

(6) Nothing in the foregoing provisions of this section shall affect any power of the court to order a fine to be recovered by civil diligence.

(7) Where time has been allowed for payment of a fine imposed by the court, it may, on an application by or on behalf of the offender, and after giving the prosecutor an opportunity of being heard, allow further time for payment.

(8) Without prejudice to subsection (2) above, where a court has imposed a fine on an offender, the court may, of its own accord or on the application of the offender, order payment of that fine by instalments of such amounts and at such time as it may think fit.

(9) Where the court has ordered payment of a fine by instalments it may—

(a) allow further time for payment of any instalment thereof;

(b) order payment thereof by instalments of lesser amounts, or at longer intervals, than those originally fixed,

and the powers conferred by this subsection shall be exercisable without requiring the attendance of the accused.

DEFINITIONS

"caution": s.227.
"fine": s.307(1).

GENERAL NOTE

Subs. (1)

Although the references are to both fines and cautions in practice it is rare for cautions to be imposed.

Subs. (2)(a) and (d)

In *Barbour v. Robertson* and *Ram v. Robertson*, 1943 J.C. 46 it was observed that in applying these provisions the nature of the offence can never be a relevant consideration when determining whether time should be allowed for payment where a substantial monetary penalty is imposed; the only relevant matters are the means of the offender and similar considerations. Where the nature of the offence is such as to warrant a sentence of imprisonment, the proper course to adopt is to impose such a sentence either without the option of a fine or with a fine in addition, and not to impose merely a pecuniary penalty of such an amount that when no time is allowed for payment the imposition of the fine is equivalent to a sentence of imprisonment without the option of a fine.

Subs. (2)(b)

A court of summary jurisdiction, when imposing a fine, has a discretion to allow or refuse time to pay and may allow time for payment where that has not been requested by the accused: *Fraser v. Herron*, 1968 S.L.T. 149.

Subs. (2)(d)
For an example of special reasons being recorded in the minutes see *Sullivan v. Mcleod*, 1980 S.L.T. (Notes) 99.

Subs. (4)
The relevant cases may be considered under the different parts of the subsection.
"*Unless the offender is before it*". The decision in *Campbell v. Jessop*, 1988 S.L.T. 160 made it clear that the accused had to be present when a sentence of imprisonment was imposed. Not least of the reasons is that the absence of the accused meant that there was no opportunity for representations to be made by or for the accused.
"*Having regard to the offence*". In *Finnie v. Mcleod*, 1983 S.C.C.R. 387 "barefaced shoplifting" justified an immediate alternative of imprisonment in default of payment of the fine by instalments but in *Dunlop v. Allan*, 1984 S.C.C.R. 329 careless driving did not allow such action nor did drunk driving in *Buchanan v. Hamilton*, 1988 S.C.C.R. 379.
"*The character of the offender*". *Paterson v. McGlennan*, 1991 S.L.T. 832 illustrates the error of proceeding under this head with only one minor road traffic previous conviction.
"*Other special reason*". Merely to have time still to serve in prison and to be unable to pay fines are not to be regarded as "special reasons"; *Robertson v. Jessop*, 1989 S.L.T. 843.

Application for further time to pay fine

215.—(1) An application by an offender for further time in which to pay a fine imposed on him by a court, or of instalments thereof, shall be made, subject to subsection (2) below, to that court.

(2) Where a transfer of fine order has been made under section 222 of this Act, section 90 of the Magistrates' Courts Act 1980 or Article 95 of the Magistrates' Courts (Northern Ireland) Order 1981, an application under subsection (1) above shall be made to the court specified in the transfer order, or to the court specified in the last transfer order where there is more than one transfer.

(3) A court to which an application is made under this section shall allow further time for payment of the fine or of instalments thereof, unless it is satisfied that the failure of the offender to make payment has been wilful or that the offender has no reasonable prospect of being able to pay if further time is allowed.

(4) An application made under this section may be made orally or in writing.

DEFINITIONS
"fine": s.307(1).

Fines: restriction on imprisonment for default

216.—(1) Where a court has imposed a fine or ordered the finding of caution without imposing imprisonment in default of payment, subject to subsection (2) below, it shall not impose imprisonment on an offender for failing to make payment of the fine or, as the case may be, to find caution, unless on an occasion subsequent to that sentence the court has enquired into in his presence the reason why the fine has not been paid or, as the case may be, caution has not been found.

(2) Subsection (1) above shall not apply where the offender is in prison.

(3) A court may, for the purpose of enabling enquiry to be made under this section—
  (a) issue a citation requiring the offender to appear before the court at a time and place appointed in the citation; or
  (b) issue a warrant of apprehension.

(4) On the failure of the offender to appear before the court in response to a citation under this section, the court may issue a warrant of apprehension.

(5) The citation of an offender to appear before a court in terms of subsection (3)(a) above shall be effected in like manner, *mutatis mutandis*, as the citation of an accused to a sitting or diet of the court under section 141 of this Act, and—

(a) the citation shall be signed by the clerk of the court before which the offender is required to appear, instead of by the prosecutor; and

(b) the forms relating to the citation of an accused shall not apply to such citation.

(6) The following matters shall be, or as nearly as may be, in such form as is prescribed by Act of Adjournal—

(a) the citation of an offender under this section;

(b) if the citation of the offender is effected by an officer of law, the written execution, if any, of that officer of law;

(c) a warrant of apprehension issued by a court under subsection (4) above; and

(d) the minute of procedure in relation to an enquiry into the means of an offender under this section.

(7) Where a child would, if he were an adult, be liable to be imprisoned in default of payment of any fine the court may, if it considers that none of the other methods by which the case may legally be dealt with is suitable, order that the child be detained for such period, not exceeding one month, as may be specified in the order in a place chosen by the local authority in whose area the court is situated.

DEFINITIONS
"caution": s.227.
"fine": s.307(1).
"officer of law": s.307(1).
"prosecutor": s.307(1).

GENERAL NOTE
The power to imprison under this authority may be constrained by statute: see *Fraser v. Herron*, 1968 S.L.T. 149. The imposition of consecutive custodial sentences in default of payment has been doubted: *Stevenson v. McGlennan*, 1990 S.L.T. 842 and *Robertson v. Jessop*, 1989 S.L.T. 843. Imprisonment under this authority must be immediate imprisonment: *Craig v. Smith*, 1990 S.C.C.R. 328.

Fines: supervision pending payment

217.—(1) Where an offender has been allowed time for payment of a fine, the court may, either on the occasion of the imposition of the fine or on a subsequent occasion, order that he be placed under the supervision of such person, in this section referred to as the "supervising officer", as the court may from time to time appoint for the purpose of assisting and advising the offender in regard to payment of the fine.

(2) An order made in pursuance of subsection (1) above shall remain in force so long as the offender to whom it relates remains liable to pay the fine or any part of it unless the order ceases to have effect or is discharged under subsection (3) below.

(3) An order under this section shall cease to have effect on the making of a transfer of fine order under section 222 of this Act in respect of the fine or may be discharged by the court that made it without prejudice, in either case, to the making of a new order.

(4) Where an offender under 21 years of age has been allowed time for payment of a fine, the court shall not order the form of detention appropriate to him in default of payment of the fine unless—

(a) he has been placed under supervision in respect of the fine; or

(b) the court is satisfied that it is impracticable to place him under supervision.

(5) Where a court, on being satisfied as mentioned in subsection (4)(b) above, orders the detention of a person under 21 years of age without an order under this section having been made, the court shall state the grounds on which it is so satisfied.

(6) Where an order under this section is in force in respect of an offender, the court shall not impose imprisonment in default of the payment of the fine unless before doing so it has—

(a) taken such steps as may be reasonably practicable to obtain from the supervising officer a report, which may be oral, on the offender's conduct and means, and has considered any such report; and

(b) in a case where an enquiry is required by section 216 of this Act, considered such enquiry.

(7) When a court appoints a different supervising officer under subsection (1) above, a notice shall be sent by the clerk of the court to the offender in such form, as nearly as may be, as is prescribed by Act of Adjournal.

(8) The supervising officer shall communicate with the offender with a view to assisting and advising him in regard to payment of the fine, and unless the fine or any instalment thereof is paid to the clerk of the court within the time allowed by the court for payment, the supervising officer shall report to the court without delay after the expiry of such time, as to the conduct and means of the offender.

DEFINITIONS
"fine": s.307(1).

Fines: supplementary provisions as to payment

218.—(1) Where under the provisions of section 214 or 217 of this Act a court is required to state a special reason for its decision or the grounds on which it is satisfied that it is undesirable or impracticable to place an offender under supervision, the reason or, as the case may be, the grounds shall be entered in the record of the proceedings along with the finding and sentence.

(2) Any reference in the said sections 214 and 217 to imprisonment shall be construed, in the case of an offender on whom by reason of his age imprisonment may not lawfully be imposed, as a reference to the lawful form of detention in default of payment of a fine appropriate to that person, and any reference to prison shall be construed accordingly.

(3) Where a warrant has been issued for the apprehension of an offender for non-payment of a fine, the offender may, notwithstanding section 211(6) of this Act, pay such fine in full to a constable; and the warrant shall not then be enforced and the constable shall remit the fine to the clerk of court.

DEFINITIONS
"fine": s.307(1).
"impose imprisonment": s.307(1).

Fines: periods of imprisonment for non-payment

219.—(1) Subject to sections 214 to 218 of this Act—

(a) a court may, when imposing a fine, impose a period of imprisonment in default of payment; or

(b) where no order has been made under paragraph (a) above and a person fails to pay a fine, or any part or instalment of a fine, by the time ordered by the court (or, where section 214(2) of this Act applies, immediately) the court may, subject to section 235(1) of this Act, impose a period of imprisonment for such failure either with immediate effect or to take effect in the event of the person failing to pay the fine or any part or instalment of it by such further time as the court may order,

whether or not the fine is imposed under an enactment which makes provision for its enforcement or recovery.

(2) Subject to the following subsections of this section, the maximum period of imprisonment which may be imposed under subsection (1) above or for failure to find caution, shall be as follows—

Amount of Fine or Caution	Maximum Period of Imprisonment
Not exceeding £200	7 days
Exceeding £200 but not exceeding £500	14 days
Exceeding £500 but not exceeding £1,000	28 days
Exceeding £1,000 but not exceeding £2,500	45 days
Exceeding £2,500 but not exceeding £5,000	3 months
Exceeding £5,000 but not exceeding £10,000	6 months
Exceeding £10,000 but not exceeding £20,000	12 months
Exceeding £20,000 but not exceeding £50,000	18 months
Exceeding £50,000 but not exceeding £100,000	2 years
Exceeding £100,000 but not exceeding £250,000	3 years
Exceeding £250,000 but not exceeding £1 Million	5 years
Exceeding £1 Million	10 years

(3) Where an offender is fined on the same day before the same court for offences charged in the same indictment or complaint or in separate indictments or complaints, the amount of the fine shall, for the purposes of this section, be taken to be the total of the fines imposed.

(4) Where a court has imposed a period of imprisonment in default of payment of a fine, and—

(a) an instalment of the fine is not paid at the time ordered; or

(b) part only of the fine has been paid within the time allowed for payment,

the offender shall be liable to imprisonment for a period which bears to the period so imposed the same proportion, as nearly as may be, as the amount outstanding at the time when warrant is issued for imprisonment of the offender in default bears to the original fine.

(5) Where no period of imprisonment in default of payment of a fine has been imposed and—

(a) an instalment of the fine is not paid at the time ordered; or

(b) part only of the fine has been paid within the time allowed for payment,

the offender shall be liable to imprisonment for a maximum period which bears, as nearly as may be, the same proportion to the maximum period of imprisonment which could have been imposed by virtue of the Table in subsection (2) above in default of payment of the original fine as the amount outstanding at the time when he appears before the court bears to the original fine.

(6) If in any sentence or extract sentence the period of imprisonment inserted in default of payment of a fine or on failure to find caution is in excess of that competent under this Part of this Act, such period of imprisonment shall be reduced to the maximum period under this Part of this Act applicable to such default or failure, and the judge who pronounced the sentence shall have power to order the sentence or extract to be corrected accordingly.

(7) The provisions of this section shall be without prejudice to the operation of section 220 of this Act.

(8) Where in any case—

(a) the sheriff considers that the imposition of imprisonment for the number of years for the time being specified in section 3(3) of this Act would be inadequate; and

(b) the maximum period of imprisonment which may be imposed under subsection (1) above (or under that subsection as read with either or both of sections 252(2) of this Act and section 14(2) of the Proceeds of Crime (Scotland) Act 1995) exceeds that number of years,

he shall remit the case to the High Court for sentence.

DEFINITIONS
"caution": s.227.
"fine": s.307(1).
"impose imprisonment": s.307(1).
"order": s.307(1).

GENERAL NOTE
Subsection (8) provides a power of remit from the sheriff court to the High Court of Justiciary in addition to that under s.195(1).

Fines: part payment by prisoners

220.—(1) Where a person committed to prison or otherwise detained for failure to pay a fine imposed by a court pays to the governor of the prison, under conditions prescribed by rules made under the Prisons (Scotland) Act 1989, any sum in part satisfaction of the fine, the term of imprisonment shall be reduced (or as the case may be further reduced) by a number of days bearing as nearly as possible the same proportion to such term as the sum so paid bears to the amount of the fine outstanding at the commencement of the imprisonment.

(2) The day on which any sum is paid as mentioned in subsection (1) above shall not be regarded as a day served by the prisoner as part of the said term of imprisonment.

(3) All sums paid under this section shall be handed over on receipt by the governor of the prison to the clerk of the court in which the conviction was obtained, and thereafter paid and applied *pro tanto* in the same manner and for the same purposes as sums adjudged to be paid by the conviction and sentence of the court, and paid and recovered in terms thereof, are lawfully paid and applied.

(4) In this section references to a prison and to the governor thereof shall include respectively references to any other place in which a person may be lawfully detained in default of payment of a fine, and to an officer in charge thereof.

DEFINITIONS
"fine": s.307(1).
"governor": s.307(1).
"prison": s.307(1).

Fines: recovery by civil diligence

221.—(1) Where any fine falls to be recovered by civil diligence in pursuance of this Act or in any case in which a court may think it expedient to order a fine to be recovered by civil diligence, there shall be added to the finding of the court imposing the fine a warrant for civil diligence in a form prescribed by Act of Adjournal which shall have the effect of authorising—

(a) the charging of the person who has been fined to pay the fine within the period specified in the charge and, in the event of failure to make such payment within that period, the execution of an earnings arrestment and the poinding of articles belonging to him and, if necessary for the purpose of executing the poinding, the opening of shut and lockfast places;

(b) an arrestment other than an arrestment of earnings in the hands of his employer,

and such diligence, whatever the amount of the fine imposed, may be executed in the same manner as if the proceedings were on an extract decree of the sheriff in a summary cause.

(2) Subject to subsection (3) below, proceedings by civil diligence under this section may be taken at any time after the imposition of the fine to which they relate.

(3) No such proceedings shall be authorised after the offender has been imprisoned in consequence of his having defaulted in payment of the fine.

(4) Where proceedings by civil diligence for the recovery of a fine or caution are taken, imprisonment for non-payment of the fine or for failure to find such caution shall remain competent and such proceedings may be authorised after the court has imposed imprisonment for, or in the event of, the non-payment or the failure but before imprisonment has followed such imposition.

DEFINITIONS
"fine": s.307(1).

Transfer of fine orders

222.—(1) Where a court has imposed a fine on a person convicted of an offence and it appears to the court that he is residing—
(a) within the jurisdiction of another court in Scotland; or
(b) in any petty sessions area in England and Wales; or
(c) in any petty sessions district in Northern Ireland,
the court may order that payment of the fine shall be enforceable by that other court or in that petty sessions area or petty sessions district as the case may be.

(2) An order under this section (in this section referred to as a "transfer of fine order") shall specify the court by which or the petty sessions area or petty sessions district in which payment is to be enforceable and, where the court to be specified in a transfer of fine order is a court of summary jurisdiction, it shall, in any case where the order is made by the sheriff court, be a sheriff court.

(3) Subject to subsections (4) and (5) below, where a transfer of fine order is made with respect to any fine under this section, any functions under any enactment relating to that sum which, if no such order had been made, would have been exercisable by the court which made the order or by the clerk of that court shall cease to be so exercisable.

(4) Where—
(a) the court specified in a transfer of fine order is satisfied, after inquiry, that the offender is not residing within the jurisdiction of that court; and
(b) the clerk of that court, within 14 days of receiving the notice required by section 223(1) of this Act, sends to the clerk of the court which made the order notice to that effect,
the order shall cease to have effect.

(5) Where a transfer of fine order ceases to have effect by virtue of subsection (4) above, the functions referred to in subsection (3) above shall again be

exercisable by the court which made the order or, as the case may be, by the clerk of that court.

(6) Where a transfer of fine order under this section, section 90 of the Magistrates' Courts Act 1980 or Article 95 of the Magistrates' Courts (Northern Ireland) Order 1981 specifies a court of summary jurisdiction in Scotland, that court and the clerk of that court shall have all the like functions under this Part of this Act in respect of the fine or the sum in respect of which that order was made (including the power to make any further order under this section) as if the fine or the sum were a fine imposed by that court and as if any order made under this section, the said Act of 1980 or the said Order of 1981 in respect of the fine or the sum before the making of the transfer of fine order had been made by that court.

(7) The functions of the court to which subsection (6) above relates shall be deemed to include the court's power to apply to the Secretary of State under any regulations made by him under section 24(1)(a) of the Criminal Justice Act 1991 (power to deduct fines etc. from income support).

(8) Where a transfer of fine order under section 90 of the Magistrates' Courts Act 1980, Article 95 of the Magistrates' Courts (Northern Ireland) Order 1981, or this section provides for the enforcement by a sheriff court in Scotland of a fine imposed by the Crown Court, the term of imprisonment which may be imposed under this Part of this Act shall be the term fixed in pursuance of section 31 of the Powers of Criminal Courts Act 1973 by the Crown Court or a term which bears the same proportion to the term so fixed as the amount of the fine remaining due bears to the amount of the fine imposed by that court, notwithstanding that the term exceeds the period applicable to the case under section 219 of this Act.

DEFINITIONS
"fine": s.307(1).
"order": s.222(2).
"transfer of fine order": s.307(1).

Transfer of fines: procedure for clerk of court

223.—(1) Where a court makes a transfer of fine order under section 222 of this Act, the clerk of the court shall send to the clerk of the court specified in the order—
   (a) a notice in the form prescribed by Act of Adjournal, or as nearly as may be in such form;
   (b) a statement of the offence of which the offender was convicted; and
   (c) a statement of the steps, if any, taken to recover the fine,
and shall give him such further information, if any, as, in his opinion, is likely to assist the court specified in the order in recovering the fine.

(2) In the case of a further transfer of fine order, the clerk of the court which made the order shall send to the clerk of the court by which the fine was imposed a copy of the notice sent to the clerk of the court specified in the order.

(3) The clerk of the court specified in a transfer of fine order shall, as soon as may be after he has received the notice mentioned in subsection (1)(a) above, send an intimation to the offender in the form prescribed by Act of Adjournal or as nearly as may be in such form.

(4) The clerk of court specified in a transfer of fine order shall remit or otherwise account for any payment received in respect of the fine to the clerk of the court by which the fine was imposed, and if the sentence has been enforced otherwise than by payment of the fine, he shall inform the clerk of court how the sentence was enforced.

DEFINITIONS
"fine": s.307(1).
"order": s.307(1).
"transfer of fine order": s.222(2).

Discharge from imprisonment to be specified

224. All warrants of imprisonment in default of payment of a fine, or on failure to find caution, shall specify a period at the expiry of which the person sentenced shall be discharged, notwithstanding the fine has not been paid, or caution found.

DEFINITIONS
"caution": s.307(1).
"fine": s.307(1).

Penalties: standard scale, prescribed sum and uprating

225.—(1) There shall be a standard scale of fines for offences triable only summarily, which shall be known as "the standard scale".
(2) The standard scale is shown below—

Level on the scale	Amount of Fine
1	£ 200
2	£ 500
3	£1,000
4	£2,500
5	£5,000

(3) Any reference in any enactment, whenever passed or made, to a specified level on the standard scale shall be construed as referring to the amount which corresponds to that level on the standard scale referred to in subsection (2) above.
(4) If it appears to the Secretary of State that there has been a change in the value of money since the relevant date, he may by order substitute for the sum or sums for the time being specified in the provisions mentioned in subsection (5) below such other sum or sums as appear to him justified by the change.
(5) The provisions referred to in subsection (4) above are—
(a) subsection (2) above;
(b) subsection (8) below;
(c) section 219(2) of this Act;
(d) column 5 or 6 of Schedule 4 to the Misuse of Drugs Act 1971 so far as the column in question relates to the offences under provisions of that Act specified in column 1 of that Schedule in respect of which the maximum fines were increased by Part II of Schedule 8 to the Criminal Justice and Public Order Act 1994.
(6) In subsection (4) above "the relevant date" means—
(a) in relation to the first order made under that subsection, the date the last order was made under section 289D(1) of the Criminal Procedure (Scotland) Act 1975; and
(b) in relation to each subsequent order, the date of the previous order.
(7) An order under subsection (4) above—
(a) shall be made by statutory instrument subject to annulment in pursuance of a resolution of either House of Parliament and may be revoked by a subsequent order thereunder; and

(b) without prejudice to Schedule 14 to the Criminal Law Act 1977, shall not affect the punishment for an offence committed before that order comes into force.

(8) In this Act "the prescribed sum" means £5,000 or such sum as is for the time being substituted in this definition by an order in force under subsection (4) above.

DEFINITIONS
  "fine": s.307(1).
  "prescribed sum": s.225(8).
  "relevant date": s.225(4).
  "standard scale": s.225(1).

Penalties: exceptionally high maximum fines

226.—(1) The Secretary of State may by order amend an enactment specifying a sum to which this subsection applies so as to substitute for that sum such other sum as appears to him—
  (a) to be justified by a change in the value of money appearing to him to have taken place since the last occasion on which the sum in question was fixed; or
  (b) to be appropriate to take account of an order altering the standard scale which has been made or is proposed to be made.

(2) Subsection (1) above applies to any sum which—
  (a) is higher than level 5 on the standard scale; and
  (b) is specified as the fine or the maximum fine which may be imposed on conviction of an offence which is triable only summarily.

(3) The Secretary of State may by order amend an enactment specifying a sum to which this subsection applies so as to substitute for that sum such other sum as appears to him—
  (a) to be justified by a change in the value of money appearing to him to have taken place since the last occasion on which the sum in question was fixed; or
  (b) to be appropriate to take account of an order made or proposed to be made altering the statutory maximum.

(4) Subsection (3) above applies to any sum which—
  (a) is higher than the statutory maximum; and
  (b) is specified as the maximum fine which may be imposed on summary conviction of an offence triable either on indictment or summarily.

(5) An order under this section—
  (a) shall be made by statutory instrument subject to annulment in pursuance of a resolution of either House of Parliament; and
  (b) shall not affect the punishment for an offence committed before that order comes into force.

(6) In this section "enactment" includes an enactment contained in an Act or subordinate instrument passed or made after the commencement of this Act.

DEFINITIONS
  "enactment": s.226(6) and s.307(1).
  "fine": s.307(1).
  "standard scale": s.225(1).

Caution

Caution

227. Where a person is convicted on indictment of an offence (other than an offence the sentence for which is fixed by law) the court may, instead of or in addition to imposing a fine or a period of imprisonment, ordain the accused to find caution for good behaviour for a period not exceeding 12 months and to such amount as the court considers appropriate.

DEFINITIONS
"fine": s.307(1).
"impose imprisonment": s.307(1).
"indictment": s.307(1).
"offence": s.307(1).

Probation

Probation orders

228.—(1) Subject to subsection (2) below, where an accused is convicted of an offence (other than an offence the sentence for which is fixed by law) the court if it is of the opinion that it is expedient to do so—
  (a) having regard to the circumstances, including the nature of the offence and the character of the offender; and
  (b) having obtained a report as to the circumstances and character of the offender,
may, instead of sentencing him, make an order requiring the offender to be under supervision for a period to be specified in the order of not less than six months nor more than three years; and such an order is, in this Act, referred to as a "probation order".

(2) A court shall not make a probation order under subsection (1) above unless it is satisfied that suitable arrangements for the supervision of the offender can be made—
  (a) in a case other than that mentioned in paragraph (b) below, by the local authority in whose area he resides or is to reside; or
  (b) in a case where, by virtue of section 234(1) of this Act, subsections (3) and (4) below would not apply, by the probation committee for the area which contains the petty sessions area which would be named in the order.

(3) A probation order shall be as nearly as may be in the form prescribed by Act of Adjournal, and shall—
  (a) name the local authority area in which the offender resides or is to reside; and
  (b) subject to subsection (4) below, make provision for the offender to be under the supervision of an officer of the local authority of that area.

(4) Where the offender resides or is to reside in a local authority area in which the court which makes the order has no jurisdiction, the court shall name the appropriate court (being such a court as could have been named in any amendment of the order in accordance with Schedule 6 to this Act) in the area of residence or intended residence, and the appropriate court shall require the local authority for that area to arrange for the offender to be under the supervision of an officer of that authority.

(5) Before making a probation order, the court shall explain to the offender in ordinary language—
  (a) the effect of the order, including any additional requirements proposed to be inserted under section 229 or 230 of this Act; and
  (b) that if he fails to comply with the order or commits another offence during the probation period he will be liable to be sentenced for the original offence,
and the court shall not make the order unless the offender expresses his willingness to comply with the requirements thereof.

(6) The clerk of the court by which a probation order is made or of the appropriate court, as the case may be, shall—
  (a) cause copies of the probation order to be given to the officer of the local authority who is to supervise the probationer and to the person in

charge of any institution or place in which the probationer is required to reside under the probation order; and
(b) cause a copy thereof to be given to the probationer or sent to him by registered post or by the recorded delivery service; and an acknowledgement or certificate of delivery of a letter containing such copy order issued by the Post Office shall be sufficient evidence of the delivery of the letter on the day specified in such acknowledgement or certificate.

DEFINITIONS
"local authority": s.307(1).
"offence": s.307(1).
"probation order": s.228(1).

GENERAL NOTE
In *Downie v. Irvine*, 1964 J.C. 52 it was held that a probation order and a sentence of imprisonment were wholly inconsistent and could not stand together.

Probation orders: additional requirements

229.—(1) Subject to section 230 of this Act, a probation order may require the offender to comply during the whole or any part of the probation period with such requirements as the court, having regard to the circumstances of the case, considers—
(a) conducive to securing the good conduct of the offender or for preventing a repetition by him of the offence or the commission of other offences; or
(b) where the probation order is to include such a requirement as is mentioned in subsection (4) or (6) below, conducive to securing or, as the case may be, preventing the matters mentioned in paragraph (a) above.
(2) Without prejudice to the generality of subsection (1) above, a probation order may, subject to subsection (3) below, include requirements relating to the residence of the offender.
(3) In relation to a probation order including a requirement such as is mentioned in subsection (2) above—
(a) before making the order, the court shall consider the home surroundings of the offender; and
(b) if the order requires the offender to reside in any institution or place, the name of the institution or place and the period for which he is so required to reside shall be specified in the order, and that period shall not extend beyond 12 months from the date of the requirement or beyond the date when the order expires.
(4) Without prejudice to the generality of subsection (1) above, where an offender has been convicted of an offence punishable by imprisonment and a court which is considering making a probation order—
(a) is satisfied that the offender is of or over 16 years of age and that the conditions specified in paragraphs (a) and (c) of section 238(2) of this Act for the making of a community service order have been met;
(b) has been notified by the Secretary of State that arrangements exist for persons who reside in the locality where the offender resides, or will be residing when the probation order comes into force, to perform unpaid work as a requirement of a probation order; and
(c) is satisfied that provision can be made under the arrangements mentioned in paragraph (b) above for the offender to perform unpaid work under the probation order,
it may include in the probation order, in addition to any other requirement, a requirement that the offender shall perform unpaid work for such number of

hours (being in total not less than 40 nor more than 240) as may be specified in the probation order.

(5) Sections 238 (except subsections (1), (2)(b) and (d) and (4)(b)), 239(1) to (3), and 240 of this Act shall apply, subject to any necessary modifications, to a probation order including a requirement such as is mentioned in subsection (4) above as they apply to a community service order, and in the application of subsection (5) of the said section 238 for the words "subsection (1) above" there shall be substituted the words "subsection (4) of section 229 of this Act".

(6) Without prejudice to the generality of subsection (1) above, where a court is considering making a probation order it may include in the probation order, in addition to any other requirement, a requirement that the offender shall pay compensation either in a lump sum or by instalments for any personal injury, loss or damage caused (whether directly or indirectly) by the acts which constituted the offence; and the following provisions of this Act shall apply to such a requirement as if any reference in them to a compensation order included a reference to a requirement to pay compensation under this subsection—

    section 249(3) to (5), (8) to (10);
    section 250(2);
    section 251(1) and (2)(b);
    section 253.

(7) Where the court imposes a requirement to pay compensation under subsection (6) above—

(a) it shall be a condition of a probation order containing such a requirement that payment of the compensation shall be completed not more than 18 months after the making of the order or not later than two months before the end of the period of probation, whichever first occurs;

(b) the court, on the application of the offender or the officer of the local authority responsible for supervising the offender, may vary the terms of the requirement, including the amount of any instalments, in consequence of any change which may have occurred in the circumstances of the offender; and

(c) in any proceedings for breach of a probation order where the breach consists only in the failure to comply with a requirement to pay compensation, a document purporting to be a certificate signed by the clerk of the court for the time being having jurisdiction in relation to the order that the compensation or, where payment by instalments has been allowed, any instalment has not been paid shall be sufficient evidence of such breach.

DEFINITIONS
   "compensation": s.229(6).
   "offence": s.307(1).
   "probation order": s.228(1).

Probation orders: requirement of treatment for mental condition

230.—(1) Where the court is satisfied, on the evidence of a registered medical practitioner approved for the purposes of section 20 or 39 of the Mental Health (Scotland) Act 1984, that the mental condition of an offender is such as requires and may be susceptible to treatment but is not such as to warrant his detention in pursuance of a hospital order under Part V of that Act, or under this Act, the court may, if it makes a probation order, include a requirement that the offender shall submit, for such period, not extending beyond 12 months from the date of the requirement, as may be specified in the order, to treatment by or under the direction of a registered medical practitioner or chartered psychologist with a view to the improvement of the offender's mental condition.

(2) The treatment required by virtue of subsection (1) above shall be such one of the following kinds of treatment as may be specified in the order, that is to say—

 (a) treatment as a resident patient in a hospital within the meaning of the said Act of 1984, not being a State hospital within the meaning of the Act;

 (b) treatment as a non-resident patient at such institution or place as may be specified in the order; or

 (c) treatment by or under the direction of such registered medical practitioner or chartered psychologist as may be specified in the order,

but otherwise the nature of the treatment shall not be specified in the order.

(3) A court shall not make a probation order containing a requirement under subsection (1) above unless it is satisfied that arrangements have been made for the treatment intended to be specified in the order, and, if the offender is to be treated as a resident patient, for his reception.

(4) Where the registered medical practitioner or chartered psychologist by whom or under whose direction a probationer is receiving any of the kinds of treatment to which he is required to submit in pursuance of a probation order is of the opinion—

 (a) that the probationer requires, or that it would be more appropriate for him to receive, a different kind of treatment (whether in whole or in part) from that which he has been receiving, being treatment of a kind which subject to subsection (5) below could have been specified in the probation order; or

 (b) that the treatment (whether in whole or in part) can be more appropriately given in or at a different institution or place from that where he has been receiving treatment in pursuance of the probation order,

he may, subject to subsection (6) below, make arrangements for the probationer to be treated accordingly.

(5) Arrangements made under subsection (4) above may provide for the probationer to receive his treatment (in whole or in part) as a resident patient in an institution or place notwithstanding that it is not one which could have been specified for that purpose in the probation order.

(6) Arrangements shall not be made under subsection (4) above unless—

 (a) the probationer and any officer responsible for his supervision agree;

 (b) the treatment will be given by or under the direction of a registered medical practitioner or chartered psychologist who has agreed to accept the probationer as his patient; and

 (c) where such treatment entails the probationer's being a resident patient, he will be received as such.

(7) Where any such arrangements as are mentioned in subsection (4) above are made for the treatment of a probationer—

 (a) any officer responsible for the probationer's supervision shall notify the appropriate court of the arrangements; and

 (b) the treatment provided for by the arrangements shall be deemed to be treatment to which he is required to submit in pursuance of the probation order.

(8) Subsections (3) to (5) of section 61 of this Act shall apply for the purposes of this section as if for the reference in subsection (3) to section 58(1)(a) of this Act there were substituted a reference to subsection (1) above.

(9) Except as provided by this section, a court shall not make a probation order requiring a probationer to submit to treatment for his mental condition.

DEFINITIONS
  "chartered psychologist": s.307(1).
  "hospital": s.307(1).
  "probation order": s.228(1).
  "registered medical practitioner": s.2 of the Medicine Act 1968.
  "State hospital": s.307(1).

Probation orders: amendment and discharge

231.—(1) Schedule 6 to this Act shall have effect in relation to the discharge and amendment of probation orders.

(2) Where, under section 232 of this Act, a probationer is sentenced for the offence for which he was placed on probation, the probation order shall cease to have effect.

DEFINITIONS
  "probation order": s.228(1).

Probation orders: failure to comply with requirement

232.—(1) If, on information from—

(a) the officer supervising the probationer;

(b) the chief social work officer of the local authority whose officer is supervising the probationer; or

(c) an officer appointed by the chief social work officer to act on his behalf for the purposes of this subsection,

it appears to the court which made the probation order or to the appropriate court that the probationer has failed to comply with any requirement of the order, that court may issue a warrant for the arrest of the probationer, or may, if it thinks fit, instead of issuing such a warrant in the first instance, issue a citation requiring the probationer to appear before the court at such time as may be specified in the citation.

(2) If it is proved to the satisfaction of the court before which a probationer appears or is brought in pursuance of subsection (1) above that he has failed to comply with a requirement of the probation order, the court may—

(a) except in the case of a failure to comply with a requirement to pay compensation and without prejudice to the continuance in force of the probation order, impose a fine not exceeding level 3 on the standard scale; or

(b) sentence the offender for the offence for which the order was made; or

(c) vary any of the requirements of the probation order, so however that any extension of the probation period shall terminate not later than three years from the date of the probation order; or

(d) without prejudice to the continuance in force of the probation order, in a case where the conditions required by sections 238 to 244 of this Act are satisfied, make a community service order, and those sections shall apply to such an order as if the failure to comply with the requirement of the probation order were the offence in respect of which the order had been made.

(3) For the purposes of subsection (2) above, evidence of one witness shall be sufficient evidence.

(4) A fine imposed under this section in respect of a failure to comply with the requirements of a probation order shall be deemed for the purposes of any enactment to be a sum adjudged to be paid by or in respect of a conviction or a penalty imposed on a person summarily convicted.

(5) A probationer who is required by a probation order to submit to treatment for his mental condition shall not be deemed for the purpose of this section to have failed to comply with that requirement on the ground only

that he has refused to undergo any surgical, electrical or other treatment if, in the opinion of the court, his refusal was reasonable having regard to all the circumstances.

(6) Without prejudice to section 233 of this Act, a probationer who is convicted of an offence committed during the probation period shall not on that account be liable to be dealt with under this section for failing to comply with any requirement of the probation order.

(7) The citation of a probationer to appear before a court of summary jurisdiction in terms of subsection (1) above or section 233(1) of this Act shall be effected in like manner, *mutatis mutandis*, as the citation of an accused to a sitting or diet of the court under section 141 of this Act.

DEFINITIONS
"community service order": s.307(1).
"court of summary jurisdiction": s.307(1).
"fine": s.307(1).
"local authority": s.307(1).
"probation order": s.228(1).
"probationer": s.307(1).
"sentence": s.307(1).
"standard scale": s.225(1).

Probation orders: commission of further offence

233.—(1) If it appears to—
(a) the court which made a probation order; or, as the case may be,
(b) the appropriate court,
in this section referred to as "the court", that the probationer to whom the order relates has been convicted by a court in any part of Great Britain of an offence committed during the probation period and has been dealt with for that offence, the court may issue a warrant for the arrest of the probationer, or may, if it thinks fit, instead of issuing such a warrant in the first instance issue a citation requiring the probationer to appear before the court at such time as may be specified in the citation, and on his appearance or on his being brought before the court, the court may, if it thinks fit, deal with him under section 232(2)(b) of this Act.

(2) Where a probationer is convicted by the court of an offence committed during the probation period, the court may, if it thinks fit, deal with him under section 232(2)(b) of this Act for the offence for which the order was made as well as for the offence committed during the period of probation.

(3) Where—
(a) a court has, under section 229(4) of this Act, included in a probation order a requirement that an offender shall perform unpaid work; and
(b) the offender is convicted of an offence committed in the circumstances mentioned in subsection (4) below,
the court which sentences him for the offence shall, in determining the appropriate sentence for that offence, have regard to the fact that the offence was committed in those circumstances.

(4) The circumstances referred to in subsection (3) above are that the offence was committed—
(a) during the period that the offender was subject to a requirement to perform unpaid work or within the period of three months following the expiry of that period; and
(b) in any place where the unpaid work was being or had previously been performed.

(5) The court shall not, under subsection (3) above, have regard to the fact that the offence was committed in the circumstances mentioned in subsection (4) above unless that fact is libelled in the indictment or, as the case may be, specified in the complaint.

Definitions
  "complaint": s.307(1).
  "indictment": s.307(1).
  "probation order": s.228(1).
  "probationer": s.307(1).

Probation orders: persons residing in England and Wales

234.—(1) Where the court which made a probation order to which this subsection applies is satisfied that the offender has attained the age of 16 years and resides or will reside in England and Wales, subsections (3) and (4) of section 228 of this Act shall not apply to the order, but—

(a) the order shall contain a requirement that he be under the supervision of a probation officer appointed for or assigned to the petty sessions area in which the offender resides or will reside; and

(b) that area shall be named in the order,

and where the order includes a requirement that the probationer performs unpaid work for a number of hours, the number specified shall not exceed one hundred.

(2) Subsection (1) above applies to a probation order which is made under the said section 228 but does not include a requirement which would, if made, correspond to a requirement mentioned in paragraph 2 or 3 of Schedule 1A to the 1973 Act, but would, if included in a probation order made under that Act, fail to accord with a restriction as to days of presentation, participation or attendance mentioned in paragraph 2(4)(a) or (6)(a), or as the case may be 3(3)(a), of that Schedule.

(3) Where a probation order has been made under the said section 228 and the court in Scotland which made the order or the appropriate court is satisfied—

(a) that the probationer has attained the age of 16 years;

(b) that he proposes to reside, or is residing, in England and Wales; and

(c) that suitable arrangements for his supervision can be made by the probation committee for the area which contains the petty sessions area in which he resides or will reside,

the power of that court to amend the order under Schedule 6 to this Act shall include power to insert the provisions required by subsection (1) above or to vary any requirement for performance of unpaid work so that such hours as remain to be worked do not exceed one hundred, and the court may so amend the order without summoning the probationer and without his consent.

(4) A probation order made or amended by virtue of this section may, notwithstanding section 230(9) of this Act, include a requirement that the probationer shall submit to treatment for his mental condition, and—

(a) subsections (1), (3) and (8) of the said section 230 and paragraph 5(3) of Schedule 1A to the 1973 Act (all of which regulate the making of probation orders which include any such requirement) shall apply to the making of an order which includes any such requirement by virtue of this subsection as they apply to the making of an order which includes any such requirement by virtue of the said section 230 and paragraph 5 of the said Schedule 1A respectively; and

(b) sub-paragraphs (5) to (7) of the said paragraph 5 (functions of supervising officer and registered medical practitioner where such a requirement has been imposed) shall apply in relation to a probationer who is undergoing treatment in England and Wales in pursuance of a requirement imposed by virtue of this subsection as they apply in relation to a probationer undergoing such treatment in pursuance of a requirement imposed by virtue of that section.

(5) Sections 231(1) and 232(1) of this Act shall not apply to any order made or amended under this section; but subject to subsection (6) below, Schedule 2 to the 1991 Act shall apply to the order—

(a) except in the case mentioned in paragraph (b) below, as if that order were a probation order made under section 2 of the 1973 Act; and

(b) in the case of an order which contains a requirement such as is mentioned in section 229(4) of this Act, as if it were a combination order made under section 11 of the 1991 Act.

(6) Part III of Schedule 2 to the 1991 Act shall not apply as mentioned in subsection (5) above; and sub-paragraphs (3) and (4) of paragraph 3 of that Schedule shall so apply as if for the first reference in the said sub-paragraph (3) to the Crown Court there were substituted a reference to a court in Scotland and for other references in those sub-paragraphs to the Crown Court there were substituted references to the court in Scotland.

(7) If it appears on information to a justice acting for the petty sessions area named in a probation order made or amended under this section that the person to whom the order relates has been convicted by a court in any part of Great Britain of an offence committed during the period specified in the order he may issue—

(a) a summons requiring that person to appear, at the place and time specified in the summons, before the court in Scotland which made the probation order; or

(b) if the information is in writing and on oath, a warrant for his arrest, directing that person to be brought before the last-mentioned court.

(8) If a warrant for the arrest of a probationer issued under section 233 of this Act by a court is executed in England and Wales and the probationer cannot forthwith be brought before that court, the warrant shall have effect as if it directed him to be brought before a magistrates' court for the place where he is arrested; and the magistrates' court shall commit him to custody or release him on bail (with or without sureties) until he can be brought or appear before the court in Scotland.

(9) The court by which a probation order is made or amended in accordance with the provisions of this section shall send three copies of the order to the clerk to the justices for the petty sessions area named in the order, together with such documents and information relating to the case as it considers likely to be of assistance to the court acting for that petty sessions area.

(10) Where a probation order which is amended under subsection (3) above is an order to which the provisions of this Act apply by virtue of section 10 of the 1973 Act (which relates to probation orders under that Act relating to persons residing in Scotland) then, notwithstanding anything in that section or this section, the order shall, as from the date of the amendment, have effect in all respects as if it were an order made under section 2 of that Act in the case of a person residing in England and Wales.

(11) In this section—

"the 1973 Act" means the Powers of Criminal Courts Act 1973; and
"the 1991 Act" means the Criminal Justice Act 1991.

DEFINITIONS
"probation order": s.307(1).
"probationer": s.307(1).

Supervised attendance

Supervised attendance orders

235.—(1) A court may make a supervised attendance order in the circumstances specified in subsection (3) below and shall, subject to paragraph 1 of Schedule 7 to this Act, make such an order where subsection (4) below applies.

(2) A supervised attendance order is an order made by a court in respect of an offender requiring him—

(a) to attend a place of supervision for such period, being a period of not less than 10 hours and not more than—

(i) where the amount of the fine, part or instalment which the offender has failed to pay does not exceed level 1 on the standard scale, 50 hours; and

(ii) in any other case, 100 hours, as is specified in the order; and

(b) during that period, to carry out such instructions as may be given to him by the supervising officer.

(3) The circumstances referred to in subsection (1) above are where—

(a) the offender is of or over 18 years of age; and

(b) having been convicted of an offence, he has had imposed on him a fine which (or any part or instalment of which) he has failed to pay and the court, but for this section, would also have imposed on him a period of imprisonment under subsection (1) of section 219 of this Act; and

(c) the court considers a supervised attendance order more appropriate than the serving of or, as the case may be, imposition of such a period of imprisonment.

(4) This subsection applies where—

(a) the court is a court prescribed for the purposes of this subsection by order made by the Secretary of State;

(b) the offender is of or over 18 years of age and is not serving a sentence of imprisonment;

(c) having been convicted of an offence, he has had imposed on him a fine which (or any part or instalment of which) he has failed to pay and the court, but for this section, would have imposed on him a period of imprisonment under section 219(1)(b) of this Act; and

(d) the fine, or as the case may be, the part or instalment, is of an amount not exceeding level 2 on the standard scale.

(5) An order under subsection (4)(a) above shall be made by statutory instrument, which shall be subject to annulment in pursuance of a resolution of either House of Parliament.

(6) The coming into force of a supervised attendance order shall have the effect of discharging the fine referred to in subsection (3)(b) or (4)(c) above or, as the case may be, section 236(3)(a) or 237(1) of this Act.

(7) Schedule 7 to this Act has effect for the purpose of making further and qualifying provision as to supervised attendance orders.

(8) In this section—

"imprisonment" includes detention;

"place of supervision" means such place as may be determined for the purposes of a supervised attendance order by the supervising officer; and

"supervising officer", in relation to a supervised attendance order, means a person appointed or assigned under Schedule 7 to this Act by the local authority whose area includes the locality in which the offender resides or will be residing when the order comes into force.

DEFINITIONS

"appropriate court": Sched. 7, para. 8.

"imprisonment": s.235(8).

"place of supervision": s.235(8).

"standard scale": s.225(1).

"supervised attendance order": s.235(2).

"supervising officer": s.235(8).

Section 62 of, and Sched. 6 to, the 1990 Act introduced supervised attendance orders ("SAOs") as an alternative to imprisonment for fine default. Under the provisions of the 1990 Act a court, with the consent of the offender, may impose an SAO where it would otherwise have imposed a term of imprisonment for fine default and where it has been notified by the Secretary of State that the appropriate arrangements exist in the area where the offender resides.

This provision extends the existing arrangements to provide that SAOs may be used as an alternative to, or replacement for, imprisonment for fine default. Under this section a court prescribed by the Secretary of State would be required to make an SAO for failure to pay a fine of less than the equivalent of level two on the standard scale (at present, £500: see s.225(2)) instead of imposing a period of imprisonment. The consent of the offender would no longer be required.

Supervised attendance orders in place of fines for 16 and 17 year olds

236.—(1) This section applies where a person of 16 or 17 years of age is convicted of an offence by a court of summary jurisdiction and the court considers that, but for this section, the appropriate sentence is a fine.

(2) Where this section applies, the court shall determine the amount of the fine and shall consider whether the person is likely to pay a fine of that amount within 28 days.

(3) If the court considers that the person is likely to pay the fine as mentioned in subsection (2) above, it shall—

(a) impose the fine; and

(b) subject to paragraph 1 of Schedule 7 to this Act, make a supervised attendance order in default of payment of the fine within 28 days.

(4) A supervised attendance order made under subsection (3)(b) above—

(a) shall come into force on such date, not earlier than 28 days after the making of the order, as may be specified in the order, unless the person pays the fine within that period;

(b) shall, for the purposes of the said Schedule 7, be deemed to be made on the date when it comes into force.

(5) Where, before the coming into force of a supervised attendance order made under subsection (3)(b) above, the person pays part of the fine, the period specified in the order shall be reduced by the proportion which the part of the fine paid bears to the whole fine, the resulting figure being rounded up or down to the nearest 10 hours; but this subsection shall not operate to reduce the period to less than 10 hours.

(6) If the court considers that the person is not likely to pay the fine as mentioned in subsection (2) above, it shall, subject to paragraph 1 of Schedule 7 to this Act, make a supervised attendance order in respect of that person.

(7) Sections 211(3), 213, 214(1) to (7), 215, 216(1) to (6), 217 to 219, 222 and 223 of this Act shall not apply in respect of a person to whom this section applies.

(8) For the purposes of any appeal or review, a supervised attendance order made under this section is a sentence.

(9) In this section "supervised attendance order" means an order made in accordance with section 235(2), (7) and (8) of this Act.

"court of summary jurisdiction": s.307(1).
"fine": s.307(1).
"sentence": s.307(1).
"supervised attendance order": s.235(2).

This section extends the use of SAOs as respects 16 and 17 year olds as a replacement for a sentence of a fine.

Supervised attendance orders where court allows further time to pay fine

237.—(1) Where a court, on an application to it under section 215(1) of this Act, allows a person further time for payment of a fine or instalments thereof it may, in addition, subject to paragraph 1 of Schedule 7 to this Act, impose a supervised attendance order in default of payment of the fine or any instalment of it on the due date.

(2) A supervised attendance order made under subsection (1) above shall—

(a) if the person fails to pay the fine or any instalment of it on the due date, come into force on the day after the due date; and

(b) for the purposes of the said Schedule 7, be deemed to be made on the date when it comes into force.

(3) Where, before the coming into force of a supervised attendance order under subsection (1) above, the person pays part of the fine, the period specified in the order shall be reduced by the proportion which the part of the fine paid bears to the whole fine, the resulting figure being rounded up or down to the nearest 10 hours; but this subsection shall not operate to reduce the period to less than 10 hours.

(4) In this section "supervised attendance order" means an order made in accordance with section 235(2), (7) and (8) of this Act.

DEFINITIONS
"fine": s.307(1).
"offence": s.307(1).
"sentence": s.307(1).
"supervised attendance order": s.235(2).

Community service by offenders

Community service orders

238.—(1) Subject to the provisions of this Act, where a person of or over 16 years of age is convicted of an offence punishable by imprisonment, other than an offence the sentence for which is fixed by law, the court may, instead of imposing on him a sentence of, or including, imprisonment or any other form of detention, make an order (in this Act referred to as "a community service order") requiring him to perform unpaid work for such number of hours (being in total not less than 40 nor more than 240) as may be specified in the order.

(2) A court shall not make a community service order in respect of any offender unless—

(a) the offender consents;

(b) the court has been notified by the Secretary of State that arrangements exist for persons who reside in the locality in which the offender resides, or will be residing when the order comes into force, to perform work under such an order;

(c) the court is satisfied, after considering a report by an officer of a local authority about the offender and his circumstances, and, if the court thinks it necessary, hearing that officer, that the offender is a suitable person to perform work under such an order; and

(d) the court is satisfied that provision can be made under the arrangements mentioned in paragraph (b) above for the offender to perform work under such an order.

(3) A copy of the report mentioned in subsection (2)(c) above shall be supplied to the offender or his solicitor.

(4) Before making a community service order the court shall explain to the offender in ordinary language—

  (a) the purpose and effect of the order and in particular the obligations on the offender as specified in subsections (1) to (3) of section 239 of this Act;

  (b) the consequences which may follow under subsections (4) to (6) of that section if he fails to comply with any of those requirements; and

  (c) that the court has under section 240 of this Act the power to review the order on the application either of the offender or of an officer of the local authority in whose area the offender for the time being resides.

(5) The Secretary of State may by order direct that subsection (1) above shall be amended by substituting, for the maximum or minimum number of hours specified in that subsection as originally enacted or as subsequently amended under this subsection, such number of hours as may be specified in the order; and an order under this subsection may specify a different maximum or minimum number of hours for different classes of case.

(6) An order under subsection (5) above shall be made by statutory instrument, but no such order shall be made unless a draft of it has been laid before, and approved by a resolution of, each House of Parliament; and any such order may be varied or revoked by a subsequent order under that subsection.

(7) Nothing in subsection (1) above shall be construed as preventing a court which makes a community service in respect of any offence from—

  (a) imposing any disqualification on the offender;

  (b) making an order for forfeiture in respect of the offence;

  (c) ordering the offender to find caution for good behaviour.

(8) A community service order shall—

  (a) specify the locality in which the offender resides or will be residing when the order comes into force;

  (b) require the local authority in whose area the locality specified under paragraph (a) above is situated to appoint or assign an officer (referred to in this section and sections 239 to 245 of this Act as "the local authority officer") who will discharge the functions assigned to him by those sections; and

  (c) state the number of hours of work which the offender is required to perform.

(9) Where, whether on the same occasion or on separate occasions, an offender is made subject to more than one community service order, or to both a community service order and a probation order which includes a requirement that that offender shall perform any unpaid work, the court may direct that the hours of work specified in any of those orders shall be concurrent with or additional to those specified in any other of those orders, but so that at no time shall the offender have an outstanding number of hours of work to perform in excess of the maximum provided for in subsection (1) above.

(10) Upon making a community service order the court shall—

  (a) give, or send by registered post or the recorded delivery service, a copy of the order to the offender;

  (b) send a copy of the order to the chief social work officer of the local authority in whose area the offender resides or will be residing where the order comes into force; and

  (c) where it is not the appropriate court, send a copy of the order (together with such documents and information relating to the case as are considered useful) to the clerk of the appropriate court.

(11) Where a copy of a community service order has, under subsection (10)(a) above, been sent by registered post or by the recorded delivery service, an acknowledgement or certificate of delivery of a letter containing the copy order issued by the Post Office shall be sufficient evidence of the delivery of the letter on the day specified in such acknowledgement or certificate.

DEFINITIONS
"caution": s.227.
"local authority": s.307(1).
"local authority officer": s.238(8)(b).
"offence": s.307(1).
"sentence": s.307(1).

Community service orders: requirements

239.—(1) An offender in respect of whom a community service order is in force shall—
(a) report to the local authority officer and notify him without delay of any change of address or in the times, if any, at which he usually works; and
(b) perform for the number of hours specified in the order such work at such times as the local authority officer may instruct.

(2) Subject to section 240(1) of this Act, the work required to be performed under a community service order shall be performed during the period of 12 months beginning with the date of the order; but, unless revoked, the order shall remain in force until the offender has worked under it for the number of hours specified in it.

(3) The instructions given by the local authority officer under this section shall, so far as practicable, be such as to avoid any conflict with the offender's religious beliefs and any interference with the times, if any, at which he normally works or attends a school or other educational establishment.

(4) If at any time while a community service order is in force in respect of any offender it appears to the appropriate court, on information from the local authority officer, that that offender has failed to comply with any of the requirements of subsections (1) to (3) above (including any failure satisfactorily to perform the work which he has been instructed to do), that court may issue a warrant for the arrest of that offender, or may, if it thinks fit, instead of issuing a warrant in the first instance issue a citation requiring that offender to appear before that court at such time as may be specified in the citation.

(5) If it is proved to the satisfaction of the court before which an offender appears or is brought in pursuance of subsection (4) above that he has failed without reasonable excuse to comply with any of the requirements of the said subsections (1) to (3), that court may—
(a) without prejudice to the continuance in force of the order, impose on him a fine not exceeding level 3 on the standard scale;
(b) revoke the order and deal with that offender in any manner in which he could have been dealt with for the original offence by the court which made the order if the order had not been made; or
(c) subject to section 238(1) of this Act, vary the number of hours specified in the order.

(6) The evidence of one witness shall, for the purposes of subsection (5) above, be sufficient evidence.

DEFINITIONS
"community service order": s.238(1).
"local authority officer": s.238(8)(b).
"standard scale": s.225(2).

Community service orders: amendment and revocation etc.

240.—(1) Where a community service order is in force in respect of any offender and, on the application of that offender or of the local authority officer, it appears to the appropriate court that it would be in the interests of justice to do so having regard to circumstances which have arisen since the order was made, that court may—

(a) extend, in relation to the order, the period of 12 months specified in section 239(2) of this Act;

(b) subject to section 238(1) of this Act, vary the number of hours specified in the order;

(c) revoke the order; or

(d) revoke the order and deal with the offender for the original offence in any manner in which he could have been dealt with for that offence by the court which made the order if the order had not been made.

(2) If the appropriate court is satisfied that the offender proposes to change, or has changed, his residence from the locality for the time being specified under section 238(8)(a) of this Act to another locality and—

(a) that court has been notified by the Secretary of State that arrangements exist for persons who reside in that other locality to perform work under community service orders; and

(b) it appears to that court that provision can be made under those arrangements for him to perform work under the order,

that court may, and on the application of the local authority officer shall, amend the order by substituting that other locality for the locality for the time being specified in the order; and sections 238 to 245 of this Act shall apply to the order as amended.

(3) Where the court proposes to exercise its powers under subsection (1)(a), (b) or (d) above otherwise than on the application of the offender, it shall issue a citation requiring him to appear before the court and, if he fails to appear, may issue a warrant for his arrest.

DEFINITIONS

"community service order": s.238(1).
"local authority officer": s.228(8)(b).

Community service order: commission of offence while order in force

241.—(1) Where—

(a) a court has made a community service order in respect of an offender; and

(b) the offender is convicted of an offence committed in the circumstances mentioned in subsection (2) below,

the court which sentences him for that offence shall, in determining the appropriate sentence for that offence, have regard to the fact that the offence was committed in those circumstances.

(2) The circumstances referred to in subsection (1) above are that the offence was committed—

(a) during the period when the community service order was in force or within the period of three months following the expiry of that order; and

(b) in any place where unpaid work under the order was being or had previously been performed.

(3) The court shall not, under subsection (1) above, have regard to the fact that the offence was committed in the circumstances mentioned in subsection (2) above unless that fact is libelled in the indictment or, as the case may be, specified in the complaint.

DEFINITIONS

"community service order": s.238(1).
"complaint": s.307(1).
"indictment": s.307(1).
"offence": s.307(1).

GENERAL NOTE
It seems a clear inference from the terms of this section that if an offence should be committed by an individual then performing unpaid work under a community service order at a relevant place, then that is an aggravation for the purposes of sentence. The court can only have regard to these facts if they have been libelled by the Crown: see subs. (3). However, reference to a community service order in the libel of a charge in itself implies previous convictions and may thus contravene ss.101(1) and 166(3) of this Act.

It would seem that for a court to have regard to the accused's behaviour in relation to this statutory aggravation the Crown will require to be particularly circumspect in drafting the charge or place the single charge on a separate indictment or complaint if there are several charges.

Community service orders: persons residing in England and Wales

242.—(1) Where a court is considering the making of a community service order and it is satisfied that the offender has attained the age of 16 years and resides, or will be residing when the order comes into force, in England or Wales, then—
> (a) section 238 of this Act shall have effect as if subsection (2) were amended as follows—
>> (i) paragraph (b) shall be omitted;
>> (ii) in paragraph (c) for the words "such an order" there shall be substituted the words "a community service order"; and
>> (iii) for paragraph (d) there shall be substituted the following paragraph—
>>> "(d) it appears to that court that provision can be made for the offender to perform work under the order made under subsection (1) above under the arrangements which exist in the petty sessions area in which he resides or will be residing for persons to perform work under community service orders made under section 14 of the Powers of Criminal Courts Act 1973;"; and
> (b) the order shall specify that the unpaid work required to be performed by the order shall be performed under the arrangements mentioned in section 238(2)(d) of this Act as substituted by paragraph (a) above.

(2) Where a community service order has been made and—
> (a) the appropriate court is satisfied that the offender has attained the age of 16 years and proposes to reside or is residing in England or Wales; and
> (b) it appears to that court that provision can be made for the offender to perform work under the order made under the arrangements which exist in the petty sessions area in which he proposes to reside or is residing for persons to perform work under community service orders made under section 14 of the Powers of Criminal Courts Act 1973,

it may amend the order by specifying that the unpaid work required to be performed by the order shall be performed under the arrangements mentioned in paragraph (b) of this subsection.

(3) A community service order made under section 238(1) as amended by or in accordance with this section shall—
> (a) specify the petty sessions area in England or Wales in which the offender resides or will be residing when the order or the amendment comes into force; and
> (b) require the probation committee for that area to appoint or assign a probation officer who will discharge in respect of the order the functions in respect of community service orders conferred on relevant officers by the Powers of Criminal Courts Act 1973.

"community service order": s.238(1).

Community service orders: persons residing in Northern Ireland

243.—(1) Where a court is considering the making of a community service order and it is satisfied that the offender resides, or will be residing when the order comes into force, in Northern Ireland, then—

(a) section 238 of this Act shall have effect as if subsection (2) were amended as follows—

    (i) paragraph (b) shall be omitted;

    (ii) for paragraph (d) there shall be substituted the following paragraph—

      "(d) it appears to the court that provision can be made by the Probation Board for Northern Ireland for him to perform work under such an order;";

(b) the order shall specify that the unpaid work required to be performed by the order shall be performed under the provision made by the Probation Board for Northern Ireland and referred to in section 238(2)(d) of this Act as substituted by paragraph (a) above.

(2) Where a community service order has been made and—

(a) the appropriate court is satisfied that the offender proposes to reside or is residing in Northern Ireland; and

(b) it appears to that court that provision can be made by the Probation Board for Northern Ireland for him to perform work under the order,

it may amend the order by specifying that the unpaid work required to be performed by the order shall be performed under the provision made by the Probation Board for Northern Ireland and referred to in paragraph (b) of this subsection.

(3) A community service order made under section 238(1) of this Act as amended by or in accordance with this section shall—

(a) specify the petty sessions district in Northern Ireland in which the offender resides or will be residing when the order or the amendment comes into force; and

(b) require the Probation Board for Northern Ireland to select an officer who will discharge in respect of the order the functions in respect of community service orders conferred on the relevant officer by the Treatment of Offenders (Northern Ireland) Order 1976.

"community service order": s.238(1).

Community service orders: general provisions relating to persons living in England and Wales or Northern Ireland

244.—(1) Where a community service order is made or amended in the circumstances specified in section 242 or 243 of this Act, the court which makes or amends the order shall send three copies of it as made or amended to the home court, together with such documents and information relating to the case as it considers likely to be of assistance to that court.

(2) In this section—

"home court" means—

    (a) if the offender resides in England or Wales, or will be residing in England or Wales at the relevant time, the magistrates' court acting for the petty sessions area in which he resides or proposes to reside; and

    (b) if he resides in Northern Ireland, or will be residing in Northern Ireland, at the relevant time, the court of summary jurisdiction acting for the petty sessions district in which he resides or proposes to reside; and

"the relevant time" means the time when the order or the amendment to it comes into force.

(3) A community service order made or amended in the circumstances specified in section 242 or 243 of this Act shall be treated, subject to the following provisions of this section, as if it were a community service order made in the part of the United Kingdom in which the offender resides, or will be residing at the relevant time; and the legislation relating to community service orders which has effect in that part of the United Kingdom shall apply accordingly.

(4) Before making or amending a community service order in those circumstances the court shall explain to the offender in ordinary language—

(a) the requirements of the legislation relating to community service orders which has effect in the part of the United Kingdom in which he resides or will be residing at the relevant time;

(b) the powers of the home court under that legislation, as modified by this section; and

(c) its own powers under this section,

and an explanation given in accordance with this section shall be sufficient without the addition of an explanation under section 238(4) of this Act.

(5) The home court may exercise in relation to the community service order any power which it could exercise in relation to a community service order made by a court in the part of the United Kingdom in which the home court exercises jurisdiction, by virtue of the legislation relating to such orders which has effect in that part of the United Kingdom, except—

(a) a power to vary the order by substituting for the number of hours' work specified in it any greater number than the court which made the order could have specified;

(b) a power to revoke the order; and

(c) a power to revoke the order and deal with the offender for the offence in respect of which it was made in any manner in which he could have been dealt with for that offence by the court which made the order if the order had not been made.

(6) If at any time while legislation relating to community service orders which has effect in one part of the United Kingdom applies by virtue of subsection (3) above to a community service order made in another part—

(a) it appears to the home court—

    (i) if that court is in England or Wales, on information to a justice of the peace acting for the petty sessions area for the time being specified in the order; or

    (ii) if it is in Northern Ireland, upon a complaint being made to a justice of the peace acting for the petty sessions district for the time being specified in the order,

that the offender has failed to comply with any of the requirements of the legislation applicable to the order; or

(b) it appears to the home court on the application of—

    (i) the offender; or

    (ii) if that court is in England and Wales, the relevant officer under the Powers of Criminal Courts Act 1973; or

    (iii) if that court is in Northern Ireland, the relevant officer under the Treatment of Offenders (Northern Ireland) Order 1976,

that it would be in the interests of justice to exercise a power mentioned in subsection (5)(b) or (c) above,

the home court may require the offender to appear before the court by which the order was made.

(7) Where an offender is required by virtue of subsection (6) above to appear before the court which made a community service order, that court—

(a) may issue a warrant for his arrest; and

(b) may exercise any power which it could exercise in respect of the community service order if the offender resided in the part of the United Kingdom where the court has jurisdiction,

and any enactment relating to the exercise of such powers shall have effect accordingly.

DEFINITIONS

"community service order": s.238(1).
"home court": s.244(2).
"relevant time": s.244(2).

Community service orders: rules, annual report and interpretation

245.—(1) The Secretary of State may make rules for regulating the performance of work under community service orders or probation orders which include a requirement that the offender shall perform unpaid work.

(2) Without prejudice to the generality of subsection (1) above, rules under this section may—

(a) limit the number of hours' work to be done by a person under such an order on any one day;

(b) make provision as to the reckoning of time worked under such orders;

(c) make provision for the payment of travelling and other expenses in connection with the performance of work under such orders;

(d) provide for records to be kept of the work done by any person under such an order.

(3) Rules under this section shall be made by statutory instrument subject to annulment in pursuance of a resolution of either House of Parliament.

(4) The Secretary of State shall lay before Parliament each year, or incorporate in annual reports he already makes, a report of the working of community service orders.

(5) In sections 238 to 243 of this Act, "the appropriate court" means—

(a) where the relevant community service order has been made by the High Court, the High Court;

(b) in any other case, the court having jurisdiction in the locality for the time being specified in the order under section 238(8)(a) of this Act, being a sheriff or district court according to whether the order has been made by a sheriff or a district court, but in a case where the order has been made by a district court and there is no district court in that locality, the sheriff court.

DEFINITIONS

"appropriate court": s.245(5).
"community service orders": s.238(1).
"probation orders": s.308(1).

Admonition and absolute discharge

Admonition and absolute discharge

246.—(1) A court may, if it appears to meet the justice of the case, dismiss with an admonition any person convicted by the court of any offence.

(2) Where a person is convicted on indictment of an offence (other than an offence the sentence for which is fixed by law), if it appears to the court, having regard to the circumstances including the nature of the offence and the character of the offender, that it is inexpedient to inflict punishment and that a probation order is not appropriate it may instead of sentencing him make an order discharging him absolutely.

(3) Where a person is charged before a court of summary jurisdiction with an offence (other than an offence the sentence for which is fixed by law) and

the court is satisfied that he committed the offence, the court, if it is of the opinion, having regard to the circumstances including the nature of the offence and the character of the offender, that it is inexpedient to inflict punishment and that a probation order is not appropriate may without proceeding to conviction make an order discharging him absolutely.

DEFINITIONS
"court of summary jurisdiction": s.307(1).
"indictment": s.307(1).
"offence": s.307(1).
"probation order": s.307(1).

Effect of probation and absolute discharge

247.—(1) Subject to the following provisions of this section, a conviction of an offence for which an order is made placing the offender on probation or discharging him absolutely shall be deemed not to be a conviction for any purpose other than the purposes of the proceedings in which the order is made and of laying it before a court as a previous conviction in subsequent proceedings for another offence.

(2) Without prejudice to subsection (1) above, the conviction of an offender who is placed on probation or discharged absolutely as aforesaid shall in any event be disregarded for the purposes of any enactment which imposes any disqualification or disability upon convicted persons, or authorises or requires the imposition of any such disqualification or disability.

(3) Subsections (1) and (2) above shall not affect any right to appeal.

(4) Where a person charged with an offence has at any time previously been discharged absolutely in respect of the commission by him of an offence it shall be competent, in the proceedings for that offence, to lay before the court the order of absolute discharge in like manner as if the order were a conviction.

(5) Where an offender is discharged absolutely by a court of summary jurisdiction, he shall have the like right of appeal against the finding that he committed the offence as if that finding were a conviction.

(6) Where an offender, being not less than 16 years of age at the time of his conviction of an offence for which he is placed on probation as mentioned in subsection (1) above, is subsequently sentenced under this Act for that offence, the provisions of that subsection shall cease to apply to the conviction.

DEFINITIONS
"court of summary jurisdiction": s.307(1).
"offence": s.307(1).
"probation": s.307(1).

Disqualification

Disqualification where vehicle used to commit offence

248.—(1) Where a person is convicted of an offence (other than one triable only summarily) and the court which passes sentence is satisfied that a motor vehicle was used for the purposes of committing or facilitating the commission of that offence, the court may order him to be disqualified for such a period as the court thinks fit from holding or obtaining a licence to drive a motor vehicle granted under Part III of the Road Traffic Act 1988.

(2) A court which makes an order under this section disqualifying a person from holding or obtaining a licence shall require him to produce any such licence held by him and its counterpart.

(3) Any reference in this section to facilitating the commission of an offence shall include a reference to the taking of any steps after it has been

committed for the purpose of disposing of any property to which it relates or of avoiding apprehension or detection.

(4) In relation to licences which came into force before 1st June 1990, the reference in subsection (2) above to the counterpart of a licence shall be disregarded.

DEFINITIONS
"offence": s.307(1).
"order": s.307(1).

Compensation

Compensation order against convicted person

249.—(1) Subject to subsections (2) and (4) below, where a person is convicted of an offence the court, instead of or in addition to dealing with him in any other way, may make an order (in this Part of this Act referred to as "a compensation order") requiring him to pay compensation for any personal injury, loss or damage caused, whether directly or indirectly, by the acts which constituted the offence.

(2) It shall not be competent for a court to make a compensation order—
  (a) where, under section 246(2) of this Act, it makes an order discharging him absolutely;
  (b) where, under section 228 of this Act, it makes a probation order; or
  (c) at the same time as, under section 202 of this Act, it defers sentence.

(3) Where, in the case of an offence involving dishonest appropriation, or the unlawful taking and using of property or a contravention of section 178(1) of the Road Traffic Act 1988 (taking motor vehicle without authority etc.) the property is recovered, but has been damaged while out of the owner's possession, that damage, however and by whomsoever it was in fact caused, shall be treated for the purposes of subsection (1) above as having been caused by the acts which constituted the offence.

(4) No compensation order shall be made in respect of—
  (a) loss suffered in consequence of the death of any person; or
  (b) injury, loss or damage due to an accident arising out of the presence of a motor vehicle on a road, except such damage as is treated, by virtue of subsection (3) above, as having been caused by the convicted person's acts.

(5) In determining whether to make a compensation order against any person, and in determining the amount to be paid by any person under such order, the court shall take into consideration his means so far as known to the court.

(6) For the purposes of subsection (5) above, in assessing the means of a person who is serving, or is to serve, a period of imprisonment or detention, no account shall be taken of earnings contingent upon his obtaining employment after release.

(7) In solemn proceedings there shall be no limit on the amount which may be awarded under a compensation order.

(8) In summary proceedings—
  (a) a sheriff, or a stipendiary magistrate appointed under section 5 of the District Courts (Scotland) Act 1975, shall have power to make a compensation order awarding in respect of each offence an amount not exceeding the prescribed sum;
  (b) a judge of a district court (other than such stipendiary magistrate) shall have power to make a compensation order awarding in respect of each offence an amount not exceeding level 4 on the standard scale.

(9) Payment of any amount under a compensation order shall be made to the clerk of the court who shall account for the amount to the person entitled thereto.

(10) Only the court shall have power to enforce a compensation order.

DEFINITIONS
    "compensation order": s.249(1).
    "offence": s.307(1).
    "probation order": s.307(1).
    "prescribed sum": s.225(8).
    "standard scale": s.225(1).

GENERAL NOTE
    Compensation orders have probably not been sought for as many offences as they might have but that may merely reflect the impecunious state of most convicted people in Scotland. Nevertheless the law to date has been clarified by several decisions: in *Stewart v. H.M. Advocate*, 1982 S.C.C.R. 203 it was held on appeal that an order made in respect of "inconvenience suffered" was not open to criticism.
    In *Carmichael v. Siddique*, 1985 S.C.C.R. 145 a sheriff rejected an argument that a compensation order was competent and appropriate only where the legal position was clear and bereft of complexities and the damage was capable of precise valuation and was not great. Such an argument has not, apparently, been put forward again. In *Collins v. Lowe*, 1990 S.C.C.R. 605 it was held on appeal that it was competent to make a compensation order in addition to custodial sentences. Further, in *Robertson v. Lees*, 1992 S.C.C.R. 545 it was observed on appeal that the court was not persuaded that the fact that the appellant was a first offender was relevant in determining the amount of compensation.
    Finally, questions of causation must be examined closely, especially from the accused's point of view, for in *Nazir v. Normand*, 1994 S.C.C.R. 265 the appellant caused and permitted another to drive an uninsured car and the appellant's appeal against a consequential compensation order was refused.

Compensation orders: supplementary provisions

    250.—(1) Where a court considers that in respect of an offence it would be appropriate to impose a fine and to make a compensation order but the convicted person has insufficient means to pay both an appropriate fine and an appropriate amount in compensation the court should prefer a compensation order.
    (2) Where a convicted person has both been fined and had a compensation order made against him in respect of the same offence or different offences in the same proceedings, a payment by the convicted person shall first be applied in satisfaction of the compensation order.
    (3) For the purposes of any appeal or review, a compensation order is a sentence.
    (4) Where a compensation order has been made against a person, a payment made to the court in respect of the order shall be retained until the determination of any appeal in relation to the order.

DEFINITIONS
    "compensation order": s.249(1).
    "offence": s.307(1).

GENERAL NOTE
    There are, having regard to subs. (3), several reported cases in which a compensation order has been appealed. For example, in *Brown v. Normand*, 1988 S.C.C.R. 229 a sentence of a fine and a compensation order was appealed on the ground that the sentence was excessive and it was allowed. Appeals were similarly allowed in *Smillie v. Wilson*, 1990 S.C.C.R. 133, *Hughes v. Brown*, 1990 G.W.D. 13–670, *Crawford v. McGlennan*, 1990 G.W.D 21–1170, *McMahon v. Hamilton*, 1990 G.W.D. 37–2124, *Wilson v. Brown*, 1992 G.W.D. 6–288, *Currie v. Webster*, 1992 G.W.D. 13–722 and *Clark v. O'Brien*, 1995 G.W.D. 20–1130. Such appeals were refused in *McPhail v. Hamilton*, 1991 G.W.D. 24–1375 and *Barclay v. Douglas*, 1994 G.W.D. 1–37.

Review of compensation order

    251.—(1) Without prejudice to the power contained in section 213 of this Act, (as applied by section 252 of this Act), at any time before a compensation order has been complied with or fully complied with, the court, on the application of the person against whom the compensation order was made, may discharge the compensation order or reduce the amount that remains to be paid if it appears to the court that—

(a) the injury, loss or damage in respect of which the compensation order was made has been held in civil proceedings to be less than it was taken to be for the purposes of the compensation order; or

(b) that property the loss of which is reflected in the compensation order has been recovered.

(2) In subsection (1) above "the court" means—

(a) in a case where, as respects the compensation order, a transfer of fine order under section 222 of this Act (as applied by the said section 252) is effective and the court by which the compensation order is enforceable is in terms of the transfer of fine order a court of summary jurisdiction in Scotland, that court; or

(b) in any other case, the court which made the compensation order or, where that court was the High Court, by which the order was first enforceable.

DEFINITIONS
"compensation order": s.249(1).
"court": s.251(2).

Enforcement of compensation orders: application of provisions relating to fines

252.—(1) The provisions of this Act specified in subsection (2) below shall, subject to any necessary modifications and to the qualifications mentioned in that subsection, apply in relation to compensation orders as they apply in relation to fines; and section 91 of the Magistrates' Courts Act 1980 and article 96 of the Magistrates' Courts (Northern Ireland) Order 1981 shall be construed accordingly.

(2) The provisions mentioned in subsection (1) above are—

section 211(3), (4) and (7) to (9) (enforcement of fines);

section 212 (fines in summary proceedings);

section 213 (power to remit fines), with the omission of the words "or (4)" in subsection (2) of that section;

section 214 (time for payment) with the omission of—
　　(a) the words from "unless" to "its decision" in subsection (4); and
　　(b) subsection (5);

section 215 (further time for payment);

section 216 (reasons for default);

section 217 (supervision pending payment of fine);

section 218 (supplementary provisions), except that subsection (1) of that section shall not apply in relation to compensation orders made in solemn proceedings;

subject to subsection (3) below, section 219(1)(b), (2), (3), (5), (6) and (8) (maximum period of imprisonment for non-payment of fine);

section 220 (payment of fine in part by prisoner);

section 221 (recovery by civil diligence);

section 222 (transfer of fine orders);

section 223 (action of clerk of court on transfer of fine order); and

section 224 (discharge from imprisonment to be specified).

(3) In the application of the provisions of section 219 of this Act mentioned in subsection (2) above for the purposes of subsection (1) above—

(a) a court may impose imprisonment in respect of a fine and decline to impose imprisonment in respect of a compensation order but not vice versa; and

(b) where a court imposes imprisonment both in respect of a fine and of a compensation order the amounts in respect of which imprisonment is imposed shall, for the purposes of subsection (2) of the said section 219, be aggregated.

DEFINITIONS
"fines": s.307(1).

Effect of compensation order on subsequent award of damages in civil proceedings

253.—(1) This section shall have effect where a compensation order or a service compensation order or award has been made in favour of any person in respect of any injury, loss or damage and a claim by him in civil proceedings for damages in respect thereof subsequently falls to be determined.

(2) The damages in the civil proceedings shall be assessed without regard to the order or award; but where the whole or part of the amount awarded by the order or award has been paid, the damages awarded in the civil proceedings shall be restricted to the amount (if any) by which, as so assessed, they exceed the amount paid under the order or award.

(3) Where the whole or part of the amount awarded by the order or award remains unpaid and damages are awarded in a judgment in the civil proceedings, then, unless the person against whom the order or award was made has ceased to be liable to pay the amount unpaid (whether in consequence of an appeal, or of his imprisonment for default or otherwise), the court shall direct that the judgment—

(a) if it is for an amount not exceeding the amount unpaid under the order or award, shall not be enforced; or

(b) if it is for an amount exceeding the amount unpaid under the order or award, shall not be enforced except to the extent that it exceeds the amount unpaid,

without the leave of the court.

(4) In this section a "service compensation order or award" means—

(a) an order requiring the payment of compensation under paragraph 11 of—

      (i) Schedule 5A to the Army Act 1955;

      (ii) Schedule 5A to the Air Force Act 1955; or

      (iii) Schedule 4A to the Naval Discipline Act 1957; or

(b) an award of stoppages payable by way of compensation under any of those Acts.

DEFINITIONS
"compensation orders": s.249(1).
"order": s.307(1).
"service compensation order": s.253(4).

GENERAL NOTE
Following *Goodhall v. Carmichael*, 1984 S.C.C.R. 247 it is clear that credible though uncorroborated evidence is sufficient to settle the value of the loss to be compensated, a practice that is now consistent with the civil law of evidence. The appeal by Goodhall was dismissed without Opinions being delivered. However, in an article following that appeal it was said that Lord Wheatley had commented during the appeal that "the whole point of compensation orders was to save victims the need to go to the civil courts": C.J. Docherty and G. Maher *Corroboration and Compensation Orders* 1984 S.L.T.(News) 125 at p. 126.

Forfeiture

Search warrant for forfeited articles

254. Where a court has made an order for the forfeiture of an article, the court or any justice may, if satisfied on information on oath—

(a) that there is reasonable cause to believe that the article is to be found in any place or premises; and

(b) that admission to the place or premises has been refused or that a refusal of such admission is apprehended,

issue a warrant of search which may be executed according to law.

PART XII

EVIDENCE

Special capacity

Special capacity

255. Where an offence is alleged to be committed in any special capacity, as by the holder of a licence, master of a vessel, occupier of a house, or the like, the fact that the accused possesses the qualification necessary to the commission of the offence shall, unless challenged—

(a) in the case of proceedings on indictment, by giving notice of a preliminary objection under paragraph (b) of section 72(1) of this Act or under that paragraph as applied by section 71(2) of this Act; or

(b) in summary proceedings, by preliminary objection before his plea is recorded,

be held as admitted.

DEFINITIONS
  "indictment": s.307(1).
  "offence": s.307(1).

GENERAL NOTE
This section relates both to solemn and summary procedure. A special capacity is a capacity which is special to the accused and is necessary to the commission of the offence.

In order to take advantage of this evidential concession, a prosecutor has to give notice in the libel of the capacity upon which he intends to found. Failure to do so will compel the prosecution to lead sufficient evidence to establish that the accused did possess the capacity essential to the commission of the offence. Furthermore if the Crown libels a special capacity and then proceeds to conduct its case by leading evidence of the fact, it risks being held to have waived the benefit of the presumption (*Wimpey Homes Holdings v. Lees*, 1991 S.C.C.R. 447; *Smith v. Ross*, 1937 J.C. 65). Note that production of an extract conviction in support of a charge of driving while disqualified does not constitute a waiver of the presumption by the Crown (*Paton v. Lees*, 1992 S.C.C.R. 212).

A special capacity is not implied in any charge so while no express formula of words is required, it must be patent that the accused was acting in that capacity at the time of the offence (*Ross v. Simpson*, 1994 S.C.C.R. 847).

Any denial of a special capacity must be stated at the first calling of a summary complaint (s.144(4)) and will only be permitted at future diets on cause shown (s.144(5)): in solemn proceedings s.72(1)(b)(iii) applies rather untidily to both sheriff and jury, the High Court, proceedings. (It will be remembered that first diets are mandatory in the case of sheriff and jury trials; while preliminary diets are normally optional in High Court cases—such a diet is essential to intimate a challenge under s.72(1)(b)(iii).)

Examples of special capacity are: being subject to bail conditions (*Aitchison v. Tudhope*, 1981 J.C. 65); being a common prostitute (*Allan v. McGraw*, 1986 S.C.C.R. 257); being a known thief as defined in s.58 of the Civic Government (Scotland) Act 1982 (c. 45) (*Newlands v. MacPhail*, 1991 S.C.C.R. 88); being a disqualified driver (*Paton v. Lees* cited above), owning a vessel (*Thomas W. Ward v. Waugh*, 1934 J.C. 13), and in certain circumstances, being the parent of a child (*Ross v. Simpson*, 1994 S.C.C.R. 847).

Agreed evidence

Agreements and admissions as to evidence

256.—(1) In any trial it shall not be necessary for the accused or for the prosecutor—
  (a) to prove any fact which is admitted by the other; or
  (b) to prove any document, the terms and application of which are not in dispute between them,
and, without prejudice to paragraph 1 of Schedule 8 to this Act, copies of any documents may, by agreement of the parties, be accepted as equivalent to the originals.
  (2) For the purposes of subsection (1) above, any admission or agreement shall be made by lodging with the clerk of court a minute in that behalf signed—
  (a) in the case of an admission, by the party making the admission or, if that party is the accused and he is legally represented, by his counsel or solicitor; and
  (b) in the case of an agreement, by the prosecutor and the accused or, if he is legally represented, his counsel or solicitor.
  (3) Where a minute has been signed and lodged as aforesaid, any facts and documents admitted or agreed thereby shall be deemed to have been duly proved.

DEFINITIONS
  "prosecutor": s.307(1).
  "trial": s.307(1).

GENERAL NOTE
  This section applies to both solemn and summary procedure and provides for the lodging of Minutes of Agreement or Minutes of Admissions describing facts accepted as established in the proceedings. Documentary evidence or copies thereof can be admitted in this way; where such evidence is not formally agreed, or is not agreed with sufficient celerity, then recourse can be had to the provisions of s.258 which permits service of a statement of what is felt to be uncontroversial evidence upon other parties or, alternatively, the use of the procedures for setting up documentary evidence contained in Sched. 8 (this preserves the terms of Sched. 3 of the Prisoners and Criminal Proceedings (Scotland) Act 1993 (c. 9)).
  It will be recalled that there is no timescale stipulated for agreement of evidence by Minutes of Agreement or Admission and, indeed, these can be prepared and lodged at any point in proceedings before evidence is closed; by contrast s.258 demands a response from the other party in seven days to any statement of facts served validly and is only available prior for use more than 14 days before trial.

Duty to seek agreement of evidence

257.—(1) Subject to subsection (2) below, the prosecutor and the accused (or each of the accused if more than one) shall each identify any facts which are facts—
  (a) which he would, apart from this section, be seeking to prove;
  (b) which he considers unlikely to be disputed by the other party (or by any of the other parties); and
  (c) in proof of which he does not wish to lead oral evidence,
and shall, without prejudice to section 258 of this Act, take all reasonable steps to secure the agreement of the other party (or each of the other parties) to them; and the other party (or each of the other parties) shall take all reasonable steps to reach such agreement.
  (2) Subsection (1) above shall not apply in relation to proceedings as respects which the accused (or any of the accused if more than one) is not legally represented.

(3) The duty under subsection (1) above applies—
(a) in relation to proceedings on indictment, from the date of service of the indictment until the swearing of the jury or, where intimation is given under section 76 of this Act, the date of that intimation; and
(b) in relation to summary proceedings, from the date on which the accused pleads not guilty until the swearing of the first witness or, where the accused tenders a plea of guilty at any time before the first witness is sworn, the date when he does so.

DEFINITIONS
"indictment": s.307(1).
"prosecutor": s.307(1).

GENERAL NOTE
This section applies to both solemn and summary proceedings. The purpose of this, and the following section, is to identify evidence which is capable of being received without the need for its introduction by parole evidence and the need for witnesses to attend court. Prior to the introduction of these provisions there was no onus upon any party to identify, or agree, formal or uncontroversial evidence and while a duty is now placed on parties to consider such material, there is no sanction for failure to do so. The prosecutor and, only where he is legally represented the accused, are each required to identify factual evidence felt to be capable of agreement and to take all reasonable steps to agree these matters before trial.

Section 256 provides a mechanism for agreement of evidence, or for the admission of facts by one party; s.258 enacts a procedure for service of statements of fact upon other parties. Subsection (3) provides two different timescales during which the duties imposed on parties persist: in solemn proceedings this is the period from service of the indictment until the commencement of trial (see s.64(9)) or, in the case of accelerated pleas, until the accused gives notice in writing of a plea which is accepted by the Crown (see s.76(1)); in summary proceedings, the period from the date of the plea being recorded (s.146(1)) until trial begins (s.147(4)) or a plea of guilty is intimated.

Uncontroversial evidence

258.—(1) This section applies where, in any criminal proceedings, a party (in this section referred to as "the first party") considers that facts which that party would otherwise be seeking to prove are unlikely to be disputed by the other parties to the proceedings.

(2) Where this section applies, the first party may prepare and sign a statement—
(a) specifying the facts concerned; or
(b) referring to such facts as set out in a document annexed to the statement,
and shall, not less than 14 days before the trial diet, serve a copy of the statement and any such document on every other party.

(3) Unless any other party serves on the first party, not more than seven days after the date of service of the copy on him under subsection (2) above or by such later time as the court may in special circumstances allow, a notice that he challenges any fact specified or referred to in the statement, the facts so specified or referred to shall be deemed to have been conclusively proved.

(4) Where a notice is served under subsection (3) above, the facts specified or referred to in the statement shall be deemed to have been conclusively proved only in so far as unchallenged in the notice.

(5) Subsections (3) and (4) above shall not preclude a party from leading evidence of circumstances relevant to, or other evidence in explanation of, any fact specified or referred to in the statement.

(6) Notwithstanding subsections (3) and (4) above, the court—
(a) may, on the application of any party, where it is satisfied that there are special circumstances; and
(b) shall, on the joint application of all the parties,

direct that the presumptions in those subsections shall not apply in relation to such fact specified or referred to in the statement as is specified in the direction.

(7) An application under subsection (6) above may be made at any time after the commencement of the trial and before the commencement of the prosecutor's address to the court on the evidence.

(8) Where the court makes a direction under subsection (6) above it shall, unless all the parties otherwise agree, adjourn the trial and may, without prejudice to section 268 of this Act, permit any party to lead evidence as to any such fact as is specified in the direction, notwithstanding that a witness or production concerned is not included in any list lodged by the parties and that the notice required by sections 67(5) and 78(4) of this Act has not been given.

(9) A copy of a statement or a notice required, under this section, to be served on any party shall be served in such manner as may be prescribed by Act of Adjournal; and a written execution purporting to be signed by the person who served such copy or notice together with, where appropriate, the relevant post office receipt shall be sufficient evidence of such service.

DEFINITIONS
    "diet": s.307(1).
    "prosecutor": s.307(1).

GENERAL NOTE
    This section applies to solemn and summary proceedings. It introduces a new procedure for evidence, which a party regards as "unlikely to be disputed", to be held as admitted after a statement of facts has been served in conformity to subs. (2) and not challenged by its recipient as provided by subs. (3). At best this provision can be seen as a further means of securing agreement of evidence but, on a cautionary note, great vigilance will have to be exercised by parties to ensure that any evidence which would be disputed does not slip through without challenge. Subsection (3) does permit a notice of challenge to be tendered late but its acceptance by the court is far from automatic.
    This procedure was introduced in the Criminal Justice (Scotland) Act 1995 (c. 20) and followed a recommendation by the Scottish Law Commission Report No. 137 "*Evidence: Report on Documentary Evidence and Proof of Undisputed Facts in Criminal Proceedings*" of such a procedure for use by the prosecution; it will be observed that s.258 is available for use by both prosecution and defence.
    It will be noted that there seems to be no limit on the number of s.258 Notices which can be served more than 14 days prior to trial, and that subs. (5) still enables the leading of evidence in clarification or explanation of the statement of facts. Subsection (6) operates as a saving provision to enable the court, or the parties, during the trial to override the terms of a statement of facts which is not in accordance with the evidence, and where the court exercises these powers, to adjourn the trial to permit parties to lead evidence struck at by that operation (see subs. (7)). Note that such evidence can be received in solemn proceedings even when it has not been specified on Crown or defence lists of witnesses or productions.
    The 1996 Act of Adjournal, Chap. 21 specifies the forms to be used to introduce a statement of facts or to challenge the same. The Act is silent as to how statements of fact, modified or unmodified by challenge, are to be introduced into the record of proceedings; they may be treated in the same way as a Minute of Agreement, being read to a jury by the clerk of court, or received by the judge in summary cases but this is not settled. It is apparent that parties serving statements of fact will need to preserve, and be able to produce to the court a copy notice and completed execution of service.

Hearsay

Exceptions to the rule that hearsay evidence is inadmissible

259.—(1) Subject to the following provisions of this section, evidence of a statement made by a person otherwise than while giving oral evidence in court in criminal proceedings shall be admissible in those proceedings as evidence of any matter contained in the statement where the judge is satisfied—

(a) that the person who made the statement will not give evidence in the proceedings of such matter for any of the reasons mentioned in sub-section (2) below;

(b) that evidence of the matter would be admissible in the proceedings if that person gave direct oral evidence of it;

(c) that the person who made the statement would have been, at the time the statement was made, a competent witness in such proceedings; and

(d) that there is evidence which would entitle a jury properly directed, or in summary proceedings would entitle the judge, to find that the statement was made and that either—

  (i) it is contained in a document; or

  (ii) a person who gave oral evidence in the proceedings as to the statement has direct personal knowledge of the making of the statement.

(2) The reasons referred to in paragraph (a) of subsection (1) above are that the person who made the statement—

(a) is dead or is, by reason of his bodily or mental condition, unfit or unable to give evidence in any competent manner;

(b) is named and otherwise sufficiently identified, but is outwith the United Kingdom and it is not reasonably practicable to secure his attendance at the trial or to obtain his evidence in any other competent manner;

(c) is named and otherwise sufficiently identified, but cannot be found and all reasonable steps which, in the circumstances, could have been taken to find him have been so taken;

(d) having been authorised to do so by virtue of a ruling of the court in the proceedings that he is entitled to refuse to give evidence in connection with the subject matter of the statement on the grounds that such evidence might incriminate him, refuses to give such evidence; or

(e) is called as a witness and either—

  (i) refuses to take the oath or affirmation; or

  (ii) having been sworn as a witness and directed by the judge to give evidence in connection with the subject matter of the statement refuses to do so,

and in the application of this paragraph to a child, the reference to a witness refusing to take the oath or affirmation or, as the case may be, to having been sworn shall be construed as a reference to a child who has refused to accept an admonition to tell the truth or, having been so admonished, refuses to give evidence as mentioned above.

(3) Evidence of a statement shall not be admissible by virtue of subsection (1) above where the judge is satisfied that the occurrence of any of the circumstances mentioned in paragraphs (a) to (e) of subsection (2) above, by virtue of which the statement would otherwise be admissible, is caused by—

(a) the person in support of whose case the evidence would be given; or

(b) any other person acting on his behalf,

for the purpose of securing that the person who made the statement does not give evidence for the purposes of the proceedings either at all or in connection with the subject matter of the statement.

(4) Where in any proceedings evidence of a statement made by any person is admitted by reference to any of the reasons mentioned in paragraphs (a) to (c) and (e)(i) of subsection (2) above—

(a) any evidence which, if that person had given evidence in connection with the subject matter of the statement, would have been admissible as relevant to his credibility as a witness shall be admissible for that purpose in those proceedings;

(b) evidence may be given of any matter which, if that person had given evidence in connection with the subject matter of the statement, could have been put to him in cross-examination as relevant to his credibility as a witness but of which evidence could not have been adduced by the cross-examining party; and

(c) evidence tending to prove that that person, whether before or after making the statement, made in whatever manner some other statement which is inconsistent with it shall be admissible for the purpose of showing that he has contradicted himself.

(5) Subject to subsection (6) below, where a party intends to apply to have evidence of a statement admitted by virtue of subsection (1) above he shall, before the trial diet, give notice in writing of—

(a) that fact;

(b) the witnesses and productions to be adduced in connection with such evidence; and

(c) such other matters as may be prescribed by Act of Adjournal,

to every other party to the proceedings and, for the purposes of this subsection, such evidence may be led notwithstanding that a witness or production concerned is not included in any list lodged by the parties and that the notice required by sections 67(5) and 78(4) of this Act has not been given.

(6) A party shall not be required to give notice as mentioned in subsection (5) above where—

(a) the grounds for seeking to have evidence of a statement admitted are as mentioned in paragraph (d) or (e) of subsection (2) above; or

(b) he satisfies the judge that there was good reason for not giving such notice.

(7) If no other party to the proceedings objects to the admission of evidence of a statement by virtue of subsection (1) above, the evidence shall be admitted without the judge requiring to be satisfied as mentioned in that subsection.

(8) For the purposes of the determination of any matter upon which the judge is required to be satisfied under subsection (1) above—

(a) except to the extent that any other party to the proceedings challenges them and insists in such challenge, it shall be presumed that the circumstances are as stated by the party seeking to introduce evidence of the statement; and

(b) where such a challenge is insisted in, the judge shall determine the matter on the balance of probabilities, and he may draw any reasonable inference—

(i) from the circumstances in which the statement was made or otherwise came into being; or

(ii) from any other circumstances, including, where the statement is contained in a document, the form and contents of the document.

(9) Where evidence of a statement has been admitted by virtue of subsection (1) above on the application of one party to the proceedings, without prejudice to anything in any enactment or rule of law, the judge may permit any party to lead additional evidence of such description as the judge may specify, notwithstanding that a witness or production concerned is not included in any list lodged by the parties and that the notice required by sections 67(5) and 78(4) of this Act has not been given.

(10) Any reference in subsections (5), (6) and (9) above to evidence shall include a reference to evidence led in connection with any determination required to be made for the purposes of subsection (1) above.

DEFINITIONS

"child": s.307(1).
"criminal proceedings": s.262(3).
"document": s.262(3).
"judge": s.307(1).
"statement": s.262(1).
"witness": s.307(1).

GENERAL NOTE

This section applies to solemn and summary proceedings. It was introduced following upon consideration by the Scottish Law Commission in its Report on Hearsay Evidence in Criminal Proceedings (No. 149) and the concerns arising from the outcome of *Perrie v. H.M. Advocate,* 1991 S.C.C.R. 255 and *McLay v. H.M. Advocate,* 1994 S.C.C.R. 397; in both these cases it had not been possible to lead evidence made to third parties by an incriminee under the then existing law.

Subsection (1) provides that hearsay evidence in criminal proceedings shall be admissible if the judge is satisfied that the maker of the statement would be a competent witness in possession of admissible evidence, but is unavailable for any of the reasons specified in subs. (2)(a) to (d), or although available, has declined to give evidence on oath in the case (subs. (2)(e)), a situation which could apply to an incriminee declining to give evidence. A party cannot use these provisions if the judge is satisfied that the party has sought to prevent direct evidence being adduced from the witness (subs. (3)).

The judge shall consider on the balance of probabilities whether hearsay evidence which is sought to be introduced, fulfils the criteria stated in subs. (1), but need only do so if other parties aver that recourse to these provisions is inappropriate. Subsection (8)(b) appears to limit the scope of any enquiry or proof to be undertaken by the judge in deciding whether to allow such hearsay evidence; however subs. (9) permits parties to amplify upon that evidence or to lead evidence in rebuttal without fulfilling the usual requirements of prior notice. While an application under subs. (1) has to be given prior to the commencement of the trial, subs. (9) which refers to "additional evidence" can plainly be utilised once the trial has begun.

In order to utilise these provisions, a party will normally be required to serve notice of such intention on all other parties prior to the trial, albeit there is no requirement to add the particulars of the witness or statement to any list of witnesses or productions (subss. (5) and (6)). The style of such a Notice is found in Form 21.3. in the 1996 Act of Adjournal.

Subsection (7) provides that in the absence of objection from other parties to the admission of the evidence, the judge need not consider whether the qualifications in subs. (1) are satisfied; it will be recalled that parties could equally have agreed or admitted such evidence in terms of s.256 without any need for recourse to s.259.

The reliability and credibility of any hearsay evidence can be challenged by reference to the grounds specified in subs. (4).

Admissibility of prior statements of witnesses

260.—(1) Subject to the following provisions of this section, where a witness gives evidence in criminal proceedings, any prior statement made by the witness shall be admissible as evidence of any matter stated in it of which direct oral evidence by him would be admissible if given in the course of those proceedings.

(2) A prior statement shall not be admissible under this section unless—

(a) the statement is contained in a document;

(b) the witness, in the course of giving evidence, indicates that the statement was made by him and that he adopts it as his evidence; and

(c) at the time the statement was made, the person who made it would have been a competent witness in the proceedings.

(3) For the purposes of this section, any reference to a prior statement is a reference to a prior statement which, but for the provisions of this section, would not be admissible as evidence of any matter stated in it.

(4) Subsections (2) and (3) above do not apply to a prior statement—

(a) contained in a precognition on oath; or

(b) made in other proceedings, whether criminal or civil and whether taking place in the United Kingdom or elsewhere,

and, for the purposes of this section, any such statement shall not be admissible unless it is sufficiently authenticated.

DEFINITIONS

"criminal proceedings": s.262(3).
"statement": s.262(1).
"witness": s.307(1).

GENERAL NOTE

This section applies to solemn and summary proceedings and permits the introduction of prior statements, as specified by subs. (2), by a witness in criminal proceedings as evidence of any matter therein of which direct oral evidence from him would have been admissible in the course of those proceedings. In essence the section permits the adoption of earlier statements, suitably authenticated, and is perceptibly influenced by the decision of the High Court in *Jamieson v. H.M. Advocate*, 1994 S.L.T. 537.

The 1996 Act of Adjournal, Rule 21.4. stipulates that any such statement shall be authenticated by means of a signed certificate on, or attached to, the first page of the statement; this would appear to preclude a statement simply being put to the witness, in the course of proceedings, and being acknowledged as accurate only then, as was allowed in *Jamieson*.

Note that the witness has both to acknowledge being the originator of the statement and adopt it as his evidence (subs. (2)(b)), circumstances which did not prevail in either *Muldoon v. Herron*, 1970 J.C. 30; 1970 S.L.T. 228 (a judgment which the court founded upon in *Jamieson*) or in *Smith v. H.M. Advocate*, 1986 S.C.C.R. 135. In both those cases police witnesses' accounts of the witness' evidence replaced the testimony of the witnesses themselves.

The effect of subs. (4) is to remove the need for a witness to adopt the terms of his precognition on oath (which of course had to be signed as an acknowledgment of its accuracy by the witness at the conclusion of the precognition proceedings) or for him to confirm the accuracy of testimony given in earlier judicial proceedings.

Statements by accused

261.—(1) Subject to the following provisions of this section, nothing in sections 259 and 260 of this Act shall apply to a statement made by the accused.

(2) Evidence of a statement made by an accused shall be admissible by virtue of the said section 259 at the instance of another accused in the same proceedings as evidence in relation to that other accused.

(3) For the purposes of subsection (2) above, the first mentioned accused shall be deemed—

(a) where he does not give evidence in the proceedings, to be a witness refusing to give evidence in connection with the subject matter of the statement as mentioned in paragraph (e) of subsection (2) of the said section 259; and

(b) to have been, at the time the statement was made, a competent witness in the proceedings.

(4) Evidence of a statement shall not be admissible as mentioned in subsection (2) above unless the accused at whose instance it is sought to be admitted has given notice of his intention to do so as mentioned in subsection (5) of the said section 259; but subsection (6) of that section shall not apply in the case of notice required to be given by virtue of this subsection.

DEFINITIONS

   "made": s.262(3).
   "statement": s.262(1).
   "witness": s.307(1).

GENERAL NOTE

This section applies to solemn and summary proceedings. Its effect is to exclude a statement made by the accused from the provisions of ss.259 and 260. However, statements made by an accused, which are hearsay, may become admissible against that accused when introduced by another accused in the same proceedings. Use of this procedure will normally require a Notice in terms of s.259(5) prior to trial (see notes to s.259 above).

Construction of sections 259 to 261

262.—(1) For the purposes of sections 259 to 261 of this Act, a "statement" includes—

(a) any representation, however made or expressed, of fact or opinion; and

(b) any part of a statement,

but does not include a statement in a precognition other than a precognition on oath.

(2) For the purposes of the said sections 259 to 261 a statement is contained in a document where the person who makes it—

(a) makes the statement in the document personally;

(b) makes a statement which is, with or without his knowledge, embodied in a document by whatever means or by any person who has direct personal knowledge of the making of the statement; or

(c) approves a document as embodying the statement.

(3) In the said sections 259 to 261—

"criminal proceedings" include any hearing by the sheriff of an application made under Chapter 3 of Part II of the Children (Scotland) Act 1995 for a finding as to whether grounds for the referral of a child's case to a children's hearing are established, in so far as the application relates to the commission of an offence by the child, or for a review of such a finding;

"document" includes, in addition to a document in writing—

(a) any map, plan, graph or drawing;

(b) any photograph;

(c) any disc, tape, sound track or other device in which sounds or other data (not being visual images) are recorded so as to be capable (with or without the aid of some other equipment) of being reproduced therefrom; and

(d) any film, negative, tape, disc or other device in which one or more visual images are recorded so as to be capable (as aforesaid) of being reproduced therefrom;

"film" includes a microfilm;

"made" includes allegedly made.

(4) Nothing in the said sections 259 to 261 shall prejudice the admissibility of a statement made by a person other than in the course of giving oral evidence in court which is admissible otherwise than by virtue of those sections.

DEFINITIONS
"child": s.307(1).
"indictment": s.307(1).
"sheriff": ss.4(4) and 5(1).

GENERAL NOTE

The section makes provision for the construction of ss.259 to 261 of the Act. Subsection (4) enacts that the section's provisions do not prejudice any other rule allowing the admissibility of statements in the course of giving oral evidence in court; see for example s.263(4) which deals with prior inconsistent statements in solemn and summary proceedings.

Witnesses

Examination of witnesses

263.—(1) In any trial, it shall be competent for the party against whom a witness is produced and sworn *in causa* to examine such witness both in cross and *in causa*.

(2) The judge may, on the motion of either party, on cause shown order that the examination of a witness for that party ("the first witness") shall be interrupted to permit the examination of another witness for that party.

(3) Where the judge makes an order under subsection (2) above he shall, after the examination of the other witness, permit the recall of the first witness.

(4) In a trial, a witness may be examined as to whether he has on any specified occasion made a statement on any matter pertinent to the issue at the trial different from the evidence given by him in the trial; and evidence may be led in the trial to prove that the witness made the different statement on the occasion specified.

(5) In any trial, on the motion of either party, the presiding judge may permit a witness who has been examined to be recalled.

DEFINITIONS
  "judge": s.307(1).
  "trial": s.307(1).
  "witness": s.307(1).

GENERAL NOTE
  This section applies to solemn and summary proceedings. Subsections (2) and (3) which permit the interruption of a witness' testimony to allow evidence to be taken from another of the party's witnesses was introduced by the Criminal Justice (Scotland) Act 1980 (c. 62), Sched. 6, para. 54. By implication such a motion could only be made during the examination or re-examination of the first witness, not during cross-examination.

  Subsection (4) repeats the familiar terms of ss.147 and 349 of the 1975 Act in relation to prior inconsistent statements by witnesses. This rule does not apply to precognitions which cannot, of course, be put to witnesses unless they are precognitions on oath (see *Kerr v. H.M. Advocate*, 1958 J.C. 14; *K.J.C. v. H.M. Advocate*, 1994 S.C.C.R. 560). See also *Coll, Petr.*, 1977 S.L.T. 58, a petition to the nobile officium by a witness to order destruction of his precognition on oath before giving evidence at the trial proceedings.

  The second part of subs. (4) does not become operative until the witness has been specifically asked whether he made the statement (*McTaggart v. H.M. Advocate*, 1934 J.C. 33) and that it was made on a specified occasion. In *Advocate, H.M. v. Hislop*, 1994 S.L.T. 333 a Crown witness, who claimed to be unable to recall events, stated that she had told the police what had happened. The prosecutor put her account to her by means of her earlier tape-recorded interview and a transcript of it, both of which were listed as productions. Objections to this use of the section's provisions were repelled.

Spouse of accused a competent witness

264.—(1) The spouse of an accused may be called as a witness—
  (a) by the accused;
  (b) by a co-accused or by the prosecutor without the consent of the accused.

(2) Nothing in this section shall—
  (a) make the spouse of an accused a compellable witness for a co-accused or for the prosecutor in a case where such spouse would not be so compellable at common law;
  (b) compel a spouse to disclose any communication made between the spouses during the marriage.

(3) The failure of the spouse of an accused to give evidence shall not be commented on by the defence or the prosecutor.

(4) The spouse of a person charged with bigamy may be called as a witness either for the prosecution or the defence and without the consent of the person charged.

DEFINITIONS
  "prosecutor": s.307(1).
  "witness": s.307(1).

GENERAL NOTE
  The term "spouse" can only be applied to persons married to each other, not to those who simply co-habit (*Casey v. H.M. Advocate*, 1993 S.L.T. 33). A spouse is a compellable witness for the accused to whom she is married, and is competent but not compellable when called by any

other party in proceedings (*Hunter v. H.M. Advocate*, 1984 S.L.T. 434); once she elects to give evidence, she must answer all relevant questions and cannot refrain from answering on the grounds that they might incriminate her spouse (see *Hunter* above and *Bates v. H.M. Advocate*, 1989 S.L.T. 701; 1989 S.C.C.R. 338).

This rule also applies to an estranged spouse who, unless she is the complainer, must be advised that she is not a compellable witness (see *Hay v. McClory*, 1993 S.C.C.R. 1040; 1994 S.L.T. 520).

Witnesses not excluded for conviction, interest, relationship, etc.

265.—(1) Every person adduced as a witness who is not otherwise by law disqualified from giving evidence, shall be admissible as a witness, and no objection to the admissibility of a witness shall be competent on the ground of—

(a) conviction of or punishment for an offence;
(b) interest;
(c) agency or partial counsel;
(d) the absence of due citation to attend; or
(e) his having been precognosced subsequently to the date of citation.

(2) Where any person who is or has been an agent of the accused is adduced and examined as a witness for the accused, it shall not be competent for the accused to object, on the ground of confidentiality, to any question proposed to be put to such witness on matter pertinent to the issue of the guilt of the accused.

(3) No objection to the admissibility of a witness shall be competent on the ground that he or she is the father, mother, son, daughter, brother or sister, by consanguinity or affinity, or uncle, aunt, nephew or niece, by consanguinity of any party adducing the witness in any trial.

(4) It shall not be competent for any witness to decline to be examined and give evidence on the ground of any relationship mentioned in subsection (3) above.

DEFINITIONS
    "conviction": s.307(5).
    "witness": s.307(1).

GENERAL NOTE
    This section permits parties' evidence to be heard irrespective of their character or interest or relationship. See generally *Dow v. McKnight*, 1949 J.C. 38. Subsection (2) provides that the accused's solicitor, or former solicitor, can be adduced as a witness by the accused; the agent cannot be objected to on the grounds that he has been present in court (*Campbell v. Cochrane*, 1928 J.C. 25).

Accused as witness

266.—(1) Subject to subsections (2) to (8) below, the accused shall be a competent witness for the defence at every stage of the case, whether the accused is on trial alone or along with a co-accused.

(2) The accused shall not be called as a witness in pursuance of this section except upon his own application or in accordance with subsection (9) or (10) below.

(3) An accused who gives evidence on his own behalf in pursuance of this section may be asked any question in cross-examination notwithstanding that it would tend to incriminate him as to the offence charged.

(4) An accused who gives evidence on his own behalf in pursuance of this section shall not be asked, and if asked shall not be required to answer, any question tending to show that he has committed, or been convicted of, or been charged with, any offence other than that with which he is then charged, or is of bad character, unless—

(a) the proof that he has committed or been convicted of such other offence is admissible evidence to show that he is guilty of the offence with which he is then charged; or

(b) the accused or his counsel or solicitor has asked questions of the witnesses for the prosecution with a view to establishing the accused's good character or impugning the character of the complainer, or the accused has given evidence of his own good character, or the nature or conduct of the defence is such as to involve imputations on the character of the prosecutor or of the witnesses for the prosecution or of the complainer; or

(c) the accused has given evidence against any other person charged in the same proceedings.

(5) In a case to which paragraph (b) of subsection (4) above applies, the prosecutor shall be entitled to ask the accused a question of a kind specified in that subsection only if the court, on the application of the prosecutor, permits him to do so.

(6) An application under subsection (5) above in proceedings on indictment shall be made in the course of the trial but in the absence of the jury.

(7) In subsection (4) above, references to the complainer include references to a victim who is deceased.

(8) Every person called as a witness in pursuance of this section shall, unless otherwise ordered by the court, give his evidence from the witness box or other place from which the other witnesses give their evidence.

(9) The accused may—

(a) with the consent of a co-accused, call that other accused as a witness on the accused's behalf; or

(b) ask a co-accused any question in cross-examination if that co-accused gives evidence,

but he may not do both in relation to the same co-accused.

(10) The prosecutor or the accused may call as a witness a co-accused who has pleaded guilty to or been acquitted of all charges against him which remain before the court (whether or not, in a case where the co-accused has pleaded guilty to any charge, he has been sentenced) or in respect of whom the diet has been deserted; and the party calling such co-accused as a witness shall not require to give notice thereof, but the court may grant any other party such adjournment or postponement of the trial as may seem just.

(11) Where, in any trial, the accused is to be called as a witness he shall be so called as the first witness for the defence unless the court, on cause shown, otherwise directs.

DEFINITIONS
  "diet": s.307(1).
  "offence": s.307(1).
  "prosecutor": s.307(1).
  "trial": s.307(1).
  "witness": s.307(1).

GENERAL NOTE
  The accused cannot be compelled to give evidence on his own behalf in his own trial, but his failure to do so can be the subject of comment, with restraint, by the trial judge in solemn proceedings when charging the jury (see *Scott (A.T.)* v. *H.M. Advocate*, 1946 J.C. 90; *Brown* v. *Macpherson*, 1918 J.C. 3): s.32 of the Criminal Justice (Scotland) Act 1995 removed the long-standing general prohibition against comment by the prosecutor upon such a failure to give evidence, which was found in the 1975 Act, s.141(1)(b) (*Dempsey* v. *H.M. Advocate*, 1995 S.C.C.R. 431 is a rare example of convictions being set aside on account of such improper comment by a prosecutor).
  There was previous authority that in some cases, the proved facts may raise a presumption that the accused committed the crime libelled, and failure by the accused to put forward an explanation sufficient to raise a reasonable doubt in the minds of the jury could occasion comment legitimately (see *Advocate, H.M.* v. *Hardy*, 1938 J.C. 144; *McIlhargey* v. *Herron*, 1972 J.C.

38; *Deacons v. H.M. Advocate*, 1994 G.W.D. 11–636). With regard to the reform which became s.32 of the Criminal Justice (Scotland) Act 1995, during the Committee Stage of the Bill (*Hansard*, H.L. Vol. 560, col. 416), the Lord Advocate observed: "Where the law itself only allows comment with restraint, and only for inferences to be drawn in narrow circumstances, it would be a foolish prosecutor indeed who went further than that."

Subss. (2) and (3)

No other party can compel an accused person to give evidence in any trial unless he has already been convicted or acquitted of all charges libelled. The accused may give evidence on his own behalf but ordinarily should do so before leading any other evidence (s.263(2) permits application to be made only for the interruption of evidence to enable the examination of another witness). Once he elects to give evidence the accused can be cross-examined on any issue subject only to the limitations imposed upon the prosecutor by subs. (4); these restrictions do not apply to co-accused who are entitled to cross-examine an accused as to his criminal record if the accused, directly or impliedly, gives evidence against them (*McCourtney v. H.M. Advocate*, 1978 S.L.T. 10; *Burton v. H.M. Advocate*, 1979 S.L.T. (Notes) 59). Much of the case law originates from the problems created by cross-incrimination of accused (see *Sandlan v. H.M. Advocate*, 1983 S.L.T. 519 which involved prejudicial evidence against first accused elicited in cross-examination of Crown witnesses by second accused without adequate opportunity for first accused to examine anew; in *Advocate, H.M. v. Ferrie*, 1983 S.C.C.R. 1 the use, by the Crown, as a witness of an accused who tendered partial pleas during trial was upheld; *Dodds v. H.M. Advocate*, 1987 S.C.C.R. 678; 1988 S.L.T. 194; an accused who had had his partial pleas accepted, then gave evidence in relation to the outstanding charge and was cross-examined by the co-accused in relation to all charges libelled, unsuccessfully appealed.

If in the conduct of his defence, either in cross-examination of prosecution witnesses or in his own evidence, the accused attacks the character of the complainer, impugns the conduct of the prosecutor or represents himself falsely to be of good character, the accused is liable to lose the customary protection of subs. (4). As subs. (5) makes clear, that protection can only properly be withdrawn by the court after the prosecutor has made that motion outwith the presence of any jury. The court must consider the motion (see *Leggate v. H.M. Advocate*, 1988 S.L.T. 665; 1988 S.C.C.R. 391).

The prosecutor has to exercise care to avoid breaching the statutory provisions, particularly in the heat of cross-examination: in *Cordiner v. H.M. Advocate*, 1991 S.C.C.R. 652; 1993 S.L.T. 2 the prosecutor challenged the accused that he had sought to instigate another witness to pervert the course of justice by false testimony, a crime not charged. No objection had been taken at the time and the Court of Appeal held that while the section had been breached technically, the appellant had waived compliance.

Note that subs. (9) has the effect of extending the protection given to the character of the complainer by subs. (4)(b) to deceased victims; it is not necessary that the deceased died as a result of being the victim of the crime charged.

Witnesses in court during trial

267.—(1) The court may, on an application by any party to the proceedings, permit a witness to be in court during the proceedings or any part of the proceedings before he has given evidence if it appears to the court that the presence of the witness would not be contrary to the interests of justice.

(2) Without prejudice to subsection (1) above, where a witness has, without the permission of the court and without the consent of the parties to the proceedings, been present in court during the proceedings, the court may, in its discretion, admit the witness, where it appears to the court that the presence of the witness was not the result of culpable negligence or criminal intent, and that the witness has not been unduly instructed or influenced by what took place during his presence, or that injustice will not be done by his examination.

Definitions
"witness": s.307(1).

GENERAL NOTE
It is a matter for the court whether the evidence of a witness present in court during the trial should be taken into account. The court should consider whether there has been any criminative intent or wilful neglect on the part of the witness, the likely effect upon his testimony of his earlier presence in court and the likelihood of injustice being done by the exclusion of that evidence in the case.

See *MacDonald v. Mackenzie*, 1947 J.C. 169; it is the task of the party tendering the witness' evidence to satisfy the court that the evidence should be admitted notwithstanding the improper presence in court. The evidence of a solicitor engaged in the case cannot be objected to on the ground of his earlier presence in court (*Campbell v. Cochrane*, 1928 J.C. 25).

Additional evidence, etc.

Additional evidence

268.—(1) Subject to subsection (2) below, the judge may, on a motion of the prosecutor or the accused made—
  (a) in proceedings on indictment, at any time before the commencement of the speeches to the jury;
  (b) in summary proceedings, at any time before the prosecutor proceeds to address the judge on the evidence,
permit him to lead additional evidence.

(2) Permission shall only be granted under subsection (1) above where the judge—
  (a) considers that the additional evidence is *prima facie* material; and
  (b) accepts that at the commencement of the trial either—
      (i) the additional evidence was not available and could not reasonably have been made available; or
      (ii) the materiality of such additional evidence could not reasonably have been foreseen by the party.

(3) The judge may permit the additional evidence to be led notwithstanding that—
  (a) in proceedings on indictment, a witness or production concerned is not included in any list lodged by the parties and that the notice required by sections 67(5) and 78(4) of this Act has not been given; or
  (b) in any case, a witness must be recalled.

(4) The judge may, when granting a motion in terms of this section, adjourn or postpone the trial before permitting the additional evidence to be led.

(5) In this section "the commencement of the trial" means—
  (a) in proceedings on indictment, the time when the jury is sworn; and
  (b) in summary proceedings, the time when the first witness for the prosecution is sworn.

DEFINITIONS
  "commencement of proceedings": s.268(5).
  "indictment": s.307(1).
  "judge": s.307(1).
  "prosecutor": s.307(1).

GENERAL NOTE
Additional evidence can be led in both solemn or summary proceedings provided that the criteria in subs. (2) are satisfied. In solemn proceedings such evidence can be received notwithstanding that the relevant productions or witnesses have not been specified in the indictment (subs. (3)(a)); in either solemn or summary trials the additional evidence can be taken from witnesses whose evidence has already been heard.

In *Cushion v. H.M. Advocate*, 1993 S.C.C.R. 356; 1994 S.L.T. 410 a review of the trial judge's refusal to admit additional evidence was appealed under the explanation that the court had not been given a full background, and that the judge's decision might have been more favourable to the application; the Appeal Court declined to review the application under s.149(1) of the 1975 Act.

Evidence in replication

269.—(1) The judge may, on a motion of the prosecutor made at the relevant time, permit the prosecutor to lead additional evidence for the purpose of—
(a) contradicting evidence given by any defence witness which could not reasonably have been anticipated by the prosecutor; or
(b) providing such proof as is mentioned in section 263(4) of this Act.
(2) The judge may permit the additional evidence to be led notwithstanding that—
(a) in proceedings on indictment, a witness or production concerned is not included in any list lodged by the parties and that the notice required by sections 67(5) and 78(4) of this Act has not been given; or
(b) in any case, a witness must be recalled.
(3) The judge may when granting a motion in terms of this section, adjourn or postpone the trial before permitting the additional evidence to be led.
(4) In subsection (1) above, "the relevant time" means—
(a) in proceedings on indictment, after the close of the defence evidence and before the commencement of the speeches to the jury; and
(b) in summary proceedings, after the close of the defence evidence and before the prosecutor proceeds to address the judge on the evidence.

DEFINITIONS
"indictment": s.307(1).
"judge": s.307(1).
"prosecutor": s.307(1).
"relevant time, the": s.269(4).

GENERAL NOTE
Evidence in replication may be led with leave of the court to contradict defence evidence which could not be anticipated by the prosecutor, or for the purpose of proving a prior statement of a witness whose evidence is now at variance (s.263(4)).

In assessing whether the prosecutor could have expected the testimony led by the defence, the court may well enquire about the preparations for trial; in both *MacGillivray v. Johnston (No. 2)*, 1994 S.L.T. 1012 and *Neizer v. Johnston*, 1993 S.C.C.R. 772 a decisive factor in refusing such a motion in each case was the Crown's awareness of the existence of witnesses who had been precognosced but had not been led in evidence.

Note that replication can only be used to counter defence evidence and cannot be used by the Crown to contradict earlier prosecution evidence (see *Campbell v. Allan*, 1988 S.C.C.R. 47).

Evidence of criminal record and character of accused

270.—(1) This section applies where—
(a) evidence is led by the defence, or the defence asks questions of a witness for the prosecution, with a view to establishing the accused's good character or impugning the character of the prosecutor, of any witness for the prosecution or of the complainer; or
(b) the nature or conduct of the defence is such as to tend to establish the accused's good character or to involve imputations on the character of the prosecutor, of any witness for the prosecution or of the complainer.
(2) Where this section applies the court may, without prejudice to section 268 of this Act, on the application of the prosecutor, permit the prosecutor to lead evidence that the accused has committed, or has been convicted of, or has been charged with, offences other than that for which he is being tried, or is of bad character, notwithstanding that, in proceedings on indictment, a witness or production concerned is not included in any list lodged by the prosecutor and that the notice required by sections 67(5) and 78(4) of this Act has not been given.
(3) In proceedings on indictment, an application under subsection (2) above shall be made in the course of the trial but in the absence of the jury.

(4) In subsection (1) above, references to the complainer include references to a victim who is deceased.

DEFINITIONS
"prosecutor": s.307(1).
"witness": s.307(1).

GENERAL NOTE
The purpose of this section is to provide a balanced picture where the defence, as a matter of tactics, elects to present the accused as being of good character or brings out the faults of witnesses or a deceased person. A cursory examination might suggest that subs. (2) is very similar to the more familiar terms of s.266(4)(b) and (c). Section 266 only enables the prosecutor or other accused to question the accused as to his history and character where such defence tactics have been pursued by the accused and the prosecutor, at least, may only do so with leave of the court (s.266(5)). It is important to note that s.266(4) is limited in scope: it is only activated when the accused gives evidence on his own behalf.

By contrast, subs. (2) is much more radical and enables the prosecution to lead evidence (without prior notice but with leave of the court) in rebuttal to demonstrate the history and character of the accused, if the defence has led evidence of his good character, or attacked the character of Crown witnesses or the prosecutor. The introduction of this provision in the Criminal Justice (Scotland) Act 1995, s.24 was not without controversy, given its nature, but it is clear that the conduct of the defence case in the future may require a good deal more circumspection than was necessary hitherto, even where the accused does not give evidence. It may also be said that subs. (1)(b) by its reference to "the nature or conduct of the defence" lacks both the familiarity and clarity of subs. (1)(a).

Evidence of children

Evidence of children: special provisions

271.—(1) Subject to subsections (7) and (8) below, where a child has been cited to give evidence in a trial the court may appoint a commissioner to take the evidence of the child if—
(a) in solemn proceedings, at any time before the oath is administered to the jury;
(b) in summary proceedings, at any time before the first witness is sworn;
(c) in exceptional circumstances in either solemn or summary proceedings, during the course of the trial,
application is made to the court in that regard; but to be so appointed a person must be, and for a period of at least five years have been, a member of the Faculty of Advocates or a solicitor.

(2) Proceedings before a commissioner appointed under subsection (1) above shall be recorded by video recorder.

(3) An accused shall not, except by leave of the commissioner, be present in the room where such proceedings are taking place but shall be entitled by such means as seem suitable to the commissioner to watch and hear the proceedings.

(4) Subsections (2) to (6), (8) and (9) of section 272 of this Act shall apply to an application under subsection (1) above and evidence taken by a commissioner appointed under that subsection as those subsections apply to an application under subsection (1) of that section and evidence taken by a commissioner appointed on such an application.

(5) Subject to subsections (7) and (8) below, where a child has been or is likely to be cited to give evidence in a trial, the court may, on an application being made to it, authorise the giving of evidence by the child by means of a live television link.

(6) Subject to subsections (7) and (8) below, where a child has been or is likely to be cited to give evidence in a trial, the court may, on application being made to it, authorise the use of a screen to conceal the accused from the

sight of the child while the child is present to give evidence; but arrangements shall be made to ensure that the accused is able to watch and hear as the evidence is given by the child.

(7) The court may grant an application under subsection (1), (5) or (6) above only on cause shown having regard in particular to—

(a) the possible effect on the child if required to give evidence, no such application having been granted;

(b) whether it is likely that the child would be better able to give evidence if such application were granted; and

(c) the views of the child.

(8) In considering whether to grant an application under subsection (1), (5) or (6) above, the court may take into account, where appropriate, any of the following—

(a) the age and maturity of the child;

(b) the nature of the alleged offence;

(c) the nature of the evidence which the child is likely to be called on to give; and

(d) the relationship, if any, between the child and the accused.

(9) Where a sheriff to whom an application has been made under subsection (1), (5) or (6) above would have granted the application but for the lack of accommodation or equipment necessary to achieve the purpose of the application, he may by order transfer the case to any sheriff court which has such accommodation and equipment available, being a sheriff court in the same sheriffdom.

(10) The sheriff court to which a case is transferred under subsection (9) above shall be deemed to have granted an application under, as the case may be, subsection (1), (5) or (6) above in relation to the case.

(11) Where a court has or is deemed to have granted an application under subsection (1), (5) or (6) above in relation to a child, and the child gives evidence that he recalls having identified, prior to the trial, a person alleged to have committed an offence, the evidence of a third party as to the identification of that person by the child prior to the trial shall be admissible as evidence as to such identification.

(12) In this section—

"child" means a person under the age of 16 years;

"court" means the High Court or the sheriff court; and

"trial" means a trial under solemn or under summary procedure.

DEFINITIONS

"child": s.271(12).
"court": s.271(12).
"offence": s.307(1).
"trial": s.271(12).
"witness": s.307(1).

GENERAL NOTE

This section re-enacts the provisions of ss.33 to 35 of the Prisoners and Criminal Proceedings (Scotland) Act 1993 (c. 9) which themselves amended the Law Reform (Miscellaneous Provisions) (Scotland) Act 1990 (c. 55). The purpose of the section is to provide protection to child witnesses from having to confront the accused in court; these provisions are in addition to the judicial power to clear the court of all disinterested observers during a child's evidence. The procedural mechanisms enacted are generally used in cases of a sexual nature but subs. (8) indicates that they can be applied in any sort of offence brought before the Sheriff and High Courts.

Where recourse is sought to use of these provisions, the court must first hear parties on the merits and apply its mind to the factors set out in subss. (7) and (8); in addition in cases (solemn or summary) before a sheriff, the judge has power to transfer the proceedings to another court in his sheriffdom if it is felt that that court is better equipped to hold the trial (subs. (9)).

Once an application has been allowed by the court it will be noted that subs. (11) can be utilised as a means of achieving the identification of the accused without the child having to confront that person: this provision only takes effect if, in the course of his or her evidence, the child speaks of having identified the person responsible for the offence prior to trial. This does not of course preclude identification by other means including *de recenti* statements.

Three distinct routes for the taking of a child's evidence can be followed under s.271 but it will be appreciated that in order to persuade the court to apply the section's provisions, the applicant party must be able to address the court on the impact of the case to date upon the child, the likely effect upon the child having to give evidence in the normal manner, and which of the three methods seems best to secure the child's evidence.

Subsection (1) provides for the appointment of a commissioner by the court to question the child whose examination has to be recorded on video tape and witnessed by the accused. Usually such an examination should be relayed to the accused but the commissioner can, if it seems appropriate, permit the accused to be present while it takes place. Subsection (2) allows the use of a closed circuit, or other, television link to relay the child's evidence to court; subs. (6) permits the use of screens in the court itself, these being positioned in such a way as to shield the child from direct sight of the accused during evidence.

Chapter 22 of the 1996 Act of Adjournal makes provision for the evidence of children. See also Form 22.1 for the style of petition to be used in applications for live television links.

Evidence on commission and from abroad

Evidence by letter of request or on commission

272.—(1) In any criminal proceedings in the High Court or the sheriff court the prosecutor or the defence may, at an appropriate time, apply to a judge of the court in which the trial is to take place (or, if that is not yet known, to a judge of the High Court) for—

    (a) the issue of a letter of request to a court, or tribunal, exercising jurisdiction in a country or territory outside the United Kingdom, Channel Islands and Isle of Man for the examination of a witness resident in that country or territory; or

    (b) the appointment of a commissioner to examine, at any place in the United Kingdom, Channel Islands, or Isle of Man, a witness who—

        (i) by reason of being ill or infirm is unable to attend the trial diet; or

        (ii) is not ordinarily resident in, and is, at the time of the trial diet, unlikely to be present in, the United Kingdom, Channel Islands or the Isle of Man.

(2) A hearing, as regards any application under subsection (1) above by a party, shall be conducted in chambers but may be dispensed with if the application is not opposed.

(3) An application under subsection (1) above may be granted only if the judge is satisfied that—

    (a) the evidence which it is averred the witness is able to give is necessary for the proper adjudication of the trial; and

    (b) there would be no unfairness to the other party were such evidence to be received in the form of the record of an examination conducted by virtue of that subsection.

(4) Any such record as is mentioned in paragraph (b) of subsection (3) above shall, without being sworn to by witnesses, be received in evidence in so far as it either accords with the averment mentioned in paragraph (a) of that subsection or can be so received without unfairness to either party.

(5) Where any such record as is mentioned in paragraph (b) of subsection (3) above, or any part of such record, is not a document in writing, that record or part shall not be received in evidence under subsection (4) above unless it is accompanied by a transcript of its contents.

(6) The procedure as regards the foregoing provisions of this section shall be prescribed by Act of Adjournal; and without prejudice to the generality of the power to make it, such an Act of Adjournal may provide for the appointment of a person before whom evidence may be taken for the purposes of this section.

(7) In subsection (1) above, "appropriate time" means as regards—

(a) solemn proceedings, any time before the oath is administered to the jury;

(b) summary proceedings, any time before the first witness is sworn,

or (but only in relation to an application under paragraph (b) of that subsection) any time during the course of the trial if the circumstances on which the application is based had not arisen, or would not have merited such application, within the period mentioned in paragraph (a) or, as the case may be, (b) of this subsection.

(8) In subsection (3) and (4) above, "record" includes, in addition to a document in writing—

(a) any disc, tape, soundtrack or other device in which sounds or other data (not being visual images) are recorded so as to be capable (with or without the aid of some other equipment) of being reproduced therefrom; and

(b) any film (including microfilm), negative, tape, disc or other device in which one or more visual images are recorded so as to be capable (as aforesaid) of being reproduced therefrom.

(9) This section is without prejudice to any existing power at common law to adjourn a trial diet to the place where a witness is.

DEFINITIONS

"appropriate time": s.272(7).
"High Court": s.307(1).
"judge": s.307(1).
"prosecutor": s.307(1).
"record": s.272(8).
"trial": s.307(1).
"witness": s.307(1).

GENERAL NOTE

This section applies to solemn and summary proceedings and can apply in circumstances in which the court might otherwise have to convene elsewhere in order to hear a witness' testimony. Chapters 23 and 24 of the 1996 Act of Adjournal regulates the form in which applications for Letters of Request of the taking of evidence on Commission are to be made. The procedures only operate in the Sheriff and High Courts.

Subsection (2) stipulates that such applications can normally only be made before trial proceedings have begun (although see the exceptional provisions available for applications which of necessity need to be made in the course of the trial). As subs. (1) states, any application should be made to a judge within whose jurisdiction the trial is due to take place, or, if no trial diet has been assigned, to a High Court judge. This requirement will be of limited applicability to summary cases since it would only rarely be necessary to seek Letters or a Commission once a trial had been fixed. The application in terms of Rule 23.1.–(4) has to be intimated to other parties and any hearing will occur in chambers if the application is opposed.

The classes of witness in relation to whom applications can be made are set out in subs. (1) but the judge has to be satisfied that the factors stipulated in subs. (3) are met before the application is allowed. Furthermore the granting of the application does not of itself mean that the testimony obtained has to be admitted as evidence: the court on receipt of the record (which must be accompanied by a written transcript) still has to consider whether its contents can be fairly admitted in accordance with the rules of evidence.

In considering the grant of an application, the court has to consider the test set out in subs. (3). It is essential that due weight is given to the potential unfairness to those in the trial who are deprived of the opportunity of oral cross-examination should Letters or a Commission be permitted (see *Muirhead v. H.M. Advocate*, 1983 S.C.C.R. 133). In *Land, Petr.*, 1991 S.L.T. 931; 1991 S.C.C.R. 138 while an application by the Crown to take the evidence on commission of a 91-year old witness was granted, and it was conceded that the sheriff's discretion was not subject to review, it was held that the issue of fairness to the accused still fell to be considered at the trial and, if necessary, on appeal.

See also *Advocate, H.M. v. Lesacher*, 1982 S.C.C.R. 418 where the trial had to be delayed to allow for the presentation of Letters of Request to West Germany through diplomatic channels.

Refer to Chap. 23 of the 1996 Act of Adjournal for provisions as to expenses, transmission of Letters and custody of documents. Note in particular that Rule 23.6. specifies that such evidence cannot be led or referred to in trial proceedings until a motion to that effect has been made and granted.

It will be observed that requests for live television links for evidence to be taken contemporaneously from abroad during proceedings (s.273 below) are initiated by way of the Letter of Request procedures described above.

Television link evidence from abroad

273.—(1) In any solemn proceedings in the High Court or the sheriff court a person other than the accused may give evidence through a live television link if—

(a) the witness is outside the United Kingdom;

(b) an application under subsection (2) below for the issue of a letter of request has been granted; and

(c) the court is satisfied as to the arrangements for the giving of evidence in that manner by that witness.

(2) The prosecutor or the defence in any proceedings referred to in subsection (1) above may apply to a judge of the court in which the trial is to take place (or, if that court is not yet known, to a judge of the High Court) for the issue of a letter of request to—

(a) a court or tribunal exercising jurisdiction in a country or territory outside the United Kingdom where a witness is ordinarily resident; or

(b) any authority which the judge is satisfied is recognised by the government of that country or territory as the appropriate authority for receiving requests for assistance in facilitating the giving of evidence through a live television link,

requesting assistance in facilitating the giving of evidence by that witness through a live television link.

(3) An application under subsection (2) above shall be granted only if the judge is satisfied that—

(a) the evidence which it is averred the witness is able to give is necessary for the proper adjudication of the trial; and

(b) the granting of the application—

(i) is in the interests of justice; and

(ii) in the case of an application by the prosecutor, is not unfair to the accused.

DEFINITIONS
"High Court": s.307(1).
"judge": s.307(1).
"prosecutor": s.307(1).
"sheriff": s.307(1).
"trial": s.307(1).
"witness": s.307(1).

GENERAL NOTE
In solemn proceedings only, application by way of the Letter of Request procedure outlined in s.272 above can be made for a live television link to take the evidence of witnesses who are outwith the United Kingdom. The factors determining whether such an application should be allowed by the court are laid out in subs. (2).

Evidence relating to sexual offences

Restrictions on evidence relating to sexual offences

274.—(1) In any trial of a person on any charge to which this section applies, subject to section 275 of this Act, the court shall not admit, or allow questioning designed to elicit, evidence which shows or tends to show that the complainer—

(a) is not of good character in relation to sexual matters;

(b) is a prostitute or an associate of prostitutes; or

(c) has at any time engaged with any person in sexual behaviour not forming part of the subject matter of the charge.

(2) This section applies to a charge of committing or attempting to commit any of the following offences, that is to say—

(a) rape;

(b) sodomy;

(c) clandestine injury to women;

(d) assault with intent to rape;

(e) indecent assault;

(f) indecent behaviour (including any lewd, indecent or libidinous practice or behaviour);

(g) an offence under section 106(1)(a) or 107 of the Mental Health (Scotland) Act 1984 (unlawful sexual intercourse with mentally handicapped female or with patient); or

(h) an offence under any of the following provisions of the Criminal Law (Consolidation) (Scotland) Act 1995—

    (i) sections 1 to 3 (incest and related offences);

    (ii) section 5 (unlawful sexual intercourse with girl under 13 or 16);

    (iii) section 6 (indecent behaviour toward girl between 12 and 16);

    (iv) section 7(2) and (3) (procuring by threats etc.);

    (v) section 8 (abduction and unlawful detention);

    (vi) section 13(5) (homosexual offences).

(3) In this section "complainer" means the person against whom the offence referred to in subsection (2) above is alleged to have been committed.

(4) This section does not apply to questioning, or evidence being adduced, by the Crown.

DEFINITIONS

"complainer": s.274(3).
"offences": s.307(1).
"trial": s.307(1).

GENERAL NOTE

This section which applies equally to summary and solemn proceedings incorporates the provisions concerning sexual offences now found in the Criminal Law (Consolidation) (Scotland) Act 1995 (c. 39). Where charges of a sexual nature as specified in subs. (2) are libelled, questions by the defence as to the sexual history or sexual preferences of the complainer are generally prohibited. The exceptions to this general rule are contained in s.275 below, where any such questioning proceeds at the discretion of the court which has the power to limit the scope of such cross-examination. In solemn proceedings any motion must be made outwith the presence of the jury.

The provisions of s.274 do not only apply to the complainer; efforts to adduce such evidence by the back door in cross-examination of other witnesses is equally prohibited. The grant or refusal of such an application rests in the discretion of the trial judge (see *Bremner v. H.M. Advocate*, 1992 S.C.C.R. 476).

Exceptions to restrictions under section 274

275.—(1) Notwithstanding section 274 of this Act, in any trial of an a accused on any charge to which that section applies, where the court is satisfied on an application by the accused—

(a) that the questioning or evidence referred to in subsection (1) of that section is designed to explain or rebut evidence adduced, or to be adduced, otherwise than by or on behalf of the accused;

(b) that the questioning or evidence referred to in paragraph (c) of that subsection—

(i) is questioning or evidence as to sexual behaviour which took place on the same occasion as the sexual behaviour forming the subject matter of the charge; or

(ii) is relevant to the defence of incrimination; or

(c) that it would be contrary to the interests of justice to exclude the questioning or evidence referred to in that subsection,

the court shall allow the questioning or, as the case may be, admit the evidence.

(2) Where questioning or evidence is or has been allowed or admitted under this section, the court may at any time limit as it thinks fit the extent of that questioning or evidence.

(3) Any application under this section shall be made in the course of the trial but in the absence of the jury, the complainer, any person cited as a witness and the public.

DEFINITIONS
"trial": s.307(1).

GENERAL NOTE
See the notes to s.274 above.

Biological material

Evidence of biological material

276.—(1) Evidence as to the characteristics and composition of any biological material deriving from human beings or animals shall, in any criminal proceedings, be admissible notwithstanding that neither the material nor a sample of it is lodged as a production.

(2) A party wishing to lead such evidence as is referred to in subsection (1) above shall, where neither the material nor a sample of it is lodged as a production, make the material or a sample of it available for inspection by the other party unless the material constitutes a hazard to health or has been destroyed in the process of analysis.

GENERAL NOTE
This section dispenses with the need to produce in court certain biological materials in relation to which evidence is to be led in proceedings. Ordinarily in solemn proceedings the accused is entitled to inspect any productions (see s.68(2)); no such provision is found in summary proceedings given their character. Section 276 arises from considerations of public health and constitutes an exception to the authority that allows an accused to see productions.

Transcripts and records

Transcript of police interview sufficient evidence

277.—(1) Subject to subsection (2) below, for the purposes of any criminal proceedings, a document certified by the person who made it as an accurate transcript made for the prosecutor of the contents of a tape (identified by means of a label) purporting to be a recording of an interview between—

(a) a police officer and an accused person; or

(b) a person commissioned, appointed or authorised under section 6(3) of the Customs and Excise Management Act 1979 and an accused person,

shall be received in evidence and be sufficient evidence of the making of the transcript and of its accuracy.

(2) Subsection (1) above shall not apply to a transcript—

(a) unless a copy of it has been served on the accused not less than 14 days before his trial; or

(b) if the accused, not less than six days before his trial, or by such later time before his trial as the court may in special circumstances allow, has served notice on the prosecutor that the accused challenges the making of the transcript or its accuracy.

(3) A copy of the transcript or a notice under subsection (2) above shall be served in such manner as may be prescribed by Act of Adjournal; and a written execution purporting to be signed by the person who served the transcript or notice, together with, where appropriate, the relevant post office receipt shall be sufficient evidence of such service.

(4) Where subsection (1) above does not apply to a transcript, if the person who made the transcript is called as a witness his evidence shall be sufficient evidence of the making of the transcript and of its accuracy.

DEFINITIONS
"prosecutor": s.307(1).

GENERAL NOTE
This section permits the admission as evidence of a transcript of any interview conducted by the police or Customs officers with the accused on tape. The transcript, prepared by a person appointed by the procurator fiscal, has to be certified by that person and a copy of it has to be served (subs. (3)) on the accused not less than 14 days before trial (subs. (2)(a)). Any challenge to the accuracy of the transcript has to be intimated to the prosecutor not less than six days before trial normally, or later on cause shown. It appears that a challenge to the accuracy of the transcript can be met conclusively by calling the person who prepared it but this would not preclude the alternative of playing the tape, provided its contents did not breach ss.101(1) and 166(3) and disclose previous convictions or contain other inadmissible material. These factors explain why the prosecution will often prepare and lodge an edited transcript deleting any such untoward references: in that event the jury, or the judge in summary proceedings, should only be referred to the edited transcript in the course of evidence.

Note that, unlike the transcript of any judicial examination, which must be lodged in solemn proceedings (see the notes to ss.36 and 37), this section does not oblige the prosecutor to lodge a transcript of taped interview.

Record of proceedings at examination as evidence

278.—(1) Subject to subsection (2) below, the record made, under section 37 of this Act (incorporating any rectification authorised under section 38(1) of this Act), of proceedings at the examination of an accused shall be received in evidence without being sworn to by witnesses, and it shall not be necessary in proceedings on indictment to insert the names of any witnesses to the record in any list of witnesses, either for the prosecution or for the defence.

(2) On the application of either an accused or the prosecutor—

(a) in proceedings on indictment, subject to sections 37(5) and 72(1)(b)(iv) of this Act, the court may determine that the record or part of the record shall not be read to the jury; and

(b) in summary proceedings, subject to the said section 37(5) and to subsection (4) below, the court may refuse to admit the record or some part of the record as evidence.

(3) At the hearing of an application under subsection (2) above, it shall be competent for the prosecutor or the defence to adduce as witnesses the persons who were present during the proceedings mentioned in subsection (1) above and for either party to examine those witnesses upon any matters regarding the said proceedings.

(4) In summary proceedings, except on cause shown, an application under subsection (2)(b) above shall not be heard unless notice of at least 10 clear days has been given to the court and to the other parties.

(5) In subsection (2) above, the "record" comprises—

(a) as regards any trial of an indictment, each record included, under section 68(1) of this Act, in the list of productions; and

(b) as regards a summary trial, each record which it is sought to have received under subsection (1) above.

DEFINITIONS

"indictment": s.307(1).
"prosecutor": s.307(1).
"record": s.278(5).
"witness": s.307(1).

GENERAL NOTE

Section 278 specifies the principles to be applied to the use of transcripts of judicial examination at trial. Section 38(1) allows for rectification of the transcript after which procedure the accuracy of the transcript is settled conclusively (see s.38(4)): s.279 is concerned with the admissibility, or otherwise, of material in the transcript. On the motion of any party, the court has to determine which parts of the transcript may be read to the jury or court in the subsequent trial. See also Chap. 25 of the 1996 Act of Adjournal in relation to the use of transcripts in evidence.

Any motion to restrict the material in a judicial examination has to be made in compliance with subs. (2), at a first or preliminary diet in solemn procedure (see s.72(1)(b)), or not less than 10 clear days before a summary trial (it is not essential that the issue be raised at the intermediate diet (see s.148) but this would obviously be a sensible time for it to be considered). Since it cannot be certain in a summary case whether the Crown intends to found upon the transcript of judicial examination until trial proceeds, there is obviously an element of anticipation involved in making such a motion.

Note that in *Hendry v. H.M. Advocate*, 1985 S.C.C.R. 275, a Five Bench decision, it was held to be illegitimate to use a self-serving statement made in a judicial examination as a substitute for parole evidence on oath. The case of *McEwan v. H.M. Advocate*, 1990 S.C.C.R. 401 gives directions as to how the contents of a judicial examination should be presented to a jury.

In considering whether a transcript of judicial examination should be admitted as evidence, a relevant factor is likely to be the similarity or otherwise between the petition charges, which formed the basis of the examination, and the charges ultimately libelled. Similar considerations will apply to any alleged admissions put to the accused at examination and their fairness and admissibility in the light of evidence. The prosecutor is now required to lodge a certified copy of the petition (and by implication any transcript of alleged admissions put to the accused at the judicial examination) as well as any transcript of judicial examination as a production.

Documentary evidence

Evidence from documents

279. Schedule 8 to this Act, which makes provision regarding the admissibility in criminal proceedings of copy documents and of evidence contained in business documents, shall have effect.

GENERAL NOTE

Schedule 8 to the Act restates the terms of Sched. 3 to the Prisoners and Criminal Proceedings (Scotland) Act 1993 which provides for the certification of documentary evidence, particularly business documents, and validates the use of certified copies of documents (as defined in Sched. (8)), which may in some instances contain hearsay material, as best evidence in criminal proceedings.

Routine evidence

Routine evidence

280.—(1) For the purposes of any proceedings for an offence under any of the enactments specified in column 1 of Schedule 9 to this Act, a certificate purporting to be signed by a person or persons specified in column 2 thereof, and certifying the matter specified in column 3 thereof shall, subject to subsection (6) below, be sufficient evidence of that matter and of the qualification or authority of that person or those persons.

(2) The Secretary of State may by order—

(a) amend or repeal the entry in Schedule 9 to this Act in respect of any enactment; or

(b) insert in that Schedule an entry in respect of a further enactment.

(3) An order under subsection (2) above may make such transitional, incidental or supplementary provision as the Secretary of State considers necessary or expedient in connection with the coming into force of the order.

(4) For the purposes of any criminal proceedings, a report purporting to be signed by two authorised forensic scientists shall, subject to subsection (5) below, be sufficient evidence of any fact or conclusion as to fact contained in the report and of the authority of the signatories.

(5) A forensic scientist is authorised for the purposes of subsection (4) above if—

(a) he is authorised for those purposes by the Secretary of State; or

(b) he—

(i) is a constable or is employed by a police authority under section 9 of the Police (Scotland) Act 1967;

(ii) possesses such qualifications and experience as the Secretary of State may for the purposes of that subsection by order prescribe; and

(iii) is authorised for those purposes by the chief constable of the police force maintained for the police area of that authority.

(6) Subsections (1) and (4) above shall not apply to a certificate or, as the case may be, report tendered on behalf of the prosecutor or the accused—

(a) unless a copy has been served on the other party not less than fourteen days before the trial; or

(b) where the other party, not more than seven days after the date of service of the copy on him under paragraph (a) above or by such later time as the court may in special circumstances allow, has served notice on the first party that the accused challenges the matter, qualification or authority mentioned in subsection (1) above or as the case may be the fact, conclusion or authority mentioned in subsection (4) above.

(7) A copy of a certificate or, as the case may be, report required by subsection (6) above, to be served on the accused or the prosecutor or of a notice required by that subsection or by subsection (1) or (2) of section 281 of this Act to be served on the prosecutor shall be served in such manner as may be prescribed by Act of Adjournal; and a written execution purporting to be signed by the person who served such certificate or notice, together with, where appropriate, the relevant post office receipt shall be sufficient evidence of service of such a copy.

(8) Where, following service of a notice under subsection (6)(b) above, evidence is given in relation to a report referred to in subsection (4) above by both of the forensic scientists purporting to have signed the report, the evidence of those forensic scientists shall be sufficient evidence of any fact (or conclusion as to fact) contained in the report.

(9) At any trial of an offence it shall be presumed that the person who appears in answer to the complaint is the person charged by the police with the offence unless the contrary is alleged.

(10) An order made under subsection (2) or (5)(b)(ii) above shall be made by statutory instrument.

(11) No order shall be made under subsection (2) above unless a draft of the order has been laid before, and approved by a resolution of, each House of Parliament.

(12) A statutory instrument containing an order under subsection (5)(b)(ii) above shall be subject to annulment pursuant to a resolution of either House of Parliament.

DEFINITIONS
"complaint": s.307(1).
"constable": s.307(1) and s.51(1) of the Police (Scotland) Act 1967 (c. 77).
"offence": s.307(1).
"prosecutor": s.307(1).
"trial": s.307(1).

GENERAL NOTE
Unlike s.26(2) of the Criminal Justice (Scotland) Act 1980 which applied only to summary proceedings, the effect of subs. (4) is to apply these provisions relating to routine evidence prepared by authorised forensic scientists to both summary and solemn proceedings. The provisions of s.281 are equally available to prosecution and defence alike provided the authors of the report are authorised scientists.

It will be noted that subs. (5) broadens the definition of "forensic scientist" to include police constables or police employees appointed by their Chief Constable. The provisions in regard to service of forensic reports are repeated in subs. (3) and the form of certificate, as provided by Chap. 27 of the 1996 Act of Adjournal, is found in Form 27.2.

Challenges to the contents of a report must be by notice served on the other party not more than seven days after service of the report (note that by contrast, s.26(3) of the 1980 Act allowed challenge up to six days before the trial). Failing such challenge, the contents of the report shall be received as sufficient evidence. Much of the case law generated by s.26 of the 1980 Act related to attacking certificated evidence, which had not been formally challenged, on the basis that the facts contained in the reports did not themselves satisfy the statutory requirements. See *Normand v. Wotherspoon*, 1993 S.C.C.R. 912; 1994 S.L.T. 487; *Straker v. Orr*, 1994 S.C.C.R. 251; *McCrindle v. Walkingshaw*, 1994 S.C.C.R. 299; *O'Brien v. McCreadie*, 1994 S.C.C.R. 516.

The section makes various other provisions intended to reduce the unnecessary attendance of witnesses at court. The Secretary of State may add to the list of matters which may be introduced into evidence by certificate, by way of subordinate legislation. This will enable suitable matters to be added to the list as they are identified without the need to wait for a suitable opportunity to incorporate them in primary legislation (subss. (2) and (3)).

This section puts it beyond doubt that the facts and conclusions as to facts spoken to either in the report or in subsequent oral evidence based on the report, are sufficient for the purpose of proving those facts. Such evidence can still be attacked on the grounds of credibility or unreliability.

Subsection (9) repeats the terms of s.26(5) and enacts a presumption that the party answering the complaint is the person charged by the police. Unless a challenge is intimated on behalf of the accused before a plea has been tendered, the presumption will hold good and it then becomes unnecessary to identify the accused in the course of the trial, always provided that it has been established that the person responsible for the offence had been charged. See *Rollo v. Wilson*, 1988 S.C.C.R. 312 where the sheriff recalled a police witness to confirm evidence of identification; on appeal it was held that the s.26(5) presumption had in any event rendered the recall unnecessary: in *Hamilton v. Ross*, 1991 S.C.C.R. 165; 1992 S.L.T. 384 the Appeal Court raised the issue of the presumption in response to a Crown appeal against a no case to answer motion; the issue had not been aired before that time but the Crown was still entitled to benefit from the provision.

Routine evidence: autopsy and forensic science reports

281.—(1) Where in a trial an autopsy report is lodged as a production by the prosecutor it shall be presumed that the body of the person identified in that report is the body of the deceased identified in the indictment or complaint, unless the accused not less than six days before the trial, or by such later time before the trial as the court may in special circumstances allow, gives notice that the contrary is alleged.

(2) At the time of lodging an autopsy or forensic science report as a production the prosecutor may intimate to the accused that it is intended that only one of the pathologists or forensic scientists (whom the prosecutor shall specify) purporting to have signed the report shall be called to give evidence in respect thereof; and the evidence of that pathologist or forensic scientist shall be sufficient evidence of any fact or conclusion as to fact contained in the report and of the qualifications of the signatories, unless the accused, not less than six days before the trial or by such later time before the trial as the court may in special circumstances allow, serves notice on the prosecutor

that he requires the attendance at the trial of the other pathologist or forensic scientist also.

(3) Where, following service of a notice by the accused under subsection (2) above, evidence is given in relation to an autopsy or forensic science report by both of the pathologists or forensic scientists purporting to have signed the report, the evidence of those pathologists or forensic scientists shall be sufficient evidence of any fact (or conclusion as to fact) contained in the report.

DEFINITIONS
"indictment": s.307(1).
"complaint": s.307(1).
"prosecutor": s.307(1).
"trial": s.307(1).

GENERAL NOTE
It is presumed, unless a challenge is notified to the prosecutor not less than six days before any trial (or later on cause shown), that the person referred to in any autopsy report founded upon in the proceedings is the same person as specified in the libel. Subsection (2) entitles the prosecutor to serve notice that he will call only one of the joint authors of a forensic of autopsy report, a concession designed to minimise inconvenience to such witnesses if their evidence is not in dispute. Again, a challenge to such a notice has to be intimated not less than six days before trial (or later on cause shown). Rule 27.1 in the 1996 Act of Adjournal requires that such notice will be in writing.

The practice has developed in solemn cases of incorporating the subs. (2) notice to the accused in the List of Productions incorporated in the indictment.

Sufficient evidence

Evidence as to controlled drugs and medicinal products

282.—(1) For the purposes of any criminal proceedings, evidence given by an authorised forensic scientist, either orally or in a report purporting to be signed by him, that a substance which satisfies either of the conditions specified in subsection (2) below is—

(a) a particular controlled drug or medicinal product; or

(b) a particular product which is listed in the British Pharmacopoeia as containing a particular controlled drug or medicinal product,

shall, subject to subsection (3) below, be sufficient evidence of that fact notwithstanding that no analysis of the substance has been carried out.

(2) Those conditions are—

(a) that the substance is in a sealed container bearing a label identifying the contents of the container; or

(b) that the substance has a characteristic appearance having regard to its size, shape, colour and manufacturer's mark.

(3) A party proposing to rely on subsection (1) above ("the first party") shall, not less than 14 days before the trial diet, serve on the other party ("the second party")—

(a) a notice to that effect; and

(b) where the evidence is contained in a report, a copy of the report,

and if the second party serves on the first party, not more than seven days after the date of service of the notice on him, a notice that he does not accept the evidence as to the identity of the substance, subsection (1) above shall not apply in relation to that evidence.

(4) A notice or copy report served in accordance with subsection (3) above shall be served in such manner as may be prescribed by Act of Adjournal; and a written execution purporting to be signed by the person who served the notice or copy together with, where appropriate, the relevant post office receipt shall be sufficient evidence of such service.

(5) In this section—

"controlled drug" has the same meaning as in the Misuse of Drugs Act 1971; and

"medicinal product" has the same meaning as in the Medicines Act 1968.

DEFINITIONS

"controlled drug": s.282(5) and s.2(1)(a) of the Misuse of Drugs Act 1971 (c. 38).
"medicinal product": s.282(5) and s.130(1) of the Medicines Act 1968 (c. 67).
"trial": s.307(1).

GENERAL NOTE

This section, introduced by the Criminal Justice (Scotland) Act 1995, s.25, enables evidence to be given, in certain circumstances, by an authorised forensic scientist in any criminal proceedings to the effect that a substance is listed in British Pharmacopoiea as being, or containing, a controlled drug or medicinal product. Instead of demanding the conduct of a chemical examination to establish identification, s.282 allows forensic identification to be achieved by reference either to the label on a sealed container or, as is more common, to the size, colour, shape and markings on the substance; this latter method is commonplace in medical practice and in the pharmaceutical industry and there seems little virtue in requiring a higher standard than that in criminal proceedings particularly when subs. (3)(b) preserves the rights of the other party to give formal notice of challenge to that evidence.

Any such forensic report can be served in accordance with subs. (3) not less than 14 days prior to trial (see Form 27.2 in the 1996 Act of Adjournal) and must be challenged within seven days of the date of service, not receipt. Such a report must be served on all other parties in the proceedings.

Evidence as to time and place of video surveillance recordings

283.—(1) For the purposes of any criminal proceedings, a certificate purporting to be signed by a person responsible for the operation of a video surveillance system and certifying—

(a) the location of the camera;
(b) the nature and extent of the person's responsibility for the system; and
(c) that visual images recorded on a particular video tape are images, recorded by the system, of events which occurred at a place specified in the certificate at a time and date so specified,

shall, subject to subsection (2) below, be sufficient evidence of the matters contained in the certificate.

(2) A party proposing to rely on subsection (1) above ("the first party") shall, not less than 14 days before the trial diet, serve on the other party ("the second party") a copy of the certificate and, if the second party serves on the first party, not more than seven days after the date of service of the copy certificate on him, a notice that he does not accept the evidence contained in the certificate, subsection (1) above shall not apply in relation to that evidence.

(3) A copy certificate or notice served in accordance with subsection (2) above shall be served in such manner as may be prescribed by Act of Adjournal; and a written execution purporting to be signed by the person who served the copy or notice together with, where appropriate, the relevant post office receipt shall be sufficient evidence of such service.

(4) In this section, "video surveillance system" means apparatus consisting of a camera mounted in a fixed position and associated equipment for transmitting and recording visual images of events occurring in any place.

DEFINITIONS

"video surveillance systems": s.283(4).

GENERAL NOTE

This section provides for evidence as to certain matters to be given by certificate by a person who is responsible for the operation of a video surveillance system, and was adopted from s.26 of the Criminal Justice (Scotland) Act 1995. The evidential matters which may be dealt with in the certificate are specified in subs. (1), and any such certificate shall be sufficient evidence of the matters stated. The form of certificate is stipulated in Chap. 27 of the 1996 Act of Adjournal (see Form 27.2). As elsewhere in Pt. XII of the Act, any certificate must be served not less than 14 days prior to trial and any challenge to the sufficiency of the evidence certified must be intimated within seven days of service.

The prime purpose of this provision is to provide a convenient means of leading the evidence of operators of city centre surveillance systems without requiring the unnecessary attendance at court of personnel. If the accused wishes to challenge this video evidence, the operator can be called upon to attend court.

Evidence in relation to fingerprints

284.—(1) For the purposes of any criminal proceedings, a certificate purporting to be signed by two constables and certifying that the fingerprints produced thereon were taken from a person designated in the certificate at a time, date and place specified therein shall, subject to subsection (2) below, be sufficient evidence of the facts contained in the certificate.

(2) A party proposing to rely on subsection (1) above ("the first party") shall, not less than 14 days before the trial diet, serve on the other party ("the second party") a copy of the certificate and, if the second party serves on the first party, not more than seven days after the date of service of the copy certificate on him, a notice that he does not accept the evidence contained in the certificate, subsection (1) above shall not apply in relation to that evidence.

(3) A copy certificate or notice served in accordance with subsection (2) above shall be served in such manner as may be prescribed by Act of Adjournal; and a written execution purporting to be signed by the person who served the copy or notice together with, where appropriate, the relevant post office receipt shall be sufficient evidence of such service.

DEFINITIONS
"constable": s.307(1) and s.51(1) of the Police (Scotland) Act 1967.

GENERAL NOTE
This section is intended to remove the need for police officers to attend court simply to give evidence as to the taking of fingerprints from an accused. Such evidence is provided by a certificate signed by both officers and in the style of Form 27.2, (Chap. 27 of the Act of Adjournal). The most effective means of certification would seem to be for the text of the certificate to be included in the body of the fingerprint and palm print forms and to be completed as accused persons are being processed at police offices.

See also s.285 (proof of previous convictions by Chief Constable's certificate) and the notes to ss.18 and 19 which provide powers to the police to obtain, *inter alia*, fresh finger and palm prints from convicted accused and persons previously detained, where the samples taken originally are found to be deficient.

Proof of previous convictions

Previous convictions: proof, general

285.—(1) A previous conviction may be proved against any person in any criminal proceedings by the production of such evidence of the conviction as is mentioned in this subsection and subsections (2) to (6) below and by showing that his fingerprints and those of the person convicted are the fingerprints of the same person.

(2) A certificate purporting to be signed by or on behalf of the Chief Constable of Strathclyde or the Commissioner of Police of the Metropolis, containing particulars relating to a conviction extracted from the criminal records kept by the person by or on whose behalf the certificate is signed, and

certifying that the copies of the fingerprints contained in the certificate are copies of the fingerprints appearing from the said records to have been taken in pursuance of rules for the time being in force under sections 12 and 39 of the Prisons (Scotland) Act 1989, or regulations for the time being in force under section 16 of the Prison Act 1952, from the person convicted on the occasion of the conviction or on the occasion of his last conviction, shall be sufficient evidence of the conviction or, as the case may be, of his last conviction and of all preceding convictions and that the copies of the fingerprints produced on the certificate are copies of the fingerprints of the person convicted.

(3) Where a person has been apprehended and detained in the custody of the police in connection with any criminal proceedings, a certificate purporting to be signed by the chief constable concerned or a person authorised on his behalf, certifying that the fingerprints produced thereon were taken from him while he was so detained, shall be sufficient evidence in those proceedings that the fingerprints produced on the certificate are the fingerprints of that person.

(4) A certificate purporting to be signed by or on behalf of the governor of a prison or of a remand centre in which any person has been detained in connection with any criminal proceedings, certifying that the fingerprints produced thereon were taken from him while he was so detained, shall be sufficient evidence in those proceedings that the fingerprints produced on the certificate are the fingerprints of that person.

(5) A certificate purporting to be signed by or on behalf of the Chief Constable of Strathclyde, and certifying that the fingerprints, copies of which are certified as mentioned in subsection (2) above by or on behalf of the Chief Constable or the Commissioner of Police of the Metropolis to be copies of the fingerprints of a person previously convicted and the fingerprints certified by or on behalf of a chief constable or a governor as mentioned in subsection (3) or (4) above, or otherwise shown, to be the fingerprints of the person against whom the previous conviction is sought to be proved, are the fingerprints of the same person, shall be sufficient evidence of the matter so certified.

(6) An extract conviction of any crime committed in any part of the United Kingdom bearing to have been issued by an officer whose duties include the issue of extract convictions shall be received in evidence without being sworn to by witnesses.

(7) It shall be competent to prove a previous conviction or any fact relevant to the admissibility of the conviction by witnesses, although the name of any such witness is not included in the list served on the accused; and the accused shall be entitled to examine witnesses with regard to such conviction or fact.

(8) An official of any prison in which the accused has been detained on such conviction shall be a competent and sufficient witness to prove its application to the accused, although he may not have been present in court at the trial to which such conviction relates.

(9) The method of proving a previous conviction authorised by this section shall be in addition to any other method of proving the conviction.

DEFINITIONS
"conviction": s.307(5).

GENERAL NOTE
This section carries over the provisions relating to proof of previous convictions by use of proved fingerprints. This procedure can be deployed to prove previous convictions which have been disputed by the accused or, in limited circumstances, as evidence in support of a substantive charge (see also s.286 below). Use is made of the fingerprint forms completed at the time of the accused's admission to a prison (subs. (4)) or when routinely detained in police custody in relation to the charges libelled (subs. (3)).

It is not necessary to list as witnesses those prison officials or court officers whose only role is to speak to the fact of a previous conviction or extract conviction.

Previous convictions: proof in support of substantive charge

286.—(1) Without prejudice to section 285(6) to (9) or, as the case may be, section 166 of this Act, where proof of a previous conviction is competent in support of a substantive charge, any such conviction or an extract of it shall, if—

    (a) it purports to relate to the accused and to be signed by the clerk of court having custody of the record containing the conviction; and

    (b) a copy of it has been served on the accused not less than 14 days before the trial diet,

be sufficient evidence of the application of the conviction to the accused unless, within seven days of the date of service of the copy on him, he serves notice on the prosecutor that he denies that it applies to him.

(2) A copy of a conviction or extract conviction served under subsection (1) above shall be served on the accused in such manner as may be prescribed by Act of Adjournal, and a written execution purporting to be signed by the person who served the copy together with, where appropriate, the relevant post office receipt shall be sufficient evidence of service of the copy.

DEFINITIONS
    "previous conviction": s.307(5).
    "trial": s.307(1).

GENERAL NOTE
    Where it is necessary to lead evidence of a conviction in support of a substantive charge, this section provides for the use in evidence, of a relevant certified extract conviction. A copy of the extract conviction has to be served on the accused not less than 14 days before trial and any challenge to it must be intimated within seven days of service. Use of a s.286 certificate may well serve to pre-empt any such challenge. In solemn proceedings the completed execution of service should be lodged as a production.

    See generally the discussion on the admissibility of evidence of previous convictions in the notes to ss.101 and 166 above.

PART XIII

MISCELLANEOUS

Lord Advocate

Demission of office by Lord Advocate

287.—(1) All indictments which have been raised by a Lord Advocate shall remain effective notwithstanding his subsequently having died or demitted office and may be taken up and proceeded with by his successor.

(2) During any period when the office of Lord Advocate is vacant it shall be lawful to indict accused persons in name of the Solicitor General then in office.

(3) The advocates depute shall not demit office when a Lord Advocate dies or demits office but shall continue in office until their successors receive commissions.

(4) The advocates depute and procurators fiscal shall have power, notwithstanding any vacancy in the office of Lord Advocate, to take up and proceed with any indictment which—

(a) by virtue of subsection (1) above, remains effective; or

(b) by virtue of subsection (2) above, is in the name of the Solicitor General.

(5) For the purposes of this Act, where, but for this subsection, demission of office by one Law Officer would result in the offices of both being vacant, he or, where both demit office on the same day, the person demitting the office of Lord Advocate shall be deemed to continue in office until the warrant of appointment of the person succeeding to the office of Lord Advocate is granted.

(6) The Lord Advocate shall enter upon the duties of his office immediately upon the grant of his warrant of appointment; and he shall as soon as is practicable thereafter take the oaths of office before the Secretary of State or any Lord Commissioner of Justiciary.

DEFINITIONS
"indictment": s.307(1).
"procurator fiscal": s.307(1).

GENERAL NOTE
The Lord Advocate has the universal and exclusive title to prosecute on indictment. This section is concerned with the consequences of the decession of office by Lord Advocate. This section puts into statutory form a variety of authorities that have evolved or been passed over the years: see Macdonald *Criminal Law of Scotland* (5th ed.) (W. Green, Edinburgh) at p. 212. In short, the section provides for the continuity of Crown business notwithstanding a change of Lord Advocate.

Two points are worth noting. First, during any period when the office of Lord Advocate is vacant it shall be lawful to indict accused persons in the name of the Solicitor General then in office: subs. (2). It is clear that such indictments may be taken up by the new Lord Advocate on his appointment: *H.M. Solicitor General v. Lavelle* (1913) 7 Adam 255. Secondly, the Lord Advocate shall enter upon the duties of his office immediately upon the grant of his warrant: subs. (6). Before this provision the Lord Advocate could not act until the Royal Warrant appointing him reached Crown Office, he was not entitled to act merely on notice of his appointment appearing in the Edinburgh Gazette: *Halliday v. Wilson* (1891) 3 White 38.

Intimation of proceedings in High Court to Lord Advocate

288.—(1) In any proceeding in the High Court (other than a proceeding to which the Lord Advocate or a procurator fiscal is a party) it shall be competent for the court to order intimation of such proceeding to the Lord Advocate.

(2) On intimation being made to the Lord Advocate under subsection (1) above, the Lord Advocate shall be entitled to appear and be heard in such proceeding.

DEFINITIONS
"High Court": s.307(1).
"procurator fiscal": s.307(1).

GENERAL NOTE
This section is probably concerned with Bill of Criminal letters which have not been presented to the Lord Advocate for concurrence or with petitions to the *Nobile Officium* of the High Court of Justiciary. The ordinary practice would be to intimate to the Lord Advocate but individuals proceeding without legal representation, for example, might not know of that practice.

Treason trials

Procedure and evidence in trials for treason

289. The procedure and rules of evidence in proceedings for treason and misprision of treason shall be the same as in proceedings according to the law of Scotland for murder.

GENERAL NOTE
It has been the rule in England since the Treason Act 1800 (see now the Criminal Law Act 1967, s.12(7)) that trials for treason and misprision should be governed by the rules applicable to trials for murder. This section restates the position in Scotland which was clarified in s.39 of the 1980 Act. The substantive law of trespass remains English, but the Treason Acts of 1800 and 1945 were repealed by s.83(3) of and Sched. 8 to the 1980 Act, along with what remained of the Treason Act 1708.

Certain rights of accused

Accused's right to request identification parade

290.—(1) Subject to subsection (2) below, the sheriff may, on an application by an accused at any time after the accused has been charged with an offence, order that, in relation to the alleged offence, the prosecutor shall hold an identification parade in which the accused shall be one of those constituting the parade.

(2) The sheriff shall make an order in accordance with subsection (1) above only after giving the prosecutor an opportunity to be heard and only if—

   (a) an identification parade, such as is mentioned in subsection (1) above, has not been held at the instance of the prosecutor;

   (b) after a request by the accused, the prosecutor has refused to hold, or has unreasonably delayed holding, such an identification parade; and

   (c) the sheriff considers the application under subsection (1) above to be reasonable.

DEFINITIONS
"offence": s.307(1).
"prosecutor": s.307(1).
"sheriff": s.4(1) and (4).

GENERAL NOTE
This section re-enacts the provisions of s.10 of the Criminal Justice (Scotland) Act 1980. It is open to the accused to make an application for an identification parade to be held by the prosecutor; (i) where no such parade has been conducted; (ii) where the prosecutor has refused a request by the accused for such a parade, or else been dilatory in organising the parade, and (iii) where the application appears reasonable to the sheriff. An application under s.290 can only be made after charges have been preferred against the accused and once the sheriff has heard the prosecutor on the merits of the charge.

The style of application is found in the 1996 Act of Adjournal, Chap. 28; note that the style applies to circumstances where either an indictment has been served or summary proceedings have begun.

In *Wilson v. Tudhope*, 1985 S.C.C.R. 339 two Crown attempts to hold an identification parade failed because witnesses were unwilling to attend. The defence craved, and were granted, an identification parade, the sheriff opining that it would be competent to cite witnesses to attend such a parade.

Precognition on oath of defence witnesses

291.—(1) The sheriff may, on the application of an accused, grant warrant to cite any person (other than a co-accused), who is alleged to be a witness in relation to any offence of which the accused has been charged, to appear before the sheriff in chambers at such time or place as shall be specified in the citation, for precognition on oath by the accused or his solicitor in relation to that offence, if the court is satisfied that it is reasonable to require such precognition on oath in the circumstances.

(2) Any person who, having been duly cited to attend for precognition under subsection (1) above and having been given at least 48 hours notice, fails without reasonable excuse to attend shall be guilty of an offence and shall be liable on summary conviction to a fine not exceeding level 3 on the standard scale or to imprisonment for a period not exceeding 21 days; and the

court may issue a warrant for the apprehension of the person concerned, ordering him to be brought before a sheriff for precognition on oath.

(3) Any person who, having been duly cited to attend for precognition under subsection (1) above, attends but—

(a) refuses to give information within his knowledge or to produce evidence in his possession; or

(b) prevaricates in his evidence,

shall be guilty of an offence and shall be liable to be summarily subjected forthwith to a fine not exceeding level 3 on the standard scale or to imprisonment for a period not exceeding 21 days.

DEFINITIONS

"enactment": s.307(1).
"imprisonment": ss.307(6) and 309.
"indictment": s.307(1).
"offence": s.307(1).

GENERAL NOTE

A warrant to cite a witness for precognition on oath may be craved by the defence once charges have been preferred and cause can be shown to justify the use of this *compulsitor*; the power should be exercised with caution (*Low v. MacNeill*, 1981 S.C.C.R. 243).

It is not competent to make an application of this sort prior to full committal on petition, since, in the period between committal for further examination and full committal the Crown are still completing enquiries; see *Cirignaco, Petr.*, 1985 S.C.C.R. 157 where precognition on oath of the complainer was sought with a view to secure early release on bail. Refusal on the part of potential witnesses to assist defence investigations, even after joint approaches by both the defence and the Crown, resulted in the grant of warrant to cite for precognition (*Brady v. Lockhart*, 1985 S.C.C.R. 349). It is likely that an application for precognition on oath without first having sought the assistance of the Crown will be treated as premature.

A warrant for precognition on oath can only be sought prior to the trial (and conviction or acquittal) of the accused (see *Gilmour, Petr.*, 1994 S.C.C.R. 872).

Failure to attend for precognition after lawful citation, prevarication, or failure to furnish information is an offence liable to peremptory punishment (subs. (3)); in such circumstances the court is not obliged to obtain social enquiry or other reports before sentencing such misconduct.

Refer to Chap. 29 of the 1996 Act of Adjournal for directions on procedures and styles.

Mode of trial

Mode of trial of certain offences

292.—(1) Subject to subsection (6) below, the offences mentioned (and broadly described) in Schedule 10 to this Act shall be triable only summarily.

(2) An offence created by statute shall be triable only summarily if—

(a) the enactment creating the offence or any other enactment expressly so provides (in whatever words); or

(b) subject to subsections (4) and (5)(a) below, the offence was created by an Act passed on or before 29 July 1977 (the date of passing of the Criminal Law Act 1977) and the penalty or maximum penalty in force immediately before that date, on any conviction of that offence, did not include any of the following—

(i) a fine exceeding £400;

(ii) subject to subsection (3) below, imprisonment for a period exceeding 3 months;

(iii) a fine exceeding £50 in respect of a specified quantity or number of things, or in respect of a specified period during which a continuing offence is committed.

(3) In the application of paragraph (b)(ii) of subsection (2) above, no regard shall be paid to the fact that section 5(3) of this Act permits the imposition of imprisonment for a period exceeding 3 months in certain circumstances.

(4) An offence created by statute which is triable only on indictment shall continue only to be so triable.

(5) An offence created by statute shall be triable either on indictment or summarily if—

(a) the enactment creating the offence or any other enactment expressly so provides (in whatever words); or

(b) it is an offence to which neither subsection (2) nor subsection (4) above applies.

(6) An offence which may under any enactment (including an enactment in this Act or passed after this Act) be tried only summarily, being an offence which, if it had been triable on indictment, could competently have been libelled as an additional or alternative charge in the indictment, may (the provisions of this or any other enactment notwithstanding) be so libelled, and tried accordingly.

(7) Where an offence is libelled and tried on indictment by virtue of subsection (6) above, the penalty which may be imposed for that offence in that case shall not exceed that which is competent on summary conviction.

DEFINITIONS
"enactment": s.307(1).
"fine": s.307(1).
"imprisonment": s.307(6).
"indictment": s.307(1).
"offence": s.307(1).

GENERAL NOTE
Offences triable summarily only are listed in Sched. 10 and in subs. (2) and can extend to offences defined in s.5(3) notwithstanding the fact that these create liability to a sentence of six months' imprisonment on a second or subsequent conviction in the sheriff court. It will be recalled that s.136(2) enacts that the six-month time limit for the commencement of statutory offences applies only to offences triable summarily only.

Offences which by statute may only be prosecuted summarily can be libelled along with other charges on an indictment but, in that event, any sentence which may be imposed on conviction of that offence shall be restricted to that which could have been passed summarily (subs. (6)).

Art and part and attempt

Statutory offences: art and part and aiding and abetting

293.—(1) A person may be convicted of, and punished for, a contravention of any enactment, notwithstanding that he was guilty of such contravention as art and part only.

(2) Without prejudice to subsection (1) above or to any express provision in any enactment having the like effect to this subsection, any person who aids, abets, counsels, procures or incites any other person to commit an offence against the provisions of any enactment shall be guilty of an offence and shall be liable on conviction, unless the enactment otherwise requires, to the same punishment as might be imposed on conviction of the first-mentioned offence.

DEFINITIONS
"enactment": s.307(1).
"offence": s.307(1).

GENERAL NOTE
Art and part guilt can apply equally to common law and statutory offences. See *Vaughan v. H.M. Advocate*, 1979 S.L.T. 49 where the accused though not himself within the forbidden degrees, was convicted under the Incest Act 1567 as an actor.

Attempt at crime

294.—(1) Attempt to commit any indictable crime is itself an indictable crime.

(2) Attempt to commit any offence punishable on complaint shall itself be an offence punishable on complaint.

Legal custody

Legal custody

295. Any person required or authorised by or under this Act or any other enactment to be taken to any place, or to be detained or kept in custody shall, while being so taken or detained or kept, be deemed to be in legal custody.

DEFINITIONS
"enactment": s.307(1).

GENERAL NOTE
The definition of legal custody applies to the status of persons either detained or arrested under the Act or other statutory powers. The anomalous position of a person suspected of committing an offence and required to remain where found by police officers (see s.13(1) and (2) above) has already been discussed; such an individual is not then in legal custody.

Warrants

Warrants for search and apprehension to be signed by judge

296. Any warrant for search or apprehension granted under this Act shall be signed by the judge granting it, and execution upon any such warrant may proceed either upon the warrant itself or upon an extract of the warrant issued and signed by the clerk of court.

DEFINITIONS
"judge": s.307(1).

GENERAL NOTE
This section applies to the grant of warrants of apprehension or search by a justice of the peace, sheriff or High Court judge. Ordinarily such warrants are craved from judges in the lower courts. See s.135 of the Act and the notes thereto.

Execution of warrants and service of complaints, etc.

297.—(1) Any warrant granted by a justice may, without being backed or endorsed by any other justice, be executed throughout Scotland in the same way as it may be executed within the jurisdiction of the justice who granted it.

(2) Any complaint, warrant, or other proceeding for the purposes of any summary proceedings under this Act may without endorsation be served or executed at any place within Scotland by any officer of law, and such service or execution may be proved either by the oath in court of the officer or by production of his written execution.

(3) A warrant issued in the Isle of Man for the arrest of a person charged with an offence may, after it has been endorsed by a justice in Scotland, be executed there by the person bringing that warrant, by any person to whom the warrant was originally directed or by any officer of law of the sheriff court

district where the warrant has been endorsed in like manner as any such warrant issued in Scotland.

(4) In subsection (3) above, "endorsed" means endorsed in the like manner as a process to which section 4 of the Summary Jurisdiction (Process) Act 1881 applies.

(5) The Indictable Offences Act Amendment Act 1868 shall apply in relation to the execution in Scotland of warrants issued in the Channel Islands.

DEFINITIONS
   "justice": s.307(1).
   "offence": s.307(1).
   "officer of law": s.307(1).

GENERAL NOTE
   This section reflects the reform introduced by s.9 of the Criminal Justice (Scotland) Act 1995 and applies to all warrants granted in Scotland. It removes the need for a warrant, granted by a justice for execution outwith his jurisdiction, to be "backed" by another justice. A degree of caution is necessary since this reform does not extend to warrants granted in Scotland for execution in England and Wales.
   Historically, a warrant granted for execution within the jurisdiction of a justice could always be executed without further ado, but matters were less straightforward when the warrant was granted for execution elsewhere in Scotland, and thoroughly byzantine when the warrant had to be executed in England and Wales: these are discussed in turn below.
   Warrants craved for execution outwith the jurisdiction of the court, but in Scotland, included a crave requesting the concurrence of judges in that other place in the granting of the warrant. This necessitated application to be made to two courts before the warrant could be executed, an anachronistic, time-consuming, and invariably unnecessary, procedure.
   Warrants craved in Scotland for execution in England or Wales will still be required to be "backed" and "endorsed" in accordance with the Summary Jurisdiction (Process) Act 1881 (c. 24): in these circumstances the warrant obtained from a Scottish court has to be docquetted in compliance with the 1881 Act and then be presented to the relevant magistrates' court having jurisdiction south of the border. It has to be emphasised that while warrant procedures in England and Wales are now regulated by Pt. II of the Police and Criminal Evidence Act 1984 (c. 60) (PACE), and the court competent to grant warrants depends upon the nature of the material to be recovered, these PACE provisions have no application at all to Scottish warrants being executed in England and Wales. Such warrants proceed by application to the relevant magistrates' court no matter what the nature of the material sought. However, warrants granted in England and Wales must be obtained under PACE and, it is submitted, cannot be craved for execution in Scotland. In such situations it would appear that the proper course is to apply direct to the Scottish court having jurisdiction for the necessary warrant.

Trial judge's report

Trial judge's report

   298.—(1) Without prejudice to sections 113 and 186(3)(b) of this Act, the High Court may, in relation to—
   (a) an appeal under section 106(1), 108 or 175(2) to (4) of this Act;
   (b) an appeal by way of bill of suspension or advocation; or
   (c) a petition to the nobile officium,
at any time before the appeal is finally determined or, as the case may be, petition finally disposed of, order the judge who presided at the trial, passed sentence or otherwise disposed of the case to provide to the Clerk of Justiciary a report in writing giving the judge's opinion on the case generally or in relation to any particular matter specified in the order.

   (2) The Clerk of Justiciary shall send a copy of a report provided under subsection (1) above to the convicted person or his solicitor, the Crown Agent and, in relation to cases referred under section 124(3) of this Act, the Secretary of State.

(3) Subject to subsection (2) above, the report of the judge shall be available only to the High Court, the parties and, on such conditions as may be prescribed by Act of Adjournal, such other persons or classes of persons as may be so prescribed.

DEFINITIONS
"Clerk of Justiciary": s.307(1).
"judge": s.307(1).

GENERAL NOTE
This new provision reinforces the statutory duty on judges at first instance to provide a report in the event of an appeal: the section allows the High Court of Justiciary to order further reports of a general or specific nature. This may be necessary because, for example, the note of appeal may not contain, as is required by s.110(3)(b), a full statement of all the grounds of appeal. Alternatively, difficulty or uncertainty in relation to a material point may have arisen at the hearing of the appeal and the trial judge's opinion may be thought necessary in the circumstances. In *Brady v. Barbour*, 1994 S.C.C.R. 890 the sheriff, for whatever reason, did not produce a draft stated case and thus placed the High Court of Justiciary in some difficulty. This provision allows further orders to be made for reports.

Correction of entries

Correction of entries

299.—(1) Subject to the provisions of this section, it shall be competent to correct any entry in—
    (a) the record of proceedings in a prosecution; or
    (b) the extract of a sentence passed or an order of court made in such proceedings,
in so far as that entry constitutes an error of recording or is incomplete.
    (2) An entry mentioned in subsection (1) above may be corrected—
    (a) by the clerk of the court, at any time before either the sentence or order of the court is executed or, on appeal, the proceedings are transmitted to the Clerk of Justiciary;
    (b) by the clerk of the court, under the authority of the court which passed the sentence or made the order, at any time after the execution of the sentence or order of the court but before such transmission as is mentioned in paragraph (a) above; or
    (c) by the clerk of the court under the authority of the High Court in the case of a remit under subsection (4)(b) below.
    (3) A correction in accordance with paragraph (b) or (c) of subsection (2) above shall be intimated to the prosecutor and to the former accused or his solicitor.
    (4) Where during the course of an appeal, the High Court becomes aware of an erroneous or incomplete entry, such as is mentioned in subsection (1) above, the court—
    (a) may consider and determine the appeal as if such entry were corrected; and
    (b) either before or after the determination of the appeal, may remit the proceedings to the court of first instance for correction in accordance with subsection (2)(c) above.
    (5) Any correction under subsections (1) and (2) above by the clerk of the court shall be authenticated by his signature and, if such correction is authorised by a court, shall record the name of the judge or judges authorising such correction and the date of such authorisation.

DEFINITIONS
"clerk of Court": s.114 of the Criminal Justice (Scotland) Act 1995.
"Clerk of Justiciary": s.307(1).

"High Court": s.307(1).
"judge": s.307(1).
"order": s.307(1).
"sentence": s.307(1).

Amendment of records of conviction and sentence in summary proceedings

300.—(1) Without prejudice to section 299 of this Act, where, on an application in accordance with subsection (2) below, the High Court is satisfied that a record of conviction or sentence in summary proceedings inaccurately records the identity of any person, it may authorise the clerk of the court which convicted or, as the case may be, sentenced the person to correct the record.

(2) An application under subsection (1) above shall be made after the determination of the summary prosecution and may be made by any party to the summary proceedings or any other person having an interest in the correction of the alleged inaccuracy.

(3) The High Court shall order intimation of an application under subsection (1) above to such persons as it considers appropriate and shall not determine the application without affording to the parties to the summary proceedings and to any other person having an interest in the correction of the alleged inaccuracy an opportunity to be heard.

(4) The power of the High Court under this section may be exercised by a single judge of the High Court in the same manner as it may be exercised by the High Court, and subject to the same provisions.

DEFINITIONS
"clerk of Court": s.114(1) of the Criminal Justice (Scotland) Act 1995.
"Clerk of Justiciary": s.308(1).

Rights of audience

Rights of audience

301.—(1) Without prejudice to section 103(8) of this Act, any solicitor who has, by virtue of section 25A (rights of audience) of the Solicitors (Scotland) Act 1980, a right of audience in relation to the High Court of Justiciary shall have the same right of audience in that court as is enjoyed by an advocate.

(2) Any person who has complied with the terms of a scheme approved under section 26 of the Law Reform (Miscellaneous Provisions) (Scotland) Act 1990 (consideration of applications made under section 25) shall have such rights of audience before the High Court of Justiciary as may be specified in an Act of Adjournal made under subsection (7)(b) of that section.

Fixed penalties

Fixed penalty: conditional offer by procurator fiscal

302.—(1) Where a procurator fiscal receives a report that a relevant offence has been committed he may send to the alleged offender a notice under this section (referred to in this section as a conditional offer); and where he issues a conditional offer the procurator fiscal shall notify the clerk of court specified in it of the issue of the conditional offer and of its terms.

(2) A conditional offer—
(a) shall give such particulars of the circumstances alleged to constitute the offence to which it relates as are necessary for giving reasonable information about the alleged offence;

(b) shall state—
        (i) the amount of the appropriate fixed penalty for that offence;
        (ii) the amount of the instalments by which the penalty may be paid; and
        (iii) the intervals at which such instalments should be paid;

(c) shall indicate that if, within 28 days of the date on which the conditional offer was issued, or such longer period as may be specified in the conditional offer, the alleged offender accepts the offer by making payment of the fixed penalty or of the first instalment thereof to the clerk of court specified in the conditional offer at the address therein mentioned, any liability to conviction of the offence shall be discharged;

(d) shall state that proceedings against the alleged offender shall not be commenced in respect of that offence until the end of a period of 28 days from the date on which the conditional offer was issued, or such longer period as may be specified in the conditional offer; and

(e) shall state that acceptance of the offer in the manner described in paragraph (c) above by the alleged offender shall not be a conviction nor be recorded as such.

(3) A conditional offer may be made in respect of more than one relevant offence and shall, in such a case, state the amount of the appropriate fixed penalty for all the offences in respect of which it is made.

(4) Where payment of the appropriate fixed penalty or of the first instalment has not been made to the clerk of court, he shall, upon the expiry of the period of 28 days referred to in subsection (2)(c) above or such longer period as may be specified in the conditional offer, notify the procurator fiscal who issued the conditional offer that no payment has been made.

(5) Proceedings shall not be brought against any person for the offence to which a conditional offer relates until the procurator fiscal receives notification from the clerk of court in accordance with subsection (4) above.

(6) Where an alleged offender makes payment of the appropriate fixed penalty or or of the first instalment to the clerk of court specified in the conditional offer no proceedings shall be brought against the alleged offender for the offence.

(7) The Secretary of State shall, by order, prescribe a scale of fixed penalties for the purpose of this section, the amount of the maximum penalty on the scale being a sum not exceeding level 1 on the standard scale.

(8) An order under subsection (7) above—
(a) may contain provision as to the payment of fixed penalties by instalments; and
(b) shall be made by statutory instrument, which shall be subject to annulment in pursuance of a resolution of either House of Parliament.

(9) In this section—
(a) "a relevant offence" means any offence in respect of which an alleged offender could competently be tried before a district court, but shall not include a fixed penalty offence within the meaning of section 51 of the Road Traffic Offenders Act 1988 nor any other offence in respect of which a conditional offer within the meaning of sections 75 to 77 of that Act may be sent; and
(b) "the appropriate fixed penalty" means such fixed penalty on the scale prescribed under subsection (7) above as the procurator fiscal thinks fit having regard to the circumstances of the case.

DEFINITIONS
"appropriate fixed penalty": s.302(9).
"offence": s.307(1).
"procurator fiscal": s.307(1).
"relevant offence": s.302(9).
"standard scale": s.225(1).

GENERAL NOTE

This section extends the range of fixed penalties which the procurator fiscal can offer to persons reported to him for offences other than Road Traffic offences. The "fiscal fine" was introduced by the Criminal Justice (Scotland) Act 1987 and then permitted procurator fiscals to use the offer of a £25 fixed fine to alleged offenders as an alternative to prosecution. Payment or part-payment of such a fine brought an end to the procurator fiscal's involvement and was not recorded as a criminal conviction. In 1987 the £25 fine, fixed by statutory instrument, equalled half the Level 1 fine on the standard scale; Level 1 is now a sum of £200. Section 302 permits the Secretary of State by statutory instrument, to set a range of fixed penalty bands from which the procurator fiscal can choose, according to the circumstances of the case as reported, when offering the option of a fiscal fine. Subsection (7) enacts that the bands must not exceed Level 1 on the standard scale.

One of the difficulties identified in the operation of the earlier fiscal fine system was that where several offences were reported against an accused as a result of an incident, the fiscal, if he chose to offer the option of such a fine, had to select one charge only from those reported. In the event of non-payment only the single charge selected previously could later be libelled against the accused; subs. (3) statutorily permits the offer of more than one fiscal fine against an accused following an incident and, hence, in the event of refusal of the offer it will be open to the prosecutor to libel several charges, not just one as before.

The administration and collection of fines remains the responsibility of the clerk of court. Whereas the old fiscal fine system required payment of the entire £25 fine within 28 days, and to an extent limited the range of offenders who could be offered that option, subs. (1)(c) enacts that payment of the full amount or a pre-determined instalment is to be made within 28 days, or a specified longer period. Once either sort of payment is received, the prosecutor is barred from prosecuting those offences. It is then the task of the clerk of court to enforce collection of any unpaid balance (see s.303 below).

It will be appreciated that the thrust of s.302 is to extend the use of fiscal fines as an alternative to prosecution. If successful, the broadened fixed penalty conditional offer scheme may reduce the pressure of criminal business in the lower courts.

Fixed penalty: enforcement

303.—(1) Subject to subsection (2) below, where an alleged offender accepts a conditional offer by paying the first instalment of the appropriate fixed penalty, any amount of the penalty which is outstanding at any time shall be treated as if the penalty were a fine imposed by the court, the clerk of which is specified in the conditional offer.

(2) In the enforcement of a penalty which is to be treated as a fine in pursuance of subsection (1) above—

(a) any reference, howsoever expressed, in any enactment whether passed or made before or after the coming into force of this section to—

(i) the imposition of imprisonment or detention in default of payment of a fine shall be construed as a reference to enforcement by means of civil diligence;

(ii) the finding or order of the court imposing the fine shall be construed as a reference to a certificate given in pursuance of subsection (3) below;

(iii) the offender shall be construed as a reference to the alleged offender;

(iv) the conviction of the offender shall be construed as a reference to the acceptance of the conditional offer by the alleged offender;

(b) the following sections of this Act shall not apply—
section 211(7);
section 213(2);
section 214(1) to (6);
section 216(7);
section 219, except subsection (1)(b);
section 220;

section 221(2) to (4);
section 222(8); and
section 224.

(3) For the purposes of any proceedings in connection with, or steps taken for, the enforcement of any amount of a fixed penalty which is outstanding, a document purporting to be a certificate signed by the clerk of court for the time being responsible for the collection or enforcement of the penalty as to any matter relating to the penalty shall be conclusive of the matter so certified.

(4) The Secretary of State may, by order made by statutory instrument subject to annulment in pursuance of a resolution of either House of Parliament, make such provision as he considers necessary for the enforcement in England and Wales or Northern Ireland of any penalty, treated in pursuance of subsection (1) above as a fine, which is transferred as a fine to a court in England and Wales or, as the case may be, Northern Ireland.

DEFINITIONS
"appropriate fixed penalty: s.302(9)(b).
"enactment": s.307(1).
"fine": s.307(1).
"impose detention": s.307(1).
"impose imprisonment": s.307(1).

GENERAL NOTE
The collection of fiscal fines remains the responsibility of the clerk of court. In the event of only partial payment of the instalments due to meet such a fine, subs. (2) allows recovery of the balance due by way of civil diligence. Subsection (3) provides that for the purpose of such enforcement the clerk of court is empowered to certify conclusively the sums due.

Subsection (2) has the effect of removing criminal sanctions for the enforcement of unpaid fiscal fines.

PART XIV

GENERAL

Criminal Courts Rules Council

304.—(1) There shall be established a body, to be known as the Criminal Courts Rules Council (in this section referred to as "the Council") which shall have the functions conferred on it by subsection (9) below.

(2) The Council shall consist of—

(a) the Lord Justice General, the Lord Justice Clerk and the Clerk of Justiciary;

(b) a further Lord Commissioner of Justiciary appointed by the Lord Justice General;

(c) the following persons appointed by the Lord Justice General after such consultation as he considers appropriate—
    (i) two sheriffs;
    (ii) two members of the Faculty of Advocates;
    (iii) two solicitors;
    (iv) one sheriff clerk; and
    (v) one person appearing to him to have a knowledge of the procedures and practices of the district court;

(d) two persons appointed by the Lord Justice General after consultation with the Lord Advocate, at least one of whom must be a procurator fiscal;

(e) two persons appointed by the Lord Justice General after consultation with the Secretary of State, at least one of whom must be a person appearing to the Lord Justice General to have—

(i) a knowledge of the procedures and practices of the courts exercising criminal jurisdiction in Scotland; and

(ii) an awareness of the interests of victims of crime and of witnesses in criminal proceedings; and

(f) any persons appointed under subsection (3) below.

(3) The Lord Justice General may appoint not more than two further persons, and the Secretary of State may appoint one person, to membership of the Council.

(4) The chairman of the Council shall be the Lord Justice General or such other member of the Council, being a Lord Commissioner of Justiciary, as the Lord Justice General may nominate.

(5) The members of the Council appointed under paragraphs (b) to (f) of subsection (2) above shall, so long as they retain the respective qualifications mentioned in those paragraphs, hold office for three years and be eligible for reappointment.

(6) Any vacancy in the membership of the Council by reason of the death or demission of office, prior to the expiry of the period for which he was appointed, of a member appointed under any of paragraphs (b) to (f) of subsection (2) above shall be filled by the appointment by the Lord Justice General or, as the case may be, the Secretary of State, after such consultation as is required by the paragraph in question, of another person having the qualifications required by that paragraph, and a person so appointed shall hold office only until the expiry of that period.

(7) The Council shall meet—

(a) at intervals of not more than 12 months; and

(b) at any time when summoned by the chairman or by three members of the Council,

but shall, subject to the foregoing, have power to regulate the summoning of its meetings and the procedure at such meetings.

(8) At any meeting of the Council six members shall be a quorum.

(9) The functions of the Council shall be—

(a) to keep under general review the procedures and practices of the courts exercising criminal jurisdiction in Scotland (including any matters incidental or relating to those procedures or practices); and

(b) to consider and comment on any draft Act of Adjournal submitted to it by the High Court, which shall, in making the Act of Adjournal, take account to such extent as it considers appropriate of any comments made by the Council under this paragraph.

(10) In the discharge of its functions under subsection (9) above the Council may invite representations on any aspect of the procedures and practices of the courts exercising criminal jurisdiction in Scotland (including any matters incidental or relating to those procedures or practices) and shall consider any such representations received by it, whether or not submitted in response to such an invitation.

DEFINITIONS
"Lord Commissioner of Justiciary": s.307(1).
"procurator fiscal": s.307(1).

GENERAL NOTE
   This innovation established a Rules Council for criminal court proceedings with functions broadly comparable to the existing Scottish Rules Council for civil court proceedings. The new body will assist the High Court of Justiciary in the discharge of its existing court procedural rule-making functions.

Acts of Adjournal

305.—(1) The High Court may by Act of Adjournal—

(a) regulate the practice and procedure in relation to criminal procedure;

(b) make such rules and regulations as may be necessary or expedient to carry out the purposes and accomplish the objects of any enactment (including an enactment in this Act) in so far as it relates to criminal procedure;

(c) subject to subsection (5) below, to fix and regulate the fees payable in connection with summary criminal proceedings; and

(d) to make provision for the application of sums paid under section 220 of this Act and for any matter incidental thereto.

(2) The High Court may by Act of Adjournal modify, amend or repeal any enactment (including an enactment in this Act) in so far as that enactment relates to matters with respect to which an Act of Adjournal may be made under subsection (1) above.

(3) No rule, regulation or provision which affects the governor or any other officer of a prison shall be made by Act of Adjournal except with the consent of the Secretary of State.

(4) The Clerk of Justiciary may, with the sanction of the Lord Justice General and the Lord Justice Clerk, vary the forms set out in an Act of Adjournal made under subsection (1) above or any other Act whether passed before or after this Act from time to time as may be found necessary for giving effect to the provisions of this Act relating to solemn procedure.

(5) Nothing in paragraph (c) of subsection (1) above shall empower the High Court to make any regulation which the Secretary of State is empowered to make by the Courts of Law Fees (Scotland) Act 1895.

DEFINITIONS
"governor": s.307(1).
"High Court": s.307(1).
"officer of a prison": s.307(1).

GENERAL NOTE
The High Court of Justiciary is best placed to know how to regulate its own procedure and it does so by Act of Adjournal on statutory authority. The previous powers of ss.282 and 457 of the 1975 Act have been combined in this single provision which relates to "criminal procedure". Variations in the wording of these sections have been removed. Differences as between other statutory powers to make Acts of Adjournal have been removed with this single provision: see, *e.g.* s.32A of the 1980 Act which allowed provisions the court thought "necessary and expedient", a wider power than that of necessity under the 1975 Act.

Information for financial and other purposes

306.—(1) The Secretary of State shall in each year publish such information as he considers expedient for the purpose of—
(a) enabling persons engaged in the administration of criminal justice to become aware of the financial implications of their decisions; or
(b) facilitating the performance by such persons of their duty to avoid discriminating against any persons on the ground of race or sex or any other improper ground.

(2) Publication under subsection (1) above shall be effected in such manner as the Secretary of State considers appropriate for the purpose of bringing the information to the attention of the persons concerned.

Interpretation

307.—(1) In this Act, unless the context otherwise requires—
"appropriate court" means a court named as such in pursuance of section 228(4) of this Act or of Schedule 6 to this Act in a probation order or in an amendment of any such order made on a change of residence of a probationer;

"bail" means release of an accused or an appellant on conditions, or conditions imposed on bail, as the context requires;

"chartered psychologist" means a person for the time being listed in the British Psychological Society's Register of Chartered Psychologists;

"child", except in section 46(3) of and Schedule 1 to this Act, has the meaning assigned to that expression for the purposes of Chapters 2 and 3 of Part II of the Children (Scotland) Act 1995;

"children's hearing" has the meaning assigned to it in Part II of the Children (Scotland) Act 1995;

"Clerk of Justiciary" shall include assistant clerk of justiciary and shall extend and apply to any person duly authorised to execute the duties of Clerk of Justiciary or assistant clerk of justiciary;

"commit for trial" means commit until liberation in due course of law;

"community service order" means an order made under section 238 of this Act;

"complaint" includes a copy of the complaint laid before the court;

"constable" has the same meaning as in the Police (Scotland) Act 1967;

"court of summary jurisdiction" means a court of summary criminal jurisdiction;

"court of summary criminal jurisdiction" includes the sheriff court and district court;

"crime" means any crime or offence at common law or under any Act of Parliament whether passed before or after this Act, and includes an attempt to commit any crime or offence;

"diet" includes any continuation of a diet;

"enactment" includes an enactment contained in a local Act and any order, regulation or other instrument having effect by virtue of an Act;

"examination of facts" means an examination of facts held under section 55 of this Act;

"existing" means existing immediately before the commencement of this Act;

"extract conviction" and "extract of previous conviction" include certified copy conviction, certificate of conviction, and any other document lawfully issued from any court of justice of the United Kingdom as evidence of a conviction;

"fine" includes—

    (a) any pecuniary penalty, (but not a pecuniary forfeiture or pecuniary compensation); and

    (b) an instalment of a fine;

"governor" means, in relation to a contracted out prison within the meaning of section 106(4) of the Criminal Justice and Public Order Act 1994, the director of the prison;

"guardian", in relation to a child, includes any person who, in the opinion of the court having cognizance of any case in relation to the child or in which the child is concerned, has for the time being the charge of or control over the child;

"guardianship order" has the meaning assigned to it by section 58 of this Act;

"High Court" and "Court of Justiciary" shall mean "High Court of Justiciary" and shall include any court held by the Lords Commissioners of Justiciary, or any of them;

"hospital" means—

    (a) any hospital vested in the Secretary of State under the National Health Service (Scotland) Act 1978;

    (b) any private hospital registered under Part IV of the Mental Health (Scotland) Act 1984; and

    (c) any State hospital;

"hospital order" has the meaning assigned to it by section 58 of this Act;

"impose detention" or "impose imprisonment" means pass a sentence of detention or imprisonment, as the case may be, or make an order for committal in default of payment of any sum of money or for contempt of court;

"indictment" includes any indictment whether in the sheriff court or the High Court framed in the form set out an Act of Adjournal or as nearly as may be in such form;

"judge", in relation to solemn procedure, means a judge of a court of solemn criminal jurisdiction and, in relation to summary procedure, means any sheriff or any judge of a district court;

"justice" includes the sheriff and any stipendiary magistrate or justice of the peace;

"justice of the peace" means any of Her Majesty's justices of the peace for any commission area in Scotland within such commission area;

"legalised police cells" has the like meaning as in the Prisons (Scotland) Act 1989;

"local authority" has the meaning assigned to it by section 1(2) of the Social Work (Scotland) Act 1968;

"Lord Commissioner of Justiciary" includes Lord Justice General and Lord Justice Clerk;

"offence" means any act, attempt or omission punishable by law;

"officer of law" includes, in relation to the service and execution of any warrant, citation, petition, indictment, complaint, list of witnesses, order, notice, or other proceeding or document—

(a) any macer, messenger-at-arms, sheriff officer or other person having authority to execute a warrant of the court;

(b) any constable;

(c) any person who is employed under section 9 of the Police (Scotland) Act 1967 for the assistance of the constables of a police force and who is authorised by the chief constable of that police force in relation to service and execution as mentioned above;

(d) where the person upon whom service or execution is effected is in prison at the time of service on him, any prison officer; and

(e) any person or class or persons authorised in that regard for the time being by the Lord Advocate or by the Secretary of State;

"order" means any order, byelaw, rule or regulation having statutory authority;

"patient" means a person suffering or appearing to be suffering from mental disorder;

"place of safety", in relation to a person not being a child, means any police station, prison or remand centre, or any hospital the board of management of which are willing temporarily to receive him, and in relation to a child means a place of safety within the meaning of Part II of the Children (Scotland) Act 1995;

"the prescribed sum" has the meaning given by section 225(8) of this Act;

"prison" does not include a naval, military or air force prison;

"prison officer" and "officer of a prison" means, in relation to a contracted out prison within the meaning of section 106(4) of the Criminal Justice and Public Order Act 1994, a prisoner custody officer within the meaning of section 114(1) of that Act;

"probationer" means a person who is under supervision by virtue of a probation order or who was under such supervision at the time of the commission of any relevant offence or failure to comply with such order;

"probation order" has the meaning assigned to it by section 228 of this Act;

"probation period" means the period for which a probationer is placed under supervision by a probation order;

"procurator fiscal" means the procurator fiscal for a sheriff court district, and includes assistant procurator fiscal and procurator fiscal depute and any person duly authorised to execute the duties of the procurator fiscal;

"prosecutor"—

(a) for the purposes of proceedings other than summary proceedings, includes Crown Counsel, procurator fiscal, any other person prosecuting in the public interest and any private prosecutor; and

(b) for the purposes of summary proceedings, includes procurator fiscal, and any other person prosecuting in the public interest and complainer and any person duly authorised to represent or act for any public prosecutor;

"remand" means an order adjourning the proceedings or continuing the case and giving direction as to detention in custody or liberation during the period of adjournment or continuation and references to remanding a person or remanding in custody or on bail shall be construed accordingly;

"remand centre" has the like meaning as in the Prisons (Scotland) Act 1989;

"residential establishment" means an establishment within the meaning of that expression for the purposes of the Social Work (Scotland) Act 1968 or, as the case may be, of Part II of the Children (Scotland) Act 1995;

"responsible medical officer" has the meaning assigned to it by section 59 of the Mental Health (Scotland) Act 1984;

"restriction order" has the meaning assigned to it by section 59 of this Act;

"sentence", whether of detention or of imprisonment, means a sentence passed in respect of a crime or offence and does not include an order for committal in default of payment of any sum of money or for contempt of court;

"sheriff clerk" includes sheriff clerk depute, and extends and applies to any person duly authorised to execute the duties of sheriff clerk;

"sheriff court district" extends to the limits within which the sheriff has jurisdiction in criminal matters whether by statute or at common law;

"State hospital" has the meaning assigned to it in Part VIII of the Mental Health (Scotland) Act 1984;

"statute" means any Act of Parliament, public general, local, or private, and any Provisional Order confirmed by Act of Parliament;

"supervision requirement" has the meaning assigned to it in Part II of the Children (Scotland) Act 1995;

"training school order" has the same meaning as in the Social Work (Scotland) Act 1968;

"witness" includes haver;

"young offenders institution" has the like meaning as in the Prisons (Scotland) Act 1989.

(2) References in this Act to a court do not include references to a court-martial; and nothing in this Act shall be construed as affecting the punishment which may be awarded by a court-martial under the Naval Discipline Act 1957, the Army Act 1955 or the Air Force Act 1955 for a civil offence within the meaning of those Acts.

(3) For the purposes of this Act, except section 228(6), where a probation order has been made on appeal, the order shall be deemed to have been made by the court from which the appeal was brought.

(4) Any reference in this Act to a previous sentence of imprisonment shall be construed as including a reference to a previous sentence of penal servitude; any such reference to a previous sentence of Borstal training shall be construed as including a reference to a previous sentence of detention in a Borstal institution.

(5) Any reference in this Act to a previous conviction or sentence shall be construed as a reference to a previous conviction by a court in any part of the United Kingdom and to a previous sentence passed by any such court.

(6) References in this Act to an offence punishable with imprisonment shall be construed, in relation to any offender, without regard to any prohibition or restriction imposed by or under any enactment, including this Act, upon the imprisonment of offenders of his age.

(7) Without prejudice to section 46 of this Act, where the age of any person at any time is material for the purposes of any provision of this Act regulating the powers of a court, his age at the material time shall be deemed to be or to have been that which appears to the court, after considering any available evidence, to be or to have been his age at that time.

(8) References in this Act to findings of guilty and findings that an offence has been committed shall be construed as including references to pleas of guilty and admissions that an offence has been committed.

Construction of enactments referring to detention etc.

308. In any enactment—

(a) any reference to a sentence of imprisonment as including a reference to a sentence of any other form of detention shall be construed as including a reference to a sentence of detention under section 207 of this Act; and

(b) any reference to imprisonment as including any other form of detention shall be construed as including a reference to detention under that section.

Short title, commencement and extent

309.—(1) This Act may be cited as the Criminal Procedure Act 1995.

(2) This Act shall come into force on 1 April 1996.

(3) Subject to subsections (4) and (5) below, this Act extends to Scotland only.

(4) The following provisions of this Act and this section extend to England and Wales—

section 44;

section 47;

section 209(3) and (7);

section 234(4) to (11);

section 244;

section 252 for the purposes of the construction mentioned in subsection (1) of that subsection;

section 303(4).

(5) The following provisions of this Act and this section extend to Northern Ireland—

section 44;

section 47;

section 244;

section 252 for the purposes of the construction mentioned in subsection (1) of that subsection;

section 303(4).

(6) Section 297(3) and (4) of this Act and this section also extend to the Isle of Man.

SCHEDULES

SCHEDULE 1

OFFENCES AGAINST CHILDREN UNDER THE AGE OF 17 YEARS TO WHICH SPECIAL PROVISIONS APPLY

1. Any offence under Part I of the Criminal Law (Consolidation) (Scotland) Act 1995.
2. Any offence under section 12, 15, 22 or 33 of the Children and Young Persons (Scotland) Act 1937.
3. Any other offence involving bodily injury to a child under the age of 17 years.
4. Any offence involving the use of lewd, indecent or libidinous practice or behaviour towards a child under the age of 17 years.

Sections 34 & 64(2)   SCHEDULE 2

EXAMPLES OF INDICTMENTS

"A.B. (*name and address, that given in the declaration being sufficient*), you are indicted at the instance of A. F. R. (*name of Lord Advocate*), Her Majesty's Advocate, and the charge against you is that on 20th 199, in a shop in George Street, Edinburgh, occupied by John Cruikshank, draper, you did steal a shawl and a boa."

"...You did rob Charles Doyle, a cattle dealer, of Biggar, Lanarkshire, of a watch and chain and £36 of money..."

"...You did break into the house occupied by Andrew Howe, banker's clerk, and did there steal twelve spoons, a ladle, and a candlestick..."

"...You did force open (*or* attempt to force open) a lockfast cupboard and did thus attempt to steal therefrom..."

"...You did place your hand in one of the packets of Thomas Kerr, commercial traveller, 115 Main Street, Perth, and did thus attempt to steal..."

"...You did assault Lewis Mann, station-master of Earlston, and compress his throat and attempt to take from him a watch and chain..."

"...You did, while in the employment of James Pentland, accountant in Frederick Street, Edinburgh, embezzle £4,075 of money..."

"...You did, while acting as commercial traveller to Brown and Company, merchants in Leith, at the times and places specified in the inventory hereto subjoined, receive from the persons therein set forth the respective sums of money therein specified for the said Brown and Company, and did embezzle the same (*or* did embezzle £470 of money, being part thereof)..."

"...You did pretend to Norah Omond, residing there, that you were a collector of subscriptions for a charitable society, and did thus induce her to deliver to you £15 of money as a subscription thereto, which you appropriated to your own use..."

"...You did reset a watch and chain, pocket book and £15.55 of money, the same having been dishonestly appropriated by theft or robbery..."

"...You did utter as genuine a bill, on which the name of John Jones bore to be signed as acceptor, such signature being forged by (*here describe in general terms how the bill was uttered, and add where the bill is produced*), and said bill of exchange is No. of the productions lodged herewith..."

"...You did utter as genuine a letter bearing to be a certificate of character of you, as a domestic servant, by Mary Watson, of 15 Bon Accord Street, Aberdeen, what was written above the signature of Mary Watson having been written there by some other person without her authority by handing it to Ellen Chisholm of Panmore Street, Forfar, to whom you were applying for a situation (*here add when the letter is produced*), and said letter is No. of the productions lodged herewith..."

"...You did utter a cheque signed by Henry Smith for £8 sterling, which had been altered without his authority by adding the letter Y to eight and the figure 0 to figure 8, so as to make it read as a cheque for XC11,480 sterling, by presenting such altered cheque for payment to Allen Brown, Cashier of the Bank of Scotland at Callander (*here add when the cheque is produced*), and said cheque is No. of the productions lodged herewith..."

"...You did, when examined under section 45 of the Bankruptcy (Scotland) Act 1985 before Hubert Hamilton Esquire, sheriff of the Lothians and Borders, depone (*here state the general nature of the false statement*), in order to defraud your creditors..."

"...You did, sequestration having been awarded on your estate on the 20th March 1991, conceal property consisting of (*here state generally the property concealed*), falling under your sequestration, in order to defraud your creditor, by burying it in the garden of your house in Troon Street, Kilmarnock (*or* by removing it to the house of James Kidd, your son, No. 17 Greek Street, Port-Glasgow)..."

"...You did set fire to a warehouse occupied by Peter Cranston in Holly Lane, Greenock, and the fire took effect on said warehouse, and this you did wilfully (*or* culpably and recklessly)..."

"...You did set fire to the shop in Brown Street, Blairgowrie, occupied by you, with intent to defraud the Liverpool, London, and Globe Insurance Company, and the fire took effect on said shop..."

"...You did assault Theresa Unwin, your wife, and did beat her and did murder her..."

"...You did stab Thomas Underwood, baker, of Shiels Place, Oban, and did murder him..."

"...You did administer poison to Vincent Wontner, your son, and did murder him..."

"...You did strangle Mary Shaw, mill-worker, daughter of John Shaw, residing at Juniper Green, in the county of Midlothian, and did murder her..."

"...You were delivered of a child now dead or amissing, and you did conceal your pregnancy and did not call for or use assistance at the birth, contrary to the Concealment of Birth (Scotland) Act 1809..."

"...You did assault Hector Morrison, carter, of 20 Buccleuch Street, Dalkeith, and did beat him with your fists and with a stick, and did break his arm..."

"...You did ravish Harriet Cowan, mill-worker, of 27 Tweed Row, Peebles..."

"...You did attempt to ravish Jane Peters, servant, at Glen House, near Dunbar..."

"...You did, when acting as railway signalman, cancel a danger signal and allow a train to enter on a part of the line protected by the signals under your charge, and did cause a collision, and did kill William Peters, commercial traveller, of Brook Street, Carlisle, a passenger in said train..."

"...You formed part of a riotous mob, which, acting of common purpose, obstructed A. B., C. D., and E. F., constables of the Northern constabulary on duty, and assaulted them, and forcibly took two persons whom they had arrested from their custody..."

"...You did, being the lawful husband of Helen Hargreaves, of 20 Teviot Row, Edinburgh, and she being still alive, bigamously marry Dorothy Rose, a widow, of 7 Blacks Row, Brechin, and did cohabit with her as her husband..."

"...You being sworn as a witness in a civil cause, then proceeding in the sheriff court, deponed (*here set forth the statements said to be false*) the truth as you knew being that (*here state the true facts*)..."

"...You did suborn James Carruthers, scavenger, 12 Hercles Street, Edinburgh, to depone as a witness in the sheriff court of Edinburgh, that (*here set forth the statements said to be false*), and he did (*time and place*) depone to that effect, the truth as you knew being (*here state the true facts*)..."

"...You did deforce John Macdonald, a sheriff officer of Renfrewshire, and prevent him serving a summons issued by the sheriff of Renfrewshire upon Peter M'Innes, market gardener in Renfrew..."

Sections 64(6) and 138(4)   SCHEDULE 3

Indictments and Complaints

1. An accused may be named and designed—
(a) according to the existing practice; or
(b) by the name given by him and designed as of the place given by him as his residence when he is examined or further examined; or
(c) by the name under which he is committed until liberated in due course of law.
2. It shall not be necessary to specify by any *nomen juris* the offence which is charged, but it shall be sufficient that the indictment or complaint sets forth facts relevant and sufficient to constitute an indictable offence or, as the case may be, an offence punishable on complaint.
3. It shall not be necessary to allege that any act or commission or omission charged was done

or omitted to be done "wilfully" or "maliciously", or "wickedly and feloniously", or "falsely and fraudulently" or "knowingly", or "culpably and recklessly", or "negligently", or in "breach of duty", or to use such words as "knowing the same to be forged", or "having good reason to know", or "well knowing the same to have been stolen", or to use any similar words or expressions qualifying any act charged, but such qualifying allegation shall be implied in every case.

4.—(1) The latitude formerly used in stating time shall be implied in all statements of time where an exact time is not of the essence of the charge.

(2) The latitude formerly used in stating any place by adding to the word "at", or to the word "in", the words "or near", or the words "or in the near neighbourhood thereof" or similar words, shall be implied in all statements of place where the actual place is not of the essence of the charge.

(3) Subject to sub-paragraph (4) below, where the circumstances of the offence charged make it necessary to take an exceptional latitude in regard to time or place it shall not be necessary to set forth the circumstances in the indictment, or to set forth that the particular time or the particular place is to the prosecutor unknown.

(4) Where exceptional latitude is taken as mentioned in sub-paragraph (3) above, the court shall, if satisfied that such exceptional latitude was not reasonable in the circumstances of the case, give such remedy to the accused by adjournment of the trial or otherwise as shall seem just.

(5) Notwithstanding sub-paragraph (4) above, nothing in any rule of law shall prohibit the amendment of an indictment or, as the case may be, a complaint to include a time outwith the exceptional latitude if it appears to the court that the amendment would not prejudice the accused.

(6) The latitude formerly used in describing quantities by the words "or thereby", or the words "or part thereof", or the words "or some other quantity to the prosecutor unknown" or similar words, shall be implied in all statements of quantities.

(7) The latitude formerly used in stating details connected with the perpetration of any act regarding persons, things or modes by inserting general alternative statements followed by the words "to the prosecutor unknown" or similar words, shall be implied in every case.

(8) In this paragraph references to latitude formerly used are references to such use before the commencement of—

(a) in the case of proceedings on indictment, the Criminal Procedure (Scotland) Act 1887; and

(b) in the case of summary proceedings, the Summary Jurisdiction (Scotland) Act 1908.

5. The word "money" shall include cheques, banknotes, postal orders, money orders and foreign currency.

6. Any document referred to shall be referred to by a general description and, where it is to be produced in proceedings on indictment, by the number given to it in the list of productions for the prosecution.

7. In an indictment which charges a crime importing personal injury inflicted by the accused, resulting in death or serious injury to the person, the accused may be lawfully convicted of the aggravation that the assault or other injurious act was committed with intent to commit such crime.

8.—(1) In an indictment or a complaint charging the resetting of property dishonestly appropriated—

(a) having been taken by theft or robbery; or

(b) by breach of trust, embezzlement or falsehood, fraud and wilful imposition,

it shall be sufficient to specify that the accused received the property, it having been dishonestly appropriated by theft or robbery, or by breach of trust and embezzlement, or by falsehood, fraud and wilful imposition, as the case may be.

(2) Under an indictment or a complaint for robbery, theft, breach of trust and embezzlement or falsehood, fraud and wilful imposition, an accused may be convicted of reset.

(3) Under an indictment or a complaint for robbery, breach of trust and embezzlement, or falsehood, fraud and wilful imposition, an accused may be convicted of theft.

(4) Under an indictment or a complaint for theft, an accused may be convicted of breach of trust and embezzlement, or of falsehood, fraud and wilful imposition, or may be convicted of theft, although the circumstances proved may in law amount to robbery.

(5) The power conferred by sub-paragraphs (2) to (4) above to convict a person of an offence other than that with which he is charged shall be exercisable by the sheriff court before which he is tried notwithstanding that the other offence was committed outside the jurisdiction of that sheriff court.

9.—(1) Where two or more crimes or acts of crime are charged cumulatively, it shall be lawful to convict of any one or more of them.

(2) Any part of the charge in an indictment or complaint which itself constitutes an indictable offence or, as the case may be an offence punishable on complaint, shall be separable and it shall be lawful to convict the accused of that offence.

(3) Where any crime is charged as having been committed with a particular intent or with particular circumstances of aggravation, it shall be lawful to convict of the crime without such intent or aggravation.

10.—(1) Under an indictment or, as the case may be, a complaint which charges a completed offence, the accused may be lawfully convicted of an attempt to commit the offence.

(2) Under an indictment or complaint charging an attempt, the accused may be convicted of such attempt although the evidence is sufficient to prove the completion of the offence said to have been attempted.

(3) Under an indictment or complaint which charges an offence involving personal injury inflicted by the accused, resulting in death or serious injury to the person, the accused may be lawfully convicted of the assault or other injurious act, and may also be lawfully convicted of the aggravation that the assault or other injurious act was committed with intent to commit such offence.

11. In an indictment or complaint charging a contravention of an enactment the description of the offence in the words of the enactment contravened, or in similar words, shall be sufficient.

12. In a complaint charging a contravention of an enactment—

(a) the statement that an act was done contrary to an enactment shall imply a statement—

(i) that the enactment applied to the circumstances existing at the time and place of the offence;

(ii) that the accused was a person bound to observe the enactment;

(iii) that any necessary preliminary procedure had been duly gone through; and

(iv) that all the circumstances necessary to a contravention existed,

and, in the case of the contravention of a subordinate instrument, such statement shall imply a statement that the instrument was duly made, confirmed, published and generally made effectual according to the law applicable, and was in force at the time and place in question; and

(b) where the offence is created by more than one section of one or more statutes or subordinate instruments, it shall be necessary to specify only the leading section or one of the leading sections.

13. In the case of an offence punishable under any enactment, it shall be sufficient to allege that the offence was committed contrary to the enactment and to refer to the enactment founded on without setting out the words of the enactment at length.

14. Where—

(a) any act alleged in an indictment or complaint as contrary to any enactment is also criminal at common law; or

(b) where the facts proved under the indictment or complaint do not amount to a contravention of the enactment, but do amount to an offence at common law,

it shall be lawful to convict of the common law offence.

15. Where the evidence in a trial is sufficient to prove the identity of any person, corporation or company, or of any place, or of anything, it shall not be a valid objection to the sufficiency of the evidence that any particulars specified in the indictment or complaint relating to such identity have not been proved.

16. Where, in relation to an offence created by or under an enactment any exception, exemption, proviso, excuse, or qualification, is expressed to have effect whether by the same or any other enactment, the exception, exemption, proviso, excuse or qualification need not be specified or negatived in the indictment or complaint, and the prosecution is not required to prove it, but the accused may do so.

17. It shall be competent to include in one indictment or complaint both common law and statutory charges.

18. In any proceedings under the Merchant Shipping Acts it shall not be necessary to produce the official register of the ship referred to in the proceedings in order to prove the nationality of the ship, but the nationality of the ship as stated in the indictment or, as the case may be, complaint shall, in the absence of evidence to the contrary, be presumed.

19. In offences inferring dishonest appropriation of property brought before a court whose power to deal with such offences is limited to cases in which the value of such property does not exceed level 4 on the standard scale it shall be assumed, and it shall not be necessary to state in the charge, that the value of the property does not exceed that sum.

SCHEDULE 4

SUPERVISION AND TREATMENT ORDERS

PART I

PRELIMINARY

1.—(1) In this Schedule "supervision and treatment order" means an order requiring the person in respect of whom it is made ("the supervised person")—

(a) to be under the supervision of a social worker who is an officer of the local authority for the area where the supervised person resides or is to reside (in this Schedule referred to as "the supervising officer") for such period, not being more than three years, as is specified in the order;

(b) to comply during that period with instructions given to him by the supervising officer regarding his supervision; and

(c) to submit during that period to treatment by or under the direction of a medical practitioner with a view to the improvement of his mental condition.

(2) The Secretary of State may by order amend sub-paragraph (1) above by substituting, for the period for the time being specified in that sub-paragraph, such period as may be specified in the order.

(3) An order under sub-paragraph (2) above may make any amendment to paragraph 8(2) below which the Secretary of State considers necessary in consequence of the order.

(4) The power of the Secretary of State to make orders under sub-paragraph (2) above shall be exercisable by statutory instrument subject to annulment in pursuance of a resolution of either House of Parliament.

PART II

MAKING AND EFFECT OF ORDERS

Circumstances in which orders may be made

2.—(1) The court shall not make a supervision and treatment order unless it is satisfied—

(a) that, having regard to all the circumstances of the case, the making of such an order is the most suitable means of dealing with the person; and

(b) on the written or oral evidence of two or more medical practitioners approved for the purposes of section 20 or 39 of the Mental Health (Scotland) Act 1984, that the mental condition of the person—

(i) is such as requires and may be susceptible to treatment; but

(ii) is not such as to warrant the making of an order under paragraph (a) of subsection (2) of section 57 of this Act (whether with or without an order under paragraph (b) of that subsection) or an order under paragraph (c) of that subsection.

(2) The court shall not make a supervision and treatment order unless it is also satisfied—

(a) that the supervising officer intended to be specified in the order is willing to undertake the supervision; and

(b) that arrangements have been made for the treatment intended to be specified in the order.

(3) Subsections (3) to (5) of section 61 of this Act shall have effect with respect to proof of a person's mental condition for the purposes of sub-paragraph (1) above as they have effect with respect to proof of an offender's mental condition for the purposes of section 58(1)(a) of this Act.

Making of orders and general requirements

3.—(1) A supervision and treatment order shall specify the local authority area in which the supervised person resides or will reside.

(2) Before making such an order, the court shall explain to the supervised person in ordinary language—

(a) the effect of the order (including any requirements proposed to be included in the order in accordance with paragraph 5 below); and

(b) that the sheriff court for the area in which the supervised person resides or will reside (in this Schedule referred to as "the relevant sheriff court") has power under paragraphs 6 to 8 below to review the order on the application either of the supervised person or of the supervising officer.

(3) After making such an order, the court shall forthwith give a copy of the order to—

(a) the supervised person;

(b) the supervising officer; and

(c) the person in charge of any institution in which the supervised person is required by the order to reside.

(4) After making such an order, the court shall also send to the relevant sheriff court—

(a) a copy of the order; and

(b) such documents and information relating to the case as it considers likely to be of assistance to that court in the exercise of its functions in relation to the order.

(5) Where such an order is made, the supervised person shall comply with such instructions as he may from time to time be given by the supervising officer regarding his supervision and shall keep in touch with that officer and notify him of any change of address.

Obligatory requirements as to medical treatment

4.—(1) A supervision and treatment order shall include a requirement that the supervised person shall submit, during the period specified in the order, to treatment by or under the direction of a medical practitioner with a view to the improvement of his mental condition.

(2) The treatment required by the order shall be such one of the following kinds of treatment as may be specified in the order, that is to say—

(a) treatment as a non-resident patient at such institution or place as may be specified in the order; and

(b) treatment by or under the direction of such medical practitioner as may be so specified; but the nature of the treatment shall not be specified in the order except as mentioned in paragraph (a) or (b) above.

(3) Where the medical practitioner by whom or under whose direction the supervised person is being treated for his mental condition in pursuance of a supervision and treatment order is of the opinion that part of the treatment can be better or more conveniently given at an institution or place which—

(a) is not specified in the order; and

(b) is one at which the treatment of the supervised person will be given by or under the direction of a medical practitioner,

he may, with the consent of the supervised person, make arrangements for him to be treated accordingly.

(4) Where any such arrangements as are mentioned in sub-paragraph (3) above are made for the treatment of a supervised person—

(a) the medical practitioner by whom the arrangements are made shall give notice in writing to the supervising officer, specifying the institution or place at which the treatment is to be carried out; and

(b) the treatment provided for by the arrangements shall be deemed to be treatment to which he is required to submit in pursuance of the supervision and treatment order.

Optional requirements as to residence

5.—(1) Subject to sub-paragraphs (2) to (4) below, a supervision and treatment order may include requirements as to the residence of the supervised person.

(2) Such an order may not require the supervised person to reside as a resident patient in a hospital.

(3) Before making such an order containing any such requirement, the court shall consider the home surroundings of the supervised person.

(4) Where such an order requires the supervised person to reside in any institution, the period for which he is so required to reside shall be specified in the order.

Part III

Revocation and Amendment of Orders

Revocation of order in interests of health or welfare

6. Where a supervision and treatment order is in force in respect of any person and, on the application of the supervised person or the supervising officer, it appears to the relevant sheriff court that, having regard to circumstances which have arisen since the order was made, it would be in the interests of the health or welfare of the supervised person that the order should be revoked, the court may revoke the order.

Amendment of order by reason of change of residence

7.—(1) This paragraph applies where, at any time while a supervision and treatment order is in force in respect of any person, the relevant sheriff court is satisfied that—

(a) the supervised person proposes to change, or has changed, his residence from the area specified in the order to the area of another local authority;

(b) a social worker who is an officer of the other local authority ("the new supervising officer") is willing to undertake the supervision; and

(c) the requirements of the order as respects treatment will continue to be complied with.

(2) Subject to sub-paragraph (3) below the court may, and on the application of the supervising officer shall, amend the supervision and treatment order by substituting the other area for the area specified in the order and the new supervising officer for the supervising officer specified in the order.

(3) Where a supervision and treatment order contains requirements which, in the opinion of the court, can be complied with only if the supervised person continues to reside in the area specified in the order, the court shall not amend the order under this paragraph unless it also, in accordance with paragraph 8 below, either—

(a) cancels those requirements; or

(b) substitutes for those requirements other requirements which can be complied with if the supervised person ceases to reside in that area.

Amendment of requirements of order

8.—(1) Without prejudice to paragraph 7 above, but subject to sub-paragraph (2) below, the relevant sheriff court may, on the application of the supervised person or the supervising officer, by order amend a supervision and treatment order—

(a) by cancelling any of the requirements of the order; or

(b) by inserting in the order (either in addition to or in substitution for any such requirement) any requirement which the court could include if it were the court by which the order was made and were then making it.

(2) The power of the court under sub-paragraph (1) above shall not include power to amend an order by extending the period specified in it beyond the end of three years from the date of the original order.

Amendment of requirements in pursuance of medical report

9.—(1) Where the medical practitioner by whom or under whose direction the supervised person is being treated for his mental condition in pursuance of any requirement of a supervision and treatment order—

(a) is of the opinion mentioned in sub-paragraph (2) below; or

(b) is for any reason unwilling to continue to treat or direct the treatment of the supervised person,

he shall make a report in writing to that effect to the supervising officer and that officer shall apply under paragraph 8 above to the relevant sheriff court for the variation or cancellation of the requirement.

(2) The opinion referred to in sub-paragraph (1) above is—

(a) that the treatment of the supervised person should be continued beyond the period specified in the supervision and treatment order;

(b) that the supervised person needs different treatment, being treatment of a kind to which he could be required to submit in pursuance of such an order;

(c) that the supervised person is not susceptible to treatment; or

(d) that the supervised person does not require further treatment.

Supplemental

10.—(1) On the making under paragraph 6 above of an order revoking a supervision and treatment order, the sheriff clerk shall forthwith give a copy of the revoking order to the supervising officer.

(2) On receipt of a copy of the revoking order the supervising officer shall give a copy to the supervised person and to the person in charge of any institution in which the supervised person was required by the order to reside.

11.—(1) On the making under paragraph 7 or 8 above of an order amending a supervision and treatment order, the sheriff clerk shall forthwith—

(a) if the order amends the supervision and treatment order otherwise than by substituting a new area or a new place for the one specified in that order, give a copy of the amending order to the supervising officer;

(b) if the order amends the supervision and treatment order in the manner excepted by paragraph (a) above, send to the new relevant sheriff court—

(i) a copy of the amending order; and

(ii) such documents and information relating to the case as he considers likely to be of assistance to that court in exercising its functions in relation to the order;

and in a case falling within paragraph (b) above, the sheriff clerk shall give a copy of the amending order to the supervising officer.

(2) On receipt of a copy of an amending order the supervising officer shall give a copy to the supervised person and to the person in charge of any institution in which the supervised person is or was required by the order to reside.

12. On the making, revocation or amendment of a supervision and treatment order the supervising officer shall give a copy of the order or, as the case may be, of the order revoking or amending it, to the Mental Welfare Commission for Scotland.

Section 138(2)   SCHEDULE 5

FORMS OF COMPLAINT AND CHARGES

The following Forms are additional to those contained in Schedule 2 to this Act, all of which, in so far as applicable to charges which may be tried summarily, are deemed to be incorporated in this Schedule:—

You did assault A.L. and strike him with your fists.

You did conduct yourself in a disorderly manner and commit a breach of the peace.

You did threaten violence to the lieges and commit a breach of the peace.

You did fight and commit a breach of the peace.

You did publicly expose your person in a shameless and indecent manner in presence of the lieges.

You did obtain from A.N. board and lodging to the value of £16 without paying and intending not to pay therefor.

You did maliciously knock down 20 metres of the coping of a wall forming the fence between two fields on the said farm.

You did maliciously place a block of wood on the railway line and attempt to obstruct a train.

You did drive a horse and cart recklessly to the danger of the lieges.

You did break into a poultry house and steal three fowls.

You did steal a coat which you obtained from R.O. on the false representation that you had been sent for it by her husband.

having received from D.G. £6 to hand to E.R., you did on (date) at (place) steal the said sum.

having received from G.R. a watch in loan, you did on at, sell it to E.G., and steal it.

having found a watch, you did, without trying to discover its owner, sell it on at, to O.R., and steal it.

You did acquire from K.O., a private in the Third Battalion a military jacket and waist belt, contrary to section 195 of the Army Act 1955.

You, being a person whose estate has been sequestrated, did obtain credit from W.A. to the extent of £260 without informing him that your estate had been sequestrated and that you had not received your discharge, contrary to section 67(9) of the Bankruptcy (Scotland) Act 1985.

You, being the occupier of the said house, did use the same for the purpose of betting with persons resorting thereto, contrary to section 1 of the Betting, Gaming and Lotteries Act 1963.

You did frequent and loiter in the said street for the purpose of betting and receiving bets, contrary to section 8 of the Betting, Gaming and Lotteries Act 1963.

You did assault L.S., a constable of the Police, while engaged in the execution of his duty, and with a stick strike him on the face to the great effusion of blood contrary to section 41 of the Police (Scotland) Act 1967.

You did cruelly ill-treat a horse by causing it to draw a cart while it was suffering from a sore on its back under the saddle, contrary to section 1 of the Protection of Animals (Scotland) Act 1912.

You did wilfully neglect your children K.I., aged seven years; J.I., aged five years; and H.I., aged three years, by failing to provide them with adequate food and clothing, and by keeping them in a filthy and verminous condition, contrary to section 12 of the Children and Young Persons (Scotland) Act 1937.

You are the owner of a dog which is dangerous and not kept under proper control, and which on in did chase a flock of sheep, contrary to section 2 of the Dogs Act 1871, section 2, as amended by section 1 of the Dogs Act 1906, whereby you are liable to be ordered to keep the said dog under proper control or to destroy it.

You, being a parent of D.U., a child of school age, aged, who has attended school, and the said child having failed, between and, without reasonable excuse, to attend regularly at the said school, you are thereby guilty of an offence against section 35 of the Education (Scotland) Act 1980.

being an unauthorised place you did keep for sale 75 kilograms of gunpowder, contrary to the Explosives Act 1875, section 5.

You did keep 78 kilograms of gunpowder, and did not keep it in a fireproof safe, contrary to the Explosives Act 1875, section 22 and section 3, subsection (1), Mode B, of the Order in Council dated 26th October 1896.

You did sell and deliver to N.C. to his prejudice an article of food namely; gallons of sweet milk which was not of the nature, substance and quality of the article demanded by him and was not genuine sweet milk in respect that it was deficient in milk fat to the extent of per cent, or thereby in that it contained only per cent, of milk fat, conform to certificate of analysis granted on (date) by A.N. analytical chemist (address), public analyst for (a copy of which certificate of analysis is annexed hereto) of a sample of the said milk taken (specify time and place) by L.O., duly appointed sampling officer for, acting under the direction of the local authority for the said burgh, while the said milk was in course of delivery to the said N.C. contrary to the Food Act 1984, and the Sale of Milk Regulations 1901.

You did take part in gaming in the street contrary to sections 5 and 8 of the Gaming Act 1968.

You did by night enter on the said land with nets for the purpose of taking game, contrary to section 1 of the Night Poaching Act 1828; or

You did by night unlawfully take six rabbits, contrary to, etc.

You did in the daytime trespass on the said land in search of pursuit of game (*or* rabbits), contrary to section 1 of the Game (Scotland) Act 1832.

You were found in the possession of five hares, a net and six net pins, which hares you had obtained by unlawfully going on land in search or pursuit of game, and which net and nets pins you had used for unlawfully killing or taking game, or you had been accessory thereto, contrary to section 2 of the Poaching Prevention Act 1862.

You did present or cause to be presented to W.E., Assessors for a return in which you falsely stated that the yearly rent of your House. No. Street, was £20, instead of £30, contrary to section 7 of the Lands Valuation (Scotland) Act 1854.

You did sell a half gill of whisky to J.M., who was then a drunken person, contrary to your certificate and section 76 of the Licensing (Scotland) Act 1976.

You were found drunk and incapable of taking care of yourself, and not under the care or protection of some suitable person, contrary to section 74(2) of the Licensing (Scotland) Act 1976.

You did drive a motor car recklessly contrary to section 2 of the Road Traffic Act 1988.

You did act as a pedlar without having obtained a certificate, contrary to section 4 of the Pedlars' Act 1871.

You did place in a Post Office letter box a lighted match, contrary to section 60 of the Post Office Act 1953.

You did travel in a railway carriage without having previously paid your fare, and with intent to avoid payment thereof, contrary to section 5(3)(a) of the Regulation of Railways Act 1889.

Having on within the house No. Street, given birth to a female child, you did fail, within twenty-one days thereafter, to attend personally and give information to C.W., registrar of births, deaths, and marriages for (Registration District), of the particulars required to be registered concerning the birth, contrary to sections 14 and 53 of the Registration of Births, Deaths, and Marriages (Scotland) Act 1965.

You did take two salmon during the annual close time by means of cobles and sweep nets, contrary to section 15 of the Salmon Fisheries (Scotland) Act 1868.

You had in your possession for use for trade a counter balance which was false, and two weights, which were unjust, contrary to the Weights and Measures Act 1985, section 17.

Section 231(1)   SCHEDULE 6

DISCHARGE OF AND AMENDMENT TO PROBATION ORDERS

Discharge

1. A probation order may on the application of the officer supervising the probationer or of the probationer be discharged—

    (a) by the appropriate court; or

(b) if no appropriate court has been named in the original or in any amending order, by the court which made the order.

Amendment

2.—(1) If the court by which a probation order was made, or the appropriate court, is satisfied that the probationer proposes to change or has changed his residence from the area of a local authority named in the order to the area of another local authority, the court may, and if application is made in that behalf by the officer supervising the probationer shall, by order, amend the probation order by—
(a) substituting for the area named therein that other area; and
(b) naming the appropriate court to which all the powers of the court by which the order was made shall be transferred and shall require the local authority for that other area to arrange for the probationer to be under the supervision of an officer of that authority.

(2) Subject to sub-paragraphs (3) and (4) below, the court to be named as the appropriate court in any amendment of a probation order in pursuance of sub-paragraph (1) above shall be a court exercising jurisdiction in the place where the probationer resides or is to reside and shall be a sheriff court or district court according to whether the probation order was made by a sheriff court or district court.

(3) If the probation order was made by a district court and there is no district court exercising jurisdiction in the place mentioned in sub-paragraph (2) above, the court to be named shall be the sheriff court.

(4) If the probation order contains requirements which in the opinion of the court cannot be complied with unless the probationer continues to reside in the local authority area named in the order, the court shall not amend the order as mentioned in sub-paragraph (2) above unless, in accordance with the following provisions of this Schedule, it cancels those requirements or substitutes therefor other requirements which can be so complied with.

(5) Where a probation order is amended under this paragraph, the clerk of the court amending it shall send to the clerk of the appropriate court four copies of the order together with such documents and information relating to the case as the court amending the order considers likely to be of assistance to the appropriate court, and the clerk of that court shall send one copy of the probation order to the local authority of the substituted local authority area and two copies to the officer supervising the probationer, one of which the supervising officer shall give to the probationer.

(6) The foregoing provisions of this paragraph shall, in a case where the probation order was made by the High Court, have effect subject to the following modifications—
(a) the court shall not name an appropriate court, but may substitute for the local authority named in the order, the local authority for the area in which the probationer is to reside;
(b) the Clerk of Justiciary shall send to the chief social work officer of that area in which the probationer is to reside three copies of the amending order together with such documents and information relating to the case as is likely to be of assistance to the chief social work officer, and the chief social work officer shall send two copies of the amending order to the officer supervising the probationer, one of which the supervising officer shall give to the probationer.

3.—(1) Without prejudice to paragraph 2 above, the court by which a probation order was made or the appropriate court may, upon application made by the officer supervising the probationer or by the probationer, subject to sub-paragraph (2) below, by order amend a probation order by cancelling any of the requirements thereof or by inserting therein (either in addition to or in substitution for any such requirement) any requirement which could be included in the order if it were then being made by that court in accordance with sections 228 to 230 of this Act.

(2) The court shall not amend a probation order under sub-paragraph (1) above—
(a) by reducing the probation period, or by extending that period beyond the end of three years from the date of the original order;
(b) so that the probationer is thereby required to reside in any institution or place, or to submit to treatment for his mental condition, for any period or periods exceeding 12 months in all;
(c) by inserting in it a requirement that the probationer shall submit to treatment for his mental condition unless the amending order is made within three months after the date of the original order.

4. Where the medical practitioner or chartered psychologist by whom or under whose direction a probationer is being treated for his mental condition in pursuance of any requirement of the probation order is of the opinion—
(a) that the treatment of the probationer should be continued beyond the period specified for that purpose in the order; or

(b) that the probationer needs a different kind of treatment (whether in whole or in part) from that which he has been receiving in pursuance of the probation order, being treatment of a kind which could have been specified in the probation order but to which the probationer or his supervising officer has not agreed under section 230(6) of this Act; or

(c) that the probationer is not susceptible to treatment; or

(d) that the probationer does not require further treatment,

or where the practitioner or psychologist is for any reason unwilling to continue to treat or direct the treatment of the probationer, he shall make a report in writing to that effect to the officer supervising the probationer and the supervising officer shall apply to the court which made the order or to the appropriate court for the variation or cancellation of the requirement.

General

5.—(1) Where the court which made the order or the appropriate court proposes to amend a probation order under this Schedule, otherwise than on the application of the probationer, it shall cite him to appear before the court; and the court shall not amend the probation order unless the probationer expresses his willingness to comply with the requirements of the order as amended.

(2) Sub-paragraph (1) above shall not apply to an order cancelling a requirement of the probation order or reducing the period of any requirement, or substituting a new area of a local authority for the area named in the probation order.

6. On the making of an order discharging or amending a probation order, the clerk of the court shall forthwith give copies of the discharging or amending order to the officer supervising the probationer; and the supervising officer shall give a copy to the probationer and to the person in charge of any institution in which the probationer is or was required by the order to reside.

Section 235 SCHEDULE 7

SUPERVISED ATTENDANCE ORDERS: FURTHER PROVISIONS

1.—(1) A court shall not make a supervised attendance order in respect of any offender unless—

(a) the court has been notified by the Secretary of State that arrangements exist for persons of a class which includes the offender who reside in the locality in which the offender resides, or will be residing when the order comes into force, to carry out the requirements of such an order.

(b) the court is satisfied that provision can be made under the arrangements mentioned in sub-sub-paragraph (a) above for the offender to carry out such requirements.

(2) Before making a supervised attendance order, the court shall explain to the offender in ordinary language—

(a) the purpose and effect of the order and in particular the obligations on the offender as specified in paragraph 3 below;

(b) the consequences which may follow under paragraph 4 below if he fails to comply with any of those requirements; and

(c) that the court has, under paragraph 5 below, the power to review the order on the application either of the offender or of an officer of the local authority in whose area the offender for the time being resides.

(3) The Secretary of State may by order direct that subsection (2) of section 235 of this Act shall be amended by substituting, for any number of hours specified in that subsection such other number of hours as may be specified in the order; and an order under this subsection may in making such amendment specify different such numbers of hours for different classes of case.

(4) An order under sub-paragraph (3) above shall be made by statutory instrument, but no such order shall be made unless a draft of it has been laid before, and approved by a resolution of, each House of Parliament.

2.—(1) A supervised attendance order shall—

(a) specify the locality in which the offender resides or will be residing when the order comes into force; and

(b) require the local authority in whose area the locality specified under sub-sub-paragraph (a) above is situated to appoint or assign a supervising officer.

(2) Where, whether on the same occasion or on separate occasions, an offender is made subject to more than one supervised attendance order, the court may direct that the requirements specified in any of those orders shall be concurrent with or additional to those specified in any

other of those orders, but so that at no time shall the offender have an outstanding number of hours during which he must carry out the requirements of these orders in excess of the largest number specified in section 235 of this Act.

(3) Upon making a supervised attendance order the court shall—

(a) give, or send by registered post or by the recorded delivery service, a copy of the order to the offender;

(b) send a copy of the order to the chief social work officer of the local authority in whose area the offender resides or will be residing when the order comes into force; and

(c) where it is not the appropriate court, send a copy of the order (together with such documents and information relating to the case as are considered useful) to the clerk of the appropriate court.

(4) Where a copy of a supervised attendance order has, under sub-paragraph (3)(a) above, been sent by registered post or by the recorded delivery service, an acknowledgement or certificate of delivery of a letter containing the copy order issued by the Post Office shall be sufficient evidence of the delivery of the letter on the day specified in such acknowledgement or certificate.

3.—(1) An offender in respect of whom a supervised attendance order is in force shall report to the supervising officer and notify him without delay of any change of address or in the times, if any, at which he usually works.

(2) Subject to paragraph 5(1) below, instructions given under a supervised attendance order shall be carried out during the period of twelve months beginning with the date of the order; but, unless revoked, the order shall remain in force until the offender has carried out the instructions given under it for the number of hours specified in it.

(3) The instructions given by the supervising officer under the order shall, so far as practicable, be such as to avoid any conflict with the offender's religious beliefs and any interference with the times, if any, at which he normally works or attends a school or other educational establishment.

4.—(1) If at any time while a supervised attendance order is in force in respect of any offender it appears to the appropriate court, on information from the supervising officer, that that offender has failed to comply with any of the requirements of paragraph 3 above or of the order (including any failure satisfactorily to carry out any instructions which he has been given by the supervising officer under the order), the court may issue a warrant for the arrest of that offender, or may, if it thinks fit, instead of issuing a warrant in the first instance issue a citation requiring the offender to appear before that court at such time as may be specified in the citation.

(2) If it is proved to the satisfaction of the court before which an offender is brought or appears in pursuance of sub-paragraph (1) above that he has failed without reasonable excuse to comply with any of the requirements of paragraph 3 above or of the order (including any failure satisfactorily to carry out any instructions which he has been given by the supervising officer under the order) the court may—

(a) revoke the order and impose such period of imprisonment not exceeding—

    (i) in the case of a sheriff court, three months; and

    (ii) in the case of a district court, 60 days,

as the court considers appropriate; or

(b) subject to section 235 of this Act and paragraph 2(2) above, vary the number of hours specified in the order.

(3) The evidence of one witness shall, for the purposes of sub-paragraph (2) above, be sufficient evidence.

5.—(1) Where a supervised attendance order is in force in respect of any offender and, on the application of that offender or of the supervising officer, it appears to the appropriate court that it would be in the interests of justice to do so having regard to circumstances which have arisen since the order was made, that court may—

(a) extend, in relation to the order, the period of twelve months specified in paragraph 3 above;

(b) subject to section 235 of this Act and paragraph 2(2) above, vary the numbers of hours specified in the order;

(c) revoke the order; or

(d) revoke the order and impose such period of imprisonment not exceeding—

    (i) in the case of a sheriff court, three months; and

    (ii) in the case of a district court, 60 days,

as the court considers appropriate.

(2) If the appropriate court is satisfied that the offender proposes to change, or has changed, his residence from the locality for the time being specified under paragraph 2(1)(a) above to another locality and—

(a) that court has been notified by the Secretary of State that arrangements exist for persons who reside in that other locality to carry out instructions under supervised attendance orders; and

(b) it appears to that court that provision can be made under those arrangements for him to carry out instructions under the order,

that court may, and on application of the supervising officer shall, amend the order by substituting that other locality for the locality for the time being specified in the order; and section 235 of this Act and this Schedule shall apply to the order as amended.

(3) Where the court proposes to exercise its powers under sub-paragraph (1)(a), (b) or (d) above otherwise than on the application of the offender, it shall issue a citation requiring him to appear before the court and, if he fails to appear, may issue a warrant for his arrest.

6.—(1) The Secretary of State may make rules for regulating the carrying out of the requirements of supervised attendance orders.

(2) Without prejudice to the generality of sub-paragraph (1) above, rules under this paragraph may—

(a) limit the number of hours during which the requirements of an order are to be met on any one day;

(b) make provision as to the reckoning of time for the purposes of the carrying out of these requirements;

(c) make provision for the payment of travelling and other expenses in connection with the carrying out of these requirements;

(d) provide for records to be kept of what has been done by any person carrying out these requirements.

(3) Rules under this paragraph shall be made by statutory instrument subject to annulment in pursuance of a resolution of either House of Parliament.

7. The Secretary of State shall lay before Parliament each year, or incorporate in annual reports he already makes, a report of the operation of section 235 of this Act and this Schedule.

8. In this Schedule—

"the appropriate court" in relation to a supervised attendance order, means the court having jurisdiction in the locality for the time being specified in the order under paragraph 2(1)(a) above, being a sheriff or district court according to whether the order has been made by a sheriff or district court, but in the case where an order has been made by a district court and there is no district court in that locality, the sheriff court;

"supervising officer" has the same meaning as in section 235 of this Act.

Section 279   SCHEDULE 8

DOCUMENTARY EVIDENCE IN CRIMINAL PROCEEDINGS

Production of copy documents

1.—(1) For the purposes of any criminal proceedings a copy of, or of a material part of, a document, purporting to be authenticated in such manner and by such person as may be prescribed, shall unless the court otherwise directs, be—

(a) deemed a true copy; and

(b) treated for evidential purposes as if it were the document, or the material part, itself, whether or not the document is still in existence.

(2) For the purposes of this paragraph it is immaterial how many removes there are between a copy and the original.

(3) In this paragraph "copy" includes a transcript or reproduction.

Statements in business documents

2.—(1) Except where it is a statement such as is mentioned in paragraph 3(b) and (c) below, a statement in a document shall be admissible in criminal proceedings as evidence of any fact or opinion of which direct oral evidence would be admissible, if the following conditions are satisfied—

(a) the document was created or received in the course of, or for the purposes of, a business or undertaking or in pursuance of the functions of the holder of a paid or unpaid office;

(b) the document is, or at any time was, kept by a business or undertaking or by or on behalf of the holder of such an office; and

(c) the statement was made on the basis of information supplied by a person (whether or not the maker of the statement) who had, or may reasonably be supposed to have had, personal knowledge of the matters dealt with in it.

(2) Sub-paragraph (1) above applies whether the information contained in the statement was supplied directly or indirectly unless, in the case of information supplied indirectly, it appears to the court that any person through whom it was so supplied did not both receive and supply it in the course of a business or undertaking or as or on behalf of the holder of a paid or unpaid office.

(3) Where in any proceedings a statement is admitted as evidence by virtue of this paragraph—

(a) any evidence which, if—

    (i) the maker of the statement; or

    (ii) where the statement was made on the basis of information supplied by another person, such supplier,

had been called as a witness, would have been admissible as relevant to the witness's credibility shall be so admissible in those proceedings;

(b) evidence may be given of any matter which, if the maker or as the case may be the supplier had been called as a witness, could have been put to him in cross-examination as relevant to his credibility but of which evidence could not have been adduced by the cross-examining party; and

(c) evidence tending to prove that the maker or as the case may be the supplier, whether before or after making the statement or supplying the information on the basis of which the statement was made, made (in whatever manner) some other representation which is inconsistent with the statement shall be admissible for the purpose of showing that he has contradicted himself.

(4) In sub-paragraph (3)(c) above, "representation" does not include a representation in a precognition.

3. A statement in a document shall be admissible in criminal proceedings as evidence of the fact that the statement was made if—

(a) the document satisfies the conditions mentioned in sub-paragraph (1)(a) and (b) of paragraph 2 above;

(b) the statement is made, whether directly or indirectly, by a person who in those proceedings is an accused; and

(c) the statement, being exculpatory only, exculpates the accused.

Documents kept by businesses etc.

4. Unless the court otherwise directs, a document may in any criminal proceedings be taken to be a document kept by a business or undertaking or by or on behalf of the holder of a paid or unpaid office if it is certified as such by a docquet in the prescribed form and purporting to be authenticated, in such manner as may be prescribed—

(a) by a person authorised to authenticate such a docquet on behalf of the business or undertaking by which; or

(b) by, or by a person authorised to authenticate such a docquet on behalf of, the office-holder by whom,

the document was kept.

Statements not contained in business documents

5.—(1) In any criminal proceedings, the evidence of an authorised person that—

(a) a document which satisfies the conditions mentioned in paragraph 2(1)(a) and (b) above does not contain a relevant statement as to a particular matter; or

(b) no document, within a category of documents satisfying those conditions, contains such a statement,

shall be admissible evidence whether or not the whole or any part of that document or of the documents within that category and satisfying those conditions has been produced in the proceedings.

(2) For the purposes of sub-paragraph (1) above, a relevant statement is a statement which is of the kind mentioned in paragraph 2(1)(c) above and which, in the ordinary course of events—

(a) the document; or

(b) a document within the category and satisfying the conditions mentioned in that sub-paragraph,

might reasonably have been expected to contain.

(3) The evidence referred to in sub-paragraph (1) above may, unless the court otherwise directs, be given by means of a certificate by the authorised person in the prescribed form and purporting to be authenticated in such manner as may be prescribed.

(4) In this paragraph, "authorised person" means a person authorised to give evidence—

(a) on behalf of the business or undertaking by which; or

(b) as or on behalf of the office-holder by or on behalf of whom,

the document is or was kept.

Additional evidence where evidence from business documents challenged

6.—(1) This sub-paragraph applies where—

(a) evidence has been admitted by virtue of paragraph 2(3) above; or

(b) the court has made a direction under paragraph 1(1), 4 or 5(3) above.

(2) Where sub-paragraph (1) above applies the judge may, without prejudice to sections 268 and 269 of this Act—

(a) in solemn proceedings, on a motion of the prosecutor or defence at any time before the commencement of the speeches to the jury;

(b) in summary proceedings, on such a motion at any time before the prosecutor proceeds to address the judge on the evidence,

permit him to lead additional evidence of such description as the judge may specify.

(3) Subsections (3) and (4) of section 268 of this Act shall apply in relation to sub-paragraph (2) above as they apply in relation to subsection (1) of that section.

General

7.—(1) Nothing in this Schedule—

(a) shall prejudice the admissibility of a statement made by a person other than in the course of giving oral evidence in court which is admissible otherwise than by virtue of this Schedule;

(b) shall affect the operation of the Bankers' Books Evidence Act 1879;

(c) shall apply to—

(i) proceedings commenced; or

(ii) where the proceedings consist of an application to the sheriff by virtue of section 42(2)(c) of the Social Work (Scotland) Act 1968, an application made,

before this Schedule comes into force.

For the purposes of sub-paragraph (1)(c)(i) above, solemn proceedings are commenced when the indictment is served.

8. In this Schedule—

"business" includes trade, profession or other occupation;

"criminal proceedings" includes any hearing by the sheriff under section 62 of the Children (Scotland) Act 1995 of an application for a finding as to whether grounds for the referral of a child's case to a children's hearing are established, in so far as the application relates to the commission of an offence by the child;

"document" includes, in addition to a document in writing—

(a) any map, plan, graph or drawing;

(b) any photograph;

(c) any disc, tape, sound track or other device in which sounds or other data (not being visual images) are recorded so as to be capable, with or without the aid of some other equipment, of being reproduced therefrom; and

(d) any film, negative, tape, disc or other device in which one or more visual images are recorded so as to be capable (as aforesaid) of being produced therefrom;

"film" includes a microfilm;

"made" includes allegedly made;

"prescribed" means prescribed by Act of Adjournal;

"statement" includes any representation (however made or expressed) of fact or opinion, including an instruction, order or request, but, except in paragraph 7(1)(a) above, does not include a statement which falls within one or more of the following descriptions—

(a) a statement in a precognition;

(b) a statement made for the purposes of or in connection with—

(i) pending or contemplated criminal proceedings; or

(ii) a criminal investigation; or

(c) a statement made by an accused person in so far as it incriminates a co-accused; and

"undertaking" includes any public or statutory undertaking, any local authority and any government department.

SCHEDULE 9

CERTIFICATES AS TO PROOF OF CERTAIN ROUTINE MATTERS

Enactment	Persons who may purport to sign certificates	Matters which may be certified
The Parks Regulations Acts 1872 to 1974.	An officer authorised to do so by the Secretary of State.	That, on a date specified in the certificate— (a) copies of regulations made under those Acts, prohibiting such activity as may be so specified, were displayed at a location so specified; (b) in so far as those regulations prohibited persons from carrying out a specified activity in the park without written permission, such permission had not been given to a person so specified.
The Wireless Telegraphy Act 1949 (c. 54) Section 1 in so far as it relates to the installation or use of a television receiver (within the meaning of that Act); and section 1A in so far as it relates to an intended such use.	A person authorised to do so by the British Broadcasting Corporation.	In relation to an address specified in the certificate, whether on a date so specified any television licence (within the meaning of that Act) was, in records maintained on behalf of the Corporation in relation to such licences, recorded as being in force; and, if so, particulars so specified of such record of that licence.
The Building (Scotland) Act 1959 (c. 24) Section 6(1) (prohibition of construction, demolition or change of use of building without warrant).	An officer of a local authority authorised to do so by the authority.	In relation to a building specified in the certificate, that on a date so specified, there had not been obtained a warrant under section 6 of that Act for construction, demolition or, as the case may be, change of use.
Section 9(5) (offence of occupying or using a building before certificate of completion issued).	An officer of a local authority authorised to do so by the authority.	That, on a date specified in the certificate— (a) a certificate of completion under section 9 of that Act had not been issued in respect of a building so specified; and (b) written permission for occupation or use of the building so specified, had not been granted under subsection (6) of that section by the local authority.

Enactment	Persons who may purport to sign certificates	Matters which may be certified
The Firearms Act 1968 (c. 27).	As respects the matters specified in paragraph (a) of column 3, a constable or a person employed by a police authority, if the constable or person is authorised to do so by the chief constable of the police force maintained for the authority's area; and as respects the matters specified in paragraph (b) of column 3, an officer authorised to do so by the Secretary of State.	In relation to a person identified in the certificate, that on a date specified therein— (a) he held, or as the case may be did not hold, a firearm certificate or shotgun certificate (within the meaning of that Act); (b) he possessed, or as the case may be did not possess, an authority (which as regards a possessed authority, shall be described in the certificate) given under section 5 of that Act by the Secretary of State.
The Misuse of Drugs Act 1971 (c. 38) Sections 4, 5, 6, 8, 9, 12, 13, 19 and 20 (various offences concerning controlled drugs).	Two analysts who have analysed the substance and each of whom is either a person possessing the qualifications (qualifying persons for appointments as public analysts) prescribed by regulations made under section 76 of the Food Safety Act 1984 (c. 30), or section 30 of the Food Safety Act 1990 (c. 16), or a person authorised by the Secretary of State to make analyses for the purposes of the provisions of the Misuse of Drugs Act 1971 mentioned in column 1.	The type, classification, purity, weight and description of any particular substance identified in the certificate by reference to a label or otherwise, which is alleged to be a controlled drug within the meaning of section 2 of the Act referred to in column 1.
The Immigration Act 1971 (c. 77) Section 24(1)(a) in so far as it relates to entry in breach of a deportation order, section 24(1)(b) and section 26(1)(f) in so far as it relates to a requirement of regulations (various offences concerning persons entering, or remaining in, the United Kingdom).	An officer authorised to do so by the Secretary of State.	In relation to a person identified in the certificate— (a) the date, place or means of his arrival in, or any removal of him from, the United Kingdom; (b) any limitation on, or condition attached to, any leave for him to enter or remain in the United Kingdom; (c) the date and method of service of any notice of, or of variations of conditions attached to, such leave.

Enactment	Persons who may purport to sign certificates	Matters which may be certified
The Control of Pollution Act 1974 (c. 40) Section 31(1) (permitting poisonous, noxious or polluting matter to enter controlled waters, etc.), 32(1) (permitting trade effluent or sewage effluent to be discharged into such waters, etc.) or 49(1)(a) (causing accumulated deposit to be carried away in suspension in inland waters) or regulations under section 31(4) (prohibition on carrying on without consent certain activities likely to pollute waters in designated areas).	Two persons authorised to do so by a river purification authority (within the meaning of that Act).	That they have analysed a sample identified in the certificate (by label or otherwise) and that the sample is of a nature and composition specified in the certificate.
The Licensing (Scotland) Act 1976 (c. 66).	A person authorised to do so by the Secretary of State.	In relation to a person identified in the certificate, that on a date specified therein he held, or as the case may be did not hold, a licence granted under that Act.
Customs and Excise Management Act 1979 The following provisions in so far as they have effect in relation to the prohibitions contained in sections 20 and 21 of the Forgery and Counterfeiting Act 1981 namely— Sections 50(2) and (3) Section 68; and Section 170 (various offences committed in connection with contraventions of prohibitions on the import and export of counterfeits or currency notes or protected coins).	Two officials authorised to do so by the Secretary of State, being officials of the authority or body which may lawfully issue the currency notes or protected coins referred to in column 3 hereof.	That the coin or note identified in the certificate by reference to a label or otherwise is a counterfeit of a currency note or protected coin; where "currency note" has the meaning assigned to it by section 27(1)(a) of the Forgery and Counterfeiting Act 1981, and "protected coin" means any coin which is customarily use as money in the United Kingdom, any of the Channel Islands, the Isle of Man or the Republic of Ireland.
The Forgery and Counterfeiting Act 1981 Sections 14 to 16 (certain offences relating to counterfeiting).	Two officials authorised to do so by the Secretary of State, being officials of the authority or body which may lawfully issue the currency notes or protected coins referred to in column 3 hereof.	That the coin or note identified in the certificate by reference to a label or otherwise is a counterfeit of a currency note or protected coin; where "currency note" has the meaning assigned to it by section 27(1)(a) of the Forgery and Counterfeiting Act 1981, and "protected coin" means any coin which is customarily used as money in the United Kingdom, any of the Channel Islands, the Isle of Man or the Republic of Ireland.

Enactment	Persons who may purport to sign certificates	Matters which may be certified
The Wildlife and Countryside Act 1981 (c. 69) Sections 1, 5, 6(1) to (3), 7, 8, 9(1), (2), (4) and (5), 11(1) and (2), 13(1) and (2) and 14 (certain offences relating to protection of wild animals or wild plants).	An officer of the appropriate authority (within the meaning of section 16(9) of that Act) authorised to do so by the authority.	In relation to a person specified in the certificate that, on a date so specified, he held, or as the case may be did not hold, a licence under section 16 of that Act and, where he held such a licence— (a) the purpose for which the licence was granted; and (b) the terms and conditions of the licence.
The Civic Government (Scotland) Act 1982 (c. 45).	A person authorised to do so by the Secretary of State.	In relation to a person identified in the certificate, that on a date specified therein he held, or as the case may be, did not hold, a licence under a provision so specified of that Act.
The Road Traffic Regulation Act 1984 (c. 27).	Two police officers who have tested the apparatus.	The accuracy of any particular— (a) speedometer fitted to a police vehicle; (b) odometer fitted to a police vehicle; (c) radar meter; or (d) apparatus for measuring speed, time or distance, identified in the certificate by reference to its number or otherwise.
The Video Recordings Act 1984 (c. 39) Sections 9 to 14 (offences relating to the supply and possession of video recordings in contravention of that Act).	A person authorised to do so by the Secretary of State, and who has— (a) in relation to the matters certified in paragraph (a), or (c) of Column 3, examined— (i) the record maintained in pursuance of arrangements made by the designated authority; and (ii) a video work (or part of a video work) contained in a video recording identified by the certificate; (b) in relation to the matters certified in paragraph (b) of Column 3 examined a video work other than the video work concerned in the proceedings.	In respect of a video work concerned in the proceedings— (a) that on the date specified in the certificate, no classification certificate had been issued; (b) where a certificate is given in respect of the matter referred to in paragraph (a) above that the video work differs in such respects as may be specified from the other video work mentioned in paragraph (b) of Column 2; (c) that on the date specified in the certificate a classification certificate in terms of a document identified by the certificate as a copy of the classification certificate was issued.

Enactment	Persons who may purport to sign certificates	Matters which may be certified
The Road Traffic Act 1988 (c. 52) Section 165(3) (offence of failure to give name and address and to produce vehicle documents when required by constable).	A constable.	In relation to a person specified in the certificate, that he failed, by such date as may be so specified, to produce such documents as may be so specified at a police station so specified.
The Control of Pollution (Amendment) Act 1989 (c. 14) Section 1 (offence of transporting controlled waste without registering).	An officer of a regulation authority within the meaning of that Act authorised to do so by the authority.	In relation to a person specified in the certificate, that on a date so specified he was not a registered carrier of controlled waste within the meaning of that Act.
The Environmental Protection Act 1990 (c. 43) Section 33(1)(a) and (b) (prohibition on harmful depositing, treatment or disposal of waste).	An officer of a waste regulation authority within the meaning of that Act authorised to do so by the authority.	In relation to a person specified in the certificate that, on a date so specified, he held, or as the case may be he did not hold, a waste management licence.
Section 34(1)(c) (duty of care as respects transfer of waste).	An officer of a waste regulation authority within the meaning of that Act authorised to do so by the authority.	In relation to a person specified in the certificate, that on a date so specified he was not an authorised person within the meaning of section 34(3)(b) or (d) of that Act.
The Social Security Administration Act 1992 (c. 5) Section 114(4) (false statements etc. to obtain payments).	Any officer authorised to do so by the Secretary of State.	In relation to a person identified in the certificate— (a) the assessment, award, or nature of any benefit applied for by him; (b) the transmission or handing over of any payment to him.

Enactment	Persons who may purport to sign certificates	Matters which may be certified
The Criminal Justice and Public Order Act 1994 (c. 33) Paragraph 5 of Schedule 6 (offence of making false statements to obtain certification as prisoner custody officer).	An officer authorised to do so by the Secretary of State.	That— (a) on a date specified in the certificate, an application for a certificate under section 114 of that Act was received from a person so specified; (b) the application contained a statement so specified; (c) a person so specified made, on a date so specified, a statement in writing in terms so specified.
This Act Sections 24(3) to (8), 25 and 27 to 29	The Clerk of Justiciary or the clerk of court.	In relation to a person specified in the certificate, that— (a) an order granting bail under that Act was made on a date so specified by a court so specified; (b) the order or a condition of it so specified was in force on a date so specified; (c) notice of the time and place appointed for a diet so specified was given to him in a manner so specified; (d) as respects a diet so specified, he failed to appear.
Section 150(8) (offence of failure of accused to appear at diet after due notice).	The clerk of court.	That, on a date specified in the certificate, he gave a person so specified, in a manner so specified, notice of the time and place appointed for a diet so specified.

Section 292(1)   SCHEDULE 10

CERTAIN OFFENCES TRIABLE ONLY SUMMARILY

Night Poaching Act 1828 (c. 69)

1. Offences under section 1 of the Night Poaching Act 1828 (taking or destroying game or rabbits by night or entering land for that purpose).

Public Meeting Act 1908 (c. 66)

2. Offences under section 1(1) of the Public Meeting Act 1908 (endeavour to break up a public meeting).

Post Office Act 1953 (c. 36)

3. Offences under section 56 of the Post Office Act 1953 (criminal diversions of letters from addressee).

Betting, Gaming and Lotteries Act 1963 (c. 2)

4. Offences under the following provisions of the Betting, Gaming and Lotteries Act 1963—
(a) section 7 (restriction of betting on dog racecourses);
(b) section 10(5) (advertising licensed betting offices);
(c) section 11(6) (person holding bookmaker's or betting agency permit employing a person disqualified from holding such a permit);
(d) section 18(2) (making unauthorised charges to bookmakers on licensed track);
(e) section 19 (occupiers of licensed tracks not to have any interest in bookmaker thereon);
(f) section 21 (betting with young persons); and
(g) section 22 (betting circulars not to be sent to young persons).

Theatres Act 1968 (c. 54)

5. Offences under section 6 of the Theatres Act 1968 (provocation of breach of the peace by means of public performance of play).

Criminal Law (Consolidation) (Scotland) Act 1995 (c. 39)

6. Offences under section 12(1) of the Criminal Law (Consolidation) (Scotland) Act 1995 (allowing child under 16 to be in brothel).

TABLE OF DERIVATIONS

Notes: 1. This Table shows the derivation of the provisions of the Bill.
2. The following abbreviations are used in the Table:

Acts of Parliament

1975	= Criminal Procedure (Scotland) Act 1975 (c. 21)
1977	= Criminal Law Act 1977 (c. 45)
1978	= Community Service by Offenders (Scotland) Act 1978 (c. 49)
1980B	= Bail (Scotland) Act 1980 (c. 4)
1980LR	= Law Reform (Miscellaneous Provisions) (Scotland) Act 1980 (c. 55)
1980CJ	= Criminal Justice (Scotland) Act 1980 (c. 62)
1982	= Criminal Justice Act 1982 (c. 48)
1983	= Mental Health (Amendment) (Scotland) Act 1983 (c. 39)
1984	= Mental Health (Scotland) Act 1984 (c. 36)
1985	= Law Reform (Miscellaneous Provisions) (Scotland) Act 1985 (c. 73)
1987	= Criminal Justice (Scotland) Act 1987 (c. 41)
1988	= Criminal Justice Act 1988 (c. 33)
1990	= Law Reform (Miscellaneous Provisions) (Scotland) Act 1990 (c. 40)
1991	= Criminal Justice Act 1991 (c. 53)
1993P	= Prisoners and Criminal Proceedings (Scotland) Act 1993 (c. 9)
1993CJ	= Criminal Justice Act 1993 (c. 36)
1994	= Criminal Justice and Public Order Act 1994 (c. 33)
1995	= Criminal Justice (Scotland) Act 1995 (c. 20)
1995C	= Children (Scotland) Act 1995 (c. 36)

Provision	Derivation
1(1)	Court of Session (Scotland) Act 1830 (11 Geo 4 & 1 Will 4 c. 69) s. 18.
(2)	1975 s.113(1).
(3)	1975 s.113(2).
(4), (5)	1975 s.113(4).
2	1975 s.114; 1987 s.57(2).
3(1)	1975 s.2(1).
(2)	1975 s.112; 1987 s.57(1).
(3) to (5)	1975 s.2(2) to (4); 1987 s.58(1).
(6)	1975 s.8; Drafting.
4(1)	1975 ss.3(1), 288(1).
(2)	1975 ss.3(4), 288(5); 1990 s.60; drafting.
(3)	1975 ss.3(2), 288(2).
(4)	1975 s.288(4); drafting.
5(1)	Drafting.
(2)	1975 s.289; 1977 Sch. 11 §44.
(3)	1975 s.290.
(4)	1975 s.291(2), (3); 1980 s.38.
6(1)	District Courts (Scotland) Act 1975 (1975 c. 20) s.2(1), (1A).
(2)	District Courts (Scotland) Act 1975 (1975 c. 20) s.2(2).
(3)	District Courts (Scotland) Act 1975 (1975 c. 20)(1) (part).
(4)	District Courts (Scotland) Act 1975 (1975 c.20) s.6(2) (part), (3) (part).
(5)	District Courts (Scotland) Act 1975 (1975 c. 20) s.6(9).
(6)	Drafting.
7(1)	District Courts (Scotland) Act 1975 (1975 c. 20) s.3(1).
(2)	District Courts (Scotland) Act 1975 (1975 c. 20) s.3(4).
(3)	1980CJ s.7(1); 1995 s.60.
(4)	1980CJ s.7(3); 1982 Sch. 7 §14.
(5)	District Courts (Scotland) Act 1975 (1975 c. 20) s.3(2).
(6)	1975 s.284; 1977 Sch. 11 §3; 1982 Sch. 7 §§4, 5.
(7)	1980CJ s.7(1A); 1995 s.60.
(8)	1975 c.285; 1980CJ s.7(3); 1982 Sch. 7 §6.
(9), (10)	1975 s.286.
8	1980B s.10; 1985 s.21.
9(1)	1975 ss.4(1), 3(3), 287(1).
(2)	1975 ss.4(2), 287(2).
(3)	1975 ss.4(3), 287(3).
(4), (5)	1975 ss.4(4), (5), 287(4), (5).
10	1975 s.5; 1987 Sch. 1 §4.
11(1), (2)	1975 s.6(1), (2).
(3)	1975 s.6(3); 1995 Sch. 6 §7.
(4)	1975 ss.7(1), (2), 292(1), (2).
12	1975 ss.9, 293.
13	1980CJ s.1.
14(1)	1980CJ s.2(1); 1994 s.129(1).
(2)	1980CJ s.2(2); 1987 Sch. 1 §16(a), (b), 1993P Sch. 7.
(3)	1980CJ s.2(3).
(4)	1980CJ s.2(3A); 1987 Sch. 1 §16(c); 1994 Sch. 10 §47; 1995 s.59.
(5)	1980CJ s.2(3B); 1994 Sch. 10 §47.
(6)	1980CJ s.2(4); 1994 s.129(2).
(7) to (9)	1980CJ s.2(5) to (7).
15(1), (2)	1980CJ s.3(1); 1994 s.129(3).
(3) to (5)	1980CJ s.3(2) to (4).
(6)	1980CJ s.3(5); 1985 Sch. 2 §23.
16	1980CJ s.5.
17(1)	1975 ss.19(1), 305; 1980CJ Sch. 7 §25; 1995 Sch. 6 §§11, 106.
(2)	1975 ss.19(2), 305; 1995 Sch. 6 §§11, 106.

Provision	Derivation
18(1), (2)	1993P s.28(1), (2).
(3)	1993P s.28(3); 1995 s.58(2), Sch. 6 §179(5).
(4)	1993P s.28(3A), (3C); 1995 s.58(3).
(5)	1993P s.28(3B); 1995 s.58(3).
(6)	1993P s.28(4); 1995 s.58(4).
(7), (8)	1993P s.28(5), (6).
19	1993P s.28A; 1995 s.58(5).
20	1993P s.28B; 1995 s.58(5).
21(1)	1975 ss.18(1), 294(1).
(2) to (5)	1975 ss.18(2) to (5), 294(2) to (5); 1980B s.7(1), (2).
22(1) to (3)	1975 s.295(1), (2); 1980B s.8.
(4), (5)	1975 ss.294(4), (5), 295(3); 1980B ss.7(2), 8.
23(1)	1975 s.26(2); 1995 Sch. 6 §15(a).
(2)	1975 s.26(3); 1995 Sch. 6 §15(b).
(3)	1975 s.26(4).
(4)	1975 s.27.
(5)	1975 s.28(1).
(6)	1975 s.298(1) (part).
(7)	1975 ss.28(2), 298(2).
(8)	1975 ss.28(3), 298(3); 1980CJ Sch. 7 §§26, 51.
24(1)	1975 ss.26(1), 298(1) (part).
(2)	1975 s.35.
(3)	1980B s.1(1); drafting.
(4) to (8)	1980B s.1(2) to (5); 1995 s.1.
25	1980B s.2.
26	1975 s.28A; 1995 s.3.
27(1), (2)	1980B s.3(1), (2); 1995 s.2(2), (3).
(3) to (6)	1980B s.3(2A) to (2D); 1995 s.2(4).
(7) to (10)	1980B s.3(3) to (6).
(11)	1980B s.3(12).
28	1980B s.3(7) to (11).
29	1980B s.4.
30(1)	1975 ss.30(1), 299(1); 1980B s.1(4).
(2)	1975 ss.30(2), 299(2); 1980B Sch. 1 §§4, 6.
(3)	1975 ss.30(3), 299(3).
(4)	1975 ss.30(4), 299(4); 1980B s.1(4).
31	1975 ss.30A, 299A; 1995 s.4.
32(1)	1975 ss.31(1), 300(1) (part).
(2)	1975 ss.31(2), 300(1) (part); 1987 s.62(4)(a).
(3), (4)	1975 ss.31(3), (4), 300(2), (3).
(5)	1975 ss.31(4A), 300(3A); 1995 Sch. 6 §§16, 105(a).
(6)	1975 ss.31(5), 300(6) (part).
(7), (8)	1975 ss.33(1), 300(4); 1995 Sch. 6 §§17(a), 105(b).
(9)	1975 s.300(4A); 1987 s.62(4)(b).
(10)	1975 s.33(2); 1995 Sch.6 §17(b).
33	1975 s.32, 300(6)(part).
34(1)	1975 s.12.
(2)	1975 s.74(7).
35(1), (2)	1975 s.19(2) (part), (3), s.305(3).
(3)	1975 s.20(1); 1980CJ s.6(1).
(4)	1975 s.20(3); 1980CJ s.6(1).
(5) to (7)	1975 s.20(3A) to (3C); 1980CJ s.6(1).
(8)	1975 s.20(4).
36(1) to (4)	1975 s.20A(1); 1980CJ s.6(2); 1995 s.10(2).
(5)	1975 s.20A(2); 1980CJ s.6(2).
(6)	1975 s.20A(3), (3A); 1980CJ s.6(2); 1995 s.10(3).

Provision	Derivation
(7)	1975 s.20A(4); 1980CJ s.6(2).
(8)	1975 s.20A(5); 1980CJ s.6(2).
(9)	1975 s.20A(6); 1980CJ s.6(2).
(10), (11)	1975 s.20A(7), (8); 1995 s.10(4).
37(1)	1975 s.20B(1); 1980CJ s.6(2); 1993P Sch. 6 §1(2).
(2) to (4)	1975 s.20B(1A) to (1C); 1993P Sch. 5 §1(2).
(5)	1975 s.20B(2); 1993P Sch. 5 §1(2).
(6)	1975 s.20B(3); 1980CJ s.6(2).
(7), (8)	1975 s.20B(5); 1980CJ s.6(2).
(9)	1975 s.20B(6); 1980CJ s.6(2).
(10)	1975 s.20B(9); 1980CJ s.6(2); 1995 Sch. 6 §13.
38	1975 s.20B(4), (7) and (8); 1980CJ s.6(2).
39	1975 s.21.
40	1975 s.22.
41	1975 ss.170, 369.
42(1)	Social Work (Scotland) Act 1968 (1968 c. 49) s.31(1); Health and Social Services and Social Security Adjudications Act 1983 (1983 c. 41) Sch. 2 §7.
(2) to (4)	1975 ss.39(1) to (3), 307(1) to (3).
(5), (6)	1975 ss.39(4), (5), 307(4), (5); 1995C Sch. 4 §24(5), (11).
(7), (8)	1975 ss.40(1), (2), 308(1), (2).
(9), (10)	1975 ss.38, 306.
43(1) to (3)	1975 s.296(1); 1980B s.9(a); 1995 Sch. 6 §104.
(4)	1975 s.296(2); 1995 Sch. 6 §104.
(5), (6)	1975 s.296(3), (4); 1995C Sch.4 §24(9).
(7), (8)	1975 s.296(5), (6); 1980B s.9(b).
44(1)	1975 s.413(1); 1987 s.59(1); 1993P Sch. 5 §1(32); 1995 Sch. 6 §141; 1995C Sch. 4 §24(17).
(2)	1975 s.413(2); 1987 s.59(1).
(3), (4)	1975 s.413(3A), (4); 1987 s.59(1); 1995C Sch. 4 §24(17).
(5)	1975 s.413(5); 1993P s.8.
(6) to (8)	1975 s.413(6A) to (6C); 1993P s.8; 1995C Sch. 4 §24(17).
(9)	1975 s.413(7); 1987 s.59(1); 1993P Sch.5 §1(32).
(10)	1975 s.413(3); 1987 s.59(1).
45(1) to (4)	1975 ss.37(1) to (3), 304(1) to (3).
(5)	1975 ss.37(4), 304(4); 1995C Sch. 4 §24(4), (10).
46(1), (2)	1975 ss.171(1), (2), 368(1), (2); 1995C Sch. 4 §24(7), (15); drafting.
(3)	1975 ss.171(3), 368(3); Sexual Offences (Scotland) Act (c. 67) Sch. 1; Incest and Related Offences (Scotland) Act 1986 (c. 36) Sch. 1 §§1, 3; 1988 Sch. 15 §48.
(4)	1975 ss.171(4), 368(4).
(5), (6)	1975 ss.171(1), (2), 368(1), (2); 1995C Sch. 4 §24(7), (15).
(7)	1975 ss.171(6), 368(6).
47(1) to (3)	1975 ss.169(1), 374(1), 1980CJ s.22.
(4)	1975 ss.169(2), 374(2); 1980CJ s.22; Cable and Broadcasting Act 1986 (c. 46) Sch. 5 §30; Broadcasting Act 1990 (c. 42) Sch. 20 §21.
(5), (6)	1975 ss.169(3), (4), 374(3), (4); 1980CJ s.22.
48	1975 ss.168, 364; 1980CJ Sch. 7 §§34, 57; 1995C Sch. 4 §24(6), (14).
49(1)	1975 ss.173(1), 372(1); Local Government etc. (Scotland) Act 1994 (c. 39) Sch. 13 §97(2).
(2)	1975 ss.173(2), 372(2).
(3)	1975 ss.173(3), 372(3); 1980CJ Sch. 7 §35; Local Government etc. (Scotland) Act 1994 (c. 39) Sch. 13 §97(2).
(4), (5)	1975 ss.173(4), (5), 372(4), (5).
(6), (7)	1975 s.373; Local Government etc. (Scotland) Act 1994 (c. 39) Sch. 13 §97(2).
50(1), (2)	1975 ss.165, 361.
(3), (4)	1975 ss.166(1), (2), 362(1), (2); 1995 Sch. 6 §64.

Provision	Derivation
(5)	1975 ss.167, 363.
(6)	1975 ss.172, 371.
51(1)	1975 ss.23(1), s.329(1); 1987 s.62(2); 1995 Sch. 6 §14; 1995C Sch. 4 §24(13).
(2) to (4)	1975 ss.23(2) to (4), 329(2) to (4); 1995 Sch. 6 §14; 1995C Sch. 4 §24(13).
52(1)	1975 ss.175(2), 376(5).
(2)	1975 ss.25(1), 330(1).
(3)	1975 ss.25(2), 330(2); 1984 Sch. 3 §§24, 31.
(4), (5)	1975 ss.25(3), (4), 330(3), (4).
(6), (7)	1975 ss.25(5), (6), 330(5), (6); 1995 s.53.
53(1)	1974 ss.174A(1) (part), 375A(1) (part); 1983 s.34(a); 1984 Sch. 3 §§25, 32.
(2) to (10)	1975 ss.174A(2) to (10), 375A(3) to (11); 1983 s.34(a).
(11), (12)	1975 ss.174A(1) (part), 375A(1) (part), (2); 1983 s.34(a).
54(1) to (4)	1975 ss.174(1) to (1C), 375(2) to (2C); 1995 s.47(1).
(5)	1975 ss.174(5), 375(4).
(6)	1975 ss.174(2), 375(3A); 1995 s.48, Sch. 6 §65.
(7)	1975 s.375(3); 1995 Sch. 6 §132.
(8)	Drafting.
55	1975 ss.174ZA, 375ZA; 1995 s.49(1), (2).
56	1975 ss.174ZB, 375ZB; 1995 s.49(1), (2).
57(1) to (4)	1975 ss.174ZC, 375ZC; 1995 s.50(1), (2).
(5)	Drafting.
58(1), (2)	1975 ss.175(1), 376(1); 1983 Sch. 2 §§31, 34(a); 1984 Sch. 3 §§26, 33.
(3)	1975 s.376(3); 1995 Sch. 6 §133(b).
(4)	1975 ss.175(3), 376(6).
(5)	1975 ss.175(4), 376(7).
(6)	1975 ss.175(5), 376(8); 1983 Sch. 2 §§31, 34.
(7)	1975 ss.175(6), 376(9); 1983 Sch. 2 §§31, 34.
(8)	1975 ss.175(7), 376(10); 1983 Sch. 2 §§31, 34.
(9)	1975 ss.177, 378; 1995C Sch. 4 §24(8), (16).
(10)	1975 s.376(4).
59(1)	1975 ss.178(1), 379(1); 1983 s.22(2); 1984 Sch. 3 §§28, 35; 1995 s.54.
(2)	1975 ss.178(2), 379(2); 1983 Sch. 2 §§33, 36; 1984 Sch. 3 §§28, 35.
(3)	1975 ss.178(3), 379(3); 1983 Sch. 2 §§33, 36; 1984 Sch. 3 §§28, 35; 1995 Sch. 6 §§67, 135.
60	1975 ss.280, 443; 1980CJ Sch. 2 §32, Sch. 3 §2; 1983 s.34(b), (d).
61(1)	1975 ss.176(1), 377(1); 1983 Sch. 2 §§32, 35; 1984 Sch. 3 §§27, 34; 1995 Sch. 6 §§66(a), 134(a).
(2)	1975 ss.176(1A), 377(1A); 1983 s.35(a), (b).
(3)	1975 ss.176(2), 377(2); 1995 Sch. 6 §§66(b), 134(b).
(4)	1975 ss.176(3), 377(3).
(5)	1975 ss.176(4), 377(4); 1995 Sch. 6 §§66(c), 134(c).
62	1975 ss.174ZD, 375ZD, 1995 s.51.
63(1) to (5)	1975 ss.174ZE, 375ZE; 1995 s.52.
(6)	Drafting.
64(1) to (4)	1975 s.41.
(5)	1975 s.57.
(6)	Drafting.
65(1) to (3)	1975 s.101(1); 1980CJ s.14(1).
(4) to (9)	1975 s.101(2) to (6); 1980CJ s.14(1).
(10)	1975 s.101(1A); 1995 s.15.
66(1), (2)	1975 s.69(1); 1980CJ Sch. 4 §2; 1995 Sch. 6 §26(a).
(3)	1975 s.69(2); 1995 Sch. 6 §26(b).
(4)	1975 s.70.
(5)	1975 s.78(1); 1980CJ Sch. 4 §8; 1995 Sch. 6 §30.
(6)	1975 s.75; 1980CJ Sch. 4 §4; 1995 s.13(1).
(7)	1975 s.71; 1980CJ Sch. 7 §27.

Provision	Derivation
(8)	1975 s.73(1); 1995 Sch. 6 §28.
(9)	1975 s.72(1); 1995 Sch. 5 §27(a), (b).
(10)	1975 s.72(2); 1995 Sch. 6 §27(c).
(11)	1975 s.73(2).
(12) to (14)	1975 s.58; 1995 Sch. 6 §22.
67(1)	1975 s.79(1) (part); 1995 Sch. 6 §31.
(2)	1975 s.79(2).
(3)	1975 s.80(1); 1980CJ Sch. 4 §9; 1995 Sch. 6 §32.
(4)	1975 s.80(2); 1980CJ Sch. 4 §9.
(5)	1975 s.81; 1980CJ Sch. 7 §28; 1995 Sch. 6 §33.
(6)	1975 s.82A; 1980CJ s.27.
68(1)	1975 s.78(2); 1980CJ Sch. 4 §8.
(2)	1975 s.83; 1980CJ Sch. 4 §11.
(3), (4)	1975 s.84; 1980CJ Sch. 4 §12; 1995 s.23.
69(1)	1975 s.68(1).
(2)	1975 s.68(2); 1995 Sch. 6 §25.
(3)	1975 s.68(3) (part); 1980CJ Sch. 4 §1.
(4)	1975 s.68(4) (part); 1995 Sch. 6 §25.
(5)	1975 s.68(3) (part) and (4) (part); 1980CJ Sch. 4 §1; 1995 Sch. 6 §25.
70(1)	Drafting.
(2), (3)	1975 s.74(1).
(4)	1975 s.74(2).
(5)	1975 s.74(4); 1980CJ Sch. 4 §3(b).
(6)	1975 s.74(5).
(7)	1975 ss.74(6), 103(4).
(8)	1975 s.74(8).
71	1975 s.75A; 1995 s.13(2).
72(1)	1975 s.76(1) (part) and (2), s.108(1) (part); 1980CJ Sch. 4 §5, §19; 1985 Sch. 2 §18; 1993P s.39(2), Sch. 5 §1(3); 1995 s.13(3)(a), Sch. 6 §39.
(2)	1975 s.76(1) (part); 1980CJ Sch. 4 §5.
(3) to (6)	1975 s.76(3) to (5), (7).
73(1), (2)	1975 s.76(6) (part).
(3) to (6)	1975 s.76(6A) to (6D); 1995 s.13(3)(b).
(7)	1975 s.109 (part).
(8)	1975 s.76(6) (part); drafting.
74	1975 s.76A; 1980CJ Sch. 4 §5; 1995 s.13(4).
75	1975 s.111A; 1980CJ Sch. 7 §31.
76	1975 s.102; 1980CJ s.16.
77(1)	1975 s.103(1) and (4), s.124 (part); 1980CJ Sch. 4 §14; 1995 Sch. 6 §38.
(2), (3)	1975 s.103(2), (3); 1980CJ Sch. 4 §14.
78(1)	1975 s.82(1) (part); Act of Adjournal (Consolidation) 1988 (S.I. 1988/110) s.68 (part); 1980CJ s.13; 1995 Sch. 6 §34(a).
(2)	1975 s.82(1A); 1995 s.11.
(3)	1975 s.82(1) (part); Act of Adjournal (Consolidation) 1988 (S.I. 1988/110) s.68 (part); 1980CJ s.13; 1995 Sch. 6 §34(a).
(4)	1975 s.82(2); 1980CJ Sch. 4 §10; 1995 Sch. 6 §34(b).
(5)	1975 s.82(3); 1980CJ Sch. 4 §10.
79(1)	1975 s.108(1) (part) and (2); 1980CJ Sch. 4 §19; 1985 Sch. 2 §18; 1995 Sch. 6 §39.
(2)	1975 s.108(1) (part); 1980CJ Sch. 4 §19; 1985 Sch. 2 §18; 1995 Sch. 6 §39.
80(1)	1975 s.77; 1980CJ Sch. 4 §6; 1995 Sch. 6 §29.
(2) to (4)	1975 s.77A(1) to (3); 1980CJ Sch. 4 §7.
(5), (6)	1975 s.77A(4), drafting; 1980CJ Sch. 4 §7.
81(1)	1975 s.127(1); 1980CJ Sch. 4 §27; 1995 Sch. 6 §44(a).
(2)	1975 s.127(1ZA); 1995 Sch. 6 §44(b).
(3)	1975 s.127(1A); 1980CJ s.18(1).

Provision	Derivation
(4) to (6)	1975 s.127(2) to (4); 1995 Sch. 6 §44(c).
(7)	1975 s.127(5); 1995 Sch. 6 §44(d).
82	1975 s.111.
83	1975 s.114A; 1995 Sch. 6 §41.
84(1)	1975 s.85; 1995 Sch. 6 §35.
(2)	1975 s.86(1); 1987 Sch. 1 §5.
(3)	1975 s.86(2); 1987 Sch. 1 §5.
(4)	1975 s.89; 1985 Sch. 2 §16.
(5)	1975 s.90; 1985 Sch. 2 §16.
(6)	1975 s.91; 1980LR Sch. 2 §6; 1985 Sch. 2 §16.
(7)	1975 s.92.
(8)	1975 s.93; 1995 Sch. 6 §36.
(9)	1975 s.94.
(10)	1975 s.95.
85(1)	1975 s.96(1); 1980CJ Sch. 4 §13.
(2)	1975 s.96(2).
(3)	1975 s.97.
(4), (5)	1975 s.98; 1980CJ Sch. 7 §29; 1985 Sch. 2 §17.
(6), (7)	1975 s.99; 1980LR s.2(3).
(8)	1975 s.100(1); 1995 Sch. 6 §37.
86(1)	1975 s.130(3A); 1995 s.8.
(2)	1975 s.130(4).
(3)	1975 s.130(5); 1980LR Sch. 2 §7.
(4)	1975 s.130(6).
87	1975 s.128; 1995 s.30(2), (3).
88(1)	1975 s.125; 1995 Sch. 6 §43.
(2)	1975 s.129 (part); 1987 Sch. 1 §7; 1995 Sch. 6 §45.
(3)	1975 s.131, drafting.
(4)	1975 s.132(1).
(5), (6)	1975 s.135(1); 1995 Sch. 6 §48(a), (b); drafting.
(7)	1975 s.133.
(8)	1975 s.137.
89	1975 s.135(2) to (4); 1995 Sch. 6 §48(c).
90	1975 s.134; 1995 Sch. 6 §47.
91	1975 s.136.
92(1), (2)	1975 s.145(1); 1980CJ s.21.
(3)	1975 s.145(3).
93	1975 s.274; 1980CJ Sch. 8; 1995 Sch. 6 §98.
94	1975 s.275; 1993P Sch. 5 §1(27).
95	1975 s.137A; 1993P Sch. 1 §1(5).
96	1975 s.123.
97(1)	1975 s.140A(1); 1980CJ s.19(1); 1995 Sch.6 §49.
(2), (3)	1975 s.140A(3), (4); 1980CJ s.19(1).
(4)	1975 s.140A(2); 1980CJ s.19(1).
98	1975 s.152.
99(1)	1975 s.153(2); 1980CJ s.24(1).
(2), (3)	1975 s.153(3); 1980CJ s.24(1); 1995 Sch. 6 §57(b).
(4)	1975 s.153(3A); 1980CJ s.24(1).
(5)	1975 s.153(4).
(6)	1975 s.155A; 1993P s.40(1).
100(1), (2)	1975 s.154; 1980CJ s.24(2).
(3)	1975 s.155 (part); drafting.
101(1)	1975 s.160(1).
(2)	1975 ss.160(2), 161(5); 1995 s.24(3).
(3)	1975 s.161(1).
(4), (5)	1975 s.161(2).

Provision	Derivation
(6)	1975 s.161(4).
(7)	1975 s.159(2)
(8)	1975 s.161(3).
102(1)	1975 s.156(1) and (2); 1995 Sch. 6 §58.
(2)	1975 s.157(1); 1995 Sch. 6 §59.
(3)	1975 ss.156(3) and 157(3).
(4)	1975 s.156(6).
(5)	1975 s.158.
103(1)	1975 s.245(2); 1987 Sch. 1 §13(2); drafting.
(2)	1975 s.245(1); 1987 Sch. 1 §13(1); 1995 s.43(1).
(3)	1975 s.245(1A); 1995 s.43(1).
(4)	1975 s.245(3); 1980CJ Sch. 8.
(5)	1975 ss.247 (part), 248; 1980CJ Sch. 2 §15, Sch. 8.
(6)	1975 s.247 (part); 1980CJ Sch. 2 §15, Sch. 8.
(7)	1975 s.249.
(8)	1975 s.250.
104(1)	1975 s.252; 1980CJ Sch. 2 §16; 1993P Sch. 5 §1(18).
(2), (3)	1975 s.253; 1980CJ Sch. 8.
105(1) to (4)	1975 s.251(1) to (4).
(5)	1975 s.251(5); 1980CJ Sch. 7 §44.
(6)	1975 s.251(6).
106(1), (2)	1975 s.228(1); 1980CJ Sch. 2 §1; 1993CJ s.68(1); 1995 s.42(1).
(3)	1975 s.228(2); 1980CJ Sch. 2 §1.
(4)	1975 s.270(1).
(5) to (9)	1975 s.270(2) to (4); 1980CJ Sch. 2 §26; 1995 Sch. 6 §96.
107	1975 s.230A; 1995 s.42(2).
108	1975 s.228A; 1993P s,42(1); 1993CJ s.68(2).
109(1)	1975 s.231(1) (part) and (2); 1980CJ Sch. 2 §3; 1987 s.45(6)(a).
(2)	1975 s.231(1) (part); 1980CJ Sch. 2 §3; 1987 s.45(6)(a).
(3)	1975 s.231(3); 1980CJ Sch. 2 §3.
(4), (5)	1975 s.231(4); 1987 s.45(6)(b).
(6)	1975 s.231(5); 1987 s.45(6)(c).
110(1), (2)	1975 s.233(1); 1980CJ Sch. 2 §5; 1993P Sch. 5 §1(9); 1993CJ Sch. 5 §2(4).
(3), (4)	1975 s.233(2), (3); 1980CJ Sch. 2 §5.
(5)	1975 s.233(3A); 1995 s.42(3).
(6)	1975 s.233(4); 1980CJ Sch. 2§5; 1993CJ Sch. 5 §2(4).
111	1975 s.236B; 1980CJ Sch. 2 §8; 1993P Sch. 5 §1(11).
112(1)	1975 s.238(1); 1993CJ Sch. 5 §2(5); 1995 s.5(2).
(2)	1975 s.2338(1A); 1995 s.5(3).
(3), (4)	1975 s.238(2); 1980CJ Sch. 2 §10(a); 1995 Sch. 6 §81.
(5)	1975 s.238(3); 1980CJ Sch. 2 §10(b).
113	1975 s.236A; 1980CJ Sch. 2 §8; 1995 Sch. 6 §78.
114	1975 s.235; 1995 Sch. 6 §77.
115(1), (2)	1975 s.234(1); 1980CJ Sch. 8.
(3), (4)	1975 s.234(2), (3); 1980CJ Sch. 8.
116(1)	1975 s.244(1); 1980CJ Sch. 2 §13.
(2)	1975 s.244(2); 1980CJ Sch. 2 §13; 1993CJ Sch. 5 §2(6).
117(1), (2)	1975 s.241; 1980CJ Sch. 7 §41.
(3)	1975 s.240; 1993P Sch. 5 §1(15); 1995 Sch. 6 §83.
(4), (5), (6)	1975 s.242; 1980CJ Sch. 7 §42.
(7)	1975 s.242A; 1993P Sch. 5 §1(16).
(8)	1975 s.243; 1980CJ Sch. 7; 1993P Sch. 5 §1(17).
(9)	1975 s.239(1); 1980CJ Sch. 2 §11; 1993 Sch. 5 §1(14); 1995 Sch. 6 §82.
118(1), (2)	1975 s.254(1); 1980CJ Sch. 2 §18; 1993CH Sch. 5 §2(7).
(3)	1975 s.254(2); 1993CJ Sch. 5 §2(7).
(4)	1975 s.254(3), (4A); 1993CJ Sch. 5 §2(7).

Provision	Derivation
(5)	1975 s.254(4); 1993CJ Sch. 5 §2(7); 1995 Sch. 6 §85.
(6)	1975 s.254(5); 1995 Sch. 6 §85.
(7)	1975 s.254A(1); 1995 s.34(1).
(8)	1975 s.254B; 1995 Sch. 6 §86.
119(1)	1975 s.255(1) (part); 1980CJ Sch. 2 §19; 1995 s.46(1).
(2)	1975 s.255(1A); 1995 s.46(1).
(3)	1975 s.255(1) (part), 1980CJ Sch. 2 §19; 1995 s.46(1).
(4)	1975 s.255(2); 1980CJ Sch. 2 §19.
(5)	1975 s.255(3) (part); 1980 Sch. 2 §19.
(6)	1975 s.255(1B); 1995 s.46(1).
(7)	1975 s.255(1C); 1995 s.46(1).
(8)	1975 s.255(3) (part); 1980CJ Sch. 2 §19.
(9)	1975 s.255(4); 1980CJ Sch. 2 §19.
(10), (11)	1975 s.255(5), (6); 1995 s.46(1)(c)
120(1)	1975 s.257; 1980CJ Sch. 8; 1995 Sch. 6 §88.
(2)	1975 s.258; 1993P Sch. 5 §1(19).
(3)	1975 s.260.
(4)	1975 s.261; 1980CJ Sch. 7 §45; 1993P Sch. 5 §1(20).
121(1), (2)	1975 s.264(1), (2); 1980CJ Sch. 2 §23; 1995 Sch. 6 §92(a).
(3)	1975 s.264(3); 1987 s.68(3).
(4)	1975 s.264(4); 1995 Sch. 6 §92(b).
122(1), (2)	1975 s.265(1), (2); 1995 Sch. 6 §93.
(3)	1975 s.265(4).
(4)	1975 s.265(4A); 1993P Sch. 5 §1(22).
123	1975 s.263A; 1980CJ s.37; 1995 Sch. 6 §91.
124(1)	1975 s.263(1) (part); 1980CJ Sch. 2 §22.
(2)	1975 ss.262, 281.
(3)	1975 s.263(1) (part); 1980CJ Sch. 2 §22.
(4)	1975 s.263(2); 1987 Sch. 2.
(5)	1975 s.263(3); 1995 Sch. 6 §90.
125(1)	1975 s.268(1); 1987 Sch. 1 §14(1); 1993P Sch. 5 §1(23); 1993CJ Sch. 5 §2(8).
(2)	1975 s.268(2); 1987 Sch. 1 §14(2); 1993P Sch. 5 §1(23); 1993CJ Sch. 5 §2(8).
(3)	1975 s.268(3); 1987 Sch. 1 §14(3); 1993P Sch. 5 §1(23).
(4)	1975 s.268(4); 1980CJ Sch. 7 §46; 1995 Sch. 6 §94.
126	1975 s.269; 1980CJ Sch. 2 §25; 1993P Sch. 5 §1(24); 1995 Sch. 6 §95.
127	1975 s.271; 1980CJ Sch. 2 §27; 1985 Sch. 2 §19.
128	1975 ss.266, 267.
129(1), (2)	1975 s.277(1); 1980CJ Sch. 8.
(3)	1975 s.277(2); 1980 CJ Sch. 2 §31, Sch. 8; 1995 Sch. 6 §100.
(4)	1975 s.277(1) (part).
130	1975 s.230.
131	1975 s.280A; 1980CJ s.35.
132	1975 s.279.
133(1)	1975 s.283(1); 1995 Sch. 6 §102.
(2)	1975 s.283(1A); 1995 Sch. 6 §102.
(3)	1975 s.283(2) (part).
(4)	1975 s.283(3); drafting.
(5)	1975 s.310A; 1995 s.63.
134	1975 s.310; 1995 Sch. 6 §108; drafting.
135(1)	1975 s.321(1); 1995 Sch. 6 §117(a).
(2)	1975 s.321(2).
(3), (4)	1975 s.321(3); 1980B Sch. 1 §7; 1995 Sch. 6 §117(b).
(5)	1975 s.321(4).
136	1975 s.331; Incest and Related Offences (Scotland) Act 1986 (1986 c. 36) Sch. 1 §2; 1995 s.62.
137(1)	1975 s.314(3); 1980CJ Sch. 8.

Provision	Derivation
(2)	1975 s.314(4); 1980CJ s.11.
(3)	1975 s.314(4A); 1995 Sch. 6 §111(b).
(4), (5)	1975 s.314(5), (6); 1980CJ s.11.
138(1)	1975 s.311(1) (part) & (2); 1995 Sch. 6 §109; drafting.
(2)	1975 s.312 (part); drafting.
(3)	1975 s.311(3).
(4)	1975 s.312(a)–(z), drafting.
139(1)	1975 s.314(1); 1995 Sch. 6 §111(a).
(2)	1975 s.314(2); 1980CJ s.11.
140	1975 s.315; 1995 Sch. 6 §112.
141(1)	1975 s.316(1) & (2) (part).
(2)	1975, s.316(2) (part).
(3), (4)	1975 s.316(3); 1995 Sch. 6 §113.
(5)	1975 s.316(4).
(6), (7)	1975 s.319; 1995 Sch. 6 §115; drafting.
142(1)	1975 s.366(1); 1995 Sch. 6 §131.
(2) to (4)	1975 s.367.
(5)	1975 s.370; 1980CJ Sch. 7 §58.
143	1975 s.333.
144(1)	1975 s.334(1) (part); 1980CJ Sch. 7 §54(a); 1993P Sch. 5 §1(30).
(2), (3)	1975 s.334(3).
(4), (5)	1975 s.334(1) (part) & (2) (part); 1980CJ Sch. 7 §54(b).
(6) to (8)	1974 s.334(4) to (6).
(9)	1975 s.334(1) (part); 1980CJ Sch. 7 §54(a); drafting.
145	1975 s.333A; 1993P s.38(1).
146(1)	1975 s.337 (part).
(2)	1975 s.337(a); 1980B Sch. 2.
(3)	1975 s.337(b).
(4), (5)	1975 s.337(c).
(6)	1975 s.337(d); 1980B Sch. 1 §8; 1987 s.62(3).
(7) to (9)	1975 s.337(f) to (h).
147	1975 s.331A; 1980CJ s.14(2).
148	1975 s.337A; 1980CJ s.15; 1995 s.14; drafting.
149	1975 s.339; 1995 Sch. 6 §121.
150(1)	1975 s.338(1) (part); 1995 Sch. 6 §120.
(2)	1975 s.338(1)(a) (part).
(3)	1975 s.338(1)(c).
(4)	1975 s.338(1)(a) (part).
(5), (6), (7)	1975 s.338(1)(b).
(8), (9), (10)	1975 s.338(2) to (4); 1980CJ s.17.
151	1975 s.331B; 1995 s.30(4).
152	1975 s.338A; 1980CJ s.18(2).
153	1975 s.337B; 1995 s.31.
154	1975 s.353.
155(1)	1975 s.344(1); 1980CJ s.46(1)(c); 1982 Sch. 7 §7; 1995 Sch. 6 §122.
(2), (3)	1975 s.344(2), (3).
(4)	1975 s.344(4); 1980CJ Sch. 7 §55.
156(1), (2)	1975 s.320; 1995 Sch. 6 §117.
(3), (4)	1975 s.321(5), (6); 1995 Sch. 6 §117.
157	1975 s.359; 1995 Sch. 6 §128.
158	1975 s.360A(1); 1993P s.40(2); 1995 Sch. 6 §130.
159	1975 s.335; 1995 Sch. 6 §118.
160	1975 345A; 1980CJ s.19(2).
161	1975 s.351.
162	1975 s.355.
163(1)	1975 s.440; 1995 Sch. 6 §145.

Provision	Derivation
(2)	1975 s.441; 1995 Sch. 6 §146.
164	1975 s.427.
165	1975 s.429.
166(1) to (6)	1975 s.357(1); 1980CJ s.40; 1995 Sch. 6 §127(a).
(7)	1975 s.356(2).
(8)	1975 s.357(5); 1995 s.24(6).
167(1)	1975 s.433.
(2), (3), (4)	1975 s.430(1); 1995 Sch. 6 §142(a).
(5), (6)	1975 s.430(2), (3).
(7)	1975 s.430(4); 1995 Sch. 6 §142(b).
(8)	1975 s.434.
168	1975 s.303(1).
169	1975 s.424; 1980CJ Sch. 7 §68.
170	1975 s.456.
171	1975 s.332.
172(1)	1975 s.309(1); 1995 Sch. 6 §107.
(2), (3)	1975 s.309(2) (part), (3).
173	1975 s.451A; 1995 s.43(2).
174	1975 s.334(2A) to (2D); 1980CJ s.36.
175(1) to (4)	1975 s.442(1); 1980 Sch. 3 §1; 1993CJ s.68(3); 1995 s.42(4).
(5), (6)	1974 s.442(2), (3); 1980 Sch. 3 §1.
(7), (8)	1975 s.442A(1), (2); 1980CJ Sch. 3 §1.
(9)	1975 s.442B; 1980CJ Sch. 3 §1; 1993CJ Sch. 5 §2(1).
(10)	1975 s.283(2) (part).
176(1)	1975 s.444(1); 1980CJ Sch. 3 §3; 1993CJ Sch. 5 §2(12); 1995 Sch. 6 §148.
(2)	1975 s.444(1A); 1980CJ Sch. 3 §3.
(3)	1975 s.444(1B); 1980CJ Sch. 3 §3.
(4)	1975 s.444(2).
(5)	1975 s.450; 1980CJ Sch. 3 §9; drafting.
177(1)	1975 s.446(1); 1980CJ Sch. 3 §5.
(2), (3)	1975 S.446(2).
(4)	1975 s.446(3).
(5) to (7)	1975 s.446(4) to (6); 1995 Sch. 6 §149.
178(1)	1975 s.447(1); 1980CJ Sch. 3 §6; 1985 Sch. 2 §20.
(2)	1975 s.447(2); 1980CJ Sch. 8.
179	1975 s.448(1)–(5); 1980CJ Sch. 3 §7; 1985 Sch. 4.
180	1975 s.442ZA; 1995 s.42(5).
181(1), (2)	1975 ss.444(3), (4), 448(6), (7); 1980CJ Sch. 3 §7.
(3)	1975 ss.444(5), 448(8); 1980B Sch. 1 §10, §12; 1980CJ Sch. 3 §3, §7.
182	1975 s.452; 1980CJ Sch. 3 §11; 1995 s.42(6).
183(1), (2)	1975 s.452A(1); 1980CJ Sch. 3 §11; 1993P Sch. 5 §1(35).
(3)	1975 s.452A(2) (part); 1980CJ Sch. 3 §11; 1993P Sch. 5 §1(35)(b); 1993CJ Sch. 5 §2(13).
(4)	1975 s.452A(3); 1980CJ Sch. 3 §11.
(5)	1975 s.452A(2) (part); 1980CJ Sch. 3 §11; 1993P Sch. 5 §1(35)(b); 1993CJ Sch. 5 §2(13).
(6), (7)	1975 s.452A(7); 1980CJ Sch. 3 §11.
(8)	1975 s.452A(4A); 1993CJ Sch. 5 §2(13).
(9)	1975 s.452A(5); 1980CJ Sch. 3 §11.
(10)	1975 s.452A(6); 1980CJ Sch. 3 §11.
184	1975 s.449; 1980CJ Sch. 3 §8.
185(1)	1975 s.452B(1) (part); 1980CJ Sch. 3 §11; 1995 s.46(2).
(2)	1975 s.452B(1A); 1995 s.46(2).
(3)	1975 s.452B(1) (part); 1980CJ Sch. 3 §11.
(4)	1975 s.452B(2); 1980CJ Sch. 3 §11.
(5)	1975 s.452B(3) (part); 1980CJ Sch. 3 §11.

Provision	Derivation
(6), (7)	1975 s.452B(1B), (1C); 1995 s.46(2).
(8)	1975 s.452B(3) (part); 1980CJ Sch. 3 §11.
(9)	1975 s.452B(4); 1980CJ Sch. 3 §11.
(10)	1975 s.452B(5); 1995 s.46(2)(c).
186(1), (2)	1975 s.453B(1), (2); 1980CJ Sch. 3 §13; 1993P Sch. 5 §1(36); 1993CJ Sch. 5 §2(14).
(3)	1975 s.453B(3); 1980CJ Sch. 3 §13; 1993CJ Sch. 5 §2(14).
(4), (5)	1975 s.453B(4); 1980CJ Sch. 3 §13; 1993CJ Sch. 5 §2(14); 1995 s.45(2).
(6)	1975 s.453B(4A); 1995 Sch. 6 §152.
(7)	1975 s.453B(5); 1980CJ Sch. 3 §13; 1993P Sch. 5 §1(36).
(8), (9)	1975 s.453B(6), (7); 1980CJ Sch. 3 §13; 1993P Sch. 5 §1(36); 1993CJ Sch. 5 §2(14).
(10)	1975 s.453B(8); 1980CJ Sch. 3 §13.
187	1975 s.453AA; 1995 s.42(7).
188(1)	1975 s.453(1); 1993P s.43; 1995 Sch. 6 §151(2).
(2), (3)	1975 s.453 (2), (3); 1993P s.43.
(4)	1975 s.453(4); 1993P s.43; 1995 Sch. 6 §151(3).
(5). (6), (7)	1975 s.453(5), (6), (7); 1993P s.43.
189(1), (2)	1975 s.453C(1); 1980CJ Sch. 3 §13.
(3)	1975 s.453C(2); 1980 Sch. 3 §13.
(4)	1975 s.453C(3); 1980CJ Sch. 3 §13; 1993P Sch. 5 §1(37); 1993CJ Sch. 5 §2(15).
(5), (6)	1975 s.453C(4), (5); 1993CJ Sch. 5 §2(15).
(7)	1975 s.455A(1); 1995 s.34(2).
190	1975 s.453D; 1980CJ Sch. 3 §13; 1995 Sch. 6 §153.
191(1), (2)	1975 s.453A(1); 1980CJ Sch. 3 §13.
(3), (4)	1975 s.453A(2), (3); 1980CJ Sch. 3 §13.
192(1), (2)	1975 s.453E; 1980CJ Sch. 3 §13.
(3)	1975 s.454(1); 1995 Sch. 6 §154.
(4), (5)	1975 s.455(1), (2).
193(1), (2)	1975 s.443A(1), (2); 1987 s.68(1); 1993CJ Sch. 5 §2(11).
(3)	1975 s.443A(3); 1995 Sch. 6 §147.
194(1)	1975 s.451(1); 1980CJ Sch. 3 §10.
(2)	1975 s.451(2); 1980CJ Sch. 3 §10; 1995 s.45(1).
(3)	1975 s.451(3); 1980CJ Sch. 3 §10; 1995 Sch. 6 §150.
195(1)	1975 s.104(1); 1980CJ Sch. 4 §15.
(2)	1975 s.104(1A); 1987 s.58(2).
(3), (4)	1975 s.104(2), (3); 1980CJ Sch. 4 §15.
196	1975 ss.217A, 430A; 1995 s.33.
197	1975 ss.254A(2), 455A(2); 1995 s.34.
198(1)	1975 s.217(1) (part); drafting.
(2), (3)	1975 s.217(2), (3); drafting.
199	1975 ss.193, 394; 1977 Sch. 13 §7; 1980CJ s.46(2), Sch. 8; 1982 Sch. 7 §10; drafting.
200(1), (2)	1975 ss.180(1) (part), 381(1) (part); 1995 s.55(2).
(3), (4), (5)	1975 ss.180(1A) to (1C), 381(1A) to (1C); 1995 s.55(3).
(6)	1975 ss.180(2), 381(2); 1980B Sch. 1 §5, Sch. 2.
(7)	1975 ss.180(4), 381(4); 1995 s.55(4).
(8)	1975 ss.180(4A), 381(4A); 1995 s.55(5).
(9)	1975 ss.180(5), 381(5); 1980B s.6(b); 1995 s.55(6).
(10), (11)	1975 ss.180(6), (7), 381(6), (7); 1995 s.55(7).
201(1) to (3)	1975 ss.179(1), 380(1); 1980B s.5(a); 1980CJ Sch. 7 §36(a), §59(a); 1995 Sch. 6 §68.
(4)	1975 s.179(2), s.380(2); 1980B s.5(b); 1980CJ Sch. 7 §36(b), §59(b).
202	1975 ss.219, 432; 1980CJ s.54; 1995 Sch. 6 §143.
203(1)	1975 ss.179A, 380A(1); 1995 s.37.

Provision	Derivation
(2)	1975 s.380A(2); 1995 s.37(2).
(3)	1975 ss.192 (part), 393 (part); 1995 Sch. 6 §74.
204(1)	1980CJ s.41(1).
(2)	1980 s.42(1).
(3)	1980CJ s.42(2).
(4)	1980CJ ss.41(2), 42(3) (part); 1987 Sch. 1 §17; 1988 Sch. 9 §5.
(5)	1980CJ ss.41(3), 42(3) (part).
(6)	1980CJ s.41(4).
205(1) to (3)	1975 s.205(1) to (3); 1980CJ s.43.
(4) to (6)	1975 s.205A(1) to (3); 1980CJ s.43.
206	1975 s.425.
207(1) to (4)	1975 ss.207(1) to (4), 415(1) to (4); 1980CJ s.45(1).
(5)	1975 ss.207(5), 415(5); 1980CJ ss.45(1); 1985 s.43(a); 1988 s.124.
208	1975 s.206; 1980CJ s.44; Prisons (Scotland) Act 1989 (1989 c.45) Sch. 2 §12.
209(1)	1975 s.212A(1); 1993P s.14(1).
(2)	1975 s.212A(1A); 1995 s.36.
(3), (4)	1975 s.212A(2), (3); 1993P s.14(1); 1995 s.132.
(5) to (7)	1975 s.212A(4) to (6).
(8)	1975 s.212A(7); 1993CJ s.69.
210(1)	1975 ss.218(1), 431(1); 1980 Sch. 7 §70, Sch. 8; 1993P s.41.
(2), (3)	1975 ss.218(2), (3), 431(2), (3); 1993P s.41.
211(1)	1975 s.193A(1); 1977 Sch. 11 §1; 1980CJ Sch. 7 §37; 1982 Sch. 15 §17.
(2)	1975 s.193A(2); 1982 Sch. 15 §17.
(3)	1975 ss.196(1), 402; 1995 Sch. 6 §75.
(4)	1975 s.196(2); 1980CJ s.48.
(5)	1975 s.203.
(6)	1975 s.412.
(7)	1975 ss.194, 395(1).
212(1), (2)	1975 s.395(2) (part); 1980CJ Sch. 7 §60.
(3) to (7)	1975 s.395(3) to (7).
(8), (9)	1975 s.395(2) (part); 1980CJ Sch. 7 §60.
213	1975 ss.194, 395A(1) to (3); 1980CJ ss.47, 49.
214(1) to (6)	1975 ss.194, 396(1) to (6); 1980CJ s.47; drafting.
(7)	1975 ss.194, 396(7); 1980CJ s.47; 1995 Sch. 6 §137.
(8)	1975 ss.194, 399(1); 1980CJ s.47.
(9)	1975 ss.194, 399(2) & (3); 1980CJ s.47, Sch. 7 §62(b).
215(1), (2)	1975 ss.194, 397; 1977 Sch. 11 §8; Magistrates' Courts Act 1980 (1980 c.43) Sch. 7 §136; 1980CJ s.47.
(3), (4)	1975 ss.194, 397(2), (3); 1980CJ s.47.
216(1), (2)	1975 ss.194, 398(1); 1980CJ s.47, Sch. 7 §61; 1995 Sch. 6 §138.
(3)	1975 ss.194, 398(2); 1980CJ s.47.
(4)	1975 ss.194, 398(3); 1980CJ s.47.
(5)	1975 ss.194, 318(1); 1980CJ s.47.
(6)	1975 ss.194, 318(2) & (3), 398(4) & (5); 1980CJ s.47; 1995 Sch. 6 §114.
(7)	1975 ss.194, 406; 1980CJ s.47; 1995 Sch. 6 §139.
217	1975 ss.194, 400; 1980CJ s.47.
218(1), (2)	1975 ss.194, 401(1), (2); 1980CJ s.47.
(3)	1975 ss.194, 401(3); 1980CJ s.47, Sch. 7 §63.
219(1)	1975 ss.194, 407(1); 1980CJ ss.47, 50; 1990 Sch. 7 §27(3).
(2)	1975 ss.194, 407(1A); 1980CJ ss.47, 50; 1985; 1987 s.67(1); 1991 s.23(2).
(3) to (5)	1975 ss.194, 407(1B) to (1D); 1980CJ s.47, 50.
(6)	1975 ss.194, 407(2); 1980CJ s.47.
(7)	1975 ss.194, 407(4); 1980CJ s.47.
(8)	1975 ss.194, 407(5); 1980CJ s.47; 1987 s.67(2).
220(1), (2)	1975 ss.194, 409(1); 1980CJ s.47, Sch. 7 §65.
(3)	1975 s.194, Sch. 7; 1980CJ s.47.

Provision	Derivation
(4)	1975 ss.194, 409(2); 1980CJ s.47.
221(1)	1975 ss.194, 411(1); 1980CJ s.47; Debtors (Scotland) Act 1987 (1987 c. 18) Sch. 6 §18.
(2), (3)	1975 ss.194, 411(3); 1980CJ s.47.
(4)	1980CJ s.52 (part).
222(1)	1975 ss.194, 403(1); 1977 Sch. 7 §2; 1980CJ s.47.
(2)	1975 ss.194, 403(2); 1980CJ s.47.
(3)	1975 ss.194, 403(3); 1980CJ s.47; 1995 s.67(2).
(4)	1975 ss.194, 403(3A); 1980CJ s.47; 1995 s.67(3).
(5)	1975 ss.194, 403(3B); 1980CJ s.47; 1995 s.67(3).
(6)	1975 ss.194, 403(4); 1977 Sch. 7 §2; 1980CJ s.47.
(7)	1975 ss.194, 403(4A); 1980CJ s.47; 1994 s.47(4).
(8)	1975 ss.194, 403(6); 1977 Sch. 7 §2; 1980CJ s.47.
223	1975 s.404.
224	1975 ss.194, 408; 1980CJ s.47; 1995 Sch. 6 §140.
225(1)	1975 s.289G(1); 1982 s.54.
(2)	1975 s.289G(2); 1982 s.54; S.I. 1984/526; 1991 s.17(1).
(3)	1975 s.289G(3); 1982 s.54.
(4)	1975 s.289D(1); 1977 Sch. 11 §5; 1982 s.53(a).
(5)	1975 s.289D(1A); 1982 s.53(a); 194 s.157(7).
(6)	1975 s.289D(1B); 1982 s.53(a); drafting.
(7)	1975 s.289D(4); 1977 Sch. 11 §5; 1987 Sch. 2.
(8)	1975 s.289B(6) (part); drafting.
226	1975 s.289GB; 1987 s.66(2).
227	1975 s.182A; 1995 Sch. 6 §69.
228(1)	1975 ss.183(1), 384(1); 1980CJ s.53(1); 1987 Sch. 1 §10; 1990 s.61(1); 1995 s.38(3)(a).
(2)	1975 ss.183(1A), 384(1A); 1990 s.61; 1991 Sch. 3 §7(2).
(3), (4)	1975 ss.183(2), 384(2).
(5)	1975 ss.183(6), 384(6); 1987 s.65(4); 1995 s.38(3)(c).
(6)	1975 ss.183(7), 384(7); 1995 Sch. 6 §70.
229(1)	1975 ss.183(4), 384(4); 1978 s.7; 1987 s.65(3); 1990 s.61(1).
(2), (3)	1975 ss.183(5), 384(5).
(4), (5)	1975 ss.183(5A), 384(5A); 1978 s.7; 1982 Sch. 13 §3; 1995 s.38(1), (3)(b); drafting.
(6), (7)	1975 ss.183(5B), (5C), 384(5B), (5C); 1987 s.65.
230(1)	1975 ss.184(1), 385(1); 1984 Sch. 3 §§29, 36; 1995 s.39(1).
(2)	1975 ss.184(2), 385(2); 1984 Sch. 3 §§29, 36; 1995 s.39(1).
(3)	1975 ss.184(3), 385(3).
(4)	1975 ss.184(5), 385(5); 1983 s.36(2); 1995 s.39(1).
(5)	1975 ss.184(5A), 385(5A); 1983 s.36(2).
(6)	1975 ss.184(5B), 385(5B); 1983 s.36(2); 1995 s.39(1).
(7)	1975 ss.184(6), 385(6); 1983 s.36(3).
(8), (9)	1975 ss.184(7), (8), 385(7), (8).
231	1975 ss.185, 386.
232(1)	1975 ss.186(1), 387(1); 1978 s.8; 1990 s.61(2); Local Government etc. (Scotland) Act 1994 (c. 39) Sch. 13 §97(3); 1995 Sch. 6 §671.
(2)	1975 ss.186(2), 387(2); 1978 s.8; 1980CJ s.46(1); 1982 Sch. 7 §§3, 9; 1987 s.65(5); 1995 s.38(2).
(3)	1975 ss.186(2A), 387(2A); 1993P Sch. 5 §1(7).
(4) to (6)	1975 ss.186(3) to (5), 387(3) to (5).
(7)	1975 s.317.
233(1), (2)	1975 ss.187(1), (2), 388(1), (2).
(3) to (5)	1975 ss.187(3) to (5), 388(3) to (5); 1995 s.40(1), (2).
234(1), (2)	1975 ss.188(1), 389(1); 1978 Sch. 2 §2, 3; 1991 Sch. 3 §7(3).

Provision	Derivation
(3) to (10)	1975 ss.188(2) to (8), 389(2) to (8); 1991 Sch. 3 §7(3).
(11)	Drafting.
235	1990 s.62; 1995 s.35(2) to (7).
236	1975 s.412A; 1995 s.35(11).
237	1975 s.412B; 1995 s.35(11).
238(1)	1978 s.1(1); 1990 s.61(3).
(2) to (7)	1978 s.1(2) to (7).
(8), (9)	1978 s.2(1), (2).
(10), (11)	1978 s.2(3), (4); 1995 Sch. 6. §161.
239(1) to (3)	1978 s.3(1) to (3).
(4)	1978 s.4(1); 1995 Sch. 6 §162.
(5)	1978 s.4(2); 1982 Sch. 7 §12.
(6)	1978 s.4(3); 1990 Sch. 8 §28.
240	1978 s.5.
241	1978 s.5A; 1995 s.40(3).
242	1978 s.6; 1982 Sch. 13 §4.
243(1)	1978 s.6A(1); 1982 Sch. 13 §5.
(2)	1978 s.6A(2); 1982 Sch. 13 §5; S.I. 1989/1345.
(3)	1978 s.6A(3); 1982 Sch. 13 §5.
244	1978 s.6B; 1982 Sch. 13 §5.
245(1) to (3)	1978 s.10(1) to (3).
(4)	1978 s.11.
(5)	1978 s.12(1).
246(1)	1975 ss.181, 382; 1993CJ Sch. 5 §2(2).
(2)	1975 s.182.
(3)	1975 s.383.
247(1)	1975 ss.191(1) (part), 392(1) (part).
(2)	1975 ss.191(2), 392(2).
(3)	1975 ss.191(3) (part), 392(3) (part), 392(3); 1993CJ Sch. 5 §2(3), (9).
(4)	1975 ss.191(4), 392(5); 1995 Sch. 6 §§73, 136.
(5)	1975 s.392(4); 1995 Sch. 6 §136.
(6)	1975 ss.191(1) (part), 392(1) (part).
248(1) to (4)	1975 ss.223A, 436A; Road Traffic Act 1991 (c. 40) s.39.
249(1), (2)	1980CJ s.58(1).
(3), (4)	1980CJ s.58(2), (3).
(5), (6)	1980CJ s.59(1).
(7), (8)	1980CJ s.59(2), (3).
(9), (10)	1980CJ s.60(1), (2).
250(1)	1980CJ s.61.
(2)	1980CJ s.62.
(3), (4)	1980CJ s.63(1), (2).
251	1980CJ s.64.
252	1980CJ s.66.
253	1980CJ s.67; Armed Forces Act 1991 (c. 62) Sch. 2) Sch. 2 §9(2).
254	1975 ss.224, 437.
255	1975 ss.67, 312(x); drafting.
256(1)	1975 ss.150(1), 354(1); 1995 Sch. 6 §§55(a), 126; drafting.
(2)	1975 ss,150(2), 354(2) (part); 1995 Sch. 6 §55(b).
(3)	1975 ss.150(3), 354(2) (part); drafting.
257	1975 ss.84A, 333B; 1995 s.12.
258	1995 s.16.
259	1995 s.17.
260	1995 s.18.
261	1995 s.19.
262	1995 s.20.
263(1) to (3)	1975 ss.148(1) to (3), 340(1) to (3); 1995 Sch. 6 §54.

Provision	Derivation
(4)	1975 ss. 147, 349.
(5)	1975 ss.148A, 349A; 1982 s.73(1), (2).
264(1) to (3)	1975 ss.143(1) to (3), 348(1) to (3); 1980CJ s.29.
(4)	Criminal Justice Administration Act 1914 (c. 58) s.28(3).
265(1)	1975 ss.138(1), (2), 341(1), (2).
(2)	1975 ss.138(4), 341(4).
(3), (4)	1975 ss.139, 342.
266(1)	1975 ss.141(1) (part), 346(1) (part); Criminal Evidence Act 1979 (1979 c. 16) s.1(1); 1980CJ s.28, Sch. 7 §56; 1995 s.24.
(2)	1975 ss.141(1)(a), 346(1)(a).
(3)	1975 ss.141(1)(e), 346(1)(e).
(4)	1975 ss.141(1)(f), 346(1)(f); Criminal Evidence Act 1979 (c. 16) s.1(1); 1995 s.24(1)(a), (4)(a).
(5)	1975 ss.141(1A), 346(1A): 1995 s.24(1)(b), (4)(b).
(6)	1975 s.141(1B); 1995 s.24(1)(b).
(7)	1975 ss.141(1C), 346(1B); 1995 s.24(1)(c), (4)(b).
(8)	1975 ss.141(1)(g), 346(1)(g).
(9)	1975 ss.141(2), 346(2); 1980CJ s.28.
(10)	1975 ss.141(3), 346(3); 1980CJ s.28.
(11)	1975 ss.142, 347; 1995 Sch. 6 §§50, 124.
267(1)	1975 ss.139A, 342A; 1987 s.63.
(2)	1975 ss.140, 343.
268(1), (2)	1975 ss.149(1), 350(1); 1980CJ s.30; 1985 s.37; 1987 Sch. 1 §9; 1993P Sch. 5 §1(31).
(3), (4)	1975 ss.149(2), (3), 350(2), (3); 1980CJ s.30.
(5)	Drafting.
269(1)	1975 ss.149A(1), 350A(2); 1980CJ s.30; 1985 s.37.
(2), (3)	1975 ss.149A(2), (3), 350A(2), (3); 1980CJ s.30.
(4)	Drafting.
270(1), (2)	1975 ss.141ZA(1), (2), 346ZA(1), (2); 1995 s.24(2), (5).
(3)	1975 s.141ZA(3); 1995 s.24(2).
(4)	1975 ss.141ZA(4), 346ZA(3); 1995 s.24(2), (5).
271(1) to (3)	1993P s.33(1) to (3).
(4)	1993P s.33(4); 1995 Sch. 6 §179(6).
(5)	1990 s.56(1); 1995 Sch. 6 §175(a).
(6)	1993P s.34; 1995 Sch. 6 §179(7).
(7)	1990 s.56(2); 1995 Sch. 6 §175(b).
(8)	1990 s.56(3).
(9)	1990 s.57(1).
(10)	1990 s.57(2).
(11)	1990 s.58; 1995 Sch. 6 §176.
(12)	1990 s.59.
272(1)	1980CJ s.32(1); 1987 s.61.
(2), (3)	1980CJ s.32(2).
(4)	1980CJ s.32(3).
(5)	1980CJ s.32(3A); 1993P s.30.
(6)	1980CJ s.32(4); 1987 s.61.
(7)	1980CJ s.32(5).
(8)	1980CJ s.32(5A); 1993P s.30
(9)	1980CJ s.32(6).
273	1980CJ s.32A; 1993P s.32.
274(1)	1975 ss.141A(1), 346A(1); 1985 s.36.
(2)	1975 ss.141A(2), 346A(2); 1985 s.36; 1995 s.28.
(3), (4)	1975 ss.141A(3), (4), 346A(3), (4); 1985 s.36.
275	1975 ss.141B, 346B; 1985 s.36.
276	1995 s.21.

Provision	Derivation
277(1)	1987 s.60(1); 1993P s.31.
(2)	1987 s.60(2).
(3)	1987 s.60(3); 1995 Sch. 6 §170.
(4)	1987 s.60(4).
278(1)	1975 ss.151(1), 352(1); 1980CJ s.6.
(2), (3)	1975 ss.151(2), 352(2); 1995 Sch. 6 §§56, 125.
(4)	1975 s.352(4).
(5)	1975 ss.151(3), 352(3).
279	1993P s.29.
280(1)	1980CJ s.26(1).
(2), (3)	1980 s.26(1A), (1B); 1995 s.22(2).
(4)	1980 CJ s.26(2); 1995 s.22(3).
(5)	1980CJ s.26(2A); 1995 s.22(4).
(6)	1980CJ s.26(3); 1995 s.22(5).
(7)	1980CJ s.26(4); 1995 s.22(6), Sch. 6 §163.
(8)	1980CJ s.26(4A); 1995 s.22(7).
(9)	1980CJ s.26(5); 1995 s.22(8).
(10) to (12)	1980 s.26(7B) to (7D); 1995 s.22(9).
281(1), (2)	1980CJ s.26(6), (7).
(3)	1980CJ s.26(7A); 1995 s.22(9).
282	1995 s.25.
283	1995 s.26.
284	1995 s.27.
285(1) to (5)	1975 ss.164(1) to (5) 358(1) to (5).
(6)	1975 ss.162(1), 357(2) (part).
(7)	1975 s.162(2).
(8)	1975 ss.162(3), 357(2) (part); 1995 Sch. 6 §§62, 127(b).
(9)	1975 ss.164(6), 357(2) (part), 358(6).
286	1975 ss.162(4), (5), 357(6), (7); 1995 s.29.
287	1975 s.42; 1995 Sch. 6 §18.
288(1)	1975 s.10.
(2)	1975 s.11.
289	1980CJ s.39.
290	1980CJ s.10(1), (2).
291(1)	1980CJ s.9(1).
(2)	1980CJ s.9(2); 1982 Sch. 6 §64.
(3)	1980CJ s.9(3); 1982 Sch. 7.
292(1)	1975 ss.283A(1), (2); 1977 Sch. 11 §2; 1980CJ Sch. 7 §49.
(2) to (7)	1975 s.457A(1) to (4); 1982 s.55(1).
293	1975 ss.216, 428; 1987 s.64(1).
294(1)	1975 s.63(1) (part).
(2)	1975 s.312(o) (part).
295	1975 ss.215, 426; 1980CJ Sch. 7 §§39, 69; 1987 Sch. 1 §12.
296	1975 ss.15A, 309(2) (part); 1995 Sch. 6 §9.
297(1)	1975 ss.15, 327; 1995 s.9.
(2)	1975 s.326(1) (part).
(3), (4)	1975 ss.16(1), (2), 324(1), (2).
(5)	1975 s.326(1) (part).
298	1995 s.44.
299	1975 ss.227A, 439; 1980CJ s.20.
300	1975 s.439A; 1995 s.41.
301(1)	1975 s.282A; 1990 Sch. 8 §27.
(2)	1975 s.282B; 1990 Sch. 8 §27.
302(1)	1987 s.56(1).
(2)	1987 s.56(3); 1995 s.61(3).
(3)	1987 s.56(3A); 1995 s.61(4).

Provision	Derivation
(4) to (6)	1987 s.56(4) to (6); 1995 s.61(5).
(7), (8)	1987 s.56(7), (7A); 1995 s.61(6).
(9)	1987 s.56(2), (2A); Road Traffic (Consequential Provisions) Act 1988 (1988 c. 54) Sch. 3 §34; 1995 s.61(2).
303(1) to (4)	1987 s.56(8) to (11); 1995 s.61(8).
304	1995 s.56(1) to (10).
305(1)	1975 ss.409(3), 457ZA(1) (part); Summary Jurisdiction (Scotland) Act 194 (c. 48) s.76(1)(d); 1995 Sch. 6 §156.
(2)	1975 s.457ZA(2); 1995 Sch. 6 §156.
(3)	1975 s.457ZA(1) (part); 1995 Sch. 6 §156.
(4)	1975 s.278.
(5)	Summary Jurisdiction (Scotland) Act 1954 (1954 c. 48) s.76(3).
306	1995 s.57.
307(1)	1975 s,462(1); 1977 Sch. 11 §10; National Health Service (Scotland) Act 1978 (1978 c. 29) Sch. 16 §41; 1980B Sch. 1 §14; 1980CJ s.25, Sch. 7 §76; 1982 Sch. 15 §19; 1983 Sch. 2 §37; 1984 Sch. 3 §37; National Health Service and Community Care Act 1990 (c. 19) Sch. 9 §14; 1995 s.39(2), Sch. 6 §157; 1995C Sch. 4 §24(18).
(2)	1975 s.462(2).
(3) to (8)	1975 s.462(4) to (9).
308	1975 ss.458, 459; 1980CJ Sch. 7 §§73, 74.
309	Drafting.
Sch. 1	1975 Sch. 1; Sexual Offences (Scotland) Act 1976 (1976 c. 67) Schs. 1, 2; 1988 Sch. 15 §§50, 51.
Sch. 2	Criminal Procedure (Scotland) Act 1887 (c. 35) Sch. 1
Sch. 3	
§1	1975 ss.43 (part), 312(a).
§2	1975 ss.44, 312(b).
§3	1975 ss.48, 312(e).
§4(1)	1975 ss.50(1), 312(f) (part).
(2)	1975 ss.50(2), 312(f) (part).
(3)	1975 ss.50(3) (part), 312(f) (part).
(4)	1975 ss.50(3) (part), 312(f) (part).
(5)	1975 ss.50(4), 312(f) (part); 1995 Sch. 6 §§20, 110(a).
(6)	1975 ss.51 (part), 312(g) (part).
(7)	1975 ss.51 (part), 312(g) (part).
(8)	Drafting.
§5	1975 ss.54, 312(j); 1995 Sch. 6 §§21, 110(b).
§6	1975 ss.55, 312(k).
§7	1975 s.63(2).
§8(1)	1975 ss.59 (part), 312(l) (part).
(2)	1975 ss.60(1), 312(m) (part).
(3)	1975 ss.60(2), 312(m) (part).
(4)	1975 ss.60(3), 312(m) (part).
(5)	1975 ss.60(4), 312(m) (part).
§9(1)	1975 ss.61(l), 312(n) (part).
(2)	1975 ss.61(2), 312(n) (part).
(3)	1975 ss.61(3), 312(n) (part).
§10(1)	1975 ss.63(1) (part), 312(o) (part).
(2)	1975 ss.63(1) (part), 312(o) (part).
(3)	1975 ss.63(2), 312(o) (part).
§11	1975 ss.48B, 312(p); 1995 Sch. 6 §19.
§12	1975 s.312(q), (r).
§13	1975 ss.49, 312(s).
§14	1975 ss.64, 312(t).
§15	1975 ss.65, 312(u).

Provision	Derivation
§16	1975 ss.66, 312(v).
§17	1975 ss.48A, 312(w); 1995 Sch. 6 §19.
§18	1975 ss.60A, 312(y); 1995 Sch. 6 §23.
§19	1975 s.312(z); 1977 Sch. 11 §6; 1980CJ s.46(b); 1982 Sch. 7 §7.
Sch. 4	1975 Sch. 5A; 1995 Sch. 2.
Sch. 5	Summary Jurisdiction (Scotland) Act 1954 (c. 48) Sch. 2 Part II.
Sch. 6	
§1	1975 Sch. 5 §1.
§2	1975 Sch. 5 §2.
§3	1975 Sch. 5 §3.
§4	1975 Sch. 5 §4; 1983 s.36(4); 1995 Sch. 6 §158.
§5	1975 Sch. 5 §5.
§6	1975 Sch. 5 §6.
Sch. 7	
§1	1990 Sch. 6 §1; 1995 s.35(8)(a).
§2	1990 Sch. 6 §2; 1995 Sch. 6 §177(a).
§3	1990 Sch. 6 §3.
§4	1990 Sch. 6 §4; 1995 s.35(8)(b), Sch. 6 §177(b).
§5	1990 Sch. 6 §5; 1995 s.35(8)(c).
§6	1990 Sch. 6 §6.
§7	1990 Sch. 6 §7.
§8	1990 Sch. 6 §9.
Sch. 8	1993P Sch. 3; 1995 Sch. 6 §179(8).
Sch. 9	1980CJ Sch. 1; Forgery and Counterfeiting Act 1981 (1981 c. 45) s.26; Road Traffic Regulation Act 1984 (1984 c. 27) Sch. 13 §37; Video Recording Act 1984 (1984 c. 39) s.20; 1987 Sch. 1 §18(2); 1993P Sch. 4; 1995 Sch. 1.
Sch. 10	1975 Sch. 7A; 1977 Sch. 11 §11.

TABLE OF DESTINATIONS

TABLE OF DESTINATIONS

SEXUAL OFFENCES (SCOTLAND) ACT 1976
(c.67)

CRIMINAL LAW ACT 1977
(c.45)

NATIONAL HEALTH SERVICE (SCOTLAND) ACT 1978
(c.29)

TABLE OF DESTINATIONS

COMMUNITY SERVICE BY OFFENDERS (SCOTLAND) ACT 1978
(c.49)

1978	1995	1978	1995	1978	1995
s.1(1)	s.238(1)	s.5A	s.241	s.8	s.232(1), (2)
(2)-(7)	238(2)-(7)	6	242	10(1)-(3)	245(1)-(3)
2(1), (2)	238(8), (9)	6A(1)	243(1)	11	245(4)
(3), (4)	238(10), (11)	(2)	243(2)	12(1)	245(5)
3(1)-(3)	239(1)-(3)	(3)	243(3)	Sched.2,	
4(1)	239(4)	6B	244	para. 2	234(1), (2)
(2)	239(5)	7	229(1), (4),	para.3	234(1), (2)
(3)	239(6)		(5)		
5	240				

CRIMINAL EVIDENCE ACT 1979
(c.16)

1979	1995
s.1(1)	s.266(1), (4)

BAIL (SCOTLAND) ACT 1980
(c.4)

1980	1995	1980	1995	1980	1995
s.1(1)	s.24(3)	s.5(a)	s.201(1)-(3)	Sched.1,	
1(2)-(3)	24(4)-(8)	5(b)	201(4)	para.4	s.30(2)
1(4)	24(4)-(8),	6(b)	200(9)	para.5	200(6)
	30(1), (4)	7(1)	21(2)-(5)	para.6	30(2)
1(5)	24(4)-(8)	7(2)	21(2)-(5),	para.7	135(3),(4)
2	25		22(4), (5)	para.8	146(6)
3(1), (2)	27(1), (2)	8	22(1)-(3), (4),	para.10	181(3)
3(2A)-(2D)	27(3)-(6)		(5)	para.12	181(3)
3(3)-(6)	27(7)-(10)	9(a)	43(1)-(3)	para.14	307(1)
3(7)-(11)	28	9(b)	43(7)-(8)	Sched.2	ss.146(2),
3(12)	27(11)	10	8		200(6)
4	29				

MAGISTRATES' COURTS ACT 1980
(c.43)

1980	1995
Sched.7,	
para.136	s.215(1), (2)

LAW REFORM (MISCELLANEOUS PROVISIONS) (SCOTAND) ACT 1980
(c.55)

1980	1995
s.2(3)	s.85(6), (7)
Sched.2,	
para.6	84(6)
para.7	86(3)

TABLE OF DESTINATIONS

CRIMINAL JUSTICE ACT (SCOTLAND) ACT 1980
(C.62)

1980	1995
s.1	s.13
2(1).........	14(1)
(2).........	14(2)
(3).........	14(3)
(3A)......	14(4)
(3B)	14(5)
(4).........	14(6)
(5)-(7)	14(7)-(9)
3(1).........	15(1), (2)
(2)-(4)	15(3)-(5)
(5).........	15(6)
5	16
6	278(1)
(1).........	35(3), (4), (5)-(7)
(2).........	ss.36(1)-(4), (5)-(9), 37(1), (6)-(10)
7(1).........	7(3)
(1A)......	7(7)
(3).........	7(4), (8)
9(1).........	291(1)
(2).........	291(2)
(3).........	291(3)
10(1), (2)....	290
11	ss.137(2), (4), (5), 139(2)
13	78(1), (3)
14(1)........	65(1)-(3), (4)-(9)
(2)........	147
15	148
16	76
17	150(8)-(10)
18(1)........	81(3)
18(2)........	152
19(1)........	97(1)-(4)
(2)........	160
20	299
21	92(1), (2)
22	47(1)-(6)
24(1)........	99(1)-(3)
(2)........	100(1), (2)
25	307(1)
26(1)........	280(1)
(2)........	280(4)
(2A)......	280(5)
(3)........	280(6)
(4)........	280(7)
(4A)......	280(8)
(5)........	280(9)
(6), (7)....	281(1), (2)
(7A)......	281(3)
(7B)-(7D).	280(10)-(12)
27	67(6)
28	266(1), (9), (10)
29	264(1)-(3)
30	268(1)-(4), 269(1)-(3)
32(1)........	272(1)
s.32(2)........	s.272(2), (3)
(3)........	272(4)
(3A)......	272(5)
(4)........	272(6)
(5)........	272(7)
(5A)......	272(8)
(6)........	272(9)
32A	273

1980	1995
s.35	s.131
36	174
37	123
39	289
40	166(1)-(6)
41(1)........	204(1)
(2)........	204(4)
(3)........	204(5)
(4)........	204(6)
42(2)........	204(3)
(3) part ...	204(4), (5)
43	205(1)-(3), (4)-(6)
44	208
45(1)........	207(1)-(4), (5)
46(1)........	232(2)
(c)....	155(1)
(2)........	199
(b)	Sched.3, para.19
47	ss.213, 214(1)-(6), (7), (8), (9), 215(1), (2), (3), (4), 216(1), (2), (3), (4), (5), (6), (7), 217, 218(1), (2), (3), 219(1), (2), (3)-(5), (6), (7), (8), 220(1), (2), (3), (4), 221(1), (2), (3), 222(1), (2), (3), (4),(5), (6), (7), (8), 224
48	211(4)
49	213
50	219(1), (2), (3)-(5)
52 part	221(4)
53(1)........	228(1)
54	202
58(1)........	249(1), (2)
2), (3)...	249(3), (4)
59(1)........	249(5), (6)
(2), (3)...	249(7), (8)
60(1), (2)....	249(9), (10)
61	250(1)
62	250(2)
63(1), (2)....	250(3), (4)
64	251
66	252
67	253
Sched.1.......	Sched.9
Sched.2,	
para.1......	s.106(1)-(3)
para.3......	109(1)-(3)
para.5......	110(1)-(4), (6)
para.8......	ss.111, 113
para.10(a)..	s.112(3), (4)
para.10(b)..	112(5)
para.11.....	117(9)
para.13.....	116(1), (2)
para.15.....	103(5), (6)
para.16.....	104(1)
para.18.....	118(1), (2)
para.19.....	119(1), (3)-(5), (8), (9)
para.22.....	124(1), (3)

1980	1995
Sched. 2—*cont.*	
para.23.....	s.121(1), (2)
para.25.....	126
para.26.....	106(5)-(9)
para.27.....	127
para.31.....	129(3)
para.32.....	61(1)
Sched.3	
para.1......	175(7)-(9)
para.2......	61(1)
para.3.....	176(1)-(3), 181(3)
para.5......	177(1)
para.6......	178(1)
para.7......	179, 181(1)-(3)
para.8......	184
para.9......	176(5)
para.10.....	194(1)-(3)
para.11.....	ss.182, 183(1)-(7), (9), (10), 185(1), (3)-(5), (8), (9)
para.13.....	186(1)-(5), (7)-(10), 189(1), (2), (4), 190, 191(1)-(4), 192(1), (2)
Sched.4,	
para.1......	s.69(3), (5)
para.2......	66(1), (2)
para.3(b)..	70(5)
para.4......	66(6)
para.5......	72(1), 72(2), 74
para.6......	80(1)
para.7......	80(2)-(6)
para.8......	66(5), 68(1)
para.9......	67(3), (4)
para.10.....	78(4), (5)
para.11.....	68(2)
para.12.....	68(3), (4)
para.13.....	85(1)
para.14.....	77(1)-(3)
para.15.....	195(1), (3), (4)
para.19.....	ss.72(1), 79(1), (2)
para.27.....	s.81(1)
Sched.6,	
para.22.....	66(12)-(14)
para.27(a)..	66(9)
para.27(b)..	66(9)
para.27(c)..	66(10)
para.28.....	66(8)
Sched.7, ...	117(8)
para.25.....	17(1)
para.26.....	23(1)
para.27.....	66(7)
para.28.....	67(5)
para.29.....	85(4), (5)
para.31.....	75
para.34.....	48
para.35.....	49(3)
para.36(a)..	201(1)-(3)
para.36(b)..	201(4)
para.37.....	211(1)
para.39.....	295
para.41.....	117(1), (2)

TABLE OF DESTINATIONS

1980	1995
Sched.7—*cont.*	
para.42	s.117(4)–(6)
para.44	105(5)
para.45	120(4)
para.46	125(4)
para.49	292(1)
para.51	23(1)
para.54(a)	144(1), (9)
para.54(b)	144(4), (5)
para.55	155(4)
para.56	266(1)

1980	1995
Sched.7—*cont.*	
para.57	s.48
para.58	142(5)
para.59(a)	201(1)-(3)
para.59(b)	201(4)
para.60	212(1), (2), (8), (9)
para.61	216(1), (2)
para.62(b)	214(9)
para.63	218(3)
para.65	220(1), (2)

1980	1995
Sched.7—*cont.*	
para.68	s.169
para.69	295
para.73	308
para.74	308
para.76	307(1)
Sched.8	ss.93, 103(4)–(6), 104(2), (3), 115(1)–(4), 120(1), 129(1)–(3), 137(1), 178(2), 199

FORGERY AND COUNTERFEITING ACT 1981
(c.45)

1981	1995
s.26	Sched.9

CRIMINAL JUSTICE ACT 1982
(c.48)

1982	1995
s.53(a)	s.225(4)–(6)
54	225(1)–(3)
55(1)	292(2)-(7)
73(1), (2)	263(5)
Sched.6	
para.64	291(2)
Sched.7	291(3)
para.4	7(6)
para.3	232(2)

1982	1995
Sched.7—*cont.*	
para.5	s.7(6)
para.6	7(8)
para.7	155(1), Sched.3, para.19
para.9	232(2)
para.10	199
para.12	239(5)
para.14	7(4)

1982	1995
Sched.13	
para.3	s.229(4), (5)
para.4	242
para.5	ss.243(1)–(3), 244
Sched.15,	
para.17	211(1), (2)
para.19	307(1)

MENTAL HEALTH (AMENDMENT) (SCOTLAND) ACT 1983
(c.39)

1983	1995
s.22(2)	s.59(1)
34(a)	53(1), (2)-(10), (11), (12), 58(1), (2)
34(b), (d)	60
35(a), (b)	61(2)
36(2)	230(4)–(6)

1983	1995
s.36(3)	s.230(7)
36(4)	Sched.6, para.4
Sched.2	
para.31	58(1), (2), (6)–(8)
para.32	61(1)

1983	1995
Sched. 2—*cont.*	
para.33	s.59(2), (3)
para.34	58(6)–(8)
para.35	61(1)
para.36	59(2), (3)
para.37	307(1)

HEALTH AND SOCIAL SERVICES AND SOCIAL SECURITIES AJUDICATIONS ACT 1983
(c.41)

1983	1995
Sched.2	
para.7	42(1)

TABLE OF DESTINATIONS

TABLE OF DESTINATIONS

CABLE AND BROADCASTING ACT 1986
(c.46)

1986	1995
Sched.5,	
para.30	s.47(4)

DEBTORS (SCOTLAND) ACT 1987
(c.18)

1987	1995
Sched.6,	
para.18	s.221(1)

CRIMINAL JUSTICE (SCOTLAND) ACT 1987
(c.41)

1987	1995	1987	1995	1987	1995
s.45(6)(a)	s.109(1), (2)	s.60(3)	s.277(3)	Sched.1,	
(6)(b)	109(4), (5)	(4)	277(4)	para.4	s.10
(6)(c)	109(6)	61	272(1), (6)	para.5	84(2), (3)
56(1)	302(1)	62(3)	146(6)	para.7	88(2)
(2), (2A)	302(9)	(4)(a)	32(2)	para.9	268(1), (2)
(3)	302(2)	(4)(b)	32(9)	para.10	228(1)
(3A)	302(3)	63	267(1)	para.12	295
(4)-(6)	302(4)-(6)	64(1)	293	para.13(1)	103(2)
(7), (7A)	302(7), (8)	65	229(6), (7)	para.13(2)	103(1)
(8)-(11)	303(1)-(4)	(3)	229(1)	para.14(1)	125(1)
57(1)	3(2)	(4)	228(5)	para.14(2)	125(2)
(2)	2	(5)	232(2)	para.14(3)	125(3)
58(1)	3(3)-(5)	66(2)	226	para.16(a),	
(2)	195(2)	67(1)	219(2)	(b)	14(2)
59(1)	44(1)–(4), (9), (10)	(2)	219(8)	para.16(c)	14(4)
		68(1)	193(1), (2)	para.17	204(4)
60(1)	277(1)	(3)	121(3)	para.18(2)	Sched.9
(2)	277(2)			Sched.2	ss.124(4), 225(7)

CRIMINAL JUSTICE ACT 1988
(c.33)

1988	1995
s.124	s.207(5)
Sched.9,	
para.5	204(4)
Sched.15,	
para.48	46(3)
para.50	Sched.1
para.51	Sched.1

ROAD TRAFFIC (CONSEQUENTIAL PROVISIONS) ACT 1988
(c.54)

1988	1995
Sched.3,	
para 34	s.302(9)

PRISONS (SCOTLAND) ACT 1989
(c.45)

1989	1995
Sched.2,	
para.12	s.208

TABLE OF DESTINATIONS

NATIONAL HEALTH SERVICE AND COMMUNITY CARE ACT 1990
(c.19)

1990	1995
Sched.9,	
para.14	s.307(1)

LAW REFORM (MISCELLANEOUS PROVISIONS) (SCOTLAND) ACT 1990
(c.40)

1990	1995	1990	1995	1990	1995
s.56(1)	s.271(5)	s.61(1)	s.229(1)	Sched.6—cont.	Sched.7—cont.
(2)	271(7)	(2)	232(1)	para.5	para.5
(3)	271(8)	(3)	238(1)	para.6	para.6
57(1)	271(9)	62	235	para.7	para.7
(2)	271(10)	Sched.6,	Sched.7	para.9	para.8
58	271(11)	para.1	para.1	Sched.8,	
59	271(12)	para.2	para.2	para.27	s.301(1), (2)
60	4(2)	para.3	para.3	para.27(3)	219(1)
61	228(1), (2)	para.4	para.4	para.28	239(6)

BROADCASTING ACT 1990
(c.42)

1990	1995
Sched.20,	
para.21	47(4)

ROAD TRAFFIC ACT 1991
(c.40)

1991	1995
s.39	s.248(1)-(4)

CRIMINAL JUSTICE ACT 1991
(c.53)

1991	1995
s.17(1)	s.225(2)
23(2)	219(2)
Sched.3,	
para.7(2)	228(2)
para.7(3)	234(1)–(10)

ARMED FORCES ACT 1991
(c.62)

1991	1995
Sched.2,	
para.9(2)	253

TABLE OF DESTINATIONS

PRISONERS AND CRIMINAL PROCEEDINGS (SCOTLAND) ACT 1993
(c.9)

1993	1995
s.8	s.44(5), (6)-(8)
14(1).	209(1), (3),
	(4)
28(1), (2). . . .	18(1), (2)
(3).	18(3)
(3A), (3C)	18(4)
(3B)	18(5)
(4).	18(6)
(5), (6). . . .	18(7), (8)
28A	19
28B.	20
29	279
30	272(5), (8)
31	277(1)
(1)-(3)	271(1)-(3)
32	273
33(4).	271(4)
34	271(6)
38(1).	145

1993	1995
s.39(2).	s.72(1)
40(1).	99(6)
(2).	158
41	210(1), (2),
	(3)
42(1).	108
43	188(1)–(7)
Sched.3.	Sched.8
Sched.4.	Sched.9
Sched.5,	
para.1(2) . . .	37(1), (2)-(4),
	(5)
para.1(3) . . .	72(1)
para.1(5) . . .	95
para.1(7) . . .	232(3)
para.1(9) . . .	110(1), (2)
para.1(11) . .	111
para.1(15) . .	117(3)
para.1(16) . .	117(7)

1993	1995
Sched.5—*cont.*	
para.1(17) . .	s.117(8)
para.1(18) . .	104(1)
para.1(19) . .	120(2)
para.1(20) . .	120(4)
para.1(22) . .	122(4)
para.1(23) . .	125(1), (2),
	(3)
para.1(24) . .	126
para.1(27) . .	94
para.1(30) . .	144(1)
para.1(31) . .	268(1), (2)
para.1(32) . .	44(1), (9)
para.1(35) . .	183(1), (2)
para.1(35)(b)	183(3), (5)
para.1(36) . .	186(1), (2),
	(7), (8), (9)
para.1(37) . .	189(4)
Sched.7.	14(2)

CRIMINAL JUSTICE ACT 1993
(c.36)

1993	1995
s.68(1).	s.106(1), (2)
(2).	108
(3).	175(1)-(4)
69	209(8)
Sched.5,	
para.2(1) . . .	175(9)
para.2(2) . . .	246(1)
para.2(3) . . .	247(3)

1993	1995
Sched.5—*cont.*	
para.2(4) . . .	s.110(1), (2),
	(6)
para.2(5) . . .	112(1)
para.2(6) . . .	116(2)
para.2(7) . . .	118(1)–(5)
para.2(8) . . .	125(1), (2)
para.2(9) . . .	247(3)

1993	1995
Sched.5—*cont.*	
para.2(11) . .	s.193(1), (2)
para.2(12) . .	176(1)
para.2(13) . .	183(3), (5),
	(8)
para.2(14) . .	186(1)–(5),
	(8), (9)
para.2(15) . .	189(4)–(6)

CRIMINAL JUSTICE AND PUBLIC ORDER ACT 1994
(c.33)

1994	1995
s.47(4).	s.222(7)
129(1)	14(1)
(2)	14(6)
(3)	15(1), (2)
132	209(3), (4)
157(7)	225(5)
Sched.10,	
para.47.	14(4), (5)

LOCAL GOVERNMENT ETC. (SCOTLAND) ACT 1994
(c.39)

1994	1995
Sched.13,	
para.97(2) . .	s.49(1), (3), (6),
	(7)
para.97(3) . .	232(1)

CRIMINAL JUSTICE (SCOTLAND) ACT 1995
(c.20)

TABLE OF DESTINATIONS

CHILDREN (SCOTLAND) ACT 1995
(c.36)

INCREASE OF CRIMINAL PENALTIES ETC. (SCOTLAND) ORDER 1984
(S.I. 1984/526)

ACT OF ADJOURNAL (CONSOLIDATION) 1988
(S.I. 1988/110)

COMMUNITY SERVICE ORDERS (NORTHERN IRELAND CONSEQUENTIAL AMENDMENTS) ORDER 1989
(S.I. 1989/1345)

INDEX